THE
WISDEN
BOOK OF
TEST
CRICKET
VOLUME II 1977-1994

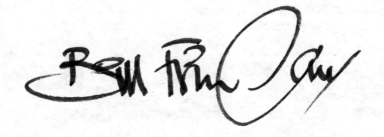

THE
WISDEN
BOOK OF
TEST
CRICKET
VOLUME II 1977-1994

Compiled and edited by
BILL FRINDALL

HEADLINE

First published in 1995
by HEADLINE BOOK PUBLISHING

10 9 8 7 6 5 4 3 2 1

A catalogue record for this book is available
from the British Library

ISBN 0 7472 1118 3

Typeset by
Letterpart Limited, Reigate, Surrey

Printed and bound in Great Britain by
Mackays of Chatham PLC, Chatham, Kent

HEADLINE BOOK PUBLISHING
A division of Hodder Headline PLC
338 Euston Road
London NW1 3BH

CONTENTS

INDIVIDUAL RECORDS – BATTING

Partnership Records

INDIVIDUAL RECORDS – BOWLING

INDIVIDUAL RECORDS – THE CAPTAINS

INDIVIDUAL RECORDS – GENERAL

INDIVIDUAL CAREER RECORDS

INDEX OF TEST CRICKETERS

FOREWORD
by
SIR DONALD BRADMAN, A.C.

One of the great joys for cricket followers is the volume of literature about the game which has been handed down to us over the years. This is not to say all of it is good. There have been some dreadful publications, obviously ghosted, and clearly produced with the box office in mind. But thankfully they are more than counterbalanced by thoughtful, intelligent and beautifully written books which are a must for the library shelves.

Not the least valuable and interesting is the statistical information which leads to so much discussion as to the merits of performers, past and present.

Bill Frindall is a leading contender for the Oscar as a statistician and the world of cricket is very much in his debt for producing *The Wisden Book of Test Cricket*.

Unfortunately the validity of statistics as a measuring stick is becoming more and more clouded by changes in rules and/or playing conditions – for instance covered versus uncovered pitches, the size of the wicket, the 'lbw' law, etc. The latest bugbear is the 'no-ball' law. Whereas for a century the bowler who delivered a 'no-ball' was in danger of being hit for six, the modern bowler is decidedly unlucky if the striker hears the call before the ball hits his bat.

Conversely the bowler's figures are debited with each violation of the 'front foot' monstrosity. I remain of the opinion that 90% of the public and the players would like to see a return to a sensible back foot control and thus rid the game of the frustrations and irritations which are etched on the bowlers' faces, especially in the limited-overs games.

The highly experienced West Indians have had such difficulty coping with the rule that 15 to 20 no-balls in a fifty-over innings are not uncommon – a percentage factor of great significance.

As I write these lines the first day-night match ever at Melbourne has just been played before an audience of over 82,000. This spectacular was followed by the results of a gallup poll showing that 57% of the people favour a multi-nation one-day series to a two-nation Test series. How long I wonder before we have day-night Test matches?

There can be no doubt that Test cricket should remain the pinnacle of achievement and the true fulfilment of cricket skill because to win you have to dismiss your opponents. No such requirement exists in the limited-overs game. It seems a travesty of justice that a team can win a match by scoring 9 for 201 against its rival's 0 for 200, simply because time has run out. But I have great sympathy for the paying customer who will not support watching 240 runs per day when next week he can see the same players in the same time amass over 500 runs – especially when he is interested in entertainment, not technique.

One thing the limited-overs game has done is to highlight good fielding. The current West Indian team is the best all-round fielding side in my memory. Another facet of great interest is the running between wickets. It is thrilling and exciting to see almost impossible singles being risked and achieved.

Of great moment to me, and I think of importance to the future conduct of the game, are two other matters. One is the 'no-ball' and/or 'wide' call. In recent years we have seen far too many short-pitched deliveries in first-class cricket without any action by umpires, probably because they were unwilling to exercise a moral judgement regarding intimidation. The rule applicable in one-day games has curbed bouncers in a sensible, realistic and practical way. I would like to see it adopted for the first-class games, with the rider that the call for an offending delivery should be 'no-ball' instead of 'wide'.

This matter is important for the game of cricket which I'm sure was never intended to be indulged in by players garbed as though they were taking part in grid-iron football. Apart from the uncomfortable helmets and voluminous padding we now find more and more players using the protective arm guard. To be fair, I think the arm guard is less of a necessity and more of a reflection on batting technique. Throughout my career I was never once hit on the forearm nor did I ever remotely feel in danger of being hit. Too many moderns are slaves to the forward prod, left elbow forward (come what may) with a resultant lack of versatility and stroke play; and may I add evasive capability. Indeed the whole gamut of protective devices must militate against mobility and speed.

The second matter is the 'wide' ball itself. This is much more severe (especially on the leg side) in one-day games and in my view could, with advantage, be adopted in first-class cricket.

There has been much speculation as to whether the current West Indian team is the best of all time. Comparisons have been made with the Australian teams of 1921 and 1948. The question provokes animated and interesting discussion but can never produce an authoritative answer.

Of course they are a great side. As I've said earlier, the best fielding team I've seen. Added to that, they have probably the best combination of fast bowlers in one side. But that particular strength immediately predicates a lack of balance when conditions don't favour speed – a fact so nakedly exposed when the West Indians were handsomely beaten in a Sydney Test, mainly through the bowling of Australia's spinners. The West Indian attack lacked adequate spin under these conditions and the batsmen (including even the great Richards) could not handle the unfamiliar spin of Holland and Bennett. Yet nobody with a knowledge of his subject and in his right mind would rate Holland and Bennett in the same class as Grimmett and O'Reilly.

Comparing great sides of different eras must be inconclusive. I always thought my 1948 side the best I saw, though conceding it would have been hard pressed to beat Armstrong's 1921 combination. Yet Armstrong, when asked whether his team was better than Joe Darling's 1902 side replied 'the 1902 side could play 22 of our chaps and give them a beating'. Armstrong played in both so he should know.

Where do we go from here?

I'm sorry for modern players who are caught up in the proliferation of Test and one-day cricket because they have to endure incessant travel, publicity and pressure. The reward is vastly increased remuneration. The corollary is, I fear, less satisfaction in personal achievement, and more subservience to commercialism. But that is the age in which we live.

Only history will be able to determine whether the scales have been tilted in the right direction. Meanwhile it is essential to chronicle events as they happen, and to that end we owe thanks to the Bill Frindalls of this world because their evidence will be valuable in the world court of jurisdiction in the 21st century.

Kensington Park,
Adelaide,
South Australia,
February 1985.

PREFACE AND ACKNOWLEDGEMENTS

The phrase 'test match' was coined during the very first cricket tour to Australia, when, in 1861-62, games between H.H.Stephenson's team and each of the Australian colonies were described as 'test matches'. Those early contests were played against odds, i.e. with the opposition batting and fielding more than 11 men. It was not until the fourth expedition to Australia, by James Lillywhite's professionals in 1876-77, that an English team played on level terms overseas. The first such encounter, against a combined eleven from Melbourne and Sydney, has become accepted as the first official Test match.

This second volume includes the full scores of the 464 official Test matches played after the Centenary Test at Melbourne in March 1977 until the end of the 1994 English season, but including the three-match Sri Lanka v Pakistan rubber played that August.

With two exceptions the matches in this second volume are arranged chronologically by rubber. To ensure that each player's Test career is shown in unbroken chronological order, the six Tests in which Australia alternately played West Indies and England in 1979-80 are set strictly in the order in which they took place. Additionally, although India's one-off Test against Sri Lanka at Chandigarh on 23 November 1990 began a few hours after the start of an Ashes campaign in Australia, it seemed illogical to place it after a five-match series which ended some three months later.

Each match has a reference number to show its position in the general order and its place in that particular series; e.g. 1265/105 is the 1,265th match listed and was the 105th in the series between England and South Africa. In this edition I have added a subsidiary set of reference numbers to show the total number of Tests played by each country involved in any particular match. In the case of Test No. 1265, these read (E707/SA189), denoting that this was the 707th Test played by England and the 189th involving South Africa. To identify a match in either the statistical notes preceding each score or in the Index of Test Cricketers, only the prefix of each reference number is given.

Ideally each score should be an exact reproduction of the match details recorded in the original scorebook. Where that document no longer survives, research has turned to contemporary match reports and I am particularly indebted to the staff of The British Library, custodians of that most comprehensive collection of newspapers and microfilm at Colindale. With the aid of Geoffrey Saulez, virtually every surviving Test match scorebook throughout the world has been checked. Apart from removing many errors of transcription, all substitute catchers have been identified and changes of batting order for the second innings determined.

In addition to features introduced in the first three editions, such as noting days when no play was possible, listing players making their first appearance at this level, denoting left-handers by annotating symbols in the career records section, showing the number of Test appearances to date for each umpire officiating in a particular match, and including the close of play and 'not out' batsmen's scores for every single day of Test cricket, this volume includes changes of bowling order for the second innings.

The use of capital letters for names including 'De', 'Du' or 'Van' is not as haphazard as it may appear. According to the late Denys Heesom, one of the outstanding chroniclers of South African cricket, the custom in the Union was to use capitals when the surname appeared alone (De Villiers) or with initials after the name (De Villiers, P.S.). Lower case was reserved for the name being qualified by initials in advance (P.S.de Villiers). This is the system I have adopted throughout.

I response to several enquiries, it should be stressed that catches and stumpings made by substitute fielders are never included in those individuals' career records.

I have not indicated the winners of match awards because I regard them merely as commercial gimmicks which detract from a team game. Nor have I listed twelfth men; frequently teams have employed several during one match and, in recent years, the officially named reserve has usually fetched and carried an assortment of drinks and protective equipment while other players have acted as emergency fielders.

In his 77th year, Sir Donald Bradman honoured the second edition by contributing a Foreword which reveals the concise mind that controlled the most successful and feared batting technique of all time. It is indeed a delight to have this work graced by 'The Don', the most esteemed name in the history of international cricket.

Besides recording my gratitude to Ian Marshall, whose unruffled enthusiasm and support has guided the fourth edition of this chronicle through all the potential hazards of book production, to Chris Leggett and his team at Letterpart for completely resetting both volumes, and to Gordon Burling and Debbie Frindall for their assiduous proof-checking, I am extremely grateful to the cricketers who made it possible and to the following friends and colleagues, some alas no longer with us, who have been unstinting with their help and kindness in assisting with some aspect of the preparation of these four editions:

John Arlott, Wilhelm Ashok, Philip Bailey, Robert Brooke, Sue Bullen, Tony Cozier, Graham Clayton, Harold de Andrado, Paula Dixon, Anandji Dossa, Graham Dowling, Ric Finlay, Michael Fordham, Christine Forrest, David Frith, Ghulam Mustafa Khan, Stephen Green, Chris Harte, Denys Heesom, Vic Isaacs, Celia Kent, Hayward Kidson, Rajesh Kumar, Syd Levey, Rex Lister, Trevor Lockett, Bapoo Mama, Christopher Martin-Jenkins, Mohandas Menon, Allan Miller, Harriet Monkhouse, Francis Payne, S.S.Perera, Ken Piesse, Jack Pollard, Qamar Ahmed, Mike Ringham, Ray Robinson, David Roylance, Dickie Rutnagur, Ashim Kumar Sarkar, Geoffrey Saulez, Peter Sichel, Bob Spence, Cheryl Styles, Sa'adi Thawfeeq, Gordon Tratalos, B.J.Wakley, Charlie Wat, Ray Webster, Roy Wilkinson, Wendy Wimbush, Mervyn Wong, Graeme Wright and Peter Wynne-Thomas.

Gratitude is also due to the assistance and facilities afforded by the following libraries, clubs and associations:

Auckland Public Library, The British Library, Lancashire County Cricket Club, Marylebone Cricket Club, New South Wales Cricket Association, Nottinghamshire County Cricket Club, Queensland Cricket Association, Royal Geographical Society, South Australia Cricket Association, State Library of South Australia, Surrey County Cricket Club, Victoria State Library, Warwickshire County Cricket Club, Western Australia Cricket Association and Yorkshire County Cricket Club.

BILL FRINDALL
Urchfont, March 1995.

Test Match Scores 1977 to 1994
(Including Sri Lanka v Pakistan 1994-95)

* denotes the Captain and   † shows the Wicket Keeper

NUMBER OF BALLS TO AN OVER IN TEST MATCHES

In England	*Balls*	**In West Indies**	*Balls*
1880 to 1888	4	1929-30 to date	6
1890 to 1899	5		
1902 to 1938	6	**In New Zealand**	
1939	8	1929-30 to 1967-68	6
1946 to date	6	1968-69 to 1978-79	8
		1979-80 to date	6
In Australia		**In India**	
1876-77 to 1887-88	4	1933-34 to date	6
1891-92 to 1920-21	6		
1924-25	8	**In Pakistan**	
1928-29 to 1932-33	6	1954-55 to 1972-73	6
1936-37 to 1978-79	8	1074-75 to 1977-78	8
1979-80 to date	6	1978-79 to date	6
In South Africa		**In Sri Lanka**	
1888-89	4	1981-82 to date	6
1891-92 to 1898-99	5		
1902-03 to 1935-36	6	**In Zimbabwe**	
1938-39 to 1957-58	8	1992-93 to date	6
1961-62 to date	6		

ENGLAND v AUSTRALIA 1977 (1st Test)

At Lord's, London, on 16, 17, 18, 20, 21 June.
Toss: England.   Result: MATCH DRAWN.
Debuts: Australia – L.S.Pascoe (*born L.S.Durtanovich*), R.D.Robinson, C.S.Serjeant.

Staged at Lord's as a Jubilee Test to commemorate 25 years of the reign of Queen Elizabeth II, this match produced the (then) record receipts for any cricket match in Britain (£220,384) and a total attendance of 101,050. Brearley began his reign as England's captain after Greig had been removed from office because of his involvement with the setting up of World Series cricket. Marsh set a new Australian catching record for this series (70) when he dismissed Old. Australia needed to score 226 runs in a minimum of 165 minutes. Old took his 100th wicket in 32 Tests when he dismissed Robinson. Five hours 43 minutes were lost to rain. Willis returned the (then) best figures of his Test career and the best against Australia at Lord's since H.Verity took 7 for 61 in 1934 (*Test No. 234*).

ENGLAND

D.L.Amiss	b Thomson	4		b Thomson	0
*J.M.Brearley	c Robinson b Thomson	9		c Robinson b O'Keeffe	49
R.A.Woolmer	run out	79		c Chappell b Pascoe	120
D.W.Randall	c Chappell b Walker	53	(7)	c McCosker b Thomson	0
A.W.Greig	b Pascoe	5	(4)	c O'Keeffe b Pascoe	91
G.D.Barlow	c McCosker b Walker	1	(5)	lbw b Pascoe	5
†A.P.E.Knott	c Walters b Thomson	8	(6)	c Walters b Walker	8
C.M.Old	c Marsh b Walker	9		c Walters b Walker	0
J.K.Lever	b Pascoe	8		c Marsh b Thomson	3
D.L.Underwood	not out	11		not out	12
R.G.D.Willis	b Thomson	17		c Marsh b Thomson	0
Extras	(B1, LB3, W1, NB7)	12		(B5, LB9, W1, NB2)	17
Total		**216**			**305**

AUSTRALIA

R.D.Robinson	b Lever	11		c Woolmer b Old	4
R.B.McCosker	b Old	23		b Willis	1
*G.S.Chappell	c Old b Willis	66		c Lever b Old	24
C.S.Serjeant	c Knott b Willis	81	(6)	c Amiss b Underwood	3
K.D.Walters	c Brearley b Willis	53		c sub‡ b Underwood	10
D.W.Hookes	c Brearley b Old	11	(4)	c and b Willis	50
†R.W.Marsh	lbw b Willis	1		not out	6
K.J.O'Keeffe	c sub (A.G.E.Ealham) b Willis	12		not out	8
M.H.N.Walker	c Knott b Willis	4			
J.R.Thomson	b Willis	6			
L.S.Pascoe	not out	3			
Extras	(LB7, W1, NB17)	25		(NB8)	8
Total		**296**		**(6 wickets)**	**114**

AUSTRALIA	O	M	R	W	O	M	R	W		FALL OF WICKETS			
										E	A	E	A
Thomson	20.5	5	41	4	24.4	3	86	4	*Wkt*	*1st*	*1st*	*2nd*	*2nd*
Pascoe	23	7	53	2	26	2	96	3	1st	12	25	0	5
Walker	30	6	66	3	35	13	56	2	2nd	13	51	132	5
O'Keeffe	10	3	32	0	(5) 15	7	26	1	3rd	111	135	224	48
Chappell	3	0	12	0	(4) 12	2	24	0	4th	121	238	263	64
									5th	134	256	286	71
ENGLAND									6th	155	264	286	102
Willis	30.1	7	78	7	10	1	40	2	7th	171	265	286	–
Lever	19	5	61	1	(4) 5	2	4	0	8th	183	284	286	–
Underwood	25	6	42	0	10	3	16	2	9th	189	290	305	–
Old	35	10	70	2	(2) 14	0	46	2	10th	216	296	305	–
Woolmer	5	1	20	0									

Umpires: H.D.Bird (11) and W.L.Budd (2).   ‡ (A.G.E.Ealham)

Close: 1st day – E(1) 216 all out; 2nd – A(1) 51-1 (McCosker 23, Chappell 11); 3rd – A(1) 278-7 (O'Keeffe 8, Walker 1); 4th – E(2) 189-2 (Woolmer 114, Greig 18).

ENGLAND v AUSTRALIA 1977 (2nd Test)

At Old Trafford, Manchester, on 7, 8, 9, 11, 12 July.
Toss: Australia.   Result: ENGLAND won by nine wickets.
Debuts: Australia – R.J.Bright.

England completed their victory at 12.34 pm on the fifth day. Woolmer (389 minutes, 338 balls, 22 fours) scored his second successive hundred in the rubber; it was the third and last of his Test career and all three centuries were made against Australia. Chappell (280 minutes, 230 balls, 1 six, 15 fours) scored 51% of his team's second innings and recorded his 14th Test hundred, six of them against England. Underwood took five or more wickets in an innings for the last time in a Test in England; it was his fourth such instance against Australia and first in any Old Trafford Test.

AUSTRALIA

R.B.McCosker	c Old b Willis	2	c Underwood b Willis		0
I.C.Davis	c Knott b Old	34	c Lever b Willis		12
*G.S.Chappell	c Knott b Greig	44	b Underwood		112
C.S.Serjeant	lbw b Lever	14	c Woolmer b Underwood		8
K.D.Walters	c Greig b Miller	88	lbw b Greig		10
D.W.Hookes	c Knott b Lever	5	c Brearley b Miller		28
†R.W.Marsh	c Amiss b Miller	36	c Randall b Underwood		1
R.J.Bright	c Greig b Lever	12	c and b Underwood		0
K.J.O'Keeffe	c Knott b Willis	12	not out		24
M.H.N.Walker	b Underwood	9	c Greig b Underwood		6
J.R.Thomson	not out	14	c Randall b Underwood		1
Extras	(LB15, NB12)	27	(LB1, W1, NB14)		16
Total		**297**			**218**

ENGLAND

D.L.Amiss	c Chappell b Walker	11	not out		28
*J.M.Brearley	c Chappell b Thomson	6	c Walters b O'Keeffe		44
R.A.Woolmer	c Davis b O'Keeffe	137	not out		0
D.W.Randall	lbw b Bright	79			
A.W.Greig	c and b Walker	76			
†A.P.E.Knott	c O'Keeffe b Thomson	39			
G.Miller	c Marsh b Thomson	6			
C.M.Old	c Marsh b Walker	37			
J.K.Lever	b Bright	10			
D.L.Underwood	b Bright	10			
R.G.D.Willis	not out	1			
Extras	(B9, LB9, NB7)	25	(LB3, NB7)		10
Total		**437**	(1 wicket)		**82**

ENGLAND	O	M	R	W	O	M	R	W	FALL OF WICKETS				
Willis	21	8	45	2	16	2	56	2		A	E	A	E
Lever	25	8	60	3	4	1	11	0	*Wkt*	*1st*	*1st*	*2nd*	*2nd*
Old	20	3	57	1	(4) 8	1	26	0	1st	4	19	0	75
Underwood	20.2	7	53	1	(3) 32.5	13	66	6	2nd	80	23	30	–
Greig	13	4	37	1	12	6	19	1	3rd	96	165	74	–
Miller	10	3	18	2	9	2	24	1	4th	125	325	92	–
									5th	140	348	146	–
									6th	238	366	147	–
AUSTRALIA									7th	246	377	147	–
Thomson	38	11	73	3	8	2	24	0	8th	272	404	202	–
Walker	54	15	131	3	7	0	17	0	9th	272	435	212	–
Bright	35.1	12	69	3	(4) 5	2	6	0	10th	297	437	218	–
O'Keeffe	36	11	114	1	(3) 9.1	4	25	1					
Chappell	6	1	25	0									

Umpires: W.E.Alley (6) and T.W.Spencer (15).

Close: 1st day – A(1) 247-7 (Bright 1, O'Keeffe 0); 2nd – E(1) 206-3 (Woolmer 82, Greig 16); 3rd – E(1) 436-9 (Underwood 10, Willis 1); 4th – E(2) 8-0 (Amiss 0, Brearley 6).

ENGLAND v AUSTRALIA 1977 (3rd Test)

At Trent Bridge, Nottingham, on 28, 29, 30 July, 1, 2 August.
Toss: Australia.   Result: ENGLAND won by seven wickets.
Debuts: England – I.T.Botham.

At 4.42 on the fifth afternoon, England gained their first win against Australia at Nottingham since 1930. Boycott returned to Test cricket after a self-imposed exile of 30 matches and scored his 13th hundred in official Tests; it was his 98th century in first-class cricket. Knott became the first wicket-keeper to score 4,000 runs in Test matches and his innings of 135 is still the highest by a 'keeper in this series. His partnership of 215 with Boycott equalled England's sixth-wicket record against Australia; it remains the only England partnership record for this series to be equalled or broken since 1938. Boycott became the second player after M.L.Jaisimha (*Test No. 486*) to bat on each day of a five-day Test. Play was suspended for eight minutes on the first evening to allow the teams to be presented to The Queen and The Duke of Edinburgh.

AUSTRALIA

R.B.McCosker	c Brearley b Hendrick	51	c Brearley b Willis		107
I.C.Davis	c Botham b Underwood	33	c Greig b Willis		9
*G.S.Chappell	b Botham	19	b Hendrick		27
D.W.Hookes	c Hendrick b Willis	17	lbw b Hendrick		42
K.D.Walters	c Hendrick b Botham	11	c Randall b Greig		28
R.D.Robinson	c Brearley b Greig	11	lbw b Underwood		34
†R.W.Marsh	lbw b Botham	0	c Greig b Willis		0
K.J.O'Keeffe	not out	48	not out		21
M.H.N.Walker	c Hendrick b Botham	0	b Willis		17
J.R.Thomson	c Knott b Botham	21	b Willis		0
L.S.Pascoe	c Greig b Hendrick	20	c Hendrick b Underwood		0
Extras	(B4, LB2, NB6)	12	(B1, LB5, W1, NB17)		24
Total		**243**			**309**

ENGLAND

*J.M.Brearley	c Hookes b Pascoe	15	b Walker		81
G.Boycott	c McCosker b Thomson	107	not out		80
R.A.Woolmer	lbw b Pascoe	0			
D.W.Randall	run out	13	(5) not out		19
A.W.Greig	b Thomson	11	(4) b Walker		0
G.Miller	c Robinson b Pascoe	13			
†A.P.E.Knott	c Davis b Thomson	135	(3) c O'Keeffe b Walker		2
I.T.Botham	b Walker	25			
D.L.Underwood	b Pascoe	7			
M.Hendrick	b Walker	1			
R.G.D.Willis	not out	2			
Extras	(B9, LB7, W3, NB16)	35	(B2, LB2, W1, NB2)		7
Total		**364**	(3 wickets)		**189**

ENGLAND	O	M	R	W	O	M	R	W	FALL OF WICKETS				
Willis	15	0	58	1	26	6	88	5		A	E	A	E
Hendrick	21.2	6	46	2	32	14	56	2	*Wkt*	*1st*	*1st*	*2nd*	*2nd*
Botham	20	5	74	5	25	5	60	0	1st	79	34	18	154
Greig	15	4	35	1	9	2	24	1	2nd	101	34	60	156
Underwood	11	5	18	1	27	15	49	2	3rd	131	52	154	158
Miller					5	2	5	0	4th	133	64	204	–
Woolmer					3	0	3	0	5th	153	82	240	–
									6th	153	297	240	–
AUSTRALIA									7th	153	326	270	–
Thomson	31	6	103	3	16	6	34	0	8th	155	357	307	–
Pascoe	32	10	80	4	22	6	43	0	9th	196	357	308	–
Walker	39.2	12	79	2	(4) 24	8	40	3	10th	243	364	309	–
Chappell	8	0	19	0									
O'Keeffe	11	4	43	0	(3) 19.2	2	65	0					
Walters	3	0	5	0									

Umpires: H.D.Bird (12) and D.J.Constant (12).

Close: 1st day – E(1) 9-0 (Brearley 5, Boycott 1); 2nd – E(1) 242-5 (Boycott 88, Knott 87); 3rd – A(2) 112-2 (McCosker 40, Hookes 31); 4th – E(2) 17-0 (Brearley 5, Boycott 12).

ENGLAND v AUSTRALIA 1977 (4th Test)

At Headingley, Leeds, on 11, 12, 13, 15 August.
Toss: England.   Result: ENGLAND won by an innings and 85 runs.
Debuts: None.

England regained the Ashes at 4.39 on the fourth afternoon when Marsh skied a drive to cover, Randall, who turned a somersault after completing the catch. At 5.49 pm on the first day, Boycott became the first batsman to score his 100th first-class hundred during a Test; last out, he batted for 629 minutes, faced 471 balls, hit a five and 23 fours, and was the fourth England player to be on the field for an entire Test match. Brearley was out to the third ball of the match. Australia were dismissed for their lowest total in a Leeds Test. Knott made his 250th dismissal in 88 Tests (Davis) and Willis took his 100th wicket in 28 Tests (Thomson).

ENGLAND

*J.M.Brearley	c Marsh b Thomson	0
G.Boycott	c Chappell b Pascoe	191
R.A.Woolmer	c Chappell b Thomson	37
D.W.Randall	lbw b Pascoe	20
A.W.Greig	b Thomson	43
G.R.J.Roope	c Walters b Thomson	34
†A.P.E.Knott	lbw b Bright	57
I.T.Botham	b Bright	0
D.L.Underwood	c Bright b Pascoe	6
M.Hendrick	c Robinson b Pascoe	4
R.G.D.Willis	not out	5
Extras	(B5, LB9, W3, NB22)	39
Total		**436**

AUSTRALIA

R.B.McCosker	run out	27	c Knott b Greig		12
I.C.Davis	lbw b Hendrick	0	c Knott b Greig		19
*G.S.Chappell	c Brearley b Hendrick	4	c Greig b Willis		36
D.W.Hookes	lbw b Botham	24	lbw b Hendrick		21
K.D.Walters	c Hendrick b Botham	4	lbw b Woolmer		15
R.D.Robinson	c Greig b Hendrick	20	b Hendrick		20
†R.W.Marsh	c Knott b Botham	2	c Randall b Hendrick		63
R.J.Bright	not out	9	c Greig b Hendrick		5
M.H.N.Walker	c Knott b Botham	7	b Willis		30
J.R.Thomson	b Botham	0	b Willis		0
L.S.Pascoe	b Hendrick	0	not out		0
Extras	(LB3, W1, NB2)	6	(B1, LB4, W4, NB18)		27
Total		**103**			**248**

AUSTRALIA	O	M	R	W	O	M	R	W	FALL OF WICKETS			
										E	A	A
Thomson	34	7	113	4					Wkt	1st	1st	2nd
Walker	48	21	97	0					1st	0	8	31
Pascoe	34.4	10	91	4					2nd	82	26	35
Walters	3	1	5	0					3rd	105	52	63
Bright	26	9	66	2					4th	201	57	97
Chappell	10	2	25	0					5th	275	66	130
									6th	398	77	167
ENGLAND									7th	398	87	179
Willis	5	0	35	0	14	7	32	3	8th	412	100	244
Hendrick	15.3	2	41	4	22.5	6	54	4	9th	422	100	245
Botham	11	3	21	5	(4) 17	3	47	0	10th	436	103	248
Greig					(3) 20	7	64	2				
Woolmer					8	4	8	1				
Underwood					8	3	16	0				

Umpires: W.E.Alley (7) and W.L.Budd (3).

Close: 1st day – E(1) 252-4 (Boycott 110, Roope 19); 2nd – A(1) 67-5 (Robinson 6, Marsh 0); 3rd – A(2) 120-4 (Chappell 29, Robinson 11).

ENGLAND v AUSTRALIA 1977 (5th Test)

At Kennington Oval, London, on 25 (*no play*), 26, 27, 29, 30 August.
Toss: Australia.   Result: MATCH DRAWN.
Debuts: Australia – K.J.Hughes, M.F.Malone.

This Test, in which 11 hours and 51 minutes were lost because of rain and a waterlogged ground, was the last before World Series cricket dominated two Australian seasons and claimed the services of twelve of its participants. Kerry Packer's schism ended Knott's record England sequence of 65 consecutive appearances (subsequently equalled by I.T.Botham), and the Test careers of Greig (58 successive matches), Malone and Walker. The last two achieved their highest first-class scores and shared a century ninth-wicket partnership in 105 minutes. Thomson took his 100th wicket in 22 Tests; Malone celebrated his only Test cap with five first innings wickets; and Boycott achieved the highest average for a rubber in this series (147.33) and scored his 5,000th run in official Tests. There were a record 22,556,000 calls to the Post Office scores service.

ENGLAND

*J.M.Brearley	c Marsh b Malone	39	c Serjeant b Thomson		4
G.Boycott	c McCosker b Walker	39	not out		25
R.A.Woolmer	lbw b Thomson	15	c Marsh b Malone		6
D.W.Randall	c Marsh b Malone	3	not out		20
A.W.Greig	c Bright b Malone	0			
G.R.J.Roope	b Thomson	38			
†A.P.E.Knott	c McCosker b Malone	6			
J.K.Lever	lbw b Malone	3			
D.L.Underwood	b Thomson	20			
M.Hendrick	b Thomson	15			
R.G.D.Willis	not out	24			
Extras	(LB6, W1, NB5)	12	(W2)		2
Total		**214**	(2 wickets)		**57**

AUSTRALIA

C.S.Serjeant	lbw b Willis	0
R.B.McCosker	lbw b Willis	32
*G.S.Chappell	c and b Underwood	39
K.J.Hughes	c Willis b Hendrick	1
D.W.Hookes	c Knott b Greig	85
K.D.Walters	b Willis	4
†R.W.Marsh	lbw b Hendrick	57
R.J.Bright	lbw b Willis	16
M.H.N.Walker	not out	78
M.F.Malone	b Lever	46
J.R.Thomson	b Willis	17
Extras	(B1, LB6, NB3)	10
Total		**385**

AUSTRALIA	O	M	R	W	O	M	R	W
Thomson	23.2	3	87	4	5	1	22	1
Malone	47	20	63	5	10	4	14	1
Walker	28	11	51	1	8	2	14	0
Bright	3	2	1	0	3	2	5	0

ENGLAND	O	M	R	W
Willis	29.3	5	102	5
Hendrick	37	5	93	2
Lever	22	6	61	1
Underwood	35	9	102	1
Greig	8	2	17	1

FALL OF WICKETS

Wkt	E 1st	A 1st	E 2nd
1st	86	0	5
2nd	88	54	16
3rd	104	67	–
4th	104	84	–
5th	106	104	–
6th	122	184	–
7th	130	236	–
8th	169	252	–
9th	174	352	–
10th	214	385	–

Umpires: D.J.Constant (13) and T.W.Spencer (16).

Close: 1st day – no play; 2nd – E(1) 181-9 (Hendrick 1, Willis 6); 3rd – A(1) 11-1 (McCosker 2, Chappell 7); 4th – A(1) 226-6 (Marsh 53, Bright 6).

AUSTRALIA v INDIA 1977-78 (1st Test)

At Woolloongabba, Brisbane, on 2, 3, 4, 6 December.
Toss: Australia.   Result: AUSTRALIA won by 16 runs.
Debuts: Australia – W.M.Clark, P.A.Hibbert, A.L.Mann, A.D.Ogilvie, S.J.Rixon, P.M.Toohey.

Australia achieved the (then) eighth-narrowest victory by a runs margin in Test cricket. With 12 of the players who appeared against England in 1977 having defected to World Series cricket, Australia recalled Simpson to play his first Test since 1967-68. Gavaskar's hundred was the first by an Indian playing his first match of this series in Australia. Mann dismissed Viswanath with his seventh ball in Test cricket. Chandrasekhar was dismissed for his third 'pair' in Test matches, equalling the world record he was to make his own two matches later.

AUSTRALIA

Batsman	Dismissal	R		Dismissal	R
P.A.Hibbert	c Kirmani b Amarnath	13	(2)	lbw b Madan Lal	2
G.J.Cosier	c Madan Lal b Amarnath	19	(1)	c Prasanna b Madan Lal	0
A.D.Ogilvie	c Viswanath b Bedi	5		b Chandrasekhar	46
C.S.Serjeant	c Gavaskar b Bedi	0		b Amarnath	0
*R.B.Simpson	c Gavaskar b Bedi	7		c Viswanath b Amarnath	89
P.M.Toohey	st Kirmani b Bedi	82		c Bedi b Chandrasekhar	57
A.L.Mann	lbw b Madan Lal	19		c Amarnath b Madan Lal	29
†S.J.Rixon	c Amarnath b Bedi	9		c Kirmani b Madan Lal	6
W.M.Clark	c Gavaskar b Chandrasekhar	4		b Madan Lal	12
J.R.Thomson	b Chandrasekhar	3		not out	41
A.G.Hurst	not out	0		run out	26
Extras	(B3, LB1, W1)	5		(B6, LB11, NB2)	19
Total		**166**			**327**

INDIA

Batsman	Dismissal	R		Dismissal	R
S.M.Gavaskar	c Cosier b Clark	3		c Rixon b Clark	113
D.B.Vengsarkar	hit wkt b Thomson	48		b Clark	1
M.Amarnath	lbw b Clark	0		c Rixon b Thomson	47
G.R.Viswanath	c Hurst b Mann	45		c Ogilvie b Thomson	35
B.P.Patel	c Serjeant b Clark	13		lbw b Thomson	3
A.V.Mankad	c Rixon b Thomson	0		b Hurst	21
Madan Lal	b Clark	4	(8)	c Rixon b Clark	2
†S.M.H.Kirmani	c Ogilvie b Thomson	11	(7)	c Serjeant b Hurst	55
E.A.S.Prasanna	c Thomson b Mann	23		c Hibbert b Clark	8
*B.S.Bedi	not out	2		not out	26
B.S.Chandrasekhar	lbw b Mann	0		c Rixon b Thomson	0
Extras	(NB 4)	4		(LB6, NB7)	13
Total		**153**			**324**

INDIA	O	M	R	W	O	M	R	W		FALL OF WICKETS			
										A	I	A	I
Madan Lal	10	3	27	1	19	2	72	5	Wkt	1st	1st	2nd	2nd
Amarnath	13	4	43	2	8	1	24	2	1st	24	11	0	7
Bedi	13.7	3	55	5	18.5	2	71	0	2nd	33	15	6	88
Prasanna	4	2	2	0	20	4	59	0	3rd	33	90	7	147
Chandrasekhar	6	1	34	2	26	6	82	2	4th	43	108	100	151
									5th	49	110	184	196
AUSTRALIA									6th	90	112	233	243
Thomson	16	1	54	3	19.7	1	76	4	7th	107	119	237	251
Clark	18	5	46	4	26	1	101	4	8th	112	149	246	275
Hurst	7	0	31	0	15	3	50	2	9th	132	151	277	318
Cosier	3	1	6	0	(6) 5	1	10	0	10th	166	153	327	324
Mann	6	0	12	3	15	3	52	0					
Simpson					(4) 4	0	22	0					

Umpires: T.F.Brooks (21) and M.G.O'Connell (11).

Close: 1st day – I(1) 13-1 (Vengsarkar 10, Amarnath 0); 2nd – A(2) 62-3 (Ogilvie 29, Simpson 27); 3rd – I(2) 51-1 (Gavaskar 15, Amarnath 32).

AUSTRALIA v INDIA 1977-78 (2nd Test)

At W.A.C.A. Ground, Perth, on 16, 17, 18, 20, 21 December.
Toss: India.   Result: AUSTRALIA won by two wickets.
Debuts: Australia – J.Dyson, J.B.Gannon.

Australia scored the highest fourth-innings total to win a Test in Australia and achieved the victory by a narrow margin for the second match running. India reached 400 for the first time in this series. Simpson, leading Australia for a record 31st time, took his 100th catch in 54 Tests – the fifth fielder to achieve this aggregate and in the fewest matches. At 41, he became the oldest Australian to score a hundred in a home Test, a record he extended in the final match of this rubber; his innings was the highest in any Perth Test until 1989-90. Mann was the second after Nasim-ul-Ghani (*Test No. 531*) to score a hundred in a Test match as a 'night-watchman'. Bedi was the first Indian to take ten wickets in a Test in Australia. The partnership of 193 between Gavaskar and Amarnath was the highest for India's second wicket against Australia until 1985-86.

INDIA

S.M.Gavaskar	c Rixon b Clark	4		b Clark	127
C.P.S.Chauhan	c Gannon b Simpson	88		c Ogilvie b Thomson	32
M.Amarnath	c Gannon b Thomson	90		c Rixon b Simpson	100
G.R.Viswanath	b Thomson	38		c Rixon b Clark	1
D.B.Vengsarkar	c Rixon b Clark	49		c Hughes b Gannon	9
B.P.Patel	c Rixon b Thomson	3		b Gannon	27
†S.M.H.Kirmani	c Rixon b Thomson	38		lbw b Gannon	2
S.Venkataraghavan	c Simpson b Gannon	37		c Hughes b Gannon	14
Madan Lal	b Gannon	43		b Thomson	3
*B.S.Bedi	b Gannon	3		not out	0
B.S.Chandrasekhar	not out	0		not out	0
Extras	(B1, NB8)	9		(B1, LB4, NB10)	15
Total		**402**		**(9 wickets declared)**	**330**

AUSTRALIA

J.Dyson	c Patel b Bedi	53		c Vengsarkar b Bedi	4
C.S.Serjeant	c Kirmani b Madan Lal	13		c Kirmani b Madan Lal	12
A.D.Ogilvie	b Bedi	27	(4)	b Bedi	47
P.M.Toohey	st Kirmani b Bedi	0	(5)	c Amarnath b Bedi	83
*R.B.Simpson	c Vengsarkar b Venkataraghavan	176	(6)	run out	39
†S.J.Rixon	c Kirmani b Amarnath	50	(8)	lbw b Bedi	23
K.J.Hughes	c Patel b Bedi	28		lbw b Madan Lal	0
A.L.Mann	c Vengsarkar b Bedi	7	(3)	c Kirmani b Bedi	105
W.M.Clark	c Patel b Chandrasekhar	15		not out	5
J.R.Thomson	c Amarnath b Venkataraghavan	0		not out	6
J.B.Gannon	not out	0			
Extras	(LB25)	25		(B8, LB10)	18
Total		**394**		**(8 wickets)**	**342**

AUSTRALIA	O	M	R	W	O	M	R	W		FALL OF WICKETS			
										I	A	I	A
Thomson	24	1	101	4	21.5	3	65	2	*Wkt*	*1st*	*1st*	*2nd*	*2nd*
Clark	17	0	95	2	(3) 18	1	83	2	1st	14	19	47	13
Gannon	16.6	1	84	3	(2) 18	2	77	4	2nd	163	61	240	33
Mann	11	0	63	0	8	0	49	0	3rd	224	65	244	172
Simpson	11	0	50	1	8	2	41	1	4th	229	149	283	195
									5th	235	250	287	295
INDIA									6th	311	321	289	296
Madan Lal	15	1	54	1	11	0	44	2	7th	319	341	327	330
Amarnath	16	2	57	1	3	0	22	0	8th	383	388	328	330
Chandrasekhar	33.6	6	114	1	(4) 15	0	67	0	9th	391	388	330	–
Bedi	31	6	89	5	(3) 30.2	6	105	5	10th	402	394	–	–
Venkataraghavan	23	4	55	2	28	9	86	0					

Umpires: R.C.Bailhache (10) and R.A.French (1).

Close: 1st day – I(1) 329-7 (Venkataraghavan 11, Madan Lal 0); 2nd – A(1) 171-4 (Simpson 52, Rixon 16); 3rd – I(2) 67-1 (Gavaskar 20, Amarnath 10); 4th – A(2) 25-1 (Serjeant 9, Mann 6).

AUSTRALIA v INDIA 1977-78 (3rd Test)

At Melbourne Cricket Ground on 30, 31 December, 2, 3, 4 January.
Toss: India.   Result: INDIA won by 222 runs.
Debuts: None.

India gained their first victory in Australia. Chandrasekhar took his 200th wicket in 48 Tests, three matches fewer than Bedi, previously the only Indian to achieve this total. Chandrasekhar's match analysis remains the best for India in Australia. He also became the first to be dismissed for a 'pair' in Test cricket on four occasions. Chauhan and Gavaskar were out to the sixth and ninth balls of the match respectively.

INDIA

S.M.Gavaskar	c Rixon b Thomson	0		c Serjeant b Gannon	118
C.P.S.Chauhan	c Mann b Clark	0		run out	20
M.Amarnath	c Simpson b Clark	72	(7)	b Cosier	41
G.R.Viswanath	c Rixon b Thomson	59		lbw b Clark	54
D.B.Vengsarkar	c Simpson b Thomson	37		c Cosier b Clark	6
A.V.Mankad	c Clark b Gannon	44		b Clark	38
†S.M.H.Kirmani	lbw b Simpson	29	(3)	c Thomson b Mann	29
K.D.Ghavri	c Rixon b Gannon	6		c Simpson b Clark	6
E.A.S.Prasanna	b Clark	0		c Rixon b Gannon	11
*B.S.Bedi	not out	2		not out	12
B.S.Chandrasekhar	b Clark	0		lbw b Cosier	0
Extras	(LB3, NB4)	7		(LB1, NB7)	8
Total		**256**			**343**

AUSTRALIA

J.Dyson	b Ghavri	0	(2)	lbw b Bedi	12
G.J.Cosier	c Chauhan b Chandrasekhar	67	(1)	b Chandrasekhar	34
A.D.Ogilvie	lbw b Ghavri	6		c Chauhan b Bedi	0
C.S.Serjeant	b Chandrasekhar	85		b Chandrasekhar	17
*R.B.Simpson	c Mankad b Chandrasekhar	2		lbw b Chandrasekhar	4
P.M.Toohey	c Viswanath b Bedi	14		c Chauhan b Chandrasekhar	14
A.L.Mann	c Gavaskar b Bedi	11		c Gavaskar b Chandrasekhar	18
†S.J.Rixon	lbw b Chandrasekhar	11		c and b Chandrasekhar	12
W.M.Clark	lbw b Chandrasekhar	3		c Ghavri b Bedi	33
J.R.Thomson	c Ghavri b Chandrasekhar	0		c and b Bedi	7
J.B.Gannon	not out	0		not out	3
Extras	(B6, LB7, NB1)	14		(B6, LB4)	10
Total		**213**			**164**

AUSTRALIA	O	M	R	W		O	M	R	W	FALL OF WICKETS				
											I	A	I	A
Thomson	16	2	78	3	(4)	18	4	47	0	*Wkt*	*1st*	*1st*	*2nd*	*2nd*
Clark	19.2	2	73	4	(1)	29	3	96	4	1st	0	0	40	42
Gannon	14	2	47	2	(2)	22	4	88	2	2nd	0	18	89	42
Cosier	12	3	25	0	(3)	12.7	2	58	2	3rd	105	122	187	52
Simpson	3	1	11	1	(6)	3	0	22	0	4th	174	124	198	60
Mann	5	1	15	0	(5)	4	0	24	1	5th	180	166	265	77
										6th	234	178	286	98
INDIA										7th	254	202	294	115
Ghavri	9	0	37	2		4	0	29	0	8th	254	211	315	122
Gavaskar	2	0	7	0						9th	256	211	343	151
Bedi	15	2	71	2	(4)	16.1	5	58	4	10th	256	213	343	164
Chandrasekhar	14.1	2	52	6	(5)	20	3	52	6					
Prasanna	10	1	32	0	(3)	8	4	5	0					
Amarnath					(2)	3	0	10	0					

Umpires: R.A.French (2) and M.G. O'Connell (12).

Close: 1st day – I(1) 234-6 (Mankad 30); 2nd – I(2) 50-1 (Gavaskar 25, Kirmani 5); 3rd – I(2) 234-4 (Gavaskar 103, Mankad 15); 4th – A(2) 123-8 (Clark 2, Thomson 0).

AUSTRALIA v INDIA 1977-78 (4th Test)

At Sydney Cricket Ground on 7, 8, 9, 11, 12 January.
Toss: Australia.   Result: INDIA won by an innings and 2 runs.
Debuts: None.

India gained their first victory by an innings margin against Australia. It was also the first time since England's tour in 1954-55 that Australia had lost successive home Tests. On a pitch still damp from pre-match torrential rain, Australia were dismissed for their (then) second-lowest total in a home Test against India. Further rain reduced the second day's play by 3½ hours. Toohey tore ankle ligaments while fielding and batted with a runner when he compiled the highest score of the match.

AUSTRALIA

J.Dyson	lbw b Chandrasekhar	26		c and b Chandrasekhar	6
G.J.Cosier	b Amarnath	17		b Bedi	68
P.M.Toohey	run out	4	(6)	c sub (Madan Lal) b Ghavri	85
C.S.Serjeant	c Ghavri b Bedi	4		b Prasanna	1
*R.B.Simpson	c Kirmani b Chandrasekhar	38		lbw b Prasanna	33
K.J.Hughes	b Bedi	17	(3)	c Vengsarkar b Bedi	19
A.L.Mann	b Bedi	0		c and b Prasanna	0
†S.J.Rixon	lbw b Chandrasekhar	17		c Viswanath b Chandrasekhar	11
W.M.Clark	c Gavaskar b Chandrasekhar	0		b Prasanna	10
J.R.Thomson	not out	1		b Ghavri	16
J.B.Gannon	c Amarnath b Prasanna	0		not out	0
Extras	(LB5, NB2)	7		(B5, LB6, NB3)	14
Total		**131**			**263**

INDIA

S.M.Gavaskar	c Rixon b Thomson	49
C.P.S.Chauhan	c Mann b Clark	42
M.Amarnath	c Gannon b Clark	9
G.R.Viswanath	b Thomson	79
D.B.Vengsarkar	c Rixon b Cosier	48
A.V.Mankad	b Thomson	16
†S.M.H.Kirmani	b Cosier	42
K.D.Ghavri	c Serjeant b Thomson	64
E.A.S.Prasanna	not out	25
*B.S.Bedi	not out	1
B.S.Chandrasekhar	did not bat	
Extras	(LB9, NB12)	21
Total	(8 wickets declared)	**396**

INDIA	O	M	R	W	O	M	R	W	FALL OF WICKETS			
Ghavri	7	1	25	0	12.7	3	42	2		A	I	A
Amarnath	7	4	6	1	5	3	9	0	*Wkt*	*1st*	*1st*	*2nd*
Bedi	13	3	49	3	(4) 28	8	62	2	1st	29	97	26
Chandrasekhar	15	3	30	4	(3) 24	3	85	2	2nd	34	102	87
Prasanna	7.4	2	14	1	29	11	51	4	3rd	46	116	88
									4th	61	241	106
AUSTRALIA									5th	84	261	171
Thomson	27	8	83	4					6th	84	263	171
Clark	21	3	66	2					7th	125	344	194
Gannon	20	4	65	0					8th	125	395	221
Mann	20	0	101	0					9th	130	–	257
Simpson	4	0	34	0					10th	131	–	263
Cosier	9	1	26	2								

Umpires: R.C.Bailhache (11) and T.F.Brooks (22).

Close: 1st day – I(1) 86-0 (Gavaskar 45, Chauhan 35); 2nd – I(1) 190-3 (Viswanath 48, Vengsarkar 23); 3rd – A(2) 40-1 (Cosier 23, Hughes 7); 4th – A(2) 243-8 (Toohey 77, Thomson 4).

AUSTRALIA v INDIA 1977-78 (5th Test)

At Adelaide Oval on 28, 29, 30 January, 1, 2, 3 February.
Toss: Australia.   Result: AUSTRALIA won by 47 runs.
Debuts: Australia – I.W.Callen, W.M.Darling, G.M.Wood, B.Yardley.

On their resurrected captain's 42nd birthday, Australia won the rubber 3-2 after India had achieved the second highest fourth-innings total in Test cricket. India's 445 also represented their (then) highest total against Australia and the highest by any side in the fourth innings to lose a Test match. Bedi set a record for either country by taking 31 wickets in the rubber. Simpson's tenth and final Test hundred was his second in successive Test innings at Adelaide separated by ten years. At 41 years 360 days, he is the oldest Australian to score a century in a home Test. Thomson strained a hamstring muscle and was unable to complete his fourth over.

AUSTRALIA

G.M.Wood	st Kirmani b Chandrasekhar	39	c Vengsarkar b Bedi		8
W.M.Darling	c Vengsarkar b Chandrasekhar	65	b Bedi		56
G.N.Yallop	c Gavaskar b Amarnath	121	b Bedi		24
P.M.Toohey	c Gavaskar b Chandrasekhar	60	c Kirmani b Prasanna		10
*R.B.Simpson	c Viswanath b Ghavri	100	lbw b Ghavri		51
G.J.Cosier	b Ghavri	1	st Kirmani b Bedi		34
†S.J.Rixon	b Bedi	32	run out		13
B.Yardley	c and b Ghavri	22	c Vengsarkar b Ghavri		26
J.R.Thomson	c Ghavri b Chandrasekhar	24	(11) c Amarnath b Ghavri		3
W.M.Clark	b Chandrasekhar	0	(9) lbw b Ghavri		1
I.W.Callen	not out	22	(10) not out		4
Extras	(B4, LB14, NB1)	19	(B5, LB15, W3, NB3)		26
Total		**505**			**256**

INDIA

S.M.Gavaskar	c Toohey b Thomson	7	c Rixon b Callen		29
C.P.S.Chauhan	c Cosier b Clark	15	c Wood b Yardley		32
M.Amarnath	c Cosier b Thomson	0	c Callen b Yardley		86
G.R.Viswanath	c Rixon b Callen	89	c Simpson b Clark		73
D.B.Vengsarkar	c Rixon b Callen	44	c Toohey b Yardley		78
A.D.Gaekwad	c Rixon b Callen	27	c and b Yardley		12
†S.M.H.Kirmani	run out	48	b Clark		51
K.D.Ghavri	c Simpson b Clark	3	c sub (K.J.Hughes) b Callen		23
E.A.S.Prasanna	not out	15	not out		10
*B.S.Bedi	c sub (K.J.Hughes) b Clark	6	c Cosier b Callen		16
B.S.Chandrasekhar	c and b Clark	2	c Rixon b Simpson		2
Extras	(B4, LB1, NB8)	13	(B6, LB11, NB16)		33
Total		**269**			**445**

INDIA	O	M	R	W	O	M	R	W	FALL OF WICKETS				
Ghavri	22	2	93	3	10.5	2	45	4		A	I	A	I
Amarnath	12	0	45	1	4	0	12	0	Wkt	1st	1st	2nd	2nd
Bedi	34	1	127	1	(4) 20	3	53	4	1st	89	23	17	40
Prasanna	10	1	48	0	(3) 34	7	68	1	2nd	110	23	84	79
Chandrasekhar	29.4	0	136	5	14	0	52	0	3rd	230	23	95	210
Gaekwad	5	0	37	0					4th	334	159	107	256
									5th	337	166	172	323
									6th	406	216	210	348
AUSTRALIA									7th	450	226	214	415
Thomson	3.3	1	12	2					8th	457	249	240	417
Clark	20.7	6	62	4	29	6	79	2	9th	458	263	248	442
Callen	22	0	83	3	(1) 33	5	108	3	10th	505	269	256	445
Cosier	4	3	4	0	(5) 13	6	21	0					
Yardley	23	6	62	0	(3) 43	6	134	4					
Simpson	9	0	33	0	(4) 23.4	6	70	1					

Umpires: R.A.French (3) and M.G.O'Connell (13).

Close: 1st day – A(1) 353-5 (Simpson 54, Rixon 8); 2nd – I(1) 131-3 (Viswanath 79, Vengsarkar 26); 3rd – A(2) 103-3 (Toohey 9, Simpson 2); 4th – I(2) 101-2 (Amarnath 21, Viswanath 9); 5th – I(2) 362-6 (Kirmani 14, Ghavri 6).

PAKISTAN v ENGLAND 1977-78 (1st Test)

At Gaddafi Stadium, Lahore, on 14, 15, 16, 18, 19 December.
Toss: Pakistan.   Result: MATCH DRAWN.
Debuts: Pakistan – Abdul Qadir; England – G.A.Cope, B.C.Rose.

A contest of monumental tedium was enlivened by two serious crowd disturbances. Not until the penultimate session of the match were the two first innings completed at a scoring rate of 31 runs per hour. Mudassar Nazar, son of Nazar Mohammad who was on the field throughout *Test No. 356*, batted for 591 minutes and took 557 minutes to score the slowest hundred in all first-class cricket. Boycott threatened this dubious record when he batted 290 minutes for his fifty – 20 minutes longer than Mudassar. The latter's partnership of 180 with Haroon remains Pakistan's highest for the third wicket against England. Cope, who dismissed Qadir and Sarfraz with successive balls, was deprived of a hat-trick in his first Test when he had Iqbal Qasim given out, caught by Brearley at slip, off the next ball. The fielder, uncertain that the catch had carried, withdrew the appeal. Miller narrowly missed his first century in first-class cricket; he was to wait another 6½ years.

PAKISTAN

Mudassar Nazar	c and b Miller	114	c Taylor b Willis		26
Sadiq Mohammad	lbw b Miller	18	b Lever		1
Shafiq Ahmed	c Rose b Old	0	lbw b Willis		7
Haroon Rashid	c and b Lever	122	not out		45
Javed Miandad	c Taylor b Lever	71	not out		19
Wasim Raja	st Taylor b Cope	24			
Abdul Qadir	lbw b Cope	11			
*†Wasim Bari	c Cope b Miller	17			
Sarfraz Nawaz	b Cope	0			
Iqbal Qasim	not out	8			
Liaquat Ali	not out	0			
Extras	(B1, LB4, NB17)	22	(NB8)		8
Total	(9 wickets declared)	**407**	(3 wickets)		**106**

ENGLAND

G.Boycott	b Qasim	63
*J.M.Brearley	run out	23
B.C.Rose	lbw b Sarfraz	1
D.W.Randall	c Qasim b Liaquat	19
G.R.J.Roope	b Qasim	19
G.Miller	not out	98
C.M.Old	c Mudassar b Qasim	2
†R.W.Taylor	b Sarfraz	32
G.A.Cope	lbw b Sarfraz	0
J.K.Lever	c Wasim Bari b Sarfraz	0
R.G.D.Willis	c Qasim b Qadir	14
Extras	(B2, LB8, NB7)	17
Total		**288**

ENGLAND	O	M	R	W		O	M	R	W				
Willis	17	3	67	0		7	0	34	2		**FALL OF WICKETS**		
Lever	16	1	47	2		3	0	13	1		P	E	P
Old	21	7	63	1	(4)	4	0	18	0	*Wkt*	*1st*	*1st*	*2nd*
Miller	37	10	102	3	(3)	10	4	24	0	1st	48	53	15
Cope	39	6	102	3		3	0	7	0	2nd	49	55	40
Boycott	3	0	4	0						3rd	229	96	45
Randall					(6)	1	0	2	0	4th	329	127	–
										5th	356	148	–
PAKISTAN										6th	378	162	–
Sarfraz	34	11	68	4						7th	387	251	–
Liaquat	27	11	43	1						8th	387	251	–
Qadir	32.7	7	82	1						9th	403	253	–
Qasim	32	12	57	3						10th	–	288	–
Wasim Raja	10	2	21	0									

Umpires: Amanullah Khan (5) and Mohammad Aslam Khokhar (3).

Close: 1st day – P(1) 164-2 (Mudassar 52, Haroon 84); 2nd – P(1) 360-5 (Wasim Raja 12, Qadir 1); 3rd – E(1) 85-2 (Boycott 38, Randall 17); 4th – E(1) 245-6 (Miller 71, Taylor 32).

PAKISTAN v ENGLAND 1977-78 (2nd Test)

At Niaz Stadium, Hyderabad, on 2, 3, 4, 6, 7 January.
Toss: Pakistan.   Result: MATCH DRAWN.
Debuts: None.

Haroon reached his hundred with his sixth six; it was his second century in successive Tests. Brearley claimed the optional last half-hour of the match to allow Boycott to complete his 15th hundred in official Tests. England were dismissed for their lowest total in Pakistan until 1983-84 (*Test No. 978*). Qadir returned Pakistan's best analysis against England until 1982 (*Test No. 931*).

PAKISTAN

Mudassar Nazar	c Edmonds b Cope	27		c Taylor b Willis	66
Sadiq Mohammad	c Taylor b Willis	9		c Edmonds b Cope	22
Shafiq Ahmed	c Miller b Edmonds	13	(6)	not out	27
Haroon Rashid	c and b Edmonds	108		c Brearley b Cope	35
Javed Miandad	not out	88		not out	61
Wasim Raja	c Brearley b Edmonds	0	(3)	c Edmonds b Willis	24
Abdul Qadir	c Brearley b Cope	4			
*†Wasim Bari	run out	10			
Iqbal Qasim	c Roope b Willis	0			
Liaquat Ali	c Edmonds b Lever	0			
Sikander Bakht	run out	3			
Extras	(B4, LB7, NB2)	13		(B13, LB11)	24
Total		**275**		**(4 wickets declared)**	**259**

ENGLAND

G.Boycott	run out	79	(2)	not out	100
*J.M.Brearley	c Wasim Bari b Qasim	17	(1)	c sub (Hasan Jamil) b Wasim Raja	74
B.C.Rose	b Qadir	27			
D.W.Randall	c and b Qadir	7			
G.R.J.Roope	c and b Qadir	1			
G.Miller	c Wasim Bari b Qasim	5			
†R.W.Taylor	b Qadir	0			
P.H.Edmonds	c Wasim Bari b Qadir	4			
G.A.Cope	c Sadiq b Wasim Raja	22			
J.K.Lever	b Qadir	4	(3)	not out	0
R.G.D.Willis	not out	8			
Extras	(B10, LB6, W1)	17		(B4, LB7, NB1)	12
Total		**191**		**(1 wicket)**	**186**

ENGLAND	O	M	R	W	O	M	R	W		FALL OF WICKETS			
Willis	16	2	40	2	11	2	26	2		P	E	P	E
Lever	16.6	7	41	1	20	2	62	0	Wkt	1st	1st	2nd	2nd
Edmonds	24	2	75	3	30	6	95	0	1st	14	40	55	185
Cope	14	6	49	2	24	9	42	2	2nd	40	123	116	–
Miller	9	0	57	0	2	0	8	0	3rd	101	137	117	–
Roope					1	0	2	0	4th	213	139	189	–
									5th	213	142	–	–
									6th	222	142	–	–
PAKISTAN									7th	247	146	–	–
Sikander	16	4	35	0	(6) 10	3	22	0	8th	248	152	–	–
Liaquat	6	0	18	0	(1) 4	1	14	0	9th	249	157	–	–
Qasim	34	11	54	2	24.4	6	42	0	10th	275	191	–	–
Miandad	5	0	21	0	(5) 4	0	10	0					
Qadir	24	8	44	6	(2) 27	5	72	0					
Wasim Raja	1.6	0	2	1	(4) 12	5	14	1					

Umpires: Mahboob Shah (2) and Shujauddin (20).

Close: 1st day – P(1) 220-5 (Miandad 48, Qadir 4); 2nd – E(1) 123-2 (Boycott 71); 3rd – P(2) 55-1 (Mudassar 32); 4th – E(2) 10-0 (Boycott 3, Brearley 7).

PAKISTAN v ENGLAND 1977-78 (3rd Test)

At National Stadium, Karachi, on 18, 19, 20, 22, 23 January.
Toss: England.   Result: MATCH DRAWN.
Debuts: Pakistan – Mohsin Khan; England – M.W.Gatting.

The sides achieved their eleventh successive draw in Pakistan. Edmonds returned the best innings analysis for England in Pakistan. The six 'lbw' decisions in England's first innings equalled the Test record. For the first time in 90 Tests Pakistan were without at least one of the Mohammad brethren. Javed Miandad kept wicket when Wasim Bari bowled. Only 108 runs were scored on the final day, shortened to 4½ hours when play was aborted an hour prematurely. Boycott took over the captaincy for the remainder of the tour after Brearley's left arm (ulna) had been fractured by a ball from Sikander Bakht in a one-day match. Boycott thus led England for the first time in his 69th Test.

ENGLAND

*G.Boycott	b Qasim	31	c Miandad b Sikander		56
B.C.Rose	c Miandad b Sarfraz	10	c Haroon b Qadir		18
D.W.Randall	lbw b Qasim	23	b Sikander		55
G.R.J.Roope	lbw b Sikander	56	not out		33
M.W.Gatting	lbw b Qadir	5	lbw b Qasim		6
G.Miller	c Mudassar b Wasim Raja	11	c Wasim Bari b Qasim		3
†R.W.Taylor	lbw b Qadir	36	not out		18
P.H.Edmonds	lbw b Qadir	6			
G.A.Cope	b Qasim	18			
J.K.Lever	not out	33			
R.G.D.Willis	lbw b Qadir	5			
Extras	(B3, LB21, NB8)	32	(B9, LB6, W3, NB15)		33
Total		**266**	(5 wickets)		**222**

PAKISTAN

Mudassar Nazar	c sub (I.T.Botham) b Edmonds	76
Shafiq Ahmed	c sub (I.T.Botham) b Willis	10
Mohsin Khan	c Willis b Cope	44
Haroon Rashid	c Taylor b Edmonds	27
Javed Miandad	c Roope b Edmonds	23
Wasim Raja	c Gatting b Edmonds	47
Abdul Qadir	c Roope b Edmonds	21
*†Wasim Bari	lbw b Miller	6
Sarfraz Nawaz	c Gatting b Edmonds	0
Iqbal Qasim	b Edmonds	8
Sikander Bakht	not out	7
Extras	(B2, LB3, NB7)	12
Total		**281**

PAKISTAN	O	M	R	W	O	M	R	W		FALL OF WICKETS		
Sarfraz	15	6	27	1	28	7	57	0		E	P	E
Sikander	15	4	39	1	17	4	40	2	*Wkt*	*1st*	*1st*	*2nd*
Qasim	40	20	56	3	29	11	51	2	1st	17	33	35
Qadir	40.1	9	81	4	8	2	26	1	2nd	69	121	125
Wasim Raja	13	3	31	1					3rd	72	167	148
Mudassar					(5) 1	0	1	0	4th	85	170	162
Miandad					(6) 2	0	5	0	5th	107	230	171
Shafiq					(7) 1	0	1	0	6th	189	243	–
Wasim Bari					(8) 1	0	2	0	7th	197	263	–
Haroon					(9) 1	0	3	0	8th	203	263	–
Mohsin					(10) 1	0	3	0	9th	232	269	–
									10th	266	281	–

ENGLAND				
Willis	8	1	23	1
Lever	12	4	32	0
Edmonds	33	7	66	7
Cope	28	8	77	1
Miller	14	0	71	1

Umpires: Amanullah Khan (6) and Shakoor Rana (4).

Close: 1st day – E(1) 152-5 (Roope 40, Taylor 17); 2nd – P(1) 54-1 (Mudassar 24, Mohsin 13); 3rd – P(1) 230-5 (Wasim Raja 38); 4th – E(2) 114-1 (Boycott 48, Randall 37).

NEW ZEALAND v ENGLAND 1977-78 (1st Test)

At Basin Reserve, Wellington, on 10, 11, 12, 14, 15 February.
Toss: England.   Result: NEW ZEALAND won by 72 runs.
Debuts: New Zealand – S.L.Boock, J.G.Wright.

New Zealand beat England for the first time in 48 matches dating back to 1929-30. England's total of 64 was their lowest since 1948 and their lowest against all countries except Australia. Collinge took his 100th wicket in 32 Tests. Hadlee (10 for 100) achieved New Zealand's best match analysis in this series until 1994. Wright survived a strong appeal for a catch by Taylor off the first ball of the match and batted throughout his first day of Test cricket (reduced by rain and light to 340 minutes). Boycott scored 77 in 442 minutes. Rose (4) retired with a bruised right arm at 14 in the second innings, and resumed at 63. Played in gale force winds, this was Wellington's last Test for three years while the ground was redeveloped and the pitch moved 30 degrees.

NEW ZEALAND

J.G.Wright	lbw b Botham	55	c Roope b Willis		19
R.W.Anderson	c Taylor b Old	28	lbw b Old		26
G.P.Howarth	c Botham b Old	13	c Edmonds b Willis		21
*M.G.Burgess	b Willis	9	c Boycott b Botham		6
B.E.Congdon	c Taylor b Old	44	c Roope b Willis		0
J.M.Parker	c Rose b Willis	16	c Edmonds b Willis		4
†W.K.Lees	c Taylor b Old	1	lbw b Hendrick		11
R.J.Hadlee	not out	27	c Boycott b Willis		2
D.R.Hadlee	c Taylor b Old	1	c Roope b Botham		2
R.O.Collinge	b Old	1	c Edmonds b Hendrick		6
S.L.Boock	b Botham	4	not out		0
Extras	(B12, LB3, W1, NB13)	29	(B2, LB9, W2, NB13)		26
Total		**228**			**123**

ENGLAND

B.C.Rose	c Lees b Collinge	21	not out		5
*G.Boycott	c Congdon b Collinge	77	b Collinge		1
G.Miller	b Boock	24	c Anderson b Collinge		4
†R.W.Taylor	c and b Collinge	8	(7) run out		0
D.W.Randall	c Burgess b R.J.Hadlee	4	(4) lbw b Collinge		9
G.R.J.Roope	c Lees b R.J.Hadlee	37	(5) c Lees b R.J.Hadlee		0
I.T.Botham	c Burgess b R.J.Hadlee	7	(6) c Boock b R.J.Hadlee		19
C.M.Old	b R.J.Hadlee	10	lbw b R.J.Hadlee		9
P.H.Edmonds	lbw b Congdon	4	c Parker b R.J.Hadlee		11
M.Hendrick	lbw b Congdon	0	c Parker b R.J.Hadlee		0
R.G.D.Willis	not out	6	c Howarth b R.J.Hadlee		3
Extras	(LB4, NB13)	17	(NB3)		3
Total		**215**			**64**

ENLAND	O	M	R	W	O	M	R	W		FALL OF WICKETS			
										NZ	E	NZ	E
Willis	25	7	65	2	15	2	32	5	*Wkt*	*1st*	*1st*	*2nd*	*2nd*
Hendrick	17	2	46	0	10	2	16	2	1st	42	39	54	2
Old	30	11	54	6	9	2	32	1	2nd	96	89	82	8
Edmonds	3	1	7	0	1	0	4	0	3rd	114	108	93	18
Botham	12.6	2	27	2	9.3	3	13	2	4th	152	126	93	18
									5th	191	183	98	38
NEW ZEALAND									6th	193	188	99	38
R.J.Hadlee	28	5	74	4	13.3	4	26	6	7th	194	203	104	53
Collinge	18	5	42	3	13	5	35	3	8th	196	205	116	53
D.R.Hadlee	21	5	47	0	1	1	0	0	9th	208	206	123	63
Boock	10	5	21	1					10th	228	215	123	64
Congdon	17.4	11	14	2									

Umpires: W.R.C.Gardiner (7) and R.L.Monteith (4).

Close: 1st day – NZ(1) 152-3 (Wright 55, Congdon 26); 2nd – E(1) 89-2 (Boycott 36, Taylor 0); 3rd – NZ(2) 12-0 (Wright 0, Anderson 2); 4th – E(2) 53-8 (Edmonds 6, Willis 0).

NEW ZEALAND v ENGLAND 1977-78 (2nd Test)

At Lancaster Park, Christchurch, on 24, 25, 26, 28 February, 1 March.
Toss: England.   Result: ENGLAND won by 174 runs.
Debuts: England – C.T.Radley.

Botham became the second England player after A.W.Greig (*Test No. 733*) to score a hundred and take five wickets in an innings of the same Test. His first Test century included a six and 12 fours and took 312 minutes. Miller (31) retired hurt at 103 after being hit on the side of the face hooking a short ball from Collinge; he returned at 288. Edmonds completed his maiden Test fifty off 68 balls. Randall was run out backing up by the bowler, Chatfield, who, without warning or reaching his delivery stride, broke the wicket underarm. This was only the third such instance in Test cricket and the first involving either of these countries. Burgess retired at 18 after offering no stroke to a ball from Willis that struck his left elbow, and resumed at 95. Willis took four of the first five second-innings wickets for nine runs in 5.5 overs.

ENGLAND

B.C.Rose	c Howarth b Chatfield	11	(2)	c Lees b Collinge	7
*G.Boycott	lbw b Collinge	8	(1)	run out	26
D.W.Randall	c Burgess b Hadlee	0		run out	13
G.R.J.Roope	c Burgess b Hadlee	50	(6)	not out	9
G.Miller	c Congdon b Collinge	89			
C.T.Radley	c Lees b Hadlee	15			
I.T.Botham	c Lees b Boock	103	(4)	not out	30
†R.W.Taylor	run out	45			
C.M.Old	b Hadlee	8	(5)	b Collinge	1
P.H.Edmonds	c Lees b Collinge	50			
R.G.D.Willis	not out	6			
Extras	(B14, LB9, NB10)	33		(B4, LB3, NB3)	10
Total		418		(4 wickets declared)	96

NEW ZEALAND

J.G.Wright	c and b Edmonds	4	c Roope b Willis	0
R.W.Anderson	b Edmonds	62	b Willis	15
G.P.Howarth	c Edmonds b Willis	5	c Edmonds b Old	1
*M.G.Burgess	c Roope b Botham	29	not out	6
B.E.Congdon	lbw b Botham	20	c Botham b Willis	0
J.M.Parker	not out	53	c Botham b Edmonds	16
†W.K.Lees	c Miller b Botham	0	b Willis	0
R.J.Hadlee	b Edmonds	1	c Botham b Edmonds	39
R.O.Collinge	c Edmonds b Botham	32	c Miller b Botham	0
S.L.Boock	c Taylor b Edmonds	2	c Taylor b Botham	0
E.J.Chatfield	c Edmonds b Botham	3	lbw b Botham	6
Extras	(B4, LB1, NB19)	24	(LB6, NB16)	22
Total		235		105

NEW ZEALAND	O	M	R	W	O	M	R	W		FALL OF WICKETS			
Hadlee	43	10	147	4	6	1	17	0		E	NZ	E	NZ
Collinge	26.5	6	89	3	9	2	29	2	*Wkt*	*1st*	*1st*	*2nd*	*2nd*
Chatfield	37	8	94	1	5	0	22	0	1st	15	37	25	2
Congdon	18	11	14	0	2	0	18	0	2nd	18	52	47	14
Boock	21	11	41	1					3rd	26	82	67	19
									4th	127	119	74	25
ENGLAND									5th	128	148	–	25
Willis	20	5	45	1	7	2	14	4	6th	288	151	–	59
Old	14	4	55	0	7	4	9	1	7th	294	153	–	81
Botham	24.7	6	73	5	7	1	38	3	8th	305	211	–	90
Edmonds	34	11	38	4	6	2	22	2	9th	375	216	–	95
									10th	418	235	–	105

Umpires: F.R.Goodall (6) and R.L.Monteith (5).

Close: 1st day – E(1) 172-5 (Botham 22, Taylor 18); 2nd – E(1) 394-9 (Miller 66, Willis 5); 3rd – NZ(1) 122-4 (Burgess 16, Parker 0); 4th – E(2) 96-4 (Botham 30, Roope 9).

NEW ZEALAND v ENGLAND 1977-78 (3rd Test)

At Eden Park, Auckland, on 4, 5, 6, 8, 9, 10 March.
Toss: New Zealand.   Result: MATCH DRAWN.
Debuts: None.

Howarth, whose first hundred took 455 minutes (307 balls), was the second New Zealand batsman after G.M.Turner (*Test No. 737*) to score two separate centuries in a Test. Radley, in his second Test, scored the slowest 150 on record until 1988-89 (594 minutes, 484 balls) and the (then) fourth-slowest Test century (487 minutes, 397 balls). In all, he batted for 648 minutes and hit 15 fours. Collinge overtook B.R.Taylor's aggregate of 111 to become New Zealand's leading wicket-taker when he dismissed Botham. Willis led England on the last two days after a contact lens had scratched Boycott's right cornea.

NEW ZEALAND

J.G.Wright	c Taylor b Lever	4		c Taylor b Edmonds	25
R.W.Anderson	c Gatting b Botham	17		c Botham b Miller	55
G.P.Howarth	c Roope b Willis	122		b Miller	102
*M.G.Burgess	c Randall b Botham	50		c Taylor b Edmonds	17
B.E.Congdon	c Miller b Botham	5		c Roope b Lever	20
J.M.Parker	lbw b Botham	14	(7)	not out	47
†G.N.Edwards	lbw b Lever	55	(6)	c Randall b Lever	54
R.J.Hadlee	c Roope b Botham	1		b Miller	10
B.L.Cairns	b Lever	11		lbw b Edmonds	20
R.O.Collinge	not out	5		not out	12
S.L.Boock	c Edmonds b Willis	1			
Extras	(B5, LB10, NB15)	30		(B6, LB4, NB10)	20
Total		**315**		(8 wickets)	**382**

ENGLAND

*G.Boycott	c Burgess b Collinge	54
D.W.Randall	lbw b Hadlee	30
C.T.Radley	c Wright b Collinge	158
G.R.J.Roope	c Burgess b Boock	68
M.W.Gatting	b Boock	0
I.T.Botham	c Edwards b Collinge	53
†R.W.Taylor	b Boock	16
G.Miller	lbw b Collinge	15
P.H.Edmonds	b Boock	8
J.K.Lever	c and b Boock	1
R.G.D.Willis	not out	0
Extras	(B6, LB6, W4, NB10)	26
Total		**429**

ENGLAND	O	M	R	W	O	M	R	W		FALL OF WICKETS		
										NZ	E	NZ
Willis	26.6	8	57	2	10	3	42	0	*Wkt*	*1st*	*1st*	*2nd*
Lever	34	5	96	3	17	4	59	2	1st	12	52	69
Botham	34	4	109	5	13	1	51	0	2nd	32	115	98
Edmonds	10	2	23	0	45	15	107	3	3rd	113	254	125
Miller	1	1	0	0	30	10	99	3	4th	129	258	185
Gatting					1	0	1	0	5th	182	355	272
Roope					1	0	2	0	6th	278	396	287
Randall					1	0	1	0	7th	285	418	305
									8th	302	427	350
NEW ZEALAND									9th	314	428	–
Hadlee	31	6	107	1					10th	315	429	–
Collinge	38	9	98	4								
Cairns	33	9	63	0								
Congdon	26	8	68	0								
Boock	28.3	4	67	5								

Umpires: W.R.C.Gardiner (8) and J.B.R.Hastie (2).

Close: 1st day – NZ(1) 162-4 (Howarth 64, Parker 7); 2nd – E(1) 30-0 (Boycott 6, Randall 21); 3rd – E(1) 172-2 (Radley 49, Roope 28); 4th – E(1) 390-5 (Radley 154, Taylor 6); 5th – NZ(2) 112-2 (Howarth 20, Burgess 7).

WEST INDIES v AUSTRALIA 1977-78 (1st Test)

At Queen's Park Oval, Port-of-Spain, Trinidad, on 3, 4, 5 March.
Toss: West Indies.   Result: WEST INDIES won by an innings and 106 runs.
Debuts: West Indies – R.A.Austin, D.L.Haynes, D.R.Parry; Australia – J.D.Higgs.

West Indies, who retained their World Series cricketers, beat Australia in Trinidad for the first time and with more than two days to spare. Australia's first innings total of 90 was the lowest in any Test at Port-of-Spain until 1993-94 and remains their lowest in the Caribbean. Only one over was possible before the first lunch interval. Its second ball removed a large divot; the third grubbed second bounce past the wicket-keeper. Toohey (15) retired at 37 for three stitches in a cut over the right eye, sustained when he missed a hook at a ball from Roberts. He returned at 84 only to have his thumb fractured by the same bowler. In the second innings, Australia's last six wickets fell for 15 runs in the course of 26 balls.

AUSTRALIA

G.M.Wood	c Haynes b Croft	2		lbw b Roberts	32
C.S.Serjeant	c Murray b Croft	3		lbw b Garner	40
G.N.Yallop	c Richards b Croft	2		b Roberts	81
P.M.Toohey	b Garner	20		absent hurt	–
*R.B.Simpson	lbw b Garner	0		b Parry	14
G.J.Cosier	c Greenidge b Croft	46	(4)	lbw b Garner	19
†S.J.Rixon	run out	1	(6)	lbw b Roberts	0
B.Yardley	c Murray b Roberts	2	(7)	not out	7
J.R.Thomson	c Austin b Roberts	0	(8)	b Parry	4
W.M.Clark	b Garner	0	(9)	b Roberts	0
J.D.Higgs	not out	0	(10)	b Roberts	2
Extras	(B4, LB6, NB4)	14		(B6, LB1, W1, NB2)	10
Total		**90**			**209**

WEST INDIES

C.G.Greenidge	b Yardley	43
D.L.Haynes	c Rixon b Higgs	61
I.V.A.Richards	lbw b Thomson	39
A.I.Kallicharran	b Yardley	127
*C.H.Lloyd	b Thomson	86
R.A.Austin	c sub (T.J.Laughlin) b Thomson	2
†D.L.Murray	c Rixon b Higgs	21
D.R.Parry	b Yardley	0
A.M.E.Roberts	st Rixon b Higgs	7
J.Garner	c Cosier b Higgs	0
C.E.H.Croft	not out	4
Extras	(LB9, NB6)	15
Total		**405**

WEST INDIES	O	M	R	W	O	M	R	W		FALL OF WICKETS		
Roberts	12	4	26	2	16.3	3	56	5		A	WI	A
Croft	9.1	5	15	4	13	1	55	0	*Wkt*	*1st*	*1st*	*2nd*
Garner	15	7	35	3	17	5	39	2	1st	7	87	59
Parry					17	1	49	2	2nd	10	143	90
									3rd	16	143	149
AUSTRALIA									4th	23	313	194
Thomson	21	6	84	3					5th	45	324	194
Clark	16	3	41	0					6th	75	385	194
Higgs	24.5	3	91	4					7th	75	385	200
Simpson	16	2	65	0					8th	84	391	201
Yardley	19	1	64	3					9th	90	391	209
Cosier	13	2	45	0					10th	90	405	–

Umpires: R.Gosein (21) and D.Sang Hue (28).

Close: 1st day – WI(1) 79-0 (Greenidge 26, Haynes 53); 2nd – WI(1) 391-9 (Roberts 2, Croft 0).

WEST INDIES v AUSTRALIA 1977-78 (2nd Test)

At Kensington Oval, Bridgetown, Barbados, on 17, 18, 19 March.
Toss: West Indies.   Result: WEST INDIES won by nine wickets.
Debuts: None.

West Indies beat Australia at Bridgetown for the first time and completed their second successive victory inside three days. Yallop was the first batsman to wear a helmet in an official Test match.

AUSTRALIA

W.M.Darling	c Richards b Croft	4		c Murray b Croft	8
G.M.Wood	lbw b Croft	69		run out	56
G.N.Yallop	c Austin b Croft	47		c Lloyd b Garner	14
C.S.Serjeant	c Murray b Parry	4		c Murray b Roberts	2
*R.B.Simpson	c Murray b Croft	9	(7)	c Murray b Roberts	17
G.J.Cosier	c Murray b Roberts	1	(5)	c Croft b Roberts	8
†S.J.Rixon	lbw b Garner	16	(6)	c Lloyd b Roberts	0
B.Yardley	b Garner	74		b Garner	43
J.R.Thomson	b Garner	12		c Richards b Garner	11
W.M.Clark	b Garner	0		lbw b Garner	0
J.D.Higgs	not out	4		not out	0
Extras	(B3, LB4, NB3)	10		(B1, LB8, NB10)	19
Total		**250**			**178**

WEST INDIES

C.G.Greenidge	c Cosier b Thomson	8		not out	80
D.L.Haynes	c Rixon b Higgs	66		c Yardley b Higgs	55
I.V.A.Richards	c Clark b Thomson	23			
A.I.Kallicharran	c Yardley b Thomson	8			
*C.H.Lloyd	c Serjeant b Clark	42			
R.A.Austin	c Serjeant b Clark	20			
†D.L.Murray	c Darling b Thomson	60			
D.R.Parry	c Serjeant b Simpson	27	(3)	not out	3
A.M.E.Roberts	lbw b Thomson	4			
J.Garner	not out	5			
C.E.H.Croft	lbw b Thomson	3			
Extras	(LB3, NB19)	22		(LB2, W1)	3
Total		**288**		(1 wicket)	**141**

WEST INDIES	O	M	R	W	O	M	R	W	FALL OF WICKETS				
Roberts	18	2	79	1	18	5	50	4		A	WI	A	WI
Croft	18	3	47	4	15	4	53	1	Wkt	1st	1st	2nd	2nd
Garner	16.1	2	65	4	15	3	56	4	1st	13	16	21	131
Parry	12	4	44	1					2nd	105	56	62	–
Austin	1	0	5	0					3rd	116	71	69	–
									4th	134	154	80	–
									5th	135	172	95	–
AUSTRALIA									6th	149	198	99	–
Thomson	13	1	77	6	6	1	22	0	7th	161	263	154	–
Clark	24	3	77	2	7	0	27	0	8th	216	269	167	–
Cosier	9	4	24	0					9th	216	282	173	–
Higgs	16	4	46	1	(3) 13	4	34	1	10th	250	288	178	–
Simpson	7	1	30	1									
Yardley	2	0	12	0	(4) 10.5	2	55	0					

Umpires: R.Gosein (22) and S.E.Parris (3).

Close: 1st day – WI(1) 71-3 (Haynes 21); 2nd – A(2) 96-5 (Wood 55, Simpson 0).

WEST INDIES v AUSTRALIA 1977-78 (3rd Test)

At Bourda, Georgetown, Guyana, on 31 March, 1, 2, 4, 5 April.
Toss: West Indies.   Result: AUSTRALIA won by three wickets.
Debuts: West Indies – S.T.Clarke, A.E.Greenidge, D.A.Murray, N.Phillip, S.Shivnarine,
A.B.Williams; Australia – T.J.Laughlin.

A pre-match dispute between the West Indies Board of Control and their captain, C.H.Lloyd, over team selection resulted in all the World Series cricketers withdrawing from the team. Australia's 362 for 7 remains the third-highest total to win any Test. Williams was the tenth to score a hundred in his first Test for West Indies; he batted for 166 minutes, faced 118 balls and hit 19 fours.

WEST INDIES

A.E.Greenidge	lbw b Thomson	56		b Clark	11
A.B.Williams	lbw b Clark	10		c Serjeant b Clark	100
H.A.Gomes	b Clark	4	(5)	c Simpson b Yardley	101
*A.I.Kallicharran	b Thomson	0	(6)	b Yardley	22
I.T.Shillingford	c Clark b Laughlin	3	(7)	c and b Thomson	16
†D.A.Murray	c Ogilvie b Clark	21	(3)	lbw b Simpson	16
S.Shivnarine	c Rixon b Thomson	53	(8)	b Cosier	63
N.Phillip	c Yardley b Simpson	15	(9)	st Rixon b Yardley	4
V.A.Holder	c Laughlin b Clark	1	(10)	lbw b Clark	31
D.R.Parry	not out	21	(4)	lbw b Clark	51
S.T.Clarke	b Thomson	6		not out	5
Extras	(LB2, NB13)	15		(B4, LB5, NB10)	19
Total		**205**			**439**

AUSTRALIA

W.M.Darling	c Greenidge b Phillip	15		c Williams b Clarke	0
G.M.Wood	lbw b Holder	50		run out	126
A.D.Ogilvie	c and b Phillip	4		lbw b Clarke	0
G.J.Cosier	lbw b Clarke	9	(6)	b Phillip	0
C.S.Serjeant	b Clarke	0		c sub (S.F.A.F.Bacchus) b Phillip	124
*R.B.Simpson	run out	67	(4)	c Murray b Clarke	4
T.J.Laughlin	c Greenidge b Parry	21	(8)	c and b Parry	24
†S.J.Rixon	c Holder b Phillip	54	(7)	not out	39
B.Yardley	b Clarke	33		not out	15
J.R.Thomson	c and b Phillip	3			
W.M.Clark	not out	2			
Extras	(LB12, W1, NB15)	28		(B8, LB4, W2, NB16)	30
Total		**286**		(7 wickets)	**362**

AUSTRALIA	O	M	R	W		O	M	R	W		FALL OF WICKETS			
											WI	A	WI	A
Thomson	16.2	1	57	4		20	2	83	1	*Wkt*	*1st*	*1st*	*2nd*	*2nd*
Clark	24	6	64	4		34.4	4	124	4	1st	31	28	36	11
Laughlin	10	4	34	1	(6) 7	1	33	0		2nd	36	36	95	13
Cosier	2	1	1	0	(5) 6	1	14	1		3rd	48	77	172	22
Simpson	8	1	34	1	(4) 19	4	70	1		4th	77	85	199	273
Yardley					(3) 30	6	96	3		5th	84	90	249	279
										6th	130	142	285	290
WEST INDIES										7th	165	237	355	338
Phillip	18	0	76	4	(2) 19	2	65	2		8th	166	256	369	–
Holder	17	1	40	1	(3) 20	3	55	0		9th	193	268	431	–
Clarke	22	3	57	3	(1) 27	5	83	3		10th	205	286	439	–
Gomes	3	0	8	0										
Parry	15	2	39	1	(4) 17	1	61	1						
Shivnarine	8	0	38	0	(5) 18	2	68	0						

Umpires: R.Gosein (23) and C.F.Vyfhuis (5).

Close: 1st day – A(1) 68-2 (Wood 31, Cosier 9); 2nd – WI(2) 98-2 (Williams 60, Parry 2); 3rd – WI(2) 439 all out; 4th – A(2) 290-6 (Rixon 9).

WEST INDIES v AUSTRALIA 1977-78 (4th Test)

At Queen's Park Oval, Port-of-Spain, Trinidad, on 15, 16, 17, 18 April.
Toss: Australia.   Result: WEST INDIES won by 198 runs.
Debuts: West Indies – S.F.A.F.Bacchus.

This win, with over a day to spare, gave West Indies victory and the Frank Worrell Trophy for only the second time in five rubbers. A boycott of the match, organised by a group in protest against the West Indies Board's schism with the World Series players, reduced attendances to under 5,000 each day. Holder achieved the best analysis of his 40-match Test career. In the final innings, Australia's last nine wickets fell for 52 runs as Parry's off-breaks claimed five wickets for six runs in 24 balls.

WEST INDIES

A.E.Greenidge	c Wood b Clark	6	c Thomson b Yardley	69
A.B.Williams	c Yallop b Higgs	87	c Yallop b Simpson	24
†D.A.Murray	c Wood b Yardley	4	lbw b Clark	4
H.A.Gomes	c Simpson b Clark	30	c Simpson b Higgs	14
*A.I.Kallicharran	c Yallop b Clark	92	c and b Clark	27
S.F.A.F.Bacchus	b Higgs	9	c Wood b Yardley	7
S.Shivnarine	c Simpson b Thomson	10	c Serjeant b Simpson	11
D.R.Parry	st Rixon b Higgs	22	c Serjeant b Yardley	65
N.Phillip	c Rixon b Thomson	3	c Wood b Yardley	46
V.A.Holder	b Thomson	7	b Simpson	0
R.R.Jumadeen	not out	0	not out	2
Extras	(B7, LB1, W2, NB12)	22	(B1, LB13, NB7)	21
Total		292		290

AUSTRALIA

G.M.Wood	c Murray b Phillip	16	lbw b Holder	17
W.M.Darling	c Jumadeen b Holder	10	b Phillip	6
P.M.Toohey	c Williams b Parry	40	c Bacchus b Jumadeen	17
G.N.Yallop	c Murray b Jumadeen	75	c Kallicharran b Parry	18
C.S.Serjeant	st Murray b Jumadeen	49	c Bacchus b Jumadeen	4
*R.B.Simpson	lbw b Holder	36	lbw b Jumadeen	6
†S.J.Rixon	c Murray b Holder	21	not out	13
B.Yardley	c Williams b Holder	22	b Parry	3
J.R.Thomson	b Holder	0	b Parry	1
W.M.Clark	b Holder	4	b Parry	0
J.D.Higgs	not out	0	b Parry	4
Extras	(B4, LB2, NB11)	17	(LB2, NB3)	5
Total		290		94

AUSTRALIA	O	M	R	W	O	M	R	W	FALL OF WICKETS			
Thomson	23	8	64	3	15	1	76	0		WI	A	WI	A
Clark	24	6	65	3	21	4	62	2	*Wkt*	*1st*	*1st*	*2nd*	*2nd*
Yardley	18	5	48	1	(5) 30.2	15	40	4	1st	7	23	36	9
Higgs	16.5	2	53	3	21	7	46	1	2nd	16	43	51	42
Simpson	15	4	40	0	(3) 14	2	45	3	3rd	111	92	79	44
									4th	166	193	134	60
WEST INDIES									5th	185	204	151	72
Phillip	17	0	73	1	7	0	24	1	6th	242	254	151	76
Holder	13	4	28	6	11	3	16	1	7th	258	275	204	80
Jumadeen	24	6	83	2	15	3	34	3	8th	262	275	273	86
Parry	30	5	77	1	10.4	4	15	5	9th	291	289	280	88
Shivnarine	6	1	12	0					10th	292	290	290	94

Umpires: R.Gosein (24) and C.F.Vyfhuis (6).

Close: 1st day – WI(1) 283-8 (Parry 22, Holder 2); 2nd – A(1) 290 all out; 3rd – WI(2) 280-9 (Phillip 39, Jumadeen 0).

WEST INDIES v AUSTRALIA 1977-78 (5th Test)

At Sabina Park, Kingston, Jamaica, on 28, 29, 30 April, 2, 3 May.
Toss: Australia.   Result: MATCH DRAWN.
Debuts: None.

Australia were denied a probable victory when spectators rioted and invaded the field after Holder had been given out 12 minutes before the close of the fifth day's play. Although 38 balls of the mandatory last 20 overs remained, attempts to complete the match on the following day were thwarted by the refusal of umpire Gosein to officiate. He cited playing conditions for the rubber which made no provision for the match to be extended unless 'in excess of one hour's play' had been lost to circumstances other than acts of God. Although umpire Malcolm was prepared to stand, no other willing official of first-class status was available. Toohey batted for 316 minutes for his only Test hundred before providing Holder with his 100th wicket in 34 matches.

AUSTRALIA

G.M.Wood	c Parry b Phillip	16	(2)	c Bacchus b Jumadeen	90
A.D.Ogilvie	c Shivnarine b Holder	0	(1)	st Murray b Parry	43
P.M.Toohey	c Williams b Holder	122		st Murray b Jumadeen	97
G.N.Yallop	c sub (H.G.Gordon) b Shivnarine	57		not out	23
C.S.Serjeant	b Holder	26		not out	32
*R.B.Simpson	c Murray b Foster	46			
T.J.Laughlin	c sub (H.G.Gordon) b Jumadeen	35			
†S.J.Rixon	not out	13			
B.Yardley	b Jumadeen	7			
J.R.Thomson	c Murray b Jumadeen	4			
J.D.Higgs	c Foster b Jumadeen	0			
Extras	(LB5, W1, NB11)	17		(B5, LB8, NB7)	20
Total		**343**		(3 wickets declared)	**305**

WEST INDIES

A.B.Williams	c Serjeant b Laughlin	17		c Wood b Yardley	19
S.F.A.F.Bacchus	c Yardley b Thomson	5		c Simpson b Thomson	21
†D.A.Murray	c Wood b Laughlin	12	(6)	b Yardley	10
H.A.Gomes	b Thomson	115	(3)	c Rixon b Higgs	1
*A.I.Kallicharran	c Ogilvie b Laughlin	6		lbw b Higgs	126
M.L.C.Foster	c Rixon b Laughlin	8	(4)	run out	5
S.Shivnarine	st Rixon b Higgs	53		c Yallop b Yardley	27
D.R.Parry	lbw b Higgs	4		c Serjeant b Yardley	0
N.Phillip	c Rixon b Simpson	26		not out	26
V.A.Holder	lbw b Laughlin	24		c Rixon b Higgs	6
R.R.Jumadeen	not out	4		not out	0
Extras	(LB1, NB5)	6		(B14, LB1, NB2)	17
Total		**280**		(9 wickets)	**258**

WEST INDIES	O	M	R	W	O	M	R	W	FALL OF WICKETS				
Phillip	32	5	90	1	17	1	64	0		A	WI	A	WI
Holder	31	8	68	3	18	2	41	0	*Wkt*	*1st*	*1st*	*2nd*	*2nd*
Parry	5	0	15	0	(4) 18	3	60	1	1st	0	13	65	42
Jumadeen	38.4	6	72	4	(3) 23	2	90	2	2nd	38	28	245	43
Foster	32	10	68	1	7	1	22	0	3rd	171	41	246	43
Shivnarine	9	2	13	1	3	1	8	0	4th	217	47	–	59
									5th	266	63	–	88
AUSTRALIA									6th	308	159	–	179
Thomson	22	4	61	2	15	1	53	1	7th	324	173	–	181
Laughlin	25.4	4	101	5	10	1	34	0	8th	335	219	–	242
Yardley	14	4	27	0	(4) 29	17	35	4	9th	343	276	–	258
Simpson	10	0	38	1	(5) 11	4	44	0	10th	343	280	–	–
Higgs	19	3	47	2	(3) 28.4	10	67	3					
Yallop					3	1	8	0					

Umpires: R.Gosein (25) and W.Malcolm (1).

Close: 1st day – A(1) 186-3 (Toohey 103, Serjeant 3); 2nd – WI(1) 30-2 (Murray 7, Gomes 0); 3rd – WI(1) 276-8 (Gomes 115, Holder 24); 4th – WI(2) 0-0 (Williams 0, Bacchus 0).

ENGLAND v PAKISTAN 1978 (1st Test)

At Edgbaston, Birmingham, on 1, 2, 3, 5 June.
Toss: Pakistan.   Result: ENGLAND won by an innings and 57 runs.
Debuts: England – D.I.Gower.

England won with a day and 75 minutes to spare. Old returned his best analysis in Tests and emulated the feat of M.J.C.Allom (*Test No. 186*) by taking the wickets of Wasim Raja, Wasim Bari, Iqbal Qasim and Sikander Bakht with five deliveries: WW no-ball WW.Radley and Botham scored hundreds in their first innings against Pakistan, Radley's being his second in successive Test innings. Gower scored four runs off his first ball in Test cricket (from Liaquat). Sarfraz strained a muscle under his ribs and retired after bowling two spells. After resisting for 42 minutes on the fourth morning, 'night-watchman' Iqbal Qasim was struck in the mouth by the first bouncer Willis bowled from round the wicket and retired at 123 for two stitches. A Pakistani spectator walked out to bat after his country's seventh second-innings wicket fell. This match launched Cornhill Insurance sponsorship of Test cricket in England.

PAKISTAN

Mudassar Nazar	c and b Botham	14		b Edmonds	30
Sadiq Mohammad	c Radley b Old	23		b Old	79
Mohsin Khan	b Willis	35	(4)	c Old b Miller	38
Javed Miandad	c Taylor b Old	15	(5)	c Brearley b Edmonds	39
Haroon Rashid	c Roope b Willis	3	(6)	b Willis	4
Wasim Raja	c Taylor b Old	17	(7)	b Edmonds	9
Sarfraz Nawaz	not out	32	(8)	not out	6
*†Wasim Bari	b Old	0	(9)	c Miller b Edmonds	3
Iqbal Qasim	c Taylor b Old	0	(3)	retired hurt	5
Sikander Bakht	c Roope b Old	0		c Roope b Miller	2
Liaquat Ali	c Brearley b Old	9		b Willis	3
Extras	(LB3, NB13)	16		(B4, LB4, W1, NB4)	13
Total		**164**			**231**

ENGLAND

*J.M.Brearley	run out	38
B.Wood	lbw b Sikander	14
C.T.Radley	lbw b Sikander	106
D.I.Gower	c Miandad b Sikander	58
G.R.J.Roope	b Sikander	32
G.Miller	c Wasim Bari b Mudassar	48
I.T.Botham	c Qasim b Liaquat	100
C.M.Old	c Mudassar b Qasim	5
P.H.Edmonds	not out	4
†R.W.Taylor	} did not bat	
R.G.D.Willis		
Extras	(LB26, W5, NB16)	47
Total	(8 wickets declared)	**452**

ENGLAND	O	M	R	W	O	M	R	W		FALL OF WICKETS		
Willis	16	2	42	2	23.4	3	70	2		P	E	P
Old	22.4	6	50	7	25	12	38	1	*Wkt*	*1st*	*1st*	*2nd*
Botham	15	4	52	1	17	3	47	0	1st	20	36	94
Wood	3	2	2	0					2nd	56	101	123
Edmonds	4	2	2	0	(4) 26	10	44	4	3rd	91	190	176
Miller					(5) 12	4	19	2	4th	94	275	193
									5th	103	276	214
PAKISTAN									6th	125	399	220
Sarfraz	6	1	12	0					7th	125	448	224
Liaquat	42	9	114	1					8th	126	452	227
Sikander	45	13	132	4					9th	126	–	231
Mudassar	27	7	59	1					10th	164	–	–
Qasim	14	2	56	1								
Wasim Raja	10	1	32	0								

Umpires: H.D.Bird (13) and K.E.Palmer (1).

Close: 1st day – P(1) 162-9 (Sarfraz 32, Liaquat 9); 2nd – E(1) 256-3 (Radley 97, Roope 22); 3rd – P(2) 95-1 (Sadiq 62, Qasim 0).

ENGLAND v PAKISTAN 1978 (2nd Test)

At Lord's, London, on 15 (*no play*), 16, 17, 19 June.
Toss: England.   Result: ENGLAND won by an innings and 120 runs.
Debuts: None.

Although rain delayed the start by a day and 45 minutes, England had completed their emphatic annihilation by lunch on the fourth day after 12 hours 42 minutes of actual playing time. Botham's third Test hundred needed only 104 balls and was his second in successive innings. England's total was scored at four runs an over in 366 minutes. Edmonds conceded only two scoring strokes in his eight-over spell. Botham's analysis is the best in any Test at Lord's, the record for England in this series, and the best of his first-class career. He was the first to score a century and take eight wickets in an innings of the same Test. By scoring a hundred and taking five or more wickets in an innings for the second time, he emulated G.St A.Sobers and Mushtaq Mohammad. During his final spell he took six wickets for 8 runs with 53 deliveries.

ENGLAND

*J.M.Brearley	lbw b Liaquat	2
G.A.Gooch	lbw b Wasim Raja	54
C.T.Radley	c Mohsin b Liaquat	8
D.I.Gower	b Qasim	56
G.R.J.Roope	c Mohsin b Qasim	69
G.Miller	c Miandad b Qasim	0
I.T.Botham	b Liaquat	108
†R.W.Taylor	c Mudassar b Sikander	10
C.M.Old	c Mohsin b Sikander	0
P.H.Edmonds	not out	36
R.G.D.Willis	b Mudassar	18
Extras	(LB2, NB1)	3
Total		**364**

PAKISTAN

Mudassar Nazar	c Edmonds b Willis	1		c Taylor b Botham	10
Sadiq Mohammad	c Botham b Willis	11		c Taylor b Willis	0
Mohsin Khan	c Willis b Edmonds	31		c Roope b Willis	46
Haroon Rashid	b Old	15	(5)	b Botham	4
Javed Miandad	c Taylor b Willis	0	(6)	c Gooch b Botham	22
Wasim Raja	b Edmonds	28	(7)	c and b Botham	1
Talat Ali	c Radley b Edmonds	2	(4)	c Roope b Botham	40
*†Wasim Bari	c Brearley b Willis	0		c Taylor b Botham	2
Iqbal Qasim	b Willis	0	(10)	b Botham	0
Sikander Bakht	c Brearley b Edmonds	4	(9)	c Roope b Botham	1
Liaquat Ali	not out	4		not out	0
Extras	(NB9)	9		(B1, LB3, W5, NB4)	13
Total		**105**			**139**

PAKISTAN	O	M	R	W	O	M	R	W
Sikander	27	3	115	2				
Liaquat	18	1	80	3				
Mudassar	4.2	0	16	1				
Qasim	30	5	101	3				
Wasim Raja	12	3	49	1				
ENGLAND								
Willis	13	1	47	5	10	2	26	2
Old	10	3	26	1	15	4	36	0
Botham	5	2	17	0	20.5	8	34	8
Edmonds	8	6	6	4	12	4	21	0
Miller					9	3	9	0

FALL OF WICKETS

Wkt	E 1st	P 1st	P 2nd
1st	5	11	1
2nd	19	22	45
3rd	120	40	100
4th	120	41	108
5th	134	84	114
6th	252	96	119
7th	290	97	121
8th	290	97	130
9th	324	97	130
10th	364	105	139

Umpires: W.L.Budd (4) and D.J.Constant (14).

Close: 1st day – no play; 2nd – E(1) 309-8 (Botham 102, Edmonds 6); 3rd – P(2) 96-2 (Mohsin 45, Talat 36).

ENGLAND v PAKISTAN 1978 (3rd Test)

At Headingley, Leeds, on 29, 30 June, 1 (*no play*), 3, 4 July.
Toss: Pakistan.   Result: MATCH DRAWN.
Debuts: None.

A total of 19 hours 28 minutes was lost to rain and a waterlogged square. Because of inadequate covering, the square and bowlers' foot marks became saturated although the pitch and outfield were playable. Saturday's play was abandoned while the surrounding districts enjoyed a full programme of league cricket. Old achieved remarkable economy during an innings which began at 5.00 pm on the first day and ended at 3.50 pm on the fourth. Sadiq made nine journeys to the middle during his 373-minute innings.

PAKISTAN

Mudassar Nazar	c Botham b Old	31
Sadiq Mohammad	c Brearley b Botham	97
Mohsin Khan	lbw b Willis	41
Talat Ali	c Gooch b Willis	0
Haroon Rashid	c Brearley b Botham	7
Javed Miandad	b Old	1
Wasim Raja	lbw b Botham	0
Sarfraz Nawaz	c Taylor b Botham	4
*†Wasim Bari	not out	7
Sikander Bakht	b Old	4
Iqbal Qasim	lbw b Old	0
Extras	(LB8, NB1)	9
Total		**201**

ENGLAND

*J.M.Brearley	c Wasim Bari b Sarfraz	0
G.A.Gooch	lbw b Sarfraz	20
C.T.Radley	b Sikander	7
D.I.Gower	lbw b Sarfraz	39
G.R.J.Roope	c Sadiq b Miandad	11
G.Miller	not out	18
†R.W.Taylor	c Wasim Bari b Sarfraz	2
I.T.Botham	lbw b Sarfraz	4
P.H.Edmonds	not out	1
C.M.Old	} did not bat	
R.G.D.Willis		
Extras	(B1, LB5, W1, NB10)	17
Total	(7 wickets)	**119**

ENGLAND	O	M	R	W
Willis	26	8	48	2
Old	41.4	22	41	4
Botham	18	2	59	4
Edmonds	11	2	22	0
Miller	9	3	22	0

PAKISTAN	O	M	R	W
Sarfraz	20	6	39	5
Sikander	15	4	26	1
Mudassar	5	2	12	0
Qasim	11	8	11	0
Miandad	3	0	14	1

FALL OF WICKETS

Wkt	P 1st	E 1st
1st	75	0
2nd	147	24
3rd	147	51
4th	169	77
5th	182	102
6th	183	110
7th	189	116
8th	190	–
9th	201	–
10th	201	–

Umpires: H.D.Bird (14) and K.E.Palmer (2).

Close: 1st day – P(1) 65-0 (Mudassar 27, Sadiq 34); 2nd – P(1) 153-3 (Sadiq 73, Haroon 1); 3rd – no play; 4th – E(1) 106-5 (Miller 13, Taylor 1).

ENGLAND v NEW ZEALAND 1978 (1st Test)

At Kennington Oval, London, on 27, 28, 29, 31 (*no play*) July, 1 August.
Toss: New Zealand.   Result: ENGLAND won by 7 wickets.
Debuts: New Zealand – B.P.Bracewell, B.A.Edgar.

Howarth was six runs from becoming the first batsman to score hundreds in three successive innings for New Zealand. Bracewell, at 18 years 316 days the fourth-youngest player to represent New Zealand, dismissed Gooch with his third ball in Test cricket. Gower's first Test hundred took 214 minutes and came off 226 balls. Edmonds conceded only four singles in his first 11 overs and 12 scoring strokes in his entire second-innings spell. Led by Gooch (175 balls, 11 fours), England won with 17.3 overs to spare. Congdon became New Zealand's most capped cricketer, his 59th appearance improving upon the record of J.R.Reid.

NEW ZEALAND

J.G.Wright	c Radley b Willis	62	lbw b Botham	25
R.W.Anderson	b Old	4	c Taylor b Botham	2
G.P.Howarth	c Edmonds b Botham	94	b Willis	0
B.A.Edgar	c and b Miller	0	b Edmonds	38
*M.G.Burgess	lbw b Willis	34	lbw b Botham	7
B.E.Congdon	run out	2	b Edmonds	36
†G.N.Edwards	b Miller	6	c Brearley b Edmonds	11
R.J.Hadlee	c Brearley b Willis	5	b Edmonds	7
B.L.Cairns	lbw b Willis	5	b Miller	27
B.P.Bracewell	c Taylor b Willis	0	b Miller	0
S.L.Boock	not out	3	not out	0
Extras	(B1, LB7, NB11)	19	(B8, LB10, NB11)	29
Total		**234**		**182**

ENGLAND

*J.M.Brearley	c Edwards b Bracewell	2	lbw b Boock	11
G.A.Gooch	lbw b Bracewell	0	not out	91
C.T.Radley	run out	49	lbw b Bracewell	2
D.I.Gower	run out	111	c Howarth b Cairns	11
G.R.J.Roope	b Boock	14	not out	10
G.Miller	lbw b Cairns	0		
I.T.Botham	c Bracewell b Boock	22		
†R.W.Taylor	c Edwards b Hadlee	8		
P.H.Edmonds	lbw b Hadlee	28		
C.M.Old	c Edwards b Cairns	16		
R.G.D.Willis	not out	3		
Extras	(B15, LB8, NB3)	26	(B2, LB3, NB8)	13
Total		**279**	(3 wickets)	**138**

ENGLAND	O	M	R	W	O	M	R	W		FALL OF WICKETS			
										NZ	E	NZ	E
Willis	20.2	9	42	5	13	2	39	1	*Wkt*	*1st*	*1st*	*2nd*	*2nd*
Old	20	7	43	1	5	2	13	0	1st	7	1	15	26
Botham	22	7	58	1	19	2	46	3	2nd	130	7	19	51
Miller	25	10	31	2	34	19	35	2	3rd	131	123	30	82
Edmonds	17	2	41	0	34.1	23	20	4	4th	191	165	70	–
									5th	197	166	86	–
NEW ZEALAND									6th	207	208	105	–
Hadlee	21.5	6	43	2	11.3	3	18	0	7th	224	212	113	–
Bracewell	17	8	46	2	13	3	26	1	8th	230	232	182	–
Cairns	40	16	65	2	(4) 7	0	21	1	9th	230	257	182	–
Boock	35	18	61	2	(3) 20	6	55	1	10th	234	279	182	–
Congdon	21	6	38	0	1	0	5	0					

Umpires: D.J.Constant (15) and B.J.Meyer (1).

Close: 1st day – NZ(1) 224-7 (Hadlee 5); 2nd – E(1) 225-7 (Taylor 6, Edmonds 8); 3rd – NZ(2) 123-7 (Congdon 15, Cairns 1); 4th – no play.

ENGLAND v NEW ZEALAND 1978 (2nd Test)

At Trent Bridge, Nottingham, on 10, 11, 12, 14 August.
Toss: England.   Result: ENGLAND won by an innings and 119 runs.
Debuts: None.

Boycott batted 417 minutes for his highest score against New Zealand and his 16th hundred in Test cricket. Howarth (7) retired at 34 after being struck on the back of the head by a bouncer from Botham; he returned on the following afternoon at the fall of the fifth wicket. When his score reached 17, Congdon passed J.R.Reid's record New Zealand aggregate of 3,428 runs. Although 196 minutes were lost, England completed their innings victory at 6.01 on the fourth evening.

ENGLAND

G.A.Gooch	c Burgess b Bracewell	55
G.Boycott	c and b Hadlee	131
C.T.Radley	lbw b Hadlee	59
D.I.Gower	c Cairns b Boock	46
*J.M.Brearley	c Parker b Bracewell	50
I.T.Botham	c Hadlee b Boock	8
G.Miller	c Howarth b Hadlee	4
†R.W.Taylor	b Hadlee	22
P.H.Edmonds	b Cairns	6
M.Hendrick	c Edwards b Bracewell	7
R.G.D.Willis	not out	1
Extras	(B16, LB12, W1, NB11)	40
Total		**429**

NEW ZEALAND

R.W.Anderson	lbw b Botham	19		run out	0
B.A.Edgar	c Taylor b Botham	6		c Botham b Edmonds	60
G.P.Howarth	not out	31		c Botham b Hendrick	34
S.L.Boock	c Taylor b Willis	8	(10)	b Edmonds	2
J.M.Parker	c Taylor b Hendrick	0	(4)	run out	38
*M.G.Burgess	c Taylor b Botham	5	(5)	c Brearley b Edmonds	7
B.E.Congdon	c Hendrick b Botham	27	(6)	c Brearley b Botham	4
†G.N.Edwards	c Taylor b Botham	0	(7)	c and b Edmonds	18
B.L.Cairns	b Edmonds	9	(8)	lbw b Botham	0
R.J.Hadlee	c Gooch b Botham	4	(9)	c Taylor b Botham	11
B.P.Bracewell	b Edmonds	0		not out	0
Extras	(LB1, W1, NB9)	11		(LB6, W1, NB9)	16
Total		**120**			**190**

NEW ZEALAND	O	M	R	W		O	M	R	W	FALL OF WICKETS			
											E	NZ	NZ
Hadlee	42	11	94	4						Wkt	1st	1st	2nd
Bracewell	33.5	2	110	3						1st	111	22	5
Cairns	38	7	85	1						2nd	240	27	63
Congdon	39	15	71	0						3rd	301	30	127
Boock	28	18	29	2						4th	342	47	148
ENGLAND										5th	350	49	152
Willis	12	5	22	1	(3) 9	0	31	0		6th	364	99	164
Hendrick	15	9	18	1	20	7	30	1		7th	374	99	168
Botham	21	9	34	6	(1) 24	7	59	3		8th	419	110	180
Edmonds	15.4	5	21	2	33.1	15	44	4		9th	427	115	190
Miller	6	1	14	0	6	3	10	0		10th	429	120	190

Umpires: D.J.Constant (16) and T.W.Spencer (17).

Close: 1st day – E(1) 252-2 (Boycott 108, Gower 6); 2nd – NZ(1) 35-3 (Boock 1, Burgess 0); 3rd – NZ(2) 0-0 (Anderson 0, Edgar 0).

ENGLAND v NEW ZEALAND 1978 (3rd Test)

At Lord's, London, on 24, 25, 26, 28 August.
Toss: New Zealand.   Result: ENGLAND won by 7 wickets.
Debuts: England – J.E.Emburey.

England gained their fifth victory of the season at 3.31 on the fourth afternoon. Emburey dismissed Edgar with his fourth ball in Test cricket. In his final Test, Bevan Congdon extended two of his New Zealand records (61 matches and 3,448 runs), and saw Howarth equal a third when he completed his third hundred against England. Botham's second innings analysis was his eighth of five or more wickets in only 11 Tests, and gave him ten or more wickets in a match for the first time. Collinge, recalled for his 35th and final Test, took his (then) national record tally of wickets to 116. The third day produced just 151 runs from 82.3 overs, the fewest of any complete day's Test cricket in England.

NEW ZEALAND

J.G.Wright	c Edmonds b Botham	17		b Botham	12
†B.A.Edgar	c Edmonds b Emburey	39		b Botham	4
G.P.Howarth	c Taylor b Botham	123	(9)	not out	14
J.M.Parker	lbw b Hendrick	14		c Taylor b Botham	3
*M.G.Burgess	lbw b Botham	68		c Hendrick b Botham	14
B.E.Congdon	c Emburey b Botham	2		c Taylor b Willis	3
R.W.Anderson	b Botham	16	(3)	c Taylor b Willis	1
R.J.Hadlee	c Brearley b Botham	0	(10)	run out	5
R.O.Collinge	c Emburey b Willis	19	(11)	b Botham	0
S.L.Boock	not out	4	(7)	c Radley b Willis	0
B.P.Bracewell	st Taylor b Emburey	4	(8)	c Hendrick b Willis	0
Extras	(B4, LB18, W4, NB7)	33		(LB3, NB8)	11
Total		**339**			**67**

ENGLAND

G.A.Gooch	c Boock b Hadlee	2		not out	42
G.Boycott	c Hadlee b Bracewell	24		b Hadlee	4
C.T.Radley	c Congdon b Hadlee	77		b Hadlee	0
D.I.Gower	c Wright b Boock	71		c Congdon b Bracewell	46
*J.M.Brearley	c Edgar b Hadlee	33		not out	8
I.T.Botham	c Edgar b Collinge	21			
†R.W.Taylor	lbw b Hadlee	1			
P.H.Edmonds	c Edgar b Hadlee	5			
J.E.Emburey	b Collinge	2			
M.Hendrick	b Bracewell	12			
R.G.D.Willis	not out	7			
Extras	(B7, LB5, NB22)	34		(LB3, W4, NB11)	18
Total		**289**		(3 wickets)	**118**

ENGLAND	O	M	R	W		O	M	R	W		FALL OF WICKETS			
Willis	29	9	79	1		16	8	16	4		NZ	E	NZ	E
Hendrick	28	14	39	1						Wkt	1st	1st	2nd	2nd
Botham	38	13	101	6	(2)	18.1	4	39	5	1st	65	2	10	14
Edmonds	12	3	19	0						2nd	70	66	14	14
Emburey	26.1	12	39	2	(3)	3	2	1	0	3rd	117	180	20	84
Gooch	10	0	29	0						4th	247	211	29	–
										5th	253	249	33	–
NEW ZEALAND										6th	290	255	37	–
Hadlee	32	9	84	5		13.5	2	31	2	7th	290	258	37	–
Collinge	30	9	58	2		6	1	26	0	8th	321	263	43	–
Bracewell	19.3	1	68	2	(4)	6	0	32	1	9th	333	274	57	–
Boock	25	10	33	1	(3)	5	1	11	0	10th	339	289	67	–
Congdon	6	1	12	0										

Umpires: H.D.Bird (15) and B.J.Meyer (2).

Close: 1st day – NZ(1) 280-5 (Howarth 105, Anderson 8); 2nd – E(1) 175-2 (Radley 75, Gower 55); 3rd – NZ(2) 37-7 (Burgess 8).

PAKISTAN v INDIA 1978-79 (1st Test)

At Iqbal Stadium, Faisalabad, on 16, 17, 18, 20, 21 October.
Toss: Pakistan.   Result: MATCH DRAWN.
Debuts: India – Kapil Dev.

Faisalabad, formerly Lyallpur and Pakistan's main textile centre, provided Test cricket with its 49th ground. The Iqbal Stadium, cricket's first ground to be named after a national poet, saw the resumption of this series exactly 26 years after its inauguration and more than 17 years after the last encounter. Zaheer became the first Pakistan batsman to score a hundred in his first innings against India; he batted for 315 minutes, hit two sixes and 24 fours, and shared in a partnership of 255 with Javed Miandad which was then the highest for any wicket by either side in this series. Pakistan's total was then their highest against India. Viswanath was the second Indian after R.H.Shodhan (*Test No. 359*) to score a century in his first innings against Pakistan, and the first to score hundreds against all five current opponents. There was an 11-minute delay at the start of the fifth morning when the umpires, reacting to language used by Gavaskar when Mohinder Amarnath was warned for damaging the pitch in his follow through, refused to go out. This was the 13th successive draw of this series.

PAKISTAN

Majid Khan	b Bedi	47	c Chauhan b Prasanna		34
Sadiq Mohammad	c and b Bedi	41	c Gavaskar b Kapil Dev		16
Zaheer Abbas	c Viswanath b Prasanna	176	c Chauhan b Gavaskar		96
*Mushtaq Mohammad	c Gavaskar b Chandrasekhar	5			
Javed Miandad	not out	154	not out		6
Asif Iqbal	c Chauhan b Bedi	0	(4) b S.Amarnath		104
Imran Khan	c Vengsarkar b Chandrasekhar	32			
†Wasim Bari	b Chandrasekhar	3			
Sarfraz Nawaz	lbw b Chandrasekhar	18			
Sikander Bakht	not out	16			
Iqbal Qasim	did not bat				
Extras	(LB5, NB6)	11	(B2, LB3, NB3)		8
Total	(8 wickets declared)	**503**	(4 wickets declared)		**264**

INDIA

S.M.Gavaskar	b Qasim	89	not out		8
C.P.S.Chauhan	c Wasim b Sarfraz	46	not out		30
S.Amarnath	c Miandad b Mushtaq	35			
G.R.Viswanath	b Mushtaq	145			
D.B.Vengsarkar	c Wasim b Imran	83			
M.Amarnath	c Wasim b Sarfraz	4			
†S.M.H.Kirmani	c Qasim b Mushtaq	1			
Kapil Dev	c sub (Haroon Rashid) b Mushtaq	8			
E.A.S.Prasanna	not out	10			
*B.S.Bedi	run out	1			
B.S.Chandrasekhar	did not bat				
Extras	(B3, LB3, NB34)	40	(B1, LB1, NB3)		5
Total	(9 wickets declared)	**462**	(0 wickets)		**43**

INDIA	O	M	R	W	O	M	R	W		FALL OF WICKETS			
Kapil Dev	16	2	71	0	12	3	25	1		P	I	P	I
M.Amarnath	7	0	44	0	10	1	43	0	Wkt	1st	1st	2nd	2nd
Prasanna	42	11	123	1	(5) 14	4	34	1	1st	84	97	54	–
Bedi	49	9	124	3	(3) 12	4	40	0	2nd	99	147	60	–
Chandrasekhar	38	6	130	4	(4) 12	1	49	0	3rd	110	248	226	–
Chauhan					5	0	26	0	4th	365	414	264	–
Gavaskar					5	0	34	1	5th	378	421	–	–
S.Amarnath					1.5	0	5	1	6th	445	425	–	–
									7th	452	445	–	–
PAKISTAN									8th	476	447	–	–
Imran	34.5	7	111	1	6	2	15	0	9th	–	462	–	–
Sarfraz	37	6	105	2	2	1	3	0	10th	–	–	–	–
Sikander	24	1	86	0									
Mushtaq	27	10	55	4									
Qasim	20	3	65	1	4	4	0	0					
Miandad					(3) 3	1	4	0					
Sadiq					(4) 4	0	16	0					

Umpires: Khalid Aziz (1) and Shakoor Rana (5).

Close: 1st day – P(1) 283-3 (Zaheer 128, Miandad 53); 2nd – I(1) 64-0 (Gavaskar 23, Chauhan 30); 3rd – I(1) 291-3 (Viswanath 77, Vengsarkar 18); 4th – P(2) 34-0 (Majid 18, Sadiq 13).

PAKISTAN v INDIA 1978-79 (2nd Test)

At Gaddafi Stadium, Lahore, on 27, 28, 29, 31 October, 1 November.
Toss: Pakistan.   Result: PAKISTAN won by 8 wickets.
Debuts: None.

After 13 successive draws, Pakistan gained their second victory in this series and achieved the first definite result since November 1952. Needing 126 in a minimum of 100 minutes, they reached their target with 8.2 overs to spare. Mohinder Amarnath retired at 106 after being hit in the face when he ducked into a short ball from Imran. He returned at 186 with Gavaskar as his runner, only to tread on his wicket attempting a hook. Zaheer recorded the highest Test innings in Pakistan until 1982-83 (*Test No. 946*). He batted for 375 minutes and hit two sixes and 29 fours, completed 2,000 runs in Tests and guided Pakistan to their (then) highest total against India. A (then) record opening stand of 192 between Gavaskar and Chauhan led to India's highest total in Pakistan until 1984-85. By playing in his 60th Test, Bedi claimed P.R.Umrigar's mantle as India's most capped cricketer; he also captured his 250th wicket. The day following this victory was declared a national holiday by the Pakistan Government.

INDIA

S.M.Gavaskar	c Majid b Salim	5		c Sarfraz b Mushtaq	97
C.P.S.Chauhan	b Imran	10		c Wasim b Miandad	93
S.Amarnath	c Asif b Imran	8		c Mudassar b Mushtaq	60
G.R.Viswanath	b Sarfraz	20		b Mudassar	83
D.B.Vengsarkar	c Wasim b Imran	76	(6)	c Wasim b Mudassar	17
M.Amarnath	hit wkt b Sarfraz	20	(7)	c Qasim b Sarfraz	7
†S.M.H.Kirmani	lbw b Mudassar	12	(8)	not out	39
Kapil Dev	lbw b Sarfraz	15	(5)	c Majid b Imran	43
E.A.S.Prasanna	not out	1		c Mushtaq b Imran	4
*B.S.Bedi	lbw b Sarfraz	4		b Sarfraz	1
B.S.Chandrasekhar	b Imran	0		b Imran	4
Extras	(B17, LB4, NB7)	28		(B8, LB4, NB5)	17
Total		**199**			**465**

PAKISTAN

Majid Khan	c Kirmani b Bedi	45		c and b M.Amarnath	38
Mudassar Nazar	c Gavaskar b Kapil Dev	12		b Kapil Dev	29
†Wasim Bari	c Kirmani b Bedi	85			
Zaheer Abbas	not out	235	(3)	not out	34
Asif Iqbal	b Chandrasekhar	29	(4)	not out	21
Javed Miandad	b M.Amarnath	35			
*Mushtaq Mohammad	run out	67			
Imran Khan	not out	9			
Sarfraz Nawaz					
Salim Altaf	did not bat				
Iqbal Qasim					
Extras	(B12, LB8, W1, NB1)	22		(LB6)	6
Total	(6 wickets declared)	**539**		(2 wickets)	**128**

PAKISTAN	O	M	R	W		O	M	R	W		FALL OF WICKETS			
Imran	18.5	2	54	4		42.3	12	110	3		I	P	I	P
Salim	13	3	34	1		16	4	36	0	Wkt	1st	1st	2nd	2nd
Sarfraz	16	4	46	4		38	7	112	2	1st	15	19	192	57
Mushtaq	6	0	32	0	(5)	30	6	106	2	2nd	19	144	202	89
Mudassar	3	2	5	1	(7)	4	1	4	2	3rd	48	161	301	–
Qasim					(4)	33	12	68	0	4th	49	216	371	–
Miandad					(6)	5	1	7	1	5th	151	356	406	–
Majid						2	1	5	0	6th	186	502	407	–
INDIA										7th	192	–	415	–
Kapil Dev	28	1	98	1		10	1	53	1	8th	194	–	437	–
Gavaskar	4	1	10	0						9th	198	–	438	–
Bedi	34	6	130	2		4	0	23	0	10th	199	–	465	–
Chandrasekhar	21	2	109	1										
M.Amarnath	21	1	76	1	(2)	6	0	39	1					
Prasanna	25	2	94	0										
Viswanath					(4)	0.4	0	7	0					

Umpires: Mahboob Shah (3) and Shujauddin (21).

Close: 1st day – P(1) 28-1 (Majid 7, Wasim 8); 2nd – P(1) 349-4 (Zaheer 128, Miandad 30); 3rd – I(2) 92-0 (Gavaskar 50, Chauhan 40); 4th – I(2) 307-3 (Viswanath 41, Kapil Dev 5).

PAKISTAN v INDIA 1978-79 (3rd Test)

At National Stadium, Karachi, on 14, 15, 17, 18, 19 November.
Toss: India.   Result: PAKISTAN won by 8 wickets.
Debuts: None.

Pakistan won their first rubber against India when Javed Miandad made the winning hit with seven balls to spare. Gavaskar overtook P.R.Umrigar's record Indian aggregate of 3,631 runs and became the first to score a century in each innings of a Test for India twice; he emulated Viswanath by making hundreds against all of India's current opponents. With 583 runs, average 194.33, Zaheer Abbas set a record aggregate for any three-match rubber, beating 558 by S.M.Nurse for West Indies against New Zealand in 1968-69. Kapil Dev scored 50 off 33 balls.

INDIA

Batsman	Dismissal	Runs	Dismissal (2nd)	Runs
S.M.Gavaskar	c Sarfraz b Imran	111	c Wasim b Sarfraz	137
C.P.S.Chauhan	c Qasim b Sarfraz	33	c Wasim b Sarfraz	0
S.Amarnath	c Mushtaq b Qasim	30	(6) run out	14
G.R.Viswanath	b Imran	0	(5) c Wasim b Sarfraz	1
D.B.Vengsarkar	c Majid b Sikander	11	(7) c Wasim b Sikander	1
M.Amarnath	lbw b Sarfraz	14	(3) b Imran	53
†S.M.H.Kirmani	c Mushtaq b Sikander	14	(4) c Qasim b Imran	4
K.D.Ghavri	c Majid b Sarfraz	42	c Miandad b Imran	35
Kapil Dev	lbw b Sarfraz	59	c Mushtaq b Sarfraz	34
*B.S.Bedi	c Majid b Imran	4	not out	0
B.S.Chandrasekhar	not out	0	b Sarfraz	0
Extras	(B10, LB6, W1, NB9)	26	(B9, LB4, W1, NB7)	21
Total		**344**		**300**

PAKISTAN

Batsman	Dismissal	Runs	Dismissal (2nd)	Runs
Majid Khan	b Kapil Dev	44	c Chauhan b Kapil Dev	14
Mudassar Nazar	c Chauhan b Chandrasekhar	57		
†Wasim Bari	c Kirmani b Ghavri	3		
Zaheer Abbas	c Viswanath b Bedi	42		
Asif Iqbal	lbw b Chandrasekhar	1	(2) c Kirmani b M.Amarnath	44
Javed Miandad	c Kirmani b Kapil Dev	100	(3) not out	62
*Mushtaq Mohammad	c sub‡ b Ghavri	78		
Imran Khan	b Chandrasekhar	32	(4) not out	31
Sarfraz Nawaz	c sub (A.D.Gaekwad) b Kapil Dev	28		
Iqbal Qasim	not out	29		
Sikander Bakht	not out	22		
Extras	(B5, LB20, W1, NB19)	45	(B3, LB9, NB1)	13
Total	(9 wickets declared)	**481**	(2 wickets)	**164**

PAKISTAN	O	M	R	W	O	M	R	W		FALL OF WICKETS			
										I	P	I	P
Imran	32	12	75	3	28	7	76	3	Wkt	1st	1st	2nd	2nd
Sarfraz	31.2	4	89	4	24	5	70	5	1st	58	84	5	21
Sikander	22	6	76	2	10	2	42	1	2nd	131	104	122	118
Qasim	23	6	67	1	7	1	27	0	3rd	132	153	143	–
Mudassar	4	2	5	0	(7) 2	0	13	0	4th	179	155	147	–
Mushtaq	3	0	6	0	(5) 9	0	36	0	5th	217	187	170	–
Miandad					(6) 2	0	15	0	6th	219	341	173	–
									7th	253	374	246	–
INDIA									8th	337	408	297	–
Kapil Dev	42	4	132	3	9	0	47	1	9th	344	447	299	–
Ghavri	24	5	66	2	6	0	36	0	10th	344	–	300	–
M.Amarnath	14	2	39	0	5.5	0	35	1					
Chandrasekhar	25	4	97	3									
Bedi	35	5	99	1	(4) 4	0	33	0					
Chauhan	1	0	3	0									

Umpires: Mahboob Shah (4) and Shujauddin (22).   ‡ (S.Venkataraghavan)

Close: 1st day – I(1) 195-4 (Gavaskar 96, M.Amarnath 6); 2nd – P(1) 92-1 (Mudassar 39, Wasim 0); 3rd – P(1) 339-5 (Miandad 80, Mushtaq 77); 4th – I(2) 131-2 (Gavaskar 67, Kirmani 1).

AUSTRALIA v ENGLAND 1978-79 (1st Test)

At Woolloongabba, Brisbane, on 1, 2, 3, 5, 6 December.
Toss: Australia.   Result: ENGLAND won by 7 wickets.
Debuts: Australia – R.M.Hogg, J.A.Maclean.

England gained their first victory in Brisbane since 1936-37 at 3.14 on the fifth afternoon. Taylor and Maclean, both making their first appearances in this series, equalled its record of five dismissals in an innings. Taylor was the first England wicket-keeper to hold five catches in an innings against Australia. After Australia had recorded their second-lowest total in any Test at 'The Gabba', Hogg returned what were to remain the best figures of his Test career at his first attempt. Hughes took 374 minutes (297 balls) to reach his first Test hundred; it was Australia's slowest century against England until 1981.

AUSTRALIA

G.M.Wood	c Taylor b Old	7	(2)	lbw b Old	19
G.J.Cosier	run out	1	(1)	b Willis	0
P.M.Toohey	b Willis	1		lbw b Botham	1
*G.N.Yallop	c Gooch b Willis	7		c and b Willis	102
K.J.Hughes	c Taylor b Botham	4		c Edmonds b Willis	129
T.J.Laughlin	c sub (J.K.Lever) b Willis	2		lbw b Old	5
†J.A.Maclean	not out	33		lbw b Miller	15
B.Yardley	c Taylor b Willis	17		c Brearley b Miller	16
R.M.Hogg	c Taylor b Botham	36		b Botham	16
A.G.Hurst	c Taylor b Botham	0		b Botham	0
J.D.Higgs	b Old	1		not out	0
Extras	(LB1, NB6)	7		(B9, LB5, NB22)	36
Total		**116**			**339**

ENGLAND

G.Boycott	c Hughes b Hogg	13		run out	16
G.A.Gooch	c Laughlin b Hogg	2		c Yardley b Hogg	2
D.W.Randall	c Laughlin b Hurst	75		not out	74
†R.W.Taylor	lbw b Hurst	20			
*J.M.Brearley	c Maclean b Hogg	6	(4)	c Maclean b Yardley	13
D.I.Gower	c Maclean b Hurst	44	(5)	not out	48
I.T.Botham	c Maclean b Hogg	49			
G.Miller	lbw b Hogg	27			
P.H.Edmonds	c Maclean b Hogg	1			
C.M.Old	not out	29			
R.G.D.Willis	c Maclean b Hurst	8			
Extras	(B7, LB4, NB1)	12		(B12, LB3, NB2)	17
Total		**286**		(3 wickets)	**170**

ENGLAND	O	M	R	W		O	M	R	W		FALL OF WICKETS			
Willis	14	2	44	4		27.6	3	69	3		A	E	A	E
Old	9.7	1	24	2	(3)	17	1	60	2	Wkt	1st	1st	2nd	2nd
Botham	12	1	40	3	(2)	26	5	95	3	1st	2	2	0	16
Gooch	1	0	1	0						2nd	5	38	2	37
Edmonds	1	1	0	0		12	1	27	0	3rd	14	111	49	74
Miller					(4)	34	12	52	2	4th	22	120	219	–
										5th	24	120	228	–
AUSTRALIA										6th	26	215	261	–
Hurst	27.4	6	93	4	(2)	10	4	17	0	7th	53	219	310	–
Hogg	28	8	74	6	(1)	12.5	2	35	1	8th	113	226	339	–
Laughlin	22	6	54	0	(4)	3	0	6	0	9th	113	266	339	–
Yardley	7	1	34	0	(3)	13	1	41	1	10th	116	286	339	–
Cosier	5	1	10	0	(6)	3	0	11	0					
Higgs	6	2	9	0	(5)	12	1	43	0					

Umpires: R.A.French (4) and M.G.O'Connell (14).

Close: 1st day – E(1) 60-2 (Randall 43, Taylor 2); 2nd – E(1) 257-8 (Miller 19, Old 17); 3rd – A(2) 157-3 (Yallop 74, Hughes 51); 4th – E(2) 16-0 (Boycott 9, Gooch 2).

AUSTRALIA v ENGLAND 1978-79 (2nd Test)

At W.A.C.A.Ground, Perth, on 15, 16, 17, 19, 20 December.
Toss: Australia.   Result: ENGLAND won by 166 runs.
Debuts: None.

For the first time since 1936-37 England won the first two Tests of a rubber in Australia. They completed an unexpected easy victory at 3.45 on the last afternoon after Australia had lost their last six wickets for 20 runs to 66 balls in 47 minutes. Boycott batted 454 minutes and faced 337 balls in scoring 77 runs. His only four included two overthrows. This marathon was rated by Lindsay Hassett as 'an exceptional innings by someone who could not find the middle of the bat'. When 47 he became the eighth England batsman to score 2,000 runs against Australia. His innings provided a perfect foil for Gower's first hundred in this series (214 minutes, 194 balls, nine fours). During the final lunch interval, Tom Brooks, then Australia's senior umpire, responded to severe criticism from various quarters by announcing his retirement.

ENGLAND

Batsman	Dismissal 1	Score	Dismissal 2	Score
G.Boycott	lbw b Hurst	77	lbw b Hogg	23
G.A.Gooch	c Maclean b Hogg	1	lbw b Hogg	43
D.W.Randall	c Wood b Hogg	0	c Cosier b Yardley	45
*J.M.Brearley	c Maclean b Dymock	17	c Maclean b Hogg	0
D.I.Gower	b Hogg	102	c Maclean b Hogg	12
I.T.Botham	lbw b Hurst	11	c Wood b Yardley	30
G.Miller	b Hogg	40	c Toohey b Yardley	25
†R.W.Taylor	c Hurst b Yardley	12	(9) c Maclean b Hogg	2
J.K.Lever	c Cosier b Hurst	14	(8) c Maclean b Hurst	10
R.G.D.Willis	c Yallop b Hogg	2	not out	3
M.Hendrick	not out	7	b Dymock	1
Extras	(B6, LB9, W3, NB8)	26	(LB6, NB8)	14
Total		**309**		**208**

AUSTRALIA

Batsman	Dismissal 1	Score	Dismissal 2	Score
G.M.Wood	lbw b Lever	5	(2) c Taylor b Lever	64
W.M.Darling	run out	25	(1) c Boycott b Lever	5
K.J.Hughes	b Willis	16	c Gooch b Willis	12
*G.N.Yallop	b Willis	3	c Taylor b Hendrick	3
P.M.Toohey	not out	81	c Taylor b Hendrick	0
G.J.Cosier	c Gooch b Willis	4	lbw b Miller	47
†J.A.Maclean	c Gooch b Miller	0	c Brearley b Miller	1
B.Yardley	c Taylor b Hendrick	12	c Botham b Lever	7
R.M.Hogg	c Taylor b Willis	18	b Miller	0
G.Dymock	b Hendrick	11	not out	6
A.G.Hurst	c Taylor b Willis	5	b Lever	5
Extras	(LB7, W1, NB2)	10	(LB3, W4, NB4)	11
Total		**190**		**161**

AUSTRALIA	O	M	R	W	O	M	R	W		FALL OF WICKETS			
										E	A	E	A
Hogg	30.5	9	65	5	17	2	57	5	*Wkt*	*1st*	*1st*	*2nd*	*2nd*
Dymock	34	4	72	1	16.3	2	53	1	1st	3	8	58	8
Hurst	26	7	70	3	17	5	43	1	2nd	3	34	93	36
Yardley	23	1	62	1	16	1	41	3	3rd	41	38	93	58
Cosier	4	2	14	0					4th	199	60	135	58
									5th	219	78	141	141
ENGLAND									6th	224	79	176	143
Lever	7	0	20	1	(2) 8.1	2	28	4	7th	253	100	201	143
Botham	11	2	46	0	(3) 11	1	54	0	8th	295	128	201	147
Willis	18.5	5	44	5	(1) 12	1	36	1	9th	300	185	206	151
Hendrick	14	1	39	2	8	3	11	2	10th	309	190	208	161
Miller	16	6	31	1	7	4	21	3					

Umpires: R.C.Bailhache (12) and T.F.Brooks (23).

Close: 1st day – E(1) 190-3 (Boycott 63, Gower 101); 2nd – A(1) 60-4 (Toohey 6); 3rd – E(2) 58-0 (Boycott 23, Gooch 26); 4th – A(2) 11-1 (Wood 2, Hughes 1).

AUSTRALIA v ENGLAND 1978-79 (3rd Test)

At Melbourne Cricket Ground on 29, 30 December, 1, 2, 3 January.
Toss: Australia.   Result: AUSTRALIA won by 103 runs.
Debuts: Australia – A.R.Border.

Australia achieved their only victory of a disastrous rubber after 23 minutes of play on the fifth day. Hogg, with the highly appropriate match figures for this pitch of 10 for 66, took his tally of wickets after three Tests to 27, with five or more in an innings on five occasions out of six. Only A.A.Mailey and C.T.B.Turner (29) enjoyed a more prolific start to their bowling careers for Australia. The square, a remarkable patchwork of green and black, had missed its second growth of couch grass. It produced a variable and progressively low bounce, giving the side batting first a strong advantage. Wood batted 392 minutes for the only score in excess of 49, his second Test hundred taking 363 minutes (264 balls). Miller batted 110 minutes for the slowest first three runs in Test match history. On the second day 14 wickets fell for 122 runs. England's defeat was their first in 16 matches under Brearley's captaincy.

AUSTRALIA

G.M.Wood	c Emburey b Miller	100	(2) b Botham		34
W.M.Darling	run out	33	(1) c Randall b Miller		21
K.J.Hughes	c Taylor b Botham	0	c Gower b Botham		48
*G.N.Yallop	c Hendrick b Botham	41	c Taylor b Miller		16
P.M.Toohey	c Randall b Miller	32	c Botham b Emburey		20
A.R.Border	c Brearley b Hendrick	29	run out		0
†J.A.Maclean	b Botham	8	c Hendrick b Emburey		10
R.M.Hogg	c Randall b Miller	0	b Botham		1
G.Dymock	b Hendrick	0	c Brearley b Hendrick		6
A.G.Hurst	b Hendrick	0	(11) not out		0
J.D.Higgs	not out	1	(10) st Taylor b Emburey		0
Extras	(LB8, NB6)	14	(B4, LB6, NB1)		11
Total		**258**			**167**

ENGLAND

G.Boycott	b Hogg	1	lbw b Hurst		38
*J.M.Brearley	lbw b Hogg	1	c Maclean b Dymock		0
D.W.Randall	lbw b Hurst	13	lbw b Hogg		2
G.A.Gooch	c Border b Dymock	25	lbw b Hogg		40
D.I.Gower	lbw b Dymock	29	lbw b Dymock		49
I.T.Botham	c Darling b Higgs	22	c Maclean b Higgs		10
G.Miller	b Hogg	7	c Hughes b Higgs		1
†R.W.Taylor	b Hogg	1	c Maclean b Hogg		5
J.E.Emburey	b Hogg	0	not out		7
R.G.D.Willis	c Darling b Dymock	19	c Yallop b Hogg		3
M.Hendrick	not out	6	b Hogg		0
Extras	(B6, LB4, NB9)	19	(B10, LB7, W1, NB6)		24
Total		**143**			**179**

ENGLAND	O	M	R	W	O	M	R	W		FALL OF WICKETS			
Willis	13	2	47	0	7	0	21	0		A	E	A	E
Botham	20.1	4	68	3	15	4	41	3	Wkt	1st	1st	2nd	2nd
Hendrick	23	3	50	3	14	4	25	1	1st	65	2	55	1
Emburey	14	1	44	0	(5) 21.2	12	30	3	2nd	65	3	81	6
Miller	19	6	35	3	(4) 14	5	39	2	3rd	126	40	101	71
									4th	189	52	136	122
AUSTRALIA									5th	247	81	136	163
Hogg	17	7	30	5	17	5	36	5	6th	250	100	152	163
Hurst	12	2	24	1	(3) 11	1	39	1	7th	250	101	157	167
Dymock	15.6	4	38	3	(2) 18	4	37	2	8th	251	101	167	171
Higgs	19	9	32	1	16	2	29	2	9th	252	120	167	179
Border					5	0	14	0	10th	258	143	167	179

Umpires: R.A.French (5) and M.G.O'Connell (15).

Close: 1st day – A(1) 243-4 (Wood 100, Border 25); 2nd – E(1) 107-8 (Miller 3, Willis 3); 3rd – A(2) 163-7 (Maclean 10, Dymock 3); 4th – E(2) 171-8 (Emburey 2).

AUSTRALIA v ENGLAND 1978-79 (4th Test)

At Sydney Cricket Ground on 6, 7, 8, 10, 11 January.
Toss: England.   Result: ENGLAND won by 93 runs.
Debuts: None.

At 5.05 on the fifth evening, when Emburey bowled Hurst, Brearley became only the second England captain after Sir Leonard Hutton to regain and then successfully defend the Ashes. Yallop kept wicket for the last 18.6 overs of England's first innings and caught Botham after Maclean had retired with heat exhaustion. Boycott, beaten by a slower breakback, was out first ball for the only time in his 193 Test innings; it was his first duck for England in 68 innings since Trent Bridge 1969. Randall's hundred in 406 minutes (353 balls) remains the slowest for either country in all Tests between England and Australia. In terms of time, Randall's 150 in 571 minutes was the second-slowest on record, 23 minutes faster than that scored by C.T.Radley in *Test No. 819*; in terms of balls received, Randall's was the slowest by 12. It was the first time that England had retained the Ashes in Australia since 1954-55.

ENGLAND

G.Boycott	c Border b Hurst	8	lbw b Hogg		0
*J.M.Brearley	b Hogg	17	b Border		53
D.W.Randall	c Wood b Hurst	0	lbw b Hogg		150
G.A.Gooch	c Toohey b Higgs	18	c Wood b Higgs		22
D.I.Gower	c Maclean b Hurst	7	c Maclean b Hogg		34
I.T.Botham	c Yallop b Hogg	59	c Wood b Higgs		6
G.Miller	c Maclean b Hurst	4	lbw b Hogg		17
†R.W.Taylor	c Border b Higgs	10	not out		21
J.E.Emburey	c Wood b Higgs	0	c Darling b Higgs		14
R.G.D.Willis	not out	7	c Toohey b Higgs		0
M.Hendrick	b Hurst	10	c Toohey b Higgs		7
Extras	(B1, LB1, W2, NB8)	12	(B5, LB3, NB14)		22
Total		**152**			**346**

AUSTRALIA

G.M.Wood	b Willis	0	(2)	run out	27
W.M.Darling	c Botham b Miller	91	(1)	c Gooch b Hendrick	13
K.J.Hughes	c Emburey b Willis	48		c Emburey b Miller	15
*G.N.Yallop	c Botham b Hendrick	44		c and b Hendrick	1
P.M.Toohey	c Gooch b Botham	1		b Miller	5
A.R.Border	not out	60		not out	45
†J.A.Maclean	lbw b Emburey	12		c Botham b Miller	0
R.M.Hogg	run out	6	(9)	c Botham b Emburey	0
G.Dymock	b Botham	5	(8)	b Emburey	0
J.D.Higgs	c Botham b Hendrick	11		lbw b Emburey	3
A.G.Hurst	run out	0		b Emburey	0
Extras	(B2, LB3, NB11)	16		(LB1, NB1)	2
Total		**294**			**111**

AUSTRALIA	O	M	R	W	O	M	R	W
Hogg	11	3	36	2	28	10	67	4
Dymock	13	1	34	0	17	4	35	0
Hurst	10.6	2	28	5	19	3	43	0
Higgs	18	4	42	3	59.6	15	148	5
Border					23	11	31	1
ENGLAND								
Willis	9	2	33	2	2	0	8	0
Botham	28	3	87	2				
Hendrick	24	4	50	2	(2) 10	3	17	2
Miller	13	2	37	1	20	7	38	3
Emburey	29	10	57	1	(3) 17.2	7	46	4
Gooch	5	1	14	0				

FALL OF WICKETS

Wkt	E 1st	A 1st	E 2nd	A 2nd
1st	18	1	0	38
2nd	18	126	111	44
3rd	35	178	169	45
4th	51	179	237	59
5th	66	210	267	74
6th	70	235	292	76
7th	94	245	307	85
8th	98	276	334	85
9th	141	290	334	105
10th	152	294	346	111

Umpires: R.C.Bailhache (13) and R.A.French (6).

Close: 1st day – A(1) 56-1 (Darling 35, Hughes 15); 2nd – A(1) 248-7 (Border 31, Dymock 0); 3rd – E(2) 133-2 (Randall 65, Gooch 6); 4th – E(2) 304-6 (Miller 16, Taylor 3).

AUSTRALIA v ENGLAND 1978-79 (5th Test)

At Adelaide Oval on 27, 28, 29, 31 January, 1 February.
Toss: Australia.   Result: ENGLAND won by 205 runs.
Debuts: Australia – P.H.Carlson, K.J.Wright.

When he dismissed Willis in the first innings, Hogg took his 37th wicket of the rubber and eclipsed the Australian record against England set by A.A.Mailey's leg-breaks and googlies in 1920-21. A frightening accident involving Darling overshadowed Australia's reply after they had dismissed England before tea on the first day. Hit under the heart by Willis's fifth ball and before a run had been scored, he was carried unconscious from the field on a stretcher. Only prompt action by Emburey and umpire O'Connell saved his life. He resumed the next morning when the fifth wicket fell in the first over. Taylor equalled his highest first-class score at that time, recorded his highest innings in Test cricket, and shared with Miller in a stand of 135 which is England's highest for the seventh wicket at Adelaide. At 2.04 on the fifth afternoon England gained their fourth win of a rubber in Australia for the first time since 1932-33.

ENGLAND

G.Boycott	c Wright b Hurst	6	c Hughes b Hurst	49
*J.M.Brearley	c Wright b Hogg	2	lbw b Carlson	9
D.W.Randall	c Carlson b Hurst	4	c Yardley b Hurst	15
G.A.Gooch	c Hughes b Hogg	1	b Carlson	18
D.I.Gower	lbw b Hurst	9	lbw b Higgs	21
I.T.Botham	c Wright b Higgs	74	c Yardley b Hurst	7
G.Miller	lbw b Hogg	31	c Wright b Hurst	64
†R.W.Taylor	run out	4	c Wright b Hogg	97
J.E.Emburey	b Higgs	4	b Hogg	42
R.G.D.Willis	c Darling b Hogg	24	c Wright b Hogg	12
M.Hendrick	not out	0	not out	3
Extras	(B1, LB4, W3, NB2)	10	(B1, LB16, W2, NB4)	23
Total		169		360

AUSTRALIA

W.M.Darling	c Willis b Botham	15	(2)	b Botham	18
G.M.Wood	c Randall b Emburey	35	(1)	run out	9
K.J.Hughes	c Emburey b Hendrick	4		c Gower b Hendrick	46
*G.N.Yallop	b Hendrick	0		b Hendrick	36
A.R.Border	c Taylor b Botham	11		b Willis	1
P.H.Carlson	c Taylor b Botham	0		c Gower b Hendrick	21
B.Yardley	b Botham	28		c Brearley b Willis	0
†K.J.Wright	lbw b Emburey	29		c Emburey b Miller	0
R.M.Hogg	b Willis	0		b Miller	2
J.D.Higgs	run out	16		not out	3
A.G.Hurst	not out	17		b Willis	13
Extras	(B1, LB3, NB5)	9		(LB1, NB10)	11
Total		164			160

AUSTRALIA	O	M	R	W	O	M	R	W	FALL OF WICKETS			
									E	A	E	A
Hogg	10.4	1	26	4	27.6	7	59	3	*1st*	*1st*	*2nd*	*2nd*
Hurst	14	1	65	3	37	9	97	4	Wkt			
Carlson	9	1	34	0	27	8	41	2	1st 10	5	31	31
Yardley	4	0	25	0	20	6	60	0	2nd 12	10	57	36
Higgs	3	1	9	2	28	4	75	1	3rd 16	22	97	115
Border					3	2	5	0	4th 18	24	106	120
									5th 27	72	130	121
ENGLAND									6th 80	94	132	121
Willis	11	1	55	1	12	3	41	3	7th 113	114	267	124
Hendrick	19	1	45	2	14	6	19	3	8th 136	116	336	130
Botham	11.4	0	42	4	14	4	37	1	9th 147	133	347	147
Emburey	12	7	13	2	(5) 9	5	16	0	10th 169	164	360	160
Miller					(4) 18	3	36	2				

Umpires: R.C.Bailhache (14) and M.G.O'Connell (16).

Close: 1st day – A(1) 69-4 (Wood 19, Yardley 28); 2nd – E(2) 82-2 (Boycott 38, Gooch 11); 3rd – E(2) 272-7 (Taylor 69, Emburey 0); 4th – A(2) 82-2 (Hughes 30, Yallop 16).

AUSTRALIA v ENGLAND 1978-79 (6th Test)

At Sydney Cricket Ground on 10, 11, 12, 14 February.
Toss: Australia.   Result: ENGLAND won by 9 wickets.
Debuts: Australia – A.M.J.Hilditch.

At 2.40 on the fourth afternoon Mike Brearley's England team became the first to gain five victories in a rubber in Australia. Both captains scored their 1,000th run in Test cricket during this match. Yallop's hundred was the fastest of the rubber when measured off the number of balls he faced (186). His innings of 121 represented 61.11% of his team's total. Only five other batsmen, led by Charles Bannerman's 67.34% in the first Test innings of all, had contributed a higher proportion of a completed Test innings involving 11 batsmen. Hogg extended his record aggregate of wickets by an Australian bowler in a home rubber against England to 41 and greeted Randall's final appearance at the crease with an artificial snake.

AUSTRALIA

G.M.Wood	c Botham b Hendrick	15	c Willis b Miller	29
A.M.J.Hilditch	run out	3	c Taylor b Hendrick	1
K.J.Hughes	c Botham b Willis	16	c Gooch b Emburey	7
*G.N.Yallop	c Gower b Botham	121	c Taylor b Miller	17
P.M.Toohey	c Taylor b Botham	8	c Gooch b Emburey	0
P.H.Carlson	c Gooch b Botham	2	c Botham b Emburey	0
B.Yardley	b Emburey	7	not out	61
†K.J.Wright	st Taylor b Emburey	3	c Boycott b Miller	5
R.M.Hogg	c Emburey b Miller	9	b Miller	7
J.D.Higgs	not out	9	c Botham b Emburey	2
A.G.Hurst	b Botham	0	c and b Miller	4
Extras	(LB3, NB2)	5	(B3, LB6, NB1)	10
Total		**198**		**143**

ENGLAND

G.Boycott	c Hilditch b Hurst	19	c Hughes b Higgs	13
*J.M.Brearley	c Toohey b Higgs	46	not out	20
D.W.Randall	lbw b Hogg	7	not out	0
G.A.Gooch	st Wright b Higgs	74		
D.I.Gower	c Wright b Higgs	65		
I.T.Botham	c Carlson b Yardley	23		
G.Miller	lbw b Hurst	18		
†R.W.Taylor	not out	36		
J.E.Emburey	c Hilditch b Hurst	0		
R.G.D.Willis	b Higgs	10		
M.Hendrick	c and b Yardley	0		
Extras	(B3, LB5, NB2)	10	(NB2)	2
Total		**308**	(1 wicket)	**35**

ENGLAND	O	M	R	W	O	M	R	W	FALL OF WICKETS				
Willis	11	4	48	1	3	0	15	0		A	E	A	E
Hendrick	12	2	21	1	7	3	22	1	*Wkt*	*1st*	*1st*	*2nd*	*2nd*
Botham	9.7	1	57	4					1st	18	37	8	31
Emburey	18	3	48	2	(3) 24	4	52	4	2nd	19	46	28	–
Miller	9	3	13	1	(4) 27.1	6	44	5	3rd	67	115	48	–
Boycott	1	0	6	0					4th	101	182	48	–
									5th	109	233	48	–
AUSTRALIA									6th	116	247	82	–
Hogg	18	6	42	1					7th	124	270	114	–
Hurst	20	4	58	3					8th	159	280	130	–
Yardley	25	2	105	2	(1) 5.2	0	21	0	9th	198	306	136	–
Carlson	10	1	24	0					10th	198	308	143	–
Higgs	30	8	69	4	(2) 5	1	12	1					

Umpires: A.R.Crafter (1) and D.G.Weser (1).

Close: 1st day – E(1) 24-0 (Boycott 6, Brearley 18); 2nd – E(1) 216-4 (Gower 47, Botham 17); 3rd – A(2) 70-5 (Yallop 13, Yardley 16).

INDIA v WEST INDIES 1978-79 (1st Test)

At Wankhede Stadium, Bombay, on 1, 2, 3, 5, 6 December.
Toss: West Indies.   Result: MATCH DRAWN.
Debuts: None.

An outfield saturated by fierce storms delayed the start by almost four hours. Kallicharran was the first captain to elect to field first in a Bombay Test and only the second visiting captain after W.M.Lawry to do so anywhere in India (*Test No. 668*). Chauhan (10) retired at 23 after ducking into a ball from Clarke and sustaining a bruised elbow; he resumed at 217. Gavaskar scored India's first double century in a home Test against West Indies, batted 400 minutes, and hit two sixes and 29 fours. It was his third hundred in successive innings. Kallicharran's highest score in Test cricket occupied 397 minutes and contained 25 fours. The opening stand of 153 between Gavaskar and Chauhan in even time remains India's best start against West Indies.

INDIA

*S.M.Gavaskar	b Clarke	205	c Murray b Clarke		73
C.P.S.Chauhan	c Greenidge b Holder	52	c Murray b Parry		84
M.Amarnath	b Clarke	4	not out		37
G.R.Viswanath	c Bacchus b Parry	52			
D.B.Vengsarkar	lbw b Phillip	11	(4) not out		10
†S.M.H.Kirmani	b Clarke	17			
Kapil Dev	c Bacchus b Holder	42			
K.D.Ghavri	not out	15			
S.Venkataraghavan	c Murray b Clarke	0			
B.S.Bedi	c and b Holder	2			
B.S.Chandrasekhar	b Holder	1			
Extras	(B6, LB4, NB13)	23	(B4, LB7, NB9)		20
Total		**424**	(2 wickets)		**224**

WEST INDIES

A.E.Greenidge	c Venkataraghavan b Ghavri	0
A.B.Williams	b Ghavri	0
H.A.Gomes	b Chandrasekhar	63
*A.I.Kallicharran	lbw b Kapil Dev	187
S.F.A.F.Bacchus	b Chandrasekhar	11
†D.A.Murray	lbw b Chandrasekhar	84
D.R.Parry	c Kirmani b Chandrasekhar	55
N.Phillip	c Vengsarkar b Venkataraghavan	26
V.A.Holder	c Vengsarkar b Chandrasekhar	14
R.R.Jumadeen	not out	2
S.T.Clarke	c Venkataraghavan b Bedi	8
Extras	(B22, LB13, NB8)	43
Total		**493**

WEST INDIES	O	M	R	W		O	M	R	W		FALL OF WICKETS		
Phillip	22	4	67	1	(2)	6	2	19	0		I	WI	I
Clarke	42	9	98	4	(1)	16	2	53	1	Wkt	1st	1st	2nd
Holder	27	3	94	4	(5)	7	2	15	0	1st	35	0	153
Parry	28	4	100	1	(3)	27	7	77	1	2nd	190	13	194
Jumadeen	17	3	39	0	(4)	21	6	32	0	3rd	217	122	–
Kallicharran	1	0	3	0		4.5	2	6	0	4th	334	150	–
Gomes						3	2	2	0	5th	344	317	–
										6th	390	387	–
INDIA										7th	408	430	–
Kapil Dev	19	3	70	1						8th	411	474	–
Ghavri	25	3	71	2						9th	414	480	–
Venkataraghavan	34	12	77	1						10th	424	493	–
Bedi	36	7	102	1									
Chandrasekhar	43	7	116	5									
Chauhan	1	0	2	0									
Amarnath	3	0	12	0									

Umpires: S.N.Hanumantha Rao (1) and B.Satyaji Rao (16).

Close: 1st day – I(1) 57-1 (Gavaskar 28, Viswanath 9); 2nd – I(1) 351-5 (Kirmani 2, Kapil Dev 4); 3rd – WI(1) 184-4 (Kallicharran 103, Murray 1); 4th – WI(1) 452-7 (Parry 45, Holder 5).

INDIA v WEST INDIES 1978-79 (2nd Test)

At Karnataka State C.A.Stadium, Bangalore, on 15, 16, 17, 19, 20 (*no play*) December.
Toss: West Indies.   Result: MATCH DRAWN.
Debuts: West Indies – M.D.Marshall.

The final day's play was cancelled on the advice of Bangalore's police chiefs who could not guarantee adequate protection at the ground following extensive rioting in the city the previous evening. This had resulted from the expulsion from Parliament and arrest in Delhi of former Prime Minister, Mrs Indira Gandhi. The match was aborted with West Indies leading by 266 runs with two wickets left against a ball only five overs old. Gavaskar was out first ball, superbly caught at gully when he slashed a short ball towards the vacant third-man area.

WEST INDIES

A.B.Williams	st Kirmani b Bedi	44		c Gavaskar b Ghavri	20
S.F.A.F.Bacchus	b Bedi	96		c Chauhan b Ghavri	4
H.A.Gomes	c and b Chandrasekhar	51		c Chauhan b Ghavri	82
*A.I.Kallicharran	c Viswanath b Ghavri	71		b Ghavri	21
†D.A.Murray	c Kirmani b Ghavri	14		b Kapil Dev	9
S.Shivnarine	b Venkataraghavan	62		c Chauhan b Kapil Dev	0
V.A.Holder	b Kapil Dev	27	(10)	not out	0
D.R.Parry	not out	41	(7)	c Kirmani b Bedi	38
M.D.Marshall	lbw b Chandrasekhar	0		b Ghavri	5
N.Phillip	run out	26	(8)	not out	13
S.T.Clarke	c and b Bedi	0			
Extras	(LB3, NB2)	5		(B1, LB3, NB4)	8
Total		**437**		**(8 wickets)**	**200**

INDIA

*S.M.Gavaskar	c Shivnarine b Clarke	0
A.D.Gaekwad	b Parry	87
D.B.Vengsarkar	c Murray b Phillip	73
G.R.Viswanath	c Kallicharran b Clarke	70
C.P.S.Chauhan	c Parry b Marshall	15
†S.M.H.Kirmani	c Kallicharran b Phillip	15
Kapil Dev	c Murray b Clarke	12
K.D.Ghavri	b Clarke	43
S.Venkataraghavan	c Phillip b Clarke	11
B.S.Bedi	c Shivnarine b Phillip	18
B.S.Chandrasekhar	not out	0
Extras	(B1, LB5, NB21)	27
Total		**371**

INDIA	O	M	R	W	O	M	R	W		FALL OF WICKETS		
										WI	I	WI
Kapil Dev	20	5	79	1	(2) 11	1	30	2	*Wkt*	*1st*	*1st*	*2nd*
Ghavri	16	1	77	2	(1) 24	8	51	5	1st	97	0	7
Bedi	29	7	98	3	19	8	33	1	2nd	164	170	38
Chandrasekhar	33	4	94	2	(5) 12	2	39	0	3rd	238	200	74
Venkataraghavan	41	15	74	1	(4) 16	5	39	0	4th	268	233	98
Gaekwad	1	0	10	0					5th	284	266	101
									6th	343	291	179
WEST INDIES									7th	383	304	181
Clarke	34.2	3	126	5					8th	384	318	192
Phillip	25	6	86	3					9th	437	369	–
Marshall	18	2	53	1					10th	437	371	–
Holder	24	3	55	0								
Parry	12	6	22	1								
Shivnarine	3	2	2	0								

Umpires: Mohammad Ghouse (3) and Swaroop Kishen (1).

Close: 1st day – WI(1) 285-5 (Shivnarine 6, Holder 0); 2nd – I(1) 129-1 (Gaekwad 57, Vengasarkar 57); 3rd – I(1) 369-8 (Ghavri 42, Bedi 18); 4th – WI(2) 200-8 (Phillip 13, Holder 0).

INDIA v WEST INDIES 1978-79 (3rd Test)

At Eden Gardens, Calcutta, on 29, 30, 31 December, 2, 3 January.
Toss: India.   Result: MATCH DRAWN.
Debuts: India – M.V.Narasimha Rao.

Gavaskar became the first batsman to score two separate hundreds in a Test match on three occasions, and the first Indian to score 4,000 runs in Tests. His unbroken partnership of 344 with Vengsarkar remains India's highest for the second wicket in all Tests and the record for any wicket in this series. West Indies were left 305 minutes plus 20 overs in which to score 335 runs. Only their last wicket separated them from defeat when bad light ended play 11 balls early, and some 15 minutes after the scheduled close when the street lighting was already shining through the gloom. Shivnarine defended stoically for 126 minutes.

INDIA

*S.M.Gavaskar	c Bacchus b Phillip	107	not out	182
C.P.S.Chauhan	b Clarke	11		
A.D.Gaekwad	c Murray b Marshall	7	(2) b Clarke	5
G.R.Viswanath	b Phillip	32		
D.B.Vengsarkar	c Williams b Parry	42	(3) not out	157
M.V.Narashimha Rao	c Gomes b Parry	1		
K.D.Ghavri	c Marshall b Phillip	5		
†S.M.H.Kirmani	lbw b Phillip	0		
Kapil Dev	b Parry	61		
S.Venkataraghavan	lbw b Holder	7		
B.S.Bedi	not out	4		
Extras	(B3, LB2, NB18)	23	(B1, LB4, NB12)	17
Total		**300**	(1 wicket declared)	**361**

WEST INDIES

A.B.Williams	c and b Ghavri	111	(7) b Ghavri	11
S.F.A.F.Bacchus	b Ghavri	26	(1) c and b Ghavri	20
H.A.Gomes	b Venkataraghavan	8	b Venkataraghavan	5
*A.I.Kallicharran	c Narasimha b Venkataraghavan	55	c Viswanath b Narasimha	46
V.A.Holder	c Narasimha b Venkataraghavan	3	(9) b Ghavri	4
†D.A.Murray	c Kapil Dev b Venkataraghavan	2	(2) st Kirmani b Venkataraghavan	66
S.Shivnarine	c sub (D.D.Parsana) b Ghavri	48	(5) not out	36
D.R.Parry	b Bedi	4	(6) c Gavaskar b Venkataraghavan	0
N.Phillip	lbw b Kapil Dev	47	(8) lbw b Ghavri	0
M.D.Marshall	c Kirmani b Kapil Dev	1	lbw b Bedi	1
S.T.Clarke	not out	4	not out	0
Extras	(B5, LB9, NB4)	18	(B2, LB4, NB2)	8
Total		**327**	(9 wickets)	**197**

WEST INDIES	O	M	R	W		O	M	R	W		FALL OF WICKETS			
												I	WI	I	WI
Clarke	27	8	70	1		28	4	104	1	*Wkt*	*1st*	*1st*	*2nd*	*2nd*
Phillip	22	6	64	4		16	0	81	0	1st	20	58	17	35
Marshall	12	3	44	1		14	3	45	0	2nd	48	95	–	45
Holder	21	5	48	1		20	3	59	0	3rd	110	197	–	133
Gomes	1	1	0	0	(7) 1	0	3	0		4th	199	210	–	143
Parry	20.3	7	51	3	(5) 13	3	50	0		5th	209	213	–	145
Shivnarine	1	1	0	0	(6) 1	0	2	0		6th	220	218	–	164
										7th	220	230	–	164
INDIA										8th	225	313	–	183
Kapil Dev	20.4	3	88	2		13	6	21	0	9th	283	318	–	197
Ghavri	29	5	74	3		23	8	46	4	10th	300	327	–	–
Venkataraghavan	33	15	55	4	(4) 30	13	47	3						
Bedi	24	4	59	1	(3) 22	14	32	1						
Narasimha Rao	11	0	33	0		17.1	6	43	1						

Umpires: S.N.Hanumantha Rao (2) and P.R.Punjabi (1).

Close: 1st day – I(1) 225-8 (Kapil Dev 0, Venkataraghavan 0); 2nd – WI(1) 209-3 (Kallicharran 54, Holder 1); 3rd – I(2) 70-1 (Gavaskar 34, Vengsarkar 27); 4th – WI(2) 15-0 (Bacchus 7, Murray 7).

INDIA v WEST INDIES 1978-79 (4th Test)

At Chepauk, Madras, on 12, 13, 14, 16 January.
Toss: West Indies.   Result: INDIA won by 3 wickets.
Debuts: West Indies – H.S.Chang; India – D.D.Parsana.

On a pitch of exaggerated bounce expected to favour the West Indian fast bowlers, India won a close match with more than a day to spare. A low-scoring contest was dominated by three innings: Kallicharran (98) batted 209 minutes, faced 155 balls and hit 16 fours; Viswanath (124) was last out in his 50th Test after 346 minutes and 17 fours; and Gomes, who scored 91 out of 135 in almost 4½ hours with 13 boundaries. Fifteen wickets fell on the third day during a bouncer war which went unchecked by the umpires.

WEST INDIES

Batsman	Dismissal 1	Runs	Dismissal 2	Runs
S.F.A.F.Bacchus	c Vengsarkar b Kapil Dev	0	c Vengsarkar b Ghavri	4
A.E.Greenidge	b Venkataraghavan	13	c Kirmani b Kapil Dev	15
H.A.Gomes	c Narasimha b Kapil Dev	14	c Gavaskar b Venkataraghavan	91
*A.I.Kallicharran	b Venkataraghavan	98	c sub ‡ b Venkataraghavan	4
H.S.Chang	c Chauhan b Kapil Dev	6	hit wkt b Ghavri	2
†D.A.Murray	hit wkt b Kapil Dev	0	c Narasimha b Kapil Dev	15
S.Shivnarine	c sub‡ b Ghavri	5	c Vengsarkar b Ghavri	9
D.R.Parry	run out	12	c sub‡ b Kapil Dev	1
N.Phillip	not out	22	not out	7
V.A.Holder	c Kapil Dev b Parsana	20	c Narasimha b Venkataraghavan	0
S.T.Clarke	lbw b Venkataraghavan	12	st Kirmani b Venkataraghavan	0
Extras	(LB9, W1, NB16)	26	(NB3)	3
Total		**228**		**151**

INDIA

Batsman	Dismissal 1	Runs	Dismissal 2	Runs
*S.M.Gavaskar	c Bacchus b Phillip	4	c Murray b Clarke	1
C.P.S.Chauhan	c Murray b Holder	20	c Bacchus b Phillip	10
D.B.Vengsarkar	c Bacchus b Clarke	0	c Shivnarine b Clarke	0
G.R.Viswanath	c Shivnarine b Clarke	124	c Kallicharran b Holder	31
A.D.Gaekwad	b Phillip	24	c Murray b Holder	21
M.V.Narasimha Rao	c Greenidge b Parry	6	c Murray b Phillip	4
Kapil Dev	c Bacchus b Clarke	0	(8) not out	26
K.D.Ghavri	c Murray b Clarke	1	(7) c Clarke b Phillip	8
†S.M.H.Kirmani	c Shivnarine b Phillip	33	not out	4
D.D.Parsana	c sub (M.D.Marshall) b Phillip	0		
S.Venkataraghavan	not out	0		
Extras	(B15, LB11, NB17)	43	(B5, LB1, NB14)	20
Total		**255**	(7 wickets)	**125**

INDIA	O	M	R	W	O	M	R	W	FALL OF WICKETS				
										WI	I	WI	I
Kapil Dev	14	0	38	4	14	3	46	3					
Ghavri	16	5	41	1	13	3	52	3	*Wkt*	*1st*	*1st*	*2nd*	*2nd*
Parsana	12	3	32	1	(4) 2	0	7	0	1st	0	10	6	16
Venkataraghavan	20.5	5	60	3	(3) 16.5	5	43	4	2nd	25	11	34	17
Narasimha Rao	10	1	31	0					3rd	45	80	87	17
									4th	55	150	100	74
WEST INDIES									5th	61	173	133	82
Clarke	29.1	3	75	4	21.2	3	46	2	6th	68	174	141	84
Phillip	22	8	48	4	15	5	37	3	7th	168	180	143	115
Holder	11	2	28	1	10	3	22	2	8th	168	250	148	–
Gomes	1	0	2	0					9th	209	255	151	–
Parry	15	2	43	1					10th	228	255	151	–
Shivnarine	5	1	16	0									

Umpires: J.D.Ghosh (1) and Swaroop Kishen (2).   ‡ (Yajurvindra Singh)

Close: 1st day – I(1) 10-1 (Chauhan 3); 2nd – I(1) 250-8 (Viswanath 120); 3rd – I(2) 31-3 (Viswanath 10, Gaekwad 4).

INDIA V WEST INDIES 1978-79 (5th Test)

At Feroz Shah Kotla, Delhi, on 24, 25, 27, 28, 29 January.
Toss: India.   Result: MATCH DRAWN.
Debuts: None.

During his 19th Test hundred, Gavaskar overtook V.L.Manjrekar's record aggregate of 586 for India in any home rubber and became the leading scorer in Tests between India and West Indies (previously G.St A.Sobers with 1,920 runs). He batted 344 minutes and hit 18 fours. Kapil Dev reached his first hundred in Tests with a six off Phillip. His 126 not out came from 124 balls and included 11 fours and that six. India's total remained their highest in all Tests until the next match. Following on 394 behind and with just over 11 hours left, West Indies were saved by rain and the Indian Board's policy of leaving pitches uncovered. Only 55 minutes of play were possible on the fourth day and more than three hours were lost on the last.

INDIA

*S.M.Gavaskar	c Murray b Clarke	120
C.P.S.Chauhan	c Parry b Phillip	60
D.B.Vengsarkar	c Murray b Clarke	109
G.R.Viswanath	c Murray b Phillip	9
A.D.Gaekwad	c Murray b Gomes	47
Kapil Dev	not out	126
†S.M.H.Kirmani	run out	30
K.D.Ghavri	c Murray b Phillip	2
D.D.Parsana	b Clarke	1
S.Venkataraghavan	not out	8
B.S.Chandrasekhar	did not bat	
Extras	(B7, LB13, NB34)	54
Total	(8 wickets declared)	**566**

WEST INDIES

A.B.Williams	b Venkataraghavan	26			
A.E.Greenidge	c Chauhan b Ghavri	0	(1)	b Chandrasekhar	32
H.A.Gomes	c Kirmani b Kapil Dev	40		b Venkataraghavan	14
*A.I.Kallicharran	c Chandrasekhar b Ghavri	7		not out	45
S.F.A.F.Bacchus	c Kapil Dev b Ghavri	0	(2)	c Gavaskar b Chandrasekhar	61
†D.A.Murray	b Chandrasekhar	20	(5)	not out	7
S.Shivnarine	b Kapil Dev	0			
D.R.Parry	lbw b Chandrasekhar	15			
N.Phillip	b Kapil Dev	26			
V.A.Holder	not out	11			
S.T.Clarke	c and b Venkataraghavan	15			
Extras	(B1, LB5, NB6)	12		(B15, LB5)	20
Total		**172**		(3 wickets)	**179**

WEST INDIES	O	M	R	W	O	M	R	W		FALL OF WICKETS		
Clarke	36	7	139	3						I	WI	WI
Phillip	38.2	3	159	3					Wkt	1st	1st	2nd
Holder	40	7	109	0					1st	119	0	89
Parry	17	4	43	0					2nd	270	48	106
Shivnarine	2	0	8	0					3rd	305	56	140
Gomes	9	0	54	1					4th	353	57	–
									5th	432	89	–
INDIA									6th	518	89	–
Kapil Dev	15	2	59	3	9	4	32	0	7th	536	106	–
Ghavri	15	3	54	3	12	2	50	0	8th	542	133	–
Venkataraghavan	10.4	5	14	2	14	8	26	1	9th	–	144	–
Chandrasekhar	16	6	33	2	15	4	32	2	10th	–	172	–
Parsana					6	3	11	0				
Gaekwad					1	0	5	0				
Vengsarkar					1	0	3	0				

Umpires: Mohammad Ghouse (4) and K.B.Ramaswami (2).

Close: 1st day – I(1) 264-1 (Gavaskar 119, Vengsarkar 55); 2nd – I(1) 523-6 (Kapil Dev 94, Ghavri 2); 3rd – WI(2) 7-0 (Greenidge 2, Bacchus 0); 4th – WI(2) 67-0 (Greenidge 21, Bacchus 41).

INDIA v WEST INDIES 1978-79 (6th Test)

At Green Park, Kanpur, on 2, 3, 4, 6, 7 (*no play*), 8 February.
Toss: India.   Result: MATCH DRAWN.
Debuts: None.

A virtually bald and lifeless pitch produced an average of 73 runs per wicket, then the third-highest scoring rate in all Test matches. For the second innings in succession India recorded a new highest total in all Tests (until 1986-87) with the aid of three individual hundreds. The partnership of 172 between Viswanath and Gaekwad remains India's highest for the fourth wicket against West Indies. Needing 445 to avoid the follow-on, West Indies began their innings on the third afternoon. Bad light ended play 50 minutes early on the fourth day, and was a prelude to rain that prevented any further activity until after lunch on the sixth day. Bacchus hit 33 fours and batted for 8½ hours spread over a five-day period for the highest score in a Kanpur Test, the second-highest score in any Test in India, and the second-highest of this series. Those latter records are held by another Guyanese, R.B.Kanhai, who scored 256 in *Test No. 461*. India's single victory gave them their first home rubber against West Indies in five attempts.

INDIA

*S.M.Gavaskar	c Murray b Marshall	40
C.P.S.Chauhan	st Murray b Parry	79
D.B.Vengsarkar	lbw b Phillip	15
G.R.Viswanath	c Phillip b Parry	179
A.D.Gaekwad	b Jumadeen	102
M.Amarnath	not out	101
Kapil Dev	c Greenidge b Jumadeen	62
†S.M.H.Kirmani	c Phillip b Jumadeen	2
K.D.Ghavri	not out	18
S.Venkataraghavan	} did not bat	
B.S.Chandrasekhar		
Extras	(B9, LB12, NB25)	46
Total	**(7 wickets declared)**	**644**

WEST INDIES

A.E.Greenidge	lbw b Ghavri	20
S.F.A.F.Bacchus	hit wkt b Venkataraghavan	250
H.A.Gomes	c Vengsarkar b Chandrasekhar	37
R.R.Jumadeen	b Kapil Dev	56
*A.I.Kallicharran	c Kirmani b Ghavri	4
†D.A.Murray	c sub‡ Ghavri	44
S.Shivnarine	c Vengsarkar b Amarnath	2
D.R.Parry	c Vengsarkar b Ghavri	4
N.Phillip	not out	10
M.D.Marshall	not out	1
V.A.Holder	did not bat	
Extras	(B9, LB9, NB6)	24
Total	**(8 wickets)**	**452**

WEST INDIES	O	M	R	W
Phillip	27	4	89	1
Marshall	34	3	123	1
Holder	43	6	118	0
Gomes	1	0	4	0
Jumadeen	45.4	4	137	3
Parry	39	6	127	2

INDIA	O	M	R	W
Kapil Dev	20	0	98	1
Ghavri	31	4	118	4
Chandrasekhar	41	10	117	1
Venkataraghavan	46.1	16	60	1
Amarnath	10	1	35	1

FALL OF WICKETS

	I	WI
Wkt	1st	1st
1st	51	37
2nd	77	134
3rd	221	263
4th	393	268
5th	502	428
6th	604	431
7th	609	440
8th	–	443
9th	–	–
10th	–	–

Umpires: P.R.Punjabi (2) and B.Satyaji Rao (17).   ‡ (Yajurvindra Singh)

Close: 1st day – I(1) 249-3 (Viswanath 94, Gaekwad 0); 2nd – I(1) 498-4 (Gaekwad 101, Amarnath 48); 3rd – WI(1) 137-2 (Bacchus 72, Jumadeen 2); 4th – WI(1) 373-4 (Bacchus 204, Murray 35); 5th – no play.

NEW ZEALAND v PAKISTAN 1978-79 (1st Test)

At Lancaster Park, Christchurch, on 2, 3, 4, 6, 7 February.
Toss: New Zealand.   Result: PAKISTAN won by 128 runs.
Debuts: Pakistan – Anwar Khan.

Pakistan, without the services of four key players who were engaged in World Series cricket, equalled their national record of winning three consecutive Tests. Edgar became the third New Zealander after G.M.Turner and R.E.Redmond to score a hundred in his first match against Pakistan. When Sarfraz dismissed Parker he became the third Pakistani after Fazal Mahmood and Intikhab Alam to take 100 wickets in Tests. Mushtaq's match analysis of 9 for 119 remained the best of his Test career. Mudassar retired hurt at 6.

PAKISTAN

Mudassar Nazar	c Edgar b Bracewell	7	retired hurt	4
Talat Ali	c Wright b Hadlee	40	c Coney b Hadlee	61
Mohsin Khan	lbw b Hadlee	12	lbw b Coney	7
Javed Miandad	b Hadlee	81	not out	160
Haroon Rashid	c Howarth b Hadlee	40	b Cairns	35
Wasim Raja	c Boock b Cairns	12	c Hadlee b Coney	17
*Mushtaq Mohammad	lbw b Hadlee	10	c Burgess b Hadlee	12
Sarfraz Nawaz	not out	31	b Hadlee	4
†Wasim Bari	b Cairns	9		
Anwar Khan	c Lees b Boock	12	(9) not out	3
Sikander Bakht	c Edgar b Boock	0		
Extras	(B5, LB8, NB4)	17	(B1, LB19)	20
Total		**271**	(6 wickets declared)	**323**

NEW ZEALAND

J.G.Wright	c Wasim Bari b Sikander	27	b Mushtaq	21
B.A.Edgar	c Wasim Bari b Sikander	129	c Sarfraz b Sikander	16
G.P.Howarth	c Wasim Raja b Mushtaq	19	(4) b Mushtaq	0
*M.G.Burgess	c Miandad b Sikander	16	(5) c Sarfraz b Wasim Raja	6
J.M.Parker	c Wasim Bari b Sarfraz	2	(6) lbw b Mushtaq	33
J.V.Coney	c Miandad b Mushtaq	6	(3) c Mohsin b Wasim Raja	36
†W.K.Lees	c and b Mushtaq	8	c Wasim Bari b Wasim Raja	19
R.J.Hadlee	c Wasim Bari b Wasim Raja	42	c Sikander b Wasim Raja	4
B.L.Cairns	lbw b Mushtaq	11	not out	23
S.L.Boock	b Wasim Raja	1	(11) c Mohsin b Mushtaq	0
B.P.Bracewell	not out	0	(10) st Wasim Bari b Mushtaq	5
Extras	(B8, LB9, NB12)	29	(B4, LB6, NB3)	13
Total		**290**		**176**

NEW ZEALAND	O	M	R	W		O	M	R	W					
Hadlee	25	2	62	5		26	4	83	3		FALL OF WICKETS			
Bracewell	12	1	50	1	(5)	7	0	53	0	*Wkt*	*1st*	*1st*	*2nd*	*2nd*
Cairns	31	5	96	2	(2)	23	7	46	1	1st	19	63	24	33
Coney	7	3	10	0	(3)	12	1	33	2	2nd	48	96	128	62
Boock	14.6	5	22	2	(4)	19	4	70	0	3rd	75	147	209	62
Howarth	3	1	14	0		6	0	18	0	4th	135	151	273	77
										5th	183	176	298	98
										6th	198	200	316	136
PAKISTAN										7th	242	254	–	142
Sarfraz	24	7	67	1		8	3	22	0	8th	255	288	–	152
Sikander	21	4	88	3		6	0	14	1	9th	271	289	–	176
Anwar	4	0	12	0						10th	271	290	–	176
Mushtaq	25	4	60	4	(3)	22	5	59	5					
Wasim Raja	10.4	5	18	2	(4)	20	3	68	4					
Mudassar	4	1	16	0										

Umpires: J.B.R.Hastie (3) and R.L.Monteith (6).

Close: 1st day – P(1) 220-6 (Mushtaq 4, Sarfraz 16); 2nd – NZ(1) 142-2 (Edgar 70, Burgess 12); 3rd – P(2) 99-1 (Talat 51, Miandad 33); 4th – NZ(2) 23-0 (Wright 8, Edgar 10).

NEW ZEALAND v PAKISTAN 1978-79 (2nd Test)

At McLean Park, Napier, on 16, 17, 18 (*no play*), 19, 20, 21 February.
Toss: Pakistan.   Result: MATCH DRAWN.
Debuts: None.

The rugby stadium at McLean Park in Napier provided Test cricket with its 50th ground. Hadlee became the fourth bowler to take 100 wickets for New Zealand when he dismissed Imran. That tally included Talat who had confused the bowler's delivery grunt with a no-ball call. Asif's tenth Test hundred included his 3,000th run for Pakistan, a career landmark also achieved by Majid in the second innings, and his 1,000th against New Zealand. The partnership of 195 between Wright and Howarth was then the highest for New Zealand's second wicket against all countries. As there was no play on the third day, the match continued on the scheduled rest day.

PAKISTAN

Majid Khan	c Lees b Cairns	29	(2)	not out	119
Talat Ali	b Hadlee	4	(1)	b Hadlee	13
Zaheer Abbas	c Parker b Cairns	2		c and b Boock	40
Javed Miandad	run out	26			
Asif Iqbal	b Cairns	104			
*Mushtaq Mohammad	c Lees b Hadlee	24	(4)	c Cairns b Boock	28
Wasim Raja	lbw b Hadlee	74			
Imran Khan	c Lees b Hadlee	3	(5)	not out	27
Sarfraz Nawaz	c Edgar b Coney	31			
†Wasim Bari	not out	37			
Sikander Bakht	lbw b Troup	19			
Extras	(B2, LB3, NB2)	7		(B2, LB1, W4)	7
Total		**360**		**(3 wickets declared)**	**234**

NEW ZEALAND

B.A.Edgar	c Mushtaq b Imran	3
J.G.Wright	c Miandad b Sikander	88
G.P.Howarth	b Sikander	114
J.M.Parker	lbw b Sikander	3
*M.G.Burgess	c Miandad b Imran	40
J.V.Coney	lbw b Sikander	69
S.L.Boock	b Imran	4
†W.K.Lees	b Imran	8
R.J.Hadlee	c Sikander b Imran	11
B.L.Cairns	c Zaheer b Mushtaq	13
G.B.Troup	not out	3
Extras	(B10, LB14, NB22)	46
Total		**402**

NEW ZEALAND	O	M	R	W		O	M	R	W		FALL OF WICKETS			
Hadlee	25	3	101	4		14	1	56	1			P	NZ	P
Cairns	19	1	86	3	(3) 11	2	23	0		Wkt	1st	1st	2nd
Troup	22.5	2	86	1	(2) 16	3	25	0		1st	19	24	27
Coney	25	9	38	1	(6) 10	2	21	0		2nd	23	219	110
Boock	12	3	41	0	(4) 30	6	77	2		3rd	42	230	188
Howarth	1	0	1	0	(5) 5	1	25	0		4th	128	241	–
										5th	180	292	–
PAKISTAN										6th	221	301	–
Imran	33	6	106	5						7th	228	318	–
Sarfraz	26	5	90	0						8th	283	351	–
Sikander	17	2	67	4						9th	313	388	–
Mushtaq	17.3	0	70	1						10th	360	402	–
Wasim Raja	3	1	10	0									
Majid	5	1	13	0									

Umpires: F.R.Goodall (7) and S.J.Woodward (1).

Close: 1st day – P(1) 206-5 (Mushtaq 23, Wasim Raja 15); 2nd – NZ(1) 25-1 (Wright 15, Howarth 0); 3rd – no play; 4th – NZ(1) 298-5 (Coney 16, Boock 4); 5th – P(2) 24-0 (Talat 13, Majid 10).

NEW ZEALAND v PAKISTAN 1978-79 (3rd Test)

At Eden Park, Auckland, on 23, 24, 25, 27, 28 February.
Toss: Pakistan.   Result: MATCH DRAWN.
Debuts: New Zealand – J.F.Reid.

Wasim Bari set a world Test record when he caught seven of the first eight wickets to fall. His performance was equalled by R.W.Taylor in February 1980 (*Test No. 876*). Curiously, Bari made no further dismissal in the match. After spending half the third day having treatment for an injured ankle and strained thigh, Hadlee took four for 12 with his last 46 balls and became the first New Zealand bowler to take five wickets in an innings six times. His total of 18 wickets is New Zealand's highest for any rubber against Pakistan.

NEW ZEALAND

J.G.Wright	c Wasim Bari b Sikander	32		b Sarfraz	10
B.A.Edgar	c Wasim Bari b Imran	1		b Imran	0
G.P.Howarth	c Wasim Bari b Sarfraz	5		c Wasim Raja b Sikander	38
J.F.Reid	c Wasim Bari b Imran	0	(5)	c Majid b Mushtaq	19
*M.G.Burgess	c Sarfraz b Sikander	3	(4)	c Asif b Sarfraz	71
J.V.Coney	c Wasim Bari b Sarfraz	82		c Mushtaq b Imran	49
†W.K.Lees	c Wasim Bari b Sarfraz	25		not out	45
B.L.Cairns	c Wasim Bari b Asif	17		b Sarfraz	4
R.J.Hadlee	not out	53		c Talat b Sarfraz	5
G.B.Troup	c Mushtaq b Sikander	7			
S.L.Boock	c Miandad b Imran	0			
Extras	(B5, LB3, W1, NB20)	29		(B8, LB13, W1, NB18)	40
Total		**254**		(8 wickets declared)	**281**

PAKISTAN

Majid Khan	b Cairns	10			
Talat Ali	c Lees b Hadlee	1	(1)	not out	8
Zaheer Abbas	c Lees b Troup	135			
Javed Miandad	lbw b Cairns	30	(2)	not out	0
Asif Iqbal	c Coney b Cairns	35			
*Mushtaq Mohammad	lbw b Hadlee	48			
Wasim Raja	c Coney b Troup	19			
Imran Khan	c Lees b Hadlee	33			
Sarfraz Nawaz	c Howarth b Hadlee	5			
†Wasim Bari	not out	25			
Sikander Bakht	c Cairns b Hadlee	6			
Extras	(B4, LB7, NB1)	12			
Total		**359**		(0 wickets)	**8**

PAKISTAN	O	M	R	W		O	M	R	W		FALL OF WICKETS			
											NZ	P	NZ	P
Imran	17.7	2	77	3		32	9	72	2	*Wkt*	*1st*	*1st*	*2nd*	*2nd*
Sarfraz	15	3	56	3		28.2	9	61	4	1st	11	5	1	–
Asif	7	1	24	1	(5)	2	0	5	0	2nd	31	22	52	–
Sikander	16	4	68	3	(3)	18	2	64	1	3rd	32	118	85	–
Mushtaq					(4)	11	2	39	1	4th	50	195	121	–
										5th	60	231	205	–
NEW ZEALAND										6th	109	273	261	–
Hadlee	27	3	104	5		0.6	0	8	0	7th	166	321	275	–
Troup	22	2	70	2						8th	209	322	281	–
Cairns	28	5	94	3						9th	251	345	–	–
Coney	19	4	51	0						10th	254	359	–	–
Boock	6	0	28	0										
Howarth	1	1	0	0										

Umpires: F.R.Goodall (8) and J.B.R.Hastie (4).

Close: 1st day – NZ(1) 229-8 (Hadlee 36, Troup 3); 2nd – P(1) 191-3 (Zaheer 113, Asif 33); 3rd – NZ(2) 51-1 (Wright 10, Howarth 27); 4th – NZ(2) 231-5 (Coney 41, Lees 18).

AUSTRALIA v PAKISTAN 1978-79 (1st Test)

At Melbourne Cricket Ground on 10, 11, 12, 14, 15 March.
Toss: Australia.   Result: PAKISTAN won by 71 runs.
Debuts: Australia – P.R.Sleep, D.F.Whatmore.

Pakistan celebrated their 100th Test match with a most improbable win, their second victory in successive Tests in Australia. At 4.30 on the final afternoon, Australia needed 77 to win with seven wickets in hand. Sarfraz Nawaz then produced one of the greatest spells of bowling in Test cricket, taking those seven wickets for one run with 33 balls. The first bowler to take nine wickets in an innings for Pakistan, his analysis was the best in any Test in Australia until 1985-86. The last seven wickets fell for five runs in the space of 65 balls. Hogg was given run out when he left his crease before the ball was dead. Although Mushtaq generously asked umpire Clarence Harvey, elder brother of Neil, to revoke his decision, his request was denied. Hogg demolished his wicket in disgust. 'I was surprised that he left one stump standing,' his captain commented. Wood (4) retired after colliding with Hilditch and injuring his wrist, and returned at the fall of the ninth wicket. Mushtaq (56) passed the record of most appearances for Pakistan held by his brother, Hanif.

PAKISTAN

Majid Khan	c Wright b Hogg	1	b Border		108
Mohsin Khan	c Hilditch b Hogg	14	c and b Hogg		14
Zaheer Abbas	b Hogg	11	b Hogg		59
Javed Miandad	b Hogg	19	c Wright b Border		16
Asif Iqbal	c Wright b Clark	9	lbw b Hogg		44
*Mushtaq Mohammad	c Wright b Hurst	36	c sub (J.D.Higgs) b Sleep		28
Wasim Raja	b Hurst	13	c Wright b Hurst		28
Imran Khan	c Wright b Hurst	33	c Clark b Hurst		28
Sarfraz Nawaz	c Wright b Sleep	35	lbw b Hurst		1
†Wasim Bari	run out	0	not out		8
Sikander Bakht	not out	5			
Extras	(B2, LB7, W1, NB10)	20	(B4, LB6, NB9)		19
Total		**196**	(9 wickets declared)		**353**

AUSTRALIA

G.M.Wood	not out	5	(6) c Wasim Bari b Sarfraz		0
A.M.J.Hilditch	c Miandad b Imran	3	b Sarfraz		62
A.R.Border	b Imran	20	b Sarfraz		105
*G.N.Yallop	b Imran	25	run out		8
K.J.Hughes	run out	19	c Mohsin b Sarfraz		84
D.F.Whatmore	lbw b Sarfraz	43	(1) b Sarfraz		15
P.R.Sleep	c Wasim Bari b Imran	10	b Sarfraz		0
†K.J.Wright	c Imran b Wasim Raja	9	not out		1
W.M.Clark	c Mushtaq b Wasim Raja	9	b Sarfraz		0
R.M.Hogg	run out	9	lbw b Sarfraz		0
A.G.Hurst	c and b Sarfraz	0	c Wasim Bari b Sarfraz		0
Extras	(B1, LB5, W2, NB8)	16	(B13, LB13, NB9)		35
Total		**168**			**310**

AUSTRALIA	O	M	R	W	O	M	R	W		FALL OF WICKETS			
Hogg	17	4	49	4	19	2	75	3		P	A	P	A
Hurst	20	4	55	3	(3) 19.5	1	115	3	Wkt	1st	1st	2nd	2nd
Clark	17	4	56	1	(2) 21	6	47	0	1st	2	11	30	49
Sleep	7.7	2	16	1	8	0	62	1	2nd	22	53	165	109
Border					14	5	35	2	3rd	28	63	204	128
									4th	40	97	209	305
									5th	83	109	261	305
PAKISTAN									6th	99	140	299	306
Imran	18	8	26	4	27	9	73	0	7th	122	152	330	308
Sarfraz	21.6	6	39	2	35.4	7	86	9	8th	173	167	332	309
Sikander	10	1	29	0	7	0	29	0	9th	177	167	353	310
Mushtaq	7	0	35	0	11	0	42	0	10th	196	168	–	310
Wasim Raja	5	0	23	2	(6) 3	0	11	0					
Majid					(5) 9	1	34	0					

Umpires: R.C.Bailhache (15) and C.E.Harvey (1).

Close: 1st day – A(1) 1-0 (Wood 1, Hilditch 0); 2nd – A(1) 168 all out; 3rd – P(2) 279-5 (Asif 41, Wasim Raja 2); 4th – A(2) 117-2 (Border 25, Yallop 3).

AUSTRALIA v PAKISTAN 1978-79 (2nd Test)

At W.A.C.A. Ground, Perth, on 24, 25, 26, 28, 29 March.
Toss: Australia.   Result: AUSTRALIA won by 7 wickets.
Debuts: Australia – J.K.Moss.

In the absence of Yallop (injured), Hughes became the first Western Australian to captain a Test team and his first act was to put Pakistan in to bat. His decision was swiftly vindicated; Majid steered the fourth ball to slip and half the side were out before lunch. After shadows across the pitch had stopped play 21 minutes early on the first evening, the Australian Board authorised play to start 30 minutes earlier on the remaining days of this late season match. Asif scored the last of his 11 Test hundreds. Mushtaq, in his final Test, became the first to play 100 innings for Pakistan. Sikander was run out by the bowler (Hurst) while he was backing up, the fourth batsman to suffer this fate in Test matches. Hilditch became the second batsman after W.R.Endean (*Test No. 435*) to be given out 'handled the ball'; the non-striker, he retrieved a wayward return and handed the ball to the bowler, Sarfraz, who appealed. This acrimonious Test was the last to feature eight-ball overs.

PAKISTAN

Majid Khan	c Hilditch b Hogg	0	c sub (T.J.Laughlin) b Hogg		0
Mudassar Nazar	c Wright b Hurst	5	c Hilditch b Hurst		25
Zaheer Abbas	c Wright b Hurst	29	c Wright b Hogg		18
Javed Miandad	not out	129	c Wright b Hurst		19
Haroon Rashid	c Border b Hurst	4	c Yardley b Dymock		47
Asif Iqbal	run out	35	not out		134
*Mushtaq Mohammad	run out	23	lbw b Yardley		1
Imran Khan	c Wright b Dymock	14	c Wright b Hurst		15
Sarfraz Nawaz	c Wright b Hurst	27	c Yardley b Hurst		3
†Wasim Bari	c Hilditch b Dymock	0	c Whatmore b Hurst		0
Sikander Bakht	b Dymock	0	run out		0
Extras	(LB3, W3, NB5)	11	(B3, LB8, NB12)		23
Total		277			285

AUSTRALIA

W.M.Darling	lbw b Mudassar	75	(2) run out		79
A.M.J.Hilditch	c Zaheer b Imran	41	(1) handled the ball		29
A.R.Border	c Majid b Miandad	85	not out		66
*K.J.Hughes	lbw b Sikander	9			
J.K.Moss	c Wasim b Mudassar	22	not out		38
D.F.Whatmore	c Asif b Imran	15			
†K.J.Wright	c Wasim b Mudassar	16			
B.Yardley	b Sarfraz	19	(4) run out		1
G.Dymock	not out	5			
R.M.Hogg	b Imran	3			
A.G.Hurst	c Wasim b Sarfraz	16			
Extras	(B3, LB4, W1, NB13)	21	(LB13, NB10)		23
Total		327	(3 wickets)		236

AUSTRALIA	O	M	R	W	O	M	R	W		FALL OF WICKETS			
Hogg	19	2	88	1	20	5	45	2		P	A	P	A
Hurst	23	4	61	4	24.7	2	94	5	*Wkt*	*1st*	*1st*	*2nd*	*2nd*
Dymock	21.6	4	65	3	23	5	72	1	1st	0	96	0	87
Yardley	14	2	52	0	14	3	42	1	2nd	27	143	35	153
Border					4	0	9	0	3rd	41	161	68	155
									4th	49	219	86	–
									5th	90	246	152	–
PAKISTAN									6th	176	273	153	–
Imran	32	5	105	3	17	1	81	0	7th	224	297	245	–
Sarfraz	35.1	7	112	2	19	1	85	0	8th	276	301	263	–
Sikander	10.5	1	33	1					9th	277	304	263	–
Mudassar	16	2	48	3	(3) 10.1	2	35	0	10th	277	327	285	–
Miandad	2	0	8	1	(4) 2	0	12	0					

Umpires: A.R.Crafter (2) and M.G.O'Connell (17).

Close: 1st day – P(1) 240-7 (Miandad 112, Sarfraz 8); 2nd – A(1) 180-3 (Border 34, Moss 11); 3rd – P(2) 19-1 (Mudassar 9, Zaheer 9); 4th – P(2) 246-7 (Asif 101, Sarfraz 0).

ENGLAND v INDIA 1979 (1st Test)

At Edgbaston, Birmingham, on 12, 13, 14, 16 July.
Toss: England.   Result: ENGLAND won by an innings and 83 runs.
Debuts: India – B.Reddy.

This four-match rubber was played after the second Prudential World Cup tournament. England completed an emphatic victory at 5.58 on the fourth evening after amassing their highest total in post-war Tests until 1984-85 and the highest in any Test at Edgbaston. Boycott completed 6,000 runs in official Tests and emulated K.F.Barrington by scoring a hundred on each of England's six current home grounds. Gower batted 365 minutes, faced 279 balls and hit 24 fours in making his first double century in first-class cricket. His unbroken partnership of 165 was then England's highest for the sixth wicket against India. Viswanath reached 4,000 runs for India when he had scored 22 in the second innings.

ENGLAND

*J.M.Brearley	c Reddy b Kapil Dev	24
G.Boycott	lbw b Kapil Dev	155
D.W.Randall	c Reddy b Kapil Dev	15
G.A.Gooch	c Reddy b Kapil Dev	83
D.I.Gower	not out	200
I.T.Botham	b Kapil Dev	33
G.Miller	not out	63
P.H.Edmonds		
†R.W.Taylor		
R.G.D.Willis	did not bat	
M.Hendrick		
Extras	(B4, LB27, W11, NB18)	60
Total	(5 wickets declared)	**633**

INDIA

S.M.Gavaskar	run out	61	c Gooch b Hendrick	68
C.P.S.Chauhan	c Gooch b Botham	4	c Randall b Willis	56
D.B.Vengsarkar	c Gooch b Edmonds	22	c Edmonds b Hendrick	7
G.R.Viswanath	c Botham b Edmonds	78	c Taylor b Botham	51
A.D.Gaekwad	c Botham b Willis	25	c Gooch b Botham	15
M.Amarnath	b Willis	31	lbw b Botham	10
Kapil Dev	lbw b Botham	1	c Hendrick b Botham	21
K.D.Ghavri	c Brearley b Willis	6	c Randall b Hendrick	4
†B.Reddy	b Hendrick	21	lbw b Hendrick	0
*S.Venkataraghavan	c Botham b Hendrick	28	lbw b Botham	0
B.S.Chandrasekhar	not out	0	not out	0
Extras	(B1, LB4, W3, NB12)	20	(B7, LB12, NB2)	21
Total		**297**		**253**

INDIA	O	M	R	W	O	M	R	W	FALL OF WICKETS			
										E	I	I
Kapil Dev	48	15	146	5					Wkt	1st	1st	2nd
Ghavri	38	5	129	0					1st	66	15	124
Amarnath	13.2	2	47	0					2nd	90	59	136
Chandrasekhar	29	1	113	0					3rd	235	129	136
Venkataraghavan	31	4	107	0					4th	426	205	182
Gaekwad	3	0	12	0					5th	468	209	227
Chauhan	3	0	19	0					6th	–	210	240
									7th	–	229	249
ENGLAND									8th	–	251	250
Willis	24	9	69	3	14	3	45	1	9th	–	294	251
Botham	26	4	86	2	29	8	70	5	10th	–	297	253
Hendrick	24.1	9	36	2	20.4	8	45	4				
Edmonds	26	11	60	2	17	6	37	0				
Boycott	5	1	8	0								
Miller	11	3	18	0	(5) 9	1	27	0				
Gooch					(6) 6	3	8	0				

Umpires: D.J.Constant (17) and B.J.Meyer (3).

Close: 1st day – E(1) 318-3 (Boycott 113, Gower 43); 2nd – I(1) 59-2 (Gavaskar 25); 3rd – I(2) 7-0 (Gavaskar 3, Chauhan 2).

ENGLAND v INDIA 1979 (2nd Test)

At Lord's, London, on 2, 3, 4, 6, 7 August.
Toss: India.   Result: MATCH DRAWN.
Debuts: India – Yashpal Sharma.

The loss of 8 hours 54 minutes to rain, allied to a third-wicket partnership of 210 in 326 minutes between Vengsarkar and Viswanath, enabled India to save the match after being 323 runs behind on first innings. Botham took five wickets for the tenth time in 34 Test innings as India lost their last four wickets for no runs. His dismissal of Gavaskar was his 100th in 2 years 9 days since his debut and was the fastest century of Test wickets until Kapil Dev eclipsed it in *Test No. 866*.

INDIA

Batsman	1st innings	R	2nd innings	R
S.M.Gavaskar	c Taylor b Gooch	42	c Brearley b Botham	59
C.P.S.Chauhan	c Randall b Botham	2	c Randall b Edmonds	31
D.B.Vengsarkar	c Botham b Hendrick	0	c Boycott b Edmonds	103
G.R.Viswanath	c Brearley b Hendrick	21	c Gower b Lever	113
A.D.Gaekwad	c Taylor b Botham	13	not out	1
Yashpal Sharma	c Taylor b Botham	11	not out	5
Kapil Dev	c Miller b Botham	4		
K.D.Ghavri	not out	3		
†B.Reddy	lbw b Botham	0		
*S.Venkataraghavan	run out	0		
B.S.Bedi	b Lever	0		
Extras		–	(B2, LB2, W1, NB1)	6
Total		96	(4 wickets)	318

ENGLAND

Batsman		R
*J.M.Brearley	c Reddy b Kapil Dev	12
G.Boycott	c Gavaskar b Ghavri	32
G.A.Gooch	b Kapil Dev	10
D.I.Gower	b Ghavri	82
D.W.Randall	run out	57
I.T.Botham	b Venkataraghavan	36
G.Miller	st Reddy b Bedi	62
P.H.Edmonds	c Reddy b Kapil Dev	20
†R.W.Taylor	c Vengsarkar b Bedi	64
J.K.Lever	not out	6
M.Hendrick	did not bat	
Extras	(B11, LB21, W2, NB4)	38
Total	(9 wickets declared)	419

ENGLAND	O	M	R	W	O	M	R	W
Lever	9.5	3	29	1	(3) 24	7	69	1
Botham	19	9	35	5	(1) 35	13	80	1
Hendrick	15	7	15	2	(2) 25	12	56	0
Edmonds	2	1	1	0	45	18	62	2
Gooch	10	5	16	1	(6) 2	0	8	0
Miller					(5) 17	6	37	0

INDIA	O	M	R	W
Kapil Dev	38	11	93	3
Ghavri	31	2	122	2
Bedi	38.5	13	87	2
Venkataraghavan	22	2	79	1

FALL OF WICKETS

Wkt	I 1st	E 1st	I 2nd
1st	12	21	79
2nd	23	60	99
3rd	51	71	309
4th	75	185	312
5th	79	226	–
6th	89	253	–
7th	96	291	–
8th	96	394	–
9th	96	419	–
10th	96	–	–

Umpires: H.D.Bird (16) and K.E.Palmer (3).

Close: 1st day – E(1) 53-1 (Boycott 26, Gooch 8); 2nd – E(1) 72-3 (Gower 9, Randall 0); 3rd – E(1) 357-7 (Miller 52, Taylor 25); 4th – I(2) 196-2 (Vengsarkar 66, Viswanath 35).

ENGLAND v INDIA 1979 (3rd Test)

At Headingley, Leeds, on 16, 17 (*no play*), 18 (*no play*), 20, 21 August.
Toss: England.   Result: MATCH DRAWN.
Debuts: None.

For the second year in succession the Headingley Test was devastated by rain, with almost three days' play (17 hours 54 minutes) being lost. Botham, who scored 9 before play was abandoned at 2.50 on the first afternoon, scored a further 99 before lunch when it resumed on the fourth day. He reached his hundred with a six off 121 balls in 170 minutes, hit the next ball for four and then blocked the last four balls before lunch, apparently unaware that another single would have enabled him to claim England's first pre-lunch century since 1935. He faced only 152 balls in an innings of savage brilliance dominated by five sixes and 16 fours.

ENGLAND

G.Boycott	c Viswanath b Kapil Dev	31
*J.M.Brearley	c Viswanath b Amarnath	15
G.A.Gooch	c Vengsarkar b Kapil Dev	4
D.I.Gower	lbw b Kapil Dev	0
D.W.Randall	b Ghavri	11
I.T.Botham	c Ghavri b Venkataraghavan	137
G.Miller	c Reddy b Amarnath	27
P.H.Edmonds	run out	18
†R.W.Taylor	c Chauhan b Bedi	1
R.G.D.Willis	not out	4
M.Hendrick	c sub (Yajurvindra Singh) b Bedi	0
Extras	(B4, LB6, W4, NB8)	22
Total		**270**

INDIA

S.M.Gavaskar	b Edmonds	78
C.P.S.Chauhan	c Botham b Willis	0
M.Amarnath	c Taylor b Willis	0
G.R.Viswanath	c Brearley b Hendrick	1
Yashpal Sharma	c Botham b Miller	40
D.B.Vengsarkar	not out	65
Kapil Dev	c Gooch b Miller	3
K.D.Ghavri	not out	20
*S.Venkataraghavan		
†B.Reddy	did not bat	
B.S.Bedi		
Extras	(B11, LB4, W1)	16
Total	(6 wickets)	**223**

INDIA	O	M	R	W		FALL OF WICKETS		
							E	I
Kapil Dev	27	7	84	3	*Wkt*	*1st*	*1st*	
Ghavri	18	4	60	1	1st	53	1	
Amarnath	20	7	53	2	2nd	57	9	
Venkataraghavan	7	2	25	1	3rd	57	12	
Bedi	8.5	2	26	2	4th	58	106	
					5th	89	156	
ENGLAND					6th	176	160	
Willis	18	5	42	2	7th	264	–	
Hendrick	14	6	13	1	8th	264	–	
Botham	13	3	39	0	9th	266	–	
Edmonds	28	8	59	1	10th	270	–	
Miller	32	13	52	2				
Gooch	3	1	2	0				
Boycott	2	2	0	0				

Umpires: H.D.Bird (17) and B.J.Meyer (4).

Close: 1st day – E(1) 80-4 (Randall 11, Botham 9); 2nd – no play; 3rd – no play; 4th – I(1) 10-2 (Gavaskar 10, Viswanath 0).

ENGLAND v INDIA 1979 (4th Test)

At Kennington Oval, London, on 30, 31 August, 1, 3, 4 September.
Toss: England.   Result: MATCH DRAWN.
Debuts: England – D.L.Bairstow, A.R.Butcher.

Set 438 runs to win in a minimum of 498 minutes, India needed 15 off the final over with two wickets left. Their superb bid to become the first visiting country to win a Cornhill Test match was launched by a stand of 213 between Gavaskar and Chauhan, which remains India's highest for the first wicket against England. Gavaskar's 20th Test hundred was then his highest score and the record for India in this series. He batted for 490 minutes, faced 443 balls and hit 21 fours. When he was fourth out, India required 49 off 7.4 overs but, in a gripping finish, lost their momentum and confidence against accurate bowling from Botham and Willey. Botham's third run was his 1,000th and brought him the Test double in 21 Tests – two matches fewer than the previous world record set by Vinoo Mankad.

ENGLAND

G.Boycott	lbw b Kapil Dev	35	b Ghavri		125
A.R.Butcher	c Yajurvindra b Venkataraghavan	14	c Venkataraghavan b Ghavri		20
G.A.Gooch	c Viswanath b Ghavri	79	lbw b Kapil Dev		31
D.I.Gower	lbw b Kapil Dev	0	c Reddy b Bedi		7
P.Willey	c Yajurvindra b Bedi	52	c Reddy b Ghavri		31
I.T.Botham	st Reddy b Venkataraghavan	38	run out		0
*J.M.Brearley	b Ghavri	34	b Venkataraghavan		11
†D.L.Bairstow	c Reddy b Kapil Dev	9	c Gavaskar b Kapil Dev		59
P.H.Edmonds	c Kapil Dev b Venkataraghavan	16	not out		27
R.G.D.Willis	not out	10			
M.Hendrick	c Gavaskar b Bedi	0			
Extras	(LB9, W4, NB5)	18	(LB14, W2, NB7)		23
Total		**305**	(8 wickets declared)		**334**

INDIA

S.M.Gavaskar	c Bairstow b Botham	13		c Gower b Botham		221
C.P.S.Chauhan	c Botham b Willis	6		c Botham b Willis		80
D.B.Vengsarkar	c Botham b Willis	0		c Botham b Edmonds		52
G.R.Viswanath	c Brearley b Botham	62	(6)	c Brearley b Willey		15
Yashpal Sharma	lbw b Willis	27		lbw b Botham		19
Yajurvindra Singh	not out	43	(7)	lbw b Botham		1
Kapil Dev	b Hendrick	16	(4)	c Gooch b Willey		0
K.D.Ghavri	c Bairstow b Botham	7	(9)	not out		3
†B.Reddy	c Bairstow b Botham	12	(10)	not out		5
*S.Venkataraghavan	c and b Hendrick	2	(8)	run out		6
B.S.Bedi	c Brearley b Hendrick	1				
Extras	(B2, LB3, W5, NB3)	13		(B11, LB15, W1)		27
Total		**202**		(8 wickets)		**429**

INDIA	O	M	R	W	O	M	R	W		FALL OF WICKETS			
Kapil Dev	32	12	83	3	28.5	4	89	2		E	I	E	I
Ghavri	26	8	61	2	34	11	76	3	Wkt	1st	1st	2nd	2nd
Bedi	29.5	4	69	2	(4) 26	4	67	1	1st	45	9	43	213
Yajurvindra	8	2	15	0	(5) 2	0	4	0	2nd	51	9	107	366
Venkataraghavan	29	9	59	3	(3) 26	4	75	1	3rd	51	47	125	367
									4th	148	91	192	389
ENGLAND									5th	203	130	194	410
Willis	18	2	53	3	28	4	89	1	6th	245	161	215	411
Botham	28	7	65	4	29	5	97	3	7th	272	172	291	419
Hendrick	22.3	7	38	3	8	2	15	0	8th	275	192	334	423
Willey	4	1	10	0	(5) 43.5	15	96	2	9th	304	200	–	–
Gooch	2	0	6	0	(6) 2	0	9	0	10th	305	202	–	–
Edmonds	5	1	17	0	(4) 38	11	87	1					
Butcher					2	0	9	0					

Umpires: D.J.Constant (18) and K.E.Palmer (4).

Close: 1st day – E(1) 245-5 (Gooch 79, Brearley 16); 2nd – I(1) 137-5 (Yajurvindra 19, Kapil Dev 0); 3rd – E(2) 177-3 (Boycott 83, Willey 26); 4th – I(2) 76-0 (Gavaskar 42, Chauhan 32).

INDIA v AUSTRALIA 1979-80 (1st Test)

At Chepauk, Madras, on 11, 12, 14, 15, 16 September.
Toss: Australia.   Result: MATCH DRAWN.
Debuts: India – D.R.Doshi.

Australia, 35 runs behind on first innings, fought a defiant rearguard action on the final day. Dymock (85 minutes) and Hogg (60 minutes) were defending grimly, when bad light followed by heavy rain ended the match two hours early, with Australia 177 runs in front. The stand of 222 between Border and Hughes is the third-wicket record for this series. Doshi took six wickets in his first innings in Test cricket. Higgs (leg-breaks and googlies) returned the best analysis of his 22-match Test career.

AUSTRALIA

A.M.J.Hilditch	c Venkataraghavan b Kapil Dev	4	(2)	lbw b Doshi	55
G.M.Wood	lbw b Doshi	33	(1)	c Chauhan b Kapil Dev	2
A.R.Border	run out	162		b Venkataraghavan	50
*K.J.Hughes	c Venkataraghavan b Doshi	100		lbw b Venkataraghavan	36
G.N.Yallop	c Yajurvindra b Doshi	18		run out	2
D.F.Whatmore	c Venkataraghavan b Doshi	20		c Chauhan b Doshi	8
†K.J.Wright	b Venkataraghavan	20		b Venkataraghavan	5
G.Dymock	lbw b Kapil Dev	16		not out	28
R.M.Hogg	c Kapil Dev b Doshi	3		not out	8
A.G.Hurst	c Kirmani b Doshi	0			
J.D.Higgs	not out	1			
Extras	(B1, LB7, W1, NB4)	13		(B11, LB4, NB3)	18
Total		**390**		**(7 wickets)**	**212**

INDIA

*S.M.Gavaskar	c Wood b Hogg	50
C.P.S.Chauhan	c Wright b Higgs	26
†S.M.H.Kirmani	c Border b Hogg	57
G.R.Viswanath	c Hughes b Higgs	17
D.B.Vengsarkar	c Whatmore b Higgs	65
Yashpal Sharma	lbw b Higgs	52
Yajurvindra Singh	c Wright b Yallop	15
Kapil Dev	c Hurst b Higgs	83
K.D.Ghavri	not out	23
S.Venkataraghavan	lbw b Higgs	4
D.R.Doshi	c Hogg b Higgs	3
Extras	(B2, LB5, NB23)	30
Total		**425**

INDIA	O	M	R	W	O	M	R	W		FALL OF WICKETS		
Kapil Dev	25.4	3	95	2	9	3	30	1		A	I	A
Ghavri	20	4	49	0	17.4	8	23	0	*Wkt*	*1st*	*1st*	*2nd*
Yajurvindra	9	1	29	0					1st	8	80	2
Venkataraghavan	46	16	101	1	45	10	77	3	2nd	75	89	103
Doshi	43	10	103	6	(3) 42	15	64	2	3rd	297	122	123
									4th	318	221	127
AUSTRALIA									5th	339	240	146
Hogg	22	1	85	2					6th	352	281	156
Hurst	23	8	51	0					7th	369	371	175
Dymock	24	6	65	0					8th	375	394	–
Higgs	41.3	12	143	7					9th	376	417	–
Border	14	4	30	0					10th	390	425	–
Yallop	6	1	21	1								

Umpires: M.V.Gothoskar (4) and Swaroop Kishen (3).

Close: 1st day – A(1) 244-2 (Border 129, Hughes 77); 2nd – I(1) 80-1 (Gavaskar 44, Kirmani 0); 3rd – I(1) 302-6 (Yashpal 29, Kapil Dev 15); 4th – A(2) 98-1 (Hilditch 44, Border 49).

INDIA v AUSTRALIA 1979-80 (2nd Test)

At Karnataka State C.A.Stadium, Bangalore, on 19, 20, 22, 23, 24 September.
Toss: Australia.   Result: MATCH DRAWN.
Debuts: India – N.S.Yadav.

The season of the southwest monsoon claimed more than seven hours of play. India's total was their highest against Australia until the fourth Test. It was founded on their record fourth-wicket partnership for this series, 159 between Vengsarkar and Viswanath. Gavaskar scored 3 off the first ball of the innings to become the first Indian to score 5,000 runs in Tests; it was his 52nd match. Hogg, in high fury at being no-balled 11 times in six overs, bowled a beamer, then plucked out a stump and hurled it to the ground before storming from the field.

AUSTRALIA

Batsman	Dismissal	R		2nd innings	R
A.M.J.Hilditch	c sub (Arun Lal) b Yadav	62	(2)	lbw b Yadav	3
W.M.Darling	b Kapil Dev	7			
A.R.Border	c Yadav b Doshi	44		b Yadav	19
*K.J.Hughes	c Ghavri b Kapil Dev	86		not out	13
G.N.Yallop	c Viswanath b Yadav	12		not out	6
B.Yardley	c and b Ghavri	47			
G.M.Wood	c Kirmani b Ghavri	18	(1)	c Viswanath b Yadav	30
†K.J.Wright	not out	16			
R.M.Hogg	lbw b Venkataraghavan	19			
J.D.Higgs	lbw b Yadav	1			
A.G.Hurst	b Yadav	0			
Extras	(B5, LB6, NB10)	21		(LB5, NB1)	6
Total		**333**		(3 wickets)	**77**

INDIA

Batsman	Dismissal	R
*S.M.Gavaskar	c Hilditch b Yardley	10
C.P.S.Chauhan	c Hilditch b Yardley	31
D.B.Vengsarkar	lbw b Yardley	112
†S.M.H.Kirmani	st Wright b Higgs	30
G.R.Viswanath	not out	161
Yashpal Sharma	c Border b Yardley	37
Kapil Dev	not out	38
K.D.Ghavri	⎫	
N.S.Yadav	⎬ did not bat	
S.Venkataraghavan		
D.R.Doshi	⎭	
Extras	(B12, LB8, W1, NB17)	38
Total	(5 wickets declared)	**457**

INDIA	O	M	R	W	O	M	R	W		FALL OF WICKETS		
										A	I	A
Kapil Dev	25	4	89	2	(2) 3	2	1	0		1st	1st	2nd
Ghavri	19	5	68	2	(1) 3	1	9	0	Wkt			
Doshi	28	6	63	1	(5) 8	4	11	0	1st	21	22	13
Venkataraghavan	20	6	43	1	(3) 8	2	18	0	2nd	99	61	53
Yadav	22.5	6	49	4	(4) 15.4	4	32	3	3rd	137	120	62
									4th	159	279	–
AUSTRALIA									5th	258	372	–
Hogg	32	6	118	0					6th	294	–	–
Hurst	29	3	93	0					7th	294	–	–
Yardley	44	16	107	4					8th	332	–	–
Higgs	37	9	95	1					9th	333	–	–
Yallop	2	0	6	0					10th	333	–	–

Umpires: P.R.Punjabi (3) and K.B.Ramaswami (3).

Close: 1st day – A(1) 182-4 (Hughes 31, Yardley 12); 2nd – I(1) 69-2 (Vengsarkar 8, Kirmani 4); 3rd – I(1) 124-3 (Vengsarkar 33, Viswanath 3); 4th – I(1) 376-5 (Viswanath 124, Kapil Dev 0)

INDIA v AUSTRALIA 1979-80 (3rd Test)

At Green Park, Kanpur, on 2, 3, 4, 6, 7 October.
Toss: India.   Result: INDIA won by 153 runs.
Debuts: None.

After looking clear favourites to win this match, Australia, needing 279 in 312 minutes, collapsed ignominiously against the fast-medium swing of Kapil Dev and off-spin of Yadav. Dymock (left-arm medium-fast) returned the best innings and match figures of his Test career and became the third bowler and the first Australian to dismiss all 11 batsmen in a Test match.

INDIA

*S.M.Gavaskar	lbw b Dymock	76	c Whatmore b Yardley	12
C.P.S.Chauhan	c and b Hogg	58	c Yardley b Dymock	84
D.B.Vengsarkar	lbw b Hogg	52	c Whatmore b Dymock	20
G.R.Viswanath	c sub (P.R.Sleep) b Dymock	44	c Whatmore b Yardley	52
Yashpal Sharma	b Hogg	0	c Wright b Dymock	0
Kapil Dev	c Hughes b Border	5	b Dymock	10
†S.M.H.Kirmani	c Whatmore b Hogg	4	b Dymock	45
K.D.Ghavri	c Whatmore b Dymock	5	c sub (P.R.Sleep) b Hogg	25
N.S.Yadav	lbw b Dymock	0	c Whatmore b Dymock	18
S.Venkataraghavan	c Border b Dymock	1	not out	4
D.R.Doshi	not out	0	b Dymock	0
Extras	(B5, LB6, NB15)	26	(B11, LB9, NB21)	41
Total		**271**		**311**

AUSTRALIA

A.M.J.Hilditch	c Chauhan b Ghavri	1	(2) b Doshi	23
B.Yardley	c Yashpal b Ghavri	29	(8) lbw b Kapil Dev	5
A.R.Border	c Viswanath b Venkataraghavan	24	(6) b Yadav	8
*K.J.Hughes	b Yadav	50	lbw b Kapil Dev	1
G.N.Yallop	hit wkt b Kapil Dev	89	(3) c Kirmani b Ghavri	15
†K.J.Wright	lbw b Kapil Dev	6	(7) b Yadav	11
D.F.Whatmore	c Gavaskar b Doshi	14	(5) b Yadav	33
W.M.Darling	c Kirmani b Ghavri	59	(1) lbw b Kapil Dev	4
G.Dymock	run out	11	st Kirmani b Yadav	6
R.M.Hogg	b Yadav	10	lbw b Kapil Dev	6
J.D.Higgs	not out	3	not out	8
Extras	(LB2, NB6)	8	(B1, LB2, NB2)	5
Total		**304**		**125**

AUSTRALIA	O	M	R	W		O	M	R	W		FALL OF WICKETS			
Dymock	35	7	99	5		28.4	5	67	7		I	A	I	A
Hogg	26	3	66	4		19	4	49	1	*Wkt*	*1st*	*1st*	*2nd*	*2nd*
Yardley	20	6	54	0		40	15	82	2	1st	114	1	24	13
Higgs	7	4	23	0	(5)	22	7	68	0	2nd	201	51	48	32
Border	3	2	3	1	(4)	2	1	4	0	3rd	206	75	161	37
										4th	214	168	163	49
INDIA										5th	231	175	177	74
Kapil Dev	27	5	78	2		16.2	5	30	4	6th	239	192	256	93
Ghavri	23.3	5	65	3		11	0	28	1	7th	246	246	261	104
Venkataraghavan	18	6	56	1		9	4	13	0	8th	246	263	302	106
Doshi	16	5	32	1		12	5	14	1	9th	256	294	311	113
Yadav	25	3	65	2		12	0	35	4	10th	271	304	311	125

Umpires: S.N.Hanumantha Rao (3) and Mohammad Ghouse (5).

Close: 1st day – I(1) 231-5 (Viswanath 19); 2nd – A(1) 175-4 (Yallop 59, Wright 6); 3rd – I(2) 67-2 (Chauhan 25, Viswanath 5); 4th – I(2) 310-8 (Yadav 17, Venkataraghavan 4).

INDIA v AUSTRALIA 1979-80 (4th Test)

At Feroz Shah Kotla, Delhi, on 13, 14, 16, 17, 18 October.
Toss: India.   Result: MATCH DRAWN.
Debuts: None.

For the second time in this rubber India compiled their highest total against Australia. The brothers-in-law, Gavaskar and Viswanath, scored their 21st and 11th hundreds in their 54th and 60th Tests respectively. Their partnership of 159 remains India's third-wicket record for this series. Australia followed-on for the first time in 34 matches against India despite a (then) record tenth-wicket partnership of 52 between Wright and Higgs. Vengsarkar kept wicket during the later stages of the second innings and caught Higgs.

INDIA

*S.M.Gavaskar	lbw b Higgs	115
C.P.S.Chauhan	c Whatmore b Dymock	19
D.B.Vengsarkar	st Wright b Higgs	26
G.R.Viswanath	st Wright b Higgs	131
Yashpal Sharma	not out	100
Kapil Dev	c Whatmore b Dymock	29
M.V.Narasimha Rao	c Wright b Dymock	5
†S.M.H.Kirmani	b Dymock	35
K.D.Ghavri	not out	8
N.S.Yadav	} did not bat	
D.R.Doshi		
Extras	(B6, LB12, NB24)	42
Total	**(7 wickets declared)**	**510**

AUSTRALIA

A.M.J.Hilditch	c Kirmani b Yadav	29		c Kirmani b Ghavri	85
W.M.Darling	c Kirmani b Kapil Dev	19		c Kirmani b Kapil Dev	7
A.R.Border	c Narasimha b Kapil Dev	24		c Narasimha b Ghavri	46
*K.J.Hughes	c Kirmani b Kapil Dev	18		c and b Ghavri	40
D.F.Whatmore	lbw b Yadav	77	(6)	lbw b Kapil Dev	54
P.R.Sleep	c Chauhan b Narasimha	17	(7)	c sub (Arun Lal) b Chauhan	64
G.N.Yallop	c Chauhan b Narasimha	21	(5)	b Doshi	25
†K.J.Wright	not out	55		b Yadav	15
G.Dymock	c Kirmani b Kapil Dev	0		not out	31
R.M.Hogg	b Kapil Dev	0		run out	0
J.D.Higgs	lbw b Doshi	11		c Vengsarkar b Viswanath	7
Extras	(B4, LB4, NB19)	27		(B13, LB9, W1, NB16)	39
Total		**298**			**413**

AUSTRALIA	O	M	R	W		O	M	R	W		FALL OF WICKETS			
Dymock	42.2	8	135	4								I	A	A
Hogg	33	8	91	0							Wkt	1st	1st	2nd
Yallop	5	0	21	0							1st	38	32	20
Border	4	2	5	0							2nd	108	72	147
Higgs	47	11	150	3							3rd	267	93	156
Sleep	13	1	66	0							4th	338	116	205
											5th	395	160	241
INDIA											6th	415	225	318
Ghavri	22	8	58	0	(2)	30	8	74	3		7th	467	228	344
Kapil Dev	32	7	82	5	(1)	20	7	48	2		8th	–	242	395
Doshi	13.3	5	29	1	(4)	34	11	69	1		9th	–	246	395
Yadav	27	10	56	2	(5)	36	10	101	1		10th	–	298	413
Narasimha Rao	12	1	46	2	(3)	19	3	50	0					
Gavaskar						4	1	10	0					
Chauhan						5	1	11	1					
Viswanath						3.3	0	11	1					

Umpires: P.R.Punjabi (4) and K.B.Ramaswami (4).

Close: 1st day – I(1) 267-3 (Viswanath 83); 2nd – A(1) 20-0 (Hilditch 8, Darling 9); 3rd – A(1) 258-9 (Wright 22, Higgs 5); 4th – A(2) 189-3 (Hughes 19, Yallop 20).

INDIA v AUSTRALIA 1979-80 (5th Test)

At Eden Gardens, Calcutta, on 26, 27, 28, 30, 31 October.
Toss: Australia.   Result: MATCH DRAWN.
Debuts: None.

A challenging declaration by Hughes failed to produce the stirring finish it deserved. Set a target of 247 runs in a minimum of 245 minutes. India were 47 short when bad light ended the match 22 balls prematurely. Vengsarkar retired at 169 because of a pulled muscle in his forearm and was out first ball when he resumed at 290. After Hilditch was caught off the fourth ball of the match, Yallop, opening a Test innings for the first time, batted 520 minutes (392 balls, 15 fours) for Australia's highest individual score in India until 1986-87.

AUSTRALIA

A.M.J.Hilditch	c Kirmani b Kapil Dev	0	b Ghavri	29
G.N.Yallop	c Gavaskar b Yadav	167	lbw b Kapil Dev	4
A.R.Border	lbw b Kapil Dev	54	st Kirmani b Doshi	6
*K.J.Hughes	lbw b Kapil Dev	92	not out	64
D.F.Whatmore	b Kapil Dev	4	c Vengsarkar b Doshi	4
W.M.Darling	st Kirmani b Doshi	39	c Gavaskar b Yadav	7
B.Yardley	not out	61	c Narasimha b Yadav	12
†K.J.Wright	lbw b Doshi	0	not out	12
G.Dymock	lbw b Doshi	3		
R.M.Hogg	c Yashpal b Doshi	0		
J.D.Higgs	lbw b Kapil Dev	1		
Extras	(B7, LB7, NB7)	21	(B9, LB4)	13
Total		**442**	(6 wickets declared)	**151**

INDIA

*S.M.Gavaskar	lbw b Hogg	14	c Hilditch b Dymock	25
C.P.S.Chauhan	c Border b Higgs	39	c Wright b Dymock	50
D.B.Vengsarkar	c Hughes b Yardley	89	c Wright b Dymock	2
G.R.Viswanath	c Wright b Yardley	96	lbw b Dymock	7
Yashpal Sharma	c Wright b Hogg	22	not out	85
M.V.Narasimha Rao	run out	10	not out	20
Kapil Dev	c Hughes b Dymock	30		
†S.M.H.Kirmani	not out	13		
K.D.Ghavri	c Wright b Yardley	1		
N.S.Yadav	c Wright b Yardley	0		
D.R.Doshi	b Dymock	0		
Extras	(B12, LB9, W4, NB8)	33	(B4, LB7)	11
Total		**347**	(4 wickets)	**200**

INDIA	O	M	R	W	O	M	R	W	FALL OF WICKETS				
Kapil Dev	32	9	74	5	11	3	33	1		A	I	A	I
Ghavri	24	3	85	0	13.3	5	39	1	*Wkt*	*1st*	*1st*	*2nd*	*2nd*
Yadav	42	8	135	1	(4) 11	6	16	2	1st	0	15	21	52
Narasimha Rao	8	0	24	0					2nd	97	132	39	54
Doshi	43	10	92	4	(3) 22	6	50	2	3rd	303	256	53	70
Chauhan	4	0	11	0					4th	311	290	62	123
									5th	347	290	81	–
AUSTRALIA									6th	396	305	115	–
Dymock	26.4	8	56	2	(2) 25	7	63	4	7th	396	341	–	–
Hogg	26	2	103	2	(1) 8.2	1	26	0	8th	418	342	–	–
Yardley	42	11	91	4	13	1	47	0	9th	426	346	–	–
Higgs	28	12	56	1	16	3	51	0	10th	442	347	–	–
Border	2	0	8	0									
Yallop	1	1	0	0	(5) 1	0	2	0					

Umpires: S.N.Hanumantha Rao (4) and Swaroop Kishen (4).

Close: 1st day – A(1) 227-2 (Yallop 114, Hughes 49); 2nd – I(1) 21-1 (Chauhan 3, Vengsarkar 3); 3rd – I(1) 221-2 (Viswanath 43, Yashpal 13); 4th – A(2) 81-5 (Hughes 23).

INDIA v AUSTRALIA 1979-80 (6th Test)

At Wankhede Stadium, Bombay, on 3, 4, 6, 7 November.
Toss: India.   Result: INDIA won by an innings and 100 runs.
Debuts: None.

India won their first rubber against Australia by inflicting their heaviest defeat of this series with more than a day to spare. Gavaskar's 22nd Test hundred placed him level with W.R.Hammond and M.C.Cowdrey: only Sir Donald Bradman (29) and Sir Garfield Sobers (26) had scored more. His partnership of 192 in 247 minutes with Chauhan remains India's highest for the first wicket in this series. Kirmani (306 minutes, 209 balls, 16 fours) was the third 'night-watchman' to score a century at this level (following Nasim-ul-Ghani in *Test No. 531* and A.L.Mann in *No. 810*). His stand of 127 in 154 minutes with Ghavri is the eighth-wicket record in these Tests. Darling was carried from the field at 154 after trying to hook a bouncer from Kapil Dev which hit him near the right temple.

INDIA

*S.M.Gavaskar	c Hughes b Border	123
C.P.S.Chauhan	b Dymock	73
D.B.Vengsarkar	c Whatmore b Border	6
G.R.Viswanath	c and b Higgs	10
†S.M.H.Kirmani	not out	101
Yashpal Sharma	c Whatmore b Hogg	8
M.Amarnath	hit wkt b Hogg	2
Kapil Dev	c Whatmore b Higgs	17
K.D.Ghavri	c sub (G.D.Porter) b Dymock	86
N.S.Yadav	not out	0
D.R.Doshi	did not bat	
Extras	(B3, LB12, NB17)	32
Total	**(8 wickets declared)**	**458**

AUSTRALIA

A.M.J.Hilditch	run out	13	b Kapil Dev		9
G.N.Yallop	c Kapil Dev b Yadav	60	c Amarnath b Ghavri		4
A.R.Border	c Vengsarkar b Yadav	23	b Doshi		61
*K.J.Hughes	c Vengsarkar b Doshi	14	c Ghavri b Kapil Dev		80
D.F.Whatmore	lbw b Doshi	6	lbw b Kapil Dev		0
W.M.Darling	c sub (R.M.H.Binny) b Yadav	16	retired hurt		0
P.R.Sleep	b Yadav	1	c Kapil Dev b Doshi		3
†K.J.Wright	not out	11	lbw b Doshi		5
G.Dymock	c Chauhan b Doshi	1	c Viswanath b Yadav		7
R.M.Hogg	c Amarnath b Doshi	5	not out		3
J.D.Higgs	b Doshi	0	b Kapil Dev		4
Extras	(B1, LB2, NB7)	10	(LB12, NB10)		22
Total		**160**			**198**

AUSTRALIA	O	M	R	W	O	M	R	W		FALL OF WICKETS		
Dymock	31	5	95	2						I	A	A
Hogg	28	14	53	2					*Wkt*	*1st*	*1st*	*2nd*
Higgs	29	4	116	2					1st	192	28	11
Border	27	7	60	2					2nd	222	77	17
Sleep	28	7	79	0					3rd	231	110	149
Whatmore	5	2	11	0					4th	240	118	154
Yallop	1	0	12	0					5th	272	124	159
									6th	281	125	176
INDIA									7th	327	144	183
Kapil Dev	8	0	26	0	14.1	5	39	4	8th	454	145	187
Ghavri	8	1	30	0	10	0	28	1	9th	–	158	198
Doshi	19.5	4	43	5	(5) 25	6	60	3	10th	–	160	–
Amarnath	5	1	11	0	(3) 2	1	1	0				
Yadav	21	7	40	4	(4) 22	9	48	1				

Umpires: J.D.Ghosh (2) and Mohammad Ghouse (6).

Close: 1st day – I(1) 231-3 (Viswanath 9, Kirmani 0); 2nd – A(1) 15-0 (Hilditch 8, Yallop 7); 3rd – A(2) 60-2 (Border 22, Hughes 19).

INDIA v PAKISTAN 1979-80 (1st Test)

At Karnataka State C.A.Stadium, Bangalore, on 21, 22, 24, 25, 26 November.
Toss: Pakistan.   Result: MATCH DRAWN.
Debuts: India – R.M.H.Binny; Pakistan – Ehteshamuddin.

Pakistan's first Test match on Indian soil for almost 19 years produced the eighth consecutive draw between the two sides in that country. Mudassar took 340 minutes to reach his hundred and emulated his father, Nazar Mohammad, who also scored a century as an opening batsman in this series (*Test No. 356*). They were only the second father/son combination after 'Dave' and Dudley Nourse (South Africa v Australia) to score hundreds in the same series. The partnership of 60 between Wasim Bari and Iqbal Qasim is Pakistan's highest for the ninth wicket against India. Play was halted for several minutes on the first day when all the players and both umpires threw themselves to the ground, face down with their hands over their ears – a swarm of bees had invaded the stadium.

PAKISTAN

Majid Khan	c Kirmani b Ghavri	1	st Kirmani b Doshi	19
Mudassar Nazar	c Doshi b Yadav	126	c Kapil Dev b Yadav	17
Zaheer Abbas	st Kirmani b Doshi	40	not out	31
Javed Miandad	lbw b Doshi	76	not out	30
Wasim Raja	lbw b Kapil Dev	36		
*Asif Iqbal	c and b Doshi	55		
Imran Khan	c Viswanath b Yadav	6		
†Wasim Bari	not out	49		
Abdul Qadir	lbw b Kapil Dev	8		
Iqbal Qasim	run out	20		
Ehteshamuddin	did not bat			
Extras	(B1, LB6, NB7)	14	(B4, NB7)	11
Total	(9 wickets declared)	**431**	(2 wickets)	**108**

INDIA

*S.M.Gavaskar	c Miandad b Qadir	88
C.P.S.Chauhan	c Majid b Imran	13
D.B.Vengsarkar	b Imran	33
G.R.Viswanath	c Wasim Bari b Ehteshamuddin	73
Yashpal Sharma	c Miandad b Majid	62
R.M.H.Binny	c Ehteshamuddin b Imran	46
†S.M.H.Kirmani	c Qasim b Ehteshamuddin	37
Kapil Dev	b Majid	38
K.D.Ghavri	b Majid	2
N.S.Yadav	not out	1
D.R.Doshi	b Imran	0
Extras	(B13, LB10)	23
Total		**416**

INDIA	O	M	R	W	O	M	R	W	FALL OF WICKETS			
Kapil Dev	24	4	67	2	4	2	6	0		P	I	P
Ghavri	24	3	83	1	8	3	30	0	*Wkt*	*1st*	*1st*	*2nd*
Binny	10	1	49	0	3	2	1	0	1st	5	17	41
Doshi	52.3	20	102	3	12	3	26	1	2nd	62	122	41
Yadav	39	5	116	2	11	2	20	1	3rd	196	164	–
Viswanath					3	1	6	0	4th	256	266	–
Gavaskar					1	0	8	0	5th	334	307	–
									6th	345	347	–
PAKISTAN									7th	348	410	–
Imran	28.4	12	53	4					8th	371	414	–
Ehteshamuddin	18	2	52	2					9th	431	415	–
Qasim	41	17	75	0					10th	–	416	–
Majid	28	9	55	3								
Qadir	35	8	114	1								
Wasim Raja	8	2	30	0								
Mudassar	6	1	14	0								

Umpires: M.V.Gothoskar (5) and Swaroop Kishen (5).

Close: 1st day – P(1) 256-4 (Mudassar 99); 2nd – I(1) 39-1 (Gavaskar 21, Vengsarkar 1); 3rd – I(1) 261-3 (Viswanath 72, Yashpal 38); 4th – I(1) 286-4 (Yashpal 56, Binny 6).

INDIA v PAKISTAN 1979-80 (2nd Test)

At Feroz Shah Kotla, Delhi, on 4, 5, 6, 8, 9 December.
Toss: Pakistan.   Result: MATCH DRAWN.
Debuts: None.

Although resulting in their ninth successive draw in India, this match produced the most dramatic contest of this series. Needing 390 runs in a minimum of 550 minutes, India required 114 off the mandatory 20 overs and were 26 runs short when the final over was abandoned. Sikander Bakht's outswing brought him the best analysis by any visiting bowler in a Test in India and the record for Pakistan in this series until 1982-83. He bowled 20.1 overs unchanged on the second day, capturing the first eight wickets that fell to a bowler after Imran (wrenched hip) had retired in mid-over. He was the first to take 11 wickets for Pakistan in a Test in India. Doshi, run out when he left his crease to complain about the shadow of a large tree which was on the pitch, was allowed to resume his innings after he had successfully entreated acting-captain Majid to withdraw the appeal. Vengsarkar's hundred took 437 minutes; during it he completed 1,000 runs in Tests for the calendar year. He went on to play the longest innings in any Test for India, his 527 minutes being just two minutes longer than 'Vinoo' Mankad required for his 231 in *Test No. 420*. Vengsarkar held the record only until the fifth Test.

PAKISTAN

Majid Khan	b Kapil Dev	0	c Kirmani b Binny	40
Mudassar Nazar	c Chauhan b Kapil Dev	18	c Kirmani b Kapil Dev	12
Zaheer Abbas	b Kapil Dev	3	c Kirmani b Binny	50
Javed Miandad	lbw b Ghavri	34	run out	0
Wasim Raja	lbw b Kapil Dev	97	c Kapil Dev b Doshi	61
*Asif Iqbal	c Vengsarkar b Ghavri	64	c Kirmani b Kapil Dev	38
Imran Khan	lbw b Binny	30	c Chauhan b Doshi	2
†Wasim Bari	b Kapil Dev	9	b Ghavri	5
Abdul Qadir	b Binny	9	c Vengsarkar b Kapil Dev	11
Iqbal Qasim	run out	2	not out	5
Sikander Bakht	not out	1	lbw b Kapil Dev	6
Extras	(LB2, NB4)	6	(B6, LB4, NB2)	12
Total		**273**		**242**

INDIA

*S.M.Gavaskar	c Wasim Bari b Sikander	31	c Wasim Bari b Sikander	21
C.P.S.Chauhan	c Wasim Bari b Sikander	11	lbw b Sikander	40
D.B.Vengsarkar	c Miandad b Sikander	1	not out	146
G.R.Viswanath	run out	4	b Qasim	34
Yashpal Sharma	not out	28	c and b Sikander	60
R.M.H.Binny	lbw b Sikander	1	(7) c Qadir b Asif	10
†S.M.H.Kirmani	b Sikander	5	(8) not out	11
Kapil Dev	b Sikander	15	(6) lbw b Mudassar	21
K.D.Ghavri	lbw b Sikander	0		
N.S.Yadav	c Qadir b Sikander	4		
D.R.Doshi	c Miandad b Asif	10		
Extras	(B2, LB5, NB9)	16	(B2, LB5, W1, NB13)	21
Total		**126**	(6 wickets)	**364**

INDIA	O	M	R	W	O	M	R	W		FALL OF WICKETS			
Kapil Dev	23.5	8	58	5	22.5	6	63	4		P	I	P	I
Ghavri	21	4	58	2	17	4	59	1	*Wkt*	*1st*	*1st*	*2nd*	*2nd*
Binny	10	3	32	2	17	3	56	2	1st	3	19	39	37
Doshi	17	3	51	0	(5) 19	6	31	2	2nd	13	35	68	92
Yadav	20	2	68	0	(4) 5	0	21	0	3rd	36	46	68	154
PAKISTAN									4th	90	52	143	276
Imran	7.3	4	11	0	1	0	2	0	5th	220	56	201	308
Sikander	21	3	69	8	38	7	121	3	6th	224	70	209	343
Asif	6.2	4	3	1	20	7	46	1	7th	250	87	210	–
Majid	1	0	12	0	(8) 4	2	8	0	8th	270	87	230	–
Qasim	3	0	7	0	(4) 30	5	87	1	9th	271	94	232	–
Mudassar	3	0	8	0	(5) 25	8	61	1	10th	273	126	242	–
Qadir					(6) 11	3	16	0					
Wasim Raja					(7) 2	1	2	0					

Umpires: Mohammad Ghouse (7) and P.R.Punjabi (5).

Close: 1st day – P(1) 217-4 (Wasim Raja 94, Asif 63); 2nd – I(1) 126-9 (Yashpal 28, Doshi 10); 3rd – P(2) 197-4 (Wasim Raja 52, Asif 38); 4th – I(2) 117-2 (Vengsarkar 32, Viswanath 13).

INDIA v PAKISTAN 1979-80 (3rd Test)

At Wankhede Stadium, Bombay, on 16, 17, 18, 20 December.
Toss: India.   Result: INDIA won by 131 runs.
Debuts: None.

India gained their first win against Pakistan since November 1952 (*Test No. 357*). The match was played on the pitch used six weeks earlier for the final Test against Australia; both matches ended in Indian victories on the fourth day. Wasim Bari became the first Pakistan wicket-keeper to complete a double of 1,000 runs and 100 dismissals when he had scored 19. Kapil Dev, with a rousing 69 off 79 balls, and Kirmani added 95 in a (then) record seventh-wicket stand for this series. Iqbal Qasim became the second Pakistan bowler after Sikander in the previous match to take ten or more wickets in a Test in India.

INDIA

Batsman	Dismissal 1	R		Dismissal 2	R
*S.M.Gavaskar	c Qadir b Sikander	4		c Zaheer b Qasim	48
C.P.S.Chauhan	c Wasim Bari b Imran	5		b Mudassar	0
D.B.Vengsarkar	c Majid b Qasim	58		c Wasim Bari b Sikander	45
G.R.Viswanath	c and b Qasim	47		lbw b Qadir	9
Yashpal Sharma	b Qasim	3		c Majid b Qasim	16
R.M.H.Binny	c Wasim Bari b Qasim	0	(9)	c and b Sikander	0
†S.M.H.Kirmani	c Asif b Sikander	41	(6)	c Asif b Qasim	15
Kapil Dev	c Wasim Raja b Sikander	69	(7)	c Wasim Bari b Qasim	3
K.D.Ghavri	c Asif b Sikander	36	(8)	c Wasim Bari b Qasim	1
N.S.Yadav	not out	29		st Wasim Bari b Qasim	1
D.R.Doshi	c Wasim Bari b Sikander	9		not out	1
Extras	(B10, LB10, W2, NB11)	33		(B9, LB7, NB5)	21
Total		**334**			**160**

PAKISTAN

Batsman	Dismissal 1	R	Dismissal 2	R
Majid Khan	c Kirmani b Binny	5	lbw b Ghavri	7
Mudassar Nazar	c Gavaskar b Doshi	25	lbw b Ghavri	13
Zaheer Abbas	b Binny	2	b Kapil Dev	11
Javed Miandad	lbw b Binny	16	lbw b Doshi	64
Wasim Raja	c Viswanath b Doshi	24	c Vengsarkar b Ghavri	4
*Asif Iqbal	c and b Yadav	14	c Viswanath b Doshi	26
Imran Khan	c Gavaskar b Doshi	15	c Gavaskar b Ghavri	19
†Wasim Bari	b Yadav	23	lbw b Doshi	3
Abdul Qadir	not out	29	c Binny b Yadav	15
Iqbal Qasim	c Kirmani b Yadav	0	c Vengsarkar b Yadav	6
Sikander Bakht	lbw b Kapil Dev	3	not out	1
Extras	(B1, LB2, NB14)	17	(B2, LB11, NB8)	21
Total		**173**		**190**

PAKISTAN	O	M	R	W		O	M	R	W		FALL OF WICKETS			
												I	P	I	P
Imran	15	7	35	1											
Sikander	22.1	5	55	5	(1)	17	6	30	2	Wkt	1st	1st	2nd	2nd
Qasim	44	15	135	4		28.5	14	40	6	1st	13	11	5	16
Majid	23	8	52	0		4	1	14	0	2nd	31	15	78	32
Qadir	3	1	16	0		11	5	27	1	3rd	111	53	97	41
Asif	2	1	1	0						4th	129	57	132	48
Mudassar	5	0	7	0	(2)	8	3	18	1	5th	129	83	146	84
Wasim Raja					(6)	1	0	10	0	6th	154	105	154	145
										7th	249	117	156	161
INDIA										8th	250	146	157	178
Kapil Dev	14.3	4	23	1		6	1	26	1	9th	310	146	157	189
Ghavri	7	2	17	0		18	4	63	4	10th	334	173	160	190
Binny	12	1	53	3	(4)	2	1	2	0					
Doshi	27	8	52	3	(3)	19	4	42	3					
Yadav	8	4	11	3		6.4	0	36	2					

Umpires: S.N.Hanumantha Rao (5) and K.B.Ramaswami (5).

Close: 1st day – I(1) 232-6 (Kirmani 39, Kapil Dev 57); 2nd – P(1) 112-6 (Imran 12, Wasim Bari 2); 3rd – I(2) 117-3 (Vengsarkar 42, Yashpal 5).

INDIA v PAKISTAN 1979-80 (4th Test)

At Green Park, Kanpur, on 25, 26, 27, 29, 30 (*no play*) December.
Toss: India.   Result: MATCH DRAWN.
Debuts: None.

Pakistan, without Imran (hip and back strain), found a well-grassed and bouncy pitch much to the liking of Sikander and Ehteshamuddin. The latter had not been included in the squad of players announced on the eve of the match. After the rest day the match continued at funereal pace on a mown and docile surface. Only 114 runs were scored in 259 minutes of play on the fourth day before bad light 19 minutes after tea effectively ended the contest. The day's highlight was a stump-kicking tantrum by Sikander. Although the final day produced cloudless conditions, overnight rain had penetrated the flimsy covers and waterlogged the pitch. Gavaskar completed 1,000 Test match runs for the second calendar year in succession. Kapil Dev achieved his best analysis for India (until the next match) and took his tally of wickets for 1979 to a (then) world record 74 from 17 Tests. That record stands tribute to his fitness and to the proliferation of Test cricket with India averaging a match every three weeks. Chauhan's 61 in 334 minutes contained the slowest recorded fifty in Indian first-class cricket – 316 minutes.

INDIA

*S.M.Gavaskar	b Sikander	2	c Mudassar b Ehteshamuddin		81
C.P.S.Chauhan	c Zaheer b Sikander	6	c Sadiq b Wasim Raja		61
D.B.Vengsarkar	c Wasim Bari b Sikander	0	not out		16
G.R.Viswanath	c Mudassar b Ehteshamuddin	2	not out		17
Yashpal Sharma	c Wasim Bari b Ehteshamuddin	16			
R.M.H.Binny	b Sikander	29			
†S.M.H.Kirmani	b Ehteshamuddin	0			
Kapil Dev	c Mudassar b Sikander	2			
K.D.Ghavri	not out	45			
N.S.Yadav	c Majid b Ehteshamuddin	25			
D.R.Doshi	c Wasim Bari b Ehteshamuddin	20			
Extras	(B1, LB1, NB13)	15	(B4, LB1, NB13)		18
Total		**162**	(2 wickets)		**193**

PAKISTAN

Mudassar Nazar	c Kirmani b Kapil Dev	6
Sadiq Mohammad	c Kirmani b Ghavri	47
Zaheer Abbas	c Gavaskar b Kapil Dev	5
Javed Miandad	lbw b Kapil Dev	8
Majid Khan	lbw b Kapil Dev	19
*Asif Iqbal	c Viswanath b Doshi	11
Wasim Raja	not out	94
†Wasim Bari	b Binny	0
Iqbal Qasim	b Kapil Dev	32
Sikander Bakht	c Kirmani b Kapil Dev	4
Ehteshamuddin	b Binny	2
Extras	(LB11, NB10)	21
Total		**249**

PAKISTAN	O	M	R	W		O	M	R	W
Sikander	24	9	56	5		23.2	5	63	0
Ehteshamuddin	26.4	11	47	5		26	9	40	1
Mudassar	10	4	22	0	(5)	3	1	19	0
Asif	8	3	22	0					
Qasim					(3)	16	7	28	0
Wasim Raja					(4)	9	2	25	1

INDIA	O	M	R	W
Kapil Dev	28	5	63	6
Ghavri	21	5	42	1
Binny	18.5	2	76	2
Doshi	17	8	26	1
Yadav	5	1	21	0

FALL OF WICKETS

	I	P	I
Wkt	1st	1st	2nd
1st	4	12	125
2nd	4	35	168
3rd	11	63	–
4th	17	92	–
5th	58	108	–
6th	67	131	–
7th	69	132	–
8th	69	214	–
9th	117	226	–
10th	162	249	–

Umpires: Mohammad Ghouse (8) and Swaroop Kishen (6).

Close: 1st day – I(1) 112-8 (Ghavri 22, Yadav 21); 2nd – P(1) 124-5 (Majid 17, Wasim Raja 12); 3rd – I(2) 79-0 (Gavaskar 48, Chauhan 23); 4th – I(2) 193-2 (Vengsarkar 16, Viswanath 17).

INDIA v PAKISTAN 1979-80 (5th Test)

At Chepauk, Madras, on 15, 16, 17, 19, 20 January.
Toss: Pakistan.   Result: INDIA won by 10 wickets.
Debuts: India – S.M.Patil.

India's resounding victory gave them their first rubber against Pakistan since 1952-53 when this series began. Gavaskar scored his 23rd hundred to move ahead of W.R.Hammond and M.C.Cowdrey. His 166 in 593 minutes (373 balls) was the longest innings for India until he himself surpassed it in 1981-82 (*Test No. 913*). Imran Khan became the fourth Pakistan bowler to take 100 Test wickets when he dismissed Kirmani. After scoring 84 off 98 balls, Kapil Dev produced the best innings (then) and match figures of his Test career.

PAKISTAN

Mudassar Nazar	c Kirmani b Kapil Dev	6	c Vengsarkar b Kapil Dev	8
Sadiq Mohammad	c Kirmani b Kapil Dev	46	c Binny b Kapil Dev	0
Majid Khan	run out	56	c Patil b Ghavri	11
Zaheer Abbas	c Kirmani b Kapil Dev	0	c Chauhan b Kapil Dev	15
Javed Miandad	c Vengsarkar b Kapil Dev	45	c Kirmani b Doshi	52
*Asif Iqbal	c Kirmani b Ghavri	34	c Kirmani b Kapil Dev	5
Wasim Raja	c Kapil Dev b Doshi	15	c Viswanath b Doshi	57
Imran Khan	run out	34	c Doshi b Kapil Dev	29
†Wasim Bari	c Binny b Ghavri	13	lbw b Kapil Dev	15
Iqbal Qasim	not out	3	not out	19
Sikander Bakht	c Vengsarkar b Ghavri	1	b Kapil Dev	2
Extras	(LB3, NB16)	19	(LB3, NB17)	20
Total		272		233

INDIA

*S.M.Gavaskar	c Qasim b Imran	166	not out	29
C.P.S.Chauhan	c Qasim b Mudassar	5	not out	46
D.B.Vengsarkar	c Miandad b Imran	17		
G.R.Viswanath	c Mudassar b Qasim	16		
S.M.Patil	c Miandad b Sikander	15		
Yashpal Sharma	b Qasim	46		
†S.M.H.Kirmani	b Imran	2		
Kapil Dev	lbw b Imran	84		
R.M.H.Binny	not out	42		
K.D.Ghavri	b Qasim	1		
D.R.Doshi	c Miandad b Imran	9		
Extras	(B1, LB2, NB24)	27	(NB3)	3
Total		430	(0 wickets)	78

INDIA	O	M	R	W	O	M	R	W	FALL OF WICKETS				
Kapil Dev	19	5	90	4	23.4	7	56	7		P	I	P	I
Ghavri	18.4	3	73	3	14	0	82	1	Wkt	1st	1st	2nd	2nd
Binny	10	1	42	0	13	2	33	0	1st	33	30	1	–
Doshi	26	6	48	1	16	3	42	2	2nd	79	88	17	–
									3rd	80	135	33	–
									4th	151	160	36	–
PAKISTAN									5th	187	265	58	–
Imran	38.2	6	114	5	5	1	20	0	6th	215	279	147	–
Sikander	32	5	105	1	6	0	37	0	7th	225	339	171	–
Mudassar	16	3	54	1	2	0	2	0	8th	266	412	197	–
Qasim	37	13	81	3	4	1	12	0	9th	268	413	229	–
Wasim Raja	2	0	19	0					10th	272	430	233	–
Majid	9	1	30	0									
Sadiq					(5)	1	0	4	0				

Umpires: M.V.Gothoskar (6) and Swaroop Kishen (7).

Close: 1st day – P(1) 254-7 (Imran 27, Wasim Bari 7); 2nd – I(1) 161-4 (Gavaskar 92, Yashpal 1); 3rd – I(1) 375-7 (Kapil Dev 68, Binny 15); 4th – P(2) 178-7 (Imran 11, Wasim Bari 5).

INDIA v PAKISTAN 1979-80 (6th Test)

At Eden Gardens, Calcutta, on 29, 30, 31 January, 2, 3 February.
Toss: India.   Result: MATCH DRAWN.
Debuts: Pakistan – Taslim Arif.

Gavaskar relinquished the captaincy as he was not available for India's imminent tour of the West Indies (subsequently cancelled). Kapil Dev, making his 25th consecutive appearance since his debut, took his 100th wicket in the record time of 1 year 105 days (beating I.T.Botham's 2 years 9 days). At 21 years 25 days he remains the youngest bowler to take 100 Test wickets (previously G.D.McKenzie). Two days later he became the youngest to score 1,000 runs (previously Javed Miandad) and to complete the Test double. Viswanath (68) and Asif Iqbal (the last of his 58) set new national records for most Test appearances. Reserve wicket-keeper Taslim Arif grafted for 424 minutes in his first Test innings. National records for a rubber between these countries were set by Gavaskar (529 runs), Kapil Dev (32 wickets), Sikander Bakht (24 wickets) and Wasim Bari (16 dismissals).

INDIA

S.M.Gavaskar	c Qasim b Imran	44	(6)	c Miandad b Imran	15
C.P.S.Chauhan	lbw b Ehteshamuddin	18	(1)	lbw b Ehteshamuddin	21
R.M.H.Binny	lbw b Imran	15	(2)	c Wasim Raja b Imran	0
*G.R.Viswanath	b Ehteshamuddin	13		b Imran	13
S.M.Patil	b Imran	62		run out	31
Yashpal Sharma	c Wasim Bari b Imran	62	(7)	b Ehteshamuddin	21
Kapil Dev	st Wasim Bari b Qasim	16	(8)	b Qasim	30
†S.M.H.Kirmani	c Qasim b Ehteshamuddin	37	(3)	c Sadiq b Imran	0
K.D.Ghavri	run out	16		not out	37
N.S.Yadav	not out	18		c and b Qasim	3
D.R.Doshi	b Ehteshamuddin	3		c Asif b Imran	6
Extras	(B3, LB9, NB15)	27		(B9, LB3, NB16)	28
Total		**331**			**205**

PAKISTAN

Taslim Arif	c Chauhan b Kapil Dev	90		c and b Binny	46
Sadiq Mohammad	lbw b Kapil Dev	5		b Ghavri	8
Majid Khan	c Kirmani b Binny	54		b Doshi	11
Javed Miandad	lbw b Ghavri	50		c and b Doshi	46
Wasim Raja	not out	50		run out	12
*Asif Iqbal	not out	5		run out	15
Imran Khan				not out	19
†Wasim Bari				not out	0
Iqbal Qasim	did not bat				
Sikander Bakht					
Ehteshamuddin					
Extras	(B1, LB8, NB9)	18		(B12, LB8, NB2)	22
Total	(4 wickets declared)	**272**		(6 wickets)	**179**

PAKISTAN	O	M	R	W	O	M	R	W		FALL OF WICKETS			
Imran	33	5	67	4	23.5	3	63	5			I	P	I	P
Sikander	22	5	87	0	6	2	18	0	Wkt	1st	1st	2nd	2nd
Ehteshamuddin	35	7	87	4	19	5	44	2	1st	48	20	7	24
Qasim	17	3	53	1	21	5	50	2	2nd	72	112	10	58
Majid	2	0	10	0					3rd	91	185	33	86
Wasim Raja					(5) 1	0	2	0	4th	99	258	48	111
									5th	187	–	88	154
INDIA									6th	218	–	92	162
Kapil Dev	26	4	65	2	20	7	49	0	7th	252	–	135	–
Ghavri	21.5	3	77	1	11	2	32	1	8th	292	–	162	–
Doshi	25	12	38	0	20	5	46	2	9th	307	–	172	–
Binny	17	3	35	1	8	2	20	1	10th	331	–	205	–
Yadav	10	0	39	0	4	3	10	0					

Umpires: P.R.Punjabi (6) and K.B.Ramaswami (6).

Close: 1st day – I(1) 205-5 (Yashpal 28, Kapil Dev 10); 2nd – P(1) 57-1 (Taslim 28, Majid 21); 3rd – P(1) 263-4 (Wasim Raja 41, Asif 5); 4th – I(2) 186-9 (Ghavri 22, Doshi 3).

AUSTRALIA v WEST INDIES 1979-80 (1st Test)

At Woolloongabba, Brisbane, on 1, 2, 3, 4, 5 December.
Toss: West Indies.   Result: MATCH DRAWN.
Debuts: Australia – B.M.Laird.

The first drawn Test in Australia for three years ended a sequence of 16 matches which had produced definite results. It was the first five-day Test without a rest day since 1956-57 (*Test No.435*), and it marked the return of players contracted to the disbanded World Series circuit. Greg Chappell celebrated his reinstatement as captain with his 15th Test hundred. Murray led West Indies for the only time while C.H.Lloyd recovered from knee surgery. Marsh became the first Australian to make 200 dismissals when he caught Haynes; only T.G.Evans and A.P.E.Knott had claimed more. The partnership of 56 between Garner (who made his highest score in first-class matches until 1980) and Croft (who batted 80 minutes for 2 runs) remains the highest for West Indies' tenth wicket in this series. Laird's match aggregate of 167 runs remains the highest without a century by any batsman in his first Test. Umpire Bailhache no-balled five of Lillee's first six deliveries on the final evening. For the first time since 1932-33, Australia reverted to six-ball overs in home Tests.

AUSTRALIA

Batsman	Dismissal	Score		2nd innings	Score
B.M.Laird	c Murray b Garner	92	(2)	c sub (M.D.Marshall) b Garner	75
R.B.McCosker	c Kallicharran b Croft	14	(1)	b Holding	33
A.R.Border	c Murray b Garner	1		c Richards b Garner	7
*G.S.Chappell	c King b Roberts	74		b Croft	124
K.J.Hughes	b Croft	3		not out	130
D.W.Hookes	c Holding b Croft	43		b Roberts	37
†R.W.Marsh	c Murray b Garner	3		c Kallicharran b King	19
R.J.Bright	b Holding	13		not out	2
D.K.Lillee	lbw b Garner	0			
R.M.Hogg	b Roberts	8			
J.R.Thomson	not out	0			
Extras	(B1, LB4, NB12)	17		(B2, LB11, W2, NB6)	21
Total		**268**		**(6 wickets declared)**	**448**

WEST INDIES

Batsman	Dismissal	Score		2nd innings	Score
C.G.Greenidge	c Marsh b Lillee	34		c McCosker b Thomson	0
D.L.Haynes	c Marsh b Thomson	42		lbw b Hogg	4
I.V.A.Richards	c Marsh b Lillee	140			
A.I.Kallicharran	c Marsh b Thomson	38		not out	10
L.G.Rowe	b Chappell	50	(3)	b Hogg	3
C.L.King	c Marsh b Lillee	0	(5)	not out	8
*†D.L.Murray	c McCosker b Thomson	21			
A.M.E.Roberts	run out	7			
J.Garner	lbw b Lillee	60			
M.A.Holding	b Bright	11			
C.E.H.Croft	not out	2			
Extras	(B5, LB3, NB28)	36		(B5, W1, NB9)	15
Total		**441**		**(3 wickets)**	**40**

WEST INDIES	O	M	R	W		O	M	R	W	FALL OF WICKETS			
Roberts	18.1	5	50	2		27	5	70	1		A	WI	A	WI
Holding	16	3	53	1		30	4	94	1	*Wkt*	*1st*	*1st*	*2nd*	*2nd*
Croft	25	6	80	3		28	3	106	1	1st	19	68	40	2
Garner	22	5	55	4		41	13	75	2	2nd	26	93	55	15
King	5	1	13	0		22	6	50	1	3rd	156	198	179	16
Kallicharran						18	0	32	0	4th	174	317	297	–
										5th	228	317	371	–
										6th	242	341	442	–
AUSTRALIA										7th	246	365	–	–
Lillee	29.1	8	104	4	(4)	2	0	3	0	8th	252	366	–	–
Hogg	25	6	55	0	(1)	5	2	11	2	9th	268	385	–	–
Thomson	24	4	90	3	(2)	3	2	3	1	10th	268	441	–	–
Chappell	12	2	25	1										
Bright	32	9	97	1	(3)	4	3	8	0					
Border	5	1	19	0										
Hookes	5	2	15	0										

Umpires: R.C.Bailhache (16) and A.R.Crafter (3).

Close: 1st day – A(1) 229-5 (Hookes 33, Marsh 1); 2nd – WI(1) 233-3 (Richards 80, Rowe 14); 3rd – A(2) 30-0 (McCosker 25, Laird 5); 4th – A(2) 240-3 (Chappell 97, Hughes 16).

AUSTRALIA v ENGLAND 1979-80 (1st Test)

At W.A.C.A.Ground, Perth, on 14, 15, 16, 18, 19 December.
Toss: England.   Result: AUSTRALIA won by 138 runs.
Debuts: Australia – J.M.Wiener; England – G.R.Dilley.

Because this rubber consisted of only three matches the Ashes were not at stake. Lillee became the eighth Australian to take 100 wickets against England when he dismissed Brearley. The previous day he had faced four balls (from Botham) and scored three runs whilst using an aluminium bat; ten minutes had been wasted in persuading him to change it. Although not a direct result of this commercial break, the 1980 code of the Laws decreed that the bat 'shall be made of wood'. Thomson took his 150th Test wicket when he had Miller caught in the first innings. Border completed Australia's quickest first 1,000 runs (354 days) before missing a hook and being struck above the left eye by a ball from Dilley. He retired with 109 at 296 and resumed, bearing five stitches and a helmet, at 303. After facing 73 balls in the second innings, Boycott scored his first boundary in a Perth Test for nine years. He was the fourth England batsman to carry his bat through a completed innings (after R.Abel, P.F.Warner and L.Hutton – twice), and the first to do so without completing a century. He became the first to score 99 not out in a Test and the second (after M.J.K.Smith) to finish one short of a century on two occasions (also *Test No. 735*). Botham took his tally of five-wicket analyses to 12 in 22 Tests.

AUSTRALIA

J.M.Wiener	run out	11	c Randall b Underwood	58
B.M.Laird	lbw b Botham	0	c Taylor b Underwood	33
A.R.Border	lbw b Botham	4	c Taylor b Willis	115
*G.S.Chappell	c Boycott b Botham	19	st Taylor b Underwood	43
K.J.Hughes	c Brearley b Underwood	99	c Miller b Botham	4
P.M.Toohey	c Underwood b Dilley	19	c Taylor b Botham	3
†R.W.Marsh	c Taylor b Dilley	42	c Gower b Botham	4
R.J.Bright	c Taylor b Botham	17	lbw b Botham	12
D.K.Lillee	c Taylor b Botham	18	c Willey b Dilley	19
G.Dymock	b Botham	5	not out	20
J.R.Thomson	not out	1	b Botham	8
Extras	(B4, LB3, NB2)	9	(B4, LB5, W2, NB7)	18
Total		**244**		**337**

ENGLAND

D.W.Randall	c Hughes b Lillee	0		lbw b Dymock	1
G.Boycott	lbw b Lillee	0		not out	99
P.Willey	c Chappell b Dymock	9		lbw b Dymock	12
D.I.Gower	c Marsh b Lillee	17		c Thomson b Dymock	23
G.Miller	c Hughes b Thomson	25		c Chappell b Thomson	8
*J.M.Brearley	c Marsh b Lillee	64	(7)	c Marsh b Bright	11
I.T.Botham	c Toohey b Thomson	15	(6)	c Marsh b Lillee	18
†R.W.Taylor	b Chappell	14		b Lillee	15
G.R.Dilley	not out	38		c Marsh b Dymock	16
D.L.Underwood	lbw b Dymock	13		c Wiener b Dymock	0
R.G.D.Willis	b Dymock	11		c Chappell b Dymock	0
Extras	(LB7, NB15)	22		(LB3, W1, NB8)	12
Total		**228**			**215**

ENGLAND	O	M	R	W	O	M	R	W		FALL OF WICKETS			
Dilley	18	1	47	2	(2) 18	3	50	1		A	E	A	E
Botham	35	9	78	6	(1) 45.5	14	98	5	*Wkt*	*1st*	*1st*	*2nd*	*2nd*
Willis	23	7	47	0	26	7	52	1	1st	2	1	91	8
Underwood	13	4	33	1	(5) 41	14	82	3	2nd	17	12	100	26
Miller	11	2	30	0	(4) 10	0	36	0	3rd	20	14	168	64
Willey					1	0	1	0	4th	88	41	183	75
									5th	127	74	191	115
AUSTRALIA									6th	186	90	204	141
Lillee	28	11	73	4	23	5	74	2	7th	219	123	225	182
Dymock	29.1	14	52	3	17.2	4	34	6	8th	219	185	303	211
Chappell	11	6	5	1	6	4	6	0	9th	243	203	323	211
Thomson	21	3	70	2	11	3	30	1	10th	244	228	337	215
Bright	2	0	6	0	23	11	30	1					
Wiener					8	3	22	0					
Border					2	0	7	0					

Umpires: M.G.O'Connell (18) and D.G.Weser (2).

Close: 1st day – A(1) 232-8 (Lillee 11, Dymock 1); 2nd – E(1) 177-7 (Brearley 56, Dilley 21); 3rd – A(2) 168-2 (Border 32, Chappell 43); 4th – E(2) 19-1 (Boycott 5, Willey 9).

AUSTRALIA v WEST INDIES 1979-80 (2nd Test)

At Melbourne Cricket Ground on 29, 30, 31 December, 1 January.
Toss: Australia.   Result: WEST INDIES won by 10 wickets.
Debuts: None.

West Indies gained their first victory at Melbourne where their seven previous encounters had all ended in defeat. They did so at 2.55 on the fourth afternoon after dismissing Australia in their first innings for their lowest total in this series at the MCG. Richards faced only 110 balls in making the highest score of the match. Hogg retired with an injured back after bowling only two overs on the second morning. Roberts completed his first Test fifty in 86 minutes.

AUSTRALIA

J.M.Wiener	lbw b Garner	40	c Murray b Croft		24
B.M.Laird	c Lloyd b Holding	16	c Garner b Holding		69
A.R.Border	c Richards b Garner	17	lbw b Holding		15
*G.S.Chappell	c Murray b Garner	19	c Murray b Roberts		22
K.J.Hughes	c Rowe b Holding	4	lbw b Roberts		70
P.M.Toohey	c Roberts b Holding	10	c Murray b Croft		7
†R.W.Marsh	c Kallicharran b Holding	0	b Croft		7
D.K.Lillee	c Lloyd b Croft	12	c and b Roberts		0
G.Dymock	c Kallicharran b Croft	7	c Lloyd b Garner		17
R.M.Hogg	c Greenidge b Croft	14	c Holding b Garner		11
J.D.Higgs	not out	0	not out		0
Extras	(B9, LB4, W2, NB2)	17	(B2, LB10, NB5)		17
Total		**156**			**259**

WEST INDIES

C.G.Greenidge	c Higgs b Dymock	48	not out		9
D.L.Haynes	c Hughes b Lillee	29	not out		9
I.V.A.Richards	c Toohey b Dymock	96			
A.I.Kallicharran	c Laird b Higgs	39			
L.G.Rowe	b Lillee	26			
*C.H.Lloyd	c Marsh b Dymock	40			
†D.L.Murray	b Dymock	24			
A.M.E.Roberts	lbw b Lillee	54			
J.Garner	c Dymock b Higgs	29			
M.A.Holding	not out	1			
C.E.H.Croft	lbw b Higgs	0			
Extras	(LB4, NB7)	11	(LB4)		4
Total		**397**	(0 wickets)		**22**

WEST INDIES	O	M	R	W	O	M	R	W	FALL OF WICKETS				
Roberts	14	1	39	0	21	1	64	3		A	WI	A	WI
Holding	14	3	40	4	23	7	61	2	*Wkt*	*1st*	*1st*	*2nd*	*2nd*
Croft	13.3	4	27	3	22	2	61	3	1st	38	46	43	–
Garner	15	7	33	3	20.4	2	56	2	2nd	69	156	88	–
									3rd	97	215	121	–
									4th	108	226	187	–
AUSTRALIA									5th	112	250	205	–
Lillee	36	7	96	3	3	0	9	0	6th	118	305	228	–
Hogg	6	0	59	0					7th	123	320	228	–
Dymock	31	2	106	4	(2) 3	0	5	0	8th	133	390	233	–
Higgs	34.4	4	122	3					9th	143	396	258	–
Chappell	5	2	3	0					10th	156	397	259	–
Hughes					(3) 1	1	0	0					
Toohey					(4) 0.2	0	4	0					

Umpires: A.R.Crafter (4) and C.E.Harvey (2).

Close: 1st day – WI(1) 103-1 (Greenidge 26, Richards 45); 2nd – WI(1) 336-7 (Roberts 13, Garner 12); 3rd – A(2) 167-3 (Laird 63, Hughes 33).

AUSTRALIA v ENGLAND 1979-80 (2nd Test)

At Sydney Cricket Ground on 4, 5, 6, 8 January.
Toss: Australia.   Result: AUSTRALIA won by 6 wickets.
Debuts: None.

Australia won at 4.46 on the fourth afternoon despite starting the match 3½ hours late following pre-match rain (the groundstaff left the pitch exposed to a violent storm). Ian Chappell returned after an absence of almost four years and completed 2,000 runs against England – the ninth to do so for Australia. He later provided Underwood with his 100th wicket in this series. Only four other England bowlers had achieved this feat: R.Peel, S.F.Barnes, W.Rhodes and A.V.Bedser. Gower and Greg Chappell made identical scores of 3 and 98 not out.

ENGLAND

G.A.Gooch	b Lillee	18		c G.S.Chappell b Dymock	4
G.Boycott	b Dymock	8		c McCosker b Pascoe	18
D.W.Randall	c G.S.Chappell b Lillee	0	(6)	c Marsh b G.S.Chappell	25
P.Willey	c Wiener b Dymock	8	(3)	b Pascoe	3
*J.M.Brearley	c Pascoe b Dymock	7	(4)	c Marsh b Pascoe	19
D.I.Gower	b G.S.Chappell	3	(7)	not out	98
I.T.Botham	c G.S.Chappell b Pascoe	27	(8)	c Wiener b G.S.Chappell	0
†R.W.Taylor	c Marsh b Lillee	10	(9)	b Lillee	8
G.R.Dilley	not out	22	(10)	b Dymock	4
R.G.D.Willis	c Wiener b Dymock	3	(11)	c G.S.Chappell b Lillee	1
D.L.Underwood	c Border b Lillee	12	(5)	c Border b Dymock	43
Extras	(NB5)	5		(B1, LB10, W1, NB2)	14
Total		**123**			**237**

AUSTRALIA

R.B.McCosker	c Gower b Willis	1	(2)	c Taylor b Underwood	41
J.M.Wiener	run out	22	(1)	b Underwood	13
I.M.Chappell	c Brearley b Gooch	42		c Botham b Underwood	9
*G.S.Chappell	c Taylor b Underwood	3		not out	98
K.J.Hughes	c Taylor b Botham	18		c Dilley b Willis	47
A.R.Border	c Gooch b Botham	15		not out	2
†R.W.Marsh	c Underwood b Gooch	7			
D.K.Lillee	c Brearley b Botham	5			
G.Dymock	c Taylor b Botham	4			
L.S.Pascoe	not out	10			
J.D.Higgs	b Underwood	2			
Extras	(B2, LB12, W2)	16		(LB8, W1)	9
Total		**145**		**(4 wickets)**	**219**

AUSTRALIA	O	M	R	W	O	M	R	W		FALL OF WICKETS			
										E	A	E	A
Lillee	13.3	4	40	4	24.3	6	63	2	Wkt	1st	1st	2nd	2nd
Dymock	17	6	42	4	28	8	48	3	1st	10	18	6	31
Pascoe	9	4	14	1	23	3	76	3	2nd	13	52	21	51
G.S.Chappell	4	1	19	1	21	10	36	2	3rd	31	71	29	98
Higgs	1	0	3	0					4th	38	92	77	203
									5th	41	100	105	–
ENGLAND									6th	74	114	156	–
Botham	17	7	29	4	(2) 23.3	12	43	0	7th	75	121	174	–
Willis	11	3	30	1	(1) 12	2	26	1	8th	90	129	211	–
Underwood	13.2	3	39	2	26	6	71	3	9th	98	132	218	–
Dilley	5	1	13	0	12	0	33	0	10th	123	145	237	–
Willey	1	0	2	0	4	0	17	0					
Gooch	11	4	16	2	8	2	20	0					

Umpires: R.C.Bailhache (17) and W.J.Copeland (1).

Close: 1st day – E(1) 90-7 (Taylor 10, Dilley 5); 2nd – E(2) 38-3 (Brearley 3, Underwood 8); 3rd – A(2) 25-0 (Wiener 8, McCosker 14).

AUSTRALIA v WEST INDIES 1979-80 (3rd Test)

At Adelaide Oval on 26, 27, 28, 29, 30 January.
Toss: Australia.   Result: WEST INDIES won by 408 runs.
Debuts: None.

West Indies won their first rubber in Australia and gained the sixth-largest victory by a margin of runs in Test cricket. Richards hit 76 off 68 balls (13 fours) before lunch on the first day; four balls after the interval he provided Marsh with a record 50th dismissal in this series. During his 12th Test century Kallicharran became the sixth batsman to score 4,000 runs for West Indies.

WEST INDIES

C.G.Greenidge	lbw b Lillee	6		st Marsh b Mallett	76
D.L.Haynes	c Lillee b Mallett	28		c Marsh b Pascoe	27
I.V.A.Richards	c Marsh b Lillee	76		b Border	74
A.I.Kallicharran	c I.M.Chappell b Mallett	9		b Mallett	106
L.G.Rowe	c Lillee b Dymock	40		c Marsh b Dymock	43
*C.H.Lloyd	lbw b Lillee	121	(7)	c Marsh b Dymock	40
†D.L.Murray	c Marsh b Dymock	4	(8)	c G.S.Chappell b Dymock	28
A.M.E.Roberts	b Lillee	9	(9)	c Laird b Dymock	8
J.Garner	c Hughes b Lillee	16	(10)	not out	1
M.A.Holding	b Pascoe	9	(11)	lbw b Dymock	1
C.E.H.Croft	not out	1	(6)	c Border b Pascoe	12
Extras	(B2, NB7)	9		(B1, LB10, NB21)	32
Total		**328**			**448**

AUSTRALIA

J.M.Wiener	c Haynes b Holding	3	c Murray b Roberts	8
B.M.Laird	c Garner b Croft	52	lbw b Garner	36
I.M.Chappell	c Greenidge b Roberts	2	c Murray b Holding	4
*G.S.Chappell	c Garner b Roberts	0	lbw b Croft	31
K.J.Hughes	c Lloyd b Croft	34	lbw b Garner	11
A.R.Border	b Roberts	54	c Greenidge b Roberts	24
†R.W.Marsh	c Murray b Croft	5	not out	23
D.K.Lillee	c Haynes b Holding	16	c Kallicharran b Croft	0
G.Dymock	c Rowe b Croft	10	c Richards b Holding	2
A.A.Mallett	c Rowe b Garner	0	b Holding	12
L.S.Pascoe	not out	5	b Holding	5
Extras	(B1, LB14, NB7)	22	(LB2, W2, NB5)	9
Total		**203**		**165**

AUSTRALIA	O	M	R	W	O	M	R	W	FALL OF WICKETS			
										WI	A	WI	A
Lillee	24	3	78	5	26	6	75	0	Wkt	1st	1st	2nd	2nd
Dymock	25	7	74	2	(3) 33.5	7	104	5	1st	11	23	48	12
Pascoe	15.3	1	90	1	(2) 25	3	93	2	2nd	115	26	184	21
Mallett	27	5	77	2	38	7	134	2	3rd	115	26	213	71
Border					4	2	10	1	4th	126	83	299	83
									5th	239	110	331	98
WEST INDIES									6th	252	127	398	130
Roberts	16.5	3	43	3	15	5	30	2	7th	300	165	417	131
Holding	15	5	31	2	13	2	40	4	8th	303	188	443	135
Garner	18	4	43	1	11	3	39	2	9th	326	189	446	159
Richards	2	0	7	0					10th	328	203	448	165
Croft	22	4	57	4	(4) 11	1	47	2					

Umpires: M.W.Johnson (1) and M.G.O'Connell (19).

Close: 1st day – WI(1) 303-8 (Garner 3); 2nd – A(1) 201-9 (Border 54, Pascoe 5); 3rd – WI(2) 303-4 (Kallicharran 56, Croft 0); 4th – A(2) 131-7 (Marsh 9, Dymock 0).

AUSTRALIA v ENGLAND 1979-80 (3rd Test)

At Melbourne Cricket Ground on 1, 2, 3, 5, 6 February.
Toss: England.   Result: AUSTRALIA won by 8 wickets.
Debuts: England – W.Larkins.

Australia completed a clean sweep of this mini-rubber with 19.2 overs to spare. That they were extended that far was due almost exclusively to a magnificent innings by Botham. Supported by Taylor (90 minutes) and Lever (105 minutes), he steered England from a position of minus 79 for 6 into a lead of 102. His first hundred against Australia took 199 minutes and came off 188 balls. Gooch missed his maiden Test hundred by a yard when he attempted a ridiculous run to mid-on. Lillee became the fifth to take 200 wickets for Australia when he bowled Lever. Greg Chappell completed 2,000 runs against England during his 16th Test hundred.

ENGLAND

G.A.Gooch	run out	99		b Mallett	51
G.Boycott	c Mallett b Dymock	44		b Lillee	7
W.Larkins	c G.S.Chappell b Pascoe	25		lbw b Pascoe	3
D.I.Gower	lbw b Lillee	0		b Lillee	11
P.Willey	lbw b Pascoe	1		c Marsh b Lillee	2
I.T.Botham	c Marsh b Lillee	8	(7)	not out	119
*J.M.Brearley	not out	60	(6)	c Border b Pascoe	10
†R.W.Taylor	b Lillee	23		c Border b Lillee	32
D.L.Underwood	c I.M.Chappell b Lillee	3		b Pascoe	0
J.K.Lever	b Lillee	22		c Marsh b Lillee	12
R.G.D.Willis	c G.S.Chappell b Lillee	4		c G.S.Chappell b Pascoe	2
Extras	(B1, LB2, NB14)	17		(B2, LB12, NB10)	24
Total		**306**			**273**

AUSTRALIA

R.B.McCosker	c Botham b Underwood	33		lbw b Botham	2
B.M.Laird	c Gower b Underwood	74		c Boycott b Underwood	25
I.M.Chappell	c and b Underwood	75		not out	26
K.J.Hughes	c Underwood b Botham	15			
A.R.Border	c and b Lever	63			
*G.S.Chappell	c Larkins b Lever	114	(4)	not out	40
†R.W.Marsh	c Botham b Lever	17			
D.K.Lillee	c Willey b Lever	8			
G.Dymock	b Botham	19			
A.A.Mallett	lbw b Botham	25			
L.S.Pascoe	not out	1			
Extras	(B13, LB12, W1, NB7)	33		(LB8, NB2)	10
Total		**477**		**(2 wickets)**	**103**

AUSTRALIA	O	M	R	W		O	M	R	W	FALL OF WICKETS				
Lillee	33.1	9	60	6		33	6	78	5		E	A	E	A
Dymock	28	6	54	1		11	2	30	0	*Wkt*	*1st*	*1st*	*2nd*	*2nd*
Mallett	35	9	104	0	(4) 14	1	45	1	1st	116	52	25	20
Pascoe	32	7	71	2	(3) 29.5	3	80	4	2nd	170	179	46	42
Border					4	0	16	0	3rd	175	196	64	–
										4th	177	219	67	–
ENGLAND										5th	177	345	88	–
Lever	53	15	111	4	(4) 7.4	3	18	0	6th	192	411	92	–
Botham	39.5	15	105	3	12	5	18	1	7th	238	421	178	–
Willis	21	4	61	0	(1) 5	3	8	0	8th	242	432	179	–
Underwood	53	19	131	3	(3) 14	2	49	1	9th	296	465	268	–
Willey	13	2	36	0						10th	306	477	273	–

Umpires: R.C.Bailhache (18) and P.M.Cronin (1).

Close: 1st day – E(1) 231-6 (Brearley 19, Taylor 21); 2nd – A(1) 155-1 (Laird 63, I.M.Chappell 53); 3rd – A(1) 399-5 (G.S.Chappell 99, Marsh 13); 4th – E(2) 157-6 (Botham 30, Taylor 28).

NEW ZEALAND v WEST INDIES 1979-80 (1st Test)

At Carisbrook, Dunedin, on 8, 9, 10, 12, 13 February.
Toss: West Indies.   Result: NEW ZEALAND won by 1 wicket.
Debuts: New Zealand – P.N.Webb.

Dunedin's first Test for seven years produced the sixth victory by a one-wicket margin and New Zealand's third win in 15 matches against West Indies. Haynes was the first to bat throughout both innings of a Test match – 276 minutes in the first innings and 435 in the second. By not fielding in the second innings, he missed becoming the first West Indian to be on the field throughout a Test. Hadlee returned the best match analysis for either side in this series and became New Zealand's leading wicket-taker when he caught and bowled Parry to overtake R.O.Collinge's total of 116. Cairns removed Parry's off-breaks from the remainder of the rubber by hitting three sixes and a two off his final over. Twelve 'lbw' decisions were given during the match, the record for any Test until 1991-92. The winning run, a scampered leg-bye off Boock's pad, precipitated much truculent behaviour from the West Indies team and management.

WEST INDIES

C.G.Greenidge	c Cairns b Hadlee	2	lbw b Hadlee	3
D.L.Haynes	c and b Cairns	55	c Webb b Troup	105
L.G.Rowe	lbw b Hadlee	1	lbw b Hadlee	12
A.I.Kallicharran	lbw b Hadlee	0	c Cairns b Troup	0
*C.H.Lloyd	lbw b Hadlee	24	c Lees b Hadlee	5
C.L.King	c Coney b Troup	14	c Boock b Cairns	41
†D.L.Murray	c Edgar b Troup	6	lbw b Hadlee	30
D.R.Parry	b Boock	17	c and b Hadlee	1
J.Garner	c Howarth b Cairns	0	b Hadlee	2
M.A.Holding	lbw b Hadlee	4	c Cairns b Troup	3
C.E.H.Croft	not out	0	not out	1
Extras	(LB8, NB9)	17	(LB4, NB5)	9
Total		**140**		**212**

NEW ZEALAND

J.G.Wright	b Holding	21		b Holding	11
B.A.Edgar	lbw b Parry	65		c Greenidge b Holding	6
*G.P.Howarth	c Murray b Croft	33		c Greenidge b Croft	11
J.M.Parker	b Croft	0		c Murray b Garner	5
P.N.Webb	lbw b Parry	5	(6)	lbw b Garner	5
J.V.Coney	b Holding	8	(5)	lbw b Croft	2
†W.K.Lees	run out	18		lbw b Garner	0
R.J.Hadlee	c Lloyd b Garner	51		b Garner	17
B.L.Cairns	b Croft	30		c Murray b Holding	19
G.B.Troup	c Greenidge b Croft	0		not out	7
S.L.Boock	not out	0		not out	2
Extras	(B5, LB2, NB11)	18		(B7, LB5, NB7)	19
Total		**249**		**(9 wickets)**	**104**

NEW ZEALAND	O	M	R	W	O	M	R	W	FALL OF WICKETS				
										WI	NZ	WI	NZ
Hadlee	20	9	34	5	36	13	68	6	*Wkt*	*1st*	*1st*	*2nd*	*2nd*
Troup	17	6	26	2	36.4	13	57	3	1st	3	42	4	15
Cairns	19.5	4	32	2	25	10	63	1	2nd	4	109	21	28
Boock	13	3	31	1	11	4	15	0	3rd	4	110	24	40
									4th	72	133	29	44
WEST INDIES									5th	91	145	117	44
Holding	22	5	50	2	16	7	24	3	6th	105	159	180	44
Croft	25	3	64	4	11	2	25	2	7th	124	168	186	54
Garner	25.5	8	51	1	23	6	36	4	8th	135	232	188	73
King	1	0	3	0					9th	136	236	209	100
Parry	22	6	63	2					10th	140	249	212	–

Umpires: F.R.Goodall (9) and J.B.R.Hastie (5).

Close: 1st day – NZ(1) 30-0 (Wright 16, Edgar 14); 2nd – NZ(1) 236-9 (Hadlee 38, Boock 0); 3rd – WI(2) 18-1 (Haynes 3, Rowe 11); 4th – WI(2) 210-9 (Haynes 103, Croft 1).

NEW ZEALAND v WEST INDIES 1979-80 (2nd Test)

At Lancaster Park, Christchurch, on 22, 23, 24, 26, 27 February.
Toss: New Zealand.　　Result: MATCH DRAWN.
Debuts: None.

As a protest against the umpiring of Fred Goodall, the West Indies team refused to take the field after tea on the third day. Although their request for a change of umpire was declined, they emerged from their locked dressing-room 12 minutes late. Howarth, then 99, had survived a confident appeal for a catch by Murray when 68. He completed his hundred off the first post-strike ball and batted on through the final work-to-rule session in which some fielders ignored balls hit in their direction. Only after lengthy rest-day conferences did the tourists agree to continue with the match and remaining itinerary. When a similar appeal against Hadlee was rejected by Goodall on the fourth morning, Croft barged into the official during his next approach. Hadlee completed 1,000 runs during his first Test century and, in his 28th match, became the first New Zealander to complete the Test double. His partnership of 99 with Coney was New Zealand's highest for the seventh wicket in this series until 1984-85. Edgar (5) retired at 14 with a bruised elbow but resumed one run later on the following day. Greenidge and Haynes shared a record West Indies opening partnership of 225 against New Zealand, before King completed his only Test hundred with a six off the last ball of the match.

WEST INDIES

C.G.Greenidge	c Boock b Troup	91	(2) c Lees b Troup		97
D.L.Haynes	c Parker b Hadlee	0	(1) c Cairns b Coney		122
L.G.Rowe	lbw b Cairns	11	c Boock b Howarth		100
C.L.King	b Cairns	0	(6) not out		100
A.I.Kallicharran	c Wright b Cairns	75	(4) c Lees b Troup		0
*C.H.Lloyd	c Howarth b Cairns	14	(5) b Boock		7
†D.L.Murray	c Webb b Cairns	6	not out		1
A.M.E.Roberts	not out	17			
J.Garner	c sub (P.E.McEwan) b Cairns	0			
M.A.Holding	lbw b Hadlee	0			
C.E.H.Croft	b Hadlee	0			
Extras	(B1, LB9, NB4)	14	(B5, LB8, W1, NB6)		20
Total		**228**	(5 wickets declared)		**447**

NEW ZEALAND

J.G.Wright	b Croft	5
B.A.Edgar	c Murray b Holding	21
P.N.Webb	b Roberts	1
*G.P.Howarth	b Holding	147
J.M.Parker	b Garner	42
J.V.Coney	c King b Roberts	80
†W.K.Lees	c Rowe b Garner	3
R.J.Hadlee	b Kallicharran	103
B.L.Cairns	run out	1
G.B.Troup	not out	13
S.L.Boock	c and b Kallicharran	6
Extras	(B18, LB6, NB14)	38
Total		**460**

NEW ZEALAND	O	M	R	W	O	M	R	W		FALL OF WICKETS		
										WI	NZ	WI
Hadlee	23.3	5	58	3	22	7	64	0	*Wkt*	*1st*	*1st*	*2nd*
Troup	21	8	38	1	27	7	84	2	1st	1	15	225
Cairns	32	8	85	6	28	8	107	0	2nd	28	18	233
Coney	13	2	33	0	19	2	71	1	3rd	28	53	234
Boock					18	3	69	1	4th	190	175	268
Howarth					5	0	32	1	5th	190	267	436
WEST INDIES									6th	210	292	–
Roberts	29	6	82	2					7th	210	391	–
Holding	29	5	97	2					8th	214	404	–
Garner	28	4	75	2					9th	224	448	–
Croft	24	3	78	1					10th	228	460	–
King	9	0	70	0								
Kallicharran	6.4	1	16	2								
Rowe	5	2	4	0								

Umpires: F.R.Goodall (10) and S.J.Woodward (2).

Close: 1st day – WI(1) 166-3 (Greenidge 86, Kallicharran 60); 2nd – NZ(1) 15-0 (Wright 5, Webb 1); 3rd – NZ(1) 248-4 (Howarth 141, Coney 20); 4th – WI(2) 157-0 (Haynes 78, Greenidge 68).

NEW ZEALAND v WEST INDIES 1979-80 (3rd Test)

At Eden Park, Auckland, on 29 February, 1, 2 (*no play*), 3, 4, 5 March.
Toss: New Zealand.   Result: MATCH DRAWN.
Debuts: New Zealand – P.E.McEwan.

Edgar's 432-minute innings and Troup's best innings and match performances at Test level enabled New Zealand, after 50 years, to win their first home rubber. Their only other successful rubber had been in Pakistan in 1969-70. In the first innings Haynes took 94 minutes over his 9 runs, including 70 minutes on 3. Garner returned his best analysis in Tests. When the third day was lost to rain, the scheduled rest day became a playing day under the tour regulations.

WEST INDIES

C.G.Greenidge	c McEwan b Hadlee	7	c Lees b Cairns	74
D.L.Haynes	c Edgar b Cairns	9	b Troup	48
L.G.Rowe	run out	50	c Lees b Troup	5
A.I.Kallicharran	c Cairns b Troup	46	lbw b Troup	25
C.H.Lloyd	c Wright b Troup	11	(6) c Lees b Troup	42
C.L.King	c Troup b Hadlee	23	(5) c Howarth b Troup	9
*D.L.Murray	c Lees b Hadlee	16	lbw b Cairns	7
A.M.E.Roberts	not out	35	c McEwan b Troup	26
J.Garner	b Troup	3	b Hadlee	7
M.A.Holding	lbw b Hadlee	5	not out	16
C.E.H.Croft	b Troup	6		
Extras	(B1, LB7, NB1)	9	(B1, LB2, NB2)	5
Total		**220**	(9 wickets declared)	**264**

NEW ZEALAND

J.G.Wright	c Greenidge b Croft	23	c Haynes b Kallicharran	23
B.A.Edgar	b Roberts	127	(5) not out	22
*G.P.Howarth	c Haynes b Croft	47	(2) run out	1
P.E.McEwan	c Murray b Croft	5	(3) b Garner	21
J.M.Parker	lbw b Garner	0	(4) run out	1
J.V.Coney	not out	49	not out	1
*W.K.Lees	b Garner	23		
R.J.Hadlee	c Murray b Garner	7		
B.L.Cairns	c Murray b Garner	1		
G.B.Troup	b Garner	0		
S.L.Boock	lbw b Garner	0		
Extras	(B4, LB11, NB8)	23	(LB3, NB1)	4
Total		**305**	(4 wickets)	**73**

NEW ZEALAND	O	M	R	W	O	M	R	W		FALL OF WICKETS			
										WI	NZ	WI	NZ
Hadlee	31	8	75	4	29	8	62	1	*Wkt*	*1st*	*1st*	*2nd*	*2nd*
Troup	31.2	11	71	4	29.1	5	95	6	1st	10	75	86	4
Cairns	20	9	56	1	30	7	76	2	2nd	36	171	92	30
Boock	2	0	9	0	6	1	26	0	3rd	116	185	137	32
									4th	116	186	147	71
WEST INDIES									5th	146	241	169	–
Roberts	34	6	90	1	9	2	24	0	6th	167	277	193	–
Holding	23	3	54	0	4	1	11	0	7th	169	299	228	–
Croft	33	5	81	3	(4) 10	4	17	0	8th	178	303	239	–
Garner	36.2	15	56	6	(3) 9	1	17	1	9th	197	303	264	–
King	2	1	1	0					10th	220	305	–	–
Kallicharran					(5) 4	4	0	1					

Umpires: W.R.C.Gardiner (9) and J.B.R.Hastie (6).

Close: 1st day – WI(1) 146-5 (Lloyd 5); 2nd – NZ(1) 43-0 (Wright 10, Edgar 28); 3rd – no play; 4th – NZ(1) 239-4 (Edgar 126, Coney 21); 5th – WI(2) 121-2 (Greenidge 56, Kallicharran 11).

INDIA v ENGLAND 1979-80 (Golden Jubilee Test)

At Wankhede Stadium, Bombay, on 15, 17, 18, 19 February.
Toss: India.   Result: ENGLAND won by 10 wickets.
Debuts: England – G.B.Stevenson.

India's 17th Test in seven months celebrated the Golden Jubilee of the formation of the Board of Control for Cricket in India. Botham, who batted for 206 minutes and hit 17 fours, was the first to score a century and take ten or more wickets in a Test match, and the first to score a hundred and take five wickets in an innings on three occasions. His match analysis of 13 for 106 remains the record for this series and for any Test in Bombay. Taylor established a world Test record by holding ten catches in the match. His seven dismissals in the first innings equalled the world record set by Wasim Bari in 1978-79 (*Test No. 848*). His stand of 171 with Botham remains England's highest for the sixth wicket against India. When they had added 85, umpire Hanumantha Rao upheld an appeal against Taylor for a catch by Kirmani. The batsman protested and the Indian captain, fielding at first slip, confirmed that he had not touched the ball and persuaded the umpire to revoke his decision. In the second innings Boycott ignored the umpire when he gave him out in response to a similar appeal and continued with his innings. Although denied these two wickets, Kirmani still managed to become the first to make 100 dismissals for India. Viswanath completed his 5,000th run in 69 Tests. The rest day was brought forward because of an eclipse of the sun.

INDIA

S.M.Gavaskar	c Taylor b Botham	49		c Taylor b Botham	24
R.M.H.Binny	run out	15		lbw b Botham	0
D.B.Vengsarkar	c Taylor b Stevenson	34		lbw b Lever	10
*G.R.Viswanath	b Lever	11		c Taylor b Botham	5
S.M.Patil	c Taylor b Botham	30		lbw b Botham	0
Yashpal Sharma	lbw b Botham	21		lbw b Botham	27
Kapil Dev	c Taylor b Botham	0	(8)	not out	45
†S.M.H.Kirmani	not out	40	(7)	c Gooch b Botham	0
K.D.Ghavri	c Taylor b Stevenson	11		c Brearley b Lever	5
N.S.Yadav	c Taylor b Botham	8		c Taylor b Botham	15
D.R.Doshi	c Taylor b Botham	6		c and b Lever	0
Extras	(B5, LB3, NB9)	17		(B4, LB8, W1, NB5)	18
Total		**242**			**149**

ENGLAND

G.A.Gooch	c Kirmani b Ghavri	8	not out	49
G.Boycott	c Kirmani b Binny	22	not out	43
W.Larkins	lbw b Ghavri	0		
D.I.Gower	lbw b Kapil Dev	16		
*J.M.Brearley	lbw b Kapil Dev	5		
I.T.Botham	lbw b Ghavri	114		
†R.W.Taylor	lbw b Kapil Dev	43		
J.E.Emburey	c Binny b Ghavri	8		
J.K.Lever	b Doshi	21		
G.B.Stevenson	not out	27		
D.L.Underwood	b Ghavri	1		
Extras	(B8, LB9, NB14)	31	(B3, LB1, NB2)	6
Total		**296**	(0 wickets)	**98**

ENGLAND	O	M	R	W	O	M	R	W		FALL OF WICKETS			
Lever	23	3	82	1	20.1	2	65	3		I	E	I	E
Botham	22.5	7	58	6	26	7	48	7	Wkt	1st	1st	2nd	2nd
Stevenson	14	1	59	2	5	1	13	0	1st	56	21	4	–
Underwood	6	1	23	0	1	0	5	0	2nd	102	21	22	–
Gooch	4	2	3	0					3rd	108	45	31	–
INDIA									4th	135	57	31	–
Kapil Dev	29	8	64	3	8	2	21	0	5th	160	58	56	–
Ghavri	20.1	5	52	5	5	0	12	0	6th	160	229	58	–
Binny	19	3	70	1					7th	181	245	102	–
Doshi	23	6	57	1	(5) 6	1	12	0	8th	197	262	115	–
Yadav	6	2	22	0	(4) 6	0	31	0	9th	223	283	148	–
Patil					(3) 3	0	8	0	10th	242	296	149	–
Gavaskar					(6) 1	0	4	0					
Viswanath					(7) 0.3	0	4	0					

Umpires: J.D.Ghosh (3) and S.N.Hanumantha Rao (6).

Close: 1st day – E(1) 3-0 (Gooch 2, Boycott 0); 2nd – E(1) 232-6 (Taylor 37, Emburey 2); 3rd – I(2) 148-8 (Kapil Dev 44, Yadav 15).

PAKISTAN v AUSTRALIA 1979-80 (1st Test)

At National Stadium, Karachi, on 27, 28, 29 February, 2 March.
Toss: Australia.   Result: PAKISTAN won by 7 wickets.
Debuts: Pakistan – Tausif Ahmed; Australia – G.R.Beard.

Australia's first Test in Pakistan for 15 years was dominated by slow bowlers, who accounted for 28 of the 33 wickets to fall. Iqbal Qasim and Bright, orthodox left-arm spinners both, recorded the best innings and match analysis of their Test careers. Bright's match figures of 10 for 111 and Qasim's innings analysis of 7 for 49 remain national records for matches within this series in Pakistan. At 22 years 260 days, Javed Miandad became Pakistan's youngest captain and the third-youngest after the Nawab of Pataudi (India) and I.D.Craig (Australia) to captain in any Test.

AUSTRALIA

Batsman	1st innings		2nd innings	
B.M.Laird	lbw b Imran	6	c Miandad b Qasim	23
G.N.Yallop	c Taslim b Tausif	12	c Majid b Qasim	16
K.J.Hughes	c Majid b Tausif	85	st Taslim b Tausif	8
G.S.Chappell	st Taslim b Qasim	20	c Taslim b Tausif	13
D.W.Hookes	c Majid b Qasim	0	lbw b Qasim	0
A.R.Border	lbw b Qasim	30	not out	58
R.W.Marsh	c Haroon b Tausif	13	c Mudassar b Qasim	1
G.R.Beard	b Imran	9	b Qasim	4
R.J.Bright	c Majid b Qasim	15	c Majid b Qasim	0
D.K.Lillee	not out	12	lbw b Qasim	5
G.Dymock	c Wasim b Tausif	3	b Tausif	0
Extras	(B8, LB9, NB3)	20	(B4, LB5, W1, NB2)	12
Total		225		140

PAKISTAN

Batsman	1st innings		2nd innings	
Taslim Arif	c Marsh b Bright	58	b Bright	8
Haroon Rashid	b Bright	6	b Bright	10
Zaheer Abbas	c Lillee b Bright	8	not out	18
Javed Miandad	c Border b Chappell	40	b Bright	21
Wasim Raja	c sub (G.F.Lawson) b Chappell	0	not out	12
Majid Khan	c Border b Bright	89		
Mudassar Nazar	c Border b Bright	29		
Imran Khan	c Border b Chappell	9		
Sarfraz Nawaz	c Chappell b Bright	17		
Iqbal Qasim	not out	14		
Tausif Ahmed	b Bright	0		
Extras	(LB12, NB10)	22	(LB3, NB4)	7
Total		292	(3 wickets)	76

PAKISTAN	O	M	R	W		O	M	R	W
Imran	16	4	28	2					
Sarfraz	13	4	20	0	(1)	7	2	7	0
Mudassar	2	0	6	0	(2)	2	0	4	0
Qasim	30	12	69	4	(3)	42	22	49	7
Tausif	30.2	9	64	4	(4)	34	11	62	3
Majid	2	0	13	0	(5)	1	1	0	0
Wasim	2	0	5	0	(6)	4	1	6	0

AUSTRALIA	O	M	R	W		O	M	R	W
Lillee	28	4	76	0		11	2	22	0
Dymock	5	2	5	0		2	0	9	0
Bright	46.5	17	87	7		11	5	24	3
Beard	17	8	39	0		1.1	0	14	0
Chappell	20	3	49	3					
Yallop	2	0	14	0					

FALL OF WICKETS

Wkt	A 1st	P 1st	A 2nd	P 2nd
1st	8	34	38	17
2nd	39	44	51	26
3rd	93	120	55	60
4th	93	121	59	–
5th	161	134	89	–
6th	177	210	90	–
7th	181	238	106	–
8th	199	266	108	–
9th	216	292	139	–
10th	225	292	140	–

Umpires: Mahboob Shah (5) and Shakoor Rana (6).

Close: 1st day – A(1) 199-7 (Beard 9, Bright 10); 2nd – P(1) 193-5 (Majid 44,Mudassar 22); 3rd – A(2) 90-6 (Border 22, Beard 0)

PAKISTAN v AUSTRALIA 1979-80 (2nd Test)

At Iqbal Stadium, Faisalabad, on 6 (*no play*), 7, 8, 10, 11 March.
Toss: Australia.   Result: MATCH DRAWN.
Debuts: None.

Australia's total of 617 was then the highest in any Test in Pakistan and the record for this series. Chappell's score of 235 remains the highest in a Faisalabad Test and was then the record for Australia v Pakistan Tests. His partnership of 217 with Yallop remains the highest for the fourth wicket in this series. Taslim Arif's score of 210 not out is still the highest by a wicket-keeper in Test cricket, a record previously held by Imtiaz Ahmed (*Test No. 414*). Taslim was on the field throughout the match and his unbroken stand of 223 with Javed Miandad was Pakistan's highest for the third wicket in all Tests until 1982-83. For the first time in any Test involving Pakistan both captains scored hundreds. Only in 1884 (*Test No. 16*) had an entire eleven previously bowled in the same innings. Chappell kept wicket after tea on the final day when Marsh had his first bowl in Test cricket. Runs were scored at an average of 83.25 per wicket – then the third-highest ratio in Tests. Javed Akhtar was the second former Pakistan Test player to umpire at this level after Mohammad Aslam Khokhar.

AUSTRALIA

J.M.Wiener	b Ehteshamuddin	5
B.M.Laird	c Taslim b Sarfraz	0
K.J.Hughes	c Ehteshamuddin b Tausif	88
*G.S.Chappell	lbw b Sarfraz	235
G.N.Yallop	b Wasim	172
A.R.Border	run out	4
†R.W.Marsh	lbw b Tausif	71
G.R.Beard	c Sarfraz b Tausif	13
R.J.Bright	b Wasim	5
D.K.Lillee	lbw b Wasim	0
G.Dymock	not out	0
Extras	(B11, LB10, NB3)	24
Total		**617**

PAKISTAN

†Taslim Arif	not out	210
Haroon Rashid	lbw b Dymock	21
Zaheer Abbas	run out	19
*Javed Miandad	not out	106
Wasim Raja		
Majid Khan		
Mudassar Nazar		
Sarfraz Nawaz	did not bat	
Iqbal Qasim		
Ehteshamuddin		
Tausif Ahmed		
Extras	(B7, LB4, NB15)	26
Total	(2 wickets)	**382**

PAKISTAN	O	M	R	W		FALL OF WICKETS		
							A	P
Sarfraz	49	13	119	2	*Wkt*	*1st*	*1st*	
Ehteshamuddin	18	2	59	1	1st	1	87	
Qasim	56	11	156	0	2nd	21	159	
Tausif	33	3	77	3	3rd	200	–	
Wasim	30	6	100	3	4th	417	–	
Majid	22	2	66	0	5th	434	–	
Miandad	3	0	16	0	6th	561	–	
AUSTRALIA					7th	585	–	
Lillee	21	4	91	0	8th	592	–	
Dymock	20	5	49	1	9th	612	–	
Bright	33	9	71	0	10th	617	–	
Border	3	2	3	0				
Beard	15	4	30	0				
Hughes	8	1	19	0				
Laird	2	1	3	0				
Chappell	6	3	5	0				
Wiener	5	1	19	0				
Marsh	10	1	51	0				
Yallop	3	0	15	0				

Umpires: Javed Akhtar (1) and Khalid Aziz (2).

Close: 1st day – no play; 2nd – A(1) 198-2 (Hughes 88, Chappell 97); 3rd – A(1) 478-5 (Yallop 108, Marsh 18); 4th – P(1) 108-1 (Taslim 67, Zaheer 7).

PAKISTAN v AUSTRALIA 1979-80 (3rd Test)

At Gaddafi Stadium, Lahore, on 18, 19, 21, 22, 23 March.
Toss: Australia.   Result: MATCH DRAWN.
Debuts: Pakistan – Azhar Khan, Azmat Rana.

This result gained Pakistan their first successful rubber against Australia. Chappell, playing in his 60th match, became the fifth batsman to score 5,000 runs for Australia. The partnership of 111 between Majid and Imran remains Pakistan's highest for the eighth wicket against Australia. Border was the first to score 150 in both innings of a Test match. Lillee took his only three Test wickets in Pakistan. Miandad kept in the final stages of the match to allow Taslim to take his only Test wicket.

AUSTRALIA

J.M.Wiener	b Qasim	93	(2) c Mudassar b Imran		4
B.M.Laird	b Tausif	17	(1) c Taslim b Tausif		63
K.J.Hughes	b Qasim	1	c Qasim b Imran		0
*G.S.Chappell	lbw b Imran	56	b Qasim		57
G.N.Yallop	lbw b Qasim	3	c and b Wasim		34
A.R.Border	not out	150	st Miandad b Azhar		153
†R.W.Marsh	b Qasim	8	run out		13
G.R.Beard	lbw b Imran	39	c sub (Sultan Rana) b Taslim		49
R.J.Bright	not out	26	not out		10
D.K.Lillee	} did not bat		not out		1
G.Dymock					
Extras	(B4, LB6, NB4)	14	(LB4, NB3)		7
Total	(7 wickets declared)	**407**	(8 wickets)		**391**

PAKISTAN

Mudassar Nazar	c Yallop b Lillee	59
†Taslim Arif	c Marsh b Bright	31
Iqbal Qasim	c Marsh b Lillee	5
Azmat Rana	c Chappell b Beard	49
*Javed Miandad	c Marsh b Bright	14
Wasim Raja	c Border b Lillee	55
Majid Khan	not out	110
Azhar Khan	b Bright	14
Imran Khan	c Chappell b Bright	56
Sarfraz Nawaz	st Marsh b Bright	5
Tausif Ahmed	did not bat	
Extras	(LB4, W1, NB17)	22
Total	(9 wickets declared)	**420**

PAKISTAN	O	M	R	W	O	M	R	W	FALL OF WICKETS			
Imran	28	7	86	2	12	3	30	2		A	P	A
Sarfraz	28	6	67	0	14	5	42	0	*Wkt*	*1st*	*1st*	*2nd*
Mudassar	6	1	16	0	(10) 2	0	20	0	1st	50	37	4
Qasim	39	10	90	4	(3) 34	8	111	1	2nd	53	53	7
Tausif	21	3	81	1	(4) 26	3	72	1	3rd	136	133	115
Wasim	14	3	45	0	(7) 9	1	42	1	4th	153	161	149
Azhar	2	1	1	0	(9) 1	0	1	1	5th	204	177	192
Miandad	2	0	5	0	(6) 4	0	14	0	6th	218	270	223
Majid	2	0	2	0	(5) 9	3	24	0	7th	298	299	357
Taslim					(8) 5	0	28	1	8th	–	410	390
									9th	–	420	–
AUSTRALIA									10th	–	–	–
Lillee	42	9	114	3								
Dymock	24	6	66	0								
Bright	56	14	172	5								
Beard	10	5	26	1								
Chappell	8	3	20	0								

Umpires: Amanullah Khan (7) and Khizer Hayat (1).

Close: 1st day – A(1) 239-6 (Border 39, Beard 15); 2nd – P(1) 42-1 (Mudassar 3, Qasim 4); 3rd – P(1) 224-5 (Wasim 27, Majid 18); 4th – A(2) 64-2 (Laird 26, Chappell 31).

ENGLAND v WEST INDIES 1980 (1st Test)

At Trent Bridge, Nottingham, on 5, 6, 7, 9, 10 June.
Toss: England.   Result: WEST INDIES won by 2 wickets.
Debuts: England – C.J.Tavaré.

The West Indies victory, gained at 2.26 on the final afternoon, featured the narrowest margin in this series. Botham, leading England for the first time, scored his only fifty in 12 matches as captain. Gooch completed 1,000 runs in Tests before he had scored a century. Roberts became the fifth West Indian to take 150 Test wickets when he dismissed Gower, and took five in an innings for the tenth time. His fellow Antiguan, Richards, scored his fifth fifty in successive Test innings. This result ended England's sequence of ten home Tests without defeat since Cornhill Insurance began their sponsorship.

ENGLAND

G.A.Gooch	c Murray b Roberts	17	run out		27
G.Boycott	c Murray b Garner	36	b Roberts		75
C.J.Tavaré	b Garner	13	c Richards b Garner		4
R.A.Woolmer	c Murray b Roberts	46	c Murray b Roberts		29
D.I.Gower	c Greenidge b Roberts	20	lbw b Garner		1
*I.T.Botham	c Richards b Garner	57	c Richards b Roberts		4
P.Willey	b Marshall	13	b Marshall		38
†A.P.E.Knott	lbw b Roberts	6	lbw b Marshall		7
J.K.Lever	c Richards b Holding	15	c Murray b Garner		4
R.G.D.Willis	b Roberts	8	b Garner		9
M.Hendrick	not out	7	not out		2
Extras	(B7, LB11, W3, NB4)	25	(B19, LB13, W10, NB10)		52
Total		**263**			**252**

WEST INDIES

C.G.Greenidge	c Knott b Hendrick	53	c Knott b Willis		6
D.L.Haynes	c Gower b Willis	12	run out		62
I.V.A.Richards	c Knott b Willis	64	lbw b Botham		48
S.F.A.F.Bacchus	c Botham b Willis	30	c Knott b Hendrick		19
A.I.Kallicharran	b Botham	17	c Knott b Willis		9
†D.L.Murray	b Willis	64	(7) c Hendrick b Willis		16
*C.H.Lloyd	c Knott b Lever	9	(6) lbw b Willis		3
M.D.Marshall	c Tavaré b Gooch	20	b Willis		7
A.M.E.Roberts	lbw b Botham	21	not out		22
J.Garner	c Lever b Botham	2			
M.A.Holding	not out	0	(10) not out		0
Extras	(B1, LB9, W2, NB4)	16	(LB8, NB9)		17
Total		**308**	(8 wickets)		**209**

WEST INDIES	O	M	R	W	O	M	R	W		FALL OF WICKETS			
Roberts	25	7	72	5	24	6	57	3		E	WI	E	WI
Holding	23.5	7	61	1	26	5	65	0	Wkt	1st	1st	2nd	2nd
Marshall	19	3	52	1	24	8	44	2	1st	27	19	46	11
Richards	1	0	9	0					2nd	72	107	68	69
Garner	23	9	44	3	(4) 34.1	20	30	4	3rd	74	151	174	109
Greenidge					(5) 3	2	4	0	4th	114	165	175	125
									5th	204	208	180	129
									6th	208	227	183	165
ENGLAND									7th	228	265	218	180
Willis	20.1	5	82	4	26	4	65	5	8th	246	306	237	205
Lever	20	2	76	1	8	2	25	0	9th	254	308	248	–
Hendrick	19	4	69	1	14	5	40	1	10th	263	308	252	–
Willey	5	3	4	0	(6) 2	0	12	0					
Botham	20	6	50	3	(4) 16.4	6	48	1					
Gooch	7	2	11	1	(5) 2	1	2	0					

Umpires: D.J.Constant (19) and D.O.Oslear (1).

Close: 1st day – E(1) 243-7 (Knott 6, Lever 14); 2nd – WI(1) 270-7 (Murray 49, Roberts 3); 3rd – E(2) 145-2 (Boycott 61, Woolmer 20); 4th – WI(2) 109-2 (Haynes 29, Bacchus 19).

ENGLAND v WEST INDIES 1980 (2nd Test)

At Lord's, London, on 19, 20, 21, 23, 24 June.
Toss: England.   Result: MATCH DRAWN.
Debuts: None.

The match was abandoned as a draw mid-way through the fifth afternoon, a total of 9 hours 55 minutes of play being lost to rain and poor light. In his 36th Test innings, Gooch scored his first century and became the first batsman to score 1,000 runs in first-class cricket that season. He scored his 123 out of 165 off 162 balls in 211 minutes with a six and 17 fours. Holding (6 for 67) and Haynes (184) recorded best performances for West Indies in Tests at Lord's. Richards completed 3,000 runs in Tests off his first ball and scored his 10th hundred for West Indies. His 145 occupied 196 minutes (159 balls), included a six and 25 fours, and took him beyond 1,000 runs against England in only six matches. Both Richards and Haynes were playing in their first Test at Lord's.

ENGLAND

G.A.Gooch	lbw b Holding	123	b Garner	47
G.Boycott	c Murray b Holding	8	not out	49
C.J.Tavaré	c Greenidge b Holding	42	lbw b Garner	6
R.A.Woolmer	c Kallicharran b Garner	15	not out	19
M.W.Gatting	b Holding	18		
*I.T.Botham	lbw b Garner	8		
D.L.Underwood	lbw b Garner	3		
P.Willey	b Holding	4		
†A.P.E.Knott	c Garner b Holding	9		
R.G.D.Willis	b Garner	14		
M.Hendrick	not out	10		
Extras	(B4, LB1, W4, NB6)	15	(LB1, NB11)	12
Total		**269**	**(2 wickets)**	**133**

WEST INDIES

C.G.Greenidge	lbw b Botham	25
D.L.Haynes	lbw b Botham	184
I.V.A.Richards	c sub (G.R.Dilley) b Willey	145
C.E.H.Croft	run out	0
A.I.Kallicharran	c Knott b Willis	15
S.F.A.F.Bacchus	c Gooch b Willis	0
*C.H.Lloyd	b Willey	56
†D.L.Murray	c Tavaré b Botham	34
A.M.E.Roberts	b Underwood	24
J.Garner	c Gooch b Willis	15
M.A.Holding	not out	0
Extras	(B1, LB9, W1, NB9)	20
Total		**518**

WEST INDIES	O	M	R	W	O	M	R	W
Roberts	18	3	50	0	13	3	24	0
Holding	28	11	67	6	15	5	51	0
Garner	24.3	8	36	4	15	6	21	2
Croft	20	3	77	0	8	2	24	0
Richards	5	1	24	0	1	0	1	0

ENGLAND	O	M	R	W
Willis	31	12	103	3
Botham	37	7	145	3
Underwood	29.2	7	108	1
Hendrick	11	2	32	0
Gooch	7	1	26	0
Willey	25	8	73	2
Boycott	7	2	11	0

FALL OF WICKETS

Wkt	E 1st	WI 1st	E 2nd
1st	20	37	71
2nd	165	260	96
3rd	190	275	–
4th	219	326	–
5th	220	330	–
6th	231	437	–
7th	232	469	–
8th	244	486	–
9th	245	518	–
10th	269	518	–

Umpires: W.E.Alley (8) and B.J.Meyer (5).

Close: 1st day – E(1) 232-7 (Willey 1); 2nd – WI(1) 265-2 (Haynes 92, Croft 0); 3rd – E(2) 33-0 (Gooch 21, Boycott 10); 4th – E(2) 51-0 (Gooch 32, Boycott 13).

ENGLAND v WEST INDIES 1980 (3rd Test)

At Old Trafford, Manchester, on 10, 11, 12 (*no play*), 14, 15 July.
Toss: West Indies.   Result: MATCH DRAWN.
Debuts: None.

Old Trafford lost its 25th day of Test cricket – almost twice the total of complete days lost by any other English ground. England recovered well after being bowled out before tea on the first day and finished 281 runs ahead, but the loss of 11 hours 10 minutes proved too great for a result. Lloyd became the third West Indian to score 5,000 runs and, in his 73rd Test, scored his 13th hundred – his only Test century on his adopted home ground.

ENGLAND

Batsman	Dismissal 1st	Runs	Dismissal 2nd	Runs
G.A.Gooch	lbw b Roberts	2	c Murray b Marshall	26
G.Boycott	c Garner b Roberts	5	lbw b Holding	86
B.C.Rose	b Marshall	70	c Kallicharran b Holding	32
W.Larkins	lbw b Garner	11	c Murray b Marshall	33
M.W.Gatting	c Richards b Marshall	33	c Kallicharran b Garner	56
*I.T.Botham	c Murray b Garner	8	lbw b Holding	35
P.Willey	b Marshall	0	not out	62
†A.P.E.Knott	run out	2	c and b Garner	6
J.E.Emburey	c Murray b Roberts	3	not out	28
G.R.Dilley	b Garner	0		
R.G.D.Willis	not out	5		
Extras	(LB4, W3, NB4)	11	(B5, LB8, W1, NB13)	27
Total		**150**	(7 wickets)	**391**

WEST INDIES

C.G.Greenidge	c Larkins b Dilley	0
D.L.Haynes	c Knott b Willis	1
I.V.A.Richards	b Botham	65
S.F.A.F.Bacchus	c Botham b Dilley	0
A.I.Kallicharran	c Knott b Botham	13
*C.H.Lloyd	c Gooch b Emburey	101
†D.L.Murray	b Botham	17
M.D.Marshall	c Gooch b Dilley	18
A.M.E.Roberts	c Knott b Emburey	11
J.Garner	lbw b Emburey	0
M.A.Holding	not out	4
Extras	(B2, LB13, W3, NB12)	30
Total		**260**

WEST INDIES	O	M	R	W		O	M	R	W
Roberts	11.2	3	23	3		14	2	36	0
Holding	14	2	46	0		34	8	100	3
Garner	11	2	34	3	(4)	40	11	73	2
Marshall	12	5	36	3	(3)	35	5	116	2
Richards						16	6	31	0
Lloyd						1	0	1	0
Bacchus						1	0	3	0
Haynes						1	0	2	0
Kallicharran						1	0	2	0

ENGLAND	O	M	R	W
Willis	14	1	99	1
Dilley	28	7	47	3
Botham	20	6	64	3
Emburey	10.3	1	20	3

FALL OF WICKETS

Wkt	E 1st	WI 1st	E 2nd
1st	3	4	32
2nd	18	25	86
3rd	35	25	181
4th	126	67	217
5th	131	100	290
6th	132	154	290
7th	142	209	309
8th	142	250	–
9th	142	250	–
10th	150	260	–

Umpires: H.D.Bird (18) and K.E.Palmer (5).

Close: 1st day – WI(1) 38-3 (Richards 32, Kallicharran 0); 2nd – WI(1) 219-7 (Lloyd 79, Roberts 4); 3rd – no play; 4th – E(2) 201-3 (Boycott 81, Gatting 12).

ENGLAND v WEST INDIES 1980 (4th Test)

At Kennington Oval, London, on 24, 25, 26 (*no play*), 28, 29 July.
Toss: England.   Result: MATCH DRAWN.
Debuts: None.

England were 197 ahead with 151 minutes and 20 overs left when their last pair joined forces at 2.09 pm. Willey, who made his first hundred in Tests, and Willis survived for 171 minutes while adding 117 runs – England's third century partnership for the tenth wicket in 560 matches. Boycott (3) retired at 9 after being hit over the right eye by a ball from Croft, and returned at 155. Lloyd pulled a leg muscle while fielding on the second afternoon and Richards took over the captaincy for the remainder of the rubber. Botham took his 150th wicket in 29 Tests, in the record time of exactly three years, when he dismissed Richards.

ENGLAND

G.A.Gooch	lbw b Holding	83		lbw b Holding	0
G.Boycott	run out	53		c Murray b Croft	5
B.C.Rose	b Croft	50		lbw b Garner	41
W.Larkins	lbw b Garner	7		b Holding	0
M.W.Gatting	b Croft	48	(6)	c Murray b Garner	15
P.Willey	c Lloyd b Holding	34	(8)	not out	100
†A.P.E.Knott	c Lloyd b Marshall	3	(9)	lbw b Holding	3
*I.T.Botham	lbw b Croft	9	(7)	c Greenidge b Garner	4
J.E.Emburey	c Holding b Marshall	24	(5)	c Bacchus b Croft	2
G.R.Dilley	b Garner	1		c sub (C.L.King) b Holding	1
R.G.D.Willis	not out	1		not out	24
Extras	(B7, LB21, W10, NB19)	57		(LB6, W1, NB7)	14
Total		**370**		(9 wickets declared)	**209**

WEST INDIES

C.G.Greenidge	lbw b Willis	6
D.L.Haynes	c Gooch b Dilley	7
I.V.A.Richards	c Willey b Botham	26
S.F.A.F.Bacchus	c Knott b Emburey	61
A.I.Kallicharran	c Rose b Dilley	11
†D.L.Murray	hit wkt b Dilley	0
M.D.Marshall	c Rose b Emburey	45
J.Garner	c Gatting b Botham	46
M.A.Holding	lbw b Dilley	22
C.E.H.Croft	not out	0
*C.H.Lloyd	absent hurt	–
Extras	(LB12, W1, NB28)	41
Total		**265**

WEST INDIES	O	M	R	W	O	M	R	W
Holding	28	5	67	2	29	7	79	4
Croft	35	9	97	3	10	6	8	2
Marshall	29.3	6	77	2	23	7	47	0
Garner	33	8	67	2	17	5	24	3
Richards	3	1	5	0	9	3	15	0
Kallicharran					6	1	22	0

ENGLAND	O	M	R	W
Willis	19	5	58	1
Dilley	23	6	57	4
Botham	18.2	8	47	2
Emburey	23	12	38	2
Gooch	1	0	2	0
Willey	11	5	22	0

FALL OF WICKETS

Wkt	E 1st	WI 1st	E 2nd
1st	155	15	2
2nd	157	34	10
3rd	182	72	13
4th	269	99	18
5th	303	105	63
6th	312	187	67
7th	336	197	73
8th	343	261	84
9th	368	265	92
10th	370	–	–

Umpires: B.J.Meyer (6) and D.O.Oslear (2).

Close: 1st day – E(1) 236-3 (Boycott 39, Gatting 18); 2nd – WI(1) 45-2 (Richards 14, Bacchus 5); 3rd – no play; 4th – E(2) 20-4 (Rose 11, Gatting 1).

ENGLAND v WEST INDIES 1980 (5th Test)

At Headingley, Leeds, on 7 (*no play*), 8, 9, 11 (*no play*), 12 August.
Toss: West Indies.   Result: MATCH DRAWN.
Debuts: None.

The first day's play was abandoned an hour before the scheduled start following two days of almost continuous rain; for the third successive year the Headingley Test was ruined by bad weather, 14 hours 7 minutes being lost in this match. West Indies retained the Wisden Trophy by virtue of their two-wicket win in the first Test. England achieved their lowest total in six matches against West Indies at Leeds. Rose, who pulled a leg muscle when he turned suddenly on the wet outfield, batted for 145 minutes with Gooch as his runner in the second innings. Botham became the first to complete the double of 1,500 runs and 150 wickets for England; the sixth player to achieve this feat, he did so in fewest matches (30).

ENGLAND

G.A.Gooch	c Marshall b Garner	14		lbw b Marshall	55
G.Boycott	c Kallicharran b Holding	4		c Kallicharran b Croft	47
B.C.Rose	b Croft	7	(5)	not out	43
W.Larkins	c Kallicharran b Garner	9	(3)	lbw b Marshall	30
M.W.Gatting	c Marshall b Croft	1	(4)	lbw b Holding	1
*I.T.Botham	c Richards b Holding	37		lbw b Marshall	7
P.Willey	c Murray b Croft	1		c Murray b Holding	10
†D.L.Bairstow	lbw b Marshall	40		not out	9
J.E.Emburey	not out	13			
C.M.Old	c Garner b Marshall	6			
G.R.Dilley	b Garner	0			
Extras	(B3, LB3, W1, NB4)	11		(B5, LB11, W2, NB7)	25
Total		**143**		(6 wickets declared)	**227**

WEST INDIES

C.G.Greenidge	lbw b Botham	34
D.L.Haynes	b Emburey	42
*I.V.A.Richards	b Old	31
S.F.A.F.Bacchus	c and b Dilley	11
A.I.Kallicharran	c Larkins b Dilley	37
C.L.King	c Bairstow b Gooch	12
†D.L.Murray	c Emburey b Dilley	14
M.D.Marshall	c Bairstow b Dilley	0
M.A.Holding	b Old	35
J.Garner	c Emburey b Gooch	0
C.E.H.Croft	not out	1
Extras	(B2, LB9, W3, NB14)	28
Total		**245**

WEST INDIES	O	M	R	W		O	M	R	W		FALL OF WICKETS		
Holding	10	4	34	2		23	2	62	2		E	WI	E
Croft	12	3	35	3		19	2	65	1	*Wkt*	*1st*	*1st*	*2nd*
Garner	14	4	41	3	(4)	1	0	1	0	1st	9	83	95
Marshall	11	3	22	2	(3)	19	5	42	3	2nd	27	105	126
King						12	3	32	0	3rd	28	133	129
Richards						1	1	0	0	4th	34	142	162
											5th	52	170	174
ENGLAND										6th	59	198	203
Dilley	23	6	79	4						7th	89	198	–
Old	28.5	9	64	2						8th	131	207	–
Botham	19	8	31	1						9th	140	207	–
Emburey	6	0	25	1						10th	143	245	–
Gooch	8	3	18	2									

Umpires: W.E.Alley (9) and K.E.Palmer (6).

Close: 1st day – no play; 2nd – WI(1) 20-0 (Greenidge 6, Haynes 13); 3rd – E(2) 22-0 (Gooch 12, Boycott 9); 4th – no play.

ENGLAND v AUSTRALIA 1980 (Centenary Test)

At Lord's, London, on 28, 29, 30 August, 1, 2 September.
Toss: Australia.   Result: MATCH DRAWN.
Debuts: England – C.W.J.Athey.

This match celebrated the centenary of the first Test played in England (*Test No. 4*). Sadly, it was disrupted by rain with over ten hours being lost (although an extra hour was added to each of the last two days), and marred by an unsavoury incident on the Saturday afternoon. When the umpires returned from the fifth inspection of two old pitches, Constant was assaulted by angry MCC members in front of the Long Room. Hughes became the third batsman after M.L.Jaisimha (*Test No. 486*) and G.Boycott (*806*) to bat on all five days of a Test. He took 346 minutes and faced 308 balls in compiling his match aggregate of 201 runs, which contained five sixes and 25 fours. Pascoe's best analysis for Australia included a spell of 5 for 10 in 32 balls. Chappell set England a target of 370 runs in a minimum of 350 minutes. Boycott became the fourth batsman after W.R.Hammond, M.C.Cowdrey and G.St A.Sobers to score 7,000 runs in Tests. On the final afternoon play ceased while everyone on the ground stood to applaud John Arlott after he had completed his 35-year career as a Test match commentator *par excellence*.

AUSTRALIA

G.M.Wood	st Bairstow b Emburey	112	(2) lbw b Old	8
B.M.Laird	c Bairstow b Old	24	(1) c Bairstow b Old	6
*G.S.Chappell	c Gatting b Old	47	b Old	59
K.J.Hughes	c Athey b Old	117	lbw b Botham	84
G.N.Yallop	lbw b Hendrick	2		
A.R.Border	not out	56	(5) not out	21
†R.W.Marsh	not out	16		
R.J.Bright				
D.K.Lillee				
A.A.Mallett	did not bat			
L.S.Pascoe				
Extras	(B1, LB8, NB2)	11	(B1, LB8, NB2)	11
Total	(5 wickets declared)	**385**	(4 wickets declared)	**189**

ENGLAND

G.A.Gooch	c Bright b Lillee	8	lbw b Lillee	16
G.Boycott	c Marsh b Lillee	62	not out	128
C.W.J.Athey	b Lillee	9	c Laird b Pascoe	1
D.I.Gower	b Lillee	45	b Mallett	35
M.W.Gatting	lbw b Pascoe	12	not out	51
*I.T.Botham	c Wood b Pascoe	0		
P.Willey	lbw b Pascoe	5		
†D.L.Bairstow	lbw b Pascoe	6		
J.E.Emburey	lbw b Pascoe	3		
C.M.Old	not out	24		
M.Hendrick	c Border b Mallett	5		
Extras	(B6, LB8, NB12)	26	(B3, LB2, NB8)	13
Total		**205**	(3 wickets)	**244**

ENGLAND	O	M	R	W	O	M	R	W	FALL OF WICKETS				
Old	35	9	91	3	20	6	47	3		A	E	A	E
Hendrick	30	6	67	1	15	4	53	0	Wkt	1st	1st	2nd	2nd
Botham	22	2	89	0	(4) 9.2	1	43	1	1st	64	10	15	19
Emburey	38	9	104	1	(3) 9	2	35	0	2nd	150	41	28	43
Gooch	8	3	16	0					3rd	260	137	139	124
Willey	1	0	7	0					4th	267	151	189	–
									5th	320	158	–	–
									6th	–	163	–	–
AUSTRALIA									7th	–	164	–	–
Lillee	15	4	43	4	19	5	53	1	8th	–	173	–	–
Pascoe	18	5	59	5	17	1	73	1	9th	–	200	–	–
Chappell	2	0	2	0					10th	–	205	–	–
Bright	21	6	50	0	(3) 25	9	44	0					
Mallett	7.2	3	25	1	(4) 21	2	61	1					

Umpires: H.D.Bird (19) and D.J.Constant (20).

Close: 1st day – A(1) 227-2 (Wood 100, Hughes 47); 2nd – A(1) 278-4 (Hughes 82, Border 2); 3rd – E(1) 1-0 (Gooch 0, Boycott 0); 4th – A(2) 106-2 (Chappell 47, Hughes 38).

PAKISTAN v WEST INDIES 1980-81 (1st Test)

At Gaddafi Stadium, Lahore, on 24, 25, 27 (*no play*), 28, 29 November.
Toss: Pakistan.   Result: MATCH DRAWN.
Debuts: Pakistan – Mansoor Akhtar.

For the first time in 15 Tests at Lahore a complete day's play was lost. Mohammad Nazir was recalled to Test cricket after an interval of 7 years 248 days – then the longest involving a Pakistan player. When he had scored 21, Imran Khan became the second Pakistani after Intikhab Alam to complete the double of 1,000 runs and 100 wickets. He went on to celebrate his 28th birthday by completing his first hundred in 30 Tests. Abdul Qadir retired at 260 after being hit on the shoulder by a ball from Croft. Taslim Arif retired when he was struck on the finger by a Clarke delivery with the total 15.

PAKISTAN

†Taslim Arif	c Murray b Garner	32	retired hurt	8
Sadiq Mohammad	c Murray b Marshall	19	lbw b Croft	28
Mansoor Akhtar	c Murray b Croft	13	b Clarke	0
*Javed Miandad	c Richards b Croft	6	run out	30
Majid Khan	c Bacchus b Garner	4	not out	62
Wasim Raja	c Kallicharran b Richards	76	lbw b Clarke	3
Imran Khan	lbw b Marshall	123	c Marshall b Richards	9
Abdul Qadir	retired hurt	18	c Haynes b Richards	1
Sarfraz Nawaz	c Richards b Croft	55	c Garner b Haynes	4
Iqbal Qasim	b Marshall	3		
Mohammad Nazir	not out	1		
Extras	(B1, LB4, W1, NB13)	19	(B2, LB2, NB7)	11
Total		**369**	(7 wickets)	**156**

WEST INDIES

D.L.Haynes	c Qasim b Nazir	40
S.F.A.F.Bacchus	lbw b Imran	0
I.V.A.Richards	b Nazir	75
A.I.Kallicharran	c Sadiq b Qadir	11
*C.H.Lloyd	c Miandad b Qasim	22
H.A.Gomes	b Wasim	43
†D.A.Murray	c Majid b Qadir	50
M.D.Marshall	b Sarfraz	9
J.Garner	c Taslim b Qadir	15
C.E.H.Croft	not out	7
S.T.Clarke	st Taslim b Qadir	15
Extras	(B3, LB6, NB1)	10
Total		**297**

WEST INDIES	O	M	R	W		O	M	R	W
Clarke	23	3	69	0		12	3	26	2
Croft	28	7	91	3	(3) 20		7	37	1
Marshall	21.5	5	88	3	(2) 15		4	30	0
Garner	27	6	71	2	(5) 9		3	17	0
Richards	7	0	31	1	(4) 11		3	20	2
Gomes						4	0	9	0
Kallicharran						1	0	4	0
Haynes						1	0	2	1

PAKISTAN	O	M	R	W
Imran	16	2	39	1
Sarfraz	13	3	40	1
Qadir	40.4	4	131	4
Qasim	12	4	18	1
Wasim	10	3	21	1
Nazir	17	4	38	2

FALL OF WICKETS			
	P	WI	P
Wkt	1st	1st	2nd
1st	31	1	15
2nd	65	118	57
3rd	67	119	101
4th	72	143	112
5th	95	158	125
6th	188	225	133
7th	356	255	156
8th	368	275	–
9th	369	276	–
10th	–	297	–

Umpires: Khizer Hayat (2) and Shakoor Rana (7).

Close: 1st day – P(1) 218-6 (Imran 53, Qadir 3); 2nd – WI(1) 64-1 (Haynes 26, Richards 34); 3rd – no play; 4th – WI(1) 297 all out.

PAKISTAN v WEST INDIES 1980-81 (2nd Test)

At Iqbal Stadium, Faisalabad, on 8, 9, 11, 12 December.
Toss: West Indies.   Result: WEST INDIES won by 156 runs.
Debuts: West Indies – R.Nanan.

West Indies included a specialist spinner for the first time in nine matches and achieved the first positive result in a Test at Faisalabad. They gained their second victory in seven matches in Pakistan and became the first visiting side to triumph there in 20 matches since November 1969 (*Test No. 663*). Clarke celebrated his 26th birthday by hitting three sixes off successive balls from Nazir, equalling the world Test record set by W.R.Hammond (*Test No. 226*), and scored 22 (006664) off the over. His partnership of 44 with Nanan was the tenth-wicket record for West Indies in this series until 1992-93. Bacchus (13) retired because of a shoulder injury at 29 in the second innings, and resumed at 171. Pakistan were dismissed for the lowest total in a Test on this ground until 1986-87.

WEST INDIES

D.L.Haynes	lbw b Qasim	15		lbw b Qadir	12
S.F.A.F.Bacchus	c Sikander b Qadir	45		b Qasim	17
I.V.A.Richards	b Nazir	72	(5)	c sub (Iqbal Sikander) b Qasim	67
A.I.Kallicharran	lbw b Qadir	8	(6)	lbw b Nazir	27
*C.H.Lloyd	c Mansoor b Nazir	20	(4)	lbw b Qasim	37
H.A.Gomes	c Qasim b Nazir	8	(7)	c Mansoor b Qasim	1
†D.A.Murray	c Majid b Qadir	31	(8)	b Nazir	19
M.D.Marshall	b Nazir	0	(9)	c Miandad b Nazir	1
R.Nanan	lbw b Nazir	8	(10)	c Wasim b Qasim	8
C.E.H.Croft	c Taslim b Qasim	2	(3)	lbw b Qasim	1
S.T.Clarke	not out	8		not out	35
Extras	(B12, LB5, NB1)	18		(B9, LB7, NB1)	17
Total		**235**			**242**

PAKISTAN

†Taslim Arif	lbw b Clarke	0	(2)	c Richards b Croft	18
Mansoor Akhtar	c Lloyd b Marshall	16	(1)	c Nanan b Marshall	7
Zaheer Abbas	b Clarke	2		lbw b Marshall	33
*Javed Miandad	c and b Clarke	50	(5)	c Lloyd b Croft	22
Majid Khan	c Murray b Marshall	26	(6)	b Clarke	3
Wasim Raja	st Murray b Nanan	21	(7)	not out	38
Imran Khan	c Richards b Croft	29	(9)	c Richards b Nanan	0
Abdul Qadir	b Nanan	4		b Croft	0
Iqbal Qasim	b Croft	0	(10)	c Richards b Nanan	5
Sikander Bakht	c Lloyd b Richards	6	(4)	c Lloyd b Marshall	1
Mohammad Nazir	not out	2		c Nanan b Marshall	0
Extras	(B4, LB7, NB9)	20		(B4, LB4, NB10)	18
Total		**176**			**145**

PAKISTAN	O	M	R	W	O	M	R	W	FALL OF WICKETS				
										WI	P	WI	P
Imran	10	0	36	0	3	0	6	0	*Wkt*	*1st*	*1st*	*2nd*	*2nd*
Sikander	7	2	22	0	4	0	9	0	1st	39	0	22	14
Qasim	19	3	54	2	(5) 32.2	5	89	6	2nd	99	2	47	43
Qadir	15.3	1	48	3	17	4	45	1	3rd	127	32	129	60
Nazir	22	7	44	5	(3) 33	13	76	3	4th	150	73	150	71
Wasim	4	0	13	0					5th	176	122	153	77
									6th	187	132	171	122
WEST INDIES									7th	187	149	186	122
Clarke	13	2	28	3	12	2	36	1	8th	207	150	189	124
Croft	16	4	35	2	(4) 13	0	29	3	9th	223	167	198	132
Marshall	9	1	39	2	(2) 9.4	0	25	4	10th	235	176	242	145
Nanan	20	1	54	2	(3) 16	6	37	2					
Richards	0.2	0	0	1									

Umpires: Amanullah Khan (8) and Javed Akhtar (2).

Close: 1st day – WI(1) 235 all out; 2nd – WI(2) 29-1 (Bacchus 13, Croft 0); 3rd – P(2) 60-2 (Zaheer 26, Sikander 1).

PAKISTAN v WEST INDIES 1980-81 (3rd Test)

At National Stadium, Karachi, on 22 (*no play*), 23, 24, 26, 27 December.
Toss: Pakistan.   Result: MATCH DRAWN.
Debuts: Pakistan – Ijaz Faqih.

Pakistan maintained their unbeaten record at Karachi but a complete day's play was lost for the first time in 17 Tests there. Pakistan's decision to bat first when the match began a day and a half late on a pitch dried by electric heaters, produced their lowest total at Karachi and the world Test record of six ducks in an innings. Zaheer (0) retired at 2 after a Clarke bouncer had left a two-inch dent in his helmet, and resumed at 111. Clarke took the wickets of Javed Miandad, Wasim Bari and Iqbal Qasim in four balls. The start of the fourth day's play was delayed by 23 minutes because umpire Shakoor Rana had left his kit at the hotel.

PAKISTAN

Shafiq Ahmed	lbw b Clarke	0		lbw b Garner	17
Sadiq Mohammad	lbw b Croft	0		c Bacchus b Clarke	36
Zaheer Abbas	not out	13	(5)	lbw b Croft	1
*Javed Miandad	c Lloyd b Clarke	60		c Haynes b Clarke	5
Majid Khan	c Bacchus b Croft	0	(3)	c Murray b Croft	18
Wasim Raja	c Bacchus b Croft	2		not out	77
Imran Khan	lbw b Garner	21		c Murray b Marshall	12
Ijaz Faqih	b Marshall	0		c Murray b Marshall	8
†Wasim Bari	c Murray b Clarke	23		b Garner	3
Iqbal Qasim	c Richards b Clarke	0		b Croft	2
Mohammad Nazir	b Garner	0		not out	2
Extras	(LB1, W1, NB7)	9		(B4, LB3, NB16)	23
Total		**128**		**(9 wickets)**	**204**

WEST INDIES

D.L.Haynes	lbw b Qasim	1
S.F.A.F.Bacchus	b Imran	16
I.V.A.Richards	c Zaheer b Qasim	18
A.I.Kallicharran	b Imran	4
*C.H.Lloyd	c Miandad b Imran	1
†D.A.Murray	c Miandad b Qasim	42
H.A.Gomes	c Miandad b Nazir	61
M.D.Marshall	b Nazir	0
S.T.Clarke	b Qasim	17
J.Garner	lbw b Imran	1
C.E.H.Croft	not out	3
Extras	(LB1, W4)	5
Total		**169**

WEST INDIES	O	M	R	W		O	M	R	W		FALL OF WICKETS		
Clarke	15	7	27	4		11	3	14	2			P	WI	P
Croft	14	5	27	3		23	6	50	3		*Wkt*	*1st*	*1st*	*2nd*
Garner	18.1	8	27	2	(4)	19	4	39	2		1st	0	19	30
Marshall	14	0	38	1	(3)	17	1	54	2		2nd	0	21	76
Richards						8	2	10	0		3rd	5	43	78
Gomes						6	0	14	0		4th	14	43	82
											5th	53	44	85
PAKISTAN											6th	57	143	122
Imran	29	5	66	4							7th	111	143	146
Qasim	34.1	11	48	4							8th	112	160	150
Nazir	9	1	21	2							9th	112	161	178
Ijaz	4	1	9	0							10th	128	169	–
Wasim Raja	1	0	8	0										
Majid	8	3	12	0										

Umpires: Javed Akhtar (3) and Shakoor Rana (8).

Close: 1st day – no play; 2nd – P(1) 68-6 (Miandad 38, Wasim Bari 3); 3rd – WI(1) 105-5 (Murray 24, Gomes 37); 4th – P(2) 70-1 (Sadiq 33, Majid 15).

PAKISTAN v WEST INDIES 1980-81 (4th Test)

At Ibn-e-Qasim Bagh Stadium, Multan, on 30, 31 December, 2, 3, 4 (*no play*) January.
Toss: West Indies.   Result: MATCH DRAWN.
Debuts: None.

The introduction of Test cricket's 51st ground coincided with Lloyd's 42nd match as captain – the most for any country, beating P.B.H.May's England record. Starting late because of the delayed arrival of an umpire, the match was ended by torrential rain after only 40 minutes on the penultimate day. It was interrupted by an embryo riot on the second afternoon when Clarke, the infuriated victim of some prolonged orange-pelting, removed a brick boundary marker and scored a direct hit on the head of the leader of a local students' union. Richards recorded his first hundred against Pakistan – the only century for West Indies on that tour. Garner took his 100th Test wicket when he bowled Sarfraz. The result gained West Indies their first rubber in three visits to Pakistan.

WEST INDIES

D.L.Haynes	b Imran	5	st Wasim Bari b Qasim		31
S.F.A.F.Bacchus	lbw b Imran	2	c Zaheer b Qasim		39
I.V.A.Richards	not out	120	c Sadiq b Nazir		12
A.I.Kallicharran	lbw b Imran	18	not out		12
H.A.Gomes	lbw b Qasim	32			
*C.H.Lloyd	run out	9	(7) not out		17
†D.A.Murray	c Wasim Bari b Qasim	0	(6) lbw b Nazir		0
S.T.Clarke	c Miandad b Imran	28			
M.D.Marshall	c Miandad b Nazir	3			
J.Garner	c Nazir b Imran	2			
C.E.H.Croft	lbw b Sarfraz	3	(5) lbw b Nazir		1
Extras	(B15, LB6, W3, NB3)	27	(LB3, W1)		4
Total		**249**	(5 wickets)		**116**

PAKISTAN

Shafiq Ahmed	c Garner b Clarke	0
Sadiq Mohammad	b Clarke	3
Majid Khan	c Richards b Garner	41
*Javed Miandad	c Haynes b Croft	57
†Wasim Bari	run out	8
Zaheer Abbas	c Murray b Marshall	8
Wasim Raja	not out	29
Imran Khan	c Haynes b Croft	10
Sarfraz Nawaz	b Garner	1
Iqbal Qasim	c Richards b Garner	1
Mohammad Nazir	lbw b Garner	0
Extras	(NB8)	8
Total		**166**

PAKISTAN	O	M	R	W	O	M	R	W	FALL OF WICKETS			
										WI	P	WI
Imran	22	6	62	5	10	0	27	0	*Wkt*	*1st*	*1st*	*2nd*
Sarfraz	15.2	6	24	1	5	1	15	0	1st	9	2	57
Qasim	28	9	61	2	12	2	35	2	2nd	22	4	84
Nazir	26	8	69	1	15	3	35	3	3rd	58	104	84
Wasim Raja	2	0	6	0					4th	134	104	85
									5th	146	120	85
WEST INDIES									6th	153	137	–
Clarke	12	1	42	2					7th	198	163	–
Croft	16	3	33	2					8th	201	164	–
Marshall	12	1	45	1					9th	208	166	–
Garner	17.2	4	38	4					10th	249	166	–

Umpires: Khizer Hayat (3) and Mahboob Shah (6).

Close: 1st day – WI(1) 198-7 (Richards 85); 2nd – P(1) 108-4 (Wasim Bari 0, Zaheer 2); 3rd – WI(2) 85-5 (Kallicharran 0); 4th – WI(2) 116-5 (Kallicharran 12, Lloyd 17).

AUSTRALIA v NEW ZEALAND 1980-81 (1st Test)

At Woolloongabba, Brisbane, on 28, 29, 30 November.
Toss: Australia.   Result: AUSTRALIA won by 10 wickets.
Debuts: Australia – G.F.Lawson; New Zealand – J.G.Bracewell, I.D.S.Smith.

New Zealand's first Test match in Brisbane ended in substantial defeat at 5.33 on the third evening. Walters was recalled after an interval of three years. Because of injuries to J.V.Coney and G.B.Troup, New Zealand recruited Brendon Bracewell from Perth, where he was playing club cricket for Melville. Lillee's analysis of 6 for 53 remains the record for Australia against New Zealand.

NEW ZEALAND

J.G.Wright	c Marsh b Pascoe	29	c Walters b Lillee	1
B.A.Edgar	c Marsh b Lawson	20	c Hughes b Lillee	51
P.E.McEwan	c Border b Lillee	6	c Hughes b Lillee	0
*G.P.Howarth	c and b Higgs	65	c Wood b Lillee	4
J.M.Parker	b Pascoe	52	c Dyson b Lawson	4
M.G.Burgess	c Chappell b Pascoe	0	c Wood b Lillee	2
†I.D.S.Smith	c Hughes b Lillee	7	c Hughes b Pascoe	7
R.J.Hadlee	c Marsh b Higgs	10	(9) not out	51
B.L.Cairns	c Border b Higgs	0	(10) c Border b Lillee	0
J.G.Bracewell	not out	6	(8) c Border b Lawson	0
B.P.Bracewell	b Higgs	0	b Pascoe	8
Extras	(LB18, W5, NB7)	30	(B4, LB4, W1, NB5)	14
Total		**225**		**142**

AUSTRALIA

G.M.Wood	c Parker b J.G.Bracewell	111	(2) not out	32
J.Dyson	lbw b Cairns	30	(1) not out	24
*G.S.Chappell	c McEwan b Cairns	35		
K.J.Hughes	c Wright b Hadlee	9		
A.R.Border	run out	36		
K.D.Walters	b Cairns	17		
†R.W.Marsh	b Hadlee	8		
D.K.Lillee	c Parker b Cairns	24		
G.F.Lawson	c sub (S.L.Boock) b Hadlee	16		
L.S.Pascoe	b Cairns	5		
J.D.Higgs	not out	1		
Extras	(B1, LB7, NB5)	13	(B2, LB2, NB3)	7
Total		**305**	(0 wickets)	**63**

AUSTRALIA	O	M	R	W		O	M	R	W		FALL OF WICKETS			
Lillee	18	7	36	2		15	1	53	6		NZ	A	NZ	A
Pascoe	19	4	41	3		13.1	2	30	2	Wkt	1st	1st	2nd	2nd
Lawson	12	2	39	1		8	0	26	2	1st	64	80	6	–
Chappell	4	1	18	0						2nd	71	145	9	–
Higgs	16.1	3	59	4	(4)	5	1	19	0	3rd	76	160	14	–
Walters	1	0	2	0						4th	193	225	30	–
										5th	193	235	34	–
NEW ZEALAND										6th	209	250	58	–
Hadlee	37	8	83	3		6	0	28	0	7th	209	258	61	–
B.P.Bracewell	22	8	71	0		3	3	0	0	8th	210	299	114	–
Cairns	38.5	11	87	5		7.3	3	16	0	9th	221	299	114	–
J.G.Bracewell	18	5	51	1		5	0	12	0	10th	225	305	142	–

Umpires: R.C.Bailhache (19) and M.W.Johnson (2).

Close: 1st day – A(1) 14-0 (Wood 4, Dyson 6); 2nd – A(1) 278-7 (Lillee 11, Lawson 9).

AUSTRALIA v NEW ZEALAND 1980-81 (2nd Test)

At W.A.C.A.Ground, Perth, on 12, 13, 14 December.
Toss: Australia.   Result: AUSTRALIA won by 8 wickets.
Debuts: None.

For the second match in succession New Zealand lost with over two days to spare, their first Test in Perth ending at 5.00 on the third evening. Walters, in his 70th Test, became the sixth Australian to score 5,000 runs. The touring side was without Howarth who injured his hand playing against Southern NSW at Wagga Wagga. New Zealand's total of 121 remains their lowest in Australia.

NEW ZEALAND

J.G.Wright	b Pascoe	10		c Marsh b Hogg	3
B.A.Edgar	c Border b Lillee	0		c Hughes b Pascoe	0
J.M.Parker	c Chappell b Hogg	3	(4)	c Hughes b Hogg	18
P.E.McEwan	c Marsh b Lillee	8	(5)	c Marsh b Lillee	16
J.V.Coney	b Hogg	71	(6)	c Marsh b Higgs	0
*M.G.Burgess	c Hughes b Lillee	43	(7)	lbw b Higgs	18
†W.K.Lees	c Marsh b Pascoe	5	(8)	not out	25
R.J.Hadlee	c Hughes b Pascoe	23	(9)	c Chappell b Higgs	0
J.G.Bracewell	lbw b Lillee	6	(3)	run out	16
B.L.Cairns	c Pascoe b Lillee	13		c Border b Higgs	6
G.B.Troup	not out	0		c Marsh b Lillee	0
Extras	(LB3, W2, NB9)	14		(LB12, W2, NB5)	19
Total		**196**			**121**

AUSTRALIA

G.M.Wood	c Bracewell b Hadlee	0	(2)	c Lees b Hadlee	0
J.Dyson	c Bracewell b Cairns	28	(1)	not out	25
*G.S.Chappell	c Cairns b Troup	12		c Lees b Hadlee	13
K.J.Hughes	c Lees b Hadlee	3		not out	16
A.R.Border	b Cairns	10			
K.D.Walters	c Coney b Hadlee	55			
†R.W.Marsh	c Coney b Hadlee	91			
D.K.Lillee	c and b Hadlee	8			
R.M.Hogg	b Cairns	3			
L.S.Pascoe	not out	30			
J.D.Higgs	c Coney b Cairns	7			
Extras	(B3, LB4, W1, NB10)	18		(LB1)	1
Total		**265**		**(2 wickets)**	**55**

AUSTRALIA	O	M	R	W		O	M	R	W		FALL OF WICKETS			
											NZ	A	NZ	A
Lillee	23.5	5	63	5		15.1	7	14	2	*Wkt*	*1st*	*1st*	*2nd*	*2nd*
Hogg	16	5	29	2	(3) 10	2	25	2	1st	6	0	0	3
Pascoe	20	3	61	3	(2) 10	1	30	1	2nd	13	22	27	31
Chappell	7	3	5	0	3	1	7	0	3rd	24	25	38	—
Higgs	5	1	13	0	(6) 8	2	25	4	4th	28	50	63	—
Walters	2	0	11	0	(5) 2	1	1	0	5th	116	68	64	—
										6th	133	156	73	—
NEW ZEALAND										7th	171	176	115	—
Hadlee	27	8	87	5	11.1	4	20	2	8th	177	187	115	—
Troup	22	5	57	1	1	0	1	0	9th	196	244	121	—
Cairns	28.1	7	88	4	5	2	17	0	10th	196	265	121	—
Bracewell	4	1	15	0	5	0	16	0					

Umpires: A.R.Crafter (5) and D.G.Weser (3).

Close: 1st day – A(1) 11-1 (Dyson 1, Chappell 6); 2nd – NZ(2) 12-1 (Wright 0, Bracewell 6).

AUSTRALIA v NEW ZEALAND 1980-81 (3rd Test)

At Melbourne Cricket Ground on 26, 27, 28, 29, 30 December.
Toss: New Zealand.   Result: MATCH DRAWN.
Debuts: None.

New Zealand, requiring 193 runs in a minimum of 205 minutes, were well placed at 95 for 1, before losing four wickets for six runs. The MCG pitch was severely criticised by both captains because of its increasingly low and difficult bounce. Burgess was the third player after J.R.Reid and B.E.Congdon to appear 50 times for New Zealand. After batting 28 minutes for one run, Higgs was caught by Lees trying to evade a medium-paced short ball from Cairns. Umpire Bailhache, invoking Law 42 (8), no-balled the delivery on the grounds of intimidation, although it was the first short-pitched ball bowled to Higgs and the law refers to 'fast' bowling. His decision allowed Walters, then 77, to complete the last of his 15 Test hundreds (his first for four years), and extend the partnership by a further 42 runs to a record last-wicket stand of 60. He batted 276 minutes and hit only six boundaries. New Zealand replied with their (then) highest total in Australia based on a third-wicket partnership of 125 between Howarth and Parker. Hadlee ended Australia's second innings by removing Chappell, Hogg and Higgs with his last four balls to return record New Zealand innings (6 for 57) and match (9 for 146) analysis against Australia until he spectacularly eclipsed them in *Test No. 1029.*

AUSTRALIA

G.M.Wood	c Lees b Hadlee	0	(2)	c Lees b Hadlee	21
J.Dyson	b Troup	13	(1)	lbw b Cairns	16
*G.S.Chappell	c Coney b Hadlee	42		b Hadlee	78
K.J.Hughes	c Parker b Hadlee	51		b Hadlee	30
A.R.Border	c Cairns b Coney	45		c Lees b Hadlee	9
K.D.Walters	b Coney	107		run out	2
†R.W.Marsh	c Parker b Coney	1		lbw b Cairns	0
D.K.Lillee	b Cairns	27		c Coney b Bracewell	8
R.M.Hogg	run out	0		b Hadlee	12
L.S.Pascoe	b Cairns	0		not out	0
J.D.Higgs	not out	6		b Hadlee	0
Extras	(B7, LB13, W3, NB6)	29		(B6, LB4, NB2)	12
Total		**321**			**188**

NEW ZEALAND

J.G.Wright	c Chappell b Higgs	4		c Wood b Hogg	44
B.A.Edgar	lbw b Higgs	21		run out	25
*G.P.Howarth	b Hogg	65		lbw b Chappell	20
J.M.Parker	c Marsh b Pascoe	56		lbw b Chappell	1
M.G.Burgess	lbw b Pascoe	49	(6)	not out	10
J.V.Coney	not out	55	(5)	lbw b Hogg	3
J.G.Bracewell	c Chappell b Pascoe	0			
†W.K.Lees	lbw b Hogg	4	(7)	b Lillee	7
R.J.Hadlee	c Border b Hogg	9	(8)	not out	5
B.L.Cairns	lbw b Higgs	18			
G.B.Troup	c Hughes b Hogg	1			
Extras	(B13, LB12, NB10)	35		(B2, LB8, W1, NB2)	13
Total		**317**		(6 wickets)	**128**

NEW ZEALAND	O	M	R	W	O	M	R	W	FALL OF WICKETS			
										A	NZ	A	NZ
Hadlee	39	8	89	3	27.2	7	57	6					
Troup	26	5	54	1	11	1	31	0	*Wkt*	*1st*	*1st*	*2nd*	*2nd*
Cairns	35	6	83	2	33	13	65	2	1st	0	27	25	50
Bracewell	9	0	38	0	15	5	22	1	2nd	32	32	64	95
Coney	12.3	6	28	3	1	0	1	0	3rd	75	157	111	97
									4th	159	163	128	101
AUSTRALIA									5th	190	247	131	101
Lillee	21	4	49	0	13	3	30	1	6th	192	247	131	121
Hogg	26.2	9	60	4	8	1	14	2	7th	261	264	149	–
Higgs	29	6	87	3	12	4	24	0	8th	261	280	185	–
Pascoe	26	6	75	3	11	1	35	0	9th	261	316	188	–
Border	4	1	6	0	(6) 2	1	5	0	10th	321	317	188	–
Chappell	2	0	5	0	(5) 7	4	7	2					
Hughes					1	1	0	0					

Umpires: R.C.Bailhache (20) and A.R.Crafter (6).

Close: 1st day – A(1) 222-6 (Walters 46, Lillee 9); 2nd – NZ(1) 139-2 (Howarth 54, Parker 47); 3rd – NZ(1) 251-6 (Coney 29, Lees 2); 4th – A(2) 121-3 (Chappell 43, Border 6).

AUSTRALIA v INDIA 1980-81 (1st Test)

At Sydney Cricket Ground on 2, 3, 4 January.
Toss: India.   Result: AUSTRALIA won by an innings and 4 runs.
Debuts: None.

India suffered the same fate as New Zealand earlier in the Australian season when they lost their opening Test on the third day. Australia thus gained their first victory by an innings margin since beating England at Edgbaston 5½ years earlier. Patil retired at 201 after being rendered unconscious by a bouncer from Pascoe. Chappell (408 minutes, 296 balls, 27 fours) compiled the highest score of this series until the next match in his first innings against India. His last 163 runs were scored after he had suffered a severe stomach upset overnight. Ghavri took his 100th wicket in 36 Tests before sharing in a then record ninth-wicket partnership of 57 with Kirmani.

INDIA

*S.M.Gavaskar	c Marsh b Lillee	0		c Marsh b Hogg	10
C.P.S.Chauhan	c Border b Pascoe	20		c Walters b Pascoe	36
D.B.Vengsarkar	c Marsh b Lillee	22		c Marsh b Pascoe	34
G.R.Viswanath	b Hogg	26		st Marsh b Higgs	24
Yashpal Sharma	c Marsh b Pascoe	6		c Walters b Lillee	4
S.M.Patil	retired hurt	65	(8)	c Wood b Lillee	4
Kapil Dev	c Marsh b Pascoe	22	(6)	c sub (S.F.Graf) b Higgs	19
†S.M.H.Kirmani	c Walters b Lillee	27	(7)	not out	43
R.M.H.Binny	c Marsh b Pascoe	3		lbw b Lillee	0
K.D.Ghavri	c Wood b Lillee	7		c Hogg b Higgs	21
D.R.Doshi	not out	0		c Lillee b Higgs	0
Extras	(LB1, NB2)	3		(B2, LB3, W1)	6
Total		**201**			**201**

AUSTRALIA

G.M.Wood	c Kirmani b Kapil Dev	9
J.Dyson	c Gavaskar b Kapil Dev	0
*G.S.Chappell	c Kapil Dev b Ghavri	204
K.J.Hughes	c Kirmani b Kapil Dev	24
A.R.Border	c Kirmani b Kapil Dev	31
K.D.Walters	c Viswanath b Ghavri	67
†R.W.Marsh	c Binny b Ghavri	12
D.K.Lillee	c Doshi b Ghavri	5
R.M.Hogg	not out	26
L.S.Pascoe	c Doshi b Ghavri	7
J.D.Higgs	b Kapil Dev	2
Extras	(B4, LB3, W3, NB9)	19
Total		**406**

AUSTRALIA	O	M	R	W	O	M	R	W		FALL OF WICKETS		
										I	A	I
Lillee	20.2	3	86	4	18	2	79	3	*Wkt*	*1st*	*1st*	*2nd*
Hogg	14	1	51	1	9	1	24	1	1st	0	3	21
Pascoe	19	6	61	4	11	2	35	2	2nd	36	14	74
Higgs					18	8	45	4	3rd	62	95	92
Walters					6	3	12	0	4th	70	169	110
									5th	78	341	120
INDIA									6th	145	355	126
Kapil Dev	36.1	7	97	5					7th	183	363	144
Ghavri	30	7	107	5					8th	186	366	144
Binny	15	1	70	0					9th	201	376	201
Doshi	27	0	103	0					10th	–	406	201
Chauhan	1	0	10	0								

Umpires: M.W.Johnson (3) and R.V.Whitehead (1).

Close: 1st day – A(1) 72-2 (Chappell 41, Hughes 18); 2nd – A(1) 388-9 (Hogg 13, Higgs 1).

AUSTRALIA v INDIA 1980-81 (2nd Test)

At Adelaide Oval on 23, 24, 25, 26, 27 January.
Toss: India.   Result: MATCH DRAWN.
Debuts: None.

Ghavri and Yadav survived the final 9.2 overs in 31 minutes after India had been left a minimum of 265 minutes in which to score 331 runs. Hughes (383 minutes, 303 balls, 21 fours) exceeded the record score for this series established by Chappell in the previous match. After being concussed by a Pascoe bouncer in the first Test, Patil (301 minutes, 240 balls, one six and 22 fours) recorded India's highest score against Australia until 1991-92. In his 65th Test Gavaskar became the first to score 6,000 runs for India.

AUSTRALIA

J.Dyson	c Gavaskar b Kapil Dev	30	(2)	lbw b Ghavri	28
G.M.Wood	c Doshi b Yadav	125	(1)	c Patil b Doshi	3
*G.S.Chappell	c Chauhan b Doshi	36		st Kirmani b Doshi	52
K.J.Hughes	c Yashpal b Yadav	213	(5)	b Kapil Dev	53
A.R.Border	c Gavaskar b Kapil Dev	57	(4)	b Doshi	7
K.D.Walters	c Viswanath b Yadav	20		not out	33
†R.W.Marsh	run out	0		c Kirmani b Yadav	23
B.Yardley	c Viswanath b Doshi	12		c Vengsarkar b Yadav	2
D.K.Lillee	c Kapil Dev b Doshi	2		not out	10
R.M.Hogg	c and b Yadav	11			
L.S.Pascoe	not out	1			
Extras	(LB13, W1, NB7)	21		(B2, LB5, NB3)	10
Total		**528**		(7 wickets declared)	**221**

INDIA

*S.M.Gavaskar	b Pascoe	23		c Chappell b Pascoe	5
C.P.S.Chauhan	c Marsh b Lillee	97		c Marsh b Pascoe	11
N.S.Yadav	c Chappell b Yardley	16	(10)	not out	0
G.R.Viswanath	lbw b Hogg	3		b Pascoe	16
D.B.Vengsarkar	lbw b Lillee	2	(3)	c Chappell b Border	37
S.M.Patil	lbw b Hogg	174	(5)	lbw b Lillee	9
Yashpal Sharma	c Marsh b Lillee	47	(6)	lbw b Yardley	13
Kapil Dev	c Border b Lillee	2	(7)	c Marsh b Lillee	7
†S.M.H.Kirmani	b Pascoe	6	(8)	c Marsh b Chappell	14
K.D.Ghavri	c Wood b Yardley	3	(9)	not out	7
D.R.Doshi	not out	6			
Extras	(B11, LB10, W2, NB17)	40		(B7, LB1, NB8)	16
Total		**419**		(8 wickets)	**135**

INDIA	O	M	R	W		O	M	R	W		FALL OF WICKETS			
Kapil Dev	32	5	112	2		17	3	55	1		A	I	A	I
Ghavri	27	3	106	0	(4)	11	2	37	1	*Wkt*	*1st*	*1st*	*2nd*	*2nd*
Doshi	48	6	146	3	(2)	33	11	49	3	1st	84	77	5	13
Yadav	42.4	6	143	4	(3)	29	6	70	2	2nd	152	112	74	16
										3rd	234	115	118	44
AUSTRALIA										4th	363	130	138	57
Lillee	34	10	80	4		19	7	38	2	5th	393	238	165	90
Hogg	28	6	100	2	(6)	3	0	11	0	6th	399	385	204	103
Pascoe	17	2	62	2	(2)	11	2	32	3	7th	435	393	208	126
Yardley	44.4	16	90	2	(5)	24	13	25	1	8th	461	399	–	128
Chappell	6	2	14	0	(4)	9	6	4	1	9th	505	409	–	–
Walters	3	0	21	0						10th	528	419	–	–
Border	4	0	11	0	(3)	9	5	9	1					
Hughes	1	0	1	0										

Umpires: A.R.Crafter (7) and R.V.Whitehead (2).

Close: 1st day – A(1) 319-3 (Hughes 85, Border 33); 2nd – I(1) 79-1 (Chauhan 49, Yadav 0); 3rd – I(1) 371-5 (Patil 150, Yashpal 47); 4th – A(2) 165-4 (Hughes 53, Walters 13).

AUSTRALIA v INDIA 1980-81 (3rd Test)

At Melbourne Cricket Ground on 7, 8, 9, 10, 11 February.
Toss: Australia.   Result: INDIA won by 59 runs.
Debuts: None.

Australia, needing only 143 to win, collapsed dramatically against an Indian attack which overcame painful leg injuries, and recorded their lowest total in any Test since 1968 (*Test No. 638*); it remains their lowest ever in this series. A courageous display by Kapil Dev (pulled thigh muscle) and Doshi (fractured instep) brought India her third victory in 17 matches in Australia and a shared rubber there for the first time in four visits. They had come close to forfeiting the match on the fourth day; Gavaskar had so vehemently disagreed with an lbw decision against himself that he urged his partner, Chauhan, to leave the field with him. India's manager, Wg Cdr S.K.Durrani, had met them at the gate and ordered Chauhan to continue his innings. Lillee (48 Tests) overtook R.Benaud's Australian record of 248 wickets in 63 Tests and became the sixth bowler to take 250. Marsh made his 250th dismissal in 68 matches to become the second wicket-keeper after A.P.E.Knott to reach that total.

INDIA

*S.M.Gavaskar	c Hughes b Pascoe	10	lbw b Lillee	70
C.P.S.Chauhan	c Yardley b Pascoe	0	c Yardley b Lillee	85
D.B.Vengsarkar	c Border b Lillee	12	c Marsh b Pascoe	41
G.R.Viswanath	c Chappell b Yardley	114	b Lillee	30
S.M.Patil	c Hughes b Lillee	23	c Chappell b Yardley	36
Yashpal Sharma	c Marsh b Lillee	4	b Pascoe	9
Kapil Dev	c Hughes b Pascoe	5	(8) b Yardley	0
†S.M.H.Kirmani	c Marsh b Lillee	25	(7) run out	9
K.D.Ghavri	run out	0	not out	11
N.S.Yadav	not out	20	absent hurt	–
D.R.Doshi	c Walters b Yardley	0	(10) b Lillee	7
Extras	(B1, LB8, W6, NB9)	24	(B11, LB8, NB7)	26
Total		**237**		**324**

AUSTRALIA

J.Dyson	c Kirmani b Kapil Dev	16	c Kirmani b Ghavri	3
G.M.Wood	c Doshi b Ghavri	10	st Kirmani b Doshi	10
*G.S.Chappell	c and b Ghavri	76	b Ghavri	0
K.J.Hughes	c Chauhan b Yadav	24	b Doshi	16
A.R.Border	b Yadav	124	(6) c Kirmani b Kapil Dev	9
K.D.Walters	st Kirmani b Doshi	78	(7) not out	18
†R.W.Marsh	c sub (K.Azad) b Doshi	45	(8) b Kapil Dev	3
B.Yardley	lbw b Doshi	0	(5) b Kapil Dev	7
D.K.Lillee	c and b Patil	19	b Kapil Dev	4
L.S.Pascoe	lbw b Patil	3	run out	6
J.D.Higgs	not out	1	lbw b Kapil Dev	0
Extras	(B12, LB6, NB5)	23	(LB5, NB2)	7
Total		**419**		**83**

AUSTRALIA	O	M	R	W	O	M	R	W	FALL OF WICKETS			
									I	A	I	A
Lillee	25	6	65	4	32.1	5	104	4	*1st*	*1st*	*2nd*	*2nd*
Pascoe	22	11	29	3	29	4	80	2	*Wkt*			
Chappell	5	2	9	0					1st	0	30	165	11
Yardley	13	3	45	2	(4) 31	11	65	2	2nd	22	32	176	11
Higgs	19	2	65	0	(3) 15	3	41	0	3rd	43	81	243	18
Border					(5) 2	0	8	0	4th	91	189	245	40
									5th	99	320	260	50
									6th	115	356	296	55
INDIA									7th	164	356	296	61
Kapil Dev	19	7	41	1	(4) 16.4	4	28	5	8th	190	413	308	69
Doshi	52	14	109	3	(3) 22	9	33	2	9th	230	413	324	79
Ghavri	39	4	110	2	(1) 8	4	10	2	10th	237	419	–	83
Yadav	32	6	100	2								
Chauhan	2	0	8	0								
Patil	12.3	4	28	2	(2) 2	0	5	0				

Umpires: M.W.Johnson (4) and R.V.Whitehead (3).

Close: 1st day – A(1) 12-0 (Dyson 9, Wood 1); 2nd – A(1) 272-4 (Border 95, Walters 36); 3rd – I(2) 108-0 (Gavaskar 59, Chauhan 41); 4th – A(2) 24-3 (Hughes 4, Yardley 4).

WEST INDIES v ENGLAND 1980-81 (1st Test)

At Queen's Park Oval, Port-of-Spain, Trinidad, on 13, 14, 16, 17, 18 February.
Toss: England.   Result: WEST INDIES won by an innings and 79 runs.
Debuts: West Indies – E.H.Mattis; England – P.R.Downton.

West Indies gained their first victory by an innings margin against England in the Caribbean since 1934-35. Vandals protesting about the omission of Deryck Murray, captain of Trinidad and Tobago, caused wet patches on the pitch and the bowlers' approaches which delayed the start by three hours. Botham, who became the second England captain after R.E.S.Wyatt to elect to field first in the West Indies, damaged a finger fielding against Lloyd on the second day and retired for repairs, leaving Miller in charge. Gomes (83 minutes) did not score during the last hour of his innings. The rest day was taken early to avoid a clash with a steel band festival. Roberts set a world Test record when he scored 24 runs off an over from Botham (462660) during his 91-minute fifty; it remains the most runs by one batsman off an over in Test cricket (equalled by S.M.Patil in 1982), and subsequently by I.T.Botham, Kapil Dev and I.D.S.Smith. England followed-on for the first time in 49 Tests since 1975. Holding and Croft took their 100th Test wickets in their 25th and 21st Tests respectively.

WEST INDIES

C.G.Greenidge	c Botham b Emburey	84
D.L.Haynes	c and b Emburey	96
I.V.A.Richards	c Gower b Miller	29
E.H.Mattis	c Miller b Emburey	0
H.A.Gomes	c Downton b Old	5
*C.H.Lloyd	b Emburey	64
†D.A.Murray	c Botham b Emburey	46
A.M.E.Roberts	not out	50
M.A.Holding	lbw b Botham	26
J.Garner	lbw b Botham	4
C.E.H.Croft	not out	4
Extras	(LB15, NB3)	18
Total	**(9 wickets declared)**	**426**

ENGLAND

G.A.Gooch	b Roberts	41	lbw b Holding		5
G.Boycott	c Richards b Croft	30	c Haynes b Holding		70
B.C.Rose	c Haynes b Garner	10	c Murray b Holding		5
D.I.Gower	lbw b Croft	48	c Murray b Roberts		27
G.Miller	c Murray b Croft	3	c Greenidge b Croft		8
*I.T.Botham	lbw b Croft	0	c Holding b Richards		16
P.Willey	lbw b Garner	13	c Lloyd b Garner		21
†P.R.Downton	b Gomes	4	c Lloyd b Roberts		5
J.E.Emburey	not out	17	b Roberts		1
G.R.Dilley	b Croft	0	not out		1
C.M.Old	b Roberts	1	c sub (S.F.A.F.Bacchus) b Garner		0
Extras	(B4, LB4, NB3)	11	(B1, LB3, NB6)		10
Total		**178**			**169**

ENGLAND	O	M	R	W	O	M	R	W		FALL OF WICKETS		
Dilley	28	4	73	0						WI	E	E
Botham	28	6	113	2					*Wkt*	*1st*	*1st*	*2nd*
Old	16	4	49	1					1st	168	45	19
Emburey	52	16	124	5					2nd	203	63	25
Miller	18	4	42	1					3rd	203	110	86
Gooch	2	0	3	0					4th	215	121	103
Willey	3	1	4	0					5th	257	127	134
WEST INDIES									6th	332	143	142
Roberts	13	3	41	2	(2) 21	7	41	3	7th	348	151	163
Holding	11	3	29	0	(1) 18	6	38	3	8th	383	163	167
Croft	22	6	40	5	(4) 16	5	26	1	9th	393	167	169
Garner	23	8	37	2	(3) 25	10	31	2	10th	–	178	169
Richards	7	2	16	0	10	6	9	1				
Gomes	2	1	4	1	9	4	14	0				

Umpires: C.E.Cumberbatch (1) and D.Sang Hue (29).

Close: 1st day – WI(1) 144-0 (Greenidge 70, Haynes 68); 2nd – WI(1) 365-7 (Roberts 15, Holding 12); 3rd – E(1) 159-7 (Gower 47, Emburey 4); 4th – E(2) 65-2 (Boycott 29, Gower 21).

The 2nd Test, scheduled to be played at Bourda, Georgetown, Guyana, on 28 February, 1, 2, 4, 5 March, was cancelled by the Cricket Council when the Guyana government withdrew R.D.Jackman's visitor's permit and served him with a deportation order (see page 466).

WEST INDIES v ENGLAND 1980-81 (3rd Test)

At Kensington Oval, Bridgetown, Barbados, on 13, 14, 15, 17, 18 March.
Toss: England.   Result: WEST INDIES won by 298 runs.
Debuts: England – R.O.Butcher, R.D.Jackman.

After prolonged deliberations on the Gleneagles Agreement, the governments of the four countries involved in the remainder of England's itinerary agreed that they would not emulate Guyana and ban Jackman because of his contacts with South Africa. The match was overshadowed by the sudden death of Ken Barrington, England's assistant manager and coach, following a heart attack on the second evening. After Botham had echoed R.E.S.Wyatt's 1934-35 action by electing to field first for the second time during a rubber in the West Indies, Jackman (aged 35) dismissed Greenidge with his fifth ball in Test cricket. Butcher, born just 14 miles from Kensington Oval, was the first black West Indian to appear for England, where he had lived since the age of 13.

WEST INDIES

C.G.Greenidge	c Gooch b Jackman	14		lbw b Dilley	0
D.L.Haynes	c Bairstow b Jackman	25		lbw b Botham	25
I.V.A.Richards	c Botham b Dilley	0	(4)	not out	182
E.H.Mattis	lbw b Botham	16	(5)	c Butcher b Jackman	24
*C.H.Lloyd	c Gooch b Jackman	100	(7)	lbw b Botham	66
H.A.Gomes	c Botham b Dilley	58		run out	34
†D.A.Murray	c Bairstow b Dilley	9	(9)	not out	5
A.M.E.Roberts	c Bairstow b Botham	14		c Bairstow b Botham	0
J.Garner	c Bairstow b Botham	15			
M.A.Holding	c Gatting b Botham	0			
C.E.H.Croft	not out	0	(3)	c Boycott b Jackman	33
Extras	(B4, LB6, W2, NB2)	14		(B3, LB7)	10
Total		**265**		**(7 wickets declared)**	**379**

ENGLAND

G.A.Gooch	b Garner	26		c Garner b Croft	116
G.Boycott	b Holding	0		c Garner b Holding	1
M.W.Gatting	c Greenidge b Roberts	2		b Holding	0
D.I.Gower	c Mattis b Croft	17		b Richards	54
R.O.Butcher	c Richards b Croft	17		lbw b Richards	2
*I.T.Botham	c Murray b Holding	26		c Lloyd b Roberts	1
P.Willey	not out	19		lbw b Croft	17
†D.L.Bairstow	c Mattis b Holding	0		c Murray b Croft	2
J.E.Emburey	c Lloyd b Roberts	0		b Garner	9
R.D.Jackman	c Roberts b Croft	7		b Garner	7
G.R.Dilley	c Gomes b Croft	0		not out	7
Extras	(B1, LB1, NB6)	8		(B1, LB3, NB4)	8
Total		**122**			**224**

ENGLAND	O	M	R	W	O	M	R	W		FALL OF WICKETS			
										WI	E	WI	E
Dilley	23	7	51	3	25	3	111	1		1st	1st	2nd	2nd
Botham	25.1	5	77	4	29	5	102	3	Wkt				
Jackman	22	4	65	3	25	5	76	2	1st	24	6	0	2
Emburey	18	4	45	0	24	7	57	0	2nd	25	11	57	2
Gooch	2	0	13	0					3rd	47	40	71	122
Willey					(5) 6	0	23	0	4th	65	55	130	134
									5th	219	72	212	139
WEST INDIES									6th	224	94	365	196
Roberts	11	3	29	2	20	6	42	1	7th	236	94	365	198
Holding	11	7	16	3	19	6	46	2	8th	258	97	–	201
Croft	13.5	2	39	4	19	1	65	3	9th	258	122	–	213
Garner	12	5	30	1	16.2	6	39	2	10th	265	122	–	224
Richards					17	6	24	2					

Umpires: D.M.Archer (1) and D.Sang Hue (30).

Close: 1st day – WI(1) 238-7 (Roberts 3, Garner 3); 2nd – WI(2) 6-1 (Haynes 6, Croft 0); 3rd – WI(2) 245-5 (Richards 102, Lloyd 19); 4th – E(2) 166-5 (Gooch 88, Willey 13).

WEST INDIES v ENGLAND 1980-81 (4th Test)

At Recreation Ground, St John's, Antigua, on 27, 28, 29, 31 (*no play*) March, 1 April.
Toss: England.   Result: MATCH DRAWN.
Debuts: None.

Antigua, an island of 108 square miles and 70,000 inhabitants, provided the West Indies with its first new Test venue since 1930. Richards scored a century in front of his home crowd at the first opportunity and just three days after his marriage. His innings of 114 included 90 in boundaries but took 305 minutes; it was his sixth hundred in 12 Tests against England. Willey (223 minutes, 15 fours and a six) scored the first century on Test cricket's 52nd ground. The unfinished partnership of 67 between Holding and Croft remains the tenth-wicket record for West Indies in this series. Boycott (345 minutes, eight fours and a five) scored his 20th Test hundred.

ENGLAND

G.A.Gooch	run out	33		c Greenidge b Richards	83
G.Boycott	c Murray b Croft	38		not out	104
C.W.J.Athey	c Lloyd b Croft	2		c Richards b Croft	1
D.I.Gower	c Mattis b Holding	32		c Murray b Croft	22
R.O.Butcher	c Greenidge b Croft	20			
*I.T.Botham	c Lloyd b Croft	1			
P.Willey	not out	102	(5)	not out	1
†P.R.Downton	c Murray b Garner	13			
J.E.Emburey	b Croft	10			
G.B.Stevenson	b Croft	1			
G.R.Dilley	c Murray b Holding	2			
Extras	(B6, LB7, W1, NB3)	17		(B11, LB3, NB9)	23
Total		**271**		(3 wickets)	**234**

WEST INDIES

C.G.Greenidge	c Athey b Stevenson	63
D.L.Haynes	c Downton b Botham	4
I.V.A.Richards	c Emburey b Dilley	114
E.H.Mattis	c Butcher b Botham	71
H.A.Gomes	c Gower b Botham	12
*C.H.Lloyd	c Downton b Stevenson	58
†D.A.Murray	c Boycott b Botham	1
A.M.E.Roberts	b Stevenson	13
J.Garner	c Butcher b Dilley	46
M.A.Holding	not out	58
C.E.H.Croft	not out	17
Extras	(B1, LB7, W1, NB2)	11
Total	(9 wickets declared)	**468**

WEST INDIES	O	M	R	W	O	M	R	W		FALL OF WICKETS		
Roberts	22	4	59	0	17	5	39	0		E	WI	E
Holding	18.2	4	51	2	9	2	21	0	*Wkt*	*1st*	*1st*	*2nd*
Garner	16	5	44	1	15	3	33	0	1st	60	12	144
Croft	25	5	74	6	16	4	39	2	2nd	70	133	146
Richards	9	4	26	0	22	7	54	1	3rd	95	241	217
Gomes					13	5	21	0	4th	135	268	–
Mattis					1	0	4	0	5th	138	269	–
									6th	138	271	–
ENGLAND									7th	176	296	–
Dilley	25	5	99	2					8th	233	379	–
Botham	37	6	127	4					9th	235	401	–
Stevenson	33	5	111	3					10th	271	–	–
Emburey	35	12	85	0								
Willey	20	8	30	0								
Gooch	2	2	0	0								
Boycott	3	2	5	0								

Umpires: D.M.Archer (2) and S.Mohammed (1).

Close: 1st day – E(1) 260-9 (Willey 91, Dilley 2); 2nd – WI(1) 236-2 (Richards 110, Mattis 56); 3rd – E(2) 7-0 (Gooch 3, Boycott 4); 4th – no play.

WEST INDIES v ENGLAND 1980-81 (5th Test)

At Sabina Park, Kingston, Jamaica, on 10, 11, 12, 14, 15 April.
Toss: West Indies.   Result: MATCH DRAWN.
Debuts: None.

Gooch scored 153 out of 249 in 315 minutes with two sixes and 21 fours; that tally included a six and 12 fours off Croft, whose 24 wickets was a record for West Indies in a home rubber against England until 1985-86. West Indies were without Marshall (strained rib muscle) on the last day when Gower (7¾ hours, a six and 16 fours) guided England to a total of 300 for the first time in eight innings. When he was joined by Downton, England's lead was only 58 and nearly four hours remained. Jackman completed an over for Dilley, who retired for boot repairs after four deliveries.

ENGLAND

G.A.Gooch	c Murray b Holding	153	c Lloyd b Marshall	3
G.Boycott	c Murray b Garner	40	c Garner b Croft	12
C.W.J.Athey	b Holding	3	c Murray b Holding	1
D.I.Gower	b Croft	22	not out	154
P.Willey	c Murray b Marshall	4	c Greenidge b Richards	67
R.O.Butcher	b Garner	32	lbw b Croft	0
*I.T.Botham	c Greenidge b Marshall	13	c Garner b Holding	16
†P.R.Downton	c Croft b Holding	0	not out	26
J.E.Emburey	b Holding	1		
R.D.Jackman	c Haynes b Holding	0		
G.R.Dilley	not out	1		
Extras	(B8, NB8)	16	(B6, LB13, NB4)	23
Total		**285**	(6 wickets declared)	**302**

WEST INDIES

C.G.Greenidge	c Botham b Dilley	62
D.L.Haynes	b Willey	84
I.V.A.Richards	c Downton b Dilley	15
E.H.Mattis	c sub (M.W.Gatting) b Dilley	34
*C.H.Lloyd	c Downton b Jackman	95
H.A.Gomes	not out	90
†D.A.Murray	c Gooch b Emburey	14
M.D.Marshall	b Emburey	15
J.Garner	c sub (D.L.Bairstow) b Dilley	19
M.A.Holding	c Downton b Botham	0
C.E.H.Croft	c sub (M.W.Gatting) b Botham	0
Extras	(LB8, W1, NB5)	14
Total		**442**

WEST INDIES	O	M	R	W	O	M	R	W
Holding	18	3	56	5	28	7	58	2
Marshall	16	2	49	2	5	0	15	1
Croft	17	4	92	1	29	7	80	2
Garner	20	4	43	2	24	7	46	0
Richards	12	2	29	0	23	8	48	1
Gomes					13	3	18	0
Mattis					5	1	10	0
Haynes					1	0	4	0

ENGLAND	O	M	R	W
Dilley	28.4	6	116	4
Botham	26.1	9	73	2
Jackman	26.2	6	57	1
Gooch	8	3	20	0
Emburey	56	23	108	2
Willey	18	3	54	1

FALL OF WICKETS

Wkt	E 1st	WI 1st	E 2nd
1st	93	116	5
2nd	148	136	10
3rd	196	179	32
4th	210	227	168
5th	249	345	168
6th	275	372	215
7th	283	415	–
8th	283	441	–
9th	284	442	–
10th	285	442	–

Umpires: C.E.Cumberbatch (2) and D.Sang Hue (31).

Close: 1st day – E(1) 278-6 (Botham 12, Downton 0); 2nd – WI(1) 193-3 (Mattis 14, Lloyd 13); 3rd – WI(1) 442 all out; 4th – E(2) 134-3 (Gower 70, Willey 44).

NEW ZEALAND v INDIA 1980-81 (1st Test)

At Basin Reserve, Wellington, on 21, 22, 23, 25 February.
Toss: India.   Result: NEW ZEALAND won by 62 runs.
Debuts: New Zealand – M.C.Snedden; India – K.Azad, R.J.Shastri, Yograj Singh.

Basin Reserve's first Test for three years involved a re-sited pitch and produced New Zealand's fourth victory in 23 matches against India. Howarth's sixth Test century was the first for New Zealand against India in three matches at Wellington. Shastri's first scoring stroke in Test cricket resulted in Kirmani being run out attempting a fourth run. Aged 18 years 270 days when the match started, the tall left-handed spinner took the wickets of Cairns, Snedden and Troup with his last four balls. Summoned to replace the injured Doshi, he had arrived from Bombay on the eve of the match. New Zealand's total of 100 remains their lowest against India. Left with two full days in which to score 253, India were all out at 5.24 on the fourth evening.

NEW ZEALAND

J.G.Wright	c Binny b Yograj	32	c Viswanath b Kapil Dev	8
B.A.Edgar	c Kirmani b Patil	39	c Patil b Binny	28
J.F.Reid	c Kirmani b Patil	46	lbw b Kapil Dev	7
*G.P.Howarth	not out	137	c Kirmani b Patil	7
J.V.Coney	c and b Shastri	4	c sub ‡ b Kapil Dev	8
G.N.Edwards	c Kirmani b Kapil Dev	23	c sub ‡ b Kapil Dev	6
†I.D.S.Smith	c Vengsarkar b Kapil Dev	20	not out	15
R.J.Hadlee	c Kirmani b Binny	20	c Kirmani b Binny	7
B.L.Cairns	c Gavaskar b Kapil Dev	13	c Vengsarkar b Shastri	0
M.C.Snedden	b Shastri	2	c Vengsarkar b Shastri	0
G.B.Troup	c Gavaskar b Shastri	0	c Vengsarkar b Shastri	0
Extras	(B4, LB17, W1, NB17)	39	(LB10, W2, NB2)	14
Total		**375**		**100**

INDIA

*S.M.Gavaskar	b Cairns	23	b Snedden	12
C.P.S.Chauhan	c Coney b Troup	17	b Hadlee	1
D.B.Vengsarkar	lbw b Cairns	39	c Smith b Hadlee	26
G.R.Viswanath	b Cairns	0	b Troup	9
S.M.Patil	c Smith b Troup	64	c Smith b Cairns	42
K.Azad	b Cairns	20	b Hadlee	16
Kapil Dev	c Smith b Troup	0	(8) c Hadlee b Troup	9
†S.M.H.Kirmani	run out	13	(7) b Cairns	11
R.M.H.Binny	b Snedden	11	not out	26
R.J.Shastri	not out	3	c Smith b Snedden	19
Yograj Singh	c Smith b Cairns	4	c Smith b Hadlee	6
Extras	(B10, LB13, NB6)	29	(B2, LB5, NB6)	13
Total		**223**		**190**

INDIA	O	M	R	W	O	M	R	W		FALL OF WICKETS			
Kapil Dev	38	9	112	3	16	4	34	4		NZ	I	NZ	I
Yograj	15	3	63	1					Wkt	1st	1st	2nd	2nd
Binny	22	4	67	1	(2) 12	4	26	2	1st	60	32	17	10
Shastri	28	9	54	3	3	0	9	3	2nd	101	70	35	30
Patil	16	3	40	2	(3) 17	10	12	1	3rd	200	70	35	30
Azad					(5) 1	0	5	0	4th	215	116	58	75
									5th	245	183	73	111
NEW ZEALAND									6th	292	183	78	117
Hadlee	16	4	62	0	22.3	7	65	4	7th	331	198	99	136
Troup	17	5	43	3	13	4	34	2	8th	364	213	100	136
Snedden	20	7	56	1	17	4	39	2	9th	375	218	100	170
Cairns	19.4	8	33	5	19	8	30	2	10th	375	223	100	190
Coney					4	1	9	0					

Umpires: F.R.Goodall (11) and S.J.Woodward (3).   ‡ (T.E.Srinivasan)

Close: 1st day – NZ(1) 241-4 (Howarth 77, Edwards 19); 2nd – I(1) 133-4 (Patil 30, Azad 6); 3rd – NZ(2) 100 all out.

NEW ZEALAND v INDIA 1980-81 (2nd Test)

At Lancaster Park, Christchurch, on 6, 7, 8 (*no play*), 9 (*no play*), 10, 11 March.
Toss: India.   Result: MATCH DRAWN.
Debuts: None.

More than 13 hours were lost, with only 50 minutes of play possible on the second day and none on the third or its replacement, the scheduled rest day. Chauhan batted 266 minutes and, in his 58th innings, became the first to amass 2,000 runs in Test cricket without scoring a century. Kirmani retired at 226 for seven stitches in his jaw after attempting to hook a Hadlee bouncer. Yashpal kept wicket until he, too, was injured, at which point a substitute, B.Reddy, took over. In his 34th Test, Hadlee became the first to take 150 wickets for New Zealand. Reid batted 445 minutes, his first hundred in Tests taking 356 minutes.

INDIA

*S.M.Gavaskar	c Smith b Hadlee	53
C.P.S.Chauhan	c Smith b Hadlee	78
D.B.Vengsarkar	b Snedden	61
G.R.Viswanath	b Hadlee	7
S.M.Patil	c Reid b Hadlee	4
Yashpal Sharma	c Howarth b Hadlee	0
†S.M.H.Kirmani	retired hurt	9
Kapil Dev	c and b Snedden	0
K.D.Ghavri	c Reid b Coney	17
R.J.Shastri	not out	12
D.R.Doshi	b Coney	0
Extras	(B4, LB5, NB5)	14
Total		**255**

NEW ZEALAND

J.G.Wright	c Vengsarkar b Ghavri	18
B.A.Edgar	lbw b Shastri	49
J.F.Reid	not out	123
*G.P.Howarth	c sub (T.E.Srinivasan) b Doshi	26
J.V.Coney	c Chauhan b Patil	15
G.N.Edwards	b Shastri	23
†I.D.S.Smith	not out	11
R.J.Hadlee		
B.L.Cairns	} did not bat	
M.C.Snedden		
G.B.Troup		
Extras	(B6, LB8, NB7)	21
Total	(5 wickets)	**286**

NEW ZEALAND	O	M	R	W
Hadlee	33	12	47	5
Troup	26	6	60	0
Cairns	33	16	57	0
Snedden	23	8	63	2
Coney	9	4	12	2
Howarth	3	2	2	0
INDIA				
Kapil Dev	22	2	60	0
Ghavri	10	4	33	1
Patil	12	4	14	1
Shastri	42	21	65	2
Chauhan	5	1	12	0
Gavaskar	3	1	11	0
Doshi	49	23	67	1
Vengsarkar	2	1	3	0

FALL OF WICKETS

	I	NZ
Wkt	1st	1st
1st	114	27
2nd	168	152
3rd	200	201
4th	210	235
5th	210	265
6th	224	–
7th	224	–
8th	255	–
9th	255	–
10th	–	–

Umpires: J.B.R.Hastie (7) and D.A.Kinsella (1).

Close: 1st day – I(1) 168-2 (Vengsarkar 32, Viswanath 0); 2nd – I(1) 174-2 (Vengsarkar 36, Viswanath 2); 3rd – no play; 4th – no play; 5th – NZ(1) 93-1 (Edgar 30, Reid 37).

NEW ZEALAND v INDIA 1980-81 (3rd Test)

At Eden Park, Auckland, on 13, 14, 15, 17, 18 March.
Toss: India.   Result: MATCH DRAWN.
Debuts: India – T.E.Srinivasan.

Although New Zealand failed to score 157 in four hours on a well-worn pitch and in fading light, the result gained them their first rubber against India at their seventh attempt. Kirmani and Yadav equalled India's highest ninth-wicket stand against New Zealand by adding 105. Wright, who endured for 460 minutes and faced 434 balls, completed his first hundred in Tests with a six. Doshi bowled 337 balls before taking his first wicket of the match.

INDIA

Batsman	Dismissal 1st	Runs		Dismissal 2nd	Runs
*S.M.Gavaskar	c Smith b Snedden	5		c Wright b Bracewell	33
C.P.S.Chauhan	c Cairns b Bracewell	36		c Cairns b Bracewell	7
D.B.Vengsarkar	c Howarth b Snedden	0	(5)	not out	52
S.M.Patil	c Smith b Cairns	19	(6)	b Bracewell	57
G.R.Viswanath	lbw b Hadlee	2	(4)	run out	46
T.E.Srinivasan	c Smith b Bracewell	29	(3)	c Wright b Cairns	19
R.J.Shastri	c and b Cairns	5	(9)	run out	9
†S.M.H.Kirmani	b Bracewell	78		b Bracewell	1
Kapil Dev	b Cairns	4	(7)	c Edgar b Cairns	14
N.S.Yadav	c Hadlee b Bracewell	43		c Smith b Bracewell	1
D.R.Doshi	not out	3		b Cairns	2
Extras	(B5, LB3, NB6)	14		(B23, LB7, NB13)	43
Total		**238**			**284**

NEW ZEALAND

Batsman	Dismissal 1st	Runs		Dismissal 2nd	Runs
J.G.Wright	c Kirmani b Chauhan	110		not out	33
B.A.Edgar	c Shastri b Patil	0		c Kirmani b Kapil Dev	1
J.F.Reid	c Viswanath b Shastri	74	(6)	lbw b Doshi	0
*G.P.Howarth	c sub (R.M.H.Binny) b Shastri	0	(5)	c Chauhan b Doshi	2
J.V.Coney	c and b Doshi	65	(7)	not out	0
G.N.Edwards	c and b Doshi	34	(3)	c and b Shastri	47
R.J.Hadlee	c Chauhan b Yadav	0	(4)	b Shastri	2
B.L.Cairns	c Gavaskar b Shastri	41			
†I.D.S.Smith	b Shastri	10			
J.G.Bracewell	lbw b Shastri	1			
M.C.Snedden	not out	0			
Extras	(B14, LB10, NB7)	31		(B3, LB4, NB3)	10
Total		**366**		**(5 wickets)**	**95**

NEW ZEALAND	O	M	R	W	O	M	R	W	FALL OF WICKETS			
									I	NZ	I	NZ
Hadlee	27	11	49	1	21	3	65	0				
Snedden	22	7	52	2	13	4	40	0	*Wkt*	*1st*	*1st*	*2nd*	*2nd*
Cairns	27	13	37	3	35.5	16	47	3	1st	9	0	43	1
Coney	9	1	14	0	(5) 4	1	3	0	2nd	10	148	50	83
Bracewell	42.3	17	61	4	(4) 41	19	75	5	3rd	43	152	93	87
Howarth	3	0	11	0	6	3	11	0	4th	50	251	143	94
									5th	97	301	236	95
INDIA									6th	100	302	260	–
Kapil Dev	20	6	34	0	10	6	15	1	7th	114	332	261	–
Patil	6	4	2	1	4	0	8	0	8th	124	354	277	–
Yadav	33	8	91	1	(5) 11	4	20	0	9th	229	365	279	–
Doshi	69	34	79	2	(3) 19	9	18	2	10th	238	366	284	–
Shastri	56	13	125	5	(4) 18	8	24	2					
Chauhan	2	0	4	1									

Umpires: F.R.Goodall (12) and S.J.Woodward (4).

Close: 1st day – I(1) 184-8 (Kirmani 42, Yadav 28); 2nd – NZ(1) 127-1 (Wright 55, Reid 66); 3rd – NZ(1) 357-8 (Cairns 34, Bracewell 0); 4th – I(2) 197-4 (Vengsarkar 20, Patil 36).

ENGLAND v AUSTRALIA 1981 (1st Test)

At Trent Bridge, Nottingham, on 18, 19, 20, 21 June.
Toss: Australia.   Result: AUSTRALIA won by 4 wickets.
Debuts: Australia – T.M.Alderman, T.M.Chappell.

This was the first Test match in England to include Sunday play; commencing at noon, it ended at 5.49 pm when Australia completed their first victory at Trent Bridge since 1948. It was also the first five-day Test in England not to include a scheduled rest day. Alderman opened his international career with a spell of 24-7-68-4. After being stranded on 198 for 11 months, Willis became the sixth bowler to take 200 wickets for England. It had taken him longer than any of the other five (10 years 5 months and 58 Tests) but only F.S.Trueman had needed fewer than Willis's 10,936 balls. Marsh became the first wicket-keeper to make 100 dismissals in this series when he caught Woolmer. That wicket also gave Marsh the record number of catches in Test cricket, previously 244 by A.P.E.Knott. The selection of Trevor Chappell provided the first instance of three brothers representing Australia in official Tests.

ENGLAND

G.A.Gooch	c Wood b Lillee	10	c Yallop b Lillee		6
G.Boycott	c Border b Alderman	27	c Marsh b Alderman		4
R.A.Woolmer	c Wood b Lillee	0	c Marsh b Alderman		0
D.I.Gower	c Yallop b Lillee	26	c sub (M.F.Kent) b Lillee		28
M.W.Gatting	lbw b Hogg	52	lbw b Alderman		15
P.Willey	c Border b Alderman	10	lbw b Lillee		13
*I.T.Botham	b Alderman	1	c Border b Lillee		33
†P.R.Downton	c Yallop b Alderman	8	lbw b Alderman		3
G.R.Dilley	b Hogg	34	c Marsh b Alderman		13
R.G.D.Willis	c Marsh b Hogg	0	c Chappell b Lillee		1
M.Hendrick	not out	6	not out		0
Extras	(LB6, W1, NB4)	11	(LB8, NB1)		9
Total		**185**			**125**

AUSTRALIA

G.M.Wood	lbw b Dilley	0	(2) c Woolmer b Willis	8
J.Dyson	c Woolmer b Willis	5	(1) c Downton b Dilley	38
G.N.Yallop	b Hendrick	13	c Gatting b Botham	6
*K.J.Hughes	lbw b Willis	7	lbw b Dilley	22
T.M.Chappell	b Hendrick	17	not out	20
A.R.Border	c and b Botham	63	b Dilley	20
†R.W.Marsh	c Boycott b Willis	19	lbw b Dilley	0
G.F.Lawson	c Gower b Botham	14	not out	5
D.K.Lillee	c Downton b Dilley	12		
R.M.Hogg	c Boycott b Dilley	0		
T.M.Alderman	not out	12		
Extras	(B4, LB8, W1, NB4)	17	(B1, LB6, NB6)	13
Total		**179**	(6 wickets)	**132**

AUSTRALIA	O	M	R	W	O	M	R	W
Lillee	13	3	34	3	16.4	2	46	5
Alderman	24	7	68	4	19	3	62	5
Hogg	11.4	1	47	3	3	1	8	0
Lawson	8	3	25	0				
ENGLAND								
Dilley	20	7	38	3	11.1	4	24	4
Willis	30	14	47	3	13	2	28	1
Hendrick	20	7	43	2	20	7	33	0
Botham	16.5	6	34	2	10	1	34	1

FALL OF WICKETS

	E	A	E	A
Wkt	1st	1st	2nd	2nd
1st	13	0	12	20
2nd	13	21	12	40
3rd	57	21	13	77
4th	67	33	39	80
5th	92	64	61	122
6th	96	89	94	122
7th	116	110	109	–
8th	159	147	113	–
9th	159	153	125	–
10th	185	179	125	–

Umpires: W.E.Alley (10) and D.J.Constant (21).

Close: 1st day – A(1) 33-4 (Chappell 5); 2nd – A(1) 166-9 (Border 57, Alderman 7); 3rd – E(2) 94-6 (Botham 21, Downton 0).

ENGLAND v AUSTRALIA 1981 (2nd Test)

At Lord's, London, on 2, 3, 4, 6, 7 July.
Toss: Australia.   Result: MATCH DRAWN.
Debuts: None.

Hughes became only the second captain after I.M.Chappell (1974-75) to elect to field first in successive Ashes Tests. Boycott emulated M.C.Cowdrey by appearing in 100 official Test matches and, after batting for 240 minutes in the second innings, equalled the latter's record of compiling 60 scores of 50 and more. Woolmer (13) retired at 83 when his arm was bruised by a ball from Lawson, and returned at 284. England's last six wickets fell for 27 runs in 59 minutes during 12.3 overs. Extras (55) achieved their highest innings total in this series until *Test No. 1125* (previously 50 in The Oval Tests of 1934 and 1938). Lillee bowled 48.4 overs before taking his first wicket of the match. Botham's 12-match reign as captain produced four defeats and eight draws to equal England's (then) longest sequence without a win (Leeds 1963 to The Oval 1964).

ENGLAND

G.A.Gooch	c Yallop b Lawson	44		lbw b Lawson	20
G.Boycott	c Alderman b Lawson	17		c Marsh b Lillee	60
R.A.Woolmer	c Marsh b Lawson	21		lbw b Alderman	9
D.I.Gower	c Marsh b Lawson	27		c Alderman b Lillee	89
M.W.Gatting	lbw b Bright	59		c Wood b Bright	16
P.Willey	c Border b Alderman	82	(7)	c Chappell b Bright	12
J.E.Emburey	run out	31			
*I.T.Botham	lbw b Lawson	0	(6)	b Bright	0
†R.W.Taylor	c Hughes b Lawson	0		b Lillee	9
G.R.Dilley	not out	7	(8)	not out	27
R.G.D.Willis	c Wood b Lawson	5			
Extras	(B2, LB3, W3, NB10)	18		(B2, LB8, NB13)	23
Total		**311**		**(8 wickets declared)**	**265**

AUSTRALIA

G.M.Wood	c Taylor b Willis	44	(2)	not out	62
J.Dyson	c Gower b Botham	7	(1)	lbw b Dilley	1
G.N.Yallop	b Dilley	1		c Botham b Willis	3
*K.J.Hughes	c Willis b Emburey	42		lbw b Dilley	4
T.M.Chappell	c Taylor b Dilley	2		c Taylor b Botham	5
A.R.Border	c Gatting b Botham	64		not out	12
†R.W.Marsh	lbw b Dilley	47			
R.J.Bright	lbw b Emburey	33			
G.F.Lawson	lbw b Willis	5			
D.K.Lillee	not out	40			
T.M.Alderman	c Taylor b Willis	5			
Extras	(B6, LB11, W6, NB32)	55		(W1, NB2)	3
Total		**345**		**(4 wickets)**	**90**

AUSTRALIA	O	M	R	W	O	M	R	W	FALL OF WICKETS				
Lillee	35.4	7	102	0	26.4	8	82	3		E	A	E	A
Alderman	30.2	7	79	1	17	2	42	1	*Wkt*	*1st*	*1st*	*2nd*	*2nd*
Lawson	43.1	14	81	7	19	6	51	1	1st	60	62	31	2
Bright	15	7	31	1	36	18	67	3	2nd	65	62	55	11
									3rd	134	69	178	17
ENGLAND									4th	187	81	217	62
Willis	27.4	9	50	3	12	3	35	1	5th	284	167	217	–
Dilley	30	8	106	3	7.5	1	18	2	6th	293	244	217	–
Botham	26	8	71	2	(4) 8	3	10	1	7th	293	257	242	–
Gooch	10	4	28	0					8th	293	268	265	–
Emburey	25	12	35	2	(3) 21	10	24	0	9th	298	314	–	–
									10th	311	345	–	–

Umpires: D.O.Oslear (3) and K.E.Palmer (7).

Close: 1st day – E(1) 191-4 (Willey 23, Emburey 0); 2nd – A(1) 10-0 (Wood 5, Dyson 3); 3rd – A(1) 253-6 (Marsh 43, Bright 3); 4th – E(2) 129-2 (Boycott 47, Gower 38).

ENGLAND v AUSTRALIA 1981 (3rd Test)

At Headingley, Leeds, on 16, 17, 18, 20, 21 July.
Toss: Australia.   Result: ENGLAND won by 18 runs.
Debuts: None.

England's victory was their first in 13 Tests since Bombay 1979-80 (*Test No. 876*). The margin of 18 runs was the narrowest in Ashes Tests since England won by 12 runs at Adelaide in 1928-29 (*179*). There had been only one previous instance of a side winning a Test after following on, England beating Australia by 10 runs in 1894-95 (*42*). Brearley, recalled to the captaincy, established an England record with his ninth victory against Australia, one more than W.G.Grace's leadership achieved. Botham became the second player after J.M.Gregory (*136*) to score a century and take five wickets in an innings of an Ashes Test; it was the fourth time he had achieved this feat in all Tests, two more than any other player. His hundred came off only 87 balls. Willis (8 for 43) returned the best analysis in any Headingley Test and the best of his career. Both wicket-keepers set world records during the match: Marsh overtook A.P.E.Knott's record of 263 dismissals in Tests when he caught Botham; and Taylor passed J.T.Murray's total of 1,270 catches in first-class cricket when he caught Lawson the second time. Lillee became the leading-wicket-taker in this series when he dismissed Willey and exceeded H.Trumble's total of 141.

AUSTRALIA

Batsman	Dismissal	Score		2nd Innings	Score
J.Dyson	b Dilley	102	(2)	c Taylor b Willis	34
G.M.Wood	lbw b Botham	34	(1)	c Taylor b Botham	10
T.M.Chappell	c Taylor b Willey	27		c Taylor b Willis	8
*K.J.Hughes	c and b Botham	89		c Botham b Willis	0
R.J.Bright	b Dilley	7	(8)	b Willis	19
G.N.Yallop	c Taylor b Botham	58	(5)	c Gatting b Willis	0
A.R.Border	lbw b Botham	8	(6)	b Old	0
†R.W.Marsh	b Botham	28	(7)	c Dilley b Willis	4
G.F.Lawson	c Taylor b Botham	13		c Taylor b Willis	1
D.K.Lillee	not out	3		c Gatting b Willis	17
T.M.Alderman	not out	0		not out	0
Extras	(B4, LB13, W3, NB12)	32		(LB3, W1, NB14)	18
Total	(9 wickets declared)	**401**			**111**

ENGLAND

Batsman	Dismissal	Score	2nd Innings	Score
G.A.Gooch	lbw b Alderman	2	c Alderman b Lillee	0
G.Boycott	b Lawson	12	lbw b Alderman	46
*J.M.Brearley	c Marsh b Alderman	10	c Alderman b Lillee	14
D.I.Gower	c Marsh b Lawson	24	c Border b Alderman	9
M.W.Gatting	lbw b Lillee	15	lbw b Alderman	1
P.Willey	b Lawson	8	c Dyson b Lillee	33
I.T.Botham	c Marsh b Lillee	50	not out	149
†R.W.Taylor	c Marsh b Lillee	5	c Bright b Alderman	1
G.R.Dilley	c and b Lillee	13	b Alderman	56
C.M.Old	c Border b Alderman	0	b Lawson	29
R.G.D.Willis	not out	1	c Border b Alderman	2
Extras	(B6, LB11, W6, NB11)	34	(B5, LB3, W3, NB5)	16
Total		**174**		**356**

ENGLAND	O	M	R	W	O	M	R	W	FALL OF WICKETS				
										A	E	E	A
Willis	30	8	72	0	(3) 15.1	3	43	8	*Wkt*	*1st*	*1st*	*2nd*	*2nd*
Old	43	14	91	0	(4) 9	1	21	1	1st	55	12	0	13
Dilley	27	4	78	2	(2) 2	0	11	0	2nd	149	40	18	56
Botham	39.2	11	95	6	(1) 7	3	14	1	3rd	196	42	37	58
Willey	13	2	31	1	3	1	4	0	4th	220	84	41	58
Boycott	3	2	2	0					5th	332	87	105	65
									6th	354	112	133	68
AUSTRALIA									7th	357	148	135	74
Lillee	18.5	7	49	4	25	6	94	3	8th	396	166	252	75
Alderman	19	4	59	3	35.3	6	135	6	9th	401	167	319	110
Lawson	13	3	32	3	23	4	96	1	10th	–	174	356	111
Bright					4	0	15	0					

Umpires: D.G.L.Evans (1) and B.J.Meyer (7).

Close: 1st day – A(1) 203-3 (Hughes 24, Bright 1); 2nd – E(1) 7-0 (Gooch 2, Boycott 0); 3rd – E(2) 6-1 (Boycott 0, Brearley 4); 4th – E(2) 351-9 (Botham 145, Willis 1).

ENGLAND v AUSTRALIA 1981 (4th Test)

At Edgbaston, Birmingham, on 30, 31 July, 1, 2 August.
Toss: England.   Result: ENGLAND won by 29 runs.
Debuts: Australia – M.F.Kent.

The second Sunday of Test match cricket in England emulated its predecessor at Trent Bridge by producing a result with more than a day to spare. Needing 142 with nine wickets left when play began at noon, Australia added 96 (for 3) before losing their last six wickets for 16 runs in 47 minutes. Botham, reluctant to bowl at that stage, took five wickets for one run in 28 balls. Gower became the first Leicestershire batsman to score 2,000 runs in Tests. For the first time in 668 Tests since West Indies played England on a rain-affected pitch at Bridgetown in January 1935 (*Test No. 238*), no batsman scored a fifty.

ENGLAND

G.Boycott	c Marsh b Alderman	13		c Marsh b Bright	29
*J.M.Brearley	c Border b Lillee	48		lbw b Lillee	13
D.I.Gower	c Hogg b Alderman	0		c Border b Bright	23
G.A.Gooch	c Marsh b Bright	21		b Bright	21
M.W.Gatting	c Alderman b Lillee	21		b Bright	39
P.Willey	b Bright	16		b Bright	5
I.T.Botham	b Alderman	26		c Marsh b Lillee	3
J.E.Emburey	b Hogg	3	(9)	not out	37
†R.W.Taylor	b Alderman	0	(10)	lbw b Alderman	8
C.M.Old	not out	11	(8)	c Marsh b Alderman	23
R.G.D.Willis	c Marsh b Alderman	13		c Marsh b Alderman	2
Extras	(B1, LB5, W1, NB10)	17		(LB6, W1, NB9)	16
Total		**189**			**219**

AUSTRALIA

G.M.Wood	run out	38	(2)	lbw b Old	2
J.Dyson	b Old	1	(1)	lbw b Willis	13
A.R.Border	c Taylor b Old	2		c Gatting b Emburey	40
R.J.Bright	lbw b Botham	27	(8)	lbw b Botham	0
*K.J.Hughes	lbw b Old	47	(4)	c Emburey b Willis	5
G.N.Yallop	b Emburey	30	(5)	c Botham b Emburey	30
M.F.Kent	c Willis b Emburey	46	(6)	b Botham	10
†R.W.Marsh	b Emburey	2	(7)	b Botham	4
D.K.Lillee	b Emburey	18		c Taylor b Botham	3
R.M.Hogg	run out	0		not out	0
T.M.Alderman	not out	3		b Botham	0
Extras	(B4, LB19, NB21)	44		(B1, LB2, NB11)	14
Total		**258**			**121**

AUSTRALIA	O	M	R	W	O	M	R	W	FALL OF WICKETS				
Lillee	18	4	61	2	26	9	51	2		E	A	E	A
Alderman	23.1	8	42	5	22	5	65	3	*Wkt*	*1st*	*1st*	*2nd*	*2nd*
Hogg	16	3	49	1	10	3	19	0	1st	29	5	18	2
Bright	12	4	20	2	34	17	68	5	2nd	29	14	52	19
									3rd	60	62	89	29
ENGLAND									4th	101	115	98	87
Willis	19	3	63	0	20	6	37	2	5th	126	166	110	105
Old	21	8	44	3	11	4	19	1	6th	145	203	115	114
Emburey	26.5	12	43	4	22	10	40	2	7th	161	220	154	114
Botham	20	1	64	1	14	9	11	5	8th	161	253	167	120
									9th	165	253	217	121
									10th	189	258	219	121

Umpires: H.D.Bird (20) and D.O.Oslear (4).

Close: 1st day – A(1) 19-2 (Wood 6, Bright 0); 2nd – E(2) 49-1 (Boycott 9, Gower 20); 3rd – A(2) 9-1 (Dyson 5, Border 2).

ENGLAND v AUSTRALIA 1981 (5th Test)

At Old Trafford, Manchester, on 13, 14, 15, 16, 17 August.
Toss: England.   Result: ENGLAND won by 103 runs.
Debuts: England – P.J.W.Allott; Australia – M.R.Whitney.

England retained the Ashes and won their third rubber against Australia under Brearley; his eleventh victory in this series equalled Sir Donald Bradman's record. Boycott, in 11 fewer matches, overtook M.C.Cowdrey's record England aggregate of 7,624 runs. Alderman eclipsed Lillee's record of 31 wickets in a rubber in England when he dismissed Emburey. Allott, who reached his maiden first-class fifty off 92 balls, and Willis added 56 (England's highest last-wicket partnership against Australia at Old Trafford), before the latter became Lillee's 150th wicket in this series. Willis dismissed Dyson (his 100th wicket against Australia), Hughes and Yallop in his third over (WO4WOW). Knott became the first wicket-keeper to make 100 dismissals against Australia when he caught Kent. Australia's first innings lasted only 30.2 overs and was their shortest in all Tests since 1902 (*Test No. 70*) when W.Rhodes and G.H.Hirst dismissed them for 36 in 23 overs. Tavaré, who took 423 minutes to score 78 runs, recorded the slowest fifty in English first-class cricket until *Test No. 932* (306 minutes). Botham (123 minutes, 102 balls) reached his century off only 86 balls; his six sixes remains the record for any Test innings in England and the most against Australia. Border, handicapped by a fractured finger, took 377 minutes to reach his hundred – the slowest recorded by an Australian in 415 Tests. Australia's total of 402 remains their second-highest in the fourth innings and their highest such to lose any Test.

ENGLAND

G.A.Gooch	lbw b Lillee	10		b Alderman	5
G.Boycott	c Marsh b Alderman	10		lbw b Alderman	37
C.J.Tavaré	c Alderman b Whitney	69		c Kent b Alderman	78
D.I.Gower	c Yallop b Whitney	23		c Bright b Lillee	1
J.M.Brearley	lbw b Alderman	2	(6)	c Marsh b Alderman	3
M.W.Gatting	c Border b Lillee	32	(5)	lbw b Alderman	11
I.T.Botham	c Bright b Lillee	0		c Marsh b Whitney	118
A.P.E.Knott	c Border b Alderman	13		c Dyson b Lillee	59
J.E.Emburey	c Border b Alderman	1		c Kent b Whitney	57
P.J.W.Allott	not out	52		c Hughes b Bright	14
R.G.D.Willis	c Hughes b Lillee	11		not out	5
Extras	(LB6, W2)	8		(B1, LB12, NB3)	16
Total		**231**			**404**

AUSTRALIA

G.M.Wood	lbw b Allott	19	(2)	c Knott b Allott	6
J.Dyson	c Botham b Willis	0	(1)	run out	5
K.J.Hughes	lbw b Willis	4		lbw b Botham	43
G.N.Yallop	c Botham b Willis	0		b Emburey	114
M.F.Kent	c Knott b Emburey	52	(6)	c Brearley b Emburey	2
A.R.Border	c Gower b Botham	11	(5)	not out	123
R.W.Marsh	c Botham b Willis	1		c Knott b Willis	47
R.J.Bright	c Knott b Botham	22		c Knott b Willis	5
D.K.Lillee	c Gooch b Botham	13		c Botham b Allott	28
M.R.Whitney	b Allott	0	(11)	c Gatting b Willis	0
T.M.Alderman	not out	2	(10)	lbw b Botham	0
Extras	(NB6)	6		(LB9, W2, NB18)	29
Total		**130**			**402**

AUSTRALIA	O	M	R	W	O	M	R	W
Lillee	24.1	8	55	4	46	13	137	2
Alderman	29	5	88	4	52	19	109	5
Whitney	17	3	50	2	27	6	74	2
Bright	16	6	30	0	26.4	12	68	1

ENGLAND	O	M	R	W	O	M	R	W
Willis	14	0	63	4	30.5	2	96	3
Allott	6	1	17	2	17	3	71	2
Botham	6.2	1	28	3	36	16	86	2
Emburey	4	0	16	1	49	9	107	2
Gatting					3	1	13	0

FALL OF WICKETS

	E	A	E	A
Wkt	*1st*	*1st*	*2nd*	*2nd*
1st	19	20	7	7
2nd	25	24	79	24
3rd	57	24	80	119
4th	62	24	98	198
5th	109	58	104	206
6th	109	59	253	296
7th	131	104	282	322
8th	137	125	356	373
9th	175	126	396	378
10th	231	130	404	402

Umpires: D.J.Constant (22) and K.E.Palmer (8).

Close: 1st day – E(1) 175-9 (Allott 9, Willis 0); 2nd – E(2) 70-1 (Boycott 31, Tavaré 29); 3rd – E(2) 345-7 (Knott 56, Emburey 27); 4th – A(2) 210-5 (Border 28, Marsh 2).

ENGLAND v AUSTRALIA 1981 (6th Test)

At Kennington Oval, London, on 27, 28, 29, 31 August, 1 September.
Toss: England.   Result: MATCH DRAWN.
Debuts: England – P.W.G.Parker; Australia – D.M.Wellham.

Australia's first innings produced an abundance of statistical highlights: their 50th century opening partnership in all Tests and their first in 54 matches since January 1977; Brearley's 50th catch in 39 Tests; Yallop's 2,000th run in 58 Test innings; Hughes's 1,000th run in 31 innings against England; Border's second undefeated hundred in successive innings; and a major series record for Willis when he bowled Lillee and became England's highest wicket-taker against Australia, passing the 109 taken by W.Rhodes. During his 21st Test hundred, Boycott (441 minutes, 321 balls) completed 1,000 runs in first-class matches for the 19th consecutive season and gained M.C.Cowdrey's world Test record by reaching 50 for the 61st time. Both wicket-keepers reached notable Test aggregates in the second innings: Knott became the second after Marsh to hold 250 catches, and Marsh became the second 'keeper after Knott to score 3,000 runs. Botham, in his 41st Test, took his 200th wicket in the record time of 4 years 34 days and at the (then) youngest age of 25 years 280 days. Wellham became the first Australian to score a hundred on Test debut, that match being in England, since H.Graham in 1893 (*Test No. 39*). Alderman ended his first Test rubber with 42 wickets, the most by any bowler for Australia in this series. Brearley retained his unbeaten record in 19 home Tests as captain.

AUSTRALIA

G.M.Wood	c Brearley b Botham	66	c Knott b Hendrick	21
M.F.Kent	c Gatting b Botham	54	c Brearley b Botham	7
*K.J.Hughes	hit wkt b Botham	31	lbw b Hendrick	6
G.N.Yallop	c Botham b Willis	26	b Hendrick	35
A.R.Border	not out	106	c Tavaré b Emburey	84
D.M.Wellham	b Willis	24	lbw b Botham	103
†R.W.Marsh	c Botham b Willis	12	c Gatting b Botham	52
R.J.Bright	c Brearley b Botham	3	b Botham	11
D.K.Lillee	b Willis	11	not out	8
T.M.Alderman	b Botham	0		
M.R.Whitney	b Botham	4	(10) c Botham b Hendrick	0
Extras	(B4, LB6, W1, NB4)	15	(B1, LB8, W1, NB7)	17
Total		**352**	(9 wickets declared)	**344**

ENGLAND

G.Boycott	c Yallop b Lillee	137	lbw b Lillee	0
W.Larkins	c Alderman b Lillee	34	c Alderman b Lillee	24
C.J.Tavaré	c Marsh b Lillee	24	c Kent b Whitney	8
M.W.Gatting	b Lillee	53	c Kent b Lillee	56
*J.M.Brearley	c Bright b Alderman	0	(6) c Marsh b Lillee	51
P.W.G.Parker	c Kent b Alderman	0	(5) c Kent b Alderman	13
I.T.Botham	c Yallop b Lillee	3	lbw b Alderman	16
†A.P.E.Knott	b Lillee	36	not out	70
J.E.Emburey	lbw b Lillee	0	not out	5
R.G.D.Willis	b Alderman	3		
M.Hendrick	not out	0		
Extras	(LB9, W3, NB12)	24	(B2, LB5, W2, NB9)	18
Total		**314**	(7 wickets)	**261**

ENGLAND	O	M	R	W	O	M	R	W		FALL OF WICKETS			
Willis	31	6	91	4	10	0	41	0		A	E	A	E
Hendrick	31	8	63	0	(3) 29.2	6	82	4	*Wkt*	*1st*	*1st*	*2nd*	*2nd*
Botham	47	13	125	6	(2) 42	9	128	4	1st	120	61	26	0
Emburey	23	2	58	0	23	3	76	1	2nd	125	131	36	18
									3rd	169	246	41	88
									4th	199	248	104	101
AUSTRALIA									5th	260	248	205	127
Lillee	31.4	4	89	7	30	10	70	4	6th	280	256	291	144
Alderman	35	4	84	3	19	6	60	2	7th	303	293	332	237
Whitney	23	3	76	0	11	4	46	1	8th	319	293	343	–
Bright	21	6	41	0	27	12	50	0	9th	320	302	344	–
Yallop					8	2	17	0	10th	352	314	–	–

Umpires: H.D.Bird (21) and B.J.Meyer (8).

Close: 1st day – A(1) 251-4 (Border 51, Wellham 19); 2nd – E(1) 100-1 (Boycott 47, Tavaré 8); 3rd – A(2) 36-2 (Wood 20); 4th – A(2) 344-9 (Lillee 8).

AUSTRALIA v PAKISTAN 1981-82 (1st Test)

At W.A.C.A.Ground, Perth, on 13, 14, 15, 16, 17 November.
Toss: Pakistan.   Result: AUSTRALIA won by 286 runs.
Debuts: Pakistan – Rizwan-uz-Zaman.

Pakistan were dismissed in 108 minutes – 21.2 overs – for their lowest total against all countries (previously 87 against England in 1954 – *Test No. 387*), and the lowest in any Test at Perth. Alderman took the wicket of Rizwan-uz-Zaman with his first ball in a Test on his home soil. Lillee took five wickets in an innings for the 20th time, a feat previously achieved only by S.F.Barnes (24) and C.V.Grimmett (21). Wasim Bari set a Pakistan record by appearing in his 59th Test. On the fourth afternoon, Lillee, who claimed that he had been provoked by abuse from Javed Miandad, deliberately impeded and then aimed a kick at the visiting captain. Umpire Crafter separated the culprits as Miandad aimed to club Lillee with his bat. Lillee's punishment was to be suspended from two one-day matches.

AUSTRALIA

B.M.Laird	c Wasim Bari b Imran	27	(2) c Wasim Bari b Imran		85
G.M.Wood	lbw b Sikander	33	(1) b Qasim		49
G.S.Chappell	lbw b Imran	22	b Imran		6
K.J.Hughes	b Sarfraz	14	c Majid b Imran		106
G.N.Yallop	c and b Qasim	20	c Imran b Sikander		38
A.R.Border	c Wasim Bari b Sarfraz	3	c Mudassar b Sikander		37
R.W.Marsh	c Qasim b Sikander	16	c Mansoor b Wasim Raja		47
B.Yardley	c Wasim Bari b Imran	9	st Wasim Bari b Qasim		22
D.K.Lillee	c Wasim Bari b Wasim Raja	16	not out		4
J.R.Thomson	b Imran	2	not out		5
T.M.Alderman	not out	0			
Extras	(LB5, W1, NB12)	18	(B1, LB9, W1, NB14)		25
Total		**180**	(8 wickets declared)		**424**

PAKISTAN

Mudassar Nazar	c Marsh b Lillee	0	lbw b Alderman	5
Rizwan-uz-Zaman	lbw b Alderman	0	c Marsh b Alderman	8
Mansoor Akhtar	c Marsh b Alderman	6	c Hughes b Thomson	36
Javed Miandad	c Hughes b Alderman	6	b Yardley	79
Majid Khan	c Marsh b Lillee	3	c Marsh b Yardley	0
Wasim Raja	c Thomson b Lillee	4	c Hughes b Yardley	48
Imran Khan	c Yardley b Lillee	4	c Alderman b Yardley	31
Sarfraz Nawaz	c Marsh b Alderman	26	c and b Yardley	9
Wasim Bari	c Marsh b Lillee	1	c Border b Yardley	20
Iqbal Qasim	c Alderman b Thomson	5	c Alderman b Lillee	4
Sikander Bakht	not out	3	not out	0
Extras	(NB4)	4	(LB1, NB15)	16
Total		**62**		**256**

PAKISTAN	O	M	R	W	O	M	R	W		FALL OF WICKETS			
Imran	31.4	8	66	4	39	12	90	3		A	P	A	P
Sarfraz	27	10	43	2	(3) 27	5	88	0	*Wkt*	*1st*	*1st*	*2nd*	*2nd*
Sikander	21	4	47	2	(2) 23	3	79	2	1st	45	1	92	8
Qasim	3	1	6	1	(5) 26	4	81	2	2nd	81	1	105	27
Wasim Raja	1	1	0	1	(4) 20	3	58	1	3rd	89	14	192	96
Miandad					1	0	2	0	4th	113	17	262	99
Mudassar					2	1	1	0	5th	119	21	327	174
									6th	136	25	360	198
AUSTRALIA									7th	154	25	412	229
Lillee	9	3	18	5	20	3	78	1	8th	165	26	416	236
Alderman	10.2	2	36	4	16	4	43	2	9th	180	57	–	254
Thomson	2	1	4	1	12	4	35	1	10th	180	62	–	256
Yardley					25.5	5	84	6					

Umpires: A.R.Crafter (8) and M.W.Johnson (5).

Close: 1st day – A(1) 159-7 (Yardley 7, Lillee 2); 2nd – A(2) 110-2 (Laird 46, Hughes 3); 3rd – A(2) 382-6 (Marsh 35, Yardley 4); 4th – P(2) 224-6 (Imran 25, Sarfraz 7).

AUSTRALIA v PAKISTAN 1981-82 (2nd Test)

At Woolloongabba, Brisbane, on 27, 28, 29, 30 November, 1 December.
Toss: Australia.   Result: AUSTRALIA won by 10 wickets.
Debuts: None.

Lillee became the third bowler after F.S.Trueman and L.R.Gibbs to take 300 Test wickets when he dismissed
Wasim Raja in the first innings. It was then the fastest 300 wickets in terms of fewest Tests (56), although
Trueman completed his in 340 fewer balls. Chappell (411 minutes, 296 balls, 22 fours) scored his fourth double
century in 69 Tests; only D.G.Bradman (12) and W.R.Hammond (7) made more. His innings of 201 was the
highest against Pakistan in Australia until 1983-84 (*Test No. 973*). During it he became the first Australian to
score 1,000 runs against Pakistan. In the second innings Majid provided Chappell with his 100th catch; he was
the sixth non-wicket-keeper to hold that many.

PAKISTAN

Mudassar Nazar	c Marsh b Lillee	36	c Laird b Lillee	3:
Mohsin Khan	c Border b Chappell	11	c Marsh b Lillee	4.
Majid Khan	c Chappell b Lillee	29	c Chappell b Yardley	1:
*Javed Miandad	b Lillee	20	lbw b Lillee	3:
Zaheer Abbas	b Lillee	80	lbw b Yardley	:
Wasim Raja	c Laird b Lillee	43	b Lillee	3:
Imran Khan	c Marsh b Alderman	0	c Wellham b Yardley	:
Ijaz Faqih	b Yardley	34	c Chappell b Thomson	2:
Sarfraz Nawaz	c Border b Alderman	4	c Alderman b Yardley	1:
†Wasim Bari	c Marsh b Thomson	7	not out	:
Sikander Bakht	not out	1	b Thomson	:
Extras	(B12, LB1, W1, NB12)	26	(B2, LB3, W1, NB9)	1.
Total		**291**		**22:**

AUSTRALIA

B.M.Laird	c Zaheer b Ijaz	44	(2) not out	
G.M.Wood	c Mudassar b Wasim Raja	72	(1) not out	(
*G.S.Chappell	c Zaheer b Sikander	201		
A.R.Border	b Imran	36		
K.J.Hughes	b Imran	28		
D.M.Wellham	b Imran	36		
†R.W.Marsh	c Zaheer b Imran	27		
B.Yardley	b Sarfraz	2		
D.K.Lillee	b Sarfraz	14		
J.R.Thomson	not out	22		
T.M.Alderman	not out	5		
Extras	(B1, LB5, W2, NB17)	25		
Total	(9 wickets declared)	**512**	(0 wickets)	**3**

AUSTRALIA	O	M	R	W	O	M	R	W	FALL OF WICKETS			
Lillee	20	3	81	5	19	4	51	4		P	A	P	A
Alderman	25	6	74	2	15	3	37	0	*Wkt*	*1st*	*1st*	*2nd*	*2nd*
Thomson	15	2	52	1	15	3	43	2	1st	40	109	72	–
Chappell	3	1	6	1					2nd	60	149	90	–
Yardley	15	1	51	1	(4) 24	4	77	4	3rd	105	219	115	–
Border	1	0	1	0					4th	111	298	115	–
									5th	236	429	177	–
									6th	237	448	178	–
PAKISTAN									7th	245	469	189	–
Imran	40	6	92	4	1.2	1	2	0	8th	263	470	216	–
Sarfraz	35	4	121	2					9th	285	492	219	–
Sikander	24	2	81	1	(2) 1	0	1	0	10th	291	–	223	–
Ijaz	22	1	76	1								
Wasim Raja	17	0	68	1								
Mudassar	2	0	10	0								
Miandad	3	0	18	0								
Majid	9	1	21	0								

Umpires: A.R.Crafter (9) and M.W.Johnson (6).

Close: 1st day – P(1) 291 all out; 2nd – A(1) 282-3 (Chappell 89, Hughes 26); 3rd – A(1) 468-6 (Marsh 27,
Yardley 1); 4th – P(2) 64-0 (Mudassar 30, Mohsin 31).

AUSTRALIA v PAKISTAN 1981-82 (3rd Test)

At Melbourne Cricket Ground on 11, 12, 13, 14, 15 December.
Toss: Pakistan.   Result: PAKISTAN won by an innings and 82 runs.
Debuts: None.

Pakistan gained their first victory by an innings against Australia after compiling the second-highest Test total without a century (see *Test No. 786*). Imran Khan became Pakistan's leading wicket-taker when he dismissed Marsh: Fazal Mahmood's record of 139 wickets had stood since 1962. Wood's sixth Test hundred took 368 minutes (298 balls). Border became the 13th batsman to be run out in both innings of a Test and the sixth to suffer this misfortune at Melbourne. After Australia had been dismissed for their lowest total in a home Test against Pakistan, both captains issued formal complaints about the pitch. Majid, partnered by Mudassar, scored an all-run 7 when he drove Lillee almost to the long-off boundary and completed four runs before Yardley, having fielded Wellham's return, overthrew the wicket.

PAKISTAN

Mudassar Nazar	c Lillee b Yardley	95		
Mohsin Khan	c Thomson b Yardley	17		
Majid Khan	c Wood b Yardley	74		
*Javed Miandad	lbw b Yardley	62		
Zaheer Abbas	c and b Yardley	90		
Wasim Raja	c Laird b Yardley	50		
Imran Khan	not out	70		
Sarfraz Nawaz	c Yardley b Chappell	0		
†Wasim Bari	b Yardley	8		
Iqbal Qasim	not out	16		
Sikander Bakht	did not bat			
Extras	(B1, LB5, NB12)	18		
Total	(8 wickets declared)	**500**		

AUSTRALIA

B.M.Laird	lbw b Qasim	35	(2) c Sarfraz b Qasim	52	
G.M.Wood	c Mohsin b Sarfraz	100	(1) c Wasim Bari b Sarfraz	1	
*G.S.Chappell	c Wasim Bari b Wasim Raja	22	c Miandad b Sarfraz	0	
A.R.Border	run out	7	run out	1	
K.J.Hughes	c and b Qasim	34	c Majid b Qasim	11	
D.M.Wellham	c Mudassar b Sarfraz	26	b Sarfraz	13	
†R.W.Marsh	c Mudassar b Imran	31	c Mohsin b Qasim	21	
B.Yardley	b Qasim	20	b Imran	0	
D.K.Lillee	lbw b Imran	1	c Wasim Bari b Qasim	4	
J.R.Thomson	not out	3	b Imran	17	
T.M.Alderman	lbw b Imran	1	not out	4	
Extras	(B4, LB6, NB3)	13	(B1)	1	
Total		**293**		**125**	

AUSTRALIA	O	M	R	W	O	M	R	W		FALL OF WICKETS		
										P	A	A
Lillee	36.3	9	104	0					Wkt	1st	1st	2nd
Alderman	27	8	62	0					1st	40	75	1
Thomson	25	2	85	0					2nd	181	118	9
Yardley	66	16	187	7					3rd	201	127	13
Border	4	1	16	0					4th	329	173	29
Chappell	9	2	17	1					5th	363	232	77
Hughes	3	1	2	0					6th	443	235	78
Laird	1	0	9	0					7th	444	286	79
									8th	456	288	92
PAKISTAN									9th	–	289	121
Imran	24.1	7	41	3	14.1	5	21	2	10th	–	293	125
Sarfraz	14	3	43	2	15	10	11	3				
Wasim Raja	37	7	73	1	(4) 13	2	34	0				
Qasim	55	17	104	3	(3) 24	11	44	4				
Sikander	2	0	9	0								
Majid	2	0	10	0	(5) 4	1	5	0				
Miandad					(6) 2	0	9	0				

Umpires: R.C.Bailhache (21) and R.A.French (7).

Close: 1st day – P(1) 245-3 (Miandad 26, Zaheer 23); 2nd – A(1) 15-0 (Laird 8, Wood 6); 3rd – A(1) 197-4 (Wood 78, Wellham 13); 4th – A(2) 78-5 (Wellham 13, Marsh 0).

INDIA v ENGLAND 1981-82 (1st Test)

At Wankhede Stadium, Bombay, on 27, 28, 29 November, 1 December.
Toss: India.   Result: INDIA won by 138 runs.
Debuts: India – K.Srikkanth.

England (102) recorded the lowest total by any visiting country in India and suffered their first defeat in eight matches on Bombay's three Test grounds. India's eighth victory in 59 Tests against England was their seventh in India in this series and their last against any country until 1984-85. Fletcher became the 62nd player to captain England but only the third from Essex after F.L.Fane and J.W.H.T.Douglas. If he had been selected for the 47 matches he had missed since his last appearance in March 1977, this would have been his 100th Test. When he had scored 23, Botham became the third player after R.Benaud and G.St A.Sobers to complete the double of 2,000 runs and 200 wickets; he did so in fewest matches (42), the shortest time (4 years 126 days) and at the (then) youngest age (26 years 7 days). Taylor made his 100th dismissal, the fourth to do so for England after T.G.Evans, J.M.Parks and A.P.E.Knott. Madan Lal, recalled after a hiatus of 35 Tests, returned his best analysis for India. His bowling partnership with Kapil Dev was within one over of becoming the first to operate unchanged throughout a completed Test innings since 1956-57 (*Test No. 430*).

INDIA

*S.M.Gavaskar	c Taylor b Botham	55		c Taylor b Botham	14
K.Srikkanth	c Fletcher b Willis	0		run out	13
D.B.Vengsarkar	c Tavaré b Dilley	17		c Tavaré b Botham	5
G.R.Viswanath	c Boycott b Botham	8		c Taylor b Botham	37
S.M.Patil	lbw b Botham	17		lbw b Botham	13
K.Azad	c sub (M.W.Gatting) b Underwood	14	(7)	lbw b Emburey	17
Kapil Dev	c Taylor b Botham	38	(8)	lbw b Willis	46
†S.M.H.Kirmani	lbw b Dilley	12	(9)	c Taylor b Emburey	0
Madan Lal	c Taylor b Dilley	0	(10)	not out	17
R.J.Shastri	not out	3	(6)	lbw b Dilley	33
D.R.Doshi	c Taylor b Dilley	0		b Botham	7
Extras	(LB5, NB10)	15		(B8, LB8, NB9)	25
Total		**179**			**227**

ENGLAND

G.A.Gooch	b Madan Lal	2		c Kirmani b Kapil Dev	1
G.Boycott	c Srikkanth b Azad	60		lbw b Madan Lal	3
C.J.Tavaré	c Shastri b Doshi	56		c Gavaskar b Kapil Dev	0
D.I.Gower	run out	5		lbw b Kapil Dev	20
*K.W.R.Fletcher	lbw b Doshi	15		lbw b Madan Lal	3
I.T.Botham	c Gavaskar b Doshi	7		c Azad b Kapil Dev	29
J.E.Emburey	lbw b Doshi	0		c Gavaskar b Madan Lal	1
G.R.Dilley	b Shastri	0		b Madan Lal	9
†R.W.Taylor	not out	9		b Madan Lal	1
D.L.Underwood	c Kirmani b Kapil Dev	8		not out	13
R.G.D.Willis	c Gavaskar b Doshi	1		c Kirmani b Kapil Dev	13
Extras	(B1, LB2)	3		(B4, LB3, NB2)	9
Total		**166**			**102**

ENGLAND	O	M	R	W	O	M	R	W		FALL OF WICKETS			
										I	E	I	E
Willis	12	5	33	1	13	4	31	1	Wkt	1st	1st	2nd	2nd
Botham	28	6	72	4	22.3	3	61	5	1st	1	3	19	2
Dilley	13	1	47	4	18	5	61	1	2nd	40	95	24	4
Underwood	4	2	12	1	11	4	14	0	3rd	70	105	43	28
Emburey					13	2	35	2	4th	104	131	72	29
									5th	112	143	90	42
INDIA									6th	164	146	138	50
Kapil Dev	22	10	29	1	13.2	0	70	5	7th	164	147	154	73
Madan Lal	12	2	24	1	12	6	23	5	8th	168	147	157	74
Doshi	29.1	12	39	5	1	1	0	0	9th	179	163	203	75
Shastri	19	6	27	1					10th	179	166	227	102
Patil	3	0	9	0									
Azad	15	4	35	1									

Umpires: K.B.Ramaswami (7) and Swaroop Kishen (8).

Close: 1st day – E(1) 15-1 (Boycott 11, Tavaré 2); 2nd – E(1) 166 all out; 3rd – I(2) 203-9 (Madan Lal 5).

INDIA v ENGLAND 1981-82 (2nd Test)

At Karnataka State C.A.Stadium, Bangalore, on 9, 10, 12, 13, 14 December.
Toss: England.   Result: MATCH DRAWN.
Debuts: None.

Gavaskar, who was on the field for all but four balls of the match, scored 172 runs off 476 balls in 708 minutes. It remains the highest innings in a Bangalore Test and he became the first Indian to score four hundreds against England. His innings was the longest in all Indian first-class cricket by 63 minutes until 1986-87, beating K.C.Ibrahim's 645-minute 219 for Bombay against Baroda in 1948-49, and surpassed his own record of 593 minutes (*Test No. 865*) as the longest for India in Test cricket. Underwood, who dismissed Nos. 1 and 11 with the second and sixth balls of his 43rd over, overtook F.S.Trueman's England record of 53 wickets in this series. Fletcher, one of a record three Essex players included in this match, became the 18th batsman to score 3,000 runs for England. Boycott celebrated passing M.C.Cowdrey's world record of 188 Test innings with his 63rd fifty. Taylor held his 100th catch for England.

ENGLAND

G.A.Gooch	c Gavaskar b Shastri	58	lbw b Kapil Dev	40
G.Boycott	c Gavaskar b Kapil Dev	36	b Doshi	50
C.J.Tavaré	lbw b Madan Lal	22	c Patil b Shastri	31
D.I.Gower	lbw b Shastri	82	not out	34
J.K.Lever	lbw b Kapil Dev	1		
*K.W.R.Fletcher	c Kirmani b Shastri	25	(5) not out	12
I.T.Botham	c Madan Lal b Doshi	55		
M.W.Gatting	lbw b Kapil Dev	29		
G.R.Dilley	c Gavaskar b Shastri	52		
†R.W.Taylor	c Kapil Dev b Doshi	33		
D.L.Underwood	not out	2		
Extras	(LB2, NB3)	5	(LB6, NB1)	7
Total		**400**	(3 wickets declared)	**174**

INDIA

*S.M.Gavaskar	c and b Underwood	172
K.Srikkanth	c Gooch b Botham	65
D.B.Vengsarkar	c Taylor b Lever	43
G.R.Viswanath	lbw b Lever	3
R.J.Shastri	lbw b Lever	1
S.M.Patil	lbw b Lever	17
K.Azad	c Fletcher b Underwood	24
Kapil Dev	c Taylor b Lever	59
†S.M.H.Kirmani	lbw b Botham	9
Madan Lal	not out	7
D.R.Doshi	c Boycott b Underwood	0
Extras	(B2, LB15, W3, NB8)	28
Total		**428**

INDIA	O	M	R	W	O	M	R	W
Kapil Dev	40	3	136	3	12	2	49	1
Madan Lal	24	7	46	1	4	2	14	0
Doshi	39	15	83	2	21	8	37	1
Azad	12	1	47	0	(5) 12	3	36	0
Shastri	43	14	83	4	(4) 20	7	31	1
ENGLAND								
Botham	47	9	137	2				
Dilley	24	4	75	0				
Lever	36	9	100	5				
Underwood	43	21	88	3				

FALL OF WICKETS

	E	I	E
Wkt	*1st*	*1st*	*2nd*
1st	88	102	59
2nd	96	195	105
3rd	180	208	152
4th	181	214	–
5th	223	242	–
6th	230	284	–
7th	278	376	–
8th	324	412	–
9th	393	428	–
10th	400	428	–

Umpires: M.V.Gothoskar (7) and P.R.Punjabi (7).

Close: 1st day – E(1) 181-4 (Gower 62, Fletcher 0); 2nd – E(1) 400 all out; 3rd – I(1) 189-1 (Gavaskar 71, Vengsarkar 42); 4th – I(1) 405-7 (Gavaskar 163, Kirmani 7).

INDIA v ENGLAND 1981-82 (3rd Test)

At Feroz Shah Kotla, Delhi, on 23, 24, 26, 27, 28 December.
Toss: England.   Result: MATCH DRAWN.
Debuts: None.

At 4.23 pm on 23 December, Boycott hit a leg-side boundary off Doshi to pass G.St A.Sobers's world Test record of 8,032 runs. He had played 30 innings more than Sobers and batted over 451 hours – the equivalent of 75 six-hour days or 15 complete five-day Tests. He also became the 13th batsman to score 40,000 runs in first-class cricket and the second Englishman after K.F.Barrington to score 1,000 runs against India. Botham's 66 included five sixes. Eight minutes were wasted on the third day when the umpires mislaid the key to the cupboard guarding the new ball. India's total of 487 was their highest against England in India until 1984-85 and provided the first instance in Test cricket of hundred partnerships for the eighth and ninth wickets in the same innings. Both stands remain records for India in this series, Shastri adding 128 for the eighth with Kirmani and 104 for the ninth with Madan Lal. Vengsarkar kept wicket throughout England's second innings.

ENGLAND

G.A.Gooch	c Kapil Dev b Doshi	71	not out	20
G.Boycott	c Madan Lal b Doshi	105	not out	34
C.J.Tavaré	b Madan Lal	149		
D.I.Gower	lbw b Madan Lal	0		
*K.W.R.Fletcher	b Patil	51		
I.T.Botham	c Azad b Madan Lal	66		
M.W.Gatting	b Madan Lal	5		
†R.W.Taylor	lbw b Madan Lal	0		
J.K.Lever	b Kapil Dev	2		
D.L.Underwood	not out	2		
R.G.D.Willis	did not bat			
Extras	(LB15, NB10)	25	(B9, NB5)	14
Total	(9 wickets declared)	476	(0 wickets declared)	68

INDIA

*S.M.Gavaskar	c Taylor b Lever	46
K.Srikkanth	b Willis	6
D.B.Vengsarkar	c Fletcher b Underwood	8
G.R.Viswanath	b Botham	107
S.M.Patil	b Willis	31
K.Azad	st Taylor b Underwood	16
Kapil Dev	c Gooch b Botham	16
R.J.Shastri	lbw b Gooch	93
†S.M.H.Kirmani	lbw b Lever	67
Madan Lal	b Gooch	44
D.R.Doshi	not out	0
Extras	(B20, LB8, W4, NB21)	53
Total		487

INDIA	O	M	R	W	O	M	R	W		FALL OF WICKETS		
Kapil Dev	40.4	5	126	1	4	1	18	0		E	I	E
Madan Lal	32	4	85	5	3	1	4	0	Wkt	1st	1st	2nd
Doshi	40	15	68	2					1st	132	11	–
Shastri	27	3	109	0					2nd	248	41	–
Azad	9	2	35	0					3rd	248	89	–
Patil	8	1	28	1	(3) 3	1	10	0	4th	368	174	–
Srikkanth					(4) 6	1	10	0	5th	459	213	–
Gavaskar					(5) 3	0	12	0	6th	465	237	–
									7th	465	254	–
ENGLAND									8th	474	382	–
Willis	26	3	99	2					9th	476	486	–
Lever	37	7	104	2					10th	–	487	–
Underwood	48	18	97	2								
Botham	41	6	122	2								
Gooch	8.1	1	12	2								

Umpires: S.N.Hanumantha Rao (7) and Swaroop Kishen (9).

Close: 1st day – E(1) 190-1 (Boycott 86, Tavaré 25); 2nd – E(1) 428-4 (Tavaré 133, Botham 47); 3rd – I(1) 172-3 (Viswanath 67, Patil 30); 4th – I(1) 376-7 (Shastri 48, Kirmani 67).

INDIA v ENGLAND 1981-82 (4th Test)

At Eden Gardens, Calcutta, on 1, 2, 3, 5, 6 January.
Toss: England.   Result: MATCH DRAWN.
Debuts: None.

An estimated 394,000 spectators attended this match to set a world record for any game of cricket. Gavaskar scored his 2,000th run against England, a total he had already achieved against West Indies. No other Indian batsman has reached that aggregate against any country, and only W.R.Hammond (Australia and South Africa) and Boycott (Australia and West Indies) had previously done so against two countries. In the last of his 108 Test matches, Boycott extended his two world records to 193 innings and 8,114 runs; the latter survived until 1983-84 when Gavaskar gained it in *Test No. 966*. Kirmani became the first Indian to hold 100 catches in Tests and Fletcher the first Essex player to hold 50. Gooch imitated Doshi and bowled slow left-arm in the closing stages.

ENGLAND

G.A.Gooch	c Viswanath b Doshi	47	b Doshi	63
G.Boycott	c Kirmani b Kapil Dev	18	lbw b Madan Lal	6
C.J.Tavaré	c Kirmani b Kapil Dev	7	run out	25
D.I.Gower	c Kirmani b Shastri	11	run out	74
*K.W.R.Fletcher	lbw b Madan Lal	69	(6) not out	60
I.T.Botham	c Gavaskar b Kapil Dev	58	(5) c Yadav b Doshi	31
D.L.Underwood	c Patil b Kapil Dev	13		
M.W.Gatting	c Kirmani b Kapil Dev	0	(7) not out	2
J.E.Emburey	lbw b Kapil Dev	1		
†R.W.Taylor	c Vengsarkar b Doshi	6		
R.G.D.Willis	not out	11		
Extras	(LB3, NB4)	7	(LB4)	4
Total		**248**	(5 wickets declared)	**265**

INDIA

*S.M.Gavaskar	b Underwood	42	not out	83
K.Srikkanth	b Underwood	10	c Botham b Emburey	25
D.B.Vengsarkar	c Taylor b Botham	70	c Tavaré b Fletcher	32
G.R.Viswanath	c and b Emburey	15	c Gooch b Emburey	0
S.M.Patil	c Fletcher b Emburey	0	not out	17
Kapil Dev	c Tavaré b Underwood	22		
R.J.Shastri	run out	8		
†S.M.H.Kirmani	b Botham	10		
Madan Lal	c Gooch b Willis	1		
N.S.Yadav	c Taylor b Willis	5		
D.R.Doshi	not out	7		
Extras	(B2, LB4, W1, NB11)	18	(LB2, NB11)	13
Total		**208**	(3 wickets)	**170**

INDIA	O	M	R	W	O	M	R	W		FALL OF WICKETS			
Kapil Dev	31	6	91	6	21	3	81	0		E	I	E	I
Madan Lal	20	4	58	1	19	3	58	1	*Wkt*	*1st*	*1st*	*2nd*	*2nd*
Doshi	19.2	8	28	2	27	5	63	2	1st	25	33	24	48
Yadav	17	7	42	0	(5) 3	0	11	0	2nd	39	83	88	117
Shastri	21	10	22	1	(4) 17	4	35	0	3rd	68	117	107	120
Patil					3	0	13	0	4th	95	117	154	–
									5th	188	143	259	–
ENGLAND									6th	216	180	–	–
Willis	14	3	28	2	6	0	21	0	7th	218	184	–	–
Botham	27	8	63	2	11	3	26	0	8th	224	187	–	–
Underwood	29	13	45	3	31	18	38	0	9th	230	196	–	–
Emburey	24	11	44	2	30	11	62	2	10th	248	208	–	–
Gooch	6	1	10	0	2	0	4	0					
Fletcher					3	1	6	1					

Umpires: M.V.Gothoskar (8) and Swaroop Kishen (10).

Close: 1st day – E(1) 198-5 (Fletcher 46, Underwood 5); 2nd – I(1) 105-2 (Vengsarkar 34, Viswanath 8); 3rd – E(2) 49-1 (Gooch 30, Tavaré 13); 4th – I(2) 5-0 (Gavaskar 2, Srikkanth 2).

INDIA v ENGLAND 1981-82 (5th Test)

At Chidambaram Stadium, Chepauk, Madras, on 13, 14, 15, 17, 18 January.
Toss: England.   Result: MATCH DRAWN.
Debuts: India – A.Malhotra, Pranab Roy. (*Roy is given his full name to differentiate him from his father, Pankaj, who made his debut in* Test No. 339)

Fletcher was the first England captain to elect to field first in a Test in India. Vengsarkar retired at 150 when he ducked into a bouncer from Willis and was struck on the back of the head. Viswanath batted 638 minutes for India's highest score against England, beating Gavaskar's 221 in 1979 (*Test No. 854*). His 31 fours equalled India's Test record set by B.K.Kunderan in 1963-64 (*553*). Viswanath's partnership of 316 with Yashpal remains the highest for any wicket by either side in this series and India's highest for the third wicket in all Tests. The partners provided the seventh instance of the same pair batting throughout an uninterrupted day of Test cricket. It was only the second time that England had failed to take a wicket during a complete day's play. Yashpal batted for 490 minutes, hitting two sixes and 18 fours. Gooch reached 50 off 46 balls and 100 off 139 deliveries, 15 of which were dispatched to the boundary. His partner, Tavaré, took 332 minutes to score 35. England employed ten bowlers in the second innings, Gooch keeping wicket for the final 12 overs. Only Allott's absence through injury prevented them from providing the third instance of an entire Test team bowling in the same innings.

INDIA

*S.M.Gavaskar	c Taylor b Willis	25		c Botham b Willis	11
Pranab Roy	c Taylor b Dilley	6		not out	60
D.B.Vengsarkar	retired hurt	71			
G.R.Viswanath	b Willis	222			
Yashpal Sharma	c Tavaré b Botham	140	(4)	c Botham b Underwood	25
Kapil Dev	not out	6	(5)	not out	15
A.Malhotra			(3)	run out	31
†S.M.H.Kirmani					
R.J.Shastri	did not bat				
Madan Lal					
D.R.Doshi					
Extras	(LB1, W1, NB9)	11		(B12, LB1, NB5)	18
Total	(4 wickets declared)	**481**		(3 wickets declared)	**160**

ENGLAND

G.A.Gooch	c and b Shastri	127
C.J.Tavaré	c Gavaskar b Doshi	35
*K.W.R.Fletcher	b Doshi	3
D.I.Gower	lbw b Shastri	64
I.T.Botham	c Kirmani b Shastri	52
M.W.Gatting	c Viswanath b Doshi	0
G.R.Dilley	c and b Kapil Dev	8
†R.W.Taylor	b Doshi	8
D.L.Underwood	c Kirmani b Kapil Dev	0
P.J.W.Allott	c Roy b Kapil Dev	6
R.G.D.Willis	not out	1
Extras	(B1, LB11, NB12)	24
Total		**328**

ENGLAND	O	M	R	W	O	M	R	W	FALL OF WICKETS			
Willis	28.1	7	79	2	7	2	15	1		I	E	I
Botham	31	10	83	1	8	1	29	0	Wkt	1st	1st	2nd
Dilley	31	4	87	1	5	1	13	0	1st	19	155	19
Allott	31	4	135	0					2nd	51	164	69
Underwood	22	7	59	0	(4) 15	8	30	1	3rd	466	195	122
Gooch	9	2	27	0	(6) 8	2	24	0	4th	481	279	–
Fletcher					(5) 1	0	9	0	5th	–	283	–
Taylor					(7) 2	0	6	0	6th	–	307	–
Tavaré					(8) 2	0	11	0	7th	–	307	–
Gower					(9) 1	0	1	0	8th	–	311	–
Gatting					(10) 1	0	4	0	9th	–	320	–
INDIA									10th	–	328	–
Kapil Dev	25.5	7	88	3								
Madan Lal	9	1	41	0								
Shastri	63	23	104	3								
Doshi	57	31	69	4								
Gavaskar	1	0	2	0								

Umpires: B.Ganguli (1) and S.N.Hanumantha Rao (8).

Close: 1st day – I(1) 178-2 (Viswanath 64, Yashpal 5); 2nd – I(1) 395-2 (Viswanath 181, Yashpal 102); 3rd – E(1) 144-0 (Gooch 117, Tavaré 26); 4th – E(1) 307-6 (Dilley 8).

INDIA v ENGLAND 1981-82 (6th Test)

At Green Park, Kanpur, on 30, 31 January, 1, 3, 4 February.
Toss: England.   Result: MATCH DRAWN.
Debuts: None.

Nearly ten hours of play were lost to mist, rain and bad light. Kapil Dev reached his second hundred in Test cricket off only 84 balls and, with Yashpal, shared in a (then) record seventh-wicket partnership against England worth 169. Taylor established a new wicket-keeping record for England against India by making 16 dismissals in the rubber. India won their fourth rubber against England by virtue of their solitary success at Bombay.

ENGLAND

G.A.Gooch	b Doshi	58
C.J.Tavaré	b Doshi	24
*K.W.R.Fletcher	b Kapil Dev	14
D.I.Gower	lbw b Kapil Dev	85
I.T.Botham	st Kirmani b Doshi	142
M.W.Gatting	c Madan Lal b Doshi	32
G.R.Dilley	lbw b Shastri	1
†R.W.Taylor	b Shastri	0
J.E.Emburey	run out	2
D.L.Underwood	not out	0
R.G.D.Willis	did not bat	
Extras	(B2, LB5, W6, NB7)	20
Total	(9 wickets declared)	**378**

INDIA

*S.M.Gavaskar	run out	52
Pranab Roy	b Botham	5
D.B.Vengsarkar	c Fletcher b Dilley	46
G.R.Viswanath	c Gower b Willis	74
Yashpal Sharma	not out	55
A.Malhotra	lbw b Willis	0
R.J.Shastri	c Taylor b Willis	2
Kapil Dev	c Dilley b Gower	116
†S.M.H.Kirmani	not out	1
Madan Lal	} did not bat	
D.R.Doshi		
Extras	(B1, LB7, W2, NB16)	26
Total	(7 wickets declared)	**377**

INDIA	O	M	R	W
Kapil Dev	34	3	147	2
Madan Lal	24	4	79	0
Doshi	34.2	8	81	4
Shastri	23	6	51	2
ENGLAND				
Willis	23	5	75	3
Botham	25	6	67	1
Dilley	14	2	67	1
Underwood	25	8	55	0
Emburey	32	7	81	0
Fletcher	2	1	5	0
Gower	1	0	1	1

FALL OF WICKETS

	E	I
Wkt	1st	1st
1st	82	12
2nd	89	79
3rd	121	166
4th	248	197
5th	349	197
6th	354	207
7th	354	376
8th	360	–
9th	378	–
10th	–	–

Umpires: D.N.Dotiwalla (1) and M.V.Gothoskar (9).

Close: 1st day – E(1) 213-3 (Gower 75, Botham 31); 2nd – E(1) 249-4 (Botham 53, Gatting 0); 3rd – I(1) 12-1 (Gavaskar 5); 4th – I(1) 193-3 (Viswanath 71, Yashpal 6).

AUSTRALIA v WEST INDIES 1981-82 (1st Test)

At Melbourne Cricket Ground on 26, 27, 28, 29, 30 December.
Toss: Australia.   Result: AUSTRALIA won by 58 runs.
Debuts: West Indies – P.J.L.Dujon.

Australia's win ended a West Indies sequence of 15 Tests without a defeat since February 1980. At 2.55 pm on 27 December, Lillee induced an edged stroke from Gomes to overhaul the world Test record of 309 wickets held by L.R.Gibbs for almost six years. He gained the record on the ground where Gibbs had claimed it from F.S.Trueman, and just four days after Boycott had broken its batting counterpart. Lillee took five wickets in an innings for the 22nd time (only S.F.Barnes achieved that feat more often with 24 instances), and returned his best analysis in Tests. He later equalled the world record of Barnes and C.V.Grimmett by taking ten wickets in a Test for the seventh time. Lillee's total of 85 wickets during 1981 established a new Test record for a calendar year, beating Kapil Dev's 74 in 1979. Holding's analysis of 11 for 107 remains the match record for West Indies against Australia. Murray's nine catches in the match set a record for West Indies and has been exceeded only by R.W.Taylor (*Test No. 876*). Hughes took his score from 71 to 100 while in partnership with the last man, Alderman.

AUSTRALIA

B.M.Laird	c Murray b Holding	4	(2)	lbw b Croft	64
G.M.Wood	c Murray b Roberts	3	(1)	c Murray b Garner	46
*G.S.Chappell	c Murray b Holding	0		c Murray b Garner	6
A.R.Border	c Murray b Holding	4		b Holding	66
K.J.Hughes	not out	100		b Holding	8
D.M.Wellham	c sub (A.L.Logie) b Croft	17		lbw b Holding	2
†R.W.Marsh	c Richards b Garner	21		c Murray b Holding	2
B.Yardley	b Garner	21		b Garner	13
D.K.Lillee	c Gomes b Holding	1		c Murray b Holding	0
G.F.Lawson	b Holding	2		not out	0
T.M.Alderman	c Murray b Croft	10		b Holding	1
Extras	(B1, LB6, NB8)	15		(B5, LB4, W1, NB4)	14
Total		**198**			**222**

WEST INDIES

D.L.Haynes	c Border b Lillee	1		c Lillee b Yardley	28
S.F.A.F.Bacchus	c Wood b Alderman	1		lbw b Alderman	0
C.E.H.Croft	lbw b Lillee	0	(11)	not out	0
I.V.A.Richards	b Lillee	2	(3)	b Alderman	0
*C.H.Lloyd	c Alderman b Yardley	29	(4)	c Border b Lawson	19
H.A.Gomes	c Chappell b Lillee	55	(5)	b Yardley	24
P.J.L.Dujon	c Hughes b Lillee	41	(6)	c Marsh b Yardley	43
†D.A.Murray	not out	32	(7)	c Marsh b Yardley	10
A.M.E.Roberts	c Marsh b Lillee	18	(8)	lbw b Lillee	10
M.A.Holding	c and b Alderman	2	(9)	lbw b Lillee	7
J.Garner	c Laird b Lillee	7	(10)	lbw b Lillee	0
Extras	(B1, LB3, NB9)	13		(B1, LB10, NB9)	20
Total		**201**			**161**

WEST INDIES	O	M	R	W		O	M	R	W		FALL OF WICKETS			
Holding	17	3	45	5		21.3	5	62	6			A	WI	A	WI
Roberts	15	6	40	1		18	4	31	0	*Wkt*	*1st*	*1st*	*2nd*	*2nd*
Garner	20	6	59	2	(4)	18	5	37	3	1st	4	3	82	4
Croft	16.1	3	39	2	(3)	20	2	61	1	2nd	4	5	106	4
Richards						5	0	17	0	3rd	8	6	139	38
										4th	26	10	184	80
AUSTRALIA										5th	59	62	190	88
Lillee	26.3	3	83	7		27.1	8	44	3	6th	115	134	199	116
Alderman	18	3	54	2		9	3	23	2	7th	149	147	215	150
Lawson	9	2	28	0		17	3	36	1	8th	153	174	218	154
Chappell	2	2	0	0						9th	155	183	220	154
Yardley	7	2	23	1	(4)	21	7	38	4	10th	198	201	222	161

Umpires: R.C.Bailhache (22) and A.R.Crafter (10).

Close: 1st day – WI(1) 10-4 (Lloyd 2); 2nd – WI(1) 187-9 (Murray 26, Garner 0); 3rd – A(2) 217-7 (Border 65, Lillee 0); 4th – WI(2) 154-9 (Holding 4).

AUSTRALIA v WEST INDIES 1981-82 (2nd Test)

At Sydney Cricket Ground on 2, 3, 4, 5, 6 January.
Toss: West Indies.   Result: MATCH DRAWN.
Debuts: None.

Left four sessions in which to score 373 to win the rubber, Australia eventually earned a draw through a 377-minute innings by Dyson. Gomes, who batted for 444 minutes, recorded his third hundred in Tests – all three against Australia. Richards completed 4,000 runs in 46 Tests and Hughes 3,000 in 44. Yardley's best analysis in Test cricket included a final spell of 7 for 37 in 77 balls.

WEST INDIES

C.G.Greenidge	c Laird b Lillee	66	c Yardley b Lillee	8
D.L.Haynes	lbw b Thomson	15	lbw b Lillee	51
I.V.A.Richards	c Marsh b Lillee	44	c Border b Alderman	22
H.A.Gomes	c Chappell b Yardley	126	c Border b Yardley	43
*C.H.Lloyd	c Marsh b Thomson	40	c Hughes b Yardley	57
P.J.L.Dujon	c and b Thomson	44	c and b Yardley	48
†D.A.Murray	b Yardley	13	c Laird b Yardley	1
M.A.Holding	lbw b Lillee	9	c Dyson b Yardley	5
S.T.Clarke	b Yardley	14	c Dyson b Yardley	5
J.Garner	c Marsh b Lillee	1	(11) b Yardley	0
C.E.H.Croft	not out	0	(10) not out	4
Extras	(LB3, NB9)	12	(LB1, W5, NB5)	11
Total		**384**		**255**

AUSTRALIA

B.M.Laird	c Dujon b Garner	14	c Murray b Croft	38
G.M.Wood	c Murray b Holding	63	(6) not out	7
J.Dyson	lbw b Holding	28	(2) not out	127
*G.S.Chappell	c Dujon b Holding	12	(3) c Murray b Croft	0
T.M.Alderman	b Clarke	0		
K.J.Hughes	b Garner	16	(4) lbw b Gomes	13
A.R.Border	not out	53	(5) b Gomes	9
†R.W.Marsh	c Holding b Gomes	17		
B.Yardley	b Holding	45		
D.K.Lillee	c Garner b Holding	4		
J.R.Thomson	run out	8		
Extras	(B1, LB2, W2, NB2)	7	(B2, LB1, NB3)	6
Total		**267**	(4 wickets)	**200**

AUSTRALIA	O	M	R	W		O	M	R	W	FALL OF WICKETS				
Lillee	39	6	119	4		20	6	50	2		WI	A	WI	A
Alderman	30	9	73	0		12	2	46	1	*Wkt*	*1st*	*1st*	*2nd*	*2nd*
Thomson	20	1	93	3	(4)	15	3	50	0	1st	37	38	29	104
Yardley	26.2	3	87	3	(3)	31.4	6	98	7	2nd	128	108	52	104
Border	1	1	0	0						3rd	133	111	112	149
										4th	229	112	179	169
WEST INDIES										5th	325	128	208	–
Holding	29	9	64	5		19	6	31	0	6th	346	141	225	–
Clarke	16	4	51	1		16	9	25	0	7th	363	172	231	–
Garner	20	4	52	2	(4)	12	3	27	0	8th	379	242	246	–
Croft	20	7	53	0	(3)	27	5	58	2	9th	380	246	255	–
Richards	13	7	21	0		13	3	33	0	10th	384	267	255	–
Gomes	9	1	19	1		15	7	20	2					

Umpires: R.A.French (8) and M.W.Johnson (7).

Close: 1st day – WI(1) 288-4 (Gomes 85, Dujon 26); 2nd – A(1) 111-3 (Chappell 3, Alderman 0); 3rd – WI(2) 93-2 (Haynes 37, Gomes 20); 4th – A(2) 54-0 (Laird 20, Dyson 32).

AUSTRALIA v WEST INDIES 1981-82 (3rd Test)

At Adelaide Oval on 30, 31 January, 1, 2, 3 February.
Toss: West Indies.   Result: WEST INDIES won by 5 wickets.
Debuts: None.

West Indies, needing 236 runs in 195 minutes and 20 overs, shared the rubber and retained the Frank Worrell Trophy when they reached their target with 17 balls to spare. For most of the match Australia were compelled to field substitutes for Hughes (bruised instep and fractured toe), Chappell (fractured finger) and Lillee (who strained a groin tendon during his fifth over). Chappell became the third Australian after D.G.Bradman and R.N.Harvey to score 6,000 runs in Tests. Marsh, whose 80th appearance took him past Harvey's record for Australia, retired at 172 in the first innings after being struck above the left eye by a ball from Croft. He resumed, with his score 37, at 206. Gomes scored his fourth Test hundred – all against Australia – and his second in successive innings. His partnership of 82 with Roberts was the West Indies eighth-wicket record against Australia until 1990-91. Yardley took his tally of wickets in the season's six home Tests to 38. Border's ninth hundred in 39 matches took him past 3,000 runs. Hughes batted for 251 minutes in the second innings with Dyson as his runner.

AUSTRALIA

B.M.Laird	c Dujon b Roberts	2	(2) c Dujon b Croft		78
G.M.Wood	c Garner b Roberts	5	(1) c and b Holding		6
J.Dyson	c Dujon b Holding	1	c Lloyd b Garner		10
K.J.Hughes	c Greenidge b Holding	5	(5) c Bacchus b Garner		84
*G.S.Chappell	c Garner b Holding	61	(7) lbw b Holding		7
A.R.Border	c Dujon b Roberts	78	(4) c Dujon b Roberts		126
†R.W.Marsh	c Dujon b Holding	39	(6) c Haynes b Holding		38
B.Yardley	b Croft	8	b Garner		6
D.K.Lillee	b Roberts	2	c Dujon b Garner		1
J.R.Thomson	not out	18	c Bacchus b Garner		0
L.S.Pascoe	b Holding	10	not out		0
Extras	(B1, LB2, W1, NB5)	9	(B7, LB10, NB13)		30
Total		**238**			**386**

WEST INDIES

C.G.Greenidge	c Border b Thomson	8	c Marsh b Thomson		52
D.L.Haynes	c Marsh b Thomson	26	c Marsh b Thomson		4
I.V.A.Richards	c Laird b Yardley	42	b Pascoe		50
H.A.Gomes	not out	124	b Pascoe		21
S.F.A.F.Bacchus	c Laird b Pascoe	0	(6) c Lillee b Pascoe		27
*C.H.Lloyd	c Marsh b Thomson	53	(5) not out		77
C.E.H.Croft	b Thomson	0			
†P.J.L.Dujon	c Thomson b Yardley	51	(7) not out		0
A.M.E.Roberts	c sub (D.W.Hookes) b Yardley	42			
M.A.Holding	b Yardley	3			
J.Garner	c Wood b Yardley	12			
Extras	(B4, LB7, W3, NB14)	28	(LB2, W1, NB5)		8
Total		**389**	(5 wickets)		**239**

WEST INDIES	O	M	R	W	O	M	R	W		FALL OF WICKETS			
Holding	25	5	72	5	29	9	70	3		A	WI	A	WI
Roberts	19	7	43	4	24	7	64	1	*Wkt*	*1st*	*1st*	*2nd*	*2nd*
Croft	23	4	60	1	(4) 32	4	90	1	1st	3	12	10	7
Garner	17	4	44	0	(3) 35	15	56	5	2nd	8	72	35	107
Gomes	7	3	10	0	14	1	38	0	3rd	8	85	201	114
Richards					18	3	38	0	4th	17	92	267	176
									5th	122	194	362	235
									6th	193	194	373	–
AUSTRALIA									7th	206	283	383	–
Lillee	4.5	3	4	0	(4) 4	0	17	0	8th	209	365	383	–
Thomson	29	1	112	4	(1) 19.1	5	62	2	9th	210	369	383	–
Yardley	40.5	10	132	5	16	0	68	0	10th	238	389	386	–
Pascoe	30	3	94	1	(2) 22	3	84	3					
Border	5	0	19	0									

Umpires: R.C.Bailhache (23) and M.W.Johnson (8).

Close: 1st day – A(1) 204-6 (Border 78, Lillee 0); 2nd – WI(1) 204-6 (Gomes 53, Dujon 4); 3rd – A(2) 100-2 (Laird 39, Border 37); 4th – A(2) 341-4 (Hughes 72, Marsh 22).

SRI LANKA v ENGLAND 1981-82 (Only Test)

At P.Saravanamuttu Stadium, Colombo, on 17, 18, 20, 21 February.
Toss: Sri Lanka.   Result: ENGLAND won by 7 wickets.
Debuts: England – G.Cook; Sri Lanka – all.

The Democratic Socialist Republic of Sri Lanka introduced Test cricket's 53rd ground for its inaugural match. Formerly the Colombo Oval, it had been renamed in 1976 in honour of P.Saravanamuttu (1892-1950). President of the Ceylon Cricket Association (1937-49) and the first President of the Board of Control for Cricket in Sri Lanka, 'P.Sara' had constructed the Colombo Oval from marshland in 1940. Fletcher, making the last of his 59 Test appearances, led England to its only victory under his seven-match tenure of captaincy with a day and five minutes to spare. Sri Lanka's first fifty was scored by the left-handed Ranatunga, their youngest Test cricketer at 18 years 78 days, who was still attending Ananda College. In their second innings, Sri Lanka lost their last seven wickets for eight runs off 68 balls, Emburey achieving a spell of 5 for 5. Along with Underwood (who took his final tally of Test wickets to 297), Gooch and 12 others, he was soon to be banned from international cricket for three years for taking part in the SAB English XI tour of South Africa.

SRI LANKA

*B.Warnapura	c Gower b Willis	2	c Gooch b Emburey	38
S.Wettimuny	c Taylor b Botham	6	b Willis	9
R.L.Dias	c Cook b Willis	0	c Taylor b Underwood	77
L.R.D.Mendis	lbw b Botham	17	c Willis b Emburey	27
R.S.Madugalle	c Gower b Underwood	65	c Cook b Emburey	3
A.Ranatunga	b Underwood	54	c Fletcher b Emburey	2
D.S.de Silva	c Gower b Underwood	3	c Fletcher b Underwood	1
A.L.F.de Mel	c Fletcher b Underwood	19	c Gower b Emburey	2
L.W.Kaluperuma	c Cook b Underwood	1	c Taylor b Emburey	0
†H.M.Goonatillake	not out	22	not out	2
G.R.A.de Silva	c Emburey b Botham	12	c Willis b Underwood	0
Extras	(B2, LB4, W2, NB9)	17	(LB6, NB8)	14
Total		**218**		**175**

ENGLAND

G.A.Gooch	lbw b De Mel	22	b G.R.A.de Silva	31
G.Cook	c Kaluperuma b De Mel	11	lbw b De Mel	0
C.J.Tavaré	b De Mel	0	st Goonatillake b G.R.A.de Silva	85
D.I.Gower	c Goonatillake b D.S.de Silva	89	not out	42
*K.W.R.Fletcher	c Warnapura b G.R.A.de Silva	45	not out	0
I.T.Botham	b De Mel	13		
†R.W.Taylor	not out	31		
J.E.Emburey	lbw b G.R.A.de Silva	0		
P.J.W.Allott	c Kaluperuma b D.S.de Silva	3		
D.L.Underwood	c Mendis b D.S.de Silva	0		
R.G.D.Willis	run out	0		
Extras	(LB3, NB6)	9	(B7, LB5, NB1)	13
Total		**223**	(3 wickets)	**171**

ENGLAND	O	M	R	W	O	M	R	W		FALL OF WICKETS			
										SL	E	SL	E
Willis	19	7	46	2	9	3	24	1	Wkt	1st	1st	2nd	2nd
Botham	12.5	1	28	3	12	1	37	0	1st	9	34	30	3
Allott	13	4	44	0					2nd	11	34	113	84
Emburey	19	3	55	0	(4) 25	9	33	6	3rd	29	40	140	167
Underwood	18	6	28	5	(3) 37.5	15	67	3	4th	34	120	167	–
SRI LANKA									5th	133	151	169	–
De Mel	17	2	70	4	13.1	4	33	1	6th	149	200	170	–
Warnapura	3	1	9	0	1	0	1	0	7th	181	207	172	–
D.S.de Silva	27.5	11	54	3	(4) 15	5	38	0	8th	183	216	173	–
Kaluperuma	9	1	29	0	(5) 12	3	40	0	9th	190	216	174	–
G.R.A.de Silva	30	12	52	2	(3) 17	6	46	2	10th	218	223	175	–

Umpires: H.C.Felsinger (1) and K.T.Francis (1).

Close: 1st day – SL(1) 183-8 (Madugalle 64); 2nd – E(1) 186-5 (Gower 79, Taylor 8); 3rd – SL(2) 152-3 (Mendis 16, Madugalle 0).

NEW ZEALAND v AUSTRALIA 1981-82 (1st Test)

At Basin Reserve, Wellington, on 26 (*no play*), 27, 28 February, 1 (*no play*), 2 March.
Toss: Australia.   Result: MATCH DRAWN.
Debuts: New Zealand – M.D.Crowe.

Rain restricted play to 9 hours 54 minutes, with only the final day escaping interruption. During the 51 minutes of play possible on the third day, Lillee retired with back muscle spasms after bowling one over, and Morrison, recalled after five years, was bowled by a ball which split two stumps, causing a five-minute delay. Wright batted 66 minutes before scoring and Edgar (336 minutes, 259 balls), took 310 minutes to reach his fifty – the slowest in first class cricket in New Zealand until 1987-88.

NEW ZEALAND

B.A.Edgar	lbw b Alderman	55
J.G.Wright	c Chappell b Yardley	38
J.F.M.Morrison	b Thomson	15
*G.P.Howarth	not out	58
J.V.Coney	lbw b Yardley	1
M.D.Crowe	run out	9
R.J.Hadlee	b Thomson	21
†I.D.S.Smith	c Chappell b Yardley	11
B.L.Cairns	not out	19
M.C.Snedden	} did not bat	
E.J.Chatfield		
Extras	(B5, LB19, W4, NB11)	39
Total	(7 wickets declared)	**266**

AUSTRALIA

G.M.Wood	b Cairns	41
B.M.Laird	not out	27
J.Dyson	not out	12
*G.S.Chappell		
K.J.Hughes		
A.R.Border		
†R.W.Marsh	} did not bat	
B.Yardley		
D.K.Lillee		
J.R.Thomson		
T.M.Alderman		
Extras	(LB2, NB3)	5
Total	(1 wicket)	**85**

AUSTRALIA	O	M	R	W		FALL OF WICKETS	
						NZ	A
Thomson	26	13	35	2	*Wkt*	*1st*	*1st*
Alderman	44	20	93	1	1st	86	65
Lillee	15	5	32	0	2nd	120	–
Chappell	8	2	18	0	3rd	149	–
Yardley	23	10	49	3	4th	162	–
					5th	186	–
NEW ZEALAND					6th	212	–
Hadlee	7	2	15	0	7th	246	–
Snedden	8	1	24	0	8th	–	–
Cairns	11	4	20	1	9th	–	–
Chatfield	8	5	7	0	10th	–	–
Crowe	4	1	14	0			

Umpires: F.R.Goodall (13) and S.J.Woodward (5).

Close: 1st day – no play; 2nd – NZ(1) 107-1 (Edgar 41, Morrison 8); 3rd – NZ(1) 127-2 (Edgar 47, Howarth 2); 4th – no play.

NEW ZEALAND v AUSTRALIA 1981-82 (2nd Test)

At Eden Park, Auckland, on 12, 13, 14, 15, 16 March.
Toss: New Zealand.   Result: NEW ZEALAND won by 5 wickets.
Debuts: None.

New Zealand gained their 13th victory in 147 Tests and their second against Australia. Edgar batted 516 minutes and faced 418 balls in recording New Zealand's highest innings in this series until 1985-86. After Laird and Wood had compiled Australia's first three-figure opening partnership in this series, Hadlee enjoyed a spell of 4 for 5 and the last six wickets fell for 39 runs off 21.2 overs in 80 minutes. Cairns scored 34 in 32 minutes off 21 balls before Hadlee concluded the match with a six.

AUSTRALIA

B.M.Laird	c Smith b Troup	38	(2)	lbw b Hadlee	39
G.M.Wood	c Smith b Cairns	9	(1)	c Snedden b Cairns	100
J.Dyson	b Snedden	33		b Cairns	33
K.J.Hughes	c Smith b Troup	0		b Cairns	17
*G.S.Chappell	run out	32		c Edgar b Hadlee	24
A.R.Border	run out	0		c Howarth b Morrison	38
†R.W.Marsh	b Troup	33		c Crowe b Hadlee	3
B.Yardley	b Hadlee	25		c Coney b Hadlee	0
J.R.Thomson	lbw b Hadlee	13		lbw b Hadlee	4
D.K.Lillee	c Crowe b Troup	9		c Smith b Morrison	5
T.M.Alderman	not out	0		not out	0
Extras	(LB2, NB16)	18		(B4, LB5, NB8)	17
Total		**210**			**280**

NEW ZEALAND

B.A.Edgar	c and b Yardley	161		c Lillee b Yardley	29
J.G.Wright	c Yardley b Lillee	4		c Laird b Alderman	4
J.F.M.Morrison	b Lillee	11		c Marsh b Lillee	8
*G.P.Howarth	run out	56		c Chappell b Yardley	19
J.V.Coney	b Yardley	73	(6)	not out	5
M.D.Crowe	c Wood b Lillee	2			
R.J.Hadlee	c Chappell b Yardley	25		not out	6
†I.D.S.Smith	lbw b Yardley	5			
B.L.Cairns	c Lillee b Alderman	14	(5)	b Border	34
M.C.Snedden	not out	18			
G.B.Troup	c Border b Alderman	4			
Extras	(B4, LB7, W1, NB2)	14		(LB4)	4
Total		**387**		(5 wickets)	**109**

NEW ZEALAND	O	M	R	W		O	M	R	W		FALL OF WICKETS			
											A	NZ	A	NZ
Hadlee	20	7	38	2		28	9	63	5	*Wkt*	*1st*	*1st*	*2nd*	*2nd*
Troup	18.3	3	82	4		15	4	31	0	1st	19	15	106	4
Cairns	17	7	38	1		44	10	85	3	2nd	75	35	167	17
Snedden	12	5	26	1		8	2	22	0	3rd	76	122	196	44
Howarth	1	0	8	0	(7)	4	2	4	0	4th	120	276	202	97
Coney					(5)	4	1	6	0	5th	120	291	241	103
Morrison					(6)	35	16	52	2	6th	131	326	254	–
										7th	173	345	254	–
AUSTRALIA										8th	187	352	260	–
Thomson	23	8	52	0						9th	203	366	277	–
Alderman	24.3	5	59	2		7	0	30	1	10th	210	387	280	–
Lillee	39	7	106	3	(1)	13	5	32	1					
Yardley	56	22	142	4	(3)	7.4	2	40	2					
Border	3	0	11	0	(4)	2	1	3	1					
Chappell	5	2	3	0										

Umpires: B.A.Bricknell (1) and S.J.Woodward (6).

Close: 1st day – NZ(1) 35-2 (Edgar 19); 2nd – NZ(1) 241-3 (Edgar 103, Coney 55); 3rd – A(2) 13-0 (Wood 9, Laird 3); 4th – A(2) 241-4 (Chappell 24, Border 14).

NEW ZEALAND v AUSTRALIA 1981-82 (3rd Test)

At Lancaster Park, Christchurch, on 19, 20, 21, 22 March.
Toss: New Zealand.   Result: AUSTRALIA won by 8 wickets.
Debuts: None.

Australia's first victory at Christchurch enabled them to share the rubber, during which they fielded an unchanged eleven. Chappell reached his 20th hundred in Tests by taking 20 off an over from Troup. He batted for 266 minutes, faced 218 balls and hit two sixes and 23 fours. On the second morning he added exactly 100 runs to his overnight score of 76, his pre-lunch century coming off 91 balls in 107 minutes. His partnership of 92 with Marsh was a record for Australia's sixth wicket in this series until 1985-86. Marsh became the first wicket-keeper to make 300 dismissals in Test cricket when he caught Crowe, his 88th catch off Lillee's bowling. The latter enjoyed a spell of 3 for 1 in 11 balls before retiring from the match with a cartilage injury to his right knee. Edgar kept wicket in the second innings and caught Laird.

AUSTRALIA

B.M.Laird	c Smith b Troup	12	c Edgar b Snedden	31
G.M.Wood	c Hadlee b Snedden	64	c Coney b Hadlee	15
J.Dyson	c Crowe b Hadlee	1	not out	14
*G.S.Chappell	c Smith b Coney	176	not out	3
K.J.Hughes	b Hadlee	12		
A.R.Border	b Snedden	6		
†R.W.Marsh	c Cairns b Hadlee	23		
B.Yardley	c Cairns b Hadlee	8		
J.R.Thomson	b Hadlee	25		
D.K.Lillee	c and b Hadlee	7		
T.M.Alderman	not out	1		
Extras	(B2, LB8, NB8)	18	(B2, LB2, NB2)	6
Total		353	(2 wickets)	69

NEW ZEALAND

B.A.Edgar	c Dyson b Alderman	22	c Marsh b Alderman	11
J.G.Wright	c Marsh b Lillee	13	b Alderman	141
J.F.M.Morrison	lbw b Thomson	8	lbw b Chappell	4
*G.P.Howarth	c Alderman b Thomson	9	c Wood b Border	41
J.V.Coney	b Lillee	0	b Border	0
M.D.Crowe	c Marsh b Lillee	0	b Yardley	9
R.J.Hadlee	c Marsh b Thomson	40	c Alderman b Yardley	0
†I.D.S.Smith	b Thomson	0	c Wood b Yardley	0
B.L.Cairns	run out	3	lbw b Yardley	16
M.C.Snedden	b Alderman	32	b Border	20
G.B.Troup	not out	0	not out	8
Extras	(B8, LB2, W1, NB11)	22	(B4, LB7, W2, NB9)	22
Total		149		272

NEW ZEALAND	O	M	R	W		O	M	R	W		FALL OF WICKETS			
Hadlee	28.5	5	100	6		8	2	10	1		A	NZ	NZ	A
Troup	11	1	53	1						Wkt	1st	1st	2nd	2nd
Snedden	18	2	89	2	(4)	4	0	15	1	1st	50	33	21	24
Cairns	21	3	74	0	(2)	9	1	28	0	2nd	57	57	36	60
Coney	8	2	15	1	(3)	1	0	2	0	3rd	82	57	129	—
Morrison	3	0	4	0	(5)	2	1	6	0	4th	128	57	133	—
Wright					(6)	1	0	2	0	5th	145	67	162	—
Crowe					(7)	0.3	0	0	0	6th	237	82	166	—
										7th	256	82	166	—
AUSTRALIA										8th	340	87	215	—
Thomson	21	5	51	4	(3)	19	5	54	0	9th	352	149	249	—
Alderman	19.2	3	63	2		23	5	66	2	10th	353	149	272	—
Lillee	12	6	13	3										
Chappell					(1)	18	5	30	1					
Yardley					(4)	27	7	80	4					
Border					(5)	10.3	4	20	3					

Umpires: F.R.Goodall (14) and D.A.Kinsella (2).

Close: 1st day – A(1) 202-5 (Chappell 76, Marsh 18); 2nd – NZ(1) 98-8 (Hadlee 22, Snedden 1); 3rd – NZ(2) 181-7 (Wright 91, Cairns 8).

PAKISTAN v SRI LANKA 1981-82 (1st Test)

At National Stadium, Karachi, on 5, 6, 7, 9, 10 March.
Toss: Pakistan.   Result: PAKISTAN won by 204 runs.
Debuts: Pakistan – Rashid Khan, Salim Malik, Salim Yousuf, Tahir Naqqash; Sri Lanka –
   J.R. Ratnayeke.

Sri Lanka, playing in their first Test overseas, were dismissed with two hours to spare after being set 354 runs in a minimum of 296 minutes. All of the side which had defeated Australia in December (*Test No. 911*) refused to play under Javed Miandad's leadership unless a new captain was appointed for Pakistan's forthcoming tour of England. Although two players subsequently withdrew their objection and were selected, the remainder declined to make themselves available until the final Test. Haroon Rashid batted for 319 minutes and hit three sixes and 16 fours in compiling the largest of his three Test centuries. Salim Malik, 18 years 328 days, became the youngest player to score a hundred in his first Test; he was the third to do so for Pakistan after Khalid Ibadulla and Miandad.

PAKISTAN

Mansoor Akhtar	c Goonatillake b De Mel	6	c Mendis b D.S.de Silva	23
Rizwan-uz-Zaman	c Goonatillake b Ratnayeke	42	c Goonatillake b De Mel	10
Salim Malik	b D.S.de Silva	12	(4) not out	100
*Javed Miandad	c Goonatillake b De Mel	4	(5) st Goonatillake b D.S.de Silva	92
Wasim Raja	c Dias b De Mel	31	(6) not out	12
Haroon Rashid	run out	153		
†Salim Yousuf	st Goonatillake b D.S.de Silva	4		
Tahir Naqqash	c Mendis b D.S.de Silva	57		
Iqbal Qasim	lbw b D.S.de Silva	1	(3) c sub‡ b D.S.de Silva	56
Rashid Khan	c Madugalle b G.R.A.de Silva	59		
Tausif Ahmed	not out	5		
Extras	(LB9, W4, NB9)	22	(B5, LB1, W1, NB1)	8
Total		**396**	(4 wickets declared)	**301**

SRI LANKA

*B.Warnapura	lbw b Tahir	13	b Tahir	0
S.Wettimuny	c Mansoor b Rashid Khan	71	c Salim Yousuf b Rashid Khan	14
R.L.Dias	lbw b Qasim	53	lbw b Tahir	19
R.S.Madugalle	c Salim Yousuf b Rashid Khan	29	c Tausif b Qasim	18
J.R.Ratnayeke	c Rizwan b Qasim	24	(10) c Salim Malik b Wasim	0
L.R.D.Mendis	c Rashid Khan b Tahir	54	(5) c Salim Yousuf b Qasim	15
A.Ranatunga	st Salim Yousuf b Tausif	13	(6) c Salim Yousuf b Tausif	33
D.S.de Silva	b Tausif	26	(7) st Salim Yousuf b Qasim	12
†H.M.Goonatillake	c Salim Yousuf b Tahir	14	c Haroon b Wasim	13
A.L.F.de Mel	run out	9	(8) c Miandad b Qasim	2
G.R.A.de Silva	not out	10	not out	0
Extras	(B1, LB12, W3, NB12)	28	(B9, LB11, W1, NB2)	23
Total		**344**		**149**

SRI LANKA	O	M	R	W	O	M	R	W		FALL OF WICKETS			
										P	SL	P	SL
De Mel	28	2	124	3	23.2	3	100	1		1st	1st	2nd	2nd
Ratnayeke	16	6	49	1	5.4	2	20	0	Wkt				
D.S.de Silva	38	8	102	4	26	3	99	3	1st	6	24	16	1
G.R.A.de Silva	17.2	2	69	1	35	5	74	0	2nd	46	120	53	27
Warnapura	2	0	9	0					3rd	53	152	107	41
Wettimuny	2	0	21	0					4th	72	199	269	68
									5th	113	221	–	91
									6th	126	242	–	121
PAKISTAN									7th	230	285	–	125
Tahir	32	11	83	3	9	1	34	2	8th	232	308	–	139
Rashid Khan	26	7	53	2	8	3	25	1	9th	359	322	–	149
Qasim	28	7	88	2	15.1	8	27	4	10th	396	344	–	149
Tausif	21.4	6	64	2	12	1	39	1					
Wasim	5	1	28	0	3	2	1	2					

Umpires: Amanullah Khan (9) and Mahboob Shah (7).   ‡ (R.G.C.E.Wijesuriya)

Close: 1st day – P(1) 240-8 (Haroon 66, Rashid Khan 5); 2nd – SL(1) 156-3 (Madugalle 9, Ratnayeke 0); 3rd – P(2) 16-1 (Mansoor 5, Qasim 0); 4th – P(2) 268-3 (Malik 79, Miandad 92).

PAKISTAN v SRI LANKA 1981-82 (2nd Test)

At Iqbal Stadium, Faisalabad, on 14, 15, 16, 18, 19 March.
Toss: Sri Lanka.   Result: MATCH DRAWN.
Debuts: Pakistan – Ashraf Ali; Sri Lanka – A.N.Ranasinghe.

Sidath Wettimuny scored Sri Lanka's first Test century, became their first player to bat throughout a complete day's play, and shared in their first hundred partnership (217 for the second wicket with Dias). For Pakistan, Iqbal Qasim became their fifth bowler to take 100 wickets and Javed Miandad their fifth batsman to score 3,000 runs. Mendis, whose first appearance as Sri Lanka's captain resulted from Warnapura's late withdrawal because of injury, set Pakistan 339 runs in a minimum of 330 minutes. They were in danger of providing a major unsolicited record as Somachandra de Silva's leg-breaks and googlies achieved Sri Lanka's first five-wicket haul, including three in the same over.

SRI LANKA

S.Wettimuny	b Wasim	157	c Ashraf b Tahir		13
†H.M.Goonatillake	c Salim b Qasim	27	b Qasim		56
R.L.Dias	c Salim b Qasim	98	c Mohsin b Tahir		7
R.S.Madugalle	not out	91	lbw b Qasim		12
*L.R.D.Mendis	b Qasim	16	run out		0
A.Ranatunga	b Qasim	0	c Ashraf b Tausif		2
A.N.Ranasinghe	c Miandad b Qasim	6	c Miandad b Tausif		5
A.L.F.de Mel	c Salim b Qasim	4	not out	(9)	25
D.S.de Silva	lbw b Rizwan	25	st Ashraf b Tausif	(8)	8
L.W.Kaluperuma	b Rizwan	0	not out		11
G.R.A.de Silva	lbw b Rizwan	5			
Extras	(LB11, W2, NB12)	25	(LB9, W1, NB5)		15
Total		454	(8 wickets declared)		154

PAKISTAN

Rizwan-uz-Zaman	b G.R.A.de Silva	36	b De Mel		16
Mohsin Khan	c Wettimuny b De Mel	12	c De Mel b D.S.de Silva		74
Salim Malik	b De Mel	23	lbw b De Mel		4
*Javed Miandad	c Ranatunga b D.S.de Silva	18	c Madugalle b D.S.de Silva		36
Wasim Raja	c Madugalle b D.S.de Silva	22	c Wettimuny b D.S.de Silva		0
Haroon Rashid	c De Mel b D.S.de Silva	25	b D.S.de Silva		0
†Ashraf Ali	b Ranasinghe	58	not out		29
Tahir Naqqash	c De Mel b G.R.A.de Silva	1	c sub‡ b D.S.de Silva		13
Iqbal Qasim	run out	5			
Rashid Khan	not out	43	not out	(9)	3
Tausif Ahmed	c Madugalle b D.S.de Silva	18			
Extras	(LB1, NB8)	9	(B3, LB7, NB1)		11
Total		270	(7 wickets)		186

PAKISTAN	O	M	R	W	O	M	R	W		FALL OF WICKETS			
Tahir	26	4	108	0	13	3	53	2		SL	P	SL	P
Rashid Khan	13	3	52	0	1	0	4	0	Wkt	1st	1st	2nd	2nd
Qasim	65	18	141	6	30	9	51	2	1st	77	19	19	24
Tausif	12	3	35	0	(5) 14	4	18	3	2nd	294	54	44	40
Wasim	26	6	66	1					3rd	304	83	82	132
Miandad	1	0	1	0					4th	341	116	82	132
Rizwan	12	3	26	3	(4) 5	2	13	0	5th	341	124	86	132
									6th	355	154	104	137
SRI LANKA									7th	385	156	114	174
De Mel	23	4	73	2	17	2	71	2	8th	446	185	114	–
Ranasinghe	7	1	23	1	5	0	17	0	9th	448	222	–	–
D.S.de Silva	32	3	103	4	18	2	59	5	10th	454	270	–	–
G.R.A.de Silva	24	10	38	2	19	4	28	0					
Kaluperuma	6	0	24	0									

Umpires: Javed Akhtar (4) and Khizer Hayat (4).   ‡ (J.B.N. Perera)

Close: 1st day – SL(1) 270-1 (Wettimuny 143, Dias 80); 2nd – P(1) 47-1 (Rizwan 13, Malik 18); 3rd – P(1) 210-8 (Ashraf 50, Rashid Khan 9); 4th – SL(2) 127-8 (De Mel 7, Kaluperuma 5).

PAKISTAN v SRI LANKA 1981-82 (3rd Test)

At Gaddafi Stadium, Lahore, on 22, 23, 24 (*no play*), 25, 26, 27 March.
Toss: Pakistan.   Result: PAKISTAN won by an innings and 102 runs.
Debuts: Sri Lanka – R.S.A.Jayasekera, R.G.C.E.Wijesuriya.

Pakistan were at full strength for the first time in the rubber, following Javed Miandad's decision to relinquish the captaincy for the 1982 tour of England. Imran Khan celebrated his return by becoming the first bowler to take 14 wickets in a match for Pakistan and the first Pakistani to take 150 wickets in Test cricket. His innings (8 for 58) and match (14 for 116) analyses remain the best of his career, the latter being the record for any Test in Pakistan. Dias (260 minutes) offered notable resistance with a chanceless maiden Test hundred. Zaheer became the sixth Pakistan batsman to score 3,000 runs and Majid equalled Wasim Bari's national record of 61 appearances. Play continued on the scheduled rest day after rain had caused the third day to be abandoned.

SRI LANKA

*B.Warnapura	c Mohsin b Imran	7		c Miandad b Tausif	26
S.Wettimuny	c Qasim b Imran	20		c Majid b Imran	41
R.S.A.Jayasekera	b Imran	0	(6)	b Imran	2
R.L.Dias	c Tausif b Imran	109	(3)	c Wasim b Tausif	9
R.S.Madugalle	c Ashraf b Imran	0	(4)	b Tausif	5
L.R.D.Mendis	c and b Tausif	26	(5)	c Mudassar b Tausif	5
D.S.de Silva	b Imran	7		not out	36
A.L.F.de Mel	st Ashraf b Qasim	34		lbw b Imran	0
†H.M.Goonatillake	b Imran	15		c and b Imran	21
J.R.Ratnayeke	not out	1		b Imran	0
R.G.C.E.Wijesuriya	lbw b Imran	0		b Imran	3
Extras	(LB11, W6, NB4)	21		(B4, LB2, W1, NB3)	10
Total		**240**			**158**

PAKISTAN

Mudassar Nazar	c Madugalle b De Silva	37
Mohsin Khan	b Ratnayeke	129
Majid Khan	c sub‡ b Ratnayeke	63
*Javed Miandad	c Goonatillake b De Mel	26
Zaheer Abbas	b Ratnayeke	134
Wasim Raja	c Goonatillake b De Mel	1
Imran Khan	c Mendis b De Mel	39
†Ashraf Ali	not out	45
Tahir Naqqash	not out	1
Iqbal Qasim	} did not bat	
Tausif Ahmed		
Extras	(B5, LB5, W5, NB10)	25
Total	(7 wickets declared)	**500**

PAKISTAN	O	M	R	W		O	M	R	W	FALL OF WICKETS			
											SL	P	SL
Imran	29.3	8	58	8		22.5	3	58	6	*Wkt*	*1st*	*1st*	*2nd*
Tahir	10	0	54	0		6	0	22	0	1st	17	79	56
Qasim	12	4	21	1	(4)	1	0	1	0	2nd	17	230	78
Mudassar	8	1	23	0						3rd	79	247	84
Tausif	12	1	50	1	(3)	25	7	58	4	4th	83	297	90
Wasim	5	1	13	0	(5)	6	4	9	0	5th	141	306	93
Majid					(6)	1	1	0	0	6th	171	406	95
										7th	209	494	96
SRI LANKA										8th	231	–	142
De Mel	28	3	120	3						9th	239	–	142
Ratnayeke	28	3	121	3						10th	240	–	158
De Silva	39	4	129	1									
Wijesuriya	24	2	105	0									

Umpires: Khizer Hayat (5) and Shakoor Rana (9).   ‡ (A.N.Ranasinghe)

Close: 1st day – SL(1) 204-6 (Dias 106, De Mel 18); 2nd – P(1) 168-1 (Mohsin 78, Majid 42); 3rd – no play; 4th – P(1) 398-5 (Zaheer 82, Imran 37); 5th – SL(2) 95-5 (Madugalle 5, De Silva 1).

ENGLAND v INDIA 1982 (1st Test)

At Lord's, London, on 10, 11, 12, 14, 15 June.
Toss: England.   Result: ENGLAND won by 7 wickets.
Debuts: England – A.J.Lamb, D.R.Pringle; India – G.A.Parkar.

This match celebrated the golden jubilee of Anglo-Indian Tests. For the first time since 1951-52 England employed four captains within a period of twelve months, with Botham, Brearley, Fletcher and Willis following the earlier sequence of F.R.Brown, N.D.Howard, D.B.Carr and L.Hutton. Willis became the fourth Warwickshire player to lead England after the Hon. F.S.G.Calthorpe, R.E.S.Wyatt and M.J.K.Smith. At 6 ft 6 in he was the tallest Test captain since A.W.Greig (6 ft 7½ in). Kirmani played in his first Test match in England after appearing in 54 elsewhere. Randall compiled his first Test hundred in England after twice reaching 150 in Australia. England's last four wickets added 267 runs and produced record seventh (125 – Randall and Edmonds) and tenth (70 – Allott and Willis) wicket partnerships for England against India. Willis and Kapil Dev took their 250th and 150th Test wickets respectively. Pringle dismissed Yashpal with his sixth ball in Test cricket.

ENGLAND

G.Cook	lbw b Kapil Dev	4		lbw b Kapil Dev	10
C.J.Tavaré	c Viswanath b Kapil Dev	4		b Kapil Dev	3
A.J.Lamb	lbw b Kapil Dev	9	(4)	not out	37
D.I.Gower	c Viswanath b Kapil Dev	37	(5)	not out	14
I.T.Botham	c Malhotra b Madan Lal	67			
D.W.Randall	c Parkar b Kapil Dev	126			
D.R.Pringle	c Gavaskar b Doshi	7			
P.H.Edmonds	c Kirmani b Madan Lal	64			
†R.W.Taylor	c Viswanath b Doshi	31	(3)	c Malhotra b Kapil Dev	1
P.J.W.Allott	not out	41			
*R.G.D.Willis	b Madan Lal	28			
Extras	(B1, LB5, NB9)	15		(LB2)	2
Total		**433**		**(3 wickets)**	**67**

INDIA

*S.M.Gavaskar	b Botham	48		c Cook b Willis	24
G.A.Parkar	lbw b Botham	6		b Willis	1
D.B.Vengsarkar	lbw b Willis	2		c Allott b Willis	157
G.R.Viswanath	b Botham	1	(5)	c Taylor b Pringle	3
Yashpal Sharma	lbw b Pringle	4	(6)	b Willis	37
A.Malhotra	lbw b Pringle	5	(7)	c Taylor b Willis	0
Kapil Dev	c Cook b Willis	41	(8)	c Cook b Botham	89
R.J.Shastri	c Cook b Willis	4	(4)	b Allott	23
†S.M.H.Kirmani	not out	6		c Gower b Willis	3
Madan Lal	c Tavaré b Botham	6		lbw b Pringle	15
D.R.Doshi	c Taylor b Botham	0		not out	4
Extras	(LB1, NB4)	5		(LB2, NB11)	13
Total		**128**			**369**

INDIA	O	M	R	W		O	M	R	W
Kapil Dev	43	8	125	5		10	1	43	3
Madan Lal	28.1	6	99	3		2	1	2	0
Shastri	34	10	73	0	(4)	2	0	9	0
Doshi	40	7	120	2	(3)	5	3	11	0
Yashpal	3	2	1	0					
ENGLAND									
Botham	19.4	3	46	5		31.5	7	103	1
Willis	16	2	41	3		28	3	101	6
Pringle	9	4	16	2		19	4	58	2
Edmonds	2	1	5	0	(5)	15	6	39	0
Allott	4	1	15	0	(4)	17	3	51	1
Cook						1	0	4	0

FALL OF WICKETS				
	E	I	I	E
Wkt	1st	1st	2nd	2nd
1st	5	17	6	11
2nd	18	21	47	13
3rd	37	22	107	18
4th	96	31	110	–
5th	149	45	252	–
6th	166	112	252	–
7th	291	116	254	–
8th	363	116	275	–
9th	363	128	341	–
10th	433	128	369	–

Umpires: D.G.L.Evans (2) and B.J.Meyer (9).

Close: 1st day – E(1) 278-6 (Randall 84, Edmonds 59); 2nd – I(1) 92-5 (Gavaskar 41, Kapil Dev 28); 3rd – I(2) 61-2 (Vengsarkar 30, Shastri 6); 4th – E(2) 23-3 (Lamb 6, Gower 2).

ENGLAND v INDIA 1982 (2nd Test)

At Old Trafford, Manchester, on 24, 25, 26, 27, 28 (*no play*) June.
Toss: England.   Result: MATCH DRAWN.
Debuts: India – S.V.Nayak.

Old Trafford lost its 26th complete day of Test cricket in 53 matches. It proved to be the last day's play to be lost in a Test in England before 1987, the number of days abandoned on the other grounds (total Tests in brackets) being: The Oval 13 (67); Lord's 13 (77); Headingley 12 (47); Trent Bridge 9 (34); Edgbaston 2 (22); Bramall Lane 0 (1). Botham celebrated his 50th Test match by scoring his 10th hundred and his second in successive innings at Old Trafford. Patil set a world Test record by scoring six boundaries off an over from Willis: 4440444 – the third delivery being a no-ball. His 24 runs equalled the Test record for the most runs off an over by one batsman established by A.M.E.Roberts in 1980-81 (*Test No. 896*). Patil's score progressed from 73 to 104 off nine balls. Kapil Dev reached 50 off only 33 balls in 44 minutes. Gavaskar surpassed the record of G.St A.Sobers by leading his country in 21 drawn Tests.

ENGLAND

G.Cook	b Doshi	66
C.J.Tavaré	b Doshi	57
A.J.Lamb	c Viswanath b Madan Lal	9
D.I.Gower	c Shastri b Madan Lal	9
I.T.Botham	b Shastri	128
D.W.Randall	c Kirmani b Doshi	0
G.Miller	c Vengsarkar b Doshi	98
D.R.Pringle	st Kirmani b Doshi	23
P.H.Edmonds	c Kirmani b Madan Lal	12
†R.W.Taylor	not out	1
*R.G.D.Willis	c Gavaskar b Doshi	6
Extras	(B2, LB5, NB9)	16
Total		**425**

INDIA

*S.M.Gavaskar	c Tavaré b Willis	2
R.J.Shastri	c Cook b Willis	0
D.B.Vengsarkar	c Randall b Pringle	12
G.R.Viswanath	c Taylor b Botham	54
†S.M.H.Kirmani	b Edmonds	58
Yashpal Sharma	b Edmonds	10
S.M.Patil	not out	129
Kapil Dev	c Taylor b Miller	65
Madan Lal	b Edmonds	26
S.V.Nayak	not out	2
D.R.Doshi	did not bat	
Extras	(B6, LB2, W3, NB10)	21
Total	(8 wickets)	**379**

INDIA	O	M	R	W
Kapil Dev	36	5	109	0
Madan Lal	35	9	104	3
Nayak	12	1	50	0
Doshi	47.1	17	102	6
Shastri	23	8	44	1
ENGLAND				
Willis	17	2	94	2
Pringle	15	4	33	1
Edmonds	37	12	94	3
Botham	19	4	86	1
Miller	16	4	51	1

FALL OF WICKETS

Wkt	E 1st	I 1st
1st	106	5
2nd	117	8
3rd	141	25
4th	161	112
5th	161	136
6th	330	173
7th	382	269
8th	413	366
9th	419	–
10th	425	–

Umpires: H.D.Bird (22) and B.J.Meyer (10).

Close: 1st day – E(1) 239-5 (Botham 60, Miller 26); 2nd – E(1) 340-6 (Miller 53, Pringle 3); 3rd – I(1) 35-3 (Viswanath 15, Kirmani 0); 4th – I(1) 379-8 (Patil 129, Nayak 2).

ENGLAND v INDIA 1982 (3rd Test)

At Kennington Oval, London, on 8, 9, 10, 12, 13 July.
Toss: England.   Result: MATCH DRAWN.
Debuts: None.

Botham (276 minutes, 226 balls, four sixes and 19 fours) scored 200 off 220 balls in 268 minutes. In terms of time it was the third-fastest for England but, calculated by fewest balls faced, it is the quickest on record. His 403 runs for the rubber set a new record for England against India in England. He also removed Gavaskar from the match at 4.25 on the first afternoon when he square-drove his fourth ball with massive power, fracturing the silly point's left fibula. Viswanath took over the captaincy. The partnership of 130 between Kirmani and Kapil Dev, who scored 97 off 93 balls, is a record for India's sixth wicket in this series. Neil Taylor, Kent's opening batsman, held a startling catch at fine-leg while substituting for Randall (strained thigh muscle). A token declaration left India to score 376 in a minimum of 160 minutes.

ENGLAND

G.Cook	c Shastri b Patil	50	c Yashpal b Kapil Dev	8
C.J.Tavaré	b Kapil Dev	39	not out	75
A.J.Lamb	run out	107	b Doshi	45
D.I.Gower	c Kirmani b Shastri	47	c and b Nayak	45
I.T.Botham	c Viswanath b Doshi	208		
D.W.Randall	st Kirmani b Shastri	95		
D.R.Pringle	st Kirmani b Doshi	9		
P.H.Edmonds	c sub (G.A.Parkar) b Doshi	14		
†R.W.Taylor	lbw b Shastri	3		
P.J.W.Allott	c Yashpal b Doshi	3		
*R.G.D.Willis	not out	1		
Extras	(B3, LB5, NB10)	18	(B6, LB8, NB4)	18
Total		**594**	(3 wickets declared)	**191**

INDIA

R.J.Shastri	c Botham b Willis	66	c Taylor b Willis	0
D.B.Vengsarkar	c Edmonds b Botham	6	(3) c Taylor b Pringle	16
G.R.Viswanath	lbw b Willis	56	(4) not out	75
Yashpal Sharma	c Gower b Willis	38	(5) not out	9
S.M.Patil	c sub (N.R.Taylor) b Botham	62		
†S.M.H.Kirmani	b Allott	43		
Kapil Dev	c Allott b Edmonds	97		
Madan Lal	c Taylor b Edmonds	5		
S.V.Nayak	b Edmonds	11	(2) c Taylor b Pringle	6
D.R.Doshi	not out	5		
*S.M.Gavaskar	absent hurt	–		
Extras	(B3, LB5, NB13)	21	(LB3, NB2)	5
Total		**410**	(3 wickets)	**111**

INDIA	O	M	R	W	O	M	R	W		FALL OF WICKETS			
Kapil Dev	25	4	109	1	19	3	53	1		E	I	E	I
Madan Lal	26	8	69	0	11	6	17	0	*Wkt*	*1st*	*1st*	*2nd*	*2nd*
Nayak	21	5	66	0	(5) 5.3	0	16	1	1st	96	21	12	0
Patil	14	1	48	1					2nd	96	134	94	18
Doshi	46	6	175	4	(3) 19	5	47	1	3rd	185	135	191	43
Shastri	41.3	8	109	3	(4) 16	3	40	0	4th	361	232	–	–
									5th	512	248	–	–
ENGLAND									6th	534	378	–	–
Willis	23	4	78	3	4	0	16	1	7th	562	394	–	–
Botham	19	2	73	2	(5) 4	0	12	0	8th	569	396	–	–
Allott	24	4	69	1	(4) 4	1	12	0	9th	582	410	–	–
Pringle	28	5	80	0	(2) 11	5	32	2	10th	594	–	–	–
Edmonds	35.2	11	89	3	(3) 13	5	34	0					

Umpires: H.D.Bird (23) and A.G.T.Whitehead (1).

Close: 1st day – E(1) 329-3 (Lamb 96, Botham 82); 2nd – E(1) 594 all out; 3rd – I(1) 284-5 (Kirmani 12, Kapil Dev 28); 4th – E(2) 30-1 (Tavaré 5, Lamb 16).

ENGLAND v PAKISTAN 1982 (1st Test)

At Edgbaston, Birmingham, on 29, 30, 31 July, 1 August.
Toss: England.   Result: ENGLAND won by 113 runs.
Debuts: England – I.A.Greig, E.E.Hemmings.

England completed their victory at 5.52 on the fourth evening. Imran (7 for 52) achieved Pakistan's best analysis in this series until 1987 (*Test No. 1077*). Hemmings (off-spin) dismissed Javed Miandad with his fourth ball in Test cricket. Randall scored 105 in 249 minutes out of a total of 188. Willis celebrated becoming the first specialist fast bowler to play 100 innings in Test cricket by making his highest score for England and sharing a record 79-run tenth-wicket partnership for this series with Taylor. Tahir Naqqash took 5 for 20 in 45 balls. Ian Greig's first appearance provided the ninth instance of brothers representing England.

ENGLAND

D.W.Randall	b Imran	17		b Imran	105
C.J.Tavaré	c Miandad b Qadir	54		c Mohsin b Imran	17
A.J.Lamb	c Wasim Bari b Sikander	6		lbw b Tahir	5
D.I.Gower	c Wasim Bari b Imran	74		c Mudassar b Tahir	13
I.T.Botham	b Imran	2	(6)	lbw b Tahir	0
M.W.Gatting	b Tahir	17	(5)	c Wasim Bari b Tahir	5
G.Miller	b Imran	47		b Tahir	5
I.A.Greig	c sub (Haroon Rashid) b Imran	14		b Qadir	7
E.E.Hemmings	lbw b Imran	2		c Mansoor b Qadir	19
†R.W.Taylor	lbw b Imran	1		c Qadir b Wasim Raja	54
*R.G.D.Willis	not out	0		not out	28
Extras	(B4, LB10, W6, NB18)	38		(B10, LB11, W7, NB5)	33
Total		**272**			**291**

PAKISTAN

Mudassar Nazar	lbw b Botham	0		lbw b Botham	0
Mohsin Khan	c Willis b Botham	26		lbw b Botham	35
Tahir Naqqash	c Taylor b Greig	12	(9)	c and b Hemmings	39
Mansoor Akhtar	c Miller b Hemmings	58	(3)	c Taylor b Botham	0
Javed Miandad	c Willis b Hemmings	30	(4)	run out	10
Zaheer Abbas	lbw b Greig	40	(5)	c Taylor b Willis	4
Wasim Raja	c Tavaré b Willis	26	(6)	c Gower b Willis	16
*Imran Khan	c Taylor b Willis	22	(7)	b Miller	65
†Wasim Bari	not out	16	(8)	c Taylor b Botham	12
Abdul Qadir	lbw b Greig	7		c Randall b Miller	9
Sikander Bakht	c Hemmings b Greig	1		not out	1
Extras	(B5, LB2, W1, NB5)	13		(LB3, NB5)	8
Total		**251**			**199**

PAKISTAN	O	M	R	W		O	M	R	W		FALL OF WICKETS			
Imran	25.3	11	52	7		32	5	84	2			E	P	E	P
Tahir	15	4	46	1	(4) 18	7	40	5		*Wkt*	*1st*	*1st*	*2nd*	*2nd*
Sikander	18	5	58	1	(2) 13	5	34	0		1st	29	0	62	0
Mudassar	5	2	8	0						2nd	37	29	98	0
Qadir	29	7	70	1	(3) 40	10	100	2		3rd	164	53	127	38
Wasim Raja					(5) 2.3	2	0	1		4th	172	110	137	54
										5th	179	164	137	66
										6th	228	198	146	77
ENGLAND										7th	263	217	170	98
Botham	24	1	86	2		21	7	70	4		8th	265	227	188	151
Greig	14.2	3	53	4	(3) 4	1	19	0		9th	271	248	212	178
Willis	15	3	42	2	(2) 14	2	49	2		10th	272	251	291	199
Hemmings	24	5	56	2		10	4	27	1						
Miller	2	1	1	0		7.4	1	26	2						

Umpires: D.G.L.Evans (3) and K.E.Palmer (9).

Close: 1st day – P(1) 4-1 (Mohsin 0, Tahir 0); 2nd – E(2) 51-0 (Randall 30, Tavaré 15); 3rd – E(2) 291 all out.

ENGLAND v PAKISTAN 1982 (2nd Test)

At Lord's, London, on 12, 13, 14, 15, 16 August.
Toss: Pakistan.   Result: PAKISTAN won by 10 wickets.
Debuts: None.

With just 29 balls to spare Pakistan gained their second victory against England, their first being in 1954 (*Test No. 390*). Gower became the second Leicestershire player after R.Illingworth to captain England, Willis withdrawing with a stiff neck. Mohsin Khan (496 minutes, 386 balls, 23 fours) recorded the first double century in a Lord's Test since 1949 and was the second after Zaheer Abbas to make 200 for Pakistan in this series. His partnership of 153 with Zaheer equalled the (then) national fourth-wicket record against England. Tavaré, who batted 404 minutes and faced 277 balls, took 350 minutes to score 50 – the second-slowest on record in all first-class cricket. By taking 67 minutes to score his first run and spending 60 minutes with his score 24, he became the first batsman in any grade of cricket to fail to score during two separate hours of an innings. In England's first innings extras were top scorer for the fifth time in Test matches and included the record number of wides for a Test innings until 1989-90.

PAKISTAN

Mohsin Khan	c Tavaré b Jackman	200		not out	39
Mudassar Nazar	c Taylor b Jackman	20			
Mansoor Akhtar	c Lamb b Botham	57			
Javed Miandad	run out	6	(2)	not out	26
Zaheer Abbas	b Jackman	75			
Haroon Rashid	lbw b Botham	1			
*Imran Khan	c Taylor b Botham	12			
Tahir Naqqash	c Gatting b Jackman	2			
†Wasim Bari	not out	24			
Abdul Qadir	not out	18			
Sarfraz Nawaz	did not bat				
Extras	(B3, LB8, NB2)	13		(B1, LB10, W1)	12
Total	(8 wickets declared)	**428**		(0 wickets)	**77**

ENGLAND

D.W.Randall	b Sarfraz	29		b Mudassar	9
C.J.Tavaré	b Sarfraz	8		c Miandad b Imran	82
A.J.Lamb	c Haroon b Tahir	33		lbw b Mudassar	0
*D.I.Gower	c Mansoor b Imran	29		c Wasim b Mudassar	0
I.T.Botham	c Mohsin b Qadir	31		c Sarfraz b Mudassar	69
M.W.Gatting	not out	32		c Wasim b Mudassar	7
D.R.Pringle	c Haroon b Qadir	5		c Miandad b Qadir	14
I.A.Greig	lbw b Qadir	3		lbw b Mudassar	2
E.E.Hemmings	b Sarfraz	6		c Wasim b Imran	14
†R.W.Taylor	lbw b Qadir	5		not out	24
R.D.Jackman	lbw b Imran	0		c Haroon b Qadir	17
Extras	(B11, LB12, W13, NB10)	46		(B10, LB19, W5, NB4)	38
Total		**227**			**276**

ENGLAND	O	M	R	W	O	M	R	W	FALL OF WICKETS				
										P	E	E	P
Botham	44	8	148	3	7	0	30	0					
Jackman	36	5	110	4	4	0	22	0	*Wkt*	*1st*	*1st*	*2nd*	*2nd*
Pringle	26	9	62	0					1st	53	16	9	–
Greig	13	2	42	0					2nd	197	69	9	–
Hemmings	20	3	53	0	(3) 2.1	0	13	0	3rd	208	89	9	–
									4th	361	157	121	–
PAKISTAN									5th	364	173	132	–
Imran	23	4	55	2	42	13	84	2	6th	380	187	171	–
Sarfraz	23	4	56	3	14	5	22	0	7th	382	197	180	–
Tahir	12	4	25	1	(5) 7	5	6	0	8th	401	217	224	–
Qadir	24	9	39	4	(3) 37.5	15	94	2	9th	–	226	235	–
Mudassar	4	1	6	0	(4) 19	7	32	6	10th	–	227	276	–

Umpires: H.D.Bird (24) and D.J.Constant (23).

Close: 1st day – P(1) 295-3 (Mohsin 159, Zaheer 44); 2nd – P(1) 428-8 (Wasim 24, Qadir 18); 3rd – E(1) 226-9 (Gatting 31, Jackman 0); 4th – E(2) 95-3 (Tavaré 24, Botham 55).

ENGLAND v PAKISTAN 1982 (3rd Test)

At Headingley, Leeds, on 26, 27, 28, 30, 31 August.
Toss: Pakistan.   Result: ENGLAND won by 3 wickets.
Debuts: England – G.Fowler, V.J.Marks.

England won the rubber after 39 minutes of play on the fifth morning. Majid overtook Hanif Mohammad's record Pakistan aggregate of 3,915 runs when he scored his 16th run. Extras contributed 221 runs to England's aggregate for the rubber – five runs more than their leading scorer, Tavaré. Imran took 21 wickets in the three Tests to set a Pakistan record for any rubber against England (equalled by himself in 1987 and surpassed by Abdul Qadir in 1987-88).

PAKISTAN

Mohsin Khan	c Taylor b Botham	10	c Taylor b Willis		0
Mudassar Nazar	b Botham	65	c Botham b Willis		0
Mansoor Akhtar	c Gatting b Willis	0	c Randall b Botham		39
Javed Miandad	c Fowler b Willis	54	c Taylor b Botham		52
Zaheer Abbas	c Taylor b Jackman	8	lbw b Botham		4
Majid Khan	lbw b Jackman	21	c Gower b Botham		10
*Imran Khan	not out	67	c Randall b Botham		46
†Wasim Bari	b Jackman	23	c Taylor b Willis		7
Abdul Qadir	c Willis b Botham	5	b Jackman		17
Sikander Bakht	c Tavare b Willis	7	c Gatting b Marks		7
Ehteshamuddin	b Botham	0	not out		0
Extras	(B1, LB7, W4, NB3)	15	(LB6, W4, NB7)		17
Total		275			199

ENGLAND

C.J.Tavaré	c sub‡ b Imran	22	c Majid b Imran		33
G.Fowler	b Ehteshamuddin	9	c Wasim b Mudassar		86
M.W.Gatting	lbw b Imran	25	lbw b Imran		25
A.J.Lamb	c Mohsin b Imran	0	lbw b Mudassar		4
D.I.Gower	c sub‡ b Sikander	74	c Wasim b Mudassar		7
I.T.Botham	c sub‡ b Sikander	57	c Majid b Mudassar		4
D.W.Randall	run out	8	lbw b Imran		0
V.J.Marks	b Qadir	7	not out		12
†R.W.Taylor	c Miandad b Imran	18	not out		6
R.D.Jackman	c Mohsin b Imran	11			
*R.G.D.Willis	not out	1			
Extras	(B4, LB10, W2, NB8)	24	(B19, LB16, W1, NB6)		42
Total		256	(7 wickets)		219

ENGLAND	O	M	R	W	O	M	R	W		FALL OF WICKETS			
										P	E	P	E
Willis	26	6	76	3	19	3	55	3	*Wkt*	*1st*	*1st*	*2nd*	*2nd*
Botham	24.5	9	70	4	30	8	74	5	1st	16	15	0	103
Jackman	37	14	74	3	28	11	41	1	2nd	19	67	3	168
Marks	5	0	23	0	2	1	8	1	3rd	119	69	81	172
Gatting	8	2	17	0	2	1	4	0	4th	128	77	85	187
									5th	160	146	108	189
PAKISTAN									6th	168	159	115	189
Imran	25.2	7	49	5	(2) 30.2	8	66	3	7th	207	170	128	199
Ehteshamuddin	14	4	46	1					8th	224	209	169	–
Sikander	24	5	47	2	(1) 20	4	40	0	9th	274	255	199	–
Qadir	22	5	87	1	(3) 8	2	16	0	10th	275	256	199	–
Mudassar	4	1	3	0	(4) 22	7	55	4					

Umpires: D.J.Constant (24) and B.J.Meyer (11).   ‡ (Haroon Rashid)

Close: 1st day – P(1) 255-8 (Imran 49, Sikander 6); 2nd – E(1) 256-9 (Jackman 11, Willis 1); 3rd – E(2) 15-0 (Tavaré 3, Fowler 3); 4th – E(2) 190-6 (Botham 0, Marks 1).

INDIA v SRI LANKA 1982-83 (Only Test)

At Chidambaram Stadium, Chepauk, Madras, on 17, 18, 19, 21, 22 September.
Toss: Sri Lanka.   Result: MATCH DRAWN.
Debuts: India – Arun Lal, R.S.Shukla.

The first official Test between these two countries produced the record aggregate of 1,441 runs for any Test in India. Gavaskar set an unfortunate Test record by losing his ninth consecutive toss. Mendis completed his first Test hundred with a six. He later became the first Sri Lankan to make two separate hundreds in a Test and the first batsman to compile an identical three-figure score in both innings at this level. Doshi's third wicket was the 100th of a Test career which began almost exactly three years earlier on the same ground. Yashpal kept wicket after tea on the first day when Kirmani retired through heat exhaustion, and again on the fourth day when he held the first two catches. Gavaskar's 25th hundred for India came in his first major innings since suffering a fractured shin and formed the basis of the highest total conceded by Sri Lanka to date. A strained neck compelled his demotion in the second innings, but this enabled him to ward off defeat after De Mel had thwarted India's attempt to score 175 runs in 53 minutes and 20 overs. A month later, Warnapura, Goonatillake, Ranasinghe and G.R.A.de Silva were among 14 players effectively banned from all Sri Lankan cricket for life for joining the clandestine Arosa tour of South Africa.

SRI LANKA

*B.Warnapura	c Yashpal b Madan Lal	4		c Yashpal b Kapil Dev	6
†H.M.Goonatillake	c Patil b Kapil Dev	7	(10)	c sub (K.Srikkanth) b Kapil Dev	0
R.L.Dias	c Arun Lal b Doshi	60		c Gavaskar b Shukla	97
L.R.D.Mendis	lbw b Doshi	105		b Shukla	105
A.Ranatunga	c Vengsarkar b Doshi	25		c Kirmani b Doshi	15
R.S.Madugalle	c Madan Lal b Doshi	46		c Patil b Doshi	4
A.N.Ranasinghe	c Arun Lal b Doshi	0		b Kapil Dev	77
D.S.de Silva	c Gavaskar b Madan Lal	49		not out	46
J.R.Ratnayeke	lbw b Kapil Dev	23	(2)	c Yashpal b Kapil Dev	6
A.L.F.de Mel	not out	18	(9)	b Doshi	12
G.R.A.de Silva	c Viswanath b Kapil Dev	0		b Kapil Dev	14
Extras	(B4, LB5)	9		(B4, LB5, W1, NB2)	12
Total		**346**			**394**

INDIA

*S.M.Gavaskar	c De Mel b D.S.de Silva	155	(9)	not out	4
Arun Lal	b De Mel	63		c Dias b De Mel	1
D.B.Vengsarkar	run out	90	(1)	c and b De Mel	5
G.R.Viswanath	c Warnapura b D.S.de Silva	9	(6)	lbw b De Mel	2
S.M.Patil	not out	114	(3)	run out	46
Yashpal Sharma	c Goonatillake b De Mel	17	(5)	not out	31
Kapil Dev	c Goonatillake b Ratnayeke	31	(4)	c Goonatillake b De Mel	30
Madan Lal	not out	37	(7)	c and b D.S.de Silva	9
†S.M.H.Kirmani			(8)	b De Mel	5
R.S.Shukla	did not bat				
D.R.Doshi					
Extras	(B11, LB8, W2, NB29)	50		(LB2)	2
Total	(6 wickets declared)	**566**		(7 wickets)	**135**

INDIA	O	M	R	W	O	M	R	W	FALL OF WICKETS			
Kapil Dev	22.5	2	97	3	24.3	3	110	5		SL	I	SL	I
Madan Lal	16	1	72	2	7	1	43	0	*Wkt*	*1st*	*1st*	*2nd*	*2nd*
Doshi	30	8	85	5	38	4	147	3	1st	11	156	6	3
Patil	2	0	13	0					2nd	11	329	47	16
Shukla	22	4	70	0	(4) 27	5	82	2	3rd	164	347	157	78
SRI LANKA									4th	203	363	198	90
De Mel	29	2	133	2	14	0	68	5	5th	204	403	202	94
Ratnayeke	19	1	75	1	5	0	36	0	6th	204	488	291	125
G.R.A.de Silva	18	2	78	0					7th	281	–	340	130
Warnapura	9	3	27	0					8th	304	–	361	–
D.S.de Silva	48	4	162	2	(3) 9	1	29	1	9th	346	–	362	–
Ranasinghe	7	0	29	0					10th	346	–	394	–
Ranatunga	1	0	12	0									

Umpires: M.V.Gothoskar (10) and Swaroop Kishen (11).

Close: 1st day – SL(1) 311-8 (Ratnayeke 6, De Mel 1); 2nd – I(1) 251-1 (Gavaskar 122, Vengsarkar 39); 3rd – I(1) 398-4 (Patil 30, Yashpal 15); 4th – SL(2) 179-3 (Mendis 59, Ranatunga 6).

PAKISTAN v AUSTRALIA 1982-83 (1st Test)

At National Stadium, Karachi, on 22, 23, 24, 26, 27 September.
Toss: Australia.   Result: PAKISTAN won by 9 wickets.
Debuts: Australia – G.M.Ritchie.

Before lunch on the fifth day Mohsin Khan struck a six to complete Pakistan's third victory against Australia; all three wins had occurred at Karachi where Pakistan remained unbeaten after 19 matches. Tahir Naqqash was on a hat-trick twice during his spell of 4 for 2 in eight balls. Mohsin played defensively to a ball from Thomson and instinctively knocked it away when it rebounded towards his stumps. He was the third batsman to be given out 'handled the ball' during a Test match, following W.R.Endean (*Test No. 435*) and A.M.J.Hilditch (*850*). Crowd disturbances on the third day caused Australia to leave the field on two occasions.

AUSTRALIA

G.M.Wood	c Wasim b Imran	0	c sub (Salim Malik) b Qadir	17
B.M.Laird	run out	32	c Mansoor b Imran	3
J.Dyson	b Qasim	87	b Qadir	6
*K.J.Hughes	c Wasim b Qasim	54	(5) c Wasim b Qadir	14
A.R.Border	not out	55	(4) c sub (Salim Malik) b Qadir	8
G.M.Ritchie	c Haroon b Qadir	4	b Qasim	17
†R.W.Marsh	b Tahir	19	lbw b Imran	32
B.Yardley	c Miandad b Tahir	0	lbw b Qadir	0
R.J.Bright	c Haroon b Tahir	2	not out	32
G.F.Lawson	c Wasim b Tahir	0	run out	11
J.R.Thomson	st Wasim b Qadir	14	c Wasim b Qasim	18
Extras	(B4, LB10, W1, NB2)	17	(B2, LB19)	21
Total		**284**		**179**

PAKISTAN

Mohsin Khan	handled the ball	58	not out	14
Mansoor Akhtar	c Bright b Thomson	32	(3) not out	26
Haroon Rashid	c Laird b Yardley	82		
Javed Miandad	b Lawson	32		
Zaheer Abbas	c Marsh b Lawson	91		
Mudassar Nazar	not out	52	(2) c Border b Thomson	5
*Imran Khan	c Yardley b Bright	1		
Tahir Naqqash	st Marsh b Bright	15		
†Wasim Bari	b Bright	0		
Abdul Qadir	run out	29		
Iqbal Qasim	not out	2		
Extras	(B4, LB8, W1, NB12)	25	(NB2)	2
Total	(9 wickets declared)	**419**	(1 wicket)	**47**

PAKISTAN	O	M	R	W	O	M	R	W
Imran	23	3	38	1	12	5	17	2
Tahir	16	3	61	4	7	3	17	0
Mudassar	13	0	33	0				
Qadir	21.4	1	80	2	26	7	76	5
Qasim	26	10	55	2	(3) 21.5	6	48	2

AUSTRALIA	O	M	R	W	O	M	R	W
Thomson	29	5	103	1	3	1	16	1
Lawson	39	10	93	2				
Bright	36	8	96	3	(2) 5	0	14	0
Yardley	23	2	98	1	(3) 3	1	9	0
Border	1	0	4	0				
Hughes					(4) 0.1	0	6	0

FALL OF WICKETS

Wkt	A 1st	P 1st	A 2nd	P 2nd
1st	0	43	10	5
2nd	71	168	29	–
3rd	169	188	32	–
4th	202	277	45	–
5th	211	328	72	–
6th	249	329	72	–
7th	249	351	73	–
8th	255	353	137	–
9th	255	404	160	–
10th	284	–	179	–

Umpires: Khizer Hayat (6) and Mahboob Shah (8).

Close: 1st day – A(1) 218-5 (Border 21, Marsh 5); 2nd – P(1) 168-2 (Haroon 65); 3rd – P(1) 330-6 (Mudassar 12, Tahir 0); 4th – A(2) 123-7 (Marsh 26, Bright 16).

PAKISTAN v AUSTRALIA 1982-83 (2nd Test)

At Iqbal Stadium, Faisalabad, on 30 September, 1, 2, 4, 5 October.
Toss: Pakistan.   Result: PAKISTAN won by an innings and 3 runs.
Debuts: None.

For the first time Pakistan won successive Tests in a rubber against Australia. Abdul Qadir returned the best innings (7 for 142) and match (11 for 218) analyses of his career to date. Mansoor Akhtar and Zaheer Abbas added 155 to set a Pakistan fourth-wicket record against Australia. Ritchie batted 295 minutes and hit three sixes and nine fours, including one off a stationary ball which had slipped from the grasp of the bowler (Qadir). Javed Akhtar and Shakoor Rana had been appointed as umpires for this match but the officials from the first Test were retained at the request of the Australian management.

PAKISTAN

Mohsin Khan	c Marsh b Lawson	76
Mudassar Nazar	c Hughes b Border	79
Mansoor Akhtar	c Marsh b Lawson	111
Javed Miandad	c Laird b Lawson	6
Zaheer Abbas	b Sleep	126
Haroon Rashid	c Laird b Lawson	51
*Imran Khan	not out	24
Tahir Naqqash	not out	15
†Wasim Bari		
Abdul Qadir	} did not bat	
Iqbal Qasim		
Extras	(B4, LB1, NB8)	13
Total	**(6 wickets declared)**	**501**

AUSTRALIA

B.M.Laird	lbw b Qadir	8		c Mudassar b Qadir	60
G.M.Wood	c Wasim b Mudassar	49	(7)	c Wasim b Qasim	22
J.Dyson	c Mudassar b Qasim	23	(2)	c Qasim b Qadir	43
A.R.Border	c Miandad b Imran	9	(3)	c Haroon b Qadir	31
*K.J.Hughes	c Imran b Qadir	11	(4)	lbw b Qadir	7
G.M.Ritchie	run out	34	(5)	not out	106
P.R.Sleep	lbw b Imran	0	(6)	c Mohsin b Qadir	29
†R.W.Marsh	b Qadir	0		run out	8
R.J.Bright	c Haroon b Qadir	0		c sub (Salim Malik) b Qasim	0
G.F.Lawson	c Zaheer b Qasim	14		lbw b Qadir	0
J.R.Thomson	not out	1		st Wasim b Qadir	11
Extras	(B8, LB6, W2, NB3)	19		(LB7, W1, NB5)	13
Total		**168**			**330**

AUSTRALIA	O	M	R	W	O	M	R	W
Thomson	23	5	79	0				
Lawson	33	6	97	4				
Sleep	36	3	158	1				
Bright	41	15	107	0				
Border	11	3	47	1				
PAKISTAN								
Tahir	15	4	21	0	9	1	25	0
Imran	14	6	16	2	10	5	20	0
Qadir	42	14	76	4	50.5	12	142	7
Qasim	24.5	11	28	2	46	18	97	2
Mudassar	7	2	8	1	9	3	26	0
Zaheer					3	0	5	0
Miandad					1	0	2	0

FALL OF WICKETS

Wkt	P 1st	A 1st	A 2nd
1st	123	20	73
2nd	181	82	125
3rd	201	96	133
4th	356	113	162
5th	428	123	218
6th	482	123	290
7th	–	124	309
8th	–	124	309
9th	–	167	310
10th	–	168	330

Umpires: Khizer Hayat (7) and Mahboob Shah (9).

Close: 1st day – P(1) 232-3 (Mansoor 44, Zaheer 19); 2nd – P(1) 501-6 (Imran 24, Tahir 15); 3rd – A(1) 141-8 (Ritchie 23, Lawson 3); 4th – A(2) 176-4 (Ritchie 21, Sleep 7).

PAKISTAN v AUSTRALIA 1982-83 (3rd Test)

At Gaddafi Stadium, Lahore, on 14, 15, 16, 18, 19 October.
Toss: Pakistan.   Result: PAKISTAN won by 9 wickets.
Debuts: Pakistan – Jalaluddin.

Pakistan won three Tests in a rubber for the first time and gained their fourth victory in successive matches in this series. For only the second time this century Australia lost every Test in a rubber, the previous occasion being their 4-0 defeat in South Africa in 1969-70. Not once did they succeed in bowling out the opposition. Lawson and Alderman equalled Australia's tenth-wicket record against Pakistan by adding 52. Abdul Qadir's 22 wickets in the rubber remains the Pakistan record against Australia.

AUSTRALIA

G.M.Wood	c Miandad b Qadir	85	(2)	c Mudassar b Jalaluddin	30
B.M.Laird	lbw b Qadir	28	(1)	lbw b Tahir	6
J.Dyson	b Jalaluddin	10		lbw b Tahir	51
A.R.Border	lbw b Imran	9		st Wasim b Qadir	6
*K.J.Hughes	b Tahir	29		st Wasim b Qadir	39
G.M.Ritchie	lbw b Imran	26		lbw b Imran	18
†R.W.Marsh	c sub (Iqbal Sikander) b Imran	1		c Mudassar b Jalaluddin	12
B.Yardley	c Haroon b Jalaluddin	40		b Imran	21
G.F.Lawson	not out	57		c sub (Iqbal Sikander) b Imran	9
J.R.Thomson	lbw b Jalaluddin	0		not out	5
T.M.Alderman	b Imran	7		c Zaheer b Imran	0
Extras	(B1, LB13, W5, NB5)	24		(B4, LB5, NB8)	17
Total		**316**			**214**

PAKISTAN

Mohsin Khan	b Border	135		lbw b Lawson	14
Mudassar Nazar	lbw b Lawson	23		not out	39
Abdul Qadir	c Laird b Yardley	1			
Mansoor Akhtar	lbw b Lawson	12	(3)	not out	2
Javed Miandad	c Hughes b Alderman	138			
Zaheer Abbas	c Yardley b Alderman	52			
Haroon Rashid	c Ritchie b Thomson	15			
*Imran Khan	not out	39			
Tahir Naqqash	not out	7			
†Wasim Bari	} did not bat				
Jalaluddin					
Extras	(B3, LB13, W2, NB27)	45		(B4, LB5)	9
Total	(7 wickets declared)	**467**		(1 wicket)	**64**

PAKISTAN	O	M	R	W		O	M	R	W		FALL OF WICKETS			
Imran	24.2	10	45	4		20	6	35	4		A	P	A	P
Tahir	18	4	65	1		16	3	39	2	*Wkt*	*1st*	*1st*	*2nd*	*2nd*
Mudassar	6	1	17	0	(5)	2	0	5	0	1st	85	92	21	55
Jalaluddin	19	4	77	3		16	8	15	2	2nd	120	93	55	–
Qadir	37	7	86	2	(3)	35	7	102	2	3rd	140	119	64	–
Zaheer	2	0	2	0		1	0	1	0	4th	140	269	138	–
										5th	197	392	157	–
										6th	202	402	170	–
AUSTRALIA										7th	203	442	189	–
Thomson	19	1	73	1		5	0	24	0	8th	264	–	203	–
Lawson	35	4	91	2		7	1	21	1	9th	264	–	214	–
Alderman	34	4	144	2		3	0	10	0	10th	316	–	214	–
Yardley	27	6	102	1										
Border	4	1	12	1										

Umpires: Javed Akhtar (5) and Shakoor Rana (10).

Close: 1st day – A(1) 188-4 (Hughes 26, Ritchie 19); 2nd – P(1) 95-2 (Mohsin 52, Mansoor 0); 3rd – P(1) 318-4 (Miandad 95, Zaheer 19); 4th – A(2) 66-3 (Dyson 20, Hughes 0).

AUSTRALIA v ENGLAND 1982-83 (1st Test)

At W.A.C.A. Ground, Perth, on 12, 13, 14, 16, 17 November.
Toss: Australia.   Result: MATCH DRAWN.
Debuts: England – N.G.Cowans.

This match, which produced only the second draw in ten Tests at Perth, was marred on the second afternoon by an invasion of the playing area by some two dozen spectators. Alderman, cuffed from behind, gave chase and, in bringing down his assailant with a flying tackle, dislocated his shoulder so severely that the injury ended his first-class season. Chappell led his team from the field for 14 minutes and 26 arrests were made. Cowans the 500th player to represent England in 586 official Tests. In his 55th match, Botham scored his 3,000th run and took his 250th wicket to achieve a (then) unique Test double. Yardley took his 100th wicket in 28 Tests. Tavaré spent 90 minutes with his score 66 in the first innings and took 63 minutes to score his first run in the second, thus emulating the previously unique feat he first achieved in *Test No. 932*. Randall's third Test century in Australia left the home side 33 overs in which to score 346.

ENGLAND

Batsman	Dismissal 1	R1	Dismissal 2	R2
G.Cook	c Dyson b Lillee	1	c Border b Lawson	7
C.J.Tavaré	c Hughes b Yardley	89	c Chappell b Yardley	9
D.I.Gower	c Dyson b Alderman	72	lbw b Lillee	28
A.J.Lamb	c Marsh b Yardley	46	c Marsh b Lawson	56
I.T.Botham	c Marsh b Lawson	12	b Lawson	0
D.W.Randall	c Wood b Yardley	78	b Lawson	115
G.Miller	c Marsh b Lillee	30	(8) c Marsh b Yardley	0
D.R.Pringle	b Lillee	0	(9) not out	47
†R.W.Taylor	not out	29	(7) b Yardley	31
*R.G.D.Willis	c Lillee b Yardley	26	b Lawson	0
N.G.Cowans	b Yardley	4	lbw b Chappell	36
Extras	(B7, LB9, W2, NB6)	24	(B5, LB11, W2, NB11)	29
Total		**411**		**358**

AUSTRALIA

Batsman	Dismissal 1	R1	Dismissal 2	R2
G.M.Wood	c and b Willis	29	c Taylor b Willis	0
J.Dyson	lbw b Miller	52	c Cowans b Willis	12
A.R.Border	c Taylor b Botham	8	not out	32
*G.S.Chappell	c Lamb b Willis	117	not out	22
K.J.Hughes	c Willis b Miller	62		
D.W.Hookes	lbw b Miller	56		
†R.W.Marsh	c Cook b Botham	0		
G.F.Lawson	b Miller	50		
B.Yardley	c Lamb b Willis	17		
D.K.Lillee	not out	2		
T.M.Alderman	did not bat			
Extras	(B4, LB1, W1, NB25)	31	(LB1, NB6)	7
Total	(9 wickets declared)	**424**	(2 wickets)	**73**

AUSTRALIA	O	M	R	W		O	M	R	W		FALL OF WICKETS			
Lillee	38	13	96	3		33	12	89	1			E	A	E	A
Alderman	43	15	84	1						Wkt	1st	1st	2nd	2nd
Lawson	29	6	89	1	(2)	32	5	108	5	1st	14	63	10	2
Chappell	3	0	11	0	(5)	2.3	1	8	1	2nd	109	76	51	22
Yardley	42.4	15	107	5	(3)	41	10	101	3	3rd	189	123	77	–
Border					(4)	7	2	21	0	4th	204	264	80	–
Hookes					(6)	1	0	2	0	5th	304	311	151	–
										6th	323	311	228	–
ENGLAND										7th	342	374	242	–
Willis	31.5	4	95	3		6	1	23	2	8th	357	414	292	–
Botham	40	10	121	2		6	1	17	0	9th	406	424	292	–
Cowans	13	2	54	0		3	1	15	0	10th	411	–	358	–
Pringle	10	1	37	0	(5)	2	0	3	0					
Miller	33	11	70	4	(4)	4	3	8	0					
Cook	4	2	16	0										
Lamb					(6)	1	1	0	0					

Umpires: A.R.Crafter (11) and M.W.Johnson (9).

Close: 1st day – E(1) 242-4 (Tavaré 66, Randall 32); 2nd – A(1) 30-0 (Wood 12, Dyson 12); 3rd – A(1) 333-6 (Hookes 35, Lawson 4); 4th – E(2) 163-5 (Randall 45, Taylor 3).

AUSTRALIA v ENGLAND 1982-83 (2nd Test)

At Woolloongabba, Brisbane, on 26, 27, 28, 30 November, 1 December.
Toss: Australia.   Result: AUSTRALIA won by 7 wickets.
Debuts: Australia – C.G.Rackemann, K.C.Wessels.

Queensland, still to win a Sheffield Shield title after 50 attempts, contributed five of Australia's team for the first time. One of them, Wessels, the first South African-born player to represent Australia, became the 13th batsman to score a century in his first Test for that country and set a record aggregate for such a debut. Marsh reached the unique total of 300 catches, set an Ashes record by holding six in an innings, and equalled G.R.A.Langley's Australian record of nine in a match (*Test No. 426*). Lawson was the first bowler to take 11 wickets in an Ashes Test at Brisbane. Gower (3,000 runs), Border (1,000 against England) and Randall (1,000 against Australia), achieved notable batting aggregates. Australia were the first side to hold 19 catches in a Test. They also established a national record by conceding 52 extras in an innings and equalled the (then) world record (*Test No. 733*) with 35 no-balls. Dyson retired at 20 with a shoulder bruised when he ducked into a ball from Willis. Miller and Yardley completed overs when Hemmings and Rackemann respectively retired injured. Australia won with 16.1 overs to spare.

ENGLAND

C.J.Tavaré	c Hughes b Lawson	1		c Marsh b Lawson	13
G.Fowler	c Yardley b Lawson	7		c Marsh b Thomson	83
D.I.Gower	c Wessels b Lawson	18		c Marsh b Thomson	34
A.J.Lamb	c Marsh b Lawson	72		c Wessels b Thomson	12
I.T.Botham	c Rackemann b Yardley	40	(6)	c Marsh b Thomson	15
D.W.Randall	c Lawson b Rackemann	37	(5)	c Yardley b Thomson	4
G.Miller	c Marsh b Lawson	0		c Marsh b Lawson	60
R.W.Taylor	c Lawson b Rackemann	1		c Hookes b Lawson	3
E.E.Hemmings	not out	15		b Lawson	18
R.G.D.Willis	c Thomson b Yardley	1		not out	10
N.G.Cowans	c Marsh b Lawson	10		c Marsh b Lawson	5
Extras	(LB2, W1, NB14)	17		(B8, LB8, W1, NB35)	52
Total		**219**			**309**

AUSTRALIA

K.C.Wessels	b Willis	162		b Hemmings	46
J.Dyson	b Botham	1		retired hurt	4
A.R.Border	c Randall b Willis	0		c Botham b Hemmings	15
G.S.Chappell	run out	53		c Lamb b Cowans	8
K.J.Hughes	c Taylor b Botham	0		not out	39
D.W.Hookes	c Taylor b Miller	28		not out	66
R.W.Marsh	c Taylor b Botham	11			
B.Yardley	c Tavaré b Willis	53			
G.F.Lawson	c Hemmings b Willis	6			
C.G.Rackemann	b Willis	4			
J.R.Thomson	not out	5			
Extras	(B2, LB8, NB8)	18		(B2, LB5, NB5)	12
Total		**341**		**(3 wickets)**	**190**

AUSTRALIA	O	M	R	W	O	M	R	W		FALL OF WICKETS			
										E	A	E	A
Lawson	18.3	4	47	6	35.3	11	87	5	Wkt	1st	1st	2nd	2nd
Rackemann	21	8	61	2	12.2	3	35	0	1st	8	4	54	60
Thomson	8	0	43	0	31	6	73	5	2nd	13	11	144	77
Yardley	17	5	51	2	40.4	21	50	0	3rd	63	94	165	83
Chappell					6	2	8	0	4th	141	99	169	–
Hookes					2	0	4	0	5th	152	130	194	–
									6th	152	171	201	–
ENGLAND									7th	178	271	226	–
Willis	29.4	3	66	5	4	1	24	0	8th	191	310	285	–
Botham	22	1	105	3	15.5	1	70	0	9th	195	332	295	–
Cowans	6	0	36	0	(4) 9	1	31	1	10th	219	341	309	–
Hemmings	33.3	6	81	0	(3) 29	9	43	2					
Miller	19.3	4	35	1	3	0	10	0					

Umpires: R.C.Bailhache (24) and M.W.Johnson (10).

Close: 1st day – E(1) 219-9 (Hemmings 15, Cowans 10); 2nd – A(1) 246-6 (Wessels 105, Yardley 35); 3rd – E(2) 71-1 (Fowler 31, Gower 5); 4th – E(2) 279-7 (Miller 50, Hemmings 18).

AUSTRALIA v ENGLAND 1982-83 (3rd Test)

At Adelaide Oval on 10, 11, 12, 14, 15 December.
Toss: England.   Result: AUSTRALIA won by 8 wickets.
Debuts: None.

Willis became the third England captain to invite Australia to bat first at Adelaide. His decision met the same fate as those of P.B.H.May in 1958-59 and M.H.Denness in 1974-75. Taylor made his 50th dismissal against Australia when he caught Wessels in the first innings; he joined the select company of A.F.A.Lilley, T.G.Evans and A.P.E.Knott. Chappell's hundred was his first in Tests at his birthplace, his 22nd for Australia, and the last of his nine against England. He became the third Australian after C.Hill and D.G.Bradman to score 2,500 runs in this series. Botham scored his 1,000th run against Australia. Both he and Gower completed 1,000 runs in Test cricket during 1982. Australia won after 85 minutes of play on the fifth day.

AUSTRALIA

K.C.Wessels	c Taylor b Botham	44	(2) c Taylor b Botham		1
J.Dyson	c Taylor b Botham	44	(1) not out		37
*G.S.Chappell	c Gower b Willis	115	(4) not out		26
K.J.Hughes	run out	88			
G.F.Lawson	c Botham b Willis	2	(3) c Randall b Willis		14
A.R.Border	c Taylor b Pringle	26			
D.W.Hookes	c Botham b Hemmings	37			
†R.W.Marsh	c Hemmings b Pringle	3			
B.Yardley	c Gower b Botham	38			
R.M.Hogg	not out	14			
J.R.Thomson	c and b Botham	3			
Extras	(LB6, NB18)	24	(NB5)		5
Total		**438**	(2 wickets)		**83**

ENGLAND

C.J.Tavaré	c Marsh b Hogg	1	c Wessels b Thomson	0
G.Fowler	c Marsh b Lawson	11	c Marsh b Lawson	37
D.I.Gower	c Marsh b Lawson	60	b Hogg	114
A.J.Lamb	c Marsh b Lawson	82	c Chappell b Yardley	8
I.T.Botham	c Wessels b Thomson	35	c Dyson b Yardley	58
D.W.Randall	b Lawson	0	c Marsh b Lawson	17
G.Miller	c Yardley b Hogg	7	lbw b Lawson	17
†R.W.Taylor	c Chappell b Yardley	2	(9) not out	3
D.R.Pringle	not out	1	(8) c Marsh b Thomson	9
E.E.Hemmings	b Thomson	0	c Wessels b Lawson	0
*R.G.D.Willis	b Thomson	1	c Marsh b Lawson	10
Extras	(LB5, NB11)	16	(B7, LB6, W3, NB15)	31
Total		**216**		**304**

ENGLAND	O	M	R	W		O	M	R	W		FALL OF WICKETS			
Willis	25	8	76	2		8	1	17	1			A	E	E	A
Botham	36.5	5	112	4		10	2	45	1	Wkt	1st	1st	2nd	2nd
Pringle	33	5	97	2	(4) 1.5	0	11	0	1st	76	1	11	3
Miller	14	2	33	0						2nd	138	21	90	37
Hemmings	48	17	96	1	(3) 4	1	5	0	3rd	264	140	118	–
										4th	270	181	236	–
										5th	315	181	247	–
AUSTRALIA										6th	355	194	272	–
Lawson	18	4	56	4		24	6	66	5	7th	359	199	277	–
Hogg	14	2	41	2	(4) 19	5	53	1	8th	391	213	289	–
Thomson	14.5	3	51	3	(2) 13	3	41	2	9th	430	213	290	–
Yardley	21	7	52	1	(3) 37	12	90	2	10th	438	216	304	–
Border						8	2	14	0					
Hookes						3	1	9	0					

Umpires: R.A.French (9) and M.W.Johnson (11).

Close: 1st day – A(1) 265-3 (Hughes 51, Lawson 0); 2nd – E(1) 66-2 (Gower 26, Lamb 23); 3rd – E(2) 90-1 (Fowler 37, Gower 43); 4th – A(2) 3-1 (Dyson 1, Lawson 0).

AUSTRALIA v ENGLAND 1982-83 (4th Test)

At Melbourne Cricket Ground on 26, 27, 28, 29, 30 December.
Toss: Australia.   Result: ENGLAND won by 3 runs.
Debuts: None.

England's victory equalled the (then) narrowest runs margin in Test cricket, established at Old Trafford in 1902 (*Test No. 73*). The first Test match to be contested on the relaid portion of the MCG square was the 250th of this series (Australia 95 wins; England 83 wins). Melbourne became the first ground to stage 75 Tests. For the first time in any rubber, the side winning the toss elected to field in each of the first four matches. Botham's vital last wicket completed his double of 100 wickets and 1,000 runs against Australia in only 22 matches. He was the fourth to achieve the double in this series after M.A.Noble (29 Tests) and G.Giffen (30) for Australia, and W.Rhodes (37) for England. Marsh, the first Australian to appear in 90 Tests, took his total of dismissals in the rubber to 27, and surpassed the world record set in South Africa in 1961-62 by J.H.B.Waite in five matches against New Zealand. During their last-wicket partnership of 70 in 128 minutes, Border and Thomson declined to run 29 comfortable singles. For the first time in any Test in which all 40 wickets fell, the four innings totals were within a range of ten runs. The match also provided the only instance in Test cricket of sides being all out at close of play on three consecutive days.

ENGLAND

G.Cook	c Chappell b Thomson	10	c Yardley b Thomson	26
G.Fowler	c Chappell b Hogg	4	b Hogg	65
C.J.Tavaré	c Yardley b Thomson	89	b Hogg	0
D.I.Gower	c Marsh b Hogg	18	c Marsh b Lawson	3
A.J.Lamb	c Dyson b Yardley	83	c Marsh b Hogg	26
I.T.Botham	c Wessels b Yardley	27	c Chappell b Thomson	46
G.Miller	c Border b Yardley	10	lbw b Lawson	14
D.R.Pringle	c Wessels b Hogg	9	c Marsh b Lawson	42
*R.W.Taylor	c Marsh b Yardley	1	lbw b Thomson	37
*R.G.D.Willis	not out	6	not out	8
N.G.Cowans	c Lawson b Hogg	3	b Lawson	10
Extras	(B3, LB6, W3, NB12)	24	(B2, LB9, NB6)	17
Total		**284**		**294**

AUSTRALIA

K.C.Wessels	b Willis	47	(2)	b Cowans	14
J.Dyson	lbw b Cowans	21	(1)	c Tavaré b Botham	31
*G.S.Chappell	c Lamb b Cowans	0		c sub (I.J.Gould) b Cowans	2
K.J.Hughes	b Willis	66		c Taylor b Miller	48
A.R.Border	b Botham	2	(6)	not out	62
D.W.Hookes	c Taylor b Pringle	53	(5)	c Willis b Cowans	68
*R.W.Marsh	b Willis	53		lbw b Cowans	13
B.Yardley	b Miller	9		b Cowans	0
G.F.Lawson	c Fowler b Miller	0		c Cowans b Pringle	7
R.M.Hogg	not out	8		lbw b Cowans	4
J.R.Thomson	b Miller	1		c Miller b Botham	21
Extras	(LB8, NB19)	27		(B5, LB9, W1, NB3)	18
Total		**287**			**288**

AUSTRALIA	O	M	R	W		O	M	R	W	FALL OF WICKETS				
											E	A	E	A
Lawson	17	6	48	0		21.4	6	66	4	Wkt	1st	1st	2nd	2nd
Hogg	23.3	6	69	4		22	5	64	3	1st	11	55	40	37
Yardley	27	9	89	4	(4)	15	2	67	0	2nd	25	55	41	39
Thomson	13	2	49	2	(3)	21	3	74	3	3rd	56	83	45	71
Chappell	1	0	5	0		1	0	6	0	4th	217	89	128	171
										5th	227	180	129	173
ENGLAND										6th	259	261	160	190
Willis	15	2	38	3		17	0	57	0	7th	262	276	201	190
Botham	18	3	69	1	(3)	25.1	4	80	2	8th	268	276	262	202
Cowans	16	0	69	2	(2)	26	6	77	6	9th	278	278	280	218
Pringle	15	2	40	1		12	4	26	1	10th	284	287	294	288
Miller	15	5	44	3		16	6	30	1					

Umpires: A.R.Crafter (12) and R.V.Whitehead (4).

Close: 1st day – E(1) 284 all out; 2nd – A(1) 287 all out; 3rd – E(2) 294 all out; 4th – A(2) 255-9 (Border 44, Thomson 8).

AUSTRALIA v ENGLAND 1982-83 (5th Test)

At Sydney Cricket Ground on 2, 3, 4, 6, 7 January.
Toss: Australia.   Result: MATCH DRAWN.
Debuts: None.

This result enabled Australia to regain the Ashes which they lost in England in 1977. At the end of the first over and before a run had been scored, Willis appeared to run out Dyson. Umpire Johnson gave Dyson the benefit of the doubt, although film confirmed the batsman to have been at least 18 inches out of his ground. Dyson eventually provided Taylor's 150th dismissal in Test cricket. Hemmings (226 minutes) was five runs from becoming the fourth 'night-watchman' to score a hundred at this level. He perished to Marsh's 28th catch of the rubber. Taylor's 18th run was his 1,000th for England and completed his wicket-keeper's double. This was only the fourth drawn Test involving these countries in 46 matches at Sydney.

AUSTRALIA

K.C.Wessels	c Willis b Botham	19	(2) lbw b Botham		53
J.Dyson	c Taylor b Hemmings	79	(1) c Gower b Willis		2
*G.S.Chappell	lbw b Willis	35	c Randall b Hemmings		11
K.J.Hughes	c Cowans b Botham	29	c Botham b Hemmings		137
D.W.Hookes	c Botham b Hemmings	17	lbw b Miller		19
A.R.Border	c Miller b Hemmings	89	c Botham b Cowans		83
†R.W.Marsh	c and b Miller	3	c Taylor b Miller		41
B.Yardley	b Cowans	24	c Botham b Hemmings		0
G.F.Lawson	c and b Botham	6	not out		13
J.R.Thomson	c Lamb b Botham	0	c Gower b Miller		12
R.M.Hogg	not out	0	run out		0
Extras	(B3, LB8, W2)	13	(LB7, NB4)		11
Total		**314**			**382**

ENGLAND

G.Cook	c Chappell b Hogg	8	lbw b Lawson		2
C.J.Tavaré	b Lawson	0	lbw b Yardley		16
D.I.Gower	c Chappell b Lawson	70	(4) c Hookes b Yardley		24
A.J.Lamb	b Lawson	0	(5) c and b Yardley		29
D.W.Randall	b Thomson	70	(6) b Thomson		44
I.T.Botham	c Wessels b Thomson	5	(7) lbw b Thomson		32
G.Miller	lbw b Thomson	34	(8) not out		21
†R.W.Taylor	lbw b Thomson	0	(9) not out		28
E.E.Hemmings	c Border b Yardley	29	(3) c Marsh b Yardley		95
*R.G.D.Willis	c Border b Thomson	1			
N.G.Cowans	not out	0			
Extras	(B4, LB4, NB12)	20	(B1, LB10, W1, NB11)		23
Total		**237**	(7 wickets)		**314**

ENGLAND	O	M	R	W	O	M	R	W
Willis	20	6	57	1	10	2	33	1
Cowans	21	3	67	1	13	1	47	1
Botham	30	8	75	4	(5) 10	0	35	1
Hemmings	27	10	68	3	(3) 47	16	116	3
Miller	17	7	34	1	(4) 49.3	12	133	3
Cook					2	1	7	0

AUSTRALIA	O	M	R	W	O	M	R	W
Lawson	20	2	70	3	15	1	50	1
Hogg	16	2	50	1	13	6	25	0
Thomson	14.5	2	50	5	(4) 12	3	30	2
Yardley	14	4	47	1	(3) 37	6	139	4
Border					16	3	36	0
Hookes					2	1	5	0
Chappell					1	0	6	0

FALL OF WICKETS

	A	E	A	E
Wkt	1st	1st	2nd	2nd
1st	39	8	23	3
2nd	96	23	38	55
3rd	150	24	82	104
4th	173	146	113	155
5th	210	163	262	196
6th	219	169	350	260
7th	262	170	357	261
8th	283	220	358	–
9th	291	232	382	–
10th	314	237	382	–

Umpires: R.A.French (10) and M.W.Johnson (12).

Close: 1st day – A(1) 138-2 (Dyson 58, Hughes 20); 2nd – E(1) 76-3 (Gower 38, Randall 21); 3rd – A(2) 90-3 (Hughes 17, Hookes 5); 4th – E(2) 8-1 (Tavaré 1, Hemmings 4).

PAKISTAN v INDIA 1982-83 (1st Test)

At Gaddafi Stadium, Lahore, on 10, 11, 12, 14, 15 December.
Toss: India.   Result: MATCH DRAWN.
Debuts. None.

Zaheer Abbas (334 minutes, 254 balls, two sixes and 23 fours) emulated G.Boycott (*Test No. 807*) by scoring his 100th first-class hundred in a Test match; he was the 20th batsman to reach that mark. Gavaskar became the fourth batsman to score 7,000 runs in Test cricket and the first to complete 1,000 in this series. Amarnath took 383 minutes to reach his hundred. Patil's 68 came from 56 balls and included 50 in boundaries, 20 of his runs coming off an over from Jalaluddin: 446420. Mohsin Khan became the first Pakistan batsman to amass 1,000 runs in Tests during a calendar year, 463 of them being scored at Lahore. Rain and bad light caused a total of 235 minutes to be lost.

PAKISTAN

Mohsin Khan	c Amarnath b Madan Lal	94	not out		101
Mudassar Nazar	c Gavaskar b Kapil Dev	50	c Arun Lal b Doshi		17
Mansoor Akhtar	c Gavaskar b Kapil Dev	3	not out		14
Javed Miandad	c Gavaskar b Madan Lal	17			
Zaheer Abbas	b Doshi	215			
Salim Malik	b Madan Lal	6			
*Imran Khan	c Madan Lal b Doshi	45			
†Wasim Bari	c Arun Lal b Doshi	12			
Tahir Naqqash	st Kirmani b Doshi	20			
Sarfraz Nawaz	c Amarnath b Doshi	18			
Jalaluddin	not out	1			
Extras	(LB3, NB1)	4	(LB3)		3
Total		**485**	(1 wicket)		**135**

INDIA

*S.M.Gavaskar	c Wasim b Sarfraz	83	
Arun Lal	c Mudassar b Imran	51	
D.B.Vengsarkar	c Mudassar b Imran	3	
G.R.Viswanath	c Wasim b Imran	1	
M.Amarnath	not out	109	
S.M.Patil	run out	68	
Kapil Dev	c Wasim b Sarfraz	9	
R.J.Shastri	lbw b Jalaluddin	7	
†S.M.H.Kirmani	c Wasim b Jalaluddin	10	
Madan Lal	c Salim b Sarfraz	7	
D.R.Doshi	b Sarfraz	0	
Extras	(B2, LB11, NB18)	31	
Total		**379**	

INDIA	O	M	R	W	O	M	R	W	FALL OF WICKETS			
Kapil Dev	39	3	149	2	8	2	27	0		P	I	P
Madan Lal	27	2	101	3	5	1	10	0	Wkt	1st	1st	2nd
Amarnath	23	5	60	0	3	1	5	0	1st	85	105	55
Doshi	32.5	6	90	5	(5) 15	2	57	1	2nd	100	111	–
Shastri	22	3	81	0	(4) 14	1	33	0	3rd	126	123	–
Gavaskar					1	1	0	0	4th	238	188	–
									5th	250	294	–
									6th	367	305	–
PAKISTAN									7th	438	322	–
Imran	27	8	68	3					8th	447	348	–
Sarfraz	31.5	11	63	4					9th	478	375	–
Jalaluddin	34	10	93	2					10th	485	379	–
Tahir	29	6	114	0								
Mudassar	3	1	10	0								

Umpires: Amanullah Khan (10) and Mahboob Shah (10).

Close: 1st day – P(1) 170-3 (Mohsin 72, Zaheer 25); 2nd – P(1) 485 all out; 3rd – I(1) 87-0 (Gavaskar 38, Arun Lal 43); 4th – I(1) 306-6 (Amarnath 63, Shastri 1).

PAKISTAN v INDIA 1982-83 (2nd Test)

At National Stadium, Karachi, on 23, 24, 25, 27 December.
Toss: Pakistan.   Result: PAKISTAN won by an innings and 86 runs.
Debuts: India – Maninder Singh.

The first Test match to be played on a recently relaid square produced an impressive victory for Pakistan after only 78 minutes' play on the fourth day. At 17 years 193 days, slow left-arm bowler Maninder Singh became the youngest player to represent India until L.Sivaramakrishnan in *Test No. 953*. Zaheer Abbas and Mudassar Nazar shared a series record fifth-wicket partnership of 213, Zaheer becoming the first Pakistan batsman to complete 1,000 runs against India. Vengsarkar took his aggregate from 45 Tests past 3,000 runs. Kapil Dev's 73 was scored off 54 balls and included 12 fours and a six; his 50 off just 30 deliveries is the fastest on record in Test cricket in terms of balls received. Imran Khan took his 200th wicket in 45 Tests when he bowled Viswanath and became the first to achieve this tally for Pakistan. He ended the match by taking five wickets for three runs with his last 25 balls, finishing with Pakistan's best innings analysis against India and the record for any Test at Karachi.

INDIA

*S.M.Gavaskar	run out	8	b Imran		42
Arun Lal	lbw b Sarfraz	35	lbw b Qadir		11
D.B.Vengsarkar	c Mohsin b Imran	0	c Wasim b Imran		79
G.R.Viswanath	c Wasim b Qadir	24	b Imran		0
M.Amarnath	lbw b Imran	5	lbw b Imran		3
S.M.Patil	c Miandad b Qadir	4	b Imran		0
Kapil Dev	c and b Sarfraz	73	(8) b Imran		1
†S.M.H.Kirmani	c Mohsin b Qadir	11	(7) c Salim b Qadir		1
Madan Lal	not out	3	not out		52
Maninder Singh	lbw b Qadir	0	lbw b Imran		0
D.R.Doshi	b Imran	0	b Imran		0
Extras	(LB4, NB2)	6	(B1, LB3, W1, NB3)		8
Total		**169**			**197**

PAKISTAN

Mohsin Khan	c Amarnath b Madan Lal	12
Mansoor Akhtar	c Kirmani b Madan Lal	0
Salim Malik	c Kirmani b Madan Lal	3
Javed Miandad	b Amarnath	39
Zaheer Abbas	lbw b Kapil Dev	186
Mudassar Nazar	c Kirmani b Kapil Dev	119
*Imran Khan	c Amarnath b Kapil Dev	33
†Wasim Bari	c Arun Lal b Doshi	30
Abdul Qadir	b Kapil Dev	0
Sarfraz Nawaz	lbw b Kapil Dev	13
Jalaluddin	not out	0
Extras	(B2, LB6, W2, NB7)	17
Total		**452**

PAKISTAN	O	M	R	W	O	M	R	W		FALL OF WICKETS		
Imran	12.1	6	19	3	20.1	4	60	8		I	P	I
Jalaluddin	10	2	28	0	7	2	31	0	*Wkt*	*1st*	*1st*	*2nd*
Sarfraz	16	2	49	2	10	2	23	0	1st	10	6	28
Qadir	15	3	67	4	23	3	75	2	2nd	10	15	102
									3rd	48	18	108
INDIA									4th	55	128	112
Kapil Dev	28.5	3	102	5					5th	70	341	112
Madan Lal	23	1	129	3					6th	130	397	113
Maninder Singh	23	2	67	0					7th	165	427	114
Amarnath	17	1	69	1					8th	168	427	197
Doshi	18	1	68	1					9th	168	452	197
									10th	169	452	197

Umpires: Khizer Hayat (8) and Shakoor Rana (11).

Close: 1st day – P(1) 57-3 (Miandad 8, Zaheer 34); 2nd – P(1) 349-5 (Mudassar 94, Imran 4); 3rd – I(2) 118-7 (Vengsarkar 53, Madan Lal 0).

PAKISTAN v INDIA 1982-83 (3rd Test)

At Iqbal Stadium, Faisalabad, on 3, 4, 5, 7, 8 January.
Toss: Pakistan.   Result: PAKISTAN won by 10 wickets.
Debuts: None.

For the first time four Pakistan batsmen scored hundreds in the same innings as they recorded their (then) highest total against India and the second-highest in all Tests without a bye. Zaheer Abbas became the first Pakistan batsman to score hundreds in three successive innings. Imran, who took 11 wickets for the second match running, emulated I.T.Botham (*Test No. 876*) by scoring a century and taking ten wickets in the same Test. His innings of 117 (192 minutes, 121 balls, five sixes and ten fours) included 21 (640461) off an over from Kapil Dev, who became the first bowler to concede 200 runs in an innings in or against Pakistan. Both captains scored hundreds, Gavaskar's 26th in Tests occupying 433 minutes as he became the first Indian to carry his bat through a completed Test innings. Four record partnerships for this series were set: 287 Miandad and Zaheer – 4th wicket; 207 Salim and Imran – 6th; 98 Patil and Kapil Dev – 6th (since beaten); and 122 Kirmani and Madan Lal – 8th. Salim Malik completed his second hundred in Tests at the age of 19 years 264 days.

INDIA

*S.M.Gavaskar	c Salim b Imran	12	not out	127
Arun Lal	b Sarfraz	0	c Zaheer b Sarfraz	3
D.B.Vengsarkar	lbw b Imran	6	lbw b Imran	1
G.R.Viswanath	b Mudassar	53	c Miandad b Sarfraz	9
M.Amarnath	b Mudassar	22	lbw b Imran	78
S.M.Patil	c Wasim b Imran	84	b Imran	6
Kapil Dev	lbw b Imran	41	c Sikander b Sarfraz	16
†S.M.H.Kirmani	lbw b Imran	66	c Wasim b Sikander	6
Madan Lal	c Salim b Imran	54	lbw b Sarfraz	10
Maninder Singh	c Mohsin b Qadir	6	lbw b Imran	2
D.R.Doshi	not out	2	b Imran	4
Extras	(B6, LB8, W4, NB8)	26	(B1, LB9, NB14)	24
Total		**372**		**286**

PAKISTAN

Mohsin Khan	c Kirmani b Kapil Dev	4	(2) not out	8
Mudassar Nazar	c Kirmani b Kapil Dev	38	(1) not out	2
Mansoor Akhtar	c Kirmani b Kapil Dev	23		
Javed Miandad	c Gavaskar b Madan Lal	126		
Zaheer Abbas	c Kirmani b Madan Lal	168		
Salim Malik	b Kapil Dev	107		
*Imran Khan	c Madan Lal b Maninder	117		
†Wasim Bari	c Kirmani b Kapil Dev	6		
Sarfraz Nawaz	c Gavaskar b Kapil Dev	4		
Abdul Qadir	not out	38		
Sikander Bakht	b Kapil Dev	9		
Extras	(LB10, NB2)	12		
Total		**652**	(0 wickets)	**10**

PAKISTAN	O	M	R	W		O	M	R	W		FALL OF WICKETS			
Imran	25	3	98	6		30.5	12	82	5			I	P	I	P
Sarfraz	23	4	95	1		33	11	79	4	*Wkt*	*1st*	*1st*	*2nd*	*2nd*
Sikander	13	1	66	0	(5)	9	3	41	1	1st	6	4	27	–
Mudassar	12	2	39	2	(3)	11	3	27	0	2nd	17	66	28	–
Qadir	12.3	1	48	1	(4)	11	1	33	0	3rd	22	79	48	–
										4th	82	366	193	–
INDIA										5th	122	367	201	–
Kapil Dev	38.4	3	220	7						6th	220	574	227	–
Madan Lal	28	5	109	2						7th	235	595	236	–
Doshi	29	2	130	0						8th	357	599	261	–
Amarnath	16	1	68	0						9th	370	612	282	–
Maninder Singh	29	3	103	1						10th	372	652	286	–
Gavaskar	2	0	10	0										
Arun Lal					(1)	1.1	0	6	0					
Vengsarkar					(2)	1	0	4	0					

Umpires: Mahboob Shah (11) and Shakil Khan (1).

Close: 1st day – I(1) 334-7 (Kirmani 57, Madan Lal 37); 2nd – P(1) 255-3 (Miandad 75, Zaheer 109); 3rd – P(1) 594-6 (Malik 102, Wasim 6); 4th – I(2) 181-3 (Gavaskar 78, Amarnath 74).

PAKISTAN v INDIA 1982-83 (4th Test)

At Niaz Stadium, Hyderabad, on 14, 15, 16, 18, 19 January.
Toss: Pakistan.   Result: PAKISTAN won by an innings and 119 runs.
Debuts: India – B.S.Sandhu.

Pakistan both completed the first hat-trick of wins in this series and won their second rubber against India. Mudassar Nazar (627 minutes, 444 balls, one six and 21 fours) and Javed Miandad (606 minutes, 460 balls, one six and 19 fours) made their highest Test scores and shared a (then) world Test record third-wicket partnership of 451 runs in 533 minutes. Their stand equalled the world record for any wicket in Test cricket: 451 in 316 minutes by W.H.Ponsford and D.G.Bradman in 1934 (*Test No. 237*). The partners achieved the fifth instance – the first involving Pakistan – of two batsmen scoring double centuries in the same Test innings. Zaheer Abbas, who had overtaken Majid Khan's record aggregate of 3,931 in the previous match, became the first to score 4,000 runs for Pakistan. Substitute Yashpal Sharma kept wicket for most of the final session on the second day when Kirmani retired with an injury. Imran took 5 for 8 in 23 balls during the first innings.

PAKISTAN

Mohsin Khan	lbw b Sandhu	24
Mudassar Nazar	c Maninder b Doshi	231
Haroon Rashid	b Sandhu	0
Javed Miandad	not out	280
Zaheer Abbas	not out	25
Salim Malik		
*Imran Khan		
†Wasim Bari	did not bat	
Sarfraz Nawaz		
Abdul Qadir		
Iqbal Qasim		
Extras	(B9, LB12)	21
Total	**(3 wickets declared)**	**581**

INDIA

*S.M.Gavaskar	c Wasim b Imran	17	c and b Qasim	60
K.Srikkanth	lbw b Sarfraz	2	c Salim b Imran	5
M.Amarnath	st Wasim b Qasim	61	c Imran b Qasim	64
G.R.Viswanath	lbw b Imran	0	lbw b Sarfraz	37
D.B.Vengsarkar	c Wasim b Imran	4	not out	58
Kapil Dev	b Imran	3	b Sarfraz	2
†S.M.H.Kirmani	b Imran	1	lbw b Sarfraz	0
S.M.Patil	c Imran b Sarfraz	2	c Imran b Qadir	9
B.S.Sandhu	b Sarfraz	71	c Imran b Qadir	12
Maninder Singh	not out	12	lbw b Sarfraz	4
D.R.Doshi	lbw b Imran	1	b Imran	14
Extras	(B1, LB7, NB7)	15	(B1, LB1, NB6)	8
Total		**189**		**273**

INDIA	O	M	R	W	O	M	R	W		FALL OF WICKETS		
Kapil Dev	27	2	111	0						P	I	I
Sandhu	33	7	107	2					Wkt	1st	1st	2nd
Amarnath	15	0	64	0					1st	60	3	8
Maninder Singh	50	10	135	0					2nd	60	44	133
Doshi	41	9	143	1					3rd	511	44	134
									4th	–	52	201
PAKISTAN									5th	–	61	203
Imran	17.2	3	35	6	24.4	14	45	2	6th	–	65	203
Sarfraz	19	4	56	3	30	4	85	4	7th	–	72	223
Qadir	11	2	35	0	(4) 26	7	77	2	8th	–	131	249
Qasim	9	3	48	1	(3) 31	9	58	2	9th	–	184	254
									10th	–	189	273

Umpires: Javed Akhtar (6) and Khizer Hayat (9).

Close: 1st day – P(1) 224-2 (Mudassar 92, Miandad 96); 2nd – P(1) 515-3 (Miandad 238, Zaheer 4); 3rd – I(1) 189 all out; 4th – I(2) 198-3 (Viswanath 37, Vengsarkar 26).

PAKISTAN v INDIA 1982-83 (5th Test)

At Gaddafi Stadium, Lahore, on 23, 24, 25, 27 (*no play*), 28 (*no play*) January.
Toss: India.   Result: MATCH DRAWN.
Debuts: India – T.A.P.Sekar.

Mudassar Nazar (495 minutes, 296 balls, 15 fours and a five) became the second Pakistan batsman to carry his bat through a completed innings; the first to do so had been his father, Nazar Mohammad, in 1952-53 (*Test No. 356*). Majid Khan failed to score in his final Test innings. Kapil Dev's best analysis to that date included three wickets with his last five balls (WWOOW). The partnership of 190 between Amarnath and Yashpal Sharma was India's highest for the third wicket against Pakistan. Viswanath set a world record by appearing in his 86th consecutive Test match, one more than the sequence achieved by G.St A.Sobers. Heavy and unseasonable storms prevented play after 33 minutes of the post-tea session on the third day.

PAKISTAN

Mohsin Khan	c Srikkanth b Kapil Dev	7
Mudassar Nazar	not out	152
Majid Khan	c Kirmani b Kapil Dev	0
Javed Miandad	c Viswanath b Maninder	85
Zaheer Abbas	c Kirmani b Kapil Dev	13
Salim Malik	b Maninder	6
*Imran Khan	c Kirmani b Kapil Dev	20
†Wasim Bari	c Amarnath b Kapil Dev	8
Sarfraz Nawaz	c Yashpal b Kapil Dev	26
Abdul Qadir	b Kapil Dev	0
Iqbal Qasim	lbw b Kapil Dev	0
Extras	(LB6)	6
Total		**323**

INDIA

*S.M.Gavaskar	lbw b Imran	13
K.Srikkanth	b Qadir	21
M.Amarnath	c Wasim b Imran	120
Yashpal Sharma	not out	63
D.B.Vengsarkar	not out	1
G.R.Viswanath		
Kapil Dev		
†S.M.H.Kirmani	did not bat	
B.S.Sandhu		
T.A.P.Sekar		
Maninder Singh		
Extras	(B6, LB5, W1, NB5)	17
Total	(3 wickets)	**235**

INDIA	O	M	R	W		FALL OF WICKETS	
Kapil Dev	30.5	7	85	8		P	I
Sandhu	21	2	56	0	Wkt	1st	1st
Sekar	20	2	86	0	1st	22	29
Maninder Singh	32	7	90	2	2nd	26	41
					3rd	174	231
PAKISTAN					4th	191	–
Imran	18	5	45	2	5th	202	–
Sarfraz	23.2	9	46	0	6th	244	–
Qadir	16	1	63	1	7th	276	–
Qasim	12	3	19	0	8th	323	–
Mudassar	11	1	41	0	9th	323	–
Majid	1	0	4	0	10th	323	–

Umpires: Javed Akhtar (7) and Khizer Hayat (10).

Close: 1st day – P(1) 224-5 (Mudassar 99, Imran 13); 2nd – I(1) 110-2 (Amarnath 52, Yashpal 15); 3rd – I(1) 235-3 (Yashpal 63, Vengsarkar 1); 4th – no play.

PAKISTAN v INDIA 1982-83 (6th Test)

At National Stadium, Karachi, on 30, 31 January, 1, 3, 4 February.
Toss: India.   Result: MATCH DRAWN.
Debuts: None.

Promoted to open the innings, Shastri reached his first Test hundred in 391 minutes off 266 balls. Vengsarkar (17) retired at 140 after being struck on the arm by a lifting ball from Sarfraz, and returned at 218. Wasim Bari became the fourth wicket-keeper to make 200 dismissals in Test cricket and set a Pakistan record with 17 dismissals in the rubber. Mudassar Nazar emulated Zaheer by scoring his third successive hundred in this rubber, his aggregate of 761 being the Pakistan record. Mudassar (761), Zaheer (650) and Miandad (594) provided the first instance of either three batsman from any country sharing an aggregate of 2,000 runs or of each averaging over 100. Imran, the first Pakistan bowler to take 40 wickets in a rubber, achieved the unique double of 40 wickets and 247 runs. Mudassar, Amarnath and Kirmani each completed 2,000 runs in Tests. Politically motivated rioting, which included an attempt to damage the pitch, caused the fourth day's play to be abandoned in mid-afternoon. Pakistan's 12 hundreds equalled the world record set by Australia in five Tests against West Indies in 1954-55.

INDIA

*S.M.Gavaskar	c Wasim Bari b Tahir	5	b Imran		67
R.J.Shastri	st Wasim Bari b Qadir	128	c Wasim Bari b Imran		17
M.Amarnath	c Wasim Bari b Imran	19	not out		103
Yashpal Sharma	c Wasim Bari b Imran	9	not out		19
D.B.Vengsarkar	c and b Tahir	89			
G.R.Viswanath	b Mudassar	10			
†S.M.H.Kirmani	c Zaheer b Sarfraz	18			
Kapil Dev	lbw b Imran	33			
B.S.Sandhu	not out	32			
T.A.P.Sekar	not out	0			
Maninder Singh	did not bat				
Extras	(B13, LB9, NB28)	50	(B10, W3, NB5)		18
Total	(8 wickets declared)	**393**	(2 wickets)		**224**

PAKISTAN

Mohsin Khan	lbw b Kapil Dev	91
Mudassar Nazar	lbw b Kapil Dev	152
Javed Miandad	c Kirmani b Sandhu	47
Zaheer Abbas	c Amarnath b Shastri	43
Wasim Raja	run out	10
*Imran Khan	not out	32
†Wasim Bari	c Kirmani b Sandhu	12
Sarfraz Nawaz	not out	6
Salim Malik		
Tahir Naqqash	} did not bat	
Abdul Qadir		
Extras	(B5, LB12, W1, NB9)	27
Total	(6 wickets declared)	**420**

PAKISTAN	O	M	R	W		O	M	R	W		FALL OF WICKETS		
Imran	32	11	65	3		16	3	41	2		I	P	I
Sarfraz	41	10	92	1		14	4	45	0	*Wkt*	*1st*	*1st*	*2nd*
Tahir	24	7	69	2	(4)	8	1	28	0	1st	47	157	43
Qadir	23	3	86	1	(3)	14	2	42	0	2nd	86	269	150
Mudassar	15	4	30	1						3rd	109	342	–
Wasim Raja	1	0	1	0	(5)	5	2	12	0	4th	178	363	–
Zaheer					(6)	8	0	24	0	5th	218	371	–
Mohsin					(7)	1	0	3	0	6th	267	411	–
Miandad					(8)	2	0	11	0	7th	316	–	–
INDIA										8th	393	–	–
Kapil Dev	33	2	137	2						9th	–	–	–
Sandhu	28.2	4	87	2						10th	–	–	–
Sekar	14	1	43	0									
Maninder Singh	16	3	49	0									
Shastri	22	1	62	1									
Amarnath	4	1	15	0									

Umpires: Javed Akhtar (8) and Khizer Hayat (11).

Close: 1st day – I(1) 188-4 (Shastri 88, Kirmani 8); 2nd – P(1) 25-0 (Mohsin 21, Mudassar 1); 3rd – P(1) 269-2 (Mudassar 109); 4th – P(1) 420-6 (Imran 32, Sarfraz 6).

WEST INDIES v INDIA 1982-83 (1st Test)

At Sabina Park, Kingston, Jamaica, on 23, 24, 26, 27 (*no play*), 28 February.
Toss: West Indies.   Result: WEST INDIES won by 4 wickets.
Debuts: West Indies – A.L.Logie.

India, 164 runs ahead with four wickets left, looked safe from defeat at tea on the final day before Roberts changed events with three wickets in his first over afterwards (W000WW) and a spell of 4 for 1 in 20 balls. With Richards making a blistering 61 off 36 balls (four sixes and five fours – 50 off 32 balls), West Indies achieved their target of 172 from 26 overs with four balls to spare, Dujon ending the chase with a six. Lloyd celebrated his 50th Test as captain by winning his 22nd toss and opting to field for the 10th time; Kapil Dev celebrated his first by scoring his 2,000th run. Gavaskar was bowled behind his legs by the first ball of the second innings.

INDIA

S.M.Gavaskar	c Dujon b Marshall	20	b Holding		0
A.D.Gaekwad	c Dujon b Holding	1	c Greenidge b Marshall		23
M.Amarnath	c Dujon b Garner	29	c Garner b Marshall		40
D.B.Vengsarkar	c Richards b Roberts	30	c Garner b Marshall		20
Yashpal Sharma	c Haynes b Garner	63	c Gomes b Holding		24
R.J.Shastri	c Dujon b Holding	1	not out		25
*Kapil Dev	c Marshall b Roberts	5	c Dujon b Roberts		12
†S.M.H.Kirmani	c Dujon b Marshall	5	c Haynes b Roberts		10
B.S.Sandhu	c Garner b Roberts	68	c Garner b Roberts		0
S.Venkataraghavan	hit wicket b Roberts	0	c Greenidge b Roberts		0
Maninder Singh	not out	3	c Holding b Roberts		2
Extras	(B1, LB15, NB10)	26	(B2, LB4, W1, NB11)		18
Total		**251**			**174**

WEST INDIES

C.G.Greenidge	c Venkataraghavan b Shastri	70	b Kapil Dev		42
D.L.Haynes	c Amarnath b Kapil Dev	25	b Kapil Dev		34
I.V.A.Richards	c Venkataraghavan b Shastri	29	(4) c Kapil Dev b Amarnath		61
H.A.Gomes	c Yashpal b Shastri	4			
A.L.Logie	run out	13	(7) lbw b Kapil Dev		10
*C.H.Lloyd	b Venkataraghavan	24	(3) c Amarnath b Kapil Dev		3
†P.J.L.Dujon	lbw b Kapil Dev	29	(6) not out		17
M.D.Marshall	c Yashpal b Kapil Dev	23	not out		0
A.M.E.Roberts	c Sandhu b Shastri	17	(5) c Kirmani b Amarnath		1
M.A.Holding	c Kirmani b Kapil Dev	1			
J.Garner	not out	0			
Extras	(B1, LB8, NB10)	19	(LB5)		5
Total		**254**	(6 wickets)		**173**

WEST INDIES	O	M	R	W	O	M	R	W		FALL OF WICKETS			
Holding	24	5	57	2	17	4	36	2		I	WI	I	WI
Roberts	22	4	61	4	24.2	9	39	5	*Wkt*	*1st*	*1st*	*2nd*	*2nd*
Garner	15.4	4	41	2	(4) 13	6	16	0	1st	10	36	0	46
Marshall	16	4	35	2	(3) 24	6	56	3	2nd	58	83	68	65
Gomes	9	0	31	0	7	2	9	0	3rd	66	91	69	131
Richards	1	1	0	0					4th	98	114	112	132
									5th	99	157	118	156
INDIA									6th	104	186	136	167
Kapil Dev	25.3	6	45	4	13	0	73	4	7th	127	228	168	–
Sandhu	11	4	30	0	3	0	22	0	8th	234	244	168	–
Venkataraghavan	25	3	66	1	7	0	39	0	9th	238	254	168	–
Maninder Singh	31	6	51	0					10th	251	254	174	–
Shastri	24	8	43	4									
Amarnath					(4) 2.2	0	34	2					

Umpires: D.M.Archer (3) and W.Malcolm (2).

Close: 1st day – I(1) 219-7 (Yashpal 46, Sandhu 62); 2nd – WI(1) 149-4 (Greenidge 50, Lloyd 20); 3rd – I(2) 81-3 (Vengsarkar 4, Yashpal 6); 4th – no play.

WEST INDIES v INDIA 1982-83 (2nd Test)

At Queen's Park Oval, Port-of-Spain, Trinidad, on 11, 12, 13, 15, 16 March.
Toss: West Indies.   Result: MATCH DRAWN.
Debuts: None.

India, 219 behind on first innings after being put in on a well-grassed pitch, earned a draw by batting 10 hours 20 minutes for their highest total in the West Indies. Yashpal Sharma (5) retired at 44 when he was concussed by a ball from Marshall; he resumed at 164. Gomes and Lloyd (who became the third West Indian to score 6,000 runs) rescued West Indies with a stand of 237 after they had made their worst start in any match. Kapil Dev, appearing in his 50th Test, became the youngest player (24 years 68 days) to take 200 wickets and complete the 'double double'. Richards, captain in the absence of Lloyd, allowed play to continue into the final half hour so that Kapil Dev could reach his hundred (142 minutes, 95 balls, three sixes, 13 fours).

INDIA

S.M.Gavaskar	c Dujon b Holding	1	c Dujon b Garner		32
A.D.Gaekwad	run out	0	c sub‡ b Gomes		35
M.Amarnath	c Lloyd b Roberts	58	lbw b Richards		117
D.B.Vengsarkar	c Holding b Marshall	7	c Dujon b Roberts		45
Yashpal Sharma	not out	11	b Roberts		50
R.J.Shastri	c Gomes b Marshall	42	lbw b Holding		9
*Kapil Dev	c Haynes b Marshall	13	not out		100
†S.M.H.Kirmani	b Roberts	7	run out		30
B.S.Sandhu	c Richards b Marshall	11	not out		0
S.Venkataraghavan	c Richards b Roberts	1			
Maninder Singh	c Dujon b Marshall	1			
Extras	(B5, LB1, W3, NB14)	23	(B10, LB20, NB21)		51
Total		**175**	(7 wickets)		**469**

WEST INDIES

C.G.Greenidge	b Sandhu	0
D.L.Haynes	c Kirmani b Sandhu	0
I.V.A.Richards	c Kirmani b Kapil Dev	1
H.A.Gomes	c Gavaskar b Venkataraghavan	123
*C.H.Lloyd	st Kirmani b Shastri	143
A.L.Logie	c Kapil Dev b Venkataraghavan	13
†P.J.L.Dujon	lbw b Kapil Dev	31
M.D.Marshall	lbw b Shastri	14
A.M.E.Roberts	b Kapil Dev	9
M.A.Holding	c Vengsarkar b Maninder	24
J.Garner	not out	21
Extras	(B4, LB7, W1, NB3)	15
Total		**394**

WEST INDIES	O	M	R	W	O	M	R	W		FALL OF WICKETS		
Holding	13	2	24	1	31	2	106	1		I	WI	I
Roberts	22	5	72	3	25	3	100	2	*Wkt*	*1st*	*1st*	*2nd*
Marshall	19.1	6	37	5	27.1	8	72	0	1st	1	0	63
Garner	10	5	17	0	30	8	81	1	2nd	5	0	132
Gomes	2	1	2	0	19	7	45	1	3rd	28	1	206
Richards					7	4	14	1	4th	131	238	312
									5th	146	255	325
INDIA									6th	147	316	329
Kapil Dev	31	6	91	3					7th	164	324	463
Sandhu	19	2	69	2					8th	166	340	–
Venkataraghavan	41	13	97	2					9th	171	346	–
Shastri	21	2	71	2					10th	175	394	–
Maninder Singh	26.3	7	51	1								

Umpires: S.E.Parris (4) and S.Mohammed (2).   ‡ (S.F.A.F.Bacchus)

Close: 1st day – I(1) 44-3 (Amarnath 21, Yashpal 5); 2nd – WI(1) 104-3 (Gomes 38, Lloyd 63); 3rd – WI(1) 335-7 (Marshall 7, Roberts 9); 4th – I(2) 169-2 (Amarnath 54, Vengsarkar 20).

WEST INDIES v INDIA 1982-83 (3rd Test)

At Bourda, Georgetown, Guyana, on 31 March, 2 (*no play*), 3, 4 (*no play*), 5 April.
Toss: West Indies.   Result: MATCH DRAWN.
Debuts: None.

Two days and a session of play were lost to overnight rain although none actually fell during the scheduled hours of the match. Even the use of a helicopter had little effect on the quagmire. Richards, in his 50th Test and 97 not out on Thursday night, had to wait until after lunch on Sunday to complete his 14th Test hundred. Gavaskar scored his 27th hundred (one more than Sobers and two fewer than Bradman) on the ground where he had made his first in 1970-71, and became the first Indian to be on the field throughout a Test match.

WEST INDIES

C.G.Greenidge	c Kirmani b Maninder	70
D.L.Haynes	c Yashpal b Venkataraghavan	46
I.V.A.Richards	c Venkataraghavan b Sandhu	109
H.A.Gomes	c Gaekwad b Kapil Dev	36
M.A.Holding	run out	0
A.L.Logie	c Kirmani b Sandhu	0
*C.H.Lloyd	c Kirmani b Shastri	81
†P.J.L.Dujon	c and b Venkataraghavan	47
M.D.Marshall	lbw b Kapil Dev	27
A.M.E.Roberts	c Gavaskar b Sandhu	36
J.Garner	not out	1
Extras	(B1, LB14, W1, NB1)	17
Total		**470**

INDIA

S.M.Gavaskar	not out	147
A.D.Gaekwad	c Dujon b Holding	8
M.Amarnath	c Richards b Marshall	13
D.B.Vengsarkar	c Richards b Garner	62
Yashpal Sharma	not out	35
R.J.Shastri		
*Kapil Dev		
†S.M.H.Kirmani	did not bat	
B.S.Sandhu		
Maninder Singh		
S.Venkataraghavan		
Extras	(B1, LB3, NB15)	19
Total	(3 wickets)	**284**

INDIA	O	M	R	W		FALL OF WICKETS	
						WI	I
Kapil Dev	30	7	68	2	*Wkt*	*1st*	*1st*
Sandhu	25.4	5	87	3	1st	89	24
Shastri	22	3	84	1	2nd	157	68
Maninder Singh	27	3	90	1	3rd	252	180
Venkataraghavan	38	4	124	2	4th	253	–
					5th	256	–
WEST INDIES					6th	299	–
Roberts	15	2	38	0	7th	387	–
Holding	16	1	72	1	8th	417	–
Garner	17	4	57	1	9th	460	–
Marshall	13	2	39	1	10th	470	–
Gomes	14	5	35	0			
Richards	4	0	24	0			

Umpires: D.M.Archer (4) and D.J.Narine (1).

Close: 1st day – WI(1) 259-5 (Richards 97, Lloyd 2); 2nd – no play; 3rd – WI(1) 470 all out; 4th – no play.

WEST INDIES v INDIA 1982-83 (4th Test)

At Kensington Oval, Bridgetown, Barbados, on 15, 16, 17, 19, 20 April.
Toss: West Indies.   Result: WEST INDIES won by 10 wickets.
Debuts: None.

On a well-grassed and bouncy pitch West Indies gained their fourth victory in five matches against India at Bridgetown. Only Amarnath coped confidently with persistent short-pitched fast bowling, and he was forced to retire (when 18) at 96 in the second innings after missing a hook at Marshall and sustaining a cut upper lip; he resumed at 139. Logie (273 minutes) recorded his first Test hundred after being dropped when 7. For the first time in Test cricket all 20 first innings wickets fell to catches. The match was concluded in uniquely bizarre fashion by a no-ball, Kirmani's second delivery in Test cricket.

INDIA

S.M.Gavaskar	c Dujon b Holding	2		c Roberts b Garner	19
A.D.Gaekwad	c Marshall b Roberts	3		b Holding	55
M.Amarnath	c Dujon b Marshall	91		c Dujon b Roberts	80
D.B.Vengsarkar	c Marshall b Holding	15		lbw b Holding	6
Yashpal Sharma	c Richards b Roberts	24		c Greenidge b Roberts	12
R.J.Shastri	c Richards b Roberts	29		c Lloyd b Marshall	19
*Kapil Dev	c Lloyd b Marshall	0	(8)	c Lloyd b Marshall	26
†S.M.H.Kirmani	c Haynes b Roberts	11	(9)	run out	33
Madan Lal	c Holding b Garner	6	(10)	lbw b Roberts	0
B.S.Sandhu	not out	8	(7)	lbw b Roberts	4
S.Venkataraghavan	c Dujon b Garner	5		not out	0
Extras	(LB1, NB14)	15		(B5, LB2, NB16)	23
Total		**209**			**277**

WEST INDIES

C.G.Greenidge	c Gavaskar b Madan Lal	57		not out	0
D.L.Haynes	c Kapil Dev b Shastri	92		not out	0
I.V.A.Richards	c Gavaskar b Venkataraghavan	80			
H.A.Gomes	c sub‡ b Venkataraghavan	6			
A.L.Logie	c Amarnath b Shastri	130			
*C.H.Lloyd	c sub‡ b Venkataraghavan	50			
†P.J.L.Dujon	c Vengsarkar b Kapil Dev	25			
M.D.Marshall	c Venkataraghavan b Kapil Dev	8			
A.M.E.Roberts	c Kapil Dev b Madan Lal	20			
M.A.Holding	c Kirmani b Kapil Dev	2			
J.Garner	not out	2			
Extras	(B1, LB11, NB2)	14		(NB1)	1
Total		**486**		(0 wickets)	**1**

WEST INDIES	O	M	R	W		O	M	R	W		FALL OF WICKETS			
Holding	14	4	46	2	(2)	21	2	75	2		I	WI	I	WI
Roberts	16	4	48	4	(1)	19.2	3	31	4	*Wkt*	*1st*	*1st*	*2nd*	*2nd*
Marshall	13	1	56	2		16	1	80	2	1st	2	98	61	–
Garner	12.2	5	41	2		15	4	48	1	2nd	10	220	108	–
Gomes	2	1	3	0		8	3	20	0	3rd	39	230	109	–
										4th	91	262	132	–
INDIA										5th	172	395	139	–
Kapil Dev	32.2	7	76	3						6th	172	454	155	–
Sandhu	5	1	21	0						7th	180	458	214	–
Madan Lal	27	2	96	2						8th	196	481	276	–
Shastri	50	13	133	2						9th	200	483	276	–
Venkataraghavan	43	6	146	3						10th	209	486	277	–
Gaekwad	1	1	0	0										
Kirmani					(1)	0.1	0	0	0					

Umpires: D.M.Archer (5) and S.E.Parris (5).   ‡ (L.Sivaramakrishnan)

Close: 1st day – I(1) 13-2 (Amarnath 8, Vengsarkar 0); 2nd – WI(1) 80-0 (Greenidge 48, Haynes 28); 3rd – WI(1) 355-4 (Logie 72, Lloyd 37); 4th – I(2) 138-4 (Shastri 13, Sandhu 4).

WEST INDIES v INDIA 1982-83 (5th Test)

At Recreation Ground, St John's, Antigua, on 28, 29, 30 April, 1, 3 May.
Toss: West Indies.   Result: MATCH DRAWN.
Debuts: West Indies – W.W.Davis; India – L.Sivaramakrishnan.

At 17 years 118 days, Laxman Sivaramakrishnan became the youngest cricketer to represent any country apart from Pakistan. Lloyd won his seventh consecutive toss and became the first captain to elect to field first four times in the same rubber. Amarnath, suffering from a viral infection, collapsed with leg cramp just before lunch on the first day, at 98; he resumed at 337 with his score 39 and with Yashpal as his runner. Greenidge flew to Barbados immediately after the third day's play to visit his two-year-old daughter critically ill in hospital; she died two days after the Test ended. His retirement (at 301) was adjudged 'not out'. His partnership of 296 with Haynes was the first-wicket record for West Indies in all Tests until 1989-90 and their highest for any wicket against India. For the first time in a home Test four West Indies batsman scored hundreds in the same innings.

INDIA

S.M.Gavaskar	c Dujon b Marshall	18	c Dujon b Davis	1
A.D.Gaekwad	c Richards b Roberts	3	lbw b Marshall	72
M.Amarnath	c Lloyd b Davis	54	c Logie b Davis	116
D.B.Vengsarkar	c Davis b Marshall	94	c Dujon b Marshall	0
Yashpal Sharma	c Gomes b Roberts	3	c sub (S.F.A.F.Bacchus) b Gomes	20
R.J.Shastri	st Dujon b Gomes	102	not out	9
*Kapil Dev	lbw b Holding	98	not out	0
†S.M.H.Kirmani	c Greenidge b Davis	2		
Madan Lal	not out	35		
L.Sivaramakrishnan	c sub (S.F.A.F.Bacchus) b Marshall	17		
S.Venkataraghavan	b Marshall	0		
Extras	(B14, LB7, W1, NB9)	31	(B11, LB8, NB10)	29
Total		**457**	(5 wickets declared)	**247**

WEST INDIES

C.G.Greenidge	retired not out	154
D.L.Haynes	c Shastri b Yashpal	136
W.W.Davis	b Madan Lal	14
I.V.A.Richards	c Gaekwad b Madan Lal	2
H.A.Gomes	lbw b Madan Lal	9
A.L.Logie	hit wkt b Kapil Dev	1
†P.J.L.Dujon	c Gaekwad b Venkataraghavan	110
*C.H.Lloyd	c Yashpal b Shastri	106
M.D.Marshall	b Venkataraghavan	2
A.M.E.Roberts	not out	1
M.A.Holding	run out	0
Extras	(B6, LB5, NB4)	15
Total		**550**

WEST INDIES	O	M	R	W		O	M	R	W	FALL OF WICKETS			
Roberts	29	3	110	2		15	3	46	0		I	WI	I
Holding	26	3	86	1						Wkt	1st	1st	2nd
Marshall	27.5	5	87	4		18	7	33	2	1st	5	296	1
Davis	29	1	121	2	(2)	23	4	54	2	2nd	28	303	201
Richards	11	3	13	0		13	1	36	0	3rd	119	323	201
Gomes	4	1	9	1		19	0	49	1	4th	181	324	235
										5th	337	334	245
INDIA										6th	372	541	–
Kapil Dev	22	6	71	1						7th	376	547	–
Madan Lal	35	7	105	3						8th	419	549	–
Sivaramakrishnan	25	1	95	0						9th	457	550	–
Shastri	46.4	5	141	1						10th	457	–	–
Venkataraghavan	36	1	114	2									
Gaekwad	1	0	3	0									
Yashpal	1	0	6	1									

Umpires: D.M.Archer (6) and A.E.Weekes (1).

Close: 1st day – I(1) 158-3 (Vengsarkar 76, Shastri 14); 2nd – WI(1) 23-0 (Greenidge 7, Haynes 14); 3rd – WI(1) 301-1 (Greenidge 154, Davis 1); 4th – I(2) 0-0 (Gavaskar 0, Gaekwad 0).

NEW ZEALAND v SRI LANKA 1982-83 (1st Test)

At Lancaster Park, Christchurch, on 4, 5, 6 March.
Toss: Sri Lanka.   Result: NEW ZEALAND won by an innings and 25 runs.
Debuts: New Zealand – J.J.Crowe; Sri Lanka – R.G.de Alwis, E.R.N.S.Fernando,
Y.Goonasekera, S.Jeganathan, V.B.John, R.J.Ratnayake, M.de S.Wettimuny.

The inaugural match of this series produced New Zealand's second victory by an innings and their first inside three days; playing time amounted to 15 hours 22 minutes. Sri Lanka were compelled to introduce seven new caps following the 25-year ban on 14 players who toured South Africa and injuries to three key members of this touring team: Mendis, captain – fractured finger; Dias, vice-captain – fractured thumb; De Mel, opening bowler – torn side muscles. Sidath Wettimuny (210 minutes, 139 balls) was the first to carry his bat through a completed innings for Sri Lanka. His partnership with Mithra Wettimuny provided Test cricket's third instance of brothers opening an innings; they followed E.M. and W.G.Grace (*Test No. 4*) and Hanif and Sadiq Mohammad (*662*). Turner returned to Test cricket after an absence of six years. De Silva, batting with a runner because of a leg injury, surrendered his wicket off the penultimate ball of the day. Howarth described the pitch as being unfit for any class of cricket.

NEW ZEALAND

G.M.Turner	c De Alwis b John	32
B.A.Edgar	c M. de S.Wettimuny b Ratnayeke	39
J.G.Wright	b Ratnayeke	13
*G.P.Howarth	c Goonasekera b Ratnayeke	0
J.J.Crowe	run out	12
J.V.Coney	run out	84
R.J.Hadlee	b John	12
B.L.Cairns	c M. de S.Wettimuny b Ratnayeke	3
†W.K.Lees	b De Silva	89
M.C.Snedden	c sub (S.A.R.Silva) b Ratnayeke	22
E.J.Chatfield	not out	10
Extras	(LB14, W2, NB12)	28
Total		**344**

SRI LANKA

M.de S.Wettimuny	c Lees b Cairns	17	c Lees b Snedden	5
S.Wettimuny	not out	63	lbw b Cairns	7
E.R.N.S.Fernando	b Cairns	0	b Cairns	46
Y.Goonasekera	c Lees b Cairns	4	c Turner b Cairns	8
R.S.Madugalle	run out	34	c Lees b Snedden	23
*D.S.de Silva	c Lees b Hadlee	7	b Chatfield	52
J.R.Ratnayeke	run out	0	lbw b Cairns	7
†R.G.de Alwis	c Turner b Hadlee	0	c Hadlee b Snedden	3
S.Jeganathan	lbw b Cairns	6	b Chatfield	8
R.J.Ratnayake	c Coney b Hadlee	1	c Howarth b Chatfield	0
V.B.John	lbw b Hadlee	0	not out	3
Extras	(B2, LB7, NB3)	12	(B1, LB6, W5, NB1)	13
Total		**144**		**175**

SRI LANKA	O	M	R	W	O	M	R	W		FALL OF WICKETS		
Ratnayake	31	8	125	2						NZ	SL	SL
John	12	2	45	2					*Wkt*	*1st*	*1st*	*2nd*
Ratnayeke	31	9	93	3					1st	59	49	14
De Silva	22.5	10	41	1					2nd	93	49	26
Jeganathan	5	2	12	0					3rd	93	56	46
									4th	93	104	95
NEW ZEALAND									5th	137	121	108
Hadlee	13.3	1	33	4	22	12	27	0	6th	159	129	124
Snedden	10	1	30	0	23	6	48	3	7th	171	133	133
Cairns	15	6	49	4	(4) 20	7	47	4	8th	250	141	168
Chatfield	15	4	20	0	(3) 16.5	3	40	3	9th	292	144	170
									10th	344	144	175

Umpires: F.R.Goodall (15) and D.A.Kinsella (3).

Close: 1st day – NZ(1) 217-7 (Coney 69, Lees 20); 2nd – SL(1) 141-8 (S.Wettimuny 62).

NEW ZEALAND v SRI LANKA 1982-83 (2nd Test)

At Basin Reserve, Wellington, on 11, 12, 13, 14, 15 March.
Toss: New Zealand.   Result: NEW ZEALAND won by 6 wickets.
Debuts: Sri Lanka – S.A.R.Silva.

New Zealand's victory was their 15th in 150 Tests, their fifth at the Basin Reserve, and, for the first time, their second in successive matches. Wright (10) retired at 33 when his nose was fractured by a bouncer from Rumesh Ratnayake. The 19-year-old bowler fainted at the sight of blood and had to be revived with smelling salts. Wright resumed his innings at 163. Goonasekera's four catches established a Sri Lankan fielding record. For New Zealand, Lees emulated R.I.Harford and K.J.Wadsworth by holding five catches in an innings, and set a national record by claiming eight in the match. Hadlee finished the rain-interrupted match with a six.

SRI LANKA

Batsman	Dismissal	Score		Dismissal	Score
S.Wettimuny	c Cairns b Hadlee	8		c Coney b Hadlee	9
M.de S.Wettimuny	c Coney b Snedden	6		c Cairns b Snedden	0
E.R.N.S.Fernando	c Wright b Hadlee	12		c Lees b Snedden	12
Y.Goonasekera	c Lees b Cairns	13	(5)	c Lees b Chatfield	23
R.S.Madugalle	run out	79	(6)	c Lees b Hadlee	13
*D.S.de Silva	lbw b Chatfield	61	(7)	c Lees b Snedden	0
†S.A.R.Silva	c Lees b Chatfield	8	(4)	c Crowe b Hadlee	0
J.R.Ratnayeke	not out	29		b Hadlee	12
S.Jeganathan	c Lees b Chatfield	5		c Lees b Chatfield	0
R.J.Ratnayake	b Snedden	12		c sub (M.D.Crowe) b Chatfield	1
V.B.John	c Wright b Chatfield	0		not out	8
Extras	(B1, LB5, NB1)	7		(B5, LB10)	15
Total		**240**			**93**

NEW ZEALAND

Batsman	Dismissal	Score		Dismissal	Score
G.M.Turner	c Goonasekera b John	10		b Ratnayeke	29
B.A.Edgar	c John b Ratnayake	10		not out	47
J.G.Wright	c De Silva b Ratnayake	14			
*G.P.Howarth	c S.Wettimuny b De Silva	36	(3)	c Silva b John	1
J.J.Crowe	c Silva b Ratnayake	36	(4)	b Ratnayake	11
J.V.Coney	c Goonasekera b John	2	(5)	c Goonasekera b De Silva	17
R.J.Hadlee	c Goonasekera b John	30	(6)	not out	17
†W.K.Lees	c Goonasekera b John	0			
B.L.Cairns	c De Silva b John	45			
M.C.Snedden	lbw b Ratnayake	5			
E.J.Chatfield	not out	2			
Extras	(B4, LB3, W3, NB1)	11		(LB11, NB1)	12
Total		**201**		**(4 wickets)**	**134**

NEW ZEALAND	O	M	R	W	O	M	R	W
Hadlee	25	9	47	2	17	5	34	4
Snedden	24	5	56	2	17	7	21	3
Chatfield	26.5	7	66	4	(4) 12	5	15	3
Cairns	20	5	53	1	(3) 7	2	8	0
Coney	5	2	11	0				
SRI LANKA								
Ratnayake	24	5	81	4	15	0	46	1
John	25.2	9	60	5	8	2	38	1
Ratnayeke	14	3	36	0	8.1	4	20	1
De Silva	9	5	13	1	6	1	18	1

FALL OF WICKETS

Wkt	SL 1st	NZ 1st	SL 2nd	NZ 2nd
1st	14	12	0	59
2nd	14	33	12	62
3rd	34	104	12	81
4th	48	107	57	116
5th	178	141	61	–
6th	191	141	61	–
7th	194	145	78	–
8th	220	163	81	–
9th	239	169	83	–
10th	240	201	93	–

Umpires: I.C.Higginson (1) and S.J.Woodward (7).

Close: 1st day – SL(1) 34-2 (Fernando 12, Goonasekera 7); 2nd – NZ(1) 12-1 (Edgar 1); 3rd – SL(2) 26-3 (Fernando 3, Goonasekera 11); 4th – NZ(2) 62-1 (Edgar 25, Howarth 1).

SRI LANKA v AUSTRALIA 1982-83 (Only Test)

At Asgiriya Stadium, Kandy, on 22, 23, 24, 26 April.
Toss: Australia.   Result: AUSTRALIA won by an innings and 38 runs.
Debuts: Australia – T.G.Hogan, R.D.Woolley; Sri Lanka – R.P.W.Guneratne.

Kandy provided a newly developed and re-landscaped 54th Test venue for the first match of this series. Shortly after 2.00 on the fourth afternoon it witnessed Sri Lanka's sixth defeat in eight official Tests. Chappell, captaining Australia for the 48th and final time, was the only right-handed batsman in the first six of his order. In his 24th Test innings, Hookes (152 balls, two sixes and 17 fours) scored his first hundred and took his score from 43 to 143 in the post-lunch session on the second day.

AUSTRALIA

K.C.Wessels	c Dias b De Silva	141
G.M.Wood	c Ratnayake b Ranatunga	4
G.N.Yallop	lbw b De Mel	98
*G.S.Chappell	lbw b De Mel	66
D.W.Hookes	not out	143
A.R.Border	not out	47
†R.D.Woolley		
T.G.Hogan		
B.Yardley	did not bat	
D.K.Lillee		
R.M.Hogg		
Extras	(LB11, W1, NB3)	15
Total	**(4 wickets declared)**	**514**

SRI LANKA

S.Wettimuny	c Woolley b Lillee	0		b Hogan	96
E.R.N.S.Fernando	c Woolley b Hogg	0		c Woolley b Lillee	3
R.L.Dias	c Border b Lillee	4		b Hogan	10
*L.R.D.Mendis	c Hookes b Yardley	74	(5)	c Border b Yardley	6
R.S.Madugalle	c and b Yardley	9	(6)	b Yardley	0
A.Ranatunga	c Lillee b Yardley	90	(7)	b Hogan	32
D.S.de Silva	c Hogan b Yardley	26	(8)	c Woolley b Hogan	5
A.L.F.de Mel	c Hookes b Hogan	29	(9)	c Yallop b Hogan	0
†R.G.de Alwis	c Border b Yardley	3	(10)	run out	9
R.J.Ratnayake	c Woolley b Border	14	(4)	run out	30
R.P.W.Guneratne	not out	0		not out	0
Extras	(B4, LB5, W1, NB12)	22		(B6, LB7, NB1)	14
Total		**271**			**205**

SRI LANKA	O	M	R	W	O	M	R	W		FALL OF WICKETS		
										A	SL	SL
De Mel	23	3	113	2					Wkt	1st	1st	2nd
Ratnayake	28	4	108	0					1st	43	1	17
Ranatunga	19	2	72	1					2nd	213	5	59
De Silva	44	7	122	1					3rd	290	9	120
Guneratne	17	1	84	0					4th	359	46	151
									5th	–	142	155
AUSTRALIA									6th	–	220	155
Lillee	19	3	67	2	11	3	40	1	7th	–	224	162
Hogg	12	4	31	1	3	2	7	0	8th	–	247	164
Chappell	1	0	2	0					9th	–	270	191
Yardley	25	7	88	5	(3) 26	6	78	2	10th	–	271	205
Hogan	11	1	50	1	(4) 25.2	6	66	5				
Border	4.5	0	11	1								

Umpires: C.E.B.Anthony (1) and H.C.Felsinger (2).

Close: 1st day – A(1) 258-2 (Yallop 91, Chappell 19); 2nd – SL (1) 65-4 (Mendis 34, Ranatunga 6); 3rd – SL(2) 71-2 (Wettimuny 45, Ratnayake 4).

ENGLAND v NEW ZEALAND 1983 (1st Test)

At Kennington Oval, London, on 14, 15, 16, 17, 18 July.
Toss: England.   Result: ENGLAND won by 189 runs.
Debuts: None.

This four-match rubber was played after the third Prudential World Cup tournament. At 2.42 on the fifth afternoon England completed their third successive win against New Zealand in Tests at The Oval. Tavaré (22) retired at 73 after being struck in the mouth by a bouncer from Hadlee, and returned at 116. Hadlee's analysis (6 for 53) was the best for New Zealand in England until the next Test. Fowler and Tavaré set a first-wicket record for England in this series by scoring 223 in 312 minutes. For the first time since 1960 (*Test No. 496*) both England's openers made hundreds in the same innings. The first joint appearance of the Crowe brothers provided New Zealand's fifth such pairing.

ENGLAND

G.Fowler	lbw b Hadlee	1	run out		105
C.J.Tavaré	run out	45	c Howarth b Bracewell		109
D.I.Gower	b Hadlee	11	c Howarth b Hadlee		25
A.J.Lamb	b Cairns	24	not out		102
I.T.Botham	b Hadlee	15	run out		26
D.W.Randall	not out	75	c Coney b Hadlee		3
V.J.Marks	c Lees b Hadlee	4	c M.D.Crowe b Bracewell		2
P.H.Edmonds	c and b Bracewell	12	not out		43
†R.W.Taylor	lbw b Hadlee	0			
*R.G.D.Willis	c J.J.Crowe b Bracewell	4			
N.G.Cowans	b Hadlee	3			
Extras	(B6, LB6, NB3)	15	(B8, LB23)		31
Total		**209**	(6 wickets declared)		**446**

NEW ZEALAND

J.G.Wright	c Gower b Willis	0	(2) run out		88
B.A.Edgar	c Taylor b Willis	12	(1) c Taylor b Willis		3
J.J.Crowe	c Randall b Willis	0	c Lamb b Willis		9
*G.P.Howarth	b Cowans	4	c Taylor b Edmonds		67
M.D.Crowe	b Willis	0	c Taylor b Edmonds		33
J.V.Coney	run out	44	lbw b Marks		2
R.J.Hadlee	c and b Botham	84	c Taylor b Marks		11
J.G.Bracewell	c and b Botham	7	(9) c Gower b Marks		0
†W.K.Lees	not out	31	(8) run out		8
B.L.Cairns	c Lamb b Botham	2	c Willis b Edmonds		32
E.J.Chatfield	c Willis b Botham	0	not out		10
Extras	(LB6, NB6)	12	(B3, LB1, NB3)		7
Total		**196**			**270**

NEW ZEALAND	O	M	R	W	O	M	R	W		FALL OF WICKETS			
										E	NZ	E	NZ
Hadlee	23.4	6	53	6	37.2	7	99	2	*Wkt*	*1st*	*1st*	*2nd*	*2nd*
Chatfield	17	3	48	0	(3) 35	9	85	0	1st	2	0	223	10
Cairns	17	3	63	1	(2) 30	7	67	0	2nd	18	1	225	26
Bracewell	8	4	16	2	(5) 54	13	115	2	3rd	67	10	269	146
M.D.Crowe	5	0	14	0	(4) 3	0	9	0	4th	104	17	322	197
Coney					27	11	39	0	5th	116	41	329	202
Howarth					3	2	1	0	6th	154	125	336	210
									7th	184	149	–	228
ENGLAND									8th	191	182	–	228
Willis	20	8	43	4	12	3	26	2	9th	202	188	–	228
Cowans	19	3	60	1	11	2	41	0	10th	209	196	–	270
Botham	16	2	62	4	4	0	17	0					
Edmonds	2	0	19	0	(5) 40.1	16	101	3					
Marks					(4) 43	20	78	3					

Umpires: H.D.Bird (25) and D.G.L.Evans (4).

Close: 1st day – NZ(1) 17-3 (Edgar 10, M.D.Crowe 0); 2nd – E(2) 146-0 (Fowler 60, Tavaré 78); 3rd – E(2) 340-6 (Lamb 48, Edmonds 4); 4th – NZ(2) 130-2 (Wright 79, Howarth 32).

ENGLAND v NEW ZEALAND 1983 (2nd Test)

At Headingley, Leeds, on 28, 29, 30 July, 1 August.
Toss: New Zealand.   Result: NEW ZEALAND won by 5 wickets.
Debuts: None.

At 4.46 on the fourth afternoon New Zealand gained their first victory in 29 Tests in England, their second of this series, and their first overseas since November 1969. Cairns recorded his best innings and match analyses in Test cricket and became the first New Zealand bowler to take seven wickets in an innings against England. Edgar (19) retired at 26, four balls after being struck on the hip attempting a hook against Botham; he resumed at 218 with Jeff Crowe as his runner. Willis, in his 81st match, became the fourth bowler to take 300 wickets in Tests when he bowled the elder Crowe; his match analysis of 9 for 92 remained his best for England.

ENGLAND

G.Fowler	c Smith b Chatfield	9	c Smith b Chatfield	19
C.J.Tavaré	c Smith b Coney	69	b Chatfield	23
D.I.Gower	c Coney b Cairns	9	not out	112
A.J.Lamb	c M.D.Crowe b Cairns	58	b Coney	28
I.T.Botham	c Howarth b Cairns	38	c Howarth b Coney	4
D.W.Randall	c Coney b Cairns	4	c Smith b Chatfield	16
P.H.Edmonds	c Smith b Cairns	8	c Smith b Chatfield	0
G.R.Dilley	b Cairns	0	c Smith b Chatfield	15
†R.W.Taylor	not out	10	b Cairns	9
*R.G.D.Willis	c J.J.Crowe b Coney	9	c Coney b Cairns	4
N.G.Cowans	c Bracewell b Cairns	0	c M.D.Crowe b Cairns	10
Extras	(B4, LB7)	11	(B8, LB3, W1)	12
Total		**225**		**252**

NEW ZEALAND

J.G.Wright	c Willis b Cowans	93	c Randall b Willis	26
B.A.Edgar	b Willis	84	c Edmonds b Willis	2
*G.P.Howarth	run out	13	c Randall b Willis	20
M.D.Crowe	lbw b Cowans	37	c Lamb b Willis	1
J.J.Crowe	run out	0	b Willis	13
J.V.Coney	c Gower b Willis	19	not out	10
R.J.Hadlee	b Cowans	75	not out	6
J.G.Bracewell	c Dilley b Edmonds	16		
†I.D.S.Smith	c Tavaré b Willis	2		
B.L.Cairns	not out	24		
E.J.Chatfield	lbw b Willis	0		
Extras	(B1, LB4, W1, NB8)	14	(B8, LB7, NB10)	25
Total		**377**	**(5 wickets)**	**103**

NEW ZEALAND	O	M	R	W	O	M	R	W		FALL OF WICKETS			
Hadlee	21	9	44	0	26	9	45	0		E	NZ	E	NZ
Chatfield	22	8	67	1	29	5	95	5	*Wkt*	*1st*	*1st*	*2nd*	*2nd*
Cairns	33.2	14	74	7	24	2	70	3	1st	18	52	39	11
Coney	12	3	21	2	8	1	30	2	2nd	35	168	44	42
Bracewell	1	0	8	0					3rd	135	169	116	60
									4th	175	169	126	61
ENGLAND									5th	185	218	142	83
Willis	23.3	6	57	4	14	5	35	5	6th	205	304	142	–
Dilley	17	4	36	0	(3) 8	2	16	0	7th	205	348	190	–
Botham	26	9	81	0	(4) 0.1	0	4	0	8th	209	351	217	–
Cowans	28	8	88	3	(2) 5	0	23	0	9th	225	377	221	–
Edmonds	45	14	101	1					10th	225	377	252	–

Umpires: D.J.Constant (25) and B.J.Meyer (12).

Close: 1st day – NZ(1) 11-0 (Wright 2, Edgar 9); 2nd – NZ(1) 252-5 (Hadlee 52, Edgar 28); 3rd – E(2) 154-6 (Gower 54, Dilley 1).

ENGLAND v NEW ZEALAND 1983 (3rd Test)

At Lord's, London, on 11, 12, 13, 15 August.
Toss: New Zealand.   Result: ENGLAND won by 127 runs.
Debuts: England – N.G.B.Cook, N.A.Foster, C.L.Smith; New Zealand – E.J.Gray.

Lord's staged its 75th official Test match, equalling the record established in December 1982 by the Melbourne Cricket Ground. England's win, their fifth in nine matches against New Zealand at Lord's, was completed at 5.12 pm on the fourth day. Smith was out to his first ball in Test cricket. Gower (227 minutes, 198 balls, 16 fours), scored his second hundred in successive innings. At his first attempt Cook achieved the first five-wicket analysis by an England slow bowler in a home Test since P.H.Edmonds in 1975 (*Test No. 762*). In his 115th innings Willis became the first to be not out 50 times in Test cricket. Having become the first Derbyshire player to appear in 50 Tests, Taylor made his 150th catch when he dismissed Wright. Lamb equalled two England fielding records by holding four catches in an innings and six in the match. Botham became the first bowler to take 50 wickets in this series.

ENGLAND

C.J.Tavaré	b Crowe	51	c Crowe b Hadlee	16
C.L.Smith	lbw b Hadlee	0	c Coney b Hadlee	43
D.I.Gower	lbw b Crowe	108	c Crowe b Gray	34
A.J.Lamb	c sub (J.J.Crowe) b Chatfield	17	c Hadlee b Gray	4
M.W.Gatting	c Wright b Hadlee	81	b Gray	15
I.T.Botham	lbw b Cairns	8	c Coney b Chatfield	61
†R.W.Taylor	b Hadlee	16	c and b Coney	7
N.A.Foster	c Smith b Hadlee	10	c Wright b Hadlee	3
N.G.B.Cook	b Chatfield	16	c Bracewell b Chatfield	5
*R.G.D.Willis	c Smith b Hadlee	7	not out	2
N.G.Cowans	not out	1	c Smith b Chatfield	1
Extras	(B3, LB3, W2, NB3)	11	(B5, LB6, NB9)	20
Total		**326**		**211**

NEW ZEALAND

J.G.Wright	c Lamb b Willis	11	c Taylor b Botham	12
B.A.Edgar	c Willis b Cook	70	c Lamb b Cowans	27
*G.P.Howarth	b Cook	25	c Taylor b Willis	0
M.D.Crowe	b Botham	46	c Foster b Cowans	12
J.V.Coney	b Cook	7	c Gatting b Foster	68
E.J.Gray	c Lamb b Botham	11	c Lamb b Cook	17
J.G.Bracewell	c Gower b Cook	0	(8) lbw b Willis	4
R.J.Hadlee	c Botham b Cook	0	(7) b Willis	30
B.L.Cairns	c Lamb b Botham	5	b Cook	16
†I.D.S.Smith	c Lamb b Botham	3	not out	17
E.J.Chatfield	not out	5	c and b Cook	2
Extras	(LB5, NB3)	8	(B3, LB4, NB7)	14
Total		**191**		**219**

NEW ZEALAND	O	M	R	W		O	M	R	W		FALL OF WICKETS			
Hadlee	40	15	93	5		26	7	42	3			E	NZ	E	NZ
Cairns	23	8	65	1	(3) 3		0	9	0	Wkt	*1st*	*1st*	*2nd*	*2nd*
Chatfield	36.3	8	116	2	(2) 13.3	4		29	3	1st	3	18	26	15
Crowe	13	1	35	2						2nd	152	49	79	17
Coney	8	7	6	0	(6) 6	4		9	1	3rd	174	147	87	57
Bracewell					(4) 11	4		29	0	4th	191	159	119	61
Gray					(5) 30	8		73	3	5th	218	176	147	108
										6th	288	176	195	154
ENGLAND										7th	290	176	199	158
Willis	13	6	28	1		12	5	24	3	8th	303	183	208	190
Foster	16	5	40	0	(5) 12	0	35	1		9th	318	184	210	206
Cowans	9	1	30	0		11	1	36	2	10th	326	191	211	219
Botham	20.4	6	50	4	(2) 7	2	20	1						
Cook	26	11	35	5	(4) 27.2	9	90	3						

Umpires: D.J.Constant (26) and D.G.L.Evans (5).

Close: 1st day – E(1) 279-5 (Gatting 74, Taylor 12); 2nd – NZ(1) 176-6 (Gray 10, Hadlee 0); 3rd – E(2) 206-7 (Foster 2, Cook 5).

ENGLAND v NEW ZEALAND 1983 (4th Test)

At Trent Bridge, Nottingham, on 25, 26, 27, 28, 29 August.
Toss: England.   Result: ENGLAND won by 165 runs.
Debuts: New Zealand – T.J.Franklin.

England won the rubber 3-1 at 2.41 on the fifth afternoon of the last Test match in England to include Sunday play until 1991. Randall (40 Tests) and Howarth (34) each completed 2,000 runs. Hadlee became the first bowler to take 200 wickets for New Zealand when he bowled Cowans; only C.V.Grimmett (36), D.K.Lillee (38) and I.T.Botham (41) had reached this total in fewer Tests than Hadlee's 44. His aggregate of 21 wickets set a New Zealand record for any rubber against England.

ENGLAND

C.J.Tavaré	c Cairns b Snedden	4	c sub (J.J.Crowe) b Bracewell		13
C.L.Smith	c Howarth b Bracewell	31	c Howarth b Snedden		4
D.I.Gower	b Cairns	72	c Cairns b Bracewell		33
A.J.Lamb	c Howarth b Bracewell	22	not out		137
M.W.Gatting	lbw b Bracewell	14	c Lees b Cairns		11
I.T.Botham	lbw b Snedden	103	c Edgar b Gray		27
D.W.Randall	c Edgar b Hadlee	83	b Hadlee		13
†R.W.Taylor	b Bracewell	21	b Hadlee		0
N.G.B.Cook	c Lees b Snedden	4	c Lees b Cairns		26
*R.G.D.Willis	not out	25	b Hadlee		16
N.G.Cowans	c Bracewell b Cairns	7	b Hadlee		0
Extras	(B11, LB14, NB9)	34	(B6, LB10, W1)		17
Total		**420**			**297**

NEW ZEALAND

T.J.Franklin	c Smith b Botham	2	b Willis		7
B.A.Edgar	c Gatting b Cook	62	c Gower b Cook		76
*G.P.Howarth	c and b Cook	36	c Tavaré b Cowans		24
J.V.Coney	c Gatting b Cook	20	(5) c Taylor b Cook		68
E.J.Gray	run out	7	(6) c Gatting b Smith		3
R.J.Hadlee	c Smith b Cowans	3	(8) not out		92
†W.K.Lees	lbw b Cook	1	c Lamb b Cowans		7
M.D.Crowe	c and b Cook	34	(4) c Taylor b Cowans		0
M.C.Snedden	b Cowans	9	c Taylor b Cook		12
B.L.Cairns	c Gower b Cowans	26	b Cook		11
J.G.Bracewell	not out	1	c Taylor b Smith		28
Extras	(LB5, NB1)	6	(B2, W1, NB14)		17
Total		**207**			**345**

NEW ZEALAND	O	M	R	W	O	M	R	W		FALL OF WICKETS			
										E	NZ	E	NZ
Hadlee	30	7	98	1	28	5	85	4	Wkt	1st	1st	2nd	2nd
Snedden	28	7	69	3	8	1	40	1	1st	5	4	5	16
Cairns	33.4	9	77	2	(4) 20	9	36	2	2nd	94	80	58	67
Bracewell	28	5	108	4	(3) 21	2	88	2	3rd	136	124	61	71
Coney	2	0	10	0					4th	156	127	92	156
Gray	3	0	24	0	(5) 15	4	31	1	5th	169	131	149	161
									6th	355	135	188	184
ENGLAND									7th	356	135	188	228
Botham	14	4	33	1	(2) 25	4	73	0	8th	379	157	252	264
Willis	10	2	23	0	(1) 19	3	37	1	9th	407	201	297	290
Cowans	21	8	74	3	(4) 21	2	95	3	10th	420	207	297	345
Cook	32	14	63	5	(3) 50	22	87	4					
Gatting	5	2	8	0	2	1	5	0					
Smith					12	2	31	2					

Umpires: H.D.Bird (26) and B.J.Meyer (13).

Close: 1st day – E(1) 362-7 (Taylor 1, Cook 4); 2nd – NZ(1) 135-7 (Crowe 0, Snedden 0); 3rd – E(2) 252-8 (Lamb 109); 4th – NZ (2) 167-5 (Coney 46, Lees 2).

INDIA v PAKISTAN 1983-84 (1st Test)

At Karnataka State C.A.Stadium, Bangalore, on 14, 15, 17, 18, 19 September.
Toss: India.   Result: MATCH DRAWN.
Debuts: Pakistan – Azeem Hafeez.

More than seven hours were lost to rain and poor light. This was the first Test match in which no-balls and wides were debited to bowlers' analyses. The seventh-wicket partnership of 155 between Binny and Madan Lal established an Indian record against Pakistan. Javed Miandad became the second Pakistan batsman after Zaheer Abbas to score 4,000 runs. After 27 minutes of confusion concerning regulations governing the number of overs to be bowled on the final day, during which time the Pakistan team left the field, Gavaskar (87) was allowed to continue his innings. He completed his 28th Test hundred off the first ball of the last of the mandatory 20 overs.

INDIA

S.M.Gavaskar	lbw b Tahir	42	not out	103
A.D.Gaekwad	b Mudassar	11	not out	66
M.Amarnath	b Mudassar	4		
Yashpal Sharma	c Wasim Bari b Mudassar	16		
S.M.Patil	c Miandad b Tahir	6		
*Kapil Dev	c Mohsin b Azeem	0		
R.M.H.Binny	not out	83		
Madan Lal	c Wasim Bari b Azeem	74		
†S.M.H.Kirmani	c Wasim Bari b Tahir	14		
S.Venkataraghavan	c Salim b Tahir	5		
D.R.Doshi	lbw b Tahir	0		
Extras	(B1, LB8, W6, NB5)	20	(LB4, W1, NB2)	7
Total		**275**	(0 wickets)	**176**

PAKISTAN

Mohsin Khan	c Kirmani b Madan Lal	17
Mudassar Nazar	c Kirmani b Kapil Dev	25
Salim Malik	c Amarnath b Kapil Dev	5
Javed Miandad	c sub (K.Srikkanth) b Madan Lal	99
*Zaheer Abbas	c Kapil Dev b Madan Lal	22
Wasim Raja	b Doshi	39
†Wasim Bari	b Kapil Dev	64
Tahir Naqqash	b Kapil Dev	1
Iqbal Qasim	c Gaekwad b Venkataraghavan	9
Azeem Hafeez	b Kapil Dev	0
Mohammad Nazir	not out	0
Extras	(B1, LB4, NB2)	7
Total		**288**

PAKISTAN	O	M	R	W	O	M	R	W		FALL OF WICKETS		
										I	P	I
Tahir	34.5	11	76	5	17	2	54	0	Wkt	1st	1st	2nd
Azeem	39	11	102	2	8	2	20	0	1st	38	32	–
Nazir	10	2	26	0	(4) 21	4	47	0	2nd	42	37	–
Mudassar	23	6	44	3	(5) 2.1	0	19	0	3rd	72	58	–
Qasim	13	7	18	0	(3) 12	2	29	0	4th	80	99	–
Zaheer					1	0	3	0	5th	81	187	–
									6th	85	243	–
INDIA									7th	240	244	–
Kapil Dev	29	6	68	5					8th	269	288	–
Madan Lal	24	5	72	3					9th	275	288	–
Binny	18	2	42	0					10th	275	288	–
Venkataraghavan	21.1	4	49	1								
Doshi	20	5	52	1								

Umpires: M.V.Gothoskar (11) and Swaroop Kishen (12).

Close: 1st day – I(1) 57-2 (Gavaskar 33, Yashpal 6); 2nd – I(1) 191-6 (Binny 50, Madan Lal 51); 3rd – P(1) 22-0 (Mohsin 13, Mudassar 9); 4th – P(1) 247-7 (Wasim Bari 30, Qasim 3).

INDIA v PAKISTAN 1983-84 (2nd Test)

At Burlton Park, Jullundur, on 24, 25, 26 (*no play*) 28, 29 September.
Toss: India.   Result: MATCH DRAWN.
Debuts: Pakistan – Qasim Omar, Shoaib Mohammad.

Burlton Park was the 55th ground to stage an official Test match and the 13th to do so in India. The game was always likely to be drawn after Zaheer had rejected a request from the ground authorities to continue the match on the rest day, following the loss of the third day to rain. Kapil Dev dismissed Mohsin Khan with the first ball of the match. By adding 95 for the eighth wicket, Wasim Raja and Tahir Naqqash set a new Pakistan record for this series (beaten in 1986-87). Gaekwad recorded India's first double century against Pakistan; it took him 652 minutes (426 balls) and was then the slowest in all first-class cricket, surpassing the Nawab of Pataudi's 622 minutes for South Zone v West Zone at Bombay in 1967-68. Gaekwad batted for 671 minutes, faced 436 balls and hit 17 fours. His partnership of 121 with Binny was India's highest for the sixth wicket against Pakistan until 1986-87.

PAKISTAN

Mohsin Khan	lbw b Kapil Dev	0	not out	7
Shoaib Mohammad	c Kirmani b Kapil Dev	6	not out	6
Qasim Omar	c Kirmani b Binny	15		
*Zaheer Abbas	b Shastri	49		
Javed Miandad	c Shastri b Kapil Dev	66		
Mudassar Nazar	c sub (K.Srikkanth) b Shastri	24		
Wasim Raja	c Kirmani b Shastri	125		
†Wasim Bari	c Kirmani b Kapil Dev	0		
Tahir Naqqash	b Binny	37		
Mohammad Nazir	run out	2		
Azeem Hafeez	not out	2		
Extras	(B3, LB6, W1, NB1)	11	(NB3)	3
Total		**337**	(0 wickets)	**16**

INDIA

S.M.Gavaskar	b Azeem	5
A.D.Gaekwad	c and b Wasim Raja	201
M.Amarnath	c Wasim Bari b Azeem	7
Yashpal Sharma	lbw b Tahir	7
S.M.Patil	c Wasim Bari b Tahir	26
R.J.Shastri	c Wasim Bari b Azeem	26
R.M.H.Binny	b Zaheer	54
*Kapil Dev	lbw b Wasim Raja	4
Madan Lal	c Wasim Bari b Wasim Raja	11
†S.M.H.Kirmani	not out	8
S.Venkataraghavan	b Wasim Raja	6
Extras	(B2, LB4, W9, NB4)	19
Total		**374**

INDIA	O	M	R	W	O	M	R	W		FALL OF WICKETS			
Kapil Dev	32	8	80	4	2	0	9	0			P	I	P
Madan Lal	20	4	61	0	1	0	1	0	Wkt	1st	1st	2nd
Binny	16	1	69	2					1st	0	5	–
Shastri	37.2	12	63	3	(3) 3	2	1	0	2nd	7	20	–
Venkataraghavan	28	5	55	0					3rd	55	73	–
Patil					(4) 2	1	2	0	4th	101	131	–
Gavaskar					(5) 1	0	3	0	5th	154	209	–
									6th	169	330	–
PAKISTAN									7th	169	345	–
Tahir	27	3	74	2					8th	264	353	–
Azeem	23	3	65	3					9th	309	368	–
Mudassar	28	6	80	0					10th	337	374	–
Nazir	52	16	76	0								
Wasim Raja	28.5	5	50	4								
Mohsin	5	2	9	0								
Zaheer	6	1	14	1								

Umpires: D.N.Dotiwalla (2) and B.Ganguli (2).

Close: 1st day – P(1) 185-7 (Wasim Raja 18, Tahir 1); 2nd – I(1) 37-2 (Gaekwad 17, Yashpal 3); 3rd – no play; 4th – I(1) 201-4 (Gaekwad 121, Shastri 21).

INDIA v PAKISTAN 1983-84 (3rd Test)

At Vidarbha C.A.Ground, Nagpur, on 5, 6, 8, 9, 10 October.
Toss: India.   Result: MATCH DRAWN.
Debuts: India – A.R.Bhat.

This match completed the third rubber between these countries in which every Test has been drawn. It began with one of its participants 600 miles away in Bombay. Patil, not in the selected squad of 14 players, was summoned when Amarnath withdrew because of a fever shortly before the start. Flown by a specially chartered Maharashtra State aircraft, Patil arrived after the first day's play had ended. Nagpur's only previous Test took place in October 1969 (*Test No. 660*).

INDIA

S.M.Gavaskar	c Mudassar b Azeem	50	c Mudassar b Nazir		64
A.D.Gaekwad	c Wasim Bari b Tahir	6	c Wasim Raja b Nazir		29
D.B.Vengsarkar	c Wasim Bari b Salim	21	c Mohsin b Nazir		40
Yashpal Sharma	lbw b Nazir	13	c Wasim Bari b Azeem		15
S.M.Patil	c Wasim Raja b Azeem	6	lbw b Wasim Raja		26
*Kapil Dev	c Wasim Bari b Mudassar	32	(8) st Wasim Bari b Wasim Raja		10
R.J.Shastri	c Mudassar b Azeem	52	(6) c Mudassar b Nazir		0
K.Azad	c Mohsin b Azeem	11	(7) c Zaheer b Nazir		0
Madan Lal	c Salim b Nazir	5	not out		32
†S.M.H.Kirmani	run out	30	not out		31
A.R.Bhat	not out	0			
Extras	(B9, LB6, W1, NB3)	19	(B7, LB7, NB1)		15
Total		**245**	(8 wickets declared)		**262**

PAKISTAN

Mohsin Khan	c Kirmani b Shastri	44			
Shoaib Mohammad	c Yashpal b Kapil Dev	9			
Salim Malik	lbw b Kapil Dev	0	not out		0
Javed Miandad	lbw b Bhat	60			
*Zaheer Abbas	c Kirmani b Kapil Dev	85			
Mudassar Nazar	st Kirmani b Bhat	78			
Wasim Raja	c Yashpal b Shastri	16			
†Wasim Bari	c Patil b Shastri	1			
Tahir Naqqash	c Gaekwad b Shastri	6	(1) not out		18
Mohammad Nazir	not out	13			
Azeem Hafeez	c Patil b Shastri	4	(2) b Kirmani		18
Extras	(B1, LB1, NB4)	6	(B4, LB1, NB1)		6
Total		**322**	(1 wicket)		**42**

PAKISTAN	O	M	R	W		O	M	R	W		FALL OF WICKETS			
Azeem	27	10	58	4		19	1	67	1			I	P	I	P
Tahir	19.3	3	72	1		23	7	55	0		*Wkt*	*1st*	*1st*	*2nd*	*2nd*
Mudassar	14	2	43	1							1st	27	20	78	42
Salim	3	0	7	1							2nd	66	26	125	–
Nazir	22	5	50	2	(3)	50	19	72	5		3rd	96	83	148	–
Zaheer					(4)	1	1	0	0		4th	103	153	172	–
Wasim Raja					(5)	10	1	46	2		5th	103	254	172	–
Mohsin					(6)	3	1	7	0		6th	171	287	188	–
Miandad					(7)	1	0	1	0		7th	190	289	188	–
											8th	205	305	207	–
INDIA											9th	242	309	–	–
Kapil Dev	27	8	68	3	(5)	1	1	0	0		10th	245	322	–	–
Madan Lal	13	2	44	0											
Bhat	39	16	65	2											
Azad	25	7	68	0											
Shastri	30.4	7	75	5											
Vengsarkar					(1)	2	0	15	0						
Yashpal					(2)	1	0	10	0						
Kirmani					(3)	2	0	9	1						
Gaekwad					(4)	1	0	3	0						
Gavaskar					(6)	1	1	0	0						

Umpires: S.R.Bose (1) and M.G.Subramaniam (1).

Close: 1st day – I(1) 92-2 (Gavaskar 46, Yashpal 12); 2nd – P(1) 9-0 (Mohsin 5, Shoaib 4); 3rd – P(1) 219-4 (Zaheer 69, Mudassar 34); 4th – I(2) 99-1 (Gavaskar 50, Vengsarkar 11).

INDIA v WEST INDIES 1983-84 (1st Test)

At Green Park, Kanpur, on 21, 22, 23, 25 October.
Toss: West Indies.   Result: WEST INDIES won by an innings and 83 runs.
Debuts: West Indies – E.A.E.Baptiste.

West Indies, with their fast bowlers claiming 19 wickets, completed their comprehensive victory soon after lunch on the fourth day. Greenidge, who batted 522 minutes for his highest Test score to that date, became the 12th batsman to score 3,000 runs for West Indies. His seventh-wicket partnership of 130 with Marshall remains a West Indies record against India. Marshall followed his career-best 92 with an opening spell of 8-5-9-4 which included Gavaskar with his second ball. Throughout this rubber no-balls and wides were debited to the bowlers' analyses.

WEST INDIES

C.G.Greenidge	c Kirmani b Amarnath	194
D.L.Haynes	c Madan Lal b Kapil Dev	6
I.V.A.Richards	c Kirmani b Kapil Dev	24
H.A.Gomes	c Gaekwad b Shastri	21
*C.H.Lloyd	c Kirmani b Bhat	23
A.L.Logie	lbw b Bhat	0
†P.J.L.Dujon	b Binny	81
M.D.Marshall	c and b Kapil Dev	92
E.A.E.Baptiste	run out	6
M.A.Holding	lbw b Kapil Dev	0
W.W.Davis	not out	0
Extras	(B4, LB2, NB1)	7
Total		**454**

INDIA

S.M.Gavaskar	c Dujon b Marshall	0		c Davis b Marshall	7
A.D.Gaekwad	c Dujon b Marshall	4		c Richards b Marshall	5
M.Amarnath	lbw b Marshall	0	(6)	b Davis	0
D.B.Vengsarkar	b Marshall	14		c Davis b Marshall	65
S.M.Patil	c Richards b Davis	19		b Davis	3
R.J.Shastri	c Dujon b Davis	0	(7)	not out	46
†S.M.H.Kirmani	b Holding	20	(9)	b Holding	14
*Kapil Dev	c Gomes b Baptiste	27		c Dujon b Holding	3
R.M.H.Binny	c Richards b Holding	39	(3)	c Dujon b Marshall	7
Madan Lal	not out	63		b Holding	0
A.R.Bhat	b Holding	0		b Davis	6
Extras	(B6, LB6, W3, NB6)	21		(B2, LB2, W1, NB3)	8
Total		**207**			**164**

INDIA	O	M	R	W	O	M	R	W	FALL OF WICKETS			
Kapil Dev	24.2	3	99	4						WI	I	I
Madan Lal	17	5	50	0					*Wkt*	*1st*	*1st*	*2nd*
Binny	17	2	74	1					1st	9	0	8
Bhat	34	6	86	2					2nd	58	0	13
Shastri	38	7	103	1					3rd	102	9	38
Gaekwad	1	0	6	0					4th	157	18	43
Amarnath	7	1	30	1					5th	157	29	43
									6th	309	49	105
WEST INDIES									7th	439	90	109
Marshall	15	7	19	4	17	7	47	4	8th	449	90	135
Holding	14.4	6	37	3	19	2	59	3	9th	451	207	143
Davis	13	2	57	2	16.3	3	46	3	10th	454	207	164
Baptiste	11	0	58	1	6	1	8	0				
Gomes	6	0	24	0								

Umpires: B.Ganguli (3) and Swaroop Kishen (13).

Close: 1st day – WI(1) 255-5 (Greenidge 130, Dujon 48); 2nd – I(1) 34-5 (Patil 10, Kirmani 4); 3rd – I(2) 73-5 (Vengsarkar 41, Shastri 7).

INDIA v WEST INDIES 1983-84 (2nd Test)

At Feroz Shah Kotla, Delhi, on 29, 30 October, 1, 2, 3 November.
Toss: India.   Result: MATCH DRAWN.
Debuts: None.

Gavaskar's hundred, scored off 94 balls, was the fastest of his 29 three-figure innings in Test cricket. It brought him level with D.G.Bradman's record tally of hundreds in 166 innings compared with the Australian's 80. Gavaskar scored 121 off 128 balls in 224 minutes, hitting two sixes and 15 fours; his first fifty came from 37 balls. When 104 he became the third batsman after G.St A.Sobers (8,032) and G.Boycott (8,114) to score 8,000 runs in Test cricket. The Indian Prime Minister, Mrs Indira Gandhi, was present at the following day's play to congratulate him. Vengsarkar's innings of 159 occupied 370 minutes (238 balls) and included a six and 20 fours. Daniel, recalled to Test cricket after a hiatus of more than seven years, took six wickets in a match for the first time. This result extended India's sequence without a win to 25 matches, a national record.

INDIA

S.M.Gavaskar	b Gomes	121	lbw b Holding	15
A.D.Gaekwad	c Richards b Holding	8	b Daniel	32
D.B.Vengsarkar	c Richards b Holding	159	b Marshall	63
Yashpal Sharma	b Holding	5	lbw b Daniel	0
R.J.Shastri	lbw b Davis	49	lbw b Holding	26
R.M.H.Binny	lbw b Holding	52	b Daniel	32
M.Amarnath	c Dujon b Daniel	1	c Davis b Marshall	0
*Kapil Dev	c Lloyd b Marshall	18	c Gomes b Marshall	0
K.Azad	lbw b Daniel	5	run out	9
Madan Lal	c sub (R.A.Harper) b Daniel	3	not out	24
†S.M.H.Kirmani	not out	1	c Logie b Gomes	3
Extras	(B4, LB9, W2, NB27)	42	(B5, LB10, W2, NB12)	29
Total		**464**		**233**

WEST INDIES

C.G.Greenidge	lbw b Azad	33		not out	72
D.L.Haynes	c Yashpal b Kapil Dev	12		b Shastri	17
W.W.Davis	b Azad	19			
I.V.A.Richards	lbw b Kapil Dev	67	(3)	c Gaekwad b Shastri	22
H.A.Gomes	c Kirmani b Shastri	19	(4)	not out	1
*C.H.Lloyd	lbw b Kapil Dev	103			
A.L.Logie	c and b Kapil Dev	63			
†P.J.L.Dujon	lbw b Kapil Dev	22			
M.D.Marshall	b Kapil Dev	17			
M.A.Holding	b Shastri	14			
W.W.Daniel	not out	1			
Extras	(B5, LB7, NB2)	14		(LB4, W1, NB3)	8
Total		**384**		**(2 wickets)**	**120**

WEST INDIES	O	M	R	W	O	M	R	W		FALL OF WICKETS			
Marshall	24	1	105	1	18	4	52	3		I	WI	I	WI
Holding	28.1	1	107	4	12	4	36	2	*Wkt*	*1st*	*1st*	*2nd*	*2nd*
Davis	25	2	87	1	12	0	45	0	1st	28	44	20	50
Daniel	21	2	86	3	15	3	38	3	2nd	206	45	73	107
Gomes	21	2	58	1	20.1	2	47	1	3rd	221	112	73	–
Richards	3	1	8	0					4th	366	143	133	–
									5th	382	173	151	–
INDIA									6th	383	304	152	–
Kapil Dev	31	2	77	6	7	2	26	0	7th	422	331	153	–
Madan Lal	15	2	59	0	7	0	15	0	8th	452	357	166	–
Binny	15	3	35	0	3	0	16	0	9th	462	370	218	–
Shastri	37.5	7	106	2	17	3	36	2	10th	464	384	233	–
Azad	26	5	84	2	14	4	22	0					
Gaekwad	3	1	11	0	(7) 1	1	0	0					
Gavaskar					(6) 1	0	1	0					

Umpires: D.N.Dotiwalla (3) and M.V.Gothoskar (12).

Close: 1st day – I(1) 299-3 (Vengsarkar 114, Shastri 23); 2nd – WI(1) 45-1 (Haynes 12, Davis 0); 3rd – WI(1) 319-6 (Lloyd 83, Dujon 14); 4th – I(2) 145-4 (Vengsarkar 58, Binny 3).

INDIA v WEST INDIES 1983-84 (3rd Test)

At Gujarat Stadium, Ahmedabad, on 12, 13, 14, 16 November.
Toss: India.   Result: WEST INDIES won by 138 runs.
Debuts: India – N.S.Sidhu. (*Sidhu has also appeared as 'Navjot Singh'.*)

Ahmedabad provided the 56th Test match ground and the 14th in India (more than any other country). When Gavaskar glanced a ball from Holding for his 83rd run soon after tea on the second day, he overtook G.Boycott's world record aggregate of 8,114 runs (108 Tests; 193 innings) in his 96th Test (168th innings). His fifty, scored out of 67 and from 58 balls, was his 65th in Tests and deprived Boycott of another world record. Gavaskar also became the first batsman to score 1,000 runs in a calendar year of Test cricket on four occasions, having already achieved this feat in 1976, 1978 and 1979. Lloyd scored his 2,000th run against India. Kapil Dev was the tenth bowler to take nine or more wickets in a Test innings, the third to do so and finish on the losing side, the third for India, and the first as captain. His analysis was then the fifth-best in Test cricket and remains the best in this series. India were dismissed for their lowest total against West Indies until the fifth Test. Gursharan Singh (20), a Delhi batsman fielding in place of Binny (torn back muscle), became the third substitute to hold three catches in a Test innings and the first to take four in a match.

WEST INDIES

C.G.Greenidge	c Maninder b Binny	7		b Kapil Dev	3
D.L.Haynes	lbw b Binny	9		c Patil b Sandhu	1
I.V.A.Richards	c Azad b Binny	8		c sub‡ b Kapil Dev	20
H.A.Gomes	c Gavaskar b Maninder	38		lbw b Kapil Dev	25
*C.H.Lloyd	c sub‡ b Maninder	68		c Gavaskar b Kapil Dev	33
A.L.Logie	c Kirmani b Maninder	0		lbw b Kapil Dev	0
†P.J.L.Dujon	c Kapil Dev b Shastri	98		c sub‡ b Kapil Dev	20
M.D.Marshall	b Maninder	10		c sub‡ b Kapil Dev	29
W.W.Daniel	run out	6	(10)	b Kapil Dev	0
M.A.Holding	b Kapil Dev	16	(9)	lbw b Kapil Dev	58
W.W.Davis	not out	3		not out	1
Extras	(B8, LB6, NB4)	18		(LB9, NB2)	11
Total		**281**			**201**

INDIA

S.M.Gavaskar	c Lloyd b Holding	90		lbw b Holding	1
A.D.Gaekwad	b Holding	39		b Davis	29
N.S.Sidhu	run out	15		c Dujon b Holding	4
S.M.Patil	c Dujon b Marshall	22		c Daniel b Marshall	1
R.J.Shastri	c Lloyd b Daniel	13		c Dujon b Holding	1
R.M.H.Binny	c Haynes b Davis	5	(8)	c Greenidge b Holding	1
*Kapil Dev	lbw b Daniel	31		b Davis	1
K.Azad	b Daniel	0	(6)	b Marshall	3
†S.M.H.Kirmani	c Haynes b Daniel	5		not out	24
B.S.Sandhu	not out	7		lbw b Davis	1
Maninder Singh	lbw b Daniel	0		lbw b Daniel	15
Extras	(B7, LB4, NB3)	14		(B6, LB12, NB4)	22
Total		**241**			**103**

INDIA	O	M	R	W	O	M	R	W		FALL OF WICKETS			
Kapil Dev	27	9	52	1	30.3	6	83	9		WI	I	WI	I
Sandhu	14	6	33	0	10	1	45	1	*Wkt*	*1st*	*1st*	*2nd*	*2nd*
Binny	6	0	18	3					1st	16	127	4	1
Maninder Singh	34	6	85	4	(3) 14	1	48	0	2nd	22	148	8	7
Azad	7	0	34	0	4	2	7	0	3rd	27	174	43	8
Shastri	16.3	2	45	1	(4) 2	0	9	0	4th	134	186	74	24
									5th	134	197	74	27
WEST INDIES									6th	158	213	107	38
Marshall	26	9	66	1	13	3	23	2	7th	168	214	114	39
Holding	26	5	80	2	17	5	30	4	8th	190	222	188	61
Daniel	11.5	0	39	5	(4) 6.1	2	11	1	9th	230	241	188	63
Davis	11	3	23	1	(3) 11	1	21	3	10th	281	241	201	103
Gomes	6	0	22	0									

Umpires: S.N.Hanumantha Rao (9) and K.B.Ramaswami (8).   ‡ (Gursharan Singh)

Close: 1st day – WI(1) 209-8 (Dujon 44, Holding 10); 2nd – I(1) 173-2 (Sidhu 14, Patil 16); 3rd – WI(2) 152-7 (Marshall 20, Holding 22).

INDIA v WEST INDIES 1983-84 (4th Test)

At Wankhede Stadium, Bombay, on 24, 26, 27, 28, 29 November.
Toss: India.   Result: MATCH DRAWN.
Debuts: West Indies – R.B.Richardson.

Set 244 runs in a minimum of 156 minutes, West Indies were content to defend on a slow, turning pitch of uneven bounce. Lloyd's 94th Test appearance deprived G.St A.Sobers of the West Indies record. Vengsarkar reached his second hundred in successive Tests after facing 135 balls in 201 minutes. Haynes was the fourth batsman to be out handling the ball in a Test match, the others being W.R.Endean (South Africa), A.M.J.Hilditch (Australia), and Mohsin Khan (Pakistan); when a ball from Kapil Dev took the inside edge and rolled slowly towards the stumps via his pad, Haynes brushed it away with his glove. Richards took 130 balls to score his 15th hundred in Tests and his sixth in 18 matches against India.

INDIA

S.M.Gavaskar	lbw b Marshall	12	c Davis b Marshall	3
A.D.Gaekwad	b Holding	48	c Richards b Holding	3
D.B.Vengsarkar	c Richards b Davis	100		
A.Malhotra	c Dujon b Holding	32	(3) not out	72
R.J.Shastri	b Holding	77	(4) run out	38
R.M.H.Binny	lbw b Marshall	65	(5) lbw b Davis	18
*Kapil Dev	b Holding	8	(6) c Dujon b Daniel	1
Madan Lal	lbw b Marshall	0	(7) not out	26
†S.M.H.Kirmani	not out	43		
N.S.Yadav	b Daniel	12		
Maninder Singh	c Lloyd b Holding	9		
Extras	(B16, LB14, W1, NB26)	57	(B1, LB6, NB5)	12
Total		**463**	(5 wickets declared)	**173**

WEST INDIES

C.G.Greenidge	b Yadav	13	b Kapil Dev	4
D.L.Haynes	handled the ball	55	b Maninder	24
R.B.Richardson	lbw b Yadav	0	b Shastri	26
I.V.A.Richards	st Kirmani b Shastri	120	c Kirmani b Shastri	4
H.A.Gomes	b Kapil Dev	26	not out	37
†P.J.L.Dujon	c Kirmani b Yadav	84		
*C.H.Lloyd	run out	67	(6) not out	9
M.D.Marshall	c Gavaskar b Yadav	4		
M.A.Holding	c and b Yadav	2		
W.W.Daniel	c Gavaskar b Shastri	0		
W.W.Davis	not out	4		
Extras	(B4, LB8, NB6)	18		
Total		**393**	(4 wickets)	**104**

WEST INDIES	O	M	R	W	O	M	R	W		FALL OF WICKETS			
										I	WI	I	WI
Marshall	32	6	88	3	13	3	47	1	*Wkt*	*1st*	*1st*	*2nd*	*2nd*
Holding	40.5	10	102	5	11	1	39	1	1st	12	47	4	4
Davis	36	3	127	1	(4) 8	0	35	1	2nd	145	47	6	40
Daniel	30	3	113	1	(3) 14	3	45	1	3rd	190	128	91	48
Gomes	4	1	3	0					4th	234	205	118	68
									5th	361	238	121	–
INDIA									6th	372	357	–	–
Kapil Dev	23	10	41	1	5	1	13	1	7th	373	377	–	–
Shastri	35	8	98	2	(5) 13	4	32	2	8th	385	383	–	–
Maninder Singh	27	7	71	0	(4) 15	7	25	1	9th	433	384	–	–
Madan Lal	13	6	29	0	(2) 3	1	8	0	10th	463	393	–	–
Binny	4	1	11	0									
Yadav	44.1	8	131	5	(3) 12	5	22	0					
Gaekwad					(6) 1	0	4	0					
Gavaskar					(7) 1	1	0	0					
Malhotra					(8) 1	1	0	0					

Umpires: M.V.Gothoskar (13) and Swaroop Kishen (14).

Close: 1st day – I(1) 259-4 (Shastri 29, Binny 14); 2nd – WI(1) 0-0 (Greenidge 0, Haynes 0); 3rd – WI(1) 204-3 (Richards 103, Gomes 26); 4th – I(2) 45-2 (Malhotra 25, Shastri 12).

Test No. 968/53 (I218/WI221)

INDIA v WEST INDIES 1983-84 (5th Test)

At Eden Gardens, Calcutta, on 10, 11, 12, 14 December.
Toss: India.   Result: WEST INDIES won by an innings and 46 runs.
Debuts: West Indies – R.A.Harper.

Armed police protected the Indian team from members of the 80,000 crowd which saw them dismissed for the lowest total of this series until 1987-88 and the lowest in any Calcutta Test. Enraged when their heroes of the 1983 Prudential World Cup lost the rubber before lunch on the fourth day, jeering spectators threw fruit, stones and bottles. They attacked the team coach, broke some of its windows and injured Malhotra and the team manager, A.A.Baig. Gavaskar became the first batsman in Test cricket to be out to the first ball of the match on more than one occasion (also *Test No. 741*). In his 46th Test Roberts became the third bowler to take 200 wickets for West Indies. Later he made his highest score in first-class cricket and shared in a national ninth-wicket record partnership of 161 with Lloyd, the latter scoring his 18th Test hundred and batting for 496 minutes.

INDIA

S.M.Gavaskar	c Dujon b Marshall	0		c Dujon b Holding	20
A.D.Gaekwad	b Marshall	2		b Holding	4
D.B.Vengsarkar	b Holding	23		lbw b Marshall	1
M.Amarnath	c and b Marshall	0		b Holding	0
A.Malhotra	c Gomes b Davis	20	(6)	c Dujon b Marshall	30
R.J.Shastri	b Holding	12	(7)	b Marshall	2
R.M.H.Binny	lbw b Roberts	44	(8)	c Harper b Marshall	6
*Kapil Dev	b Holding	69	(9)	c Dujon b Marshall	0
†S.M.H.Kirmani	b Roberts	49	(10)	b Roberts	13
N.S.Yadav	c Greenidge b Roberts	10	(5)	b Marshall	4
Maninder Singh	not out	0		not out	0
Extras	(LB6, NB6)	12		(B1, LB5, NB4)	10
Total		**241**			**90**

WEST INDIES

C.G.Greenidge	c Yadav b Binny	25
D.L.Haynes	lbw b Kapil Dev	5
I.V.A.Richards	c Kirmani b Kapil Dev	9
H.A.Gomes	b Yadav	18
†P.J.L.Dujon	c Gaekwad b Kapil Dev	0
*C.H.Lloyd	not out	161
M.D.Marshall	lbw b Maninder	54
M.A.Holding	c Shastri b Maninder	17
R.A.Harper	lbw b Kapil Dev	0
A.M.E.Roberts	c Amarnath b Yadav	68
W.W.Davis	lbw b Yadav	0
Extras	(B8, LB7, W1, NB4)	20
Total		**377**

WEST INDIES	O	M	R	W		O	M	R	W		FALL OF WICKETS		
Marshall	22	7	65	3		15	4	37	6		I	WI	I
Roberts	23.4	9	56	3	(4)	4	1	11	1	*Wkt*	*1st*	*1st*	*2nd*
Davis	14	1	39	1		2	0	7	0	1st	0	32	14
Holding	20	4	59	3	(2)	9	3	29	3	2nd	9	41	29
Harper	8	2	16	0						3rd	13	42	29
										4th	41	42	33
INDIA										5th	63	88	36
Kapil Dev	35	5	91	4						6th	63	175	50
Binny	13	2	62	1						7th	145	213	77
Amarnath	7	1	19	0						8th	212	213	77
Yadav	27	1	80	3						9th	240	374	80
Shastri	18	2	56	0						10th	241	377	90
Maninder Singh	28	7	54	2									

Umpires: M.V.Gothoskar (14) and Swaroop Kishen (15).

Close: 1st day – I(1) 231-8 (Kirmani 42, Yadav 8); 2nd – WI(1) 179-6 (Lloyd 58, Holding 0); 3rd – I(2) 36-5 (Malhotra 2).

INDIA v WEST INDIES 1983-84 (6th Test)

At Chidambaram Stadium, Chepauk, Madras, on 24 (*no play*), 26, 27, 28, 29 December.
Toss: West Indies.   Result: MATCH DRAWN.
Debuts: None.

Incessant rain for two days before the match left the ground waterlogged for the first day. Gavaskar (644 minutes, 425 balls, 23 fours) scored his 30th hundred in Test cricket to surpass D.G.Bradman's world record. His score of 236 not out remains the highest for India in all Tests, beating 'Vinoo' Mankad's 231 in *Test No. 420*. He became the first batsman to score either 13 hundreds or three double centuries against West Indies. His stands of 170 for the sixth wicket with Shastri and 143 unfinished for the ninth with Kirmani remain records for India in this series. Gavaskar's century partnership with Shastri was the 48th in which he had shared in Test cricket and deprived G.Boycott of another world record. Holding's innings included four sixes. Marshall equalled the national record of 33 wickets in a rubber shared by A.L.Valentine (v England 1950) and C.E.H.Croft (v Pakistan 1976-77).

WEST INDIES

C.G.Greenidge	c Gavaskar b Shastri	34	not out		26
D.L.Haynes	b Maninder	23	c Vengsarkar b Shastri		24
I.V.A.Richards	c Kirmani b Maninder	32			
H.A.Gomes	b Yadav	28	(3) not out		10
†P.J.L.Dujon	c Kapil Dev b Binny	62			
*C.H.Lloyd	lbw b Kapil Dev	32			
W.W.Davis	c Sidhu b Binny	12			
M.D.Marshall	lbw b Kapil Dev	38			
M.A.Holding	lbw b Kapil Dev	34			
A.M.E.Roberts	not out	0			
R.A.Harper	c and b Maninder	0			
Extras	(LB12, NB6)	18	(LB2, NB2)		4
Total		**313**	(1 wicket)		**64**

INDIA

A.D.Gaekwad	c Harper b Marshall	0
N.S.Sidhu	c Richards b Roberts	20
D.B.Vengsarkar	c Harper b Marshall	0
S.M.Gavaskar	not out	236
A.Malhotra	c sub (R.B.Richardson) b Harper	9
N.S.Yadav	c Dujon b Marshall	3
R.J.Shastri	lbw b Davis	72
R.M.H.Binny	c sub (E.A.E.Baptiste) b Marshall	1
*Kapil Dev	c sub (E.A.E.Baptiste) b Marshall	26
†S.M.H.Kirmani	not out	63
Maninder Singh	did not bat	
Extras	(B1, LB5, W9, NB6)	21
Total	(8 wickets declared)	**451**

INDIA	O	M	R	W		O	M	R	W	FALL OF WICKETS			
											WI	I	WI
Kapil Dev	15	3	44	3		6	2	11	0		*1st*	*1st*	*2nd*
Binny	12	1	48	2		2	0	14	0	*Wkt*			
Shastri	28	6	72	1	(4)	6	3	10	1	1st	47	0	38
Yadav	28	4	96	1						2nd	91	0	–
Maninder Singh	29.3	9	41	3	(3)	6	2	10	0	3rd	100	54	–
Sidhu					(5)	1	0	9	0	4th	136	67	–
Kirmani					(6)	1	0	4	0	5th	200	92	–
Vengsarkar					(7)	1	0	4	0	6th	226	262	–
										7th	232	269	–
WEST INDIES										8th	303	308	–
Marshall	26	8	72	5						9th	312	–	–
Roberts	28	4	81	1						10th	313	–	–
Davis	30	4	75	1									
Holding	26	2	85	0									
Harper	42	7	108	1									
Gomes	8	0	24	0									

Umpires: M.G.Subramaniam (2) and Swaroop Kishen (16).

Close: 1st day – no play; 2nd – WI(1) 207-5 (Dujon 48, Davis 4); 3rd – I(1) 69-4 (Gavaskar 36, Yadav 1); 4th – I(1) 262-6 (Gavaskar 149).

AUSTRALIA v PAKISTAN 1983-84 (1st Test)

At W.A.C.A.Ground, Perth, on 11, 12, 13, 14 November.
Toss: Pakistan.   Result: AUSTRALIA won by an innings and 9 runs.
Debuts: Australia – W.B.Phillips.

Phillips (307 minutes, 246 balls, 20 fours) became the ninth batsman to score a hundred in his first innings for Australia; his partnership of 259 in 267 minutes with Yallop set an all-wicket record for this series. Hogg took the wickets of Mohsin, Miandad and Zaheer for no runs in ten balls, Miandad's nought ending a sequence of 763 runs in seven Test innings. Rackemann's match analysis of 11 for 118 remains the record for Australia against Pakistan and was the best in Tests at Perth until 1988-89. This was the first Test in Australia where no-balls and wides were debited to the bowlers' analyses.

AUSTRALIA

K.C.Wessels	c Wasim Bari b Azeem	12
W.B.Phillips	c Tahir b Nazir	159
G.N.Yallop	b Azeem	141
*K.J.Hughes	b Qadir	16
A.R.Border	c Wasim Raja b Azeem	32
G.S.Chappell	c Azeem b Qadir	17
†R.W.Marsh	c Wasim Bari b Azeem	24
G.F.Lawson	c Nazir b Qadir	9
D.K.Lillee	c Wasim Raja b Azeem	0
R.M.Hogg	not out	7
C.G.Rackemann	did not bat	
Extras	(LB9, W3, NB7)	19
Total	(9 wickets declared)	**436**

PAKISTAN

Mohsin Khan	c Marsh b Hogg	8	c Border b Rackemann	24
Mudassar Nazar	c Phillips b Lillee	1	c Chappell b Rackemann	27
Qasim Omar	c Yallop b Rackemann	48	c Marsh b Rackemann	65
Javed Miandad	c Phillips b Hogg	0	lbw b Rackemann	46
*Zaheer Abbas	c Phillips b Hogg	0	c Marsh b Rackemann	30
Wasim Raja	c Chappell b Rackemann	14	c Marsh b Lawson	4
†Wasim Bari	c Chappell b Rackemann	0	c Marsh b Lawson	7
Tahir Naqqash	not out	29	c Marsh b Rackemann	26
Abdul Qadir	b Rackemann	5	run out	18
Mohammad Nazir	c Chappell b Rackemann	16	c Border b Hogg	18
Azeem Hafeez	c Border b Lawson	1	not out	0
Extras	(LB3, NB4)	7	(B4, LB7, W2, NB20)	33
Total		**129**		**298**

PAKISTAN	O	M	R	W	O	M	R	W		FALL OF WICKETS		
Tahir	22	6	76	0						A	P	P
Azeem	27.3	5	100	5					*Wkt*	*1st*	*1st*	*2nd*
Mudassar	15	1	39	0					1st	34	7	62
Nazir	29	5	91	1					2nd	293	13	63
Qadir	32	4	121	3					3rd	321	15	188
									4th	369	15	197
AUSTRALIA									5th	386	65	206
Lillee	13	3	26	1	29	6	56	0	6th	404	68	218
Hogg	12	4	20	3	21.1	2	72	1	7th	424	90	257
Rackemann	8	0	32	5	26	6	86	6	8th	424	105	267
Lawson	7.2	0	48	1	13	1	53	2	9th	436	124	281
Chappell					9	1	20	0	10th	–	129	298

Umpires: M.W.Johnson (13) and P.J.McConnell (1).

Close: 1st day – A(1) 330-3 (Yallop 122, Border 5); 2nd – P(1) 28-4 (Omar 9, Wasim Raja 8); 3rd – P(2) 155-2 (Omar 53, Miandad 25).

AUSTRALIA v PAKISTAN 1983-84 (2nd Test)

At Woolloongabba, Brisbane, on 25, 26, 27, 28, 29 (*no play*) November.
Toss: Pakistan.   Result: MATCH DRAWN.
Debuts: None.

Pakistan were saved from a second successive defeat by an innings when torrential rain flooded the ground after lunch on the fourth day. Hogg became the 20th bowler to take 100 wickets for Australia. The partnership of 171 between Border and Chappell equalled the fifth-wicket record for this series (set by Chappell and G.J.Cosier in *Test No. 794*). Chappell (334 minutes, 250 balls, 17 fours) recorded his 23rd hundred in Tests and Border his tenth. Chappell's seven Test matches in his adopted home state of Queensland produced 1,006 runs, average 111.77.

PAKISTAN

Mohsin Khan	c Chappell b Lawson	2	b Lawson		37
Mudassar Nazar	c Marsh b Lawson	24	c Wessels b Rackemann		18
Qasim Omar	c Hughes b Lawson	17	not out		11
Javed Miandad	c Marsh b Hogg	6	c Phillips b Rackemann		5
Zaheer Abbas	c Border b Lawson	56	not out		3
Wasim Raja	c Hughes b Rackemann	27			
Wasim Bari	c Border b Rackemann	2			
Abdul Qadir	b Rackemann	0			
Rashid Khan	not out	13			
Mohammad Nazir	c Marsh b Hogg	1			
Azeem Hafeez	b Lawson	2			
Extras	(LB3, W1, NB2)	6	(LB6, NB2)		8
Total		**156**	(3 wickets)		**82**

AUSTRALIA

K.C.Wessels	c Omar b Azeem	35
W.B.Phillips	b Rashid	46
G.N.Yallop	c Wasim Bari b Rashid	33
K.J.Hughes	c Nazir b Azeem	53
A.R.Border	c Wasim Bari b Rashid	118
G.S.Chappell	not out	150
R.W.Marsh	b Azeem	1
G.F.Lawson	b Qadir	49
D.K.Lillee		
R.M.Hogg	did not bat	
C.G.Rackemann		
Extras	(B2, LB6, W1, NB15)	24
Total	(7 wickets declared)	**509**

AUSTRALIA	O	M	R	W	O	M	R	W		FALL OF WICKETS		
Lawson	17.1	1	49	5	(2) 10	3	24	1		P	A	P
Hogg	15	2	43	2	(1) 3	0	11	0	*Wkt*	*1st*	*1st*	*2nd*
Rackemann	10	3	28	3	8	1	31	2	1st	10	56	57
Lillee	8	1	33	0	2	0	10	0	2nd	39	120	59
									3rd	46	124	74
PAKISTAN									4th	62	232	–
Azeem	37	7	152	3					5th	124	403	–
Rashid	43	10	129	3					6th	128	406	–
Mudassar	16	2	47	0					7th	128	509	–
Qadir	32	5	112	1					8th	146	–	–
Nazir	24	6	50	0					9th	147	–	–
Wasim Raja	3	0	11	0					10th	156	–	–

Umpires: R.A.French (11) and M.W.Johnson (14).

Close: 1st day – P(1) 156 all out; 2nd – A(1) 273-4 (Border 63, Chappell 26); 3rd – P(2) 42-0 (Mohsin 25, Mudassar 15); 4th – P(2) 82-3 (Omar 11, Zaheer 3).

AUSTRALIA v PAKISTAN 1983-84 (3rd Test)

At Adelaide Oval on 9, 10, 11, 12, 13 December.
Toss: Australia.   Result: MATCH DRAWN.
Debuts: None.

Pakistan's total of 624 was the highest by either country in this series, their second-highest in all Tests, the fifth-highest by any country against Australia, and the highest in all Test cricket since 1979 (*Test No. 851*). It was also the highest total made against Australia since England amassed their world record 903 for 7 declared at The Oval in 1938 (*266*). Pakistan set partnership records against Australia for the second wicket (233 by Mohsin Khan and Qasim Omar) and the fifth wicket (186 by Javed Miandad and Salim Malik). Wessels (340 minutes, 233 balls, a six and 23 fours) made his highest Test score. Marsh retired at 288 after sustaining a triple fracture of the left cheekbone attempting to hook Azeem Hafeez. Lillee took five wickets in an innings for the 23rd and last time, just one instance short of the Test record held by S.F.Barnes.

AUSTRALIA

Batsman	Dismissal 1st	R		Dismissal 2nd	R
K.C.Wessels	c Zaheer b Qadir	179	(2)	c Wasim b Sarfraz	2
W.B.Phillips	c Wasim b Azeem	12	(1)	c Mudassar b Qadir	54
G.N.Yallop	c Omar b Sarfraz	68		c Miandad b Qadir	14
*K.J.Hughes	c Wasim b Azeem	30		c Mudassar b Azeem	106
A.R.Border	not out	117		lbw b Azeem	66
G.S.Chappell	c Wasim b Sarfraz	6		run out	4
†R.W.Marsh	c Mohsin b Sarfraz	2		retired hurt	33
T.G.Hogan	run out	2		c Omar b Salim	8
G.F.Lawson	c Wasim b Azeem	4		not out	7
D.K.Lillee	c Sarfraz b Azeem	25		not out	4
R.M.Hogg	c Miandad b Azeem	5			
Extras	(LB7, W4, NB4)	15		(B3, LB4, W1, NB4)	12
Total		**465**		**(7 wickets)**	**310**

PAKISTAN

Batsman	Dismissal	R
Mohsin Khan	c Phillips b Lawson	149
Mudassar Nazar	c Marsh b Lillee	44
Qasim Omar	c Marsh b Lillee	113
Javed Miandad	lbw b Lawson	131
*Zaheer Abbas	c Yallop b Hogg	46
Salim Malik	c Lawson b Hogan	77
Sarfraz Nawaz	c Yallop b Lillee	32
Abdul Qadir	b Lillee	10
†Wasim Bari	c Marsh b Lillee	0
Mohammad Nazir	not out	5
Azeem Hafeez	c Wessels b Lillee	5
Extras	(B1, LB4, NB7)	12
Total		**624**

PAKISTAN	O	M	R	W		O	M	R	W
Azeem	38.2	8	167	5	(2)	19	4	50	2
Sarfraz	42	7	105	3	(1)	30	8	69	1
Qadir	20	1	96	1		47	9	132	2
Mudassar	10	2	45	0					
Nazir	9	0	37	0	(4)	27	14	39	0
Mohsin	3	0	8	0		1	1	0	0
Miandad					(5)	3	0	10	0
Salim					(7)	1	0	3	1
Omar					(8)	1	1	0	0

AUSTRALIA	O	M	R	W
Lawson	37	7	127	2
Hogg	34	3	123	1
Lillee	50.2	8	171	6
Hogan	37	8	107	1
Chappell	32	6	82	0
Border	1	0	9	0

FALL OF WICKETS

Wkt	A 1st	P 1st	A 2nd
1st	21	73	3
2nd	163	306	44
3rd	219	314	121
4th	353	371	216
5th	376	557	228
6th	378	590	293
7th	383	604	305
8th	394	612	–
9th	451	613	–
10th	465	624	–

Umpires: A.R.Crafter (13) and R.A.French (12).

Close: 1st day – A(1) 376-5 (Border 76); 2nd – P(1) 184-1 (Mohsin 78, Omar 60); 3rd – P(1) 431-4 (Miandad 50, Malik 19); 4th – A(2) 94-2 (Phillips 48, Hughes 27).

AUSTRALIA v PAKISTAN 1983-84 (4th Test)

At Melbourne Cricket Ground on 26, 27, 28, 29, 30 December.
Toss: Pakistan.   Result: MATCH DRAWN.
Debuts: Australia – J.N.Maguire, G.R.J.Matthews.

Yallop (716 minutes, 517 balls, 29 fours) made the highest score of his first-class career, the highest for either country in this series, and the third-highest by any batsman against Pakistan. It was the seventh-longest recorded innings in all first-class cricket, the third-longest for Australia in Tests, and the longest in Tests by any batsman scoring under 300. His innings enabled him to eclipse D.G.Bradman's record Australian first-class aggregate for a calendar year (1,763 in 1929), and to become the sixth batsman to score 1,000 runs in the Australian first-class season before January. Yallop shared Australian record partnerships against Pakistan of 203 for the third wicket with Hughes (who completed 4,000 runs), and 185 with Matthews for the seventh. Returning as a batsman for his 50th match, Imran became the fifth player and first Pakistani to score 2,000 runs and take 200 wickets in Tests.

PAKISTAN

Mohsin Khan	lbw b Lillee	152		c Hughes b Lillee	3
Mudassar Nazar	c Marsh b Lawson	7		lbw b Matthews	35
Qasim Omar	b Maguire	23		b Lawson	9
Javed Miandad	c Marsh b Maguire	27		lbw b Lillee	11
Zaheer Abbas	run out	44	(6)	b Matthews	50
Salim Malik	c Maguire b Lawson	35	(8)	b Lillee	14
Imran Khan	c Marsh b Lillee	83		not out	72
Sarfraz Nawaz	c Hughes b Maguire	22	(9)	not out	11
Abdul Qadir	c Lawson b Matthews	45	(5)	b Lawson	12
Wasim Bari	not out	6			
Azeem Hafeez	c Maguire b Matthews	7			
Extras	(LB11, NB8)	19		(B10, LB9, W2)	21
Total		**470**		**(7 wickets)**	**238**

AUSTRALIA

K.C.Wessels	c Wasim b Azeem	11
W.B.Phillips	lbw b Azeem	35
G.N.Yallop	c Wasim b Sarfraz	268
K.J.Hughes	lbw b Azeem	94
A.R.Border	lbw b Qadir	32
G.S.Chappell	c Salim b Qadir	5
R.W.Marsh	c Mudassar b Qadir	0
G.R.J.Matthews	lbw b Sarfraz	75
G.F.Lawson	c Mudassar b Qadir	0
J.N.Maguire	c Wasim b Qadir	4
D.K.Lillee	not out	2
Extras	(B15, LB9, W2, NB3)	29
Total		**555**

AUSTRALIA	O	M	R	W		O	M	R	W		FALL OF WICKETS		
Lawson	38	8	125	2		21	8	47	2		P	A	P
Lillee	38	11	113	2		29	7	71	3	Wkt	1st	1st	2nd
Maguire	29	7	111	3		12	3	26	0	1st	13	21	3
Matthews	28.4	7	95	2		21	8	48	2	2nd	64	70	18
Chappell	7	3	15	0	(6)	8	3	13	0	3rd	112	273	37
Border					(5)	5	3	9	0	4th	244	342	73
Marsh						2	0	3	0	5th	294	354	81
Wessels						2	1	2	0	6th	321	354	160
										7th	349	539	213
PAKISTAN										8th	457	540	–
Sarfraz	51	12	106	2						9th	459	553	–
Azeem	35	8	115	3						10th	470	555	–
Qadir	54.3	12	166	5									
Mudassar	20	0	76	0									
Miandad	5	0	16	0									
Zaheer	22	5	42	0									
Salim	2	1	10	0									

Umpires: A.R.Crafter (14) and P.J.McConnell (2).

Close: 1st day – P(1) 308-5 (Malik 28, Imran 10); 2nd – A(1) 88-2 (Yallop 24, Hughes 14); 3rd – A(1) 379-6 (Yallop 173, Matthews 14); 4th – P(2) 38-3 (Mudassar 11, Qadir 0).

AUSTRALIA v PAKISTAN 1983-84 (5th Test)

At Sydney Cricket Ground on 2, 3, 4, 5, 6 January.
Toss: Australia.   Result: AUSTRALIA won by 10 wickets.
Debuts: None.

Chappell became the sixth player to score 7,000 runs in Test cricket and exceeded D.G.Bradman's Australian record of 6,996. His innings (530 minutes, 400 balls, 17 fours) enabled him to become the first batsman to score hundreds in his first and last Test innings; R.A.Duff and W.H.Ponsford had done so in their first and last matches. Later, he broke M.C.Cowdrey's world record of 120 catches by a non-wicket-keeper. Lillee became the first bowler to take 350 wickets and Marsh the first wicket-keeper to make 350 dismissals; their 95 shared dismissals (c Marsh b Lillee) also constitutes a world Test record. The three Australian world record holders (Lillee 355 wickets, Marsh 355 dismissals, Chappell 122 catches) all announced their retirements either during or immediately after this match. Wasim Bari, also playing in his last Test, became the third to hold 200 catches after A.P.E.Knott and Marsh.

PAKISTAN

Mohsin Khan	c Border b Lillee	14	c Chappell b Lawson	
Mudassar Nazar	c Chappell b Lawson	84	b Lawson	2
Qasim Omar	c Border b Lillee	15	c Marsh b Lawson	2
Abdul Qadir	c Hughes b Lawson	4	(9) c Marsh b Lillee	
Javed Miandad	c Lillee b Matthews	16	(4) c Marsh b Lawson	6
Zaheer Abbas	c Yallop b Lawson	61	(5) c Marsh b Hogg	3
*Imran Khan	c Yallop b Lawson	5	(6) c Marsh b Hogg	1
Salim Malik	c Lillee b Lawson	54	(7) c Chappell b Lillee	
Sarfraz Nawaz	lbw b Lillee	5	(8) c Phillips b Lillee	2
†Wasim Bari	not out	7	c Phillips b Lillee	2
Azeem Hafeez	c Marsh b Lillee	4	not out	
Extras	(B2, LB7)	9	(LB4, NB1)	
Total		**278**		**210**

AUSTRALIA

K.C.Wessels	c Wasim b Azeem	3	not out	1
W.B.Phillips	c Salim b Sarfraz	37	not out	19
G.N.Yallop	c Wasim b Mudassar	30		
G.S.Chappell	lbw b Mudassar	182		
*K.J.Hughes	lbw b Sarfraz	76		
A.R.Border	c Wasim b Mudassar	64		
G.R.J.Matthews	not out	22		
†R.W.Marsh	not out	15		
G.F.Lawson				
R.M.Hogg	did not bat			
D.K.Lillee				
Extras	(LB15, W1, NB9)	25	(NB2)	2
Total	(6 wickets declared)	**454**	(0 wickets)	**35**

AUSTRALIA	O	M	R	W		O	M	R	W		FALL OF WICKETS			
Lillee	31.2	10	65	4		29.5	5	88	4		P	A	P	A
Hogg	18	1	61	0	(4)	14	2	53	2	Wkt	1st	1st	2nd	2nd
Chappell	8	0	25	0						1st	18	11	5	
Lawson	25	5	59	5	(2)	20	7	48	4	2nd	57	66	47	
Matthews	18	4	59	1	(3)	7	4	17	0	3rd	67	83	56	
										4th	131	254	104	
PAKISTAN										5th	150	407	132	
Sarfraz	53	13	132	2		3	1	7	0	6th	158	436	163	
Azeem	36	7	121	1		2.4	0	28	0	7th	254	–	163	
Mudassar	31	9	81	3						8th	267	–	173	
Qadir	34	9	105	0						9th	267	–	191	
										10th	278	–	210	

Umpires: R.A.French (13) and M.W.Johnson (15).

Close: 1st day – P(1) 61-2 (Mudassar 26, Qadir 2); 2nd – A(1) 6-0 (Wessels 2, Phillips 4); 3rd – A(1) 242-3 (Chappell 79, Hughes 76); 4th – P(2) 47-1 (Mudassar 21, Omar 23).

NEW ZEALAND v ENGLAND 1983-84 (1st Test)

At Basin Reserve, Wellington, on 20, 21, 22, 23, 24 January.
Toss: New Zealand.   Result: MATCH DRAWN.
Debuts: None.

Howarth won his ninth toss in 18 Tests as captain and chose to bat for the first time. Willis took his 308th wicket in 84 Tests to supersede F.S.Trueman (67 Tests) as England's leading wicket taker. Botham scored a hundred and took five wickets in an innings of the same Test for the fifth time – he is alone in achieving this feat more than twice. Cairns, who took the first six wickets to fall, including his 100th (Lamb) in 33 Tests, recorded the best analysis (7 for 143) for New Zealand in a home Test in this series. Coney's innings (490 minutes, 373 balls, a six and 26 fours) was the highest of his career, the record against England in New Zealand and for New Zealand in all Wellington Tests, and his first first-class century in 131 innings since 1976-77. His partnership of 118 with Cairns was New Zealand's ninth-wicket record against all countries until 1989-90. Their total of 537 was their highest in New Zealand and the record for any Test at the Basin Reserve until 1990-91.

NEW ZEALAND

J.G.Wright	c Cook b Botham	17	c Foster b Cook	35
B.A.Edgar	c Taylor b Botham	9	c Taylor b Willis	30
*G.P.Howarth	c Gower b Botham	15	run out	34
M.D.Crowe	b Willis	13	c Botham b Gatting	100
J.J.Crowe	c Taylor b Foster	52	lbw b Botham	3
J.V.Coney	c Gower b Cook	27	not out	174
R.J.Hadlee	c Gatting b Botham	24	c Lamb b Foster	18
M.C.Snedden	c Taylor b Willis	11	c Taylor b Foster	16
†I.D.S.Smith	lbw b Botham	24	b Cook	29
B.L.Cairns	c Gatting b Willis	3	c sub (G.Fowler) b Willis	64
E.J.Chatfield	not out	4	b Cook	0
Extras	(B4, LB9, NB7)	20	(B4, LB14, W2, NB14)	34
Total		**219**		**537**

ENGLAND

C.J.Tavaré	b Cairns	9	not out	36
C.L.Smith	c Hadlee b Cairns	27	not out	30
D.I.Gower	c Hadlee b Cairns	33		
A.J.Lamb	c M.D.Crowe b Cairns	13		
M.W.Gatting	lbw b Cairns	19		
I.T.Botham	c J.J.Crowe b Cairns	138		
D.W.Randall	c M.D.Crowe b Hadlee	164		
†R.W.Taylor	run out	14		
N.G.B.Cook	c Smith b Cairns	7		
N.A.Foster	c Howarth b Hadlee	10		
*R.G.D.Willis	not out	5		
Extras	(LB8, NB16)	24	(NB3)	3
Total		**463**	(0 wickets)	**69**

ENGLAND	O	M	R	W	O	M	R	W		FALL OF WICKETS			
										NZ	E	NZ	E
Willis	19	7	37	3	37	8	102	2	*Wkt*	*1st*	*1st*	*2nd*	*2nd*
Botham	27.4	8	59	5	36	6	137	1	1st	34	41	62	–
Foster	24	9	60	1	37	12	91	2	2nd	39	51	79	–
Cook	23	11	43	1	66.3	26	153	3	3rd	56	84	153	–
Gatting					8	4	14	1	4th	71	92	165	–
Smith					3	1	6	0	5th	114	115	279	–
									6th	160	347	302	–
NEW ZEALAND									7th	174	372	334	–
Hadlee	31.5	6	97	2					8th	200	386	402	–
Snedden	21	3	101	0	(1) 7	2	28	0	9th	208	426	520	–
Cairns	45	10	143	7					10th	219	463	537	–
Chatfield	28	6	68	0	(2) 5	0	24	0					
M.D.Crowe	3	0	20	0	(3) 6	1	11	0					
Coney	4	1	10	0									
Edgar					(4) 3	1	3	0					
J.J.Crowe					(5) 1	1	0	0					

Umpires: F.R.Goodall (16) and S.J.Woodward (8).

Close: 1st day – NZ(1) 212-9 (Smith 22, Chatfield 0); 2nd – E(1) 293-5 (Botham 103, Randall 71); 3rd – NZ(2) 93-2 (Howarth 11, M.D.Crowe 8); 4th – NZ(2) 335-7 (Coney 76, Smith 1).

NEW ZEALAND v ENGLAND 1983-84 (2nd Test)

At Lancaster Park, Christchurch, on 3, 4, 5 February.
Toss: New Zealand.   Result: NEW ZEALAND won by an innings and 132 runs.
Debuts: England – A.C.S.Pigott.

Failing to include a specialist spin bowler for only the third time in 596 Tests, England's defeat echoed the result of both previous instances (Melbourne 1932-33 and Brisbane 1954-55). New Zealand, who were able to enforce the follow-on for the first time in 59 matches in this series, gained their 17th victory (third v England) and by their largest margin. It was England's heaviest defeat since 1973 (*Test No. 727*). For the first time since 1894-95 (*45*), England failed to total 100 in either innings; the last of the previous 14 instances in Test cricket was inflicted upon New Zealand by England in 1958 (*455*). The match was completed at 4.31 on the third afternoon after 11 hours 41 minutes of play. Pigott, then playing for Wellington, was summoned when Foster and Dilley were injured, delayed his wedding and took a wicket with his seventh ball. Hadlee scored 99 off 81 balls in 111 minutes with 18 fours.

NEW ZEALAND

J.G.Wright	c Taylor b Cowans	25
B.A.Edgar	c Randall b Pigott	1
*G.P.Howarth	b Cowans	9
M.D.Crowe	c Tavaré b Botham	19
J.J.Crowe	lbw b Cowans	47
J.V.Coney	c Botham b Pigott	41
R.J.Hadlee	c Taylor b Willis	99
†I.D.S.Smith	not out	32
B.L.Cairns	c Taylor b Willis	2
S.L.Boock	c Taylor b Willis	5
E.J.Chatfield	lbw b Willis	0
Extras	(B8, LB11, W2, NB6)	27
Total		**307**

ENGLAND

G.Fowler	b Boock	4		c Howarth b Boock	10
C.J.Tavaré	c J.J.Crowe b Hadlee	3		c Smith b Hadlee	6
D.I.Gower	lbw b Hadlee	2		c Cairns b Hadlee	8
A.J.Lamb	c Smith b Chatfield	11		c Coney b Chatfield	9
D.W.Randall	c Coney b Hadlee	0	(7)	c Cairns b Hadlee	25
I.T.Botham	c Chatfield b Cairns	18		c M.D.Crowe b Boock	0
M.W.Gatting	not out	19	(5)	c Hadlee b Boock	0
†R.W.Taylor	c J.J.Crowe b Cairns	2		run out	15
A.C.S.Pigott	lbw b Cairns	4		not out	8
*R.G.D.Willis	b Chatfield	6		c Howarth b Hadlee	0
N.G.Cowans	c Coney b Chatfield	4		c Smith b Hadlee	7
Extras	(LB6, NB3)	9		(LB2, NB3)	5
Total		**82**			**93**

ENGLAND	O	M	R	W	O	M	R	W		FALL OF WICKETS		
Willis	22.1	5	51	4						NZ	E	E
Botham	17	1	88	1					*Wkt*	*1st*	*1st*	*2nd*
Pigott	17	7	75	2					1st	30	7	15
Cowans	14	2	52	3					2nd	42	9	23
Gatting	2	0	14	0					3rd	53	10	25
									4th	87	10	31
NEW ZEALAND									5th	137	41	31
Hadlee	17	9	16	3	18	6	28	5	6th	203	41	33
Cairns	19	5	35	3	(3) 9	3	21	0	7th	281	47	72
Boock	6	3	12	1	(4) 13	3	25	3	8th	291	58	76
Chatfield	8.2	3	10	3	(2) 11	1	14	1	9th	301	72	80
									10th	307	82	93

Umpires: F.R.Goodall (17) and S.J.Woodward (9).

Close: 1st day – E(1) 7-1 (Tavaré 2); 2nd – E(1) 53-7 (Gatting 4, Pigott 3).

NEW ZEALAND v ENGLAND 1983-84 (3rd Test)

At Eden Park, Auckland, on 10, 11, 12, 14, 15 February.
Toss: New Zealand.   Result: MATCH DRAWN.
Debuts: None.

Howarth became the first New Zealand captain to win three successive tosses in a home rubber. The fourth-wicket partnership of 154 by Wright and Jeff Crowe surpassed New Zealand's record against England set by M.L.Page and R.C.Blunt in 1931 (*Test No. 209*). Ian Smith improved his highest Test score for the fourth time in successive innings and celebrated his maiden Test hundred by hitting the last two balls in the innings for six before catching Fowler off the first ball of England's reply. Smith's five dismissals equalled the New Zealand record. Chris Smith batted for 457 minutes (396 balls) and took 294 minutes (264 balls) to reach his maiden Test fifty. After 54 years, and at their 21st attempt, New Zealand won their first rubber against England.

NEW ZEALAND

J.G.Wright	b Willis	130	not out	11
B.A.Edgar	lbw b Willis	0	not out	0
*G.P.Howarth	c Randall b Cowans	35		
M.D.Crowe	c Botham b Willis	16		
J.J.Crowe	b Marks	128		
J.V.Coney	b Cowans	9		
R.J.Hadlee	b Marks	3		
†I.D.S.Smith	not out	113		
B.L.Cairns	c Cowans b Foster	28		
S.L.Boock	lbw b Marks	2		
E.J.Chatfield	not out	6		
Extras	(LB19, NB7)	26	(LB1, NB4)	5
Total	**(9 wickets declared)**	**496**	**(0 wickets)**	**16**

ENGLAND

G.Fowler	c Smith b Hadlee	0
C.L.Smith	c Smith b Cairns	91
D.I.Gower	b Boock	26
A.J.Lamb	lbw b Cairns	49
D.W.Randall	c Wright b Chatfield	104
†R.W.Taylor	st Smith b Boock	23
I.T.Botham	run out	70
V.J.Marks	c Smith b Chatfield	6
N.A.Foster	not out	18
*R.G.D.Willis	c Smith b Hadlee	3
N.G.Cowans	c Cairns b Boock	21
Extras	(B7, LB13, NB8)	28
Total		**439**

ENGLAND	O	M	R	W	O	M	R	W		FALL OF WICKETS		
										NZ	E	NZ
Willis	34	7	109	3	3	1	7	0		*1st*	*1st*	*2nd*
Botham	29	10	70	0					Wkt			
Cowans	36	11	98	2	(2) 2	1	4	0	1st	3	0	–
Foster	30	8	78	1					2nd	74	48	–
Marks	40.2	9	115	3					3rd	111	143	–
									4th	265	234	–
									5th	293	284	–
NEW ZEALAND									6th	302	371	–
Hadlee	43	12	91	2					7th	385	387	–
Cairns	40	19	52	2					8th	451	391	–
Boock	61.3	28	103	3					9th	461	396	–
Chatfield	46	23	72	2					10th	–	439	–
M.D.Crowe	17	5	62	0								
Coney	13	8	13	0								
Howarth	7	1	18	0								

Umpires: F.R.Goodall (18) and S.J.Woodward (10).

Close: 1st day – NZ(1) 140-3 (Wright 71, J.J.Crowe 10); 2nd – NZ(1) 354-6 (J.J.Crowe 115, Smith 26); 3rd – E(1) 54-2 (Smith 16, Lamb 4); 4th – E(1) 238-4 (Randall 54, Taylor 0).

PAKISTAN v ENGLAND 1983-84 (1st Test)

At National Stadium, Karachi, on 2, 3, 4, 6 March.
Toss: England.   Result: PAKISTAN won by 3 wickets.
Debuts: Pakistan – Anil Dalpat, Ramiz Raja.

Pakistan beat England in a home Test for the first time in 13 attempts and ended a sequence of 11 drawn matches. They maintained their unbeaten record at Karachi: played 21, won 10, drawn 11. England's totals were then their two lowest in Pakistan. Botham made the last of 65 consecutive Test appearances to equal A.P.E. Knott's England record. Anil Dalpat was the first Hindu to represent Pakistan at cricket. Ramiz and Wasim Raja were the second set of brothers to appear for Pakistan, following the four Mohammads. Cook (11 for 83) became the first bowler to take more than eight wickets in a Test for England in Pakistan. He took his total of wickets after his first four Tests to 32, exceeding T.Richardson's England record by one. Mohsin Khan scored his 2,000th run in 31 Tests.

ENGLAND

C.L.Smith	c Wasim b Sarfraz	28	(2) lbw b Sarfraz	5
M.W.Gatting	b Tausif	26	(1) lbw b Sarfraz	4
D.I.Gower	lbw b Qadir	58	c Mohsin b Tausif	57
A.J.Lamb	c Ramiz b Sarfraz	4	c Anil b Qadir	20
D.W.Randall	b Qadir	8	b Qadir	16
I.T.Botham	c Ramiz b Qadir	22	b Tausif	10
V.J.Marks	c Ramiz b Sarfraz	5	b Qadir	1
†R.W.Taylor	lbw b Qadir	4	c Mohsin b Tausif	19
N.G.B.Cook	c Salim b Qadir	9	c Mohsin b Wasim	5
*R.G.D.Willis	c Wasim b Sarfraz	6	c Tausif b Wasim	2
N.G.Cowans	not out	1	not out	0
Extras	(LB6, NB5)	11	(B6, LB6, NB8)	20
Total		**182**		**159**

PAKISTAN

Mohsin Khan	c Botham b Cook	54	b Cook	10
Qasim Omar	lbw b Cook	29	c Botham b Cook	7
Ramiz Raja	c Smith b Cook	1	c Botham b Marks	1
*Zaheer Abbas	c Lamb b Botham	0	b Cook	8
Salim Malik	lbw b Willis	74	run out	11
Wasim Raja	c Cowans b Cook	3	c Cowans b Cook	0
†Anil Dalpat	c Taylor b Willis	12	not out	16
Abdul Qadir	c Lamb b Botham	40	b Cook	7
Sarfraz Nawaz	c Botham b Cook	8	not out	4
Tausif Ahmed	not out	17		
Azeem Hafeez	c Willis b Cook	24		
Extras	(LB5, NB10)	15	(B1, NB1)	2
Total		**277**	(7 wickets)	**66**

PAKISTAN	O	M	R	W	O	M	R	W		FALL OF WICKETS			
Azeem	11	3	21	0	8	3	14	0		E	P	E	P
Sarfraz	25.5	8	42	4	15	1	27	2	Wkt	1st	1st	2nd	2nd
Tausif	24	11	33	1	(4) 21	6	37	3	1st	41	67	6	17
Wasim	3	2	1	0	(5) 3.3	1	2	2	2nd	90	79	21	18
Qadir	31	12	74	5	(3) 31	4	59	3	3rd	94	80	63	26
									4th	108	96	94	38
ENGLAND									5th	154	105	121	38
Willis	17	6	33	2	2	0	13	0	6th	159	138	128	40
Cowans	12	3	34	0	2.3	1	10	0	7th	164	213	128	59
Botham	30	5	90	2					8th	165	229	157	–
Cook	30	12	65	6	(3) 14	8	18	5	9th	180	240	159	–
Marks	13	4	40	0	(4) 12	5	23	1	10th	182	277	159	–

Umpires: Khizer Hayat (12) and Shakoor Rana (12).

Close: 1st day – E(1) 147-4 (Gower 52, Botham 21); 2nd – P(1) 131-5 (Malik 27, Dalpat 10); 3rd – E(2) 54-2 (Gower 28, Lamb 14).

PAKISTAN v ENGLAND 1983-84 (2nd Test)

At Iqbal Stadium, Faisalabad, on 12, 13, 14, 16, 17 March.
Toss: Pakistan.   Result: MATCH DRAWN.
Debuts: None.

England marked their first Test in Faisalabad by compiling their highest total in Pakistan. Gower (426 minutes, 318 balls, 16 fours) became the 14th batsman to score 4,000 runs for England; leading in the absence through illness of Willis, he was the first England captain to score a Test hundred since A.W.Greig in 1976-77 (*Test No. 789*). Gower's partnership of 167 with Marks remains England's highest for the seventh wicket in this series. Salim Malik emulated G.A.Headley (West Indies) and R.G.Pollock (South Africa) by scoring a third Test hundred before his 21st birthday. Dilley was no-balled six times in his first over.

PAKISTAN

Mohsin Khan	c Lamb b Dilley	20	b Dilley	2
Mudassar Nazar	c Gatting b Cook	12	lbw b Foster	4
Qasim Omar	c Gatting b Foster	16	c Taylor b Dilley	17
Salim Malik	c Lamb b Cook	116	c sub (N.G.Cowans) b Marks	76
*Zaheer Abbas	lbw b Gatting	68	not out	32
Wasim Raja	b Marks	112	not out	5
Abdul Qadir	c Foster b Dilley	50		
†Anil Dalpat	lbw b Dilley	8		
Sarfraz Nawaz	not out	16		
Tausif Ahmed	not out	1		
Azeem Hafeez	did not bat			
Extras	(LB11, W2, NB17)	30	(LB1)	1
Total	(8 wickets declared)	**449**	(4 wickets)	**137**

ENGLAND

C.L.Smith	b Sarfraz	66
M.W.Gatting	c Salim b Tausif	75
D.W.Randall	b Sarfraz	65
A.J.Lamb	c Anil b Azeem	19
*D.I.Gower	st Anil b Mudassar	152
G.Fowler	c Omar b Wasim	57
†R.W.Taylor	c Salim b Qadir	0
V.J.Marks	b Sarfraz	83
G.R.Dilley	not out	2
N.G.B.Cook	not out	1
N.A.Foster	did not bat	
Extras	(B10, LB4, NB12)	26
Total	(8 wickets declared)	**546**

ENGLAND	O	M	R	W		O	M	R	W		FALL OF WICKETS		
Foster	30	7	109	1	(2)	5	1	10	1		P	E	P
Dilley	28	6	101	3	(1)	9	0	41	2	Wkt	1st	1st	2nd
Cook	54	14	133	2		16	6	38	0	1st	35	127	6
Marks	27	9	59	1		8	2	26	1	2nd	53	163	6
Gatting	3	0	17	1		2	0	18	0	3rd	70	214	56
Fowler						1	0	3	0	4th	200	245	123
										5th	323	361	–
PAKISTAN										6th	416	361	–
Azeem	19	3	71	1						7th	430	528	–
Sarfraz	50	11	129	3						8th	433	545	–
Wasim	26	6	61	1						9th	–	–	–
Qadir	51	14	124	1						10th	–	–	–
Tausif	30	8	96	1									
Mudassar	13	1	39	1									

Umpires: Javed Akhtar (9) and Mahboob Shah (12).

Close: 1st day – P(1) 257-4 (Malik 92, Wasim 28); 2nd – E(1) 26-0 (Smith 3, Gatting 22); 3rd – E (1) 233-3 (Randall 57, Gower 9); 4th – E(1) 461-6 (Gower 113, Marks 45).

PAKISTAN v ENGLAND 1983-84 (3rd Test)

At Gaddafi Stadium, Lahore, on 19, 20, 21, 23, 24 March.
Toss: Pakistan.   Result: MATCH DRAWN.
Debuts: Pakistan – Mohsin Kamal.

After 12 attempts during a period of 30 years, Pakistan won their first rubber against England. For the first time England lost two rubbers in the same season. This was England's 600th official Test match (won 222, lost 152, drawn 226). Mohsin Kamal was the 100th Test cricketer to represent Pakistan. During his highest Test innings, Sarfraz Nawaz, in his 55th match, became the third after Intikhab Alam and Imran Khan to complete the double of 1,000 runs and 100 wickets for Pakistan. Gower (423 minutes, 284 balls, 16 fours) set a record aggregate of 449 runs for this series in Pakistan. Abdul Qadir (10 for 194) was the first to take more than seven wickets in a Test against England in Pakistan; his tally of 19 wickets was a series record in his own country. The stand of 173 between Mohsin and Shoaib remains Pakistan's highest for the first wicket against England. Cowans took five wickets in 22 balls, including three in his eleventh over (2W2W0W). Zaheer (strained groin) batted with a runner in both innings.

ENGLAND

C.L.Smith	c Salim b Sarfraz	18	(2)	run out	15
M.W.Gatting	lbw b Sarfraz	0	(3)	run out	53
*D.I.Gower	c Anil b Mohsin Kamal	9	(4)	not out	173
A.J.Lamb	c Ramiz b Qadir	29	(5)	c and b Qadir	6
D.W.Randall	c Salim b Qadir	14	(6)	c Salim b Qadir	0
G.Fowler	c Omar b Qadir	58	(1)	c Anil b Mohsin Kamal	19
V.J.Marks	c Mohsin Khan b Qadir	74		c sub (Akram Raza) b Qadir	55
†R.W.Taylor	lbw b Sarfraz	1	(10)	b Sarfraz	5
N.A.Foster	lbw b Qadir	6	(8)	lbw b Qadir	0
N.G.B.Cook	c Anil b Sarfraz	3			
N.G.Cowans	not out	3	(9)	st Anil b Qadir	3
Extras	(B4, LB5, W9, NB8)	26		(B6, LB3, W1, NB5)	15
Total		**241**		(9 wickets declared)	**344**

PAKISTAN

Mohsin Khan	lbw b Foster	1		c Smith b Cowans	104
Shoaib Mohammad	lbw b Cowans	7		c Gatting b Cowans	80
Qasim Omar	c Fowler b Foster	73		run out	0
Salim Malik	b Marks	38		c Gatting b Cowans	7
Ramiz Raja	c Smith b Foster	26	(8)	not out	6
Wasim Raja	c Gower b Cowans	12		lbw b Cowans	0
*Zaheer Abbas	not out	82	(5)	c Gatting b Cowans	5
Abdul Qadir	c Taylor b Foster	3			
†Anil Dalpat	c Gower b Foster	2			
Sarfraz Nawaz	c Gatting b Smith	90	(7)	not out	10
Mohsin Kamal	c Gower b Cook	0			
Extras	(LB9)	9		(LB5)	5
Total		**343**		(6 wickets)	**217**

PAKISTAN	O	M	R	W	O	M	R	W	FALL OF WICKETS				
Mohsin Kamal	15	0	66	1	17	3	59	1		E	P	E	P
Sarfraz	22.5	5	49	4	27.4	1	112	1	*Wkt*	*1st*	*1st*	*2nd*	*2nd*
Qadir	30	7	84	5	42	5	110	5	1st	5	9	35	173
Wasim	11	4	16	0	21	5	48	0	2nd	20	13	38	175
									3rd	47	99	175	187
ENGLAND									4th	77	138	189	197
Cowans	29	5	89	2	14	2	42	5	5th	83	151	189	199
Foster	32	8	67	5	15	4	44	0	6th	203	166	308	199
Cook	46	12	117	1	18.3	2	73	0	7th	205	175	309	–
Marks	20	4	59	1	10	0	53	0	8th	222	181	327	–
Smith	1	0	2	1	1	1	0	0	9th	237	342	344	–
									10th	241	343	–	–

Umpires: Amanullah Khan (11) and Khizer Hayat (13).

Close: 1st day – E(1) 241-9 (Cook 3, Cowans 3); 2nd – P(1) 173-6 (Zaheer 13, Qadir 2); 3rd – E(2) 65-2 (Gatting 9, Gower 18); 4th – E(2) 273-5 (Gower 124, Marks 41).

WEST INDIES v AUSTRALIA 1983-84 (1st Test)

At Bourda, Georgetown, Guyana, on 2, 3, 4, 6, 7 March.
Toss: Australia.   Result: MATCH DRAWN.
Debuts: Australia – S.B.Smith.

Set 323 runs in a minimum of 260 minutes, West Indies responded with their highest opening partnership against Australia. Rain allowed only 71 minutes of play on the first day. None of the Australian team had previously appeared in a Test in the Caribbean. For the first time since December 1980 (*Test No. 887*), West Indies included only three fast bowlers. Hogan and Hogg, who scored his first fifty in Test cricket, shared a record tenth-wicket series partnership of 97 in 150 minutes. Border (4,000 runs in 57 Tests) and Haynes (2,000 runs in 36 Tests) completed notable career aggregates. Lawson was fined $US200 (£136) by the tour management committee for showing dissent over umpire Narine's decision concerning his 'lbw' appeal on the second day. This was the first Test in the West Indies to debit no-balls and wides to bowlers' analyses.

AUSTRALIA

S.B.Smith	c Dujon b Garner	3	(2)	c Dujon b Garner	12
K.C.Wessels	c Lloyd b Garner	4	(1)	c Lloyd b Daniel	20
G.M.Ritchie	c Davis b Harper	78		lbw b Garner	3
K.J.Hughes	b Garner	18		c Haynes b Daniel	0
A.R.Border	b Garner	5		run out	54
D.W.Hookes	c Dujon b Harper	32		b Garner	10
W.B.Phillips	c Greenidge b Harper	16		b Daniel	76
G.F.Lawson	c Richards b Harper	11		not out	35
T.G.Hogan	not out	42		lbw b Davis	18
T.M.Alderman	lbw b Garner	1	(11)	not out	3
R.M.Hogg	lbw b Garner	52	(10)	b Davis	6
Extras	(B2, LB3, W1, NB11)	17		(B10, LB15, NB11)	36
Total		**279**		**(9 wickets declared)**	**273**

WEST INDIES

C.G.Greenidge	c Wessels b Lawson	16	not out	120
D.L.Haynes	lbw b Hogg	60	not out	103
R.B.Richardson	lbw b Lawson	19		
I.V.A.Richards	c Phillips b Hogg	8		
H.A.Gomes	c Border b Hogan	10		
C.H.Lloyd	c Phillips b Alderman	36		
P.J.L.Dujon	b Hogan	21		
R.A.Harper	b Hogan	10		
J.Garner	not out	16		
W.W.Davis	c Ritchie b Hogan	11		
W.W.Daniel	lbw b Lawson	4		
Extras	(LB3, NB16)	19	(B10, LB13, NB4)	27
Total		**230**	**(0 wickets)**	**250**

WEST INDIES	O	M	R	W		O	M	R	W		FALL OF WICKETS			
											A	WI	A	WI
Garner	27.2	10	75	6		24	5	67	3		*1st*	*1st*	*2nd*	*2nd*
Daniel	12	3	60	0		27	4	86	3	Wkt				
Davis	19	2	45	0		14	3	35	2	1st	6	29	37	–
Harper	24	7	56	4		15	4	27	0	2nd	23	72	41	–
Gomes	15	1	35	0		11	2	25	0	3rd	55	93	42	–
Richards	5	2	3	0		6	2	8	0	4th	63	110	50	–
										5th	139	154	60	–
AUSTRALIA										6th	166	181	185	–
Lawson	20.4	4	59	3	(3)	18	0	54	0	7th	180	191	209	–
Alderman	21	3	64	1		11	0	43	0	8th	181	203	249	–
Hogg	12	0	48	2	(1)	13	0	56	0	9th	182	225	263	–
Hogan	25	9	56	4		19	2	74	0	10th	279	230	–	–

Umpires: D.M.Archer (7) and D.J.Narine (2).

Close: 1st day – A(1) 55-3 (Ritchie 23); 2nd – WI(1) 20-0 (Greenidge 8, Haynes 10); 3rd – A(2) 23-0 (Wessels 11, Smith 5); 4th – A(2) 202-6 (Phillips 71, Lawson 7).

WEST INDIES v AUSTRALIA 1983-84 (2nd Test)

At Queen's Park Oval, Port-of-Spain, Trinidad, on 16, 17, 18, 20, 21 March.
Toss: West Indies.   Result: MATCH DRAWN.
Debuts: Australia – D.M.Jones; West Indies – M.A.Small.

Australia were saved from defeat by two courageous innings by Border. The left-hander scored 198 runs in the match without being dismissed; he batted for a total of 634 minutes and survived 535 balls. Alderman partnered him for the final 105 minutes of the match, negotiating 83 balls and sharing an unfinished last-wicket partnership of 61. Six hours of play were lost to rain and poor light during the first two days. For the second time (also *Test No. 884*), Richards led West Indies in the absence of Lloyd with a pulled hamstring.

AUSTRALIA

K.C.Wessels	c Gomes b Garner	4		lbw b Garner	4
†W.B.Phillips	c Dujon b Garner	4		run out	0
G.M.Ritchie	b Garner	1		b Small	26
*K.J.Hughes	c Dujon b Garner	24		lbw b Marshall	33
A.R.Border	not out	98	(6)	not out	100
D.W.Hookes	b Garner	23	(7)	c Richardson b Gomes	21
D.M.Jones	c and b Richards	48	(8)	b Richards	5
G.F.Lawson	c and b Daniel	14	(9)	b Marshall	20
T.G.Hogan	c Greenidge b Daniel	0	(5)	c Logie b Daniel	38
R.M.Hogg	c Marshall b Daniel	11		c Garner b Richards	9
T.M.Alderman	c Richardson b Garner	1		not out	21
Extras	(B6, LB4, NB17)	27		(B6, LB1, W1, NB14)	22
Total		**255**		(9 wickets)	**299**

WEST INDIES

C.G.Greenidge	c Phillips b Hogg	24
D.L.Haynes	run out	53
R.B.Richardson	c Wessels b Alderman	23
*I.V.A.Richards	c Phillips b Alderman	76
H.A.Gomes	b Lawson	3
A.L.Logie	lbw b Hogg	97
†P.J.L.Dujon	b Hogan	130
M.D.Marshall	lbw b Lawson	10
J.Garner	not out	24
W.W.Daniel	not out	6
M.A.Small	did not bat	
Extras	(B7, LB12, W2, NB1)	22
Total	(8 wickets declared)	**468**

WEST INDIES	O	M	R	W		O	M	R	W		FALL OF WICKETS		
Garner	28.1	9	60	6	(2)	15	4	35	1		A	WI	A
Marshall	19	4	73	0	(1)	22	3	73	2	*Wkt*	*1st*	*1st*	*2nd*
Daniel	15	2	40	3	(4)	9	3	11	1	1st	4	35	1
Small	10	3	24	0	(3)	14	2	51	1	2nd	7	93	35
Gomes	10	0	33	0	(6)	27	5	53	1	3rd	16	124	41
Richards	10	4	15	1	(5)	25	5	65	2	4th	50	129	114
Logie						0.1	0	4	0	5th	85	229	115
										6th	185	387	153
AUSTRALIA										7th	233	430	162
Lawson	32	3	132	2						8th	233	462	196
Hogg	31	2	103	1						9th	253	–	238
Alderman	35	9	91	2						10th	255	–	–
Hogan	28	3	123	2									

Umpires: D.M.Archer (8) and C.E.Cumberbatch (3).

Close: 1st day – A(1) 55-4 (Border 12, Hookes 0); 2nd – A(1) 241-8 (Border 92, Hogg 5); 3rd – WI(1) 218-4 (Richards 69, Logie 39); 4th – A(2) 55-3 (Hughes 12, Hogan 6).

WEST INDIES v AUSTRALIA 1983-84 (3rd Test)

At Kensington Oval, Bridgetown, Barbados, on 30, 31 March, 1, 3, 4 April.
Toss: West Indies.   Result: WEST INDIES won by 10 wickets.
Debuts: None.

West Indies took a lead in the rubber just before lunch on the fifth day after dismissing Australia for the (then) lowest total in any Bridgetown Test. Phillips (227 minutes, 197 balls, four sixes and 14 fours) was the second Australian wicket-keeper after R.W.Marsh to score a Test century. He contributed 80 of the 99 runs added for the last two wickets, his score being 40 when Hogg joined him and 70 when Alderman (35 balls) shared the last 81 minutes. Earlier, Wood, flown in the previous week as replacement for Wessels (injured knee), had batted impressively for 4¾ hours. Lloyd's 77-ball innings included three sixes.

AUSTRALIA

S.B.Smith	c Dujon b Marshall	10	(2)	b Marshall	7
G.M.Wood	c Dujon b Holding	68	(1)	lbw b Garner	20
G.M.Ritchie	c and b Harper	57		c Haynes b Marshall	0
*K.J.Hughes	c Lloyd b Holding	20		c Lloyd b Holding	25
A.R.Border	c Richardson b Marshall	38	(6)	c Dujon b Holding	8
D.W.Hookes	c Dujon b Garner	30	(7)	b Holding	9
T.G.Hogan	b Garner	40	(5)	c Richardson b Holding	2
†W.B.Phillips	c Dujon b Garner	120		b Marshall	1
G.F.Lawson	b Baptiste	10		c Harper b Marshall	2
R.M.Hogg	c Garner b Harper	3		not out	5
T.M.Alderman	not out	2		b Marshall	0
Extras	(B14, LB8, NB9)	31		(B1, LB6, NB11)	18
Total		**429**			**97**

WEST INDIES

C.G.Greenidge	run out	64	not out	10
D.L.Haynes	b Hogg	145	not out	11
R.B.Richardson	not out	131		
I.V.A.Richards	b Lawson	6		
E.A.E.Baptiste	b Lawson	11		
†P.J.L.Dujon	b Alderman	2		
*C.H.Lloyd	b Hogg	76		
M.D.Marshall	b Hogg	10		
R.A.Harper	b Hogg	19		
J.Garner	c Phillips b Hogg	9		
M.A.Holding	c Smith b Hogg	0		
Extras	(LB25, NB11)	36		
Total		**509**	(0 wickets)	**21**

WEST INDIES	O	M	R	W		O	M	R	W		FALL OF WICKETS			
Garner	33.5	6	110	3	(2)	8	4	9	1		A	WI	A	WI
Marshall	26	2	83	2	(1)	15.5	1	42	5	*Wkt*	*1st*	*1st*	*2nd*	*2nd*
Holding	30	5	94	2		15	4	24	4	1st	11	132	13	–
Baptiste	17	5	34	1	(5)	3	0	14	0	2nd	114	277	13	–
Harper	43	9	86	2	(4)	2	1	1	0	3rd	158	289	63	–
										4th	171	313	65	–
										5th	223	316	68	–
AUSTRALIA										6th	263	447	80	–
Lawson	33.2	4	150	2		2	1	3	0	7th	307	465	85	–
Alderman	42.4	6	152	1		1.4	0	18	0	8th	330	493	85	–
Hogg	32.4	4	77	6						9th	366	509	92	–
Hogan	34	8	97	0						10th	429	509	97	–
Border	3	1	8	0										

Umpires: D.M.Archer (9) and L.H.Barker (1).

Close: 1st day – A(1) 227-5 (Border 23, Hogan 3); 2nd – WI(1) 57-0 (Greenidge 22, Haynes 32); 3rd – WI(1) 301-3 (Richardson 61, Baptiste 6); 4th – A(2) 68-4 (Hogan 2, Border 1).

WEST INDIES v AUSTRALIA 1983-84 (4th Test)

At Recreation Ground, St John's, Antigua, on 7, 8, 9, 11 April.
Toss: Australia.   Result: WEST INDIES won by an innings and 36 runs.
Debuts: None.

West Indies retained the Frank Worrell Trophy by completing an emphatic victory 50 minutes before the end of the fourth day. Australia were without Wood (fractured right index finger) and Hogg (strained side). Richards (375 minutes, 30 fours) and Richardson (468 minutes, a six and 22 fours), playing on their home ground, shared a partnership of 308 – the highest for the third wicket by either side in this series. Richards compiled the highest score in a Test at St John's until 1992-93. Marshall took his 100th wicket in 26 Tests when he dismissed Woolley. In Australia's second innings extras were the main contributor in a completed Test innings for the sixth time.

AUSTRALIA

W.B.Phillips	c Dujon b Garner	5	(2)	b Garner	22
G.M.Ritchie	c Holding b Marshall	6	(1)	c Dujon b Garner	23
A.R.Border	c Dujon b Baptiste	98		c Greenidge b Baptiste	19
*K.J.Hughes	c Marshall b Harper	24		c Richards b Marshall	29
D.M.Jones	b Harper	1		c Dujon b Garner	11
D.W.Hookes	c Richardson b Baptiste	51		c Greenidge b Holding	29
†R.D.Woolley	c Dujon b Baptiste	13		lbw b Marshall	8
T.G.Hogan	c Harper b Holding	14		c Baptiste b Garner	6
G.F.Lawson	b Holding	4		not out	17
J.N.Maguire	not out	15		b Marshall	0
C.G.Rackemann	b Holding	12		b Garner	0
Extras	(B5, LB4, NB10)	19		(B19, LB7, NB10)	36
Total		**262**			**200**

WEST INDIES

C.G.Greenidge	c Ritchie b Lawson	0
D.L.Haynes	b Lawson	21
R.B.Richardson	c Woolley b Rackemann	154
I.V.A.Richards	c Woolley b Rackemann	178
†P.J.L.Dujon	c Hughes b Rackemann	28
*C.H.Lloyd	c Jones b Rackemann	38
M.D.Marshall	c Hookes b Maguire	6
E.A.E.Baptiste	b Maguire	6
R.A.Harper	c Ritchie b Maguire	27
J.Garner	c Hogan b Rackemann	10
M.A.Holding	not out	3
Extras	(B13, LB13, NB1)	27
Total		**498**

WEST INDIES	O	M	R	W		O	M	R	W		FALL OF WICKETS		
Marshall	18	2	70	1		17	5	51	3		A	WI	A
Garner	18	5	34	1		20.5	2	63	5	*Wkt*	*1st*	*1st*	*2nd*
Holding	19.5	3	42	3		14	2	22	1	1st	14	0	50
Harper	19	4	58	2	(5) 6	0	24	0		2nd	14	43	57
Baptiste	17	2	42	3	(4) 8	2	14	1		3rd	67	351	97
Richards	5	0	7	0						4th	78	390	116
										5th	202	405	150
AUSTRALIA										6th	208	426	167
Lawson	29	4	125	2						7th	217	442	176
Rackemann	42.4	8	161	5						8th	224	468	185
Maguire	44	9	121	3						9th	246	491	185
Hogan	30	9	65	0						10th	262	498	200

Umpires: D.M.Archer (10) and A.E.Weekes (2).

Close: 1st day – A(1) 238-8 (Hogan 11, Maguire 7); 2nd – WI(1) 273-2 (Richardson 111, Richards 127); 3rd – WI(1) 493-9 (Garner 6, Holding 2).

WEST INDIES v AUSTRALIA 1983-84 (5th Test)

At Sabina Park, Kingston, Jamaica, on 28, 29, 30 April, 2 May.
Toss: West Indies.   Result: WEST INDIES won by 10 wickets.
Debuts: None.

West Indies achieved their largest margin of victory (3-0) in a rubber against Australia, completing a decisive victory before lunch on the fourth day for the second match in succession. They also became the first side not to lose a single second-innings wicket during a five-Test rubber. Lloyd became the first West Indian to appear in 100 Test matches; only M.C.Cowdrey (114) and G.Boycott (108) had played in more. By coincidence, this was the 100th Test match to be staged in the Caribbean, West Indies winning 33, losing 18 and drawing 49. Smith's left little finger was fractured by a ball from Garner, who set a West Indies record against Australia by taking 31 wickets in the rubber. Hogg was allowed to bowl 12 bouncers in two overs against the West Indies opening batsmen; his tactics were in retaliation for the quantity of similar deliveries which Marshall and Garner had been permitted the previous day.

AUSTRALIA

†W.B.Phillips	c Dujon b Garner	12		b Garner	2
S.B.Smith	c Greenidge b Marshall	9		absent hurt	–
A.R.Border	c Dujon b Marshall	41		not out	60
G.M.Ritchie	c Dujon b Marshall	5		b Holding	8
*K.J.Hughes	c Harper b Holding	19		c Greenidge b Marshall	23
D.W.Hookes	b Harper	36		c Dujon b Marshall	7
G.R.J.Matthews	st Dujon b Harper	7	(2)	b Holding	7
T.G.Hogan	c and b Garner	25	(7)	b Marshall	10
G.F.Lawson	c Harper b Garner	15	(8)	b Marshall	4
R.M.Hogg	not out	1	(9)	b Marshall	14
J.N.Maguire	b Baptiste	9	(10)	b Garner	0
Extras	(B8, LB3, W1, NB8)	20		(B17, LB4, NB4)	25
Total		**199**			**160**

WEST INDIES

C.G.Greenidge	c Ritchie b Hogan	127		not out	32
D.L.Haynes	b Hogan	60		not out	15
R.B.Richardson	c Phillips b Lawson	0			
I.V.A.Richards	run out	2			
*C.H.Lloyd	c Phillips b Lawson	20			
†P.J.L.Dujon	c Phillips b Maguire	23			
M.D.Marshall	c Hookes b Maguire	19			
E.A.E.Baptiste	c Lawson b Maguire	27			
R.A.Harper	c Phillips b Maguire	0			
J.Garner	c Phillips b Lawson	7			
M.A.Holding	not out	0			
Extras	(B1, LB11, NB8)	20		(B2, LB3, NB3)	8
Total		**305**		(0 wickets)	**55**

WEST INDIES	O	M	R	W	O	M	R	W	FALL OF WICKETS			
										A	WI	A	WI
Marshall	18	4	37	3	23	3	51	5					
Garner	17	4	42	3	16.4	6	28	2	*Wkt*	*1st*	*1st*	*2nd*	*2nd*
Holding	12	2	43	1	11	4	20	2	1st	22	162	7	–
Baptiste	11	3	40	1	6	3	11	0	2nd	23	169	15	–
Harper	20	8	26	2	9	2	25	0	3rd	34	174	27	–
Richards					2	0	4	0	4th	73	213	89	–
									5th	113	228	109	–
									6th	124	260	125	–
AUSTRALIA													
Lawson	30	6	91	3	5	0	24	0	7th	142	274	131	–
Hogg	16	2	67	0	5.2	0	18	0	8th	181	274	159	–
Hogan	30	8	68	2					9th	190	297	160	–
Maguire	16.4	2	57	4	(3) 1	0	8	0	10th	199	305	–	–
Matthews	2	0	10	0									

Umpires: D.M.Archer (11) and L.H.Barker (2).

Close: 1st day – WI(1) 25-0 (Greenidge 17, Haynes 0); 2nd – WI(1) 263-6 (Dujon 19, Baptiste 0); 3rd – A(2) 135-7 (Border 55, Hogg 0).

SRI LANKA v NEW ZEALAND 1983-84 (1st Test)

At Asgiriya Stadium, Kandy, on 9 (*no play*), 10, 11, 13, 14 March.
Toss: New Zealand.   Result: NEW ZEALAND won by 165 runs.
Debuts: Sri Lanka – M.J.G.Amerasinghe, S.M.S.Kaluperuma.

New Zealand's first Test match in Sri Lanka saw Howarth open the batting in both innings for the first time for seven years. Hadlee was warned by umpire Vidanagamage for intimidation after bowling successive bouncers at John. The latter's partnership of 60 with Amerasinghe was a tenth-wicket record for Sri Lanka in all Tests until 1988. Needing 263 runs to win in 140 minutes plus 20 overs, Sri Lanka were bowled out in exactly two hours for their lowest total in a home Test until 1994-95. It was also the lowest total (in which all 11 have batted) to include an individual fifty, Ranatunga receiving only 45 balls for his 51. Riot police were called to quell angry demonstrations after the match.

NEW ZEALAND

*G.P.Howarth	c De Alwis b John	62	lbw b John	60
J.G.Wright	lbw b John	45	c De Alwis b John	4
J.F.Reid	c Kaluperuma b Amerasinghe	26	c Ranatunga b De Silva	30
M.D.Crowe	c Ratnayake b De Silva	26	(5) st De Alwis b De Silva	8
J.J.Crowe	c sub ‡ b John	20	(8) c Amerasinghe b Kaluperuma	9
J.V.Coney	lbw b Ratnayake	25	(10) not out	3
R.J.Hadlee	c Ranatunga b John	29	(6) c sub‡ b Kaluperuma	27
†I.D.S.Smith	b Ranatunga	30	(9) not out	31
B.L.Cairns	c De Alwis b Ranatunga	0	(7) c Wettimuny b De Silva	2
J.G.Bracewell	c De Silva b John	2	(4) c Amerasinghe b John	21
S.L.Boock	not out	4		
Extras	(B1, LB1, W5)	7	(B3, W3)	6
Total		**276**	**(8 wickets declared)**	**201**

SRI LANKA

S.Wettimuny	c Coney b Hadlee	0	c Smith b Hadlee	5
E.R.N.S.Fernando	c Hadlee b Boock	29	lbw b Hadlee	2
S.M.S.Kaluperuma	c Howarth b Bracewell	18	c J.J.Crowe b Boock	5
R.J.Ratnayake	c Smith b Hadlee	6	(9) lbw b Boock	12
*L.R.D.Mendis	c Bracewell b Hadlee	5	(4) b Hadlee	0
R.S.Madugalle	c M.D.Crowe b Hadlee	33	(5) c Bracewell b Hadlee	2
A.Ranatunga	c Bracewell b Cairns	20	(6) c and b Bracewell	51
D.S.de Silva	b Bracewell	11	(7) c Coney b Boock	0
†R.G.de Alwis	lbw b Boock	26	(8) c Howarth b Boock	19
V.B.John	not out	27	c Wright b Boock	0
M.J.G.Amerasinghe	run out	34	not out	0
Extras	(LB2, NB4)	6	(NB1)	1
Total		**215**		**97**

SRI LANKA	O	M	R	W	O	M	R	W	FALL OF WICKETS				
John	29.1	7	86	5	17.5	1	73	3		NZ	SL	NZ	SL
Ratnayake	15	4	45	1					*Wkt*	*1st*	*1st*	*2nd*	*2nd*
Ranatunga	9	3	17	2	(2) 4	0	14	0	1st	97	0	14	3
De Silva	29	6	69	1	21	2	59	3	2nd	124	38	75	12
Amerasinghe	12	3	45	1	(3) 8	2	32	0	3rd	165	55	111	12
Kaluperuma	6	3	7	0	(5) 4	0	17	2	4th	169	55	126	14
									5th	210	61	133	18
NEW ZEALAND									6th	236	89	137	18
Hadlee	20.5	7	35	4	7	4	8	4	7th	266	120	167	55
Cairns	18	3	71	1	4	1	6	0	8th	266	132	167	97
M.D.Crowe	3	1	4	0					9th	272	155	–	97
Boock	23	7	63	2	(3) 9.3	4	28	5	10th	276	215	–	97
Bracewell	15	4	36	2	(4) 7	1	54	1					

Umpires: H.C.Felsinger (3) and P.W.Vidanagamage (1).   ‡ (U.S.H.Karnain).

Close: 1st day – no play; 2nd – NZ(1) 120-1 (Wright 41, Reid 10); 3rd – SL(1) 50-2 (Fernando 26, Ratnayake 4); 4th – NZ(2) 77-2 (Howarth 38, Bracewell 0).

SRI LANKA v NEW ZEALAND 1983-84 (2nd Test)

At Sinhalese Sports Club Ground, Colombo, on 16, 17, 18, 20, 21 March.
Toss: New Zealand.   Result: MATCH DRAWN.
Debuts: None.

The Sinhalese Sports Club provided Test cricket with its 57th ground. 'Ravi' Ratnayeke (5 for 42) recorded Sri Lanka's best analysis in ten Tests to that date. For the first time Sri Lanka dismissed their opponents for under 200. Dias (272 minutes, 215 balls, 18 fours) scored Sri Lanka's first hundred in a home Test. Before Wettimuny (65) retired at 172 after being hit in the groin by a ball from Hadlee, he shared an unbroken partnership of 159 with Dias which is Sri Lanka's highest for the third wicket in all Tests. He resumed at 244 but failed to add to his score. New Zealand were set 266 runs to win in 350 minutes. After losing two early wickets and handicapped by illness and injury, they settled for a draw. Martin Crowe, restricted by a damaged thumb, scored 19 in 217 minutes off 157 balls, eight of those runs coming from his last three balls. Only 117 runs were scored off 81 overs in 330 minutes on the fifth day, a record for the final day of any Test.

SRI LANKA

S.Wettimuny	c Coney b Chatfield	26		c Hadlee b Chatfield	65
E.R.N.S.Fernando	b M.D.Crowe	8		c J.J.Crowe b Hadlee	0
S.M.S.Kaluperuma	b Boock	23		c Cairns b Hadlee	2
R.L.Dias	run out	16		b Cairns	108
*L.R.D.Mendis	b Hadlee	1	(6)	b Chatfield	36
R.S.Madugalle	not out	44	(7)	c J.J.Crowe b Chatfield	36
A.Ranatunga	c Smith b Cairns	6	(8)	run out	7
J.R.Ratnayeke	lbw b Hadlee	22	(5)	c and b Hadlee	12
D.S.de Silva	c Coney b Cairns	0		not out	13
†R.G.de Alwis	c Smith b Cairns	2		b Chatfield	2
V.B.John	c Smith b Cairns	0		not out	3
Extras	(B5, LB7, W8, NB6)	26		(LB4, NB1)	5
Total		**174**		(9 wickets declared)	**289**

NEW ZEALAND

*G.P.Howarth	b John	24		c Kaluperuma b John	10
J.G.Wright	c Dias b John	20		c De Silva b Ranatunga	48
J.F.Reid	c De Alwis b John	7		lbw b John	0
J.J.Crowe	b Ratnayeke	50		c De Alwis b Ranatunga	16
J.V.Coney	c John b De Silva	30	(6)	not out	20
R.J.Hadlee	b Ratnayeke	19			
S.L.Boock	c Madugalle b Ratnayeke	4			
M.D.Crowe	c Kaluperuma b Ratnayeke	0	(5)	not out	19
†I.D.S.Smith	c Kaluperuma b Ratnayeke	7			
B.L.Cairns	lbw b De Silva	14			
E.J.Chatfield	not out	9			
Extras	(B4, LB6, W1, NB3)	14		(B4, LB4, NB2)	10
Total		**198**		(4 wickets)	**123**

NEW ZEALAND	O	M	R	W	O	M	R	W		FALL OF WICKETS			
Hadlee	22	12	27	2	30	14	58	3		SL	NZ	SL	NZ
Cairns	24.5	6	47	4	(3) 22	3	79	1	*Wkt*	*1st*	*1st*	*2nd*	*2nd*
Chatfield	20	7	35	1	(2) 29	9	78	4	1st	25	38	3	10
M.D.Crowe	13	5	21	1					2nd	66	53	13	10
Boock	11	2	18	1	(4) 42	16	65	0	3rd	68	66	176	48
Coney					(5) 4	3	4	0	4th	69	127	209	89
									5th	99	151	234	–
SRI LANKA									6th	111	166	244	–
John	24	1	89	3	21	11	26	2	7th	152	166	245	–
Ratnayeke	21	8	42	5	21	11	17	0	8th	153	171	278	–
Kaluperuma	1	0	3	0	(4) 6	3	10	0	9th	165	178	282	–
Ranatunga	4	1	11	0	(5) 18	7	29	2	10th	174	198	–	–
De Silva	14.3	6	39	2	(3) 19	10	31	0					
Madugalle					1	1	0	0					

Umpires: D.P.Buultjens (1) and H.C.Felsinger (4).

Close: 1st day – SL(1) 145-6 (Madugalle 25, Ratnayeke 19); 2nd – NZ(1) 164-5 (Hadlee 17, Boock 3); 3rd – SL(2) 133-2 (Wettimuny 56, Dias 74); 4th – NZ(2) 6-0 (Howarth 6, Wright 0).

SRI LANKA v NEW ZEALAND 1983-84 (3rd Test)

At Colombo Cricket Club Ground on 24, 25, 26, 28, 29 March.
Toss: Sri Lanka.   Result: NEW ZEALAND won by an innings and 61 runs.
Debuts: None.

Colombo became the first city to boast three current Test match venues by staging this match at the Colombo Cricket Club Ground. Although Johannesburg and Bombay have both played Test cricket on three different grounds, neither city used more than one venue during a rubber or returned to a discarded one. Reid (685 minutes, 445 balls, 16 fours) scored New Zealand's first hundred in this series and compiled the highest innings by any batsman against Sri Lanka so far. Boock, who equalled his highest score in first-class cricket, reached double figures for the first time in 24 Test innings. Hadlee's match analysis of 10 for 102 was a record for any Test in Sri Lanka. In the first innings, Madugalle (87) retired at 172 after being hit behind the left ear by a ball from Hadlee. His partnership of 109, unbroken, was Sri Lanka's highest for the sixth wicket until 1984 (*Test No. 994*). He resumed his innings at 249. Dias split the webbing between the first and second fingers of his right hand while fielding. New Zealand gained their first victory by an innings overseas.

SRI LANKA

S.Wettimuny	b Hadlee	4		c Coney b Hadlee	2
S.M.S.Kaluperuma	b Hadlee	16		c Coney b Hadlee	18
J.R.Ratnayeke	lbw b Hadlee	0	(7)	b Boock	2
R.L.Dias	c Smith b Chatfield	10		absent hurt	–
*L.R.D.Mendis	c J.J.Crowe b Chatfield	19	(6)	b Boock	10
R.S.Madugalle	not out	89	(3)	c Wright b Bracewell	38
A.Ranatunga	c sub (B.A.Edgar) b Chatfield	37	(4)	c Wright b Boock	50
D.S.de Silva	c Smith b Hadlee	17	(5)	c Smith b Hadlee	1
†R.G.de Alwis	c Boock b Hadlee	28	(8)	c Bracewell b Hadlee	10
M.J.G.Amerasinghe	c Wright b Chatfield	15	(9)	b Hadlee	5
V.B.John	c and b Chatfield	12	(10)	not out	0
Extras	(LB4, NB5)	9		(W1, NB5)	6
Total		**256**			**142**

NEW ZEALAND

*G.P.Howarth	lbw b Ratnayeke	7
J.G.Wright	c De Alwis b Ratnayeke	18
J.F.Reid	c and b Amerasinghe	180
M.D.Crowe	c De Alwis b Ratnayeke	45
S.L.Boock	b John	35
J.J.Crowe	lbw b John	18
J.V.Coney	c De Alwis b Amerasinghe	92
R.J.Hadlee	c Kaluperuma b De Silva	0
†I.D.S.Smith	b John	42
J.G.Bracewell	c Kaluperuma b De Silva	0
E.J.Chatfield	not out	1
Extras	(B5, LB8, W2, NB6)	21
Total		**459**

NEW ZEALAND	O	M	R	W	O	M	R	W	FALL OF WICKETS			
Hadlee	22	4	73	5	16	7	29	5		SL	NZ	SL
Chatfield	22	5	63	5	9	2	27	0	*Wkt*	*1st*	*1st*	*2nd*
M.D.Crowe	6	2	22	0	5	2	13	0	1st	4	13	6
Boock	20	9	51	0	(5) 16	2	32	3	2nd	4	32	63
Bracewell	9	2	31	0	(4) 11	4	35	1	3rd	22	132	63
Coney	3	0	7	0					4th	32	214	79
									5th	63	253	101
SRI LANKA									6th	182	386	105
John	37	8	99	3					7th	222	391	136
Ratnayeke	40	9	128	3					8th	227	429	138
Ranatunga	16	5	18	0					9th	249	436	142
De Silva	42	4	95	2					10th	256	459	–
Amerasinghe	30	4	73	2								
Kaluperuma	10	2	25	0								

Umpires: K.T. Francis (2) and P.W. Vidanagamage (2).

Close: 1st day – SL(1) 230-8 (Amerasinghe 1, John 2); 2nd – NZ(1) 135-3 (Reid 56, Boock 3); 3rd – NZ(1) 322-5 (Reid 156, Coney 26); 4th – SL(2) 69-3 (Ranatunga 6, De Silva 0).

ENGLAND v WEST INDIES 1984 (1st Test)

At Edgbaston, Birmingham, on 14, 15, 16, 18 June.
Toss: England.   Result: WEST INDIES won by an innings and 180 runs.
Debuts: England – T.A.Lloyd.

At 1.56 on the fourth afternoon, West Indies became only the second side to defeat England in 22 Tests at Edgbaston (also *Test No. 760*). Andy Lloyd, the first Shropshire-born cricketer to represent England in a home Test, retired at 20, after 33 minutes, when he was struck on the temple of his helmet by a sharply lifting ball from Marshall. Hospitalised for several days with blurred vision, he was unable to play again during 1984. West Indies compiled their highest total against England since 1976. Richards became the fourth batsman to score 5,000 runs for West Indies. Only D.G.Bradman (11) among overseas batsmen has exceeded his tally of seven hundreds in England. Baptiste and Holding shared a record West Indies ninth-wicket partnership against England of 150 in 114 minutes.

ENGLAND

G.Fowler	c Dujon b Garner	0	lbw b Garner		7
T.A.Lloyd	retired hurt	10	absent hurt		–
D.W.Randall	b Garner	0	c Lloyd b Garner		1
*D.I.Gower	c Harper b Holding	10	c Dujon b Garner		12
A.J.Lamb	c Lloyd b Baptiste	15	c Richards b Marshall		13
I.T.Botham	c Garner b Harper	64	lbw b Garner		38
G.Miller	c Dujon b Garner	22	c Harper b Marshall		11
D.R.Pringle	c Dujon b Holding	4	not out		46
†P.R.Downton	lbw b Garner	33	c Greenidge b Harper	(2)	56
N.G.B.Cook	c Lloyd b Marshall	2	run out	(9)	9
R.G.D.Willis	not out	10	c Dujon b Garner	(10)	22
Extras	(B8, LB5, NB8)	21	(B1, LB5, W4, NB10)		20
Total		**191**			**235**

WEST INDIES

C.G.Greenidge	lbw b Willis	19
D.L.Haynes	lbw b Willis	8
H.A.Gomes	c Miller b Pringle	143
I.V.A.Richards	c Randall b Cook	117
†P.J.L.Dujon	c Gower b Miller	23
*C.H.Lloyd	c Pringle b Botham	71
M.D.Marshall	lbw b Pringle	2
R.A.Harper	b Pringle	14
E.A.E.Baptiste	not out	87
M.A.Holding	c Willis b Pringle	69
J.Garner	c Lamb b Pringle	0
Extras	(B6, LB17, W2, NB28)	53
Total		**606**

WEST INDIES	O	M	R	W		O	M	R	W		FALL OF WICKETS		
Marshall	14	4	37	1		23	7	65	2		E	WI	E
Garner	14.3	2	53	4		23.5	7	55	5	*Wkt*	*1st*	*1st*	*2nd*
Holding	16	4	44	2		12	3	29	0	1st	1	34	17
Baptiste	11	3	28	1	(5)	5	1	18	0	2nd	5	35	21
Harper	4	1	8	1	(4)	13	3	48	1	3rd	45	241	37
										4th	49	294	65
ENGLAND										5th	89	418	127
Willis	25	3	108	2						6th	103	418	138
Botham	34	7	127	1						7th	168	421	181
Pringle	31	5	108	5						8th	173	455	193
Cook	38	6	127	1						9th	191	605	235
Miller	15	1	83	1						10th	–	606	–

Umpires: H.D.Bird (27) and B.J.Meyer (14).

Close: 1st day – WI(1) 53-2 (Gomes 4, Richards 14); 2nd – WI(1) 421-7 (Harper 0); 3rd – E(2) 112-4 (Downton 34, Botham 30).

ENGLAND v WEST INDIES 1984 (2nd Test)

At Lord's, London, on 28, 29, 30 June, 2, 3 July.
Toss: West Indies.   Result: WEST INDIES won by 9 wickets.
Debuts: England – B.C.Broad.   .

Lord's celebrated its centenary of Test cricket. England employed their seventh different opening pair of batsmen in eight matches. Lloyd became the second West Indies batsman after G.St A.Sobers to score 7,000 runs. Other notable Test career landmarks were reached by Botham and Greenidge (both 4,000 runs) and Gomes (2,000). Botham was the first bowler to take eight wickets in an innings against West Indies in England. Greenidge (300 minutes, 241 balls, two sixes, 29 fours) scored the first West Indies double century at Lord's, his unbroken stand of 287 in 236 minutes with Gomes setting a second-wicket record for either side in this series, and achieving victory with 11.5 overs to spare. West Indies lost a second-innings wicket for the first time in seven matches. Their total of 344 was the fifth-highest in a fourth innings to win a Test. For the first time since 1948 (*Test No. 302*) England lost after declaring their second innings closed. Lamb became the fourth player to bat on each day of a five-day Test. The total of 12 'lbw' decisions by umpires Meyer (7) and Evans (5) equalled the record set in 1979-80 (*Test No. 873*).

ENGLAND

G.Fowler	c Harper b Baptiste	106	lbw b Small		11
B.C.Broad	c Dujon b Marshall	55	c Harper b Garner		0
*D.I.Gower	lbw b Marshall	3	c Lloyd b Small		21
A.J.Lamb	lbw b Marshall	23	c Dujon b Marshall		110
M.W.Gatting	lbw b Marshall	1	lbw b Marshall		29
I.T.Botham	c Richards b Baptiste	30	lbw b Garner		81
†P.R.Downton	not out	23	lbw b Small		4
G.Miller	run out	0	b Harper		9
D.R.Pringle	lbw b Garner	2	lbw b Garner		8
N.A.Foster	c Harper b Marshall	6	not out		9
R.G.D.Willis	b Marshall	2			
Extras	(B4, LB14, W2, NB15)	35	(B4, LB7, W1, NB6)		18
Total		**286**	(9 wickets declared)		**300**

WEST INDIES

C.G.Greenidge	c Miller b Botham	1	not out		214
D.L.Haynes	lbw b Botham	12	run out		17
H.A.Gomes	c Gatting b Botham	10	not out		92
I.V.A.Richards	lbw b Botham	72			
*C.H.Lloyd	lbw b Botham	39			
†P.J.L.Dujon	c Fowler b Botham	8			
M.D.Marshall	c Pringle b Willis	29			
E.A.E.Baptiste	c Downton b Willis	44			
R.A.Harper	c Gatting b Botham	8			
J.Garner	c Downton b Botham	6			
M.A.Small	not out	3			
Extras	(LB5, W1, NB7)	13	(B4, LB4, NB13)		21
Total		**245**	(1 wicket)		**344**

WEST INDIES	O	M	R	W	O	M	R	W		FALL OF WICKETS			
Garner	32	10	67	1	30.3	3	91	3		E	WI	E	WI
Small	9	0	38	0	(3) 12	2	40	3	*Wkt*	*1st*	*1st*	*2nd*	*2nd*
Marshall	36.5	10	85	6	(2) 22	6	85	2	1st	101	1	5	57
Baptiste	20	6	36	2	26	8	48	0	2nd	106	18	33	–
Harper	8	0	25	0	8	1	18	1	3rd	183	35	36	–
									4th	185	138	88	–
ENGLAND									5th	243	147	216	–
Willis	19	5	48	2	15	5	48	0	6th	248	173	230	–
Botham	27.4	6	103	8	20.1	2	117	0	7th	251	213	273	–
Pringle	11	0	54	0	8	0	44	0	8th	255	231	290	–
Foster	6	2	13	0	12	0	69	0	9th	264	241	300	–
Miller	2	0	14	0	11	0	45	0	10th	286	245	–	–

Umpires: D.G.L. Evans (6) and B.J.Meyer (15).

Close: 1st day – E(1) 167-2 (Fowler 70, Lamb 13); 2nd – WI(1) 119-3 (Richards 60, Lloyd 32); 3rd – E(2) 114-4 (Lamb 30, Botham 17); 4th – E(2) 287-7 (Lamb 109, Pringle 6).

ENGLAND v WEST INDIES 1984 (3rd Test)

At Headingley, Leeds, on 12, 13, 14, 16 July.
Toss: England.   Result: WEST INDIES won by 8 wickets.
Debuts: England – V.P.Terry.

Boundaries by Richards off successive balls enabled West Indies to retain the Wisden Trophy at 2.48 on the fourth afternoon. On only one previous occasion – against Australia in 1921 – had England lost the first three matches of a home rubber. Holding became the fourth West Indies bowler to take 200 wickets when he dismissed Pringle. Marshall batted (one-handed) and returned his (then) best innings analysis in Tests with his doubly-fractured left thumb encased in plaster. Willis, in the last of his 90 Test matches (easily the record for a fast bowler), extended his world record of 'not out' innings to 55 and his record number of wickets by an England bowler to 325.

ENGLAND

Batsman	Dismissal 1	R	Dismissal 2	R
G.Fowler	lbw b Garner	10	c and b Marshall	50
B.C.Broad	c Lloyd b Harper	32	c Baptiste b Marshall	2
V.P.Terry	c Harper b Holding	8	lbw b Garner	1
*D.I.Gower	lbw b Garner	2	c Dujon b Harper	43
A.J.Lamb	b Harper	100	lbw b Marshall	3
I.T.Botham	c Dujon b Baptiste	45	c Dujon b Garner	14
†P.R.Downton	c Lloyd b Harper	17	c Dujon b Marshall	27
D.R.Pringle	c Haynes b Holding	19	(9) lbw b Marshall	2
P.J.W.Allott	b Holding	3	(10) lbw b Marshall	4
N.G.B.Cook	b Holding	1	(8) c Lloyd b Marshall	0
R.G.D.Willis	not out	4	not out	5
Extras	(B4, LB7, NB18)	29	(LB6, NB2)	8
Total		**270**		**159**

WEST INDIES

Batsman	Dismissal 1	R	Dismissal 2	R
C.G.Greenidge	c Botham b Willis	10	c Terry b Cook	49
D.L.Haynes	b Allott	18	c Fowler b Cook	43
H.A.Gomes	not out	104	not out	2
I.V.A.Richards	c Pringle b Allott	15	not out	22
*C.H.Lloyd	c Gower b Cook	48		
†P.J.L.Dujon	lbw b Allott	26		
E.A.E.Baptiste	c Broad b Allott	0		
R.A.Harper	c Downton b Allott	0		
M.A.Holding	c Allott b Willis	59		
J.Garner	run out	0		
M.D.Marshall	c Botham b Allott	4		
Extras	(LB3, NB15)	18	(LB2, NB13)	15
Total		**302**	(2 wickets)	**131**

WEST INDIES	O	M	R	W	O	M	R	W
Garner	30	11	73	2	(2) 16	7	37	2
Marshall	6	4	6	0	(1) 26	9	53	7
Holding	29.2	8	70	4	7	1	31	0
Baptiste	13	1	45	1				
Harper	19	6	47	3	(4) 16	8	30	1

ENGLAND	O	M	R	W	O	M	R	W
Willis	18	1	123	2	8	1	40	0
Allott	26.5	7	61	6	7	2	24	0
Botham	7	0	45	0				
Pringle	13	3	26	0	(4) 8.3	2	25	0
Cook	9	1	29	1	(3) 9	2	27	2

FALL OF WICKETS

Wkt	E 1st	WI 1st	E 2nd	WI 2nd
1st	13	16	10	106
2nd	43	43	13	108
3rd	53	78	104	–
4th	87	148	106	–
5th	172	201	107	–
6th	236	206	135	–
7th	237	206	138	–
8th	244	288	140	–
9th	254	290	146	–
10th	270	302	159	–

Umpires: D.J.Constant (27) and D.G.L.Evans (7).

Close: 1st day – E(1) 237-6 (Lamb 100, Pringle 1); 2nd – WI(1) 239-7 (Gomes 79, Holding 28); 3rd – E(2) 135-6 (Downton 14, Cook 0).

ENGLAND v WEST INDIES 1984 (4th Test)

At Old Trafford, Manchester, on 26, 27, 28, 30, 31 July.
Toss: West Indies.   Result: WEST INDIES won by an innings and 64 runs.
Debuts: None.

Old Trafford, like Lord's, celebrated its centenary of Test cricket. At 12.11 pm on the final day, West Indies became the first visiting team to win the first four Tests of a rubber in England. Pocock returned to Test cricket after missing 86 matches. Greenidge (588 minutes, 425 balls, 30 fours) recorded his highest Test score and the first double century for West Indies at Old Trafford. He emulated Richards (1976) by scoring two double centuries for West Indies in the same rubber. Terry (7) retired at 105 when his left ulna was fractured by a ball from Davis. He resumed at the fall of the ninth wicket (Lamb 98), batting one-handed with his left arm be-slinged under his sweater, in his last innings until 1985. Lamb became the first England batsman to score hundreds in three successive Tests within a rubber since K.F.Barrington did so against Pakistan in 1967.

WEST INDIES

C.G.Greenidge	c Downton b Pocock	223
D.L.Haynes	c Cowans b Botham	2
H.A.Gomes	c Botham b Allott	30
I.V.A.Richards	c Cook b Allott	1
*C.H.Lloyd	c Downton b Allott	1
†P.J.L.Dujon	c Downton b Botham	101
W.W.Davis	b Pocock	77
E.A.E.Baptiste	b Pocock	6
R.A.Harper	not out	39
M.A.Holding	b Cook	0
J.Garner	c Terry b Pocock	7
Extras	(B4, LB6, W2, NB1)	13
Total		**500**

ENGLAND

G.Fowler	b Baptiste	38		b Holding	0
B.C.Broad	c Harper b Davis	42		lbw b Harper	21
V.P.Terry	b Garner	7		absent hurt	–
*D.I.Gower	c Dujon b Baptiste	4		not out	57
A.J.Lamb	not out	100		b Harper	9
I.T.Botham	c Garner b Baptiste	6		c Haynes b Harper	1
†P.R.Downton	c Harper b Garner	0	(3)	b Harper	24
P.J.W.Allott	c Gomes b Davis	26	(7)	b Garner	14
N.G.B.Cook	b Holding	13	(8)	c Dujon b Garner	0
P.I.Pocock	b Garner	0	(9)	c Garner b Harper	0
N.G.Cowans	b Garner	0	(10)	b Harper	14
Extras	(B5, LB21, NB18)	44		(B9, LB3, W1, NB3)	16
Total		**280**			**156**

ENGLAND	O	M	R	W	O	M	R	W		FALL OF WICKETS		
										WI	E	E
Botham	29	5	100	2					Wkt	1st	1st	2nd
Cowans	19	2	76	0					1st	11	90	0
Allott	28	9	76	3					2nd	60	112	39
Cook	39	6	114	1					3rd	62	117	77
Pocock	45.3	14	121	4					4th	70	138	99
									5th	267	147	101
WEST INDIES									6th	437	228	125
Garner	22.2	7	51	4	(2) 12	4	25	2	7th	443	257	127
Davis	20	2	71	2	(4) 3	1	6	0	8th	470	278	128
Harper	23	10	33	0	28.4	12	57	6	9th	471	278	156
Holding	21	2	50	1	(1) 11	2	21	1	10th	500	280	–
Baptiste	19	8	31	3	(6) 11	5	29	0				
Richards					(5) 1	0	2	0				

Umpires: H.D.Bird (28) and D.O.Oslear (5).

Close: 1st day – WI(1) 273-5 (Greenidge 128, Davis 2); 2nd – WI(1) 500 all out; 3rd – E(1) 163-5 (Lamb 27, Allott 10); 4th – E(2) 120-5 (Gower 43, Allott 10).

ENGLAND v WEST INDIES 1984 (5th Test)

At Kennington Oval, London, on 9, 10, 11, 13, 14 August.
Toss: West Indies.   Result: WEST INDIES won by 172 runs.
Debuts: England – J.P.Agnew, R.M.Ellison.

At one minute past noon on the final day, Ellison edged Garner to gully and West Indies had completed a unique 'blackwash'. They were the fifth side to win every Test of a five-match rubber and the first to do so against England at home. They equalled the world record of eight successive wins by Australia against England in 1920-21 and 1921, and extended their unbeaten run to 23 Tests. Only one of their last 38 matches had resulted in defeat. Botham became the fifth bowler to take 300 wickets in Tests when he dismissed Dujon, and, in his 72nd match, the first to complete the 'triple double' of 3,000 runs and 300 wickets. Marshall claimed five wickets in an innings for the seventh time in his last ten Tests. His tally from his last four rubbers, played within only 18 months, was 99 wickets, average 20.53. Pocock became the second England player after R.Peel (1894-95) to be dismissed for a 'pair' twice in consecutive matches. Fowler (12) retired at 21 when a ball from Marshall struck him on the arm, and resumed at 83.

WEST INDIES

C.G.Greenidge	lbw b Botham	22		c Botham b Agnew	34
D.L.Haynes	b Allott	10		b Botham	125
H.A.Gomes	c Botham b Ellison	18		c Tavaré b Ellison	1
I.V.A.Richards	c Allott b Botham	8		lbw b Agnew	15
†P.J.L.Dujon	c Tavaré b Botham	3	(6)	c Lamb b Ellison	49
*C.H.Lloyd	not out	60	(5)	c Downton b Ellison	36
M.D.Marshall	c Gower b Ellison	0	(8)	c Lamb b Botham	12
E.A.E.Baptiste	c Fowler b Allott	32	(7)	c Downton b Allott	5
R.A.Harper	b Botham	18		c Downton b Allott	17
M.A.Holding	lbw b Botham	0		lbw b Botham	30
J.Garner	c Downton b Allott	6		not out	10
Extras	(B1, LB4, W7, NB1)	13		(LB12)	12
Total		**190**			**346**

ENGLAND

G.Fowler	c Richards b Baptiste	31		c Richards b Marshall	7
B.C.Broad	b Garner	4		c Greenidge b Holding	39
P.I.Pocock	c Greenidge b Marshall	0	(10)	c and b Holding	0
C.J.Tavaré	c Dujon b Holding	16	(3)	c Richards b Garner	49
*D.I.Gower	c Dujon b Holding	12	(4)	lbw b Holding	7
A.J.Lamb	lbw b Marshall	12	(5)	c Haynes b Holding	1
I.T.Botham	c Dujon b Marshall	14	(6)	c Marshall b Garner	54
†P.R.Downton	c Lloyd b Garner	16	(7)	lbw b Garner	10
R.M.Ellison	not out	20	(8)	c Holding b Garner	13
P.J.W.Allott	b Marshall	16	(9)	c Lloyd b Holding	4
J.P.Agnew	b Marshall	5		not out	2
Extras	(B2, LB4, NB10)	16		(LB2, W1, NB13)	16
Total		**162**			**202**

ENGLAND	O	M	R	W		O	M	R	W		FALL OF WICKETS			
											WI	E	WI	E
Agnew	12	3	46	0	(4)	14	1	51	2	Wkt	1st	1st	2nd	2nd
Allott	17	7	25	3		26	1	96	2	1st	19	10	51	15
Botham	23	8	72	5	(1)	22.3	2	103	3	2nd	45	22	52	75
Ellison	18	3	34	2	(5)	26	7	60	3	3rd	64	45	69	88
Pocock					(3)	8	3	24	0	4th	64	64	132	90
										5th	67	83	214	135
WEST INDIES										6th	70	84	237	181
Garner	18	6	37	2	(2)	18.4	3	51	4	7th	124	116	264	186
Marshall	17.5	5	35	5	(1)	22	5	71	1	8th	154	133	293	200
Holding	13	2	55	2		13	2	43	5	9th	154	156	329	200
Baptiste	12	4	19	1		8	3	11	0	10th	190	162	346	202
Harper	1	1	0	0		8	5	10	0					

Umpires: D.J.Constant (28) and B.J.Meyer (16).

Close: 1st day – E(1) 10-1 (Fowler 4, Pocock 0); 2nd – WI(2) 15-0 (Greenidge 10, Haynes 4); 3rd – WI(2) 284-7 (Haynes 111, Harper 14); 4th – E(2) 151-5 (Botham 32, Downton 2).

ENGLAND v SRI LANKA 1984 (Only Test)

At Lord's, London, on 23, 24, 25, 27, 28 August.
Toss: England.   Result: MATCH DRAWN.
Debuts: Sri Lanka – P.A.de Silva.

Sri Lanka's first innings in England produced the highest total of their 12-match history. Wettimuny (636 minutes, 471 balls, 21 fours) recorded Sri Lanka's highest score until 1986-87, the sixth-highest score against England at Lord's and the longest Test innings at Lord's. Mendis became the first Sri Lankan captain to score a Test hundred while in office. His century came in 144 minutes off 112 balls and was the fastest of the eight scored for Sri Lanka so far. His three sixes also set a national record. Lamb's fourth Test hundred of the English season equalled the record shared by H.Sutcliffe (1929), D.G.Bradman (1930) and D.C.S.Compton (1947). Botham equalled S.F.Barnes's world record by taking five or more wickets in an innings for the 24th time. Silva scored his first hundred in first-class cricket. Three record Sri Lankan partnerships were set in this match; 148 (4th wicket) by Wettimuny and Ranatunga; 150 (5th) by Wettimuny and Mendis; and 138 (6th) by Silva and Mendis. England's 12th match without victory equalled their longest run of non-success.

SRI LANKA

S.Wettimuny	c Downton b Allott	190		c Gower b Botham	13
†S.A.R.Silva	lbw b Botham	8		not out	102
R.S.Madugalle	b Ellison	5		b Botham	3
R.L.Dias	c Lamb b Pocock	32		lbw b Botham	38
A.Ranatunga	b Agnew	84		lbw b Botham	0
*L.R.D.Mendis	c Fowler b Pocock	111	(7)	c Fowler b Botham	94
P.A.de Silva	c Downton b Agnew	16	(6)	c Downton b Pocock	3
A.L.F.de Mel	not out	20		c Ellison b Botham	14
J.R.Ratnayeke	not out	5		not out	7
D.S.de Silva	} did not bat				
V.B.John					
Extras	(B2, LB8, W2, NB8)	20		(B5, LB4, NB11)	20
Total	(7 wickets declared)	**491**		(7 wickets declared)	**294**

ENGLAND

G.Fowler	c Madugalle b John	25
B.C.Broad	c Silva b De Mel	86
C.J.Tavaré	c Ranatunga b D.S.de Silva	14
*D.I.Gower	c Silva b De Mel	55
A.J.Lamb	c Dias b John	107
I.T.Botham	c sub (D.M.Vonhagt) b John	6
R.M.Ellison	c Ratnayeke b D.S.de Silva	41
†P.R.Downton	c Dias b De Mel	10
P.J.W.Allott	b De Mel	0
P.I.Pocock	c Silva b John	2
J.P.Agnew	not out	1
Extras	(B5, LB7, W5, NB6)	23
Total		**370**

ENGLAND	O	M	R	W		O	M	R	W	FALL OF WICKETS			
Agnew	32	3	123	2		11	3	54	0		SL	E	SL
Botham	29	6	114	1	(3)	27	6	90	6	*Wkt*	*1st*	*1st*	*2nd*
Ellison	28	6	70	1	(5)	7	0	36	0	1st	17	49	19
Pocock	41	17	75	2		29	10	78	1	2nd	43	105	27
Allott	36	7	89	1	(2)	1	0	2	0	3rd	144	190	111
Lamb						1	0	6	0	4th	292	210	115
Tavaré						3	3	0	0	5th	442	218	118
Fowler						1	0	8	0	6th	456	305	256
SRI LANKA										7th	464	354	276
De Mel	37	10	110	4						8th	–	354	–
John	39.1	12	98	4						9th	–	369	–
Ratnayeke	22	5	50	0						10th	–	370	–
D.S.de Silva	45	16	85	2									
Ranatunga	1	1	0	0									
Madugalle	3	0	4	0									

Umpires: H.D.Bird (29) and D.G.L.Evans (8).

Close: 1st day – SL(1) 226-3 (Wettimuny 116, Ranatunga 54); 2nd – SL(1) 434-4 (Wettimuny 187, Mendis 100); 3rd – E(1) 139-2 (Broad 69, Gower 16); 4th – E(1) 370 all out.

PAKISTAN v INDIA 1984-85 (1st Test)

At Gaddafi Stadium, Lahore, on 17, 18, 19, 21, 22 October.
Toss: Pakistan.   Result: MATCH DRAWN.
Debuts: India – C.Sharma.

Gavaskar (35) became the first Indian and the fourth and youngest player after M.C.Cowdrey, G.Boycott and C.H.Lloyd to play in 100 Test matches. Chetan Sharma, aged 18 years 288 days, bowled Mohsin with his fifth ball in Test cricket – the third Indian to take a wicket in his first over at this level. Zaheer and Amarnath each recorded their third hundreds at Lahore in this series; Zaheer's was his 12th in Tests (equalling Hanif Mohammad's Pakistan record) and sixth against India, while Amarnath's eighth Test century was his fourth against Pakistan. Zaheer's partnership of 142 with Ashraf was Pakistan's highest for the seventh wicket against India until 1986-87. Azeem's analysis of 6 for 46 was his best in Test cricket and included a spell of 4 for 5.

PAKISTAN

Mohsin Khan	b Sharma	4
Mudassar Nazar	c Gavaskar b Sharma	15
Qasim Omar	c Amarnath b Shastri	46
Javed Miandad	c Amarnath b Sharma	34
*Zaheer Abbas	not out	168
Salim Malik	c and b Shastri	45
Wasim Raja	c Amarnath b Kapil Dev	3
†Ashraf Ali	c Gavaskar b Gaekwad	65
Tausif Ahmed	c Gavaskar b Maninder	10
Jalaluddin	lbw b Shastri	2
Azeem Hafeez	not out	17
Extras	(LB7, W1, NB11)	19
Total	**(9 wickets declared)**	**428**

INDIA

*S.M.Gavaskar	c Salim b Azeem	48		lbw b Jalaluddin	37
A.D.Gaekwad	b Jalaluddin	4		c Salim b Tausif	60
D.B.Vengsarkar	c Ashraf b Azeem	41		c Mudassar b Azeem	28
M.Amarnath	b Wasim	36		not out	101
S.M.Patil	c Salim b Azeem	0		b Jalaluddin	7
R.J.Shastri	lbw b Azeem	0		lbw b Salim	71
Kapil Dev	lbw b Azeem	3	(8)	not out	33
R.M.H.Binny	lbw b Mudassar	0	(7)	lbw b Wasim	13
†S.M.H.Kirmani	c sub (Ramiz Raja) b Mudassar	2			
C.Sharma	b Azeem	4			
Maninder Singh	not out	4			
Extras	(B2, LB7, W1, NB4)	14		(B6, LB7, W4, NB4)	21
Total		**156**		**(6 wickets)**	**371**

INDIA	O	M	R	W	O	M	R	W	FALL OF WICKETS			
Kapil Dev	30	4	104	1						P	I	I
Sharma	29	2	94	3					Wkt	1st	1st	2nd
Binny	8	1	20	0					1st	6	7	85
Maninder	40	10	90	1					2nd	54	94	114
Shastri	46	13	90	3					3rd	100	112	147
Amarnath	4	0	19	0					4th	110	114	164
Gaekwad	1	0	4	1					5th	195	114	290
									6th	212	119	315
PAKISTAN									7th	354	120	–
Jalaluddin	16.3	5	40	1	24	3	61	2	8th	394	130	–
Azeem	23	7	46	6	43	12	114	1	9th	397	135	–
Mudassar	16.3	3	32	2	14	3	34	0	10th	–	156	–
Tausif	13	3	19	0	50	19	93	1				
Wasim	3.5	0	10	1	19	4	46	1				
Salim					5	2	6	1				
Miandad					1	0	4	0				

Umpires: Khizer Hayat (14) and Shakoor Rana (13).

Close: 1st day – P(1) 211-5 (Zaheer 51, Wasim 3); 2nd – P(1) 428-9 (Zaheer 168, Azeem 17); 3rd – I(1) 156 all out; 4th – I(2) 180-4 (Amarnath 28, Shastri 6).

PAKISTAN v INDIA 1984-85 (2nd Test)

At Iqbal Stadium, Faisalabad, on 24, 25, 26, 28, 29 October.
Toss: India.   Result: MATCH DRAWN.
Debuts: Pakistan – Manzoor Elahi.

The 35th encounter between these countries was the 25th to be drawn. Pakistan gained a first innings lead on the final day while amassing their highest total in Test cricket until 1987. India's highest score in Pakistan until 1989-90 included a fifth-wicket partnership of 200 between Patil and Shastri – the highest (since equalled) by India for any wicket in this series. Qasim Omar (685 minutes, 442 balls, 27 fours) played the longest Test innings in Pakistan and compiled the highest score by a Kenyan in Test cricket; his partnership of 250 with Mudassar remains Pakistan's record for the second wicket against India. Mudassar (552 minutes, 408 balls, 24 fours), the first to be dismissed for 199 in Test cricket, registered his seventh century in Tests and his sixth against India, while Salim Malik's fourth Test hundred was his third at the Iqbal Stadium. In his 28th match, Qadir became the sixth Pakistan bowler to take 100 Test wickets.

INDIA

*S.M.Gavaskar	c Omar b Qadir	35
A.D.Gaekwad	c and b Manzoor	74
D.B.Vengsarkar	c Mohsin b Qadir	5
M.Amarnath	hit wkt b Azeem	37
S.M.Patil	c Zaheer b Mudassar	127
R.J.Shastri	c Ashraf b Qadir	139
Kapil Dev	c Manzoor b Azeem	16
Madan Lal	c Ashraf b Azeem	0
†S.M.H.Kirmani	c sub‡ b Azeem	6
N.S.Yadav	c Salim b Qadir	29
C.Sharma	not out	18
Extras	(B1, LB6, NB7)	14
Total		**500**

PAKISTAN

Mohsin Khan	c Gavaskar b Sharma	59
Mudassar Nazar	c Kirmani b Yadav	199
Qasim Omar	c Yadav b Gaekwad	210
Javed Miandad	st Kirmani b Shastri	16
*Zaheer Abbas	c Kirmani b Madan Lal	26
Salim Malik	not out	102
Manzoor Elahi	run out	26
†Ashraf Ali	not out	9
Abdul Qadir		
Jalaluddin	} did not bat	
Azeem Hafeez		
Extras	(B7, LB6, W1, NB13)	27
Total	(6 wickets)	**674**

PAKISTAN	O	M	R	W
Jalaluddin	34	5	103	0
Azeem	44	9	137	4
Mudassar	25	5	74	1
Manzoor	21	3	74	1
Qadir	38	8	104	4
Salim	1	0	1	0
INDIA				
Kapil Dev	4.5	0	22	0
Sharma	32	0	139	1
Madan Lal	27	3	94	1
Yadav	75	18	196	1
Shastri	50.1	17	99	1
Gaekwad	27	5	75	1
Amarnath	8.5	0	36	0

FALL OF WICKETS

	I	P
Wkt	1st	1st
1st	88	141
2nd	100	391
3rd	148	430
4th	170	494
5th	370	608
6th	412	650
7th	420	–
8th	441	–
9th	461	–
10th	500	–

Umpires: Amanullah Khan (12) and Mahboob Shah (13).   ‡ (Shoaib Mohammad)

Close: 1st day – I(1) 216-4 (Patil 42, Shastri 18); 2nd – I(1) 484-9 (Yadav 25, Sharma 7); 3rd – P(1) 216-1 (Mudassar 112, Omar 35); 4th – P(1) 443-3 (Omar 147, Zaheer 3).

The 3rd Test, scheduled to be played at the National Stadium, Karachi, on 4, 5, 6, 8, 9 November, was abandoned along with the remainder of India's tour following the assassination of Mrs Indira Gandhi on 31 October.

AUSTRALIA v WEST INDIES 1984-85 (1st Test)

At W.A.C.A.Ground, Perth, on 9, 10, 11, 12 November.
Toss: Australia.   Result: WEST INDIES won by an innings and 112 runs.
Debuts: West Indies – C.A.Walsh.

With only their fourth victory by an innings in 58 Tests against Australia (completed with a day and two sessions in hand), West Indies became the first side to win nine Test matches in succession. Gomes, who batted for 472 minutes (297 balls) registered his eighth century in 41 Tests and his fifth against Australia, while Dujon's fourth Test hundred remains his highest score. Dujon (35) retired at 154 with blurred vision, after being struck by a ball from Alderman, and resumed at 186. Australia followed on 340 runs in arrears after being dismissed in 100 minutes for 76, their lowest total against West Indies (previously 82 at Adelaide in 1951-52). The victims of outstanding fast bowling (and catching) on a pitch of erratic bounce following two days of rain which had curtailed its preparation, Australia also registered the lowest total of this series, surpassing the 78 by West Indies at Sydney in 1951-52. Alderman's best analysis to date included a spell of 4 for 5 in 26 balls.

WEST INDIES

C.G.Greenidge	c Rackemann b Alderman	30
D.L.Haynes	c Yallop b Hogg	56
R.B.Richardson	b Alderman	0
H.A.Gomes	b Hogg	127
I.V.A.Richards	c Phillips b Alderman	10
*C.H.Lloyd	c Phillips b Alderman	0
†P.J.L.Dujon	c Phillips b Alderman	139
M.D.Marshall	c Hughes b Hogg	21
M.A.Holding	c Wood b Alderman	1
J.Garner	c Phillips b Hogg	17
C.A.Walsh	not out	9
Extras	(B1, LB1, NB4)	6
Total		**416**

AUSTRALIA

K.C.Wessels	c Holding b Garner	13	(2)	c Lloyd b Garner	0
J.Dyson	c Lloyd b Marshall	0	(1)	b Marshall	30
G.M.Wood	c Lloyd b Garner	6		c Richardson b Walsh	56
A.R.Border	c Dujon b Holding	15		c Haynes b Marshall	6
*K.J.Hughes	c Marshall b Holding	4		lbw b Marshall	37
G.N.Yallop	c Greenidge b Holding	2		c Haynes b Walsh	1
†W.B.Phillips	c Marshall b Holding	22		c Dujon b Garner	16
G.F.Lawson	c Dujon b Marshall	1		not out	38
R.M.Hogg	b Holding	0		b Marshall	0
C.G.Rackemann	c Richardson b Holding	0		b Garner	0
T.M.Alderman	not out	0		c Richardson b Holding	23
Extras	(B4, LB2, NB7)	13		(LB7, NB14)	21
Total		**76**			**228**

AUSTRALIA	O	M	R	W	O	M	R	W		FALL OF WICKETS		
										WI	A	A
Lawson	24	3	79	0					Wkt	1st	1st	2nd
Rackemann	28	3	106	0					1st	83	1	4
Hogg	32	6	101	4					2nd	83	18	94
Alderman	39	12	128	6					3rd	89	28	107
									4th	104	40	107
WEST INDIES									5th	104	46	124
Marshall	15	5	25	2	(2) 21	4	68	4	6th	186	53	166
Garner	7	0	24	2	(1) 16	5	52	3	7th	335	58	168
Holding	9.2	3	21	6	11.3	1	53	1	8th	337	63	168
Walsh					20	4	43	1	9th	387	63	169
Gomes					1	0	1	0	10th	416	76	228
Richards					1	0	4	0				

Umpires: A.R.Crafter (15) and P.J.McConnell (3).

Close: 1st day – WI(1) 211-6 (Gomes 38, Dujon 52); 2nd – A(1) 36-3 (Border 8, Hughes 2); 3rd – A(2) 158-5 (Hughes 34, Phillips 11).

Test No. 998/59 (A446/WI234)

AUSTRALIA v WEST INDIES 1984-85 (2nd Test)

At Woolloongabba, Brisbane, on 23, 24, 25, 26 November.
Toss: West Indies.   Result: WEST INDIES won by eight wickets.
Debuts: Australia – D.C.Boon, R.G.Holland.

Lloyd (208 minutes, 154 balls, three sixes and 14 fours) scored the last of his 19 Test hundreds and became the first West Indian to score six centuries against Australia. Richardson scored his third hundred in just nine Test innings and hit 24 fours. Playing in his 44th Test, Garner became the fifth West Indian after Gibbs, Sobers, Roberts and Holding to take 200 wickets. Lawson took his 100th Test wicket in 25 matches. After West Indies had completed another four-day victory to extend their record number of consecutive wins to ten, Hughes tearfully resigned the captaincy having led Australia to only four victories in 28 matches during an intermittent reign which began in 1979-80. In his second innings, Alderman (1) retired hurt (bruised ribs) at 134 and resumed at 271 for 9.

AUSTRALIA

J.Dyson	c Dujon b Holding	13	(2) c Dujon b Marshall		21
K.C.Wessels	b Garner	0	(1) c Gomes b Walsh		61
G.M.Wood	c Marshall b Walsh	20	c Richardson b Holding		3
A.R.Border	c Lloyd b Marshall	17	c sub (R.A.Harper) b Holding		24
*K.J.Hughes	c Marshall b Garner	34	lbw b Holding		4
D.C.Boon	c Richardson b Marshall	11	c Holding b Marshall		51
†W.B.Phillips	c Dujon b Walsh	44	(8) c sub (R.A.Harper) b Holding		54
G.F.Lawson	b Garner	14	(9) c Richards b Marshall		14
T.M.Alderman	c Lloyd b Walsh	0	(7) c Richardson b Marshall		1
R.G.Holland	c Dujon b Garner	6	b Marshall		0
R.M.Hogg	not out	0	not out		21
Extras	(B4, LB1, NB11)	16	(B4, LB5, NB8)		17
Total		**175**			**271**

WEST INDIES

C.G.Greenidge	c Border b Lawson	44			
D.L.Haynes	b Alderman	21	(1) b Lawson		7
R.B.Richardson	c Phillips b Alderman	138	(2) c Alderman b Hogg		5
H.A.Gomes	b Holland	13	(3) not out		9
I.V.A.Richards	c Boon b Lawson	6	(4) not out		3
†P.J.L.Dujon	c Phillips b Holland	14			
*C.H.Lloyd	c Hughes b Alderman	114			
M.D.Marshall	b Lawson	57			
M.A.Holding	b Lawson	1			
J.Garner	not out	0			
C.A.Walsh	c Phillips b Lawson	0			
Extras	(B2, LB6, NB8)	16	(LB2)		2
Total		**424**	(2 wickets)		**26**

WEST INDIES	O	M	R	W		O	M	R	W		FALL OF WICKETS			
Garner	18.4	5	67	4	(2)	20	4	80	0			A	WI	A	WI
Marshall	14.4	5	39	2	(1)	34	7	82	5	Wkt	1st	1st	2nd	2nd
Holding	6.2	2	9	1		30	7	92	4	1st	1	36	88	6
Walsh	16	5	55	3		5	2	7	1	2nd	33	99	88	18
Richards						1	0	1	0	3rd	33	129	99	–
										4th	81	142	106	–
										5th	97	184	131	–
AUSTRALIA										6th	102	336	212	–
Lawson	30.4	8	116	5		5	0	10	1	7th	122	414	236	–
Alderman	29	10	107	3						8th	136	423	236	–
Hogg	21	3	71	0	(2)	4.1	0	14	1	9th	173	424	271	–
Holland	27	5	97	2						10th	175	424	271	–
Border	5	0	25	0										

Umpires: R.A.French (14) and M.W.Johnson (16).

Close: 1st day – WI(1) 65-1 (Greenidge 27, Richardson 13); 2nd – WI(1) 396-6 (Lloyd 109, Marshall 35); 3rd – A(2) 134-5 (Boon 8, Alderman 1).

AUSTRALIA v WEST INDIES 1984-85 (3rd Test)

At Adelaide Oval on 7, 8, 9, 10, 11 December.
Toss: West Indies.   Result: WEST INDIES won by 191 runs.
Debuts: None.

Six minutes before tea on the fifth day, West Indies celebrated the centenary of Test cricket at the Adelaide Oval by gaining their 36th victory in 72 Tests under the leadership of Clive Lloyd. This result extended their world record of successive wins to eleven and equalled England's record of 26 matches without defeat (set between 1968 and 1971). It also ensured their retention of the Frank Worrell Trophy, regained in 1977-78 and now successfully defended for the fourth time. Lawson's analysis of 8 for 112 remained his best in first-class cricket. Gomes became the seventh West Indian to score 1,000 runs against Australia and emulated Lloyd by scoring his sixth hundred against them. Marshall, who took five wickets in an innings for the tenth time, reached 150 wickets in his 34th Test. Wessels, who batted for 398 minutes in the match, retired at 90 (when 36) in the first innings after being hit on the right forearm by a ball from Walsh; he resumed at 138. Border began his record reign of 93 consecutive matches as a Test captain.

WEST INDIES

C.G.Greenidge	c Hogg b Lawson	95		lbw b Lawson	4
D.L.Haynes	c Hughes b Hogg	0		c Wood b Lawson	50
R.B.Richardson	c Border b Lawson	8	(4)	lbw b Hogg	3
H.A.Gomes	c Rixon b Lawson	60	(5)	not out	120
I.V.A.Richards	c Rixon b Lawson	0	(6)	c Rixon b Hogg	42
*C.H.Lloyd	b Lawson	78	(7)	c Rixon b Lawson	6
†P.J.L.Dujon	lbw b Lawson	77	(8)	c Boon b Holland	32
M.D.Marshall	c Rixon b Lawson	9			
R.A.Harper	c Rixon b Lawson	9	(3)	c Rixon b Hogg	26
J.Garner	not out	8			
C.A.Walsh	b Holland	0			
Extras	(B5, LB4, NB3)	12		(LB2, NB7)	9
Total		**356**		**(7 wickets declared)**	**292**

AUSTRALIA

G.M.Wood	c Greenidge b Harper	41	(7)	c Dujon b Harper	19
J.Dyson	c Dujon b Walsh	8		lbw b Marshall	5
K.C.Wessels	b Marshall	98	(1)	c Dujon b Harper	70
†S.J.Rixon	c Richards b Marshall	0	(6)	lbw b Harper	16
K.J.Hughes	c Dujon b Garner	0	(4)	b Marshall	2
*A.R.Border	c Garner b Marshall	21	(3)	b Marshall	18
D.C.Boon	c Dujon b Marshall	12	(5)	c Harper b Garner	9
G.F.Lawson	c Dujon b Garner	49		c Dujon b Marshall	2
R.G.Holland	c Haynes b Walsh	2		not out	7
R.M.Hogg	not out	7		b Harper	7
T.M.Alderman	c Richardson b Marshall	10		b Marshall	0
Extras	(B2, LB8, NB26)	36		(B7, LB7, NB4)	18
Total		**284**			**173**

AUSTRALIA	O	M	R	W		O	M	R	W		FALL OF WICKETS			
											WI	A	WI	A
Lawson	40	7	112	8		24	6	69	3	*Wkt*	*1st*	*1st*	*2nd*	*2nd*
Hogg	28	7	75	1		21	2	77	3	1st	4	28	4	22
Alderman	19	8	38	0	(4) 12	1	66	0	2nd	25	91	70
Holland	30.2	5	109	1	(3) 18.1	1	54	1	3rd	157	91	45	78
Wessels	5	0	13	0						4th	157	122	121	97
Border					(5) 4	0	24	0	5th	172	138	218	126
										6th	322	145	225	150
WEST INDIES										7th	331	232	292	153
Marshall	26	8	69	5		15.5	4	38	5	8th	348	241	–	153
Garner	26	5	61	2		16	2	58	1	9th	355	265	–	170
Walsh	24	8	88	2		4	0	20	0	10th	356	284	–	173
Harper	21	4	56	1		15	6	43	4					

Umpires: A.R.Crafter (16) and M.W.Johnson (17).

Close: 1st day – WI(1) 244-5 (Lloyd 36, Dujon 41); 2nd – A(1) 91-1 (Wood 34, Rixon 0); 3rd – WI(2) 13-1 (Haynes 1, Harper 8); 4th – WI(2) 292-7 (Gomes 120).

AUSTRALIA v WEST INDIES 1984-85 (4th Test)

At Melbourne Cricket Ground on 22, 23, 24, 26, 27 December.
Toss: Australia.   Result: MATCH DRAWN.
Debuts: Australia – M.J.Bennett, C.J.McDermott.

Although a defiant 339-minute vigil by Hilditch (recalled after a five-year interval) ended their record run of victories, West Indies set a world record by avoiding defeat for the 27th consecutive match. After debutant McDermott (19) had taken the wickets of Richardson, Gomes and Dujon for one run in seven balls, Richards, (374 minutes, 376 balls, three sixes and 22 fours) compiled his 18th Test hundred. His third Test double century was the first for West Indies in Australia. During a brief interlude as wicket-keeper he caught Border. Garner's second over in the first innings began with six successive no-balls and a seventh call by umpire Randell ensured that it lasted a full ten minutes. Marshall gained five wickets for the fourth successive time. Lawson was fined $500 and bonded $1,500 for his overall behaviour on the field following an incident with Greenidge and an official protest from the tourists.

WEST INDIES

C.G.Greenidge	c Bennett b Lawson	10	lbw b Lawson		1
D.L.Haynes	c Border b Lawson	13	b McDermott		63
R.B.Richardson	b McDermott	51	b Lawson		3
H.A.Gomes	c Matthews b McDermott	68	c Bennett b McDermott		18
I.V.A.Richards	c Hughes b Matthews	208	lbw b McDermott		0
†P.J.L.Dujon	b McDermott	0	not out		49
*C.H.Lloyd	c Lawson b Matthews	19	not out		34
M.D.Marshall	c Rixon b Hogg	55			
R.A.Harper	c and b Hogg	5			
J.Garner	lbw b Lawson	8			
C.A.Walsh	not out	18			
Extras	(B1, LB11, NB12)	24	(B4, LB9, NB5)		18
Total		**479**	(5 wickets declared)		**186**

AUSTRALIA

A.M.J.Hilditch	b Harper	70	(2) b Gomes		113
G.M.Wood	lbw b Garner	12	(1) c Dujon b Garner		5
K.C.Wessels	c Dujon b Marshall	90	b Garner		0
K.J.Hughes	c Dujon b Walsh	0	lbw b Garner		0
*A.R.Border	c Richards b Walsh	35	c Dujon b Richards		41
G.R.J.Matthews	b Marshall	5	b Harper		2
†S.J.Rixon	c Richardson b Marshall	0	c Richardson b Harper		17
M.J.Bennett	not out	22	not out		3
G.F.Lawson	c Walsh b Garner	8	b Walsh		0
C.J.McDermott	b Marshall	0			
R.M.Hogg	lbw b Marshall	19			
Extras	(B5, LB7, W1, NB22)	35	(B6, LB2, NB9)		17
Total		**296**	(8 wickets)		**198**

AUSTRALIA	O	M	R	W	O	M	R	W	FALL OF WICKETS				
										WI	A	WI	A
Lawson	37	9	108	3	19	4	54	2	*Wkt*	*1st*	*1st*	*2nd*	*2nd*
Hogg	27	2	96	2	14	3	40	0	1st	27	38	2	17
McDermott	27	2	118	3	21	6	65	3	2nd	30	161	12	17
Bennett	20	0	78	0	3	0	12	0	3rd	153	163	63	17
Matthews	14.3	2	67	2					4th	154	220	63	128
Wessels					(5) 1	0	2	0	5th	154	238	100	131
									6th	223	238	–	162
WEST INDIES									7th	362	240	–	198
Marshall	31.5	6	86	5	20	4	36	0	8th	376	253	–	198
Garner	24	6	74	2	19	1	49	3	9th	426	253	–	–
Walsh	21	5	57	2	18	4	44	1	10th	479	296	–	–
Harper	14	1	58	1	22	4	54	2					
Richards	1	0	9	0	6	2	7	1					
Gomes					2	2	0	1					

Umpires: P.J.McConnell (4) and S.G.Randell (1).

Close: 1st day – WI(1) 280-6 (Richards 82, Marshall 18); 2nd – A(1) 115-1 (Hilditch 46, Wessels 44); 3rd – A(1) 281-9 (Bennett 17, Hogg 12); 4th – WI(2) 163-5 (Dujon 40, Lloyd 22).

AUSTRALIA v WEST INDIES 1984-85 (5th Test)

At Sydney Cricket Ground on 30, 31 December, 1, 2 January.
Toss: Australia.   Result: AUSTRALIA won by an innings and 55 runs.
Debuts: None.

West Indies suffered their first defeat since Australia gained a 58-run victory at Melbourne in December 1981. Their last defeat by an innings had also been at the MCG in 1968-69. It was Lloyd's 11th defeat (set against 36 wins) in a record 74 Tests as captain; he retired after amassing 7,515 runs (average 46.67), with 19 hundreds, in 110 Tests. Only M.C.Cowdrey (114) had then appeared in more matches. Wessels (481 minutes, 352 balls) made his fourth hundred in 17 Tests. Holland, a 38-year-old leg-spinner playing in his third Test, exploited a turning pitch to return match figures of 10 for 144, a record against West Indies at Sydney until 1988-89. Marshall's 28 wickets was the West Indies record for a rubber in Australia until 1992-93. Ritchie, struck on the cheek by a lifter from Walsh, retired at 194 (when 30) and resumed at 342.

AUSTRALIA

A.M.J.Hilditch	c Dujon b Holding	2
G.M.Wood	c Haynes b Gomes	45
K.C.Wessels	b Holding	173
G.M.Ritchie	run out	37
*A.R.Border	c Greenidge b Walsh	69
D.C.Boon	b Garner	49
†S.J.Rixon	c Garner b Holding	20
M.J.Bennett	c Greenidge b Garner	23
G.F.Lawson	not out	5
C.J.McDermott	c Greenidge b Walsh	4
R.G.Holland	did not bat	
Extras	(B7, LB20, NB17)	44
Total	(9 wickets declared)	**471**

WEST INDIES

C.G.Greenidge	c Rixon b McDermott	18	b Holding	12
D.L.Haynes	c Wessels b Holland	34	lbw b McDermott	3
R.B.Richardson	b McDermott	2	c Wood b Bennett	26
H.A.Gomes	c Bennett b Holland	28	c Wood b Lawson	8
I.V.A.Richards	c Wessels b Holland	15	b Bennett	58
*C.H.Lloyd	c Wood b Holland	33	c Border b McDermott	72
†P.J.L.Dujon	c Hilditch b Bennett	22	c and b Holland	8
M.D.Marshall	st Rixon b Holland	0	not out	32
M.A.Holding	c McDermott b Bennett	0	c Wessels b Holland	0
J.Garner	c Rixon b Holland	0	c Rixon b Bennett	8
C.A.Walsh	not out	1	c Bennett b Holland	4
Extras	(LB3, NB7)	10	(B2, LB12, NB8)	22
Total		**163**		**253**

WEST INDIES	O	M	R	W	O	M	R	W		FALL OF WICKETS		
Marshall	37	2	111	0						A	WI	WI
Garner	31	5	101	2					Wkt	1st	1st	2nd
Holding	31	7	74	3					1st	12	26	7
Walsh	38.2	1	118	2					2nd	126	34	31
Gomes	12	2	29	1					3rd	338	72	46
Richards	7	2	11	0					4th	342	103	93
									5th	350	106	153
AUSTRALIA									6th	392	160	180
Lawson	9	1	27	0	6	1	14	1	7th	450	160	231
McDermott	9	0	34	2	12	0	56	2	8th	463	160	231
Bennett	22.5	7	45	2	33	9	79	3	9th	471	161	244
Holland	22	7	54	6	33	8	90	4	10th	–	163	253

Umpires: R.C.Isherwood (1) and M.W.Johnson (18).

Close: 1st day – A(1) 235-2 (Wessels 120, Border 19); 2nd – A(1) 414-6 (Boon 29, Bennett 8); 3rd – WI(2) 31-1 (Greenidge 12, Richardson 11).

PAKISTAN v NEW ZEALAND 1984-85 (1st Test)

At Gaddafi Stadium, Lahore, on 16, 17, 18, 19, 20 November.
Toss: New Zealand.   Result: PAKISTAN won by six wickets.
Debuts: New Zealand – D.A.Stirling.

Pakistan completed their ninth victory in 22 Tests against New Zealand after just 20 minutes of play on the fifth day. Coney captained New Zealand for the first time, Howarth being unavailable for the tour. Iqbal Qasim, although not included among the originally selected 16 players, was recalled from Karachi on the eve of the match after missing 13 Tests. On a grassless pitch, his left-arm leg-breaks returned match figures of 8 for 106. In his 72nd match, Zaheer became the first Pakistani to score 5,000 runs in Test cricket.

NEW ZEALAND

J.J.Crowe	c Anil b Mudassar	0	(5)	b Iqbal Qasim	43
B.A.Edgar	b Mudassar	3		lbw b Azeem	26
M.D.Crowe	c Qasim Omar b Qadir	55		c sub (Ramiz Raja) b Iqbal Qasim	33
J.G.Wright	c Anil b Azeem	1	(1)	run out	65
J.F.Reid	lbw b Mudassar	2	(4)	b Qadir	6
*J.V.Coney	c Mohsin b Iqbal Qasim	7		c Anil b Azeem	26
E.J.Gray	c sub (Ramiz Raja) b Iqbal Qasim	12	(8)	c Mudassar b Qadir	6
†I.D.S.Smith	c Iqbal Qasim b Azeem	41	(9)	not out	11
D.A.Stirling	b Iqbal Qasim	16	(10)	c Anil b Iqbal Qasim	10
S.L.Boock	c Miandad b Iqbal Qasim	13	(7)	c Miandad b Qadir	0
E.J.Chatfield	not out	6		c Qasim Omar b Iqbal Qasim	0
Extras	(B1)	1		(B8, LB2, W1, NB4)	15
Total		**157**			**241**

PAKISTAN

Mudassar Nazar	c Reid b Stirling	26		b Boock	16
Mohsin Khan	c Reid b Gray	58		c and b Gray	38
Qasim Omar	c J.J.Crowe b Boock	13		lbw b Stirling	20
Javed Miandad	c Reid b Gray	11		not out	48
*Zaheer Abbas	c M.D.Crowe b Boock	43		c Smith b Gray	31
Salim Malik	lbw b Stirling	10		not out	24
Abdul Qadir	c Coney b Chatfield	14			
†Anil Dalpat	b M.D.Crowe	11			
Iqbal Qasim	c Coney b Chatfield	22			
Azeem Hafeez	c Boock b Chatfield	11			
Tausif Ahmed	not out	0			
Extras	(NB2)	2		(LB4)	4
Total		**221**		**(4 wickets)**	**181**

PAKISTAN	O	M	R	W	O	M	R	W		FALL OF WICKETS			
Mudassar	11	5	8	3	10	1	30	0		NZ	P	NZ	P
Azeem	18	9	40	2	13	5	37	2	Wkt	1st	1st	2nd	2nd
Qadir	21	6	58	1	(5) 26	4	82	3	1st	0	54	66	33
Iqbal Qasim	22.4	10	41	4	30	10	65	4	2nd	11	84	123	77
Tausif	2	0	9	0	(3) 4	0	17	0	3rd	28	103	138	77
									4th	31	114	140	138
NEW ZEALAND									5th	50	144	208	–
Stirling	27	7	71	2	15.1	2	60	1	6th	76	165	210	–
M.D.Crowe	7	1	21	1					7th	120	188	220	–
Gray	8	1	19	2	(4) 18	0	45	2	8th	124	189	220	–
Chatfield	27.2	7	57	3	(2) 13	7	12	0	9th	146	212	235	–
Boock	24	7	53	2	(3) 17	2	56	1	10th	157	221	241	–
Coney					(5) 2	1	4	0					

Umpires: Mahboob Shah (14) and Shakil Khan (2).

Close: 1st day – P(1) 26-0 (Mudassar 11, Mohsin 15); 2nd – P(1) 189-7 (Qadir 14, Iqbal Qasim 1); 3rd – NZ(2) 212-6 (J.J.Crowe 40, Gray 1); 4th – P(2) 153-4 (Miandad 41, Salim 3).

PAKISTAN v NEW ZEALAND 1984-85 (2nd Test)

At Niaz Stadium, Hyderabad, on 25, 26, 27, 29 November.
Toss: New Zealand.   Result: PAKISTAN won by seven wickets.
Debuts: None.

Pakistan celebrated staging Test cricket's 1,000th match by clinching the rubber with more than a day to spare. Javed Miandad became the second Pakistani after Hanif Mohammad (v England at Dacca in 1961-62) to score a century in each innings of a Test. This feat took his tally of hundreds to 13, five of them against New Zealand. With Mudassar, who scored his eighth century, Miandad shared a partnership of 212 – the third-wicket record by either side in this series until 1988-89. For New Zealand, Reid (291 minutes, 325 balls) scored his third hundred. Boock's analysis of 7 for 87 remains the best by a New Zealand spinner in Test cricket. Following complaints by the tourists' management about the standard of umpiring, the BCCP ordered an enquiry which found that six poor decisions had been made, including four in Pakistan's favour, but no action was taken.

NEW ZEALAND

J.G.Wright	c Anil b Iqbal Qasim	18	c Anil b Iqbal Qasim		22
B.A.Edgar	c Salim b Qadir	11	lbw b Mudassar		1
M.D.Crowe	b Qadir	19	(4) st Anil b Iqbal Qasim		21
J.F.Reid	lbw b Azeem	106	(3) lbw b Qadir		21
*J.V.Coney	c Manzoor b Qadir	6	b Iqbal Qasim		5
J.J.Crowe	c Salim b Zaheer	39	lbw b Iqbal Qasim		57
†I.D.S.Smith	c Iqbal Qasim b Zaheer	6	c Mudassar b Azeem		34
E.J.Gray	lbw b Mudassar	25	c Qasim Omar b Iqbal Qasim		5
J.G.Bracewell	c Mudassar b Qadir	0	c and b Qadir		0
D.A.Stirling	not out	11	b Qadir		11
S.L.Boock	lbw b Qadir	12	not out		4
Extras	(B13, NB1)	14	(B1, LB4, NB3)		8
Total		267			189

PAKISTAN

Mudassar Nazar	c M.D.Crowe b Bracewell	28	c Coney b Boock		106
Mohsin Khan	c Gray b Boock	9	b M.D.Crowe		2
Qasim Omar	c Coney b Boock	45	lbw b M.D.Crowe		0
Javed Miandad	c J.J.Crowe b Boock	104	not out		103
†Anil Dalpat	b Bracewell	1			
*Zaheer Abbas	st Smith b Boock	2			
Salim Malik	b Boock	1			
Manzoor Elahi	c J.J.Crowe b Boock	19	(5) not out		4
Abdul Qadir	lbw b Boock	11			
Iqbal Qasim	c J.J.Crowe b Bracewell	8			
Azeem Hafeez	not out	0			
Extras	(LB2)	2	(B5, LB7, NB3)		15
Total		230	(3 wickets)		230

PAKISTAN	O	M	R	W	O	M	R	W	FALL OF WICKETS			
										NZ	P	NZ	P
Mudassar	7	4	14	1	5	2	8	1	Wkt	1st	1st	2nd	2nd
Azeem	18	4	29	1	8	2	34	1	1st	30	26	2	14
Iqbal Qasim	33	6	80	1	24.1	7	78	5	2nd	30	50	34	14
Qadir	40.3	11	108	5	18	3	59	3	3rd	74	153	58	226
Manzoor	2	1	2	0					4th	88	154	71	–
Zaheer	8	0	21	2	(5) 1	0	5	0	5th	150	159	80	–
									6th	164	169	125	–
NEW ZEALAND									7th	238	191	149	–
Stirling	3	1	11	0	4	0	26	0	8th	239	215	149	–
M.D.Crowe	3	0	8	0	8	1	29	2	9th	243	230	167	–
Coney	10	4	8	0	(6) 4	1	9	0	10th	267	230	189	–
Boock	37	13	87	7	(3) 23.4	4	69	1					
Bracewell	16.1	3	44	3	14	3	36	0					
Gray	22	4	70	0	(4) 11	0	49	0					

Umpires: Khizer Hayat (15) and Mian Mohammad Aslam (1).

Close: 1st day – NZ(1) 239-7 (Reid 101, Bracewell 0); 2nd – P (1) 159-5 (Miandad 73); 3rd – NZ (2) 158-8 (J.J.Crowe 35, Stirling 7).

PAKISTAN v NEW ZEALAND 1984-85 (3rd Test)

At National Stadium, Karachi, on 10, 11, 12, 14, 15 December.
Toss: Pakistan.   Result: MATCH DRAWN.
Debuts: None.

In his 21st Test, Salim Malik passed 1,000 runs (in the first innings) and completed his fifth Test hundred in 173 minutes – the fastest century of the rubber. The stand of 89 between Anil Dalpat and Iqbal Qasim remains a Pakistan eighth-wicket record for this series. Wright scored his fourth hundred in 214 minutes off 191 balls, while Boock took his 50th wicket and Smith held his 50th catch. Qadir (1) retired hurt at 212 and resumed at 319. In the final session of the fourth day heated exchanges, following Shakoor Rana's rejection of an appeal (caught Smith) against Miandad, resulted in Coney threatening to take his team off the field.

PAKISTAN

Mudassar Nazar	c Smith b Stirling	5	c McEwan b Stirling		0
Shoaib Mohammad	c Smith b Stirling	31	c McEwan b Boock		34
Qasim Omar	lbw b Boock	45	c and b M.D.Crowe		17
Javed Miandad	c Smith b M.D.Crowe	13	c J.J.Crowe b Boock		58
*Zaheer Abbas	c Smith b Stirling	14	c Smith b Bracewell		3
Salim Malik	c and b M.D.Crowe	50	not out		119
Wasim Raja	lbw b Stirling	51	not out		60
Abdul Qadir	c Wright b Boock	7			
†Anil Dalpat	b Boock	52			
Iqbal Qasim	not out	45			
Azeem Hafeez	lbw b Boock	0			
Extras	(B5, LB6, W1, NB3)	15	(B2, LB8, NB7)		17
Total		**328**	(5 wickets)		**308**

NEW ZEALAND

J.G.Wright	c Anil b Iqbal Qasim	107
B.A.Edgar	run out	15
J.F.Reid	c Iqbal Qasim b Azeem	97
M.D.Crowe	lbw b Wasim	45
J.J.Crowe	c Miandad b Azeem	62
*J.V.Coney	c and b Iqbal Qasim	16
P.E.McEwan	not out	40
†I.D.S.Smith	c Salim b Iqbal Qasim	0
D.A.Stirling	c Qasim Omar b Iqbal Qasim	7
J.G.Bracewell	c Anil b Azeem	30
S.L.Boock	c Anil b Azeem	0
Extras	(B1, LB5, NB1)	7
Total		**426**

NEW ZEALAND	O	M	R	W		O	M	R	W		FALL OF WICKETS		
Stirling	29	5	88	4		14	1	82	1		P	NZ	P
M.D.Crowe	21	4	81	2		10	3	26	1	*Wkt*	*1st*	*1st*	*2nd*
McEwan	4	1	6	0	(6)	2	0	7	0	1st	14	83	5
Boock	41	9	83	4		30	10	83	2	2nd	80	163	37
Coney	5	3	5	0						3rd	92	258	119
Bracewell	20	5	54	0	(3)	33	12	83	1	4th	102	292	126
Reid					(5)	2	0	7	0	5th	124	338	130
J.J.Crowe					(7)	2	0	9	0	6th	204	352	–
Wright					(8)	1	0	1	0	7th	226	353	–
										8th	315	361	–
PAKISTAN										9th	319	426	–
Mudassar	15.4	2	45	0						10th	328	426	–
Azeem	46.4	9	132	4									
Iqbal Qasim	57	13	133	4									
Wasim	33	8	97	1									
Zaheer	5.2	1	13	0									

Umpires: Javed Akhtar (10) and Shakoor Rana (14).

Close: 1st day – P(1) 203-5 (Salim 50, Wasim 38); 2nd – NZ(1) 99-1 (Wright 81, Reid 3); 3rd – NZ(1) 316-4 (J.J.Crowe 39, Coney 8); 4th – P(2) 77-2 (Shoaib 22, Miandad 25).

INDIA v ENGLAND 1984-85 (1st Test)

At Wankhede Stadium, Bombay, on 28, 29 November, 1, 2, 3 December.
Toss: England.   Result: INDIA won by eight wickets.
Debuts: England – C.S.Cowdrey, R.T.Robinson.

India's win ended a barren sequence of 31 matches. England's eighth defeat of 1984 equalled the unprecedented fate of India in 1959. Kapil Dev became the second Indian after B.S.Bedi to take 250 Test wickets. The partnership of 235 between Shastri and Kirmani remains India's seventh-wicket record against all countries. Gavaskar completed 1,000 runs in Tests at the Wankhede Stadium. Sivaramakrishnan (12 for 181) returned the second-best Indian match analysis against England after 'Vinoo' Mankad's 12 for 108 in *Test No. 343*. In his 54th innings Gatting scored his first Test hundred. The selection of Christopher Cowdrey enabled Pocock to become only the second England player after Wilfred Rhodes (who appeared with Fred and Maurice Tate), to take the field with two generations of the same family. His dismissal of Kapil Dev with his fourth ball caused his astonished father, Colin, listening in London to the radio commentary, to drive in the wrong direction along a one-way street.

ENGLAND

G.Fowler	c and b Sivaramakrishnan	28		lbw b Sivaramakrishnan	55
R.T.Robinson	c Kirmani b Sivaramakrishnan	22		lbw b Kapil Dev	1
M.W.Gatting	c and b Sivaramakrishnan	15		c Patil b Sivaramakrishnan	136
D.I.Gower	b Kapil Dev	13		c Vengsarkar b Shastri	2
A.J.Lamb	c Shastri b Kapil Dev	9		st Kirmani b Sivaramakrishnan	1
C.S.Cowdrey	c Kirmani b Yadav	13		c Vengsarkar b Yadav	14
R.M.Ellison	b Sivaramakrishnan	1	(8)	c Vengsarkar b Yadav	0
P.R.Downton	not out	37	(7)	lbw b Sivaramakrishnan	62
P.H.Edmonds	c Gaekwad b Shastri	48		c Kapil Dev b Sivaramakrishnan	8
P.I.Pocock	c Kirmani b Sivaramakrishnan	8		not out	22
N.G.Cowans	c Shastri b Sivaramakrishnan	0		c Vengsarkar b Sivaramakrishnan	0
Extras	(B1)	1		(B4, LB8, NB4)	16
Total		**195**			**317**

INDIA

S.M.Gavaskar	c Downton b Cowans	27		c Gower b Cowans	5
A.D.Gaekwad	run out	24		st Downton b Edmonds	1
D.B.Vengsarkar	c Lamb b Cowans	34		not out	21
M.Amarnath	c Cowdrey b Pocock	49		not out	22
S.M.Patil	c Gower b Edmonds	20			
R.J.Shastri	c Lamb b Pocock	142			
Kapil Dev	b Cowdrey	42			
S.M.H.Kirmani	c Lamb b Pocock	102			
C.Sharma	not out	5			
N.S.Yadav	not out	7			
L.Sivaramakrishnan	did not bat				
Extras	(B4, LB2, NB7)	13		(B2)	2
Total	(8 wickets declared)	**465**		(2 wickets)	**51**

INDIA	O	M	R	W	O	M	R	W		FALL OF WICKETS			
										E	I	E	I
Kapil Dev	22	8	44	2	21	8	34	1	*Wkt*	*1st*	*1st*	*2nd*	*2nd*
Sharma	11	4	28	0	9	2	39	0	1st	46	47	3	5
Shastri	17	8	23	1	(5) 29	8	50	1	2nd	51	59	138	7
Amarnath	3	2	1	0					3rd	78	116	145	–
Sivaramakrishnan	31.2	10	64	6	(3) 46	10	117	6	4th	78	156	152	–
Yadav	12	2	34	1	(4) 29	9	64	2	5th	93	156	199	–
Gaekwad					(6) 1	0	1	0	6th	94	218	222	–
									7th	114	453	228	–
ENGLAND									8th	175	453	255	–
Ellison	18	3	85	0					9th	193	–	317	–
Cowans	28	6	109	2	5	2	18	1	10th	195	–	317	–
Edmonds	33	6	82	1	(1) 8	3	21	1					
Pocock	46	10	133	3	(3) 2.1	0	10	0					
Cowdrey	5	0	30	1									
Gatting	7	0	20	0									

Umpires: B Ganguli (4) and Swaroop Kishen (17).

Close: 1st day – E(1) 190-8 (Downton 32, Pocock 8); 2nd – I(1) 268-6 (Shastri 45, Kirmani 20); 3rd – E(2) 37-1 (Fowler 19, Gatting 14); 4th – E(2) 228-7 (Downton 9).

INDIA v ENGLAND 1984-85 (2nd Test)

At Feroz Shah Kotla, Delhi, on 12, 13, 15, 16, 17 December.
Toss: India.   Result: ENGLAND won by eight wickets.
Debuts: India – M.Prabhakar.

Gower led England to victory for the first time in 11 attempts and ended their record sequence of 13 matches without a win. Playing in his second Test, Robinson recorded the 100th century in this series, batting for 8¼ hours. His partnership of 110 with Lamb was England's first of three figures for the third wicket in India. Downton (74) registered his highest Test score for the second innings in succession. Amarnath completed 3,000 runs in his 46th Test.

INDIA

*S.M.Gavaskar	c Downton b Ellison	1	b Pocock	6.
A.D.Gaekwad	b Pocock	28	(8) c Downton b Edmonds	
D.B.Vengsarkar	st Downton b Edmonds	24	b Cowans	
M.Amarnath	c Gower b Pocock	42	b Edmonds	6
S.M.Patil	c Pocock b Edmonds	30	c Lamb b Edmonds	4
R.J.Shastri	c Fowler b Pocock	2	not out	2
Kapil Dev	c Downton b Ellison	60	c Lamb b Pocock	
†S.M.H.Kirmani	c Gatting b Ellison	27	(9) b Pocock	
M.Prabhakar	c Downton b Ellison	25	(2) c Downton b Cowans	
N.S.Yadav	not out	28	c Lamb b Edmonds	
L.Sivaramakrishnan	run out	25	c and b Pocock	
Extras	(B1, LB12, NB2)	15	(B6, LB10, W1, NB3)	2
Total		**307**		**235**

ENGLAND

G.Fowler	c Gaekwad b Prabhakar	5	c Vengsarkar b Sivaramakrishnan	2
R.T.Robinson	c Gavaskar b Kapil Dev	160	run out	1
M.W.Gatting	b Yadav	26	not out	3
A.J.Lamb	c Vengsarkar b Yadav	52	not out	3
*D.I.Gower	lbw b Sivaramakrishnan	5		
C.S.Cowdrey	c Gavaskar b Sivaramakrishnan	38		
†P.R.Downton	c Kapil Dev b Sivaramakrishnan	74		
P.H.Edmonds	c Shastri b Sivaramakrishnan	26		
R.M.Ellison	b Sivaramakrishnan	10		
P.I.Pocock	b Sivaramakrishnan	0		
N.G.Cowans	not out	0		
Extras	(B6, LB13, NB3)	22	(B4, LB7, NB2)	1
Total		**418**	(2 wickets)	**127**

ENGLAND	O	M	R	W	O	M	R	W		FALL OF WICKETS			
Cowans	20	5	70	0	13	2	43	2		I	E	I	E
Ellison	26	6	66	4	7	1	20	0	Wkt	1st	1st	2nd	2nd
Edmonds	44.2	16	83	2	44	24	60	4	1st	3	15	12	41
Pocock	33	8	70	3	38.4	9	93	4	2nd	56	60	15	68
Gatting	2	0	5	0	1	0	3	0	3rd	68	170	136	–
									4th	129	181	172	–
INDIA									5th	131	237	207	–
Kapil Dev	32	5	87	1	6	0	20	0	6th	140	343	214	–
Prabhakar	21	3	68	1	3	0	18	0	7th	208	398	216	–
Sivaramakrishnan	49.1	17	99	6	8	0	41	1	8th	235	411	225	–
Yadav	36	6	95	2	2	0	7	0	9th	258	415	234	–
Shastri	29	4	44	0	4	0	20	0	10th	307	418	235	–
Amarnath	2	0	6	0									
Gavaskar					(6) 0.4	0	10	0					

Umpires: D.N.Dotiwalla (4) and P.D.Reporter (1).

Close: 1st day – I(1) 208-6 (Kapil Dev 60, Kirmani 16); 2nd – E(1) 107-2 (Robinson 53, Lamb 12); 3rd – E(1) 337-5 (Robinson 157, Downton 35); 4th – I(2) 128-2 (Gavaskar 51, Amarnath 57).

INDIA v ENGLAND 1984-85 (3rd Test)

At Eden Gardens, Calcutta, on 31 December, 1, 3, 4, 5 January.
Toss: India.   Result: MATCH DRAWN.
Debuts: India – M.Azharuddin.

Gavaskar appeared in his 88th successive Test to claim the world record from his brother-in-law, G.R.Viswanath. Azharuddin (21) became the seventh batsman to score a century in his first Test for India; it took 382 minutes (288 balls). Shastri's fifth Test hundred took 422 minutes (330 balls) and was then the second-slowest in all Tests for India after that of Vengsarkar (437 minutes) in *Test No. 862*. Within a week Shastri was to score the fastest 200 in all first-class cricket and equal another world record by hitting six sixes in one over. He was the fifth batsman to bat on all five days of a Test match and his partnership of 214 with Azharuddin remains India's highest for the fifth wicket against all countries. Fowler scored his 1,000th run in 19 Tests. Robinson (17) retired with contact lens problems at 31 and resumed at 71. Kapil Dev's omission ended an unbroken run of 65 Tests and was the only gap in his 131-match career.

INDIA

*S.M.Gavaskar	c Gatting b Edmonds	13			
A.D.Gaekwad	c Downton b Cowans	18			
D.B.Vengsarkar	b Edmonds	48			
M.Amarnath	c Cowdrey b Edmonds	42			
M.Azharuddin	c Gower b Cowans	110			
R.J.Shastri	b Cowans	111	(1) not out	7
†S.M.H.Kirmani	c Fowler b Pocock	35			
M.Prabhakar	not out	35	(2) lbw b Lamb	21
C.Sharma	not out	13			
N.S.Yadav	} did not bat		(3) not out	0
L.Sivaramakrishnan				
Extras	(LB8, W1, NB3)	12	(NB1)	1
Total	(7 wickets declared)	437	(1 wicket)	29

ENGLAND

G.Fowler	c Vengsarkar b Sivaramakrishnan	49
R.T.Robinson	b Yadav	36
*D.I.Gower	c Shastri b Yadav	19
P.I.Pocock	c Azharuddin b Sivaramakrishnan	5
M.W.Gatting	b Yadav	48
A.J.Lamb	c Kirmani b Sharma	67
C.S.Cowdrey	lbw b Yadav	27
†P.R.Downton	not out	6
P.H.Edmonds	c Gavaskar b Sharma	8
R.M.Ellison	c and b Sharma	1
N.G.Cowans	b Sharma	1
Extras	(LB2, NB7)	9
Total		276

ENGLAND	O	M	R	W	O	M	R	W		FALL OF WICKETS		
Cowans	41	12	103	3	4	1	6	0		I	E	I
Ellison	53	14	117	0	(4) 1	0	1	0	Wkt	1st	1st	2nd
Edmonds	47	22	72	3	4	3	2	0	1st	28	71	29
Pocock	52	14	108	1	(5) 2	1	4	0	2nd	35	98	–
Gatting	2	1	1	0					3rd	126	110	–
Cowdrey	2	0	15	0	(2) 4	0	10	0	4th	127	152	–
Gower	3	0	13	0					5th	341	163	–
Lamb					(6) 1	0	6	1	6th	356	229	–
Robinson					(7) 1	1	0	0	7th	407	261	–
Fowler					(8) 1	1	0	0	8th	–	270	–
INDIA									9th	–	273	–
Sharma	12.3	0	38	4					10th	–	276	–
Prabhakar	5	1	16	0								
Sivaramakrishnan	28	7	90	2								
Yadav	32	10	86	4								
Shastri	23	6	44	0								

Umpires: B.Ganguli (5) and V.Vikramraju (1).

Close: 1st day – I(1) 168-4 (Azharuddin 13, Shastri 26); 2nd – I(1) 176-4 (Azharuddin 21, Shastri 26); 3rd – I(1) 348-5 (Shastri 108, Kirmani 0); 4th – E(1) 99-2 (Robinson 25, Pocock 0).

INDIA v ENGLAND 1984-85 (4th Test)

At Chidambaram Stadium, Chepauk, Madras, on 13, 14, 15, 17, 18 January.
Toss: India.   Result: ENGLAND won by nine wickets.
Debuts: None.

For the first time a visiting team in India took the lead in a rubber after being a match down. England's total of 652 for 7 declared was their highest against India (until 1990), their fifth-highest against all countries and their highest since 1938-39. It was the highest total in any Test in India until 1986-87. Fowler and Gatting were the first pair to score double hundreds in the same innings for England in 610 Test matches since 1877; it was the sixth such instance in all Test cricket. The previous highest score for England in India was 179 by D.L.Amiss in *Test No. 788*. Fowler's partnerships of 178 with Robinson (surpassed in 1990) and 241 with Gatting were records for England's first two wickets in this series. Azharuddin was only the fourth batsman after W.H.Ponsford, K.D.Walters and A.I.Kallicharran to score hundreds in each of his first two Tests. The tenth-wicket partnership of 51 between Kirmani and Sharma equalled India's record against England set in *Test No.555*. Foster became the second bowler after A.V.Bedser (*Test No. 276*) to take 11 wickets in his first Test against India.

INDIA

*S.M.Gavaskar	b Foster	17		c Gatting b Foster	3
K.Srikkanth	c Downton b Cowans	0		c Cowdrey b Foster	16
D.B.Vengsarkar	c Lamb b Foster	17		c Downton b Foster	2
M.Amarnath	c Downton b Foster	78		c Cowans b Foster	95
M.Azharuddin	b Cowdrey	48		c Gower b Pocock	105
R.J.Shastri	c Downton b Foster	2		c Cowdrey b Edmonds	33
Kapil Dev	c Cowans b Cowdrey	53		c Gatting b Cowans	49
†S.M.H.Kirmani	not out	30		c Lamb b Edmonds	75
N.S.Yadav	b Foster	2	(10)	c Downton b Cowans	5
L.Sivaramakrishnan	c Cowdrey b Foster	13	(9)	lbw b Foster	5
C.Sharma	c Lamb b Cowans	5		not out	17
Extras	(LB3, NB4)	7		(B1, LB4, NB2)	7
Total		**272**			**412**

ENGLAND

G.Fowler	c Kirmani b Kapil Dev	201	c Kirmani b Sivaramakrishnan	2
R.T.Robinson	c Kirmani b Sivaramakrishnan	74	not out	21
M.W.Gatting	c sub (G.Sharma) b Shastri	207	not out	10
A.J.Lamb	b Amarnath	62		
P.H.Edmonds	lbw b Shastri	36		
N.A.Foster	b Amarnath	5		
*D.I.Gower	b Kapil Dev	18		
C.S.Cowdrey	not out	3		
†P.R.Downton	not out	3		
P.I.Pocock	} did not bat			
N.G.Cowans				
Extras	(B7, LB19, NB17)	43	(LB1, W1)	2
Total	(7 wickets declared)	**652**	(1 wicket)	**35**

ENGLAND	O	M	R	W	O	M	R	W		FALL OF WICKETS			
Cowans	12.5	3	39	2	15	1	73	2		I	E	I	E
Foster	23	2	104	6	28	8	59	5	Wkt	1st	1st	2nd	2nd
Edmonds	6	1	33	0	(4) 41.5	13	119	2	1st	17	178	7	7
Cowdrey	19	1	65	2	(3) 5	0	26	0	2nd	17	419	19	–
Pocock	7	1	28	0	33	8	130	1	3rd	45	563	22	–
									4th	155	599	212	–
									5th	167	604	212	–
INDIA									6th	167	640	259	–
Kapil Dev	36	5	131	2	3	0	20	0	7th	241	646	341	–
Sharma	18	0	95	0					8th	243	–	350	–
Sivaramakrishnan	44	6	145	1	(2) 4	0	12	1	9th	263	–	361	–
Yadav	23	4	76	0					10th	272	–	412	–
Shastri	42	7	143	2	(3) 1	0	2	0					
Amarnath	12	1	36	2									

Umpires: M.Y.Gupte (1) and V.K.Ramaswamy (1).

Close: 1st day – E(1) 32-0 (Fowler 10, Robinson 18); 2nd – E(1) 293-1 (Fowler 149, Gatting 50); 3rd – E(1) 611-5 (Edmonds 15, Gower 5); 4th – I(2) 246-4 (Azharuddin 103, Shastri 22).

INDIA v ENGLAND 1984-85 (5th Test)

At Green Park, Kanpur, on 31 January, 1, 3, 4, 5 February.
Toss: India.   Result: MATCH DRAWN.
Debuts: India – G.Sharma.

Gower became the third captain after D.R.Jardine and A.W.Greig to lead England to victory in India, and the first to do so from any country after being a match down. Not since 1954-55 in Australia had England won a rubber overseas after losing the first Test. It was England's first victorious expedition since they beat Australia in 1978-79. Azharuddin, whose second fifty occupied only 38 balls, became the first batsman to score hundreds in each of his first three Test matches. India's total of 553 for 8 declared was then their highest against England, exceeding 510 at Leeds in 1967. Gopal Sharma was the first Uttar Pradesh cricketer to represent India since 1936 when the Maharajkumar of Vizianagram led his country in their first three-match rubber in England. Vengsarkar reached his ninth hundred in 307 minutes (219 balls). Robinson (more contact lens trouble) retired at 36.

INDIA

*S.M.Gavaskar	b Cowans	9		
K.Srikkanth	c Downton b Foster	84	not out	41
M.Azharuddin	c sub (R.M.Ellison) b Cowdrey	122	not out	54
M.Amarnath	b Cowans	15		
D.B.Vengsarkar	c Downton b Foster	137		
A.Malhotra	lbw b Pocock	27		
R.J.Shastri	b Edmonds	59	(1) run out	2
Kapil Dev	c Gower b Foster	42		
†S.M.H.Kirmani	not out	16		
L.Sivaramakrishnan	not out	16		
G.Sharma	did not bat			
Extras	(B9, LB12, W5)	26		
Total	**(8 wickets declared)**	**553**	**(1 wicket declared)**	**97**

ENGLAND

G.Fowler	c Kirmani b Shastri	69		
R.T.Robinson	lbw b Kapil Dev	96	retired hurt	16
M.W.Gatting	c and b Sharma	62	not out	41
A.J.Lamb	c Srikkanth b Shastri	13		
*D.I.Gower	lbw b Shastri	78	(1) not out	32
C.S.Cowdrey	c Kirmani b Sharma	1		
†P.R.Downton	b Sharma	1		
P.H.Edmonds	lbw b Kapil Dev	49		
N.A.Foster	c Kirmani b Kapil Dev	8		
P.I.Pocock	not out	4		
N.G.Cowans	b Kapil Dev	9		
Extras	(B10, LB17)	27	(LB2)	2
Total		**417**	**(0 wickets)**	**91**

ENGLAND	O	M	R	W	O	M	R	W	FALL OF WICKETS			
									I	E	I	E
Cowans	36	9	115	2	7	0	51	0	Wkt	1st	1st	2nd	2nd
Foster	36	8	123	3					1st	19	156	2	–
Pocock	24	2	79	1					2nd	169	196	–	–
Edmonds	48	16	112	1					3rd	209	222	–	–
Cowdrey	21	1	103	1	(2) 5	0	39	0	4th	277	276	–	–
Gatting					(3) 1	0	7	0	5th	362	278	–	–
									6th	457	286	–	–
INDIA									7th	511	386	–	–
Kapil Dev	36.5	7	81	4	5	0	19	0	8th	533	402	–	–
Amarnath	4	1	6	0					9th	–	404	–	–
Sharma	60	16	115	3	11	4	17	0	10th	–	417	–	–
Sivaramakrishnan	54	11	133	0	10	2	22	0					
Shastri	32	13	52	3	(2) 7	2	12	0					
Malhotra	2	0	3	0									
Srikkanth					(5) 2	0	11	0					
Azharuddin					(6) 1	0	8	0					

Umpires: V.K.Ramaswamy (2) and P.D.Reporter (2).

Close: 1st day – I(1) 228-3 (Azharuddin 98, Vengsarkar 11); 2nd – I(1) 525-7 (Kapil Dev 41, Kirmani 5); 3rd – E(1) 163-1 (Robinson 84, Gatting 3); 4th – E(1) 373-6 (Gower 66, Edmonds 42).

NEW ZEALAND v PAKISTAN 1984-85 (1st Test)

At Basin Reserve, Wellington, on 18, 19, 20, 21, 22 (*no play*) January.
Toss: New Zealand.   Result: MATCH DRAWN.
Debuts: None.

New Zealand recorded their highest total against Pakistan after the tourists had retained the original ball throughout the first two days for 172 overs. Reid batted 572 minutes (427 balls), reaching his fourth hundred in 404 minutes off 311 balls. His partnership of 145 in 190 minutes with Hadlee remains a New Zealand sixth-wicket record against Pakistan. Boock was the first New Zealand slow bowler to take five wickets in a Wellington Test. Qadir's second Test fifty took 90 minutes. Torrential rain flooded parts of the Basin Reserve and prevented play on the last day.

NEW ZEALAND

Batsman	Dismissal	Runs	Dismissal 2	Runs 2
*G.P.Howarth	run out	33	c Anil b Azeem	17
J.G.Wright	c Shoaib b Azeem	11	lbw b Mudassar	11
J.F.Reid	b Azeem	148	c Qadir b Iqbal Qasim	3
M.D.Crowe	c Anil b Iqbal Qasim	37	c Qadir b Iqbal Qasim	33
J.J.Crowe	c Shoaib b Iqbal Qasim	4	not out	19
J.V.Coney	b Qadir	48	not out	18
R.J.Hadlee	c Miandad b Azeem	89		
†I.D.S.Smith	c and b Mudassar	65		
B.L.Cairns	b Azeem	36		
S.L.Boock	c Anil b Azeem	0		
E.J.Chatfield	not out	3		
Extras	(B5, LB12, NB1)	18	(LB2)	2
Total		**492**	(4 wickets)	**103**

PAKISTAN

Mudassar Nazar	c and b Boock	38
Mohsin Khan	c Wright b Boock	40
Shoaib Mohammad	run out	7
Qasim Omar	b Boock	8
*Javed Miandad	c Smith b Boock	30
Salim Malik	c Cairns b Hadlee	66
Wasim Raja	c M.D.Crowe b Boock	14
Abdul Qadir	c Smith b Hadlee	54
†Anil Dalpat	c Smith b Chatfield	15
Iqbal Qasim	not out	27
Azeem Hafeez	c Boock b Cairns	3
Extras	(B9, LB9, NB2)	20
Total		**322**

PAKISTAN	O	M	R	W		O	M	R	W		FALL OF WICKETS		
											NZ	P	NZ
Mudassar	29	5	80	1	(2)	6	3	13	1	*Wkt*	*1st*	*1st*	*2nd*
Azeem	48	12	127	5	(1)	15	3	51	1	1st	24	62	24
Qadir	51	13	142	1	(4)	8	1	18	0	2nd	61	85	30
Iqbal Qasim	41	5	105	2	(3)	16	8	19	2	3rd	126	95	42
Wasim	2	0	10	0						4th	138	102	73
Shoaib	1	0	4	0						5th	230	161	–
Miandad	3	1	7	0						6th	375	187	–
										7th	414	223	–
NEW ZEALAND										8th	488	288	–
Hadlee	32	11	70	2						9th	488	309	–
Cairns	27.3	5	65	1						10th	492	322	–
Chatfield	25	10	52	1									
Boock	45	18	117	5									

Umpires: G.C.Morris (1) and S.J.Woodward (11).

Close: 1st day – NZ(1) 220-4 (Reid 86, Coney 42); 2nd – NZ(1) 485-7 (Smith 63, Cairns 34); 3rd – P(1) 236-7 (Qadir 23, Anil 0); 4th – NZ(2) 103-4 (J.J.Crowe 19, Coney 18).

NEW ZEALAND v PAKISTAN 1984-85 (2nd Test)

At Eden Park, Auckland, on 25, 26, 27, 28 January.
Toss: New Zealand.   Result: NEW ZEALAND won by an innings and 99 runs.
Debuts: Pakistan – Wasim Akram.

Just before tea on the fourth day, New Zealand gained their first victory in 11 home Tests against Pakistan; it was only their second win in 26 contests in this series and their first by an innings. Reid's fifth hundred (his second in successive innings) took him past 1,000 runs in 20 innings. He retired when 123 (at 322) for five stitches after his chin had been gashed by a bouncer from Azeem, resuming at 359. His innings lasted 486 minutes (318 balls). Mudassar batted throughout the second innings and completed 3,000 runs in 51 Tests. Chatfield, playing in his 22nd match, took his 50th Test wicket.

PAKISTAN

Mudassar Nazar	lbw b Hadlee	12		b Cairns	89
Mohsin Khan	c Coney b Cairns	26		c Coney b Hadlee	1
Qasim Omar	c M.D.Crowe b Cairns	33		c Cairns b Chatfield	22
*Javed Miandad	c Smith b Chatfield	26	(5)	c Smith b Chatfield	1
Zaheer Abbas	c J.J.Crowe b Cairns	6	(6)	c sub (J.G.Bracewell) b Hadlee	12
Salim Malik	not out	41	(4)	c Cairns b Chatfield	0
Wasim Raja	c Smith b Chatfield	4		c Wright b Boock	11
Abdul Qadir	run out	0		lbw b Cairns	10
†Anil Dalpat	c J.J.Crowe b Hadlee	7		lbw b Cairns	6
Wasim Akram	c M.D.Crowe b Hadlee	0	(11)	not out	0
Azeem Hafeez	c Boock b Hadlee	6	(10)	lbw b Cairns	17
Extras	(LB5, NB3)	8		(LB11, NB3)	14
Total		**169**			**183**

NEW ZEALAND

*G.P.Howarth	c Miandad b Mudassar	13
J.G.Wright	c Salim b Wasim Akram	66
J.F.Reid	not out	158
M.D.Crowe	c sub‡ b Qadir	84
S.L.Boock	c Wasim Raja b Azeem	10
J.J.Crowe	run out	30
J.V.Coney	c Anil b Mudassar	25
R.J.Hadlee	c Mohsin b Azeem	13
†I.D.S.Smith	c Miandad b Wasim Akram	7
B.L.Cairns	b Azeem	23
E.J.Chatfield	not out	1
Extras	(B6, LB9, NB6)	21
Total	(9 wickets declared)	**451**

NEW ZEALAND	O	M	R	W	O	M	R	W		FALL OF WICKETS		
										P	NZ	P
Hadlee	19.5	3	60	4	17	1	66	2	*Wkt*	*1st*	*1st*	*2nd*
Cairns	29	10	73	3	(3) 19.5	8	49	4	1st	33	60	13
Chatfield	14	5	24	2	(2) 19	5	47	3	2nd	58	108	54
Coney	4	1	7	0					3rd	93	245	54
Boock					(4) 4	2	10	1	4th	105	278	57
									5th	111	359	79
PAKISTAN									6th	115	366	122
Azeem	47	10	157	3					7th	123	387	140
Wasim Akram	34.4	4	105	2					8th	147	411	152
Mudassar	34	5	85	2					9th	151	447	178
Qadir	22	5	52	1					10th	169	–	183
Wasim Raja	1	0	3	0								
Salim	8.2	3	34	0								

Umpires: F.R.Goodall (19) and S.J.Woodward (12).   ‡ (Shoaib Mohammad)

Close: 1st day – P(1) 147-8 (Salim 28, Wasim Akram 0); 2nd – NZ(1) 248-3 (Reid 73, Boock 1); 3rd – NZ(1) 451-9 (Reid 158, Chatfield 1).

NEW ZEALAND v PAKISTAN 1984-85 (3rd Test)

At Carisbrook, Dunedin, on 9, 10, 11, 13, 14 February.
Toss: New Zealand.   Result: NEW ZEALAND won by two wickets.
Debuts: None.

Test cricket returned to Carisbrook after a five-year break. New Zealand's margin of victory was just one wicket in reality as Cairns had retired hurt at 217 and been hospitalised with a suspected hairline fracture of the skull. They thus narrowly avenged their recent identical 2-0 defeat in the rubber in Pakistan. Javed Miandad completed 5,000 runs in his 68th Test – four matches fewer than Zaheer, then the only other batsman to achieve this aggregate for Pakistan. Hadlee (53 Tests) became the first bowler to take 250 wickets for New Zealand. Wasim Akram, an 18-year-old left-arm fast-medium swing bowler playing in only his second Test, almost snatched victory with Pakistan's second ten-wicket analysis in New Zealand. Coney (385 minutes, 243 balls) and Chatfield (104 minutes, 84 balls) inched their way to their target, scoring 50 off 132 balls. It was Chatfield's longest first-class innings and highest score in Test cricket.

PAKISTAN

Mudassar Nazar	c J.J.Crowe b Hadlee	18		c Coney b Bracewell	5
Mohsin Khan	run out	39		c M.D.Crowe b Hadlee	27
Qasim Omar	c J.J.Crowe b Coney	96		c Smith b Chatfield	89
*Javed Miandad	c Smith b Hadlee	79		c Reid b Hadlee	2
Zaheer Abbas	c Reid b Hadlee	6		lbw b Cairns	0
Rashid Khan	c M.D.Crowe b Hadlee	0	(9)	b Bracewell	37
†Anil Dalpat	b Bracewell	16		b Chatfield	21
Salim Malik	lbw b Hadlee	0	(6)	b Cairns	9
Tahir Naqqash	c Wright b Hadlee	0	(8)	run out	1
Azeem Hafeez	c Smith b Bracewell	4		b Chatfield	7
Wasim Akram	not out	1		not out	8
Extras	(B1, LB2, NB12)	15		(B1, LB9, NB7)	17
Total		**274**			**223**

NEW ZEALAND

*G.P.Howarth	b Wasim	23		c Mohsin b Wasim	17
J.G.Wright	c Omar b Azeem	32		c Mohsin b Azeem	1
J.F.Reid	b Wasim	24		c Anil b Wasim	0
M.D.Crowe	c Miandad b Wasim	57		c Mudassar b Tahir	84
J.J.Crowe	lbw b Wasim	6		lbw b Wasim	0
J.V.Coney	c Anil b Rashid	24		not out	111
R.J.Hadlee	c Anil b Rashid	18		b Azeem	11
†I.D.S.Smith	lbw b Tahir	12		c Miandad b Wasim	6
B.L.Cairns	c Anil b Wasim	6		retired hurt	0
B.P.Bracewell	c Rashid b Tahir	3		c Tahir b Wasim	4
E.J.Chatfield	not out	2		not out	21
Extras	(B7, LB5, NB1)	13		(B5, LB6, W1, NB11)	23
Total		**220**		(8 wickets)	**278**

NEW ZEALAND	O	M	R	W	O	M	R	W		FALL OF	WICKETS		
Hadlee	24	5	51	6	26	9	59	2		P	NZ	P	NZ
Bracewell	18.2	1	81	2	14.4	2	48	2	Wkt	1st	1st	2nd	2nd
Cairns	22	0	77	0	22	4	41	2	1st	25	41	5	4
Chatfield	24	6	46	0	26	5	65	3	2nd	100	81	72	5
Coney	6	1	16	1					3rd	241	84	75	23
									4th	243	92	76	23
PAKISTAN									5th	245	149	103	180
Rashid	23	7	64	2	(3) 9	2	33	0	6th	251	185	157	208
Azeem	20	6	65	1	(1) 32	9	84	2	7th	251	203	166	217
Wasim	26	7	56	5	(2) 33	10	72	5	8th	255	205	169	228
Tahir	16.4	4	23	2	16.4	1	58	1	9th	273	216	181	–
Mudassar					9	2	20	0	10th	274	220	223	–

Umpires: F.R.Goodall (20) and G.C.Morris (2).

Close: 1st day – P(1) 251-7 (Anil 0, Salim 0); 2nd – NZ (1) 201-6 (M.D.Crowe 56, Smith 10); 3rd – P(2) 109-5 (Omar 50, Anil 5); 4th – NZ(2) 114-4 (M.D.Crowe 41, Coney 46).

WEST INDIES v NEW ZEALAND 1984-85 (1st Test)

At Queen's Park Oval, Port-of-Spain, Trinidad, on 29, 30, 31 March, 2, 3 April.
Toss: West Indies.   Result: MATCH DRAWN.
Debuts: New Zealand – K.R.Rutherford.

After an interlude of 13 years, New Zealand paid only their second visit to the Caribbean. Hadlee dismissed Haynes and Gomes in his third over. The partnership of 185 between Greenidge, who compiled his 12th Test hundred (316 minutes, 235 balls), and Richardson is the third-wicket record for West Indies in this series. Chatfield returned the first ten-wicket analysis for New Zealand in the West Indies. Almost four hours were lost on the third day when rain seeped through a frayed tarpaulin covering the pitch. New Zealand were set 307 to win in a minimum of five hours on a pitch of uneven bounce. Rutherford was run out without facing a ball to complete a 'pair' on debut. Dujon made his 100th dismissal to complete the wicket-keepers' double in his 30th Test. When he had scored 31 during his match-saving partnership with Coney, Hadlee (186 minutes, 150 balls) became the sixth player and first New Zealander to complete the Test double of 2,000 runs and 200 wickets.

WEST INDIES

C.G.Greenidge	b Boock	100			
D.L.Haynes	c Rutherford b Hadlee	0	(1) c M.D.Crowe b Chatfield		78
H.A.Gomes	c Smith b Hadlee	0	c and b Chatfield		25
R.B.Richardson	c Hadlee b Coney	78	(2) c Smith b Chatfield		3
I.V.A.Richards	b Hadlee	57	(4) b Cairns		78
A.L.Logie	b Chatfield	24	(5) b Cairns		42
P.J.L.Dujon	b Chatfield	15	(6) b Chatfield		5
M.D.Marshall	c sub (J.G.Bracewell) b Chatfield	0	(7) c Coney b Chatfield		1
R.A.Harper	c Howarth b Chatfield	0	(8) not out		11
M.A.Holding	lbw b Hadlee	12	(9) c J.J.Crowe b Chatfield		8
J.Garner	not out	0			
Extras	(B1, LB16, NB4)	21	(LB3, NB7)		10
Total		**307**	(8 wickets declared)		**261**

NEW ZEALAND

J.G.Wright	c Richardson b Harper	40	lbw b Holding		19
K.R.Rutherford	c Haynes b Marshall	0	run out		0
J.J.Crowe	c and b Harper	64	c Garner b Marshall		27
M.D.Crowe	lbw b Holding	3	c Haynes b Marshall		2
G.P.Howarth	c sub (P.V.Simmons) b Holding	45	b Marshall		14
J.V.Coney	lbw b Marshall	25	c Dujon b Marshall		44
R.J.Hadlee	c Garner b Holding	18	not out		39
I.D.S.Smith	c Logie b Holding	10	not out		11
B.L.Cairns	c Harper b Garner	8			
S.L.Boock	c sub (P.V.Simmons) b Garner	3			
E.J.Chatfield	not out	4			
Extras	(B12, LB11, NB19)	42	(B17, LB6, NB8)		31
Total		**262**	(6 wickets)		**187**

NEW ZEALAND	O	M	R	W	O	M	R	W
Hadlee	24.3	6	82	4	17	2	58	0
Chatfield	28	11	51	4	22	4	73	6
Cairns	26	3	93	0	19	2	70	2
Boock	19	5	47	1	14	4	57	0
Coney	9	3	17	1				

WEST INDIES	O	M	R	W	O	M	R	W
Marshall	25	3	78	2	26	4	65	4
Garner	21.3	8	41	2	18	2	41	0
Holding	29	8	79	4	17	6	36	1
Harper	22	11	33	2	14	7	19	0
Richards	2	0	7	0	2	1	1	0
Gomes	1	0	1	0	2	1	2	0
Richardson					1	1	0	0
Logie					1	1	0	0

FALL OF WICKETS

	WI	NZ	WI	NZ
Wkt	1st	1st	2nd	2nd
1st	5	1	10	0
2nd	9	110	58	40
3rd	194	113	172	59
4th	196	132	226	76
5th	236	182	239	83
6th	267	223	240	158
7th	267	225	241	–
8th	269	248	261	–
9th	302	250	–	–
10th	307	262	–	–

Umpires: D.M.Archer (12) and C.E.Cumberbatch (4).

Close: 1st day – WI(1) 231-4 (Richards 14, Logie 20); 2nd – NZ(1) 166-4 (Howarth 25, Coney 16); 3rd – NZ(1) 223-5 (Howarth 44, Hadlee 18); 4th – WI(2) 228-4 (Logie 35, Dujon 1).

WEST INDIES v NEW ZEALAND 1984-85 (2nd Test)

At Bourda, Georgetown, Guyana, on 6, 7, 8, 10, 11 April.
Toss: West Indies.   Result: MATCH DRAWN.
Debuts: West Indies – C.G.Butts.

Bourda revived memories of New Zealand's earlier visit (*Test No. 696*) by providing 1,219 runs at an average of 55.40 per wicket. Richardson batted 455 minutes (346 balls) in the first innings, his fourth Test hundred taking 194 minutes despite his reaching 50 in just 65 minutes. His progress was hampered by Howarth's tactics which involved retaining the old ball and dispensing with all close fielders. During his second Test hundred, an innings occupying 571 minutes (462 balls) overall, Martin Crowe completed 1,000 runs in 21 Tests. His partnerships with Coney (142) and Smith (143) are fifth and seventh-wicket New Zealand records for this series respectively.

WEST INDIES

C.G.Greenidge	b Chatfield	10		c and b Coney	69
D.L.Haynes	b Hadlee	90		c Smith b Hadlee	9
R.B.Richardson	run out	185	(4)	c J.J.Crowe b Cairns	60
H.A.Gomes	lbw b Cairns	53	(5)	c sub‡ b Rutherford	35
*I.V.A.Richards	st Smith b Coney	40	(8)	not out	7
A.L.Logie	c Howarth b Hadlee	52		not out	41
†P.J.L.Dujon	not out	60		b Cairns	3
C.G.Butts			(3)	c Smith b Hadlee	9
M.D.Marshall					
M.A.Holding	did not bat				
J.Garner					
Extras	(B1, LB16, W1, NB3)	21		(B7, LB25, W1, NB2)	35
Total	(6 wickets declared)	**511**		(6 wickets declared)	**268**

NEW ZEALAND

J.G.Wright	run out	27
K.R.Rutherford	c Dujon b Garner	4
J.J.Crowe	b Marshall	22
M.D.Crowe	lbw b Garner	188
*G.P.Howarth	c Haynes b Marshall	4
J.V.Coney	c Richards b Holding	73
R.J.Hadlee	c Dujon b Marshall	16
†I.D.S.Smith	lbw b Marshall	53
B.L.Cairns	b Holding	3
S.L.Boock	b Holding	0
E.J.Chatfield	not out	3
Extras	(B12, LB2, W6, NB27)	47
Total		**440**

NEW ZEALAND	O	M	R	W		O	M	R	W
Hadlee	25.5	5	83	2		16	3	32	2
Chatfield	30	3	122	1		16	3	43	0
Cairns	32	5	105	1	(4)	18	4	47	2
Boock	43	11	107	0	(3)	18	3	52	0
Coney	18	2	62	1		10	3	20	1
Howarth	4	1	15	0	(7)	5	4	2	0
Rutherford					(6)	9	1	38	1
Wright						3	1	2	0

WEST INDIES	O	M	R	W
Marshall	33	3	110	4
Garner	27.5	5	72	2
Holding	28	6	89	3
Butts	47	12	113	0
Richards	8	1	22	0
Gomes	8	2	20	0

FALL OF WICKETS

Wkt	WI 1st	NZ 1st	WI 2nd
1st	30	8	22
2nd	221	45	46
3rd	327	81	150
4th	394	98	191
5th	407	240	207
6th	511	261	225
7th	–	404	–
8th	–	415	–
9th	–	415	–
10th	–	440	–

Umpires: L.H.Barker (3) and D.J.Narine (3).   ‡ (J.G.Bracewell)

Close: 1st day – WI(1) 271-2 (Richardson 140, Gomes 18); 2nd – WI(1) 511-6 dec; 3rd – NZ(1) 230-4 (M.D.Crowe 72, Coney 65); 4th – WI(2) 41-1 (Greenidge 21, Butts 5).

WEST INDIES v NEW ZEALAND 1984-85 (3rd Test)

At Kensington Oval, Bridgetown, Barbados, on 26, 27, 28, 30 April, 1 May.
Toss: West Indies.   Result: WEST INDIES won by ten wickets.
Debuts: None.

Although almost eight hours were lost to rain, Greenidge made the winning hit just 37 minutes into the fifth day to secure the first outright result in eight Tests between these teams in the Caribbean. On a lively pitch, New Zealand, 1 for 3 after 13 balls, were dismissed for their lowest total in the Caribbean and the lowest by any side at Bridgetown. Jeff Crowe batted 175 minutes for his 21 and remained on 1 for 91 minutes (65 balls). Richards (192 minutes, 147 balls) included three sixes and 13 fours in his 19th Test hundred – his first as captain. Before returning the best match analysis in any Bridgetown Test and achieving the first ten-wicket haul for West Indies in this series, Marshall shared in record West Indies eighth- and ninth-wicket partnerships against New Zealand with Richards (83) and Garner (70) respectively. In the second innings, Smith (14) retired at 132 with a bruised forearm, resuming at 235 when Stirling was bowled off his helmet.

NEW ZEALAND

*G.P.Howarth	c Greenidge b Garner	1	(2)	c Haynes b Marshall	5
J.G.Wright	c Dujon b Marshall	0	(1)	c Richardson b Davis	64
K.R.Rutherford	c Richards b Marshall	0		c Holding b Marshall	2
M.D.Crowe	hit wkt b Holding	14		c Dujon b Marshall	2
J.J.Crowe	c Dujon b Davis	21		b Davis	4
J.V.Coney	c Richardson b Marshall	12		c Logie b Marshall	83
†I.D.S.Smith	c Greenidge b Marshall	2		c and b Marshall	26
R.J.Hadlee	c Logie b Davis	29		c Greenidge b Davis	3
D.A.Stirling	c Logie b Davis	6		b Marshall	3
S.L.Boock	c Dujon b Garner	1		c Haynes b Marshall	22
E.J.Chatfield	not out	0		not out	4
Extras	(NB8)	8		(B8, LB1, W2, NB19)	30
Total		**94**			**248**

WEST INDIES

C.G.Greenidge	c J.J.Crowe b Hadlee	2		not out	4
D.L.Haynes	c Smith b Hadlee	62		not out	5
R.B.Richardson	lbw b M.D.Crowe	22			
H.A.Gomes	c J.J.Crowe b M.D.Crowe	0			
W.W.Davis	c Smith b Stirling	16			
*I.V.A.Richards	c M.D.Crowe b Boock	105			
A.L.Logie	c J.J.Crowe b Chatfield	7			
†P.J.L.Dujon	b Hadlee	3			
M.D.Marshall	c J.J.Crowe b Chatfield	63			
J.Garner	not out	37			
M.A.Holding	c Smith b Stirling	1			
Extras	(B2, LB8, W6, NB2)	18		(W1)	1
Total		**336**		(0 wickets)	**10**

WEST INDIES	O	M	R	W		O	M	R	W		FALL OF WICKETS			
											NZ	WI	NZ	WI
Marshall	15	3	40	4		25.3	6	80	7	Wkt	1st	1st	2nd	2nd
Garner	15	9	14	2		19	5	56	0	1st	1	12	26	–
Holding	7	4	12	1	(4)	1	0	2	0	2nd	1	91	35	–
Davis	10.4	5	28	3	(3)	18	0	66	3	3rd	1	91	45	–
Richards						13	3	25	0	4th	18	95	60	–
Gomes						4	0	10	0	5th	37	142	108	–
										6th	44	161	141	–
NEW ZEALAND										7th	80	174	149	–
Hadlee	26	5	86	3						8th	87	257	226	–
Chatfield	28	10	57	2						9th	90	327	235	–
Stirling	14.1	0	82	2						10th	94	336	248	–
M.D.Crowe	10	2	25	2										
Boock	15	1	76	1	(1)	1	1	0	0					
Rutherford					(2)	0.4	0	10	0					

Umpires: D.M.Archer (13) and L.H.Barker (4).

Close: 1st day – NZ(1) 18-4 (J.J.Crowe 1, Coney 0); 2nd – WI(1) 113-4 (Davis 6, Richards 11); 3rd – NZ(2) 15-0 (Wright 12, Howarth 1); 4th – NZ(2) 228-8 (Coney 81, Chatfield 0).

WEST INDIES v NEW ZEALAND 1984-85 (4th Test)

At Sabina Park, Kingston, Jamaica, on 4, 5, 6, 8 May.
Toss: New Zealand.   Result: WEST INDIES won by ten wickets.
Debuts: None.

West Indies, undefeated at home since 1978, completed their second successive victory by ten wickets, this time with more than a day to spare. It was gained at the expense of much criticism of their intimidatory bowling tactics and the failure of the umpires to invoke the law in this respect. Coney retired at 51, his left forearm fractured below its protector by a short-pitched ball from Garner. After New Zealand had followed on, Howarth, playing his final Test innings, batted 301 minutes and shared a stand of 210 in 294 minutes with Jeff Crowe to establish a New Zealand second-wicket record against all countries until 1991-92. Marshall's tally of 27 wickets in the rubber equalled the record set by B.R.Taylor for New Zealand in 1971-72. Greenidge kept wicket for the later part of New Zealand's second innings after Dujon had been injured and Martin Crowe deputised when Smith bowled.

WEST INDIES

C.G.Greenidge	c J.J.Crowe b M.D.Crowe	46	not out	33
D.L.Haynes	c J.J.Crowe b Coney	76	not out	24
R.B.Richardson	c M.D.Crowe b Coney	30		
H.A.Gomes	c Wright b Hadlee	45		
*I.V.A.Richards	lbw b Hadlee	23		
A.L.Logie	c M.D.Crowe b Hadlee	0		
†P.J.L.Dujon	c Bracewell b Troup	70		
M.D.Marshall	lbw b Bracewell	26		
W.W.Davis	c M.D.Crowe b Troup	0		
J.Garner	c M.D.Crowe b Hadlee	12		
C.A.Walsh	not out	12		
Extras	(B7, LB9, W1, NB6)	23	(B1, LB1)	2
Total		**363**	(0 wickets)	**59**

NEW ZEALAND

*G.P.Howarth	c Gomes b Marshall	5	(2) c Garner b Walsh		84
J.G.Wright	b Davis	53	(1) c Dujon b Garner		10
J.J.Crowe	c Richardson b Garner	2	c Marshall b Richards		112
M.D.Crowe	c Davis b Walsh	6	c Dujon b Walsh		1
J.V.Coney	retired hurt	4	absent hurt		–
K.R.Rutherford	c Dujon b Marshall	1	(5) lbw b Marshall		5
†I.D.S.Smith	b Garner	0	(6) b Marshall		9
R.J.Hadlee	c Dujon b Davis	18	(7) c Walsh b Marshall		14
J.G.Bracewell	not out	25	(8) c Gomes b Marshall		27
G.B.Troup	c Marshall b Davis	0	(9) c Richardson b Garner		2
E.J.Chatfield	b Davis	2	(10) not out		0
Extras	(B4, LB1, W2, NB15)	22	(B7, LB4, NB8)		19
Total		**138**			**283**

NEW ZEALAND	O	M	R	W		O	M	R	W
Hadlee	28.4	11	53	4		5	1	15	0
Troup	17	1	87	2		3	0	13	0
Chatfield	26	5	85	0		2	0	10	0
M.D.Crowe	10	2	30	1					
Bracewell	21	5	54	1	(4)	4	0	14	0
Coney	14	3	38	2					
Smith					(5)	3	1	5	0
WEST INDIES									
Marshall	17	3	47	2		28.4	8	66	4
Garner	16	0	37	2		19	8	41	2
Davis	13.5	5	19	4	(4)	21	1	75	0
Walsh	9	1	30	1	(3)	16	4	45	2
Richards						14	2	34	1
Gomes						3	0	11	0
Richardson						1	1	0	0

FALL OF WICKETS

	WI	NZ	NZ	WI
Wkt	1st	1st	2nd	2nd
1st	82	11	13	–
2nd	144	15	223	–
3rd	164	37	223	–
4th	207	65	228	–
5th	207	68	238	–
6th	273	106	242	–
7th	311	113	259	–
8th	311	122	281	–
9th	339	138	283	–
10th	363	–	–	–

Umpires: D.M.Archer (14) and J.R.Gayle (2).

Close: 1st day – WI(1) 273-6 (Dujon 41); 2nd – NZ(1) 65-4 (Wright 30); 3rd – NZ(2) 211-1 (Howarth 78, J.J.Crowe 108).

ENGLAND v AUSTRALIA 1985 (1st Test)

At Headingley, Leeds, on 13, 14, 15, 17, 18 June.
Toss: Australia.   Result: ENGLAND won by five wickets.
Debuts: Australia – S.P.O'Donnell.

England completed their victory with 13.2 overs in hand to achieve only their second defeat of Australia since 1930 in the initial match of a home rubber. Headingley staged the opening Test of an Ashes series for the first time. The first Test to have a standby umpire (R.Julian) in attendance, it was also the first in England in which no-balls and wides were debited to bowlers' analyses. Botham became only the second England bowler after W.Voce (*Test No. 256*) to take three wickets in four balls against Australia when he dismissed Ritchie, O'Donnell and McDermott. Robinson (413 minutes, 270 balls, 27 fours) was the 15th England batsman to score a hundred in his first Test against Australia; only R.E.Foster (287 in *Test No. 78*) had made a higher score on such a debut. England's total of 533 was their highest against Australia at Leeds. Lamb scored his 2,000th run in 33 Tests.

AUSTRALIA

G.M.Wood	lbw b Allott	14	(2)	c Lamb b Botham	3
A.M.J.Hilditch	c Downton b Gooch	119	(1)	c Robinson b Emburey	80
K.C.Wessels	c Botham b Emburey	36		b Emburey	64
*A.R.Border	c Botham b Cowans	32		c Downton b Botham	8
D.C.Boon	lbw b Gooch	14		b Cowans	22
G.M.Ritchie	b Botham	46		b Emburey	1
†W.B.Phillips	c Gower b Emburey	30		c Lamb b Botham	91
C.J.McDermott	b Botham	18	(10)	c Gooch b Emburey	6
S.P.O'Donnell	lbw b Botham	0	(8)	c Downton b Botham	24
G.F.Lawson	c Downton b Allott	0	(9)	c Downton b Emburey	15
J.R.Thomson	not out	4		not out	2
Extras	(LB13, W4, NB1)	18		(B4, LB3, W1)	8
Total		**331**			**324**

ENGLAND

G.A.Gooch	lbw b McDermott	5	lbw b O'Donnell	28
R.T.Robinson	c Boon b Lawson	175	b Lawson	21
*D.I.Gower	c Phillips b McDermott	17	c Border b O'Donnell	5
M.W.Gatting	c Hilditch b McDermott	53	c Phillips b Lawson	12
A.J.Lamb	b O'Donnell	38	not out	31
I.T.Botham	b Thomson	60	b O'Donnell	12
P.Willey	c Hilditch b Lawson	36	not out	3
†P.R.Downton	c Border b McDermott	54		
J.E.Emburey	b Lawson	21		
P.J.W.Allott	c Boon b Thomson	12		
N.G.Cowans	not out	22		
Extras	(B5, LB16, W5, NB14)	40	(LB7, W1, NB3)	11
Total		**533**	(5 wickets)	**123**

ENGLAND	O	M	R	W		O	M	R	W		FALL OF WICKETS			
Cowans	20	4	78	1	(4)	13	2	50	1		A	E	A	E
Allott	22	3	74	2		17	4	57	0	Wkt	1st	1st	2nd	2nd
Botham	29.1	8	86	3	(1)	33	7	107	4	1st	23	14	5	44
Gooch	21	4	57	2	(5)	9	3	21	0	2nd	155	50	144	59
Emburey	6	1	23	2	(3)	43.4	14	82	5	3rd	201	186	151	71
										4th	229	264	159	83
										5th	229	344	160	110
AUSTRALIA										6th	284	417	192	–
Lawson	26	4	117	3	(2)	16	4	51	2	7th	326	422	272	–
McDermott	32	2	134	4	(1)	4	0	20	0	8th	326	462	307	–
Thomson	34	3	166	2	(4)	3	0	8	0	9th	327	484	318	–
O'Donnell	27	8	77	1	(3)	15.4	5	37	3	10th	331	533	324	–
Border	3	0	16	0										
Wessels	3	2	2	0										

Umpires: B.J.Meyer (17) and K.E.Palmer (10).

Close: 1st day – A(1) 284-6 (Ritchie 22, McDermott 0); 2nd – E(1) 134-2 (Robinson 66, Gatting 31); 3rd – E(1) 484-9 (Downton 28, Cowans 0); 4th – A(2) 190-5 (Boon 20, Phillips 11).

ENGLAND v AUSTRALIA 1985 (2nd Test)

At Lord's, London, on 27, 28, 29 June, 1, 2 July.
Toss: Australia.　Result: AUSTRALIA won by four wickets.
Debuts: None.

Australia achieved the first victory in an Ashes Test at Lord's since 1972 after Gower had lost his sixth successive toss in Tests. Border (450 minutes, 318 balls, 22 fours) recorded the highest score by an Australian captain at Lord's (beating 155 by W.M.Woodfull in 1930), and completed 5,000 Test runs in the record time of 6 years 186 days. In taking five or more wickets in an innings for the 25th time, Botham gained the world Test record held by S.F.Barnes since 1914. When Wood became his 326th victim, Botham succeeded R.G.D.Willis as England's leading wicket-taker. Edmonds and Emburey, having played a combined total of 51 Tests, appeared together for England for only the second time (also *Test No. 830*).

ENGLAND

G.A.Gooch	lbw b McDermott	30		c Phillips b McDermott	17
R.T.Robinson	lbw b McDermott	6		b Holland	12
*D.I.Gower	c Border b McDermott	86	(5)	c Phillips b McDermott	22
M.W.Gatting	lbw b Lawson	14	(6)	not out	75
A.J.Lamb	c Phillips b Lawson	47	(7)	c Holland b Lawson	9
I.T.Botham	c Ritchie b Lawson	5	(8)	c Border b Holland	85
†P.R.Downton	c Wessels b McDermott	21	(9)	c Boon b Holland	0
J.E.Emburey	lbw b O'Donnell	33	(3)	b Lawson	20
P.H.Edmonds	c Border b McDermott	21	(10)	c Boon b Holland	1
N.A.Foster	c Wessels b McDermott	3	(11)	c Border b Holland	0
P.J.W.Allott	not out	1	(4)	b Lawson	0
Extras	(B1, LB4, W1, NB17)	23		(B1, LB12, W4, NB3)	20
Total		**290**			**261**

AUSTRALIA

G.M.Wood	c Emburey b Allott	8	(2)	c Lamb b Botham	6
A.M.J.Hilditch	b Foster	14	(1)	c Lamb b Botham	0
K.C.Wessels	lbw b Botham	11		run out	28
*A.R.Border	c Gooch b Botham	196	(5)	not out	41
D.C.Boon	c Downton b Botham	4	(6)	b Edmonds	1
G.M.Ritchie	lbw b Botham	94	(4)	b Allott	2
†W.B.Phillips	c Edmonds b Botham	21		c Edmonds b Emburey	29
S.P.O'Donnell	c Lamb b Edmonds	48		not out	9
G.F.Lawson	not out	5			
C.J.McDermott	run out	9			
R.G.Holland	b Edmonds	0			
Extras	(LB10, W1, NB4)	15		(LB11)	11
Total		**425**		**(6 wickets)**	**127**

AUSTRALIA	O	M	R	W		O	M	R	W	FALL OF WICKETS				
Lawson	25	2	91	3	(2)	23	0	86	3		E	A	E	A
McDermott	29.2	5	70	6	(1)	20	2	84	2	*Wkt*	*1st*	*1st*	*2nd*	*2nd*
O'Donnell	22	3	82	1	(4)	5	0	10	0	1st	26	11	32	0
Holland	23	6	42	0	(3)	32	12	68	5	2nd	51	24	34	9
										3rd	99	80	38	22
ENGLAND										4th	179	101	57	63
Foster	23	1	83	1						5th	184	317	77	65
Allott	30	4	70	1		7	4	8	1	6th	211	347	98	116
Botham	24	2	109	5	(1)	15	0	49	2	7th	241	398	229	–
Edmonds	25.4	5	85	2	(3)	16	5	35	1	8th	273	414	229	–
Gooch	3	1	11	0						9th	283	425	261	–
Emburey	19	3	57	0	(4)	8	4	24	1	10th	290	425	261	–

Umpires: H.D.Bird (30) and D.G.L.Evans (9).

Close: 1st day – E(1) 273-8 (Edmonds 9, Foster 0); 2nd – A(1) 183-4 (Border 92, Ritchie 46); 3rd – E(2) 37-2 (Emburey 4, Allott 0); 4th – A(2) 46-3 (Wessels 23, Border 12).

ENGLAND v AUSTRALIA 1985 (3rd Test)

At Trent Bridge, Nottingham, on 11, 12, 13, 15, 16 July.
Toss: England.   Result: MATCH DRAWN.
Debuts: England – A.Sidebottom.

Sidebottom was the first Yorkshire player to appear for England since January 1982 when G.Boycott played in the last of his 108 matches. England scored 358 before losing their third wicket – their best start against Australia since Old Trafford in 1964. Gower (381 minutes, 283 balls, 17 fours) recorded his first Test century for 23 innings and the highest score by an England captain at Trent Bridge (previously 149 by R.E.S.Wyatt in *Test No. 242*). Wood completed 1,000 runs against England and 3,000 runs in Tests during his eighth hundred; his 599-minute innings (448 balls) was the second-longest for Australia in England after R.B.Simpson's 762 minutes (*564*). Australia achieved their highest total at Trent Bridge and the highest in this series since 1965-66 (*601*). Robinson compiled the highest score by a Nottinghamshire batsman against Australia on his home ground.

ENGLAND

G.A.Gooch	c Wessels b Lawson	70	c Ritchie b McDermott	48
R.T.Robinson	c Border b Lawson	38	not out	77
*D.I.Gower	c Phillips b O'Donnell	166	c Phillips b McDermott	17
M.W.Gatting	run out	74	not out	35
A.J.Lamb	lbw b Lawson	17		
I.T.Botham	c O'Donnell b McDermott	38		
†P.R.Downton	c Ritchie b McDermott	0		
A.Sidebottom	c O'Donnell b Lawson	2		
J.E.Emburey	not out	16		
P.H.Edmonds	b Holland	12		
P.J.W.Allott	c Border b Lawson	7		
Extras	(LB12, W1, NB3)	16	(B1, LB16, NB2)	19
Total		**456**	(2 wickets)	**196**

AUSTRALIA

G.M.Wood	c Robinson b Botham	172
A.M.J.Hilditch	lbw b Allott	47
R.G.Holland	lbw b Sidebottom	10
K.C.Wessels	c Downton b Emburey	33
*A.R.Border	c Botham b Edmonds	23
D.C.Boon	c and b Emburey	15
G.M.Ritchie	b Edmonds	146
†W.B.Phillips	b Emburey	2
S.P.O'Donnell	c Downton b Botham	46
G.F.Lawson	c Gooch b Botham	18
C.J.McDermott	not out	0
Extras	(B6, LB7, W2, NB12)	27
Total		**539**

AUSTRALIA	O	M	R	W	O	M	R	W	FALL OF WICKETS			
										E	A	E
Lawson	39.4	10	103	5	13	4	32	0	**Wkt**	*1st*	*1st*	*2nd*
McDermott	35	3	147	2	16	2	42	2	1st	55	87	79
O'Donnell	29	4	104	1	(4) 10	2	26	0	2nd	171	128	107
Holland	26	3	90	1	(3) 28	9	69	0	3rd	358	205	–
Ritchie					1	0	10	0	4th	365	234	–
									5th	416	263	–
ENGLAND									6th	416	424	–
Botham	34.2	3	107	3					7th	419	437	–
Sidebottom	18.4	3	65	1					8th	419	491	–
Allott	18	4	55	1					9th	443	539	–
Edmonds	66	18	155	2					10th	456	539	–
Emburey	55	15	129	3								
Gooch	8.2	2	13	0								
Gatting	1	0	2	0								

Umpires: D.J.Constant (29) and A.G.T.Whitehead (2).

Close: 1st day – E(1) 279-2 (Gower 107, Gatting 53); 2nd – A(1) 94-1 (Wood 38, Holland 4); 3rd – A(1) 366-5 (Wood 152, Ritchie 65); 4th – E(2) 8-0 (Gooch 4, Robinson 3).

ENGLAND v AUSTRALIA 1985 (4th Test)

At Old Trafford, Manchester, on 1, 2, 3, 5, 6 August.
Toss: England.   Result: MATCH DRAWN.
Debuts: None.

Cheshire provided the birthplaces of England's first three bowlers for the first time. Gower completed 5,000 runs in 74 Tests in 7 years 62 days – the fastest of England's nine instances. Gatting (357 minutes, 266 balls, 21 fours) completed his first hundred against Australia and his first in 40 Test innings in England. At 20 years 113 days McDermott became the youngest Australian to take eight wickets in a Test innings. During his 14th Test hundred, Border (346 minutes, 334 balls) completed 1,000 runs in first-class matches on the tour – the first left-handed Australian captain to do so since J.Darling in 1905. Earlier he had succumbed to England's first stumping in a home Test since 1980. Phillips scored his 1,000th run in 16 Tests.

AUSTRALIA

K.C.Wessels	c Botham b Emburey	34	(3)	c and b Emburey	50
A.M.J.Hilditch	c Gower b Edmonds	49	(1)	b Emburey	40
D.C.Boon	c Lamb b Botham	61	(5)	b Emburey	7
*A.R.Border	st Downton b Edmonds	8		not out	146
G.M.Ritchie	c and b Edmonds	4	(6)	b Emburey	31
†W.B.Phillips	c Downton b Botham	36	(7)	not out	39
G.R.J.Matthews	b Botham	4	(2)	c and b Edmonds	17
S.P.O'Donnell	b Edmonds	45			
G.F.Lawson	c Downton b Botham	4			
C.J.McDermott	lbw b Emburey	0			
R.G.Holland	not out	5			
Extras	(LB3, W1, NB3)	7		(B1, LB6, NB3)	10
Total		**257**		**(5 wickets)**	**340**

ENGLAND

G.A.Gooch	lbw b McDermott	74
R.T.Robinson	c Border b McDermott	10
*D.I.Gower	c Hilditch b McDermott	47
M.W.Gatting	c Phillips b McDermott	160
A.J.Lamb	run out	67
I.T.Botham	c O'Donnell b McDermott	20
†P.R.Downton	b McDermott	23
J.E.Emburey	not out	31
P.H.Edmonds	b McDermott	1
P.J.W.Allott	b McDermott	7
J.P.Agnew	not out	2
Extras	(B7, LB16, NB17)	40
Total	**(9 wickets declared)**	**482**

ENGLAND	O	M	R	W		O	M	R	W		FALL OF WICKETS		
Botham	23	4	79	4		15	3	50	0		A	E	A
Agnew	14	0	65	0	(5)	9	2	34	0	*Wkt*	*1st*	*1st*	*2nd*
Allott	13	1	29	0	(2)	6	2	4	0	1st	71	21	38
Emburey	24	7	41	2		51	17	99	4	2nd	97	142	85
Edmonds	15.1	4	40	4	(3)	54	12	122	1	3rd	118	148	126
Gatting						4	0	14	0	4th	122	304	138
Lamb						1	0	10	0	5th	193	339	213
										6th	198	430	–
AUSTRALIA										7th	211	448	–
Lawson	37	7	114	0						8th	223	450	–
McDermott	36	3	141	8						9th	224	470	–
Holland	38	7	101	0						10th	257	–	–
O'Donnell	21	6	82	0									
Matthews	9	2	21	0									

Umpires: H.D.Bird (31) and D.R.Shepherd (1).

Close: 1st day – A(1) 257 all out; 2nd – E(1) 233-3 (Gatting 45, Lamb 38); 3rd – E(1) 448-6 (Downton 23, Emburey 12); 4th – A(2) 192-4 (Border 49, Ritchie 22).

ENGLAND v AUSTRALIA 1985 (5th Test)

At Edgbaston, Birmingham, on 15, 16, 17, 19, 20 August.
Toss: England.   Result: ENGLAND won by an innings and 118 runs.
Debuts: England – L.B.Taylor.

England completed a remarkable victory with 11.5 overs to spare after Ellison had captured the wickets of Wessels, Wood, Holland and Border in 15 balls. Gower became the first England captain to put Australia in to bat in successive Tests. His score of 215 (452 minutes, 314 balls, one six and 25 fours) was the highest against Australia at Edgbaston (beating 180 by E.R.Dexter in 1961) and the second highest by an England captain against Australia after W.R.Hammond's 240 at Lord's in 1938; he also exceeded D.C.S.Compton's record aggregate for a home Ashes series of 562 in 1948. The second-wicket partnership of 331 in 343 minutes between Robinson and Gower was England's second highest for any wicket against Australia. Gatting's second hundred in successive innings (off 127 balls) enabled him to complete 1,000 runs in ten Tests since 28 November 1984. Thomson's 200th wicket in 51 Tests was also his 100th in 21 matches against England. Botham (28 Tests) succeeded R.G.D.Willis (128 wickets in 35 matches) as the leading wicket-taker against Australia. Hilditch completed 1,000 runs in his 16th Test. In the second innings, the left-handed Phillips was caught at silly mid-off via Lamb's instep at silly point.

AUSTRALIA

G.M.Wood	c Edmonds b Botham	19	(2)	c Robinson b Ellison	10
A.M.J.Hilditch	c Downton b Edmonds	39	(1)	c Ellison b Botham	10
K.C.Wessels	c Downton b Ellison	83		c Downton b Ellison	10
*A.R.Border	c Edmonds b Ellison	45	(5)	b Ellison	2
G.M.Ritchie	c Botham b Ellison	8	(6)	c Lamb b Emburey	20
†W.B.Phillips	c Robinson b Ellison	15	(7)	c Gower b Edmonds	59
S.P.O'Donnell	c Downton b Taylor	1	(8)	b Botham	11
G.F.Lawson	run out	53	(9)	c Gower b Edmonds	3
C.J.McDermott	c Gower b Ellison	35	(10)	c Edmonds b Botham	8
J.R.Thomson	not out	28	(11)	not out	4
R.G.Holland	c Edmonds b Ellison	0	(4)	lbw b Ellison	0
Extras	(LB4, W1, NB4)	9		(B1, LB3, NB1)	5
Total		**335**			**142**

ENGLAND

G.A.Gooch	c Phillips b Thomson	19
R.T.Robinson	b Lawson	148
*D.I.Gower	c Border b Lawson	215
M.W.Gatting	not out	100
A.J.Lamb	c Wood b McDermott	46
I.T.Botham	c Thomson b McDermott	18
†P.R.Downton	not out	0
J.E.Emburey		
R.M.Ellison	did not bat	
P.H.Edmonds		
L.B.Taylor		
Extras	(B7, LB20, NB22)	49
Total	(5 wickets declared)	**595**

ENGLAND	O	M	R	W	O	M	R	W	FALL OF WICKETS			
Botham	27	1	108	1	14.1	2	52	3		A	E	A
Taylor	26	5	78	1	13	4	27	0	Wkt	1st	1st	2nd
Ellison	31.5	9	77	6	9	3	27	4	1st	44	38	10
Edmonds	20	4	47	1	15	9	13	2	2nd	92	369	32
Emburey	9	2	21	0	13	5	19	1	3rd	189	463	32
									4th	191	572	35
									5th	207	592	36
AUSTRALIA									6th	208	–	113
Lawson	37	1	135	2					7th	218	–	117
McDermott	31	2	155	2					8th	276	–	120
Thomson	19	1	101	1					9th	335	–	137
Holland	25	4	95	0					10th	335	–	142
O'Donnell	16	3	69	0								
Border	6	1	13	0								

Umpires: D.J.Constant (30) and D.R.Shepherd (2).

Close: 1st day – A(1) 181-2 (Wessels 76, Border 43); 2nd – A(1) 335-8 (Lawson 53, Thomson 28); 3rd – E(1) 355-1 (Robinson 140, Gower 169); 4th – A(2) 37-5 (Ritchie 0, Phillips 1).

ENGLAND v AUSTRALIA 1985 (6th Test)

At Kennington Oval, London, on 29, 30, 31 August, 2 September.
Toss: England.   Result: ENGLAND won by an innings and 94 runs.
Debuts: Australia – D.R.Gilbert.

After compelling them to follow on for the first time since 1977 (Leeds), England recorded successive innings victories against Australia for the first time since 1956 and regained the Ashes lost at Sydney in January 1983. England (376 for 3) achieved their highest total in a single day's play against Australia since 1938 (409 for 5 at Lord's) and their highest in all Tests since 1962 (406 for 2 at The Oval). Gower (337 minutes, 215 balls, 20 fours) recorded his 12th Test hundred (5th v Australia), took his aggregate for the rubber to 732 (the fourth-highest for England against all countries), and became the ninth England batsman to complete 2,000 runs against Australia. For the second consecutive innings he shared in a triple-century stand, the 351 he added in 337 minutes with Gooch succeeding the 331 with Robinson in the previous Test as England's second-highest for any wicket against Australia. Gooch's fifth hundred was his first in 40 innings against Australia, his highest Test score occupying 424 minutes (310 balls) and including 27 fours. Physiotherapist Bernard Thomas ended his 17-year association with England teams. Receipts from the six Cornhill Tests were £2,467,030 (total attendance 373,000).

ENGLAND

G.A.Gooch	c and b McDermott	196
R.T.Robinson	b McDermott	3
*D.I.Gower	c Bennett b McDermott	157
M.W.Gatting	c Border b Bennett	4
J.E.Emburey	c Wellham b Lawson	9
A.J.Lamb	c McDermott b Lawson	1
I.T.Botham	c Phillips b Lawson	12
†P.R.Downton	b McDermott	16
R.M.Ellison	c Phillips b Gilbert	3
P.H.Edmonds	lbw b Lawson	12
L.B.Taylor	not out	1
Extras	(B13, LB11, NB26)	50
Total		**464**

AUSTRALIA

G.M.Wood	lbw b Botham	22	(2)	b Botham	6
A.M.J.Hilditch	c Gooch b Botham	17	(1)	c Gower b Taylor	9
K.C.Wessels	b Emburey	12		c Downton b Botham	7
*A.R.Border	b Edmonds	38		c Botham b Ellison	58
D.M.Wellham	c Downton b Ellison	13		lbw b Ellison	5
G.M.Ritchie	not out	64		c Downton b Ellison	6
†W.B.Phillips	b Edmonds	18		c Downton b Botham	10
M.J.Bennett	c Robinson b Ellison	12		c and b Taylor	11
G.F.Lawson	c Botham b Taylor	14		c Downton b Ellison	7
C.J.McDermott	run out	25		c Botham b Ellison	2
D.R.Gilbert	b Botham	1		not out	0
Extras	(LB3, W2)	5		(B4, NB4)	8
Total		**241**			**129**

AUSTRALIA	O	M	R	W	O	M	R	W		FALL OF WICKETS		
Lawson	29.2	6	101	4						E	A	A
McDermott	31	2	108	4					*Wkt*	*1st*	*1st*	*2nd*
Gilbert	21	2	96	1					1st	20	35	13
Bennett	32	8	111	1					2nd	371	52	16
Border	2	0	8	0					3rd	376	56	37
Wessels	3	0	16	0					4th	403	101	51
									5th	405	109	71
ENGLAND									6th	418	144	96
Botham	20	3	64	3	17	3	44	3	7th	425	171	114
Taylor	13	1	39	1	11.3	1	34	2	8th	447	192	127
Ellison	18	5	35	2	17	3	46	5	9th	452	235	129
Emburey	19	7	48	1	1	0	1	0	10th	464	241	129
Edmonds	14	2	52	2								

Umpires: H.D.Bird (32) and K.E.Palmer (11).

Close: 1st day – E(1) 376-3 (Gooch 179, Emburey 0); 2nd – A(1) 145-6 (Ritchie 20, Bennett 0); 3rd – A(2) 62-4 (Border 26, Ritchie 6).

SRI LANKA v INDIA 1985-86 (1st Test)

At Sinhalese Sports Club Ground, Colombo, on 30, 31 August, 1, 3, 4 September.
Toss: India.   Result: MATCH DRAWN.
Debuts: Sri Lanka – F.S.Ahangama, E.A.R.de Silva; India – L.S.Rajput, S.Viswanath.

A tenacious 406-minute innings by Vengsarkar, abetted by the loss of 116 minutes of play to rain on the final day, enabled India to avoid defeat in their first official Test in Sri Lanka. Ahangama became the first Sri Lankan to take a wicket in his first over in Test cricket when he dismissed Azharuddin with his fourth ball. Thus was ended the Indian's unique sequence of hundreds in each of his first three Tests. Madugalle and Ranatunga recorded their first Test hundreds. Sri Lanka dismissed their opponents twice for the first time, Rumesh Ratnayake (6 for 85) and Amal Silva (nine catches, including six in the first innings) sharing three national records. With Sri Lanka needing 123 off 11 overs for their first victory, Aravinda de Silva struck the first ball of the innings for six and 17 runs came from Kapil Dev's opening over. Their heroic attempt was abandoned when India took three wickets in eight balls and bad light ended play three overs early.

INDIA

L.S.Rajput	c Silva b Ahangama	32	c Silva b Ratnayake		61
K.Srikkanth	b Ratnayake	2	c Silva b Ratnayake		9
M.Azharuddin	c Silva b Ahangama	3	lbw b Ahangama		16
D.B.Vengsarkar	c Silva b De Mel	6	not out		98
S.M.Gavaskar	run out	51	c De Mel b Ratnayake		0
R.J.Shastri	c Silva b De Mel	9	lbw b Ratnayake		40
*Kapil Dev	c Silva b De Mel	36	c sub (S.D.Anurasiri) b Ratnayake		6
†S.Viswanath	c E.A.R.de Silva b De Mel	20	c Silva b Ratnayake		0
C.Sharma	c Silva b De Mel	38	run out		4
G.Sharma	not out	10	lbw b Ahangama		1
Maninder Singh	lbw b Ratnayake	0	b Ahangama		3
Extras	(LB5, W1, NB5)	11	(B4, LB3, NB6)		13
Total		**218**			**251**

SRI LANKA

S.Wettimuny	c Viswanath b C.Sharma	13			
†S.A.R.Silva	c Azharuddin b C.Sharma	7	(6) not out		1
R.S.Madugalle	c and b Maninder	103	(5) not out		5
R.L.Dias	c Azharuddin b C.Sharma	4	(3) c Srikkanth b Kapil Dev		0
*L.R.D.Mendis	c Gavaskar b Maninder	51	(2) c Kapil Dev b C.Sharma		18
A.Ranatunga	b Shastri	111	(4) run out		15
P.A.de Silva	c Azharuddin b Shastri	33	(1) c Maninder b Kapil Dev		21
A.L.F.de Mel	c Viswanath b Kapil Dev	16			
R.J.Ratnayake	lbw b Kapil Dev	2			
E.A.R.de Silva	not out	1			
F.S.Ahangama	c Viswanath b Kapil Dev	0			
Extras	(LB5, NB1)	6	(LB1)		1
Total		**347**	(4 wickets)		**61**

SRI LANKA	O	M	R	W	O	M	R	W	FALL OF WICKETS				
De Mel	28	8	64	5	30	3	84	0		I	SL	I	SL
Ratnayake	24.2	7	64	2	41	10	85	6	*Wkt*	*1st*	*1st*	*2nd*	*2nd*
Ahangama	23	3	60	2	27.3	10	49	3	1st	19	18	23	38
E.A.R.de Silva	12	5	18	0	15	6	20	0	2nd	30	29	54	39
Ranatunga	10	8	7	0	6	2	6	0	3rd	47	33	130	44
									4th	49	118	130	58
INDIA									5th	65	262	188	–
Kapil Dev	30.4	8	74	3	4	0	36	2	6th	101	317	206	–
C.Sharma	25	3	81	3	4	0	24	1	7th	143	342	206	–
Shastri	34	9	70	2					8th	202	346	220	–
Maninder	40	12	82	2					9th	218	346	229	–
G.Sharma	15	6	35	0					10th	218	347	251	–

Umpires: H.C.Felsinger (5) and K.T.Francis (3).

Close: 1st day – I(1) 184-7 (Gavaskar 43, C.Sharma 23); 2nd – SL(1) 148-4 (Madugalle 55, Ranatunga 16); 3rd – SL(1) 342-7 (Ranatunga 109, Ratnayake 0); 4th – I(2) 153-4 (Vengsarkar 42, Shastri 17).

SRI LANKA v INDIA 1985-86 (2nd Test)

At P.Saravanamuttu Stadium, Colombo, on 6, 7, 8, 10, 11 September.
Toss: Sri Lanka.   Result: SRI LANKA won by 149 runs.
Debuts: Sri Lanka – C.D.U.S.Weerasinghe.

After 4½ years and at their 14th attempt, Sri Lanka gained their first victory in the first of the final 20 overs. Amal Silva set two world records, becoming the first wicket-keeper to score a hundred and make nine dismissals in the same Test, and the first to make 18 dismissals within two successive Tests (including only the second stumping of Gavaskar in 188 Test innings). Set a target of 348 in a minimum of 393 minutes, India collapsed against the medium pace of Rumesh Ratnayake, whose match analysis of 9 for 125 remains the best by a Sri Lankan bowler. Weerasinghe (17 years 189 days) became the (then) seventh youngest Test cricketer and he remains the youngest to represent Sri Lanka.

SRI LANKA

S.Wettimuny	run out	19	c Rajput b Sharma		32
†S.A.R.Silva	c Viswanath b Shastri	111	c Vengsarkar b Kapil Dev		11
R.S.Madugalle	lbw b Sharma	54			
R.L.Dias	c Viswanath b Sharma	95	not out		60
*L.R.D.Mendis	c Shastri b Amarnath	51	not out		13
A.Ranatunga	lbw b Sharma	21			
P.A.de Silva	c Azharuddin b Sharma	2	(3) b Shastri		75
A.L.F.de Mel	lbw b Shastri	0			
R.J.Ratnayake	c Sivaramakrishnan b Shastri	7			
C.D.U.S.Weerasinghe	b Sharma	3			
F.S.Ahangama	not out	0			
Extras	(LB3, W4, NB15)	22	(B4, LB6, NB5)		15
Total		**385**	(3 wickets declared)		**206**

INDIA

L.S.Rajput	c Silva b De Mel	0	lbw b De Mel		12
K.Srikkanth	c Mendis b Ahangama	64	lbw b Ratnayake		25
M.Azharuddin	c Silva b Ratnayake	0	c Silva b De Mel		25
D.B.Vengsarkar	c Ranatunga b Ratnayake	1	c Silva b Ratnayake		0
L.Sivaramakrishnan	c Wettimuny b Ratnayake	18	(9) c Silva b De Mel		21
S.M.Gavaskar	st Silva b Ranatunga	52	(5) c Silva b Ratnayake		19
M.Amarnath	c Ahangama b De Mel	60	(6) c De Silva b Ratnayake		10
R.J.Shastri	c Silva b Ahangama	17	(7) c Silva b Ahangama		4
*Kapil Dev	c Ratnayake b Ahangama	6	(8) c and b Ratnayake		78
†S.Viswanath	c Wettimuny b Ratnayake	7	lbw b Ahangama		0
C.Sharma	not out	4	not out		0
Extras	(B4, LB6, W1, NB4)	15	(LB2, NB2)		4
Total		**244**			**198**

INDIA	O	M	R	W	O	M	R	W	FALL OF WICKETS				
Kapil Dev	32	10	69	0	20	4	73	1		SL	I	SL	I
Sharma	33	3	118	5	13	1	55	1	*Wkt*	*1st*	*1st*	*2nd*	*2nd*
Shastri	45.3	11	74	3	13	4	41	1	1st	74	0	46	39
Sivaramakrishnan	31	4	90	0	7	1	27	0	2nd	169	1	48	39
Amarnath	15	2	31	1					3rd	229	3	180	41
									4th	328	79	–	84
SRI LANKA									5th	368	88	–	84
De Mel	31	8	63	2	22	4	64	3	6th	372	178	–	98
Ratnayake	25.1	5	76	4	23.2	6	49	5	7th	375	218	–	98
Ahangama	18	3	59	3	14	3	56	2	8th	375	229	–	168
Weerasinghe	16	7	28	0	3	1	8	0	9th	379	238	–	169
Ranatunga	5	1	8	1	4	0	19	0	10th	385	244	–	198

Umpires: S.Ponnadurai (1) and P.W.Vidanagamage (3).

Close: 1st day – SL(1) 168-1 (Silva 82, Madugalle 54); 2nd – I(1) 6-3 (Srikkanth 4, Sivaramakrishnan 0); 3rd – I(1) 210-6 (Amarnath 48, Shastri 15); 4th – I(2) 16-0 (Rajput 6, Srikkanth 9).

SRI LANKA v INDIA 1985-86 (3rd Test)

At Asgiriya Stadium, Kandy, on 14, 15, 16, 18, 19 September.
Toss: India.   Result: MATCH DRAWN.
Debuts: Sri Lanka – B.R.Jurangpathy.

A 216-run partnership in 285 minutes between Dias and Mendis earned Sri Lanka an honourable draw and their first victorious rubber. Besides establishing a national fourth-wicket record, both batsmen completed 1,000 runs in Tests and off successive balls, Mendis being the first to do so for his country. Amal Silva set a world record for a three-Test rubber by making 22 dismissals, while Rumesh Ratnayake established a national series record with 20 wickets. Amarnath's ninth hundred in 51 Tests enabled India to set a target of 377 runs in a minimum of 480 minutes. The decisive stand began after three wickets had fallen for 34 runs. Kapil Dev (71 Tests) became India's leading wicket-taker when he dismissed Silva and passed B.S.Bedi's aggregate of 266 in four fewer matches; that achievement was clouded by his own barren run as captain being extended to 17 Tests. In 34 matches since December 1981, India had gained only one win and suffered 12 defeats. Sharma (4) retired hurt at 237 in the first innings and resumed at 242. Viswanath equalled India's Test record by making six dismissals in the match. Jurangpathy began his Test career at the age of 18 years 81 days.

INDIA

R.J.Shastri	c Madugalle b De Mel	6		c Silva b Ahangama	81
K.Srikkanth	b Ahangama	40		lbw b Ahangama	47
M.Amarnath	lbw b Ahangama	30		not out	116
D.B.Vengsarkar	run out	62		lbw b Ahangama	10
M.Azharuddin	c Silva b Ahangama	25	(6)	b Ratnayake	43
S.M.Gavaskar	c Silva b Ratnayake	49	(7)	not out	15
*Kapil Dev	lbw b Ahangama	0	(5)	b Ranatunga	2
R.M.H.Binny	c De Mel b Ahangama	19			
C.Sharma	c Wettimuny b De Mel	11			
†S.Viswanath	c Silva b Ratnayake	4			
Maninder Singh	not out	0			
Extras	(LB1, W1, NB1)	3		(LB5, W4, NB2)	11
Total		249		(5 wickets declared)	325

SRI LANKA

S.Wettimuny	c Viswanath b Kapil Dev	34		c Vengsarkar b Sharma	5
†S.A.R.Silva	lbw b Binny	19		c Viswanath b Kapil Dev	2
R.S.Madugalle	c and b Binny	5		c Viswanath b Kapil Dev	10
R.L.Dias	c Viswanath b Sharma	8		run out	106
*L.R.D.Mendis	c sub‡ b Maninder	53		c Gavaskar b Sharma	124
A.Ranatunga	c Vengsarkar b Maninder	38		b Sharma	0
F.S.Ahangama	c Gavaskar b Maninder	11			
P.A.de Silva	run out	8	(7)	not out	29
B.R.Jurangpathy	c Viswanath b Kapil Dev	1	(8)	lbw b Kapil Dev	0
A.L.F.de Mel	c Viswanath b Maninder	1	(9)	not out	9
R.J.Ratnayake	not out	0			
Extras	(LB4, NB16)	20		(B8, LB4, W4, NB6)	22
Total		198		(7 wickets)	307

SRI LANKA	O	M	R	W	O	M	R	W		FALL OF WICKETS			
De Mel	26.3	5	97	2	13	2	66	0		I	SL	I	SL
Ratnayake	26	5	88	2	23	2	97	1	Wkt	1st	1st	2nd	2nd
Ahangama	24	7	52	5	27	6	72	3	1st	10	36	74	5
Ranatunga	8	5	11	0	16	4	51	1	2nd	66	44	178	8
Jurangpathy					4	0	24	0	3rd	111	68	206	34
Madugalle					1	0	10	0	4th	161	80	211	250
									5th	180	153	289	250
INDIA									6th	180	173	–	266
Kapil Dev	19	4	46	2	24	4	74	3	7th	212	196	–	267
Binny	12	0	49	2					8th	241	197	–	–
Sharma	14	1	40	1	(2) 20	4	65	3	9th	242	198	–	–
Shastri	6	2	28	0	24	5	57	0	10th	249	198	–	–
Maninder	12.3	4	31	4	(3) 34	11	99	0					

Umpires: D.P.Buultjens (2) and M.D.D.N.Gooneratne (1).   ‡ (L.Sivaramakrishnan)

Close: 1st day – I(1) 197-6 (Gavaskar 22, Binny 10); 2nd – SL(1) 153-5 (Mendis 30, Ahangama 0); 3rd – I(2) 149-1 (Shastri 68, Amarnath 28); 4th – SL(2) 78-3 (Dias 24, Mendis 29).

PAKISTAN v SRI LANKA 1985-86 (1st Test)

At Iqbal Stadium, Faisalabad, on 16, 17, 18, 20, 21 October.
Toss: Sri Lanka.   Result: MATCH DRAWN.
Debuts: None.

Sri Lanka's second series in Pakistan began with a high-scoring and meaningless draw on a typically dead Iqbal Stadium pitch, 1,034 runs being scored for the loss of 13 wickets. The captains agreed to abandon the game when Omar was dismissed soon after tea on the last day. Pakistan's captain and Hanif Mohammad (Chairman of Selectors) chose an old pitch in preference to a more lively relaid one. Aravinda de Silva's maiden Test hundred was completed a day after his 20th birthday with a six off Imran, the latter returning to Test cricket after a two-year absence. De Silva batted 510 minutes, hitting 17 fours and three sixes; his stand of 121 with Ranatunga established a sixth-wicket national record against Pakistan. Miandad and Omar added 397 for the third wicket, the eighth-highest stand in Test history and highest against Sri Lanka, and registered their third and second double centuries respectively.

SRI LANKA

S.Wettimuny	lbw b Qadir	52
†S.A.R.Silva	c Shoaib b Imran	17
R.S.Madugalle	b Mudassar	5
R.L.Dias	c Ashraf b Jalaluddin	48
*L.R.D.Mendis	lbw b Imran	15
A.Ranatunga	c Shoaib b Qadir	79
P.A.de Silva	c Ashraf b Imran	122
J.R.Ratnayeke	run out	34
A.L.F. de Mel	c Ashraf b Wasim	17
R.J.Ratnayake	lbw b Qadir	56
R.G.C.E.Wijesuriya	not out	7
Extras	(B4, LB11, W2, NB10)	27
Total		**479**

PAKISTAN

Mudassar Nazar	lbw b Ratnayake	78
Shoaib Mohammad	c Silva b Ratnayake	33
Qasim Omar	b Ratnayeke	206
*Javed Miandad	not out	203
Zaheer Abbas		
Salim Malik		
Imran Khan		
†Ashraf Ali	did not bat	
Abdul Qadir		
Wasim Akram		
Jalaluddin		
Extras	(B6, LB17, W1, NB11)	35
Total	(3 wickets)	**555**

PAKISTAN	O	M	R	W	O	M	R	W		FALL OF WICKETS	
										SL	P
Imran	49	15	112	3					*Wkt*	*1st*	*1st*
Wasim	42.3	12	98	1					1st	23	86
Jalaluddin	39	12	89	1					2nd	40	158
Mudassar	13.3	3	29	1					3rd	125	555
Qadir	54.3	17	132	3					4th	129	–
Shoaib	2	1	4	0					5th	165	–
									6th	286	–
SRI LANKA									7th	352	–
De Mel	27	3	106	0					8th	391	–
Ratnayake	32	4	93	2					9th	443	–
Ratnayeke	29.5	3	117	1					10th	479	–
Wijesuriya	44	13	102	0							
Ranatunga	18	1	74	0							
Madugalle	7	1	18	0							
De Silva	5	0	22	0							

Umpires: Khizer Hayat (16) and Mahboob Shah (15).

Close: 1st day – SL(1) 180-5 (Ranatunga 26, De Silva 8); 2nd – SL(1) 363-7 (De Silva 93, De Mel 0); 3rd – P(1) 86-0 (Mudassar 42, Shoaib 33); 4th – P(1) 313-2 (Omar 95, Miandad 81).

PAKISTAN v SRI LANKA 1985-86 (2nd Test)

At Jinnath Stadium, Sialkot, on 27, 28, 29, 31 October.
Toss: Pakistan.   Result: PAKISTAN won by eight wickets.
Debuts: None.

Jinnah Stadium provided Test cricket's 59th venue and Pakistan's 11th. Taking full advantage of a pitch which encouraged seam bowling, Ravi Ratnayeke returned Sri Lanka's best analysis in Test cricket. Pakistan completed their victory on the fourth morning. In the last of his 78 appearances, Zaheer Abbas extended his aggregate to 5,062 runs (average 44.79). Dias (5) retired for an X-ray on his left wrist at 49 and resumed at 110. Following scores of 203 not out and 40, Javed Miandad resigned the captaincy with effect from the end of this series 'to concentrate on his batting'. This 'self-imposed' interregnum was to last just two years.

SRI LANKA

S.Wettimuny	c Salim Yousuf b Imran	45	lbw b Imran	0
†S.A.R.Silva	c Omar b Mudassar	12	c Wasim b Mudassar	35
R.S.Madugalle	c Salim Yousuf b Mohsin Kamal	0	c Miandad b Mohsin Kamal	65
R.L.Dias	c Omar b Mohsin Kamal	21	lbw b Mudassar	7
*L.R.D.Mendis	c Mudassar b Mohsin Kamal	20	c Salim Yousuf b Wasim	3
A.Ranatunga	not out	25	c Salim Malik b Imran	28
P.A.de Silva	hit wkt b Imran	2	c Salim Yousuf b Wasim	8
J.R.Ratnayeke	c Salim Yousuf b Imran	0	not out	17
A.L.F.de Mel	lbw b Wasim	1	b Imran	0
R.J.Ratnayake	b Imran	1	c sub (Ramiz Raja) b Imran	2
R.G.C.E.Wijesuriya	lbw b Wasim	8	lbw b Imran	0
Extras	(B6, LB2, W3, NB11)	22	(B9, LB10, NB16)	35
Total		**157**		**200**

PAKISTAN

Mudassar Nazar	c Silva b Ratnayake	78	not out	24
Mohsin Khan	lbw b Ratnayake	50	run out	44
Qasim Omar	c Wijesuriya b Ratnayeke	1	c Ranatunga b De Mel	3
*Javed Miandad	lbw b Ratnayeke	40		
Zaheer Abbas	b Ratnayeke	4		
Salim Malik	lbw b Ratnayeke	22		
Imran Khan	c sub‡ b Ratnayeke	6		
†Salim Yousuf	lbw b Ratnayeke	23	(4) not out	13
Abdul Qadir	c Silva b Ratnayeke	10		
Wasim Akram	c Silva b Ratnayeke	4		
Mohsin Kamal	not out	4		
Extras	(B5, LB3, W1, NB8)	17	(B4, LB4, NB8)	16
Total		**259**	(2 wickets)	**100**

PAKISTAN	O	M	R	W		O	M	R	W		FALL OF WICKETS			
											SL	P	SL	P
Imran	19	3	55	4		18.3	5	40	5	Wkt	1st	1st	2nd	2nd
Wasim	14.2	4	38	2	(3)	19	4	74	2	1st	41	88	0	76
Mohsin Kamal	17	3	50	3	(2)	12	2	38	1	2nd	41	93	98	82
Mudassar	6	1	6	1	(5)	11.5	1	28	2	3rd	81	181	111	–
Qadir					(4)	1.1	0	1	0	4th	99	185	121	–
										5th	101	209	147	–
SRI LANKA										6th	101	216	163	–
De Mel	15	3	63	0	(2)	10	1	43	1	7th	110	216	188	–
Ratnayake	18	2	77	2	(1)	6	0	24	0	8th	130	245	188	–
Ratnayeke	23.2	5	83	8		7.4	1	25	0	9th	131	252	200	–
Ranatunga	3	0	18	0						10th	157	259	200	–
Wijesuriya	4	1	10	0										

Umpires: Javed Akhtar (11) and Mian Mohammad Aslam (2).   ‡ (A.P.Gurusinha)

Close: 1st day – P(1) 4-0 (Mudassar 2, Mohsin Khan 1); 2nd – P(1) 259 all out; 3rd – P(2) 1-0 (Mudassar 1, Mohsin Khan 0).

PAKISTAN v SRI LANKA 1985-86 (3rd Test)

At National Stadium, Karachi, on 7, 8, 9, 11 November.
Toss: Sri Lanka.   Result: PAKISTAN won by ten wickets.
Debuts: Sri Lanka – A.P.Gurusinha.

On a closely shaved pitch which took spin from the first morning, Pakistan completed their second decisive victory in succession before lunch on the fourth day. De Silva's second Test hundred took 265 minutes and was completed with his 16th four; a remarkable innings, it was achieved on a pitch where mere survival was often difficult. Imran took over the captaincy in the second innings after Miandad had sustained a hairline fracture to his right thumb while batting on the second day. On the fourth morning Pakistan were led by their third captain, Mudassar, after Imran had strained a thigh muscle soon after taking his 249th Test wicket. Play was halted for 20 minutes on the third day when spectators hurled fruit and other missiles on to the square. Wijesuriya (left-arm orthodox spin) usurped J.J.Warr as the most expensive wicket-taker in Test cricket: 1 for 294.

SRI LANKA

S.Wettimuny	b Wasim	17		c Salim Yousuf b Imran	10
J.R.Ratnayeke	b Qadir	36		c Salim Yousuf b Imran	3
R.S.Madugalle	lbw b Wasim	0	(8)	b Tausif	5
R.L.Dias	c Salim Yousuf b Imran	7		c Salim Malik b Qadir	4
*L.R.D.Mendis	c Miandad b Qadir	15	(7)	b Imran	2
A.Ranatunga	c Miandad b Tausif	12	(5)	c Salim Yousuf b Wasim	25
P.A.de Silva	c and b Qadir	13	(3)	c Salim Yousuf b Tausif	105
†A.P.Gurusinha	lbw b Imran	17	(6)	c Salim Yousuf b Tausif	12
A.L.F.de Mel	st Salim Yousuf b Qadir	3		b Tausif	18
R.J.Ratnayake	not out	21		c Omar b Tausif	22
R.G.C.E.Wijesuriya	lbw b Qadir	2		not out	2
Extras	(B5, LB10, W1, NB3)	19		(B5, LB11, NB6)	22
Total		**162**			**230**

PAKISTAN

Mudassar Nazar	c Gurusinha b De Mel	16		not out	57
Mohsin Khan	c Gurusinha b De Mel	13		not out	36
Qasim Omar	c Ranatunga b De Mel	8			
*Javed Miandad	lbw b De Mel	63			
Salim Malik	b De Mel	4			
Ramiz Raja	c and b De Mel	52			
Imran Khan	c Ratnayake b Ratnayeke	63			
†Salim Yousuf	lbw b Ratnayeke	27			
Abdul Qadir	c Wettimuny b Wijesuriya	19			
Tausif Ahmed	b Ratnayeke	1			
Wasim Akram	not out	5			
Extras	(B13, LB8, W2, NB1)	24		(B1, LB3, NB1)	5
Total		**295**		(0 wickets)	**98**

PAKISTAN	O	M	R	W	O	M	R	W	FALL OF WICKETS				
Imran	20	9	36	2	14.1	5	28	3		SL	P	SL	P
Wasim	14	7	17	2	14	4	24	1	*Wkt*	*1st*	*1st*	*2nd*	*2nd*
Tausif	22	10	50	1	(5) 23.2	8	54	5	1st	27	27	14	–
Qadir	20.5	5	44	5	(3) 25.5	4	102	1	2nd	28	43	15	–
Mudassar					(4) 3	0	6	0	3rd	60	60	57	–
									4th	89	68	104	–
SRI LANKA									5th	90	153	132	–
De Mel	22	1	109	6	3	0	28	0	6th	106	228	139	–
Ratnayake	15	2	48	2	4	0	33	0	7th	122	259	157	–
Ratnayeke	15	4	48	1	6	1	24	0	8th	125	288	191	–
Wijesuriya	22	5	68	1	3.4	2	9	0	9th	151	290	221	–
Ranatunga	1	0	1	0					10th	162	295	230	–

Umpires: Khizer Hayat (17) and Mahboob Shah (16).

Close: 1st day – SL(1) 162 all out; 2nd – P(1) 294-9 (Tausif 1, Wasim 4); 3rd – SL(2) 216-8 (De Silva 103, Ratnayake 13).

AUSTRALIA v NEW ZEALAND 1985-86 (1st Test)

At Woolloongabba, Brisbane, on 8, 9, 10, 11, 12 November.
Toss: New Zealand.   Result: NEW ZEALAND won by an innings and 41 runs.
Debuts: New Zealand – V.R.Brown.

At their seventh attempt New Zealand gained their first victory in Australia. Hadlee's innings (9 for 52) and match (15 for 123) analyses are records for New Zealand. Only J.C.Laker (twice) and G.A.Lohmann had achieved better innings analyses in Tests. New Zealand's record total surpassed their 551 for 9 declared at Lord's in 1973. Reid's sixth hundred took 341 minutes while Martin Crowe's third required 261 minutes; their partnership of 224 was a national third-wicket record against all countries until 1986-87. Crowe batted 472 minutes, faced 328 balls and hit 26 fours. Border and Matthews added 197 to set a national sixth-wicket partnership against New Zealand, the latter reaching his maiden hundred with a six in 198 minutes. Border's 15th three-figure innings occupied 468 minutes (301 balls) and included two sixes and 20 fours. Wessels announced his retirement from Test cricket after contractual differences with the ACB.

AUSTRALIA

K.C.Wessels	lbw b Hadlee	70	(2) c Brown b Chatfield		3
A.M.J.Hilditch	c Chatfield b Hadlee	0	(1) c Chatfield b Hadlee		12
D.C.Boon	c Coney b Hadlee	31	c Smith b Chatfield		1
*A.R.Border	c Edgar b Hadlee	1	not out		152
G.M.Ritchie	c M.D.Crowe b Hadlee	8	c Coney b Snedden		20
*W.B.Phillips	b Hadlee	34	b Hadlee		2
G.R.J.Matthews	b Hadlee	2	c Coney b Hadlee		115
G.F.Lawson	c Hadlee b Brown	8	(9) c Brown b Chatfield		7
C.J.McDermott	c Coney b Hadlee	9	(8) c and b Hadlee		5
D.R.Gilbert	not out	0	c Chatfield b Hadlee		10
R.G.Holland	c Brown b Hadlee	0	b Hadlee		0
Extras	(B9, LB5, NB2)	16	(LB3, NB3)		6
Total		**179**			**333**

NEW ZEALAND

B.A.Edgar	c Phillips b Gilbert	17
J.G.Wright	lbw b Matthews	46
J.F.Reid	c Border b Gilbert	108
M.D.Crowe	b Matthews	188
*J.V.Coney	c Phillips b Lawson	22
J.J.Crowe	c Holland b Matthews	35
V.R.Brown	not out	36
R.J.Hadlee	c Phillips b McDermott	54
*I.D.S.Smith	not out	2
M.C.Snedden	} did not bat	
E.J.Chatfield		
Extras	(B2, LB11, NB32)	45
Total	(7 wickets declared)	**553**

NEW ZEALAND	O	M	R	W	O	M	R	W			FALL OF WICKETS	
Hadlee	23.4	4	52	9	28.5	9	71	6		A	NZ	A
Chatfield	18	6	29	0	32	9	75	3	*Wkt*	*1st*	*1st*	*2nd*
Snedden	11	1	45	0	19	3	66	1	1st	1	36	14
M.D.Crowe	5	0	14	0	9	2	19	0	2nd	70	85	16
Brown	12	5	17	1	25	5	96	0	3rd	72	309	16
Coney	7	5	8	0	3	1	3	0	4th	82	362	47
									5th	148	427	67
AUSTRALIA									6th	150	471	264
Lawson	36.5	8	96	1					7th	159	549	272
McDermott	31	3	119	1					8th	175	–	291
Gilbert	39	4	102	2					9th	179	–	333
Matthews	31	5	110	3					10th	179	–	333
Holland	22	3	106	0								
Border	0.1	0	0	0								
Wessels	1	0	7	0								

Umpires: A.R.Crafter (17) and R.A.French (15).

Close: 1st day – A(1) 146-4 (Wessels 69, Phillips 25); 2nd – NZ(1) 209-2 (Reid 71, M.D.Crowe 58); 3rd – NZ(1) 553-7 (Brown 36, Smith 2); 4th – A(2) 266-6 (Border 106, McDermott 1).

AUSTRALIA v NEW ZEALAND 1985-86 (2nd Test)

At Sydney Cricket Ground on 22, 23, 24, 25, 26 November.
Toss: Australia.   Result: AUSTRALIA won by four wickets.
Debuts: Australia – R.B.Kerr.

With just 23 balls to spare, Australia levelled the series on a slow, turning pitch after Border had astounded most pundits by opting to field first. New Zealand were rescued by a last-wicket partnership of 124 in 137 minutes between spin bowlers Bracewell (hastily summoned from home because of the pitch) and Boock. The latter contributed his highest first-class score to Test cricket's 11th and sixth-highest three-figure tenth-wicket partnership. Australia needed 260 to win in almost a day and a half but rain prevented play after tea on the fourth day. The pitch 'sweated' under the covers that night and, bound together by that moisture, became its most placid on the crucial final day. Boon, fighting for his Test place, achieved his highest score to date. Holland was the first to be dismissed for nought in five successive Test innings.

NEW ZEALAND

Batsman	Dismissal 1	Score 1	Dismissal 2	Score 2
J.G.Wright	c O'Donnell b Bright	38	c and b Matthews	43
B.A.Edgar	c Border b Holland	50	c and b Holland	52
J.F.Reid	c Kerr b Holland	7	b Matthews	19
M.D.Crowe	run out	8	b Holland	0
*J.V.Coney	c Border b Holland	8	b Holland	7
J.J.Crowe	b Holland	13	c and b Holland	6
V.R.Brown	lbw b Holland	0	b Bright	15
†I.D.S.Smith	c Hookes b Bright	28	c and b Bright	12
R.J.Hadlee	lbw b Holland	5	lbw b Gilbert	26
J.G.Bracewell	not out	83	not out	2
S.L.Boock	lbw b Gilbert	37	c Boon b Bright	3
Extras	(B6, LB8, NB2)	16	(B1, LB4, NB3)	8
Total		**293**		**193**

AUSTRALIA

Batsman	Dismissal 1	Score 1	Dismissal 2	Score 2
†W.B.Phillips	b Bracewell	31	c Bracewell b Boock	63
R.B.Kerr	lbw b Hadlee	7	c Wright b Bracewell	7
D.C.Boon	lbw b Hadlee	0	c Reid b Bracewell	81
*A.R.Border	b Bracewell	20	st Smith b Bracewell	11
G.M.Ritchie	c J.J.Crowe b Hadlee	89	c M.D.Crowe b Hadlee	13
D.W.Hookes	run out	0	not out	38
G.R.J.Matthews	c Smith b Hadlee	50	lbw b Hadlee	32
S.P.O'Donnell	not out	20	not out	2
R.J.Bright	lbw b Boock	1		
D.R.Gilbert	c Smith b Hadlee	0		
R.G.Holland	st Smith b Boock	0		
Extras	(B5, LB2, NB2)	9	(B3, LB9, NB1)	13
Total		**227**	(6 wickets)	**260**

AUSTRALIA	O	M	R	W	O	M	R	W		FALL OF WICKETS			
										NZ	A	NZ	A
Gilbert	20.3	6	41	1	9	2	22	1	Wkt	1st	1st	2nd	2nd
O'Donnell	6	2	13	0	5	4	4	0	1st	79	19	100	27
Bright	34	12	87	2	(5) 17.5	3	39	3	2nd	92	22	106	132
Matthews	17	3	32	0	30	11	55	2	3rd	109	48	107	144
Holland	47	19	106	6	(3) 41	16	68	4	4th	112	71	119	163
									5th	128	71	131	192
NEW ZEALAND									6th	128	186	137	258
Hadlee	24	2	65	5	27.1	10	58	2	7th	161	224	162	–
M.D.Crowe	5	2	15	0	2	1	7	0	8th	166	225	163	–
Bracewell	25	9	51	2	30	7	91	3	9th	169	226	190	–
Boock	29.5	14	53	2	22	4	49	1	10th	293	227	193	–
Brown	13	3	35	0	7	0	28	0					
Coney	1	0	1	0	9	1	15	0					

Umpires: M.W.Johnson (19) and B.E.Martin (1).

Close: 1st day – NZ(1) 217-9 (Bracewell 35, Boock 11); 2nd – A(1) 175-5 (Ritchie 60, Matthews 48); 3rd – NZ(2) 119-3 (Reid 10, Coney 7); 4th – A(2) 36-1 (Phillips 17, Boon 6).

AUSTRALIA v NEW ZEALAND 1985-86 (3rd Test)

At W.A.C.A.Ground, Perth, on 30 November, 1, 2, 3, 4 December.
Toss: New Zealand.   Result: NEW ZEALAND won by six wickets.
Debuts: None.

New Zealand won their first series against Australia and became the first holders of the Trans-Tasman Trophy. An intricately designed award featuring fans comprising 11 bats and 11 balls of diminishing sizes, the largest ball bearing raised maps of the two countries, it was presented at the start of this rubber by the Australia New Zealand Foundation. Their victory was achieved with ten overs to spare and on a newly repositioned square, the pitch being relaid only two months previously. Hadlee took his career aggregate to 299 wickets and his tally for the series to 33, a record for New Zealand; only G.A.Lohmann (35 on South African mats in 1895-96) has claimed more wickets in a three-match rubber.

AUSTRALIA

†W.B.Phillips	c Smith b Chatfield	37	c Smith b Chatfield		10
R.B.Kerr	c Smith b Chatfield	17	b Hadlee		0
D.C.Boon	c Bracewell b Hadlee	12	b Hadlee		50
*A.R.Border	c Smith b Hadlee	12	b Hadlee		83
G.M.Ritchie	lbw b Coney	6	c M.D.Crowe b Coney		44
D.W.Hookes	c Bracewell b Coney	14	b Bracewell		7
G.R.J.Matthews	b Hadlee	34	lbw b Hadlee		14
G.F.Lawson	c J.J.Crowe b Hadlee	11	c J.J.Crowe b Hadlee		21
C.J.McDermott	b Chatfield	36	lbw b Bracewell		11
D.R.Gilbert	not out	12	b Hadlee		3
R.G.Holland	c M.D.Crowe b Hadlee	4	not out		0
Extras	(LB6, NB2)	8	(B2, LB5, NB9)		16
Total		**203**			**259**

NEW ZEALAND

J.G.Wright	c Phillips b Lawson	20	b Gilbert		35
B.A.Edgar	c Hookes b McDermott	74	c Border b Matthews		16
J.F.Reid	b Gilbert	7	c Phillips b Gilbert		28
M.D.Crowe	lbw b McDermott	71	not out		42
*J.V.Coney	c Phillips b Lawson	19	b Gilbert		16
J.J.Crowe	lbw b Holland	17	not out		2
R.J.Hadlee	c Hookes b Holland	26			
†I.D.S.Smith	c Matthews b Lawson	12			
J.G.Bracewell	not out	28			
B.L.Cairns	c Ritchie b Holland	0			
E.J.Chatfield	c Phillips b Lawson	3			
Extras	(B1, LB7, NB14)	22	(B7, LB7, NB11)		25
Total		**299**	(4 wickets)		**164**

NEW ZEALAND	O	M	R	W	O	M	R	W		FALL OF WICKETS			
Hadlee	26.5	6	65	5	39	11	90	6		A	NZ	A	NZ
Cairns	14	1	50	0	26	6	59	0	Wkt	1st	1st	2nd	2nd
Chatfield	16	6	33	3	30	9	47	1	1st	38	43	3	47
Coney	21	11	43	2	(5) 8	5	9	1	2nd	63	55	28	77
Bracewell	6	3	6	0	(4) 28.5	8	47	2	3rd	78	184	109	121
									4th	85	191	195	149
AUSTRALIA									5th	85	215	207	–
Lawson	47	12	79	4	21	7	35	0	6th	114	253	214	–
McDermott	33	9	66	2	(3) 13	1	27	0	7th	131	256	234	–
Gilbert	31	9	75	1	(2) 23	5	48	3	8th	159	273	251	–
Holland	40	12	63	3	(5) 8	1	27	0	9th	190	276	255	–
Matthews	5	3	6	0	(4) 9	3	13	1	10th	203	299	259	–
Hookes	1	0	2	0									

Umpires: R.C.Isherwood (2) and P.J.McConnell (5).

Close: 1st day – NZ(1) 8-0 (Wright 3, Edgar 4); 2nd – NZ(1) 184-2 (Edgar 74, M.D.Crowe 70); 3rd – A(2) 38-2 (Boon 18, Border 5); 4th – A(2) 239-7 (Lawson 15, McDermott 2).

AUSTRALIA v INDIA 1985-86 (1st Test)

At Adelaide Oval on 13, 14, 15, 16, 17 December.
Toss: Australia.   Result: MATCH DRAWN.
Debuts: Australia – M.G.Hughes, G.R.Marsh, B.A.Reid.

A bland pitch and the loss of five hours to rain combined to produce a tame draw. Australia introduced three new caps, including their tallest-ever representative, Bruce Reid, a 6ft 8in cousin of New Zealand's J.F.Reid. Boon took 285 minutes to reach the first hundred in Test cricket by a resident Tasmanian, while Ritchie's third century took 44 minutes longer. Kapil Dev finished with a spell of 5 for 4 from 21 balls to achieve India's best analysis in Australia and the second-best in Tests at Adelaide after A.E.Trott's 8 for 43 in *Test No. 44*. Gavaskar, who retired overnight at 97 (when 39) after being struck on the elbow, resumed at 247 and extended his world record number of Test hundreds to 31. After completing his sixth hundred against Australia in 368 minutes (286 balls), he became the first batsman to reach 9,000 runs (when 160) having earlier completed 1,000 runs against Australia. His series record tenth-wicket partnership of 94 with Yadav took India to their highest total against Australia until the third Test.

AUSTRALIA

†W.B.Phillips	c Yadav b Kapil Dev	11			
D.C.Boon	c Vengsarkar b Kapil Dev	123	(1)	not out	11
G.R.Marsh	c Sharma b Binny	5	(2)	not out	2
*A.R.Border	b Kapil Dev	49			
G.M.Ritchie	c Kirmani b Kapil Dev	128			
D.W.Hookes	b Yadav	34			
G.R.J.Matthews	lbw b Kapil Dev	18			
R.J.Bright	not out	5			
C.J.McDermott	lbw b Kapil Dev	0			
B.A.Reid	c Gavaskar b Kapil Dev	2			
M.G.Hughes	c Vengsarkar b Kapil Dev	0			
Extras	(LB4, NB2)	6	(LB3, NB1)		4
Total		**381**	(0 wickets)		**17**

INDIA

S.M.Gavaskar	not out	166
K.Srikkanth	c Ritchie b McDermott	51
C.Sharma	c Phillips b Reid	54
D.B.Vengsarkar	c Phillips b Hughes	7
M.Azharuddin	c Phillips b Reid	17
M.Amarnath	c Marsh b McDermott	37
R.J.Shastri	b Reid	42
*Kapil Dev	lbw b Bright	38
R.M.H.Binny	c Phillips b McDermott	38
†S.M.H.Kirmani	c Boon b Reid	7
N.S.Yadav	c Hughes b Hookes	41
Extras	(B2, LB7, W1, NB12)	22
Total		**520**

INDIA	O	M	R	W	O	M	R	W		FALL OF WICKETS		
Kapil Dev	38	6	106	8	3	1	3	0		A	I	A
Binny	24	7	56	1					*Wkt*	*1st*	*1st*	*2nd*
Sharma	19	3	70	0	(2) 2	0	9	0	1st	19	95	–
Yadav	27	6	66	1	(3) 2	1	2	0	2nd	33	131	–
Shastri	38	11	70	0	(4) 1	1	1	0	3rd	124	171	–
Amarnath	3	0	9	0					4th	241	187	–
									5th	318	247	–
AUSTRALIA									6th	374	273	–
McDermott	48	14	131	3					7th	375	333	–
Hughes	38	6	123	1					8th	375	409	–
Reid	53	22	113	4					9th	381	426	–
Bright	44	15	80	1					10th	381	520	–
Matthews	17	2	60	0								
Hookes	2	0	4	1								

Umpires: A.R.Crafter (18) and S.G.Randell (2).

Close: 1st day – A(1) 248-4 (Ritchie 55, Hookes 2); – I(1) 97-1 (Gavaskar 39, Sharma 1); 3rd – I(1) 176-3 (Azharuddin 12, Amarnath 4); 4th – I(1) 391-7 (Gavaskar 94, Binny 34).

AUSTRALIA v INDIA 1985-86 (2nd Test)

At Melbourne Cricket Ground on 26, 27, 28, 29, 30 December.
Toss: India.   Result: MATCH DRAWN.
Debuts: Australia – S.R.Waugh.

Thunderstorms at tea on the final day left India 67 runs short of their target with eight wickets in hand and prevented Kapil Dev from leading India to victory for the first time in 19 Tests. When he had scored 46 in this, his 73rd Test, he became the third player after G.St A.Sobers (80 Tests) and I.T.Botham (55) to achieve the double of 3,000 runs and 200 wickets. Matthews scored the last 41 runs of his second Test hundred in 49 minutes after being joined by last man Gilbert. On the final day the latter survived for 115 minutes in what was to prove a match-saving tenth-wicket stand of 77 (an Australia record v India) with Border (163 in 410 minutes off 358 balls with 16 fours). Srikkanth's swashbuckling 86 had included the same number of boundaries and required only 89 balls.

AUSTRALIA

†W.B.Phillips	b Yadav	7	(7)	c Srikkanth b Yadav	13
D.C.Boon	lbw b Shastri	14		c and b Kapil Dev	19
G.R.Marsh	c Sivaramakrishnan b Yadav	30	(1)	c Sivaramakrishnan b Shastri	19
*A.R.Border	c and b Sivaramakrishnan	11	(3)	st Kirmani b Yadav	163
D.W.Hookes	b Shastri	42	(4)	c Srikkanth b Shastri	0
S.R.Waugh	c Kapil Dev b Sivaramakrishnan	13	(5)	b Shastri	5
G.R.J.Matthews	not out	100	(6)	c Azharuddin b Sivaramakrishnan	16
R.J.Bright	b Shastri	28		lbw b Kapil Dev	20
C.J.McDermott	c Kapil Dev b Shastri	1		c and b Shastri	2
B.A.Reid	c Srikkanth b Kapil Dev	1		c Sivaramakrishnan b Yadav	13
D.R.Gilbert	c Kirmani b Yadav	4		not out	10
Extras	(B5, LB6)	11		(B11, LB16, NB1)	28
Total		**262**			**308**

INDIA

S.M.Gavaskar	b Gilbert	6	b Reid	8
K.Srikkanth	lbw b Gilbert	86	c Bright b Reid	38
M.Amarnath	c Phillips b Reid	45	not out	3
D.B.Vengsarkar	c and b Matthews	75	not out	1
M.Azharuddin	b Matthews	37		
R.J.Shastri	c Phillips b Waugh	49		
*Kapil Dev	c Hookes b Reid	55		
R.M.H.Binny	c Matthews b Reid	0		
†S.M.H.Kirmani	c Phillips b Waugh	35		
L.Sivaramakrishnan	c Phillips b Reid	15		
N.S.Yadav	not out	6		
Extras	(B4, LB15, NB17)	36	(B4, LB1, NB4)	9
Total		**445**	**(2 wickets)**	**59**

INDIA	O	M	R	W	O	M	R	W		FALL OF WICKETS			
Kapil Dev	23	6	38	1	22	7	53	2		A	I	A	I
Binny	3	0	11	0					Wkt	1st	1st	2nd	2nd
Shastri	37	13	87	4	47	13	92	4	1st	22	15	32	39
Yadav	27.5	10	64	3	38.5	15	84	3	2nd	26	116	54	57
Sivaramakrishnan	13	2	51	2	13	1	43	1	3rd	41	172	54	–
Amarnath					(2) 3	0	9	0	4th	90	246	84	–
									5th	109	291	126	–
AUSTRALIA									6th	127	370	161	–
McDermott	15	5	52	0	6	1	17	0	7th	193	372	202	–
Gilbert	22	1	81	2	4	0	9	0	8th	195	420	205	–
Reid	38.2	11	100	4	8	1	23	2	9th	216	425	231	–
Bright	31	8	76	0	7	4	5	0	10th	262	445	308	–
Matthews	31	7	81	2									
Waugh	11	5	36	2									

Umpires: R.A.French (16) and R.C.Isherwood (3).

Close: 1st day – A(1) 210-8 (Matthews 54, Reid 0); 2nd – I(1) 187-3 (Vengsarkar 38, Azharuddin 5); 3rd – I(1) 431-9 (Sivaramakrishnan 6, Yadav 2); 4th – A(2) 228-8 (Border 98, Reid 11).

AUSTRALIA v INDIA 1985-86 (3rd Test)

At Sydney Cricket Ground on 2, 3, 4, 5, 6 January.
Toss: India.   Result: MATCH DRAWN.
Debuts: None.

For the second match running Australia were fortunate to avoid what would have been their fourth home defeat by India who again achieved a new record total for this series. Srikkanth, aided by a runner for most of his innings, hit 22 (046444) off an over from Holland and needed only 97 balls (152 minutes) for his first Test hundred. With Gavaskar and Amarnath, who scored their 32nd and tenth Test hundreds respectively, he had benefited from some poor fielding, five chances going astray on the first day. Boon, who registered his second hundred in three matches as an opener, shared in Australia's first century opening partnership since 1981-82 (*Test No. 923*) and their highest against India. After Border had completed 1,000 runs against India, Australia lost their last five wickets for nine runs and followed on. That they managed to survive for 77 overs was mainly due to Ritchie who defended for 166 minutes, the last 20 with Bright.

INDIA

S.M.Gavaskar	b Holland	172
K.Srikkanth	b Reid	116
M.Amarnath	c Bright b Gilbert	138
*Kapil Dev	b Gilbert	42
D.B.Vengsarkar	not out	37
M.Azharuddin	not out	59
R.J.Shastri		
†S.M.H.Kirmani		
C.Sharma	did not bat	
L.Sivaramakrishnan		
N.S.Yadav		
Extras	(B5, LB9, NB22)	36
Total	**(4 wickets declared)**	**600**

AUSTRALIA

D.C.Boon	b Kapil Dev	131	(2)	run out	25
G.R.Marsh	c Gavaskar b Shastri	92	(1)	lbw b Yadav	28
*A.R.Border	c Sharma b Shastri	71	(7)	c Sivaramakrishnan b Yadav	4
G.M.Ritchie	c Kapil Dev b Yadav	14	(3)	not out	17
†W.B.Phillips	c Srikkanth b Shastri	14		c Srikkanth b Shastri	22
G.R.J.Matthews	c Amarnath b Yadav	40		c Kapil Dev b Yadav	17
S.R.Waugh	c Sivaramakrishnan b Yadav	8	(4)	lbw b Shastri	0
R.J.Bright	c Kirmani b Shastri	3		not out	0
D.R.Gilbert	c Azharuddin b Yadav	1			
B.A.Reid	st Kirmani b Yadav	4			
R.G.Holland	not out	1			
Extras	(LB14, NB3)	17		(B3, LB2, NB1)	6
Total		**396**		**(6 wickets)**	**119**

AUSTRALIA	O	M	R	W	O	M	R	W		FALL OF WICKETS		
										I	A	A
Gilbert	37	3	135	2					Wkt	1st	1st	2nd
Reid	34	8	89	1					1st	191	217	57
Bright	41	7	121	0					2nd	415	258	57
Holland	21	6	113	1					3rd	485	277	60
Matthews	29	2	95	0					4th	510	302	87
Waugh	7	0	33	0					5th	–	369	111
									6th	–	387	115
INDIA									7th	–	388	–
Kapil Dev	25	8	65	1	7	3	11	0	8th	–	390	–
Shastri	57	21	101	4	(4) 25	12	36	2	9th	–	395	–
Yadav	62.3	2	99	5	(2) 33	22	19	3	10th	–	396	–
Sivaramakrishnan	22	2	79	0	(5) 9	0	37	0				
Sharma	13	2	38	0	(3) 3	0	11	0				

Umpires: P.J.McConnell (6) and S.G.Randell (3).

Close: 1st day – I(1) 334-1 (Gavaskar 132, Amarnath 72); 2nd – A(1) 4-0 (Boon 2, Marsh 1); 3rd – A(1) 169-0 (Boon 100, Marsh 54); 4th – A(1) 347-4 (Border 64, Matthews 15).

NEW ZEALAND v AUSTRALIA 1985-86 (1st Test)

At Basin Reserve, Wellington, on 21, 22, 23, 24, 25 (*no play*) February.
Toss: New Zealand.   Result: MATCH DRAWN.
Debuts: New Zealand – S.R.Gillespie; Australia – S.P.Davis, T.J.Zoehrer.

At 4.07 on the first afternoon, with his 15,400th ball in 61 matches, Richard Hadlee became the sixth bowler (first New Zealander) to take 300 Test wickets. Only D.K.Lillee (56) had reached the mark in fewer matches, and only F.S.Trueman (14,584) and Lillee (14,942) had achieved it with fewer deliveries. After Ritchie and Matthews had added 213 in 275 minutes to set a new record for Australia's fifth wicket against New Zealand, the last six wickets fell for 56 runs in 87 minutes. Coney, leading New Zealand for the first time at home, emulated Matthews by scoring his third Test hundred, and shared in record sixth (109) and seventh-wicket (132 unbroken) stands with Rutherford (who advanced his Test average from 1.71) and Hadlee respectively. Rain allowed only 81 minutes of play on the fourth day and none on the fifth.

AUSTRALIA

D.C.Boon	c Smith b Troup	70
G.R.Marsh	c Coney b Chatfield	43
W.B.Phillips	b Gillespie	32
*A.R.Border	lbw b Hadlee	13
G.M.Ritchie	b Troup	92
G.R.J.Matthews	c Rutherford b Coney	130
S.R.Waugh	c Smith b Coney	11
†T.J.Zoehrer	c sub (J.G.Bracewell) b Coney	18
C.J.McDermott	b Hadlee	2
B.A.Reid	not out	0
S.P.Davis	c and b Hadlee	0
Extras	(B2, LB9, W4, NB9)	24
Total		**435**

NEW ZEALAND

T.J.Franklin	c Border b McDermott	0
B.A.Edgar	c Waugh b Matthews	38
J.F.Reid	c Phillips b Reid	32
S.R.Gillespie	c Border b Reid	28
M.D.Crowe	b Matthews	19
K.R.Rutherford	c sub (R.J.Bright) b Reid	65
*J.V.Coney	not out	101
R.J.Hadlee	not out	72
†I.D.S.Smith		
G.B.Troup	} did not bat	
E.J.Chatfield		
Extras	(B2, LB6, W1, NB15)	24
Total	(6 wickets)	**379**

NEW ZEALAND	O	M	R	W
Hadlee	37.1	5	116	3
Chatfield	36	10	96	1
Troup	28	6	86	2
Gillespie	27	2	79	1
Coney	18	7	47	3

AUSTRALIA	O	M	R	W
McDermott	25.3	5	80	1
Davis	25	4	70	0
Reid	31	6	104	3
Matthews	37	10	107	2
Border	4	3	1	0
Waugh	4	1	9	0

FALL OF WICKETS

Wkt	A 1st	NZ 1st
1st	104	0
2nd	143	57
3rd	166	94
4th	166	115
5th	379	138
6th	414	247
7th	418	–
8th	435	–
9th	435	–
10th	435	–

Umpires: F.R.Goodall (21) and S.J.Woodward (13).

Close: 1st day – A(1) 285-4 (Ritchie 55, Matthews 55); 2nd – NZ(1) 70-2 (Edgar 28, Gillespie 6); 3rd – NZ (1) 311-6 (Coney 79, Hadlee 27); 4th – NZ(1) 379-6 (Coney 101, Hadlee 72).

NEW ZEALAND v AUSTRALIA 1985-86 (2nd Test)

At Lancaster Park, Christchurch, on 28 February, 1, 2, 3, 4 March.
Toss: New Zealand.   Result: MATCH DRAWN.
Debuts: None.

Marsh and Boon achieved their fourth successive half-century opening partnership: 217, 57, 104, 57. When 78 Border became the fourth Australian after D.G.Bradman, R.N.Harvey and G.S.Chappell to score 6,000 runs in Tests. Batting for a total of 682 minutes in the match (538 balls) Border later became the second Australian after Greg Chappell to score hundreds in both innings of Tests on two occasions. In his 62nd Test (overtaking B.E.Congdon's New Zealand record), Hadlee equalled Botham's world record of 25 instances of five wickets in an innings. When he dismissed Phillips he became the first New Zealand bowler to take 100 wickets against another country. For the first time in ten Tests, Australia achieved a first innings lead. Crowe batted 292 minutes (226 balls, 21 fours). Struck on the chin by a Reid bouncer he retired when 51 (at 117), resuming at 190 to complete his fourth hundred.

AUSTRALIA

G.R.Marsh	b Hadlee	28	(2)	lbw b Bracewell	15
D.C.Boon	c Coney b Hadlee	26	(1)	c Coney b Troup	6
W.B.Phillips	c Smith b Chatfield	1		b Hadlee	25
*A.R.Border	b Chatfield	140		not out	114
G.M.Ritchie	lbw b Hadlee	4		c Smith b Bracewell	11
G.R.J.Matthews	c Smith b Hadlee	6		c sub (J.J.Crowe) b Hadlee	3
S.R.Waugh	lbw b Hadlee	74		c Smith b Bracewell	1
†T.J.Zoehrer	c Coney b Hadlee	30		c Rutherford b Bracewell	13
R.J.Bright	c Smith b Bracewell	21		not out	21
D.R.Gilbert	b Hadlee	15			
B.A.Reid	not out	1			
Extras	(B1, LB9, NB8)	18		(LB6, W1, NB3)	10
Total		**364**		**(7 wickets declared)**	**219**

NEW ZEALAND

B.A.Edgar	lbw b Reid	8		c and b Matthews	9
J.G.Wright	c Zoehrer b Gilbert	10		not out	4
J.F.Reid	c Zoehrer b Waugh	2		not out	0
M.D.Crowe	c Waugh b Reid	137			
K.R.Rutherford	lbw b Gilbert	0			
*J.V.Coney	c Reid b Waugh	98			
R.J.Hadlee	c Zoehrer b Reid	0			
†I.D.S.Smith	b Waugh	22			
J.G.Bracewell	c Marsh b Reid	20			
G.B.Troup	lbw b Waugh	10			
E.J.Chatfield	not out	2			
Extras	(B6, LB8, NB16)	30		(NB3)	3
Total		**339**		**(1 wicket)**	**16**

NEW ZEALAND	O	M	R	W		O	M	R	W		FALL OF WICKETS			
Hadlee	44.4	8	116	7		25	4	47	2			A	NZ	A	NZ
Troup	34	4	104	0		15	0	50	1		Wkt	1st	1st	2nd	2nd
Chatfield	36	13	56	2		17	6	29	0		1st	57	17	15	13
Coney	9	0	28	0	(6)	3	1	10	0		2nd	58	29	32	–
Bracewell	27	9	46	1	(4)	33	12	77	4		3rd	58	29	76	–
Crowe	2	1	4	0							4th	64	48	120	–
Reid					(5)	1	1	0	0		5th	74	124	129	–
											6th	251	190	130	–
AUSTRALIA											7th	319	263	166	–
Reid	34.3	8	90	4	(2)	4	0	7	0		8th	334	311	–	–
Gilbert	26	4	106	2	(1)	7	4	9	0		9th	358	331	–	–
Waugh	23	6	56	4							10th	364	339	–	–
Bright	18	6	51	0											
Matthews	6	1	22	0	(3)	3	3	0	1						

Umpires: B.L.Aldridge (1) and F.R.Goodall (22).

Close: 1st day – A(1) 224-5 (Border 84, Waugh 65); 2nd – NZ(1) 48-3 (Crowe 14, Rutherford 0); 3rd – NZ(1) 339 all out; 4th – A(2) 49-2 (Phillips 11, Border 15).

NEW ZEALAND v AUSTRALIA 1985-86 (3rd Test)

At Eden Park, Auckland, on 13, 14, 15, 16, 17 March.
Toss: Australia.   Result: NEW ZEALAND won by eight wickets.
Debuts: New Zealand – G.K.Robertson.

New Zealand retained the Trans-Tasman Trophy and became the first side to defeat Australia in two rubbers in the same season. Marsh, who reached his first Test hundred in 258 minutes off 224 balls, added 168 with Phillips to register a record Australian second-wicket partnership against New Zealand. Coney achieved his third successive score in excess of 90 to average 146 in the series. Australia lost the series between 11.30 and 2.10 pm on the fourth day when five wickets fell for 12 runs, their total of 103 being their lowest against New Zealand. Bracewell became the first spin bowler to take ten wickets in a Test for New Zealand. Boon, who batted 241 minutes, faced 174 balls and hit six fours, provided Australia's tenth instance of an opener carrying his bat through a Test innings. Earlier Zoehrer had become the first batsman to officiate as night-watchman in both innings of a Test.

AUSTRALIA

D.C.Boon	c Coney b Hadlee	16	(2)	not out	58
G.R.Marsh	c Coney b Hadlee	118	(1)	lbw b Hadlee	0
W.B.Phillips	c Smith b Bracewell	62		c Bracewell b Chatfield	15
A.R.Border	c Smith b Chatfield	17	(5)	b Bracewell	6
T.J.Zoehrer	c Coney b Robertson	9	(4)	lbw b Chatfield	1
G.M.Ritchie	c Smith b Chatfield	56		lbw b Chatfield	1
G.R.J.Matthews	b Bracewell	5		st Smith b Bracewell	4
S.R.Waugh	c Reid b Bracewell	1		b Bracewell	0
R.J.Bright	c Smith b Hadlee	5		b Bracewell	0
C.J.McDermott	lbw b Bracewell	9		b Bracewell	6
B.A.Reid	not out	0		c Hadlee b Bracewell	8
Extras	(B2, LB11, NB3)	16		(LB4)	4
Total		**314**			**103**

NEW ZEALAND

J.G.Wright	c Zoehrer b McDermott	56	c Boon b Matthews	59
B.A.Edgar	lbw b Matthews	24	b Reid	1
K.R.Rutherford	b Matthews	0	not out	50
M.D.Crowe	lbw b Matthews	0	not out	23
J.F.Reid	c Phillips b Bright	16		
J.V.Coney	c Border b McDermott	93		
R.J.Hadlee	b Reid	33		
I.D.S.Smith	b Waugh	3		
J.G.Bracewell	c Boon b Bright	4		
G.K.Robertson	st Zoehrer b Matthews	12		
E.J.Chatfield	not out	1		
Extras	(B7, LB8, NB1)	16	(B18, LB4, NB5)	27
Total		**258**	(2 wickets)	**160**

NEW ZEALAND	O	M	R	W		O	M	R	W			FALL OF WICKETS			
Hadlee	31	12	60	3		20	7	48	1			A	NZ	A	NZ
Robertson	24	6	91	1							*Wkt*	*1st*	*1st*	*2nd*	*2nd*
Chatfield	29	10	54	2	(2)	18	9	19	3		1st	25	73	0	6
Crowe	3	2	4	0							2nd	193	73	28	106
Bracewell	43.3	19	74	4	(3)	22	8	32	6		3rd	225	73	35	–
Coney	5	0	18	0							4th	225	103	59	–
											5th	278	107	62	–
											6th	293	170	71	–
AUSTRALIA											7th	294	184	71	–
McDermott	17	2	47	2		14	3	29	0		8th	301	203	71	–
Reid	19	2	63	1		12.4	2	30	1		9th	309	250	85	–
Matthews	34	15	61	4		31	18	46	1		10th	314	258	103	–
Bright	22	4	58	2		23	12	29	0						
Waugh	5	1	14	1		4	1	4	0						

Umpires: R.L.McHarg (1) and S.J.Woodward (14).

Close: 1st day – A(1) 227-4 (Zoehrer 0, Ritchie 2); 2nd – NZ(1) 75-3 (Wright 44, Reid 0); 3rd – A(2) 32-2 (Boon 13, Zoehrer 0); 4th – NZ(2) 85-1 (Wright 46, Rutherford 22).

WEST INDIES v ENGLAND 1985-86 (1st Test)

At Sabina Park, Kingston, Jamaica, on 21, 22, 23 February.
Toss: England.   Result: WEST INDIES won by ten wickets.
Debuts: West Indies – C.A.Best, B.P.Patterson; England – D.M.Smith, J.G.Thomas.

At 4.39 on the third afternoon West Indies completed their sixth successive victory against England. In his firs
Test, Patterson achieved match figures of 7 for 74 on a hard, uneven pitch. His express pace and vicious bounce
had been carefully concealed during 17 undramatic first-class appearances during two seasons with Lancashire
Although the umpires did nothing to restrict a barrage of short-pitched bowling, they did decline an appeal for h
wicket when Edmonds was struck over the heart by a beamer. Thomas and Smith provided Glamorgan an
Worcestershire with their first England caps since 1973. Best's first scoring stroke was a hooked six off his thir
ball. Six lbw decisions in the West Indies first innings equalled the Test record. After 22 Tests and almost ten year
Willey, top scorer of the match with a typically courageous 71, completed 1,000 runs. Greenidge (47) retired at 7
for three stitches in an eyebrow cut when he mishooked Botham; he resumed at 247.

ENGLAND

G.A.Gooch	c Garner b Marshall	51		b Marshall	
R.T.Robinson	c Greenidge b Patterson	6		b Garner	
*D.I.Gower	lbw b Holding	16		c Best b Patterson	
D.M.Smith	c Dujon b Patterson	1	(7)	c Gomes b Marshall	
A.J.Lamb	b Garner	49		c sub (R.A.Harper) b Patterson	1.
I.T.Botham	c Patterson b Marshall	15		b Marshall	2
P.Willey	c Dujon b Holding	0	(4)	b Garner	7
†P.R.Downton	c Dujon b Patterson	2		c Haynes b Holding	
R.M.Ellison	c Haynes b Patterson	9		b Garner	1
P.H.Edmonds	not out	5		lbw b Patterson	
J.G.Thomas	b Garner	0		not out	
Extras	(NB5)	5		(B5, NB3)	
Total		**159**			**15**

WEST INDIES

C.G.Greenidge	lbw b Ellison	58		
D.L.Haynes	c Downton b Thomas	32	(1)	not out
J.Garner	c Edmonds b Botham	24		
R.B.Richardson	lbw b Botham	7	(2)	not out
H.A.Gomes	lbw b Ellison	56		
C.A.Best	lbw b Willey	35		
*I.V.A.Richards	lbw b Ellison	23		
†P.J.L.Dujon	c Gooch b Thomas	54		
M.D.Marshall	c sub (J.E.Emburey) b Ellison	6		
M.A.Holding	lbw b Ellison	3		
B.P.Patterson	not out	0		
Extras	(B2, LB4, NB3)	9		(NB1)
Total		**307**		(0 wickets)

WEST INDIES	O	M	R	W		O	M	R	W		FALL OF WICKETS				
Marshall	11	1	30	2		11	4	29	3			E	WI	E	W.
Garner	14.3	0	58	2		9	2	22	3		Wkt	1st	1st	2nd	2nd
Patterson	11	4	30	4	(4)	10.5	0	44	3		1st	32	95	1	
Holding	7	1	36	2	(3)	12	1	52	1		2nd	53	112	3	
Richards	1	1	0	0							3rd	54	115	19	
Richardson	1	0	5	0							4th	83	183	40	
											5th	120	222	95	
ENGLAND											6th	127	241	103	
Botham	19	4	67	2							7th	138	247	106	
Thomas	28.5	6	82	2	(1)	1	0	4	0		8th	142	299	140	
Ellison	33	12	78	5							9th	158	303	146	
Edmonds	21	6	53	0							10th	159	307	152	
Willey	4	0	15	1											
Gooch	2	1	6	0											
Lamb					(2)	0‡	0	1	0						

Umpires: D.M.Archer (15) and J.R.Gayle (3).   ‡ One no-ball

Close: 1st day – WI(1) 85-0 (Haynes 30, Garner 5); 2nd – WI(1) 268-7 (Dujon 26, Greenidge 54).

WEST INDIES v ENGLAND 1985-86 (2nd Test)

At Queen's Park Oval, Port-of-Spain, Trinidad, on 7, 8, 9, 11, 12 March.
Toss: West Indies.   Result: WEST INDIES won by seven wickets.
Debuts: West Indies – T.R.O.Payne; England – W.N.Slack.

On a slower pitch England managed to avert defeat until 10.29 on the fifth morning. Their second innings of 315 set one of Test cricket's more subtle records: the highest total without an individual contribution of 50 or more (discounting extras which top-scored for only the seventh time in 1,039 matches). Playing in his 42nd Test, Marshall became the sixth West Indian to take 200 wickets, achieving the feat in fewer matches than his predecessors. Richardson completed 1,000 runs in 17 Tests, reaching his fifth hundred in 157 minutes off 111 balls. Emburey became the first spinner from any country to take five wickets in an innings of a Caribbean Test since February 1981 when he had himself taken 5 for 124 in 52 overs on the same ground. The partnership of 72 between Ellison and Thomas was England's highest for the tenth wicket in the West Indies.

ENGLAND

G.A.Gooch	c Best b Marshall	2	lbw b Walsh	43
W.N.Slack	c Payne b Marshall	2	run out	0
*D.I.Gower	lbw b Garner	66	b Walsh	47
P.Willey	c Payne b Patterson	5	b Marshall	26
A.J.Lamb	c Marshall b Garner	62	lbw b Walsh	40
I.T.Botham	c Richardson b Marshall	2	c Payne b Marshall	1
J.E.Emburey	c Payne b Garner	0	c Best b Walsh	14
†P.R.Downton	c Marshall b Walsh	8	lbw b Marshall	5
R.M.Ellison	lbw b Marshall	4	lbw b Marshall	36
P.H.Edmonds	not out	3	c Payne b Garner	13
J.G.Thomas	b Patterson	4	not out	31
Extras	(LB4, NB14)	18	(B20, LB11, W1, NB27)	59
Total		176		315

WEST INDIES

C.G.Greenidge	c Lamb b Thomas	37	c Lamb b Edmonds	45
D.L.Haynes	st Downton b Emburey	67	not out	39
R.B.Richardson	c Downton b Emburey	102	c Gooch b Emburey	9
H.A.Gomes	st Downton b Emburey	30	b Emburey	0
C.A.Best	b Edmonds	22	not out	0
*I.V.A.Richards	c Botham b Edmonds	34		
†T.R.O.Payne	c Gower b Emburey	5		
M.D.Marshall	not out	62		
J.Garner	c Gooch b Emburey	12		
C.A.Walsh	c Edmonds b Thomas	3		
B.P.Patterson	c Gooch b Botham	9		
Extras	(LB11, W1, NB4)	16	(LB2)	2
Total		399	(3 wickets)	95

WEST INDIES	O	M	R	W		O	M	R	W		FALL OF WICKETS			
											E	WI	E	WI
Marshall	15	3	38	4	(2)	32.2	9	94	4		1st	1st	2nd	2nd
Garner	15	4	45	3	(1)	21	5	44	1	Wkt				
Patterson	8.4	0	60	2	(5)	16	0	65	0	1st	2	59	2	72
Walsh	6	2	29	1		27	4	74	4	2nd	11	209	82	89
Richards					(3)	7	4	7	0	3rd	30	242	109	91
Gomes						1	1	0	0	4th	136	257	190	–
										5th	147	298	192	–
ENGLAND										6th	148	303	197	–
Botham	9.4	0	68	1						7th	153	327	214	–
Thomas	20	4	86	2	(1)	5	1	21	0	8th	163	342	214	–
Ellison	18	3	58	0	(2)	3	1	12	0	9th	165	364	243	–
Edmonds	30	5	98	2	(3)	12.3	3	24	1	10th	176	399	315	–
Emburey	27	5	78	5	(4)	10	1	36	2					

Umpires: D.M.Archer (16) and C.E.Cumberbatch (5).

Close: 1st day – WI(1) 67-1 (Haynes 22, Richardson 6); 2nd – WI(1) 347-8 (Marshall 22, Walsh 1); 3rd – E(2) 168-3 (Willey 19, Lamb 26); 4th – WI(2) 76-1 (Haynes 29, Richardson 0).

WEST INDIES v ENGLAND 1985-86 (3rd Test)

At Kensington Oval, Bridgetown, Barbados, on 21, 22, 23, 25 March.
Toss: England.   Result: WEST INDIES won by an innings and 30 runs.
Debuts: None.

At 12.20 pm on the fourth day, West Indies completed their eighth consecutive victory against England, including three by an innings. They thus retained the Wisden Trophy which they had held since 1973, England's last series win against them being in 1969. It was their sixth consecutive victory at Kensington Oval, their only defeat there in 23 Tests occurring against England in 1934-35. Richardson's sixth hundred in 18 Tests included an initial 50 runs off 44 balls. Dujon's five catches in an innings equalled the West Indies record, the first of six previous instances being achieved by F.C.M.Alexander against England at the same venue in 1959-60.

WEST INDIES

C.G.Greenidge	c Botham b Foster	21
D.L.Haynes	c Botham b Foster	84
R.B.Richardson	lbw b Emburey	160
H.A.Gomes	c Gower b Thomas	33
*I.V.A.Richards	c Downton b Thomas	51
C.A.Best	lbw b Foster	21
†P.J.L.Dujon	c sub (W.N.Slack) b Botham	5
M.A.Holding	b Thomas	23
M.D.Marshall	run out	4
J.Garner	c Gooch b Thomas	0
B.P.Patterson	not out	0
Extras	(B2, LB9, W3, NB2)	16
Total		**418**

ENGLAND

G.A.Gooch	c Dujon b Garner	53		b Patterson	11
R.T.Robinson	c Dujon b Marshall	3		b Patterson	43
*D.I.Gower	c Dujon b Marshall	66		c Marshall b Garner	23
P.Willey	c Dujon b Marshall	5		lbw b Garner	17
A.J.Lamb	c Richardson b Marshall	5		c and b Holding	6
I.T.Botham	c Dujon b Patterson	14	(7)	c Dujon b Garner	21
†P.R.Downton	lbw b Holding	11	(8)	c Dujon b Holding	26
J.E.Emburey	c Best b Patterson	0	(9)	not out	35
P.H.Edmonds	c Richardson b Patterson	4	(6)	lbw b Garner	4
N.A.Foster	lbw b Holding	0		c Richardson b Holding	0
J.G.Thomas	not out	4		b Patterson	0
Extras	(B4, LB8, W2, NB10)	24		(LB1, NB12)	13
Total		**189**			**199**

ENGLAND	O	M	R	W	O	M	R	W		FALL OF WICKETS		
Botham	24	3	80	1							WI	E	E
Thomas	16.1	2	70	4					*Wkt*	*1st*	*1st*	*2nd*
Foster	19	0	76	3					1st	34	6	48
Edmonds	29	2	85	0					2nd	228	126	71
Emburey	38	7	96	1					3rd	286	134	94
									4th	361	141	108
WEST INDIES									5th	362	151	108
Marshall	14	1	42	4	13	1	47	0	6th	367	168	132
Garner	14	4	35	1	17	2	69	4	7th	406	172	138
Patterson	15	5	54	3	8.4	2	28	3	8th	413	181	188
Holding	13	4	37	2	10	1	47	3	9th	418	185	188
Richards	3	0	9	0	4	1	7	0	10th	418	189	199

Umpires: D.M.Archer (17) and L.H.Barker (5).

Close: 1st day – WI(1) 269-2 (Richardson 150, Gomes 6); 2nd – E(1) 110-1 (Gooch 46, Gower 51); 3rd – E(2) 132-6 (Edmonds 3).

WEST INDIES v ENGLAND 1985-86 (4th Test)

At Queen's Park Oval, Port-of-Spain, Trinidad, on 3, 4, 5 April.
Toss: West Indies.   Result: WEST INDIES won by ten wickets.
Debuts: None.

West Indies' ninth successive victory against England, completed at 4.22 on the third afternoon, established a new record, surpassing Australia's run of eight Ashes victories in 1920-21 and 1921. Although no England batsman reached 50 in the match there was some compensation in Botham's first innings analysis; it was his 26th of five or more wickets in 83 Tests and enabled him to reclaim his world record from R.J.Hadlee. When he bowled Holding he became the second bowler after D.K.Lillee (70 Tests) to take 350 wickets. Three West Indies batsmen achieved notable career totals: Richards (6,000 runs in 81 Tests), Greenidge (5,000 in 70) and Gomes (3,000 in 53).

ENGLAND

G.A.Gooch	c Richards b Garner	14	c Dujon b Marshall	0
R.T.Robinson	c Marshall b Garner	0	b Garner	5
*D.I.Gower	c Dujon b Garner	10	lbw b Patterson	22
D.M.Smith	c Greenidge b Patterson	47	lbw b Holding	32
A.J.Lamb	b Holding	36	b Patterson	11
I.T.Botham	b Holding	38	c Gomes b Marshall	25
P.Willey	c Richardson b Garner	10	lbw b Marshall	2
†P.R.Downton	c Garner b Marshall	7	not out	11
J.E.Emburey	c Haynes b Marshall	8	b Holding	0
N.A.Foster	c Richards b Holding	0	b Garner	14
J.G.Thomas	not out	5	b Garner	0
Extras	(LB3, W1, NB21)	25	(B5, LB7, NB16)	28
Total		**200**		**150**

WEST INDIES

C.G.Greenidge	lbw b Emburey	42		
D.L.Haynes	c Botham b Foster	25	(1) not out	17
R.B.Richardson	b Emburey	32	(2) not out	22
H.A.Gomes	c Downton b Foster	48		
*I.V.A.Richards	lbw b Botham	87		
†P.J.L.Dujon	c Downton b Botham	5		
M.D.Marshall	b Emburey	5		
R.A.Harper	lbw b Botham	21		
M.A.Holding	b Botham	25		
J.Garner	not out	5		
B.P.Patterson	c Downton b Botham	3		
Extras	(LB10, W3, NB1)	14		
Total		**312**	(0 wickets)	**39**

WEST INDIES	O	M	R	W		O	M	R	W		FALL OF WICKETS			
Marshall	23	4	71	2		10	2	42	3			E	WI	E	WI
Garner	18	3	43	4		9	3	15	3		Wkt	1st	1st	2nd	2nd
Patterson	10	2	31	1	(4)	9	1	36	2		1st	8	58	0	–
Holding	14.4	3	52	3	(3)	10	1	45	2		2nd	29	74	30	–
											3rd	31	111	30	–
											4th	123	213	75	–
ENGLAND											5th	124	244	105	–
Botham	24.1	3	71	5		3	0	24	0		6th	151	249	109	–
Thomas	15	0	101	0							7th	168	249	115	–
Foster	24	3	68	2	(2)	2.5	0	15	0		8th	181	300	126	–
Emburey	27	10	62	3							9th	190	306	150	–
											10th	200	312	150	–

Umpires: C.E.Cumberbatch (6) and S.Mohammed (3).

Close: 1st day – WI(1) 12-0 (Greenidge 4, Haynes 8); 2nd – WI(1) 271-7 (Harper 3, Holding 15)

WEST INDIES v ENGLAND 1985-86 (5th Test)

At Recreation Ground, St John's, Antigua, on 11, 12, 13, 15, 16 April.
Toss: England.   Result: WEST INDIES won by 240 runs.
Debuts: None.

Although England, assisted by 94 extras, including a record 40 no-balls in the first innings, gave their most impressive display of the series and took the match well into the final hour of the fifth day, they could not prevent West Indies from completing their tenth successive win against them with their second successive 'blackwash'. In a sensational display of batting on the fourth afternoon, Richards scored the fastest hundred in terms of fewest balls received (56): 00361261410211 (tea: 28 off 14 balls) 04121112021110001016 (53 – 34 balls, 46 minutes) 2404411200664612021004 (103 – 56 balls, 81 minutes) 61 (110 – 58 balls, 83 minutes). This extraordinary innings included seven sixes, a total then exceeded only by W.R.Hammond (ten in *Test No. 226*). Earlier Haynes had scored his eighth hundred in 59 Tests, Richards had completed 2,000 runs against England, Holding had made his highest Test score, and Robinson had scored his 1,000th run in 15 Tests. Garner and Marshall shared a new West Indies home record against England with 27 wickets apiece.

WEST INDIES

C.G.Greenidge	b Botham	14		
D.L.Haynes	c Gatting b Ellison	131	(1) run out	70
R.B.Richardson	c Slack b Emburey	24	(2) c Robinson b Emburey	31
H.A.Gomes	b Emburey	24		
*I.V.A.Richards	c Gooch b Botham	26	(3) not out	110
†P.J.L.Dujon	b Foster	21		
M.D.Marshall	c Gatting b Gooch	76		
R.A.Harper	c Lamb b Foster	60	(4) not out	19
M.A.Holding	c Gower b Ellison	73		
J.Garner	run out	11		
B.P.Patterson	not out	0		
Extras	(B2, LB11, W1)	14	(B4, LB9, W1, NB2)	16
Total		**474**	(2 wickets declared)	**246**

ENGLAND

G.A.Gooch	lbw b Holding	51	lbw b Holding	51
W.N.Slack	c Greenidge b Patterson	52	b Garner	8
R.T.Robinson	b Marshall	12	run out	3
*D.I.Gower	c Dujon b Marshall	90	(5) c Dujon b Harper	21
A.J.Lamb	c and b Harper	1	(6) b Marshall	1
M.W.Gatting	c Dujon b Garner	15	(7) b Holding	1
I.T.Botham	c Harper b Garner	10	(8) b Harper	13
†P.R.Downton	c Holding b Garner	5	(9) lbw b Marshall	13
R.M.Ellison	c Dujon b Marshall	6	(4) lbw b Garner	16
J.E.Emburey	not out	7	c Richardson b Harper	0
N.A.Foster	c Holding b Garner	10	not out	0
Extras	(B5, LB6, NB40)	51	(B10, LB10, W2, NB21)	43
Total		**310**		**170**

ENGLAND	O	M	R	W	O	M	R	W	FALL OF WICKETS				
Botham	40	6	147	2	15	0	78	0		WI	E	WI	E
Foster	28	5	86	2	10	0	40	0	*Wkt*	*1st*	*1st*	*2nd*	*2nd*
Ellison	24.3	3	114	2	(4) 4	0	32	0	1st	23	127	100	14
Emburey	37	11	93	2	(3) 14	0	83	1	2nd	63	132	161	29
Gooch	5	2	21	1					3rd	137	157	–	84
									4th	178	159	–	101
WEST INDIES									5th	232	205	–	112
Marshall	24	5	64	3	16.1	6	25	2	6th	281	213	–	124
Garner	21.4	2	67	4	17	5	38	2	7th	351	237	–	147
Patterson	14	2	49	1	15	3	29	0	8th	401	289	–	166
Holding	20	3	71	1	16	3	45	2	9th	450	290	–	168
Harper	26	7	45	1	12	8	10	3	10th	474	310	–	170
Richards	2	0	3	0	3	1	3	0					

Umpires: L.H.Barker (6) and C.E.Cumberbatch (7).

Close: 1st day – WI(1) 228-4 (Haynes 117, Dujon 17); 2nd – E(1) 40-0 (Gooch 9, Slack 20); 3rd – E(1) 263-7 (Gower 70, Ellison 2); 4th – E(2) 33-2 (Gooch 14, Ellison 2).

SRI LANKA v PAKISTAN 1985-86 (1st Test)

At Asgiriya Stadium, Kandy, on 23, 24, 25, 27 February.
Toss: Sri Lanka.   Result: PAKISTAN won by an innings and 20 runs.
Debuts: Sri Lanka – K.P.J.Warnaweera; Pakistan – Zulqarnain.

Although rain allowed only 65 minutes (12.2 overs) of play on the third day, Pakistan celebrated their first Test in Sri Lanka with an innings victory achieved with more than a day to spare on a turning pitch. The final stages were marred by an outrageous display of abuse by the Pakistanis when the umpire declined an appeal for a bat/pad catch at short-leg against Ranatunga. The batsmen and umpires left the field and there was a 30-minute suspension of play. This was Sri Lanka's 19th official Test and the first without R.S.Madugalle. De Mel became the first Sri Lankan bowler to take 50 wickets as Pakistan recorded their lowest total against his country. Tausif Ahmed returned his best innings and match analyses. After Silva was injured on the first day, Aravinda de Silva kept wicket and caught Salim Malik. Imran, whose first wicket was his 250th in 55 Tests, bowled three successive wides in the second innings.

SRI LANKA

S.Wettimuny	lbw b Imran	0		c Ramiz b Wasim	8
†S.A.R.Silva	c Zulqarnain b Wasim	3		absent hurt	–
P.A.de Silva	c Zulqarnain b Imran	11		b Tausif	5
R.L.Dias	b Tausif	11		b Tausif	26
*L.R.D.Mendis	c Mudassar b Imran	6		c Mudassar b Tausif	4
A.Ranatunga	b Tausif	18		st Zulqarnain b Tausif	33
J.R.Ratnayeke	b Qadir	4	(2)	b Imran	7
A.L.F.de Mel	b Tausif	23	(7)	b Tausif	0
R.J.Ratnayake	c Salim b Qadir	4	(8)	st Zulqarnain b Tausif	4
E.A.R.de Silva	not out	10	(9)	not out	4
K.P.J.Warnaweera	c Imran b Qadir	3	(10)	b Imran	0
Extras	(LB7, W2, NB7)	16		(LB3, W6, NB1)	10
Total		**109**			**101**

PAKISTAN

Mudassar Nazar	c Mendis b Ratnayeke	81
Mohsin Khan	lbw b De Mel	1
Qasim Omar	lbw b Ratnayeke	11
Javed Miandad	lbw b E.A.R.de Silva	4
Ramiz Raja	lbw b Warnaweera	3
Salim Malik	c P.A.de Silva b De Mel	54
*Imran Khan	c sub‡ b Ranatunga	7
Abdul Qadir	b Ratnayeke	11
†Zulqarnain	b De Mel	5
Tausif Ahmed	not out	23
Wasim Akram	run out	19
Extras	(B4, W7)	11
Total		**230**

PAKISTAN	O	M	R	W		O	M	R	W		FALL OF WICKETS		
Imran	9	0	20	3		16	5	29	2		SL	P	SL
Wasim	8	3	21	1		5	3	5	1	*Wkt*	*1st*	*1st*	*2nd*
Tausif	13	4	32	3	(4)	15	7	45	6	1st	0	1	14
Qadir	12.4	3	29	3	(3)	7	1	19	0	2nd	14	28	19
										3rd	25	49	31
SRI LANKA										4th	37	52	43
De Mel	16.2	5	50	3						5th	44	154	74
Ratnayeke	10	1	26	0						6th	59	167	74
Ratnayake	23	2	57	3						7th	69	173	80
Warnaweera	8.3	2	26	1						8th	78	181	100
E.A.R.de Silva	18	7	37	1						9th	100	191	101
Ranatunga	14.3	6	30	1						10th	109	230	–

Umpires: A.C.Felsinger (1) and S.Ponnadurai (2).   ‡ (R.S.Mahanama)

Close: 1st day – P(1) 58-4 (Mudassar 34, Salim 3); 2nd – SL(2) 7-0 (Wettimuny 3, Ratnayeke 4); 3rd – SL(2) 31-2 (P.A.de Silva 5, Dias 7).

SRI LANKA v PAKISTAN 1985-86 (2nd Test)

At Colombo Cricket Club Ground on 14, 15, 16, 18 March.
Toss: Sri Lanka.   Result: SRI LANKA won by eight wickets.
Debuts: Sri Lanka – S.D.Anurasiri, A.K.Kuruppuarachchi, R.S.Mahanama.

Sri Lanka's 20th Test match brought their second victory. It was achieved with the aid of three debutants and with more than a day to spare. Kosala Kuruppuarachchi (left-arm fast-medium) celebrated his first appearance with five wickets as Pakistan recorded the lowest total by any country against Sri Lanka. Mudassar's wicket was his 50th in 57 Tests. When he reached 74, Ranatunga, top-scorer of the match, became the fourth Sri Lankan batsman after Mendis, R.L.Dias and Sidath Wettimuny to score 1,000 runs. The match was marred by further incidents involving Pakistani fielders incensed by various umpiring decisions. When members and VIPs responded with what Imran described as 'vile and obnoxious language and gestures' and a spectator threw a stone at Miandad after the latter had disputed his dismissal, Pakistan threatened to abandon the tour.

PAKISTAN

Mudassar Nazar	c De Alwis b Kuruppuarachchi	3		lbw b Kuruppuarachchi	1
Mohsin Khan	lbw b Kuruppuarachchi	35		c De Silva b De Mel	2
Qasim Omar	lbw b De Mel	3		c De Alwis b Ratnayeke	52
Javed Miandad	c De Alwis b De Mel	0	(5)	lbw b Ratnayeke	36
Ramiz Raja	lbw b De Mel	32	(4)	c De Alwis b Ratnayeke	21
Salim Malik	c Mahanama b Kuruppuarachchi	42		c Wettimuny b Ratnayeke	30
*Imran Khan	c Mendis b Ratnayeke	8		c De Silva b De Mel	0
Tausif Ahmed	b Ratnayeke	0	(9)	lbw b Ratnayeke	1
Wasim Akram	c De Mel b Kuruppuarachchi	0	(8)	c Ranatunga b De Mel	0
†Zulqarnain	c De Silva b Kuruppuarachchi	1		lbw b Kuruppuarachchi	5
Mohsin Kamal	not out	1		not out	13
Extras	(LB4, W2, NB1)	7		(B1, LB6, NB4)	11
Total		**132**			**172**

SRI LANKA

S.Wettimuny	c Zulqarnain b Mudassar	37		c Salim b Imran	7
R.S.Mahanama	run out	10		c Zulqarnain b Imran	8
A.P.Gurusinha	c Imran b Wasim	23		not out	9
P.A.de Silva	c sub‡ b Mohsin Kamal	37		not out	1
A.Ranatunga	c Omar b Wasim	77			
*L.R.D.Mendis	c Mohsin Khan b Imran	5			
J.R.Ratnayeke	c Imran b Wasim	38			
†R.G.de Alwis	c Miandad b Mohsin Kamal	10			
A.L.F.de Mel	c Zulqarnain b Imran	11			
S.D.Anurasiri	c Ramiz b Wasim	4			
A.K.Kuruppuarachchi	not out	0			
Extras	(B7, LB3, W4, NB7)	21		(B2, LB2, W1, NB2)	7
Total		**273**		(2 wickets)	**32**

SRI LANKA	O	M	R	W	O	M	R	W		FALL OF WICKETS			
De Mel	16	6	39	3	16	1	79	3		P	SL	P	SL
Kuruppuarachchi	14.5	2	44	5	10.3	1	41	2	Wkt	1st	1st	2nd	2nd
Ratnayeke	17.4	6	29	2	17	3	37	5	1st	3	40	6	19
Ranatunga	1	0	12	0					2nd	12	69	6	31
Anurasiri	2	1	4	0	(4) 2	0	8	0	3rd	12	82	72	–
									4th	74	130	93	–
PAKISTAN									5th	78	137	131	–
Imran	27	5	78	2	7	2	18	2	6th	124	227	136	–
Wasim	27.3	9	55	4	6	1	10	0	7th	124	248	136	–
Mohsin Kamal	15	0	52	2					8th	130	265	145	–
Mudassar	14	2	36	1					9th	131	272	154	–
Tausif	11	2	40	0					10th	132	273	172	–
Salim	1	0	2	0									

Umpires: K.T.Francis (4) and D.C.C.Perera (1).   ‡ (Shoaib Mohammad)

Close: 1st day – SL(1) 21-0 (Wettimuny 11, Mahanama 7); 2nd – SL(1) 248-6 (Ranatunga 69, De Alwis 10); 3rd – P(2) 154-9 (Zulqarnain 0, Mohsin Kamal 0).

SRI LANKA v PAKISTAN 1985-86 (3rd Test)

At P.Saravanamuttu Stadium, Colombo, on 22, 23, 24, 26, 27 March.
Toss: Sri Lanka.   Result: MATCH DRAWN.
Debuts: Sri Lanka – K.N.Amalean; Pakistan – Zakir Khan.

An historic unbroken record fourth-wicket partnership of 240 between two left-handers, Gurusinha and Ranatunga, enabled Sri Lanka to draw this final Test and the series after Mendis had won his fourth successive toss. The stand remains the highest for any wicket by Sri Lanka. Both batsmen recorded their highest scores and became the eighth pair to bat throughout an uninterrupted day of Test cricket. Gurusinha (19) reached his maiden hundred in 437 minutes and continued for a further 58 minutes, hitting 14 boundaries in a chanceless innings. Ranatunga's second Test century included four sixes but was by permission of Miandad, Salim and Zulqarnain who conspired to drop him five times behind the wicket before he had scored 30. Earlier a maiden hundred by Ramiz (122 in 388 minutes off 242 balls with 17 fours) had earned Pakistan a first innings lead of 37. Rain and bad light reduced play to 140 minutes on the fourth day.

SRI LANKA

S.Wettimuny	c Ramiz b Wasim	0		c Ramiz b Wasim	14
R.S.Mahanama	c Zulqarnain b Qadir	41		b Imran	4
A.P.Gurusinha	c Zulqarnain b Imran	39		not out	116
A.Ranatunga	c Imran b Zakir	53	(5)	not out	135
P.A.de Silva	c Mohsin b Zakir	16	(4)	c Miandad b Imran	25
*L.R.D.Mendis	c Zulqarnain b Imran	58			
J.R.Ratnayeke	c Miandad b Zakir	7			
†R.G.de Alwis	b Imran	18			
A.L.F.de Mel	not out	14			
S.D.Anurasiri	b Imran	8			
K.N.Amalean	lbw b Qadir	2			
Extras	(B7, LB9, W6, NB3)	25		(B19, LB7, W1, NB2)	29
Total		281		(3 wickets)	323

PAKISTAN

Mudassar Nazar	c De Alwis b De Mel	8
Mohsin Khan	lbw b Amalean	12
Qasim Omar	c De Alwis b Ratnayeke	19
Javed Miandad	lbw b Amalean	23
Ramiz Raja	lbw b Ratnayeke	122
Salim Malik	c sub‡ b Ratnayeke	29
*Imran Khan	c De Alwis b Ratnayeke	33
Abdul Qadir	b Amalean	20
†Zulqarnain	c De Alwis b Ratnayeke	13
Wasim Akram	run out	11
Zakir Khan	not out	0
Extras	(B10, LB7, W1, NB10)	28
Total		318

PAKISTAN	O	M	R	W	O	M	R	W	FALL OF WICKETS			
										SL	P	SL
Imran	32	11	69	4	(2) 25	4	56	2	Wkt	1st	1st	2nd
Wasim	22	8	41	1	(1) 29	11	72	1	1st	12	24	18
Zakir	24	6	80	3	21	4	70	0	2nd	79	32	18
Mudassar	7	2	19	0	(5) 10	2	29	0	3rd	109	49	83
Qadir	23.5	3	56	2	(4) 22	5	70	0	4th	149	87	–
Salim					1	1	0	0	5th	202	158	–
									6th	218	234	–
SRI LANKA									7th	251	278	–
De Mel	27	3	91	1					8th	260	305	–
Amalean	18.2	1	59	3					9th	272	318	–
Ratnayeke	30	4	116	4					10th	281	318	–
Anurasiri	15	11	9	0								
Ranatunga	11	5	26	1								

Umpires: D.P.Buultjens (3) and H.C.Felsinger (6).   ‡ (S.M.S.Kaluperuma)

Close: 1st day – SL(1) 191-4 (Ranatunga 51, Mendis 24); 2nd – P(1) 180-5 (Ramiz 73, Imran 3); 3rd – SL(2) 24-2 (Gurusinha 1, De Silva 5); 4th – SL(2) 83-3 (Gurusinha 34, Ranatunga 0).

Test No. 1046/73 (E623/I233)

ENGLAND v INDIA 1986 (1st Test)

At Lord's, London, on 5, 6, 7, 9, 10 June.
Toss: India.   Result: INDIA won by five wickets.
Debuts: India – K.S.More.

At 2.55pm on the fifth day India gained their first victory in 11 Tests at Lord's, their second in 33 matches in England, their first after 19 instances of putting the opposition in, and their first in 21 Tests under the captaincy of Kapil Dev. In 42 matches since defeating England at Bombay in December 1981, India had won only once (v England at Bombay in 1984-85) and lost 12 times. Gooch (355 minutes, 280 balls, one six and 12 fours) recorded his sixth hundred in 54 Tests. Vengsarkar (327 minutes, 213 balls, 16 fours) scored his tenth hundred in 83 Tests and became the first to score three hundreds against England at Lord's. Only 132 runs were scored off 83.2 overs in 5½ hours on the second day. This was the earliest start (by five days) of Lord's 79 Tests, an aggregate which surpassed the record previously shared with Melbourne Cricket Ground. After this defeat, England's sixth in succession, Gower's two-year reign as England's captain was terminated.

ENGLAND

G.A.Gooch	b Sharma	114	lbw b Kapil Dev		8
R.T.Robinson	c Azharuddin b Maninder	35	c Amarnath b Kapil Dev		11
*D.I.Gower	c More b Sharma	18	lbw b Kapil Dev		8
M.W.Gatting	b Sharma	0	b Sharma		40
A.J.Lamb	c Srikkanth b Sharma	6	c More b Shastri		39
D.R.Pringle	b Binny	63	c More b Kapil Dev		6
J.E.Emburey	c Amarnath b Kapil Dev	7	(9) c and b Maninder		1
†P.R.Downton	lbw b Sharma	5	(7) c Shastri b Maninder		29
R.M.Ellison	c Kapil Dev b Binny	12	(8) c More b Binny		19
G.R.Dilley	c More b Binny	4	not out		2
P.H.Edmonds	not out	7	c Binny b Maninder		7
Extras	(LB15, W1, NB7)	23	(LB6, W1, NB3)		10
Total		**294**			**180**

INDIA

S.M.Gavaskar	c Emburey b Dilley	34	c Downton b Dilley		22
K.Srikkanth	c Gatting b Dilley	20	c Gooch b Dilley		0
M.Amarnath	c Pringle b Edmonds	69	lbw b Pringle		8
D.B.Vengsarkar	not out	126	b Edmonds		33
M.Azharuddin	c and b Dilley	33	run out		14
R.J.Shastri	c Edmonds b Dilley	1	not out		20
R.M.H.Binny	lbw b Pringle	9			
*Kapil Dev	c Lamb b Ellison	1	(7) not out		23
C.Sharma	b Pringle	2			
†K.S.More	lbw b Pringle	25			
Maninder Singh	c Lamb b Emburey	6			
Extras	(LB5, W1, NB9)	15	(B1, LB9, W1, NB5)		16
Total		**341**	(5 wickets)		**136**

INDIA	O	M	R	W	O	M	R	W		FALL OF WICKETS			
Kapil Dev	31	8	67	1	22	7	52	4		E	I	E	I
Binny	18.2	4	55	3	(3) 15	3	44	1	Wkt	1st	1st	2nd	2nd
Sharma	32	10	64	5	(2) 17	4	48	1	1st	66	31	18	10
Maninder	30	15	45	1	(5) 20.4	12	9	3	2nd	92	90	23	31
Amarnath	7	1	18	0	(6) 2	2	0	0	3rd	92	161	35	76
Shastri	10	3	30	0	(4) 20	8	21	1	4th	98	232	108	78
									5th	245	238	113	110
ENGLAND									6th	264	252	121	–
Dilley	34	7	146	4	10	3	28	2	7th	269	253	164	–
Ellison	29	11	63	1	6	0	17	0	8th	271	264	170	–
Emburey	27	13	28	1					9th	287	303	170	–
Edmonds	22	7	41	1	11	2	51	1	10th	294	341	180	–
Pringle	25	7	58	3	(3) 15	5	30	1					

Umpires: K.E.Palmer (12) and D.R.Shepherd (3).

Close: 1st day – E(1) 245-5 (Pringle 51, Emburey 0); 2nd – I(1) 83-1 (Gavaskar 30, Amarnath 27); 3rd – E(2) 8-0 (Gooch 5, Robinson 3); 4th – E(2) 180 all out.

ENGLAND v INDIA 1986 (2nd Test)

At Headingley, Leeds, on 19, 20, 21, 23 June.
Toss: India.   Result: INDIA won by 279 runs.
Debuts: England – B.N.French; India – C.S.Pandit.

A change of leadership, with Gatting captaining England for the first time, could not prevent a seventh successive disaster. After just 77 minutes of play on the fourth morning, India gained their largest victory by a runs margin against all countries and won their second rubber in England. Vengsarkar batted 327 minutes (213 balls), his 11th hundred being his fifth against England. Gavaskar equalled M.C.Cowdrey's world record of 114 Test match appearances, reaching the landmark in 15 years 3 months – five years faster than the MCC President Elect. Athey became the first Gloucestershire player to win an England cap since June 1966 when D.A.Allen played the last of his 39 Tests.

INDIA

S.M.Gavaskar	c French b Pringle	35		c French b Lever	1
K.Srikkanth	c Emburey b Pringle	31		b Dilley	8
R.J.Shastri	c Pringle b Dilley	32		lbw b Lever	3
D.B.Vengsarkar	c French b Lever	61		not out	102
M.Azharuddin	lbw b Gooch	15		lbw b Lever	2
C.S.Pandit	c Emburey b Pringle	23		b Pringle	17
*Kapil Dev	lbw b Lever	0	(8)	c Gatting b Lever	31
R.M.H.Binny	c Slack b Emburey	6	(10)	lbw b Pringle	26
Madan Lal	c Gooch b Dilley	20		run out	22
†K.S.More	not out	36	(7)	c Slack b Pringle	16
Maninder Singh	c Gooch b Dilley	3		c Gatting b Pringle	1
Extras	(LB5, NB5)	10		(B4, LB4)	8
Total		**272**			**237**

ENGLAND

G.A.Gooch	c Binny b Kapil Dev	8		c Srikkanth b Kapil Dev	5
W.N.Slack	b Madan Lal	0		c Gavaskar b Binny	19
C.L.Smith	b Madan Lal	6		c More b Shastri	28
A.J.Lamb	c Pandit b Binny	10		c More b Binny	10
*M.W.Gatting	c More b Binny	13		not out	31
C.W.J.Athey	c More b Madan Lal	32		c More b Maninder	8
D.R.Pringle	c Srikkanth b Binny	8	(8)	lbw b Maninder	8
J.E.Emburey	c Kapil Dev b Binny	0	(9)	c Azharuddin b Kapil Dev	1
†B.N.French	b Binny	8	(10)	c Vengsarkar b Maninder	5
G.R.Dilley	b Shastri	10	(11)	run out	2
J.K.Lever	not out	0	(7)	c More b Maninder	0
Extras	(B1, LB2, NB4)	7		(LB9, NB2)	11
Total		**102**			**128**

ENGLAND	O	M	R	W	O	M	R	W	FALL OF WICKETS				
										I	E	I	E
Dilley	24.2	7	54	3	17	2	71	1	*Wkt*	*1st*	*1st*	*2nd*	*2nd*
Lever	30	4	102	2	23	5	64	4	1st	64	4	9	12
Pringle	27	6	47	3	22.3	6	73	4	2nd	75	14	9	46
Emburey	17	4	45	1	7	3	9	0	3rd	128	14	29	63
Gooch	6	0	19	1	7	2	12	0	4th	163	38	35	77
									5th	203	41	70	90
INDIA									6th	203	63	102	90
Kapil Dev	18	7	36	1	19.2	7	24	2	7th	211	63	137	101
Madan Lal	11.1	3	18	3	9.4	2	30	0	8th	213	71	173	104
Binny	13	1	40	5	(4) 8	1	18	2	9th	267	100	233	109
Shastri	3	1	5	1	(5) 10	3	21	1	10th	272	102	237	128
Maninder					(3) 16.3	6	26	4					

Umpires: J.Birkenshaw (1) and D.J.Constant (31).

Close: 1st day – I(1) 235-8 (Madan Lal 12, More 11); 2nd – I(2) 70-5 (Vengsarkar 33, More 0); 3rd – E(2) 90-6 (Gatting 10).

ENGLAND v INDIA 1986 (3rd Test)

At Edgbaston, Birmingham, on 3, 4, 5, 7, 8 July.
Toss: England.   Result: MATCH DRAWN.
Debuts: England – M.R.Benson, N.V.Radford.

For only the fourth time in 1,048 Tests since 1877 both sides were dismissed for identical first innings totals (also *Tests Nos. 107, 460*, and *713*). England ended their run of seven defeats by drawing the first Edgbaston Test since 1973; the previous eight Birmingham Tests had all been decided in under four days of actual play, six of them by an innings. Gatting (387 minutes, 294 balls, two sixes and 20 fours) scored his fifth Test hundred and his third against India. Sharma achieved his best innings and match analyses and became the first Indian bowler to take ten wickets in a Test in England. Gavaskar celebrated his world record 115th Test appearance by becoming the first to play 200 innings and the first Indian fielder to hold 100 catches (Gower). At the end of the match his other world records stood as follows: most runs (9,367), most hundreds (32), most innings of 50 and over (72), and most hundred partnerships (52).

ENGLAND

G.A.Gooch	c More b Kapil Dev	0	lbw b Sharma		40
M.R.Benson	b Maninder	21	b Shastri		30
C.W.J.Athey	c More b Kapil Dev	0	c More b Sharma		38
D.I.Gower	lbw b Sharma	49	c Gavaskar b Sharma		26
*M.W.Gatting	not out	183	lbw b Sharma		26
D.R.Pringle	c Amarnath b Shastri	44	c More b Maninder		7
J.E.Emburey	c Shastri b Maninder	38	not out		27
N.A.Foster	b Binny	17	run out		0
P.H.Edmonds	b Sharma	18	c Binny b Maninder		10
†B.N.French	b Sharma	8	c More b Sharma		1
N.V.Radford	c Gavaskar b Sharma	0	c Azharuddin b Sharma		1
Extras	(LB7, NB5)	12	(B10, LB6, W2, NB11)		29
Total		**390**			**235**

INDIA

S.M.Gavaskar	b Pringle	29	c French b Foster		54
K.Srikkanth	c Pringle b Radford	23	c Pringle b Edmonds		23
M.Amarnath	b Edmonds	79	c French b Edmonds		16
D.B.Vengsarkar	c Gooch b Radford	38	c French b Edmonds		0
M.Azharuddin	c French b Foster	64	not out		29
R.J.Shastri	c Gooch b Foster	18	c Emburey b Edmonds		0
*Kapil Dev	c French b Foster	26			
†K.S.More	c French b Emburey	48	(7) not out		31
R.M.H.Binny	c Gower b Emburey	40			
C.Sharma	c Gower b Pringle	9			
Maninder Singh	not out	0			
Extras	(B3,LB7, W1, NB5)	16	(B1, LB15, W1, NB4)		21
Total		**390**	(5 wickets)		**174**

INDIA	O	M	R	W	O	M	R	W	FALL OF WICKETS				
Kapil Dev	31	6	89	2	7	1	38	0		E	I	E	I
Binny	17	1	53	1	16	1	41	0	Wkt	1st	1st	2nd	2nd
Sharma	29.3	2	130	4	24	4	58	6	1st	0	53	49	58
Maninder	25	3	66	2	(5) 22	5	41	2	2nd	0	58	102	101
Shastri	14	1	45	1	(6) 23	8	39	1	3rd	61	139	152	101
Amarnath					(4) 2	1	2	0	4th	88	228	163	104
									5th	184	266	190	105
ENGLAND									6th	278	275	190	–
Radford	35	3	131	2	(2) 3	0	17	0	7th	327	302	190	–
Foster	41	9	93	3	(1) 22	9	48	1	8th	367	370	217	–
Pringle	21	2	61	2	16	5	33	0	9th	384	385	229	–
Edmonds	24	7	55	1	28	11	31	4	10th	390	390	235	–
Emburey	18.5	7	40	2	7	1	19	0					
Gatting					2	0	10	0					

Umpires: H.D.Bird (33) and B.J.Meyer (18).

Close: 1st day – E(1) 315-6 (Gatting 141, Foster 13); 2nd – I(1) 182-3 (Amarnath 59, Azharuddin 20); 3rd – I(1) 390 all out; 4th – E(2) 231-9 (Emburey 24, Radford 1).

ENGLAND v NEW ZEALAND 1986 (1st Test)

At Lord's, London, on 24, 25, 26, 28, 29 July.
Toss: England.   Result: MATCH DRAWN.
Debuts: England – M.D.Moxon; New Zealand – W.Watson.

Hadlee took five or more wickets in a Test innings for the 26th time to equal I.T.Botham's world record. French retired hurt at 259. In New Zealand's first innings a bizarre record was set when the wicket-keeping duties were shared by four players: Athey (first two overs), R.W.Taylor (overs 3 to 76), R.J.Parks (overs 77 to 140) and French (the final ball). Playing in his 39th Test, Edmonds became the second Middlesex bowler after F.J.Titmus to take 100 wickets for England. Martin Crowe (340 minutes, 247 balls, 11 fours) recorded his fifth hundred in 30 Tests; his partnership of 210 with Edgar remains New Zealand's highest for the third wicket against England. Gooch (441 minutes, 368 balls, 22 fours) achieved the highest score against New Zealand at Lord's (previously 178 by K.W.R.Fletcher in 1973). Wright, who deputised as captain in England's first innings when Coney (strained side) left the field after 22 overs, bagged his first 'pair' in 47 Tests.

ENGLAND

Player	Dismissal	Score	Dismissal	Score
G.A.Gooch	c Smith b Hadlee	18	c Watson b Bracewell	183
M.D.Moxon	lbw b Hadlee	74	lbw b Hadlee	5
C.W.J.Athey	c J.J.Crowe b Hadlee	44	b Gray	16
D.I.Gower	c M.D.Crowe b Bracewell	62	b Gray	3
*M.W.Gatting	b Hadlee	2	c M.D.Crowe b Gray	26
P.Willey	lbw b Watson	44	b Bracewell	42
P.H.Edmonds	c M.D.Crowe b Hadlee	6	not out	9
†B.N.French	retired hurt	0		
G.R.Dilley	c Smith b Hadlee	17		
N.A.Foster	b Watson	8		
N.V.Radford	not out	12		
Extras	(B6, LB7, NB7)	20	(LB6, W1, NB4)	11
Total		**307**	(6 wickets declared)	**295**

NEW ZEALAND

Player	Dismissal	Score		Dismissal	Score
J.G.Wright	b Dilley	0	(2)	c Gower b Dilley	0
B.A.Edgar	c Gatting b Gooch	83	(1)	c Gower b Foster	0
K.R.Rutherford	c Gooch b Dilley	0		not out	24
M.D.Crowe	c and b Edmonds	106		not out	11
J.J.Crowe	c Gatting b Edmonds	18			
*J.V.Coney	c Gooch b Radford	51			
E.J.Gray	c Gower b Edmonds	11			
R.J.Hadlee	b Edmonds	19			
†I.D.S.Smith	c Edmonds b Dilley	18			
J.G.Bracewell	not out	1			
W.Watson	lbw b Dilley	1			
Extras	(B4, LB9, W6, NB15)	34		(LB4, NB2)	6
Total		**342**		(2 wickets)	**41**

NEW ZEALAND	O	M	R	W		O	M	R	W
Hadlee	37.5	11	80	6		27	3	78	1
Watson	30	7	70	2		17	2	50	0
M.D.Crowe	8	1	38	0	(4)	4	0	13	0
Coney	4	0	12	0					
Bracewell	26	8	65	1		23.4	7	57	2
Gray	13	9	29	0	(3)	46	14	83	3
Rutherford					(6)	3	0	8	0
ENGLAND									
Dilley	35.1	9	82	4	(2)	6	3	5	1
Foster	25	6	56	0	(1)	3	1	13	1
Radford	25	4	71	1					
Edmonds	42	10	97	4	(3)	5	0	18	0
Gooch	13	6	23	1					
Gower					(4)	1	0	1	0

	FALL OF WICKETS			
	E	NZ	E	NZ
Wkt	1st	1st	2nd	2nd
1st	27	2	9	0
2nd	102	5	68	8
3rd	196	215	72	–
4th	198	218	136	–
5th	237	274	262	–
6th	258	292	295	–
7th	271	310	–	–
8th	285	340	–	–
9th	307	340	–	–
10th	–	342	–	–

Umpires: H.D.Bird (34) and A.G.T.Whitehead (3).

Close: 1st day – E(1) 248-5 (Willey 27, Edmonds 6); 2nd – NZ(1) 127-2 (Edgar 52, M.D.Crowe 52); 3rd – NZ(1) 342-9 (Bracewell 1, Watson 1); 4th – E(2) 110-3 (Gooch 64, Gatting 21).

ENGLAND v NEW ZEALAND 1986 (2nd Test)

At Trent Bridge, Nottingham, on 7, 8, 9, 11, 12 August.
Toss: New Zealand.   Result: NEW ZEALAND won by eight wickets.
Debuts: England – G.C.Small.

At 5.44 on the fifth evening, with eight overs to spare, New Zealand gained their second victory in 33 Tests in England. Hadlee surpassed I.T.Botham's world record of 26 five-wicket hauls and went on to achieve his seventh ten-wicket analysis to equal the world record shared by S.F.Barnes, C.V.Grimmett and D.K.Lillee. His 10 for 140 equalled Jack Cowie's record New Zealand match analysis in England set at Manchester in 1937. Bracewell (270 minutes, 200 balls, 10 fours) completed his first hundred in 19 Tests and his second in successive first-class innings. Smith overtook K.J.Wadsworth's New Zealand wicket-keeping record of 96 dismissals. Gower became the sixth batsman to score 6,000 runs for England. He also became the first England bowler to be called for throwing in a Test in England when he deliberately chucked the final ball of the match. The Secretary of the TCCB, D.B.Carr, ruled that the boundary hit by Martin Crowe off that historic delivery should stand.

ENGLAND

G.A.Gooch	lbw b Hadlee	18		c Coney b Bracewell	17
M.D.Moxon	b Hadlee	9		c Smith b Hadlee	23
C.W.J.Athey	lbw b Watson	55	(4)	c Smith b Bracewell	6
D.I.Gower	lbw b Gray	71	(5)	c J.J.Crowe b Bracewell	26
*M.W.Gatting	b Hadlee	17	(6)	c Smith b Gray	4
D.R.Pringle	c Watson b Stirling	21	(7)	c Gray b Stirling	9
J.E.Emburey	c Smith b Hadlee	8	(8)	c M.D.Crowe b Hadlee	75
P.H.Edmonds	c Smith b Hadlee	0	(3)	lbw b Hadlee	20
J.G.Thomas	b Hadlee	28		c Gray b Stirling	10
†B.N.French	c Coney b Watson	21		not out	12
G.C.Small	not out	2		lbw b Hadlee	12
Extras	(B1, LB3, NB2)	6		(B4, LB9, W1, NB2)	16
Total		**256**			**230**

NEW ZEALAND

J.G.Wright	c Athey b Small	58		b Emburey	7
B.A.Edgar	lbw b Thomas	8			
J.J.Crowe	c French b Small	23	(2)	lbw b Small	2
M.D.Crowe	c Edmonds b Emburey	28	(3)	not out	48
*J.V.Coney	run out	24	(4)	not out	20
E.J.Gray	c Athey b Edmonds	50			
R.J.Hadlee	c Gooch b Thomas	68			
J.G.Bracewell	c Moxon b Emburey	110			
†I.D.S.Smith	lbw b Edmonds	2			
D.A.Stirling	b Small	26			
W.Watson	not out	8			
Extras	(LB4, W2, NB2)	8			
Total		**413**		**(2 wickets)**	**77**

NEW ZEALAND	O	M	R	W		O	M	R	W		FALL OF WICKETS			
											E	NZ	E	NZ
Hadlee	32	7	80	6		33.1	15	60	4		*1st*	*1st*	*2nd*	*2nd*
Stirling	17	3	62	1		18	5	48	2	*Wkt*				
Gray	13	4	30	1	(5)	24	9	55	1	1st	18	39	23	5
Watson	16.5	6	51	2		9	3	25	0	2nd	43	85	47	19
Coney	7	1	18	0						3rd	126	92	63	–
Bracewell	4	1	11	0	(3)	11	5	29	3	4th	170	142	87	–
										5th	176	144	98	–
ENGLAND										6th	191	239	104	–
Small	38	12	88	3		8	3	10	1	7th	191	318	178	–
Thomas	39	5	124	2		4	0	16	0	8th	205	326	203	–
Pringle	20	1	58	0	(5)	2	0	16	0	9th	240	391	203	–
Edmonds	28	11	52	2		4	1	16	0	10th	256	413	230	–
Emburey	42.5	17	87	2	(3)	6	1	15	1					
Gooch	2	2	0	0										
Gower					(6)	0‡	0	4	0					

Umpires: D.J.Constant (32) and K.E.Palmer (13).   ‡ One no-ball.

Close: 1st day – E(1) 240-9 (French 7, Small 0); 2nd – NZ(1) 211-5 (Gray 14, Hadlee 53); 3rd – E(2) 31-1 (Moxon 14, Edmonds 0); 4th – E(2) 64-3 (Edmonds 13, Gower 0).

ENGLAND v NEW ZEALAND 1986 (3rd Test)

At Kennington Oval, London, on 21, 22, 23, 25, 26 August.
Toss: England.   Result: MATCH DRAWN.
Debuts: New Zealand – T.E.Blain.

After nine unsuccessful missions New Zealand won their first rubber in England when rain limited play to a total of 15.5 overs on the last two days, including just two 3-ball interludes on the final one. With the first and 12th balls since his suspension from Test cricket, Botham equalled and passed (at 12.28pm) D.K.Lillee's world record of 355 Test wickets. It had stood since 2.55 pm on 27 December 1981 (*Test No. 918*). Botham's 355 wickets came from 19,201 balls in 85 Tests played over nine years; Lillee's came from 18,467 balls in 70 Tests during a period of 13 years. This was the fifth major landmark in Botham's career to have been achieved at The Oval, following 1,000 runs and the double (1979), 200 wickets (1981) and 300 wickets (1984). Wright (424 minutes, 343 balls) scored his fifth hundred and the first for New Zealand in eight Tests at The Oval. Botham scored 59 off 36 balls, reaching his fifty off 32 balls in 48 minutes. His onslaught included 24 (464604) off Stirling's ninth over to equal the 6-ball over Test record shared by A.M.E.Roberts and S.M.Patil.

NEW ZEALAND

J.G.Wright	b Edmonds	119	not out	7
B.A.Edgar	c Gooch b Botham	1	not out	0
J.J.Crowe	lbw b Botham	8		
M.D.Crowe	lbw b Dilley	13		
*J.V.Coney	c Gooch b Botham	38		
E.J.Gray	b Dilley	30		
R.J.Hadlee	c French b Edmonds	6		
J.G.Bracewell	c Athey b Emburey	3		
†T.E.Blain	c Gooch b Dilley	37		
D.A.Stirling	not out	18		
E.J.Chatfield	c French b Dilley	5		
Extras	(B1, W1, NB7)	9		
Total		**287**	(0 wickets)	**7**

ENGLAND

G.A.Gooch	c Stirling b Hadlee	32
C.W.J.Athey	lbw b Hadlee	17
D.I.Gower	b Chatfield	131
A.J.Lamb	b Chatfield	0
*M.W.Gatting	b Chatfield	121
I.T.Botham	not out	59
J.E.Emburey	not out	9
†B.N.French		
P.H.Edmonds	did not bat	
G.R.Dilley		
G.C.Small		
Extras	(LB9, W5, NB5)	19
Total	(5 wickets declared)	**388**

ENGLAND	O	M	R	W	O	M	R	W	FALL OF WICKETS		
									NZ	E	NZ
Dilley	28.2	4	92	4							
Small	18	5	36	0					Wkt	1st	1st	2nd
Botham	25	4	75	3	(1) 1	0	7	0	1st	17	38	–
Emburey	31	15	39	1					2nd	31	62	–
Edmonds	22	10	29	2					3rd	59	62	–
Gooch	4	1	15	0					4th	106	285	–
									5th	175	326	–
NEW ZEALAND									6th	192	–	–
Hadlee	23.5	6	92	2					7th	197	–	–
Stirling	9	0	71	0					8th	251	–	–
Chatfield	21	7	73	3					9th	280	–	–
Gray	21	4	74	0					10th	287	–	–
Bracewell	11	1	51	0								
Coney	5	0	18	0								

Umpires: H.D.Bird (35) and D.R.Shepherd (4).

Close: 1st day – NZ(1) 142-4 (Wright 63, Gray 15); 2nd – NZ(1) 257-8 (Blain 27, Stirling 5); 3rd – E(1) 281-3 (Gower 129, Gatting 86); 4th – E(1) 388-5 (Botham 59, Emburey 9).

INDIA v AUSTRALIA 1986-87 (1st Test)

At Chidambaram Stadium, Chepauk, Madras, on 18, 19, 20, 21, 22 September.
Toss: Australia.   Result: MATCH TIED.
Debuts: None.

At 5.18pm, with the penultimate ball of the final over, off-spinner Greg Matthews claimed an lbw decision against Maninder Singh to gain only the second tie in 1,052 Test matches since 1877 (also *Test No. 502*). It was the climax to an astonishing fight-back by Australia after India, set 348 at the start of the final day, had reached the relative safety of first 158 for 1 and later 331 for 6. Matthews achieved the only five-wicket analyses of his career. Gavaskar became the first to make 100 consecutive Test appearances. Australia recorded their highest total in India. Shastri completed 2,000 runs and 100 wickets in his 44th Test. Jones (503 minutes, 330 balls, 27 fours and two sixes) recorded Australia's highest score in India (previously 167 by G.N.Yallop in *Test No. 859*). Totally exhausted after his marathon innings in intense humidity, Jones required hospitalisation for saline treatment. Boon completed 1,000 runs in 17 Tests during his third hundred – all against India. Pandit deputised as wicket-keeper after More (mild food poisoning) retired after 50 minutes of the first morning's play.

AUSTRALIA

D.C.Boon	c Kapil Dev b Sharma	122	(2) lbw b Maninder	49
G.R.Marsh	c Kapil Dev b Yadav	22	(1) b Shastri	11
D.M.Jones	b Yadav	210	c Azharuddin b Maninder	24
R.J.Bright	c Shastri b Yadav	30		
*A.R.Border	c Gavaskar b Shastri	106	(4) b Maninder	27
G.M.Ritchie	run out	13	(5) c Pandit b Shastri	28
G.R.J.Matthews	c Pandit b Yadav	44	(6) not out	27
S.R.Waugh	not out	12	(7) not out	2
†T.J.Zoehrer				
C.J.McDermott	did not bat			
B.A.Reid				
Extras	(B1, LB7, W1, NB6)	15	(LB1, NB1)	2
Total	(7 wickets declared)	**574**	(5 wickets declared)	**170**

INDIA

S.M.Gavaskar	c and b Matthews	8	c Jones b Bright	90
K.Srikkanth	c Ritchie b Matthews	53	c Waugh b Matthews	39
M.Amarnath	run out	1	c Boon b Matthews	51
M.Azharruddin	c and b Bright	50	c Ritchie b Bright	42
R.J.Shastri	c Zoehrer b Matthews	62	(7) not out	48
C.S.Pandit	c Waugh b Matthews	35	(5) b Matthews	39
*Kapil Dev	c Border b Matthews	119	(6) c Bright b Matthews	1
†K.S.More	c Zoehrer b Waugh	4	(9) lbw b Bright	0
C.Sharma	c Zoehrer b Reid	30	(8) c McDermott b Bright	23
N.S.Yadav	c Border b Bright	19	b Bright	8
Maninder Singh	not out	0	lbw b Matthews	0
Extras	(B1, LB9, NB6)	16	(B1, LB3, NB2)	6
Total		**397**		**347**

INDIA	O	M	R	W	O	M	R	W	FALL OF WICKETS			
										A	I	A	I
Kapil Dev	18	5	52	0	(2) 1	0	5	0	Wkt	1st	1st	2nd	2nd
Sharma	16	1	70	1	(1) 6	0	19	0	1st	48	62	31	55
Maninder	39	8	135	0	(4) 19	2	60	3	2nd	206	65	81	158
Yadav	49.5	9	142	4	(5) 9	0	35	0	3rd	282	65	94	204
Shastri	47	8	161	1	(3) 14	2	50	2	4th	460	142	125	251
Srikkanth	1	0	6	0					5th	481	206	165	253
									6th	544	220	–	291
AUSTRALIA									7th	574	245	–	331
McDermott	14	2	59	0	5	0	27	0	8th	–	330	–	334
Reid	18	4	93	1	10	2	48	0	9th	–	387	–	344
Matthews	28.2	3	103	5	39.5	7	146	5	10th	–	397	–	347
Bright	23	3	88	2	25	3	94	5					
Waugh	11	2	44	1	(6) 4	1	16	0					
Border					(5) 3	0	12	0					

Umpires: D.N.Dotiwalla (5) and V.Vikramraju (2).

Close: 1st day – A(1) 211-2 (Jones 56, Bright 1); 2nd – A(1) 556-6 (Matthews 34, Waugh 5); 3rd – I(1) 270-7 (Kapil Dev 33, Sharma 14); 4th – A(2) 170-5 (Matthews 27, Waugh 2).

INDIA v AUSTRALIA 1986-87 (2nd Test)

At Feroz Shah Kotla, Delhi, on 26 (*no play*), 27 (*no play*), 28 (*no play*), 29, 30 September.
Toss: Australia.   Result: MATCH DRAWN.
Debuts: None.

A succession of unseasonal bouts of heavy rain, allied to inadequate covering, prevented a start until after tea on the fourth day. Vengsarkar completed 5,000 runs in his 86th Test, the third to do so for India following Gavaskar and G.R.Viswanath.

AUSTRALIA

G.R.Marsh	c Pandit b Sharma	11
D.C.Boon	c Maninder b Shastri	67
D.M.Jones	st Pandit b Shastri	29
S.R.Waugh	not out	39
†T.J.Zoehrer	not out	52
*A.R.Border		
G.M.Ritchie		
G.R.J.Matthews		
R.J.Bright	did not bat	
C.J.McDermott		
D.R.Gilbert		
Extras	(LB2, W4, NB3)	9
Total	(3 wickets declared)	**207**

INDIA

S.M.Gavaskar	b Gilbert	4
K.Srikkanth	run out	26
M.Azharuddin	c Zoehrer b Waugh	24
D.B.Vengsarkar	not out	22
†C.S.Pandit	not out	26
M.Amarnath		
R.J.Shastri		
*Kapil Dev	did not bat	
C.Sharma		
N.S.Yadav		
Maninder Singh		
Extras	(LB5)	5
Total	(3 wickets)	**107**

INDIA	O	M	R	W
Kapil Dev	14	5	27	0
Sharma	8	1	34	1
Shastri	21.4	4	44	2
Maninder	19	4	54	0
Yadav	13	1	46	0

AUSTRALIA	O	M	R	W
McDermott	6	1	24	0
Gilbert	11	1	44	1
Waugh	6	0	29	1
Boon	2	1	5	0
Jones	1	1	0	0

FALL OF WICKETS

	A	I
Wkt	*1st*	*1st*
1st	34	9
2nd	110	57
3rd	118	59
4th	–	–
5th	–	–
6th	–	–
7th	–	–
8th	–	–
9th	–	–
10th	–	–

Umpires: V.K.Ramaswamy (3) and P.D.Reporter (3).

Close: 1st day – no play; 2nd – no play; 3rd – no play; 4th – A(1) 58-1 (Boon 37, Jones 3).

INDIA v AUSTRALIA 1986-87 (3rd Test)

At Wankhede Stadium, Bombay, on 15, 16, 17, 18, 19 October.
Toss: Australia.   Result: MATCH DRAWN.
Debuts: India – R.R.Kulkarni.

India compiled their highest total in a home Test against Australia. Gavaskar scored his 33rd hundred and completed 1,500 runs (eight hundreds) against Australia. Vengsarkar, who completed 1,000 runs against Australia, and Shastri shared an unbroken partnership of 298 in 388 minutes to set an Indian sixth-wicket record against all countries and the record for any wicket by either country in this series. Shastri became the first Indian to hit six sixes in a Test innings. The match produced 1,078 runs at an average of 63.41 per wicket.

AUSTRALIA

Player	Dismissal	Runs		2nd innings	Runs
G.R.Marsh	c Gavaskar b Kulkarni	101	(2)	b Shastri	20
D.C.Boon	c Gavaskar b Kulkarni	47	(1)	c More b Shastri	40
D.M.Jones	c sub‡ b Yadav	35		not out	73
*A.R.Border	st More b Maninder	46		not out	66
G.M.Ritchie	run out	31			
G.R.J.Matthews	b Yadav	20			
S.R.Waugh	b Yadav	6			
†T.J.Zoehrer	c and b Maninder	21			
R.J.Bright	lbw b Kulkarni	8			
D.R.Gilbert	c sub ‡ b Yadav	1			
B.A.Reid	not out	2			
Extras	(B5, LB12, NB10)	27		(B5, LB5, NB7)	17
Total		345		(2 wickets)	216

INDIA

S.M.Gavaskar	c Ritchie b Matthews	103
K.Srikkanth	c Marsh b Bright	24
†K.S.More	c Jones b Matthews	15
M.Amarnath	c sub# b Matthews	35
D.B.Vengsarkar	not out	164
M.Azharuddin	c sub# b Matthews	10
R.J.Shastri	not out	121
*Kapil Dev		
N.S.Yadav	did not bat	
R.R.Kulkarni		
Maninder Singh		
Extras	(B9, LB15, NB21)	45
Total	(5 wickets declared)	517

INDIA	O	M	R	W		O	M	R	W		FALL OF WICKETS		
Kulkarni	23	2	85	3	(5)	6	0	29	0		A	I	A
Kapil Dev	6	1	16	0	(1)	6	1	24	0	Wkt	1st	1st	2nd
Shastri	42	16	68	0		30	8	60	2	1st	76	53	64
Yadav	41.4	8	84	4		23	7	52	0	2nd	151	119	70
Maninder	33	10	72	2	(2)	20	6	31	0	3rd	241	194	–
Srikkanth	2	0	3	0		3	0	10	0	4th	252	205	–
										5th	295	219	–
AUSTRALIA										6th	304	–	–
Reid	32	5	81	0						7th	308	–	–
Gilbert	24	3	75	0						8th	340	–	–
Matthews	52	8	158	4						9th	340	–	–
Bright	38	6	109	1						10th	345	–	–
Border	10	3	29	0									
Waugh	14	2	41	0									

‡ (L.Sivaramakrishnan)
Umpires: J.D.Ghosh (4) and R.B.Gupta (1).   # (M.R.J.Veletta)

Close: 1st day – A(1) 217-2 (Marsh 89, Border 34); 2nd – I(1) 61-1 (Gavaskar 30, More 0); 3rd – I(1) 291-5 (Vengsarkar 41, Shastri 37); 4th – A(2) 9-0 (Boon 5, Marsh 2).

PAKISTAN v WEST INDIES 1986-87 (1st Test)

At Iqbal Stadium, Faisalabad, on 24, 26, 27, 28, 29 October.
Toss: Pakistan.   Result: PAKISTAN won by 186 runs.
Debuts: West Indies – A.H.Gray.

After 25 minutes of the fifth morning, Pakistan gained their fifth victory in 20 Tests against the West Indies and their first since 1976-77. This defeat, the first under the captaincy of Richards, ended a run of seven wins and was only the second inflicted upon the touring side in their last 38 Tests and the third in their last 54. West Indies were dismissed for their lowest total in 247 Tests (previously 76, also at the hands of Pakistan (*Test No. 470*)), and the lowest total in 73 Tests by all countries in Pakistan, previously 70 by New Zealand (*415*). There had been only five lower totals in 772 Test matches since 1946. Abdul Qadir returned the best analysis for Pakistan against West Indies (until 1987-88) and obtained his tenth five-wicket haul, nine of which had occurred in Pakistan. Salim Malik retired at 90 when his left arm was fractured above the wrist by a lifting ball from Walsh. Batting last in the second innings with his arm in plaster, Malik survived 15 balls from Walsh and Gray in a brave stand of 32 with Wasim Akram. After facing the first ball left-handed he reverted to his normal stance.

PAKISTAN

Mohsin Khan	lbw b Marshall	2		c Haynes b Walsh	40
Mudassar Nazar	c Richardson b Marshall	26		c Haynes b Marshall	2
Ramiz Raja	lbw b Marshall	0		c Gray b Patterson	13
Javed Miandad	c Dujon b Patterson	1	(6)	c sub (A.L.Logie) b Gray	30
Qasim Omar	hit wkt b Gray	3		lbw b Walsh	48
Salim Malik	retired hurt	21	(11)	not out	3
*Imran Khan	c and b Gray	61		c Harper b Marshall	23
Abdul Qadir	c and b Patterson	14		lbw b Gray	2
†Salim Yousuf	lbw b Gray	0	(4)	c Greenidge b Harper	61
Wasim Akram	c Richardson b Gray	0	(9)	st Dujon b Harper	66
Tausif Ahmed	not out	9	(10)	b Walsh	8
Extras	(B1, LB11, NB10)	22		(B7, LB8, W2, NB15)	32
Total		**159**			**328**

WEST INDIES

C.G.Greenidge	lbw b Wasim	10		lbw b Imran	12
D.L.Haynes	lbw b Imran	40		lbw b Imran	0
R.B.Richardson	b Tausif	54		c Ramiz b Qadir	14
H.A.Gomes	c sub (Manzoor Elahi) b Qadir	33		b Qadir	2
†P.J.L.Dujon	c Ramiz b Tausif	0	(6)	lbw b Imran	0
R.A.Harper	c Salim Yousuf b Wasim	28	(7)	c sub‡ b Qadir	2
M.D.Marshall	c Salim Yousuf b Wasim	5	(8)	c and b Qadir	10
*I.V.A.Richards	c Salim Yousuf b Wasim	33	(5)	c Ramiz b Qadir	0
A.H.Gray	not out	12		b Qadir	5
C.A.Walsh	lbw b Wasim	4		b Imran	0
B.P.Patterson	lbw b Wasim	0		not out	6
Extras	(B9, LB8, NB12)	29		(LB2)	2
Total		**248**			**53**

WEST INDIES	O	M	R	W		O	M	R	W		FALL OF WICKETS			
Marshall	10	2	48	3		26	3	83	2		P	WI	P	WI
Patterson	12	1	38	2		19	3	63	1	Wkt	*1st*	*1st*	*2nd*	*2nd*
Gray	11.5	3	39	4	(4)	22	4	82	2	1st	12	12	2	5
Walsh	5	0	22	0	(5)	23	6	49	3	2nd	12	103	19	16
Harper					(3)	27.5	9	36	2	3rd	19	124	113	19
										4th	37	124	124	19
PAKISTAN										5th	37	178	208	20
Wasim	25	3	91	6	(2)	3	0	5	0	6th	119	192	218	23
Imran	21	8	32	1	(1)	13	5	30	4	7th	120	223	224	36
Qadir	15	1	58	1		9.3	1	16	6	8th	120	243	258	42
Tausif	22	5	50	2						9th	159	247	296	43
										10th	–	248	328	53

Umpires: Khizer Hayat (18) and Mian Mohammad Aslam (3).   ‡ (Shoaib Mohammad)

Close: 1st day – WI(1) 54-1 (Haynes 18, Richardson 20); 2nd – P(2) 28-2 (Mohsin 3, Salim Yousuf 9); 3rd – P(2) 183-4 (Omar 38, Miandad 15); 4th – WI(2) 43-9 (Marshall 6).

PAKISTAN v WEST INDIES 1986-87 (2nd Test)

At Gaddafi Stadium, Lahore, on 7, 8, 9, November.
Toss: Pakistan.   Result: WEST INDIES won by an innings and 10 runs.
Debuts: Pakistan – Asif Mujtaba.

With their third three-day victory of 1986 West Indies exacted immediate revenge for their humiliating defeat at Faisalabad. This contest produced an aggregate of 426 runs for 29 wickets (an average of 14.68 runs per wicket) and a highest partnership of only 49. The West Indies total of 218 is the third-lowest to achieve an innings victory in Test cricket following 153 by Australia (*Test No. 216*) and 172 by England (*30*). Pakistan were dismissed for their lowest total against West Indies and their lowest in any home Test. Marshall took five wickets in an innings for the 14th time and achieved a record analysis for West Indies in Pakistan. Although West Indies included two specialist spin bowlers for the first time since 1978-79 (*845*) they shared but a single over. Qasim Omar retired at 26 after being struck in the face by a bouncer from Walsh.

PAKISTAN

Batsman	Dismissal 1st	Runs		Dismissal 2nd	Runs
Mohsin Khan	b Marshall	0		lbw b Gray	1
Rizwan-uz-Zaman	c Richardson b Marshall	2		b Marshall	1
Qasim Omar	lbw b Marshall	4		retired hurt	10
Javed Miandad	c Greenidge b Walsh	46		b Walsh	19
Ramiz Raja	b Gray	15		lbw b Gray	1
Asif Mujtaba	b Marshall	8		lbw b Richards	6
†Salim Yousuf	lbw b Walsh	8	(8)	lbw b Gray	13
Abdul Qadir	run out	12	(9)	b Walsh	2
Wasim Akram	lbw b Marshall	1	(11)	c Harper b Walsh	0
*Imran Khan	not out	13	(7)	c Dujon b Walsh	2
Tausif Ahmed	c Dujon b Walsh	0	(10)	not out	6
Extras	(B9, LB4, NB9)	22		(B4, LB9, W1, NB2)	16
Total		**131**			**77**

WEST INDIES

C.G.Greenidge	lbw b Qadir	75
D.L.Haynes	b Tausif	18
R.B.Richardson	lbw b Qadir	4
H.A.Gomes	lbw b Imran	9
*I.V.A.Richards	c Salim b Qadir	44
†P.J.L.Dujon	b Imran	2
R.A.Harper	lbw b Qadir	6
M.D.Marshall	not out	13
C.G.Butts	c Salim b Imran	6
A.H.Gray	b Imran	10
C.A.Walsh	b Imran	8
Extras	(B15, LB5, NB3)	23
Total		**218**

WEST INDIES	O	M	R	W	O	M	R	W
Marshall	18	5	33	5	8	3	14	1
Gray	13	0	28	1	17	7	20	3
Walsh	21.4	3	56	3	14.5	5	21	4
Harper	1	0	1	0				
Richards					(4) 5	2	9	1

PAKISTAN	O	M	R	W
Imran	30.5	4	59	5
Wasim	9	2	16	0
Qadir	32	5	96	4
Tausif	19	8	27	1

FALL OF WICKETS

Wkt	P 1st	WI 1st	P 2nd
1st	0	49	3
2nd	6	71	3
3rd	9	107	33
4th	46	153	44
5th	75	160	54
6th	95	172	63
7th	98	179	69
8th	99	189	71
9th	129	204	77
10th	131	218	–

Umpires: V.K.Ramaswamy (4) and P.D.Reporter (4).

Close: 1st day – WI(1) 15-0 (Greenidge 9, Haynes 6); 2nd – WI(1) 185-7 (Marshall 3, Butts 4).

PAKISTAN v WEST INDIES 1986-87 (3rd Test)

At National Stadium, Karachi, on 20, 21, 22, 24, 25 November.
Toss: West Indies.   Result: MATCH DRAWN.
Debuts: Pakistan – Salim Jaffer.

The umpires' decision to abandon play because of unfit light with nine overs unbowled ensured that Pakistan kept their unbeaten record at Karachi, their 25 matches at the National Stadium having produced 11 wins and 14 draws. Ramiz Raja scored 62 in 408 minutes, his fifty (318 minutes) being then the third-slowest in Tests. Imran Khan achieved his 19th five-wicket haul as Haynes became the third West Indian after F.M.M.Worrell and C.C.Hunte to carry his bat through a completed Test innings; only S.M.Gavaskar and Mudassar Nazar had previously achieved this feat in Pakistan. Despite a fractured bone in his left hand Abdul Qadir bowled 75.5 overs. Harper and Butts provided the first instance since February 1979 of specialist spin bowlers operating in the same innings for West Indies – an interlude embracing 59 Tests and 14 series. For only the second time since 1888 no player scored a hundred during a series involving three or more Tests; the last series barren of centuries was that between India and New Zealand in 1969-70.

WEST INDIES

C.G.Greenidge	c Salim Yousuf b Mudassar	27		b Qadir	8
D.L.Haynes	lbw b Imran	3		not out	88
R.B.Richardson	c Asif b Salim Jaffer	44		c Ramiz b Qadir	32
H.A.Gomes	lbw b Qadir	18		lbw b Qadir	5
*I.V.A.Richards	c Ramiz b Tausif	70		c Salim Yousuf b Imran	28
†P.J.L.Dujon	c Salim Yousuf b Qadir	19		c Salim Yousuf b Salim Jaffer	6
R.A.Harper	lbw b Imran	9		b Imran	4
M.D.Marshall	b Tausif	4		lbw b Imran	0
C.G.Butts	lbw b Qadir	17		c Mohsin b Imran	12
A.H.Gray	c Imran b Qadir	0		b Imran	0
C.A.Walsh	not out	0		b Imran	0
Extras	(B14, LB11, W1, NB3)	29		(B7, LB13, W1, NB7)	28
Total		**240**			**211**

PAKISTAN

Mudassar Nazar	b Gray	16	(6)	lbw b Butts	25
Mohsin Khan	c Richards b Marshall	1		c Greenidge b Marshall	4
Ramiz Raja	c Harper b Butts	62	(4)	b Butts	29
Javed Miandad	run out	76	(5)	b Marshall	4
*Imran Khan	lbw b Butts	1	(8)	not out	15
Asif Mujtaba	c Dujon b Marshall	12	(7)	c Dujon b Walsh	6
Qasim Omar	c Richardson b Butts	5	(1)	c Dujon b Gray	1
†Salim Yousuf	c Walsh b Butts	22	(3)	c Haynes b Marshall	10
Tausif Ahmed	c Richardson b Gray	3		not out	7
Salim Jaffer	b Gray	9			
Abdul Qadir	not out	8			
Extras	(B9, LB12, W1, NB2)	24		(B17, LB6, W1)	24
Total		**239**		(7 wickets)	**125**

PAKISTAN	O	M	R	W		O	M	R	W		FALL OF WICKETS			
											WI	P	WI	P
Imran	19	4	32	2		22.3	2	46	6		*Wkt*	*1st*	*1st*	*2nd*	*2nd*
Salim Jaffer	15	5	34	1		14	4	23	1		*Wkt*	*1st*	*1st*	*2nd*	*2nd*
Mudassar	4	0	15	1							1st	14	19	36	3
Qadir	31.5	3	107	4		44	9	84	3		2nd	55	29	107	16
Tausif	17	7	27	2	(3)	12	2	36	0		3rd	94	140	128	19
Asif					(5)	3	2	2	0		4th	110	145	159	25
											5th	172	172	171	73
WEST INDIES											6th	204	179	185	95
Marshall	33	9	57	2		19	5	31	3		7th	210	215	185	95
Gray	21.1	6	40	3		14	7	18	1		8th	227	218	209	–
Harper	7	0	31	0	(5)	1	0	1	0		9th	234	222	211	–
Walsh	11	2	17	0	(3)	22	11	30	1		10th	240	239	211	–
Butts	38	15	73	4	(4)	22	9	22	2						

Umpires: V.K.Ramaswamy (5) and P.D.Reporter (5).

Close: 1st day – WI(1) 212-7 (Harper 6, Butts 1); 2nd – P(1) 157-4 (Ramiz 42, Asif 6); 3rd – WI(2) 84-1 (Haynes 46, Richardson 21); 4th – P(2) 16-2 (Mohsin 4).

AUSTRALIA v ENGLAND 1986-87 (1st Test)

At Woolloongabba, Brisbane, on 14, 15, 16, 18, 19 November.
Toss: Australia. Result: ENGLAND won by seven wickets.
Debuts: Australia – C.D.Matthews; England – P.A.J.DeFreitas, C.J.Richards.

The first English team ever to visit Australia without a current Yorkshire or Lancashire player ended a sequence of 11 Tests without victory. Gatting became the first England captain to enforce the follow-on while playing his first Test match in Australia. It was also the first time Australia had suffered this indignity in a home Ashes Test since 1965-66. Emburey, playing his 38th Test, completed 50 wickets against Australia before becoming the third Middlesex bowler after F.J.Titmus and P.H.Edmonds to take 100 Test wickets. At 6ft 8in Reid became the tallest player to appear in Ashes Tests, surpassing England's A.W.Greig (6ft 7½in) and Australia's G.J.Bonnor and L.E.Nagel (both 6ft 6in). Botham (249 minutes, 174 balls, four sixes and 13 fours) registered England's highest innings at the 'Gabba' and set a record for one batsman in Ashes Tests by hitting 22 (224644) off one over from Hughes. Marsh scored 56 and 110 in his first Test against England. DeFreitas (20 years 269 days) was England's fourth-youngest representative against Australia (after D.B.Close, D.C.S.Compton and G.R.Dilley) and their first from Dominica.

ENGLAND

Batsman	Dismissal	Runs		Dismissal (2nd)	Runs
B.C.Broad	c Zoehrer b Reid	8		not out	35
C.W.J.Athey	c Zoehrer b C.D.Matthews	76		c Waugh b Hughes	1
*M.W.Gatting	b Hughes	61		c G.R.J.Matthews b Hughes	12
A.J.Lamb	lbw b Hughes	40		lbw b Reid	9
D.I.Gower	c Ritchie b C.D.Matthews	51		not out	15
I.T.Botham	c Hughes b Waugh	138			
†C.J.Richards	b C.D.Matthews	0			
J.E.Emburey	c Waugh b Hughes	8			
P.A.J.DeFreitas	c C.D.Matthews b Waugh	40			
P.H.Edmonds	not out	9			
G.R.Dilley	c Boon b Waugh	0			
Extras	(B3, LB19, NB3)	25		(B2, NB3)	5
Total		456		(3 wickets)	77

AUSTRALIA

Batsman	Dismissal	Runs		Dismissal (2nd)	Runs
G.R.Marsh	c Richards b Dilley	56	(2)	b DeFreitas	110
D.C.Boon	c Broad b DeFreitas	10	(1)	lbw b Botham	14
†T.J.Zoehrer	lbw b Dilley	38	(8)	not out	16
D.M.Jones	lbw b DeFreitas	8	(3)	st Richards b Emburey	18
*A.R.Border	c DeFreitas b Edmonds	7	(4)	c Lamb b Emburey	23
G.M.Ritchie	c Edmonds b Dilley	41	(5)	lbw b DeFreitas	45
G.R.J.Matthews	not out	56	(6)	c and b Dilley	13
S.R.Waugh	c Richards b Dilley	0	(7)	b Emburey	28
C.D.Matthews	c Gatting b Botham	11		lbw b Emburey	0
M.G.Hughes	b Botham	0		b DeFreitas	0
B.A.Reid	c Richards b Dilley	3		c Broad b Emburey	2
Extras	(B2, LB8, W2, NB6)	18		(B5, LB6, NB2)	13
Total		248			282

AUSTRALIA	O	M	R	W		O	M	R	W
Reid	31	4	86	1	(3)	6	1	20	1
Hughes	36	7	134	3		5.3	0	28	2
C.D.Matthews	35	10	95	3	(1)	4	0	11	0
Waugh	21	3	76	3					
G.R.J.Matthews	11	2	43	0	(4)	7	1	16	0

ENGLAND	O	M	R	W		O	M	R	W
DeFreitas	16	5	32	2	(4)	17	2	62	3
Dilley	25.4	7	68	5		19	6	47	1
Emburey	34	11	66	0		42.5	14	80	5
Edmonds	12	6	12	1	(5)	24	8	46	0
Botham	16	1	58	2	(1)	12	0	34	1
Gatting	1	0	2	0		2	0	2	0

FALL OF WICKETS

Wkt	E 1st	A 1st	A 2nd	E 2nd
1st	15	27	24	6
2nd	116	97	44	25
3rd	198	114	92	40
4th	198	126	205	–
5th	316	159	224	–
6th	324	198	262	–
7th	351	204	266	–
8th	443	239	266	–
9th	451	239	275	–
10th	456	248	282	–

Umpires: A.R.Crafter (19) and M.W.Johnson (20).

Close: 1st day – E(1) 198-2 (Athey 76, Lamb 40); 2nd – A(1) 33-1 (Marsh 17, Zoehrer 0); 3rd – A(2) 2-0 (Boon 1, Marsh 1); 4th – A(2) 243-5 (Marsh 108, Waugh 12).

AUSTRALIA v ENGLAND 1986-87 (2nd Test)

At W.A.C.A.Ground, Perth, on 28, 29, 30 November, 2, 3 December.
Toss: England.   Result: MATCH DRAWN.
Debuts: None.

Australia were set 391 runs on the final day after England had registered their second-highest total in Australia – exceeded only by their 636 at Sydney in December 1928. Gatting, playing in his 50th Test, became the first England captain to declare in Australia since R.Illingworth (*Test No. 678*). Broad (435 minutes, 303 balls, 25 fours) made England's highest score at Perth, his opening partnership of 223 with Athey being the highest for any England wicket on that ground. Richards, the second Cornishman to represent England, became the third England wicket-keeper after L.E.G.Ames and A.P.E.Knott to score a hundred against Australia, Knott's 106 not out (*754*) being the only other such hundred in Australia. Border recorded Australia's 200th hundred against England and his 20th in 86 Tests; he also became the 11th Australian to complete 2,000 runs against England. When he caught Boon, Botham emulated G.St A.Sobers by completing the Test treble of 1,000 runs, 100 wickets and 100 catches.

ENGLAND

B.C.Broad	c Zoehrer b Reid	162		lbw b Waugh	16
C.W.J.Athey	b Reid	96		c Border b Reid	6
A.J.Lamb	c Zoehrer b Reid	0	(4)	lbw b Reid	2
*M.W.Gatting	c Waugh b C.D.Matthews	14	(3)	b Waugh	70
D.I.Gower	c Waugh b G.R.J.Matthews	136		c Zoehrer b Waugh	48
I.T.Botham	c Border b Reid	0		c G.R.J.Matthews b Reid	6
†C.J.Richards	c Waugh b C.D.Matthews	133		c Lawson b Waugh	15
P.A.J.DeFreitas	lbw b C.D.Matthews	11		b Waugh	15
J.E.Emburey	not out	5		not out	4
P.H.Edmonds	did not bat				
G.R.Dilley					
Extras	(B4, LB15, W3, NB13)	35		(B4, LB9, NB4)	17
Total	(8 wickets declared)	**592**		(8 wickets declared)	**199**

AUSTRALIA

G.R.Marsh	c Broad b Botham	15	(2)	lbw b Emburey	49
D.C.Boon	b Dilley	2	(1)	c Botham b Dilley	0
S.R.Waugh	c Botham b Emburey	71			
D.M.Jones	c Athey b Edmonds	27	(3)	run out	69
*A.R.Border	c Richards b Dilley	125	(4)	c Lamb b Edmonds	16
G.M.Ritchie	c Botham b Edmonds	33	(5)	not out	24
G.R.J.Matthews	c Botham b Dilley	45	(6)	not out	14
†T.J.Zoehrer	lbw b Dilley	29			
G.F.Lawson	b DeFreitas	13			
C.D.Matthews	c Broad b Emburey	10			
B.A.Reid	not out	2			
Extras	(B9, LB9, NB11)	29		(B9, LB6, NB10)	25
Total		**401**		(4 wickets)	**197**

AUSTRALIA	O	M	R	W		O	M	R	W		FALL OF WICKETS			
Lawson	41	8	126	0	(2)	9	1	44	0		E	A	E	A
C.D.Matthews	29.1	4	112	3	(4)	2	0	15	0	*Wkt*	*1st*	*1st*	*2nd*	*2nd*
Reid	40	8	115	4	(1)	21	3	58	3	1st	223	4	8	0
Waugh	24	4	90	0	(3)	21.3	4	69	5	2nd	227	64	47	126
G.R.J.Matthews	34	3	124	1						3rd	275	114	50	142
Border	2	0	6	0						4th	333	128	123	152
										5th	339	198	140	–
ENGLAND										6th	546	279	172	–
Botham	22	4	72	1	(2)	7.2	4	13	0	7th	585	334	190	–
Dilley	24.4	4	79	4	(1)	15	1	53	1	8th	592	360	199	–
Emburey	43	9	110	2	(4)	28	11	41	1	9th	–	385	–	–
DeFreitas	24	4	67	1	(3)	13.4	2	47	0	10th	–	401	–	–
Edmonds	21	4	55	2		27	13	25	1					
Gatting						5	3	3	0					
Lamb						1	1	0	0					

Umpires: R.A.French (17) and P.J.McConnell (7).

Close: 1st day – E(1) 272-2 (Broad 146, Gatting 11); 2nd – A(1) 19-1 (Marsh 6, Waugh 8); 3rd – A(1) 309-6 (Border 81, Zoehrer 15); 4th – E(2) 199-8 (Emburey 4).

Test No. 1060/260 (A470/E631)

AUSTRALIA v ENGLAND 1986-87 (3rd Test)

At Adelaide Oval on 12, 13, 14, 15, 16 December.
Toss: Australia.   Result: MATCH DRAWN.
Debuts: Australia – G.C.Dyer; England – J.J.Whitaker.

A benign pitch resulted in a match aggregate of 1,209 runs for 20 wickets and the fourth-highest average (60.45) in this series. Botham (torn left intercostal muscle) ended an unbroken sequence of 29 Tests against Australia since 1978. England exceeded 400 for a record seventh successive time in first innings against Australia. Marsh and Boon shared an opening partnership of 113, Australia's first three-figure start in a home Test against England since *Test No. 755*. Boon and Gatting each scored a century and a duck. Border's 21st Test hundred was his ninth as captain and seventh against England. Sleep made his first Test appearance since October 1982. England included three Leicestershire players for the first time. A female spectator set up an ironing board and attended to her laundry throughout the fifth day's play.

AUSTRALIA

G.R.Marsh	b Edmonds	43	(2) c and b Edmonds		41
D.C.Boon	c Whitaker b Emburey	103	(1) lbw b DeFreitas		0
D.M.Jones	c Richards b Dilley	93	c Lamb b Dilley		2
*A.R.Border	c Richards b Edmonds	70	not out		100
G.M.Ritchie	c Broad b DeFreitas	36	not out		46
G.R.J.Matthews	not out	73			
S.R.Waugh	not out	79			
P.R.Sleep					
†G.C.Dyer					
M.G.Hughes	} did not bat				
B.A.Reid					
Extras	(LB2, NB15)	17	(B4, LB6, NB2)		12
Total	(5 wickets declared)	**514**	(3 wickets declared)		**201**

ENGLAND

B.C.Broad	c Marsh b Waugh	116	not out		15
C.W.J.Athey	b Sleep	55	c Dyer b Hughes		12
*M.W.Gatting	c Waugh b Sleep	100	b Matthews		0
A.J.Lamb	c Matthews b Hughes	14	not out		9
D.I.Gower	lbw b Reid	38			
J.E.Emburey	c Dyer b Reid	49			
J.J.Whitaker	c Matthews b Reid	11			
†C.J.Richards	c Jones b Sleep	29			
P.A.J.DeFreitas	not out	4			
P.H.Edmonds	c Border b Sleep	13			
G.R.Dilley	b Reid	0			
Extras	(B4, LB14, W4, NB4)	26	(B2, LB1)		3
Total		**455**	(2 wickets)		**39**

ENGLAND	O	M	R	W	O	M	R	W
Dilley	32	3	111	1	21	8	38	1
DeFreitas	32	4	128	1	16	5	36	1
Emburey	46	11	117	1	22	6	50	0
Edmonds	52	14	134	2	29	7	63	1
Gatting	9	1	22	0	2	1	4	0

AUSTRALIA	O	M	R	W		O	M	R	W
Hughes	30	8	82	1		7	2	16	1
Reid	28.4	8	64	4					
Sleep	47	14	132	4	(4)	5	5	0	0
Matthews	23	1	102	0	(3)	8	4	10	1
Border	1	0	1	0					
Waugh	19	4	56	1	(2)	3	1	10	0

FALL OF WICKETS

Wkt	A 1st	E 1st	A 2nd	E 2nd
1st	113	112	1	21
2nd	185	273	8	22
3rd	311	283	77	–
4th	333	341	–	–
5th	368	341	–	–
6th	–	361	–	–
7th	–	422	–	–
8th	–	439	–	–
9th	–	454	–	–
10th	–	455	–	–

Umpires: A.R.Crafter (20) and S.G.Randell (4).

Close: 1st day – A(1) 207-2 (Jones 27, Border 19); 2nd – E(1) 29-0 (Broad 18, Athey 10); 3rd – E(1) 349-5 (Emburey 5, Whitaker 3); 4th – A(2) 82-3 (Border 31, Ritchie 4).

AUSTRALIA v ENGLAND 1986-87 (4th Test)

At Melbourne Cricket Ground on 26, 27, 28 December.
Toss: England.   Result: ENGLAND won by an innings and 14 runs.
Debuts: None.

England retained the Ashes through their first three-day victory in Australia since 1901-02 (*Test No. 65*). Gatting, leading his first overseas mission and one of ten players making their maiden tour of Australia, became only the fourth England captain this century (after A.P.F.Chapman, L.Hutton and J.M.Brearley) to defend the Ashes successfully abroad, and only the third (after J.W.H.T.Douglas at Melbourne in 1911-12, and D.I.Gower at Birmingham in 1985) to insert Australia and win. He also exceeded 3,000 runs in Test cricket. Broad joined the elite of J.B.Hobbs (who achieved the feat twice), H.Sutcliffe and W.R.Hammond as the only England batsmen to score three hundreds in a rubber in Australia. Botham, playing in his 88th Test, equalled R.J.Hadlee's world record by taking five wickets in an innings for the 27th time; only S.F.Barnes (12) and T.Richardson (11) exceeded Botham's nine instances against Australia. Richards equalled the England record for the most dismissals in an Australian innings.

AUSTRALIA

G.R.Marsh	c Richards b Botham	17	(2) run out	60
D.C.Boon	c Botham b Small	7	(1) c Gatting b Small	8
D.M.Jones	c Gower b Small	59	c Gatting b DeFreitas	21
*A.R.Border	c Richards b Botham	15	c Emburey b Small	34
S.R.Waugh	c Botham b Small	10	b Edmonds	49
G.R.J.Matthews	c Botham b Small	14	b Emburey	0
P.R.Sleep	c Richards b Small	0	run out	6
†T.J.Zoehrer	b Botham	5	c Athey b Edmonds	1
C.J.McDermott	c Richards b Botham	0	b Emburey	1
M.G.Hughes	c Richards b Botham	2	c Small b Edmonds	8
B.A.Reid	not out	2	not out	0
Extras	(B1, LB1, W1, NB7)	10	(LB3, W1, NB2)	6
Total		**141**		**194**

ENGLAND

B.C.Broad	c Zoehrer b Hughes	112
C.W.J.Athey	lbw b Reid	21
*M.W.Gatting	c Hughes b Reid	40
A.J.Lamb	c Zoehrer b Reid	43
D.I.Gower	c Matthews b Sleep	7
I.T.Botham	c Zoehrer b McDermott	29
†C.J.Richards	c Marsh b Reid	3
P.A.J.DeFreitas	c Matthews b McDermott	7
J.E.Emburey	c and b McDermott	22
P.H.Edmonds	lbw b McDermott	19
G.C.Small	not out	21
Extras	(B6, LB7, W1, NB11)	25
Total		**349**

ENGLAND	O	M	R	W	O	M	R	W		FALL OF WICKETS		
Small	22.4	7	48	5	(2) 15	3	40	2		A	E	A
DeFreitas	11	1	30	0	(1) 12	1	44	1	Wkt	1st	1st	2nd
Emburey	4	0	16	0	(5) 20	5	43	2	1st	16	58	13
Botham	16	4	41	5	(3) 7	1	19	0	2nd	44	163	48
Gatting	1	0	4	0					3rd	80	198	113
Edmonds					(4) 19.4	5	45	3	4th	108	219	153
									5th	118	251	153
									6th	118	273	175
AUSTRALIA									7th	129	277	180
McDermott	26.5	4	83	4					8th	133	289	185
Hughes	30	3	94	1					9th	137	319	189
Reid	28	5	78	4					10th	141	349	194
Waugh	8	4	16	0								
Sleep	28	4	65	1								

Umpires: A.R.Crafter (21) and R.A.French (18).

Close: 1st day – E(1) 95-1 (Broad 56, Gatting 8); 2nd – E(1) 349 all out.

AUSTRALIA v ENGLAND 1986-87 (5th Test)

At Sydney Cricket Ground on 10, 11, 12, 14, 15 January.
Toss: Australia.   Result: AUSTRALIA won by 55 runs.
Debuts: Australia – P.L.Taylor.

Australia ended their record barren run of 14 matches when Sleep bowled Emburey with the last ball of the penultimate available over. Taylor made his decisive Test debut after playing six first-class matches, only one of them during the current season. Emburey achieved his best analysis in Tests. Jones (540 minutes, 420 balls, one six and 12 fours) made Australia's highest score at Sydney since S.G.Barnes and D.G.Bradman each scored 234 in 1946-47.

AUSTRALIA

G.R.Marsh	c Gatting b Small	24	(2)	c Emburey b Dilley	14
G.M.Ritchie	lbw b Dilley	6	(1)	c Botham b Edmonds	13
D.M.Jones	not out	184		c Richards b Emburey	30
*A.R.Border	c Botham b Edmonds	34		b Edmonds	49
D.M.Wellham	c Richards b Small	17		c Lamb b Emburey	1
S.R.Waugh	c Richards b Small	0		c Athey b Emburey	73
P.R.Sleep	c Richards b Small	9		c Lamb b Emburey	10
†T.J.Zoehrer	c Gatting b Small	12		lbw b Emburey	1
P.L.Taylor	c Emburey b Edmonds	11		c Lamb b Emburey	42
M.G.Hughes	c Botham b Edmonds	16		b Emburey	5
B.A.Reid	b Dilley	4		not out	1
Extras	(B12, LB4, W2, NB8)	26		(B5, LB7)	12
Total		**343**			**251**

ENGLAND

B.C.Broad	lbw b Hughes	6		c and b Sleep	17
C.W.J.Athey	c Zoehrer b Hughes	5		b Sleep	31
*M.W.Gatting	lbw b Reid	0	(5)	c and b Waugh	96
A.J.Lamb	c Zoehrer b Taylor	24		c Waugh b Taylor	3
D.I.Gower	c Wellham b Taylor	72	(3)	c Marsh b Taylor	37
I.T.Botham	c Marsh b Taylor	16		c Wellham b Taylor	0
†C.J.Richards	c Wellham b Reid	46		b Sleep	38
J.E.Emburey	b Taylor	69		b Sleep	22
P.H.Edmonds	c Marsh b Taylor	3		lbw b Sleep	0
G.C.Small	b Taylor	14		c Border b Reid	2
G.R.Dilley	not out	4		not out	0
Extras	(B9, LB3, W2, NB2)	16		(B8, LB6, W1, NB3)	18
Total		**275**			**264**

ENGLAND	O	M	R	W		O	M	R	W		FALL OF WICKETS			
Dilley	23.5	5	67	2		15	4	48	1		A	E	A	E
Small	33	11	75	5		8	2	17	0	Wkt	1st	1st	2nd	2nd
Botham	23	10	42	0	(5)	3	0	17	0	1st	8	16	29	24
Emburey	30	4	62	0		46	15	78	7	2nd	58	17	31	91
Edmonds	34	5	79	3	(3)	43	16	79	2	3rd	149	17	106	91
Gatting	1	0	2	0		2	2	0	0	4th	184	89	110	102
										5th	184	119	115	102
AUSTRALIA										6th	200	142	141	233
Hughes	16	3	58	2		12	3	32	0	7th	232	213	145	257
Reid	25	7	74	2		19	8	32	1	8th	271	219	243	257
Waugh	6	4	6	0	(6)	6	2	13	1	9th	338	270	248	262
Taylor	26	7	78	6		29	10	76	2	10th	343	275	251	264
Sleep	21	6	47	0	(3)	35	14	72	5					
Border					(5)	13	6	25	1					

Umpires: P.J.McConnell (8) and S.G.Randell (5)

Close: 1st day – A(1) 236-7 (Jones 119, Taylor 0); 2nd – E(1) 132-5 (Gower 62, Richards 8); 3rd – A(2) 74-2 (Jones 6, Border 38); 4th – E(2) 39-1 (Athey 11, Gower 7).

INDIA v SRI LANKA 1986-87 (1st Test)

At Green Park, Kanpur, on 17, 18 (*no play*), 20, 21, 22 December.
Toss: Sri Lanka.   Result: MATCH DRAWN.
Debuts: India – B.Arun, R.Lamba; Sri Lanka – G.F.Labrooy.

Despite the loss of the second day to rain and fog this match produced 1,096 runs at a rate of 64.47 per wicket. India amassed their highest total against all countries (and the highest by any Test side in India) while Sri Lanka recorded their highest total against India. Gavaskar scored his 34th hundred. Azharuddin, who batted 500 minutes and completed 1,000 runs, became only the second batsman to be dismissed for 199 in Test cricket (following Mudassar Nazar in *Test No. 996*) and partnered Kapil Dev (240 minutes, 165 balls, 19 fours and a six) in a sixth-wicket stand of 272 in 49.3 overs to set a record for any wicket in this series. Kapil Dev's hundred, off 74 balls, was the fastest on record for India. For only the second time, three batsmen scored over 150 in the same Test innings (also for England v Australia at The Oval in 1938). Earlier Wettimuny and Ratnayeke had shared Sri Lanka's first three-figure opening partnership against any country.

SRI LANKA

S.Wettimuny	lbw b Sharma	79
J.R.Ratnayeke	lbw b Kapil Dev	93
P.A.de Silva	b Arun	26
A.P.Gurusinha	b Kapil Dev	19
R.L.Dias	c Azharuddin b Arun	50
*L.R.D.Mendis	lbw b Sharma	1
A.Ranatunga	lbw b Maninder	52
†R.G.de Alwis	b Maninder	13
A.L.F.de Mel	c Arun b Shastri	25
E.A.R.de Silva	lbw b Arun	21
G.F.Labrooy	not out	5
Extras	(B1, LB10, W6, NB19)	36
Total		**420**

INDIA

S.M.Gavaskar	c Wettimuny b Labrooy	176
K.Srikkanth	c De Alwis b Ratnayeke	18
R.Lamba	run out	24
D.B.Vengsarkar	c Gurusinha b De Mel	57
M.Azharuddin	lbw b Ratnayeke	199
R.J.Shastri	lbw b Ratnayeke	6
*Kapil Dev	lbw b Ratnayeke	163
B.Arun	not out	2
†K.S.More		
C.Sharma	} did not bat	
Maninder Singh		
Extras	(B1, LB11, W1, NB18)	31
Total	(7 wickets)	**676**

INDIA	O	M	R	W		FALL OF WICKETS	
Kapil Dev	30	11	81	2		SL	I
Arun	27	7	76	3	*Wkt*	*1st*	*1st*
Sharma	31	4	122	2	1st	159	50
Maninder	32	12	89	2	2nd	217	100
Shastri	17	6	37	1	3rd	217	217
Srikkanth	1	0	4	0	4th	286	380
					5th	292	399
SRI LANKA					6th	355	671
De Mel	31	4	119	1	7th	355	676
Labrooy	35	4	164	1	8th	389	–
Ratnayeke	37.1	2	132	4	9th	394	–
E.A.R.de Silva	40	7	133	0	10th	420	–
Ranatunga	15	4	58	0			
Gurusinha	7	0	42	0			
Wettimuny	2	0	16	0			

Umpires: R.B.Gupta (2) and V.K.Ramaswamy (6).

Close: 1st day – SL(1) 217-2 (Ratnayeke 93, Gurusinha 0); 2nd – no play; 3rd – I(1) 74-1 (Gavaskar 39, Lamba 13); 4th – I(1) 321-3 (Gavaskar 148, Azharuddin 59).

INDIA v SRI LANKA 1986-87 (2nd Test)

At Vidarbha C.A.Ground, Nagpur, on 27, 28, 30, 31 December.
Toss: Sri Lanka.   Result: INDIA won by an innings and 106 runs.
Debuts: None.

On a pitch that gave generous assistance to spin, India gained their first victory in six Tests against Sri Lanka and their first victory in a home Test since they defeated England in December 1984. Sri Lanka were dismissed for their lowest total in this series until 1990-91. Amarnath's 11th hundred in 60 Tests enabled him to become the fourth to score 4,000 runs for India. Maninder Singh returned the first ten-wicket match analysis of this series. Gurusinha (right-arm medium pace) captured his first Test wickets during a dramatic 11-ball spell: 6W12414610W.

SRI LANKA

S.Wettimuny	c Amarnath b Sharma	6		c Srikkanth b Kapil Dev	6
J.R.Ratnayeke	c Shastri b Kapil Dev	17		c Gavaskar b Maninder	54
A.P.Gurusinha	c Amarnath b Yadav	29		c and b Yadav	15
R.L.Dias	b Maninder	6		b Maninder	2
P.A.de Silva	lbw b Yadav	33		c sub (Arun Lal) b Maninder	6
A.Ranatunga	c Amarnath b Yadav	59	(7)	c Gavaskar b Maninder	5
*L.R.D.Mendis	c Srikkanth b Maninder	1	(6)	b Maninder	38
B.R.Jurangpathy	b Maninder	0		c Vengsarkar b Yadav	0
†R.G.de Alwis	c Vengsarkar b Yadav	1	(11)	c More b Maninder	0
R.J.Ratnayeke	not out	32		not out	4
E.A.R.de Silva	c Shastri b Yadav	16	(9)	c Srikkanth b Maninder	0
Extras	(B2, LB1, NB1)	4		(B4, LB5, NB2)	11
Total		204			141

INDIA

K.Srikkanth	c De Alwis b Ratnayake	4
R.Lamba	c Jurangpathy b E.A.R.de Silva	53
M.Amarnath	c sub‡ b Jurangpathy	131
D.B.Vengsarkar	c Jurangpathy b Ratnayake	153
S.M.Gavaskar	c E.A.R.de Silva b Gurusinha	74
*Kapil Dev	not out	11
R.J.Shastri	c sub‡ b Gurusinha	12
†K.S.More		
C.Sharma		
N.S.Yadav	} did not bat	
Maninder Singh		
Extras	(LB4, W1, NB8)	13
Total	(6 wickets declared)	451

INDIA	O	M	R	W	O	M	R	W		FALL OF WICKETS		
Kapil Dev	10	3	29	1	6	1	16	1		SL	I	SL
Sharma	5	0	26	1	5	0	14	0	Wkt	1st	1st	2nd
Maninder	20	6	56	3	(4) 17.4	4	51	7	1st	7	5	15
Yadav	19.1	4	76	5	(3) 14	6	21	2	2nd	38	131	42
Shastri	5	2	14	0	6	0	30	0	3rd	52	304	47
									4th	66	420	57
SRI LANKA									5th	105	428	122
Ratnayake	35	4	139	2					6th	110	451	132
Ratnayeke	28	4	89	0					7th	110	–	137
Ranatunga	6	1	34	0					8th	129	–	137
E.A.R.de Silva	38	5	91	1					9th	160	–	141
Jurangpathy	21	3	69	1					10th	204	–	141
Gurusinha	1.5	0	25	2								

Umpires: R.Mehra (1) and P.D.Reporter (6).   ‡ (R.S.Mahanama)

Close: 1st day – I(1) 0-0 (Srikkanth 0, Lamba 0); 2nd – I(1) 54-1 (Lamba 19, Amarnath 26); 3rd – I(1) 324-3 (Vengsarkar 115, Gavaskar 10).

INDIA v SRI LANKA 1986-87 (3rd Test)

At Barabati Stadium, Cuttack, on 4, 5, 6, 7 January.
Toss: India.   Result: INDIA won by an innings and 67 runs.
Debuts: None.

The Barabati Stadium, scene of India's first-ever victory in one-day internationals (January 1982), provided Test cricket with its 60th venue. An underprepared pitch helped India complete their second successive innings victory with more than a day to spare and record their first home series win since 1981-82. One day after his 28th birthday and playing in his 83rd Test, Kapil Dev became the youngest of seven bowlers to take 300 wickets in Test cricket – although he required most matches. He thus emulated I.T.Botham's feat (achieved in 72 matches) of scoring 3,000 runs and taking 300 wickets in Tests. Vengsarkar batted seven hours (279 balls, 14 fours) for his 14th hundred and highest Test score.

INDIA

S.M.Gavaskar	lbw b Ratnayeke	5
K.Srikkanth	b Ratnayeke	40
M.Amarnath	b Anurasiri	39
D.B.Vengsarkar	lbw b Ratnayeke	166
R.Lamba	lbw b Ratnayeke	24
R.J.Shastri	c E.A.R.de Silva b Ratnayeke	19
*Kapil Dev	b Anurasiri	60
B.Arun	c Ranatunga b Anurasiri	2
†K.S.More	not out	6
N.S.Yadav	st De Alwis b Anurasiri	3
Maninder Singh	lbw b Ratnayeke	2
Extras	(B8, LB19, NB7)	34
Total		**400**

SRI LANKA

S.Wettimuny	c Kapil Dev b Maninder	6		b Shastri	12
J.R.Ratnayeke	c Srikkanth b Yadav	20		c Srikkanth b Yadav	22
A.P.Gurusinha	c Lamba b Arun	40		c Arun b Yadav	10
E.A.R.de Silva	b Kapil Dev	1	(9)	st More b Yadav	19
*L.R.D.Mendis	b Kapil Dev	9		lbw b Shastri	27
A.Ranatunga	lbw b Kapil Dev	30		lbw b Maninder	2
R.L.Dias	c Kapil Dev b Maninder	49		b Shastri	9
P.A.de Silva	lbw b Maninder	21		c Shastri b Maninder	8
R.J.Ratnayeke	lbw b Maninder	0	(4)	b Kapil Dev	24
†R.G.de Alwis	c Srikkanth b Kapil Dev	0		lbw b Shastri	0
S.D.Anurasiri	not out	0		not out	0
Extras	(B1, LB11, NB3)	15		(B2, LB5, NB2)	9
Total		**191**			**142**

SRI LANKA	O	M	R	W	O	M	R	W		FALL OF WICKETS		
Ratnayeke	30	5	98	1						I	SL	SL
Ratnayeke	27.3	3	85	5					*Wkt*	*1st*	*1st*	*2nd*
E.A.R.de Silva	40	6	114	0					1st	18	27	35
Anurasiri	26	3	71	4					2nd	70	33	45
Ranatunga	4	2	5	0					3rd	164	38	51
									4th	225	56	91
INDIA									5th	272	96	94
Kapil Dev	26	3	69	4	16	4	36	1	6th	383	125	112
Arun	13	5	26	1	2	0	14	0	7th	385	188	121
Maninder	17.1	6	41	4	(4) 17	5	42	2	8th	387	190	121
Yadav	15	6	21	1	(3) 13	3	32	3	9th	397	191	124
Shastri	5	0	22	0	11	4	11	4	10th	400	191	142

Umpires: R.B.Gupta (3) and V.K.Ramaswamy (7).

Close: 1st day – I(1) 224-3 (Vengsarkar 98, Lamba 24); 2nd – SL(1) 37-2 (Gurusinha 4, E.A.R.de Silva 1); 3rd – SL(2) 51-3 (Ratnayeke 0).

INDIA v PAKISTAN 1986-87 (1st Test)

At Chidambaram Stadium, Chepauk, Madras, on 3, 4, 6, 7, 8 February.
Toss: Pakistan.   Result: MATCH DRAWN.
Debuts: Pakistan – Ijaz Ahmed.

Shoaib's painstaking maiden Test hundred enabled the Mohammad father/son combination to emulate that of the family Nazar in scoring centuries against India. Imran, on 68 when the ninth wicket fell, completed his third Test hundred with a six and he went on to his highest score, hitting five sixes and 14 fours. His stand of 112 with Wasim Akram (who also struck five sixes) established an eighth-wicket record against India and enabled Pakistan to reach their highest total in India. A crowd of 50,000 saw Srikkanth race to his second Test hundred off 118 balls (two sixes, 14 fours), with his second fifty requiring only 32 balls. His opening partnership of 200 with Gavaskar remains the highest by either side in this series. Ijaz Ahmed began his Test career at the age of 18 years 136 days.

PAKISTAN

Rizwan-uz-Zaman	c More b Kulkarni	1	(3) not out		54
Shoaib Mohammad	lbw b Maninder	101	c Vengsarkar b Maninder		45
Ramiz Raja	c Srikkanth b Maninder	24	(1) c Azharuddin b Kulkarni		14
Javed Miandad	run out	94	st More b Maninder		54
Salim Malik	b Maninder	19	not out		6
Ijaz Ahmed	c Vengsarkar b Maninder	3			
Abdul Qadir	c Azharuddin b Shastri	21			
*Imran Khan	not out	135			
Wasim Akram	c Gavaskar b Yadav	62			
†Salim Yousuf	c Kulkarni b Maninder	1			
Tausif Ahmed	not out	13			
Extras	(LB11, W1, NB1)	13	(LB3, NB6)		9
Total	(9 wickets declared)	487	(3 wickets)		182

INDIA

S.M.Gavaskar	c Tausif b Qadir	91
K.Srikkanth	c Wasim b Tausif	123
M.Amarnath	run out	89
D.B.Vengsarkar	st Salim Yousuf b Tausif	96
M.Azharuddin	st Salim Yousuf b Tausif	20
R.J.Shastri	c Salim Yousuf b Imran	41
*Kapil Dev	c Ramiz b Qadir	5
†K.S.More	lbw b Wasim	28
R.R.Kulkarni	c Salim Yousuf b Imran	2
N.S.Yadav	not out	6
Maninder Singh	not out	7
Extras	(B9, LB5, NB5)	19
Total	(9 wickets declared)	527

INDIA	O	M	R	W	O	M	R	W		FALL OF WICKETS		
Kapil Dev	18	1	68	0	9	1	36	0		P	I	P
Kulkarni	7	0	41	1	5	0	15	1	Wkt	1st	1st	2nd
Maninder	59	16	135	5	(4) 26	10	47	2	1st	2	200	17
Yadav	41	3	127	1	(5) 15	4	29	0	2nd	60	220	70
Shastri	38	8	105	1	(3) 18	5	42	0	3rd	215	405	160
Srikkanth					3	0	6	0	4th	237	424	–
Gavaskar					1	0	4	0	5th	244	429	–
									6th	257	453	–
PAKISTAN									7th	273	494	–
Wasim	34	10	78	1					8th	385	498	–
Imran	27	4	103	2					9th	406	515	–
Qadir	39	4	130	2					10th	–	–	–
Tausif	67	6	189	3								
Shoaib	3	0	13	0								

Umpires: R.Mehra (2) and V.K.Ramaswamy (8).

Close: 1st day – P(1) 247-5 (Salim Malik 14, Qadir 2); 2nd – I(1) 15-0 (Gavaskar 10, Srikkanth 5); 3rd – I(1) 290-2 (Amarnath 33, Vengsarkar 39); 4th – I(1) 527-9 (Yadav 6, Maninder Singh 7).

INDIA v PAKISTAN 1986-87 (2nd Test)

At Eden Gardens, Calcutta, on 11, 12, 14, 15, 16 February.
Toss: Pakistan.   Result: MATCH DRAWN.
Debuts: None.

Set 356 to win in 285 minutes plus 20 overs, Pakistan settled for a draw, night-watchman Salim Yousuf batting 216 minutes for 43 and Javed Miandad 235 minutes for 63 not out. Gavaskar ended his record run of 106 consecutive Test appearances when he refused to play in Calcutta because of the crowd's abuse in earlier matches. Azharuddin (400 minutes) scored his fifth hundred in Tests, his partnership of 143 with Kapil Dev setting a sixth-wicket record for India against Pakistan. Rizwan-uz-Zaman took 294 minutes to reach 60, his highest Test score, his fifty occupying 275 minutes. Binny's best analysis in Test included a spell of 4 for 9 in 30 balls. The attendance exceeded 70,000 each day.

INDIA

K.Srikkanth	c Salim Malik b Wasim	22	lbw b Imran		21
Arun Lal	c Tausif b Salim Jaffer	52	c Wasim b Imran		70
M.Amarnath	run out	9	b Tausif		31
D.B.Vengsarkar	c Salim Yousuf b Wasim	38	not out		41
M.Azharuddin	b Wasim	141			
R.J.Shastri	b Qadir	5			
*Kapil Dev	c Miandad b Salim Jaffer	66			
R.M.H.Binny	not out	52			
†K.S.More	run out	0			
R.R.Kulkarni	lbw b Wasim	0			
Maninder Singh	b Wasim	3			
Extras	(B1, LB8, W1, NB5)	15	(B4, LB12, NB2)		18
Total		**403**	(3 wickets declared)		**181**

PAKISTAN

Shoaib Mohammad	run out	24	(2) lbw b Binny		5
Ramiz Raja	c sub (S.Viswanath) b Shastri	69	(1) c More b Binny		29
Rizwan-uz-Zaman	b Kapil Dev	60	(4) b Shastri		8
Javed Miandad	c More b Binny	17	(5) not out		63
Salim Malik	lbw b Binny	0	(6) lbw b Kapil Dev		20
*Imran Khan	c Kapil Dev b Binny	1	(7) not out		5
†Salim Yousuf	lbw b Kapil Dev	33	(3) b Maninder		43
Wasim Akram	b Binny	1			
Abdul Qadir	b Binny	2			
Tausif Ahmed	c Vengsarkar b Binny	0			
Salim Jaffer	not out	0			
Extras	(B4, LB4, W1, NB13)	22	(B1, LB2, W2, NB1)		6
Total		**229**	(5 wickets)		**179**

PAKISTAN	O	M	R	W		O	M	R	W	FALL OF WICKETS				
Imran	27	2	93	0		7.1	0	28	2		I	P	I	P
Wasim	31	6	96	5		18	4	46	0	Wkt	1st	1st	2nd	2nd
Salim Jaffer	36	2	115	2	(5)	7	0	33	0	1st	30	57	37	12
Tausif	10	1	39	0	(3)	18	2	50	1	2nd	73	136	100	37
Qadir	14	3	51	1	(4)	2	0	8	0	3rd	104	178	181	73
										4th	144	178	–	116
										5th	149	191	–	170
INDIA										6th	292	195	–	–
Kapil Dev	29	5	88	2		19	7	41	1	7th	393	207	–	–
Binny	25.1	8	56	6		21	4	45	2	8th	393	215	–	–
Maninder	20.1	11	21	0	(5)	16	6	30	1	9th	395	229	–	–
Shastri	20.5	10	18	1		24	6	41	1	10th	403	229	–	–
Kulkarni	13	1	38	0	(3)	7	2	19	0					

Umpires: R.B.Gupta (4) and P.D.Reporter (7).

Close: 1st day – I(1) 225-5 (Azharuddin 51, Kapil Dev 39); 2nd – P(1) 57-1 (Ramiz 25, Rizwan 0); 3rd – P(1) 215-7 (Salim Yousuf 21, Qadir 2); 4th – P(2) 16-1 (Ramiz 7, Salim Yousuf 4).

INDIA v PAKISTAN 1986-87 (3rd Test)

At Sawai Mansingh Stadium, Jaipur, 21, 22, 24 (*no play*), 25, 26 February.
Toss: India.   Result: MATCH DRAWN.
Debuts: None.

Rajasthan provided Test cricket with its 61st venue, the 16th in India. The left-handed Younis Ahmed (39) was recalled by Pakistan 17 years 111 days after his previous appearance; only G.Gunn (17 years 316 days) had endured a longer hiatus, although, in terms of Tests missed, Younis exceeded the previous record (103 by England's D.Shackleton) by one. For the third time in his Test career Gavaskar was dismissed by the first ball of the match (bowled by Imran); no other batsman has suffered this fate more than once. Pakistan's President, General Zia ul-Haq, watched part of the second day as part of his 'Cricket for Peace' mission as Shastri appropriately took 424 minutes to reach his seventh Test hundred. Azharuddin completed his second hundred in successive innings. Torrential rain, which seeped under the covers on the rest day and resulted in controversial pitch repairs involving sawdust, led to the third day being abandoned when Imran threatened to refuse to bat.

INDIA

Batsman	Dismissal	R	Dismissal 2	R2
S.M.Gavaskar	c Miandad b Imran	0	c Ramiz b Tausif	24
K.Srikkanth	lbw b Wasim	45	c sub (Ijaz Ahmed) b Qasim	51
M.Amarnath	b Imran	49	not out	15
D.B.Vengsarkar	c Qasim b Shoaib	30	not out	21
M.Azharuddin	c Salim Yousuf b Tausif	110		
R.J.Shastri	c Ramiz b Qasim	125		
*Kapil Dev	c Salim Yousuf b Rizwan	50		
†K.S.More	c Miandad b Tausif	22		
R.M.H.Binny	not out	6		
N.S.Yadav	not out	8		
G.Sharma	did not bat			
Extras	(B2, LB10, W1, NB7)	20	(LB2, NB1)	3
Total	(8 wickets declared)	**465**	(2 wickets)	**114**

PAKISTAN

Batsman	Dismissal	R
Ramiz Raja	b Kapil Dev	114
Shoaib Mohammad	c Gavaskar b Amarnath	0
Rizwan-uz-Zaman	c More b Kapil Dev	10
Javed Miandad	lbw b Shastri	50
Younis Ahmed	c sub (Arun Lal) b Sharma	14
Salim Malik	c Srikkanth b Sharma	10
*Imran Khan	c Kapil Dev b Sharma	66
†Salim Yousuf	run out	14
Wasim Akram	c Kapil Dev b Yadav	11
Iqbal Qasim	c Srikkanth b Sharma	20
Tausif Ahmed	not out	10
Extras	(B8, LB2, NB12)	22
Total		**341**

PAKISTAN	O	M	R	W		O	M	R	W
Imran	35	7	93	2	(2)	5	2	8	0
Wasim	36.3	5	88	1	(1)	5	1	17	0
Qasim	44	5	149	1		13	4	34	1
Tausif	38	3	97	2		13	3	47	1
Shoaib	5	0	19	1	(6)	1	1	0	0
Rizwan	5	2	7	1					
Younis					(5)	1	0	6	0

INDIA	O	M	R	W
Kapil Dev	27	7	84	2
Amarnath	8	4	15	1
Shastri	36	11	79	1
Yadav	25	7	65	1
Sharma	32.5	2	88	4

FALL OF WICKETS

Wkt	I 1st	P 1st	I 2nd
1st	0	0	72
2nd	74	28	88
3rd	114	122	–
4th	156	162	–
5th	286	174	–
6th	384	228	–
7th	444	282	–
8th	451	302	–
9th	–	318	–
10th	–	341	–

Umpires: V.K.Ramaswamy (9) and P.D.Reporter (8).

Close: 1st day – I(1) 228-4 (Azharuddin 72, Shastri 22); 2nd – I(1) 459-8 (Binny 3, Yadav 5); 3rd – no play; 4th – P(1) 228-6 (Imran 21).

INDIA v PAKISTAN 1986-87 (4th Test)

At Gujarat Stadium, Ahmedabad, on 4, 5, 7, 8, 9 March.
Toss: Pakistan.   Result: MATCH DRAWN.
Debuts: None.

Shortly after tea on the third day, Gavaskar, playing his 212th innings in his 124th Test, late cut a two to take his score to 58 and became the first batsman to score 10,000 runs in Test cricket. A jubilant crowd invasion delayed play for more than 20 minutes. Ijaz Faqih reached both his fifty and hundred (241 balls) with sixes and added 154 with Imran to set a Pakistan seventh-wicket record against India. Yadav took his 100th wicket in 34 Tests. Kapil Dev scored 50 off 52 balls. Abdul Qadir acquired his 150th Test wicket before Wasim Akram claimed the last three wickets in five balls. On the fourth afternoon play was suspended for 50 minutes after a section of the crowd had pelted Pakistan's fielders with stones. Play resumed after tea with six of the visitors wearing helmets. The fifth day, mercifully aborted after ten of the final 20 overs, produced just 110 runs.

PAKISTAN

Ramiz Raja	b Kapil Dev	41		c Azharuddin b Maninder	21
Salim Yousuf	st More b Amarnath	2			
Rizwan-uz-Zaman	c Kapil Dev b Maninder	5	(2)	c Azharuddin b Sharma	58
Younis Ahmed	st More b Yadav	40	(3)	not out	34
Salim Malik	c More b Yadav	20	(4)	not out	14
Manzoor Elahi	c Kapil Dev b Yadav	52			
Imran Khan	b Sharma	72			
Ijaz Faqih	lbw b Kapil Dev	105			
Abdul Qadir	b Kapil Dev	25			
Wasim Akram	not out	4			
Iqbal Qasim	c More b Yadav	0			
Extras	(B6, LB20, NB3)	29		(NB8)	8
Total		**395**		**(2 wickets)**	**135**

INDIA

S.M.Gavaskar	lbw b Imran	63
K.Srikkanth	b Ijaz	22
M.Amarnath	c and b Qasim	7
D.B.Vengsarkar	c Salim Malik b Wasim	109
K.S.More	c Qasim b Qadir	23
M.Azharuddin	b Imran	12
R.J.Shastri	c Qasim b Manzoor	15
Kapil Dev	not out	50
N.S.Yadav	b Wasim	0
G.Sharma	lbw b Wasim	0
Maninder Singh	b Wasim	0
Extras	(B11, LB6, NB5)	22
Total		**323**

INDIA	O	M	R	W		O	M	R	W
Kapil Dev	27	9	46	3		10	3	19	0
Amarnath	9	3	14	1		2	0	6	0
Maninder	54	21	106	1	(5)	23	16	13	1
Sharma	36	8	62	1		26	9	36	1
Yadav	48.3	13	109	4	(3)	14	4	18	0
Shastri	11	3	26	0		18	6	23	0
Srikkanth	2	0	6	0	(8)	2	0	5	0
Gavaskar					(7)	4	1	15	0

PAKISTAN	O	M	R	W
Imran	17	6	41	2
Wasim	21.5	2	60	4
Ijaz	27	3	81	1
Qasim	30	11	63	1
Qadir	13	1	53	1
Manzoor	3	2	8	1

FALL OF WICKETS			
	P	I	P
Wkt	1st	1st	2nd
1st	2	34	43
2nd	23	46	107
3rd	62	157	–
4th	99	204	–
5th	149	218	–
6th	176	246	–
7th	330	306	–
8th	391	322	–
9th	394	322	–
10th	395	323	–

Umpires: R.B.Gupta (5) and S.R.Ramachandra Rao (1).

Close: 1st day – P(1) 130-4 (Salim Malik 17, Manzoor 19); 2nd – P(1) 379-7 (Ijaz 104, Qadir 20); 3rd – I(1) 165-3 (Vengsarkar 62, More 1); 4th – P(2) 25-0 (Ramiz 14, Rizwan 10).

INDIA v PAKISTAN 1986-87 (5th Test)

At Chinnaswamy Stadium, Bangalore, on 13, 14, 15, 17 March.
Toss: Pakistan.   Result: PAKISTAN won by 16 runs.
Debuts: None.

Pakistan gained their first series win in five visits to India with only their second victory there, the first being i
October 1952 (*Test No. 356*). This remarkable result, which broke a stalemate of 11 successive draws, wa
achieved after the tourists had been dismissed for their lowest total against India. This was India's first defea
in 18 matches since September 1985. Maninder Singh's best analysis in Tests to date included a spell of fou
wickets in 13 balls. In his final Test innings, with India requiring 221 for victory on a turning pitch of eccentri
bounce, Gavaskar gave a supreme exhibition of temperament and technique lasting 323 minutes, during whic
he completed 2,000 runs against Pakistan. The next highest contributor was extras with 27. He ended hi
career holding the following world Test records: most matches (125); most consecutive matches (106); mos
innings (214); most runs (10,122); most hundreds (34); most scores of 50 or more (79); and most hundre
partnerships (58).

PAKISTAN

Ramiz Raja	c Vengsarkar b Kapil Dev	22	b Yadav	4
Rizwan-uz-Zaman	b Kapil Dev	0	(3) b Shastri	
Salim Malik	b Maninder	33	(4) b Kapil Dev	3
Javed Miandad	c Shastri b Maninder	7	(2) c Srikkanth b Shastri	1
Manzoor Elahi	c Azharuddin b Maninder	0	(7) c More b Maninder	
*Imran Khan	c Amarnath b Maninder	6	c Srikkanth b Shastri	3
Wasim Akram	b Maninder	0	(8) lbw b Maninder	1
†Salim Yousuf	c and b Shastri	0	(9) not out	4
Iqbal Qasim	b Maninder	19	(5) c Srikkanth b Yadav	2
Tausif Ahmed	not out	15	c Yadav b Shastri	1
Salim Jaffer	c Vengsarkar b Maninder	8	c Gavaskar b Maninder	
Extras	(B2, LB1, NB3)	6	(B7, LB8, NB1)	1
Total		**116**		**24**

INDIA

S.M.Gavaskar	b Tausif	21	c Rizwan b Qasim	9
K.Srikkanth	b Tausif	21	lbw b Wasim	
M.Amarnath	b Tausif	13	c Salim Yousuf b Wasim	
D.B.Vengsarkar	c Manzoor b Tausif	50	b Tausif	1
M.Azharuddin	c Manzoor b Qasim	6	(6) c and b Qasim	2
R.J.Shastri	c Salim Malik b Tausif	7	(7) c and b Qasim	
*Kapil Dev	c Salim Malik b Qasim	9	(8) b Qasim	
R.M.H.Binny	c Tausif b Qasim	1	(9) c Salim Yousuf b Tausif	1
†K.S.More	not out	9	(5) lbw b Tausif	
N.S.Yadav	b Qasim	0	b Tausif	
Maninder Singh	c Salim Yousuf b Qasim	0	not out	
Extras	(B4, LB4)	8	(B22, LB5)	2
Total		**145**		**20**

INDIA	O	M	R	W	O	M	R	W		FALL OF WICKETS			
Kapil Dev	11	2	23	2	12	2	25	1		P	I	P	I
Binny	3	0	25	0					Wkt	1st	1st	2nd	2n
Amarnath	3	1	7	0					1st	3	39	45	1
Maninder	18.2	8	27	7	(2) 43.5	8	99	3	2nd	39	56	57	1
Shastri	11	1	19	1	(3) 24	3	69	4	3rd	60	71	89	6
Yadav	3	0	12	0	(4) 15	3	41	2	4th	60	102	121	8
									5th	68	126	142	12
PAKISTAN									6th	68	130	166	15
Imran	5	0	26	0					7th	73	135	184	16
Wasim	2	0	9	0	(1) 11	3	19	2	8th	74	137	198	18
Qasim	30	15	48	5	37	11	73	4	9th	98	143	249	18
Tausif	27	7	54	5	(2) 45.5	12	85	4	10th	116	145	249	20

Umpires: R.B.Gupta (6) and V.K.Ramaswamy (10).

Close: 1st day – I(1) 68-2 (Amarnath 12, Vengsarkar 9); 2nd – P(2) 155-5 (Imran 18, Manzoor 1); 3rd – I(2)
99-4 (Gavaskar 51, Azharuddin 7).

NEW ZEALAND v WEST INDIES 1986-87 (1st Test)

At Basin Reserve, Wellington, on 20, 21, 22, 23, 24 February.
Toss: West Indies.   Result: MATCH DRAWN.
Debuts: New Zealand – D.N.Patel.

New Zealand were rescued by a partnership of 241 in 385 minutes (their highest for the third wicket in all Tests until 1990-91) between Wright and Martin Crowe. Both scored their sixth hundreds, Wright's 582-minute innings (465 balls) being the longest by a New Zealander in a home Test until 1990-91. He batted 828 minutes in the match. Richards, hampered by the loss of Marshall and Holding, not to mention one of Wellington's infamous northerly winds, countered by retaining the original ball throughout New Zealand's second innings (177 overs). Earlier, Garner had taken his 250th Test wicket in 57 Tests, Haynes (307 minutes, 269 balls, 20 fours) had completed his ninth Test hundred, Smith had become the first wicket-keeper to make 100 dismissals for New Zealand, and Marshall had scored his 1,000th run to complete the double in his 49th Test. Holding (injured back) announced his retirement from Test cricket after taking 249 wickets in 60 matches.

NEW ZEALAND

Batsman	Dismissal	Runs	Dismissal 2	Runs 2
J.G.Wright	c Garner b Richards	75	c and b Gomes	138
K.R.Rutherford	c Logie b Garner	6	lbw b Garner	6
*J.V.Coney	c Logie b Marshall	3	c Richards b Garner	4
M.D.Crowe	lbw b Walsh	3	c Holding b Richards	119
D.N.Patel	c Garner b Walsh	18	b Walsh	20
J.J.Crowe	c Logie b Garner	37	not out	27
J.G.Bracewell	lbw b Garner	17	not out	28
R.J.Hadlee	not out	35		
†I.D.S.Smith	lbw b Garner	0		
S.L.Boock	c Garner b Marshall	3		
E.J.Chatfield	lbw b Garner	0		
Extras	(LB7, NB24)	31	(B10, LB10, NB24)	44
Total		**228**	(5 wickets declared)	**386**

WEST INDIES

Batsman	Dismissal	Runs	Dismissal 2	Runs 2
C.G.Greenidge	c Rutherford b Chatfield	78	c Rutherford b Boock	25
D.L.Haynes	b Bracewell	121	c Hadlee b Boock	13
H.A.Gomes	c Smith b Hadlee	18	not out	8
R.B.Richardson	b Boock	37	not out	0
*I.V.A.Richards	c Smith b Chatfield	24		
A.L.Logie	c Coney b Hadlee	3		
†P.J.L.Dujon	c Smith b Chatfield	22		
M.D.Marshall	c and b Boock	30		
M.A.Holding	c sub (T.D.Ritchie) b Chatfield	0		
J.Garner	c Hadlee b Boock	0		
C.A.Walsh	not out	1		
Extras	(B1, LB8, W1, NB1)	11	(B3, LB1)	4
Total		**345**	(2 wickets)	**50**

WEST INDIES	O	M	R	W	O	M	R	W
Marshall	22	3	57	2	20	6	43	0
Garner	27	5	51	5	30	9	72	2
Walsh	12	1	46	2	(4) 34	13	59	1
Holding	16	4	34	0	(3) 21	4	65	0
Richards	11	3	32	1	47	13	86	1
Gomes	1	0	1	0	21	6	37	1
Richardson					4	1	4	0

NEW ZEALAND	O	M	R	W	O	M	R	W
Hadlee	31	9	77	2	4	0	12	0
Chatfield	39	14	102	4	4	0	13	0
Coney	3	0	8	0				
Bracewell	14	5	47	1	7	2	13	0
Boock	35	14	76	3	(3) 7	4	8	2
M.D.Crowe	3	1	13	0				
Patel	3	0	13	0				

FALL OF WICKETS

Wkt	NZ 1st	WI 1st	NZ 2nd	WI 2nd
1st	10	150	13	33
2nd	19	208	20	46
3rd	46	232	261	–
4th	107	278	301	–
5th	153	287	331	–
6th	181	289	–	–
7th	192	339	–	–
8th	192	343	–	–
9th	226	344	–	–
10th	228	345	–	–

Umpires: B.L.Aldridge (2) and S.J.Woodward (15).

Close: 1st day – NZ(1) 205-8 (Hadlee 16, Boock 2); 2nd – WI(1) 218-2 (Haynes 110, Richardson 6); 3rd – NZ(2) 91-2 (Wright 35, M.D.Crowe 28); 4th – NZ(2) 272-3 (Wright 102, Patel 4).

NEW ZEALAND v WEST INDIES 1986-87 (2nd Test)

At Eden Park, Auckland, on 27, 28 February, 1, 2, 3 March.
Toss: West Indies: Result: WEST INDIES won by ten wickets.
Debuts: None.

Despite the loss of 494 minutes (involving 14 interruptions) to rain and bad light, West Indies gained their first victory in New Zealand since 1968-69 with 4.3 overs in hand. Greenidge (534 minutes, 384 balls, seven sixes and 20 fours) wore sun-glasses to score his 13th hundred and third double-hundred in Tests; only W.R.Hammond (10) has struck more sixes in a Test innings. Hadlee took five wickets in a Test innings for the 28th time to reclaim his world record from I.T.Botham. Martin Crowe (382 minutes, 264 balls) completed 2,000 runs in 34 Tests; his seventh Test hundred (reached with a six) equalled the New Zealand record tally shared by B.E.Congdon and G.M.Turner.

WEST INDIES

C.G.Greenidge	b Hadlee	213	not out	10
D.L.Haynes	c M.D.Crowe b Hadlee	1	not out	6
H.A.Gomes	c Smith b Chatfield	5		
R.B.Richardson	c Smith b Hadlee	41		
*I.V.A.Richards	b Hadlee	14		
A.L.Logie	c M.D.Crowe b Hadlee	34		
†P.J.L.Dujon	b Boock	77		
M.D.Marshall	c J.J.Crowe b Boock	6		
C.G.Butts	not out	8		
A.H.Gray	lbw b Hadlee	8		
C.A.Walsh	did not bat			
Extras	(B4, LB3, NB4)	11		
Total	(9 wickets declared)	**418**	(0 wickets)	**16**

NEW ZEALAND

J.G.Wright	c Richardson b Marshall	11	c Logie b Walsh	7
K.R.Rutherford	b Marshall	12	c Richardson b Marshall	5
J.J.Crowe	c Dujon b Walsh	1	c Gray b Walsh	21
M.D.Crowe	c Dujon b Marshall	10	c Logie b Gray	104
D.N.Patel	c Greenidge b Butts	21	lbw b Marshall	5
*J.V.Coney	c Logie b Gray	15	c Dujon b Gray	17
J.G.Bracewell	c Richardson b Gray	7	lbw b Gomes	43
R.J.Hadlee	c Dujon b Butts	0	c Richardson b Walsh	14
†I.D.S.Smith	not out	40	c Richards b Walsh	10
S.L.Boock	c Dujon b Gray	0	c Dujon b Walsh	4
E.J.Chatfield	c Logie b Marshall	4	not out	0
Extras	(B12, LB2, NB22)	36	(B7, LB8, NB28)	43
Total		**157**		**273**

NEW ZEALAND	O	M	R	W	O	M	R	W		FALL OF WICKETS			
										WI	NZ	NZ	WI
Hadlee	41.4	7	105	6	1	0	9	0	*Wkt*	*1st*	*1st*	*2nd*	*2nd*
Chatfield	37	14	88	1	0.3	0	7	0	1st	7	30	10	–
Boock	25	6	96	2					2nd	14	38	14	–
Bracewell	17	2	53	0					3rd	109	39	83	–
Coney	11	2	22	0					4th	131	69	91	–
M.D.Crowe	5	1	9	0					5th	219	81	126	–
Patel	6	0	38	0					6th	384	95	233	–
									7th	400	101	250	–
WEST INDIES									8th	402	109	260	–
Marshall	17	3	43	4	33	7	71	2	9th	418	118	269	–
Walsh	14	5	34	1	30.2	6	73	5	10th	–	157	273	–
Butts	12	4	21	2	26	6	61	0					
Gray	10	1	45	3	18	4	44	2					
Gomes					4	1	9	1					

Umpires: F.R.Goodall (23) and G.C.Morris (3).

Close: 1st day – WI(1) 211-4 (Greenidge 112, Logie 33); 2nd – WI(1) 415-8 (Butts 7, Gray 6); 3rd – NZ(2) 1-0 (Wright 0, Rutherford 0); 4th – NZ(2) 64-2 (J.J.Crowe 17, M.D.Crowe 18).

NEW ZEALAND v WEST INDIES 1986-87 (3rd Test)

At Lancaster Park, Christchurch, on 12 (*no play*), 13, 14, 15 March.
Toss: New Zealand.   Result: NEW ZEALAND won by five wickets.
Debuts: New Zealand – P.A.Horne.

New Zealand levelled the series in under three days of play and retained their record of being unbeaten in any home rubber since 1978-79. It was the first three-day defeat to be inflicted upon West Indies since 1964-65 when Australia won at Port-of-Spain. Two days of heavy rain immediately before the scheduled start left part of the outfield waterlogged and prevented a start until the second morning. Put in on a slightly damp pitch by Coney in his final Test, West Indies were 67 for 6 at lunch and dismissed in under three hours for their second-lowest total against New Zealand. Hadlee became the third bowler after D.K.Lillee and I.T.Botham to claim 350 Test wickets and he also took his world record of five-wicket hauls to 29. Haynes (4,000 runs), Dujon (2,000 runs), Smith (100 catches) and Hadlee (350 wickets) all reached notable Test aggregates.

WEST INDIES

C.G.Greenidge	b Chatfield	2	c Smith b Hadlee	16
D.L.Haynes	b Hadlee	0	c Horne b Chatfield	19
R.B.Richardson	c M.D.Crowe b Hadlee	37	c M.D.Crowe b Hadlee	19
H.A.Gomes	c J.J.Crowe b Chatfield	8	c Coney b M.D.Crowe	33
*I.V.A.Richards	c Smith b Chatfield	1	c Smith b Snedden	38
A.L.Logie	c Coney b Hadlee	6	c J.J.Crowe b Snedden	19
†P.J.L.Dujon	c Coney b Hadlee	6	c M.D.Crowe b Snedden	39
M.D.Marshall	c Snedden b Chatfield	2	b Hadlee	45
J.Garner	c Coney b Hadlee	0	c Wright b Snedden	11
A.H.Gray	not out	10	c M.D.Crowe b Snedden	3
C.A.Walsh	b Hadlee	14	not out	8
Extras	(LB6, NB8)	14	(B2, LB4, NB8)	14
Total		**100**		**264**

NEW ZEALAND

J.G.Wright	c Richards b Walsh	6	c Richards b Gray	2
P.A.Horne	c Richards b Garner	9	c Gray b Walsh	0
J.J.Crowe	c Dujon b Gray	55	c Gray b Walsh	2
M.D.Crowe	b Marshall	83	not out	9
D.N.Patel	c Dujon b Gray	0	c Richardson b Walsh	9
*J.V.Coney	run out	36	c Gray b Garner	2
J.G.Bracewell	c Haynes b Garner	66	not out	2
R.J.Hadlee	not out	25		
†I.D.S.Smith	c Dujon b Garner	7		
M.C.Snedden	c Logie b Garner	7		
E.J.Chatfield	not out	1		
Extras	(B6, LB2, W1, NB28)	37	(NB7)	7
Total	(9 wickets declared)	**332**	(5 wickets)	**33**

NEW ZEALAND	O	M	R	W		O	M	R	W		FALL OF WICKETS			
											WI	NZ	WI	NZ
Hadlee	12.3	2	50	6		23	2	101	3	*Wkt*	*1st*	*1st*	*2nd*	*2nd*
Chatfield	18	8	30	4		16	3	42	1					
Snedden	6	1	14	0	(5)	18.3	2	68	5	1st	2	12	37	1
Bracewell					(3)	7	0	34	0	2nd	6	23	37	3
M.D.Crowe					(4)	6	0	13	1	3rd	44	179	80	13
										4th	56	180	129	27
WEST INDIES										5th	56	181	133	30
Marshall	27	2	75	1						6th	64	270	160	–
Garner	19	2	79	4	(3)	1	0	3	1	7th	67	294	237	–
Walsh	24.5	3	78	1	(1)	5.1	0	16	3	8th	70	307	241	–
Gray	17	4	47	2	(2)	4	1	14	1	9th	75	330	255	–
Richards	9	3	29	0						10th	100	–	264	–
Gomes	4	1	16	0										

Umpires: G.C.Morris (4) and S.J.Woodward (16).

Close: 1st day – no play; 2nd – NZ(1) 117-2 (J.J.Crowe 38, M.D.Crowe 44); 3rd – WI(2) 35-0 (Greenidge 16, Haynes 17).

SRI LANKA v NEW ZEALAND 1986-87 (1st Test)

At Colombo Cricket Club Ground on 16, 18, 19, 20, 21 April.
Toss: New Zealand.   Result: MATCH DRAWN.
Debuts: Sri Lanka – D.S.B.P.Kuruppu; New Zealand – A.H.Jones.

Kuruppu took 776 minutes to reach Sri Lanka's first double century and the slowest 200 in all first-class cricket. His innings (777 minutes, 548 balls, 24 fours) was then the third-longest in Test and first-class matches. The first wicket-keeper – and Sri Lankan – to score a hundred in his first Test, he was the third to score 200 on debut and the second to be on the field throughout his maiden Test. It was his maiden first-class hundred. Chatfield took his 100th wicket in 33 Tests spread over 12 years. Batting throughout a final day aborted with 16 overs remaining, Jeff Crowe (609 minutes, 398 balls) marked his first Test as captain by scoring the slowest hundred for New Zealand (515 minutes), while Hadlee (406 minutes, 240 balls) recorded his country's 100th century and his own highest score. Their unbroken partnership of 246 established a national sixth-wicket record.

SRI LANKA

R.S.Mahanama	c Smith b Chatfield	16
†D.S.B.P.Kuruppu	not out	201
A.P.Gurusinha	lbw b Hadlee	22
R.L.Dias	c Bracewell b Hadlee	25
A.Ranatunga	c Smith b Bracewell	15
*L.R.D.Mendis	c Bracewell b Hadlee	12
R.S.Madugalle	c Hadlee b Gray	60
J.R.Ratnayeke	c M.D.Crowe b Bracewell	12
R.J.Ratnayake	c Bracewell b Hadlee	17
S.D.Anurasiri	c Smith b Chatfield	1
A.K.Kuruppuarachchi	not out	0
Extras	(LB4, W1, NB11)	16
Total	(9 wickets declared)	**397**

NEW ZEALAND

K.R.Rutherford	c Madugalle b Ratnayeke	11
P.A.Horne	c Kuruppu b Anurasiri	16
A.H.Jones	lbw b Ratnayeke	38
M.D.Crowe	c Mendis b Ratnayeke	27
*J.J.Crowe	not out	120
E.J.Gray	c Ranatunga b Kuruppuarachchi	31
R.J.Hadlee	not out	151
J.G.Bracewell		
†I.D.S.Smith	did not bat	
M.C.Snedden		
E.J.Chatfield		
Extras	(LB2, W4, NB6)	12
Total	(5 wickets)	**406**

NEW ZEALAND	O	M	R	W
Hadlee	38.5	10	102	4
Chatfield	38	11	104	2
M.D.Crowe	7	4	13	0
Snedden	16	4	41	0
Bracewell	47	14	98	2
Gray	27	12	35	1

SRI LANKA	O	M	R	W
Ratnayake	32	7	79	1
Kuruppuarachchi	20	3	64	1
Ranatunga	23	10	43	0
Ratnayeke	37	6	111	2
Anurasiri	36	13	67	1
Gurusinha	9	1	17	0
Madugalle	2	0	6	0
Dias	4	0	17	0

FALL OF WICKETS

Wkt	SL 1st	NZ 1st
1st	29	20
2nd	70	51
3rd	129	90
4th	166	99
5th	210	160
6th	319	–
7th	342	–
8th	382	–
9th	383	–
10th	–	–

Umpires: P.W.Vidanagamage (4) and W.A.U.Wickramsinghe (1).

Close: 1st day – SL(1) 141-3 (Kuruppu 66, Ranatunga 3); 2nd – SL(1) 317-5 (Kuruppu 153, Madugalle 59); 3rd – NZ(1) 51-2 (Jones 19, M.D.Crowe 0); 4th – NZ(1) 214-5 (J.J.Crowe 42, Hadlee 40).

The 2nd and 3rd Test matches, scheduled to be played at the Asgiriya Stadium, Kandy (24, 25, 26, 28, 29 April) and at the Sinhalese Sports Club Ground, Colombo (5, 6, 7, 9, 10 May) respectively, were abandoned along with the remainder of New Zealand's tour following intensive political unrest.

ENGLAND v PAKISTAN 1987 (1st Test)

At Old Trafford, Manchester, on 4, 5, 6, 8, 9 (*no play*) June.
Toss: Pakistan.   Result: MATCH DRAWN.
Debuts: England – N.H.Fairbrother.

England's strong position was rendered impotent by Manchester's infamous 'local forces', which permitted only 13 hours 53 minutes of actual playing time and saw Old Trafford's 27th abandoned day in 55 Tests. Surprisingly, this was the first day to be washed out in any Test in England since 28 June 1982 (Manchester). Making his debut against Pakistan, Robinson (528 minutes, 366 balls, 16 fours) took full advantage of an attack weakened by Imran's inability to bowl and recorded England's highest score of this series at Old Trafford. His main ally was night-watchman French who reached his only Test fifty. Miandad deputised as captain when Imran left the field for nine overs on the second evening. No play was possible after 12.54 pm on the fourth day. J.Birkenshaw deputised for H.D.Bird (struck on the shin by a return) for seven overs on the second afternoon.

ENGLAND

C.W.J.Athey	b Wasim	19
R.T.Robinson	c Salim Yousuf b Mohsin	166
*M.W.Gatting	b Mohsin	42
N.H.Fairbrother	lbw b Mohsin	0
†B.N.French	c Imran b Wasim	59
D.I.Gower	c Salim Yousuf b Wasim	22
I.T.Botham	c Wasim b Tausif	48
J.E.Emburey	c Shoaib b Mohsin	19
P.A.J.DeFreitas	b Wasim	11
N.A.Foster	b Tausif	8
P.H.Edmonds	not out	23
Extras	(B9, LB15, W1, NB5)	30
Total		**447**

PAKISTAN

Ramiz Raja	c Emburey b DeFreitas	15
Shoaib Mohammad	c French b Foster	0
Mansoor Akhtar	c Fairbrother b Edmonds	75
Javed Miandad	c French b Botham	21
Salim Malik	run out	6
*Imran Khan	not out	10
Mudassar Nazar	not out	0
†Salim Yousuf		
Wasim Akram	} did not bat	
Tausif Ahmed		
Mohsin Kamal		
Extras	(B9, LB2, W1, NB1)	13
Total	(5 wickets)	**140**

PAKISTAN	O	M	R	W
Wasim	46	11	111	4
Mohsin	39	4	127	4
Tausif	21.4	4	52	2
Mudassar	37	8	133	0

ENGLAND	O	M	R	W
Foster	15	3	34	1
DeFreitas	12	4	36	1
Botham	14	7	29	1
Emburey	16	3	28	0
Edmonds	7	5	2	1

FALL OF WICKETS

	E	P
Wkt	1st	1st
1st	50	9
2nd	133	21
3rd	133	74
4th	246	100
5th	284	139
6th	373	–
7th	397	–
8th	413	–
9th	413	–
10th	447	–

Umpires: H.D.Bird (36) and B.J.Meyer (19).

Close: 1st day – E(1) 145-3 (Robinson 62, French 6); 2nd – E(1) 402-7 (Emburey 14, DeFreitas 5); 3rd – P(1) 93-3 (Mansoor 42, Salim Malik 3); 4th – P(1) 140-5 (Imran 10, Mudassar 0).

ENGLAND v PAKISTAN 1987 (2nd Test)

At Lord's, London, on 18, 19 (*no play*), 20, 22 (*no play*), 23 (*no play*) June.
Toss: England.   Result: MATCH DRAWN.
Debuts: None.

Not since Pakistan's very first tour had three days of a Test been lost in England. The insurance which allowed advance ticket holders to reclaim their outlay (less a 50p handling charge) was activated for the first time. Not since 1931 (*Test No. 211*) had England failed to take the field in a home Test. After two Tests England's bowlers had a return of four wickets from just 64 overs. Almost two thirds of the total playing time available to date had been lost: 38 hours out of a possible 60 or 579 overs out of 900. There was time for Broad and Robinson to become the first all-Nottinghamshire opening pairing since March 1885 when W.Barnes partnered W.H.Scotton against Australia in the fifth Test at Melbourne. Not since 1967 (Surrey's J.H.Edrich and K.F.Barrington in *Test No. 619*) had one county provided England's opening pair. Athey (315 minutes, 203 balls, 14 fours) scored his first Test century in his 26th innings. It was England's first hundred by a player registered with Gloucestershire since C.A.Milton's debut innings against New Zealand at Leeds in 1958.

ENGLAND

B.C.Broad	b Mudassar	55
R.T.Robinson	c Salim Yousuf b Mohsin	7
C.W.J.Athey	b Imran	123
D.I.Gower	c Salim Yousuf b Mudassar	8
*M.W.Gatting	run out	43
†B.N.French	b Wasim	42
I.T.Botham	c Miandad b Wasim	6
J.E.Emburey	run out	12
N.A.Foster	b Qadir	21
P.H.Edmonds	not out	17
G.R.Dilley	c Salim Yousuf b Imran	17
Extras	(LB12, W1, NB4)	17
Total		**368**

PAKISTAN

Mudassar Nazar
Shoaib Mohammad
Mansoor Akhtar
Javed Miandad
Salim Malik
Ijaz Ahmed
*Imran Khan
†Salim Yousuf
Wasim Akram
Abdul Qadir
Mohsin Kamal

PAKISTAN	O	M	R	W
Imran	34.5	7	90	2
Wasim	28	1	98	2
Mohsin	9	2	42	1
Qadir	25	1	100	1
Mudassar	16	6	26	2

FALL OF WICKETS

Wkt	E 1st
1st	29
2nd	118
3rd	128
4th	230
5th	272
6th	294
7th	305
8th	329
9th	340
10th	368

Umpires: D.J.Constant (33) and A.G.T.Whitehead (4).

Close: 1st day – E(1) 231-4 (Athey 107, French 1); 2nd – no play; 3rd – E(1) 368 all out; 4th – no play.

ENGLAND v PAKISTAN 1987 (3rd Test)

At Headingley, Leeds, on 2, 3, 4, 6 July.
Toss: England.　Result: PAKISTAN won by an a innings and 18 runs.
Debuts: England – D.J.Capel.

After just 24 minutes of play on the fourth day Pakistan completed their fourth victory in 42 Tests against England. It was their first by an innings and their first at Headingley. Imran Khan inspired his young team and became the eighth bowler (and first Pakistani) to take 300 Test wickets when he dismissed Richards. His second innings analysis was his 20th of five or more wickets in 68 Tests (and a Pakistan record against England) while his match analysis was his fifth of ten or more wickets. Foster, whose analysis was his best in first-class cricket, became the third bowler after C.Blythe (1907) and R.G.D.Willis (1981) to take eight wickets for England at Leeds. Wasim Akram's 43 included four sixes. Capel was the fourth Northamptonshire-born cricketer to gain a Test cap for England and the first from Northampton itself. Pakistan gained five byes when Richards allowed a ball to torpedo him and hit a parked fielding helmet.

ENGLAND

B.C.Broad	c Salim Yousuf b Wasim	8	c Salim Yousuf b Imran	4
R.T.Robinson	lbw b Imran	0	c Salim Malik b Imran	2
C.W.J.Athey	c Salim Yousuf b Imran	4	lbw b Imran	26
D.I.Gower	b Imran	10	b Imran	55
*M.W.Gatting	lbw b Wasim	8	c Miandad b Wasim	9
I.T.Botham	c Salim Yousuf b Mudassar	26	(8) c Mudassar b Mohsin	24
D.J.Capel	c and b Mohsin	53	(6) c Ijaz b Imran	28
C.J.Richards	lbw b Wasim	6	(7) c Ijaz b Imran	2
N.A.Foster	c Salim Malik b Mohsin	9	b Wasim	22
P.H.Edmonds	c Salim Yousuf b Mohsin	0	not out	0
G.R.Dilley	not out	1	b Imran	0
Extras	(B1, LB8, W1, NB1)	11	(B5, LB12, W7, NB3)	27
Total		**136**		**199**

PAKISTAN

Mudassar Nazar	lbw b Foster	24	
Shoaib Mohammad	c Richards b Foster	16	
Mansoor Akhtar	lbw b Foster	29	
*Salim Yousuf	c Athey b Foster	37	
Javed Miandad	c Gatting b Foster	0	
Salim Malik	c Gower b Edmonds	99	
*Imran Khan	c Richards b Foster	26	
Ijaz Ahmed	c Athey b Foster	50	
Wasim Akram	c Edmonds b Foster	43	
Abdul Qadir	b Dilley	2	
Mohsin Kamal	not out	3	
Extras	(B5, LB13, W1, NB5)	24	
Total		**353**	

PAKISTAN	O	M	R	W		O	M	R	W
Imran	19	3	37	3		19.1	5	40	7
Wasim	14	4	36	3		21	5	55	2
Qadir	5	0	14	0		27	5	60	0
Mudassar	14	5	18	1	(5)	2	0	8	0
Mohsin	8.4	2	22	3	(4)	9	4	19	1
ENGLAND									
Dilley	33	7	89	1					
Foster	46.2	15	107	8					
Capel	18	1	64	0					
Edmonds	25	10	59	1					
Gatting	9	3	16	0					

FALL OF WICKETS

	E	P	E
Wkt	1st	1st	2nd
1st	1	22	4
2nd	13	60	9
3rd	13	86	60
4th	31	86	94
5th	31	152	120
6th	85	208	122
7th	113	280	160
8th	133	318	197
9th	133	328	197
10th	136	353	199

Umpires: K.E.Palmer (14) and D.R.Shepherd (5).

Close: 1st day – P(1) 76-2 (Mansoor 24, Yousuf 4); 2nd – P(1) 280-7 (Ijaz 33, Wasim 0); 3rd – E(2) 186-7 (Capel 26, Foster 13).

ENGLAND v PAKISTAN 1987 (4th Test)

At Edgbaston, Birmingham, on 23, 24, 25, 27, 28 July.
Toss: England.   Result: MATCH DRAWN.
Debuts: None.

Edgbaston's 25th Test produced one of the most exciting final sessions at this level after a draw had seemed inevitable. By taking nine second innings wickets after lunch on the final day, England earned an outside chance of squaring the rubber, their target being 124 runs from 18 overs. Although they were exactly on course at the halfway mark with just three wickets down, Imran and Wasim Akram managed narrowly to preserve Pakistan's lead. Gatting became only the third England captain after M.H.Denness (1975) and Gower (1985) to insert the opposition in a Birmingham Test. Mudassar (417 minutes, 361 balls) seemed to safeguard the tourists' lead with his ninth hundred but, propelled by Gatting (401 minutes, 281 balls), England gained a lead of 82 from 22 fewer balls than their opponents. Broad and Robinson were the fourth pair from the same county to share a century opening stand for England. Botham became the first bowler to concede 10,000 runs in Tests.

PAKISTAN

Mudassar Nazar	lbw b Dilley	124		b Dilley	10
Shoaib Mohammad	c Foster b Edmonds	18		lbw b Foster	50
Mansoor Akhtar	b Foster	26		lbw b Foster	17
Javed Miandad	lbw b Dilley	75		c Emburey b Foster	4
Salim Malik	c French b Dilley	24		c and b Botham	17
Ijaz Ahmed	lbw b Botham	20		b Botham	11
*Imran Khan	c Emburey b Dilley	0		lbw b Foster	37
†Salim Yousuf	not out	91		c Gatting b Edmonds	17
Wasim Akram	c Botham b Foster	26		c Edmonds b Dilley	6
Abdul Qadir	c Edmonds b Dilley	6		run out	20
Mohsin Kamal	run out	10		not out	0
Extras	(B4, LB11, W1, NB3)	19		(LB13, W1, NB2)	16
Total		**439**			**205**

ENGLAND

B.C.Broad	c Salim Yousuf b Imran	54		c Mudassar b Imran	30
R.T.Robinson	c Salim Yousuf b Wasim	80		c Imran b Wasim	4
C.W.J.Athey	b Imran	0	(6)	not out	14
D.I.Gower	c Salim Yousuf b Imran	61	(3)	b Imran	18
*M.W.Gatting	c Wasim b Imran	124		run out	8
†B.N.French	b Imran	0	(9)	not out	1
I.T.Botham	c and b Wasim	37	(4)	c Mohsin b Wasim	6
J.E.Emburey	lbw b Wasim	58	(7)	run out	20
N.A.Foster	run out	29			
P.H.Edmonds	not out	24	(8)	run out	0
G.R.Dilley	b Imran	2			
Extras	(B1, LB24, W11, NB16)	52		(LB7, W1)	8
Total		**521**		(7 wickets)	**109**

ENGLAND	O	M	R	W	O	M	R	W		FALL OF WICKETS			
Dilley	35	6	92	5	(2) 18	3	53	2		P	E	P	E
Foster	37	8	107	2	(1) 27	7	59	4	Wkt	1st	1st	2nd	2nd
Emburey	26	7	48	0	4	1	3	0	1st	44	119	47	37
Edmonds	24.3	12	50	1	(5) 4	1	11	1	2nd	83	132	80	39
Botham	48	13	121	1	(4) 20.3	3	66	2	3rd	218	157	85	53
Gatting	3	0	6	0					4th	284	251	104	72
									5th	289	251	104	73
PAKISTAN									6th	289	300	116	108
Imran	41.5	8	129	6	9	0	61	2	7th	317	443	156	108
Wasim	43	12	83	3	8.4	0	41	2	8th	360	484	165	–
Qadir	21	4	65	0					9th	384	512	204	–
Mudassar	35	7	97	0					10th	439	521	205	–
Mohsin	29	2	122	0									

Umpires: B.J.Meyer (20) and A.G.T.Whitehead (5).

Close: 1st day – P(1) 250-3 (Mudassar 102, Salim Malik 13); 2nd – E(1) 18-0 (Broad 14, Robinson 2); 3rd – E(1) 273-5 (Gatting 35, Botham 16); 4th – P(2) 38-0 (Mudassar 6, Shoaib 32).

ENGLAND v PAKISTAN 1987 (5th Test)

At Kennington Oval, London, on 6, 7, 8, 10, 11 August.
Toss: Pakistan.   Result: MATCH DRAWN.
Debuts: None.

Pakistan's total of 708 was their highest in Test matches, the highest in any post-war Test in England, the sixth-highest in all Tests, the second-highest against England, and the fourth-highest in post-war first-class cricket in Britain. It was ended by Dilley's final spell of 4 for 1 in 16 balls. Javed Miandad's 260 (613 minutes, 520 balls, one six and 28 fours) was the fourth-highest Test innings at The Oval; he became only the seventh batsman to score four or more double hundreds in Test cricket and the first to score 6,000 runs for Pakistan. It was his 15th hundred but his first against England. His partnership of 234 with Salim Malik was a fourth-wicket record for the series until 1992. Botham conceded more runs in a Test innings than any England bowler in 638 matches. He also completed 5,000 runs to acquire a unique treble when allied to his record 373 wickets and 109 catches. Emburey completed 1,000 runs in 46 Tests and became the eighth to achieve the 'double' for England.

PAKISTAN

Mudassar Nazar	c Moxon b Botham	73
Ramiz Raja	b Botham	14
Mansoor Akhtar	c French b Dilley	5
Javed Miandad	c and b Dilley	260
Salim Malik	c Gower b Botham	102
*Imran Khan	run out	118
Ijaz Ahmed	c Moxon b Dilley	69
†Salim Yousuf	c and b Dilley	42
Wasim Akram	c Botham b Dilley	5
Abdul Qadir	c Moxon b Dilley	0
Tausif Ahmed	not out	0
Extras	(B2, LB18)	20
Total		**708**

ENGLAND

B.C.Broad	c Salim Yousuf b Imran	0	c Ijaz b Qadir	42
M.D.Moxon	c Miandad b Qadir	8	c Salim Yousuf b Tausif	15
R.T.Robinson	b Qadir	30	c Wasim b Qadir	10
D.I.Gower	b Tausif	28	c Mudassar b Qadir	34
*M.W.Gatting	c Imran b Qadir	61	not out	150
I.T.Botham	b Qadir	34	not out	51
J.E.Emburey	c Salim Malik b Qadir	53		
†B.N.French	c Salim Malik b Qadir	1		
N.A.Foster	c Ijaz b Tausif	4		
P.H.Edmonds	lbw b Qadir	2		
G.R.Dilley	not out	0		
Extras	(B4, LB3, W1, NB3)	11	(B4, LB5, W1, NB3)	13
Total		**232**	(4 wickets)	**315**

ENGLAND	O	M	R	W	O	M	R	W		FALL OF WICKETS		
										P	E	E
Dilley	47.3	10	154	6					Wkt	1st	1st	2nd
Foster	12	3	32	0					1st	40	0	22
Botham	52	7	217	3					2nd	45	32	40
Emburey	61	10	143	0					3rd	148	54	89
Edmonds	32	8	97	0					4th	382	78	139
Gatting	10	2	18	0					5th	573	165	–
Moxon	6	2	27	0					6th	601	166	–
									7th	690	184	–
PAKISTAN									8th	707	198	–
Imran	18	2	39	1	26.3	8	59	0	9th	707	223	–
Wasim	14	2	37	0	6	3	3	0	10th	708	232	–
Qadir	44.4	15	96	7	53	21	115	3				
Tausif	23	9	53	2	46.3	15	98	1				
Mudassar					6	0	21	0				
Miandad					4	2	10	0				

Umpires: D.J.Constant (34) and K.E.Palmer (15).

Close: 1st day – P(1) 297-3 (Miandad 131, Salim Malik 64); 2nd – P(1) 616-6 (Ijaz 22, Salim Yousuf 6); 3rd – E(1) 144-4 (Gatting 50, Botham 23); 4th – E(2) 95-3 (Broad 26, Gatting 5).

INDIA v WEST INDIES 1987-88 (1st Test)

At Feroz Shah Kotla, Delhi, on 25, 26, 28, 29 November.
Toss: India.   Result: WEST INDIES won by five wickets.
Debuts: India – Arshad Ayub, S.V.Manjrekar; West Indies – W.K.M.Benjamin.

Uncharacteristic bowling conditions which encouraged excessive swing and lively bounce conspired to produce a dramatically fluctuating contest after both sides had been dismissed for their lowest total of this series and 18 wickets had fallen on the first day. India's 145-minute innings produced the lowest Test total in that country. Haynes batted throughout West Indies' 3½-hour reply. In his 96th Test, Vengsarkar, the most senior cricketer in terms of matches to be first appointed a Test captain, batted 405 minutes for his 16th hundred and exceeded 6,000 runs. Manjrekar, struck over the left eye by a lifting ball from Benjamin, retired at 105. Left to score 276 on a pitch now favouring spin, West Indies were led to victory by their captain, who played an outstanding innings of 109 not out off 102 balls in 156 minutes; his 21st hundred was his seventh against India.

INDIA

K.Srikkanth	c Dujon b Patterson	0	c Harper b Patterson		5
Arun Lal	c Greenidge b Davis	20	c Benjamin b Walsh		40
R.Lamba	b Davis	1	b Patterson		0
*D.B.Vengsarkar	c Harper b Davis	10	c Greenidge b Walsh		102
R.J.Shastri	c Richardson b Benjamin	6	c Harper b Patterson		4
S.V.Manjrekar	c Harper b Patterson	5	retired hurt		10
Kapil Dev	c Dujon b Walsh	7	lbw b Benjamin		44
†K.S.More	not out	12	c Dujon b Walsh		49
Arshad Ayub	c Harper b Patterson	7	lbw b Walsh		17
C.Sharma	c Richardson b Patterson	0	b Walsh		24
Maninder Singh	b Patterson	0	not out		2
Extras	(LB1, W3, NB3)	7	(B17, LB7, W5, NB1)		30
Total		**75**			**327**

WEST INDIES

C.G.Greenidge	lbw b Kapil Dev	0	lbw b Ayub		33
D.L.Haynes	c Lamba b Sharma	45	hit wicket b Ayub		27
R.B.Richardson	lbw b Kapil Dev	4	c Lamba b Kapil Dev		31
*I.V.A.Richards	c More b Sharma	9	(5) not out		109
A.L.Logie	lbw b Sharma	4	(6) lbw b Ayub		46
†P.J.L.Dujon	c Lamba b Kapil Dev	5	(7) not out		12
R.A.Harper	run out	4			
W.W.Davis	c and b Sharma	6	(4) c sub (C.S.Pandit) b Ayub		1
W.K.M.Benjamin	b Ayub	19			
C.A.Walsh	c Lamba b Sharma	16			
B.P.Patterson	not out	5			
Extras	(B3, LB1, W1, NB5)	10	(B1, LB9, NB7)		17
Total		**127**	(5 wickets)		**276**

WEST INDIES	O	M	R	W	O	M	R	W	FALL OF WICKETS				
										I	WI	I	WI
Patterson	8.5	1	24	5	29	6	100	3		*1st*	*1st*	*2nd*	*2nd*
Davis	11	2	20	3	20	3	60	0	*Wkt*				
Benjamin	7	0	17	1	23	3	76	1	1st	0	0	6	62
Walsh	4	0	13	1	29.3	9	54	5	2nd	7	4	6	69
Harper					12	3	13	0	3rd	32	13	66	91
									4th	42	17	82	111
INDIA									5th	42	25	178	203
Kapil Dev	18	8	41	3	20	8	44	1	6th	52	29	274	–
Sharma	13.1	2	55	5	11	1	44	0	7th	58	49	277	–
Maninder	7	3	13	0	20	4	75	0	8th	75	102	318	–
Ayub	9	4	14	1	25	4	72	4	9th	75	122	327	–
Shastri					9	2	30	0	10th	75	127	–	–
Arun Lal					0.3	0	1	0					

Umpires: D.N.Dotiwalla (6) and V.K.Ramaswamy (11).

Close: 1st day – WI(1) 118-8 (Haynes 45, Walsh 12); 2nd – I(2) 210-5 (Vengsarkar 74, More 18); 3rd – WI(2) 80-2 (Richardson 15, Davis 1).

INDIA v WEST INDIES 1987-88 (2nd Test)

At Wankhede Stadium, Bombay, on 11, 12 (*no play*), 13, 15, 16 December.
Toss: India.   Result: MATCH DRAWN.
Debuts: West Indies – C.L.Hooper.

West Indies finished tantalisingly close to victory (needing 114 runs with nine wickets in hand) despite the loss of more than 613 minutes (156 overs) during the first three days. In reality they required 118 from the game's final 11 overs but rejected the challenge after 12 balls. Srikkanth challenged the fast bowlers with fearless hooking and driving to complete 50 off only 39 balls in the first innings, his 71 (63 balls) including 11 fours and a six. He followed this with 65 off 78 balls in 128 minutes with 10 fours.

INDIA

K.Srikkanth	b Walsh	71	b Patterson		65
Arun Lal	c Richardson b Walsh	3	c Greenidge b Patterson		1
M.Amarnath	c Butts b Walsh	1	c Richards b Walsh		8
*D.B.Vengsarkar	st Dujon b Butts	51	not out		40
M.Azharuddin	run out	34	c Davis b Patterson		5
R.J.Shastri	c Richards b Davis	0	c Butts b Davis		5
Kapil Dev	c Greenidge b Butts	47	c Dujon b Patterson		5
†K.S.More	c Dujon b Patterson	9	c Richardson b Patterson		0
Arshad Ayub	c Richards b Walsh	8	b Walsh		18
C.Sharma	not out	22	b Walsh		0
Maninder Singh	c Richardson b Walsh	0	c Richardson b Walsh		0
Extras	(B4, LB15, NB16)	35	(B1, LB5, W8, NB12)		26
Total		**281**			**173**

WEST INDIES

C.G.Greenidge	c Arun Lal b Shastri	15	c Kapil Dev b Sharma	2
D.L.Haynes	c sub (C.S.Pandit) b Shastri	58	not out	0
R.B.Richardson	lbw b Sharma	89	not out	0
*I.V.A.Richards	b Maninder	37		
A.L.Logie	run out	0		
C.L.Hooper	lbw b Kapil Dev	37		
†P.J.L.Dujon	c and b Shastri	14		
C.G.Butts	c More b Shastri	18		
W.W.Davis	c and b Sharma	30		
C.A.Walsh	c Srikkanth b Sharma	5		
B.P.Patterson	not out	21		
Extras	(LB8, W1, NB4)	13	(LB1, NB1)	2
Total		**337**	(1 wicket)	**4**

WEST INDIES	O	M	R	W	O	M	R	W					
Patterson	17	3	78	1	16	1	68	5					
Davis	15	0	71	1	15	2	59	1					
Walsh	17.4	2	54	5	14	2	40	4					
Butts	18	5	59	2	1	1	0	0					

									FALL OF WICKETS				
										I	WI	I	WI
INDIA									*Wkt*	*1st*	*1st*	*2nd*	*2nd*
Kapil Dev	25	8	72	1	1	0	2	0	1st	60	55	16	3
Sharma	13	1	64	3	1	0	1	1	2nd	74	99	58	–
Ayub	20	1	54	0					3rd	85	146	105	–
Maninder	17	5	68	1					4th	157	146	112	–
Shastri	28.3	9	71	4					5th	162	210	126	–
									6th	222	258	132	–
									7th	241	258	132	–
									8th	247	300	173	–
									9th	271	308	173	–
									10th	281	337	173	–

Umpires: R.B.Gupta (7) and P.D.Reporter (9).

Close: 1st day – I(1) 99-3 (Vengsarkar 7, Azharuddin 6); 2nd – no play; 3rd – WI(1) 49-0 (Greenidge 11, Haynes 36); 4th – WI(1) 327-9 (Butts 17, Patterson 12).

INDIA v WEST INDIES 1987-88 (3rd Test)

At Eden Gardens, Calcutta, on 26, 27, 28, 30, 31 December.
Toss: West Indies.   Result: MATCH DRAWN.
Debuts: None.

A benign pitch produced 1,252 runs, only 16 wickets and extended the tally of recently drawn Tests at Eden Gardens to seven out of eight. Greenidge (265 balls, five sixes and 14 fours) reached 50 off 62 balls and recorded his 14th hundred. Logie scored his second Test hundred off 134 balls. At 21 years 12 days, Hooper became the third-youngest West Indian century-maker after G.A.Headley and O.G.Smith. Five balls after Vengsarkar (332 minutes, 261 balls, 11 fours) had completed his 17th hundred (sixth against West Indies) his left hand was fractured by a ball from Davis. He retired at 426, Shastri deputising as captain.

WEST INDIES

C.G.Greenidge	c More b Kapil Dev	141	c sub (S.K.Sharma) b Shastri	69
D.L.Haynes	c Srikkanth b Kapil Dev	5	c and b Shastri	47
R.B.Richardson	c Azharuddin b Shastri	51	not out	8
*I.V.A.Richards	c Kapil Dev b Sharma	68		
A.L.Logie	c and b Maninder	101	(4) not out	20
C.L.Hooper	not out	100		
†P.J.L.Dujon	not out	40		
C.G.Butts				
W.W.Davis	} did not bat			
C.A.Walsh				
B.P.Patterson				
Extras	(B2, LB12, NB10)	24	(B4, LB2, NB7)	13
Total	(5 wickets declared)	**530**	(2 wickets)	**157**

INDIA

K.Srikkanth	c Dujon b Walsh	23
Arun Lal	lbw b Walsh	93
M.Amarnath	b Davis	43
*D.B.Vengsarkar	retired hurt	102
M.Azharuddin	c Logie b Walsh	60
R.J.Shastri	b Davis	47
Kapil Dev	lbw b Davis	4
†K.S.More	c Richardson b Richards	44
Arshad Ayub	c Richardson b Patterson	57
C.Sharma	b Walsh	27
Maninder Singh	not out	1
Extras	(B12, LB25, NB27)	64
Total		**565**

INDIA	O	M	R	W	O	M	R	W	FALL OF WICKETS			
										WI	I	WI
Kapil Dev	28	6	103	2	10	2	19	0	*Wkt*	*1st*	*1st*	*2nd*
Sharma	15.1	0	80	1	4	0	24	0	1st	13	56	114
Maninder	36.5	5	111	1	16	2	43	0	2nd	160	152	129
Ayub	46	5	146	0	14	5	34	0	3rd	284	201	–
Shastri	22	4	60	1	(6) 10	3	13	2	4th	288	305	–
Amarnath	3.5	0	16	0	(5) 4	0	11	0	5th	457	403	–
Srikkanth					3	0	7	0	6th	–	410	–
Arun Lal					1	1	0	0	7th	–	505	–
									8th	–	553	–
WEST INDIES									9th	–	565	–
Patterson	22.2	0	107	1					10th	–	–	–
Walsh	29	3	136	4								
Davis	27	4	84	3								
Butts	50	13	122	0								
Richards	24	6	39	1								
Hooper	20	5	40	0								

Umpires: R.B.Gupta (8) and P.D.Reporter (10).

Close: 1st day – WI(1) 263-2 (Greenidge 133, Richards 55); 2nd – I(1) 20-0 (Srikkanth 7, Arun Lal 11); 3rd – I(1) 304-3 (Vengsarkar 53, Azharuddin 60); 4th – I(1) 521-7 (Ayub 43, Sharma 5).

INDIA v WEST INDIES 1987-88 (4th Test)

At Chidambaram Stadium, Chepauk, Madras, on 11, 12, 14, 15 January.
Toss: India.   Result: INDIA won by 255 runs.
Debuts: India – N.D.Hirwani, W.V.Raman, A.K.Sharma; West Indies – P.V.Simmons.

An astonishing debut by Narendra Hirwani, a 19-year-old leg break bowler who exacted maximum turn from an underprepared pitch, enabled India to draw the series with an emphatic victory. After Shastri, captain in the absence of Vengsarkar, had won an important toss, Kapil Dev scored a spectacular sixth Test hundred off 105 balls (153 minutes, 17 fours). Hirwani's first innings analysis (8 for 61) is the third-best by any bowler in their first Test. After his fellow debutant, Raman, had consolidated India's lead by enduring 257 minutes for the second-highest score of the match, he completed a match analysis of 16 for 136. Only J.C.Laker (19) and S.F.Barnes (17) have taken more wickets in a Test match. Remarkably, the only other bowler to take 16 wickets in a Test, R.A.L.Massie (*Test No. 699*), also did so in his first match but at a cost of one run more. Hirwani owed much to More who set world Test stumping records by making five in an innings and six in the match.

INDIA

K.Srikkanth	c Davis b Walsh	23	lbw b Davis	17
Arun Lal	c Logie b Hooper	69	lbw b Walsh	1
M.Amarnath	c Dujon b Walsh	3	(4) c Richardson b Walsh	1
W.V.Raman	c Dujon b Davis	9	(3) c Dujon b Walsh	83
M.Azharuddin	c Haynes b Hooper	47	c Davis b Richards	39
A.K.Sharma	lbw b Richards	30	lbw b Patterson	23
Kapil Dev	c Richards b Walsh	109	lbw b Patterson	5
*R.J.Shastri	b Davis	23	not out	20
†K.S.More	b Davis	17	c Dujon b Walsh	0
Arshad Ayub	not out	23	not out	3
N.D.Hirwani	c Richardson b Davis	1		
Extras	(B15, LB4, NB9)	28	(B8, LB7, NB10)	25
Total		**382**	(8 wickets declared)	**217**

WEST INDIES

D.L.Haynes	c Kapil Dev b Shastri	13	lbw b Hirwani	6
P.V.Simmons	c and b Kapil Dev	8	c Amarnath b Hirwani	14
R.B.Richardson	c Azharuddin b Hirwani	36	c Amarnath b Ayub	7
*I.V.A.Richards	b Hirwani	68	c Kapil Dev b Hirwani	4
A.L.Logie	c Azharuddin b Hirwani	12	st More b Hirwani	67
C.L.Hooper	lbw b Hirwani	2	st More b Hirwani	8
†P.J.L.Dujon	st More b Hirwani	24	st More b Hirwani	2
C.G.Butts	c Raman b Hirwani	0	c Sharma b Hirwani	38
W.W.Davis	lbw b Hirwani	1	st More b Hirwani	7
C.A.Walsh	c More b Hirwani	8	st More b Raman	0
B.P.Patterson	not out	0	not out	0
Extras	(B8, LB2, NB2)	12	(B4, LB1, NB2)	7
Total		**184**		**160**

WEST INDIES	O	M	R	W	O	M	R	W	FALL OF WICKETS			
										I	WI	I	WI
Patterson	15	1	62	0	9	2	17	2	*Wkt*	*1st*	*1st*	*2nd*	*2nd*
Walsh	27	3	85	3	16	5	55	4	1st	30	17	3	22
Davis	18.1	0	76	4	6	0	20	1	2nd	38	47	36	24
Butts	24	4	62	0	21	1	62	0	3rd	64	98	37	33
Richards	8	1	36	1	(6) 18	4	28	1	4th	153	128	124	41
Hooper	12	3	42	2	(5) 6	1	20	0	5th	156	132	185	61
									6th	269	163	185	79
INDIA									7th	313	175	190	138
Kapil Dev	7	0	20	1	4	3	8	0	8th	342	175	194	153
Amarnath	3	0	8	0	2	0	7	0	9th	369	183	–	160
Shastri	13	6	29	1	5	0	25	0	10th	382	184	–	160
Ayub	28	10	47	0	14	5	33	1					
Hirwani	18.3	3	61	8	15.2	3	75	8					
Sharma	4	0	9	0									
Raman					(6) 1	0	7	1					

Umpires: R.B.Gupta (9) and P.D.Reporter (11).

Close: 1st day – I(1) 308-6 (Kapil Dev 104, Shastri 5); 2nd – WI(1) 147-5 (Richards 62, Dujon 4); 3rd – I(2) 181-4 (Raman 82, Sharma 22).

PAKISTAN v ENGLAND 1987-88 (1st Test)

At Gaddafi Stadium, Lahore, on 25, 26, 27, 28 November.
Toss: England.　　Result: PAKISTAN won by an innings and 87 runs.
Debuts: None.

It is one of the tragedies of Test cricket that an epic display of leg-spin and googly bowling, which totally dominated the match from its 11th over, should have occurred in one of the most unsavoury games of cricket ever played. Sadly, the match is doomed to be remembered for its controversies: an under-prepared pitch that proffered an extravagant degree of turn from the start; some appalling umpiring by Shakil Khan; and by Broad's refusal to leave the crease when given out in the second innings. Abdul Qadir's first innings analysis of 9 for 56 remains the record for Pakistan, the fifth-best in all Test cricket and the best by any bowler in all Tests against England. Only two other bowlers had taken nine wickets in an England innings: A.A.Mailey (1920-21) and H.J.Tayfield (1956-57). It was also the first nine-wicket analysis to be achieved in a Test in Pakistan. His career-best match analysis of 13 for 101 remains the best by Pakistan in this series. He also became the fourth bowler to dismiss all 11 batsmen in a Test. Broad completed 1,000 runs in his 15th Test, batting over four hours in the first innings. England's second innings total equalled their lowest of this series: 130 at The Oval in 1954. Mudassar's 10th hundred was his third against England.

ENGLAND

G.A.Gooch	b Qadir	12		c Ashraf b Qasim	15
B.C.Broad	c Asif b Qadir	41		c Ashraf b Qasim	13
R.T.Robinson	c Ashraf b Qadir	6		lbw b Qadir	1
*M.W.Gatting	lbw b Qadir	0		lbw b Qadir	23
C.W.J.Athey	lbw b Qadir	5		c Ashraf b Tausif	2
D.J.Capel	c Asif b Tausif	0	(7)	c Miandad b Qadir	0
P.A.J.DeFreitas	lbw b Qadir	5	(8)	c Tausif b Qasim	15
J.E.Emburey	b Qadir	0	(9)	not out	38
N.A.Foster	lbw b Qadir	39	(10)	c sub (Akram Raza) b Tausif	1
†B.N.French	not out	38	(6)	lbw b Qadir	9
N.G.B.Cook	c Miandad b Qadir	10		b Tausif	5
Extras	(B4, LB14, NB1)	19		(B4, LB4)	8
Total		**175**			**130**

PAKISTAN

Mudassar Nazar	lbw b Foster	120
Ramiz Raja	b Emburey	35
Salim Malik	b Emburey	0
*Javed Miandad	c Gooch b Cook	65
Ijaz Ahmed	b DeFreitas	44
Asif Mujtaba	b Foster	7
†Ashraf Ali	b Emburey	7
Wasim Akram	c Broad b Cook	40
Abdul Qadir	st French b Cook	38
Iqbal Qasim	run out	1
Tausif Ahmed	not out	5
Extras	(B18, LB8, NB4)	30
Total		**392**

PAKISTAN	O	M	R	W	O	M	R	W	FALL OF WICKETS			
Wasim	14	4	32	0	2	0	6	0		E	P	E
Mudassar	5	3	9	0	1	0	4	0	Wkt	1st	1st	2nd
Qadir	37	13	56	9	36	14	45	4	1st	22	71	23
Tausif	23	9	38	1	20.2	7	28	3	2nd	36	71	24
Qasim	4	0	22	0	20	10	39	3	3rd	36	213	38
									4th	44	272	43
ENGLAND									5th	55	290	66
DeFreitas	29	7	84	1					6th	70	301	70
Foster	23	6	58	2					7th	81	328	73
Emburey	48	16	109	3					8th	94	360	105
Cook	31	10	87	3					9th	151	370	116
Capel	3	0	28	0					10th	175	392	130

Umpires: Amanullah Khan (13) and Shakil Khan (3).

Close: 1st day – P(1) 13-0 (Mudassar 11, Ramiz 0); 2nd – P(1) 277-4 (Ijaz 27, Asif 2); 3rd – E(2) 47-4 (Gatting 6, French 4).

PAKISTAN v ENGLAND 1987-88 (2nd Test)

At Iqbal Stadium, Faisalabad, on 7, 8, 9 (*no play*), 11, 12 December.
Toss: England.   Result: MATCH DRAWN.
Debuts: Pakistan – Aamer Malik.

With Pakistan 106 for 5 and still 186 behind England's first innings total, square-leg umpire Shakoor Rana invoked Law 42 on the grounds of unfair play by Gatting (backward short-leg), who, quite legally having advised the batsman, had surreptitiously moved a fielder as Hemmings was starting his approach. The consequent abusive confrontation between captain and official resulted in the loss of the next day's play (when that umpire refused to restart the match without an apology from Gatting), the near cancellation of the tour, intervention from the Foreign Office and TCCB, and a mutinous statement from England's team. When the BCCP refused to make up the lost day, Pakistan, although dismissed for their lowest home total against England, were able to avoid their first home defeat in this series since 1961-62. Broad's hundred was his fourth in Tests (all overseas). Gatting's furious 79 was made off 81 balls. Miandad called his batsmen in when the mandatory 20 overs were about to start.

ENGLAND

G.A.Gooch	c Aamer b Qasim	28	lbw b Qadir		65
B.C.Broad	b Tausif	116	st Ashraf b Qadir		14
C.W.J.Athey	c Aamer b Qadir	27	b Mudassar		20
*M.W.Gatting	b Qadir	79	c Qadir b Qasim		8
R.T.Robinson	c Ashraf b Qadir	2	(8) not out		7
N.G.B.Cook	c Ashraf b Qasim	2			
D.J.Capel	c Aamer b Qadir	1	lbw b Qasim		2
J.E.Emburey	st Ashraf b Qasim	15	(5) not out		10
N.A.Foster	c Aamer b Qasim	0	(6) c Miandad b Qadir		0
†B.N.French	st Ashraf b Qasim	2			
E.E.Hemmings	not out	1			
Extras	(B10, LB5, W1, NB3)	19	(B1, LB9, NB1)		11
Total		**292**	(6 wickets declared)		**137**

PAKISTAN

Mudassar Nazar	c French b Foster	1	b Cook		4
Ramiz Raja	c Gooch b Foster	12	not out		13
Salim Malik	b Cook	60	not out		28
*Javed Miandad	b Emburey	19			
Ijaz Ahmed	c Robinson b Emburey	11			
Shoaib Mohammad	b Emburey	0			
Aamer Malik	c French b Foster	5			
†Ashraf Ali	c French b Foster	4			
Abdul Qadir	c Gooch b Cook	38			
Iqbal Qasim	lbw b Hemmings	24			
Tausif Ahmed	not out	5			
Extras	(LB5, NB7)	12	(B4, LB1, NB1)		6
Total		**191**	(1 wicket)		**51**

PAKISTAN	O	M	R	W	O	M	R	W	FALL OF WICKETS				
										E	P	E	P
Aamer	5	0	19	0	(2) 3	0	20	0	Wkt	*1st*	*1st*	*2nd*	*2nd*
Mudassar	3	0	8	0	(1) 12	1	33	1	1st	73	11	47	15
Qadir	42	7	105	4	15	3	45	3	2nd	124	22	102	–
Tausif	28	9	62	1					3rd	241	58	107	–
Qasim	35.2	7	83	5	(4) 10	2	29	2	4th	249	77	115	–
Shoaib	1	1	0	0					5th	258	77	115	–
									6th	259	115	120	–
ENGLAND									7th	288	122	–	–
Foster	18	4	42	4	3	0	4	0	8th	288	123	–	–
Capel	7	1	23	0					9th	288	175	–	–
Hemmings	18	5	35	1	(5) 7	3	16	0	10th	292	191	–	–
Emburey	21	8	49	3	(3) 2	0	3	0					
Cook	20.3	10	37	2	(4) 9	3	15	1					
Gooch					(2) 2	1	4	0					
Broad					(6) 1	0	4	0					

Umpires: Khizer Hayat (19) and Shakoor Rana (15).

Close: 1st day – E(1) 254-4 (Broad 101, Cook 1); 2nd – P(1) 106-5 (Salim Malik 54, Aamer Malik 1); 3rd – no play; 4th – P(1) 191 all out.

PAKISTAN v ENGLAND 1987-88 (3rd Test)

At National Stadium, Karachi, on 16, 17, 18, 20, 21 December.
Toss: England.   Result: MATCH DRAWN.
Debuts: None.

Pakistan won their third successive series against England and, gaining the better of a draw on a well-prepared flat pitch, maintained their unbeaten record at the National Stadium where 26 Tests have produced 11 victories and 15 draws. Abdul Qadir extended his five-wicket tallies to 14, his ten-wicket match hauls to five and his 30 wickets in these three matches set a record for an England-Pakistan rubber. Capel batted 373 minutes before misreading a googly while Aamer Malik needed 416 minutes for the same score. Dilley took his 100th wicket in 31 Tests.

ENGLAND

Batsman	Dismissal	Runs	Dismissal 2	Runs 2
G.A.Gooch	c Ashraf b Wasim	12	b Mudassar	93
B.C.Broad	lbw b Wasim	7	lbw b Qadir	13
C.W.J.Athey	b Qadir	26	c Ashraf b Salim Jaffer	12
*M.W.Gatting	b Qadir	18	lbw b Salim Jaffer	0
N.H.Fairbrother	c sub ‡ b Salim Jaffer	3	c sub‡ b Qadir	1
D.J.Capel	b Qadir	98	c Qasim b Qadir	24
P.A.J.DeFreitas	b Qadir	12	(9) lbw b Qadir	6
J.E.Emburey	c Qadir b Salim Jaffer	70	(7) not out	74
†B.N.French	c Miandad b Salim Malik	31	(8) lbw b Salim Jaffer	0
N.G.B.Cook	lbw b Qadir	2	b Qadir	14
G.R.Dilley	not out	0	not out	0
Extras	(LB8, W1, NB6)	15	(B9, LB5, W1, NB6)	21
Total		**294**	(9 wickets)	**258**

PAKISTAN

Mudassar Nazar	lbw b DeFreitas	6
Ramiz Raja	c French b Cook	50
Salim Malik	c Gatting b DeFreitas	55
*Javed Miandad	lbw b Emburey	4
Ijaz Ahmed	run out	0
Aamer Malik	not out	98
†Ashraf Ali	c French b Dilley	12
Wasim Akram	c French b DeFreitas	37
Abdul Qadir	b Capel	61
Iqbal Qasim	c French b DeFreitas	11
Salim Jaffer	lbw b DeFreitas	0
Extras	(LB11, NB8)	19
Total		**353**

PAKISTAN	O	M	R	W		O	M	R	W
Wasim	24.1	3	64	2					
Salim Jaffer	23.5	6	74	2	(1)	42	9	79	3
Qadir	49.4	15	88	5		55	16	98	5
Qasim	18	4	51	0		27	10	44	0
Mudassar	1	1	0	0	(6)	4	3	2	1
Salim Malik	5	2	9	1	(5)	7	2	14	0
Aamer					(2)	2	0	7	0

ENGLAND	O	M	R	W
Dilley	21	2	102	1
DeFreitas	23.5	3	86	5
Emburey	53	24	90	1
Cook	33	12	56	1
Capel	3	0	8	1

FALL OF WICKETS

Wkt	E 1st	P 1st	E 2nd
1st	20	18	34
2nd	41	105	54
3rd	55	110	54
4th	72	110	61
5th	72	122	115
6th	85	146	175
7th	199	222	176
8th	274	316	187
9th	291	349	246
10th	294	353	–

Umpires: Khizer Hayat (20) and Mahboob Shah (17).   ‡ (Asif Mujtaba)

Close: 1st day – E(1) 222-7 (Capel 53, French 10); 2nd – P(1) 122-4 (Salim Malik 55, Aamer Malik 1); 3rd – P(1) 345-8 (Aamer Malik 91, Qasim 10); 4th – E(2) 150-5 (Gooch 79, Emburey 9).

AUSTRALIA v NEW ZEALAND 1987-88 (1st Test)

At Woolloongabba, Brisbane, on 4, 5, 6, 7 December.
Toss: Australia.   Result: AUSTRALIA won by nine wickets.
Debuts: Australia – M.R.J.Veletta; New Zealand – D.K.Morrison.

At 3.47 on the fourth afternoon, Australia completed a comprehensive victory to avenge their first home defeat in this series on the same ground two years previously. Having beaten England at Sydney in January, it gave Australia their first pair of successive Test wins for four years. Their success was founded on winning the toss to gain first bowl on a surface which had had its preparation hampered by torrential rain. Equally vital was its effect in preventing Hadlee from gaining first use of conditions highly favourable to his bowling. After New Zealand had been dismissed for a modest total, their downfall started by Veletta taking a short-leg catch from his first touch of the ball as a Test cricketer, Boon's fifth Test hundred ensured Australia retained control. He batted for 342 minutes (255 balls) and hit 15 fours. Marsh exceeded 1,000 runs in his 15th Test. Hadlee's consolation was to move ahead of D.K.Lillee's total of 355 Test wickets.

NEW ZEALAND

K.R.Rutherford	c Veletta b Reid	0	(2) c Dyer b McDermott		2
J.G.Wright	c Dyer b Hughes	38	(1) lbw b Reid		15
A.H.Jones	b McDermott	4	c Border b Reid		45
M.D.Crowe	c Waugh b Hughes	67	c Jones b Hughes		23
*J.J.Crowe	lbw b Waugh	16	lbw b Reid		12
D.N.Patel	c Dyer b McDermott	17	c Dyer b Hughes		62
R.J.Hadlee	c Boon b Hughes	8	c Marsh b McDermott		24
J.G.Bracewell	c Veletta b McDermott	11	c Dyer b McDermott		0
†I.D.S.Smith	lbw b Reid	2	c Veletta b Reid		9
D.K.Morrison	c Waugh b McDermott	0	c Dyer b Waugh		2
E.J.Chatfield	not out	0	not out		1
Extras	(B1, LB7, W4, NB11)	23	(B6, LB1, W1, NB9)		17
Total		**186**			**212**

AUSTRALIA

G.R.Marsh	c Bracewell b Hadlee	25	(2) not out		31
D.C.Boon	run out	143	(1) lbw b Bracewell		24
D.M.Jones	b Hadlee	2	not out		38
*A.R.Border	lbw b Morrison	9			
M.R.J.Veletta	c Rutherford b Bracewell	4			
S.R.Waugh	c Jones b Morrison	21			
P.R.Sleep	c and b Bracewell	39			
†G.C.Dyer	lbw b Hadlee	8			
C.J.McDermott	c Wright b Morrison	22			
M.G.Hughes	c Smith b Morrison	5			
B.A.Reid	not out	8			
Extras	(B3, LB5, W2, NB9)	19	(LB1, W1, NB2)		4
Total		**305**	(1 wicket)		**97**

AUSTRALIA	O	M	R	W	O	M	R	W	FALL OF WICKETS			
										NZ	A	NZ	A
Reid	25	10	40	2	25	6	53	4	Wkt	1st	1st	2nd	2nd
McDermott	22.2	6	43	4	21	2	79	3	1st	0	65	18	37
Hughes	18	5	40	3	17	7	57	2	2nd	28	72	20	–
Waugh	22	9	35	1	(5) 2	1	2	1	3rd	80	110	66	–
Sleep	6	1	20	0	(4) 14	5	14	0	4th	133	131	103	–
									5th	143	219	104	–
NEW ZEALAND									6th	153	219	142	–
Hadlee	31	5	95	3	8	3	14	0	7th	175	250	142	–
Morrison	28	7	86	4	8	0	32	0	8th	180	286	152	–
Chatfield	34	11	58	0					9th	181	291	204	–
Bracewell	24.5	3	58	2	(3) 13	3	32	1	10th	186	305	212	–
Patel					(4) 3.1	0	18	0					

Umpires: A.R.Crafter (22) and M.W.Johnson (21).

Close: 1st day – NZ(1) 181-9 (Bracewell 6); 2nd – A(1) 219-6 (Sleep 0); 3rd – NZ(2) 131-5 (Patel 8, Hadlee 17).

AUSTRALIA v NEW ZEALAND 1987-88 (2nd Test)

At Adelaide Oval on 11, 12, 13, 14, 15 December.
Toss: New Zealand.   Result: MATCH DRAWN.
Debuts: Australia – T.B.A.May.

Enacted in stifling heat, this match was played on a bland pitch ideally suited to a timeless Test. Playing in only his third match, Andrew Jones batted 444 minutes to become only the 19th New Zealander to reach 150 in Tests and sharing with Wright in a (then) series record second-wicket stand of 128. Martin Crowe (184 balls, a six and 17 fours) became the first to score eight hundreds for New Zealand, reaching that mark off 130 balls. Border (599 minutes, 485 balls, 20 fours) recorded his 22nd hundred (first double) in 91 Tests, completed 7,000 runs, overtook G.S.Chappell's record Australian aggregate of 7,110 and, with Waugh, shared a series record fourth-wicket partnership of 116. When 66 he was taken low at wide mid-on by Jeff Crowe but reprieved when the fielder signalled 'no catch'. Hadlee overcame the flat surface and extreme temperatures to claim five wickets in an innings for the 30th time.

NEW ZEALAND

*J.J.Crowe	c Veletta b Reid	0		c Boon b May	19
J.G.Wright	c Waugh b May	45		b McDermott	8
A.H.Jones	run out	150		c Border b Sleep	64
M.D.Crowe	c sub (M.G.Hughes) b Sleep	137		c Border b Sleep	8
D.N.Patel	c Marsh b McDermott	35		c Boon b May	40
E.J.Gray	c Boon b McDermott	23		c Border b May	14
R.J.Hadlee	c and b Jones	36	(9)	not out	3
J.G.Bracewell	c Sleep b McDermott	32			
†I.D.S.Smith	not out	8	(8)	c Dyer b Sleep	5
M.C.Snedden	c Veletta b McDermott	0	(7)	not out	8
D.K.Morrison	did not bat				
Extras	(B3, LB7, W1, NB8)	19		(B2, LB4, NB7)	13
Total	(9 wickets declared)	**485**		(7 wickets)	**182**

AUSTRALIA

G.R.Marsh	c Gray b Hadlee	30
D.C.Boon	b Hadlee	6
D.M.Jones	c Smith b Hadlee	0
*A.R.Border	st Smith b Bracewell	205
S.R.Waugh	lbw b Snedden	61
P.R.Sleep	c Smith b Morrison	62
M.R.J.Veletta	c sub‡ b Bracewell	10
†G.C.Dyer	run out	60
C.J.McDermott	lbw b Hadlee	18
T.B.A.May	not out	14
B.A.Reid	c Smith b Hadlee	5
Extras	(B2, LB13, W1, NB9)	25
Total		**496**

AUSTRALIA	O	M	R	W		O	M	R	W		FALL OF WICKETS		
											NZ	A	NZ
Reid	7	0	21	1						Wkt	1st	1st	2nd
McDermott	45.5	10	135	4	(1) 10	3	29	1		1st	0	29	16
Waugh	31	11	71	0	(2) 10	4	17	0		2nd	128	29	57
May	54	13	134	1	30	10	68	3		3rd	341	85	77
Sleep	34	5	109	1	(3) 32	14	61	3		4th	346	201	139
Jones	3	1	5	1	(5) 3	2	1	0		5th	398	355	153
										6th	405	380	170
NEW ZEALAND										7th	473	417	179
Hadlee	42	16	68	5						8th	481	451	–
Morrison	22	0	89	1						9th	485	489	–
Bracewell	48	8	122	2						10th	–	496	–
Snedden	32	6	89	1									
Gray	44	10	102	0									
Patel	7	3	11	0									

Umpires: R.C.Bailhache (25) and S.G.Randell (6).   ‡ (K.R.Rutherford)

Close: 1st day – NZ(1) 268-2 (Jones 128, M.D.Crowe 88); 2nd – A(1) 17-0 (Marsh 5, Boon 6); 3rd – A(1) 225-4 (Border 105, Sleep 6); 4th – A(1) 496-9 (May 14, Reid 5).

AUSTRALIA v NEW ZEALAND 1987-88 (3rd Test)

At Melbourne Cricket Ground on 26, 27, 28, 29, 30 December.
Toss: Australia.   Result: MATCH DRAWN.
Debuts: Australia – A.I.C.Dodemaide.

Australia's last pair survived the final 29 balls to secure the Trans-Tasman Trophy and provide Border with his first series victory in eight attempts. Wright (310 minutes) completed 3,000 runs in 55 Tests. A.H.Jones was out in controversial circumstances, replays appearing to show the ball bouncing before being caught by Dyer. Dodemaide, who celebrated his debut with 50 and a six-wicket analysis, added 61 with McDermott to set an Australian ninth-wicket record in this series. Martin Crowe took his aggregate for this rubber to a record 396 and became only the seventh batsman (the first since L.Hutton in 1948) to score 4,000 first-class runs in a calendar year. He was dismissed by Border's 100th catch in 92 Tests. With Australia requiring 247 from a minimum of 92 overs, Hadlee bowled unchanged from 5.17 until the finish at 6.49pm, equalled I.T.Botham's world record of 373 wickets, extended his world record of five-wicket hauls to 32 and became the first to take ten wickets in a Test eight times. He was the first to congratulate Whitney after the tail-ender had miraculously played out his final over. Horne deputised for the injured Smith from overs 2 to 24 in the second innings.

NEW ZEALAND

P.A.Horne	c Dyer b Dodemaide	7		c Boon b Dodemaide	27
J.G.Wright	c Dyer b McDermott	99		b Sleep	43
A.H.Jones	c Dyer b McDermott	40		run out	20
M.D.Crowe	c Veletta b McDermott	82		c Border b Dodemaide	79
*J.J.Crowe	lbw b McDermott	6		c Boon b Sleep	25
D.N.Patel	b McDermott	0		c Dyer b Dodemaide	38
J.G.Bracewell	c Dyer b Whitney	9	(8)	c Veletta b Dodemaide	1
R.J.Hadlee	c Dodemaide b Whitney	11	(7)	lbw b Sleep	29
†I.D.S.Smith	c Jones b Whitney	44		c Dyer b Dodemaide	12
D.K.Morrison	c Border b Whitney	0		b Dodemaide	0
E.J.Chatfield	not out	6		not out	1
Extras	(B1, LB4, NB8)	13		(B2, LB8, NB1)	11
Total		317			286

AUSTRALIA

D.C.Boon	lbw b Hadlee	10	(2)	c M.D.Crowe b Morrison	54
G.R.Marsh	c sub (K.R.Rutherford) b Hadlee	13	(1)	c Bracewell b Hadlee	23
D.M.Jones	c Smith b Hadlee	4		c M.D.Crowe b Chatfield	8
*A.R.Border	c J.J.Crowe b Bracewell	31		lbw b Hadlee	43
M.R.J.Veletta	lbw b Hadlee	31		c Patel b Bracewell	39
S.R.Waugh	c Jones b Bracewell	55		c Patel b Chatfield	10
P.R.Sleep	lbw b Hadlee	90		lbw b Hadlee	20
†G.C.Dyer	run out	21		c Smith b Hadlee	4
A.I.C.Dodemaide	c Smith b Morrison	50		lbw b Hadlee	3
C.J.McDermott	b Morrison	33		not out	10
M.R.Whitney	not out	0		not out	2
Extras	(LB8, NB11)	19		(B1, LB9, NB4)	14
Total		357		(9 wickets)	230

AUSTRALIA	O	M	R	W	O	M	R	W		FALL OF WICKETS			
										NZ	A	NZ	A
McDermott	35	8	97	5	10	3	43	0	Wkt	1st	1st	2nd	2nd
Whitney	33.3	6	92	4	20	5	45	0	1st	32	24	73	45
Dodemaide	20	4	48	1	28.3	10	58	6	2nd	119	30	76	59
Waugh	10	1	44	0					3rd	187	31	158	103
Sleep	12	1	31	0	(4) 26	5	107	3	4th	221	78	178	147
Jones					(5) 8	3	23	0	5th	223	121	220	176
									6th	254	170	272	209
NEW ZEALAND									7th	254	213	272	209
Hadlee	44	11	109	5	31	9	67	5	8th	280	293	281	216
Morrison	27.4	5	93	2	16	2	54	1	9th	294	354	285	227
Chatfield	30	10	55	0	21	6	41	2	10th	317	357	286	–
Bracewell	32	8	69	2	24	5	58	1					
Patel	12	6	23	0									

Umpires: A.R.Crafter (23) and R.A.French (19).

Close: 1st day – NZ(1) 242-5 (M.D.Crowe 76, Bracewell 4); 2nd – A(1) 170-5 (Waugh 55, Sleep 16); 3rd – NZ (2) 0-0 (Horne 0, Wright 0); 4th – NZ(2) 285-9 (Smith 12, Chatfield 0).

AUSTRALIA v ENGLAND 1987-88 (Bicentenary Test)

At Sydney Cricket Ground on 29, 30, 31 January, 1, 2 February.
Toss: England.   Result: MATCH DRAWN.
Debuts: None.

Although the Ashes were not at stake for this commemorative Test, it proved an attritional contest rather than the anticipated festival match to celebrate 200 years of Australian white settlement. Broad (434 minutes, 361 balls) scored his fourth hundred – all on different grounds – in six Tests in Australia before indulging in a display of stump abuse which attracted a £500 fine from the tour management. Jones completed 1,000 runs in 14 Tests but could not prevent the follow-on. Boon (491 minutes, 431 balls) played a match-saving innings, completing his sixth hundred and sharing with Marsh in the highest first-wicket partnership against England at Sydney. The aggregate crowd of 103,831 fell substantially short of expectations. The highlight of the final day was a press box presentation to W.J.('Tiger') O'Reilly (82) at the end of his Test match reporting career with the *Sydney Morning Herald*. Veletta kept wicket for the last 18 balls of England's innings after Dyer had been hit on the nose.

ENGLAND

B.C.Broad	b Waugh	139
M.D.Moxon	b Sleep	40
R.T.Robinson	c Veletta b Dodemaide	43
*M.W.Gatting	c Dyer b Waugh	13
C.W.J.Athey	c and b Taylor	37
D.J.Capel	c Sleep b Taylor	21
J.E.Emburey	st Dyer b Sleep	23
†B.N.French	st Dyer b Taylor	47
N.A.Foster	c Border b Taylor	19
E.E.Hemmings	not out	8
G.R.Dilley	b Waugh	13
Extras	(B4, LB9, W1, NB8)	22
Total		**425**

AUSTRALIA

D.C.Boon	c French b Foster	12	(2) not out		184
G.R.Marsh	c French b Capel	5	(1) c Athey b Emburey		56
D.M.Jones	c Emburey b Hemmings	56	c Moxon b Capel		24
*A.R.Border	c Broad b Capel	2	not out		48
M.R.J.Veletta	c Emburey b Hemmings	22			
S.R.Waugh	c French b Dilley	27			
P.R.Sleep	c Athey b Foster	41			
†G.C.Dyer	lbw b Dilley	0			
P.L.Taylor	c French b Hemmings	20			
A.I.C.Dodemaide	not out	12			
C.J.McDermott	c Foster b Dilley	1			
Extras	(LB10, W1, NB5)	16	(B3, LB7, NB6)		16
Total		**214**	(2 wickets)		**328**

AUSTRALIA	O	M	R	W	O	M	R	W		FALL OF WICKETS			
McDermott	35	8	65	0							E	A	A
Dodemaide	36	10	98	1						Wkt	1st	1st	2nd
Taylor	34	10	84	4						1st	93	18	162
Waugh	22.5	5	51	3						2nd	192	25	218
Sleep	45	8	114	2						3rd	245	34	–
										4th	262	82	–
ENGLAND										5th	313	116	–
Dilley	19.1	4	54	3	(3) 13	1	48	0		6th	314	147	–
Foster	19	6	27	2	(1) 15	6	27	0		7th	346	153	–
Emburey	30	10	57	0	(5) 38	5	98	1		8th	387	183	–
Capel	6	3	13	2	(2) 17	4	38	1		9th	410	209	–
Hemmings	22	3	53	3	(4) 52	15	107	0		10th	425	214	–

Umpires: A.R.Crafter (24) and P.J.McConnell (9).

Close: 1st day – E(1) 221-2 (Broad 116, Gatting 3); 2nd – A(1) 14-0 (Boon 12, Marsh 1); 3rd – A(1) 164-7 (Sleep 20, Taylor 7); 4th – A(2) 101-0 (Marsh 41, Boon 54).

NEW ZEALAND v ENGLAND 1987-88 (1st Test)

At Lancaster Park, Christchurch, on 12, 13, 14, 16, 17 February.
Toss: New Zealand.   Result: MATCH DRAWN.
Debuts: England – P.W.Jarvis.

Left the final day to score 304 to win, New Zealand settled for a draw and, as the pitch dried, achieved their objective comfortably with the aid of an hour lost to poor light. Hadlee, needing one wicket to break I.T.Botham's world Test record of 373, sprained his calf muscle during his 18th over, completing the last two balls off a short run; it was his last bowl of the series, although, batting with a runner, he later withstood England's attack for 183 valuable minutes. Broad (341 minutes, 244 balls) scored a hundred on his debut against New Zealand; his six Test hundreds were all scored overseas and in the course of ten Tests. Dilley took the first five wickets and his analysis remained his best in Test cricket. Some terrace-rending expletives when an appeal was rejected on the last afternoon earned him a £250 fine. A total of 4 hours 55 minutes was lost in the match.

ENGLAND

B.C.Broad	c Smith b Snedden	114	c sub ‡ b Chatfield		20
M.D.Moxon	c Jones b Morrison	1	c Jones b Chatfield		27
R.T.Robinson	c Smith b Morrison	70	c Wright b Chatfield		2
*M.W.Gatting	c sub‡ b Morrison	8	b Snedden		23
C.W.J.Athey	c sub‡ b Morrison	22	c Smith b Snedden		19
D.J.Capel	c Bracewell b Chatfield	11	c M.D.Crowe b Chatfield		0
J.E.Emburey	c Jones b Morrison	42	run out		19
†B.N.French	c Smith b Chatfield	7	c J.J.Crowe b Snedden		3
P.A.J.DeFreitas	c Morrison b Chatfield	4	lbw b Snedden		16
P.W.Jarvis	c Smith b Chatfield	14	not out		10
G.R.Dilley	not out	7	c Jones b Morrison		2
Extras	(LB11, W1, NB7)	19	(LB7, NB4)		11
Total		**319**			**152**

NEW ZEALAND

J.G.Wright	c Moxon b Dilley	10	lbw b Dilley		23
T.J.Franklin	c Athey b Dilley	10	lbw b Dilley		12
A.H.Jones	c French b Dilley	8	not out		54
M.D.Crowe	c Moxon b Dilley	5	c French b Jarvis		6
*J.J.Crowe	c French b DeFreitas	28	lbw b DeFreitas		0
J.G.Bracewell	c French b Dilley	31	not out		20
R.J.Hadlee	c French b Dilley	37			
†I.D.S.Smith	c Capel b Jarvis	13			
M.C.Snedden	lbw b DeFreitas	0			
D.K.Morrison	b Jarvis	0			
E.J.Chatfield	not out	0			
Extras	(B2, LB12, NB12)	26	(B6, LB4, NB5)		15
Total		**168**	(4 wickets)		**130**

NEW ZEALAND	O	M	R	W	O	M	R	W		FALL OF WICKETS			
										E	NZ	E	NZ
Hadlee	18	3	50	0					Wkt	1st	1st	2nd	2nd
Morrison	21.1	3	69	5	(1) 21.1	4	64	1	1st	7	20	32	37
Chatfield	42	13	87	4	(2) 30	13	36	4	2nd	175	25	38	43
Snedden	33	9	86	1	(3) 23	8	45	4	3rd	186	32	55	61
Bracewell	6	1	16	0					4th	219	40	95	78
									5th	237	96	96	–
ENGLAND									6th	241	131	99	–
DeFreitas	22	6	39	2	(2) 19	6	26	1	7th	248	151	118	–
Dilley	24.5	9	38	6	(1) 18	5	32	2	8th	260	155	125	–
Capel	10	2	32	0	(5) 13	5	16	0	9th	285	156	147	–
Jarvis	21	8	43	2	(3) 17	7	30	1	10th	319	168	152	–
Emburey	4	3	2	0	(4) 10	4	16	0					

Umpires: B.L.Aldridge (3) and S.J.Woodward (17).   ‡ (M.J.Greatbatch)

Close: 1st day – E(1) 235-4 (Athey 18, Capel 10); 2nd – NZ(1) 83-4 (J.J.Crowe 15, Bracewell 22); 3rd – E(2) 55-2 (Moxon 27, Gatting 3); 4th – E(2) 152 all out.

NEW ZEALAND v ENGLAND 1987-88 (2nd Test)

At Eden Park, Auckland, on 25, 26, 27, 28, 29 February.
Toss: England.   Result: MATCH DRAWN.
Debuts: New Zealand – M.J.Greatbatch.

A staunch hundred by Greatbatch, who withstood England's attack for 407 minutes (326 balls, 12 fours), removed any chance of an England victory after their hopes had been raised by the seizure of five wickets for 36 runs on the fourth evening. He was the fourth New Zealander after J.E.Mills, B.R.Taylor and R.E.Redmond to celebrate his Test debut with a century, all four being left-handed. Wright (353 minutes, 276 balls) scored his seventh hundred (third against England) after being missed by French off the first ball of the match, and completed 1,000 runs against England in the second innings. Moxon (348 minutes, 269 balls) became the ninth England batsman to be dismissed for 99; early in his innings a well-timed sweep had been signalled as three leg-byes. Smith scored his 1,000th run in 42 Tests and completed the wicket-keepers' double. This was the first Test match to end on a Leap Day.

NEW ZEALAND

J.G.Wright	c French b Dilley	103	(2) c French b Radford	49
T.J.Franklin	b Jarvis	27	(1) b Dilley	62
*J.J.Crowe	c Capel b Dilley	11	lbw b Dilley	1
M.D.Crowe	c Capel b Emburey	36	lbw b Jarvis	26
M.J.Greatbatch	c French b Dilley	11	not out	107
K.R.Rutherford	b Capel	29	b Emburey	2
J.G.Bracewell	c Moxon b Dilley	9	(8) lbw b Gatting	38
†I.D.S.Smith	c French b Jarvis	23	(9) not out	23
M.C.Snedden	c Moxon b Dilley	14	(7) c French b Capel	20
D.K.Morrison	not out	14		
E.J.Chatfield	c French b Capel	10		
Extras	(B1, LB2, W2, NB9)	14	(B8, LB8, NB6)	22
Total		**301**	(7 wickets declared)	**350**

ENGLAND

B.C.Broad	c M.D.Crowe b Bracewell	9
M.D.Moxon	c J.J.Crowe b Chatfield	99
R.T.Robinson	c Morrison b Bracewell	54
*M.W.Gatting	c Smith b Morrison	42
N.H.Fairbrother	c Smith b Chatfield	1
D.J.Capel	c Bracewell b Morrison	5
J.E.Emburey	c Smith b Chatfield	45
†B.N.French	c Franklin b Bracewell	13
P.W.Jarvis	c Smith b Snedden	10
N.V.Radford	b Chatfield	8
G.R.Dilley	not out	8
Extras	(B12, LB12, NB5)	29
Total		**323**

ENGLAND	O	M	R	W	O	M	R	W		FALL OF WICKETS		
										NZ	E	NZ
Dilley	28	9	60	5	23	9	44	2	Wkt	1st	1st	2nd
Jarvis	33	9	74	2	27	7	54	1	1st	77	27	117
Radford	30	4	79	0	20	4	53	1	2nd	98	135	119
Capel	26.2	4	57	2	(5) 21	4	40	1	3rd	169	211	119
Emburey	17	7	28	1	(4) 57	24	91	1	4th	191	220	150
Gatting					17	4	40	1	5th	207	222	153
Fairbrother					2	0	9	0	6th	219	234	232
Moxon					2	0	3	0	7th	254	267	296
									8th	262	282	–
NEW ZEALAND									9th	279	308	–
Morrison	32	7	95	2					10th	301	323	–
Chatfield	31.1	15	37	4								
Bracewell	39	8	88	3								
Snedden	34	14	71	1								
Rutherford	5	1	8	0								

Umpires: F.R.Goodall (24) and R.L.McHarg (2).

Close: 1st day – NZ(1) 186-3 (Wright 101, Greatbatch 5); 2nd – E(1) 97-1 (Moxon 42, Robinson 37); 3rd – E(1) 302-8 (Emburey 40, Radford 5); 4th – NZ(2) 154-5 (Greatbatch 6, Snedden 0).

NEW ZEALAND v ENGLAND 1987-88 (3rd Test)

At Basin Reserve, Wellington, on 3, 4, 5, 6 (*no play*), 7 (*no play*) March.
Toss: New Zealand.   Result: MATCH DRAWN.
Debuts: New Zealand – R.H.Vance.

Heavy rain brought this lacklustre series to a merciful conclusion after a grassless pitch of rolled mud had produced another potential stalemate. Wright captained for the first time, Jeff Crowe having become the first New Zealand leader to be removed from office during a home series. Martin Crowe (403 minutes, 333 balls), who recorded his ninth Test hundred and highest score against England, shared a record series fourth-wicket partnership of 155 with Greatbatch. Rutherford (265 minutes, 181 balls) completed his first hundred after achieving an aggregate of 224 (average 11.20) in his first 13 Tests, and shared a (then) series record sixth-wicket stand of 134 with Bracewell. England's sixth successive draw extended their run of matches without victory to a record-equalling 13.

NEW ZEALAND

J.G.Wright	c Fairbrother b Capel	36
T.J.Franklin	lbw b DeFreitas	14
R.H.Vance	run out	47
M.D.Crowe	lbw b Gatting	143
M.J.Greatbatch	c DeFreitas b Emburey	68
K.R.Rutherford	not out	107
J.G.Bracewell	c Fairbrother b Capel	54
I.D.S.Smith	not out	33
S.L.Boock		
D.K.Morrison	did not bat	
E.J.Chatfield		
Extras	(LB10)	10
Total	(6 wickets declared)	**512**

ENGLAND

B.C.Broad	b Boock	61
M.D.Moxon	not out	81
R.T.Robinson	c Smith b Chatfield	0
M.W.Gatting	not out	33
N.H.Fairbrother		
D.J.Capel		
J.E.Emburey		
B.N.French	did not bat	
P.A.J.DeFreitas		
E.E.Hemmings		
G.R.Dilley		
Extras	(LB6, NB2)	8
Total	(2 wickets)	**183**

ENGLAND	O	M	R	W
Dilley	11	1	36	0
DeFreitas	50.1	21	110	1
Capel	39	7	129	2
Emburey	45.5	10	99	1
Hemmings	45	15	107	0
Gatting	6	1	21	1

NEW ZEALAND	O	M	R	W
Morrison	6	0	41	0
Chatfield	23	10	38	1
Bracewell	23	9	44	0
Boock	26	9	53	1
Rutherford	1	0	1	0

FALL OF WICKETS

	NZ	E
Wkt	1st	1st
1st	33	129
2nd	70	132
3rd	132	–
4th	287	–
5th	336	–
6th	470	–
7th	–	–
8th	–	–
9th	–	–
10th	–	–

Umpires: B.L.Aldridge (4) and S.J.Woodward (18).

Close: 1st day – NZ(1) 192-3 (Crowe 57, Greatbatch 34); 2nd – NZ(1) 451-5 (Rutherford 91, Bracewell 43); 3rd – E(1) 183-2 (Moxon 81, Gatting 33); 4th – no play.

AUSTRALIA v SRI LANKA 1987-88 (Only Test)

At W.A.C.A.Ground, Perth, on 12, 13, 14, 15 February.
Toss: Australia.   Result: AUSTRALIA won by an innings and 108 runs.
Debuts: Sri Lanka – C.P.H.Ramanayake.

Sri Lanka's comprehensive defeat in their first Test in Australia was completed after just 75 minutes of the fourth day. Unable to host tours because of continued civil unrest and without a domestic first-class competition, Madugalle's side was desperately short of recent experience of the 'long game' and unfamiliar with bouncy pitches. Jones, who completed his third Test hundred when he ran two off a dropped catch, added 156 in 151 minutes with Border. The latter was leading Australia for the 31st time, a tally exceeded only by G.S.Chappell (48). Ratnayeke, playing in his 19th Test, became the second Sri Lankan after A.L.F.de Mel to take 50 wickets and the first to have also scored 500 runs. Madugalle celebrated his debut as captain by completing 1,000 runs in his 20th Test.

AUSTRALIA

G.R.Marsh	b Labrooy	53
D.C.Boon	b Ratnayeke	64
D.M.Jones	lbw b Labrooy	102
*A.R.Border	b Ratnayeke	88
M.R.J.Veletta	c De Alwis b Ratnayeke	21
S.R.Waugh	c Labrooy b Amalean	20
†G.C.Dyer	c Ramanayake b Amalean	38
P.L.Taylor	c Amalean b Ratnayeke	18
A.I.C.Dodemaide	not out	16
C.J.McDermott	c De Alwis b Amalean	4
M.G.Hughes	b Amalean	8
Extras	(LB12, W5, NB6)	23
Total		**455**

SRI LANKA

R.S.Mahanama	c Dyer b Dodemaide	41	run out	28
D.S.B.P.Kuruppu	c Marsh b McDermott	19	c Dyer b Dodemaide	3
S.M.S.Kaluperuma	lbw b McDermott	0	c and b Hughes	6
P.A.de Silva	lbw b Waugh	6	lbw b Dodemaide	7
A.Ranatunga	c and b Waugh	55	lbw b Dodemaide	45
*R.S.Madugalle	c Border b Dodemaide	6	c Waugh b Hughes	7
J.R.Ratnayeke	c Marsh b McDermott	24	c Dyer b Dodemaide	38
†R.G.de Alwis	c Dyer b Waugh	0	c Waugh b Hughes	8
C.P.H.Ramanayake	c Dyer b Waugh	9	c Veletta b Hughes	0
G.F.Labrooy	c Dyer b Dodemaide	4	b Hughes	4
K.N.Amalean	not out	7	not out	0
Extras	(B1, LB6, W2, NB14)	23	(LB6, NB1)	7
Total		**194**		**153**

SRI LANKA	O	M	R	W	O	M	R	W		FALL OF WICKETS		
										A	SL	SL
Ratnayeke	40	6	98	4					*Wkt*	*1st*	*1st*	*2nd*
Labrooy	36	5	108	2					1st	120	51	36
Ramanayake	17	2	58	0					2nd	133	51	42
Amalean	22.2	1	97	4					3rd	289	60	42
Kaluperuma	13	0	62	0					4th	346	93	66
Ranatunga	8	2	18	0					5th	346	107	83
De Silva	1	0	2	0					6th	380	147	111
									7th	418	148	130
AUSTRALIA									8th	434	181	131
McDermott	20	3	50	3	4	2	8	0	9th	443	182	153
Hughes	18	2	61	0	21	7	67	5	10th	455	194	153
Dodemaide	22.3	6	40	3	(4) 19.1	7	58	4				
Waugh	20	7	33	4	(3) 8	4	14	0				
Taylor	2	1	3	0								

Umpires: R.C.Bailhache (26) and P.J.McConnell (10).

Close: 1st day – A(1) 333-3 (Jones 100, Veletta 10); 2nd – SL(1) 85-3 (Mahanama 37, Ranatunga 11); 3rd – SL(2) 78-4 (Ranatunga 24, Madugalle 5).

WEST INDIES v PAKISTAN 1987-88 (1st Test)

At Bourda, Georgetown, Guyana, on 2, 3, 4, 6 April.
Toss: West Indies.   Result: PAKISTAN won by 9 wickets.
Debuts: West Indies – C.E.L.Ambrose.

Before tea on the fourth day, Pakistan became the first visiting side to win a Test in the Caribbean since the 1977-78 Australians defeated a side devastated by defections to World Series cricket. Leading West Indies for the first time in the absence of I.V.A.Richards (convalescing from surgery), Greenidge elected to bat on a newly relaid pitch. Imran Khan celebrated the end of his 'retirement' from Test cricket with his sixth ten-wicket haul. Pakistan's best innings and match analyses in the West Indies included the record match analysis for any Test in Guyana. Miandad (405 minutes, 234 balls) scored his 16th Test hundred and his first against West Indies. Salim Malik completed 2,000 runs in 45 Tests. The total of 71 extras set a new Test record, surpassing the 68, also conceded by West Indies against Pakistan, at Kingston in 1976-77; 53 no-balls were called in the innings.

WEST INDIES

D.L.Haynes	c Salim Yousuf b Imran	1	b Ijaz Faqih	5
P.V.Simmons	b Ijaz Faqih	16	b Qadir	11
R.B.Richardson	c Shoaib b Imran	75	c Salim Yousuf b Qadir	16
*C.G.Greenidge	c Salim Malik b Wasim	17	b Imran	43
A.L.Logie	lbw b Qadir	80	c Salim Yousuf b Imran	24
C.L.Hooper	c Wasim b Imran	33	c Salim Malik b Qadir	30
†P.J.L.Dujon	lbw b Imran	15	c Imran b Shoaib	11
W.K.M.Benjamin	lbw b Imran	2	c Miandad b Shoaib	0
C.A.Walsh	b Imran	7	c Salim Yousuf b Imran	14
C.E.L.Ambrose	not out	25	not out	1
B.P.Patterson	b Imran	10	b Imran	0
Extras	(B2, LB3, NB6)	11	(B4, LB8, NB5)	17
Total		292		172

PAKISTAN

Mudassar Nazar	b Ambrose	29	lbw b Patterson	0
Ramiz Raja	c Haynes b Patterson	5	not out	18
Shoaib Mohammad	c Greenidge b Walsh	46	not out	13
Javed Miandad	b Patterson	114		
Salim Malik	c Greenidge b Patterson	27		
Ijaz Ahmed	c Haynes b Ambrose	31		
*Imran Khan	c Simmons b Benjamin	24		
†Salim Yousuf	lbw b Walsh	62		
Ijaz Faqih	b Hooper	5		
Abdul Qadir	b Walsh	19		
Wasim Akram	not out	2		
Extras	(B21, LB8, W4, NB38)	71	(NB1)	1
Total		435	(1 wicket)	32

PAKISTAN	O	M	R	W	O	M	R	W	FALL OF WICKETS			
Imran	22.4	2	80	7	(2) 14.4	0	41	4		WI	P	WI	P
Wasim	14	5	41	1	(1) 6	1	7	0	Wkt	1st	1st	2nd	2nd
Ijaz Faqih	14	0	60	1	15	4	38	1	1st	7	20	18	0
Qadir	24	2	91	1	25	5	66	3	2nd	41	57	34	–
Mudassar	5	2	9	0					3rd	95	127	44	–
Salim Malik	1	0	6	0					4th	144	217	109	–
Shoaib					(5) 2	0	8	2	5th	220	297	120	–
									6th	244	300	145	–
WEST INDIES									7th	248	364	145	–
Patterson	24	1	82	3	2	0	19	1	8th	249	383	166	–
Ambrose	28	5	108	2	1.3	0	13	0	9th	258	423	172	–
Walsh	27	4	80	3					10th	292	435	172	–
Benjamin	31	3	99	1									
Hooper	12	0	37	1									

Umpires: D.M.Archer (18) and L.H.Barker (7).

Close: 1st day – WI(1) 292 all out; 2nd – P(1) 249-4 (Miandad 96, Ijaz Ahmed 10); 3rd – WI(2) 25-1 (Simmons 11, Richardson 6).

Test No. 1096/24 (WI258/P175)

WEST INDIES v PAKISTAN 1987-88 (2nd Test)

At Queen's Park Oval, Port-of-Spain, Trinidad, on 14, 15, 16, 17, 19 April.
Toss: Pakistan.   Result: MATCH DRAWN.
Debuts: None.

A magnificent attempt at a victory target of 372 ended in one of Test cricket's most dramatic finales with last man, Abdul Qadir, having to survive the last five balls from Richards. Surprisingly the match went the distance after 15 wickets had fallen on the first day. Pakistan's slender lead was the product of their highest eighth-wicket partnership of the series: 94 between Salim Malik and Salim Yousuf. Richardson completed 2,000 runs in 32 Tests. Richards, who had scored 49 off 43 balls in the first innings, reached his 22nd hundred off 134 balls in 232 minutes. Dujon (315 minutes) scored his fifth hundred as Qadir took his tally of wickets beyond 200 in 53 Tests. A chanceless 17th hundred by Miandad (427 minutes, 240 balls) kept Pakistan in touch with victory. When he was out 84 runs were needed from the last 20 overs and the task proved beyond even the gifted lower order.

WEST INDIES

C.G.Greenidge	c Ijaz Ahmed b Imran	1	c sub (Naved Anjum) b Imran		29
D.L.Haynes	lbw b Wasim	17	c Ijaz Ahmed b Imran		0
R.B.Richardson	c Qadir b Wasim	42	c Salim Yousuf b Imran		40
A.L.Logie	c Miandad b Qadir	18	b Imran		1
*I.V.A.Richards	c Miandad b Qadir	49	lbw b Wasim		123
C.L.Hooper	c Salim Yousuf b Qadir	0	c Ijaz Ahmed b Imran		26
†P.J.L.Dujon	c Salim Yousuf b Imran	24	not out		106
M.D.Marshall	not out	10	b Qadir		2
C.E.L.Ambrose	lbw b Imran	4	lbw b Qadir		9
W.K.M.Benjamin	b Qadir	0	lbw b Qadir		16
C.A.Walsh	b Imran	5	st Salim Yousuf b Qadir		12
Extras	(LB2, NB2)	4	(B9, LB14, NB4)		27
Total		**174**			**391**

PAKISTAN

Mudassar Nazar	c Haynes b Marshall	14	c Dujon b Benjamin		13
Ramiz Raja	c Richardson b Marshall	1	c Richards b Marshall		44
Shoaib Mohammad	c Richards b Ambrose	12	b Benjamin		0
Javed Miandad	b Benjamin	18	c Richards b Ambrose		102
Ijaz Faqih	c Richards b Benjamin	0	(10) not out		10
Salim Malik	c Logie b Hooper	66	(5) lbw b Walsh		30
Ijaz Ahmed	c Logie b Benjamin	3	st Dujon b Richards		43
*Imran Khan	c Logie b Marshall	4	(6) c Dujon b Benjamin		1
†Salim Yousuf	c Dujon b Marshall	39	(8) lbw b Richards		35
Wasim Akram	run out	7	(9) c Hooper b Marshall		2
Abdul Qadir	not out	17	not out		0
Extras	(B1, LB4, NB8)	13	(B17, LB17, W2, NB25)		61
Total		**194**	(9 wickets)		**341**

PAKISTAN	O	M	R	W	O	M	R	W		FALL OF WICKETS			
										WI	P	WI	P
Imran	16.3	2	38	4	45	9	115	5	Wkt	1st	1st	2nd	2nd
Wasim	14	4	35	2	25	4	75	1	1st	2	3	1	60
Ijaz Faqih	3	0	13	0	(4) 4	0	22	0	2nd	25	25	55	62
Mudassar	1	0	3	0					3rd	80	46	66	67
Qadir	19	2	83	4	(3) 47.4	6	148	4	4th	89	49	81	153
Shoaib					(5) 3	0	8	0	5th	89	50	175	169
									6th	147	62	272	282
WEST INDIES									7th	157	68	284	288
Marshall	20	4	55	4	30	4	85	2	8th	166	162	301	311
Ambrose	14	3	44	1	30	7	62	1	9th	167	170	357	341
Walsh	8	0	23	0	(4) 29	8	52	1	10th	174	194	391	–
Benjamin	8	0	32	3	(3) 32	9	73	3					
Hooper	9.1	1	35	1	4	1	18	0					
Richards					4	1	17	2					

Umpires: L.H.Barker (8) and C.E.Cumberbatch (8).

Close: 1st day – P(1) 55-5 (Salim Malik 5, Ijaz Ahmed 1); 2nd – WI(2) 78-3 (Richardson 39, Richards 7); 3rd – WI(2) 329-8 (Dujon 70, Benjamin 4); 4th – P(2) 107-3 (Miandad 19, Salim Malik 17).

WEST INDIES v PAKISTAN 1987-88 (3rd Test)

At Kensington Oval, Bridgetown, Barbados, on 22, 23, 24, 26, 27 April.
Toss: West Indies.   Result: WEST INDIES won by two wickets.
Debuts: None.

Another epic match gave West Indies the narrow victory sufficient to prevent them losing a home rubber for the first time since Australia defeated them in 1972-73. Until Benjamin joined Dujon in a match-winning series record ninth-wicket unbroken stand of 61, Pakistan seemed certain to become the first visiting country ever to win at Bridgetown in 23 matches since 1934-35. Salim Yousuf retired at 285 when he top-edged a hook against Marshall (who later took his 250th wicket in 53 Tests) and fractured his nose in two places. Aamer Malik kept wicket in both innings. Playing in his 94th Test, Richards scored 50 off 51 balls and, when 61, became the ninth batsman to complete 7,000 runs. Benjamin scored the winning boundary off Qadir who had earlier been involved in exchanges, verbal and physical, with a heckler on the boundary. An out-of-court settlement of $1,000 was paid to the punched spectator to avoid Qadir having to remain in Barbados to face prosecution.

PAKISTAN

Mudassar Nazar	b Ambrose	18	c Greenidge b Hooper		41
Ramiz Raja	c Greenidge b Benjamin	54	c Logie b Marshall		4
Shoaib Mohammad	c Greenidge b Ambrose	54	c and b Richards		64
Javed Miandad	c Richardson b Marshall	14	c Dujon b Marshall		34
Salim Malik	b Marshall	15	lbw b Benjamin		9
Aamer Malik	c Hooper b Benjamin	32	c Logie b Marshall		2
*Imran Khan	c Dujon b Benjamin	18	not out		43
†Salim Yousuf	retired hurt	32	(9) c Richardson b Benjamin		28
Wasim Akram	c Benjamin b Marshall	38	(8) lbw b Marshall		0
Abdul Qadir	c Walsh b Marshall	17	c Greenidge b Marshall		2
Salim Jaffer	not out	1	b Ambrose		4
Extras	(LB7, NB9)	16	(B3, LB14, NB14)		31
Total		**309**			**262**

WEST INDIES

C.G.Greenidge	lbw b Imran	10	c Shoaib b Salim Jaffer		35
D.L.Haynes	c Aamer b Mudassar	48	c Salim Malik b Wasim		4
R.B.Richardson	c Aamer b Wasim	3	st Aamer b Qadir		64
C.L.Hooper	b Wasim	54	run out		13
*I.V.A.Richards	c Mudassar b Wasim	67	b Wasim		39
A.L.Logie	c Miandad b Mudassar	0	b Qadir		3
†P.J.L.Dujon	run out	0	(8) not out		29
M.D.Marshall	c Aamer b Imran	48	(9) lbw b Wasim		15
C.E.L.Ambrose	lbw b Imran	7	(7) c Salim Jaffer b Wasim		1
W.K.M.Benjamin	run out	31	not out		40
C.A.Walsh	not out	14			
Extras	(B5, LB11, NB8)	24	(B9, LB6, NB10)		25
Total		**306**	(8 wickets)		**268**

WEST INDIES	O	M	R	W	O	M	R	W	FALL OF WICKETS			
									P	WI	P	WI
Marshall	18.4	3	79	4	23	3	65	5	*Wkt*	*1st*	*1st*	*2nd*	*2nd*
Ambrose	14	0	64	2	26.5	3	74	1	1st	46	18	6	21
Benjamin	14	3	52	3	(4) 15	1	37	2	2nd	99	21	100	78
Walsh	10	1	53	0	(3) 12	1	22	0	3rd	128	100	153	118
Richards	6	0	19	0	(6) 7	3	8	1	4th	155	198	165	128
Hooper	12	3	35	0	(5) 10	1	39	1	5th	186	198	167	150
									6th	215	199	169	159
PAKISTAN									7th	218	201	182	180
Imran	25	3	108	3	(2) 6	0	34	0	8th	297	225	234	207
Wasim	27	1	88	3	(1) 31	7	73	4	9th	309	283	245	–
Qadir	15	1	35	0	32	5	115	2	10th	–	306	262	–
Salim Jaffer	7	1	35	0	5	0	25	1					
Mudassar	10	4	24	2									
Shoaib					(5) 3	1	6	0					

Umpires: D.M.Archer (19) and L.H.Barker (9).

Close: 1st day – P(1) 309 all out; 2nd – WI(1) 226-8 (Marshall 15, Benjamin 0); 3rd – P(2) 177-6 (Imran 6, Wasim 0); 4th – WI(2) 154-5 (Richards 26, Ambrose 0).

ENGLAND v WEST INDIES 1988 (1st Test)

At Trent Bridge, Nottingham, on 2, 3, 4, 6, 7 June.
Toss: England.   Result: MATCH DRAWN.
Debuts: None.

England celebrated the 150th anniversary of Trent Bridge Cricket Ground by ending a sequence of ten successive defeats in this series, but were unable to avoid registering a record 14th Test without victory. After Gooch (who exceeded 4,000 runs) and Broad had posted England's 16th three-figure opening partnership in 91 Tests against West Indies, all ten wickets fell for 120 runs. Marshall, who utilised a damp pitch by swinging the ball at reduced pace and repeatedly varying his angle of attack from over to around the stumps, took six of the first seven wickets to fall. Although Saturday's capacity crowd of 13,000 was deprived of nearly four hours of play, their patience was rewarded by an awesome display from Richards who needed only 60 balls (80 minutes) to reach his 54th fifty in 142 Test innings. England began the final day with nine wickets available and 95 overs to survive. Their rearguard action, considerably eased by a rib-muscle injury to Marshall, featured a steadfast display from Gooch (410 minutes, 303 balls, 15 fours), whose eighth hundred was his fourth against West Indies, and Gower, who completed 1,000 runs against them.

ENGLAND

G.A.Gooch	b Marshall	73	c Dujon b Patterson		146
B.C.Broad	b Marshall	54	c Dujon b Ambrose		16
*M.W.Gatting	c Logie b Marshall	5	b Marshall		29
D.I.Gower	c Dujon b Ambrose	18	not out		88
A.J.Lamb	lbw b Marshall	0	not out		6
D.R.Pringle	b Marshall	39			
†P.R.Downton	not out	16			
J.E.Emburey	c Dujon b Marshall	0			
P.A.J.DeFreitas	b Ambrose	3			
P.W.Jarvis	b Ambrose	6			
G.R.Dilley	b Ambrose	2			
Extras	(LB13, W5, NB11)	29	(LB10, NB6)		16
Total		**245**	(3 wickets)		**301**

WEST INDIES

C.G.Greenidge	c Downton b Jarvis	25
D.L.Haynes	c Downton b Jarvis	60
R.B.Richardson	c Gatting b Emburey	17
*I.V.A.Richards	c Gooch b DeFreitas	80
C.L.Hooper	c Downton b DeFreitas	84
A.L.Logie	c Gooch b Pringle	20
†P.J.L.Dujon	c and b Dilley	16
M.D.Marshall	b Emburey	72
C.E.L.Ambrose	run out	43
C.A.Walsh	not out	3
B.P.Patterson	did not bat	
Extras	(B6, LB8, NB14)	28
Total	(9 wickets declared)	**448**

WEST INDIES	O	M	R	W	O	M	R	W		FALL OF	WICKETS	
										E	WI	E
Marshall	30	4	69	6	13	4	23	1	Wkt	1st	1st	2nd
Patterson	16	2	49	0	24	6	69	1	1st	125	54	39
Ambrose	26	10	53	4	23	4	56	1	2nd	141	84	116
Walsh	20	4	39	0	25	5	84	0	3rd	161	159	277
Hooper	8	1	20	0	(6) 14	1	33	0	4th	161	231	—
Richards	1	0	2	0	(5) 9	1	26	0	5th	186	271	—
									6th	223	309	—
ENGLAND									7th	223	334	—
Dilley	34	5	101	1					8th	235	425	—
DeFreitas	27	5	93	2					9th	243	448	—
Jarvis	18.1	1	63	2					10th	245	—	—
Pringle	34	11	82	1								
Emburey	16	4	95	2								

Umpires: H.D.Bird (37) and J.Birkenshaw (2).

Close: 1st day – E(1) 220-5 (Pringle 39, Downton 9); 2nd – WI(1) 126-2 (Haynes 53, Richards 22); 3rd – WI(1) 264-4 (Hooper 47, Logie 18); 4th – E(2) 67-1 (Gooch 38, Gatting 8).

ENGLAND v WEST INDIES 1988 (2nd Test)

At Lord's, London, on 16, 17, 18, 20, 21 June.
Toss: West Indies.   Result: WEST INDIES won by 134 runs.
Debuts: None.

At 1.59 on the fifth afternoon, West Indies extended their run of success at Lord's to six wins in eight visits and England's abysmal record there to two victories in their last 15 matches. England were led by their 66th captain, Emburey becoming the eleventh Middlesex player to gain the honour (four more than has been bestowed upon any other county), the tenth having been removed from office as a result of extra-curricular activities during the previous Test being reported in the seedier press. After enjoying their best session of the rubber, reducing West Indies to 66 for 5 with Dilley bowling unchanged (and uninjured) to earn figures of 13-4-35-4, they were gradually overpowered yet again. Greenidge (242 minutes, 192 balls) reached his 15th hundred (sixth against England) and became the fifth West Indian to score 6,000 runs. Although Lamb (338 minutes, 213 balls) scored his eighth Test hundred (fourth against West Indies and a record second against them at Lord's), he could not prevent the inevitable Marshall from taking ten wickets for the third time. For the first time in England, the match receipts exceeded six figures: £1,031,262 (attendance 77,923).

WEST INDIES

C.G.Greenidge	c Downton b Dilley	22	c Emburey b Dilley	103
D.L.Haynes	c Moxon b Dilley	12	c Downton b Dilley	5
R.B.Richardson	c Emburey b Dilley	5	lbw b Pringle	26
I.V.A.Richards	c Downton b Dilley	6	b Pringle	72
C.L.Hooper	c Downton b Small	3	c Downton b Jarvis	11
A.L.Logie	c Emburey b Small	81	not out	95
P.J.L.Dujon	b Emburey	53	b Jarvis	52
M.D.Marshall	c Gooch b Dilley	11	b Jarvis	6
C.E.L.Ambrose	c Gower b Small	0	b Dilley	0
C.A.Walsh	not out	9	b Dilley	0
B.P.Patterson	b Small	0	c Downton b Jarvis	2
Extras	(LB6, NB1)	7	(LB19, W1, NB5)	25
Total		**209**		**397**

ENGLAND

G.A.Gooch	b Marshall	44	lbw b Marshall	16
B.C.Broad	lbw b Marshall	0	c Dujon b Marshall	1
M.D.Moxon	c Richards b Ambrose	26	run out	14
D.I.Gower	c sub (K.L.T.Arthurton) b Walsh	46	c Richardson b Patterson	1
A.J.Lamb	lbw b Marshall	10	run out	113
D.R.Pringle	c Dujon b Walsh	1	lbw b Walsh	0
P.R.Downton	lbw b Marshall	11	lbw b Marshall	27
J.E.Emburey	b Patterson	7	b Ambrose	30
G.C.Small	not out	5	c Richards b Marshall	7
P.W.Jarvis	c Haynes b Marshall	7	not out	29
G.R.Dilley	b Marshall	0	c Richardson b Patterson	28
Extras	(LB6, NB2)	8	(B5, LB20, W2, NB14)	41
Total		**165**		**307**

ENGLAND	O	M	R	W	O	M	R	W		FALL OF WICKETS			
										WI	E	WI	E
Dilley	23	6	55	5	27	6	73	4	*Wkt*	*1st*	*1st*	*2nd*	*2nd*
Jarvis	13	2	47	0	(3) 26	3	107	4	1st	21	13	32	27
Small	18.5	5	64	4	(2) 19	1	76	0	2nd	40	58	115	29
Pringle	7	3	20	0	(5) 21	4	60	2	3rd	47	112	198	31
Emburey	6	2	17	1	(4) 15	1	62	0	4th	50	129	226	104
									5th	54	134	240	105
WEST INDIES									6th	184	140	371	161
Marshall	18	5	32	6	25	5	60	4	7th	199	153	379	212
Patterson	13	3	52	1	21.5	2	100	2	8th	199	157	380	232
Ambrose	12	1	39	1	(4) 20	4	47	1	9th	199	165	384	254
Walsh	16	6	36	2	(3) 20	1	75	1	10th	209	165	397	307

Umpires: K.E.Palmer (16) and D.R.Shepherd (6).

Close: 1st day – E(1) 20-1 (Gooch 17, Moxon 3); 2nd – WI(2) 16-0 (Greenidge 12, Haynes 4); 3rd – WI(2) 354-5 (Logie 69, Dujon 45); 4th – E(2) 214-7 (Lamb 99, Small 0).

ENGLAND v WEST INDIES 1988 (3rd Test)

At Old Trafford, Manchester, on 30 June, 1, 2, 4, 5 July.
Toss: England. Result: WEST INDIES won by an innings and 156 runs.
Debuts: England – J.H.Childs.

Taking into account the loss of 125 overs during the first four days, West Indies achieved their overwhelming victory in under three days of actual play. England lost their 20 wickets for just 228 runs in 103 overs (451 minutes). Once again, Marshall was the chief architect of victory, returning his best analysis in Tests. At this stage of his career, his 281 wickets had been taken more cheaply (20.29 runs apiece) and at a greater frequency (every 44.5 balls) than any of the nine bowlers ranged above him on the list of leading Test wicket-takers. Childs became the fourth Devon-born England cricketer, following E.G.Arnold (Exmouth), L.J.Coldwell (Newton Abbot) and R.W.Tolchard (Torquay); at 36 years 320 days, he was the oldest English debutant since 1947 (R.Howorth). A damaged hamstring caused Haynes to end an unbroken run of Test appearances embracing 72 matches and nearly nine years. Harper batted 307 minutes (245 balls) for his highest Test score.

ENGLAND

G.A.Gooch	c Dujon b Benjamin	27	lbw b Marshall	1
M.D.Moxon	b Marshall	0	c Richards b Benjamin	15
M.W.Gatting	lbw b Marshall	0	c Richardson b Marshall	4
D.I.Gower	c Harper b Walsh	9	c Richardson b Marshall	34
A.J.Lamb	c Greenidge b Ambrose	33	c Logie b Ambrose	9
D.J.Capel	b Benjamin	1	c sub ‡ b Marshall	0
†P.R.Downton	c Greenidge b Walsh	24	c Harper b Marshall	6
*J.E.Emburey	c Dujon b Walsh	1	c Logie b Ambrose	8
P.A.J.DeFreitas	c Greenidge b Ambrose	15	c Harper b Marshall	0
G.R.Dilley	c Harper b Walsh	14	b Marshall	4
J.H.Childs	not out	2	not out	0
Extras	(LB4, NB5)	9	(B1, LB10, NB1)	12
Total		**135**		**93**

WEST INDIES

C.G.Greenidge	lbw b DeFreitas	45
R.B.Richardson	b Dilley	23
C.L.Hooper	lbw b Childs	15
*I.V.A.Richards	b Capel	47
A.L.Logie	lbw b Dilley	39
†P.J.L.Dujon	c Capel b Dilley	67
R.A.Harper	b Dilley	74
M.D.Marshall	not out	43
C.E.L.Ambrose	not out	7
W.K.M.Benjamin	} did not bat	
C.A.Walsh		
Extras	(LB21, NB3)	24
Total	(7 wickets declared)	**384**

WEST INDIES	O	M	R	W	O	M	R	W
Marshall	12	5	19	2	15.4	5	22	7
Ambrose	17	5	35	2	16	4	36	2
Walsh	18.2	4	46	4	4	1	10	0
Benjamin	13	4	31	2	4	1	6	1
Harper					2	1	4	0
Hooper					1	0	4	0
ENGLAND								
Dilley	28.1	4	99	4				
Emburey	25	7	54	0				
DeFreitas	35	5	81	1				
Capel	12	2	38	1				
Childs	40	12	91	1				

FALL OF WICKETS

	E	WI	E
Wkt	1st	1st	2nd
1st	12	35	6
2nd	14	77	22
3rd	33	101	36
4th	55	175	73
5th	61	187	73
6th	94	281	73
7th	98	373	87
8th	113	–	87
9th	123	–	93
10th	135	–	93

Umpires: D.J.Constant (35) and N.T.Plews (1).

‡ (K.L.T.Arthurton)

Close: 1st day – WI(1) 4-0 (Greenidge 4, Richardson 0); 2nd – WI(1) 242-5 (Dujon 35, Harper 23); 3rd – WI(1) 357-6 (Harper 61, Marshall 37); 4th – E(2) 60-3 (Gower 24, Lamb 6).

ENGLAND v WEST INDIES 1988 (4th Test)

At Headingley, Leeds, on 21, 22, 23, 25, 26 July.

Toss: West Indies.   Result: WEST INDIES won by ten wickets.

Debuts: England – T.S.Curtis, R.A.Smith; West Indies – K.L.T.Arthurton.

England made seven changes to the side humiliated at Old Trafford but, defeated in under 17 hours of actual playing time, they conceded their sixth successive series victory to West Indies. Cowdrey's appointment completed England's second father/son captaincy double after F.T. and F.G.Mann. Gower became the fifth player to appear in 100 Tests; at 31 he was the youngest by four years. He also became the fourth batsman to score 7,000 runs for England. Commencing 50 minutes late because of overnight rain, the match was suspended until 2.30 pm after just two overs because of a mysterious water seepage into the bowler's approach at the Main Stand End. A resolute fifth-wicket partnership of 103 between Lamb and Smith was ended only when Lamb tore a calf muscle when setting off for a quick single. That injury marked the game's turning point, heralding a collapse (from 183 for 4) which saw four wickets fall for two runs. Pringle enjoyed a spell of 3 for 11 in 16 balls and recorded only the fourth five-wicket analysis against West Indies at Leeds. England lost all ten wickets for 82 after a brave opening partnership of 56 between Curtis, who survived for over 90 minutes in each innings, and Gooch, who scored his third fifty of the rubber. Marshall took his 100th wicket against England while Ambrose celebrated his 20th first-class match by winning the Cornhill Award; a year earlier he had made only one appearance at first-class level.

ENGLAND

G.A.Gooch	c Dujon b Marshall	9	c Hooper b Walsh		50
T.S.Curtis	lbw b Benjamin	12	b Ambrose		12
C.W.J.Athey	lbw b Ambrose	16	c Dujon b Walsh		11
D.I.Gower	c Dujon b Benjamin	13	c Dujon b Marshall		2
A.J.Lamb	retired hurt	64	(8) c Dujon b Ambrose		19
R.A.Smith	c Dujon b Ambrose	38	(5) lbw b Marshall		11
C.S.Cowdrey	lbw b Marshall	0	(6) b Walsh		5
C.J.Richards	b Ambrose	2	(7) b Ambrose		8
D.R.Pringle	c Dujon b Marshall	0	b Benjamin		3
N.A.Foster	not out	8	c Hooper b Benjamin		0
G.R.Dilley	c Hooper b Ambrose	8	not out		2
Extras	(B1, LB18, W6, NB6)	31	(B3, LB8, NB4)		15
Total		**201**			**138**

WEST INDIES

D.L.Haynes	lbw b Pringle	54	not out	25
P.J.L.Dujon	c Smith b Dilley	13	not out	40
C.L.Hooper	lbw b Foster	19		
I.V.A.Richards	c Curtis b Foster	18		
A.L.Logie	c Foster b Pringle	44		
K.L.T.Arthurton	c Richards b Pringle	27		
R.A.Harper	c Gower b Foster	56		
M.D.Marshall	c Gooch b Pringle	3		
C.E.L.Ambrose	lbw b Pringle	8		
W.K.M.Benjamin	run out	9		
C.A.Walsh	not out	9		
Extras	(LB15)	15	(LB2)	2
Total		**275**	**(0 wickets)**	**67**

WEST INDIES	O	M	R	W		O	M	R	W		FALL OF WICKETS			
												E	WI	E	WI
Marshall	23	8	55	3		17	4	47	2			1st	1st	2nd	2nd
Ambrose	25.1	8	58	4		19.5	4	40	3		Wkt				
Benjamin	9	2	27	2	(4)	5	4	2	2		1st	14	15	56	–
Walsh	12	4	42	0	(3)	20	9	38	3		2nd	43	61	80	–
											3rd	58	97	85	–
ENGLAND											4th	80	137	85	–
Dilley	20	5	59	1		4	0	16	0		5th	183	156	105	–
Foster	32.2	6	98	3		7	1	36	0		6th	183	194	105	–
Pringle	27	7	95	5							7th	185	210	127	–
Cowdrey	2	0	8	0	(3)	3.3	0	13	0		8th	185	222	132	–
											9th	201	245	132	–
											10th	–	275	138	–

Umpires: H.D.Bird (38) and D.R.Shepherd (7).

Close: 1st day – E(1) 137-4 (Lamb 45, Smith 23); 2nd – WI(1) 156-5 (Arthurton 1, Harper 0); 3rd – WI(1) 238-8 (Harper 31, Benjamin 7); 4th – WI(2) 27-0 (Haynes 10, Dujon 17).

ENGLAND v WEST INDIES 1988 (5th Test)

At Kennington Oval, London, on 4, 5, 6, 8 August.
Toss: England.   Result: WEST INDIES won by eight wickets.
Debuts: England – R.J.Bailey, M.P.Maynard.

A fourth successive drubbing, completed 20 minutes after tea on the fourth day, extended England's reco
sequence of matches without victory to 18. A foot injury to C.S.Cowdrey had led to the appointment of Goo
as their fourth captain of the summer. It was only the fourth time in Test history that a side had employed fou
captains in one series: Australia v England 1884-85, West Indies v England 1929-30, and India v West Indi
1958-59. The acquisition of two more debutants brought the number of players used in the rubber to 2
Thanks to a lion-hearted display of bowling in extreme heat by Foster, who removed the first five batsme
England gained a first innings lead over the West Indies for the first time in 13 Tests. Gooch, the only Englan
player to appear in all five Tests, batted throughout the second innings (422 minutes, 240 balls). Marshall too
his tally for the rubber to 35, a West Indies record in any series. Greenidge completed 2,000 runs in 28 Tes
against England. Pringle deputised as captain in the second innings after Gooch dislocated his finger off th
first ball of the second over.

ENGLAND

*G.A.Gooch	c Logie b Ambrose	9	c Greenidge b Ambrose	8
T.S.Curtis	c Dujon b Benjamin	30	lbw b Marshall	1
R.J.Bailey	c Dujon b Ambrose	43	b Benjamin	
R.A.Smith	c Harper b Marshall	57	lbw b Benjamin	
M.P.Maynard	c Dujon b Ambrose	3	(6) c and b Benjamin	1
D.J.Capel	c Marshall b Harper	16	(7) lbw b Walsh	1
†C.J.Richards	c Logie b Harper	0	(8) c Dujon b Walsh	
D.R.Pringle	c Dujon b Marshall	1	(9) b Harper	
P.A.J.DeFreitas	c Haynes b Harper	18	(10) c Haynes b Harper	
N.A.Foster	c sub‡ b Marshall	7	(5) c Logie b Benjamin	3
J.H.Childs	not out	0	not out	
Extras	(LB6, NB15)	21	(B3, LB15, NB15)	3
Total		**205**		**20**

WEST INDIES

C.G.Greenidge	c DeFreitas b Foster	10	c Richards b Childs	7
D.L.Haynes	c Richards b Foster	2	not out	7
C.L.Hooper	c Gooch b Foster	11	b Foster	2
*I.V.A.Richards	c Curtis b Foster	0		
A.L.Logie	c Gooch b Foster	47	(4) not out	3
†P.J.L.Dujon	lbw b Pringle	64		
R.A.Harper	run out	17		
M.D.Marshall	c and b Childs	0		
C.E.L.Ambrose	not out	17		
W.K.M.Benjamin	b Pringle	0		
C.A.Walsh	c DeFreitas b Pringle	5		
Extras	(LB7, W1, NB2)	10	(B2, LB3, NB6)	1
Total		**183**	(2 wickets)	**22**

WEST INDIES	O	M	R	W	O	M	R	W	FALL OF WICKETS			
										E	WI	E	W
Marshall	24.3	3	64	3	25	6	52	1					
Ambrose	20	6	31	3	24.1	10	50	1	Wkt	1st	1st	2nd	2n
Walsh	10	1	21	0	(4) 12	5	21	2	1st	12	9	50	13
Benjamin	14	2	33	1	(3) 22	4	52	4	2nd	77	16	55	16
Harper	21	7	50	3	6	3	9	2	3rd	116	16	55	
Hooper	1	1	0	0					4th	121	57	108	
									5th	160	126	125	
ENGLAND									6th	160	155	139	
Foster	16	2	64	5	18	3	52	1	7th	165	156	157	
DeFreitas	13	4	33	0	17	2	46	0	8th	196	167	175	
Pringle	17	4	45	3	(4) 13	4	24	0	9th	198	168	177	
Capel	7	0	21	0	(5) 3	0	20	0	10th	205	183	202	
Childs	6	1	13	1	(3) 40	16	79	1					

Umpires: H.D.Bird (39) and K.E.Palmer (17).   ‡ (K.L.T.Arthurton

Close: 1st day – E(1) 203-9 (Foster 5, Childs 0); 2nd – E(2) 64-3 (Gooch 38, Foster 1); 3rd – WI(2) 71-
(Greenidge 53, Haynes 15).

ENGLAND v SRI LANKA 1988 (Only Test)

At Lord's, London, on 25, 26, 27, 29, 30 August.
Toss: England.   Result: ENGLAND won by seven wickets.
Debuts: England – K.J.Barnett, D.V.Lawrence, P.J.Newport, R.C.Russell; Sri Lanka – A.W.R.Madurasinghe, M.A.R.Samarasekera.

Four balls after lunch on the fifth day, after employing 28 players in the summer's six Tests, including nine first-timers, England gained their first victory since Melbourne 1986-87 and ended a record run of 18 Tests without success. Their last win in England had been three years previously against Australia at The Oval and five years had elapsed since their last victory at Lord's. Even this belated victory was achieved in bizarre circumstances, when, with the scores level, storms brewing and two players planning hectic dashes to join their counties for matches starting that day, Robinson played out the last three balls before lunch. Lawrence (Gloucester) and Russell (Stroud) were the first Gloucestershire-born players from that county to represent England since 1966 and not since 1961-62 had an England team included two Gloucestershire players. Russell's 94 (277 minutes, 202 balls, 11 fours) was then the highest score of his first-class career and it remains the third-highest score by an England night-watchman after H.Larwood's 98 (*Test No. 224*) and E.E.Hemmings's 95 (*942*). Ratnayeke and Labrooy's partnership of 64 remains the highest for Sri Lanka's tenth wicket in all Tests.

SRI LANKA

D.S.B.P.Kuruppu	c Gooch b Newport	46	c Barnett b Foster		25
†S.A.R.Silva	c Russell b Foster	1	c Russell b Newport		16
M.A.R.Samarasekera	c Russell b Foster	0	lbw b Emburey		57
P.A.de Silva	c Gooch b Newport	3	lbw b Lawrence		18
*R.S.Madugalle	lbw b Foster	3	b Foster		20
A.Ranatunga	lbw b Newport	5	b Newport		78
L.R.D.Mendis	c Smith b Lawrence	21	lbw b Pringle		56
J.R.Ratnayeke	not out	59	c Lamb b Lawrence		32
A.W.R.Madurasinghe	run out	4	b Newport		2
C.P.H.Ramanayake	lbw b Pringle	0	(11) c Gooch b Newport		2
G.F.Labrooy	lbw b Pringle	42	(10) not out		9
Extras	(B1, LB7, NB2)	10	(LB8, NB8)		16
Total		**194**			**331**

ENGLAND

*G.A.Gooch	lbw b Ratnayeke	75	c Silva b Samarasekera		36
R.T.Robinson	c Samarasekera b Ratnayeke	19	not out		34
†R.C.Russell	c Samarasekera b Labrooy	94			
K.J.Barnett	c Ranatunga b Labrooy	66	(3) c Silva b Samarasekera		0
A.J.Lamb	b Labrooy	63	(4) c De Silva b Ranatunga		8
R.A.Smith	b Ranatunga	31	(5) not out		8
D.R.Pringle	c Silva b Labrooy	14			
J.E.Emburey	c De Silva b Samarasekera	0			
P.J.Newport	c De Silva b Ramanayake	26			
N.A.Foster	not out	14			
D.V.Lawrence	c Mendis b Ramanayake	4			
Extras	(B1, LB3, W2, NB17)	23	(LB8, W2, NB4)		14
Total		**429**	(3 wickets)		**100**

ENGLAND	O	M	R	W	O	M	R	W		FALL OF WICKETS			
											SL	E	SL	E
Foster	21	5	51	3	33	10	98	2	*Wkt*	*1st*	*1st*	*2nd*	*2nd*
Lawrence	15	4	37	1	21	5	74	2	1st	7	40	43	73
Newport	21	4	77	3	26.3	7	87	4	2nd	44	171	51	73
Pringle	6.5	1	17	2	11	2	30	1	3rd	52	233	96	82
Emburey	2	1	4	0	18	9	34	1	4th	53	320	145	–
									5th	61	358	147	–
SRI LANKA									6th	63	373	251	–
Ratnayeke	32	3	107	2	(2) 7	1	16	0	7th	122	378	309	–
Labrooy	40	7	119	4	(1) 9	0	24	0	8th	127	383	311	–
Ramanayake	27.2	3	86	2					9th	130	420	323	–
Madurasinghe	16	4	41	0					10th	194	429	331	–
Samarasekera	22	5	66	1	(3) 10	0	38	2					
Ranatunga	6	3	6	1	(4) 8.4	4	14	1					

Umpires: D.J.Constant (36) and J.W.Holder (1).

Close: 1st day – E(1) 47-1 (Gooch 24, Russell 2); 2nd – E(1) 278-3 (Barnett 55, Lamb 20); 3rd – SL(2) 92-2 (Samarasekera 30, De Silva 15); 4th – E(2) 8-0 (Gooch 1, Robinson 4).

PAKISTAN v AUSTRALIA 1988-89 (1st Test)

At National Stadium, Karachi, on 15, 16, 17, 19, 20 September.
Toss: Pakistan.   Result: PAKISTAN won by an innings and 188 runs.
Debuts: Australia – I.A.Healy.

The staple Pakistani formula produced inevitable results: an under-prepared pitch plus a succession of controversial umpiring decisions equals acrimony plus very substantial victory for home side. Despite a revamped administration, this series was almost immediately in turmoil with the Australians threatening to abort their impossible mission against conspiracy to defraud. Pakistan's fourth victory against Australia in six Karachi Tests was completed after 90 minutes of the last day and by their largest margin in this series. Javed Miandad, restored to the captaincy when Imran Khan refused to take part in the series, amassed Pakistan's highest score against Australia after being dropped when 126 and 186. Batting 590 minutes on a sharply turning pitch, he faced 439 balls and hit a six and 29 fours in recording his fifth double century. He reached his 18th hundred (fifth against Australia) in 315 minutes, adding 196 in 279 minutes with Shoaib.

PAKISTAN

Mudassar Nazar	b Reid	0
Ramiz Raja	c Healy b Reid	9
Shoaib Mohammad	b Waugh	94
*Javed Miandad	c Boon b Reid	211
Tausif Ahmed	c Boon b May	35
Salim Malik	c Boon b May	45
Ijaz Ahmed	c Boon b Reid	12
Aamer Malik	not out	17
†Salim Yousuf	c Wood b May	5
Abdul Qadir	c Marsh b May	8
Iqbal Qasim	did not bat	
Extras	(B16, LB12, NB5)	33
Total	**(9 wickets declared)**	**469**

AUSTRALIA

G.R.Marsh	b Qasim	8		lbw b Tausif	17
D.C.Boon	b Qadir	14	(3)	b Qasim	4
D.M.Jones	lbw b Qasim	3	(4)	c Ijaz b Qadir	4
G.M.Wood	c Qasim b Tausif	23	(5)	lbw b Qasim	15
*A.R.Border	c Aamer Malik b Qasim	4	(6)	b Qasim	18
S.R.Waugh	lbw b Qasim	0	(7)	st Salim Yousuf b Qasim	13
P.L.Taylor	not out	54	(2)	c Ijaz b Aamer Malik	2
†I.A.Healy	c Ijaz b Mudassar	26		c Shoaib b Qadir	21
A.I.C.Dodemaide	c Ijaz b Salim Malik	8		st Salim Yousuf b Tausif	2
T.B.A.May	c Salim Yousuf b Qadir	6		lbw b Qadir	0
B.A.Reid	lbw b Qasim	0		not out	8
Extras	(B12, LB7)	19		(B6, LB6)	12
Total		**165**			**116**

AUSTRALIA	O	M	R	W	O	M	R	W
Reid	41	10	109	4				
Dodemaide	29	13	35	0				
Waugh	26	3	94	1				
May	40.5	10	97	4				
Taylor	16	2	73	0				
Border	17	7	33	0				
PAKISTAN								
Mudassar	10	3	15	1	3	0	5	0
Aamer Malik	2	0	6	0	2	2	0	1
Qasim	39	24	35	5	25	14	49	4
Qadir	37	16	54	2	13	4	34	3
Tausif	26	15	28	1	21.4	13	16	2
Shoaib	2	1	1	0				
Salim Malik	6	4	7	1				

FALL OF WICKETS

	P	A	A
Wkt	1st	1st	2nd
1st	0	19	4
2nd	21	23	10
3rd	217	40	15
4th	284	48	46
5th	398	54	50
6th	428	64	80
7th	444	106	93
8th	457	139	104
9th	469	162	104
10th	–	165	116

Umpires: Khizer Hayat (21) and Mahboob Shah (18).

Close: 1st day – P(1) 227-3 (Miandad 95, Tausif 7); 2nd – P(1) 438-6 (Ijaz 8, Aamer Malik 5); 3rd – A(1) 116-7 (Taylor 22, Dodemaide 4); 4th – A(2) 66-5 (Border 5, Waugh 11).

PAKISTAN v AUSTRALIA 1988-89 (2nd Test)

At Iqbal Stadium, Faisalabad, on 23, 24, 25, 27, 28 September.
Toss: Pakistan.   Result: MATCH DRAWN.
Debuts: None.

Despite being four wickets down in the first 50 minutes of play, Pakistan were able to recover through a maiden hundred by Ijaz Ahmed (20) who batted for 290 minutes and hit 17 fours and two sixes. Playing in his 73rd Test, Mudassar became the third Pakistani after Miandad and Zaheer Abbas to score 4,000 runs. Border, who batted nearly six hours, compiled his 23rd hundred. It was his sixth in this series, as was Miandad's 19th century, scored in 240 minutes, which removed any thoughts of an Australian victory. The Pakistan captain was given out lbw for only the fourth time in 63 Test innings on his home soil and delayed his declaration until 45 minutes after lunch.

PAKISTAN

Mudassar Nazar	c Marsh b Reid	9		c Border b May	27
Ramiz Raja	lbw b Dodemaide	0		c Boon b Waugh	32
Shoaib Mohammad	b Dodemaide	11		st Healy b May	74
*Javed Miandad	c Boon b May	43		lbw b Reid	107
Salim Malik	b Dodemaide	0		c Border b Reid	10
Ijaz Ahmed	b Reid	122		c Healy b Reid	0
†Salim Yousuf	c Boon b Dodemaide	62		not out	66
Abdul Qadir	b Reid	6	(10)	c Reid b May	13
Tausif Ahmed	not out	35	(8)	c Waugh b Dodemaide	2
Iqbal Qasim	c and b Sleep	16	(9)	lbw b Reid	28
Salim Jaffer	lbw b Sleep	0			
Extras	(B2, LB6, NB4)	12		(LB6, NB13)	19
Total		**316**		**(9 wickets declared)**	**378**

AUSTRALIA

D.C.Boon	b Mudassar	13	(2)	c Mudassar b Tausif	15
G.R.Marsh	b Tausif	51	(1)	b Qadir	9
D.M.Jones	lbw b Qadir	16		not out	21
G.M.Wood	lbw b Salim Jaffer	32	(5)	not out	2
A.I.C.Dodemaide	c Ijaz b Mudassar	19			
*A.R.Border	not out	113			
S.R.Waugh	st Salim Yousuf b Tausif	1	(4)	c and b Shoaib	19
P.R.Sleep	b Tausif	12			
†I.A.Healy	c Qasim b Salim Jaffer	27			
T.B.A.May	c sub (Moin-ul-Atiq) b Qadir	14			
B.A.Reid	c Salim Yousuf b Qasim	1			
Extras	(B4, LB15, W1, NB2)	22		(B1)	1
Total		**321**		**(3 wickets)**	**67**

AUSTRALIA	O	M	R	W	O	M	R	W	FALL OF WICKETS			
Reid	31	8	92	3	30	6	100	4		P	A	P	A
Dodemaide	34	6	87	4	20	4	48	1	Wkt	1st	1st	2nd	2nd
Waugh	11	3	36	0	18	6	44	1	1st	4	24	64	18
Sleep	5.5	1	24	2	(5) 13	4	51	0	2nd	20	65	64	30
May	19	3	58	1	(4) 34.4	7	126	3	3rd	24	122	236	65
Border	6	1	11	0	1	0	3	0	4th	25	122	264	–
									5th	144	167	265	–
									6th	255	170	269	–
PAKISTAN									7th	255	204	274	–
Salim Jaffer	29	7	69	2	2	0	8	0	8th	267	256	344	–
Mudassar	17	4	39	2	2	0	5	0	9th	316	318	378	–
Qadir	34	5	84	2	10	1	34	1	10th	316	321	–	–
Tausif	35	10	73	3	11	4	17	1					
Qasim	14.5	4	37	1									
Shoaib					(5) 1	0	2	1					

Umpires: Mahboob Shah (19) and Tariq Ata (1).

Close: 1st day – P(1) 244-5 (Ijaz 122, Salim Yousuf 52); 2nd – A(1) 128-4 (Dodemaide 5, Border 0); 3rd – A(1) 321 all out; 4th – P(2) 264-3 (Miandad 107, Salim Malik 9).

PAKISTAN v AUSTRALIA 1988-89 (3rd Test)

At Gaddafi Stadium, Lahore, on 7, 8, 9, 10, 11 October.
Toss: Australia.   Result: MATCH DRAWN.
Debuts: None.

Pakistan were made to fight tenaciously to complete their third successive home series win against Australia. Set 269 in a minimum of 75 overs, this unfortunate series ended with Iqbal Qasim and Tausif grimly surviving the last five dramatic overs. Miandad, in his 95th Test, became the first to score 7,000 runs for Pakistan and his 412 runs in this rubber set a Pakistan record for the series.

AUSTRALIA

D.C.Boon	c Shoaib b Salim Jaffer	43	(2)	c Miandad b Salim Jaffer	28
G.R.Marsh	st Salim Yousuf b Qasim	64	(1)	not out	84
D.M.Jones	lbw b Tausif	0		lbw b Salim Jaffer	0
*A.R.Border	c Salim Yousuf b Tausif	75		c Salim Yousuf b Tausif	20
G.M.Wood	lbw b Mudassar	15			
P.L.Taylor	st Salim Yousuf b Qadir	29	(5)	not out	25
S.R.Waugh	c Ijaz b Qasim	59			
†I.A.Healy	lbw b Qadir	0			
A.I.C.Dodemaide	c Qasim b Qadir	14			
T.B.A.May	not out	13			
B.A.Reid	c Mudassar b Tausif	8			
Extras	(B4, LB12, NB4)	20		(LB4)	4
Total		**340**		(3 wickets declared)	**161**

PAKISTAN

Mudassar Nazar	c Boon b May	27		c Border b Taylor	49
Ramiz Raja	c Healy b Reid	64		c Boon b May	21
Shoaib Mohammad	run out	13		lbw b May	3
*Javed Miandad	c Healy b Reid	27		c Border b May	24
Salim Malik	c and b Dodemaide	26		c Healy b Taylor	13
Ijaz Ahmed	lbw b Dodemaide	23		c Taylor b Dodemaide	15
†Salim Yousuf	c Healy b Reid	1		c Waugh b Taylor	2
Abdul Qadir	lbw b Dodemaide	18		st Healy b Taylor	6
Iqbal Qasim	lbw b May	14		not out	10
Tausif Ahmed	c Boon b May	3		not out	1
Salim Jaffer	not out	0			
Extras	(LB6, NB11)	17		(B6, LB1, NB2)	9
Total		**233**		(8 wickets)	**153**

PAKISTAN	O	M	R	W		O	M	R	W		FALL OF WICKETS			
Salim Jaffer	33	9	82	1		14	2	60	2		A	P	A	P
Mudassar	15	6	23	1		3	0	8	0	*Wkt*	*1st*	*1st*	*2nd*	*2nd*
Qadir	37	10	88	3	(4)	4	1	26	0	1st	87	80	71	36
Tausif	50	20	85	3	(3)	17	2	48	1	2nd	88	104	71	48
Qasim	22	6	42	2		3	0	15	0	3rd	155	118	108	86
Shoaib	1	0	4	0						4th	200	172	–	107
										5th	231	172	–	123
AUSTRALIA										6th	241	173	–	125
Reid	23	3	53	3						7th	241	206	–	131
Waugh	18	4	34	0	(2)	5	1	8	0	8th	294	228	–	147
Dodemaide	26	6	56	3	(1)	12	5	20	1	9th	331	232	–	–
May	27.2	6	73	3	(3)	35	20	39	3	10th	340	233	–	–
Taylor	4	2	11	0	(4)	28	9	78	4					
Border					(5)	4	3	1	0					

Umpires: Khizer Hayat (22) and Salim Badar (1).

Close: 1st day – A(1) 175-3 (Border 54, Wood 5); 2nd – P(1) 6-0 (Mudassar 1, Ramiz 4); 3rd – P(1) 165-3 (Miandad 24, Salim Malik 22); 4th – A(2) 132-3 (Marsh 75, Taylor 5).

INDIA v NEW ZEALAND 1988-89 (1st Test)

At Chinnaswamy Stadium, Bangalore, on 12, 13, 14, 16, 17 November.
Toss: India.   Result: INDIA won by 172 runs.
Debuts: New Zealand – C.M.Kuggeleijn.

Struck down by a mystery virus and at one point compelled to field a record five substitutes, New Zealand were spun to defeat half an hour after lunch on the fifth day. With the first ball of the third over of his 75th Test, Hadlee found the edge of Arun Lal's bat and leapt high in jubilation as victim number 374 was safely caught at third slip by Kuggeleijn, whose own Test career was just 18 minutes old. Hadlee had waited 318 days since equalling Botham's world record to become the leading wicket-taker in Test cricket in his own right. He went on to extend another world record – most instances of five wickets in an innings – to 33 and also exceeded C.V.Grimmett's total of 1,424 first-class wickets (the record by a New Zealand-born bowler). Recalled after a five-year interlude, Sidhu (295 minutes, 195 balls, four sixes and 12 fours) added 174 in a 210-minute unbroken third-wicket stand with Vengsarkar which ended when the Indian captain retired with a cramped arm at 184 (when 73); he resumed at 254. Hadlee, who had retired ill at 145 (when 1), was forced to return at 183-9 to save the follow-on. Hirwani's third analysis of five or more wickets brought his tally of dismissals to 24 in his first two Tests.

INDIA

K.Srikkanth	b Hadlee	1	not out		58
Arun Lal	c Kuggeleijn b Hadlee	6	c and b Gray		33
N.S.Sidhu	c Jones b Gray	116	not out		43
*D.B.Vengsarkar	b Hadlee	75			
M.Azharuddin	c Smith b Hadlee	42			
W.V.Raman	b Hadlee	3			
R.J.Shastri	c Rutherford b Gray	54			
Kapil Dev	c Jones b Chatfield	24			
†K.S.More	lbw b Kuggeleijn	46			
Arshad Ayub	not out	2			
N.D.Hirwani	not out	0			
Extras	(B4, LB4, NB7)	15	(B5, LB2)		7
Total	(9 wickets declared)	**384**	(1 wicket declared)		**141**

NEW ZEALAND

T.J.Franklin	c Azharuddin b Ayub	28	b Hirwani		16
*J.G.Wright	c Arun Lal b Ayub	22	lbw b Hirwani		58
A.H.Jones	c Srikkanth b Ayub	45	lbw b Hirwani		17
M.J.Greatbatch	c Srikkanth b Raman	14	c Kapil Dev b Ayub		10
K.R.Rutherford	c Arun Lal b Hirwani	14	(6) lbw b Hirwani		0
E.J.Gray	lbw b Hirwani	1	(5) c Srikkanth b Hirwani		2
R.J.Hadlee	b Kapil Dev	5	(8) not out		13
J.G.Bracewell	c More b Ayub	3	(10) c Arun Lal b Ayub		11
†I.D.S.Smith	lbw b Kapil Dev	30	lbw b Hirwani		25
E.J.Chatfield	not out	4	(11) c Vengsarkar b Ayub		0
C.M.Kuggeleijn	lbw b Kapil Dev	0	(7) c More b Ayub		0
Extras	(B6, LB8, NB9)	23	(B10, NB2)		12
Total		**189**			**164**

NEW ZEALAND	O	M	R	W		O	M	R	W		FALL OF WICKETS			
											I	NZ	I	NZ
Hadlee	30	10	65	5						*Wkt*	*1st*	*1st*	*2nd*	*2nd*
Chatfield	30	12	53	1	(1) 14	0	61	0		1st	9	58	64	77
Kuggeleijn	13	2	50	1						2nd	10	62	–	92
Gray	45	8	128	2	(3) 6	0	39	1		3rd	236	118	–	107
Bracewell	24	1	80	0	(2) 8	0	34	0		4th	244	128	–	113
										5th	254	135	–	113
INDIA										6th	258	140	–	113
Kapil Dev	9.3	4	24	3	4	0	16	0		7th	294	149	–	113
Ayub	48	21	51	4	35.4	12	53	4		8th	378	183	–	143
Hirwani	31	12	62	2	30	10	59	6		9th	384	183	–	164
Shastri	14	8	11	0	7	1	21	0		10th	–	189	–	164
Raman	17	8	26	1	2	0	5	0						
Srikkanth	3	2	1	0										

Umpires: S.K.Ghosh (1) and P.D.Reporter (12).

Close: 1st day – I(1) 243-3 (Azharuddin 33, Raman 2); 2nd – NZ(1) 9-0 (Franklin 5, Wright 4); 3rd – NZ(1) 145-6 (Hadlee 1, Bracewell 3); 4th – NZ(2) 73-0 (Franklin 16, Wright 49).

INDIA v NEW ZEALAND 1988-89 (2nd Test)

At Wankhede Stadium, Bombay, on 24, 25, 26, 27, 29 November.
Toss: New Zealand.   Result: NEW ZEALAND won by 136 runs.
Debuts: India – R.Patel.

New Zealand needed only 21 minutes (34 balls) of the fifth day to complete their second victory in 17 Tests in India and draw level in the rubber. Hadlee's immense contribution involved returning record innings and match analyses for New Zealand in India. He also extended his world records of five wickets in an innings and ten wickets in a match instances to 34 and nine respectively. Vengsarkar became the sixth (second Indian) to play in 100 Test matches. Wright, in his 60th Test, became New Zealand's most prolific batsman when he overtook B.E.Congdon's aggregate of 3,448 runs in 61 matches. Bracewell provided New Zealand's tenth instance of a fifty and five wickets in an innings of the same Test. His ninth-wicket stand of 76 with Morrison was New Zealand's highest against India until 1989-90.

NEW ZEALAND

T.J.Franklin	st More b Ayub	18	c More b Kapil Dev		2
*J.G.Wright	c More b Hirwani	33	lbw b Hirwani		36
A.H.Jones	lbw b Kapil Dev	3	lbw b Ayub		78
M.J.Greatbatch	lbw b Shastri	46	b Hirwani		31
K.R.Rutherford	c Srikkanth b Hirwani	6	c Arun Lal b Ayub		17
T.E.Blain	c Kapil Dev b Shastri	16	lbw b Ayub		5
R.J.Hadlee	c Patel b Hirwani	10	c Vengsarkar b Hirwani		1
†I.D.S.Smith	b Shastri	13	c Vengsarkar b Ayub		54
J.G.Bracewell	c More b Shastri	52	c and b Ayub	(10)	32
D.K.Morrison	not out	27	c More b Hirwani	(9)	0
E.J.Chatfield	b Kapil Dev	0	not out		2
Extras	(LB5, NB7)	12	(B4, LB8, W1, NB8)		21
Total		**236**			**279**

INDIA

K.Srikkanth	c Franklin b Hadlee	94	lbw b Hadlee	0
Arun Lal	lbw b Hadlee	9	c Greatbatch b Hadlee	47
N.S.Sidhu	lbw b Chatfield	6	b Bracewell	14
*D.B.Vengsarkar	c Blain b Bracewell	25	b Bracewell	0
M.Azharuddin	c Greatbatch b Bracewell	9	c Rutherford b Bracewell	21
R.J.Shastri	b Chatfield	32	c Smith b Hadlee	6
Kapil Dev	b Hadlee	7	c Wright b Bracewell	36
†K.S.More	b Hadlee	28	b Bracewell	2
Arshad Ayub	c Bracewell b Hadlee	10	not out	4
R.Patel	c Rutherford b Hadlee	0	c Smith b Hadlee	0
N.D.Hirwani	not out	2	c Chatfield b Bracewell	3
Extras	(LB5, NB7)	12	(B5, LB4, NB3)	12
Total		**234**		**145**

INDIA	O	M	R	W	O	M	R	W		FALL OF WICKETS			
										NZ	I	NZ	I
Kapil Dev	15.3	4	48	2	24	5	52	1	*Wkt*	*1st*	*1st*	*2nd*	*2nd*
Patel	4	0	14	0	10	0	37	0	1st	36	26	2	0
Ayub	25	10	42	1	33	11	50	5	2nd	43	34	73	48
Hirwani	31	6	82	3	38	7	93	4	3rd	67	134	149	54
Shastri	18	1	45	4	10	1	35	0	4th	83	150	163	89
									5th	110	150	169	89
NEW ZEALAND									6th	121	172	176	134
Hadlee	20.5	8	49	6	16	3	39	4	7th	141	209	176	134
Morrison	16	1	58	0	6	1	27	0	8th	158	224	181	141
Chatfield	18	6	41	2	10	1	19	0	9th	234	229	250	142
Bracewell	21	6	81	2	17.4	3	51	6	10th	236	234	279	145

Umpires: R.B.Gupta (10) and V.K.Ramaswamy (12).

Close: 1st day – NZ(1) 231-8 (Bracewell 51, Morrison 25); 2nd – I(1) 232-9 (More 27, Hirwani 2); 3rd – NZ(2) 182-8 (Smith 5, Bracewell 1); 4th – I(2) 137-7 (More 0, Ayub 2).

INDIA v NEW ZEALAND 1988-89 (3rd Test)

At Lal Bahadur Stadium, Hyderabad, on 2, 3, 4, 6 December.
Toss: New Zealand.   Result: INDIA won by ten wickets.
Debuts: India – S.K.Sharma.

Hyderabad's first Test match for 19 years was completed 12 minutes after lunch with India winning their fourth home series out of five against New Zealand. On pitches tailored for spin Arshad Ayub and Hirwani shared 41 of New Zealand's 60 wickets, the latter's first four Tests having produced 36 dismissals. Wright (231 minutes, 189 balls) batted throughout New Zealand's lowest innings in India. Hadlee took his world record wickets tally to 391 and set a New Zealand record in India with 18 wickets at 14 runs apiece.

NEW ZEALAND

Batsman	Dismissal 1	Score		Dismissal 2	Score
T.J.Franklin	c Arun Lal b Ayub	7		c Kapil Dev b Hirwani	15
J.G.Wright	c and b Ayub	17		c and b Shastri	62
A.H.Jones	c Kapil Dev b Ayub	8		c Vengsarkar b Ayub	5
M.J.Greatbatch	not out	90	(5)	lbw b Hirwani	5
T.E.Blain	b Hirwani	15	(6)	c Arun Lal b Hirwani	0
C.M.Kuggeleijn	c Vengsarkar b Hirwani	7	(7)	c Sharma b Ayub	0
R.J.Hadlee	c Azharuddin b Ayub	1	(8)	c More b Kapil Dev	31
I.D.S.Smith	c Srikkanth b Kapil Dev	79	(9)	b Kapil Dev	0
J.G.Bracewell	c Vengsarkar b Sharma	3	(10)	lbw b Kapil Dev	0
M.C.Snedden	lbw b Sharma	0	(4)	lbw b Ayub	0
E.J.Chatfield	c Srikkanth b Sharma	0		not out	0
Extras	(B8, LB11, W1, NB7)	27		(LB1, W5)	6
Total		**254**			**124**

INDIA

Batsman	Dismissal 1	Score		Dismissal 2	Score
K.Srikkanth	c Bracewell b Snedden	69		not out	18
Arun Lal	c Greatbatch b Hadlee	8		not out	0
N.S.Sidhu	c Franklin b Snedden	19			
D.B.Vengsarkar	c Hadlee b Chatfield	32			
R.J.Shastri	c Franklin b Chatfield	42			
M.Azharuddin	c Smith b Chatfield	81			
Kapil Dev	c Wright b Hadlee	40			
K.S.More	c Bracewell b Snedden	0			
Arshad Ayub	c Smith b Hadlee	19			
S.K.Sharma	not out	18			
N.D.Hirwani	c and b Snedden	17			
Extras	(LB9, NB4)	13		(NB4)	4
Total		**358**		(0 wickets)	**22**

INDIA	O	M	R	W	O	M	R	W		FALL OF WICKETS			
										NZ	I	NZ	I
Kapil Dev	26	6	71	1	10	3	21	3	*Wkt*	*1st*	*1st*	*2nd*	*2nd*
Sharma	17	4	37	3	4	0	13	0	1st	25	17	49	–
Ayub	30	9	55	4	(4) 25	12	36	3	2nd	33	48	58	–
Shastri	6	2	15	0	(5) 3.3	1	10	1	3rd	38	116	60	–
Hirwani	15	2	51	2	(3) 23	10	43	3	4th	82	150	71	–
Srikkanth	1	0	6	0					5th	90	217	75	–
									6th	91	279	80	–
NEW ZEALAND									7th	230	281	118	–
Hadlee	34	7	99	3					8th	246	310	118	–
Chatfield	33	6	82	3	(1) 1	0	5	0	9th	248	322	124	–
Snedden	18.3	3	69	4	(2) 1	0	13	0	10th	254	358	124	–
Bracewell	18	1	86	0									
Kuggeleijn	3	0	13	0	(3) 0.1	0	4	0					

Umpires: S.K.Ghosh (2) and R.B.Gupta (11).

Close: 1st day – NZ(1) 226-6 (Greatbatch 76, Smith 78); 2nd – I(1) 211-4 (Shastri 41, Azharuddin 35); 3rd – NZ(2) 65-3 (Wright 39, Greatbatch 1).

AUSTRALIA v WEST INDIES 1988-89 (1st Test)

At Woolloongabba, Brisbane, on 18, 19, 20, 21 November.
Toss: Australia.   Result: WEST INDIES won by nine wickets.
Debuts: None.

Richards celebrated his 100th Test (the seventh instance and second West Indian after C.H.Lloyd) by leading West Indies to victory with a day and a half to spare and, appropriately, by becoming the 10th fielder to hold 100 catches. Greenidge and Haynes shared their 13th three-figure opening partnership in Tests. Walsh achieved the 18th hat-trick at this level when he had Dodemaide caught off his last ball in the first innings and dismissed Veletta and Wood with his first two balls in the second. It was the first Test hat-trick since 1976-77, the first in Australia since 1960-61 and the first to involve both innings.

AUSTRALIA

G.R.Marsh	c Logie b Ambrose	27	(2)	lbw b Ambrose	
D.C.Boon	lbw b Marshall	10	(1)	c Dujon b Marshall	1
M.R.J.Veletta	b Hooper	37		c Hooper b Walsh	1
G.M.Wood	c Greenidge b Ambrose	6	(5)	lbw b Walsh	
*A.R.Border	c Dujon b Ambrose	4	(6)	c Haynes b Ambrose	4
S.R.Waugh	lbw b Marshall	4	(4)	c Haynes b Marshall	9
†I.A.Healy	c Logie b Walsh	27		c Ambrose b Marshall	
A.I.C.Dodemaide	c Richards b Walsh	22		c Richards b Marshall	
C.J.McDermott	c Logie b Walsh	2		not out	3
C.D.Matthews	c Dujon b Walsh	1		c sub (K.L.T.Arthurton) b Walsh	3
T.B.A.May	not out	4		c Hooper b Ambrose	
Extras	(B1, LB5, W1, NB16)	23		(B4, LB5, NB21)	3
Total		**167**			**28**

WEST INDIES

C.G.Greenidge	b May	80		c Healy b Dodemaide	1
D.L.Haynes	c Healy b Waugh	40		not out	3
R.B.Richardson	lbw b Dodemaide	81		not out	
C.L.Hooper	c Border b Waugh	1			
*I.V.A.Richards	c McDermott b May	68			
A.L.Logie	c Border b May	19			
†P.J.L.Dujon	c May b McDermott	27			
M.D.Marshall	c Border b McDermott	11			
C.E.L.Ambrose	not out	19			
C.A.Walsh	lbw b McDermott	0			
B.P.Patterson	lbw b Dodemaide	0			
Extras	(B5, LB9, W6, NB28)	48		(LB4, W3, NB3)	1
Total		**394**		(1 wicket)	**63**

WEST INDIES	O	M	R	W		O	M	R	W		FALL OF WICKETS			
Marshall	18	3	39	2		26	2	92	4			A	WI	A	W
Patterson	3.1	1	5	0						*Wkt*	*1st*	*1st*	*2nd*	*2nd*
Ambrose	16.5	5	30	3	(2)	26.1	5	78	3	1st	19	135	14	43
Walsh	18.3	3	62	4	(3)	19	3	61	3	2nd	52	156	16	–
Hooper	12	2	24	1		4	0	23	0	3rd	64	162	65	–
Richards	1	0	1	0	(4)	11	4	26	0	4th	76	270	65	–
										5th	86	307	157	–
AUSTRALIA										6th	126	359	199	–
McDermott	28	3	99	3		4	0	12	0	7th	138	361	212	–
Matthews	21	3	62	0		3.5	1	18	0	8th	140	389	212	–
Dodemaide	16.4	2	60	2		5.2	1	15	1	9th	150	393	270	–
May	29	6	90	3						10th	167	394	289	–
Waugh	18	2	61	2	(4)	6	0	14	0					
Border	1	0	8	0										

Umpires: A.R.Crafter (25) and P.J.McConnell (11).

Close: 1st day – WI(1) 39-0 (Greenidge 24, Haynes 5); 2nd – WI(1) 366-7 (Marshall 3, Ambrose 2); 3rd – A(2) 200-6 (Healy 25, Dodemaide 0).

AUSTRALIA v WEST INDIES 1988-89 (2nd Test)

At W.A.C.A.Ground, Perth, on 2, 3, 4, 5, 6 December.
Toss: Australia.   Result: WEST INDIES won by 169 runs.
Debuts: None.

Richards (146 off 150 balls, with three sixes and 21 fours) scored his 23rd hundred (his fifth against Australia), Haynes his tenth, and Wood, who shared a fifth-wicket stand of 200 with Waugh, his ninth. Lawson sustained a fractured jaw when he lost sight of a lifting ball from Ambrose; he disturbed his wicket but was ruled 'retired hurt'. Border declared as Lawson was being stretchered from the field. Hughes achieved the most convoluted hat-trick in Test history; having ended the first innings by dismissing Ambrose with the last ball of his 36th over and Patterson with his first ball of the 37th, he had Greenidge lbw with the first of the second innings. His second innings analysis is the record for Tests at Perth, while his match figures of 13 for 217 surpassed H.Ironmonger's 11 for 79 at Melbourne in 1930-31 as Australia's best against West Indies anywhere.

WEST INDIES

C.G.Greenidge	b Lawson	40	lbw b Hughes		0
D.L.Haynes	lbw b Hughes	11	c Healy b Hughes		100
R.B.Richardson	c Boon b Hughes	66	c Healy b Hughes		48
C.L.Hooper	c Boon b Lawson	26	c Dodemaide b Hughes		64
*I.V.A.Richards	c Dodemaide b Lawson	146	lbw b Hughes		5
A.L.Logie	c Waugh b May	93	b Hughes		30
†P.J.L.Dujon	c Veletta b May	32	c Dodemaide b Hughes		9
M.D.Marshall	c Veletta b Hughes	4	c Healy b Dodemaide		23
C.E.L.Ambrose	c Healy b Hughes	8	c Wood b Hughes		15
C.A.Walsh	not out	0	not out		17
B.P.Patterson	c Dodemaide b Hughes	1	not out		6
Extras	(B1, LB12, NB9)	22	(B14, LB9, NB9)		32
Total		**449**	(9 wickets declared)		**349**

AUSTRALIA

G.R.Marsh	c Richardson b Walsh	30	(2) c Logie b Marshall		6
D.C.Boon	c Logie b Ambrose	80	(1) b Patterson		4
M.R.J.Veletta	run out	11	c Dujon b Marshall		13
G.M.Wood	c Richardson b Ambrose	111	c Greenidge b Walsh		42
*A.R.Border	c Dujon b Ambrose	6	b Hooper		26
S.R.Waugh	c Dujon b Ambrose	91	c Hooper b Patterson		26
†I.A.Healy	lbw b Marshall	8	c Logie b Ambrose		52
A.I.C.Dodemaide	not out	7	lbw b Ambrose		11
T.B.A.May	c Richards b Ambrose	2	not out		8
G.F.Lawson	retired hurt	0	absent hurt		–
M.G.Hughes	did not bat		(10) c Logie b Ambrose		0
Extras	(B5, LB9, NB35)	49	(B5, LB4, NB37)		46
Total	(8 wickets declared)	**395**			**234**

AUSTRALIA	O	M	R	W		O	M	R	W		FALL OF WICKETS			
											WI	A	WI	A
Lawson	32	7	97	3						Wkt	1st	1st	2nd	2nd
Hughes	36.1	7	130	5	(1) 37	9	87	8		1st	16	83	0	14
Dodemaide	17	1	79	0	(2) 24	2	101	1		2nd	82	138	103	14
Waugh	28	3	90	0	(3) 23	1	70	0		3rd	126	152	216	46
May	10	3	40	2	(4) 14	1	68	0		4th	180	167	236	93
WEST INDIES										5th	343	367	246	138
Marshall	23	3	84	1	12	0	50	2		6th	421	374	259	140
Patterson	16	1	95	0	14	2	58	2		7th	426	388	300	190
Walsh	19	3	58	1	(4) 15	1	46	1		8th	440	395	310	232
Ambrose	23.3	3	72	5	(3) 17	1	66	3		9th	448	–	341	234
Richards	14	0	43	0						10th	449	–	–	–
Hooper	5	0	29	0	(5) 5	2	5	1						

Umpires: R.C.Bailhache (27) and T.A.Prue (1).

Close: 1st day – WI(1) 280-4 (Richards 95, Logie 30); 2nd – A(1) 119-1 (Boon 65, Veletta 7); 3rd – WI(2) 2-1 (Haynes 0, Richardson 2); 4th – WI(2) 331-8 (Ambrose 8, Walsh 12).

AUSTRALIA v WEST INDIES 1988-89 (3rd Test)

At Melbourne Cricket Ground on 24, 26, 27, 28, 29 December.
Toss: Australia.   Result: WEST INDIES won by 285 runs.
Debuts: None.

West Indies retained the Frank Worrell Trophy with their third emphatic victory. Border became the first Australian to play in 100 Tests. Waugh reached 1,000 runs in 24 Tests. Richardson (391 minutes, 288 balls, 14 fours) scored his seventh Test hundred and his fourth against Australia. In his 61st Test, Marshall became the ninth bowler (the second West Indian after L.R.Gibbs) to take 300 wickets. In the second innings, Greenidge (25) retired hurt at 69, his eye swollen from an edged hook, and resumed at 335.

WEST INDIES

C.G.Greenidge	c Healy b Alderman	49		not out	36
D.L.Haynes	c Boon b McDermott	17		lbw b Alderman	23
R.B.Richardson	c Taylor b Alderman	26		c and b Waugh	122
C.L.Hooper	c Border b McDermott	38		lbw b Alderman	4
*I.V.A.Richards	c Border b Waugh	12	(6)	lbw b Waugh	63
A.L.Logie	lbw b Alderman	10	(10)	c Border b Waugh	17
†P.J.L.Dujon	c Healy b Waugh	26	(5)	c Wood b Alderman	46
M.D.Marshall	c Jones b Waugh	7	(7)	c Alderman b Waugh	19
C.E.L.Ambrose	lbw b McDermott	44	(8)	c Marsh b McDermott	5
C.A.Walsh	not out	30	(9)	c Marsh b Waugh	6
B.P.Patterson	lbw b Alderman	13		not out	3
Extras	(B1, LB4, NB3)	8		(LB1, NB16)	17
Total		**280**		**(9 wickets declared)**	**361**

AUSTRALIA

D.C.Boon	run out	23	(2)	lbw b Marshall	20
G.R.Marsh	b Patterson	36	(1)	b Patterson	1
D.M.Jones	b Ambrose	28		c sub (R.A.Harper) b Ambrose	18
G.M.Wood	c Haynes b Patterson	12		c Ambrose b Walsh	7
*A.R.Border	b Ambrose	0		c Haynes b Patterson	20
S.R.Waugh	c Greenidge b Ambrose	42		c sub (R.A.Harper) b Ambrose	3
†I.A.Healy	lbw b Patterson	4		c Hooper b Walsh	8
P.L.Taylor	c Greenidge b Ambrose	14		not out	18
C.J.McDermott	c Marshall b Patterson	28		c sub ‡ b Patterson	0
M.G.Hughes	not out	21		c Dujon b Patterson	4
T.M.Alderman	b Walsh	3		c Dujon b Patterson	0
Extras	(B2, LB14, NB15)	31		(B4, LB5, NB6)	15
Total		**242**			**114**

AUSTRALIA	O	M	R	W	O	M	R	W	FALL OF WICKETS			
										WI	A	WI	A
Hughes	14	3	52	0	24	8	71	0	*Wkt*	*1st*	*1st*	*2nd*	*2nd*
Alderman	32.1	9	68	4	36	12	78	3					
McDermott	19	3	62	3	(4) 26	3	78	1	1st	68	40	38	7
Waugh	21	3	77	3	(3) 24	5	92	5	2nd	68	103	92	30
Taylor	7	3	16	0	(6) 9	1	41	0	3rd	114	117	191	56
Border					(5) 1	1	0	0	4th	137	117	284	58
									5th	147	155	317	64
WEST INDIES									6th	166	161	324	75
Marshall	30	8	68	0	9	3	12	1	7th	185	186	324	104
Ambrose	27	7	60	4	(3) 13	5	21	2	8th	199	190	335	104
Walsh	17.3	3	49	1	(4) 16	7	21	2	9th	256	234	356	114
Patterson	20	2	49	4	(2) 15.1	3	39	5	10th	280	242	–	114
Richards					4	1	12	0					

Umpires: A.R.Crafter (26) and P.J.McConnell (12).   ‡ (K.L.T.Arthurton)

Close: 1st day – WI(1) 246-8 (Ambrose 37, Walsh 16); 2nd – A(1) 121-4 (Wood 4, Waugh 4); 3rd – WI(2) 69-1 (Greenidge 25, Richardson 17); 4th – WI(2) 361-9 (Greenidge 36, Patterson 3).

AUSTRALIA v WEST INDIES 1988-89 (4th Test)

At Sydney Cricket Ground on 26, 27, 28, 29, 30 January.
Toss: West Indies.   Result: AUSTRALIA won by seven wickets.
Debuts: Australia – T.V.Hohns, M.A.Taylor.

West Indies lost their second successive Test at Sydney as Australia gained the fourth win in their last six Tests there. Border was the astonished architect of victory. His left-arm finger spin having claimed 16 wickets in his first 100 Tests (best 3 for 20), he finished with the record match analysis by an Australian captain: 11 for 96. He also grafted 310 minutes (262 balls) for the slowest Test fifty by an Australian, scoring 75 in 386 minutes. Boon (499 minutes) scored his seventh Test hundred and Haynes his 11th. Walsh took his 100th wicket in 29 Tests and Marshall captured five wickets in an innings for the 19th time.

WEST INDIES

C.G.Greenidge	c Waugh b P.L.Taylor	56	c and b Hughes		4
D.L.Haynes	c Boon b Hohns	75	c M.A.Taylor b Border		143
R.B.Richardson	c P.L.Taylor b Border	28	c Hughes b P.L.Taylor		22
C.L.Hooper	c Marsh b Border	0	c Jones b Hohns		35
*I.V.A.Richards	c Boon b Border	11	c Jones b Hohns		4
A.L.Logie	b Border	0	c P.L.Taylor b Hohns		6
†P.J.L.Dujon	c Hughes b Border	18	run out		9
R.A.Harper	c P.L.Taylor b Border	17	lbw b Border		12
M.D.Marshall	c Marsh b Border	9	c P.L.Taylor b Border		3
C.E.L.Ambrose	c Jones b P.L.Taylor	1	c Boon b Border		5
C.A.Walsh	not out	4	not out		7
Extras	(B1, W1, NB3)	5	(B1, W1, NB4)		6
Total		**224**			**256**

AUSTRALIA

G.R.Marsh	c Dujon b Marshall	2	(2) b Richards		23
M.A.Taylor	b Ambrose	25	(1) c Haynes b Ambrose		3
D.C.Boon	c Dujon b Walsh	149	c Harper b Marshall		10
D.M.Jones	b Richards	29	not out		24
*A.R.Border	b Marshall	75	not out		16
S.R.Waugh	not out	55			
†I.A.Healy	c Logie b Marshall	11			
P.L.Taylor	lbw b Marshall	0			
T.V.Hohns	b Marshall	0			
M.G.Hughes	c Dujon b Walsh	12			
T.M.Alderman	run out	9			
Extras	(B6, LB14, NB14)	34	(B3, LB1, NB2)		6
Total		**401**	(3 wickets)		**82**

AUSTRALIA	O	M	R	W		O	M	R	W		FALL OF WICKETS			
												WI	A	WI	A
Alderman	10	2	17	0	(2)	2	0	6	0	Wkt	1st	1st	2nd	2nd
Hughes	10	3	28	0	(1)	18	6	29	1	1st	90	14	17	3
P.L.Taylor	25.2	8	65	2	(4)	29	4	91	1	2nd	144	43	56	16
Hohns	24	8	49	1	(5)	34	11	69	3	3rd	156	114	167	55
Border	26	10	46	7	(6)	18.4	3	50	4	4th	174	284	188	–
Waugh	4	0	18	0	(3)	3	0	10	0	5th	174	335	198	–
										6th	174	355	225	–
WEST INDIES										7th	199	357	232	–
Marshall	31	16	29	5		8	2	17	1	8th	213	357	244	–
Ambrose	33	5	78	1		7	1	16	1	9th	220	388	247	–
Harper	37	9	86	0						10th	224	401	256	–
Walsh	22.5	5	48	2		3	0	9	0					
Hooper	37	10	72	0	(3)	10.3	2	24	0					
Richards	31	1	68	1	(5)	7	2	12	1					

Umpires: L.J.King (1) and T.A.Prue (2).

Close: 1st day – WI(1) 224 all out; 2nd – A(1) 200-3 (Boon 110, Border 18); 3rd – A(1) 401 all out; 4th – WI(1) 254-9 (Ambrose 4, Walsh 6).

AUSTRALIA v WEST INDIES 1988-89 (5th Test)

At Adelaide Oval on 3, 4, 5, 6, 7 February.
Toss: Australia.   Result: MATCH DRAWN.
Debuts: None.

Jones (538 minutes, 346 balls, 16 fours) scored Australia's seventh double century against West Indies and the first at Adelaide. His partnership of 114 with Hughes, who recorded his highest first-class score off 118 balls, is Australia's record for the ninth wicket in this series. Richardson reached his eighth Test hundred off 137 balls, adding 167 with Haynes in a West Indies record second-wicket stand against Australia until 1990-91. Greenidge, at his 32nd attempt in five tours, scored his first hundred in Australia (the 16th of his Test career). Haynes exceeded 5,000 runs in his 81st Test and set a new record aggregate for West Indies in Australia with 537 (beating R.B.Kanhai's 503 in 1960-61). West Indies equalled their own world record by conceding 40 no-balls during their first innings.

AUSTRALIA

G.R.Marsh	c Dujon b Ambrose	21	(2)	c Dujon b Ambrose	79
M.A.Taylor	run out	3	(1)	run out	36
D.C.Boon	c Richardson b Ambrose	34		not out	55
D.M.Jones	run out	216		lbw b Richards	6
*A.R.Border	b Marshall	64	(6)	not out	6
S.R.Waugh	c Dujon b Walsh	12	(5)	run out	8
†I.A.Healy	lbw b Walsh	0			
T.V.Hohns	c Hooper b Walsh	9			
T.B.A.May	c Richardson b Ambrose	24			
M.G.Hughes	not out	72			
M.R.Whitney	c Dujon b Patterson	2			
Extras	(LB18, NB40)	58		(B11, LB13, NB10)	34
Total		**515**		**(4 wickets declared)**	**224**

WEST INDIES

C.G.Greenidge	b Whitney	12		c Boon b May	104
D.L.Haynes	run out	83		c Healy b Whitney	15
R.B.Richardson	c Jones b Whitney	106		c Border b Whitney	22
C.L.Hooper	c Healy b Whitney	2		b May	0
*I.V.A.Richards	c Boon b Whitney	69		not out	68
A.L.Logie	c Healy b Hohns	21		not out	2
†P.J.L.Dujon	b Hohns	28			
M.D.Marshall	c Marsh b Whitney	0			
C.E.L.Ambrose	c Boon b Whitney	9			
C.A.Walsh	c Healy b Whitney	4			
B.P.Patterson	not out	9			
Extras	(B6, LB10, NB10)	26		(B3, LB7, W1, NB11)	22
Total		**369**		**(4 wickets)**	**233**

WEST INDIES	O	M	R	W	O	M	R	W		FALL OF WICKETS			
										A	WI	A	WI
Marshall	23	3	67	1	12	2	30	0					
Patterson	30.5	1	130	1	(4) 8	1	29	0	Wkt	1st	1st	2nd	2nd
Ambrose	26	4	93	3	(2) 15	2	44	1	1st	7	19	98	21
Walsh	33	5	120	3	(3) 13	2	26	0	2nd	64	186	176	87
Hooper	3	0	14	0	(6) 3	1	7	0	3rd	75	190	187	89
Richards	25	1	73	0	(5) 24	3	64	1	4th	289	231	213	212
									5th	311	293	–	–
									6th	311	315	–	–
AUSTRALIA									7th	333	315	–	–
Hughes	15	0	86	0	9	5	20	0	8th	383	331	–	–
Whitney	30	6	89	7	20	4	60	2	9th	497	346	–	–
May	16	6	42	0	(5) 23	3	60	2	10th	515	369	–	–
Waugh	3	0	17	0	(3) 9	3	23	0					
Hohns	47.4	9	106	2	(4) 15	3	56	0					
Border	10	2	13	0	5	3	4	0					

Umpires: R.J.Evans (1) and P.J.McConnell (13).

Close: 1st day – A(1) 283-3 (Jones 131, Border 61); 2nd – WI(1) 74-1 (Haynes 22, Richardson 39); 3rd – WI(1) 338-8 (Dujon 12, Walsh 2); 4th – A(2) 224-4 (Boon 55, Border 6).

NEW ZEALAND v PAKISTAN 1988-89 (2nd Test)

At Basin Reserve, Wellington, on 10, 11, 12, 13, 14 February.
Toss: Pakistan.   Result: MATCH DRAWN.
Debuts: Pakistan – Aqib Javed.

Aqib Javed (16 years 189 days) became the second youngest Test cricketer after Mushtaq Mohammad (15 years 124 days). Martin Crowe (592 minutes, 410 balls, 16 fours), the first to score ten Test hundreds for New Zealand, registered his country's highest score against Pakistan and equalled the record score by a New Zealander in a Wellington Test. Shoaib batted 720 minutes (the sixth-longest innings in Tests) for his highest Test score; the longest first-class innings in New Zealand (beating C.T.Radley's 648 minutes in *Test No. 819*), it came from 516 balls and included a six and 17 fours. He also recorded the slowest 150 in Tests (624 minutes). Shoaib's second Test hundred came from 273 balls in 379 minutes and he joined Miandad in a series record third-wicket stand of 220 as his partner completed his 20th Test hundred in 276 minutes from 219 balls.

NEW ZEALAND

R.H.Vance	c Salim Yousuf b Mudassar	5	(2) lbw b Imran		44
*J.G.Wright	c Salim Yousuf b Mudassar	7	(1) c Miandad b Imran		19
A.H.Jones	c Shoaib b Salim Jaffer	86	c sub (Ramiz Raja) b Salim Jaffer		39
M.D.Crowe	c Miandad b Salim Jaffer	174	lbw b Salim Jaffer		0
D.N.Patel	lbw b Imran	0	c Salim Yousuf b Salim Jaffer		2
J.J.Crowe	b Qadir	39	b Salim Jaffer		23
J.G.Bracewell	b Imran	15	lbw b Salim Jaffer		0
R.J.Hadlee	c Rizwan b Salim Jaffer	32	c sub (Ijaz Ahmed) b Imran		7
†I.D.S.Smith	not out	40	not out		29
D.K.Morrison	lbw b Imran	0	not out		1
E.J.Chatfield	run out	14			
Extras	(B10, LB14, NB11)	35	(B10, LB6, NB6)		22
Total		**447**	(8 wickets)		**186**

PAKISTAN

Mudassar Nazar	c and b Morrison	6
Rizwan-uz-Zaman	lbw b Hadlee	18
Shoaib Mohammad	b Hadlee	163
Javed Miandad	lbw b Hadlee	118
Salim Malik	c Smith b Bracewell	38
*Imran Khan	b Chatfield	71
Aamer Malik	not out	8
†Salim Yousuf	c Jones b Hadlee	4
Abdul Qadir	not out	0
Salim Jaffer	} did not bat	
Aqib Javed		
Extras	(B1, LB8, NB3)	12
Total	(7 wickets declared)	**438**

PAKISTAN	O	M	R	W	O	M	R	W		FALL OF WICKETS		
										NZ	P	NZ
Imran	46.4	18	75	3	17	8	34	3	*Wkt*	*1st*	*1st*	*2nd*
Salim Jaffer	34	5	94	3	(4) 17	4	40	5	1st	13	14	36
Mudassar	22	5	59	2					2nd	18	54	107
Aqib	34	5	103	0	(2) 13	1	57	0	3rd	167	274	108
Qadir	29	4	83	1	(3) 14	3	39	0	4th	168	325	117
Aamer	4	1	9	0					5th	282	422	128
									6th	321	430	132
NEW ZEALAND									7th	389	437	140
Hadlee	54	14	101	4					8th	398	–	180
Morrison	36	10	96	1					9th	399	–	–
Chatfield	53	21	82	1					10th	447	–	–
Bracewell	40	8	123	1								
Patel	12	3	27	0								

Umpires: R.S.Dunne (1) and S.J.Woodward (19).

Close: 1st day – NZ(1) 229-4 (M.D.Crowe 89, J.J.Crowe 22); 2nd – NZ(1) 447 all out; 3rd – P(1) 205-2 (Shoaib 89, Miandad 87); 4th – P(1) 401-4 (Shoaib 159, Imran 52).

The 1st Test at Carisbrook, Dunedin, scheduled for 3, 4, 5, 6, 7 February, was abandoned without a ball being bowled (see page 466).

NEW ZEALAND v PAKISTAN 1988-89 (3rd Test)

At Eden Park, Auckland, on 24, 25, 26, 27, 28 February.
Toss: Pakistan.   Result: MATCH DRAWN.
Debuts: None.

Their fifth successive draw in home Tests ensured that New Zealand had not lost a series in their own country during the 1980s. Pakistan's total, amassed in 808 minutes, was the highest in all Tests in New Zealand until 1990-91 and the record by either country in this series. Miandad (558 minutes, 465 balls, five sixes and 28 fours) registered his 21st century, his sixth double century, the second-highest Test score in New Zealand and the record score for this series. His stand of 248 with Shoaib (350 minutes, 254 balls, 17 fours) broke Pakistan's third-wicket record for this series set in the previous match. Imran completed 3,000 runs in his 75th Test and became the third player after I.T.Botham and Kapil Dev to score 3,000 runs and take 300 wickets. Boock, whose 70 overs was the second-longest spell for New Zealand in Test cricket, returned the most expensive analysis by a New Zealander in first-class cricket, while Chatfield's 65 overs represented the longest spell by a medium-pace bowler for New Zealand. Martin Crowe completed 3,000 runs in his 44th Test. Qadir took five or more wickets in a Test innings for the 15th time. Hadlee extended his record of Test wickets to 396 from 79 matches.

PAKISTAN

Mudassar Nazar	lbw b Hadlee	5
Rizwan-uz-Zaman	c J.J.Crowe b Boock	15
Shoaib Mohammad	run out	112
Javed Miandad	c Smith b Chatfield	271
Aamer Malik	c J.J.Crowe b Bracewell	56
Salim Malik	not out	80
*Imran Khan	not out	69
†Salim Yousuf		
Abdul Qadir		
Tausif Ahmed	did not bat	
Salim Jaffer		
Extras	(LB7, NB1)	8
Total	(5 wickets declared)	**616**

NEW ZEALAND

R.H.Vance	c Shoaib b Qadir	68	(2)	c Salim Yousuf b Mudassar	31
*J.G.Wright	c Rizwan b Tausif	2	(1)	c Salim Yousuf b Qadir	36
A.H.Jones	run out	47		c Salim Yousuf b Mudassar	0
M.D.Crowe	c Salim Yousuf b Salim Jaffer	78		not out	9
S.L.Boock	c Mudassar b Qadir	8			
M.J.Greatbatch	b Qadir	76	(5)	not out	13
J.J.Crowe	c Miandad b Qadir	33			
J.G.Bracewell	b Qadir	0			
†I.D.S.Smith	c Mudassar b Imran	58			
R.J.Hadlee	not out	14			
E.J.Chatfield	c Aamer b Qadir	0			
Extras	(B7, LB2, NB10)	19		(NB10)	10
Total		**403**		(3 wickets)	**99**

NEW ZEALAND	O	M	R	W	O	M	R	W
Hadlee	28	7	68	1				
Chatfield	65	14	158	1				
Boock	70	10	229	1				
Bracewell	37	4	138	1				
Jones	3	0	16	0				
PAKISTAN								
Salim Jaffer	18	6	44	1	8	4	18	0
Imran	34	9	76	1	5.4	1	13	0
Tausif	69	28	106	1	12	4	23	0
Qadir	58.1	18	160	6	16	7	27	1
Shoaib	2	1	1	0	1	0	5	0
Mudassar	3	1	7	0	8	2	13	2

FALL OF WICKETS

Wkt	P 1st	NZ 1st	NZ 2nd
1st	10	13	68
2nd	44	122	71
3rd	292	123	76
4th	439	132	–
5th	480	286	–
6th	–	294	–
7th	–	294	–
8th	–	388	–
9th	–	388	–
10th	–	403	–

Umpires: B.L.Aldridge (5) and S.J.Woodward (20).

Close: 1st day – P(1) 289-2 (Shoaib 110, Miandad 154); 2nd – P(1) 497-5 (Salim Malik 22, Imran 8); 3rd – NZ(1) 133-4 (M.D.Crowe 3, Greatbatch 0); 4th – NZ(1) 360-7 (J.J.Crowe 26, Smith 37).

WEST INDIES v INDIA 1988-89 (1st Test)

At Bourda, Georgetown, Guyana, on 25, 26, 27 (*no play*), 28 (*no play*), 29 (*no play*), 30 (*no play*) March.
Toss: India.   Result: MATCH DRAWN.
Debuts: West Indies – I.R.Bishop.

Even the conversion of the rest day (28 March) to a playing day could not prevent this Test, at the venue closest to the equator, from becoming the worst affected by weather in the Caribbean (until the following season). Richardson (459 minutes, 367 balls, 20 fours) recorded his highest first-class score and his ninth Test hundred. Arshad Ayub (off-spin) took five wickets in his first Test innings outside India.

WEST INDIES

C.G.Greenidge	b Sharma	82
D.L.Haynes	b Ayub	20
R.B.Richardson	c Shastri b Ayub	194
K.L.T.Arthurton	run out	9
*I.V.A.Richards	b Kapil Dev	5
I.R.Bishop	lbw b Kapil Dev	0
A.L.Logie	c and b Hirwani	46
†P.J.L.Dujon	lbw b Ayub	31
C.E.L.Ambrose	not out	12
W.K.M.Benjamin	c Sharma b Ayub	7
C.A.Walsh	b Ayub	6
Extras	(LB6, W4, NB15)	25
Total		**437**

INDIA

Arun Lal	c Richards b Walsh	9
N.S.Sidhu	not out	42
R.J.Shastri	not out	29
*D.B.Vengsarkar		
M.Azharuddin		
S.V.Manjrekar		
Kapil Dev	did not bat	
†K.S.More		
Arshad Ayub		
C.Sharma		
N.D.Hirwani		
Extras	(LB1, NB5)	6
Total	(1 wicket)	**86**

INDIA	O	M	R	W
Kapil Dev	28	8	66	2
Sharma	20	2	68	1
Shastri	33	6	87	0
Ayub	31	4	104	5
Hirwani	29	2	106	1

WEST INDIES	O	M	R	W
Ambrose	3	2	6	0
Bishop	9	3	15	0
Benjamin	11	2	27	0
Walsh	6	0	12	1
Richards	7	1	17	0
Arthurton	3	0	8	0

FALL OF WICKETS

Wkt	WI 1st	I 1st
1st	41	14
2nd	219	–
3rd	231	–
4th	270	–
5th	270	–
6th	357	–
7th	412	–
8th	413	–
9th	423	–
10th	437	–

Umpires: D.M.Archer (20) and L.H.Barker (10).

Close: 1st day – WI(1) 273-5 (Richardson 143, Logie 2); 2nd – I(1) 86-1 (Sidhu 42, Shastri 29); no further play.

WEST INDIES v INDIA 1988-89 (2nd Test)

At Kensington Oval, Bridgetown, Barbados, on 7, 8, 9, 11, 12 April.
Toss: West Indies.   Result: WEST INDIES won by eight wickets.
Debuts: None.

West Indies required only 35 minutes of the fifth day to complete their eighth successive victory in Bridgetown and protect their unbeaten record there since 1934-35. Sanjay Manjrekar (343 minutes, 221 balls, 15 fours), son of Vijay, scored his maiden hundred in his third Test. Kapil Dev's fourth run during a 26-ball innings of 34 enabled him to emulate I.T.Botham's achievement in scoring 4,000 runs and taking 300 wickets. Bishop's fast late out-swingers brought him six wickets in his second Test innings. Greenidge (236 minutes, 182 balls) scored his 17th Test hundred; it was his first in nine matches on his native island. Marshall overtook L.R.Gibbs' tally of 309 to become the leading West Indian Test wicket-taker. Shastri (441 minutes, 255 balls) contributed his eighth hundred. Haynes (177 minutes, 128 balls, 11 fours and three sixes) completed his 12th hundred and, with Richardson (who passed 3,000 runs in his 43rd Test), added 128 in 106 minutes.

INDIA

Arun Lal	c Dujon b Bishop	8	(2)	c Haynes b Walsh	15
N.S.Sidhu	c Richards b Walsh	9	(1)	c Logie b Marshall	0
R.J.Shastri	c Richardson b Bishop	6		c sub (W.Herbert) b Ambrose	107
*D.B.Vengsarkar	run out	20		c Dujon b Bishop	6
M.Azharuddin	c Ambrose b Bishop	61		c Dujon b Marshall	14
S.V.Manjrekar	c Greenidge b Bishop	108		c Logie b Ambrose	3
Kapil Dev	c Richardson b Bishop	34		c Dujon b Marshall	1
†K.S.More	c Dujon b Marshall	1		b Marshall	50
Arshad Ayub	c Richards b Bishop	32		b Marshall	0
C.Sharma	not out	12		c Dujon b Ambrose	21
N.D.Hirwani	c Haynes b Walsh	1		not out	1
Extras	(B2, LB5, NB22)	29		(B16, LB4, NB13)	33
Total		**321**			**251**

WEST INDIES

C.G.Greenidge	c Hirwani b Sharma	117		lbw b Sharma	6
D.L.Haynes	c Manjrekar b Shastri	27		not out	112
R.B.Richardson	c Sidhu b Ayub	93		b Ayub	59
K.L.T.Arthurton	b Hirwani	0		not out	11
*I.V.A.Richards	c sub (R.R.Singh) b Hirwani	1			
A.L.Logie	c Manjrekar b Shastri	26			
†P.J.L.Dujon	c Manjrekar b Shastri	33			
M.D.Marshall	not out	40			
C.E.L.Ambrose	c Kapil Dev b Shastri	3			
I.R.Bishop	lbw b Kapil Dev	8			
C.A.Walsh	b Kapil Dev	0			
Extras	(LB7, NB22)	29		(LB5, NB3)	8
Total		**377**		(2 wickets)	**196**

WEST INDIES	O	M	R	W		O	M	R	W	FALL OF WICKETS			
Marshall	22	0	56	1		26	5	60	5		I	WI	I	WI
Ambrose	26	5	84	0		20.3	3	66	3	*Wkt*	*1st*	*1st*	*2nd*	*2nd*
Bishop	25	5	87	6	(4)	24	7	55	1	1st	14	84	0	14
Walsh	23.2	5	69	2	(3)	20	6	34	1	2nd	22	201	23	142
Richards	9	3	18	0		6	0	16	0	3rd	27	201	32	–
Arthurton						1	1	0	0	4th	68	203	53	–
										5th	139	246	62	–
INDIA										6th	218	325	63	–
Kapil Dev	24.5	3	68	2		8	0	42	0	7th	219	325	195	–
Sharma	18	1	86	1		4	0	19	1	8th	303	354	195	–
Ayub	17	1	55	1		14	4	26	1	9th	320	377	245	–
Shastri	28	7	78	4	(5)	11	2	41	0	10th	321	377	251	–
Hirwani	24	1	83	2	(4)	10	0	56	0					
Manjrekar						1	0	7	0					

Umpires: D.M.Archer (21) and L.H.Barker (11).

Close: 1st day – I(1) 281-7 (Manjrekar 93, Ayub 25); 2nd – WI(1) 246-5 (Richardson 55); 3rd – I(2) 81-6 (Shastri 17, More 14); 4th – WI(2) 154-2 (Haynes 80, Arthurton 2).

WEST INDIES v INDIA 1988-89 (3rd Test)

At Queen's Park Oval, Port-of-Spain, Trinidad, on 15, 16, 17, 19, 20 April.
Toss: India.   Result: WEST INDIES won by 217 runs.
Debuts: None.

Marshall's outstanding match analysis of 11 for 89, his fourth of ten or more in a match, ensured that West Indies clinched this rubber before lunch on the fifth day. It was the first time India had been beaten in Port-of-Spain in six Tests since 1961-62. Dujon became the fifth wicket-keeper (the first West Indian) to make 200 dismissals. Richardson (352 minutes, 277 balls), bowled behind his legs, was the fifth West Indian to be dismissed for 99 in Test cricket. Kapil Dev claimed five wickets in a Test innings for the 20th time. In the second innings, Arun Lal (16) retired at 20 (hit behind the right ear when he turned his back on a short ball from Bishop) and resumed at 75.

WEST INDIES

C.G.Greenidge	c More b Kapil Dev	21	c More b Sharma		5
D.L.Haynes	c Raman b Shastri	65	c Shastri b Sharma		6
R.B.Richardson	c Hirwani b Ayub	15	b Kapil Dev		99
K.L.T.Arthurton	c sub (R.R.Singh) b Ayub	37	lbw b Kapil Dev		1
*I.V.A.Richards	b Ayub	19	c Manjrekar b Sharma		0
A.L.Logie	c More b Hirwani	87	c and b Hirwani		38
†P.J.L.Dujon	c Raman b Ayub	5	b Shastri		3
M.D.Marshall	st More b Ayub	18	lbw b Kapil Dev		26
C.E.L.Ambrose	c More b Kapil Dev	12	c More b Kapil Dev		16
I.R.Bishop	not out	11	not out		30
C.A.Walsh	c Sharma b Hirwani	6	b Kapil Dev		4
Extras	(B7, LB5, NB6)	18	(B3, LB24, W1, NB10)		38
Total		**314**			**266**

INDIA

Arun Lal	c Richards b Marshall	30	(2) c Dujon b Marshall		18
N.S.Sidhu	b Marshall	11	(1) c Dujon b Ambrose		1
R.J.Shastri	c Logie b Marshall	8	c Dujon b Bishop		15
*D.B.Vengsarkar	b Richards	2	(5) c Logie b Marshall		62
W.V.Raman	c Dujon b Walsh	17	(4) lbw b Marshall		15
S.V.Manjrekar	lbw b Marshall	0	lbw b Marshall		1
Kapil Dev	c Dujon b Marshall	16	c Dujon b Bishop		4
†K.S.More	b Walsh	2	lbw b Marshall		42
Arshad Ayub	b Walsh	29	c Richards b Bishop		1
C.Sharma	not out	19	b Marshall		7
N.D.Hirwani	lbw b Walsh	0	not out		1
Extras	(B2, LB5, W1, NB8)	16	(B7, LB15, NB24)		46
Total		**150**			**213**

INDIA	O	M	R	W	O	M	R	W
Kapil Dev	19	6	45	2	25	5	58	5
Sharma	6	1	23	0	13	0	54	3
Ayub	52	11	117	5	18	1	50	0
Shastri	27	8	58	1	18	3	32	1
Hirwani	19.3	1	59	2	19	4	40	1
Raman					4	1	5	0

WEST INDIES	O	M	R	W	O	M	R	W
Ambrose	9	1	28	0	15	8	23	1
Bishop	11	4	16	0	25	8	81	3
Walsh	18	5	37	4	10	4	15	0
Marshall	17	7	34	5	19.5	2	55	6
Richards	12	3	28	1	8	0	13	0
Arthurton					4	2	4	0

FALL OF WICKETS

Wkt	WI 1st	I 1st	WI 2nd	I 2nd
1st	33	32	17	20
2nd	80	48	19	60
3rd	118	51	23	64
4th	146	61	26	67
5th	216	68	100	75
6th	238	88	119	92
7th	269	93	180	190
8th	294	99	204	194
9th	302	148	250	212
10th	314	150	266	213

Umpires: C.E.Cumberbatch (9) and A.E.Weekes (3).

Close: 1st day – WI(1) 237-5 (Logie 63, Dujon 5); 2nd – I(1) 122-8 (Ayub 18, Sharma 7); 3rd – WI(2) 199-7 (Richardson 77, Ambrose 13); 4th – I(2) 161-6 (Vengsarkar 40, More 25).

WEST INDIES v INDIA 1988-89 (4th Test)

At Sabina Park, Kingston, Jamaica, on 28, 29, 30 April, 2, 3 May.
Toss: West Indies.   Result: WEST INDIES won by seven wickets.
Debuts: India – M.Venkataramana.

On a pitch of unpredictable bounce, India extended another unequal contest into the final morning only with the assistance of a cloudburst which washed out the final session of the fourth day. Sidhu (358 minutes, 237 balls), whose 286 against Jamaica on an adjacent pitch the previous weekend was the highest score for an Indian team overseas, retired hurt (when 116) with a bruised right hand at 219 and resumed at 252. Richardson (482 minutes, 314 balls, 20 fours) scored his tenth hundred (the sixth innings of over 90 in his last seven Tests) and finished the rubber with an aggregate of 619 runs. His fourth-wicket stand of 235 with Richards (305 minutes, 178 balls, 13 fours and a six) was ended by a controversial dismissal which resulted in a 35-minute mini riot. The West Indies captain's 24th hundred was his first in eight Tests at Kingston. Walsh returned his best innings and match analyses. Logie ended the series with a six over long-on.

INDIA

N.S.Sidhu	c Richards b Walsh	116	(2) c Greenidge b Walsh		0
Arun Lal	c Richards b Marshall	7	(1) c Greenidge b Bishop		26
R.J.Shastri	c Richards b Bishop	5	lbw b Bishop		0
*D.B.Vengsarkar	c Dujon b Bishop	12	(5) b Bishop		8
M.Azharuddin	c Richards b Walsh	25	(6) b Walsh		13
S.V.Manjrekar	c Logie b Walsh	47	(4) c Haynes b Walsh		41
†K.S.More	b Walsh	6	(8) c Dujon b Walsh		2
Kapil Dev	c Ambrose b Walsh	23	(7) c Richards b Bishop		13
Arshad Ayub	c Arthurton b Walsh	2	run out		14
C.Sharma	c Arthurton b Ambrose	6	b Marshall		21
M.Venkataramana	not out	0	not out		0
Extras	(B1, LB7, W1, NB31)	40	(B1, LB2, NB11)		14
Total		**289**			**152**

WEST INDIES

C.G.Greenidge	c Arun Lal b Kapil Dev	0	c More b Kapil Dev		12
D.L.Haynes	c Shastri b Kapil Dev	15	st More b Venkataramana		35
R.B.Richardson	b Kapil Dev	156	st More b Shastri		3
K.L.T.Arthurton	c Azharuddin b Sharma	20	not out		0
*I.V.A.Richards	c More b Kapil Dev	110			
A.L.Logie	lbw b Kapil Dev	11	(5) not out		6
†P.J.L.Dujon	b Ayub	11			
M.D.Marshall	b Kapil Dev	0			
C.E.L.Ambrose	c More b Sharma	10			
I.R.Bishop	not out	6			
C.A.Walsh	c Venkataramana b Ayub	4			
Extras	(B10, LB9, W3, NB19)	41	(LB3, NB1)		4
Total		**384**	(3 wickets)		**60**

WEST INDIES	O	M	R	W		O	M	R	W		FALL OF WICKETS			
Ambrose	13.2	1	46	1	(4)	7	0	20	0		I	WI	I	WI
Bishop	26	8	55	2	(1)	17	3	61	4	Wkt	1st	1st	2nd	2nd
Walsh	29	8	62	6	(2)	17	7	39	4	1st	35	1	0	31
Marshall	19	4	56	1	(3)	7.3	0	29	1	2nd	64	32	1	50
Richards	9	1	36	0						3rd	97	86	75	54
Arthurton	6	0	26	0						4th	142	321	75	–
										5th	252	343	88	–
INDIA										6th	252	344	100	–
Kapil Dev	33	7	84	6		9	2	22	1	7th	256	344	107	–
Sharma	27	2	100	2		2	0	16	0	8th	279	364	113	–
Ayub	39.5	12	99	2						9th	285	378	151	–
Venkataramana	11	1	48	0		0.4	0	10	1	10th	289	384	152	–
Shastri	13	1	34	0	(3)	7	2	9	1					

Umpires: D.M.Archer (22) and S.A.Bucknor (1).

Close: 1st day – I(1) 226-4 (Manjrekar 24, More 3); 2nd – WI(1) 170-3 (Richardson 85, Richards 28); 3rd – I(2) 32-2 (Arun Lal 15, Manjrekar 14); 4th – WI(2) 31-1 (Haynes 17).

ENGLAND v AUSTRALIA 1989 (1st Test)

At Headingley, Leeds, on 8, 9, 10, 12, 13 June.
Toss: England.   Result: AUSTRALIA won by 210 runs.
Debuts: Australia – G.D.Campbell.

Omitting their specialist slow bowler and ignoring the groundsman's pitch predictions, England conspired to lose to Australia at Leeds for the first time since 1964. This was the ninth consecutive Yorkshire Test to produce an outright result with England losing six times in seven years. Australia's total has been exceeded only once in all first-class matches at Headingley, Somerset scoring 630 in 1901. Taylor (393 minutes, 315 balls, 16 fours) became the 16th Australian to score a hundred in his first Test against England. Waugh (309 minutes, 242 balls, 24 fours) reached his hundred off 124 balls and completed the first instance of two Australians scoring their first centuries against England in the same Test innings since 1978-79. Lamb (279 minutes, 205 balls, 24 fours) completed 3,000 runs in his 57th Test. His first hundred against Australia was his ninth in Tests (all scored in England). Alderman captured ten wickets in a Test for the first time. Border exceeded the world record of G.St A.Sobers by captaining his country for the 40th consecutive match. Gower became the first to survive a sequence of 100 Test innings without a 'duck'.

AUSTRALIA

G.R.Marsh	lbw b DeFreitas	16	(2)	c Russell b Foster	6
M.A.Taylor	lbw b Foster	136	(1)	c Broad b Pringle	60
D.C.Boon	c Russell b Foster	9		lbw b DeFreitas	43
*A.R.Border	c Foster b DeFreitas	66		not out	60
D.M.Jones	c Russell b Newport	79		not out	40
S.R.Waugh	not out	177			
†I.A.Healy	c and b Newport	16			
M.G.Hughes	c Russell b Foster	71			
G.F.Lawson	not out	10			
G.D.Campbell	} did not bat				
T.M.Alderman					
Extras	(LB13, W1, NB7)	21		(B2, LB5, W9, NB5)	21
Total	**(7 wickets declared)**	**601**		**(3 wickets declared)**	**230**

ENGLAND

G.A.Gooch	lbw b Alderman	13	lbw b Hughes	68
B.C.Broad	b Hughes	37	lbw b Alderman	7
K.J.Barnett	lbw b Alderman	80	c Taylor b Alderman	34
A.J.Lamb	c Boon b Alderman	125	c Boon b Alderman	4
*D.I.Gower	c Healy b Lawson	26	c Healy b Lawson	34
R.A.Smith	lbw b Alderman	66	c Border b Lawson	0
D.R.Pringle	lbw b Campbell	6	c Border b Alderman	0
P.J.Newport	c Boon b Lawson	36	c Marsh b Alderman	8
†R.C.Russell	c Marsh b Lawson	15	c Healy b Hughes	2
P.A.J.DeFreitas	lbw b Alderman	1	b Hughes	21
N.A.Foster	not out	2	not out	1
Extras	(B5, LB7, W1, NB10)	23	(B4, LB3, NB5)	12
Total		**430**		**191**

ENGLAND	O	M	R	W		O	M	R	W		FALL OF WICKETS			
DeFreitas	45.3	8	140	2	(2)	18	2	76	1		A	E	A	E
Foster	46	14	109	3	(1)	19	4	65	1	Wkt	1st	1st	2nd	2nd
Newport	39	5	153	2	(4)	5	2	22	0	1st	44	35	14	17
Pringle	33	5	123	0	(3)	12.5	1	60	1	2nd	57	81	97	67
Gooch	9	1	31	0						3rd	174	195	129	77
Barnett	6	0	32	0						4th	273	243	–	134
										5th	411	323	–	134
AUSTRALIA										6th	441	338	–	153
Alderman	37	7	107	5		20	7	44	5	7th	588	392	–	153
Lawson	34.5	6	105	3		11	2	58	2	8th	–	421	–	166
Campbell	14	0	82	1		10	0	42	0	9th	–	424	–	170
Hughes	28	7	92	1		9.2	2	36	3	10th	–	430	–	191
Waugh	6	2	27	0										
Border	2	1	5	0	(5)	5	3	4	0					

Umpires: J.W.Holder (2) and D.R.Shepherd (8)

Close: 1st day – A(1) 207-3 (Taylor 96, Jones 10); 2nd – A(1) 580-6 (Waugh 174, Hughes 63); 3rd – E(1) 284-4 (Lamb 103, Smith 16); 4th – A(2) 158-3 (Border 31, Jones 12).

ENGLAND v AUSTRALIA 1989 (2nd Test)

At Lord's, London, on 22, 23, 24, 26, 27 June.
Toss: England.   Result: AUSTRALIA won by six wickets.
Debuts: None.

For the first time since 1948 Australia won successive matches of a series in England. Despite an heroic fightback on the last two days, England again succumbed to the hoodoo which affects Ashes encounters at Lord's, this defeat being their 11th in 19 matches in this series there and the sixth since their last victory in 1934. Waugh (329 minutes, 249 balls, 17 fours) exceeded 150 for the second time in successive innings. Australia's last five wickets amassed 293 runs, with Lawson plundering his highest score in first-class cricket. The stand of 130 in 108 minutes between Waugh and Lawson was Australia's second-highest for the ninth wicket in all Test cricket. Alderman took his 100th wicket in 26 Tests. Gower (269 minutes, 198 balls, 16 fours), having stormed out of Saturday evening's press conference to attend the theatre, defiantly recorded his 15th hundred in Tests and his seventh against Australia. Waugh completed the victory with a boundary which took his undefeated aggregate for the series to 350. Border, whose second innings ended with a catch by a member of the MCC groundstaff at long-leg, became the first to captain Australia to victory at Lord's twice. An attendance of 89,042 attracted (then) record receipts of £1,273,826.

ENGLAND

G.A.Gooch	c Healy b Waugh	60	lbw b Alderman	0
B.C.Broad	lbw b Alderman	18	b Lawson	20
K.J.Barnett	c Boon b Hughes	14	c Jones b Alderman	3
M.W.Gatting	c Boon b Hughes	0	lbw b Alderman	22
*D.I.Gower	b Lawson	57	c Border b Hughes	106
R.A.Smith	c Hohns b Lawson	32	b Alderman	96
J.E.Emburey	b Alderman	0	(8) not out	36
†R.C.Russell	not out	64	(7) c Boon b Lawson	29
N.A.Foster	c Jones b Hughes	16	lbw b Alderman	4
P.W.Jarvis	c Marsh b Hughes	6	lbw b Alderman	5
G.R.Dilley	c Border b Alderman	7	c Boon b Hughes	24
Extras	(LB9, NB3)	12	(B6, LB6, NB2)	14
Total		**286**		**359**

AUSTRALIA

G.R.Marsh	c Russell b Dilley	3	(2) b Dilley	1
M.A.Taylor	lbw b Foster	62	(1) c Gooch b Foster	27
D.C.Boon	c Gooch b Dilley	94	not out	58
*A.R.Border	c Smith b Emburey	35	c sub (R.J.Sims) b Foster	1
D.M.Jones	lbw b Foster	27	c Russell b Foster	0
S.R.Waugh	not out	152	not out	21
†I.A.Healy	c Russell b Jarvis	3		
M.G.Hughes	c Gooch b Foster	30		
T.V.Hohns	b Emburey	21		
G.F.Lawson	c Broad b Emburey	74		
T.M.Alderman	lbw b Emburey	8		
Extras	(LB11, NB8)	19	(B3, LB4, NB4)	11
Total		**528**	(4 wickets)	**119**

AUSTRALIA	O	M	R	W		O	M	R	W		FALL OF WICKETS			
Alderman	20.5	4	60	3		38	6	128	6		E	A	E	A
Lawson	27	8	88	2		39	10	99	2	*Wkt*	*1st*	*1st*	*2nd*	*2nd*
Hughes	23	6	71	4		24	8	44	2	1st	31	6	0	9
Waugh	9	3	49	1	(6) 7		2	20	0	2nd	52	151	18	51
Hohns	7	3	9	0		13	6	33	0	3rd	58	192	28	61
Border					(4) 9			23	0	4th	131	221	84	67
										5th	180	235	223	–
ENGLAND										6th	185	265	274	–
Dilley	34	3	141	2		10	2	27	1	7th	191	331	300	–
Foster	45	7	129	3		18	3	39	3	8th	237	381	304	–
Jarvis	31	3	150	1	(4) 9.2		0	38	0	9th	253	511	314	–
Emburey	42	12	88	4	(3) 3		3	8	0	10th	286	528	359	–
Gooch	6	2	9	0										

Umpires: H.D.Bird (40) and N.T.Plews (2).

Close: 1st day – A(1) 4-0 (Marsh 3, Taylor 1); 2nd – A(1) 276-6 (Waugh 35, Hughes 2); 3rd – E(2) 58-3 (Gatting 16, Gower 15); 4th – E(2) 322-9 (Emburey 21, Dilley 4).

ENGLAND v AUSTRALIA 1989 (3rd Test)

At Edgbaston, Birmingham, on 6, 7, 8, 10, 11 July.
Toss: Australia.   Result: MATCH DRAWN.
Debuts: England – A.R.C.Fraser.

The loss of 9 hours 38 minutes of play (142 overs) prevented England from even threatening to reduce their two-nil deficit. A bizarre variety of injuries and misfortunes removed Lamb, Foster, Gatting and Smith. The return of Tavaré, Botham and Curtis (after intervals of 47, 15 and 3 Tests respectively), plus the introduction of Fraser, amounted to the employment of 19 players in the first three Tests with England fielding three current Worcestershire representatives for the first time. Russell achieved England's first stumping for 14 matches. Border became the fourth batsman after Sobers, Boycott and Gavaskar to amass 8,000 runs in Tests. Batting on four separate days, Jones (396 minutes, 293 balls, 17 fours) compiled the highest innings for Australia at Birmingham, Australia's only previous hundred there being R.N.Harvey's 114 in 1961. Friday's 67 minutes of play included Waugh's first dismissal of the rubber, his tally of 393 runs without being dismissed being a record for Anglo-Australian Tests. Saturday's 127 minutes saw the first known instance of a ball producing seven leg-byes.

AUSTRALIA

G.R.Marsh	lbw b Botham	42	(2) b Jarvis		42
M.A.Taylor	st Russell b Emburey	43	(1) c Botham b Gooch		51
D.C.Boon	run out	38	not out		22
*A.R.Border	b Emburey	8			
D.M.Jones	c sub (I.Folley) b Fraser	157			
S.R.Waugh	b Fraser	43			
†I.A.Healy	b Fraser	2	(4) not out		33
M.G.Hughes	c Botham b Dilley	2			
T.V.Hohns	c Gooch b Dilley	40			
G.F.Lawson	b Fraser	12			
T.M.Alderman	not out	0			
Extras	(LB20, NB17)	37	(B4, LB4, NB2)		10
Total		**424**	(2 wickets)		**158**

ENGLAND

G.A.Gooch	lbw b Lawson	8
T.S.Curtis	lbw b Hughes	41
*D.I.Gower	lbw b Alderman	8
C.J.Tavaré	c Taylor b Alderman	2
K.J.Barnett	c Healy b Waugh	10
I.T.Botham	b Hughes	46
†R.C.Russell	c Taylor b Hohns	42
J.E.Emburey	c Boon b Lawson	26
A.R.C.Fraser	run out	12
G.R.Dilley	not out	11
P.W.Jarvis	lbw b Alderman	22
Extras	(B1, LB2, NB11)	14
Total		**242**

ENGLAND	O	M	R	W		O	M	R	W	FALL OF WICKETS			
Dilley	31	3	123	2		10	4	27	0		A	E	A
Jarvis	23	4	82	0	(4)	6	1	20	1	Wkt	1st	1st	2nd
Fraser	33	8	63	4	(2)	12	0	29	0	1st	88	17	81
Botham	26	5	75	1						2nd	94	42	109
Emburey	29	5	61	2	(3)	20	8	37	0	3rd	105	47	–
Gooch					(5)	14	5	30	1	4th	201	75	–
Curtis					(6)	3	0	7	0	5th	272	75	–
										6th	289	171	–
AUSTRALIA										7th	299	171	–
Alderman	26.3	6	61	3						8th	391	185	–
Lawson	21	4	54	2						9th	421	215	–
Waugh	11	3	38	1						10th	424	242	–
Hughes	22	4	68	2									
Hohns	16	8	18	1									

Umpires: H.D.Bird (41) and J.W.Holder (3).

Close: 1st day – A(1) 232-4 (Jones 71, Waugh 17); 2nd – A(1) 294-6 (Jones 101, Hughes 1); 3rd – A(1) 391-7 (Jones 141, Hohns 40); 4th – E(1) 185-7 (Emburey 2, Fraser 12).

ENGLAND v AUSTRALIA 1989 (4th Test)

At Old Trafford, Manchester, on 27, 28, 29, 31 July, 1 August.
Toss: England.   Result: AUSTRALIA won by nine wickets.
Debuts: None.

At 5.42 pm on the fifth evening Boon swept Cook to the boundary to reclaim the Ashes lost at The Oval on 2 September 1985. Border thus became only the second Australian captain to regain the urn in England, emulating W.M.Woodfull who achieved this feat in 1930 and 1934 on his 33rd and 37th birthdays. By coincidence, this Test, which brought Australia their 100th victory of the series, began on Border's 34th birthday. Before play on the final morning, the names were announced of 16 players (including Emburey, Foster and Robinson) who had accepted two-year contracts from the SACU to tour South Africa during the early weeks of 1990 and 1991. Smith (355 minutes, 285 balls, 15 fours) scored 55% of England's total. Russell and Emburey added 142 in 220 minutes (63.2 overs) to equal England's highest seventh-wicket partnership against Australia in any home Test but fell one run short of England's record for the series. Russell (351 minutes, 293 balls, 14 fours) was the fourth to score his maiden first-class century in a Test match for England (after H.Wood, A.J.L.Hill and S.C.Griffith), the first to do so against Australia, and the first to achieve this feat at home.

ENGLAND

G.A.Gooch	b Lawson	11	c Alderman b Lawson	13
T.S.Curtis	b Lawson	22	c Boon b Alderman	0
R.T.Robinson	lbw b Lawson	0	lbw b Lawson	12
R.A.Smith	c Hohns b Hughes	143	c Healy b Alderman	1
*D.I.Gower	lbw b Hohns	35	c Marsh b Lawson	15
I.T.Botham	b Hohns	0	lbw b Alderman	4
†R.C.Russell	lbw b Lawson	1	not out	128
J.E.Emburey	lbw b Hohns	5	b Alderman	64
N.A.Foster	c Border b Lawson	39	b Alderman	6
A.R.C.Fraser	lbw b Lawson	2	c Marsh b Hohns	3
N.G.B.Cook	not out	0	c Healy b Hughes	5
Extras	(LB2)	2	(LB6, W2, NB5)	13
Total		**260**		**264**

AUSTRALIA

M.A.Taylor	st Russell b Emburey	85	(2) not out	37
G.R.Marsh	c Russell b Botham	47	(1) c Robinson b Emburey	31
D.C.Boon	b Fraser	12	not out	10
*A.R.Border	c Russell b Foster	80		
D.M.Jones	b Botham	69		
S.R.Waugh	c Curtis b Fraser	92		
†I.A.Healy	lbw b Foster	0		
T.V.Hohns	c Gower b Cook	17		
M.G.Hughes	b Cook	3		
G.F.Lawson	b Fraser	17		
T.M.Alderman	not out	6		
Extras	(B5, LB7, W1, NB6)	19	(NB3)	3
Total		**447**	(1 wicket)	**81**

AUSTRALIA	O	M	R	W		O	M	R	W		FALL OF WICKETS			
												E	A	E	A
Alderman	25	13	49	0	(2)	27	7	66	5			E	A	E	A
Lawson	33	11	72	6	(1)	31	8	81	3	*Wkt*	*1st*	*1st*	*2nd*	*2nd*
Hughes	17	6	55	1	(4)	14.4	2	45	1	1st	23	135	10	62
Hohns	22	7	59	3	(3)	26	15	37	1	2nd	23	143	25	–
Waugh	6	1	23	0	(6)	4	0	17	0	3rd	57	154	27	–
Border					(5)	8	2	12	0	4th	132	274	28	–
										5th	140	362	38	–
ENGLAND										6th	147	362	59	–
Foster	34	12	74	2		5	2	5	0	7th	158	413	201	–
Fraser	36.5	4	95	3		10	0	28	0	8th	232	423	223	–
Emburey	45	9	118	1		13	3	30	1	9th	252	423	255	–
Cook	28	6	85	2		4.5	0	18	0	10th	260	447	264	–
Botham	24	6	63	2										

Umpires: J.H.Hampshire (1) and B.J.Meyer (21).

Close: 1st day – E(1) 224-7 (Smith 112, Foster 36); 2nd – A(1) 219-3 (Border 19, Jones 49); 3rd – A(1) 441-9 (Lawson 13, Alderman 5); 4th – E(2) 123-6 (Russell 47, Emburey 23).

ENGLAND v AUSTRALIA 1989 (5th Test)

At Trent Bridge, Nottingham, on 10, 11, 12, 14 August.
Toss: Australia.   Result: AUSTRALIA won by an innings and 180 runs.
Debuts: England – M.A.Atherton, D.E.Malcolm.

At 4.18 on the fourth afternoon Border's underrated team emulated the 1948 Australians by completing their fourth victory on English soil. It was the largest of only four innings defeats in this series achieved by Australia in the course of 128 Tests in England. Australia batted until 11.56 on the third morning in compiling their highest total at Trent Bridge. The partnership of 329 between Marsh (430 minutes, 382 balls, 15 fours) and Taylor (550 minutes, 461 balls, 23 fours) set first-wicket records for all Tests in England (beating 290 by G.Pullar and M.C.Cowdrey in *Test No. 496*) and for all Anglo-Australian Tests, surpassing 323 by J.B.Hobbs and W.Rhodes (*119*). The ninth pair to bat throughout an uninterrupted day of Test cricket, they were the first to do so in England. Taylor recorded his first double century in first-class cricket (509 minutes, 430 balls) and Australia's first against England since 1970-71. Border overtook Boycott's aggregate of 8,114 runs in Test cricket to take second position behind Gavaskar's 10,122. The 61 extras conceded by England constituted a record for this series and for any Test in England.

AUSTRALIA

G.R.Marsh	c Botham b Cook	138
M.A.Taylor	st Russell b Cook	219
D.C.Boon	st Russell b Cook	73
A.R.Border	not out	65
D.M.Jones	c Gower b Fraser	22
S.R.Waugh	c Gower b Malcolm	0
I.A.Healy	b Fraser	5
T.V.Hohns	not out	19
M.G.Hughes		
G.F.Lawson	} did not bat	
T.M.Alderman		
Extras	(B6, LB23, W3, NB29)	61
Total	(6 wickets declared)	**602**

ENGLAND

T.S.Curtis	lbw b Alderman	2	(2)	lbw b Alderman	6
M.D.Moxon	c Waugh b Alderman	0	(5)	b Alderman	18
M.A.Atherton	lbw b Alderman	0		c and b Hohns	47
R.A.Smith	c Healy b Alderman	101		b Hughes	26
D.I.Gower	c Healy b Lawson	11	(1)	b Lawson	5
R.C.Russell	c Healy b Lawson	20		b Lawson	1
E.E.Hemmings	b Alderman	38		lbw b Hughes	35
A.R.C.Fraser	b Hohns	29		b Hohns	1
I.T.Botham	c Waugh b Hohns	12		absent hurt	–
N.G.B.Cook	not out	2	(9)	not out	7
D.E.Malcolm	c Healy b Hughes	9	(10)	b Hughes	5
Extras	(LB18, NB13)	31		(B3, LB6, W1, NB6)	16
Total		**255**			**167**

ENGLAND	O	M	R	W	O	M	R	W	FALL OF WICKETS			
										A	E	E
Fraser	52.3	18	108	2					Wkt	1st	1st	2nd
Malcolm	44	2	166	1					1st	329	1	5
Botham	30	4	103	0					2nd	430	1	13
Hemmings	33	9	81	0					3rd	502	14	67
Cook	40	10	91	3					4th	543	37	106
Atherton	7	0	24	0					5th	553	119	114
									6th	560	172	120
AUSTRALIA									7th	–	214	134
Alderman	19	2	69	5	16	6	32	2	8th	–	243	160
Lawson	21	5	57	2	15	3	51	2	9th	–	244	167
Hohns	18	8	48	2	(4) 12	3	29	2	10th	–	255	–
Hughes	7.5	0	40	1	(3) 12.3	1	46	3				
Waugh	11	4	23	0								

Umpires: N.T.Plews (3) and D.R.Shepherd (9).

Close: 1st day – A(1) 301-0 (Marsh 125, Taylor 141); 2nd – A(1) 560-5 (Border 46, Healy 5); 3rd – E(1) 246-9 (Cook 1, Malcolm 1).

ENGLAND v AUSTRALIA 1989 (6th Test)

At Kennington Oval, London, on 24, 25, 26, 28, 29 August.
Toss: Australia.   Result: MATCH DRAWN.
Debuts: England – A.P.Igglesden, J.P.Stephenson.

A draw was the most likely outcome after rain had reduced the second and third days by a total of 96.4 overs and Border had delayed his declaration until lunch on the final day. England's total of 29 representatives in the six-match rubber has been exceeded only by their 30 in the five-match Ashes series of 1921; it extended the list of England Test players to 541 (235 still living). For the first time in the series England managed to take seven wickets in a day but they were unable to prevent Australia from becoming the first side to score 400 in eight successive Tests. Marsh and Jones completed 2,000 runs in Tests. When Gooch was lbw for the fifth time in the series, it was also the fifth time that Alderman had taken a wicket in his opening over. The latter took his tally for the summer to 41 (including 19 lbws and six instances of five or more in an innings) and he became the first bowler to take 40 wickets in a series twice, having taken 42 in England in 1981. Taylor's total of 839 runs (11 innings) has been bettered in an Ashes series only by Bradman and Hammond. The series produced (then) record receipts of £4,251,425 from an attendance of 342,954.

AUSTRALIA

G.R.Marsh	c Igglesden b Small	17	(2)	lbw b Igglesden	4
M.A.Taylor	c Russell b Igglesden	71	(1)	c Russell b Small	48
D.C.Boon	c Atherton b Small	46		run out	37
*A.R.Border	c Russell b Capel	76		not out	51
D.M.Jones	c Gower b Small	122		b Capel	50
S.R.Waugh	b Igglesden	14		not out	7
†I.A.Healy	c Russell b Pringle	44			
T.V.Hohns	c Russell b Pringle	30			
M.G.Hughes	lbw b Pringle	21			
G.F.Lawson	b Pringle	2			
T.M.Alderman	not out	6			
Extras	(B1, LB9, NB9)	19		(B2, LB7, NB13)	22
Total		**468**		(4 wickets declared)	**219**

ENGLAND

G.A.Gooch	lbw b Alderman	0		c and b Alderman	10
J.P.Stephenson	c Waugh b Alderman	25		lbw b Alderman	11
M.A.Atherton	c Healy b Hughes	12		b Lawson	14
R.A.Smith	b Lawson	11		not out	77
*D.I.Gower	c Healy b Alderman	79		c Waugh b Lawson	7
D.J.Capel	lbw b Alderman	4		c Taylor b Hohns	17
†R.C.Russell	c Healy b Alderman	12		not out	0
D.R.Pringle	c Taylor b Hohns	27			
G.C.Small	c Jones b Lawson	59			
N.G.B.Cook	c Jones b Lawson	31			
A.P.Igglesden	not out	2			
Extras	(B2, LB7, W1, NB13)	23		(LB1, W1, NB5)	7
Total		**285**		(5 wickets)	**143**

ENGLAND	O	M	R	W		O	M	R	W		FALL OF WICKETS			
Small	40	8	141	3		20	4	57	1			A	E	A	E
Igglesden	24	2	91	2		13	1	55	1	Wkt	1st	1st	2nd	2nd
Pringle	24.3	6	70	4	(4)	16	0	53	0	1st	48	1	7	20
Capel	16	2	66	1	(3)	8	0	35	1	2nd	130	28	100	27
Cook	25	5	78	0		6	2	10	0	3rd	149	47	101	51
Atherton	1	0	10	0						4th	345	80	189	67
Gooch	2	1	2	0						5th	347	84	–	138
										6th	386	98	–	–
AUSTRALIA										7th	409	169	–	–
Alderman	27	7	66	5		13	3	30	2	8th	447	201	–	–
Lawson	29.1	9	85	3		15.1	2	41	2	9th	453	274	–	–
Hughes	23	3	84	1		8	2	34	0	10th	468	285	–	–
Hohns	10	1	30	1		10	2	37	1					
Waugh	3	0	11	0										

Umpires: H.D.Bird (42) and K.E.Palmer (18).

Close: 1st day – A(1) 325-3 (Border 66, Jones 114); 2nd – E(1) 1-1 (Stephenson 0, Atherton 0); 3rd – E(1) 124-6 (Gower 43, Pringle 6); 4th – A(2) 87-1 (Taylor 43, Boon 29).

PAKISTAN v INDIA 1989-90 (1st Test)

At National Stadium, Karachi, on 15, 16, 17, 19, 20 November.
Toss: India.   Result: MATCH DRAWN.
Debuts: Pakistan – Shahid Saeed, Waqar Younis; India – S.A.Ankola, S.R.Tendulkar.

At 16 years 205 days, Tendulkar became the third youngest Test cricketer after Mushtaq Mohammad and Aqib Javed of Pakistan. Srikkanth began his four-match reign as captain by electing to field. Kapil Dev, the first bowler, third Indian and ninth player overall to play in 100 Tests, remains, at 30 years 313 days, the youngest to achieve this mark. He also became the fourth (and youngest) bowler to take 350 Test wickets. Azharuddin's five catches in that innings equalled the world record shared by V.Y.Richardson and Yajurvindra Singh. Manjrekar scored a hundred on his first appearance against Pakistan, his stand of 135 with Sidhu setting a second-wicket record for India in this series. Shoaib spent 60 minutes on 45 in the second innings. After Salim Yousuf was injured in the second innings, Aamer Malik kept wicket and caught Azharuddin. For the first time two independent umpires officiated in a Test.

PAKISTAN

Aamer Malik	c Azharuddin b Kapil Dev	0		c Manjrekar b Kapil Dev	15
Ramiz Raja	c Shastri b Prabhakar	44		b Prabhakar	2
Shoaib Mohammad	c Azharuddin b Kapil Dev	67		lbw b Kapil Dev	95
Javed Miandad	c Azharuddin b Kapil Dev	78		b Kapil Dev	36
Salim Malik	c Azharuddin b Ankola	36	(6)	not out	102
*Imran Khan	not out	109	(7)	not out	28
Shahid Saeed	c More b Kapil Dev	12			
†Salim Yousuf	c More b Prabhakar	36	(5)	c More b Ankola	4
Wasim Akram	c Azharuddin b Prabhakar	0			
Abdul Qadir	c More b Prabhakar	4			
Waqar Younis	c More b Prabhakar	0			
Extras	(B4, LB9, W3, NB7)	23		(B3, LB11, NB9)	23
Total		409		(5 wickets declared)	305

INDIA

*K.Srikkanth	lbw b Wasim	4		lbw b Wasim	31
N.S.Sidhu	b Wasim	0		c Ramiz b Imran	85
S.V.Manjrekar	c Salim Yousuf b Waqar	3		not out	113
M.Azharuddin	lbw b Imran	35		c Aamer b Qadir	35
M.Prabhakar	b Waqar	9			
S.R.Tendulkar	b Waqar	15			
R.J.Shastri	c Imran b Qadir	45	(5)	not out	22
Kapil Dev	c Miandad b Waqar	55			
†K.S.More	not out	58			
Arshad Ayub	lbw b Wasim	1			
S.A.Ankola	b Wasim	6			
Extras	(B5, LB10, W5, NB11)	31		(B9, LB4, W1, NB3)	17
Total		262		(3 wickets)	303

INDIA	O	M	R	W		O	M	R	W		FALL OF WICKETS			
Kapil Dev	24	5	69	4		36	15	82	3			P	I	P	I
Prabhakar	34.5	6	104	5		30	4	107	1	*Wkt*	*1st*	*1st*	*2nd*	*2nd*
Ankola	19	1	93	1		11	6	35	1	1st	4	1	2	43
Shastri	10	1	37	0	(5) 5	0	15	0		2nd	83	13	24	178
Ayub	27	3	81	0	(4) 10	1	37	0		3rd	158	13	92	256
Srikkanth	1	0	2	0						4th	233	41	109	–
Tendulkar	1	0	10	0	(6) 4	0	15	0		5th	271	73	250	–
										6th	307	85	–	–
PAKISTAN										7th	398	163	–	–
Wasim	26.2	4	83	4	(2) 25	7	68	1		8th	398	220	–	–
Waqar	19	1	80	4	(4) 2	0	11	0		9th	409	241	–	–
Imran	15	4	44	1	(1) 28	11	56	1		10th	409	262	–	–
Shahid	2	0	7	0	(5) 13	0	36	0						
Qadir	10	1	33	1	(3) 28	3	119	1						

Umpires: J.H.Hampshire (*England*) (2) and J.W.Holder (*England*) (4).

Close: 1st day – P(1) 259-4 (Miandad 76, Imran 17); 2nd – I(1) 157-6 (Shastri 25, Kapil Dev 49); 3rd – P(2) 106-3 (Shoaib 46, Salim Yousuf 3); 4th – I(2) 86-1 (Sidhu 34, Manjrekar 14).

PAKISTAN v INDIA 1989-90 (2nd Test)

At Iqbal Stadium, Faisalabad, on 23, 24, 25, 27, 28 November.
Toss: Pakistan.   Result: MATCH DRAWN.
Debuts: Pakistan – Nadeem Abbasi, Naved Anjum; India – V.Razdan.

Razdan appeared in Test cricket after two first-class matches, just 20 days after making his debut at that level and before he had played in a Ranji Trophy match. At 16 years 214 days, Tendulkar became the youngest either to score a fifty or to share in a hundred partnership in Test cricket. Azharuddin, whose seventh Test hundred was his first outside India, completed 2,000 runs in his 32nd Test (48th innings). Pakistan's bowlers established a Test record by bowling 15 wides in an innings.

INDIA

*K.Srikkanth	lbw b Wasim	36	b Wasim	13
N.S.Sidhu	c Nadeem b Wasim	20	run out	51
S.V.Manjrekar	c Salim Malik b Naved	76	lbw b Naved	83
M.Azharuddin	lbw b Wasim	0	b Naved	109
R.J.Shastri	c Nadeem b Salim Jaffer	11	c Nadeem b Wasim	5
S.R.Tendulkar	lbw b Imran	59	run out	8
M.Prabhakar	not out	24	not out	54
Kapil Dev	lbw b Naved	0	c Ramiz b Qadir	49
†K.S.More	lbw b Imran	4	not out	2
Maninder Singh	c Ramiz b Imran	3		
V.Razdan	c sub (Ijaz Ahmed) b Imran	0		
Extras	(B2, LB16, W15, NB22)	55	(B7, LB7, W7, NB3)	24
Total		**288**	(7 wickets)	**398**

PAKISTAN

Aamer Malik	c and b Prabhakar	117
Ramiz Raja	c Srikkanth b Prabhakar	58
Shoaib Mohammad	lbw b Kapil Dev	24
Javed Miandad	lbw b Prabhakar	13
Salim Malik	lbw b Prabhakar	63
*Imran Khan	c Azharuddin b Prabhakar	34
Naved Anjum	c More b Kapil Dev	12
†Nadeem Abbasi	c More b Kapil Dev	36
Wasim Akram	c Tendulkar b Prabhakar	28
Abdul Qadir	not out	5
Salim Jaffer	not out	0
Extras	(B2, LB9, W8, NB14)	33
Total	(9 wickets declared)	**423**

PAKISTAN	O	M	R	W	O	M	R	W	FALL OF WICKETS		
Imran	26.1	7	45	4	27	5	100	0		I	P	I
Wasim	38	4	107	3	31	6	86	2	Wkt	1st	1st	2nd
Salim Jaffer	17	4	54	1					1st	68	105	33
Naved	29	6	57	2	(3) 22	4	92	2	2nd	74	157	91
Qadir	3	1	7	0	(4) 31	3	90	1	3rd	85	193	249
Aamer					(5) 2	0	9	0	4th	101	289	258
Shoaib					(6) 3	0	7	0	5th	244	307	274
									6th	252	331	290
INDIA									7th	253	368	385
Kapil Dev	45	11	106	3					8th	278	409	–
Prabhakar	42.3	4	132	6					9th	284	419	–
Razdan	13	1	62	0					10th	288	–	–
Maninder	21	4	70	0								
Shastri	9	0	29	0								
Srikkanth	2	0	13	0								

Umpires: J.H.Hampshire (*England*) (3) and J.W.Holder (*England*) (5).

Close: 1st day – I(1) 200-4 (Manjrekar 58, Tendulkar 35); 2nd – P(1) 82-0 (Aamer 26, Ramiz 45); 3rd – P(1) 338-6 (Imran 16, Nadeem 5); 4th – I(2) 164-2 (Manjrekar 43, Azharuddin 48).

PAKISTAN v INDIA 1989-90 (3rd Test)

At Gaddafi Stadium, Lahore, on 1, 2, 3, 5, 6 December.
Toss: India.   Result: MATCH DRAWN.
Debuts: Pakistan – Akram Raza, Shahid Mahboob.

On the ground where he made his Test debut, Javed Miandad became the first Pakistani and tenth player overall to appear in 100 Tests. He emulated M.C.Cowdrey (*Test No. 639*) by celebrating the event with a hundred but was the first to score hundreds in his first and his 100th Tests. Both sides registered their highest totals for this series in Pakistan, with Pakistan's being the highest for all Tests in Lahore. Manjrekar's 218 (511 minutes, 401 balls, a five and 28 fours) was the highest Test score by a visiting batsman in Pakistan and India's record for this series. With Shastri, who completed 3,000 runs in his 68th Test (102nd innings), he shared an Indian record fourth-wicket partnership of 186 against Pakistan. Shoaib's undefeated 203 took 486 minutes, 335 balls and included 19 fours. He and Hanif Mohammad are the only son and father to each score double hundreds in Tests. Qadir scored his 1,000th run, completed the slowest Test double (62 matches), and emulated Imran by achieving the rarer double of 1,000 runs and 200 wickets for Pakistan. The match average of 80.5 runs per wicket was then the fifth highest in Test cricket.

INDIA

*K.Srikkanth	b Wasim	0
N.S.Sidhu	lbw b Imran	4
S.V.Manjrekar	run out	218
M.Azharuddin	c Nadeem b Shahid	77
R.J.Shastri	c Miandad b Shahid	61
M.Prabhakar	run out	45
S.R.Tendulkar	b Qadir	41
Kapil Dev	b Qadir	1
*K.S.More	not out	26
Arshad Ayub	c sub (Ijaz Ahmed) b Qadir	10
Maninder Singh	c Akram Raza b Imran	0
Extras	(B4, LB19, W1, NB2)	26
Total		**509**

PAKISTAN

Aamer Malik	c sub (W.V.Raman) b Maninder	113
Ramiz Raja	c More b Prabhakar	63
Salim Malik	c Manjrekar b Maninder	55
Javed Miandad	b Shastri	145
Shoaib Mohammad	not out	203
*Imran Khan	c Manjrekar b Shastri	66
Abdul Qadir	not out	39
*Nadeem Abbasi		
Wasim Akram	did not bat	
Akram Raza		
Shahid Mahboob		
Extras	(B3, LB4, NB8)	15
Total	(5 wickets)	**699**

PAKISTAN	O	M	R	W
Imran	50.2	13	130	2
Wasim	24	6	65	1
Shahid	49	12	131	2
Akram Raza	18	3	58	0
Qadir	35	8	97	3
Salim	1	0	2	0
Aamer	1	0	3	0
INDIA				
Kapil Dev	28	2	77	0
Prabhakar	34	2	107	1
Maninder	61	7	191	2
Ayub	49	4	182	0
Srikkanth	3	0	19	0
Shastri	26.4	2	104	2
More	2	0	12	0

FALL OF WICKETS

Wkt	I 1st	P 1st
1st	1	100
2nd	5	223
3rd	154	248
4th	340	494
5th	375	628
6th	466	–
7th	466	–
8th	469	–
9th	508	–
10th	509	–

Umpires: J.H.Hampshire (*England*) (4) and J.W.Holder (*England*) (6).

Close: 1st day – I(1) 255-3 (Manjrekar 132, Shastri 33); 2nd – I(1) 458-5 (Prabhakar 44, Tendulkar 34); 3rd – P(1) 159-1 (Aamer 60, Salim 30); 4th – P(1) 416-3 (Miandad 84, Shoaib 90).

PAKISTAN v INDIA 1989-90 (4th Test)

At Jinnah Stadium, Sialkot, on 9, 10, 11, 13, 14 December.
Toss: Pakistan.   Result: MATCH DRAWN.
Debuts: None.

Sialkot's second Test match was the 44th (and last to date) between these two countries and produced the 33rd stalemate. India gained a first innings lead in Pakistan for only the second time. In his 79th Test, Imran became the fifth bowler to take 350 wickets. Kapil Dev took his aggregate of wickets against Pakistan to 99, the highest for India against any other country (previously 95 by B.S.Chandrasekhar against England). Razdan, who has not made a subsequent appearance in Test cricket, returned a five-wicket analysis in his fourth first-class match. The match was called off at tea on the final day, ostensibly because of poor light.

INDIA

*K.Srikkanth	lbw b Wasim	10	c Wasim b Imran		3
N.S.Sidhu	c Ramiz b Wasim	12	c Imran b Zakir		97
S.V.Manjrekar	lbw b Waqar	72	lbw b Imran		4
M.Azharuddin	run out	52	c Shoaib b Wasim		4
R.J.Shastri	c and b Imran	20	lbw b Wasim		0
S.R.Tendulkar	lbw b Wasim	35	c Nadeem b Imran		57
Kapil Dev	b Wasim	27	lbw b Zakir		27
M.Prabhakar	c Shoaib b Imran	25	not out		11
†K.S.More	c Zakir b Waqar	15	not out		17
Maninder Singh	c Nadeem b Wasim	8			
V.Razdan	not out	6			
Extras	(B6, LB14, W8, NB14)	42	(B5, LB7, NB2)		14
Total		**324**	(7 wickets)		**234**

PAKISTAN

Aamer Malik	lbw b Prabhakar	9
Ramiz Raja	b Razdan	56
Shoaib Mohammad	b Razdan	23
Javed Miandad	c More b Kapil Dev	7
Salim Malik	c Shastri b Razdan	34
*Imran Khan	c More b Prabhakar	25
†Nadeem Abbasi	b Prabhakar	10
Wasim Akram	b Razdan	30
Abdul Qadir	c Azharuddin b Razdan	7
Zakir Khan	not out	9
Waqar Younis	c More b Kapil Dev	4
Extras	(B7, LB24, W1, NB4)	36
Total		**250**

PAKISTAN	O	M	R	W		O	M	R	W
Wasim	28.2	6	101	5		32	17	41	2
Waqar	21	2	83	2	(4)	16	1	63	0
Zakir	16	3	59	0	(5)	13	0	50	2
Imran	17	3	61	2	(2)	22	4	68	3
Qadir	2	2	0	0					
Shoaib					(3)	1	1	0	0
INDIA									
Kapil Dev	35.4	17	44	2					
Prabhakar	40	10	92	3					
Razdan	27	5	79	5					
Maninder	1	0	4	0					

FALL OF WICKETS

	I	P	I
Wkt	1st	1st	2nd
1st	20	11	10
2nd	39	76	33
3rd	167	87	38
4th	181	133	38
5th	225	170	139
6th	251	185	198
7th	270	194	207
8th	296	222	–
9th	314	233	–
10th	324	250	–

Umpires: J.H.Hampshire (*England*) (5) and J.W.Holder (*England*) (7).

Close: 1st day – I(1) 181-3 (Manjrekar 72, Shastri 5); 2nd – P(1) 23-1 (Ramiz 9, Shoaib 2); 3rd – P(1) 181-5 (Imran 21, Nadeem 7); 4th – I(2) 102-4 (Sidhu 54, Tendulkar 33).

AUSTRALIA v NEW ZEALAND 1989-90 (Only Test)

At W.A.C.A.Ground, Perth, on 24, 25, 26, 27, 28 November.
Toss: New Zealand.   Result: MATCH DRAWN.
Debuts: Australia – T.M.Moody; New Zealand – C.L.Cairns.

Put in to bat, Australia overcame a bouncy pitch and soaring temperatures to post their highest total in a home Test against New Zealand, Boon (451 minutes, 326 balls, 28 fours) recording the first Test double hundred in 17 Tests at Perth and completing 3,000 runs in his 43rd Test. It was Australia's ninth first innings total in excess of 400 in successive matches. The left-handed Greatbatch, making his debut in this series, thwarted Australia with two memorable defensive innings, 76 (221 minutes, 139 balls, 13 fours) followed by an epic 146 not out (655 minutes, 485 balls, 17 fours). During the latter innings, the third longest by a New Zealander, he shared in New Zealand's highest eighth-wicket stand against Australia, 88 unbroken with Snedden. His hundred took 462 minutes and was then the slowest in first-class cricket in Australia. Rackemann was recalled after a hiatus of five years (46 matches).

AUSTRALIA

M.A.Taylor	c Wright b Morrison	9
D.C.Boon	c Wright b Snedden	200
T.M.Moody	c Smith b Snedden	61
*A.R.Border	b Morrison	50
D.M.Jones	lbw b Morrison	99
S.R.Waugh	c Greatbatch b Snedden	17
†I.A.Healy	c J.J.Crowe b Patel	28
M.G.Hughes	c Wright b Snedden	16
G.F.Lawson	b Morrison	1
C.G.Rackemann	not out	15
T.M.Alderman	did not bat	
Extras	(B1, LB9, W2, NB13)	25
Total	**(9 wickets declared)**	**521**

NEW ZEALAND

*J.G.Wright	b Rackemann	34	c Border b Lawson	3
R.H.Vance	b Alderman	4	c Alderman b Rackemann	8
M.J.Greatbatch	c Healy b Hughes	76	not out	146
M.D.Crowe	lbw b Alderman	62	c Taylor b Moody	30
D.N.Patel	c Boon b Hughes	0	lbw b Alderman	7
J.J.Crowe	c Healy b Rackemann	7	lbw b Hughes	49
†I.D.S.Smith	c Lawson b Hughes	11	c Border b Hughes	0
C.L.Cairns	c Healy b Hughes	1	lbw b Hughes	28
M.C.Snedden	not out	13	not out	33
D.K.Morrison	c Border b Lawson	3		
W.Watson	lbw b Alderman	4		
Extras	(B1, LB6, W4, NB5)	16	(LB14, NB4)	18
Total		**231**	**(7 wickets)**	**322**

NEW ZEALAND	O	M	R	W	O	M	R	W		FALL OF WICKETS		
Morrison	39.1	8	145	4						A	NZ	NZ
Cairns	12	2	60	0					*Wkt*	*1st*	*1st*	*2nd*
Snedden	42	10	108	4					1st	28	28	11
Watson	37	7	118	0					2nd	177	84	11
Patel	28	5	80	1					3rd	316	173	79
									4th	361	178	107
AUSTRALIA									5th	395	191	189
Alderman	25.4	7	73	3	32	14	59	1	6th	449	204	189
Lawson	22	5	54	1	38	12	88	1	7th	489	206	234
Rackemann	20	4	39	2	31	21	23	1	8th	490	212	–
Hughes	20	7	51	4	36	8	92	3	9th	521	226	–
Moody	4	1	6	0	17	6	23	1	10th	–	231	–
Border	1	0	1	0	5	2	17	0				
Jones					3	2	6	0				

Umpires: R.J.Evans (2) and P.J.McConnell (14).

Close: 1st day – A(1) 296-2 (Boon 169, Border 45); 2nd – NZ(1) 25-0 (Wright 12, Vance 4); 3rd – NZ(1) 218-8 (Snedden 7, Morrison 0); 4th – NZ(2) 168-4 (Greatbatch 69, J.J.Crowe 42).

AUSTRALIA v SRI LANKA 1989-90 (1st Test)

At Woolloongabba, Brisbane, on 8, 9, 10, 11, 12 December.
Toss: Sri Lanka.   Result: MATCH DRAWN.
Debuts: Sri Lanka – D.Ranatunga, A.G.D.Wickremasinghe.

'The Gabba' became the first Australian ground to host Tests against seven different opponent countries. Border surpassed S.M.Gavaskar's record of 106 consecutive Test appearances. Ratnayeke (side strain) was unable to complete his ninth over. Despite Moody's maiden Test hundred, an innings subjected to five interruptions by rain, Sri Lanka ended Australia's sequence of nine successive first innings scores over 400, each of which had produced a first innings lead. De Silva (491 minutes, 361 balls, a six and 17 fours) scored Sri Lanka's first hundred against Australia. His partnership of 144 with Ratnayeke was Sri Lanka's highest for the seventh wicket in all Tests. During his third Test hundred, Taylor became the first batsman to complete 1,000 Test match runs in the year of his debut. Although four fine days followed the loss of 160 minutes on the first, the match attendance (16,187) was the lowest for any Brisbane Test.

AUSTRALIA

D.C.Boon	c Samarasekera b Labrooy	0	(2)	lbw b Ramanayake	26
M.A.Taylor	c Wickremasinghe b Ramanayake	9	(1)	lbw b Ramanayake	164
T.M.Moody	c Wickremasinghe b Labrooy	106		c A.Ranatunga b E.A.R.de Silva	30
*A.R.Border	c A.Ranatunga b Labrooy	56			
D.M.Jones	lbw b Labrooy	15	(4)	c Ramanayake b P.A.de Silva	23
S.R.Waugh	c A.Ranatunga b Ramanayake	60	(5)	b Gurusinha	57
†I.A.Healy	lbw b Gurusinha	21	(6)	not out	26
M.G.Hughes	run out	25		not out	23
G.F.Lawson	c Wickremasinghe b Labrooy	22			
C.G.Rackemann	not out	5	(7)	b Gurusinha	0
T.M.Alderman	c P.A.de Silva b Gurusinha	18			
Extras	(B1, LB8, NB21)	30		(B5, LB4, NB17)	26
Total		**367**		**(6 wickets)**	**375**

SRI LANKA

R.S.Mahanama	lbw b Alderman	5
D.Ranatunga	c Waugh b Lawson	40
A.P.Gurusinha	c Healy b Rackemann	43
E.A.R.de Silva	b Alderman	22
P.A.de Silva	c Lawson b Rackemann	167
*A.Ranatunga	lbw b Hughes	25
M.A.R.Samarasekera	c Moody b Rackemann	18
J.R.Ratnayeke	lbw b Hughes	56
†A.G.D.Wickremasinghe	c Boon b Hughes	2
G.F.Labrooy	lbw b Alderman	1
C.P.H.Ramanayake	not out	10
Extras	(LB23, W2, NB4)	29
Total		**418**

SRI LANKA	O	M	R	W	O	M	R	W		FALL OF WICKETS		
Ratnayeke	8.5	1	17	0						A	SL	A
Labrooy	31.1	5	133	5	(1) 24	4	69	0	Wkt	1st	1st	2nd
Ramanayake	26	2	101	2	(2) 28	3	81	2	1st	1	10	60
A.Ranatunga	13	1	49	0	(6) 6	0	25	0	2nd	27	80	124
E.A.R.de Silva	8	1	21	0	(3) 39	8	112	1	3rd	185	114	167
Gurusinha	8.3	1	37	2	(5) 10	3	31	2	4th	197	148	316
P.A.de Silva					(4) 15	2	45	1	5th	210	201	324
Mahanama					(7) 1	0	3	0	6th	247	238	324
AUSTRALIA									7th	295	382	–
Alderman	40	13	81	3					8th	339	386	–
Lawson	33	10	51	1					9th	339	391	–
Rackemann	30.3	6	88	3					10th	367	418	–
Hughes	39	8	123	3								
Moody	16	8	15	0								
Border	7	0	36	0								
Jones	1	0	1	0								

Umpires: A.R.Crafter (27) and C.D.Timmins (1).

Close: 1st day – A(1) 178-2 (Moody 101, Border 54); 2nd – SL(1) 81-2 (Gurusinha 28, E.A.R.de Silva 1); 3rd – SL(1) 275-6 (P.A.de Silva 75, Ratnayeke 22); 4th – A(2) 94-1 (Taylor 36, Moody 22).

AUSTRALIA v SRI LANKA 1989-90 (2nd Test)

At Bellerive Oval, Hobart, on 16, 17, 18, 19, 20 December.
Toss: Sri Lanka.   Result: AUSTRALIA won by 173 runs.
Debuts: Sri Lanka – H.P.Tillekeratne.

Formerly the Clarence Cricket Club's ground, the Tasmanian Cricket Council's new headquarters beside the Derwent River provided Test cricket with its 62nd venue and Australia with its seventh. Appropriately the first ball was bowled to David Boon while his fellow Tasmanians Steve Randell and Neville Oliver officiated at the bowler's end and on the ABC microphone respectively. Australia were dismissed for their lowest total in this series, Ratnayake being the first bowler to take six wickets in an innings for either country. Border overhauled G.S.Chappell's world record of 122 catches in the field when he caught Ratnayake. Jones, who completed 1,000 runs in 1989, and Waugh shared an unbroken partnership of 260 in 234 minutes, Australia's second-highest for the sixth wicket.

AUSTRALIA

D.C.Boon	c Mahanama b Ratnayake	41	(2)	c Ratnayake b Labrooy	0
M.A.Taylor	c Tillekeratne b Ratnayake	23	(1)	c Gurusinha b P.A.de Silva	108
T.M.Moody	c Gurusinha b Ratnayake	6		c Tillekeratne b Ratnayake	5
A.R.Border	c E.A.R.de Silva b Ratnayeke	24	(5)	b P.A.de Silva	85
D.M.Jones	c Tillekeratne b Ratnayake	3	(6)	not out	118
S.R.Waugh	c Tillekeratne b Labrooy	16	(7)	not out	134
P.R.Sleep	not out	47			
I.A.Healy	c Tillekeratne b Gurusinha	17			
M.G.Hughes	b E.A.R.de Silva	27	(4)	c Gurusinha b Ratnayake	30
G.D.Campbell	c Mahanama b Ratnayake	6			
T.M.Alderman	b Ratnayake	0			
Extras	(LB7, W1, NB6)	14		(B2, LB5, W4, NB22)	33
Total		224		(5 wickets declared)	513

SRI LANKA

R.S.Mahanama	c Healy b Sleep	85		lbw b Campbell	5
D.Ranatunga	c Moody b Alderman	2		c Healy b Hughes	45
A.P.Gurusinha	c Taylor b Alderman	0		c sub (R.J.Tucker) b Hughes	20
E.A.R.de Silva	c Border b Campbell	2	(8)	b Campbell	50
P.A.de Silva	lbw b Campbell	75	(4)	c Campbell b Sleep	72
A.Ranatunga	c Moody b Sleep	21	(5)	c Jones b Hughes	38
H.P.Tillekeratne	c Taylor b Sleep	0	(6)	c Waugh b Sleep	6
J.R.Ratnayeke	c Taylor b Hughes	9	(7)	c Healy b Campbell	75
G.F.Labrooy	b Hughes	11		b Hughes	5
C.P.H.Ramanayake	not out	4		not out	2
R.J.Ratnayake	c Border b Hughes	0		lbw b Hughes	5
Extras	(LB4, NB3)	7		(B9, LB12, NB4)	25
Total		216			348

SRI LANKA	O	M	R	W		O	M	R	W
Ratnayeke	15	2	39	1	(3) 19	1	86	0
Labrooy	19	3	61	1	(1) 22	3	100	1
Ratnayake	19.4	2	66	6	(2) 35	5	123	2
Ramanayake	4	0	21	0	(6) 10	0	49	0
Gurusinha	6	0	20	1				
E.A.R.de Silva	9	6	10	1	(4) 21	2	83	0
P.A.de Silva					(5) 18	1	65	2

AUSTRALIA	O	M	R	W		O	M	R	W
Alderman	23	2	71	2	30	12	48	0
Campbell	23	9	41	2	33	8	102	3
Hughes	21.4	6	68	3	(4) 31.4	8	88	5
Sleep	10	4	26	0	(3) 36	16	73	2
Waugh	6	3	6	0				
Moody					(5) 2	0	9	0
Jones					(6) 4	2	5	0
Border					(7) 5	4	2	0

FALL OF WICKETS

Wkt	A 1st	SL 1st	A 2nd	SL 2nd
1st	50	11	1	6
2nd	68	15	10	53
3rd	83	18	77	94
4th	89	146	240	187
5th	112	188	253	187
6th	123	192	–	208
7th	166	193	–	332
8th	207	201	–	337
9th	224	216	–	337
10th	224	216	–	348

Umpires: L.J.King (2) and S.G.Randell (7).

Close: 1st day – SL(1) 27-3 (Mahanama 18, P.A.de Silva 5); 2nd – A(2) 25-2 (Taylor 11, Hughes 9); 3rd – A(2) 387-5 (Jones 51, Waugh 77); 4th – SL(2) 166-3 (P.A.de Silva 64, A.Ranatunga 25).

AUSTRALIA v PAKISTAN 1989-90 (1st Test)

At Melbourne Cricket Ground on 12, 13, 14, 15, 16 January.
Toss: Pakistan.   Result: AUSTRALIA won by 92 runs.
Debuts: None.

Border surpassed G.S.Chappell's Australian record by captaining for the 49th time. Wasim, who took hi
100th wicket in 30 Tests when he dismissed Alderman, and Imran each took two wickets with successive balls
Taylor scored his third hundred in successive Tests and top-scored in both innings. Ijaz emulated this latte
feat for Pakistan, resisting Australia's attack for 450 minutes (331 balls, 11 fours) before falling to a
astonishing catch by Marsh, who dived full length at point to hold a well-timed square cut with his left hand
For the fifth time six batsmen were adjudged lbw in a Test innings. Australia completed their win with 2
minutes, or a minimum of 9.1 overs, to spare.

AUSTRALIA

G.R.Marsh	c Salim b Wasim	30	(2) c Wasim b Aqib	2
M.A.Taylor	c Aqib b Imran	52	(1) c Aamer b Tausif	10
D.C.Boon	lbw b Wasim	0	run out	2
*A.R.Border	c Miandad b Wasim	24	not out	6
D.M.Jones	c Salim b Imran	0	lbw b Wasim	1
S.R.Waugh	c Salim b Aqib	20	c Salim b Wasim	
P.R.Sleep	lbw b Wasim	23	b Wasim	
†I.A.Healy	c Shoaib b Aqib	48	c Ijaz b Wasim	2
M.G.Hughes	c Mansoor b Wasim	8	c Mansoor b Wasim	3
T.M.Alderman	c Aamer b Wasim	0	not out	
C.G.Rackemann	not out	0		
Extras	(LB9, NB9)	18	(B2, LB10, W1, NB20)	3
Total		223	(8 wickets declared)	31

PAKISTAN

Aamer Malik	lbw b Alderman	7	c Taylor b Hughes	
Shoaib Mohammad	c Healy b Alderman	6	(3) c Boon b Hughes	1
Mansoor Akhtar	c Taylor b Rackemann	5	(2) lbw b Alderman	1
Javed Miandad	c Healy b Alderman	3	lbw b Waugh	6
Ijaz Ahmed	c Taylor b Hughes	19	c Marsh b Hughes	12
*Imran Khan	c Alderman b Rackemann	3	lbw b Alderman	4
†Salim Yousuf	c Taylor b Hughes	16	lbw b Alderman	3
Wasim Akram	c Healy b Hughes	6	c Taylor b Sleep	
Tausif Ahmed	not out	9	not out	1
Waqar Younis	lbw b Sleep	18	lbw b Alderman	
Aqib Javed	c Healy b Rackemann	0	lbw b Alderman	
Extras	(B1, LB4, NB10)	15	(B1, LB7, W2, NB9)	1
Total		107		33

PAKISTAN	O	M	R	W		O	M	R	W		FALL OF WICKETS			
Imran	18	6	53	2	(2)	8	2	21	0		A	P	A	P
Wasim	30	9	62	6	(1)	41.4	12	98	5	Wkt	1st	1st	2nd	2n
Aqib	22.1	7	47	2		21	1	55	1	1st	90	12	73	
Waqar	12	3	27	0		22	4	68	0	2nd	90	20	116	2.
Tausif	8	1	25	0		16	3	58	1	3rd	98	20	204	3
										4th	98	44	216	13.
										5th	131	44	220	21.
AUSTRALIA										6th	148	65	220	29
Alderman	19	6	30	3	(3)	33.5	6	105	5	7th	201	71	260	30.
Rackemann	21.5	8	32	3		38	13	67	0	8th	223	71	305	32.
Hughes	17	7	34	3	(1)	42	14	79	3	9th	223	106	–	33.
Sleep	8	5	6	1		21	7	64	1	10th	223	107	–	33
Waugh						3	0	13	1					

Umpires: R.J.Evans (3) and P.J.McConnell (15).

Close: 1st day – A(1) 198-6 (Sleep 23, Healy 33); 2nd – A(2) 1-0 (Taylor 0, Marsh 0); 3rd – A(2) 260-7 (Border 51); 4th – P(2) 159-4 (Ijaz 46, Imran 13).

AUSTRALIA v PAKISTAN 1989-90 (2nd Test)

At Adelaide Oval on 19, 20, 21, 22, 23 January.
Toss: Pakistan.   Result: MATCH DRAWN.
Debuts: Pakistan – Mushtaq Ahmed.

Border became the first to captain in 50 successive Tests. Rackemann took three wickets in four balls, including that of Mushtaq, out first ball on debut. Healy held five catches in succession. Marsh, who fractured his thumb catching Ijaz, retired (6) overnight at 10 and resumed at 328 for 7. Led on first innings by 84 runs and having collapsed to 22 for 4 in their second, Pakistan were rescued by an epic stand of 191 in 244 minutes between Imran, who compiled the highest of his six Test hundreds (136 in 485 minutes, 361 balls, 10 fours) and Wasim (244 minutes, 195 balls, a six and 18 fours). It was the highest sixth-wicket partnership by either side in this series. Wasim emulated Mushtaq Mohammad (twice) and Imran by scoring a hundred and taking five wickets in an innings of a Test for Pakistan. Jones became the tenth Australian to score hundreds in both innings of a Test. Before play on the second day, Sir Donald Bradman (81) opened the new stand bearing his name.

PAKISTAN

Shoaib Mohammad	lbw b Hughes	43		c Healy b Hughes	0
Ramiz Raja	c P.L.Taylor b Campbell	9		c Waugh b Hughes	2
†Salim Yousuf	lbw b Rackemann	38		c M.A.Taylor b Hughes	1
Javed Miandad	c Healy b Campbell	52	(6)	c P.L.Taylor b Hughes	21
Ijaz Ahmed	c Marsh b Border	28	(4)	c P.L.Taylor b Hughes	4
Salim Malik	c Healy b Hughes	11	(8)	not out	65
*Imran Khan	c Healy b Rackemann	13	(5)	b P.L.Taylor	136
Wasim Akram	c Border b Campbell	52	(7)	b Campbell	123
Tausif Ahmed	c Healy b Rackemann	0		c Healy b Rackemann	18
Mushtaq Ahmed	c Healy b Rackemann	0		b P.L.Taylor	4
Waqar Younis	not out	1			
Extras	(B4, LB4, W1, NB1)	10		(B4, LB5, W1, NB3)	13
Total		**257**		(9 wickets declared)	**387**

AUSTRALIA

G.R.Marsh	c Salim Yousuf b Wasim	13			
M.A.Taylor	lbw b Imran	77	(1)	c sub (Saeed Anwar) b Mushtaq	59
D.C.Boon	lbw b Wasim	29	(2)	c Ramiz b Wasim	5
*A.R.Border	b Waqar	13	(3)	c Salim Yousuf b Waqar	8
D.M.Jones	c Wasim b Imran	116	(4)	not out	121
S.R.Waugh	lbw b Wasim	17	(5)	b Tausif	4
†I.A.Healy	c sub (Maqsood Rana) b Waqar	12	(6)	c sub (Aamer Malik) b Tausif	27
P.L.Taylor	run out	33	(7)	c Shoaib b Tausif	1
M.G.Hughes	not out	6	(8)	not out	2
G.D.Campbell	lbw b Wasim	0			
C.G.Rackemann	b Wasim	0			
Extras	(LB12, NB13)	25		(LB3, NB3)	6
Total		**341**		(6 wickets)	**233**

AUSTRALIA	O	M	R	W	O	M	R	W	FALL OF WICKETS				
Hughes	18	5	63	2	32	9	111	5		P	A	P	A
Campbell	21.3	2	79	3	29	5	83	1	*Wkt*	*1st*	*1st*	*2nd*	*2nd*
P.L.Taylor	12	0	57	0	(4) 41.5	13	94	2	1st	27	82	0	9
Rackemann	21	3	40	4	(3) 37	11	85	1	2nd	91	113	2	33
Border	4	0	10	1	4	0	5	0	3rd	95	156	7	106
									4th	166	188	22	129
PAKISTAN									5th	187	216	90	213
Wasim	43	10	100	5	11	3	29	1	6th	187	328	281	229
Waqar	26	4	66	2	14	4	42	1	7th	241	328	316	–
Mushtaq	23	4	69	0	(4) 25	5	72	1	8th	251	341	380	–
Imran	27	6	61	2					9th	251	341	387	–
Tausif	14	1	33	0	(3) 32	6	80	3	10th	257	341	–	–
Shoaib					(5) 1	0	7	0					

Umpires: A.R.Crafter (28) and L.J.King (3).

Close: 1st day – A(1) 10-0 (Marsh 6, M.A.Taylor 3); 2nd – A(1) 259-5 (Jones 67, P.L.Taylor 14); 3rd – P(2) 73-4 (Imran 43, Miandad 16); 4th – P(2) 357-7 (Salim Malik 46, Tausif 11).

AUSTRALIA v PAKISTAN 1989-90 (3rd Test)

At Sydney Cricket Ground on 3 (*no play*), 4 (*no play*), 5, 6, 7 (*no play*), 8 February.
Toss: Australia.   Result: MATCH DRAWN.
Debuts: Pakistan – Nadeem Ghauri.

Even the addition of an extra day to compensate for the loss of the first two could not rescue this match from the effects of Cyclone Nancy as 20 inches of rain fell during Sydney's wettest week for 100 years. But for the Herculean efforts of Peter Leroy's groundstaff, this could easily have become the fifth Test to be abandoned without a ball bowled. It was a tribute to their labours that 11 hours 19 minutes of play were salvaged. Taylor's sixth hundred in 14 Tests was his fourth in this convoluted season's six matches. After catching Moody at short-leg in the second innings, Aamer deputised for Salim Yousuf as wicket-keeper from tea (115 for 2) until the match was abandoned.

PAKISTAN

Aamer Malik	c Healy b Alderman	7
Ramiz Raja	c and b Hughes	0
Shoaib Mohammad	lbw b Alderman	9
Javed Miandad	c Jones b Hughes	49
Ijaz Ahmed	c M.A.Taylor b Rackemann	8
*Imran Khan	not out	82
Wasim Akram	c M.A.Taylor b Alderman	10
†Salim Yousuf	c Jones b Rackemann	6
Tausif Ahmed	b Alderman	0
Waqar Younis	c Veletta b Hughes	16
Nadeem Ghauri	b Alderman	0
Extras	(B1, LB7, NB4)	12
Total		**199**

AUSTRALIA

M.A.Taylor	not out	101
M.R.J.Veletta	lbw b Waqar	9
T.M.Moody	c Aamer b Tausif	26
*A.R.Border	not out	27
D.M.Jones		
S.R.Waugh		
†I.A.Healy		
P.L.Taylor	did not bat	
M.G.Hughes		
T.M.Alderman		
C.G.Rackemann		
Extras	(B4, LB5, NB4)	13
Total	(2 wickets)	**176**

AUSTRALIA	O	M	R	W		FALL OF WICKETS		
Alderman	33.5	10	65	5			P	A
Hughes	31	16	70	3		*Wkt*	*1st*	*1st*
Rackemann	22	8	33	2		1st	2	33
P.L.Taylor	8	1	23	0		2nd	15	106
						3rd	20	–
PAKISTAN						4th	51	–
Wasim	10	3	29	0		5th	106	–
Imran	17	2	32	0		6th	128	–
Tausif	19	3	62	1		7th	154	–
Nadeem	8	1	20	0		8th	160	–
Waqar	9	4	21	1		9th	191	–
Ijaz	2	0	3	0		10th	199	–

Umpires: A.R.Crafter (29) and P.J.McConnell (16).

Close: 1st day – no play; 2nd – no play; 3rd – P(1) 110-5 (Imran 27, Wasim 4); 4th – A(1) 0-0 (M.A.Taylor 0, Veletta 0); 5th – no play.

NEW ZEALAND v INDIA 1989-90 (1st Test)

At Lancaster Park, Christchurch, on 2, 3, 4, 5 February.
Toss: New Zealand.   Result: NEW ZEALAND won by ten wickets.
Debuts: India – S.L.V.Raju (*sometimes given as S.L.Venkatapathy Raju*), A.S.Wassan.

Azharuddin began his reign as India's 25th Test captain, the fourth Muslim to gain this honour after the two Nawabs of Pataudi and Ghulam Ahmed. At 3.01 on the third afternoon Richard Hadlee, playing his 80th match, bowled Manjrekar to become the first to take 400 Test wickets. Earlier Wright had batted 553 minutes for the highest of his eight Test hundreds (443 balls, 23 fours). His partnership of 125 with Greatbatch was New Zealand's highest for the fourth wicket against India. Morrison took 5 for 12 in 27 balls and ended Sidhu's tour with a fractured knuckle. At 1.15 on the fourth afternoon New Zealand gained their 28th Test victory and their sixth at Lancaster Park.

NEW ZEALAND

T.J.Franklin	c Prabhakar b Kapil Dev	20			
*J.G.Wright	b Raju	185			
A.H.Jones	c Raju b Hirwani	52			
M.D.Crowe	lbw b Raju	24			
M.J.Greatbatch	b Wassan	46			
K.R.Rutherford	b Kapil Dev	69			
J.G.Bracewell	b Hirwani	0			
†I.D.S.Smith	lbw b Raju	9			
R.J.Hadlee	c Hirwani b Prabhakar	28			
M.C.Snedden	lbw b Kapil Dev	3	(1) not out		1
D.K.Morrison	not out	1	(2) not out		1
Extras	(B3, LB12, NB7)	22			
Total		**459**	(0 wickets)		**2**

INDIA

W.V.Raman	lbw b Hadlee	0	c Jones b Morrison		96
N.S.Sidhu	lbw b Morrison	51	absent hurt		–
S.V.Manjrekar	c Jones b Hadlee	5	b Hadlee		4
*M.Azharuddin	lbw b Hadlee	48	b Bracewell		30
S.L.V.Raju	c Crowe b Snedden	31	(8) c Smith b Snedden		21
S.R.Tendulkar	c Smith b Morrison	0	c Smith b Bracewell		24
M.Prabhakar	c Smith b Snedden	1	(2) b Snedden		40
Kapil Dev	c Snedden b Morrison	4	(7) lbw b Hadlee		25
†K.S.More	c Smith b Morrison	1	(5) b Hadlee		11
A.S.Wassan	c Smith b Morrison	2	(9) not out		24
N.D.Hirwani	not out	1	(10) c Bracewell b Hadlee		0
Extras	(B5, LB5, NB10)	20	(B6, LB2, NB13)		21
Total		**164**			**296**

INDIA	O	M	R	W	O	M	R	W	FALL OF WICKETS				
										NZ	I	I	NZ
Kapil Dev	28.3	4	89	3					Wkt	1st	1st	2nd	2nd
Prabhakar	38	8	114	1	(1) 0.5	0	2	0	1st	26	0	80	–
Wassan	25	3	95	1					2nd	141	27	85	–
Raju	35	12	86	3					3rd	182	88	135	–
Hirwani	29	9	60	2					4th	307	146	160	–
									5th	374	146	206	–
NEW ZEALAND									6th	375	148	242	–
Hadlee	14	1	45	3	22.5	3	69	4	7th	394	153	254	–
Morrison	16	2	75	5	19	0	94	1	8th	448	158	289	–
Bracewell	3	0	14	0	(5) 20	4	45	2	9th	454	161	296	–
Snedden	12.5	4	20	2	(3) 25	5	59	2	10th	459	164	–	–
Rutherford					(4) 5	1	21	0					

Umpires: R.S.Dunne (2) and S.J.Woodward (21).

Close: 1st day – NZ(1) 255-3 (Wright 127, Greatbatch 21); 2nd – I(1) 97-3 (Sidhu 27, Raju 7); 3rd – I(2) 210-5 (Raman 85, Kapil Dev 4).

NEW ZEALAND v INDIA 1989-90 (2nd Test)

At McLean Park, Napier, on 9 (*no play*), 10, 11, 12, 13 (*no play*) February.
Toss: India.   Result: MATCH DRAWN.
Debuts: None.

Napier's first Test for eleven years was reduced to a three-day match by rain. Hadlee dismissed Raman with the first ball of the match, the 16th instance of this feat in Test cricket; he emulated England's G.G.Arnold by achieving it twice (also *Test No. 738*). Tendulkar, who fell 12 runs short of becoming the youngest scorer of a Test hundred, and More shared India's highest seventh-wicket partnership against New Zealand (128). Wright completed his second hundred in successive innings and with Franklin shared New Zealand's highest opening partnership in this series.

INDIA

W.V.Raman	lbw b Hadlee	0
M.Prabhakar	c Smith b Hadlee	95
S.V.Manjrekar	c Smith b Morrison	42
*M.Azharuddin	b Morrison	33
D.B.Vengsarkar	c Smith b Morrison	0
S.R.Tendulkar	c Wright b Morrison	88
Kapil Dev	lbw b Hadlee	4
†K.S.More	c Franklin b Snedden	73
S.L.V.Raju	not out	3
A.S.Wassan	b Morrison	0
N.D.Hirwani	not out	1
Extras	(LB5, NB14)	19
Total	**(9 wickets declared)**	**358**

NEW ZEALAND

T.J.Franklin	c Kapil Dev b Wassan	50
*J.G.Wright	not out	113
A.H.Jones	not out	4
M.D.Crowe		
M.J.Greatbatch		
K.R.Rutherford		
†I.D.S.Smith	did not bat	
R.J.Hadlee		
J.G.Bracewell		
M.C.Snedden		
D.K.Morrison		
Extras	(B5, LB3, W1, NB2)	11
Total	**(1 wicket)**	**178**

NEW ZEALAND	O	M	R	W		FALL OF WICKETS		
Hadlee	35	11	73	3			I	NZ
Morrison	38	8	98	5	Wkt	*1st*	*1st*	
Snedden	42	10	104	1	1st	0	149	
Bracewell	22	2	50	0	2nd	92	–	
Rutherford	9	0	28	0	3rd	150	–	
					4th	152	–	
INDIA					5th	210	–	
Prabhakar	13	3	25	0	6th	218	–	
Kapil Dev	14	4	30	0	7th	346	–	
Wassan	15	2	48	1	8th	356	–	
Hirwani	18	7	40	0	9th	356	–	
Raju	11	4	27	0	10th	–	–	

Umpires: B.L.Aldridge (6) and S.J.Woodward (22).

Close: 1st day – no play; 2nd – I(1) 126-2 (Prabhakar 54, Azharuddin 19); 3rd – I(1) 348-7 (Tendulkar 80, Raju 2); 4th – NZ(1) 178-1 (Wright 113, Jones 4).

NEW ZEALAND v INDIA 1989-90 (3rd Test)

At Eden Park, Auckland, on 22, 23, 24, 25, 26 February.
Toss: India.   Result: MATCH DRAWN.
Debuts: New Zealand – S.A.Thomson; India – Gursharan Singh.

An exceptional innings by Ian Smith dominated this match after India had taken six wickets in the first session. His 173 (237 minutes, 136 balls, 3 sixes and 23 fours) is the highest score by anyone batting number nine in Tests, beating C.Hill's 160 in 1907-08 (*Test No. 98*). It was New Zealand's highest score at Eden Park and their highest by a wicket-keeper. His hundred took 95 balls and his 150 came from just 118. He equalled the Test record with 24 runs off an over (244266 off Wassan) and shared in two record New Zealand stands against India: 103 for the eighth wicket with Hadlee and 136 for the ninth with Snedden. Azharuddin led India to their highest total in New Zealand with the highest score (192) by an Indian captain abroad (259 balls, 421 minutes, 26 fours). In his 67th Test, Wright became the first New Zealander to score 4,000 runs. Jones (636 minutes, 448 balls, 2 sixes and 15 fours) and Crowe (227 minutes, 174 balls, 17 fours) confirmed the eventual ascendancy of the bat in a match which produced the highest aggregate for a Test in New Zealand: 1,505 runs for an average of 60.2 per wicket.

NEW ZEALAND

T.J.Franklin	c Tendulkar b Wassan	4	lbw b Prabhakar		2
*J.G.Wright	c Gursharan b Kapil Dev	3	c Wassan b Hirwani		74
A.H.Jones	c More b Prabhakar	19	not out		170
M.D.Crowe	c More b Wassan	24	lbw b Hirwani		113
M.J.Greatbatch	b Wassan	4	c Gursharan b Wassan		43
K.R.Rutherford	c Prabhakar b Wassan	20	c More b Hirwani		8
S.A.Thomson	c More b Kapil Dev	22	not out		43
R.J.Hadlee	b Hirwani	87			
†I.D.S.Smith	lbw b Prabhakar	173			
M.C.Snedden	c More b Prabhakar	22			
D.K.Morrison	not out	0			
Extras	(LB9, NB4)	13	(B4, LB14, NB12)		30
Total		**391**	(5 wickets declared)		**483**

INDIA

W.V.Raman	c Franklin b Hadlee	8	not out		72
M.Prabhakar	lbw b Snedden	36	not out		63
S.V.Manjrekar	b Morrison	16			
D.B.Vengsarkar	c Smith b Morrison	47			
*M.Azharuddin	c Rutherford b Thomson	192			
S.R.Tendulkar	c Smith b Morrison	5			
Gursharan Singh	c and b Thomson	18			
Kapil Dev	c Jones b Hadlee	22			
†K.S.More	lbw b Morrison	50			
A.S.Wassan	b Morrison	53			
N.D.Hirwani	not out	0			
Extras	(B1, LB11, W1, NB22)	35	(LB9, NB5)		14
Total		**482**	(0 wickets)		**149**

INDIA	O	M	R	W	O	M	R	W	FALL OF WICKETS			
										NZ	I	NZ	I
Kapil Dev	29.2	6	85	2	31	4	101	0	*Wkt*	*1st*	*1st*	*2nd*	*2nd*
Prabhakar	29.2	3	123	3	38	6	118	1	1st	8	15	7	–
Wassan	16.4	1	108	4	25	5	80	1	2nd	29	65	155	–
Hirwani	17	1	66	1	46	11	143	3	3rd	29	71	334	–
Raman					19	10	23	0	4th	51	215	396	–
									5th	64	223	406	–
NEW ZEALAND									6th	85	263	–	–
Hadlee	30	8	123	2	4	1	9	0	7th	131	308	–	–
Morrison	30	3	145	5	7	1	34	0	8th	234	396	–	–
Snedden	26	4	110	1	12	1	29	0	9th	370	482	–	–
Thomson	18.3	3	92	2	9	1	30	0	10th	391	482	–	–
Jones					9	1	28	0					
Rutherford					3	0	10	0					
Greatbatch					1	1	0	0					

Umpires: B.L.Aldridge (7) and R.S.Dunne (3).

Close: 1st day – NZ(1) 387-9 (Smith 169, Morrison 0); 2nd – I(1) 316-7 (Azharuddin 130, More 6); 3rd – NZ(2) 135-1 (Wright 58, Jones 62); 4th – NZ(2) 416-5 (Jones 144, Thomson 8).

WEST INDIES v ENGLAND 1989-90 (1st Test)

At Sabina Park, Kingston, Jamaica, on 24, 25, 26, 28 (*no play*) February, 1 March.
Toss: West Indies.   Result: ENGLAND won by nine wickets.
Debuts: England – N.Hussain, A.J.Stewart.

England won their first Test against West Indies since 1973-74 (5th Test), a wait of 16 years and 24 matches, and their first in Kingston since 1953-54. West Indies, who were dismissed for their lowest score in this series since 1969, had not been defeated in Jamaica since Australia won in 1954-55. Inspired by Lamb's tenth Test hundred (his first overseas and his fifth against West Indies), England made their highest total in this series for 41 innings (since their 370 at The Oval in 1980). Larkins celebrated his first Test appearance since August 1981, an interlude of 85 matches, with his highest score and, later, the winning hit.

WEST INDIES

C.G.Greenidge	run out	32	c Hussain b Malcolm		36
D.L.Haynes	c and b Small	36	b Malcolm		14
R.B.Richardson	c Small b Capel	10	lbw b Fraser		25
C.A.Best	c Russell b Capel	4	c Gooch b Small		64
C.L.Hooper	c Capel b Fraser	20	c Larkins b Small		8
*I.V.A.Richards	lbw b Malcolm	21	b Malcolm		37
†P.J.L.Dujon	not out	19	b Malcolm		15
M.D.Marshall	b Fraser	0	not out		8
I.R.Bishop	c Larkins b Fraser	0	c Larkins b Small		3
C.A.Walsh	b Fraser	6	b Small		2
B.P.Patterson	b Fraser	0	run out		2
Extras	(B9, LB3, NB4)	16	(B14, LB10, W1, NB1)		26
Total		**164**			**240**

ENGLAND

*G.A.Gooch	c Dujon b Patterson	18	c Greenidge b Bishop		8
W.Larkins	lbw b Walsh	46	not out		29
A.J.Stewart	c Best b Bishop	13	not out		0
A.J.Lamb	c Hooper b Walsh	132			
R.A.Smith	c Best b Bishop	57			
N.Hussain	c Dujon b Bishop	13			
D.J.Capel	c Richardson b Walsh	5			
†R.C.Russell	c Patterson b Walsh	26			
G.C.Small	lbw b Marshall	4			
A.R.C.Fraser	not out	2			
D.E.Malcolm	lbw b Walsh	0			
Extras	(B23, LB12, W1, NB12)	48	(LB1, NB3)		4
Total		**364**	(1 wicket)		**41**

ENGLAND	O	M	R	W	O	M	R	W		FALL OF WICKETS			
										WI	E	WI	E
Small	15	6	44	1	22	6	58	4	*Wkt*	*1st*	*1st*	*2nd*	*2nd*
Malcolm	16	4	49	1	21.3	2	77	4	1st	62	40	26	35
Fraser	20	8	28	5	(4) 14	4	31	1	2nd	81	60	69	–
Capel	13	4	31	2	(3) 15	1	50	0	3rd	92	116	87	–
									4th	92	288	112	–
WEST INDIES									5th	124	315	192	–
Patterson	18	2	74	1	3	1	11	0	6th	144	315	222	–
Bishop	27	5	72	3	7.3	2	17	1	7th	144	325	222	–
Marshall	18	3	46	1					8th	150	339	227	–
Walsh	27.2	4	68	5	(3) 6	0	12	0	9th	164	364	237	–
Hooper	6	0	28	0					10th	164	364	240	–
Richards	9	1	22	0									
Best	4	0	19	0									

Umpires: L.H.Barker (12) and S.A.Bucknor (2).

Close: 1st day – E(1) 80-2 (Larkins 28, Lamb 10); 2nd – E(1) 342-8 (Russell 12, Fraser 1); 3rd – WI(2) 229-8 (Marshall 2, Walsh 0); 4th – no play.

The 2nd Test at Bourda, Georgetown, Guyana, scheduled for 9, 10, 11, 13, 14 March, was abandoned without a ball bowled (see page 466).

WEST INDIES v ENGLAND 1989-90 (3rd Test)

At Queen's Park Oval, Port-of-Spain, Trinidad, on 23, 24, 25, 27, 28 March.
Toss: England.   Result: MATCH DRAWN.
Debuts: West Indies – E.A.Moseley.

Malcolm, who dismissed Haynes, Best and Logie in four balls and improved his best bowling analysis in each of the first four innings of this rubber, took ten wickets in a first-class match for the first time. It was the first ten-wicket return for England since 1985 (R.M.Ellison in *Test No. 1021*). Requiring 151 for victory, England reached 73 for 1 at lunch on the final day, despite having lost Gooch at 37 when his left hand was fractured by a lifting ball from Moseley. The latter was making his debut at the age of 32 years 76 days. Rain removed the middle session and the ground was barely fit when play resumed, theoretically with 30 overs remaining. Haynes, captaining West Indies for the first time in his 87th Test in the absence of Richards (ill), ensured that his reluctant bowlers delivered only 16.5 overs in 1 hour 55 minutes to leave England 31 runs short of their target when dire light ended this tense contest. In the first innings, Greenidge kept wicket after Dujon was injured.

WEST INDIES

C.G.Greenidge	c Stewart b Malcolm	5	lbw b Fraser		42
D.L.Haynes	c Lamb b Small	0	c Lamb b Malcolm		45
R.B.Richardson	c Russell b Fraser	8	c Gooch b Small		34
C.A.Best	c Lamb b Fraser	10	lbw b Malcolm		0
P.J.L.Dujon	lbw b Small	4	b Malcolm		0
A.L.Logie	c Lamb b Fraser	98	c Larkins b Malcolm		20
C.L.Hooper	c Russell b Capel	32	run out		10
E.A.Moseley	c Russell b Malcolm	0	c Lamb b Malcolm		26
C.E.L.Ambrose	c Russell b Malcolm	7	c Russell b Fraser		18
I.R.Bishop	b Malcolm	16	not out		15
C.A.Walsh	not out	8	lbw b Malcolm		1
Extras	(LB4, NB7)	11	(B2, LB13, W1, NB12)		28
Total		**199**			**239**

ENGLAND

G.A.Gooch	c Dujon b Bishop	84	retired hurt		18
W.Larkins	c Dujon b Ambrose	54	c Dujon b Moseley		7
A.J.Stewart	c Dujon b Ambrose	9	c Bishop b Walsh		31
A.J.Lamb	b Bishop	32	lbw b Bishop		25
R.A.Smith	c Dujon b Moseley	5	lbw b Walsh		2
R.J.Bailey	c Logie b Moseley	0	b Walsh		0
D.J.Capel	c Moseley b Ambrose	40	not out		17
R.C.Russell	c Best b Walsh	15	not out		5
G.C.Small	lbw b Bishop	0			
A.R.C.Fraser	c Hooper b Ambrose	11			
D.E.Malcolm	not out	0			
Extras	(B10, LB9, W3, NB16)	38	(B2, LB7, NB6)		15
Total		**288**	(5 wickets)		**120**

ENGLAND	O	M	R	W	O	M	R	W		FALL OF WICKETS			
										WI	E	WI	E
Small	17	4	41	2	(2) 21	8	56	1	*Wkt*	*1st*	*1st*	*2nd*	*2nd*
Malcolm	20	2	60	4	(1) 26.2	4	77	6	1st	5	112	96	27
Fraser	13.1	2	41	3	(4) 24	4	61	2	2nd	5	152	100	74
Capel	15	2	53	1	(3) 13	3	30	0	3rd	22	195	100	79
									4th	27	214	100	85
WEST INDIES									5th	29	214	142	106
Ambrose	36.2	8	59	4	(2) 6	0	20	0	6th	92	214	167	–
Bishop	31	6	69	3	(1) 10	1	31	1	7th	93	243	200	–
Walsh	22	5	45	1	(4) 7	0	27	3	8th	103	244	200	–
Hooper	18	5	26	0					9th	177	284	234	–
Moseley	30	5	70	2	(3) 10	2	33	1	10th	199	288	239	–

Umpires: L.H.Barker (13) and C.E.Cumberbatch (10).

Close: 1st day – E(1) 43-0 (Gooch 19, Larkins 19); 2nd – E(1) 189-2 (Gooch 83, Lamb 20); 3rd – WI(2) 11-0 (Greenidge 6, Haynes 0); 4th – WI(2) 234-9 (Bishop 11, Walsh 0).

WEST INDIES v ENGLAND 1989-90 (4th Test)

At Kensington Oval, Bridgetown, Barbados, on 5, 6, 7, 8, 10 April.
Toss: England.   Result: WEST INDIES won by 164 runs.
Debuts: None.

West Indies gained their ninth consecutive victory in Tests at Kensington Oval at 5.15 on the final afternoon when fading light would have allowed barely 40 more minutes of play. When Richards claimed the new ball 80 minutes earlier, England were 165 for 5 having lost only two wickets in the previous 4 hours 50 minutes. Ambrose then produced a devastating display of accurate fast bowling to return the best analysis (8 for 45) in all Tests between these two sides. Lamb became only the second England captain after A.C.MacLaren in 1897-98 (*Test No. 53*) to score a hundred in his first match as leader. His fourth-wicket partnership of 193 with Smith was England's highest for any wicket at Bridgetown and he equalled M.C.Cowdrey's record of six hundreds against West Indies. Russell was the first England wicket-keeper to hold five catches in an innings in this series.

WEST INDIES

C.G.Greenidge	c Russell b DeFreitas	41		lbw b Small	3
D.L.Haynes	c Stewart b Small	0		c Malcolm b Small	109
R.B.Richardson	c Russell b Small	45		lbw b DeFreitas	39
C.A.Best	c Russell b Small	164			
*I.V.A.Richards	c Russell b Capel	70	(4)	c Small b Capel	12
A.L.Logie	c Russell b Capel	31	(5)	lbw b DeFreitas	48
†P.J.L.Dujon	b Capel	31	(8)	not out	15
M.D.Marshall	c Lamb b Small	4	(7)	c Smith b Small	7
C.E.L.Ambrose	not out	20		c Capel b DeFreitas	1
I.R.Bishop	run out	10		not out	11
E.A.Moseley	b DeFreitas	4	(6)	b Small	5
Extras	(LB8, NB18)	26		(LB12, W1, NB4)	17
Total		**446**		**(8 wickets declared)**	**267**

ENGLAND

A.J.Stewart	c Richards b Moseley	45		c Richards b Ambrose	37
W.Larkins	c Richardson b Bishop	0		c Dujon b Bishop	0
R.J.Bailey	b Bishop	17		c Dujon b Ambrose	6
*A.J.Lamb	lbw b Ambrose	119	(6)	c Dujon b Moseley	10
R.A.Smith	b Moseley	62	(7)	not out	40
N.Hussain	lbw b Marshall	18	(8)	lbw b Ambrose	0
D.J.Capel	c Greenidge b Marshall	2	(9)	lbw b Ambrose	6
†R.C.Russell	lbw b Bishop	7	(5)	b Ambrose	55
P.A.J.DeFreitas	c and b Ambrose	24	(10)	lbw b Ambrose	0
G.C.Small	not out	1	(4)	lbw b Ambrose	0
D.E.Malcolm	b Bishop	12		lbw b Ambrose	4
Extras	(B14, LB9, W3, NB25)	51		(B8, LB9, W1, NB15)	33
Total		**358**			**191**

ENGLAND	O	M	R	W	O	M	R	W		FALL OF WICKETS			
Malcolm	33	6	142	0	10	0	46	0		WI	E	WI	E
Small	35	5	109	4	20	1	74	4	Wkt	1st	1st	2nd	2nd
DeFreitas	29.5	5	99	2	22	2	69	3	1st	6	1	13	1
Capel	24	5	88	3	16	1	66	1	2nd	69	46	80	10
									3rd	108	75	109	10
WEST INDIES									4th	227	268	223	71
Bishop	24.3	8	70	4	20	7	40	1	5th	291	297	228	97
Ambrose	25	2	82	2	22.4	10	45	8	6th	395	301	239	166
Moseley	28	3	114	2	(4) 19	3	44	1	7th	406	308	239	173
Marshall	23	6	55	2	(3) 18	8	31	0	8th	411	340	239	181
Richards	9	4	14	0	10	5	11	0	9th	431	340	–	181
Richardson					2	1	3	0	10th	446	358	–	191

Umpires: D.M.Archer (23) and L.H.Barker (14).

Close: 1st day – WI(1) 311-5 (Best 102, Dujon 2); 2nd – E(1) 155-3 (Lamb 63, Smith 17); 3rd – WI(2) 19-1 (Haynes 10, Richardson 6); 4th – E(2) 15-3 (Stewart 4, Russell 3).

WEST INDIES v ENGLAND 1989-90 (5th Test)

At Recreation Ground, St John's, Antigua, on 12, 14, 15, 16 April.
Toss: England.   Result: WEST INDIES won by an innings and 32 runs.
Debuts: None.

Still bereft of the services of Gooch but granted the best batting pitch of the rubber, England were unable to avoid a comprehensive defeat with four sessions to spare. Greenidge became the third West Indian (11th player overall) to appear in 100 Tests and emulated Pakistan's Javed Miandad by scoring hundreds in both his first and his 100th Test. His partnership of 298 with Haynes was the highest by a West Indian opening pair in all Tests. Greenidge, who also completed 7,000 runs, scored his 18th hundred (7th against England), while Haynes registered his 14th (5th against England). Richards overtook C.H.Lloyd's West Indies record of 110 Test appearances. Smith, subjected to a barrage of bouncers without intervention from the umpires, retired hurt at 61 for 4 with a fractured hand.

ENGLAND

A.J.Stewart	c Richards b Walsh	27		c Richardson b Bishop	8
W.Larkins	c Hooper b Ambrose	30		b Ambrose	10
R.J.Bailey	c Dujon b Bishop	42	(4)	c Dujon b Bishop	8
*A.J.Lamb	c Richards b Ambrose	37	(5)	b Baptiste	35
R.A.Smith	lbw b Walsh	12	(6)	retired hurt	8
N.Hussain	c Dujon b Bishop	35	(7)	c Dujon b Bishop	34
D.J.Capel	c Haynes b Bishop	10	(8)	run out	1
†R.C.Russell	c Dujon b Bishop	7	(9)	c Richardson b Ambrose	24
P.A.J.DeFreitas	lbw b Bishop	21	(10)	c Greenidge b Ambrose	0
G.C.Small	lbw b Walsh	8	(3)	b Ambrose	4
D.E.Malcolm	not out	0		not out	1
Extras	(B5, LB11, NB15)	31		(B1, LB8, W1, NB11)	21
Total		**260**			**154**

WEST INDIES

C.G.Greenidge	run out	149
D.L.Haynes	c Russell b Small	167
R.B.Richardson	c Russell b Malcolm	34
C.L.Hooper	b Capel	1
*I.V.A.Richards	c Smith b Malcolm	1
A.L.Logie	c Lamb b DeFreitas	15
†P.J.L.Dujon	run out	25
E.A.E.Baptiste	c Russell b Malcolm	9
C.E.L.Ambrose	c DeFreitas b Capel	5
I.R.Bishop	not out	14
C.A.Walsh	b Malcolm	8
Extras	(LB5, NB13)	18
Total		**446**

WEST INDIES	O	M	R	W	O	M	R	W		FALL OF WICKETS		
Bishop	28.1	6	84	5	14	2	36	3		E	WI	E
Ambrose	29	5	79	2	13	7	22	4	*Wkt*	*1st*	*1st*	*2nd*
Walsh	21	4	51	3	10	1	40	0	1st	42	298	16
Baptiste	13	4	30	0	10	1	47	1	2nd	101	357	20
									3rd	143	358	33
ENGLAND									4th	167	359	37
Small	31	3	123	1					5th	167	382	86
Malcolm	34.5	3	126	4					6th	195	384	96
Capel	28	1	118	2					7th	212	415	148
DeFreitas	27	4	74	1					8th	242	417	148
									9th	259	433	154
									10th	260	446	–

Umpires: D.M.Archer (24) and A.E.Weekes (4).

Close: 1st day – E(1) 203-6 (Hussain 16, Russell 4); 2nd – WI(1) 228-0 (Greenidge 118, Haynes 101); 3rd – E(2) 16-1 (Stewart 4).

NEW ZEALAND v AUSTRALIA 1989-90 (Only Test)

At Basin Reserve, Wellington, on 15, 16, 17, 18, 19 March.
Toss: Australia.   Result: NEW ZEALAND won by nine wickets.
Debuts: None.

New Zealand's sixth win of this series ended Australia's run of 14 matches without defeat. Outstanding work by the groundstaff enabled play to start at 2 pm following torrential storms two days earlier. Electing to bat on a slow pitch, Australia were bowled out in 198 minutes, Hadlee, playing his final Test at home, taking five or more wickets in an innings for the 100th time in first-class matches and extending his world Test record of such hauls to 35. Later he scored his 3,000th run in 83 Tests and became the first player to combine that tally with 400 wickets. Snedden set a Test record for the longest time without adding to a score by remaining on 6 for 94 minutes. Jones completed 1,000 runs in his 14th Test and shared with Wright an unbroken partnership of 128 to establish a new second-wicket record for New Zealand against Australia. Bracewell became the leading wicket-taker among New Zealand's slow bowlers when he dismissed Healy and passed H.J.Howarth's total of 86. Wright scored his 10th hundred in 68 Tests.

AUSTRALIA

M.A.Taylor	lbw b Morrison	4	(2)	lbw b Hadlee	5
G.R.Marsh	b Morrison	4	(1)	c Rutherford b Bracewell	41
D.C.Boon	lbw b Hadlee	0		c Smith b Bracewell	12
*A.R.Border	lbw b Morrison	1	(5)	not out	78
D.M.Jones	c Wright b Snedden	20	(6)	lbw b Morrison	0
S.R.Waugh	b Hadlee	25	(7)	c Greatbatch b Hadlee	25
†I.A.Healy	b Snedden	0	(8)	c Rutherford b Bracewell	10
P.L.Taylor	c Wright b Hadlee	29	(4)	c Smith b Morrison	87
G.D.Campbell	lbw b Hadlee	4		b Bracewell	0
C.G.Rackemann	not out	6		b Bracewell	1
T.M.Alderman	b Hadlee	4		st Smith b Bracewell	1
Extras	(LB6, NB7)	13		(LB6, NB3)	9
Total		**110**			**269**

NEW ZEALAND

T.J.Franklin	c Marsh b P.L.Taylor	28	c Healy b Campbell	18
*J.G.Wright	c Healy b Alderman	36	not out	117
A.H.Jones	c and b Border	18	not out	33
M.C.Snedden	b Alderman	23		
M.J.Greatbatch	c Healy b P.L.Taylor	16		
K.R.Rutherford	c Healy b P.L.Taylor	12		
J.J.Crowe	lbw b Alderman	9		
R.J.Hadlee	lbw b Campbell	18		
†I.D.S.Smith	c M.A.Taylor b Campbell	1		
J.G.Bracewell	not out	19		
D.K.Morrison	c M.A.Taylor b Alderman	12		
Extras	(B2, LB5, NB3)	10	(B2, LB10, NB1)	13
Total		**202**	(1 wicket)	**181**

NEW ZEALAND	O	M	R	W	O	M	R	W	FALL OF WICKETS			
										A	NZ	A	NZ
Hadlee	16.2	5	39	5	25	3	70	2		A	NZ	A	NZ
Morrison	10	4	22	3	24	8	58	2	*Wkt*	*1st*	*1st*	*2nd*	*2nd*
Snedden	15	2	33	2	25	5	46	0	1st	4	48	27	53
Rutherford	2	0	8	0					2nd	9	89	54	–
Bracewell	2	1	2	0	(4) 34.2	11	85	6	3rd	9	89	91	–
Jones					(5) 1	0	4	0	4th	12	111	194	–
									5th	38	123	194	–
AUSTRALIA									6th	44	150	232	–
Alderman	29	9	46	4	14	8	27	0	7th	70	151	261	–
Rackemann	32	17	42	0	15	4	39	0	8th	87	152	261	–
P.L.Taylor	33	19	44	3	11	3	39	0	9th	103	171	267	–
Campbell	21	3	51	2	7	2	23	1	10th	110	202	269	–
Border	6	3	12	1	(6) 10.4	5	27	0					
Jones					(5) 6	3	14	0					

Umpires: R.S.Dunne (4) and S.J.Woodward (23).

Close: 1st day – NZ(1) 18-0 (Franklin 12, Wright 5); 2nd – NZ(1) 93-3 (Snedden 0, Greatbatch 4); 3rd – A(2) 57-2 (Marsh 33, P.L.Taylor 1); 4th – NZ(2) 4-0 (Franklin 2, Wright 1).

ENGLAND v NEW ZEALAND 1990 (1st Test)

At Trent Bridge, Nottingham, on 7, 8, 9, 11, 12 June.
Toss: New Zealand.   Result: MATCH DRAWN.
Debuts: New Zealand – M.W.Priest.

A fifth successive draw in this series was inevitable after 13 hours 43 minutes (211 overs) were lost, play on the second and third days being restricted to 5 and 11.1 overs respectively. Hadlee dismissed Gooch with the first ball of his final series. Atherton (22) became England's youngest century-maker since D.I.Gower in 1978; it was the first hundred by a Cambridge blue since A.R.Lewis scored 125 at Kanpur in January 1973. His hundred, completed off 310 balls in 405 minutes with his ninth boundary, was the 20th by an England batsman in his first Test against New Zealand. When he caught Stewart, Ian Smith became the tenth wicket-keeper and the first New Zealander to make 150 dismissals in Test matches.

NEW ZEALAND

T.J.Franklin	b Malcolm	33		not out	22
*J.G.Wright	c Stewart b Small	8		c Russell b Small	1
A.H.Jones	c Stewart b Malcolm	39		c Russell b DeFreitas	13
M.D.Crowe	b DeFreitas	59			
M.J.Greatbatch	b Hemmings	1			
M.W.Priest	c Russell b DeFreitas	26			
M.C.Snedden	c Gooch b DeFreitas	0			
J.G.Bracewell	c Gooch b Small	28			
R.J.Hadlee	b DeFreitas	0			
†I.D.S.Smith	not out	2			
D.K.Morrison	lbw b DeFreitas	0	(4)	not out	0
Extras	(B1, LB10, W1)	12			
Total		**208**		(2 wickets)	**36**

ENGLAND

*G.A.Gooch	lbw b Hadlee	0
M.A.Atherton	c Snedden b Priest	151
A.J.Stewart	c Smith b Hadlee	27
A.J.Lamb	lbw b Hadlee	0
R.A.Smith	c Smith b Bracewell	55
N.H.Fairbrother	c Franklin b Snedden	19
†R.C.Russell	c Snedden b Morrison	28
P.A.J.DeFreitas	lbw b Bracewell	14
G.C.Small	c Crowe b Hadlee	26
E.E.Hemmings	not out	13
D.E.Malcolm	not out	4
Extras	(B2, LB3, NB3)	8
Total	(9 wickets declared)	**345**

ENGLAND	O	M	R	W		O	M	R	W		FALL OF WICKETS		
											NZ	E	NZ
Small	29	9	49	2	(2)	6	2	14	1	*Wkt*	*1st*	*1st*	*2nd*
Malcolm	19	7	48	2	(1)	7	2	22	0	1st	16	0	8
Hemmings	19	6	47	1	(4)	2	2	0	0	2nd	75	43	36
DeFreitas	22	6	53	5	(3)	2	2	0	1	3rd	110	45	–
										4th	121	141	–
NEW ZEALAND										5th	170	168	–
Hadlee	33	6	89	4						6th	174	260	–
Morrison	22	3	96	1						7th	191	302	–
Snedden	36	17	54	1						8th	191	306	–
Bracewell	35	8	75	2						9th	203	340	–
Priest	12	4	26	1						10th	208	–	–

Umpires: H.D.Bird (43) and J.H.Hampshire (6).

Close: 1st day – NZ(1) 171-5 (Priest 23, Snedden 0); 2nd – NZ(1) 189-6 (Snedden 0, Bracewell 15); 3rd – E(1) 4-1 (Atherton 3, Stewart 1); 4th – E(1) 187-5 (Atherton 78, Russell 4).

ENGLAND v NEW ZEALAND 1990 (2nd Test)

At Lord's, London, on 21, 22, 23, 25, 26 June.
Toss: New Zealand.   Result: MATCH DRAWN.
Debuts: None.

The loss of 118 overs to rain, combined with a placid pitch, made the draw an inevitable result. Put in under leaden skies, England salvaged just 27 runs from an opening day reduced to 11.3 overs in 51 minutes. Atherton was dismissed for his only score under 50 in the series. Robin Smith completed 1,000 runs in his 14th Test. Franklin (432 minutes, 310 balls, 8 fours) laboured diligently for his maiden Test hundred and shared with Wright New Zealand's highest opening partnership in England (185 in 278 minutes). The highlight of the tourists' innings was a belligerent 84-ball innings of 86 by Sir Richard Hadlee whose knighthood had been announced in the Queen's Birthday Honours nine days before this match began. He was the third knight to play Test cricket after gaining his title, although the others, Sir Timothy O'Brien and Sir Vijaya Vizianagram, were not honoured for their services to cricket. He was also the first knight to receive a match award. Crowe deputised as captain for the last 12 overs of the second day after Wright had sprained his left wrist in the field. In the final session, New Zealand fielded substitutes for Hadlee, Greatbatch and Snedden.

ENGLAND

*G.A.Gooch	c and b Bracewell	85	b Hadlee		37
M.A.Atherton	b Morrison	0	c Bracewell b Jones		54
A.J.Stewart	lbw b Hadlee	54	c sub (M.W.Priest) b Bracewell		42
A.J.Lamb	lbw b Snedden	39	not out		84
R.A.Smith	c Bracewell b Morrison	64	hit wicket b Bracewell		0
N.H.Fairbrother	c Morrison b Bracewell	2	not out		33
†R.C.Russell	b Hadlee	13			
P.A.J.DeFreitas	c Franklin b Morrison	38			
G.C.Small	b Morrison	3			
E.E.Hemmings	b Hadlee	0			
D.E.Malcolm	not out	0			
Extras	(LB13, W1, NB22)	36	(B8, LB8, NB6)		22
Total		**334**	(4 wickets declared)		**272**

NEW ZEALAND

T.J.Franklin	c Russell b Malcolm	101
*J.G.Wright	c Stewart b Small	98
A.H.Jones	c Stewart b Malcolm	49
M.D.Crowe	c Russell b Hemmings	1
M.J.Greatbatch	b Malcolm	47
K.R.Rutherford	c Fairbrother b Malcolm	0
Sir R.J.Hadlee	b Hemmings	86
J.G.Bracewell	run out	4
†I.D.S.Smith	c Small b Malcolm	27
M.C.Snedden	not out	13
D.K.Morrison	not out	2
Extras	(B12, LB15, W2, NB5)	34
Total	(9 wickets declared)	**462**

NEW ZEALAND	O	M	R	W		O	M	R	W		FALL OF WICKETS		
											E	NZ	E
Hadlee	29	5	113	3		13	2	32	1				
Morrison	18.4	4	64	4		16	0	81	0	Wkt	*1st*	*1st*	*2nd*
Snedden	21	4	72	1						1st	3	185	68
Bracewell	21	3	72	2	(3)	34	13	85	2	2nd	151	278	135
Jones					(4)	12	3	40	1	3rd	178	281	171
Rutherford					(5)	3	0	18	0	4th	216	284	175
										5th	226	285	–
ENGLAND										6th	255	408	–
Malcolm	43	14	94	5						7th	319	415	–
Small	35	4	127	1						8th	322	425	–
DeFreitas	35.4	1	122	0						9th	332	448	–
Hemmings	30	13	67	2						10th	334	–	–
Gooch	13	7	25	0									
Atherton	1	1	0	0									

Umpires: M.J.Kitchen (1) and D.R.Shepherd (10).

Close: 1st day – E(1) 27-1 (Gooch 16, Stewart 3); 2nd – E(1) 329-8 (DeFreitas 33, Hemmings 0); 3rd – NZ(1) 156-0 (Franklin 60, Wright 84); 4th – NZ(1) 440-8 (Smith 20, Snedden 0).

ENGLAND v NEW ZEALAND 1990 (3rd Test)

At Edgbaston, Birmingham, on 5, 6, 7, 9, 10 July.
Toss: New Zealand.   Result: ENGLAND won by 114 runs.
Debuts: England – C.C.Lewis; New Zealand – A.C.Parore.

At 19 years 163 days, Parore became New Zealand's youngest wicket-keeper. Gooch (394 minutes, 281 balls, a six and 19 fours) became the 11th to score 5,000 runs for England during his ninth Test hundred in 140 innings and his first as captain. His stand of 170 with Atherton was the first-wicket record for England in all Tests at Edgbaston. Hemmings (41) returned his best analysis in Tests and the best by a slow bowler in a home Test for England since 1974. England's second innings total was their lowest against New Zealand in a home Test (previously 187 at Old Trafford in 1937). Having completed 1,000 runs on the third day of his 41st Test, Bracewell took his 100th wicket when he dismissed Lamb on the fourth day to become the 26th player to complete the Test double, the second after Hadlee (28 matches) to do so for New Zealand, and the second after Kapil Dev (25 matches) to complete both sections in the same Test. Needing four wickets to average five per Test throughout his 86-match career, Hadlee extended his (then) world record tally to 431 wickets, his (record) 36th five-wicket return being captured during a final 50-ball sequence which included Hemmings and Malcolm with the third and sixth deliveries of his last over.

ENGLAND

*G.A.Gooch	c Hadlee b Morrison	154	b Snedden	30
M.A.Atherton	lbw b Snedden	82	c Rutherford b Bracewell	70
A.J.Stewart	c Parore b Morrison	9	lbw b Bracewell	15
A.J.Lamb	c Parore b Hadlee	2	st Parore b Bracewell	4
R.A.Smith	c Jones b Bracewell	19	c and b Hadlee	14
N.H.Fairbrother	lbw b Snedden	2	lbw b Bracewell	3
†R.C.Russell	b Snedden	43	c sub (J.J.Crowe) b Hadlee	0
C.C.Lewis	c Rutherford b Bracewell	32	c Parore b Hadlee	1
G.C.Small	not out	44	not out	11
E.E.Hemmings	c Parore b Hadlee	20	b Hadlee	0
D.E.Malcolm	b Hadlee	0	lbw b Hadlee	0
Extras	(B4, LB15, NB9)	28	(LB6, NB4)	10
Total		**435**		**158**

NEW ZEALAND

T.J.Franklin	c Smith b Hemmings	66	lbw b Malcolm	5
*J.G.Wright	c Russell b Malcolm	24	c Smith b Lewis	46
A.H.Jones	c Russell b Malcolm	2	c Gooch b Small	40
M.D.Crowe	lbw b Lewis	11	lbw b Malcolm	25
M.J.Greatbatch	b Malcolm	45	c Atherton b Hemmings	22
K.R.Rutherford	c Stewart b Hemmings	29	c Lamb b Lewis	18
Sir R.J.Hadlee	c Atherton b Hemmings	8	b Malcolm	13
J.G.Bracewell	b Hemmings	25	(9) c Atherton b Malcolm	0
†A.C.Parore	not out	12	(8) c Lamb b Lewis	20
M.C.Snedden	lbw b Hemmings	2	not out	21
D.K.Morrison	b Hemmings	1	b Malcolm	6
Extras	(B9, LB11, W2, NB2)	24	(LB9, W1, NB4)	14
Total		**249**		**230**

NEW ZEALAND	O	M	R	W	O	M	R	W
Hadlee	37.5	8	97	3	21	3	53	5
Morrison	26	7	81	2	3	1	29	0
Snedden	35	9	106	3	9	0	32	1
Bracewell	42	12	130	2	16	5	38	4
Jones	1	0	2	0				
ENGLAND								
Small	18	7	44	0	(2) 16	5	56	1
Malcolm	25	7	59	3	(1) 24.4	8	46	5
Lewis	19	5	51	1	22	3	76	3
Hemmings	27.3	10	58	6	29	13	43	1
Atherton	9	5	17	0				

FALL OF WICKETS

Wkt	E 1st	NZ 1st	E 2nd	NZ 2nd
1st	170	45	50	25
2nd	193	67	87	85
3rd	198	90	99	111
4th	245	161	129	125
5th	254	163	136	155
6th	316	185	141	163
7th	351	223	146	180
8th	381	230	157	180
9th	435	243	158	203
10th	435	249	158	230

Umpires: J.W.Holder (8) and B.J.Meyer (22).

Close: 1st day – E(1) 191-1 (Gooch 95, Stewart 8); 2nd – NZ(1) 9-0 (Franklin 8, Wright 1); 3rd – NZ(1) 249 all out; 4th – NZ(2) 101-2 (Jones 37, Crowe 10).

ENGLAND v INDIA 1990 (1st Test)

At Lord's, London, on 26, 27, 28, 30, 31 July.
Toss: India.   Result: ENGLAND won by 247 runs.
Debuts: England – J.E.Morris.

Gooch dominated a match overflowing with records and outstanding cricket. His 333 (627 minutes, 485 balls, 3 sixes and 43 fours) was the sixth-highest Test score, the third-highest score for England, the highest by any Test captain, the highest score against India and the highest score in any match at Lord's. By adding 123 in the second innings (148 minutes, 113 balls, 4 sixes and 13 fours), he became the first to score a triple hundred and a hundred in any first-class match and set a record Test match aggregate of 456 runs. Only Hanif Mohammad (499) had exceeded that tally in a first-class match. He also completed 35,000 first-class runs and his third-wicket stand of 308 with Lamb was England's highest for any wicket against India. England's total is their highest against India and the record for any country put in by the opposition. His opening partnership of 204 with Atherton was also a series record (until their next innings). Kapil Dev averted the follow-on when he became the first to hit four successive balls (from Hemmings) for six. Fraser returned figures of 8 for 143 from 61.1 overs during a match which produced the highest aggregate of any Lord's Test (1,603 runs).

ENGLAND

*G.A.Gooch	b Prabhakar	333	c Azharuddin b Sharma	123
M.A.Atherton	b Kapil Dev	8	c Vengsarkar b Sharma	72
D.I.Gower	c Manjrekar b Hirwani	40	not out	32
A.J.Lamb	c Manjrekar b Sharma	139	c Tendulkar b Hirwani	19
R.A.Smith	not out	100	b Prabhakar	15
J.E.Morris	not out	4		
†R.C.Russell				
C.C.Lewis				
E.E.Hemmings	did not bat			
A.R.C.Fraser				
D.E.Malcolm				
Extras	(B2, LB21, W2, NB4)	29	(LB11)	11
Total	(4 wickets declared)	**653**	(4 wickets declared)	**272**

INDIA

R.J.Shastri	c Gooch b Hemmings	100	c Russell b Malcolm	12
N.S.Sidhu	c Morris b Fraser	30	c Morris b Fraser	1
S.V.Manjrekar	c Russell b Gooch	18	c Russell b Malcolm	33
D.B.Vengsarkar	c Russell b Fraser	52	c Russell b Hemmings	35
*M.Azharuddin	b Hemmings	121	c Atherton b Lewis	37
S.R.Tendulkar	b Lewis	10	c Gooch b Fraser	27
M.Prabhakar	c Lewis b Malcolm	25	lbw b Lewis	8
Kapil Dev	not out	77	c Lewis b Hemmings	7
†K.S.More	c Morris b Fraser	8	lbw b Fraser	16
S.K.Sharma	c Russell b Fraser	0	run out	38
N.D.Hirwani	lbw b Fraser	0	not out	0
Extras	(LB1, W4, NB8)	13	(B3, LB1, NB6)	10
Total		**454**		**224**

INDIA	O	M	R	W	O	M	R	W		FALL OF WICKETS			
Kapil Dev	34	5	120	1	10	0	53	0		E	I	E	I
Prabhakar	43	6	187	1	11.2	2	45	1	Wkt	1st	1st	2nd	2nd
Sharma	33	5	122	1	(4) 15	0	75	2	1st	14	63	204	9
Shastri	22	0	99	0	(3) 7	0	38	0	2nd	141	102	207	23
Hirwani	30	1	102	1	11	0	50	1	3rd	449	191	250	63
									4th	641	241	272	114
ENGLAND									5th	–	288	–	127
Malcolm	25	1	106	1	(2) 10	0	65	2	6th	–	348	–	140
Fraser	39.1	9	104	5	(1) 22	7	39	3	7th	–	393	–	158
Lewis	24	3	108	1	(5) 8	1	26	2	8th	–	430	–	181
Gooch	6	3	26	1					9th	–	430	–	206
Hemmings	20	3	109	2	(3) 21	2	79	2	10th	–	454	–	224
Atherton					(4) 1	0	11	0					

Umpires: H.D.Bird (44) and N.T.Plews (4).

Close: 1st day – E(1) 359-2 (Gooch 194, Lamb 104); 2nd – I(1) 48-0 (Shastri 27, Sidhu 20); 3rd – I(1) 376-6 (Azharuddin 117, Kapil Dev 14); 4th – I(2) 57-2 (Manjrekar 29, Vengsarkar 14).

ENGLAND v INDIA 1990 (2nd Test)

At Old Trafford, Manchester, on 9, 10, 11, 13, 14 August.
Toss: England.   Result: MATCH DRAWN.
Debuts: India – A.Kumble.

Batsmen continued to have the upper hand, exceeding the record Lord's match aggregate by 11 runs. Gooch scored his 12th hundred in 80 Tests, became the fourth to score three in successive innings for England and completed 1,000 runs for the year (in 12 innings). He and Atherton became the first pair to record successive opening partnerships of 200 and surpassed their own record for this series. Atherton was only the second Lancashire player after G.Pullar (*Test No. 477*) to score a Test hundred for England at Old Trafford. India retained the same ball throughout the 160.5 overs of the first innings, a record in England. Azharuddin's tenth hundred was his fifth in eight matches against England and his third in successive Tests; he scored 103 between lunch and tea on the third day. He and Gooch became the first pair of opposing captains to each score hundreds in the same Test in successive matches. England's eight hundreds in successive Tests also established a record beating Australia's seven in the Caribbean in 1954-55. Manjrekar completed 1,000 runs in his 14th Test. At 17 years 112 days, Tendulkar became the second-youngest after Mushtaq Mohammad (17 years 82 days) to score a Test hundred. Morris retired at 290.

ENGLAND

*G.A.Gooch	c More b Prabhakar	116	c More b Prabhakar		7
M.A.Atherton	c More b Hirwani	131	lbw b Kapil Dev		74
D.I.Gower	c Tendulkar b Kapil Dev	38	b Hirwani		16
A.J.Lamb	c Manjrekar b Kumble	38	b Kapil Dev		109
†R.C.Russell	c More b Hirwani	8	(7) not out		16
R.A.Smith	not out	121	(5) not out		61
J.E.Morris	b Kumble	13	(6) retired hurt		15
C.C.Lewis	b Hirwani	3			
E.E.Hemmings	lbw b Hirwani	19			
A.R.C.Fraser	c Tendulkar b Kumble	1			
D.E.Malcolm	b Shastri	13			
Extras	(B2, LB9, W1, NB6)	18	(LB15, NB7)		22
Total		**519**	(4 wickets declared)		**320**

INDIA

R.J.Shastri	c Gooch b Fraser	25	b Malcolm		12
N.S.Sidhu	c Gooch b Fraser	13	c sub (C.J.Adams) b Fraser		0
S.V.Manjrekar	c Smith b Hemmings	93	c sub (C.J.Adams) b Hemmings		50
D.B.Vengsarkar	c Russell b Fraser	6	b Lewis		32
*M.Azharuddin	c Atherton b Fraser	179	c Lewis b Hemmings		11
S.R.Tendulkar	c Lewis b Hemmings	68	not out		119
M.Prabhakar	c Russell b Malcolm	4	(8) not out		67
Kapil Dev	lbw b Lewis	0	(7) b Hemmings		26
†K.S.More	b Fraser	6			
A.Kumble	run out	2			
N.D.Hirwani	not out	15			
Extras	(B5, LB4, NB12)	21	(B17, LB3, NB6)		26
Total		**432**	(6 wickets)		**343**

INDIA	O	M	R	W	O	M	R	W		FALL OF WICKETS			
Kapil Dev	13	2	67	1	22	4	69	2		E	I	E	I
Prabhakar	25	2	112	1	18	1	80	1	Wkt	1st	1st	2nd	2nd
Kumble	43	7	105	3	(4) 17	3	65	0	1st	225	26	15	4
Hirwani	62	10	174	4	(3) 15	0	52	1	2nd	292	48	46	35
Shastri	17.5	2	50	1	9	0	39	0	3rd	312	57	180	109
									4th	324	246	248	109
ENGLAND									5th	366	358	–	127
Malcolm	26	3	96	1	14	5	59	1	6th	392	364	–	183
Fraser	35	5	124	5	21	3	81	1	7th	404	365	–	–
Hemmings	29.2	8	74	2	31	10	75	3	8th	434	396	–	–
Lewis	13	1	61	1	(5) 20	3	86	1	9th	459	401	–	–
Atherton	16	3	68	0	(4) 4	0	22	0	10th	519	432	–	–

Umpires: J.H.Hampshire (7) and J.W.Holder (9).

Close: 1st day – E(1) 322-3 (Lamb 20, Russell 7); 2nd – I(1) 77-3 (Manjrekar 21, Azharuddin 4); 3rd – I(1) 432 all out; 4th – E(2) 290-4 (Smith 49, Morris 15).

ENGLAND v INDIA 1990 (3rd Test)

At Kennington Oval, London, on 23, 24, 25, 27, 28 August.
Toss: India.   Result: MATCH DRAWN.
Debuts: England – N.F.Williams.

India's highest total against England was founded upon the highest of Shastri's ten Test hundreds (187 in 561 minutes, 435 balls, 23 fours). At 17 years 123 days, Tendulkar became the youngest to score 2,000 runs in first-class cricket (when 9). India compelled England to follow on for only the second time in 78 matches (also *Test No. 514*). With 752 runs, Gooch established a record for any three-match rubber, beating 583 by Zaheer Abbas (Pakistan v India 1978-79) and he became the first to score 1,000 runs in a season's Test matches (1,058 runs in 11 innings). Gower (366 minutes, 271 balls, 21 fours) scored his 16th hundred and his last in England. Pausing only for scheduled intervals, Hirwani bowled 59 overs unchanged from the Vauxhall End.

INDIA

R.J.Shastri	c Lamb b Malcolm	187			
N.S.Sidhu	c Russell b Fraser	12			
S.V.Manjrekar	c Russell b Malcolm	22			
D.B.Vengsarkar	c and b Atherton	33			
*M.Azharuddin	c Russell b Williams	78			
M.Prabhakar	lbw b Fraser	28			
S.R.Tendulkar	c Lamb b Williams	21			
Kapil Dev	st Russell b Hemmings	110			
†K.S.More	not out	61			
A.S.Wassan	b Hemmings	15			
N.D.Hirwani	not out	2			
Extras	(B7, LB8, W6, NB16)	37			
Total	(9 wickets declared)	**606**			

ENGLAND

*G.A.Gooch	c Shastri b Hirwani	85	c Vengsarkar b Hirwani		88
M.A.Atherton	c More b Prabhakar	7	lbw b Kapil Dev		86
N.F.Williams	lbw b Prabhakar	38			
D.I.Gower	lbw b Wassan	8	(3) not out		157
J.E.Morris	c More b Wassan	7	(4) c More b Wassan		32
A.J.Lamb	b Kapil Dev	7	(5) c Shastri b Kapil Dev		52
R.A.Smith	c Manjrekar b Shastri	57	(6) not out		7
†R.C.Russell	run out	35			
E.E.Hemmings	c Vengsarkar b Prabhakar	51			
A.R.C.Fraser	c More b Prabhakar	0			
D.E.Malcolm	not out	15			
Extras	(B8, LB9, W4, NB9)	30	(B16, LB22, W5, NB12)		55
Total		**340**	(4 wickets declared)		**477**

ENGLAND	O	M	R	W	O	M	R	W		FALL OF WICKETS		
Malcolm	35	7	110	2						I	E	E
Fraser	42	17	112	2					Wkt	1st	1st	2nd
Williams	41	5	148	2					1st	16	18	176
Gooch	12	1	44	0					2nd	61	92	251
Hemmings	36	3	117	2					3rd	150	111	334
Atherton	7	0	60	1					4th	289	120	463
									5th	335	139	–
INDIA									6th	368	231	–
Kapil Dev	25	7	70	1	(2) 24	5	66	2	7th	478	233	–
Prabhakar	32.4	9	74	4	(1) 25	8	56	0	8th	552	295	–
Wassan	19	3	79	2	18	2	94	1	9th	576	299	–
Hirwani	35	12	71	1	59	18	137	1	10th	–	340	–
Shastri	12	2	29	1	28	2	86	0				

Umpires: N.T.Plews (5) and D.R.Shepherd (11).

Close: 1st day – I(1) 324-4 (Shastri 135, Prabhakar 20); 2nd – E(1) 36-1 (Gooch 5, Williams 15); 3rd – E(1) 293-7 (Russell 34, Hemmings 26); 4th – E(2) 215-1 (Atherton 71, Gower 32).

PAKISTAN v NEW ZEALAND 1990-91 (1st Test)

At National Stadium, Karachi, on 10, 11, 12, 14, 15 October.
Toss: Pakistan.   Result: PAKISTAN won by an innings and 43 runs.
Debuts: New Zealand – G.E.Bradburn, C.Pringle, D.J.White.

On a pitch favouring seam bowling, Pakistan needed only ten balls on the fifth day to maintain their unbeaten record in Karachi. Shoaib (656 minutes, 411 balls, 23 fours) equalled his highest score and recorded his third hundred in successive innings against New Zealand. His stand of 172 with Ramiz established a series record for the first wicket. Crowe, in his first Test as captain, batted for 250 minutes (143 balls) in the second innings.

NEW ZEALAND

T.J.Franklin	c Salim Yousuf b Waqar	16		b Wasim	0
D.J.White	c Salim Yousuf b Wasim	9		b Wasim	18
M.J.Greatbatch	c and b Ijaz	43		lbw b Aqib	21
*M.D.Crowe	c Ramiz b Waqar	7		not out	68
K.R.Rutherford	b Aqib	79		lbw b Aqib	0
D.N.Patel	lbw b Waqar	2		lbw b Wasim	19
D.K.Morrison	lbw b Wasim	4	(9)	b Wasim	0
G.E.Bradburn	not out	11	(7)	c Salim Yousuf b Waqar	2
†I.D.S.Smith	lbw b Wasim	4	(8)	b Waqar	14
C.Pringle	b Waqar	0		lbw b Qadir	20
W.Watson	lbw b Wasim	0		lbw b Waqar	11
Extras	(B5, LB11, W2, NB3)	21		(B7, LB9, NB5)	21
Total		196			194

PAKISTAN

Ramiz Raja	c Crowe b Bradburn	78
Shoaib Mohammad	not out	203
Salim Malik	c Rutherford b Pringle	43
*Javed Miandad	lbw b Morrison	27
Wasim Akram	run out	28
Ijaz Ahmed	b Watson	9
†Salim Yousuf	c Crowe b Morrison	13
Abdul Qadir	not out	6
Tausif Ahmed	⎫	
Waqar Younis	⎬ did not bat	
Aqib Javed	⎭	
Extras	(B3, LB11, W1, NB11)	26
Total	(6 wickets declared)	433

PAKISTAN	O	M	R	W		O	M	R	W		FALL OF WICKETS		
Wasim	29.5	12	44	4		24	5	60	4		NZ	P	NZ
Waqar	22	7	40	4	(3)	15.4	4	39	3	*Wkt*	*1st*	*1st*	*2nd*
Aqib	16	4	37	1	(2)	12	1	45	2	1st	28	172	4
Qadir	7	1	32	0		10	2	32	1	2nd	37	239	23
Tausif	5	0	18	0		1	0	2	0	3rd	51	288	56
Ijaz	5	0	9	1						4th	167	360	57
										5th	174	384	96
NEW ZEALAND										6th	181	413	103
Morrison	28.3	5	86	2						7th	181	–	119
Pringle	25	3	68	1						8th	194	–	120
Watson	40	8	125	1						9th	195	–	173
Bradburn	17	3	56	1						10th	196	–	194
Patel	24	6	62	0									
Crowe	6	1	22	0									

Umpires: Feroze Butt (1) and Mahboob Shah (20).

Close: 1st day – NZ(1) 175-5 (Patel 2, Morrison 0); 2nd – P(1) 159-0 (Ramiz 68, Shoaib 82); 3rd – P(1) 386-5 (Shoaib 175, Salim Yousuf 1); 4th – NZ(2) 192-9 (Crowe 67, Watson 11).

PAKISTAN v NEW ZEALAND 1990-91 (2nd Test)

At Gaddafi Stadium, Lahore, on 18, 19, 20, 22, 23 October.
Toss: New Zealand.   Result: PAKISTAN won by nine wickets.
Debuts: None.

Pakistan completed another comprehensive victory with more than a session to spare after New Zealand had opted to bat on another pitch favouring fast bowling. In New Zealand's first innings, extras contributed the highest score for the eighth time. Shoaib (351 minutes, 223 balls, a six and 15 fours) scored his fourth hundred in successive innings against New Zealand. Crowe (552 minutes, 306 balls, a six and 14 fours), who recorded his 12th hundred in 53 Tests, rated the bowling of Waqar (match analysis 10 for 106) as the highest quality of pace and swing he had ever faced.

NEW ZEALAND

T.J.Franklin	c Wasim b Salim Jaffer	11		c Salim Yousuf b Salim Jaffer	25
D.J.White	c Salim Yousuf b Wasim	3		b Waqar	1
M.J.Greatbatch	b Waqar	11		b Waqar	6
*M.D.Crowe	c Salim Malik b Aqib	20		not out	108
K.R.Rutherford	lbw b Wasim	23	(6)	lbw b Waqar	60
D.N.Patel	b Waqar	4	(7)	c Salim Yousuf b Salim Jaffer	7
G.E.Bradburn	lbw b Salim Jaffer	8	(8)	c sub (Aamir Sohail) b Waqar	14
†I.D.S.Smith	c Salim Yousuf b Qadir	33	(9)	c Salim Jaffer b Qadir	8
C.Pringle	c Ramiz b Waqar	9	(10)	b Waqar	7
D.K.Morrison	c Salim Yousuf b Qadir	0	(5)	b Waqar	7
W.Watson	not out	0		lbw b Waqar	0
Extras	(B5, LB13, W5, NB15)	38		(B17, LB10, NB17)	44
Total		**160**			**287**

PAKISTAN

Ramiz Raja	c Greatbatch b Watson	48		c Crowe b Morrison	11
Shoaib Mohammad	b Morrison	105		not out	42
Salim Malik	lbw b Watson	6		not out	19
*Javed Miandad	c Smith b Bradburn	43			
Ijaz Ahmed	c Greatbatch b Watson	86			
†Salim Yousuf	c Rutherford b Pringle	33			
Wasim Akram	c Bradburn b Watson	1			
Waqar Younis	b Watson	17			
Salim Jaffer	not out	10			
Aqib Javed	c Crowe b Watson	7			
Abdul Qadir	did not bat				
Extras	(B4, LB1, NB12)	17		(LB1, W1, NB3)	5
Total	(9 wickets declared)	**373**		(1 wicket)	**77**

PAKISTAN	O	M	R	W		O	M	R	W		FALL OF WICKETS			
Wasim	16	3	43	2		9	4	15	0			NZ	P	NZ	P
Waqar	15	7	20	3		37.5	11	86	7	*Wkt*	*1st*	*1st*	*2nd*	*2nd*
Salim Jaffer	12	2	37	2	(4)	25	8	62	2	1st	7	98	10	27
Aqib	13	2	37	1	(3)	21	9	40	0	2nd	30	117	18	–
Qadir	3	1	5	2		19	4	43	1	3rd	39	192	57	–
Shoaib						2	0	8	0	4th	79	246	74	–
Ijaz						2	0	6	0	5th	99	317	206	–
										6th	103	337	228	–
NEW ZEALAND										7th	143	342	264	–
Morrison	29	9	103	1		8	2	36	1	8th	147	363	277	–
Pringle	31	6	112	1		7	4	10	0	9th	154	373	287	–
Watson	36	10	78	6	(4)	2	0	12	0	10th	160	–	287	–
Patel	16	5	43	0	(3)	3	0	13	0					
Bradburn	13	4	32	1										
White					(5)	0.3	0	5	0					

Umpires: Athar Zaidi (1) and Salim Badar (2).

Close: 1st day – P(1) 43-0 (Ramiz 23, Shoaib 17); 2nd – P(1) 252-4 (Ijaz 33, Salim Yousuf 4); 3rd – NZ(2) 69-3 (Crowe 17, Morrison 7); 4th – NZ(2) 253-6 (Crowe 100, Bradburn 5).

PAKISTAN v NEW ZEALAND 1990-91 (3rd Test)

At Iqbal Stadium, Faisalabad, on 26, 28, 29, 30, 31 October.
Toss: New Zealand.   Result: PAKISTAN won by 65 runs.
Debuts: None.

Pakistan overcame the ignominy of being dismissed for their lowest total against New Zealand to gain three wins in a rubber for only the third time (also v Australia and v India in 1982-83). Shoaib's third hundred of the rubber (142 in 527 minutes off 368 balls with 20 fours) was his fifth hundred in seven innings against New Zealand. During his second innings, Javed Miandad became the fifth batsman to score 8,000 runs in Tests. Waqar, who claimed 29 wickets in the rubber, improved upon his best innings analysis for the third match in succession, and returned Pakistan's record match figures in this series. Pringle returned New Zealand's best innings and match analyses against Pakistan and became only the second New Zealand bowler to take 11 wickets in a Test. In contrast to Morrison's 242-minute vigil for 25, Smith's 42-ball innings of 61 included 50 off 34 balls. In the first innings, Horne retired at 7 after ducking into a ball from Waqar and resumed at 166 but, when Smith was taken ill, he kept wicket for five overs before A.C.Parore substituted for the remainder of that second innings. Waqar became only the fifth bowler to dismiss all eleven batsmen in a Test.

PAKISTAN

Ramiz Raja	c Smith b Pringle	20		lbw b Watson	16
Shoaib Mohammad	c Crowe b Pringle	15		c sub (A.C.Parore) b Pringle	142
Salim Malik	c Smith b Pringle	4	(4)	c and b Crowe	71
*Javed Miandad	c Smith b Pringle	25	(5)	c Bradburn b Pringle	55
Ijaz Ahmed	c Horne b Watson	5	(6)	c Horne b Pringle	6
†Salim Yousuf	c Morrison b Watson	14	(3)	c Crowe b Pringle	13
Naved Anjum	c Smith b Pringle	10		b Morrison	22
Tausif Ahmed	c Rutherford b Pringle	1		not out	12
Waqar Younis	b Pringle	0		c Rutherford b Morrison	0
Salim Jaffer	lbw b Watson	0		b Morrison	2
Aqib Javed	not out	0		c sub (A.C.Parore) b Morrison	4
Extras	(LB3, NB5)	8		(B1, LB8, NB5)	14
Total		**102**			**357**

NEW ZEALAND

T.J.Franklin	b Waqar	25		c Ijaz b Aqib	12
P.A.Horne	c Ramiz b Salim Jaffer	0		lbw b Waqar	12
M.J.Greatbatch	c Salim Yousuf b Waqar	8	(4)	b Aqib	0
*M.D.Crowe	c Tausif b Salim Jaffer	31	(5)	c Salim Yousuf b Waqar	10
K.R.Rutherford	b Waqar	0	(6)	c Salim Yousuf b Salim Jaffer	25
D.N.Patel	lbw b Waqar	0	(7)	c Salim Yousuf b Salim Jaffer	45
D.K.Morrison	c Shoaib b Waqar	25	(3)	c Salim Yousuf b Aqib	0
†I.D.S.Smith	c Salim Malik b Tausif	61	(9)	c and b Waqar	21
G.E.Bradburn	c Salim Yousuf b Waqar	18	(8)	not out	30
C.Pringle	not out	24		c Salim Yousuf b Waqar	0
W.Watson	lbw b Waqar	2		lbw b Waqar	2
Extras	(B12, LB8, NB3)	23		(B10, LB5, W1, NB4)	20
Total		**217**			**177**

NEW ZEALAND	O	M	R	W	O	M	R	W	FALL OF WICKETS				
Morrison	9	3	18	0	29.5	3	105	4		P	NZ	P	NZ
Pringle	16	4	52	7	43	13	100	4	*Wkt*	*1st*	*1st*	*2nd*	*2nd*
Watson	15.3	5	29	3	44	23	77	1	1st	35	36	33	23
Patel					6	0	21	0	2nd	37	37	61	25
Crowe					11	5	22	1	3rd	42	37	192	28
Bradburn					6	1	23	0	4th	65	37	309	31
									5th	82	89	314	45
PAKISTAN									6th	92	166	321	64
Waqar	30.2	13	76	7	23.5	9	54	5	7th	98	171	349	148
Aqib	10	5	24	0	(3) 17	1	57	3	8th	102	178	349	171
Naved	6	4	13	0					9th	102	207	353	171
Salim Jaffer	20	5	47	2	(2) 18	4	51	2	10th	102	217	357	177
Tausif	10	2	37	1									

Umpires: Athar Zaidi (2) and Salim Badar (3).

Close: 1st day – NZ(1) 40-4 (Crowe 1, Morrison 2); 2nd – P(2) 43-1 (Shoaib 24, Salim Yousuf 0); 3rd – P(2) 252-3 (Shoaib 122, Miandad 22); 4th – NZ(2) 31-4 (Crowe 3, Rutherford 0).

PAKISTAN v WEST INDIES 1990-91 (1st Test)

At National Stadium, Karachi, on 15, 16, 17, 19, 20 November.
Toss: West Indies.   Result: PAKISTAN won by eight wickets.
Debuts: Pakistan – Zahid Fazal.

Imran Khan returned to the helm for this three-match rubber (billed as the 'unofficial world championship of cricket') and led Pakistan to their fourth successive win of the season. Haynes, captain while Richards was convalescing from surgery, chose to bat first on a grassless pitch of variable bounce. Although he recorded his 15th hundred in 90 Tests, he received scant support as Waqar returned his fourth successive innings haul of five or more wickets. Shoaib and Salim Malik, whose eighth Test hundred occupied 268 minutes (208 balls), retrieved a dismal start by adding 174, Pakistan's record for the fourth wicket against West Indies.

WEST INDIES

C.G.Greenidge	lbw b Waqar	3	st Salim Yousuf b Qadir		11
*D.L.Haynes	lbw b Wasim	117	c Salim Yousuf b Waqar		47
R.B.Richardson	st Salim Yousuf b Mushtaq	26	lbw b Waqar		11
C.A.Best	c Ramiz b Mushtaq	1	lbw b Mushtaq		8
C.L.Hooper	lbw b Waqar	8	lbw b Wasim		0
A.L.Logie	c Salim Yousuf b Wasim	25	not out		58
†P.J.L.Dujon	c Miandad b Waqar	17	b Shoaib		1
M.D.Marshall	b Waqar	13	b Wasim		21
C.E.L.Ambrose	lbw b Waqar	2	lbw b Waqar		0
I.R.Bishop	c Salim Yousuf b Wasim	22	b Waqar		0
C.A.Walsh	not out	6	b Wasim		0
Extras	(B6, LB6, NB9)	21	(B10, LB8, NB6)		24
Total		**261**			**181**

PAKISTAN

Shoaib Mohammad	c Richardson b Marshall	86	not out		32
Ramiz Raja	b Bishop	0	lbw b Walsh		7
Zahid Fazal	c Logie b Ambrose	7	c Richardson b Walsh		12
Javed Miandad	c Dujon b Bishop	7			
Salim Malik	c Dujon b Marshall	102	(4) not out		30
*Imran Khan	not out	73			
†Salim Yousuf	b Ambrose	5			
Wasim Akram	c Richardson b Walsh	9			
Mushtaq Ahmed	c Richardson b Ambrose	3			
Abdul Qadir	c Dujon b Ambrose	0			
Waqar Younis	c Hooper b Bishop	5			
Extras	(B7, LB14, W1, NB26)	48	(LB8, NB9)		17
Total		**345**	(2 wickets)		**98**

PAKISTAN	O	M	R	W	O	M	R	W		FALL OF WICKETS			
										WI	P	WI	P
Wasim	23.3	1	61	3	20.3	6	39	3	*Wkt*	*1st*	*1st*	*2nd*	*2nd*
Waqar	22	0	76	5	17	3	44	4	1st	4	2	47	15
Qadir	20	2	56	0	8	1	22	1	2nd	77	16	85	56
Mushtaq	18	3	56	2	15	5	38	1	3rd	81	27	86	–
Shoaib					6	1	15	1	4th	96	201	90	–
Salim Malik					1	0	5	0	5th	151	281	111	–
									6th	178	298	127	–
WEST INDIES									7th	200	313	166	–
Ambrose	34	7	78	4	(2) 2	0	4	0	8th	204	318	174	–
Bishop	27.2	3	81	3	(1) 7	0	21	0	9th	243	318	174	–
Marshall	24	5	48	2	5	1	8	0	10th	261	345	181	–
Walsh	19	0	50	1	12	2	27	2					
Hooper	28	6	65	0	11	2	30	0					
Best	1	0	2	0									

Umpires: Khizer Hayat (23) and Riazuddin (1).

Close: 1st day – WI(1) 237-8 (Haynes 113, Bishop 12); 2nd – P(1) 171-3 (Shoaib 48, Salim Malik 88); 3rd – P(1) 332-9 (Imran 60, Waqar 5); 4th – WI(2) 172-7 (Logie 51, Ambrose 0).

PAKISTAN v WEST INDIES 1990-91 (2nd Test)

At Iqbal Stadium, Faisalabad, on 23, 24, 25 November.
Toss: Pakistan.   Result: WEST INDIES won by seven wickets.
Debuts: Pakistan – Moin Khan, Saeed Anwar.

Just five days later, West Indies gained full revenge for their defeat in Karachi, a cavalier innings by Richardson sealing victory with more than six sessions to spare. Although devoid of pace, another pitch of variable bounce, this time providing ample lateral movement, was fully exploited by the fast bowlers. Marshall took four wickets in 13 balls while Waqar returned his fifth five-wicket analysis in six innings and set a Pakistan record by reaching 50 wickets in only his tenth Test. Left-hander Saeed Anwar faced only five balls in being dismissed for a pair before his Test career was two days old.

PAKISTAN

Saeed Anwar	c Best b Ambrose	0		lbw b Bishop	0
Shoaib Mohammad	c Dujon b Bishop	7		b Ambrose	15
Zahid Fazal	run out	32		b Bishop	5
Javed Miandad	c Dujon b Walsh	7	(6)	c Dujon b Ambrose	9
Salim Malik	c Richardson b Bishop	74	(4)	b Marshall	71
*Imran Khan	lbw b Walsh	3	(7)	c Dujon b Marshall	0
Wasim Akram	run out	4	(8)	run out	0
†Moin Khan	c Greenidge b Ambrose	24	(5)	c Logie b Walsh	32
Akram Raza	b Bishop	5		b Marshall	0
Mushtaq Ahmed	not out	2		not out	5
Waqar Younis	c Dujon b Bishop	1		c Dujon b Marshall	3
Extras	(LB3, NB8)	11		(LB4, NB10)	14
Total		**170**			**154**

WEST INDIES

C.G.Greenidge	lbw b Waqar	12	(4)	lbw b Wasim	10
*D.L.Haynes	lbw b Akram Raza	19	(1)	c Akram Raza b Wasim	0
R.B.Richardson	c Saeed b Akram Raza	44		not out	70
C.A.Best	c Moin b Waqar	6	(2)	b Wasim	7
C.L.Hooper	lbw b Waqar	5		not out	33
A.L.Logie	c Moin b Waqar	12			
†P.J.L.Dujon	lbw b Wasim	9			
M.D.Marshall	b Wasim	20			
C.E.L.Ambrose	b Waqar	15			
I.R.Bishop	lbw b Wasim	0			
C.A.Walsh	not out	14			
Extras	(B8, LB20, NB11)	39		(B4, LB2, NB4)	10
Total		**195**		**(3 wickets)**	**130**

WEST INDIES	O	M	R	W	O	M	R	W		FALL OF WICKETS			
										P	WI	P	WI
Bishop	17.2	6	47	4	11	1	53	2	*Wkt*	*1st*	*1st*	*2nd*	*2nd*
Ambrose	17	3	47	2	13	5	32	2	1st	1	26	0	0
Walsh	10	1	38	2	9	0	32	1	2nd	15	78	10	11
Marshall	8	1	30	0	4.2	0	24	4	3rd	29	101	38	34
Hooper	2	1	5	0	3	1	9	0	4th	76	101	127	–
									5th	91	108	145	–
PAKISTAN									6th	99	121	146	–
Wasim	17	1	63	3	12	0	46	3	7th	146	143	146	–
Waqar	16	3	46	5	9	2	41	0	8th	157	162	146	–
Akram Raza	19	4	52	2	7.2	0	37	0	9th	169	162	146	–
Mushtaq	4	1	6	0	1	1	0	0	10th	170	195	154	–

Umpires: Khizer Hayat (24) and Riazuddin (2).

Close: 1st day – P(1) 170 all out; 2nd – P(2) 38-3 (Salim 16, Moin 0).

PAKISTAN v WEST INDIES 1990-91 (3rd Test)

At Gaddafi Stadium, Lahore, on 6, 7, 8, 10, 11 December.
Toss: West Indies.   Result: MATCH DRAWN.
Debuts: Pakistan – Masood Anwar; West Indies – B.C.Lara.

After conceding a first innings lead of 172 on yet another paceless pitch of uneven bounce, Pakistan showed great tenacity in thwarting the West Indies attack for the final five sessions. Brian Charles Lara began his Test career by providing Hooper with his only major support during only his second hundred in 22 matches. Bishop completed 50 wickets in his 11th Test and hit Moin Khan in the face with a bouncer. Aamer Malik deputised as wicket-keeper in the second innings which Wasim terminated in dramatic style by taking four wickets in five balls to emulate the feats of M.J.C.Allom and C.M.Old. The dismissals of Dujon and Ambrose were followed by an edged single to Bishop and the wickets of Marshall and Walsh. A resolute Imran (196 balls) and night-watchman Masood Anwar (130 balls) defied a cracked and ragged surface to ensure that the third successive rubber in this series ended in a 1-1 draw.

WEST INDIES

C.G.Greenidge	lbw b Imran	21	c Zahid b Waqar		1
*D.L.Haynes	c Moin b Imran	3	c Shoaib b Masood		12
R.B.Richardson	lbw b Wasim	5	c Aamer b Imran		6
B.C.Lara	c Aamer b Qadir	44	c Salim b Imran		5
C.L.Hooper	c Zahid b Masood	134	run out		49
A.L.Logie	lbw b Waqar	16	lbw b Wasim		59
†P.J.L.Dujon	st Moin b Masood	0	c Moin b Wasim		3
M.D.Marshall	b Wasim	27	b Wasim		11
C.E.L.Ambrose	lbw b Wasim	0	lbw b Wasim		0
I.R.Bishop	c Moin b Wasim	9	not out		1
C.A.Walsh	not out	5	lbw b Wasim		0
Extras	(B8, LB12, NB10)	30	(B14, LB4, NB8)		26
Total		294			173

PAKISTAN

Aamer Malik	b Bishop	3	c Logie b Ambrose		0
Shoaib Mohammad	b Bishop	0	(3) b Bishop		49
Zahid Fazal	c Haynes b Ambrose	13	(7) b Walsh		6
Ramiz Raja	c Logie b Ambrose	6	(2) b Walsh		41
Salim Malik	c Greenidge b Bishop	8	b Bishop		0
*Imran Khan	c Logie b Ambrose	17	not out		58
Wasim Akram	b Ambrose	38	(8) not out		21
†Moin Khan	c Logie b Ambrose	7			
Masood Anwar	c Logie b Bishop	2	(4) c Lara b Hooper		37
Abdul Qadir	lbw b Bishop	1			
Waqar Younis	not out	0			
Extras	(B4, LB12, W1, NB10)	27	(LB4, NB26)		30
Total		122	(6 wickets)		242

PAKISTAN	O	M	R	W		O	M	R	W	FALL OF WICKETS				
											WI	P	WI	P
Imran	6	0	22	2		13	5	32	2	*Wkt*	*1st*	*1st*	*2nd*	*2nd*
Wasim	24	4	61	4	(4)	9	0	28	5	1st	13	2	1	0
Waqar	17	0	57	1	(2)	8	0	32	1	2nd	24	11	13	90
Qadir	18	1	75	1	(5)	4	0	19	0	3rd	37	33	27	107
Masood	13.5	3	59	2	(3)	13	1	43	1	4th	132	34	47	110
Shoaib						1	0	1	0	5th	185	48	155	177
										6th	186	93	155	187
WEST INDIES										7th	247	108	172	–
Ambrose	20	5	35	5		20.5	5	43	1	8th	249	120	172	–
Bishop	20.2	7	41	5		23	6	59	2	9th	278	121	173	–
Marshall	5	2	8	0	(4)	19	5	48	0	10th	294	122	173	–
Walsh	5	1	22	0	(3)	19	3	53	2					
Hooper						15	4	35	1					

Umpires: Khizer Hayat (25) and Riazuddin (3).

Close: 1st day – WI(1) 250-8 (Hooper 107, Bishop 0); 2nd – P(1) 93-6 (Wasim 21, Moin 0); 3rd – WI(2) 128-4 (Hooper 39, Logie 43); 4th – P(2) 90-2 (Shoaib 36, Masood 0).

INDIA v SRI LANKA 1990-91 (Only Test)

At Sector 16 Stadium, Chandigarh, on 23, 24, 25, 27 November.
Toss: India.   Result: INDIA won by an innings and 8 runs.
Debuts: Sri Lanka – M.S.Atapattu.

Although this solitary match began a few hours after the start of an Ashes campaign, it seemed illogical to place it after a series which ended some three months later. Chandigarh, India's equivalent of Milton Keynes, provided Test cricket with its 63rd ground and staged the country's first home Test for two years. Because of the cancellation of Pakistan's tour it was India's sole Test of the season. Their victory ended a barren sequence of 14 matches, all overseas, six of them under the captaincy of Azharuddin. The toss proved all-important on an under-prepared pitch favouring spin, the match having been transferred from Jullundur at a late stage. Sri Lanka failed to avoid the follow-on target of 89 and were dismissed for their lowest total until 1994-95 and the lowest by any country against India. Gurusinha (181 minutes, 169 balls) carried his bat through the innings and contributed 63.4% of the total, the third highest portion of any completed Test innings. Raju returned the extraordinary figures of 6 for 12 in 17.5 overs, including a spell of 5 for 2 in 39 balls.

INDIA

R.J.Shastri	c De Silva b Warnaweera	88
M.Prabhakar	lbw b Warnaweera	31
S.V.Manjrekar	lbw b Madurasinghe	39
D.B.Vengsarkar	lbw b Ratnayake	7
M.Azharuddin	c Labrooy b Madurasinghe	23
S.R.Tendulkar	lbw b Madurasinghe	11
Kapil Dev	c De Silva b Warnaweera	4
K.S.More	not out	37
S.L.V.Raju	lbw b Ratnayake	14
G.Sharma	lbw b Ratnayake	0
N.D.Hirwani	run out	0
Extras	(B5, LB10, NB19)	34
Total		**288**

SRI LANKA

R.S.Mahanama	c More b Kapil Dev	1		c More b Kapil Dev	48
M.A.R.Samarasekera	lbw b Prabhakar	13		c More b Prabhakar	5
A.P.Gurusinha	not out	52		c Sharma b Prabhakar	0
P.A.de Silva	b Raju	5		lbw b Hirwani	7
A.Ranatunga	b Raju	1		c Azharuddin b Raju	42
H.P.Tillekeratne	b Raju	0	(7)	c Shastri b Kapil Dev	55
M.S.Atapattu	c More b Raju	0	(6)	lbw b Kapil Dev	0
R.J.Ratnayake	lbw b Raju	0		lbw b Raju	0
G.F.Labrooy	b Sharma	0		b Kapil Dev	0
A.W.R.Madurasinghe	run out	2		b Prabhakar	11
K.P.J.Warnaweera	b Raju	0		not out	0
Extras	(B1, LB2, NB5)	8		(B5, LB15, NB10)	30
Total		**82**			**198**

SRI LANKA	O	M	R	W		O	M	R	W		FALL OF WICKETS		
Ratnayake	21.5	3	60	3							I	SL	SL
Labrooy	12	1	59	0						*Wkt*	*1st*	*1st*	*2nd*
Warnaweera	46	17	90	3						1st	58	4	14
Ranatunga	5	2	4	0						2nd	134	34	14
Madurasinghe	26	6	60	3						3rd	158	50	47
										4th	208	54	110
INDIA										5th	210	54	110
Kapil Dev	8	3	14	1		29.4	15	36	4	6th	220	54	135
Prabhakar	9	0	27	1		15	4	44	3	7th	240	60	135
Raju	17.5	13	12	6	(4)	36	25	25	2	8th	276	65	136
Sharma	17	5	26	1	(3)	20	7	39	0	9th	276	77	196
Hirwani						20	9	34	1	10th	288	82	198

Umpires: S.B.Kulkarni (1) and R.S.Rathore (1).

Close: 1st day – I(1) 220-6 (Tendulkar 7, More 0); 2nd – SL(1) 75-8 (Gurusinha 47, Madurasinghe 0); 3rd – SL(2) 125-5 (Ranatunga 36, Tillekeratne 11).

AUSTRALIA v ENGLAND 1990-91 (1st Test)

At Woolloongabba, Brisbane, on 23, 24, 25 November.
Toss: Australia.   Result: AUSTRALIA won by ten wickets.
Debuts: None.

Australia overcame a first innings deficit of 42 to win by ten wickets, an unbroken partnership of 157 between Taylor and Marsh (then the record for any Brisbane Test) sealing victory on the third day. Gooch's absence following surgery on a poisoned hand proved crucial when England had to bat first in conditions favouring swing and seam movement. Leading England for the first time, Lamb passed 4,000 runs in Tests and 25,000 in first-class matches. Border became the second batsman after Gavaskar to play 200 Test innings. Some outstanding catching earned England their slender lead but Alderman's best analysis in Tests condemned them to their lowest total at Brisbane.

ENGLAND

Batsman	Dismissal	R		Dismissal	R
M.A.Atherton	lbw b Reid	13		b Alderman	15
W.Larkins	c Healy b Hughes	12		lbw b Reid	0
D.I.Gower	c Healy b Reid	61		b Hughes	27
*A.J.Lamb	c Hughes b Matthews	32		lbw b Alderman	14
R.A.Smith	b Reid	7	(6)	c Taylor b Alderman	1
A.J.Stewart	lbw b Reid	4	(7)	c sub (P.E.Cantrell) b Alderman	6
†R.C.Russell	c and b Alderman	16	(5)	lbw b Waugh	15
C.C.Lewis	c Border b Hughes	20		lbw b Alderman	14
G.C.Small	not out	12		c Alderman b Hughes	15
A.R.C.Fraser	c Healy b Alderman	1		c sub (P.E.Cantrell) b Alderman	0
D.E.Malcolm	c Waugh b Hughes	5		not out	0
Extras	(B1, LB7, NB3)	11		(LB3, NB4)	7
Total		**194**			**114**

AUSTRALIA

Batsman	Dismissal	R		Dismissal	R
G.R.Marsh	lbw b Fraser	9	(2)	not out	72
M.A.Taylor	c Lewis b Fraser	10	(1)	not out	67
D.C.Boon	lbw b Small	18			
*A.R.Border	c Atherton b Small	9			
D.M.Jones	c Small b Lewis	17			
S.R.Waugh	c Smith b Small	1			
G.R.J.Matthews	c Small b Malcolm	35			
†I.A.Healy	c Atherton b Lewis	22			
M.G.Hughes	c Russell b Fraser	9			
B.A.Reid	b Lewis	0			
T.M.Alderman	not out	0			
Extras	(B1, LB10, NB11)	22		(B3, LB2, W3, NB10)	18
Total		**152**		(0 wickets)	**157**

AUSTRALIA	O	M	R	W		O	M	R	W
Alderman	18	5	44	2		22	7	47	6
Reid	18	3	53	4		14	3	40	1
Hughes	19	5	39	3		12.1	5	17	2
Waugh	7	2	20	0	(5)	4	2	7	1
Matthews	16	8	30	1	(4)	1	1	0	0
ENGLAND									
Malcolm	17	2	45	1	(3)	9	5	22	0
Fraser	21	6	33	3	(1)	14	2	49	0
Small	16	4	34	3	(2)	15	2	36	0
Lewis	9	0	29	3		6	0	29	0
Atherton						2	0	16	0

FALL OF WICKETS				
	E	A	E	A
Wkt	1st	1st	2nd	2nd
1st	23	22	0	–
2nd	43	35	42	–
3rd	117	49	46	–
4th	123	60	60	–
5th	134	64	78	–
6th	135	89	84	–
7th	167	135	93	–
8th	181	150	112	–
9th	187	150	114	–
10th	194	152	114	–

Umpires: A.R.Crafter (30) and P.J.McConnell (17).

Close: 1st day – A(1) 16-0 (Marsh 6, Taylor 4); 2nd – E(2) 56-3 (Lamb 10, Russell 1).

AUSTRALIA v ENGLAND 1990-91 (2nd Test)

At Melbourne Cricket Ground on 26, 27, 28, 29, 30 December.
Toss: England.   Result: AUSTRALIA won by eight wickets.
Debuts: England – P.C.R.Tufnell.

This match, played on a slow pitch of low bounce, followed a similar pattern to its predecessor with Australia again countering first innings arrears (46) by inflicting a startling collapse (6 wickets for 3 runs) before romping home with a vast unbroken partnership (187 between Marsh and Boon, the latter completing 1,000 runs against England). Gower (254 minutes, 170 balls), burdened by a bruised right wrist, became the second England batsman after Hobbs to score 3,000 runs against Australia. His second innings duck ended a world record sequence of 119 Test innings without one. Russell was the first England wicket-keeper to make six dismissals in an innings against Australia. The left-handed Reid improved his best Test analysis in each innings, returning match figures of 13 for 148. Fraser sustained the hip injury which threatened to end his career. Waugh completed 2,000 runs in 41 Tests and Border captained Australia for a record 20th time in this series.

ENGLAND

*G.A.Gooch	lbw b Alderman	20	c Alderman b Reid	58
M.A.Atherton	c Boon b Reid	0	c Healy b Reid	4
W.Larkins	c Healy b Reid	64	c Healy b Reid	54
R.A.Smith	c Healy b Hughes	30	c Taylor b Reid	8
D.I.Gower	c and b Reid	100	c Border b Matthews	0
A.J.Stewart	c Healy b Reid	79	c Marsh b Reid	8
†R.C.Russell	c Healy b Hughes	15	c Jones b Matthews	1
P.A.J.DeFreitas	c Healy b Reid	3	lbw b Reid	0
A.R.C.Fraser	c Jones b Alderman	24	c Taylor b Reid	0
D.E.Malcolm	c Taylor b Reid	6	lbw b Matthews	1
P.C.R.Tufnell	not out	0	not out	0
Extras	(LB2, NB9)	11	(B7, LB3, NB6)	16
Total		352		150

AUSTRALIA

G.R.Marsh	c Russell b DeFreitas	36	not out	79
M.A.Taylor	c Russell b DeFreitas	61	c Atherton b Malcolm	5
D.C.Boon	c Russell b Malcolm	28	(4) not out	94
*A.R.Border	c Russell b Fraser	62		
D.M.Jones	c Russell b Fraser	44		
S.R.Waugh	b Fraser	19		
G.R.J.Matthews	lbw b Fraser	12		
†I.A.Healy	c Russell b Fraser	5	(3) c Atherton b Fraser	1
M.G.Hughes	lbw b Malcolm	4		
T.M.Alderman	b Fraser	0		
B.A.Reid	not out	3		
Extras	(B4, LB12, NB16)	32	(B4, LB12, NB2)	18
Total		306	(2 wickets)	197

AUSTRALIA	O	M	R	W	O	M	R	W	FALL OF WICKETS				
Alderman	30.4	7	86	2	10	2	19	0		E	A	E	A
Reid	39	8	97	6	22	12	51	7	*Wkt*	*1st*	*1st*	*2nd*	*2nd*
Hughes	29	7	83	2	9	4	26	0	1st	12	63	17	9
Matthews	27	8	65	0	25	9	40	3	2nd	30	133	103	10
Waugh	6	2	19	0	7	6	4	0	3rd	109	149	115	–
									4th	152	224	122	–
									5th	274	264	147	–
ENGLAND									6th	303	281	148	–
Malcolm	25.5	4	74	2	23	7	52	1	7th	307	289	148	–
Fraser	39	10	82	6	20	4	33	1	8th	324	298	148	–
Tufnell	21	5	62	0	24	12	36	0	9th	344	302	150	–
DeFreitas	25	5	69	2	16	3	46	0	10th	352	306	150	–
Atherton	2	1	3	0	3	0	14	0					

Umpires: A.R.Crafter (31) and P.J.McConnell (18).

Close: 1st day – E(1) 239-4 (Gower 73, Stewart 42); 2nd – A(1) 109-1 (Taylor 42, Boon 18); 3rd – A(1) 306 all out; 4th – A(2) 28-2 (Marsh 11, Boon 8).

AUSTRALIA v ENGLAND 1990-91 (3rd Test)

At Sydney Cricket Ground on 4, 5, 6, 7, 8 January.
Toss: Australia.   Result: MATCH DRAWN.
Debuts: None.

When England failed to score 255 at nine runs an over, Australia retained the Ashes at home for the first time since 1965-66. England were briefly on course when Gooch (54 off 42 balls) and Gower, who became the second Englishman after Boycott to score 8,000 runs in Tests, struck 81 off 11 overs. Gaining first use of a placid pitch, Australia amassed their highest total in a home Test against England since 1965-66, the innovative Matthews (242 minutes, 175 balls) contributing their first hundred of the rubber. Gooch completed 6,000 runs in 150 innings and Atherton (424 minutes) scored the slowest hundred in Anglo-Australian Tests, batting 451 minutes (349 balls) for his 105. Gower (312 minutes, 236 balls) scored the last of his 18 Test hundreds; only Hobbs (12) has exceeded his tally of nine against Australia. Tufnell, who took his first Test wicket after bowling 440 balls and conceding 191 runs, narrowly missed a hat-trick when Gower failed to hold a sharp chance at silly point. Border (3,000 runs in 39 Tests) and Taylor (1,000 runs in nine) achieved notable landmarks in this series. The defence of Rackemann (72 minutes on 0) was crucial to the final equation. Reid (calloused heel) was unable to complete his 17th over.

AUSTRALIA

G.R.Marsh	c Larkins b Malcolm	13	(2)	c Stewart b Malcolm	4
M.A.Taylor	c Russell b Malcolm	11	(1)	lbw b Hemmings	19
D.C.Boon	c Atherton b Gooch	97	(4)	c Gooch b Tufnell	29
*A.R.Border	b Hemmings	78	(5)	c Gooch b Tufnell	20
D.M.Jones	st Russell b Small	60	(6)	c and b Tufnell	0
S.R.Waugh	c Stewart b Malcolm	48	(7)	c Russell b Hemmings	14
G.R.J.Matthews	c Hemmings b Tufnell	128	(8)	b Hemmings	19
†I.A.Healy	c Small b Hemmings	35	(3)	c Smith b Tufnell	69
C.G.Rackemann	b Hemmings	1		b Malcolm	9
T.M.Alderman	not out	26		c Gower b Tufnell	1
B.A.Reid	c Smith b Malcolm	0		not out	5
Extras	(B5, LB8, NB8)	21		(LB16)	16
Total		**518**			**205**

ENGLAND

*G.A.Gooch	c Healy b Reid	59		c Border b Matthews	54
M.A.Atherton	c Boon b Matthews	105	(6)	not out	3
W.Larkins	run out	11		lbw b Border	0
R.A.Smith	c Healy b Reid	18	(5)	not out	10
D.I.Gower	c Marsh b Reid	123	(2)	c Taylor b Matthews	36
A.J.Stewart	lbw b Alderman	91	(4)	run out	7
†R.C.Russell	not out	30			
G.C.Small	lbw b Alderman	10			
E.E.Hemmings	b Alderman	0			
P.C.R.Tufnell	not out	5			
D.E.Malcolm	did not bat				
Extras	(B1, LB8, NB8)	17		(LB1, NB2)	3
Total	(8 wickets declared)	**469**		(4 wickets)	**113**

ENGLAND	O	M	R	W	O	M	R	W		FALL OF WICKETS			
Malcolm	45	12	128	4	6	1	19	2		A	E	A	E
Small	31	5	103	1	2	1	6	0	*Wkt*	*1st*	*1st*	*2nd*	*2nd*
Hemmings	32	7	105	3	41	9	94	3	1st	21	95	21	84
Tufnell	30	6	95	1	37	18	61	5	2nd	38	116	29	84
Gooch	14	3	46	1					3rd	185	156	81	100
Atherton	5	0	28	0	(5) 3	1	9	0	4th	226	295	129	100
AUSTRALIA									5th	292	394	129	–
Alderman	20.1	4	62	3	4	0	29	0	6th	347	426	166	–
Reid	35.1	9	79	3					7th	442	444	166	–
Rackemann	25.5	5	89	0	(2) 3	0	20	0	8th	457	444	189	–
Matthews	58	16	145	1	(3) 9	2	26	2	9th	512	–	192	–
Border	19	5	45	0	(4) 9	1	37	1	10th	518	–	205	–
Waugh	14	3	40	0									

Umpires: A.R.Crafter (32) and P.J.McConnell (19).

Close: 1st day – A(1) 259-4 (Jones 27, Waugh 22); 2nd – E(1) 1-0 (Gooch 1, Atherton 0); 3rd – E(1) 227-3 (Atherton 94, Gower 33); 4th – A(2) 38-2 (Healy 9, Boon 3).

AUSTRALIA v ENGLAND 1990-91 (4th Test)

At Adelaide Oval on 25, 26, 27, 28, 29 January.
Toss: Australia.   Result: MATCH DRAWN.
Debuts: Australia – M.E.Waugh.

The highlight of a thrilling contest in one of the world's most beautiful settings was a classic innings by the younger Waugh twin (236 minutes, 186 balls). Having provided the first instance of twins both playing Test cricket, he became the 15th Australian to score a hundred on debut and the eighth to do so in the first innings of a Test against England. He reached his 100 off 126 balls and sped from 21 to 116 after tea on the first day, failing by five runs to become the first to score 100 in his first full batting session of Test cricket. Boon (448 minutes, 276 balls) contributed his ninth Test hundred and his third against England. Taylor became the first batsman to be run out in both innings of a Test twice (both instances at Adelaide). England made a valiant bid to score 472 and laid the base for what would have been a substantial world record fourth-innings winning score when Gooch (214 minutes, 188 balls) and Atherton notched their third opening stand of 200 or more in nine Tests. Gooch's 13th Test hundred was destined to be his only one in Australia.

AUSTRALIA

G.R.Marsh	c Gooch b Small	37	(2)	c Gooch b Small	0
M.A.Taylor	run out	5	(1)	run out	4
D.C.Boon	c Fraser b Malcolm	49		b Tufnell	121
A.R.Border	b DeFreitas	12	(7)	not out	83
D.M.Jones	lbw b DeFreitas	0	(4)	lbw b DeFreitas	8
M.E.Waugh	b Malcolm	138	(5)	b Malcolm	23
G.R.J.Matthews	c Stewart b Gooch	65	(8)	not out	34
I.A.Healy	c Stewart b DeFreitas	1			
C.J.McDermott	not out	42			
M.G.Hughes	lbw b Small	1	(6)	c Gooch b Fraser	30
B.A.Reid	c Lamb b DeFreitas	5			
Extras	(B2, LB23, W2, NB4)	31		(B1, LB7, W1, NB2)	11
Total		**386**		(6 wickets declared)	**314**

ENGLAND

G.A.Gooch	c Healy b Reid	87		c Marsh b Reid	117
M.A.Atherton	lbw b McDermott	0		c Waugh b Reid	87
A.J.Lamb	c Healy b McDermott	0		b McDermott	53
R.A.Smith	c and b Hughes	53	(5)	not out	10
D.I.Gower	c Hughes b McDermott	11	(4)	lbw b Hughes	16
A.J.Stewart	c Healy b Reid	11		c Jones b McDermott	9
P.A.J.DeFreitas	c Matthews b McDermott	45		not out	19
G.C.Small	b McDermott	1			
A.R.C.Fraser	c Healy b Reid	2			
D.E.Malcolm	c Healy b Reid	2			
P.C.R.Tufnell	not out	0			
Extras	(B1, LB3, NB13)	17		(B5, LB9, W1, NB9)	24
Total		**229**		(5 wickets)	**335**

ENGLAND	O	M	R	W	O	M	R	W
Malcolm	38	7	104	2	21	0	87	1
Fraser	23	6	48	0	(4) 26	3	66	1
Small	34	10	92	2	(2) 18	3	64	1
DeFreitas	26.2	6	56	4	(3) 23	6	61	1
Tufnell	5	0	38	0	16	3	28	1
Gooch	9	2	23	1				

AUSTRALIA	O	M	R	W	O	M	R	W
Reid	29	9	53	4	23	5	59	2
McDermott	26.3	3	97	5	27	5	106	2
Hughes	22	4	62	1	(4) 14	3	52	1
Waugh	4	1	13	0	(5) 1	0	4	0
Matthews					(3) 31	7	100	0

FALL OF WICKETS

Wkt	A 1st	E 1st	A 2nd	E 2nd
1st	11	10	1	203
2nd	62	11	8	246
3rd	104	137	25	287
4th	104	160	64	287
5th	124	176	130	297
6th	295	179	240	–
7th	298	198	–	–
8th	358	215	–	–
9th	373	219	–	–
10th	386	229	–	–

Umpires: L.J.King (4) and T.A.Prue (3).

Close: 1st day – A(1) 269-5 (Waugh 116, Matthews 29); 2nd – E(1) 95-2 (Gooch 50, Smith 36); 3rd – A(2) 68-4 (Boon 24, Hughes 3); 4th – E(2) 19-0 (Gooch 14, Atherton 1).

AUSTRALIA v ENGLAND 1990-91 (5th Test)

At W.A.C.A.Ground, Perth, on 1, 2, 3, 5 February.
Toss: England.   Result: AUSTRALIA won by nine wickets.
Debuts: None.

Australia won after 87 minutes play on the fourth morning to gain a 3-0 victory in the rubber, their most impressive margin in a home Ashes tournament since 1974-75. On the eve of the match Perth had registered its highest recorded temperature of 45.8°C (114°F) but it had dropped to 27 when play began. England produced another startling collapse, McDermott's best analysis in Tests including a spell of 4 for 8 in 13 balls. In the second innings, Hughes took his 100th wicket in 27 Tests and Alderman became the tenth Australian bowler to take 100 wickets against England. For the first time since 1958-59 England failed to win a Test during a five-match rubber in Australia.

ENGLAND

*G.A.Gooch	c Healy b McDermott	13	c Alderman b Hughes		18
M.A.Atherton	c Healy b McDermott	27	c Boon b Hughes		25
A.J.Lamb	c Border b McDermott	91	lbw b McDermott		5
R.A.Smith	c Taylor b McDermott	58	lbw b Alderman		43
D.I.Gower	not out	28	c Taylor b Alderman		5
†A.J.Stewart	lbw b McDermott	2	c Healy b McDermott		7
P.A.J.DeFreitas	c Marsh b McDermott	5	c Healy b Alderman		5
P.J.Newport	c Healy b McDermott	0	not out		40
G.C.Small	c Boon b Hughes	0	c Taylor b Hughes		4
P.C.R.Tufnell	c Healy b Hughes	0	c Healy b Hughes		8
D.E.Malcolm	c Marsh b McDermott	7	c Jones b McDermott		6
Extras	(B1, LB6, W1, NB5)	13	(B5, LB5, NB6)		16
Total		**244**			**182**

AUSTRALIA

G.R.Marsh	c Stewart b Small	1	(2) not out		63
M.A.Taylor	c Stewart b Malcolm	12	(1) c Stewart b DeFreitas		19
D.C.Boon	c Stewart b Malcolm	64	not out		30
*A.R.Border	lbw b DeFreitas	17			
D.M.Jones	b Newport	34			
M.E.Waugh	c Small b Malcolm	26			
G.R.J.Matthews	not out	60			
†I.A.Healy	c Lamb b Small	42			
C.J.McDermott	b Tufnell	25			
M.G.Hughes	c Gooch b Tufnell	0			
T.M.Alderman	lbw b DeFreitas	7			
Extras	(B2, LB8, W1, NB8)	19	(LB5, W2, NB1)		8
Total		**307**	(1 wicket)		**120**

AUSTRALIA	O	M	R	W		O	M	R	W		FALL OF WICKETS			
Alderman	22	5	66	0	(2)	22	3	75	3		E	A	E	A
McDermott	24.4	2	97	8	(1)	19.3	2	60	3	*Wkt*	*1st*	*1st*	*2nd*	*2nd*
Hughes	17	3	49	2		20	7	37	4	1st	27	1	41	39
Waugh	1	0	9	0						2nd	50	44	49	–
Matthews	2	0	16	0						3rd	191	90	75	–
										4th	212	113	80	–
ENGLAND										5th	220	161	114	–
Malcolm	30	4	94	3		9	0	40	0	6th	226	168	118	–
Small	23	3	65	2		10	5	24	0	7th	226	230	125	–
DeFreitas	16.5	2	57	2		6.2	0	29	1	8th	227	281	134	–
Newport	14	0	56	1		6	0	22	0	9th	227	283	144	–
Tufnell	7	1	25	2						10th	244	307	182	–

Umpires: S.G.Randell (8) and C.D.Timmins (2).

Close: 1st day – A(1) 19-1 (Taylor 9, Boon 9); 2nd – A(1) 307 all out; 3rd – A(2) 39-1 (Marsh 19).

NEW ZEALAND v SRI LANKA 1990-91 (1st Test)

At Basin Reserve, Wellington, on 31 January, 1, 2, 3, 4 February.
Toss: Sri Lanka.   Result: MATCH DRAWN.
Debuts: Sri Lanka – C.P.Senanayake.

An extraordinary match in which Sri Lanka, having gained a first innings lead of 323 and with more than two days in which to dismiss New Zealand again, managed to capture only four wickets in the next 14 hours. De Silva (509 minutes, 380 balls, 40 fours) completed 1,000 runs in Tests and contributed Sri Lanka's highest score to their (then) record total. New Zealand responded with the highest second-innings score in Test cricket and their own record total. It was based on a partnership of 467 in 548 minutes off 924 balls between Andrew Jones (562 minutes, 454 balls, 15 fours) and Martin Crowe (610 minutes, 523 balls, three sixes, 29 fours), the world record for the third wicket in first-class cricket and the record for any wicket at Test level. Crowe's score of 299 was the highest for New Zealand in Tests and the record in any match at Basin Reserve. Tillekeratne set a Test record by not conceding a bye while 671 runs were scored.

NEW ZEALAND

T.J.Franklin	c sub‡ b Labrooy	3	lbw b Ramanayake	39
J.G.Wright	c Gurusinha b Labrooy	15	c Tillekeratne b Ramanayake	88
A.H.Jones	c Tillekeratne b Ratnayake	5	c sub# b Ranatunga	186
*M.D.Crowe	c Tillekeratne b Ramanayake	30	c Tillekeratne b Ranatunga	299
M.J.Greatbatch	c Gurusinha b Labrooy	13	not out	14
K.R.Rutherford	c Tillekeratne b Ratnayake	25		
G.E.Bradburn	c Tillekeratne b Ramanayake	14		
†I.D.S.Smith	c Senanayake b Ratnayake	28		
C.Pringle	lbw b Labrooy	0		
D.K.Morrison	b Ratnayake	13		
W.Watson	not out	10		
Extras	(B1, LB7, W1, NB9)	18	(LB9, W1, NB35)	45
Total		174	(4 wickets)	671

SRI LANKA

C.P.Senanayake	c Smith b Watson	0
†H.P.Tillekeratne	c Greatbatch b Morrison	21
A.P.Gurusinha	c Crowe b Watson	70
P.A.de Silva	c Bradburn b Morrison	267
*A.Ranatunga	hit wkt b Morrison	55
E.A.R.de Silva	c Smith b Morrison	26
G.F.Labrooy	c Wright b Morrison	0
R.J.Ratnayake	b Watson	26
C.P.H.Ramanayake	not out	14
K.P.J.Warnaweera	b Watson	3
R.S.Mahanama	absent hurt	–
Extras	(LB7, NB8)	15
Total		497

SRI LANKA	O	M	R	W	O	M	R	W
Ratnayake	18.2	6	45	4	30	1	101	0
Labrooy	23	5	68	4	26	1	88	0
Ramanayake	11	3	39	2	40	5	122	2
Warnaweera	6	1	14	0	(6) 34	8	75	0
Ranatunga					(4) 19.3	4	60	2
E.A.R.de Silva					(5) 56	14	141	0
P.A.de Silva					8	0	59	0
Gurusinha					7	0	16	0
NEW ZEALAND								
Morrison	44	6	153	5				
Watson	46.1	10	121	4				
Pringle	31	4	116	0				
Bradburn	26	5	83	0				
Rutherford	2	0	11	0				
Jones	2	0	6	0				

FALL OF WICKETS

Wkt	NZ 1st	SL 1st	NZ 2nd
1st	5	8	134
2nd	18	41	148
3rd	33	184	615
4th	75	362	671
5th	78	449	–
6th	108	449	–
7th	124	454	–
8th	131	487	–
9th	150	497	–
10th	174	–	–

‡ (S.T.Jayasuriya)
# (A.W.R.Madurasinghe)

Umpires: B.L.Aldridge (8) and S.J.Woodward (24).

Close: 1st day – SL(1) 41-2 (Gurusinha 17, P.A.de Silva 0); 2nd – SL(1) 359-3 (P.A.de Silva 203, Ranatunga 52); 3rd – NZ(2) 91-0 (Franklin 24, Wright 55); 4th – NZ(2) 369-2 (Jones 82, Crowe 126).

NEW ZEALAND v SRI LANKA 1990-91 (2nd Test)

At Trust Bank Park, Hamilton, on 22, 23, 24, 25, 26 February.
Toss: Sri Lanka.   Result: MATCH DRAWN.
Debuts: Sri Lanka – U.C.Hathurusinghe, S.T.Jayasuriya.

Hamilton provided Test cricket's 64th venue, the ground being formerly known as Seddon Park (named after New Zealand's Lancashire-born, longest-serving prime minister). Ratnayake gained his fourth five-wicket haul and became Sri Lanka's leading wicket-taker. Smith equalled the world Test record with seven catches in an innings. Jones and Gurusinha each scored hundreds in both innings - the second occasion that a batsman on each side has achieved this feat in the same Test match (also *Test No. 282*). Jones was the first to score hundreds in three successive innings for New Zealand. Sri Lanka finished just 74 runs short of their target of 418. Injuries to both captains led to Smith and Aravinda de Silva deputising in the field for the last three days.

NEW ZEALAND

Batsman	Dismissal 1		Dismissal 2	
T.J.Franklin	c P.A.de Silva b Gurusinha	15	b Ratnayake	69
J.G.Wright	c Hathurusinghe b Labrooy	21	c Tillekeratne b Ramanayake	101
A.H.Jones	c Tillekeratne b Ratnayake	122	(4) not out	100
*M.D.Crowe	c Tillekeratne b Ranatunga	36		
K.R.Rutherford	c Tillekeratne b Ramanayake	0	b E.A.R.de Silva	6
S.A.Thomson	b Ramanayake	36	c Tillekeratne b E.A.R.de Silva	55
D.N.Patel	not out	26	b Labrooy	9
†I.D.S.Smith	c Senanayake b Ratnayake	7	not out	6
D.K.Morrison	c Tillekeratne b Ratnayake	0	(3) c Jayasuriya b Ramanayake	0
C.Pringle	b Ratnayake	9		
W.Watson	c Tillekeratne b Ratnayake	4		
Extras	(B4, LB12, NB4)	20	(B3, LB9, W2, NB14)	28
Total		**296**	(6 wickets declared)	**374**

SRI LANKA

Batsman	Dismissal 1		Dismissal 2	
C.P.Senanayake	c Smith b Pringle	5	c Jones b Watson	64
U.C.Hathurusinghe	c Smith b Morrison	23	c sub‡ b Thomson	81
A.P.Gurusinha	c Thomson b Morrison	119	(4) c Smith b Morrison	102
P.A.de Silva	c Smith b Watson	1	(5) c and b Patel	6
†H.P.Tillekeratne	c Smith b Pringle	12	(6) c sub (G.E.Bradburn) b Patel	26
S.T.Jayasuriya	lbw b Patel	35		
C.P.H.Ramanayake	run out	13	(3) c sub‡ b Watson	11
*A.Ranatunga	c Smith b Morrison	21	(7) not out	20
E.A.R.de Silva	c Smith b Watson	0	(8) not out	11
G.F.Labrooy	c Smith b Watson	6		
R.J.Ratnayake	not out	1		
Extras	(LB4, NB13)	17	(B4, LB11, NB8)	23
Total		**253**	(6 wickets)	**344**

SRI LANKA	O	M	R	W	O	M	R	W
Ratnayake	30.4	10	77	5	27	4	70	1
Labrooy	22	6	46	1	20	2	65	1
Ramanayake	27	9	52	2	26	5	97	2
Gurusinha	14.2	3	36	1	4	1	12	0
E.A.R.de Silva	14	2	35	0	24	6	89	2
Ranatunga	13.4	1	34	1				
Hathurusinghe					(6) 2	0	15	0
P.A.de Silva					(7) 2	0	14	0

NEW ZEALAND	O	M	R	W	O	M	R	W
Morrison	26	6	77	3	25	4	85	1
Pringle	20	5	64	2	12	2	46	0
Watson	26.4	8	65	3	37	8	75	2
Patel	15	4	33	1	39	13	90	2
Thomson	6	1	10	0	8	3	18	1
Jones					4	1	15	0

FALL OF WICKETS

Wkt	NZ 1st	SL 1st	NZ 2nd	SL 2nd
1st	40	8	161	95
2nd	40	38	162	121
3rd	125	41	209	238
4th	126	83	222	245
5th	239	163	327	300
6th	239	185	359	320
7th	258	240	–	–
8th	270	246	–	–
9th	288	246	–	–
10th	296	253	–	–

Umpires: B.L.Aldridge (9) and R.S.Dunne (5).

‡ (M.J.Greatbatch)

Close: 1st day – NZ(1) 221-4 (Jones 109, Thomson 32); 2nd – SL(1) 180-5 (Gurusinha 81, Ramanayake 13); 3rd – NZ(2) 170-2 (Franklin 56, Jones 2); 4th – SL(2) 109-1 (Hathurusinghe 30, Ramanayake 11).

NEW ZEALAND v SRI LANKA 1990-91 (3rd Test)

At Eden Park, Auckland, on 1, 2, 3, 4, 5 March.
Toss: New Zealand.   Result: MATCH DRAWN.
Debuts: None.

Crowe's knee injury resulted in Smith becoming the first wicket-keeper to captain New Zealand. De Silva, who struck five sixes in the second innings, took his aggregate for the rubber to 493. Labrooy's highest score in first-class cricket, 70 not out off 80 balls in 89 minutes (two sixes, 12 fours), included 16 off his first three balls, and 50 off 45 balls. He set a world Test record by reaching 50 from fewest scoring strokes - 13. A fifth-wicket partnership of 100 (214 balls) between Jones and Thomson ensured a drawn series and extended New Zealand's unbeaten home record. The aggregate of 513 by Jones set a record for New Zealand in any home series.

SRI LANKA

C.P.Senanayake	c Smith b Cairns	20		c Greatbatch b Cairns	8
J.C.Hathurusinghe	b Watson	13		c Smith b Cairns	74
A.P.Gurusinha	lbw b Cairns	50		c and b Cairns	29
P.A.de Silva	c Smith b Cairns	96		c Morrison b Thomson	123
A.Ranatunga	c Smith b Cairns	34		c Thomson b Cairns	30
H.P.Tillekeratne	lbw b Morrison	31		c Cairns b Thomson	3
S.T.Jayasuriya	c Smith b Watson	18		not out	12
E.A.R.de Silva	c Jones b Patel	2	(9)	c Greatbatch b Thomson	0
G.F.Labrooy	not out	70	(8)	c Morrison b Cairns	1
R.J.Ratnayake	c Greatbatch b Watson	18		c Greatbatch b Morrison	20
C.P.H.Ramanayake	c Smith b Morrison	1		b Morrison	0
Extras	(B2, LB15, W1, NB9)	27		(B1, LB5, NB13)	19
Total		**380**			**319**

NEW ZEALAND

T.J.Franklin	lbw b Ratnayake	13	c Tillekeratne b Labrooy	31
J.G.Wright	c Ranatunga b Ramanayake	84	c Tillekeratne b Ramanayake	20
A.H.Jones	c Ratnayake b E.A.R.de Silva	27	lbw b Labrooy	73
M.J.Greatbatch	lbw b Labrooy	65	b Labrooy	7
K.R.Rutherford	c Gurusinha b E.A.R.de Silva	15	lbw b Labrooy	6
S.A.Thomson	lbw b Ratnayake	1	not out	80
D.N.Patel	c Labrooy b Ramanayake	41	not out	16
I.D.S.Smith	b Ratnayake	3		
C.L.Cairns	c P.A.de Silva b Labrooy	17		
D.K.Morrison	lbw b Labrooy	7		
W.Watson	not out	5		
Extras	(B1, LB7, NB31)	39	(B1, LB9, NB18)	28
Total		**317**	(5 wickets)	**261**

NEW ZEALAND	O	M	R	W	O	M	R	W		FALL OF WICKETS			
										SL	NZ	SL	NZ
Morrison	21	5	87	2	20	2	74	2	*Wkt*	*1st*	*1st*	*2nd*	*2nd*
Cairns	32	5	136	4	27	6	75	5	1st	34	63	9	39
Watson	31.5	11	81	3	9	1	23	0	2nd	61	139	56	80
Thomson	12.1	6	22	0	19	5	63	3	3rd	132	140	201	95
Patel	8	2	37	1	23	6	78	0	4th	223	170	276	117
									5th	234	172	282	217
SRI LANKA									6th	255	247	282	–
Labrooy	21.3	6	48	3	(4) 19	6	42	4	7th	273	257	285	–
Ramanayake	26	7	96	2	19	4	62	1	8th	325	299	288	–
Ratnayake	33	3	83	3	(1) 21	3	44	0	9th	356	304	319	–
E.A.R.de Silva	29	8	67	2	(3) 25	4	61	0	10th	380	317	319	–
Gurusinha	6	2	15	0	(7) 2	1	1	0					
Ranatunga					(5) 7	1	23	0					
Jayasuriya					(6) 6	1	18	0					

Umpires: B.L.Aldridge (10) and R.L.McHarg (3).

Close: 1st day – SL(1) 325-8 (Labrooy 41); 2nd – NZ(1) 194-5 (Greatbatch 18, Patel 9); 3rd – SL(2) 64-2 (Hathurusinghe 16, P.A.de Silva 5); 4th – NZ(2) 18-0 (Franklin 5, Wright 12).

WEST INDIES v AUSTRALIA 1990-91 (1st Test)

At Sabina Park, Kingston, Jamaica, on 1, 2, 3, 5 (*no play*), 6 March.
Toss: West Indies.   Result: MATCH DRAWN.
Debuts: None.

For the second year in succession lack of adequate covering allowed heavy rain to leak on to the pitch and cause the fourth day's play to be abandoned. On the final day, the umpires protected their decision to restart play b issuing an extraordinary edict: 'should the pitch prove too difficult to bat on, play could be called off.' In the fir innings, McDermott had caused two West Indian casualties, Haynes (4) retiring at 9 after being yorked on the to and resuming at 69 for 4 when Logie (9) retired having been struck under the right eye. Logie, sporting nin stitches, returned at 166 to contribute a brave unbeaten 77 off 110 balls with 12 fours, mostly straight drives. Boo scored a chanceless tenth Test hundred, Border became the second batsman to reach 9,000 Test runs, Richard posted 8,000 and then exceeded the Sobers West Indian record of 8,032, Haynes made his 6,000th an McDermott, with 26 in three matches since his recall, took his 100th wicket in 27 Tests.

WEST INDIES

Batsman	Dismissal 1	Score	Dismissal 2	Score
C.G.Greenidge	c and b McDermott	27	c Healy b McDermott	3
D.L.Haynes	b McDermott	8	c Healy b McDermott	8
R.B.Richardson	c Healy b Hughes	15	not out	10
C.L.Hooper	c Marsh b Hughes	0	b McDermott	3
*I.V.A.Richards	c Hughes b McDermott	11	not out	5
A.L.Logie	not out	77		
†P.J.L.Dujon	c Marsh b Hughes	59		
M.D.Marshall	lbw b McDermott	0		
C.E.L.Ambrose	c and b Waugh	33		
C.A.Walsh	lbw b McDermott	10		
B.P.Patterson	b Hughes	4		
Extras	(LB6, W1, NB13)	20	(B15, LB6, W1, NB6)	2
Total		264	(3 wickets declared)	33

AUSTRALIA

G.R.Marsh	c Dujon b Ambrose	69
M.A.Taylor	c Hooper b Patterson	58
D.C.Boon	not out	109
*A.R.Border	c Dujon b Ambrose	31
D.M.Jones	c and b Hooper	0
M.E.Waugh	lbw b Marshall	39
G.R.J.Matthews	c Dujon b Patterson	10
†I.A.Healy	lbw b Walsh	0
C.J.McDermott	b Patterson	1
M.G.Hughes	c Hooper b Patterson	0
M.R.Whitney	b Patterson	2
Extras	(B4, LB23, W4, NB21)	52
Total		371

AUSTRALIA	O	M	R	W	O	M	R	W
McDermott	23	3	80	5	24	10	48	3
Whitney	21	4	58	0	17	3	55	0
Hughes	21.3	4	67	4	22	5	79	0
Matthews	11	3	28	0	25	2	90	0
Waugh	6	1	25	1	(6) 13	6	20	0
Border					(5) 10	3	21	0

WEST INDIES	O	M	R	W
Ambrose	30	3	94	2
Patterson	24	1	83	5
Marshall	22	3	57	1
Walsh	23	4	73	1
Hooper	21	7	37	1

	FALL OF WICKETS		
	WI	A	WI
Wkt	1st	1st	2nd
1st	33	139	118
2nd	37	159	134
3rd	57	227	216
4th	69	228	–
5th	75	329	–
6th	75	357	–
7th	144	358	–
8th	166	365	–
9th	234	365	–
10th	264	371	

Umpires: D.M.Archer (25) and S.A.Bucknor (3).

Close: 1st day – A(1) 4-0 (Marsh 0, Taylor 2); 2nd – A(1) 296-4 (Boon 71, Waugh 22); 3rd – WI(2) 187-2 (Richardson 33, Hooper 11); 4th – no play.

WEST INDIES v AUSTRALIA 1990-91 (2nd Test)

At Bourda, Georgetown, Guyana, on 23, 24, 25, 27, 28 March.
Toss: Australia.   Result: WEST INDIES won by ten wickets.
Debuts: None.

Thanks largely to new over-rate legislation for Tests in the Caribbean which provided an extra three hours of play over the first four days, West Indies gained their first victory at Bourda since 1964-65. Their chief executioner was Richardson (344 minutes, 260 balls, two sixes and 26 fours) who played a spectacular innings which included only one chance (at 127). His (series) record second-wicket partnership of 297 with Haynes included 198 off 41 overs in the second day's protracted final session (Richardson 106). Haynes (318 minutes, 211 balls) scored his 16th Test hundred. Border enjoyed a spell of 4 for 0 in nine balls, including the wickets of Dujon, Logie and Ambrose in four balls. Jones was incorrectly adjudged run out by Cumberbatch after leaving for the pavilion (in the direction of extra-cover) unaware that the delivery which bowled him had been called 'no ball'. Law 38.2 states: 'If a no-ball has been called, the striker shall not be given run out unless he attempts to run.' Ambrose took his 100th wicket in 25 Tests.

AUSTRALIA

M.A.Taylor	lbw b Patterson	0	(2)	lbw b Ambrose	15
G.R.Marsh	c Hooper b Patterson	94	(1)	b Walsh	22
D.C.Boon	c Dujon b Marshall	7		c Dujon b Marshall	2
*A.R.Border	b Marshall	47		c Dujon b Marshall	34
D.M.Jones	b Marshall	34		run out	3
M.E.Waugh	c Dujon b Patterson	71		c Richards b Ambrose	31
G.R.J.Matthews	c Dujon b Ambrose	1		c Dujon b Marshall	16
†I.A.Healy	run out	53		run out	47
C.J.McDermott	lbw b Patterson	1		c Dujon b Patterson	4
M.G.Hughes	b Ambrose	0		c Patterson b Walsh	21
M.R.Whitney	not out	1		not out	0
Extras	(B6, LB8, W2, NB23)	39		(B17, LB6, W2, NB28)	53
Total		**348**			**248**

WEST INDIES

C.G.Greenidge	lbw b McDermott	2		not out	5
D.L.Haynes	c Waugh b Border	111		not out	23
R.B.Richardson	lbw b McDermott	182			
C.L.Hooper	c Waugh b Matthews	62			
*I.V.A.Richards	b Matthews	50			
A.L.Logie	c Healy b Border	54			
†P.J.L.Dujon	lbw b Border	29			
M.D.Marshall	not out	22			
C.E.L.Ambrose	b Border	0			
C.A.Walsh	b Border	1			
B.P.Patterson	lbw b Matthews	15			
Extras	(B5, LB13, NB23)	41		(LB2, NB1)	3
Total		**569**		(0 wickets)	**31**

WEST INDIES	O	M	R	W	O	M	R	W	FALL OF WICKETS			
									A	WI	A	WI
Ambrose	31.4	9	64	2	24	5	44	2	*Wkt*	*1st*	*1st*	*2nd*	*2nd*
Patterson	24	1	80	4	14	5	47	1	*Wkt*	*1st*	*1st*	*2nd*	*2nd*
Walsh	24	2	81	0	23	4	55	2	1st	3	10	32	–
Marshall	23	3	67	3	15	2	31	3	2nd	24	307	43	–
Hooper	13	3	37	0	18	6	35	0	3rd	124	353	67	–
Richards	1	0	5	0	4	2	13	0	4th	188	443	73	–
									5th	237	444	130	–
AUSTRALIA									6th	238	529	161	–
McDermott	36	2	114	2	4	1	10	0	7th	339	530	172	–
Whitney	28	4	103	0					8th	346	530	187	–
Matthews	37.5	6	155	3					9th	346	532	241	–
Hughes	20	4	93	0	(2) 3.5	0	19	0	10th	348	569	248	–
Waugh	2	0	18	0								
Border	30	11	68	5								

Umpires: C.E.Cumberbatch (11) and C.R.Duncan (1).

Close: 1st day – A(1) 249-6 (Waugh 30, Healy 3); 2nd – WI(1) 226-1 (Haynes 87, Richardson 114); 3rd – WI(1) 532-9 (Marshall 1, Patterson 0); 4th – A(2) 178-7 (Healy 10, McDermott 0).

Test No. 1168/70 (WI283/A506)

WEST INDIES v AUSTRALIA 1990-91 (3rd Test)

At Queen's Park Oval, Port-of-Spain, Trinidad, on 5, 6, 8, 9, 10 April.
Toss: West Indies.   Result: MATCH DRAWN.
Debuts: None.

The loss of nearly ten hours to torrential rain on the first two days and a 55-minute delay on the third made a draw inevitable. If the rest day had not been brought forward, the third day would have been abandoned, the ground being completely flooded. The recall of Steve Waugh created the first instance of twins appearing together in a Test match. Dujon and Ambrose, who scored his first fifty in Tests, shared a record West Indies eighth-wicket partnership of 87 for this series. Richardson took his Test aggregate past 4,000 runs.

AUSTRALIA

G.R.Marsh	c Hooper b Ambrose	10	(2) lbw b Marshall		12
M.A.Taylor	c Walsh b Marshall	61	(1) b Patterson		2
D.C.Boon	c Logie b Patterson	27	b Walsh		29
*A.R.Border	run out	43	(5) not out		27
D.M.Jones	lbw b Patterson	21	(4) not out		39
M.E.Waugh	lbw b Marshall	64			
S.R.Waugh	c Dujon b Walsh	26			
†I.A.Healy	c Dujon b Marshall	9			
C.J.McDermott	c Richardson b Patterson	0			
M.G.Hughes	lbw b Patterson	0			
B.A.Reid	not out	0			
Extras	(B6, LB14, NB13)	33	(B1, LB9, NB4)		14
Total		**294**	(3 wickets declared)		**123**

WEST INDIES

C.G.Greenidge	c M.E.Waugh b Reid	12
D.L.Haynes	b McDermott	1
R.B.Richardson	c Taylor b Hughes	30
C.L.Hooper	lbw b Hughes	12
A.L.Logie	c M.E.Waugh b Hughes	1
*I.V.A.Richards	c S.R.Waugh b Hughes	2
†P.J.L.Dujon	lbw b McDermott	70
M.D.Marshall	c McDermott b Border	12
C.E.L.Ambrose	c Border b M.E.Waugh	53
C.A.Walsh	not out	12
B.P.Patterson	b McDermott	0
Extras	(B6, LB7, NB9)	22
Total		**227**

WEST INDIES	O	M	R	W	O	M	R	W		FALL OF WICKETS		
										A	WI	A
Ambrose	29	7	51	1	10	4	11	0	*Wkt*	*1st*	*1st*	*2nd*
Patterson	26	2	50	4	7	0	27	1	1st	24	16	3
Marshall	18.1	3	55	3	10	3	24	1	2nd	93	18	49
Walsh	30	9	45	1	12	6	11	1	3rd	116	46	53
Hooper	25	5	73	0	13	3	38	0	4th	174	52	–
Richardson					1	0	2	0	5th	210	56	–
									6th	268	86	–
AUSTRALIA									7th	293	110	–
McDermott	14.2	2	36	3					8th	294	197	–
Reid	22	0	79	1					9th	294	225	–
Border	19	5	28	1					10th	294	227	–
Hughes	17	5	48	4								
S.R.Waugh	5	0	10	0								
M.E.Waugh	6	2	9	1								
Jones	1	0	4	0								

Umpires: D.M.Archer (26) and L.H.Barker (15).

Close: 1st day – A(1) 55-1 (Taylor 28, Boon 6); 2nd – A(1) 75-1 (Taylor 35, Boon 18); 3rd – A(1) 279-6 (M.E.Waugh 57, Healy 2); 4th – WI(1) 220-8 (Dujon 70, Walsh 6).

WEST INDIES v AUSTRALIA 1990-91 (4th Test)

At Kensington Oval, Bridgetown, Barbados, on 19, 20, 21, 23, 24 April.
Toss: Australia.   Result: WEST INDIES won by 343 runs.
Debuts: None.

West Indies achieved their most comprehensive victory by a runs margin in this series, retained the Frank Worrell Trophy and recorded their tenth successive win at Bridgetown. Few would have predicted that result when West Indies, put in on an evenly grassed surface, were literally caught out in 61.1 overs for their lowest home score since 1972-73. West Indies recovered the initiative, their hostile attack requiring only 50.1 overs to claim a lead of 15 before Greenidge (677 minutes, 480 balls, 32 fours) celebrated his imminent 40th birthday with his fourth double century. It was the highest (and last) of his 19 Test hundreds, his fourth against Australia and, until Lara scored 277 in 1992-93 (*Test No. 1206*), it was the highest West Indies innings in this series. He also shared the last of his 16 hundred partnerships with Haynes. Border batted with a fractured left thumb in the second innings. Marshall became the first to take 350 wickets for West Indies.

WEST INDIES

C.G.Greenidge	c Reid b McDermott	10		lbw b Hughes	226
D.L.Haynes	c M.E.Waugh b Hughes	28		c Healy b M.E.Waugh	40
R.B.Richardson	c Boon b McDermott	1	(4)	lbw b M.E.Waugh	99
C.L.Hooper	c Jones b Hughes	0	(5)	c Healy b M.E.Waugh	57
*I.V.A.Richards	c Hughes b McDermott	32	(6)	lbw b M.E.Waugh	25
A.L.Logie	c Taylor b Reid	11	(7)	not out	33
†P.J.L.Dujon	c Healy b Hughes	10	(8)	c M.E.Waugh b McDermott	4
M.D.Marshall	c Marsh b Reid	17	(3)	c Healy b McDermott	15
C.E.L.Ambrose	not out	19		b Reid	2
C.A.Walsh	c M.E.Waugh b McDermott	10		c Marsh b Reid	0
B.P.Patterson	c M.E.Waugh b Hughes	1		not out	4
Extras	(LB3, NB7)	10		(LB19, NB12)	31
Total		**149**		(9 wickets declared)	**536**

AUSTRALIA

M.A.Taylor	lbw b Ambrose	26	(2)	lbw b Marshall	76
G.R.Marsh	c Logie b Ambrose	12	(1)	lbw b Ambrose	0
D.C.Boon	c Hooper b Marshall	0		b Ambrose	57
*A.R.Border	b Marshall	29		c Dujon b Ambrose	0
D.M.Jones	lbw b Marshall	22	(6)	b Hooper	37
M.E.Waugh	not out	20	(7)	b Hooper	3
S.R.Waugh	c Dujon b Patterson	2	(8)	not out	4
†I.A.Healy	c Dujon b Walsh	2	(9)	lbw b Marshall	0
M.G.Hughes	c Logie b Walsh	3	(5)	c Dujon b Marshall	3
C.J.McDermott	b Walsh	2		c sub (R.I.C.Holder) b Walsh	2
B.A.Reid	b Walsh	0		b Walsh	0
Extras	(LB2, NB14)	16		(B3, LB5, NB18)	26
Total		**134**			**208**

AUSTRALIA	O	M	R	W		O	M	R	W		FALL OF WICKETS			
											WI	A	WI	A
McDermott	22	6	49	4		37.3	8	130	2	*Wkt*	*1st*	*1st*	*2nd*	*2nd*
Reid	21	8	50	2		30	4	100	2	1st	17	24	129	0
Hughes	16.1	2	44	4		36	6	125	1	2nd	21	27	153	111
S.R.Waugh	2	0	3	0		28	6	77	0	3rd	22	59	352	111
M.E.Waugh						28	6	80	4	4th	72	95	454	122
Jones						3	1	5	0	5th	89	97	470	190
										6th	96	100	512	200
WEST INDIES										7th	103	106	522	200
Ambrose	16	5	36	2		19	7	36	3	8th	125	121	525	200
Patterson	13	6	22	1		15	3	56	0	9th	148	127	525	208
Marshall	16	1	60	3	(4)	17	5	35	3	10th	149	134	–	208
Walsh	5.1	1	14	4	(3)	15.3	4	37	2					
Hooper						18	4	28	2					
Richards						3	0	8	0					

Umpires: D.M.Archer (27) and L.H.Barker (16).

Close: 1st day – A(1) 56-2 (Taylor 23, Border 17); 2nd – WI(2) 138-1 (Greenidge 85, Marshall 5); 3rd – WI(2) 407-3 (Greenidge 209, Hooper 25); 4th – A(2) 122-3 (Taylor 46, Hughes 3).

WEST INDIES v AUSTRALIA 1990-91 (5th Test)

At Recreation Ground, St John's, Antigua, on 27, 28, 29 April, 1 May.
Toss: Australia.   Result: AUSTRALIA won by 157 runs.
Debuts: None.

Adopting a more positive approach, their first-day total of 355 for 5 off 87 overs being the highest in any Caribbean Test, Australia became the first visiting team to win a Test in Antigua. West Indies became only the third team to remain unchanged throughout a five-match rubber. Border ignored his fractured thumb to make his 125th Test appearance and equal Gavaskar's record. Waugh (307 minutes, 188 balls, 11 fours and three sixes) scored 110 runs in the first day's final session and repeatedly adopted Bradman's technique against 'bodyline' bowling by moving to leg and cutting the short-pitched balls. Taylor (361 minutes, 227 balls) contributed 54% of Australia's second innings total. Richards, who had announced that this would be his final home international, was dismissed for his only duck in a Test in the West Indies. Greenidge played his final Test innings on his 40th birthday.

AUSTRALIA

G.R.Marsh	c Richards b Patterson	6	(2) c Dujon b Ambrose		1
M.A.Taylor	c Dujon b Hooper	59	(1) c and b Ambrose		144
D.C.Boon	c Greenidge b Ambrose	0	(4) b Walsh		35
*A.R.Border	c Dujon b Hooper	59	(5) b Walsh		5
D.M.Jones	lbw b Marshall	81	(6) b Walsh		8
M.E.Waugh	not out	139	(7) lbw b Walsh		0
†I.A.Healy	c Dujon b Marshall	12	(3) c Logie b Patterson		32
P.L.Taylor	c Dujon b Ambrose	2	lbw b Marshall		4
M.G.Hughes	b Ambrose	1	c Walsh b Ambrose		13
C.J.McDermott	c Dujon b Walsh	7	c Dujon b Marshall		1
T.M.Alderman	b Walsh	0	not out		0
Extras	(B1, LB12, W6, NB18)	37	(B11, LB7, NB4)		22
Total		**403**			**265**

WEST INDIES

C.G.Greenidge	lbw b McDermott	6	run out	43
D.L.Haynes	lbw b McDermott	84	run out	33
R.B.Richardson	b McDermott	3	c Jones b Waugh	41
C.L.Hooper	lbw b Hughes	2	c Waugh b P.L.Taylor	35
*I.V.A.Richards	lbw b McDermott	0	c Alderman b Border	2
A.L.Logie	c Jones b P.L.Taylor	24	lbw b Alderman	61
†P.J.L.Dujon	c Jones b Hughes	33	lbw b McDermott	4
M.D.Marshall	c Healy b Waugh	28	lbw b Hughes	51
C.E.L.Ambrose	c M.A.Taylor b Hughes	8	run out	0
C.A.Walsh	not out	11	c Healy b Hughes	0
B.P.Patterson	b Hughes	2	not out	7
Extras	(LB2, NB11)	13	(B5, LB7, NB8)	20
Total		**214**		**297**

WEST INDIES	O	M	R	W		O	M	R	W	FALL OF WICKETS				
											A	WI	A	WI
Ambrose	30	6	92	3		16	1	64	3		1st	1st	2nd	2nd
Patterson	12	1	44	1	(4)	1	0	1	1	Wkt	1st	1st	2nd	2nd
Walsh	22	1	54	2	(2)	26	2	56	4	1st	10	10	4	76
Marshall	22	1	72	2	(5)	13.1	4	36	2	2nd	13	22	49	92
Hooper	15	1	82	2	(3)	27	6	61	0	3rd	129	35	142	142
Richards	7	0	46	0		8	0	29	0	4th	158	46	168	145
										5th	342	114	184	182
										6th	370	136	184	193
AUSTRALIA										7th	381	188	237	271
McDermott	15	4	42	4		17	2	55	1	8th	385	195	258	271
Alderman	7	0	42	0		15.4	4	63	1	9th	403	206	265	271
Hughes	17	2	65	4		19	5	49	2	10th	403	214	265	297
P.L.Taylor	11	2	40	1		10	0	39	1					
Waugh	5	0	23	1	(6)	5	3	8	1					
Border					(5)	15	2	71	1					

Umpires: L.H.Barker (17) and S.A.Bucknor (4).

Close: 1st day – A(1) 355-5 (Waugh 117, Healy 1); 2nd – A(2) 6-1 (M.A.Taylor 2, Healy 1); 3rd – WI(2) 2-0 (Greenidge 2, Haynes 0).

ENGLAND v WEST INDIES 1991 (1st Test)

At Headingley, Leeds, on 6, 7, 8, 9, 10 June.
Toss: West Indies.   Result: ENGLAND won by 115 runs.
Debuts: England – G.A.Hick, M.R.Ramprakash, S.L.Watkin.

Inspired by their captain's finest innings, England celebrated the 100th Test of this series by gaining their first win in 24 home matches against West Indies since 1969. In alien conditions strongly favouring seam and swing bowling, Gooch (449 minutes, 331 balls, 18 fours) gave a monumental exhibition of concentration and stamina in joining K.F.Barrington, I.T.Botham and G.Boycott with hundreds on each of England's six current Test grounds. He became only the second after L.Hutton to carry his bat throughout an England innings at home and the third after Hutton and G.M.Turner (New Zealand) to do so against West Indies anywhere. His 14th Test hundred remained his highest score in this series and his share of 61.11% of the total is the record for any completed England innings. Ambrose took the first six wickets to fall in England's second innings. For the first time the selected England party assembled two days prior to the start of the match.

ENGLAND

*G.A.Gooch	c Dujon b Marshall	34	not out	154
M.A.Atherton	b Patterson	2	c Dujon b Ambrose	6
G.A.Hick	c Dujon b Walsh	6	b Ambrose	6
A.J.Lamb	c Hooper b Marshall	11	c Hooper b Ambrose	0
M.R.Ramprakash	c Hooper b Marshall	27	c Dujon b Ambrose	27
R.A.Smith	run out	54	lbw b Ambrose	0
†R.C.Russell	lbw b Patterson	5	c Dujon b Ambrose	4
D.R.Pringle	c Logie b Patterson	16	c Dujon b Marshall	27
P.A.J.DeFreitas	c Simmons b Ambrose	15	lbw b Walsh	3
S.L.Watkin	b Ambrose	2	c Hooper b Marshall	0
D.E.Malcolm	not out	5	b Marshall	4
Extras	(LB5, W2, NB14)	21	(B4, LB9, W1, NB7)	21
Total		**198**		**252**

WEST INDIES

P.V.Simmons	c Ramprakash b DeFreitas	38	b DeFreitas	0
D.L.Haynes	c Russell b Watkin	7	c Smith b Pringle	19
R.B.Richardson	run out	29	c Lamb b DeFreitas	68
C.L.Hooper	run out	0	c Lamb b Watkin	5
*I.V.A.Richards	c Lamb b Pringle	73	c Gooch b Watkin	3
A.L.Logie	c Lamb b DeFreitas	6	c Gooch b Watkin	3
†P.J.L.Dujon	c Ramprakash b Watkin	6	lbw b DeFreitas	33
M.D.Marshall	c Hick b Pringle	0	lbw b Pringle	1
C.E.L.Ambrose	c Hick b DeFreitas	0	c Pringle b DeFreitas	14
C.A.Walsh	c Gooch b DeFreitas	3	c Atherton b Malcolm	9
B.P.Patterson	not out	5	not out	0
Extras	(LB1, NB5)	6	(LB1, NB6)	7
Total		**173**		**162**

WEST INDIES	O	M	R	W	O	M	R	W	FALL OF WICKETS			
										E	WI	E	WI
Ambrose	26	8	49	2	28	6	52	6					
Patterson	26.2	8	67	3	15	1	52	0	*Wkt*	*1st*	*1st*	*2nd*	*2nd*
Walsh	14	7	31	1	(4) 30	5	61	1	1st	13	36	22	0
Marshall	13	4	46	3	(3) 25	4	58	3	2nd	45	54	38	61
Hooper					4	1	11	0	3rd	45	58	38	77
Richards					4	1	5	0	4th	64	102	116	85
									5th	129	139	116	88
ENGLAND									6th	149	156	124	136
Malcolm	14	0	69	0	(2) 6.4	0	26	1	7th	154	160	222	137
DeFreitas	17.1	5	34	4	(1) 21	4	59	4	8th	177	165	236	139
Watkin	14	2	55	2	(4) 7	0	38	3	9th	181	167	238	162
Pringle	9	3	14	2	(3) 22	6	38	2	10th	198	173	252	162

Umpires: H.D.Bird (45) and D.R.Shepherd (12).

Close: 1st day – E(1) 174-7 (Pringle 6, DeFreitas 13); 2nd – WI(1) 166-8 (Richards 73, Walsh 1); 3rd – E(2) 143-6 (Gooch 82, Pringle 10); 4th – WI(2) 11-1 (Haynes 3, Richardson 8).

ENGLAND v WEST INDIES 1991 (2nd Test)

At Lord's, London, on 20, 21, 22, 23 (*no play*), 24 June.
Toss: West Indies.   Result: MATCH DRAWN.
Debuts: West Indies – I.B.A.Allen.

An absorbing contest, played to capacity attendances on the first three days, was wrecked by rain which allowed only 25 minutes of play during the final two. Pringle's third five-wicket analysis, all achieved against the West Indies in England, prevented the tourists from capitalising on their first day total of 317 for 3. Hooper (280 minutes, 202 balls, a six and 14 fours) scored his first hundred against England. Smith (412 minutes, 271 balls, 20 fours) dominated England's response with the highest of his five Test hundreds to date as the last five wickets produced 270 runs.

WEST INDIES

P.V.Simmons	c Lamb b Hick	33	lbw b DeFreitas		2
D.L.Haynes	c Russell b Pringle	60	not out		4
R.B.Richardson	c DeFreitas b Hick	57	c Hick b Malcolm		1
C.L.Hooper	c Lamb b Pringle	111	not out		1
*I.V.A.Richards	lbw b DeFreitas	63			
A.L.Logie	b DeFreitas	5			
†P.J.L.Dujon	c Lamb b Pringle	20			
M.D.Marshall	lbw b Pringle	25			
C.E.L.Ambrose	c and b Malcolm	5			
C.A.Walsh	c Atherton b Pringle	10			
I.B.A.Allen	not out	1			
Extras	(B3, LB7, NB19)	29	(LB2, NB2)		4
Total		**419**	(2 wickets)		**12**

ENGLAND

*G.A.Gooch	b Walsh	37
M.A.Atherton	b Ambrose	5
G.A.Hick	c Richardson b Ambrose	0
A.J.Lamb	c Haynes b Marshall	1
M.R.Ramprakash	c Richards b Allen	24
R.A.Smith	not out	148
†R.C.Russell	c Dujon b Hooper	46
D.R.Pringle	c Simmons b Allen	35
P.A.J.DeFreitas	c Dujon b Marshall	29
S.L.Watkin	b Ambrose	6
D.E.Malcolm	b Ambrose	0
Extras	(LB1, NB22)	23
Total		**354**

ENGLAND	O	M	R	W	O	M	R	W		FALL OF WICKETS		
										WI	E	WI
DeFreitas	31	6	93	2	3	2	1	1		*1st*	*1st*	*2nd*
Malcolm	19	3	76	1	2.5	0	9	1	*Wkt*			
Watkin	15	2	60	0					1st	90	5	9
Pringle	35.1	6	100	5					2nd	102	6	10
Hick	18	4	77	2					3rd	198	16	–
Gooch	2	0	3	0					4th	322	60	–
									5th	332	84	–
WEST INDIES									6th	366	180	–
Ambrose	34	10	87	4					7th	382	269	–
Marshall	30	4	78	2					8th	402	316	–
Walsh	26	4	90	1					9th	410	353	–
Allen	23	2	88	2					10th	419	354	–
Hooper	5	2	10	1								

Umpires: B.J.Meyer (23) and K.E.Palmer (19).

Close: 1st day – WI(1) 317-3 (Hooper 87, Richards 60); 2nd – E(1) 110-5 (Smith 23, Russell 16); 3rd – WI(2) 0-0 (Simmons 0, Haynes 0); 4th – no play.

ENGLAND v WEST INDIES 1991 (3rd Test)

At Trent Bridge, Nottingham, on 4, 5, 6, 8, 9 July.
Toss: England.   Result: WEST INDIES won by nine wickets.
Debuts: England – R.K.Illingworth.

Despite England scoring 106 for 0 in the first session, West Indies drew level in the rubber by completing a substantial victory four balls before lunch on the fifth day. Gooch joined S.M.Gavaskar (2,749) and G.Boycott (2,205) by completing 2,000 runs against West Indies. Illingworth became the eleventh bowler to take a wicket with his first ball in Test cricket, the first since 1959-60 and the first for England since a fellow Worcestershire left-arm spinner, R.Howorth, in 1947. Haynes celebrated his 100th Test match (the 12th to reach this mark and the fourth West Indian) by becoming the sixth to score 2,000 runs for West Indies in this series.

ENGLAND

Batsman	Dismissal	Runs	Dismissal	Runs
G.A.Gooch	lbw b Marshall	68	b Ambrose	13
M.A.Atherton	lbw b Ambrose	32	b Marshall	4
G.A.Hick	c Dujon b Ambrose	43	c Dujon b Ambrose	0
A.J.Lamb	lbw b Ambrose	13	lbw b Marshall	29
M.R.Ramprakash	b Ambrose	13	c Dujon b Ambrose	21
R.A.Smith	not out	64	c Richards b Walsh	15
R.C.Russell	c Logie b Allen	3	b Walsh	3
D.R.Pringle	c sub (C.B.Lambert) b Allen	0	c Simmons b Walsh	3
P.A.J.DeFreitas	b Walsh	8	not out	55
R.K.Illingworth	c Hooper b Ambrose	13	c Simmons b Walsh	13
D.V.Lawrence	c Allen b Marshall	4	c Hooper b Allen	34
Extras	(LB17, W1, NB21)	39	(LB14, W3, NB4)	21
Total		**300**		**211**

WEST INDIES

Batsman	Dismissal	Runs	Dismissal	Runs
P.V.Simmons	b Illingworth	12	c Russell b Lawrence	1
D.L.Haynes	c Smith b Lawrence	18	not out	57
R.B.Richardson	b Lawrence	43	not out	52
C.L.Hooper	c Russell b DeFreitas	11		
I.V.A.Richards	b Illingworth	80		
A.L.Logie	c Ramprakash b DeFreitas	78		
P.J.L.Dujon	c Hick b Pringle	19		
M.D.Marshall	c Illingworth b DeFreitas	67		
C.E.L.Ambrose	b Illingworth	17		
C.A.Walsh	lbw b Pringle	12		
I.B.A.Allen	not out	4		
Extras	(B2, LB13, W1, NB20)	36	(NB5)	5
Total		**397**	**(1 wicket)**	**115**

WEST INDIES	O	M	R	W	O	M	R	W	FALL OF WICKETS				
										E	WI	E	WI
Ambrose	34	7	74	5	27	7	61	3	Wkt	1st	1st	2nd	2nd
Marshall	21.5	6	54	2	21	6	49	2	1st	108	32	4	1
Walsh	24	4	75	1	(4) 24	7	64	4	2nd	113	32	8	–
Allen	17	0	69	2	(3) 7	2	23	1	3rd	138	45	25	–
Hooper	6	4	10	0					4th	186	118	63	–
Richards	1	0	1	0					5th	192	239	100	–
									6th	212	272	106	–
ENGLAND									7th	217	324	106	–
DeFreitas	31.1	9	67	3	11	3	29	0	8th	228	358	115	–
Lawrence	24	2	116	2	12.2	0	61	1	9th	270	392	153	–
Illingworth	33	8	110	3	(4) 2	0	5	0	10th	300	397	211	–
Pringle	25	6	71	2	(3) 7	2	20	0					
Hick	5	0	18	0									

Umpires: J.H.Hampshire (8) and M.J.Kitchen (2).

Close: 1st day – E(1) 269-8 (Smith 40, Illingworth 13); 2nd – WI(1) 262-5 (Logie 72, Dujon 3); 3rd – E(2) 54-3 (Lamb 25, Ramprakash 7); 4th – WI(2) 20-1 (Haynes 8, Richardson 10).

ENGLAND v WEST INDIES 1991 (4th Test)

At Edgbaston, Birmingham, on 25, 26, 27, 28 July.
Toss: West Indies.   Result: WEST INDIES won by seven wickets.
Debuts: England – H.Morris.

A straight driven six by Richards at 5.52 on the fourth evening ensured that West Indies would not lose any of the dozen series under his captaincy. In an innings of supreme technical skill and application on an inconsistent pitch, Richardson (269 minutes, 229 balls, 13 fours) overcame a viral infection to record his 13th Test hundred; it was his first in three tours of England. The last six of Hick's first seven innings at this level were terminated by Ambrose. England's opening bowlers were both the product of Willesden High School, London.

ENGLAND

*G.A.Gooch	b Marshall	45	b Patterson	40
H.Morris	c Dujon b Patterson	3	lbw b Patterson	1
M.A.Atherton	lbw b Walsh	16	c Hooper b Patterson	1
G.A.Hick	c Richards b Ambrose	19	b Ambrose	1
A.J.Lamb	lbw b Marshall	9	c Dujon b Walsh	25
M.R.Ramprakash	c Logie b Walsh	29	c Dujon b Marshall	25
†R.C.Russell	c Richardson b Ambrose	12	c Dujon b Patterson	0
D.R.Pringle	b Ambrose	2	c Logie b Marshall	45
P.A.J.DeFreitas	c Richardson b Marshall	10	b Patterson	7
C.C.Lewis	lbw b Marshall	13	c sub (C.B.Lambert) b Ambrose	65
R.K.Illingworth	not out	0	not out	5
Extras	(B4, LB3, NB23)	30	(B5, LB21, NB14)	40
Total		**188**		**255**

WEST INDIES

P.V.Simmons	c Hick b Lewis	28	lbw b DeFreitas	16
D.L.Haynes	c Russell b DeFreitas	32	c Hick b DeFreitas	8
R.B.Richardson	lbw b Lewis	104	c Hick b DeFreitas	0
C.L.Hooper	b Illingworth	31	not out	55
*I.V.A.Richards	c Lewis b Pringle	22	not out	73
A.L.Logie	c Atherton b Lewis	28		
†P.J.L.Dujon	lbw b DeFreitas	6		
M.D.Marshall	not out	6		
C.E.L.Ambrose	c Hick b Lewis	1		
C.A.Walsh	c and b Lewis	18		
B.P.Patterson	b Lewis	3		
Extras	(LB7, NB6)	13	(LB4, NB1)	5
Total		**292**	(3 wickets)	**157**

WEST INDIES	O	M	R	W	O	M	R	W		FALL OF WICKETS			
										E	WI	E	WI
Ambrose	23	6	64	3	33	16	42	2	*Wkt*	*1st*	*1st*	*2nd*	*2nd*
Patterson	11	2	39	1	31	6	81	5	1st	6	52	2	23
Walsh	21	6	43	2	(4) 7	1	20	1	2nd	53	93	4	23
Marshall	12.4	1	33	4	(3) 19.4	3	53	2	3rd	88	148	5	24
Hooper	3	2	2	0	(6) 12	3	26	0	4th	108	194	71	–
Simmons					(5) 3	0	7	0	5th	129	257	94	–
									6th	159	258	96	–
ENGLAND									7th	163	266	127	–
DeFreitas	25.3	9	40	2	13	2	54	3	8th	163	267	144	–
Lewis	35	10	111	6	16	7	45	0	9th	184	285	236	–
Pringle	23	9	48	1	7	1	31	0	10th	188	292	255	–
Illingworth	17	2	75	1	4.4	0	23	0					
Gooch	6	1	11	0									
Hick	1	1	0	0									

Umpires: B.Dudleston (1) and D.R.Shepherd (13).

Close: 1st day – E(1) 184-9 (DeFreitas 7, Illingworth 0); 2nd – WI(1) 253-4 (Richardson 103, Logie 24); 3rd – E(2) 156-8 (Pringle 26, Lewis 7).

ENGLAND v WEST INDIES 1991 (5th Test)

At Kennington Oval, London, on 8, 9, 10, 11, 12 August.
Toss: England.　Result: ENGLAND won by five wickets.
Debuts: West Indies – C.B.Lambert.

At 3.46 on the fifth afternoon, England drew a rubber against West Indies for the first time since 1973-74. This match marked the final Test appearances for Richards, who suffered his eighth defeat in 50 matches as captain, Marshall and Dujon. Smith (353 minutes, 257 balls, 13 fours) passed 2,000 runs during his sixth hundred in 51 Test innings. Haynes became the first West Indian to carry his bat through a Test innings on two occasions. Tufnell's spell of 6 for 4 in 33 balls included three wickets in his 14th over and 4 for 0 with his last nine balls. West Indies followed on against England for the first time since 1969 (*Test No. 653*). Richardson (458 minutes, 312 balls, a six and 11 fours) scored his 14th hundred in 107 innings. Lambert took a wicket with his third ball in Tests. Botham, who faced just one ball in making the final hit, finished on the winning side for the first time in 20 matches against West Indies.

ENGLAND

*G.A.Gooch	lbw b Ambrose	60	lbw b Marshall		29
H.Morris	c Lambert b Ambrose	44	c Dujon b Patterson		2
M.A.Atherton	c Hooper b Walsh	0	c Hooper b Patterson		13
R.A.Smith	lbw b Marshall	109	c Patterson b Walsh		26
M.R.Ramprakash	c Lambert b Hooper	25	lbw b Lambert		19
†A.J.Stewart	c Richardson b Patterson	31	not out		38
I.T.Botham	hit wicket b Ambrose	31	not out		4
C.C.Lewis	not out	47			
P.A.J.DeFreitas	c Dujon b Walsh	7			
D.V.Lawrence	c Richardson b Walsh	9			
P.C.R.Tufnell	c Haynes b Patterson	2			
Extras	(B8, LB10, W1, NB35)	54	(B4, W1, NB10)		15
Total		**419**	(5 wickets)		**146**

WEST INDIES

P.V.Simmons	lbw b Lawrence	15	c Lewis b Botham		36
D.L.Haynes	not out	75	lbw b Lawrence		43
R.B.Richardson	c Stewart b Botham	20	(4) c Gooch b Lawrence		121
C.L.Hooper	c Stewart b DeFreitas	3	(5) c Gooch b Tufnell		54
C.B.Lambert	c Ramprakash b Tufnell	39	(3) lbw b Botham		14
†P.J.L.Dujon	lbw b Lawrence	0	(7) c Stewart b Lawrence		5
M.D.Marshall	c Botham b Tufnell	0	(8) b DeFreitas		17
*I.V.A.Richards	c Stewart b Tufnell	2	(6) c Morris b Lawrence		60
C.E.L.Ambrose	c Botham b Tufnell	0	lbw b DeFreitas		0
C.A.Walsh	c Gooch b Tufnell	0	lbw b Lawrence		14
B.P.Patterson	c Botham b Tufnell	2	not out		1
Extras	(LB9, NB11)	20	(B7, LB5, W2, NB6)		20
Total		**176**			**385**

WEST INDIES	O	M	R	W		O	M	R	W
Ambrose	36	8	83	3		8	0	48	0
Patterson	25.1	3	87	2		9	0	63	2
Walsh	32	5	91	3	(4)	9	3	18	1
Marshall	24	5	62	1	(3)	5	3	9	1
Hooper	34	1	78	1					
Lambert					(5)	0.4	0	4	1

ENGLAND	O	M	R	W		O	M	R	W
DeFreitas	13	6	38	1		20	9	42	2
Lawrence	16	1	67	2		25.5	4	106	5
Tufnell	14.3	3	25	6	(4)	46	6	150	1
Botham	11	4	27	1	(5)	16	4	40	2
Lewis	3	1	10	0	(3)	25	12	35	0

FALL OF WICKETS

	E	WI	WI	E
Wkt	1st	1st	2nd	2nd
1st	112	52	53	3
2nd	114	95	71	40
3rd	120	98	125	80
4th	188	158	208	80
5th	263	160	305	142
6th	336	161	311	–
7th	351	172	356	–
8th	386	172	356	–
9th	411	172	378	–
10th	419	176	385	–

Umpires: J.W.Holder (10) and M.J.Kitchen (3).

Close: 1st day – E(1) 231-4 (Smith 54, Stewart 19); 2nd – WI(1) 90-1 (Haynes 46, Richardson 20); 3rd – WI(2) 152-3 (Richardson 39, Hooper 11); 4th – WI(2) 356-6 (Richardson 108, Marshall 17).

ENGLAND v SRI LANKA 1991 (Only Test)

At Lord's, London, on 22, 23, 24, 26, 27 August.
Toss: England.   Result: ENGLAND won by 137 runs.
Debuts: Sri Lanka – K.I.W.Wijegunawardene.

England completed their third victory in four Tests against Sri Lanka at 4.33 on the final afternoon. Stewart (305 minutes, 240 balls, 14 fours) rescued a struggling innings with England's highest score against Sri Lanka. His record was comfortably exceeded by Gooch's second innings when England's captain batted 328 minutes, faced 252 balls, hit 19 fours, and passed 7,000 runs during the last of his record six hundreds at Lord's. Ratnayake was the first Sri Lankan to score a fifty and take five wickets in an innings of the same Test. DeFreitas returned his best analysis in Tests and established the record for England in this brief series.

ENGLAND

*G.A.Gooch	c and b Ramanayake	38	b Anurasiri	174
H.Morris	lbw b Ratnayake	42	c Mahanama b Anurasiri	23
A.J.Stewart	not out	113	c De Silva b Anurasiri	43
R.A.Smith	c Tillekeratne b Ratnayake	4	not out	63
M.R.Ramprakash	c Mahanama b Hathurusinghe	0		
I.T.Botham	c Mahanama b Ramanayake	22		
C.C.Lewis	c De Silva b Anurasiri	11		
†R.C.Russell	b Anurasiri	17	(5) not out	12
P.A.J.DeFreitas	b Ratnayake	1		
D.V.Lawrence	c and b Ratnayake	3		
P.C.R.Tufnell	lbw b Ratnayake	0		
Extras	(B9, LB8, NB14)	31	(B15, LB23, W1, NB10)	49
Total		282	(3 wickets declared)	364

SRI LANKA

D.S.B.P.Kuruppu	b DeFreitas	5	lbw b Lewis	21
U.C.Hathurusinghe	c Tufnell b DeFreitas	66	c Morris b Tufnell	25
A.P.Gurusinha	lbw b DeFreitas	4	b Tufnell	34
*P.A.de Silva	c Lewis b DeFreitas	42	c Russell b Lawrence	18
R.S.Mahanama	c Russell b Botham	2	c Botham b Tufnell	15
S.T.Jayasuriya	c Smith b DeFreitas	11	c Russell b Lewis	66
†H.P.Tillekeratne	c Morris b Lawrence	20	b Tufnell	16
R.J.Ratnayake	b DeFreitas	52	c sub (I.D.K.Salisbury) b Lawrence	17
C.P.H.Ramanayake	lbw b DeFreitas	0	not out	34
K.I.W.Wijegunawardene	not out	6	c Botham b DeFreitas	4
S.D.Anurasiri	b Lawrence	1	lbw b Tufnell	16
Extras	(LB15)	15	(B1, LB16, NB2)	19
Total		224		285

SRI LANKA	O	M	R	W	O	M	R	W
Ratnayake	27	4	69	5	26	4	91	0
Ramanayake	24	5	75	2	20	2	86	0
Wijegunawardene	10	1	36	0	2	0	13	0
Hathurusinghe	17	6	40	1				
Anurasiri	17	4	45	2	(4) 36.1	8	135	3
Jayasuriya					(5) 1	0	1	0

ENGLAND	O	M	R	W	O	M	R	W
DeFreitas	26	8	70	7	22	8	45	1
Lawrence	15.1	3	61	2	23	7	83	2
Lewis	10	5	29	0	(4) 18	4	31	2
Botham	10	3	26	1	(3) 6	2	15	0
Tufnell	7	2	23	0	34.3	14	94	5

FALL OF WICKETS

	E	SL	E	SL
Wkt	1st	1st	2nd	2nd
1st	70	12	78	50
2nd	114	22	217	50
3rd	119	75	322	111
4th	120	86	–	119
5th	160	105	–	159
6th	183	139	–	212
7th	246	213	–	212
8th	258	213	–	241
9th	276	220	–	253
10th	282	224	–	285

Umpires: H.D.Bird (46) and J.H.Hampshire (9).

Close: 1st day – E(1) 229-6 (Stewart 76, Russell 11); 2nd – SL(1) 75-2 (Hathurusinghe 19, De Silva 42); 3rd – E(2) 100-1 (Gooch 60, Stewart 7); 4th – SL(2) 79-2 (Gurusinha 16, De Silva 7).

AUSTRALIA v INDIA 1991-92 (1st Test)

At Woolloongabba, Brisbane, on 29, 30 November, 1, 2 December.
Toss: Australia.   Result: AUSTRALIA won by ten wickets.
Debuts: India – J.Srinath.

Border celebrated his usurping of S.M.Gavaskar's record 125 Test match appearances by leading Australia to a comprehensive four-day victory in his 63rd successive match as captain. In his 107th Test innings, Boon became the eleventh Australian to score 4,000 runs. Prabhakar was the first bowler to be no-balled under new ICC legislation prohibiting more than one bouncer at each batsman in the same over. This was also the first Test match played under the jurisdiction of a referee appointed from an ICC panel, former England captain M.J.K.Smith being the first to hold this office.

INDIA

R.J.Shastri	c Waugh b McDermott	8	c Healy b McDermott	41
K.Srikkanth	c Boon b McDermott	13	c Boon b Hughes	0
S.V.Manjrekar	c and b Hughes	17	c Boon b Hughes	5
D.B.Vengsarkar	c Waugh b Hughes	5	lbw b Hughes	0
*M.Azharuddin	c Hughes b Whitney	10	c Boon b Hughes	12
S.R.Tendulkar	b Whitney	16	c Healy b McDermott	7
Kapil Dev	b McDermott	44	c Waugh b McDermott	25
M.Prabhakar	not out	54	c Healy b Whitney	39
†K.S.More	c Whitney b Hughes	19	lbw b McDermott	1
S.L.V.Raju	c Healy b McDermott	12	c Healy b Whitney	2
J.Srinath	c Healy b McDermott	21	not out	12
Extras	(B1, LB6, NB13)	20	(LB4, NB8)	12
Total		**239**		**156**

AUSTRALIA

G.R.Marsh	b Srinath	47	(2) not out	17
M.A.Taylor	c Vengsarkar b Raju	94	(1) not out	35
D.C.Boon	c More b Prabhakar	66		
*A.R.Border	b Kapil Dev	28		
D.M.Jones	b Kapil Dev	0		
M.E.Waugh	c More b Srinath	11		
†I.A.Healy	lbw b Prabhakar	12		
P.L.Taylor	c Raju b Srinath	31		
M.G.Hughes	b Kapil Dev	11		
C.J.McDermott	c Azharuddin b Kapil Dev	8		
M.R.Whitney	not out	7		
Extras	(LB15, W1, NB9)	25	(LB4, NB2)	6
Total		**340**	(0 wickets)	**58**

AUSTRALIA	O	M	R	W	O	M	R	W	FALL OF WICKETS			
										I	A	I	A
McDermott	28.1	11	54	5	25	7	47	4					
Whitney	21	2	82	2	(3) 17.2	3	55	2	Wkt	1st	1st	2nd	2nd
Hughes	20	5	34	3	(2) 16	4	50	4	1st	21	95	0	–
Waugh	1	0	6	0					2nd	24	178	14	–
P.L.Taylor	18	3	56	0					3rd	50	244	14	–
									4th	53	244	32	–
									5th	67	265	47	–
INDIA													
Kapil Dev	34	9	80	4	9	0	23	0	6th	83	278	87	–
Prabhakar	37	10	88	2	2	1	3	0	7th	141	280	136	–
Srinath	24.4	4	59	3	9	5	6	0	8th	186	301	140	–
Raju	31	5	90	1	3	1	13	0	9th	206	316	142	–
Tendulkar	1	0	8	0	1	0	5	0	10th	239	340	156	–
Manjrekar					0.5	0	4	0					

Umpires: P.J.McConnell (20) and S.G.Randell (9). Referee: M.J.K.Smith (*England*) (1).

Close: 1st day – I(1) 239 all out; 2nd – A(1) 235-2 (Boon 59, Border 24); 3rd – I(2) 104-6 (Shastri 37, Prabhakar 9).

AUSTRALIA v INDIA 1991-92 (2nd Test)

At Melbourne Cricket Ground on 26, 27, 28, 29 December.
Toss: India.   Result: AUSTRALIA won by eight wickets.
Debuts: None.

Australia's substantial victory was based on another outstanding performance by Reid. He followed his 13-wicket haul against England at Melbourne a year earlier with a match analysis of 12 for 126 which set a record for Australia in home Tests against India and included his 100th wicket (Srinath) in 25 Tests. Azharuddin completed 3,000 runs in 64 Test innings. When he dismissed Boon, Kapil Dev passed I.T.Botham's tally of 380 wickets and moved into second place behind Sir Richard Hadlee's record of 431. Healy became the fourth Australian wicket-keeper to make 100 dismissals. Umpire King failed to uphold an appeal for obstruction or handling the ball when Jones, attempting a stroke, wedged the ball between his thigh and his left hand which was holding the bat. He prevented More from gathering the ball by slapping it away with his other hand. The ball had not been ruled 'dead'. Border scored the winning run off the last possible ball of the fourth day.

INDIA

R.J.Shastri	c Healy b Reid	23		c Healy b Reid	22
K.Srikkanth	c Boon b Reid	5		lbw b Reid	6
M.Prabhakar	b Reid	0	(9)	c Healy b Reid	17
S.V.Manjrekar	c Waugh b Reid	25	(3)	c M.A.Taylor b McDermott	30
D.B.Vengsarkar	c Reid b Hughes	23	(4)	c sub‡ b McDermott	54
*M.Azharuddin	c Jones b McDermott	22	(5)	c M.A.Taylor b Reid	2
S.R.Tendulkar	c Waugh b Reid	15		c Border b P.L.Taylor	40
Kapil Dev	c Hughes b McDermott	19		c Healy b Reid	12
†K.S.More	not out	67	(10)	lbw b Reid	12
S.L.V.Raju	c Border b Hughes	31	(6)	c and b McDermott	1
J.Srinath	c Border b Reid	14		not out	0
Extras	(B1, LB8, W6, NB4)	19		(B1, LB6, NB10)	17
Total		**263**			**213**

AUSTRALIA

G.R.Marsh	c Vengsarkar b Kapil Dev	86	(2)	lbw b Prabhakar	10
M.A.Taylor	c Tendulkar b Prabhakar	13	(1)	st More b Raju	60
D.C.Boon	c Srikkanth b Kapil Dev	11		not out	44
*A.R.Border	b Kapil Dev	0		not out	5
D.M.Jones	c More b Prabhakar	59			
M.E.Waugh	c More b Shastri	34			
†I.A.Healy	lbw b Kapil Dev	60			
P.L.Taylor	c More b Prabhakar	11			
M.G.Hughes	c Tendulkar b Kapil Dev	36			
C.J.McDermott	not out	16			
B.A.Reid	c Kapil Dev b Prabhakar	3			
Extras	(LB9, NB11)	20		(LB3, NB6)	9
Total		**349**		**(2 wickets)**	**128**

AUSTRALIA	O	M	R	W	O	M	R	W	FALL OF WICKETS			
McDermott	30	6	100	2	29	8	63	3		I	A	I	A
Reid	26.2	7	66	6	29	9	60	6	*Wkt*	*1st*	*1st*	*2nd*	*2nd*
Hughes	23	6	52	2	19	6	43	0	1st	11	24	13	16
Waugh	8	1	16	0					2nd	11	55	48	122
P.L.Taylor	6	0	20	0	(4) 11	3	40	1	3rd	61	55	75	–
									4th	64	163	78	–
INDIA									5th	109	211	79	–
Kapil Dev	35	9	97	5	12	1	30	0	6th	109	229	141	–
Prabhakar	34	7	84	4	11	0	38	1	7th	128	262	155	–
Srinath	25	3	71	0	8	0	28	0	8th	151	326	173	–
Raju	17	3	52	0	6	0	17	1	9th	228	337	213	–
Tendulkar	4	1	16	0					10th	263	349	213	–
Shastri	7	1	20	1	(5) 3	1	12	0					

Umpires: L.J.King (5) and T.A.Prue (4). Referee: M.J.K.Smith (*England*) (2).   ‡ (M.R.Whitney)

Close: 1st day – I(1) 243-9 (More 50, Srinath 12); 2nd – A(1) 215-5 (Marsh 79, Healy 4); 3rd – I(2) 92-5 (Vengsarkar 14, Tendulkar 8).

AUSTRALIA v INDIA 1991-92 (3rd Test)

At Sydney Cricket Ground on 2, 3, 4, 5, 6 January.
Toss: India.   Result: MATCH DRAWN.
Debuts: Australia – S.K.Warne; India – S.T.Banerjee.

Despite gaining a first innings lead of 170, India, hampered by the loss of five hours to rain and bad light on the third and fourth days, were unable to complete a notable victory when Australia managed to survive for 84 overs on the last day. Boon (444 minutes, 361 balls, 13 fours) scored his 11th Test hundred and his fourth in Sydney. In an innings spread over three days, Shastri (572 minutes, 478 balls, two sixes and 17 fours) scored India's first double hundred against Australia. His partnership of 196 with Tendulkar (298 minutes, 215 balls, 14 fours), who, at 18 years 256 days became the youngest to score a Test hundred in Australia, was a fifth-wicket record for India in this series. After a baptism of just seven first-class matches, the first analysis of 22-year-old Shane Warne at this level provided no hint of the havoc his leg-spin was to wreak.

AUSTRALIA

G.R.Marsh	b Banerjee	8	(2)	c Pandit b Kapil Dev	4
M.A.Taylor	c Pandit b Banerjee	56	(1)	c Kapil Dev b Shastri	35
D.C.Boon	not out	129		c Azharuddin b Srinath	7
M.E.Waugh	c Prabhakar b Banerjee	5		lbw b Prabhakar	18
D.M.Jones	run out	35		c Pandit b Shastri	18
*A.R.Border	c Pandit b Kapil Dev	19		not out	53
†I.A.Healy	c sub (K.Srikkanth) b Prabhakar	1		c Prabhakar b Shastri	7
M.G.Hughes	c Pandit b Prabhakar	2		c Prabhakar b Tendulkar	21
C.J.McDermott	b Prabhakar	1		c Vengsarkar b Shastri	0
S.K.Warne	c Pandit b Kapil Dev	20		not out	1
B.A.Reid	c Tendulkar b Kapil Dev	0			
Extras	(B4, LB14, W1, NB18)	37		(LB4, W1, NB4)	9
Total		**313**		(8 wickets)	**173**

INDIA

R.J.Shastri	c Jones b Warne	206
N.S.Sidhu	c Waugh b McDermott	0
S.V.Manjrekar	c Waugh b Hughes	34
D.B.Vengsarkar	c Waugh b McDermott	54
*M.Azharuddin	c Boon b McDermott	4
S.R.Tendulkar	not out	148
M.Prabhakar	c Taylor b Hughes	14
Kapil Dev	c Marsh b Hughes	0
†C.S.Pandit	run out	9
S.T.Banerjee	c Border b McDermott	3
J.Srinath	run out	1
Extras	(B1, LB4, NB5)	10
Total		**483**

INDIA	O	M	R	W	O	M	R	W
Kapil Dev	33	9	60	3	19	5	41	1
Prabhakar	39	12	82	3	27	10	53	1
Banerjee	18	4	47	3				
Srinath	21	5	69	0	(3) 12	0	28	1
Shastri	13	1	37	0	(4) 25	8	45	4
Tendulkar					(5) 1	0	2	1

AUSTRALIA	O	M	R	W
McDermott	51	12	147	4
Reid	4	0	10	0
Hughes	41.4	8	104	3
Waugh	14	5	28	0
Warne	45	7	150	1
Border	13	3	39	0

FALL OF WICKETS

	A	I	A
Wkt	1st	1st	2nd
1st	22	7	9
2nd	117	86	31
3rd	127	197	55
4th	210	201	85
5th	248	397	106
6th	251	434	114
7th	259	434	164
8th	269	458	171
9th	313	474	–
10th	313	483	–

Umpires: P.J.McConnell (21) and S.G.Randell (10). Referee: P.B.H.May (*England*) (1).

Close: 1st day – A(1) 234-4 (Boon 89, Border 14); 2nd – I(1) 103-2 (Shastri 52, Vengsarkar 13); 3rd – I(1) 178-2 (Shastri 95, Vengsarkar 43); 4th –I(1) 445-7 (Tendulkar 120, Pandit 3).

AUSTRALIA v INDIA 1991-92 (4th Test)

At Adelaide Oval on 25, 26, 27, 28, 29 January.
Toss: India.   Result: AUSTRALIA won by 38 runs.
Debuts: None.

A highly absorbing match, in which 21 wickets fell on the first two days and only one on the third, ended with India narrowly failing to reach their target of 372. Australia overcame a first innings deficit of 80 through a second-wicket partnership of 221 between Taylor (395 minutes, 303 balls, nine fours) and Boon (465 minutes, 352 balls, 16 fours), the latter completing 1,000 runs against India and becoming the first Australian to score five hundreds against them. Azharuddin (185 minutes, 162 balls, 17 fours) scored his first hundred in ten Tests against Australia, before McDermott ended his 101-run partnership with Prabhakar and claimed the last four wickets with the new ball to return match figures of 10 for 168.

AUSTRALIA

G.R.Marsh	b Prabhakar	8	(2)	b Kapil Dev	5
M.A.Taylor	b Tendulkar	11	(1)	c Raju b Kapil Dev	100
D.C.Boon	b Kapil Dev	19		run out	135
*A.R.Border	c Pandit b Tendulkar	0		not out	91
D.M.Jones	c Azharuddin b Raju	41		c Pandit b Kapil Dev	0
M.E.Waugh	lbw b Prabhakar	15		c Tendulkar b Kapil Dev	0
†I.A.Healy	c Pandit b Kapil Dev	1		c Srikkanth b Kapil Dev	41
M.G.Hughes	c Manjrekar b Kapil Dev	26		lbw b Srinath	23
S.K.Warne	st Pandit b Raju	7		c Pandit b Srinath	0
C.J.McDermott	b Raju	0		b Raju	21
M.R.Whitney	not out	0		c Srinath b Raju	12
Extras	(LB10, NB7)	17		(LB15, NB8)	23
Total		**145**			**451**

INDIA

K.Srikkanth	c Healy b McDermott	17		b McDermott	22
N.S.Sidhu	c Healy b Hughes	27		lbw b Hughes	35
S.V.Manjrekar	lbw b Hughes	2		run out	45
D.B.Vengsarkar	c Waugh b McDermott	13	(5)	lbw b Hughes	4
*M.Azharuddin	lbw b McDermott	1	(6)	c Taylor b McDermott	106
S.R.Tendulkar	lbw b McDermott	6	(4)	lbw b Waugh	17
Kapil Dev	c Border b Hughes	56		c Marsh b Hughes	5
M.Prabhakar	lbw b Whitney	33		lbw b McDermott	64
†C.S.Pandit	c Boon b McDermott	15		c Waugh b McDermott	7
S.L.V.Raju	not out	19		not out	8
J.Srinath	c Healy b Whitney	21		c Warne b McDermott	3
Extras	(LB5, NB10)	15		(B3, LB9, NB5)	17
Total		**225**			**333**

INDIA	O	M	R	W	O	M	R	W	FALL OF WICKETS			
Kapil Dev	23	11	33	3	51	12	130	5		A	I	A	I
Prabhakar	18	3	55	2	21	5	60	0	*Wkt*	*1st*	*1st*	*2nd*	*2nd*
Srinath	10	2	26	0	(4) 37	13	76	2	1st	13	30	10	52
Tendulkar	4	2	10	2	(6) 20	5	44	0	2nd	36	33	231	72
Raju	11.4	7	11	3	(3) 56	15	121	2	3rd	39	55	277	97
Srikkanth					(5) 1	0	5	0	4th	50	64	277	102
									5th	77	70	277	172
AUSTRALIA									6th	81	70	348	182
McDermott	31	9	76	5	29.1	8	92	5	7th	117	135	383	283
Whitney	26.2	6	68	2	17	3	59	0	8th	141	174	383	291
Hughes	18	5	55	3	23	4	66	3	9th	145	192	409	327
Warne	7	1	18	0	(5) 16	1	60	0	10th	145	225	451	333
Waugh	2	1	3	0	(4) 12	2	36	1					
Border					3	0	8	0					

Umpires: D.B.Hair (1) and P.J.McConnell (22). Referee: P.B.H.May (*England*) (2).

Close: 1st day – I(1) 45-2 (Sidhu 15, Vengsarkar 8); 2nd – A(2) 36-1 (Taylor 18, Boon 11); 3rd – A(2) 245-2 (Boon 121, Border 6); 4th – I(2) 31-0 (Srikkanth 13, Sidhu 13).

AUSTRALIA v INDIA 1991-92 (5th Test)

At W.A.C.A.Ground, Perth, on 1, 2, 3, 4, 5 February.
Toss: Australia.   Result: AUSTRALIA won by 300 runs.
Debuts: Australia – W.N.Phillips, P.R.Reiffel.

Border's side emulated the 4-0 series successes of the 1947-48 and 1967-68 Australian teams against India when India collapsed from 82 for 0 to 141 all out. Boon (377 minutes, 304 balls) scored his third hundred in successive Tests. Healy became the third Australian wicket-keeper after W.A.S.Oldfield and R.W.Marsh to achieve the double of 100 dismissals and 1,000 runs when he had scored 19. Srikkanth, who also completed 2,000 runs, equalled the Test record by holding five catches in an innings; a record 33 wickets fell to catches in the match. Tendulkar (228 minutes, 161 balls) shared an Indian record ninth-wicket partnership of 81 for this series with More. Kapil Dev became the second bowler to take 400 wickets when he dismissed Taylor in the second innings. Jones (395 minutes, 265 balls) and Moody (186 minutes, 149 balls) added 173 for the fourth wicket. Whitney returned Australia's best innings analysis against India. McDermott's tally of 31 wickets equalled B.S.Bedi's record for this series. Umpire Crafter's 33rd Test appearance surpassed R.M.Crockett's Australian record.

AUSTRALIA

M.A.Taylor	c Srikkanth b Kapil Dev	2	(2) lbw b Kapil Dev		16
W.N.Phillips	c More b Prabhakar	8	(1) c Kapil Dev b Srinath		14
D.C.Boon	c Sidhu b Prabhakar	107	c Kapil Dev b Prabhakar		38
A.R.Border	c Srikkanth b Kapil Dev	59	(8) not out		20
D.M.Jones	c Srikkanth b Raju	7	(4) not out		150
T.M.Moody	c Vengsarkar b Prabhakar	50	(5) c More b Kapil Dev		101
I.A.Healy	c More b Srinath	28	(6) c More b Raju		7
M.G.Hughes	c Srikkanth b Srinath	24	(7) c Tendulkar b Srinath		11
P.R.Reiffel	c More b Prabhakar	9			
C.J.McDermott	c Srikkanth b Prabhakar	31			
M.R.Whitney	not out	1			
Extras	(B1, LB7, NB12)	20	(LB4, NB6)		10
Total		**346**	(6 wickets declared)		**367**

INDIA

K.Srikkanth	c Boon b McDermott	34	c Jones b Whitney		38
N.S.Sidhu	c Healy b Hughes	5	c Jones b Reiffel		35
S.V.Manjrekar	c Jones b Hughes	31	c Healy b Whitney		8
S.R.Tendulkar	c Moody b Whitney	114	c Moody b Reiffel		5
D.B.Vengsarkar	c Taylor b Hughes	1	c Moody b Whitney		4
M.Azharuddin	c Healy b McDermott	11	lbw b Whitney		24
S.L.V.Raju	c Taylor b Whitney	1	(10) c Healy b Whitney		8
Kapil Dev	c Hughes b Whitney	4	(7) lbw b Whitney		0
M.Prabhakar	c Reiffel b Whitney	0	(8) c Healy b McDermott		3
K.S.More	c Healy b Hughes	43	(9) c Taylor b Whitney		1
J.Srinath	not out	5	not out		1
Extras	(LB14, NB9)	23	(LB11, NB3)		14
Total		**272**			**141**

INDIA	O	M	R	W	O	M	R	W		FALL OF WICKETS			
										A	I	A	I
Kapil Dev	40	12	103	2	28	8	48	2	*Wkt*	*1st*	*1st*	*2nd*	*2nd*
Prabhakar	32.5	9	101	5	32	4	116	1	1st	10	25	27	82
Srinath	25	5	69	2	29.3	4	121	2	2nd	21	69	31	90
Tendulkar	5	2	9	0					3rd	138	100	113	97
Raju	23	6	56	1	(4) 24	5	78	1	4th	145	109	286	103
									5th	232	130	298	111
AUSTRALIA									6th	259	135	315	111
McDermott	21	6	47	2	20	8	44	1	7th	290	159	–	126
Hughes	26.5	5	82	4	12	2	25	0	8th	303	159	–	129
Reiffel	17	5	46	0	11	2	34	2	9th	338	240	–	134
Whitney	23	4	68	4	12.1	3	27	7	10th	346	272	–	141
Moody	2	0	15	0									

Umpires: A.R.Crafter (33) and T.A.Prue (5). Referee: P.B.H.May (*England*) (3).

Close: 1st day – A(1) 222-4 (Boon 91, Moody 42); 2nd –I(1) 135-5 (Tendulkar 31, Raju 1); 3rd – A(2) 104-2 (Boon 35, Jones 34); 4th – I(2) 55-0 (Srikkanth 26, Sidhu 24).

PAKISTAN v SRI LANKA 1991-92 (1st Test)

At Jinnah Stadium, Sialkot, on 12, 13, 14, 16, 17 December.
Toss: Sri Lanka.   Result: MATCH DRAWN.
Debuts: Sri Lanka – G.P.Wickremasinghe.

Fading early winter light in this northern city, which curtailed the match by 285 minutes, 175 of them on the final day, prevented Pakistan from winning after gaining a first innings lead of 153. Waqar Younis recorded his sixth five-wicket analysis in 12 Tests. Salim Malik (298 minutes, 212 balls) scored his ninth hundred in 91 innings. Imran's 93 not out was the highest innings ended by a declaration, in this instance his own decision, until 1994-95. Ranatunga was dismissed for a 'pair' in his first Test since being relieved of the captaincy.

SRI LANKA

M.A.R.Samarasekera	c Moin b Waqar	19	b Waqar	6
U.C.Hathurusinghe	c Akram Raza b Aqib	17	c Ramiz b Wasim	7
A.P.Gurusinha	b Aqib	33	lbw b Aqib	23
*P.A.de Silva	b Waqar	31	c sub‡ b Akram Raza	19
A.Ranatunga	lbw b Aqib	0	c Moin b Waqar	0
S.T.Jayasuriya	b Akram Raza	77	not out	35
†H.P.Tillekeratne	c Akram Raza b Waqar	49	not out	42
R.J.Ratnayake	b Waqar	13		
C.P.H.Ramanayake	b Akram Raza	0		
S.D.Anurasiri	not out	3		
G.P.Wickremasinghe	b Waqar	0		
Extras	(B5, LB11, NB12)	28	(NB5)	5
Total		**270**	**(5 wickets)**	**137**

PAKISTAN

Ramiz Raja	c Tillekeratne b Anurasiri	98
Shoaib Mohammad	c and b Wickremasinghe	43
Zahid Fazal	c and b Ratnayake	36
Salim Malik	c Gurusinha b Anurasiri	101
Javed Miandad	c Jayasuriya b Anurasiri	1
*Imran Khan	not out	93
Wasim Akram	not out	20
†Moin Khan		
Akram Raza	did not bat	
Waqar Younis		
Aqib Javed		
Extras	(LB6, NB25)	31
Total	**(5 wickets declared)**	**423**

PAKISTAN	O	M	R	W		O	M	R	W		FALL OF WICKETS		
Wasim	32	7	47	0	(2)	13	4	31	1		SL	P	SL
Waqar	30.5	5	84	5	(1)	14.4	1	43	2	*Wkt*	*1st*	*1st*	*2nd*
Akram Raza	24	10	37	2	(4)	11	3	34	1	1st	21	128	6
Aqib	23	4	70	3	(3)	7	3	22	1	2nd	70	169	33
Imran	9	1	16	0						3rd	89	232	58
Salim					(5)	1	0	7	0	4th	89	233	58
										5th	128	365	58
SRI LANKA										6th	229	–	–
Ratnayake	31	4	100	1						7th	244	–	–
Ramanayake	33	9	75	0						8th	245	–	–
Wickremasinghe	27	3	120	1						9th	270	–	–
Hathurusinghe	1	0	3	0						10th	270	–	–
Anurasiri	61	21	106	3									
De Silva	4	0	13	0									

Umpires: Ikram Rabbani (1) and Khizer Hayat (26). Referee: D.B.Carr (*England*) (1).   ‡ (Ijaz Ahmed)

Close: 1st day – SL(1) 191-5 (Jayasuriya 60, Tillekeratne 14); 2nd – P(1) 72-0 (Ramiz 43, Shoaib 19); 3rd – P(1) 243-4 (Salim 36, Imran 5); 4th – SL (2) 13-1 (Hathurusinghe 2, Gurusinha 2).

PAKISTAN v SRI LANKA 1991-92 (2nd Test)

At Municipal Stadium, Gujranwala, on 20, 21 (*no play*), 22 (*no play*), 24 (*no play*) 25 (*no play*) December.
Toss: Sri Lanka.   Result: MATCH DRAWN.
Debuts: None.

Play on the 65th ground to stage Test cricket was restricted by poor light to 152 minutes on an interrupted first day. Showers and persistent drizzle subsequently turned into mud areas of the outfield damaged by an October public meeting. Play was finally abandoned early on Christmas morning. Ironically, Gujranwala currently boasted one of the best playing surfaces in Pakistan and a capacity crowd attended the first day.

PAKISTAN

Ramiz Raja	not out	51
Shoaib Mohammad	c Tillekeratne b Ratnayake	1
Zahid Fazal	c Tillekeratne b Wickremasinghe	21
Javed Miandad	not out	20
Salim Malik		
*Imran Khan		
†Moin Khan		
Wasim Akram	did not bat	
Waqar Younis		
Aqib Javed		
Salim Jaffer		
Extras	(LB10, NB6)	16
Total	(2 wickets)	**109**

SRI LANKA

R.S.Mahanama
U.C.Hathurusinghe
A.P.Gurusinha
*P.A.de Silva
A.Ranatunga
S.T.Jayasuriya
†H.P.Tillekeratne
R.J.Ratnayake
C.P.H.Ramanayake
S.D.Anurasiri
G.P.Wickremasinghe
Extras
Total

SRI LANKA	O	M	R	W		FALL OF WICKETS	
Ratnayake	13	3	39	1			P
Ramanayake	10	2	16	0	Wkt	1st	
Wickremasinghe	7	2	27	1	1st	3	
Hathurusinghe	2	1	6	0	2nd	59	
Anurasiri	1	0	2	0	3rd	–	
Gurusinha	2	0	9	0	4th	–	
Ranatunga	1	1	0	0	5th	–	
					6th	–	
					7th	–	
					8th	–	
					9th	–	
					10th	–	

Umpires: Athar Zaidi (3) and Khizer Hayat (27). Referee: D.B.Carr (*England*) (2).

Close: 1st day – P(1) 109-2 (Ramiz 51, Miandad 20); 2nd – no play; 3rd – no play; 4th – no play.

PAKISTAN v SRI LANKA 1991-92 (3rd Test)

At Iqbal Stadium, Faisalabad, on 2, 3, 4, 6, 7 January.
Toss: Pakistan.   Result: PAKISTAN won by three wickets.
Debuts: None.

In what transpired to be their captain's final Test, Pakistan narrowly deprived Sri Lanka of their first win overseas. The consistent Jayasuriya again improved his highest Test score and Waqar claimed his seventh five-wicket analysis in 14 matches. Gurusinha led Sri Lanka on the third day when De Silva was absent ill. Umpires Shakoor Rana, standing in his first Test since his infamous confrontation with England's captain in 1987-88, and Khalid Aziz, whose last Test had been in 1979-80, combined to uphold a record total (until 1992-93) of 14 lbw decisions.

SRI LANKA

Batsman	Dismissal 1	Score 1		Dismissal 2	Score 2
R.S.Mahanama	c Moin b Salim Jaffer	58		lbw b Waqar	8
U.C.Hathurusinghe	b Waqar	49		c Zahid b Waqar	20
A.P.Gurusinha	c Zahid b Wasim	3		lbw b Aqib	14
*P.A.de Silva	c Moin b Salim Jaffer	12		lbw b Waqar	38
A.Ranatunga	lbw b Salim Jaffer	0	(8)	c Miandad b Wasim	6
S.T.Jayasuriya	run out	81		c Salim Malik b Waqar	45
†H.P.Tillekeratne	c Shoaib b Waqar	11		c Moin b Aqib	14
R.J.Ratnayake	lbw b Waqar	4	(9)	not out	5
S.D.Anurasiri	c Shoaib b Waqar	0	(10)	b Wasim	0
K.I.W.Wijegunawardene	lbw b Wasim	2	(5)	b Waqar	2
G.P.Wickremasinghe	not out	1		b Wasim	0
Extras	(B3, LB6, W2, NB8)	19		(LB3, NB10)	13
Total		**240**			**165**

PAKISTAN

Batsman	Dismissal 1	Score 1		Dismissal 2	Score 2
Ramiz Raja	lbw b Wickremasinghe	63		lbw b Wickremasinghe	8
Shoaib Mohammad	lbw b Wickremasinghe	30	(7)	b Ratnayake	7
Zahid Fazal	lbw b Wijegunawardene	13	(2)	c Anurasiri b Gurusinha	78
Javed Miandad	c Gurusinha b Wickremasinghe	14	(3)	c Gurusinha b Wijegunawardene	2
Salim Malik	c Tillekeratne b Gurusinha	4	(4)	c Gurusinha b Wijegunawardene	4
*Imran Khan	b Wijegunawardene	22	(5)	lbw b Wijegunawardene	0
Wasim Akram	lbw b Gurusinha	13	(6)	c De Silva b Wijegunawardene	54
†Moin Khan	lbw b Wickremasinghe	3		not out	22
Waqar Younis	lbw b Wickremasinghe	6		not out	1
Salim Jaffer	not out	8			
Aqib Javed	c sub‡ b Wijegunawardene	10			
Extras	(LB8, W1, NB26)	35		(B2, LB3, NB7)	12
Total		**221**		(7 wickets)	**188**

PAKISTAN	O	M	R	W	O	M	R	W	FALL OF WICKETS				
										SL	P	SL	P
Wasim	22	8	62	2	18	2	71	3	*Wkt*	*1st*	*1st*	*2nd*	*2nd*
Salim Jaffer	17	4	36	3	(3) 8	2	19	0	1st	81	102	28	31
Waqar	21	1	87	4	(2) 17	3	65	5	2nd	89	110	43	52
Aqib	12.1	3	46	0	8	4	7	2	3rd	130	141	67	60
									4th	130	146	72	60
SRI LANKA									5th	150	162	105	149
Ratnayake	13	2	40	0	9.3	0	43	1	6th	179	186	136	156
Wijegunawardene	31.2	13	47	3	(3) 17.2	2	51	4	7th	185	196	146	179
Wickremasinghe	32	9	73	5	(2) 26	6	53	1	8th	193	197	160	–
Anurasiri	10	2	28	0	(5) 6	1	18	0	9th	205	205	165	–
Gurusinha	15	9	19	2	(4) 12	5	18	1	10th	240	221	165	–
Ranatunga	3	2	2	0									
Hathurusinghe	2	0	4	0									

Umpires: Khalid Aziz (3) and Shakoor Rana (16).   Referee: D.B.Carr (*England*) (3).   ‡ (M.S.Atapattu)

Close: 1st day – SL(1) 205-9 (Jayasuriya 50, Wickremasinghe 0); 2nd – P(1) 117-2 (Zahid 6, Miandad 0); 3rd – SL (2) 68-3 (De Silva 18, Wijegunawardene 1); 4th – P(2) 95-4 (Zahid 55, Wasim 19).

NEW ZEALAND v ENGLAND 1991-92 (1st Test)

At Lancaster Park, Christchurch, on 18, 19, 20, 21, 22 January.
Toss: New Zealand.   Result: ENGLAND won by an innings and 4 runs.
Debuts: New Zealand – B.R.Hartland; England – D.A.Reeve.

England, capitalising on the record Test total at Christchurch, gained their first victory in New Zealand since 1977-78 and, having beaten West Indies and Sri Lanka in the final Tests of 1991, became the first country to win successive matches against three different opponents. With his side 4 runs in arrears and just three more overs possible, Crowe gambled on lofting a match-saving boundary but miscued a skier to extra-cover. Stewart (357 minutes, 265 balls, 17 fours) scored his second hundred in successive Tests. In his 93rd Test innings, Crowe became the second New Zealander after Wright to score 4,000 runs. Patel (189 minutes, 134 balls) and Cairns added 117 in a record New Zealand seventh-wicket partnership for this series. Wright (400 minutes, 323 balls), marooned on 99 for 16 balls, became the third player to be out twice for that score in Tests. His dismissal triggered a collapse in which seven wickets fell for 53 runs in 25.4 overs. Tufnell took five or more wickets for the fourth time in seven Tests, his analysis being a record for this series in New Zealand. For the first time at this level, four batsmen were dismissed in the nineties. Reeve was the first Test cricketer to have been born in Hong Kong.

ENGLAND

*G.A.Gooch	c Smith b Morrison	2
A.J.Stewart	c Crowe b Morrison	148
G.A.Hick	lbw b Cairns	35
R.A.Smith	c Greatbatch b Pringle	96
A.J.Lamb	b Patel	93
†R.C.Russell	run out	36
D.A.Reeve	c Jones b Pringle	59
C.C.Lewis	b Pringle	70
D.R.Pringle	c Greatbatch b Patel	10
P.A.J.DeFreitas	not out	7
P.C.R.Tufnell	did not bat	
Extras	(B5, LB10, W1, NB8)	24
Total	(9 wickets declared)	**580**

NEW ZEALAND

B.R.Hartland	c Smith b Tufnell	22		c Smith b Tufnell	45
J.G.Wright	c Lamb b Tufnell	28		st Russell b Tufnell	99
A.H.Jones	lbw b Lewis	16	(4)	c Russell b Pringle	39
M.J.Greatbatch	c Stewart b Tufnell	11	(6)	c Smith b Tufnell	0
S.A.Thomson	b Tufnell	5	(7)	lbw b Tufnell	0
D.N.Patel	run out	99	(8)	c Pringle b Tufnell	6
*M.D.Crowe	c Stewart b Pringle	20	(5)	c Pringle b Tufnell	48
C.L.Cairns	c Hick b Reeve	61	(9)	c Smith b Tufnell	0
†I.D.S.Smith	lbw b DeFreitas	20	(10)	c Russell b Lewis	1
D.K.Morrison	not out	8	(3)	c Russell b Lewis	0
C.Pringle	c Hick b DeFreitas	6		not out	5
Extras	(B1, LB7, NB8)	16		(B1, LB7, NB13)	21
Total		**312**			**264**

NEW ZEALAND	O	M	R	W	O	M	R	W		FALL OF WICKETS		
										E	NZ	NZ
Morrison	33	5	133	2					Wkt	1st	1st	2nd
Cairns	30	3	118	1					1st	6	51	81
Pringle	36	4	127	3					2nd	95	52	81
Thomson	15	3	47	0					3rd	274	73	182
Patel	46	5	132	2					4th	310	87	211
Jones	3	0	8	0					5th	390	91	222
ENGLAND									6th	466	139	222
DeFreitas	32.4	16	54	2	23	6	54	0	7th	544	256	236
Lewis	30	9	69	1	(5) 22	3	66	2	8th	571	279	241
Pringle	15	2	54	1	(2) 21	5	64	1	9th	580	306	250
Tufnell	39	10	100	4	(3) 46.1	25	47	7	10th	–	312	264
Hick	3	0	11	0	(4) 14	8	11	0				
Reeve	8	4	16	1	2	0	8	0				
Smith					4	2	6	0				

Umpires: B.L.Aldridge (11) and R.S.Dunne (6). Referee: P.J.P.Burge (*Australia*) (1).

Close: 1st day – E(1) 310-4 (Lamb 17, Russell 0); 2nd – NZ(1) 3-0 (Hartland 0, Wright 2); 3rd – NZ(1) 169-6 (Patel 55, Cairns 3); 4th – NZ(2) 81-1 (Wright 28, Morrison 0).

NEW ZEALAND v ENGLAND 1991-92 (2nd Test)

At Eden Park, Auckland, on 30, 31 January, 1, 2, 3 February.
Toss: New Zealand.   Result: ENGLAND won by 168 runs.
Debuts: New Zealand – M.L.Su'a.

At 11.06 on the fifth morning, England won their first series in New Zealand since 1974-75 and the first by any visiting team there since Pakistan's success in 1978-79. Not since 1979 had England won four Tests in succession. Torrential overnight rain delayed the start until 2.15pm. Gooch (294 minutes, 220 balls, two sixes and 15 fours; his 16th hundred) played an exceptional innings on a pitch assisting seam movement. Lamb's 60 included 46 in boundaries, his fifty coming from 33 balls. In the first innings, Wright (5) retired at 13 and resumed at 91.

ENGLAND

*G.A.Gooch	c Parore b Morrison	4	run out		114
A.J.Stewart	c Parore b Cairns	4	c Parore b Su'a		8
G.A.Hick	lbw b Cairns	30	lbw b Su'a		4
R.A.Smith	c Parore b Cairns	0	b Morrison		35
A.J.Lamb	b Su'a	13	c Watson b Patel		60
D.A.Reeve	c Parore b Watson	22	lbw b Watson		25
C.C.Lewis	c Cairns b Watson	33	run out		23
†R.C.Russell	c Parore b Cairns	33	c Hartland b Cairns		24
D.R.Pringle	lbw b Cairns	41	lbw b Cairns		2
P.A.J.DeFreitas	c Crowe b Cairns	1	c Wright b Morrison		0
P.C.R.Tufnell	not out	6	not out		0
Extras	(LB11, NB5)	16	(B8, LB16, NB2)		26
Total		**203**			**321**

NEW ZEALAND

B.R.Hartland	lbw b Lewis	0	c Russell b DeFreitas		0
J.G.Wright	b Pringle	15	lbw b Lewis		0
A.H.Jones	c Smith b DeFreitas	14	lbw b DeFreitas		5
*M.D.Crowe	c Hick b Lewis	45	c Lamb b DeFreitas		56
K.R.Rutherford	c Russell b DeFreitas	26	c Stewart b Pringle		32
D.N.Patel	lbw b Lewis	24	c and b Tufnell		17
C.L.Cairns	c Hick b Tufnell	1	c Russell b Tufnell		24
†A.C.Parore	lbw b Pringle	0	lbw b Lewis		15
M.L.Su'a	not out	0	lbw b DeFreitas		36
D.K.Morrison	lbw b Lewis	0	run out		12
W.Watson	b Lewis	2	not out		5
Extras	(NB15)	15	(LB1, NB11)		12
Total		**142**			**214**

NEW ZEALAND	O	M	R	W	O	M	R	W		FALL OF WICKETS			
										E	NZ	E	NZ
Morrison	17	2	55	1	21.4	6	66	2	Wkt	1st	1st	2nd	2nd
Cairns	21	4	52	6	19	6	86	2	1st	9	2	29	0
Watson	24	13	41	2	26	10	59	1	2nd	9	35	33	0
Su'a	21	8	44	1	10	3	43	2	3rd	9	91	93	7
Patel					22	7	43	1	4th	34	102	182	77
									5th	72	123	263	109
ENGLAND									6th	91	124	269	118
DeFreitas	16	2	53	2	27	11	62	4	7th	128	139	319	153
Lewis	21	7	31	5	27	4	83	2	8th	165	139	321	173
Pringle	15	7	21	2	7	2	23	1	9th	171	139	321	203
Reeve	7	1	21	0					10th	203	142	321	214
Tufnell	4	2	16	1	(4) 17	5	45	2					
Hick					(5) 1	1	0	0					

Umpires: B.L.Aldridge (12) and R.S.Dunne (7). Referee: P.J.P.Burge (*Australia*) (2).

Close: 1st day – E(1) 146-7 (Russell 23, Pringle 8); 2nd – NZ(1) 141-9 (Su'a 0, Watson 1); 3rd – E(2) 272-6 (Lewis 3, Russell 0); 4th – NZ(2) 203-8 (Su'a 36, Morrison 6).

NEW ZEALAND v ENGLAND 1991-92 (3rd Test)

At Basin Reserve, Wellington, on 6, 7, 8, 9, 10 February.
Toss: England.   Result: MATCH DRAWN.
Debuts: New Zealand – R.T.Latham.

The most evenly contested match of an entertaining series will inevitably be remembered for the tragic injury which ended 'Syd' Lawrence's first-class career. At 3.40 on the final afternoon, his left kneecap fractured horizontally as he delivered the first ball of his third over. Unlike the previous two pitches, Basin Reserve's favoured batsmen and spin bowlers. After Stewart (321 minutes, 241 balls) had recorded his third hundred in four Tests and completed 1,000 runs in 31 innings, New Zealand gained a lead of 127 largely through a national record second-wicket partnership of 241 in 380 minutes between Wright (404 minutes, 334 balls) and Jones (460 minutes, 398 balls), each hitting 15 fours. Lamb (305 minutes, 231 balls, two sixes and 19 fours) scored the highest and last of his 14 Test hundreds before being caught off a reverse sweep. Botham became the fourth England player to appear in 100 Tests, Russell scored his 1,000th run in his 45th innings, and Tufnell's 71-over marathon in the first innings set a record for all first-class cricket in New Zealand.

ENGLAND

*G.A.Gooch	b Patel	30	c Rutherford b Cairns		11
A.J.Stewart	b Morrison	107	c Smith b Patel		63
G.A.Hick	b Patel	43	c Smith b Su'a		22
R.A.Smith	c Rutherford b Patel	6	c and b Su'a		76
A.J.Lamb	c Smith b Patel	30	c Latham b Patel		142
D.A.Reeve	c Latham b Su'a	18	b Su'a		0
D.V.Lawrence	c Rutherford b Cairns	6			
I.T.Botham	c Cairns b Su'a	15	(7) lbw b Patel		1
†R.C.Russell	lbw b Morrison	18	(8) not out		24
P.A.J.DeFreitas	lbw b Morrison	3			
P.C.R.Tufnell	not out	2			
Extras	(B4, LB12, NB11)	27	(LB13, NB7)		20
Total		305	(7 wickets declared)		359

NEW ZEALAND

B.R.Hartland	c Botham b Lawrence	2	lbw b Botham	19
J.G.Wright	c Reeve b Tufnell	116	c Russell b Botham	0
A.H.Jones	b Hick	143	(4) lbw b Reeve	9
*M.D.Crowe	b Tufnell	30	(3) not out	13
K.R.Rutherford	run out	8	not out	2
R.T.Latham	b Hick	25		
D.N.Patel	lbw b Hick	9		
C.L.Cairns	c Russell b Botham	33		
†I.D.S.Smith	b Hick	21		
M.L.Su'a	not out	20		
D.K.Morrison	not out	0		
Extras	(B1, LB15, W1, NB8)	25		
Total	(9 wickets declared)	432	(3 wickets)	43

NEW ZEALAND	O	M	R	W	O	M	R	W	FALL OF WICKETS			
Morrison	22.1	6	44	3	23	5	63	0		E	NZ	E	NZ
Cairns	25	3	89	1	22	4	84	1	Wkt	1st	1st	2nd	2nd
Su'a	36	10	62	2	33	10	87	3	1st	83	3	17	4
Patel	34	10	87	4	41.3	12	112	3	2nd	159	244	52	24
Jones	1	0	7	0					3rd	169	308	127	41
									4th	215	312	249	–
									5th	235	327	249	–
ENGLAND									6th	248	340	254	–
DeFreitas	8	4	12	0					7th	277	369	359	–
Lawrence	27	7	67	1	(1) 2.1	1	4	0	8th	286	404	–	–
Tufnell	71	22	147	2	(4) 9	5	12	0	9th	298	430	–	–
Hick	69	27	126	4					10th	305	–	–	–
Botham	14	4	53	1	(2) 8	1	23	2					
Reeve	3	1	11	0	(3) 4.5	2	4	1					

Umpires: B.L.Aldridge (13) and R.S.Dunne (8). Referee: P.J.P.Burge (*Australia*) (3).

Close: 1st day – E(1) 239-5 (Reeve 9, Lawrence 0); 2nd – NZ(1) 104-1 (Wright 44, Jones 51); 3rd – NZ(1) 340-6 (Latham 12, Cairns 0); 4th – E(2) 171-3 (Smith 41, Lamb 24).

WEST INDIES v SOUTH AFRICA 1991-92 (Only Test)

At Kensington Oval, Bridgetown, Barbados, on 18, 19, 20, 22, 23 April.
Toss: South Africa.   Result: WEST INDIES won by 52 runs.
Debuts: West Indies – J.C.Adams, K.C.G.Benjamin, D.Williams; South Africa – all except K.C.Wessels who had previously appeared for Australia.

Returning to the Test arena after being ostracised since March 1970, South Africa came close to ending their hosts' 57-year-old unbeaten sequence at Bridgetown. Having dominated the previous days, they began the fifth with eight wickets in hand and just 79 runs required for victory. On that dramatic morning their lack of experience of the five-day game was brutally exploited by outstanding fast bowling on a worn pitch providing minimal bounce. Ambrose (4 for 16 in 10.4 overs) and Walsh (4 for 8 in 11) bowled unchanged to produce one of Test cricket's most dramatic collapses. This historic inaugural Test match encounter between South Africa and a non-white team was marred by a local boycott which restricted the match attendance to 6,500, a mere 300 witnessing the epic finale. Wessels was the 13th player to play Test cricket for two countries, having appeared in 24 matches for Australia. Hudson (520 minutes, 384 balls, 20 fours) became the first to score a hundred on debut for South Africa. Adams dismissed Cronje with his fourth ball in Tests.

WEST INDIES

D.L.Haynes	c Wessels b Snell	58	c Richardson b Snell		23
P.V.Simmons	c Kirsten b Snell	35	c Kirsten b Bosch		3
B.C.Lara	c Richardson b Bosch	17	c Richardson b Donald		64
*R.B.Richardson	c Richardson b Snell	44	lbw b Snell		2
K.L.T.Arthurton	c Kuiper b Pringle	59	b Donald		22
J.C.Adams	b Donald	11	not out		79
†D.Williams	c Hudson b Donald	1	lbw b Snell		5
C.E.L.Ambrose	not out	6	c Richardson b Donald		6
K.C.G.Benjamin	b Snell	1	lbw b Donald		7
C.A.Walsh	b Pringle	6	c Richardson b Snell		13
B.P.Patterson	run out	0	b Bosch		11
Extras	(LB7, NB17)	24	(B17, LB11, NB20)		48
Total		**262**			**283**

SOUTH AFRICA

M.W.Rushmere	c Lara b Ambrose	3	(2) b Ambrose		3
A.C.Hudson	b Benjamin	163	(1) c Lara b Ambrose		0
*K.C.Wessels	c Adams b Ambrose	59	c Lara b Walsh		74
P.N.Kirsten	c Lara b Benjamin	11	b Walsh		52
W.J.Cronje	c Lara b Adams	5	c Williams b Ambrose		2
A.P.Kuiper	c Williams b Patterson	34	c Williams b Walsh		0
†D.J.Richardson	c Ambrose b Adams	8	c Williams b Ambrose		2
R.P.Snell	run out	6	c Adams b Walsh		0
M.W.Pringle	c Walsh b Adams	15	b Ambrose		4
A.A.Donald	st Williams b Adams	0	(11) b Ambrose		0
T.Bosch	not out	5	(10) not out		0
Extras	(B4, LB6, W1, NB25)	36	(B4, LB3, NB4)		11
Total		**345**			**148**

SOUTH AFRICA	O	M	R	W	O	M	R	W	FALL OF WICKETS			
										WI	SA	WI	SA
Donald	20	1	67	2	25	3	77	4	*Wkt*	*1st*	*1st*	*2nd*	*2nd*
Bosch	15	2	43	1	24.3	7	61	2	1st	99	14	10	0
Pringle	18.4	2	62	2	(4) 16	0	43	0	2nd	106	139	66	27
Snell	18	3	83	4	(3) 16	1	74	4	3rd	137	168	68	123
									4th	219	187	120	130
WEST INDIES									5th	240	279	139	131
Ambrose	36	19	47	2	24.4	7	34	6	6th	241	293	164	142
Patterson	23	4	79	1	7	1	26	0	7th	250	312	174	142
Walsh	27	7	71	0	(4) 22	10	31	4	8th	255	316	196	147
Benjamin	25	3	87	2	(3) 9	2	21	0	9th	262	336	221	148
Arthurton	3	0	8	0					10th	262	345	283	148
Adams	21.5	5	43	4	(5) 5	0	16	0					
Simmons					(6) 5	1	13	0					

Umpires: D.M.Archer (28) and S.A.Bucknor (5). Referee: R.Subba Row (*England*) (1).

Close: 1st day – SA(1) 13-0 (Rushmere 2, Hudson 9); 2nd – SA(1) 254-4 (Hudson 135, Kuiper 19); 3rd – WI(2) 184-7 (Adams 23, Benjamin 6); 4th – SA(2) 122-2 (Wessels 74, Kirsten 36).

ENGLAND v PAKISTAN 1992 (1st Test)

At Edgbaston, Birmingham, on 4 (*no play*), 5, 6, 7, 8 June.
Toss: England.   Result: MATCH DRAWN.
Debuts: Pakistan – Aamir Sohail, Ata-ur-Rehman, Inzamam-ul-Haq.

The combination of a bland pitch and the loss of the first two days condemned this match to a certain draw. Not quite all of the second day was lost, the two balls being bowled at 2.45pm being sufficient to nullify the no-play refunded admission clause. Angry protests were eventually to persuade the TCCB to modify the regulations. Javed Miandad (416 minutes, 336 balls, 19 fours) scored the last of his 23 hundreds, became the fourth Pakistani to score 1,000 runs against England and, with Salim Malik (370 minutes, 297 balls, a six and 19 fours), added 322 in the highest partnership for any wicket by either side in this series. Stewart (351 minutes, 261 balls, 31 fours) scored his fourth hundred in five Tests and with Smith (323 minutes, 231 balls, 18 fours) shared a record third-wicket stand of 227 for this series.

PAKISTAN

Aamir Sohail	c Stewart b DeFreitas	18
Ramiz Raja	lbw b DeFreitas	47
Asif Mujtaba	c Russell b DeFreitas	29
*Javed Miandad	not out	153
Salim Malik	lbw b DeFreitas	165
Inzamam-ul-Haq	not out	8
†Moin Khan		
Mushtaq Ahmed		
Waqar Younis	did not bat	
Aqib Javed		
Ata-ur-Rehman		
Extras	(B2, LB5, NB19)	26
Total	(4 wickets declared)	**446**

ENGLAND

*G.A.Gooch	c Asif b Aqib	8
A.J.Stewart	c Salim b Rehman	190
G.A.Hick	c Miandad b Waqar	51
R.A.Smith	lbw b Mushtaq	127
M.R.Ramprakash	c Moin b Rehman	0
A.J.Lamb	c Miandad b Rehman	12
C.C.Lewis	b Mushtaq	24
†R.C.Russell	not out	29
D.R.Pringle	not out	0
I.T.Botham	did not bat	
P.A.J.DeFreitas		
Extras	(B5, LB5, W1, NB7)	18
Total	(7 wickets declared)	**459**

ENGLAND	O	M	R	W
DeFreitas	33	6	121	4
Lewis	33	3	116	0
Pringle	28	2	92	0
Botham	19	6	52	0
Hick	13	1	46	0
Gooch	10	5	9	0
Ramprakash	1	0	3	0

PAKISTAN	O	M	R	W
Waqar	24	2	96	1
Aqib	16	3	86	1
Mushtaq	50	8	156	2
Rehman	18	5	69	3
Asif	8	1	29	0
Aamir	2	0	8	0
Salim	1	0	5	0

FALL OF WICKETS

	P	E
Wkt	1st	1st
1st	33	28
2nd	96	121
3rd	110	348
4th	432	348
5th	–	378
6th	–	415
7th	–	446
8th	–	–
9th	–	–
10th	–	–

Umpires: M.J.Kitchen (4) and B.J.Meyer (24). Referee: R.M.Cowper (*Australia*) (1).

Close: 1st day – no play; 2nd – P(1) 3-0 (Aamir 3, Ramiz 0); 3rd – P(1) 290-3 (Miandad 99, Salim 80); 4th – E(1) 170-2 (Stewart 94, Smith 10).

ENGLAND v PAKISTAN 1992 (2nd Test)

At Lord's, London, on 18, 19, 20, 21 June.
Toss: England.   Result: PAKISTAN won by two wickets.
Debuts: England – I.D.K.Salisbury.

After four days of enthralling cricket played to capacity crowds, Pakistan gained the narrowest victory in any Lord's Test. Throughout this rubber, England's middle order frequently subsided against late swing, often achieved with a 'reverse' grip on an old ball. Waqar's eighth instance of five or more wickets in an innings, all within his last ten Tests, included a spell of 5 for 34 in 58 balls. Wasim ended the second innings with three wickets in four balls, Stewart becoming the sixth to carry his bat through an England innings but the first to do so at Lord's. Botham, playing in the last of his 102 matches, equalled M.C.Cowdrey's England record of 120 catches in the field. After 17 wickets had fallen on the fourth day, Wasim and Waqar took Pakistan to a breathtaking victory with the largest stand of the innings, 46 (unbroken) in 57 minutes.

ENGLAND

*G.A.Gooch	b Wasim	69		lbw b Aqib	13
A.J.Stewart	c Miandad b Asif	74		not out	69
G.A.Hick	c Miandad b Waqar	13	(4)	c Moin b Mushtaq	11
R.A.Smith	c sub (Rashid Latif) b Wasim	9	(5)	b Mushtaq	8
A.J.Lamb	b Waqar	30	(6)	lbw b Mushtaq	12
I.T.Botham	b Waqar	2	(7)	lbw b Waqar	6
C.C.Lewis	lbw b Waqar	2	(8)	b Waqar	15
†R.C.Russell	not out	22	(9)	b Wasim	1
P.A.J.DeFreitas	c Inzamam b Waqar	3	(10)	c Inzamam b Wasim	0
I.D.K.Salisbury	hit wkt b Mushtaq	4	(3)	lbw b Wasim	12
D.E.Malcolm	lbw b Mushtaq	0		b Wasim	0
Extras	(B6, LB12, NB9)	27		(B5, LB8, NB15)	28
Total		**255**			**175**

PAKISTAN

Aamir Sohail	c Russell b DeFreitas	73	b Salisbury	39
Ramiz Raja	b Lewis	24	c Hick b Lewis	0
Asif Mujtaba	c Smith b Malcolm	59	c Russell b Lewis	0
*Javed Miandad	c Botham b Salisbury	9	c Russell b Lewis	0
Salim Malik	c Smith b Malcolm	55	c Lewis b Salisbury	12
Inzamam-ul-Haq	c and b Malcolm	0	run out	8
Wasim Akram	b Salisbury	24	not out	45
†Moin Khan	c Botham b DeFreitas	12	c Smith b Salisbury	3
Mushtaq Ahmed	c Russell b DeFreitas	4	c Hick b Malcolm	5
Waqar Younis	b Malcolm	14	not out	20
Aqib Javed	not out	5		
Extras	(B4, LB3, NB7)	14	(B2, LB5, W1, NB1)	9
Total		**293**	**(8 wickets)**	**141**

PAKISTAN	O	M	R	W	O	M	R	W	FALL OF WICKETS			
									E	P	E	P
Wasim	19	5	49	2	17.4	2	66	4				
Aqib	14	3	40	0	12	3	23	1	*Wkt*	*1st*	*1st*	*2nd* *2nd*
Waqar	21	4	91	5	13	3	40	2	1st	123	43	40 6
Mushtaq	19.1	5	57	2	9	1	32	3	2nd	153	123	73 10
Asif	3	3	0	1	1	0	1	0	3rd	172	143	108 18
									4th	197	228	120 41
ENGLAND									5th	213	228	137 62
DeFreitas	26	8	58	3					6th	221	235	148 68
Malcolm	15.5	1	70	4	(1) 15	2	42	1	7th	232	263	174 81
Lewis	29	7	76	1	(2) 16	3	43	3	8th	242	271	175 95
Salisbury	23	3	73	2	(3) 14.1	0	49	3	9th	247	276	175 –
Botham	5	2	9	0					10th	255	293	175 –

Umpires: B.Dudleston (2) and J.H.Hampshire (10). Referee: R.M.Cowper (*Australia*) (2).

Close: 1st day – P(1) 31-0 (Aamir 10, Ramiz 20); 2nd – P(1) 123-1 (Aamir 73, Asif 22); 3rd – E(2) 52-1 (Stewart 21, Salisbury 1).

ENGLAND v PAKISTAN 1992 (3rd Test)

At Old Trafford, Manchester, on 2, 3 (*no play*), 4, 6, 7 July.
Toss: Pakistan.   Result: MATCH DRAWN.
Debuts: England – T.A.Munton.

Pakistan's 200th Test and the 50th in this series was marred by rain, which, by eliminating the second day, extended Manchester's world record of abandoned Test match days to 28, and by the churlish behaviour of Aqib and his captain on the third evening. Aamir Sohail (342 minutes, 284 balls, 32 fours) became the first left-hander to score a double hundred for Pakistan. He was chiefly responsible for a first day total of 388 for 3, the most conceded by England in a day's play since West Indies amassed 437 for 9 at Leeds in 1976. For the eighth time in Test cricket, the first three wickets each produced hundred partnerships. Recalled after an 11-match absence, Gower celebrated his record 115th appearance for England by exceeding G.Boycott's record England aggregate of 8,114 runs and becoming the third batsman after S.M.Gavaskar and A.R.Border to play 200 Test innings. Ramiz scored his 2,000th run in 67 innings. Wasim's tenth five-wicket analysis was his first against England.

PAKISTAN

Aamir Sohail	b Lewis	205	c Smith b Lewis		1
Ramiz Raja	c Russell b Malcolm	54	c Hick b Lewis		88
Asif Mujtaba	c Atherton b Lewis	57	c Atherton b Lewis		40
*Javed Miandad	c Hick b Munton	88	not out		45
†Moin Khan	c Gower b Malcolm	15	(7) not out		11
Salim Malik	b Gooch	34	(5) b Gooch		16
Inzamam-ul-Haq	c Gooch b Malcolm	26			
Wasim Akram	st Russell b Gooch	0	(6) c Atherton b Gooch		13
Waqar Younis	not out	2			
Mushtaq Ahmed	c Lewis b Gooch	6			
Aqib Javed	did not bat				
Extras	(B9, LB4, W2, NB3)	18	(B8, LB5, W5, NB7)		25
Total	**(9 wickets declared)**	**505**	**(5 wickets declared)**		**239**

ENGLAND

*G.A.Gooch	c Moin b Waqar	78
A.J.Stewart	c Inzamam b Wasim	15
M.A.Atherton	c Moin b Wasim	0
R.A.Smith	lbw b Aqib	11
D.I.Gower	c Moin b Wasim	73
G.A.Hick	b Aqib	22
C.C.Lewis	c Moin b Wasim	55
†R.C.Russell	c Aamir b Aqib	4
I.D.K.Salisbury	c Aamir b Wasim	50
T.A.Munton	not out	25
D.E.Malcolm	b Aqib	4
Extras	(B8, LB8, W2, NB35)	53
Total		**390**

ENGLAND	O	M	R	W	O	M	R	W	FALL OF WICKETS			
Malcolm	31	3	117	3	12	2	57	0		P	E	P
Lewis	24	5	90	2	17	5	46	3	*Wkt*	*1st*	*1st*	*2nd*
Munton	30	6	112	1	17	6	26	0	1st	115	41	1
Salisbury	20	0	117	0	(5) 13	0	67	0	2nd	241	42	143
Gooch	18	2	39	3	(4) 16	5	30	2	3rd	378	93	148
Hick	3	0	17	0	2	2	0	0	4th	428	186	195
									5th	432	200	217
PAKISTAN									6th	492	252	–
Wasim	36	4	128	5					7th	497	256	–
Waqar	32	6	96	1					8th	497	315	–
Aqib	21.4	1	100	4					9th	505	379	–
Asif	1	1	0	0					10th	–	390	–
Mushtaq	10	1	50	0								

Umpires: R.Palmer (1) and D.R.Shepherd (14). Referee: C.L.Walcott (*West Indies*) (1).

Close: 1st day – P(1) 388-3 (Miandad 59, Moin 7); 2nd – no play; 3rd – E(1) 72-2 (Gooch 39, Smith 5); 4th – E(1) 390 all out.

ENGLAND v PAKISTAN 1992 (4th Test)

At Headingley, Leeds, on 23, 24, 25, 26 July.
Toss: Pakistan.   Result: ENGLAND won by six wickets.
Debuts: England – N.A.Mallender.

At 5.46 on the fourth evening Headingley produced its eleventh successive result when England drew level in the rubber by completing their first win in this series since 1982. Gooch (414 minutes, 301 balls, a six and 19 fours) scored his 17th hundred and his first in 13 innings against Pakistan. His partnership of 168 with Atherton was England's first for the first wicket in a home match of this series. Waqar's ninth five-wicket haul, all in his last dozen Tests, contributed to nine wickets falling for 50 runs. Salim became the fifth Pakistani to score 1,000 runs against England. Hick equalled the England fielding records for most catches in an innings (4) and in a match (6). Mallender was the first England bowler to achieve a five-wicket analysis on debut since N.G.B.Cook in 1983 (*Test No. 959*).

PAKISTAN

Aamir Sohail	c Atherton b Mallender	23		c Stewart b Mallender	1
Ramiz Raja	b Pringle	17		c Atherton b Munton	63
Asif Mujtaba	b Mallender	7		c Hick b Mallender	11
*Javed Miandad	c Smith b Pringle	6		c Stewart b Mallender	4
Salim Malik	not out	82		not out	84
Inzamam-ul-Haq	c Hick b Munton	5		c Smith b Pringle	19
Wasim Akram	run out	12		c Ramprakash b Pringle	17
†Moin Khan	c Hick b Lewis	2		c Hick b Mallender	3
Waqar Younis	c Hick b Mallender	6	(10)	b Mallender	3
Mushtaq Ahmed	b Lewis	11	(9)	lbw b Pringle	0
Aqib Javed	c Hick b Munton	0		run out	0
Extras	(B1, LB2, W7, NB16)	26		(B4, LB1, W2, NB9)	16
Total		**197**			**221**

ENGLAND

*G.A.Gooch	b Mushtaq	135		c Asif b Mushtaq	37
M.A.Atherton	b Wasim	76		lbw b Waqar	5
R.A.Smith	c Miandad b Aqib	42		c sub (Zahid Fazal) b Waqar	0
†A.J.Stewart	lbw b Waqar	8	(5)	c Moin b Mushtaq	2
D.I.Gower	not out	18	(4)	not out	31
M.R.Ramprakash	lbw b Mushtaq	0		not out	12
G.A.Hick	b Waqar	1			
C.C.Lewis	lbw b Waqar	0			
D.R.Pringle	b Waqar	0			
N.A.Mallender	b Waqar	1			
T.A.Munton	c Inzamam b Mushtaq	0			
Extras	(B1, LB14, W1, NB23)	39		(B5, LB3, NB4)	12
Total		**320**		(4 wickets)	**99**

ENGLAND	O	M	R	W	O	M	R	W		FALL OF WICKETS			
										P	E	P	E
Lewis	23	6	48	2	16	3	55	0	Wkt	*1st*	*1st*	*2nd*	*2nd*
Mallender	23	7	72	3	23	7	50	5	1st	34	168	11	27
Pringle	17	6	41	2	(4) 19	2	66	3	2nd	54	270	53	27
Munton	10.3	3	22	2	(3) 10	0	40	1	3rd	60	292	64	61
Gooch	6	3	11	0	1	0	5	0	4th	68	298	96	65
									5th	80	298	147	–
PAKISTAN									6th	111	303	177	–
Wasim	36	12	80	1	17	4	36	0	7th	117	305	205	–
Aqib	16	3	48	1					8th	128	305	206	–
Waqar	30	3	117	5	(2) 12	2	28	2	9th	192	313	213	–
Mushtaq	29.5	6	60	3	(3) 13.4	3	27	2	10th	197	320	221	–
Aamir	2	2	0	0									

Umpires: M.J.Kitchen (5) and K.E.Palmer (20). Referee: C.L.Walcott (*West Indies*) (2).

Close: 1st day – P(1) 165-8 (Salim 57, Mushtaq 6); 2nd – E(1) 216-1 (Gooch 93, Smith 22); 3rd – P(2) 98-4 (Salim 13, Inzamam 2).

ENGLAND v PAKISTAN 1992 (5th Test)

At Kennington Oval, London, on 6, 7, 8, 9 August.
Toss: England.   Result: PAKISTAN won by ten wickets.
Debuts: Pakistan – Rashid Latif.

At 12.45pm on the fourth day, Pakistan won their fourth rubber against England. For the first time since 1955, the final Test of a five-match home series began with the teams level. Fast bowlers dominated the match on a pitch with pace and even bounce. Although six batsmen scored fifties, only Smith progressed beyond 60. Wasim's spell of 5 for 8 in 22 balls precipitated another spectacular collapse in which seven wickets fell for 25 runs. Salim Malik's aggregate of 488 in the rubber was a record for either side in this series, while Waqar's tally of 22 wickets equalled the record set by F.S.Trueman in 1962.

ENGLAND

*G.A.Gooch	c Asif b Aqib	20	c Aamir b Waqar	24
†A.J.Stewart	c Ramiz b Wasim	31	lbw b Waqar	8
M.A.Atherton	c Rashid b Waqar	60	c Rashid b Waqar	4
R.A.Smith	b Mushtaq	33	not out	84
D.I.Gower	b Aqib	27	b Waqar	1
M.R.Ramprakash	lbw b Wasim	2	c Asif b Mushtaq	17
C.C.Lewis	lbw b Wasim	4	st Rashid b Mushtaq	14
D.R.Pringle	b Wasim	1	b Wasim	1
N.A.Mallender	b Wasim	4	c Mushtaq b Wasim	3
P.C.R.Tufnell	not out	0	b Wasim	0
D.E.Malcolm	b Wasim	2	b Waqar	0
Extras	(B4, LB8, W1, NB10)	23	(B1, LB8, NB9)	18
Total		207		174

PAKISTAN

Aamir Sohail	c Stewart b Malcolm	49	not out	4
Ramiz Raja	b Malcolm	19	not out	0
Shoaib Mohammad	c and b Tufnell	55		
*Javed Miandad	c and b Lewis	59		
Salim Malik	b Malcolm	40		
Asif Mujtaba	run out	50		
Wasim Akram	c Stewart b Malcolm	7		
†Rashid Latif	c Smith b Mallender	50		
Waqar Younis	c Gooch b Malcolm	6		
Mushtaq Ahmed	c Lewis b Mallender	9		
Aqib Javed	not out	0		
Extras	(B2, LB6, W4, NB24)	36	(W1)	1
Total		380	(0 wickets)	5

PAKISTAN	O	M	R	W	O	M	R	W	FALL OF WICKETS			
Wasim	22.1	3	67	6	21	6	36	3				
Waqar	16	4	37	1	(3) 18	5	52	5	Wkt	1st	1st	2nd 2nd
Aqib	16	6	44	2	(2) 9	2	25	0		E	P	E P
Mushtaq	24	7	47	1	23	6	46	2	1st	39	64	29 –
Aamir					1	0	6	0	2nd	57	86	47 –
									3rd	138	197	55 –
ENGLAND									4th	182	214	59 –
Mallender	28.5	6	93	2					5th	190	278	92 –
Malcolm	29	6	94	5					6th	196	292	153 –
Lewis	30	8	70	1					7th	199	332	159 –
Tufnell	34	9	87	1					8th	203	342	173 –
Pringle	6	0	28	0					9th	205	359	173 –
Ramprakash					(1) 0.1	0	5	0	10th	207	380	174 –

Umpires: H.D.Bird (47) and D.R.Shepherd (15). Referee: C.L.Walcott (*West Indies*) (3).

Close: 1st day – P(1) 16-0 (Aamir 9, Ramiz 7); 2nd – P(1) 275-4 (Salim 38, Asif 31); 3rd – E(2) 137-5 (Smith 59, Lewis 8).

SRI LANKA v AUSTRALIA 1992-93 (1st Test)

At Sinhalese Sports Club, Colombo, on 17, 18, 19, 21, 22 August.
Toss: Sri Lanka.   Result: AUSTRALIA won by 16 runs.
Debuts: Sri Lanka – R.S.Kaluwitharana.

Australia's recovery, from a first innings deficit of 291 runs, to achieve a sensational victory represents the greatest revival in Test cricket, surpassing England's victory against Australia in 1894-95 (*Test No. 42*) after following on 261 runs behind. Gurusinha (525 minutes, 399 balls) and Ranatunga (266 minutes, 192 balls) added 230 in Sri Lanka's second highest partnership to date. Kaluwitharana (203 minutes, 158 balls, 26 fours) became the second Sri Lankan wicket-keeper after D.S.B.P.Kuruppu to score a hundred on debut and enabled Sri Lanka to declare at their highest total so far. Australia achieved the ninth instance of all eleven reaching double figures. With Sri Lanka 54 short of victory with eight wickets in hand, Border courageously gambled on the leg-spin of Warne (1 for 335 in 90 overs of Test cricket at that point) who responded with a spell of 3 for 0.

AUSTRALIA

M.A.Taylor	lbw b Wickremasinghe	42	(2)	c Gurusinha b Anurasiri	43
T.M.Moody	lbw b Ramanayake	1	(1)	b Ramanayake	13
D.C.Boon	c Ramanayake b Hathurusinghe	32		c Ranatunga b Anurasiri	68
D.M.Jones	lbw b Hathurusinghe	10		run out	57
M.E.Waugh	c Kaluwitharana b Hathurusinghe	5		c Kaluwitharana b Wickremasinghe	56
*A.R.Border	b Hathurusinghe	3		c Gurusinha b Anurasiri	15
G.R.J.Matthews	lbw b Ramanayake	6		c Kaluwitharana b Ramanayake	64
†I.A.Healy	not out	66		lbw b Hathurusinghe	12
C.J.McDermott	c Ranatunga b Ramanayake	22		lbw b Ramanayake	40
S.K.Warne	c and b Anurasiri	24		b Anurasiri	35
M.R.Whitney	c and b Wickremasinghe	13		not out	10
Extras	(LB10, W3, NB19)	32		(LB23, W1, NB34)	58
Total		**256**			**471**

SRI LANKA

R.S.Mahanama	c Healy b Waugh	78	c Boon b Matthews	39
U.C.Hathurusinghe	c Taylor b Waugh	18	run out	36
A.P.Gurusinha	c Jones b Whitney	137	not out	31
P.A.de Silva	lbw b Matthews	6	c Border b McDermott	37
*A.Ranatunga	c Warne b Matthews	127	c Border b McDermott	0
M.S.Atapattu	b Matthews	0	b Matthews	1
†R.S.Kaluwitharana	not out	132	b Matthews	4
C.P.H.Ramanayake	c Healy b McDermott	0	lbw b Matthews	6
G.P.Wickremasinghe	c Matthews b McDermott	21	c Waugh b Warne	2
A.W.R.Madurasinghe	not out	5	(11) c Matthews b Warne	0
S.D.Anurasiri	did not bat		(10) c Waugh b Warne	1
Extras	(B2, LB7, W1, NB13)	23	(B2, LB3, NB2)	7
Total	(8 wickets declared)	**547**		**164**

SRI LANKA	O	M	R	W		O	M	R	W		FALL OF WICKETS			
											A	SL	A	SL
Ramanayake	20	4	51	3		37	10	113	3	*Wkt*	*1st*	*1st*	*2nd*	*2nd*
Wickremasinghe	18	4	69	2		19	0	79	1	1st	8	36	41	76
Hathurusinghe	22	5	66	4		27	7	79	1	2nd	84	128	107	79
Madurasinghe	10	1	21	0	(5)	14	1	50	0	3rd	94	137	195	127
Gurusinha	2	0	17	0						4th	96	367	233	132
Anurasiri	12	2	22	1	(4)	35	3	127	4	5th	109	367	269	133
										6th	118	463	319	137
AUSTRALIA										7th	124	472	361	147
McDermott	40	9	125	2		14	4	43	2	8th	162	503	417	150
Whitney	32	10	84	1		5	2	13	0	9th	207	–	431	156
Moody	17	3	44	0		5	0	10	0	10th	256	–	471	164
Waugh	17	3	77	2	(5)	2	0	6	0					
Warne	22	2	107	0	(6)	5.1	3	11	3					
Matthews	38	11	93	3	(4)	20	2	76	4					
Border	4	1	8	0										

Umpires: K.T.Francis (5) and T.M.Samarasinghe (1). Referee: F.J.Cameron (*New Zealand*) (1).

Close: 1st day – SL(1) 9-0 (Mahanama 6, Hathurusinghe 3); 2nd – SL(1) 265-3 (Gurusinha 87, Ranatunga 69); 3rd – A(2) 26-0 (Moody 8, Taylor 9); 4th – A(2) 393-7 (Matthews 51, McDermott 28).

SRI LANKA v AUSTRALIA 1992-93 (2nd Test)

At Khettarama Stadium, Colombo, on 28, 29, 30 August, 1, 2 September.
Toss: Sri Lanka.   Result: MATCH DRAWN.
Debuts: Sri Lanka – D.K.Liyanage, M.Muralitharan.

Colombo created a unique Test record by providing a fourth ground to host Test cricket. This 66th venue was built on drained marshland and had its turf laid by female staff. Frequent showers and inadequate drainage led to the loss of almost a full day's play. Jones (281 minutes, 213 balls) scored the last of his 11 Test hundreds. Border's lunchtime declaration set Sri lanka 286 runs in a minimum of 62 overs.

AUSTRALIA

T.M.Moody	c Kaluwitharana b Liyanage	1	(2) b Muralitharan		54
M.A.Taylor	c Jayasuriya b Hathurusinghe	15	(1) lbw b Hathurusinghe		26
D.C.Boon	c Jayasuriya b Liyanage	28	c Mahanama b Anurasiri		15
D.M.Jones	lbw b Gurusinha	77	not out		100
M.E.Waugh	c Jayasuriya b Ramanayake	0	lbw b Muralitharan		0
*A.R.Border	b Liyanage	13	lbw b Anurasiri		28
G.R.J.Matthews	c Muralitharan b Ramanayake	55	c Mahanama b Anurasiri		51
†I.A.Healy	lbw b Gurusinha	0	not out		4
C.J.McDermott	lbw b Muralitharan	9			
A.I.C.Dodemaide	not out	16			
M.R.Whitney	lbw b Ramanayake	1			
Extras	(B10, LB14, W2, NB6)	32	(B4, LB9, NB5)		18
Total		247	(6 wickets declared)		296

SRI LANKA

R.S.Mahanama	c Moody b Dodemaide	14	lbw b McDermott		69
U.C.Hathurusinghe	b Moody	67	c Moody b McDermott		49
A.P.Gurusinha	c Healy b Whitney	29	not out		8
P.A.de Silva	c Healy b McDermott	85			
*A.Ranatunga	c sub (D.R.Martyn) b Dodemaide	18			
S.T.Jayasuriya	c Healy b McDermott	19	(4) not out		1
†R.S.Kaluwitharana	c sub (D.R.Martyn) b Border	1			
C.P.H.Ramanayake	b McDermott	8			
D.K.Liyanage	c Healy b McDermott	4			
S.D.Anurasiri	not out	2			
M.Muralitharan	not out	0			
Extras	(LB6, NB5)	11	(LB6, NB3)		9
Total	(9 wickets declared)	258	(2 wickets)		136

SRI LANKA	O	M	R	W	O	M	R	W	FALL OF WICKETS			
										A	SL	A	SL
Ramanayake	23.3	7	64	3	12	0	49	0	Wkt	1st	1st	2nd	2nd
Liyanage	30	10	66	3	13	1	47	0	1st	1	26	61	110
Hathurusinghe	9	1	26	1	12	4	12	1	2nd	34	67	102	129
Gurusinha	9	2	18	2					3rd	69	174	104	–
Anurasiri	8	0	17	0	(4) 44	11	66	3	4th	72	211	104	–
Muralitharan	17	2	32	1	(5) 34	7	109	2	5th	109	240	149	–
									6th	181	243	280	–
AUSTRALIA									7th	183	243	–	–
McDermott	20	4	53	4	19	7	32	2	8th	200	255	–	–
Whitney	16	1	49	1	5	2	13	0	9th	239	258	–	–
Dodemaide	25	4	74	2	(4) 5	2	11	0	10th	247	–	–	–
Matthews	10	2	20	0	(3) 21	5	59	0					
Waugh	4	0	11	0									
Moody	6	1	17	1									
Border	11	3	28	1	(5) 4	0	15	0					

Umpires: I.Anandappa (1) and W.A.U.Wickremasinghe (2). Referee: F.J.Cameron (*New Zealand*) (2).

Close: 1st day – A(1) 177-5 (Jones 77, Matthews 18); 2nd – SL(1) 0-0 (Mahanama 0, Hathurusinghe 0); 3rd – SL(1) 258-9 (Anurasiri 2, Muralitharan 0); 4th – A(2) 206-5 (Jones 48, Matthews 23).

SRI LANKA v AUSTRALIA 1992-93 (3rd Test)

At Tyronne Fernando Stadium, Moratuwa, on 8, 9, 10, 12, 13 September.
Toss: Australia.   Result: MATCH DRAWN.
Debuts: None.

Test cricket's 67th venue (Sri Lanka's sixth) provided Border (217 minutes, 169 balls, 16 fours) with his 24th hundred; it was his first for four years and 36 matches, during which period he had scored 21 fifties. Ranatunga became the first Sri Lankan to score 2,000 Test runs. Waugh was dismissed for a 'pair' for the second Test in succession, the sixth instance of this fate but the first by a specialist batsman. Rain caused the loss of more than nine hours of play. I.Anandappa deputised for umpire Francis (ill) for the middle session of the second day.

AUSTRALIA

T.M.Moody	b Ramanayake	0	(2)	c Tillekeratne b Ramanayake	2
M.A.Taylor	c Ranatunga b Anurasiri	19	(1)	c Mahanama b Liyanage	3
D.C.Boon	c De Silva b Ramanayake	18		lbw b Liyanage	0
D.M.Jones	lbw b Liyanage	11		b Anurasiri	21
M.E.Waugh	b Ramanayake	0		c Tillekeratne b Liyanage	0
*A.R.Border	b Ramanayake	106		lbw b Ramanayake	78
G.R.J.Matthews	run out	57		b Ramanayake	96
†I.A.Healy	c Jayasuriya b Muralitharan	71		c Jayasuriya b Liyanage	49
C.J.McDermott	c Tillekeratne b Hathurusinghe	10			
S.K.Warne	c Gurusinha b Ramanayake	7			
A.I.C.Dodemaide	not out	13	(9)	not out	2
Extras	(B3, LB9, W3, NB10)	25		(LB4, W1, NB15)	20
Total		**337**		**(8 wickets)**	**271**

SRI LANKA

R.S.Mahanama	lbw b Matthews	50
U.C.Hathurusinghe	c Boon b McDermott	2
A.P.Gurusinha	c Healy b McDermott	0
P.A.de Silva	b Dodemaide	58
†H.P.Tillekeratne	c Waugh b Dodemaide	82
*A.Ranatunga	c Jones b McDermott	48
S.T.Jayasuriya	c Boon b McDermott	2
C.P.H.Ramanayake	not out	15
D.K.Liyanage	c Moody b Dodemaide	1
S.D.Anurasiri	b Dodemaide	0
M.Muralitharan	did not bat	
Extras	(LB8, W3, NB5)	16
Total	**(9 wickets declared)**	**274**

SRI LANKA	O	M	R	W		O	M	R	W		FALL OF WICKETS			
Ramanayake	31	3	82	5		22.1	4	75	3			A	SL	A
Liyanage	17	0	54	1		16	3	56	4	Wkt	1st	1st	2nd
Hathurusinghe	21	8	50	1		4	2	3	0	1st	0	4	6
Anurasiri	22	2	57	1	(5)	29	5	49	1	2nd	42	4	6
Muralitharan	15.1	2	58	1	(6)	7	1	26	0	3rd	46	111	6
Jayasuriya	2	0	9	0	(8)	7	1	17	0	4th	57	116	9
Gurusinha	3	0	15	0	(4)	1	0	5	0	5th	58	232	60
Ranatunga					(7)	1	0	9	0	6th	185	234	132
Mahanama						5	0	27	0	7th	252	262	261
										8th	283	274	271
AUSTRALIA										9th	302	274	–
McDermott	31	6	89	4						10th	337	–	–
Dodemaide	23.5	9	65	4									
Moody	3	0	8	0									
Matthews	31	8	64	1									
Warne	11	3	40	0									

Umpires: B.C.Cooray (1) and K.T.Francis (6). Referee: F.J.Cameron (*New Zealand*) (3).

Close: 1st day – A(1) 287-8 (Healy 43, Warne 1); 2nd – SL(1) 143-4 (Tillekeratne 18, Ranatunga 9); 3rd – SL(1) 215-4 (Tillekeratne 52, Ranatunga 45); 4th – A(2) 147-6 (Matthews 20, Healy 8).

ZIMBABWE v INDIA 1992-93 (Only Test)

At Harare Sports Club on 18, 19, 20, 21, 22 October.
Toss: Zimbabwe.   Result: MATCH DRAWN.
Debuts: Zimbabwe – all except A.J.Traicos who had previously appeared for South Africa.

Zimbabwe, the ninth ICC full member, amassed the highest total and largest partnership by a debutant, and became the first to avoid defeat in its inaugural Test match since Australia in 1876-77. Their captain, Houghton (414 minutes, 322 balls, 15 fours), emulated C.Bannerman in that match by scoring a hundred and, at 35 years 118 days, was the oldest to achieve that feat on debut. High temperatures, a lifeless pitch at Test cricket's 68th venue and an ultra-defensive approach by the former Rhodesians, always favoured a draw and provided scant entertainment for a miniscule crowd. Traicos (45), the 14th player to represent two countries, set a new record for the longest interval between appearances, the last of his three Tests for South Africa having been 22 years 222 days earlier. More became the second Indian after S.M.H.Kirmani to make 100 Test dismissals. Bird, the first umpire to appear under National Grid's sponsorship, equalled F.Chester's record by officiating in his 48th Test, while the two local umpires stood on alternate days. Manjrekar's hundred (500 minutes, 397 balls) was the fourth slowest in Tests.

ZIMBABWE

K.J.Arnott	c Raman b Kumble	40		b Prabhakar	32
G.W.Flower	c More b Srinath	82		c More b Kapil Dev	6
A.D.R.Campbell	lbw b Kapil Dev	45		b Kapil Dev	0
A.J.Pycroft	c Azharuddin b Prabhakar	39		lbw b Shastri	46
M.G.Burmester	c Azharuddin b Prabhakar	7			
D.L.Houghton	c More b Srinath	121	(5)	not out	41
A.Flower	b Prabhakar	59	(6)	not out	1
G.J.Crocker	not out	23			
E.A.Brandes	lbw b Srinath	0			
A.J.Traicos	b Kumble	5			
M.P.Jarvis	c Raman b Kumble	0			
Extras	(B1, LB19, NB15)	35		(B13, LB2, NB5)	20
Total		**456**		**(4 wickets declared)**	**146**

INDIA

R.J.Shastri	c Pycroft b Burmester	11
W.V.Raman	b Crocker	43
S.V.Manjrekar	c sub (S.G.Davies) b Jarvis	104
S.R.Tendulkar	c and b Traicos	0
M.Azharuddin	c G.W.Flower b Traicos	9
S.L.V.Raju	c Arnott b Traicos	7
Kapil Dev	b Traicos	60
M.Prabhakar	c Arnott b Traicos	14
K.S.More	c Traicos b Burmester	41
A.Kumble	c A.Flower b Burmester	0
J.Srinath	not out	6
Extras	(B2, LB9, NB1)	12
Total		**307**

INDIA	O	M	R	W		O	M	R	W		FALL OF WICKETS		
											Z	I	Z
Kapil Dev	39	13	71	1	(2)	15	4	22	2	Wkt	1st	1st	2nd
Prabhakar	45	15	66	3	(1)	14	4	22	1	1st	100	29	16
Srinath	39	12	89	3	(4)	5	1	15	0	2nd	175	77	16
Raju	39	15	79	0	(6)	7	2	17	0	3rd	186	78	93
Kumble	35.2	11	79	3	(5)	9	1	15	0	4th	199	93	119
Shastri	17	3	52	0	(7)	12	4	32	1	5th	252	101	–
Tendulkar					(3)	4	3	8	0	6th	417	197	–
ZIMBABWE										7th	445	219	–
Brandes	2	0	3	0						8th	445	287	–
Burmester	39.4	18	78	3						9th	454	294	–
Jarvis	38	17	73	1						10th	456	307	–
Crocker	35	18	41	1									
Traicos	50	16	86	5									
G.W.Flower	5	0	15	0									

Umpires: H.D.Bird (*England*) (48), K.Kanjee (1) and I.D.Robinson (1). Referee: P.L.van der Merwe (*South Africa*) (1).

Close: 1st day – Z(1) 188-3 (Pycroft 6, Burmester 2); 2nd – Z(1) 406-5 (Houghton 110, A.Flower 55); 3rd – I(1) 93-4 (Manjrekar 27, Raju 0); 4th – I(1) 278-7 (Manjrekar 100, More 23).

ZIMBABWE v NEW ZEALAND 1992-93 (1st Test)

At Bulawayo Athletic Club on 1, 2, 3, 4, 5 November.
Toss: New Zealand.   Result: MATCH DRAWN.
Debuts: Zimbabwe – A.H.Omarshah (*known as A.H.Shah*); New Zealand – S.B.Doull, M.J.Haslam.

The arrival of Test cricket at its 69th venue, combined with rain-maker Bird's record 49th match, ended months of drought. The loss of ten hours to rain and the inadequate covering of another extremely slow pitch ensured that the hosts would become the first country to avoid defeat in its first two Test matches. Greatbatch who hit 50 off 39 balls in the first innings, and Latham, who celebrated his second Test with 119 (282 minutes, 214 balls, a six and 14 fours), were the first New Zealand openers to produce a hundred partnership in both innings. Crowe declared on the third day when Zimbabwe, already deprived of Traicos (strained back Houghton completed his 24th over), were reluctant to bowl on wet run-ups. Jones scored his 2,000th run in 4 innings before retiring with a thigh strain at 175. Set 329 in 75 overs, Zimbabwe made no attempt at the target Arnott (248 minutes, 200 balls, 12 fours) registering his country's second hundred.

NEW ZEALAND

M.J.Greatbatch	c Campbell b Shah	87	c Houghton b Jarvis	8?
R.T.Latham	run out	119	c Houghton b G.W.Flower	4?
A.H.Jones	not out	67	retired hurt	3?
*M.D.Crowe	c Jarvis b Traicos	42	(5) c A.Flower b Jarvis	?
K.R.Rutherford	not out	7	(7) not out	1
†A.C.Parore			(4) c Houghton b Jarvis	1?
S.B.Doull			(6) b Traicos	
D.N.Patel	did not bat		(8) not out	1
M.L.Su'a				
W.Watson				
M.J.Haslam				
Extras	(LB3)	3	(B1, LB3, NB1)	?
Total	(3 wickets declared)	**325**	(5 wickets declared)	**22?**

ZIMBABWE

K.J.Arnott	c Crowe b Patel	30	not out	10?
G.W.Flower	c Rutherford b Patel	29	c Latham b Patel	4?
M.G.Burmester	c Haslam b Patel	0		
A.D.R.Campbell	run out	0	(3) not out	4?
A.J.Pycroft	b Doull	2		
*D.L.Houghton	b Patel	36		
†A.Flower	c Haslam b Su'a	81		
A.H.Shah	c Parore b Su'a	28		
G.J.Crocker	b Patel	1		
A.J.Traicos	b Patel	4		
M.P.Jarvis	not out	2		
Extras	(LB4, NB2)	6	(LB2, W1)	?
Total		**219**	(1 wicket)	**19?**

ZIMBABWE	O	M	R	W	O	M	R	W
Jarvis	26.1	4	87	0	11	0	38	3
Burmester	14	1	71	0				
Shah	14	6	46	1	(2) 7	0	36	0
Traicos	23.1	4	56	1	17	1	82	1
Crocker	14	1	57	0	(3) 5	0	30	0
Houghton	0.5	0	0	0				
G.W.Flower	4	2	5	0	(5) 8	0	32	1
NEW ZEALAND								
Su'a	9	3	18	2	6.1	2	9	0
Patel	40.4	12	113	6	(3) 28	7	60	1
Doull	15	6	29	1	(2) 4	1	8	0
Watson	7	3	10	0	(6) 7	2	21	0
Haslam	21	8	44	0	(4) 19	4	76	0
Jones	1	0	1	0				
Latham					(5) 3	2	6	0
Crowe					(7) 4	0	15	0

FALL OF WICKETS

Wkt	NZ 1st	Z 1st	NZ 2nd	Z 2n?
1st	116	54	102	9?
2nd	243	56	181	
3rd	314	59	193	
4th	–	62	196	
5th	–	64	204	
6th	–	134	–	
7th	–	194	–	
8th	–	213	–	
9th	–	213	–	
10th	–	219	–	

Umpires: H.D.Bird (*England*) (49), K.Kanjee (2) and I.D.Robinson (2). Referee: D.J.McGlew (*South Africa*) (1?)

Close: 1st day – NZ(1) 205-1 (Latham 86, Jones 30); 2nd – NZ(1) 325-3 (Jones 67, Rutherford 7); 3rd – Z(1) 54-1 (Arnott 25, Burmester 0); 4th – NZ(2) 163-1 (Greatbatch 80, Jones 31).

ZIMBABWE v NEW ZEALAND 1992-93 (2nd Test)

At Harare Sports Club on 7, 9, 10, 11, 12 November.
Toss: New Zealand.   Result: NEW ZEALAND won by 177 runs.
Debuts: Zimbabwe – D.H.Brain; New Zealand – D.J.Nash.

New Zealand's victory ended a 13-match drought since March 1990 and was their first in ten Tests under Crowe's leadership. Set to score 315 from 71 overs, Zimbabwe were lured to their first defeat by off-spinner Patel, who claimed his second six-wicket analysis in successive Tests. Crowe (182 minutes, 163 balls, three sixes and 17 fours) scored his 14th hundred in 101 innings, 96 coming in a post-lunch session. Rutherford completed 1,000 runs in 53 innings. Robinson deputised for Bird (ill, but not as a result of celebrating his 50th Test) on the final afternoon. This was the first Test to be absurdly interrupted by a limited-overs international.

NEW ZEALAND

M.J.Greatbatch	c A.Flower b Brain	55	c Brandes b Brain		13
R.T.Latham	c A.Flower b Crocker	15	c Houghton b Brandes		10
A.H.Jones	c Pycroft b Brandes	8	st A.Flower b Traicos		28
*M.D.Crowe	c Burmester b Crocker	140	lbw b Traicos		61
K.R.Rutherford	c A.Flower b Traicos	74	c Arnott b Brandes		89
D.N.Patel	c Campbell b Traicos	6	not out		58
†A.C.Parore	run out	2			
D.J.Nash	not out	11			
M.L.Su'a	c Arnott b Brandes	1			
W.Watson	b Brain	3			
M.J.Haslam	c A.Flower b Brain	3			
Extras	(LB11, NB6)	17	(LB2, W1)		3
Total		**335**	(5 wickets declared)		**262**

ZIMBABWE

K.J.Arnott	b Watson	68	c Watson b Nash		10
G.W.Flower	lbw b Su'a	5	c Latham b Su'a		1
A.D.R.Campbell	c Su'a b Patel	52	c Greatbatch b Patel		35
A.J.Pycroft	b Su'a	60	c Latham b Watson		5
*D.L.Houghton	c Parore b Su'a	21	c Nash b Patel		2
†A.Flower	c Patel b Nash	14	c Parore b Patel		9
E.A.Brandes	c Parore b Su'a	0	c and b Patel		6
G.J.Crocker	b Su'a	12	c Greatbatch b Haslam		33
D.H.Brain	c Su'a b Patel	11	c Su'a b Patel		17
M.G.Burmester	not out	30	not out		17
A.J.Traicos	not out	1	lbw b Patel		0
Extras	(LB7, NB2)	9	(LB2)		2
Total	(9 wickets declared)	**283**			**137**

ZIMBABWE	O	M	R	W	O	M	R	W	FALL OF WICKETS			
									NZ	Z	NZ	Z
Brandes	22	4	49	2	19.4	3	59	2	*Wkt*	*1st*	*1st*	*2nd*	*2nd*
Brain	18	5	49	3	16	2	52	1	1st	44	7	21	3
Crocker	15	1	65	2	7	0	24	0	2nd	73	114	27	15
Burmester	10	2	34	0	(6) 9	1	44	0	3rd	131	136	77	28
Traicos	23	1	82	2	(4) 27	8	70	2	4th	299	210	132	34
G.W.Flower	6	0	45	0	(5) 4	0	11	0	5th	306	211	262	56
									6th	313	211	–	62
NEW ZEALAND									7th	321	239	–	71
Su'a	37	8	85	5	12	3	30	1	8th	327	239	–	91
Nash	28	10	59	1	8	3	19	1	9th	330	275	–	137
Watson	25	6	51	1	3	2	3	1	10th	335	–	–	137
Patel	33	7	81	2	17.3	5	50	6					
Haslam					10	2	33	1					

Umpires: H.D.Bird (*England*) (50), K.Kanjee (3) and I.D.Robinson (3). Referee: D.J.McGlew (*South Africa*) (2).

Close: 1st day – NZ(1) 314-6 (Rutherford 72, Nash 0); 2nd – Z(1) 173-3 (Pycroft 38, Houghton 7); 3rd – Z(1) 228-6 (A.Flower 8, Crocker 8); 4th – NZ(2) 187-4 (Rutherford 57, Patel 16).

SOUTH AFRICA v INDIA 1992-93 (1st Test)

At Kingsmead, Durban, on 13, 14, 15, 16 (*no play*), 17 November.
Toss: India.   Result: MATCH DRAWN.
Debuts: South Africa – S.J.Cook, O.Henry, B.M.McMillan, J.N.Rhodes, B.N.Schultz; India –
P.K.Amre, A.D.Jadeja.

South Africa's first home Test match for 22 years, condemned to a draw by the loss of a day and 80 minutes to rain and bad light, was launched dramatically by the very first ball of this inaugural match against India. Cook (39), having waited two decades for an official Test cap and uniquely having played in all 19 unofficial matches against rebel sides, edged a late outswinger to third slip to become the first debutant to be dismissed by the first ball of a match. Omar Henry became the first non-white cricketer to represent South Africa and, at 40 years 295 days, the oldest to do so. Wessels, who represented ten different first-class teams based in three countries, became the first to score hundreds for two of them; his fifth Test hundred came from 205 balls, in 260 minutes and included 17 fours. Amre (374 minutes, 298 balls, 10 fours) was the ninth to score a hundred in his first Test for India. This was the first Test in which television replays monitored by a third umpire off the field were called upon to adjudicate in line decisions, Tendulkar becoming the system's first victim. As in Zimbabwe's first three Tests, the overseas umpire (Bucknor) stood on all five days while the local officials alternated daily. Schultz (strained hamstring) was unable to complete his 15th over.

SOUTH AFRICA

S.J.Cook	c Tendulkar b Kapil Dev	0	c and b Kumble		43
A.C.Hudson	b Kapil Dev	14	c More b Srinath		55
*K.C.Wessels	c Azharuddin b Kumble	118	c More b Srinath		32
P.N.Kirsten	c More b Srinath	13	not out		11
J.N.Rhodes	c Azharuddin b Kumble	41	not out		26
B.M.McMillan	c Prabhakar b Shastri	3			
†D.J.Richardson	lbw b Prabhakar	15			
O.Henry	c Tendulkar b Shastri	3			
M.W.Pringle	lbw b Kapil Dev	33			
A.A.Donald	lbw b Prabhakar	1			
B.N.Schultz	not out	0			
Extras	(LB6, NB7)	13	(B1, LB2, NB6)		9
Total		**254**	(3 wickets)		**176**

INDIA

R.J.Shastri	lbw b Pringle	14
A.D.Jadeja	c McMillan b Schultz	3
S.V.Manjrekar	lbw b McMillan	0
S.R.Tendulkar	run out	11
*M.Azharuddin	run out	36
P.K.Amre	c Rhodes b McMillan	103
Kapil Dev	c Richardson b McMillan	2
M.Prabhakar	c McMillan b Donald	13
†K.S.More	lbw b Henry	55
A.Kumble	b Henry	8
J.Srinath	not out	1
Extras	(B1, LB7, W4, NB19)	31
Total		**277**

INDIA	O	M	R	W	O	M	R	W		FALL OF WICKETS		
Kapil Dev	22	6	43	3	19	11	19	0		SA	I	SA
Prabhakar	24.4	7	47	2	14	3	47	0	Wkt	1st	1st	2nd
Srinath	18	3	69	1	16	3	42	2	1st	0	18	68
Kumble	28	8	51	2	16	4	36	1	2nd	41	22	129
Shastri	11	1	38	2	14	2	22	0	3rd	101	38	138
Tendulkar					2	1	3	0	4th	183	38	–
Manjrekar					1	0	4	0	5th	194	125	–
SOUTH AFRICA									6th	206	127	–
Donald	29	6	69	1					7th	215	146	–
Schultz	14.5	7	25	1					8th	251	247	–
McMillan	37	18	52	3					9th	253	274	–
Pringle	34	10	67	1					10th	254	277	–
Henry	19.1	3	56	2								

Umpires: S.A.Bucknor (*West Indies*) (6), K.E.Liebenberg (1) and C.J.Mitchley (1). Referee: C.H.Lloyd (*West Indies*) (1).

Close: 1st day – SA(1) 215-7 (Richardson 11); 2nd – I(1) 128-6 (Amre 39, Prabhakar 0); 3rd – I(1) 277 all out; 4th – no play.

SOUTH AFRICA v INDIA 1992-93 (2nd Test)

At The Wanderers, Johannesburg, on 26, 27, 28, 29, 30 November.
Toss: South Africa.   Result: MATCH DRAWN.
Debuts: South Africa – C.R.Matthews.

Defensive tactics by both sides on the final day condemned this match to a draw. Prabhakar caused an early collapse with a spell of three wickets in six balls. Rhodes, when 28, was fortunate to escape being run out when Bucknor refused to call for the third umpire's verdict on a replay which showed him to be out by six inches. Pringle retired at 261 when a Srinath bouncer squeezed past his visor and fractured his left eye socket. At 19 years 217 days, Tendulkar (375 minutes, 270 balls, 19 fours), in the course of his fourth hundred in 28 Test innings, became the youngest to complete 1,000 runs (displacing Kapil Dev). Shastri took 89 minutes to advance his score from 9 on the last morning as India added just 41 runs before lunch.

SOUTH AFRICA

S.J.Cook	c More b Prabhakar	2	c More b Srinath		31
A.C.Hudson	c Azharuddin b Prabhakar	8	b Kumble		53
*K.C.Wessels	c Azharuddin b Srinath	5	(4) run out		11
P.N.Kirsten	lbw b Prabhakar	0	(5) b Kumble		26
J.N.Rhodes	lbw b Kumble	91	(6) b Kumble		13
W.J.Cronje	c and b Kapil Dev	8	(7) b Kumble		15
B.M.McMillan	c Manjrekar b Srinath	98	(8) c Prabhakar b Kumble		5
†D.J.Richardson	lbw b Kumble	9	(3) b Kumble		50
C.R.Matthews	b Prabhakar	31	c Tendulkar b Prabhakar		18
M.W.Pringle	retired hurt	3	absent hurt		–
A.A.Donald	not out	14	(10) not out		7
Extras	(LB10, W4, NB9)	23	(B1, LB14, W1, NB7)		23
Total		**292**			**252**

INDIA

R.J.Shastri	c Wessels b Matthews	7	b Matthews		23
A.D.Jadeja	lbw b McMillan	14	c Wessels b Donald		43
S.V.Manjrekar	b McMillan	7	(5) not out		32
S.R.Tendulkar	c Hudson b Cronje	111	lbw b Donald		1
*M.Azharuddin	c Wessels b Matthews	9	(3) c Richardson b Matthews		1
P.K.Amre	lbw b McMillan	7	not out		35
M.Prabhakar	c Richardson b Donald	2			
Kapil Dev	c McMillan b Donald	25			
†K.S.More	c Richardson b McMillan	10			
A.Kumble	not out	21			
J.Srinath	c Richardson b Donald	5			
Extras	(LB4, W4, NB1)	9	(B2, LB2, NB2)		6
Total		**227**	(4 wickets)		**141**

INDIA	O	M	R	W	O	M	R	W		FALL OF WICKETS			
										SA	I	SA	I
Kapil Dev	25	4	62	1	24	6	50	0	*Wkt*	*1st*	*1st*	*2nd*	*2nd*
Prabhakar	29	3	90	4	23.2	3	74	1	1st	10	27	73	68
Srinath	26.5	6	60	2	26	2	58	1	2nd	11	27	108	70
Kumble	26	8	60	2	44	22	53	6	3rd	11	44	138	71
Shastri	4	0	10	0					4th	26	77	170	73
Tendulkar					(5) 1	0	2	0	5th	73	124	194	–
									6th	158	127	199	–
SOUTH AFRICA									7th	186	155	209	–
Donald	31	9	78	3	20	6	43	2	8th	251	174	239	–
McMillan	29	11	74	4	21	6	34	0	9th	292	212	252	–
Matthews	29	13	41	2	20	10	23	2	10th	–	227	–	–
Cronje	17	10	22	1	18	7	32	0					
Kirsten	2	0	8	0	3	1	5	0					

Umpires: S.A.Bucknor (*West Indies*) (7), S.B.Lambson (1) and C.J.Mitchley (2). Referee: C.H.Lloyd (*West Indies*) (2).

Close: 1st day – SA(1) 226-7 (McMillan 69, Matthews 15); 2nd – I(1) 128-6 (Tendulkar 75, Kapil Dev 1); 3rd – SA(2) 75-1 (Hudson 35, Richardson 2); 4th – I(2) 15-0 (Shastri 7, Jadeja 8).

SOUTH AFRICA v INDIA 1992-93 (3rd Test)

At St George's Park, Port Elizabeth, on 26, 27, 28, 29 December.
Toss: South Africa.   Result: SOUTH AFRICA won by nine wickets.
Debuts: None.

Spearheaded by Donald's match analysis of 12 for 139, South Africa gained their first Test win since March 1970, on the same ground. Azharuddin scored his only fifty in nine first-class innings on the tour. Cronje (531 minutes, 411 balls, a six and 12 fours) took 419 minutes to complete South Africa's second slowest hundred. Beginning his innings when India were 27 for 5, Kapil Dev, batting with an injured right hand, scored the last of his eight Test hundreds: 129 out of 188 off 177 balls with a six and 14 fours. Richardson set a national record with nine catches in the match. Wessels, with an undefeated 95 off 167 balls, took his side to victory with a day and seven minutes to spare.

INDIA

Batsman	Dismissal 1	Score 1	Dismissal 2	Score 2
R.J.Shastri	c Henry b McMillan	10	c Richardson b McMillan	5
W.V.Raman	c Richardson b Donald	21	b Donald	0
S.V.Manjrekar	c Henry b McMillan	23	lbw b Donald	6
S.R.Tendulkar	c Richardson b Donald	6	c Richardson b Schultz	0
*M.Azharuddin	c Richardson b Donald	60	c Wessels b Donald	7
P.K.Amre	c McMillan b Donald	11	c Richardson b Schultz	7
Kapil Dev	c Kirsten b McMillan	12	c McMillan b Donald	129
M.Prabhakar	c McMillan b Matthews	11	c Richardson b Donald	17
†K.S.More	c Richardson b Donald	20	b Donald	17
A.Kumble	c McMillan b Schultz	14	c Richardson b Donald	17
S.L.V.Raju	not out	0	not out	2
Extras	(LB13, W4, NB7)	24	(LB4, W1, NB3)	8
Total		**212**		**215**

SOUTH AFRICA

Batsman	Dismissal 1	Score 1	Dismissal 2	Score 2
A.C.Hudson	b Raju	52	(2) c Azharuddin b Tendulkar	33
*K.C.Wessels	b Prabhakar	0	(1) not out	95
W.J.Cronje	b Kumble	135	not out	16
P.N.Kirsten	c More b Raju	0		
B.M.McMillan	lbw b Raju	25		
J.N.Rhodes	c Prabhakar b Kumble	2		
†D.J.Richardson	run out	1		
O.Henry	lbw b Kapil Dev	16		
C.R.Matthews	c Azharuddin b Kapil Dev	17		
A.A.Donald	b Kumble	6		
B.N.Schultz	not out	0		
Extras	(B2, LB13, NB6)	21	(B8, LB3)	11
Total		**275**	**(1 wicket)**	**155**

SOUTH AFRICA	O	M	R	W	O	M	R	W
Donald	27	11	55	5	28	4	84	7
Schultz	20.5	4	39	1	16	5	37	2
McMillan	20	9	41	3	12	2	30	1
Matthews	17	7	34	1	9	1	43	0
Henry	11	2	30	0	8	2	17	0

INDIA	O	M	R	W	O	M	R	W
Kapil Dev	24	6	45	2	5	1	9	0
Prabhakar	15	3	57	1	5	2	7	0
Kumble	50.3	16	81	3	(4) 20	5	65	0
Raju	46	15	73	3	(3) 18	5	50	0
Tendulkar	1	1	0	0	3	0	9	1
Shastri	2	1	4	0				
Azharuddin					(6) 0.1	0	4	0

FALL OF WICKETS

Wkt	I 1st	SA 1st	I 2nd	SA 2nd
1st	43	0	1	98
2nd	49	117	10	–
3rd	59	117	11	–
4th	98	171	20	–
5th	143	182	27	–
6th	152	185	31	–
7th	160	215	88	–
8th	185	259	120	–
9th	208	274	197	–
10th	212	275	215	–

Umpires: W.Diedricks (1), R.E.Koertzen (1) and D.R.Shepherd (*England*) (16). Referee: M.J.K.Smith (*England*) (3).

Close: 1st day – I(1) 197-8 (More 15, Kumble 5); 2nd – SA(1) 163-3 (Cronje 75, McMillan 19); 3rd – I(2) 71-6 (Kapil Dev 33, Prabhakar 10).

SOUTH AFRICA v INDIA 1992-93 (4th Test)

At Newlands, Cape Town, on 2, 3, 4, 5, 6 January.
Toss: South Africa.   Result: MATCH DRAWN.
Debuts: South Africa – D.J.Cullinan.

An abysmal scoring rate on a pitch devoid of pace and bounce did nothing to promote Test cricket to a new audience reared on the limited-overs game. Five days produced a miserly 795 runs at 1.83 per over. Hudson equalled the South African fielding record with four catches in an innings.

SOUTH AFRICA

A.C.Hudson	c and b Srinath	19	(2)	c More b Srinath	11
*K.C.Wessels	b Prabhakar	0	(1)	c and b Srinath	34
W.J.Cronje	c Manjrekar b Kumble	33		c More b Srinath	0
P.N.Kirsten	c More b Kapil Dev	13		c Manjrekar b Kapil Dev	13
D.J.Cullinan	c Prabhakar b Raju	46		c More b Srinath	28
J.N.Rhodes	c More b Srinath	86		c Srinath b Kumble	16
B.M.McMillan	c sub (V.Yadav) b Kumble	52		not out	11
†D.J.Richardson	c Tendulkar b Kumble	21		not out	10
O.Henry	run out	34			
C.R.Matthews	not out	28			
A.A.Donald	not out	1			
Extras	(B2, LB22, W2, NB1)	27		(LB4, NB3)	7
Total	(9 wickets declared)	360		(6 wickets declared)	130

INDIA

A.D.Jadeja	c Kirsten b McMillan	19		not out	20
M.Prabhakar	c Wessels b Henry	62		c Richardson b Matthews	7
S.V.Manjrekar	c Hudson b Donald	46		not out	2
P.K.Amre	c McMillan b Donald	6			
S.R.Tendulkar	c Hudson b Cronje	73			
*M.Azharuddin	c Richardson b McMillan	7			
S.L.V.Raju	c Cullinan b Matthews	18			
Kapil Dev	c Hudson b Cronje	34			
†K.S.More	lbw b Matthews	0			
A.Kumble	c Hudson b Matthews	0			
J.Srinath	not out	0			
Extras	(LB7, W3, NB1)	11			–
Total		276		(1 wicket)	29

INDIA	O	M	R	W	O	M	R	W		FALL OF WICKETS			
										SA	I	SA	I
Kapil Dev	29	8	42	1	17	4	29	1	Wkt	1st	1st	2nd	2nd
Prabhakar	23	6	48	1	10	4	19	0	1st	0	44	20	21
Raju	47	15	94	1	(5) 20	8	25	0	2nd	28	129	28	–
Srinath	25	6	51	2	(3) 27	10	33	4	3rd	57	138	61	–
Kumble	47	13	101	3	(4) 23	11	20	1	4th	78	144	61	–
									5th	177	153	95	–
SOUTH AFRICA									6th	245	200	107	–
Donald	36	13	58	2	4	0	7	0	7th	282	275	–	–
McMillan	36	9	76	2					8th	319	276	–	–
Matthews	28	12	32	3	(2) 6	1	17	1	9th	345	276	–	–
Cronje	18.4	8	17	2	(3) 3	3	0	0	10th	–	276	–	–
Henry	33	8	86	1									
Rhodes					(4) 1	0	5	0					

Umpires: S.B.Lambson (2), K.E.Liebenberg (2) and D.R.Shepherd (*England*) (17). Referee: M.J.K.Smith (*England*) (4).

Close: 1st day – SA(1) 189-5 (Rhodes 61, McMillan 4); 2nd – I(1) 13-0 (Jadeja 4, Prabhakar 7); 3rd – I(1) 161-5 (Tendulkar 9, Raju 2); 4th – SA(2) 48-2 (Wessels 29, Kirsten 7).

AUSTRALIA v WEST INDIES 1992-93 (1st Test)

At Woolloongabba, Brisbane, on 27, 28, 29, 30 November, 1 December.
Toss: Australia.   Result: MATCH DRAWN.
Debuts: Australia – D.R.Martyn.

This evenly contested overture heralded a notable series. West Indies, needing 231 from a minimum of 63 overs, were reduced to 9 for 4 by McDermott but clung on for a draw when Bishop blocked out the last 107 minutes. In his first appearance against Australia, Arthurton (447 minutes, 343 balls, a six and 16 fours) recorded his first Test hundred in his 11th Test innings. Boon (325 minutes, 259 balls, 13 fours) recorded his fourth hundred in successive home Tests; it was his 14th in 123 Test innings and third against West Indies. Border needed a runner after straining a hamstring when 5 in the second innings. Ambrose's seventh five-wicket analysis included three wickets in eleven deliveries with the second new ball. Williams became the fifth West Indian to make five dismissals in an innings. Walsh pulled a hamstring and was unable to complete his first over. Border and Hughes were fined for dissent when several lbw appeals were rejected in the frenzied final session.

AUSTRALIA

M.A.Taylor	c Williams b Bishop	7	(2)	c Williams b Walsh	34
D.C.Boon	c Simmons b Hooper	48	(1)	c Arthurton b Bishop	111
S.R.Waugh	c Williams b Ambrose	10		c Williams b Ambrose	20
M.E.Waugh	c and b Hooper	39		c Haynes b Ambrose	60
D.R.Martyn	c Lara b Ambrose	36		lbw b Ambrose	15
*A.R.Border	run out	73		c Williams b Walsh	17
G.R.J.Matthews	c Arthurton b Bishop	30		lbw b Ambrose	0
†I.A.Healy	c Lara b Hooper	17		c Williams b Bishop	18
M.G.Hughes	c Bishop b Hooper	10		c Williams b Ambrose	1
C.J.McDermott	c Hooper b Patterson	3		not out	16
B.A.Reid	not out	1		c Richardson b Hooper	1
Extras	(B3, LB4, NB12)	19		(B4, LB2, NB9)	15
Total		**293**			**308**

WEST INDIES

D.L.Haynes	c Taylor b Reid	8		c Healy b McDermott	1
P.V.Simmons	b Reid	27		c Healy b Reid	1
*R.B.Richardson	c Matthews b Hughes	17	(5)	c Healy b Hughes	66
B.C.Lara	st Healy b Matthews	58	(3)	c Taylor b McDermott	0
K.L.T.Arthurton	not out	157	(4)	b McDermott	0
C.L.Hooper	b S.R.Waugh	47		c Boon b Matthews	32
†D.Williams	c Hughes b Reid	15		lbw b McDermott	0
I.R.Bishop	b McDermott	5		not out	16
C.E.L.Ambrose	lbw b Reid	4		c Hughes b Reid	4
B.P.Patterson	c M.E.Waugh b Reid	0			
C.A.Walsh	b Hughes	17	(10)	not out	0
Extras	(LB6, NB10)	16		(LB7, NB6)	13
Total		**371**		**(8 wickets)**	**133**

WEST INDIES	O	M	R	W		O	M	R	W	FALL OF WICKETS				
											A	WI	A	WI
Ambrose	29.1	12	53	2		32	8	66	5	*Wkt*	*1st*	*1st*	*2nd*	*2nd*
Bishop	23	3	51	2		27	6	58	2	1st	8	25	64	2
Patterson	19	0	83	1	(5)	7	0	44	0	2nd	21	50	114	2
Walsh	0.5	0	2	0		24	3	64	2	3rd	88	58	224	3
Hooper	30.1	4	75	4	(3)	28.2	8	63	1	4th	125	170	250	9
Simmons	7	2	16	0	(7)	1	0	5	0	5th	180	265	255	95
Arthurton	3	0	6	0	(6)	1	0	2	0	6th	252	293	255	96
										7th	264	307	280	123
AUSTRALIA										8th	285	321	287	128
McDermott	25	4	93	1		18	7	35	4	9th	288	331	295	–
Reid	37	2	112	5		16	7	39	2	10th	293	371	308	–
Hughes	18.3	3	58	2		13	4	28	1					
Matthews	27	12	41	1		13	4	18	1					
Border	1	0	7	0										
S.R.Waugh	14	2	46	1	(5)	5	2	6	0					
M.E.Waugh	2	0	8	0										

Umpires: T.A.Prue (6) and S.G.Randell (11). Referee: R.Subba Row (*England*) (2).

Close: 1st day – A(1) 259-6 (Matthews 28, Healy 2); 2nd – WI(1) 195-4 (Arthurton 61, Hooper 14); 3rd – A(2) 21-0 (Boon 6, Taylor 14); 4th – A(2) 266-6 (Border 6, Healy 5).

AUSTRALIA v WEST INDIES 1992-93 (2nd Test)

At Melbourne Cricket Ground, on 26, 27, 28, 29, 30 December.
Toss: Australia.   Result: AUSTRALIA won by 139 runs.
Debuts: None.

A devastating spell of leg-spin bowling by Warne on his first appearance against West Indies gave Australia a comfortable victory after the tourists, chasing 359 on a worn pitch, had reached an impressive 143 for 1. Boon completed 1,000 runs against West Indies. Waugh (328 minutes, 234 balls) and Border (350 minutes, 274 balls) added 204 in a fifth-wicket record for this series in Australia, Border's 25th hundred being his first at home for five years. Simmons (253 minutes, 178 balls) scored a chanceless maiden hundred in his 20th Test innings. On the final afternoon, Warne improved Test career figures of 5 for 451 from 130.1 overs with a spell of 7 for 21 in 14.4 overs.

AUSTRALIA

M.A.Taylor	c Lara b Walsh	13	(2) b Bishop		42
D.C.Boon	c Williams b Walsh	46	(1) b Simmons		11
S.R.Waugh	c Lara b Ambrose	38	(4) c Simmons b Bishop		1
M.E.Waugh	c Williams b Ambrose	112	(5) c Adams b Walsh		16
D.R.Martyn	c Simmons b Ambrose	7	(6) not out		67
*A.R.Border	c Williams b Bishop	110	(7) b Bishop		4
†I.A.Healy	c Hooper b Walsh	24	(8) c and b Walsh		8
S.K.Warne	c Adams b Bishop	1	(3) c Arthurton b Ambrose		5
M.G.Hughes	not out	9	c Williams b Ambrose		15
C.J.McDermott	b Walsh	17	c Arthurton b Simmons		4
M.R.Whitney	lbw b Bishop	0	run out		13
Extras	(LB14, W1, NB3)	18	(B1, LB8, NB1)		10
Total		**395**			**196**

WEST INDIES

D.L.Haynes	b Hughes	7	c Healy b Hughes		5
P.V.Simmons	c Boon b Hughes	6	c Boon b Warne		110
*R.B.Richardson	c Healy b Hughes	15	b Warne		52
B.C.Lara	lbw b Whitney	52	c Boon b Whitney		4
K.L.T.Arthurton	c Healy b McDermott	71	st Healy b Warne		13
C.L.Hooper	c and b S.R.Waugh	3	c Whitney b Warne		0
J.C.Adams	c Boon b McDermott	47	c Taylor b McDermott		16
†D.Williams	c Healy b McDermott	0	c M.E.Waugh b Warne		0
I.R.Bishop	b McDermott	9	c Taylor b Warne		7
C.E.L.Ambrose	c McDermott b Warne	7	not out		6
C.A.Walsh	not out	0	c Hughes b Warne		0
Extras	(LB10, NB6)	16	(B3, LB2, NB1)		6
Total		**233**			**219**

WEST INDIES	O	M	R	W		O	M	R	W		FALL OF WICKETS			
Ambrose	35	10	70	3		30	9	57	2		A	WI	A	WI
Bishop	29	2	84	3		20	5	45	3	Wkt	1st	1st	2nd	2nd
Simmons	10	2	23	0	(4)	18	6	34	2	1st	38	11	22	9
Walsh	39	10	91	4	(3)	21	7	42	2	2nd	100	28	40	143
Hooper	36	3	95	0		2.4	1	9	0	3rd	104	33	41	148
Adams	4	0	18	0						4th	115	139	73	165
										5th	319	144	90	177
AUSTRALIA										6th	362	192	102	198
McDermott	25.1	8	66	4		17	2	66	1	7th	366	192	121	206
Hughes	19	5	51	3		18	7	41	1	8th	369	206	154	206
Whitney	13	4	27	1		10	2	32	1	9th	394	233	167	219
Warne	24	7	65	1		23.2	8	52	7	10th	395	233	196	219
S.R.Waugh	4	1	14	1										
M.E.Waugh					(5)	3	0	23	0					

Umpires: S.G.Randell (12) and C.D.Timmins (3). Referee: R.Subba Row (*England*) (3).

Close: 1st day – A(1) 227-4 (M.E.Waugh 63, Border 51); 2nd – WI(1) 62-3 (Lara 14, Arthurton 13); 3rd – A(2) 26-1 (Taylor 9, Warne 1); 4th – WI(2) 32-1 (Simmons 14, Richardson 12).

AUSTRALIA v WEST INDIES 1992-93 (3rd Test)

At Sydney Cricket Ground, on 2, 3, 4, 5, 6 January.
Toss: Australia.   Result: MATCH DRAWN.
Debuts: West Indies – J.R.Murray.

A batting feast which produced the highest average of runs per wicket (64.5) for any Test in Australia and the sixth instance of both teams exceeding 500 runs in the first innings of any Test. Steve Waugh (269 minutes, 207 balls) scored his fourth hundred in 47 Tests and exceeded 48 for the first time since 1989-90 (17 innings). When he had made 21, Border, playing his 136th Test, became the second batsman after S.M.Gavaskar, who achieved the mark in 124 matches, to score 10,000 runs. When 42, Border became the first Australian to score 2,000 runs against West Indies. Lara's prodigious 277 (474 minutes, 372 balls, 38 fours) was the highest score in this series, the second highest by a visiting batsman in Australia, the third highest against Australia, the fourth highest in Australia and the fourth highest maiden Test hundred. Richardson (330 minutes, 253 balls) scored his 15th Test hundred and a record eighth (and his 1,000th run) against Australia. Taylor scored his 3,000th run in Tests while Boon reached his 5,000th and his 1,000th at Sydney. Junior Murray was the first Test cricketer to have been born in Grenada.

AUSTRALIA

M.A.Taylor	c Murray b Bishop	20	(2) not out		46
D.C.Boon	c Murray b Adams	76	(1) not out		63
S.R.Waugh	c Simmons b Ambrose	100			
M.E.Waugh	run out	57			
D.R.Martyn	b Ambrose	0			
*A.R.Border	c Murray b Hooper	74			
G.R.J.Matthews	c Murray b Hooper	79			
†I.A.Healy	not out	36			
M.G.Hughes	c Haynes b Bishop	17			
S.K.Warne	c Simmons b Hooper	14			
C.J.McDermott	did not bat	–			
Extras	(B2, LB23, NB5)	30	(B1, LB2, NB5)		8
Total	(9 wickets declared)	**503**	(0 wickets)		**117**

WEST INDIES

D.L.Haynes	b Matthews	22
P.V.Simmons	c Taylor b McDermott	3
*R.B.Richardson	c Warne b Hughes	109
B.C.Lara	run out	277
K.L.T.Arthurton	c Healy b Matthews	47
C.L.Hooper	b Warne	21
J.C.Adams	not out	77
†J.R.Murray	c Healy b Hughes	11
I.R.Bishop	run out	1
C.E.L.Ambrose	c Martyn b M.E.Waugh	16
C.A.Walsh	c Healy b Hughes	0
Extras	(B4, LB9, W1, NB8)	22
Total		**606**

WEST INDIES	O	M	R	W		O	M	R	W		FALL OF WICKETS		
Ambrose	35	8	87	2		6	2	10	0			A	WI	A
Bishop	36	6	87	2		4	1	9	0		Wkt	1st	1st	2nd
Walsh	30	8	86	0	(4)	8	3	13	0		1st	42	13	–
Hooper	45.4	6	137	3	(5)	10	2	22	0		2nd	160	31	–
Adams	15	2	56	1	(6)	8	1	29	0		3rd	254	324	–
Simmons	10	2	25	0	(3)	3	2	9	0		4th	261	448	–
Arthurton						5	1	14	0		5th	270	481	–
Lara						2	0	4	0		6th	425	537	–
Richardson						1	0	4	0		7th	440	573	–
											8th	469	577	–
AUSTRALIA											9th	503	603	–
McDermott	33	3	119	1							10th	–	606	–
Hughes	16.4	1	76	3										
Matthews	59	12	169	2										
S.R.Waugh	11	1	43	0										
Warne	41	6	116	1										
Border	14	1	41	0										
M.E.Waugh	10	1	29	1										

Umpires: D.B.Hair (2) and T.A.Prue (7). Referee: D.B.Carr (*England*) (4).

Close: 1st day – A(1) 272-5 (Border 0, Matthews 0); 2nd – WI(1) 24-1 (Haynes 16, Richardson 3); 3rd – WI(1) 248-2 (Richardson 94, Lara 121); 4th – WI(1) 488-5 (Hooper 7, Adams 5).

AUSTRALIA v WEST INDIES 1992-93 (4th Test)

At Adelaide Oval on 23, 24, 25, 26 January.
Toss: West Indies.   Result: WEST INDIES won by 1 run.
Debuts: Australia – J.L.Langer.

An enthralling match produced an inappropriate Australia Day ending, West Indies retaining the Frank Worrell Trophy through this victory by the narrowest margin in Test history. Boon, when 2, retired hurt at 16 with a bruised elbow and returned at 108 for 5. In his 67th Test Richardson became the sixth West Indian to score 5,000 runs. May celebrated his recall after a four-year absence with his best Test batting and bowling performances to date. His 32-ball spell of 5 for 5 left Australia two days to score 186 and regain the Trophy. Ambrose swung the match with his second ten-wicket match analysis before Langer (253 minutes, 146 balls) bravely accumulated Australia's only fifty of the game. May, on his 31st birthday, sustained a fractured finger but added 40 for the last wicket with McDermott before the latter failed to evade a lifting ball from Walsh which just flicked his glove and exacted a brave decision from umpire Hair.

WEST INDIES

D.L.Haynes	st Healy b May	45	c Healy b McDermott		11
P.V.Simmons	c Hughes b S.R.Waugh	46	b McDermott		10
*R.B.Richardson	lbw b Hughes	2	c Healy b Warne		72
B.C.Lara	c Healy b McDermott	52	c S.R.Waugh b Hughes		7
K.L.T.Arthurton	c S.R.Waugh b May	0	c Healy b McDermott		0
C.L.Hooper	c Healy b Hughes	2	c Hughes b May		25
†J.R.Murray	not out	49	c M.E.Waugh b May		0
I.R.Bishop	c M.E.Waugh b Hughes	13	c M.E.Waugh b May		6
C.E.L.Ambrose	c Healy b Hughes	0	st Healy b May		1
K.C.G.Benjamin	b M.E.Waugh	15	c Warne b May		0
C.A.Walsh	lbw b Hughes	5	not out		0
Extras	(LB11, NB12)	23	(LB2, NB12)		14
Total		**252**			**146**

AUSTRALIA

M.A.Taylor	c Hooper b Bishop	1	(2) c Murray b Benjamin	7
D.C.Boon	not out	39	(1) lbw b Ambrose	0
J.L.Langer	c Murray b Benjamin	20	c Murray b Bishop	54
M.E.Waugh	c Simmons b Ambrose	0	c Hooper b Walsh	26
S.R.Waugh	c Murray b Ambrose	42	c Arthurton b Ambrose	4
*A.R.Border	c Hooper b Ambrose	19	c Haynes b Ambrose	1
†I.A.Healy	c Hooper b Ambrose	0	b Walsh	0
M.G.Hughes	c Murray b Hooper	43	lbw b Ambrose	1
S.K.Warne	lbw b Hooper	0	lbw b Bishop	9
T.B.A.May	c Murray b Ambrose	6	not out	42
C.J.McDermott	b Ambrose	14	c Murray b Walsh	18
Extras	(B7, LB3, NB19)	29	(B1, LB8, NB13)	22
Total		**213**		**184**

AUSTRALIA	O	M	R	W	O	M	R	W
McDermott	16	1	85	1	11	0	66	3
Hughes	21.3	3	64	5	13	1	43	1
S.R.Waugh	13	4	37	1	5	1	8	0
May	14	1	41	2	6.5	3	9	5
Warne	2	0	11	0	6	2	18	1
M.E.Waugh	1	0	3	1				

WEST INDIES	O	M	R	W	O	M	R	W
Ambrose	28.2	6	74	6	26	5	46	4
Bishop	18	3	48	1	17	3	41	2
Benjamin	6	0	22	1	12	2	32	1
Walsh	10	3	34	0	19	4	44	3
Hooper	13	4	25	2	5	1	12	0

FALL OF WICKETS

Wkt	WI 1st	A 1st	WI 2nd	A 2nd
1st	84	1	14	5
2nd	99	16	49	16
3rd	129	46	63	54
4th	130	108	65	64
5th	134	108	124	72
6th	189	112	137	73
7th	206	181	145	74
8th	206	181	146	102
9th	247	197	146	144
10th	252	213	146	184

Umpires: D.B.Hair (3) and L.J.King (6). Referee: D.B.Carr (*England*) (5).

Close: 1st day – A(1) 2-1 (Boon 1, Langer 0); 2nd – A(1) 100-3 (S.R.Waugh 35, Border 18); 3rd – WI(2) 146 all out.

AUSTRALIA v WEST INDIES 1992-93 (5th Test)

At W.A.C.A.Ground, Perth, on 30, 31 January, 1 February.
Toss: Australia.   Result: WEST INDIES won by an innings and 25 runs.
Debuts: Australia – J.Angel; West Indies – A.C.Cummins.

At 12.58pm on the third day, West Indies completed their fourth win in as many Tests in Perth. It was the earliest finish to any Test since 1945-46 (*Test No. 275*) and in Australia since 1931-32 (*Test No. 216*), the actual playing time totalling 14 hours 4 minutes. Ambrose, aided by a fast, bouncy pitch and with the 'Fremantle Doctor' behind him, effectively decided this contest on the first afternoon with a fearsome spell of 7 for 1 off 32 balls and returned the best West Indian analysis against Australia. West Indies gained a first innings lead on the first day. Haynes (21) retired at 34 when struck in the face hooking and resumed at 195. Border celebrated his record 75th appearance as a Test captain with his only 'pair' in first-class cricket. Bishop returned his best analysis in Tests and Ambrose set a West Indies record for this series with 33 wickets. The WACA curator was subsequently dismissed for producing this pitch.

AUSTRALIA

J.L.Langer	c Murray b Bishop	10	(2)	c sub (A.L.Logie) b Ambrose	1
D.C.Boon	c Richardson b Ambrose	44	(1)	b Bishop	52
S.R.Waugh	c Murray b Bishop	13		c sub (A.L.Logie) b Bishop	0
M.E.Waugh	c Murray b Ambrose	9		c Richardson b Bishop	21
D.R.Martyn	c Simmons b Ambrose	13	(6)	c Ambrose b Cummins	31
*A.R.Border	c Murray b Ambrose	0	(7)	b Bishop	0
†I.A.Healy	c Lara b Ambrose	0	(8)	c Murray b Bishop	27
M.G.Hughes	c Arthurton b Ambrose	0	(9)	c Murray b Walsh	22
S.K.Warne	run out	13	(5)	c Murray b Ambrose	0
J.Angel	c Murray b Ambrose	0		not out	4
C.J.McDermott	not out	2		c Lara b Bishop	8
Extras	(LB8, W1, NB6)	15		(B1, LB6, NB5)	12
Total		**119**			**178**

WEST INDIES

D.L.Haynes	c Healy b Hughes	24
P.V.Simmons	c S.R.Waugh b Angel	80
*R.B.Richardson	c Langer b McDermott	47
B.C.Lara	c Warne b McDermott	16
K.L.T.Arthurton	c S.R.Waugh b McDermott	77
J.C.Adams	b Hughes	8
†J.R.Murray	c Healy b M.E.Waugh	37
I.R.Bishop	c Healy b M.E.Waugh	0
A.C.Cummins	c M.E.Waugh b Hughes	3
C.E.L.Ambrose	not out	9
C.A.Walsh	b Hughes	1
Extras	(B4, LB10, NB6)	20
Total		**322**

WEST INDIES	O	M	R	W	O	M	R	W		FALL OF WICKETS		
Ambrose	18	9	25	7	21	8	54	2		A	WI	A
Bishop	11	6	17	2	16	4	40	6	*Wkt*	*1st*	*1st*	*2nd*
Walsh	11.2	2	45	0	12	2	46	1	1st	27	111	13
Cummins	7	0	24	0	8	3	31	1	2nd	58	136	14
									3rd	85	184	66
AUSTRALIA									4th	90	195	67
McDermott	22	4	85	3					5th	90	205	95
Hughes	25.4	6	71	4					6th	100	280	95
Angel	19	4	72	1					7th	102	286	130
Warne	12	0	51	0					8th	104	301	162
S.R.Waugh	6	3	8	0					9th	104	319	170
M.E.Waugh	6	1	21	2					10th	119	322	178

Umpires: S.G.Randell (13) and C.D.Timmins (4). Referee: D.B.Carr (*England*) (6).

Close: 1st day – WI(1) 135-1 (Simmons 45, Lara 16); 2nd – A(2) 75-4 (Boon 45, Martyn 3).

SRI LANKA v NEW ZEALAND 1992-93 (1st Test)

At Tyronne Fernando Stadium, Moratuwa, on 27, 28, 29 November, 1, 2 December.
Toss: Sri Lanka.   Result: MATCH DRAWN.
Debuts: New Zealand – C.Z.Harris, M.B.Owens, J.T.C.Vaughan.

New Zealand's third Test tour of Sri Lanka was close to being abandoned when a suicide bomb attack left five dead outside their Colombo hotel soon after their arrival from Zimbabwe. Five players accepted the New Zealand Board's offer to return home and the tour was restructured with two Tests instead of three. Rutherford (277 minutes, 227 balls, two sixes and 13 fours) registered only his second hundred in 54 Test innings. His partnership of 151 with Harris, whose fifty came in 296 minutes off 176 balls, set a fifth-wicket record for this series. Mahanama (361 minutes, 297 balls, 18 fours) dominated Sri Lanka's innings with his maiden Test hundred and highest first-class score to date before rain on the fourth day compelled Ranatunga to declare just 39 ahead and reduced their chance of victory. Wright, recalled (as one of four replacements) after retiring from international cricket, became the first New Zealander to score 5,000 Test runs.

NEW ZEALAND

B.R.Hartland	c De Silva b Liyanage	3	lbw b Ramanayake		52
J.G.Wright	c Gurusinha b Ramanayake	11	st Wickremasinghe b Anurasiri		42
A.H.Jones	c Mahanama b Liyanage	35	c Wickremasinghe b Ramanayake		14
*M.D.Crowe	c Ranatunga b Warnaweera	19	c Tillekeratne b Anurasiri		11
K.R.Rutherford	c Wickremasinghe b Hathurusinghe	105	lbw b Warnaweera		53
C.Z.Harris	b Warnaweera	56	(7) not out		0
J.T.C.Vaughan	b Liyanage	17	(6) not out		0
†A.C.Parore	c Wickremasinghe b Anurasiri	3			
D.J.Nash	c Wickremasinghe b Liyanage	4			
M.L.Su'a	b Anurasiri	0			
M.B.Owens	not out	0			
Extras	(B5, LB12, W2, NB16)	35	(LB8, W1, NB14)		23
Total		**288**	(5 wickets)		**195**

SRI LANKA

R.S.Mahanama	run out	153
U.C.Hathurusinghe	c Jones b Nash	10
A.P.Gurusinha	c Vaughan b Su'a	43
P.A.de Silva	c Nash b Su'a	62
H.P.Tillekeratne	b Owens	1
*A.Ranatunga	c Parore b Owens	3
†A.G.D.Wickremasinghe	not out	13
C.P.H.Ramanayake	not out	10
D.K.Liyanage	⎫	
S.D.Anurasiri	⎬ did not bat	
K.P.J.Warnaweera	⎭	
Extras	(LB7, W9, NB16)	32
Total	(6 wickets declared)	**327**

SRI LANKA	O	M	R	W	O	M	R	W	FALL OF WICKETS		
									NZ	SL	NZ
Ramanayake	23	2	57	1	17	6	27	2	*Wkt*	*1st*	*1st*	*2nd*
Liyanage	26.5	4	82	4	17	4	48	0	1st	6	26	110
Hathurusinghe	8	4	12	1	10	6	22	0	2nd	44	164	122
Anurasiri	34	11	55	2	(5) 26	11	32	2	3rd	77	297	136
Warnaweera	34	15	46	2	(6) 25	15	31	1	4th	87	299	160
De Silva	4	2	8	0					5th	238	300	194
Gurusinha	1	0	6	0					6th	265	309	–
Ranatunga	3	2	5	0	(4) 7	2	26	0	7th	273	–	–
Tillekeratne					(7) 1	0	1	0	8th	283	–	–
NEW ZEALAND									9th	286	–	–
Su'a	25	6	62	2					10th	288	–	–
Owens	17	3	63	2								
Nash	18	2	62	1								
Vaughan	14	0	56	0								
Harris	15	5	64	0								
Jones	1	0	3	0								
Crowe	2	0	10	0								

Umpires: K.T.Francis (7) and T.M.Samarasinghe (2). Referee: S.Venkataraghavan (*India*) (1).

Close: 1st day – NZ(1) 139-4 (Rutherford 46, Harris 11); 2nd – SL(1) 10-0 (Mahanama 3, Hathurusinghe 0); 3rd – SL(1) 299-4 (Tillekeratne 0, Ranatunga 0); 4th – NZ(2) 104-0 (Hartland 50, Wright 38).

SRI LANKA v NEW ZEALAND 1992-93 (2nd Test)

At Sinhalese Sports Club Ground, Colombo, on 6, 7, 8, 9 December.
Toss: Sri Lanka.   Result: SRI LANKA won by nine wickets.
Debuts: None.

With four sessions to spare, Sri Lanka gained their third victory in 42 Tests and their first against New Zealand. Mahanama (217 minutes, 154 balls, 14 fours) scored his second hundred in successive innings. On a pitch that began to disintegrate on the first day, New Zealand lost all ten first innings wickets for 45 runs to be dismissed for their lowest total against Sri Lanka. In an inspired display of furious hitting, Crowe, (159 minutes, 121 balls, four sixes and 10 fours) scored his 15th Test hundred in 106 Test innings. When 39, he stood his ground after Anandappa upheld silly point's appeal for a catch that had not carried. Samarasinghe at square-leg asked his colleague to rescind his decision. Having registered his highest score to date, former wicket-keeper Tillekeratne equalled the Test record for fielders by holding seven catches in the match.

SRI LANKA

R.S.Mahanama	c Bradburn b Owens	109	c Parore b Owens		29
U.C.Hathurusinghe	c Harris b Owens	27	not out		26
A.P.Gurusinha	st Parore b Bradburn	22	not out		14
P.A.de Silva	c Parore b Pringle	3			
*A.Ranatunga	c Parore b Su'a	76			
H.P.Tillekeratne	c Parore b Bradburn	93			
†A.G.D.Wickremasinghe	c Rutherford b Owens	2			
D.K.Liyanage	c Parore b Su'a	16			
S.D.Anurasiri	c Su'a b Owens	24			
M.Muralitharan	not out	4			
K.P.J.Warnaweera	c Crowe b Bradburn	5			
Extras	(B3, LB4, W3, NB3)	13	(LB2, NB2)		4
Total		**394**	(1 wicket)		**73**

NEW ZEALAND

B.R.Hartland	c Gurusinha b Warnaweera	21	c Muralitharan b Gurusinha		21
J.G.Wright	c Wickremasinge b Warnaweera	30	c Mahanama b Muralitharan		50
A.H.Jones	c Tillekeratne b Warnaweera	20	c Tillekeratne b Warnaweera		5
*M.D.Crowe	b Muralitharan	0	c Tillekeratne b Muralitharan		107
K.R.Rutherford	c Tillekeratne b Warnaweera	0	c sub‡ b Warnaweera		38
C.Z.Harris	run out	9	lbw b Anurasiri		19
†A.C.Parore	lbw b Muralitharan	5	c Tillekeratne b Muralitharan		60
G.E.Bradburn	c Tillekeratne b Liyanage	1	c Wickremasinghe b Anurasiri		7
M.L.Su'a	not out	2	b Muralitharan		0
C.Pringle	b Liyanage	0	c Tillekeratne b Liyanage		23
M.B.Owens	c Anurasiri b Muralitharan	0	not out		8
Extras	(LB4, W1, NB9)	14	(B2, LB8, NB13)		23
Total		**102**			**361**

NEW ZEALAND	O	M	R	W		O	M	R	W		FALL OF WICKETS			
Su'a	26	7	50	2	(3)	2	0	14	0		SL	NZ	NZ	SL
Owens	30	7	101	4	(1)	6	1	36	1	*Wkt*	*1st*	*1st*	*2nd*	*2nd*
Pringle	32	7	85	1	(2)	2	1	5	0	1st	102	57	23	36
Bradburn	37.3	4	134	3		3	1	8	0	2nd	160	60	30	–
Harris	3	0	17	0						3rd	167	63	189	–
Jones					(5)	1.4	1	8	0	4th	182	64	196	–
										5th	274	88	240	–
SRI LANKA										6th	287	97	261	–
Liyanage	9	3	9	2		12	2	35	1	7th	316	99	285	–
Gurusinha	4	1	15	0		8	1	19	1	8th	385	100	286	–
Anurasiri	6	1	13	0	(5)	22	4	54	2	9th	385	100	317	–
Hathurusinge	7	3	14	0	(6)	3	2	2	0	10th	394	102	361	–
Warnaweera	14	3	25	4	(3)	34	4	107	2					
Muralitharan	12.1	3	22	3	(4)	40	6	134	4					

‡ (S.T.Jayasuriya)

Umpires: I.Anandappa (2) and T.M.Samarasinghe (3). Referee: S.Venkataraghavan (*India*) (2).

Close: 1st day – SL(1) 303-6 (Tillekeratne 43, Liyanage 10); 2nd – NZ(1) 100-7 (Bradburn 1, Su'a 1); 3rd – NZ(2) 277-6 (Parore 17, Bradburn 5).

NEW ZEALAND v PAKISTAN 1992-93 (Only Test)

At Trust Bank Park, Hamilton, on 2, 3, 4, 5 January.
Toss: New Zealand.   Result: PAKISTAN won by 33 runs.
Debuts: None.

Inspired fast bowling by Waqar, who took his 100th wicket in 20 Tests, and Wasim earned Pakistan a remarkable victory after New Zealand had required only 127 to win an ill-tempered encounter. Rutherford became New Zealand's 22nd Test captain after Wright and Crowe had withdrawn through injury. A tenacious hundred by Greatbatch (133 in 427 minutes, 317 balls, 16 fours), his third in 38 Test innings, contributed most to the hosts' first innings lead of 48. Wasim completed 1,000 runs and the Test 'double' in his 45th Test. For the tenth time extras were the main contributor to a Test innings.

PAKISTAN

Ramiz Raja	c Rutherford b Su'a	4	(2)	c Parore b Morrison	8
Aamir Sohail	c Owens b Morrison	0	(1)	b Morrison	0
Asif Mujtaba	c Owens b Su'a	0		lbw b Morrison	11
*Javed Miandad	b Su'a	92		lbw b Su'a	12
Salim Malik	c Parore b Morrison	14		c Su'a b Morrison	0
Inzamam-ul-Haq	c Morrison b Su'a	23		lbw b Owens	75
Wasim Akram	c Greatbatch b Patel	27	(8)	b Patel	15
†Rashid Latif	not out	32	(7)	c Rutherford b Su'a	33
Waqar Younis	run out	13		not out	4
Mushtaq Ahmed	lbw b Su'a	2		c Rutherford b Morrison	10
Aqib Javed	c Greatbatch b Morrison	1		c Hartland b Patel	2
Extras	(W4, NB4)	8		(LB2, NB2)	4
Total		**216**			**174**

NEW ZEALAND

M.J.Greatbatch	lbw b Waqar	133	(2)	c Aamir b Wasim	8
B.R.Hartland	st Rashid b Mushtaq	43	(1)	b Wasim	9
A.H.Jones	lbw b Wasim	2		c Asif b Waqar	19
R.T.Latham	lbw b Wasim	2	(6)	b Waqar	0
*K.R.Rutherford	c Rashid b Mushtaq	14	(7)	c Aamir b Wasim	9
C.Z.Harris	lbw b Waqar	6	(8)	b Waqar	9
D.N.Patel	lbw b Mushtaq	12	(9)	b Waqar	4
†A.C.Parore	lbw b Wasim	16	(5)	c Rashid b Wasim	13
M.L.Su'a	c Rashid b Waqar	0	(10)	lbw b Waqar	0
D.K.Morrison	not out	3	(4)	lbw b Wasim	0
M.B.Owens	b Waqar	0		not out	0
Extras	(B1, LB15, W1, NB16)	33		(B1, LB11, NB10)	22
Total		**264**			**93**

NEW ZEALAND	O	M	R	W	O	M	R	W		FALL OF WICKETS			
										P	NZ	P	NZ
Morrison	19.3	4	42	3	15	2	41	5	Wkt	1st	1st	2nd	2nd
Su'a	24	2	73	5	13	1	47	2	1st	4	108	0	19
Owens	12	3	48	0	7	0	19	1	2nd	4	111	20	31
Patel	14	2	53	1	20.1	5	65	2	3rd	12	117	25	32
									4th	45	147	25	65
PAKISTAN									5th	87	164	39	67
Wasim Akram	31	9	66	3	22	4	45	5	6th	158	193	119	71
Waqar Younis	28	11	59	4	(3) 13.3	4	22	5	7th	176	254	158	88
Mushtaq Ahmed	38	10	87	3					8th	202	256	158	88
Aqib	7	2	24	0	(2) 8	2	14	0	9th	208	257	171	88
Aamir	5	2	12	0					10th	216	264	174	93

Umpires: B.L.Aldridge (14) and R.S.Dunne (9). Referee: P.J.P.Burge (*Australia*) (4).

Close: 1st day – NZ(1) 23-0 (Greatbatch 8, Hartland 7); 2nd – NZ(1) 256-8 (Parore 16); 3rd – NZ(2) 39-3 (Jones 11, Parore 3).

INDIA v ENGLAND 1992-93 (1st Test)

At Eden Gardens, Calcutta, on 29, 30, 31 January, 1, 2 February.
Toss: India.   Result: INDIA won by eight wickets.
Debuts: India – R.K.Chauhan, V.G.Kambli; England – J.P.Taylor.

After 66 minutes of play on the fifth day, India won their first Test in ten matches since defeating Sri Lanka on an underprepared Chandigarh pitch in November 1990. That success had been Azharuddin's only victory in 17 matches as captain. On a slow pitch responsive to spin, he played an outstanding innings (324 minutes, 197 balls, a six and 26 fours) to record his 12th hundred. It was the highest of his record six against England and his fourth in successive home matches in this series, the last having been played in 1984-85. Gatting celebrated his return to Test cricket, after missing 33 matches through leading an unofficial tour to South Africa, by top scoring in both innings. Gooch became the fifth England player to appear in 100 Tests; in the second innings he allowed himself to be stumped when he grounded his foot on the crease line and not behind it. Venkataraghavan was the first former Indian Test cricketer (or captain, or manager) to umpire at this level. The match attracted an estimated total attendance of 270,000, most of them armed with fireworks.

INDIA

M.Prabhakar	c Lewis b Salisbury	46	b Hick		13
N.S.Sidhu	c Hick b Taylor	13	st Stewart b Hick		37
V.G.Kambli	c Hick b Jarvis	16	not out		18
S.R.Tendulkar	c Hick b Malcolm	50	not out		9
*M.Azharuddin	c Gooch b Hick	182			
P.K.Amre	c Hick b Jarvis	12			
Kapil Dev	c Lewis b Hick	13			
†K.S.More	not out	4			
A.Kumble	b Malcolm	0			
R.K.Chauhan	b Malcolm	2			
S.L.V.Raju	c Salisbury b Hick	1			
Extras	(B6, LB6, W10, NB10)	32	(LB4, NB1)		5
Total		**371**	(2 wickets)		**82**

ENGLAND

*G.A.Gooch	c Azharuddin b Raju	17	st More b Kumble		18
†A.J.Stewart	b Prabhakar	0	c Tendulkar b Kumble		49
M.W.Gatting	c Chauhan	33	b Chauhan		81
R.A.Smith	c Amre b Kumble	1	c More b Chauhan		8
G.A.Hick	b Kumble	1	lbw b Raju		25
N.H.Fairbrother	c More b Kumble	17	c sub (W.V.Raman) b Kumble		25
I.D.K.Salisbury	c More b Chauhan	28	(9) c More b Kapil Dev		26
C.C.Lewis	b Raju	21	(7) c Amre b Raju		16
P.W.Jarvis	c Prabhakar b Raju	4	(8) lbw b Raju		6
J.P.Taylor	st More b Chauhan	17	not out		17
D.E.Malcolm	not out	4	lbw b Kapil Dev		0
Extras	(B8, LB8, W4)	20	(LB13, NB2)		15
Total		**163**			**286**

ENGLAND	O	M	R	W	O	M	R	W	FALL OF WICKETS			
Malcolm	24	3	67	3	6	1	16	0		I	E	E	I
Jarvis	27	5	72	2	5.2	1	23	0	*Wkt*	*1st*	*1st*	*2nd*	*2nd*
Lewis	23	5	64	0	(5) 3	1	5	0	1st	49	8	48	51
Taylor	19	2	65	1	(3) 3	1	9	0	2nd	78	37	111	62
Salisbury	17	2	72	1	(4) 6	3	16	0	3rd	93	38	145	–
Hick	12.5	5	19	3	6	1	9	2	4th	216	40	192	–
									5th	280	87	192	–
INDIA									6th	346	89	216	–
Kapil Dev	6	1	18	0	8.2	5	12	2	7th	362	111	234	–
Prabhakar	9	3	10	1	9	4	26	0	8th	368	119	254	–
Kumble	29	8	50	3	(5) 40	16	76	3	9th	370	149	286	–
Raju	27	14	39	3	35	9	80	3	10th	371	163	286	–
Chauhan	29.1	15	30	3	(3) 45	17	79	2					

Umpires: P.D.Reporter (13) and S.Venkataraghavan (1). Referee: C.W.Smith (*West Indies*) (1).

Close: 1st day – I(1) 263-4 (Azharuddin 114, Amre 7); 2nd – E(1) 88-5 (Fairbrother 17, Salisbury 0); 3rd – E(2) 128-2 (Gatting 48, Smith 2); 4th – I(2) 36-0 (Prabhakar 12, Sidhu 20).

INDIA v ENGLAND 1992-93 (2nd Test)

At M.A.Chidambaram Stadium, Madras, on 11, 12, 13, 14, 15 February.
Toss: India.   Result: INDIA won by an innings and 22 runs.
Debuts: England – R.J.Blakey.

India won their first rubber since 1988-89 when they completed only their second victory by an innings in this series. Stewart captained England for the first time when Gooch withdrew through illness on the morning of the match. Sidhu (401 minutes, 273 balls, 9 fours) scored his first hundred for four years and completed 1,000 runs in his 36th innings. Tendulkar (361 minutes, 296 balls, a six and 24 fours) completed his first Test hundred in India and became the first to score five Test hundreds before his 20th birthday. Kapil Dev was the fourth to score 5,000 runs for India; his 'double' of 5,000 runs and 400 wickets remains unique. England followed on in successive Tests in this series for the first time after conceding their highest total in India. Gatting completed 4,000 runs in 121 Test innings. Lewis (172 minutes, 140 balls, two sixes and 15 fours) celebrated his 25th birthday by reaching his first Test hundred with a straight six.

INDIA

M.Prabhakar	c Blakey b Lewis	27
N.S.Sidhu	c Hick b Jarvis	106
V.G.Kambli	lbw b Hick	59
S.R.Tendulkar	c and b Salisbury	165
M.Azharuddin	c Smith b Jarvis	6
P.K.Amre	c Jarvis b Salisbury	78
Kapil Dev	not out	66
K.S.More	not out	26
A.Kumble		
R.K.Chauhan	} did not bat	
S.L.V.Raju		
Extras	(LB10, W2, NB15)	27
Total	(6 wickets declared)	**560**

ENGLAND

R.A.Smith	lbw b Kumble	17	c Amre b Kumble		56
A.J.Stewart	c sub (W.V.Raman) b Raju	74	lbw b Kapil Dev		0
G.A.Hick	lbw b Chauhan	64	c Tendulkar b Kapil Dev		0
M.W.Gatting	run out	2	lbw b Raju		19
N.H.Fairbrother	c Kapil Dev b Chauhan	83	c Prabhakar b Kumble		9
R.J.Blakey	b Raju	0	b Kumble		6
C.C.Lewis	c Azharuddin b Raju	0	c and b Kumble		117
I.D.K.Salisbury	lbw b Kumble	4	b Kumble		12
P.W.Jarvis	c sub (W.V.Raman) b Raju	8	c Tendulkar b Kumble		2
P.C.R.Tufnell	c Azharuddin b Chauhan	2	not out		22
D.E.Malcolm	not out	0	c sub (W.V.Raman) b Raju		0
Extras	(B14, LB16, NB2)	32	(B4, LB5)		9
Total		**286**			**252**

ENGLAND	O	M	R	W	O	M	R	W	FALL OF WICKETS
Malcolm	27	7	87	0					
Jarvis	28	7	72	2					
Lewis	11	1	40	1					
Tufnell	41	3	132	0					
Hick	29	2	77	1					
Salisbury	29	1	142	2					

	I	E	E
Wkt	1st	1st	2nd
1st	41	46	10
2nd	149	157	12
3rd	296	166	71
4th	324	175	82
5th	442	179	99
6th	499	179	99
7th	–	220	172
8th	–	277	186
9th	–	279	241
10th	–	286	252

INDIA	O	M	R	W	O	M	R	W
Prabhakar	3	2	7	0	3	2	4	0
Kumble	25	9	61	2	(5) 21	7	64	6
Chauhan	39.3	16	69	3	(4) 21	4	59	0
Raju	54	21	103	4	(3) 23.1	3	76	2
Kapil Dev	4	0	11	0	(2) 11	5	36	2
Tendulkar	2	1	5	0	2	1	4	0

Umpires: V.K.Ramaswamy (13) and R.S.Rathore (2). Referee: C.W.Smith (*West Indies*) (2).

Close: 1st day –I(1) 275-2 (Sidhu 104, Tendulkar 70); 2nd – E(1) 19-0 (Smith 6, Stewart 10); 3rd – E(1) 221-7 (Fairbrother 38, Jarvis 0); 4th – E(2) 231-8 (Lewis 108, Tufnell 10).

INDIA v ENGLAND 1992-93 (3rd Test)

At Wankhede Stadium, Bombay, on 19, 20, 21, 22, 23 February.
Toss: England.   Result: INDIA won by an innings and 15 runs.
Debuts: None.

At 12.44pm on the fifth day, India gained their second successive innings victory to win three matches in a series for the first time. Hick (390 minutes, 319 balls, a six and 20 fours) contributed 51.3% of England's highest total of the rubber; it was his first hundred in 22 Test innings, his 68th in first-class cricket and England's highest individual score in Bombay. Tufnell survived for 81 minutes, the slowest Test innings of two runs. India again improved upon their highest home total against England, Kambli (603 minutes, 411 balls, 23 fours) amassing India's highest score against England, their third highest in all Tests and the 12th highest maiden hundred. He added 194 for the third wicket with his former schoolmate, Tendulkar. Five years earlier, this pair had each scored triple hundreds as they established a world record for any wicket by putting on 664 (unbroken), also for the third wicket, for Sharadashram Vidyamandir against St Xavier's High School in a Harris Shield match at Bombay's Sassanian Ground. England's poor technique against the turning ball accounted for the loss of 46 wickets in six innings.

ENGLAND

*G.A.Gooch	c More b Kapil Dev	4	b Prabhakar		8
A.J.Stewart	run out	13	lbw b Prabhakar		10
M.A.Atherton	c Prabhakar b Kumble	37	c More b Prabhakar		11
R.A.Smith	c More b Raju	2	b Kumble		62
M.W.Gatting	c Kapil Dev b Raju	23	st More b Chauhan		61
G.A.Hick	c Kapil Dev b Prabhakar	178	c Amre b Kumble		47
†R.J.Blakey	lbw b Kumble	1	b Kumble		0
C.C.Lewis	lbw b Kumble	49	c More b Raju		3
J.E.Emburey	c More b Kapil Dev	12	c Tendulkar b Kumble		1
P.A.J.DeFreitas	lbw b Kapil Dev	11	st More b Raju		12
P.C.R.Tufnell	not out	2	not out		2
Extras	(B4, LB5, W2, NB4)	15	(B4, LB6, W1, NB1)		12
Total		**347**			**229**

INDIA

N.S.Sidhu	c Smith b Tufnell	79
M.Prabhakar	c Blakey b Hick	44
V.G.Kambli	c Gatting b Lewis	224
S.R.Tendulkar	lbw b Tufnell	78
*M.Azharuddin	lbw b Lewis	26
P.K.Amre	c DeFreitas b Hick	57
Kapil Dev	c DeFreitas b Emburey	22
†K.S.More	c Lewis b Emburey	0
A.Kumble	c Atherton b Tufnell	16
R.K.Chauhan	c Atherton b Tufnell	15
S.L.V.Raju	not out	0
Extras	(B5, LB14, W5, NB6)	30
Total		**591**

INDIA	O	M	R	W	O	M	R	W		FALL OF WICKETS		
Kapil Dev	15	3	35	3	7	1	21	0		E	I	E
Prabhakar	13	2	52	1	11	4	28	3	*Wkt*	*1st*	*1st*	*2nd*
Raju	44	8	102	2	26.5	7	68	2	1st	11	109	17
Kumble	40	4	95	3	26	9	70	4	2nd	25	174	26
Chauhan	23	7	54	0	12	5	32	1	3rd	30	368	34
									4th	58	418	155
ENGLAND									5th	116	519	181
DeFreitas	20	4	75	0					6th	118	560	181
Lewis	42	9	114	2					7th	211	560	206
Emburey	59	14	144	2					8th	262	563	214
Tufnell	39.3	6	142	4					9th	279	591	215
Hick	29	3	97	2					10th	347	591	229

Umpires: P.D.Reporter (14) and S.Venkataraghavan (2). Referee: C.W.Smith (*West Indies*) (3).

Close: 1st day – E(1) 239-7 (Hick 99, Emburey 5); 2nd – I(1) 144-1 (Sidhu 69, Kambli 20); 3rd – I(1) 397-3 (Kambli 164, Azharuddin 14); 4th – E(2) 108-3 (Smith 39, Gatting 31).

NEW ZEALAND v AUSTRALIA 1992-93 (1st Test)

At Lancaster Park, Christchurch, on 25, 26, 27, 28 February.
Toss: New Zealand.   Result: AUSTRALIA won by an innings and 60 runs.
Debuts: None.

Put in on a wet pitch, Australia dominated this match after compiling the third highest total in Test cricket not to include an individual hundred. When top scorer Border (88 in 236 minutes off 182 balls with 13 fours) pulled Patel to the mid-wicket boundary at 1.51pm on the second day, he completed his 84th fifty in 240 innings (139 Tests) and overtook S.M.Gavaskar's record Test aggregate of 10,122 runs from 214 innings. Hughes hit four sixes in his 46-ball innings of 45. Wright's 39 occupied 270 minutes and 201 balls. Even Rutherford (260 minutes, 215 balls, a six and 9 fours), who added his third hundred in 61 innings to a first innings fifty, could not prevent Australia from gaining their first victory in New Zealand since 1981-82 at 4.14 on the fourth afternoon.

AUSTRALIA

D.C.Boon	c Parore b Owens	15
M.A.Taylor	c Crowe b Morrison	82
J.L.Langer	lbw b Morrison	63
M.E.Waugh	c Parore b Patel	13
S.R.Waugh	lbw b Owens	62
*A.R.Border	c Parore b Morrison	88
†I.A.Healy	c Morrison b Owens	54
M.G.Hughes	c Cairns b Patel	45
P.R.Reiffel	c Greatbatch b Su'a	18
S.K.Warne	not out	22
C.J.McDermott	c Jones b Cairns	4
Extras	(B2, LB6, W5, NB6)	19
Total		**485**

NEW ZEALAND

M.J.Greatbatch	c Healy b McDermott	4	c Reiffel b Hughes	0
J.G.Wright	lbw b Warne	39	b McDermott	14
A.H.Jones	lbw b McDermott	8	c Border b McDermott	10
*M.D.Crowe	c Taylor b Hughes	15	lbw b Hughes	14
K.R.Rutherford	b Warne	57	c Healy b Warne	102
C.L.Cairns	c Boon b McDermott	0	c Taylor b Warne	21
†A.C.Parore	c Boon b Reiffel	6	c Boon b Warne	5
D.N.Patel	c McDermott b Hughes	35	b Warne	8
M.L.Su'a	c Healy b Reiffel	0	b Hughes	44
D.K.Morrison	not out	4	c Healy b Hughes	19
M.B.Owens	lbw b Warne	0	not out	0
Extras	(B2, LB4, W4, NB4)	14	(LB2, NB4)	6
Total		**182**		**243**

NEW ZEALAND	O	M	R	W	O	M	R	W
Morrison	36	11	81	3				
Su'a	33	5	106	1				
Cairns	31.3	9	87	1				
Owens	26	9	58	3				
Patel	31	3	145	2				
AUSTRALIA								
McDermott	21	4	73	3	(2) 19	6	45	2
Hughes	21	10	44	2	(1) 24.5	6	62	4
Reiffel	18	8	27	2	18	3	59	0
S.R.Waugh	4	2	9	0	2	2	0	0
Warne	22	12	23	3	26	7	63	4
M.E.Waugh					5	1	12	0

FALL OF WICKETS

Wkt	A 1st	NZ 1st	NZ 2nd
1st	33	4	0
2nd	149	18	19
3rd	170	53	24
4th	217	124	51
5th	264	128	92
6th	363	138	110
7th	435	150	144
8th	441	152	190
9th	480	181	242
10th	485	182	243

Umpires: B.L.Aldridge (15) and C.E.King (1). Referee: Javed Burki (*Pakistan*) (1).

Close: 1st day – A(1) 217-3 (Langer 63, S.R.Waugh 33); 2nd – NZ(1) 30-2 (Wright 4, Crowe 7); 3rd – NZ (2) 37-3 (Crowe 5, Rutherford 4).

NEW ZEALAND v AUSTRALIA 1992-93 (2nd Test)

At Basin Reserve, Wellington, on 4, 5, 6, 7, 8 March.
Toss: Australia.   Result: MATCH DRAWN.
Debuts: None.

Rain reduced the first day to 49 minutes (12.1 overs). Greatbatch and Wright shared a series record opening partnership of 111 in 211 minutes after New Zealand had been put in. Crowe's score was increased from 97 after stumps on the third day when the umpires ruled that a hit for three had crossed the boundary. Morrison's career-best analysis of 7 for 89 was a New Zealand record for this series in home matches. Wright, who twisted his ankle when catching Hughes, batted with a runner in the second innings. His two innings totalled 581 minutes and were chiefly responsible for New Zealand drawing the match. When he reached 42 on the last day he became the second New Zealander after G.M.Turner to score 25,000 first-class runs.

NEW ZEALAND

M.J.Greatbatch	c Taylor b Reiffel	61		b McDermott	0
J.G.Wright	c Healy b Hughes	72	(6)	not out	46
A.H.Jones	b Reiffel	4	(2)	lbw b Warne	42
*M.D.Crowe	b McDermott	98	(3)	lbw b McDermott	3
K.R.Rutherford	c Healy b Hughes	32	(4)	c Healy b Reiffel	11
†T.E.Blain	b Hughes	1	(5)	c Healy b Warne	51
C.L.Cairns	c Border b McDermott	13		lbw b McDermott	14
D.N.Patel	not out	13		c Healy b M.E.Waugh	25
D.K.Morrison	c Warne b McDermott	2		not out	0
W.Watson	c Taylor b Warne	3			
M.B.Owens	b Warne	0			
Extras	(B7, LB11, W2, NB10)	30		(B8, LB8, W1, NB1)	18
Total		**329**		(7 wickets)	**210**

AUSTRALIA

M.A.Taylor	run out	50
D.C.Boon	c and b Morrison	37
J.L.Langer	c Blain b Watson	24
M.E.Waugh	c and b Owens	12
S.R.Waugh	c Blain b Morrison	75
*A.R.Border	lbw b Morrison	30
†I.A.Healy	c Rutherford b Morrison	8
M.G.Hughes	c Wright b Morrison	8
P.R.Reiffel	lbw b Morrison	7
S.K.Warne	c Greatbatch b Morrison	22
C.J.McDermott	not out	7
Extras	(LB14, NB4)	18
Total		**298**

AUSTRALIA	O	M	R	W		O	M	R	W	FALL OF WICKETS			
											NZ	A	NZ
McDermott	31	8	66	3		23	9	54	3	*Wkt*	*1st*	*1st*	*2nd*
Hughes	35	9	100	3		11	5	22	0	1st	111	92	4
Reiffel	23	8	55	2	(4) 16		7	27	1	2nd	120	105	9
S.R.Waugh	15	7	28	0						3rd	191	128	30
Warne	29	9	59	2	(3) 40		25	49	2	4th	287	154	101
M.E.Waugh	2	1	3	0		8	3	12	1	5th	289	229	131
Border					(5) 12		5	15	0	6th	307	237	154
Taylor					(7) 4		2	15	0	7th	308	251	202
Boon					(8) 1		1	0	0	8th	314	258	–
										9th	329	271	–
NEW ZEALAND										10th	329	298	–
Morrison	26.4	5	89	7									
Cairns	24	3	77	0									
Watson	29	12	60	1									
Owens	21	3	54	1									
Patel	1	0	4	0									

Umpires: B.L.Aldridge (16) and R.S.Dunne (10). Referee: Javed Burki (*Pakistan*) (2).

Close: 1st day – NZ(1) 28-0 (Greatbatch 13, Wright 10); 2nd – NZ(1) 237-3 (Crowe 62, Rutherford 14); 3rd – A(1) 107-2 (Langer 8, M.E.Waugh 0); 4th – NZ(2) 40-3 (Jones 20, Blain 2).

NEW ZEALAND v AUSTRALIA 1992-93 (3rd Test)

At Eden Park, Auckland, on 12, 13, 14, 15, 16 March.
Toss: Australia.   Result: NEW ZEALAND won by five wickets.
Debuts: None.

A gradually improving New Zealand team ensured that Australia never recovered from being bowled out for 139 in conditions increasingly favouring swing bowling. Morrison became the eighth bowler to take 100 wickets for New Zealand when he dismissed Healy during his eighth analysis of five or more wickets in 29 Tests. Requiring 201 for the victory which would draw the series and retain the Trans-Tasman Trophy, New Zealand reached their objective after 29 minutes on the fifth day and in front of the largest crowd of the match, close on 10,000 having been granted free entry. In the last of his 82 Test matches, John Wright batted with his customary tenacity for a total of 266 minutes.

AUSTRALIA

D.C.Boon	lbw b Watson	20	(2)	lbw b Su'a	53
M.A.Taylor	lbw b Morrison	13	(1)	st Blain b Patel	3
J.L.Langer	c Blain b Morrison	0		lbw b Patel	0
D.R.Martyn	c Blain b Watson	1		c Greatbatch b Patel	74
S.R.Waugh	c Jones b Watson	41		lbw b Patel	0
*A.R.Border	c Blain b Morrison	0		c Harris b Watson	71
†I.A.Healy	c Jones b Morrison	0		c Blain b Patel	24
M.G.Hughes	c Morrison b Patel	33		not out	31
P.R.Reiffel	c Blain b Morrison	9		b Watson	1
S.K.Warne	not out	3		c Jones b Morrison	2
C.J.McDermott	b Morrison	6		c Wright b Watson	10
Extras	(LB7, NB6)	13		(B1, LB7, NB8)	16
Total		**139**			**285**

NEW ZEALAND

J.G.Wright	c Taylor b McDermott	33	run out	33
M.J.Greatbatch	c Border b Hughes	32	b Hughes	29
A.H.Jones	c Healy b Hughes	20	b Warne	26
*M.D.Crowe	c Taylor b Waugh	31	c Langer b Warne	25
K.R.Rutherford	st Healy b Warne	43	not out	53
C.Z.Harris	c Taylor b Warne	13	lbw b Waugh	0
†T.E.Blain	c Healy b McDermott	15	not out	24
D.N.Patel	c Healy b Warne	2		
M.L.Su'a	c Waugh b Warne	3		
D.K.Morrison	not out	10		
W.Watson	lbw b Hughes	0		
Extras	(B7, LB10, NB5)	22	(LB10, NB1)	11
Total		**224**	(5 wickets)	**201**

NEW ZEALAND	O	M	R	W	O	M	R	W	FALL OF WICKETS			
									A	NZ	A	NZ
Morrison	18.4	5	37	6	33	8	81	1	*Wkt*	*1st*	*1st*	*2nd*	*2nd*
Su'a	14	3	27	0	(4) 18	4	56	1	1st	38	60	5	44
Watson	19	9	47	3	19	5	43	3	2nd	38	91	8	65
Patel	4	0	21	1	(2) 34	10	93	5	3rd	39	97	115	109
Harris					2	1	4	0	4th	39	144	119	129
									5th	43	178	160	134
AUSTRALIA									6th	48	200	225	–
McDermott	19	6	50	2	12	3	38	0	7th	101	205	261	–
Hughes	24.5	6	67	3	15.4	2	54	1	8th	121	206	271	–
Reiffel	22	6	63	0	6	1	19	0	9th	133	224	274	–
Warne	15	12	8	4	27	8	54	2	10th	139	224	285	–
Waugh	14	6	19	1	(6) 6	1	15	1					
Martyn	1	1	0	0									
Border					(5) 6	3	11	0					

Umpires: B.L.Aldridge (17) and C.E.King (2). Referee: Javed Burki (*Pakistan*) (3).

Close: 1st day – A(1) 139-9 (Warne 3, McDermott 6); 2nd – NZ(1) 206-8 (Su'a 0, Morrison 0); 3rd – A(2) 226-6 (Border 61, Hughes 0); 4th – NZ(2) 168-5 (Rutherford 31, Blain 19).

INDIA v ZIMBABWE 1992-93 (Only Test)

At Feroz Shah Kotla, Delhi, on 13, 14, 15, 16, 17 March.
Toss: India.   Result: INDIA won by an innings and 13 runs.
Debuts: India – V.Yadav; Zimbabwe – G.A.Briant, U.Ranchod.

India achieved their fourth successive victory of the season and their third by an innings despite rain allowing only 71 minutes (16.4 overs) of play on the second day. Their third successive total in excess of 500 was built around another remarkable batting display by Kambli (413 minutes, 301 balls, 28 fours), who emulated Hammond (twice) and Bradman by scoring double hundreds in successive innings. Arnott was dismissed by the first ball bowled to a Zimbabwe batsman in a Test overseas. Grant (425 minutes, 359 balls, 8 fours) and Andy Flower (289 minutes, 236 balls, 15 fours) added 192 for the fourth wicket in Zimbabwe's highest partnership to date and came close to emulating the feats of the brothers Chappell (Ian and Greg) and Mohammad (Mushtaq and Sadiq) by each scoring hundreds in the same innings. Kumble's third five-wicket haul took his career tally to 53 wickets in ten Tests, the fewest Tests in which an Indian bowler has reached 50 wickets.

INDIA

M.Prabhakar	c A.Flower b Brain	3
N.S.Sidhu	lbw b Traicos	61
V.G.Kambli	c and b Traicos	227
S.R.Tendulkar	c Traicos b Ranchod	62
*M.Azharuddin	run out	42
P.K.Amre	not out	52
Kapil Dev	st A.Flower b Traicos	16
†V.Yadav	b Brain	30
A.Kumble	not out	18
R.K.Chauhan	} did not bat	
Maninder Singh		
Extras	(B17, LB6, W2)	25
Total	**(7 wickets declared)**	**536**

ZIMBABWE

K.J.Arnott	lbw b Kapil Dev	0	b Maninder	21
G.W.Flower	lbw b Maninder	96	lbw b Prabhakar	0
A.D.R.Campbell	b Chauhan	32	c Amre b Kumble	61
*D.L.Houghton	lbw b Kumble	18	c Amre b Kumble	1
†A.Flower	st Yadav b Maninder	115	not out	62
G.A.Briant	st Yadav b Kumble	1	c Kambli b Maninder	16
A.H.Shah	run out	25	lbw b Kumble	6
E.A.Brandes	c Sidhu b Kumble	8	c Chauhan b Maninder	1
D.H.Brain	c Kambli b Maninder	0	lbw b Kumble	0
U.Ranchod	b Chauhan	7	c Yadav b Maninder	1
A.J.Traicos	not out	0	lbw b Kumble	1
Extras	(B4, LB10, W1, NB5)	20	(B10, LB16, W2, NB3)	31
Total		**322**		**201**

ZIMBABWE	O	M	R	W	O	M	R	W		FALL OF WICKETS			
Brandes	26	4	93	0							I	Z	Z
Brain	34	1	146	2					*Wkt*	*1st*	*1st*	*2nd*
Shah	10	3	43	0					1st	19	0	2
Traicos	50	4	186	3					2nd	126	53	53
Ranchod	12	0	45	1					3rd	263	83	62
									4th	370	275	126
INDIA									5th	434	276	159
Kapil Dev	13	4	37	1	4	1	4	0	6th	464	276	167
Prabhakar	14	4	23	0	4	3	5	1	7th	507	286	176
Chauhan	28.1	4	68	2	14	5	30	0	8th	–	287	177
Kumble	43	12	90	3	38.5	16	70	5	9th	–	318	188
Maninder	32	4	79	3	35	8	66	4	10th	–	322	201
Tendulkar	5	1	11	0								

Umpires: S.K.Bansal (1) and S.Venkataraghavan (3). Referee: Asif Iqbal (*Pakistan*) (1).

Close: 1st day – I(1) 340-3 (Kambli 176, Azharuddin 29); 2nd – I(1) 411-4 (Kambli 207, Amre 12); 3rd – Z(1) 152-3 (G.W.Flower 47, A.Flower 46); 4th – Z(2) 62-2 (Campbell 31, Houghton 1).

SRI LANKA v ENGLAND 1992-93 (Only Test)

At Sinhalese Sports Club Ground, Colombo, on 13, 14, 15, 17, 18 March.
Toss: England.   Result: SRI LANKA won by five wickets.
Debuts: Sri Lanka – A.M.de Silva.

England's nightmare winter ended in their first defeat by Sri Lanka, who gained successive Test victories for the first time when Jayasuriya pulled his first ball for six. Opening England's innings for the third time, Smith (446 minutes, 338 balls, 20 fours) scored his eighth hundred in 73 innings and his first overseas. Tillekeratne (280 minutes, 208 balls) reached 93 for the second time in Tests and shared in a record Sri Lankan ninth-wicket stand of 83 with Muralitharan.

ENGLAND

R.A.Smith	b Muralitharan	128	b Jayasuriya		35
M.A.Atherton	lbw b Ramanayake	13	c Tillekeratne b Gurusinha		2
M.W.Gatting	c Jayasuriya b Muralitharan	29	c Tillekeratne b Warnaweera		18
G.A.Hick	c Tillekeratne b Muralitharan	68	c Ramanayake b Warnaweera		26
†A.J.Stewart	c Tillekeratne b Warnaweera	63	c Mahanama b Warnaweera		3
N.H.Fairbrother	b Warnaweera	18	run out		3
C.C.Lewis	run out	22	c Jayasuriya b Muralitharan		45
J.E.Emburey	not out	1	b Gurusinha		59
P.W.Jarvis	lbw b Warnaweera	0	st A.M.de Silva b Jayasuriya		3
P.C.R.Tufnell	lbw b Muralitharan	1	c A.M.de Silva b Warnaweera		1
D.E.Malcolm	c Gurusinha b Warnaweera	13	not out		8
Extras	(B5, LB3, W1, NB15)	24	(B4, LB2, W1, NB18)		25
Total		**380**			**228**

SRI LANKA

R.S.Mahanama	c Smith b Emburey	64	c Stewart b Lewis		6
U.C.Hathurusinghe	c Stewart b Lewis	59	c Stewart b Tufnell		14
A.P.Gurusinha	st Stewart b Tufnell	43	b Emburey		29
P.A.de Silva	c Stewart b Jarvis	80	c Jarvis b Emburey		7
*A.Ranatunga	c Stewart b Lewis	64	c Gatting b Tufnell		35
H.P.Tillekeratne	not out	93	not out		36
S.T.Jayasuriya	c Atherton b Lewis	4	not out		6
†A.M.de Silva	c Gatting b Emburey	9			
C.P.H.Ramanayake	c Lewis b Jarvis	1			
M.Muralitharan	b Lewis	19			
K.P.J.Warnaweera	b Jarvis	1			
Extras	(B2, LB13, W2, NB15)	32	(B1, LB2, NB6)		9
Total		**469**	(5 wickets)		**142**

SRI LANKA	O	M	R	W	O	M	R	W
Ramanayake	17	2	66	1	3	0	16	0
Gurusinha	5	1	12	0	6	3	7	2
Warnaweera	40.1	11	90	4	25	4	98	4
Hathurusinghe	8	2	22	0				
Muralitharan	45	12	118	4	(4) 16	3	55	1
Jayasuriya	12	1	53	0	(5) 16	3	46	2
Ranatunga	3	0	11	0				
ENGLAND								
Malcolm	25	7	60	0	(3) 3	1	11	0
Jarvis	25.5	1	76	3	8	2	14	0
Lewis	31	5	66	4	(1) 8	1	21	1
Tufnell	33	5	108	1	(5) 7.4	1	34	2
Emburey	34	6	117	2	(4) 14	2	48	2
Hick	8	0	27	0	2	0	11	0

FALL OF WICKETS

	E	SL	E	SL
Wkt	1st	1st	2nd	2nd
1st	40	99	16	8
2nd	82	153	38	48
3rd	194	203	83	61
4th	316	330	91	61
5th	323	339	96	136
6th	358	349	130	–
7th	366	371	153	–
8th	366	376	173	–
9th	367	459	188	–
10th	380	469	228	–

Umpires: K.T.Francis (8) and T.M.Samarasinghe (4). Referee: C.W.Smith (*West Indies*) (4).

Close: 1st day – E(1) 245-3 (Smith 91, Stewart 26); 2nd – SL(1) 140-1 (Hathurusinghe 53, Gurusinha 12); 3rd – SL(1) 408-8 (Tillekeratne 51, Muralitharan 7); 4th – E(2) 226-9 (Emburey 57, Malcolm 8).

WEST INDIES v PAKISTAN 1992-93 (1st Test)

At Queen's Park Oval, Port-of-Spain, Trinidad, on 16, 17, 18 April.
Toss: West Indies.   Result: WEST INDIES won by 204 runs.
Debuts: Pakistan – Basit Ali.

The start of this match was postponed a day to allow the tourists to recover from the trauma of four of their players, including the captain and vice-captain, being arrested and charged with 'constructive possession' of marijuana. They recovered sufficiently to dismiss West Indies for their lowest home total in this series as a remarkable opening day to this three-match rubber produced 17 wickets. Aggressive bowling by Ambrose and Bishop, who recorded his fifth five-wicket analysis in 17 Tests, restricted Pakistan's lead to 13. Haynes (459 minutes, 288 balls, 20 fours) became the first to carry his bat through a completed Test innings on three occasions and the fifth to score 7,000 runs for West Indies. His partnership of 169 with Lara (96 off 135 balls) set a third-wicket record for West Indies in this series. Hooper's off-spin returned its best analysis in 37 Tests as Pakistan failed to take the contest beyond a third day on which another 17 wickets fell. Umpires Bucknor (12) and Bird (5) upheld a record total of 17 lbw appeals in this Test, a tribute to the pitch's exceptionally low bounce on the first and third days.

WEST INDIES

D.L.Haynes	c Moin b Rehman	31		not out	143
P.V.Simmons	c Moin b Rehman	27		c Asif b Aamir	22
*R.B.Richardson	b Mushtaq	7		c Wasim b Waqar	68
B.C.Lara	c Aamir b Waqar	6		b Asif	96
K.L.T.Arthurton	run out	3	(6)	lbw b Wasim	1
C.L.Hooper	lbw b Waqar	9	(7)	lbw b Waqar	0
†J.R.Murray	lbw b Waqar	0	(8)	lbw b Waqar	0
I.R.Bishop	c Inzamam b Rehman	4	(5)	c Moin b Wasim	3
C.E.L.Ambrose	lbw b Wasim	4		lbw b Wasim	5
A.C.Cummins	not out	14		lbw b Wasim	0
C.A.Walsh	b Wasim	0		run out	6
Extras	(B6, LB3, W2, NB11)	22		(B1, LB18, W2, NB17)	38
Total		**127**			**382**

PAKISTAN

Aamir Sohail	c Hooper b Bishop	55	lbw b Walsh	15
Ramiz Raja	lbw b Bishop	9	lbw b Ambrose	11
Inzamam-ul-Haq	lbw b Walsh	10	lbw b Walsh	6
Javed Miandad	lbw b Ambrose	20	c Murray b Bishop	4
Basit Ali	lbw b Bishop	0	c Richardson b Hooper	37
Asif Mujtaba	c Lara b Bishop	10	lbw b Hooper	20
*Wasim Akram	c Richardson b Ambrose	2	st Murray b Hooper	4
†Moin Khan	c Murray b Ambrose	0	c Bishop b Hooper	18
Waqar Younis	c Lara b Ambrose	16	lbw b Walsh	1
Mushtaq Ahmed	c Hooper b Bishop	3	not out	12
Ata-ur-Rehman	not out	3	c Ambrose b Hooper	19
Extras	(LB6, NB6)	12	(LB10, NB8)	18
Total		**140**		**165**

PAKISTAN	O	M	R	W	O	M	R	W		FALL OF WICKETS			
										WI	P	WI	P
Wasim	10.2	2	32	2	27	6	75	4	*Wkt*	*1st*	*1st*	*2nd*	*2nd*
Waqar	11	3	37	3	23	2	88	3	1st	63	17	57	17
Mushtaq	8	1	21	1	(4) 13	1	45	0	2nd	76	52	160	34
Rehman	9	1	28	3	(3) 19	0	82	0	3rd	85	100	329	41
Aamir					5	1	30	1	4th	85	100	342	42
Asif					10	1	43	1	5th	95	102	356	109
									6th	95	104	358	111
WEST INDIES									7th	102	108	358	114
Ambrose	17	6	34	4	13	3	37	1	8th	102	120	371	127
Bishop	15.5	6	43	5	11	2	28	1	9th	127	136	371	134
Walsh	7	4	13	1	12	3	29	3	10th	127	140	382	165
Cummins	5	0	19	0	5	1	16	0					
Hooper	4	0	25	0	11.5	3	40	5					
Simmons					1	0	5	0					

Umpires: H.D.Bird (*England*) (51) and S.A.Bucknor (8). Referee: R.Subba Row (*England*) (4).

Close: 1st day – P(1) 113-7 (Asif 8, Waqar 1); 2nd – WI(2) 333-3 (Haynes 115, Bishop 1).

WEST INDIES v PAKISTAN 1992-93 (2nd Test)

At Kensington Oval, Bridgetown, Barbados, on 23, 24, 25, 27 April.
Toss: Pakistan.   Result: WEST INDIES won by ten wickets.
Debuts: Pakistan – Aamir Nazir.

West Indies clinched this mini series in four days with their twelfth successive victory in Bridgetown. Pakistan chose to bowl on a hard pitch with patches of grass on a fast bowler's length at each end. Simmons, reprieved by being dropped twice in Waqar's second over, scored 87 off 90 balls. Haynes (351 minutes, 206 balls, two sixes and 14 fours) scored the last of his 18 hundreds to date. Basit Ali (228 minutes, 174 balls, a six and 11 fours) played an outstanding innings against a formidable attack. Miandad was caught off the penultimate ball of the third day attempting a second successive six. In his 58th Test, Walsh became the seventh West Indian to take 200 wickets. Aamir Nazir's only previous first-class match had been on this tour.

WEST INDIES

D.L.Haynes	b Aamir Nazir	125	not out	16
P.V.Simmons	c Moin b Rehman	87	not out	8
R.B.Richardson	lbw b Waqar	31		
B.C.Lara	c Moin b Rehman	51		
K.L.T.Arthurton	b Wasim	56		
C.L.Hooper	c Moin b Waqar	15		
J.R.Murray	st Moin b Aamir Sohail	35		
I.R.Bishop	c Moin b Aamir Nazir	11		
C.E.L.Ambrose	not out	12		
W.K.M.Benjamin	b Waqar	0		
C.A.Walsh	c and b Waqar	3		
Extras	(B1, LB1, W2, NB25)	29	(W3, NB2)	5
Total		**455**	(0 wickets)	**29**

PAKISTAN

Aamir Sohail	c Murray b Ambrose	10		c Benjamin b Ambrose	4
Ramiz Raja	c Haynes b Ambrose	37		lbw b Walsh	25
Asif Mujtaba	c Richardson b Walsh	13		lbw b Benjamin	41
Javed Miandad	c Richardson b Benjamin	22		c Arthurton b Hooper	43
Inzamam-ul-Haq	lbw b Bishop	7	(7)	lbw b Benjamin	26
Basit Ali	not out	92		lbw b Walsh	37
Wasim Akram	c Simmons b Hooper	29	(8)	b Benjamin	0
Moin Khan	c Murray b Walsh	0	(5)	c Murray b Hooper	17
Waqar Younis	c Murray b Walsh	0		c Lara b Hooper	29
Ata-ur-Rehman	c Benjamin b Walsh	0		c Simmons b Walsh	13
Aamir Nazir	c Arthurton b Benjamin	1		not out	6
Extras	(LB3, NB7)	10		(B12, LB5, NB4)	21
Total		**221**			**262**

PAKISTAN	O	M	R	W		O	M	R	W	FALL OF WICKETS				
Wasim	32	2	95	1		2.3	0	18	0		WI	P	P	WI
Waqar	25.5	3	132	4						Wkt	1st	1st	2nd	2nd
Aamir Nazir	20	1	79	2	(2)	2	0	11	0	1st	122	12	4	–
Rehman	21	1	103	2						2nd	200	31	47	–
Asif	3	0	30	0						3rd	303	62	113	–
Aamir Sohail	4	1	14	1						4th	337	79	133	–
										5th	363	109	141	–
WEST INDIES										6th	426	189	207	–
Ambrose	16	5	42	2		26	10	55	1	7th	440	190	207	–
Bishop	16	5	43	1		4	1	13	0	8th	440	190	215	–
Walsh	18	2	56	4	(4)	24	7	51	3	9th	445	200	238	–
Benjamin	19	5	55	2	(3)	17	7	30	3	10th	455	221	262	–
Hooper	7	0	22	1		32.3	6	96	3					

Umpires: L.H.Barker (18) and H.D.Bird (*England*) (52). Referee: R.Subba Row (*England*) (5).

Close: 1st day – WI(1) 351-4 (Arthurton 19, Hooper 11); 2nd – P(1) 131-5 (Basit 33, Wasim 3); 3rd – P(2) 113-3 (Asif 36, Moin 0).

WEST INDIES v PAKISTAN 1992-93 (3rd Test)

At Recreation Ground, St John's, Antigua, on 1, 2, 4, 5, 6 (*no play*) May.
Toss: West Indies.   Result: MATCH DRAWN.
Debuts: Pakistan – Nadeem Khan, Shakil Ahmed.

Rain reduced this match by more than five sessions, the final day being abandoned after an overnight downpour. Hooper's exhilarating and chanceless innings (293 minutes, 247 balls, four sixes and 19 fours) was his fourth hundred in Tests but his first in 23 innings in the Caribbean. He manoeuvred his tenth-wicket partnership of 106 in 103 minutes with Walsh, a West Indies record against all countries, so successfully that Walsh faced only 31 balls in 23 overs. Waqar took five wickets for the twelfth time in 23 Tests. Inzamam (314 minutes, 225 balls, a six and 11 fours) scored his first Test hundred in his 13th innings. Clancy Mack deputised for umpire Bird (bruised back) on the fourth afternoon.

WEST INDIES

D.L.Haynes	c Rashid b Nadeem	23	not out	64
P.V.Simons	c Wasim b Rehman	28	b Waqar	17
*R.B.Richardson	c Wasim b Waqar	52	lbw b Waqar	0
B.C.Lara	st Rashid b Nadeem	44	lbw b Waqar	19
K.L.T.Arthurton	lbw b Waqar	30	lbw b Waqar	0
C.L.Hooper	not out	178	not out	29
†J.R.Murray	lbw b Waqar	4		
C.E.L.Ambrose	lbw b Wasim	1		
A.C.Cummins	lbw b Waqar	14		
W.K.M.Benjamin	c Wasim b Waqar	12		
C.A.Walsh	c Asif b Wasim	30		
Extras	(LB6, NB16)	22	(B8, LB5, NB11)	24
Total		**438**	(4 wickets)	**153**

PAKISTAN

Shakil Ahmed	lbw b Ambrose	0
Ramiz Raja	c Murray b Walsh	0
Asif Mujtaba	c Haynes b Hooper	59
Javed Miandad	lbw b Benjamin	31
Basit Ali	b Cummins	56
Inzamam-ul-Haq	c Haynes b Cummins	123
†Rashid Latif	lbw b Cummins	2
*Wasim Akram	c Hooper b Benjamin	9
Waqar Younis	c Hooper b Benjamin	4
Nadeem Khan	c Murray b Cummins	25
Ata-ur-Rehman	not out	1
Extras	(LB6, NB10)	16
Total		**326**

PAKISTAN	O	M	R	W		O	M	R	W		FALL OF WICKETS		
											WI	P	WI
Wasim	26.2	5	108	2		10	2	30	0	*Wkt*	*1st*	*1st*	*2nd*
Waqar	28	4	104	5	(4)	11	1	23	4	1st	35	0	36
Rehman	17	1	66	1	(2)	9	1	24	0	2nd	77	4	36
Nadeem	38	5	147	2	(3)	14	0	48	0	3rd	153	85	68
Asif	1	0	7	0		4	1	9	0	4th	159	108	68
Basit						1	0	6	0	5th	218	196	–
										6th	241	206	–
WEST INDIES										7th	252	221	–
Ambrose	23	9	40	1						8th	312	227	–
Walsh	19	3	58	1						9th	332	323	–
Benjamin	20	4	53	3						10th	438	326	–
Cummins	20	4	54	4									
Hooper	28	2	98	1									
Simmons	5	0	17	0									

Umpires: H.D.Bird (*England*) (53) and S.A.Bucknor (9). Referee: R.Subba Row (*England*) (6).

Close: 1st day – WI(1) 344-9 (Hooper 116, Walsh 0); 2nd – P(1) 85-3 (Asif 50, Basit 0); 3rd – P(1) 326 all out; 4th – WI(2) 153-4 (Haynes 64, Hooper 29).

ENGLAND v AUSTRALIA 1993 (1st Test)

At Old Trafford, Manchester, on 3, 4, 5, 6, 7 June.
Toss: England.   Result: AUSTRALIA won by 179 runs.
Debuts: England – A.R.Caddick, P.M.Such; Australia – B.P.Julian, M.J.Slater.

Australia's victory with 9.4 overs to spare condemned England to their sixth successive defeat in a sequence involving four countries. Taylor (323 minutes, 234 balls, two sixes and 12 fours) defied a damp pitch to record his ninth Test hundred. Such returned the best analysis by an England bowler on debut in this series since F.Martin took 6 for 50 and 6 for 52 in 1890 (*Test No. 34*). Warne's first ball in an Ashes Test was an unplayable leg-break, subsequently dubbed 'the ball from hell', which pitched outside Gatting's legs and hit the top of his off stump. Border became the third fielder after G.S.Chappell and I.T.Botham to hold 50 catches in this series. Healy (164 minutes, 133 balls, 12 fours) became the fifth to complete his maiden first-class hundred in a Test for Australia. Gooch (307 minutes, 247 balls, two sixes and 21 fours) completed his 18th hundred, but only his third against Australia, before becoming the fifth batsman to be out 'handled the ball' in Test cricket. Having played the ball down into his crease, he fended it away with his right glove when it bounced up and was about to fall on his stumps.

AUSTRALIA

M.A.Taylor	c and b Such	124	(2)	lbw b Such	9
M.J.Slater	c Stewart b DeFreitas	58	(1)	c Caddick b Such	27
D.C.Boon	c Lewis b Such	21		c Gatting b DeFreitas	93
M.E.Waugh	c and b Tufnell	6		b Tufnell	64
*A.R.Border	st Stewart b Such	17		c and b Caddick	31
S.R.Waugh	b Such	3		not out	78
†I.A.Healy	c Such b Tufnell	12		not out	102
B.P.Julian	c Gatting b Such	0			
M.G.Hughes	c DeFreitas b Such	2			
S.K.Warne	not out	15			
C.J.McDermott	run out	8			
Extras	(B8, LB8, NB7)	23		(B6, LB14, NB8)	28
Total		**289**		(5 wickets declared)	**432**

ENGLAND

*G.A.Gooch	c Julian b Warne	65	handled the ball	133
M.A.Atherton	c Healy b Hughes	19	c Taylor b Warne	25
M.W.Gatting	b Warne	4	b Hughes	23
R.A.Smith	c Taylor b Warne	4	b Warne	18
G.A.Hick	c Border b Hughes	34	c Healy b Hughes	22
†A.J.Stewart	b Julian	27	c Healy b Warne	11
C.C.Lewis	c Boon b Hughes	9	c Taylor b Warne	43
P.A.J.DeFreitas	lbw b Julian	5	lbw b Julian	7
A.R.Caddick	c Healy b Warne	7	c Warne b Hughes	25
P.M.Such	not out	14	c Border b Hughes	9
P.C.R.Tufnell	c Healy b Hughes	1	not out	0
Extras	(B6, LB10, NB5)	21	(LB11, W1, NB4)	16
Total		**210**		**332**

ENGLAND	O	M	R	W		O	M	R	W		FALL OF WICKETS			
Caddick	15	4	38	0		20	3	79	1		A	E	A	E
DeFreitas	23	8	46	1		24	1	80	1	*Wkt*	*1st*	*1st*	*2nd*	*2nd*
Lewis	13	2	44	0	(6)	9	0	43	0	1st	128	71	23	73
Such	33.3	9	67	6	(3)	31	6	78	2	2nd	183	80	46	133
Tufnell	28	5	78	2	(4)	37	4	112	1	3rd	221	84	155	171
Hick					(5)	9	1	20	0	4th	225	123	234	223
										5th	232	148	252	230
										6th	260	168	–	238
AUSTRALIA										7th	264	178	–	260
McDermott	18	2	50	0		30	9	76	0	8th	266	183	–	299
Hughes	20.5	5	59	4		27.2	4	92	4	9th	267	203	–	331
Julian	11	2	30	2	(4)	14	1	67	1	10th	289	210	–	332
Warne	24	10	51	4	(3)	49	26	86	4					
Border	1	0	4	0										

Umpires: H.D.Bird (54) and K.E.Palmer (21). Referee: Nawab of Pataudi, jr (*India*) (1).

Close: 1st day – A(1) 242-5 (Border 9, Healy 6); 2nd – E(1) 202-8 (Caddick 6, Such 9); 3rd – A(2) 231-3 (Boon 85, Border 29); 4th – E(2) 133-2 (Gooch 82).

ENGLAND v AUSTRALIA 1993 (2nd Test)

At Lord's, London, on 17, 18, 19, 20, 21 June.
Toss: Australia.   Result: AUSTRALIA won by an innings and 62 runs.
Debuts: None.

Capitalising on their highest total against England since 1964 and their second highest at Lord's, Australia extended their hosts' run of defeats to seven, three of them by an innings. For the fifth time in Tests, the first three batsmen in the order scored hundreds: Taylor 111 (322 minutes, 245 balls, a six and 10 fours, his tenth hundred in 77 innings); Slater 152 (293 minutes, 263 balls, 18 fours, his first in three innings); Boon 164 not out (471 minutes, 378 balls, 15 fours, his 15th in 138 innings and his first in England). Taylor completed 1,000 runs in eight Tests in England and with Slater shared a partnership of 260, the second highest opening stand in this series and the record for any wicket by either country in Ashes Tests at Lord's. Border extended his Test batting record at Lord's to 503 runs, average 100.60. Smith completed 3,000 runs in 78 innings and, in the first innings, became the first to be adjudged out on the evidence of a television replay in a Test in England.

AUSTRALIA

M.A.Taylor	st Stewart b Tufnell	111	
M.J.Slater	c sub (B.F.Smith) b Lewis	152	
D.C.Boon	not out	164	
M.E.Waugh	b Tufnell	99	
*A.R.Border	b Lewis	77	
S.R.Waugh	not out	13	
†I.A.Healy			
M.G.Hughes			
S.K.Warne	did not bat		
T.B.A.May			
C.J.McDermott			
Extras	(LB1, W1, NB14)	16	
Total	**(4 wickets declared)**	**632**	

ENGLAND

*G.A.Gooch	c May b Hughes	12	c Healy b Warne	29	
M.A.Atherton	b Warne	80	run out	99	
M.W.Gatting	b May	5	lbw b Warne	59	
R.A.Smith	st Healy b May	22	c sub (M.L.Hayden) b May	5	
G.A.Hick	c Healy b Hughes	20	c Taylor b May	64	
†A.J.Stewart	lbw b Hughes	3	lbw b May	62	
C.C.Lewis	lbw b Warne	0	st Healy b May	0	
N.A.Foster	c Border b Warne	16	c M.E.Waugh b Border	20	
A.R.Caddick	c Healy b Hughes	21	not out	0	
P.M.Such	c Taylor b Warne	7	b Warne	4	
P.C.R.Tufnell	not out	2	b Warne	0	
Extras	(LB8, NB9)	17	(B10, LB13)	23	
Total		**205**		**365**	

ENGLAND	O	M	R	W	O	M	R	W	FALL OF WICKETS		
										A	E	E
Caddick	38	5	120	0					Wkt	1st	1st	2nd
Foster	30	4	94	0					1st	260	33	71
Such	36	6	90	0					2nd	277	50	175
Tufnell	39	3	129	2					3rd	452	84	180
Lewis	36	5	151	2					4th	591	123	244
Gooch	9	1	26	0					5th	–	131	304
Hick	8	3	21	0					6th	–	132	312
									7th	–	167	361
AUSTRALIA									8th	–	174	361
Hughes	20	5	52	4	31	9	75	0	9th	–	189	365
M.E.Waugh	6	1	16	0	17	4	55	0	10th	–	205	365
S.R.Waugh	4	1	5	0	(4) 2	0	13	0				
May	31	12	64	2	(3) 51	23	81	4				
Warne	35	12	57	4	48.5	17	102	4				
Border	3	1	3	0	16	9	16	1				

Umpires: M.J.Kitchen (6) and D.R.Shepherd (18). Referee: Nawab of Pataudi, jr (*India*) (2).

Close: 1st day – A(1) 292-2 (Boon 11, M.E.Waugh 6); 2nd – A(1) 592-4 (Boon 138, S.R.Waugh 0); 3rd – E(1) 193-9 (Caddick 11, Tufnell 0); 4th – E(2) 237-3 (Gatting 58, Hick 30).

ENGLAND v AUSTRALIA 1993 (3rd Test)

At Trent Bridge, Nottingham, on 1, 2, 3, 5, 6 July.
Toss: England.   Result: MATCH DRAWN.
Debuts: England – M.C.Ilott, M.N.Lathwell, M.J.McCague, G.P.Thorpe.

Introducing four debutants, England ended their seven-match run of defeats. Warne took his 50th wicket in 13 Tests when he dismissed Hussain. McCague and Ilott were the first newly capped pair to open England's bowling since 1961-62 (A.Brown and D.W.White at Lahore in *Test No. 512*). Boon (259 minutes, 177 balls, 17 fours) scored his 16th Test hundred and his second in successive innings. Gooch (325 minutes, 265 balls, a six and 18 fours) made his 19th Test hundred in 189 innings, became the third to score 8,000 runs for England and the tenth to score 2,000 runs for England against Australia. Thorpe (335 minutes, 280 balls, 11 fours) became the 14th to score a hundred on debut for England, the first since F.C.Hayes in 1973 and the sixth to do so in a Test against Australia. England's first declaration for eleven matches set Australia 371 runs in a minimum of 77 overs. Steve Waugh took 63 minutes to advance his score from 27.

ENGLAND

M.N.Lathwell	c Healy b Hughes	20		lbw b Warne	33
M.A.Atherton	c Boon b Warne	11		c Healy b Hughes	9
R.A.Smith	c and b Julian	86		c Healy b Warne	50
†A.J.Stewart	c M.E.Waugh b Warne	25		lbw b Hughes	6
*G.A.Gooch	c Border b Hughes	38		c Taylor b Warne	120
G.P.Thorpe	c S.R.Waugh b Hughes	6	(7)	not out	114
N.Hussain	c Boon b Warne	71	(8)	not out	47
A.R.Caddick	lbw b Hughes	15	(6)	c Boon b Julian	12
M.J.McCague	c M.E.Waugh b Hughes	9			
M.C.Ilott	c Taylor b May	6			
P.M.Such	not out	0			
Extras	(B5, LB23, W4, NB2)	34		(B11, LB11, NB9)	31
Total		**321**		(6 wickets declared)	**422**

AUSTRALIA

M.J.Slater	lbw b Caddick	40	(2)	b Such	26
M.A.Taylor	c Stewart b McCague	28	(1)	c Atherton b Such	28
D.C.Boon	b McCague	101		c Stewart b Caddick	18
M.E.Waugh	c McCague b Such	70		b Caddick	1
S.R.Waugh	c Stewart b McCague	13	(6)	not out	47
†I.A.Healy	c Thorpe b Ilott	9	(7)	lbw b Ilott	5
B.P.Julian	c Stewart b Ilott	5	(8)	not out	56
*A.R.Border	c Smith b Such	38	(5)	c Thorpe b Caddick	2
M.G.Hughes	b Ilott	17			
S.K.Warne	not out	35			
T.B.A.May	lbw b McCague	1			
Extras	(B4, LB8, W4)	16		(B5, LB5, W4, NB5)	19
Total		**373**		(6 wickets)	**202**

AUSTRALIA	O	M	R	W		O	M	R	W		FALL OF WICKETS			
Hughes	31	7	92	5		22	8	41	2			E	A	E	A
Julian	24	3	84	1		33	10	110	1		*Wkt*	*1st*	*1st*	*2nd*	*2nd*
Warne	40	17	74	3	(4)	50	21	108	3		1st	28	55	11	46
May	14.4	7	31	1	(3)	38	6	112	0		2nd	63	74	100	74
S.R.Waugh	8	4	12	0		1	0	3	0		3rd	153	197	109	75
M.E.Waugh	1	1	0	0	(7)	6	3	15	0		4th	159	239	117	81
Border					(6)	5	0	11	0		5th	174	250	159	93
											6th	220	262	309	115
ENGLAND											7th	290	284	–	–
McCague	32.3	5	121	4		19	6	58	0		8th	304	311	–	–
Ilott	34	8	108	3		18	5	44	1		9th	321	356	–	–
Such	20	7	51	2		23	6	58	2		10th	321	373	–	–
Caddick	22	5	81	1		16	6	32	3						

Umpires: B.J.Meyer (25) and R.Palmer (2). Referee: C.H.Lloyd (*West Indies*) (3).

Close: 1st day – E(1) 276-6 (Hussain 50, Caddick 10); 2nd – A(1) 262-5 (Boon 88, Julian 5); 3rd – E(2) 122-4 (Gooch 12, Caddick 0); 4th – E(2) 362-6 (Thorpe 88, Hussain 16).

ENGLAND v AUSTRALIA 1993 (4th Test)

At Headingley, Leeds, on 22, 23, 24, 25, 26 July.
Toss: Australia.   Result: AUSTRALIA won by an innings and 148 runs.
Debuts: England – M.P.Bicknell.

At 2.23 on the fifth afternoon, Australia completed their second innings victory of the summer and retained the Ashes. Gooch immediately resigned the England captaincy after 34 matches (10 wins, 12 defeats) in which he scored 3,582 runs, an England record. Boon (312 minutes, 225 balls, 17 fours) scored his 50th first-class hundred, completed 500 runs in this rubber and 1,000 in the series, and became the first Australian to score hundreds in three successive Ashes Tests since Bradman in 1938. Border (569 minutes, 399 balls, 26 fours) and Steve Waugh (409 minutes, 305 balls, 19 fours) added 332 (unbroken) to register the second highest fifth-wicket partnership in Test cricket and take Australia to the highest total in any first-class match at Headingley. Border's second Test double hundred was the highest, and last, of his eight hundreds against England. In his 49th Test, Hughes became the seventh bowler to take 200 wickets for Australia.

AUSTRALIA

M.J.Slater	b Ilott	67
M.A.Taylor	lbw b Bicknell	27
D.C.Boon	lbw b Ilott	107
M.E.Waugh	b Ilott	52
*A.R.Border	not out	200
S.R.Waugh	not out	157
†I.A.Healy		
M.G.Hughes		
P.R.Reiffel	} did not bat	
S.K.Warne		
T.B.A.May		
Extras	(B8, LB22, W4, NB9)	43
Total	(4 wickets declared)	**653**

ENGLAND

M.N.Lathwell	c Healy b Hughes	0	b May	25
M.A.Atherton	b Reiffel	55	st Healy b May	63
R.A.Smith	c and b May	23	lbw b Reiffel	35
†A.J.Stewart	c Slater b Reiffel	5	c M.E.Waugh b Reiffel	78
*G.A.Gooch	lbw b Reiffel	59	st Healy b May	26
G.P.Thorpe	c Healy b Reiffel	0	c Taylor b Reiffel	13
N.Hussain	b Reiffel	15	not out	18
A.R.Caddick	c M.E.Waugh b Hughes	9	lbw b Hughes	12
M.P.Bicknell	c Border b Hughes	12	lbw b Hughes	0
M.J.McCague	c Taylor b Warne	0	b Hughes	11
M.C.Ilott	not out	0	c Border b May	4
Extras	(B2, LB3, NB17)	22	(B5, LB3, W1, NB11)	20
Total		**200**		**305**

ENGLAND	O	M	R	W	O	M	R	W	FALL OF WICKETS		
									A	E	E
McCague	28	2	115	0					*Wkt*	*1st*	*1st*	*2nd*
Ilott	51	11	161	3					1st	86	0	60
Caddick	42	5	138	0					2nd	110	43	131
Bicknell	50	8	155	1					3rd	216	50	149
Gooch	16	5	40	0					4th	321	158	202
Thorpe	6	1	14	0					5th	–	158	256
									6th	–	169	263
AUSTRALIA									7th	–	184	279
Hughes	15.5	3	47	3	30	10	79	3	8th	–	195	279
Reiffel	26	6	65	5	28	8	87	3	9th	–	200	295
May	15	3	33	1	(4) 27	6	65	4	10th	–	200	305
Warne	23	9	43	1	(3) 40	16	63	0				
M.E.Waugh	3	0	7	0	2	1	3	0				

Umpires: H.D.Bird (55) and N.T.Plews (6). Referee: C.H.Lloyd (*West Indies*) (4).

Close: 1st day – A(1) 307-3 (Boon 102, Border 38); 2nd – A(1) 613-4 (Border 175, S.R.Waugh 144); 3rd – E(1) 195-7 (Caddick 9, Bicknell 7); 4th – E(2) 237-4 (Stewart 59, Thorpe 10).

ENGLAND v AUSTRALIA 1993 (5th Test)

At Edgbaston, Birmingham, on 5, 6, 7, 8, 9 August.
Toss: England.   Result: AUSTRALIA won by eight wickets.
Debuts: None.

Atherton, England's 71st captain, contributed England's highest score of the match but could not avert the fourth defeat of this rubber. Reiffel was the first Australian to take six wickets in a Test innings at Edgbaston. Mark Waugh (240 minutes, 219 balls, 18 fours) scored his fourth hundred in 41 Test innings. It was Australia's tenth hundred of the rubber, their record in England. In his 146th match, Border became the first to play 250 Test innings. Warne's first five-wicket analysis against England took his total of wickets in the rubber to 29, equalling Australia's record by a leg-break bowler in England set by C.V.Grimmett in 1930.

ENGLAND

G.A.Gooch	c Taylor b Reiffel	8	b Warne	48
*M.A.Atherton	b Reiffel	72	c Border b Warne	28
R.A.Smith	b M.E.Waugh	21	lbw b Warne	19
M.P.Maynard	c S.R.Waugh b May	0	c Healy b May	10
†A.J.Stewart	c and b Warne	45	lbw b Warne	5
G.P.Thorpe	c Healy b May	37	st Healy b Warne	60
N.Hussain	b Reiffel	3	c S.R.Waugh b May	0
J.E.Emburey	not out	55	c Healy b May	37
M.P.Bicknell	c M.E.Waugh b Reiffel	14	c S.R.Waugh b May	0
P.M.Such	b Reiffel	1	not out	7
M.C.Ilott	c Healy b Reiffel	3	b May	15
Extras	(B4, LB6, NB7)	17	(B11, LB9, NB2)	22
Total		276		251

AUSTRALIA

M.A.Taylor	run out	19	(2) c Thorpe b Such	4
M.J.Slater	c Smith b Such	22	(1) c Thorpe b Emburey	8
D.C.Boon	lbw b Emburey	0	not out	38
M.E.Waugh	c Thorpe b Ilott	137	not out	62
*A.R.Border	c Hussain b Such	3		
S.R.Waugh	c Stewart b Bicknell	59		
†I.A.Healy	c Stewart b Bicknell	80		
M.G.Hughes	b Bicknell	38		
P.R.Reiffel	b Such	20		
S.K.Warne	c Stewart b Emburey	10		
T.B.A.May	not out	3		
Extras	(B7, LB8, NB2)	17	(B3, LB5)	8
Total		408	(2 wickets)	120

AUSTRALIA	O	M	R	W		O	M	R	W	FALL OF WICKETS			
											E	A	E	A
Hughes	19	4	53	0		18	7	24	0					
Reiffel	22.5	3	71	6		11	2	30	0	Wkt	1st	1st	2nd	2nd
M.E.Waugh	15	5	43	1	(6)	5	2	5	0	1st	17	34	60	12
S.R.Waugh	5	2	4	0						2nd	71	39	104	12
May	19	9	32	2	(3)	48.2	15	89	5	3rd	76	69	115	–
Warne	21	7	63	1	(4)	49	23	82	5	4th	156	80	115	–
Border					(5)	2	1	1	0	5th	156	233	124	–
										6th	160	263	125	–
ENGLAND										7th	215	370	229	–
Bicknell	34	9	99	3		3	0	9	0	8th	262	379	229	–
Ilott	24	4	85	1	(4)	2	0	14	0	9th	264	398	229	–
Such	52.5	18	90	3	(2)	20.3	4	58	1	10th	276	408	251	–
Emburey	39	9	119	2	(3)	18	4	31	1					

Umpires: J.H.Hampshire (11) and D.R.Shepherd (19). Referee: C.H.Lloyd (*West Indies*) (5).

Close: 1st day – E(1) 276-9 (Emburey 55, Ilott 3); 2nd – A(1) 258-5 (S.R.Waugh 57, Healy 12); 3rd – E(2) 89-1 (Gooch 44, Smith 7); 4th – A(2) 9-0 (Slater 7, Taylor 2).

ENGLAND v AUSTRALIA 1993 (6th Test)

At Kennington Oval, London, on 19, 20, 21, 22, 23 August.
Toss: England.   Result: ENGLAND won by 161 runs.
Debuts: None.

At 5.16 on the fifth evening, with 13.5 overs to spare, England closed their barren sequence of ten matches involving four countries, and ended an unprecedented run of 18 matches since their last victory over Australia (Melbourne 1986-87). Stewart scored his 2,000th run in 59 Test innings. When he had scored 18 in the second innings, Gooch (195 innings) overtook D.I.Gower's England record aggregate of 8,231 runs from 204 innings. Atherton's aggregate of 553 runs was the highest in any Ashes rubber without a hundred (previously 521 by C.Hill in five Tests in 1901-02). Healy's tally of 26 dismissals was the second highest in any rubber. Warne's total of 34 wickets was the fourth highest by an Australian in England but his combined total of 55 wickets with May represented the most successful harvest by any pair of Australian spinners there. Sadly, this proved to be Brian Johnston's final Test, ending 48 summers of lively commentary for the BBC; he was 81 years young when he died on 5 January 1994.

ENGLAND

Player	Dismissal 1	R	Dismissal 2	R
G.A.Gooch	c Border b S.R.Waugh	56	c Healy b Warne	79
*M.A.Atherton	lbw b S.R.Waugh	50	c Warne b Reiffel	42
G.A.Hick	c Warne b May	80	c Boon b May	36
M.P.Maynard	b Warne	20	c Reiffel b Hughes	9
N.Hussain	c Taylor b Warne	30	c M.E.Waugh b Hughes	0
†A.J.Stewart	c Healy b Hughes	76	c M.E.Waugh b Reiffel	35
M.R.Ramprakash	c Healy b Hughes	6	c Slater b Hughes	64
A.R.C.Fraser	b Reiffel	28	c Healy b Reiffel	13
S.L.Watkin	c S.R.Waugh b Reiffel	13	lbw b Warne	4
P.M.Such	c M.E.Waugh b Hughes	4	lbw b Warne	10
D.E.Malcolm	not out	0	not out	0
Extras	(LB7, W1, NB9)	17	(B5, LB12, W1, NB3)	21
Total		**380**		**313**

AUSTRALIA

Player	Dismissal 1	R	Dismissal 2	R
M.A.Taylor	c Hussain b Malcolm	70	(2) b Watkin	8
M.J.Slater	c Gooch b Malcolm	4	(1) c Stewart b Watkin	12
D.C.Boon	c Gooch b Malcolm	13	lbw b Watkin	0
M.E.Waugh	c Stewart b Fraser	10	c Ramprakash b Malcolm	49
*A.R.Border	c Stewart b Fraser	48	c Stewart b Malcolm	17
S.R.Waugh	b Fraser	20	lbw b Malcolm	26
†I.A.Healy	not out	83	c Maynard b Watkin	5
M.G.Hughes	c Ramprakash b Watkin	7	c Watkin b Fraser	12
P.R.Reiffel	c Maynard b Watkin	0	c and b Fraser	42
S.K.Warne	c Stewart b Fraser	16	lbw b Fraser	37
T.B.A.May	c Stewart b Fraser	15	not out	4
Extras	(B5, LB6, W2, NB4)	17	(B2, LB6, W2, NB7)	17
Total		**303**		**229**

AUSTRALIA	O	M	R	W	O	M	R	W
Hughes	30	7	121	3	31.2	9	110	3
Reiffel	28.5	4	88	2	24	8	55	3
S.R.Waugh	12	2	45	2				
Warne	20	5	70	2	(3) 40	15	78	3
M.E.Waugh	1	0	17	0				
May	10	3	32	1	(4) 24	6	53	1

ENGLAND	O	M	R	W	O	M	R	W
Malcolm	26	5	86	3	20	3	84	3
Watkin	28	4	87	2	25	9	65	4
Fraser	26.4	4	87	5	19.1	5	44	3
Such	14	4	32	0	9	4	17	0
Hick					8	3	11	0

FALL OF WICKETS

Wkt	E 1st	A 1st	E 2nd	A 2nd
1st	88	9	77	23
2nd	143	30	157	23
3rd	177	53	180	30
4th	231	132	180	92
5th	253	164	186	95
6th	272	181	254	106
7th	339	196	276	142
8th	363	196	283	143
9th	374	248	313	217
10th	380	303	313	229

Umpires: M.J.Kitchen (7) and B.J.Meyer (26). Referee: C.H.Lloyd (*West Indies*) (6).

Close: 1st day – E(1) 353-7 (Fraser 15, Watkin 8); 2nd – A(1) 239-8 (Healy 39, Warne 14); 3rd – E(2) 210-5 (Stewart 14, Ramprakash 12); 4th – A(2) 1-0 (Slater 1, Taylor 0).

SRI LANKA v INDIA 1993-94 (1st Test)

At Asgiriya Stadium, Kandy, on 17 (*no play*), 18, 19 (*no play*), 21 (*no play*), 22 (*no play*) July.
Toss: India.   Result: MATCH DRAWN.
Debuts: None.

The wisdom of staging a Test in Kandy during the Perehara, a festival which attracts tourists and rain in equal measure, was called into question when the rains permitted a grand total of 50 minutes' play, just 12 overs being bowled, all after lunch on the second day. Kapil Dev removed Mahanama with his fifth ball to claim his 121st wicket, ten short of Sir Richard Hadlee's world record.

SRI LANKA

R.S.Mahanama	c More b Kapil Dev	0
U.C.Hathurusinghe	c Kumble b Prabhakar	4
A.P.Gurusinha	not out	10
P.A.de Silva	c Kumble b Prabhakar	1
A.Ranatunga	not out	7
H.P.Tillekeratne		
A.M.de Silva		
D.K.Liyanage	} did not bat	
C.P.H.Ramanayake		
M.Muralitharan		
K.P.J.Warnaweera		
Extras	(LB1, NB1)	2
Total	(3 wickets)	**24**

INDIA

M.Prabhakar
N.S.Sidhu
V.G.Kambli
S.R.Tendulkar
M.Azharuddin
P.K.Amre
Kapil Dev
K.S.More
A.Kumble
R.K.Chauhan
J.Srinath
Extras
Total

INDIA	O	M	R	W
Kapil Dev	5	1	10	1
Prabhakar	6	1	13	2
Srinath	1	1	0	0

	FALL OF WICKETS	
		SL
Wkt		*1st*
1st		0
2nd		6
3rd		8
4th		–
5th		–
6th		–
7th		–
8th		–
9th		–
10th		–

Umpires: K.T.Francis (9) and T.M.Samarasinghe (5). Referee: P.J.P.Burge (*Australia*) (5).

Close: 1st day – no play; 2nd – SL(1) 24-3 (Gurusinha 10, Ranatunga 7); 3rd – no play; 4th – no play.

SRI LANKA v INDIA 1993-94 (2nd Test)

At Sinhalese Sports Club Ground, Colombo, on 27, 28, 29, 31 July, 1 August.
Toss: India.   Result: INDIA won by 235 runs.
Debuts: Sri Lanka – R.S.Kalpage.

By winning this ill-tempered contest with 70 minutes to spare, India terminated a seven-year sequence of matches since their last victory overseas. Kambli (358 minutes, 220 balls, a six and 13 fours) scored his thi(rd) hundred in successive innings. He was reprimanded by referee Burge for disputing his dismissal in the seco(nd) innings. De Silva became the second Sri Lankan after Ranatunga to score 2,000 runs. Sidhu (384 minutes, 2(?) balls, 7 fours) scored his fourth hundred in 40 Test innings, while Tendulkar (217 minutes, 163 balls, a six a(nd) 11 fours) recorded his sixth hundred in 39 innings. Kapil Dev made his 126th appearance to pa(ss) S.M.Gavaskar's Indian record. Kumble returned his fourth five-wicket analysis in 12 Tests.

INDIA

Batsman	1st innings	R	2nd innings	R
M.Prabhakar	lbw b Gurusinha	4	c Tillekeratne b Kalpage	(?)
N.S.Sidhu	c Tillekeratne b Warnaweera	82	c A.M.de Silva b Hathurusinghe	1(?)
V.G.Kambli	c Mahanama b Hathurusinghe	125	c A.M.de Silva b Warnaweera	
S.R.Tendulkar	c Tillekeratne b Kalpage	28	not out	1(?)
*M.Azharuddin	lbw b Wickremasinghe	26	c Tillekeratne b Kalpage	
P.K.Amre	c Kalpage b Warnaweera	21	not out	
Kapil Dev	lbw b Gurusinha	35		
†K.S.More	c Mahanama b Warnaweera	4		
A.Kumble	lbw b Wickremasinghe	1		
R.K.Chauhan	c A.M.de Silva b Wickremasinghe	2		
J.Srinath	not out	0		
Extras	(B9, LB3, W10, NB16)	38	(B5, LB1, W2, NB8)	
Total		366	(4 wickets declared)	3(?)

SRI LANKA

Batsman	1st innings	R	2nd innings
R.S.Mahanama	c More b Prabhakar	22	lbw b Kapil Dev
U.C.Hathurusinghe	b Kumble	37	c Azharuddin b Prabhakar
A.P.Gurusinha	lbw b Prabhakar	4	c Chauhan b Kumble
P.A.de Silva	c Azharuddin b Kumble	22	c Azharuddin b Kumble
*A.Ranatunga	c Srinath b Kumble	88	c More b Prabhakar
H.P.Tillekeratne	c More b Srinath	28	c sub (W.V.Raman) b Prabhakar
†A.M.de Silva	c Amre b Kumble	0	b Kapil Dev
R.S.Kalpage	c More b Srinath	1	c Amre b Srinath
D.K.Liyanage	lbw b Kumble	2	c Azharuddin b Chauhan
G.P.Wickremasinghe	not out	11	lbw b Kumble
K.P.J.Warnaweera	b Prabhakar	20	not out
Extras	(B9, LB5, W4, NB1)	19	(B6, LB6, W3, NB1)
Total		254	

SRI LANKA	O	M	R	W		O	M	R	W				
Liyanage	19	3	64	0	(2)	10	2	31	0				
Wickremasinghe	27	6	83	3	(1)	22	4	58	0				
Hathurusinghe	17	2	48	1	(5)	12	1	35	1				
Gurusinha	16	2	49	2		7	0	24	0				
Warnaweera	20.1	1	76	3	(3)	20	1	86	1				
Kalpage	8	1	34	1		38	3	97	2				
Ranatunga						2	1	5	0				
P.A.de Silva						7	0	17	0				

INDIA	O	M	R	W	O	M	R	W
Kapil Dev	11	4	26	0	26	13	34	2
Prabhakar	15.5	5	43	3	18	4	49	3
Srinath	17	5	42	2	15	2	36	1
Kumble	24	3	87	5	38.1	14	85	3
Chauhan	10	1	42	0	24	18	20	1

FALL OF WICKETS

Wkt	I 1st	SL 1st	I 2nd	S(L 2n)
1st	25	48	171	2(?)
2nd	151	60	176	(?)
3rd	219	85	263	12
4th	282	96	316	18
5th	311	207	–	18
6th	352	208	–	1(?)
7th	362	209	–	19
8th	363	218	–	2(?)
9th	366	218	–	22
10th	366	254	–	2(?)

Umpires: I.Anandappa (3) and S.Ponnadurai (3). Referee: P.J.P.Burge (*Australia*) (6).

Close: 1st day – I(1) 300-4 (Kambli 119, Amre 6); 2nd – SL(1) 200-4 (Ranatunga 82, Tillekeratne (?)) 3rd – I(2) 205-2 (Sidhu 85, Tendulkar 13); 4th – SL(2) 86-2 (Gurusinha 19, P.A. de Silva 10).

SRI LANKA v INDIA 1993-94 (3rd Test)

At P.Saravanamuttu Stadium, Colombo, on 4, 5, 7, 8, 9 August.
Toss: Sri Lanka.   Result: MATCH DRAWN.
Debuts: None.

India won their first rubber overseas since defeating England in 1986. De Silva (388 minutes, 297 balls, two sixes and 17 fours) scored his sixth Test hundred but his first at home. Kambli (315 minutes, 241 balls, 2 sixes and 15 fours) extended his sequence of hundreds to four in five innings. Mahanama (531 minutes, 362 balls, 19 fours) completed his third hundred in 31 Test innings. Kapil Dev passed the record number of balls bowled in Test cricket (27,115 by West Indies off-spinner L.R.Gibbs) and ended the match with 425 Test wickets, needing seven to break the record. Arguments between batsmen and fielders, disputes of umpiring decisions, 'sledging', time-wasting and ball-tampering all featured in a lamentable display by players on both sides during these two Colombo Tests.

SRI LANKA

R.S.Mahanama	lbw b Prabhakar	6	c Chauhan b Prabhakar		151
U.C.Hathurusinghe	c Amre b Kapil Dev	6	c sub (W.V.Raman) b Raju		22
A.P.Gurusinha	c Tendulkar b Kumble	56	c sub (W.V.Raman) b Kumble		35
P.A.de Silva	c Raju b Kumble	148	c Kambli b Kumble		2
*A.Ranatunga	c Kapil Dev b Raju	9	c Tendulkar b Prabhakar		13
H.P.Tillekeratne	b Chauhan	51	c and b Kumble		86
S.T.Jayasuriya	lbw b Chauhan	0	not out		31
†R.S.Kaluwitharana	b Prabhakar	40			
G.P.Wickremasinghe	c Tendulkar b Chauhan	0			
M.Muralitharan	b Kapil Dev	7			
K.P.J.Warnaweera	not out	1			
Extras	(B3, LB20, W1, NB3)	27	(B6, LB4, W1, NB1)		12
Total		351	(6 wickets)		352

INDIA

M.Prabhakar	c Jayasuriya b Wickremasinghe	55
N.S.Sidhu	c Kaluwitharana b Wickremasinghe	39
V.G.Kambli	lbw b Warnaweera	120
S.R.Tendulkar	c Ranatunga b Hathurusinghe	71
*M.Azharuddin	c Wickremasinghe b Muralitharan	50
P.K.Amre	c Kaluwitharana b Wickremasinghe	21
A.Kumble	b Muralitharan	9
Kapil Dev	lbw b Warnaweera	27
†K.S.More	c and b Muralitharan	4
R.K.Chauhan	not out	15
S.L.V.Raju	c Jayasuriya b Muralitharan	1
Extras	(B5, LB12, W1, NB16)	34
Total		446

INDIA	O	M	R	W	O	M	R	W	FALL OF WICKETS			
										SL	I	SL
Kapil Dev	27.1	11	56	2	24	11	33	0	Wkt	1st	1st	2nd
Prabhakar	21	7	59	2	31	14	59	2	1st	13	86	75
Raju	25	5	55	1	(4) 27	5	66	1	2nd	29	109	142
Tendulkar	3	0	4	0					3rd	165	271	144
Kumble	40	12	95	2	(3) 38.2	7	108	3	4th	182	334	157
Chauhan	26	7	59	3	(5) 33	5	76	0	5th	281	384	289
									6th	286	388	352
SRI LANKA									7th	309	397	–
Wickremasinghe	38	8	95	3					8th	309	409	–
Gurusinha	11	1	27	0					9th	347	437	–
Warnaweera	23	2	86	2					10th	351	446	–
Hathurusinghe	20	6	53	1								
Ranatunga	4	2	2	0								
Muralitharan	47.1	12	136	4								
Jayasuriya	8	2	30	0								

Umpires: B.C.Cooray (2) and P.Manuel (1). Refree: P.J.P.Burge (*Australia*) (7).

Close: 1st day – SL(1) 226-4 (P.A.de Silva 118, Tillekeratne 14); 2nd – I(1) 84-0 (Prabhakar 37, Sidhu 39); 3rd – I(1) 384-5 (Azharuddin 47, Kumble 0); 4th – SL(2) 132-1 (Mahanama 67, Gurusinha 34).

SRI LANKA v SOUTH AFRICA 1993-94 (1st Test)

At Tyronne Fernando Stadium, Moratuwa, on 25, 26, 28, 29, 30 August.
Toss: Sri Lanka.   Result: MATCH DRAWN.
Debuts: Sri Lanka – P.B.Dassanayake, P.K.Wijetunge; South Africa – C.E.Eksteen, P.L.Symcox.

Drifting at 138 for 6 having been set 365 to win in a minimum of 115 overs, South Africa were rescued from defeat in the inaugural Test of this series by the resolute defiance of Rhodes (262 minutes, 193 balls, a six and 14 fours, his maiden hundred coming in his ninth innings) and the tenacity of Eksteen (4 in 92 minutes). Donald secured his third five-wicket haul in five innings and subsequently achieved a hole-in-one at the 320-yard 10th hole on the Royal Colombo course. Muralitharan became only the second slow bowler after D.S.de Silva (*Test No. 926*) to take five wickets in a Test innings for Sri Lanka. Ranatunga (204 minutes, 140 balls, a six and 18 fours) completed the fastest hundred for Sri Lanka from 114 balls. Aldridge was the first umpire to officiate as a member of the ICC international panel.

SRI LANKA

R.S.Mahanama	b Schultz	53		lbw b Symcox	17
U.C.Hathurusinghe	c Richardson b Donald	1		b Donald	9
A.P.Gurusinha	c Richardson b Donald	26	(4)	b Schultz	27
P.A.de Silva	c Wessels b Schultz	27	(5)	c Richardson b Symcox	68
*A.Ranatunga	c Richardson b Donald	44	(6)	b Schultz	131
H.P.Tillekeratne	lbw b Schultz	92	(7)	not out	33
R.S.Kalpage	c Richardson b Cronje	42	(8)	not out	0
†P.B.Dassanayake	b Schultz	7			
P.K.Wijetunge	b Donald	10	(3)	c Hudson b Symcox	0
G.P.Wickremasinghe	c Rhodes b Donald	11			
M.Muralitharan	not out	2			
Extras	(LB11, W1, NB4)	16		(B3, LB6, NB6)	15
Total		**331**		**(6 wickets declared)**	**300**

SOUTH AFRICA

*K.C.Wessels	c Tillekeratne b Muralitharan	47	(2)	c Wickremasinghe b Muralitharan	16
A.C.Hudson	c Gurusinha b Wijetunge	90	(1)	c Dassanayake b Hathurusinghe	4
W.J.Cronje	b Muralitharan	17		c sub‡ b Wickremasinghe	1
D.J.Cullinan	lbw b Hathurusinghe	33		lbw b Wickremasinghe	46
S.J.Cook	b Wickremasinghe	7		c Tillekeratne b Wijetunge	24
J.N.Rhodes	c Tillekeratne b Muralitharan	8		not out	101
†D.J.Richardson	c and b Wickremasinghe	2		c Tillekeratne b De Silva	4
P.L.Symcox	c Mahanama b Muralitharan	48		c Hathurusinghe b De Silva	21
C.E.Eksteen	b Muralitharan	1		not out	4
A.A.Donald	not out	0			
B.N.Schultz	lbw b Kalpage	0			
Extras	(LB4, W1, NB9)	14		(B10, LB4, W1, NB15)	30
Total		**267**		**(7 wickets)**	**251**

SOUTH AFRICA	O	M	R	W		O	M	R	W
Donald	28	5	69	5		22	5	73	1
Schultz	31.2	12	75	4		20	2	82	2
Eksteen	14	4	44	0	(5) 9	2	34	0
Cronje	26	14	32	1	(3) 8	2	27	0
Symcox	28	3	100	0	(4) 21	2	75	3

SRI LANKA	O	M	R	W		O	M	R	W
Wickremasinghe	19	4	58	2		22	6	59	2
Gurusinha	3	0	3	0					
Kalpage	17.5	6	23	1	(5) 8	2	21	0
Wijetunge	29	2	58	1		23	3	60	1
Muralitharan	39	8	104	5	(3) 31	11	48	1
De Silva	1	0	3	0		17	3	35	2
Hathurusinghe	4	0	14	1	(2) 9	5	9	1
Tillekeratne					(7) 2	0	5	0

FALL OF WICKETS

	SL	SA	SL	SA
Wkt	1st	1st	2nd	2nd
1st	5	104	26	13
2nd	77	152	26	15
3rd	100	179	34	47
4th	157	203	75	92
5th	168	203	196	126
6th	258	206	299	138
7th	273	240	–	199
8th	285	262	–	–
9th	313	267	–	–
10th	331	267	–	–

‡ (S.T.Jayasuriya)

Umpires: B.L.Aldridge (*New Zealand*) (18) and K.T.Francis (10). Referee: J.R.Reid (*New Zealand*) (1).

Close: 1st day – SL(1) 241-5 (Tillekeratne 37, Kalpage 39); 2nd – SA(1) 81-0 (Wessels 39, Hudson 39); 3rd – SL(2) 26-2 (Hathurusinghe 6, Gurusinha 0); 4th – SA(2) 25-2 (Wessels 9, Cullinan 4).

SRI LANKA v SOUTH AFRICA 1993-94 (2nd Test)

At Sinhalese Sports Club Ground, Colombo, on 6, 7, 8, 10 September.
Toss: Sri Lanka.   Result: SOUTH AFRICA won by an innings and 208 runs.
Debuts: Sri Lanka – H.D.P.K.Dharmasena.

South Africa gained their first Test win overseas since 1965 and with a day and 67 overs to spare. It was their largest margin of victory until 1994 (*Test No. 1263*) and Sri Lanka's biggest defeat. Wessels batted 304 minutes for his 92. Cronje (412 minutes, 297 balls, 11 fours) scored his second Test hundred in his eleventh innings. The left-handed Schultz, playing his fourth Test, returned his best innings and match analyses. Richardson was the first overseas wicket-keeper to make eight dismissals in a Test in Sri Lanka.

SRI LANKA

R.S.Mahanama	c Richardson b Schultz	7		b Schultz	0
U.C.Hathurusinghe	c McMillan b Donald	34		c Cronje b Donald	0
H.P.Tillekeratne	c Cronje b McMillan	9		c Richardson b Snell	9
P.A.de Silva	c Richardson b Schultz	34		c and b Donald	24
*A.Ranatunga	c Cullinan b Snell	11	(6)	c Richardson b Schultz	14
*P.B.Dassanayake	b Schultz	44	(7)	b Schultz	16
P.B.Dassanayake	c Richardson b Donald	0	(8)	c Richardson b Snell	10
H.D.P.K.Dharmasena	c Richardson b Schultz	5	(9)	c Richardson b Schultz	2
C.P.H.Ramanayake	not out	3	(5)	lbw b McMillan	0
G.P.Wickremasinghe	b Schultz	17		c Donald b Snell	21
M.Muralitharan	c Rhodes b Snell	0		not out	14
Extras	(LB3, NB1)	4		(LB4, NB5)	9
Total		**168**			**119**

SOUTH AFRICA

*K.C.Wessels	c Dassanayake b Muralitharan	92
A.C.Hudson	lbw b Wickremasinghe	58
W.J.Cronje	b De Silva	122
D.J.Cullinan	c and b Muralitharan	52
J.N.Rhodes	run out	10
B.M.McMillan	b Muralitharan	0
†D.J.Richardson	c Jayasuriya b Muralitharan	11
P.L.Symcox	st Dassanayake b De Silva	50
R.P.Snell	st Dassanayake b De Silva	48
A.A.Donald	not out	4
B.N.Schultz	st Dassanayake b Muralitharan	6
Extras	(B5, LB20, W1, NB16)	42
Total		**495**

SOUTH AFRICA	O	M	R	W	O	M	R	W		FALL OF WICKETS		
										SL	SA	SL
Donald	12	4	22	2	10	7	6	2	*Wkt*	*1st*	*1st*	*2nd*
Schultz	20	8	48	5	16	4	58	4	1st	7	137	1
Snell	19	3	57	2	12	4	32	3	2nd	27	179	1
McMillan	9	1	38	1	4	0	11	1	3rd	72	284	30
Symcox	2	2	0	0	1	0	8	0	4th	85	306	31
									5th	117	307	49
SRI LANKA									6th	119	333	54
Ramanayake	20	5	63	0					7th	145	401	69
Wickremasinghe	31	6	111	1					8th	147	480	76
Hathurusinghe	7	4	12	0					9th	167	487	101
Dharmasena	45	12	91	0					10th	168	495	119
Muralitharan	54	17	101	5								
Jayasuriya	9	1	47	0								
De Silva	13	1	39	3								
Ranatunga	2	0	6	0								

Umpires: B.L.Aldridge (*New Zealand*) (19) and T.M.Samarasinghe (6). Referee: J.R.Reid (*New Zealand*) (2).

Close: 1st day – SA(1) 48-0 (Wessels 19, Hudson 19); 2nd – SA(1) 280-2 (Cronje 54, Cullinan 52); 3rd – SL(2) 49-4 (De Silva 22, Ranatunga 14).

SRI LANKA v SOUTH AFRICA 1993-94 (3rd Test)

At P.Saravanamuttu Stadium, Colombo, on 14, 15, 16, 18, 19 (*no play*) September.
Toss: South Africa.   Result: MATCH DRAWN.
Debuts: None.

Winning the toss on his 36th birthday proved a good omen for Wessels, exceptionally defensive batting by Sri Lanka and the loss of the last day ensuring that South Africa won its first overseas rubber since emerging from isolation. Cullinan (358 minutes, 222 balls, 17 fours) scored his maiden Test hundred in his sixth innings. Donald dismissed Hathurusinghe for the fifth successive time. Sri Lanka managed only 128 runs from 73 overs on the third day, the sessions producing 36, 44 and 48 runs, their innings occupying 628 minutes (139.5 overs). Schultz took his tally of wickets for the three-match rubber to 20 at 16.30.

SOUTH AFRICA

A.C.Hudson	c Tillekeratne b Dharmasena	22	(2)	b Ramanayake	28
*K.C.Wessels	b Liyanage	26	(1)	c Mahanama b Hathurusinghe	7
W.J.Cronje	b Ramanayake	24		not out	73
D.J.Cullinan	c Ramanayake b Jayasuriya	102		c sub‡ b Dharmasena	4
J.N.Rhodes	st Dassanayake b Muralitharan	7		b Muralitharan	19
B.M.McMillan	c Jayasuriya b Muralitharan	2		not out	0
†D.J.Richardson	c De Silva b Muralitharan	62			
P.L.Symcox	c Tillekeratne b Ramanayake	30			
R.P.Snell	not out	13			
A.A.Donald	lbw b Ramanayake	1			
B.N.Schultz	c De Silva b Muralitharan	0			
Extras	(B6, LB10, NB11)	27		(B4, LB17, NB7)	28
Total		**316**		**(4 wickets declared)**	**159**

SRI LANKA

R.S.Mahanama	c McMillan b Schultz	25
U.C.Hathurusinghe	c Richardson b Donald	1
†P.B.Dassanayake	run out	8
P.A.de Silva	lbw b Symcox	82
*A.Ranatunga	c Richardson b Schultz	50
H.P.Tillekeratne	c Richardson b Schultz	37
S.T.Jayasuriya	c Cronje b Schultz	65
H.D.P.K.Dharmasena	c Richardson b Schultz	5
D.K.Liyanage	b Donald	0
C.P.H.Ramanayake	not out	0
M.Muralitharan	did not bat	
Extras	(B7, LB9, NB7)	23
Total	**(9 wickets declared)**	**296**

SRI LANKA	O	M	R	W		O	M	R	W		FALL OF WICKETS		
Ramanayake	25	4	75	3		10	1	26	1		SA	SL	SA
Liyanage	21	4	58	1	(3)	4	1	17	0	*Wkt*	*1st*	*1st*	*2nd*
Hathurusinghe	6	4	6	0	(2)	8	4	7	1	1st	51	1	11
Dharmasena	28	5	79	1	(5)	18	8	29	1	2nd	53	27	58
Muralitharan	35.1	8	64	4	(4)	15	3	39	1	3rd	96	55	65
De Silva	1	0	9	0	(7)	3	1	3	0	4th	108	156	159
Jayasuriya	5	1	9	1	(6)	3	1	17	0	5th	128	202	–
										6th	250	263	–
SOUTH AFRICA										7th	281	273	–
Donald	30	12	62	2						8th	311	294	–
Schultz	36.5	9	63	5						9th	315	296	–
McMillan	30	8	64	0						10th	316	–	–
Snell	25	8	44	0									
Symcox	18	5	47	1									

‡ (D.P.Samaraweera)

Umpires: B.L.Aldridge (*New Zealand*) (20) and B.C.Cooray (3). Referee: J.R.Reid (*New Zealand*) (3).

Close: 1st day – SA(1) 231-5 (Cullinan 85, Richardson 51); 2nd – SL(1) 117-3 (De Silva 44, Ranatunga 30); 3rd – SL(1) 245-5 (Tillekeratne 29, Jayasuriya 35); 4th – SA(2) 159-4 (Cronje 73, McMillan 0).

AUSTRALIA v NEW ZEALAND 1993-94 (1st Test)

At W.A.C.A.Ground, Perth, on 12, 13, 14, 15, 16 November.
Toss: New Zealand.   Result: MATCH DRAWN.
Debuts: Australia – G.D.McGrath; New Zealand – B.A.Pocock.

Set 303 in 263 minutes, New Zealand secured an honourable draw but at considerable cost. Their captain, Crowe, who defied Australia's last-day blitz for 132 minutes, aggravated a knee injury, flew home for surgery and took no further part in the tour. Healy (262 minutes, 181 balls, 11 fours) recorded the higher of his two Test hundreds, Reiffel reached his first Test fifty off 60 balls and Australia's last four wickets added 200. McDermott, playing his 50th Test, became the eighth to take 200 wickets for Australia when he dismissed Rutherford. Jones (351 minutes, 283 balls, 11 fours) scored the last of his seven Test hundreds in his 59th innings. Slater (243 minutes, 181 balls, 13 fours) and Taylor (360 minutes, 255 balls, 8 fours) took heavy toll of an attack devoid of Watson (hamstring) and Cairns (heel), putting on 198, the highest opening stand by either side in this series. It was Taylor's eleventh hundred in 86 innings and he became the first to score hundreds on each of Australia's six Test grounds.

AUSTRALIA

M.A.Taylor	b Cairns	64	(2)	not out	142
M.J.Slater	c Patel b Cairns	10	(1)	c Blain b Patel	99
D.C.Boon	c Rutherford b Cairns	0		not out	67
M.E.Waugh	lbw b Morrison	36			
*A.R.Border	c Rutherford b Morrison	16			
S.R.Waugh	c Blain b Patel	44			
†I.A.Healy	not out	113			
P.R.Reiffel	c Jones b Watson	51			
S.K.Warne	c Patel b Cairns	11			
C.J.McDermott	b Su'a	35			
G.D.McGrath	lbw b Su'a	0			
Extras	(B4, LB7, NB7)	18		(LB6, NB9)	15
Total		398		(1 wicket declared)	323

NEW ZEALAND

M.J.Greatbatch	c Healy b McGrath	18	c Healy b McDermott	0
B.A.Pocock	c Boon b McDermott	34	c Healy b McGrath	28
A.H.Jones	c Healy b M.E.Waugh	143	lbw b M.E.Waugh	45
*M.D.Crowe	c Taylor b Reiffel	42	not out	31
K.R.Rutherford	c Healy b McDermott	17	lbw b S.R.Waugh	39
D.N.Patel	c S.R.Waugh b Reiffel	20	not out	18
C.L.Cairns	b Warne	78		
†T.E.Blain	lbw b McDermott	36		
M.L.Su'a	not out	14		
D.K.Morrison	lbw b McGrath	0		
W.Watson	not out	0		
Extras	(B1, LB6, NB10)	17	(LB1, NB4)	5
Total	(9 wickets declared)	419	(4 wickets)	166

NEW ZEALAND	O	M	R	W	O	M	R	W	FALL OF WICKETS			
									A	NZ	A	NZ
Morrison	35	4	113	2	25	5	80	0				
Cairns	28	4	113	4	(3) 1	0	12	0	*Wkt*	*1st*	*1st*	*2nd*	*2nd*
Watson	24	11	52	1					1st	37	25	198	0
Su'a	19.5	2	72	2	20	0	71	0	2nd	37	100	–	66
Patel	8	0	37	1	(2) 39	4	144	1	3rd	100	199	–	85
Pocock					(5) 2	0	10	0	4th	129	239	–	145
									5th	164	275	–	–
									6th	198	292	–	–
AUSTRALIA									7th	291	394	–	–
McDermott	40	10	127	3	13	3	40	1	8th	329	413	–	–
McGrath	39	12	92	2	16	6	50	1	9th	398	418	–	–
Reiffel	24	2	75	2	7	2	25	0	10th	398	–	–	–
Warne	37.1	6	90	1	(5) 13	6	23	0					
M.E.Waugh	13	5	18	1	(4) 6	4	17	1					
S.R.Waugh	4	0	10	0	7	2	10	1					
Border	2	2	0	0									

Umpires: D.B.Hair (4) and A.J.McQuillan (1). Referee: S.Venkataraghavan (*India*) (3).

Close: 1st day – A(1) 229-6 (Healy 30, Reiffel 16); 2nd – NZ(1) 123-2 (Jones 62, Crowe 2); 3rd – NZ(1) 390-6 (Cairns 66, Blain 35); 4th – A(2) 218-1 (Taylor 94, Boon 15).

AUSTRALIA v NEW ZEALAND 1993-94 (2nd Test)

At Bellerive Oval, Hobart, on 26, 27, 28, 29 November.
Toss: Australia.   Result: AUSTRALIA won by an innings and 222 runs.
Debuts: New Zealand – R.P.de Groen.

Australia amassed their highest home total of this series (until the next match) before May and Warne spun New Zealand to their heaviest defeat in all Tests, each claiming their third five-wicket spoil. Slater (328 minutes, 235 balls, 17 fours) and Boon (317 minutes, 242 balls, 9 fours) shared a series record second-wicket stand of 235, Boon completing his 18th Test hundred (the first in his native Tasmania) and, in his 148th innings, completing 1,000 runs against New Zealand and becoming the fifth to score 6,000 runs for Australia. Mark Waugh (187 minutes, 139 balls, 15 fours) scored his fifth hundred in 46 innings. Warne concluded the match at 12.22pm on the fourth day with a spell of 4 for 3 from 14 balls.

AUSTRALIA

M.A.Taylor	c Jones b Su'a	27
M.J.Slater	c Morrison b Patel	168
D.C.Boon	c Jones b Doull	106
M.E.Waugh	c Doull b De Groen	111
*A.R.Border	c and b Morrison	60
S.R.Waugh	not out	25
†I.A.Healy	c Doull b De Groen	1
P.R.Reiffel	not out	23
S.K.Warne	⎫	
T.B.A.May	⎬ did not bat	
C.J.McDermott	⎭	
Extras	(B7, LB2, NB14)	23
Total	**(6 wickets declared)**	**544**

NEW ZEALAND

M.J.Greatbatch	c May b McDermott	12	c M.E.Waugh b McDermott	0
B.A.Pocock	lbw b M.E.Waugh	9	st Healy b Warne	15
A.H.Jones	c Healy b May	47	c Border b M.E.Waugh	18
*K.R.Rutherford	c Taylor b May	17	b Warne	55
D.N.Patel	c Taylor b Warne	18	lbw b May	16
C.Z.Harris	c M.E.Waugh b May	0	b May	4
†T.E.Blain	c Warne b May	40	c and b Warne	29
M.L.Su'a	c Taylor b Warne	6	b Warne	5
D.K.Morrison	c M.E.Waugh b May	0	b Warne	0
S.B.Doull	lbw b Warne	0	c May b Warne	1
R.P.de Groen	not out	0	not out	3
Extras	(B2, LB1, NB9)	12	(B2, LB5, NB8)	15
Total		**161**		**161**

NEW ZEALAND	O	M	R	W	O	M	R	W
Morrison	33	4	125	1				
Su'a	24	3	102	1				
Doull	21	0	99	1				
De Groen	36	9	113	2				
Patel	23	3	78	1				
Harris	2	0	18	0				
AUSTRALIA								
McDermott	15	3	29	1	17	8	42	1
Reiffel	5	1	13	0	12	1	28	0
S.R.Waugh	4	1	8	0				
M.E.Waugh	9	4	7	1	(3) 4	0	8	1
May	31.3	10	65	5	(4) 25	13	45	2
Warne	18	5	36	3	(5) 19.5	9	31	6

FALL OF WICKETS

Wkt	A 1st	NZ 1st	NZ 2nd
1st	65	15	1
2nd	300	47	29
3rd	335	84	84
4th	485	105	103
5th	501	107	111
6th	502	117	133
7th	–	137	149
8th	–	138	149
9th	–	139	158
10th	–	161	161

Umpires: D.B.Hair (5) and W.P.Sheahan (1). Referee: S.Venkataraghavan (*India*) (4).

Close: 1st day – A(1) 329-2 (Boon 105, M.E.Waugh 18); 2nd – NZ(1) 81-2 (Jones 34, Rutherford 15); 3rd – NZ(2) 127-5 (Harris 4, Blain 9).

AUSTRALIA v NEW ZEALAND 1993-94 (3rd Test)

At Woolloongabba, Brisbane, on 3, 4, 5, 6, 7 December.
Toss: New Zealand.   Result: AUSTRALIA won by an innings and 96 runs.
Debuts: New Zealand – B.A.Young.

Border (275 minutes, 193 balls, 15 fours) celebrated becoming the first to appear in 150 Tests by scoring the last of his 27 hundreds, including a record 15 as captain, holding his 150th catch (another record) and leading Australia to a second successive innings defeat of New Zealand to regain the Trans-Tasman Trophy. Steve Waugh (380 minutes, 281 balls, 15 fours) completed 3,000 Test runs in 92 innings during his sixth hundred. Warne batted 133 minutes for his highest score, reached 50 off 82 balls and took Australia to the highest total by either side in this series. It was the highest total conceded by New Zealand overseas and for only the second time in Test cricket (also *Test No. 407*), five bowlers conceded 100 runs. Warne took his record- breaking tally for the series to 18 at 16.94.

NEW ZEALAND

B.A.Pocock	c Healy b McDermott	0	(2)	c Healy b McDermott	11
B.A.Young	c Healy b M.E.Waugh	38	(1)	b Warne	53
A.H.Jones	b Warne	56		c Border b Warne	15
K.R.Rutherford	c Boon b McDermott	36		c Warne b McGrath	86
M.J.Greatbatch	c Healy b McDermott	35		lbw b McDermott	2
C.L.Cairns	c and b Warne	5		c Healy b McGrath	16
D.N.Patel	c Boon b May	1	(8)	b Warne	3
T.E.Blain	not out	42	(7)	b McGrath	18
D.K.Morrison	c Healy b Warne	0		not out	20
S.B.Doull	c Healy b McDermott	10		c Taylor b Warne	24
R.P.de Groen	c Border b Warne	3		b May	6
Extras	(B2, LB3, NB2)	7		(B7, LB12, NB5)	24
Total		**233**			**278**

AUSTRALIA

M.J.Slater	c Blain b Patel	28
M.A.Taylor	c Pocock b Doull	53
D.C.Boon	c Blain b Doull	89
M.E.Waugh	c Greatbatch b Cairns	68
A.R.Border	c Patel b De Groen	105
S.R.Waugh	not out	147
I.A.Healy	run out	15
S.K.Warne	not out	74
C.J.McDermott		
T.B.A.May	} did not bat	
G.D.McGrath		
Extras	(B6, LB13, NB9)	28
Total	(6 wickets declared)	**607**

AUSTRALIA	O	M	R	W		O	M	R	W	FALL OF WICKETS			
											NZ	A	NZ
McDermott	23	11	39	4		25	4	63	2	*Wkt*	*1st*	*1st*	*2nd*
McGrath	20	7	45	0		21	1	66	3	1st	2	80	34
S.R.Waugh	3	0	13	0						2nd	96	102	80
M.E.Waugh	10	4	14	1	(5)	6	1	30	0	3rd	98	227	81
May	21	7	51	1	(3)	16	3	41	1	4th	167	277	84
Warne	28.3	12	66	4	(4)	35	11	59	4	5th	170	436	138
										6th	174	465	187
NEW ZEALAND										7th	174	–	218
Morrison	33	3	104	0						8th	178	–	230
Cairns	36	7	128	1						9th	193	–	265
Doull	33	5	105	2						10th	233	–	278
De Groen	46	14	120	1									
Patel	33	4	125	1									
Jones	2	0	6	0									

Umpires: P.D.Parker (1) and S.G.Randell (14). Referee: S.Venkataraghavan (*India*) (5).

Close: 1st day – NZ (1) 208-9 (Blain 20, De Groen 1); 2nd – A(1) 241-3 (Boon 72, Border 5); 3rd – A(2) 533-6 (S.R.Waugh 113, Warne 37); 4th – NZ(2) 158-5 (Rutherford 40, Blain 7).

PAKISTAN v ZIMBABWE 1993-94 (1st Test)

At Defence Stadium, Karachi, on 1, 2, 3, 5, 6 December.
Toss: Pakistan.   Result: PAKISTAN won by 131 runs.
Debuts: Zimbabwe – G.K.Bruk-Jackson, M.H.Dekker, S.G.Peall, J.A.Rennie, H.H.Streak, G.J.Whittall.

With Wasim Akram recovering from a fractured wrist, Waqar Younis, at 22 years 15 days, became Pakistan's youngest captain and returned his best match figures to date, 13 for 135. That all but one of his dismissals were bowled or lbw was testimony to his accuracy. Zimbabwe, with six new caps, were set 266 in 68 overs and came within 31 balls of drawing this inaugural Test played on Test cricket's 70th ground. Peall took the wicket of Aamir Sohail with his fourth ball.

PAKISTAN

Aamir Sohail	b Peall	63	run out	29
Shoaib Mohammad	c A.Flower b Rennie	81		
Inzamam-ul-Haq	c A.Flower b Brandes	21	(2) not out	57
Javed Miandad	lbw b Brandes	70	run out	12
Basit Ali	c A.Flower b Whittall	36	(3) c and b Brandes	13
Asif Mujtaba	c Dekker b Brandes	4	(5) not out	10
†Rashid Latif	not out	68		
*Waqar Younis	c Peall b G.W.Flower	13		
Mushtaq Ahmed	c A.Flower b Peall	18		
Tausif Ahmed	not out	21		
Ata-ur-Rehman	did not bat			
Extras	(B15, LB12, NB1)	28	(B6, LB2, W1, NB1)	10
Total	(8 wickets declared)	**423**	(3 wickets declared)	**131**

ZIMBABWE

G.W.Flower	b Waqar	24	b Rehman	25
M.H.Dekker	lbw b Waqar	5	lbw b Waqar	0
A.D.R.Campbell	lbw b Mushtaq	53	c Inzamam b Mushtaq	8
D.L.Houghton	lbw b Waqar	46	lbw b Waqar	18
*†A.Flower	lbw b Rehman	63	c Inzamam b Mushtaq	21
G.J.Whittall	run out	33	b Rehman	2
G.K.Bruk-Jackson	b Waqar	31	lbw b Waqar	4
S.G.Peall	c Aamir b Waqar	0	b Waqar	0
H.H.Streak	b Waqar	0	not out	19
E.A.Brandes	not out	0	b Waqar	17
J.A.Rennie	lbw b Waqar	3	lbw b Waqar	0
Extras	(B5, LB24, W1, NB1)	31	(B12, LB5, NB3)	20
Total		**289**		**134**

ZIMBABWE	O	M	R	W		O	M	R	W		FALL OF WICKETS			
Brandes	35	4	106	3		13	0	59	1		P	Z	P	Z
Streak	29	6	77	0	(3)	10	1	40	0	*Wkt*	*1st*	*1st*	*2nd*	*2nd*
Rennie	32	6	90	1	(2)	3	0	24	0	1st	95	16	47	1
Whittall	12	4	26	1						2nd	134	71	76	17
Peall	41	10	89	2						3rd	217	132	108	61
G.W.Flower	6	2	8	1						4th	268	153	–	63
										5th	280	230	–	65
PAKISTAN										6th	305	280	–	78
Waqar	34.1	8	91	7		21.5	7	44	6	7th	332	284	–	80
Rehman	15	5	28	1		16	6	20	2	8th	363	284	–	92
Mushtaq	39	11	89	1		17	7	24	2	9th	–	285	–	130
Tausif	23	7	49	0		6	2	13	0	10th	–	289	–	134
Shoaib	1	0	1	0										
Aamir	1	0	1	0	(5)	2	0	16	0					
Asif	3	2	1	0										

Umpires: Mahboob Shah (21) and Shakil Khan (4). Referee: R.S.Madugalle (*Sri Lanka*) (1).

Close: 1st day – P(1) 197-2 (Shoaib 71, Miandad 37); 2nd – P(1) 388-8 (Rashid 52, Tausif 8); 3rd – Z(1) 179-4 (A.Flower 21, Whittall 12); 4th – P(2) 111-3 (Inzamam 47, Asif 2).

PAKISTAN v ZIMBABWE 1993-94 (2nd Test)

At Pindi Stadium, Rawalpindi, on 9, 10, 11, 13, 14 December.
Toss: Zimbabwe.   Result: PAKISTAN won by 52 runs.
Debuts: Pakistan – Ashfaq Ahmed.

Having held their own for three-quarters of the match and even gained a slender first-innings lead, Zimbabwe were undone by Pakistan's formidable pace attack on the final day, their last wicket falling with 28 balls remaining. With the Pindi Stadium, the 71st ground to stage Test matches, providing a pitch favouring fast bowling, the inexperienced tourists lost their last nine wickets for 52 runs after Dekker and Campbell had shared their second three-figure partnership of the match. In the first innings, Campbell scored 63 off 55 balls with a six and 11 fours, reaching his fifty off 40 balls. Streak was the first bowler to take eight wickets in a match for Zimbabwe. Dekker (289 minutes) became the first to carry his bat through a completed innings for Zimbabwe. Inzamam equalled Pakistan's fielding record with four catches in the first innings and five in the match.

PAKISTAN

Aamir Sohail	c Houghton b Streak	8		lbw b Streak	9
Shoaib Mohammad	lbw b Brain	18		c A.Flower b Streak	13
Inzamam-ul-Haq	b Brain	38		b Brandes	14
Javed Miandad	b Streak	20	(5)	b Streak	10
Basit Ali	c Streak b Brandes	25	(6)	lbw b Brandes	40
Asif Mujtaba	not out	54	(7)	c A.Flower b Brain	51
†Rashid Latif	lbw b Brain	33	(8)	c Houghton b Streak	61
*Wasim Akram	c Campbell b Brandes	11	(9)	lbw b Brandes	15
Waqar Younis	lbw b Brandes	7	(10)	c Campbell b Streak	17
Ata-ur-Rehman	lbw b Brain	10	(4)	lbw b Brain	0
Ashfaq Ahmed	c A.Flower b Streak	0		not out	1
Extras	(B4, LB12, W2, NB3)	21		(B1, LB11, W3, NB2)	17
Total		**245**			**248**

ZIMBABWE

G.W.Flower	c Inzamam b Wasim	0		b Wasim	0
M.H.Dekker	c Inzamam b Waqar	68		not out	68
A.D.R.Campbell	lbw b Rehman	63		c Aamir b Rehman	75
D.L.Houghton	c Asif b Ashfaq	5		lbw b Waqar	4
*†A.Flower	c Wasim b Waqar	12		c Rashid b Waqar	0
H.H.Streak	c Inzamam b Waqar	2	(8)	b Waqar	0
G.J.Whittall	c Inzamam b Ashfaq	29	(6)	lbw b Wasim	0
G.K.Bruk-Jackson	c Aamir b Waqar	0	(7)	c Rashid b Wasim	4
D.H.Brain	c Rehman b Waqar	16		b Waqar	2
E.A.Brandes	c Basit b Wasim	18		lbw b Wasim	1
S.G.Peall	not out	11		c Inzamam b Wasim	10
Extras	(B9, LB10, W1, NB10)	30		(B1, LB11, W1, NB10)	23
Total		**254**			**187**

ZIMBABWE	O	M	R	W	O	M	R	W		FALL OF WICKETS			
Brandes	32	5	82	3	31	9	71	3		P	Z	P	Z
Brain	32	9	41	4	34	6	73	2	Wkt	1st	1st	2nd	2nd
Streak	23.2	5	58	3	20.3	3	56	5	1st	29	0	25	0
Whittall	17	6	39	0	(5) 4	1	10	0	2nd	33	102	38	135
Peall	6	3	9	0	(4) 8	4	13	0	3rd	99	110	39	140
G.W.Flower					4	0	13	0	4th	101	126	54	144
									5th	131	131	58	147
PAKISTAN									6th	187	203	132	152
Wasim	21	4	68	2	23.2	3	65	5	7th	209	203	209	153
Waqar	19	3	88	5	21	4	50	4	8th	225	204	219	164
Rehman	14	4	40	1	8	1	22	1	9th	241	225	240	168
Ashfaq	17	8	31	2	6	1	22	0	10th	245	254	248	187
Aamir	3	0	8	0									
Shoaib					(5) 4	1	16	0					

Umpires: Javed Akhtar (12) and Shakoor Rana (17). Referee: R.S.Madugalle (*Sri Lanka*) (2).

Close: 1st day – P(1) 185-5 (Asif 25, Rashid 32); 2nd – Z(1) 129-4 (Dekker 37, Streak 0); 3rd – P(2) 40-3 (Inzamam 9, Miandad 1); 4th – P(2) 221-8 (Wasim 5, Waqar 1).

PAKISTAN v ZIMBABWE 1993-94 (3rd Test)

At Gaddafi Stadium, Lahore, on 16, 17, 18, 20, 21 December.
Toss: Zimbabwe.   Result: MATCH DRAWN.
Debuts: Zimbabwe – W.R.James.

Lahore's seasonal fog and mist extracted 120 overs from the match after Zimbabwe had elected to bowl and had dismissed their hosts in 51.4 overs for 147, comfortably the lowest total against them in seven matches to date. Rashid became the sixth Pakistan wicket-keeper to make five dismissals in an innings. Waqar's 16th five-wicket prize in 26 Tests took his tally for the series to 27 at 13.81. Shoaib (325 minutes, 236 balls, 4 fours) took 315 minutes to complete his fifty, the sixth slowest recorded in Test cricket. His 81 in Karachi proved to be the highest individual score of a rubber dominated by bowlers.

PAKISTAN

Aamir Sohail	c Campbell b Brain	2	c James b Brain		32
Shoaib Mohammad	c Brandes b Rennie	14	not out		53
Inzamam-ul-Haq	b Brandes	33			
Javed Miandad	lbw b Brain	31			
Basit Ali	b Brain	29			
Asif Mujtaba	c James b Brain	0	(3) not out		65
†Rashid Latif	c Houghton b Brandes	7			
*Wasim Akram	not out	16			
Waqar Younis	b Brain	0			
Mushtaq Ahmed	b Brandes	1			
Ata-ur-Rehman	c James b Rennie	0			
Extras	(B4, LB6, NB4)	14	(B7, LB13, W1, NB3)		24
Total		**147**	(1 wicket)		**174**

ZIMBABWE

G.W.Flower	c Rashid b Rehman	30
M.H.Dekker	c Rashid b Wasim	2
A.D.R.Campbell	c Rashid b Waqar	6
D.L.Houghton	c Rashid b Waqar	50
*A.Flower	not out	62
G.J.Whittall	c Asif b Wasim	2
†W.R.James	c Shoaib b Waqar	8
H.H.Streak	b Waqar	0
D.H.Brain	c Aamir b Wasim	28
E.A.Brandes	lbw b Wasim	9
J.A.Rennie	c Rashid b Waqar	2
Extras	(B10, LB13, W1, NB7)	31
Total		**230**

ZIMBABWE	O	M	R	W	O	M	R	W	FALL OF WICKETS			
Brandes	14	3	45	3	16	5	31	0		P	Z	P
Brain	15	3	42	5	14	6	28	1	*Wkt*	*1st*	*1st*	*2nd*
Streak	12	3	28	0	16	4	25	0	1st	3	17	56
Rennie	10.4	3	22	2	14	6	35	0	2nd	50	35	–
G.W.Flower					10	2	15	0	3rd	54	88	–
Whittall					10.5	4	17	0	4th	107	121	–
Campbell					1	0	3	0	5th	111	126	–
A.Flower					0.1	0	0	0	6th	130	141	–
									7th	130	141	–
PAKISTAN									8th	135	187	–
Wasim	32	7	70	4					9th	140	215	–
Waqar	34.4	9	100	5					10th	147	230	–
Rehman	13	6	24	1								
Mushtaq	5	1	13	0								

Umpires: Athar Zaidi (4) and Khizer Hayat (28). Referee: R.S.Madugalle (*Sri Lanka*) (3).

Close: 1st day – Z(1) 15-0 (G.W.Flower 10, Dekker 2); 2nd – Z(1) 110-3 (Houghton 47, A.Flower 10); 3rd – Z(1) 121-3 (Houghton 50, A.Flower 15); 4th – P(2) 37-0 (Aamir 19, Shoaib 8).

SRI LANKA v WEST INDIES 1993-94 (Only Test)

At Tyronne Fernando Stadium, Moratuwa, on 8 (*no play*), 9, 10, 11, 12 (*no play*), 13 (*no play*) December.
Toss: Sri Lanka.   Result: MATCH DRAWN.
Debuts: Sri Lanka – D.P.Samaraweera.

Sri Lanka had waited more than twelve years since being elected to full membership of the ICC before West Indies played a Test match against them. Regrettably this inaugural match (Sri Lanka's 50th and West Indies' 300th) was staged on Sri Lanka's worst-appointed major ground. Named after the president of the Sri Lanka Cricket Board (who also happened to be MP for Moratuwa, a borough some dozen miles south of Colombo), the stadium boasts the most meagre of amenities, a barren, uneven pitch and no drainage. Inadequate pitch-covering and drying facilities restricted play to 11½ hours, even though the match was extended to include the scheduled rest day (11 December) after the opening day had been abandoned. Ironically, play would have been possible on any of Colombo's other grounds on the days when it proved to be impossible at Moratuwa. Harper, recalled to Test cricket after a five-year hiatus, opened with a seven-over spell of 1 for 1.

SRI LANKA

R.S.Mahanama	c Murray b Benjamin	11	c Simmons b Benjamin		11
D.P.Samaraweera	c Harper b Hooper	16	run out		5
H.P.Tillekeratne	c Lara b Harper	0	not out		9
P.A.de Silva	b Benjamin	53	not out		15
*A.Ranatunga	c Lara b Walsh	31			
S.T.Jayasuriya	lbw b Benjamin	0			
R.S.Kalpage	c Richardson b Ambrose	39			
†P.B.Dassanayake	c Murray b Benjamin	18			
G.P.Wickremasinghe	c Lara b Ambrose	0			
S.D.Anurasiri	b Ambrose	1			
M.Muralitharan	not out	1			
Extras	(B1, LB9, NB10)	20	(LB2, NB1)		3
Total		**190**	(2 wickets)		**43**

WEST INDIES

D.L.Haynes	lbw b Anurasiri	20
P.V.Simmons	c Dassanayake b Kalpage	17
*R.B.Richardson	c Dassanayake b Kalpage	51
B.C.Lara	c Dassanayake b Muralitharan	18
K.L.T.Arthurton	c Jayasuriya b Anurasiri	0
C.L.Hooper	c Samaraweera b Muralitharan	62
R.A.Harper	lbw b Jayasuriya	3
†J.R.Murray	lbw b Anurasiri	7
W.K.M.Benjamin	b Muralitharan	2
C.E.L.Ambrose	not out	7
C.A.Walsh	c Kalpage b Muralitharan	0
Extras	(LB5, NB12)	17
Total		**204**

WEST INDIES	O	M	R	W		O	M	R	W		FALL OF WICKETS		
Ambrose	12.2	5	14	3		6	2	13	0		SL	WI	SL
Walsh	21	6	40	1		9.1	4	20	0	*Wkt*	*1st*	*1st*	*2nd*
Harper	24	12	36	1	(4) 1	0	3	0	1st	18	42	17
Hooper	20	5	44	1						2nd	20	42	18
Benjamin	20	8	46	4	(3) 6	5	5	1	3rd	57	78	–
Arthurton	1	1	0	0						4th	106	84	–
										5th	106	168	–
SRI LANKA										6th	130	178	–
Wickremasinghe	11	0	35	0						7th	181	191	–
Ranatunga	4	1	6	0						8th	182	191	–
Anurasiri	35	6	77	3						9th	188	204	–
Kalpage	10	2	27	2						10th	190	204	–
Muralitharan	15.5	4	47	4									
Jayasuriya	3	0	7	1									

Umpires: K.T.Francis (11) and T.M.Samarasinghe (7). Referee: Zaheer Abbas (*Pakistan*) (1).

Close: 1st day – no play; 2nd – SL(1) 66-3 (De Silva 29, Ranatunga 6); 3rd – WI(1) 99-4 (Richardson 26, Hooper 9); 4th – SL(2) 43-2 (Tillekeratne 9, De Silva 15); 5th – no play.

AUSTRALIA v SOUTH AFRICA 1993-94 (1st Test)

At Melbourne Cricket Ground on 26, 27 (*no play*), 28, 29, 30 December.
Toss: Australia.   Result: MATCH DRAWN.
Debuts: South Africa – P.S.de Villiers, G.Kirsten.

Rain ruined South Africa's first Test in Australia since February 1964, restricting actual playing time to 15 hours 43 minutes. Wessels became the first player since W.E.Midwinter in 1881-82 to appear for and against Australia. Playing his 50th Test, Taylor (495 minutes, 349 balls, 12 fours) scored his 12th hundred in 89 innings and became the twelfth Australian to score 4,000 runs. He also became the first to score hundreds in his first matches against four different countries and the second, after M.D.Crowe, to score Test hundreds against seven different opponents. With Waugh he shared a series record fourth-wicket partnership of 169. Hudson retired at 152.

AUSTRALIA

M.A.Taylor	b Symcox	170
M.J.Slater	c Kirsten b Donald	32
S.K.Warne	lbw b De Villiers	0
D.C.Boon	b Matthews	25
M.E.Waugh	lbw b Matthews	84
*A.R.Border	c Richardson b Matthews	2
D.R.Martyn	b Symcox	8
†I.A.Healy	not out	7
P.R.Reiffel		
T.B.A.May	} did not bat	
C.J.McDermott		
Extras	(B2, LB7, NB5)	14
Total	**(7 wickets declared)**	**342**

SOUTH AFRICA

A.C.Hudson	retired hurt	64
G.Kirsten	c Taylor b Waugh	16
W.J.Cronje	c Boon b Warne	71
D.J.Cullinan	c Border b McDermott	0
J.N.Rhodes	not out	35
*K.C.Wessels	not out	63
†D.J.Richardson		
P.L.Symcox		
C.R.Matthews	} did not bat	
P.S.de Villiers		
A.A.Donald		
Extras	(LB2, NB7)	9
Total	**(3 wickets)**	**258**

SOUTH AFRICA	O	M	R	W		FALL OF WICKETS		
Donald	30	4	108	1			A	SA
De Villiers	32	6	83	1	Wkt	1st	1st
Matthews	24	5	68	3	1st	57	49
Cronje	13	4	25	0	2nd	58	157
Symcox	16.5	3	49	2	3rd	127	157
					4th	296	–
AUSTRALIA					5th	300	–
McDermott	23	5	60	1	6th	327	–
Reiffel	21	4	55	0	7th	342	–
Waugh	12	3	20	1	8th	–	–
May	28	7	58	0	9th	–	–
Warne	31	8	63	1	10th	–	–

Umpires: D.B.Hair (6) and T.A.Prue (8). Referee: J.L.Hendriks (*West Indies*) (1).

Close: 1st day – A(1) 71-2 (Taylor 30, Boon 4); 2nd – no play; 3rd – A(1) 140-3 (Taylor 63, Waugh 11); 4th – SA(1) 59-1 (Hudson 35, Cronje 3).

AUSTRALIA v SOUTH AFRICA 1993-94 (2nd Test)

At Sydney Cricket Ground on 2, 3, 4, 5, 6 January.
Toss: South Africa.   Result: SOUTH AFRICA won by 5 runs.
Debuts: None.

A crowd of 12,000, admitted free to watch Australia, with six wickets in hand, attain their modest target of 54 runs, unexpectedly witnessed an epic finish as South Africa snatched an astonishing victory by the fourth narrowest runs margin in Test history. Warne's first innings analysis included a spell of 5 for 5 in 22 balls and was a record against South Africa in Australia. His match figures of 12 for 128 were the second best in 80 Tests at Sydney. De Villiers, who bowled throughout the last morning (117 minutes), returned a match analysis of 10 for 123 in his second Test. Cronje deputised for Wessels (faulty knee) in the second innings. Australia were dismissed for their lowest total in a home Test in this series. That same total, the dreaded 'Nelson' (111), had proved to be their nemesis at Headingley in 1981.

SOUTH AFRICA

A.C.Hudson	lbw b McGrath	0		c Healy b McDermott	1
G.Kirsten	st Healy b Warne	67		b McDermott	41
W.J.Cronje	c Waugh b McDermott	41		b McDermott	38
D.J.Cullinan	b Warne	9	(5)	lbw b Warne	2
J.N.Rhodes	lbw b Warne	4	(6)	not out	76
*K.C.Wessels	c and b Warne	3	(4)	b Warne	18
†D.J.Richardson	c Taylor b Warne	4		lbw b McGrath	24
P.L.Symcox	b Warne	7		c Healy b McDermott	4
C.R.Matthews	c Taylor b Warne	0		c Waugh b Warne	4
P.S.de Villiers	c Waugh b McDermott	18		lbw b Warne	2
A.A.Donald	not out	0		c Healy b Warne	10
Extras	(B1, LB4, NB11)	16		(B13, LB1, NB5)	19
Total		**169**			**239**

AUSTRALIA

M.J.Slater	b Donald	92	(2)	b De Villiers	1
M.A.Taylor	c Richardson b Donald	7	(1)	c Richardson b De Villiers	27
D.C.Boon	b De Villiers	19		c Kirsten b De Villiers	24
M.E.Waugh	lbw b Symcox	7	(5)	lbw b Donald	11
*A.R.Border	c Richardson b De Villiers	49	(6)	b Donald	7
D.R.Martyn	c Richardson b De Villiers	59	(7)	c Hudson b Donald	6
†I.A.Healy	c Richardson b Donald	19	(8)	b De Villiers	1
S.K.Warne	c Rhodes b Symcox	11	(9)	run out	1
C.J.McDermott	c Cronje b De Villiers	6	(10)	not out	29
T.B.A.May	not out	8	(4)	lbw b De Villiers	0
G.D.McGrath	b Donald	9		c and b De Villiers	1
Extras	(B1, LB2, NB3)	6		(LB3)	3
Total		**292**			**111**

AUSTRALIA	O	M	R	W	O	M	R	W		FALL OF WICKETS			
McDermott	18.1	2	42	2	28	9	62	4		SA	A	SA	A
McGrath	19	5	32	1	14	3	30	1	*Wkt*	*1st*	*1st*	*2nd*	*2nd*
Warne	27	8	56	7	(4) 42	17	72	5	1st	1	10	2	4
May	10	1	34	0	(3) 22	4	53	0	2nd	91	58	75	51
Border					3	1	8	0	3rd	110	75	101	51
									4th	133	179	107	56
									5th	134	179	110	63
SOUTH AFRICA									6th	141	229	182	72
Donald	31.2	8	83	4	17	5	34	3	7th	142	250	188	73
De Villiers	36	12	80	4	23.3	8	43	6	8th	142	266	197	75
Matthews	28	11	44	0	6	5	9	0	9th	152	281	203	110
Symcox	46	11	82	2	10	3	22	0	10th	169	292	239	111

Umpires: S.G.Randell (15) and W.P.Sheahan (2). Referee: J.L.Hendriks (*West Indies*) (2).

Close: 1st day – A(1) 20-1 (Slater 5, Boon 7); 2nd – A(1) 200-5 (Martyn 15, Healy 6); 3rd – SA(2) 94-2 (Cronje 37, Wessels 7); 4th – A(2) 63-4 (Waugh 4, Border 7).

AUSTRALIA v SOUTH AFRICA 1993-94 (3rd Test)

At Adelaide Oval on 28, 29, 30, 31 January, 1 February.
Toss: Australia.   Result: AUSTRALIA won by 191 runs.
Debuts: None.

Australia squared this mini-rubber with an emphatic win based on outstanding first innings contributions from Steve Waugh. Having missed the first two Tests through a hamstring injury he made his highest score in a home Test (379 minutes, 276 balls, 19 fours), his seventh hundred (second in successive innings) coming in his first innings against South Africa, produced a spell of 4 for 15 in 8.5 overs and added a run out for good measure. With Border he shared a partnership of 208 to set a fifth-wicket record for this series. Border, playing in his last home Test, became the first to score 11,000 runs (in 259 innings) when his score reached 66. Despite a fractured thumb, 'nightwatchman' De Villiers survived for 197 minutes and contributed his (then) highest score to a stand of 82 which threatened to save the match. His partner, Peter Kirsten, batted for 568 minutes in the match but was fined twice for dissent involving decisions by umpire Hair, his liabilities allegedly being met from an appeal fund organised by a Johannesburg radio station. Playing in his 59th Test, Healy became the sixth 'keeper to make 200 dismissals. Warne, who took his 100th Test wicket in 23 matches, sealed Australia's first victory in this series since 1966-67 with 73 minutes to spare.

AUSTRALIA

M.A.Taylor	b G.Kirsten	62	(2) b Snell		38
M.J.Slater	c Rhodes b Donald	53	(1) lbw b Donald		7
D.C.Boon	c De Villiers b Donald	50	c Hudson b McMillan		38
M.E.Waugh	c Snell b McMillan	2	c Richardson b Donald		12
*A.R.Border	c Richardson b McMillan	84	run out		4
S.R.Waugh	c Richardson b Donald	164	c Richardson b Snell		1
†I.A.Healy	c Rhodes b McMillan	0	not out		14
P.R.Reiffel	not out	32	not out		2
S.K.Warne	not out	4			
C.J.McDermott	} did not bat				
T.B.A.May					
Extras	(LB9, NB9)	18	(LB7, NB1)		8
Total	(7 wickets declared)	**469**	(6 wickets declared)		**124**

SOUTH AFRICA

A.C.Hudson	lbw b S.R.Waugh	90	c S.R.Waugh b McDermott		2
G.Kirsten	c May b McDermott	43	b Warne		7
*W.J.Cronje	c Healy b Reiffel	0	lbw b Warne		3
P.N.Kirsten	c M.E.Waugh b Warne	79	lbw b McDermott		42
J.N.Rhodes	b S.R.Waugh	5	(6) lbw b May		4
D.J.Cullinan	b S.R.Waugh	10	(7) c Healy b McDermott		5
B.M.McMillan	lbw b S.R.Waugh	2	(8) lbw b Warne		4
†D.J.Richardson	lbw b McDermott	6	(9) c Taylor b May		10
R.P.Snell	c Healy b McDermott	10	(10) c and b Warne		1
P.S.de Villiers	run out	4	(5) c Reiffel b McDermott		30
A.A.Donald	not out	1	not out		0
Extras	(B3, LB10, W1, NB9)	23	(B9, LB7, W2, NB3)		21
Total		**273**			**129**

SOUTH AFRICA	O	M	R	W	O	M	R	W	FALL OF WICKETS				
Donald	38	7	122	3	11	2	26	2					
De Villiers	41	11	105	0						Wkt	A 1st	SA 1st	A 2nd	SA 2nd
Snell	19	6	44	0	(4) 12	3	38	2	1st	83	100	23	12
McMillan	30	3	89	3	(2) 11	0	33	1	2nd	152	103	79	17
Cronje	9	3	21	0	(3) 6	1	20	0	3rd	159	173	91	18
G.Kirsten	23	8	62	1					4th	183	179	99	100
P.N.Kirsten	4	0	17	0					5th	391	195	103	105
AUSTRALIA									6th	391	203	109	113
McDermott	27	9	49	3	19	8	33	4	7th	464	222	–	116
Reiffel	15	4	36	1	11	4	15	0	8th	–	243	–	128
May	25	9	57	0	(4) 32	20	26	2	9th	–	270	–	128
Warne	44.2	15	85	1	(3) 30.5	15	31	4	10th	–	273	–	129
M.E.Waugh	3	1	7	0	(7) 3	2	3	0					
S.R.Waugh	18	7	26	4	(5) 6	3	4	0					
Border					(6) 4	3	1	0					

Umpires: D.B.Hair (7) and T.A.Prue (9). Referee: J.L.Hendriks (*West Indies*) (3).

Close: 1st day – A(1) 240-4 (Border 28, S.R.Waugh 32); 2nd – SA(1) 39-0 (Hudson 17, G.Kirsten 16); 3rd – SA(1) 235-7 (P.N.Kirsten 52, Snell 7); 4th – SA(2) 18-3 (P.N.Kirsten 1, De Villiers 0).

INDIA v SRI LANKA 1993-94 (1st Test)

At K.D.'Babu' Singh Stadium, Lucknow, on 18, 19, 20, 22 January.
Toss: India.   Result: INDIA won by an innings and 119 runs.
Debuts: India – N.R.Mongia.

Named after India's gold medal-winning 1948 Olympic hockey captain, this was the 72nd ground to stage Test cricket. Sidhu (236 minutes, 172 balls, 8 sixes and 9 fours) recorded the highest of his five hundreds in 42 innings; only W.R.Hammond (10) has hit more sixes in a Test innings. Tendulkar (260 minutes, 224 balls, 22 fours) became the first to score seven hundreds before his 21st birthday. Tillekeratne completed 1,000 runs in 33 innings. Kumble, whose match analysis was the record for this series only until the third Test, returned his best analysis in first-class cricket to date as India won with a day and 45 minutes to spare.

INDIA

M.Prabhakar	lbw b Liyanage	21
N.S.Sidhu	c Kalpage b Muralitharan	124
V.G.Kambli	run out	5
S.R.Tendulkar	c Samaraweera b Anurasiri	142
M.Azharuddin	c Tillekeratne b Anurasiri	47
S.V.Manjrekar	c and b Muralitharan	61
Kapil Dev	c Wickremasinghe b Muralitharan	42
N.R.Mongia	c Samaraweera b Muralitharan	44
A.Kumble	b Wickremasinghe	4
R.K.Chauhan	c Tillekeratne b Muralitharan	3
S.L.V.Raju	not out	5
Extras	(LB3, W2, NB8)	13
Total		**511**

SRI LANKA

R.S.Mahanama	c Mongia b Kumble	73	c Azharuddin b Kumble	45
D.P.Samaraweera	lbw b Chauhan	42	lbw b Kumble	12
H.P.Tillekeratne	c Mongia b Kumble	7	c Prabhakar b Kumble	47
P.A.de Silva	c Azharuddin b Kumble	13	b Kumble	11
A.Ranatunga	c Chauhan b Raju	9	c Mongia b Kumble	0
R.S.Kalpage	c Azharuddin b Kumble	2	c Kumble b Raju	2
P.B.Dassanayake	st Mongia b Raju	36	b Prabhakar	15
D.K.Liyanage	lbw b Prabhakar	12	c Mongia b Chauhan	23
S.D.Anurasiri	b Prabhakar	2	lbw b Kumble	4
G.P.Wickremasinghe	lbw b Kapil Dev	6	not out	0
M.Muralitharan	not out	9	b Kumble	0
Extras	(LB7)	7	(B5, LB6, W4)	15
Total		**218**		**174**

SRI LANKA	O	M	R	W	O	M	R	W	FALL OF WICKETS			
Wickremasinghe	20	3	84	1						I	SL	SL
Liyanage	17	6	55	1					*Wkt*	*1st*	*1st*	*2nd*
Ranatunga	3	2	1	0					1st	63	120	29
Anurasiri	58	13	147	2					2nd	84	120	100
Kalpage	22	2	59	0					3rd	205	132	109
Muralitharan	41.5	3	162	5					4th	347	149	109
									5th	370	149	122
INDIA									6th	446	158	122
Prabhakar	16.4	7	36	2	16	3	38	1	7th	459	191	162
Kapil Dev	10	3	27	1	3	0	8	0	8th	482	197	174
Raju	20	10	25	2	14	5	28	1	9th	501	208	174
Kumble	37	10	69	4	27.3	9	59	7	10th	511	218	174
Chauhan	23	7	54	1	13	2	30	1				

Umpires: R.C.Sharma (1) and S.Venkataraghavan (4). Referee: E.de C.Weekes (*West Indies*) (1).

Close: 1st day – I(1) 269-3 (Tendulkar 88, Azharuddin 20); 2nd – I(1) 511 all out; 3rd – SL(1) 197-7 (Liyanage 6, Anurasiri 2).

INDIA v SRI LANKA 1993-94 (2nd Test)

At Chinnaswamy Stadium, Bangalore, on 26, 27, 29, 30 January.
Toss: India.   Result: INDIA won by an innings and 95 runs.
Debuts: None.

In virtually a repeat of the previous match, India gained another emphatic victory, this time after only 34 minutes of the fourth day. Azharuddin (289 minutes, 217 balls, a six and 11 fours) recorded his 13th Test hundred as India exceeded 500 for the fifth successive time in home Tests. With the final wicket, his 431st, Kapil Dev (27,506 balls in 129 Tests) equalled the world record held by Sir Richard Hadlee since November 1988 (21,918 balls in 86 Tests). Significantly, 64 of Kapil's matches were on India's slow surfaces. When he dismissed Samaraweera he passed another Hadlee record by removing 67 of his victims for ducks.

INDIA

M.Prabhakar	c Dassanayake b Wickremasinghe	14
N.S.Sidhu	lbw b Muralitharan	99
V.G.Kambli	c Wickremasinghe b Muralitharan	82
S.R.Tendulkar	b Anurasiri	96
*M.Azharuddin	lbw b Muralitharan	108
S.V.Manjrekar	c Mahanama b Muralitharan	39
Kapil Dev	not out	53
†N.R.Mongia	not out	18
A.Kumble		
R.K.Chauhan	did not bat	
S.L.V.Raju		
Extras	(B6, LB6, NB20)	32
Total	(6 wickets declared)	**541**

SRI LANKA

R.S.Mahanama	c and b Kumble	47		c Azharuddin b Raju	36
D.P.Samaraweera	c Prabhakar b Kapil Dev	0		c Tendulkar b Prabhakar	4
P.A.de Silva	c Chauhan b Prabhakar	17	(4)	lbw b Raju	8
*A.Ranatunga	lbw b Kapil Dev	26	(5)	c Sidhu b Kumble	28
S.T.Jayasuriya	c Prabhakar b Kumble	22	(6)	c sub (A.D.Jadeja) b Chauhan	1
H.P.Tillekeratne	c Raju b Kumble	0	(3)	c and b Chauhan	80
R.S.Kalpage	lbw b Kapil Dev	63		lbw b Kumble	18
†P.B.Dassanayake	lbw b Prabhakar	16		lbw b Kumble	0
S.D.Anurasiri	c Tendulkar b Prabhakar	4		c Azharuddin b Kapil Dev	7
G.P.Wickremasinghe	c Mongia b Prabhakar	8		c Sidhu b Kapil Dev	1
M.Muralitharan	not out	8		not out	20
Extras	(LB12, NB8)	20		(B9, LB3)	12
Total		**231**			**215**

SRI LANKA	O	M	R	W	O	M	R	W		FALL OF WICKETS		
Wickremasinghe	20	0	98	1							I	SL	SL
Jayasuriya	8	2	26	0					*Wkt*	*1st*	*1st*	*2nd*
Muralitharan	65	11	179	4					1st	34	7	5
Ranatunga	4	0	14	0					2nd	182	36	69
Anurasiri	45	2	158	1					3rd	248	94	97
Kalpage	19	1	54	0					4th	372	116	164
									5th	459	132	168
INDIA									6th	468	132	176
Prabhakar	20	4	82	4	3	0	18	1	7th	–	189	179
Kapil Dev	21.1	5	73	3	8.3	1	41	2	8th	–	196	188
Kumble	13	2	50	3	16	3	64	3	9th	–	208	189
Raju	4	0	14	0	12	2	36	2	10th	–	231	215
Chauhan					16	3	44	2				

Umpires: S.K.Bansal (2) and K.Parthasarathy (1). Referee: E.de C.Weekes (*West Indies*) (2).

Close: 1st day – I(1) 339-3 (Tendulkar 90, Azharuddin 32); 2nd – SL(1) 59-2 (Mahanama 25, Ranatunga 11); 3rd – SL(2) 179-7 (Kalpage 10).

INDIA v SRI LANKA 1993-94 (3rd Test)

At Gujarat Stadium, Ahmedabad, on 8, 9, 10, 12 February.
Toss: Sri Lanka.   Result: INDIA won by an innings and 17 runs.
Debuts: None.

India's achievement in winning their ninth successive home match dating back to 1988-89, the last six by an innings, was overshadowed by Kapil Dev's long-awaited world record. With most of India at a standstill monitoring his progress, he reached the landmark at 10.34am after 64 minutes of play, when Tillekeratne was taken at short-leg to become his 432nd victim and his 217th in India. His feat was saluted by 432 balloons and a minute's standing ovation from a crowd of 6,000. Azharuddin (361 minutes, 260 balls, a six and 16 fours) scored his 14th Test hundred (second in succession) in 87 innings. With Chauhan (9 in 132 minutes off 96 balls; 84 minutes before scoring) he added a series record 67 for the ninth wicket. In his third Test, Atapattu was dismissed for his fifth duck, including two 'pairs', in six innings. Azharuddin's ninth win in 27 Tests as captain equalled India's record held by Pataudi jr (40 Tests) and S.M.Gavaskar (47). Venkatapathy Raju's match figures of 11 for 125 marginally eclipsed the series record set by Kumble at Lucknow.

SRI LANKA

Batsman	Dismissal	Runs	Dismissal (2nd)	Runs
R.S.Mahanama	lbw b Kumble	18	lbw b Raju	63
D.P.Samaraweera	b Chauhan	16	run out	20
H.P.Tillekeratne	c Manjrekar b Kapil Dev	5	c Azharuddin b Raju	40
P.A.de Silva	lbw b Raju	7	c Azharuddin b Chauhan	14
*A.Ranatunga	c Azharuddin b Raju	15	c Sidhu b Raju	29
M.S.Atapattu	b Chauhan	0	c Mongia b Chauhan	0
R.S.Kalpage	c Azharuddin b Chauhan	2	c Azharuddin b Chauhan	9
†P.B.Dassanayake	c Kambli b Raju	10	not out	21
S.D.Anurasiri	b Raju	4	c Prabhakar b Raju	6
G.P.Wickremasinghe	st Mongia b Raju	22	c Prabhakar b Raju	0
M.Muralitharan	not out	5	c Mongia b Raju	4
Extras	(B8, LB7)	15	(B4, LB11, NB1)	16
Total		**119**		**222**

INDIA

M.Prabhakar	b Anurasiri	14
N.S.Sidhu	c Kalpage b Muralitharan	43
V.G.Kambli	c Ranatunga b Wickremasinghe	57
S.R.Tendulkar	b Wickremasinghe	6
*M.Azharuddin	b Muralitharan	152
S.V.Manjrekar	c Ranatunga b De Silva	16
Kapil Dev	lbw b De Silva	4
†N.R.Mongia	lbw b Anurasiri	14
A.Kumble	c Kalpage b De Silva	15
R.K.Chauhan	b Muralitharan	9
S.L.V.Raju	not out	1
Extras	(B17, LB5, NB5)	27
Total		**358**

INDIA	O	M	R	W	O	M	R	W		FALL OF WICKETS		
Prabhakar	5	0	13	0	5	2	11	0		SL	I	SL
Kapil Dev	9	4	15	1	5	1	12	0	*Wkt*	*1st*	*1st*	*2nd*
Kumble	15	3	30	1	(4) 28	9	45	0	1st	34	27	67
Raju	23.5	7	38	5	(3) 32.3	9	87	6	2nd	39	110	98
Chauhan	11	8	8	3	30	14	45	3	3rd	47	123	149
Tendulkar					4	1	7	0	4th	59	123	149
									5th	59	169	153
SRI LANKA									6th	71	203	167
Wickremasinghe	36	9	108	2					7th	79	249	193
Ranatunga	8	1	15	0					8th	89	288	214
Anurasiri	28	3	75	2					9th	108	355	214
Muralitharan	36.3	7	79	3					10th	119	358	222
Kalpage	7	2	9	0								
De Silva	23	5	50	3								

Umpires: A.L.Narasimhan (1) and V.K.Ramaswamy (14). Referee: E.de C.Weekes (*West Indies*) (3).

Close: 1st day – I(1) 90-1 (Sidhu 29, Kambli 45); 2nd – I(1) 329-8 (Azharuddin 134, Chauhan 0); 3rd – SL(1) 154-5 (Ranatunga 5, Kalpage 0).

NEW ZEALAND v PAKISTAN 1993-94 (1st Test)

At Eden Park, Auckland, on 10, 11, 12 February.
Toss: Pakistan.   Result: PAKISTAN won by five wickets.
Debuts: None.

A match dominated by fast bowlers ended shortly after lunch on the third day, 30 wickets having fallen on the first two. The highest partnership of the match was 75 from only 47 balls for the fourth wicket by Jones and Greatbatch (48 off 34 balls with a six and 8 fours). In his 51st Test, Wasim became the third Pakistan bowler to take 200 wickets. Subsequently, he bowled unchanged for 16.1 overs to return a career-best (then) 6 for 43. Earlier, Waqar had claimed his 150th wicket in 27 matches. Salim Malik, captaining Pakistan for the first time in his 72nd Test, held his 50th catch. Rashid's nine catches in the match created a Pakistan record, while Young's six catches set a match fielding record for New Zealand. Both umpires were guilty of some rare miscounting: Dunne managed an eight, two fives and two sevens, while Bird permitted a five-ball over.

NEW ZEALAND

B.A.Young	c Rashid b Waqar	29	c Rashid b Wasim		0
B.A.Pocock	c Rashid b Wasim	0	c Asif b Wasim		10
A.H.Jones	c Rashid b Mushtaq	66	c Rashid b Wasim		6
*K.R.Rutherford	b Waqar	14	b Waqar		18
M.J.Greatbatch	c Salim b Mushtaq	48	c Inzamam b Wasim		0
S.A.Thomson	c Rashid b Waqar	29	c Rashid b Waqar		0
C.L.Cairns	c Salim b Mushtaq	6	c Asif b Rehman		31
†T.E.Blain	c Mushtaq b Wasim	26	c Rashid b Rehman		4
S.B.Doull	c and b Waqar	0	c Salim b Wasim		29
R.P.de Groen	c Mushtaq b Wasim	2	not out		0
M.B.Owens	not out	2	c Rashid b Wasim		0
Extras	(B4, LB8, W1, NB7)	20	(B4, LB5, NB3)		12
Total		**242**			**110**

PAKISTAN

Saeed Anwar	c Blain b Cairns	16	c Young b De Groen		7
Aamir Sohail	c Jones b De Groen	16	c Young b Thomson		78
Asif Mujtaba	c Blain b Doull	8	c and b Doull		0
Mushtaq Ahmed	c Young b Doull	0			
*Salim Malik	c Young b Doull	18	(4) c Young b De Groen		11
Basit Ali	c Blain b Cairns	25	(5) c and b Doull		7
Inzamam-ul-Haq	c Young b De Groen	43	(6) not out		20
†Rashid Latif	lbw b Doull	30	(7) not out		13
Wasim Akram	c Blain b De Groen	35			
Waqar Younis	c Cairns b Doull	11			
Ata-ur-Rehman	not out	2			
Extras	(LB6, NB5)	11	(LB3, NB2)		5
Total		**215**	(5 wickets)		**141**

PAKISTAN	O	M	R	W	O	M	R	W		FALL OF WICKETS			
										NZ	P	NZ	P
Wasim	22.3	9	50	3	16.1	4	43	6		1st	1st	2nd	2nd
Waqar	15	2	46	4	10	3	35	2	Wkt				
Rehman	14	3	55	0	6	1	23	2	1st	3	17	0	21
Mushtaq	17	1	79	3					2nd	67	36	8	25
									3rd	95	48	31	56
NEW ZEALAND									4th	170	50	35	73
Cairns	18	2	75	2	6	1	15	0	5th	175	87	40	119
Owens	7	1	28	0	(4) 2	0	10	0	6th	185	93	44	–
Doull	15	2	66	5	16	0	48	2	7th	228	141	67	–
De Groen	17.4	5	40	3	(2) 13	3	48	2	8th	228	176	103	–
Thomson					4	1	17	1	9th	233	207	110	–
									10th	242	215	110	–

Umpires: H.D.Bird (*England*) (56) and R.S.Dunne (11). Referee: R.Subba Row (*England*) (7).

Close: 1st day – P(1) 61-4 (Salim 5, Basit 8); 2nd – P(2) 3-0 (Saeed 1, Aamir 1).

NEW ZEALAND v PAKISTAN 1993-94 (2nd Test)

At Basin Reserve, Wellington, on 17, 18, 19, 20 February.
Toss: New Zealand.   Result: PAKISTAN won by an innings and 12 runs.
Debuts: New Zealand – M.N.Hart.

Pakistan, their fast bowlers accounting for all 20 wickets on a blameless pitch, secured the match and the series after tea on the fourth day. Wasim, who dismissed Young with the fourth ball of the match, took seven wickets in an innings for the first time to claim his third ten-wicket match analysis. Pakistan recorded the highest total against New Zealand at Basin Reserve. Saeed (307 minutes, 248 balls, 26 fours) scored his maiden hundred in his fifth innings, Salim (286 minutes, 200 balls, 20 fours) his 11th in 106, and Inzamam (251 minutes, 195 balls, a six and 19 fours) his second in 21.

NEW ZEALAND

B.A.Young	lbw b Wasim	0	(2)	b Wasim	4
B.A.Pocock	b Rehman	16	(1)	b Waqar	0
A.H.Jones	lbw b Rehman	43		b Wasim	76
*K.R.Rutherford	c Raza b Rehman	7		c Raza b Rehman	63
M.J.Greatbatch	c Rashid b Waqar	45		c Rashid b Wasim	10
S.A.Thomson	b Wasim	7		c Rehman b Wasim	47
†T.E.Blain	c Saeed b Waqar	8		c Basit b Wasim	78
M.N.Hart	not out	12		b Wasim	7
D.K.Morrison	c Rashid b Wasim	5	(10)	lbw b Waqar	42
S.B.Doull	c Basit b Waqar	17	(9)	c Salim b Wasim	15
R.P.de Groen	b Wasim	4		not out	1
Extras	(LB7, NB4)	11		(B1, LB5, NB12)	18
Total		**175**			**361**

PAKISTAN

Saeed Anwar	run out	169
Aamir Sohail	lbw b Morrison	2
Akram Raza	c Blain b Morrison	0
Basit Ali	b Thomson	85
*Salim Malik	c and b Hart	140
Inzamam-ul-Haq	not out	135
Asif Mujtaba		
†Rashid Latif		
Wasim Akram	did not bat	
Waqar Younis		
Ata-ur-Rehman		
Extras	(B5, LB6, NB6)	17
Total	(5 wickets declared)	**548**

PAKISTAN	O	M	R	W	O	M	R	W	FALL OF WICKETS		
									NZ	P	NZ
Wasim	24	10	60	4	37	7	119	7	*Wkt*	*1st*	*1st*	*2nd*
Waqar	22	5	51	3	25.2	4	111	2	1st	0	34	3
Rehman	15	4	50	3	18	1	86	1	2nd	40	36	6
Raza	6	4	7	0	(5) 12	4	25	0	3rd	49	233	120
Aamir					(4) 1	0	1	0	4th	100	290	143
Salim					2	0	13	0	5th	126	548	209
									6th	128	–	216
NEW ZEALAND									7th	140	–	244
Morrison	31	4	139	2					8th	149	–	276
De Groen	31	8	104	0					9th	170	–	350
Doull	27	6	112	0					10th	175	–	361
Hart	31.2	9	102	1								
Thomson	17	3	80	1								

Umpires: B.L.Aldridge (21) and H.D.Bird (*England*) (57). Referee: R.Subba Row (*England*) (8).

Close: 1st day – P(1) 35-1 (Saeed 30, Raza 0); 2nd – P(1) 398-4 (Salim 62, Inzamam 63); 3rd – NZ(2) 189-4 (Jones 66, Thomson 37).

NEW ZEALAND v PAKISTAN 1993-94 (3rd Test)

At Lancaster Park, Christchurch, on 24, 25, 26, 27, 28 February.
Toss: New Zealand.   Result: NEW ZEALAND won by five wickets.
Debuts: Pakistan – Atif Rauf.

New Zealand mustered their highest fourth innings winning total to end their run of four successive defeats. Saeed was dropped off the first ball of the match. Basit (197 minutes, 139 balls, three sixes and 9 fours) scored his maiden Test hundred in his 14th innings. Jones, who was run out in both innings of his final Test before a retirement that was subsequently reduced to a sabbatical, reached his 50 off 46 balls. Waqar acquired his 17th five-wicket prize in 29 Tests as 15 wickets fell on the second day. With just over two days to score 324, Young (416 minutes, 314 balls, 7 fours) and Thomson (233 minutes, 167 balls, two sixes and 15 fours) shared a fifth-wicket stand of 154 and made their first Test hundreds as New Zealand completed their demanding task with more than five hours to spare. Wasim set a series record for Pakistan in New Zealand with his tally of 25 wickets at 17.24.

PAKISTAN

Saeed Anwar	c Young b Doull	69		c Blain b Morrison	0
Aamir Sohail	c Hartland b Doull	60		c Young b Doull	3
Atif Rauf	c Greatbatch b Morrison	16		c Young b Doull	9
*Salim Malik	b Hart	18	(5)	c Pringle b Morrison	23
Basit Ali	c Hartland b Pringle	103	(6)	run out	67
Inzamam-ul-Haq	c Greatbatch b Doull	5	(7)	c sub (M.A.Hastings) b Morrison	20
†Rashid Latif	c Hartland b Thomson	27	(8)	c and b Hart	3
Wasim Akram	c Greatbatch b Morrison	5	(9)	b Hart	17
Akram Raza	not out	29	(4)	st Blain b Hart	26
Waqar Younis	c Doull b Morrison	2		c Blain b Morrison	10
Aamir Nazir	b Morrison	0		not out	0
Extras	(LB6, W1, NB3)	10		(NB1)	1
Total		**344**			**179**

NEW ZEALAND

B.R.Hartland	c Basit b Waqar	3	(2)	c Inzamam b Wasim	10
B.A.Young	lbw b Aamir Nazir	38	(1)	b Wasim	120
A.H.Jones	run out	81		run out	26
*K.R.Rutherford	c Inzamam b Waqar	7		lbw b Wasim	13
M.J.Greatbatch	lbw b Wasim	1		c Inzamam b Waqar	1
S.A.Thomson	c Rashid b Waqar	3		not out	120
†T.E.Blain	lbw b Waqar	0		not out	11
M.N.Hart	lbw b Wasim	6			
S.B.Doull	lbw b Waqar	17			
D.K.Morrison	not out	6			
C.Pringle	b Waqar	0			
Extras	(B5, LB9, NB24)	38		(LB5, NB18)	23
Total		**200**		(5 wickets)	**324**

NEW ZEALAND	O	M	R	W	O	M	R	W		FALL OF WICKETS			
										P	NZ	P	NZ
Morrison	24	3	105	4	21.3	5	66	4	*Wkt*	*1st*	*1st*	*2nd*	*2nd*
Doull	25	3	93	3	(3) 5	0	13	2	1st	125	12	0	22
Pringle	33	6	83	1	(2) 17	3	41	0	2nd	147	109	4	76
Hart	9	2	37	1	18	5	47	3	3rd	169	124	26	119
Thomson	6	0	20	1	4	0	12	0	4th	195	139	53	133
PAKISTAN									5th	206	147	77	287
Wasim	22	5	54	2	38	6	105	3	6th	254	147	133	–
Waqar	19	1	78	6	27	6	84	1	7th	261	171	152	–
Aamir Nazir	15	2	54	1	16	0	59	0	8th	339	186	154	–
Raza					19	5	49	0	9th	344	198	171	–
Aamir Sohail					2	1	5	0	10th	344	200	179	–
Salim					4	1	13	0					
Saeed					1	0	4	0					

Umpires: R.S.Dunne (12) and K.T.Francis (*Sri Lanka*) (12). Referee: R.Subba Row (*England*) (9).

Close: 1st day – P(1) 334-7 (Basit 98, Raza 27); 2nd – P(2) 8-2 (Atif 3, Raza 2); 3rd – NZ(2) 9-0 (Young 3, Hartland 3); 4th – NZ(2) 277-4 (Young 115, Thomson 93).

WEST INDIES v ENGLAND 1993-94 (1st Test)

At Sabina Park, Kingston, Jamaica, on 19, 20, 21, 23, 24 February.
Toss: England.   Result: WEST INDIES won by eight wickets.
Debuts: None.

West Indies needed only 14 minutes on the fifth morning to complete another emphatic victory. England flattered to deceive, an opening partnership of 121 preluding the loss of all ten wickets for 113 runs as Kenneth Benjamin returned his best Test analysis. Arthurton (322 minutes, 232 balls, two sixes and 11 fours) completing his second hundred (the 100th for West Indies against England) in 25 innings on the eve of his 29th birthday. Adams (341 minutes, 226 balls, 10 fours) nursed the later order to a decisive lead of 173. He subsequently equalled the West Indies fielding record by holding six catches in the match. Atherton completed 2,000 runs in 57 innings. Hick (308 minutes, 187 balls, 12 fours) completed 1,000 runs in 33 innings during his highest score against West Indies.

ENGLAND

*M.A.Atherton	c Murray b K.C.G.Benjamin	55		c Adams b Walsh	28
A.J.Stewart	c Murray b K.C.G.Benjamin	70		run out	19
G.P.Thorpe	b K.C.G.Benjamin	16	(7)	b W.K.M.Benjamin	14
R.A.Smith	b Walsh	0	(3)	c Adams b Walsh	2
G.A.Hick	b Adams	23	(4)	c sub‡ b K.C.G.Benjamin	96
M.P.Maynard	lbw b K.C.G.Benjamin	35	(5)	c Murray b W.K.M.Benjamin	0
†R.C.Russell	lbw b K.C.G.Benjamin	0	(6)	c Adams b W.K.M.Benjamin	32
C.C.Lewis	c Adams b Ambrose	8		lbw b Ambrose	21
A.R.Caddick	c Adams b K.C.G.Benjamin	3		not out	29
A.P.Igglesden	not out	3		c Adams b K.C.G.Benjamin	0
D.E.Malcolm	run out	6		b Walsh	18
Extras	(B2, LB5, W4, NB4)	15		(B1, LB3, W2, NB2)	8
Total		**234**			**267**

WEST INDIES

D.L.Haynes	c Thorpe b Malcolm	4		not out	43
P.V.Simmons	c Russell b Caddick	8		lbw b Igglesden	12
*R.B.Richardson	c Maynard b Malcolm	5	(4)	not out	4
B.C.Lara	b Hick	83	(3)	b Caddick	28
K.L.T.Arthurton	c Lewis b Malcolm	126			
J.C.Adams	not out	95			
†J.R.Murray	lbw b Igglesden	34			
W.K.M.Benjamin	b Caddick	38			
C.E.L.Ambrose	b Caddick	0			
K.C.G.Benjamin	b Lewis	0			
C.A.Walsh	lbw b Lewis	0			
Extras	(LB10, W1, NB3)	14		(B5, LB3)	8
Total		**407**		**(2 wickets)**	**95**

WEST INDIES	O	M	R	W	O	M	R	W		FALL OF WICKETS			
Ambrose	22	8	46	1	24	4	67	1		E	WI	E	WI
Walsh	23	6	41	1	24.5	6	67	3	*Wkt*	*1st*	*1st*	*2nd*	*2nd*
K.C.G.Benjamin	24	7	66	6	(4) 18	2	60	2	1st	121	12	34	38
W.K.M.Benjamin	19.1	7	43	0	(3) 20	3	56	3	2nd	133	12	39	87
Adams	10	1	31	1	2	0	9	0	3rd	134	23	58	–
Simmons					3	1	4	0	4th	172	167	63	–
									5th	172	256	126	–
									6th	172	319	155	–
ENGLAND									7th	194	389	213	–
Malcolm	23	3	113	3	5	1	19	0	8th	209	389	226	–
Caddick	29	5	94	3	6	1	19	1	9th	227	390	228	–
Lewis	26	4	82	2	3	0	6	0	10th	234	407	267	–
Igglesden	24	5	53	1	7	0	36	1					
Hick	21	4	55	1	3	1	2	0					
Stewart					2.2	0	5	0					

‡ (R.A.Harper)

Umpires: S.A.Bucknor (10) and I.D.Robinson (*Zimbabwe*) (4). Referee: S.M.Gavaskar (*India*) (1).

Close: 1st day – E(1) 209-7 (Maynard 24, Caddick 3); 2nd – WI(1) 238-4 (Arthurton 113, Adams 21); 3rd – E(2) 80-4 (Hick 24, Russell 6); 4th – WI(2) 87-2 (Haynes 40).

WEST INDIES v ENGLAND 1993-94 (2nd Test)

At Bourda, Georgetown, Guyana, on 17, 18, 19, 20, 22 March.
Toss: West Indies.   Result: WEST INDIES won by an innings and 44 runs.
Debuts: West Indies – S.Chanderpaul.

Despite a resolute hundred by Atherton (411 minutes, 296 balls, 17 fours), his fourth in 58 innings and his first as captain, West Indies completed a substantial victory at 2.08pm on the fifth afternoon. It was England's first defeat at Bourda since 1947-48, their last appearance there being in 1973-74. Lara (256 minutes, 210 balls, two sixes and 25 fours) completed 1,000 runs in 21 innings during his first hundred in ten innings in the Caribbean. Adams (413 minutes, 262 balls, 21 fours) scored his maiden hundred in his eighth innings. Ambrose bowled Atherton with his fourth ball of the second innings to secure his 200th wicket from 10,922 balls in 45 Tests and become the eighth West Indies bowler to achieve this mark. Chanderpaul, Guyana's 19-year-old left-hander, was the first teenager to represent West Indies since E.T.Willett in 1972-73 and the first East Indian since A.I.Kallicharran in 1980-81.

ENGLAND

*M.A.Atherton	c Murray b Ambrose	144		b Ambrose	0
A.J.Stewart	b Walsh	0		b K.C.G.Benjamin	79
M.R.Ramprakash	lbw b Walsh	2		b Ambrose	5
R.A.Smith	c Lara b K.C.G.Benjamin	84		c Richardson b Ambrose	24
G.A.Hick	c Richardson b Ambrose	33		b K.C.G.Benjamin	5
G.P.Thorpe	b Ambrose	0		b Walsh	20
I.D.K.Salisbury	lbw b W.K.M.Benjamin	8	(9)	b Walsh	19
†R.C.Russell	c Richardson b Ambrose	13	(7)	c Murray b Ambrose	6
C.C.Lewis	c Richardson b K.C.G.Benjamin	17	(8)	c Adams b K.C.G.Benjamin	24
A.R.C.Fraser	not out	0		b K.C.G.Benjamin	0
A.P.Igglesden	b K.C.G.Benjamin	0		not out	1
Extras	(LB14, NB7)	21		(B2, LB2, W1, NB2)	7
Total		**322**			**190**

WEST INDIES

D.L.Haynes	c Russell b Salisbury	63
*R.B.Richardson	c Lewis b Fraser	35
B.C.Lara	c Atherton b Lewis	167
K.L.T. Arthurton	c Thorpe b Salisbury	5
J.C.Adams	lbw b Igglesden	137
S.Chanderpaul	b Salisbury	62
†J.R.Murray	lbw b Salisbury	0
W.K.M.Benjamin	b Fraser	44
C.E.L.Ambrose	c Russell b Lewis	10
K.C.G.Benjamin	c Russell b Lewis	1
C.A.Walsh	not out	10
Extras	(B2, LB6, W1, NB13)	22
Total		**556**

WEST INDIES	O	M	R	W	O	M	R	W		FALL OF WICKETS		
Ambrose	30	8	58	4	23	5	37	4		E	WI	E
Walsh	26	7	69	2	25	4	71	2	*Wkt*	*1st*	*1st*	*2nd*
K.C.G.Benjamin	23.5	5	60	3	(4) 19	6	34	4	1st	0	63	0
W.K.M.Benjamin	26	9	62	1	(3) 16	4	44	0	2nd	2	177	30
Adams	3	1	10	0	2	2	0	0	3rd	173	203	91
Chanderpaul	16	2	49	0					4th	245	315	96
									5th	253	441	129
ENGLAND									6th	276	441	140
Lewis	28	1	110	3					7th	281	505	150
Igglesden	24.3	3	94	1					8th	322	520	185
Fraser	29	5	85	2					9th	322	532	186
Salisbury	37	4	163	4					10th	322	556	190
Hick	20	1	61	0								
Ramprakash	15	1	35	0								

Umpires: C.R.Duncan (2) and S.Venkataraghavan (*India*) (5). Referee: J.R.Reid (*New Zealand*) (4).

Close: 1st day – E(1) 258-5 (Atherton 131, Salisbury 2); 2nd – WI(1) 152-1 (Haynes 53, Lara 57); 3rd – WI(1) 487-6 (Adams 102, W.K.M. Benjamin 37); 4th – E(2) 119-4 (Stewart 72, Thorpe 10).

WEST INDIES v ENGLAND 1993-94 (3rd Test)

At Queen's Park Oval, Port-of-Spain, Trinidad, on 25, 26, 27, 29, 30 March.
Toss: West Indies.   Result: WEST INDIES won by 147 runs.
Debuts: None.

Having held the upper hand for three days, England began their quest for the modest target of 194 with 15 overs remaining on the fourth evening. Atherton fell to Ambrose's first ball, Ramprakash ran himself out off the fifth and Smith was bowled by his eighth. In one of Test cricket's most sensational - and accurate - spells of sustained fast bowling, Ambrose destroyed England's slim hopes of recovering the Wisden Trophy. Desolate at 40 for 8 overnight, they were finally eliminated after 19 minutes (26 balls) the following morning, avoiding their lowest total in 699 Tests by a single run. This electrifying piece of demolition brought Ambrose record match figures for a home Test against England, ten wickets in a Test for the third time, and a bonus of £50,000 from a London company. It also provided West Indies with their first instance of two bowlers operating unchanged throughout a completed innings.

WEST INDIES

D.L.Haynes	b Salisbury	38	b Lewis		19
*R.B.Richardson	lbw b Salisbury	63	c and b Caddick		3
B.C.Lara	lbw b Lewis	43	c Salisbury b Caddick		12
K.L.T.Arthurton	lbw b Lewis	1	c Stewart b Caddick		42
J.C.Adams	c Smith b Lewis	2	c Russell b Salisbury		43
S.Chanderpaul	b Fraser	19	c Fraser b Caddick		50
†J.R.Murray	not out	27	c Russell b Caddick		14
W.K.M.Benjamin	b Fraser	10	c Fraser b Lewis		35
C.E.L.Ambrose	c Thorpe b Fraser	13	b Caddick		12
K.C.G.Benjamin	b Fraser	9	not out		5
C.A.Walsh	lbw b Lewis	0	lbw b Lewis		1
Extras	(B1, LB13, W1, NB12)	27	(B8, LB13, NB12)		33
Total		**252**			**269**

ENGLAND

*M.A.Atherton	c Murray b W.K.M.Benjamin	48	lbw b Ambrose		0
A.J.Stewart	b Ambrose	6	b Ambrose		18
M.R.Ramprakash	c and b W.K.M.Benjamin	23	run out		1
R.A.Smith	lbw b Ambrose	12	b Ambrose		0
G.A.Hick	lbw b Walsh	40	c Murray b Ambrose		6
G.P.Thorpe	c Lara b Ambrose	86	b Ambrose		3
†R.C.Russell	b Ambrose	23	(8) c sub (P.V.Simmons) b Ambrose		4
C.C.Lewis	b Ambrose	9	(9) c W.K.M.Benjamin b Walsh		6
I.D.K.Salisbury	c Lara b Walsh	36	(7) c Lara b Walsh		0
A.R.Caddick	c Lara b W.K.M.Benjamin	6	c Lara b Walsh		1
A.R.C.Fraser	not out	8	not out		0
Extras	(B10, LB9, W1, NB11)	31	(LB6, NB1)		7
Total		**328**			**46**

ENGLAND	O	M	R	W	O	M	R	W	FALL OF WICKETS			
										WI	E	WI	E
Fraser	24	9	49	4	25	6	71	0	Wkt	1st	1st	2nd	2nd
Caddick	19	5	43	0	26	5	65	6	1st	66	16	15	0
Lewis	25.2	3	61	4	27.5	6	71	3	2nd	158	82	37	1
Salisbury	22	4	72	2	9	1	41	1	3rd	158	87	51	5
Ramprakash	2	1	8	0					4th	163	115	131	21
Hick	3	1	5	0					5th	164	167	143	26
									6th	201	249	167	27
WEST INDIES									7th	212	273	227	37
Ambrose	29	6	60	5	10	1	24	6	8th	241	281	247	40
Walsh	27.2	3	77	2	9.1	1	16	3	9th	251	294	267	45
K.C.G.Benjamin	20	5	70	0					10th	252	328	269	46
W.K.M.Benjamin	24	3	66	3									
Adams	4	0	18	0									
Chanderpaul	5	0	13	0									
Arthurton	3	0	5	0									

Umpires: S.A.Bucknor (11) and S.Venkataraghavan (*India*) (6). Referee: J.R.Reid (*New Zealand*) (5).

Close: 1st day – WI(1) 227-7 (Murray 22, Ambrose 5); 2nd – E(1) 236-5 (Thorpe 64, Russell 17); 3rd – WI(2) 143-5 (Chanderpaul 1); 4th – E(2) 40-8 (Lewis 1).

WEST INDIES v ENGLAND 1993-94 (4th Test)

At Kensington Oval, Bridgetown, Barbados, on 8, 9, 10, 12, 13 April.
Toss: West Indies.   Result: ENGLAND won by 208 runs.
Debuts: None.

After their abysmal collapse in Trinidad and defeat in a subsequent four-day match, England extended their recent eccentric form by inflicting only the second defeat on their hosts in 30 Tests at Bridgetown. The last victorious tourists had been R.E.S.Wyatt's England side who won a low-scoring contest on a rain-affected pitch in January 1935. For the 13th consecutive Test at Bridgetown, the winner of the toss elected to bowl. Stewart (347 minutes, 221 balls, 18 fours) scored his fifth hundred on his 31st birthday. Three days later he added another, in his 68th innings (476 minutes, 319 balls, 20 fours), to become the first England P.V.batsman to score a hundred in each innings against West Indies. His stand of 150 with Thorpe was a fifth-wicket series record. Fraser's outstanding eight-wicket analysis included a 17-ball spell of 4 for 1, was England's best against West Indies and his best in first-class cricket. Requiring 446 in a minimum of 112 overs, West Indies were all out at 2.54 on the fifth afternoon. In the first innings, Haynes (cut finger) retired at 51, when 35, and resumed at 126 for 4. Richardson (pulled hamstring) retired at 32 in the second innings, when 18, and resumed at 150. Walsh hit Tufnell for three sixes in five balls before England completed their historic win to the vociferous delight of thousands of their touring supporters.

ENGLAND

*M.A.Atherton	c Lara b K.C.G.Benjamin	85		c Lara b Walsh	15
A.J.Stewart	b W.K.M.Benjamin	118		b Walsh	143
M.R.Ramprakash	c Murray b W.K.M.Benjamin	20		c Chanderpaul b Walsh	3
R.A.Smith	c Murray b W.K.M.Benjamin	10		lbw b K.C.G.Benjamin	13
G.A.Hick	c Murray b Ambrose	34		c Lara b Walsh	59
G.P.Thorpe	c sub‡ b K.C.G.Benjamin	7		c Arthurton b Walsh	84
†R.C.Russell	c Chanderpaul b Ambrose	38		not out	17
C.C.Lewis	c Murray b Ambrose	0		c Walsh b Adams	10
A.R.Caddick	b Ambrose	8			
A.R.C.Fraser	c Chanderpaul b Walsh	3			
P.C.R.Tufnell	not out	0			
Extras	(LB8, NB24)	32		(B8, LB6, NB36)	50
Total		**355**		**(7 wickets declared)**	**394**

WEST INDIES

D.L.Haynes	c Atherton b Fraser	35	(8)	c Thorpe b Tufnell	15
*R.B.Richardson	c Atherton b Fraser	20	(1)	c Ramprakash b Caddick	33
B.C.Lara	c sub (N.Hussain) b Lewis	26		c Tufnell b Caddick	64
K.L.T.Arthurton	c Russell b Fraser	0	(5)	b Tufnell	52
J.C.Adams	c Thorpe b Fraser	26	(2)	c Russell b Caddick	12
S.Chanderpaul	c Ramprakash b Tufnell	77		c sub (N.Hussain) b Hick	5
†J.R.Murray	c Thorpe b Fraser	0		c Thorpe b Caddick	5
W.K.M.Benjamin	c Hick b Fraser	8	(9)	c Stewart b Tufnell	3
C.E.L.Ambrose	c Hick b Fraser	44	(10)	b Lewis	12
K.C.G.Benjamin	not out	43	(4)	c Hick b Caddick	0
C.A.Walsh	c Tufnell b Fraser	13		not out	18
Extras	(LB1, NB11)	12		(B1, LB7, NB10)	18
Total		**304**			**237**

WEST INDIES	O	M	R	W	O	M	R	W		FALL OF WICKETS			
Ambrose	24.2	5	86	4	22	4	75	0		E	WI	E	WI
Walsh	24	3	88	1	28	5	94	5	*Wkt*	*1st*	*1st*	*2nd*	*2nd*
W.K.M.Benjamin	22	4	76	3	22	3	58	0	1st	171	55	33	43
K.C.G.Benjamin	20	5	74	2	20	1	92	1	2nd	223	55	43	43
Chanderpaul	10	4	23	0	10	3	30	0	3rd	242	95	79	128
Adams					6.5	0	31	1	4th	265	126	194	150
									5th	290	126	344	164
ENGLAND									6th	307	126	382	179
Fraser	28.5	7	75	8	17	7	40	0	7th	307	134	394	195
Caddick	24	2	92	0	17	3	63	5	8th	327	205	–	199
Lewis	17	2	60	1	(4) 8.2	1	23	1	9th	351	263	–	216
Tufnell	32	12	76	1	(3) 36	12	100	3	10th	355	304	–	237
Hick					4	2	3	1					

‡ (P.V.Simmons)

Umpires: L.H.Barker (19) and D.B.Hair (*Australia*) (8). Referee: J.R.Reid (*New Zealand*) (6).

Close: 1st day – E(1) 299-5 (Hick 26, Russell 3); 2nd – WI(1) 188-7 (Chanderpaul 31, Ambrose 35); 3rd – E(2) 171-3 (Stewart 62, Hick 52); 4th – WI(2) 47-2 (Lara 10, Arthurton 0).

WEST INDIES v ENGLAND 1993-94 (5th Test)

At Recreation Ground, St John's, Antigua, on 16, 17, 18, 20, 21 April.
Toss: West Indies.   Result: MATCH DRAWN.
Debuts: West Indies – S.C.Williams.

Determined to capitalise upon perfect batting conditions, Brian Charles Lara set his sights on the world record Test score of 365 not out by a 21-year-old Garfield Sobers against Pakistan at Kingston in February/March 1958. Starting his innings in the seventh over at 10.32 on the first morning, he broke the record with a pulled boundary off Lewis in the 178th over at 11.46am two days later. The ensuing crowd invasion, led by Sir Garfield himself, lasted six minutes. Lara's complete innings, the highest first-class score by a West Indian, occupied 768 minutes, 536 balls, and produced 45 fours, 10 threes, 33 twos and 99 singles. It took his series aggregate to a record 798 at 99.75. After 797 minutes in the field, England showed great resilience in equalling their hosts' mammoth total. Atherton (538 minutes, 383 balls, 13 fours) scored his fifth hundred and passed 500 runs for the series, while Smith (415 minutes, 315 balls, three sixes and 26 fours) made the highest of his nine hundreds. Their partnership of 303 was a third-wicket record for this series. In Richardson's absence, Walsh, in his 65th Test, became the first specialist bowler to captain West Indies, who, for the first time in their 305 Tests, were without a Barbados representative.

WEST INDIES

P.V.Simmons	lbw b Caddick	8	not out	22
S.C.Williams	c Caddick b Fraser	3	not out	21
B.C.Lara	c Russell b Caddick	375		
J.C.Adams	c sub (N.Hussain) b Fraser	59		
K.L.T.Arthurton	c Russell b Caddick	47		
S.Chanderpaul	not out	75		
†J.R.Murray				
W.K.M.Benjamin				
C.E.L.Ambrose	did not bat			
K.C.G.Benjamin				
*C.A.Walsh				
Extras	(LB3, NB23)	26		
Total	(5 wickets declared)	**593**	(0 wickets)	**43**

ENGLAND

*M.A.Atherton	c Murray b Ambrose	135
A.J.Stewart	c Ambrose b K.C.G.Benjamin	24
M.R.Ramprakash	lbw b K.C.G.Benjamin	19
R.A.Smith	lbw b K.C.G.Benjamin	175
G.A.Hick	b K.C.G.Benjamin	20
G.P.Thorpe	c Adams b Chanderpaul	9
†R.C.Russell	c Murray b W.K.M.Benjamin	62
C.C.Lewis	not out	75
A.R.Caddick	c W.K.M.Benjamin b Adams	22
A.R.C.Fraser	b Adams	0
P.C.R.Tufnell	lbw b W.K.M.Benjamin	0
Extras	(B9, LB20, NB23)	52
Total		**593**

ENGLAND	O	M	R	W	O	M	R	W
Fraser	43	4	121	2	2	1	2	0
Caddick	47.2	8	158	3	2	1	11	0
Tufnell	39	8	110	0	6	4	5	0
Lewis	33	1	140	0				
Hick	18	3	61	0	(4) 8	2	11	0
Ramprakash					(5) 3	1	5	0
Thorpe					(6) 2	1	1	0
Stewart					(7) 1	0	8	0
WEST INDIES								
Ambrose	40	18	66	1				
Walsh	40	9	123	0				
W.K.M.Benjamin	41.1	15	93	2				
K.C.G.Benjamin	37	7	110	4				
Chanderpaul	24	1	94	1				
Adams	22	4	74	2				
Arthurton	2	1	4	0				

FALL OF WICKETS

Wkt	WI 1st	E 1st	WI 2nd
1st	11	40	–
2nd	12	70	–
3rd	191	373	–
4th	374	393	–
5th	593	401	–
6th	–	417	–
7th	–	535	–
8th	–	585	–
9th	–	589	–
10th	–	593	–

Umpires: S.A.Bucknor (12) and D.B.Hair (*Australia*) (9). Referee: J.R.Reid (*New Zealand*) (7).

Close: 1st day – WI(1) 274-3 (Lara 164, Arthurton 25); 2nd – WI(1) 502-4 (Lara 320, Chanderpaul 41); 3rd – E(1) 185-2 (Atherton 63, Smith 68); 4th – E(1) 442-6 (Russell 18, Lewis 12).

SOUTH AFRICA v AUSTRALIA 1993-94 (1st Test)

At The Wanderers, Johannesburg, on 4, 5, 6, 7, 8 March.
Toss: South Africa.   Result: SOUTH AFRICA won by 197 runs.
Debuts: Australia – M.L.Hayden.

South Africa extended their successful, if considerably interrupted, home record against Australia with their seventh win (and one draw) in the last eight Tests. Despite its wide margin, victory was completed as light rain fell and thunderstorms threatened. With his first run, Hughes completed 1,000 in 68 innings and the Test double in his 52nd Test, thus becoming the eighth Australian to achieve this feat. Cronje (250 minutes, 192 balls, a six and 16 fours) scored his third Test hundred in 20 innings. Richardson surpassed R.W.Marsh's record by one match when he made his 50th dismissal in only his 12th Test. The referee fined Hughes and Warne for violating the ICC code of discipline, meagre penalties which were subsequently dramatically increased by the ACB.

SOUTH AFRICA

A.C.Hudson	c Healy b McDermott	17		b Warne	60
G.Kirsten	b Hughes	47		c Hughes b May	35
W.J.Cronje	c Border b S.R.Waugh	21		c S.R.Waugh b Hughes	122
*K.C.Wessels	c Hayden b Hughes	18		c Border b Warne	50
P.N.Kirsten	b May	12		c Boon b May	53
J.N.Rhodes	c M.E.Waugh b McDermott	69		c Healy b S.R.Waugh	14
B.M.McMillan	c Boon b May	0	(8)	b Warne	24
†D.J.Richardson	lbw b Warne	31	(9)	c Border b Warne	20
C.R.Matthews	c Boon b Hughes	6	(10)	not out	31
P.S.de Villiers	b McDermott	16	(7)	b McDermott	4
A.A.Donald	not out	0		not out	15
Extras	(B1, LB10, NB3)	14		(B13, LB4, NB5)	22
Total		**251**		(9 wickets declared)	**450**

AUSTRALIA

M.J.Slater	c Hudson b De Villiers	26	(2)	b De Villiers	41
M.L.Hayden	c Richardson b Donald	15	(1)	b De Villiers	5
D.C.Boon	c De Villiers b Donald	17		b Matthews	83
M.E.Waugh	run out	42		c Richardson b Donald	28
*A.R.Border	run out	34		c G.Kirsten b McMillan	14
S.R.Waugh	not out	45		c Richardson b Matthews	0
†I.A.Healy	b Matthews	11		c and b Donald	30
M.G.Hughes	c G.Kirsten b McMillan	7		not out	26
S.K.Warne	lbw b Matthews	15		lbw b McMillan	1
C.J.McDermott	lbw b Donald	31		b McMillan	10
T.B.A.May	lbw b De Villiers	2		c G.Kirsten b Cronje	11
Extras	(B1, LB1, NB1)	3		(LB5, NB2)	7
Total		**248**			**256**

AUSTRALIA	O	M	R	W	O	M	R	W	FALL OF WICKETS				
										SA	A	SA	A
McDermott	15.2	3	63	3	35	3	112	1	Wkt	1st	1st	2nd	2nd
Hughes	20	6	59	3	25	5	86	1	1st	21	35	76	18
May	22	5	62	2	39	11	107	2	2nd	70	56	123	95
S.R.Waugh	9	2	14	1	10	3	28	1	3rd	103	70	258	136
Warne	14	4	42	1	(6) 44.5	14	86	4	4th	116	136	289	164
M.E.Waugh					(5) 6	2	14	0	5th	126	142	324	164
									6th	126	169	343	191
SOUTH AFRICA									7th	194	176	366	219
Donald	19	0	86	3	23	3	71	2	8th	203	201	403	225
DeVilliers	19.3	1	74	2	30	11	70	2	9th	249	245	406	235
McMillan	14	3	46	1	19	2	61	3	10th	251	248	–	256
Matthews	15	4	40	2	20	6	42	2					
G.Kirsten					4	0	7	0					
Cronje					0.3	0	0	1					

Umpires: S.B.Lambson (3) and D.R.Shepherd (*England*) (20). Referee: D.B.Carr (*England*) (7).

Close: 1st day – A(1) 34-0 (Slater 26, Hayden 6); 2nd – SA(2) 42-0 (Hudson 22, G.Kirsten 17); 3rd – SA(2) 335-5 (P.N.Kirsten 32, De Villiers 4); 4th – A(2) 123-2 (Boon 56, M.E.Waugh 16).

SOUTH AFRICA v AUSTRALIA 1993-94 (2nd Test)

At Newlands, Cape Town, on 17, 18, 19, 20, 21 March.
Toss: South Africa.　　Result: AUSTRALIA won by nine wickets.
Debuts: None.

Australia squared the rubber with their seventh win in eight Tests at Newlands. Firm pre-match counsel from ICC and ACB administrators produced a marked change of attitude and behaviour from a stunned Australian team. Hudson (249 minutes, 175 balls, 13 fours) celebrated his 29th birthday with his second hundred. Steve Waugh and Healy added a series record 108 for the sixth wicket, with Healy completing 2,000 runs in his 89th innings and, in his 61st Test, becoming the fifth wicket-keeper to score 2,000 runs and make 200 dismissals. Waugh then returned the most remarkably economic of his three five-wicket analyses. Slater completed 1,000 Test runs in his 23rd innings. The third day (Saturday) produced a record attendance of 18,326.

SOUTH AFRICA

A.C.Hudson	run out	102	lbw b S.R.Waugh		49
G.Kirsten	run out	29	lbw b Warne		10
W.J.Cronje	b McGrath	2	c and b S.R.Waugh		19
*K.C.Wessels	c M.E.Waugh b McDermott	11	run out		9
P.N.Kirsten	lbw b Warne	70	c Taylor b Warne		3
J.N.Rhodes	lbw b McGrath	5	c Border b S.R.Waugh		27
B.M.McMillan	b Warne	74	(8) lbw b S.R.Waugh		3
†D.J.Richardson	lbw b McDermott	34	(9) c Healy b McGrath		31
C.R.Matthews	not out	7	(10) not out		0
P.S.de Villiers	c Taylor b Warne	7	(7) lbw b Warne		0
A.A.Donald	c Healy b McGrath	7	b S.R.Waugh		0
Extras	(LB6, NB7)	13	(B4, LB6, NB3)		13
Total		**361**			**164**

AUSTRALIA

M.J.Slater	c P.N.Kirsten b De Villiers	26	(2) not out		43
M.A.Taylor	c Richardson b De Villiers	70	(1) b Donald		14
D.C.Boon	c Richardson b De Villiers	96	not out		32
M.E.Waugh	c P.N.Kirsten b McMillan	7			
*A.R.Border	c Richardson b Matthews	45			
S.R.Waugh	b Matthews	86			
†I.A.Healy	c De Villiers b Matthews	61			
M.G.Hughes	lbw b Matthews	0			
S.K.Warne	c McMillan b De Villiers	11			
C.J.McDermott	c P.N.Kirsten b Matthews	1			
G.D.McGrath	not out	1			
Extras	(B6, LB17, W1, NB7)	31	(B1, NB2)		3
Total		**435**	(1 wicket)		**92**

AUSTRALIA	O	M	R	W	O	M	R	W	FALL OF WICKETS			
										SA	A	SA	A
McDermott	27	6	80	2	13	3	39	0	Wkt	1st	1st	2nd	2nd
Hughes	20	1	80	0	5	1	12	0	1st	71	40	33	30
McGrath	26.1	4	65	3	(4) 16	6	26	1	2nd	78	145	69	–
S.R.Waugh	9	3	20	0	(5) 22.3	9	28	5	3rd	100	153	94	–
Warne	47	18	78	3	(3) 30	13	38	3	4th	189	244	97	–
M.E.Waugh	10	3	23	0	(7) 3	1	11	0	5th	198	310	97	–
Border	5	2	9	0	(6) 1	1	0	0	6th	260	418	97	–
									7th	335	418	103	–
SOUTH AFRICA									8th	339	430	164	–
Donald	35	10	111	0	(3) 5	0	20	1	9th	348	434	164	–
De Villiers	44.4	11	117	4	6	0	20	0	10th	361	435	164	–
Matthews	36	12	80	5	(1) 6	1	14	0					
McMillan	29	8	82	1	5	0	23	0					
G.Kirsten	4	0	13	0	(6) 1.1	0	10	0					
Cronje	11	4	9	0	(5) 2	0	4	0					

Umpires: K.E.Liebenberg (3) and D.R.Shepherd (*England*) (21). Referee: D.B.Carr (*England*) (8).

Close: 1st day – SA(1) 237-5 (P.N.Kirsten 62, McMillan 16); 2nd – A(1) 112-1 (Taylor 57, Boon 26); 3rd – A(1) 336-5 (S.R.Waugh 50, Healy 15); 4th – SA(2) 100-6 (Rhodes 1, McMillan 1).

SOUTH AFRICA v AUSTRALIA 1993-94 (3rd Test)

At Kingsmead, Durban, on 25, 26, 27, 28, 29 March.
Toss: South Africa.   Result: MATCH DRAWN.
Debuts: None.

As a public relations exercise in a country starved of Test cricket for two decades, this attritional match on a lifeless pitch was a disaster. Wessels won few admirers for his grossly defensive strategy whereby, having put Australia in and dismissed them before lunch on the second day, his batsmen grafted to a decisive lead in the hope that Australia would collapse in the time left. Having drawn level, it took South Africa a further five hours to gain a lead of only 153, their total of 422 requiring 205.2 overs and 832 minutes. Hudson became the first South African to complete 1,000 runs (in his 25th innings) since his country's restoration. Mark Waugh (283 minutes, 222 balls, 13 fours) scored his sixth hundred and shared an unbroken fifth-wicket partnership with his captain to draw the rubber. Border subsequently announced his retirement after a record-breaking career which brought him most caps (156), most innings (265), most runs (11,174), most scores of 50 or more (90), most catches in the field (156), most matches as captain (93; 32 wins, 22 defeats, 38 draws, 1 tie), and the longest unbroken sequences as a player (153) and as a captain (93).

AUSTRALIA

M.J.Slater	c Rhodes b Matthews	20	(2)	lbw b Donald	95
M.A.Taylor	lbw b Donald	1	(1)	lbw b De Villiers	12
D.C.Boon	c G.Kirsten b Donald	37		c P.N.Kirsten b Donald	12
M.E.Waugh	c Richardson b Donald	43	(5)	not out	113
*A.R.Border	c Rhodes b McMillan	17	(6)	not out	42
S.R.Waugh	c Wessels b Matthews	64			
†I.A.Healy	b Matthews	55			
P.R.Reiffel	lbw b De Villiers	13			
S.K.Warne	c Wessels b Matthews	2	(4)	c McMillan b Donald	12
C.J.McDermott	c Donald b DeVilliers	6			
G.D.McGrath	not out	0			
Extras	(LB1, W1, NB9)	11		(LB6, W1, NB4)	11
Total		**269**		**(4 wickets)**	**297**

SOUTH AFRICA

A.C.Hudson	lbw b Reiffel	65
G.Kirsten	c Healy b Reiffel	41
W.J.Cronje	c S.R.Waugh b Warne	26
*K.C.Wessels	lbw b McDermott	1
P.N.Kirsten	lbw b S.R.Waugh	49
J.N.Rhodes	lbw b Warne	78
B.M.McMillan	c Slater b S.R.Waugh	84
†D.J.Richardson	c Reiffel b Warne	59
C.R.Matthews	lbw b Warne	1
P.S.de Villiers	lbw b S.R.Waugh	0
A.A.Donald	not out	0
Extras	(B3, LB10, NB5)	18
Total		**422**

SOUTH AFRICA	O	M	R	W	O	M	R	W		FALL OF WICKETS		
Donald	18	1	71	3	28	7	66	3		A	SA	A
De Villiers	24.2	5	55	2	24	5	69	1	Wkt	1st	1st	2nd
Matthews	29	9	65	4	(4) 28	12	56	0	1st	7	100	55
McMillan	19	5	56	1	(3) 22	6	53	0	2nd	45	117	81
Cronje	5	1	8	0	18	5	40	0	3rd	81	118	109
G.Kirsten	6	1	13	0	3	1	7	0	4th	123	155	157
Rhodes					1	1	0	0	5th	123	256	–
									6th	215	274	–
AUSTRALIA									7th	250	417	–
McDermott	38	11	76	1					8th	256	422	–
Reiffel	30	7	77	2					9th	269	422	–
McGrath	41	11	78	0					10th	269	422	–
Warne	55	20	92	4								
S.R.Waugh	27.2	12	40	3								
M.E.Waugh	11	3	38	0								
Border	3	1	8	0								

Umpires: Mahboob Shah (*Pakistan*) (22) and C.J.Mitchley (3). Referee: D.B.Carr (*England*) (9).

Close: 1st day – A(1) 241-6 (S.R.Waugh 50, Reiffel 8); 2nd – SA(1) 143-3 (Cronje 16, P.N.Kirsten 14); 3rd – SA(1) 322-6 (McMillan 35, Richardson 16); 4th – A(2) 89-2 (Slater 56, Warne 4).

NEW ZEALAND v INDIA 1993-94 (Only Test)

At Trust Bank Park, Hamilton, on 19, 20, 21, 22, 23 March.
Toss: New Zealand.   Result: MATCH DRAWN.
Debuts: New Zealand – S.P.Fleming.

India were set 310 to win from a minimum of 66 overs but they aborted the chase after Sidhu's dismissal. With his first innings score 31, Tendulkar, at 20 years 331 days and playing his 44th innings, became the youngest to score 2,000 runs. Rutherford subsequently reached the same mark in his 79th innings. During his 88th innings, Azharuddin became the sixth Indian to compile 4,000 runs. The left-handed Fleming (250 minutes, 177 balls, 12 fours) looked set for a hundred on debut when he edged to slip.

NEW ZEALAND

B.A.Hartland	c Chauhan b Kapil Dev	0	(2)	c Mongia b Srinath	25
B.A.Young	c Kumble b Srinath	13	(1)	c Mongia b Chauhan	85
*K.R.Rutherford	b Kumble	63		b Chauhan	59
M.J.Greatbatch	c Azharuddin b Srinath	12		c Manjrekar b Kumble	27
S.P.Fleming	c Kambli b Srinath	16		c Kapil b Chauhan	92
S.A.Thomson	c Manjrekar b Raju	12		b Raju	26
†A.C.Parore	c and b Chauhan	9		c Mongia b Kapil Dev	17
M.N.Hart	b Chauhan	17		not out	20
D.J.Nash	not out	10		not out	9
D.K.Morrison	lbw b Srinath	3			
C.Pringle	b Raju	18			
Extras	(LB9, NB5)	14		(B2, LB1, NB5)	8
Total		**187**		**(7 wickets declared)**	**368**

INDIA

†N.R.Mongia	run out	45		b Hart	38
N.S.Sidhu	b Morrison	10		c Parore b Hart	98
V.G.Kambli	c Young b Pringle	9		b Pringle	19
S.R.Tendulkar	c Nash b Thomson	43		not out	11
*M.Azharuddin	b Thomson	63			
S.V.Manjrekar	c Young b Morrison	29	(5)	not out	8
Kapil Dev	c Fleming b Nash	18			
A.Kumble	c Fleming b Morrison	7			
R.K.Chauhan	not out	12			
S.L.V.Raju	c Young b Morrison	2			
J.Srinath	c Parore b Pringle	1			
Extras	(LB6, W1)	7		(LB3)	3
Total		**246**		**(3 wickets)**	**177**

INDIA	O	M	R	W	O	M	R	W	FALL OF WICKETS			
									NZ	I	NZ	I
Srinath	31	8	60	4	33	4	104	1				
Kapil Dev	9	2	29	1	16	2	43	1	Wkt	1st	1st	2nd	2nd
Kumble	23	8	34	1	(4) 27	6	68	1	1st	1	25	56	102
Raju	13.2	5	14	2	(3) 24	6	53	1	2nd	21	38	172	140
Chauhan	21	6	41	2	29	5	97	3	3rd	49	89	176	167
									4th	100	138	220	–
NEW ZEALAND									5th	122	183	265	–
Morrison	30	9	52	4	8	1	15	0	6th	124	216	317	–
Nash	20	5	57	1	13	6	25	0	7th	154	226	355	–
Pringle	22.3	8	52	2	(4) 12	2	29	1	8th	155	227	–	–
Hart	19	5	33	0	(5) 15	2	66	2	9th	158	237	–	–
Thomson	11	1	46	2	(3) 11	1	39	0	10th	187	246	–	–

Umpires: B.L.Aldridge (22) and Khizer Hayat (*Pakistan*) (29). Referee: R.Subba Row (*England*) (10).

Close: 1st day – NZ(1) 81-3 (Rutherford 43, Fleming 10); 2nd – I(1) 104-3 (Mongia 33, Azharuddin 8); 3rd – NZ(2) 39-0 (Young 19, Hartland 18); 4th – NZ(2) 306-5 (Fleming 67, Parore 10).

ENGLAND v NEW ZEALAND 1994 (1st Test)

At Trent Bridge, Nottingham, on 2, 3, 4, 5, 6 June.
Toss: New Zealand.   Result: ENGLAND won by an innings and 90 runs.
Debuts: England – S.J.Rhodes, C.White; New Zealand – H.T.Davis, G.R.Larsen.

At 12.30pm on the fifth day, England gained their first win by an innings margin since 1991-92 and their first at home since 1985. Atherton (325 minutes, 264 balls, 13 fours) compiled his sixth hundred in 65 innings and his second in successive innings. Gooch (418 minutes, 317 balls, 29 fours) scored the last of his 20 hundreds, completed 1,000 runs against New Zealand, became England's highest scorer in this series, overtook G.Boycott's England record of 64 scores of 50 or more and was the fourth oldest player to score 200 in a Test. England's total was their highest against New Zealand. DeFreitas became the 100th bowler to take 100 wickets and recorded his fourth five-wicket analysis in 34 Tests. Larsen made his Test debut after appearing in 55 limited-overs internationals. Bucknor was the first overseas umpire to officiate in a Test in England since Australian 'Dimboola Jim' Phillips stood in eleven Tests between 1893 and 1905.

NEW ZEALAND

B.A.Young	c Hick b DeFreitas	15	(2) c Rhodes b Fraser		53
B.R.Hartland	c Hick b DeFreitas	6	(1) lbw b DeFreitas		22
*K.R.Rutherford	lbw b DeFreitas	25	c Atherton b Such		14
M.D.Crowe	c Rhodes b White	16	lbw b DeFreitas		28
S.P.Fleming	c White b DeFreitas	54	c White b Hick		11
S.A.Thomson	c Hick b Fraser	14	c White b Such		6
†A.C.Parore	c Rhodes b Malcolm	38	c Rhodes b DeFreitas		42
G.R.Larsen	c Fraser b Such	8	c Stewart b DeFreitas		2
M.N.Hart	c Hick b Fraser	36	lbw b Fraser		22
D.J.Nash	c Rhodes b Malcolm	19	c Rhodes b DeFreitas		5
H.T.Davis	not out	0	not out		0
Extras	(LB6, NB14)	20	(LB1, NB20)		21
Total		**251**			**226**

ENGLAND

*M.A.Atherton	c Parore b Larsen	101
A.J.Stewart	c Larsen b Davis	8
G.A.Gooch	c Crowe b Thomson	210
G.A.Hick	b Nash	18
R.A.Smith	run out	78
C.White	c Larsen b Hart	19
†S.J.Rhodes	c Thomson b Nash	49
P.A.J.DeFreitas	not out	51
A.R.C.Fraser	c Fleming b Larsen	8
P.M.Such	} did not bat	
D.E.Malcolm		
Extras	(LB9, W6, NB10)	25
Total	(8 wickets declared)	**567**

ENGLAND	O	M	R	W	O	M	R	W	FALL OF WICKETS			
Malcolm	17.4	5	45	2	10	2	39	0		NZ	E	NZ
Fraser	21	10	40	2	23	8	53	2	*Wkt*	*1st*	*1st*	*2nd*
DeFreitas	23	4	94	4	22.3	4	71	5	1st	13	16	59
Such	19	7	28	1	34	12	50	2	2nd	37	279	95
White	13	3	38	1	(6) 3	3	0	0	3rd	66	314	95
Hick					(5) 14	6	12	1	4th	78	375	122
									5th	108	414	141
									6th	168	482	141
NEW ZEALAND									7th	188	528	147
Davis	21	0	93	1					8th	194	567	201
Nash	36	5	153	2					9th	249	–	224
Larsen	44.4	11	116	2					10th	251	–	226
Hart	35	7	123	1								
Thomson	38	6	73	1								

Umpires: H.D.Bird (58) and S.A.Bucknor (*West Indies*) (13). Referee: C.H.Lloyd (*West Indies*) (7).

Close: 1st day – NZ(1) 236-8 (Hart 28, Nash 13); 2nd – E(1) 277-1 (Atherton 101, Gooch 152); 3rd – E(1) 516-6 (Rhodes 41, DeFreitas 17); 4th – NZ(2) 184-7 (Parore 20, Hart 15).

ENGLAND v NEW ZEALAND 1994 (2nd Test)

At Lord's, London, on 16, 17, 18, 19, 20 June.
Toss: New Zealand.   Result: MATCH DRAWN.
Debuts: None.

Almost unrecognisable as the side that was so badly mauled at Trent Bridge, New Zealand came close to squaring the rubber. England scrambled a draw through Stewart's second hundred at Lord's and a highly determined rearguard action led by Rhodes (129 minutes, 114 balls). Crowe (368 minutes, 255 balls, three sixes and 20 fours) scored his 16th hundred in 117 innings and became the second after J.G.Wright to score 5,000 runs for New Zealand. His partnership of 180 in 174 minutes with Thomson was a fifth-wicket series record. Stewart (288 minutes, 229 balls, 20 fours) contributed his seventh hundred in 72 innings. Nash became the first New Zealand bowler to take eleven wickets in a Test against England; his analysis of 6 for 76 was a record for New Zealand at Lord's and he was also the first to take ten or more wickets and score 50 in a Test there.

NEW ZEALAND

B.A.Young	lbw b Fraser	0	(2)	c Hick b Such	94
B.A.Pocock	c Smith b Such	10	(1)	lbw b DeFreitas	2
K.R.Rutherford	c Stewart b DeFreitas	37		lbw b DeFreitas	0
M.D.Crowe	c Smith b DeFreitas	142		b DeFreitas	9
S.P.Fleming	lbw b Fraser	41		lbw b Taylor	39
S.A.Thomson	run out	69		not out	38
A.C.Parore	c Rhodes b Taylor	40		not out	15
M.N.Hart	b Such	25			
D.J.Nash	b White	56			
C.Pringle	c Hick b DeFreitas	14			
M.B.Owens	not out	2			
Extras	(B3, LB15, W1, NB21)	40		(LB4, NB10)	14
Total		**476**		(5 wickets declared)	**211**

ENGLAND

M.A.Atherton	lbw b Hart	28	c Young b Nash	33
A.J.Stewart	c Parore b Nash	45	c Crowe b Nash	119
G.A.Gooch	lbw b Nash	13	lbw b Nash	0
R.A.Smith	c and b Nash	6	c Parore b Nash	23
G.A.Hick	c Young b Pringle	58	lbw b Pringle	37
C.White	run out	51	c Thomson b Nash	9
S.J.Rhodes	not out	32	not out	24
P.A.J.DeFreitas	c Parore b Thomson	11	lbw b Owens	3
A.R.C.Fraser	c and b Nash	10	lbw b Hart	2
J.P.Taylor	c Parore b Nash	0	not out	0
P.M.Such	c Parore b Nash	4		
Extras	(B4, LB12, NB7)	23	(B2, LB1, NB1)	4
Total		**281**	(8 wickets)	**254**

ENGLAND	O	M	R	W	O	M	R	W		FALL OF WICKETS			
										NZ	E	NZ	E
Fraser	36	9	102	2	15	0	50	0	Wkt	1st	1st	2nd	2nd
DeFreitas	35	8	102	3	16	0	63	3	1st	0	65	9	60
Taylor	20	4	64	1	(6) 6	2	18	1	2nd	39	95	9	60
Such	30	8	84	2	(3) 25	5	55	1	3rd	67	95	29	136
White	21.1	4	84	1	(4) 4	1	21	0	4th	138	101	144	210
Gooch	5	1	13	0					5th	318	193	170	217
Hick	2	0	9	0	(5) 2	2	0	0	6th	350	225	–	240
									7th	391	241	–	244
NEW ZEALAND									8th	397	265	–	250
Owens	7	0	34	0	(2) 10	3	35	1	9th	434	271	–	–
Nash	25	6	76	6	(1) 29	8	93	5	10th	476	281	–	–
Pringle	23	5	65	1	(4) 16	5	41	1					
Hart	44	21	50	1	(3) 41	23	55	1					
Thomson	22	8	40	1	12	4	27	0					

Umpires: S.A.Bucknor (*West Indies*) (14) and N.T.Plews (7). Referee: C.H.Lloyd (*West Indies*) (8).

Close: 1st day – NZ(1) 316-4 (Crowe 133, Thomson 68); 2nd – E(1) 94-1 (Atherton 27, Gooch 13); 3rd – E(1) 281 all out; 4th – E(2) 56-0 (Atherton 29, Stewart 25).

ENGLAND v NEW ZEALAND 1994 (3rd Test)

At Old Trafford, Manchester, on 30 June, 1, 2, 4, 5 July.
Toss: England.   Result: MATCH DRAWN.
Debuts: England – D.Gough.

Despite a fine all-round debut by Gough, England's attempts to gain a second victory in this rubber were thwarted by two high-class innings from Crowe and seasonal Mancunian weather which, after several interruptions, prevented further play after 3.20 on the last afternoon. Atherton (408 minutes, 307 balls, 1 fours) scored his seventh hundred in 68 innings and his fourth in ten Tests as captain. He was the first Lancashire player to captain England at Old Trafford since A.C.MacLaren in 1909. DeFreitas (69 off 107 balls with 8 fours) and debutant Gough (65 off 126 balls with 10 fours) added 130 in 134 minutes for the eighth wicket. Gough dismissed Greatbatch with his fifth (legitimate) ball in Tests. In his 110th Test, Gooch became the fourth England fieldsman to hold 100 catches. Crowe (335 minutes, 237 balls, 15 fours) reached his 17th hundred in 120 Test innings and his fifth against England. His partnership of 141 with Parore was sixth-wicket record against England. This was New Zealand's first Test at Old Trafford since 1958.

ENGLAND

*M.A.Atherton	lbw b Nash	111
A.J.Stewart	c Pringle b Nash	24
G.A.Gooch	c Young b Nash	0
R.A.Smith	b Owens	13
G.A.Hick	c Nash b Owens	20
C.White	c Hart b Owens	42
†S.J.Rhodes	c Parore b Nash	12
P.A.J.DeFreitas	b Owens	69
D.Gough	c sub (H.T.Davis) b Pringle	65
A.R.C.Fraser	c Thomson b Hart	10
P.M.Such	not out	5
Extras	(LB8, W1, NB2)	11
Total		**382**

NEW ZEALAND

B.A.Young	c Rhodes b DeFreitas	25		lbw b DeFreitas	
M.J.Greatbatch	c Hick b Gough	0		c DeFreitas b White	2
*K.R.Rutherford	c Gooch b DeFreitas	7		c Rhodes b Gough	1
S.P.Fleming	c Rhodes b Gough	14		c Hick b Fraser	1
M.D.Crowe	c Gooch b White	70		c Hick b DeFreitas	11
M.N.Hart	c Atherton b Gough	0	(8)	not out	1
S.A.Thomson	c Rhodes b DeFreitas	9	(6)	c Smith b Gough	2
†A.C.Parore	c Rhodes b White	7	(7)	c Gooch b DeFreitas	7
D.J.Nash	not out	8		not out	
C.Pringle	b White	0			
M.B.Owens	c Stewart b Gough	4			
Extras	(NB7)	7		(B8, LB13, NB5)	2
Total		**151**		**(7 wickets)**	**30**

NEW ZEALAND	O	M	R	W		O	M	R	W		FALL OF WICKETS		
Nash	39	9	107	4								E	NZ	NZ
Owens	34	12	99	4						Wkt	1st	1st	2nd
Pringle	39	12	95	1						1st	37	2	8
Hart	27.3	9	50	1						2nd	37	12	34
Thomson	7	1	23	0						3rd	68	47	48
										4th	104	82	73
ENGLAND										5th	203	93	132
Fraser	12	3	17	0	(3)	19	7	34	1	6th	224	113	273
Gough	16.3	2	47	4		31.2	5	105	2	7th	235	125	287
DeFreitas	17	2	61	3	(1)	30	6	60	3	8th	365	140	–
Such	5	2	8	0	(5)	10	2	39	0	9th	372	140	–
White	7	1	18	3	(4)	14	3	36	1	10th	382	151	–
Gooch						2	0	13	0				

Umpires: S.B.Lambson (*South Africa*) (4) and D.R.Shepherd (22). Referee: E.de C.Weekes (*West Indies*) (4).

Close: 1st day – E(1) 199-4 (Atherton 96, White 42); 2nd – NZ(1) 84-4 (Crowe 33, Hart 0); 3rd – NZ(2) 205-? (Crowe 65, Parore 50); 4th – NZ(2) 253-5 (Crowe 94, Parore 66).

ENGLAND v SOUTH AFRICA 1994 (1st Test)

At Lord's, London, on 21, 22, 23, 24 July.
Toss: South Africa.   Result: SOUTH AFRICA won by 356 runs.
Debuts: England – J.P.Crawley.

South Africa celebrated their return to England after a hiatus of 29 years with their biggest victory by a runs margin in all Tests. Their second win in eleven Tests at Lord's, the other being in 1935, was completed at 5.39 on the fourth day when they dismissed England for their lowest total at Lord's since 1888 (53 and 62 against Australia). Wessels (299 minutes, 217 balls, 15 fours) scored his sixth hundred in Tests and his second for South Africa. He achieved the unique feat of twice scoring a hundred in his first Test against England, following his 162 on his debut for Australia at Brisbane in 1982-83. Donald contributed his fourth five-wicket analysis in 15 Tests. Gooch was the second batsman after D.I.Gower to play 200 innings for England. In his 21st innings at Lord's he became the first to score 2,000 runs in Tests on a single ground. Atherton was fined £2,000 by the England management for allegedly using dirt from his pocket to tamper with the ball and not disclosing the true facts to the referee.

SOUTH AFRICA

A.C.Hudson	c Gooch b Gough	6	(2)	lbw b Fraser	3
G.Kirsten	c DeFreitas b Hick	72	(1)	st Rhodes b Hick	44
W.J.Cronje	c Crawley b Fraser	7		c Fraser b Gough	32
*K.C.Wessels	c Rhodes b Gough	105		c Crawley b Salisbury	28
P.N.Kirsten	c Rhodes b Gough	8		b Gough	42
J.N.Rhodes	b White	32		b Gough	32
B.M.McMillan	c Rhodes b Fraser	29		not out	39
†D.J.Richardson	lbw b Gough	26		c Rhodes b Fraser	3
C.R.Matthews	b White	41		b Gough	25
P.S.de Villiers	c Rhodes b Fraser	8			
A.A.Donald	not out	5			
Extras	(LB9, NB9)	18		(B8, LB10, NB12)	30
Total		**357**		**(8 wickets declared)**	**278**

ENGLAND

*M.A.Atherton	c Wessels b Donald	20		c McMillan b De Villiers	8
A.J.Stewart	b Donald	12		c Richardson b Matthews	27
J.P.Crawley	c Hudson b De Villiers	9		c Hudson b McMillan	7
G.A.Hick	c Richardson b De Villiers	38		lbw b McMillan	11
G.A.Gooch	lbw b De Villiers	20		lbw b Donald	28
C.White	c Richardson b Donald	10		c Wessels b Matthews	0
†S.J.Rhodes	b McMillan	15		not out	14
I.D.K.Salisbury	not out	6	(10)	lbw b Donald	0
P.A.J.DeFreitas	c Wessels b Donald	20	(8)	c G.Kirsten b Matthews	1
D.Gough	c and b Donald	12	(9)	retired hurt	0
A.R.C.Fraser	run out	3		lbw b McMillan	1
Extras	(B2, LB5, NB8)	15		(B1, LB1)	2
Total		**180**			**99**

ENGLAND	O	M	R	W	O	M	R	W		FALL OF WICKETS			
DeFreitas	18	5	67	0	(3) 14	3	43	0		SA	E	SA	E
Gough	28	6	76	4	19.3	5	46	4	Wkt	1st	1st	2nd	2nd
Salisbury	25	2	68	0	(5) 19	4	53	1	1st	18	19	14	16
Fraser	24.5	7	72	3	(1) 23	5	62	2	2nd	35	41	73	29
Hick	10	5	22	1	(4) 24	14	38	1	3rd	141	68	101	45
White	13	2	43	2	3	0	18	0	4th	164	107	141	74
									5th	239	119	208	74
									6th	241	136	209	82
SOUTH AFRICA									7th	281	141	220	85
Donald	19.3	5	74	5	12	5	29	2	8th	334	161	278	88
De Villiers	16	5	28	3	12	4	26	1	9th	348	176	–	99
Matthews	16	6	46	0	14	6	25	3	10th	357	180	–	–
McMillan	10	1	25	1	6.5	2	16	3					
Cronje					1	0	1	0					

Umpires: H.D.Bird (59) and S.G.Randell (*Australia*) (16). Referee: P.J.P.Burge (*Australia*) (8).

Close: 1st day – SA(1) 244-6 (McMillan 2, Richardson 1); 2nd – E(1) 141-7 (Salisbury 3); 3rd – SA(2) 195-4 (P.N.Kirsten 40, Rhodes 23).

Test No. 1264/104 (E706/SA188)

ENGLAND v SOUTH AFRICA 1994 (2nd Test)

At Headingley, Leeds, on 4, 5, 6, 7, 8 August.
Toss: England.   Result: MATCH DRAWN.
Debuts: None.

Despite amassing the highest total against South Africa since their readmission, England were unable to press home their advantage. It was the fourth highest total without an individual hundred. Atherton (321 minutes, 224 balls, a six and 9 fours) became the fifth batsman to score 99 twice in Test cricket. Peter Kirsten (294 minutes, 226 balls, 13 fours) scored his maiden Test hundred in his 19th innings and his 53rd in first-class cricket. At 39 years 84 days he was the sixth oldest to score a maiden Test hundred. South Africa's last five wickets added 342 runs. Hick (271 minutes, 192 balls, two sixes and 9 fours) registered his first Test hundred in 26 innings in England, his second overall and his 76th in first-class matches. It was the first drawn Test at Headingley since 1980.

ENGLAND

G.A.Gooch	c McMillan b De Villiers	23	c Richardson b Matthews		27
*M.A.Atherton	c and b McMillan	99	c sub (D.J.Cullinan) b De Villiers		17
G.A.Hick	c McMillan b De Villiers	25	lbw b McMillan		110
G.P.Thorpe	c Rhodes b McMillan	72	run out		73
A.J.Stewart	b McMillan	89	not out		36
J.P.Crawley	lbw b Matthews	38	c Cronje b McMillan		0
†S.J.Rhodes	not out	65			
P.A.J.DeFreitas	b Donald	15			
D.Gough	run out	27			
A.R.C.Fraser	c Cronje b De Villiers	6			
P.C.R.Tufnell	did not bat				
Extras	(B1, LB5, NB12)	18	(LB1, NB3)		4
Total	(9 wickets declared)	**477**	(5 wickets declared)		**267**

SOUTH AFRICA

A.C.Hudson	c Atherton b Gough	9	(2) c and b Tufnell		12
G.Kirsten	c Rhodes b DeFreitas	7	(1) c Rhodes b DeFreitas		65
†D.J.Richardson	b Fraser	48			
W.J.Cronje	b DeFreitas	0	(3) not out		13
*K.C.Wessels	c Crawley b Fraser	25	(4) b Tufnell		7
P.N.Kirsten	c Stewart b DeFreitas	104	(5) not out		8
J.N.Rhodes	c Rhodes b Gough	46			
B.M.McMillan	b Tufnell	78			
C.R.Matthews	not out	62			
P.S.de Villiers	st Rhodes b Tufnell	13			
A.A.Donald	c Crawley b DeFreitas	27			
Extras	(B8, LB7, NB13)	28	(B2, LB2, NB7)		11
Total		**447**	(3 wickets)		**116**

SOUTH AFRICA	O	M	R	W	O	M	R	W		FALL OF WICKETS			
										E	SA	E	SA
Donald	29	2	135	1					Wkt	*1st*	*1st*	*2nd*	*2nd*
De Villiers	39.3	12	108	3	(1) 25	3	98	1	1st	34	13	39	43
Matthews	39	7	97	1	24	8	53	1	2nd	84	31	57	93
McMillan	37	12	93	3	(2) 15.3	0	66	2	3rd	226	31	190	104
Cronje	16	3	38	0	12	3	39	0	4th	235	91	267	–
G.Kirsten					(4) 2	1	10	0	5th	350	105	267	–
									6th	367	199	–	–
ENGLAND									7th	394	314	–	–
Gough	37	3	153	2	(2) 10	5	15	0	8th	447	391	–	–
DeFreitas	29.1	6	89	4	(1) 14	3	41	1	9th	477	410	–	–
Fraser	31	5	92	2	(4) 7	2	19	0	10th	–	447	–	–
Tufnell	32	13	81	2	(3) 23	8	31	2					
Gooch	3	0	9	0									
Hick	1	0	8	0	(5) 6	3	6	0					

Umpires: R.S.Dunne (*New Zealand*) (13) and D.R.Shepherd (23). Referee: P.J.P.Burge (*Australia*) (9).

Close: 1st day – E(1) 268-4 (Stewart 24, Crawley 12); 2nd – SA(1) 31-1 (G.Kirsten 7, Richardson 13); 3rd – SA(1) 318-7 (McMillan 57, Matthews 0); 4th – E(2) 144-2 (Hick 48, Thorpe 51).

ENGLAND v SOUTH AFRICA 1994 (3rd Test)

At Kennington Oval, London, on 18, 19, 20, 21 August.
Toss: South Africa.   Result: ENGLAND won by eight wickets.
Debuts: England – J.E.Benjamin.

England gained their first win against South Africa since 1964-65 and their first at home since 1960. A frenetic eighth-wicket partnership of 70 in 52 minutes between DeFreitas (37 off 31 balls) and Gough (42 not out off 47 balls) transformed this match after England had subsided to 222 for 7, still 110 behind. Malcolm, incensed by being struck on the helmet by a bouncer from De Villiers, tore in and demolished some extremely apprehensive batsmen on a fast, bouncy pitch. His analysis of 9 for 57 was the sixth best in Test cricket, a record against South Africa in England and a record for all Tests at The Oval. Only Cullinan (221 minutes, 134 balls, 12 fours) batted with any degree of confidence. Wessels completed 1,000 runs in his 29th innings for South Africa and became the first to score 1,000 runs for two countries. When England required 204 to win in over two days, Gooch struck 33, including seven fours, off 20 balls and 50 runs were scored from 4.3 overs. In four successive overs spread over the two innings, Donald was savaged for 57 runs. England completed their task at 12.41 on the fourth day and shared their second rubber of the summer.

SOUTH AFRICA

G.Kirsten	c Rhodes b DeFreitas	2	(2) c and b Malcolm		0
P.N.Kirsten	b Malcolm	16	(1) c DeFreitas b Malcolm		1
W.J.Cronje	lbw b Benjamin	38	b Malcolm		0
*K.C.Wessels	lbw b Benjamin	45	c Rhodes b Malcolm		28
D.J.Cullinan	c Rhodes b DeFreitas	7	c Thorpe b Gough		94
J.N.Rhodes	retired hurt	8	(9) c Rhodes b Malcolm		10
B.M.McMillan	c Hick b DeFreitas	93	(6) c Thorpe b Malcolm		25
†D.J.Richardson	c Rhodes b Benjamin	58	(7) lbw b Malcolm		3
C.R.Matthews	c Hick b Benjamin	0	(8) c Rhodes b Malcolm		0
P.S.de Villiers	c Stewart b DeFreitas	14	not out		0
A.A.Donald	not out	14	b Malcolm		0
Extras	(B8, LB10, W1, NB18)	37	(LB5, NB9)		14
Total		**332**			**175**

ENGLAND

G.A.Gooch	c Richardson b Donald	8	b Matthews		33
*M.A.Atherton	lbw b De Villiers	0	c Richardson b Donald		63
G.A.Hick	b Donald	39	not out		81
G.P.Thorpe	b Matthews	79	not out		15
A.J.Stewart	b De Villiers	62			
J.P.Crawley	c Richardson b Donald	5			
†S.J.Rhodes	lbw b De Villiers	11			
P.A.J.DeFreitas	run out	37			
D.Gough	not out	42			
J.E.Benjamin	lbw b De Villiers	0			
D.E.Malcolm	c sub (T.G.Shaw) b Matthews	4			
Extras	(B1, W1, NB15)	17	(LB6, NB7)		13
Total		**304**	(2 wickets)		**205**

ENGLAND	O	M	R	W	O	M	R	W	FALL OF WICKETS			
										SA	E	SA	E
DeFreitas	26.2	5	93	4	12	3	25	0				
Malcolm	25	5	81	1	16.3	2	57	9	*Wkt*	*1st*	*1st*	*2nd*	*2nd*
Gough	19	1	85	0	9	1	39	1	1st	2	1	0	56
Benjamin	17	2	42	4	11	1	38	0	2nd	43	33	1	180
Hick	5	1	13	0	2	0	11	0	3rd	73	93	1	–
									4th	85	145	73	–
SOUTH AFRICA									5th	136	165	137	–
Donald	17	2	76	3	12	1	96	1	6th	260	219	143	–
De Villiers	19	3	62	4	12	0	66	0	7th	266	222	143	–
Matthews	21	4	82	2	11.3	4	37	1	8th	301	292	175	–
McMillan	12	1	67	0					9th	332	293	175	–
Cronje	8	3	16	0					10th	–	304	175	–

Umpires: R.S.Dunne (*New Zealand*) (14) and K.E.Palmer (22). Referee: P.J.P.Burge (*Australia*) (10).

Close: 1st day – SA(1) 326-8 (McMillan 91, Donald 11); 2nd – E(1) 281-7 (DeFreitas 37, Gough 25); 3rd – E(2) 107-1 (Atherton 42, Hick 27).

SRI LANKA v PAKISTAN 1994-95 (1st Test)

At P.Saravanamuttu Stadium, Colombo, on 9, 10, 11, 13 August.
Toss: Pakistan.   Result: PAKISTAN won by 301 runs.
Debuts: None.

Pakistan inflicted a fourth successive four-day defeat upon Sri Lanka. Ranatunga was the first to appear in 50 Tests for Sri Lanka. Off-spinner Dharmasena returned a remarkably economical six-wicket analysis in his third Test. De Silva (211 minutes, 156 balls, a six and 19 fours) completed his hundred (his seventh) with a six (off his 122nd ball) for the third time. Saeed (319 minutes, 218 balls, 12 fours) registered his second hundred and the highest score for Pakistan in Sri Lanka. In his 100th innings, Salim became the fourth Pakistani to score 4,000 runs. On a pitch totally unsuited to fast bowling, Wasim took five wickets in an innings for the 16th time in 54 Tests.

PAKISTAN

Saeed Anwar	c Jayasuriya b Warnaweera	94	c Dassanayake b Warnaweera	136
Aamir Sohail	b Dharmasena	41	c Jayasuriya b Dharmasena	65
Asif Mujtaba	c Dassanayake b Dharmasena	44	c Dassanayake b Warnaweera	31
*Salim Malik	c Tillekeratne b Dharmasena	1	not out	50
Basit Ali	lbw b Warnaweera	27	b Dharmasena	11
Inzamam-ul-Haq	c Tillekeratne b Dharmasena	81	not out	7
†Rashid Latif	c Dassanayake b Muralitharan	0		
Wasim Akram	c Jayasuriya b Dharmasena	37		
Akram Raza	c Tillekeratne b Warnaweera	25		
Mushtaq Ahmed	not out	5		
Waqar Younis	c Gurusinha b Dharmasena	2		
Extras	(B11, LB6, NB16)	33	(LB6, NB12)	18
Total		**390**	**(4 wickets declared)**	**318**

SRI LANKA

R.S.Mahanama	b Mushtaq	21		c sub (Zahid Fazal) b Raza	37
S.T.Jayasuriya	c Aamir b Wasim	9		c Rashid b Wasim	1
A.P.Gurusinha	c Rashid b Mushtaq	11		c Asif b Waqar	8
P.A.de Silva	c Aamir b Raza	127		c and b Waqar	5
*A.Ranatunga	c and b Mushtaq	9	(6)	st Rashid b Raza	41
H.P.Tillekeratne	lbw b Waqar	34	(5)	c and b Raza	8
†P.B.Dassanayake	c Rashid b Wasim	3		b Wasim	24
H.D.P.K.Dharmasena	c Aamir b Wasim	1		lbw b Wasim	30
G.P.Wickremasinghe	not out	0		b Wasim	4
M.Muralitharan	c Asif b Raza	0		not out	20
K.P.J.Warnaweera	c and b Raza	4		b Wasim	0
Extras	(B1, LB5, NB1)	7		(LB2, NB1)	3
Total		**226**			**181**

SRI LANKA	O	M	R	W	O	M	R	W		FALL OF WICKETS			
Wickremasinghe	12	0	59	0	5	0	25	0		P	SL	P	SL
Gurusinha	4	1	24	0					Wkt	1st	1st	2nd	2nd
Dharmasena	45.3	13	99	6	(2) 31	2	84	2	1st	65	13	128	1
Muralitharan	36	6	123	1	11	0	42	0	2nd	180	41	202	30
Warnaweera	28	5	63	3	(3) 31	1	108	2	3rd	181	42	273	38
De Silva	1	0	5	0					4th	221	60	298	52
Jayasuriya					(5) 13	0	53	0	5th	247	179	–	59
									6th	260	215	–	118
PAKISTAN									7th	345	218	–	135
Wasim	17	4	30	3	18	4	43	5	8th	354	222	–	160
Waqar	16	1	84	1	7	0	28	2	9th	387	222	–	181
Mushtaq	14	2	57	3	(4) 6	1	25	0	10th	390	226	–	181
Raza	19	7	46	3	(3) 16	3	83	3					
Aamir	2	0	3	0									

Umpires: K.T.Francis (13) and I.D.Robinson (*Zimbabwe*) (5). Referee: C.W.Smith (*West Indies*) (5).

Close: 1st day – P(1) 297-6 (Inzamam 46, Wasim 22); 2nd – SL(1) 152-4 (De Silva 74, Tillekeratne 25); 3rd – P(2) 238-2 (Saeed 110, Salim 15).

The 2nd Test at Sinhalese Sports Club Ground, Colombo, scheduled for 18, 19, 20, 22, 23 August, was cancelled because of civil unrest following a general election.

SRI LANKA v PAKISTAN 1994-95 (3rd Test)

At Asgiriya Stadium, Kandy, on 26, 27, 28 August.
Toss: Pakistan.   Result: PAKISTAN won by an innings and 52 runs.
Debuts: Sri Lanka – K.R.Pushpakumara, S.Ranatunga, W.P.U.C.J.Vaas; Pakistan – Kabir Khan.

Dismissed for their lowest score, 71 in 145 minutes off 28.2 overs, Sri Lanka suffered their fifth successive defeat, this time in only three days. The hosts' final total represented a recovery from 46 for 9 as Wasim and Waqar became only the second Pakistan pair to bowl unchanged through a completed innings (also *Test No. 430*). Inzamam (197 minutes, 125 balls, 13 fours) scored his third hundred in 26 innings. Tillekeratne made his eighth Test score between 80 and 93 inclusive. Waqar claimed his 18th and 19th five-wicket analyses in 31 Tests and his fourth haul of ten wickets in a match (his first outside Pakistan).

SRI LANKA

R.S.Mahanama	c Rashid b Waqar	2		c Inzamam b Waqar	10
D.P.Samaraweera	c Rashid b Wasim	6		lbw b Waqar	13
S.Ranatunga	c Rashid b Waqar	5	(4)	c Wasim b Waqar	4
P.A.de Silva	lbw b Wasim	7	(5)	c Rashid b Wasim	5
*A.Ranatunga	c Saeed b Waqar	0	(6)	c Rashid b Waqar	34
H.P.Tillekeratne	b Waqar	9	(7)	not out	83
R.S.Kalpage	c Aamir b Wasim	6	(8)	c sub (Ramiz Raja) b Kabir	62
†P.B.Dassanayake	not out	19	(3)	lbw b Waqar	1
H.D.P.K.Dharmasena	lbw b Waqar	0		c sub (Zahid Fazal) b Mushtaq	3
W.P.U.C.J.Vaas	c Wasim b Waqar	0		lbw b Mushtaq	4
K.R.Pushpakumara	c Aamir b Wasim	6		lbw b Mushtaq	0
Extras	(B1, LB4, W5, NB1)	11		(LB6, NB9)	15
Total		**71**			**234**

PAKISTAN

Saeed Anwar	lbw b Pushpakumara	31
Aamir Sohail	c Tillekeratne b Pushpakumara	74
Mushtaq Ahmed	run out	0
Asif Mujtaba	c Dassanayake b Pushpakumara	17
*Salim Malik	c Dassanayake b Dharmasena	22
Basit Ali	c and b Dharmasena	53
Inzamam-ul-Haq	not out	100
†Rashid Latif	c Samaraweera b Dharmasena	7
Wasim Akram	c De Silva b Pushpakumara	12
Waqar Younis	c Kalpage b Dharmasena	20
Kabir Khan	did not bat	
Extras	(B4, LB3, W1, NB13)	21
Total	(9 wickets declared)	**357**

PAKISTAN	O	M	R	W	O	M	R	W	FALL OF WICKETS			
										SL	P	SL
Wasim	14.2	4	32	4	26	12	70	1	*Wkt*	*1st*	*1st*	*2nd*
Waqar	14	4	34	6	18	1	85	5	1st	12	94	11
Kabir					10	1	39	1	2nd	20	94	13
Mushtaq					7.3	1	34	3	3rd	22	117	17
									4th	28	158	22
SRI LANKA									5th	28	158	42
Vaas	22	2	80	0					6th	43	256	78
Pushpakumara	26	3	145	4					7th	45	264	209
Dharmasena	28.5	7	75	4					8th	46	297	221
Kalpage	11	0	50	0					9th	46	357	234
									10th	71	–	234

Umpires: B.C.Cooray (4) and I.D.Robinson (*Zimbabwe*) (6). Referee: C.W.Smith (*West Indies*) (6).

Close: 1st day – P(1) 109-2 (Aamir 68, Asif 1); 2nd – SL(2) 17-3 (Samaraweera 2).

CANCELLED TEST MATCH

WEST INDIES v ENGLAND 1980-81 (2nd Test)

Scheduled to be played at Bourda, Georgetown, Guyana, on 28 February, 1, 2, 4, 5 March.

The match was cancelled by the Cricket Council when permission for R.D.Jackman to stay in Guyana was revoked by the Government of that country because he had played and coached in South Africa during the previous 11 years.

Extract from the statement of the Cricket Council:

'The Guyanese Minister of Foreign Affairs has informed the British High Commissioner that Mr. Jackman's permission to stay in Guyana is being revoked.

'The Cricket Council has informed the Manager of the England touring team that, as Robin Jackman has been asked to leave Guyana, it is no longer possible for the Test team to be chosen without restrictions being imposed.

'It is therefore with deep regret that England cannot take part in the second Test due to start on Saturday.'

Unpires appointed for the Test were C.E.Cumberbatch and C.F.Vyfhuis.

ABANDONED TEST MATCHES

NEW ZEALAND v PAKISTAN 1988-89 (1st Test)

At Carisbrook, Dunedin, on 3, 4, 5, 6, 7 February. No toss.

NEW ZEALAND
(From) J.W.Wright*, R.H.Vance, A.H.Jones, M.D.Crowe, J.J.Crowe, D.N.Patel, R.J.Hadlee, I.D.S.Smith†, J.G.Bracewell, M.C.Snedden, W.Watson, E.J.Chatfield.

PAKISTAN
(From) Shoaib Mohammad, Rizwan-uz-Zaman, Aamer Malik, Javed Miandad, Salim Malik, Mudassar Nazar, Imran Khan*, Salim Yousuf†, Abdul Qadir, Salim Jaffer, Aqib Javed, Ramiz Raja, Ijaz Ahmed.

Umpires: R.S.Dunne and S.J.Woodward.

WEST INDIES v ENGLAND 1989-90 (2nd Test)

At Bourda, Georgetown, Guyana, scheduled for 10, 11, 12, 14, 15 March. No toss.

WEST INDIES
C.G.Greenidge, D.L.Haynes, R.B.Richardson, C.A.Best, C.L.Hooper, I.V.A.Richards*, P.J.L.Dujon†, C.E.L.Ambrose, E.A.Moseley, I.R.Bishop, C.A.Walsh. (B.P.Patterson and K.L.T.Arthurton were omitted from selected XIII).

ENGLAND
(From) G.A.Gooch*, W.Larkins, A.J.Stewart, A.J.Lamb, R.A.Smith, N.Hussain, D.J.Capel, R.C.Russell†, G.C.Small, A.R.C.Fraser, D.E.Malcolm, E.E.Hemmings.

Umpires: D.M.Archer and C.R.Duncan.

Test Match Records 1876-77 to 1994

TEST MATCH RECORDS

KEY TO SYMBOLS
* denotes a 'not out' innings or an unbroken partnership.
All other symbols are explained within the section in which they appear.

KEY TO TEST MATCH GROUNDS
(Where more than one ground has been used in a city)

Bombay[1]	Gymkhana Ground
Bombay[2]	Brabourne Stadium
Bombay[3]	Wankhede Stadium
Brisbane[1]	Exhibition Ground
Brisbane[2]	Woolloongabba
Colombo (PSS)	P.Saravanamuttu Stadium
Colombo (SSC)	Sinhalese Sports Club Ground
Colombo (CCC)	Colombo Cricket Club Ground
Colombo (KS)	Khettarama Stadium
Durban[1]	Lord's
Durban[2]	Kingsmead
Johannesburg[1]	Old Wanderers
Johannesburg[2]	Ellis Park
Johannesburg[3]	Wanderers Stadium
Karachi[1]	National Stadium
Karachi[2]	Defence Stadium
Lahore[1]	Bagh-i-Jinnah
Lahore[2]	Gaddafi Stadium
Lucknow[1]	University Ground
Lucknow[2]	K.D.'Babu' Singh Stadium
Madras[1]	Chepauk Stadium
Madras[2]	Corporation (Nehru) Stadium
Rawalpindi[1]	Pindi Club Ground
Rawalpindi[2]	Cricket Stadium

This system has not been applied to London where Test cricket has been staged on two grounds concurrently since 1884.

TEST MATCH GROUNDS

TEST MATCH GROUNDS

Official Test matches have been played on 72 grounds and at 58 centres – if the two London grounds, Lord's and The Oval, are treated as separate Test centres. Ten centres, excluding London, have staged Test matches on more than one ground; Colombo has employed four, Johannesburg and Bombay have used three, while Brisbane, Durban, Lucknow, Madras, Karachi, Lahore and Rawalpindi have each played Test cricket on two different grounds.

Where any of these ten centres appears in this Records section, the exact ground is denoted by an indicator number (e.g. Bombay[3]) except for Colombo, where the ground appears in brackets. This number refers to the key included in the following tables and which is summarised in the key to Test match grounds in the introduction to this section.

The following tables show the full title, date of the first day's play and number of Tests staged for each ground. The records are those for each centre.

Test Match Centres	Grounds	First Test Match Day	No. of Tests
ENGLAND			**(359)**
Birmingham	Edgbaston	29.5.1902	30
Leeds	Headingley	29.6.1899	56
Lord's, London	Lord's Cricket Ground	21.7.1884	92
Manchester	Old Trafford	10.7.1884†	61
Nottingham	Trent Bridge	1.6.1899	42
Oval, London	Kennington Oval	6.9.1880	77
Sheffield	Bramall Lane	3.7.1902	1
AUSTRALIA			**(279)**
Adelaide	Adelaide Oval	12.12.1884	52
Brisbane	[1]Exhibition Ground (1928-29 to 1930-31)	30.11.1928	2
	[2]Woolloongabba	27.11.1931	36
Hobart	Bellerive Oval	16.12.1989	2
Melbourne	Melbourne Cricket Ground	15.3.1877	86
Perth	Western Australia Cricket Association (WACA) Ground	11.12.1970	21
Sydney	Sydney Cricket Ground (No. 1)	17.2.1882	80
SOUTH AFRICA			**(105)**
Cape Town	Newlands	25.3.1889	26
Durban	[1]Lord's (1909-10 to 1921-22)	21.1.1910	4
	[2]Kingsmead	18.1.1923	21
Johannesburg	[1]Old Wanderers (1895-96 to 1938-39)	2.3.1896	22
	[2]Ellis Park (1948-49 to 1953-54)	27.12.1948	6
	[3]Wanderers Stadium	24.12.1956	13
Port Elizabeth	St George's Park	12.3.1889	13
WEST INDIES			**(134)**
Bridgetown, Barbados	Kensington Oval	11.1.1930	30
Georgetown, Guyana	Bourda	21.2.1930	23
Kingston, Jamaica	Sabina Park	3.4.1930	30
Port-of-Spain, Trinidad	Queen's Park Oval	1.2.1930	43
St John's, Antigua	Recreation Ground	27.3.1981	8
NEW ZEALAND			**(110)**
Auckland	Eden Park	14.2.1930‡	36
Christchurch	Lancaster Park	10.1.1930	32
Dunedin	Carisbrook	11.3.1955	8
Hamilton	Trust Bank (Seddon) Park	22.2.1991	3
Napier	McLean Park	16.2.1979	2
Wellington	Basin Reserve	24.1.1930	29

The Grounds

Test Match Centres	Grounds	First Test Match Day	No. of Tests
INDIA			(153)
Ahmedabad	Gujarat Stadium	12.11.1983	3
Bangalore	Karnataka State Cricket Association Stadium (Chinnaswamy Stadium)	22.11.1974	10
Bombay	[1]Gymkhana (1933-34 only)	15.12.1933	1
	[2]Brabourne Stadium (1948-49 to 1972-73)	9.12.1948	17
	[3]Wankhede Stadium	23.1.1975	14
Calcutta	Eden Gardens	5.1.1934	27
Chandigarh	Sector 16 Stadium	23.11.1990	1
Cuttack	Barabati Stadium	4.1.1987	1
Delhi	Feroz Shah Kotla	10.11.1948	23
Hyderabad (Deccan)	Fateh Maidan (Lal Bahadur Stadium)	19.11.1955	3
Jaipur	Sawai Mansingh Stadium	21.2.1987	1
Jullundur	Burlton Park	24.9.1983	1
Kanpur	Green Park (Modi Stadium)	12.1.1952	16
Lucknow	[1]University Ground	23.10.1952	1
	[2]K.D.'Babu' Singh Stadium	18.1.1994	1
Madras	[1]Chepauk (Chidambaram Stadium)	10.2.1934	21
	[2]Corporation (Nehru) Stadium (1955-56 to 1964-65)	6.1.1956	9
Nagpur	Vidarbha Cricket Association Ground	3.10.1969	3
PAKISTAN			(97)
Bahawalpur	Dring Stadium	15.1.1955	1
Dacca	Dacca Stadium	1.1.1955	7
Faisalabad	Iqbal Stadium	16.10.1978	16
Gujranwala	Municipal Stadium	20.12.1991	1
Hyderabad (Sind)	Niaz Stadium	16.3.1973	5
Karachi	[1]National Stadium	26.2.1955	30
	[2]Defence Stadium	1.12.1993	1
Lahore	[1]Lawrence Gardens (Bagh-i-Jinnah) (1954-55 to 1958-59)	29.1.1955	3
	[2]Lahore (Gaddafi) Stadium	21.11.1959	26
Multan	Ibn-e-Qasim Bagh Stadium	30.12.1980	1
Peshawar	Services Ground	13.2.1955	1
Rawalpindi	[1]Pindi Club Ground	27.3.1965	1
	[2]Cricket Stadium	9.12.1993	1
Sialkot	Jinnah Stadium	27.10.1985	3
SRI LANKA			(27)
Colombo	P.Saravanamuttu Stadium (PSS)	17.2.1982	6
	Sinhalese Sports Club Ground (SSC)	16.3.1984	7
	Colombo Cricket Club Ground (CCC)	24.3.1984	3
	Khettarama Stadium (KS)	28.8.1992	1
Kandy	Asgiriya Stadium	22.4.1983	6
Moratuwa	Tyronne Fernando Stadium	8.9.1992	4
ZIMBABWE			(3)
Bulawayo	Bulawayo Athletic Club	1.11.1992	1
Harare	Harare Sports Club	18.10.1992	2

† Rain prevented play until 11.7.1884.
‡ Rain prevented play until 17.2.1930.
The 1890 and 1938 Tests at Manchester, the 1970-71 Third Test at Melbourne, the 1988-89 Test at Dunedin and the 1989-90 Test at Georgetown, all abandoned without a ball being bowled, plus the cancelled 1980-81 Second Test at a Georgetown and 1994-95 Second Test at Colombo (SCC), are excluded from these figures.

RECORD TOTALS FOR EACH TEST MATCH CENTRE

Centre	Highest Total			Lowest Total‡		
Birmingham	633-5d	England v India	1979	30	S Africa v England	1924
Leeds	653-4d	Australia v England	1993	67	N Zealand v England	1958
Lord's	729-6d	Australia v England	1930	42	India v England	1974
Manchester	656-8d	Australia v England	1964	58	India v England	1952
Nottingham	658-8d	England v Australia	1938	88	S Africa v England	1960
Oval	903-7d	England v Australia	1938	44	Australia v England	1896
Sheffield	289	Australia v England	1902	145	England v Australia	1902
Adelaide	674	Australia v India	1947-48	82	Australia v W Indies	1951-52
Brisbane	645	Australia v England	1946-47	58	{ Australia v England India v Australia	1936-37 1947-48
Hobart	544-6d	Australia v N Zealand	1993-94	161	N Zealand v Australia	1993-94
Melbourne	604	Australia v England	1936-37	36	S Africa v Australia	1931-32
Perth	592-8d	England v Australia	1986-87	62	Pakistan v Australia	1981-82
Sydney	659-8d	Australia v England	1946-47	42	Australia v England	1887-88
Cape Town	559-9d	England v S Africa	1938-39	35	S Africa v England	1898-99
Durban	654-5	England v S Africa	1938-39	75	Australia v S Africa	1949-50
Johannesburg	620	S Africa v Australia	1966-67	72	S Africa v England	1956-57
Port Elizabeth	549-7d	Australia v S Africa	1949-50	30	S Africa v England	1895-96
Bridgetown	668	Australia v W Indies	1954-55	94	N Zealand v W Indies	1984-85
Georgetown	569	W Indies v Australia	1990-91	109	W Indies v Australia	1972-73
Kingston	849	England v W Indies	1929-30	97†	India v W Indies	1975-76
Port-of-Spain	681-8d	W Indies v England	1953-54	46	England v W Indies	1993-94
St John's	593-5d	W Indies v England	1993-94	154	England v W Indies	1989-90
Auckland	616-5d	Pakistan v N Zealand	1988-89	26	N Zealand v England	1954-55
Christchurch	580-9d	England v N Zealand	1991-92	65	N Zealand v England	1970-71
Dunedin	507-6d	Pakistan v N Zealand	1972-73	74	N Zealand v W Indies	1955-56
Hamilton	374-6d	N Zealand v Sri Lanka	1990-91	93	N Zealand v Pakistan	1992-93
Napier	402	N Zealand v Pakistan	1978-79	360	Pakistan v N Zealand	1978-79
Wellington	671-4	N Zealand v Sri Lanka	1990-91	42	N Zealand v Australia	1945-46
Ahmedabad	395	Pakistan v India	1986-87	103	India v W Indies	1983-84
Bangalore	541-6d	India v Sri Lanka	1993-94	116	Pakistan v India	1986-87
Bombay	629-6d	W Indies v India	1948-49	88	India v N Zealand	1964-65
Calcutta	614-5d	W Indies v India	1958-59	90	India v W Indies	1983-84
Chandigarh	288	India v Sri Lanka	1990-91	82	Sri Lanka v India	1990-91
Cuttack	400	India v Sri Lanka	1986-87	142	Sri Lanka v India	1986-87
Delhi	644-8d	W Indies v India	1958-59	75	India v W Indies	1987-88
Hyderabad	498-4d	India v N Zealand	1955-56	89	India v N Zealand	1969-70
Jaipur	465-8d	India v Pakistan	1986-87	341	Pakistan v India	1986-87
Jullundur	374	India v Pakistan	1983-84	337	Pakistan v India	1983-84
Kanpur	676-7	India v Sri Lanka	1986-87	105	Australia v India	1959-60
Lucknow	511	India v Sri Lanka	1993-94	106	India v Pakistan	1952-53
Madras	652-7d	England v India	1984-85	83	India v England	1976-77
Nagpur	451-6d	India v Sri Lanka	1986-87	109	India v N Zealand	1969-70
Bahawalpur	312-9d	Pakistan v India	1954-55	235	India v Pakistan	1954-55
Dacca	439	England v Pakistan	1961-62	70	N Zealand v Pakistan	1955-56
Faisalabad	674-6	Pakistan v India	1984-85	53	W Indies v Pakistan	1986-87
Gujranwala	109-2	Pakistan v Sri Lanka	1991-92	–		
Hyderabad	581-3d	Pakistan v India	1982-83	189	{ India v Pakistan N Zealand v Pakistan	1982-83 1984-85
Karachi	565-9d	Pakistan v N Zealand	1976-77	80	Australia v Pakistan	1956-57
Lahore	699-5	Pakistan v India	1989-90	77	Pakistan v W Indies	1986-87
Multan	249	W Indies v Pakistan	1980-81	166	Pakistan v W Indies	1980-81
Peshawar	245	India v Pakistan	1954-55	182	Pakistan v India	1954-55
Rawalpindi	318	Pakistan v N Zealand	1964-65	79	N Zealand v Pakistan	1964-65
Sialkot	423-5d	Pakistan v Sri Lanka	1991-92	157	Sri Lanka v Pakistan	1985-86
Colombo (PSS)	446	India v Sri Lanka	1993-94	175	Sri Lanka v England	1981-82
Colombo (SSC)	547-8d	Sri Lanka v Australia	1992-93	102	N Zealand v Sri Lanka	1992-93
Colombo (CCC)	459	N Zealand v Sri Lanka	1983-84	132	Pakistan v Sri Lanka	1985-86
Colombo (KS)	296-6d	Australia v Sri Lanka	1992-93	247	Australia v Sri Lanka	1992-93
Kandy	514-4d	Australia v Sri Lanka	1982-83	71	Sri Lanka v Australia	1994-95
Moratuwa	337	Australia v Sri Lanka	1992-93	190	Sri Lanka v W Indies	1993-94
Bulawayo	325-3d	N Zealand v Zimbabwe	1992-93	219	Zimbabwe v N Zealand	1992-93
Harare	456	Zimbabwe v India	1992-93	137	Zimbabwe v N Zealand	1992-93

†*Five men were absent hurt. The second lowest total at Kingston is 103 by England in 1934-35.* ‡*Completed innings.*

HIGHEST INDIVIDUAL SCORE FOR EACH CENTRE

Birmingham	285*	P.B.H.May	England v West Indies	1957
Leeds	334	D.G.Bradman	Australia v England	1930
Lord's	333	G.A.Gooch	England v India	1990
Manchester	311	R.B.Simpson	Australia v England	1964
Nottingham	278	D.C.S.Compton	England v Pakistan	1954
Oval	364	L.Hutton	England v Australia	1938
Sheffield	119	C.Hill	Australia v England	1902
Adelaide	299*	D.G.Bradman	Australia v South Africa	1931-32
Brisbane	226	D.G.Bradman	Australia v South Africa	1931-32
Hobart	168	M.J.Slater	Australia v New Zealand	1993-94
Melbourne	307	R.M.Cowper	Australia v England	1965-66
Perth	200	D.C.Boon	Australia v New Zealand	1989-90
Sydney	287	R.E.Foster	England v Australia	1903-04
Cape Town	209	R.G.Pollock	South Africa v Australia	1966-67
Durban	274	R.G.Pollock	South Africa v Australia	1969-70
Johannesburg	231	A.D.Nourse	South Africa v Australia	1935-36
Port Elizabeth	167	A.L.Hassett	Australia v South Africa	1949-50
Bridgetown	337	Hanif Mohammad	Pakistan v West Indies	1957-58
Georgetown	259	G.M.Turner	New Zealand v West Indies	1971-72
Kingston	365*	G.St A.Sobers	West Indies v Pakistan	1957-58
Port-of-Spain	220	S.M.Gavaskar	India v West Indies	1970-71
St John's	375	B.C.Lara	West Indies v England	1993-94
Auckland	336*	W.R.Hammond	England v New Zealand	1932-33
Christchurch	258	S.M.Nurse	West Indies v New Zealand	1968-69
Dunedin	201	Mushtaq Mohammad	Pakistan v New Zealand	1972-73
Hamilton	135	M.J.Greatbatch	New Zealand v Pakistan	1992-93
Napier	119*	Majid Khan	Pakistan v New Zealand	1978-79
Wellington	299	M.D.Crowe	New Zealand v Sri Lanka	1990-91
Ahmedabad	152	M.Azharuddin	India v Sri Lanka	1993-94
Bangalore	172	S.M.Gavaskar	India v England	1981-82
Bombay	242*	C.H.Lloyd	West Indies v India	1974-75
Calcutta	256	R.B.Kanhai	West Indies v India	1958-59
Chandigarh	88	R.J.Shastri	India v Sri Lanka	1990-91
Cuttack	166	D.B.Vengsarkar	India v Sri Lanka	1986-87
Delhi	230*	B.Sutcliffe	New Zealand v India	1955-56
Hyderabad	223	P.R.Umrigar	India v New Zealand	1955-56
Jaipur	125	R.J.Shastri	India v Pakistan	1986-87
Jullundur	201	A.D.Gaekwad	India v Pakistan	1983-84
Kanpur	250	S.F.A.F.Bacchus	West Indies v India	1978-79
Lucknow	142	S.R.Tendulkar	India v Sri Lanka	1993-94
Madras	236*	S.M.Gavaskar	India v West Indies	1983-84
Nagpur	153	D.B.Vengsarkar	India v Sri Lanka	1986-87
Bahawalpur	142	Hanif Mohammad	Pakistan v India	1954-55
Dacca	165	G.Pullar	England v Pakistan	1961-62
Faisalabad	235	G.S.Chappell	Australia v Pakistan	1979-80
Gujranwala	51*	Ramiz Raja	Pakistan v Sri Lanka	1991-92
Hyderabad	280*	Javed Miandad	Pakistan v India	1982-83
Karachi	211	Javed Miandad	Pakistan v Australia	1988-89
Lahore	235*	Zaheer Abbas	Pakistan v India	1978-79
Multan	120*	I.V.A.Richards	West Indies v Pakistan	1980-81
Peshawar	108	P.R.Umrigar	India v Pakistan	1954-55
Rawalpindi	76	B.R.Taylor	New Zealand v Pakistan	1964-65
Sialkot	101	Salim Malik	Pakistan v Sri Lanka	1991-92
Colombo (PSS)	151	R.S.Mahanama	Sri Lanka v India	1993-94
Colombo (SSC)	137	A.P.Gurusinha	Sri Lanka v Australia	1992-93
Colombo (CCC)	201*	D.S.B.P.Kuruppu	Sri Lanka v New Zealand	1986-87
Colombo (KS)	100*	D.M.Jones	Australia v Sri Lanka	1992-93
Kandy	143*	D.W.Hookes	Australia v Sri Lanka	1982-83
Moratuwa	153	R.S.Mahanama	Sri Lanka v New Zealand	1992-93
Bulawayo	119	R.T.Latham	New Zealand v Zimbabwe	1992-93
Harare	140	M.D.Crowe	New Zealand v Zimbabwe	1992-93

HIGHEST PARTNERSHIPS FOR EACH TEST MATCH CENTRE

	Runs	Wkt			
Birmingham	411	4th	P.B.H.May, M.C.Cowdrey	E v WI	1957
Leeds	388	4th	W.H.Ponsford, D.G.Bradman	A v E	1934
Lord's	370	3rd	W.J.Edrich, D.C.S.Compton	E v SA	1947
Manchester	246	3rd	E.R.Dexter, K.F.Barrington	E v A	1964
Nottingham	329	1st	G.R.Marsh, M.A.Taylor	A v E	1989
Oval	451	2nd	W.H.Ponsford, D.G.Bradman	A v E	1934
Sheffield	107	4th	C.Hill, S.E.Gregory	A v E	1902
Adelaide	341	3rd	E.J.Barlow, R.G.Pollock	SA v A	1963-64
Brisbane	276	3rd	D.G.Bradman, A.L.Hassett	A v E	1946-47
Hobart	260*	6th	D.M.Jones, S.R.Waugh	A v SL	1989-90
Melbourne	346	6th	J.H.W.Fingleton, D.G.Bradman	A v E	1936-37
Perth	259	2nd	W.B.Phillips, G.N.Yallop	A v P	1983-84
Sydney	405	5th	S.G.Barnes, D.G.Bradman	A v E	1946-47
Cape Town	260	1st	B.Mitchell, I.J.Siedle	SA v E	1930-31
Durban	280	2nd	P.A.Gibb, W.J.Edrich	E v SA	1938-39
Johannesburg	359	1st	L.Hutton, C.Washbrook	E v SA	1948-49
Port Elizabeth	187	3rd	A.R.Morris, R.N.Harvey	A v SA	1949-50
Bridgetown	399	4th	G.St A.Sobers, F.M.M.Worrell	WI v E	1959-60
Georgetown	387	1st	G.M.Turner, T.W.Jarvis	NZ v WI	1971-72
Kingston	446	2nd	C.C.Hunte, G.St A.Sobers	WI v P	1957-58
Port-of-Spain	338	3rd	E.de C.Weekes, F.M.M.Worrell	WI v E	1953-54
St John's	308	3rd	R.B.Richardson, I.V.A.Richards	WI v A	1983-84
Auckland	266	4th	M.H.Denness, K.W.R.Fletcher	E v NZ	1974-75
Christchurch	242	5th	W.R.Hammond, L.E.G.Ames	E v NZ	1932-33
Dunedin	350	4th	Mushtaq Mohammad, Asif Iqbal	P v NZ	1972-73
Hamilton	161	1st	T.J.Franklin, J.G.Wright	NZ v SL	1990-91
Napier	195	2nd	J.G.Wright, G.P.Howarth	NZ v P	1978-79
Wellington	467	3rd	A.H.Jones, M.D.Crowe	NZ v SL	1990-91
Ahmedabad	154	7th	Imran Khan, Ijaz Faqih	P v I	1986-87
Bangalore	207	4th	C.G.Greenidge, C.H.Lloyd	WI v I	1974-75
Bombay	298*	6th	D.B.Vengsarkar, R.J.Shastri	I v A	1986-87
Calcutta	344*	2nd	S.M.Gavaskar, D.B.Vengsarkar	I v WI	1978-79
Chandigarh	76	2nd	R.J.Shastri, S.V.Manjrekar	I v SL	1990-91
Cuttack	111	6th	D.B.Vengsarkar, Kapil Dev	I v SL	1986-87
Delhi	267	4th	C.L.Walcott, G.E.Gomez	WI v I	1948-49
Hyderabad	238	3rd	P.R.Umrigar, V.L.Manjrekar	I v NZ	1955-56
Jaipur	130	5th	M.Azharuddin, R.J.Shastri	I v P	1986-87
Jullundur	121	6th	A.D.Gaekwad, R.M.H.Binny	I v P	1983-84
Kanpur	272	6th	M.Azharuddin, Kapil Dev	I v SL	1986-87
Lucknow	142	4th	S.R.Tendulkar, M.Azharuddin	I v SL	1993-94
Madras	413	1st	M.H.Mankad, P.Roy	I v NZ	1955-56
Nagpur	173	3rd	M.Amarnath, D.B.Vengsarkar	I v SL	1986-87
Bahawalpur	127	1st	Hanif Mohammad, Alimuddin	P v I	1954-55
Dacca	198	1st	G.Pullar, R.W.Barber	E v P	1961-62
Faisalabad	397	3rd	Qasim Omar, Javed Miandad	P v SL	1985-86
Gujranwala	56	2nd	Ramiz Raja, Zahid Fazal	P v SL	1991-92
Hyderabad	451	3rd	Mudassar Nazar, Javed Miandad	P v I	1982-83
Karachi	252	4th	Javed Miandad, Mushtaq Mohammad	P v NZ	1976-77
Lahore	308	7th	Waqar Hassan, Imtiaz Ahmed	P v NZ	1955-56
Multan	100	3rd	Majid Khan, Javed Miandad	P v WI	1980-81
Peshawar	91	3rd	P.R.Umrigar, V.L.Manjrekar	I v P	1954-55
Rawalpindi	135	2nd	M.H.Dekker, A.D.R.Campbell	Z v P	1993-94
Sialkot	132	5th	Salim Malik, Imran Khan	P v SL	1991-92
Colombo (PSS)	240*	4th	A.P.Gurusinha, A.Ranatunga	SL v P	1985-86.
Colombo (SSC)	230	4th	A.P.Gurusinha, A.Ranatunga	SL v A	1992-93
Colombo (CCC)	246*	6th	J.J.Crowe, R.J.Hadlee	NZ v SL	1986-87
Colombo (KS)	131	6th	D.M.Jones, G.R.J.Matthews	A v SL	1992-93
Kandy	216	4th	R.L.Dias, L.R.D.Mendis	SL v I	1985-86
Moratuwa	151	5th	K.R.Rutherford, C.Z.Harris	NZ v SL	1992-93
Bulawayo	127	2nd	R.T.Latham, A.H.Jones	NZ v Z	1992-93
Harare	168	4th	M.D.Crowe, K.R.Rutherford	NZ v Z	1992-93

BEST INNINGS BOWLING ANALYSIS FOR EACH CENTRE

Birmingham	7-17	W.Rhodes	England v Australia	1902
Leeds	8-43	R.G.D.Willis	England v Australia	1981
Lord's	8-34	I.T.Botham	England v Pakistan	1978
Manchester	10-53	J.C.Laker	England v Australia	1956
Nottingham	8-107	B.J.T.Bosanquet	England v Australia	1905
Oval	9-57	D.E.Malcolm	England v South Africa	1994
Sheffield	6-49	S.F.Barnes	England v Australia	1902
Adelaide	8-43	A.E.Trott	Australia v England	1894-95
Brisbane	9-52	R.J.Hadlee	New Zealand v Australia	1985-86
Hobart	6-31	S.K.Warne	Australia v New Zealand	1993-94
Melbourne	9-86	Sarfraz Nawaz	Pakistan v Australia	1978-79
Perth	8-87	M.G.Hughes	Australia v West Indies	1988-89
Sydney	8-35	G.A.Lohmann	England v Australia	1886-87
Cape Town	8-11	J.Briggs	England v South Africa	1888-89
Durban	8-69	H.J.Tayfield	South Africa v England	1956-57
Johannesburg	9-28	G.A.Lohmann	England v South Africa	1895-96
Port Elizabeth	8-7	G.A.Lohmann	England v South Africa	1895-96
Bridgetown	8-38	L.R.Gibbs	West Indies v India	1961-62
Georgetown	7-44	I.W.Johnson	Australia v West Indies	1954-55
Kingston	7-34	T.E.Bailey	England v West Indies	1953-54
Port-of-Spain	9-95	J.M.Noreiga	West Indies v India	1970-71
St John's	6-74	C.E.H.Croft	West Indies v England	1980-81
Auckland	8-76	E.A.S.Prasanna	India v New Zealand	1975-76
Christchurch	7-47	P.C.R.Tufnell	England v New Zealand	1991-92
Dunedin	7-52	Intikhab Alam	Pakistan v New Zealand	1972-73
Hamilton	5-22	Waqar Younis	Pakistan v New Zealand	1992-93
Napier	5-98	D.K.Morrison	New Zealand v India	1989-90
Wellington	7-23	R.J.Hadlee	New Zealand v India	1975-76
Ahmedabad	9-83	Kapil Dev	India v West Indies	1983-84
Bangalore	7-27	Maninder Singh	India v Pakistan	1986-87
Bombay	7-48	I.T.Botham	England v India	1979-80
Calcutta	7-49	Ghulam Ahmed	India v Australia	1956-57
Chandigarh	6-12	S.L.V.Raju	India v Sri Lanka	1990-91
Cuttack	5-85	J.R.Ratnayeke	Sri Lanka v India	1986-87
Delhi	8-52	M.H.Mankad	India v Pakistan	1952-53
Hyderabad	7-128	S.P.Gupte	India v New Zealand	1955-56
Jaipur	4-88	G.Sharma	India v Pakistan	1986-87
Jullundur	4-50	Wasim Raja	Pakistan v India	1983-84
Kanpur	9-69	J.M.Patel	India v Australia	1959-60
Lucknow	7-42	Fazal Mahmood	Pakistan v India	1952-53
Madras	8-55	M.H.Mankad	India v England	1951-52
Nagpur	7-51	Maninder Singh	India v Sri Lanka	1986-87
Bahawalpur	6-74	P.R.Umrigar	India v Pakistan	1954-55
Dacca	6-21	Khan Mohammad	Pakistan v New Zealand	1955-56
Faisalabad	7-52	C.Pringle	New Zealand v Pakistan	1990-91
Gujranwala	1-27	G.P.Wickremasinghe	Sri Lanka v Pakistan	1991-92
Hyderabad	7-87	S.L.Boock	New Zealand v Pakistan	1984-85
Karachi	8-60	Imran Khan	Pakistan v India	1982-83
Lahore	9-56	Abdul Qadir	Pakistan v England	1987-88
Multan	5-62	Imran Khan	Pakistan v West Indies	1980-81
Peshawar	5-63	S.P.Gupte	India v Pakistan	1954-55
Rawalpindi	5-56	H.H.Streak	Zimbabwe v Pakistan	1993-94
Sialkot	8-83	J.R.Ratnayeke	Sri Lanka v Pakistan	1985-86
Colombo (PSS)	6-33	J.E.Emburey	England v Sri Lanka	1981-82
Colombo (SSC)	6-85	R.J.Ratnayake	Sri Lanka v India	1985-86
Colombo (CCC)	5-29	R.J.Hadlee	New Zealand v Sri Lanka	1983-84
Colombo (KS)	4-53	C.J.McDermott	Australia v Sri Lanka	1992-93
Kandy	6-34	Waqar Younis	Pakistan v Sri Lanka	1994-95
Moratuwa	5-69	A.A.Donald	South Africa v Sri Lanka	1993-94
Bulawayo	6-113	D.N.Patel	New Zealand v Zimbabwe	1992-93
Harare	6-50	D.N.Patel	New Zealand v Zimbabwe	1992-93

BEST MATCH BOWLING ANALYSIS FOR EACH CENTRE

Birmingham	12-119	F.S.Trueman	England v West Indies	1963
Leeds	15-99	C.Blythe	England v South Africa	1907
Lord's	16-137	R.A.L.Massie	Australia v England	1972
Manchester	19-90	J.C.Laker	England v Australia	1956
Nottingham	14-99	A.V.Bedser	England v Australia	1953
Oval	14-90	F.R.Spofforth	Australia v England	1882
Sheffield	11-103	M.A.Noble	Australia v England	1902
Adelaide	14-199	C.V.Grimmett	Australia v South Africa	1931-32
Brisbane	15-123	R.J.Hadlee	New Zealand v Australia	1985-86
Hobart	9-67	S.K.Warne	Australia v New Zealand	1993-94
Melbourne	15-124	W.Rhodes	England v Australia	1903-04
Perth	13-217	M.G.Hughes	Australia v West Indies	1988-89
Sydney	12-87	C.T.B.Turner	Australia v England	1887-88
Cape Town	15-28	J.Briggs	England v South Africa	1888-89
Durban	14-144	S.F.Barnes	England v South Africa	1913-14
Johannesburg	17-159	S.F.Barnes	England v South Africa	1913-14
Port Elizabeth	15-45	G.A.Lohmann	England v South Africa	1895-96
Bridgetown	11-120	M.D.Marshall	West Indies v New Zealand	1984-85
Georgetown	11-121	Imran Khan	Pakistan v West Indies	1987-88
Kingston	10-96	H.H.H.Johnson	West Indies v England	1947-48
Port-of-Spain	13-156	A.W.Greig	England v West Indies	1973-74
St John's	9-127	Waqar Younis	Pakistan v West Indies	1992-93
Auckland	11-123	D.K.Lillee	Australia v New Zealand	1976-77
Christchurch	12-97	D.L.Underwood	England v New Zealand	1970-71
Dunedin	11-102	R.J.Hadlee	New Zealand v West Indies	1979-80
Hamilton	9-81	Waqar Younis	Pakistan v New Zealand	1992-93
Napier	5-98	D.K.Morrison	New Zealand v India	1989-90
Wellington	11-58	R.J.Hadlee	New Zealand v India	1975-76
Ahmedabad	11-125	S.L.V.Raju	India v Sri Lanka	1993-94
Bangalore	10-126	Maninder Singh	India v Pakistan	1986-87
Bombay	13-106	I.T.Botham	England v India	1979-80
Calcutta	11-105	R.Benaud	Australia v India	1956-57
Chandigarh	8-37	S.L.V.Raju	India v Sri Lanka	1990-91
Cuttack	6-83	Maninder Singh	India v Sri Lanka	1986-87
Delhi	13-131	M.H.Mankad	India v Pakistan	1952-53
Hyderabad	8-109	E.A.S.Prasanna	India v New Zealand	1969-70
Jaipur	4-88	G.Sharma	India v Pakistan	1986-87
Jullundur	4-50	Wasim Raja	Pakistan v India	1983-84
Kanpur	14-124	J.M.Patel	India v Australia	1959-60
Lucknow	12-94	Fazal Mahmood	Pakistan v India	1952-53
Madras	16-136	N.D.Hirwani	India v West Indies	1987-88
Nagpur	10-107	Maninder Singh	India v Sri Lanka	1986-87
Bahawalpur	7-124	Khan Mohammad	Pakistan v India	1954-55
Dacca	12-100	Fazal Mahmood	Pakistan v West Indies	1958-59
Faisalabad	12-130	Waqar Younis	Pakistan v New Zealand	1990-91
Gujranwala	1-27	G.P.Wickremasinghe	Sri Lanka v Pakistan	1991-92
Hyderabad	8-80	Imran Khan	Pakistan v India	1982-83
Karachi	13-114	Fazal Mahmood	Pakistan v Australia	1956-57
Lahore	14-116	Imran Khan	Pakistan v Sri Lanka	1981-82
Multan	5-89	Imran Khan	Pakistan v West Indies	1980-81
Peshawar	6-115	S.P.Gupte	India v Pakistan	1954-55
Rawalpindi	9-138	Waqar Younis	Pakistan v Zimbabwe	1993-94
Sialkot	9-95	Imran Khan	Pakistan v Sri Lanka	1985-86
Colombo (PSS)	9-125	R.J.Ratnayake	Sri Lanks v India	1985-86
Colombo (SSC)	9-106	B.N.Schultz	South Africa v Sri Lanka	1993-94
Colombo (CCC)	10-102	R.J.Hadlee	New Zealand v Sri Lanka	1983-84
Colombo (KS)	6-85	C.J.McDermott	Australia v Sri Lanka	1992-93
Kandy	11-119	Waqar Younis	Pakistan v Sri Lanka	1994-95
Moratuwa	8-157	C.P.H.Ramanayake	Sri Lanka v Australia	1992-93
Bulawayo	7-173	D.N.Patel	New Zealand v Zimbabwe	1992-93
Harare	8-131	D.N.Patel	New Zealand v Zimbabwe	1992-93

RESULTS SUMMARY

RESULTS SUMMARY OF ALL TEST MATCHES 1876-77 to 1994
To 27 September 1994 (Including Sri Lanka v Pakistan 1994-95)

Opponents		Tests	Won by										Tied	Drawn
			E	A	SA	WI	NZ	I	P	SL	Z		
England	Australia	280	89	108	–	–	–	–	–	–	–	–	–	83
	South Africa	105	47	–	19	–	–	–	–	–	–	–	–	39
	West Indies	109	25	–	–	46	–	–	–	–	–	–	–	38
	New Zealand	75	34	–	–	–	4	–	–	–	–	–	–	37
	India	81	31	–	–	–	–	14	–	–	–	–	–	36
	Pakistan	52	14	–	–	–	–	–	7	–	–	–	–	31
	Sri Lanka	5	3	–	–	–	–	–	–	1	–	–	–	1
Australia	South Africa	59	–	31	13	–	–	–	–	–	–	–	–	15
	West Indies	77	–	30	–	26	–	–	–	–	–	–	1	20
	New Zealand	32	–	13	–	–	7	–	–	–	–	–	–	12
	India	50	–	24	–	–	–	8	–	–	–	–	1	17
	Pakistan	34	–	12	–	–	–	–	9	–	–	–	–	13
	Sri Lanka	7	–	4	–	–	–	–	–	0	–	–	–	3
South Africa	West Indies	1	–	–	0	1	–	–	–	–	–	–	–	–
	New Zealand	17	–	–	9	–	2	–	–	–	–	–	–	6
	India	4	–	–	1	–	–	0	–	–	–	–	–	3
	Sri Lanka	3	–	–	1	–	–	–	–	0	–	–	–	2
West Indies	New Zealand	24	–	–	–	8	4	–	–	–	–	–	–	12
	India	62	–	–	–	26	–	6	–	–	–	–	–	30
	Pakistan	31	–	–	–	12	–	–	7	–	–	–	–	12
	Sri Lanka	1	–	–	–	0	–	–	–	0	–	–	–	1
New Zealand	India	32	–	–	–	–	6	12	–	–	–	–	–	14
	Pakistan	36	–	–	–	–	4	–	16	–	–	–	–	16
	Sri Lanka	11	–	–	–	–	4	–	–	1	–	–	–	6
	Zimbabwe	2	–	–	–	–	1	–	–	–	0	–	–	1
India	Pakistan	44	–	–	–	–	–	4	7	–	–	–	–	33
	Sri Lanka	14	–	–	–	–	–	7	–	1	–	–	–	6
	Zimbabwe	2	–	–	–	–	–	1	–	–	0	–	–	1
Pakistan	Sri Lanka	14	–	–	–	–	–	–	8	1	–	–	–	5
	Zimbabwe	3	–	–	–	–	–	–	2	–	0	–	–	1
		1267	243	222	43	119	32	52	56	4	0	2		494

	Tests	Won	Lost	Drawn	Tied	Toss Won
England	707	243	199	265	–	348
Australia	539	222	152	163	2	271
South Africa	189	43	81	65	–	91
West Indies	305	119	72	113	1	158
New Zealand	229	32	93	104	–	116
India	289	52	96	140	1	144
Pakistan	214	56	47	111	–	108
Sri Lanka	55	4	27	24	–	28
Zimbabwe	7	0	4	3	–	3

SERIES RECORDS – ENGLAND v AUSTRALIA

HIGHEST INNINGS TOTALS

England	in England	903-7d		Oval	1938
	in Australia	636		Sydney	1928-29
Australia	in England	729-6d		Lord's	1930
	in Australia	659-8d		Sydney	1946-47

LOWEST INNINGS TOTALS

England	in England	52		Oval	1948
	in Australia	45		Sydney	1886-87
Australia	in England	36		Birmingham	1902
	in Australia	42		Sydney	1887-88

HIGHEST MATCH AGGREGATE	1753 for 40 wickets	Adelaide	1920-21
LOWEST MATCH AGGREGATE	291 for 40 wickets	Lord's	1888

HIGHEST INDIVIDUAL INNINGS

England	in England	364	L.Hutton	Oval	1938
	in Australia	287	R.E.Foster	Sydney	1903-04
Australia	in England	334	D.G.Bradman	Leeds	1930
	in Australia	307	R.M.Cowper	Melbourne	1965-66

HIGHEST AGGREGATE OF RUNS IN A SERIES

England	in England	732 (av 81.33)	D.I.Gower		1985
	in Australia	905 (av 113.12)	W.R.Hammond		1928-29
Australia	in England	974 (av 139.14)	D.G.Bradman		1930
	in Australia	810 (av 90.00)	D.G.Bradman		1936-37

RECORD WICKET PARTNERSHIPS – ENGLAND

1st	323	J.B.Hobbs (178), W.Rhodes (179)	Melbourne	1911-12
2nd	382	L.Hutton (364), M.Leyland (187)	Oval	1938
3rd	262	W.R.Hammond (177), D.R.Jardine (98)	Adelaide	1928-29
4th	222	W.R.Hammond (240), E.Paynter (99)	Lord's	1938
5th	206	E.Paynter (216*), D.C.S.Compton (102)	Nottingham	1938
6th	215	L.Hutton (364), J.Hardstaff, jr (169*)	Oval	1938
	215	G.Boycott (107), A.P.E.Knott (135)	Nottingham	1977
7th	143	F.E.Woolley (133*), J.Vine (36)	Sydney	1911-12
8th	124	E.H.Hendren (169), H.Larwood (70)	Brisbane[1]	1928-29
9th	151	W.H.Scotton (90), W.W.Read (117)	Oval	1884
10th	130	R.E.Foster (287), W.Rhodes (40*)	Sydney	1903-04

RECORD WICKET PARTNERSHIPS – AUSTRALIA

1st	329	G.R.Marsh (138), M.A.Taylor (219)	Nottingham	1989
2nd	451	W.H.Ponsford (266), D.G.Bradman (244)	Oval	1934
3rd	276	D.G.Bradman (187), A.L.Hassett (128)	Brisbane[2]	1946-47
4th	388	W.H.Ponsford (181), D.G.Bradman (304)	Leeds	1934
5th	405	S.G.Barnes (234), D.G.Bradman (234)	Sydney	1946-47
6th	346	J.H.W.Fingleton (136), D.G.Bradman (270)	Melbourne	1936-37
7th	165	C.Hill (188), H.Trumble (46)	Melbourne	1897-98
8th	243	R.J.Hartigan (113), C.Hill (160)	Adelaide	1907-08
9th	154	S.E.Gregory (201), J.M.Blackham (74)	Sydney	1894-95
10th	127	J.M.Taylor (108), A.A.Mailey (46*)	Sydney	1924-25

BEST INNINGS BOWLING ANALYSIS

England	in England	10-53	J.C.Laker	Manchester	1956
	in Australia	8-35	G.A.Lohmann	Sydney	1886-87
Australia	in England	8-31	F.Laver	Manchester	1909
	in Australia	9-121	A.A.Mailey	Melbourne	1920-21

BEST MATCH BOWLING ANALYSIS

England	in England	19-90	J.C.Laker	Manchester	1956
	in Australia	15-124	W.Rhodes	Melbourne	1903-04
Australia	in England	16-137	R.A.L.Massie	Lord's	1972
	in Australia	13-77	M.A.Noble	Melbourne	1901-02

HIGHEST AGGREGATE OF WICKETS IN A SERIES

England	in England	46 (av 9.60)	J.C.Laker		1956
	in Australia	38 (av 23.18)	M.W.Tate		1924-25
Australia	in England	42 (av 21.26)	T.M.Alderman		1981
	in Australia	41 (av 12.85)	R.M.Hogg		1978-79

MOST RUNS

	Tests	I	NO	HS	Runs	Avge
D.G.Bradman (A)	37	63	7	334	**5028**	89.78
J.B.Hobbs (E)	41	71	4	187	**3636**	54.26
A.R.Border (A)	47	82	19	200*	**3548**	56.31
D.I.Gower (E)	42	77	4	215	**3269**	44.78
G.Boycott (E)	38	71	9	191	**2945**	47.50
W.R.Hammond (E)	33	58	3	251	**2852**	51.85
H.Sutcliffe (E)	27	46	5	194	**2741**	66.85
C.Hill (A)	41	76	1	188	**2660**	35.46
J.H.Edrich (E)	32	57	3	175	**2644**	48.96
G.S.Chappell (A)	35	65	8	144	**2619**	45.94
M.C.Cowdrey (E)	43	75	4	113	**2433**	34.26
L.Hutton (E)	27	49	6	364	**2428**	56.46
R.N.Harvey (A)	37	68	5	167	**2416**	38.34
G.A.Gooch (E)	37	69	0	196	**2387**	34.59
V.T.Trumper (A)	40	74	5	185*	**2263**	32.79
W.M.Lawry (A)	29	51	5	166	**2233**	48.54
S.E.Gregory (A)	52	92	7	201	**2193**	25.80
W.W.Armstrong (A)	42	71	9	158	**2172**	35.03
I.M.Chappell (A)	30	56	4	192	**2138**	41.11
K.F.Barrington (E)	23	39	6	256	**2111**	63.96
A.R.Morris (A)	24	43	2	206	**2080**	50.73

D.G.Bradman holds the unique record of scoring 2000 runs in both countries in this series (2674 runs in England and 2354 in Australia). J.B.Hobbs is the only other batsman to score 2000 runs in either country (2493 runs in Australia).

MOST WICKETS

	Tests	Balls	Runs	Wkts	BB	5wI	Avge
D.K.Lillee (A)	29	8516	3507	**167**	7-89	11	21.00
I.T.Botham (E)	36	8479	4093	**148**	6-78	9	27.65
H.Trumble (A)	31	7895	2945	**141**	8-65	9	20.88
R.G.D.Willis (E)	35	7294	3346	**128**	8-43	7	26.14
M.A.Noble (A)	39	6845	2860	**115**	7-17	9	24.86
R.R.Lindwall (A)	29	6728	2559	**114**	7-63	6	22.44
W.Rhodes (E)	41	5791	2616	**109**	8-68	6	24.00
S.F.Barnes (E)	20	5749	2288	**106**	7-60	12	21.58
C.V.Grimmett (A)	22	9224	3439	**106**	6-37	11	32.44
D.L.Underwood (E)	29	8000	2770	**105**	7-50	4	26.38
A.V.Bedser (E)	21	7065	2859	**104**	7-44	7	27.49
G.Giffen (A)	31	6457	2791	**103**	7-117	7	27.09
W.J.O'Reilly (A)	19	7864	2587	**102**	7-54	8	25.36
R.Peel (E)	20	5216	1715	**102**	7-31	6	16.98
C.T.B.Turner (A)	17	5195	1670	**101**	7-43	11	16.53
T.M.Alderman (A)	17	4717	2117	**100**	6-47	11	21.17
J.R.Thomson (A)	21	4951	2418	**100**	6-46	5	24.18

MOST WICKET-KEEPING DISMISSALS

	Tests	Ct	St	Total
R.W.Marsh (A)	42	141	7	**148**
A.P.E.Knott (E)	34	97	8	**105**
W.A.S.Oldfield (A)	38	59	31	**90**
A.F.A.Lilley (E)	32	65	19	**84**
A.T.W.Grout (A)	22	69	7	**76**
T.G.Evans (E)	31	63	12	**75**

R.W.Marsh (141 catches) and W.A.S.Oldfield (31 stumpings) hold the respective individual records in Anglo-Australian Tests.

SERIES RECORDS – ENGLAND v SOUTH AFRICA

HIGHEST INNINGS TOTALS

England	in England	554-8d	Lord's	1947
	in South Africa	654-5	Durban[2]	1938-39
South Africa	in England	538	Leeds	1951
	in South Africa	530	Durban[2]	1938-39

LOWEST INNINGS TOTALS

England	in England	76	Leeds	1907
	in South Africa	92	Cape Town	1898-99
South Africa	in England	30	Birmingham	1924
	in South Africa	30	Port Elizabeth	1895-96

HIGHEST MATCH AGGREGATE 1981 for 35 wickets		Durban[2]	1938-39
LOWEST MATCH AGGREGATE 378 for 30 wickets		Oval	1912

HIGHEST INDIVIDUAL INNINGS

England	in England	211	J.B.Hobbs	Lord's	1924
	in South Africa	243	E.Paynter	Durban[2]	1938-39
South Africa	in England	236	E.A.B.Rowan	Leeds	1951
	in South Africa	176	H.W.Taylor	Johannesburg[1]	1922-23

HIGHEST AGGREGATE OF RUNS IN A SERIES

England	in England	753 (av 94.12)	D.C.S.Compton		1947
	in South Africa	653 (av 81.62)	E.Paynter		1938-39
South Africa	in England	621 (av 69.00)	A.D.Nourse		1947
	in South Africa	582 (av 64.66)	H.W.Taylor		1922-23

RECORD WICKET PARTNERSHIPS – ENGLAND

1st	359	L.Hutton (158), C.Washbrook (195)	Johannesburg[2]	1948-49
2nd	280	P.A.Gibb (120), W.J.Edrich (219)	Durban[2]	1938-39
3rd	370	W.J.Edrich (189), D.C.S.Compton (208)	Lord's	1947
4th	197	W.R.Hammond (181), L.E.G.Ames (115)	Cape Town	1938-39
5th	237	D.C.S.Compton (163), N.W.D.Yardley (99)	Nottingham	1947
6th	206*	K.F.Barrington (148*), J.M.Parks (108*)	Durban[2]	1964-65
7th	115	J.W.H.T.Douglas (119), M.C.Bird (61)	Durban[1]	1913-14
8th	154	C.W.Wright (71), H.R.Bromley-Davenport (84)	Johannesburg[1]	1895-96
9th	71	H.Wood (134*), J.T.Hearne (40)	Cape Town	1891-92
10th	92	C.A.G.Russell (111), A.E.R.Gilligan (39*)	Durban[2]	1922-23

RECORD WICKET PARTNERSHIPS – SOUTH AFRICA

1st	260	B.Mitchell (123), I.J.Siedle (141)	Cape Town	1930-31
2nd	198	E.A.B.Rowan (236), C.B.van Ryneveld (83)	Leeds	1951
3rd	319	A.Melville (189), A.D.Nourse (149)	Nottingham	1947
4th	214	H.W.Taylor (121), H.G.Deane (93)	Oval	1929
5th	157	A.J.Pithey (95), J.H.B.Waite (64)	Johannesburg[3]	1964-65
6th	171	J.H.B.Waite (113), P.L.Winslow (108)	Manchester	1955
7th	123	H.G.Deane (73), E.P.Nupen (69)	Durban[2]	1927-28
8th	109*	B.Mitchell (189*), L.Tuckett (40*)	Oval	1947
9th	137	E.L.Dalton (117), A.B.C.Langton (73*)	Oval	1935
10th	103	H.G.Owen-Smith (129), A.J.Bell (26*)	Leeds	1929

BEST INNINGS BOWLING ANALYSIS

England	in England	9-57	D.E.Malcolm	Oval	1994
	in South Africa	9-28	G.A.Lohmann	Johannesburg[1]	1895-96
South Africa	in England	7-65	S.J.Pegler	Lord's	1912
	in South Africa	9-113	H.J.Tayfield	Johannesburg[3]	1956-57

BEST MATCH BOWLING ANALYSIS

England	in England	15-99	C.Blythe	Leeds	1907
	in South Africa	17-159	S.F.Barnes	Johannesburg[1]	1913-14
South Africa	in England	10-87	P.M.Pollock	Nottingham	1965
	in South Africa	13-192	H.J.Tayfield	Johannesburg[3]	1956-57

HIGHEST AGGREGATE OF WICKETS IN A SERIES

England	in England	34 (av 8.29)	S.F.Barnes	1912
	in South Africa	49 (av 10.93)	S.F.Barnes	1913-14
South Africa	in England	26 (av 21.84)	H.J.Tayfield	1955
		26 (av 22.57)	N.A.T.Adcock	1960
	in South Africa	37 (av 17.18)	H.J.Tayfield	1956-57

SERIES RECORDS – ENGLAND v WEST INDIES

HIGHEST INNINGS TOTALS

England	in England	619-6d		Nottingham	1957
	in West Indies	849		Kingston	1929-30
West Indies	in England	687-8d		Oval	1976
	in West Indies	681-8d		Port-of-Spain	1953-54

LOWEST INNINGS TOTALS

England	in England	71		Manchester	1976
	in West Indies	46		Port-of-Spain	1993-94
West Indies	in England	86		Oval	1957
	in West Indies	102		Bridgetown	1934-35

HIGHEST MATCH AGGREGATE 1815 for 34 wickets   Kingston   1929-30
LOWEST MATCH AGGREGATE   309 for 29 wickets   Bridgetown   1934-35

HIGHEST INDIVIDUAL INNINGS

England	in England	285*	P.B.H.May	Birmingham	1957
	in West Indies	325	A.Sandham	Kingston	1929-30
West Indies	in England	291	I.V.A.Richards	Oval	1976
	in West Indies	375	B.C.Lara	St John's	1993-94

HIGHEST AGGREGATE OF RUNS IN A SERIES

England	in England	489 (av 97.80)	P.B.H.May		1957
	in West Indies	693 (av 115.50)	E.H.Hendren		1929-30
West Indies	in England	829 (av 118.42)	I.V.A.Richards		1976
	in West Indies	798 (av 99.75)	B.C.Lara		1993-94

RECORD WICKET PARTNERSHIPS – ENGLAND

1st	212	C.Washbrook (102), R.T.Simpson (94)	Nottingham	1950
2nd	266	P.E.Richardson (126), T.W.Graveney (258)	Nottingham	1957
3rd	303	M.A.Atherton (135), R.A.Smith (175)	St John's	1993-94
4th	411	P.B.H.May (285*), M.C.Cowdrey (154)	Birmingham	1957
5th	150	A.J.Stewart (143), G.P.Thorpe (84)	Bridgetown	1993-94
6th	163	A.W.Greig (148), A.P.E.Knott (87)	Bridgetown	1973-74
7th	197	M.J.K.Smith (96), J.M.Parks (101*)	Port-of-Spain	1959-60
8th	217	T.W.Graveney (165), J.T.Murray (112)	Oval	1966
9th	109	G.A.R.Lock (89), P.I.Pocock (13)	Georgetown	1967-68
10th	128	K.Higgs (63), J.A.Snow (59*)	Oval	1966

RECORD WICKET PARTNERSHIPS – WEST INDIES

1st	298	C.G.Greenidge (149), D.L.Haynes (167)	St John's	1989-90
2nd	287*	C.G.Greenidge (214*), H.A.Gomes (92*)	Lord's	1984
3rd	338	E.de C.Weekes (206), F.M.M.Worrell (167)	Port-of-Spain	1953-54
4th	399	G.St A.Sobers (226), F.M.M. Worrell (197*)	Bridgetown	1959-60
5th	265	S.M.Nurse (137), G.St A.Sobers (174)	Leeds	1966
6th	274*	G.St A.Sobers (163*), D.A.J.Holford (105*)	Lord's	1966
7th	155*†	G.St A.Sobers (150*), B.D.Julien (121)	Lord's	1973
8th	99	C.A.McWatt (54), J.K.Holt (48*)	Georgetown	1953-54
9th	150	E.A.E.Baptiste (87*), M.A.Holding (69)	Birmingham	1984
10th	67*	M.A.Holding (58*), C.E.H.Croft (17*)	St John's	1980-81

BEST INNINGS BOWLING ANALYSIS

England	in England	8-103	I.T.Botham	Lord's	1984
	in West Indies	8-75	A.R.C.Fraser	Bridgetown	1993-94
West Indies	in England	8-92	M.A.Holding	Oval	1976
	in West Indies	8-45	C.E.L.Ambrose	Bridgetown	1989-90

BEST MATCH BOWLING ANALYSIS

England	in England	12-119	F.S.Trueman	Birmingham	1963
	in West Indies	13-156	A.W.Greig	Port-of-Spain	1973-74
West Indies	in England	14-149	M.A.Holding	Oval	1976
	in West Indies	11-84	C.E.L.Ambrose	Port-of-Spain	1993-94

HIGHEST AGGREGATE OF WICKETS IN A SERIES

England	in England	34 (av 17.47)	F.S.Trueman		1963
	in West Indies	27 (av 18.66)	J.A.Snow		1967-68
West Indies	in England	35 (av 12.65)	M.D.Marshall		1988
	in West Indies	{27 (av 16.14)	J.Garner		1985-86
		{27 (av 17.65)	M.D.Marshall		1985-86

† 231 runs were added for this wicket; G.St A.Sobers retired ill and was succeeded by K.D.Boyce after 155 had been scored.

SERIES RECORDS – ENGLAND v NEW ZEALAND

HIGHEST INNINGS TOTALS
England	in England	567-8d	Nottingham	1994
	in New Zealand	593-6d	Auckland	1974-75
New Zealand	in England	551-9d	Lord's	1973
	in New Zealand	537	Wellington	1983-84

LOWEST INNINGS TOTALS
England	in England	158	Birmingham	1990
	in New Zealand	64	Wellington	1977-78
New Zealand	in England	47	Lord's	1958
	in New Zealand	26	Auckland	1954-55

HIGHEST MATCH AGGREGATE 1293 for 34 wickets		Lord's	1931
LOWEST MATCH AGGREGATE 390 for 30 wickets		Lord's	1958

HIGHEST INDIVIDUAL INNINGS
England	in England	310*	J.H.Edrich	Leeds	1965
	in New Zealand	336*	W.R.Hammond	Auckland	1932-33
New Zealand	in England	206	M.P.Donnelly	Lord's	1949
	in New Zealand	174*	J.V.Coney	Wellington	1983-84

HIGHEST AGGREGATE OF RUNS IN A SERIES
England	in England	469 (av 78.16)	L.Hutton		1949
	in New Zealand	563 (av 563.00)	W.R.Hammond		1932-33
New Zealand	in England	462 (av 77.00)	M.P.Donnelly		1949
	in New Zealand	341 (av 85.25)	C.S.Dempster		1929-30

RECORD WICKET PARTNERSHIPS – ENGLAND
1st	223	G.Fowler (105), C.J.Tavaré (109)	Oval	1983
2nd	369	J.H.Edrich (310*), K.F.Barrington (163)	Leeds	1965
3rd	245	J.Hardstaff, jr (114), W.R.Hammond (140)	Lord's	1937
4th	266	M.H.Denness (188), K.W.R.Fletcher (216)	Auckland	1974-75
5th	242	W.R.Hammond (227), L.E.G.Ames (103)	Christchurch	1932-33
6th	240	P.H.Parfitt (131*), B.R.Knight (125)	Auckland	1962-63
7th	149	A.P.E.Knott (104), P.Lever (64)	Auckland	1970-71
8th	246	L.E.G.Ames (137), G.O.B.Allen (122)	Lord's	1931
9th	163*	M.C.Cowdrey (128*), A.C.Smith (69*)	Wellington	1962-63
10th	59	A.P.E.Knott (49), N.Gifford (25*)	Nottingham	1973

RECORD WICKET PARTNERSHIPS – NEW ZEALAND
1st	276	C.S.Dempster (136), J.E.Mills (117)	Wellington	1929-30
2nd	241	J.G.Wright (116), A.H.Jones (143)	Wellington	1991-92
3rd	210	B.A.Edgar (83), M.D.Crowe (106)	Lord's	1986
4th	155	M.D.Crowe (143), M.J.Greatbatch (68)	Wellington	1987-88
5th	180	M.D.Crowe (142), S.A.Thomson (69)	Lord's	1994
6th	141	M.D.Crowe (115), A.C.Parore (71)	Manchester	1994
7th	117	D.N.Patel (99), C.L.Cairns (61)	Christchurch	1991-92
8th	104	D.A.R.Moloney (64), A.W.Roberts (66*)	Lord's	1937
9th	118	J.V.Coney (174*), B.L.Cairns (64)	Wellington	1983-84
10th	57	F.L.H.Mooney (46), J.Cowie (26*)	Leeds	1949

BEST INNINGS BOWLING ANALYSIS
England	in England	7-32	D.L.Underwood	Lord's	1969
	in New Zealand	7-47	P.C.R.Tufnell	Christchurch	1991-92
New Zealand	in England	7-74	B.L.Cairns	Leeds	1983
	in New Zealand	7-143	B.L.Cairns	Wellington	1983-84

BEST MATCH BOWLING ANALYSIS
England	in England	12-101	D.L.Underwood	Oval	1969
	in New Zealand	12-97	D.L.Underwood	Christchurch	1970-71
New Zealand	in England	11-169	D.J.Nash	Lord's	1994
	in New Zealand	10-100	R.J.Hadlee	Wellington	1977-78

HIGHEST AGGREGATE OF WICKETS IN A SERIES
England	in England	34 (av 7.47)	G.A.R.Lock		1958
	in New Zealand	17 (av 9.34)	K.Higgs		1965-66
		17 (av 12.05)	D.L.Underwood		1970-71
		17 (av 18.29)	I.T.Botham		1977-78
New Zealand	in England	21 (av 26.61)	R.J.Hadlee		1983
	in New Zealand	15 (av 19.53)	R.O.Collinge		1977-78
		15 (av 24.73)	R.J.Hadlee		1977-78

SERIES RECORDS – ENGLAND v INDIA

HIGHEST INNINGS TOTALS

England	in England	653-4d	Lord's	1990
	in India	652-7d	Madras[1]	1984-85
India	in England	606-9d	Oval	1990
	in India	591	Bombay[3]	1992-93

LOWEST INNINGS TOTALS

England	in England	101	Oval	1971
	in India	102	Bombay[3]	1981-82
India	in England	42	Lord's	1974
	in India	83	Madras[1]	1976-77

HIGHEST MATCH AGGREGATE	1614 for 30 wickets	Lord's	1990
LOWEST MATCH AGGREGATE	482 for 31 wickets	Lord's	1936

HIGHEST INDIVIDUAL INNINGS

England	in England	333	G.A.Gooch	Lord's	1990
	in India	207	M.W.Gatting	Madras[1]	1984-85
India	in England	221	S.M.Gavaskar	Oval	1979
	in India	224	V.G.Kambli	Bombay[3]	1992-93

HIGHEST AGGREGATE OF RUNS IN A SERIES

England	in England	752 (av 125.33)	G.A.Gooch		1990
	in India	594 (av 99.00)	K.F.Barrington		1961-62
India	in England	542 (av 77.42)	S.M.Gavaskar		1979
	in India	586 (av 83.71)	V.L.Manjrekar		1961-62

RECORD WICKET PARTNERSHIPS – ENGLAND

1st	225	G.A.Gooch (116), M.A.Atherton (131)	Manchester	1990
2nd	241	G.Fowler (201), M.W.Gatting (207)	Madras[1]	1984-85
3rd	308	G.A.Gooch (333), A.J.Lamb (139)	Lord's	1990
4th	266	W.R.Hammond (217), T.S.Worthington (128)	Oval	1936
5th	254	K.W.R.Fletcher (113), A.W.Greig (148)	Bombay[2]	1972-73
6th	171	I.T.Botham (114), R.W.Taylor (43)	Bombay[3]	1979-80
7th	125	D.W.Randall (126), P.H.Edmonds (64)	Lord's	1982
8th	168	R.Illingworth (107), P.Lever (88*)	Manchester	1971
9th	83	K.W.R.Fletcher (97*), N.Gifford (19)	Madras[1]	1972-73
10th	70	P.J.W.Allott (41*), R.G.D.Willis (28)	Lord's	1982

RECORD WICKET PARTNERSHIPS – INDIA

1st	213	S.M.Gavaskar (221), C.P.S.Chauhan (80)	Oval	1979
2nd	192	F.M.Engineer (121), A.L.Wadekar (87)	Bombay[2]	1972-73
3rd	316†	G.R.Viswanath (222), Yashpal Sharma (140)	Madras[1]	1981-82
4th	222	V.S.Hazare (89), V.L.Manjrekar (133)	Leeds	1952
5th	214	M.Azharuddin (110), R.J.Shastri (111)	Calcutta	1984-85
6th	130	S.M.H.Kirmani (43), Kapil Dev (97)	Oval	1982
7th	235	R.J.Shastri (142), S.M.H.Kirmani (102)	Bombay[3]	1984-85
8th	128	R.J.Shastri (93), S.M.H.Kirmani (67)	Delhi	1981-82
9th	104	R.J.Shastri (93), Madan Lal (44)	Delhi	1981-82
10th	{51	R.G.Nadkarni (43*), B.S.Chandrasekhar (16)	Calcutta	1963-64
	{51	S.M.H.Kirmani (75), C.Sharma (17*)	Madras[1]	1984-85

BEST INNINGS BOWLING ANALYSIS

England	in England	8-31	F.S.Trueman	Manchester	1952
	in India	7-46	J.K.Lever	Delhi	1976-77
India	in England	6-35	L.Amar Singh	Lord's	1936
	in India	8-55	M.H.Mankad	Madras[1]	1951-52

BEST MATCH BOWLING ANALYSIS

England	in England	11-93	A.V.Bedser	Manchester	1946
	in India	13-106	I.T.Botham	Bombay[3]	1979-80
India	in England	10-188	C. Sharma	Birmingham	1986
	in India	12-108	M.H.Mankad	Madras[1]	1951-52

HIGHEST AGGREGATE OF WICKETS IN A SERIES

England	in England	29 (av 13.31)	F.S.Trueman		1952
	in India	29 (av 17.55)	D.L.Underwood		1976-77
India	in England	17 (av 34.64)	S.P.Gupte		1959
	in India	35 (av 18.91)	B.S.Chandrasekhar		1972-73

†415 runs were added for this wicket. D.B.Vengsarkar retired hurt and was replaced by Yashpal Sharma after 99 had been scored.

HIGHEST INNINGS TOTALS

England	in England	558-6d	Nottingham	1954
	in Pakistan	546-8d	Faisalabad	1983-84
Pakistan	in England	708	Oval	1987
	in Pakistan	569-9d	Hyderabad	1972-73

LOWEST INNINGS TOTALS

England	in England	130	Oval	1954
	in Pakistan	130	Lahore[2]	1987-88
Pakistan	in England	87	Lord's	1954
	in Pakistan	191	Faisalabad	1987-88

HIGHEST MATCH AGGREGATE

HIGHEST MATCH AGGREGATE	1274 for 25 wickets	Hyderabad	1972-73
	1274 for 37 wickets	Birmingham	1987
LOWEST MATCH AGGREGATE	509 for 28 wickets	Nottingham	1967

HIGHEST INDIVIDUAL INNINGS

England	in England	278	D.C.S.Compton	Nottingham	1954
	in Pakistan	205	E.R.Dexter	Karachi[1]	1961-62
Pakistan	in England	274	Zaheer Abbas	Birmingham	1971
	in Pakistan	157	Mushtaq Mohammad	Hyderabad	1972-73

HIGHEST AGGREGATE OF RUNS IN A SERIES

England	in England	453 (av 90.60)	D.C.S.Compton		1954
	in Pakistan	449 (av 112.25)	D.I.Gower		1983-84
Pakistan	in England	488 (av 81.33)	Salim Malik		1992
	in Pakistan	407 (av 67.83)	Hanif Mohammad		1961-62

RECORD WICKET PARTNERSHIPS – ENGLAND

1st	198	G.Pullar (165), R.W.Barber (86)	Dacca	1961-62
2nd	248	M.C.Cowdrey (182), E.R.Dexter (172)	Oval	1962
3rd	227	A.J.Stewart (190), R.A.Smith (127)	Birmingham	1992
4th	188	E.R.Dexter (205), P.H.Parfitt (111)	Karachi[1]	1961-62
5th	192	D.C.S.Compton (278), T.E.Bailey (36*)	Nottingham	1954
6th	153*	P.H.Parfitt (101*), D.A.Allen (79*)	Birmingham	1962
7th	167	D.I.Gower (152), V.J.Marks (83)	Faisalabad	1983-84
8th	99	P.H.Parfitt (119), D.A.Allen (62)	Leeds	1962
9th	76	T.W.Graveney (153), F.S.Trueman (29)	Lord's	1962
10th	79	R.W.Taylor (54), R.G.D.Willis (28*)	Birmingham	1982

RECORD WICKET PARTNERSHIPS – PAKISTAN

1st	173	Mohsin Khan (104), Shoaib Mohammad (80)	Lahore[2]	1983-84
2nd	291	Zaheer Abbas (274), Mushtaq Mohammad (100)	Birmingham	1971
3rd	180	Mudassar Nazar (114), Haroon Rashid (122)	Lahore[2]	1977-78
4th	322	Javed Miandad (153*), Salim Malik (165)	Birmingham	1992
5th	197	Javed Burki (101), Nasim-ul-Ghani (101)	Lord's	1962
6th	145	Mushtaq Mohammad (157), Intikhab Alam (138)	Hyderabad	1972-73
7th	89	Ijaz Ahmed (69), Salim Yousuf (42)	Oval	1987
8th	130	Hanif Mohammad (187*), Asif Iqbal (76)	Lord's	1967
9th	190	Asif Iqbal (146), Intikhab Alam (51)	Oval	1967
10th	62	Sarfraz Nawaz (53), Asif Masood (4*)	Leeds	1974

BEST INNINGS BOWLING ANALYSIS

England	in England	8-34	I.T.Botham	Lord's	1978
	in Pakistan	7-66	P.H.Edmonds	Karachi[1]	1977-78
Pakistan	in England	7-40	Imran Khan	Leeds	1987
	in Pakistan	9-56	Abdul Qadir	Lahore[2]	1987-88

BEST MATCH BOWLING ANALYSIS

England	in England	13-71	D.L.Underwood	Lord's	1974
	in Pakistan	11-83	N.G.B.Cook	Karachi[1]	1983-84
Pakistan	in England	12-99	Fazal Mahmood	Oval	1954
	in Pakistan	13-101	Abdul Qadir	Lahore[2]	1987-88

HIGHEST AGGREGATE OF WICKETS IN A SERIES

England	in England	22 (av 19.95)	F.S.Trueman	1962
	in Pakistan	14 (av 31.71)	N.G.B.Cook	1983-84
Pakistan	in England	22 (av 25.31)	Waqar Younis	1992
	in Pakistan	30 (av 14.56)	Abdul Qadir	1987-88

SERIES RECORDS – ENGLAND v SRI LANKA

HIGHEST INNINGS TOTALS

England	in England	429		Lord's	1988
	in Sri Lanka	380		Colombo (SSC)	1992-93
Sri Lanka	in England	491-7d		Lord's	1984
	in Sri Lanka	469		Colombo (SSC)	1992-93

LOWEST INNINGS TOTALS

England	in England	282		Lord's	1991
	in Sri Lanka	223		Colombo (PSS)	1981-82
Sri Lanka	in England	194		Lord's	1988
	in Sri Lanka	175		Colombo (PSS)	1981-82

HIGHEST MATCH AGGREGATE 1219 for 35 wickets   Colombo (SSC)   1992-93
LOWEST MATCH AGGREGATE   787 for 33 wickets   Colombo (PSS)   1981-82

HIGHEST INDIVIDUAL INNINGS

England	in England	174	G.A.Gooch	Lord's	1991
	in Sri Lanka	128	R.A.Smith	Colombo (SSC)	1992-93
Sri Lanka	in England	190	S.Wettimuny	Lord's	1984
	in Sri Lanka	93*	H.P.Tillekeratne	Colombo (SSC)	1992-93

HIGHEST AGGREGATE OF RUNS IN A SERIES

England	in England	212 (av 106.00)	G.A.Gooch		1991
	in Sri Lanka	163 (av 81.50)	R.A.Smith		1992-93
Sri Lanka	in England	205 (av 102.50)	L.R.D.Mendis		1984
	in Sri Lanka	129 (av ∞)	H.P.Tillekeratne		1992-93

RECORD WICKET PARTNERSHIPS – ENGLAND

1st	78	G.A.Gooch (174), H.Morris (23)	Lord's	1991
2nd	139	G.A.Gooch (174), A.J.Stewart (43)	Lord's	1991
3rd	112	R.A.Smith (128), G.A.Hick (68)	Colombo (SSC)	1992-93
4th	122	R.A.Smith (128), A.J.Stewart (63)	Colombo (SSC)	1992-93
5th	40	A.J.Stewart (113*), I.T.Botham (22)	Lord's	1991
6th	87	A.J.Lamb (107), R.M.Ellison (41)	Lord's	1984
7th	63	A.J.Stewart (113*), R.C.Russell (17)	Lord's	1991
8th	20	J.E.Emburey (59), P.W.Jarvis (3)	Colombo (SSC)	1992-93
9th	37	P.J.Newport (26), N.A.Foster (14*)	Lord's	1988
10th	40	J.E.Emburey (59), D.E.Malcolm (8*)	Colombo (SSC)	1992-93

RECORD WICKET PARTNERSHIPS – SRI LANKA

1st	99	R.S.Mahanama (64), U.C.Hathurusinghe (59)	Colombo (SSC)	1992-93
2nd	83	B.Warnapura (38), R.L.Dias (77)	Colombo (PSS)	1981-82
3rd	101	S.Wettimuny (190), R.L.Dias (32)	Lord's	1984
4th	148	S.Wettimuny (190), A.Ranatunga (84)	Lord's	1984
5th	150	S.Wettimuny (190), L.R.D.Mendis (111)	Lord's	1984
6th	138	S.A.R.Silva (102*), L.R.D.Mendis (94)	Lord's	1984
7th	74	U.C.Hathurusinghe (66), R.J.Ratnayake (52)	Lord's	1991
8th	29	R.J.Ratnayake (17), C.P.H.Ramanayake (34*)	Lord's	1991
9th	83	H.P.Tillekeratne (93*), M.Muralitharan (19)	Colombo (SSC)	1992-93
10th	64	J.R.Ratnayeke (59*), G.F.Labrooy (42)	Lord's	1988

BEST INNINGS BOWLING ANALYSIS

England	in England	7-70	P.A.J.DeFreitas	Lord's	1991
	in Sri Lanka	6-33	J.E.Emburey	Colombo (PSS)	1981-82
Sri Lanka	in England	5-69	R.J.Ratnayake	Lord's	1991
	in Sri Lanka	4-70	A.L.F.de Mel	Colombo (PSS)	1981-82

BEST MATCH BOWLING ANALYSIS

England	in England	8-115	P.A.J.DeFreitas	Lord's	1991
	in Sri Lanka	8-95	D.L.Underwood	Colombo (PSS)	1981-82
Sri Lanka	in England	5-160	R.J.Ratnayake	Lord's	1991
	in Sri Lanka	8-188	K.P.J.Warnaweera	Colombo (SSC)	1992-93

HIGHEST WICKET AGGREGATE IN A SERIES

England	in England	8 (av 14.37)	P.A.J.DeFreitas		1991
	in Sri Lanka	8 (av 11.87)	D.L.Underwood		1981-82
Sri Lanka	in England	5 (av 32.00)	R.J.Ratnayake		1991
		5 (av 36.00)	S.D.Anurasiri		1991
	in Sri Lanka	8 (av 23.50)	K.P.J.Warnaweera		1992-93

SERIES RECORDS – AUSTRALIA v SOUTH AFRICA

HIGHEST INNINGS TOTALS

Australia	in Australia	578		Melbourne	1910-11
	in South Africa	549-7d		Port Elizabeth	1949-50
South Africa	in Australia	595		Adelaide	1963-64
	in South Africa	622-9d		Durban[2]	1969-70

LOWEST INNINGS TOTALS

Australia	in Australia	111		Sydney	1993-94
	in South Africa	75		Durban[2]	1949-50
South Africa	in Australia	36		Melbourne	1931-32
	in South Africa	85		Johannesburg[1]	1902-03
		85		Cape Town	1902-03

HIGHEST MATCH AGGREGATE	1646 for 40 wickets	Adelaide	1910-11
LOWEST MATCH AGGREGATE	234 for 29 wickets	Melbourne	1931-32

HIGHEST INDIVIDUAL INNINGS

Australia	in Australia	299*	D.G.Bradman	Adelaide	1931-32
	in South Africa	203	H.L.Collins	Johannesburg[1]	1921-22
South Africa	in Australia	204	G.A.Faulkner	Melbourne	1910-11
	in South Africa	274	R.G.Pollock	Durban[2]	1969-70

HIGHEST AGGREGATE OF RUNS IN A SERIES

Australia	in Australia	834 (av 92.66)	R.N.Harvey		1952-53
	in South Africa	660 (av 132.00)	R.N.Harvey		1949-50
South Africa	in Australia	732 (av 73.20)	G.A.Faulkner		1910-11
	in South Africa	606 (av 86.57)	D.T.Lindsay		1966-67

RECORD WICKET PARTNERSHIPS – AUSTRALIA

1st	233	J.H.W.Fingleton (112), W.A.Brown (121)	Cape Town	1935-36
2nd	275	C.C.McDonald (154), A.L.Hassett (163)	Adelaide	1952-53
3rd	242	C.Kelleway (102), W.Bardsley (164)	Lord's	1912
4th	169	M.A.Taylor (170), M.E.Waugh (84)	Melbourne	1993-94
5th	208	A.R.Border (84), S.R.Waugh (164)	Adelaide	1993-94
6th	108	S.R.Waugh (86), I.A.Healy (61)	Cape Town	1993-94
7th	160	R.Benaud (90), G.D.McKenzie (76)	Sydney	1963-64
8th	83	A.G.Chipperfield (109), C.V.Grimmett (15)	Durban[2]	1935-36
9th	78	D.G.Bradman (299*), W.J.O'Reilly (23)	Adelaide	1931-32
	78	K.D.Mackay (83*), I.Meckiff (26)	Johannesburg[3]	1957-58
10th	82	V.S.Ransford (95), W.J.Whitty (39*)	Melbourne	1910-11

RECORD WICKET PARTNERSHIPS – SOUTH AFRICA

1st	176	D.J.McGlew (108), T.L.Goddard (90)	Johannesburg[3]	1957-58
2nd	173	L.J.Tancred (97), C.B.Llewellyn (90)	Johannesburg[1]	1902-03
3rd	341	E.J.Barlow (201), R.G.Pollock (175)	Adelaide	1963-64
4th	206	C.N.Frank (152), A.W.Nourse (111)	Johannesburg[1]	1921-22
5th	129	J.H.B.Waite (59), W.R.Endean (77)	Johannesburg[3]	1957-58
6th	200	R.G.Pollock (274), H.R.Lance (61)	Durban[2]	1969-70
7th	221	D.T.Lindsay (182), P.L.van der Merwe (76)	Johannesburg[3]	1966-67
8th	124	A.W.Nourse (72), E.A.Halliwell (57)	Johannesburg[1]	1902-03
9th	85	R.G.Pollock (209), P.M.Pollock (41)	Cape Town	1966-67
10th	53	L.A.Stricker (48), S.J.Pegler (24*)	Adelaide	1910-11

BEST INNINGS BOWLING ANALYSIS

Australia	in Australia	7-56	S.K.Warne	Sydney	1993-94
	in South Africa	7-34	J.V.Saunders	Johannesburg[1]	1902-03
South Africa	in Australia	7-81	H.J.Tayfield	Melbourne	1952-53
	in South Africa	7-23	H.J.Tayfield	Durban[2]	1949-50

BEST MATCH BOWLING ANALYSIS

Australia	in Australia	14-199	C.V.Grimmett	Adelaide	1931-32
	in South Africa	13-173	C.V.Grimmett	Durban[2]	1935-36
South Africa	in Australia	13-165	H.J.Tayfield	Melbourne	1952-53
	in South Africa	10-116	C.B.Llewellyn	Johannesburg[1]	1902-03

HIGHEST AGGREGATE OF WICKETS IN A SERIES

Australia	in Australia	37 (av 17.08)	W.J.Whitty	1910-11
	in South Africa	44 (av 14.59)	C.V.Grimmett	1935-36
South Africa	in Australia	30 (av 28.10)	H.J.Tayfield	1952-53
	in South Africa	26 (av 16.23)	T.L.Goddard	1966-67
		26 (av 13.57)	M.J.Procter	1969-70

SERIES RECORDS – AUSTRALIA v WEST INDIES

HIGHEST INNINGS TOTALS
Australia	in Australia	619		Sydney	1968-69
	in West Indies	758-8d		Kingston	1954-55
West Indies	in Australia	616		Adelaide	1968-69
	in West Indies	573		Bridgetown	1964-65

LOWEST INNINGS TOTALS
Australia	in Australia	76		Perth	1984-85
	in West Indies	90		Port-of-Spain	1977-78
West Indies	in Australia	78		Sydney	1951-52
	in West Indies	109		Georgetown	1972-73

HIGHEST MATCH AGGREGATE 1764 for 39 wickets   Adelaide   1968-69
LOWEST MATCH AGGREGATE   534 for 28 wickets   Melbourne   1930-31

HIGHEST INDIVIDUAL INNINGS
Australia	in Australia	242	K.D.Walters	Sydney	1968-69
	in West Indies	210	W.M.Lawry	Bridgetown	1964-65
West Indies	in Australia	277	B.C.Lara	Sydney	1992-93
	in West Indies	226	C.G.Greenidge	Bridgetown	1990-91

HIGHEST AGGREGATE OF RUNS IN A SERIES
Australia	in Australia	702 (av 117.00)	G.S.Chappell		1975-76
	in West Indies	650 (av 108.33)	R.N.Harvey		1954-55
West Indies	in Australia	537 (av 59.66)	D.L.Haynes		1988-89
	in West Indies	827 (av 82.70)	C.L.Walcott		1954-55

RECORD WICKET PARTNERSHIPS – AUSTRALIA
1st	382	W.M.Lawry (210), R.B.Simpson (201)	Bridgetown	1964-65
2nd	298	W.M.Lawry (205), I.M.Chappell (165)	Melbourne	1968-69
3rd	295	C.C.McDonald (127), R.N.Harvey (204)	Kingston	1954-55
4th	336	W.M.Lawry (151), K.D.Walters (242)	Sydney	1968-69
5th	220	K.R.Miller (109), R.G.Archer (128)	Kingston	1954-55
6th	206	K.R.Miller (137), R.G.Archer (98)	Bridgetown	1954-55
7th	134	A.K.Davidson (80), R.Benaud (52)	Brisbane[2]	1960-61
8th	137	R.Benaud (128), I.W.Johnson (27*)	Kingston	1954-55
9th	114	D.M.Jones (216), M.G.Hughes (72*)	Adelaide	1988-89
10th	97	T.G.Hogan (42*), R.M.Hogg (52)	Georgetown	1983-84

RECORD WICKET PARTNERSHIPS – WEST INDIES
1st	250*	C.G.Greenidge (120*), D.L.Haynes (103*)	Georgetown	1983-84
2nd	297	D.L.Haynes (111), R.B.Richardson (182)	Georgetown	1990-91
3rd	308	R.B.Richardson (154), I.V.A.Richards (178)	St John's	1983-84
4th	198	L.G.Rowe (107), A.I.Kallicharran (101)	Brisbane[2]	1975-76
5th	210	R.B.Kanhai (84), M.L.C.Foster (125)	Kingston	1972-73
6th	165	R.B.Kanhai (105), D.L.Murray (90)	Bridgetown	1972-73
7th	347	D.St E.Atkinson (219), C.C.Depeiza (122)	Bridgetown	1954-55
8th	87	P.J.L.Dujon (70), C.E.L.Ambrose (53)	Port-of-Spain	1990-91
9th	122	D.A.J.Holford (80), J.L.Hendriks (37*)	Adelaide	1968-69
10th	56	J.Garner (60), C.E.H.Croft (2*)	Brisbane[2]	1979-80

BEST INNINGS BOWLING ANALYSIS
Australia	in Australia	8-71	G.D.McKenzie	Melbourne	1968-69
	in West Indies	7-44	I.W.Johnson	Georgetown	1954-55
West Indies	in Australia	7-25	C.E.L.Ambrose	Perth	1992-93
	in West Indies	6-28	V.A.Holder	Port-of-Spain	1977-78

BEST MATCH BOWLING ANALYSIS
Australia	in Australia	13-217	M.G.Hughes	Perth	1988-89
	in West Indies	10-115	N.J.N.Hawke	Georgetown	1964-65
West Indies	in Australia	11-107	M.A.Holding	Melbourne	1981-82
	in West Indies	9-80	L.R.Gibbs	Georgetown	1964-65

HIGHEST AGGREGATE OF WICKETS IN A SERIES
Australia	in Australia	33 (av 17.96)	C.V.Grimmett		1930-31
		33 (av 18.54)	A.K.Davidson		1960-61
	in West Indies	26 (av 20.73)	M.H.N.Walker		1972-73
West Indies	in Australia	33 (av 16.42)	C.E.L.Ambrose		1992-93
	in West Indies	31 (av 16.87)	J.Garner		1983-84

SERIES RECORDS – AUSTRALIA v NEW ZEALAND

HIGHEST INNINGS TOTALS

Australia	in Australia	607-6d		Brisbane[2]	1993-94
	in New Zealand	552		Christchurch	1976-77
New Zealand	in Australia	553-7d		Brisbane[2]	1985-86
	in New Zealand	484		Wellington	1973-74

LOWEST INNINGS TOTALS

Australia	in Australia	162		Sydney	1973-74
	in New Zealand	103		Auckland	1985-86
New Zealand	in Australia	121		Perth	1980-81
	in New Zealand	42		Wellington	1945-46

HIGHEST MATCH AGGREGATE	1455 for 24 wickets		Wellington	1973-74
LOWEST MATCH AGGREGATE	295 for 28 wickets		Wellington	1945-46

HIGHEST INDIVIDUAL INNINGS

Australia	in Australia	205	A.R.Border	Adelaide	1987-88
	in New Zealand	250	K.D.Walters	Christchurch	1976-77
New Zealand	in Australia	188	M.D.Crowe	Brisbane[2]	1985-86
	in New Zealand	161	B.A.Edgar	Auckland	1981-82

HIGHEST AGGREGATE OF RUNS IN A SERIES

Australia	in Australia	305 (av 76.25)	M.J.Slater		1993-94
	in New Zealand	449 (av 89.80)	G.S.Chappell		1973-74
New Zealand	in Australia	396 (av 66.00)	M.D.Crowe		1987-88
	in New Zealand	403 (av 100.75)	G.M.Turner		1973-74

RECORD WICKET PARTNERSHIPS – AUSTRALIA

1st	198	M.J.Slater (99), M.A.Taylor (142*)	Perth	1993-94
2nd	235	M.J.Slater (168), D.C.Boon (106)	Hobart	1993-94
3rd	264	I.M.Chappell (145), G.S.Chappell (247*)	Wellington	1973-74
4th	150	M.E.Waugh (111), A.R.Border (60)	Hobart	1993-94
5th	213	G.M.Ritchie (92), G.R.J.Matthews (130)	Wellington	1985-86
6th	197	A.R.Border (152*), G.R.J.Matthews (115)	Brisbane[2]	1985-86
7th	217	K.D.Walters (250), G.J.Gilmour (101)	Christchurch	1976-77
8th	93	G.J.Gilmour (64), K.J.O'Keeffe (32)	Auckland	1976-77
9th	69	I.A.Healy (113*), C.J.McDermott (35)	Perth	1993-94
10th	60	K.D.Walters (107), J.D.Higgs (6*)	Melbourne	1980-81

RECORD WICKET PARTNERSHIPS – NEW ZEALAND

1st	111	M.J.Greatbatch (61), J.G.Wright (72)	Wellington	1992-93
2nd	128*	J.G.Wright (117*), A.H.Jones (33*)	Wellington	1989-90
3rd	224	J.F.Reid (108), M.D.Crowe (188)	Brisbane[2]	1985-86
4th	229	B.E.Congdon (132), B.F.Hastings (101)	Wellington	1973-74
5th	88	J.V.Coney (71), M.G.Burgess (43)	Perth	1980-81
6th	109	K.R.Rutherford (65), J.V.Coney (101*)	Wellington	1985-86
7th	132*	J.V.Coney (101*), R.J.Hadlee (72*)	Wellington	1985-86
8th	88*	M.J.Greatbatch (146*), M.C.Snedden (33*)	Perth	1989-90
9th	73	H.J.Howarth (61), D.R.Hadlee (37)	Christchurch	1976-77
10th	124	J.G.Bracewell (83*), S.L.Boock (37)	Sydney	1985-86

BEST INNINGS BOWLING ANALYSIS

Australia	in Australia	6-31	S.K.Warne	Hobart	1993-94
	in New Zealand	6-72	D.K.Lillee	Auckland	1976-77
New Zealand	in Australia	9-52	R.J.Hadlee	Brisbane[2]	1985-86
	in New Zealand	7-89	D.K.Morrison	Wellington	1992-93

BEST MATCH BOWLING ANALYSIS

Australia	in Australia	10-174	R.G.Holland	Sydney	1985-86
	in New Zealand	11-123	D.K.Lillee	Auckland	1976-77
New Zealand	in Australia	15-123	R.J.Hadlee	Brisbane[2]	1985-86
	in New Zealand	10-106	J.G.Bracewell	Auckland	1985-86

HIGHEST AGGREGATE OF WICKETS IN A SERIES

Australia	in Australia	18 (av 16.94)	S.K.Warne	1993-94
	in New Zealand	17 (av 15.05)	S.K.Warne	1992-93
New Zealand	in Australia	33 (av 12.15)	R.J.Hadlee	1985-86
	in New Zealand	17 (av 25.64)	R.O.Collinge	1973-74
		17 (av 16.94)	D.K.Morrison	1992-93

SERIES RECORDS – AUSTRALIA v INDIA

HIGHEST INNINGS TOTALS

Australia	in Australia	674	Adelaide	1947-48
	in India	574-7d	Madras[1]	1986-87
India	in Australia	600-4d	Sydney	1985-86
	in India	517-5d	Bombay[3]	1986-87

LOWEST INNINGS TOTALS

Australia	in Australia	83	Melbourne	1980-81
	in India	105	Kanpur	1959-60
India	in Australia	58	Brisbane[2]	1947-48
	in India	135	Delhi	1959-60

HIGHEST MATCH AGGREGATE 1488 for 32 wickets — Madras[1] — 1986-87
LOWEST MATCH AGGREGATE 538 for 28 wickets — Brisbane[2] — 1947-48

HIGHEST INDIVIDUAL INNINGS

Australia	in Australia	213	K.J.Hughes	Adelaide	1980-81
	in India	210	D.M.Jones	Madras[1]	1986-87
India	in Australia	206	R.J.Shastri	Sydney	1991-92
	in India	164*	D.B.Vengsarkar	Bombay[3]	1986-87

HIGHEST AGGREGATE OF RUNS IN A SERIES

Australia	in Australia	715 (av 178.75)	D.G.Bradman		1947-48
	in India	594 (av 59.40)	K.J.Hughes		1979-80
India	in Australia	473 (av 52.55)	G.R.Viswanath		1977-78
	in India	518 (av 74.00)	G.R.Viswanath		1979-80

RECORD WICKET PARTNERSHIPS – AUSTRALIA

1st	217	D.C.Boon (131), G.R.Marsh (92)	Sydney	1985-86
2nd	236	S.G.Barnes (112), D.G.Bradman (201)	Adelaide	1947-48
3rd	222	A.R.Border (162), K.J.Hughes (100)	Madras[1]	1979-80
4th	178	D.M.Jones (210), A.R.Border (106)	Madras[1]	1986-87
5th	223*	A.R.Morris (100*), D.G.Bradman (127*)	Melbourne	1947-48
6th	151	T.R.Veivers (67), B.N.Jarman (78)	Bombay[2]	1964-65
7th	66	G.R.J.Matthews (100*), R.J.Bright (28)	Melbourne	1985-86
8th	73	T.R.Veivers (74), G.D.McKenzie (27)	Madras[2]	1964-65
9th	87	I.W.Johnson (73), W.P.A.Crawford (34)	Madras[2]	1956-57
10th	77	A.R.Border (163), D.R.Gilbert (10*)	Melbourne	1985-86

RECORD WICKET PARTNERSHIPS – INDIA

1st	192	S.M.Gavaskar (123), C.P.S.Chauhan (73)	Bombay[3]	1979-80
2nd	224	S.M.Gavaskar (172), M.Amarnath (138)	Sydney	1985-86
3rd	159	S.M.Gavaskar (115), G.R.Viswanath (131)	Delhi	1979-80
4th	159	D.B.Vengsarkar (112), G.R.Viswanath (161*)	Bangalore	1979-80
5th	196	R.J.Shastri (206), S.R.Tendulkar (148*)	Sydney	1991-92
6th	298*	D.B.Vengsarkar (164*), R.J.Shastri (121*)	Bombay[3]	1986-87
7th	132	V.S.Hazare (145), H.R.Adhikari (51)	Adelaide	1947-48
8th	127	S.M.H.Kirmani (101*), K.D.Ghavri (86)	Bombay[3]	1979-80
9th	81	S.R.Tendulkar (114), K.S.More (43)	Perth	1991-92
10th	94	S.M.Gavaskar (166*), N.S.Yadav (41)	Adelaide	1985-86

BEST INNINGS BOWLING ANALYSIS

Australia	in Australia	7-27	M.R.Whitney	Perth	1991-92
	in India	7-43	R.R.Lindwall	Madras[2]	1956-57
India	in Australia	8-106	Kapil Dev	Adelaide	1985-86
	in India	9-69	J.M.Patel	Kanpur	1959-60

BEST MATCH BOWLING ANALYSIS

Australia	in Australia	12-126	B.A.Reid	Melbourne	1991-92
	in India	12-124	A.K.Davidson	Kanpur	1959-60
India	in Australia	12-104	B.S.Chandrasekhar	Melbourne	1977-78
	in India	14-124	J.M.Patel	Kanpur	1959-60

HIGHEST AGGREGATE OF WICKETS IN A SERIES

Australia	in Australia	31 (av 21.61)	C.J.McDermott		1991-92
	in India	29 (av 14.86)	A.K.Davidson		1959-60
		29 (av 19.58)	R.Benaud		1959-60
India	in Australia	31 (av 23.87)	B.S.Bedi		1977-78
	in India	28 (av 22.32)	Kapil Dev		1979-80

HIGHEST INNINGS TOTALS

Australia	in Australia	585	Adelaide	1972-73
	in Pakistan	617	Faisalabad	1979-80
Pakistan	in Australia	624	Adelaide	1983-84
	in Pakistan	501-6d	Faisalabad	1982-83

LOWEST INNINGS TOTALS

Australia	in Australia	125	Melbourne	1981-82
	in Pakistan	80	Karachi[1]	1956-57
Pakistan	in Australia	62	Perth	1981-82
	in Pakistan	134	Dacca	1959-60

HIGHEST MATCH AGGREGATE 1640 for 33 wickets — Melbourne 1972-73
LOWEST MATCH AGGREGATE 535 for 31 wickets — Karachi[1] 1956-57

HIGHEST INDIVIDUAL INNINGS

Australia	in Australia	268	G.N.Yallop	Melbourne	1983-84
	in Pakistan	235	G.S.Chappell	Faisalabad	1979-80
Pakistan	in Australia	158	Majid Khan	Melbourne	1972-73
	in Pakistan	211	Javed Miandad	Karachi[1]	1988-89

HIGHEST AGGREGATE OF RUNS IN A SERIES

Australia	in Australia	554 (av 92.33)	G.N.Yallop	1983-84
	in Pakistan	395 (av 131.66)	A.R.Border	1979-80
Pakistan	in Australia	390 (av 43.33)	Mohsin Khan	1983-84
	in Pakistan	412 (av 82.40)	Javed Miandad	1988-89

RECORD WICKET PARTNERSHIPS – AUSTRALIA

1st	134	I.C.Davis (56), A.Turner (82)	Melbourne	1976-77
2nd	259	W.B.Phillips (159), G.N.Yallop (141)	Perth	1983-84
3rd	203	G.N.Yallop (268), K.J.Hughes (94)	Melbourne	1983-84
4th	217	G.S.Chappell (235), G.N.Yallop (172)	Faisalabad	1979-80
5th	171	G.S.Chappell (121), G.J.Cosier (168)	Melbourne	1976-77
	171	A.R.Border (118), G.S.Chappell (150*)	Brisbane[2]	1983-84
6th	139	R.M.Cowper (83), T.R.Veivers (88)	Melbourne	1964-65
7th	185	G.N.Yallop (268), G.R.J.Matthews (75)	Melbourne	1983-84
8th	117	G.J.Cosier (168), K.J.O'Keeffe (28*)	Melbourne	1976-77
9th	83	J.R.Watkins (36), R.A.L.Massie (42)	Sydney	1972-73
10th	52	D.K.Lillee (14), M.H.N.Walker (34*)	Sydney	1976-77
	52	G.F.Lawson (57*), T.M.Alderman (7)	Lahore[2]	1982-83

RECORD WICKET PARTNERSHIPS – PAKISTAN

1st	249	Khalid Ibadulla (166), Abdul Kadir (95)	Karachi[1]	1964-65
2nd	233	Mohsin Khan (149), Qasim Omar (113)	Adelaide	1983-84
3rd	223*	Taslim Arif (210*), Javed Miandad (106*)	Faisalabad	1979-80
4th	155	Mansoor Akhtar (111), Zaheer Abbas (126)	Faisalabad	1982-83
5th	186	Javed Miandad (131), Salim Malik (77)	Adelaide	1983-84
6th	191	Imran Khan (136), Wasim Akram (123)	Adelaide	1989-90
7th	104	Intikhab Alam (64), Wasim Bari (72)	Adelaide	1972-73
8th	111	Majid Khan (110*), Imran Khan (56)	Lahore[2]	1979-80
9th	56	Intikhab Alam (61), Afaq Hussain (13*)	Melbourne	1964-65
10th	87	Asif Iqbal (152*), Iqbal Qasim (4)	Adelaide	1976-77

BEST INNINGS BOWLING ANALYSIS

Australia	in Australia	8-59	A.A.Mallett	Adelaide	1972-73
	in Pakistan	7-75	L.F.Kline	Lahore[2]	1959-60
Pakistan	in Australia	9-86	Sarfraz Nawaz	Melbourne	1978-79
	in Pakistan	7-49	Iqbal Qasim	Karachi[1]	1979-80

BEST MATCH BOWLING ANALYSIS

Australia	in Australia	11-118	C.G.Rackemann	Perth	1983-84
	in Pakistan	10-111	R.J.Bright	Karachi[1]	1979-80
Pakistan	in Australia	12-165	Imran Khan	Sydney	1976-77
	in Pakistan	13-114	Fazal Mahmood	Karachi[1]	1956-57

HIGHEST AGGREGATE OF WICKETS IN A SERIES

Australia	in Australia	24 (av 24.16)	G.F.Lawson	1983-84
	in Pakistan	18 (av 21.05)	R.Benaud	1959-60
Pakistan	in Australia	19 (av 38.52)	Azeem Hafeez	1983-84
	in Pakistan	22 (av 25.54)	Abdul Qadir	1982-83

SERIES RECORDS – AUSTRALIA v SRI LANKA

HIGHEST INNINGS TOTALS

Australia	in Australia	513-5d	Hobart	1989-90
	in Sri Lanka	514-4d	Kandy	1982-83
Sri Lanka	in Australia	418	Brisbane[2]	1989-90
	in Sri Lanka	547-8d	Colombo (SSC)	1992-93

LOWEST INNINGS TOTALS

Australia	in Australia	224	Hobart	1989-90
	in Sri Lanka	247	Colombo (KS)	1992-93
Sri Lanka	in Australia	153	Perth	1987-88
	in Sri Lanka	164	Colombo (SSC)	1992-93

HIGHEST MATCH AGGREGATE 1438 for 38 wickets		Colombo (SSC)	1992-93
LOWEST MATCH AGGREGATE 802 for 30 wickets		Perth	1987-88

HIGHEST INDIVIDUAL INNINGS

Australia	in Australia	164	M.A.Taylor	Brisbane[2]	1989-90
	in Sri Lanka	143*	D.W.Hookes	Kandy	1982-83
Sri Lanka	in Australia	167	P.A.de Silva	Brisbane[2]	1989-90
	in Sri Lanka	137	A.P.Gurusinha	Colombo (SSC)	1992-93

HIGHEST AGGREGATE OF RUNS IN A SERIES

Australia	in Australia	304 (av 76.00)	M.A.Taylor	1989-90
	in Sri Lanka	329 (av 54.83)	G.R.J.Matthews	1992-93
Sri Lanka	in Australia	314 (av 104.66)	P.A.de Silva	1989-90
	in Sri Lanka	250 (av 50.00)	R.S.Mahanama	1992-93

RECORD WICKET PARTNERSHIPS – AUSTRALIA

1st	120	G.R.Marsh (53), D.C.Boon (64)	Perth	1987-88
2nd	170	K.C.Wessels (141), G.N.Yallop (98)	Kandy	1982-83
3rd	158	T.M.Moody (106), A.R.Border (56)	Brisbane[2]	1989-90
4th	163	M.A.Taylor (108), A.R.Border (85)	Hobart	1989-90
5th	155*	D.W.Hookes (143*), A.R.Border (47*)	Kandy	1982-83
6th	260*	D.M.Jones (118*), S.R.Waugh (134*)	Hobart	1989-90
7th	129	G.R.J.Matthews (96), I.A.Healy (49)	Moratuwa	1992-93
8th	56	G.R.J.Matthews (64), C.J.McDermott (40)	Colombo (SSC)	1992-93
9th	45	I.A.Healy (66*), S.K.Warne (24)	Colombo (SSC)	1992-93
10th	49	I.A.Healy (66*), M.R.Whitney (13)	Colombo (SSC)	1992-93

RECORD WICKET PARTNERSHIPS – SRI LANKA

1st	110	R.S.Mahanama (69), U.C.Hathurusinghe (49)	Colombo (KS)	1992-93
2nd	92	R.S.Mahanama (78), A.P.Gurusinha (137)	Colombo (SSC)	1992-93
3rd	107	U.C.Hathurusinghe (67), P.A.de Silva (85)	Colombo (KS)	1992-93
	107	R.S.Mahanama (50), P.A.de Silva (58)	Moratuwa	1992-93
4th	230	A.P.Gurusinha (137), A.Ranatunga (127)	Colombo (SSC)	1992-93
5th	116	H.P.Tillekeratne (82), A.Ranatunga (48)	Moratuwa	1992-93
6th	96	A.Ranatunga (127), R.S.Kaluwitharana (132*)	Colombo (SSC)	1992-93
7th	144	P.A.de Silva (167), J.R.Ratnayeke (56)	Brisbane[2]	1989-90
8th	33	A.Ranatunga (55), C.P.H.Ramanayake (9)	Perth	1987-88
9th	44*	R.S.Kaluwitharana (132*), A.W.R.Madurasinghe (5*)	Colombo (SSC)	1992-93
10th	27	P.A.de Silva (167), C.P.H.Ramanayake (10*)	Brisbane[2]	1989-90

BEST INNINGS BOWLING ANALYSIS

Australia	in Australia	5-67	M.G.Hughes	Perth	1987-88
	in Sri Lanka	5-66	T.G.Hogan	Kandy	1982-83
Sri Lanka	in Australia	6-66	R.J.Ratnayake	Hobart	1989-90
	in Sri Lanka	5-82	C.P.H.Ramanayake	Moratuwa	1992-93

BEST MATCH BOWLING ANALYSIS

Australia	in Australia	8-156	M.G.Hughes	Hobart	1989-90
	in Sri Lanka	7-166	B.Yardley	Kandy	1982-83
Sri Lanka	in Australia	8-189	R.J.Ratnayake	Hobart	1989-90
	in Sri Lanka	8-157	C.P.H.Ramanayake	Moratuwa	1992-93

HIGHEST AGGREGATE OF WICKETS IN A SERIES

Australia	in Australia	11 (av 25.36)	M.G.Hughes	1989-90
	in Sri Lanka	14 (av 24.42)	C.J.McDermott	1992-93
Sri Lanka	in Australia	8 (av 23.62)	R.J.Ratnayake	1989-90
	in Sri Lanka	17 (av 25.52)	C.P.H.Ramanayake	1992-93

HIGHEST INNINGS TOTALS

South Africa	in South Africa				
	in West Indies	345		Bridgetown	1991-92
West Indies	in South Africa				
	in West Indies	283		Bridgetown	1991-92

LOWEST INNINGS TOTALS

South Africa	in South Africa				
	in West Indies	148		Bridgetown	1991-92
West Indies	in South Africa				
	in West Indies	262		Bridgetown	1991-92

HIGHEST MATCH AGGREGATE 1038 for 40 wickets		Bridgetown	1991-92
LOWEST MATCH AGGREGATE 1038 for 40 wickets		Bridgetown	1991-92

HIGHEST INDIVIDUAL INNINGS

South Africa	in South Africa				
	in West Indies	163	A.C.Hudson	Bridgetown	1991-92
West Indies	in South Africa				
	in West Indies	79*	J.C.Adams	Bridgetown	1991-92

HIGHEST AGGREGATE OF RUNS IN A SERIES

South Africa	in South Africa				
	in West Indies	163 (av 81.50)	A.C.Hudson	Bridgetown	1991-92
West Indies	in South Africa				
	in West Indies	90 (av 90.00)	J.C.Adams	Bridgetown	1991-92

RECORD WICKET PARTNERSHIPS – SOUTH AFRICA

1st	14	M.W.Rushmere (3), A.C.Hudson (163)	Bridgetown	1991-92
2nd	125	A.C.Hudson (163), K.C.Wessels (59)	Bridgetown	1991-92
3rd	96	K.C.Wessels (74), P.N.Kirsten (52)	Bridgetown	1991-92
4th	19	A.C.Hudson (163), W.J.Cronje (5)	Bridgetown	1991-92
5th	92	A.C.Hudson (163), A.P.Kuiper (34)	Bridgetown	1991-92
6th	14	A.C.Hudson (163), D.J.Richardson (8)	Bridgetown	1991-92
7th	19	A.C.Hudson (163), R.P.Snell (6)	Bridgetown	1991-92
8th	5	D.J.Richardson (2), M.W.Pringle (4)	Bridgetown	1991-92
9th	20	M.W.Pringle (15), A.A.Donald (0)	Bridgetown	1991-92
10th	9	M.W.Pringle (15), T.Bosch (5*)	Bridgetown	1991-92

RECORD WICKET PARTNERSHIPS – WEST INDIES

1st	99	D.L.Haynes (58), P.V.Simmons (35)	Bridgetown	1991-92
2nd	56	D.L.Haynes (23), B.C.Lara (64)	Bridgetown	1991-92
3rd	31	B.C.Lara (17), R.B.Richardson (44)	Bridgetown	1991-92
4th	82	R.B.Richardson (44), K.L.Arthurton (59)	Bridgetown	1991-92
5th	21	K.L.T.Arthurton (59), J.C.Adams (11)	Bridgetown	1991-92
6th	25	J.C.Adams (79*), D.Williams (5)	Bridgetown	1991-92
7th	10	J.C.Adams (79*), C.E.L.Ambrose (6)	Bridgetown	1991-92
8th	22	J.C.Adams (79*), K.C.G.Benjamin (7)	Bridgetown	1991-92
9th	25	J.C.Adams (79*), C.A.Walsh (13)	Bridgetown	1991-92
10th	62	J.C.Adams (79*), B.P.Patterson (11)	Bridgetown	1991-92

BEST INNINGS BOWLING ANALYSIS

South Africa	in South Africa				
	in West Indies	4-74	R.P.Snell	Bridgetown	1991-92
West Indies	in South Africa				
	in West Indies	6-34	C.E.L.Ambrose	Bridgetown	1991-92

BEST MATCH BOWLING ANALYSIS

South Africa	in South Africa				
	in West Indies	8-157	R.P.Snell	Bridgetown	1991-92
West Indies	in South Africa				
	in West Indies	8-81	C.E.L.Ambrose	Bridgetown	1991-92

HIGHEST AGGREGATE OF WICKETS IN A SERIES

South Africa	in South Africa			
	in West Indies	8 (av 19.62)	R.P.Snell	1991-92
West Indies	in South Africa			
	in West Indies	8 (av 10.12)	C.E.L.Ambrose	1991-92

SERIES RECORDS – SOUTH AFRICA v NEW ZEALAND

HIGHEST INNINGS TOTALS

South Africa	in South Africa	464		Johannesburg[3]	1961-6
	in New Zealand	524-8d		Wellington	1952-5
New Zealand	in South Africa	505		Cape Town	1953-5
	in New Zealand	364		Wellington	1931-3

LOWEST INNINGS TOTALS

South Africa	in South Africa	148		Johannesburg[2]	1953-5
	in New Zealand	223		Dunedin	1963-6
New Zealand	in South Africa	79		Johannesburg[2]	1953-5
	in New Zealand	138		Dunedin	1963-6

HIGHEST MATCH AGGREGATE 1122 for 39 wickets   Cape Town   1961-6

LOWEST MATCH AGGREGATE   535 for 31 wickets   Johannesburg[2]   1953-5

HIGHEST INDIVIDUAL INNINGS

South Africa	in South Africa	127*	D.J.McGlew	Durban[2]	1961-6
	in New Zealand	255*	D.J.McGlew	Wellington	1952-5
New Zealand	in South Africa	142	J.R.Reid	Johannesburg[3]	1961-6
	in New Zealand	138	B.W.Sinclair	Auckland	1963-6

HIGHEST AGGREGATE OF RUNS IN A SERIES

South Africa	in South Africa	426 (av 60.85)	D.J.McGlew		1961-62
	in New Zealand	323 (av 161.50)	D.J.McGlew		1952-5
New Zealand	in South Africa	546 (av 60.66)	J.R.Reid		1961-6
	in New Zealand	264 (av 44.00)	B.W.Sinclair		1963-6

RECORD WICKET PARTNERSHIPS – SOUTH AFRICA

1st	196	J.A.J.Christy (103), B.Mitchell (113)	Christchurch	1931-3
2nd	76	J.A.J.Christy (62), H.B.Cameron (44)	Wellington	1931-3
3rd	112	D.J.McGlew (120), R.A.McLean (78)	Johannesburg[3]	1961-6
4th	135	K.J.Funston (39), R.A.McLean (101)	Durban[2]	1953-5
5th	130	W.R.Endean (116), J.E.Cheetham (54)	Auckland	1952-5
6th	83	K.C.Bland (83), D.T.Lindsay (37)	Auckland	1963-6
7th	246	D.J.McGlew (255*), A.R.A.Murray (109)	Wellington	1952-5
8th	95	J.E.Cheetham (89), H.J.Tayfield (34)	Cape Town	1953-5
9th	60	P.M.Pollock (54*), N.A.T.Adcock (24)	Port Elizabeth	1961-6
10th	47	D.J.McGlew (28*), H.D.Bromfield (21)	Port Elizabeth	1961-6

RECORD WICKET PARTNERSHIPS – NEW ZEALAND

1st	126	G.O.Rabone (56), M.E.Chapple (76)	Cape Town	1953-5
2nd	51	W.P.Bradburn (32), B.W.Sinclair (52)	Dunedin	1963-6
3rd	94	M.B.Poore (44), B.Sutcliffe (66)	Cape Town	1953-5
4th	171	B.W.Sinclair (138), S.N.McGregor (62)	Auckland	1963-6
5th	174	J.R.Reid (135), J.E.F.Beck (99)	Cape Town	1953-5
6th	100	H.G.Vivian (100), F.T.Badcock (53)	Wellington	1931-3
7th	84	J.R.Reid (142), G.A.Bartlett (33)	Johannesburg[2]	1961-6
8th	73	P.G.Z.Harris (74), G.A.Bartlett (40)	Durban[2]	1961-6
9th	69	C.F.W.Allcott (26), I.B.Cromb (51*)	Wellington	1931-3
10th	49*	A.E.Dick (50*), F.J.Cameron (10*)	Cape Town	1961-6

BEST INNINGS BOWLING ANALYSIS

South Africa	in South Africa	8-53	G.B.Lawrence	Johannesburg[3]	1961-62
	in New Zealand	6-47	P.M.Pollock	Wellington	1963-6
New Zealand	in South Africa	6-68	G.O.Rabone	Cape Town	1953-5
	in New Zealand	6-60	J.R.Reid	Dunedin	1963-64

BEST MATCH BOWLING ANALYSIS

South Africa	in South Africa	11-196	S.F.Burke	Cape Town	1961-62
	in New Zealand	9-127	Q.McMillan	Christchurch	1931-32
New Zealand	in South Africa	8-180	J.C.Alabaster	Cape Town	1961-62
	in New Zealand	7-142	R.W.Blair	Auckland	1963-64

HIGHEST AGGREGATE OF WICKETS IN A SERIES

South Africa	in South Africa	28 (av 18.28)	G.B.Lawrence		1961-62
	in New Zealand	16 (av 20.18)	Q.McMillan		1931-32
New Zealand	in South Africa	22 (av 20.63)	A.R.MacGibbon		1953-54
		22 (av 28.04)	J.C.Alabaster		1961-62
	in Zealand	12 (av 23.16)	J.R.Reid		1963-64
		12 (av 27.16)	R.W.Blair		1963-64

SERIES RECORDS – SOUTH AFRICA v INDIA

HIGHEST INNINGS TOTALS
South Africa	in South Africa	360-9d		Cape Town	1992-93
	in India				
India	in South Africa	277		Durban	1992-93
	in India				

LOWEST INNINGS TOTALS
South Africa	in South Africa	252		Johannesburg	1992-93
	in India				
India	in South Africa	212		Port Elizabeth	1992-93
	in India				

HIGHEST MATCH AGGREGATE	912 for 32 wickets		Johannesburg	1992-93
LOWEST MATCH AGGREGATE	707 for 23 wickets		Durban	1992-93

HIGHEST INDIVIDUAL INNINGS
South Africa	in South Africa	135	W.J.Cronje	Port Elizabeth	1992-93
	in India				
India	in South Africa	129	Kapil Dev	Port Elizabeth	1992-93
	in India				

HIGHEST AGGREGATE OF RUNS IN A SERIES
South Africa	in South Africa	295 (av 42.14)	K.C.Wessels		1992-93
	in India				
India	in South Africa	202 (av 40.40)	Kapil Dev		1992-93
		202 (av 33.66)	S.R.Tendulkar		1992-93
	in India				

RECORD WICKET PARTNERSHIPS – SOUTH AFRICA
1st	98	K.C.Wessels (95*), A.C.Hudson (33)	Port Elizabeth	1992-93
2nd	117	A.C.Hudson (52), W.J.Cronje (135)	Port Elizabeth	1992-93
3rd	60	K.C.Wessels (118), P.N.Kirsten (13)	Durban	1992-93
4th	82	K.C.Wessels (118), J.N.Rhodes (41)	Durban	1992-93
5th	99	D.J.Cullinan (46), J.N.Rhodes (86)	Cape Town	1992-93
6th	85	J.N.Rhodes (91), B.M.McMillan (98)	Johannesburg	1992-93
7th	37	B.M.McMillan (52), D.J.Richardson (21)	Cape Town	1992-93
8th	65	B.M.McMillan (98), C.R.Matthews (31)	Johannesburg	1992-93
9th	31†	B.M.McMillan (98), A.A.Donald (14*)	Johannesburg	1992-93
10th	15*	C.R.Matthews (28*), A.A.Donald (1*)	Cape Town	1992-93

RECORD WICKET PARTNERSHIPS – INDIA
1st	68	R.J.Shastri (23), A.D.Jadeja (43)	Johannesburg	1992-93
2nd	85	M.Prabhakar (62), S.V.Manjrekar (46)	Cape Town	1992-93
3rd	17	S.V.Manjrekar (7), S.R.Tendulkar (111)	Johannesburg	1992-93
4th	39	S.V.Manjrekar (23), M.Azharuddin (60)	Port Elizabeth	1992-93
5th	87	M.Azharuddin (36), P.K.Amre (103)	Durban	1992-93
6th	47	S.R.Tendulkar (73), S.L.V.Raju (18)	Cape Town	1992-93
7th	75	S.R.Tendulkar (73), Kapil Dev (34)	Cape Town	1992-93
8th	101	P.K.Amre (103), K.S.More (55)	Durban	1992-93
9th	77	Kapil Dev (129), A.Kumble (17)	Port Elizabeth	1992-93
10th	18	Kapil Dev (129), S.L.V.Raju (2*)	Port Elizabeth	1992-93

BEST INNINGS BOWLING ANALYSIS
South Africa	in South Africa	7-84	A.A.Donald	Port Elizabeth	1992-93
	in India				
India	in South Africa	6-53	A.Kumble	Johannesburg	1992-93
	in India				

BEST MATCH BOWLING ANALYSIS
South Africa	in South Africa	12-139	A.A.Donald	Port Elizabeth	1992-93
	in India				
India	in South Africa	8-113	A.Kumble	Johannesburg	1992-93
	in India				

HIGHEST AGGREGATE OF WICKETS IN A SERIES
South Africa	in South Africa	20 (av 19.70)	A.A.Donald		1992-93
	in India				
India	in South Africa	18 (av 25.94)	A.Kumble		1992-93
	India				

† 41 runs were added for this wicket. M.W.Pringle retired hurt and was replaced by A.A.Donald after 10 had been scored.

SERIES RECORDS – SOUTH AFRICA v SRI LANKA

HIGHEST INNINGS TOTALS
South Africa	in South Africa				
	in Sri Lanka	495		Colombo (SSC)	1993-94
Sri Lanka	in South Africa				
	in Sri Lanka	331		Moratuwa	1993-94

LOWEST INNINGS TOTALS
South Africa	in South Africa				
	in Sri Lanka	267		Moratuwa	1993-94
Sri Lanka	in South Africa				
	in Sri Lanka	119		Colombo (SSC)	1993-94

HIGHEST MATCH AGGREGATE 1149 for 33 wickets		Moratuwa	1993-94
LOWEST MATCH AGGREGATE 771 for 23 wickets		Colombo (PSS)	1993-94

HIGHEST INDIVIDUAL INNINGS
South Africa	in South Africa				
	in Sri Lanka	122	W.J.Cronje	Colombo (SSC)	1993-94
Sri Lanka	in South Africa				
	in Sri Lanka	131	A.Ranatunga	Moratuwa	1993-94

HIGHEST AGGREGATE OF RUNS IN A SERIES
South Africa	in South Africa				
	in Sri Lanka	237 (av 59.25)	W.J.Cronje		1993-94
		237 (av 47.40)	D.J.Cullinan		1993-94
Sri Lanka	in South Africa				
	in Sri Lanka	250 (av 50.00)	A.Ranatunga		1993-94

RECORD WICKET PARTNERSHIPS – SOUTH AFRICA
1st	137	K.C.Wessels (92), A.C.Hudson (58)	Colombo (SSC)	1993-94
2nd	48	A.C.Hudson (90), W.J.Cronje (17)	Moratuwa	1993-94
3rd	105	W.J.Cronje (122), D.J.Cullinan (52)	Colombo (SSC)	1993-94
4th	94	W.J.Cronje (73*), J.N.Rhodes (19)	Colombo (PSS)	1993-94
5th	34	S.J.Cook (24), J.N.Rhodes (101*)	Moratuwa	1993-94
6th	122	D.J.Cullinan (102), D.J.Richardson (62)	Colombo (PSS)	1993-94
7th	68	W.J.Cronje (122), P.L.Symcox (50)	Colombo (SSC)	1993-94
8th	79	P.L.Symcox (50), R.P.Snell (48)	Colombo (SSC)	1993-94
9th	7	R.P.Snell (48), A.A.Donald (4*)	Colombo (SSC)	1993-94
10th	8	A.A.Donald (4*), B.N.Schultz (6)	Colombo (SSC)	1993-94

RECORD WICKET PARTNERSHIPS – SRI LANKA
1st	26	R.S.Mahanama (17), U.C.Hathurusinghe (9)	Moratuwa	1993-94
2nd	72	R.S.Mahanama (53), A.P.Gurusinha (26)	Moratuwa	1993-94
3rd	45	U.C.Hathurusinghe (34), P.A.de Silva (34)	Colombo (SSC)	1993-94
4th	101	P.A.de Silva (82), A.Ranatunga (50)	Colombo (PSS)	1993-94
5th	121	P.A.de Silva (68), A.Ranatunga (131)	Moratuwa	1993-94
6th	103	A.Ranatunga (131), H.P.Tillekeratne (33*)	Moratuwa	1993-94
7th	26	S.T.Jayasuriya (44), H.D.P.K.Dharmasena (5)	Colombo (SSC)	1993-94
8th	21	S.T.Jayasuriya (65), D.K.Liyanage (0)	Colombo (PSS)	1993-94
9th	28	H.P.Tillekeratne (92), G.P.Wickremasinghe (11)	Moratuwa	1993-94
10th	18	H.P.Tillekeratne (92), M.Muralitharan (2*)	Moratuwa	1993-94
	18	P.B.Dassanayake (10), M.Muralitharan (14*)	Colombo (SSC)	1993-94

BEST INNINGS BOWLING ANALYSIS
South Africa	in South Africa				
	in Sri Lanka	5-48	B.N.Schultz	Colombo (SSC)	1993-94
Sri Lanka	in South Africa				
	in Sri Lanka	5-101	M.Muralitharan	Colombo (SSC)	1993-94

BEST MATCH BOWLING ANALYSIS
South Africa	in South Africa				
	in Sri Lanka	9-106	B.N.Schultz	Colombo (SSC)	1993-94
Sri Lanka	in South Africa				
	in Sri Lanka	6-152	M.Muralitharan	Moratuwa	1993-94

HIGHEST AGGREGATE OF WICKETS IN A SERIES
South Africa	in South Africa				
	in Sri Lanka	20 (av 16.30)	B.N.Schultz		1993-94
Sri Lanka	in South Africa				
	Sri Lanka	16 (av 22.25)	M.Muralitharan		1993-94

SERIES RECORDS – WEST INDIES v NEW ZEALAND

HIGHEST INNINGS TOTALS
West Indies	in West Indies	564-8		Bridgetown	1971-72
	in New Zealand	546-6d		Auckland	1951-52
New Zealand	in West Indies	543-3d		Georgetown	1971-72
	in New Zealand	460		Christchurch	1979-80

LOWEST INNINGS TOTALS
West Indies	in West Indies	133		Bridgetown	1971-72
	in New Zealand	77		Auckland	1955-56
New Zealand	in West Indies	94		Bridgetown	1984-85
	in New Zealand	74		Dunedin	1955-56

HIGHEST MATCH AGGREGATE 1348 for 23 wickets — Kingston — 1971-72
LOWEST MATCH AGGREGATE 634 for 39 wickets — Auckland — 1955-56

HIGHEST INDIVIDUAL INNINGS
West Indies	in West Indies	214	L.G.Rowe	Kingston	1971-72
	in New Zealand	258	S.M.Nurse	Christchurch	1968-69
New Zealand	in West Indies	259	G.M.Turner	Georgetown	1971-72
	in New Zealand	147	G.P.Howarth	Christchurch	1979-80

HIGHEST AGGREGATE OF RUNS IN A SERIES
West Indies	in West Indies	487 (av 54.11)	R.C.Fredericks		1971-72
	in New Zealand	558 (av 111.60)	S.M.Nurse		1968-69
New Zealand	in West Indies	672 (av 96.00)	G.M.Turner		1971-72
	in New Zealand	328 (av 65.60)	M.D.Crowe		1986-87

RECORD WICKET PARTNERSHIPS – WEST INDIES
1st	225	C.G.Greenidge (97), D.L.Haynes (122)	Christchurch	1979-80
2nd	269	R.C.Fredericks (163), L.G.Rowe (214)	Kingston	1971-72
3rd	185	C.G.Greenidge (100), R.B.Richardson (78)	Port-of-Spain	1984-85
4th	162	E.de C.Weekes (123), O.G.Smith (64)	Dunedin	1955-56
	162	C.G.Greenidge (91), A.I.Kallicharran (75)	Christchurch	1979-80
5th	189	F.M.M.Worrell (100), C.L.Walcott (115)	Auckland	1951-52
6th	254	C.A.Davis (183), G.St A.Sobers (142)	Bridgetown	1971-72
7th	143	D.St E.Atkinson (85), J.D.C.Goddard (83*)	Christchurch	1955-56
8th	83	I.V.A.Richards (105), M.D.Marshall (63)	Bridgetown	1984-85
9th	70	M.D.Marshall (63), J.Garner (37*)	Bridgetown	1984-85
10th	31	T.M.Findlay (44*), G.C.Shillingford (15)	Bridgetown	1971-72

RECORD WICKET PARTNERSHIPS – NEW ZEALAND
1st	387	G.M.Turner (259), T.W.Jarvis (182)	Georgetown	1971-72
2nd	210	G.P.Howarth (84), J.J.Crowe (112)	Kingston	1984-85
3rd	241	J.G.Wright (138), M.D.Crowe (119)	Wellington	1986-87
4th	175	B.E.Congdon (126), B.F.Hastings (105)	Bridgetown	1971-72
5th	142	M.D.Crowe (188), J.V.Coney (73)	Georgetown	1984-85
6th	220	G.M.Turner (223*), K.J.Wadsworth (78)	Kingston	1971-72
7th	143	M.D.Crowe (188), I.D.S.Smith (53)	Georgetown	1984-85
8th	136	B.E.Congdon (166*), R.S.Cunis (51)	Port-of-Spain	1971-72
9th	62*	V.Pollard (51*), R.S.Cunis (20*)	Auckland	1968-69
10th	41	B.E.Congdon (166*), J.C.Alabaster (18)	Port-of-Spain	1971-72

BEST INNINGS BOWLING ANALYSIS
West Indies	in West Indies	7-80	M.D.Marshall	Bridgetown	1984-85
	in New Zealand	7-53	D.St E.Atkinson	Auckland	1955-56
New Zealand	in West Indies	7-74	B.R.Taylor	Bridgetown	1971-72
	in New Zealand	6-50	R.J.Hadlee	Christchurch	1986-87

BEST MATCH BOWLING ANALYSIS
West Indies	in West Indies	11-120	M.D.Marshall	Bridgetown	1984-85
	in New Zealand	9-81	S.Ramadhin	Dunedin	1955-56
New Zealand	in West Indies	10-124	E.J.Chatfield	Port-of-Spain	1984-85
	in New Zealand	11-102	R.J.Hadlee	Dunedin	1979-80

HIGHEST AGGREGATE OF WICKETS IN A SERIES
West Indies	in West Indies	27 (av 18.00)	M.D.Marshall		1984-85
	in New Zealand	20 (av 15.80)	S.Ramadhin		1955-56
New Zealand	in West Indies	27 (av 17.70)	B.R.Taylor		1971-72
	in New Zealand	19 (av 19.00)	R.J.Hadlee		1979-80

SERIES RECORDS – WEST INDIES v INDIA

HIGHEST INNINGS TOTALS

West Indies	in West Indies	631-8d		Kingston	1961-62
	in India	644-8d		Delhi	1958-59
India	in West Indies	469-7		Port-of-Spain	1982-83
	in India	644-7d		Kanpur	1978-79

LOWEST INNINGS TOTALS

West Indies	in West Indies	214		Port-of-Spain	1970-71
	in India	127		Delhi	1987-88
India	in West Indies	97		Kingston	1975-76
	in India	75		Delhi	1987-88

HIGHEST MATCH AGGREGATE 1478 for 38 wickets		Port-of-Spain	1970-71
LOWEST MATCH AGGREGATE 605 for 30 wickets		Port-of-Spain	1961-62

HIGHEST INDIVIDUAL INNINGS

West Indies	in West Indies	237	F.M.M.Worrell	Kingston	1952-53
	in India	256	R.B.Kanhai	Calcutta	1958-59
India	in West Indies	220	S.M.Gavaskar	Port-of-Spain	1970-71
	in India	236*	S.M.Gavaskar	Madras[1]	1983-84

HIGHEST AGGREGATE OF RUNS IN A SERIES

West Indies	in West Indies	716 (av 102.28)	E.de C.Weekes		1952-53
	in India	779 (av 111.28)	E.de C.Weekes		1948-49
India	in West Indies	774 (av 154.80)	S.M.Gavaskar		1970-71
	in India	732 (av 91.50)	S.M.Gavaskar		1978-79

RECORD WICKET PARTNERSHIPS – WEST INDIES

1st	296	C.G.Greenidge (154*), D.L.Haynes (136)	St John's	1982-83
2nd	255	E.D.A.St J.McMorris (125), R.B.Kanhai (158)	Kingston	1961-62
3rd	220	I.V.A.Richards (142), A.I.Kallicharran (93)	Bridgetown	1975-76
4th	267	C.L.Walcott (152), G.E.Gomez (101)	Delhi	1948-49
5th	219	E.de C.Weekes (207), B.H.Pairaudeau (115)	Port-of-Spain	1952-53
6th	250	C.H.Lloyd (242*), D.L.Murray (91)	Bombay[3]	1974-75
7th	130	C.G.Greenidge (194), M.D.Marshall (92)	Kanpur	1983-84
8th	124	I.V.A.Richards (192*), K.D.Boyce (68)	Delhi	1974-75
9th	161	C.H.Lloyd (161*), A.M.E.Roberts (68)	Calcutta	1983-84
10th	98*	F.M.M.Worrell (73*), W.W.Hall (50*)	Port-of-Spain	1961-62

RECORD WICKET PARTNERSHIPS – INDIA

1st	153	S.M.Gavaskar (73), C.P.S.Chauhan (84)	Bombay[3]	1978-79
2nd	344*	S.M.Gavaskar (182*), D.B.Vengsarkar (157*)	Calcutta	1978-79
3rd	159	M.Amarnath (85), G.R.Viswanath (112)	Port-of-Spain	1975-76
4th	172	G.R.Viswanath (179), A.D.Gaekwad (102)	Kanpur	1978-79
5th	204	S.M.Gavaskar (156), B.P.Patel (115*)	Port-of-Spain	1975-76
6th	170	S.M.Gavaskar (236*), R.J.Shastri (72)	Madras[1]	1983-84
7th	186	D.N.Sardesai (150), E.D.Solkar (65)	Bridgetown	1970-71
8th	107	Yashpal Sharma (63), B.S.Sandhu (68)	Kingston	1982-83
9th	143*	S.M.Gavaskar (236*), S.M.H.Kirmani (63*)	Madras[1]	1983-84
10th	62	D.N.Sardesai (150), B.S.Bedi (20*)	Bridgetown	1970-71

BEST INNINGS BOWLING ANALYSIS

West Indies	in West Indies	9-95	J.M.Noreiga	Port-of-Spain	1970-71
	in India	7-64	A.M.E.Roberts	Madras[1]	1974-75
India	in West Indies	7-162	S.P.Gupte	Port-of-Spain	1952-53
	in India	9-83	Kapil Dev	Ahmedabad	1983-84

BEST MATCH BOWLING ANALYSIS

West Indies	in West Indies	11-89	M.D.Marshall	Port-of-Spain	1988-89
	in India	12-121	A.M.E.Roberts	Madras[1]	1974-75
India	in West Indies	8-118	Kapil Dev	Kingston	1982-83
	in India	16-136	N.D.Hirwani	Madras[1]	1987-88

HIGHEST AGGREGATE OF WICKETS IN A SERIES

West Indies	in West Indies	28 (av 29.57)	A.L.Valentine		1952-53
	in India	33 (av 18.81)	M.D.Marshall		1983-84
India	in West Indies	27 (av 29.22)	S.P.Gupte		1952-53
	in India	29 (av 18.51)	Kapil Dev		1983-84

SERIES RECORDS – WEST INDIES v PAKISTAN

HIGHEST INNINGS TOTALS

West Indies	in West Indies	790-3d		Kingston	1957-58
	in Pakistan	493		Karachi[1]	1974-75
Pakistan	in West Indies	657-8d		Bridgetown	1957-58
	in Pakistan	406-8d		Karachi[1]	1974-75

LOWEST INNINGS TOTALS

West Indies	in West Indies	127		Port-of-Spain	1992-93
	in Pakistan	53		Faisalabad	1986-87
Pakistan	in West Indies	106		Bridgetown	1957-58
	in Pakistan	77		Lahore[2]	1986-87

HIGHEST MATCH AGGREGATE 1453 for 32 wickets		Georgetown	1957-58
LOWEST MATCH AGGREGATE 426 for 29 wickets		Lahore[2]	1986-87

HIGHEST INDIVIDUAL INNINGS

West Indies	in West Indies	365*	G.St A.Sobers	Kingston	1957-58
	in Pakistan	217	R.B.Kanhai	Lahore[1]	1958-59
Pakistan	in West Indies	337	Hanif Mohammad	Bridgetown	1957-58
	in Pakistan	{123	Mushtaq Mohammad	Lahore[2]	1974-75
		{123	Imran Khan	Lahore[2]	1980-81

HIGHEST AGGREGATE OF RUNS IN A SERIES

West Indies	in West Indies	824 (av 137.33)	G.St A.Sobers		1957-58
	in Pakistan	364 (av 72.80)	I.V.A.Richards		1980-81
Pakistan	in West Indies	628 (av 69.77)	Hanif Mohammad		1957-58
	in Pakistan	285 (av 57.00)	Salim Malik		1990-91

RECORD WICKET PARTNERSHIPS – WEST INDIES

1st	182	R.C.Fredericks (83), C.G.Greenidge (82)	Kingston	1976-77
2nd	446	C.C.Hunte (260), G.St A.Sobers (365*)	Kingston	1957-58
3rd	169	D.L.Haynes (143*), B.C.Lara (96)	Port-of-Spain	1992-93
4th	188*	G.St A.Sobers (365*), C.L.Walcott (88*)	Kingston	1957-58
5th	185	E.de C.Weekes (197), O.G.Smith (78)	Bridgetown	1957-58
6th	151	C.H.Lloyd (157), D.L.Murray (52)	Bridgetown	1976-77
7th	70	C.H.Lloyd (157), J.Garner (43)	Bridgetown	1976-77
8th	60	C.L.Hooper (178*), A.C.Cummins (14)	St John's	1992-93
9th	61*	P.J.L.Dujon (29*), W.K.M.Benjamin (40*)	Bridgetown	1987-88
10th	106	C.L.Hooper (178*), C.A.Walsh (30)	St John's	1992-93

RECORD WICKET PARTNERSHIPS – PAKISTAN

1st	159†	Majid Khan (167), Zaheer Abbas (80)	Georgetown	1976-77
2nd	178	Hanif Mohammad (103), Saeed Ahmed (78)	Karachi[1]	1958-59
3rd	169	Saeed Ahmed (97), Wazir Mohammad (189)	Port-of-Spain	1957-58
4th	174	Shoaib Mohammad (86), Salim Malik (102)	Karachi[1]	1990-91
5th	88	Basit Ali (56), Inzamam-ul-Haq (123)	St John's	1992-93
6th	166	Wazir Mohammad (106), A.H.Kardar (57)	Kingston	1957-58
7th	128	Wasim Raja (107*), Wasim Bari (58)	Karachi[1]	1974-75
8th	94	Salim Malik (66), Salim Yousuf (39)	Port-of-Spain	1987-88
9th	96	Inzamam-ul-Haq (123), Nadeem Khan (25)	St John's	1992-93
10th	133	Wasim Raja (71), Wasim Bari (60*)	Bridgetown	1976-77

BEST INNINGS BOWLING ANALYSIS

West Indies	in West Indies	8-29	C.E.H.Croft	Port-of-Spain	1976-77
	in Pakistan	5-33	M.D.Marshall	Lahore[2]	1986-87
Pakistan	in West Indies	7-80	Imran Khan	Georgetown	1987-88
	in Pakistan	6-16	Abdul Qadir	Faisalabad	1986-87

BEST MATCH BOWLING ANALYSIS

West Indies	in West Indies	9-95	C.E.H.Croft	Port-of-Spain	1976-77
	in Pakistan	9-187	A.M.E.Roberts	Lahore[2]	1974-75
Pakistan	in West Indies	11-121	Imran Khan	Georgetown	1987-88
	in Pakistan	12-100	Fazal Mahmood	Dacca	1958-59

HIGHEST AGGREGATE OF WICKETS IN A SERIES

West Indies	in West Indies	33 (av 20.48)	C.E.H.Croft		1976-77
	in Pakistan	17 (av 17.76)	C.E.H.Croft		1980-81
Pakistan	in West Indies	25 (av 31.60)	Imran Khan		1976-77
	in Pakistan	{21 (av 15.85)	Fazal Mahmood		1958-59
		{21 (av 14.19)	Wasim Akram		1990-91

†219 runs were added for this wicket in two separate partnerships, Sadiq Mohammad retired hurt and was succeeded by Zaheer Abbas when 60 had been scored.

SERIES RECORDS – WEST INDIES v SRI LANKA

HIGHEST INNINGS TOTALS

West Indies	in West Indies				
	in Sri Lanka	204		Moratuwa	1993-94
Sri Lanka	in West Indies				
	in Sri Lanka	190		Moratuwa	1993-94

LOWEST INNINGS TOTALS

West Indies	in West Indies				
	in Sri Lanka	204		Moratuwa	1993-94
Sri Lanka	in West Indies				
	in Sri Lanka	190		Moratuwa	1993-94

HIGHEST MATCH AGGREGATE	437 for 22 wickets	Moratuwa	1993-94
LOWEST MATCH AGGREGATE	437 for 22 wickets	Moratuwa	1993-94

HIGHEST INDIVIDUAL INNINGS

West Indies	in West Indies				
	in Sri Lanka	62	C.L.Hooper	Moratuwa	1993-94
Sri Lanka	in West Indies				
	in Sri Lanka	53	P.A.de Silva	Moratuwa	1993-94

HIGHEST AGGREGATE OF RUNS IN A SERIES

West Indies	in West Indies				
	in Sri Lanka	62 (av 62.00)	C.L.Hooper	Moratuwa	1993-94
Sri Lanka	in West Indies				
	in Sri Lanka	68 (av 68.00)	P.A.de Silva	Moratuwa	1993-94

RECORD WICKET PARTNERSHIPS – WEST INDIES

1st	42	D.L.Haynes (20), P.V.Simmons (17)	Moratuwa	1993-94
2nd	0	P.V.Simmons (17), R.B.Richardson (51)	Moratuwa	1993-94
3rd	36	R.B.Richardson (51), B.C.Lara (18)	Moratuwa	1993-94
4th	6	R.B.Richardson (51), K.L.T.Arthurton (0)	Moratuwa	1993-94
5th	84	R.B.Richardson (51), C.L.Hooper (62)	Moratuwa	1993-94
6th	10	C.L.Hooper (62), R.A.Harper (3)	Moratuwa	1993-94
7th	13	C.L.Hooper (62), J.R.Murray (7)	Moratuwa	1993-94
8th	0	C.L.Hooper (62), W.K.M.Benjamin (2)	Moratuwa	1993-94
9th	13	W.K.M.Benjamin (2), C.E.L.Ambrose (7*)	Moratuwa	1993-94
10th	0	C.E.L.Ambrose (7*), C.A.Walsh (0)	Moratuwa	1993-94

RECORD WICKET PARTNERSHIPS – SRI LANKA

1st	18	R.S.Mahanama (11), D.P.Samaraweera (16)	Moratuwa	1993-94
2nd	2	D.P.Samaraweera (16), H.P.Tillekeratne (0)	Moratuwa	1993-94
3rd	37	D.P.Samaraweera (16), P.A.de Silva (53)	Moratuwa	1993-94
4th	49	P.A.de Silva (53), A.Ranatunga (31)	Moratuwa	1993-94
5th	0	A.Ranatunga (31), S.T.Jayasuriya (0)	Moratuwa	1993-94
6th	24	A.Ranatunga (31), R.S.Kalpage (39)	Moratuwa	1993-94
7th	51	R.S.Kalpage (39), P.B.Dassanayake (18)	Moratuwa	1993-94
8th	1	R.S.Kalpage (39), G.P.Wickremasinghe (0)	Moratuwa	1993-94
9th	6	R.S.Kalpage (39), S.D.Anurasiri (1)	Moratuwa	1993-94
10th	2	S.D.Anurasiri (1), M.Muralitharan (1*)	Moratuwa	1993-94

BEST INNINGS BOWLING ANALYSIS

West Indies	in West Indies				
	in Sri Lanka	4-46	W.K.M.Benjamin	Moratuwa	1993-94
Sri Lanka	in West Indies				
	in Sri Lanka	4-47	M.Muralitharan	Moratuwa	1993-94

BEST MATCH BOWLING ANALYSIS

West Indies	in West Indies				
	in Sri Lanka	5-51	W.K.M.Benjamin	Moratuwa	1993-94
Sri Lanka	in West Indies				
	in Sri Lanka	4-47	M.Muralitharan	Moratuwa	1993-94

HIGHEST AGGREGATE OF WICKETS IN A SERIES

West Indies	in West Indies				
	in Sri Lanka	5 (av 10.20)	W.K.M.Benjamin		1993-94
Sri Lanka	in West Indies				
	in Sri Lanka	4 (av 11.75)	M.Muralitharan		1993-94

SERIES RECORDS – NEW ZEALAND v INDIA

HIGHEST INNINGS TOTALS

New Zealand	in New Zealand	502		Christchurch	1967-68
	in India	462-9d		Calcutta	1964-65
India	in New Zealand	482		Auckland	1989-90
	in India	537-3d		Madras^2	1955-56

LOWEST INNINGS TOTALS

New Zealand	in New Zealand	100		Wellington	1980-81
	in India	124		Hyderabad	1988-89
India	in New Zealand	81		Wellington	1975-76
	in India	88		Bombay^2	1964-65

HIGHEST MATCH AGGREGATE	1505 for 25 wickets	Auckland	1989-90
LOWEST MATCH AGGREGATE	635 for 29 wickets	Wellington	1975-76

HIGHEST INDIVIDUAL INNINGS

New Zealand	in New Zealand	239	G.T.Dowling	Christchurch	1967-68
	in India	230*	B.Sutcliffe	Delhi	1955-56
India	in New Zealand	192	M.Azharuddin	Auckland	1989-90
	in India	231	M.H.Mankad	Madras^2	1955-56

HIGHEST AGGREGATE OF RUNS IN A SERIES

New Zealand	in New Zealand	471 (av 58.87)	G.T.Dowling	1967-68
	in India	611 (av 87.28)	B.Sutcliffe	1955-56
India	in New Zealand	330 (av 47.14)	A.L.Wadekar	1967-68
	in India	526 (av 105.20)	M.H.Mankad	1955-56

RECORD WICKET PARTNERSHIPS – NEW ZEALAND

1st	149	T.J.Franklin (50), J.G.Wright (113*)	Napier	1989-90
2nd	155	G.T.Dowling (143), B.E.Congdon (58)	Dunedin	1967-68
3rd	222*	B.Sutcliffe (230*), J.R.Reid (119*)	Delhi	1955-56
4th	125	J.G.Wright (185), M.J.Greatbatch (46)	Christchurch	1989-90
5th	119	G.T.Dowling (239), K.Thomson (69)	Christchurch	1967-68
6th	87	J.W.Guy (102), A.R.MacGibbon (59)	Hyderabad	1955-56
7th	163	B.Sutcliffe (151*), B.R.Taylor (105)	Calcutta	1964-65
8th	103	R.J.Hadlee (87), I.D.S.Smith (173)	Auckland	1989-90
9th	136	I.D.S.Smith (173), M.C.Snedden (22)	Auckland	1989-90
10th	61	J.T.Ward (35*), R.O.Collinge (34)	Madras^2	1964-65

RECORD WICKET PARTNERSHIPS – INDIA

1st	413	M.H.Mankad (231), P.Roy (173)	Madras^2	1955-56
2nd	204	S.M.Gavaskar (116), S.Amarnath (124)	Auckland	1975-76
3rd	238	P.R.Umrigar (223), V.L.Manjrekar (118)	Hyderabad	1955-56
4th	171	P.R.Umrigar (223), A.G.Kripal Singh (100*)	Hyderabad	1955-56
5th	127	V.L.Manjrekar (177), G.S.Ramchand (72)	Delhi	1955-56
6th	193*	D.N.Sardesai (200*), Hanumant Singh (75*)	Bombay^2	1964-65
7th	128	S.R.Tendulkar (88), K.S.More (73)	Napier	1989-90
8th	143	R.G.Nadkarni (75), F.M.Engineer (90)	Madras^2	1964-65
9th	105	S.M.H.Kirmani (88), B.S.Bedi (36)	Bombay^3	1976-77
	105	S.M.H.Kirmani (78), N.S.Yadav (43)	Auckland	1980-81
10th	57	R.B.Desai (32*), B.S.Bedi (22)	Dunedin	1967-68

BEST INNINGS BOWLING ANALYSIS

New Zealand	in New Zealand	7-23	R.J.Hadlee	Wellington	1975-76
	in India	6-49	R.J.Hadlee	Bombay^3	1988-89
India	in New Zealand	8-76	E.A.S.Prasanna	Auckland	1975-76
	in India	8-72	S.Venkataraghavan	Delhi	1964-65

BEST MATCH BOWLING ANALYSIS

New Zealand	in New Zealand	11-58	R.J.Hadlee	Wellington	1975-76
	in India	10-88	R.J.Hadlee	Bombay^3	1988-89
India	in New Zealand	11-140	E.A.S.Prasanna	Auckland	1975-76
	in India	12-152	S.Venkataraghavan	Delhi	1964-65

HIGHEST AGGREGATE OF WICKETS IN A SERIES

New Zealand	in New Zealand	16 (av 27.87)	D.K.Morrison	1989-90
	in India	18 (av 14.00)	R.J.Hadlee	1988-89
India	in New Zealand	24 (av 18.79)	E.A.S.Prasanna	1967-68
	in India	34 (av 19.67)	S.P.Gupte	1955-56

SERIES RECORDS – NEW ZEALAND v PAKISTAN

HIGHEST INNINGS TOTALS
New Zealand	in New Zealand	492	Wellington	1984-85
	in Pakistan	482-6d	Lahore[2]	1964-65
Pakistan	in New Zealand	616-5d	Auckland	1988-89
	in Pakistan	565-9d	Karachi[1]	1976-77

LOWEST INNINGS TOTALS
New Zealand	in New Zealand	93	Hamilton	1992-93
	in Pakistan	70	Dacca	1955-56
Pakistan	in New Zealand	169	Auckland	1984-85
	in Pakistan	102	Faisalabad	1990-91

HIGHEST MATCH AGGREGATE 1585 for 31 wickets		Karachi[1]	1976-77
LOWEST MATCH AGGREGATE 572 for 30 wickets		Rawalpindi[1]	1964-65

HIGHEST INDIVIDUAL INNINGS
New Zealand	in New Zealand	174	M.D.Crowe	Wellington	1988-89
	in Pakistan	152	W.K.Lees	Karachi[1]	1976-77
Pakistan	in New Zealand	271	Javed Miandad	Auckland	1988-89
	in Pakistan	209	Imtiaz Ahmed	Lahore[1]	1955-56

HIGHEST AGGREGATE OF RUNS IN A SERIES
New Zealand	in New Zealand	333 (av 83.25)	J.F.Reid		1984-85
	in Pakistan	296 (av 59.20)	J.R.Reid		1964-65
Pakistan	in New Zealand	389 (av 194.50)	Javed Miandad		1988-89
	in Pakistan	507 (av 169.00)	Shoaib Mohammad		1990-91

RECORD WICKET PARTNERSHIPS – NEW ZEALAND
1st	159	R.E.Redmond (107), G.M.Turner (58)	Auckland	1972-73
2nd	195	J.G.Wright (88), G.P.Howarth (114)	Napier	1978-79
3rd	178	B.W.Sinclair (130), J.R.Reid (88)	Lahore[2]	1964-65
4th	128	B.F.Hastings (72), M.G.Burgess (79)	Wellington	1972-73
5th	183	M.G.Burgess (111), R.W.Anderson (92)	Lahore[2]	1976-77
6th	145	J.F.Reid (148), R.J.Hadlee (89)	Wellington	1984-85
7th	186	W.K.Lees (152), R.J.Hadlee (87)	Karachi[1]	1976-77
8th	100	B.W.Yuile (47*), D.R.Hadlee (56)	Karachi[1]	1969-70
9th	96	M.G.Burgess (119*), R.S.Cunis (23)	Dacca	1969-70
10th	151	B.F.Hastings (110), R.O.Collinge (68*)	Auckland	1972-73

RECORD WICKET PARTNERSHIPS – PAKISTAN
1st	172	Ramiz Raja (78), Shoaib Mohammad (203*)	Karachi[1]	1990-91
2nd	114	Mohammad Ilyas (56), Saeed Ahmed (68)	Rawalpindi[1]	1964-65
3rd	248	Shoaib Mohammad (112), Javed Miandad (271)	Auckland	1988-89
4th	350	Mushtaq Mohammad (201), Asif Iqbal (175)	Dunedin	1972-73
5th	281	Javed Miandad (163), Asif Iqbal (166)	Lahore[2]	1976-77
6th	217	Hanif Mohammad (203*), Majid Khan (80)	Lahore[2]	1964-65
7th	308	Waqar Hassan (189), Imtiaz Ahmed (209)	Lahore[1]	1955-56
8th	89	Anil Dalpat (52), Iqbal Qasim (45*)	Karachi[1]	1984-85
9th	52	Intikhab Alam (45), Arif Butt (20)	Auckland	1964-65
10th	65	Salahuddin (34*), Mohammad Farooq (47)	Rawalpindi[1]	1964-65

BEST INNINGS BOWLING ANALYSIS
New Zealand	in New Zealand	6-51	R.J.Hadlee	Dunedin	1984-85
	in Pakistan	7-52	C.Pringle	Faisalabad	1990-91
Pakistan	in New Zealand	7-52	Intikhab Alam	Dunedin	1972-73
	in Pakistan	7-74	Pervez Sajjad	Lahore[2]	1969-70

BEST MATCH BOWLING ANALYSIS
New Zealand	in New Zealand	9-70	F.J.Cameron	Auckland	1964-65
	in Pakistan	11-152	C.Pringle	Faisalabad	1990-91
Pakistan	in New Zealand	11-130	Intikhab Alam	Dunedin	1972-73
	in Pakistan	12-130	Waqar Younis	Faisalabad	1990-91

HIGHEST AGGREGATE OF WICKETS IN A SERIES
New Zealand	in New Zealand	18 (av 23.00)	R.J.Hadlee		1978-79
	in Pakistan	17 (av 25.35)	S.L.Boock		1984-85
Pakistan	in New Zealand	25 (av 17.24)	Wasim Akram		1993-94
	in Pakistan	29 (av 10.86)	Waqar Younis		1990-91

SERIES RECORDS – NEW ZEALAND v SRI LANKA

HIGHEST INNINGS TOTALS
New Zealand	in New Zealand	671-4		Wellington	1990-91
	in Sri Lanka	459		Colombo (CCC)	1983-84
Sri Lanka	in New Zealand	497		Wellington	1990-91
	in Sri Lanka	397-9d		Colombo (CCC)	1986-87

LOWEST INNINGS TOTALS
New Zealand	in New Zealand	174		Wellington	1990-91
	in Sri Lanka	102		Colombo (SSC)	1992-93
Sri Lanka	in New Zealand	93		Wellington	1982-83
	in Sri Lanka	97		Kandy	1983-84

HIGHEST MATCH AGGREGATE	1342 for 23 wickets		Wellington	1990-91
LOWEST MATCH AGGREGATE	663 for 30 wickets		Christchurch	1982-83

HIGHEST INDIVIDUAL INNINGS
New Zealand	in New Zealand	299	M.D.Crowe	Wellington	1990-91
	in Sri Lanka	180	J.F.Reid	Colombo (CCC)	1983-84
Sri Lanka	in New Zealand	267	P.A.de Silva	Wellington	1990-91
	in Sri Lanka	201*	D.S.B.P.Kuruppu	Colombo (CCC)	1986-87

HIGHEST AGGREGATE OF RUNS IN A SERIES
New Zealand	in New Zealand	513 (av 102.60)	A.H.Jones		1990-91
	in Sri Lanka	243 (av 48.60)	J.F.Reid		1983-84
Sri Lanka	in New Zealand	493 (av 98.60)	P.A.de Silva		1990-91
	in Sri Lanka	291 (av 97.00)	R.S.Mahanama		1992-93

RECORD WICKET PARTNERSHIPS – NEW ZEALAND
1st	161	T.J.Franklin (69), J.G.Wright (101)	Hamilton	1990-91
2nd	76	J.G.Wright (84), A.H.Jones (27)	Auckland	1990-91
3rd	467	A.H.Jones (186), M.D.Crowe (299)	Wellington	1990-91
4th	82	J.F.Reid (180), S.L.Boock (35)	Colombo (CCC)	1983-84
5th	151	K.R.Rutherford (105), C.J.Harris (56)	Moratuwa	1992-93
6th	246*	J.J.Crowe (120*), R.J.Hadlee (151*)	Colombo (CCC)	1986-87
7th	{30	R.J.Hadlee (29), I.D.S.Smith (30)	Kandy	1983-84
	{30	R.J.Hadlee (27), J.J.Crowe (9)	Kandy	1983-84
8th	79	J.V.Coney (84), W.K.Lees (89)	Christchurch	1982-83
9th	42	W.K.Lees (89), M.C.Snedden (22)	Christchurch	1982-83
10th	52	W.K.Lees (89), E.J.Chatfield (10*)	Christchurch	1982-83

RECORD WICKET PARTNERSHIPS – SRI LANKA
1st	102	R.S.Mahanama (109), U.C.Hathurusinghe (27)	Colombo (SSC)	1992-93
2nd	138	R.S.Mahanama (153), A.P.Gurusinha (43)	Moratuwa	1992-93
3rd	159*†	S.Wettimuny (65), R.L.Dias (108)	Colombo (SSC)	1983-84
4th	178	P.A.de Silva (267), A.Ranatunga (55)	Wellington	1990-91
5th	130	R.S.Madugalle (79), D.S.de Silva (61)	Wellington	1982-83
6th	109*‡	R.S.Madugalle (89*), A.Ranatunga (37)	Colombo (CCC)	1983-84
7th	55	A.P.Gurusinha (119), A.Ranatunga (21)	Hamilton	1990-91
8th	69	H.P.Tillekeratne (93), S.D.Anurasiri (24)	Colombo (SSC)	1992-93
9th	{31	G.F.Labrooy (70*), R.J.Ratnayake (18)	Auckland	1990-91
	{31	S.T.Jayasuriya (12*), R.J.Ratnayake (20)	Auckland	1990-91
10th	60	V.B.John (27*), M.J.G.Amerasinghe (34)	Kandy	1983-84

BEST INNINGS BOWLING ANALYSIS
New Zealand	in New Zealand	5-75	C.L.Cairns	Auckland	1990-91
	in Sri Lanka	5-28	S.L.Boock	Kandy	1983-84
Sri Lanka	in New Zealand	5-60	V.B.John	Wellington	1982-83
	in Sri Lanka	5-42	J.R.Ratnayeke	Colombo (SSC)	1983-84

BEST MATCH BOWLING ANALYSIS
New Zealand	in New Zealand	9-211	C.L.Cairns	Auckland	1990-91
	in Sri Lanka	10-102	R.J.Hadlee	Colombo (CCC)	1983-84
Sri Lanka	in New Zealand	7-90	G.F.Labrooy	Auckland	1990-91
	in Sri Lanka	8-159	V.B.John	Kandy	1983-84

HIGHEST AGGREGATE OF WICKETS IN A SERIES
New Zealand	in New Zealand	13 (av 36.61)	D.K.Morrison		1990-91
	in Sri Lanka	23 (av 10.00)	R.J.Hadlee		1983-84
Sri Lanka	in New Zealand	{13 (av 27.46)	G.F.Labrooy		1990-91
		{13 (av 32.30)	R.J.Ratnayake		1990-91
	in Sri Lanka	16 (av 23.31)	V.B.John		1983-84

†163 runs were added for this wicket, S.Wettimuny retiring hurt and being succeeded by L.R.D.Mendis after 159 had been scored.

‡119 runs were added for this wicket, R.S.Madugalle retiring hurt and being succeeded by D.S.de Silva after 109 had been scored.

SERIES RECORDS – NEW ZEALAND v ZIMBABWE

HIGHEST INNINGS TOTALS

New Zealand	in New Zealand				
	in Zimbabwe	335		Harare	1992-93
Zimbabwe	in New Zealand				
	in Zimbabwe	283-9d		Harare	1992-93

LOWEST INNINGS TOTALS

New Zealand	in New Zealand				
	in Zimbabwe	335		Harare	1992-93
Zimbabwe	in New Zealand				
	in Zimbabwe	137		Harare	1992-93

HIGHEST MATCH AGGREGATE 1017 for 34 wickets		Harare	1992-93
LOWEST MATCH AGGREGATE 963 for 19 wickets		Bulawayo	1992-93

HIGHEST INDIVIDUAL INNINGS

New Zealand	in New Zealand				
	in Zimbabwe	140	M.D.Crowe	Harare	1992-93
Zimbabwe	in New Zealand				
	in Zimbabwe	101*	K.J.Arnott	Bulawayo	1992-93

HIGHEST AGGREGATE OF RUNS IN A SERIES

New Zealand	in New Zealand				
	in Zimbabwe	249 (av 62.25)	M.D.Crowe		1992-93
Zimbabwe	in New Zealand				
	in Zimbabwe	209 (av 69.66)	K.J.Arnott		1992-93

RECORD WICKET PARTNERSHIPS – NEW ZEALAND

1st	116	M.J.Greatbatch (87), R.T.Latham (119)	Bulawayo	1992-93
2nd	127	R.T.Latham (119), A.H.Jones (67*)	Bulawayo	1992-93
3rd	71	A.H.Jones (67*), M.D.Crowe (42)	Bulawayo	1992-93
4th	168	M.D.Crowe (140), K.R.Rutherford (74)	Harare	1992-93
5th	130	K.R.Rutherford (89), D.N.Patel (58*)	Harare	1992-93
6th	18*	K.R.Rutherford (11*), D.N.Patel (11*)	Bulawayo	1992-93
7th	8	K.R.Rutherford (74), D.J.Nash (11*)	Harare	1992-93
8th	6	D.J.Nash (11*), M.L.Su'a (1)	Harare	1992-93
9th	3	D.J.Nash (11*), W.Watson (3)	Harare	1992-93
10th	5	D.J.Nash (11*), M.J.Haslam (3)	Harare	1992-93

RECORD WICKET PARTNERSHIPS – ZIMBABWE

1st	92	K.J.Arnott (101*), G.W.Flower (45)	Bulawayo	1992-93
2nd	107	K.J.Arnott (68), A.D.R.Campbell (52)	Harare	1992-93
3rd	22	K.J.Arnott (68), A.J.Pycroft (60)	Harare	1992-93
4th	74	A.J.Pycroft (60), D.L.Houghton (21)	Harare	1992-93
5th	22	A.D.R.Campbell (35), A.Flower (9)	Harare	1992-93
6th	70	D.L.Houghton (36), A.Flower (81)	Bulawayo	1992-93
7th	60	A.Flower (81), A.H.Shah (28)	Bulawayo	1992-93
8th	20	G.J.Crocker (33), D.H.Brain (17)	Harare	1992-93
9th	46	G.J.Crocker (33), M.G.Burmester (17*)	Harare	1992-93
10th	8*	M.G.Burmester (30*), A.J.Traicos (1*)	Harare	1992-93

BEST INNINGS BOWLING ANALYSIS

New Zealand	in New Zealand				
	in Zimbabwe	6-50	D.N.Patel	Harare	1992-93
Zimbabwe	in New Zealand				
	in Zimbabwe	3-38	M.P.Jarvis	Bulawayo	1992-93

BEST MATCH BOWLING ANALYSIS

New Zealand	in New Zealand				
	in Zimbabwe	8-131	D.N.Patel	Harare	1992-93
Zimbabwe	in New Zealand				
	in Zimbabwe	4-101	D.H.Brain	Harare	1992-93

HIGHEST AGGREGATE OF WICKETS IN A SERIES

New Zealand	in New Zealand				
	in Zimbabwe	15 (av 20.26)	D.N.Patel		1992-93
Zimbabwe	in New Zealand				
	in Zimbabwe	6 (av 48.33)	A.J.Traicos		1992-93

SERIES RECORDS – INDIA v PAKISTAN

HIGHEST INNINGS TOTALS

India	in India	539-9d	Madras[2]	1960-61
	in Pakistan	509	Lahore[2]	1989-90
Pakistan	in India	487-9d	Madras[1]	1986-87
	in Pakistan	699-5	Lahore[2]	1989-90

LOWEST INNINGS TOTALS

India	in India	106	Lucknow[1]	1952-53
	in Pakistan	145	Karachi[1]	1954-55
Pakistan	in India	116	Bangalore	1986-87
	in Pakistan	158	Dacca	1954-55

HIGHEST MATCH AGGREGATE	1331 for 28 wickets	Lahore[2]	1978-79
LOWEST MATCH AGGREGATE	619 for 30 wickets	Lucknow[1]	1952-53

HIGHEST INDIVIDUAL INNINGS

India	in India	201	A.D.Gaekwad	Jullundur	1983-84
	in Pakistan	218	S.V.Manjrekar	Lahore[2]	1989-90
Pakistan	in India	160	Hanif Mohammad	Bombay[2]	1960-61
	in Pakistan	280*	Javed Miandad	Hyderabad	1982-83

HIGHEST AGGREGATE OF RUNS IN A SERIES

India	in India	529 (av 52.90)	S.M.Gavaskar		1979-80
	in Pakistan	584 (av 73.00)	M.Amarnath		1982-83
Pakistan	in India	460 (av 51.11)	Saeed Ahmed		1960-61
	in Pakistan	761 (av 126.83)	Mudassar Nazar		1982-83

RECORD WICKET PARTNERSHIPS – INDIA

1st	200	S.M.Gavaskar (91), K.Srikkanth (123)	Madras[1]	1986-87
2nd	135	N.S.Sidhu (85), S.V.Manjrekar (113*)	Karachi[1]	1989-90
3rd	190	M.Amarnath (120), Yashpal Sharma (63*)	Lahore[2]	1982-83
4th	186	S.V.Manjrekar (218), R.J.Shastri (61)	Lahore[2]	1989-90
5th	200	S.M.Patil (127), R.J.Shastri (139)	Faisalabad	1984-85
6th	143	M.Azharuddin (141), Kapil Dev (66)	Calcutta	1986-87
7th	155	R.M.H.Binny (83*), Madan Lal (74)	Bangalore	1983-84
8th	122	S.M.H.Kirmani (66), Madan Lal (54)	Faisalabad	1982-83
9th	149	P.G.Joshi (52*), R.B.Desai (85)	Bombay[2]	1960-61
10th	109	H.R.Adhikari (81*), Ghulam Ahmed (50)	Delhi	1952-53

RECORD WICKET PARTNERSHIPS – PAKISTAN

1st	162	Hanif Mohammad (62), Imtiaz Ahmed (135)	Madras[2]	1960-61
2nd	250	Mudassar Nazar (199), Qasim Omar (210)	Faisalabad	1984-85
3rd	451	Mudassar Nazar (230), Javed Miandad (280*)	Hyderabad	1982-83
4th	287	Javed Miandad (126), Zaheer Abbas (168)	Faisalabad	1982-83
5th	213	Zaheer Abbas (186), Mudassar Nazar (119)	Karachi[1]	1982-83
6th	207	Salim Malik (107), Imran Khan (117)	Faisalabad	1982-83
7th	154	Imran Khan (72), Ijaz Faqih (105)	Ahmedabad	1986-87
8th	112	Imran Khan (135*), Wasim Akram (62)	Madras[1]	1986-87
9th	60	Wasim Bari (49*), Iqbal Qasim (20)	Bangalore	1979-80
10th	104	Zulfiqar Ahmed (63*), Amir Elahi (47)	Madras[1]	1952-53

BEST INNINGS BOWLING ANALYSIS

India	in India	8-52	M.H.Mankad	Delhi	1952-53
	in Pakistan	8-85	Kapil Dev	Lahore[2]	1982-83
Pakistan	in India	8-69	Sikander Bakht	Delhi	1979-80
	in Pakistan	8-60	Imran Khan	Karachi[1]	1982-83

BEST MATCH BOWLING ANALYSIS

India	in India	13-131	M.H.Mankad	Delhi	1952-53
	in Pakistan	8-85	Kapil Dev	Lahore[2]	1982-83
Pakistan	in India	12-94	Fazal Mahmood	Lucknow[1]	1952-53
	in Pakistan	11-79	Imran Khan	Karachi[1]	1982-83

HIGHEST AGGREGATE OF WICKETS IN A SERIES

India	in India	32 (av 17.68)	Kapil Dev		1979-80
	in Pakistan	24 (av 34.62)	Kapil Dev		1982-83
Pakistan	in India	24 (av 26.70)	Sikander Bakht		1979-80
	in Pakistan	40 (av 13.95)	Imran Khan		1982-83

SERIES RECORDS – INDIA v SRI LANKA

HIGHEST INNINGS TOTALS

India	in India	676-7		Kanpur	1986-87
	in Sri Lanka	446		Colombo (PSS)	1993-94
Sri Lanka	in India	420		Kanpur	1986-87
	in Sri Lanka	385		Colombo (PSS)	1985-86

LOWEST INNINGS TOTALS

India	in India	288		Chandigarh	1990-91
	in Sri Lanka	198		Colombo (PSS)	1985-86
Sri Lanka	in India	82		Chandigarh	1990-91
	in Sri Lanka	198		Kandy	1985-86

HIGHEST MATCH AGGREGATE 1441 for 33 wickets		Madras[1]	1982-83
LOWEST MATCH AGGREGATE 568 for 30 wickets		Chandigarh	1990-91

HIGHEST INDIVIDUAL INNINGS

India	in India	199	M.Azharuddin	Kanpur	1986-87
	in Sri Lanka	125	V.G.Kambli	Colombo (SSC)	1993-94
Sri Lanka	in India	105 (twice)	L.R.D.Mendis	Madras[1]	1982-83
	in Sri Lanka	151	R.S.Mahanama	Colombo (PSS)	1993-94

HIGHEST AGGREGATE OF RUNS IN A SERIES

India	in India	376 (av 125.33)	D.B.Vengsarkar		1986-87
	in Sri Lanka	249 (av 83.00)	V.G.Kambli		1993-94
Sri Lanka	in India	282 (av 47.00)	R.S.Mahanama		1993-94
	in Sri Lanka	310 (av 62.00)	L.R.D.Mendis		1985-86

RECORD WICKET PARTNERSHIPS – INDIA

1st	171	M.Prabhakar (95), N.S.Sidhu (104)	Colombo (SSC)	1993-94
2nd	173	S.M.Gavaskar (155), D.B.Vengsarkar (90)	Madras[1]	1982-83
3rd	173	M.Amarnath (131), D.B.Vengsarkar (153)	Nagpur	1986-87
4th	163	S.M.Gavaskar (176), M.Azharuddin (199)	Kanpur	1986-87
5th	87	M.Azharuddin (108), S.V.Manjrekar (39)	Bangalore	1993-94
6th	272	M.Azharuddin (199), Kapil Dev (163)	Kanpur	1986-87
7th	78*	S.M.Patil (114*), Madan Lal (37*)	Madras[1]	1982-83
8th	70	Kapil Dev (78), L.Sivaramakrishnan (21)	Colombo (PSS)	1985-86
9th	67	M.Azharuddin (152), R.K.Chauhan (9)	Ahmedabad	1993-94
10th	29	Kapil Dev (78), C.Sharma (0*)	Colombo (PSS)	1985-86

RECORD WICKET PARTNERSHIPS – SRI LANKA

1st	159	S.Wettimuny (79), J.R.Ratnayeke (93)	Kanpur	1986-87
2nd	95	S.A.R.Silva (111), R.S.Madugalle (54)	Colombo (PSS)	1985-86
3rd	153	R.L.Dias (60), L.R.D.Mendis (105)	Madras[1]	1982-83
4th	216	R.L.Dias (106), L.R.D.Mendis (124)	Kandy	1985-86
5th	144	R.S.Madugalle (103), A.Ranatunga (111)	Colombo (SSC)	1985-86
6th	89	L.R.D.Mendis (105), A.N.Ranasinghe (77)	Madras[1]	1982-83
7th	77	R.S.Madugalle (46), D.S.de Silva (49)	Madras[1]	1982-83
8th	40*	P.A.de Silva (29*), A.L.F.de Mel (9*)	Kandy	1985-86
9th	60	H.P.Tillekeratne (55), A.W.R.Madurasinghe (11)	Chandigarh	1990-91
10th	44	R.J.Ratnayake (32*), E.A.R.de Silva (16)	Nagpur	1986-87

BEST INNINGS BOWLING ANALYSIS

India	in India	7-51	Maninder Singh	Nagpur	1986-87
	in Sri Lanka	5-87	A.Kumble	Colombo (SSC)	1993-94
Sri Lanka	in India	5-68	A.L.F.de Mel	Madras[1]	1982-83
	in Sri Lanka	6-85	R.J.Ratnayake	Colombo (SSC)	1985-86

BEST MATCH BOWLING ANALYSIS

India	in India	11-125	S.L.V.Raju	Ahmedabad	1993-94
	in Sri Lanka	8-172	A.Kumble	Colombo (SSC)	1993-94
Sri Lanka	in India	7-201	A.L.F.de Mel	Madras[1]	1982-83
	in Sri Lanka	9-125	R.J.Ratnayake	Colombo (PSS)	1985-86

HIGHEST AGGREGATE OF WICKETS IN A SERIES

India	in India	18 (av 15.50)	Maninder Singh		1986-87
		18 (av 17.61)	A.Kumble		1993-94
	in Sri Lanka	14 (av 27.35)	C.Sharma		1985-86
Sri Lanka	in India	12 (av 35.00)	M.Muralitharan		1993-94
	in Sri Lanka	20 (av 22.95)	R.J.Ratnayake		1985-86

SERIES RECORDS – INDIA v ZIMBABWE

HIGHEST INNINGS TOTALS
India	in India	536-7d		Delhi	1992-93
	in Zimbabwe	307		Harare	1992-93
Zimbabwe	in India	322		Delhi	1992-93
	in Zimbabwe	456		Harare	1992-93

LOWEST INNINGS TOTALS
India	in India	536-7d		Delhi	1992-93
	in Zimbabwe	307		Harare	1992-93
Zimbabwe	in India	201		Delhi	1992-93
	in Zimbabwe	456		Harare	1992-93

HIGHEST MATCH AGGREGATE 1059 for 27 wickets — Delhi — 1992-93
LOWEST MATCH AGGREGATE 909 for 24 wickets — Harare — 1992-93

HIGHEST INDIVIDUAL INNINGS
India	in India	227	V.G.Kambli	Delhi	1992-93
	in Zimbabwe	104	S.V.Manjrekar	Harare	1992-93
Zimbabwe	in India	115	A.Flower	Delhi	1992-93
	in Zimbabwe	121	D.L.Houghton	Harare	1992-93

HIGHEST AGGREGATE OF RUNS IN A SERIES
India	in India	227 (av 227.00)	V.G.Kambli	1992-93
	in Zimbabwe	104 (av 104.00)	S.V.Manjrekar	1992-93
Zimbabwe	in India	177 (av 177.00)	A.Flower	1992-93
	in Zimbabwe	162 (av 162.00)	D.L.Houghton	1992-93

RECORD WICKET PARTNERSHIPS – INDIA
1st	29	R.J.Shastri (11), W.V.Raman (43)	Harare	1992-93
2nd	107	N.S.Sidhu (61), V.G.Kambli (227)	Delhi	1992-93
3rd	137	V.G.Kambli (227), S.R.Tendulkar (62)	Delhi	1992-93
4th	107	V.G.Kambli (227), M.Azharuddin (42)	Delhi	1992-93
5th	69	V.G.Kambli (227), P.K.Amre (52*)	Delhi	1992-93
6th	96	S.V.Manjrekar (104), Kapil Dev (60)	Harare	1992-93
7th	43	P.K.Amre (52*), V.Yadav (30)	Delhi	1992-93
8th	68	S.V.Manjrekar (104), K.S.More (41)	Harare	1992-93
9th	7	K.S.More (41), A.Kumble (0)	Harare	1992-93
10th	13	K.S.More (41), J.Srinath (6*)	Harare	1992-93

RECORD WICKET PARTNERSHIPS – ZIMBABWE
1st	100	K.J.Arnott (40), G.W.Flower (82)	Harare	1992-93
2nd	75	G.W.Flower (82), A.D.R.Campbell (45)	Harare	1992-93
3rd	77	K.J.Arnott (32), A.J.Pycroft (46)	Harare	1992-93
4th	192	G.W.Flower (96), A.Flower (115)	Delhi	1992-93
5th	53	A.J.Pycroft (39), D.L.Houghton (121)	Harare	1992-93
6th	165	D.L.Houghton (121), A.Flower (59)	Harare	1992-93
7th	28	D.L.Houghton (121), G.J.Crocker (23*)	Harare	1992-93
8th	1	A.H.Shah (25), D.H.Brain (0)	Delhi	1992-93
8th	1	A.Flower (62*), D.H.Brain (0)	Delhi	1992-93
9th	31	A.H.Shah (25), U.Ranchod (7)	Delhi	1992-93
10th	13	A.Flower (62*), A.J.Traicos (1)	Delhi	1992-93

BEST INNINGS BOWLING ANALYSIS
India	in India	5-70	A.Kumble	Delhi	1992-93
	in Zimbabwe	3-66	M.Prabhakar	Harare	1992-93
Zimbabwe	in India	3-186	A.J.Traicos	Delhi	1992-93
	in Zimbabwe	5-86	A.J.Traicos	Harare	1992-93

BEST MATCH BOWLING ANALYSIS
India	in India	8-160	A.Kumble	Delhi	1992-93
	in Zimbabwe	4-88	M.Prabhakar	Harare	1992-93
Zimbabwe	in India	3-186	A.J.Traicos	Delhi	1992-93
	in Zimbabwe	5-86	A.J.Traicos	Harare	1992-93

HIGHEST AGGREGATE OF WICKETS IN A SERIES
India	in India	8 (av 20.00)	A.Kumble	1992-93
	in Zimbabwe	4 (av 22.00)	M.Prabhakar	1992-93
Zimbabwe	in India	3 (av 62.00)	A.J.Traicos	1992-93
	in Zimbabwe	5 (av 17.20)	A.J.Traicos	1992-93

SERIES RECORDS – PAKISTAN v SRI LANKA

HIGHEST INNINGS TOTALS
Pakistan	in Pakistan	555-3	Faisalabad	1985-86
	in Sri Lanka	390	Colombo (PSS)	1994-95
Sri Lanka	in Pakistan	479	Faisalabad	1985-86
	in Sri Lanka	323-3	Colombo (PSS)	1985-86

LOWEST INNINGS TOTALS
Pakistan	in Pakistan	221	Faisalabad	1991-92
	in Sri Lanka	132	Colombo (CCC)	1985-86
Sri Lanka	in Pakistan	149	Karachi[1]	1981-82
	in Sri Lanka	71	Kandy	1994-95

HIGHEST MATCH AGGREGATE	1190 for 34 wickets	Karachi[1]	1981-82
LOWEST MATCH AGGREGATE	440 for 29 wickets	Kandy	1985-86

HIGHEST INDIVIDUAL INNINGS
Pakistan	in Pakistan	206	Qasim Omar	Faisalabad	1985-86
	in Sri Lanka	136	Saeed Anwar	Colombo (PSS)	1994-95
Sri Lanka	in Pakistan	157	S.Wettimuny	Faisalabad	1981-82
	in Sri Lanka	135*	A.Ranatunga	Colombo (PSS)	1985-86

HIGHEST AGGREGATE OF RUNS IN A SERIES
Pakistan	in Pakistan	306 (av 153.00)	Javed Miandad		1985-86
	in Sri Lanka	261 (av 87.00)	Saeed Anwar		1994-95
Sri Lanka	in Pakistan	316 (av 52.66)	S.Wettimuny		1981-82
	in Sri Lanka	316 (av 79.00)	A.Ranatunga		1985-86

RECORD WICKET PARTNERSHIPS – PAKISTAN
1st	128	Ramiz Raja (98), Shoaib Mohammad (43)	Sialkot	1991-92
	128	Saeed Anwar (136), Aamir Sohail (65)	Colombo (PSS)	1994-95
2nd	151	Mohsin Khan (129), Majid Khan (63)	Lahore[2]	1981-82
3rd	397	Qasim Omar (206), Javed Miandad (203*)	Faisalabad	1985-86
4th	162	Salim Malik (100*), Javed Miandad (92)	Karachi[1]	1981-82
5th	132	Salim Malik (101), Imran Khan (93*)	Sialkot	1991-92
6th	100	Zaheer Abbas (134), Imran Khan (39)	Lahore[2]	1981-82
7th	104	Haroon Rashid (153), Tahir Naqqash (57)	Karachi[1]	1981-82
8th	33	Inzamam-ul-Haq (100*), Wasim Akram (12)	Kandy	1994-95
9th	127	Haroon Rashid (153), Rashid Khan (59)	Karachi[1]	1981-82
10th	48	Rashid Khan (43*), Tausif Ahmed (18)	Faisalabad	1981-82

RECORD WICKET PARTNERSHIPS – SRI LANKA
1st	81	R.S.Mahanama (58), U.C.Hathurusinghe (49)	Faisalabad	1991-92
2nd	217	S.Wettimuny (157), R.L.Dias (98)	Faisalabad	1981-82
3rd	85	S.Wettimuny (52), R.L.Dias (48)	Faisalabad	1985-86
4th	240*	A.P.Gurusinha (116*), A.Ranatunga (135*)	Colombo (PSS)	1985-86
5th	119	P.A.de Silva (127), H.P.Tillekeratne (34)	Colombo (PSS)	1994-95
6th	121	A.Ranatunga (79), P.A.de Silva (122)	Faisalabad	1985-86
7th	131	H.P.Tillekeratne (83*), R.S.Kalpage (62)	Kandy	1994-95
8th	61	R.S.Madugalle (91*), D.S.de Silva (25)	Faisalabad	1981-82
9th	52	P.A.de Silva (122), R.J.Ratnayake (56)	Faisalabad	1985-86
10th	36	R.J.Ratnayake (56), R.G.C.E.Wijesuriya (7*)	Faisalabad	1985-86

BEST INNINGS BOWLING ANALYSIS
Pakistan	in Pakistan	8-58	Imran Khan	Lahore[2]	1981-82
	in Sri Lanka	6-34	Waqar Younis	Kandy	1994-95
Sri Lanka	in Pakistan	8-83	J.R.Ratnayeke	Sialkot	1985-86
	in Sri Lanka	6-99	H.D.P.K.Dharmasena	Colombo (PSS)	1994-95

BEST MATCH BOWLING ANALYSIS
Pakistan	in Pakistan	14-116	Imran Khan	Lahore[2]	1981-82
	in Sri Lanka	11-119	Waqar Younis	Kandy	1994-95
Sri Lanka	in Pakistan	9-162	D.S.de Silva	Faisalabad	1981-82
	in Sri Lanka	8-183	H.D.P.K.Dharmasena	Colombo (PSS)	1994-95

HIGHEST AGGREGATE OF WICKETS IN A SERIES
Pakistan	in Pakistan	17 (av 15.94)	Imran Khan		1985-86
	in Sri Lanka	15 (av 18.00)	Imran Khan		1985-86
Sri Lanka	in Pakistan	17 (av 28.94)	D.S.de Silva		1981-82
	in Sri Lanka	12 (av 21.50)	H.D.P.K.Dharmasena		1994-95

SERIES RECORDS – PAKISTAN v ZIMBABWE

HIGHEST INNINGS TOTALS

Pakistan	in Pakistan	423-8d		Karachi[2]	1993-94
	in Zimbabwe				
Zimbabwe	in Pakistan	289		Karachi[2]	1993-94
	in Zimbabwe				

LOWEST INNINGS TOTALS

Pakistan	in Pakistan	147		Lahore[2]	1993-94
	in Zimbabwe				
Zimbabwe	in Pakistan	134		Karachi[2]	1993-94
	in Zimbabwe				

HIGHEST MATCH AGGREGATE	977 for 31 wickets	Karachi[2]	1993-94
LOWEST MATCH AGGREGATE	551 for 21 wickets	Lahore[2]	1993-94

HIGHEST INDIVIDUAL INNINGS

Pakistan	in Pakistan	81	Shoaib Mohammad	Karachi[2]	1993-94
	in Zimbabwe				
Zimbabwe	in Pakistan	75	A.D.R.Campbell	Rawalpindi[2]	1993-94
	in Zimbabwe				

HIGHEST AGGREGATE OF RUNS IN A SERIES

Pakistan	in Pakistan	184 (av 61.33)	Asif Mujtaba		1993-94
	in Zimbabwe				
Zimbabwe	in Pakistan	205 (av 41.00)	A.D.R.Campbell		1993-94
	in Zimbabwe				

RECORD WICKET PARTNERSHIPS – PAKISTAN

1st	95	Aamir Sohail (63), Shoaib Mohammad (81)	Karachi[2]	1993-94
2nd	118*	Shoaib Mohammad (53*), Asif Mujtaba (65*)	Lahore[2]	1993-94
3rd	83	Shoaib Mohammad (81), Javed Miandad (70)	Karachi[2]	1993-94
4th	53	Javed Miandad (31), Basit Ali (29)	Lahore[2]	1993-94
5th	30	Basit Ali (25), Asif Mujtaba (54*)	Rawalpindi[2]	1993-94
6th	74	Basit Ali (40), Asif Mujtaba (51)	Rawalpindi[2]	1993-94
7th	77	Asif Mujtaba (51), Rashid Latif (61)	Rawalpindi[2]	1993-94
8th	31	Rashid Latif (68*), Mushtaq Ahmed (18)	Karachi[2]	1993-94
9th	60*	Rashid Latif (68*), Tausif Ahmed (21*)	Karachi[2]	1993-94
10th	8	Waqar Younis (17), Ashfaq Ahmed (1*)	Rawalpindi[2]	1993-94

RECORD WICKET PARTNERSHIPS – ZIMBABWE

1st	17	G.W.Flower (30), M.H.Dekker (2)	Lahore[2]	1993-94
2nd	135	M.H.Dekker (68*), A.D.R.Campbell (75)	Rawalpindi[2]	1993-94
3rd	61	A.D.R.Campbell (53), D.L.Houghton (46)	Karachi[2]	1993-94
4th	33	D.L.Houghton (50), A.Flower (62*)	Lahore[2]	1993-94
5th	77	A.Flower (63), G.J.Whittall (33)	Karachi[2]	1993-94
6th	72	M.H.Dekker (68), G.J.Whittall (29)	Rawalpindi[2]	1993-94
7th	4	G.K.Bruk-Jackson (31), S.G.Peall (0)	Karachi[2]	1993-94
8th	46	A.Flower (62*), D.H.Brain (28)	Lahore[2]	1993-94
9th	38	H.H.Streak (19*), E.A.Brandes (17)	Karachi[2]	1993-94
10th	29	E.A.Brandes (18), S.G.Peall (11*)	Rawalpindi[2]	1993-94

BEST INNINGS BOWLING ANALYSIS

Pakistan	in Pakistan	7-91	Waqar Younis	Karachi[2]	1993-94
	in Zimbabwe				
Zimbabwe	in Pakistan	5-42	D.H.Brain	Lahore[2]	1993-94
	in Zimbabwe				

BEST MATCH BOWLING ANALYSIS

Pakistan	in Pakistan	13-135	Waqar Younis	Karachi[2]	1993-94
	in Zimbabwe				
Zimbabwe	in Pakistan	8-114	H.H.Streak	Rawalpindi[2]	1993-94
	in Zimbabwe				

HIGHEST AGGREGATE OF WICKETS IN A SERIES

Pakistan	in Pakistan	27 (av 13.81)	Waqar Younis		1993-94
	in Zimbabwe				
Zimbabwe	in Pakistan	13 (av 30.30)	E.A.Brandes		1993-94
	in Zimbabwe				

TEAM RECORDS
HIGHEST INNINGS TOTALS

903-7d	England v Australia	Oval	1938
849	England v West Indies	Kingston	1929-30
790-3d	West Indies v Pakistan	Kingston	1957-58
758-8d	Australia v West Indies	Kingston	1954-55
729-6d	Australia v England	Lord's	1930
708	Pakistan v England	Oval	1987
701	Australia v England	Oval	1934
699-5	Pakistan v India	Lahore[2]	1989-90
695	Australia v England	Oval	1930
687-8d	West Indies v England	Oval	1976
681-8d	West Indies v England	Port-of-Spain	1953-54
676-7	India v Sri Lanka	Kanpur	1986-87
674-6	Pakistan v India	Faisalabad	1984-85
674	Australia v India	Adelaide	1947-48
671-4	New Zealand v Sri Lanka	Wellington	1990-91
668	Australia v West Indies	Bridgetown	1954-55
659-8d	Australia v England	Sydney	1946-47
658-8d	England v Australia	Nottingham	1938
657-8d	Pakistan v West Indies	Bridgetown	1957-58
656-8d	Australia v England	Manchester	1964
654-5	England v South Africa	Durban[2]	1938-39
653-4d	England v India	Lord's	1990
653-4d	Australia v England	Leeds	1993
652-7d	England v India	Madras[1]	1984-85
652-8d	West Indies v England	Lord's	1973
652	Pakistan v India	Faisalabad	1982-83
650-6d	Australia v West Indies	Bridgetown	1964-65
645	Australia v England	Brisbane[2]	1946-47
644-7d	India v West Indies	Kanpur	1978-79
644-8d	West Indies v India	Delhi	1958-59
636	England v Australia	Sydney	1928-29
633-5d	England v India	Birmingham	1979
632-4d	Australia v England	Lord's	1993
631-8d	West Indies v India	Kingston	1961-62
631	West Indies v India	Delhi	1948-49
629-6d	West Indies v India	Bombay[2]	1948-49
629	England v India	Lord's	1974
627-9d	England v Australia	Manchester	1934
624	Pakistan v Australia	Adelaide	1983-84
622-9d	South Africa v Australia	Durban[2]	1969-70
620	South Africa v Australia	Johannesburg[3]	1966-67
619-6d	England v West Indies	Nottingham	1957
619	Australia v West Indies	Sydney	1968-69
617	Australia v Pakistan	Faisalabad	1979-80
616-5d	Pakistan v New Zealand	Auckland	1988-89
616	West Indies v Australia	Adelaide	1968-69
614-5d	West Indies v India	Calcutta	1958-59
611	England v Australia	Manchester	1964
608-7d	Pakistan v England	Birmingham	1971
608	England v South Africa	Johannesburg[2]	1948-49
607-6d	Australia v New Zealand	Brisbane[2]	1993-94
606-9d	India v England	Oval	1990
606	West Indies v England	Birmingham	1984
606	West Indies v Australia	Sydney	1992-93
604-6d	West Indies v India	Bombay[3]	1974-75
604	Australia v England	Melbourne	1936-37
602-6d	Australia v England	Nottingham	1989
601-7d	Australia v England	Leeds	1989
601-8d	Australia v England	Brisbane[2]	1954-55
600-4d	India v Australia	Sydney	1985-86
600-7d	Pakistan v England	Oval	1974
600-9d	Australia v West Indies	Port-of-Spain	1954-55
600	Australia v England	Melbourne	1924-25

The highest totals by Sri Lanka and Zimbabwe are:

547-8d	Sri Lanka v Australia	Colombo (SSC)	1992-93
456	Zimbabwe v India	Harare	1992-93

BOTH TEAMS SCORING 600

Australia (656-8d) v England (611)	Manchester	1964

HIGHEST SECOND INNINGS TOTALS

First innings in brackets

671-4	(174)	New Zealand v Sri Lanka	Wellington	1990-91
657-8d†	(106)	Pakistan v West Indies	Bridgetown	1957-58
654-5	(316)	England v South Africa	Durban[2]	1938-39
620	(199)	South Africa v Australia	Johannesburg[3]	1966-67
616	(276)	West Indies v Australia	Adelaide	1968-69
583-4d	(186)	England v West Indies	Birmingham	1957
582	(354)	Australia v England	Adelaide	1920-21
581	(267)	Australia v England	Sydney	1920-21
578	(328)	Australia v South Africa	Melbourne	1910-11
564-8	(133)	West Indies v New Zealand	Bridgetown	1971-72
564	(200-9d)	Australia v England	Melbourne	1936-37
554	(198)	Australia v South Africa	Melbourne	1931-32
551†	(208)	England v South Africa	Nottingham	1947

†*After following on.*

HIGHEST FOURTH INNINGS TOTALS

TO WIN

				Runs set in 4th innings
406-4	India v West Indies	Port-of-Spain	1975-76	403
404-3	Australia v England	Leeds	1948	404
362-7	Australia v West Indies	Georgetown	1977-78	359
348-5	West Indies v New Zealand	Auckland	1968-69	345
344-1	West Indies v England	Lord's	1984	342
342-8	Australia v India	Perth	1977-78	339
336-5	Australia v South Africa	Durban[2]	1949-50	336
332-7	England v Australia	Melbourne	1928-29	332
324-5	New Zealand v Pakistan	Christchurch	1993-94	324
317-2	West Indies v Pakistan	Georgetown	1957-58	317
315-6	Australia v England	Adelaide	1901-02	315

TO TIE

347	India v Australia	Madras[1]	1986-87	

TO DRAW

				Runs set in 4th innings
654-5	England v South Africa	Durban[2]	1938-39	696
429-8	India v England	Oval	1979	438
423-7	South Africa v England	Oval	1947	451
408-5	West Indies v England	Kingston	1929-30	836
364-6	India v Pakistan	Delhi	1979-80	390
355-8	India v West Indies	Bombay[2]	1948-49	361
344-6	Sri Lanka v New Zealand	Hamilton	1990-91	418
343-6	India v England	Manchester	1990	408
341-9	Pakistan v West Indies	Port-of-Spain	1987-88	372
339-9	Australia v West Indies	Adelaide	1968-69	360
335-5	England v Australia	Adelaide	1990-91	472
329-3	Australia v England	Lord's	1975	484
328-3	Australia v England	Adelaide	1970-71	469
326-5	South Africa v Australia	Sydney	1963-64	409
325-3	India v West Indies	Calcutta	1948-49	431
314-7	England v Australia	Sydney	1982-83	460
310-7	England v Australia	Melbourne	1946-47	551
308-4	England v South Africa	Oval	1965	399
307-7	Sri Lanka v India	Kandy	1985-86	377
303-3	India v Pakistan	Karachi[1]	1989-90	453

TO LOSE

				Losing Margin
445	India v Australia	Adelaide	1977-78	47
440	New Zealand v England	Nottingham	1973	38
417	England v Australia	Melbourne	1976-77	45
411	England v Australia	Sydney	1924-25	193
402	Australia v England	Manchester	1981	103
376	India v England	Manchester	1959	171
370	England v Australia	Adelaide	1920-21	119

				Losing Margin
TO LOSE *continued*				
363	England v Australia	Adelaide	1924-25	11†
355	India v Australia	Brisbane[2]	1967-68	39
352	West Indies v Australia	Sydney	1968-69	382
348	Sri Lanka v Australia	Hobart	1989-90	173
345	New Zealand v England	Nottingham	1983	165
339	Australia v South Africa	Adelaide	1910-11	38
336	Australia v England	Adelaide	1928-29	12
336	Pakistan v Australia	Melbourne	1989-90	92
335	Australia v England	Nottingham	1930	93
335	South Africa v New Zealand	Cape Town	1961-62	72
333	Australia v England	Melbourne	1894-95	94
333	India v Australia	Adelaide	1991-92	38
332	England v Australia	Manchester	1993	179
327	England v West Indies	Georgetown	1929-30	289
326	West Indies v Australia	Melbourne	1975-76	165
324	India v Australia	Brisbane[2]	1977-78	16
323	England v Australia	Melbourne	1936-37	365
316	England v West Indies	Kingston	1953-54	140
313	England v West Indies	Bridgetown	1953-54	181
310	Australia v Pakistan	Melbourne	1978-79	71
307	England v West Indies	Lord's	1988	134
304	South Africa v England	Johannesburg[1]	1913-14	91
301	Pakistan v West Indies	Kingston	1976-77	140

HIGHEST MATCH AGGREGATES

BOTH SIDES

Runs	Wkts				Days Played
1981	35	South Africa v England	Durban[2]	1938-39	10†
1815	34	West Indies v England	Kingston	1929-30	9‡
1764	39	Australia v West Indies	Adelaide	1968-69	5
1753	40	Australia v England	Adelaide	1920-21	6
1723	31	England v Australia	Leeds	1948	5
1661	36	West Indies v Australia	Bridgetown	1954-55	6
1646	40	Australia v South Africa	Adelaide	1910-11	6
1644	38	Australia v West Indies	Sydney	1968-69	6
1640	24	West Indies v Australia	Bridgetown	1964-65	6
1640	33	Australia v Pakistan	Melbourne	1972-73	5
1619	40	Australia v England	Melbourne	1924-25	7
1614	30	England v India	Manchester	1990	5
1611	40	Australia v England	Sydney	1924-25	7
1603	28	England v India	Lord's	1990	5
1601	29	England v Australia	Lord's	1930	4
1585	31	Pakistan v New Zealand	Karachi[1]	1976-77	5
1562	37	Australia v England	Melbourne	1946-47	6
1554	35	Australia v England	Melbourne	1928-29	8
1541	35	Australia v England	Sydney	1903-04	6
1528	24	West Indies v England	Port-of-Spain	1953-54	6
1514	40	Australia v England	Sydney	1894-95	6
1507	28	England v West Indies	Oval	1976	5
1505	25	New Zealand v India	Auckland	1989-90	5
1502	29	Australia v England	Adelaide	1946-47	6

†*No play on one day*   ‡*No play on two days*

ONE SIDE

Runs	Wkts			
1121	19	England v West Indies	Kingston	1929-30
1028	20	Australia v England	Oval	1934
1013	18	Australia v West Indies	Sydney	1968-69
1011	20	South Africa v England	Durban[2]	1938-39

LOWEST INNINGS TOTALS

26	New Zealand v England	Auckland	1954-55
30	South Africa v England	Port Elizabeth	1895-96
30	South Africa v England	Birmingham	1924
35	South Africa v England	Cape Town	1898-99
36	Australia v England	Birmingham	1902
36	South Africa v Australia	Melbourne	1931-32
42	Australia v England	Sydney	1887-88
42	New Zealand v Australia	Wellington	1945-46
42†	India v England	Lord's	1974
43	South Africa v England	Cape Town	1888-89
44	Australia v England	Oval	1896
45	England v Australia	Sydney	1886-87
45	South Africa v Australia	Melbourne	1931-32
46	England v West Indies	Port-of-Spain	1993-94
47	South Africa v England	Cape Town	1888-89
47	New Zealand v England	Lord's	1958
52	England v Australia	Oval	1948
53	England v Australia	Lord's	1988
53	Australia v England	Lord's	1896
53	West Indies v Pakistan	Faisalabad	1986-87
54	New Zealand v Australia	Wellington	1945-46
58	South Africa v England	Lord's	1912
58†	Australia v England	Brisbane[2]	1936-37
58	India v Australia	Brisbane[2]	1947-48
58	India v England	Manchester	1952
60	Australia v England	Lord's	1888

†*One batsman absent hurt/ill.*

The lowest innings totals by Pakistan, Sri Lanka and Zimbabwe are:

62	Pakistan v Australia	Perth	1981-82
71	Sri Lanka v Pakistan	Kandy	1994-95
134	Zimbabwe v Pakistan	Karachi[2]	1993-94

The following innings closed at a low total:

32-7d	Australia v England	Brisbane[2]	1950-51
35-8	Australia v England	Manchester	1953
48-8	New Zealand v England	Christchurch	1965-66
51-6d	West Indies v England	Bridgetown	1934-35

DISMISSED FOR UNDER 100 IN BOTH INNINGS

42 & 82	Australia v England	Sydney	1887-88
53 & 62	England v Australia	Lord's	1888
81 & 70	Australia v England	Manchester	1888
47 & 43	South Africa v England	Cape Town	1888-89
97 & 83	South Africa v England	Cape Town	1891-92
65 & 72	England v Australia	Sydney	1894-95
93 & 30	South Africa v England	Port Elizabeth	1895-96
95 & 93	South Africa v England	Oval	1912
36 & 45	South Africa v Australia	Melbourne	1931-32
42 & 54	New Zealand v Australia	Wellington	1945-46
58 & 98	India v Australia	Brisbane[2]	1947-48
58 & 82	India v England	Manchester	1952
89 & 86	West Indies v England	Oval	1957
47 & 74	New Zealand v England	Lord's	1958
82 & 93	England v New Zealand	Christchurch	1983-84

LOWEST MATCH AGGREGATES

Completed match

Runs	Wkts				Days Played
234	29	Australia v South Africa	Melbourne	1931-32	3†
291	40	England v Australia	Lord's	1888	2
295	28	New Zealand v Australia	Wellington	1945-46	2
309	29	West Indies v England	Bridgetown	1934-35	3

Runs	Wkts				Days Played
323	30	England v Australia	Manchester	1888	2
363	40	England v Australia	Oval	1882	2
374	40	Australia v England	Sydney	1887-88	5‡
378	30	England v South Africa	Oval	1912	2
382	30	South Africa v England	Cape Town	1888-89	2
289	38	England v Australia	Oval	1890	2
390	30	England v New Zealand	Lord's	1958	3
392	40	England v Australia	Oval	1896	3

†*No play on one day*   ‡*No play on two days*

LARGEST MARGINS OF VICTORY

Inns and 579 runs	England v Australia	Oval	1938
Inns and 336 runs	West Indies v India	Calcutta	1958-59
Inns and 332 runs	Australia v England	Brisbane[2]	1946-47
Inns and 285 runs	England v India	Lord's	1974
Inns and 259 runs	Australia v South Africa	Port Elizabeth	1949-50
Inns and 237 runs	England v West Indies	Oval	1957
Inns and 230 runs	England v Australia	Adelaide	1891-92
Inns and 226 runs	Australia v India	Brisbane[2]	1947-48
Inns and 226 runs	West Indies v England	Lord's	1973
Inns and 225 runs	England v Australia	Melbourne	1911-12
Inns and 222 runs	Australia v New Zealand	Hobart	1993-94
Inns and 217 runs	England v Australia	Oval	1886
Inns and 217 runs	Australia v West Indies	Brisbane[1]	1930-31
Inns and 215 runs	England v New Zealand	Auckland	1962-63
Inns and 208 runs	South Africa v Sri Lanka	Colombo (SSC)	1993-94
Inns and 207 runs	England v India	Manchester	1952
Inns and 202 runs	England v South Africa	Cape Town	1888-89
Inns and 200 runs	Australia v England	Melbourne	1936-37
675 runs	England v Australia	Brisbane[1]	1928-29
562 runs	Australia v England	Oval	1934
530 runs	Australia v South Africa	Melbourne	1910-11
425 runs	West Indies v England	Manchester	1976
409 runs	Australia v England	Lord's	1948
408 runs	West Indies v Australia	Adelaide	1979-80
382 runs	Australia v England	Adelaide	1894-95
382 runs	Australia v West Indies	Sydney	1968-69
377 runs	Australia v England	Sydney	1920-21
365 runs	Australia v England	Melbourne	1936-37
356 runs	South Africa v England	Lord's	1994
348 runs	Australia v Pakistan	Melbourne	1976-77
343 runs	West Indies v Australia	Bridgetown	1990-91
338 runs	England v Australia	Adelaide	1932-33
326 runs	West Indies v England	Lord's	1950
323 runs	South Africa v Australia	Port Elizabeth	1969-70
322 runs	England v Australia	Brisbane[2]	1936-37
312 runs	England v South Africa	Cape Town	1956-57
308 runs	Australia v England	Melbourne	1907-08
307 runs	Australia v England	Sydney	1924-25
307 runs	South Africa v Australia	Johannesburg[3]	1969-70
301 runs	Pakistan v Sri Lanka	Colombo (PSS)	1994-95
300 runs	Australia v India	Perth	1991-92

VICTORY LOSING FEWEST WICKETS

TWO WICKETS

England (531-2d) v South Africa (273 & 240)	Lord's	1924
England (267-2d) v New Zealand (67 & 129)	Leeds	1958
England (459-2d) v India (165 & 216)	Birmingham	1974

RESULTS BY NARROW MARGINS

TIED

Australia v West Indies	Brisbane[2]	1960-61
India v Australia	Madras[1]	1986-87

WON BY ONE WICKET

		10th Wicket Partnership	
England v Australia	Oval	15*	1902
South Africa v England	Johannesburg[1]	48*	1905-06
England v Australia	Melbourne	39*	1907-08
England v South Africa	Cape Town	5*	1922-23
Australia v West Indies	Melbourne	38*	1951-52
New Zealand v West Indies	Dunedin	4*	1979-80
		(*unbroken)	

WON BY TWO WICKETS

England v Australia	Oval	1890
Australia v England	Sydney	1907-08
†England v South Africa	Durban[2]	1948-49
Australia v West Indies	Melbourne	1960-61
India v Australia	Bombay[2]	1964-65
Australia v India	Perth	1977-78
West Indies v England	Nottingham	1980
New Zealand v Pakistan	Dunedin	1984-85
West Indies v Pakistan	Bridgetown	1987-88
Pakistan v England	Lord's	1992

†*England won by a leg bye off the last possible ball*

FEWER THAN TWENTY RUNS

1	West Indies v Australia	Adelaide	1992-93
3	Australia v England	Manchester	1902
3	England v Australia	Melbourne	1982-83
5	South Africa v Australia	Sydney	1993-94
6	Australia v England	Sydney	1884-85
7	Australia v England	Oval	1882
10	England v Australia	Sydney	1894-95
11	Australia v England	Adelaide	1924-25
12	England v Australia	Adelaide	1928-29
13	England v Australia	Sydney	1886-87
16	Australia v India	Brisbane[2]	1977-78
16	Pakistan v India	Bangalore	1986-87
16	Australia v Sri Lanka	Colombo (SSC)	1992-93
17	South Africa v England	Johannesburg[3]	1956-57
18	England v Australia	Leeds	1981
19	South Africa v England	Johannesburg[1]	1909-10

At Port-of-Spain in 1934-35, West Indies took England's last second innings wicket with the fifth ball of the last possible over to win by 217 runs.

DRAWS

	Total	Target	Opponents		
India	355-8	361	West Indies	Bombay[2]	1948-49
England	228-9	234	West Indies	Lord's	1963
Australia	339-9	360	West Indies	Adelaide	1968-69
Australia	238-8	246	England	Melbourne	1974-75
India	429-8	438	England	Oval	1979
Australia	230-9	247	New Zealand	Melbourne	1987-88
Pakistan	341-9	372	West Indies	Port-of-Spain	1987-88

VICTORY AFTER FOLLOWING ON

England (325 & 437) beat Australia (586 & 166) by 10 runs	Sydney	1894-95
England (174 & 356) beat Australia (401-9d & 111) by 18 runs	Leeds	1981

LONGEST MATCHES

10 days	South Africa v England	Durban[2]	1938-39
9 days	West Indies v England	Kingston	1929-30
8 days	Australia v England	Melbourne	1928-29

MATCHES COMPLETED IN TWO DAYS

England (101 & 77) v Australia (63 & 122)	Oval	1882
England (53 & 62) v Australia (116 & 60)	Lord's	1888
England (317) v Australia (80 & 100)	Oval	1888
England (172) v Australia (81 & 70)	Manchester	1888
South Africa (83 & 129) v England (148 & 67-2)	Port Elizabeth	1888-89
South Africa (47 & 43) v England (292)	Cape Town	1888-89
England (100 & 95-8) v Australia (92 & 102)	Oval	1890
South Africa (93 & 30) v England (185 & 226)	Port Elizabeth	1895-96
South Africa (115 & 117) v England (265)	Cape Town	1895-96
England (176 & 14-0) v South Africa (95 & 93)	Oval	1912
Australia (448) v South Africa (265 & 95)	Manchester	1912
England (112 & 147) v Australia (232 & 30-0)	Nottingham	1921
Australia (328-8d) v West Indies (99 & 107)	Melbourne	1930-31
South Africa (157 & 98) v Australia (439)	Johannesburg[1]	1935-36
New Zealand (42 & 54) v Australia (199-8d)	Wellington	1945-46

COMPLETE SIDE DISMISSED TWICE IN A DAY

		Day	
India (58 & 82) v England	Manchester	3rd	1952

MOST RUNS IN ONE DAY

BY ONE TEAM

			Day	
503-2	England v South Africa	Lord's	2nd	1924
494-6	Australia v South Africa	Sydney	1st	1910-11
475-2	Australia v England	Oval	1st	1934
471-8	England v India	Oval	1st	1936
458-3	Australia v England	Leeds	1st	1930
455-1	Australia v England	Leeds	2nd	1934
450-10	Australia v South Africa	Johannesburg[1]	1st	1921-22

BY BOTH TEAMS

588-6	England (398-6) v India (190-0)	Manchester	2nd	1936
522-2	England (503-2) v South Africa (19-0)	Lord's	2nd	1924
508-8	England (221-2) v South Africa (287-6)	Oval	3rd	1935
496-4	England (437-4) v Pakistan (59-0)	Nottingham	2nd	1954
491-7	New Zealand (29-1 & 195-2) v England (267-4d)	Leeds	3rd	1949
473-4	England (264-1) v South Africa (209-3)	Oval	3rd	1929
471-9	England (244-2) v Australia (227-7)	Oval	3rd	1921
469-7	England (366-3) v West Indies (103-4)	Oval	3rd	1939
464-11	Australia (448) v South Africa (16-1)	Manchester	1st	1912
458-12	Australia (155-5) v West Indies (303-7)	Sydney	5th	1968-69

FEWEST RUNS IN A FULL DAY'S PLAY

			Day	
95	Australia (80) v Pakistan (15-2)	Karachi[1]	1st	1956-57
104	Pakistan (104-5) v Australia	Karachi[1]	4th	1959-60
106	England (92-2 to 198 out) v Australia	Brisbane[2]	4th	1958-59
112	Australia (138-6 to 187 out) v Pakistan (63-1)	Karachi[1]	4th	1956-57
115	Australia (116-7 to 165 out & 66-5) v Pakistan	Karachi[1]	4th	1988-89
117	India (117-5) v Australia	Madras[2]	1st	1956-57
117	New Zealand (6-0 to 123-4) v Sri Lanka	Colombo (SSC)	5th	1983-84

In England:

151	England (175-2 to 289 out) v New Zealand (37-7)	Lord's	3rd	1978

MOST WICKETS IN ONE DAY

			Day	
27	England (18-3 to 53 out & 62) v Australia (60)	Lord's	2nd	1888
25	Australia (112 & 48-5) v England (61)	Melbourne	1st	1901-02

MOST WICKETS BEFORE LUNCH

			Day	
18	Australia (35-2 to 81 out & 70) v England	Manchester	2nd	1888

NO WICKETS IN A FULL DAY'S PLAY

		Day	
England (283-0) v Australia	Melbourne	3rd	1924-25
West Indies (187-6 to 494-6) v Australia	Bridgetown	4th	1954-55
India (234-0) v New Zealand	Madras²	1st	1955-56
West Indies (147-1 to 504-1) v Pakistan	Kingston	3rd	1957-58
West Indies (279-3 to 486-3) v England†	Bridgetown	5th	1959-60
Australia (263-0) v West Indies	Bridgetown	1st	1964-65
West Indies (310-7 to 365-7d) v New Zealand (163-0)	Georgetown	3rd	1971-72
India (70-1 to 361-1d) v West Indies (15-0)	Calcutta	4th	1978-79
India (178-2 to 395-2) v England	Madras¹	2nd	1981-82
Sri Lanka (83-3 to 323-3) v Pakistan	Colombo (PSS)	5th	1985-86
Australia (310-0) v England	Nottingham	1st	1989

†*G.St A.Sobers (226) and F.M.M.Worrell (197*) added 399 for the fourth wicket in the longest partnership in Test cricket (579 minutes) and remain the only pair of batsmen to bat throughout two consecutive days of Test cricket, although the final hour of the fourth day was lost to rain and a rest day intervened.*

The following pairs of batsmen have batted throughout one full day's play in the above matches: J.B.Hobbs and H.Sutcliffe (1924-25), D.St E.Atkinson and C.C.Depeiza (1954-55), M.H.Mankad and Pankaj Roy (1955-56), C.C.Hunte and G.St A.Sobers (1957-58), W.M.Lawry and R.B.Simpson (1964-65), G.R.Viswanath and Yashpal Sharma (1981-82), A.P.Gurusinha and A.Ranatunga (1985-86), and G.R.Marsh and M.A.Taylor (1989).

BATSMEN'S MATCHES

Over 60 runs per wicket

Runs/Wkt	Runs-Wkts			
109.30	1093-10	India v New Zealand	Delhi	1955-56
99.40	994-10	West Indies v New Zealand	Georgetown	1971-72
86.87	695-8	New Zealand v England	Wellington	1987-88
83.25	999-12	Pakistan v Australia	Faisalabad	1979-80
82.27	905-11	England v Pakistan	Birmingham	1992
81.93	1229-15	West Indies v England	St John's	1993-94
80.53	1208-15	Pakistan v India	Lahore²	1989-90
79.53	1034-13	Pakistan v Sri Lanka	Faisalabad	1985-86
78.25	1252-16	India v West Indies	Calcutta	1987-88
73.37	1174-16	Pakistan v India	Faisalabad	1984-85
73.06	1096-15	India v West Indies	Kanpur	1978-79
70.61	1271-18	England v Australia	Manchester	1964
68.33	1640-24	West Indies v Australia	Bridgetown	1964-65
66.95	1406-21	West Indies v Pakistan	Kingston	1957-58
65.35	1307-20	England v Australia	Manchester	1934
65.00	1235-19	India v West Indies	Bombay²	1948-49
64.75	1036-16	India v New Zealand	Hyderabad	1955-56
64.52	1226-19	Australia v West Indies	Sydney	1992-93
64.47	1096-17	India v Sri Lanka	Kanpur	1986-87
63.66	1528-24	West Indies v England	Port-of-Spain	1953-54
63.41	1078-17	India v Australia	Bombay	1986-87
62.33	1496-24	England v Australia	Nottingham	1938
62.11	1118-18	New Zealand v Pakistan	Auckland	1988-89
62.00	1116-18	West Indies v England	Bridgetown	1959-60
61.86	1423-23	England v India	Oval	1990
61.52	1046-17	India v Pakistan	Madras²	1960-61

Runs/Wkt	Runs-Wkts			
60.94	1158-19	India v England	Kanpur	1984-85
60.62	1455-24	New Zealand v Australia	Wellington	1973-74
60.57	1272-21	Pakistan v India	Faisalabad	1978-79
60.45	1209-20	Australia v England	Adelaide	1986-87
60.20	1505-25	New Zealand v India	Auckland	1989-90
60.00	600-10	Australia v South Africa	Melbourne	1993-94

HIGHEST SCORES FOR EACH BATTING POSITION

No.					
1	364	L.Hutton	England v Australia	Oval	1938
2	325	A.Sandham	England v West Indies	Kingston	1929-30
3	375	B.C.Lara	West Indies v England	St John's	1993-94
4	307	R.M.Cowper	Australia v England	Melbourne	1965-66
5	304	D.G.Bradman	Australia v England	Leeds	1934
6	250	K.D.Walters	Australia v New Zealand	Christchurch	1976-77
7	270	D.G.Bradman	Australia v England	Melbourne	1936-37
8	209	Imtiaz Ahmed	Pakistan v New Zealand	Lahore[1]	1955-56
9	173	I.D.S.Smith	New Zealand v India	Auckland	1989-90
10	117	W.W.Read	England v Australia	Oval	1884
11	68*	R.O.Collinge	New Zealand v Pakistan	Auckland	1972-73

HIGHEST SCORE AT THE FALL OF EACH WICKET

1st	413	India (537-3d) v New Zealand	Madras[2]	1955-56
2nd	533	West Indies (790-3d) v Pakistan	Kingston	1957-58
3rd	615	New Zealand (671-4) v Sri Lanka	Wellington	1990-91
4th	671	New Zealand (671-4) v Sri Lanka	Wellington	1990-91
5th	720	England (849) v West Indies	Kingston	1929-30
6th	770	England (903-7d) v Australia	Oval	1938
7th	876	England (903-7d) v Australia	Oval	1938
8th	813	England (849) v West Indies	Kingston	1929-30
9th	821	England (849) v West Indies	Kingston	1929-30
10th	849	England (849) v West Indies	Kingston	1929-30

LOWEST SCORE AT THE FALL OF EACH WICKET

1st	0	Numerous instances		
2nd	0			
3rd	0	Australia (32-7d) v England	Brisbane[2]	1950-51
		India (165) v England	Leeds	1952
4th	0	India (165) v England	Leeds	1952
5th	6	India (98) v England	Oval	1952
6th	7	Australia (70) v England	Manchester	1888
7th	14	Australia (44) v England	Oval	1896
8th	19	Australia (44) v England	Oval	1896
9th	25	Australia (44) v England	Oval	1896
10th	26	New Zealand (26) v England	Auckland	1954-55

MOST HUNDREDS IN AN INNINGS

5	Australia (758-8d) v West Indies	Kingston	1954-55
4	England (658-8d) v Australia	Nottingham	1938
4	West Indies (631) v India	Delhi	1948-49
4	Pakistan (652) v India	Faisalabad	1982-83
4	West Indies (550) v India	St John's	1982-83

The record number of fifties in a Test innings is seven by England (627-9d) v Australia at Manchester in 1934.

MOST HUNDREDS IN A MATCH (BOTH TEAMS)

7	England (4) v Australia (3)	Nottingham	1938
7	West Indies (2) v Australia (5)	Kingston	1954-55

The record number of fifties in a Test match is 17 by Australia (10) and West Indies (7) at Adelaide in 1968-69.

MOST HUNDREDS IN A SERIES (ONE TEAM)

		Venue	Tests	
12	Australia v West Indies	West Indies	5	1954-55
12	Pakistan v India	Pakistan	6	1982-83
11	England v South Africa	South Africa	5	1938-39
11	West Indies v India	India	5	1948-49
11	Australia v South Africa	South Africa	5	1949-50
11	India v West Indies	India	6	1978-79

MOST HUNDREDS IN A SERIES (BOTH TEAMS)

		Venue	Tests	
21	West Indies (9) v Australia (12)	West Indies	5	1954-55
17	Australia (9) v England (8)	Australia	5	1928-29
17	South Africa (6) v England (11)	South Africa	5	1938-39
17	Pakistan (12) v India (5)	Pakistan	6	1982-83
16	India (5) v West Indies (11)	India	5	1948-49
16	Australia (10) v West Indies (6)	Australia	5	1968-69
16	Australia (10) v West Indies (6)	Australia	6	1975-76
15	Australia (10) v England (5)	Australia	5	1946-47
15	England (9) v India (6)	England	3	1990

TEAM UNCHANGED THROUGHOUT A SERIES

Tests		Venue	
5	England v Australia	Australia	1884-85
5	South Africa v England	South Africa	1905-06
5	West Indies v Australia	West Indies	1990-91
4	England v Australia	Australia	1881-82
3	Australia v England	England	1884
3	Australia v England	England	1893
3	Pakistan v New Zealand	Pakistan	1964-65
3	India v England	England	1971
3	Australia v New Zealand	New Zealand	1981-82
3	India v England	India	1992-93
3	India v Sri Lanka	India	1993-94
3	South Africa v Australia	South Africa	1993-94

MOST PLAYERS ENGAGED BY ONE SIDE IN A SERIES

		Venue	
30 in 5 Tests	England v Australia	England	1921
29 in 6 Tests	England v Australia	England	1989
28 in 5 Tests	Australia v England	Australia	1884-85
27 in 4 Tests	West Indies v England	West Indies	1929-30
26 in 5 Tests	India v Pakistan	India	1952-53
25 in 4 Tests	England v West Indies	England	1950
25 in 5 Tests	England v Australia	England	1909
25 in 5 Tests	England v South Africa	England	1935
25 in 5 Tests	England v South Africa	England	1955

South Africa used 20 players in the three-match rubber of 1895-96 against England in South Africa.

WINNING EVERY TEST IN A SERIES

Minimum: 4 matches		Venue	Tests
1920-21	Australia v England	Australia	5
1931-32	Australia v South Africa	Australia	5
1959	England v India	England	5
1961-62	West Indies v India	West Indies	5
1967-68	Australia v India	Australia	4
1969-70	South Africa v Australia	South Africa	4
1984	West Indies v England	England	5
1985-86	West Indies v England	West Indies	5

The following countries won six-match series in Australia by five Tests to one: Australia (v West Indies 1975-76); England (v Australia 1978-79).

MOST CONSECUTIVE WINS

11	West Indies	Bridgetown 1983-84 to Adelaide 1984-85
8	Australia	Sydney 1920-21 to Leeds 1921
7	England	Melbourne 1884-85 to Sydney 1887-88
7	England	Lord's 1928 to Adelaide 1928-29
7	West Indies	Bridgetown 1984-85 to St John's 1985-86
7	West Indies	Lord's 1988 to Melbourne 1988-89
6	England	Oval 1888 to Oval 1890
6	England	Leeds 1957 to Manchester 1958
6	West Indies	Port-of-Spain 1961-62 to Manchester 1963

MOST CONSECUTIVE MATCHES WITHOUT DEFEAT

27	West Indies	Sydney 1981-82 to Melbourne 1984-85
26	England	Lord's 1968 to Manchester 1971
25	Australia	Wellington 1945-46 to Adelaide 1950-51
18	England	Christchurch 1958-59 to Birmingham 1961
17	Australia	Madras[2] 1956-57 to Delhi 1959-60
17	India	Kandy 1985-86 to Ahmedabad 1986-87
16	Australia	Sydney 1920-21 to Adelaide 1924-25
16	Pakistan	Karachi[1] 1986-87 to Port-of-Spain 1987-88
15	England	Melbourne 1911-12 to Port Elizabeth 1913-14
15	Pakistan	Wellington 1972-73 to Adelaide 1976-77
15	India	Lord's 1979 to Calcutta 1979-80
15	West Indies	Christchurch 1979-80 to Kingston 1980-81
14	Australia	Sydney 1988-89 to Sydney 1989-90
13	India	Port-of-Spain 1952-53 to Madras[2] 1955-56
13	Australia	Oval 1972 to Wellington 1973-74
12	England	Oval 1938 to Oval 1946
12	Pakistan	Manchester 1954 to Bridgetown 1957-58
12	England	Oval 1966 to Georgetown 1967-68
12	Pakistan	Karachi[1] 1982-83 to Nagpur 1983-84
12	India	Cape Town 1992-93 to Hamilton 1993-94

MOST CONSECUTIVE DEFEATS

8	South Africa	Port Elizabeth 1888-89 to Cape Town 1898-99 (*their first 8 Tests*)
8	England	Sydney 1920-21 to Leeds 1921
7	Australia	Melbourne 1884-85 to Sydney 1887-88
7	England	Lord's 1950 to Adelaide 1950-51
7	India	Leeds 1967 to Sydney 1967-68
7	England	Kingston 1985-86 to Leeds 1986
7	England	Oval 1992 to Lord's 1993
6	South Africa	Melbourne 1910-11 to Lord's 1912
6	New Zealand	Johannesburg[2] 1953-54 to Lahore[1] 1955-56
6	India	Nottingham 1959 to Delhi 1959-60
6	Australia	Bridgetown 1983-84 to Adelaide 1984-85

MOST CONSECUTIVE MATCHES WITHOUT VICTORY

44	New Zealand	Christchurch 1929-30 to Wellington 1955-56
31	India	Bangalore 1981-82 to Faisalabad 1984-85
28	South Africa	Leeds 1935 to Port Elizabeth 1949-50
24	India	Lord's 1932 to Kanpur 1951-52
23	New Zealand	Auckland 1962-63 to Dunedin 1967-68
22	Pakistan	Lahore[1] 1958-59 to Christchurch 1964-65
21	Sri Lanka	Colombo (PSS) 1985-86 to Moratuwa 1992-93
20	West Indies	Wellington 1968-69 to Port-of-Spain 1972-73
18	New Zealand	Dacca 1969-70 to Wellington 1973-74
18	England	Sydney 1986-87 to Oval 1988
16	South Africa	Melbourne 1910-11 to Cape Town 1921-22
16	Pakistan	Lord's 1967 to Wellington 1972-73
14	India	Madras[2] 1956-57 to Delhi 1959-60
14	Australia	Perth 1985-86 to Melbourne 1986-87
14	India	Georgetown 1988-89 to Oval 1990
13	India	Madras[1] 1952-53 to Hyderabad 1955-56
13	England	Wellington 1983-84 to Bombay[3] 1984-85
13	Sri Lanka	Colombo (PSS) 1981-82 to Colombo (SSC) 1985-86
12	South Africa	Cape Town 1922-23 to Durban[2] 1927-28
12	England	Leeds 1963 to Oval 1964
12	England	Nottingham 1980 to Lord's 1981
12	New Zealand	Nottingham 1990 to Wellington 1991-92

MOST CONSECUTIVE DRAWS

10	West Indies	Georgetown 1970-71 to Bridgetown 1972-73
9	India	Port-of-Spain 1952-53 to Hyderabad 1955-56
9	India	Calcutta 1959-60 to Delhi 1961-62

DRAWING EVERY TEST IN A FIVE-MATCH SERIES

1954-55	Pakistan v India
1960-61	India v Pakistan
1963-64	India v England
1971-72	West Indies v New Zealand

ELEVEN BATSMEN REACHING DOUBLE FIGURES IN AN INNINGS

		Venue	Lowest Score
1894-95	England (475) v Australia	Melbourne	11
1905-06	South Africa (385) v England	Johannesburg[1]	10
1928-29	England (636) v Australia	Sydney	11
1931-32	South Africa (358) v Australia	Melbourne	10*
1947-48	Australia (575-9d) v India	Melbourne	11
1952-53	India (397) v Pakistan	Calcutta	11
1967-68	India (359) v New Zealand	Dunedin	12
1976-77	India (524-9d) v New Zealand	Kanpur	10*
1992-93	Australia (471) v Sri Lanka	Colombo (SSC)	10*

NO BATSMAN REACHING DOUBLE FIGURES IN A COMPLETED INNINGS

South Africa (30 – highest score 7) v England	Birmingham	1924

ONLY FOUR BOWLERS IN AN INNINGS OF OVER 400 RUNS

	Opponents		
Australia	England (403-8d)	Oval	1921
South Africa	England (421-8)	Oval	1924

Only Four Bowlers in an Innings of Over 400 Runs

	Opponents		
Australia	England (403-8d)	Oval	1921
New Zealand	England (482)	Oval	1949
England	Australia (426)	Sydney	1950-51
India	England (419-9d)	Lord's	1979
India	Australia (528)	Adelaide	1980-81
Australia	England (404)	Manchester	1981
England	India (428)	Bangalore	1981-82
Sri Lanka	Pakistan (500-7d)	Lahore[2]	1981-82
Pakistan	Australia (454-6d)	Sydney	1983-84
Australia	West Indies (468-8d)	Port-of-Spain	1983-84
Australia	West Indies (498)	St John's	1983-84
Australia	West Indies (416)	Perth	1984-85
Australia	England (456)	Nottingham	1985
Pakistan	England (447)	Manchester	1987
New Zealand	India (482)	Auckland	1989-90
England	West Indies (446)	Bridgetown	1989-90
England	West Indies (446)	St John's	1989-90
England	Australia (408)	Birmingham	1993

ELEVEN BOWLERS IN AN INNINGS

England	Australia (551)	Oval	1884
Australia	Pakistan (382-2)	Faisalabad	1979-80

TWENTY BOWLERS IN A MATCH

South Africa (501-7d, 346) v England (442, 15-0)	Cape Town	1964-65

EXTRAS BEING HIGHEST SCORER IN A COMPLETED INNINGS

	Total	*Highest Score*	Extras	*Opponents*		
South Africa	58	13	17	England	Lord's	1912
South Africa	30	7	11	England	Birmingham	1924
New Zealand	97	19	20	England	Nottingham	1973
England	126	24	25	West Indies	Manchester	1976
England	227	33	46	Pakistan	Lord's	1982
Australia	200	29	36	West Indies	St John's	1983-84
England	315	47	59	West Indies	Port-of-Spain	1985-86
New Zealand	160	33	38	Pakistan	Lahore[2]	1990-91
Australia	248	47	53	West Indies	Georgetown	1990-91
New Zealand	93	19	22	Pakistan	Hamilton	1992-93

MOST EXTRAS IN AN INNINGS

71 (B 21, LB 8, W 4, NB 38) Pakistan (435) v West Indies	Georgetown	1987-88

MOST BYES

37	Australia (327) v England	Oval	1934

MOST LEG BYES

30	West Indies (411-5d) v England	Manchester	1976

MOST WIDES

15	India (288) v Pakistan	Faisalabad	1989-90
13	England (227) v Pakistan	Lord's	1982

MOST NO-BALLS (Off which no runs were scored by batsmen)

40	England (310) v West Indies	St John's	1985-86
40	Australia (515) v West Indies	Adelaide	1988-89

MOST EXTRAS IN A MATCH

173 (B 37, LB 31, W 2, NB 103) West Indies v Pakistan   Bridgetown   1976-77

The highest total without an extra is Pakistan's 328 v India at Lahore in 1954-55.

UNUSUAL DISMISSALS

HANDLED THE BALL

W.R.Endean (3)	SA v E	Cape Town	1956-57
A.M.J.Hilditch (29)	A v P	Perth	1978-79
Mohsin Khan (58)	P v A	Karachi[1]	1982-83
D.L.Haynes (55)	WI v I	Bombay[3]	1983-84
G.A.Gooch (133)	E v A	Manchester	1993

HIT THE BALL TWICE
No instance

OBSTRUCTING THE FIELD

L.Hutton (27)	E v SA	Oval	1951

RUN OUT BY THE BOWLER (while backing up before the ball had been bowled)

W.A.Brown (18) by M.H.Mankad	A v I	Sydney	1947-48
I.R.Redpath (9) by C.C.Griffith	A v WI	Adelaide	1968-69
D.W.Randall (13) by E.J.Chatfield	E v NZ	Christchurch	1977-78
Sikander Bakht (0) by A.G.Hurst	P v A	Perth	1978-79

STUMPED BY A SUBSTITUTE

S.J.Snooke by N.C.Tufnell (sub for H. Strudwick)	SA v E	Durban[1]	1909-10
Pervez Sajjad by B.E.Congdon (sub for A.E.Dick)	P v NZ	Lahore[2]	1964-65

SIMILARITY OF DISMISSAL

TEN BATSMEN CAUGHT IN AN INNINGS

Australia v England	Melbourne	1903-04
South Africa v Australia	Melbourne	1931-32
England v South Africa	Durban[2]	1948-49
New Zealand v England	Leeds	1949
England v Pakistan	Oval	1954
England v Australia	Melbourne	1958-59
West Indies v Australia	Sydney	1960-61
New Zealand v India	Wellington	1967-68
New Zealand v West Indies	Auckland	1968-69
New Zealand v India	Bombay[2]	1969-70
India v West Indies	Port-of-Spain	1970-71
India v England	Lord's	1971
Australia v England	Nottingham	1972
England v India	Madras[1]	1972-73
England v West Indies	Lord's	1973
Australia v New Zealand	Auckland	1973-74
New Zealand v Pakistan	Auckland	1978-79
†England v Australia	Brisbane[2]	1982-83
England v Australia	Melbourne	1982-83
India v West Indies	Bridgetown	1982-83
West Indies v India	Bridgetown	1982-83
Sri Lanka v Australia	Kandy	1982-83
England v New Zealand	Christchurch	1987-88
England v West Indies	Oval	1988
India v New Zealand	Hyderabad	1988-89
West Indies v Australia	Bridgetown	1990-91
Australia v India	Perth	1991-92
India v Australia	Perth	1991-92
India v South Africa	Port Elizabeth	1992-93
West Indies v England	Bridgetown	1993-94

†Australia held nine catches in England's second innings to become the only side to hold 19 catches in a Test.

Similarity of Dismissal

MOST BATSMEN CAUGHT IN A MATCH
33	Australia v India	Perth	1991-92
32	England v Pakistan	Leeds	1971

MOST BATSMEN BOWLED IN AN INNINGS
9	South Africa v England	Cape Town	1888-89

MOST BATSMEN BOWLED IN A MATCH
23	South Africa v England	Port Elizabeth	1895-96

MOST BATSMEN LBW IN AN INNINGS
6	England v South Africa	Leeds	1955
6	England v West Indies	Kingston	1959-60
6	England v Pakistan	Karachi[1]	1977-78
6	West Indies v England	Kingston	1985-86
6	Pakistan v Australia	Melbourne	1989-90
6	India v Sri Lanka	Chandigarh	1990-91
6	Pakistan v Sri Lanka	Faisalabad	1991-92
6	New Zealand v Pakistan	Hamilton	1992-93
6	South Africa v Australia	Durban[2]	1993-94

MOST BATSMEN LBW IN A MATCH
17	West Indies v Pakistan	Port-of-Spain	1992-93
14	Pakistan v Sri Lanka	Faisalabad	1991-92
13	New Zealand v England	Auckland	1991-92
12	New Zealand v West Indies	Dunedin	1979-80
12	England v West Indies	Lord's	1984

MOST BATSMEN RUN OUT IN AN INNINGS
4	India v Pakistan	Peshawar	1954-55
4	Australia v West Indies	Adelaide	1968-69

MOST BATSMEN RUN OUT IN A MATCH
7	Australia v Pakistan	Melbourne	1972-73

MOST BATSMEN STUMPED IN AN INNINGS
5	West Indies v India (by K.S.More)	Madras[1]	1987-88

MOST BATSMEN STUMPED IN A MATCH
6	Australia v England	Sydney	1894-95
6	India v England	Madras[1]	1951-52
6	West Indies v India (by K.S.More)	Madras[1]	1987-88

INDIVIDUAL RECORDS – BATTING

2000 RUNS IN TESTS

ENGLAND

	M	I	Runs	Opponents A	SA	WI	NZ	I	P	SL
G.A.Gooch	113	205	**8655**	2387	139	2197	1148	1725	683	376
D.I.Gower	117	204	**8231**	3269	–	1149	1051	1391	1185	186
G.Boycott	108	193	**8114**	2945	373	2205	916	1084	591	–
M.C.Cowdrey	114	188	**7624**	2433	1021	1751	1133	653	633	–
W.R.Hammond	85	140	**7249**	2852	2188	639	1015	555	–	–
L.Hutton	79	138	**6971**	2428	1564	1661	777	522	19	–
K.F.Barrington	82	131	**6806**	2111	989	1042	594	1355	715	–
D.C.S.Compton	78	131	**5807**	1842	2205	592	510	205	453	–
J.B.Hobbs	61	102	**5410**	3636	1562	212	–	–	–	–
I.T.Botham	102	161	**5200**	1673	–	792	846	1201	647	41
J.H.Edrich	77	127	**5138**	2644	7	792	840	494	361	–
T.W.Graveney	79	123	**4882**	1075	234	1532	293	805	943	–
A.J.Lamb	79	139	**4656**	1138	–	1342	941	877	180	178
H.Sutcliffe	54	84	**4555**	2741	1336	206	250	22	–	–
P.B.H.May	66	106	**4537**	1566	906	986	603	356	120	–
E.R.Dexter	62	102	**4502**	1358	585	866	477	467	749	–
A.P.E.Knott	95	149	**4389**	1682	–	994	352	685	676	–
M.W.Gatting	74	129	**4227**	1479	–	258	435	1155	853	47
R.A.Smith	53	97	**3677**	1074	–	1028	485	507	314	269
D.L.Amiss	50	88	**3612**	305	–	1130	433	965	779	–
A.W.Greig	58	93	**3599**	1303	–	795	267	883	351	–
E.H.Hendren	51	83	**3525**	1740	876	909	–	–	–	–
F.E.Woolley	64	98	**3283**	1664	1354	–	235	30	–	–
K.W.R.Fletcher	59	96	**3272**	661	–	528	578	874	586	45
A.J.Stewart	43	78	**2982**	602	226	716	673	146	397	222
M.A.Atherton	40	74	**2917**	905	207	589	630	426	145	15
M.Leyland	41	65	**2764**	1705	936	37	–	86	–	–
C.Washbrook	37	66	**2569**	996	938	255	234	146	–	–
B.L.D'Oliveira	44	70	**2484**	865	–	555	258	254	552	–
D.W.Randall	47	79	**2470**	1161	–	1	543	390	375	–
W.J.Edrich	39	63	**2440**	1184	792	94	366	–	4	–
T.G.Evans	91	133	**2439**	783	511	625	142	315	63	–
L.E.G.Ames	47	72	**2434**	675	530	748	410	71	–	–
W.Rhodes	58	98	**2325**	1706	568	51	–	–	–	–
T.E.Bailey	61	91	**2290**	875	552	343	439	–	81	–
M.J.K.Smith	50	78	**2278**	248	561	319	312	639	199	–
P.E.Richardson	34	56	**2061**	526	369	427	317	304	118	–

AUSTRALIA

	M	I	Runs	Opponents E	SA	WI	NZ	I	P	SL
A.R.Border	156	265	**11174**	3548	298	2052	1500	1567	1666	543
G.S.Chappell	87	151	**7110**	2619	–	1400	1076	368	1581	66
D.G.Bradman	52	80	**6996**	5028	806	447	–	715	–	–
D.C.Boon	89	160	**6564**	1991	433	1285	1187	1204	172	292
R.N.Harvey	79	137	**6149**	2416	1625	1054	–	775	279	–
K.D.Walters	74	125	**5357**	1981	258	1196	901	756	265	–
I.M.Chappell	75	136	**5345**	2138	288	1545	486	536	352	–
W.M.Lawry	67	123	**5234**	2233	985	1035	–	892	89	–
R.B.Simpson	62	111	**4869**	1405	980	1043	–	1125	316	–
I.R.Redpath	66	120	**4737**	1512	791	1247	413	475	299	–
K.J.Hughes	70	124	**4415**	1499	–	774	138	988	1016	–
M.A.Taylor	54	97	**4275**	1480	401	678	452	422	390	452
R.W.Marsh	96	150	**3633**	1633	–	707	486	83	724	–
D.M.Jones	52	89	**3631**	1320	–	631	171	681	291	537
A.R.Morris	46	79	**3533**	2080	792	452	–	209	–	–
S.R.Waugh	65	98	**3495**	1341	360	591	695	85	136	287
C.Hill	49	89	**3412**	2660	752	–	–	–	–	–
G.M.Wood	59	112	**3374**	1063	–	1077	393	287	550	4
V.T.Trumper	48	89	**3163**	2263	900	–	–	–	–	–
C.C.McDonald	47	83	**3107**	1043	786	880	–	224	174	–

AUSTRALIA *continued*

	M	I	Runs	Opponents						
				E	SA	WI	NZ	I	P	SI
A.L.Hassett	43	69	3073	1572	748	402	19	332	–	
K.R.Miller	55	87	2958	1511	399	801	30	185	32	
W.W.Armstrong	50	84	2863	2172	691	–	–	–	–	
G.R.Marsh	50	93	2854	1151	–	453	371	526	300	5
K.R.Stackpole	43	80	2807	1164	441	600	197	368	37	
N.C.O'Neill	42	69	2779	1072	285	788	–	416	218	
G.N.Yallop	39	70	2756	709	–	499	–	568	882	9
S.J.McCabe	39	62	2748	1922	621	205	–	–	–	
W.Bardsley	41	66	2469	1487	982	–	–	–	–	
W.M.Woodfull	35	54	2300	1684	421	195	–	–	–	
P.J.P.Burge	42	68	2290	1179	331	229	–	457	94	
S.E.Gregory	58	100	2282	2193	89	–	–	–	–	
R.Benaud	63	97	2201	767	684	462	–	144	144	
M.E.Waugh	36	57	2177	737	349	707	240	83	–	6
C.G.Macartney	35	55	2131	1640	491	–	–	–	–	
W.H.Ponsford	29	48	2122	1558	97	467	–	–	–	
R.M.Cowper	27	46	2061	686	255	417	–	604	99	
I.A.Healy	62	90	2057	574	198	423	253	157	186	26

SOUTH AFRICA

	M	I	Runs	Opponents					
				E	A	WI	NZ	I	SL
B.Mitchell	42	80	3471	2732	573	–	166	–	–
A.D.Nourse	34	62	2960	2037	923	–	–	–	–
H.W.Taylor	42	76	2936	2287	640	–	9	–	–
E.J.Barlow	30	57	2516	742	1149	–	625	–	–
T.L.Goddard	41	78	2516	1193	1090	–	233	–	–
D.J.McGlew	34	64	2440	736	604	–	1100	–	–
J.H.B.Waite	50	86	2405	923	839	–	643	–	–
R.G.Pollock	23	41	2256	750	1453	–	53	–	–
A.W.Nourse	45	83	2234	1415	819	–	–	–	–
R.A.McLean	40	73	2120	1068	480	–	572	–	–

K.C.Wessels has scored 2788 runs in 40 Tests: 1761 runs in 24 Tests for Australia and 1027 runs in 16 Tests for South Africa.

WEST INDIES

	M	I	Runs	Opponents						
				E	A	SA	NZ	I	P	SL
I.V.A.Richards	121	182	8540	2869	2266	–	387	1927	1091	
G.St A.Sobers	93	160	8032	3214	1510	–	404	1920	984	
C.G.Greenidge	108	185	7558	2318	1819	–	882	1678	861	
C.H.Lloyd	110	175	7515	2120	2211	–	234	2344	606	
D.L.Haynes	116	202	7487	2392	2233	81	843	990	928	2
R.B.Kanhai	79	137	6227	2267	1694	–	–	1693	573	
R.B.Richardson	76	130	5445	1311	1946	46	512	871	708	5
E.de C.Weekes	48	81	4455	1313	714	–	478	1495	455	
A.I.Kallicharran	66	109	4399	891	1325	–	365	1229	589	
R.C.Fredericks	59	109	4334	1369	1069	–	537	767	592	
F.M.M.Worrell	51	87	3860	1979	918	–	233	730	–	
C.L.Walcott	44	74	3798	1391	914	–	199	909	385	
P.J.L.Dujon	81	115	3322	798	1176	–	300	806	242	
C.C.Hunte	44	78	3245	1005	927	–	–	670	643	
H.A.Gomes	60	91	3171	801	1122	–	230	806	212	
B.F.Butcher	44	78	3104	1373	810	–	216	572	133	
S.M.Nurse	29	54	2523	1016	820	–	558	129	–	
A.L.Logie	52	78	2470	696	556	–	228	694	296	
G.A.Headley	22	40	2190	1852	336	–	–	2		
J.B.Stollmeyer	32	56	2159	858	417	–	188	696	–	
L.G.Rowe	30	49	2047	742	528	–	598	179	–	

NEW ZEALAND

	M	I	Runs	Opponents							
				E	A	SA	WI	I	P	SL	Z
J.G.Wright	82	148	5334	1518	1277	–	535	804	576	624	–
M.D.Crowe	70	120	5230	1421	1255	–	544	161	973	627	249
B.E.Congdon	61	114	3448	1143	456	–	764	713	372	–	–
J.R.Reid	58	108	3428	953	–	914	212	691	658	–	–
R.J.Hadlee	86	134	3124	798	783	–	389	310	559	285	–

NEW ZEALAND *continued*

	M	I	Runs	Opponents E	A	SA	WI	I	P	SL	Z
G.M.Turner	41	73	2991	510	541	–	855	583	431	71	–
A.H.Jones	37	70	2898	431	808	–	–	401	491	625	142
B.Sutcliffe	42	76	2727	1049	–	455	196	885	142	–	–
M.G.Burgess	50	92	2684	610	279	–	317	725	753	–	–
J.V.Coney	52	85	2668	622	695	–	458	92	528	273	–
G.P.Howarth	47	83	2531	910	468	–	397	216	340	200	–
G.T.Dowling	39	77	2306	517	–	271	277	964	277	–	–
K.R.Rutherford	48	85	2119	373	677	–	41	256	332	259	181

INDIA

	M	I	Runs	Opponents E	A	SA	WI	NZ	P	SL	Z
S.M.Gavaskar	125	214	10122	2483	1550	–	2749	651	2089	600	–
D.B.Vengasarkar	116	185	6868	1589	1304	–	1596	440	1284	655	–
G.R.Viswanath	91	155	6080	1880	1538	–	1455	585	611	11	–
Kapil Dev	131	184	5248	1355	687	202	1079	207	1054	588	76
M.Amarnath	69	113	4378	656	773	–	1076	407	1080	386	–
M.Azharuddin	62	88	4020	1236	431	120	298	519	627	738	51
R.J.Shastri	80	121	3830	1026	622	59	847	182	801	282	11
P.R.Umrigar	59	94	3631	770	227	–	1372	351	911	–	–
V.L.Manjrekar	55	92	3208	1181	377	–	569	507	574	–	–
C.G.Borde	55	97	3061	746	502	–	870	613	330	–	–
Nawab of Pataudi, jr	46	83	2793	946	829	–	352	666	–	–	–
S.M.H.Kirmani	88	124	2759	707	756	–	469	400	422	5	–
F.M.Engineer	46	87	2611	1113	449	–	465	584	–	–	–
Pankaj Roy	43	79	2442	620	432	–	717	301	372	–	–
V.S.Hazare	30	52	2192	803	429	–	737	–	223	–	–
A.L.Wadekar	37	71	2113	840	548	–	230	495	–	–	–
M.H.Mankad	44	72	2109	618	388	–	397	526	180	–	–
C.P.S.Chauhan	40	68	2084	213	878	–	331	224	438	–	–
K.Srikkanth	43	72	2062	365	568	–	204	240	436	249	–
M.L.Jaisimha	39	71	2056	852	434	–	276	268	226	–	–
S.R.Tendulkar	32	45	2023	547	368	202	–	171	215	458	62
D.N.Sardesai	30	55	2001	674	156	–	811	360	–	–	–

PAKISTAN

	M	I	Runs	Opponents E	A	WI	NZ	I	SL	Z
Javed Miandad	124	189	8832	1329	1797	834	1919	2228	582	143
Zaheer Abbas	78	124	5062	1086	1411	259	428	1740	138	–
Mudassar Nazar	76	116	4114	858	893	184	365	1431	383	–
Salim Malik	77	111	4040	1201	357	456	805	719	502	–
Majid Khan	63	106	3931	751	915	821	936	445	63	–
Hanif Mohammad	55	97	3915	1039	548	736	622	970	–	–
Imran Khan	88	126	3807	500	862	775	308	1091	271	–
Mushtaq Mohammad	57	100	3643	1554	409	488	779	413	–	–
Asif Iqbal	58	99	3575	822	758	416	1113	466	–	–
Saeed Ahmed	41	78	2991	791	611	707	422	460	–	–
Wasim Raja	57	92	2821	488	334	919	371	643	66	–
Mohsin Khan	48	79	2709	736	786	48	259	472	408	–
Shoaib Mohammad	42	63	2622	226	263	378	854	608	114	179
Sadiq Mohammad	41	74	2579	820	400	456	740	163	–	–
Ramiz Raja	48	78	2243	485	137	382	185	604	450	–
Imtiaz Ahmed	41	72	2079	488	131	423	284	753	–	–

SRI LANKA

	M	I	Runs	Opponents E	A	SA	WI	NZ	I	P
A.Ranatunga	52	86	2804	322	499	250	31	425	654	623
P.A.de Silva	43	74	2760	187	513	235	68	558	610	589

ZIMBABWE
The leading scorer is A.Flower with 499 runs in 7 Tests.

1000 RUNS IN A CALENDAR YEAR

	Country	Year	Tests	I	NO	HS	Runs	Avge	100
I.V.A.Richards	West Indies	1976	11	19	–	291	1710	90.00	7
S.M.Gavaskar	India	1979	18	27	1	221	1555	59.80	5
G.R.Viswanath	India	1979	17	26	3	179	1388	60.34	5
R.B.Simpson	Australia	1964	14	26	3	311	1381	60.04	3
D.L.Amiss	England	1974	13	22	2	262*	1379	68.95	5
S.M.Gavaskar	India	1983	18	32	4	236*	1310	46.78	5
G.A.Gooch	England	1990	9	17	1	333	1264	79.00	4
D.C.Boon	Australia	1993	16	25	5	164*	1241	62.05	4
M.A.Taylor	Australia	1989†	11	20	1	219	1219	64.15	4
G.St A.Sobers	West Indies	1958	7	12	3	365*	1193	132.55	5
D.B.Vengsarkar	India	1979	18	27	4	146*	1174	51.04	5
K.J.Hughes	Australia	1979	15	28	4	130*	1163	48.45	2
D.C.S.Compton	England	1947	9	15	1	208	1159	82.78	6
C.G.Greenidge	West Indies	1984	14	22	4	223	1149	63.83	4
M.A.Taylor	Australia	1993	15	23	2	170	1106	52.66	4
A.R.Border	Australia	1985	11	20	3	196	1099	64.64	4
D.M.Jones	Australia	1989†	11	18	3	216	1099	73.26	4
I.T.Botham	England	1982	14	22	–	208	1095	49.77	3
K.W.R.Fletcher	England	1973	13	22	4	178	1090	60.55	2
M.Amarnath	India	1983	14	24	1	120	1077	46.82	4
A.R.Border	Australia	1979	14	27	3	162	1073	44.70	3
C.Hill	Australia	1902	12	21	2	142	1061	55.78	2
D.I.Gower	England	1982	14	25	2	114	1061	46.13	1
D.I.Gower	England	1986	14	25		136	1059	44.12	2
W.M.Lawry	Australia	1964	14	27	2	157	1056	42.24	2
S.M.Gavaskar	India	1978	9	15	2	205	1044	80.30	4
G.A.Gooch	England	1991	9	17	1	174	1040	65.00	3
K.F.Barrington	England	1963	12	22	2	132*	1039	51.95	3
E.R.Dexter	England	1962	11	15	1	205	1038	74.14	2
K.F.Barrington	England	1961	10	17	4	172	1032	79.38	4
Mohsin Khan	Pakistan	1982	10	17	3	200	1029	73.50	4
D.G.Bradman	Australia	1948	8	13	4	201	1025	113.88	5
S.M.Gavaskar	India	1976	11	20	1	156	1024	53.89	4
A.R.Border	Australia	1986	11	19	3	140	1000	62.50	5

The earliest date for reaching 1000 runs is 3 May (1983) by M.Amarnath.
†*The year of his debut.*

HIGHEST CAREER BATTING AVERAGES

Qualification: 20 innings

	Country	Tests	I	NO	HS	Runs	Avge	100	50
D.G.Bradman	Australia	52	80	10	334	6996	99.94	29	13
B.C.Lara	West Indies	16	26	–	375	1628	62.61	3	8
R.G.Pollock	South Africa	23	41	4	274	2256	60.97	7	11
G.A.Headley	West Indies	22	40	4	270*	2190	60.83	10	5
H.Sutcliffe	England	54	84	9	194	4555	60.73	16	23
E.Paynter	England	20	31	5	243	1540	59.23	4	7
K.F.Barrington	England	82	131	15	256	6806	58.67	20	35
E.de C.Weekes	West Indies	48	81	5	207	4455	58.61	15	19
W.R.Hammond	England	85	140	16	336*	7249	58.45	22	24
G.St A.Sobers	West Indies	93	160	21	365*	8032	57.78	26	30
J.B.Hobbs	England	61	102	7	211	5410	56.94	15	28
C.L.Walcott	West Indies	44	74	7	220	3798	56.68	15	14
L.Hutton	England	79	138	15	364	6971	56.67	19	33
G.E.Tyldesley	England	14	20	2	122	990	55.00	3	6
C.A.Davis	West Indies	15	29	5	183	1301	54.20	4	4
G.S.Chappell	Australia	87	151	19	247*	7110	53.86	24	31
A.D.Nourse	South Africa	34	62	7	231	2960	53.81	9	14
Javed Miandad	Pakistan	124	189	21	280*	8832	52.57	23	43
J.Ryder	Australia	20	32	5	201*	1394	51.62	3	9
S.M.Gavaskar	India	125	214	16	236*	10122	51.12	34	45
S.R.Tendulkar	India	32	45	5	165	2023	50.57	7	10
A.R.Border	Australia	156	265	44	205	11174	50.56	27	63
I.V.A.Richards	West Indies	121	182	12	291	8540	50.23	24	45
D.C.S.Compton	England	78	131	15	278	5807	50.06	17	28

HIGHEST AGGREGATES IN A SERIES

			Tests	I	NO	HS	Runs	Avge	100	50
D.G.Bradman	A v E	1930	5	7	–	334	974	139.14	4	–
W.R.Hammond	E v A	1928-29	5	9	1	251	905	113.12	4	–
M.A.Taylor	A v E	1989	6	11	1	219	839	83.90	2	5
R.N.Harvey	A v SA	1952-53	5	9	–	205	834	92.66	4	3
I.V.A.Richards	WI v E	1976	4	7	–	291	829	118.42	3	2
C.L.Walcott	WI v A	1954-55	5	10	–	155	827	82.70	5	2
G.St A.Sobers	WI v P	1957-58	5	8	2	365*	824	137.33	3	3
D.G.Bradman	A v E	1936-37	5	9	–	270	810	90.00	3	1
D.G.Bradman	A v SA	1931-32	5	5	1	299*	806	201.50	4	–
B.C.Lara	WI v E	1993-94	5	8	–	375	798	99.75	2	2
E.de C.Weekes	WI v I	1948-49	5	7	–	194	779	111.28	4	2
S.M.Gavaskar	I v WI	1970-71	4	8	3	220	774	154.80	4	3
Mudassar Nazar	P v I	1982-83	6	8	2	231	761	126.83	4	1
D.G.Bradman	A v E	1934	5	8	–	304	758	94.75	2	1
D.C.S.Compton	E v SA	1947	5	8	–	208	753	94.12	4	2
G.A.Gooch	E v I	1990	3	6	–	333	752	125.33	3	2
H.Sutcliffe	E v A	1924-25	5	9	–	176	734	81.55	4	2
G.A.Faulkner	SA v A	1910-11	5	10	–	204	732	73.20	2	5
S.M.Gavaskar	I v WI	1978-79	6	9	1	205	732	91.50	4	1
D.I.Gower	E v A	1985	6	9	–	215	732	81.33	3	1
G.St A.Sobers	WI v E	1966	5	8	1	174	722	103.14	3	2
E.de C.Weekes	WI v I	1952-53	5	8	1	207	716	102.28	3	2
D.G.Bradman	A v I	1947-48	5	6	2	201	715	178.75	4	1
G.St A.Sobers	WI v E	1959-60	5	8	1	226	709	101.28	3	1
G.A.Headley	WI v E	1929-30	4	8	–	223	703	87.87	4	–
G.S.Chappell	A v WI	1975-76	6	11	5	182*	702	117.00	3	3
K.D.Walters	A v WI	1968-69	4	6	–	242	699	116.50	4	2
C.L.Walcott	WI v E	1953-54	5	10	2	220	698	87.25	3	3
A.R.Morris	A v E	1948	5	9	1	196	696	87.00	3	3
E.H.Hendren	E v WI	1929-30	4	8	2	205*	693	115.50	2	5
D.G.Bradman	A v E	1946-47	5	8	1	234	680	97.14	2	3
L.Hutton	E v WI	1953-54	5	8	1	205	677	96.71	2	3
G.A.Gooch	E v A	1993	6	12	–	133	673	56.08	2	4
G.M.Turner	NZ v WI	1971-72	5	8	1	259	672	96.00	2	2
W.M.Lawry	A v WI	1968-69	5	8	–	205	667	83.37	3	2
D.L.Amiss	E v WI	1973-74	5	9	1	262*	663	82.87	3	–
J.B.Hobbs	E v A	1911-12	5	9	1	187	662	82.75	3	1
V.T.Trumper	A v SA	1910-11	5	9	2	214*	661	94.42	2	2
R.N.Harvey	A v SA	1949-50	5	8	3	178	660	132.00	4	1
G.Boycott	E v A	1970-71	5	10	3	142*	657	93.85	2	5
E.Paynter	E v SA	1938-39	5	8	–	243	653	81.62	3	2
R.N.Harvey	A v WI	1954-55	5	7	–	204	650	108.33	3	1
Zaheer Abbas	P v I	1982-83	6	6	1	215	650	130.00	3	–
J.H.Edrich	E v A	1970-71	6	11	2	130	648	72.00	2	4
D.N.Sardesai	I v WI	1970-71	5	8	–	212	642	80.25	3	1
C.H.Lloyd	WI v I	1974-75	5	9	1	242*	636	79.20	2	1
Hanif Mohammad	P v WI	1957-58	5	9	–	337	628	69.77	1	3
K.R.Stackpole	A v E	1970-71	6	12	–	207	627	52.25	2	2
C.C.Hunte	WI v P	1957-58	5	9	1	260	622	77.75	3	–
A.D.Nourse	SA v E	1947	5	9	–	149	621	69.00	2	5
R.B.Richardson	WI v I	1988-89	4	7	–	194	619	88.42	2	3
L.G.Rowe	WI v E	1973-74	5	7	–	302	616	88.00	3	–
B.Sutcliffe	NZ v I	1955-56	5	9	2	230*	611	87.28	2	1
W.R.Hammond	E v SA	1938-39	5	8	1	181	609	87.00	3	2
G.S.Chappell	A v E	1974-75	6	11	–	144	608	55.27	2	5
D.T.Lindsay	SA v A	1966-67	5	7	–	182	606	86.57	3	2
E.J.Barlow	SA v A	1963-64	5	10	2	201	603	75.37	3	1

MOST RUNS IN A MATCH

456	G.A.Gooch (333, 123)	England v India	Lord's	1990
380	G.S.Chappell (247*, 133)	Australia v New Zealand	Wellington	1973-74
375	A.Sandham (325, 50)	England v West Indies	Kingston	1929-30
375	B.C.Lara (375)	West Indies v England	St John's	1993-94
365	G.St A.Sobers (365*)	West Indies v Pakistan	Kingston	1957-58
364	L.Hutton (364)	England v Australia	Oval	1938
354	Hanif Mohammad (17, 337)	Pakistan v West Indies	Bridgetown	1957-58

CARRYING BAT THROUGH A COMPLETED INNINGS

ENGLAND	Score	Total	Opponents		
R.Abel	132*	307	Australia	Sydney	1891-92
P.F.Warner†	132*	237	South Africa	Johannesburg[1]	1898-99
L.Hutton	202*	344	West Indies	Oval	1950
L.Hutton	156*	272	Australia	Adelaide	1950-51
G.Boycott	99*	215	Australia	Perth	1979-80
G.A.Gooch	154*	252	West Indies	Leeds	1991
A.J.Stewart	69*	175	Pakistan	Lord's	1992
AUSTRALIA					
J.E.Barrett†	67*	176	England	Lord's	1890
W.W.Armstrong	159*	309	South Africa	Johannesburg[1]	1902-03
W.Bardsley	193*	383	England	Lord's	1926
W.M.Woodfull	30*	66‡	England	Brisbane[1]	1928-29
W.M.Woodfull	73*	193‡	England	Adelaide	1932-33
W.A.Brown	206*	422	England	Lord's	1938
W.M.Lawry	49*	107	India	Delhi	1969-70
W.M.Lawry	60*	116‡	England	Sydney	1970-71
I.R.Redpath	159*	346	New Zealand	Auckland	1973-74
D.C.Boon	58*	103	New Zealand	Auckland	1985-86
SOUTH AFRICA					
A.B.Tancred	26*	47	England	Cape Town	1888-89
J.W.Zulch	43*	103	England	Cape Town	1909-10
T.L.Goddard	56*	99	Australia	Cape Town	1957-58
D.J.McGlew	127*	292	New Zealand	Durban[2]	1961-62
WEST INDIES					
F.M.M.Worrell	191*	372	England	Nottingham	1957
C.C.Hunte	60*	131	Australia	Port-of-Spain	1964-65
D.L.Haynes	88*	211	Pakistan	Karachi[1]	1986-87
D.L.Haynes	75*	176	England	Oval	1991
D.L.Haynes	143*	382	Pakistan	Port-of-Spain	1992-93
NEW ZEALAND					
G.M.Turner	43*	131	England	Lord's	1969
G.M.Turner	223*	386	West Indies	Kingston	1971-72
INDIA					
S.M.Gavaskar	127*	286	Pakistan	Faisalabad	1982-83
PAKISTAN					
Nazar Mohammad	124*	331	India	Lucknow	1952-53
Mudassar Nazar	152*	323	India	Lahore[2]	1982-83
SRI LANKA					
S.Wettimuny	63*	144	New Zealand	Christchurch	1982-83
ZIMBABWE					
M.H.Dekker	68*	187	Pakistan	Rawalpindi[2]	1993-94

†On debut in Test cricket.
‡Completed innings in which one or more batsmen were retired or absent.
G.M.Turner is the youngest player to carry his bat through a Test match innings; he was 22 years and 63 days old when he first achieved this feat.
Nazar Mohammad and his son Mudassar Nazar are the only related players to achieve this feat at Test level.
D.L.Amiss (262*) batted throughout England's innings of 439-9 against West Indies at Kingston in 1973-74. His unbroken tenth-wicket partnership with R.G.D.Willis (3*) added 40 runs in 53 minutes.
D.L.Haynes (55 and 105) batted throughout both innings for West Indies v New Zealand at Dunedin in 1979-80.

HIGHEST INDIVIDUAL INNINGS

375	B.C.Lara	West Indies v England	St John's	1993-94
365*	G.St A.Sobers	West Indies v Pakistan	Kingston	1957-58
364	L.Hutton	England v Australia	Oval	1938
337	Hanif Mohammad	Pakistan v West Indies	Bridgetown	1957-58
336*	W.R.Hammond	England v New Zealand	Auckland	1932-33

334	D.G.Bradman	Australia v England	Leeds	1930
333	G.A.Gooch	England v India	Lord's	1990
325	A.Sandham	England v West Indies	Kingston	1929-30
311	R.B.Simpson	Australia v England	Manchester	1964
310*	J.H.Edrich	England v New Zealand	Leeds	1965
307	R.M.Cowper	Australia v England	Melbourne	1965-66
304	D.G.Bradman	Australia v England	Leeds	1934
302	L.G.Rowe	West Indies v England	Bridgetown	1973-74
299*	D.G.Bradman	Australia v South Africa	Adelaide	1931-32
299	M.D.Crowe	New Zealand v Sri Lanka	Wellington	1990-91
291	I.V.A.Richards	West Indies v England	Oval	1976
287	R.E.Foster	England v Australia	Sydney	1903-04
285*	P.B.H.May	England v West Indies	Birmingham	1957
280*	Javed Miandad	Pakistan v India	Hyderabad (Pak)	1982-83
278	D.C.S.Compton	England v Pakistan	Nottingham	1954
277	B.C.Lara	West Indies v Australia	Sydney	1992-93
274	R.G.Pollock	South Africa v Australia	Durban[2]	1969-70
274	Zaheer Abbas	Pakistan v England	Birmingham	1971
271	Javed Miandad	Pakistan v New Zealand	Auckland	1988-89
270*	G.A.Headley	West Indies v England	Kingston	1934-35
270	D.G.Bradman	Australia v England	Melbourne	1936-37
268	G.N.Yallop	Australia v Pakistan	Melbourne	1983-84
267	P.A.de Silva	Sri Lanka v New Zealand	Wellington	1990-91
266	W.H.Ponsford	Australia v England	Oval	1934
262*	D.L.Amiss	England v West Indies	Kingston	1973-74
261	F.M.M.Worrell	West Indies v England	Nottingham	1950
260	C.C.Hunte	West Indies v Pakistan	Kingston	1957-58
260	Javed Miandad	Pakistan v England	Oval	1987
259	G.M.Turner	New Zealand v West Indies	Georgetown	1971-72
258	T.W.Graveney	England v West Indies	Nottingham	1957
258	S.M.Nurse	West Indies v New Zealand	Christchurch	1968-69
256	R.B.Kanhai	West Indies v India	Calcutta	1958-59
256	K.F.Barrington	England v Australia	Manchester	1964
255*	D.J.McGlew	South Africa v New Zealand	Wellington	1952-53
254	D.G.Bradman	Australia v England	Lord's	1930
251	W.R.Hammond	England v Australia	Sydney	1928-29
250	K.D.Walters	Australia v New Zealand	Christchurch	1976-77
250	S.F.A.F.Bacchus	West Indies v India	Kanpur	1978-79
247*	G.S.Chappell	Australia v New Zealand	Wellington	1973-74
246*	G.Boycott	England v India	Leeds	1967
244	D.G.Bradman	Australia v England	Oval	1934
243	E.Paynter	England v South Africa	Durban[2]	1938-39
242*	C.H.Lloyd	West Indies v India	Bombay[3]	1974-75
242	K.D.Walters	Australia v West Indies	Sydney	1968-69
240	W.R.Hammond	England v Australia	Lord's	1938
240	Zaheer Abbas	Pakistan v England	Oval	1974
239	G.T.Dowling	New Zealand v India	Christchurch	1967-68
237	F.M.M.Worrell	West Indies v India	Kingston	1952-53
236*	S.M.Gavaskar	India v West Indies	Madras[1]	1983-84
236	E.A.B.Rowan	South Africa v England	Leeds	1951
235*	Zaheer Abbas	Pakistan v India	Lahore[2]	1978-79
235	G.S.Chappell	Australia v Pakistan	Faisalabad	1979-80
234	D.G.Bradman	Australia v England	Sydney	1946-47
234	S.G.Barnes	Australia v England	Sydney	1946-47
232	D.G.Bradman	Australia v England	Oval	1930
232	S.J.McCabe	Australia v England	Nottingham	1938
232	I.V.A.Richards	West Indies v England	Nottingham	1976
231*	W.R.Hammond	England v Australia	Sydney	1936-37
231	A.D.Nourse	South Africa v Australia	Johannesburg[1]	1935-36
231	M.H.Mankad	India v New Zealand	Madras[2]	1955-56
231	Mudassar Nazar	Pakistan v India	Hyderabad	1982-83
230*	B.Sutcliffe	New Zealand v India	Delhi	1955-56
227	W.R.Hammond	England v New Zealand	Christchurch	1932-33
227	V.G.Kambli	India v Zimbabwe	Delhi	1992-93
226	D.G.Bradman	Australia v South Africa	Brisbane[2]	1931-32
226	G.St A.Sobers	West Indies v England	Bridgetown	1959-60
226	C.G.Greenidge	West Indies v Australia	Bridgetown	1990-91
225	R.B.Simpson	Australia v England	Adelaide	1965-66
224	V.G.Kambli	India v England	Bombay[3]	1992-93
223*	G.M.Turner	New Zealand v West Indies	Kingston	1971-72

223	G.A.Headley	West Indies v England	Kingston	1929-30
223	D.G.Bradman	Australia v West Indies	Brisbane[1]	1930-31
223	P.R.Umrigar	India v New Zealand	Hyderabad	1955-56
223	M.H.Mankad	India v New Zealand	Bombay[2]	1955-56
223	C.G.Greenidge	West Indies v England	Manchester	1984
222	G.R.Viswanath	India v England	Madras[1]	1981-82
221	S.M.Gavaskar	India v England	Oval	1979
220	C.L.Walcott	West Indies v England	Bridgetown	1953-54
220	S.M.Gavaskar	India v West Indies	Port-of-Spain	1970-71
219	W.J.Edrich	England v South Africa	Durban[2]	1938-39
219	D.St E.Atkinson	West Indies v Australia	Bridgetown	1954-55
219	M.A.Taylor	Australia v England	Nottingham	1989
218	S.V.Manjrekar	India v Pakistan	Lahore[2]	1989-90
217	W.R.Hammond	England v India	Oval	1936
217	R.B.Kanhai	West Indies v Pakistan	Lahore[1]	1958-59
216*	E.Paynter	England v Australia	Nottingham	1938
216	K.W.R.Fletcher	England v New Zealand	Auckland	1974-75
216	D.M.Jones	Australia v West Indies	Adelaide	1988-89
215	Zaheer Abbas	Pakistan v India	Lahore[2]	1982-83
215	D.I.Gower	England v Australia	Birmingham	1985
214*	V.T.Trumper	Australia v South Africa	Adelaide	1910-11
214*	D.Lloyd	England v India	Birmingham	1974
214*	C.G.Greenidge	West Indies v England	Lord's	1984
214	L.G.Rowe	West Indies v New Zealand	Kingston	1971-72
213	K.J.Hughes	Australia v India	Adelaide	1980-81
213	C.G.Greenidge	West Indies v New Zealand	Auckland	1986-87
212	D.G.Bradman	Australia v England	Adelaide	1936-37
212	D.N.Sardesai	India v West Indies	Kingston	1970-71
211	W.L.Murdoch	Australia v England	Oval	1884
211	J.B.Hobbs	England v South Africa	Lord's	1924
211	Javed Miandad	Pakistan v Australia	Karachi[1]	1988-89
210*	Taslim Arif	Pakistan v Australia	Faisalabad	1979-80
210	W.M.Lawry	Australia v West Indies	Bridgetown	1964-65
210	Qasim Omar	Pakistan v India	Faisalabad	1984-85
210	D.M.Jones	Australia v India	Madras[1]	1986-87
210	G.A.Gooch	England v New Zealand	Nottingham	1994
209*	B.F.Butcher	West Indies v England	Nottingham	1966
209	C.A.Roach	West Indies v England	Georgetown	1929-30
209	Imtiaz Ahmed	Pakistan v New Zealand	Lahore[1]	1955-56
209	R.G.Pollock	South Africa v Australia	Cape Town	1966-67
208	D.C.S.Compton	England v South Africa	Lord's	1947
208	A.D.Nourse	South Africa v England	Nottingham	1951
208	I.T.Botham	England v India	Oval	1982
208	I.V.A.Richards	West Indies v Australia	Melbourne	1984-85
207	E.de C.Weekes	West Indies v India	Port-of-Spain	1952-53
207	K.R.Stackpole	Australia v England	Brisbane[2]	1970-71
207	M.W.Gatting	England v India	Madras[1]	1984-85
206*	W.A.Brown	Australia v England	Lord's	1938
206	M.P.Donnelly	New Zealand v England	Lord's	1949
206	L.Hutton	England v New Zealand	Oval	1949
206	A.R.Morris	Australia v England	Adelaide	1950-51
206	E.de C.Weekes	West Indies v England	Port-of-Spain	1953-54
206	Javed Miandad	Pakistan v New Zealand	Karachi[1]	1976-77
206	Qasim Omar	Pakistan v Sri Lanka	Faisalabad	1985-86
206	R.J.Shastri	India v Australia	Sydney	1991-92
205*	E.H.Hendren	England v West Indies	Port-of-Spain	1929-30
205*	J.Hardstaff, jr	England v India	Lord's	1946
205	R.N.Harvey	Australia v South Africa	Melbourne	1952-53
205	L.Hutton	England v West Indies	Kingston	1953-54
205	E.R.Dexter	England v Pakistan	Karachi[1]	1961-62
205	W.M.Lawry	Australia v West Indies	Melbourne	1968-69
205	S.M.Gavaskar	India v West Indies	Bombay[3]	1978-79
205	A.R.Border	Australia v New Zealand	Adelaide	1987-88
205	Aamir Sohail	Pakistan v England	Manchester	1992
204	G.A.Faulkner	South Africa v Australia	Melbourne	1910-11
204	R.N.Harvey	Australia v West Indies	Kingston	1954-55
204	G.S.Chappell	Australia v India	Sydney	1980-81
203*	Nawab of Pataudi, jr	India v England	Delhi	1963-64
203*	Hanif Mohammad	Pakistan v New Zealand	Lahore[2]	1964-65
203*	Javed Miandad	Pakistan v Sri Lanka	Faisalabad	1985-86

203*	Shoaib Mohammad	Pakistan v India	Lahore[2]	1989-90
203*	Shoaib Mohammad	Pakistan v New Zealand	Karachi[1]	1990-91
203	H.L.Collins	Australia v South Africa	Johannesburg[1]	1921-22
203	D.L.Amiss	England v West Indies	Oval	1976
202*	L.Hutton	England v West Indies	Oval	1950
201*	J.Ryder	Australia v England	Adelaide	1924-25
201*	D.S.B.P.Kuruppu	Sri Lanka v New Zealand	Colombo (CCC)	1986-87
201	S.E.Gregory	Australia v England	Sydney	1894-95
201	D.G.Bradman	Australia v India	Adelaide	1947-48
201	E.J.Barlow	South Africa v Australia	Adelaide	1963-64
201	R.B.Simpson	Australia v West Indies	Bridgetown	1964-65
201	S.M.Nurse	West Indies v Australia	Bridgetown	1964-65
201	Mushtaq Mohammad	Pakistan v New Zealand	Dunedin	1972-73
201	G.S.Chappell	Australia v Pakistan	Brisbane[2]	1981-82
201	A.D.Gaekwad	India v Pakistan	Jullundur	1983-84
201	G.Fowler	England v India	Madras[1]	1984-85
200*	D.N.Sardesai	India v New Zealand	Bombay[2]	1964-65
200*	D.I.Gower	England v India	Birmingham	1979
200*	A.R.Border	Australia v England	Leeds	1993
200	W.R.Hammond	England v Australia	Melbourne	1928-29
200	Mohsin Khan	Pakistan v England	Lord's	1982
200	D.C.Boon	Australia v New Zealand	Perth	1989-90

MOST HUNDREDS

		Total	200s	I	E	A	SA	Opponents WI	NZ	I	P	SL	Z
S.M.Gavaskar	India	34	4	214	4	8	–	13	2	–	5	2	–
D.G.Bradman	Australia	29	12	80	19	–	4	2	–	4	–	–	–
A.R.Border	Australia	27	2	265	8	–	–	3	5	4	6	1	–
G.St A.Sobers	West Indies	26	2	160	10	4	–	–	1	8	3	–	–
G.S.Chappell	Australia	24	4	151	9	–	–	5	3	1	6	–	–
I.V.A.Richards	West Indies	24	3	182	8	5	–	–	1	8	2	–	–
Javed Miandad	Pakistan	23	6	177	2	6	–	2	7	5	–	1	–
G.Boycott	England	22	1	193	–	7	1	5	2	4	3	–	–
M.C.Cowdrey	England	22	–	188	–	5	3	6	2	3	3	–	–
W.R.Hammond	England	22	7	140	–	9	6	1	4	2	–	–	–
R.N.Harvey	Australia	21	2	137	6	–	8	3	–	4	–	–	–
K.F.Barrington	England	20	1	131	–	5	2	3	3	3	4	–	–
G.A.Gooch	England	20	2	205	–	4	–	5	4	5	1	1	–
C.G.Greenidge	West Indies	19	4	185	7	4	–	–	2	5	1	–	–
L.Hutton	England	19	4	138	–	5	4	5	3	2	–	–	–
C.H.Lloyd	West Indies	19	1	175	5	6	–	–	–	7	1	–	–
D.C.Boon	Australia	18	1	160	6	–	–	3	3	6	–	–	–
D.I.Gower	England	18	2	204	–	9	–	1	4	2	2	–	–
D.L.Haynes	West Indies	18	–	202	5	5	–	–	3	2	3	–	–
D.C.S.Compton	England	17	2	131	–	5	7	2	2	–	1	–	–
M.D.Crowe	New Zealand	17	1	120	5	3	–	3	–	1	2	2	1
D.B.Vengsarkar	India	17	–	185	5	2	–	6	–	–	2	2	–
H.Sutcliffe	England	16	–	84	–	8	6	–	2	–	–	–	–
J.B.Hobbs	England	15	1	102	–	12	2	1	–	–	–	–	–
R.B.Kanhai	West Indies	15	2	137	5	5	–	–	–	4	1	–	–
R.B.Richardson	West Indies	15	–	122	4	8	–	1	2	–	–	–	–
C.L.Walcott	West Indies	15	1	74	4	5	–	–	1	4	1	–	–
K.D.Walters	Australia	15	2	125	4	–	–	6	3	1	1	–	–
E.de C.Weekes	West Indies	15	2	81	3	1	–	–	3	7	1	–	–

The most hundreds for countries not included above is: South Africa – 9 in 62 innings by A.D.Nourse; Sri Lanka – 7 in 74 innings by P.A.de Silva; Zimbabwe – 1 in 12 innings by A.Flower and D.L.Houghton.

The most double undreds by batsmen not qualifying for the above list is four by Zaheer Abbas (12 hundreds for Pakistan) and three by R.B.Simpson (12 hundreds for Australia).

MOST HUNDREDS IN A SERIES

FIVE

C.L.Walcott		West Indies v Australia	1954-55

FOUR

D.G.Bradman	(3)	Australia v England	1930
		Australia v South Africa	1931-32
		Australia v India	1947-48
D.C.S.Compton		England v South Africa	1947
S.M.Gavaskar	(2)	India v West Indies	1970-71
		India v West Indies	1978-79
W.R.Hammond		England v Australia	1928-29
R.N.Harvey	(2)	Australia v South Africa	1949-50
		Australia v South Africa	1952-53
G.A.Headley		West Indies v England	1929-30
Mudassar Nazar		Pakistan v India	1982-83
H.Sutcliffe	(2)	England v Australia	1924-25
		England v South Africa	1929
K.D.Walters		Australia v West Indies	1968-69
E.de C.Weekes		West Indies v India	1948-49

MOST DOUBLE HUNDREDS IN A SERIES

THREE

D.G.Bradman		Australia v England	1930

TWO

D.G.Bradman	(3)	Australia v South Africa	1931-32
		Australia v England	1934
		Australia v England	1936-37
C.G.Greenidge		West Indies v England	1984
W.R.Hammond	(2)	England v Australia	1928-29
		England v New Zealand	1932-33
M.H.Mankad		India v New Zealand	1955-56
I.V.A.Richards		West Indies v England	1976
G.M.Turner		New Zealand v West Indies	1971-72

HUNDREDS IN MOST CONSECUTIVE INNINGS

FIVE

			Opponents		
E.de C.Weekes	West Indies	141	England	Kingston	1947-48
		128	India	Delhi	1948-49
		194	India	Bombay[2]	1948-49
		162 } 101 }	India	Calcutta	1948-49

Weekes was run out for 90 in his next innings (Madras[1] 1948-49).

FOUR

J.H.W.Fingleton	Australia	112	South Africa	Cape Town	1935-36
		108	South Africa	Johannesburg[1]	1935-36
		118	South Africa	Durban[2]	1935-36
		100	England	Brisbane[2]	1936-37
A.Melville	South Africa	103	England	Durban[2]	1938-39
		189 } 104* }	England	Nottingham	1947
		117	England	Lord's	1947

THREE

W.Bardsley	Australia	136 } 130 }	England	Oval	1909
		132	South Africa	Sydney	1910-11
G.Boycott	England	119*	Australia	Adelaide	1970-71
		121*	Pakistan	Lord's	1971
		112	Pakistan	Leeds	1971

			Opponents		
D.G.Bradman	Australia	132 127*}	India	Melbourne	1947-48
		201	India	Adelaide	1947-48
D.C.S.Compton	England	163	South Africa	Nottingham	1947
		208	South Africa	Lord's	1947
		115	South Africa	Manchester	1947
S.M.Gavaskar (2)	India	117*	West Indies	Bridgetown	1970-71
		124 220}	West Indies	Port-of-Spain	1970-71
		111 137}	Pakistan	Karachi[1]	1978-79
		205	West Indies	Bombay[3]	1978-79
G.A.Gooch	England	333 123}	India	Lord's	1990
		116	India	Manchester	1990
C.G.Greenidge	West Indies	134 101}	England	Manchester	1976
		115	England	Leeds	1976
V.S.Hazare	India	122	West Indies	Bombay[2]	1948-49
		164*	England	Delhi	1951-52
		155	England	Bombay[2]	1951-52
D.L.Haynes	West Indies	109	England	Bridgetown	1989-90
		167	England	St John's	1989-90
		117	Pakistan	Karachi[1]	1990-91
G.A.Headley	West Indies	270*	England	Kingston	1934-35
		106 107}	England	Lord's	1939
A.H.Jones	New Zealand	186	Sri Lanka	Wellington	1990-91
		122 100*}	Sri Lanka	Hamilton	1990-91
V.G.Kambli	India	224	England	Bombay	1992-93
		227	Zimbabwe	Delhi	1992-93
		125	Sri Lanka	Colombo (SSC)	1993-94
C.G.Macartney	Australia	133*	England	Lord's	1926
		151	England	Leeds	1926
		109	England	Manchester	1926
A.R.Morris	Australia	155	England	Melbourne	1946-47
		122 124*}	England	Adelaide	1946-47
Mudassar Nazar	Pakistan	231	India	Hyderabad	1982-83
		152*	India	Lahore[2]	1982-83
		152	India	Karachi[1]	1982-83
G.St A.Sobers	West Indies	365*	Pakistan	Kingston	1957-58
		125 109*}	Pakistan	Georgetown	1957-58
H.Sutcliffe	England	115	Australia	Sydney	1924-25
		176 127}	Australia	Melbourne	1924-25
P.R.Umrigar	India	117	Pakistan	Madras[2]	1960-61
		112	Pakistan	Delhi	1960-61
		147*	England	Kanpur	1961-62
E.de C.Weekes	West Indies	123	New Zealand	Dunedin	1955-56
		103	New Zealand	Christchurch	1955-56
		156	New Zealand	Wellington	1955-56
Zaheer Abbas	Pakistan	215	India	Lahore[2]	1982-83
		186	India	Karachi[1]	1982-83
		168	India	Faisalabad	1982-83

HUNDRED IN EACH INNINGS OF A MATCH

ENGLAND

			Opponents		
C.A.G.Russell	140	111	South Africa	Durban[2]	1922-23
H.Sutcliffe	176	127	Australia	Melbourne	1924-25
W.R.Hammond	119*	177	Australia	Adelaide	1928-29
H.Sutcliffe	104	109*	South Africa	Oval	1929
E.Paynter	117	100	South Africa	Johannesburg[1]	1938-39
D.C.S.Compton	147	103*	Australia	Adelaide	1946-47

Hundreds in Each Innings

			Opponents		
G.A.Gooch	333	123	India	Lord's	1990
A.J.Stewart	118	143	West Indies	Bridgetown	1993-94

AUSTRALIA

W.Bardsley	136	130	England	Oval	1909
A.R.Morris	122	124*	England	Adelaide	1946-47
D.G.Bradman	132	127*	India	Melbourne	1947-48
J.Moroney	118	101*	South Africa	Johannesburg[2]	1949-50
R.B.Simpson	153	115	Pakistan	Karachi[1]	1964-65
K.D.Walters	242	103	West Indies	Sydney	1968-69
I.M.Chappell	145	121	New Zealand	Wellington	1973-74
G.S.Chappell	247*	133	New Zealand	Wellington	1973-74
G.S.Chappell	123	109*	West Indies	Brisbane[2]	1975-76
A.R.Border	150*	153	Pakistan	Lahore[2]	1979-80
A.R.Border	140	114*	New Zealand	Christchurch	1985-86
D.M.Jones	116	121*	Pakistan	Adelaide	1989-90

SOUTH AFRICA

A.Melville	189	104*	England	Nottingham	1947
B.Mitchell	120	189*	England	Oval	1947

WEST INDIES

G.A.Headley	114	112	England	Georgetown	1929-30
G.A.Headley	106	107	England	Lord's	1939
E.de C.Weekes	162	101	India	Calcutta	1948-49
C.L.Walcott	126	110	Australia	Port-of-Spain	1954-55
C.L.Walcott	155	110	Australia	Kingston	1954-55
G.St A.Sobers	125	109*	Pakistan	Georgetown	1957-58
R.B.Kanhai	117	115	Australia	Adelaide	1960-61
L.G.Rowe	214	100*	New Zealand	Kingston	1971-72
C.G.Greenidge	134	101	England	Manchester	1976

NEW ZEALAND

G.M.Turner	101	110*	Australia	Christchurch	1973-74
G.P.Howarth	122	102	England	Auckland	1977-78
A.H.Jones	122	100*	Sri Lanka	Hamilton	1990-91

INDIA

V.S.Hazare	116	145	Australia	Adelaide	1947-48
S.M.Gavaskar	124	220	West Indies	Port-of-Spain	1970-71
S.M.Gavaskar	111	137	Pakistan	Karachi[1]	1978-79
S.M.Gavaskar	107	182*	West Indies	Calcutta	1978-79

PAKISTAN

Hanif Mohammad	111	104	England	Dacca	1961-62
Javed Miandad	104	103*	New Zealand	Hyderabad	1984-85

SRI LANKA

L.R.D.Mendis	105	105	India	Madras[1]	1982-83
A.P.Gurusinha	119	102	New Zealand	Hamilton	1990-91

L.G.Rowe achieved this feat in his first Test match.
V.S.Hazare scored two separate hundreds on successive days – 108 (3rd day) and 102* (4th day).*
L.R.D.Mendis is alone in making the same three-figure score twice in a Test match.
G.Boycott scored 99 and 112 for England v West Indies at Port-of-Spain in 1973-74.

HUNDREDS IN MOST CONSECUTIVE MATCHES

SIX

D.G.Bradman	Australia	270, 212, 169, 144*, 102*, 103	1936-37 to 1938

Because of injury Bradman was unable to bat in his next Test but scored 187 and 234 in his following two matches in 1946-47.

HUNDRED ON DEBUT

IN BOTH INNINGS

L.G.Rowe	214 } 100* }	West Indies v New Zealand	Kingston	1971-72

IN FIRST INNINGS

C.Bannerman	165*	Australia v England	Melbourne	1876-77
W.G.Grace	152	England v Australia	Oval	1880
H.Graham	107	Australia v England	Lord's	1893
R.E.Foster	287	England v Australia	Sydney	1903-04
G.Gunn	119	England v Australia	Sydney	1907-08
W.H.Ponsford	110	Australia v England	Sydney	1924-25
A.A.Jackson	164	Australia v England	Adelaide	1928-29
J.E.Mills	117	New Zealand v England	Wellington	1929-30
Nawab of Pataudi, sr	102	England v Australia	Sydney	1932-33
B.H.Valentine	136	England v India	Bombay[1]	1933-34
S.C.Griffith	140	England v West Indies	Port-of-Spain	1947-48
A.G.Ganteaume	112	West Indies v England	Port-of-Spain	1947-48
P.B.H.May	138	England v South Africa	Leeds	1951
R.H.Shodhan	110	India v Pakistan	Calcutta	1952-53
B.H.Pairaudeau	115	West Indies v India	Port-of-Spain	1952-53
A.G.Kripal Singh	100*	India v New Zealand	Hyderabad	1955-56
C.C.Hunte	142	West Indies v Pakistan	Bridgetown	1957-58
C.A.Milton	104*	England v New Zealand	Leeds	1958
Hanumant Singh	105	India v England	Delhi	1963-64
Khalid Ibadulla	166	Pakistan v Australia	Karachi[1]	1964-65
B.R.Taylor	105	New Zealand v India	Calcutta	1964-65
K.D.Walters	155	Australia v England	Brisbane[2]	1965-66
J.H.Hampshire	107	England v West Indies	Lord's	1969
G.S.Chappell	108	Australia v England	Perth	1970-71
A.I.Kallicharran	100*	West Indies v New Zealand	Georgetown	1971-72
R.E.Redmond	107	New Zealand v Pakistan	Auckland	1972-73
G.J.Cosier	109	Australia v West Indies	Melbourne	1975-76
S.Amarnath	124	India v New Zealand	Auckland	1975-76
Javed Miandad	163	Pakistan v New Zealand	Lahore[2]	1976-77
K.C.Wessels	162	Australia v England	Brisbane[2]	1982-83
W.B.Phillips	159	Australia v Pakistan	Perth	1983-84
M.Azharuddin	110	India v England	Calcutta	1984-85
D.S.B.P.Kuruppu	201*	Sri Lanka v New Zealand	Colombo (CCC)	1986-87
M.E.Waugh	138	Australia v England	Adelaide	1990-91
A.C.Hudson	163	South Africa v West Indies	Bridgetown	1991-92
R.S.Kaluwitharana	132*	Sri Lanka v Australia	Colombo (SSC)	1992-93
D.L.Houghton	121	Zimbabwe v India	Harare	1992-93
P.K.Amre	103	India v South Africa	Durban	1992-93

IN SECOND INNINGS

K.S.Ranjitsinhji	154*	England v Australia	Manchester	1896
P.F.Warner	132*	England v South Africa	Johannesburg[1]	1898-99
R.A.Duff	104	Australia v England	Melbourne	1901-02
R.J.Hartigan	116	Australia v England	Adelaide	1907-08
H.L.Collins	104	Australia v England	Sydney	1920-21
G.A.Headley	176	West Indies v England	Bridgetown	1929-30
L.Amarnath	118	India v England	Bombay[1]	1933-34
P.A.Gibb	106	England v South Africa	Johannesburg[1]	1938-39
J.W.Burke	101*	Australia v England	Adelaide	1950-51
O.G.Smith	104	West Indies v Australia	Kingston	1954-55
A.A.Baig	112	India v England	Manchester	1959
G.R.Viswanath	137	India v Australia	Kanpur	1969-70
F.C.Hayes	106*	England v West Indies	Oval	1973
C.G.Greenidge	107	West Indies v India	Bangalore	1974-75
L.Baichan	105*	West Indies v Pakistan	Lahore[2]	1974-75
A.B.Williams	100	West Indies v Australia	Georgetown	1977-78
D.M.Wellham	103	Australia v England	Oval	1981
Salim Malik	100*	Pakistan v Sri Lanka	Karachi[1]	1981-82
M.J.Greatbatch	107*	New Zealand v England	Auckland	1987-88
G.P.Thorpe	114*	England v Australia	Nottingham	1993

L.Amarnath and S.Amarnath are the only father and son each to score a hundred on debut.

A.I.Kallicharran also scored a hundred in his second Test innings – 101 v New Zealand at Port-of-Spain, 1971-72.

M.Azharuddin scored hundreds in each of his first three Test matches, v England in 1984-85, his full scoring sequence being 110 at Calcutta, 48 and 105 at Madras[1], and 122 and 54 at Kanpur.*

The following scored 99 in their first Test:

A.G.Chipperfield	(1st innings)	Australia v England	Nottingham	1934
R.J.Christiani	(2nd innings)	West Indies v England	Bridgetown	1947-48

MOST RUNS IN FIRST TEST MATCH

314	L.G.Rowe	(214, 100*)	West Indies v New Zealand	Kingston	1971-72
306	R.E.Foster	(287, 19)	England v Australia	Sydney	1903-04

B.M.Laird (92 and 75) scored 167 runs for Australia v West Indies at Brisbane[2] in 1979-80 – the highest aggregate without a hundred by any player in his first Test.

MAIDEN FIRST-CLASS HUNDRED IN A TEST MATCH

C.Bannerman†‡	165*	Australia v England	Melbourne	1876-77
W.L.Murdoch	153*	Australia v England	Oval	1880
P.S.McDonnell	147	Australia v England	Sydney	1881-82
H.Wood‡	134*	England v South Africa	Cape Town	1891-92
H.Graham†	107	Australia v England	Lord's	893
A.J.L.Hill	124	England v South Africa	Cape Town	1895-96
J.H.Sinclair	106	South Africa v England	Cape Town	1898-99
P.W.Sherwell	115	South Africa v England	Lord's	1907
H.G.Owen-Smith	129	South Africa v England	Leeds	1929
C.A.Roach	122	West Indies v England	Bridgetown	1929-30
S.C.Griffith†	140	England v West Indies	Port-of-Spain	1947-48
V.L.Manjrekar	133	India v England	Leeds	1952
C.C.Depeiza‡	122	West Indies v Australia	Bridgetown	1954-55
P.L.Winslow	108	South Africa v England	Manchester	1955
S.N.McGregor	111	New Zealand v Pakistan	Lahore[1]	1955-56
F.C.M.Alexander‡	108	West Indies v Australia	Sydney	1960-61
Nasim-ul-Ghani	101	Pakistan v England	Lord's	1962
B.R.Taylor†	105	New Zealand v India	Calcutta	1964-65
B.D.Julien	121	West Indies v England	Lord's	1973
W.K.Lees	152	New Zealand v Pakistan	Karachi[1]	1976-77
Kapil Dev	126*	India v West Indies	Delhi	1978-79
S.Wettimuny	157	Sri Lanka v Pakistan	Faisalabad	1981-82
S.A.R.Silva	102*	Sri Lanka v England	Lord's	1984
D.S.B.P.Kuruppu†	201*	Sri Lanka v New Zealand	Colombo (CCC)	1986-87
R.C.Russell	128*	England v Australia	Manchester	1989

†On Test debut   ‡Only hundred in first-class cricket
H.Graham (105 v England at Sydney in 1894-95), C.A.Roach (209 v England at Georgetown in 1929-30) and B.R.Taylor (124 v West Indies at Auckland in 1968-69) also scored their second first-class hundred in a Test match.

YOUNGEST PLAYERS TO SCORE A HUNDRED

Years	Days				
17	82	Mushtaq Mohammad	101	Pakistan v India	Delhi	1960-61
17	112	S.R.Tendulkar	119*	India v England	Manchester	1990
18	328	Salim Malik	100*	Pakistan v Sri Lanka	Karachi[1]	1981-82
19	26	Mohammad Ilyas	126	Pakistan v New Zealand	Karachi[1]	1964-65
19	119	Javed Miandad	163	Pakistan v New Zealand	Lahore[2]	1976-77
19	121	H.G.Vivian	100	New Zealand v South Africa	Wellington	1931-32
19	121	R.N.Harvey	153	Australia v India	Melbourne	1947-48
19	152	A.A.Jackson	164	Australia v England	Adelaide	1928-29
19	192	A.P.Gurusinha	116*	Sri Lanka v Pakistan	Colombo (PSS)	1985-86
19	318	R.G.Pollock	122	South Africa v Australia	Sydney	1963-64
19	357	K.D.Walters	155	Australia v England	Brisbane[2]	1965-66
20	1	P.A.de Silva	122	Sri Lanka v Pakistan	Faisalabad	1985-86
20	3	Ijaz Ahmed	122	Pakistan v Australia	Faisalabad	1988-89
20	19	D.C.S.Compton	102	England v Australia	Nottingham	1938
20	21	Kapil Dev	126*	India v West Indies	Delhi	1978-79
20	58	Hanif Mohammad	142	Pakistan v India	Bahawalpur	1954-55
20	129	D.G.Bradman	112	Australia v England	Melbourne	1928-29
20	131	A.A.Baig	112	India v England	Manchester	1959
20	148	H.G.Owen-Smith	129	South Africa v England	Leeds	1929
20	154	Saeed Ahmed	150	Pakistan v West Indies	Georgetown	1957-58
20	230	G.A.Headley	176	West Indies v England	Bridgetown	1929-30
20	240	J.W.Burke	101*	Australia v England	Adelaide	1950-51
20	249	R.J.Shastri	128	India v Pakistan	Karachi[1]	1982-83
20	253	V.L.Manjrekar	133	India v England	Leeds	1952

Years	Days					
20	281	G.R.Viswanath	137	India v Australia	Kanpur	1969-70
20	317	C.Hill	188	Australia v England	Melbourne	1897-98
20	324	J.W.Hearne	114	England v Australia	Melbourne	1911-12
20	330	O.G.Smith	104	West Indies v Australia	Kingston	1954-55

Only the first hundred is listed for each player. S.R.Tendulkar scored three hundreds before his 19th birthday, five before his 20th and seven before his 21st. Mushtaq Mohammad scored two before his 19th birthday. R.N.Harvey, R.G.Pollock, Javed Miandad and Salim Malik each scored two before their 20th and G.A.Headley scored four before his 21st.

YOUNGEST PLAYERS TO SCORE A DOUBLE HUNDRED

Years	Days					
19	141	Javed Miandad	206	Pakistan v New Zealand	Karachi[1]	1976-77
20	315	G.A.Headley	223	West Indies v England	Kingston	1929-30

YOUNGEST PLAYERS TO SCORE A TRIPLE HUNDRED

Years	Days					
21	216	G.St A.Sobers	365*	West Indies v Pakistan	Kingston	1957-58
21	318	D.G.Bradman	334	Australia v England	Leeds	1930

OLDEST PLAYERS TO SCORE A HUNDRED

Years	Days					
46	82	J.B.Hobbs	142	England v Australia	Melbourne	1928-29
45	240	J.B.Hobbs	159	England v West Indies	Oval	1928
45	151	E.H.Hendren	132	England v Australia	Manchester	1934

The ages of Indian and Pakistani players have not been confirmed.

DISTRIBUTION OF TEST MATCH HUNDREDS

Conceded By	E	A	SA	WI	NZ	I	P	SL	Z	Total Conceded
England	–	224	60	103	38	60	33	3	–	521
Australia	199	–	38	77	19	35	31	4	–	403
South Africa	88	58	–	0	7	3	–	1	–	157
West Indies	93	74	1	–	17	55	18	0	–	258
New Zealand	79	30	11	25	–	22	37	7	1	212
India	72	51	2	76	21	–	41	9	2	274
Pakistan	44	37	–	24	21	31	–	8	0	165
Sri Lanka	4	10	3	0	10	17	10	–	–	54
Zimbabwe	–	–	–	–	2	2	0	–	–	4
Total Scored	579	484	115	305	135	225	170	32	3	2048

HUNDREDS IN TEST CRICKET

† *Denotes hundred on first appearance against that country.*

ENGLAND (579)

				Opponents		
Abel, R.	(2)	120		South Africa	Cape Town	1888-89
		132*		Australia	Sydney	1891-92
Allen, G.O.B.		122†		New Zealand	Lord's	1931
Ames, L.E.G.	(8)	105		West Indies	Port-of-Spain	1929-30
		149		West Indies	Kingston	1929-30
		137†		New Zealand	Lord's	1931
		103		New Zealand	Christchurch	1932-33
		120		Australia	Lord's	1934
		126		West Indies	Kingston	1934-35
		148*		South Africa	Oval	1935

537

		Opponents		
Ames, L.E.G. *continued*		115	South Africa	Cape Town	1938-39
Amiss, D.L.	(11)	112	Pakistan	Lahore[2]	1972-73
		158	Pakistan	Hyderabad	1972-73
		138*†	New Zealand	Nottingham	1973
		174	West Indies	Port-of-Spain	1973-74
		262*	West Indies	Kingston	1973-74
		118	West Indies	Georgetown	1973-74
		188	India	Lord's	1974
		183	Pakistan	Oval	1974
		164*	New Zealand	Christchurch	1974-75
		203	West Indies	Oval	1976
		179	India	Delhi	1976-77
Atherton, M.A.	(7)	151†	New Zealand	Nottingham	1990
		131	India	Manchester	1990
		105	Australia	Sydney	1990-91
		144	West Indies	Georgetown	1993-94
		135	West Indies	St John's	1993-94
		101	New Zealand	Nottingham	1994
		111	New Zealand	Manchester	1994
Athey, C.W.J.		123	Pakistan	Lord's	1987
Bailey, T.E.		134*	New Zealand	Christchurch	1950-51
Bakewell, A.H.		107†	West Indies	Oval	1933
Barber, R.W.		185	Australia	Sydney	1965-66
Barnes, W.		134	Australia	Adelaide	1884-85
Barnett, C.J.	(2)	129	Australia	Adelaide	1936-37
		126	Australia	Nottingham	1938
Barrington, K.F.	(20)	128†	West Indies	Bridgetown	1959-60
		121	West Indies	Port-of-Spain	1959-60
		139†	Pakistan	Lahore[2]	1961-62
		151*	India	Bombay[2]	1961-62
		172	India	Kanpur	1961-62
		113*	India	Delhi	1961-62
		132*	Australia	Adelaide	1962-63
		101	Australia	Sydney	1962-63
		126†	New Zealand	Auckland	1962-63
		256	Australia	Manchester	1964
		148*	South Africa	Durban[2]	1964-65
		121	South Africa	Johannesburg[3]	1964-65
		137	New Zealand	Birmingham	1965
		163	New Zealand	Leeds	1965
		102	Australia	Adelaide	1965-66
		115	Australia	Melbourne	1965-66
		148	Pakistan	Lord's	1967
		109*	Pakistan	Nottingham	1967
		142	Pakistan	Oval	1967
		143	West Indies	Port-of-Spain	1967-68
Botham, I.T.	(14)	103	New Zealand	Christchurch	1977-78
		100†	Pakistan	Birmingham	1978
		108	Pakistan	Lord's	1978
		137	India	Leeds	1979
		119*	Australia	Melbourne	1979-80
		114	India	Bombay[3]	1979-80
		149*	Australia	Leeds	1981
		118	Australia	Manchester	1981
		142	India	Kanpur	1981-82
		128	India	Manchester	1982
		208	India	Oval	1982
		103	New Zealand	Nottingham	1983
		138	New Zealand	Wellington	1983-84
		138	Australia	Brisbane[2]	1986-87
Bowley, E.H.		109	New Zealand	Auckland	1929-30
Boycott, G.	(22)	113	Australia	Oval	1964
		117	South Africa	Port Elizabeth	1964-65
		246*†	India	Leeds	1967
		116	West Indies	Georgetown	1967-68
		128	West Indies	Manchester	1969
		106	West Indies	Lord's	1969
		142*	Australia	Sydney	1970-71
		119*	Australia	Adelaide	1970-71

			Opponents		
Boycott, G. *continued*		121*	Pakistan	Lord's	1971
		112	Pakistan	Leeds	1971
		115	New Zealand	Leeds	1973
		112	West Indies	Port-of-Spain	1973-74
		107	Australia	Nottingham	1977
		191	Australia	Leeds	1977
			(His 100th first-class hundred)		
		100*	Pakistan	Hyderabad	1977-78
		131	New Zealand	Nottingham	1978
		155	India	Birmingham	1979
		125	India	Oval	1979
		128*	Australia	Lord's	1980
		104*	West Indies	St John's	1980-81
		137	Australia	Oval	1981
		105	India	Delhi	1981-82
Braund, L.C.	(3)	103*	Australia	Adelaide	1901-02
		102	Australia	Sydney	1903-04
		104†	South Africa	Lord's	1907
Briggs, J.		121	Australia	Melbourne	1884-85
Broad, B.C.	(6)	162	Australia	Perth	1986-87
		116	Australia	Adelaide	1986-87
		112	Australia	Melbourne	1986-87
		116	Pakistan	Faisalabad	1987-88
		139	Australia	Sydney	1987-88
		114†	New Zealand	Christchurch	1987-88
Brown, J.T.		140	Australia	Melbourne	1894-95
Chapman, A.P.F.		121	Australia	Lord's	1930
Compton, D.C.S.	(17)	102†	Australia	Nottingham	1938
		120†	West Indies	Lord's	1939
		147 103* }	Australia	Adelaide	1946-47
		163†	South Africa	Nottingham	1947
		208	South Africa	Lord's	1947
		115	South Africa	Manchester	1947
		113	South Africa	Oval	1947
		184	Australia	Nottingham	1948
		145*	Australia	Manchester	1948
		114	South Africa	Johannesburg[2]	1948-49
		114	New Zealand	Leeds	1949
		116	New Zealand	Lord's	1949
		112	South Africa	Nottingham	1951
		133	West Indies	Port-of-Spain	1953-54
		278	Pakistan	Nottingham	1954
		158	South Africa	Manchester	1955
Cowdrey, M.C.	(22)	102	Australia	Melbourne	1954-55
		101	South Africa	Cape Town	1956-57
		154†	West Indies	Birmingham	1957
		152	West Indies	Lord's	1957
		100*	Australia	Sydney	1958-59
		160	India	Leeds	1959
		114	West Indies	Kingston	1959-60
		119	West Indies	Port-of-Spain	1959-60
		155	South Africa	Oval	1960
		159†	Pakistan	Birmingham	1962
		182	Pakistan	Oval	1962
		113	Australia	Melbourne	1962-63
		128*	New Zealand	Wellington	1962-63
		107	India	Calcutta	1963-64
		151	India	Delhi	1963-64
		119	New Zealand	Lord's	1965
		105	South Africa	Nottingham	1965
		104	Australia	Melbourne	1965-66
		101	West Indies	Kingston	1967-68
		148	West Indies	Port-of-Spain	1967-68
		104	Australia	Birmingham	1968
			(In his 100th Test match)		
		100	Pakistan	Lahore[2]	1968-69
Denness, M.H.	(4)	118	India	Lord's	1974
		100	India	Birmingham	1974

				Opponents		
Denness, M.H. *continued*			188	Australia	Melbourne	1974-75
			181	New Zealand	Auckland	1974-75
Denton, D.			104	South Africa	Johannesburg[1]	1909-10
Dexter, E.R.		(9)	141	New Zealand	Christchurch	1958-59
			136*†	West Indies	Bridgetown	1959-60
			110	West Indies	Georgetown	1959-60
			180	Australia	Birmingham	1961
			126*	India	Kanpur	1961-62
			205	Pakistan	Karachi[1]	1961-62
			172	Pakistan	Oval	1962
			174	Australia	Manchester	1964
			172	South Africa	Johannesburg[3]	1964-65
D'Oliveira, B.L.		(5)	109†	India	Leeds	1967
			158	Australia	Oval	1968
			114*	Pakistan	Dacca	1968-69
			117	Australia	Melbourne	1970-71
			100	New Zealand	Christchurch	1970-71
Douglas, J.W.H.T.			119†	South Africa	Durban[1]	1913-14
Duleepsinhji, K.S.		(3)	117	New Zealand	Auckland	1929-30
			173†	Australia	Lord's	1930
			109	New Zealand	Oval	1931
Edrich, J.H.		(12)	120†	Australia	Lord's	1964
			310*†	New Zealand	Leeds	1965
			109	Australia	Melbourne	1965-66
			103	Australia	Sydney	1965-66
			146	West Indies	Bridgetown	1967-68
			164	Australia	Oval	1968
			115	New Zealand	Lord's	1969
			115	New Zealand	Nottingham	1969
			115*	Australia	Perth	1970-71
			130	Australia	Adelaide	1970-71
			100*	India	Manchester	1974
			175	Australia	Lord's	1975
Edrich, W.J.		(6)	219	South Africa	Durban[2]	1938-39
			119	Australia	Sydney	1946-47
			189	South Africa	Lord's	1947
			191	South Africa	Manchester	1947
			111	Australia	Leeds	1948
			100	New Zealand	Oval	1949
Evans, T.G.		(2)	104	West Indies	Manchester	1950
			104	India	Lord's	1952
Fane, F.L.			143	South Africa	Johannesburg[1]	1905-06
Fletcher, K.W.R.		(7)	113	India	Bombay[2]	1972-73
			178	New Zealand	Lord's	1973
			129*	West Indies	Bridgetown	1973-74
			123*	India	Manchester	1974
			122	Pakistan	Oval	1974
			146	Australia	Melbourne	1974-75
			216	New Zealand	Auckland	1974-75
Foster, R.E.			287†	Australia	Sydney	1903-04
Fowler, G.		(3)	105†	New Zealand	Oval	1983
			106	West Indies	Lord's	1984
			201	India	Madras[1]	1984-85
Fry, C.B.		(2)	144	Australia	Oval	1905
			129	South Africa	Oval	1907
Gatting, M.W.		(9)	136	India	Bombay[3]	1984-85
			207	India	Madras[1]	1984-85
			160	Australia	Manchester	1985
			100*	Australia	Birmingham	1985
			183*	India	Birmingham	1986
			121	New Zealand	Oval	1986
			100	Australia	Adelaide	1986-87
			124	Pakistan	Birmingham	1987
			150*	Pakistan	Oval	1987
Gibb, P.A.		(2)	106†	South Africa	Johannesburg[1]	1938-39
			120	South Africa	Durban[2]	1938-39
Gooch, G.A.		(20)	123	West Indies	Lord's	1980
			116	West Indies	Bridgetown	1980-81
			153	West Indies	Kingston	1980-81

			Opponents		
Gooch, G.A. *continued*		127	India	Madras[1]	1981-82
		196	Australia	Oval	1985
		114	India	Lord's	1986
		183	New Zealand	Lord's	1986
		146	West Indies	Nottingham	1988
		154	New Zealand	Birmingham	1990
		333 ⎫ 123 ⎭	India	Lord's	1990
		116	India	Manchester	1990
		117	Australia	Adelaide	1990-91
		154*	West Indies	Leeds	1991
		174	Sri Lanka	Lord's	1991
		114	New Zealand	Auckland	1991-92
		135	Pakistan	Leeds	1992
		133	Australia	Manchester	1993
		120	Australia	Nottingham	1993
		210	New Zealand	Nottingham	1994
Gower, D.I.	(18)	111†	New Zealand	Oval	1978
		102	Australia	Perth	1978-79
		200*†	India	Birmingham	1979
		154*	West Indies	Kingston	1980-81
		114	Australia	Adelaide	1982-83
		112*	New Zealand	Leeds	1983
		108	New Zealand	Lord's	1983
		152	Pakistan	Faisalabad	1983-84
		173*	Pakistan	Lahore[2]	1983-84
		166	Australia	Nottingham	1985
		215	Australia	Birmingham	1985
		157	Australia	Oval	1985
		131	New Zealand	Oval	1986
		136	Australia	Perth	1986-87
		106	Australia	Lord's	1989
		157*	India	Oval	1990
		100	Australia	Melbourne	1990-91
		123	Australia	Sydney	1990-91
Grace, W.G.	(2)	152†	Australia	Oval	1880
		170	Australia	Oval	1886
Graveney, T.W.	(11)	175†	India	Bombay[2]	1951-52
		111	Australia	Sydney	1954-55
		258	West Indies	Nottingham	1957
		164	West Indies	Oval	1957
		153	Pakistan	Lord's	1962
		114	Pakistan	Nottingham	1962
		109	West Indies	Nottingham	1966
		165	West Indies	Oval	1966
		151	India	Lord's	1967
		118	West Indies	Port-of-Spain	1967-68
		105	Pakistan	Karachi[1]	1968-69
Greig, A.W.	(8)	148	India	Bombay[2]	1972-73
		139†	New Zealand	Nottingham	1973
		148	West Indies	Bridgetown	1973-74
		121	West Indies	Georgetown	1973-74
		106	India	Lord's	1974
		110	Australia	Brisbane[2]	1974-75
		116	West Indies	Leeds	1976
		103	India	Calcutta	1976-77
Griffith, S.C.		140†	West Indies	Port-of-Spain	1947-48
Gunn, G.	(2)	119†	Australia	Sydney	1907-08
		122*	Australia	Sydney	1907-08
Gunn, W.		102*	Australia	Manchester	1893
Hammond, W.R.	(22)	251	Australia	Sydney	1928-29
		200	Australia	Melbourne	1928-29
		119* ⎫ 177 ⎭	Australia	Adelaide	1928-29
		138*	South Africa	Birmingham	1929
		101*	South Africa	Oval	1929
		113	Australia	Leeds	1930
		136*	South Africa	Durban[2]	1930-31
		100*	New Zealand	Oval	1931

			Opponents		
Hammond, W.R. *continued*		112	Australia	Sydney	1932-33
		101	Australia	Sydney	1932-33
		227	New Zealand	Christchurch	1932-33
		336*	New Zealand	Auckland	1932-33
		167	India	Manchester	1936
		217	India	Oval	1936
		231*	Australia	Sydney	1936-37
		140	New Zealand	Lord's	1937
		240	Australia	Lord's	1938
		181	South Africa	Cape Town	1938-39
		120	South Africa	Durban[2]	1938-39
		140	South Africa	Durban[2]	1938-39
		138	West Indies	Oval	1939
Hampshire, J.H.		107†	West Indies	Lord's	1969
Hardstaff, J., jr	(4)	114†	New Zealand	Lord's	1937
		103	New Zealand	Oval	1937
		169*	Australia	Oval	1938
		205*	India	Lord's	1946
Hayes, F.C.		106*†	West Indies	Oval	1973
Hayward, T.W.	(3)	122	South Africa	Johannesburg[1]	1895-96
		130	Australia	Manchester	1899
		137	Australia	Oval	1899
Hearne, J.W.		114	Australia	Melbourne	1911-12
Hendren, E.H.	(7)	132	South Africa	Leeds	1924
		142	South Africa	Oval	1924
		127*	Australia	Lord's	1926
		169	Australia	Brisbane[1]	1928-29
		205*	West Indies	Port-of-Spain	1929-30
		123	West Indies	Georgetown	1929-30
		132	Australia	Manchester	1934
Hick, G.A.	(2)	178	India	Bombay[3]	1992-93
		110	South Africa	Leeds	1994
Hill, A.J.L.		124	South Africa	Cape Town	1895-96
Hobbs, J.B.	(15)	187	South Africa	Cape Town	1909-10
		126*	Australia	Melbourne	1911-12
		187	Australia	Adelaide	1911-12
		178	Australia	Melbourne	1911-12
		107	Australia	Lord's	1912
		122	Australia	Melbourne	1920-21
		123	Australia	Adelaide	1920-21
		211	South Africa	Lord's	1924
		115	Australia	Sydney	1924-25
		154	Australia	Melbourne	1924-25
		119	Australia	Adelaide	1924-25
		119	Australia	Lord's	1926
		100	Australia	Oval	1926
		159	West Indies	Oval	1928
		142	Australia	Melbourne	1928-29
Hutchings, K.L.		126	Australia	Melbourne	1907-08
Hutton, L.	(19)	100	New Zealand	Manchester	1937
		100†	Australia	Nottingham	1938
		364	Australia	Oval	1938
		196†	West Indies	Lord's	1939
		165*	West Indies	Oval	1939
		122*	Australia	Sydney	1946-47
		100	South Africa	Leeds	1947
		158	South Africa	Johannesburg[2]	1948-49
		123	South Africa	Johannesburg[2]	1948-49
		101	New Zealand	Leeds	1949
		206	New Zealand	Oval	1949
		202*	West Indies	Oval	1950
		156*	Australia	Adelaide	1950-51
		100	South Africa	Leeds	1951
		150	India	Lord's	1952
		104	India	Manchester	1952
		145	Australia	Lord's	1953
		169	West Indies	Georgetown	1953-54
		205	West Indies	Kingston	1953-54
Illingworth, R.	(2)	113	West Indies	Lord's	1969

		Opponents		
Illingworth, R. *continued*		107	India	Manchester	1971
Insole, D.J.		110*	South Africa	Durban[2]	1956-57
Jackson, Hon. F.S.	(5)	103	Australia	Oval	1893
		118	Australia	Oval	1899
		128	Australia	Manchester	1902
		144*	Australia	Leeds	1905
		113	Australia	Manchester	1905
Jardine, D.R.		127	West Indies	Manchester	1933
Jessop, G.L.		104	Australia	Oval	1902
Knight, B.R.	(2)	125†	New Zealand	Auckland	1962-63
		127	India	Kanpur	1963-64
Knott, A.P.E.	(5)	101	New Zealand	Auckland	1970-71
		116	Pakistan	Birmingham	1971
		106*	Australia	Adelaide	1974-75
		116	West Indies	Leeds	1976
		135	Australia	Nottingham	1977
Lamb, A.J.	(14)	107	India	Oval	1982
		102*†	New Zealand	Oval	1983
		137*	New Zealand	Nottingham	1983
		110	West Indies	Lord's	1984
		100	West Indies	Leeds	1984
		100*	West Indies	Manchester	1984
		107†	Sri Lanka	Lord's	1984
		113	West Indies	Lord's	1988
		125	Australia	Leeds	1989
		132	West Indies	Kingston	1989-90
		119	West Indies	Bridgetown	1989-90
		139	India	Lord's	1990
		109	India	Manchester	1990
		142	New Zealand	Wellington	1991-92
Legge, G.B.		196	New Zealand	Auckland	1929-30
Lewis, A.R.		125	India	Kanpur	1972-73
Lewis, C.C.		117	India	Madras[1]	1992-93
Leyland, M.	(9)	137†	Australia	Melbourne	1928-29
		102	South Africa	Lord's	1929
		109	Australia	Lord's	1934
		153	Australia	Manchester	1934
		110	Australia	Oval	1934
		161	South Africa	Oval	1935
		126	Australia	Brisbane[2]	1936-37
		111*	Australia	Melbourne	1936-37
		187	Australia	Oval	1938
Lloyd, D.		214*	India	Birmingham	1974
Luckhurst, B.W.	(4)	131	Australia	Perth	1970-71
		109	Australia	Melbourne	1970-71
		108*†	Pakistan	Birmingham	1971
		101	India	Manchester	1971
MacLaren, A.C.	(5)	120	Australia	Melbourne	1894-95
		109	Australia	Sydney	1897-98
		124	Australia	Adelaide	1897-98
		116	Australia	Sydney	1901-02
		140	Australia	Nottingham	1905
Makepeace, J.W.H.		117	Australia	Melbourne	1920-21
Mann, F.G.		136*	South Africa	Port Elizabeth	1948-49
May, P.B.H.	(13)	138†	South Africa	Leeds	1951
		135	West Indies	Port-of-Spain	1953-54
		104	Australia	Sydney	1954-55
		112	South Africa	Lord's	1955
		117	South Africa	Manchester	1955
		101	Australia	Leeds	1956
		285*	West Indies	Birmingham	1957
		104	West Indies	Nottingham	1957
		113*	New Zealand	Leeds	1958
		101	New Zealand	Manchester	1958
		113	Australia	Melbourne	1958-59
		124*	New Zealand	Auckland	1958-59
		106	India	Nottingham	1959
Mead, C.P.	(4)	102	South Africa	Johannesburg[1]	1913-14
		117	South Africa	Port Elizabeth	1913-14

			Opponents		
Mead, C.P. *continued*		182*	Australia	Oval	1921
		181	South Africa	Durban[2]	1922-23
Milburn, C.	(2)	126*	West Indies	Lord's	1966
		139	Pakistan	Karachi[1]	1968-69
Milton, C.A.		104*†	New Zealand	Leeds	1958
Murray, J.T.		112†	West Indies	Oval	1966
Parfitt, P.H.	(7)	111	Pakistan	Karachi[1]	1961-62
		101*	Pakistan	Birmingham	1962
		119	Pakistan	Leeds	1962
		101*	Pakistan	Nottingham	1962
		131*†	New Zealand	Auckland	1962-63
		121	India	Kanpur	1963-64
		122*	South Africa	Johannesburg[3]	1964-65
Parks, J.M.	(2)	101*†	West Indies	Port-of-Spain	1959-60
		108*	South Africa	Durban[2]	1964-65
Pataudi, Nawab of, sr		102†	Australia	Sydney	1932-33
Paynter, E.	(4)	216*	Australia	Nottingham	1938
		117† } 100† }	South Africa	Johannesburg[1]	1938-39
		243	South Africa	Durban[2]	1938-39
Place, W.		107	West Indies	Kingston	1947-48
Pullar, G.	(4)	131	India	Manchester	1959
		175	South Africa	Oval	1960
		119	India	Kanpur	1961-62
		165	Pakistan	Dacca	1961-62
Radley, C.T.	(2)	158	New Zealand	Auckland	1977-78
		106†	Pakistan	Birmingham	1978
Randall, D.W.	(7)	174†	Australia	Melbourne	1976-77
		150	Australia	Sydney	1978-79
		126	India	Lord's	1982
		105	Pakistan	Birmingham	1982
		115	Australia	Perth	1982-83
		164	New Zealand	Wellington	1983-84
		104	New Zealand	Auckland	1983-84
Ranjitsinhji, K.S.	(2)	154*†	Australia	Manchester	1896
		175	Australia	Sydney	1897-98
Read, W.W.		117	Australia	Oval	1884
Rhodes, W.	(2)	179	Australia	Melbourne	1911-12
		152	South Africa	Johannesburg[1]	1913-14
Richards, C.J.		133	Australia	Perth	1986-87
Richardson, P.E.	(5)	104	Australia	Manchester	1956
		117†	South Africa	Johannesburg[3]	1956-57
		126	West Indies	Nottingham	1957
		107	West Indies	Oval	1957
		100†	New Zealand	Birmingham	1958
Robertson, J.D.B.	(2)	133	West Indies	Port-of-Spain	1947-48
		121†	New Zealand	Lord's	1949
Robins, R.W.V.		108	South Africa	Manchester	1935
Robinson, R.T.	(4)	160	India	Delhi	1984-85
		175†	Australia	Leeds	1985
		148	Australia	Birmingham	1985
		166†	Pakistan	Manchester	1987
Russell, C.A.G.	(5)	135*	Australia	Adelaide	1920-21
		101	Australia	Manchester	1921
		102*	Australia	Oval	1921
		140 } 111 }	South Africa	Durban[2]	1922-23
Russell, R.C.		128*	Australia	Manchester	1989
Sandham, A.	(2)	152†	West Indies	Bridgetown	1929-30
		325	West Indies	Kingston	1929-30
Sharp, J.		105	Australia	Oval	1909
Sharpe, P.J.		111	New Zealand	Nottingham	1969
Sheppard, Rev. D.S.	(3)	119	India	Oval	1952
		113	Australia	Manchester	1956
		113	Australia	Melbourne	1962-63
Shrewsbury, A.	(3)	105*	Australia	Melbourne	1884-85
		164	Australia	Lord's	1886
		106	Australia	Lord's	1893
Simpson, R.T.	(4)	103†	New Zealand	Manchester	1949

			Opponents		
Simpson, R.T. *continued*		156*	Australia	Melbourne	1950-51
		137	South Africa	Nottingham	1951
		101	Pakistan	Nottingham	1954
Smith, M.J.K.	(3)	100†	India	Manchester	1959
		108	West Indies	Port-of-Spain	1959-60
		121	South Africa	Cape Town	1964-65
Smith, R.A.	(9)	143	Australia	Manchester	1989
		101	Australia	Nottingham	1989
		100*†	India	Lord's	1990
		121*	India	Manchester	1990
		148*	West Indies	Lord's	1991
		109	West Indies	Oval	1991
		127†	Pakistan	Birmingham	1992
		128	Sri Lanka	Colombo (SSC)	1992-93
		175	West Indies	St John's	1993-94
Spooner, R.H.		119†	South Africa	Lord's	1912
Steel, A.G.	(2)	135*	Australia	Sydney	1882-83
		148	Australia	Lord's	1884
Steele, D.S.		106†	West Indies	Nottingham	1976
Stewart, A.J.	(7)	113*†	Sri Lanka	Lord's	1991
		148	New Zealand	Christchurch	1991-92
		107	New Zealand	Wellington	1991-92
		190†	Pakistan	Birmingham	1992
		118 } 143	West Indies	Bridgetown	1993-94
		119	New Zealand	Lord's	1994
Stoddart, A.E.	(2)	134	Australia	Adelaide	1891-92
		173	Australia	Melbourne	1894-95
Subba Row, R.	(3)	100†	West Indies	Georgetown	1959-60
		112†	Australia	Birmingham	1961
		137	Australia	Oval	1961
Sutcliffe, H.	(16)	122	South Africa	Lord's	1924
		115†	Australia	Sydney	1924-25
		176 } 127	Australia	Melbourne	1924-25
		143	Australia	Melbourne	1924-25
		161	Australia	Oval	1926
		102	South Africa	Johannesburg[1]	1927-28
		135	Australia	Melbourne	1928-29
		114	South Africa	Birmingham	1929
		100	South Africa	Lord's	1929
		104 } 109*	South Africa	Oval	1929
		161	Australia	Oval	1930
		117†	New Zealand	Oval	1931
		109*	New Zealand	Manchester	1931
		194	Australia	Sydney	1932-33
Tate, M.W.		100*	South Africa	Lord's	1929
Tavaré, C.J.	(2)	149	India	Delhi	1981-82
		109†	New Zealand	Oval	1983
Thorpe, G.P.		114*†	Australia	Nottingham	1993
Tyldesley, G.E.	(3)	122	South Africa	Johannesburg[1]	1927-28
		100	South Africa	Durban[2]	1927-28
		122†	West Indies	Lord's	1928
Tyldesley, J.T.	(4)	112	South Africa	Cape Town	1898-99
		138	Australia	Birmingham	1902
		100	Australia	Leeds	1905
		112*	Australia	Oval	1905
Ulyett, G.		149	Australia	Melbourne	1881-82
Valentine, B.H.	(2)	136†	India	Bombay[1]	1933-34
		112	South Africa	Cape Town	1938-39
Walters, C.F.		102	India	Madras[1]	1933-34
Ward, Albert		117	Australia	Sydney	1894-95
Warner, P.F.		132*†	South Africa	Johannesburg[1]	1898-99
Washbrook, C.	(6)	112	Australia	Melbourne	1946-47
		143	Australia	Leeds	1948
		195	South Africa	Johannesburg[2]	1948-49
		103*	New Zealand	Leeds	1949
		114†	West Indies	Lord's	1950

			Opponents		
Washbrook, C. *continued*		102	West Indies	Nottingham	1950
Watkins, A.J.	(2)	111	South Africa	Johannesburg[2]	1948-49
		137*†	India	Delhi	1951-52
Watson, W.	(2)	109†	Australia	Lord's	1953
		116†	West Indies	Kingston	1953-54
Willey, P.	(2)	100*	West Indies	Oval	1980
		102*	West Indies	St John's	1980-81
Wood, H.		134*	South Africa	Cape Town	1891-92
Woolley, F.E.	(5)	133*	Australia	Sydney	1911-12
		115*	South Africa	Johannesburg[1]	1922-23
		134*	South Africa	Lord's	1924
		123	Australia	Sydney	1924-25
		154	South Africa	Manchester	1929
Woolmer, R.A.	(3)	149	Australia	Oval	1975
		120	Australia	Lord's	1977
		137	Australia	Manchester	1977
Worthington, T.S.		128	India	Oval	1936
Wyatt, R.E.S.	(2)	113	South Africa	Manchester	1929
		149	South Africa	Nottingham	1935

AUSTRALIA (484)

Archer, R.G.		128	West Indies	Kingston	1954-55
Armstrong, W.W.	(6)	159*	South Africa	Johannesburg[1]	1902-03
		133*	England	Melbourne	1907-08
		132	South Africa	Melbourne	1910-11
		158	England	Sydney	1920-21
		121	England	Adelaide	1920-21
		123*	England	Melbourne	1920-21
Badcock, C.L.		118	England	Melbourne	1936-37
Bannerman, C.		165*†	England	Melbourne	1876-77
			(The first hundred in Test cricket)		
Bardsley, W.	(6)	136 } 130 }	England	Oval	1909
		132†	South Africa	Sydney	1910-11
		121	South Africa	Manchester	1912
		164	South Africa	Lord's	1912
		193*	England	Lord's	1926
Barnes, S.G.	(3)	234	England	Sydney	1946-47
		112	India	Adelaide	1947-48
		141	England	Lord's	1948
Benaud, J.		142	Pakistan	Melbourne	1972-73
Benaud, R.	(3)	121	West Indies	Kingston	1954-55
		122	South Africa	Johannesburg[3]	1957-58
		100	South Africa	Johannesburg[3]	1957-58
Bonnor, G.J.		128	England	Sydney	1884-85
Boon, D.C.	(18)	123†	India	Adelaide	1985-86
		131	India	Sydney	1985-86
		122	India	Madras[1]	1986-87
		103	England	Adelaide	1986-87
		143	New Zealand	Brisbane[2]	1987-88
		184*	England	Sydney	1987-88
		149	West Indies	Sydney	1988-89
		200	New Zealand	Perth	1989-90
		121	England	Adelaide	1990-91
		109*	West Indies	Kingston	1990-91
		129*	India	Sydney	1991-92
		135	India	Adelaide	1991-92
		107	India	Perth	1991-92
		111	West Indies	Brisbane[2]	1992-93
		164*	England	Lord's	1993
		101	England	Nottingham	1993
		107	England	Leeds	1993
		106	New Zealand	Hobart	1993-94
Booth, B.C.	(5)	112	England	Brisbane[2]	1962-63
		103	England	Melbourne	1962-63
		169†	South Africa	Brisbane[2]	1963-64
		102*	South Africa	Sydney	1963-64
		117	West Indies	Port-of-Spain	1964-65

			Opponents		
Border, A.R.	(27)	105†	Pakistan	Melbourne	1978-79
		162†	India	Madras[1]	1979-80
		115	England	Perth	1979-80
		150* } 153	Pakistan	Lahore[2]	1979-80
		124	India	Melbourne	1980-81
		123*	England	Manchester	1981
		106*	England	Oval	1981
		126	West Indies	Adelaide	1981-82
		118	Pakistan	Brisbane[2]	1983-84
		117*	Pakistan	Adelaide	1983-84
		100*	West Indies	Port-of-Spain	1983-84
		196	England	Lord's	1985
		146*	England	Manchester	1985
		152*	New Zealand	Brisbane[2]	1985-86
		163	India	Melbourne	1985-86
		140 } 114*	New Zealand	Christchurch	1985-86
		106	India	Madras[1]	1986-87
		125	England	Perth	1986-87
		100*	England	Adelaide	1986-87
		205	New Zealand	Adelaide	1987-88
		113*	Pakistan	Faisalabad	1988-89
		106	Sri Lanka	Moratuwa	1992-93
		110	West Indies	Melbourne	1992-93
		200*	England	Leeds	1993
		105	New Zealand	Brisbane[2]	1993-94
Bradman, D.G.	(29)	112	England	Melbourne	1928-29
		123	England	Melbourne	1928-29
		131	England	Nottingham	1930
		254	England	Lord's	1930
		334	England	Leeds	1930
		232	England	Oval	1930
		223	West Indies	Brisbane[1]	1930-31
		152	West Indies	Melbourne	1930-31
		226†	South Africa	Brisbane[2]	1931-32
		112	South Africa	Sydney	1931-32
		167	South Africa	Melbourne	1931-32
		299*	South Africa	Adelaide	1931-32
		103*	England	Melbourne	1932-33
		304	England	Leeds	1934
		244	England	Oval	1934
		270	England	Melbourne	1936-37
		212	England	Adelaide	1936-37
		169	England	Melbourne	1936-37
		144*	England	Nottingham	1938
		102*	England	Lord's	1938
		103	England	Leeds	1938
		187	England	Brisbane[2]	1946-47
		234	England	Sydney	1946-47
		185†	India	Brisbane[2]	1947-48
		132 } 127*	India	Melbourne	1947-48
		201	India	Adelaide	1947-48
		138	England	Nottingham	1948
		173*	England	Leeds	1948
Brown, W.A.	(4)	105	England	Lord's	1934
		121	South Africa	Cape Town	1935-36
		133	England	Nottingham	1938
		206*	England	Lord's	1938
Burge, P.J.P.	(4)	181	England	Oval	1961
		103	England	Sydney	1962-63
		160	England	Leeds	1964
		120	England	Melbourne	1965-66
Burke, J.W.	(3)	101*†	England	Adelaide	1950-51
		161	India	Bombay[2]	1956-57
		189	South Africa	Cape Town	1957-58
Chappell, G.S.	(24)	108†	England	Perth	1970-71
		131	England	Lord's	1972

		Opponents		
Chappell, G.S. *continued*		113	England	Oval	1972
		116*	Pakistan	Melbourne	1972-73
		106	West Indies	Bridgetown	1972-73
		247* ⎫ 133 ⎭	New Zealand	Wellington	1973-74
		144	England	Sydney	1974-75
		102	England	Melbourne	1974-75
		123 ⎫ 109* ⎭	West Indies	Brisbane²	1975-76
		182*	West Indies	Sydney	1975-76
		121	Pakistan	Melbourne	1976-77
		112	England	Manchester	1977
		124	West Indies	Brisbane²	1979-80
		114	England	Melbourne	1979-80
		235	Pakistan	Faisalabad	1979-80
		204†	India	Sydney	1980-81
		201	Pakistan	Brisbane²	1981-82
		176	New Zealand	Christchurch	1981-82
		117	England	Perth	1982-83
		115	England	Adelaide	1982-83
		150*	Pakistan	Brisbane²	1983-84
		182	Pakistan	Sydney	1983-84
Chappell, I.M.	(14)	151	India	Melbourne	1967-68
		117†	West Indies	Brisbane²	1968-69
		165	West Indies	Melbourne	1968-69
		138	India	Delhi	1969-70
		111	England	Melbourne	1970-71
		104	England	Adelaide	1970-71
		118	England	Oval	1972
		196	Pakistan	Adelaide	1972-73
		106*	West Indies	Bridgetown	1972-73
		109	West Indies	Georgetown	1972-73
		145 ⎫ 121 ⎭	New Zealand	Wellington	1973-74
		192	England	Oval	1975
		156	West Indies	Perth	1975-76
Chipperfield, A.G.		109†	South Africa	Durban²	1935-36
Collins, H.L.	(4)	104†	England	Sydney	1920-21
		162	England	Adelaide	1920-21
		203	South Africa	Johannesburg¹	1921-22
		114	England	Sydney	1924-25
Cosier, G.J.	(2)	109†	West Indies	Melbourne	1975-76
		168	Pakistan	Melbourne	1976-77
Cowper, R.M.	(5)	143	West Indies	Port-of-Spain	1964-65
		102	West Indies	Bridgetown	1964-65
		307	England	Melbourne	1965-66
		108	India	Adelaide	1967-68
		165	India	Sydney	1967-68
Darling, J.	(3)	101	England	Sydney	1897-98
		178	England	Adelaide	1897-98
		160	England	Sydney	1897-98
Davis, I.C.		105†	Pakistan	Adelaide	1976-77
Duff, R.A.	(2)	104†	England	Melbourne	1901-02
		146	England	Oval	1905
Dyson, J.	(2)	102	England	Leeds	1981
		127*†	West Indies	Sydney	1981-82
Edwards, R.	(2)	170*	England	Nottingham	1972
		115	England	Perth	1974-75
Favell, L.E.		101	India	Madras²	1959-60
Fingleton, J.H.W.	(5)	112	South Africa	Cape Town	1935-36
		108	South Africa	Johannesburg¹	1935-36
		118	South Africa	Durban²	1935-36
		100	England	Brisbane²	1936-37
		136	England	Melbourne	1936-37
Giffen, G.		161	England	Sydney	1894-95
Gilmour, G.J.		101	New Zealand	Christchurch	1976-77
Graham, H.	(2)	107†	England	Lord's	1893
		105	England	Sydney	1894-95
Gregory, J.M.	(2)	100	England	Melbourne	1920-21

			Opponents		
Gregory, J.M. *continued*		119	South Africa	Johannesburg[1]	1921-22
			(Including the fastest Test hundred in 70 minutes)		
Gregory, S.E.	(4)	201	England	Sydney	1894-95
		103	England	Lord's	1896
		117	England	Oval	1899
		112	England	Adelaide	1903-04
Hartigan, R.J.		116†	England	Adelaide	1907-08
Harvey, R.N.	(21)	153	India	Melbourne	1947-48
		112†	England	Leeds	1948
		178	South Africa	Cape Town	1949-50
		151*	South Africa	Durban[2]	1949-50
		100	South Africa	Johannesburg[2]	1949-50
		116	South Africa	Port Elizabeth	1949-50
		109	South Africa	Brisbane[2]	1952-53
		190	South Africa	Sydney	1952-53
		116	South Africa	Adelaide	1952-53
		205	South Africa	Melbourne	1952-53
		122	England	Manchester	1953
		162	England	Brisbane[2]	1954-55
		133	West Indies	Kingston	1954-55
		133	West Indies	Port-of-Spain	1954-55
		204	West Indies	Kingston	1954-55
		140	India	Bombay[2]	1956-57
		167	England	Melbourne	1958-59
		114	India	Delhi	1959-60
		102	India	Bombay[2]	1959-60
		114	England	Birmingham	1961
		154	England	Adelaide	1962-63
Hassett, A.L.	(10)	128	England	Brisbane[2]	1946-47
		198*	India	Adelaide	1947-48
		137	England	Nottingham	1948
		112†	South Africa	Johannesburg[2]	1949-50
		167	South Africa	Port Elizabeth	1949-50
		132	West Indies	Sydney	1951-52
		102	West Indies	Melbourne	1951-52
		163	South Africa	Adelaide	1952-53
		115	England	Nottingham	1953
		104	England	Lord's	1953
Healy, I.A.	(2)	102*	England	Manchester	1993
		113*	New Zealand	Perth	1993-94
Hendry, H.S.T.L.		112	England	Sydney	1928-29
Hilditch, A.M.J.	(2)	113†	West Indies	Melbourne	1984-85
		119	England	Leeds	1985
Hill, C.	(7)	188	England	Melbourne	1897-98
		135	England	Lord's	1899
		119	England	Sheffield	1902
		142†	South Africa	Johannesburg[1]	1902-03
		160	England	Adelaide	1907-08
		191	South Africa	Sydney	1910-11
		100	South Africa	Melbourne	1910-11
Hookes, D.W.		143*†	Sir Lanka	Kandy	1982-83
Horan, T.P.		124	England	Melbourne	1881-82
Hughes, K.J.	(9)	129	England	Brisbane[2]	1978-79
		100	India	Madras[1]	1979-80
		130*†	West Indies	Brisbane[2]	1979-80
		117	England	Lord's	1980
		213	India	Adelaide	1980-81
		106	Pakistan	Perth	1981-82
		100*	West Indies	Melbourne	1981-82
		137	England	Sydney	1982-83
		106	Pakistan	Adelaide	1983-84
Iredale, F.A.	(2)	140	England	Adelaide	1894-95
		108	England	Manchester	1896
Jackson, A.A.		164†	England	Adelaide	1928-29
Jones, D.M.	(11)	210†	India	Madras[1]	1986-87
		184*	England	Sydney	1986-87
		102†	Sri Lanka	Perth	1987-88
		216	West Indies	Adelaide	1988-89
		157	England	Birmingham	1989

		Score	Opponents	Venue	Year
Jones, D.M. *continued*		122	England	Oval	1989
		118*	Sri Lanka	Hobart	1989-90
		116 } 121*	Pakistan	Adelaide	1989-90
		150*	India	Perth	1991-92
		100*	Sri Lanka	Colombo (KS)	1992-93
Kelleway, C.	(3)	114	South Africa	Manchester	1912
		102	South Africa	Lord's	1912
		147	England	Adelaide	1920-21
Kippax, A.F.	(2)	100	England	Melbourne	1928-29
		146†	West Indies	Adelaide	1930-31
Lawry, W.M.	(13)	130	England	Lord's	1961
		102	England	Manchester	1961
		157	South Africa	Melbourne	1963-64
		106	England	Manchester	1964
		210	West Indies	Bridgetown	1964-65
		166	England	Brisbane[2]	1965-66
		119	England	Adelaide	1965-66
		108	England	Melbourne	1965-66
		100	India	Melbourne	1967-68
		135	England	Oval	1968
		105	West Indies	Brisbane[2]	1968-69
		205	West Indies	Melbourne	1968-69
		151	West Indies	Sydney	1968-69
Lindwall, R.R.	(2)	100	England	Melbourne	1946-47
		118	West Indies	Bridgetown	1954-55
Loxton, S.J.E.		101†	South Africa	Johannesburg[2]	1949-50
Lyons, J.J.		134	England	Sydney	1891-92
Macartney, C.G.	(7)	137	South Africa	Sydney	1910-11
		170	England	Sydney	1920-21
		115	England	Leeds	1921
		116	South Africa	Durban[1]	1921-22
		133*	England	Lord's	1926
		151	England	Leeds	1926
		109	England	Manchester	1926
McCabe, S.J.	(6)	187*	England	Sydney	1932-33
		137	England	Manchester	1934
		149	South Africa	Durban[2]	1935-36
		189*	South Africa	Johannesburg[1]	1935-36
		112	England	Melbourne	1936-37
		232	England	Nottingham	1938
McCool, C.L.		104*	England	Melbourne	1946-47
McCosker, R.B.	(4)	127	England	Oval	1975
		109*	West Indies	Melbourne	1975-76
		105	Pakistan	Melbourne	1976-77
		107	England	Nottingham	1977
McDonald, C.C.	(5)	154	South Africa	Adelaide	1952-53
		110	West Indies	Port-of-Spain	1954-55
		127	West Indies	Kingston	1954-55
		170	England	Adelaide	1958-59
		133	England	Melbourne	1958-59
McDonnell, P.S.	(3)	147	England	Sydney	1881-82
		103	England	Oval	1884
		124	England	Adelaide	1884-85
McLeod, C.E.		112	England	Melbourne	1897-98
Mann, A.L.		105	India	Perth	1977-78
Marsh, G.R.	(4)	118	New Zealand	Auckland	1985-86
		101	India	Bombay[3]	1986-87
		110†	England	Brisbane[2]	1986-87
		138	England	Nottingham	1989
Marsh, R.W.	(3)	118†	Pakistan	Adelaide	1972-73
		132	New Zealand	Adelaide	1973-74
		110*	England	Melbourne	1976-77
Matthews, G.R.J.	(4)	115†	New Zealand	Brisbane[2]	1985-86
		100*	India	Melbourne	1985-86
		130	New Zealand	Wellington	1985-86
		128	England	Sydney	1990-91
Miller, K.R.	(7)	141*	England	Adelaide	1946-47
		145*	England	Sydney	1950-51

			Opponents		
Miller, K.R. *continued*		129	West Indies	Sydney	1951-52
		109	England	Lord's	1953
		147	West Indies	Kingston	1954-55
		137	West Indies	Bridgetown	1954-55
		109	West Indies	Kingston	1954-55
Moody, T.M.	(2)	106†	Sri Lanka	Brisbane[2]	1989-90
		101†	India	Perth	1991-92
Moroney, J.	(2)	118 } 101* }	South Africa	Johannesburg[2]	1949-50
Morris, A.R.	(12)	155	England	Melbourne	1946-47
		122 } 124* }	England	Adelaide	1946-47
		100*	India	Melbourne	1947-48
		105	England	Lord's	1948
		182	England	Leeds	1948
		196	England	Oval	1948
		111	South Africa	Johannesburg[2]	1949-50
		157	South Africa	Port Elizabeth	1949-50
		206	England	Adelaide	1950-51
		153	England	Brisbane[2]	1954-55
		111	West Indies	Port-of-Spain	1954-55
Murdoch, W.L.	(2)	153*	England	Oval	1880
		211	England	Oval	1884
Noble, M.A.		133	England	Sydney	1903-04
O'Neill, N.C.	(6)	134	Pakistan	Lahore[2]	1959-60
		163	India	Bombay[2]	1959-60
		113	India	Calcutta	1959-60
		181†	West Indies	Brisbane[2]	1960-61
		117	England	Oval	1961
		100	England	Adelaide	1962-63
Pellew, C.E.	(2)	116	England	Melbourne	1920-21
		104	England	Adelaide	1920-21
Phillips, W.B.	(2)	159†	Pakistan	Perth	1983-84
		120	West Indies	Bridgetown	1983-84
Ponsford, W.H.	(7)	110†	England	Sydney	1924-25
		128	England	Melbourne	1924-25
		110	England	Oval	1930
		183	West Indies	Sydney	1930-31
		109	West Indies	Brisbane[1]	1930-31
		181	England	Leeds	1934
		266	England	Oval	1934
Ransford, V.S.		143*	England	Lord's	1909
Redpath, I.R.	(8)	132	West Indies	Sydney	1968-69
		171	England	Perth	1970-71
		135	Pakistan	Melbourne	1972-73
		159*	New Zealand	Auckland	1973-74
		105	England	Sydney	1974-75
		102	West Indies	Melbourne	1975-76
		103	West Indies	Adelaide	1975-76
		101	West Indies	Melbourne	1975-76
Richardson, A.J.		100	England	Leeds	1926
Richardson, V.Y.		138	England	Melbourne	1924-25
Rigg, K.E.		127†	South Africa	Sydney	1931-32
Ritchie, G.M.	(3)	106*	Pakistan	Faisalabad	1982-83
		146	England	Nottingham	1985
		128†	India	Adelaide	1985-86
Ryder, J.	(3)	142	South Africa	Cape Town	1921-22
		201*	England	Adelaide	1924-25
		112	England	Melbourne	1928-29
Scott, H.J.H.		102	England	Oval	1884
Serjeant, C.S.		124	West Indies	Georgetown	1977-78
Sheahan, A.P.	(2)	114	India	Kanpur	1969-70
		127	Pakistan	Melbourne	1972-73
Simpson, R.B.	(10)	311	England	Manchester	1964
		153† } 115† }	Pakistan	Karachi[1]	1964-65
		201	West Indies	Bridgetown	1964-65
		225	England	Adelaide	1965-66
		153	South Africa	Cape Town	1966-67

			Score	Opponents	Venue	Season
Simpson, R.B. *continued*			103	India	Adelaide	1967-68
			109	India	Melbourne	1967-68
			176	India	Perth	1977-78
			100	India	Adelaide	1977-78
Slater, M.J.		(2)	152	England	Lord's	1993
			168	New Zealand	Hobart	1993-94
Stackpole, K.R.		(7)	134	South Africa	Cape Town	1966-67
			103†	India	Bombay[2]	1969-70
			207	England	Brisbane[2]	1970-71
			136	England	Adelaide	1970-71
			114	England	Nottingham	1972
			142	West Indies	Kingston	1972-73
			122†	New Zealand	Melbourne	1973-74
Taylor, J.M.			108	England	Sydney	1924-25
Taylor, M.A.		(12)	136†	England	Leeds	1989
			219	England	Nottingham	1989
			164†	Sri Lanka	Brisbane[2]	1989-90
			108	Sri Lanka	Hobart	1989-90
			101†	Pakistan	Melbourne	1989-90
			101*	Pakistan	Sydney	1989-90
			144	West Indies	St John's	1990-91
			100	India	Adelaide	1991-92
			124	England	Manchester	1993
			111	England	Lord's	1993
			142*	New Zealand	Perth	1993-94
			170†	South Africa	Melbourne	1993-94
Toohey, P.M.			122	West Indies	Kingston	1977-78
Trott, G.H.S.			143	England	Lord's	1896
Trumper, V.T.		(8)	135*	England	Lord's	1899
			104	England	Manchester	1902
			185*	England	Sydney	1903-04
			113	England	Adelaide	1903-04
			166	England	Sydney	1907-08
			159	South Africa	Melbourne	1910-11
			214*	South Africa	Adelaide	1910-11
			113	England	Sydney	1911-12
Turner, A.			136	West Indies	Adelaide	1975-76
Walters, K.D.		(15)	155†	England	Brisbane[2]	1965-66
			115	England	Melbourne	1965-66
			118	West Indies	Sydney	1968-69
			110	West Indies	Adelaide	1968-69
			242 } 103	West Indies	Sydney	1968-69
			102	India	Madras[1]	1969-70
			112	England	Brisbane[2]	1970-71
			102*	West Indies	Bridgetown	1972-73
			112	West Indies	Port-of-Spain	1972-73
			104*	New Zealand	Auckland	1973-74
			103	England	Perth	1974-75
			107	Pakistan	Adelaide	1976-77
			250	New Zealand	Christchurch	1976-77
			107	New Zealand	Melbourne	1980-81
Waugh, M.E.		(6)	138†	England	Adelaide	1990-91
			139*	West Indies	St John's	1990-91
			112	West Indies	Melbourne	1992-93
			137	England	Birmingham	1993
			111	New Zealand	Hobart	1993-94
			113*	South Africa	Durban[2]	1993-94
Waugh, S.R.		(7)	177*	England	Leeds	1989
			152*	England	Lord's	1989
			134*	Sri Lanka	Hobart	1989-90
			100	West Indies	Sydney	1992-93
			157*	England	Leeds	1993
			147*	New Zealand	Brisbane[2]	1993-94
			164†	South Africa	Adelaide	1993-94
Wellham, D.M.			103†	England	Oval	1981
Wessels, K.C.		(4)	162†	England	Brisbane[2]	1982-83
			141†	Sri Lanka	Kandy	1982-83
			179	Pakistan	Adelaide	1983-84

			Opponents		
Wessels, K.C. *continued*		173	West Indies	Sydney	1984-85
Wood, G.M.	(9)	126	West Indies	Georgetown	1977-78
		100	England	Melbourne	1978-79
		112	England	Lord's	1980
		111†	New Zealand	Brisbane[2]	1980-81
		125	India	Adelaide	1980-81
		100	Pakistan	Melbourne	1981-82
		100	New Zealand	Auckland	1981-82
		172	England	Nottingham	1985
		111	West Indies	Perth	1988-89
Woodfull, W.M.	(7)	141	England	Leeds	1926
		117	England	Manchester	1926
		111	England	Sydney	1928-29
		107	England	Melbourne	1928-29
		102	England	Melbourne	1928-29
		155	England	Lord's	1930
		161	South Africa	Melbourne	1931-32
Yallop, G.N.	(8)	121†	India	Adelaide	1977-78
		102†	England	Brisbane[2]	1978-79
		121	England	Sydney	1978-79
		167	India	Calcutta	1979-80
		172	Pakistan	Faisalabad	1979-80
		114	England	Manchester	1981
		141	Pakistan	Perth	1983-84
		268	Pakistan	Melbourne	1983-84

SOUTH AFRICA (115)

Balaskas, X.C.		122*	New Zealand	Wellington	1931-32
Barlow, E.J.	(6)	114†	Australia	Brisbane[2]	1963-64
		109	Australia	Melbourne	1963-64
		201	Australia	Adelaide	1963-64
		138	England	Cape Town	1964-65
		127	Australia	Cape Town	1969-70
		110	Australia	Johannesburg[3]	1969-70
Bland, K.C.	(3)	126	Australia	Sydney	1963-64
		144*	England	Johannesburg[3]	1964-65
		127	England	Oval	1965
Catterall, R.H.	(3)	120	England	Birmingham	1924
		120	England	Lord's	1924
		119	England	Durban[2]	1927-28
Christy, J.A.J.		103†	New Zealand	Christchurch	1931-32
Cronje, W.J.	(3)	135	India	Port Elizabeth	1992-93
		122	Sri Lanka	Colombo (SSC)	1993-94
		122	Australia	Johannesburg[3]	1993-94
Cullinan, D.J.		102	Sri Lanka	Colombo (PSS)	1993-94
Dalton, E.L.	(2)	117	England	Oval	1935
		102	England	Johannesburg[1]	1938-39
Endean, W.R.	(3)	162*	Australia	Melbourne	1952-53
		116	New Zealand	Auckland	1952-53
		116*	England	Leeds	1955
Faulkner, G.A.	(4)	123	England	Johannesburg[1]	1909-10
		204	Australia	Melbourne	1910-11
		115	Australia	Adelaide	1910-11
		122*	Australia	Manchester	1912
Frank, C.N.		152	Australia	Johannesburg[1]	1921-22
Goddard, T.L.		112	England	Johannesburg[3]	1964-65
Hathorn, C.M.H.		102	England	Johannesburg[1]	1905-06
Hudson, A.C.	(2)	163†	West Indies	Bridgetown	1991-92
		102	Australia	Cape Town	1993-94
Irvine, B.L.		102	Australia	Port Elizabeth	1969-70
Kirsten, P.N.		104	England	Leeds	1994
Lindsay, D.T.	(3)	182	Australia	Johannesburg[3]	1966-67
		137	Australia	Durban[2]	1966-67
		131	Australia	Johannesburg[3]	1966-67
McGlew, D.J.	(7)	255*†	New Zealand	Wellington	1952-53
		104*	England	Manchester	1955
		133	England	Leeds	1955
		108	Australia	Johannesburg[3]	1957-58

			Opponents		
McGlew, D.J. *continued*		105	Australia	Durban[2]	1957-58
		127*	New Zealand	Durban[2]	1961-62
		120	New Zealand	Johannesburg[3]	1961-62
McLean, R.A.	(5)	101	New Zealand	Durban[2]	1953-54
		142	England	Lord's	1955
		100	England	Durban[2]	1956-57
		109	England	Manchester	1960
		113	New Zealand	Cape Town	1961-62
Melville, A.	(4)	103	England	Durban[2]	1938-39
		189 } 104* }	England	Nottingham	1947
		117	England	Lord's	1947
Mitchell, B.	(8)	123	England	Cape Town	1930-31
		113†	New Zealand	Christchurch	1931-32
		164*	England	Lord's	1935
		128	England	Oval	1935
		109	England	Durban[2]	1938-39
		120 } 189* }	England	Oval	1947
		120	England	Cape Town	1948-49
Murray, A.R.A.		109†	New Zealand	Wellington	1952-53
Nourse, A.D.	(9)	231	Australia	Johannesburg[1]	1935-36
		120	England	Cape Town	1938-39
		103	England	Durban[2]	1938-39
		149	England	Nottingham	1947
		115	England	Manchester	1947
		112	England	Cape Town	1948-49
		129*	England	Johannesburg[2]	1948-49
		114	Australia	Cape Town	1949-50
		208	England	Nottingham	1951
Nourse, A.W.		111	Australia	Johannesburg[1]	1921-22
Owen-Smith, H.G.		129	England	Leeds	1929
Pithey, A.J.		154	England	Cape Town	1964-65
Pollock, R.G.	(7)	122	Australia	Sydney	1963-64
		175	Australia	Adelaide	1963-64
		137	England	Port Elizabeth	1964-65
		125	England	Nottingham	1965
		209	Australia	Cape Town	1966-67
		105	Australia	Port Elizabeth	1966-67
		274	Australia	Durban[2]	1969-70
Rhodes, J.N.		101*†	Sri Lanka	Moratuwa	1993-94
Richards, B.A.	(2)	140	Australia	Durban[2]	1969-70
		126	Australia	Port Elizabeth	1969-70
Rowan, E.A.B.	(3)	156*	England	Johannesburg[2]	1948-49
		143	Australia	Durban[2]	1949-50
		236	England	Leeds	1951
Sherwell, P.W.		115	England	Lord's	1907
Siedle, I.J.		141	England	Cape Town	1930-31
Sinclair, J.H.	(3)	106	England	Cape Town	1898-99
		101	Australia	Johannesburg[1]	1902-03
		104	Australia	Cape Town	1902-03
Snooke, S.J.		103	Australia	Adelaide	1910-11
Taylor, H.W.	(7)	109	England	Durban[1]	1913-14
		176	England	Johannesburg[1]	1922-23
		101	England	Johannesburg[1]	1922-23
		102	England	Durban[2]	1922-23
		101	England	Johannesburg[1]	1927-28
		121	England	Oval	1929
		117	England	Cape Town	1930-31
Van der Bijl, P.G.V.		125	England	Durban[2]	1938-39
Viljoen, K.G.	(2)	111	Australia	Melbourne	1931-32
		124	England	Manchester	1935
Wade, W.W.		125	England	Port Elizabeth	1948-49
Waite, J.H.B.	(4)	113	England	Manchester	1955
		115	Australia	Johannesburg[3]	1957-58
		134	Australia	Durban[2]	1957-58
		101	New Zealand	Johannesburg[3]	1961-62
Wessels, K.C.	(2)	118†	India	Durban[2]	1992-93
		105	England	Lord's	1994

			Opponents		
White, G.C.	(2)	147	England	Johannesburg[1]	1905-06
		118	England	Durban[1]	1909-10
Winslow, P.L.		108	England	Manchester	1955
Zulch, J.W.	(2)	105	Australia	Adelaide	1910-11
		150	Australia	Sydney	1910-11

WEST INDIES (305)

Adams, J.C.		137	England	Georgetown	1993-94
Alexander, F.C.M.		108	Australia	Sydney	1960-61
Arthurton, K.L.T.	(2)	157*†	Australia	Brisbane[2]	1992-93
		126	England	Kingston	1993-94
Atkinson, D.St E.		219	Australia	Bridgetown	1954-55
Bacchus, S.F.A.F.		250	India	Kanpur	1978-79
Baichan, L.		105*†	Pakistan	Lahore[2]	1974-75
Barrow, I.		105	England	Manchester	1933
Best, C.A.		164	England	Bridgetown	1989-90
Butcher, B.F.	(7)	103	India	Calcutta	1958-59
		142	India	Madras[2]	1958-59
		133	England	Lord's	1963
		117	Australia	Port-of-Spain	1964-65
		209*	England	Nottingham	1966
		101	Australia	Sydney	1968-69
		118	Australia	Adelaide	1968-69
Carew, G.M.		107	England	Port-of-Spain	1947-48
Carew, M.C.		109†	New Zealand	Auckland	1968-69
Christiani, R.J.		107†	India	Delhi	1948-49
Davis, C.A.	(4)	103	England	Lord's	1969
		125*	India	Georgetown	1970-71
		105	India	Port-of-Spain	1970-71
		183	New Zealand	Bridgetown	1971-72
Depeiza, C.C.		122	Australia	Bridgetown	1954-55
Dujon, P.J.L.	(5)	110	India	St John's	1982-83
		130	Australia	Port-of-Spain	1983-84
		101	England	Manchester	1984
		139	Australia	Perth	1984-85
		106*	Pakistan	Port-of-Spain	1987-88
Foster, M.L.C.		125†	Australia	Kingston	1972-73
Fredericks, R.C.	(8)	163	New Zealand	Kingston	1971-72
		150	England	Birmingham	1973
		100	India	Calcutta	1974-75
		104	India	Bombay[3]	1974-75
		169	Australia	Perth	1975-76
		138	England	Lord's	1976
		109	England	Leeds	1976
		120	Pakistan	Port-of-Spain	1976-77
Ganteaume, A.G.		112†	England	Port-of-Spain	1947-48
Gomes, H.A.	(9)	101†	Australia	Georgetown	1977-78
		115	Australia	Kingston	1977-78
		126	Australia	Sydney	1981-82
		124*	Australia	Adelaide	1981-82
		123	India	Port-of-Spain	1982-83
		143	England	Birmingham	1984
		104*	England	Leeds	1984
		127	Australia	Perth	1984-85
		120*	Australia	Adelaide	1984-85
Gomez, G.E.		101†	India	Delhi	1948-49
Greenidge, C.G.	(19)	107†	India	Bangalore	1974-75
		134 / 101	England	Manchester	1976
		115	England	Leeds	1976
		100	Pakistan	Kingston	1976-77
		154*	India	St John's	1982-83
		194	India	Kanpur	1983-84
		120*	Australia	Georgetown	1983-84
		127	Australia	Kingston	1983-84
		214*	England	Lord's	1984
		223	England	Manchester	1984
		100	New Zealand	Port-of-Spain	1984-85

			Opponents		
Greenidge, C.G. *continued*		213	New Zealand	Auckland	1986-87
		141	India	Calcutta	1987-88
		103	England	Lord's	1988
		104	Australia	Adelaide	1988-89
		117	India	Bridgetown	1988-89
		149	England	St John's	1989-90
		226	Australia	Bridgetown	1990-91
Haynes, D.L.	(18)	105†	New Zealand	Dunedin	1979-80
		122	New Zealand	Christchurch	1979-80
		184	England	Lord's	1980
		136	India	St John's	1982-83
		103*	Australia	Georgetown	1983-84
		145	Australia	Bridgetown	1983-84
		125	England	Oval	1984
		131	England	St John's	1985-86
		121	New Zealand	Wellington	1986-87
		100	Australia	Perth	1988-89
		143	Australia	Sydney	1988-89
		112*	India	Bridgetown	1988-89
		109	England	Bridgetown	1989-90
		167	England	St John's	1989-90
		117	Pakistan	Karachi[1]	1990-91
		111	Australia	Georgetown	1990-91
		143*	Pakistan	Port-of-Spain	1992-93
		125	Pakistan	Bridgetown	1992-93
Headley, G.A.	(10)	176†	England	Bridgetown	1929-30
		114 112 }	England	Georgetown	1929-30
		223	England	Kingston	1929-30
		102*	Australia	Brisbane[1]	1930-31
		105	Australia	Sydney	1930-31
		169*	England	Manchester	1933
		270*	England	Kingston	1934-35
		106 107 }	England	Lord's	1939
Holford, D.A.J.		105*	England	Lord's	1966
Holt, J.K.	(2)	166	England	Bridgetown	1953-54
		123	India	Delhi	1958-59
Hooper, C.L.	(4)	100*	India	Calcutta	1987-88
		134	Pakistan	Lahore[2]	1990-91
		111	England	Lord's	1991
		178*	Pakistan	St John's	1992-93
Hunte, C.C.	(8)	142†	Pakistan	Bridgetown	1957-58
		260	Pakistan	Kingston	1957-58
		114	Pakistan	Georgetown	1957-58
		110	Australia	Melbourne	1960-61
		182	England	Manchester	1963
		108*	England	Oval	1963
		135	England	Manchester	1966
		101	India	Bombay[2]	1966-67
Julien, B.D.	(2)	121	England	Lord's	1973
		101	Pakistan	Karachi[1]	1974-75
Kallicharran, A.I.	(12)	100*†	New Zealand	Georgetown	1971-72
		101	New Zealand	Port-of-Spain	1971-72
		158	England	Port-of-Spain	1973-74
		119	England	Bridgetown	1973-74
		124†	India	Bangalore	1974-75
		115	Pakistan	Karachi[1]	1974-75
		101	Australia	Brisbane[2]	1975-76
		103*	India	Port-of-Spain	1975-76
		127	Australia	Port-of-Spain	1977-78
		126	Australia	Kingston	1977-78
		187	India	Bombay[3]	1978-79
		106	Australia	Adelaide	1979-80
Kanhai, R.B.	(15)	256	India	Calcutta	1958-59
		217	Pakistan	Lahore[1]	1958-59
		110	England	Port-of-Spain	1959-60
		117 115 }	Australia	Adelaide	1960-61

			Opponents		
Kanhai, R.B. *continued*		138	India	Kingston	1961-62
		139	India	Port-of-Spain	1961-62
		129	Australia	Bridgetown	1964-65
		121	Australia	Port-of-Spain	1964-65
		104	England	Oval	1966
		153	England	Port-of-Spain	1967-68
		150	England	Georgetown	1967-68
		158*	India	Kingston	1970-71
		105	Australia	Bridgetown	1972-73
		157	England	Lord's	1973
King, C.L.		100*	New Zealand	Christchurch	1979-80
Lara, B.C.	(3)	277	Australia	Sydney	1992-93
		167	England	Georgetown	1993-94
		375	England	St John's	1993-94
Lloyd, C.H.	(19)	118†	England	Port-of-Spain	1967-68
		113*	England	Bridgetown	1967-68
		129†	Australia	Brisbane[2]	1968-69
		178	Australia	Georgetown	1972-73
		132	England	Oval	1973
		163	India	Bangalore	1974-75
		242*	India	Bombay[3]	1974-75
		149	Australia	Perth	1975-76
		102	Australia	Melbourne	1975-76
		102	India	Bridgetown	1975-76
		157	Pakistan	Bridgetown	1976-77
		121	Australia	Adelaide	1979-80
		101	England	Manchester	1980
		100	England	Bridgetown	1980-81
		143	India	Port-of-Spain	1982-83
		106	India	St John's	1982-83
		103	India	Delhi	1983-84
		161*	India	Calcutta	1983-84
		114	Australia	Brisbane[2]	1984-85
Logie, A.L.	(2)	130	India	Bridgetown	1982-83
		101	India	Calcutta	1987-88
McMorris, E.D.A.St J.		125†	India	Kingston	1961-62
Martin, F.R.		123*	Australia	Sydney	1930-31
Nurse, S.M.	(6)	201	Australia	Bridgetown	1964-65
		137	England	Leeds	1966
		136	England	Port-of-Spain	1967-68
		137	Australia	Sydney	1968-69
		168†	New Zealand	Auckland	1968-69
		258	New Zealand	Christchurch	1968-69
Pairaudeau, B.H.		115†	India	Port-of-Spain	1952-53
Rae, A.F.	(4)	104	India	Bombay[2]	1948-49
		109	India	Madras[1]	1948-49
		106	England	Lord's	1950
		109	England	Oval	1950
Richards, I.V.A.	(24)	192*	India	Delhi	1974-75
		101	Australia	Adelaide	1975-76
		142	India	Bridgetown	1975-76
		130	India	Port-of-Spain	1975-76
		177	India	Port-of-Spain	1975-76
		232†	England	Nottingham	1976
		135	England	Manchester	1976
		291	England	Oval	1976
		140	Australia	Brisbane[2]	1979-80
		145	England	Lord's	1980
		120	Pakistan	Multan	1980-81
		182*	England	Bridgetown	1980-81
		114	England	St John's	1980-81
		109	India	Georgetown	1982-83
		120	India	Bombay[3]	1983-84
		178	Australia	St John's	1983-84
		117	England	Birmingham	1984
		208	Australia	Melbourne	1984-85
		105	New Zealand	Bridgetown	1984-85
		110*	England	St John's	1985-86
		109*	India	Delhi	1987-88

			Opponents		
Richards, I.V.A. *continued*		123	Pakistan	Port-of-Spain	1987-88
		146	Australia	Perth	1988-89
		110	India	Kingston	1988-89
Richardson, R.B.	(15)	131*	Australia	Bridgetown	1983-84
		154	Australia	St John's[2]	1983-84
		138	Australia	Brisbane[2]	1984-85
		185	New Zealand	Georgetown	1984-85
		102	England	Port-of-Spain	1985-86
		160	England	Bridgetown	1985-86
		122	Australia	Melbourne	1988-89
		106	Australia	Adelaide	1988-89
		194	India	Georgetown	1988-89
		156	India	Kingston	1988-89
		104*	Australia	Kingston	1990-91
		182	Australia	Georgetown	1990-91
		104	England	Birmingham	1991
		121	England	Oval	1991
		109	Australia	Sydney	1992-93
Roach, C.A.	(2)	122	England	Bridgetown	1929-30
		209	England	Georgetown	1929-30
Rowe, L.G.	(7)	214† 100*† }	New Zealand	Kingston	1971-72
		120	England	Kingston	1973-74
		302	England	Bridgetown	1973-74
		123	England	Port-of-Spain	1973-74
		107	Australia	Brisbane[2]	1975-76
		100	New Zealand	Christchurch	1979-80
Shillingford, I.T.		120	Pakistan	Georgetown	1976-77
Simmons, P.V.		110	Australia	Melbourne	1992-93
Smith, O.G.	(4)	104†	Australia	Kingston	1954-55
		161†	England	Birmingham	1957
		168	England	Nottingham	1957
		100	India	Delhi	1958-59
Sobers, G.St A.	(26)	365*	Pakistan	Kingston	1957-58
		125 109* }	Pakistan	Georgetown	1957-58
		142*†	India	Bombay[2]	1958-59
		198	India	Kanpur	1958-59
		106*	India	Calcutta	1958-59
		226	England	Bridgetown	1959-60
		147	England	Kingston	1959-60
		145	England	Georgetown	1959-60
		132	Australia	Brisbane[2]	1960-61
		168	Australia	Sydney	1960-61
		153	India	Kingston	1961-62
		104	India	Kingston	1961-62
		102	England	Leeds	1963
		161	England	Manchester	1966
		163*	England	Lord's	1966
		174	England	Leeds	1966
		113*	England	Kingston	1967-68
		152	England	Georgetown	1967-68
		110	Australia	Adelaide	1968-69
		113	Australia	Sydney	1968-69
		108*	India	Georgetown	1970-71
		178	India	Bridgetown	1970-71
		132	India	Port-of-Spain	1970-71
		142	New Zealand	Bridgetown	1971-72
		150*	England	Lord's	1973
Solomon, J.S.		100*	India	Delhi	1958-59
Stollmeyer, J.B.	(4)	160	India	Madras[2]	1948-49
		104	Australia	Sydney	1951-52
		152	New Zealand	Auckland	1951-52
		104*	India	Port-of-Spain	1952-53
Walcott, C.L.	(15)	152†	India	Delhi	1948-49
		108	India	Calcutta	1948-49
		168*	England	Lord's	1950
		115	New Zealand	Auckland	1951-52
		125	India	Georgetown	1952-53

			Opponents		
Walcott, C.L. *continued*		118	India	Kingston	1952-53
		220	England	Bridgetown	1953-54
		124	England	Port-of-Spain	1953-54
		116	England	Kingston	1953-54
		108	Australia	Kingston	1954-55
		126 } 110 }	Australia	Port-of-Spain	1954-55
		155 } 110 }	Australia	Kingston	1954-55
		145	Pakistan	Georgetown	1957-58
Weekes, E.de C.	(15)	141	England	Kingston	1947-48
		128†	India	Delhi	1948-49
		194	India	Bombay[2]	1948-49
		162 } 101 }	India	Calcutta	1948-49
		129	England	Nottingham	1950
		207	India	Port-of-Spain	1952-53
		161	India	Port-of-Spain	1952-53
		109	India	Kingston	1952-53
		206	England	Port-of-Spain	1953-54
		139	Australia	Port-of-Spain	1954-55
		123	New Zealand	Dunedin	1955-56
		103	New Zealand	Christchurch	1955-56
		156	New Zealand	Wellington	1955-56
		197†	Pakistan	Bridgetown	1957-58
Weekes, K.H.		137	England	Oval	1939
Williams, A.B.	(2)	100†	Australia	Georgetown	1977-78
		111	India	Calcutta	1978-79
Worrell, F.M.M.	(9)	131*	England	Georgetown	1947-48
		261	England	Nottingham	1950
		138	England	Oval	1950
		108	Australia	Melbourne	1951-52
		100	New Zealand	Auckland	1951-52
		237	India	Kingston	1952-53
		167	England	Port-of-Spain	1953-54
		191*	England	Nottingham	1957
		197*	England	Bridgetown	1959-60

NEW ZEALAND (135)					
Barton, P.T.		109	South Africa	Port Elizabeth	1961-62
Bracewell, J.G.		110	England	Nottingham	1986
Burgess, M.G.	(5)	119*	Pakistan	Dacca	1969-70
		104	England	Auckland	1970-71
		101	West Indies	Kingston	1971-72
		105	England	Lord's	1973
		111	Pakistan	Lahore[2]	1976-77
Coney, J.V.	(3)	174*	England	Wellington	1983-84
		111*	Pakistan	Dunedin	1984-85
		101*	Australia	Wellington	1985-86
Congdon, B.E.	(7)	104	England	Christchurch	1965-66
		166*	West Indies	Port-of-Spain	1971-72
		126	West Indies	Bridgetown	1971-72
		176	England	Nottingham	1973
		175	England	Lord's	1973
		132	Australia	Wellington	1973-74
		107*	Australia	Christchurch	1976-77
Crowe, J.J.	(3)	128	England	Auckland	1983-84
		112	West Indies	Kingston	1984-85
		120*	Sri Lanka	Colombo (CCC)	1986-87
Crowe, M.D.	(17)	100	England	Wellington	1983-84
		188	West Indies	Georgetown	1984-85
		188	Australia	Brisbane[2]	1985-86
		137	Australia	Christchurch	1985-86
		106	England	Lord's	1986
		119	West Indies	Wellington	1986-87
		104	West Indies	Auckland	1986-87
		137	Australia	Adelaide	1987-88
		143	England	Wellington	1987-88
		174	Pakistan	Wellington	1988-89

			Opponents		
Crowe, M.D. *continued*		113	India	Auckland	1989-90
		108*	Pakistan	Lahore[2]	1990-91
		299	Sri Lanka	Wellington	1990-91
		140	Zimbabwe	Harare	1992-93
		107	Sri Lanka	Colombo (SSC)	1992-93
		142	England	Lord's	1994
		115	England	Manchester	1994
Dempster, C.S.	(2)	136	England	Wellington	1929-30
		120	England	Lord's	1931
Donnelly, M.P.		206	England	Lord's	1949
Dowling, G.T.	(3)	129	India	Bombay[2]	1964-65
		143	India	Dunedin	1967-68
		239	India	Christchurch	1967-68
Edgar, B.A.	(3)	129†	Pakistan	Christchurch	1978-79
		127	West Indies	Auckland	1979-80
		161	Australia	Auckland	1981-82
Franklin, T.J.		101	England	Lord's	1990
Greatbatch, M.J.	(3)	107*†	England	Auckland	1987-88
		146*†	Australia	Perth	1989-90
		133	Pakistan	Hamilton	1992-93
Guy, J.W.		102†	India	Hyderabad	1955-56
Hadlee, R.J.	(2)	103	West Indies	Christchurch	1979-80
		151*	Sri Lanka	Colombo (CCC)	1986-87
Hadlee, W.A.		116	England	Christchurch	1946-47
Harris, P.G.Z.		101	South Africa	Cape Town	1961-62
Hastings, B.F.	(4)	117*	West Indies	Christchurch	1968-69
		105	West Indies	Bridgetown	1971-72
		110	Pakistan	Auckland	1972-73
		101	Australia	Wellington	1973-74
Howarth, G.P.	(6)	122 } 102 }	England	Auckland	1977-78
		123	England	Lord's	1978
		114	Pakistan	Napier	1978-79
		147	West Indies	Christchurch	1979-80
		137*	India	Wellington	1980-81
Jarvis, T.W.		182	West Indies	Georgetown	1971-72
Jones, A.H.	(7)	150	Australia	Adelaide	1987-88
		170*	India	Auckland	1989-90
		186	Sri Lanka	Wellington	1990-91
		122 } 100* }	Sri Lanka	Hamilton	1990-91
		143	England	Wellington	1991-92
		143	Australia	Perth	1993-94
Latham, R.T.		119†	Zimbabwe	Bulawayo	1992-93
Lees, W.K.		152	Pakistan	Karachi[1]	1976-77
McGregor, S.N.		111	Pakistan	Lahore[1]	1955-56
Mills, J.E.		117†	England	Wellington	1929-30
Morrison, J.F.M.		117	Australia	Sydney	1973-74
Page, M.L.		104	England	Lord's	1931
Parker, J.M.	(3)	108	Australia	Sydney	1973-74
		121	England	Auckland	1974-75
		104	India	Bombay[3]	1976-77
Pollard, V.	(2)	116	England	Nottingham	1973
		105*	England	Lord's	1973
Rabone, G.O.		107	South Africa	Durban[2]	1953-54
Redmond, R.E.		107†	Pakistan	Auckland	1972-73
Reid, J.F.	(6)	123*	India	Christchurch	1980-81
		180	Sri Lanka	Colombo (CCC)	1983-84
		106	Pakistan	Hyderabad	1984-85
		148	Pakistan	Wellington	1984-85
		158*	Pakistan	Auckland	1984-85
		108†	Australia	Brisbane[2]	1985-86
Reid, J.R.	(6)	135	South Africa	Cape Town	1953-54
		119*	India	Delhi	1955-56
		120	India	Calcutta	1955-56
		142	South Africa	Johannesburg[3]	1961-62
		100	England	Christchurch	1962-63
		128	Pakistan	Karachi[1]	1964-65
Rutherford, K.R.	(3)	107*	England	Wellington	1987-88

560

			Opponents		
Rutherford, K.R. *continued*		105	Sri Lanka	Moratuwa	1992-93
		102	Australia	Christchurch	1992-93
Sinclair, B.W.	(3)	138	South Africa	Auckland	1963-64
		130	Pakistan	Lahore[2]	1964-65
		114	England	Auckland	1965-66
Smith, I.D.S.	(2)	113*	England	Auckland	1983-84
		173	India	Auckland	1989-90
Sutcliffe, B.	(5)	101	England	Manchester	1949
		116	England	Christchurch	1950-51
		137*†	India	Hyderabad	1955-56
		230*	India	Delhi	1955-56
		151*	India	Calcutta	1964-65
Taylor, B.R.	(2)	105†	India	Calcutta	1964-65
		124†	West Indies	Auckland	1968-69
Thomson, S.A.		120*	Pakistan	Christchurch	1993-94
Turner, G.M.	(7)	110†	Pakistan	Dacca	1969-70
		223*	West Indies	Kingston	1971-72
		259	West Indies	Georgetown	1971-72
		101 } 110* }	Australia	Christchurch	1973-74
		117	India	Christchurch	1975-76
		113	India	Kanpur	1976-77
Vivian, H.G.		100†	South Africa	Wellington	1931-32
Wright, J.G.	(12)	110	India	Auckland	1980-81
		141	Australia	Christchurch	1981-82
		130	England	Auckland	1983-84
		107	Pakistan	Karachi[1]	1984-85
		119	England	Oval	1986
		138	West Indies	Wellington	1986-87
		103	England	Auckland	1987-88
		185	India	Christchurch	1989-90
		113*	India	Napier	1989-90
		117*	Australia	Wellington	1989-90
		101	Sri Lanka	Hamilton	1990-91
		116	England	Wellington	1991-92
Young, B.A.		120	Pakistan	Christchurch	1993-94

INDIA (225)

Adhikari, H.R.		114*†	West Indies	Delhi	1948-49
Amarnath, L.		118†	England	Bombay[1]	1933-34
Amarnath, M.	(11)	100	Australia	Perth	1977-78
		101*	West Indies	Kanpur	1978-79
		109*	Pakistan	Lahore[2]	1982-83
		120	Pakistan	Lahore[2]	1982-83
		103*	Pakistan	Karachi[1]	1982-83
		117	West Indies	Port-of-Spain	1982-83
		116	West Indies	St John's	1982-83
		101*	Pakistan	Lahore[2]	1984-85
		116*	Sri Lanka	Kandy	1985-86
		138	Australia	Sydney	1985-86
		131	Sri Lanka	Nagpur	1986-87
Amarnath, S.		124†	New Zealand	Auckland	1975-76
Amre, P.K.		103†	South Africa	Durban[2]	1992-93
Apte, M.L.		163*	West Indies	Port-of-Spain	1952-53
Azharuddin, M.	(14)	110†	England	Calcutta	1984-85
		105	England	Madras[1]	1984-85
		122	England	Kanpur	1984-85
		199	Sri Lanka	Kanpur	1986-87
		141	Pakistan	Calcutta	1986-87
		110	Pakistan	Jaipur	1986-87
		109	Pakistan	Faisalabad	1989-90
		192	New Zealand	Auckland	1989-90
		121	England	Lord's	1990
		179	England	Manchester	1990
		106	Australia	Adelaide	1991-92
		182	England	Calcutta	1992-93
		108	Sri Lanka	Bangalore	1993-94
		152	Sri Lanka	Ahmedabad	1993-94
Baig, A.A.		112†	England	Manchester	1959

Hundreds (India)

		Opponents		
Borde, C.G.	(5)	109	West Indies	Delhi	1958-59
		177*	Pakistan	Madras[2]	1960-61
		109	New Zealand	Bombay[2]	1964-65
		121	West Indies	Bombay[2]	1966-67
		125	West Indies	Madras[1]	1966-67
Contractor, N.J.		108	Australia	Bombay[2]	1959-60
Durani, S.A.		104	West Indies	Port-of-Spain	1961-62
Engineer, F.M.	(2)	109	West Indies	Madras[1]	1966-67
		121	England	Bombay[2]	1972-73
Gaekwad, A.D.	(2)	102	West Indies	Kanpur	1978-79
		201	Pakistan	Jullundur	1983-84
Gavaskar, S.M.	(34)	116	West Indies	Georgetown	1970-71
		117*	West Indies	Bridgetown	1970-71
		124 } 220	West Indies	Port-of-Spain	1970-71
		101	England	Manchester	1974
		116†	New Zealand	Auckland	1975-76
		156	West Indies	Port-of-Spain	1975-76
		102	West Indies	Port-of-Spain	1975-76
		119	New Zealand	Bombay[3]	1976-77
		108	England	Bombay[3]	1976-77
		113†	Australia	Brisbane[2]	1977-78
		127	Australia	Perth	1977-78
		118	Australia	Melbourne	1977-78
		111 } 137	Pakistan	Karachi[1]	1978-79
		205	West Indies	Bombay[3]	1978-79
		107 } 182*	West Indies	Calcutta	1978-79
		120	West Indies	Delhi	1978-79
		221	England	Oval	1979
		115	Australia	Delhi	1979-80
		123	Australia	Bombay[3]	1979-80
		166	Pakistan	Madras[1]	1979-80
		172	England	Bangalore	1981-82
		155†	Sri Lanka	Madras[1]	1982-83
		127*	Pakistan	Faisalabad	1982-83
		147*	West Indies	Georgetown	1982-83
		103*	Pakistan	Bangalore	1983-84
		121	West Indies	Delhi	1983-84
		236*	West Indies	Madras[1]	1983-84
		166*	Australia	Adelaide	1985-86
		172	Australia	Sydney	1985-86
		103	Australia	Bombay[3]	1986-87
		176	Sri Lanka	Kanpur	1986-87
Hanumant Singh		105†	England	Delhi	1963-64
Hazare, V.S.	(7)	116 } 145	Australia	Adelaide	1947-48
		134*	West Indies	Bombay[2]	1948-49
		122	West Indies	Bombay[2]	1948-49
		164*	England	Delhi	1951-52
		155	England	Bombay[2]	1951-52
		146*	Pakistan	Bombay[2]	1952-53
Jaisimha, M.L.	(3)	127	England	Delhi	1961-62
		129	England	Calcutta	1963-64
		101	Australia	Brisbane[2]	1967-68
Kambli, V.G.	(4)	224	England	Bombay[3]	1992-93
		227†	Zimbabwe	Delhi	1992-93
		125	Sri Lanka	Colombo (SSC)	1993-94
		120	Sri Lanka	Colombo (PSS)	1993-94
Kapil Dev	(8)	126*	West Indies	Delhi	1978-79
		116	England	Kanpur	1981-82
		100*	West Indies	Port-of-Spain	1982-83
		119	Australia	Madras[1]	1986-87
		163	Sri Lanka	Kanpur	1986-87
		109	West Indies	Madras[1]	1987-88
		110	England	Oval	1990
		129	South Africa	Port Elizabeth	1992-93
Kirmani, S.M.H.	(2)	101*	Australia	Bombay[3]	1979-80

			Opponents		
Kirmani, S.M.H. *continued*		102	England	Bombay[3]	1984-85
Kripal Singh, A.G		100*†	New Zealand	Hyderabad	1955-56
Kunderan, B.K.	(2)	192	England	Madras[2]	1963-64
		100	England	Delhi	1963-64
Manjrekar, S.V.	(4)	108	West Indies	Bridgetown	1988-89
		113*†	Pakistan	Karachi[1]	1989-90
		218	Pakistan	Lahore[2]	1989-90
		104†	Zimbabwe	Harare	1992-93
Manjrekar, V.L.	(7)	133	England	Leeds	1952
		118	West Indies	Kingston	1952-53
		118†	New Zealand	Hyderabad	1955-56
		177	New Zealand	Delhi	1955-56
		189*	England	Delhi	1961-62
		108	England	Madras[2]	1963-64
		102*	New Zealand	Madras[2]	1964-65
Mankad, M.H.	(5)	116	Australia	Melbourne	1947-48
		111	Australia	Melbourne	1947-48
		184	England	Lord's	1952
		223	New Zealand	Bombay[2]	1955-56
		231	New Zealand	Madras[2]	1955-56
Merchant, V.M.	(3)	114	England	Manchester	1936
		128	England	Oval	1946
		154	England	Delhi	1951-52
Modi, R.S.		112	West Indies	Bombay[2]	1948-49
Mushtaq Ali	(2)	112	England	Manchester	1936
		106†	West Indies	Calcutta	1948-49
Nadkarni, R.G.		122*	England	Kanpur	1963-64
Pataudi, Nawab of, jr	(6)	103	England	Madras[2]	1961-62
		203*	England	Delhi	1963-64
		128*†	Australia	Madras[2]	1964-65
		153	New Zealand	Calcutta	1964-65
		113	New Zealand	Delhi	1964-65
		148	England	Leeds	1967
Patel, B.P.		115*	West Indies	Port-of-Spain	1975-76
Patil, S.M.	(4)	174	Australia	Adelaide	1980-81
		129*	England	Manchester	1982
		114*†	Sri Lanka	Madras[1]	1982-83
		127	Pakistan	Faisalabad	1984-85
Phadkar, D.G.	(2)	123	Australia	Adelaide	1947-48
		115	England	Calcutta	1951-52
Ramchand, G.S.	(2)	106*	New Zealand	Calcutta	1955-56
		109	Australia	Bombay[2]	1956-57
Roy, Pankaj	(5)	140	England	Bombay[2]	1951-52
		111	England	Madras[1]	1951-52
		150	West Indies	Kingston	1952-53
		100	New Zealand	Calcutta	1955-56
		173	New Zealand	Madras[2]	1955-56
Sardesai, D.N.	(5)	200*	New Zealand	Bombay[2]	1964-65
		106	New Zealand	Delhi	1964-65
		212	West Indies	Kingston	1970-71
		112	West Indies	Port-of-Spain	1970-71
		150	West Indies	Bridgetown	1970-71
Shastri, R.J.	(11)	128	Pakistan	Karachi[1]	1982-83
		102	West Indies	St John's	1982-83
		139	Pakistan	Faisalabad	1984-85
		142	England	Bombay[3]	1984-85
		111	England	Calcutta	1984-85
		121*	Australia	Bombay[3]	1986-87
		125	Pakistan	Jaipur	1986-87
		107	West Indies	Bridgetown	1988-89
		100	England	Lord's	1990
		187	England	Oval	1990
		206	Australia	Sydney	1991-92
Shodhan, R.H.		110†	Pakistan	Calcutta	1952-53
Sidhu, N.S.	(5)	116†	New Zealand	Bangalore	1988-89
		116	West Indies	Kingston	1988-89
		106	England	Madras[1]	1992-93
		104	Sri Lanka	Colombo (SSC)	1993-94
		124	Sri Lanka	Lucknow[2]	1993-94

Hundreds (India)

			Opponents		
Solkar, E.D.		102	West Indies	Bombay[3]	1974-75
Srikkanth, K.	(2)	116	Australia	Sydney	1985-86
		123	Pakistan	Madras[1]	1986-87
Tendulkar, S.R.	(7)	119*	England	Manchester	1990
		148*	Australia	Sydney	1991-92
		114	Australia	Perth	1991-92
		111	South Africa	Johannesburg[3]	1992-93
		165	England	Madras[1]	1992-93
		104*	Sri Lanka	Colombo (SSC)	1993-94
		142	Sri Lanka	Lucknow[2]	1993-94
Umrigar, P.R.	(12)	130*	England	Madras[1]	1951-52
		102	Pakistan	Bombay[2]	1952-53
		130	West Indies	Port-of-Spain	1952-53
		117	West Indies	Kingston	1952-53
		108	Pakistan	Peshawar	1954-55
		223†	New Zealand	Hyderabad	1955-56
		118	England	Manchester	1959
		115	Pakistan	Kanpur	1960-61
		117	Pakistan	Madras[2]	1960-61
		112	Pakistan	Delhi	1960-61
		147*	England	Kanpur	1961-62
		172*	West Indies	Port-of-Spain	1961-62
Vengsarkar, D.B.	(17)	157*	West Indies	Calcutta	1978-79
		109	West Indies	Delhi	1978-79
		103	England	Lord's	1979
		112	Australia	Bangalore	1979-80
		146*	Pakistan	Delhi	1979-80
		157	England	Lord's	1982
		159	West Indies	Delhi	1983-84
		100	West Indies	Bombay[3]	1983-84
		137	England	Kanpur	1984-85
		126*	England	Lord's	1986
		102*	England	Leeds	1986
		164*	Australia	Bombay[3]	1986-87
		153	Sri Lanka	Nagpur	1986-87
		166	Sri Lanka	Cuttack	1986-87
		109	Pakistan	Ahmedabad	1986-87
		102	West Indies	Delhi	1987-88
		102*	West Indies	Calcutta	1987-88
Viswanath, G.R.	(14)	137†	Australia	Kanpur	1969-70
		113	England	Bombay[2]	1972-73
		139	West Indies	Calcutta	1974-75
		112	West Indies	Port-of-Spain	1975-76
		103*	New Zealand	Kanpur	1976-77
		145†	Pakistan	Faisalabad	1978-79
		124	West Indies	Madras[1]	1978-79
		179	West Indies	Kanpur	1978-79
		113	England	Lord's	1979
		161*	Australia	Bangalore	1979-80
		131	Australia	Delhi	1979-80
		114	Australia	Melbourne	1980-81
		107	England	Delhi	1981-82
		222	England	Madras[1]	1981-82
Wadekar, A.L.		143	New Zealand	Wellington	1967-68
Yashpal Sharma	(2)	100*	Australia	Delhi	1979-80
		140	England	Madras[1]	1981-82

PAKISTAN (170)

Aamer Malik	(2)	117	India	Faisalabad	1989-90
		113	India	Lahore[2]	1989-90
Aamir Sohail		205	England	Manchester	1992
Alimuddin	(2)	103*	India	Karachi[1]	1954-55
		109	England	Karachi[1]	1961-62
Asif Iqbal	(11)	146	England	Oval	1967
		104*	England	Birmingham	1971
		175	New Zealand	Dunedin	1972-73
		102	England	Lahore[2]	1972-73
		166	New Zealand	Lahore[2]	1976-77

			Opponents		
Asif Iqbal *continued*		152*	Australia	Adelaide	1976-77
		120	Australia	Sydney	1976-77
		135	West Indies	Kingston	1976-77
		104†	India	Faisalabad	1978-79
		104	New Zealand	Napier	1978-79
		134*	Australia	Perth	1978-79
Basit Ali		103	New Zealand	Christchurch	1993-94
Hanif Mohammad	(12)	142	India	Bahawalpur	1954-55
		103	New Zealand	Dacca	1955-56
		337†	West Indies	Bridgetown	1957-58
		103	West Indies	Karachi[1]	1958-59
		101*	Australia	Karachi[1]	1959-60
		160	India	Bombay[2]	1960-61
		111 104 }	England	Dacca	1961-62
		104	Australia	Melbourne	1964-65
		100*	New Zealand	Christchurch	1964-65
		203*	New Zealand	Lahore[2]	1964-65
		187*	England	Lord's	1967
Haroon Rashid	(3)	122†	England	Lahore[2]	1977-78
		108	England	Hyderabad	1977-78
		153†	Sri Lanka	Karachi[1]	1981-82
Ijaz Ahmed	(2)	122	Australia	Faisalabad	1988-89
		121	Australia	Melbourne	1989-90
Ijaz Faqih		105†	India	Ahmedabad	1986-87
Imran Khan	(6)	123	West Indies	Lahore[2]	1980-81
		117	India	Faisalabad	1982-83
		135*	India	Madras[1]	1986-87
		118	England	Oval	1987
		109*	India	Karachi[1]	1989-90
		136	Australia	Adelaide	1989-90
Imtiaz Ahmed	(3)	209	New Zealand	Lahore[1]	1955-56
		122	West Indies	Kingston	1957-58
		135	India	Madras[2]	1960-61
Intikhab Alam		138	England	Hyderabad	1972-73
Inzamam-ul-Haq	(3)	123	West Indies	St John's	1992-93
		135*	New Zealand	Wellington	1993-94
		100*	Sri Lanka	Kandy	1994-95
Javed Burki	(3)	138†	England	Lahore[2]	1961-62
		140	England	Dacca	1961-62
		101	England	Lord's	1962
Javed Miandad	(23)	163†	New Zealand	Lahore[2]	1976-77
		206	New Zealand	Karachi[1]	1976-77
		154*†	India	Faisalabad	1978-79
		100	India	Karachi[1]	1978-79
		160*	New Zealand	Christchurch	1978-79
		129*	Australia	Perth	1978-79
		106*	Australia	Faisalabad	1979-80
		138	Australia	Lahore[2]	1982-83
		126	India	Faisalabad	1982-83
		280*	India	Hyderabad	1982-83
		131	Australia	Adelaide	1983-84
		104 103* }	New Zealand	Hyderabad	1984-85
		203*	Sri Lanka	Faisalabad	1985-86
		260	England	Oval	1987
		114	West Indies	Georgetown	1987-88
		102	West Indies	Port-of-Spain	1987-88
		211	Australia	Karachi[1]	1988-89
		107	Australia	Faisalabad	1988-89
		118	New Zealand	Wellington	1988-89
		271	New Zealand	Auckland	1988-89
		145	India	Lahore[2]	1989-90
		153*	England	Birmingham	1992
Khalid Ibadulla		166†	Australia	Karachi[1]	1964-65
Majid Khan	(8)	158	Australia	Melbourne	1972-73
		110	New Zealand	Auckland	1972-73
		100	West Indies	Karachi[1]	1974-75
		112	New Zealand	Karachi[1]	1976-77

Hundreds (Pakistan)

			Opponents		
Majid Khan *continued*		167	West Indies	Georgetown	1976-77
		119*	New Zealand	Napier	1978-79
		108	Australia	Melbourne	1978-79
		110*	Australia	Lahore²	1979-80
Mansoor Akhtar		111	Australia	Faisalabad	1982-83
Mohammad Ilyas		126	New Zealand	Karachi¹	1964-65
Mohsin Khan	(7)	129	Sri Lanka	Lahore²	1981-82
		200	England	Lord's	1982
		135	Australia	Lahore²	1982-83
		101*†	India	Lahore²	1982-83
		149	Australia	Adelaide	1983-84
		152	Australia	Melbourne	1983-84
		104	England	Lahore²	1983-84
Mudassar Nazar	(10)	114†	England	Lahore²	1977-78
		126	India	Bangalore	1979-80
		119	India	Karachi¹	1982-83
		231	India	Hyderabad	1982-83
		152*	India	Lahore²	1982-83
		152	India	Karachi¹	1982-83
		199	India	Faisalabad	1984-85
		106	New Zealand	Hyderabad	1984-85
		124	England	Birmingham	1987
		120	England	Lahore²	1987-88
Mushtaq Mohammad	(10)	101	India	Delhi	1960-61
		100*	England	Nottingham	1962
		100	England	Birmingham	1971
		121	Australia	Sydney	1972-73
		201	New Zealand	Dunedin	1972-73
		157	England	Hyderabad	1972-73
		123	West Indies	Lahore²	1974-75
		101	New Zealand	Hyderabad	1976-77
		107	New Zealand	Karachi¹	1976-77
		121	West Indies	Port-of-Spain	1976-77
Nasim-ul-Ghani		101	England	Lord's	1962
Nazar Mohammad		124*	India	Lucknow¹	1952-53
Qasim Omar	(3)	113	Australia	Adelaide	1983-84
		210	India	Faisalabad	1984-85
		206†	Sri Lanka	Faisalabad	1985-86
Ramiz Raja	(2)	122	Sri Lanka	Colombo (PSS)	1985-86
		114	India	Jaipur	1986-87
Sadiq Mohammad	(5)	137	Australia	Melbourne	1972-73
		166	New Zealand	Wellington	1972-73
		119	England	Lahore²	1972-73
		103*	New Zealand	Hyderabad	1976-77
		105	Australia	Melbourne	1976-77
Saeed Ahmed	(5)	150	West Indies	Georgetown	1957-58
		166	Australia	Lahore²	1959-60
		121†	India	Bombay²	1960-61
		103	India	Madras²	1960-61
		172	New Zealand	Karachi¹	1964-65
Saeed Anwar	(2)	169	New Zealand	Wellington	1993-94
		136†	Sri Lanka	Colombo (PSS)	1994-95
Salim Malik	(11)	100*†	Sri Lanka	Karachi¹	1981-82
		107	India	Faisalabad	1982-83
		116	England	Faisalabad	1983-84
		102*	India	Faisalabad	1984-85
		119*	New Zealand	Karachi¹	1984-85
		102	England	Oval	1987
		102*	India	Karachi¹	1989-90
		102	West Indies	Karachi¹	1990-91
		101	Sri Lanka	Sialkot	1991-92
		165	England	Birmingham	1992
		140	New Zealand	Wellington	1993-94
Shoaib Mohammad	(7)	101	India	Madras¹	1986-87
		163	New Zealand	Wellington	1988-89
		112	New Zealand	Auckland	1988-89
		203*	India	Lahore²	1989-90
		203*	New Zealand	Karachi¹	1990-91
		105	New Zealand	Lahore²	1990-91

		Opponents		
Shoaib Mohammad *continued*		142	New Zealand	Faisalabad	1990-91
Taslim Arif		210*	Australia	Faisalabad	1979-80
Waqar Hassan		189	New Zealand	Lahore[1]	1955-56
Wasim Akram		123	Australia	Adelaide	1989-90
Wasim Raja	(4)	107*	West Indies	Karachi[1]	1974-75
		117*	West Indies	Bridgetown	1976-77
		125	India	Jullundur	1983-84
		112	England	Faisalabad	1983-84
Wazir Mohammad	(2)	106	West Indies	Kingston	1957-58
		189	West Indies	Port-of-Spain	1957-58
Zaheer Abbas	(12)	274†	England	Birmingham	1971
		240	England	Oval	1974
		101	Australia	Adelaide	1976-77
		176†	India	Faisalabad	1978-79
		235*	India	Lahore[2]	1978-79
		135	New Zealand	Auckland	1978-79
		134†	Sri Lanka	Lahore[2]	1981-82
		126	Australia	Faisalabad	1982-83
		215	India	Lahore[2]	1982-83
		186	India	Karachi[1]	1982-83
		168	India	Faisalabad	1982-83
		168*	India	Lahore[2]	1984-85

SRI LANKA (32)

De Silva, P.A.	(7)	122†	Pakistan	Faisalabad	1985-86
		105	Pakistan	Karachi[1]	1985-86
		167	Australia	Brisbane[2]	1989-90
		267†	New Zealand	Wellington	1990-91
		123	New Zealand	Auckland	1990-91
		148	India	Colombo (PSS)	1993-94
		127	Pakistan	Colombo (PSS)	1994-95
Dias, R.L.	(3)	109	Pakistan	Lahore[2]	1981-82
		108†	New Zealand	Colombo (SSC)	1983-84
		106	India	Kandy	1985-86
Gurusinha, A.P.	(4)	116*	Pakistan	Colombo (PSS)	1985-86
		119 102 }	New Zealand	Hamilton	1990-91
		137	Australia	Colombo (SSC)	1992-93
Kaluwitharana, R.S.		132*†	Australia	Colombo (SSC)	1992-93
Kuruppu, D.S.B.P.		201*†	New Zealand	Colombo (CCC)	1986-87
Madugalle, R.S.		103	India	Colombo (SSC)	1985-86
Mahanama, R.S.	(3)	153	New Zealand	Moratuwa	1992-93
		109	New Zealand	Colombo (SSC)	1992-93
		151	India	Colombo (PSS)	1993-94
Mendis, L.R.D.	(4)	105† 105† }	India	Madras[1]	1982-83
		111	England	Lord's	1984
		124	India	Kandy	1985-86
Ranatunga, A.	(4)	111	India	Colombo (SSC)	1985-86
		135*	Pakistan	Colombo (PSS)	1985-86
		127	Australia	Colombo (SSC)	1992-93
		131†	South Africa	Moratuwa	1993-94
Silva, S.A.R.	(2)	102*†	England	Lord's	1984
		111	India	Colombo (PSS)	1985-86
Wettimuny, S.	(2)	157	Pakistan	Faisalabad	1981-82
		190	England	Lord's	1984

ZIMBABWE (3)

Arnott, K.J.		101*†	New Zealand	Bulawayo	1992-93
Flower, A.		115	India	Delhi	1992-93
Houghton, D.L.		121†	India	Harare	1992-93

MOST FIFTIES

All scores of 50 and over

			Opponents								
		50	E	A	SA	WI	NZ	I	P	SL	Z
A.R.Border	Australia	90	29	–	1	17	11	13	14	5	–
S.M.Gavaskar	India	79	20	12	–	20	5	–	17	5	–
I.V.A.Richards	West Indies	69	23	19	–	–	3	16	8	–	–
Javed Miandad	Pakistan	66	11	13	–	6	13	19	–	3	1
G.A.Gooch	England	65	–	19	–	18	7	13	6	2	–
G.Boycott	England	64	–	21	3	20	8	6	6	–	–
M.C.Cowdrey	England	60	–	16	10	16	10	5	3	–	–
C.H.Lloyd	West Indies	58	18	18	–	–	–	19	3	–	–
D.I.Gower	England	57	–	21	–	7	8	8	11	2	–
D.L.Haynes	West Indies	57	17	19	1	–	8	6	6	–	–
G.St A.Sobers	West Indies	56	23	10	–	–	1	15	7	–	–
K.F.Barrington	England	55	–	18	8	7	4	12	6	–	–
G.S.Chappell	Australia	55	21	–	–	12	6	3	12	1	–
C.G.Greenidge	West Indies	53	15	12	–	–	7	16	3	–	–
L.Hutton	England	52	–	19	11	11	7	4	–	–	–
D.B.Vengsarkar	India	52	11	9	–	13	3	–	10	6	–

MOST CONSECUTIVE FIFTIES

SEVEN

E.de C.Weekes	West Indies	141	128	194	162	101	90	56	1947-48 to 1948-49

SIX

J.Ryder	Australia	78*	58	56	142	201*	88		1921-22 to 1924-25
E.H.Hendren	England	77	205*	56	123	61	55		1929-30
G.A.Headley	West Indies	93	53	270*	106	107	51		1934-35 to 1939
A.Melville	South Africa	67	78	103	189	104*	117		1938-39 to 1947
G.St A.Sobers	West Indies	52	52	80	365*	125	109*		1957-58
E.R.Dexter	England	85	172	70	99	93	52		1962 to 1962-63
K.F.Barrington	England	63	132*	101	94	126	76		1962-63
K.D.Walters	Australia	76	118	110	50	242	103		1968-69
G.S.Chappell	Australia	68	54*	52	70	121	67		1975-76 to 1976-77
G.R.Viswanath	India	59	54	79	89	73	145		1977-78 to 1978-79
Zaheer Abbas	Pakistan	91	126	52	215	186	168		1982-83
A.R.Border	Australia	80	65*	76	51*	50	56		1989 to 1989-90

G.Boycott (England) scored nine fifties in ten innings in 1970-71 and 1971: 70, 50, 77, 142*, 12, 76*, 58, 119*, 121*, 112.

M.A.Noble (Australia) is the only player to score two separate fifties on the same day: 60* and 59* v England at Manchester in 1899 on the second day.

OVER 60% OF A COMPLETED INNINGS TOTAL

%					
67.34	C.Bannerman	165*/245	Australia v England	Melbourne	1876-77
63.50	C.G.Greenidge	134/211	West Indies v England	Manchester	1976
63.41	A.P.Gurusinha	52*/82	Sri Lanka v India	Chandigarh	1990-91
62.89	J.R.Reid	100/159	New Zealand v England	Christchurch	1962-63
61.87	S.M.Nurse	258/417	West Indies v New Zealand	Christchurch	1968-69
61.85	M.Amarnath	60/97†	India v West Indies	Kingston	1975-76
61.11	G.N.Yallop	121/198	Australia v England	Sydney	1978-79
61.11	G.A.Gooch	154*/252	England v West Indies	Leeds	1991
60.65	V.T.Trumper	74/122	Australia v England	Melbourne	1903-04
60.26	H.A.Gomes	91/151	West Indies v India	Madras[1]	1978-79
60.19	J.T.Tyldesley	62/103	England v Australia	Melbourne	1903-04

†Five men were absent hurt.

D.L.Amiss (262*) scored 60.64% of England's total of 432 for 9 against West Indies at Kingston in 1973-74.

OVER 50% OF COMPLETED INNINGS TOTALS IN A MATCH

%					
51.88	J.H.Sinclair	106/177 4/35 }	South Africa v England	Cape Town	1898-99

OVER 600 RUNS ADDED DURING ONE BATSMAN'S INNINGS

770	L.Hutton	364	England v Australia	Oval	1938
720	A.Sandham	325	England v West Indies	Kingston	1929-30
703	G.St A.Sobers	365*	West Indies v Pakistan	Kingston	1957-58
646	R.B.Simpson	311	Australia v England	Manchester	1964
641	G.A.Gooch	333	England v India	Lord's	1990
628	Hanif Mohammad	337	Pakistan v West Indies	Bridgetown	1957-58

LONGEST INNINGS FOR EACH COUNTRY

For	Min		Opponents		
England	797	L.Hutton (364)	Australia	Oval	1938
Australia	762	R.B.Simpson (311)	England	Manchester	1964
South Africa	575	D.J.McGlew (105)	Australia	Durban[2]	1957-58
West Indies	768	B.C.Lara (375)	England	St John's	1993-94
New Zealand	704	G.M.Turner (259)	West Indies	Georgetown	1971-72
India	708	S.M.Gavaskar (172)	England	Bangalore	1981-82
Pakistan	970	Hanif Mohammad (337)	West Indies	Bridgetown	1957-58
Sri Lanka	777	D.S.B.P.Kuruppu (201*)	New Zealand	Colombo (CCC)	1986-87
Zimbabwe	425	G.W.Flower (96)	India	Delhi	1992-93

BATTED ON EACH DAY OF A FIVE-DAY MATCH

	Scores				
M.L.Jaisimha	20*	74	I v A	Calcutta	1959-60
G.Boycott	107	80*	E v A	Nottingham	1977
K.J.Hughes	117	84	A v E	Lord's	1980
A.J.Lamb	23	110	E v WI	Lord's	1984
R.J.Shastri	111	7*	I v E	Calcutta	1984-85

MOST RUNS FROM STROKES WORTH FOUR OR MORE IN AN INNINGS

	6s	5s	4s					
238	5	–	52	J.H.Edrich	310*	E v NZ	Leeds	1965
196	10	–	34	W.R.Hammond	336*	E v NZ	Auckland	1932-33
190	3	–	43	G.A.Gooch	333	E v I	Lord's	1990
184	–	–	46	D.G.Bradman	334	A v E	Leeds	1930
184	2	–	43	D.G.Bradman	304	A v E	Leeds	1934
180	–	–	45	B.C.Lara	375	WI v E	St John's	1993-94
177	–	1	43	R.G.Pollock	274	SA v A	Durban[2]	1969-70
168	–	–	42	R.B.Kanhai	256	WI v I	Calcutta	1958-59
166	1	–	40	D.L.Amiss	262*	E v WI	Kingston	1973-74
160	–	–	40	P.A.de Silva	267	SL v NZ	Wellington	1990-91
157	–	1	38	G.St A.Sobers	365*	WI v P	Kingston	1957-58
152	2	–	35	F.M.M.Worrell	261	WI v E	Nottingham	1950
152	–	–	38	Zaheer Abbas	274	P v E	Birmingham	1971
152	–	–	38	I.V.A.Richards	291	WI v E	Oval	1976
152	–	–	38	B.C.Lara	277	WI v A	Sydney	1992-93
150	1	–	36	L.G.Rowe	302	WI v E	Bridgetown	1973-74

MOST SIXES IN AN INNINGS

TEN	W.R.Hammond (336*)	E v NZ	Auckland	1932-33
EIGHT	N.S.Sidhu (124)	I v SL	Lucknow[2]	1993-94
SEVEN	B.Sutcliffe (80*)	NZ v SA	Johannesburg[2]	1953-54
	I.V.A.Richards (110*)	WI v E	St John's	1985-86
	C.G.Greenidge (213)	WI v NZ	Auckland	1986-87

SIX	J.H.Sinclair (104)	SA v A	Cape Town	1902-03
	I.V.A.Richards (192*)	WI v I	Delhi	1974-75
	Haroon Rashid (108)	P v E	Hyderabad	1977-78
	I.T.Botham (118)	E v A	Manchester	1981
	R.J.Shastri (121*)	I v A	Bombay[3]	1986-87

MOST SIXES OFF CONSECUTIVE BALLS

FOUR	Kapil Dev (77*) off E.E.Hemmings	I v E	Lord's	1990
THREE	W.R.Hammond (336*) off J.Newman	E v NZ	Auckland	1932-33
	S.T.Clarke (35*) off Mohammad Nazir	WI v P	Faisalabad	1980-81

MOST FOURS OFF CONSECUTIVE BALLS

FIVE	D.T.Lindsay (60) off J.W.Gleeson	SA v A	Port Elizabeth	1969-70
	R.E.Redmond (107) off Majid Khan	NZ v P	Auckland	1972-73
	D.W.Hookes (56) off A.W.Greig	A v E	Melbourne	1976-77

MOST RUNS OFF ONE OVER

EIGHT-BALL				
25 (66061600)	B.Sutcliffe and R.W.Blair (off H.J.Tayfield)	NZ v SA	Johannesburg[2]	1953-54
SIX-BALL				
24 (462660†) (†1 leg-bye)	A.M.E.Roberts (off I.T.Botham)	WI v E	Port-of-Spain	1980-81
24 (444†0444) (†no-ball)	S.M.Patil (off R.G.D.Willis)	I v E	Manchester	1982
24 (464604)	I.T.Botham (off D.A.Stirling)	E v NZ	Oval	1986
24 (006666)	Kapil Dev (off E.E.Hemmings)	I v E	Lord's	1990
24 (244266)	I.D.S.Smith (off A.S.Wassan)	NZ v I	Auckland	1989-90

FASTEST FIFTIES

Min	Balls				
28		J.T.Brown (140)	England v Australia	Melbourne	1894-95
29		S.A.Durani (61*)	India v England	Kanpur	1963-64
30		E.A.V.Williams (72)	West Indies v England	Bridgetown	1947-48
30	36	B.R.Taylor (124)	New Zealand v West Indies	Auckland	1968-69
33		C.A.Roach (56)	West Indies v England	Oval	1933
34		C.R.Browne (70*)	West Indies v England	Georgetown	1929-30
35		J.H.Sinclair (104)	South Africa v Australia	Cape Town	1902-03
35		C.G.Macartney (56)	Australia v South Africa	Sydney	1910-11
35		J.W.Hitch (51*)	England v Australia	Oval	1921

F.G.Mann scored 49* in 24 minutes for England v New Zealand at Leeds in 1949.

The fastest fifties in terms of fewest balls received (where recorded) are:

Balls	Min				
30	50	Kapil Dev (73)	India v Pakistan	Karachi[1]	1982-83
32		I.V.A.Richards (61)	West Indies v India	Kingston	1982-83
32	48	I.T.Botham (59*)	England v New Zealand	Oval	1986
33	45	R.C.Fredericks (169)	West Indies v Australia	Perth	1975-76
33		Kapil Dev (59)	India v Pakistan	Karachi[1]	1978-79
33	44	Kapil Dev (65)	India v England	Manchester	1982
33	48	A.J.Lamb (60)	England v New Zealand	Auckland	1991-92

G.F.Labrooy reached his fifty in 13 scoring strokes for Sri Lanka v New Zealand at Auckland in 1990-91.

FASTEST HUNDREDS

Min	Balls				
70	67	J.M.Gregory (119)	Australia v South Africa	Johannesburg[1]	1921-22
75	76	G.L.Jessop (104)	England v Australia	Oval	1902
78		R.Benaud (121)	Australia v West Indies	Kingston	1954-55
80		J.H.Sinclair (104)	South Africa v Australia	Cape Town	1902-03
81	56	I.V.A.Richards (110*)	West Indies v England	St John's	1985-86
86	83	B.R.Taylor (124)	New Zealand v West Indies	Auckland	1968-69
91		J.Darling (160)	Australia v England	Sydney	1897-98
91	120	S.J.McCabe (189*)	Australia v South Africa	Johannesburg[1]	1935-36
94	c105	V.T.Trumper (185*)	Australia v England	Sydney	1903-04
95		J.T.Brown (140)	England v Australia	Melbourne	1894-95
95		P.W.Sherwell (115)	South Africa v England	Lord's	1907

The fastest hundreds in terms of fewest balls received (where recorded) are:

Balls	Min				
56	81	I.V.A.Richards (110*)	West Indies v England	St John's	1985-86
67	70	J.M.Gregory (119)	Australia v South Africa	Johannesburg[1]	1921-22
71	116	R.C.Fredericks (169)	West Indies v Australia	Perth	1975-76
74	113	Majid Khan (112)	Pakistan v New Zealand	Karachi[1]	1976-77
74		Kapil Dev (163)	India v Sri Lanka	Kanpur	1986-87
76	75	G.L.Jessop (104)	England v Australia	Oval	1902

HUNDRED BEFORE LUNCH

FIRST DAY	Lunch score			
V.T.Trumper (104)	103*	Australia v England	Manchester	1902
C.G.Macartney (151)	112*	Australia v England	Leeds	1926
D.G.Bradman (334)	105*	Australia v England	Leeds	1930
Majid Khan (112)	108*	Pakistan v New Zealand	Karachi[1]	1976-77

OTHER DAYS	Overnight score	Lunch score		Day		
K.S.Ranjitsinhji (154*)	41*	154*	E v A	3	Manchester	1896
C.Hill (142)	22*	138*	A v SA	3	Johannesburg[1]	1902-03
W.Bardsley (164)	32*	150*	A v SA	2	Lord's	1912
C.P.Mead (182*)	19*	128*	E v A	2	Oval	1921
J.B.Hobbs (211)	12*	114*	E v SA	2	Lord's	1924
H.G.Owen-Smith (129)	27*	129	SA v E	3	Leeds	1929
W.R.Hammond (336*)	41*	152*	E v NZ	2	Auckland	1932-33
L.E.G.Ames (148*)	25*	148*	E v SA	3	Oval	1935
S.J.McCabe (189*)	59*	159*	A v SA	4	Johannesburg[1]	1935-36
G.S.Chappell (176)	76*	176	A v NZ	2	Christchurch	1981-82

I.T.Botham (9 to 108*) scored 99 before lunch on the 4th day for England v India at Leeds in 1979.*

FASTEST DOUBLE HUNDREDS

Minutes				
214	D.G.Bradman (334)	Australia v England	Leeds	1930
223	S.J.McCabe (232)	Australia v England	Nottingham	1938
226	V.T.Trumper (214*)	Australia v South Africa	Adelaide	1910-11
234	D.G.Bradman (254)	Australia v England	Lord's	1930
240	W.R.Hammond (336*)	England v New Zealand	Auckland	1932-33
241	S.E.Gregory (201)	Australia v England	Sydney	1894-95
245	D.C.S.Compton (278)	England v Pakistan	Nottingham	1954
251	D.G.Bradman (223)	Australia v West Indies	Brisbane[1]	1930-31
253	D.G.Bradman (226)	Australia v South Africa	Brisbane[2]	1931-32

The fastest double hundreds in terms of fewest balls received (where recorded) are:

Balls	Min				
220	268	I.T.Botham (208)	England v India	Oval	1982
232	289	C.G.Greenidge (214*)	West Indies v England	Lord's	1984
240		C.H.Lloyd (242*)	West Indies v India	Bombay[3]	1974-75
241		Zaheer Abbas (215)	Pakistan v India	Lahore[2]	1982-83
242		D.G.Bradman (244)	Australia v England	Oval	1934
242		I.V.A.Richards (208)	West Indies v Australia	Melbourne	1984-85

FASTEST TRIPLE HUNDREDS

Minutes

288	W.R.Hammond (336*)	England v New Zealand	Auckland	1932-33
336	D.G.Bradman (334)	Australia v England	Leeds	1930

W.R.Hammond's third hundred was scored in 48 minutes.
D.G.Bradman scored his three hundreds in 99, 115 and 122 minutes respectively and reached 309* at the end of the first day.

MOST RUNS IN A DAY

309	(0-309*)	D.G.Bradman (334)	A v E	Leeds	1930
295	(41*-336*)	W.R.Hammond (336*)	E v NZ	Auckland	1932-33
273	(5*-278)	D.C.S.Compton (278)	E v P	Nottingham	1954
271	(0-271*)	D.G.Bradman (304)	A v E	Leeds	1934
244	(0-244)	D.G.Bradman (244)	A v E	Oval	1934
239	(0-239*)	F.M.M.Worrell (261)	WI v E	Nottingham	1950
223	(0-223*)	W.R.Hammond (227)	E v NZ	Christchurch	1932-33
223	(0-223*)	D.G.Bradman (223)	A v WI	Brisbane[1]	1930-31
217	(0-217)	W.R.Hammond (217)	E v I	Oval	1936
214	(73*-287)	R.E.Foster (287)	E v A	Sydney	1903-04
213	(19*-232)	S.J.McCabe (232)	A v E	Nottingham	1938
210	(0-210*)	W.R.Hammond (240)	E v A	Lord's	1938
209	(0-209)	C.A.Roach (209)	WI v E	Georgetown	1929-30
208	(20*-228*)	G.St A.Sobers (365*)	WI v P	Kingston	1957-58
208	(0-208*)	V.T.Trumper (214*)	A v SA	Adelaide	1910-11
206	(0-206)	L.Hutton (206)	E v NZ	Oval	1949
205	(0-205*)	W.H.Ponsford (266)	A v E	Oval	1934
205	(0-205)	Aamir Sohail (205)	P v E	Manchester	1992
203	(0-203)	H.L.Collins (203)	A v SA	Johannesburg[1]	1921-22
203	(0-203*)	R.B.Kanhai (256)	WI v I	Calcutta	1958-59
203	(0-203*)	P.A.de Silva (267)	SL v NZ	Wellington	1990-91
201	(0-201)	D.G.Bradman (201)	A v I	Adelaide	1947-48
200	(0-200*)	D.G.Bradman (226)	A v SA	Brisbane[2]	1931-32
200	(0-200*)	I.V.A.Richards (291)	WI v E	Oval	1976

FAST INNINGS

Runs	Min				
35	14	W.P.Howell	A v E	Sydney	1901-02
49*	24	F.G.Mann	E v NZ	Leeds	1949
61*	34	S.A.Durani	I v E	Kanpur	1963-64
63	50	V.T.Trumper	A v SA	Johannesburg[1]	1902-03
72	63	E.A.V.Williams	WI v E	Bridgetown	1947-48
104	77	G.L.Jessop	E v A	Oval	1902
119	97	J.M.Gregory	A v SA	Johannesburg[1]	1921-22
124	110	B.R.Taylor	NZ v WI	Auckland	1968-69
128	115	G.J.Bonnor	A v E	Sydney	1884-85
137	135	K.H.Weekes	WI v E	Oval	1939
189*	165	S.J.McCabe	A v SA	Johannesburg[1]	1935-36
191	202	C.Hill	A v SA	Sydney	1910-11
232	235	S.J.McCabe	A v E	Nottingham	1938
278	290	D.C.S.Compton	E v P	Nottingham	1954
336*	318	W.R.Hammond	E v NZ	Auckland	1932-33

FAST PARTNERSHIPS

Runs	Min	Wkt				
42*	16	9th	F.W.Freer (28*), G.E.Tribe (25*)	A v E	Sydney	1946-47
66*	24	5th	C.Washbrook (103*), F.G.Mann (49*)	E v NZ	Leeds	1949
77	28	10th	S.J.McCabe (232), L.O'B.Fleetwood-Smith (5*)	A v E	Nottingham	1938
80	41	7th	B.W.Yuile (20), B.R.Taylor (124)	NZ v WI	Auckland	1968-69
86	44	3rd	I.M.Chappell (121), G.S.Chappell (133)	A v NZ	Wellington	1973-74
108	45	7th	F.R.Brown (74), W.Voce (66)	E v NZ	Christchurch	1932-33
121*	55	3rd	F.E.Woolley (134*), E.H.Hendren (50*)	E v SA	Lord's	1924
144	64	3rd	C.Hill (191), D.R.A.Gehrs (67)	A v SA	Sydney	1910-11
154	73	9th	S.E.Gregory (201), J.M.Blackham (74)	A v E	Sydney	1894-95
158	90	6th	J.T.Tyldesley (112*), R.H.Spooner (79)	E v A	Oval	1905

209	97	3rd	H.L.Collins (203), J.M.Gregory (119)	A v SA	Johannesburg[1]	1921-22
224	115	2nd	W.Bardsley (132), C.Hill (191)	A v SA	Sydney	1910-11
248	140	4th	L.Hutton (196), D.C.S.Compton (120)	E v WI	Lord's	1939
249	163	3rd	D.G.Bradman (169), S.J.McCabe (112)	A v E	Melbourne	1936-37
264	180	3rd	L.Hutton (165*), W.R.Hammond (138)	E v WI	Oval	1939
301	217	2nd	A.R.Morris (182), D.G.Bradman (173*)	A v E	Leeds	1948
350	274	4th	Mushtaq Mohammad (201), Asif Iqbal (175)	P v NZ	Dunedin	1972-73
451	316	2nd	W.H.Ponsford (266), D.G.Bradman (244)	A v E	Oval	1934

SLOWEST FIFTIES

Min	Balls				
357	350	T.E.Bailey (68)	E v A	Brisbane[2]	1958-59
350	236	C.J.Tavaré (82)	E v P	Lord's	1982
326		S.M.Gavaskar (51)	I v SL	Colombo (SSC)	1985-86
318	209	Ramiz Raja (62)	P v WI	Karachi[1]	1986-87
316		C.P.S.Chauhan (61)	I v P	Kanpur	1979-80
315		Shoaib Mohammad (53*)	P v Z	Lahore[2]	1993-94
313		D.J.McGlew (70)	SA v A	Johannesburg[3]	1957-58
312	212	J.J.Crowe (120*)	NZ v SL	Colombo (CCC)	1986-87
310		B.A.Edgar (55)	NZ v A	Wellington	1981-82
310	262	A.R.Border (75)	A v WI	Sydney	1988-89
306	219	C.J.Tavaré (78)	E v A	Manchester	1981
304	235	P.L.Taylor (54*)	A v P	Karachi[1]	1988-89
302		D.N.Sardesai (60)	I v WI	Bridgetown	1961-62
301	238	E.J.Gray (50)	NZ v E	Nottingham	1986
300		G.S.Camacho (57)	WI v E	Bridgetown	1967-68

SLOWEST HUNDREDS

Min	Balls				
557	420	Mudassar Nazar (114)	P v E	Lahore[2]	1977-78
545		D.J.McGlew (105)	SA v A	Durban[2]	1957-58
516	331	J.J.Crowe (120*)	NZ v SL	Colombo (CCC)	1986-87
500	397	S.V.Manjrekar (104)	I v Z	Harare	1992-93
488		P.E.Richardson (117)	E v SA	Johannesburg[3]	1956-57
487	397	C.T.Radley (158)	E v NZ	Auckland	1977-78
468		Hanif Mohammad (142)	P v I	Bahawalpur	1954-55
462	341	M.J.Greatbatch (146*)	NZ v A	Perth	1989-90
461	265	M.D.Crowe (108*)	NZ v P	Lahore[2]	1990-91
460		Hanif Mohammad (111)	P v E	Dacca	1961-62
458	329	K.W.R.Fletcher (122)	E v P	Oval	1974
457		S.A.R.Silva (111)	SL v I	Colombo (PSS)	1985-86
455	307	G.P.Howarth (122)	NZ v E	Auckland	1977-78
440		A.J.Watkins (137*)	E v I	Delhi	1951-52
437		D.B.Vengsarkar (146*)	I v P	Delhi	1979-80
437		A.P.Gurusinha (116*)	SL v P	Colombo (PSS)	1985-86
435		J.W.Guy (102)	NZ v I	Hyderabad	1955-56
434		M.C.Cowdrey (154)	E v WI	Birmingham	1957
431	309	T.J.Franklin (101)	NZ v E	Lord's	1990
428	280	S.M.Gavaskar (172)	I v E	Bangalore	1981-82
427		R.J.Shastri (109)	I v P	Bridgetown	1988-89
425		H.A.Gomes (127)	WI v A	Perth	1984-85
424		R.J.Shastri (125)	I v P	Jaipur	1986-87
424	326	M.A.Atherton (105)	E v A	Sydney	1990-91
422	330	R.J.Shastri (111)	I v E	Calcutta	1984-85
420		M.D.Crowe (188)	NZ v WI	Georgetown	1984-85

SLOWEST DOUBLE HUNDREDS

Min	Balls				
777	548	D.S.B.P.Kuruppu (201*)	SL v NZ	Colombo (CCC)	1986-87
656	411	Shoaib Mohammad (203*)	P v NZ	Karachi[1]	1990-91
652	426	A.D.Gaekwad (201)	I v P	Jullundur	1983-84
608		R.B.Simpson (311)	A v E	Manchester	1964
596		A.R.Border (205)	A v NZ	Adelaide	1987-88
595		G.St A.Sobers (226)	WI v E	Bridgetown	1959-60
584		Hanif Mohammad (337)	P v WI	Bridgetown	1957-58
570		S.G.Barnes (234)	A v E	Sydney	1946-47
570		Javed Miandad (211)	P v A	Karachi[1]	1988-89

SLOWEST TRIPLE HUNDREDS

Min

858	Hanif Mohammad (337)	P v WI	Bridgetown	1957-58
753	R.B.Simpson (311)	A v E	Manchester	1964

SLOWEST INNINGS

Runs	Min				
2*	81	P.C.R.Tufnell	E v I	Bombay³	1992-93
3*	100	J.T.Murray (*injured*)	E v A	Sydney	1962-63
5	102	Nawab of Pataudi, jr	I v E	Bombay²	1972-73
7	123	G.Miller	E v A	Melbourne	1978-79
9	132	R.K.Chauhan	I v SL	Ahmedabad	1993-94
10*	133	T.G.Evans	E v A	Adelaide	1946-47
16*	147	D.B.Vengsarkar	I v P	Kanpur	1979-80
17*	166	G.M.Ritchie	A v I	Sydney	1985-86
18	194	W.R.Playle	NZ v E	Leeds	1958
19	217	M.D.Crowe	NZ v SL	Colombo (SSC)	1983-84
25	242	D.K.Morrison	NZ v P	Faisalabad	1990-91
28*	250	J.W.Burke	A v E	Brisbane²	1958-59
31	264	K.D.Mackay	A v E	Lord's	1956
34*	271	Younis Ahmed	P v I	Ahmedabad	1986-87
35	332	C.J.Tavaré	E v I	Madras¹	1981-82
55	336	B.A.Edgar	NZ v A	Wellington	1981-82
57	346	G.S.Camacho	WI v E	Bridgetown	1967-68
58	367	Ijaz Butt	P v A	Karachi¹	1959-60
60	390	D.N.Sardesai	I v WI	Bridgetown	1961-62
62	408	Ramiz Raja	P v WI	Karachi¹	1986-87
68	458	T.E.Bailey	E v A	Brisbane²	1958-59
86	474	Shoaib Mohammad	P v WI	Karachi¹	1990-91
99	505	M.L.Jaisimha	I v P	Kanpur	1960-61
105	575	D.J.McGlew	SA v A	Durban²	1957-58
114	591	Mudassar Nazar	P v E	Lahore²	1977-78
120*	609	J.J.Crowe	NZ v SL	Colombo (CCC)	1986-87
146*	655	M.J.Greatbatch	NZ v A	Perth	1989-90
163	720	Shoaib Mohammad	P v NZ	Wellington	1988-89
201*	777	D.S.B.P.Kuruppu	SL v NZ	Colombo (CCC)	1986-87
337	970	Hanif Mohammad	P v WI	Bridgetown	1957-58

FEWEST BOUNDARIES IN AN INNINGS

Runs	Fours				
84	0	W.M.Lawry	A v E	Brisbane²	1970-71
77	0†	G.Boycott	E v A	Perth	1978-79
67	0	E.A.B.Rowan	SA v E	Durban²	1938-39
65	0‡	G.R.J.Matthews	A v E	Adelaide	1990-91
120	2	P.A.Gibb	E v SA	Durban²	1938-39
94	2	K.F.Barrington	E v A	Sydney	1962-63
102	3	W.M.Woodfull	A v E	Melbourne	1928-29
161	5	W.M.Woodfull	A v SA	Melbourne	1931-32

†*Including an all-run four with two runs from an overthrow.*
‡*Including three all-run fours.*

AN HOUR BEFORE SCORING FIRST RUN

Min

97	T.G.Evans (10*)	E v A	Adelaide	1946-47
84	R.K.Chauhan (9)	I v SL	Ahmedabad	1993-94
82	P.I.Pocock (13)	E v WI	Georgetown	1967-68
74	J.T.Murray (3*)	E v A	Sydney	1962-63
72	C.G.Rackemann (9)	A v E	Sydney	1990-91
70	W.L.Murdoch (17)	A v E	Sydney	1882-83
69	R.M.Hogg (7*)	A v WI	Adelaide	1984-85
67	C.J.Tavaré (82)	E v P	Lord's	1982
66	J.G.Wright (38)	NZ v A	Wellington	1981-82
65	Shujauddin (45)	P v A	Lahore²	1959-60
63	C.J.Tavaré (9)	E v A	Perth	1982-83
63	P.C.R.Tufnell (2*)	E v I	Bombay³	1992-93

AN HOUR WITHOUT ADDING TO A SCORE

Min				
94	M.C.Snedden (23)	NZ v A	Wellington	1989-90
91	J.J.Crowe (21)	NZ v WI	Bridgetown	1984-85
90	B.Mitchell (58)	SA v A	Brisbane[2]	1931-32
90	C.J.Tavaré (89)	E v A	Perth	1982-83
89	R.J.Shastri (23)	I v SA	Johannesburg[3]	1992-93
79	T.E.Bailey (8)	E v SA	Leeds	1955
77	D.B.Close (20)	E v WI	Manchester	1976
75	A.Ranatunga (37)	SL v NZ	Colombo (CCC)	1983-84
70	D.L.Haynes (9)	WI v NZ	Auckland	1979-80
69	G.A.Gooch (84)	E v WI	Oval	1988
67	W.H.Scotton (34)	E v A	Oval	1886
66	S.M.Gavaskar (52)	I v SL	Colombo (PSS)	1985-86
65	Nawab of Pataudi, jr (5)	I v E	Bombay[2]	1972-73
64	Anil Dalpat (15)	P v NZ	Wellington	1984-85
63	D.R.Jardine (24)	E v A	Brisbane[2]	1932-33
63	W.R.Endean (18)	SA v E	Johannesburg[3]	1956-57
63	W.R.Playle (18)	NZ v E	Leeds	1958
63	J.M.Brearley (48)	E v A	Birmingham	1981
63	S.R.Waugh (47*)	A v E	Nottingham	1993
62	K.F.Barrington (137)	E v NZ	Birmingham	1965
61	J.F.Reid (148)	NZ v P	Wellington	1984-85
61	M.D.Marshall (6*)	WI v E	Birmingham	1991
60	B.Mitchell (73)	SA v E	Johannesburg[1]	1938-39
60	T.E.Bailey (80)	E v SA	Durban[2]	1956-57
60	C.J.Tavaré (82)	E v P	Lord's	1982
60	A.R.Border (9)	A v P	Faisalabad	1982-83
60	S.M.Gavaskar (51)	I v SL	Colombo (SSC)	1985-86
60	J.J.Crowe (120*)	NZ v SL	Colombo (CCC)	1986-87

FEWEST RUNS IN A DAY

49	(5*-54*)	M.L.Jaisimha (99)	I v P	Kanpur	1960-61
52	(0-52*)	Mudassar Nazar (114)	P v E	Lahore[2]	1977-78
56	(1*-57*)	D.J.McGlew (70)	SA v A	Johannesburg[3]	1957-58
59	(0*-59*)	M.L.Jaisimha (74)	I v A	Calcutta	1959-60

DISMISSED BY THE FIRST BALL OF A MATCH

Batsman	Bowler			
A.C.MacLaren	A.Coningham	E v A	Melbourne	1894-95
T.W.Hayward	A.E.E.Vogler	E v SA	Oval	1907
W.Bardsley	M.W.Tate	A v E	Leeds	1926
H.Sutcliffe	F.T.Badcock	E v NZ	Christchurch	1932-33
T.S.Worthington	E.L.McCormick	E v A	Brisbane[2]	1936-37
C.C.Hunte	Fazal Mahmood	WI v P	Port-of-Spain	1957-58
E.J.Barlow	G.D.McKenzie	SA v A	Durban[2]	1966-67
R.C.Fredericks	S.Abid Ali	WI v I	Port-of-Spain	1970-71
K.R.Stackpole	R.J.Hadlee	A v NZ	Auckland	1973-74
S.M.Gavaskar	G.G.Arnold	I v E	Birmingham	1974
S.S.Naik	A.M.E.Roberts	I v WI	Calcutta	1974-75
J.F.M.Morrison	G.G.Arnold	NZ v E	Christchurch	1974-75
Mohsin Khan	Kapil Dev	P v I	Jullundur	1983-84
S.M.Gavaskar	M.D.Marshall	I v WI	Calcutta	1983-84
S.M.Gavaskar	Imran Khan	I v P	Jaipur	1986-87
W.V.Raman	R.J.Hadlee	I v NZ	Napier	1989-90
S.J.Cook	Kapil Dev	SA v I	Durban[2]	1992-93

BATSMEN DISMISSED FOR A PAIR

FOUR TIMES

B.S.Chandrasekhar (India): v E 1976-77; v A 1977-78 (twice); v NZ 1975-76.

THREE TIMES

R.Peel (England): v A 1894-95 (twice), 1896.
R.W.Blair (New Zealand): v E 1962-63; v SA 1963-64; v WI 1955-56.
D.L.Underwood (England): v A 1974-75; v WI 1966, 1976.
B.S.Bedi (India): v E 1974, 1976-77; v WI 1974-75.
A.G.Hurst (Australia): v E 1978-79 (twice); v P 1978-79.
C.E.L.Ambrose (West Indies): v E 1988, 1991; v P 1990-91.
D.K.Morrison (New Zealand): v A 1987-88, 1993-94; v SL 1990-91.

TWICE

ENGLAND: A.V.Bedser v A 1948; v WI 1950. D.L.Amiss v A 1968, 1974-75. P.I.Pocock v WI 1984 (twice). N.A.Foster v WI 1985-86; v P 1987-88. D.E.Malcolm v NZ 1990; v P 1992.

AUSTRALIA: K.D.Mackay v E 1956; v I 1959-60. G.D.McKenzie v E 1968; v SA 1963-64. J.W.Gleeson v E 1970-71; v SA 1969-70. W.M.Clark v WI 1977-78 (twice). R.M.Hogg v I 1979-80; v WI 1984-85. R.G.Holland v E 1985; v NZ 1985-86. M.E.Waugh v SL 1992-93 (twice).

SOUTH AFRICA: L.J.Tancred v E 1907, 1912. Q.McMillan v A 1931-32 (twice). R.J.Crisp v A 1935-36 (twice).

WEST INDIES: C.A.Roach v E 1929-30, 1933. A.L. Valentine v E 1950, 1953-54. A.I.Kallicharran v E 1973-74, v NZ 1979-80.

INDIA: M.Amarnath v WI 1983-84 (twice). Maninder Singh v P 1982-83; v WI 1987-88.

PAKISTAN: Aqib Javed v A 1989-90; v E 1992.

SRI LANKA: M.S.Atapattu v I 1990-91, 1993-94.

ONCE

ENGLAND: G.F.Grace v A 1880. W.Attewell v A 1891-92. G.A.Lohmann v SA 1895-96. E.G.Arnold v A 1903-04. A.E.Knight v A 1903-04. E.G.Hayes v SA 1905-06. M.C.Bird v SA 1909-10. H.Strudwick v A 1921. P.Holmes v SA 1927-28. C.I.J.Smith v WI 1934-35. J.T.Ikin v A 1946-47. J.J.Warr v A 1950-51. F.Ridgway v I 1951-52. R.T.Spooner v SA 1955. J.H.Wardle v A 1956. F.S.Trueman v A 1958-59. T.E.Bailey v A 1958-59. G.Pullar v P 1961-62. M.J.K.Smith v I 1961-62. J.T.Murray v P 1967. B.W.Luckhurst v P 1971. A.P.E.Knott v NZ 1973. G.G.Arnold v A 1974-75. G.A.Gooch v A 1975. A.Ward v WI 1976. J.C.Balderstone v WI 1976. M.Hendrick v NZ 1977-78. R.A.Woolmer v A 1981. I.T.Botham v A 1981. E.E.Hemmings v A 1982-83. N.G.Cowans v I 1984-85. D.J.Capel v P 1987-88. R.J.Bailey v WI 1989-90. W.Larkins v WI 1989-90. C.C.Lewis v A 1993.

AUSTRALIA: P.S.McDonnell v E 1882-83. T.W.Garrett v E 1882-83. E.Evans v E 1886. P.G. McShane v E 1887-88. A.C.Bannerman v E 1888. M.A.Noble v E 1899. S.E.Gregory v E 1899. C.E.McLeod v E 1901-02. J.Darling v E 1902. J.J.Kelly v E 1902. H.Trumble v E 1903-04. V.T.Trumper v E 1907-08. J.V.Saunders v E 1907-08. C.V.Grimmett v E 1930. W.A.S.Oldfield v SA 1931-32. J.H.W.Fingleton v E 1932-33. V.Y.Richardson v E 1932-33. C.L.Badcock v E 1938. I.W.Johnson v E 1946-47. J.Moroney v E 1950-51. J.B.Iverson v E 1950-51. L.V.Maddocks v E 1956. R.N.Harvey v E 1956. A.T.W.Grout v WI 1960-61. R.Benaud v E 1961. A.N.Connolly v WI 1968-69. R.Edwards v E 1972. K.R.Stackpole v NZ 1973-74. G.Dymock v E 1974-75. R.W.Marsh v E 1977. J.R.Thomson v E 1977. C.S.Serjeant v I 1977-78. A.L.Mann v I 1977-78. D.W.Hookes v P 1979-80. G.M.Wood v NZ 1980-81. M.R.Whitney v E 1981. B.Yardley v P 1982-83. R.J.Bright v P 1982-83 C.G.Rackemann v WI 1984-85. K.J.Hughes v WI 1984-85. M.G.Hughes v E 1986-87. D.M.Jones v P 1988-89. B.A.Reid v WI 1990-91. I.A.Healy v E 1992-93. A.R.Border v WI 1992-93. J.L.Langer v NZ 1992-93.

SOUTH AFRICA: C.S.Wimble v E 1891-92. J.T.Willoughby v E 1895-96. J.J.Kotze v A 1902-03. P.S.T.Jones v A 1902-03. A.E.E.Vogler v A 1910-11. T.A.Ward v A 1912. C.B.Llewellyn v E 1912. P.T.Lewis v E 1913-14. J.L.Cox v E 1913-14. C.D.Dixon v E 1913-14.G.A.L. Hearne v E 1922-23. A.E.Hall v E 1922-23. F.Nicholson v A 1935-36. X.C.Balaskas v A 1935-36. C.N.McCarthy v E 1948-49. D.J.McGlew v E 1955. W.R.Endean v E 1955. P.S.Heine v E 1956-57. C.Wesley v E 1960. M.A.Seymour v A 1969-70. A.A.Donald v WI 1991-92. C.R.Matthews v E 1994.

WEST INDIES: C.R.Browne v E 1929-30. H.C.Griffith v E 1933. E.E.Achong v E 1934-35. J.Trim v A 1951-52. A.P.Binns v A 1954-55. O.G.Smith v A 1954-55. S.Ramadhin v E 1957. E.de C.Weekes v E 1957. F.C.M.Alexander v E 1957. L.R.Gibbs v P 1958-59. F.M.M.Worrell v A 1960-61. J.S.Solomon v I 1961-62. J.L.Hendriks v E 1966. W.W.Hall v E 1967-68. D.L.Murray v I 1974-75. C.G.Greenidge v A 1975-76. J.Garner v P 1976-77. D.A.Murray v P 1980-81. A.L.Logie v I 1983-84. M.A.Holding v A 1984-85. P.J.L.Dujon v P 1986-87. A.H.Gray v P 1986-87. D.Williams v A 1992-93. K.L.T.Arthurton v A 1992-93. J.R.Murray v P 1992-93.

NEW ZEALAND: K.C.James v E 1929-30. F.T.Badcock v E 1929-30. J.Cowie v E 1937. C.G.Rowe v A 1945-46. L.A.Butterfield v A 1945-46. L.S.M.Miller v SA 1953-54. M.B.Poore v E 1954-55. I.A.Colquhoun v E 1954-55. J.A.Hayes v E 1954-55. A.R.MacGibbon v I 1955-56. H.B.Cave v WI 1955-56. N.S.Harford v E 1958. R.C.Motz v SA 1961-62. M.J.F.Shrimpton v SA 1963-64. A.E.Dick v P 1964-65. G.A.Bartlett v E 1965-66. T.W.Jarvis v P 1972-73. W.K.Lees v E 1977-78. B.P.Bracewell v E 1978. B.L.Cairns v A 1980-81. B.A.Edgar v A 1980-81. G.B.Troup v I 1980-81. J.V.Coney v A 1981-82. I.D.S.Smith v A 1981-82. J.G.Bracewell v P 1984-85. K.R.Rutherford v WI 1984-85. J.G.Wright v E 1986. C.M.Kuggeleijn v I 1988-89. M.C.Snedden v I 1988-89. B.R.Hartland v E 1991-92. M.L.Su'a v P 1992-93.

INDIA: V.S.Hazare v E 1951-52. G.S.Ramchand v E 1952. Pankaj Roy v E 1952. P.G.Joshi v WI 1952-53. C.V.Gadkari v WI 1952-53. N.S.Tamhane v WI 1958-59. Surendranath v E 1959. R.B.Desai v A 1959-60. D.N.Sardesai v WI 1961-62. M.L.Jaisimha v NZ 1969-70. E.A.S.Prasanna v WI 1974-75. F.M.Engineer v WI 1974-75. D.B.Vengsarkar v WI 1978-79. Yashpal Sharma v A 1979-80. R.M.H.Binny v P 1979-80. D.R.Doshi v P 1982-83. S.Venkataraghavan v WI 1982-83. R.Patel v NZ 1988-89.

PAKISTAN: M.E.Z.Ghazali v E 1954. Nasim-ul-Ghani v WI 1957-58. Wazir Mohammad v WI 1957-58. Imtiaz Ahmed v E 1961-62. Javed Burki v NZ 1964-65. Salim Altaf v A 1976-77. Iqbal Qasim v E 1978. Majid Khan v A 1978-79. Wasim Bari v A 1978-79. Sikander Bakht v A 1978-79. Mudassar Nazar v E 1982. Wasim Akram v SL 1985-86. Waqar Younis v NZ 1990-91. Saeed Anwar v WI 1990-91. Aamir Sohail v NZ 1992-93.

SRI LANKA: B.R.Jurangpathy v I 1986-87. R.G.de Alwis v I 1986-87. R.J.Ratnayake v I 1990-91. G.F.Labrooy v I 1990-91. A.Ranatunga v P 1991-92. S.D.Anurasiri v P 1991-92.

ZIMBABWE: D.H.Brain v I 1992-93. S.G.Peall v P 1993-94. G.W.Flower v P 1993-94.

FASTEST PAIRS

Timed from the start of their first innings to their dismissal in the second innings.

Min				
120	M.E.Z.Ghazali	Pakistan v England	Manchester	1954
124	R.N.Harvey	Australia v England	Manchester	1956
164	Pankaj Roy	India v England	Manchester	1952

DISMISSED FOR A PAIR BY THE SAME FIELDING COMBINATION

R.Peel	st Jarvis b Turner	E v A	Sydney	1894-95
J.Darling	c Braund b Barnes	A v E	Sheffield	1902
P.T.Lewis	c Woolley b Barnes	SA v E	Durban[1]	1913-14
Q.McMillan	st/c Oldfield b Ironmonger	SA v A	Melbourne	1931-32
P.G.Joshi	c Worrell b Valentine	I v WI	Bridgetown	1952-53
K.D.Mackay	c Oakman b Laker	A v E	Manchester	1956
Maninder Singh	c Richardson b Walsh	I v WI	Bombay[3]	1987-88

THREE PAIRS IN A MATCH BY THE SAME TEAM

M.B.Poore, I.A.Colquhoun, J.A.Hayes	NZ v E	Auckland	1954-55
D.L.Amiss, D.L.Underwood, G.G.Arnold	E v A	Adelaide	1974-75
Majid Khan, Wasim Bari, Sikander Bakht	P v A	Perth	1978-79
M.S.Atapattu, R.J.Ratnayake, G.F.Labrooy	SL v I	Chandigarh	1990-91

MOST CONSECUTIVE DUCKS

FIVE			
R.G.Holland	(including two pairs in consecutive Tests)	A v E	1985
		A v NZ	1985-86
FOUR			
R.Peel	(two pairs in consecutive Tests)	E v A	1894-95
R.J.Crisp	(two pairs in consecutive Tests)	SA v A	1935-36

Pankaj Roy	(including one pair)	I v E	1952
L.S.M.Miller	(including one pair)	NZ v SA	1953-54
W.M.Clark	(two pairs in consecutive Tests)	A v WI	1977-78
P.I.Pocock	(two pairs in consecutive Tests)	E v WI	1984
R.G.de Alwis	(including one pair)	SL v I	1986-87
		SL v A	1987-88
M.E.Waugh	(two pairs in consecutive Tests)	A v SL	1992-93

R.J.Crisp was dismissed four times in five balls.

MOST DUCKS IN A SERIES

				Innings	
SIX	A.G.Hurst	Australia v England		12	1978-79
FIVE	Pankaj Roy	India v England		7	1952
	R.C.Motz	New Zealand v South Africa		9	1961-62
	W.M.Clark	Australia v West Indies		7	1977-78
	M.Amarnath	India v West Indies		6	1983-84

FEWEST DUCKS IN A CAREER

Ducks	Innings			
1	74	C.L.Walcott	West Indies	1947-48 to 1959-60
1	73	G.M.Turner	New Zealand	1968-69 to 1982-83
2	84	H.Sutcliffe	England	1924 to 1935
2	83	C.C.McDonald	Australia	1951-52 to 1961
4	175	C.H.Lloyd	West Indies	1966-67 to 1984-85
4	140	W.R.Hammond	England	1927-28 to 1946-47
5	131	K.F.Barrington	England	1955 to 1968

MOST INNINGS BEFORE FIRST DUCK

58	C.H.Lloyd	West Indies	1966-67 to 1973-74
51	A.K.Davidson	Australia	1953 to 1961
46	B.F.Butcher	West Indies	1958-59 to 1966-67
41	R.N.Harvey	Australia	1947-48 to 1953
41	K.D.Ghavri	India	1974-75 to 1979-80
40	W.H.Ponsford	Australia	1924-25 to 1932-33

MOST CONSECUTIVE INNINGS WITHOUT A DUCK

119	D.I.Gower	England	1982 to 1990-91
89	A.R.Border	Australia	1982-83 to 1988-89
78	K.F.Barrington	England	1962 to 1967-68
74	C.H.Lloyd	West Indies	1976 to 1984
72	H.W.Taylor	South Africa	1912 to 1931-32
72	G.M.Turner	New Zealand	1968-69 to 1982-83
68	K.D.Walters	Australia	1969-70 to 1976-77
67	W.R.Hammond	England	1929 to 1936
67	G.Boycott	England	1969 to 1978-79

PARTNERSHIP RECORDS

Throughout these records, partnerships involving more than two batsmen are excluded unless two of the partners added at least 100 runs together.

PARTNERSHIPS OF 300 AND OVER

Runs	Wkt				
467	3rd	A.H.Jones (186), M.D.Crowe (299)	NZ v SL	Wellington	1990-91
451	2nd	W.H.Ponsford (266), D.G.Bradman (244)	A v E	Oval	1934
451	3rd	Mudassar Nazar (231), Javed Miandad (280*)	P v I	Hyderabad	1982-83
446	2nd	C.C.Hunte (260), G.St A.Sobers (365*)	WI v P	Kingston	1957-58
413	1st	M.H.Mankad (231), Pankaj Roy (173)	I v NZ	Madras[2]	1955-56
411	4th	P.B.H.May (285*), M.C.Cowdrey (154)	E v WI	Birmingham	1957
405	5th	S.G.Barnes (234), D.G.Bradman (234)	A v E	Sydney	1946-47
399	4th	G.St A.Sobers (226), F.M.M.Worrell (197*)	WI v E	Bridgetown	1959-60
397	3rd	Qasim Omar (206), Javed Miandad (203*)	P v SL	Faisalabad	1985-86

Runs	Wkt				
388	4th	W.H.Ponsford (181), D.G.Bradman (304)	A v E	Leeds	1934
387	1st	G.M.Turner (259), T.W.Jarvis (182)	NZ v WI	Georgetown	1971-72
382	2nd	L.Hutton (364), M.Leyland (187)	E v A	Oval	1938
382	1st	W.M.Lawry (210), R.B.Simpson (201)	A v WI	Bridgetown	1964-65
370	3rd	W.J.Edrich (189), D.C.S.Compton (208)	E v SA	Lord's	1947
369	2nd	J.H.Edrich (310*), K.F.Barrington (163)	E v NZ	Leeds	1965
359	1st	L.Hutton (158), C.Washbrook (195)	E v SA	Johannesburg[2]	1948-49
351	2nd	G.A.Gooch (196), D.I.Gower (157)	E v A	Oval	1985
350	4th	Mushtaq Mohammad (201), Asif Iqbal (175)	P v NZ	Dunedin	1972-73
347	7th	D.St E.Atkinson (219), C.C.Depeiza (122)	WI v A	Bridgetown	1954-55
346	6th	J.H.W.Fingleton (136), D.G.Bradman (270)	A v E	Melbourne	1936-37
344*	2nd	S.M.Gavaskar (182*), D.B.Vengsarkar (157*)	I v WI	Calcutta	1978-79
341	3rd	E.J.Barlow (201), R.G.Pollock (175)	SA v A	Adelaide	1963-64
338	3rd	E.de C.Weekes (206), F.M.M.Worrell (167)	WI v E	Port-of-Spain	1953-54
336	4th	W.M.Lawry (151), K.D.Walters (242)	A v WI	Sydney	1968-69
332*	5th	A.R.Border (200*), S.R.Waugh (157*)	A v E	Leeds	1993
331	2nd	R.T.Robinson (148), D.I.Gower (215)	E v A	Birmingham	1985
329	1st	G.R.Marsh (138), M.A.Taylor (219)	A v E	Nottingham	1989
323	1st	J.B.Hobbs (178), W.Rhodes (179)	E v A	Melbourne	1911-12
322	4th	Javed Miandad (153*), Salim Malik (165)	P v E	Birmingham	1992
319	3rd	A.Melville (189), A.D.Nourse (149)	SA v E	Nottingham	1947
316†	3rd	G.R.Viswanath (222), Yashpal Sharma (140)	I v E	Madras[1]	1981-82
308	7th	Waqar Hassan (189), Imtiaz Ahmed (209)	P v NZ	Lahore[1]	1955-56
308	3rd	R.B.Richardson (154), I.V.A.Richards (178)	WI v A	St John's	1983-84
308	3rd	G.A.Gooch (333), A.J.Lamb (139)	E v I	Lord's	1990
303	3rd	I.V.A.Richards (232), A.I.Kallicharran (97)	WI v E	Nottingham	1976
303	3rd	M.A.Atherton (135), R.A.Smith (175)	E v WI	St John's	1993-94
301	2nd	A.R.Morris (182), D.G.Bradman (173*)	A v E	Leeds	1948

†415 runs were scored for this wicket in two separate partnerships, D.B.Vengsarkar retiring hurt and being succeeded by Yashpal Sharma when 99 runs had been added.

BATSMEN SHARING IN MOST HUNDRED PARTNERSHIPS

		Total	1st	2nd	3rd	4th	5th	6th	7th	8th	9th	10th
A.R.Border	A	63	–	2	15	20	16	8	1	1	–	–
S.M.Gavaskar	I	58	22	18	8	6	2	1	–	–	1	–
Javed Miandad	P	50	–	2	22	15	8	3	–	–	–	–
G.Boycott	E	47	20	8	9	8	–	2	–	–	–	–
C.G.Greenidge	WI	46	22	9	5	4	2	3	1	–	–	–
G.S.Chappell	A	44	–	2	15	13	11	2	1	–	–	–
I.V.A.Richards	WI	44	–	11	12	12	5	2	1	1	–	–
G.St A.Sobers	WI	43	–	3	4	12	12	10	2	–	–	–
M.C.Cowdrey	E	42	5	9	6	13	4	3	1	–	1	–
G.A.Gooch	E	41	18	11	7	2	2	1	–	–	–	–
L.Hutton	E	41	17	13	7	1	–	2	1	–	–	–
C.H.Lloyd	WI	41	–	–	6	14	9	10	1	–	1	–
D.L.Haynes	WI	40	17	16	5	1	–	1	–	–	–	–
D.I.Gower	E	38	–	7	10	11	6	2	2	–	–	–
D.C.Boon	A	37	6	12	13	4	1	1	–	–	–	–
K.F.Barrington	E	35	–	6	10	14	4	1	–	–	–	–
D.G.Bradman	A	35	–	14	11	3	6	1	–	–	–	–
R.B.Kanhai	WI	34	2	9	11	7	3	2	–	–	–	–
W.R.Hammond	E	33	1	6	12	11	2	1	–	–	–	–
H.Sutcliffe	E	33	21	10	1	–	–	1	–	–	–	–
J.H.Edrich	E	32	9	11	6	5	1	–	–	–	–	–
R.N.Harvey	A	32	–	6	13	9	3	1	–	–	–	–
J.B.Hobbs	E	32	24	6	1	–	–	–	1	–	–	–
I.M.Chappell	A	30	–	18	8	1	1	2	–	–	–	–
D.C.S.Compton	E	30	–	–	14	7	7	1	–	1	–	–
D.B.Vengsarkar	I	30	–	9	9	9	1	2	–	–	–	–

MOST HUNDRED PARTNERSHIPS IN ONE INNINGS

		Opponents			
FOUR					
England	382 (2nd), 135 (3rd), 215 (6th), 106 (7th)	Australia	Oval	1938
West Indies	267 (4th), 101 (6th), 118 (7th), 106 (9th)	India	Delhi	1948-49
Pakistan	152 (1st), 112 (2nd), 154 (3rd), 121 (4th)	West Indies	Bridgetown	1957-58
India	144 (3rd), 172 (4th), 109 (5th), 102 (6th)	West Indies	Kanpur	1978-79

HUNDRED PARTNERSHIPS

ENGLAND – (674) – 1st Wicket

			A	SA	WI	NZ	I	P	SL
L.Hutton (158), C.Washbrook (195)	Johannesburg[2]	1948-49	–	359	–	–	–	–	–
J.B.Hobbs (178), W.Rhodes (179)	Melbourne	1911-12	323	–	–	–	–	–	–
G.Pullar (175), M.C.Cowdrey (155)	Oval	1960	–	290	–	–	–	–	–
J.B.Hobbs (154), H.Sutcliffe (176)	Melbourne	1924-25	283	–	–	–	–	–	–
J.B.Hobbs (211), H.Sutcliffe (122)	Lord's	1924	–	268	–	–	–	–	–
G.Boycott (84), R.W.Barber (185)	Sydney	1965-66	234	–	–	–	–	–	–
G.A.Gooch (116), M.A.Atherton (131)	Manchester	1990	–	–	–	–	225	–	–
G.Fowler (105), C.J.Tavaré (109)	Oval	1983	–	–	–	223	–	–	–
B.C.Broad (162), C.W.J.Athey (96)	Perth	1986-87	223	–	–	–	–	–	–
J.B.Hobbs (187), W.Rhodes (77)	Cape Town	1909-10	–	221	–	–	–	–	–
C.J.Barnett (126), L.Hutton (100)	Nottingham	1938	219	–	–	–	–	–	–
C.Washbrook (102), R.T.Simpson (94)	Nottingham	1950	–	–	212	–	–	–	–
G.Boycott (93), D.L.Amiss (174)	Port-of-Spain	1973-74	–	–	209	–	–	–	–
G.A.Gooch (123), M.A.Atherton (72)	Lord's	1990	–	–	–	–	204	–	–
G.A.Gooch (117), M.A.Atherton (87)	Adelaide	1990-91	203	–	–	–	–	–	–
G.Pullar (165), R.W.Barber (86)	Dacca	1961-62	–	–	–	–	–	198	–
T.W.Hayward (137), F.S.Jackson (118)	Oval	1899	185	–	–	–	–	–	–
G.Boycott (100*), J.M.Brearley (74)	Hyderabad	1977-78	–	–	–	–	–	185	–
J.B.Hobbs (119), H.Sutcliffe (82)	Lord's	1926	182	–	–	–	–	–	–
G.Fowler (201), R.T.Robinson (74)	Madras[1]	1984-85	–	–	–	–	178	–	–
M.C.Cowdrey (97), G.Pullar (66)	Kingston	1959-60	–	–	177	–	–	–	–
G.A.Gooch (88), M.A.Atherton (86)	Oval	1990	–	–	–	–	176	–	–
P.E.Richardson (104), M.C.Cowdrey (80)	Manchester	1956	174	–	–	–	–	–	–
G.Gunn (85), A.Sandham (325)	Kingston	1929-30	–	–	173	–	–	–	–
J.B.Hobbs (100), H.Sutcliffe (161)	Oval	1926	172	–	–	–	–	–	–
J.H.Edrich (146), G.Boycott (90)	Bridgetown	1967-68	–	–	172	–	–	–	–
G.Boycott (70), B.W.Luckhurst (131)	Perth	1970-71	171	–	–	–	–	–	–
M.A.Atherton (85), A.J.Stewart (118)	Bridgetown	1993-94	–	–	171	–	–	–	–
W.G.Grace (170), W.H.Scotton (34)	Oval	1886	170	–	–	–	–	–	–
G.A.Gooch (154), M.A.Atherton (82)	Birmingham	1990	–	–	–	170	–	–	–
L.Hutton (81), C.Washbrook (143)	Leeds	1948	168	–	–	–	–	–	–
G.A.Gooch (135), M.A.Atherton (76)	Leeds	1992	–	–	–	–	168	–	–
G.Boycott (76*), J.H.Edrich (74*)	Melbourne	1970-71	161*	–	–	–	–	–	–
R.E.S.Wyatt (54), W.R.Hammond (136*)	Durban[2]	1930-31	–	160	–	–	–	–	–
J.B.Hobbs (89), W.Rhodes (66)	Johannesburg[1]	1909-10	–	159	–	–	–	–	–
P.E.Richardson (71), G.Pullar (83)	Bombay[2]	1961-62	–	–	–	–	159	–	–
C.A.G.Russell (102*), G.Brown (84)	Oval	1921	158	–	–	–	–	–	–
J.B.Hobbs (115), H.Sutcliffe (59)	Sydney	1924-25	157	–	–	–	–	–	–
D.L.Amiss (79), D.Lloyd (214*)	Birmingham	1974	–	–	–	–	157	–	–
J.B.Hobbs (88), H.Sutcliffe (94)	Leeds	1926	156	–	–	–	–	–	–
G.Fowler (69), R.T.Robinson (96)	Kanpur	1984-85	–	–	–	–	156	–	–
J.B.Hobbs (159), H.Sutcliffe (63)	Oval	1928	–	–	155	–	–	–	–
G.A.Gooch (127), C.J.Tavaré (35)	Madras[1]	1981-82	–	–	–	–	155	–	–
A.C.MacLaren (116), T.W.Hayward (69)	Sydney	1901-02	154	–	–	–	–	–	–
J.M.Brearley (81), G.Boycott (80*)	Nottingham	1977	154	–	–	–	–	–	–
A.Sandham (58), C.A.G.Russell (96)	Johannesburg[1]	1922-23	–	153	–	–	–	–	–
W.G.Grace (68), A.E.Stoddart (83)	Oval	1893	151	–	–	–	–	–	–
P.E.Richardson (73), M.C.Cowdrey (81)	Nottingham	1956	151	–	–	–	–	–	–
T.W.Hayward (90), A.C.MacLaren (67)	Adelaide	1901-02	149	–	–	–	–	–	–
T.W.Hayward (67), P.F.Warner (79)	Adelaide	1903-04	148	–	–	–	–	–	–
J.B.Hobbs (187), W.Rhodes (59)	Adelaide	1911-12	147	–	–	–	–	–	–
L.Hutton (66), R.T.Simpson (68)	Oval	1949	–	–	–	147	–	–	–
W.G.A.Parkhouse (78), G.Pullar (75)	Leeds	1959	–	–	–	–	146	–	–
D.L.Amiss (50), J.M.Brearley (91)	Bombay[3]	1976-77	–	–	–	–	146	–	–
G.A.Gooch (83), B.C.Rose (50)	Oval	1980	–	–	146†	–	–	–	–
T.W.Hayward (47), A.C.MacLaren (140)	Nottingham	1905	145	–	–	–	–	–	–
G.A.Gooch (83), G.Boycott (104*)	St John's	1980-81	–	–	144	–	–	–	–
J.B.Hobbs (74), H.Sutcliffe (64)	Adelaide	1928-29	143	–	–	–	–	–	–
L.Hutton (66), J.D.B.Robertson (121)	Lord's	1949	–	–	–	143	–	–	–
L.Hutton (86), D.S.Sheppard (119)	Oval	1952	–	–	–	–	143	–	–
W.Rhodes (152), A.E.Relf (63)	Johannesburg[1]	1913-14	–	141	–	–	–	–	–
L.Hutton (100), C.Washbrook (75)	Leeds	1947	–	141	–	–	–	–	–
P.Holmes (88), H.Sutcliffe (99)	Cape Town	1927-28	–	140	–	–	–	–	–
L.Hutton (40), C.Washbrook (112)	Melbourne	1946-47	138	–	–	–	–	–	–
L.Hutton (94), C.Washbrook (65)	Adelaide	1946-47	137	–	–	–	–	–	–
J.B.Hobbs (76), H.Sutcliffe (64)	Birmingham	1924	–	136	–	–	–	–	–
J.B.Hobbs (97), W.Rhodes (35)	Durban[1]	1913-14	–	133	–	–	–	–	–

1st Wicket *continued*

			A	SA	WI	NZ	I	P	SL
G.A.Gooch (71), G.Boycott (105)	Delhi	1981-82	–	–	–	–	132	–	–
L.Hutton (56), W.Watson (116)	Kingston	1953-54	–	–	130	–	–	–	–
L.Hutton (56), J.D.B.Robertson (64)	Kingston	1947-48	–	–	129	–	–	–	–
L.Hutton (57), C.Washbrook (65)	Leeds	1948	129	–	–	–	–	–	–
B.C.Broad (61), M.D.Moxon (81*)	Wellington	1987-88	–	–	–	129	–	–	–
D.Smith (57), A.Mitchell (72)	Leeds	1935	–	128	–	–	–	–	–
C.L.Smith (66), M.W.Gatting (75)	Faisalabad	1983-84	–	–	–	–	–	127	–
G.A.Gooch (51), W.N.Slack (52)	St John's	1985-86	–	–	127	–	–	–	–
J.B.Hobbs (66), H.Sutcliffe (143)	Melbourne	1924-25	126	–	–	–	–	–	–
P.E.Richardson (74), W.Watson (66)	Manchester	1958	–	–	–	126	–	–	–
J.B.Hobbs (74), H.Sutcliffe (58*)	Nottingham	1930	125	–	–	–	–	–	–
J.B.Bolus (57), J.G.Binks (55)	Bombay[2]	1963-64	–	–	–	–	125	–	–
G.Boycott (47), J.H.Edrich (115)	Lord's	1969	–	–	–	125	–	–	–
G.A.Gooch (73), B.C.Broad (54)	Nottingham	1988	–	–	125	–	–	–	–
G.Boycott (121*), B.W.Luckhurst (46)	Lord's	1971	–	–	–	–	–	124	–
C.F.Walters (50*), H.Sutcliffe (69*)	Manchester	1934	123*	–	–	–	–	–	–
J.H.Edrich (62), R.M.Prideaux (64)	Leeds	1968	123	–	–	–	–	–	–
G.A.Gooch (69), A.J.Stewart (74)	Lord's	1992	–	–	–	–	–	123	–
R.G.Barlow (62), G.Ulyett (67)	Sydney	1881-82	122	–	–	–	–	–	–
P.F.Warner (68), T.W.Hayward (58)	Melbourne	1903-04	122	–	–	–	–	–	–
L.Hutton (98*), J.T.Ikin (38)	Manchester	1951	–	121	–	–	–	–	–
M.A.Atherton (55), A.J.Stewart (70)	Kingston	1993-94	–	–	121	–	–	–	–
G.Boycott (73), R.W.Barber (74)	Durban[2]	1964-65	–	120	–	–	–	–	–
J.B.Hobbs (53), H.Sutcliffe (54)	Manchester	1928	–	–	119	–	–	–	–
B.C.Broad (54), R.T.Robinson (80)	Birmingham	1987	–	–	–	–	–	119	–
H.Sutcliffe (61), R.E.S.Wyatt (149)	Nottingham	1935	–	118	–	–	–	–	–
B.W.Luckhurst (53*), R.A.Hutton (58*)	Lord's	1971	–	–	–	–	–	117*	–
Rev D.S.Sheppard (57), M.C.Cowdrey (182)	Oval	1962	–	–	–	–	–	117	–
G.Boycott (77), B.W.Luckhurst (38)	Sydney	1970-71	116	–	–	–	–	–	–
D.L.Amiss (188), D.Lloyd (46)	Lord's	1974	–	–	–	–	116	–	–
G.A.Gooch (99), G.Boycott (44)	Melbourne	1979-80	116	–	–	–	–	–	–
P.E.Richardson (68), T.E.Bailey (80)	Durban[2]	1956-57	–	115	–	–	–	–	–
D.L.Amiss (90), D.Lloyd (44)	Melbourne	1974-75	115	–	–	–	–	–	–
H.Sutcliffe (86), D.R.Jardine (46)	Brisbane[2]	1932-33	114	–	–	–	–	–	–
Rev D.S.Sheppard (57), G.Pullar (56)	Brisbane[2]	1962-63	114	–	–	–	–	–	–
J.B.Hobbs (107), W.Rhodes (59)	Lord's	1912	112	–	–	–	–	–	–
H.Sutcliffe (194), R.E.S.Wyatt (38)	Sydney	1932-33	112	–	–	–	–	–	–
J.H.Edrich (58), G.Boycott (128)	Manchester	1969	–	–	112	–	–	–	–
G.Boycott (92), D.Amiss (53)	Lord's	1973	–	–	–	112	–	–	–
B.C.Broad (116), C.W.J.Athey (55)	Adelaide	1986-87	112	–	–	–	–	–	–
G.A.Gooch (84), W.Larkins (54)	Port-of-Spain	1989-90	–	–	112	–	–	–	–
G.A.Gooch (60), H.Morris (44)	Oval	1991	–	–	112	–	–	–	–
A.C.MacLaren (65), E.Wainwright (49)	Sydney	1897-98	111	–	–	–	–	–	–
A.H.Bakewell (85), C.F.Walters (59)	Madras[1]	1933-34	–	–	–	–	111	–	–
B.Wood (52), J.H.Edrich (175)	Lord's	1975	111	–	–	–	–	–	–
G.A.Gooch (55), G.Boycott (131)	Nottingham	1978	–	–	–	111	–	–	–
J.B.Hobbs (57), H.Sutcliffe (115)	Sydney	1924-25	110	–	–	–	–	–	–
J.B.Hobbs (31), H.Sutcliffe (74)	Manchester	1930	108	–	–	–	–	–	–
G.A.Gooch (68), M.A.Atherton (32)	Nottingham	1991	–	–	108	–	–	–	–
J.B.Hobbs (66), W.Rhodes (49)	Oval	1912	107	–	–	–	–	–	–
G.Boycott (58), J.H.Edrich (130)	Adelaide	1970-71	107	–	–	–	–	–	–
L.Hutton (150), R.T.Simpson (53)	Lord's	1952	–	–	–	–	106	–	–
G.Cook (66), C.J.Tavaré (57)	Manchester	1982	–	–	–	–	106	–	–
J.B.Hobbs (62*), C.B.Fry (35*)	Birmingham	1909	105*	–	–	–	–	–	–
G.Boycott (56*), D.L.Amiss (56)	Birmingham	1973	–	–	105*‡	–	–	–	–
J.B.Hobbs (49), H.Sutcliffe (135)	Melbourne	1928-29	105	–	–	–	–	–	–
M.H.Denness (50), D.L.Amiss (112)	Lahore[2]	1972-73	–	–	–	–	–	105	–
C.F.Walters (64), H.Sutcliffe (38)	Oval	1934	104	–	–	–	–	–	–
L.Hutton (73), C.Washbrook (44)	Manchester	1949	–	–	–	103	–	–	–
G.Boycott (119*), J.H.Edrich (40)	Adelaide	1970-71	103	–	–	–	–	–	–
C.J.Tavaré (33), G.Fowler (86)	Leeds	1982	–	–	–	–	–	103	–
J.B.Bolus (58), J.H.Edrich (41)	Delhi	1963-64	–	–	–	–	101	–	–
G.Fowler (106), B.C.Broad (55)	Lord's	1984	–	–	101	–	–	–	–
J.B.Hobbs (92), W.Rhodes (35)	Johannesburg[1]	1913-14	–	100	–	–	–	–	–
L.Hutton (100), C.J.Barnett (62)	Manchester	1937	–	–	–	100	–	–	–
L.Hutton (76), C.Washbrook (39)	Adelaide	1946-47	100	–	–	–	–	–	–
Totals:		*(133)*	54	18	21	11	18	11	–

Hundred Partnerships (England)

†155 *runs were added for this wicket in two separate partnerships, G.Boycott retiring hurt and being succeeded by B.C.Rose when the score was 9.*

‡119 *runs were added for this wicket in two partnerships, G.Boycott retiring hurt and being succeeded by B.W.Luckhurst when 105 runs had been scored.*

ENGLAND – 2nd Wicket

			A	SA	WI	NZ	I	P	SL
L.Hutton (364), M.Leyland (187)	Oval	1938	382	–	–	–	–	–	–
J.H.Edrich (310*), K.F.Barrington (163)	Leeds	1965	–	–	–	369	–	–	–
G.A.Gooch (196), D.I.Gower (157)	Oval	1985	351	–	–	–	–	–	–
R.T.Robinson (148), D.I.Gower (215)	Birmingham	1985	351	–	–	–	–	–	–
P.A.Gibb (120), W.J.Edrich (219)	Durban[2]	1938-39	–	280	–	–	–	–	–
P.E.Richardson (126), T.W.Graveney (258)	Nottingham	1957	–	–	266	–	–	–	–
M.A.Atherton (101), G.A.Gooch (210)	Nottingham	1994	–	–	–	263	–	–	–
J.H.Edrich (155), P.J.Sharpe (111)	Nottingham	1969	–	–	–	249	–	–	–
M.C.Cowdrey (182), E.R.Dexter (172)	Oval	1962	–	–	–	–	248	–	–
G.Fowler (201), M.W.Gatting (207)	Madras[1]	1984-85	–	–	–	–	241	–	–
H.Sutcliffe (102), G.E.Tyldesley (122)	Johannesburg[1]	1927-28	–	230	–	–	–	–	–
H.Sutcliffe (114), W.R.Hammond (138*)	Birmingham	1929	–	221	–	–	–	–	–
D.L.Amiss (188), J.H.Edrich (96)	Lord's	1974	–	–	–	–	221	–	–
L.Hutton (206), W.J.Edrich (100)	Oval	1949	–	–	–	218	–	–	–
D.Lloyd (214*), M.H.Denness (100)	Birmingham	1974	–	–	–	–	211	–	–
M.C.Cowdrey (119), E.R.Dexter (76)	Port-of-Spain	1959-60	–	–	191	–	–	–	–
H.Sutcliffe (194), W.R.Hammond (112)	Sydney	1932-33	188	–	–	–	–	–	–
H.Sutcliffe (109*), W.R.Hammond (101*)	Oval	1929	–	187*	–	–	–	–	–
P.A.Gibb (93), E.Paynter (117)	Johannesburg[1]	1938-39	–	184	–	–	–	–	–
T.W.Graveney (111), P.B.H.May (79)	Sydney	1954-55	182	–	–	–	–	–	–
H.Sutcliffe (117), K.S.Duleepsinhji (109)	Oval	1931	–	–	–	178	–	–	–
G.Boycott (116), M.C.Cowdrey (59)	Georgetown	1967-68	–	–	172	–	–	–	–
J.H.Edrich (130), K.W.R.Fletcher (80)	Adelaide	1970-71	169	–	–	–	–	–	–
P.A.Gibb (106), E.Paynter (100)	Johannesburg[1]	1938-39	–	168	–	–	–	–	–
L.Hutton (145), T.W.Graveney (78)	Lord's	1953	168	–	–	–	–	–	–
D.L.Amiss (158), K.W.R.Fletcher (78)	Hyderabad	1972-73	–	–	–	–	168	–	–
B.C.Broad (114), R.T.Robinson (70)	Christchurch	1987-88	–	–	–	168	–	–	–
M.C.Cowdrey (159), E.R.Dexter (72)	Birmingham	1962	–	–	–	–	166	–	–
G.Pullar (89), K.F.Barrington (113*)	Delhi	1961-62	–	–	–	–	164	–	–
Rev D.S.Sheppard (83), E.R.Dexter (85)	Nottingham	1962	–	–	–	–	161	–	–
B.C.Broad (116), M.W.Gatting (100)	Adelaide	1986-87	161	–	–	–	–	–	–
L.Hutton (150), P.B.H.May (74)	Lord's	1952	–	–	–	–	158	–	–
C.Milburn (139), T.W.Graveney (105)	Karachi[1]	1968-69	–	–	–	–	–	156	–
A.Shrewsbury (81), W.Gunn (77)	Lord's	1893	152	–	–	–	–	–	–
L.Hutton (122*), W.J.Edrich (60)	Sydney	1946-47	150	–	–	–	–	–	–
C.J.Tavaré (51), D.I.Gower (108)	Lord's	1983	–	–	–	149	–	–	–
A.Sandham (325), R.E.S.Wyatt (58)	Kingston	1929-30	–	–	148	–	–	–	–
G.A.Gooch (85), A.J.Stewart (54)	Lord's	1990	–	–	–	148	–	–	–
C.Washbrook (62), W.J.Edrich (89)	Melbourne	1946-47	147	–	–	–	–	–	–
G.Pullar (165), K.F.Barrington (84)	Dacca	1961-62	–	–	–	–	–	147	–
P.E.Richardson (107), T.W.Graveney (164)	Oval	1957	–	–	146	–	–	–	–
G.A.Gooch (123), C.J.Tavaré (42)	Lord's	1980	–	–	145	–	–	–	–
L.Hutton (63), R.T.Simpson (137)	Nottingham	1951	–	144	–	–	–	–	–
A.C.MacLaren (124), K.S.Ranjitsinhji (77)	Adelaide	1897-98	142	–	–	–	–	–	–
J.B.Hobbs (211), F.E.Woolley (134*)	Lord's	1924	–	142	–	–	–	–	–
G.Pullar (119), K.F.Barrington (172)	Kanpur	1961-62	–	–	–	–	139	–	–
G.Boycott (246*), K.F.Barrington (93)	Leeds	1967	–	–	–	–	139	–	–
G.A.Gooch (174), A.J.Stewart (43)	Lord's	1991	–	–	–	–	–	–	139
G.Ulyett (87), J.Selby (55)	Melbourne	1881-82	137	–	–	–	–	–	–
A.C.MacLaren (109), T.W.Hayward (72)	Sydney	1897-98	136	–	–	–	–	–	–
R.W.Barber (97), E.R.Dexter (172)	Johannesburg[3]	1964-65	–	136	–	–	–	–	–
G.Fowler (55), M.W.Gatting (136)	Bombay[3]	1984-85	–	–	–	–	135	–	–
J.B.Hobbs (72), G.Gunn (122*)	Sydney	1907-08	134	–	–	–	–	–	–
A.E.Fagg (39), W.R.Hammond (167)	Manchester	1936	–	–	–	–	134	–	–
L.Hutton (87), J.F.Crapp (54)	Cape Town	1948-49	–	134	–	–	–	–	–
H.Sutcliffe (58), W.R.Hammond (200)	Melbourne	1928-29	133	–	–	–	–	–	–
T.W.Graveney (60), P.B.H.May (112)	Lord's	1955	–	132	–	–	–	–	–
G.Boycott (49), C.Milburn (83)	Lord's	1968	132	–	–	–	–	–	–
J.M.Brearley (49), R.A.Woolmer (120)	Lord's	1977	132	–	–	–	–	–	–
T.W.Hayward (137), K.S.Ranjitsinhji (54)	Oval	1899	131	–	–	–	–	–	–
L.Hutton (73), N.Oldfield (80)	Oval	1939	–	131	–	–	–	–	–
L.Hutton (79), R.T.Simpson (156*)	Melbourne	1950-51	131	–	–	–	–	–	–
G.Pullar (131), M.C.Cowdrey (67)	Manchester	1959	–	–	–	–	131	–	–
G.A.Gooch (75), R.C.Russell (94)	Lord's	1988	–	–	–	–	–	–	131

2nd Wicket *continued*

			A	SA	WI	NZ	I	P	SL
H.Sutcliffe (51), G.E.Tyldesley (100)	Durban[2]	1927-28	–	130	–	–	–	–	–
D.L.Amiss (99), K.W.R.Fletcher (54)	Karachi[1]	1972-73	–	–	–	–	–	130	–
J.B.Hobbs (159), G.E.Tyldesley (73)	Oval	1928	–	–	129	–	–	–	–
L.Hutton (100), P.B.H.May (138)	Leeds	1951	–	129	–	–	–	–	–
J.H.Edrich (96), M.C.Cowdrey (101)	Kingston	1967-68	–	–	129	–	–	–	–
D.L.Amiss (183), D.L.Underwood (43)	Oval	1974	–	–	–	–	–	129	–
G.Boycott (131), C.T.Radley (59)	Nottingham	1978	–	–	–	129	–	–	–
L.Hutton (100), J.Hardstaff, jr (58)	Manchester	1937	–	–	–	128	–	–	–
W.Rhodes (61), J.W.Hearne (114)	Melbourne	1911-12	127	–	–	–	–	–	–
G.A.Gooch (333), D.I.Gower (40)	Lord's	1990	–	–	–	–	127	–	–
H.Sutcliffe (109*), K.S.Duleepsinhji (63)	Manchester	1931	–	–	126	–	–	–	–
J.H.Edrich (96), D.S.Steele (66)	Oval	1975	125	–	–	–	–	–	–
W.Rhodes (36), R.H.Spooner (119)	Lord's	1912	–	124	–	–	–	–	–
C.Washbrook (85*), W.J.Edrich (53)	Manchester	1948	124	–	–	–	–	–	–
Rev D.S.Sheppard (113), E.R.Dexter (52)	Melbourne	1962-63	124	–	–	–	–	–	–
M.A.Atherton (63), G.A.Hick (81*)	Oval	1994	–	124	–	–	–	–	–
B.W.Luckhurst (101), J.H.Edrich (59)	Manchester	1971	–	–	–	–	123	–	–
H.Sutcliffe (56), W.R.Hammond (101)	Sydney	1932-33	122	–	–	–	–	–	–
G.A.Gooch (74), D.I.Gower (47)	Manchester	1985	121	–	–	–	–	–	–
W.G.Grace (152), A.P.Lucas (55)	Oval	1880	120	–	–	–	–	–	–
C.Washbrook (97), J.F.Crapp (51)	Johannesburg[2]	1948-49	–	120	–	–	–	–	–
G.A.Gooch (53), D.I.Gower (66)	Bridgetown	1985-86	–	–	120	–	–	–	–
D.L.Amiss (174), M.H.Denness (44)	Port-of-Spain	1973-74	–	–	119	–	–	–	–
C.Washbrook (103*), W.J.Edrich (70)	Leeds	1949	–	–	–	118	–	–	–
Rev D.S.Sheppard (119), J.T.Ikin (53)	Oval	1952	–	–	–	–	118	–	–
W.E.Russell (56), M.C.Cowdrey (59)	Auckland	1965-66	–	–	–	118	–	–	–
G.Boycott (80*), M.C.Cowdrey (71)	Port-of-Spain	1967-68	–	–	118	–	–	–	–
B.W.Luckhurst (96), P.H.Parfitt (46)	Nottingham	1972	117	–	–	–	–	–	–
A.Shrewsbury (72), W.Barnes (58)	Melbourne	1884-85	116	–	–	–	–	–	–
G.Boycott (105), C.J.Tavaré (149)	Delhi	1981-82	–	–	–	–	116	–	–
G.A.Gooch (70), D.I.Gower (166)	Nottingham	1985	116	–	–	–	–	–	–
P.A.Gibb (38), E.Paynter (243)	Durban[2]	1938-39	–	115	–	–	–	–	–
G.Boycott (60), T.W.Graveney (96)	Lord's	1966	–	–	115	–	–	–	–
W.Rhodes (73), J.W.H.Makepeace (54)	Melbourne	1920-21	113	–	–	–	–	–	–
J.B.Hobbs (126*), G.Gunn (43)	Melbourne	1911-12	112	–	–	–	–	–	–
J.H.Edrich (62), D.S.Steele (73)	Leeds	1975	112	–	–	–	–	–	–
E.H.Bowley (109), K.S.Duleepsinhji (117)	Auckland	1929-30	–	–	–	111	–	–	–
G.Boycott (58), E.R.Dexter (174)	Manchester	1964	111	–	–	–	–	–	–
J.M.Brearley (53), D.W.Randall (150)	Sydney	1978-79	111	–	–	–	–	–	–
A.J.Stewart (74), G.A.Hick (64)	Madras[1]	1992-93	–	–	–	–	111	–	–
R.Subba Row (49), E.R.Dexter (76)	Manchester	1961	110	–	–	–	–	–	–
R.Subba Row (112), E.R.Dexter (180)	Birmingham	1961	109	–	–	–	–	–	–
H.Gimblett (67*), M.J.L.Turnbull (37*)	Lord's	1936	–	–	–	–	108*	–	–
J.H.Edrich (88), M.C.Cowdrey (104)	Birmingham	1968	108	–	–	–	–	–	–
M.D.Moxon (99), R.T.Robinson (54)	Auckland	1987-88	–	–	–	108	–	–	–
L.Hutton (77), P.B.H.May (62)	Bridgetown	1953-54	–	–	107	–	–	–	–
A.C.MacLaren (92), J.T.Tyldesley (79)	Sydney	1901-02	106	–	–	–	–	–	–
H.Sutcliffe (143), J.W.Hearne (44)	Melbourne	1924-25	106	–	–	–	–	–	–
J.A.Jameson (82), J.H.Edrich (41)	Oval	1971	–	–	–	–	106	–	–
W.G.Grace (66), R.Abel (94)	Lord's	1896	105	–	–	–	–	–	–
J.B.Hobbs (123), J.W.H.Makepeace (30)	Adelaide	1920-21	105	–	–	–	–	–	–
B.C.Broad (112), M.W.Gatting (40)	Melbourne	1986-87	105	–	–	–	–	–	–
Albert Ward (32), A.E.Stoddart (68)	Melbourne	1894-95	104	–	–	–	–	–	–
J.H.Edrich (175), D.S.Steele (45)	Lord's	1975	104	–	–	–	–	–	–
M.A.Atherton (99), M.W.Gatting (59)	Lord's	1993	104	–	–	–	–	–	–
G.Pullar (65), K.F.Barrington (128)	Bridgetown	1959-60	–	–	103	–	–	–	–
W.Rhodes (179), G.Gunn (75)	Melbourne	1911-12	102	–	–	–	–	–	–
P.Holmes (56), G.E.Tyldesley (62*)	Durban[2]	1927-28	–	102	–	–	–	–	–
G.A.Gooch (135), R.A.Smith (42)	Leeds	1992	–	–	–	–	–	102	–
C.W.J.Athey (76), M.W.Gatting (61)	Brisbane[2]	1986-87	101	–	–	–	–	–	–
J.B.Hobbs (59), J.W.Hearne (57)	Sydney	1920-21	100	–	–	–	–	–	–
C.Washbrook (143), W.J.Edrich (111)	Leeds	1948	100	–	–	–	–	–	–
L.Hutton (82), P.B.H.May (39)	Oval	1953	100	–	–	–	–	–	–
D.L.Amiss (203), D.S.Steele (44)	Oval	1976	–	–	100	–	–	–	–
	Totals: (128)		51	18	16	15	17	9	2

ENGLAND – 3rd Wicket

			A	SA	WI	NZ	I	P	SL
W.J.Edrich (189), D.C.S.Compton (208)	Lord's	1947	–	370	–	–	–	–	–
G.A.Gooch (333), A.J.Lamb (139)	Lord's	1990	–	–	–	–	308	–	–
M.A.Atherton (135), R.A.Smith (175)	St John's	1993-94	–	–	303	–	–	–	–
L.Hutton (165*), W.R.Hammond (138)	Oval	1939	–	–	264	–	–	–	–
W.R.Hammond (177), D.R.Jardine (98)	Adelaide	1928-29	262	–	–	–	–	–	–
E.R.Dexter (174), K.F.Barrington (256)	Manchester	1964	246	–	–	–	–	–	–
R.E.S.Wyatt (113), F.E.Woolley (154)	Manchester	1929	–	245	–	–	–	–	–
J.Hardstaff, jr (114), W.R.Hammond (140)	Lord's	1937	–	–	–	245	–	–	–
E.Paynter (243), W.R.Hammond (120)	Durban[2]	1938-39	–	242	–	–	–	–	–
W.J.Edrich (191), D.C.S.Compton (115)	Manchester	1947	–	228	–	–	–	–	–
A.J.Stewart (190), R.A.Smith (127)	Birmingham	1992	–	–	–	–	–	227	–
Albert Ward (93), J.T.Brown (140)	Melbourne	1894-95	210	–	–	–	–	–	–
T.W.Graveney (258), P.B.H.May (104)	Nottingham	1957	–	–	207	–	–	–	–
K.F.Barrington (148), T.W.Graveney (81)	Lord's	1967	–	–	–	–	–	201	–
C.A.Milton (104*), P.B.H.May (113*)	Leeds	1958	–	–	–	194*	–	–	–
K.F.Barrington (139), M.J.K.Smith (99)	Lahore[2]	1961-62	–	–	–	–	–	192	–
E.R.Dexter (172), K.F.Barrington (121)	Johannesburg[3]	1964-65	–	191	–	–	–	–	–
D.I.Gower (166), M.W.Gatting (74)	Nottingham	1985	187	–	–	–	–	–	–
A.J.Stewart (148), R.A.Smith (96)	Christchurch	1991-92	–	–	–	179	–	–	–
J.H.Edrich (85), K.F.Barrington (115)	Melbourne	1965-66	178	–	–	–	–	–	–
W.H.Scotton (82), W.Barnes (134)	Adelaide	1884-85	175	–	–	–	–	–	–
E.R.Dexter (93), M.C.Cowdrey (113)	Melbourne	1962-63	175	–	–	–	–	–	–
M.A.Atherton (144), R.A.Smith (84)	Georgetown	1993-94	–	–	171	–	–	–	–
R.Subba Row (94), M.J.K.Smith (98)	Oval	1959	–	–	–	169	–	–	–
A.Sandham (152), E.H.Hendren (80)	Bridgetown	1929-30	–	–	168	–	–	–	–
P.B.H.May (135), D.C.S.Compton (133)	Port-of-Spain	1953-54	–	–	166	–	–	–	–
D.W.Randall (174), D.L.Amiss (64)	Melbourne	1976-77	166	–	–	–	–	–	–
G.A.Gooch (146), D.I.Gower (88*)	Nottingham	1988	–	–	161	–	–	–	–
W.J.Edrich (111), A.V.Bedser (79)	Leeds	1948	155	–	–	–	–	–	–
W.Rhodes (152), C.P.Mead (102)	Johannesburg[1]	1913-14	–	152	–	–	–	–	–
D.L.Amiss (164*), M.H.Denness (59*)	Christchurch	1974-75	–	–	–	151*	–	–	–
J.F.Crapp (56), D.C.S.Compton (114)	Johannesburg[2]	1948-49	–	150	–	–	–	–	–
L.Hutton (169), D.C.S.Compton (64)	Georgetown	1953-54	–	–	150	–	–	–	–
W.R.Hammond (336*), E.Paynter (36)	Auckland	1932-33	–	–	–	149	–	–	–
J.H.Edrich (70), M.H.Denness (188)	Melbourne	1974-75	149	–	–	–	–	–	–
E.R.Dexter (110), R.Subba Row (100)	Georgetown	1959-60	–	–	148	–	–	–	–
G.Boycott (155), G.A.Gooch (83)	Birmingham	1979	–	–	–	145	–	–	–
M.W.Gatting (207), A.J.Lamb (62)	Madras[1]	1984-85	–	–	–	–	144	–	–
E.R.Dexter (205), M.J.K.Smith (56)	Karachi[1]	1961-62	–	–	–	–	–	143	–
J.B.Hobbs (122), E.H.Hendren (67)	Melbourne	1920-21	142	–	–	–	–	–	–
R.A.Woolmer (137), D.W.Randall (79)	Manchester	1977	142	–	–	–	–	–	–
M.A.Atherton (99), G.P.Thorpe (72)	Leeds	1994	–	142	–	–	–	–	–
K.F.Barrington (142), T.W.Graveney (77)	Oval	1967	–	–	–	–	–	141	–
A.J.Lamb (91), R.A.Smith (58)	Perth	1990-91	141	–	–	–	–	–	–
F.E.Woolley (87), E.H.Hendren (127*)	Lord's	1926	140	–	–	–	–	–	–
C.A.G.Russell (140), C.P.Mead (66)	Durban[2]	1922-23	–	139	–	–	–	–	–
C.T.Radley (158), G.R.J.Roope (68)	Auckland	1977-78	–	–	–	139	–	–	–
A.Shrewsbury (106), Hon F.S.Jackson (91)	Lord's	1893	137	–	–	–	–	–	–
M.W.Gatting (53), D.I.Gower (173*)	Lahore[2]	1983-84	–	–	–	–	–	137	–
R.T.Robinson (175), M.W.Gatting (53)	Leeds	1985	136	–	–	–	–	–	–
L.Hutton (364), W.R.Hammond (59)	Oval	1938	135	–	–	–	–	–	–
M.C.Cowdrey (72), K.F.Barrington (143)	Port-of-Spain	1967-68	–	–	134	–	–	–	–
M.A.Atherton (74), A.J.Lamb (109)	Manchester	1990	–	–	–	134	–	–	–
M.C.Cowdrey (148), K.F.Barrington (48)	Port-of-Spain	1967-68	–	–	133	–	–	–	–
G.A.Hick (110), G.P.Thorpe (73)	Leeds	1994	–	133	–	–	–	–	–
W.R.Hammond (231*), M.Leyland (42)	Sydney	1936-37	129	–	–	–	–	–	–
R.T.Simpson (81), D.C.S.Compton (79)	Christchurch	1950-51	–	–	–	129	–	–	–
G.Boycott (128), T.W.Graveney (73)	Manchester	1969	–	–	128	–	–	–	–
G.E.Tyldesley (78), W.R.Hammond (90)	Durban[2]	1927-28	–	127	–	–	–	–	–
W.R.Hammond (167), T.S.Worthington (87)	Manchester	1936	–	–	–	–	127	–	–
C.J.Tavaré (54), D.I.Gower (74)	Birmingham	1982	–	–	–	–	–	127	–
G.Boycott (76), E.R.Dexter (80*)	Lord's	1965	–	–	–	126	–	–	–
G.A.Gooch (87), R.A.Smith (53)	Adelaide	1990-91	126	–	–	–	–	–	–
R.E.S.Wyatt (61*), W.R.Hammond (75*)	Sydney	1932-33	125*	–	–	–	–	–	–
W.J.Edrich (88), P.B.H.May (44)	Brisbane[2]	1954-55	124	–	–	–	–	–	–
P.B.H.May (117), D.C.S.Compton (71)	Manchester	1955	–	124	–	–	–	–	–
H.Sutcliffe (194), Nawab of Pataudi, sr (102)	Sydney	1932-33	123	–	–	–	–	–	–
G.Boycott (60), D.I.Gower (89)	Lord's	1981	123	–	–	–	–	–	–

3rd Wicket *continued*

			A	SA	WI	NZ	I	P	SL
F.E.Woolley (134*), E.H.Hendren (50*)	Lord's	1924	–	121*	–	–	–	–	–
G.A.Gooch (116), D.I.Gower (54)	Bridgetown	1980-81	–	–	120	–	–	–	–
T.W.Hayward (122), C.B.Fry (64)	Johannesburg[1]	1895-96	–	119	–	–	–	–	–
W.R.Hammond (75), E.H.Hendren (64)	Johannesburg[1]	1930-31	–	119	–	–	–	–	–
G.Boycott (115), K.W.R.Fletcher (81)	Leeds	1973	–	–	–	119	–	–	–
D.I.Gower (60), A.J.Lamb (82)	Adelaide	1982-83	119	–	–	–	–	–	–
J.H.Edrich (109), K.F.Barrington (63)	Melbourne	1965-66	118	–	–	–	–	–	–
J.H.Edrich (64), M.H.Denness (181)	Auckland	1974-75	–	–	–	117	–	–	–
B.C.Broad (116), M.W.Gatting (79)	Faisalabad	1987-88	–	–	–	–	–	117	–
C.T.Radley (49), D.I.Gower (111)	Oval	1978	–	–	–	116	–	–	–
G.Boycott (137), M.W.Gatting (53)	Oval	1981	115	–	–	–	–	–	–
C.T.Radley (77), D.I.Gower (71)	Lord's	1978	–	–	–	114	–	–	–
K.J.Barnett (80), A.J.Lamb (125)	Leeds	1989	114	–	–	–	–	–	–
W.Place (107), J.Hardstaff, jr (64)	Kingston	1947-48	–	–	113	–	–	–	–
R.A.Smith (128), G.A.Hick (68)	Colombo (SSC)	1992-93	–	–	–	–	–	–	112
L.Hutton (74), D.C.S.Compton (184)	Nottingham	1948	111	–	–	–	–	–	–
G.Pullar (63), P.B.H.May (95)	Manchester	1961	111	–	–	–	–	–	–
R.T.Robinson (160), A.J.Lamb (52)	Delhi	1984-85	–	–	–	–	110	–	–
P.A.Gibb (58), W.R.Hammond (181)	Cape Town	1938-39	–	109	–	–	–	–	–
L.Hutton (202*), D.C.S.Compton (44)	Oval	1950	–	–	109	–	–	–	–
A.P.E.Knott (73), J.H.Edrich (79)	Brisbane[2]	1970-71	109	–	–	–	–	–	–
P.E.Richardson (81), P.B.H.May (73)	Nottingham	1956	108	–	–	–	–	–	–
M.C.Cowdrey (159), T.W.Graveney (97)	Birmingham	1962	–	–	–	–	–	107	–
G.Boycott (246*), T.W.Graveney (59)	Leeds	1967	–	–	–	–	107	–	–
J.T.Tyldesley (55), J.Sharp (61)	Leeds	1909	106	–	–	–	–	–	–
W.J.Edrich (57), D.C.S.Compton (65)	Nottingham	1947	–	106	–	–	–	–	–
W.G.A.Parkhouse (69), J.G.Dewes (67)	Nottingham	1950	–	–	106	–	–	–	–
G.Boycott (75), R.A.Woolmer (29)	Nottingham	1980	–	–	106	–	–	–	–
G.A.Gooch (174), R.A.Smith (63*)	Lord's	1991	–	–	–	–	–	–	105
W.Rhodes (66), C.B.Fry (62)	Oval	1909	104	–	–	–	–	–	–
J.Hardstaff, jr (64), C.J.Barnett (83*)	Lord's	1937	–	–	–	104	–	–	–
Rev D.S.Sheppard (113), M.C.Cowdrey (58*)	Melbourne	1962-63	104	–	–	–	–	–	–
W.J.Edrich (54), D.C.S.Compton (66)	Leeds	1948	103	–	–	–	–	–	–
A.C.MacLaren (47*), Hon F.S.Jackson (55*)	Lord's	1902	102*	–	–	–	–	–	–
Albert Ward (117), J.T.Brown (53)	Sydney	1894-95	102	–	–	–	–	–	–
W.J.Edrich (119), D.C.S.Compton (54)	Sydney	1946-47	102	–	–	–	–	–	–
L.Hutton (101), D.C.S.Compton (114)	Leeds	1949	–	–	–	102	–	–	–
L.Hutton (145), D.C.S.Compton (57)	Lord's	1953	102	–	–	–	–	–	–
J.H.Edrich (76*), D.B.Close (36*)	Nottingham	1976	–	–	101*	–	–	–	–
P.B.H.May (97), D.J.Insole (47)	Leeds	1955	–	101	–	–	–	–	–
M.C.Cowdrey (101), K.F.Barrington (63)	Kingston	1967-68	–	–	101	–	–	–	–
G.Boycott (112), K.W.R.Fletcher (45)	Port-of-Spain	1973-74	–	–	101	–	–	–	–
G.A.Gooch (54), D.I.Gower (56)	Lord's	1978	–	–	–	–	–	101	–
T.W.Hayward (59), C.B.Fry (144)	Oval	1905	100	–	–	–	–	–	–
D.L.Amiss (118), K.W.R.Fletcher (41)	Georgetown	1973-74	–	–	100	–	–	–	–
C.J.Tavaré (69), A.J.Lamb (58)	Leeds	1983	–	–	–	100	–	–	–
Totals: *(114)*			40	18	21	15	8	10	2

Although the 3rd wicket added 145 against Australia (2nd Test – Melbourne) in 1903-04, this consisted of two partnerships: J.T.Tyldesley added 89* with R.E.Foster (retired ill) and a further 56 with L.C.Braund.

ENGLAND – 4th Wicket

			A	SA	WI	NZ	I	P	SL
P.B.H.May (285*), M.C.Cowdrey (154)	Birmingham	1957	–	–	411	–	–	–	–
W.R.Hammond (217), T.S.Worthington (128)	Oval	1936	–	–	–	–	266	–	–
M.H.Denness (181), K.W.R.Fletcher (216)	Auckland	1974-75	–	–	–	266	–	–	–
G.Boycott (246*), B.L.D'Oliveira (109)	Leeds	1967	–	–	–	–	252	–	–
A.Sandham (325), L.E.G.Ames (149)	Kingston	1929-30	–	–	249	–	–	–	–
L.Hutton (196), D.C.S.Compton (120)	Lord's	1939	–	–	248	–	–	–	–
E.H.Hendren (205*), L.E.G.Ames (105)	Port-of-Spain	1929-30	–	–	237	–	–	–	–
D.I.Gower (131), M.W.Gatting (121)	Oval	1986	–	–	–	223	–	–	–
W.R.Hammond (240), E.Paynter (99)	Lord's	1938	222	–	–	–	–	–	–
K.F.Barrington (172), E.R.Dexter (126*)	Kanpur	1961-62	–	–	–	–	206	–	–
W.R.Hammond (181), L.E.G.Ames (115)	Cape Town	1938-39	–	197	–	–	–	–	–
M.C.Cowdrey (160), K.F.Barrington (80)	Leeds	1959	–	–	–	–	193	–	–
A.J.Lamb (119), R.A.Smith (62)	Bridgetown	1989-90	–	–	193	–	–	–	–
M.H.Denness (188), K.W.R.Fletcher (146)	Melbourne	1974-75	192	–	–	–	–	–	–
G.A.Gooch (333), R.A.Smith (100*)	Lord's	1990	–	–	–	–	192	–	–
B.R.Knight (127), P.H.Parfitt (121)	Kanpur	1963-64	–	–	–	–	191	–	–

4th Wicket *continued*

			A	SA	WI	NZ	I	P	SL
G.Boycott (155), D.I.Gower (200*)	Birmingham	1979	–	–	–	–	191	–	–
E.R.Dexter (205), P.H.Parfitt (111)	Karachi[1]	1961-62	–	–	–	–	–	188	–
K.F.Barrington (143), T.W.Graveney (118)	Port-of-Spain	1967-68	–	–	188	–	–	–	–
P.B.H.May (101), C.Washbrook (98)	Leeds	1956	187	–	–	–	–	–	–
T.W.Graveney (114), P.H.Parfitt (101*)	Nottingham	1962	–	–	–	–	–	184	–
P.B.H.May (92), M.C.Cowdrey (100*)	Sydney	1958-59	182	–	–	–	–	–	–
A.J.Lamb (107), I.T.Botham (208)	Oval	1982	–	–	–	–	176	–	–
A.J.Lamb (132), R.A.Smith (57)	Kingston	1989-90	–	–	172	–	–	–	–
T.W.Graveney (109), M.C.Cowdrey (96)	Nottingham	1966	–	–	169	–	–	–	–
T.W.Graveney (114), P.H.Parfitt (101*)	Oval	1982	–	–	–	–	176	–	–
K.F.Barrington (126), M.C.Cowdrey (86)	Auckland	1962-63	–	–	–	166	–	–	–
W.R.Hammond (140), E.Paynter (75)	Durban[2]	1938-39	–	164	–	–	–	–	–
E.R.Dexter (180), K.F.Barrington (48*)	Birmingham	1961	161	–	–	–	–	–	–
K.F.Barrington (151*), E.R.Dexter (85)	Bombay[2]	1961-62	–	–	–	–	161	–	–
C.J.Tavaré (89), A.J.Lamb (83)	Melbourne	1982-83	161	–	–	–	–	–	–
R.A.Woolmer (137), A.W.Greig (76)	Manchester	1977	160	–	–	–	–	–	–
A.J.Watkins (137*), D.B.Carr (76)	Delhi	1951-52	–	–	–	–	158	–	–
G.Boycott (77), D.I.Gower (102)	Perth	1978-79	158	–	–	–	–	–	–
G.Boycott (117), K.F.Barrington (72)	Port Elizabeth	1964-65	–	157	–	–	–	–	–
P.B.H.May (83*), D.C.S.Compton (94)	Oval	1956	156	–	–	–	–	–	–
M.W.Gatting (160), A.J.Lamb (67)	Manchester	1985	156	–	–	–	–	–	–
D.C.S.Compton (278), T.W.Graveney (84)	Nottingham	1954	–	–	–	–	154	–	–
C.B.Fry (144), Hon F.S.Jackson (76)	Oval	1905	151	–	–	–	–	–	–
W.R.Hammond (65), M.Leyland (161)	Oval	1935	–	151	–	–	–	–	–
W.R.Hammond (251), E.H.Hendren (74)	Sydney	1928-29	145	–	–	–	–	–	–
A.R.Lewis (125), K.W.R.Fletcher (58)	Kanpur	1972-73	–	–	–	–	144	–	–
K.F.Barrington (121), E.R.Dexter (77)	Port-of-Spain	1959-60	–	–	142	–	–	–	–
D.C.S.Compton (112), W.Watson (57)	Nottingham	1951	–	141	–	–	–	–	–
B.W.Luckhurst (109), B.L.D'Oliveira (117)	Melbourne	1970-71	140	–	–	–	–	–	–
R.E.S.Wyatt (149), M.Leyland (69)	Nottingham	1935	–	139	–	–	–	–	–
M.A.Atherton (105), D.I.Gower (123)	Sydney	1990-91	139	–	–	–	–	–	–
K.F.Barrington (73), M.C.Cowdrey (85)	Birmingham	1965	–	–	–	136	–	–	–
D.I.Gower (154*), P.Willey (67)	Kingston	1980-81	–	–	136	–	–	–	–
K.F.Barrington (73), M.C.Cowdrey (78*)	Oval	1965	–	135	–	–	–	–	–
G.Boycott (112), B.L.D'Oliveira (74)	Leeds	1971	–	–	–	–	–	135	–
G.Boycott (142*), B.L.D'Oliveira (56)	Sydney	1970-71	133	–	–	–	–	–	–
W.R.Hammond (100*), L.E.G.Ames (41)	Oval	1931	–	–	–	130	–	–	–
W.R.Hammond (87*), R.E.S.Wyatt (44)	Leeds	1935	–	129	–	–	–	–	–
D.I.Gower (157*), A.J.Lamb (52)	Oval	1990	–	–	–	129	–	–	–
D.L.Amiss (203), P.Willey (33)	Oval	1976	–	–	128	–	–	–	–
D.I.Gower (85), I.T.Botham (142)	Kanpur	1981-82	–	–	–	–	127	–	–
G.Boycott (106), P.J.Sharpe (86)	Lord's	1969	–	–	126	–	–	–	–
D.C.S.Compton (65), J.Hardstaff, jr (103)	Oval	1937	–	–	–	125	–	–	–
P.B.H.May (106), K.F.Barrington (56)	Nottingham	1959	–	–	–	–	125	–	–
J.H.Edrich (164), T.W.Graveney (63)	Oval	1968	125	–	–	–	–	–	–
T.W.Hayward (122), A.J.L.Hill (65)	Johannesburg[1]	1895-96	–	122	–	–	–	–	–
D.C.S.Compton (79), W.Watson (79)	Lord's	1951	–	122	–	–	–	–	–
T.W.Graveney (151), B.L.D'Oliveira (33)	Lord's	1967	–	–	–	–	122	–	–
G.R.J.Roope (77), R.A.Woolmer (149)	Oval	1975	122	–	–	–	–	–	–
D.I.Gower (70), D.W.Randall (70)	Sydney	1982-83	122	–	–	–	–	–	–
R.A.Smith (76), A.J.Lamb (142)	Wellington	1991-92	–	–	–	122	–	–	–
R.A.Smith (128), A.J.Stewart (63)	Colombo (SSC)	1992-93	–	–	–	–	–	–	122
P.E.Richardson (117), M.C.Cowdrey (59)	Johannesburg[3]	1956-57	–	121	–	–	–	–	–
P.B.H.May (84), M.C.Cowdrey (81)	Birmingham	1958	–	–	–	121	–	–	–
D.S.Steele (106), R.A.Woolmer (82)	Nottingham	1976	–	–	121	–	–	–	–
R.A.Smith (62), M.W.Gatting (61)	Bombay[3]	1992-93	–	–	–	–	121	–	–
G.Boycott (128*), M.W.Gatting (51*)	Lord's	1980	120*	–	–	–	–	–	–
W.R.Hammond (63), D.R.Jardine (83)	Manchester	1928	–	–	120	–	–	–	–
C.J.Tavaré (149), K.W.R.Fletcher (51)	Delhi	1981-82	–	–	–	–	120	–	–
J.B.Bolus (88), K.F.Barrington (80)	Madras[2]	1963-64	–	–	–	–	119	–	–
D.I.Gower (114), I.T.Botham (58)	Adelaide	1982-83	118	–	–	–	–	–	–
G.Gunn (119), L.C.Braund (30)	Sydney	1907-08	117	–	–	–	–	–	–
E.H.Hendren (127*), A.P.F.Chapman (50*)	Lord's	1926	116*	–	–	–	–	–	–
P.B.H.May (104), M.C.Cowdrey (54)	Sydney	1954-55	116	–	–	–	–	–	–
A.J.Stewart (143), G.A.Hick (59)	Bridgetown	1993-94	–	–	115	–	–	–	–
D.I.Gower (82), D.W.Randall (57)	Lord's	1979	–	–	–	–	114	–	–
G.Gunn (74), J.Hardstaff, sr (63)	Sydney	1907-08	113	–	–	–	–	–	–
L.C.Braund (47), J.Hardstaff, sr (72)	Adelaide	1907-08	113	–	–	–	–	–	–
R.T.Robinson (166), B.N.French (59)	Manchester	1987	–	–	–	–	113	–	–

4th Wicket *continued*

			A	SA	WI	NZ	I	P	SL
C.J.Tavaré (82), I.T.Botham (69)	Lord's	1982	–	–	–	–	112	–	–
D.C.S.Compton (51*), A.J.Watkins (64*)	Cape Town	1948-49	–	111*	–	–	–	–	–
C.B.Fry (60), A.C.MacLaren (49)	Oval	1899	110	–	–	–	–	–	–
J.H.Edrich (100*), M.H.Denness (45*)	Manchester	1974	–	–	–	–	109*	–	–
M.J.K.Smith (100), K.F.Barrington (87)	Manchester	1959	–	–	–	–	109	–	–
J.H.Edrich (310*), P.H.Parfitt (32)	Leeds	1965	–	–	–	109	–	–	–
J.H.Edrich (146), T.W.Graveney (55)	Bridgetown	1967-68	–	–	109	–	–	–	–
J.M.Brearley (59), A.W.Greig (54)	Madras[1]	1976-77	–	–	–	–	109†	–	–
M.W.Gatting (100*), A.J.Lamb (46)	Birmingham	1985	109	–	–	–	–	–	–
K.L.Hutchings (126), L.C.Braund (49)	Melbourne	1907-08	108	–	–	–	–	–	–
P.B.H.May (117), M.C.Cowdrey (50)	Manchester	1955	–	108	–	–	–	–	–
M.A.Atherton (55), G.A.Gooch (59)	Leeds	1993	108	–	–	–	–	–	–
D.I.Gower (66), A.J.Lamb (62)	Port-of-Spain	1985-86	–	–	106	–	–	–	–
J.H.Edrich (109), M.C.Cowdrey (104)	Melbourne	1965-66	105	–	–	–	–	–	–
K.S.Duleepsinhji (173), E.H.Hendren (48)	Lord's	1930	104	–	–	–	–	–	–
W.R.Hammond (231*), L.E.G.Ames (29)	Sydney	1936-37	104	–	–	–	–	–	–
P.E.Richardson (100), M.C.Cowdrey (70)	Birmingham	1958	–	–	–	104	–	–	–
A.Shrewsbury (66), Albert Ward (55)	Oval	1893	103	–	–	–	–	–	–
C.W.J.Athey (123), M.W.Gatting (43)	Lord's	1987	–	–	–	–	102	–	–
W.R.Hammond (63), M.J.L.Turnbull (61)	Johannesburg[1]	1930-31	–	101	–	–	–	–	–
F.L.Fane (37), F.E.Woolley (64)	Cape Town	1909-10	–	100	–	–	–	–	–
K.F.Barrington (93), P.H.Parfitt (122*)	Johannesburg[3]	1964-65	–	100	–	–	–	–	–
		Totals: (107)	33	16	17	10	23	7	1

†*111 runs were added for this wicket in two partnerships, R.W.Tolchard retiring hurt and being succeeded by A.W.Greig after 2 runs had been scored.*

Although the 4th wicket added 101 against New Zealand (Christchurch) in 1977-78, this consisted of two partnerships: G.R.J.Roope added 77* with G.Miller (retired hurt) and a further 24 with C.T.Radley.

ENGLAND – 5th Wicket

			A	SA	WI	NZ	I	P	SL
K.W.R.Fletcher (113), A.W.Greig (148)	Bombay[2]	1972-73	–	–	–	–	254	–	–
W.R.Hammond (227), L.E.G.Ames (103)	Christchurch	1932-33	–	–	–	242	–	–	–
D.C.S.Compton (163), N.W.D.Yardley (99)	Nottingham	1947	–	237	–	–	–	–	–
D.L.Amiss (138*), A.W.Greig (139)	Nottingham	1973	–	–	–	210	–	–	–
E.Paynter (216*), D.C.S.Compton (102)	Nottingham	1938	206	–	–	–	–	–	–
M.H.Denness (118), A.W.Greig (106)	Lord's	1974	–	–	–	–	202	–	–
R.E.Foster (287), L.C.Braund (102)	Sydney	1903-04	192	–	–	–	–	–	–
D.C.S.Compton (278), T.E.Bailey (36*)	Nottingham	1954	–	–	–	–	–	192	–
E.H.Hendren (132), M.Leyland (153)	Manchester	1934	191	–	–	–	–	–	–
G.B.Legge (196), M.S.Nichols (75)	Auckland	1929-30	–	–	–	184	–	–	–
J.Hardstaff, jr (205*), P.A.Gibb (60)	Lord's	1946	–	–	–	–	182	–	–
M.Leyland (161), L.E.G.Ames (148*)	Oval	1935	–	179	–	–	–	–	–
M.W.Gatting (150*), I.T.Botham (51*)	Oval	1987	–	–	–	–	176*	–	–
R.Subba Row (137), K.F.Barrington (83)	Oval	1961	172	–	–	–	–	–	–
W.Watson (109), T.E.Bailey (71)	Lord's	1953	163	–	–	–	–	–	–
A.C.MacLaren (164), R.Peel (73)	Melbourne	1894-95	162	–	–	–	–	–	–
A.Shrewsbury (164), W.Barnes (58)	Lord's	1886	161	–	–	–	–	–	–
M.Leyland (83), R.E.S.Wyatt (78)	Adelaide	1932-33	156	–	–	–	–	–	–
C.P.Mead (181), P.G.H.Fender (60)	Durban[2]	1922-23	–	154	–	–	–	–	–
I.T.Botham (208), D.W.Randall (95)	Oval	1982	–	–	–	–	151	–	–
A.J.Stewart (143), G.P.Thorpe (84)	Bridgetown	1993-94	–	–	150	–	–	–	–
T.W.Graveney (175), A.J.Watkins (80)	Bombay[2]	1951-52	–	–	–	–	148	–	–
K.W.R.Fletcher (146), A.W.Greig (89)	Melbourne	1974-75	148	–	–	–	–	–	–
G.A.Gooch (114), D.R.Pringle (63)	Lord's	1986	–	–	–	–	147	–	–
D.R.Jardine (61), B.H.Valentine (136)	Bombay[1]	1933-34	–	–	–	–	145	–	–
D.C.S.Compton (158), T.E.Bailey (44)	Manchester	1955	–	144	–	–	–	–	–
K.F.Barrington (256), J.M.Parks (60)	Manchester	1964	143	–	–	–	–	–	–
R.W.Tolchard (67), A.W.Greig (103)	Calcutta	1976-77	–	–	–	–	142	–	–
D.I.Gower (106), R.A.Smith (96)	Lord's	1989	139	–	–	–	–	–	–
D.C.S.Compton (84), T.E.Bailey (72)	Sydney	1954-55	134	–	–	–	–	–	–
C.Milburn (126*), T.W.Graveney (30*)	Lord's	1966	–	–	130*	–	–	–	–
A.J.Lamb (110), I.T.Botham (81)	Lord's	1984	–	–	128	–	–	–	–
M.C.Cowdrey (93*), K.F.Barrington (54*)	Oval	1964	126*	–	–	–	–	–	–
W.R.Hammond (200), D.R.Jardine (62)	Melbourne	1928-29	126	–	–	–	–	–	–
G.A.Gooch (183), P.Willey (42)	Lord's	1986	–	–	–	126	–	–	–
Hon F.S.Jackson (113), R.H.Spooner (52)	Manchester	1905	125	–	–	–	–	–	–
M.J.K.Smith (87), P.H.Parfitt (46*)	Christchurch	1965-66	–	–	–	125	–	–	–
D.I.Gower (100), A.J.Stewart (79)	Melbourne	1990-91	122	–	–	–	–	–	–

Hundred Partnerships (England)

5th Wicket continued

			A	SA	WI	NZ	I	P	SL
J.H.Edrich (164), B.L.D'Oliveira (158)	Oval	1968	121	–	–	–	–	–	–
D.C.S.Compton (147), J.Hardstaff, jr (67)	Adelaide	1946-47	118	–	–	–	–	–	–
P.B.H.May (113), M.C.Cowdrey (44)	Melbourne	1958-59	118	–	–	–	–	–	–
D.I.Gower (51), I.T.Botham (138)	Brisbane[2]	1986-87	118	–	–	–	–	–	–
D.I.Gower (152), G.Fowler (57)	Faisalabad	1983-84	–	–	–	–	–	116	–
P.H.Parfitt (67), M.C.Cowdrey (151)	Delhi	1963-64	–	–	–	–	115	–	–
A.J.Stewart (89), J.P.Crawley (38)	Leeds	1994	–	115	–	–	–	–	–
P.F.Warner (39), F.E.Woolley (73)	Lord's	1912	–	113	–	–	–	–	–
M.J.K.Smith (54), P.H.Parfitt (54)	Christchurch	1965-66	–	–	–	113	–	–	–
R.Abel (70), W.Barnes (62)	Oval	1888	112	–	–	–	–	–	–
J.W.Hearne (45), F.E.Woolley (57)	Leeds	1912	–	111	–	–	–	–	–
D.C.S.Compton (133), T.W.Graveney (92)	Port-of-Spain	1953-54	–	–	110	–	–	–	–
A.J.Watkins (68), C.J.Poole (55)	Calcutta	1951-52	–	–	–	–	107	–	–
J.W.H.Makepeace (117), J.W.H.T.Douglas (50)	Melbourne	1920-21	106	–	–	–	–	–	–
R.Abel (120), H.Wood (59)	Cape Town	1888-89	–	105	–	–	–	–	–
R.T.Simpson (103), T.E.Bailey (72*)	Manchester	1949	–	–	–	105	–	–	–
M.C.Cowdrey (119), M.J.K.Smith (44)	Lord's	1965	–	–	–	105	–	–	–
D.I.Gower (74), K.W.R.Fletcher (60*)	Calcutta	1981-82	–	–	–	–	105	–	–
C.P.Mead (117), F.E.Woolley (54)	Port Elizabeth	1913-14	–	104	–	–	–	–	–
B.L.D'Oliveira (81*), D.B.Close (36)	Lord's	1967	–	–	–	–	104	–	–
A.J.Lamb (64*), R.A.Smith (38)	Leeds	1988	–	–	103*‡	–	–	–	–
G.E.Tyldesley (78*), P.G.H.Fender (44*)	Manchester	1921	102*	–	–	–	–	–	–
K.F.Barrington (132*), T.W.Graveney (36*)	Adelaide	1962-63	101*	–	–	–	–	–	–
A.R.Lewis (70*), A.W.Greig (40*)	Delhi	1972-73	–	–	–	–	101*	–	–
A.Sandham (46), E.H.Hendren (142)	Oval	1924	–	101	–	–	–	–	–
E.R.Dexter (57), P.J.Sharpe (85*)	Birmingham	1963	–	–	101	–	–	–	–
D.B.Close (46), P.J.Sharpe (63)	Oval	1963	–	–	101	–	–	–	–
I.T.Botham (142), M.W.Gatting (32)	Kanpur	1981-82	–	–	–	–	101	–	–
A.R.Lewis (88), A.W.Greig (48)	Karachi[1]	1972-73	–	–	–	–	–	100†	–
C.J.Tavaré (89), D.W.Randall (78)	Perth	1982-83	100	–	–	–	–	–	–
	Totals: (68)		25	10	7	8	13	5	–

‡A.J.Lamb retired hurt after a stand of 103; his successor, C.S.Cowdrey, was dismissed without addition to the total.

†103 runs were added for this wicket in two partnerships, P.I.Pocock retiring hurt after 3 runs had been scored. Although the 5th wicket added 115 v Australia in 1884-85 (5th Test – Melbourne), this consisted of two partnerships: A.Shrewsbury added 73* with W.Bates (retired ill) and a further 42 with W.Flowers. Similarly, in the Oval Test v Pakistan in 1974, 139 runs were added in two partnerships for the 5th wicket. K.W.R.Fletcher added 61* with D.L.Amiss (retired hurt) and a further 78 with A.W.Greig.

ENGLAND – 6th Wicket

			A	SA	WI	NZ	I	P	SL
P.H.Parfitt (131*), B.R.Knight (125)	Auckland	1962-63	–	–	–	240	–	–	–
I.T.Botham (138), D.W.Randall (164)	Wellington	1983-84	–	–	–	232	–	–	–
L.Hutton (364), J.Hardstaff, jr (169*)	Oval	1938	215	–	–	–	–	–	–
G.Boycott (107), A.P.E.Knott (135)	Nottingham	1977	215	–	–	–	–	–	–
D.I.Gower (136), C.J.Richards (133)	Perth	1986-87	207	–	–	–	–	–	–
K.F.Barrington (148*), J.M.Parks (108*)	Durban[2]	1964-65	–	206*	–	–	–	–	–
D.C.S.Compton (116), T.E.Bailey (93)	Lord's	1949	–	–	–	189	–	–	–
W.R.Hammond (240), L.E.G.Ames (83)	Lord's	1938	186	–	–	–	–	–	–
I.T.Botham (103), D.W.Randall (83)	Nottingham	1983	–	–	–	186	–	–	–
I.T.Botham (114), R.W.Taylor (43)	Bombay[3]	1979-80	–	–	–	–	171	–	–
H.Sutcliffe (161), R.E.S.Wyatt (64)	Oval	1930	170	–	–	–	–	–	–
I.T.Botham (128), G.Miller (98)	Manchester	1982	–	–	–	–	169	–	–
D.I.Gower (200*), G.Miller (63*)	Birmingham	1979	–	–	–	–	165*	–	–
A.W.Greig (148), A.P.E.Knott (87)	Bridgetown	1973-74	–	–	163	–	–	–	–
T.E.Bailey (82*), T.G.Evans (104)	Manchester	1950	–	–	161	–	–	–	–
I.T.Botham (103), R.W.Taylor (45)	Christchurch	1977-78	–	–	–	160	–	–	–
T.W.Graveney (73), T.G.Evans (104)	Lord's	1952	–	–	–	159	–	–	–
J.T.Tyldesley (112*), R.H.Spooner (79)	Oval	1905	158	–	–	–	–	–	–
L.E.G.Ames (126), J.Iddon (54)	Kingston	1934-35	–	157	–	–	–	–	–
C.P.Mead (181), F.T.Mann (84)	Durban[2]	1922-23	–	156	–	–	–	–	–
P.H.Parfitt (101*), D.A.Allen (79*)	Birmingham	1962	–	–	–	–	153*	–	–
A.W.Greig (116), A.P.E.Knott (116)	Leeds	1976	–	152	–	–	–	–	–
R.A.Woolmer (149), A.P.E.Knott (64)	Oval	1975	151	–	–	–	–	–	–
G.A.Gooch (120), G.P.Thorpe (114*)	Nottingham	1993	150	–	–	–	–	–	–
C.J.Tavaré (78), I.T.Botham (118)	Manchester	1981	149	–	–	–	–	–	–
L.C.Braund (104), G.L.Jessop (93)	Lord's	1907	–	145	–	–	–	–	–
M.Leyland (153), L.E.G.Ames (72)	Manchester	1934	142	–	–	–	–	–	–

6th Wicket *continued*

			A	SA	WI	NZ	I	P	SL
K.W.R.Fletcher (129*), A.P.E.Knott (67)	Bridgetown	1973-74	–	–	142	–	–	–	–
Hon F.S.Jackson (128), L.C.Braund (65)	Manchester	1902	141	–	–	–	–	–	–
E.H.Hendren (95), M.Leyland (137)	Melbourne	1928-29	140	–	–	–	–	–	–
M.C.Cowdrey (79), J.M.Parks (89)	Melbourne	1965-66	138	–	–	–	–	–	–
W.W.Read (52), Hon F.S.Jackson (103)	Oval	1893	131	–	–	–	–	–	–
M.W.Gatting (96), C.J.Richards (38)	Sydney	1986-87	131	–	–	–	–	–	–
M.Leyland (102), M.W.Tate (100*)	Lord's	1929	–	129	–	–	–	–	–
M.Leyland (109), L.E.G.Ames (120)	Lord's	1934	129	–	–	–	–	–	–
J.H.Hampshire (107), A.P.E.Knott (53)	Lord's	1969	–	–	128	–	–	–	–
M.C.Cowdrey (82), A.P.E.Knott (73*)	Georgetown	1967-68	–	–	127	–	–	–	–
A.P.F.Chapman (121), G.O.B.Allen (57)	Lord's	1930	125	–	–	–	–	–	–
G.H.Hirst (62), K.S.Ranjitsinhji (175)	Sydney	1897-98	124	–	–	–	–	–	–
C.A.G.Russell (135*), J.W.H.T.Douglas (60)	Adelaide	1920-21	124	–	–	–	–	–	–
F.E.Woolley (115*), F.T.Mann (59)	Johannesburg[1]	1922-23	–	124	–	–	–	–	–
G.Boycott (191), A.P.E.Knott (57)	Leeds	1977	123	–	–	–	–	–	–
G.Miller (48), I.T.Botham (100)	Birmingham	1978	–	–	–	–	–	123	–
C.P.Mead (182), Hon L.H.Tennyson (51)	Oval	1921	121	–	–	–	–	–	–
M.J.K.Smith (99), P.M.Walker (52)	Lord's	1960	–	120	–	–	–	–	–
G.Fowler (58), V.J.Marks (74)	Lahore[2]	1983-84	–	–	–	–	–	120	–
A.W.Greig (121), A.P.E.Knott (61)	Georgetown	1973-74	–	–	119	–	–	–	–
D.I.Gower (173*), V.J.Marks (55)	Lahore[2]	1983-84	–	–	–	–	–	119	–
G.R.J.Roope (69), I.T.Botham (108)	Lord's	1978	–	–	–	–	–	118	–
M.J.K.Smith (121), J.M.Parks (59)	Cape Town	1964-65	–	117	–	–	–	–	–
W.W.Read (66), E.F.S.Tylecote (66)	Sydney	1882-83	116	–	–	–	–	–	–
Hon F.S.Jackson (82*), W.Rhodes (39*)	Nottingham	1905	113*	–	–	–	–	–	–
J.T.Ikin (48), N.W.D.Yardley (61)	Melbourne	1946-47	113	–	–	–	–	–	–
M.C.Cowdrey (148), A.P.E.Knott (69*)	Port-of-Spain	1967-68	–	–	113	–	–	–	–
A.W.Greig (64), A.P.E.Knott (63*)	Hyderabad	1972-73	–	–	–	–	112	–	–
Hon F.S.Jackson (49), G.L.Jessop (104)	Oval	1902	109	–	–	–	–	–	–
W.G.Quaife (68), L.C.Braund (103*)	Adelaide	1901-02	108	–	–	–	–	–	–
L.Hutton (205), T.G.Evans (28)	Kingston	1953-54	–	–	108	–	–	–	–
F.E.Woolley (83), M.Leyland (45)	Leeds	1929	–	106	–	–	–	–	–
M.J.Horton (58), T.G.Evans (73)	Nottingham	1959	–	–	–	–	106	–	–
B.L.D'Oliveira (72), R.Illingworth (45)	Leeds	1971	–	–	–	–	–	106	–
R.T.Robinson (160), P.R.Downton (74)	Delhi	1984-85	–	–	–	–	106	–	–
M.Leyland (53), R.W.V.Robins (108)	Manchester	1935	–	105	–	–	–	–	–
J.W.H.T.Douglas (60), P.G.H.Fender (59)	Melbourne	1920-21	104	–	–	–	–	–	–
K.W.R.Fletcher (123*), A.W.Greig (53)	Manchester	1974	–	–	–	–	104	–	–
E.R.Dexter (66*), R.W.Barber (39*)	Lahore[2]	1961-62	–	–	–	–	–	101*	–
D.L.Amiss (179), A.P.E.Knott (75)	Delhi	1976-77	–	–	–	–	101	–	–
F.G.Mann (136*), R.O.Jenkins (29)	Port Elizabeth	1948-49	–	100	–	–	–	–	–
	Totals: (68)		27	10	10	5	8	8	–

Although the 6th wicket added 121 v Australia (Oval) 1934, this consisted of two partnerships: M.Leyland added 85* with L.E.G.Ames (retired hurt) and a further 36 with G.O.B.Allen.

ENGLAND – 7th Wicket

			A	SA	WI	NZ	I	P	SL
M.J.K.Smith (96), J.M.Parks (101*)	Port-of-Spain	1959-60	–	–	197	–	–	–	–
M.C.Cowdrey (152), T.G.Evans (82)	Lord's	1957	–	–	174	–	–	–	–
D.I.Gower (152), V.J.Marks (83)	Faisalabad	1983-84	–	–	–	–	–	167	–
A.P.E.Knott (116), P.Lever (47)	Birmingham	1971	–	–	–	–	–	159	–
A.P.E.Knott (104), P.Lever (64)	Auckland	1970-71	–	–	–	149	–	–	–
F.E.Woolley (133*), J.Vine (36)	Sydney	1911-12	143	–	–	–	–	–	–
M.W.Gatting (124), J.E.Emburey (58)	Birmingham	1987	–	–	–	–	–	143	–
J.Sharp (105), K.L.Hutchings (59)	Oval	1909	142	–	–	–	–	–	–
R.C.Russell (128*), J.E.Emburey (64)	Manchester	1989	142	–	–	–	–	–	–
D.R.Jardine (128), R.W.V.Robins (55)	Manchester	1933	–	–	140	–	–	–	–
G.Miller (64), R.W.Taylor (97)	Adelaide	1978-79	135	–	–	–	–	–	–
W.W.Whysall (76), R.Kilner (74)	Melbourne	1924-25	133	–	–	–	–	–	–
M.W.Gatting (75*), I.T.Botham (85)	Lord's	1985	131	–	–	–	–	–	–
K.W.R.Fletcher (122), C.M.Old (65)	Oval	1974	–	–	–	–	–	130	–
D.W.Randall (126), P.H.Edmonds (64)	Lord's	1982	–	–	–	–	125	–	–
A.F.A.Lilley (84), L.C.Braund (58)	Sydney	1901-02	124	–	–	–	–	–	–
E.R.Dexter (136*), R.Swetman (45)	Bridgetown	1959-60	–	–	123	–	–	–	–
J.B.Hobbs (119), E.H.Hendren (92)	Adelaide	1924-25	117	–	–	–	–	–	–
J.W.H.T.Douglas (119), M.C.Bird (61)	Durban[1]	1913-14	–	115	–	–	–	–	–
D.J.Capel (98), J.E.Emburey (70)	Karachi[1]	1987-88	–	–	–	–	–	114	–
G.P.Thorpe (114*), N.Hussain (47*)	Nottingham	1993	113*	–	–	–	–	–	–

Hundred Partnerships (England)

7th Wicket *continued*

			A	SA	WI	NZ	I	P	SL
T.W.Hayward (130), A.F.A.Lilley (58)	Manchester	1899	113	–	–	–	–	–	–
M.Leyland (111*), R.W.V.Robins (61)	Melbourne	1936-37	111	–	–	–	–	–	–
A.J.Lamb (102*), P.H.Edmonds (43*)	Oval	1983	–	–	–	110*	–	–	–
F.R.Brown (74), W.Voce (66)	Christchurch	1932-33	–	–	–	108	–	–	–
J.Hardstaff, jr (169*), A.Wood (53)	Oval	1938	106	–	–	–	–	–	–
L.Hutton (205), J.H.Wardle (66)	Kingston	1953-54	–	–	105	–	–	–	–
A.J.Lamb (142), R.C.Russell (24*)	Wellington	1991-92	–	–	–	105	–	–	–
G.P.Thorpe (60), J.E.Emburey (37)	Birmingham	1993	104	–	–	–	–	–	–
A.P.E.Knott (90), R.A.Hutton (81)	Oval	1971	–	–	–	–	103	–	–
W.Flowers (56), J.M.Read (56)	Sydney	1884-85	102	–	–	–	–	–	–
R.Illingworth (50), R.Swetman (65)	Oval	1959	–	–	–	–	102	–	–
E.H.Hendren (79), G.Geary (53)	Nottingham	1934	101	–	–	–	–	–	–
D.I.Gower (78), P.H.Edmonds (49)	Kanpur	1984-85	–	–	–	–	100	–	–
Totals:	*(34)*		15	1	5	4	4	5	–

ENGLAND – 8th Wicket

			A	SA	WI	NZ	I	P	SL
L.E.G.Ames (137), G.O.B.Allen (122)	Lord's	1931	–	–	–	246	–	–	–
T.W.Graveney (165), J.T.Murray (112)	Oval	1966	–	–	217	–	–	–	–
R.Illingworth (107), P.Lever (88*)	Manchester	1971	–	–	–	–	168	–	–
C.W.Wright (71), H.R.Bromley-Davenport (84)	Johannesburg[1]	1895-96	–	154	–	–	–	–	–
R.W.V.Robins (76), H.Verity (66*)	Manchester	1936	–	–	–	–	138	–	–
P.A.J.DeFreitas (69), D.Gough (65)	Manchester	1994	–	–	–	130	–	–	–
E.H.Hendren (169), H.Larwood (70)	Brisbane[1]	1928-29	124	–	–	–	–	–	–
D.C.S.Compton (145*), A.V.Bedser (37)	Manchester	1948	121	–	–	–	–	–	–
I.T.Botham (149*), G.R.Dilley (56)	Leeds	1981	117	–	–	–	–	–	–
D.A.Allen (88), D.J.Brown (44)	Christchurch	1965-66	–	–	–	107	–	–	–
R.Illingworth (57), J.A.Snow (48)	Leeds	1972	104	–	–	–	–	–	–
G.Miller (62), R.W.Taylor (64)	Lord's	1979	–	–	–	–	103	–	–
Totals:	*(12)*		4	1	1	3	3	–	–

ENGLAND – 9th Wicket

			A	SA	WI	NZ	I	P	SL
M.C.Cowdrey (128*), A.C.Smith (69*)	Wellington	1962-63	–	–	–	163*	–	–	–
W.H.Scotton (90), W.W.Read (117)	Oval	1884	151	–	–	–	–	–	–
F.E.Woolley (123), A.P.Freeman (50*)	Sydney	1924-25	128	–	–	–	–	–	–
T.E.Bailey (134*), D.V.P.Wright (45)	Christchurch	1950-51	–	–	–	117	–	–	–
R.E.Foster (287), A.E.Relf (31)	Sydney	1903-04	115	–	–	–	–	–	–
G.A.R.Lock (89), P.I.Pocock (13)	Georgetown	1967-68	–	–	109	–	–	–	–
G.Geary (35*), G.G.Macaulay (76)	Leeds	1926	108	–	–	–	–	–	–
Totals:	*(7)*		4	–	1	2	–	–	–

ENGLAND – 10th Wicket

			A	SA	WI	NZ	I	P	SL
R.E.Foster (287), W.Rhodes (40*)	Sydney	1903-04	130	–	–	–	–	–	–
K.Higgs (63), J.A.Snow (59*)	Oval	1966	–	–	128	–	–	–	–
P.Willey (100*), R.G.D.Willis (24*)	Oval	1980	–	–	117*	–	–	–	–
Totals:	*(3)*		1	–	2	–	–	–	–

AUSTRALIA – (525) – 1st Wicket

			E	SA	WI	NZ	I	P	SL
W.M.Lawry (210), R.B.Simpson (201)	Bridgetown	1964-65	–	–	382	–	–	–	–
G.R.Marsh (138), M.A.Taylor (219)	Nottingham	1989	329	–	–	–	–	–	–
M.A.Taylor (111), M.J.Slater (152)	Lord's	1993	260	–	–	–	–	–	–
R.B.Simpson (225), W.M.Lawry (119)	Adelaide	1965-66	244	–	–	–	–	–	–
J.H.W.Fingleton (112), W.A.Brown (121)	Cape Town	1935-36	–	233	–	–	–	–	–
W.M.Lawry (157), I.R.Redpath (97)	Melbourne	1963-64	–	219	–	–	–	–	–
D.C.Boon (131), G.R.Marsh (92)	Sydney	1985-86	–	–	–	–	217	–	–
A.R.Morris (111), J.Moroney (118)	Johannesburg[2]	1949-50	–	214	–	–	–	–	–
W.M.Lawry (106), R.B.Simpson (311)	Manchester	1964	201	–	–	–	–	–	–
M.J.Slater (99), M.A.Taylor (142*)	Perth	1993-94	–	–	–	198	–	–	–
C.C.McDonald (110), A.R.Morris (111)	Port-of-Spain	1954-55	–	–	191	–	–	–	–
R.B.Simpson (109), W.M.Lawry (100)	Melbourne	1967-68	–	–	–	–	191	–	–
C.C.McDonald (99), J.W.Burke (189)	Cape Town	1957-58	–	190	–	–	–	–	–
W.Bardsley (130), S.E.Gregory (74)	Oval	1909	180	–	–	–	–	–	–
W.H.Ponsford (92*), A.A.Jackson (70*)	Adelaide	1930-31	–	–	172*	–	–	–	–
C.C.McDonald (170), J.W.Burke (66)	Adelaide	1958-59	171	–	–	–	–	–	–
W.M.Woodfull (155), W.H.Ponsford (81)	Lord's	1930	162	–	–	–	–	–	–
J.H.W.Fingleton (118), W.A.Brown (84)	Durban[2]	1935-36	–	162	–	–	–	–	–

1st Wicket *continued*

			E	SA	WI	NZ	I	P	SL
G.R.Marsh (56), D.C.Boon (184*)	Sydney	1987-88	162	–	–	–	–	–	–
K.R.Stackpole (142), I.R.Redpath (60)	Kingston	1972-73	–	–	161	–	–	–	–
W.M.Woodfull (54), W.H.Ponsford (110)	Oval	1930	159	–	–	–	–	–	–
G.R.Marsh (72*), M.A.Taylor (67*)	Brisbane[2]	1990-91	157*	–	–	–	–	–	–
I.R.Redpath (65), A.Turner (136)	Adelaide	1975-76	–	–	148	–	–	–	–
C.C.McDonald (91), R.B.Simpson (75)	Melbourne	1960-61	–	–	146	–	–	–	–
G.R.Marsh (69), M.A.Taylor (58)	Kingston	1990-91	–	–	139	–	–	–	–
C.C.McDonald (78), J.W.Burke (65)	Lord's	1956	137	–	–	–	–	–	–
W.M.Lawry (98), R.B.Simpson (71)	Brisbane[2]	1962-63	136	–	–	–	–	–	–
K.P.Stackpole (76*), I.R.Redpath (57*)	Georgetown	1972-73	–	–	135*	–	–	–	–
V.T.Trumper (104), R.A.Duff (54)	Manchester	1902	135	–	–	–	–	–	–
M.A.Taylor (85), G.R.Marsh (47)	Manchester	1989	135	–	–	–	–	–	–
I.C.Davis (56), A.Turner (82)	Melbourne	1976-77	–	–	–	–	134	–	–
W.M.Woodfull (67), V.Y.Richardson (83)	Brisbane[2]	1932-33	133	–	–	–	–	–	–
V.T.Trumper (113), R.A.Duff (79)	Adelaide	1903-04	129	–	–	–	–	–	–
M.A.Taylor (124), M.J.Slater (58)	Manchester	1993	128	–	–	–	–	–	–
V.T.Trumper (63), M.A.Noble (64)	Melbourne	1907-08	126	–	–	–	–	–	–
S.G.Barnes (71), A.R.Morris (57)	Sydney	1946-47	126	–	–	–	–	–	–
H.L.Collins (104), W.Bardsley (57)	Sydney	1920-21	123	–	–	–	–	–	–
S.G.Barnes (141), A.R.Morris (57)	Lord's	1948	122	–	–	–	–	–	–
C.C.McDonald (41), A.R.Morris (99)	Melbourne	1952-53	–	122	–	–	–	–	–
R.B.Simpson (67), W.M.Lawry (78)	Melbourne	1965-66	120	–	–	–	–	–	–
G.M.Wood (66), M.F.Kent (54)	Oval	1981	120	–	–	–	–	–	–
G.R.Marsh (53), D.C.Boon (64)	Perth	1987-88	–	–	–	–	–	–	120
R.B.Simpson (65), W.M.Lawry (98)	Johannesburg[3]	1966-67	–	118	–	–	–	–	–
D.C.Boon (63*), M.A.Taylor (46*)	Sydney	1992-93	–	–	117*	–	–	–	–
H.L.Collins (59), W.Bardsley (56)	Melbourne	1920-21	117	–	–	–	–	–	–
S.G.Barnes (61), A.R.Morris (196)	Oval	1948	117	–	–	–	–	–	–
C.E.McLeod (77), J.Worrall (75)	Oval	1899	116	–	–	–	–	–	–
H.L.Collins (64), W.Bardsley (51)	Melbourne	1920-21	116	–	–	–	–	–	–
A.R.Morris (124*), M.R.Harvey (31)	Adelaide	1946-47	116	–	–	–	–	–	–
W.M.Lawry (45), I.R.Redpath (79)	Brisbane[2]	1967-68	–	–	–	–	116	–	–
W.M.Lawry (47*), R.B.Simpson (71)	Calcutta	1964-65	–	–	–	–	115	–	–
W.M.Lawry (102), R.B.Simpson (51)	Manchester	1961	113	–	–	–	–	–	–
G.R.Marsh (43), D.C.Boon (103)	Adelaide	1986-87	113	–	–	–	–	–	–
W.M.Lawry (52), R.M.Cowper (165)	Sydney	1967-68	–	–	–	–	111	–	–
I.R.Redpath (83), R.B.McCosker (76)	Melbourne	1974-75	111	–	–	–	–	–	–
A.C.Bannerman (37), W.L.Murdoch (85)	Melbourne	1881-82	110	–	–	–	–	–	–
B.M.Laird (44), G.M.Wood (72)	Brisbane[2]	1981-82	–	–	–	–	–	109	–
C.C.McDonald (46), L.E.Favell (72)	Bridgetown	1954-55	–	–	108	–	–	–	–
W.M.Woodfull (54), W.H.Ponsford (83)	Manchester	1930	106	–	–	–	–	–	–
B.M.Laird (39), G.M.Wood (100)	Auckland	1981-82	–	–	–	106	–	–	–
J.H.W.Fingleton (62), W.A.Brown (51)	Johannesburg[1]	1935-36	–	105	–	–	–	–	–
B.M.Laird (38), J.Dyson (127*)	Sydney	1981-82	–	–	104	–	–	–	–
D.C.Boon (70), G.R.Marsh (43)	Wellington	1985-86	–	–	–	104	–	–	–
W.Bardsley (63*), T.J.E.Andrews (49)	Lord's	1921	103	–	–	–	–	–	–
C.C.McDonald (50), A.R.Morris (65)	Kingston	1954-55	–	–	102	–	–	–	–
V.T.Trumper (70), R.A.Duff (34)	Cape Town	1902-03	–	100	–	–	–	–	–
	Totals: (66)		34	9	12	3	5	2	1

AUSTRALIA – 2nd Wicket

			E	SA	WI	NZ	I	P	SL
W.H.Ponsford (266), D.G.Bradman (244)	Oval	1934	451	–	–	–	–	–	–
A.R.Morris (182), D.G.Bradman (173*)	Leeds	1948	301	–	–	–	–	–	–
W.M.Lawry (205), I.M.Chappell (165)	Melbourne	1968-69	–	–	298	–	–	–	–
R.B.McCosker (127), I.M.Chappell (192)	Oval	1975	277	–	–	–	–	–	–
C.C.McDonald (154), A.L.Hassett (163)	Adelaide	1952-53	–	275	–	–	–	–	–
W.M.Woodfull (161), D.G.Bradman (167)	Melbourne	1931-32	–	274	–	–	–	–	–
W.B.Phillips (159), G.N.Yallop (141)	Perth	1983-84	–	–	–	–	–	259	–
S.G.Barnes (112), D.G.Bradman (201)	Adelaide	1947-48	–	–	–	–	236	–	–
W.M.Woodfull (141), C.G.Macartney (151)	Leeds	1926	235	–	–	–	–	–	–
M.J.Slater (168), D.C.Boon (106)	Hobart	1993-94	–	–	–	235	–	–	–
A.P.Sheahan (127), J.Benaud (142)	Melbourne	1972-73	–	–	–	–	–	233	–
W.M.Woodfull (155), D.G.Bradman (254)	Lord's	1930	231	–	–	–	–	–	–
W.H.Ponsford (109), D.G.Bradman (223)	Brisbane[1]	1930-31	–	–	229	–	–	–	–
W.Bardsley (132), C.Hill (191)	Sydney	1910-11	–	224	–	–	–	–	–
M.A.Taylor (100), D.C.Boon (135)	Adelaide	1991-92	–	–	–	–	221	–	–
I.R.Redpath (105), G.S.Chappell (144)	Sydney	1974-75	220	–	–	–	–	–	–
W.M.Lawry (105), I.M.Chappell (117)	Brisbane[2]	1968-69	–	–	217	–	–	–	–

Hundred Partnerships (Australia)

2nd Wicket *continued*

			E	SA	WI	NZ	I	P	SL
W.M.Woodfull (111), H.S.T.L.Hendry (112)	Sydney	1928-29	215	–	–	–	–	–	–
J.W.Burke (161), R.N.Harvey (140)	Bombay²	1956-57	–	–	–	–	204	–	–
K.R.Stackpole (136), I.M.Chappell (104)	Adelaide	1970-71	202	–	–	–	–	–	–
W.A.Brown (72), S.J.McCabe (137)	Manchester	1934	196	–	–	–	–	–	–
W.M.Woodfull (117), C.G.Macartney (109)	Manchester	1926	192	–	–	–	–	–	–
W.M.Woodfull (50), D.G.Bradman (334)	Leeds	1930	192	–	–	–	–	–	–
H.L.Collins (114), W.H.Ponsford (110)	Sydney	1924-25	190	–	–	–	–	–	–
I.R.Redpath (72), I.M.Chappell (111)	Melbourne	1970-71	180†	–	–	–	–	–	–
G.M.Wood (90), P.M.Toohey (97)	Kingston	1977-78	–	–	180	–	–	–	–
J.H.W.Fingleton (40), S.J.McCabe (189*)	Johannesburg¹	1935-36	–	177	–	–	–	–	–
W.M.Woodfull (82), D.G.Bradman (299*)	Adelaide	1931-32	–	176	–	–	–	–	–
I.C.Davis (88), R.B.McCosker (105)	Melbourne	1976-77	–	–	–	–	176	–	–
A.C.Bannerman (91), J.J.Lyons (134)	Sydney	1891-92	174	–	–	–	–	–	–
S.G.Barnes (141), D.G.Bradman (89)	Lord's	1948	174	–	–	–	–	–	–
W.A.Brown (133), D.G.Bradman (144*)	Nottingham	1938	170	–	–	–	–	–	–
J.Moroney (101*), R.N.Harvey (100)	Johannesburg²	1949-50	–	170	–	–	–	–	–
K.C.Wessels (141), G.N.Yallop (98)	Kandy	1982-83	–	–	–	–	–	–	170
G.R.Marsh (118), W.B.Phillips (62)	Auckland	1985-86	–	–	–	168	–	–	–
A.R.Morris (89), K.R.Miller (109)	Lord's	1953	165	–	–	–	–	–	–
W.M.Woodfull (76), D.G.Bradman (226)	Brisbane²	1931-32	–	163	–	–	–	–	–
W.A.Brown (66), S.J.McCabe (149)	Durban²	1935-36	–	161	–	–	–	–	–
R.B.Simpson (91), R.N.Harvey (64)	Sydney	1962-63	160	–	–	–	–	–	–
D.C.Boon (122), D.M.Jones (210)	Madras¹	1986-87	–	–	–	–	158	–	–
A.R.Morris (77), R.N.Harvey (116)	Adelaide	1952-53	–	157	–	–	–	–	–
W.M.Woodfull (83), D.G.Bradman (152)	Melbourne	1930-31	–	–	156	–	–	–	–
K.R.Stackpole (207), I.M.Chappell (59)	Brisbane²	1970-71	151	–	–	–	–	–	–
D.C.Boon (200), T.M.Moody (61)	Perth	1989-90	–	–	–	149	–	–	–
J.Darling (178), C.Hill (81)	Adelaide	1897-98	148	–	–	–	–	–	–
C.Kelleway (61), C.G.Macartney (99)	Lord's	1912	146	–	–	–	–	–	–
M.A.Taylor (62), D.C.Boon (94)	Lord's	1989	145	–	–	–	–	–	–
P.S.McDonnell (103), W.L.Murdoch (211)	Oval	1884	143	–	–	–	–	–	–
V.T.Trumper (113), C.Hill (88)	Adelaide	1903-04	143	–	–	–	–	–	–
K.C.Wessels (179), G.N.Yallop (68)	Adelaide	1983-84	–	–	–	–	–	142	–
I.R.Redpath (93), I.M.Chappell (121)	Wellington	1973-74	–	–	–	141	–	–	–
W.M.Lawry (89), N.C.O'Neill (88)	Sydney	1963-64	–	140	–	–	–	–	–
W.M.Lawry (210), R.M.Cowper (102)	Bridgetown	1964-65	–	–	140	–	–	–	–
A.M.J.Hilditch (80), K.C.Wessels (64)	Leeds	1985	139	–	–	–	–	–	–
R.B.Simpson (72), R.M.Cowper (69)	Port-of-Spain	1964-65	–	–	138	–	–	–	–
V.T.Trumper (65), C.Hill (98)	Adelaide	1901-02	137	–	–	–	–	–	–
W.M.Woodfull (58), K.E.Rigg (127)	Sydney	1931-32	–	137	–	–	–	–	–
A.M.J.Hilditch (119), K.C.Wessels (36)	Leeds	1985	132	–	–	–	–	–	–
F.A.Iredale (108), G.Giffen (80)	Manchester	1896	131	–	–	–	–	–	–
W.M.Lawry (135), I.R.Redpath (67)	Oval	1968	129	–	–	–	–	–	–
K.R.Stackpole (122), I.M.Chappell (54)	Melbourne	1973-74	–	–	–	128	–	–	–
I.R.Redpath (103), G.N.Yallop (47)	Adelaide	1975-76	–	–	128	–	–	–	–
A.M.J.Hilditch (85), A.R.Border (46)	Delhi	1979-80	–	–	–	–	127	–	–
B.M.Laird (74), I.M.Chappell (75)	Melbourne	1979-80	127	–	–	–	–	–	–
C.C.McDonald (47), R.N.Harvey (167)	Melbourne	1958-59	126	–	–	–	–	–	–
G.R.Marsh (49), D.M.Jones (69)	Perth	1986-87	126	–	–	–	–	–	–
M.A.Taylor (142*), D.C.Boon (67*)	Perth	1993-94	–	–	125*	–	–	–	–
A.L.Hassett (104), R.N.Harvey (59)	Lord's	1953	125	–	–	–	–	–	–
I.C.Davis (105), R.B.McCosker (65)	Adelaide	1976-77	–	–	–	–	125	–	–
W.M.Darling (91), K.J.Hughes (48)	Sydney	1978-79	125	–	–	–	–	–	–
C.E.McLeod (112), C.Hill (58)	Melbourne	1897-98	124	–	–	–	–	–	–
C.G.Macartney (137), H.V.Hordern (50)	Sydney	1910-11	–	124	–	–	–	–	–
J.H.W.Fingleton (73), D.G.Bradman (82)	Sydney	1936-37	124	–	–	–	–	–	–
R.Edwards (170*), I.M.Chappell (50)	Nottingham	1972	124	–	–	–	–	–	–
H.L.Collins (24), C.G.Macartney (133*)	Lord's	1926	123	–	–	–	–	–	–
I.R.Redpath (135), I.M.Chappell (66)	Melbourne	1972-73	–	–	–	–	123	–	–
A.M.J.Hilditch (70), K.C.Wessels (90)	Melbourne	1984-85	–	–	123	–	–	–	–
A.R.Morris (67), A.L.Hassett (115)	Nottingham	1953	122	–	–	–	–	–	–
D.C.Boon (76), S.R.Waugh (100)	Sydney	1992-93	–	–	122	–	–	–	–
C.Kelleway (70), C.Hill (65)	Sydney	1911-12	121	–	–	–	–	–	–
K.A.Archer (48), A.L.Hassett (70)	Sydney	1950-51	121	–	–	–	–	–	–
R.B.Simpson (115), I.R.Redpath (40*)	Karachi¹	1964-65	–	–	–	–	–	119	–
R.B.McCosker (79), I.M.Chappell (86)	Lord's	1975	119	–	–	–	–	–	–
R.B.Simpson (153), I.R.Redpath (54)	Cape Town	1966-67	–	117	–	–	–	–	–
K.R.Stackpole (79), I.M.Chappell (37)	Oval	1972	116	–	–	–	–	–	–
M.A.Taylor (82), J.L.Langer (63)	Christchurch	1992-93	–	–	–	116	–	–	–

2nd Wicket *continued*

			E	SA	WI	NZ	I	P	SL
W.M.Woodfull (67), D.G.Bradman (71)	Sydney	1932-33	115	–	–	–	–	–	–
G.M.Wood (45), K.C.Wessels (173)	Sydney	1984-85	–	–	114	–	–	–	–
H.L.Collins (203), J.Ryder (56)	Johannesburg[1]	1921-22	–	113	–	–	–	–	–
H.L.Collins (104), C.G.Macartney (69)	Sydney	1920-21	111	–	–	–	–	–	–
R.M.Cowper (57), I.M.Chappell (71)	Birmingham	1968	111	–	–	–	–	–	–
M.A.Taylor (76), D.C.Boon (57)	Bridgetown	1990-91	–	–	111	–	–	–	–
W.A.Brown (67), S.G.Barnes (54)	Wellington	1945-46	–	–	–	109	–	–	–
R.Edwards (74), I.M.Chappell (56)	Port-of-Spain	1972-73	–	–	109	–	–	–	–
I.R.Redpath (66), G.S.Chappell (56)	Port-of-Spain	1972-73	–	–	107	–	–	–	–
M.A.Noble (50), C.Hill (54)	Nottingham	1905	106‡	–	–	–	–	–	–
R.B.McCosker (95*), I.M.Chappell (62)	Leeds	1975	106	–	–	–	–	–	–
M.A.Taylor (60), D.C.Boon (44*)	Melbourne	1991-92	–	–	–	–	106	–	–
A.Turner (136), G.N.Yallop (43)	Adelaide	1975-76	–	–	105	–	–	–	–
W.B.Phillips (63), D.C.Boon (81)	Sydney	1985-86	–	–	–	105	–	–	–
M.A.Taylor (70), D.C.Boon (96)	Cape Town	1993-94	–	105	–	–	–	–	–
J.Moroney (87), K.R.Miller (58)	Cape Town	1949-50	–	104	–	–	–	–	–
I.R.Redpath (83), I.M.Chappell (50)	Melbourne	1974-75	104	–	–	–	–	–	–
G.M.Wood (68), G.M.Ritchie (57)	Bridgetown	1983-84	–	–	103	–	–	–	–
W.Bardsley (85), C.Hill (39)	Melbourne	1910-11	–	101	–	–	–	–	–
A.M.J.Hilditch (55), A.R.Border (50)	Madras[1]	1979-80	–	–	–	–	101	–	–
M.A.Taylor (219), D.C.Boon (73)	Nottingham	1989	101	–	–	–	–	–	–
A.P.Sheahan (44), I.M.Chappell (196)	Adelaide	1972-73	–	–	–	–	–	100	–
	Totals: (108)		50	17	16	9	7	8	1

†*202 runs were added for this wicket, W.M.Lawry retiring hurt and being succeeded by I.R.Redpath after 22 runs had been scored.*

‡*128 runs were added for this wicket, V.T.Trumper retiring hurt and being succeeded by M.A.Noble after 22 runs had been scored.*

Although the 2nd wicket added 134 v India at Melbourne in 1947-48, this consisted of two partnerships: W.A.Brown added 92* with D.G.Bradman (retired hurt) and a further 42 with K.R.Miller. Similarly, 105 were added v England at Adelaide in 1958-59, R.N.Harvey scoring 97* with C.C.McDonald (retired hurt) and a further 8 with N.C.O'Neill.

AUSTRALIA – 3rd Wicket

			E	SA	WI	NZ	I	P	SL
C.C.McDonald (127), R.N.Harvey (204)	Kingston	1954-55	–	295	–	–	–	–	–
D.G.Bradman (187), A.L.Hassett (128)	Brisbane[2]	1946-47	276	–	–	–	–	–	–
I.M.Chappell (145), G.S.Chappell (247*)	Wellington	1973-74	–	–	–	264	–	–	–
D.G.Bradman (169), S.J.McCabe (112)	Melbourne	1936-37	249	–	–	–	–	–	–
C.Kelleway (102), W.Bardsley (164)	Lord's	1912	–	242	–	–	–	–	–
D.G.Bradman (334), A.F.Kippax (77)	Leeds	1930	229	–	–	–	–	–	–
R.M.Cowper (143), B.C.Booth (117)	Port-of-Spain	1964-65	–	–	225†	–	–	–	–
R.N.Harvey (133), K.R.Miller (147)	Kingston	1954-55	–	–	224	–	–	–	–
A.R.Border (162), K.J.Hughes (100)	Madras[1]	1979-80	–	–	–	–	222	–	–
W.M.Lawry (108), R.M.Cowper (307)	Melbourne	1965-66	212	–	–	–	–	–	–
H.L.Collins (203), J.M.Gregory (119)	Johannesburg[1]	1921-22	–	209	–	–	–	–	–
K.R.Stackpole (207), K.D.Walters (112)	Brisbane[2]	1970-71	209	–	–	–	–	–	–
W.L.Murdoch (211), H.J.H.Scott (102)	Oval	1884	207	–	–	–	–	–	–
R.N.Harvey (102), N.C.O'Neill (163)	Bombay[2]	1959-60	–	–	–	–	207	–	–
G.N.Yallop (167), K.J.Hughes (92)	Calcutta	1979-80	–	–	–	–	206	–	–
G.N.Yallop (268), K.J.Hughes (94)	Melbourne	1983-84	–	–	–	–	203	–	–
C.Kelleway (114), W.Bardsley (121)	Manchester	1912	–	202	–	–	–	–	–
A.R.Morris (153), R.N.Harvey (162)	Brisbane[2]	1954-55	202	–	–	–	–	–	–
I.M.Chappell (118), G.S.Chappell (113)	Oval	1972	201	–	–	–	–	–	–
J.Darling (160), J.Worrall (62)	Sydney	1897-98	193	–	–	–	–	–	–
D.G.Bradman (223), A.F.Kippax (84)	Brisbane[1]	1930-31	–	–	193	–	–	–	–
I.M.Chappell (106*), K.D.Walters (102*)	Bridgetown	1972-73	–	–	192*	–	–	–	–
D.G.Bradman (254), A.F.Kippax (83)	Lord's	1930	192	–	–	–	–	–	–
A.R.Morris (122), A.L.Hassett (78)	Adelaide	1946-47	189	–	–	–	–	–	–
G.R.Marsh (79*), D.C.Boon (94*)	Melbourne	1990-91	187*	–	–	–	–	–	–
A.R.Morris (157), R.N.Harvey (116)	Port Elizabeth	1949-50	–	187	–	–	–	–	–
K.J.Hughes (88), G.S.Chappell (235)	Faisalabad	1979-80	–	–	–	–	–	179	–
D.C.Boon (164*), M.E.Waugh (99)	Lord's	1993	175	–	–	–	–	–	–
R.B.Simpson (103), R.M.Cowper (108)	Adelaide	1967-68	–	–	–	–	172	–	–
D.G.Bradman (132), A.L.Hassett (80)	Melbourne	1947-48	–	–	–	–	169	–	–
B.M.Laird (78), A.R.Border (126)	Adelaide	1981-82	–	–	166	–	–	–	–
W.W.Armstrong (59), C.Hill (142)	Johannesburg[1]	1902-03	–	164	–	–	–	–	–
I.M.Chappell (74*), G.S.Chappell (109*)	Brisbane[2]	1975-76	–	–	159*	–	–	–	–
J.W.Burke (81), R.Benaud (100)	Johannesburg[3]	1957-58	–	158	–	–	–	–	–

Hundred Partnerships (Australia)

3rd Wicket *continued*

			E	SA	WI	NZ	I	P	SL
T.M.Moody (106), A.R.Border (56)	Brisbane[2]	1989-90	–	–	–	–	–	–	158
H.Carter (72), C.Hill (98)	Adelaide	1911-12	157	–	–	–	–	–	–
D.M.Jones (102), A.R.Border (88)	Perth	1987-88	–	–	–	–	–	–	156
R.N.Harvey (109), A.L.Hassett (55)	Brisbane[2]	1952-53	–	155	–	–	–	–	–
D.G.Bradman (77), S.J.McCabe (70)	Oval	1934	150	–	–	–	–	–	–
D.C.Boon (97), A.R.Border (78)	Sydney	1990-91	147	–	–	–	–	–	–
D.M.Jones (73*), A.R.Border (66*)	Bombay[3]	1986-87	–	–	–	–	146*	–	–
R.N.Harvey (114), N.C.O'Neill (82)	Birmingham	1961	146	–	–	–	–	–	–
R.Edwards (170*), G.S.Chappell (72)	Nottingham	1972	146	–	–	–	–	–	–
C.G.Macartney (137), W.Bardsley (94)	Sydney	1910-11	–	145	–	–	–	–	–
C.Hill (191), D.R.A.Gehrs (67)	Sydney	1910-11	–	144	–	–	–	–	–
W.M.Lawry (81), K.D.Walters (81)	Manchester	1968	144	–	–	–	–	–	–
K.C.Wessels (173), A.R.Border (69)	Sydney	1984-85	–	–	144‡	–	–	–	–
A.L.Mann (105), A.D.Ogilvie (47)	Perth	1977-78	–	–	–	–	139	–	–
D.C.Boon (200), A.R.Border (50)	Perth	1989-90	–	–	–	139	–	–	–
J.W.Burke (161), P.J.P.Burge (83)	Bombay[2]	1956-57	–	–	–	–	137	–	–
R.B.Simpson (71), B.C.Booth (77)	Adelaide	1962-63	133	–	–	–	–	–	–
P.M.Toohey (122), G.N.Yallop (57)	Kingston	1977-78	–	133	–	–	–	–	–
A.R.Border (61), K.J.Hughes (80)	Bombay[3]	1979-80	–	–	–	–	132	–	–
J.Ryder (52*), J.M.Gregory (76*)	Melbourne	1920-21	130*	–	–	–	–	–	–
B.M.Laird (92), G.S.Chappell (74)	Brisbane[2]	1979-80	–	–	130	–	–	–	–
I.M.Chappell (72), G.S.Chappell (106)	Bridgetown	1972-73	–	–	129	–	–	–	–
W.M.Lawry (58*), N.C.O'Neill (74*)	Bridgetown	1964-65	–	–	126*§	–	–	–	–
G.S.Chappell (115), K.J.Hughes (88)	Adelaide	1982-83	126	–	–	–	–	–	–
D.M.Jones (93), A.R.Border (70)	Adelaide	1986-87	126	–	–	–	–	–	–
D.C.Boon (89), M.E.Waugh (68)	Brisbane[2]	1993-94	–	–	–	125	–	–	–
B.M.Laird (75), G.S.Chappell (124)	Brisbane[2]	1979-80	–	–	124	–	–	–	–
W.M.Lawry (205), K.D.Walters (76)	Melbourne	1968-69	–	–	123	–	–	–	–
D.C.Boon (101), M.E.Waugh (70)	Nottingham	1993	123	–	–	–	–	–	–
I.M.Chappell (109), G.S.Chappell (51)	Georgetown	1972-73	–	–	121	–	–	–	–
G.N.Yallop (121), P.M.Toohey (60)	Adelaide	1967-68	–	–	–	–	120	–	–
R.N.Harvey (167), N.C.O'Neill (37)	Melbourne	1958-59	118	–	–	–	–	–	–
A.P.Sheahan (81), R.M.Cowper (92)	Adelaide	1967-68	–	–	–	–	118	–	–
M.A.Taylor (136), A.R.Border (66)	Leeds	1989	117	–	–	–	–	–	–
D.C.Boon (107), A.R.Border (59)	Perth	1991-92	–	–	–	–	117	–	–
R.B.Simpson (153), P.J.P.Burge (54)	Karachi[1]	1964-65	–	–	–	–	–	116	–
M.A.Taylor (59), A.R.Border (59)	St John's	1990-91	–	–	116	–	–	–	–
R.A.Duff (146), M.A.Noble (25)	Oval	1905	115	–	–	–	–	–	–
R.B.McCosker (84), G.S.Chappell (58)	Auckland	1976-77	–	–	–	115	–	–	–
V.T.Trumper (166), S.E.Gregory (56)	Sydney	1907-08	114	–	–	–	–	–	–
C.C.McDonald (67), R.N.Harvey (190)	Sydney	1952-53	–	113	–	–	–	–	–
K.E.Rigg (127), D.G.Bradman (112)	Sydney	1931-32	–	111	–	–	–	–	–
G.S.Chappell (59), K.J.Hughes (84)	Lord's	1980	111	–	–	–	–	–	–
D.C.Boon (184*), A.R.Border (48*)	Sydney	1987-88	110*	–	–	–	–	–	–
A.R.Morris (206), R.N.Harvey (43)	Adelaide	1950-51	110	–	–	–	–	–	–
G.M.Wood (112), K.J.Hughes (117)	Lord's	1980	110	–	–	–	–	–	–
D.C.Boon (111), M.E.Waugh (60)	Brisbane[2]	1992-93	–	–	110	–	–	–	–
D.G.Bradman (212), S.J.McCabe (55)	Adelaide	1936-37	109	–	–	–	–	–	–
A.R.Morris (196), A.L.Hassett (37)	Oval	1948	109	–	–	–	–	–	–
D.C.Boon (93), M.E.Waugh (64)	Manchester	1993	109	–	–	–	–	–	–
D.C.Boon (38*), M.E.Waugh (62*)	Birmingham	1993	108*	–	–	–	–	–	–
C.G.Macartney (61), T.J.E.Andrews (94)	Oval	1921	108	–	–	–	–	–	–
R.N.Harvey (85), N.C.O'Neill (70)	Sydney	1960-61	–	–	108	–	–	–	–
B.M.Laird (63), G.S.Chappell (57)	Lahore[2]	1979-80	–	–	–	–	–	108	–
D.C.Boon (53), D.R.Martyn (74)	Auckland	1992-93	–	–	–	107	–	–	–
D.C.Boon (107), M.E.Waugh (52)	Leeds	1993	106	–	–	–	–	–	–
D.G.Bradman (201), A.L.Hassett (198*)	Adelaide	1947-48	–	–	–	–	105	–	–
R.B.Simpson (78), P.J.P.Burge (81)	Adelaide	1963-64	–	104	–	–	–	–	–
G.J.Cosier (67), C.S.Serjeant (85)	Melbourne	1977-78	–	–	–	–	104	–	–
R.N.Harvey (205), A.L.Hassett (40)	Melbourne	1952-53	–	103	–	–	–	–	–
W.Bardsley (82), W.W.Armstrong (48)	Melbourne	1910-11	–	102	–	–	–	–	–
C.G.Macartney (115), C.E.Pellew (52)	Leeds	1921	101	–	–	–	–	–	–
D.G.Bradman (185), A.L.Hassett (48)	Brisbane[2]	1947-48	–	–	–	–	101	–	–
I.M.Chappell (99), K.D.Walters (56)	Calcutta	1969-70	–	–	–	–	101	–	–
I.R.Redpath (39), G.S.Chappell (61)	Melbourne	1974-75	101	–	–	–	–	–	–
R.N.Harvey (74), W.J.Watson (30)	Bridgetown	1954-55	–	–	100	–	–	–	–
I.M.Chappell (90), G.S.Chappell (58)	Brisbane[2]	1974-75	100	–	–	–	–	–	–
G.R.Marsh (94), A.R.Border (47)	Georgetown	1990-91	–	–	100	–	–	–	–
Totals: (102)			41	14	20	5	16	4	2

†*128 runs were added for this wicket, N.C.O'Neill retiring hurt and being succeeded by B.C.Booth after 3 runs had been scored.*
‡*212 runs were added for this wicket, G.M.Ritchie retiring hurt and being succeeded by A.R.Border after 68 runs had been scored.*
§*147 runs were added for this wicket, W.M.Lawry retiring hurt and being succeeded by B.C.Booth after 126 runs had been scored.*

AUSTRALIA – 4th Wicket			E	SA	WI	NZ	I	P	SL
W.H.Ponsford (181), D.G.Bradman (304)	Leeds	1934	388	–	–	–	–	–	–
W.M.Lawry (151), K.D.Walters (242)	Sydney	1968-69	–	–	336	–	–	–	–
G.M.Wood (126), C.S.Serjeant (124)	Georgetown	1977-78	–	–	251	–	–	–	–
D.G.Bradman (232), A.A.Jackson (73)	Oval	1930	243	–	–	–	–	–	–
A.L.Hassett (132), K.R.Miller (129)	Sydney	1951-52	–	–	235	–	–	–	–
G.H.S.Trott (143), S.E.Gregory (103)	Lord's	1896	221	–	–	–	–	–	–
G.S.Chappell (235), G.N.Yallop (172)	Faisalabad	1979-80	–	–	–	–	–	217	–
D.M.Jones (216), A.R.Border (64)	Adelaide	1988-89	–	–	214	–	–	–	–
I.R.Redpath (132), K.D.Walters (103)	Sydney	1968-69	–	–	210	–	–	–	–
A.C.Bannerman (70), P.S.McDonnell (147)	Sydney	1881-82	199	–	–	–	–	–	–
C.G.Macartney (170), J.M.Gregory (93)	Sydney	1920-21	198	–	–	–	–	–	–
A.R.Border (76), D.M.Jones (122)	Oval	1989	196	–	–	–	–	–	–
C.Kelleway (147), W.W.Armstrong (121)	Adelaide	1920-21	194	–	–	–	–	–	–
R.N.Harvey (154), N.C.O'Neill (100)	Adelaide	1962-63	194	–	–	–	–	–	–
A.F.Kippax (146), S.J.McCabe (90)	Adelaide	1930-31	–	–	182	–	–	–	–
D.M.Jones (210), A.R.Border (106)	Madras[1]	1986-87	–	–	–	–	178	–	–
A.R.Border (105), K.J.Hughes (84)	Melbourne	1978-79	–	–	–	–	–	177	–
R.N.Harvey (122), G.B.Hole (66)	Manchester	1953	173	–	–	–	–	–	–
D.M.Jones (150*), T.M.Moody (101)	Perth	1991-92	–	–	–	–	173	–	–
R.M.Cowper (307), K.D.Walters (60)	Melbourne	1965-66	172	–	–	–	–	–	–
I.M.Chappell (196), R.Edwards (89)	Adelaide	1972-73	–	–	–	–	172	–	–
G.Giffen (161), F.A.Iredale (81)	Sydney	1894-95	171	–	–	–	–	–	–
G.S.Chappell (182), K.J.Hughes (76)	Sydney	1983-84	–	–	–	–	–	171	–
G.N.Yallop (102), K.J.Hughes (129)	Brisbane[2]	1978-79	170	–	–	–	–	–	–
D.C.Boon (149), A.R.Border (75)	Sydney	1988-89	–	–	170	–	–	–	–
M.A.Taylor (170), M.E.Waugh (84)	Melbourne	1993-94	–	169	–	–	–	–	–
R.N.Harvey (190), K.R.Miller (55)	Sydney	1952-53	–	168	–	–	–	–	–
M.A.Taylor (108), A.R.Border (85)	Hobart	1989-90	–	–	–	–	–	–	163
M.A.Noble (65), S.E.Gregory (112)	Adelaide	1903-04	162	–	–	–	–	–	–
W.H.Ponsford (128), J.M.Taylor (72)	Melbourne	1924-25	161	–	–	–	–	–	–
A.F.Kippax (100), J.Ryder (112)	Melbourne	1928-29	161	–	–	–	–	–	–
R.N.Harvey (153), S.J.E.Loxton (80)	Melbourne	1947-48	–	–	–	–	159	–	–
W.W.Armstrong (132), C.Hill (100)	Melbourne	1910-11	–	154	–	–	–	–	–
N.C.O'Neill (113), P.J.P.Burge (60)	Calcutta	1959-60	–	–	–	–	150	–	–
M.E.Waugh (111), A.R.Border (60)	Hobart	1993-94	–	–	–	150	–	–	–
M.A.Taylor (164), S.R.Waugh (57)	Brisbane[2]	1989-90	–	–	–	–	–	–	149
R.N.Harvey (205), I.D.Craig (53)	Melbourne	1952-53	–	148	–	–	–	–	–
A.L.Hassett (198*), K.R.Miller (67)	Adelaide	1947-48	–	–	–	–	142	–	–
G.S.Chappell (117), K.J.Hughes (62)	Perth	1982-83	141	–	–	–	–	–	–
D.C.Boon (164*), A.R.Border (77)	Lord's	1993	139	–	–	–	–	–	–
A.F.Kippax (51), J.Ryder (87)	Adelaide	1928-29	137	–	–	–	–	–	–
K.C.Wessels (179), A.R.Border (117*)	Adelaide	1983-84	–	–	–	–	–	134	–
R.N.Harvey (114), K.D.Mackay (78)	Delhi	1959-60	–	–	–	–	132	–	–
R.N.Harvey (162), G.B.Hole (57)	Brisbane[2]	1954-55	131	–	–	–	–	–	–
C.Hill (135), M.A.Noble (54)	Lord's	1899	130	–	–	–	–	–	–
J.W.Burke (189), K.D.Mackay (63)	Cape Town	1957-58	–	130	–	–	–	–	–
W.M.Woodfull (141), A.J.Richardson (100)	Leeds	1926	129	–	–	–	–	–	–
K.J.Hughes (213), A.R.Border (57)	Adelaide	1980-81	–	–	–	–	129	–	–
A.A.Jackson (164), J.Ryder (63)	Adelaide	1928-29	126	–	–	–	–	–	–
R.M.Cowper (81), B.C.Booth (74)	Bombay[2]	1964-65	–	–	–	–	125	–	–
A.R.Border (100*), G.M.Ritchie (46*)	Adelaide	1986-87	124*	–	–	–	–	–	–
W.A.Brown (206*), A.L.Hassett (56)	Lord's	1938	124	–	–	–	–	–	–
R.N.Harvey (83), K.R.Miller (47)	Melbourne	1951-52	–	124	–	–	–	–	–
I.R.Redpath (101), G.S.Chappell (68)	Melbourne	1975-76	–	–	124	–	–	–	–
N.C.O'Neill (117), P.J.P.Burge (181)	Oval	1961	123	–	–	–	–	–	–
K.R.Miller (58), R.N.Harvey (112)	Leeds	1948	121	–	–	–	–	–	–
D.G.Bradman (185), K.R.Miller (58)	Brisbane[2]	1947-48	–	–	–	–	120	–	–
N.C.O'Neill (82), B.C.Booth (169)	Brisbane[2]	1963-64	–	120	–	–	–	–	–
A.R.Border (80), D.M.Jones (69)	Manchester	1989	120	–	–	–	–	–	–
W.Bardsley (54), V.T.Trumper (214*)	Adelaide	1910-11	–	118	–	–	–	–	–
K.D.Walters (48), I.R.Redpath (77)	Bombay[2]	1969-70	–	–	–	–	118	–	–

4th Wicket *continued*

			E	SA	WI	NZ	I	P	SL
G.S.Chappell (124), K.J.Hughes (130*)	Brisbane²	1979-80	–	–	118	–	–	–	–
D.C.Boon (123), G.M.Ritchie (128)	Adelaide	1985-86	–	–	–	–	117	–	–
A.R.Border (205), S.R.Waugh (61)	Adelaide	1987-88	–	–	–	116	–	–	–
A.R.Morris (157), A.L.Hassett (167)	Port Elizabeth	1949-50	–	114	–	–	–	–	–
G.S.Chappell (71), R.Edwards (53)	Brisbane²	1974-75	114	–	–	–	–	–	–
G.R.Marsh (110), G.M.Ritchie (45)	Brisbane²	1986-87	113	–	–	–	–	–	–
W.A.Brown (73), S.J.McCabe (88)	Nottingham	1934	112	–	–	–	–	–	–
A.F.Kippax (67), S.J.McCabe (71)	Melbourne	1931-32	–	111	–	–	–	–	–
G.S.Chappell (41), K.D.Walters (70)	Port-of-Spain	1972-73	–	–	111	–	–	–	–
A.M.J.Hilditch (113), A.R.Border (41)	Melbourne	1984-85	–	–	111	–	–	–	–
R.B.McCosker (109*), G.S.Chappell (54*)	Melbourne	1975-76	–	–	110*	–	–	–	–
N.C.O'Neill (77), L.E.Favell (54)	Sydney	1958-59	110	–	–	–	–	–	–
C.G.Macartney (115), J.M.Taylor (50)	Leeds	1921	109	–	–	–	–	–	–
K.R.Miller (84), A.L.Hassett (53)	Johannesburg²	1949-50	–	109	–	–	–	–	–
A.L.Hassett (115), K.R.Miller (55)	Nottingham	1953	109	–	–	–	–	–	–
N.C.O'Neill (73), P.J.P.Burge (103)	Sydney	1962-63	109	–	–	–	–	–	–
G.S.Chappell (76), A.R.Border (124)	Melbourne	1980-81	–	–	–	–	108	–	–
K.J.Hughes (53), A.R.Border (118)	Brisbane²	1983-84	–	–	–	–	–	108	–
G.R.Marsh (86), D.M.Jones (59)	Melbourne	1991-92	–	–	–	–	108	–	–
G.S.Chappell (73*), R.Edwards (52*)	Lord's	1975	107*	–	–	–	–	–	–
K.J.Hughes (39*), D.W.Hookes (66*)	Brisbane²	1982-83	107*	–	–	–	–	–	–
C.Hill (119), S.E.Gregory (29)	Sheffield	1902	107	–	–	–	–	–	–
M.A.Noble (133), W.W.Armstrong (48)	Sydney	1903-04	106	–	–	–	–	–	–
C.G.Macartney (116), J.Ryder (58)	Durban¹	1921-22	–	106	–	–	–	–	–
A.L.Hassett (128), K.R.Miller (79)	Brisbane²	1946-47	106	–	–	–	–	–	–
W.M.Lawry (94), B.C.Booth (74)	Oval	1964	106	–	–	–	–	–	–
I.R.Redpath (58), I.C.Davis (50)	Christchurch	1973-74	–	–	–	106	–	–	–
G.S.Chappell (98*), K.J.Hughes (47)	Sydney	1979-80	105	–	–	–	–	–	–
D.C.Boon (107), A.R.Border (200*)	Leeds	1993	105	–	–	–	–	–	–
G.N.Yallop (121), R.B.Simpson (100)	Adelaide	1977-78	–	–	–	–	104	–	–
M.J.Slater (92), A.R.Border (49)	Sydney	1993-94	–	–	104	–	–	–	–
C.S.Serjeant (81), K.D.Walters (53)	Lord's	1977	103	–	–	–	–	–	–
P.L.Taylor (87), A.R.Border (78*)	Wellington	1989-90	–	–	–	103	–	–	–
A.R.Border (60*), D.M.Jones (40*)	Leeds	1989	101*	–	–	–	–	–	–
G.S.Chappell (70), K.D.Walters (51)	Adelaide	1976-77	–	–	–	–	–	101	–
G.N.Yallop (75), C.S.Serjeant (49)	Port-of-Spain	1977-78	–	–	101	–	–	–	–
G.S.Chappell (42), K.D.Walters (94)	Adelaide	1973-74	–	–	–	100	–	–	–
K.J.Hughes (48), D.W.Hookes (68)	Melbourne	1982-83	100	–	–	–	–	–	–
	Totals:	(99)	45	12	14	5	14	7	2

AUSTRALIA – 5th Wicket

			E	SA	WI	NZ	I	P	SL
S.G.Barnes (234), D.G.Bradman (234)	Sydney	1946-47	405	–	–	–	–	–	–
A.R.Border (200*), S.R.Waugh (157*)	Leeds	1993	332*	–	–	–	–	–	–
A.R.Morris (100*), D.G.Bradman (127*)	Melbourne	1947-48	–	–	–	–	223*	–	–
K.R.Miller (109), R.G.Archer (128)	Kingston	1954-55	–	–	220	–	–	–	–
R.B.Simpson (311), B.C.Booth (98)	Manchester	1964	219	–	–	–	–	–	–
A.R.Border (196), G.M.Ritchie (94)	Lord's	1985	216	–	–	–	–	–	–
G.M.Ritchie (92), G.R.J.Matthews (130)	Wellington	1985-86	–	–	–	213	–	–	–
A.R.Border (84), S.R.Waugh (164)	Adelaide	1993-94	–	208	–	–	–	–	–
M.E.Waugh (112), A.R.Border (110)	Melbourne	1992-93	–	–	204	–	–	–	–
G.M.Wood (111), S.R.Waugh (91)	Perth	1988-89	–	–	200	–	–	–	–
P.J.P.Burge (120), K.D.Walters (115)	Melbourne	1965-66	198	–	–	–	–	–	–
W.M.Lawry (166), K.D.Walters (155)	Brisbane²	1965-66	187	–	–	–	–	–	–
P.J.P.Burge (181), B.C.Booth (71)	Oval	1961	185	–	–	–	–	–	–
D.M.Jones (81), M.E.Waugh (139*)	St John's	1990-91	–	–	184	–	–	–	–
D.G.Bradman (123), A.G.Fairfax (65)	Melbourne	1928-29	183	–	–	–	–	–	–
W.H.Ponsford (183), W.M.Woodfull (58)	Sydney	1930-31	–	–	183	–	–	–	–
G.S.Chappell (204), K.D.Walters (67)	Sydney	1980-81	–	–	–	–	172	–	–
G.S.Chappell (121), G.J.Cosier (168)	Melbourne	1976-77	–	–	–	–	–	171	–
A.R.Border (118), G.S.Chappell (150*)	Brisbane²	1983-84	–	–	–	–	–	171	–
R.Edwards (115), K.D.Walters (103)	Perth	1974-75	170	–	–	–	–	–	–
C.L.Badcock (118), R.G.Gregory (80)	Melbourne	1936-37	161	–	–	–	–	–	–
A.R.Border (105), S.R.Waugh (147*)	Brisbane²	1993-94	–	–	159	–	–	–	–
D.W.Hookes (143*), A.R.Border (47*)	Kandy	1982-83	–	–	–	–	–	–	155*
A.R.Border (205), P.R.Sleep (62)	Adelaide	1987-88	–	–	154	–	–	–	–
G.S.Chappell (182), A.R.Border (64)	Sydney	1983-84	–	–	–	–	–	153	–
M.E.Waugh (137), S.R.Waugh (59)	Birmingham	1993	153	–	–	–	–	–	–
A.P.Sheahan (88), I.M.Chappell (73)	Manchester	1968	152	–	–	–	–	–	–

5th Wicket *continued*

			E	SA	WI	NZ	I	P	SL
K.R.Miller (141*), I.W.Johnson (52)	Adelaide	1946-47	150	–	–	–	–	–	–
K.J.Hughes (137), A.R.Border (83)	Sydney	1982-83	149	–	–	–	–	–	–
G.S.Chappell (116*), R.W.Marsh (74)	Melbourne	1972-73	–	–	–	–	–	146	–
W.W.Armstrong (132), V.T.Trumper (87)	Melbourne	1910-11	–	143	–	–	–	–	–
S.E.Gregory (70), J.Darling (74)	Melbourne	1894-95	142	–	–	–	–	–	–
M.E.Waugh (113*), A.R.Border (42*)	Durban[2]	1993-94	–	140*	–	–	–	–	–
R.N.Harvey (178), S.J.E.Loxton (35)	Cape Town	1949-50	–	140	–	–	–	–	–
G.Giffen (161), S.E.Gregory (201)	Sydney	1894-95	139	–	–	–	–	–	–
D.M.Jones (79), S.R.Waugh (177*)	Leeds	1989	138	–	–	–	–	–	–
D.G.Bradman (212), R.G.Gregory (50)	Adelaide	1936-37	135	–	–	–	–	–	–
R.N.Harvey (151*), S.J.E.Loxton (54)	Durban[2]	1949-50	–	135	–	–	–	–	–
I.R.Redpath (70), A.P.Sheahan (114)	Kanpur	1969-70	–	–	–	–	131	–	–
A.R.Border (124), K.D.Walters (78)	Melbourne	1980-81	–	–	–	–	131	–	–
G.S.Chappell (201), D.M.Wellham (36)	Brisbane[2]	1981-82	–	–	–	–	131	–	–
S.J.McCabe (187*), V.Y.Richardson (49)	Sydney	1932-33	129	–	–	–	–	–	–
A.R.Border (63), G.S.Chappell (114)	Melbourne	1979-80	126	–	–	–	–	–	–
F.A.Iredale (89), G.H.S.Trott (79)	Melbourne	1897-98	124	–	–	–	–	–	–
A.R.Border (98), D.W.Hookes (51)	St John's	1983-84	–	–	124	–	–	–	–
G.S.Chappell (123), R.W.Marsh (48)	Brisbane[2]	1975-76	–	–	122	–	–	–	–
D.G.Bradman (138), A.L.Hassett (137)	Nottingham	1948	120	–	–	–	–	–	–
W.Bardsley (136), V.T.Trumper (73)	Oval	1909	118	–	–	–	–	–	–
D.G.Bradman (299*), K.E.Rigg (35)	Adelaide	1931-32	–	114	–	–	–	–	–
G.S.Chappell (52), G.J.Cosier (109)	Melbourne	1975-76	–	–	114	–	–	–	–
K.D.Walters (71*), R.W.Marsh (55)	Adelaide	1974-75	112	–	–	–	–	–	–
K.J.Hughes (89), G.N.Yallop (58)	Leeds	1981	112	–	–	–	–	–	–
K.D.Walters (118), A.P.Sheahan (47)	Sydney	1968-69	–	–	110	–	–	–	–
V.T.Trumper (166), C.Hill (44)	Sydney	1907-08	108	–	–	–	–	–	–
T.P.Horan (124), G.Giffen (30)	Melbourne	1881-82	107	–	–	–	–	–	–
G.H.S.Trott (92), H.Graham (42)	Oval	1893	106	–	–	–	–	–	–
W.W.Armstrong (77), C.G.Macartney (54)	Melbourne	1907-08	106	–	–	–	–	–	–
G.S.Chappell (131), R.Edwards (28)	Lord's	1972	106	–	–	–	–	–	–
R.N.Harvey (112), S.J.E.Loxton (93)	Leeds	1948	105	–	–	–	–	–	–
G.S.Chappell (61), A.R.Border (78)	Adelaide	1981-82	–	–	105	–	–	–	–
N.C.O'Neill (181), K.D.Mackay (35)	Brisbane[2]	1960-61	–	–	103	–	–	–	–
B.C.Booth (169), R.Benaud (43)	Brisbane[2]	1963-64	–	102	–	–	–	–	–
K.D.Walters (102), I.R.Redpath (33)	Madras[1]	1969-70	–	–	–	–	102	–	–
J.Ryder (79), O.E.Nothling (44)	Sydney	1928-29	101	–	–	–	–	–	–
R.B.Simpson (176), S.J.Rixon (50)	Perth	1977-78	–	–	–	–	101	–	–
A.R.Border (84), D.M.Wellham (103)	Oval	1981	101	–	–	–	–	–	–
D.C.Boon (109*), M.E.Waugh (39)	Kingston	1990-91	–	–	101	–	–	–	–
J.Darling (71), S.E.Gregory (117)	Oval	1899	100	–	–	–	–	–	–
P.M.Toohey (83), R.B.Simpson (39)	Perth	1977-78	–	–	–	–	100	–	–
Totals:	(69)		34	7	12	3	7	5	1

AUSTRALIA – 6th Wicket

			E	SA	WI	NZ	I	P	SL
J.H.W.Fingleton (136), D.G.Bradman (270)	Melbourne	1936-37	346	–	–	–	–	–	–
D.M.Jones (118*), S.R.Waugh (134*)	Hobart	1989-90	–	–	–	–	–	–	260*
I.R.Redpath (171), G.S.Chappell (108)	Perth	1970-71	219	–	–	–	–	–	–
K.R.Miller (137), R.G.Archer (98)	Bridgetown	1954-55	–	–	206	–	–	–	–
A.R.Border (152*), G.R.J.Matthews (115)	Brisbane[2]	1985-86	–	–	–	197	–	–	–
C.Kelleway (78), W.W.Armstrong (158)	Sydney	1920-21	187	–	–	–	–	–	–
S.R.Waugh (78*), I.A.Healy (102*)	Manchester	1993	180*	–	–	–	–	–	–
A.R.Border (140), S.R.Waugh (74)	Christchurch	1985-86	–	–	–	177	–	–	–
M.E.Waugh (138), G.R.J.Matthews (65)	Adelaide	1990-91	171	–	–	–	–	–	–
G.M.Wood (172), G.M.Ritchie (146)	Nottingham	1985	161	–	–	–	–	–	–
A.R.Border (74), G.R.J.Matthews (79)	Sydney	1992-93	–	–	155	–	–	–	–
T.R.Veivers (67), B.N.Jarman (78)	Bombay[2]	1964-65	–	–	–	–	151	–	–
G.R.J.Matthews (73*), S.R.Waugh (79*)	Adelaide	1986-87	146*	–	–	–	–	–	–
J.M.Gregory (77), W.W.Armstrong (123*)	Melbourne	1920-21	145	–	–	–	–	–	–
S.E.Gregory (57), H.Graham (107)	Lord's	1893	142	–	–	–	–	–	–
R.M.Cowper (83), T.R.Veivers (88)	Melbourne	1964-65	–	–	–	–	–	139	–
I.M.Chappell (151), B.N.Jarman (65)	Melbourne	1967-68	–	–	–	134	–	–	–
C.L.McCool (95), I.W.Johnson (47)	Brisbane[2]	1946-47	131	–	–	–	–	–	–
D.M.Jones (100*), G.R.J.Matthews (51)	Colombo (KS)	1992-93	–	–	–	–	–	–	131
A.R.Border (146*), W.B.Phillips (39*)	Manchester	1985	127*	–	–	–	–	–	–
G.N.Yallop (172), R.W.Marsh (71)	Faisalabad	1979-80	–	–	–	–	–	127	–
A.R.Border (106), G.R.J.Matthews (57)	Moratuwa	1992-93	–	–	–	–	–	–	127
C.Kelleway (147), C.E.Pellew (104)	Adelaide	1920-21	126	–	–	–	–	–	–

Hundred Partnerships (Australia)

6th Wicket *continued*

			E	SA	WI	NZ	I	P	SL
A.R.Border (54), W.B.Phillips (76)	Georgetown	1983-84	–	–	125	–	–	–	–
V.Y.Richardson (138), C.Kelleway (32)	Melbourne	1924-25	123	–	–	–	–	–	–
K.D.Walters (155), T.R.Veivers (56*)	Brisbane[2]	1965-66	119	–	–	–	–	–	–
I.M.Chappell (138), H.B.Taber (46)	Delhi	1969-70	–	–	–	–	118	–	–
G.S.Chappell (182*), R.W.Marsh (38)	Sydney	1975-76	–	–	117	–	–	–	–
G.M.Ritchie (89), G.R.J.Matthews (50)	Sydney	1985-86	–	–	115	–	–	–	–
D.M.Jones (116), P.L.Taylor (33)	Adelaide	1989-90	–	–	–	–	–	112	–
D.C.Boon (121), A.R.Border (83*)	Adelaide	1990-91	110	–	–	–	–	–	–
V.T.Trumper (113), R.B.Minnett (90)	Sydney	1911-12	109	–	–	–	–	–	–
S.R.Waugh (86), I.A.Healy (61)	Cape Town	1993-94	–	108	–	–	–	–	–
C.Kelleway (59), V.S.Ransford (75)	Melbourne	1910-11	–	107	–	–	–	–	–
R.N.Harvey (151*), C.L.McCool (39*)	Durban[2]	1949-50	–	106*	–	–	–	–	–
W.H.Ponsford (80), A.F.Kippax (42)	Sydney	1924-25	105	–	–	–	–	–	–
B.C.Booth (75), R.Benaud (43)	Sydney	1963-64	–	100	–	–	–	–	–
A.R.Border (98*), D.M.Jones (48)	Port-of-Spain	1983-84	–	–	100	–	–	–	–
Totals:	*(38)*		17	4	5	3	3	3	3

AUSTRALIA – 7th Wicket

			E	SA	WI	NZ	I	P	SL
K.D.Walters (250), G.J.Gilmour (101)	Christchurch	1976-77	–	–	–	217	–	–	–
G.N.Yallop (268), G.R.J.Matthews (75)	Melbourne	1983-84	–	–	–	–	–	185	–
R.W.Marsh (132), K.J.O'Keeffe (85)	Adelaide	1973-74	–	–	–	168	–	–	–
C.Hill (188), H.Trumble (46)	Melbourne	1897-98	165	–	–	–	–	–	–
R.Benaud (90), G.D.McKenzie (76)	Sydney	1963-64	–	160	–	–	–	–	–
K.R.Miller (145*), I.W.Johnson (77)	Sydney	1950-51	150	–	–	–	–	–	–
S.R.Waugh (177*), M.G.Hughes (71)	Leeds	1989	147	–	–	–	–	–	–
J.Ryder (201*), T.J.E.Andrews (72)	Adelaide	1924-25	134	–	–	–	–	–	–
A.K.Davidson (80), R.Benaud (52)	Brisbane[2]	1960-61	–	–	134	–	–	–	–
A.R.Border (153), G.R.Beard (49)	Lahore[2]	1979-80	–	–	–	–	–	134	–
G.R.J.Matthews (96), I.A.Healy (49)	Moratuwa	1992-93	–	–	–	–	–	–	129
K.R.Stackpole (134), G.D.Watson (50)	Cape Town	1966-67	–	128	–	–	–	–	–
R.W.Marsh (118), K.J.O'Keeffe (40)	Adelaide	1972-73	–	–	–	–	–	120	–
K.D.Mackay (31), R.Benaud (97)	Lord's	1956	117	–	–	–	–	–	–
K.D.Mackay (57), A.K.Davidson (71)	Sydney	1958-59	115	–	–	–	–	–	–
R.Benaud (64), A.T.W.Grout (74)	Melbourne	1958-59	115	–	–	–	–	–	–
H.L.Collins (61), J.M.Gregory (73)	Oval	1926	107	–	–	–	–	–	–
I.A.Healy (80), M.G.Hughes (38)	Birmingham	1993	107	–	–	–	–	–	–
B.C.Booth (112), K.D.Mackay (86*)	Brisbane[2]	1962-63	103	–	–	–	–	–	–
G.S.Chappell (150*), G.F.Lawson (49)	Brisbane[2]	1983-84	–	–	–	–	–	103	–
M.E.Waugh (71), I.A.Healy (53)	Georgetown	1990-91	–	–	101	–	–	–	–
K.C.Wessels (162), B.Yardley (53)	Brisbane[2]	1982-83	100	–	–	–	–	–	–
Totals:	*(22)*		11	2	2	2	–	4	1

AUSTRALIA – 8th Wicket

			E	SA	WI	NZ	I	P	SL
R.J.Hartigan (116), C.Hill (160)	Adelaide	1907-08	243	–	–	–	–	–	–
C.E.Pellew (116), J.M.Gregory (100)	Melbourne	1920-21	173	–	–	–	–	–	–
G.J.Bonnor (128), S.P.Jones (40)	Sydney	1884-85	154	–	–	–	–	–	–
D.Tallon (92), R.R.Lindwall (100)	Melbourne	1946-47	154	–	–	–	–	–	–
R.Benaud (128), I.W.Johnson (27*)	Kingston	1954-55	–	–	137	–	–	–	–
G.J.Cosier (168), K.J.O'Keeffe (28*)	Melbourne	1976-77	–	–	–	–	–	117	–
C.Kelleway (73), W.A.S.Oldfield (65*)	Sydney	1924-25	116	–	–	–	–	–	–
H.Graham (105), A.E.Trott (85*)	Sydney	1894-95	112	–	–	–	–	–	–
W.W.Armstrong (133*), H.Carter (66)	Melbourne	1907-08	112	–	–	–	–	–	–
A.R.Border (150*), R.J.Bright (26*)	Lahore[2]	1979-80	–	–	–	–	–	109*	–
A.L.Hassett (137), R.R.Lindwall (42)	Nottingham	1948	107	–	–	–	–	–	–
P.J.P.Burge (160), N.J.N.Hawke (37)	Leeds	1964	105	–	–	–	–	–	–
Totals:	*(12)*		9	–	1	–	–	2	–

AUSTRALIA – 9th Wicket

			E	SA	WI	NZ	I	P	SL
S.E.Gregory (201), J.M.Blackham (74)	Sydney	1894-95	154	–	–	–	–	–	–
S.R.Waugh (152*), G.F.Lawson (74)	Lord's	1989	130	–	–	–	–	–	–
D.M.Jones (216), M.G.Hughes (72*)	Adelaide	1988-89	–	–	114	–	–	–	–
J.Ryder (201*), W.A.S.Oldfield (47)	Adelaide	1924-25	108	–	–	–	–	–	–
R.W.Marsh (91), J.W.Gleeson (30)	Manchester	1972	104	–	–	–	–	–	–
A.E.V.Hartkopf (80), W.A.S.Oldfield (39*)	Melbourne	1924-25	100	–	–	–	–	–	–
M.H.N.Walker (78*), M.F.Malone (46)	Oval	1977	100	–	–	–	–	–	–
Totals:	*(7)*		6	–	1	–	–	–	–

AUSTRALIA – 10th Wicket

			E	SA	WI	NZ	I	P	SL
J.M.Taylor (108), A.A.Mailey (46*)	Sydney	1924-25	127	–	–	–	–	–	–
R.A.Duff (104), W.W.Armstrong (45*)	Melbourne	1901-02	120	–	–	–	–	–	–
	Totals:	*(2)*	2	–	–	–	–	–	–

SOUTH AFRICA – (150) – 1st Wicket

			E	A	WI	NZ	I	SL
B.Mitchell (123), I.J.Siedle (141)	Cape Town	1930-31	260	–	–	–	–	–
J.A.J.Christy (103), B.Mitchell (113)	Christchurch	1931-32	–	–	–	196	–	–
B.Mitchell (89), P.G.V.van der Bijl (97)	Durban²	1938-39	191	–	–	–	–	–
D.J.McGlew (133), T.L.Goddard (74)	Leeds	1955	176	–	–	–	–	–
D.J.McGlew (108), T.L.Goddard (90)	Johannesburg³	1957-58	–	176	–	–	–	–
B.Mitchell (61*), R.H.Catterall (98)	Birmingham	1929	171	–	–	–	–	–
B.A.Richards (81), E.J.Barlow (73)	Port Elizabeth	1969-70	–	157	–	–	–	–
H.W.Taylor (70), J.W.Zulch (82)	Johannesburg¹	1913-14	153	–	–	–	–	–
D.J.McGlew (104*), T.L.Goddard (62)	Manchester	1955	147	–	–	–	–	–
K.C.Wessels (92), A.C.Hudson (58)	Colombo (SSC)	1993-94	–	–	–	–	–	137
D.J.McGlew (120), E.J.Barlow (67)	Johannesburg³	1961-62	–	–	–	134	–	–
T.L.Goddard (60), E.J.Barlow (96)	Johannesburg³	1964-65	134	–	–	–	–	–
A.Melville (78), P.G.V.van der Bijl (125)	Durban²	1938-39	131	–	–	–	–	–
H.W.Taylor (87), J.W.Zulch (60)	Port Elizabeth	1913-14	129	–	–	–	–	–
B.Mitchell (73), I.J.Siedle (57)	Durban²	1930-31	127	–	–	–	–	–
B.Mitchell (88), R.H.Catterall (67)	Birmingham	1929	119	–	–	–	–	–
T.L.Goddard (40), E.J.Barlow (92)	Wellington	1963-64	–	–	–	117	–	–
T.L.Goddard (63), E.J.Barlow (49)	Dunedin	1963-64	–	–	–	117	–	–
B.Mitchell (128), I.J.Siedle (35)	Oval	1935	116	–	–	–	–	–
H.W.Taylor (71), J.M.M.Commaille (47)	Cape Town	1927-28	115	–	–	–	–	–
T.L.Goddard (73), E.J.Barlow (61)	Auckland	1963-64	–	–	–	115	–	–
T.L.Goddard (61), E.J.Barlow (69)	Port Elizabeth	1964-65	114	–	–	–	–	–
D.J.McGlew (84), J.H.B.Waite (43)	Durban²	1953-54	–	–	–	113	–	–
T.L.Goddard (74), E.J.Barlow (46)	Port Elizabeth	1966-67	–	112	–	–	–	–
H.W.Taylor (91), R.H.Catterall (52)	Durban²	1922-23	110	–	–	–	–	–
A.Melville (67), P.G.V.van der Bijl (31)	Johannesburg¹	1938-39	108	–	–	–	–	–
B.Mitchell (53), J.A.J.Christy (53)	Wellington	1931-32	–	–	–	104	–	–
D.J.McGlew (61), R.J.Westcott (43)	Johannesburg²	1953-54	–	–	–	104	–	–
K.C.Wessels (47), A.C.Hudson (90)	Moratuwa	1993-94	–	–	–	–	–	104
B.Mitchell (56), E.A.B.Rowan (37)	Port Elizabeth	1948-49	101	–	–	–	–	–
A.C.Hudson (90), G.Kirsten (43)	Adelaide	1993-94	–	100	–	–	–	–
A.C.Hudson (65), G.Kirsten (41)	Durban²	1993-94	–	100	–	–	–	–
	Totals:	*(32)*	17	5	–	8	–	2

SOUTH AFRICA – 2nd Wicket

			E	A	WI	NZ	I	SL
E.A.B.Brown (236), C.B.van Ryneveld (83)	Leeds	1951	198	–	–	–	–	–
L.J.Tancred (97), C.B.Llewellyn (90)	Johannesburg¹	1902-03	–	173	–	–	–	–
E.J.Barlow (138), A.J.Pithey (154)	Cape Town	1964-65	172	–	–	–	–	–
R.H.Catterall (76), H.W.Taylor (68)	Cape Town	1922-23	155	–	–	–	–	–
P.G.V.van der Bijl (87), E.A.B.Rowan (89*)	Cape Town	1938-39	147	–	–	–	–	–
A.Melville (104*), K.G.Viljoen (51*)	Nottingham	1947	145*	–	–	–	–	–
P.W.Sherwell (115), C.M.H.Hathorn (30)	Lord's	1907	139	–	–	–	–	–
J.W.Zulch (105), G.A.Faulkner (56)	Adelaide	1910-11	–	135	–	–	–	–
B.A.Richards (126), A.Bacher (73)	Port Elizabeth	1969-70	–	126	–	–	–	–
A.C.Hudson (163), K.C.Wessels (59)	Bridgetown	1991-92	–	–	125	–	–	–
T.L.Goddard (93), A.J.Pithey (49)	Sydney	1963-64	–	124	–	–	–	–
B.Mitchell (109), E.A.B.Rowan (67)	Durban²	1938-39	119	–	–	–	–	–
A.C.Hudson (52), W.J.Cronje (135)	Port Elizabeth	1992-93	–	–	–	–	117	–
T.L.Goddard (112), A.J.Pithey (39)	Johannesburg³	1964-65	115	–	–	–	–	–
E.A.B.Rowan (86*), K.G.Viljoen (53)	Johannesburg²	1948-49	113	–	–	–	–	–
T.L.Goddard (67), J.H.B.Waite (61)	Johannesburg³	1956-57	112	–	–	–	–	–
J.H.B.Waite (62), W.R.Endean (162*)	Melbourne	1952-53	–	111	–	–	–	–
L.J.Tancred (73), G.C.White (147)	Johannesburg¹	1905-06	110	–	–	–	–	–
J.W.Zulch (42), G.A.Faulkner (204)	Melbourne	1910-11	–	107	–	–	–	–
B.Mitchell (164*), E.A.B.Rowan (44)	Lord's	1935	104	–	–	–	–	–
A.C.Hudson (64*), W.J.Cronje (71)	Melbourne	1993-94	–	103*†	–	–	–	–
B.Mitchell (46), J.A.J.Christy (63)	Melbourne	1931-32	–	102	–	–	–	–
	Totals:	*(22)*	12	8	1	–	1	–

†108 runs were added for this wicket, A.C.Hudson retiring hurt and being succeeded by D.J.Cullinan after 103 runs had been scored.

Hundred Partnerships (South Africa)

SOUTH AFRICA – 3rd Wicket

			E	A	WI	NZ	I	SL
E.J.Barlow (201), R.G.Pollock (175)	Adelaide	1963-64	–	341	–	–	–	–
A.Melville (189), A.D.Nourse (149)	Nottingham	1947	319	–	–	–	–	–
D.J.McGlew (105), J.H.B.Waite (134)	Durban[2]	1957-58	–	231	–	–	–	–
B.Mitchell (120), A.D.Nourse (112)	Cape Town	1948-49	190	–	–	–	–	–
B.Mitchell (189*), A.D.Nourse (97)	Oval	1947	184	–	–	–	–	–
E.A.B.Rowan (143), A.D.Nourse (66)	Durban[2]	1949-50	–	167	–	–	–	–
E.A.B.Rowan (156*), A.D.Nourse (56*)	Johannesburg[2]	1948-49	162*	–	–	–	–	–
J.W.Zulch (150), G.A.Faulkner (92)	Sydney	1910-11	–	143	–	–	–	–
E.J.Barlow (110), R.G.Pollock (87)	Johannesburg[3]	1969-70	–	139	–	–	–	–
W.J.Cronje (122), K.C.Wessels (50)	Johannesburg[3]	1993-94	–	135	–	–	–	–
H.W.Taylor (101), A.W.Nourse (63)	Johannesburg[1]	1922-23	134	–	–	–	–	–
A.Bacher (60*), R.G.Pollock (67*)	Durban[2]	1966-67	–	127*	–	–	–	–
B.Mitchell (72), R.H.Catterall (54)	Johannesburg[1]	1930-31	122	–	–	–	–	–
B.Mitchell (95), H.W.Taylor (84)	Adelaide	1931-32	–	121	–	–	–	–
G.C.White (147), A.W.Nourse (55)	Johannesburg[1]	1905-06	120	–	–	–	–	–
B.Mitchell (75), H.W.Taylor (78)	Adelaide	1931-32	–	120	–	–	–	–
A.Melville (117), A.D.Nourse (61)	Lord's	1947	118	–	–	–	–	–
B.Mitchell (73), A.D.Nourse (73)	Johannesburg[1]	1938-39	116	–	–	–	–	–
E.A.B.Rowan (85), B.Mitchell (63)	Johannesburg[1]	1938-39	116	–	–	–	–	–
D.J.McGlew (120), R.A.McLean (78)	Johannesburg[3]	1961-62	–	–	–	112	–	–
G.A.Faulkner (204), A.W.Nourse (33)	Melbourne	1910-11	–	110	–	–	–	–
G.Kirsten (72), K.C.Wessels (105)	Lord's	1994	106	–	–	–	–	–
C.N.Frank (152), H.W.Taylor (80)	Johannesburg[1]	1921-22	–	105	–	–	–	–
W.J.Cronje (122), D.J.Cullinan (52)	Colombo (SSC)	1993-94	–	–	–	–	–	105
D.J.McGlew (127), R.A.McLean (63)	Durban[2]	1961-62	–	–	–	103	–	–
B.A.Richards (140), R.G.Pollock (274)	Durban[2]	1969-70	–	103	–	–	–	–
B.Mitchell (99), A.D.Nourse (73)	Port Elizabeth	1948-49	101	–	–	–	–	–
G.A.Faulkner (78), A.W.Nourse (53)	Johannesburg[1]	1909-10	100	–	–	–	–	–
H.W.Taylor (91), A.W.Nourse (52)	Durban[2]	1922-23	100	–	–	–	–	–
Totals:	*(29)*		14	12	–	2	–	1

SOUTH AFRICA – 4th Wicket

			E	A	WI	NZ	I	SL
H.W.Taylor (121), H.G.Deane (93)	Oval	1929	214	–	–	–	–	–
C.N.Frank (152), A.W.Nourse (111)	Johannesburg[1]	1921-22	–	206	–	–	–	–
B.Mitchell (99), W.W.Wade (125)	Port Elizabeth	1948-49	150	–	–	–	–	–
H.W.Taylor (117), R.H.Catterall (56)	Cape Town	1930-31	148	–	–	–	–	–
G.C.White (118), A.W.Nourse (69)	Durban[1]	1909-10	143	–	–	–	–	–
K.J.Funston (39), R.A.McLean (101)	Durban[2]	1953-54	–	–	–	135	–	–
B.Mitchell (45), A.D.Nourse (231)	Johannesburg[1]	1935-36	–	129	–	–	–	–
A.J.Pithey (76), J.H.B.Waite (77)	Melbourne	1963-64	–	128	–	–	–	–
A.D.Nourse (115), K.G.Viljoen (32)	Manchester	1947	121	–	–	–	–	–
S.J.Snooke (47), G.A.Faulkner (99)	Cape Town	1909-10	120	–	–	–	–	–
E.A.B.Rowan (49), A.D.Nourse (91)	Durban[2]	1935-36	–	118	–	–	–	–
A.J.Pithey (154), K.C.Bland (78)	Cape Town	1964-65	117	–	–	–	–	–
T.L.Goddard (99), J.H.B.Waite (77)	Oval	1960	115	–	–	–	–	–
G.C.White (72), G.A.Faulkner (76)	Johannesburg[1]	1909-10	114	–	–	–	–	–
M.J.Susskind (64), R.H.Catterall (120)	Lord's	1924	112	–	–	–	–	–
H.W.Taylor (176), W.V.S.Ling (38)	Johannesburg[1]	1922-23	111	–	–	–	–	–
J.H.B.Waite (44), K.J.Funston (92)	Adelaide	1952-53	–	108	–	–	–	–
J.F.W.Nicolson (78), R.H.Catterall (76)	Durban[2]	1927-28	107	–	–	–	–	–
W.R.Endean (87), J.C.Watkins (45)	Port Elizabeth	1953-54	–	–	–	107	–	–
A.D.Nourse (129*), W.W.Wade (54)	Johannesburg[2]	1948-49	106	–	–	–	–	–
J.H.B.Waite (115), W.R.Endean (50)	Johannesburg[3]	1957-58	–	104	–	–	–	–
J.N.Rhodes (35*), K.C.Wessels (58*)	Melbourne	1993-94	–	101*	–	–	–	–
D.J.McGlew (63), R.A.McLean (113)	Cape Town	1961-62	–	–	–	101	–	–
Totals:	*(23)*		13	7	–	3	–	–

SOUTH AFRICA – 5th Wicket

			E	A	WI	NZ	I	SL
A.J.Pithey (95), J.H.B.Waite (64)	Johannesburg[3]	1964-65	157	–	–	–	–	–
R.H.Catterall (119), H.B.Cameron (53)	Durban[2]	1927-28	135	–	–	–	–	–
W.R.Endean (116), J.E.Cheetham (54)	Auckland	1952-53	–	–	–	130	–	–
J.H.B.Waite (59), W.R.Endean (77)	Johannesburg[3]	1957-58	–	129	–	–	–	–
A.D.Nourse (208), G.M.Fullerton (54)	Nottingham	1951	121	–	–	–	–	–
H.R.Lance (53), D.T.Lindsay (81)	Cape Town	1966-67	–	119	–	–	–	–
R.H.Catterall (120), J.M.Blanckenberg (56)	Birmingham	1924	114	–	–	–	–	–
G.A.Faulkner (115), C.B.Llewellyn (80)	Adelaide	1910-11	–	109	–	–	–	–
E.A.B.Rowan (236), R.A.McLean (67)	Leeds	1951	108	–	–	–	–	–

5th Wicket *continued*

			E	A	WI	NZ	I	SL
H.J.Keith (40*), R.A.McLean (76*)	Melbourne	1952-53	–	106*	–	–	–	–
K.G.Viljoen (74), A.Melville (103)	Durban[2]	1938-39	104	–	–	–	–	–
P.N.Kirsten (49), J.N.Rhodes (78)	Durban[2]	1993-94	–	101	–	–	–	–
	Totals:	(12)	6	5	–	1	–	–

SOUTH AFRICA – 6th Wicket

			E	A	WI	NZ	I	SL
R.G.Pollock (274), H.R.Lance (61)	Durban[2]	1969-70	–	200	–	–	–	–
J.H.B.Waite (113), P.L.Winslow (108)	Manchester	1955	171	–	–	–	–	–
K.C.Bland (144*), G.D.Varnals (23)	Johannesburg[3]	1964-65	124	–	–	–	–	–
B.M.McMillan (93), D.J.Richardson (58)	Oval	1994	124	–	–	–	–	–
D.J.Cullinan (102), D.J.Richardson (62)	Colombo (PSS)	1993-94	–	–	–	–	–	122
K.C.Bland (126), D.T.Lindsay (65)	Sydney	1963-64	–	118	–	–	–	–
R.G.Pollock (137), P.L.van der Merwe (66)	Port Elizabeth	1964-65	113	–	–	–	–	–
R.G.Pollock (209), P.L.van der Merwe (50)	Cape Town	1966-67	–	112	–	–	–	–
H.R.Lance (44), D.T.Lindsay (69)	Johannesburg[3]	1966-67	–	110	–	–	–	–
R.A.McLean (142), H.J.Keith (57)	Lord's	1955	109	–	–	–	–	–
A.D.Nourse (231), F.Nicholson (29)	Johannesburg[1]	1935-36	–	106	–	–	–	–
R.A.McLean (109), S.O'Linn (27)	Manchester	1960	102	–	–	–	–	–
	Totals:	(12)	6	5	–	–	–	1

SOUTH AFRICA – 7th Wicket

			E	A	WI	NZ	I	SL
D.J.McGlew (255*), A.R.A.Murray (109)	Wellington	1952-53	–	–	–	246	–	–
D.T.Lindsay (182), P.L.van der Merwe (76)	Johannesburg[3]	1966-67	–	221	–	–	–	–
B.M.McMillan (84), D.J.Richardson (59)	Durban[2]	1993-94	–	143	–	–	–	–
H.G.Deane (73), E.P.Nupen (69)	Durban[2]	1927-28	123	–	–	–	–	–
G.C.White (81), A.W.Nourse (93*)	Johannesburg[1]	1905-06	121	–	–	–	–	–
P.N.Kirsten (104), B.M.McMillan (78)	Leeds	1994	115	–	–	–	–	–
J.E.Cheetham (66), P.N.F.Mansell (52)	Melbourne	1952-53	–	111	–	–	–	–
S.O'Linn (98), J.H.B.Waite (60)	Nottingham	1960	109	–	–	–	–	–
K.G.Viljoen (50), E.L.Dalton (102)	Johannesburg[1]	1938-39	108	–	–	–	–	–
A.D.Nourse (103), R.E.Grieveson (75)	Durban[2]	1938-39	107	–	–	–	–	–
X.C.Balaskas (122*), C.L.Vincent (33)	Wellington	1931-32	–	–	–	105	–	–
D.T.Lindsay (137), P.L.van der Merwe (42)	Durban[2]	1966-67	–	103	–	–	–	–
B.Mitchell (164*), A.B.C.Langton (44)	Lord's	1935	101	–	–	–	–	–
	Totals:	(13)	7	4	–	2	–	–

SOUTH AFRICA – 8th Wicket

			E	A	WI	NZ	I	SL
A.W.Nourse (72), E.A.Halliwell (57)	Johannesburg[1]	1902-03	–	124	–	–	–	–
B.Mitchell (189*), L.Tuckett (40*)	Oval	1947	109*	–	–	–	–	–
K.G.Viljoen (111), Q.McMillan (29)	Melbourne	1931-32	–	104	–	–	–	–
H.J.Tayfield (75), N.B.F.Mann (46)	Cape Town	1949-50	–	102	–	–	–	–
G.A.Faulkner (62), R.O.Schwarz (61)	Sydney	1910-11	–	100	–	–	–	–
	Totals:	(5)	1	4	–	–	–	–

SOUTH AFRICA – 9th Wicket

			E	A	WI	NZ	I	SL
E.L.Dalton (117), A.B.C.Langton (73*)	Oval	1935	137	–	–	–	–	–

SOUTH AFRICA – 10th Wicket

			E	A	WI	NZ	I	SL
H.G.Owen-Smith (129), A.J.Bell (26*)	Leeds	1929	103	–	–	–	–	–

WEST INDIES – (334) – 1st Wicket

			E	A	SA	NZ	I	P	SL
C.G.Greenidge (149), D.L.Haynes (167)	St John's	1989-90	298	–	–	–	–	–	–
C.G.Greenidge (154*), D.L.Haynes (136)	St John's	1982-83	–	–	–	–	296	–	–
C.G.Greenidge (120*), D.L.Haynes (103*)	Georgetown	1983-84	–	250*	–	–	–	–	–
J.B.Stollmeyer (160), A.F.Rae (109)	Madras[1]	1948-49	–	–	–	–	239	–	–
C.G.Greenidge (97), D.L.Haynes (122)	Christchurch	1979-80	–	–	–	225	–	–	–
R.C.Fredericks (94), L.G.Rowe (120)	Kingston	1973-74	206	–	–	–	–	–	–
J.B.Stollmeyer (152), A.F.Rae (99)	Auckland	1951-52	–	–	–	197	–	–	–
R.C.Fredericks (109), C.G.Greenidge (115)	Leeds	1976	192	–	–	–	–	–	–
R.C.Fredericks (86*), C.G.Greenidge (85*)	Oval	1976	182*	–	–	–	–	–	–
R.C.Fredericks (83), C.G.Greenidge (82)	Kingston	1976-77	–	–	–	–	182	–	–
G.M.Carew (107), A.G.Ganteaume (112)	Port-of-Spain	1947-48	173	–	–	–	–	–	–
C.G.Greenidge (84), D.L.Haynes (96)	Port-of-Spain	1980-81	168	–	–	–	–	–	–
C.G.Greenidge (127), D.L.Haynes (60)	Kingston	1983-84	–	162	–	–	–	–	–
C.C.Hunte (92), J.K.Holt (123)	Delhi	1958-59	–	–	–	–	159	–	–
R.C.Fredericks (52*), C.G.Greenidge (96)	Georgetown	1976-77	–	–	–	–	154	–	–

Hundred Partnerships (West Indies)

1st Wicket *continued*

			E	A	SA	NZ	I	P	SL
C.G.Greenidge (78), D.L.Haynes (121)	Wellington	1986-87	–	–	–	150	–	–	–
C.C.Hunte (81), B.A.Davis (68)	Bridgetown	1964-65	–	145	–	–	–	–	–
C.A.Roach (209), E.A.C.Hunte (53)	Georgetown	1929-30	144	–	–	–	–	–	–
J.B.Stollmeyer (76*), A.F.Rae (63*)	Port-of-Spain	1952-53	–	–	–	–	142*	–	–
C.G.Greenidge (93), A.I.Kallicharan (124)	Bangalore	1974-75	–	–	–	–	139†	–	–
C.G.Greenidge (80), D.L.Haynes (40)	Brisbane²	1988-89	–	135	–	–	–	–	–
J.B.Stollmeyer (66), A.F.Rae (104)	Bombay²	1948-49	–	–	–	–	134	–	–
C.G.Greenidge (64), D.L.Haynes (145)	Bridgetown	1983-84	–	132	–	–	–	–	–
C.G.Greenidge (80*), D.L.Haynes (55)	Bridgetown	1977-78	–	131	–	–	–	–	–
C.G.Greenidge (77), D.L.Haynes (77*)	Oval	1988	131	–	–	–	–	–	–
C.G.Greenidge (226), D.L.Haynes (40)	Bridgetown	1990-91	–	129	–	–	–	–	–
R.C.Fredericks (32), L.G.Rowe (302)	Bridgetown	1973-74	126	–	–	–	–	–	–
C.C.Hunte (114), R.B.Kanhai (62)	Georgetown	1957-58	–	–	–	–	–	125	–
C.C.Hunte (142), R.B.Kanhai (27)	Bridgetown	1957-58	–	–	–	–	–	122	–
D.L.Haynes (125), P.V.Simmons (87)	Bridgetown	1992-93	–	–	–	–	–	122	–
G.S.Camacho (87), M.C.Carew (36)	Port-of-Spain	1967-68	119	–	–	–	–	–	–
C.G.Greenidge (35), D.L.Haynes (84)	Kingston	1990-91	–	118	–	–	–	–	–
C.C.Hunte (89), B.A.Davis (54)	Port-of-Spain	1964-65	–	116	–	–	–	–	–
R.C.Fredericks (50), C.G.Greenidge (101)	Manchester	1976	116	–	–	–	–	–	–
C.G.Greenidge (62), D.L.Haynes (84)	Kingston	1980-81	116	–	–	–	–	–	–
C.G.Greenidge (69), D.L.Haynes (47)	Calcutta	1987-88	–	–	–	–	114	–	–
R.C.Fredericks (67), L.G.Rowe (123)	Port-of-Spain	1973-74	110	–	–	–	–	–	–
R.C.Fredericks (63), G.S.Camacho (67)	Lord's	1969	106	–	–	–	–	–	–
C.G.Greenidge (49), D.L.Haynes (43)	Leeds	1984	106	–	–	–	–	–	–
R.C.Fredericks (82), L.G.Rowe (47)	Kingston	1975-76	–	–	–	–	105	–	–
J.B.Stollmeyer (52*), A.F.Rae (46*)	Nottingham	1950	103*	–	–	–	–	–	–
S.M.Nurse (73), G.S.Camacho (25)	Kingston	1967-68	102	–	–	–	–	–	–
R.C.Fredericks (39), M.C.Carew (64)	Sydney	1968-69	–	100	–	–	–	–	–
D.L.Haynes (70), R.B.Richardson (31)	St John's	1985-86	100	–	–	–	–	–	–
Totals: (44)			18	10	–	3	8	5	–

†177 runs were added for this wicket, R.C.Fredericks retiring hurt and being succeeded by A.I.Kallicharran after 38 runs had been scored.

Although the 1st wicket added 111 against Australia (5th Test – Perth) in 1992-93, this consisted of two partnerships: P.V.Simmons added 34* with D.L.Haynes (retired hurt) and a further 77 with R.B.Richardson.

WEST INDIES – 2nd Wicket

			E	A	SA	NZ	I	P	SL
C.C.Hunte (260), G.St.A.Sobers (365*)	Kingston	1957-58	–	–	–	–	–	446	–
D.L.Haynes (111), R.B.Richardson (182)	Georgetown	1990-91	–	297	–	–	–	–	–
C.G.Greenidge (214*), H.A.Gomes (92*)	Lord's	1984	287*	–	–	–	–	–	–
G.St A.Sobers (125), C.L.Walcott (145)	Georgetown	1957-58	–	–	–	–	–	269	–
R.C.Fredericks (163), L.G.Rowe (214)	Kingston	1971-72	–	–	–	269	–	–	–
E.D.A.St J.McMorris (125), R.B.Kanhai (158)	Kingston	1961-62	–	–	–	–	255	–	–
L.G.Rowe (302), A.I.Kallicharran (119)	Bridgetown	1973-74	249	–	–	–	–	–	–
M.C.Carew (91), S.M.Nurse (258)	Christchurch	1968-69	–	–	–	231	–	–	–
R.K.Nunes (92), G.A.Headley (223)	Kingston	1929-30	227	–	–	–	–	–	–
D.L.Haynes (184), I.V.A.Richards (145)	Lord's	1980	223	–	–	–	–	–	–
J.K.Holt (166), F.M.M.Worrell (76*)	Bridgetown	1953-54	222	–	–	–	–	–	–
I.Barrow (105), G.A.Headley (169)	Manchester	1933	200	–	–	–	–	–	–
D.L.Haynes (84), R.B.Richardson (160)	Bridgetown	1985-86	194	–	–	–	–	–	–
C.A.Roach (209), G.A.Headley (114)	Georgetown	1929-30	192	–	–	–	–	–	–
D.L.Haynes (90), R.B.Richardson (185)	Georgetown	1984-85	–	–	–	191	–	–	–
C.G.Greenidge (82), R.B.Richardson (194)	Georgetown	1988-89	–	–	–	–	178	–	–
A.F.Rae (109), F.M.M.Worrell (138)	Oval	1950	172	–	–	–	–	–	–
M.C.Carew (109), S.M.Nurse (95)	Auckland	1968-69	–	–	–	172	–	–	–
D.L.Haynes (83), R.B.Richardson (106)	Adelaide	1988-89	–	167	–	–	–	–	–
D.M.Lewis (88), R.B.Kanhai (85)	Bridgetown	1970-71	–	–	–	–	166	–	–
M.C.Carew (83), R.B.Kanhai (94)	Brisbane²	1968-69	–	165	–	–	–	–	–
C.C.Hunte (79), R.B.Kanhai (115)	Adelaide	1960-61	–	163	–	–	–	–	–
C.A.Roach (77), G.A.Headley (176)	Bridgetown	1929-30	156	–	–	–	–	–	–
R.C.Fredericks (71), I.V.A.Richards (291)	Oval	1976	154	–	–	–	–	–	–
F.R.Martin (123), G.A.Headley (105)	Sydney	1930-31	–	152	–	–	–	–	–
C.C.Hunte (182), R.B.Kanhai (90)	Manchester	1963	151	–	–	–	–	–	–
D.L.Haynes (67), R.B.Richardson (102)	Port-of-Spain	1985-86	150	–	–	–	–	–	–
C.G.Greenidge (141), R.B.Richardson (51)	Calcutta	1987-88	–	–	–	–	147	–	–
D.L.Haynes (145), R.B.Richardson (131*)	Bridgetown	1983-84	–	145	–	–	–	–	–
C.G.Greenidge (76), I.V.A.Richards (74)	Adelaide	1979-80	–	136	–	–	–	–	–
C.C.Hunte (114), G.St A.Sobers (109*)	Georgetown	1957-58	–	–	–	–	–	135	–

2nd Wicket *continued*

			E	A	SA	NZ	I	P	SL
J.B.Stollmeyer (60), J.K.Holt (94)	Kingston	1953-54	134	–	–	–	–	–	–
P.V.Simmons (110), R.B.Richardson (52)	Melbourne	1992-93	–	134	–	–	–	–	–
M.C.Carew (90), R.B.Kanhai (80)	Adelaide	1968-69	–	132	–	–	–	–	–
R.C.Fredericks (52), I.V.A.Richards (91)	Bridgetown	1976-77	–	–	–	–	–	130	–
D.L.Haynes (112*), R.B.Richardson (59)	Bridgetown	1988-89	–	–	–	–	128	–	–
D.L.Haynes (92), I.V.A.Richards (80)	Bridgetown	1982-83	–	–	–	–	122	–	–
C.G.Greenidge (63), I.V.A.Richards (114)	St John's	1980-81	121	–	–	–	–	–	–
E.D.A.St J.McMorris (50), R.B.Kanhai (139)	Port-of-Spain	1961-62	–	–	–	–	119	–	–
J.B.Stollmeyer (59), G.A.Headley (106)	Lord's	1939	118	–	–	–	–	–	–
D.L.Haynes (40), I.V.A.Richards (75)	Lahore[2]	1980-81	–	–	–	–	–	117	–
C.G.Greenidge (117), R.B.Richardson (93)	Bridgetown	1988-89	–	–	–	–	117	–	–
D.L.Haynes (57*), R.B.Richardson (52*)	Nottingham	1991	114*	–	–	–	–	–	–
D.L.Haynes (63), B.C.Lara (167)	Georgetown	1993-94	114	–	–	–	–	–	–
J.B.Stollmeyer (59), G.A.Headley (65)	Oval	1939	113	–	–	–	–	–	–
C.C.Hunte (180*), R.B.Kanhai (77)	Oval	1963	113	–	–	–	–	–	–
R.C.Fredericks (138), A.I.Kallicharran (34)	Lord's	1976	113	–	–	–	–	–	–
R.C.Fredericks (104), A.I.Kallicharran (98)	Bombay[3]	1974-75	–	–	–	–	113	–	–
C.G.Greenidge (48), I.V.A.Richards (96)	Melbourne	1979-80	–	110	–	–	–	–	–
C.G.Greenidge (101), I.V.A.Richards (135)	Manchester	1976	108	–	–	–	–	–	–
D.L.Haynes (28), I.V.A.Richards (76)	Adelaide	1979-80	–	104	–	–	–	–	–
R.C.Fredericks (43), R.B.Kanhai (69)	Sydney	1968-69	–	103	–	–	–	–	–
M.C.Carew (45), C.A.Davis (125*)	Georgetown	1970-71	–	–	–	–	103	–	–
D.L.Haynes (100), R.B.Richardson (48)	Perth	1988-89	–	103	–	–	–	–	–
D.L.Haynes (143*), R.B.Richardson (68)	Port-of-Spain	1992-93	–	–	–	–	–	103	–
J.K.Holt (60), O.G.Smith (104)	Kingston	1954-55	–	102	–	–	–	–	–
R.C.Fredericks (76), A.I.Kallicharran (91)	Port-of-Spain	1972-73	–	102	–	–	–	–	–
C.G.Greenidge (52), I.V.A.Richards (50)	Adelaide	1981-82	–	100	–	–	–	–	–
	Totals:	*(58)*	22	16	–	4	10	6	–

WEST INDIES – 3rd Wicket

			E	A	SA	NZ	I	P	SL
E.de C.Weekes (206), F.M.M.Worrell (167)	Port-of-Spain	1953-54	338	–	–	–	–	–	–
R.B.Richardson (154), I.V.A.Richards (178)	St John's	1983-84	–	308	–	–	–	–	–
I.V.A.Richards (232), A.I.Kallicharran (97)	Nottingham	1976	303	–	–	–	–	–	–
R.B.Richardson (109), B.C.Lara (277)	Sydney	1992-93	–	293	–	–	–	–	–
S.M.Nurse (136), R.B.Kanhai (153)	Port-of-Spain	1967-68	273	–	–	–	–	–	–
C.L.Walcott (126), E.de C.Weekes (139)	Port-of-Spain	1954-55	–	242	–	–	–	–	–
I.V.A.Richards (142), A.I.Kallicharran (93)	Bridgetown	1975-76	–	–	–	–	220	–	–
H.A.Gomes (143), I.V.A.Richards (117)	Birmingham	1984	206	–	–	–	–	–	–
G.A.Headley (270*), J.E.D.Sealy (91)	Kingston	1934-35	202	–	–	–	–	–	–
R.B.Kanhai (129), S.M.Nurse (201)	Bridgetown	1964-65	–	200	–	–	–	–	–
C.G.Greenidge (226), R.B.Richardson (99)	Bridgetown	1990-91	–	199	–	–	–	–	–
F.M.M.Worrell (237), E.de C.Weekes (109)	Kingston	1952-53	–	–	–	–	197	–	–
I.V.A.Richards (291), L.G.Rowe (70)	Oval	1976	191	–	–	–	–	–	–
C.G.Greenidge (100), R.B.Richardson (78)	Port-of-Spain	1984-85	–	–	–	185	–	–	–
B.C.Lara (375), J.C.Adams (59)	St John's	1993-94	179	–	–	–	–	–	–
S.M.Nurse (168), B.F.Butcher (78*)	Auckland	1968-69	–	–	–	174	–	–	–
D.L.Haynes (143*), B.C.Lara (96)	Port-of-Spain	1992-93	–	–	–	–	–	169	–
R.B.Kanhai (217), G.St A.Sobers (72)	Lahore[1]	1958-59	–	–	–	–	–	162	–
A.F.Rae (62), F.M.M.Worrell (261)	Nottingham	1950	143	–	–	–	–	–	–
G.A.Headley (176), F.I.de Caires (70)	Bridgetown	1929-30	142	–	–	–	–	–	–
R.B.Kanhai (157), C.H.Lloyd (63)	Lord's	1973	138	–	–	–	–	–	–
R.B.Kanhai (89), B.F.Butcher (49)	Georgetown	1964-65	–	135	–	–	–	–	–
E.D.A.St J.McMorris (73), G.St A.Sobers (147)	Kingston	1959-60	133*†	–	–	–	–	–	–
I.V.A.Richards (135), C.H.Lloyd (43)	Manchester	1976	132	–	–	–	–	–	–
C.G.Greenidge (95), H.A.Gomes (60)	Adelaide	1984-85	–	132	–	–	–	–	–
S.F.A.F.Bacchus (250), R.R.Jumadeen (56)	Kanpur	1978-79	–	–	–	–	129	–	–
J.B.Stollmeyer (104*), E.de C.Weekes (55*)	Port-of-Spain	1952-53	–	–	–	–	127*	–	–
C.L.Walcott (110), E.de C.Weekes (87*)	Port-of-Spain	1954-55	–	127	–	–	–	–	–
I.V.A.Richards (101), A.I.Kallicharran (67)	Adelaide	1975-76	–	127	–	–	–	–	–
R.C.Fredericks (169), A.I.Kallicharran (57)	Perth	1975-76	–	124	–	–	–	–	–
C.G.Greenidge (141), I.V.A.Richards (68)	Calcutta	1987-88	–	–	–	–	124	–	–
S.M.Nurse (70), R.B.Kanhai (84)	Melbourne	1960-61	–	123	–	–	–	–	–
R.B.Richardson (51), H.A.Gomes (68)	Melbourne	1984-85	–	123	–	–	–	–	–
I.V.A.Richards (98), A.I.Kallicharran (44)	Melbourne	1975-76	–	117	–	–	–	–	–
C.C.Hunte (81), B.F.Butcher (71)	Kingston	1964-65	–	116	–	–	–	–	–
L.G.Rowe (76), A.I.Kallicharran (50)	Kingston	1972-73	–	116	–	–	–	–	–
J.B.Stollmeyer (152), E.de C.Weekes (51)	Auckland	1951-52	–	–	–	115	–	–	–
R.B.Kanhai (55), G.St A.Sobers (145)	Georgetown	1959-60	115	–	–	–	–	–	–

Hundred Partnerships (West Indies)

3rd Wicket *continued*

			E	A	SA	NZ	I	P	SL
R.B.Kanhai (158*), C.H.Lloyd (57)	Kingston	1970-71	–	–	–	–	115	–	–
D.L.Haynes (78), I.V.A.Richards (78)	Port-of-Spain	1984-85	–	–	–	114	–	–	–
D.L.Haynes (100), C.L.Hooper (64)	Perth	1988-89	–	113	–	–	–	–	–
A.I.Kallicharran (93), C.H.Lloyd (49)	Kingston	1973-74	112	–	–	–	–	–	–
D.L.Haynes (143), C.L.Hooper (35)	Sydney	1988-89	–	111	–	–	–	–	–
F.R.Martin (123*), G.C.Grant (62)	Sydney	1930-31	–	110	–	–	–	–	–
J.B.Stollmeyer (85), E.de C.Weekes (56)	Bombay²	1948-49	–	–	–	–	110	–	–
G.St A.Sobers (147), S.M.Nurse (70)	Kingston	1959-60	110†	–	–	–	–	–	–
R.B.Kanhai (63), B.F.Butcher (209*)	Nottingham	1966	110	–	–	–	–	–	–
F.M.M.Worrell (191*), R.B.Kanhai (42)	Nottingham	1957	109	–	–	–	–	–	–
H.A.Gomes (63), A.I.Kallicharran (187)	Bombay³	1978-79	–	–	–	–	109	–	–
R.B.Kanhai (256), O.G.Smith (34)	Calcutta	1958-59	–	–	–	–	108	–	–
G.S.Camacho (71), B.F.Butcher (91)	Leeds	1969	108	–	–	–	–	–	–
I.V.A.Richards (114), E.H.Mattis (71)	St John's	1980-81	108	–	–	–	–	–	–
R.B.Richardson (185), H.A.Gomes (53)	Georgetown	1984-85	–	–	–	106	–	–	–
A.F.Rae (106), E.de C.Weekes (63)	Lord's	1950	105	–	–	–	–	–	–
I.V.A.Richards (140), A.I.Kallicharran (38)	Brisbane²	1979-80	–	105	–	–	–	–	–
J.B.Stollmeyer (78), G.E.Gomez (86)	Bridgetown	1947-48	104	–	–	–	–	–	–
A.I.Kallicharran (98), C.H.Lloyd (242*)	Bombay³	1974-75	–	–	–	–	104	–	–
C.G.Greenidge (69), R.B.Richardson (60)	Georgetown	1984-85	–	–	–	104	–	–	–
D.L.Haynes (125), B.C.Lara (51)	Bridgetown	1992-93	–	–	–	–	–	103	–
L.G.Rowe (123), C.H.Lloyd (52)	Port-of-Spain	1973-74	102	–	–	–	–	–	–
A.B.Williams (111), A.I.Kallicharran (55)	Calcutta	1978-79	–	–	–	–	102	–	–
A.I.Kallicharran (101), C.A.Davis (40)	Port-of-Spain	1971-72	–	–	–	101	–	–	–
	Totals:	(62)	22	19	–	7	11	3	–

†243 runs were added for this wicket, E.D.A.St J.McMorris retiring hurt and being succeeded by S.M.Nurse after 133 runs had been scored.

WEST INDIES – 4th Wicket

			E	A	SA	NZ	I	P	SL
G.St A.Sobers (226), F.M.M.Worrell (197*)	Bridgetown	1959-60	399	–	–	–	–	–	–
F.M.M.Worrell (261), E.de C.Weekes (129)	Nottingham	1950	283	–	–	–	–	–	–
C.L.Walcott (152), G.E.Gomez (101)	Delhi	1948-49	–	–	–	–	267	–	–
R.B.Kanhai (150), G.St A.Sobers (152)	Georgetown	1967-68	250	–	–	–	–	–	–
H.A.Gomes (123), C.H.Lloyd (143)	Port-of-Spain	1982-83	–	–	–	–	237	–	–
R.B.Richardson (156), I.V.A.Richards (110)	Kingston	1988-89	–	–	–	–	235	–	–
R.B.Kanhai (256), B.F.Butcher (103)	Calcutta	1958-59	–	–	–	–	217	–	–
F.M.M.Worrell (237), C.L.Walcott (118)	Kingston	1952-53	–	–	–	–	213	–	–
C.H.Lloyd (132), A.I.Kallicharran (80)	Oval	1973	208	–	–	–	–	–	–
C.G.Greenidge (107), C.H.Lloyd (163)	Bangalore	1974-75	–	–	–	–	207	–	–
L.G.Rowe (107), A.I.Kallicharran (101)	Brisbane²	1975-76	–	198	–	–	–	–	–
G.St A.Sobers (365*), C.L.Walcott (88*)	Kingston	1957-58	–	–	–	–	–	188*	–
C.H.Lloyd (178), R.B.Kanhai (57)	Georgetown	1972-73	–	187	–	–	–	–	–
B.C.Lara (375), K.L.T.Arthurton (47)	St John's	1993-94	183	–	–	–	–	–	–
C.L.Walcott (110), G.St A.Sobers (64)	Kingston	1954-55	–	179	–	–	–	–	–
G.St A.Sobers (132), F.M.M.Worrell (65)	Brisbane²	1960-61	–	174	–	–	–	–	–
I.V.A.Richards (291), C.H.Lloyd (84)	Oval	1976	174	–	–	–	–	–	–
R.B.Kanhai (158*), G.St A.Sobers (93)	Kingston	1970-71	–	–	–	–	173	–	–
C.A.Davis (125*), G.St A.Sobers (108*)	Georgetown	1970-71	–	–	–	–	170*	–	–
A.I.Kallicharran (127), C.H.Lloyd (86)	Port-of-Spain	1977-78	–	170	–	–	–	–	–
C.A.Davis (79), G.St A.Sobers (178*)	Bridgetown	1970-71	–	–	–	–	167	–	–
C.L.Walcott (220), B.H.Pairaudeau (71)	Bridgetown	1953-54	165	–	–	–	–	–	–
L.Baichan (105*), C.H.Lloyd (83)	Lahore²	1974-75	–	–	–	–	–	164	–
E.de C.Weekes (123), O.G.Smith (64)	Dunedin	1955-56	–	–	–	162	–	–	–
C.G.Greenidge (91), A.I.Kallicharran (75)	Christchurch	1979-80	–	–	–	162	–	–	–
B.F.Butcher (117), G.St A.Sobers (69)	Port-of-Spain	1964-65	–	160	–	–	–	–	–
S.M.Nurse (201), C.C.Hunte (75)	Bridgetown	1964-65	–	146	–	–	–	–	–
B.C.Lara (83), K.L.T.Arthurton (126)	Kingston	1993-94	144	–	–	–	–	–	–
R.B.Kanhai (92), G.St A.Sobers (102)	Leeds	1963	143	–	–	–	–	–	–
A.I.Kallicharran (115), C.H.Lloyd (73)	Karachi¹	1974-75	–	–	–	–	–	139	–
C.L.Hooper (55*), I.V.A.Richards (73*)	Birmingham	1991	133*	–	–	–	–	–	–
E.de C.Weekes (86), C.L.Walcott (125)	Georgetown	1952-53	–	–	–	–	130	–	–
F.M.M.Worrell (71), C.L.Walcott (65)	Christchurch	1951-52	–	–	–	129	–	–	–
B.F.Butcher (71), O.G.Smith (100)	Delhi	1958-59	–	–	–	–	127	–	–
C.L.Walcott (73), F.M.M.Worrell (56)	Georgetown	1954-55	–	125	–	–	–	–	–
F.I.de Caires (80), J.E.D.Sealy (58)	Bridgetown	1929-30	124	–	–	–	–	–	–
I.V.A.Richards (177), C.H.Lloyd (68)	Port-of-Spain	1975-76	–	–	–	–	124	–	–
C.L.Hooper (111), I.V.A.Richards (63)	Lord's	1991	124	–	–	–	–	–	–

4th Wicket *continued*

	Venue	Season	E	A	SA	NZ	I	P	SL
B.C.Lara (277), K.L.T.Arthurton (47)	Sydney	1992-93	–	124	–	–	–	–	–
C.G.Greenidge (104), I.V.A.Richards (68*)	Adelaide	1988-89	–	123	–	–	–	–	–
C.C.Hunte (182), G.St A.Sobers (64)	Manchester	1963	120	–	–	–	–	–	–
G.St A.Sobers (142*), O.G.Smith (58)	Bombay²	1958-59	–	–	–	–	119	–	–
I.V.A.Richards (140), L.G.Rowe (50)	Brisbane²	1979-80	–	119	–	–	–	–	–
C.A.Best (164), I.V.A.Richards (70)	Bridgetown	1989-90	119	–	–	–	–	–	–
R.B.Richardson (104*), I.V.A.Richards (52*)	Kingston	1990-91	–	118*	–	–	–	–	–
R.B.Kanhai (85), C.H.Lloyd (118)	Port-of-Spain	1967-68	116	–	–	–	–	–	–
D.L.Haynes (109), A.L.Logie (48)	Bridgetown	1989-90	114	–	–	–	–	–	–
B.C.Lara (58), K.L.T.Arthurton (157*)	Brisbane²	1992-93	–	112	–	–	–	–	–
B.C.Lara (167), J.C.Adams (137)	Georgetown	1993-94	112	–	–	–	–	–	–
C.C.Hunte (101), C.H.Lloyd (82)	Bombay²	1966-67	–	–	–	–	110	–	–
C.L.Walcott (155), F.M.M.Worrell (61)	Kingston	1954-55	–	109	–	–	–	–	–
R.B.Richardson (81), I.V.A.Richards (68)	Brisbane²	1988-89	–	108	–	–	–	–	–
R.B.Kanhai (117), F.M.M.Worrell (71)	Adelaide	1960-61	–	107	–	–	–	–	–
B.F.Butcher (209*), S.M.Nurse (53)	Nottingham	1966	107	–	–	–	–	–	–
H.A.Gomes (38), C.H.Lloyd (68)	Ahmedabad	1983-84	–	–	–	–	107	–	–
B.C.Lara (52), K.L.T.Arthurton (71)	Melbourne	1992-93	–	106	–	–	–	–	–
I.V.A.Richards (72), C.H.Lloyd (39)	Lord's	1984	103	–	–	–	–	–	–
H.A.Gomes (48), I.V.A.Richards (87)	Port-of-Spain	1985-86	102	–	–	–	–	–	–
C.G.Greenidge (226), C.L.Hooper (57)	Bridgetown	1990-91	–	102	–	–	–	–	–
E.de C.Weekes (207), C.L.Walcott (47)	Port-of-Spain	1952-53	–	–	–	–	101	–	–
C.W.Smith (55), F.M.M.Worrell (82)	Sydney	1960-61	–	101	–	–	–	–	–
B.F.Butcher (60), C.H.Lloyd (113*)	Bridgetown	1967-68	101	–	–	–	–	–	–
Totals: (62)			21	19	–	3	16	3	–

WEST INDIES – 5th Wicket

	Venue	Season	E	A	SA	NZ	I	P	SL
S.M.Nurse (137), G.St A.Sobers (174)	Leeds	1966	265	–	–	–	–	–	–
E.de C.Weekes (207), B.H.Pairaudeau (115)	Port-of-Spain	1952-53	–	–	–	–	219	–	–
B.C.Lara (375), S.Chanderpaul (75*)	St John's	1993-94	219	–	–	–	–	–	–
R.B.Kanhai (84), M.L.C.Foster (125)	Kingston	1972-73	–	210	–	–	–	–	–
C.G.Greenidge (223), P.J.L.Dujon (101)	Manchester	1984	197	–	–	–	–	–	–
F.M.M.Worrell (100), C.L.Walcott (115)	Auckland	1951-52	–	–	–	189	–	–	–
E.de C.Weekes (197), O.G.Smith (78)	Bridgetown	1957-58	–	–	–	–	–	185	–
C.A.Davis (105), G.St A.Sobers (132)	Port-of-Spain	1970-71	–	–	–	–	177	–	–
B.F.Butcher (209*), S.M.Nurse (94)	Nottingham	1966	173	–	–	–	–	–	–
E.de C.Weekes (194), R.J.Christiani (74)	Bombay²	1948-49	–	–	–	–	170	–	–
A.L.Logie (101), C.L.Hooper (100*)	Calcutta	1987-88	–	–	–	–	169	–	–
L.G.Rowe (100), C.L.King (100*)	Christchurch	1979-80	–	–	–	168	–	–	–
A.I.Kallicharran (187), D.A.Murray (84)	Bombay³	1978-79	–	–	–	–	167	–	–
C.H.Lloyd (149), D.L.Murray (63)	Perth	1975-76	–	164	–	–	–	–	–
V.H.Stollmeyer (96), K.H.Weekes (137)	Oval	1939	163	–	–	–	–	–	–
I.V.A.Richards (146), A.L.Logie (93)	Perth	1988-89	–	163	–	–	–	–	–
S.F.A.F.Bacchus (250), D.A.Murray (44)	Kanpur	1978-79	–	–	–	–	160	–	–
C.H.Lloyd (100), H.A.Gomes (58)	Bridgetown	1980-81	154	–	–	–	–	–	–
G.St A.Sobers (142*), B.F.Butcher (64*)	Bombay²	1958-59	–	–	–	–	134*	–	–
S.M.Nurse (74), G.St A.Sobers (67)	Melbourne	1968-69	–	134	–	–	–	–	–
A.L.Logie (130), C.H.Lloyd (50)	Bridgetown	1982-83	–	–	–	–	133	–	–
G.St A.Sobers (168), S.M.Nurse (43)	Sydney	1960-61	–	128	–	–	–	–	–
J.C.Adams (137), S.Chanderpaul (62)	Georgetown	1993-94	126	–	–	–	–	–	–
H.A.Gomes (143), C.H.Lloyd (71)	Birmingham	1984	124	–	–	–	–	–	–
R.B.Kanhai (104), G.St A.Sobers (81)	Oval	1966	122	–	–	–	–	–	–
I.V.A.Richards (130), D.L.Murray (46)	Port-of-Spain	1975-76	–	–	–	–	122	–	–
G.St A.Sobers (145), F.M.M.Worrell (38)	Georgetown	1959-60	121	–	–	–	–	–	–
I.V.A.Richards (80), A.L.Logie (78)	Nottingham	1991	121	–	–	–	–	–	–
E.de C.Weekes (156), D.St E.Atkinson (60)	Wellington	1955-56	–	–	–	120	–	–	–
I.V.A.Richards (192*), C.H.Lloyd (71)	Delhi	1974-75	–	–	–	–	120	–	–
C.H.Lloyd (95), H.A.Gomes (90*)	Kingston	1980-81	118	–	–	–	–	–	–
E.de C.Weekes (141), K.R.Rickards (67)	Kingston	1947-48	116	–	–	–	–	–	–
G.St A.Sobers (198), B.F.Butcher (60)	Kanpur	1958-59	–	–	–	–	114	–	–
L.G.Rowe (40), C.H.Lloyd (121)	Adelaide	1979-80	–	113	–	–	–	–	–
C.G.Greenidge (134), C.L.King (32)	Manchester	1976	111	–	–	–	–	–	–
C.L.Hooper (49), A.L.Logie (59)	Lahore²	1990-91	–	–	–	–	–	108	–
R.B.Kanhai (90), S.M.Nurse (56)	Calcutta	1966-67	–	–	–	–	105	–	–
C.H.Lloyd (78*), G.St A.Sobers (53*)	Bombay²	1966-67	–	–	–	–	102*	–	–
H.A.Gomes (124*), C.H.Lloyd (53)	Adelaide	1981-82	–	102	–	–	–	–	–
C.L.Walcott (51*), D.St E.Atkinson (53*)	Port-of-Spain	1953-54	101*	–	–	–	–	–	–
F.C.M.Alexander (57), G.St A.Sobers (80)	Port-of-Spain	1957-58	–	–	–	–	–	101	–

Hundred Partnerships (West Indies)

5th Wicket *continued*

			E	A	SA	NZ	I	P	SL
G.St A.Sobers (66), E.de C.Weekes (90)	Lord's	1957	100	–	–	–	–	–	–
I.V.A.Richards (76), A.L.Logie (97)	Port-of-Spain	1983-84	–	100	–	–	–	–	–
	Totals:	(43)	16	8	–	3	13	3	–

WEST INDIES – 6th Wicket

			E	A	SA	NZ	I	P	SL
G.St A.Sobers (163*), D.A.J.Holford (105*)	Lord's	1966	274*	–	–	–	–	–	–
C.A.Davis (183), G.St A.Sobers (142)	Bridgetown	1971-72	–	–	–	254	–	–	–
C.H.Lloyd (242*), D.L.Murray (91)	Bombay[3]	1974-75	–	–	–	–	250	–	–
C.L.Walcott (168*), G.E.Gomez (70)	Lord's	1950	211	–	–	–	–	–	–
P.J.L.Dujon (110), C.H.Lloyd (106)	St John's	1982-83	–	–	–	–	207	–	–
F.M.M.Worrell (161), O.G.Smith (81)	Birmingham	1957	190	–	–	–	–	–	–
C.G.Greenidge (223), W.W.Davis (77)	Manchester	1984	170	–	–	–	–	–	–
R.B.Kanhai (105), D.L.Murray (90)	Bridgetown	1972-73	–	165	–	–	–	–	–
C.G.Greenidge (213), P.J.L.Dujon (77)	Auckland	1986-87	–	–	–	165	–	–	–
G.St A.Sobers (198), J.S.Solomon (86)	Kanpur	1958-59	–	–	–	–	163	–	–
G.St A.Sobers (106*), J.S.Solomon (69*)	Calcutta	1958-59	–	–	–	–	160*	–	–
A.L.Logie (97), P.J.L.Dujon (130)	Port-of-Spain	1983-84	–	158	–	–	–	–	–
I.V.A.Richards (182*), C.H.Lloyd (66)	Bridgetown	1980-81	153	–	–	–	–	–	–
C.G.Greenidge (194), P.J.L.Dujon (81)	Kanpur	1983-84	–	–	–	–	152	–	–
R.B.Richardson (138), C.H.Lloyd (114)	Brisbane[2]	1984-85	–	152	–	–	–	–	–
C.H.Lloyd (157), D.L.Murray (52)	Bridgetown	1976-77	–	–	–	–	–	151	–
C.H.Lloyd (78), P.J.L.Dujon (77)	Adelaide	1984-85	–	150	–	–	–	–	–
C.L.Walcott (108), O.G.Smith (44)	Kingston	1954-55	–	138	–	–	–	–	–
C.H.Lloyd (103), A.L.Logie (63)	Delhi	1983-84	–	–	–	–	131	–	–
R.B.Richardson (131*), C.H.Lloyd (76)	Bridgetown	1983-84	–	131	–	–	–	–	–
A.L.Logie (95*), P.J.L.Dujon (52)	Lord's	1988	131	–	–	–	–	–	–
A.L.Logie (81), P.J.L.Dujon (53)	Lord's	1988	130	–	–	–	–	–	–
G.St A.Sobers (161), D.A.J.Holford (32)	Manchester	1966	127	–	–	–	–	–	–
I.T.Shillingford (120), D.L.Murray (42)	Georgetown	1976-77	–	–	–	–	–	123	–
P.J.L.Dujon (84), C.H.Lloyd (67)	Bombay[3]	1983-84	–	–	–	–	119	–	–
G.St A.Sobers (113), S.M.Nurse (137)	Sydney	1968-69	–	118	–	–	–	–	–
G.C.Grant (53*), E.L.Bartlett (84)	Adelaide	1930-31	–	114	–	–	–	–	–
R.C.Fredericks (150), D.L.Murray (25)	Birmingham	1973	114	–	–	–	–	–	–
F.M.M.Worrell (53), F.C.M.Alexander (87*)	Adelaide	1960-61	–	113	–	–	–	–	–
G.St A.Sobers (57), B.D.Julien (66)	Kingston	1973-74	112	–	–	–	–	–	–
G.St A.Sobers (153), F.M.M.Worrell (58)	Kingston	1961-62	–	–	–	–	110	–	–
B.F.Butcher (133), F.M.M.Worrell (33)	Lord's	1963	110	–	–	–	–	–	–
G.St A.Sobers (113*), D.A.J.Holford (35)	Kingston	1967-68	110	–	–	–	–	–	–
G.E.Gomez (74), J.D.C.Goddard (58*)	Oval	1950	109	–	–	–	–	–	–
G.St A.Sobers (178*), M.L.C.Foster (36*)	Bridgetown	1970-71	–	–	–	107*	–	–	–
I.V.A.Richards (177), B.D.Julien (47)	Port-of-Spain	1975-76	–	–	–	–	107	–	–
D.L.Haynes (184), C.H.Lloyd (56)	Lord's	1980	107	–	–	–	–	–	–
E.de C.Weekes (156), A.P.Binns (27)	Wellington	1955-56	–	–	–	106	–	–	–
O.G.Smith (168), D.St E.Atkinson (46)	Nottingham	1957	105	–	–	–	–	–	–
A.L.Logie (52), P.J.L.Dujon (60*)	Georgetown	1984-85	–	–	–	104	–	–	–
C.A.Best (164), P.J.L.Dujon (31)	Bridgetown	1989-90	104	–	–	–	–	–	–
J.D.C.Goddard (44), E.de C.Weekes (128)	Delhi	1948-49	–	–	–	–	101	–	–
B.F.Butcher (142), J.S.Solomon (43)	Madras[2]	1958-59	–	–	–	–	101	–	–
R.B.Kanhai (217), J.S.Solomon (56)	Lahore[1]	1958-59	–	–	–	–	–	100	–
	Totals:	(44)	16	9	–	4	12	3	–

WEST INDIES – 7th Wicket

			E	A	SA	NZ	I	P	SL
D.St E.Atkinson (219), C.C.Depeiza (122)	Bridgetown	1954-55	–	347	–	–	–	–	–
G.St A.Sobers (150*), B.D.Julien (121)	Lord's	1973	155*†	–	–	–	–	–	–
O.G.Smith (168), J.D.C.Goddard (61)	Nottingham	1957	154	–	–	–	–	–	–
H.A.Gomes (127), P.J.L.Dujon (139)	Perth	1984-85	–	149	–	–	–	–	–
G.A.Headley (270*), R.S.Grant (77)	Kingston	1934-35	147	–	–	–	–	–	–
D.St E.Atkinson (85), J.D.C.Goddard (83*)	Christchurch	1955-56	–	–	–	143	–	–	–
I.V.A.Richards (208), M.D.Marshall (55)	Melbourne	1984-85	–	139	–	–	–	–	–
C.G.Greenidge (194), M.D.Marshall (92)	Kanpur	1983-84	–	–	–	–	130	–	–
G.St A.Sobers (153), I.L.Mendonça (78)	Kingston	1961-62	–	–	–	–	127	–	–
C.H.Lloyd (129), M.C.Carew (71*)	Brisbane[2]	1968-69	–	120	–	–	–	–	–
E.de C.Weekes (128), R.J.Christiani (107)	Delhi	1948-49	–	–	–	–	118	–	–
D.L.Murray (71), M.A.Holding (55)	Kingston	1975-76	–	–	–	–	107	–	–
J.S.Solomon (45), F.C.M.Alexander (70)	Kanpur	1958-59	–	–	–	–	100	–	–

7th Wicket *continued*

			E	A	SA	NZ	I	P	SL
A.I.Kallicharan (158), B.D.Julien (86*)	Port-of- Spain	1973-74	100	–	–	–	–	–	–
A.I.Kallicharan (98), D.R.Parry (12)	Madras[1]	1978-79	–	–	–	–	100	–	–
	Totals: (15)		4	4	–	1	6	–	–

†231 runs were added for this wicket, G.St A.Sobers retiring ill and being succeeded by K.D.Boyce after 155 runs had been scored.

WEST INDIES – 8th Wicket

			E	A	SA	NZ	I	P	SL
I.V.A.Richards (192*), K.D.Boyce (68)	Delhi	1974-75	–	–	–	–	124	–	–

WEST INDIES – 9th Wicket

			E	A	SA	NZ	I	P	SL
C.H.Lloyd (161*), A.M.E.Roberts (68)	Calcutta	1983-84	–	–	–	–	161	–	–
E.A.E.Baptiste (87*), M.A.Holding (69)	Birmingham	1984	150	–	–	–	–	–	–
D.A.J.Holford (80), J.L.Hendriks (37*)	Adelaide	1968-69	–	122	–	–	–	–	–
R.J.Christiani (107), D.St E.Atkinson (45)	Delhi	1948-49	–	–	–	–	106	–	–
	Totals: (4)		1	1	–	–	2	–	–

WEST INDIES – 10th Wicket

			E	A	SA	NZ	I	P	SL
C.L.Hooper (178*), C.A.Walsh (30)	St John's	1992-93	–	–	–	–	106	–	–

NEW ZEALAND – (154) – 1st Wicket

			E	A	SA	WI	I	P	SL	Z
G.M.Turner (259), T.W.Jarvis (182)	Georgetown	1971-72	–	–	–	387	–	–	–	–
C.S.Dempster (136), J.E.Mills (117)	Wellington	1929-30	276	–	–	–	–	–	–	–
T.J.Franklin (101), J.G.Wright (98)	Lord's	1990	185	–	–	–	–	–	–	–
T.J.Franklin (69), J.G.Wright (101)	Hamilton	1990-91	–	–	–	–	–	–	161	–
R.E.Redmond (107), G.M.Turner (58)	Auckland	1972-73	–	–	–	–	–	–	159	–
T.J.Franklin (50), J.G.Wright (113*)	Napier	1989-90	–	–	–	149	–	–	–	–
G.T, Dowling (83), T.W.Jarvis (55)	Lahore[2]	1964-65	–	–	–	–	–	136	–	–
T.J.Franklin (39), J.G.Wright (88)	Wellington	1990-91	–	–	–	–	–	–	134	–
B.Sutcliffe (58), W.A.Hadlee (116)	Christchurch	1946-47	133	–	–	–	–	–	–	–
G.O.Rabone (56), M.E.Chapple (76)	Cape Town	1953-54	–	–	126	–	–	–	–	–
B.A.G.Murray (74), G.T.Dowling (239)	Christchurch	1967-68	–	–	–	–	126	–	–	–
B.Sutcliffe (88), V.J.Scott (60)	Oval	1949	121	–	–	–	–	–	–	–
T.J.Franklin (62), J.G.Wright (49)	Auckland	1987-88	117	–	–	–	–	–	–	–
M.J.Greatbatch (87), R.T.Latham (119)	Bulawayo	1992-93	–	–	–	–	–	–	–	116
G.T.Dowling (76), G.M.Turner (38)	Christchurch	1968-69	–	–	–	115	–	–	–	–
B.Sutcliffe (82), V.J.Scott (43)	Leeds	1949	112	–	–	–	–	–	–	–
G.T.Dowling (71), G.M.Turner (40)	Auckland	1968-69	–	–	–	112	–	–	–	–
M.J.Greatbatch (61), J.G.Wright (72)	Wellington	1992-93	–	111	–	–	–	–	–	–
B.R.Hartland (52), J.G.Wright (42)	Moratuwa	1992-93	–	–	–	–	–	–	110	–
M.J.Greatbatch (133), B.R.Hartland (43)	Hamilton	1992-93	–	–	–	–	–	108	–	–
G.M.Turner (72), J.M.Parker (34)	Auckland	1973-74	–	107	–	–	–	–	–	–
G.T.Dowling (42), B.A.G.Murray (80)	Hyderabad	1969-70	–	–	–	–	106	–	–	–
M.J.Greatbatch (88), R.T.Latham (48)	Bulawayo	1992-93	–	–	–	–	–	–	–	102
S.N.McGregor (49), J.G.Leggat (50*)	Delhi	1955-56	–	–	–	–	101	–	–	–
J.G.Wright (43), B.A.Edgar (52)	Sydney	1985-86	–	100	–	–	–	–	–	–
	Totals: (25)		6	3	1	3	4	3	3	2

NEW ZEALAND – 2nd Wicket

			E	A	SA	WI	I	P	SL	Z
J.G.Wright (116), A.H.Jones (143)	Wellington	1991-92	241	–	–	–	–	–	–	–
G.P.Howarth (84), J.J.Crowe (112)	Kingston	1984-85	–	–	–	210	–	–	–	–
J.G.Wright (88), G.P.Howarth (114)	Napier	1978-79	–	–	–	–	–	195	–	–
G.T.Dowling (143), B.E.Congdon (58)	Dunedin	1967-68	–	–	–	–	155	–	–	–
J.G.Wright (110), J.F.Reid (74)	Auckland	1980-81	–	–	–	–	148	–	–	–
J.G.Wright (74), A.H.Jones (170*)	Auckland	1989-90	–	–	–	–	148	–	–	–
G.M.Turner (95), B.E.Congdon (82)	Port-of-Spain	1971-72	–	–	–	139	–	–	–	–
B.Sutcliffe (116), J.R.Reid (50)	Christchurch	1950-51	131	–	–	–	–	–	–	–
B.Sutcliffe (230*), J.W.Guy (52)	Delhi	1955-56	–	–	–	–	130	–	–	–
J.G.Wright (117*), A.H.Jones (33*)	Wellington	1989-90	–	128*	–	–	–	–	–	–
J.G.Wright (45), A.H.Jones (150)	Adelaide	1987-88	–	128	–	–	–	–	–	–
R.T.Latham (119), A.H.Jones (67*)	Bulawayo	1992-93	–	–	–	–	–	–	–	127
B.A.Edgar (49), J.F.Reid (123*)	Christchurch	1980-81	–	–	–	–	–	125	–	–
J.G.Wright (62), G.P.Howarth (94)	Oval	1978	123	–	–	–	–	–	–	–
J.F.M.Morrison (58), J.M.Parker (121)	Auckland	1974-75	116	–	–	–	–	–	–	–
J.G.Wright (93), M.D.Crowe (37)	Leeds	1983	116	–	–	–	–	–	–	–
B.A.Young (85), K.R.Rutherford (59)	Hamilton	1993-94	–	–	–	–	116	–	–	–

2nd Wicket *continued*

			E	A	SA	WI	I	P	SL	Z
G.M.Turner (117), B.E.Congdon (58)	Christchurch	1975-76	–	–	–	–	114	–	–	–
J.G.Wright (40), J.J.Crowe (64)	Port-of-Spain	1984-85	–	–	–	109	–	–	–	–
R.H.Vance (68), A.H.Jones (47)	Auckland	1988-89	–	–	–	–	–	109	–	–
G.M.Turner (79), J.F.M.Morrison (66)	Wellington	1973-74	–	108	–	–	–	–	–	–
G.M.Turner (65), J.M.Parker (104)	Bombay[3]	1976-77	–	–	–	–	106	–	–	–
J.G.Wright (185), A.H.Jones (52)	Christchurch	1989-90	–	–	–	–	105	–	–	–
J.G.Wright (59), K.R.Rutherford (50*)	Auckland	1985-86	–	100	–	–	–	–	–	–
	Totals: (24)		5	4	–	3	9	2	–	1

NEW ZEALAND – 3rd Wicket

			E	A	SA	WI	I	P	SL	Z
A.H.Jones (186), M.D.Crowe (299)	Wellington	1990-91	–	–	–	–	–	–	467	–
J.G.Wright (138), M.D.Crowe (119)	Wellington	1986-87	–	–	–	241	–	–	–	–
J.F.Reid (108), M.D.Crowe (188)	Brisbane[2]	1985-86	–	224	–	–	–	–	–	–
B.Sutcliffe (230*), J.R.Reid (119*)	Delhi	1955-56	–	–	–	–	222*	–	–	–
A.H.Jones (150), M.D.Crowe (137)	Adelaide	1987-88	–	213	–	–	–	–	–	–
B.A.Edgar (83), M.D.Crowe (106)	Lord's	1986	210	–	–	–	–	–	–	–
B.E.Congdon (175), B.F.Hastings (86)	Lord's	1973	190	–	–	–	–	–	–	–
J.W.Guy (91), J.R.Reid (120)	Calcutta	1955-56	–	–	–	–	184	–	–	–
A.H.Jones (170*), M.D.Crowe (113)	Auckland	1989-90	–	–	–	–	179	–	–	–
B.W.Sinclair (130), J.R.Reid (88)	Lahore[2]	1964-65	–	–	–	–	–	178	–	–
J.G.Wright (50), M.D.Crowe (107)	Colombo (SSC)	1992-93	–	–	–	–	–	–	159	–
J.J.Crowe (55), M.D.Crowe (83)	Christchurch	1986-87	–	–	–	156	–	–	–	–
B.E.Congdon (66), B.F.Hastings (83)	Nottingham	1969	150	–	–	–	–	–	–	–
A.H.Jones (86), M.D.Crowe (174)	Wellington	1988-89	–	–	–	–	–	149	–	–
J.F.Reid (158*), M.D.Crowe (84)	Auckland	1984-85	–	–	–	–	–	137	–	–
G.T.Dowling (129), R.W.Morgan (71)	Bombay[2]	1964-65	–	–	–	–	134	–	–	–
B.A.Edgar (74), M.D.Crowe (71)	Perth	1985-86	–	129	–	–	–	–	–	–
G.P.Howarth (65), J.M.Parker (56)	Melbourne	1980-81	–	125	–	–	–	–	–	–
B.E.Congdon (54), J.M.Parker (70)	Auckland	1975-76	–	–	–	–	122	–	–	–
J.G.Wright (88), G.P.Howarth (67)	Oval	1983	120	–	–	–	–	–	–	–
C.S.Dempster (120), M.L.Page (104)	Lord's	1931	118	–	–	–	–	–	–	–
A.H.Jones (76), K.R.Rutherford (63)	Wellington	1993-94	–	–	–	–	–	114	–	–
B.Sutcliffe (137*), J.R.Reid (45*)	Hyderabad	1955-56	–	–	–	–	108*	–	–	–
G.M.Turner (113), M.G.Burgess (54)	Kanpur	1976-77	–	–	–	–	106	–	–	–
G.T.Dowling (27), J.R.Reid (82)	Calcutta	1964-65	–	–	–	–	101	–	–	–
B.A.G.Murray (90), B.F.Hastings (80*)	Lahore[2]	1969-70	–	–	–	–	–	101	–	–
J.G.Wright (99), A.H.Jones (39)	Christchurch	1991-92	101	–	–	–	–	–	–	–
J.F.Reid (180), M.D.Crowe (45)	Colombo (CCC)	1983-84	–	–	–	–	–	–	100	–
	Totals: (28)		6	4	–	2	8	5	3	–

NEW ZEALAND – 4th Wicket

			E	A	SA	WI	I	P	SL	Z
B.E.Congdon (132), B.F.Hastings (101)	Wellington	1973-74	–	229	–	–	–	–	–	–
B.E.Congdon (126), B.F.Hastings (105)	Bridgetown	1971-72	–	–	–	175	–	–	–	–
B.W.Sinclair (138), S.N.McGregor (62)	Auckland	1963-64	–	–	171	–	–	–	–	–
M.D.Crowe (140), K.R.Rutherford (74)	Harare	1992-93	–	–	–	–	–	–	–	168
M.D.Crowe (143), M.J.Greatbatch (68)	Wellington	1987-88	155	–	–	–	–	–	–	–
B.A.Edgar (161), J.V.Coney (73)	Auckland	1981-82	–	154	–	–	–	–	–	–
J.G.Wright (130), J.J.Crowe (128)	Auckland	1983-84	154⁻	–	–	–	–	–	–	–
M.L.Page (104), R.C.Blunt (96)	Lord's	1931	142	–	–	–	–	–	–	–
G.P.Howarth (123), M.G.Burgess (68)	Lord's	1978	130	–	–	–	–	–	–	–
B.F.Hastings (72), M.G.Burgess (79)	Wellington	1972-73	–	–	–	–	–	128	–	–
G.T.Dowling (78), J.R.Reid (69)	Port Elizabeth	1961-62	–	–	125	–	–	–	–	–
J.G.Wright (185), M.J.Greatbatch (46)	Christchurch	1989-90	–	–	–	–	125	–	–	–
J.F.M.Morrison (117), B.F.Hastings (83)	Sydney	1973-74	–	124	–	–	–	–	–	–
G.P.Howarth (147), J.M.Parker (42)	Christchurch	1979-80	–	–	–	122	–	–	–	–
G.P.Howarth (65), J.M.Parker (52)	Brisbane[2]	1980-81	–	117	–	–	–	–	–	–
M.J.Greatbatch (43), K.R.Rutherford (79)	Karachi[1]	1990-91	–	–	–	–	–	116	–	–
G.M.Turner (110*), B.F.Hastings (46)	Christchurch	1973-74	–	115	–	–	–	–	–	–
G.M.Turner (98), J.M.Parker (41)	Christchurch	1974-75	115	–	–	–	–	–	–	–
B.A.Young (94), S.P.Fleming (39)	Lord's	1994	115	–	–	–	–	–	–	–
B.E.Congdon (42), J.R.Reid (97)	Wellington	1964-65	–	–	–	–	109	–	–	–
G.T.Dowling (239), M.G.Burgess (26)	Christchurch	1967-68	–	–	–	–	103	–	–	–
	Totals: (21)		6	5	2	2	2	3	–	1

NEW ZEALAND – 5th Wicket

			E	A	SA	WI	I	P	SL	Z
M.G.Burgess (111), R.W.Anderson (92)	Lahore[2]	1976-77	–	–	–	–	–	183	–	–
M.D.Crowe (142), S.A.Thomson (69)	Lord's	1994	180	–	–	–	–	–	–	–

5th Wicket *continued*

			E	A	SA	WI	I	P	SL	Z
B.E.Congdon (176), V.Pollard (116)	Nottingham	1973	177	–	–	–	–	–	–	–
J.R.Reid (135), J.E.F.Beck (99)	Cape Town	1953-54	–	–	176	–	–	–	–	–
M.D.Crowe (84), J.V.Coney (111*)	Dunedin	1984-85	–	–	–	–	–	157	–	–
M.D.Crowe (78), M.J.Greatbatch (76)	Auckland	1988-89	–	–	–	–	–	154	–	–
B.A.Young (120), S.A.Thomson (120*)	Christchurch	1993-94	–	–	–	–	–	154	–	–
K.R.Rutherford (105), C.Z.Harris (56)	Moratuwa	1992-93	–	–	–	–	–	–	151	–
S.N.McGregor (111), N.S.Harford (93)	Lahore[1]	1955-56	–	–	–	–	–	150	–	–
P.G.Z.Harris (101), M.E.Chapple (69)	Cape Town	1961-62	–	–	148	–	–	–	–	–
M.D.Crowe (188), J.V.Coney (73)	Georgetown	1984-85	–	–	–	142	–	–	–	–
M.G.Burgess (104), M.J.F.Shrimpton (46)	Auckland	1970-71	141	–	–	–	–	–	–	–
M.D.Crowe (108*), K.R.Rutherford (60)	Lahore[2]	1990-91	–	–	–	–	–	132	–	–
K.R.Rutherford (89), D.N.Patel (58*)	Harare	1992-93	–							130
M.P.Donnelly (64), F.B.Smith (96)	Leeds	1949	120	–	–	–	–	–	–	–
G.T.Dowling (239), K.Thomson (69)	Christchurch	1967-68	–	–	–	–	119	–	–	–
M.P.Donnelly (75), J.R.Reid (50)	Manchester	1949	116	–	–	–	–	–	–	–
M.D.Crowe (100), J.V.Coney (174*)	Wellington	1983-84	114	–	–	–	–	–	–	–
M.D.Crowe (174), J.J.Crowe (39)	Wellington	1988-89	–	–	–	–	–	114	–	–
A.H.Jones (122), S.A.Thomson (36)	Hamilton	1990-91	–	–	–	–	–	–	113	–
B.F.Hastings (117*), V.Pollard (44)	Christchurch	1968-69	–	–	–	110	–	–	–	–
M.G.Burgess (87), V.Pollard (62)	Leeds	1973	106	–	–	–	–	–	–	–
A.H.Jones (100*), S.A.Thomson (55)	Hamilton	1990-91	–	–	–	–	–	–	105	–
J.R.Reid (84), J.E.F.Beck (38)	Auckland	1955-56	–	–	–	104	–	–	–	–
T.W.Jarvis (77), B.Sutcliffe (54)	Delhi	1964-65	–	–	–	–	104	–	–	–
A.H.Jones (73), S.A.Thomson (80*)	Auckland	1990-91	–	–	–	–	–	–	100	–
Totals: (26)			7	–	2	3	2	7	4	1

NEW ZEALAND – 6th Wicket

			E	A	SA	WI	I	P	SL	Z
J.J.Crowe (120*), R.J.Hadlee (151*)	Colombo (CCC)	1986-87	–	–	–	–	–	–	246*	–
G.M.Turner (223*), K.J.Wadsworth (78)	Kingston	1971-72	–	–	–	220	–	–	–	–
J.F.Reid (148), R.J.Hadlee (89)	Wellington	1984-85	–	–	–	–	–	145	–	–
M.D.Crowe (115), A.C.Parore (71)	Manchester	1994	141	–	–	–	–	–	–	–
K.R.Rutherford (107*), J.G.Bracewell (54)	Wellington	1987-88	134	–	–	–	–	–	–	–
J.F.Reid (180), J.V.Coney (92)	Colombo (CCC)	1983-84	–	–	–	–	–	–	133	–
M.J.Greatbatch (47), R.J.Hadlee (86)	Lord's	1990	123	–	–	–	–	–	–	–
M.G.Burgess (105), V.Pollard (105*)	Lord's	1973	117	–	–	–	–	–	–	–
J.M.Parker (121), K.J.Wadsworth (58)	Auckland	1974-75	112	–	–	–	–	–	–	–
K.R.Rutherford (65), J.V.Coney (101*)	Wellington	1985-86	–	109	–	–	–	–	–	–
M.D.Crowe (104), J.G.Bracewell (43)	Auckland	1986-87	–	–	–	107	–	–	–	–
M.G.Burgess (38), R.J.Hadlee (81)	Auckland	1976-77	–	105	–	–	–	–	–	–
H.G.Vivian (100), F.T.Badcock (53)	Wellington	1931-32	–	–	100	–	–	–	–	–
Totals: (13)			5	2	1	2	–	1	2	–

NEW ZEALAND – 7th Wicket

			E	A	SA	WI	I	P	SL	Z
W.K.Lees (152), R.J.Hadlee (87)	Karachi[1]	1976-77	–	–	–	–	–	186	–	–
B.Sutcliffe (151*), B.R.Taylor (105)	Calcutta	1964-65	–	–	–	–	163	–	–	–
M.D.Crowe (188), I.D.S.Smith (53)	Georgetown	1984-85	–	–	–	143	–	–	–	–
M.J.Greatbatch (90*), I.D.S.Smith (79)	Hyderabad	1988-89	–	–	–	–	–	139	–	–
J.V.Coney (101*), R.J.Hadlee (72*)	Wellington	1985-86	–	132*	–	–	–	–	–	–
D.N.Patel (99), C.L.Cairns (61)	Christchurch	1991-92	117	–	–	–	–	–	–	–
B.Sutcliffe (53), V.Pollard (81*)	Birmingham	1965	104	–	–	–	–	–	–	–
C.L.Cairns (78), T.E.Blain (36)	Perth	1993-94	–	102	–	–	–	–	–	–
T.C.Lowry (80), H.M.McGirr (51)	Auckland	1929-30	100	–	–	–	–	–	–	–
Totals: (9)			3	2	–	1	2	1	–	–

NEW ZEALAND – 8th Wicket

			E	A	SA	WI	I	P	SL	Z
B.E.Congdon (166*), R.S.Cunis (51)	Port-of-Spain	1971-72	–	–	–	136	–	–	–	–
D.A.R.Moloney (64), A.W.Roberts (66*)	Lord's	1937	104	–	–	–	–	–	–	–
R.J.Hadlee (87), I.D.S.Smith (173)	Auckland	1989-90	–	–	–	–	103	–	–	–
B.W.Yuile (47*), D.R.Hadlee (56)	Karachi[1]	1969-70	–	–	–	–	–	100	–	–
Totals: (4)			1	–	–	1	1	1	–	–

NEW ZEALAND – 9th Wicket

			E	A	SA	WI	I	P	SL	Z
I.D.S.Smith (173), M.C.Snedden (22)	Auckland	1989-90	–	–	–	–	136	–	–	–
J.V.Coney (174*), B.L.Cairns (64)	Wellington	1983-84	118	–	–	–	–	–	–	–
Totals: (2)			1	–	–	–	1	–	–	–

NEW ZEALAND – 10th Wicket

			E	A	SA	WI	NZ	P	SL	Z
B.F.Hastings (110), R.O.Collinge (68*)	Auckland	1972-73	–	–	–	–	–	151	–	–
J.G.Bracewell (83*), S.L.Boock (37)	Sydney	1985-86	–	124	–	–	–	–	–	–
	Totals: (2)		–	1	–	–	–	1	–	–

INDIA – (261) – 1st Wicket

			E	A	SA	WI	NZ	P	SL	Z
M.H.Mankad (231), Pankaj Roy (173)	Madras²	1955-56	–	–	–	–	413	–	–	–
S.M.Gavaskar (221), C.P.S.Chauhan (80)	Oval	1979	213	–	–	–	–	–	–	–
V.M.Merchant (114), Mushtaq Ali (112)	Manchester	1936	203	–	–	–	–	–	–	–
S.M.Gavaskar (91), K.Srikkanth (123)	Madras¹	1986-87	–	–	–	–	–	200	–	–
S.M.Gavaskar (97), C.P.S.Chauhan (93)	Lahore²	1978-79	–	–	–	–	–	192	–	–
S.M.Gavaskar (123), C.P.S.Chauhan (73)	Bombay³	1979-80	–	192	–	–	–	–	–	–
S.M.Gavaskar (172), K.Srikkanth (116)	Sydney	1985-86	–	191	–	–	–	–	–	–
S.M.Gavaskar (103*), A.D.Gaekwad (66*)	Bangalore	1983-84	–	–	–	–	–	176*	–	–
M.Prabhakar (95), N.S.Sidhu (104)	Colombo (SSC)	1993-94	–	–	–	–	–	–	171	–
S.M.Gavaskar (70), C.P.S.Chauhan (85)	Melbourne	1980-81	–	165	–	–	–	–	–	–
S.M.Gavaskar (155), Arun Lal (63)	Madras¹	1982-83	–	–	–	–	–	–	156	–
S.M.Gavaskar (73), C.P.S.Chauhan (84)	Bombay³	1978-79	–	–	–	153	–	–	–	–
W.V.Raman (72*), M.Prabhakar (63*)	Auckland	1989-90	–	–	–	–	149*	–	–	–
S.M.Gavaskar (66), A.D.Gaekwad (81*)	Kingston	1975-76	–	–	–	136	–	–	–	–
F.M.Engineer (66), S.M.Gavaskar (67)	Bombay²	1972-73	135	–	–	–	–	–	–	–
S.M.Gavaskar (49), F.M.Engineer (86)	Lord's	1974	131	–	–	–	–	–	–	–
D.N.Sardesai (28), F.M.Engineer (109)	Madras¹	1966-67	–	–	–	129	–	–	–	–
S.M.Gavaskar (90), A.D.Gaekwad (39)	Ahmedabad	1983-84	–	–	–	127	–	–	–	–
S.M.Gavaskar (81), C.P.S.Chauhan (61)	Kanpur	1979-80	–	–	–	–	–	125	–	–
V.M.Merchant (78), Mushtaq Ali (46)	Manchester	1946	124	–	–	–	–	–	–	–
M.H.Mankad (116), C.T.Sarwate (36)	Melbourne	1947-48	–	124	–	–	–	–	–	–
S.M.Gavaskar (68), C.P.S.Chauhan (56)	Birmingham	1979	124	–	–	–	–	–	–	–
A.M.Mankad (53*), S.M.Gavaskar (64*)	Georgetown	1970-71	–	–	–	123*	–	–	–	–
Pankaj Roy (99), N.J.Contractor (34)	Delhi	1959-60	–	121	–	–	–	–	–	–
M.L.Jaisimha (127), N.J.Contractor (39)	Delhi	1961-62	121	–	–	–	–	–	–	–
S.M.Gavaskar (119), A.D.Gaekwad (42)	Bombay³	1976-77	–	–	–	–	120	–	–	–
S.M.Gavaskar (120), C.P.S.Chauhan (60)	Delhi	1978-79	–	–	–	119	–	–	–	–
S.M.Gavaskar (76), C.P.S.Chauhan (58)	Kanpur	1979-80	–	114	–	–	–	–	–	–
S.M.Gavaskar (53), C.P.S.Chauhan (78)	Christchurch	1980-81	–	–	–	–	114	–	–	–
F.M.Engineer (77), A.M.Mankad (64)	Kanpur	1969-70	–	111	–	–	–	–	–	–
N.S.Sidhu (79), M.Prabhakar (44)	Bombay³	1992-93	109							
M.H.Mankad (72), Pankaj Roy (35)	Lords	1952	106							
S.M.Gavaskar (83), Arun Lal (51)	Lahore²	1982-83	–	–	–	–	–	105	–	–
Pankaj Roy (31*), M.H.Mankad (71*)	Calcutta	1951-52	103*							
S.M.Gavaskar (172), K.Srikkanth (65)	Bangalore	1981-82	102							
N.R.Mongia (38), N.S.Sidhu (98)	Hamilton	1993-94	–	–	–	–	102	–	–	–
	Totals: (36)		11	7	–	6	5	5	2	–

INDIA – 2nd Wicket

			E	A	SA	WI	NZ	P	SL	Z
S.M.Gavaskar (182*), D.B.Vengsarkar (157*)	Calcutta	1978-79	–	–	–	344*	–	–	–	–
Pankaj Roy (150), V.L.Manjrekar (118)	Kingston	1952-53	–	–	–	237	–	–	–	–
S.M.Gavaskar (172), M.Amarnath (138)	Sydney	1985-86	–	224	–	–	–	–	–	–
S.M.Gavaskar (116), S.Amarnath (124)	Auckland	1975-76	–	–	–	–	204	–	–	–
A.D.Gaekwad (72), M.Amarnath (116)	St John's	1982-83	–	–	–	200	–	–	–	–
S.M.Gavaskar (127), M.Amarnath (100)	Perth	1977-78	–	193	–	–	–	–	–	–
F.M.Engineer (121), A.L.Wadekar (87)	Bombay²	1972-73	192	–	–	–	–	–	–	–
S.M.Gavaskar (121), D.B.Vengsarkar (159)	Delhi	1983-84	–	–	–	178	–	–	–	–
S.M.Gavaskar (155), D.B.Vengsarkar (90)	Madras¹	1982-83	–	–	–	–	–	–	173	–
A.D.Gaekwad (87), D.B.Vengsarkar (73)	Bangalore	1978-79	–	–	–	170	–	–	–	–
F.M.Engineer (87), A.L.Wadekar (91)	Leeds	1967	168	–	–	–	–	–	–	–
S.M.Gavaskar (86), E.D.Solkar (102)	Bombay³	1974-75	–	–	–	168	–	–	–	–
S.M.Gavaskar (205), G.R.Viswanath (52)	Bombay³	1978-79	–	–	–	155	–	–	–	–
S.M.Gavaskar (221), D.B.Vengsarkar (52)	Oval	1979	153	–	–	–	–	–	–	–
S.M.Gavaskar (120), D.B.Vengsarkar (109)	Delhi	1978-79	–	–	–	151	–	–	–	–
K.Srikkanth (84), M.Azharuddin (122)	Kanpur	1984-85	150	–	–	–	–	–	–	–
C.P.S.Chauhan (88), M.Amarnath (90)	Perth	1977-78	–	149	–	–	–	–	–	–
S.M.Gavaskar (220), A.L.Wadekar (54)	Port-of-Spain	1970-71	–	–	–	148	–	–	–	–
N.S.Sidhu (99), V.G.Kambli (82)	Bangalore	1993-94	–	–	–	–	–	–	148	–
V.L.Mehra (62), S.A.Durani (104)	Port-of-Spain	1961-62	–	–	–	144	–	–	–	–
B.K.Kunderan (192), D.N.Sardesai (65)	Madras²	1963-64	143	–	–	–	–	–	–	–
N.J.Contractor (92), P.R.Umrigar (76)	Delhi	1958-59	–	–	–	137	–	–	–	–
N.S.Sidhu (85), S.V.Manjrekar (113*)	Karachi¹	1989-90	–	–	–	–	–	135	–	–

2nd Wicket *continued*

			E	A	SA	WI	NZ	P	SL	Z
A.D.Gaekwad (48), D.B.Vengsarkar (100)	Bombay[3]	1983-84	–	–	133	–	–	–	–	–
M.L.Jaisimha (51), V.L.Manjrekar (84)	Bombay[2]	1961-62	131	–	–	–	–	–	–	–
R.Lamba (53), M.Amarnath (131)	Nagpur	1986-87	–	–	–	–	–	–	126	–
N.S.Sidhu (82), V.G.Kambli (125)	Colombo (SSC)	1993-94	–	–	–	–	–	–	126	–
S.M.Gavaskar (60), M.Amarnath (64)	Hyderabad	1982-83	–	–	–	–	–	125	–	–
M.H.Mankad (111), H.R.Adhikari (38)	Melbourne	1947-48	–	124	–	–	–	–	–	–
D.N.Sardesai (106), Hanumant Singh (82)	Delhi	1964-65	–	–	–	–	123	–	–	–
K.C.Ibrahim (85), R.S.Modi (63)	Delhi	1948-49	–	–	121	–	–	–	–	–
S.M.Gavaskar (137), M.Amarnath (53)	Karachi[1]	1978-79	–	–	–	–	–	117	–	–
C.P.S.Chauhan (39), D.B.Vengsarkar (89)	Calcutta	1979-80	–	117	–	–	–	–	–	–
S.M.Gavaskar (66), M.Amarnath (70)	Kanpur	1976-77	–	–	–	–	114	–	–	–
R.J.Shastri (66), G.R.Viswanath (56)	Oval	1982	113	–	–	–	–	–	–	–
N.J.Contractor (56), A.A.Baig (112)	Manchester	1959	109	–	–	–	–	–	–	–
M.L.Jaisimha (70), V.L.Manjrekar (96)	Kanpur	1961-62	109	–	–	–	–	–	–	–
B.K.Kunderan (55), R.G.Nadkarni (122*)	Kanpur	1963-64	109	–	–	–	–	–	–	–
S.M.Gavaskar (102), M.Amarnath (85)	Port-of-Spain	1975-76	–	–	–	108	–	–	–	–
N.S.Sidhu (106), V.G.Kambli (59)	Madras[1]	1992-93	108	–	–	–	–	–	–	–
N.J.Contractor (92), R.F.Surti (64)	Delhi	1960-61	–	–	–	–	–	107	–	–
S.M.Gavaskar (67), M.Amarnath (103*)	Karachi[1]	1982-83	–	–	–	–	–	107	–	–
N.S.Sidhu (61), V.G.Kambli (227)	Delhi	1992-93	–	–	–	–	–	–	–	107
S.M.Gavaskar (88), D.B.Vengsarkar (33)	Bangalore	1979-80	–	–	–	–	–	105	–	–
R.J.Shastri (81), M.Amarnath (116*)	Kandy	1985-86	–	–	–	–	–	–	104	–
S.M.Gavaskar (90), M.Amarnath (51)	Madras[1]	1986-87	–	103	–	–	–	–	–	–
K.Srikkanth (86), M.Amarnath (45)	Melbourne	1985-86	–	101	–	–	–	–	–	–
	Totals: (47)		11	7	–	14	3	6	5	1

INDIA – 3rd Wicket

			E	A	SA	WI	NZ	P	SL	Z
G.R.Viswanath (222), Yashpal Sharma (140)	Madras[1]	1981-82	316†	–	–	–	–	–	–	–
P.R.Umrigar (223), V.L.Manjrekar (118)	Hyderabad	1955-56	–	–	–	–	–	238	–	–
V.M.Merchant (154), V.S.Hazare (164*)	Delhi	1951-52	211	–	–	–	–	–	–	–
M.H.Mankad (184), V.S.Hazare (49)	Lord's	1952	211	–	–	–	–	–	–	–
D.B.Vengsarkar (103), G.R.Viswanath (113)	Lord's	1979	210	–	–	–	–	–	–	–
V.G.Kambli (224), S.R.Tendulkar (78)	Bombay[3]	1992-93	194	–	–	–	–	–	–	–
M.Amarnath (120), Yashpal Sharma (63*)	Lahore[2]	1982-83	–	–	–	–	–	190	–	–
Pankaj Roy (140), V.S.Hazare (155)	Bombay[2]	1951-52	187	–	–	–	–	–	–	–
L.Amarnath (118), C.K.Nayudu (67)	Bombay[1]	1933-34	186	–	–	–	–	–	–	–
M.Amarnath (89), D.B.Vengsarkar (96)	Madras[1]	1986-87	–	–	–	–	185	–	–	–
N.S.Sidhu (116), D.B.Vengsarkar (75)	Bangalore	1988-89	–	–	–	–	174*†	–	–	–
M.Amarnath (131), D.B.Vengsarkar (153)	Nagpur	1986-87	–	–	–	–	–	–	173	–
A.D.Gaekwad (77*), G.R.Viswanath (103*)	Kanpur	1976-77	–	–	–	–	163*	–	–	–
V.G.Kambli (120), S.R.Tendulkar (71)	Colombo (PSS)	1993-94	–	–	–	–	–	–	162	–
M.Amarnath (85), G.R.Viswanath (112)	Port-of-Spain	1975-76	–	–	–	159	–	–	–	–
S.M.Gavaskar (115), G.R.Viswanath (131)	Delhi	1979-80	–	159	–	–	–	–	–	–
S.V.Manjrekar (83), M.Azharuddin (109)	Faisalabad	1989-90	–	–	–	–	–	158	–	–
R.M.Modi (112), V.S.Hazare (134*)	Bombay[2]	1948-49	–	–	156	–	–	–	–	–
S.V.Manjrekar (218), M.Azharuddin (77)	Lahore[2]	1989-90	–	–	–	–	–	149	–	–
N.S.Sidhu (106), S.R.Tendulkar (165)	Madras[1]	1992-93	147	–	–	–	–	–	–	–
Pankaj Roy (100), V.L.Manjrekar (90)	Calcutta	1955-56	–	–	–	–	144	–	–	–
R.G.Nadkarni (122*), D.N.Sardesai (87)	Kanpur	1963-64	144	–	–	–	–	–	–	–
C.P.S.Chauhan (79), G.R.Viswanath (179)	Kanpur	1978-79	–	–	–	144	–	–	–	–
V.G.Kambli (227), S.R.Tendulkar (62)	Delhi	1992-93	–	–	–	–	–	–	–	137
N.J.Contractor (108), A.A.Baig (50)	Bombay[2]	1959-60	–	133	–	–	–	–	–	–
M.Amarnath (86), G.R.Viswanath (73)	Adelaide	1977-78	–	131	–	–	–	–	–	–
Pankaj Roy (67*), V.L.Manjrekar (74*)	Dacca	1954-55	–	–	–	–	–	130*	–	–
R.S.Modi (80), V.S.Hazare (59)	Calcutta	1948-49	–	–	–	129	–	–	–	–
S.V.Manjrekar (72), M.Azharuddin (52)	Sialkot	1989-90	–	–	–	–	–	128	–	–
B.K.Kunderan (100), Nawab of Pataudi, jr (203*)	Delhi	1963-64	125	–	–	–	–	–	–	–
Pankaj Roy (78), V.L.Manjrekar (59)	Bahawalpur	1954-55	–	–	–	–	–	123	–	–
S.M.Gavaskar (124), D.N.Sardesai (75)	Port-of-Spain	1970-71	–	–	–	122	–	–	–	–
S.M.Gavaskar (65), M.Amarnath (64)	Delhi	1984-85	121	–	–	–	–	–	–	–
N.S.Sidhu (124), S.R.Tendulkar (142)	Lucknow[2]	1993-94	–	–	–	–	–	–	121	–
S.M.Gavaskar (176), D.B.Vengsarkar (57)	Kanpur	1986-87	–	–	–	–	–	–	117	–
A.L.Wadekar (99), R.F.Surti (43)	Melbourne	1967-68	–	116	–	–	–	–	–	–
C.P.S.Chauhan (84), G.R.Viswanath (52)	Kanpur	1979-80	–	113	–	–	–	–	–	–
M.L.Apte (64), V.S.Hazare (63)	Bridgetown	1952-53	–	–	–	112	–	–	–	–
M.L.Jaisimha (66), V.L.Manjrekar (59)	Bombay[2]	1964-65	–	112	–	–	–	–	–	–
S.M.Gavaskar (116), G.R.Viswanath (50)	Georgetown	1970-71	–	–	–	112	–	–	–	–
S.M.Gavaskar (147*), D.B.Vengsarkar (62)	Georgetown	1982-83	–	–	–	112	–	–	–	–

Hundred Partnerships (India)

3rd Wicket continued			E	A	SA	WI	NZ	P	SL	Z
S.M.Gavaskar (63), D.B.Vengsarkar (109)	Ahmedabad	1986-87	–	–	–	–	–	111	–	–
R.J.Shastri (206), D.B.Vengsarkar (54)	Sydney	1991-92	–	111	–	–	–	–	–	–
R.S.Modi (87), V.S.Hazare (58*)	Calcutta	1948-49	–	–	–	108	–	–	–	–
M.Amarnath (72), G.R.Viswanath (59)	Melbourne	1977-78	–	105	–	–	–	–	–	–
N.J.Contractor (86), Nawab of Pataudi, jr (103)	Madras²	1961-62	104	–	–	–	–	–	–	–
A.L.Wadekar (71), R.F.Surti (44)	Dunedin	1967-68	–	–	–	–	103	–	–	–
A.L.Wadekar (55), G.R.Viswanath (59)	Madras¹	1969-70	–	102	–	–	–	–	–	–
S.M.Gavaskar (89), G.R.Viswanath (145)	Faisalabad	1978-79	–	–	–	–	–	101	–	–
K.Srikkanth (94), D.B.Vengsarkar (25)	Bombay³	1988-89	–	–	–	–	100	–	–	–
	Totals: (50)		12	9	–	9	6	9	4	1

†415 runs were added for this wicket in two separate partnerships, D.B.Vengsarkar retiring hurt and being succeeded by Yashpal Sharma when 99 runs had been scored.

‡226 runs were added for this wicket in two separate partnerships, D.B.Vengsarkar retiring hurt and being succeeded by M.Azharuddin after 174 runs had been scored.

Although the 3rd wicket added 124 v Australia at Calcutta in 1979-80, this consisted of two partnerships: G.R.Viswanath added 37 with D.B.Vengsarkar (retired hurt) and a further 87 with Yashpal Sharma.

INDIA – 4th Wicket			E	A	SA	WI	NZ	P	SL	Z
V.S.Hazare (89), V.L.Manjrekar (133)	Leeds	1952	222	–	–	–	–	–	–	–
M.Amarnath (95), M.Azharuddin (105)	Madras¹	1984-85	190	–	–	–	–	–	–	–
S.V.Manjrekar (93), M.Azharuddin (179)	Manchester	1990	189	–	–	–	–	–	–	–
S.V.Manjrekar (218), R.J.Shastri (61)	Lahore²	1989-90	–	–	–	–	–	186	–	–
V.S.Hazare (146*), P.R.Umrigar (102)	Bombay²	1952-53	–	–	–	–	–	183	–	–
G.R.Viswanath (179), A.D.Gaekwad (102)	Kanpur	1978-79	–	–	–	172	–	–	–	–
P.R.Umrigar (223), A.G.Kripal Singh (100*)	Hyderabad	1955-56	–	–	–	–	171	–	–	–
M.H.Mankad (223), A.G.Kripal Singh (63)	Bombay²	1955-56	–	–	–	–	167	–	–	–
G.R.Viswanath (145), D.B.Vengsarkar (83)	Faisalabad	1978-79	–	–	–	–	–	166	–	–
S.M.Gavaskar (176), M.Azharuddin (199)	Kanpur	1986-87	–	–	–	–	–	–	163	–
D.B.Vengsarkar (112), G.R.Viswanath (161*)	Bangalore	1979-80	–	159	–	–	–	–	–	–
D.N.Sardesai (200*), C.G.Borde (109)	Bombay²	1964-65	–	–	–	154	–	–	–	–
Pankaj Roy (85), P.R.Umrigar (117)	Kingston	1952-53	–	–	–	150	–	–	–	–
A.V.Mankad (74), Nawab of Pataudi, jr (95)	Bombay²	1969-70	–	146	–	–	–	–	–	–
S.M.Gavaskar (127*), M.Amarnath (78)	Faisalabad	1982-83	–	–	–	–	–	145	–	–
D.B.Vengsarkar (159), R.J.Shastri (49)	Delhi	1983-84	–	–	–	145	–	–	–	–
V.S.Hazare (134*), L.Amarnath (58*)	Bombay²	1948-49	–	–	–	144*	–	–	–	–
D.B.Vengsarkar (47), M.Azharuddin (192)	Auckland	1989-90	–	–	–	–	144	–	–	–
S.R.Tendulkar (142), M.Azharuddin (47)	Lucknow²	1993-94	–	–	–	–	–	–	142	–
R.S.Modi (86), V.S.Hazare (122)	Bombay²	1948-49	–	–	–	139	–	–	–	–
S.M.Gavaskar (108), B.P.Patel (83)	Bombay³	1976-77	139	–	–	–	–	–	–	–
R.J.Shastri (187), M.Azharuddin (78)	Oval	1990	139	–	–	–	–	–	–	–
C.G.Borde (87), Nawab of Pataudi, jr (113)	Delhi	1964-65	–	–	–	–	138	–	–	–
G.R.Viswanath (89), D.B.Vengsarkar (44)	Adelaide	1977-78	–	136	–	–	–	–	–	–
M.L.Apte (163*), P.R.Umrigar (67)	Port-of-Spain	1952-53	–	–	–	135	–	–	–	–
R.F.Surti (52), Nawab of Pataudi, jr (74)	Brisbane²	1967-68	–	128	–	–	–	–	–	–
G.R.Viswanath (79), D.B.Vengsarkar (48)	Sydney	1977-78	–	125	–	–	–	–	–	–
S.R.Tendulkar (96), M.Azharuddin (108)	Bangalore	1993-94	–	–	–	–	–	–	124	–
S.R.Tendulkar (50), M.Azharuddin (182)	Calcutta	1992-93	123	–	–	–	–	–	–	–
D.B.Vengsarkar (146*), Yashpal Sharma (60)	Delhi	1979-80	–	–	–	–	–	122	–	–
C.G.Borde (69), R.F.Surti (70)	Adelaide	1967-68	–	121	–	–	–	–	–	–
A.L.Wadekar (91*), G.R.Viswanath (44*)	Delhi	1969-70	–	120*	–	–	–	–	–	–
S.M.Gavaskar (205), C.P.S.Chauhan (52)	Bombay³	1978-79	–	–	–	117	–	–	–	–
D.B.Vengsarker (153), S.M.Gavaskar (74)	Nagpur	1986-87	–	–	–	–	–	–	116	–
M.Amarnath (78), M.Azharuddin (48)	Madras¹	1984-85	110	–	–	–	–	–	–	–
C.G.Borde (96), H.R.Adhikari (40)	Delhi	1958-59	–	–	–	108	–	–	–	–
P.R.Umrigar (112), C.G.Borde (45)	Delhi	1960-61	–	–	–	–	–	107†	–	–
V.G.Kambli (227), M.Azharuddin (42)	Delhi	1992-93	–	–	–	–	–	–	–	107
M.Amarnath (117), Yashpal Sharma (50)	Port-of-Spain	1982-83	–	–	–	106	–	–	–	–
S.M.Gavaskar (147*), Yashpal Sharma (35*)	Georgetown	1982-83	–	–	–	104*	–	–	–	–
D.B.Vengsarkar (102*), M.Azharuddin (60)	Calcutta	1987-88	–	–	–	104	–	–	–	–
R.F.Surti (67), Nawab of Pataudi, jr (52)	Christchurch	1967-68	–	–	–	–	103	–	–	–
G.R.Viswanath (73), Yashpal Sharma (62)	Bangalore	1979-80	–	–	–	–	–	102	–	–
F.M.Engineer (75), P.Sharma (49)	Delhi	1974-75	–	–	–	–	101	–	–	–
	Totals: (44)		7	7	–	12	6	7	4	1

†123 runs were added for this wicket, N.J.Contractor retiring hurt and being succeeded by C.G.Borde after 16 runs had been scored.

Although the 4th wicket added 103 runs in the first innings v West Indies at Port-of-Spain in 1982-83, this consisted of two partnerships, M.Amarnath adding 16 with Yashpal Sharma (retired hurt) and a further 87 with R.J.Shastri.

INDIA – 5th Wicket

			E	A	SA	WI	NZ	P	SL	Z
M.Azharuddin (110), R.J.Shastri (111)	Calcutta	1984-85	214	–	–	–	–	–	–	–
S.M.Gavaskar (156), B.P.Patel (115*)	Port-of-Spain	1975-76	–	–	–	204	–	–	–	–
S.M.Patil (127), R.J.Shastri (139)	Faisalabad	1984-85	–	–	–	–	–	200	–	–
R.J.Shastri (206), S.R.Tendulkar (148*)	Sydney	1991-92	–	196	–	–	–	–	–	–
Nawab of Pataudi, jr (203*), C.G.Borde (67*)	Delhi	1963-64	190*	–	–	–	–	–	–	–
P.R.Umrigar (117), C.G.Borde (177*)	Madras²	1960-61	–	–	–	–	–	177	–	–
R.J.Shastri (102), Kapil Dev (98)	St John's	1982-83	–	–	–	156	–	–	–	–
S.A.Durani (73), G.R.Viswanath (113)	Bombay²	1972-73	150	–	–	–	–	–	–	–
S.V.Manjrekar (76), S.R.Tendulkar (59)	Faisalabad	1989-90	–	–	–	–	–	143	–	–
C.G.Borde (69), S.A.Durani (71)	Bombay²	1961-62	142	–	–	–	–	–	–	–
D.B.Vengsarkar(157), Yashpal Sharma (37)	Lord's	1982	142	–	–	–	–	–	–	–
Hanumant Singh (73), Nawab of Pataudi, jr (148)	Leeds	1967	134	–	–	–	–	–	–	–
V.L.Manjrekar (189*), C.G.Borde (45)	Delhi	1961-62	132	–	–	–	–	–	–	–
P.R.Umrigar (69), D.G.Phadkar (65)	Port-of-Spain	1952-53	–	–	–	131	–	–	–	–
M.Azharaddin (110), R.J.Shastri (125)	Jaipur	1986-87	–	–	–	–	–	130	–	–
V.L.Manjrekar (177), G.S.Ramchand (72)	Delhi	1955-56	–	–	–	–	127	–	–	–
R.J.Shastri (77), R.M.H.Binny (65)	Bombay³	1983-84	–	–	–	127	–	–	–	–
R.F.Surti (99), C.G.Borde (65*)	Auckland	1967-68	–	–	–	–	126	–	–	–
M.Amarnath (101*), R.J.Shastri (71)	Lahore²	1984-85	–	–	–	–	–	126	–	–
G.R.Viswanath (95), A.D.Gaekwad (51)	Bombay³	1974-75	–	–	–	121	–	–	–	–
S.R.Tendulkar (165), P.K.Amre (78)	Madras¹	1992-93	118	–	–	–	–	–	–	–
D.N.Sardesai (112), E.D.Solkar (55)	Port-of-Spain	1970-71	–	–	–	114	–	–	–	–
M.Azharuddin (179), S.R.Tendulkar (68)	Manchester	1990	112	–	–	–	–	–	–	–
C.G.Borde (62), Nawab of Pataudi, jr (153)	Calcutta	1964-65	–	–	–	–	110	–	–	–
A.A.Baig (58), R.B.Kenny (55*)	Bombay²	1959-60	–	109	–	–	–	–	–	–
A.D.Gaekwad (102), M.Amarnath (101*)	Kanpur	1978-79	–	–	–	109	–	–	–	–
C.P.S.Chauhan (97), S.M.Patil (174)	Adelaide	1980-81	–	108	–	–	–	–	–	–
M.Amarnath (109*), S.M.Patil (68)	Lahore²	1982-83	–	–	–	–	–	106	–	–
S.M.Gavaskar (166), Yashpal Sharma (46)	Madras¹	1979-80	–	–	–	–	–	105	–	–
N.S.Sidhu (97), S.R.Tendulkar (57)	Sialkot	1989-90	–	–	–	–	–	101	–	–
V.G.Kambli (224), P.K.Amre (57)	Bombay³	1992-93	101	–	–	–	–	–	–	–
Totals: (31)			10	3	–	7	3	8	–	–

Although the 5th wicket added 102 v Pakistan at Lahore in 1978-79, this consisted of two partnerships: D.B.Vengsarkar added 57 with M.Amarnath (retired hurt) and a further 45 with S.M.H.Kirmani.
Although the 5th wicket added 110 v West Indies at Kingston in 1988-89, this comprised two partnerships: S.V.Manjrekar added 77* with N.S.Sidhu (retired hurt) and a further 33 with K.S.More.

INDIA – 6th Wicket

			E	A	SA	WI	NZ	P	SL	Z
D.B.Vengsarkar (164*), R.J.Shastri (121*)	Bombay³	1986-87	–	298*	–	–	–	–	–	–
M.Azharuddin (199), Kapil Dev (163)	Kanpur	1986-87	–	–	–	–	–	272	–	–
D.N.Sardesai (200*), Hanumant Singh (75*)	Bombay²	1964-65	–	–	–	–	193*	–	–	–
V.S.Hazare (116), D.G.Phadkar (123)	Adelaide	1947-48	–	188	–	–	–	–	–	–
S.M.Gavaskar (236*), R.J.Shastri (72)	Madras¹	1983-84	–	–	–	170	–	–	–	–
S.M.Patil (174), Yashpal Sharma (47)	Adelaide	1980-81	–	147	–	–	–	–	–	–
M.Azharuddin (141), Kapil Dev (66)	Calcutta	1986-87	–	–	–	–	–	143	–	–
Nawab of Pataudi, jr (128*), C.G.Borde (49)	Madras²	1964-65	–	142	–	–	–	–	–	–
D.N.Sardesai (212), E.D.Solkar (61)	Kingston	1970-71	–	–	–	137	–	–	–	–
C.G.Borde (109), H.R.Adhikari (63)	Delhi	1958-59	–	–	–	134	–	–	–	–
S.M.H.Kirmani (43), Kapil Dev (97)	Oval	1982	130	–	–	–	–	–	–	–
V.L.Manjrekar (177), R.G.Nadkarni (68*)	Delhi	1955-56	–	–	–	–	123	–	–	–
A.D.Gaekwad (201), R.M.H.Binny (54)	Jullundur	1983-84	–	–	–	–	–	121	–	–
M.L.Jaisimha (101), C.G.Borde (63)	Brisbane²	1967-68	–	119	–	–	–	–	–	–
P.R.Umrigar (130), D.K.Gaekwad (43)	Port-of-Spain	1952-53	–	–	–	118	–	–	–	–
A.K.Sharma (30), Kapil Dev (109)	Madras¹	1987-88	–	–	–	113	–	–	–	–
D.B.Vengsarkar (166), Kapil Dev (60)	Cuttack	1986-87	–	–	–	–	–	111	–	–
G.R.Viswanath (137), E.D.Solkar (35)	Kanpur	1969-70	–	110	–	–	–	–	–	–
V.S.Hazare (56), D.G.Phadkar (64)	Leeds	1952	105	–	–	–	–	–	–	–
D.G.Phadkar (61), P.R.Umrigar (130*)	Madras¹	1951-52	104	–	–	–	–	–	–	–
E.D.Solkar (75), F.M.Engineer (63)	Delhi	1972-73	103	–	–	–	–	–	–	–
C.G.Borde (121), S.A.Durani (55)	Bombay²	1966-67	–	–	–	102	–	–	–	–
M.Amarnath (101*), Kapil Dev (62)	Kanpur	1978-79	–	–	–	102	–	–	–	–
Totals: (23)			4	6	–	7	2	2	2	–

Hundred Partnerships (India)

INDIA – 7th Wicket

			E	A	SA	WI	NZ	P	SL	Z
R.J.Shastri (142), S.M.H.Kirmani (102)	Bombay³	1984-85	235	–	–	–	–	–	–	–
D.N.Sardesai (150), E.D.Solkar (65)	Bridgetown	1970-71	–	–	–	186	–	–	–	–
Yashpal Sharma (55*), Kapil Dev (116)	Kanpur	1981-82	169	–	–	–	–	–	–	–
S.R.Tendulkar (119*), M.Prabhakar (67*)	Manchester	1990	160*	–	–	–	–	–	–	–
R.M.H.Binny (83*), Madan Lal (74)	Bangalore	1983-84	–	–	–	–	–	155	–	–
M.L.Apte (163*), M.H.Mankad (96)	Port-of-Spain	1952-53	–	–	–	153	–	–	–	–
C.G.Borde (84), S.A.Durani (90)	Bombay²	1963-64	153	–	–	–	–	–	–	–
Kapil Dev (100*), S.M.H.Kirmani (30)	Port-of-Spain	1982-83	–	–	–	134	–	–	–	–
V.S.Hazare (145), H.R.Adhikari (51)	Adelaide	1947-48	–	132	–	–	–	–	–	–
R.J.Shastri (107), K.S.More (50)	Bridgetown	1988-89	–	–	–	132	–	–	–	–
S.R.Tendulkar (88), K.S.More (73)	Napier	1989-90	–	–	–	–	128	–	–	–
B.P.Patel (81), S.M.H.Kirmani (49)	Wellington	1975-76	–	–	–	–	116	–	–	–
R.J.Shastri (187), Kapil Dev (110)	Oval	1990	110	–	–	–	–	–	–	–
M.Azharuddin (141), R.M.H.Binny (52*)	Calcutta	1986-87	–	–	–	–	–	101	–	–
M.Azharuddin (106), M.Prabhakar (64)	Adelaide	1991-92	–	101	–	–	–	–	–	–
	Total: (15)		5	2	–	4	2	2	–	–

INDIA – 8th Wicket

			E	A	SA	WI	NZ	P	SL	Z
R.G.Nadkarni (75), F.M.Engineer (90)	Madras²	1964-65	–	–	–	–	143	–	–	–
R.J.Shastri (93), S.M.H.Kirmani (67)	Delhi	1981-82	128	–	–	–	–	–	–	–
S.M.H.Kirmani (101*), K.D.Ghavri (86)	Bombay³	1979-80	–	127	–	–	–	–	–	–
S.M.H.Kirmani (66), Madan Lal (54)	Faisalabad	1982-83	–	–	–	–	–	122	–	–
Yashpal Sharma (63), B.S.Sandhu (68)	Kingston	1982-83	–	–	–	107	–	–	–	–
R.G.Nadkarni (63), F.M.Engineer (65)	Madras²	1961-62	101	–	–	–	–	–	–	–
P.K.Amre (103), K.S.More (55)	Durban²	1992-93	–	–	101	–	–	–	–	–
	Totals: (7)		2	1	1	1	1	1	–	–

INDIA – 9th Wicket

			E	A	SA	WI	NZ	P	SL	Z
P.G.Joshi (52*), R.B.Desai (85)	Bombay²	1960-61	–	–	–	–	–	149	–	–
S.M.Gavaskar (236*), S.M.H.Kirmani (63*)	Madras¹	1983-84	–	–	–	143*	–	–	–	–
D.N.Sardesai (212), E.A.S.Prasanna (25)	Kingston	1970-71	–	–	–	122	–	–	–	–
R.M.H.Binny (39), Madan Lal (63*)	Kanpur	1983-84	–	–	–	117	–	–	–	–
S.M.H.Kirmani (88), B.S.Bedi (36)	Bombay³	1976-77	–	–	–	–	105	–	–	–
S.M.H.Kirmani (78), N.S.Yadav (43)	Auckland	1980-81	–	–	–	–	105	–	–	–
R.J.Shastri (93), Madan Lal (44)	Delhi	1981-82	104	–	–	–	–	–	–	–
	Totals: (7)		1	–	–	3	2	1	–	–

INDIA – 10th Wicket

			E	A	SA	WI	NZ	P	SL	Z
H.R.Adhikari (81*), Ghulam Ahmed (50)	Delhi	1952-53	–	–	–	–	–	109	–	–

PAKISTAN – (178) – 1st Wicket

			E	A	WI	NZ	I	SL	Z
Khalid Ibadulla (166), Abdul Kadir (95)	Karachi¹	1964-65	–	249	–	–	–	–	–
Mohsin Khan (104), Shoaib Mohammad (80)	Lahore²	1983-84	173	–	–	–	–	–	–
Ramiz Raja (78), Shoaib Mohammad (203*)	Karachi¹	1990-91	–	–	–	172	–	–	–
Hanif Mohammad (62), Imtiaz Ahmed (135)	Madras²	1960-61	–	–	–	–	162	–	–
Majid Khan (167), Zaheer Abbas (80)	Georgetown	1976-77	–	–	159†	–	–	–	–
Mohsin Khan (91), Mudassar Nazar (152)	Karachi¹	1982-83	–	–	–	–	157	–	–
Hanif Mohammad (337), Imtiaz Ahmed (91)	Bridgetown	1957-58	–	–	152	–	–	–	–
Sadiq Mohammad (34), Majid Khan (112)	Karachi¹	1976-77	–	–	–	147	–	–	–
Mohsin Khan (59), Mudassar Nazar (199)	Faisalabad	1984-85	–	–	–	–	141	–	–
Sadiq Mohammad (103*), Majid Khan (98)	Hyderabad	1976-77	–	–	–	136*‡	–	–	–
Ramiz Raja (98), Shoaib Mohammad (43)	Sialkot	1991-92	–	–	–	–	–	128	–
Saeed Anwar (136), Aamir Sohail (65)	Colombo (PSS)	1994-95	–	–	–	–	–	128	–
Hanif Mohammad (142), Alimuddin (64)	Bahawalpur	1954-55	–	–	–	–	127	–	–
Saeed Anwar (69), Aamir Sohail (60)	Christchurch	1993-94	–	–	–	125	–	–	–
Majid Khan (54), Sadiq Mohammad (81)	Port-of-Spain	1976-77	–	–	123	–	–	–	–
Mohsin Khan (76), Mudassar Nazar (79)	Faisalabad	1982-83	–	123	–	–	–	–	–
Hanif Mohammad (104), Alimuddin (50)	Dacca	1961-62	122	–	–	–	–	–	–
Mohammad Ilyas (126), Naushad Ali (39)	Karachi¹	1964-65	–	–	–	–	121	–	–
Aamir Sohail (205), Ramiz Raja (54)	Manchester	1992	115	–	–	–	–	–	–
Majid Khan (76), Sadiq Mohammad (105)	Melbourne	1976-77	–	113	–	–	–	–	–
Aamer Malik (117), Ramiz Raja (58)	Faisalabad	1989-90	–	–	–	–	105	–	–
Ramiz Raja (63), Shoaib Mohammad (30)	Faisalabad	1991-92	–	–	–	–	–	102	–
Aamer Malik (113), Ramiz Raja (63)	Lahore²	1989-90	–	–	–	100	–	–	–
	Totals: (23)		3	3	3	5	6	3	–

†*219 runs were added for this wicket, Sadiq Mohammad retiring hurt and being succeeded by Zaheer Abbas after 60 runs had been scored.*
‡*164 runs were added for this wicket, Sadiq Mohammad retiring hurt and being succeeded by Zaheer Abbas after 136 runs had been scored.*
Although the 1st wicket added 128 v Australia at Melbourne in 1972-73, this consisted of two partnerships: Sadiq Mohammad added 31* with Saeed Ahmed (retired hurt) and a further 97 with Zaheer Abbas.

PAKISTAN – 2nd Wicket

			E	A	WI	NZ	I	SL	Z
Zaheer Abbas (274), Mushtaq Mohammad (100)	Birmingham	1971	291	–	–	–	–	–	–
Mudassar Nazar (199), Qasim Omar (210)	Faisalabad	1984-85	–	–	–	–	250	–	–
Hanif Mohammad (160), Saeed Ahmed (121)	Bombay²	1960-61	–	–	–	–	246	–	–
Mohsin Khan (149), Qasim Omar (113)	Adelaide	1983-84	–	233	–	–	–	–	–
Sadiq Mohammad (137), Majid Khan (158)	Melbourne	1972-73	–	195	–	–	–	–	–
Hanif Mohammad (103), Saeed Ahmed (78)	Karachi¹	1958-59	–	–	178	–	–	–	–
Hanif Mohammad (96), Waqar Hassan (65)	Bombay²	1952-53	–	–	–	–	165	–	–
Mohsin Khan (129), Majid Khan (63)	Lahore²	1981-82	–	–	–	–	–	151	–
Mohsin Khan (200), Mansoor Akhtar (57)	Lord's	1982	144	–	–	–	–	–	–
Ramiz Raja (88), Asif Mujtaba (40)	Manchester	1992	142	–	–	–	–	–	–
Mudassar Nazar (95), Majid Khan (74)	Melbourne	1981-82	–	141	–	–	–	–	–
Imtiaz Ahmed (98), Mushtaq Mohammad (72)	Oval	1962	137	–	–	–	–	–	–
Majid Khan (108), Zaheer Abbas (59)	Melbourne	1978-79	–	135	–	–	–	–	–
Hanif Mohammad (81), Saeed Ahmed (64)	Port-of-Spain	1957-58	–	–	130	–	–	–	–
Sadiq Mohammad (105), Zaheer Abbas (90)	Melbourne	1976-77	–	128	–	–	–	–	–
Aamer Sohail (205), Asif Mujtaba (57)	Manchester	1992	126	–	–	–	–	–	–
Majid Khan (45), Wasim Bari (85)	Lahore²	1978-79	–	–	–	–	125	–	–
Mohsin Khan (58), Haroon Rashid (82)	Karachi¹	1982-83	–	125	–	–	–	–	–
Aamer Malik (113), Salim Malik (55)	Lahore²	1989-90	–	–	–	–	123	–	–
Shoaib Mohammad (53*), Asif Mujtaba (65*)	Lahore²	1993-94	–	–	–	–	–	–	118*
Imtiaz Ahmed (122), Saeed Ahmed (52)	Kingston	1957-58	–	–	118	–	–	–	–
Saeed Anwar (94), Asif Mujtaba (44)	Colombo (PSS)	1994-95	–	–	–	–	–	115	–
Mohammad Ilyas (56), Saeed Ahmed (68)	Rawalpindi¹	1964-65	–	–	114	–	–	–	–
Hanif Mohammad (111), Saeed Ahmed (69)	Dacca	1961-62	113	–	–	–	–	–	–
Hanif Mohammad (337), Alimuddin (37)	Bridgetown	1957-58	–	–	112	–	–	–	–
Mudassar Nazar (152), Javed Miandad (47)	Karachi¹	1982-83	–	–	–	–	112	–	–
Talat Ali (61), Javed Miandad (160*)	Christchurch	1978-79	–	–	–	104	–	–	–
Majid Khan (98), Zaheer Abbas (240)	Oval	1974	100	–	–	–	–	–	–
	Totals:	*(28)*	7	6	4	2	6	2	1

PAKISTAN – 3rd Wicket

			E	A	WI	NZ	I	SL	Z
Mudassar Nazar (231), Javed Miandad (280*)	Hyderabad	1982-83	–	–	–	–	451	–	–
Qasim Omar (206), Javed Miandad (203*)	Faisalabad	1985-86	–	–	–	–	–	397	–
Shoaib Mohammad (112), Javed Miandad (271)	Auckland	1988-89	–	–	–	248	–	–	–
Taslim Arif (210*), Javed Miandad (106*)	Faisalabad	1979-80	–	223*	–	–	–	–	–
Shoaib Mohammad (163), Javed Miandad (118)	Wellington	1988-89	–	–	–	220	–	–	–
Mudassar Nazar (106), Javed Miandad (103)	Hyderabad	1984-85	–	–	–	212	–	–	–
Saeed Anwar (169), Basit Ali (85)	Wellington	1993-94	–	–	–	197	–	–	–
Shoaib Mohammad (94), Javed Miandad (211)	Karachi¹	1988-89	–	196	–	–	–	–	–
Mudassar Nazar (114), Haroon Rashid (122)	Lahore²	1977-78	180	–	–	–	–	–	–
Zaheer Abbas (240), Mushtaq Mohammad (76)	Oval	1974	172	–	–	–	–	–	–
Shoaib Mohammad (74), Javed Miandad (107)	Faisalabad	1988-89	–	172	–	–	–	–	–
Sadiq Mohammad (166), Majid Khan (79)	Wellington	1972-73	–	–	–	171	–	–	–
Saeed Ahmed (97), Wazir Mohammad (189)	Port-of-Spain	1957-58	–	–	169	–	–	–	–
Saeed Ahmed (166), Shujauddin (45)	Lahore²	1959-60	–	169	–	–	–	–	–
Zaheer Abbas (96), Asif Iqbal (104)	Faisalabad	1978-79	–	–	–	–	166	–	–
Hanif Mohammad (111), Javed Burki (140)	Dacca	1961-62	156	–	–	–	–	–	–
Shoaib Mohammad (101), Javed Miandad (94)	Madras¹	1986-87	–	–	–	–	155	–	–
Hanif Mohammad (337), Saeed Ahmed (65)	Bridgetown	1957-58	–	–	154	–	–	–	–
Mudassar Nazar (152*), Javed Miandad (85)	Lahore²	1982-83	–	–	–	–	148	–	–
Mudassar Nazar (120), Javed Miandad (65)	Lahore²	1987-88	142	–	–	–	–	–	–
Qasim Omar (96), Javed Miandad (79)	Dunedin	1984-85	–	–	–	141	–	–	–
Saeed Ahmed (74), Javed Burki (138)	Lahore²	1961-62	138	–	–	–	–	–	–
Aamir Sohail (205), Javed Miandad (88)	Manchester	1992	137	–	–	–	–	–	–
Saeed Ahmed (150), Hanif Mohammad (79)	Georgetown	1957-58	–	–	136	–	–	–	–
Mudassar Nazar (124), Javed Miandad (75)	Birmingham	1987	135	–	–	–	–	–	–
Mudassar Nazar (126), Javed Miandad (76)	Bangalore	1979-80	–	–	–	–	134	–	–
Shoaib Mohammad (142), Salim Malik (71)	Faisalabad	1990-91	–	–	–	131	–	–	–
Zaheer Abbas (72), Mushtaq Mohammad (57)	Leeds	1971	129	–	–	–	–	–	–
Qasim Omar (65), Javed Miandad (46)	Perth	1983-84	–	125	–	–	–	–	–
Majid Khan (99), Mushtaq Mohammad (99)	Karachi¹	1972-73	121	–	–	–	–	–	–

Hundred Partnerships (Pakistan)

3rd Wicket *continued*

			E	A	WI	NZ	I	SL	Z
Saeed Ahmed (172), Javed Burki (29)	Karachi[1]	1964-65	–	–	–	114	–	–	–
Ramiz Raja (62), Javed Miandad (76)	Karachi[1]	1986-87	–	–	111	–	–	–	–
Shoaib Mohammad (55), Javed Miandad (59)	Oval	1992	111	–	–	–	–	–	–
Majid Khan (110), Mushtaq Mohammad (61)	Auckland	1972-73	–	–	–	104	–	–	–
Qasim Omar (45), Javed Miandad (104)	Hyderabad	1984-85	–	–	–	103	–	–	–
Mudassar Nazar (73), Javed Miandad (260)	Oval	1987	103	–	–	–	–	–	–
Imtiaz Ahmed (122), W.Mathias (77)	Kingston	1957-58	–	–	101	–	–	–	–
Majid Khan (41), Javed Miandad (57)	Multan	1980-81	–	–	100	–	–	–	–
Mudassar Nazar (65), Javed Miandad (54)	Leeds	1982	100	–	–	–	–	–	–
Totals:	*(39)*		12	5	6	10	5	1	–

PAKISTAN – 4th Wicket

			E	A	WI	NZ	I	SL	Z
Mushtaq Mohammad (201), Asif Iqbal (175)	Dunedin	1972-73	–	–	–	350	–	–	–
Javed Miandad (153*), Salim Malik (165)	Birmingham	1992	322	–	–	–	–	–	–
Javed Miandad (126), Zaheer Abbas (168)	Faisalabad	1982-83	–	–	–	–	287	–	–
Zaheer Abbas (176), Javed Miandad (154*)	Faisalabad	1978-79	–	–	–	–	255	–	–
Javed Miandad (206), Mushtaq Mohammad (107)	Karachi[1]	1976-77	–	–	–	252	–	–	–
Javed Miandad (145), Shoaib Mohammad (203*)	Lahore[2]	1989-90	–	–	–	–	246	–	–
Javed Miandad (260), Salim Malik (102)	Oval	1987	234	–	–	–	–	–	–
Shoaib Mohammad (86), Salim Malik (102)	Karachi[1]	1990-91	–	–	174	–	–	–	–
Mushtaq Mohammad (101), Asif Iqbal (73)	Hyderabad	1976-77	–	–	–	164	–	–	–
Salim Malik (100*), Javed Miandad (92)	Karachi[1]	1981-82	–	–	–	–	–	162	–
Mansoor Akhtar (111), Zaheer Abbas (126)	Faisalabad	1982-83	–	155	–	–	–	–	–
Wazir Mohammad (189), Hanif Mohammad (54)	Port-of-Spain	1957-58	–	–	154	–	–	–	–
Javed Burki (138), Mushtaq Mohammad (76)	Lahore[2]	1961-62	153	–	–	–	–	–	–
Mohsin Khan (200), Zaheer Abbas (75)	Lord's	1982	153	–	–	–	–	–	–
Mohsin Khan (135), Javed Miandad (138)	Lahore[2]	1982-83	–	150	–	–	–	–	–
Javed Miandad (271), Aamer Malik (56)	Auckland	1988-89	–	–	–	147	–	–	–
Maqsood Ahmed (99), A.H.Kardar (44)	Lahore[1]	1954-55	–	–	–	–	136	–	–
Mohsin Khan (152), Zaheer Abbas (44)	Melbourne	1983-84	–	132	–	–	–	–	–
Salim Malik (116), Zaheer Abbas (68)	Faisalabad	1983-84	130	–	–	–	–	–	–
Javed Miandad (62), Zaheer Abbas (90)	Melbourne	1981-82	–	128	–	–	–	–	–
Hanif Mohammad (337), Wazir Mohammad (35)	Bridgetown	1957-58	–	–	121	–	–	–	–
Shoaib Mohammad (142), Javed Miandad (55)	Faisalabad	1990-91	–	–	–	117	–	–	–
Mushtaq Mohammad (76), Wasim Raja (53)	Lord's	1974	115	–	–	–	–	–	–
Haroon Rashid (108), Javed Miandad (88*)	Hyderabad	1977-78	112	–	–	–	–	–	–
Mohsin Khan (94), Zaheer Abbas (215)	Lahore[2]	1982-83	–	–	–	–	112	–	–
Javed Miandad (39), Zaheer Abbas (186)	Karachi[1]	1982-83	–	–	–	–	110	–	–
Majid Khan (92), Mushtaq Mohammad (121)	Port-of-Spain	1976-77	–	–	108	–	–	–	–
Mushtaq Mohammad (100*), Saeed Ahmed (64)	Nottingham	1962	107	–	–	–	–	–	–
Javed Miandad (65), Ijaz Ahmed (121)	Melbourne	1989-90	–	103	–	–	–	–	–
Majid Khan (75), Zaheer Abbas (48)	Leeds	1974	100	–	–	–	–	–	–
Mudassar Nazar (114), Javed Miandad (71)	Lahore[2]	1977-78	100	–	–	–	–	–	–
Totals:	*(31)*		10	5	4	5	6	1	–

PAKISTAN – 5th Wicket

			E	A	WI	NZ	I	SL	Z
Javed Miandad (163), Asif Iqbal (166)	Lahore[2]	1976-77	–	–	–	281	–	–	–
Salim Malik (140), Inzamam-ul-Haq (135*)	Wellington	1993-94	–	–	–	258	–	–	–
Zaheer Abbas (186), Mudassar Nazar (119)	Karachi[1]	1982-83	–	–	–	–	213	–	–
Javed Burki (101), Nasim-ul-Ghani (101)	Lord's	1962	197	–	–	–	–	–	–
Javed Miandad (260), Imran Khan (118)	Oval	1987	191	–	–	–	–	–	–
Javed Miandad (131), Salim Malik (77)	Adelaide	1983-84	–	186	–	–	–	–	–
Alimuddin (103*), A.H.Kardar (93)	Karachi[1]	1954-55	–	–	–	–	155	–	–
Mushtaq Mohammad (157), Asif Iqbal (68)	Hyderabad	1972-73	153	–	–	–	–	–	–
Shoaib Mohammad (95), Salim Malik (102*)	Karachi[1]	1989-90	–	–	–	141	–	–	–
Zaheer Abbas (235*), Javed Miandad (35)	Lahore[2]	1978-79	–	–	–	140	–	–	–
Mushtaq Mohammad (121), Asif Iqbal (65)	Sydney	1972-73	–	139	–	–	–	–	–
Javed Miandad (85), Mushtaq Mohammad (67*)	Karachi[1]	1976-77	–	–	–	138	–	–	–
Javed Burki (61), Mushtaq Mohammad (101)	Delhi	1960-61	–	–	–	–	136	–	–
Shoaib Mohammad (203*), Imran Khan (66)	Lahore[2]	1989-90	–	–	–	–	134	–	–
Salim Malik (101), Imran Khan (93*)	Sialkot	1991-92	–	–	–	–	–	132	–
Wasim Raja (97), Asif Iqbal (64)	Delhi	1979-80	–	–	–	–	130	–	–
Zaheer Abbas (80), Wasim Raja (43)	Brisbane[2]	1981-82	–	125	–	–	–	–	–
Javed Miandad (138), Zaheer Abbas (52)	Lahore[2]	1982-83	–	123	–	–	–	–	–
Salim Malik (116), Wasim Raja (112)	Faisalabad	1983-84	123	–	–	–	–	–	–

5th Wicket *continued*

			E	A	WI	NZ	I	SL	Z
Javed Miandad (43), Ijaz Ahmed (122)	Faisalabad	1988-89	–	119	–	–	–	–	–
Qasim Omar (210), Salim Malik (102*)	Faisalabad	1984-85	–	–	–	–	114	–	–
Javed Miandad (211), Salim Malik (45)	Karachi[1]	1988-89	–	114	–	–	–	–	–
Mudassar Nazar (81), Salim Malik (54)	Kandy	1985-86	–	–	–	–	–	102	–
Zaheer Abbas (85), Mudassar Nazar (78)	Nagpur	1983-84	–	–	–	–	101	–	–
	Totals: (24)		4	6	–	3	9	2	–

PAKISTAN – 6th Wicket

			E	A	WI	NZ	I	SL	Z
Hanif Mohammad (203*), Majid Khan (80)	Lahore[2]	1964-65	–	–	–	217	–	–	–
Salim Malik (107), Imran Khan (117)	Faisalabad	1982-83	–	–	–	–	207	–	–
Imran Khan (136), Wasim Akram (123)	Adelaide	1989-90	–	191	–	–	–	–	–
Salim Malik (119*), Wasim Raja (60*)	Karachi[1]	1984-85	–	–	–	178*	–	–	–
Wazir Mohammad (106), A.H.Kardar (57)	Kingston	1957-58	–	–	166	–	–	–	–
Javed Miandad (100), Mushtaq Mohammad (78)	Karachi[1]	1978-79	–	–	–	–	154	–	–
Zaheer Abbas (235*), Mushtaq Mohammad (67)	Lahore[2]	1978-79	–	–	–	–	146	–	–
Mushtaq Mohammad (157), Intikhab Alam (138)	Hyderabad	1972-73	145	–	–	–	–	–	–
Salim Malik (80*), Imran Khan (69*)	Auckland	1988-89	–	–	–	136*	–	–	–
Zaheer Abbas (215), Imran Khan (45)	Lahore[2]	1982-83	–	–	–	–	117	–	–
Mushtaq Mohammad (123), Aftab Baloch (60*)	Lahore[2]	1974-75	–	116	–	–	–	–	–
Mushtaq Mohammad (56), Wasim Raja (70)	Port-of-Spain	1976-77	–	116	–	–	–	–	–
Asif Iqbal (120), Javed Miandad (64)	Sydney	1976-77	–	115	–	–	–	–	–
Asif Iqbal (135), Wasim Raja (64)	Kingston	1976-77	–	–	115	–	–	–	–
Javed Miandad (102), Ijaz Ahmed (43)	Port-of-Spain	1987-88	–	–	113	–	–	–	–
Ijaz Ahmed (122), Salim Yousuf (62)	Faisalabad	1988-89	–	111	–	–	–	–	–
Wazir Mohammad (67), A.H.Kardar (69)	Karachi[1]	1956-57	–	104	–	–	–	–	–
Zaheer Abbas (134), Imran Khan (39)	Lahore[2]	1981-82	–	–	–	–	–	100	–
	Totals: (18)		1	4	5	3	4	1	–

PAKISTAN – 7th Wicket

			E	A	WI	NZ	I	SL	Z
Waqar Hassan (189), Imtiaz Ahmed (209)	Lahore[1]	1955-56	–	–	–	308	–	–	–
Imran Khan (72), Ijaz Faqih (105)	Ahmedabad	1986-87	–	–	–	–	154	–	–
Zaheer Abbas (168*), Ashraf Ali (65)	Lahore[2]	1984-85	–	–	–	–	142	–	–
Wasim Raja (107*), Wasim Bari (58)	Karachi[1]	1974-75	–	–	128	–	–	–	–
Intikhab Alam (64), Wasim Bari (72)	Adelaide	1972-73	–	104	–	–	–	–	–
Haroon Rashid (153), Tahir Naqqash (57)	Karachi[1]	1981-82	–	–	–	–	–	104	–
	Totals: (6)		–	1	1	1	2	1	–

*Although the 7th wicket added 168 v West Indies at Lahore[2] in 1980-81, this consisted of two partnerships:
Imran Khan added 72 with Abdul Qadir (retired hurt) and a further 96 with Sarfraz Nawaz.*

PAKISTAN – 8th Wicket

			E	A	WI	NZ	I	SL	Z
Hanif Mohammad (187*), Asif Iqbal (76)	Lord's	1967	130	–	–	–	–	–	–
Imran Khan (135*), Wasim Akram (62)	Madras[1]	1986-87	–	–	–	–	112	–	–
Majid Khan (110*), Imran Khan (56)	Lahore[2]	1979-80	–	111	–	–	–	–	–
Imran Khan (83), Abdul Qadir (45)	Melbourne	1983-84	–	108	–	–	–	–	–
	Totals: (4)		1	2	–	–	1	–	–

PAKISTAN – 9th Wicket

			E	A	WI	NZ	I	SL	Z
Asif Iqbal (146), Intikhab Alam (51)	Oval	1967	190	–	–	–	–	–	–
Zaheer Abbas (82*), Sarfraz Nawaz (90)	Lahore[2]	1983-84	161	–	–	–	–	–	–
Haroon Rashid (153), Rashid Khan (59)	Karachi[1]	1981-82	–	–	–	–	–	127	–
	Totals: (3)		2	–	–	–	–	1	–

PAKISTAN – 10th Wicket

			E	A	WI	NZ	I	SL	Z
Wasim Raja (71), Wasim Bari (60*)	Bridgetown	1976-77	–	133	–	–	–	–	–
Zulfiqar Ahmed (63*), Amir Elahi (47)	Madras[1]	1952-53	–	–	–	–	104	–	–
	Totals: (2)		–	–	1	–	1	–	–

Hundred Partnerships (Sri Lanka)

SRI LANKA – (43) – 1st Wicket

			E	A	SA	WI	NZ	I	P
S.Wettimuny (79), J.R.Ratnayeke (93)	Kanpur	1986-87	–	–	–	–	–	159	–
R.S.Mahanama (73), D.P.Samaraweera (42)	Lucknow[2]	1993-94	–	–	–	–	–	120	–
R.S.Mahanama (69), U.C.Hathurusinghe (49)	Colombo (KS)	1992-93	–	110	–	–	–	–	–
	Totals:	(3)	–	1	–	–	–	2	–

SRI LANKA – 2nd Wicket

			E	A	SA	WI	NZ	I	P
S.Wettimuny (157), R.L.Dias (98)	Faisalabad	1981-82	–	–	–	–	–	–	217
R.S.Mahanama (153), A.P.Gurusinha (43)	Moratuwa	1992-93	–	–	–	–	138	–	–
	Totals:	(2)	–	–	–	–	1	–	1

SRI LANKA – 3rd Wicket

			E	A	SA	WI	NZ	I	P
S.Wettimuny (65), R.L.Dias (108)	Colombo (SSC)	1983-84	–	–	–	–	159*†	–	–
R.L.Dias (60), L.R.D.Mendis (105)	Madras[1]	1982-83	–	–	–	–	–	153	–
U.C.Hathurusinghe (74), P.A.de Silva (123)	Auckland	1990-91	–	–	–	–	145	–	–
A.P.Gurusinha (70), P.A.de Silva (267)	Wellington	1990-91	–	–	–	–	143	–	–
A.P.Gurusinha (56), P.A.de Silva (148)	Colombo (PSS)	1993-94	–	–	–	–	–	136	–
R.S.Mahanama (153), P.A.de Silva (62)	Moratuwa	1992-93	–	–	–	–	133	–	–
P.A.de Silva (75), R.L.Dias (60*)	Colombo (PSS)	1985-86	–	–	–	–	–	132	–
U.C.Hathurusinghe (81), A.P.Gurusinha (102)	Hamilton	1990-91	–	–	–	–	117	–	–
R.L.Dias (97), L.R.D.Mendis (105)	Madras[1]	1982-83	–	–	–	–	–	110	–
U.C.Hathurusinghe (67), P.A.de Silva (85)	Colombo (KS)	1992-93	–	107	–	–	–	–	–
R.S.Mahanama (50), P.A.de Silva (58)	Moratuwa	1992-93	–	107	–	–	–	–	–
S.Wettimuny (190), R.L.Dias (32)	Lord's	1984	101	–	–	–	–	–	–
	Totals:	(12)	1	2	–	–	5	4	–

†163 runs were added for this wicket, S.Wettimuny retiring hurt and being succeeded by J.R.Ratnayake after 159 runs had been added.

SRI LANKA – 4th Wicket

			E	A	SA	WI	NZ	I	P
A.P.Gurusinha (116*), A.Ranatunga (135*)	Colombo (PSS)	1985-86	–	–	–	–	–	–	240
A.P.Gurusinha (137), A.Ranatunga (127)	Colombo (SSC)	1992-93	–	230	–	–	–	–	–
R.L.Dias (106), L.R.D.Mendis (124)	Kandy	1985-86	–	–	–	–	–	216	–
P.A.de Silva (267), A.Ranatunga (55)	Wellington	1990-91	–	–	–	–	178	–	–
S.Wettimuny (190), A.Ranatunga (84)	Lord's	1984	148	–	–	–	–	–	–
R.S.Mahanama (85), P.A.de Silva (75)	Hobart	1989-90	–	128	–	–	–	–	–
P.A.de Silva (80), A.Ranatunga (64)	Colombo (SSC)	1992-93	127	–	–	–	–	–	–
P.A.de Silva (82), A.Ranatunga (50)	Colombo (PSS)	1993-94	–	–	101	–	–	–	–
	Totals:	(8)	2	2	1	–	1	1	1

SRI LANKA – 5th Wicket

			E	A	SA	WI	NZ	I	P
S.Wettimuny (190), L.R.D.Mendis (111)	Lord's	1984	150	–	–	–	–	–	–
R.S.Madugalle (103), A.Ranatunga (111)	Colombo (SSC)	1985-86	–	–	–	–	–	144	–
R.S.Mahanama (151), H.P.Tillekeratne (86)	Colombo (PSS)	1993-94	–	–	–	–	–	132	–
R.S.Madugalle (79), D.S.de Silva (61)	Wellington	1982-83	–	–	–	–	130	–	–
P.A.de Silva (68), A.Ranatunga (131)	Moratuwa	1993-94	–	–	121	–	–	–	–
P.A.de Silva (127), H.P.Tillekeratne (34)	Colombo (PSS)	1994-95	–	–	–	–	–	–	119
H.P.Tillekeratne (82), A.Ranatunga (48)	Moratuwa	1992-93	–	116	–	–	–	–	–
A.Ranatunga (88), H.P.Tillekeratne (28)	Colombo (SSC)	1993-94	–	–	–	–	–	111	–
	Totals:	(8)	1	1	1	–	1	3	1

SRI LANKA – 6th Wicket

			E	A	SA	WI	NZ	I	P
S.A.R.Silva (102*), L.R.D.Mendis (94)	Lord's	1984	138	–	–	–	–	–	–
A.Ranatunga (79), P.A.de Silva (122)	Faisalabad	1985-86	–	–	–	–	–	–	121
R.S.Madugalle (89*), A.Ranatunga (37)	Colombo (CCC)	1983-84	–	–	–	–	109*†	–	–
D.S.B.P.Kuruppu (201*), R.S.Madugalle (60)	Colombo (CCC)	1986-87	–	–	–	–	109	–	–
A.Ranatunga (78), L.R.D.Mendis (56)	Lord's	1988	104	–	–	–	–	–	–
A.Ranatunga (131), H.P.Tillekeratne (33)	Moratuwa	1993-94	–	–	103	–	–	–	–
S.T.Jayasuriya (77), H.P.Tillekeratne (49)	Sialkot	1991-92	–	–	–	–	–	–	101
	Totals:	(7)	2	–	1	–	2	–	2

†119 runs were added for the 6th wicket, R.S.Madugalle retiring hurt and being succeeded by D.S.de Silva after 109 runs had been scored.

RI LANKA – 7th Wicket

			E	A	SA	WI	NZ	I	P
.A.de Silva (167), J.R.Ratnayeke (56)	Brisbane[2]	1989-90	–	144	–	–	–	–	–
I.P.Tillekeratne (83*), R.S.Kalpage (62)	Kandy	1994- 95	–	–	–	–	–	–	131
.R.Ratnayeke (75), E.A.R.de Silva (50)	Hobart	1989-90	–	124	–	–	–	–	–
		Totals: (3)	–	2	–	–	–	–	1

RI LANKA – 8th Wicket
No instance – highest partnership

			E	A	SA	WI	NZ	I	P
R.S.Madugalle (91*), D.S.de Silva (25)	Faisalabad	1981-82	–	–	–	–	–	–	61

RI LANKA – 9th Wicket
No instance – highest partnership

			E	A	SA	WI	NZ	I	P
H.P.Tillekeratne (93*), M.Muralitharan (19)	Colombo (SSC)	1992-93	83	–	–	–	–	–	–

RI LANKA – 10th Wicket
No instance – highest partnership

			E	A	SA	WI	NZ	I	P
.R.Ratnayeke (59*), G.F.Labrooy (42)	Lord's	1988	64	–	–	–	–	–	–

ZIMBABWE – (7) – 1st Wicket

			NZ	I	P
K.J.Arnott (40), G.W.Flower (82)	Harare	1992-93	–	100	–

ZIMBABWE – 2nd Wicket

			NZ	I	P
M.H.Dekker (68*), A.D.R.Campbell (75)	Rawalpindi[2]	1993-94	–	–	135
K.J.Arnott (68), A.D.R.Campbell (52)	Harare	1992-93	107	–	–
K.J.Arnott (101*), A.D.R.Campbell (48*)	Bulawayo	1992-93	105*	–	–
M.H.Dekker (68), A.D.R.Campbell (63)	Rawalpindi[2]	1993-94	–	–	102
		Totals: (4)	2	–	2

ZIMBABWE – 3rd Wicket
No instance – highest partnership

			NZ	I	P
K.J.Arnott (32), A.J.Pycroft (46)	Harare	1992-93	–	77	–

ZIMBABWE – 4th Wicket

			NZ	I	P
G.W.Flower (96), A.Flower (115)	Delhi	1992-93	–	192	–

ZIMBABWE – 5th Wicket
No instance – highest partnership

			NZ	I	P
A.Flower (63), G.J.Whittall (33)	Karachi[2]	1993-94	–	–	77

ZIMBABWE – 6th Wicket

			NZ	I	P
D.L.Houghton (121), A.Flower (59)	Harare	1992-93	–	165	–

ZIMBABWE – 7th Wicket
No instance – highest partnership

			NZ	I	P
A.Flower (81), A.H.Shah (28)	Bulawayo	1992-93	60	–	–

ZIMBABWE – 8th Wicket
No instance – highest partnership

			NZ	I	P
A.Flower (62*), D.H.Brain (28)	Lahore[2]	1993-94	–	–	46

ZIMBABWE – 9th Wicket
No instance – highest partnership

			NZ	I	P
G.J.Crocker (33), M.G.Burmester (17*)	Harare	1992-93	46	–	–

ZIMBABWE – 10th Wicket
No instance – highest partnership

			NZ	I	P
E.A.Brandes (18), S.G.Peall (11*)	Rawalpindi[2]	1993-94	–	–	29

SUMMARY OF HUNDRED PARTNERSHIPS

	1st	2nd	3rd	4th	5th	6th	7th	8th	9th	10th	Tot
England	133	128	114	107	68	68	34	12	7	3	67
Australia	66	108	102	99	69	38	22	12	7	2	52
South Africa	32	22	29	23	12	12	13	5	1	1	15
West Indies	44	58	62	62	43	44	15	1	4	1	33
New Zealand	25	24	28	21	26	13	9	4	2	2	15
India	36	47	50	44	31	23	15	7	7	1	26
Pakistan	23	28	39	31	24	18	6	4	3	2	17
Sri Lanka	3	2	12	8	8	7	3	–	–	–	4
Zimbabwe	1	4	–	1	–	1	–	–	–	–	
Totals	363	421	436	396	281	224	117	45	31	12	232

INDIVIDUAL RECORDS – BOWLING

100 WICKETS IN TESTS

ENGLAND	Tests	Wkts	Avge	Opponents A	SA	WI	NZ	I	P	SL
I.T.Botham	102	383	28.40	148	–	61	64	59	40	11
R.G.D.Willis	90	325	25.20	128	–	38	60	62	34	3
F.S.Trueman	67	307	21.57	79	27	86	40	53	22	–
D.L.Underwood	86	297	25.83	105	–	38	48	62	36	8
J.B.Statham	70	252	24.84	69	69	42	20	25	27	–
A.V.Bedser	51	236	24.89	104	54	11	13	44	10	–
J.A.Snow	49	202	26.66	83	4	72	20	16	7	–
J.C.Laker	46	193	21.24	79	32	51	21	8	2	–
S.F.Barnes	27	189	16.43	106	83	–	–	–	–	–
G.A.R.Lock	49	174	25.58	31	15	39	47	26	16	–
M.W.Tate	39	155	26.16	83	53	13	6	–	–	–
F.J.Titmus	53	153	32.22	47	27	15	28	27	9	–
J.E.Emburey	63	147	37.85	78	–	30	9	12	7	11
H.Verity	40	144	24.37	59	31	9	7	38	–	–
C.M.Old	46	143	28.11	40	–	18	21	43	21	–
A.W.Greig	58	141	32.20	44	–	36	20	27	14	–
G.R.Dilley	41	138	29.76	41	–	36	24	17	20	–
T.E.Bailey	61	132	29.21	42	28	29	32	–	1	–
W.Rhodes	58	127	26.96	109	8	10	–	–	–	–
P.A.J.DeFreitas	39	125	32.21	24	9	31	39	–	14	8
P.H.Edmonds	51	125	34.18	36	–	3	31	33	22	–
D.A.Allen	39	122	30.97	28	21	15	13	21	24	–
R.Illingworth	61	122	31.20	34	6	19	22	31	10	–
J.Briggs	33	118	17.75	97	21	–	–	–	–	–
G.G.Arnold	34	115	28.29	30	–	17	20	27	21	–
G.A.Lohmann	18	112	10.75	77	35	–	–	–	–	–
D.V.P.Wright	34	108	39.11	48	37	11	8	4	–	–
J.H.Wardle	28	102	20.39	24	46	7	5	–	20	–
R.Peel	20	101	16.98	101	–	–	–	–	–	–
C.Blythe	19	100	18.63	41	59	–	–	–	–	–

AUSTRALIA	Tests	Wkts	Avge	Opponents E	SA	WI	NZ	I	P	SL
D.K.Lillee	70	355	23.92	167	–	55	38	21	71	3
R.Benaud	63	248	27.03	83	52	42	–	52	19	–
G.D.McKenzie	60	246	29.78	96	41	47	–	47	15	–
C.J.McDermott	58	231	28.97	52	21	59	48	34	–	17
R.R.Lindwall	61	228	23.03	114	31	41	2	36	4	–
C.V.Grimmett	37	216	24.21	106	77	33	–	–	–	–
M.G.Hughes	53	212	28.38	75	4	53	25	23	16	16
J.R.Thomson	51	200	28.00	100	–	62	6	22	10	–
A.K.Davidson	44	186	20.53	84	25	33	–	30	14	–
G.F.Lawson	46	180	30.56	97	–	39	10	–	33	1
T.M.Alderman	41	170	27.15	100	–	26	16	–	23	5
K.R.Miller	55	170	22.97	87	30	40	2	9	2	–
W.A.Johnston	40	160	23.91	75	44	25	–	16	–	–
W.J.O'Reilly	27	144	22.59	102	34	–	8	–	–	–
H.Trumble	32	141	21.78	141	–	–	–	–	–	–
M.H.N.Walker	34	138	27.47	56	–	37	28	–	17	–
A.A.Mallett	38	132	29.84	50	6	16	19	28	13	–
B.Yardley	33	126	31.63	29	–	35	13	21	21	7
R.M.Hogg	38	123	28.44	56	–	22	10	15	19	1
M.A.Noble	42	121	25.00	115	6	–	–	–	–	–
S.K.Warne	26	116	23.96	34	33	10	35	1	–	3
B.A.Reid	27	113	24.63	47	–	12	16	24	14	–
I.W.Johnson	45	109	29.19	42	22	22	–	19	4	–
G.Giffen	31	103	27.09	103	–	–	–	–	–	–
A.N.Connolly	29	102	29.22	25	26	20	–	31	–	–
C.T.B.Turner	17	101	16.53	101	–	–	–	–	–	–

621

SOUTH AFRICA

	Tests	Wkts	Avge	E	A	WI	NZ	I	SL
H.J.Tayfield	37	170	25.91	75	64	–	31	–	–
T.L.Goddard	41	123	26.22	63	53	–	7	–	–
P.M.Pollock	28	116	24.18	32	52	–	32	–	–
N.A.T.Adcock	26	104	21.10	57	14	–	33	–	–

WEST INDIES

	Tests	Wkts	Avge	E	A	SA	NZ	I	P	SL
M.D.Marshall	81	376	20.94	127	87	–	36	76	50	–
L.R.Gibbs	79	309	29.09	100	103	–	11	63	32	–
J.Garner	58	259	20.97	92	89	–	36	7	35	–
M.A.Holding	60	249	23.68	96	76	–	16	61	–	–
G.St A.Sobers	93	235	34.03	102	51	–	19	59	4	–
C.A.Walsh	65	222	26.23	75	47	4	16	44	35	1
C.E.L.Ambrose	48	219	21.07	96	77	8	–	5	30	3
A.M.E.Roberts	47	202	25.61	50	51	–	3	67	31	–
W.W.Hall	48	192	26.38	65	45	–	1	65	16	–
S.Ramadhin	43	158	28.98	80	22	–	32	15	9	–
A.L.Valentine	36	139	30.32	40	43	–	23	30	3	–
C.E.H.Croft	27	125	23.30	33	32	–	10	–	50	–
V.A.Holder	40	109	33.27	33	28	–	12	31	5	–

NEW ZEALAND

	Tests	Wkts	Avge	E	A	SA	WI	I	P	SL	Z
R.J.Hadlee	86	431	22.29	97	130	–	51	65	51	37	–
B.L.Cairns	43	130	32.92	32	23	–	17	22	21	15	–
E.J.Chatfield	43	123	32.17	34	24	–	23	6	14	22	–
D.K.Morrison	35	120	34.84	23	37	–	–	20	27	13	–
R.O.Collinge	35	116	29.24	48	17	–	–	23	28	–	–
B.R.Taylor	30	111	26.60	28	–	–	32	29	22	–	–
J.G.Bracewell	41	102	35.81	31	38	–	2	19	6	6	–
R.C.Motz	32	100	31.48	28	–	21	17	22	12	–	–

INDIA

	Tests	Wkts	Avge	E	A	SA	WI	NZ	P	SL	Z
Kapil Dev	131	434	29.64	85	79	8	89	25	99	45	4
B.S.Bedi	67	266	28.71	85	56	–	62	57	6	–	–
B.S.Chandrasekhar	58	242	29.74	95	38	–	65	36	8	–	–
E.A.S.Prasanna	49	189	30.38	41	57	–	34	55	2	–	–
M.H.Mankad	44	162	32.32	54	23	–	36	12	37	–	–
S.Venkataraghavan	57	156	36.11	23	20	–	68	44	1	–	–
R.J.Shastri	80	151	40.96	30	26	2	37	20	24	11	1
S.P.Gupte	36	149	29.55	24	8	–	49	34	34	–	–
D.R.Doshi	33	114	30.71	36	38	–	–	5	27	8	–
K.D.Ghavri	39	109	33.54	19	32	–	36	5	17	–	–
N.S.Yadav	35	102	35.09	9	55	–	9	1	17	11	–

PAKISTAN

	Tests	Wkts	Avge	E	A	WI	NZ	I	SL	Z
Imran Khan	88	362	22.81	47	64	80	31	94	46	–
Abdul Qadir	67	236	32.80	82	45	42	26	27	14	–
Wasim Akram	55	235	22.88	39	17	47	55	31	35	11
Waqar Younis	31	180	18.78	22	4	35	56	6	30	27
Sarfraz Nawaz	55	177	32.75	37	52	26	26	36	–	–
Iqbal Qasim	50	171	28.11	24	57	19	22	34	15	–
Fazal Mahmood	34	139	24.70	25	24	41	5	44	–	–
Intikhab Alam	47	125	35.93	49	9	8	54	5	–	–

SRI LANKA
The leading wicket-taker is R.J.Ratnayake with 73 wickets in 23 Tests.

ZIMBABWE
The leading wicket-taker is D.H.Brain with 18 wickets in 4 Tests.

BEST BOWLING AVERAGES

Qualification: 25 wickets

		Tests	Balls	Runs	Wkts	Avge	5wI	10wM
G.A.Lohmann	E	18	3821	1205	112	**10.75**	9	5
J.J.Ferris	A/E	9	2302	775	61	**12.70**	6	1
A.E.Trott	A/E	5	948	390	26	**15.00**	2	–
M.J.Procter	SA	7	1514	616	41	**15.02**	1	–
W.Barnes	E	21	2289	793	51	**15.54**	3	–
W.Bates	E	15	2364	821	50	**16.42**	4	1
S.F.Barnes	E	27	7873	3106	189	**16.43**	24	7
C.T.B.Turner	A	17	5179	1670	101	**16.53**	11	2
R.Peel	E	20	5216	1715	101	**16.98**	5	2
J.Briggs	E	33	5332	2095	118	**17.75**	9	4
R.Appleyard	E	9	1596	534	31	**17.87**	1	–
W.S.Lees	E	5	1256	467	26	**17.96**	2	–
H.Ironmonger	A	14	4695	1330	74	**17.97**	4	2
G.B.Lawrence	SA	5	1334	512	28	**18.28**	2	–
F.R.Spofforth	A	18	4185	1731	94	**18.41**	7	4
F.H.Tyson	E	17	3452	1411	76	**18.56**	4	1
C.Blythe	E	19	4446	1863	100	**18.63**	9	4
G.F.Bissett	SA	4	989	469	25	**18.76**	2	–
Waqar Younis	P	31	6411	3382	180	**18.78**	19	4
A.S.Kennedy	E	5	1683	599	31	**19.32**	2	–

MOST FREQUENT WICKET-TAKERS

Qualification: 25 wickets

		Balls/wkt	Tests	Balls	Runs	Wkts	Avge
G.A.Lohmann	E	**34.11**	18	3821	1205	112	10.75
Waqar Younis	P	**35.61**	31	6411	3382	180	18.78
A.E.Trott	A/E	**36.46**	5	948	390	26	15.00
M.J.Procter	SA	**36.92**	7	1514	616	41	15.02
J.J.Ferris	A/E	**37.73**	9	2302	775	61	12.70
B.J.T.Bosanquet	E	**38.80**	7	970	604	25	24.16
G.F.Bissett	SA	**39.56**	4	989	469	25	18.76
S.F.Barnes	E	**41.65**	27	7873	3106	189	16.43

MOST ECONOMICAL CAREER FIGURES

Qualification: 2000 balls

		Runs/100 balls	Tests	Balls	Runs	Wkts	Avge
W.Attewell	E	**21.96**	10	2850	626	28	22.35
C.Gladwin	E	**26.82**	8	2129	571	15	38.06
T.L.Goddard	SA	**27.48**	41	11736	3226	123	26.22
R.G.Nadkarni	I	**27.92**	41	9165	2559	88	29.07
H.Ironmonger	A	**28.32**	14	4695	1330	74	17.97
J.C.Watkins	SA	**29.09**	15	2805	816	29	28.13
K.D.Mackay	A	**29.71**	37	5792	1721	50	34.42
A.R.A.Murray	SA	**29.90**	10	2374	710	18	39.44

25 WICKETS IN A SERIES

ENGLAND		Venue	Tests	Opponents A	SA	WI	NZ	I	P	SL
S.F.Barnes	1913-14	SA	4	–	49	–	–	–	–	–
J.C.Laker	1956	E	5	46	–	–	–	–	–	–
A.V.Bedser	1953	E	5	39	–	–	–	–	–	–
M.W.Tate	1924-25	A	5	38	–	–	–	–	–	–
G.A.Lohmann	1895-96	SA	3	–	35	–	–	–	–	–
S.F.Barnes	1911-12	A	5	34	–	–	–	–	–	–
S.F.Barnes	1912	E	3	–	34	–	–	–	–	–
G.A.R.Lock	1958	E	5	–	–	–	34	–	–	–
F.S.Trueman	1963	E	5	–	–	34	–	–	–	–
I.T.Botham	1981	E	6	34	–	–	–	–	–	–
H.Larwood	1932-33	A	5	33	–	–	–	–	–	–

ENGLAND continued		Venue	Tests	Opponents A	SA	WI	NZ	I	P	SL
T.Richardson	1894-95	A	5	32	–	–	–	–	–	–
F.R.Foster	1911-12	A	5	32	–	–	–	–	–	–
W.Rhodes	1903-04	A	5	31	–	–	–	–	–	–
A.S.Kennedy	1922-23	SA	5	–	31	–	–	–	–	–
J.A.Snow	1970-71	A	6	31	–	–	–	–	–	–
I.T.Botham	1985	E	6	31	–	–	–	–	–	–
J.N.Crawford	1907-08	A	5	30	–	–	–	–	–	–
A.V.Bedser	1950-51	A	5	30	–	–	–	–	–	–
A.V.Bedser	1951	E	5	–	30	–	–	–	–	–
F.S.Trueman	1952	E	4	–	–	–	–	29	–	–
D.L.Underwood	1976-77	I	5	–	–	–	–	29	–	–
R.G.D.Willis	1981	E	6	29	–	–	–	–	–	–
F.H.Tyson	1954-55	A	5	28	–	–	–	–	–	–
R.Peel	1894-95	A	5	27	–	–	–	–	–	–
M.W.Tate	1924	E	5	–	27	–	–	–	–	–
J.B.Statham	1960	E	5	–	27	–	–	–	–	–
F.J.Titmus	1963-64	I	5	–	–	–	–	27	–	–
J.A.Snow	1967-68	WI	4	–	–	27	–	–	–	–
R.G.D.Willis	1977	E	5	27	–	–	–	–	–	–
W.S.Lees	1905-06	SA	5	–	26	–	–	–	–	–
C.Blythe	1907	E	3	–	26	–	–	–	–	–
W.Voce	1936-37	A	5	26	–	–	–	–	–	–
J.H.Wardle	1956-57	SA	4	–	26	–	–	–	–	–
J.K.Lever	1976-77	I	5	–	–	–	–	26	–	–
A.Fielder	1907-08	A	4	25	–	–	–	–	–	–
J.C.White	1928-29	A	5	25	–	–	–	–	–	–
F.S.Trueman	1960	SA	5	–	25	–	–	–	–	–

AUSTRALIA		Venue	Tests	Opponents E	SA	WI	NZ	I	P	SL
C.V.Grimmett	1935-36	SA	5	–	44	–	–	–	–	–
T.M.Alderman	1981	E	6	42	–	–	–	–	–	–
R.M.Hogg	1978-79	A	6	41	–	–	–	–	–	–
T.M.Alderman	1989	E	6	41	–	–	–	–	–	–
D.K.Lillee	1981	E	6	39	–	–	–	–	–	–
W.J.Whitty	1910-11	A	5	–	37	–	–	–	–	–
A.A.Mailey	1920-21	A	5	36	–	–	–	–	–	–
G.Giffen	1894-95	A	5	34	–	–	–	–	–	–
G.F.Lawson	1982-83	A	5	34	–	–	–	–	–	–
S.K.Warne	1993	E	6	34	–	–	–	–	–	–
C.V.Grimmett	1930-31	A	5	–	–	33	–	–	–	–
C.V.Grimmett	1931-32	A	5	–	33	–	–	–	–	–
A.K.Davidson	1960-61	A	4	–	–	33	–	–	–	–
J.R.Thomson	1974-75	A	5	33	–	–	–	–	–	–
M.A.Noble	1901-02	A	5	32	–	–	–	–	–	–
H.V.Hordern	1911-12	A	5	32	–	–	–	–	–	–
J.V.Saunders	1907-08	A	5	31	–	–	–	–	–	–
H.Ironmonger	1931-32	A	4	–	31	–	–	–	–	–
R.Benaud	1958-59	A	5	31	–	–	–	–	–	–
D.K.Lillee	1972	E	5	31	–	–	–	–	–	–
C.J.McDermott	1991-92	A	5	–	–	–	–	31	–	–
M.G.Hughes	1993	E	6	31	–	–	–	–	–	–
R.Benaud	1957-58	SA	5	–	30	–	–	–	–	–
G.D.McKenzie	1968-69	A	5	–	–	30	–	–	–	–
C.J.McDermott	1985	E	6	30	–	–	–	–	–	–
C.V.Grimmett	1930	E	5	29	–	–	–	–	–	–
A.K.Davidson	1959-60	I	5	–	–	–	–	29	–	–
R.Benaud	1959-60	I	5	–	–	–	–	29	–	–
G.D.McKenzie	1964	E	5	29	–	–	–	–	–	–
J.R.Thomson	1975-76	A	6	–	–	29	–	–	–	–
G.F.Lawson	1989	E	6	29	–	–	–	–	–	–
H.Trumble	1901-02	A	5	28	–	–	–	–	–	–
W.J.O'Reilly	1934	E	5	28	–	–	–	–	–	–
A.A.Mallett	1969-70	I	5	–	–	–	–	28	–	–
W.M.Clark	1977-78	A	5	–	–	–	–	28	–	–
E.A.McDonald	1921	E	5	27	–	–	–	–	–	–
W.J.O'Reilly	1932-33	A	5	27	–	–	–	–	–	–
W.J.O'Reilly	1935-36	SA	5	–	27	–	–	–	–	–

AUSTRALIA *continued*		Venue	Tests	*Opponents*						
				E	SA	WI	NZ	I	P	SL
R.R.Lindwall	1948	E	5	27	–	–	–	–	–	–
W.A.Johnston	1948	E	5	27	–	–	–	–	–	–
D.K.Lillee	1975-76	A	5	–	–	27	–	–	–	–
B.A.Reid	1990-91	A	4	27	–	–	–	–	–	–
E.Jones	1899	E	5	26	–	–	–	–	–	–
H.Trumble	1902	E	3	26	–	–	–	–	–	–
R.R.Lindwall	1953	E	5	26	.	–	–	–	–	–
J.W.Gleeson	1968-69	A	5	–	–	–	26	–	–	–
M.H.N.Walker	1972-73	WI	5	–	–	–	26	–	–	–
C.V.Grimmett	1934	E	5	25	–	–	–	–	–	–
W.J.O'Reilly	1936-37	A	5	25	–	–	–	–	–	–
A.K.Davidson	1957-58	SA	5	–	25	–	–	–	–	–
D.K.Lillee	1974-75	A	6	25	–	–	–	–	–	–
A.G.Hurst	1978-79	A	6	25	–	–	–	–	–	–

SOUTH AFRICA		Venue	Tests	*Opponents*					
				E	A	WI	NZ	I	SL
H.J.Tayfield	1956-57	SA	5	37	–	–	–	–	–
A.E.E.Vogler	1909-10	SA	5	36	–	–	–	–	–
H.J.Tayfield	1952-53	A	5	–	30	–	–	–	–
G.A.Faulkner	1909-10	SA	5	29	–	–	–	–	–
G.B.Lawrence	1961-62	SA	5	–	–	–	28	–	–
A.E.Hall	1922-23	SA	4	27	–	–	–	–	–
H.J.Tayfield	1955	E	5	26	–	–	–	–	–
N.A.T.Adcock	1960	E	5	26	–	–	–	–	–
T.L.Goddard	1966-67	SA	5	–	26	–	–	–	–
M.J.Procter	1969-70	SA	4	–	26	–	–	–	–
C.B.Llewellyn	1902-03	SA	3	–	25	–	–	–	–
R.O.Schwarz	1910-11	A	5	–	25	–	–	–	–
J.M.Blankenberg	1922-23	SA	5	25	–	–	–	–	–
G.F.Bissett	1927-28	SA	4	25	–	–	–	–	–
T.L.Goddard	1955	E	5	25	–	–	–	–	–
P.M.Pollock	1963-64	A	5	–	25	–	–	–	–
J.T.Partridge	1963-64	A	5	–	25	–	–	–	–

WEST INDIES		Venue	Tests	*Opponents*						
				E	A	SA	NZ	I	P	SL
M.D.Marshall	1988	E	5	35	–	–	–	–	–	–
A.L.Valentine	1950	E	4	33	–	–	–	–	–	–
C.E.H.Croft	1976-77	WI	5	–	–	–	–	–	33	–
M.D.Marshall	1983-84	I	6	–	–	–	–	33	–	–
C.E.L.Ambrose	1992-93	A	5	–	33	–	–	–	–	–
C.C.Griffith	1963	E	5	32	–	–	–	–	–	–
A.M.E.Roberts	1974-75	I	5	–	–	–	–	32	–	–
J.Garner	1983-84	WI	5	–	31	–	–	–	–	–
W.W.Hall	1958-59	I	5	–	–	–	–	30	–	–
M.A.Holding	1983-84	I	6	–	–	–	–	30	–	–
J.Garner	1984	E	5	29	–	–	–	–	–	–
A.L.Valentine	1952-53	WI	5	–	–	–	–	28	–	–
M.A.Holding	1976	E	4	28	–	–	–	–	–	–
A.M.E.Roberts	1976	E	5	28	–	–	–	–	–	–
M.D.Marshall	1984-85	A	5	–	28	–	–	–	–	–
C.E.L.Ambrose	1991	E	5	28	–	–	–	–	–	–
W.W.Hall	1961-62	WI	5	–	–	–	–	27	–	–
M.D.Marshall	1984-85	WI	4	–	–	–	27	–	–	–
J.Garner	1985-86	WI	5	27	–	–	–	–	–	–
M.D.Marshall	1985-86	WI	5	27	–	–	–	–	–	–
S.Ramadhin	1950	E	4	26	–	–	–	–	–	–
R.Gilchrist	1958-59	I	4	–	–	–	–	26	–	–
L.R.Gibbs	1963	E	5	26	–	–	–	–	–	–
L.R.Gibbs	1972-73	WI	5	–	26	–	–	–	–	–
J.Garner	1980	E	5	26	–	–	–	–	–	–
C.A.Walsh	1987-88	I	4	–	–	–	–	26	–	–
C.E.L.Ambrose	1988-89	A	5	–	26	–	–	–	–	–
C.E.L.Ambrose	1993-94	WI	5	26	–	–	–	–	–	–
J.Garner	1976-77	WI	5	–	–	–	–	–	25	–

NEW ZEALAND		Venue	Tests	Opponents							
				E	A	SA	WI	I	P	SL	Z
R.J.Hadlee	1985-86	A	3	–	33	–	–	–	–	–	–
B.R.Taylor	1971-72	WI	4	–	–	–	27	–	–	–	–

INDIA		Venue	Tests	Opponents							
				E	A	SA	WI	NZ	P	SL	Z
B.S.Chandrasekhar	1972-73	I	5	35	–	–	–	–	–	–	–
M.H.Mankad	1951-52	I	5	34	–	–	–	–	–	–	–
S.P.Gupte	1955-56	I	5	–	–	–	34	–	–	–	–
Kapil Dev	1979-80	I	6	–	–	–	–	–	32	–	–
B.S.Bedi	1977-78	A	5	–	31	–	–	–	–	–	–
Kapil Dev	1983-84	I	6	–	–	–	29	–	–	–	–
B.S.Chandrasekhar	1977-78	A	5	–	28	–	–	–	–	–	–
Kapil Dev	1979-80	I	6	–	28	–	–	–	–	–	–
S.P.Gupte	1952-53	WI	5	–	–	–	27	–	–	–	–
K.D.Ghavri	1978-79	I	6	–	–	–	27	–	–	–	–
D.R.Doshi	1979-80	I	6	–	27	–	–	–	–	–	–
E.A.S.Prasanna	1969-70	I	5	–	26	–	–	–	–	–	–
M.H.Mankad	1952-53	I	5	–	–	–	–	–	–	25	–
E.A.S.Prasanna	1967-68	A	4	–	25	–	–	–	–	–	–
B.S.Bedi	1972-73	I	5	25	–	–	–	–	–	–	–
B.S.Bedi	1976-77	I	5	25	–	–	–	–	–	–	–
Kapil Dev	1991-92	A	5	–	25	–	–	–	–	–	–

PAKISTAN		Venue	Tests	Opponents						
				E	A	WI	NZ	I	SL	Z
Imran Khan	1982-83	P	6	–	–	–	–	40	–	–
Abdul Qadir	1987-88	P	3	30	–	–	–	–	–	–
Waqar Younis	1990-91	P	3	–	–	–	29	–	–	–
Waqar Younis	1993-94	P	3	–	–	–	–	–	–	27
Imran Khan	1976-77	WI	5	–	–	25	–	–	–	–
Wasim Akram	1993-94	NZ	3	–	–	–	25	–	–	–

SRI LANKA
The most wickets in a series is 20 (av 22.95) by R.J.Ratnayake v India (3 Tests) in Sri Lanka in 1985-86.

ZIMBABWE
The most wickets in a series is 13 (av 30.30) by E.A.Brandes (3 Tests) in Pakistan in 1993-94.

TEN WICKETS IN A MATCH
†*On debut*

ENGLAND (88)			Opponents						
			A	SA	WI	NZ	I	P	SL
J.C.Laker	1956	Manchester	19-90	–	–	–	–	–	–
S.F.Barnes	1913-14	Johannesburg[1]	–	17-159	–	–	–	–	–
J.Briggs	1888-89	Cape Town	–	15-28	–	–	–	–	–
G.A.Lohmann	1895-96	Port Elizabeth	–	15-45	–	–	–	–	–
C.Blythe	1907	Leeds	–	15-99	–	–	–	–	–
H.Verity	1934	Lord's	15-104	–	–	–	–	–	–
W.Rhodes	1903-04	Melbourne	15-124	–	–	–	–	–	–
A.V.Bedser	1953	Nottingham	14-99	–	–	–	–	–	–
W.Bates	1882-83	Melbourne	14-102	–	–	–	–	–	–
S.F.Barnes	1913-14	Durban[1]	–	14-144	–	–	–	–	–
S.F.Barnes	1912	Oval	–	13-57	–	–	–	–	–
D.L.Underwood	1974	Lord's	–	–	–	–	–	13-71	–
J.J.Ferris	1891-92	Cape Town	–	13-91	–	–	–	–	–
I.T.Botham	1979-80	Bombay[3]	–	–	–	–	13-106	–	–
A.W.Greig	1973-74	Port-of-Spain	–	–	13-156	–	–	–	–
S.F.Barnes	1901-02	Melbourne	13-163	–	–	–	–	–	–
T.Richardson	1896	Manchester	13-244	–	–	–	–	–	–
J.C.White	1928-29	Adelaide	13-256	–	–	–	–	–	–
G.A.Lohmann	1895-96	Johannesburg[1]	–	12-71	–	–	–	–	–
J.H.Wardle	1956-57	Cape Town	–	12-89	–	–	–	–	–
D.L.Underwood	1970-71	Christchurch	–	–	–	12-97	–	–	–
R.Tattersall	1951	Lord's	–	12-101	–	–	–	–	–
D.L.Underwood	1969	Oval	–	–	–	12-101	–	–	–

			Opponents						
			A	SA	WI	NZ	I	P	SL
ENGLAND (continued)									
F.Martin†	1890	Oval	12-102	–	–	–	–	–	–
G.A.Lohmann	1886	Oval	12-104	–	–	–	–	–	–
A.V.Bedser	1951	Manchester	–	12-112	–	–	–	–	–
F.S.Trueman	1963	Birmingham	–	–	12-119	–	–	–	–
G.Geary	1927-28	Johannesburg[1]	–	12-130	–	–	–	–	–
J.Briggs	1891-92	Adelaide	12-136	–	–	–	–	–	–
A.P.Freeman	1929	Manchester	–	12-171	–	–	–	–	–
G.A.R.Lock	1957	Oval	–	–	11-48	–	–	–	–
G.A.R.Lock	1958	Leeds	–	–	–	11-65	–	–	–
R.Peel	1888	Manchester	11-68	–	–	–	–	–	–
D.L.Underwood	1969	Lord's	–	–	–	11-70	–	–	–
J.Briggs	1886	Lord's	11-74	–	–	–	–	–	–
W.H.Lockwood	1902	Manchester	11-76	–	–	–	–	–	–
N.G.B.Cook	1983-84	Karachi[1]	–	–	–	–	–	11-83	–
G.A.R.Lock	1958-59	Christchurch	–	–	–	11-84	–	–	–
F.S.Trueman	1961	Leeds	11-88	–	–	–	–	–	–
A.E.R.Gilligan	1924	Birmingham	–	11-90	–	–	–	–	–
A.V.Bedser	1946	Manchester	–	–	–	–	11-93	–	–
C.S.Marriott†	1933	Oval	–	–	11-96	–	–	–	–
J.B.Statham	1960	Lord's	–	11-97	–	–	–	–	–
T.E.Bailey	1957	Lord's	–	–	11-98	–	–	–	–
C.Blythe	1909	Birmingham	11-102	–	–	–	–	–	–
S.F.Barnes	1912	Lord's	–	11-110	–	–	–	–	–
J.C.Laker	1956	Leeds	11-113	–	–	–	–	–	–
C.Blythe	1905-06	Cape Town	–	11-118	–	–	–	–	–
I.T.Botham	1978	Lord's	–	–	–	11-140	–	–	–
A.V.Bedser†	1946	Lord's	–	–	–	–	11-145	–	–
P.C.R.Tufnell	1991-92	Christchurch	–	–	–	11-147	–	–	–
W.Voce	1929-30	Port-of-Spain	–	–	11-149	–	–	–	–
F.S.Trueman	1963	Lord's	–	–	11-152	–	–	–	–
H.Verity	1933-34	Madras[1]	–	–	–	–	11-153	–	–
N.A.Foster	1984-85	Madras[1]	–	–	–	–	11-163	–	–
T.Richardson	1896	Lord's	11-173	–	–	–	–	–	–
I.T.Botham	1979-80	Perth	11-176	–	–	–	–	–	–
D.L.Underwood	1974-75	Adelaide	11-215	–	–	–	–	–	–
M.W.Tate	1924-25	Sydney	11-228	–	–	–	–	–	–
F.E.Woolley	1912	Oval	10-49	–	–	–	–	–	–
W.Voce	1936-37	Brisbane[2]	10-57	–	–	–	–	–	–
J.T.Hearne	1896	Oval	10-60	–	–	–	–	–	–
J.K.Lever†	1976-77	Delhi	–	–	–	–	10-70	–	–
G.O.B.Allen	1936	Lord's	–	–	–	–	10-78	–	–
D.L.Underwood	1972	Leeds	10-82	–	–	–	–	–	–
G.A.Lohmann	1886-87	Sydney	10-87	–	–	–	–	–	–
A.P.Freeman	1928	Manchester	–	–	10-93	–	–	–	–
C.Blythe	1909-10	Cape Town	–	10-104	–	–	–	–	–
R.M.Ellison	1985	Birmingham	10-104	–	–	–	–	–	–
A.V.Bedser	1950-51	Melbourne	10-105	–	–	–	–	–	–
S.F.Barnes	1913-14	Durban[1]	–	10-105	–	–	–	–	–
S.F.Barnes	1912	Leeds	–	10-115	–	–	–	–	–
J.C.Laker	1951	Oval	–	10-119	–	–	–	–	–
H.Larwood	1932-33	Sydney	10-124	–	–	–	–	–	–
F.H.Tyson	1954-55	Sydney	10-130	–	–	–	–	–	–
D.E.Malcolm	1989-90	Port-of-Spain	–	–	10-137	–	–	–	–
D.E.Malcolm	1994	Oval	–	10-138	–	–	–	–	–
G.A.Lohmann	1891-92	Sydney	10-142	–	–	–	–	–	–
J.A.Snow	1967-68	Georgetown	–	–	10-142	–	–	–	–
J.Briggs	1893	Oval	10-148	–	–	–	–	–	–
A.W.Greig	1974-75	Auckland	–	–	–	10-149	–	–	–
T.Richardson†	1893	Manchester	10-156	–	–	–	–	–	–
D.V.P.Wright	1947	Lord's	–	10-175	–	–	–	–	–
K.Farnes†	1934	Nottingham	10-179	–	–	–	–	–	–
G.T.S.Stevens	1929-30	Bridgetown	–	–	10-195	–	–	–	–
T.Richardson	1897-98	Sydney	10-204	–	–	–	–	–	–
A.P.Freeman	1929	Leeds	–	10-207	–	–	–	–	–
I.T.Botham	1981	Oval	10-253	–	–	–	–	–	–

			Opponents						
AUSTRALIA (71)			E	SA	WI	NZ	I	P	SL
R.A.L.Massie†	1972	Lord's	16-137	–	–	–	–	–	–
F.R.Spofforth	1882	Oval	14-90	–	–	–	–	–	–
C.V.Grimmett	1931-32	Adelaide	–	14-199	–	–	–	–	–
M.A.Noble	1901-02	Melbourne	13-77	–	–	–	–	–	–
F.R.Spofforth	1878-79	Melbourne	13-110	–	–	–	–	–	–
B.A.Reid	1990-91	Melbourne	13-148	–	–	–	–	–	–
C.V.Grimmett	1935-36	Durban[2]	–	13-173	–	–	–	–	–
M.G.Hughes	1988-89	Perth	–	–	13-217	–	–	–	–
A.A.Mailey	1920-21	Melbourne	13-236	–	–	–	–	–	–
C.T.B.Turner	1887-88	Sydney	12-87	–	–	–	–	–	–
H.Trumble	1896	Oval	12-89	–	–	–	–	–	–
A.K.Davidson	1959-60	Kanpur	–	–	–	–	12-124	–	–
B.A.Reid	1991-92	Melbourne	–	–	–	–	12-126	–	–
S.K.Warne	1993-94	Sydney	–	12-128	–	–	–	–	–
G.Dymock	1979-80	Kanpur	–	–	–	–	12-166	–	–
H.Trumble	1902	Oval	12-173	–	–	–	–	–	–
H.V.Hordern	1911-12	Sydney	12-175	–	–	–	–	–	–
H.Ironmonger	1931-32	Melbourne	–	11-24	–	–	–	–	–
E.R.H.Toshack	1947-48	Brisbane[2]	–	–	–	–	11-31	–	–
H.Ironmonger	1930-31	Melbourne	–	–	11-79	–	–	–	–
C.V.Grimmett†	1924-25	Sydney	11-82	–	–	–	–	–	–
C.G.Macartney	1909	Leeds	11-85	–	–	–	–	–	–
M.R.Whitney	1991-92	Perth	–	–	–	–	11-95	–	–
A.R.Border	1988-89	Sydney	–	–	11-96	–	–	–	–
M.A.Noble	1902	Sheffield	11-103	–	–	–	–	–	–
R.Benaud	1956-57	Calcutta	–	–	–	–	11-105	–	–
F.R.Spofforth	1882-83	Sydney	11-117	–	–	–	–	–	–
C.G.Rackemann	1983-84	Perth	–	–	–	–	–	11-118	–
D.K.Lillee	1976-77	Auckland	–	–	–	11-123	–	–	–
W.J.O'Reilly	1934	Nottingham	11-129	–	–	–	–	–	–
G.F.Lawson	1982-83	Brisbane[2]	11-134	–	–	–	–	–	–
D.K.Lillee	1979-80	Melbourne	11-138	–	–	–	–	–	–
C.J.McDermott	1990-91	Perth	11-157	–	–	–	–	–	–
D.K.Lillee	1981	Oval	11-159	–	–	–	–	–	–
G.E.Palmer	1881-82	Sydney	11-165	–	–	–	–	–	–
D.K.Lillee	1976-77	Melbourne	11-165	–	–	–	–	–	–
G.F.Lawson	1984-85	Adelaide	–	–	11-181	–	–	–	–
C.V.Grimmett	1930-31	Adelaide	–	–	11-183	–	–	–	–
A.K.Davidson	1960-61	Brisbane[2]	–	–	11-222	–	–	–	–
C.T.B.Turner	1888	Lord's	10-63	–	–	–	–	–	–
R.M.Hogg	1978-79	Melbourne	10-66	–	–	–	–	–	–
C.V.Grimmett	1935-36	Cape Town	–	10-88	–	–	–	–	–
G.D.McKenzie	1964-65	Madras[2]	–	–	–	–	10-91	–	–
C.V.Grimmett	1935-36	Johannesburg[1]	–	10-110	–	–	–	–	–
R.J.Bright	1979-80	Karachi[1]	–	–	–	–	–	10-111	–
N.J.N.Hawke	1964-65	Georgetown	–	–	10-115	–	–	–	–
W.J.O'Reilly	1938	Leeds	10-122	–	–	–	–	–	–
R.M.Hogg	1978-79	Perth	10-122	–	–	–	–	–	–
G.E.Palmer	1882-83	Melbourne	10-126	–	–	–	–	–	–
D.K.Lillee	1981-82	Melbourne	–	–	10-127	–	–	–	–
H.Trumble	1902	Manchester	10-128	–	–	–	–	–	–
W.J.O'Reilly	1932-33	Melbourne	10-129	–	–	–	–	–	–
D.K.Lillee	1976-77	Melbourne	–	–	–	–	–	10-135	–
F.R.Spofforth	1884-85	Sydney	10-144	–	–	–	–	–	–
A.A.Mallett	1969-70	Madras[1]	–	–	–	–	10-144	–	–
R.G.Holland	1984-85	Sydney	–	–	10-144	–	–	–	–
G.D.McKenzie	1967-68	Melbourne	–	–	–	–	10-151	–	–
T.M.Alderman	1989	Leeds	10-151	–	–	–	–	–	–
K.R.Miller	1956	Lord's	10-152	–	–	–	–	–	–
G.D.McKenzie	1968-69	Melbourne	–	–	10-159	–	–	–	–
G.Giffen	1891-92	Sydney	10-160	–	–	–	–	–	–
H.V.Hordern	1911-12	Sydney	10-161	–	–	–	–	–	–
E.Jones	1899	Lord's	10-164	–	–	–	–	–	–
C.J.McDermott	1991-92	Adelaide	–	–	–	–	10-168	–	–
R.G.Holland	1985-86	Sydney	–	–	–	10-174	–	–	–
D.K.Lillee	1972	Oval	10-181	–	–	–	–	–	–
B.Yardley	1981-82	Sydney	–	–	10-185	–	–	–	–
C.V.Grimmett	1930	Nottingham	10-201	–	–	–	–	–	–

AUSTRALIA (continued)

			Opponents						
			E	SA	WI	NZ	I	P	SL
L.O'B.Fleetwood-Smith	1936-37	Adelaide	10-239	–	–	–	–	–	–
G.R.J.Matthews	1986-87	Madras[1]	–	–	–	10-249	–	–	–
A.A.Mailey	1920-21	Adelaide	10-302	–	–	–	–	–	–

SOUTH AFRICA (11)

			E	A	WI	NZ	I	SL
H.J.Tayfield	1952-53	Melbourne	–	13-165	–	–	–	–
H.J.Tayfield	1956-57	Johannesburg[3]	13-192	–	–	–	–	–
S.J.Snooke	1905-06	Johannesburg[1]	12-127	–	–	–	–	–
A.A.Donald	1992-93	Port Elizabeth	–	–	–	–	12-139	–
A.E.E.Vogler	1909-10	Johannesburg[1]	12-181	–	–	–	–	–
A.E.Hall†	1922-23	Cape Town	11-112	–	–	–	–	–
E.P.Nupen	1930-31	Johannesburg[1]	11-150	–	–	–	–	–
S.F.Burke†	1961-62	Cape Town	–	–	–	11-196	–	–
P.M.Pollock	1965	Nottingham	10-87	–	–	–	–	–
C.B.Llewellyn	1902-03	Johannesburg[1]	–	10-116	–	–	–	–
P.S.de Villiers	1993-94	Sydney	–	10-123	–	–	–	–

WEST INDIES (22)

			E	A	SA	NZ	I	P	SL
M.A.Holding	1976	Oval	14-149	–	–	–	–	–	–
A.M.E.Roberts	1974-75	Madras[1]	–	–	–	–	12-121	–	–
C.E.L.Ambrose	1993-94	Port-of-Spain	11-84	–	–	–	–	–	–
M.D.Marshall	1988-89	Port-of-Spain	–	–	–	–	11-89	–	–
M.A.Holding	1981-82	Melbourne	–	11-107	–	–	–	–	–
M.D.Marshall	1984-85	Bridgetown	–	–	–	11-120	–	–	–
W.W.Hall	1958-59	Kanpur	–	–	–	–	11-126	–	–
K.D.Boyce	1973	Oval	11-147	–	–	–	–	–	–
S.Ramadhin	1950	Lord's	11-152	–	–	–	–	–	–
L.R.Gibbs	1963	Manchester	11-157	–	–	–	–	–	–
A.L.Valentine†	1950	Manchester	11-204	–	–	–	–	–	–
W.Ferguson	1947-48	Port-of-Spain	11-229	–	–	–	–	–	–
M.D.Marshall	1988	Lord's	10-92	–	–	–	–	–	–
H.H.H.Johnson†	1947-48	Kingston	10-96	–	–	–	–	–	–
C.A.Walsh	1988-89	Kingston	–	–	–	10-101	–	–	–
L.R.Gibbs	1966	Manchester	10-106	–	–	–	–	–	–
M.D.Marshall	1984-85	Adelaide	–	10-107	–	–	–	–	–
G.E.Gomez	1951-52	Sydney	–	10-113	–	–	–	–	–
C.E.L.Ambrose	1992-93	Adelaide	–	10-120	–	–	–	–	–
A.M.E.Roberts	1976	Lord's	10-123	–	–	–	–	–	–
C.E.L.Ambrose	1989-90	Bridgetown	10-127	–	–	–	–	–	–
A.L.Valentine	1950	Oval	10-160	–	–	–	–	–	–

NEW ZEALAND (16)

			E	A	SA	WI	I	P	SL	Z
R.J.Hadlee	1985-86	Brisbane[2]	–	15-123	–	–	–	–	–	–
R.J.Hadlee	1975-76	Wellington	–	–	–	–	11-58	–	–	–
R.J.Hadlee	1979-80	Dunedin	–	–	–	11-102	–	–	–	–
C.Pringle	1990-91	Faisalabad	–	–	–	–	–	11-152	–	–
R.J.Hadlee	1985-86	Perth	–	11-155	–	–	–	–	–	–
D.J.Nash	1994	Lord's	11-169	–	–	–	–	–	–	–
R.J.Hadlee	1988-89	Bombay[3]	–	–	–	–	10-88	–	–	–
R.J.Hadlee	1977-78	Wellington	10-100	–	–	–	–	–	–	–
R.J.Hadlee	1983-84	Colombo (CCC)	–	–	–	–	–	–	10-102	–
J.G.Bracewell	1985-86	Auckland	–	10-106	–	–	–	–	–	–
E.J.Chatfield	1984-85	Port-of-Spain	–	–	–	10-124	–	–	–	–
J.Cowie	1937	Manchester	10-140	–	–	–	–	–	–	–
R.J.Hadlee	1986	Nottingham	10-140	–	–	–	–	–	–	–
B.L.Cairns	1983	Leeds	10-144	–	–	–	–	–	–	–
G.B.Troup	1979-80	Auckland	–	–	–	10-166	–	–	–	–
R.J.Hadlee	1987-88	Melbourne	–	10-176	–	–	–	–	–	–

INDIA (22)

			E	A	SA	WI	NZ	P	SL	Z
N.D.Hirwani†	1987-88	Madras[1]	–	–	–	16-136	–	–	–	–
J.M.Patel	1959-60	Kanpur	–	14-124	–	–	–	–	–	–
M.H.Mankad	1952-53	Delhi	–	–	–	–	–	13-131	–	–
B.S.Chandrasekhar	1977-78	Melbourne	–	12-104	–	–	–	–	–	–
M.H.Mankad	1951-52	Madras[1]	12-108	–	–	–	–	–	–	–
S.Venkataraghavan	1964-65	Delhi	–	–	–	–	12-152	–	–	–
L.Sivaramakrishnan	1984-85	Bombay[3]	12-181	–	–	–	–	–	–	–
R.G.Nadkarni	1964-65	Madras[2]	–	11-122	–	–	–	–	–	–
S.L.V.Raju	1993-94	Ahmedabad	–	–	–	–	–	–	11-125	–

Ten Wickets in a Match

INDIA (continued)

			Opponents							
			E	A	SA	WI	NZ	P	SL	Z
A.Kumble	1993-94	Lucknow[2]	–	–	–	–	–	–	11-128	–
E.A.S.Prasanna	1975-76	Auckland	–	–	–	–	11-140	–	–	–
Kapil Dev	1979-80	Madras[1]	–	–	–	–	–	11-146	–	–
B.S.Chandrasekhar	1966-67	Bombay[2]	–	–	–	11-235	–	–	–	–
Maninder Singh	1986-87	Nagpur	–	–	–	–	–	–	10-107	–
Maninder Singh	1986-87	Bangalore	–	–	–	–	10-126	–	–	–
Ghulam Ahmed	1956-57	Calcutta	–	10-130	–	–	–	–	–	–
Kapil Dev	1983-84	Ahmedabad	–	–	–	10-135	–	–	–	–
E.A.S.Prasanna	1969-70	Madras[1]	–	10-174	–	–	–	–	–	–
S.A.Durani	1961-62	Madras[2]	10-177	–	–	–	–	–	–	–
C.Sharma	1986	Birmingham	10-188	–	–	–	–	–	–	–
B.S.Bedi	1977-78	Perth	–	10-194	–	–	–	–	–	–
S.P.Gupte	1958-59	Kanpur	–	–	–	10-223	–	–	–	–

PAKISTAN (29)

			E	A	WI	NZ	I	SL	Z
Imran Khan	1981-82	Lahore[2]	–	–	–	–	–	14-116	–
Abdul Qadir	1987-88	Lahore[2]	13-101	–	–	–	–	–	–
Fazal Mahmood	1956-57	Karachi[1]	–	13-114	–	–	–	–	–
Waqar Younis	1993-94	Karachi[2]	–	–	–	–	–	–	13-135
Fazal Mahmood	1952-53	Lucknow	–	–	–	–	12-94	–	–
Fazal Mahmood	1954	Oval	12-99	–	–	–	–	–	–
Fazal Mahmood	1958-59	Dacca	–	–	12-100	–	–	–	–
Waqar Younis	1990-91	Faisalabad	–	–	–	12-130	–	–	–
Imran Khan	1976-77	Sydney	–	12-165	–	–	–	–	–
Zulfiqar Ahmed	1955-56	Karachi[1]	–	–	11-79	–	–	–	–
Imran Khan	1982-83	Karachi[1]	–	–	–	11-79	–	–	–
Iqbal Qasim	1979-80	Karachi[1]	–	11-118	–	–	–	–	–
Waqar Younis	1994-95	Kandy	–	–	–	–	–	11-119	–
Imran Khan	1987-88	Georgetown	–	–	11-121	–	–	–	–
Sarfraz Nawaz	1978-79	Melbourne	–	11-125	–	–	–	–	–
Intikhab Alam	1972-73	Dunedin	–	–	–	11-130	–	–	–
Wasim Akram	1989-90	Melbourne	–	11-160	–	–	–	–	–
Wasim Akram	1993-94	Wellington	–	–	–	11-179	–	–	–
Imran Khan	1982-83	Faisalabad	–	–	–	–	11-180	–	–
Sikander Bakht	1979-80	Delhi	–	–	–	–	11-190	–	–
Abdul Qadir	1982-83	Faisalabad	–	11-218	–	–	–	–	–
Imran Khan	1987	Leeds	10-77	–	–	–	–	–	–
Waqar Younis	1990-91	Lahore[2]	–	–	–	10-106	–	–	–
Wasim Akram	1984-85	Dunedin	–	–	–	10-128	–	–	–
Iqbal Qasim	1979-80	Bombay[3]	–	–	–	–	10-175	–	–
Intikhab Alam	1969-70	Dacca	–	–	–	10-182	–	–	–
Abdul Qadir	1987-88	Karachi[1]	10-186	–	–	–	–	–	–
Abdul Qadir	1983-84	Lahore[2]	10-194	–	–	–	–	–	–
Abdul Qadir	1987	Oval	10-211	–	–	–	–	–	–

SRI LANKA
No instance of ten wickets in a match.
Best analysis: R.J.Ratnayake 9-125 v India at Colombo (PSS) in 1985–86.

ZIMBABWE
No instance of ten wickets in a match.
Best analysis: H.H.Streak 8-114 v Pakistan at Rawalpindi[2] in 1993-94.

EIGHT WICKETS IN AN INNINGS
†On debut

ENGLAND (26)			Opponents A	SA	WI	NZ	I	P	SL
J.C.Laker	1956	Manchester	10-53	–	–	–	–	–	–
G.A.Lohmann	1895-96	Johannesburg[1]	–	9-28	–	–	–	–	–
J.C.Laker	1956	Manchester	9-37	–	–	–	–	–	–
D.E.Malcolm	1994	Oval	–	9-57	–	–	–	–	–
S.F.Barnes	1913-14	Johannesburg[1]	–	9-103	–	–	–	–	–
G.A.Lohmann	1895-96	Port Elizabeth	–	8-7	–	–	–	–	–
J.Briggs	1888-89	Cape Town	–	8-11	–	–	–	–	–
S.F.Barnes	1912	Oval	–	8-29	–	–	–	–	–
F.S.Trueman	1952	Manchester	–	–	–	–	8-31	–	–
I.T.Botham	1978	Lord's	–	–	–	–	–	8-34	–
G.A.Lohmann	1886-87	Sydney	8-35	–	–	–	–	–	–
H.Verity	1934	Lord's	8-43	–	–	–	–	–	–
R.G.D.Willis	1981	Leeds	8-43	–	–	–	–	–	–
D.L.Underwood	1974	Lord's	–	–	–	–	–	8-51	–
S.F.Barnes	1913-14	Johannesburg[1]	–	8-56	–	–	–	–	–
G.A.Lohmann	1891-92	Sydney	8-58	–	–	–	–	–	–
C.Blythe	1907	Leeds	–	8-59	–	–	–	–	–
W.Rhodes	1903-04	Melbourne	8-68	–	–	–	–	–	–
A.R.C.Fraser	1993-94	Bridgetown	–	–	8-75	–	–	–	–
L.C.Braund	1903-04	Melbourne	8-81	–	–	–	–	–	–
A.W.Greig	1973-74	Port-of-Spain	–	–	8-86	–	–	–	–
T.Richardson	1897-98	Sydney	8-94	–	–	–	–	–	–
I.T.Botham	1984	Lord's	–	–	8-103	–	–	–	–
B.J.T.Bosanquet	1905	Nottingham	8-107	–	–	–	–	–	–
N.A.Foster	1987	Leeds	–	–	–	–	–	8-107	–
J.C.White	1928-29	Adelaide	8-126	–	–	–	–	–	–

AUSTRALIA (13)			E	SA	WI	NZ	I	P	SL
A.A.Mailey	1920-21	Melbourne	9-121	–	–	–	–	–	–
F.Laver	1909	Manchester	8-31	–	–	–	–	–	–
A.E.Trott†	1894-95	Adelaide	8-43	–	–	–	–	–	–
R.A.L.Massie†	1972	Lord's	8-53	–	–	–	–	–	–
A.A.Mallett	1972-73	Adelaide	–	–	–	–	–	8-59	–
H.Trumble	1902	Oval	8-65	–	–	–	–	–	–
G.D.McKenzie	1968-69	Melbourne	–	–	8-71	–	–	–	–
R.A.L.Massie†	1972	Lord's	8-84	–	–	–	–	–	–
M.G.Hughes	1988-89	Perth	–	–	8-87	–	–	–	–
C.J.McDermott	1990-91	Perth	8-97	–	–	–	–	–	–
G.F.Lawson	1984-85	Adelaide	–	–	8-112	–	–	–	–
C.J.McDermott	1985	Manchester	8-141	–	–	–	–	–	–
M.H.N.Walker	1974-75	Melbourne	8-143	–	–	–	–	–	–

SOUTH AFRICA (4)			E	A	WI	NZ	I	SL	
H.J.Tayfield	1956-57	Johannesburg[3]	9-113	–	–	–	–	–	
G.B.Lawrence	1961-62	Johannesburg[3]	–	–	–	8-53	–	–	
H.J.Tayfield	1956-57	Durban[2]	8-69	–	–	–	–	–	
S.J.Snooke	1905-06	Johannesburg[1]	8-70	–	–	–	–	–	

WEST INDIES (6)			E	A	SA	NZ	I	P	SL
J.M.Noreiga	1970-71	Port-of-Spain	–	–	–	–	9-95	–	–
C.E.H.Croft	1976-77	Port-of-Spain	–	–	–	–	–	8-29	–
L.R.Gibbs	1961-62	Bridgetown	–	–	–	–	8-38	–	–
C.E.L.Ambrose	1989-90	Bridgetown	8-45	–	–	–	–	–	–
M.A.Holding	1976	Oval	8-92	–	–	–	–	–	–
A.L.Valentine†	1950	Manchester	8-104	–	–	–	–	–	–

NEW ZEALAND (1)			E	A	SA	WI	I	P	SL	Z
R.J.Hadlee	1985-86	Brisbane[2]	–	9-52	–	–	–	–	–	–

INDIA (12)			E	A	SA	WI	NZ	P	SL	Z
J.M.Patel	1959-60	Kanpur	–	9-69	–	–	–	–	–	–
Kapil Dev	1983-84	Ahmedabad	–	–	–	9-83	–	–	–	–
S.P.Gupte	1958-59	Kanpur	–	–	–	9-102	–	–	–	–
M.H.Mankad	1952-53	Delhi	–	–	–	–	–	8-52	–	–
M.H.Mankad	1951-52	Madras[1]	8-55	–	–	–	–	–	–	–

			Opponents							
INDIA *(continued)*			E	A	SA	WI	NZ	P	SL	Z
N.D.Hirwani†	1987-88	Madras¹	–	–	–	8-61	–	–	–	–
S.Venkataraghavan	1964-65	Delhi	–	–	–	–	8-72	–	–	–
N.D.Hirwani†	1987-88	Madras¹	–	–	–	8-75	–	–	–	–
E.A.S.Prasanna	1975-76	Auckland	–	–	–	–	8-76	–	–	–
B.S.Chandrasekhar	1972-73	Delhi	8-79	–	–	–	–	–	–	–
Kapil Dev	1982-83	Lahore²	–	–	–	–	–	8-85	–	–
Kapil Dev	1985-86	Adelaide	–	8-106	–	–	–	–	–	–
PAKISTAN (5)			E	A	WI	NZ	I	SL	Z	
Abdul Qadir	1987-88	Lahore²	9-56	–	–	–	–	–	–	
Sarfraz Nawaz	1978-79	Melbourne	–	9-86	–	–	–	–	–	
Imran Khan	1981-82	Lahore²	–	–	–	–	–	8-58	–	
Imran Khan	1982-83	Karachi¹	–	–	–	–	8-60	–	–	
Sikander Bakht	1979-80	Delhi	–	–	–	–	8-69	–	–	
SRI LANKA (1)			E	A	SA	WI	NZ	I	P	
J.R.Ratnayeke	1985-86	Sialkot	–	–	–	–	–	–	8-83	

ZIMBABWE
No instance of eight wickets in an innings.
Best analysis: D.H.Brain 5-42 v Pakistan at Lahore² in 1993-94.

OUTSTANDING INNINGS ANALYSES

O	M	R	W				
51.2	23	53	10	J.C.Laker	E v A	Manchester	1956
14.2	6	28	9	G.A.Lohmann	E v SA	Johannesburg¹	1895-96
16.4	4	37	9	J.C.Laker	E v A	Manchester	1956
9.4	5	7	8	G.A.Lohmann	E v SA	Port Elizabeth	1895-96
14.2	5	11	8	J.Briggs	E v SA	Cape Town	1888-89
19.1	11	17	7	J.Briggs	E v SA	Cape Town	1888-89
7.4	2	17	7	M.A.Noble	A v E	Melbourne	1901-02
11	3	17	7	W.Rhodes	E v A	Birmingham	1902
6.3	4	7	6	A.E.R.Gilligan	E v SA	Birmingham	1924
11.4	6	11	6	S.Haigh	E v SA	Cape Town	1898-99
11.6	7	12	6	D.L.Underwood	E v NZ	Christchurch	1970-71
17.5	13	12	6	S.L.V.Raju	I v SL	Chandigarh	1990-91
14	7	13	6	H.J.Tayfield	SA v NZ	Johannesburg²	1953-54
18	11	15	6	C.T.B.Turner	A v E	Sydney	1886-87
16	8	15	6	M.H.N.Walker	A v P	Sydney	1972-73
2.3	1	2	5	E.R.H.Toshack	A v I	Brisbane²	1947-48
7.2	5	6	5	H.Ironmonger	A v SA	Melbourne	1931-32
6.5	3	9	5	T.B.A.May	A v WI	Adelaide	1992-93
12	8	5	4	Pervez Sajjad	P v NZ	Rawalpindi¹	1964-65
9	7	5	4	K.Higgs	E v NZ	Christchurch	1965-66
8	6	6	4	P.H.Edmonds	E v P	Lord's	1978
6.3	2	7	4	J.C.White	E v A	Brisbane¹	1928-29
5	2	7	4	J.H.Wardle	E v A	Manchester	1953
6	3	7	4	R.Appleyard	E v NZ	Auckland	1954-55
3.4	3	0	3	R.Benaud	A v I	Delhi	1959-60

HAT-TRICKS

F.R.Spofforth	Australia v England	Melbourne	1878-79
W.Bates	England v Australia	Melbourne	1882-83
J.Briggs	England v Australia	Sydney	1891-92
G.A.Lohmann	England v South Africa	Port Elizabeth	1895-96
J.T.Hearne	England v Australia	Leeds	1899
H.Trumble	Australia v England	Melbourne	1901-02
H.Trumble‡	Australia v England	Melbourne	1903-04
T.J.Matthews (2)	Australia v South Africa	Manchester	1912
M.J.C.Allom†	England v New Zealand	Christchurch	1929-30
T.W.J.Goddard	England v South Africa	Johannesburg¹	1938-39
P.J.Loader	England v West Indies	Leeds	1957
L.F.Kline	Australia v South Africa	Cape Town	1957-58
W.W.Hall	West Indies v Pakistan	Lahore¹	1958-59
G.M.Griffin‡	South Africa v England	Lord's	1960
L.R.Gibbs	West Indies v Australia	Adelaide	1960-61
P.J.Petherick†	New Zealand v Pakistan	Lahore²	1976-77
C.A.Walsh#	West Indies v Australia	Brisbane²	1988-89
M.G.Hughes#	Australia v West Indies	Perth	1988-89

†On debut   ‡On final appearance   #Involving both innings

T.J.Matthews aid the hat-trick in each innings on the second afternoon of the match and took all six wickets without assistance from fielders.

FOUR WICKETS IN FIVE BALLS

M.J.C.Allom	England v New Zealand	Christchurch	1929-30
	On debut – in his eighth over – W●WWW		
C.M.Old	England v Pakistan	Birmingham	1978
	In the same over – WW●WW – his third ball was a no-ball		
Wasim Akram	Pakistan v West Indies	Lahore²	1990-91
	In the same over – WW●WW		

THREE WICKETS IN FOUR BALLS

F.R.Spofforth (2)	Australia v England	Oval	1882
	Australia v England	Sydney	1884-85
J.Briggs	England v South Africa	Cape Town	1888-89
W.P.Howell	Australia v South Africa	Cape Town	1902-03
J.M.Gregory	Australia v England	Nottingham	1921
E.P.Nupen	South Africa v England	Johannesburg¹	1930-31
W.J.O'Reilly	Australia v England	Manchester	1934
B.Mitchell	South Africa v England	Johannesburg¹	1935-36
W.Voce	England v Australia	Sydney	1936-37
R.R.Lindwall	Australia v England	Adelaide	1946-47
K.Cranston	England v South Africa	Leeds	1947
R.Appleyard	England v New Zealand	Auckland	1954-55
R.Benaud	Australia v West Indies	Georgetown	1954-55
Fazal Mahmood	Pakistan v Australia	Karachi¹	1956-57
J.W.Martin	Australia v West Indies	Melbourne	1960-61
L.R.Gibbs	West Indies v Australia	Sydney	1960-61
K.D.Mackay	Australia v England	Birmingham	1961
W.W.Hall	West Indies v India	Port-of-Spain	1961-62
D.Shackleton	England v West Indies	Lord's	1963
G.D.McKenzie	Australia v West Indies	Port-of-Spain	1964-65
F.J.Titmus	England v New Zealand	Leeds	1965
P.Lever	England v Pakistan	Leeds	1971
D.K.Lillee (2)	Australia v England	Manchester	1972
	Australia v England	Oval	1972
C.M.Old	England v Pakistan	Birmingham	1978
S.T.Clarke	West Indies v Pakistan	Karachi¹	1980-81
R.J.Hadlee	New Zealand v Australia	Melbourne	1980-81
R.J.Shastri	India v New Zealand	Wellington	1980-81
I.T.Botham	England v Australia	Leeds	1985
D.E.Malcolm	England v West Indies	Port-of-Spain	1989-90
A.R.Border	Australia v West Indies	Georgetown	1990-91
Wasim Akram	Pakistan v England	Lord's	1992

K.Cranston, F.J.Titmus and C.M.Old each took four wickets in an over.

WICKET WITH FIRST BALL IN TEST CRICKET

	Batsman dismissed			
A.Coningham	A.C.MacLaren	A v E	Melbourne	1894-95
W.M.Bradley	F.Laver	E v A	Manchester	1899
E.G.Arnold	V.T.Trumper	E v A	Sydney	1903-04
G.G.Macaulay	G.A.L.Hearne	E v SA	Cape Town	1922-23
M.W.Tate	M.J.Susskind	E v SA	Birmingham	1924
M.Henderson	E.W.Dawson	NZ v E	Christchurch	1929-30
H.D.Smith	E.Paynter	NZ v E	Christchurch	1932-33
T.F.Johnson	W.W.Keeton	WI v E	Oval	1939
R.Howorth	D.V.Dyer	E v SA	Oval	1947
Intikhab Alam	C.C.McDonald	P v A	Karachi[1]	1959-60
R.K.Illingworth	P.V.Simmons	E v WI	Nottingham	1991

MOST WICKETS BY A BOWLER IN ONE DAY

15	J.Briggs	15-28	England v South Africa	Cape Town	1888-89
14	H.Verity	14-80	England v Australia	Lord's	1934

OVER 200 RUNS CONCEDED IN AN INNINGS

O	M	R	W				
87	11	298	1	L.O'B.Fleetwood-Smith	A v E	Oval	1938
80.2	13	266	5	O.C.Scott	WI v E	Kingston	1929-30
54	5	259	0	Khan Mohammad	P v WI	Kingston	1957-58
85.2	20	247	2	Fazal Mahmood	P v WI	Kingston	1957-58
70	10	229	1	S.L.Boock	NZ v P	Auckland	1988-89
82	17	228	5	M.H.Mankad	I v WI	Kingston	1952-53
64.2	8	226	6	B.S.Bedi	I v E	Lord's	1974
38.4	3	220	7	Kapil Dev	I v P	Faisalabad	1982-83
52	7	217	3	I.T.Botham	E v P	Oval	1987
71	8	204	6	I.A.R.Peebles	E v A	Oval	1930
75	16	202	3	M.H.Mankad	I v WI	Bombay[2]	1948-49
84	19	202	6	Haseeb Ahsan	P v I	Madras[2]	1960-61

OVER 300 RUNS CONCEDED IN A MATCH

O	M	R	W				
105.2	13	374	9	O.C.Scott	WI v E	Kingston	1929-30
63	3	308	7	A.A.Mailey	A v E	Sydney	1924-25
61.3	6	302	10	A.A.Mailey	A v E	Adelaide	1920-21

BOWLERS UNCHANGED IN A COMPLETED INNINGS

ENGLAND		*Opponents*		
F.Morley (2-34)	R.G.Barlow (7-40)	Australia (83)	Sydney	1882-83
G.A.Lohmann (7-36)	J.Briggs (3-28)	Australia (68)	Oval	1886
G.A.Lohmann (5-17)	R.Peel (5-18)	Australia (42)	Sydney	1887-88
J.Briggs (8-11)	A.J.Fothergill (1-30)	South Africa (43)	Cape Town	1888-89
J.J.Ferris (7-37)	F.Martin (2-39)	South Africa (83)	Cape Town	1891-92
J.Briggs (6-49)	G.A.Lohmann (3-46)	Australia (100)	Adelaide	1891-92
T.Richardson (6-39)	G.A.Lohmann (3-13)	Australia (53)	Lord's	1896
S.Haigh (6-11)	A.E.Trott (4-19)	South Africa (35)	Cape Town	1898-99
S.F.Barnes (6-42)	C.Blythe (4-64)	Australia (112)	Melbourne	1901-02
G.H.Hirst (4-28)	C.Blythe (6-44)	Australia (74)	Birmingham	1909
F.R.Foster (5-16)	S.F.Barnes (5-25)	South Africa (58)	Lord's	1912
A.E.R.Gilligan (6-7)	M.W.Tate (4-12)	South Africa (30)	Birmingham	1924
G.O.B.Allen (5-36)	W.Voce (4-16)	Australia (58)	Brisbane[2]	1936-37

AUSTRALIA		*Opponents*		
G.E.Palmer (7-68)	E.Evans (3-64)	England (133)	Sydney	1881-82
F.R.Spofforth (5-30)	G.E.Palmer (4-32)	England (77)	Sydney	1884-85
C.T.B.Turner (6-15)	J.J.Ferris (4-27)	England (45)	Sydney	1886-87
C.T.B.Turner (5-36)	J.J.Ferris (5-26)	England (62)	Lord's	1888
G.Giffen (5-26)	C.T.B.Turner (4-33)	England (72)	Sydney	1894-95
H.Trumble (3-38)	M.A.Noble (7-17)	England (61)	Melbourne	1901-02
M.A.Noble (5-54)	J.V.Saunders (5-43)	England (99)	Sydney	1901-02

WEST INDIES		*Opponents*		
C.E.L.Ambrose (6-24)	C.A.Walsh (3-16)	England (46)	Port-of-Spain	1993-94

PAKISTAN		*Opponents*		
Fazal Mahmood (6-34)	Khan Mohammad (4-43)	Australia (80)	Karachi[1]	1956-57
Wasim Akram (4-32)	Waqar Younis (6-34)	Sri Lanka (71)	Kandy	1994-95

500 BALLS IN AN INNINGS

588	S.Ramadhin	98	35	179	2	WI v E	Birmingham	1957
571	T.R.Veivers	95.1	36	155	3	A v E	Manchester	1964
552	A.L.Valentine	92	49	140	3	WI v E	Nottingham	1950
522	L.O'B.Fleetwood-Smith	87	11	298	1	A v E	Oval	1938
512	Fazal Mahmood	85.2	20	247	2	P v WI	Kingston	1957-58
510	W.J.O'Reilly	85	26	178	3	A v E	Oval	1938
504	Haseeb Ahsan	84	19	202	6	P v I	Madras[2]	1960-61

700 BALLS IN A MATCH

774	S.Ramadhin	129	51	228	9	WI v E	Birmingham	1957
766	H.Verity	95.6	23	184	4	E v SA	Durban[2]	1938-39
749	J.C.White	124.5	37	256	13	E v A	Adelaide	1928-29
738	N.Gordon	92.2	17	256	1	SA v E	Durban[2]	1938-39
728	A.B.C.Langton	91	24	203	4	SA v E	Durban[2]	1938-39
712	M.W.Tate	89	19	228	11	E v A	Sydney	1924-25
708	G.Giffen	118	42	239	8	A v E	Sydney	1894-95

DISMISSING ALL ELEVEN BATSMEN IN A MATCH

J.C.Laker	19-90	E v A	Manchester	1956
S.Venkataraghavan	12-152	I v NZ	Delhi	1964-65
G.Dymock	12-166	A v I	Kanpur	1979-80
Abdul Qadir	13-101	P v E	Lahore[2]	1987-88
Waqar Younis	12-130	P v NZ	Faisalabad	1990-91

INDIVIDUAL RECORDS – WICKET-KEEPING

100 DISMISSALS IN TESTS

		Tests	Dis	Ct	St	Opponents E	A	SA	WI	NZ	I	P	SL	Z
R.W.Marsh	A	96	**355**	343	12	148	–	–	65	58	16	68	–	–
P.J.L.Dujon	WI	81	**272**	267‡	5	84	86	–	–	20	60	22	–	–
A.P.E.Knott	E	95	**269**	250	19	–	105	–	43	26	54	41	–	–
Wasim Bari	P	81	**228**	201	27	54	66	–	21	32	55	–	–	–
T.G.Evans	E	91	**219**	173	46	–	76	59	37	28	12	7	–	–
I.A.Healy	A	62	**205**	191	14	64	–	12	45	34	19	20	11	–
S.M.H.Kirmani	I	88	**198**	160	38	42	41	–	36	28	–	50	1	–
D.L.Murray	WI	62	**189**	181	8	94	40	–	–	7	27	21	–	–
A.T.W.Grout	A	51	**187**	163	24	76	–	33	41	–	20	17	–	–
I.D.S.Smith	NZ	63	**176**	168	8	42	39	–	16	–	29	23	27	–
R.W.Taylor	E	57	**174**	167	7	–	57	–	–	45	40	29	3	–
J.H.B.Waite	SA	50	**141**	124	17	56	28	–	–	57	–	–	–	–
K.S.More	I	49	**130**	110	20	37	13	11	21	13	–	21	11	3
W.A.S.Oldfield	A	54	**130**	78	52	90	–	27	13	–	–	–	–	–
J.M.Parks	E	46	**114**	103†	11	–	21	30	31	22	9	1	–	–
Salim Yousuf	P	32	**104**	91	13	15	15	–	22	22	11	–	19	–

The most dismissals by a wicket-keeper for Sri Lanka and Zimbabwe are:

S.A.R.Silva	SL	9	**34**	33	1	6	–	–	–	2	22	4	–	–
A.Flower	Z	7††	**16**	14	2	–	–	–	–	6	3	7	–	–

†*Including two catches in three Tests when not keeping wicket.*
‡*Including two catches in two Tests when not keeping wicket.*
††*Including one Test in which he did not keep wicket.*

20 DISMISSALS IN A SERIES

ENGLAND		Venue	Tests	St	Opponents A	SA	WI	NZ	I	P	SL
A.P.E.Knott	1970-71	A	6	3	24	–	–	–	–	–	–
A.P.E.Knott	1974-75	A	6	1	23	–	–	–	–	–	–
H.Strudwick	1913-14	SA	5	6	–	21	–	–	–	–	–
T.G.Evans	1956-57	SA	5	2	–	20	–	–	–	–	–
R.W.Taylor	1978-79	A	6	2	20	–	–	–	–	–	–
P.R.Downton	1985	E	6	1	20	–	–	–	–	–	–

AUSTRALIA		Venue	Tests	St	E	SA	WI	NZ	I	P	SL
R.W.Marsh	1982-83	A	5	–	28	–	–	–	–	–	–
R.W.Marsh	1975-76	A	6	–	–	–	26	–	–	–	–
I.A.Healy	1993	A	6	5	26	–	–	–	–	–	–
I.A.Healy	1990-91	A	5	–	24	–	–	–	–	–	–
A.T.W.Grout	1960-61	A	5	3	–	–	23	–	–	–	–
R.W.Marsh	1972	E	5	2	23	–	–	–	–	–	–
R.W.Marsh	1981	E	6	–	23	–	–	–	–	–	–
I.A.Healy	1992-93	A	5	4	–	–	23	–	–	–	–
S.J.Rixon	1977-78	A	5	–	–	–	–	–	22	–	–
R.A.Saggers	1949-50	SA	5	8	–	21	–	–	–	–	–
G.R.A.Langley	1951-52	A	5	5	–	–	21	–	–	–	–
A.T.W.Grout	1961	E	5	1	21	–	–	–	–	–	–
R.W.Marsh	1983-84	A	5	–	–	–	–	–	–	21	–
D.Tallon	1946-47	A	5	4	20	–	–	–	–	–	–
G.R.A.Langley	1954-55	WI	4	4	–	–	20	–	–	–	–
A.T.W.Grout	1958-59	A	5	3	20	–	–	–	–	–	–
H.B.Taber	1966-67	SA	5	1	–	20	–	–	–	–	–

SOUTH AFRICA		Venue	Tests	St	E	A	WI	NZ	I	SL
J.H.B.Waite	1961-62	SA	5	3	–	–	–	26	–	–
D.T.Lindsay	1966-67	SA	5	–	–	24	–	–	–	–
J.H.B.Waite	1953-54	SA	5	7	–	–	–	23	–	–

WEST INDIES		Venue	Tests	St	Opponents E	A	SA	NZ	I	P	SL
D.L.Murray	1963	E	5	2	24	–	–	–	–	–	–
F.C.M.Alexander	1959-60	WI	5	1	23	–	–	–	–	–	–
P.J.L.Dujon	1990-91	WI	5	–	–	23	–	–	–	–	–
P.J.L.Dujon	1983-84	WI	5	1	–	20	–	–	–	–	–
P.J.L.Dujon	1988	E	5	–	20	–	–	–	–	–	–

NEW ZEALAND		Venue	Tests	St	E	A	SA	WI	I	P	SL	Z
A.E.Dick	1961-62	SA	5	2	–	–	23	–	–	–	–	–

SRI LANKA		Venue	Tests	St	E	A	SA	WI	NZ	I	P
S.A.R.Silva	1985-86	SL	3	1	–	–	–	–	–	22	–

The most dismissals in a series for India is 19 by N.S.Tamhane (7 st) in five Tests in Pakistan in 1954-55 and S.M.H. Kirmani (2 st) in six home Tests v Pakistan in 1979-80; for Pakistan 17 by Wasim Bari (2 st) in six home Tests v India in 1982-83; for Zimbabwe 7 by A.Flower in two Tests in Pakistan in 1993-94.

MOST STUMPINGS IN A SERIES

9	P.W.Sherwell	SA v A	5 Tests in Australia	1910-11

EIGHT DISMISSALS IN A MATCH

†On debut

ENGLAND			St	Opponents A	SA	WI	NZ	I	P	SL
R.W.Taylor	1979-80	Bombay³	–	–	–	–	–	10	–	–
L.E.G.Ames	1933	Oval	2	–	–	8	–	–	–	–
J.M.Parks	1965-66	Christchurch	–	–	–	–	8	–	–	–

AUSTRALIA			St	E	SA	WI	NZ	I	P	SL
G.R.A.Langley	1956	Lord's	1	9	–	–	–	–	–	–
R.W.Marsh	1982-83	Brisbane²	–	9	–	–	–	–	–	–
J.J.Kelly	1901-02	Sydney	–	8	–	–	–	–	–	–
G.R.A.Langley	1954-55	Kingston	–	–	–	8	–	–	–	–
A.T.W.Grout	1959-60	Lahore²	2	–	–	–	–	–	8	–
A.T.W.Grout	1961	Lord's	–	8	–	–	–	–	–	–
H.B.Tabert†	1966-67	Johannesburg³	1	–	8	–	–	–	–	–
R.W.Marsh	1975-76	Melbourne	–	–	–	8	–	–	–	–
R.W.Marsh	1976-77	Christchurch	–	–	–	–	8	–	–	–
R.W.Marsh	1980-81	Sydney	1	–	–	–	8	–	–	–
R.W.Marsh	1982-83	Adelaide	–	8	–	–	–	–	–	–
I.A.Healy	1992-93	Adelaide	2	–	–	8	–	–	–	–

SOUTH AFRICA			St	E	A	WI	NZ	I	SL
D.J.Richardson	1992-93	Port Elizabeth	–	–	–	–	–	9	–
D.T.Lindsay	1966-67	Johannesburg³	–	–	8	–	–	–	–
D.J.Richardson	1993-94	Colombo (SSC)	–	–	–	–	–	–	8

WEST INDIES			St	E	A	SA	NZ	I	P	SL
D.A.Murray	1981-82	Melbourne	–	–	9	–	–	–	–	–
J.R.Murray	1992-93	Perth	–	–	8	–	–	–	–	–

NEW ZEALAND			St	E	A	SA	WI	I	P	SL	Z
W.K.Lees	1982-83	Wellington	–	–	–	–	–	–	–	8	–
I.D.S.Smith	1990-91	Hamilton	–	–	–	–	–	–	–	8	–

PAKISTAN			St	E	A	WI	NZ	I	SL	Z
Rashid Latif	1993-94	Auckland	–	–	–	–	9	–	–	–
Wasim Bari	1971	Leeds	–	8	–	–	–	–	–	–

SRI LANKA			St	E	A	SA	WI	NZ	I	P
S.A.R.Silva	1985-86	Colombo (SSC)	–	–	–	–	–	–	9	–
S.A.R.Silva	1985-86	Colombo (PSS)	1	–	–	–	–	–	9	–

The most dismissals in a match for India is 7 (1 ct, 6 st) by K.S. More v West Indies at Madras¹ in 1987-88; and for Zimbabwe 5 (4 ct, 1 st) by A.Flower v New Zealand at Harare in 1992-93.

MOST STUMPINGS IN A MATCH

| 6 | K.S.More | I v WI | Madras[1] | 1987-88 |

FIVE DISMISSALS IN AN INNINGS
†*On debut*

						Opponents					
ENGLAND			St	A	SA	WI	NZ	I	P	SL
R.W.Taylor	1979-80	Bombay[3]	–	–	–	–	–	7	–	–
J.T.Murray	1967	Lord's	–	–	–	–	–	6	–	–
R.C.Russell	1990-91	Melbourne	–	6	–	–	–	–	–	–
J.G.Binks	1963-64	Calcutta	–	–	–	–	–	5	–	–
J.M.Parks	1965-66	Sydney	2	5	–	–	–	–	–	–
J.M.Parks	1965-66	Christchurch	–	–	–	–	5	–	–	–
A.P.E.Knott	1974	Manchester	1	–	–	–	–	5	–	–
R.W.Taylor	1978	Nottingham	–	–	–	–	5	–	–	–
R.W.Taylor	1978-79	Brisbane[2]	–	5	–	–	–	–	–	–
C.J.Richards	1986-87	Melbourne	–	5	–	–	–	–	–	–
R.C.Russell	1989-90	Bridgetown	–	–	–	5	–	–	–	–

			St	E	SA	WI	NZ	I	P	SL
AUSTRALIA										
A.T.W.Grout†	1957-58	Johannesburg[3]	–	–	6	–	–	–	–	–
R.W.Marsh	1982-83	Brisbane[2]	–	6	–	–	–	–	–	–
W.A.S.Oldfield	1924-25	Melbourne	4	5	–	–	–	–	–	–
G.R.A.Langley	1954-55	Georgetown	3	–	–	5	–	–	–	–
G.R.A.Langley	1954-55	Kingston	–	–	–	5	–	–	–	–
G.R.A.Langley	1956	Lord's	–	5	–	–	–	–	–	–
A.T.W.Grout	1957-58	Durban[2]	1	–	5	–	–	–	–	–
A.T.W.Grout	1959-60	Lahore[2]	–	–	–	–	–	–	5	–
A.T.W.Grout	1960-61	Brisbane[2]	1	–	–	5	–	–	–	–
A.T.W.Grout	1961	Lord's	–	5	–	–	–	–	–	–
A.T.W.Grout	1965-66	Sydney	–	5	–	–	–	–	–	–
H.B.Taber†	1966-67	Johannesburg[3]	–	–	5	–	–	–	–	–
H.B.Taber	1968-69	Sydney	–	–	–	5	–	–	–	–
H.B.Taber	1969-70	Port Elizabeth	–	–	5	–	–	–	–	–
R.W.Marsh	1972	Manchester	–	5	–	–	–	–	–	–
R.W.Marsh	1972	Nottingham	–	5	–	–	–	–	–	–
R.W.Marsh	1973-74	Sydney	–	–	–	–	5	–	–	–
R.W.Marsh	1973-74	Christchurch	–	–	–	–	5	–	–	–
R.W.Marsh	1975-76	Melbourne	–	–	–	5	–	–	–	–
R.W.Marsh	1976-77	Christchurch	–	–	–	–	5	–	–	–
J.A.Maclean†	1978-79	Brisbane[2]	–	5	–	–	–	–	–	–
K.J.Wright	1978-79	Melbourne	–	–	–	–	–	–	5	–
R.W.Marsh	1979-80	Brisbane[2]	–	–	–	5	–	–	–	–
R.W.Marsh	1980-81	Sydney	–	–	–	–	–	5	–	–
R.W.Marsh	1981-82	Perth	–	–	–	–	–	–	5	–
R.W.Marsh	1983-84	Perth	–	–	–	–	–	–	5	–
R.W.Marsh	1983-84	Sydney	–	–	–	–	–	–	5	–
W.B.Phillips	1983-84	Kingston	–	–	–	5	–	–	–	–
I.A.Healy	1989-90	Adelaide	–	–	–	–	–	–	5	–
I.A.Healy	1990-91	Melbourne	–	5	–	–	–	–	–	–
I.A.Healy	1990-91	Adelaide	–	5	–	–	–	–	–	–
I.A.Healy	1993-94	Brisbane[2]	–	–	–	–	5	–	–	–

			St	E	A	WI	NZ	I	SL	
SOUTH AFRICA										
D.T.Lindsay	1966-67	Johannesburg[3]	–	–	6	–	–	–	–	
D.J.Richardson	1992-93	Port Elizabeth	–	–	–	–	–	5	–	

			St	E	A	SA	NZ	I	P	SL
WEST INDIES										
F.C.M.Alexander	1959-60	Bridgetown	–	5	–	–	–	–	–	–
D.L.Murray	1976	Leeds	–	5	–	–	–	–	–	–
D.L.Murray	1976-77	Georgetown	–	–	–	–	–	–	5	–
D.A.Murray	1978-79	Delhi	–	–	–	–	–	5	–	–
D.A.Murray	1981-82	Melbourne	–	–	5	–	–	–	–	–
P.J.L.Dujon	1982-83	Kingston	–	–	–	–	–	5	–	–
P.J.L.Dujon	1985-86	Bridgetown	–	5	–	–	–	–	–	–
P.J.L.Dujon	1990-91	St John's	–	–	5	–	–	–	–	–
D.Williams	1992-93	Brisbane[2]	–	–	5	–	–	–	–	–
J.R.Murray	1992-93	Perth	–	–	5	–	–	–	–	–

			St	Opponents							
NEW ZEALAND				*E*	*A*	*SA*	*WI*	*I*	*P*	*SL*	*Z*
I.D.S.Smith	1990-91	Hamilton	–	–	–	–	–	–	–	7	–
R.I.Harford	1967-68	Wellington	–	–	–	–	–	5	–	–	–
K.J.Wadsworth	1972-73	Auckland	–	–	–	–	–	–	5	–	–
W.K.Lees	1982-83	Wellington	–	–	–	–	–	–	–	5	–
I.D.S.Smith	1983-84	Auckland	1	5	–	–	–	–	–	–	–
I.D.S.Smith	1990-91	Auckland	–	–	–	–	–	–	–	5	–
A.C.Parore	1991-92	Auckland	–	5	–	–	–	–	–	–	–
A.C.Parore	1992-93	Colombo (SSC)	1	–	–	–	–	–	–	5	–
INDIA			*St*	*E*	*A*	*SA*	*WI*	*NZ*	*P*	*SL*	*Z*
S.M.H.Kirmani	1975-76	Christchirch	1	–	–	–	–	6	–	–	–
B.K.Kunderan	1961-62	Bombay²	2	5	–	–	–	–	–	–	–
S.M.H.Kirmani	1982-83	Faisalabad	–	–	–	–	–	–	5	–	–
K.S.More	1987-88	Madras¹	5	–	–	–	5	–	–	–	–
PAKISTAN			*St*	*E*	*A*	*WI*	*NZ*	*I*	*SL*	*Z*	
Wasim Bari	1978-79	Auckland	–	–	–	–	7	–	–	–	
Imtiaz Ahmed	1959-60	Lahore²	1	–	5	–	–	–	–	–	
Wasim Bari	1971	Leeds	–	5	–	–	–	–	–	–	
Salim Yousuf	1985-86	Karachi¹	–	–	–	–	–	–	5	–	
Salim Yousuf	1990-91	Faisalabad	–	–	–	–	5	–	–	–	
Moin Khan	1992-93	Bridgetown	1	–	–	5	–	–	–	–	
Rashid Latif	1993-94	Lahore²	–	–	–	–	–	–	–	5	
Rashid Latif	1993-94	Auckland	–	–	–	–	5	–	–	–	
SRI LANKA			*St*	*E*	*A*	*SA*	*WI*	*NZ*	*I*	*P*	
S.A.R.Silva	1985-86	Colombo (SSC)	–	–	–	–	–	–	6	–	
S.A.R.Silva	1985-86	Colombo (PSS)	–	–	–	–	–	–	5	–	
H.P.Tillekeratne	1990-91	Hamilton	–	–	–	–	–	5	–	–	

MOST STUMPINGS IN AN INNINGS

5	K.S.More	I v WI	Madras¹	1987-88

NO BYES CONCEDED IN TOTAL OF 500 RUNS

671-4	H.P.Tillekeratne	SL v NZ	Wellington	1990-91
659-8d	T.G.Evans	E v A	Sydney	1946-47
652	S.M.H.Kirmani	I v P	Faisalabad	1982-83
632-4d	A.J.Stewart	E v A	Lord's	1993
619	J.L.Hendriks	WI v A	Sydney	1968-69
616-5d	I.D.S.Smith	NZ v P	Auckland	1988-89
601-7d	R.C.Russell	E v A	Leeds	1989
593-5d	R.C.Russell	E v WI	St John's	1993-94
567-8d	A.C.Parore	NZ v E	Nottingham	1994
560-6d	R.J.Blakey	E v I	Madras¹	1992-93
559-9d	W.W.Wade	SA v E	Cape Town	1938-39
551	J.J.Kelly	A v E	Sydney	1897-98
551-9d	A.P.E.Knott	E v NZ	Lord's	1973
544-5d	Imtiaz Ahmed	P v E	Birmingham	1962
543-3d	T.M.Findlay	WI v NZ	Georgetown	1971-72
536-9d	I.A.Healy	A v WI	Bridgetown	1990-91
532-9d	A.P.E.Knott	E v A	Oval	1975
531	D.T.Lindsay	SA v E	Johannesburg³	1964-65
528	S.M.H.Kirmani	I v A	Adelaide	1980-81
528	R.C.Russell	E v A	Lord's	1989
526-7d	A.P.E.Knott	E v WI	Port-of-Spain	1967-68
521	W.A.S.Oldfield	A v E	Brisbane¹	1928-29
520	J.H.B.Waite	SA v A	Melbourne	1952-53
515	P.J.L.Dujon	WI v A	Adelaide	1988-89
514-4d	R.G.de Alwis	SL v A	Kandy	1982-83
514-5d	C.J.Richards	E v A	Adelaide	1986-87
512-6d	B.N.French	E v NZ	Wellington	1987-88
511	P.B.Dassanayake	SL v I	Lucknow²	1993-94
510	J.L.Hendriks	WI v A	Melbourne	1968-69

No Byes Conceded in Total of 500 Runs

509	W.B.Phillips	A v WI	Bridgetown	1983-84
507-6d	K.J.Wadsworth	NZ v P	Dunedin	1972-73
503-8d	S.M.H.Kirmani	I v P	Faisalabad	1978-79

MOST BYES CONCEDED IN AN INNINGS

37	F.E.Woolley	E v A	Oval	1934
	At the age of 47, deputising for L.E.G.Ames (injured).			
33	J.T.Murray	E v I	Bombay[2]	1961-62
33	J.M.Parks	E v WI	Kingston	1967-68

INDIVIDUAL RECORDS – FIELDING

100 CATCHES IN TESTS

		Tests	Ct	Opponents E	A	SA	WI	NZ	I	P	SL	Z
A.R.Border	A	156	**156**	57	–	5	19	31	14	22	8	–
G.S.Chappell	A	87	**122**	61	–	–	16	18	5	22	–	–
I.V.A.Richards	WI	121	**122**	29	24	–	–	7	39	23	–	–
I.T.Botham	E	102	**120**	–	61	–	15	14	14	14	2	–
M.C.Cowdrey	E	114	**120**	–	40	22	21	15	11	11	–	–
R.B.Simpson	A	62	**110**	30	–	27	29	–	21	3	–	–
W.R.Hammond	E	85	**110**	–	43	30	22	9	6	–	–	–
G.St A.Sobers	WI	93	**109**	40	27	–	–	11	27	4	–	–
S.M.Gavaskar	I	125	**108**	35	19	–	17	11	–	19	7	–
I.M.Chappell	A	75	**105**	31	–	11	24	16	17	6	–	–
G.A.Gooch	E	113	**103**	–	29	1	28	13	21	7	4	–

The records for South Africa, New Zealand, Pakistan, Sri Lanka and Zimbabwe are:

		Tests	Ct	E	A	SA	WI	NZ	I	P	SL	Z
B.Mitchell	SA	42	**56**	43	10	–	–	3	–	–	–	–
J.V.Coney	NZ	52	**64**	12	24	–	8	–	1	10	9	–
Javed Miandad	P	124	**93**	22	10	–	12	20	18	–	11	–
H.P.Tillekeratne	SL	15†	**28**	4	–	6	–	8	6	4	–	–
D.L.Houghton	Z	7	**7**	–	–	–	–	4	–	3	–	–

† *Excluding ten Tests in which he made 28 dismissals as a wicket-keeper.*

12 CATCHES IN A SERIES

ENGLAND		Venue	Tests	Opponents A	SA	WI	NZ	I	P	SL
L.C.Braund	1901-02	A	5	12	–	–	–	–	–	–
W.R.Hammond	1934	E	5	12	–	–	–	–	–	–
J.T.Ikin	1951	E	3	–	12	–	–	–	–	–
A.W.Greig	1974-75	A	6	12	–	–	–	–	–	–
I.T.Botham	1981	E	6	12	–	–	–	–	–	–

AUSTRALIA		Venue	Tests	E	SA	WI	NZ	I	P	SL
J.M.Gregory	1920-21	A	5	15	–	–	–	–	–	–
G.S.Chappell	1974-75	A	6	14	–	–	–	–	–	–
R.B.Simpson	1957-58	SA	5	–	13	–	–	–	–	–
R.B.Simpson	1960-61	A	5	–	–	13	–	–	–	–
D.F.Whatmore	1979-80	I	5	–	–	–	–	12	–	–
A.R.Border	1981	E	6	12	–	–	–	–	–	–

SOUTH AFRICA		Venue	Tests	E	A	WI	NZ	I	SL
A.E.E.Vogler	1909-10	SA	5	12	–	–	–	–	–
B.Mitchell	1930-31	SA	5	12	–	–	–	–	–
T.L.Goddard	1956-57	SA	5	12	–	–	–	–	–

WEST INDIES		Venue	Tests	E	A	SA	NZ	I	P	SL
G.St A.Sobers	1960-61	A	5	–	12	–	–	–	–	–

INDIA		Venue	Tests	E	A	SA	WI	NZ	P	SL	Z
E.D.Solkar	1972-73	I	5	12	–	–	–	–	–	–	–

The most catches by non-wicket-keepers in a series for New Zealand is 9 by B.A.Young in three home Tests v Pakistan in 1993-94; for Pakistan 9 by W.Mathias in five Tests in West Indies 1957-58; for Sri Lanka 8 by H.P.Tillekeratne in two home Tests v New Zealand in 1992-93; and for Zimbabwe 4 by D.L.Houghton in two home Tests in New Zealand in 1992-93.

SIX CATCHES IN A MATCH

†On debut

			Opponents						
ENGLAND			A	SA	WI	NZ	I	P	SL
A.Shrewsbury	1887-88	Sydney	6	–	–	–	–	–	–
F.E.Woolley	1911-12	Sydney	6	–	–	–	–	–	–
M.C.Cowdrey	1963	Lord's	–	–	6	–	–	–	–
A.W.Greig	1974	Leeds	–	–	–	–	–	6	–
A.J.Lamb	1983	Lord's	–	–	–	6	–	–	–
G.A.Hick	1992	Leeds	–	–	–	–	–	6	–
AUSTRALIA			E	SA	WI	NZ	I	P	SL
G.S.Chappell	1974-75	Perth	7	–	–	–	–	–	–
J.M.Gregory	1920-21	Sydney	6	–	–	–	–	–	–
V.Y.Richardson	1935-36	Durban[2]	–	6	–	–	–	–	–
R.N.Harvey	1962-63	Sydney	6	–	–	–	–	–	–
I.M.Chappell	1973-74	Adelaide	–	–	–	6	–	–	–
D.F.Whatmore	1979-80	Kanpur	–	–	–	–	6	–	–
SOUTH AFRICA			E	A	WI	NZ	I	SL	
A.E.E.Vogler	1909-10	Durban[1]	6	–	–	–	–	–	
B.Mitchell	1931-32	Melbourne	–	6	–	–	–	–	
WEST INDIES			E	A	SA	NZ	I	P	SL
G.St A.Sobers	1973	Lord's	6	–	–	–	–	–	–
R.B.Richardson	1991-92	Bridgetown	–	–	6	–	–	–	–
J.C.Adams	1993-94	Kingston	6	–	–	–	–	–	–
NEW ZEALAND			E	A	SA	WI	I	P	SL	Z
B.A.Young	1993-94	Auckland	–	–	–	–	–	6	–	–
INDIA			E	A	SA	WI	NZ	P	SL	Z
Yajurvindra Singh†	1976-77	Bangalore	7	–	–	–	–	–	–	–
E.D.Solkar	1970-71	Port-of-Spain	–	–	–	6	–	–	–	–
SRI LANKA			E	A	SA	WI	NZ	I	P	
H.P.Tillekeratne	1992-93	Colombo (SSC)	–	–	–	–	7	–	–	

FIVE CATCHES IN AN INNINGS

V.Y.Richardson	Australia v South Africa	Durban[2]	1935-36
Yajurvindra Singh	India v England	Bangalore	1976-77
M.Azharuddin	India v Pakistan	Karachi	1989-90
K.Srikkanth	India v Australia	Perth	1991-92

Richardson was playing in his last Test and Yajurvindra in his first.

MOST SUBSTITUTE CATCHES BY ONE FIELDER IN A MATCH

FOUR

Gursharan Singh	India v West Indies	Ahmedabad	1983-84

THREE

H.Strudwick	England v Australia	Melbourne	1903-04
J.E.D.Sealy	West Indies v England	Port-of-Spain	1929-30
W.V.Rodriguez	West Indies v India	Port-of-Spain	1961-62
Yajurvindra Singh	India v West Indies	Madras[1]	1978-79
Haroon Rashid	Pakistan v England	Leeds	1982
M.J.Greatbatch	New Zealand v England	Christchurch	1987-88

MOST SUBSTITUTE CATCHES BY ONE FIELDER IN AN INNINGS

THREE

H.Strudwick	England v Australia	Melbourne	1903-04
Haroon Rashid	Pakistan v England	Leeds	1982
Gursharan Singh	India v West Indies	Ahmedabad	1983-84

INDIVIDUAL RECORDS –
ALL-ROUND PERFORMANCES

1000 RUNS AND 100 WICKETS

ENGLAND	Tests	Runs	Wkts	Tests for Double
T.E.Bailey	61	2290	132	47
I.T.Botham	102	5200	383	21
J.E.Emburey	63	1705	147	46
A.W.Greig	58	3599	141	37
R.Illingworth	61	1836	122	47
W.Rhodes	58	2325	127	44
M.W.Tate	39	1198	155	33
F.J.Titmus	53	1449	153	40
AUSTRALIA				
R.Benaud	63	2201	248	32
A.K.Davidson	44	1328	186	34
G.Giffen	31	1238	103	30
M.G.Hughes	53	1032	212	52
I.W.Johnson	45	1000	109	45
R.R.Lindwall	61	1502	228	38
K.R.Miller	55	2958	170	33
M.A.Noble	42	1997	121	27
SOUTH AFRICA				
T.L.Goddard	41	2516	123	36
WEST INDIES				
M.D.Marshall	81	1810	376	49
G.St A.Sobers	93	8032	235	48
NEW ZEALAND				
J.G.Bracewell	41	1001	102	41
R.J.Hadlee	86	3124	431	28
INDIA				
Kapil Dev	131	5248	434	25
M.H.Mankad	44	2109	162	23
R.J.Shastri	80	3830	151	44
PAKISTAN				
Abdul Qadir	67	1029	236	62
Imran Khan	88	3807	362	30
Intikhab Alam	47	1493	125	41
Sarfraz Nawaz	55	1045	177	55
Wasim Akram	55	1205	235	45

1000 RUNS, 50 WICKETS AND 50 CATCHES

ENGLAND	Tests	Runs	Wkts	Catches
I.T.Botham	102	5200	383	120
A.W.Greig	58	3599	141	87
W.R.Hammond	85	7249	83	110
W.Rhodes	58	2325	127	60
F.E.Woolley	64	3283	83	64
AUSTRALIA				
R.Benaud	63	2201	248	65
R.B.Simpson	62	4869	71	110
WEST INDIES				
G.St A.Sobers	93	8032	235	109
INDIA				
Kapil Dev	131	5248	434	64

1000 RUNS AND 100 WICKET-KEEPING DISMISSALS

ENGLAND	Tests	Runs	Dismissals	Tests for Double
T.G.Evans	91	2439	219	42
A.P.E.Knott	95	4389	269	30
J.M.Parks	46	1962	114	41
R.W.Taylor	57	1156	174	47
AUSTRALIA				
I.A.Healy	62	2057	205	36
R.W.Marsh	96	3633	355	25
W.A.S.Oldfield	54	1427	130	41
SOUTH AFRICA				
J.H.B.Waite	50	2405	141	36
WEST INDIES				
P.J.L.Dujon	81	3322	272	30
D.L.Murray	62	1993	189	33
NEW ZEALAND				
I.D.S.Smith	63	1815	176	42
INDIA				
S.M.H.Kirmani	88	2759	198	42
K.S.More	49	1285	130	39
PAKISTAN				
Salim Yousuf	32	1055	104	32
Wasim Bari	81	1366	228	53

250 RUNS AND 20 WICKETS IN A SERIES

	Tests	Runs	Wkts		
G.Giffen	5	475	34	Australia v England	1894-95
L.C.Braund	5	256	21	England v Australia	1901-02
G.A.Faulkner	5	545	29	South Africa v England	1909-10
G.J.Thompson	5	267	23	England v South Africa	1909-10
J.M.Gregory	5	442	23	Australia v England	1920-21
K.R.Miller	5	362	20	Australia v West Indies	1951-52
K.R.Miller	5	439	20	Australia v West Indies	1954-55
R.Benaud	5	329	30	Australia v South Africa	1957-58
G.St A.Sobers	5	424	23	West Indies v India	1961-62
G.St A.Sobers	5	322	20	West Indies v England	1963
G.St A.Sobers	5	722	20	West Indies v England	1966
T.L.Goddard	5	294	26	South Africa v Australia	1966-67
A.W.Greig	5	430	24	England v West Indies	1973-74
I.T.Botham	6	291	23	England v Australia	1978-79
Kapil Dev	6	278	32	India v Pakistan	1979-80
I.T.Botham	6	399	34	England v Australia	1981
Kapil Dev	6	318	22	India v England	1981-82
R.J.Hadlee	4	301	21	New Zealand v England	1983
I.T.Botham	6	250	31	England v Australia	1985

250 RUNS AND 20 WICKET-KEEPING DISMISSALS IN A SERIES

	Tests	Runs	Dis		
J.H.B.Waite	5	263	26	South Africa v New Zealand	1961-62
D.T.Lindsay	5	606	24	South Africa v Australia	1966-67
A.P.E.Knott	6	364	23	England v Australia	1974-75
P.I.L.Dujon	5	305	20	West Indies v England	1988
I.A.Healy	6	296	26	Australia v England	1993

500 RUNS IN A SERIES BY A WICKET-KEEPER

	Tests	Runs	Avge		
B.K.Kunderan	5	525	52.50	India v England	1963-64
D.T.Lindsay	5	606	86.57	South Africa v Australia	1966-67

MATCH DOUBLE – 100 RUNS AND 10 WICKETS

A.K.Davidson	44	5-135	A v WI	Brisbane[2]	1960-61
	80	6-87			
I.T.Botham	114	6-58	E v I	Bombay[3]	1979-80
		7-48			
Imran Khan	117	6-98	P v I	Faisalabad	1982-83
		5-82			

A HUNDRED AND FIVE WICKETS IN AN INNINGS

†*On debut*

ENGLAND			Opponents		
A.W.Greig	148	6-164	West Indies	Bridgetown	1973-74
I.T.Botham	103	5-73	New Zealand	Christchurch	1977-78
I.T.Botham	108	8-34	Pakistan	Lord's	1978
I.T.Botham	114	6-58	India	Bombay[3]	1979-80
		7-48			
I.T.Botham	149*	6-95	Australia	Leeds	1981
I.T.Botham	138	5-59	New Zealand	Wellington	1983-84
AUSTRALIA					
C.Kelleway	114	5-33	South Africa	Manchester	1912
J.M.Gregory	100	7-69	England	Melbourne	1920-21
K.R.Miller	109	6-107	West Indies	Kingston	1954-55
R.Benaud	100	5-84	South Africa	Johannesburg[3]	1957-58
SOUTH AFRICA					
J.H.Sinclair	106	6-26	England	Cape Town	1898-99
G.A.Faulkner	123	5-120	England	Johannesburg[1]	1909-10
WEST INDIES					
D.St E.Atkinson	219	5-56	Australia	Bridgetown	1954-55
O.G.Smith	100	5-90	India	Delhi	1958-59
G.St A.Sobers	104	5-63	India	Kingston	1961-62
G.St A.Sobers	174	5-41	England	Leeds	1966
NEW ZEALAND					
B.R.Taylor†	105	5-86	India	Calcutta	1964-65
INDIA					
M.H.Mankad	184	5-196	England	Lord's	1952
P.R.Umrigar	172*	5-107	West Indies	Port-of-Spain	1961-62
PAKISTAN					
Mushtaq Mohammad	201	5-49	New Zealand	Dunedin	1972-73
Mushtaq Mohammad	121	5-28	West Indies	Port-of-Spain	1976-77
Imran Khan	117	6-98	India	Faisalabad	1982-83
		5-82			
Wasim Akram	123	5-100	Australia	Adelaide	1989-90

A HUNDRED AND FIVE DISMISSALS IN AN INNINGS

D.T.Lindsay	182	6 ct	SA v A	Johannesburg[3]	1966-67
I.D.S.Smith	113*	4 ct, 1 st	NZ v E	Auckland	1983-84
S.A.R.Silva	111	5 ct	SL v I	Colombo (PSS)	1985-86

INDIVIDUAL RECORDS – THE CAPTAINS

RESULTS SUMMARY

ENGLAND (71)	Tests as Captain	Opponents A	SA	WI	NZ	I	P	SL	Results W	L	D	Toss Won
James Lillywhite	2	2	–	–	–	–	–	–	1	1	–	–
Lord Harris	4	4	–	–	–	–	–	–	2	1	1	2
A.Shaw	4	4	–	–	–	–	–	–	–	2	2	4
A.N.Hornby	2	2	–	–	–	–	–	–	–	1	1	1
Hon I.F.W.Bligh	4	4	–	–	–	–	–	–	2	2	–	3
A.Shrewsbury	7	7	–	–	–	–	–	–	5	2	–	3
A.G.Steel	4	4	–	–	–	–	–	–	3	1	–	2
W.W.Read	2	1	1	–	–	–	–	–	2	–	–	–
W.G.Grace	13	13	–	–	–	–	–	–	8	3	2	4
C.A.Smith	1	–	1	–	–	–	–	–	1	–	–	–
M.P.Bowden	1	–	1	–	–	–	–	–	1	–	–	1
A.E.Stoddart	8	8	–	–	–	–	–	–	3	4	1	2
T.C.O'Brien	1	–	1	–	–	–	–	–	1	–	–	–
Lord Hawke	4	–	4	–	–	–	–	–	4	–	–	4
A.C.MacLaren	22	22	–	–	–	–	–	–	4	11	7	11
P.F.Warner	10	5	5	–	–	–	–	–	4	6	–	5
Hon F.S.Jackson	5	5	–	–	–	–	–	–	2	–	3	5
R.E.Foster	3	–	3	–	–	–	–	–	1	–	2	3
F.L.Fane	5	3	2	–	–	–	–	–	2	3	–	3
A.O.Jones	2	2	–	–	–	–	–	–	–	2	–	1
H.D.G.Leveson Gower	3	–	3	–	–	–	–	–	1	2	–	–
J.W.H.T.Douglas	18	12	6	–	–	–	–	–	8	8	2	7
C.B.Fry	6	3	3	–	–	–	–	–	4	–	2	4
Hon L.H.Tennyson	3	3	–	–	–	–	–	–	–	1	2	2
F.T.Mann	5	–	5	–	–	–	–	–	2	1	2	3
A.E.R.Gilligan	9	5	4	–	–	–	–	–	4	4	1	4
A.W.Carr	6	4	2	–	–	–	–	–	1	–	5	3
A.P.F.Chapman	17	9	5	3	–	–	–	–	9	2	6	9
R.T.Stanyforth	4	–	4	–	–	–	–	–	2	1	1	–
G.T.S.Stevens	1	–	1	–	–	–	–	–	–	1	–	–
J.C.White	4	1	3	–	–	–	–	–	1	1	2	3
A.H.H.Gilligan	4	–	–	–	4	–	–	–	1	–	3	1
Hon F.S.G.Calthorpe	4	–	–	4	–	–	–	–	1	1	2	2
R.E.S.Wyatt	16	5	5	5	1	–	–	–	3	5	8	12
D.R.Jardine	15	5	–	2	4	4	–	–	9	1	5	7
C.F.Walters	1	1	–	–	–	–	–	–	–	1	–	–
G.O.B.Allen	11	5	–	5	–	3	–	–	4	5	2	6
R.W.V.Robins	3	–	–	–	3	–	–	–	1	–	2	2
W.R.Hammond	20	8	5	3	1	3	–	–	4	3	13	12
N.W.D.Yardley	14	6	5	3	–	–	–	–	4	7	3	9
K.Cranston	1	–	–	1	–	–	–	–	–	–	1	–
F.G.Mann	7	–	5	–	2	–	–	–	2	–	5	5
F.R.Brown	15	5	5	1	4	–	–	–	5	6	4	3
N.D.Howard	4	–	–	–	–	4	–	–	1	–	3	2
D.B.Carr	1	–	–	–	–	1	–	–	–	1	–	1
L.Hutton	23	10	–	5	2	4	2	–	11	4	8	7
Rev D.S.Sheppard	2	–	–	–	–	–	2	–	1	–	1	1
P.B.H.May	41	13	10	8	7	3	–	–	20	10	11	26
M.C.Cowdrey	27	6	5	10	–	2	4	–	8	4	15	17
E.R.Dexter	30	10	–	5	3	5	7	–	9	7	14	13
M.J.K.Smith	25	5	8	1	6	5	–	–	5	3	17	10
D.B.Close	7	–	–	1	–	5	3	–	6	–	1	4
T.W.Graveney	1	1	–	–	–	–	–	–	–	–	1	–
R.Illingworth	31	11	–	6	8	3	3	–	12	5	14	15‡
A.R.Lewis	8	–	–	–	–	5	3	–	1	2	5	3
M.H.Denness	19	6	–	5	2	3	3	–	6	5	8	9

ENGLAND continued	Tests as Captain	Opponents							Results			Toss Won
		A	SA	WI	NZ	I	P	SL	W	L	D	
J.H.Edrich	1	1	–	–	–	–	–	–	–	1	–	–
A.W.Greig	14	4	–	5	–	5	–	–	3	5	6	6
J.M.Brearley	31	18	–	–	3	5	5	–	18	4	9	13
G.Boycott	4	–	–	–	3	–	1	–	1	1	2	3
I.T.Botham	12	3	–	9					–	4	8	6
K.W.R.Fletcher	7	–	–	–	–	6	–	1	1	1	5	5
R.G.D.Willis	18	5	–	–	7	3	3	–	7	5	6	8
D.I.Gower	32	12	–	10	–	6	3	1	5	18	9	14
M.W.Gatting	23	6	–	1	6	2	8	–	2	5	16	14
J.E.Emburey	2	–	–	2	–	–	–	–	–	2	–	1
C.S.Cowdrey	1	–	–	1	–	–	–	–	–	1	–	–
G.A.Gooch	34	8	–	8	6	5	5	2	10	12	12	16
A.J.Lamb	3	1	–	2	–	–	–	–	–	3	–	2
A.J.Stewart	2	–	–	–	–	1	–	1	–	2	–	1
M.A.Atherton	13	2	3	5	3	–	–	–	4	5	4	5
	707	280	105	109	75	81	52	5	243	199	265	348

‡Excluding toss won in abandoned Melbourne Test of 1970-71.

AUSTRALIA (38)	Tests as Captain	Opponents							Results				Toss Won
		E	SA	WI	NZ	I	P	SL	W	L	D	Tie	
D.W.Gregory	3	3	–	–	–	–	–	–	2	1	–	–	2
W.L.Murdoch	16	16	–	–	–	–	–	–	5	7	4	–	7
T.P.Horan	2	2	–	–	–	–	–	–	–	2	–	–	1
H.H.Massie	1	1	–	–	–	–	–	–	1	–	–	–	1
J.M.Blackham	8	8	–	–	–	–	–	–	3	3	2	–	4
H.J.H.Scott	3	3	–	–	–	–	–	–	–	3	–	–	1
P.S.McDonnell	6	6	–	–	–	–	–	–	1	5	–	–	4
G.Giffen	4	4	–	–	–	–	–	–	2	2	–	–	3
G.H.S.Trott	8	8	–	–	–	–	–	–	5	3	–	–	5
J.Darling	21	18	3	–	–	–	–	–	7	4	10	–	7
H.Trumble	2	2	–	–	–	–	–	–	2	–	–	–	1
M.A.Noble	15	15	–	–	–	–	–	–	8	5	2	–	11
C.Hill	10	5	5	–	–	–	–	–	5	5	–	–	5
S.E.Gregory	6	3	3	–	–	–	–	–	2	1	3	–	1
W.W.Armstrong	10	10	–	–	–	–	–	–	8	–	2	–	4
H.L.Collins	11	8	3	–	–	–	–	–	5	2	4	–	7
W.Bardsley	2	2	–	–	–	–	–	–	–	–	2	–	1
J.Ryder	5	5	–	–	–	–	–	–	1	4	–	–	2
W.M.Woodfull	25	15	5	5	–	–	–	–	14	7	4	–	12
V.Y.Richardson	5	–	5	–	–	–	–	–	4	–	1	–	1
D.G.Bradman	24	19	–	–	–	5	–	–	15	3	6	–	10
W.A.Brown	1	–	–	–	1	–	–	–	1	–	–	–	–
A.L.Hassett	24	10	10	4	–	–	–	–	14	4	6	–	18
A.R.Morris	2	1	–	1	–	–	–	–	–	2	–	–	2
I.W.Johnson	17	9	–	5	–	2	1	–	7	5	5	–	6
R.R.Lindwall	1	–	–	–	–	1	–	–	–	–	1	–	–
I.D.Craig	5	–	5	–	–	–	–	–	3	–	2	–	3
R.Benaud	28	14	1	5	–	5	3	–	12	4	11	1	11
R.N.Harvey	1	1	–	–	–	–	–	–	1	–	–	–	–
R.B.Simpson	39	8	9	10	–	10	2	–	12	12	15	–	19
B.C.Booth	2	2	–	–	–	–	–	–	–	1	1	–	1
W.M.Lawry	25	9	4	5	–	7	–	–	9	8	8	–	8
B.N.Jarman	1	1	–	–	–	–	–	–	–	–	1	–	1
I.M.Chappell	30	16	–	5	6	–	3	–	15	5	10	–	17
G.S.Chappell	48	15	–	12	8	3	9	1	21	13	14	–	29
G.N.Yallop	7	6	–	–	–	–	1	–	1	6	–	–	6
K.J.Hughes	28	6	–	7	–	6	9	–	4	13	11	–	13
A.R.Border	93	29	6	18	17	11	6	6	32	22	38	1	47
	539	280	59	77	32	50	34	7	222	152	163	2	271

Captains' Results Summary

SOUTH AFRICA (26)	Tests as Captain	Opponents						Results			Toss Won
		E	A	WI	NZ	I	SL	W	L	D	
O.R.Dunell	1	1	–	–	–	–	–	–	1	–	1
W.H.Milton	2	2	–	–	–	–	–	–	2	–	1
E.A.Halliwell	3	2	1	–	–	–	–	–	3	–	1
A.R.Richards	1	1	–	–	–	–	–	–	1	–	–
M.Bisset	2	2	–	–	–	–	–	–	2	–	–
H.M.Taberer	1	–	1	–	–	–	–	–	–	1	1
J.H.Anderson	1	–	1	–	–	–	–	–	1	–	–
P.W.Sherwell	13	8	5	–	–	–	–	5	6	2	5
S.J.Snooke	5	5	–	–	–	–	–	3	2	–	3
F.Mitchell	3	1	2	–	–	–	–	–	3	–	2
L.J.Tancred	3	2	1	–	–	–	–	–	2	1	2
H.W.Taylor	18	15	3	–	–	–	–	1	10	7	11
H.G.Deane	12	12	–	–	–	–	–	2	4	6	9
E.P.Nupen	1	1	–	–	–	–	–	1	–	–	–
H.B.Cameron	9	2	5	–	2	–	–	2	5	2	3
H.F.Wade	10	5	5	–	–	–	–	1	4	5	5
A.Melville	10	10	–	–	–	–	–	–	4	6	4
A.D.Nourse	15	10	5	–	–	–	–	1	9	5	7
J.E.Cheetham	15	3	5	–	7	–	–	7	5	3	6
D.J.McGlew	14	8	1	–	5	–	–	4	6	4	4
C.B.van Ryneveld	8	4	4	–	–	–	–	2	4	2	3
T.L.Goddard	13	5	5	–	3	–	–	1	2	10	4
P.L.van der Merwe	8	3	5	–	–	–	–	4	1	3	4
A.Bacher	4	–	4	–	–	–	–	4	–	–	4
K.C.Wessels	16	3	5	1	–	4	3	5	3	8	11
W.J.Cronje	1	–	1	–	–	–	–	–	1	–	–
	189	105	59	1	17	4	3	43	81	65	91

WEST INDIES (23)	Tests as Captain	Opponents							Results				Toss Won
		E	A	SA	NZ	I	P	SL	W	L	D	Tie	
R.K.Nunes	4	4	–	–	–	–	–	–	–	3	1	–	2
E.L.G.Hoad	1	1	–	–	–	–	–	–	–	–	1	–	1
N.Betancourt	1	1	–	–	–	–	–	–	–	1	–	–	1
M.P.Fernandes	1	1	–	–	–	–	–	–	1	–	–	–	1
G.C.Grant	12	7	5	–	–	–	–	–	3	7	2	–	5
R.S.Grant	3	3	–	–	–	–	–	–	–	1	2	–	2
G.A.Headley	1	1	–	–	–	–	–	–	–	–	1	–	1
G.E.Gomez	1	1	–	–	–	–	–	–	–	–	1	–	–
J.D.C.Goddard	22	11	4	–	2	5	–	–	8	7	7	–	12
J.B.Stollmeyer	13	5	3	–	–	5	–	–	3	4	6	–	7
D.St E.Atkinson	7	–	3	–	4	–	–	–	3	3	1	–	3
F.C.M.Alexander	18	5	–	–	5	8	–	–	7	4	7	–	9
F.M.M.Worrell	15	5	5	–	–	5	–	–	9	3	2	1	9
G.St A.Sobers	39	13	10	–	8	8	–	–	9	10	20	–	27
R.B.Kanhai	13	8	5	–	–	–	–	–	3	3	7	–	6
C.H.Lloyd	74	18	22	–	3	20	11	–	36	12	26	–	35
A.I.Kallicharran	9	–	3	–	–	6	–	–	1	2	6	–	4
D.L.Murray	1	–	1	–	–	–	–	–	–	–	1	–	1
I.V.A.Richards	50	19	11	–	7	8	5	–	27	8	15	–	23
C.G.Greenidge	1	–	–	–	–	–	1	–	–	1	–	–	1
D.L.Haynes	4	1	–	–	–	–	3	–	1	1	2	–	2
R.B.Richardson	14	4	5	1	–	–	3	1	8	2	4	–	6
C.A.Walsh	1	1	–	–	–	–	–	–	–	–	1	–	1
	305	109	77	1	24	62	31	1	119	72	113	1	158

NEW ZEALAND (22)	Tests as Captain	Opponents E	A	SA	WI	I	P	SL	Z	Results W	L	D	Toss Won
T.C.Lowry	7	7	–	–	–	–	–	–	–	–	2	5	5
M.L.Page	7	5	–	2	–	–	–	–	–	–	3	4	4
W.A.Hadlee	8	7	1	–	–	–	–	–	–	–	2	6	4
B.Sutcliffe	4	–	–	2	2	–	–	–	–	–	3	1	4
W.M.Wallace	2	–	–	2	–	–	–	–	–	–	1	1	–
G.O.Rabone	5	2	–	3	–	–	–	–	–	–	4	1	2
H.B.Cave	9	–	–	–	1	5	3	–	–	–	5	4	5
J.R.Reid	34	13	–	8	3	4	6	–	–	3	18	13	17
M.E.Chapple	1	1	–	–	–	–	–	–	–	–	–	1	–
B.W.Sinclair	3	2	–	–	–	1	–	–	–	–	1	2	3
G.T.Dowling	19	5	–	–	5	6	3	–	–	4	7	8	10
B.E.Congdon	17	5	6	–	3	–	3	–	–	1	7	9	4
G.M.Turner	10	–	2	–	–	6	2	–	–	1	6	3	2
J.M.Parker	1	–	–	–	–	–	1	–	–	–	–	1	–
M.G.Burgess	10	6	1	–	–	–	3	–	–	1	6	3	4
G.P.Howarth	30	7	5	–	7	3	3	5	–	11	7	12	17
J.V.Coney	15	3	6	–	3	–	3	–	–	5	4	6	8
J.J.Crowe	6	2	3	–	–	–	–	1	–	–	1	5	3
J.G.Wright	14	4	2	–	–	6	2	–	–	3	3	8	8
M.D.Crowe	16	3	4	–	–	–	3	4	2	2	7	7	8
I.D.S.Smith	1	–	–	–	–	–	–	1	–	–	–	1	1
K.R.Rutherford	10	3	2	–	–	1	4	–	–	1	6	3	7
	229	75	32	17	24	32	36	11	2	32	93	104	116

INDIA (25)	Tests as Captain	Opponents E	A	SA	WI	NZ	P	SL	Z	Results W	L	D	Tie	Toss Won
C.K.Nayudu	4	4	–	–	–	–	–	–	–	–	3	1	–	1
Maharajkumar of Vizianagram	3	3	–	–	–	–	–	–	–	–	2	1	–	1
Nawab of Pataudi, sr	3	3	–	–	–	–	–	–	–	–	1	2	–	3
L.Amarnath	15	–	5	–	5	–	5	–	–	2	6	7	–	4
V.S.Hazare	14	9	–	–	5	–	–	–	–	1	5	8	–	8
M.H.Mankad	6	–	–	–	1	–	5	–	–	–	1	5	–	1
Ghulam Ahmed	3	–	–	–	2	1	–	–	–	–	2	1	–	1
P.R.Umrigar	8	–	3	–	1	4	–	–	–	2	2	4	–	6
H.R.Adhikari	1	–	–	–	1	–	–	–	–	–	–	1	–	1
D.K.Gaekwad	4	4	–	–	–	–	–	–	–	–	4	–	–	2
Pankaj Roy	1	1	–	–	–	–	–	–	–	–	1	–	–	1
G.S.Ramchand	5	–	5	–	–	–	–	–	–	1	2	2	–	4
N.J.Contractor	12	5	–	–	2	–	5	–	–	2	2	8	–	7
Nawab of Pataudi, jr	40	8	11	–	10	11	–	–	–	9	19	12	–	20
C.G.Borde	1	–	1	–	–	–	–	–	–	–	1	–	–	–
A.L.Wadekar	6	11	–	–	5	–	–	–	–	4	4	8	–	7
S.Venkataraghavan	5	4	–	–	1	–	–	–	–	–	2	3	–	2
S.M.Gavaskar	47	14	9	–	6	4	13	1	–	9	8	30	–	22
B.S.Bedi	22	5	5	–	4	5	3	–	–	6	11	5	–	13
G.R.Viswanath	2	1	–	–	–	–	1	–	–	–	1	1	–	2
Kapil Dev	34	3	6	–	11	–	8	6	–	4	7	22	1	15
D.B.Vengsarkar	10	–	–	–	7	3	–	–	–	2	5	3	–	4
R.J.Shastri	1	–	–	–	1	–	–	–	–	1	–	–	–	1
K.Srikkanth	4	–	–	–	–	4	–	–	–	–	–	4	–	2
M.Azharuddin	28	6	5	4	–	4	–	7	2	9	7	12	–	16
	289	81	50	4	62	32	44	14	2	52	96	140	1	144

PAKISTAN (17)	Tests as Captain	Opponents							Results			Toss Won
		E	A	WI	NZ	I	SL	Z	W	L	D	
A.H.Kardar	23	4	1	5	3	10	–	–	6	6	11	10
Fazal Mahmood	10	–	2	3	–	5	–	–	2	2	6	6
Imtiaz Ahmed	4	3	1	–	–	–	–	–	–	2	2	4
Javed Burki	5	5	–	–	–	–	–	–	–	4	1	3
Hanif Mohammad	11	3	2	–	6	–	–	–	2	2	7	6
Saeed Ahmed	3	3	–	–	–	–	–	–	–	–	3	1
Intikhab Alam	17	6	3	2	6	–	–	–	1	5	11	12
Majid Khan	3	3	–	–	–	–	–	–	–	–	3	1
Mushtaq Mohammad	19	–	5	5	6	3	–	–	8	4	7	10
Wasim Bari	6	6	–	–	–	–	–	–	–	2	4	4
Asif Iqbal	6	–	–	–	–	6	–	–	–	2	4	3
Javed Miandad	34	8	9	4	7	–	6	–	14	6	14	12
Imran Khan	48	8	8	9	2	15	6	–	14	8	26	25
Zaheer Abbas	14	3	3	–	3	5	–	–	3	1	10	6
Wasim Akram	5	–	–	3	–	–	–	2	1	2	2	1
Salim Malik	5	–	–	–	3	–	2	–	4	1	–	3
Waqar Younis	1	–	–	–	–	–	–	1	1	–	–	1
	214	52	34	31	36	44	14	3	56	47	111	108

SRI LANKA (6)	Tests as Captain	Opponents							Results			Toss Won
		E	A	SA	WI	NZ	I	P	W	L	D	
B.Warnapura	4	1	–	–	–	–	1	2	–	3	1	2
L.R.D.Mendis	19	1	1	–	–	4	6	7	2	8	9	10
D.S.de Silva	2	–	–	–	–	2	–	–	–	2	–	1
R.S.Madugalle	2	1	1	–	–	–	–	–	–	2	–	–
A.Ranatunga	24	1	5	3	1	5	7	2	2	10	12	13
P.A.de Silva	4	1	–	–	–	–	–	3	–	2	2	2
	55	5	7	3	1	11	14	14	4	27	24	28

ZIMBABWE (2)	Tests as Captain	Opponents			Results			Toss Won
		NZ	I	P	W	L	D	
D.L.Houghton	4	2	2	–	–	2	2	1
A.Flower	3	–	–	3	–	2	1	2
	7	2	2	3	–	4	3	3

MOST CONSECUTIVE MATCHES AS CAPTAIN

			From	To
England	35	P.B.H.May	1955	1959
Australia	93	A.R.Border	1984-85	1993-94
South Africa	18	H.W.Taylor	1913-14	1924
West Indies	39	G.St A.Sobers	1964-65	1971-72
New Zealand	34	J.R.Reid	1955-56	1965
India	28	M.Azharuddin	1989-90	1993-94
Pakistan	23	A.H.Kardar	1952-53	1957-58
Sri Lanka	18	L.R.D.Mendis	1982-83	1986-87
	18	A.Ranatunga	1992-93	1994-95
Zimbabwe	4	D.L.Houghton	1992-93	1992-93

In addition to those listed above, the following had unbroken captaincy runs of 20 or more matches: 30 – I.M.Chappell (A); 29 – C.H.Lloyd (WI); 25 – W.M.Woodfull (A), R.Illingworth (E), D.I.Gower (E); 23 – C.H.Lloyd (WI), M.W.Gatting (E); 21 – Nawab of Pataudi, jr (I); 20 – M.J.K.Smith (E), W.M.Lawry (A), J.M.Brearley (E), Kapil Dev (I).

WINNING ALL FIVE TOSSES IN A SERIES

Captains		*Venue*	
Hon F.S.Jackson	England v Australia	England	1905
M.A.Noble	Australia v England	England	1909
H.G.Deane	South Africa v England	South Africa	1927-28
J.D.C.Goddard	West Indies v India	India	1948-49
A.L.Hassett	Australia v England	England	1953
P.B.H.May (3) ⎫ M.C.Cowdrey (2) ⎭	England v West Indies	West Indies	1959-60
M.C.Cowdrey	England v South Africa	England	1960
Nawab of Pataudi, jr	India v England	India	1963-64
G.St A.Sobers	West Indies v England	England	1966
G.St A.Sobers	West Indies v New Zealand	West Indies	1971-72
C.H.Lloyd	West Indies v India	West Indies	1982-83

The following Australian captains won five tosses during six-match series in Australia: I.M.Chappell v England 1974-75; G.S.Chappell v West Indies 1975-76; G.N.Yallop v England 1978-79.
K.W.R.Fletcher (England) won five successive tosses during the six-match series in India in 1981-82.
M.C.Cowdrey won the toss for England in nine consecutive Tests from 1959-60 to 1961.

YOUNGEST CAPTAINS

Years	*Days*				
21	77	Nawab of Pataudi, jr	I v WI	Bridgetown	1961-62
22	194	J.D.Craig	A v SA	Johannesburg[3]	1957-58
22	260	Javed Miandad	P v A	Karachi[1]	1979-80
22	306	M.Bisset	SA v E	Johannesburg[1]	1898-99
23	144	M.P.Bowden	E v SA	Cape Town	1888-89
23	217	G.C.Grant	WI v A	Adelaide	1930-31
23	292	Hon I.F.W.Bligh	E v A	Melbourne	1882-83

The youngest New Zealand captain is J.M.Parker who was 25 years 251 days when he led his country against Pakistan in Karachi in 1976-77.

OLDEST CAPTAINS

Years	*Days*				
50	220	W.G.Grace	E v A	Nottingham	1899
45	245	G.O.B.Allen	E v WI	Kingston	1947-48

INDIVIDUAL RECORDS – GENERAL

MOST APPEARANCES FOR EACH COUNTRY

For	Total		Opponents								
			E	A	SA	WI	NZ	I	P	SL	Z
England	117	D.I.Gower	–	42	–	19	13	24	17	2	–
Australia	156	A.R.Border	47	–	6	31	23	20	22	7	–
South Africa	50	J.H.B.Waite	21	14	–	–	15	–	–	–	–
West Indies	121	I.V.A.Richards	36	34	–	–	7	28	16	–	–
New Zealand	86	R.J.Hadlee	21	23	–	10	–	11	15	6	–
India	131	Kapil Dev	27	20	4	25	10	–	29	14	2
Pakistan	124	Javed Miandad	22	25	–	16	18	28	–	12	3
Sri Lanka	51	A.Ranatunga	4	7	3	1	9	14	13	–	–

The most appearances for Zimbabwe is 7 by A.D.R.Campbell, A.Flower, G.W.Flower and D.L.Houghton.

MOST CONSECUTIVE APPEARANCES

			From			To		
153	A.R.Border	A	Melbourne	1978-79		Durban	1993-94	
106	S.M.Gavaskar	I	Bombay[3]	1974-75		Madras[1]	1986-87	
87	G.R.Viswanath	I	Georgetown	1970-71		Karachi[1]	1982-83	
85	G.St A.Sobers	WI	Port-of-Spain	1954-55		Port-of-Spain	1971-72	
72	D.L.Haynes	WI	Brisbane[2]	1979-80		Lord's	1988	
71	I.M.Chappell	A	Adelaide	1965-66		Melbourne	1975-76	
66	Kapil Dev	I	Faisalabad	1978-79		Delhi	1984-85	
65	A.P.E.Knott	E	Auckland	1970-71		Oval	1977	
65	I.T.Botham	E	Wellington	1977-78		Karachi[1]	1983-84	
65	Kapil Dev	I	Madras[1]	1984-85		Hamilton	1993-94	
61	R.B.Kanhai	WI	Birmingham	1957		Sydney	1968-69	
61	I.V.A.Richards	WI	Nottingham	1980		Madras[1]	1987-88	
58†	J.R.Reid	NZ	Manchester	1949		Leeds	1965	
58†	A.W.Greig	E	Manchester	1972		Oval	1977	
56	S.M.H.Kirmani	I	Madras[1]	1979-80		Kanpur	1984-85	
53	K.J.Hughes	A	Brisbane[2]	1978-79		Sydney	1982-83	
53	Javed Miandad	P	Lahore[2]	1977-78		Sydney	1983-84	
52	F.E.Woolley	E	Oval	1909		Oval	1926	
52	P.B.H.May	E	Oval	1953		Leeds	1959	
52	R.W.Marsh	A	Brisbane[2]	1970-71		Oval	1977	
51	G.S.Chappell	A	Perth	1970-71		Oval	1977	
51	D.I.Gower	E	Bombay[3]	1981-82		Lord's	1986	

The most for South Africa is 45† by A.W.Nourse, and for Sri Lanka 30 by P.A.de Silva.
†His entire Test career.

PLAYERS WHO REPRESENTED TWO COUNTRIES

		Total Tests
Amir Elahi	I (1) 1947-48 and P (5) 1952-53	6
J.J.Ferris	A (8) 1886-87 to 1890 and E (1) 1891-92	9
S.C.Guillen	WI (5) 1951-52 and NZ (3) 1955-56	8
Gul Mahomed	I (8) 1946 to 1952-53 and P (1) 1956-57	9
F.Hearne	E (2) 1888-89 and SA (4) 1891-92 to 1895-96	6
A.H.Kardar	I (3) 1946† and P (23) 1952-53 to 1957-58	26
W.E.Midwinter	A (8) 1876-77 to 1886-87 and E (4) 1881-82	12
F.Mitchell	E (2) 1898-99 and SA (3) 1912	5
W.L.Murdoch	A (18) 1876-77 to 1890 and E (1) 1891-92	19
Nawab of Pataudi, sr	E (3) 1932-33 to 1934 and I (3) 1946	6
A.J.Traicos	SA (3) 1969-70 and Zimbabwe (4) 1992-93	7
A.E.Trott	A (3) 1894-95 and E (2) 1898-99	5
K.C.Wessels	A (24) 1982-83 to 1985-86 and SA (16) 1991-92 to 1994	40
S.M.J.Woods	A (3) 1888 and E (3) 1895-96	6

†As 'Abdul Hafeez'

652

RELATED TEST PLAYERS

FATHER AND TWO SONS
L.Amarnath and his sons M. and S. (India)
W.A.Hadlee and his sons D.R. and R.J. (New Zealand)

FATHERS AND SONS
W.M. and R.W.Anderson (New Zealand)
W.P. and G.E.Bradburn (New Zealand)
B.L. and C.L.Cairns (New Zealand)
M.C. and C.S.Cowdrey (England)
D.K. and A.D.Gaekwad (India)
E.J. and S.E.Gregory (Australia)
J.Hardstaff, sr and J.Hardstaff, jr (England)
P.G.Z. and C.Z.Harris (New Zealand)
G.A. and R.G.A.Headley (West Indies)
F.Hearne (England and South Africa) and G.A.L.Hearne (South Africa)
L. and R.A.Hutton (England)
Jahangir Khan (India) and Majid Khan (Pakistan)
J.D. and D.T.Lindsay (South Africa)
V.L. and S.V.Manjrekar (India)
M.H. and A.V.Mankad (India)
F.T. and F.G.Mann (England)
Hanif Mohammad and Shoaib Mohammad (Pakistan)
Nazar Mohammad and Mudassar Nazar (Pakistan)
A.W. and A.D.Nourse (South Africa)
J.H. and J.M.Parks (England)
Nawab of Pataudi, sr (England and India) and Nawab of Pataudi, jr (India)
Pankaj and Pranab Roy (India)
O.C. and A.P.H.Scott (West Indies)
M.J. and A.J.Stewart (England)
F.W. and M.W.Tate (England)
C.L. and D.C.H.Townsend (England)
L.R. and L.Tuckett (South Africa)
H.G. and G.E.Vivian (New Zealand)
S.Wazir Ali (India) and Khalid Wazir (Pakistan)

FOUR BROTHERS
Hanif, Mushtaq, Sadiq and Wazir Mohammad (Pakistan)

Hanif, Mushtaq and Sadiq all played against New Zealand at Karachi in 1969-70.

THREE BROTHERS
G.S., I.M. and T.M.Chappell (Australia)
E.M., G.F. and W.G.Grace (England)
A., F. and G.G.Hearne (England) – F.Hearne also played for South Africa.
A., D. and S.Ranatunga (Sri Lanka)
A.B., L.J. and V.M.Tancred (South Africa)

All three Grace brothers played against Australia at The Oval in 1880.
A. and G.G.Hearne (E) and F.Hearne (SA) all played in the match between South Africa and England at Cape Town in 1891-92.

TWO BROTHERS

ENGLAND
A.E.R. and A.H.H.Gilligan
A.W. and I.A.Greig
G. and J.R.Gunn
D.W. and P.E.Richardson
C.L. and R.A.Smith
C.T. and G.B.Studd
G.E. and J.T.Tyldesley
C.E.M. and E.R.Wilson

WEST INDIES
D.St E. and E.St E.Atkinson
F.J. and J.H.Cameron
C.M. and R.J.Christiani
B.A. and C.A.Davis
G.C. and R.S.Grant
N.E. and R.E.Marshall
E.L. and W.H.St Hill
J.B. and V.H.Stollmeyer

AUSTRALIA	NEW ZEALAND	PAKISTAN
K.A. and R.G.Archer	B.P. and J.G.Bracewell	Ramiz Raja and Wasim Raja
A.C. and C.Bannerman	J.J. and M.D.Crowe	Azmat Rana and Shafqat Rana
J. and R.Benaud	D.R. and R.J.Hadlee	Pervez Sajjad and Waqar Hassan
G. and W.F.Giffen	G.P. and H.J.Howarth	Saeed Ahmed and Younis Ahmed
D.W. and E.J.Gregory	J.M. and N.M.Parker	Moin Khan and Nadeem Khan
M.R. and R.N.Harvey		
C.E. and R.W.McLeod		
A.E. and G.H.S.Trott		
H. and J.W.Trumble		
M.E. and S.R.Waugh		

SOUTH AFRICA	INDIA	SRI LANKA
P.A.M. and R.H.M.Hands	M. and S.Amarnath	M.de S. and S.Wettimuny
G. and P.N.Kirsten	L. Amar Singh and L.Ramji	
A.J. and D.B.Pithey	A.L. and M.L.Apte	ZIMBABWE
P.M. and R.G.Pollock	B.P. and S.P.Gupte	A. and G.W.Flower
A.R. and W.H.M.Richards	A.G.Kripal Singh and	
A.M.B. and E.A.B.Rowan	A.G.Milkha Singh	
S.D. and S.J.Snooke	C.K. and C.S.Nayudu	
G.L. and L.E.Tapscott	S.Nazir Ali and S.Wazir Ali	
D. and H.W.Taylor		
H.F. and W.W.Wade		

YOUNGEST TEST PLAYERS

Years	Days				
15	124	Mushtaq Mohammad	P v WI	Lahore[1]	1958-59
16	189	Aqib Javed	P v NZ	Wellington	1988-89
16	205	S.R.Tendulkar	I v P	Karachi[1]	1989-90
16	221	Aftab Baloch	P v NZ	Dacca	1969-70
16	248	Nasim-ul-Ghani	P v WI	Bridgetown	1957-58
16	352	Khalid Hassan	P v E	Nottingham	1954
17	5	Zahid Fazal	P v WI	Karachi[1]	1990-91
17	69	Ata-ur-Rehman	P v E	Birmingham	1992
17	118	L.Sivaramakrishnan	I v WI	St John's	1982-83
17	122	J.E.D.Sealy	WI v E	Bridgetown	1929-30
17	189	C.D.U.S.Weerasinghe	SL v I	Colombo (PSS)	1985-86
17	193	Maninder Singh	I v P	Karachi[1]	1982-83
17	239	I.D.Craig	A v SA	Melbourne	1952-53
17	245	G.St A.Sobers	WI v E	Kingston	1953-54
17	265	V.L.Mehra	I v NZ	Bombay[2]	1955-56
17	300	Hanif Mohammad	P v I	Delhi	1952-53
17	341	Intikhab Alam	P v A	Karachi[1]	1959-60
17	364	Waqar Younis	P v I	Karachi[1]	1989-90

The youngest to represent countries not included above are:

18	149	D.B.Close	E v NZ	Manchester	1949
18	197	D.L.Freeman	NZ v E	Christchurch	1932-33
19	1	A.E.Ochse	SA v E	Port Elizabeth	1888-89
19	260	H.H.Streak	Z v P	Karachi[2]	1993-94

OLDEST PLAYERS ON TEST DEBUT

Years	Days				
49	119	J.Southerton	E v A	Melbourne	1876-77
47	284	Miran Bux	P v I	Lahore[1]	1954-55
46	253	D.D.Blackie	A v E	Sydney	1928-29
46	237	H.Ironmonger	A v E	Brisbane[2]	1928-29
42	242	N.Betancourt	WI v E	Port-of-Spain	1929-30
41	337	E.R.Wilson	E v A	Sydney	1920-21
41	27	R.J.D.Jamshedji	I v E	Bombay[1]	1933-34
40	345	C.A.Wiles	WI v E	Manchester	1933
40	295	O.Henry	SA v I	Durban[2]	1992-93
40	216	S.Kinneir	E v A	Sydney	1911-12
40	110	H.W.Lee	E v SA	Johannesburg[1]	1930-31
40	56	G.W.A.Chubb	SA v E	Nottingham	1951
40	37	C.Ramaswami	I v E	Manchester	1936

The oldest to make their debut for countries not included above are:

39	251	D.S.de Silva	SL v E	Colombo (PSS)	1981-82
38	101	H.M.McGirr	NZ v E	Auckland	1929-30
36	317	M.P.Jarvis	Z v I	Harare	1992-93

A.J.Traicos was 45 years 154 days old when he made his debut for Zimbabwe (v India at Harare in 1992-93) having played three Tests for South Africa in 1969-70.

OLDEST TEST PLAYERS

Age on final day of their last Test match

Years	Days				
52	165	W.Rhodes	E v WI	Kingston	1929-30
50	327	H.Ironmonger	A v E	Sydney	1932-33
50	320	W.G.Grace	E v A	Nottingham	1899
50	303	G.Gunn	E v WI	Kingston	1929-30
49	139	J.Southerton	E v A	Melbourne	1876-77
47	302	Miran Bux	P v I	Peshawar	1954-55
47	249	J.B.Hobbs	E v A	Oval	1930
47	87	F.E.Woolley	E v A	Oval	1934
46	309	D.D.Blackie	A v E	Adelaide	1928-29
46	206	A.W.Nourse	SA v E	Oval	1924
46	202	H.Strudwick	E v A	Oval	1926
46	41	E.H.Hendren	E v WI	Kingston	1934-35
45	304	A.J.Traicos	Z v I	Durban[2]	1992-93
45	245	G.O.B.Allen	E v WI	Kingston	1947-48
45	215	P.Holmes	E v I	Lord's	1932
45	140	D.B.Close	E v WI	Manchester	1976
44	341	E.G.Wynyard	E v SA	Johannesburg[1]	1905-06
44	317	J.M.M.Commaille	SA v E	Cape Town	1927-28
44	238	R.Abel	E v A	Manchester	1902
44	236	G.A.Headley	WI v E	Kingston	1953-54
44	105	Amir Elahi	P v I	Calcutta	1952-53

The ages of Indian and Pakistani players have not been confirmed.

LONGEST CAREERS

From debut to final day of last match

Years	Days			From		To	
30	315	W.Rhodes	E	Nottingham	1899	Kingston	1929-30
26	355	D.B.Close	E	Manchester	1949	Manchester	1976
25	13	F.E.Woolley	E	Oval	1909	Oval	1934
24	10	G.A.Headley	WI	Bridgetown	1929-30	Kingston	1953-54
23	40	A.J.Traicos	SA/Z	Durban[2]	1969-70	Delhi	1992-93
22	233	J.B.Hobbs	E	Melbourne	1907-08	Oval	1930
22	120	G.Gunn	E	Sydney	1907-08	Kingston	1929-30
22	18	S.E.Gregory	A	Lord's	1890	Oval	1912

LONGEST INTERVALS BETWEEN APPEARANCES

Years	Days			From		To	
22	222	A.J.Traicos	SA/Z	Port Elizabeth	1969-70	Harare	1992-93
17	316	G.Gunn	E	Sydney	1911-12	Bridgetown	1929-30
17	111	Younis Ahmed	P	Lahore[2]	1969-70	Jaipur	1986-87
14	92	J.M.M.Commaille	SA	Cape Town	1909-10	Birmingham	1924
14	28	D.C.Cleverley	NZ	Christchurch	1931-32	Wellington	1945-46
13	53	F.Mitchell	E/SA	Cape Town	1898-99	Manchester	1912
13	32	G.M.Carew	WI	Bridgetown	1934-35	Port-of-Spain	1947-48
12	160	L.Amarnath	I	Madras[1]	1933-34	Lord's	1946
12	81	W.E.Hollies	E	Kingston	1934-35	Nottingham	1947
12	14	Nawab of Pataudi, sr	E/I	Nottingham	1934	Lord's	1946

The most matches between appearances is 104 by Younis Ahmed (as above).

ON THE FIELD THROUGHOUT A MATCH

				Days
Nazar Mohammad	P v I	Lucknow	1952-53	4
D.J.McGlew	SA v NZ	Wellington	1952-53	4
C.A.Milton†	E v NZ	Leeds	1958	5‡
J.H.Edrich	E v NZ	Leeds	1965	5
D.Lloyd	E v I	Birmingham	1974	3
G.Boycott	E v A	Leeds	1977	4
Taslim Arif	P v A	Faisalabad	1979-80	4
S.M.Gavaskar	I v WI	Georgetown	1982-83	5‡
D.S.B.P.Kuruppu†	SL v NZ	Colombo (CCC)	1986-87	5

†On debut
‡Rain prevented play on two days

UMPIRES' RECORDS

MOST TEST MATCHES

Tests		Venue	From	To
59	H.D.Bird	England (51)	1973	1994
		Zimbabwe (3)	1992-93	
		West Indies (3)	1992-93	
		New Zealand (2)	1993-94	
48	F.Chester	England	1924	1955
42	C.S.Elliott	England (41)	1957	1974
		New Zealand (1)	1970-71	
36	D.J.Constant	England	1971	1988
33	J.S.Buller	England	1956	1969
33	A.R.Crafter	Australia	1978-79	1991-92
32	R.W.Crockett	Australia	1901-02	1924-25
31	D.Sang Hue	West Indies	1961-62	1980-81
29	Khizer Hayat	Pakistan (28)	1979-80	1993-94
		New Zealand (1)	1993-94	
29	J.Phillips	England (11)	1893	1905
		Australia (13)	1884-85	1897-98
		South Africa (5)	1905-06	
29	F.S.Lee	England	1949	1962
29	C.J.Egar	Australia	1960-61	1968-69
28	D.M.Archer	West Indies	1978-79	1991-92
27	R.C.Bailhache	Australia	1974-75	1988-89
26	B.J.Meyer	England	1978	1993
25	R.Gosein	West Indies	1964-65	1977-78
25	L.P.Rowan	Australia	1962-63	1970-71

Most in other countries:

24	F.R.Goodall	New Zealand	1964-65	1987-88
24	S.J.Woodward	New Zealand	1978-79	1990-91
17	B.Satyaji Rao	India	1960-61	1978-79
17	Swaroop Kishen	India	1978-79	1984-85
14	R.G.A.Ashman	South Africa	1935-36	1949-50
12	K.T.Francis	Sri Lanka	1981-82	1994-95
3	I.D.Robinson	Zimbabwe	1992-93	

C.J.Egar and L.P.Rowan stood together in 19 Test matches, four more than the partnership of R.Gosein and D.Sang Hue.

Individual Career Records 1876-77 to 1994

INDIVIDUAL CAREER RECORDS

These career records for all players appearing in official Test matches are complete to the end of the 1994 English season.
Symbols: *not out; †left-handed batsman; ‡left-handed bowler.

ENGLAND (570 players)	Tests	I	NO	BATTING AND FIELDING HS	Runs	Avge	100	50	Ct/St	BOWLING Balls	Runs	Wkts	Avge	BB	5wI	10wM
Abel, R.	13	22	2	132*	744	37.20	2	2	13	–	–	–	–	–	–	–
Absolom, C.A.	1	1	–	52	58	29.00	–	1	–							
Agnew, J.P.	3	4	3	5	10	10.00	–	–	–	552	373	4	93.25	2-51	–	–
Allen, D.A.	39	51	15	88	918	25.50	–	5	10	11297	3779	122	30.97	5-30	4	–
Allen, G.O.B.	25	33	2	122	750	24.19	1	3	20	4386	2379	81	29.37	7-80	5	1
Allom, M.J.C.	5	3	2	8*	14	14.00	–	–	–	817	265	14	18.92	5-38	1	–
Allott, P.J.W.	13	18	3	52*	213	14.20	–	1	4	2225	1084	26	41.69	6-61	1	–
Ames, L.E.G.	47	72	12	149	2434	40.56	8	7	74/23							
Amiss, D.L.	50	88	10	262*	3612	46.30	11	11	24	–						
Andrew, K.V.	2	4	1	15	29	9.66	–	–	1							
Appleyard, R.	9	9	6	19*	51	17.00	–	–	4	1596	554	31	17.87	5-51	1	–
Archer, A.G.	1	2	1	24*	31	31.00	–	–	1							
Armitage, T.	2	3	–	21	33	11.00	–	–	–	12	15	0	–	–	–	–
Arnold, E.G.	10	15	3	40	160	13.33	–	1	8	1677	788	31	25.41	5-37	1	–
Arnold, G.G.	34	46	11	59	421	12.02	–	1	9	7650	3254	115	28.29	6-45	6	–
Arnold, J.	1	2	–	34	34	17.00	–	–	–	–						
Astill, W.E.	9	15	1	40	190	12.66	–	–	7	2182	856	25	34.24	4-58	–	–
Atherton, M.A.	40	74	1	151	2917	39.95	7	19	30	366	282	1	282.00	1-60	–	–
Athey, C.W.J.	23	41	1	123	919	22.97	1	4	13	–						
Attewell, W.	10	15	6	43*	150	16.66	–	–	9	2850	626	28	22.35	4-42	–	–
Bailey, R.J.	4	8	–	43	119	14.87	–	–	–							
Bailey, T.E.	61	91	14	134*	2290	29.74	1	10	32	9712	3856	132	29.21	7-34	5	1
Bairstow, D.L.	4	7	1	59	125	20.83	–	1	12/1							
Bakewell, A.H.	6	9	–	107	409	45.44	1	3	3	18	8	0	–	–	–	–
Balderstone, J.C.	2	4	–	35	39	9.75	–	–	1	96‡	80	1	80.00	1-80	–	–
Barber, R.W.	28	45†	3	185	1495	35.59	1	9	21	3426	1806	42	43.00	4-132	–	–
Barber, W.	2	4	–	44	83	20.75	–	–	1							
Barlow, G.D.	3	5†	1	7*	17	4.25	–	–	1	2	0	1	0.00	1-0	–	–
Barlow, R.G.	17	30	4	62	591	22.73	–	2	14	2456‡	767	34	22.55	7-40	3	–
Barnes, S.F.	27	39	9	38*	242	8.06	–	–	12	7873	3106	189	16.43	9-103	24	7
Barnes, W.	21	33	2	134	725	23.38	1	5	19	2289	793	51	15.54	6-28	3	–
Barnett, C.J.	20	35	4	129	1098	35.41	2	5	14	256	93	0	–	–	–	–
Barnett, K.J.	4	7	–	80	207	29.57	–	2	1	36	32	0	–	–	–	–

INDIVIDUAL CAREER RECORDS – ENGLAND *continued*

	Tests	I	NO	HS	Runs	Avge	100	50	Ct/St	Balls	Runs	Wkts	Avge	BB	5wI	10wM
				BATTING AND FIELDING								*BOWLING*				
Barratt, F.	5	4	1	17	28	9.33	–	–	2	750	235	5	47.00	1-8	–	–
Barrington, K.F.	82	131	15	256	6806	58.67	20	35	58	2715	1300	29	44.82	3-4	–	–
Barton, V.A.	1	1	–	23	23	23.00	–	–	9	–	–	–	–	–	–	–
Bates, W.	15	26	2	64	656	27.33	–	5	9	2364	821	50	16.42	7-28	4	1
Bean, G.	3	5	–	50	92	18.40	–	1	4	–	–	–	–	–	–	–
Bedser, A.V.	51	71	15	79	714	12.75	–	1	26	15918	5876	236	24.89	7-44	15	5
Benjamin, J.E.	1	1	–	0	0	0.00	–	–	–	168	80	4	20.00	4-42	–	–
Benson, M.R.	1	2†	–	30	51	25.50	–	–	1	–	–	–	–	–	–	–
Berry, R.	2	4†	2	4*	6	3.00	–	–	2	653‡	228	9	25.33	5-63	1	–
Bicknell, M.P.	2	4	–	14	26	6.50	–	–	–	522	263	4	65.75	3-99	–	–
Binks, J.G.	2	4	–	55	91	22.75	–	–	8	–	–	–	–	–	–	–
Bird, M.C.	10	16	1	61	280	18.66	–	2	5	264	120	8	15.00	3-11	1	–
Birkenshaw, J.	5	7†	1	64	148	21.14	–	1	3	1017	469	13	36.07	5-57	1	–
Blakey, R.J.	2	4	–	6	7	1.75	–	–	2	–	–	–	–	–	–	–
Bligh, *Hon* I.F.W.	4	7	1	19	62	10.33	–	–	7	–	–	–	–	–	–	–
Blythe, C.	19	31	12	27	183	9.63	–	–	6	4546‡	1863	100	18.63	8-59	9	4
Board, J.H.	6	12	2	29	108	10.80	–	–	8/3	–	–	–	–	–	–	–
Bolus, J.B.	7	12	–	88	496	41.33	–	4	2	18‡	16	0	–	–	–	–
Booth, M.W.	2	2	–	32	46	23.00	–	–	–	312	130	7	18.57	4-49	–	–
Bosanquet, B.J.T.	7	14	3	27	147	13.36	–	–	9	970	604	25	24.16	8-107	2	–
Botham, I.T.	102	161	6	208	5200	33.54	14	22	120	21815	10878	383	28.40	8-34	27	4
Bowden, M.P.	2	2	–	25	25	12.50	–	–	1	–	–	–	–	–	–	–
Bowes, W.E.	15	11	5	10*	28	4.66	–	–	2	3655	1519	68	22.33	6-33	6	–
Bowley, E.H.	5	7	–	109	252	36.00	1	2	2	252	116	0	–	–	–	–
Boycott, G.	108	193	23	246*	8114	47.72	22	42	33	944	382	7	54.57	3-47	–	–
Bradley, W.M.	2	2	1	23*	23	23.00	–	–	–	625	233	6	38.83	5-67	1	–
Braund, L.C.	23	41	3	104	987	25.97	3	2	39	3805	1810	47	38.51	8-81	3	–
Brearley, J.M.	39	66	3	91	1442	22.88	–	9	52	–	–	–	–	–	–	–
Brearley, W.	4	5	2	11*	21	7.00	–	–	–	705	359	17	21.11	5-110	1	–
Brennan, D.V.	2	2	–	16	16	8.00	–	–	–/1	–	–	–	–	–	–	–
Briggs, J.	33	50	5	121	815	18.11	1	2	12	5332‡	2095	118	17.75	8-11	9	4
Broad, B.C.	25	44†	2	162	1661	39.54	6	6	10	6	4	0	–	–	–	–
Brockwell, W.	7	12	–	49	202	16.83	–	1	6	582	309	5	61.80	3-33	–	–
Bromley-Davenport, H.R.	4	6	–	84	128	21.33	–	1	1	155‡	98	4	24.50	2-46	–	–
Brookes, D.	1	2	–	10	17	8.50	–	–	1	–	–	–	–	–	–	–
Brown, A.	2	1	1	3*	3	–	–	–	1	323	150	3	50.00	3-27	–	–
Brown, D.J.	26	34	5	44*	342	11.79	–	–	7	5098	2237	79	28.31	5-42	2	–
Brown, F.R.	22	30	1	79	734	25.31	–	5	22	3260	1398	45	31.06	5-49	1	–

INDIVIDUAL CAREER RECORDS – ENGLAND continued

	Tests	I	NO	HS	Runs	Avge	100	50	Ct/St	Balls	Runs	Wkts	Avge	BB	5wI	10wM
				BATTING AND FIELDING						BOWLING						
Brown, G.	7	12†	2	84	299	29.90	–	2	9/3	–	–	–	–	–	–	–
Brown, J.T.	8	16	3	140	470	36.15	1	1	7	35	22	0	–	–	–	–
Buckenham, C.P.	4	7	1	17	43	6.14	–	–	2	1182	593	21	28.23	5-115	1	–
Butcher, A.R.	1	2†	–	20	34	17.00	–	–	–	12‡	9	0	–	–	–	–
Butcher, R.O.	3	5	–	32	71	14.20	–	–	3	–	–	–	–	–	–	–
Butler, H.J.	2	2	1	15*	15	15.00	–	–	1	552	215	12	17.91	4-34	–	–
Butt, H.R.	3	4	1	13	22	7.33	–	–	1/1	–	–	–	–	–	–	–
Caddick, A.R.	8	14	2	29*	170	14.16	–	–	4	1940	1033	23	44.91	6-65	2	–
Calthorpe, Hon F.S.G.	4	7	–	49	129	18.42	–	–	3	204	91	1	91.00	1-38	–	–
Capel, D.J.	15	25	1	98	374	15.58	–	2	6	2000	1064	21	50.66	3-88	–	–
Carr, A.W.	11	13	–	63	237	19.75	–	1	3	–	–	–	–	–	–	–
Carr, D.B.	2	4	–	76	135	33.75	–	1	–	210‡	140	2	70.00	2-84	–	–
Carr, D.W.	1	1	–	0	0	0.00	–	–	–	414	282	7	40.28	5-146	1	–
Cartwright, T.W.	5	7	2	9	26	5.20	–	–	2	1611	544	15	36.26	6-94	1	–
Chapman, A.P.F.	26	36†	4	121	925	28.90	1	5	32	40‡	20	0	–	–	–	–
Charlwood, H.R.J.	2	4	–	36	63	15.75	–	–	–	–	–	–	–	–	–	–
Chatterton, W.	1	1	–	48	48	48.00	–	–	1	–	–	–	–	–	–	–
Childs, J.H.	2	4†	4	2*	2	–	–	–	1	516‡	183	3	61.00	1-13	–	–
Christopherson, S.	1	2	–	17	17	17.00	–	–	–	136	69	1	69.00	1-52	–	–
Clark, E.W.	8	9†	5	10	36	9.00	–	–	1	1931‡	899	32	28.09	5-98	1	–
Clay, J.C.	1	–	–	–	–	–	–	–	1	192	75	0	–	–	–	–
Close, D.B.	22	37†	2	70	887	25.34	–	4	24	1212	532	18	29.55	4-35	–	–
Coldwell, L.J.	7	7	5	6*	9	4.50	–	–	1	1668	610	22	27.72	6-85	1	–
Compton, D.C.S.	78	131	15	278	5807	50.06	17	28	49	2716‡	1410	25	56.40	5-70	1	–
Cook, C.	1	2	1	4	4	2.00	–	–	–	180‡	127	0	–	–	–	–
Cook, G.	7	13	–	66	203	15.61	–	2	9	42‡	27	0	–	–	–	–
Cook, N.G.B.	15	25	4	31	179	8.52	–	–	5	4174‡	1689	52	32.48	6-65	4	1
Cope, G.A.	3	3	–	22	40	13.33	–	–	1	864	277	8	34.62	3-102	–	–
Copson, W.H.	3	1	–	6	6	6.00	–	–	1	762	297	15	19.80	5-85	1	–
Cornford, W.L.	4	4	–	18	36	9.00	–	–	5/3	–	–	–	–	–	–	–
Cottam, R.M.H.	4	5	1	13	27	6.75	–	–	2	903	327	14	23.35	4-50	–	–
Coventry, Hon C.J.	2	2	–	12	13	13.00	–	–	–	–	–	–	–	–	–	–
Cowans, N.G.	19	29	7	36	175	7.95	–	–	9	3452	2003	51	39.27	6-77	2	–
Cowdrey, C.S.	6	8	1	38	101	14.42	–	–	5	399	309	4	77.25	2-65	–	–
Cowdrey, M.C.	114	188	15	182	7624	44.06	22	38	120	119	104	0	–	–	–	–
Coxon, A.	1	2	–	19	19	9.50	–	–	–	378	172	3	57.33	2-90	–	–
Cranston, J.	1	2†	–	16	31	15.50	–	–	1	–	–	–	–	–	–	–

INDIVIDUAL CAREER RECORDS – ENGLAND *continued*

				BATTING AND FIELDING						BOWLING						
	Tests	I	NO	HS	Runs	Avge	100	50	Ct/St	Balls	Runs	Wkts	Avge	BB	5wI	10wM
Cranston, K.	8	14	1	45	209	14.92	–	–	3	1010	461	18	25.61	4-12	–	–
Crapp, J.F.	7	13†	2	56	319	29.00	–	3	7						–	–
Crawford, J.N.	12	23	2	74	469	22.33	–	2	13	2203	1150	39	29.48	5-48	3	–
Crawley, J.P.	3	5	–	38	59	11.80	–	–	4						–	–
Curtis, T.S.	5	9	–	41	140	15.55	–	–	3	18	7	0	–	–	–	–
Cuttell, W.R.	2	4	–	21	65	16.25	–	–	2	285	73	6	12.16	3-17	–	–
Dawson, E.W.	5	9	–	55	175	19.44	–	1	–						–	–
Dean, H.	3	4†	2	8	10	5.00	–	–	2	447‡	153	11	13.90	4-19	–	–
DeFreitas, P.A.J.	39	58	5	69	769	14.50	–	3	12	8572	4027	125	32.21	7-70	4	–
Denness, M.H.	28	45	3	188	1667	39.69	4	7	28						–	–
Denton, D.	11	22	1	104	424	20.19	1	1	8						–	–
Dewes, J.G.	5	10†	–	67	121	12.10	–	1	–						–	–
Dexter, E.R.	62	102	8	205	4502	47.89	9	27	29	5317	2306	66	34.93	4-10	–	–
Dilley, G.R.	41	58†	19	56	521	13.35	–	2	10	8192	4107	138	29.76	6-38	6	–
Dipper, A.E.	1	2	–	40	51	25.50	–	–	–						–	–
Doggart, G.H.G.	2	4	–	29	76	19.00	–	–	3						–	–
D'Oliveira, B.L.	44	70	8	158	2484	40.06	5	15	29	5706	1859	47	39.55	3-46	–	–
Dollery, H.E.	4	7	–	37	72	10.28	–	–	1						–	–
Dolphin, A.	1	2	–	1	1	0.50	–	–	1						–	–
Douglas, J.W.H.T.	23	35	2	119	962	29.15	1	6	9	2812	1486	45	33.02	5-46	1	–
Downton, P.R.	30	48	8	74	785	19.62	–	4	70/5						–	–
Druce, N.F.	5	9	–	64	252	28.00	–	1	5						–	–
Ducat, A.	1	2	–	3	5	2.50	–	–	1						–	–
Duckworth, G.	24	28	12	39*	234	14.62	–	–	45/15						–	–
Duleepsinhji, K.S.	12	19	2	173	995	58.52	3	5	10	6	7	0	–	–	–	–
Durston, F.J.	1	2	1	6*	8	8.00	–	–	–	202	136	5	27.20	4-102	–	–
Edmonds, P.H.	51	65	15	64	875	17.50	–	2	42	12028‡	4273	125	34.18	7-66	2	–
Edrich, J.H.	77	127†	9	310*	5138	43.54	12	24	43	30	23	0	–	–	–	–
Edrich, W.J.	39	63	2	219	2440	40.00	6	13	39	3234	1693	41	41.29	4-68	–	–
Elliott, H.	4	5	1	37*	61	15.25	–	–	8/3						–	–
Ellison, R.M.	11	16†	1	41	202	13.46	–	–	2	2264	1048	35	29.94	6-77	3	–
Emburey, J.E.	63	95	20	75	1705	22.73	–	10	33	15211	5564	147	37.85	7-78	6	1
Emmett, G.M.	1	2	–	10	10	5.00	–	–	–						–	–
Emmett, T.	7	13†	1	48	160	13.33	–	–	9	728‡	284	9	31.55	7-68	1	–
Evans, A.J.	1	2	–	14	18	9.00	–	–	–						–	–
Evans, T.G.	91	133	14	104	2439	20.49	2	8	173/46						–	–

INDIVIDUAL CAREER RECORDS – ENGLAND continued

	Tests	I	NO	HS	Runs	Avge	100	50	Ct/St	Balls	Runs	Wkts	Avge	BB	5wI	10wM
					BATTING AND FIELDING					BOWLING						
Fagg, A.E.	5	8	1	39	150	18.75	–	–	5	–	–	–	–	–	–	–
Fairbrother, N.H.	10	15†	1	83	219	15.64	–	1	4	12‡	9	0	–	–	–	–
Fane, F.L.	14	27	–	143	682	26.23	1	3	6	–	–	–	–	–	–	–
Farnes, K.	15	17	5	20	58	4.83	–	–	–	3932	1719	60	28.65	6-96	3	1
Farrimond, W.	4	7	1	35	116	16.57	–	–	5/2	–	–	–	–	–	–	–
Fender, P.G.H.	13	21	1	60	380	19.00	–	2	14	2178	1185	29	40.86	5-90	2	–
Ferris, J.J.	1	1†	–	16	16	16.00	–	–	–	272‡	91	13	7.00	7-37	2	1
Fielder, A.	6	12	5	20	78	11.14	–	–	4	1491	711	26	27.34	6-82	1	–
Fishlock, L.B.	4	5†	1	19*	47	11.75	–	–	1	–	–	–	–	–	–	–
Flavell, J.A.	4	6†	2	14	31	7.75	–	–	–	792	367	7	52.42	2-65	–	–
Fletcher, K.W.R.	59	96	14	216	3272	39.90	7	19	54	285	193	2	96.50	1-6	–	–
Flowers, W.	8	14	–	56	254	18.14	–	1	2	858	296	14	21.14	5-46	1	–
Ford, F.G.J.	5	9†	–	48	168	18.66	–	–	5	204‡	129	1	129.00	1-47	–	–
Foster, F.R.	11	15	1	71	330	23.57	–	3	11	2447‡	926	45	20.57	6-91	4	–
Foster, N.A.	29	45	7	39	446	11.73	–	–	7	6261	2891	88	32.85	8-107	5	1
Foster, R.E.	8	14	1	287	602	46.30	1	1	13	–	–	–	–	–	–	–
Fothergill, A.J.	2	2†	–	32	33	16.50	–	–	–	321‡	90	8	11.25	4-19	–	–
Fowler, G.	21	37†	4	201	1307	35.32	3	8	10	18	11	0	–	–	–	–
Fraser, A.R.C.	21	29	5	29	180	7.20	–	–	6	5665	2370	85	27.88	8-75	6	–
Freeman, A.P.	12	16	4	50*	154	14.00	–	1	4	3732	1707	66	25.86	7-71	5	3
French, B.N.	16	21	4	59	308	18.11	–	1	38/1	–	–	–	–	–	–	–
Fry, C.B.	26	41	3	144	1223	32.18	2	7	17	10	3	0	–	–	–	–
Gatting, M.W.	74	129	14	207	4227	36.75	9	21	56	752	317	4	79.25	1-14	–	–
Gay, L.H	1	2	–	33	37	18.50	–	–	3/1	–	–	–	–	–	–	–
Geary, G.	14	20	4	66	249	15.56	–	2	13	3810	1353	46	29.41	7-70	4	1
Gibb, P.A.	8	13	–	120	581	44.69	2	3	3/1	–	–	–	–	–	–	–
Gifford, N.	15	20†	9	25*	179	16.27	–	–	8	3084‡	1026	33	31.09	5-55	1	–
Gilligan, A.E.R.	11	16	3	39*	209	16.07	–	–	3	2404	1046	36	29.05	6-7	2	–
Gilligan, A.H.H.	4	4	–	32	71	17.75	–	–	1	–	–	–	–	–	–	–
Gimblett, H.	3	5	1	67*	129	32.25	–	1	1	–	–	–	–	–	–	–
Gladwin, C.	8	11	5	51*	170	28.33	–	1	2	2129	571	15	38.06	3-21	–	–
Goddard, T.W.J.	8	5	3	8	13	6.50	–	–	3	1563	588	22	26.72	6-29	1	–
Gooch, G.A.	113	205	6	333	8655	43.49	20	45	103	2505	995	22	45.22	3-39	–	–
Gough, D.	4	5	2	65	146	48.66	–	1	1	1022	566	17	33.29	4-46	–	–
Gover, A.R.	4	1	1	2*	2	–	–	–	1	816	359	8	44.87	3-85	–	–
Gower, D.I.	117	204†	18	215	8231	44.25	18	39	74	36	20	1	20.00	1-1	–	–
Grace, E.M.	1	2	–	36	36	18.00	–	–	1	–	–	–	–	–	–	–

INDIVIDUAL CAREER RECORDS – ENGLAND *continued*

				BATTING AND FIELDING					BOWLING						
	Tests	I	NO	HS	Runs	Avge	100	50	Ct/St	Balls	Runs	Wkts	Avge	BB	5wI	10wM
Grace, G.F.	1	2	–	0	0	0.00	–	–	2	–					–	–
Grace, W.G.	22	36	2	170	1098	32.29	2	5	39	666	236	9	26.22	2-12	–	–
Graveney, T.W.	79	123	13	258	4882	44.38	11	20	80	260	167	1	167.00	1-34	–	–
Greenhough, T.	4	4	1	4	4	1.33	–	–	1	1129	357	16	22.31	5-35	1	–
Greenwood, A.	2	4	–	49	77	19.25	–	–	2							
Greig, A.W.	58	93	4	148	3599	40.43	8	20	87	9802	4541	141	32.20	8-86	6	2
Greig, I.A.	2	4	1	14	26	6.50	–	–	–	188	114	4	28.50	4-53	–	–
Grieve, B.A.F.	2	3	2	14*	40	40.00	–	–	5							
Griffith, S.C.	3	5	–	140	157	31.40	1	–	15							
Gunn, G.	15	29	1	122*	1120	40.00	2	7	15	12	8	0	–	–	–	–
Gunn, J.R.	6	10†	2	24	85	10.62	–	–	3	999‡	387	18	21.50	5-76	1	–
Gunn, W.	11	20	2	102*	392	21.77	1	1	5							
Haigh, N.E.	5	9	–	47	126	14.00	–	–	4	1026	448	13	34.46	3-73	–	–
Haigh, S.	11	18	3	25	113	7.53	–	–	8	1294	622	24	25.91	6-11	1	–
Hallows, C.	2†	2	–	26	42	42.00	–	–	–							
Hammond, W.R.	85	140	16	336*	7249	58.45	22	24	110	7969	3138	83	37.80	5-36	2	–
Hampshire, J.H.	8	16	1	107	403	26.86	1	2	9							
Hardinge, H.T.W.	1	2	–	25	30	15.00	–	–	1							
Hardstaff, J., *sr*	5	10	–	72	311	31.10	–	3	1							
Hardstaff, J., *jr*	23	38	3	205*	1636	46.74	4	10	9							
Harris, *Lord*	4	6	1	52	145	29.00	–	1	2	32	29	0	–	–	–	–
Hartley, J.C.	2	4	–	9	15	3.75	–	–	2	192	115	1	115.00	1-62	–	–
Hawke, *Lord*	5	8	1	30	55	7.85	–	–	3							
Hayes, E.G.	5	9	–	35	86	10.75	–	–	2	90	52	1	52.00	1-28	–	–
Hayes, F.C.	9	17	1	106*	244	15.25	1	–	7							
Hayward, T.W.	35	60	2	137	1999	34.46	3	12	19	893	514	14	36.71	4-22	–	–
Hearne, A.	1	1	–	9	9	9.00	–	–	1							
Hearne, F.	2	2	–	27	47	23.50	–	–	1							
Hearne, G.G.	1†	1†	–	0	0	0.00	–	–	–							
Hearne, J.T.	12	18	4	40	126	9.00	–	–	4	2976	1082	49	22.08	6-41	4	1
Hearne, J.W.	24	36	5	114	806	26.00	1	2	13	2926	1462	30	48.73	5-49	1	–
Hemmings, E.E.	16	21	4	95	383	22.52	–	2	5	4437	1825	43	42.44	6-58	1	–
Hendren, E.H.	51	83	9	205*	3525	47.63	7	21	33	47	31	1	31.00	1-27	–	–
Hendrick, M.	30	35	15	15	128	6.40	–	–	25	6208	2248	87	25.83	4-28	–	–
Heseltine, C.	2	2	1	18	18	9.00	–	–	3	157	84	5	16.80	5-38	1	–
Hick, G.A.	29	50	1	178	1725	35.20	2	9	41	2303	915	19	48.15	4-126	1	–
Higgs, K.	15	19†	3	63	185	11.56	–	1	4	4112	1473	71	20.74	6-91	2	–

INDIVIDUAL CAREER RECORDS – ENGLAND *continued*

	Tests	I	NO	HS	Runs	Avge	100	50	Ct/St	Balls	Runs	Wkts	Avge	BB	5wI	10wM
Hill, A.	2	4	2	49	101	50.50	–	1	1	340	130	7	18.57	4-27	–	–
Hill, A.J.L.	3	4	1	124	251	62.75	1	1	1	40	8	4	2.00	4-8	–	–
Hilton, M.J.	4	6	1	15	37	7.40	–	–	1	1244‡	477	14	34.07	5-61	1	–
Hirst, G.H.	24	38	3	85	790	22.57	–	5	18	4010‡	1770	59	30.00	5-48	3	–
Hitch, J.W.	7	10	3	51*	103	14.71	–	–	4	462	325	7	46.42	2-31	–	–
Hobbs, J.B.	61	102	7	211	5410	56.94	15	28	17	376	165	1	165.00	1-19	–	–
Hobbs, R.N.S.	7	8	3	15*	34	6.80	–	–	8	1291	481	12	40.08	3-25	–	–
Hollies, W.E.	13	15	8	18*	37	5.28	–	–	2	3554	1332	44	30.27	7-50	5	–
Holmes, E.R.T.	5	9	2	85*	114	16.28	–	1	4	108	76	2	38.00	1-10	–	–
Holmes, P.	7	14	1	88	357	27.46	–	4	3	–						
Hone, L.	1	2	–	13	13	6.50	–	–	2							
Hopwood, J.L.	2	3	1	8	12	6.00	–	–	–	462‡	155	0	–	–	–	–
Hornby, A.N.	3	6	–	9	21	3.50	–	–	–	28	0	1	0.00	1-0	–	–
Horton, M.J.	2	2	–	58	60	30.00	–	1	2	238	59	2	29.50	2-24	–	–
Howard, N.D.	4	6	1	23	86	17.20	–	1	4	–						
Howell, H.	5	8	6	5	15	7.50	–	–	–	918	559	7	79.85	4-115	–	–
Howorth, R.	5	10†	2	45*	145	18.12	–	1	2	1536‡	635	19	33.42	6-124	1	–
Humphries, J.	3	6	1	16	44	8.80	–	–	7	–						
Hunter, J.	5	7	2	39*	93	18.60	–	–	8/3	–						
Hussain, N.	7	13	2	71	284	25.81	–	1	3	–						
Hutchings, K.L.	7	12	1	126	341	28.41	1	1	9	90	81	1	81.00	1-5	–	–
Hutton, L.	79	138	15	364	6971	56.67	19	33	57	260	232	3	77.33	1-2	–	–
Hutton, R.A.	5	8	2	81	219	36.50	–	2	9	738	257	9	28.55	3-72	–	–
Iddon, J.	5	7	1	73	170	28.33	–	2	–	66‡	27	0	–	–	–	–
Igglesden, A.P.	3	5	3	3*	6	3.00	–	–	1	555	329	6	54.83	2-91	–	–
Ikin, J.T.	18	31†	2	60	606	20.89	–	3	31	572	354	3	118.00	1-38	–	–
Illingworth, R.	61	90	11	113	1836	23.24	2	5	45	11934	3807	122	31.20	6-29	3	–
Illingworth, R.K.	2	4	1	13	31	15.50	–	–	1	340‡	213	4	53.25	3-110	–	–
Ilott, M.C.	3	5†	1	15	28	7.00	–	–	–	774‡	412	8	51.50	3-108	–	–
Insole, D.J.	9	17	2	110*	408	27.20	1	1	8	–						
Jackman, R.D.	4	6	–	17	42	7.00	–	–	–	1070	445	14	31.78	4-110	–	–
Jackson, *Hon* F.S.	20	33	4	144*	1415	48.79	5	6	10	1587	799	24	33.29	5-52	1	–
Jackson, H.L.	2	2	1	8	15	15.00	–	1	1	498	155	7	22.14	2-26	–	–
Jameson, J.A.	4	8	–	82	214	26.75	–	1	–	42	17	1	17.00	1-17	–	–
Jardine, D.R.	22	33	6	127	1296	48.00	1	10	26	6	10	0	–	–	–	–
Jarvis, P.W.	9	15	2	29*	132	10.15	–	–	2	1912	965	21	45.95	4-107	–	–

INDIVIDUAL CAREER RECORDS – ENGLAND *continued*

	Tests	I	NO	BATTING AND FIELDING HS	Runs	Avge	100	50	Ct/St	BOWLING Balls	Runs	Wkts	Avge	BB	5wI	10wM
Jenkins, R.O.	9	12	1	39	198	18.00	–	–	4	2118	1098	32	34.31	5-116	1	–
Jessop, G.L.	18	26	–	104	569	21.88	1	3	11	732	354	10	35.40	4-68	–	–
Jones, A.O.	12	21	–	34	291	13.85	–	–	15	228	133	3	44.33	3-73	1	–
Jones, I.J.	15	17	9	16	38	4.75	–	–	4	3546‡	1769	44	40.20	6-118	1	–
Jupp, H.	2	4	–	63	68	17.00	–	1	2	–	–	–	–	–	–	–
Jupp, V.W.C.	8	13	1	38	208	17.33	–	–	5	1301	616	28	22.00	4-37	–	–
Keeton, W.W.	2	4	–	25	57	14.25	–	–	–	–	–	–	–	–	–	–
Kennedy, A.S.	5	8	2	41*	93	15.50	–	–	5	1683	599	31	19.32	5-76	2	–
Kenyon, D.	8	15	–	87	192	12.80	–	1	5	–	–	–	–	–	–	–
Killick, E.T.	2	4	–	31	81	20.25	–	–	2	–	–	–	–	–	–	–
Kilner, R.	9	8†	1	74	233	33.28	–	2	6	2368‡	734	24	30.58	4-51	1	–
King, J.H.	1	2†	1	60	64	32.00	–	1	–	162‡	99	1	99.00	1-99	–	–
Kinneir, S.P.	1	2†	–	30	52	26.00	–	–	–	–	–	–	–	–	–	–
Knight, A.E.	3	6	1	70*	81	16.20	–	1	1	–	–	–	–	–	–	–
Knight, B.R.	29	38	7	127	812	26.19	2	–	14	5377	2223	70	31.75	4-38	–	–
Knight, D.J.	2	4	–	38	54	13.50	–	–	–	–	–	–	–	–	–	–
Knott, A.P.E.	95	149	15	135	4389	32.75	5	30	250/19	–	–	–	–	–	–	–
Knox, N.A.	2	4	1	8*	24	8.00	–	–	–	126	105	3	35.00	2-39	–	–
Laker, J.C.	46	63	15	63	676	14.08	–	2	12	12027	4101	193	21.24	10-53	9	3
Lamb, A.J.	79	139	10	142	4656	36.09	14	18	75	30	23	1	23.00	1-6	–	–
Langridge, James	8	9†	–	70	242	26.88	–	1	6	1074‡	413	19	21.73	7-56	2	–
Larkins, W.	13	25	1	64	493	20.54	–	3	8	–	–	–	–	–	–	–
Larter, J.D.F.	10	7	2	10	16	3.20	–	–	5	2172	941	37	25.43	5-57	2	–
Larwood, H.	21	28	3	98	485	19.40	–	2	15	4969	2212	78	28.35	6-32	4	1
Lathwell, M.N.	2	4	–	33	78	19.50	–	–	–	–	–	–	–	–	–	–
Lawrence, D.V.	5	6	–	34	60	10.00	–	–	–	1089	676	18	37.55	5-106	1	–
Leadbeater, E.	2	2	–	38	40	20.00	–	–	3	289	218	2	109.00	1-38	–	–
Lee, H.W.	1	2	–	18	19	9.50	–	–	–	–	–	–	–	–	–	–
Lees, W.S.	5	9	3	25*	66	11.00	–	–	2	1256	467	26	17.96	6-78	2	–
Legge, G.B.	5	7	1	196	299	49.83	1	1	1	30	34	0	–	–	–	–
Leslie, C.F.H.	4	7	–	54	106	15.14	–	1	1	96	44	4	11.00	3-31	–	–
Lever, J.K.	21	31	5	53	306	11.76	–	1	11	4433‡	1951	73	26.72	7-46	3	1
Lever, P.	17	18	2	88*	350	21.87	–	2	11	3571	1509	41	36.80	6-38	2	–
Leveson Gower, H.D.G.	3	6	2	31	95	23.75	–	–	1	–	–	–	–	–	–	–
Levett, W.H.V.	1	2	1	5	7	7.00	–	–	3	–	–	–	–	–	–	–
Lewis, A.R.	9	16	2	125	457	32.64	1	3	–	–	–	–	–	–	–	–

INDIVIDUAL CAREER RECORDS – ENGLAND continued

	Tests	I	NO	HS	BATTING AND FIELDING Runs	Avge	100	50	Ct/St	Balls	Runs	BOWLING Wkts	Avge	BB	5wI	10wM
Lewis, C.C.	25	40	2	117	941	24.76	1	4	20	5163	2621	66	39.71	6-111	2	—
Leyland, M.	41	65†	5	187	2764	46.06	9	10	13	1103‡	585	6	97.50	3-91	—	—
Lilley, A.F.A.	35	52	8	84	903	20.52	—	4	70/22	25	23	1	23.00	1-23	—	—
Lillywhite, James	2	3†	1	10	16	8.00	—	—	1	340‡	126	8	15.75	4-70	—	—
Lloyd, D.	9	15†	2	214*	552	42.46	1	—	11	24‡	17	0	—	—	—	—
Lloyd, T.A.	1	1†	1	10*	10	—	—	—	—							
Loader, P.J.	13	19	6	17	76	5.84	—	—	2	2662	878	39	22.51	6-36	1	—
Lock, G.A.R.	49	63	9	89	742	13.74	—	3	59	13147‡	4451	174	25.58	7-35	9	3
Lockwood, W.H.	12	16	3	52*	231	17.76	—	1	4	1970	883	43	20.53	7-71	5	1
Lohmann, G.A.	18	26	2	62*	213	8.87	—	1	28	3830	1205	112	10.75	9-28	9	5
Lowson, F.A.	7	13	—	68	245	18.84	—	2	5							
Lucas, A.P.	5	9	1	55	157	19.62	—	1	1	120	54	0	—	—	—	—
Luckhurst, B.W.	21	41	5	131	1298	36.05	4	5	14	57‡	32	1	32.00	1-9	—	—
Lyttelton, Hon A.	4	7	1	31	94	15.66	—	—	2	48	19	4	4.75	4-19	—	—
Macaulay, G.G	8	10	4	76	112	18.66	—	1	5	1701	662	24	27.58	5-64	1	—
MacBryan, J.C.W.	1	1	—	—	—	—	—	—	—							
McCague, M.J.	2	3	—	11	20	6.66	—	—	1	477	294	4	73.50	4-121	—	—
McConnon, J.E.	2	3	1	11	18	9.00	—	—	4	216	74	4	18.50	3-19	—	—
McGahey, C.P.	2	4	—	18	38	9.50	—	—	—							
MacGregor, G.	8	11	3	31	96	12.00	—	—	14/3	—						
McIntyre, A.J.W.	3	6	—	7	19	3.16	—	—	8	—						
MacKinnon, F.A.	1	2	—	5	5	2.50	—	—	—							
MacLaren, A.C.	35	61	4	140	1931	33.87	5	8	29	—						
McMaster, J.E.P.	1	1	—	0	0	0.00	—	—	—							
Makepeace, J.W.H.	4	8	1	117	279	34.87	1	2	4	—						
Malcolm, D.E.	28	40	13	18	158	5.85	—	—	4	6190	3438	98	35.08	9-57	5	2
Mallender, N.A.	2	3	—	4	8	2.66	—	—	3	449	215	10	21.50	5-50	1	—
Mann, F.G.	7	12	2	136*	376	37.60	1	3	3	—						
Mann, F.T.	5	9	1	84	281	35.12	—	2	4	—						
Marks, V.J.	6	10	1	83	249	27.66	—	3	1	1082	484	11	44.00	3-78	—	—
Marriott, C.S.	1	1	—	0	0	0.00	—	—	—	247	96	11	8.72	6-59	2	1
Martin, F.	2	2†	—	13	14	7.00	—	—	2	410‡	141	14	10.07	6-50	2	1
Martin, J.W.	1	2	—	26	26	13.00	—	—	1	270	129	1	129.00	1-111	—	—
Mason, J.R.	5	10	1	32*	129	12.90	—	—	3	324	149	2	74.50	1-8	—	—
Matthews, A.D.G.	1	1	1	2*	2	—	—	—	1	180	65	2	32.50	1-13	—	—
May, P.B.H.	66	106	9	285*	4537	46.77	13	22	42	—						
Maynard, M.P.	4	8	—	35	87	10.87	—	—	3	—						

INDIVIDUAL CAREER RECORDS – ENGLAND *continued*

	Tests	I	NO	BATTING AND FIELDING HS	Runs	Avge	100	50	Ct/St	BOWLING Balls	Runs	Wkts	Avge	BB	5wI	10wM
Mead, C.P.	17	26†	2	182*	1185	49.37	4	3	4	–	–	–	–	–	–	–
Mead, W.	1	2	–	7	7	3.50	–	–	1	265	91	1	91.00	1-91	–	–
Midwinter, W.E.	4	7	–	36	95	13.57	–	–	5	776	272	10	27.20	4-81	–	–
Milburn, C.	9	16	2	139	654	46.71	2	2	7	–	–	–	–	–	–	–
Miller, A.M.	1	2	2	20*	24	–	–	–	1	–	–	–	–	–	–	–
Miller, G.	34	51	4	98*	1213	25.80	–	7	17	5149	1859	60	30.98	5-44	1	–
Milligan, F.W.	2	4	–	38	58	14.50	–	–	1	45	29	0	–	–	–	–
Millman, G.	6	7	2	32*	60	12.00	–	–	13/2	–	–	–	–	–	–	–
Milton, C.A.	6	9	1	104*	204	25.50	1	2	5	24	12	0	–	–	–	–
Mitchell, A.	6	10	–	72	298	29.80	–	2	9	6	4	0	–	–	–	–
Mitchell, F.	2	4	–	41	88	22.00	–	–	2	–	–	–	–	–	–	–
Mitchell, T.B.	5	6	2	9	20	5.00	–	–	1	894	498	8	62.25	2-49	–	–
Mitchell-Innes, N.S.	1	1	–	5	5	5.00	–	–	1	–	–	–	–	–	–	–
Mold, A.W.	3	3	1	0*	0	0.00	–	–	4	491	234	7	33.42	3-44	–	–
Moon, L.J.	4	8	–	36	182	22.75	–	1	4	–	–	–	–	–	–	–
Morley, F.	4	6†	2	2*	6	1.50	–	–	4	972‡	296	16	18.50	5-56	1	–
Morris, H.	3	5	–	44	115	19.16	–	–	3	–	–	–	–	–	–	–
Morris, J.E.	3	5	–	32	71	23.66	–	–	3	–	–	–	–	–	–	–
Mortimore, J.B.	9	12	2	73*	243	24.30	–	1	3	2162	733	13	56.38	3-36	–	–
Moss, A.E.	9	7	1	26	61	10.16	–	–	1	1657	626	21	29.80	4-35	–	–
Moxon, M.D.	10	17	1	99	455	28.43	–	3	10	48	30	0	–	–	–	–
Munton, T.A.	2	2	1	25*	25	25.00	–	–	–	405	200	4	50.00	2-22	–	–
Murdoch, W.L.	1	1	–	12	12	12.00	–	–	–/1	–	–	–	–	–	–	–
Murray, J.T.	21	28	5	112	506	22.00	1	2	52/3	–	–	–	–	–	–	–
Newham, W.	1	2	–	17	26	13.00	–	–	1	–	–	–	–	–	–	–
Newport, P.J.	3	5	1	40*	110	27.50	–	–	1	669	417	10	41.70	4-87	–	–
Nichols, M.S.	14	19†	7	78*	355	29.58	–	2	11	2565	1152	41	28.09	6-35	2	–
Oakman, A.S.M.	2	2	–	10	14	7.00	–	–	7	48	21	0	–	–	–	–
O'Brien, T.C.	5	8	–	20	59	7.37	–	–	4	–	–	–	–	–	–	–
O'Connor, J.	4	7	–	51	153	21.85	–	1	2	162	72	1	72.00	1-31	–	–
Old, C.M.	46	66†	9	65	845	14.82	–	2	22	8858	4020	143	28.11	7-50	4	–
Oldfield, N.	1	2	–	80	99	49.50	–	1	–	–	–	–	–	–	–	–
Padgett, D.E.V.	2	4	–	31	51	12.75	–	–	–	12	8	0	–	–	–	–
Paine, G.A.E.	4	7	1	49	97	16.16	–	–	5	1044‡	467	17	27.47	5-168	1	–
Palairet, L.C.H.	2	4	–	20	49	12.25	–	–	2	–	–	–	–	–	–	–

INDIVIDUAL CAREER RECORDS – ENGLAND continued

	Tests	I	NO	HS	BATTING AND FIELDING Runs	Avge	100	50	Ct/St	Balls	BOWLING Runs	Wkts	Avge	BB	5wI	10wM
Palmer, C.H.	1	2	–	22	22	11.00	–	–	–	30	15	0	–	–	–	–
Palmer, K.E.	1	1	–	10	10	10.00	–	–	–	378	189	1	189.00	1-113	–	–
Parfitt, P.H.	37	52†	6	131*	1882	40.91	7	6	42	1326	574	12	47.83	2-5	–	–
Parker, C.W.L.	1	1	1	3*	3	–	–	–	–	168‡	32	2	16.00	2-32	–	–
Parker, P.W.G.	1	2	–	13	13	6.50	–	–	2	–						
Parkhouse, W.G.A.	7	13	–	78	373	28.69	–	2	3							
Parkin, C.H.	10	16	3	36	160	12.30	–	–	3	2095	1128	32	35.25	5-38	2	–
Parks, J.H.	1	2	–	22	29	14.50	–	–	3	126	36	3	12.00	2-26	–	–
Parks, J.M.	46	68	7	108*	1962	32.16	2	9	103/11	54	51	1	51.00	1-43	–	–
Pataudi, Nawab of, sr	3	5	–	102	144	28.80	1	–	–							
Paynter, E.	20	31†	5	243	1540	59.23	4	7	7	–						
Peate, E.	9	14†	8	13	70	11.66	–	–	2	2096‡	683	31	22.03	6-85	2	–
Peebles, I.A.R.	13	17	8	26	98	10.88	–	–	5	2882	1391	45	30.91	6-63	3	–
Peel, R.	20	33†	4	83	427	14.72	–	3	17	5216‡	1715	101	16.98	7-31	5	1
Penn, F.	1	2	–	27*	50	50.00	–	–	–	12	2	0	–	–	–	–
Perks, R.T.D.	2	2†	2	2*	3	–	–	–	1	829	355	11	32.27	5-100	2	–
Philipson, H.	5	8	1	30	63	9.00	–	–	8/3							
Pigott, A.C.S.	1	2	1	8*	12	12.00	–	–	–	102	75	2	37.50	2-75	–	–
Pilling, R.	8	13	1	23	91	7.58	–	–	10/4							
Place, W.	3	6	1	107	144	28.80	1	–	–							
Pocock, P.I.	25	37	4	33	206	6.24	–	–	15	6650	2976	67	44.41	6-79	3	–
Pollard, R.	4	3	2	10*	13	13.00	–	–	3	1102	378	15	25.20	5-24	1	–
Poole, C.J.	3	5†	1	69*	161	40.25	–	2	1	30‡	9	0	–	–	–	–
Pope, G.H.	1	1	–	8*	8	–	–	–	–	218	85	1	85.00	1-49	–	–
Pougher, A.D.	1	1	–	17	17	17.00	–	–	2	105	26	3	8.66	3-26	–	–
Price, J.S.E.	15	15†	6	32	66	7.33	–	–	7	2724	1401	40	35.02	5-73	1	–
Price, W.F.F.	1	2	–	6	6	3.00	–	–	2							
Prideaux, R.M.	3	6	–	64	102	20.40	–	1	–	12	0	0	–	–	–	–
Pringle, D.R.	30	50	4	63	695	15.10	–	1	10	5287	2518	70	35.97	5-95	3	–
Pullar, G.	28	49†	4	175	1974	43.86	4	12	2	66	37	1	37.00	1-1	–	–
Quaife, W.G.	7	13	1	68	228	19.00	–	1	4	15	6	0	–	–	–	–
Radford, N.V.	3	4	1	12*	21	7.00	–	–	–	678	351	4	87.75	2-131	–	–
Radley, C.T.	8	10	–	158	481	48.10	2	2	4							
Ramprakash, M.R.	14	24	–	64	384	16.69	–	1	9	127	56	0	–	–	–	–
Randall, D.W.	47	79	5	174	2470	33.37	7	12	31	16	3	0	–	–	–	–
Ranjitsinhji, K.S.	15	26	4	175	989	44.95	2	6	13	97	39	1	39.00	1-23	–	–

INDIVIDUAL CAREER RECORDS – ENGLAND *continued*

				BATTING AND FIELDING						BOWLING						
	Tests	I	NO	HS	Runs	Avge	100	50	Ct/St	Balls	Runs	Wkts	Avge	BB	5wI	10wM
Read, H.D.	1	–	1	–	–	–	–	–	–	270	200	6	33.33	4-136	–	–
Read, J.M.	17	29	2	57	461	17.07	–	2	8	–	63	–	–	–	–	–
Read, W.W.	18	27	1	117	720	27.69	1	5	16	60	63	0	–	–	–	–
Reeve, D.A.	3	5	–	59	124	24.80	–	1	1	149	60	2	30.00	1-4	–	–
Relf, A.E.	13	21	3	63	416	23.11	–	1	14	1764	624	25	24.96	5-85	1	–
Rhodes, H.J.	2	1	1	0*	0	–	–	–	–	449	244	9	27.11	4-50	–	–
Rhodes, S.J.	6	8	4	65*	222	55.50	–	1	26/2	–	–	–	–	–	–	–
Rhodes, W.	58	98	21	179	2325	30.19	2	11	60	8231‡	3425	127	26.96	8-68	6	1
Richards, C.J.	8	13	–	133	285	21.92	1	–	20/1	–	–	–	–	–	–	–
Richardson, D.W.	1	1†	–	33	33	33.00	–	–	1	–	–	–	–	–	–	–
Richardson, P.E.	34	56†	1	126	2061	37.47	5	9	6	120	48	3	16.00	2-10	–	–
Richardson, T.	14	24	8	25*	177	11.06	–	–	5	4498	2220	88	25.22	8-94	11	4
Richmond, T.L.	1	2	–	4	6	3.00	–	–	–	114	86	2	43.00	2-69	–	–
Ridgway, F.	5	6	–	24	49	8.16	–	–	3	793	379	7	54.14	4-83	–	–
Robertson, J.D.B.	11	21	–	133	881	46.36	2	6	6	138	58	2	29.00	2-17	–	–
Robins, R.W.V.	19	27	4	108	612	26.60	1	4	12	3318	1758	64	27.46	6-32	1	–
Robinson, R.T.	29	49	5	175	1601	36.38	4	6	8	6	0	0	–	–	–	–
Roope, G.R.J.	21	32	4	77	860	30.71	–	7	35	172	76	0	–	–	–	–
Root, C.F.	3	3	–	–	–	–	–	–	1	642	194	8	24.25	4-84	–	–
Rose, B.C.	9	16†	2	70	358	25.57	–	2	4	16	6	0	–	–	–	–
Royle, V.P.F.A.	1	2	–	18	21	10.50	–	–	2	–	–	–	–	–	–	–
Rumsey, F.E.	5	5	3	21*	30	15.00	–	–	–	1145‡	461	17	27.11	4-25	–	–
Russell, C.A.G.	10	18	2	140	910	56.87	5	2	8	144	44	0	–	–	–	–
Russell, R.C.	36	58†	11	128*	1255	26.70	1	4	90/8	–	–	–	–	–	–	–
Russell, W.E.	10	18	1	70	362	21.29	–	2	4	–	–	–	–	–	–	–
Salisbury, I.D.K.	7	13	1	50	205	17.08	–	1	3	1405	933	16	58.31	4-163	–	–
Sandham, A.	14	23	1	325	879	38.21	2	3	4	–	–	–	–	–	–	–
Schultz, S.S.	1	2	1	20	20	20.00	–	–	–	34	26	1	26.00	1-16	–	–
Scotton, W.H.	15	25†	2	90	510	22.17	–	3	4	20‡	20	0	–	–	–	–
Selby, J.	6	12	–	70	256	23.27	–	2	1	–	–	–	–	–	–	–
Selvey, M.W.W.	3	5	3	5*	15	7.50	–	–	1	492	343	6	57.16	4-41	–	–
Shackleton, D.	7	13	7	42	113	18.83	–	–	1	2078	768	18	42.66	4-72	–	–
Sharp, J.	3	6	2	105	188	47.00	1	1	1	183	111	3	37.00	3-67	–	–
Sharpe, J.W.	3	6	4	26	44	22.00	–	–	2	975	305	11	27.72	6-84	1	–
Sharpe, P.J.	12	21	4	111	786	46.23	1	4	17	–	–	–	–	–	–	–
Shaw, A.	7	12	1	40	111	10.09	–	–	4	1096	285	12	23.75	5-38	1	–
Sheppard, Rev D.S.	22	33	2	119	1172	37.80	3	6	12	–	–	–	–	–	–	–

INDIVIDUAL CAREER RECORDS – ENGLAND continued

	Tests	I	NO	HS	Runs	Avge	100	50	Ct/St	Balls	Runs	Wkts	Avge	BB	5wI	10wM
						BATTING AND FIELDING							*BOWLING*			
Sherwin, M.	3	6	4	21*	30	15.00	–	–	5/2	–	–	–	–	–	–	–
Shrewsbury, A.	23	40	4	164	1277	35.47	3	4	29	12	2	0	–	–	–	–
Shuter, J.	1	1	–	28	28	28.00	–	–	–	–	–	–	–	–	–	–
Shuttleworth, K.	5	6	1	21	46	7.66	–	–	1	1071	427	12	35.58	5-47	1	–
Sidebottom, A.	1	1	–	2	2	2.00	–	–	–	112	65	1	65.00	1-65	–	–
Simpson, R.T.	27	45	3	156*	1401	33.35	4	6	5	45	22	2	11.00	2-4	–	–
Simpson-Hayward, G.H.T.	5	8	1	29*	105	15.00	–	–	1	898	420	23	18.26	6-43	2	–
Sims, J.M.	4	4	–	12	16	4.00	–	–	5	887	480	11	43.63	5-73	1	–
Sinfield, R.A.	1	1	–	6	6	6.00	–	–	6	378	123	2	61.50	1-51	–	–
Slack, W.N.	3	6†	–	52	81	13.50	–	1	3	–	–	–	–	–	–	–
Smailes, T.F.	1	1†	–	25	25	25.00	–	–	–	120	62	3	20.66	3-44	–	–
Small, G.C.	17	24	7	59*	263	15.47	–	1	9	3927	1871	55	34.01	5-48	2	–
Smith, A.C.	6	7	3	69*	118	29.50	–	1	20	–	–	–	–	–	–	–
Smith, C.A.	1	1	–	3	3	3.00	–	–	1	154	61	7	8.71	5-19	1	–
Smith, C.I.J.	5	10	1	27	102	10.20	–	–	1	930	393	15	26.20	5-16	1	–
Smith, C.L.	8	14	1	91	392	30.15	–	2	5	102	39	3	13.00	2-31	–	–
Smith, D.	2	4†	–	57	128	32.00	–	1	1	–	–	–	–	–	–	–
Smith, D.M.	2	4†	1	47	80	20.00	–	–	–	–	–	–	–	–	–	–
Smith, D.R.	5	5	1	34	38	9.50	–	–	2	972	359	6	59.83	2-60	–	–
Smith, D.V.	3	4†	1	16*	25	8.33	–	–	–	270‡	97	1	97.00	1-12	–	–
Smith, E.J.	11	14	1	22	113	8.69	–	–	17/3	–	–	–	–	–	–	–
Smith, H.	1	1	–	7	7	7.00	–	–	1	–	–	–	–	–	–	–
Smith, M.J.K.	50	78	6	121	2278	31.63	3	11	53	214	128	1	128.00	1-10	–	–
Smith, R.A.	53	97	14	175	3677	44.30	9	24	35	24	6	0	–	–	–	–
Smith, T.P.B.	4	5	–	24	33	6.60	–	–	1	538	319	3	106.33	2-172	–	–
Smithson, G.A.	2	3†	–	35	70	23.33	–	–	–	–	–	–	–	–	–	–
Snow, J.A.	49	71	14	73	772	13.54	–	2	16	12021	5387	202	26.66	7-40	8	1
Southerton, J.	2	3	1	6	7	3.50	–	–	2	263	107	7	15.28	4-46	–	–
Spooner, R.H.	10	15	–	119	481	32.06	1	4	4	–	–	–	–	–	–	–
Spooner, R.T.	7	14†	1	92	354	27.23	–	3	10/2	–	–	–	–	–	–	–
Stanyforth, R.T.	4	6	–	6*	13	2.60	–	–	7/2	–	–	–	–	–	–	–
Staples, S.J.	3	5	–	39	65	13.00	–	–	–	1149	435	15	29.00	3-50	–	–
Statham, J.B.	70	87†	28	38	675	11.44	–	–	28	16056	6261	252	24.84	7-39	9	1
Steel, A.G.	13	20	3	148	600	35.29	2	–	5	1360	605	29	20.86	3-27	–	–
Steele, D.S.	8	16	1	106	673	42.06	1	5	7	88‡	39	2	19.50	1-1	–	–
Stephenson, J.P.	1	2	–	25	36	18.00	–	–	–	–	–	–	–	–	–	–
Stevens, G.T.S.	10	17	1	69	263	15.47	–	1	9	1186	648	20	32.40	5-90	2	1
Stevenson, G.B.	2	2	1	27*	28	28.00	–	–	–	312	183	5	36.60	3-111	–	–

INDIVIDUAL CAREER RECORDS – ENGLAND continued

				BATTING AND FIELDING						BOWLING					
	Tests	I	NO	HS	Runs	Avge	100	50	Ct/St	Balls	Runs	Wkts	Avge	BB	5wI	10wM
Stewart, A.J.	43	78	5	190	2982	40.84	7	15	53/4	20	13	0	–	–	–	–
Stewart, M.J.	8	12	1	87	385	35.00	–	2	6						–	–
Stoddart, A.E.	16	30	2	173	996	35.57	2	3	6	162	94	2	47.00	1-10		
Storer, W.	6	11	–	51	215	19.54	–	1	11	168	108	2	54.00	1-24		
Street, G.B.	1	2	1	7*	11	11.00	!	–	1	–						
Strudwick, H.	28	42	13	24	230	7.93	–	–	60/12	–						
Studd, C.T.	5	9	1	48	160	20.00	–	–	5	384	98	3	32.66	2-35	–	
Studd, G.B.	4	7	–	9	31	4.42	–	–	8							
Subba Row, R.	13	22†	1	137	984	46.85	3	4	5	6	2	0	–	–		
Such, P.M.	8	11	4	14*	65	9.28	–	–	2	2177	805	22	36.59	6-67	1	
Sugg, F.H.	2	2	–	31	55	27.50	–	–	–							
Sutcliffe, H.	54	84	9	194	4555	60.73	16	23	23	–						
Swetman, R.	11	17	2	65	254	16.93	–	1	24/2	–						
Tate, F.W.	1	2	1	5*	9	9.00	–	–	2	96	51	2	25.50	2-7	–	–
Tate, M.W.	39	52	5	100*	1198	25.48	1	5	11	12523	4055	155	26.16	6-42	7	1
Tattersall, R.	16	17†	7	10*	50	5.00	–	–	8	4228	1513	58	26.08	7-52	4	1
Tavaré, C.J.	31	56	2	149	1755	32.50	2	12	20	30	11	0	–	–	–	–
Taylor, J.P.	2	4†	2	17*	34	17.00	–	–	–	288‡	156	3	52.00	1-18	–	–
Taylor, K.	3	5	–	24	57	11.40	–	–	1	12	6	0	–	–	–	–
Taylor, L.B.	2	1	1	1*	1	–	–	–	1	381	178	4	44.50	2-34	–	–
Taylor, R.W.	57	83	12	97	1156	16.28	–	3	167/7	12	6	0	–	–	–	–
Tennyson, Hon L.H.	9	12	1	74*	345	31.36	–	4	6	6	6	0	–	–		
Terry, V.P.	2	3	–	8	16	5.33	–	–	2	–						
Thomas, J.G.	5	10	4	31*	83	13.83	–	–	5	774	504	10	50.40	4-70	–	–
Thompson, G.J.	6	10	1	63	273	30.33	–	2	5	1367	638	23	27.73	4-50	–	–
Thomson, N.I.	5	4	1	39	69	23.00	–	–	3	1488	568	9	63.11	2-55	–	–
Thorpe, G.P.	10	19†	2	114*	708	41.64	1	6	14	48	15	0	–	–	–	–
Titmus, F.J.	53	76	11	84*	1449	22.29	–	10	35	15118	4931	153	32.22	7-79	7	–
Tolchard, R.W.	4	7	2	67	129	25.80	–	1	5	–						
Townsend, C.L.	2	3†	–	38	51	17.00	–	–	1	140	75	3	25.00	3-50	–	–
Townsend, D.C.H.	3	6	–	36	77	12.83	–	–	–	6	9	0	–	–	–	–
Townsend, L.F.	4	6	–	40	97	16.16	–	–	2	399	205	6	34.16	2-22	–	–
Tremlett, M.F.	3	5	2	18*	20	6.66	–	–	–	492	226	4	56.50	2-98	–	–
Trott, A.E.	2	4	–	16	23	5.75	–	–	–	474	198	17	11.64	5-49	1	–
Trueman, F.S.	67	85	14	39*	981	13.81	–	–	64	15178	6625	307	21.57	8-31	17	3
Tufnell, N.C.	1	1	–	14	14	14.00	–	–	–/1	–						
Tufnell, P.C.R.	18	25	14	22*	56	5.09	–	–	8	5132‡	2229	58	38.43	7-47	4	1

INDIVIDUAL CAREER RECORDS – ENGLAND continued

				BATTING AND FIELDING						BOWLING						
	Tests	I	NO	HS	Runs	Avge	100	50	Ct/St	Balls	Runs	Wkts	Avge	BB	5wI	10wM
Turnbull, M.J.L.	9	13	2	61	224	20.36	–	1	1	–						
Tyldesley, G.E.	14	20	2	122	990	55.00	3	6	2	3	2	0	–	–	–	–
Tyldesley, J.T.	31	55	1	138	1661	30.75	4	9	16	–						
Tyldesley, R.K.	6	7	1	29	47	7.83	–	–	1	1615	619	19	32.57	3-50	–	–
Tylecote, E.F.S.	6	9	1	66	152	19.00	–	1	5/5	–						
Tyler, E.J.	1	1†	–	0	0	0.00	–	–	–	145‡	65	4	16.25	3-49	–	–
Tyson, F.H.	17	24	3	37*	230	10.95	–	–	4	3452	1411	76	18.56	7-27	4	1
Ulyett, G.	25	39	–	149	949	24.33	1	7	19	2627‡	1020	50	20.40	7-36	1	–
Underwood, D.L.	86	116	35	45*	937	11.56	–	–	44	21862‡	7674	297	25.83	8-51	17	6
Valentine, B.H.	7	9	2	136	454	64.85	2	1	2	–						
Verity, H.	40	44	12	66*	669	20.90	–	3	30	11173‡	3510	144	24.37	8-43	5	2
Vernon, G.F.	1	2	1	11*	14	14.00	–	–	–	–						
Vine, J	2	3	2	36	46	46.00	–	–	–	–						
Voce, W.	27	38	15	66	308	13.39	–	1	15	6360‡	2733	98	27.88	7-70	3	2
Waddington, A.	2	4	–	7	16	4.00	–	–	1	276‡	119	1	119.00	1-35	–	–
Wainwright, E.	5	9	–	49	132	14.66	–	1	2	127	73	0	–	–	–	–
Walker, P.M.	3	4	–	52	128	32.00	–	1	5	78‡	34	0	–	–	–	–
Walters, C.F.	11	18	3	102	784	52.26	1	7	6	–						
Ward, Alan	5	6	1	21	40	8.00	–	–	3	761	453	14	32.35	4-61	–	–
Ward, Albert	7	13	–	117	487	37.46	1	3	1	–						
Wardle, J.H.	28	41†	8	66	653	19.78	–	2	12	6597‡	2080	102	20.39	7-36	5	1
Warner, P.F.	15	28	2	132*	622	23.92	1	3	3	–						
Warr, J.J.	2	4	–	4	4	1.00	–	–	1	584	281	1	281.00	1-76	–	–
Warren, A.	1	1	–	7	7	7.00	–	–	1	236	113	6	18.83	5-57	1	–
Washbrook, C.	37	66	6	195	2569	42.81	6	12	12	36	33	1	33.00	1-25	–	–
Watkin, S.L.	3	5	–	13	25	5.00	–	–	1	534	305	11	27.72	4-65	–	–
Watkins, A.J.	15	24†	4	137*	810	40.50	2	4	17	1364‡	554	11	50.36	3-20	–	–
Watson, W.	23	37†	3	116	879	25.85	2	3	8	–						
Webbe, A.J.	1	2	–	4	2	2.00	–	–	2	–						
Wellard, A.W.	2	4	–	38	47	11.75	–	–	2	456	237	7	33.85	4-81	–	–
Wharton, A.	1	2†	–	13	20	10.00	–	–	1	–						
Whitaker, J.J.	1	1	–	11	11	11.00	–	–	–	–						
White, C.	4	6	–	51	131	21.83	–	1	3	469	258	8	32.25	3-18	–	–
White, D.W.	2	2†	–	0	0	0.00	–	–	–	220	119	4	29.75	3-65	–	–
White, J.C.	15	22	9	29	239	18.38	–	1	6	4801‡	1581	49	32.26	8-126	3	1

INDIVIDUAL CAREER RECORDS – ENGLAND continued

				BATTING AND FIELDING						BOWLING						
	Tests	I	NO	HS	Runs	Avge	100	50	Ct/St	Balls	Runs	Wkts	Avge	BB	5wI	10wM
Whysall, W.W.	4	7	–	76	209	29.85	–	2	7	16	9	0	–	–	–	–
Wilkinson, L.L.	3	2	1	2	3	3.00	–	–	1	573	271	7	38.71	2-12	–	–
Willey, P.	26	50	6	102*	1184	26.90	2	5	3	1091	456	7	65.14	2-73	–	–
Williams, N.F.	1	1	–	38	38	38.00	–	–	–	246	148	2	74.00	2-148	–	–
Willis, R.G.D.	90	128	55	28*	840	11.50	–	–	39	17357	8190	325	25.20	8-43	16	–
Wilson, C.E.M.	2	4	1	18	42	14.00	–	–	1	–	–	–	–	–	–	–
Wilson, D.	6	7†	1	42	75	12.50	–	–	1	1472‡	466	11	42.36	2-17	–	–
Wilson, E.R.	1	2	1	5	10	5.00	–	–	–	123	36	3	12.00	2-28	–	–
Wood, A.	4	5	1	53	80	20.00	–	–	10/1	–	–	–	–	–	–	–
Wood, B.	12	21	–	90	454	21.61	–	2	6	98	50	0	–	–	–	–
Wood, G.E.C.	3	2	–	6	7	3.50	–	–	5/1	–	–	–	–	–	–	–
Wood, H.	4	2†	1	134*	204	68.00	1	1	2/1	–	–	–	–	–	–	–
Wood, R.	1	2†	–	6	6	3.00	–	–	–	–	–	–	–	–	–	–
Woods, S.M.J.	3	4	–	53	122	30.50	–	1	4	195	129	5	25.80	3-28	–	–
Woolley, F.E.	64	98†	7	154	3283	36.07	5	23	64	6495‡	2815	83	33.91	7-76	4	1
Woolmer, R.A.	19	34	2	149	1059	33.09	3	2	10	546	299	4	74.75	1-8	–	–
Worthington, T.S.	9	11	–	128	321	29.18	1	1	8	633	316	8	39.50	2-19	–	–
Wright, C.W.	3	4	–	71	125	31.25	–	1	–	–	–	–	–	–	–	–
Wright, D.V.P.	34	39	13	45	289	11.11	–	–	10	8135	4224	108	39.11	7-105	6	1
Wyatt, R.E.S.	40	64	6	149	1839	31.70	2	12	16	1395	642	18	35.66	3-4	–	–
Wynyard, E.G.	3	6	–	30	72	12.00	–	–	–	24	17	0	–	–	–	–
Yardley, N.W.D.	20	34	2	99	812	25.37	–	4	14	1662	707	21	33.66	3-67	–	–
Young, H.I.	2	2	–	43	43	21.50	–	–	1	556‡	262	12	21.83	4-30	–	–
Young, J.A.	8	10	5	10*	28	5.60	–	–	5	2368‡	757	17	44.52	3-65	–	–
Young, R.A.	2	4	–	13	27	6.75	–	–	6	–	–	–	–	–	–	–

INDIVIDUAL CAREER RECORDS – AUSTRALIA

AUSTRALIA (350 players)	Tests	I	NO	BATTING AND FIELDING HS	Runs	Avge	100	50	Ct/St	BOWLING Balls	Runs	Wkts	Avge	BB	5wI	10wM
A'Beckett, E.L.	4	7	–	41	143	20.42	–	–	4	1062	317	3	105.66	1-41	–	–
Alderman, T.M.	41	53	22	26*	203	6.54	–	–	27	10181	4616	170	27.15	6-47	14	1
Alexander, G.	2	4	–	33	52	13.00	–	–	2	168	93	2	46.50	2-69	–	–
Alexander, H.H.	1	2	1	17*	17	17.00	–	–	–	276	154	1	154.00	1-129	–	–
Allan, F.E.	1	1†	–	5	5	5.00	–	–	–	180‡	80	4	20.00	2-30	–	–
Allan, P.J.	1	–	–	–	–	–	–	–	–	192	83	2	41.50	2-58	–	–
Allen, R.C.	1	2	–	30	44	22.00	–	–	2	–	–	–	–	–	–	–
Andrews, T.J.E.	16	23	1	94	592	26.90	–	4	12	156	116	1	116.00	1-23	–	–
Angel, J.	1	2†	1	4*	4	4.00	–	–	–	114	72	1	72.00	1-72	–	–
Archer, K.A.	5	9	–	48	234	26.00	–	–	–	–	–	–	–	–	–	–
Archer, R.G.	19	30	1	128	713	24.58	1	2	20	3576	1318	48	27.45	5-53	1	–
Armstrong, W.W.	50	84	10	159*	2863	38.68	6	8	44	8022	2923	87	33.59	6-35	3	–
Badcock, C.L.	7	12	1	118	160	14.54	1	–	3	–	–	–	–	–	–	–
Bannerman, A.C.	28	50	2	94	1108	23.08	–	8	21	292	163	4	40.75	3-111	–	–
Bannerman, C.	3	6	2	165*	239	59.75	1	–	–	–	–	–	–	–	–	–
Bardsley, W.	41	66†	5	193*	2469	40.47	6	14	12	–	–	–	–	–	–	–
Barnes, S.G.	13	19	2	234	1072	63.05	3	5	14	594	218	4	54.50	2-25	–	–
Barnett, B.A.	4	8†	1	57	195	27.85	–	1	3/2	–	–	–	–	–	–	–
Barrett, J.E.	2	4†	1	67*	80	26.66	–	1	1	–	–	–	–	–	–	–
Beard, G.R.	3	5	–	49	114	22.80	–	–	–	259	109	1	109.00	1-26	–	–
Benaud, J.	3	5	–	142	223	44.60	1	–	–	24	12	2	6.00	2-12	–	–
Benaud, R.	63	97	7	122	2201	24.45	3	9	65	19108	6704	248	27.03	7-72	16	1
Bennett, M.J.	3	5	2	23	71	23.66	–	–	5	665‡	325	6	54.16	3-79	–	–
Blackham, J.M.	35	62	11	74	800	15.68	–	4	37/24	–	–	–	–	–	–	–
Blackie, D.D.	3	6†	3	11*	24	8.00	–	–	2	1260	444	14	31.71	6-94	1	–
Bonnor, G.J.	17	30	–	128	512	17.06	1	2	16	164	84	2	42.00	1-5	–	–
Boon, D.C.	89	160	18	200	6564	46.22	18	30	85	18	5	0	–	–	–	–
Booth, B.C.	29	48	6	169	1773	42.21	5	10	17	436	146	3	48.66	2-33	–	–
Border, A.R.	156	265†	44	205	11174	50.56	27	63	156	4009‡	1525	39	39.10	7-46	2	1
Boyle, H.F.	12	16	4	36*	153	12.75	–	–	10	1743	641	32	20.03	6-42	1	–
Bradman, D.G.	52	80	10	334	6996	99.94	29	13	32	160	72	2	36.00	1-8	–	–
Bright, R.J.	25	39	8	33	445	14.35	–	–	13	5541‡	2180	53	41.13	7-87	4	1
Bromley, E.H.	2	4†	–	26	38	9.50	–	–	2	60‡	19	0	–	–	–	–
Brown, W.A.	22	35	1	206*	1592	46.82	4	9	14	–	–	–	–	–	–	–

INDIVIDUAL CAREER RECORDS – AUSTRALIA continued

| | | | | BATTING AND FIELDING | | | | | | BOWLING | | | | | | |
	Tests	I	NO	HS	Runs	Avge	100	50	Ct/St	Balls	Runs	Wkts	Avge	BB	5wI	10wM
Bruce, W.	14	26†	2	80	702	29.25	4	5	12	998‡	440	12	36.66	3-88	–	–
Burge, P.J.P.	42	68	8	181	2290	38.16	4	12	23	–	–	–	–	–	–	–
Burke, J.W.	24	44	7	189	1280	34.59	3	5	18	814	230	8	28.75	4-37	–	–
Burn, E.J.K.	2	4	1	19	41	10.25	–	–	–	–	–	–	–	–	–	–
Burton, F.J.	2	4	2	2*	4	2.00	–	–	1/1	–	–	–	–	–	–	–
Callaway, S.T.	3	6	1	41	87	17.40	–	–	–	471	142	6	23.66	5-37	1	–
Callen, I.W.	1	2†	2	22*	26	–	–	–	1	440	191	6	31.83	3-83	–	–
Campbell, G.D.	4	4	–	6*	10	2.50	–	–	1	951	503	13	38.69	3-79	–	–
Carkeek, W.	6	5†	2	6*	16	5.33	–	–	6	–	–	–	–	–	–	–
Carlson, P.H.	2	4	–	21	23	5.75	–	–	2	368	99	2	49.50	2-41	–	–
Carter, H.	28	47	9	72	873	22.97	–	4	44/21	–	–	–	–	–	–	–
Chappell, G.S.	87	151	19	247*	7110	53.86	24	31	122	5327	1913	47	40.70	5-61	1	–
Chappell, I.M.	75	136	10	196	5345	42.42	14	26	105	2873	1316	20	65.80	2-21	–	–
Chappell, T.M.	3	6	1	27	79	15.80	–	–	2	–	–	–	–	–	–	–
Charlton, P.C.	2	4	–	11	29	7.25	–	–	–	45	24	3	8.00	3-18	–	–
Chipperfield, A.G.	14	20	3	109	552	32.47	1	2	15	924	437	5	87.40	3-91	–	–
Clark, W.M.	10	19	2	33	98	5.76	–	1	6	2793	1265	44	28.75	4-46	–	–
Colley, D.J.	3	4	–	54	84	21.00	–	1	1	729	312	6	52.00	3-83	–	–
Collins, H.L.	19	31	1	203	1352	45.06	4	6	13	654‡	252	4	63.00	2-47	–	–
Coningham, A.	1	2†	–	10	13	6.50	–	–	–	186‡	76	2	38.00	2-17	–	–
Connolly, A.N.	29	45	20	37	260	10.40	–	–	17	7818	2981	102	29.22	6-47	4	–
Cooper, B.B.	1	2	–	15	18	9.00	–	–	2	–	–	–	–	–	–	–
Cooper, W.H.	2	3	1	7	13	6.50	–	–	1	466	226	9	25.11	6-120	1	–
Corling, G.E.	5	4	1	3	5	1.66	–	–	–	1159	447	12	37.25	4-60	–	–
Cosier, G.J.	18	32	1	168	897	28.93	2	3	14	899	341	5	68.20	2-26	–	–
Cottam, J.T.	1	2	–	3	4	2.00	–	–	1	–	–	–	–	–	–	–
Cotter, A.	21	37	2	45	457	13.05	–	–	8	4639	2549	89	28.64	7-148	7	–
Coulthard, G.	1	1	–	6*	6	–	–	–	–	–	–	–	–	–	–	–
Cowper, R.M.	27	46†	2	307	2061	46.84	5	10	21	3005	1139	36	31.63	4-48	–	–
Craig, I.D.	11	18	–	53	358	19.88	–	2	2	–	–	–	–	–	–	–
Crawford, W.P.A.	4	5	2	34	53	17.66	–	–	1	437	107	7	15.28	3-38	–	–
Darling, J.	34	60†	2	178	1657	28.56	3	8	27	–	–	–	–	–	–	–
Darling, L.S.	12	18†	1	85	474	27.88	–	3	8	162	65	0	–	–	–	–
Darling, W.M.	14	27	1	91	697	26.80	–	6	5	–	–	–	–	–	–	–
Davidson, A.K.	44	61†	7	80	1328	24.59	–	5	42	11587‡	3819	186	20.53	7-93	14	2
Davis, I.C.	15	27	1	105	692	26.61	1	4	9	–	–	–	–	–	–	–

INDIVIDUAL CAREER RECORDS – AUSTRALIA *continued*

	Tests	I	NO	HS	Runs	Avge	100	50	Ct/St	Balls	Runs	Wkts	Avge	BB	5wI	10wM
				BATTING AND FIELDING									*BOWLING*			
Davis, S.P.	1	1	0	0	0	0.00	–	–	–	150	70	0	–	–	–	–
De Courcy, J.H.	3	6	1	41	81	16.20	–	–	3	–	–	–	–	–	–	–
Dell, A.R.	2	2	2	3*	6	–	–	–	–	559‡	160	6	26.66	3-65	–	–
Dodemaide, A.I.C.	10	15	6	50	202	22.44	–	1	6	2184	953	34	28.02	6-58	1	–
Donnan, H.	5	10	1	15	75	8.33	–	–	1	54	22	0	–	–	–	–
Dooland, B.	3	5	1	29	76	19.00	–	–	3	880	419	9	46.55	4-69	–	–
Duff, R.A.	22	40	3	146	1317	35.59	2	6	14	180	85	4	21.25	2-43	–	–
Duncan, J.R.F.	1	1	–	3	3	3.00	–	–	–	112	30	0	–	–	–	–
Dyer, G.C.	6	6	1	60	131	21.83	–	1	22/2	–	–	–	–	–	–	–
Dymock, G.	21	32†	7	31*	236	9.44	–	–	1	5545‡	2116	78	27.12	7-67	5	1
Dyson, J.	30	58	7	127*	1359	26.64	2	5	10	–	–	–	–	–	–	–
Eady, C.J.	2	4	1	10*	20	6.66	–	–	2	223	112	7	16.00	3-30	–	–
Eastwood, K.H.	1	2†	–	5	5	2.50	–	–	–	40‡	21	1	21.00	1-21	–	–
Ebeling, H.I.	1	2	–	41	43	21.50	–	–	1	186	89	3	29.66	3-74	–	–
Edwards, J.D.	3	6	1	26	48	9.60	–	–	1	12	20	0	–	–	–	–
Edwards, R.	20	32	3	170*	1171	40.37	2	9	7	–	–	–	–	–	–	–
Edwards, W.J.	3	6‡	–	30	68	11.33	–	–	–	–	–	–	–	–	–	–
Emery, S.H.	4	2	–	5	6	3.00	–	–	2	462	249	5	49.80	2-46	–	–
Evans, E.	6	10	2	33	82	10.25	–	–	5	1237	332	7	47.42	3-64	–	–
Fairfax, A.G.	10	12	4	65	410	51.25	–	4	15	1520	645	21	30.71	4-31	–	–
Favell, L.E.	19	31	3	101	757	27.03	1	5	9	–	–	–	–	–	–	–
Ferris, J.J.	8	16†	4	20*	98	8.16	–	–	4	2030‡	684	48	14.25	5-26	4	–
Fingleton, J.H.W.	18	29	1	136	1189	42.46	5	3	13	–	–	–	–	–	–	–
Fleetwood-Smith, L.O'B.	10	11	5	16*	54	9.00	–	–	1	3093‡	1570	42	37.38	6-110	2	1
Francis, B.C.	3	5	–	27	52	10.40	–	–	1	–	–	–	–	–	–	–
Freeman, E.W.	11	18	1	76	345	19.16	–	2	5	2183	1128	34	33.17	4-52	–	–
Freer, F.W.	1	1	1	28*	28	–	–	–	–	160	74	3	24.66	2-49	–	–
Gannon, J.B.	3	5	4	3*	3	3.00	–	–	3	726‡	361	11	32.81	4-77	–	–
Garrett, T.W.	19	33	6	51*	339	12.55	–	1	7	2728	970	36	26.94	6-78	2	–
Gaunt, R.A.	3	4†	2	3	6	3.00	–	–	1	716	310	7	44.28	3-53	–	–
Gehrs, D.R.A.	6	11	1	67	221	20.09	–	2	6	6	4	0	–	–	–	–
Giffen, G.	31	53	–	161	1238	23.35	1	6	24	6391	2791	103	27.09	7-117	7	1
Giffen, W.F.	3	6	–	3	11	1.83	–	–	1	–	–	–	–	–	–	–
Gilbert, D.R.	9	12†	4	15	57	7.12	–	–	4	1647	843	16	52.68	3-48	–	–
Gilmour, G.J.	15	22†	1	101	483	23.00	1	3	8	2661‡	1406	54	26.03	6-85	3	–

INDIVIDUAL CAREER RECORDS – AUSTRALIA continued

				BATTING AND FIELDING						BOWLING						
	Tests	I	NO	HS	Runs	Avge	100	50	Ct/St	Balls	Runs	Wkts	Avge	BB	5wI	10wM
Gleeson, J.W.	29	46	8	45	395	10.39	-	-	17	8857	3367	93	36.20	5-61	3	-
Graham, H.	6	10	-	107	301	30.10	2	-	3	-	-	-	-	-	-	-
Gregory, D.W.	3	5	2	43	60	20.00	-	-	-	20	9	0	-	-	-	-
Gregory, E.J.	1	2	-	11	11	5.50	-	-	1	-	-	-	-	-	-	-
Gregory, J.M.	24	34†	3	119	1146	36.96	2	7	37	5582	2648	85	31.15	7-69	4	-
Gregory, R.G.	2	3	-	80	153	51.00	-	2	1	24	14	0	-	-	-	-
Gregory, S.E.	58	100	7	201	2282	24.53	4	8	25	30	33	0	-	-	-	-
Grimmett, C.V.	37	50	10	50	557	13.92	-	1	17	14513	5231	216	24.21	7-40	21	7
Groube, T.U.	1	2	-	11	11	5.50	-	-	-	-	-	-	-	-	-	-
Grout, A.T.W.	51	67	8	74	890	15.08	-	3	163/24	-	-	-	-	-	-	-
Guest, C.E.J.	1	1	-	11	11	11.00	-	-	-	144	59	0	-	-	-	-
Hamence, R.A.	3	4	1	30*	81	27.00	-	-	1	-	-	-	-	-	-	-
Hammond, J.R.	5	5	2	19	28	9.33	-	-	2	1031	488	15	32.53	4-38	-	-
Harry, J.	1	2	-	6	8	4.00	-	-	1	-	-	-	-	-	-	-
Hartigan, R.J.	2	4	-	116	170	42.50	1	-	1	12	7	0	-	-	-	-
Hartkopf, A.E.V.	1	2	-	80	80	40.00	-	1	-	240	134	1	134.00	1-120	-	-
Harvey, M.R.	1	2	-	31	43	21.50	-	-	-	-	-	-	-	-	-	-
Harvey, R.N.	79	137†	10	205	6149	48.41	21	24	64	414	120	3	40.00	1-8	-	-
Hassett, A.L.	43	69	3	198*	3073	46.56	10	11	30	111	78	0	-	-	-	-
Hawke, N.J.N.	27	37	15	45*	365	16.59	-	-	9	6974	2677	91	29.41	7-105	6	1
Hayden, M.L.	1	2†	-	15	20	10.00	-	-	1	-	-	-	-	-	-	-
Hazlitt, G.R.	9	12	4	34*	89	11.12	-	-	4	1563	623	23	27.08	7-25	1	-
Healy, I.A.	62	90	10	113*	2057	25.71	2	11	191/14	-	-	-	-	-	-	-
Hendry, H.S.T.L.	11	18	2	112	335	20.93	1	-	10	1706	640	16	40.00	3-36	-	-
Hibbert, P.A.	1	2†	-	13	15	7.50	-	-	1	-	-	-	-	-	-	-
Higgs, J.D.	22	36	16	16	111	5.55	-	-	3	4752	2057	66	31.16	7-143	2	-
Hilditch, A.M.J.	18	34	-	119	1073	31.55	2	6	13	-	-	-	-	-	-	-
Hill, C.	49	89†	2	191	3412	39.21	7	19	33	-	-	-	-	-	-	-
Hill, J.C.	3	6	3	8*	21	7.00	-	-	2	606	273	8	34.12	3-35	-	-
Hoare, D.E.	1	2	-	35	35	17.50	-	-	2	232	156	2	78.00	2-68	-	-
Hodges, J.H.	2	4†	1	8	10	3.33	-	-	-	136‡	84	6	14.00	2-7	-	-
Hogan, T.G.	7	12	1	42*	205	18.63	-	1	2	1436‡	706	15	47.06	5-66	1	-
Hogg, R.M.	38	58	13	52	439	9.75	-	1	7	7633	3503	123	28.47	6-74	6	2
Hohns, T.V.	7	7†	1	40	136	22.66	-	1	7	1528	580	17	34.11	3-59	-	-
Hole, G.B.	18	33	2	66	789	25.45	-	6	21	398	126	3	42.00	1-9	-	-
Holland, R.G.	11	15	4	10	35	3.18	-	-	5	2889	1352	34	39.76	6-54	3	2
Hookes, D.W.	23	41†	3	143*	1306	34.36	1	8	12	96‡	41	1	41.00	1-4	-	-

INDIVIDUAL CAREER RECORDS – AUSTRALIA *continued*

	Tests	I	NO	HS	Runs	Avge	100	50	Ct/St	Balls	Runs	Wkts	Avge	BB	5wI	10wM
						BATTING AND FIELDING							BOWLING			
Hopkins, A.J.Y.	20	33	2	43	509	16.42	—	1	11	1327	696	26	26.76	4-81	1	—
Horan, T.P.	15	27	2	124	471	18.84	1	1	6	373	143	11	13.00	6-40	1	—
Hordern, H.V.	7	13	—	50	254	23.09	—	1	6	2148	1075	46	23.36	7-90	5	2
Hornibrook, P.M.	6	7†	1	26	60	10.00	—	—	7	1579‡	664	17	39.05	7-92	1	—
Howell, W.P.	18	27†	6	35	158	7.52	—	—	12	3892	1407	49	28.71	5-81	1	—
Hughes, K.J.	70	124	6	213	4415	37.41	9	22	50	85	28	0	—	—	—	—
Hughes, M.G.	53	70	8	72*	1032	16.64	—	2	23	12285	6017	212	28.38	8-87	7	1
Hunt, W.A.	1	1†	—	0	0	0.00	—	—	—	96‡	39	0	—	—	—	—
Hurst, A.G.	12	20	3	26	102	6.00	—	—	3	3054	1200	43	27.90	5-28	2	—
Hurwood, A.	2	2	—	5	5	2.50	—	—	2	517	170	11	15.45	4-22	—	—
Inverarity, R.J.	6	11	1	56	174	17.40	—	1	4	372‡	93	4	23.25	3-26	—	—
Iredale, F.A.	14	23	1	140	807	36.68	2	4	16	12	3	0	—	—	—	—
Ironmonger, H.	14	21†	5	12	42	2.62	—	—	3	4695‡	1330	74	17.97	7-23	4	2
Iverson, J.B.	5	7	3	1*	3	0.75	—	—	2	1108	320	21	15.23	6-27	1	—
Jackson, A.A.	8	11	1	164	474	47.40	1	2	7	–						
Jarman, B.N.	19	30	3	78	400	14.81	—	2	50/4	–						
Jarvis, A.H.	11	21	3	82	303	16.83	—	1	9/9							
Jenner, T.J.	9	14	5	74	208	23.11	—	1	5	1881	749	24	31.20	5-90	1	—
Jennings, C.B.	6	8	2	32	107	17.83	—	—	5							
Johnson, I.W.	45	66	12	77	1000	18.51	—	6	30	8780	3182	109	29.19	7-44	3	—
Johnson, L.J.	1	1	—	25*	25	–	—	—	—	282	74	6	12.33	3-8	—	—
Johnston, W.A.	40	49†	25	29	273	11.37	—	—	16	11048‡	3826	160	23.91	6-44	7	—
Jones, D.M.	52	89	11	216	3631	46.55	11	14	34	198	64	1	64.00	1-5	—	—
Jones, E.	19	26	1	20	126	5.04	—	—	21	3754	1857	64	29.01	7-88	3	1
Jones, S.P.	12	24	4	87	428	21.40	—	1	12	262	112	6	18.66	4-47	—	—
Joslin, L.R.	1	2†	—	7	9	4.50	—	—	—							
Julian, B.P.	2	3	1	56*	61	30.50	—	1	2	492‡	291	5	58.20	2-30	—	—
Kelleway, C.	26	42	4	147	1422	37.42	3	6	24	4363	1683	52	32.36	5-33	1	—
Kelly, J.J.	36	56	17	46*	664	17.02	—	—	43/20							
Kelly, T.J.D.	2	3	—	35	64	21.33	—	—	1							
Kendall, T.	2	4†	1	17*	39	13.00	—	—	2	563‡	215	14	15.35	7-55	1	—
Kent, M.F.	3	6	—	54	171	28.50	—	2	6							
Kerr, R.B.	2	4	—	17	31	7.75	—	—	1							
Kippax, A.F.	22	34	1	146	1192	36.12	2	8	13	72	19	0	—	–	—	—
Kline, L.F.	13	16†	9	15*	58	8.28	—	1	9	2373‡	776	34	22.82	7-75	1	—

INDIVIDUAL CAREER RECORDS – AUSTRALIA *continued*

			BATTING AND FIELDING							*BOWLING*						
	Tests	I	NO	HS	Runs	Avge	100	50	Ct/St	Balls	Runs	Wkts	Avge	BB	5wI	10wM
Laird, B.M.	21	40	2	92	1341	35.28	–	11	16	18	12	0	–	–	–	–
Langley, J.L.	5	8†	–	63	172	21.50	–	2	2	–	–	–	–	–	–	–
Langley, G.R.A.	26	37	12	53	374	14.96	–	1	83/15	–	–	–	–	–	–	–
Laughlin, T.J.	3	5†	–	35	87	17.40	–	–	3	516	262	6	43.66	5-101	1	–
Laver, F.	15	23	6	45	196	11.52	–	–	8	2361	964	37	26.05	8-31	2	–
Lawry, W.M.	67	123†	12	210	5234	47.15	13	27	30	14‡	6	0	–	–	–	–
Lawson, G.F.	46	68	12	74	894	15.96	–	4	10	11118	5501	180	30.56	8-112	11	2
Lee, P.K.	2	3	–	42	57	19.00	–	–	1	436	212	5	42.40	4-111	–	–
Lillee, D.K.	70	90	24	73*	905	13.71	–	1	23	18467	8493	355	23.92	7-83	23	7
Lindwall, R.R.	61	84	13	118	1502	21.15	2	5	26	13650	5251	228	23.03	7-38	12	–
Love, H.S.B.	1	2	–	5	8	4.00	–	–	3	–	–	–	–	–	–	–
Loxton, S.J.E.	12	15	–	101	554	36.93	1	3	7	906	349	8	43.62	3-55	–	–
Lyons, J.J.	14	27	–	134	731	27.07	1	3	3	316	149	6	24.83	5-30	1	–
McAlister, P.A.	8	16	1	41	252	16.80	–	–	10	–	–	–	–	–	–	–
Macartney, C.G.	35	55	4	170	2131	41.78	7	9	17	3561‡	1240	45	27.55	7-58	2	1
McCabe, S.J.	39	62	5	232	2748	48.21	6	13	41	3746	1543	36	42.86	4-13	–	–
McCool, C.L.	14	17	4	104*	459	35.30	1	1	14	2504	958	36	26.61	5-41	3	–
McCormick, E.L.	12	14†	5	17*	54	6.00	–	–	8	2107	1079	36	29.97	4-101	–	–
McCosker, R.B.	25	46	5	127	1622	39.56	4	9	21	–	–	–	–	–	–	–
McDermott, C.J.	58	74	9	42*	817	12.56	–	–	11	13400	6694	231	28.97	8-97	9	2
McDonald, C.C.	47	83	4	170	3107	39.32	5	17	14	8	3	0	–	–	–	–
McDonald, E.A.	11	12	5	36	116	16.57	–	–	3	2885	1431	43	33.27	5-32	2	–
McDonnell, P.S.	19	34	1	147	955	28.93	3	2	6	52	53	0	–	–	–	–
McGrath, G.D.	5	5	2	9	11	3.66	–	–	1	1273	484	12	40.33	3-65	–	–
McIlwraith, J.	1	2	–	7	9	4.50	–	–	1	–	–	–	–	–	–	–
Mackay, K.D.	37	52†	7	89	1507	33.48	–	13	16	5792	1721	50	34.42	6-42	2	–
McKenzie, G.D.	60	89	12	76	945	12.27	–	2	34	17681	7328	246	29.78	8-71	16	3
McKibbin, T.R.	5	8†	2	28*	88	14.66	–	–	4	1032	496	17	29.17	3-35	–	–
McLaren, J.W.	1	2	2	0*	0	–	–	–	–	144	70	1	70.00	1-23	–	–
Maclean, J.A.	4	8	1	33*	79	11.28	–	–	18	–	–	–	–	–	–	–
McLeod, C.E.	17	29	5	112	573	23.87	1	4	9	3374	1325	33	40.15	5-65	2	–
McLeod, R.W.	6	11†	1	31	146	13.27	–	–	3	1089	382	12	31.83	5-53	1	–
McShane, F.G.	3	6†	1	12*	26	5.20	–	–	2	108‡	48	1	48.00	1-39	–	–
Maddocks, L.V.	7	12	2	69	177	17.70	–	1	18/1	–	–	–	–	–	–	–
Maguire, J.N.	3	5	1	15*	28	7.00	–	–	2	616	323	10	32.30	4-57	–	–
Mailey, A.A.	21	29	9	46*	222	11.10	–	–	14	6119	3358	99	33.91	9-121	6	2
Mallett, A.A.	38	50	13	43*	430	11.62	–	–	30	9990	3940	132	29.84	8-59	6	1

INDIVIDUAL CAREER RECORDS – AUSTRALIA continued

	Tests	I	NO	HS	Runs	Avge	100	50	Ct/St	Balls	Runs	Wkts	Avge	BB	5wI	10wM
				BATTING AND FIELDING						BOWLING						
Malone, M.F.	1	1	1	46	46	46.00	–	–	1	342	77	6	12.83	5-63	1	–
Mann, A.L.	4	8†	–	105	189	23.62	1	–	2	552	316	4	79.00	3-12	–	–
Marr, A.P.	1	2	–	5	5	2.50	–	–	–	48	14	0	–	–	–	–
Marsh, G.R.	50	93	7	138	2854	33.18	4	15	38	–						
Marsh, R.W.	96	150†	13	132	3633	26.51	3	16	343/12	72	54	0	–	–	–	–
Martin, J.W.	8	13†	1	55	214	17.83	–	1	5	1846‡	832	17	48.94	3-56	–	–
Martyn, D.R.	7	12	1	74	317	28.81	–	3	1	6	0	0	–	–	–	–
Massie, H.H.	9	16	–	55	249	15.56	–	1	5							
Massie, R.A.L.	6	8†	1	42	78	11.14	–	–	1	1739	647	31	20.87	8-53	2	1
Matthews, C.D.	3	5†	–	32	54	10.80	–	–	1	570‡	313	6	52.16	3-95	–	–
Matthews, G.R.J.	33	53†	8	130	1849	41.08	4	12	17	6271	2942	61	48.22	5-103	2	1
Matthews, T.J.	8	10	1	53	153	17.00	–	1	7	1081	419	16	26.18	4-29	–	–
May, T.B.A.	19	20	8	42*	182	15.16	–	–	6	5419	2136	68	31.41	5-9	3	–
Mayne, E.R.	4	4	1	25*	64	21.33	–	–	2	6	1	0	–	–	–	–
Mayne, L.C.	6	11†	3	13	76	9.50	–	–	3	1251	628	19	33.05	4-43	–	–
Meckiff, I.	18	20	7	45*	154	11.84	–	–	9	3734‡	1423	45	31.62	6-38	2	–
Meuleman, K.D.	1	1	–	0	0	0.00	–	–	1							
Midwinter, W.E.	8	14	1	37	174	13.38	–	–	5	949	333	14	23.78	5-78	1	1
Miller, K.R.	55	87	7	147	2958	36.97	7	13	38	10461	3906	170	22.97	7-60	7	1
Minnett, R.B.	9	15	–	90	391	26.06	–	3	–	589	290	11	26.36	4-34	–	–
Misson, F.M.	5	5	3	25*	38	19.00	–	–	6	1197	616	16	38.50	4-58	–	–
Moody, T.M.	8	14	–	106	456	32.57	2	3	9	432	147	2	73.50	1-17	–	–
Moroney, J.	7	12	1	118	383	34.81	2	1	–	111‡	50	2	25.00	1-5	–	–
Morris, A.R.	46	79†	3	206	3533	46.48	12	12	15	136	73	2	36.50	2-73	–	–
Morris, S.	1	2	1	10*	14	14.00	–	–	1							
Moses, H.	6	10†	–	33	198	19.80	–	1	1							
Moss, J.K.	1	2†	–	38*	60	60.00	–	1	–							
Moule, W.H.	1	2	–	34	40	20.00	–	–	1	51	23	3	7.66	3-23	–	–
Murdoch, W.L.	18	33	5	211	896	32.00	2	1	14/-	–						
Musgrove, H.	1	2	–	9	13	6.50	–	–	–	–						
Nagel, L.E.	1	2	1	21*	21	21.00	–	–	–	262	110	2	55.00	2-110	–	–
Nash, L.J.	2	2	–	17	30	15.00	–	–	6	311	126	10	12.60	4-18	–	–
Nitschke, H.C.	2	2†	–	47	53	26.50	–	–	3							
Noble, M.A.	42	73	7	133	1997	30.25	1	16	26	7159	3025	121	25.00	7-17	9	2
Noblet, G.	3	4	1	13*	22	7.33	–	–	1	774	183	7	26.14	3-21	–	–
Nothling, O.E.	1	2	–	44	52	26.00	–	–	–	276	72	0	–	–	–	–

INDIVIDUAL CAREER RECORDS – AUSTRALIA continued

	Tests	I	NO	HS	Runs	Avge	100	50	Ct/St	Balls	Runs	Wkts	Avge	BB	5wI	10wM
					BATTING AND FIELDING								*BOWLING*			
O'Brien, L.P.J.	5	8†	–	61	211	26.37	–	2	3	–	–	–	–	–	–	–
O'Connor, J.D.A.	4	8†	1	20	86	12.28	–	–	3	692	340	13	26.15	5-40	1	–
O'Donnell, S.P.	6	10	3	48	206	29.42	–	–	4	940	504	6	84.00	3-37	–	–
Ogilvie, A.D.	5	10	–	47	178	17.80	–	1	5	–						
O'Keeffe, K.J.	24	34	9	85	644	25.76	–	1	15	5384	2018	53	38.07	5-101	1	–
Oldfield, W.A.S.	54	80	17	65*	1427	22.65	–	4	78/52	–						
O'Neill, N.C.	42	69	8	181	2779	45.55	6	15	21	1392	667	17	39.23	4-41	–	–
O'Reilly, W.J.	27	39†	7	56*	410	12.81	–	1	7	10024	3254	144	22.59	7-54	11	3
Oxenham, R.K.	7	10	–	48	151	15.10	–	–	4	1802	522	14	37.28	4-39	–	–
Palmer, G.E.	17	25	4	48	296	14.09	–	–	13	4517	1678	78	21.51	7-65	6	2
Park, R.L.	1	1	–	0	0	0.00	–	–	–	6	9	0	–	–	–	–
Pascoe, L.S.	14	19	9	30*	106	10.60	–	–	2	3403	1668	64	26.06	5-59	1	–
Pellew, C.E.	10	14	1	116	484	37.23	2	1	4	78	34	0	–	–	–	–
Phillips, W.B.	27	48†	2	159	1485	32.28	2	7	52	–						
Phillips, W.N.	1	2	–	14	22	11.00	–	–	–	–						
Philpott, P.I.	8	10	1	22	93	10.33	–	–	5	2262	1000	26	38.46	5-90	1	–
Ponsford, W.H.	29	48	4	266	2122	48.22	7	6	21	–						
Pope, R.J.	1	2	–	3	3	1.50	–	–	–	–						
Rackemann, C.G.	12	14	4	15*	53	5.30	–	–	2	2719	1137	39	29.15	6-86	3	1
Ransford, V.S.	20	38†	6	143*	1211	37.84	1	7	10	43‡	28	1	28.00	1-9	–	–
Redpath, I.R.	66	120	11	171	4737	43.45	8	31	83	64	41	0	–	–	–	–
Reedman, J.C.	1	2	–	17	21	10.50	–	–	1	57	24	1	24.00	1-12	–	–
Reid, B.A.	27	34†	14	13	93	4.65	–	–	5	6244‡	2784	113	24.63	7-51	5	2
Reiffel, P.R.	12	13	3	51	227	22.70	–	1	5	2380	1050	31	33.87	6-71	2	1
Renneberg, D.A.	8	13	7	9	22	3.66	–	–	2	1598	830	23	36.08	5-39	2	–
Richardson, A.J.	9	13	–	100	403	31.00	1	2	1	1812	521	12	43.41	2-20	–	–
Richardson, V.Y.	19	30	–	138	706	23.53	1	1	24	–						
Rigg, K.E.	8	12	–	127	401	33.41	1	1	5	–						
Ring, D.T.	13	21	2	67	426	22.42	–	4	5	3024	1305	35	37.28	6-72	2	–
Ritchie, G.M.	30	53	5	146	1690	35.20	3	7	14	6	10	0	–	–	–	–
Rixon, S.J.	13	24	3	54	394	18.76	–	2	42/5	–						
Robertson, W.R.	1	2	–	2	2	1.00	–	–	–	44	24	0	–	–	–	–
Robinson, R.D.	3	6	–	34	100	16.66	–	–	4	–						
Robinson, R.H.	1	2	–	3	5	2.50	–	–	1	–						
Rorke, G.F.	4	4†	2	7	9	4.50	–	–	1	703	203	10	20.30	3-23	–	–

INDIVIDUAL CAREER RECORDS – AUSTRALIA *continued*

				BATTING AND FIELDING						BOWLING						
	Tests	I	NO	HS	Runs	Avge	100	50	Ct/St	Balls	Runs	Wkts	Avge	BB	5wi	10wM
Rutherford, J.W.	1	1	–	30	30	30.00	–	–	–	36	15	1	15.00	1-11	–	–
Ryder, J.	20	32	5	201*	1394	51.62	3	9	17	1897	743	17	43.70	2-20	–	–
Saggers, R.A.	6	5	2	14	30	10.00	–	–	16/8	–	–	–	–	–	–	–
Saunders, J.V.	14	23†	6	11*	39	2.29	–	–	5	3565‡	1796	79	22.73	7-34	6	–
Scott, H.J.H.	8	14	1	102	359	27.61	1	1	8	28	26	0	–	–	–	–
Sellers, R.H.D.	1	1	–	0	0	0.00	–	–	1	30	17	0	–	–	–	–
Serjeant, C.S.	12	23	1	124	522	23.72	1	2	13	–	–	–	–	–	–	–
Sheahan, A.P.	31	53	6	127	1594	33.91	2	7	17	–	–	–	–	–	–	–
Shepherd, B.K.	9	14†	2	96	502	41.83	–	5	2	–	–	–	–	–	–	–
Sievers, M.W.	3	6	1	25*	67	13.40	–	–	4	602	161	9	17.88	5-21	1	–
Simpson, R.B.	62	111	7	311	4869	46.81	10	27	110	6881	3001	71	42.26	5-57	2	–
Sincock, D.J.	3	4	1	29	80	26.66	–	–	2	724‡	410	8	51.25	3-67	–	–
Slater, K.N.	1	1	1	1*	1	–	–	–	–	256	101	2	50.50	2-40	–	–
Slater, M.J.	15	25	1	168	1157	48.20	2	6	3	–	–	–	–	–	–	–
Sleep, P.R.	14	21	1	90	483	24.15	–	3	4	2982	1397	31	45.06	5-72	1	–
Slight, J.	1	2	–	11	11	5.50	–	–	–	–	–	–	–	–	–	–
Smith, D.B.M.	2	3	1	24*	30	15.00	–	–	1	–	–	–	–	–	–	–
Smith, S.B.	3	5	–	12	41	8.20	–	–	1	–	–	–	–	–	–	–
Spofforth, F.R.	18	29	6	50	217	9.43	–	1	11	4185	1731	94	18.41	7-44	7	4
Stackpole, K.R.	43	80	5	207	2807	37.42	7	14	47	2321	1001	15	66.73	2-33	–	–
Stevens, G.B.	4	7	–	28	112	16.00	–	–	2	–	–	–	–	–	–	–
Taber, H.B.	16	27	5	48	353	16.04	–	–	56/4	–	–	–	–	–	–	–
Tallon, D.	21	26	3	92	394	17.13	–	2	50/8	–	–	–	–	–	–	–
Taylor, J.M.	20	28	–	108	997	35.60	1	8	11	114	45	1	45.00	1-25	–	–
Taylor, M.A.	54	97†	6	219	4275	46.97	12	24	73	24	15	0	–	–	–	–
Taylor, P.L.	13	19†	3	87	431	26.93	–	2	10	2227	1068	27	39.55	6-78	1	–
Thomas, G.	8	12	1	61	325	29.54	–	3	3	112	31	1	31.00	1-14	–	–
Thompson, N.	2	4	–	41	67	16.75	–	–	3	–	–	–	–	–	–	–
Thoms, G.R.	1	2	–	28	44	22.00	–	–	–	–	–	–	–	–	–	–
Thomson, A.L.	4	5	4	12*	22	22.00	–	–	–	1519	654	12	54.50	3-79	–	–
Thomson, J.R.	51	73	20	49	679	12.81	–	–	20	10535	5601	200	28.00	6-46	8	–
Thurlow, H.M.	1	1	–	0	0	0.00	–	–	–	234	86	0	–	–	–	–
Toohey, P.M.	15	29	1	122	893	31.89	1	7	9	2	4	0	–	–	–	–
Toshack, E.R.H.	12	11	6	20*	73	14.60	–	–	4	3140‡	989	47	21.04	6-29	4	1
Travers, J.P.F.	1	2†	–	9	10	5.00	–	–	1	48‡	14	1	14.00	1-14	–	–
Tribe, G.E.	3	3†	1	25*	35	17.50	–	–	–	760‡	330	2	165.00	2-48	–	–

INDIVIDUAL CAREER RECORDS – AUSTRALIA continued

				BATTING AND FIELDING						BOWLING						
	Tests	I	NO	HS	Runs	Avge	100	50	Ct/St	Balls	Runs	Wkts	Avge	BB	5wI	10wM
Trott, A.E.	3	5	3	85*	205	102.50	–	2	4	474	192	9	21.33	8-43	1	–
Trott, G.H.S.	24	42	–	143	921	21.92	1	4	21	1890	1019	29	35.13	4-71	–	3
Trumble, H.	32	57	14	70	851	19.79	–	4	45	8099	3072	141	21.78	8-65	9	3
Trumble, J.W.	7	13	1	59	243	20.25	–	1	3	600	222	10	22.20	3-29	–	–
Trumper, V.T.	48	89	8	214*	3163	39.04	8	13	31	546	317	8	39.62	3-60	–	–
Turner, A.	14	27†	1	136	768	29.53	1	3	15	–	–	–				
Turner, C.T.B.	17	32	4	29	323	11.53	–	–	8	5179	1670	101	16.53	7-43	11	2
Veivers, T.R.	21	30†	4	88	813	31.26	–	7	7	4191	1375	33	41.66	4-68	–	–
Veletta, M.R.J.	8	11	–	39	207	18.81	–	–	12	–	–	–				
Waite, M.G.	2	3	–	8	11	3.66	–	–	1	552	190	1	190.00	1-150	–	–
Walker, M.H.N.	34	43	13	78*	586	19.53	–	1	12	10094	3792	138	27.47	8-143	6	–
Wall, T.W.	18	24	5	20	121	6.36	–	–	11	4812	2010	56	35.89	5-14	3	–
Walters, F.H.	1	2	–	7	12	6.00	–	–	2							
Walters, K.D.	74	125	14	250	5357	48.26	15	33	43	3295	1425	49	29.08	5-66	1	–
Ward, F.A.	4	8	2	18	36	6.00	–	–	1	1268	574	11	52.18	6-102	1	–
Warne, S.K.	26	34	7	74*	440	16.29	–	1	16	7985	2780	116	23.96	7-52	5	1
Watkins, J.R.	1	2	1	36	39	39.00	–	–	1	48	21	0	–	–	–	–
Watson, G.D.	5	9	–	50	97	10.77	–	–	1	552	254	6	42.33	2-67	–	–
Watson, W.J.	4	7	1	30	106	7.66	–	–	2	6	5	0	–	–	–	–
Waugh, M.E.	36	57	4	139*	2177	41.07	6	12	48	1920	874	23	38.00	4-80	–	–
Waugh, S.R.	65	98	18	177*	3495	43.68	7	19	48	5580	2496	66	37.81	5-28	3	–
Wellham, D.M.	6	11	–	103	257	23.36	1	–	5							
Wessels, K.C.	24	42†	1	179	1761	42.95	4	9	18	90	42	0	–	–	–	–
Whatmore, D.C.	7	13	–	77	293	22.53	–	2	13	30	11	0	–	–	–	–
Whitney, M.R.	12	19	8	13	68	6.18	–	–	2	2672‡	1325	39	33.97	7-27	2	1
Whitty, W.J	14	19	7	39*	161	13.41	–	–	4	3357‡	1373	65	21.12	6-17	3	–
Wiener, J.M.	6	11	–	93	281	25.64	–	2	4	78	41	0	–	–	–	–
Wilson, J.W.	1	–	–	–	–	–	–	–	–	216‡	64	1	64.00	1-25	–	–
Wood, G.M.	59	112†	6	172	3374	31.83	9	13	41							
Woodcock, A.J.	1	1	–	27	27	27.00	–	–	1	–	–	–				
Woodfull, W.M.	35	54	4	161	2300	46.00	7	13	7	–	–	–				
Woods, S.M.J.	3	6	–	18	32	5.33	–	–	1	217	121	5	24.20	2-35	–	–
Woolley, R.D.	2	2	0	13	21	10.50	–	–	7	–	–	–				
Worrall, J.	11	22	3	76	478	25.15	–	5	13	255	127	1	127.00	1-97	–	–

INDIVIDUAL CAREER RECORDS – AUSTRALIA *continued*

	Tests	I	NO	HS	BATTING AND FIELDING Runs	Avge	100	50	Ct/St	Balls	Runs	Wkts	BOWLING Avge	BB	5wI	10wM
Wright, K.J.	10	18	5	55*	219	16.84	–	1	31/4	–						
Yallop, G.N.	39	70†	3	268	2756	41.13	8	9	23	192‡	116	1	116.00	1-21	–	–
Yardley, B.	33	54	4	74	978	19.56	–	4	31	8909	3986	126	31.63	7-98	6	1
Zoehrer, T.J.	10	14	2	52*	246	20.50	–	1	18/1	–						

INDIVIDUAL CAREER RECORDS – SOUTH AFRICA

SOUTH AFRICA (257 players)	Tests	I	NO	BATTING AND FIELDING HS	Runs	Avge	100	50	Ct/St	BOWLING Balls	Runs	Wkts	Avge	BB	5wI	10wM
Adcock, N.A.T.	26	39	12	24	146	5.40	–	–	4	6391	2195	104	21.10	6-43	5	–
Anderson, J.H.	1	2	–	32	43	21.50	–	–	1	–						
Ashley, W.H.	1	2	–	1	1	0.50	–	–	–	173‡	95	7	13.57	7-95	1	–
Bacher, A.	12	22	1	73	679	32.33	–	6	10	–						
Balaskas, X.C.	9	13	1	122*	174	14.50	1	–	5	1572	806	22	36.63	5-49	1	–
Barlow, E.J.	30	57	2	201	2516	45.74	6	15	35	3021	1362	40	34.05	5-85	1	–
Baumgartner, H.V.	1	2	–	16	19	9.50	–	–	1	166‡	99	2	49.50	2-99	–	–
Beaumont, R.	5	9	–	31	70	7.77	–	–	2	6	0	0	–	–	–	–
Begbie, D.W.	5	7	–	48	138	19.71	–	–	2	160	130	1	130.00	1-38	–	–
Bell, A.J.	16	23	12	26*	69	6.27	–	–	6	3342	1567	48	32.64	6-99	4	–
Bisset, M.	3	6	2	35	103	25.75	–	–	2/1	–						
Bissett, G.F.	4	4	2	23	38	19.00	–	–	–	989	469	25	18.76	7-29	2	–
Blanckenberg, J.M.	18	30	7	59	455	19.78	–	2	9	3888	1817	60	30.28	6-76	4	–
Bland, K.C.	21	39	5	144*	1669	49.08	3	9	10	394	125	2	62.50	2-16	–	–
Bock, E.G.	1	2	–	9*	11	–	–	–	–	138	91	0	–	–	–	–
Bond, G.E.	1	1	–	0	0	0.00	–	–	–	16	16	0	–	–	–	–
Bosch, T.	1	2	2	5*	5	–	–	–	–	237	104	3	34.66	2-61	–	–
Botten, J.T.	3	6	–	33	65	10.83	–	–	1	828	337	8	42.12	2-56	–	–
Brann, W.H.	3	5	–	50	71	14.20	–	1	2	–						
Briscoe, A.W.	3	3	–	16	33	11.00	–	–	1	–						
Bromfield, H.D.	9	12	7	21	59	11.80	–	–	13	1810	599	17	35.23	5-88	1	–
Brown, L.S.	2	3	–	8	17	5.66	–	–	–	318	189	3	63.00	1-30	–	–
Burger, C.G.de V.	2	4	1	37*	62	20.66	–	–	1	–						
Burke, S.F.	2	4	1	20	42	14.00	–	–	–	660	257	11	23.36	6-128	2	1
Buys, I.D.	1	2	1	4*	4	4.00	–	–	–	144	52	0	–	–	–	–
Cameron, H.B.	26	45	4	90	1239	30.21	–	10	39/12	–						
Campbell, T.	5	9	3	48	90	15.00	–	–	7/1	–						
Carlstein, P.R.	8	14	–	42	190	14.61	–	–	3	–						
Carter, C.P.	10	15	5	45	181	18.10	–	–	2	1475‡	694	28	24.78	6-50	2	–
Catterall, R.H.	24	43	2	120	1555	37.92	3	11	12	342	162	7	23.14	3-15	–	–
Chapman, H.W.	2	4	1	17	39	13.00	–	–	1	126	104	1	104.00	1-51	–	–
Cheetham, J.E.	24	43	6	89	883	23.86	–	5	13	6	2	0	–	–	–	–
Chevalier, G.A.	1	2	1	0*	0	0.00	–	–	1	253‡	100	5	20.00	3-68	–	–

INDIVIDUAL CAREER RECORDS – SOUTH AFRICA *continued*

	Tests	I	NO	HS	Runs	Avge	100	50	Ct/St	Balls	Runs	Wkts	Avge	BB	5wI	10wM
Christy, J.A.J.	10	18	—	103	618	34.33	1	5	3	138	92	2	46.00	1-15	—	—
Chubb, G.W.A.	5	9	3	15*	63	10.50	—	—	—	1425	577	21	27.47	6-51	2	—
Cochran, J.A.K.	1	1	—	4	4	4.00	—	—	—	138	47	0	—	—	—	—
Coen, S.K.	2	4	2	41*	101	50.50	—	—	1	12	7	0	—	—	—	—
Commaille, J.M.M.	12	22	1	47	355	16.90	—	—	1	—						
Conyngham, D.P.	1	2	2	3*	6	—	—	—	1	366	103	2	51.50	1-40	—	—
Cook, F.J.	1	2	—	7	7	3.50	—	—	—							
Cook, S.J.	3	6	—	43	107	17.83	—	—	1	—						
Cooper, A.H.C.	1	2	—	6	6	3.00	—	—	1							
Cox, J.L.	3	6	1	12*	17	3.40	—	—	1	576	245	4	61.25	2-74	—	—
Cripps, G.	1	2	—	18	21	10.50	—	—	—	15	23	0	—	—	—	—
Crisp, R.J.	9	13	1	35	123	10.25	—	—	3	1428	747	20	37.35	5-99	1	—
Cronje, W.J.	16	29	3	135	884	34.00	3	2	6	1153	351	5	70.20	2-17	—	—
Cullinan, D.J.	8	14	—	102	438	31.28	1	2	2	—						
Curnow, S.H.	7	14	—	47	168	12.00	—	—	5	—						
Dalton, E.L.	15	24	2	117	698	31.72	2	3	5	864	490	12	40.83	4-59	—	—
Davies, E.Q.	5	8	3	3	9	1.80	—	—	—	768	481	7	68.71	4-75	—	—
Dawson, O.C.	9	15	1	55	293	20.92	—	1	10	1294	578	10	57.80	2-57	—	—
Deane, H.G.	17	27	2	93	628	25.12	—	3	8	—						
De Villiers, P.S.	9	13	1	30	116	9.66	—	—	4	2427	1104	34	32.47	6-43	1	1
Dixon, C.D.	1	2	—	0	0	0.00	—	—	—	240	118	3	39.33	2-62	—	—
Donald, A.A.	17	23	13	27	113	11.30	—	—	5	4001	1978	75	26.37	7-84	4	1
Dower, R.R.	1	2	—	9	9	4.50	—	—	2							
Draper, R.G.	2	3	—	15	25	8.33	—	—	—							
Duckworth, C.A.R.	2	4	—	13	28	7.00	—	—	3							
Dumbrill, R.	5	10	1	36	153	15.30	—	—	3	816	336	9	37.33	4-30	—	—
Duminy, J.P.	3	6†	—	12	30	5.00	—	—	2	60‡	39	1	39.00	1-17	—	—
Dunell, O.R.	2	4	1	26*	42	14.00	—	—	1							
Du Preez, J.H.	2	2	2	0*	0	0.00	—	—	2	144	51	3	17.00	2-22	—	—
Du Toit, J.F.	1	2	2	2*	2	—	—	—	—	85	47	1	47.00	1-47	—	—
Dyer, D.V.	3	6	—	62	96	16.00	—	1	1							
Eksteen, C.E.	1	2	1	4*	5	5.00	—	—	—	138‡	78	0	—	—	—	—
Elgie, M.K.	3	6	—	56	75	12.50	—	1	4	66‡	46	0	—	—	—	—
Endean, W.R.	28	52	4	162*	1630	33.95	3	8	41	—						
Farrer, W.S.	6	10	2	40	221	27.62	—	—	2	—						

INDIVIDUAL CAREER RECORDS – SOUTH AFRICA *continued*

	Tests	I	NO	BATTING AND FIELDING HS	Runs	Avge	100	50	Ct/St	BOWLING Balls	Runs	Wkts	Avge	BB	5wI	10wM
Faulkner, G.A.	25	47	4	204	1754	40.79	4	8	20	4227	2180	82	26.58	7-84	4	–
Fellows-Smith, J.P.	4	8	2	35	166	27.66	–	–	2	114	61	0	–	–	–	–
Fichardt, C.G.	2	4	–	10	15	3.75	–	–	2	–				–	–	–
Finlason, C.E.	1	2	–	6	6	3.00	–	–	–	12	7	0	–	–	–	–
Floquet, C.E.	1	2	1	11*	12	12.00	–	–	–	48	24	0	–	–	–	–
Francis, H.H.	2	4	–	29	39	9.75	–	–	1	–				–	–	–
Francois, C.M.	5	9	1	72	252	31.50	–	1	5	684	225	6	37.50	3-23	–	–
Frank, C.N.	3	6	–	152	236	39.33	1	1	–	–				–	–	–
Frank, W.H.B.	1	2	–	7	7	3.50	–	–	–	–				–	–	–
Fuller, E.R.H.	7	9	1	17	64	8.00	–	–	3	58	52	1	52.00	1-52	–	–
Fullerton, G.M.	7	13	1	88	325	25.00	–	3	10/2	1898	668	22	30.36	5-66	1	–
Funston, K.J.	18	33	1	92	824	25.75	–	5	7	–				–	–	–
Gamsy, D.	2	3	1	30*	39	19.50	–	–	5	–				–	–	–
Gleeson, R.A.	1	2	1	3	4	4.00	–	–	2	–				–	–	–
Glover, G.K.	1	2	1	18*	21	21.00	–	–	–	65	28	1	28.00	1-28	–	–
Goddard, T.L.	41	78†	5	112	2516	34.46	1	18	48	11736‡	3226	123	26.22	6-53	5	–
Gordon, N.	5	6	2	7*	8	2.00	–	–	1	1966	807	20	40.35	5-103	2	–
Graham, R.	2	4	–	4	6	1.50	–	–	2	240	127	3	42.33	2-22	–	–
Grieveson, R.E.	2	2	–	75	114	57.00	–	1	7/3	–				–	–	–
Griffin, G.M.	2	4	–	14	25	6.25	–	–	–	432	192	8	24.00	4-87	–	–
Hall, A.E.	7	8	2	5	11	1.83	–	–	4	2361‡	886	40	22.15	7-63	3	–
Hall, G.G.	1	1	–	0	0	0.00	–	–	–	186	94	1	94.00	1-94	–	1
Halliwell, E.A.	8	15	–	57	188	12.53	–	1	9/2	–				–	–	–
Halse, C.G.	3	3	3	19*	30	–	–	–	1	587	260	6	43.33	3-50	–	–
Hands, P.A.M.	7	12	–	83	300	25.00	–	2	3	37	18	0	–	–	–	–
Hands, R.H.M.	1	1	–	7	7	3.50	–	–	–	–				–	–	–
Hanley, M.A.	1	1	–	0	0	0.00	–	–	–	232	88	1	88.00	1-57	–	–
Harris, T.A.	3	5	1	60	100	25.00	–	1	1	–				–	–	–
Hartigan, G.P.D.	5	10	–	51	114	11.40	–	1	1	252	141	1	141.00	1-72	–	–
Harvey, R.L.	2	4	–	28	51	12.75	–	–	5	–				–	–	–
Hathorn, C.M.H.	12	20	1	102	325	17.10	1	–	2	–				–	–	–
Hearne, F.	4	8	1	30	121	15.12	–	–	3	62	40	2	20.00	2-40	–	–
Hearne, G.A.L.	3	5	–	28	59	11.80	–	–	8	–				–	–	–
Heine, P.S.	14	24	3	31	209	9.95	–	–	8	3890	1455	58	25.08	6-58	4	–
Henry, O.	3	3†	–	34	53	17.66	–	–	2	427‡	189	3	63.00	2-56	–	–
Hime, C.F.W.	1	2	–	8	8	4.00	–	–	–	55	31	1	31.00	1-20	–	–

INDIVIDUAL CAREER RECORDS – SOUTH AFRICA *continued*

				BATTING AND FIELDING						BOWLING						
	Tests	I	NO	HS	Runs	Avge	100	50	Ct/St	Balls	Runs	Wkts	Avge	BB	5wI	10wM
Hudson, A.C.	16	29	1	163	1090	38.92	2	9	12	–	–	–	–	–	–	–
Hutchinson, P.	2	4	–	11	14	3.50	–	–	3	–	–	–	–	–	–	–
Ironside, D.E.J.	3	4	2	13	37	18.50	–	–	1	985	275	15	18.33	5-51	1	–
Irvine, B.L.	4	7†	–	102	353	50.42	1	2	2	–	–	–	–	–	–	–
Johnson, C.L.	1	2	–	7	10	5.00	–	–	1	140	57	0	–	–	–	–
Keith, H.J.	8	16†	1	73	318	21.20	–	2	9	108‡	63	0	–	–	–	–
Kempis, G.A.	1	2	1	0*	0	0.00	–	–	–	168‡	76	4	19.00	3-53	–	–
Kirsten, G.	9	16†	2	72	526	32.87	–	3	7	259	122	1	122.00	1-62	–	–
Kirsten, P.N.	12	22	2	104	626	31.30	1	4	8	54	30	0	–	–	–	–
Kotze, J.J.	3	5	–	2	2	0.40	–	–	3	413	243	6	40.50	3-64	–	–
Kuiper, A.P.	1	2	–	34	34	17.00	–	–	1	–	–	–	–	–	–	–
Kuys, F.	1	2	–	26	26	13.00	–	–	–	60	31	2	15.50	2-31	–	–
Lance, H.R.	13	22	1	70	591	28.14	–	5	7	948	479	12	39.91	3-30	–	–
Langton, A.B.C.	15	23	4	73*	298	15.68	–	2	8	4199	1827	40	45.67	5-58	1	–
Lawrence, G.B.	5	8	–	43	141	17.62	–	–	2	1334	512	28	18.28	8-53	2	–
Le Roux, F.L.	1	2	–	1	1	0.50	–	–	–	54	24	0	–	–	–	–
Lewis, P.T.	1	2	–	0	0	0.00	–	–	–	–	–	–	–	–	–	–
Lindsay, D.T.	19	31	1	182	1130	37.66	3	5	57/2	–	–	–	–	–	–	–
Lindsay, J.D.	3	5	2	9*	21	7.00	–	–	4/1	–	–	–	–	–	–	–
Lindsay, N.V.	1	2	–	29	35	17.50	–	–	1	–	–	–	–	–	–	–
Ling, W.V.S.	6	10	–	38	168	16.80	–	–	1	18	20	0	–	–	–	–
Llewellyn, C.B.	15	28†	1	90	544	20.14	–	4	7	2292‡	1421	48	29.60	6-92	4	1
Lundie, E.B.	1	2	1	1	1	1.00	–	–	–	286	107	4	26.75	4-101	–	–
Macaulay, M.J.	1	2	–	21	33	16.50	–	–	–	276‡	73	2	36.50	1-10	–	–
McCarthy, C.N.	15	24	15	5	28	3.11	–	–	6	3499	1510	36	41.94	6-43	2	–
McGlew, D.J.	34	64	6	255*	2440	42.06	7	10	18	32	23	0	–	–	–	–
McKinnon, A.H.	8	13	7	27	107	17.83	–	–	1	2546‡	925	26	35.57	4-128	–	–
McLean, R.A.	40	73	3	142	2120	30.28	5	10	23	4	1	0	–	–	–	–
McMillan, B.M.	13	21	3	98	651	36.16	–	6	16	2570	1130	34	33.23	4-74	–	–
McMillan, Q.	13	21	4	50*	306	18.00	–	1	8	2021	1243	36	34.52	5-66	2	–
Mann, N.B.F.	19	31	1	52	400	13.33	–	–	3	5796†	1920	58	33.10	6-59	1	–
Mansell, P.N.F.	13	22	2	90	355	17.75	–	1	15	1506	736	11	66.90	3-58	–	–
Markham, L.A.	1	1	–	20	20	20.00	–	–	–	104	72	1	72.00	1-34	–	–

INDIVIDUAL CAREER RECORDS – SOUTH AFRICA *continued*

	Tests	I	NO	BATTING AND FIELDING HS	Runs	Avge	100	50	Ct/St	BOWLING Balls	Runs	Wkts	Avge	BB	5wI	10wM
Marx, W.F.E.	3	6†	–	36	125	20.83	–	1	–	2228‡	144	4	36.00	3-85	–	–
Matthews, C.R.	11	16	5	62*	271	24.63	–	1	3	2559	948	33	28.72	5-80	1	–
Meintjes, D.J.	2	3	1	21	43	14.33	–	–	3	246	115	6	19.16	3-38	–	–
Melle, M.G.	7	12	4	17	68	8.50	–	–	4	1667	851	26	32.73	6-71	2	–
Melville, A.	11	19	2	189	894	52.58	4	3	8	–	–	–	–	–	–	–
Middleton, J.	6	12	5	22	52	7.42	–	–	1	1064‡	442	24	18.41	5-51	2	–
Mills, C.	1	2	–	21	25	12.50	–	–	2	140	83	2	41.50	2-83	–	–
Milton, W.H.	3	6	–	21	68	11.33	–	–	1	79	48	2	24.00	1-5	–	–
Mitchell, B.	42	80	9	189*	3471	48.88	8	21	56	2519	1380	27	51.11	5-87	1	–
Mitchell, F.	3	6	–	12	28	4.66	–	–	1	–	–	–	–	–	–	–
Morkel, D.P.B.	16	28	1	88	663	24.55	–	4	13	1704	821	18	45.61	4-93	–	–
Murray, A.R.A.	10	14	1	109	289	22.23	1	1	3	2374	710	18	39.44	4-169	–	–
Nel, J.D.	6	11	–	38	150	13.63	–	–	1	–	–	–	–	–	–	–
Newberry, C.	4	8	–	16	62	7.75	–	–	3	558	268	11	24.36	4-72	–	–
Newson, E.S.	3	5	1	16	30	7.50	–	–	3	874	265	4	66.25	2-58	–	–
Nicholson, F.	4	8	–	29	76	10.85	–	–	3	–	–	–	–	–	–	–
Nicolson, J.F.W.	3	5†	–	78	179	35.80	–	1	–	24	17	0	–	–	–	–
Norton, N.O.	1	2	–	7	9	4.50	–	–	–	90	47	4	11.75	4-47	–	–
Nourse, A.D.	34	62	7	231	2960	53.81	9	14	12	20	9	0	–	–	–	–
Nourse, A.W.	45	83†	8	111	2234	29.78	1	15	43	3234	1553	41	37.87	4-25	–	–
Nupen, E.P.	17	31	7	69	348	14.50	–	2	9	4159	1788	50	35.76	6-46	5	1
Ochse, A.E.	2	4	–	8	16	4.00	–	–	1	–	–	–	–	–	–	–
Ochse, A.L.	3	4	1	4*	11	3.66	–	–	1	649	362	10	36.20	4-79	–	–
O'Linn, S.	7	12†	1	98	297	27.00	–	2	4	–	–	–	–	–	–	–
Owen-Smith, H.G.	5	8	2	129	252	42.00	1	1	4	156	113	0	–	–	–	–
Palm, A.W.	1	2	–	13	15	7.50	–	–	1	–	–	–	–	–	–	–
Parker, G.M.	2	4	3	2*	3	1.50	–	–	–	366	273	8	34.12	6-152	1	–
Parkin, D.C.	2	2	–	6	6	3.00	–	–	1	130	82	3	27.33	3-82	–	–
Partridge, J.T.	11	12	5	13*	73	10.42	–	–	6	3684	1373	44	31.20	7-91	3	–
Pearse, C.O.C.	3	6	–	31	55	9.16	–	–	1	144	106	3	35.33	3-56	–	–
Pegler, S.J.	16	28	5	35*	356	15.47	–	–	5	2989	1572	47	33.44	7-65	2	–
Pithey, A.J.	17	27	1	154	819	31.50	1	4	3	–	–	–	–	–	–	–
Pithey, D.B.	8	12	1	55	138	12.54	–	1	6	1424	577	12	48.08	6-58	1	–
Plimsoll, J.B.	1	2	1	8*	16	16.00	–	–	–	237‡	143	3	47.66	3-128	–	–
Pollock, P.M.	28	41	13	75*	607	21.67	–	2	9	6522	2806	116	24.18	6-38	9	1

INDIVIDUAL CAREER RECORDS – SOUTH AFRICA *continued*

	Tests	I	NO	HS	Runs	Avge	100	50	Ct/St	Balls	Runs	Wkts	Avge	BB	5wI	10wM
				BATTING AND FIELDING						*BOWLING*						
Pollock, R.G.	23	41†	4	274	2256	60.97	7	11	17	414	204	4	51.00	2-50	—	—
Poore, R.M.	3	6	1	20	76	12.66	—	—	3	9	4	1	4.00	1-4	—	—
Pothecary, J.E.	3	4	—	12	26	6.50	—	—	2	828	354	9	39.33	4-58	—	—
Powell, A.W.	1	2	—	11	16	8.00	—	—	2	20	10	1	10.00	1-10	—	—
Prince, C.F.H.	1	2	—	5	6	3.00	—	—	—							
Pringle, M.W.	3	4	1	33	55	18.33	—	—	—	412	172	3	57.33	2-62	—	—
Procter, M.J.	7	10	1	48	226	25.11	—	—	4	1514	616	41	15.02	6-73	1	—
Promnitz, H.L.E.	2	4	—	5	14	3.50	—	—	2	528	161	8	20.12	5-58	1	—
Quinn, N.A.	12	18	3	28	90	6.00	—	—	1	2922‡	1145	35	32.71	6-92	1	—
Reid, N.	1	2	—	11	17	8.50	—	—	—	126	63	2	31.50	2-63	—	—
Rhodes, J.N.	16	27	4	101*	865	39.31	1	5	9	12	5	0	—	—	—	—
Richards, A.R.	1	2	—	6	6	3.00	—	—	3							
Richards, B.A.	4	7	—	140	508	72.57	2	2	3	72	26	1	26.00	1-12	—	—
Richards, W.H.M.	1	2	—	4	4	2.00	—	—	—							
Richardson, D.J.	17	26	1	62	552	22.08	—	4	63							
Robertson, J.B.	3	6	1	17	51	10.20	—	—	2	738	321	6	53.50	3-143	—	—
Rose-Innes, A.	2	4	1	13	14	3.50	—	—	2	128‡	89	5	17.80	5-43	1	—
Routledge, T.W.	4	8	—	24	72	9.00	—	—	2							
Rowan, A.M.B.	15	23	6	41	290	17.05	—	—	7	5193	2084	54	38.59	5-68	4	—
Rowan, E.A.B.	26	50	5	236	1965	43.66	3	12	14	19	7	0	—	—	—	—
Rowe, G.A.	5	9	3	13*	26	4.33	—	—	4	998‡	456	15	30.40	5-115	1	—
Rushmere, M.W.	1	2	—	3	6	3.00	—	—	—							
Samuelson, S.V.	1	2	—	15	22	11.00	—	—	1	108	64	0	—	—	—	—
Schultz, B.N.	5	5†	2	6	6	2.00	—	—	—	1055‡	427	24	17.79	5-48	2	—
Schwarz, R.O.	20	35	8	61	374	13.85	—	1	18	2639	1417	55	25.76	6-47	2	—
Seccull, A.W.	1	2	1	17*	23	23.00	—	—	1	60	37	2	18.50	2-37	—	—
Seymour, M.A.	7	10	3	36	84	12.00	—	—	2	1458	588	9	65.33	3-80	—	—
Shalders, W.A.	12	23	1	42	355	16.13	—	—	3	48	6	1	6.00	1-6	—	—
Shepstone, G.H.	2	4	—	21	38	9.50	—	—	—	115	47	0	—	—	—	—
Sherwell, P.W.	13	22	4	115	427	23.72	1	1	20/16							
Siedle, I.J.	18	34	1	141	977	28.73	1	5	7	19	7	1	7.00	1-7	—	—
Sinclair, J.H.	25	47	1	106	1069	23.23	3	3	9	3598	1996	63	31.68	6-26	1	—
Smith, C.J.E.	3	6	1	45	106	21.20	—	—	2							
Smith, F.W.	3	6	1	12	45	9.00	—	—	2							
Smith, V.I.	9	16	6	11*	39	3.90	—	—	3	1655	769	12	64.08	4-143	—	—

INDIVIDUAL CAREER RECORDS – SOUTH AFRICA continued

				BATTING AND FIELDING						BOWLING						
	Tests	I	NO	HS	Runs	Avge	100	50	Ct/St	Balls	Runs	Wkts	Avge	BB	5wI	10wM
Snell, R.P.	4	6	1	48	78	15.60	–	–	1	726	372	15	24.80	4-74	–	–
Snooke, S.D.	1	1	1	0	0	0.00	–	–	2	–	–	–	–	–	–	–
Snooke, S.J.	26	46	1	103	1008	22.40	1	5	24	1620	702	35	20.05	8-70	1	1
Solomon, W.R.T.	1	2	–	2	4	2.00	–	–	1	–	–	–	–	–	–	–
Stewart, R.B.	1	2	–	9	13	6.50	–	–	2	–	–	–	–	–	–	–
Stricker, L.A.	13	24	–	48	342	14.25	–	–	3	174	105	1	105.00	1-36	–	–
Susskind, M.J.	5	8	–	65	268	33.50	–	4	1	–	–	–	–	–	–	–
Symcox, P.L.	5	6	–	50	160	26.66	–	1	–	857	383	8	47.87	3-75	–	–
Taberer, H.M.	1	1	–	2	2	2.00	–	–	–	60	48	1	48.00	1-25	–	–
Tancred, A.B.	2	4	1	29	87	29.00	–	–	2	–	–	–	–	–	–	–
Tancred, L.J.	14	26	–	97	530	21.20	–	2	3	–	–	–	–	–	–	–
Tancred, V.M.	1	2	–	18	25	12.50	–	–	1	–	–	–	–	–	–	–
Tapscott, G.L.	1	2	–	4	5	2.50	–	–	–	–	–	–	–	–	–	–
Tapscott, L.E.	2	3	1	50*	58	29.00	–	1	1	12	2	0	–	–	–	–
Tayfield, H.J.	37	60	9	75	862	16.90	–	2	26	13568	4405	170	25.91	9-113	14	2
Taylor, A.I.	1	2	–	12	18	9.00	–	–	–	–	–	–	–	–	–	–
Taylor, D.	2	4	–	36	85	21.25	–	–	–	–	–	–	–	–	–	–
Taylor, H.W.	42	76	4	176	2936	40.77	7	17	19	342	156	5	31.20	3-15	–	–
Theunissen, N.H.	1	2	1	2*	2	2.00	–	–	1	80	51	0	–	–	–	–
Thornton, P.G.	1	1†	–	1*	1	–	–	–	–	24‡	20	1	20.00	1-20	–	–
Tomlinson, D.S.	1	1	–	9	9	9.00	–	–	–	60	38	0	–	–	–	–
Traicos, A.J.	3	4	2	5*	8	4.00	–	–	4	470	207	4	51.75	2-70	–	–
Trimborn, P.H.J.	4	4	2	11*	13	6.50	–	–	7	747	257	11	23.36	3-12	–	–
Tuckett, L.	9	14	3	40*	131	11.90	–	–	9	2104	980	19	51.57	5-68	2	–
Tuckett, L.R.	1	2	1	0*	0	0.00	–	–	2	120	69	0	–	–	–	–
Twentyman-Jones, P.S.	1	2	–	0	0	0.00	–	–	–	–	–	–	–	–	–	–
Van der Bijl, P.G.V.	5	9	–	125	460	51.11	1	2	1	–	–	–	–	–	–	–
Van der Merwe, E.A.	2	4	1	19	27	9.00	–	–	3	–	–	–	–	–	–	–
Van der Merwe, P.L.	15	23	2	76	533	25.38	–	3	11	79†	22	1	22.00	1-6	–	–
Van Ryneveld, C.B.	19	33	6	83	724	26.81	–	3	14	1554	671	17	39.47	4-67	–	–
Varnals, G.D.	3	6	–	23	97	16.16	–	–	–	12	2	0	–	–	–	–
Viljoen, K.G.	27	50	2	124	1365	28.43	2	9	5	48	23	0	–	–	–	–
Vincent, C.L.	25	38†	12	60	526	20.23	–	2	27	5851‡	2631	84	31.32	6-51	3	–
Vincent, C.H.	3	6†	–	9	26	4.33	–	–	1	369‡	193	4	48.25	3-88	–	–
Vogler, A.E.E.	15	26	6	65	340	17.00	–	2	20	2764	1455	64	22.73	7-94	5	1

INDIVIDUAL CAREER RECORDS – SOUTH AFRICA *continued*

	Tests	I	NO	HS	Runs	Avge	100	50	Ct/St	Balls	Runs	Wkts	Avge	BB	5wI	10wM
						BATTING AND FIELDING						*BOWLING*				
Wade, H.F.	10	18	2	40*	327	20.43	–	–	4	–	–					–
Wade, W.W.	11	19	1	125	511	28.38	1	3	15/2	–						–
Waite, J.H.B.	50	86	7	134	2405	30.44	4	16	124/17	–						
Walter, K.A.	2	3	–	10	11	3.66	–	–	3	495	197	6	32.83	4-63	–	–
Ward, T.A.	23	42	9	64	459	13.90	–	2	19/13	–						
Watkins, J.C.	15	27	1	92	612	23.53	–	3	12	2805	816	29	28.13	4-22	–	–
Wesley, C.	3	5†	–	35	49	9.80	–	–	1	–						
Wessels, K.C.	16	29†	2	118	1027	38.03	2	6	12	–						
Westcott, R.J.	5	9	–	62	166	18.44	–	1	–	32	22	0	–	–		
White, G.C.	17	31	2	147	872	30.06	2	4	10	498	301	9	33.44	4-47	–	–
Willoughby, J.T.	2	4	–	5	8	2.00	–	–	–	275	159	6	26.50	2-37	–	–
Wimble, C.S.	1	2	–	0	0	0.00	–	–	–	–						
Winslow, P.L.	5	9	–	108	186	20.66	1	–	1	–						
Wynne, O.E.	6	12	–	50	219	18.25	–	1	3	–						
Zulch, J.W.	16	32	2	150	985	32.83	2	4	4	24	28	0	–	–	–	–

INDIVIDUAL CAREER RECORDS – WEST INDIES

WEST INDIES (205 players)	Tests	I	NO	BATTING AND FIELDING						BOWLING						
				HS	Runs	Avge	100	50	Ct/St	Balls	Runs	Wkts	Avge	BB	5wI	10wM
Achong, E.E.	6	11†	1	22	81	8.10	1	—	6	918‡	378	8	47.25	2-64	—	—
Adams, J.C.	9	13†	3	137	612	61.20	1	4	12	622‡	335	9	37.22	4-43	—	—
Alexander, F.C.M.	25	38	6	108	961	30.03	—	7	85/5	—	—	—	—	—	—	—
Ali, Imtiaz	1	1	1	1*	1	—	—	—	—	204	89	2	44.50	2-37	—	—
Ali, Inshan	12	18†	2	25	172	10.75	—	—	7	3718‡	1621	34	47.67	5-59	1	—
Allan, D.W.	5	7	1	40*	75	12.50	—	—	15/3	—	—	—	—	—	—	—
Allen, I.B.A.	2	2	2	4*	5	—	—	—	1	282	180	5	36.00	2-69	—	—
Ambrose, C.E.L.	48	70†	13	53	680	11.92	—	1	10	11809	4616	219	21.07	8-45	11	3
Arthurton, K.L.T.	20	31†	3	157*	914	32.64	2	5	11	192‡	77	0	—	—	—	—
Asgarali, N.R.	2	4	—	29	62	15.50	—	—	—	—	—	—	—	—	—	—
Atkinson, D.St E.	22	35	6	219	922	31.79	1	5	11	5201	1647	47	35.04	7-53	3	1
Atkinson, E.St E.	8	9	1	37	126	15.75	—	—	2	1634	589	25	23.56	5-42	1	—
Austin, R.A.	2	2	—	20	22	11.00	—	—	2	6	5	0	—	—	—	—
Bacchus, S.F.A.F.	19	30	—	250	782	26.06	1	3	17	6	3	0	—	—	—	—
Baichan, L.	3	6†	2	105*	184	46.00	1	1	2	—	—	—	—	—	—	—
Baptiste, E.A.E.	10	11	1	87*	233	23.30	—	1	2	1362	563	16	35.18	3-31	—	—
Barrett, A.G.	6	7	1	19	40	6.66	—	—	2	1612	603	13	46.38	3-43	—	—
Barrow, I.	11	19	2	105	276	16.23	1	1	17/5	—	—	—	—	—	—	—
Bartlett, E.L.	5	8	1	84	131	18.71	—	1	2	—	—	—	—	—	—	—
Benjamin, K.C.G.	7	10	2	43*	81	10.12	—	—	—	1403	728	26	28.00	6-66	1	—
Benjamin, W.K.M.	16	19	1	44	276	15.33	—	1	8	2882	1251	51	24.52	4-46	—	—
Best, C.A.	8	13	1	164	342	28.50	1	1	8	30	21	0	—	—	—	—
Betancourt, N.	1	2	—	39	52	26.00	—	—	14/3	—	—	—	—	—	—	—
Binns, A.P.	5	8	1	27	64	9.14	—	—	4	—	—	—	—	—	—	—
Birkett, L.S.	4	8	—	64	136	17.00	—	1	4	126	71	1	71.00	1-16	—	—
Bishop, I.R.	18	28	8	30*	231	11.55	—	—	3	3918	1698	83	20.45	6-40	5	1
Boyce, K.D.	21	30	3	95*	657	24.33	—	4	5	3501	1801	60	30.01	6-77	2	—
Browne, C.R.	4	8	1	70*	176	25.14	—	1	1	840	288	6	48.00	2-72	—	—
Butcher, B.F.	44	78	6	209*	3104	43.11	7	16	15	256	90	5	18.00	5-34	1	—
Butler, L.S.	1	1	—	16	16	16.00	—	—	—	240	151	2	75.50	2-151	—	—
Butts, C.G.	7	8	1	38	108	15.42	—	—	2	1554	595	10	59.50	4-73	—	—
Bynoe, M.R.	4	6	—	48	111	18.50	—	—	4	30‡	5	1	5.00	1-5	—	—
Camacho, G.S.	11	22	—	87	640	29.09	—	4	4	18	12	0	—	—	—	—

INDIVIDUAL CAREER RECORDS – WEST INDIES *continued*

				BATTING AND FIELDING						BOWLING						
	Tests	I	NO	HS	Runs	Avge	100	50	Ct/St	Balls	Runs	Wkts	Avge	BB	5wI	10wM
Cameron, F.J.	5	7	1	75*	151	25.16	–	1	–	786	278	3	92.66	2-74	–	–
Cameron, J.H.	2	3	–	5	6	2.00	–	–	–	232	88	3	29.33	3-66	–	–
Carew, G.M.	4	7	1	107	170	28.33	1	–	1	18‡	2	0	–	–	–	–
Carew, M.C.	19	36†	3	109	1127	34.15	1	5	13	1174	437	8	54.62	1-11	–	–
Challenor, G.	3	6	–	46	101	16.83	–	–	–							
Chanderpaul, S.	4	6†	1	77	288	57.60	–	4	3	390	209	1	209.00	1-94	–	–
Chang, H.S.	1	2†	–	6	8	4.00	–	–	–							
Christiani, C.M.	4	7	2	32*	98	19.60	–	–	6/1							
Christiani, R.J.	22	37	3	107	896	26.35	1	4	19/2	234	108	3	36.00	3-52	–	–
Clarke, C.B.	3	4	1	2	3	1.00	–	–	–	456	261	6	43.50	3-59	–	–
Clarke, S.T.	11	16	5	35*	172	15.63	–	–	2	2477	1170	42	27.85	5-126	1	–
Constantine, L.N.	18	33	–	90	635	19.24	–	4	28	3583	1746	58	30.10	5-75	2	–
Croft, C.E.H.	27	37	22	33	158	10.53	–	–	8	6165	2913	125	23.30	8-29	3	–
Cummins, A.C.	3	4	1	14*	31	10.33	–	–	–	270	144	5	28.80	4-54	–	–
Da Costa, O.C.	5	9	1	39	153	19.12	–	–	5	372	175	3	58.33	1-14	–	–
Daniel, W.W.	10	11	4	11	46	6.57	–	–	4	1754	910	36	25.27	5-39	1	–
Davis, B.A.	4	8	–	68	245	30.62	–	3	1							
Davis, C.A.	15	29	5	183	1301	54.20	4	4	4	894	330	2	165.00	1-27	–	–
Davis, W.W.	15	17	4	77	202	15.53	–	1	10	2773	1472	45	32.71	4-19	–	–
De Caires, F.I.	3	6	–	80	232	38.66	–	2	1	12	9	0	–	–	–	–
Depeiza, C.C.	5	8	2	122	187	31.16	1	–	7/4	30	15	0	–	–	–	–
Dewdney, D.T.	9	12	5	5*	17	2.42	–	–	1	1641	807	21	38.42	5-21	1	–
Dowe, U.G.	4	3	2	5*	8	8.00	–	–	3	1014	534	12	44.50	4-69	–	–
Dujon, P.J.L.	81	115	11	139	3322	31.94	5	16	267/5							
Edwards, R.M.	5	8	1	22	65	9.28	–	–	–	1311	626	18	34.77	5-84	1	–
Ferguson, W.	8	10	3	75	200	28.57	–	2	11	2568	1165	34	34.26	6-92	3	1
Fernandes, M.P.	2	4	–	22	49	12.25	–	–	–							
Findlay, T.M.	10	16	3	44*	212	16.30	–	–	19/2							
Foster, M.L.C.	14	24	5	125	580	30.52	1	1	3	1776	600	9	66.66	2-41	–	–
Francis, G.N.	10	18	4	19*	81	5.78	–	–	7	1619	763	23	33.17	4-40	–	–
Frederick, M.C.	1	2	–	30	30	15.00	–	–	–							
Fredericks, R.C.	59	109†	7	169	4334	42.49	8	26	62	1187‡	548	7	78.28	1-12	–	–
Fuller, R.L.	1	1	–	1	1	1.00	–	–	–	48	12	0	–	–	–	–
Furlonge, H.A.	3	5	–	64	99	19.80	–	1	–							

INDIVIDUAL CAREER RECORDS – WEST INDIES *continued*

	Tests	I	NO	HS	Runs	Avge	100	50	Ct/St	Balls	Runs	Wkts	Avge	BB	5wI	10wM
				BATTING AND FIELDING									BOWLING			
Ganteaume, A.G.	1	1	–	112	112	112.00	1	–	–	–	–	–	–	–	–	–
Garner, J.	58	68	14	60	672	12.44	–	1	42	13169	5433	259	20.97	6-56	7	1
Gaskin, B.B.M.	2	3	–	10	17	5.66	–	–	1	474	158	2	79.00	1-15	–	–
Gibbs, G.L.	1	2†	–	12	12	6.00	–	–	1	24‡	7	0	–	–	–	–
Gibbs, L.R.	79	109	39	25	488	6.97	–	–	52	27115	8989	309	29.09	8-38	18	2
Gilchrist, R.	13	14	3	60	60	5.45	–	–	4	3227	1521	57	26.68	6-55	1	–
Gladstone, G.	1	1†	1	12*	12	–	–	–	–	300‡	189	1	189.00	1-139	–	–
Goddard, J.D.C.	27	39†	11	83*	859	30.67	–	4	22	2931	1050	33	31.81	5-31	1	–
Gomes, H.A.	60	91†	11	143	3171	39.63	9	13	18	2401	930	15	62.00	2-20	–	–
Gomez, G.E.	29	46	5	101	1243	30.31	1	8	18	5236	1590	58	27.41	7-55	1	1
Grant, G.C.	12	21	5	71*	413	25.81	–	3	10	24	18	0	–	–	–	–
Grant, R.S.	7	11	1	77	220	22.00	–	1	13	986	353	11	32.09	3-68	–	–
Gray, A.H.	5	8	2	12*	48	8.00	–	–	6	888	377	22	17.13	4-39	–	–
Greenidge, A.E.	6	10	–	69	222	22.20	–	2	5	26	4	0	–	–	–	–
Greenidge, C.G.	108	185	16	226	7558	44.72	19	34	96	156	75	0	–	–	–	–
Greenidge, G.A.	5	9	2	50	209	29.85	–	1	3	30	17	1	17.00	–	–	–
Grell, M.G.	1	2	–	21	34	17.00	–	–	1	–	–	–	–	–	–	–
Griffith, C.C.	28	42	10	54	530	16.56	–	1	16	5631	2683	94	28.54	6-36	5	–
Griffith, H.C.	13	23	5	18	91	5.05	–	–	4	2663	1243	44	28.25	6-103	2	–
Guillen, S.C.	5	6	2	54	104	26.00	–	1	9/2	–	–	–	–	–	–	–
Hall, W.W.	48	66	14	50*	818	15.73	–	2	11	10421	5066	192	26.38	7-69	9	1
Harper, R.A.	25	32	3	74	535	18.44	–	3	36	3615	1291	46	28.06	6-57	1	–
Haynes, D.L.	116	202	25	184	7487	42.29	18	39	65	18	8	1	8.00	1-2	–	–
Headley, G.A.	22	40	4	270*	2190	60.83	10	5	14	398	230	0	–	–	–	–
Headley, R.G.A.	2	4†	–	42	62	15.50	–	–	2	–	–	–	–	–	–	–
Hendriks, J.L.	20	32	8	64	447	18.62	–	2	42/5	–	–	–	–	–	–	–
Hoad, E.L.G.	4	8	–	36	98	12.25	–	–	1	–	–	–	–	–	–	–
Holder, V.A.	40	59	11	42	682	14.20	–	–	16	9095	3627	109	33.27	6-28	3	–
Holding, M.A.	60	76	10	73	910	13.78	–	6	22	12680	5898	249	23.68	8-92	13	2
Holford, D.A.J.	24	39	5	105*	768	22.58	1	3	18	4816	2009	51	39.39	5-23	1	–
Holt, J.K.	17	31	2	166	1066	36.75	2	5	8	30	20	1	20.00	1-20	–	–
Hooper, C.L.	40	67	6	178*	1832	30.03	4	8	40	4559	2010	36	55.83	5-40	1	–
Howard, A.B.	1	–†	–	–	–	–	–	–	–	372	140	2	70.00	2-140	–	–
Hunte, C.C.	44	78	6	260	3245	45.06	8	13	16	270	110	2	55.00	1-17	–	–
Hunte, E.A.C.	3	6	1	58	166	33.20	–	2	5	–	–	–	–	–	–	–
Hylton, L.G.	6	8	2	19	70	11.66	–	1	1	965	418	16	26.12	4-27	–	–

INDIVIDUAL CAREER RECORDS – WEST INDIES *continued*

				BATTING AND FIELDING							BOWLING					
	Tests	I	NO	HS	Runs	Avge	100	50	Ct/St	Balls	Runs	Wkts	Avge	BB	5wI	10wM
Johnson, H.H.H.	3	4	1	22	38	9.50	–	–	1	789	238	13	18.30	5-41	2	1
Johnson, T.F.	1	1†	1	9*	9	–	–	–	1	240‡	129	3	43.00	2-53	–	–
Jones, C.E.L.	4	7†	–	19	63	9.00	–	–	3	102‡	11	0	–	–	–	–
Jones, P.E.	9	11	2	10*	47	5.22	–	–	4	1842	751	25	30.04	5-85	1	–
Julien, B.D.	24	34	6	121	866	30.92	2	3	14	4542‡	1868	50	37.36	5-57	1	–
Jumadeen, R.R.	12	14	10	56	84	21.00	–	1	4	3140‡	1141	29	39.34	4-72	–	–
Kallicharran, A.I.	66	109†	10	187	4399	44.43	12	21	51	406	158	4	39.50	2-16	–	–
Kanhai, R.B.	79	137	6	256	6227	47.53	15	28	50	183	85	0	–	–	–	–
Kentish, E.S.M.	2	2	1	1*	1	1.00	–	–	1	540	178	8	22.25	5-49	1	–
King, C.L.	9	16	3	100*	418	32.15	1	2	5	582	282	3	94.00	1-30	–	–
King, F.M.	14	17	3	21	116	8.28	–	–	5	2869	1159	29	39.96	5-74	1	–
King, L.A.	2	4	–	20	41	10.25	–	–	2	476	154	9	17.11	5-46	1	–
Lambert, C.B.	1	2†	–	39	53	26.50	–	–	2	4	4	1	14.00	1-4	–	–
Lara, B.C.	16	26†	–	375	1628	62.61	3	8	27	12	4	0	–	–	–	–
Lashley, P.D.	4	7†	–	49	159	22.71	–	–	4	18	1	1	1.00	1-1	–	–
Legall, R.A.	4	5	–	23	50	10.00	–	–	8/1	–	–	–	–	–	–	–
Lewis, D.M.	3	5	2	88	259	86.33	–	3	8	–	–	–	–	–	–	–
Lloyd, C.H.	110	175†	14	242*	7515	46.67	19	39	90	1716	622	10	62.20	2-13	–	–
Logie, A.L.	52	78	9	130	2470	35.79	2	16	57	7	4	0	–	–	–	–
McMorris, E.D.A.St J.	13	21	2	125	564	26.85	1	3	5	24	16	1	16.00	1-16	–	–
McWatt, C.A.	6	9†	2	54	202	28.85	–	2	9/1	–						
Madray, I.S.	2	3	–	2	3	1.00	–	–	2	210	108	0	–	–	–	–
Marshall, M.D.	81	107	11	92	1810	18.85	–	10	25	17584	7876	376	20.94	7-22	22	4
Marshall, N.E.	1	2	–	8	8	4.00	–	–	1	279	62	2	31.00	1-22	–	–
Marshall, R.E.	4	7	–	30	143	20.42	–	–	1	52	15	0	–	–	–	–
Martin, F.R.	9	18†	1	123*	486	28.58	1	–	2	1346‡	619	8	77.37	3-91	–	–
Martindale, E.A.	10	14	3	22	58	5.27	–	–	5	1605	804	37	21.72	5-22	3	–
Mattis, E.H.	4	5	1	71	145	29.00	–	1		36	14	0	–	–	–	–
Mendonca, I.L.	2	2	–	78	81	40.50	–	1	8/2	–						
Merry, C.A.	2	2	–	13	34	8.50	–	–	1	–						
Miller, R.	1	1	–	23	23	23.00	–	–	1	96	28	0	–	–	–	–
Moseley, E.A	2	4	–	26	35	8.75	–	–		522	261	6	43.50	2-70	–	–
Mudie, G.H.	1	1†	–	5	5	5.00	–	–	1	174‡	40	3	13.33	2-23	–	–
Murray, D.A.	19	31	3	84	601	21.46	–	3	57/5	–						
Murray, D.L.	62	96	9	91	1993	22.90	–	11	181/8	–						

INDIVIDUAL CAREER RECORDS – WEST INDIES *continued*

	Tests	I	NO	HS	Runs	Avge	100	50	Ct/St	Balls	Runs	Wkts	Avge	BB	5wI	10wM
					BATTING AND FIELDING								*BOWLING*			
Murray, J.R.	12	15	2	49*	223	17.15	–	–	42/1	–						
Nanan, R.	1	2	–	8	16	8.00	–	–	2	216	91	4	22.75	2-37	–	–
Neblett, J.M.	1	2†	1	11*	16	16.00	–	–	–	216‡	75	1	75.00	1-44	–	–
Noreiga, J.M.	4	5	2	9	11	3.66	–	–	2	1322	493	17	29.00	9-95	2	–
Nunes, R.K.	4	8†	–	92	245	30.62	–	2	2	–						
Nurse, S.M.	29	54	1	258	2523	47.60	6	10	21	42	7	0	–			
Padmore, A.L.	2	2	1	8*	8	8.00	–	–	–	474	135	1	135.00	1-36	–	–
Pairaudeau, B.H.	13	21	–	115	454	21.61	1	3	6	6	3	0	–	–	–	–
Parry, D.R.	12	20	3	65	381	22.41	–	3	4	1909	936	23	40.69	5-15	1	–
Passailaigue, C.C.	1	2	1	44	46	46.00	–	–	3	12	15	0	–	–	–	–
Patterson, B.P.	28	38	16	21*	145	6.59	–	–	5	4829	2875	93	30.91	5-24	5	–
Payne, T.R.O.	1	1†	–	5	5	5.00	–	–	5	–						
Philip, N.	9	15	5	47	297	29.70	–	–	5	1820	1041	28	37.17	4-48	–	–
Pierre, L.R.	1	–	–	–	–	–	–	–	1	42	28	0	–	–	–	–
Rae, A.F.	15	24†	2	109	1016	46.18	4	4	10	–						
Ramadhin, S.	43	58	14	44	361	8.20	–	–	9	13939	4579	158	28.98	7-49	10	1
Richards, I.V.A.	121	182	12	291	8540	50.23	24	45	122	5170	1964	32	61.37	2-17	–	–
Richardson, R.B.	76	130	11	194	5445	45.75	15	25	82	66	18	0	–	–	–	–
Rickards, K.R.	2	3	–	67	104	34.66	–	1	–	–						
Roach, C.A.	16	32	1	209	952	30.70	2	6	5	222	103	2	51.50	1-18	–	–
Roberts, A.M.E.	47	62	11	68	762	14.94	–	3	9	11135	5174	202	25.61	7-54	11	2
Roberts, A.T.	1	2	–	28	28	14.00	–	–	–	–						
Rodriguez, W.V.	5	7	–	50	96	13.71	–	1	3	573	374	7	53.42	3-51	–	–
Rowe, L.G.	30	49	2	302	2047	43.55	7	7	17	86	44	0	–	–	–	–
St Hill, E.L.	2	4	–	12	18	4.50	–	–	–	558	221	3	73.66	2-110	–	–
St Hill, W.H.	3	6	–	38	117	19.50	–	–	1	12	9	0	–	–	–	–
Scarlett, R.O.	3	4	1	29*	54	18.00	–	–	2	804	209	2	104.50	1-46	–	–
Scott, A.P.H.	1	1	–	5	5	5.00	–	–	–	264	140	0	–	–	–	–
Scott, O.C.	8	13	3	35	171	17.10	–	–	–	1405	925	22	42.04	5-266	1	–
Sealey, B.J.	1	2	–	29	41	20.50	–	–	–	30	10	1	10.00	1-10	–	–
Sealy, J.E.D.	11	19	2	92	478	28.11	–	3	6/1	156	94	3	31.33	2-7	–	–
Shepherd, J.N.	5	8	–	32	77	9.62	–	–	4	1445	479	19	25.21	5-104	1	–
Shillingford, G.C.	7	8†	1	25	57	8.14	–	–	2	1181	537	15	35.80	3-63	–	–
Shillingford, I.T.	4	7	–	120	218	31.14	1	–	1	–						

INDIVIDUAL CAREER RECORDS – WEST INDIES continued

	Tests	I	NO	HS	Runs	Avge	100	50	Ct/St	Balls	Runs	Wkts	Avge	BB	5wI	10wM
													BOWLING			
				BATTING AND FIELDING												
Shivnarine, S.	8	14	1	63	379	29.15	–	4	6	336‡	167	1	167.00	1-13	–	–
Simmons, P.V.	19	35	2	110	807	24.45	1	2	15	396	158	2	79.00	2-34	–	–
Singh, C.K.	2	3†	–	11	11	3.66	–	–	2	506‡	166	5	33.20	2-28	–	–
Small, J.A.	3	6	1	52	79	13.16	–	1	2	366	184	3	61.33	2-67	–	–
Small, M.A.	2	1	1	3*	3	–	–	–	3	270	153	4	38.25	3-40	–	–
Smith, C.W.	5	10	1	55	222	24.66	–	1	4/1	–	–	–	–	–	–	–
Smith, O.G.	26	42	0	168	1331	31.69	4	6	9	4431	1625	48	33.85	5-90	1	–
Sobers, G.St A.	93	160†	21	365*	8032	57.78	26	30	109	21599‡	7999	235	34.03	6-73	6	–
Solomon, J.S.	27	46	7	100*	1326	34.00	1	9	13	702	268	4	67.00	1-20	–	–
Stayers, S.C.	4	4	1	35*	58	19.33	–	–	–	636	364	9	40.44	3-65	–	–
Stollmeyer, J.B.	32	56	5	160	2159	42.33	4	12	20	990	507	13	39.00	3-32	–	–
Stollmeyer, V.H.	1	1	–	96	96	96.00	–	1	–	–	–	–	–	–	–	–
Taylor, J.	3	5	3	4*	4	2.00	–	–	–	672	273	10	27.30	5-109	1	–
Trim, J.	4	5	1	12	21	5.25	–	–	2	794	291	18	16.16	5-34	1	–
Valentine, A.L.	36	51	21	14	141	4.70	–	–	13	12953‡	4215	139	30.32	8-104	8	2
Valentine, V.A.	2	4	1	19*	35	11.66	–	–	–	288	104	1	104.00	1-55	–	–
Walcott, C.L.	44	74	7	220	3798	56.68	15	14	53/11	1194	408	11	37.09	3-50	–	–
Walcott, L.A.	1	2	1	24	40	40.00	–	–	–	48	32	1	32.00	1-17	–	–
Walsh, C.A.	65	88	27	30*	560	9.18	–	–	9	13197	5824	222	26.23	6-62	6	1
Watson, C.D.	7	6	1	5	12	2.40	–	–	1	1458	724	19	38.10	4-62	–	–
Weekes, E.de C.	48	81	5	207	4455	58.61	15	19	49	122	77	1	77.00	1-8	–	–
Weekes, K.H.	2	3†	–	137	173	57.66	1	–	–	–	–	–	–	–	–	–
White, A.W.	2	4	1	57*	71	23.66	–	1	1	491	152	3	50.66	2-34	–	–
Wight, C.V.	2	4	1	23	67	22.33	–	1	1	30	6	0	–	–	–	–
Wight, G.L.	1	1	–	21	21	21.00	–	–	–	–	–	–	–	–	–	–
Wiles, C.A.	1	2	–	2	2	1.00	–	–	–	–	–	–	–	–	–	–
Willett, E.T.	5	8†	3	26	74	14.80	–	–	5	1326‡	482	11	43.81	3-33	–	–
Williams, A.B.	7	12	–	111	469	39.08	2	1	5	–	–	–	–	–	–	–
Williams, D.	3	6	–	15	21	3.50	–	–	15/1	–	–	–	–	–	–	–
Williams, E.A.V.	4	6	1	72	113	18.83	–	1	2	796	241	9	26.77	3-51	–	–
Williams, S.C.	1	2	1	21*	24	24.00	–	–	–	–	–	–	–	–	–	–
Wishart, K.L.	1	2†	–	52	52	26.00	–	1	–	–	–	–	–	–	–	–
Worrell, F.M.M.	51	87	9	261	3860	49.48	9	22	43	7141‡	2672	69	38.72	7-70	2	–

INDIVIDUAL CAREER RECORDS – NEW ZEALAND

NEW ZEALAND (190 players)	Tests	I	NO	HS	Runs	Avge	100	50	Ct/St	Balls	Runs	Wkts	Avge	BB	5wI	10wM
Alabaster, J.C.	21	34	6	34	272	9.71	–	–	7	3992	1863	49	38.02	4-46	–	–
Allcott, C.F.W.	6	7†	2	33	113	22.60		–	3	1206‡	541	6	90.16	2-102	–	–
Anderson, R.W.	9	18	–	92	423	23.50		3	1	–						
Anderson, W.M.	1	2†	–	4	5	2.50		–	1	–						
Andrews, B.	2	3	2	17	22	22.00		–	1	256	154	2	77.00	2-40		–
Badcock, F.T.	7	9	2	64	137	19.57	–	2	1	1608	610	16	38.12	4-80		–
Barber, R.T.	1	2	–	12	17	8.50		–	1	–						
Bartlett, G.A.	10	18	1	40	263	15.47	–	–	8	1768	792	24	33.00	6-38	1	–
Barton, P.T.	7	14	–	109	285	20.35	1	1	4	–						
Beard, D.D.	4	7	2	31	101	20.20	–	–	2	806	302	9	33.55	3-22		–
Beck, J.E.F.	8	15†	–	99	394	26.26	–	3	2	–						
Bell, W.	2	3	3	21*	21	–		–	1	491	235	2	117.50	1-54		–
Bilby, G.P.	2	4	–	28	55	13.75	–	–	3							
Blain, T.E.	11	20	3	78	456	26.82	–	2	19/2							
Blair, R.W.	19	34	6	64*	189	6.75	–	1	5	3525	1515	43	35.23	4-85	–	–
Blunt, R.C.	9	13	1	96	330	27.50	–	1	5	936	472	12	39.33	3-17	–	–
Bolton, B.A.	2	3	–	33	59	19.66		–	1							
Boock, S.L.	30	41	8	37	207	6.27	–	–	14	6598‡	2564	74	34.64	7-87	4	–
Bracewell, B.P.	6	12	2	8	24	2.40	–	–	1	1036	585	14	41.78	3-110	–	–
Bracewell, J.G.	41	60	11	110	1001	20.42	1	4	31	8403	3653	102	35.81	6-32	4	1
Bradburn, G.E.	5	9	2	30*	105	15.00	–	–	4	615	336	5	67.20	3-134	–	–
Bradburn, W.P.	2	4	–	32	62	15.50		–	2							
Brown, V.R.	2	3†	1	36*	51	25.50		–	3	342	176	1	176.00	1-17	–	–
Burgess, M.G.	50	92	6	119*	2684	31.20	5	14	34	498	212	6	35.33	3-23	–	–
Burke, C.	1	2	–	3	4	2.00	–	–	–	66	30	2	15.00	2-30	–	–
Burtt, T.B.	10	15	3	42	252	21.00	–	–	2	2593‡	1170	33	35.45	6-162	3	–
Butterfield, L.A.	1	2	–	0	0	0.00		–	–	78	24	0	–	–	–	–
Cairns, B.L.	43	65	8	64	928	16.28	–	2	30	10628	4280	130	32.91	7-74	6	1
Cairns, C.L.	10	17	–	78	349	20.52	–	2	6	1995	1207	28	43.10	6-52	2	–
Cameron, F.J.	19	30	20	27*	116	11.60	–	–	2	4570	1849	62	29.82	5-34	3	–
Cave, H.B.	19	31	5	22*	229	8.80	–	–	8	4074	1467	34	43.14	4-21	–	–
Chapple, M.E.	14	27	1	76	497	19.11	–	3	10	248‡	84	1	84.00	1-24	–	–
Chatfield, E.J.	43	54	33	21*	180	8.57	–	–	7	10360	3958	123	32.17	6-73	3	1

INDIVIDUAL CAREER RECORDS – NEW ZEALAND continued

	Tests	I	NO	HS	Runs	Avge	100	50	Ct/St	Balls	Runs	Wkts	Avge	BB	5wI	10wM
				BATTING AND FIELDING							BOWLING					
Cleverley, D.C.	2	4†	3	10*	19	19.00	–	–	–	222	130	0	–	–	–	–
Collinge, R.O.	35	50	13	68*	533	14.40	–	2	10	7689‡	3392	116	29.25	6-63	3	–
Colquhoun, I.A.	2	4	2	1*	1	0.50	–	–	4	–	–	–	–	–	–	–
Coney, J.V.	52	85	14	174*	2668	37.57	3	16	64	2835	966	27	35.77	3-28	–	–
Congdon, B.E.	61	114	7	176	3448	32.22	7	19	44	5620	2154	59	36.50	5-65	1	–
Cowie, J.	9	13	4	45	90	10.00	–	–	3	2028	969	45	21.53	6-40	4	1
Cresswell, G.F.	3	5†	3	12*	14	7.00	–	–	–	650	292	13	22.46	6-168	1	1
Cromb, I.B.	5	8	2	51*	123	20.50	–	1	1	960	442	8	55.25	3-113	–	–
Crowe, J.J.	39	65	4	128	1601	26.24	3	6	41	18	9	0	–	–	–	–
Crowe, M.D.	70	120	11	299	5230	47.98	17	17	63	1377	676	14	48.28	2-25	–	–
Cunis, R.S.	20	31	8	51	295	12.82	–	1	1	4250	1887	51	37.00	6-76	1	–
D'Arcy, J.W.	5	10	–	33	136	13.60	–	–	–	126	93	1	93.00	1-93	–	–
Davis, H.T.	1	2	2	0*	0	–	–	–	–	862	425	8	53.12	3-40	–	–
De Groen, R.P.	4	8	4	6	19	4.75	–	–	–	5	10	0	–	–	–	–
Dempster, C.S.	10	15	4	136	723	65.72	2	5	2	–	–	–	–	–	–	–
Dempster, E.W.	5	8†	2	47	106	17.66	–	–	1	544‡	219	2	109.50	1-24	–	–
Dick, A.E.	17	30	4	50*	370	14.23	–	1	47/4	–	–	–	–	–	–	–
Dickinson, G.R.	3	5	1	11	31	6.20	–	–	3	451	245	8	30.62	3-66	–	–
Donnelly, M.P.	7	12†	1	206	582	52.90	1	4	7	30‡	20	0	–	–	–	–
Doull, S.B.	6	10	2	29	115	11.50	–	–	5	966	573	16	35.81	5-66	1	–
Dowling, G.T.	39	77	3	239	2306	31.16	3	11	23	36	19	1	19.00	1-19	–	–
Dunning, J.A.	4	6	1	19	38	7.60	–	–	2	830	493	5	98.60	2-35	–	–
Edgar, B.A.	39	68†	4	161	1958	30.59	3	12	14	18	3	0	–	–	–	–
Edwards, G.N.	8	15	1	55	377	25.13	–	3	7	–	–	–	–	–	–	–
Emery, R.W.G.	2	4	–	28	46	11.50	–	–	–	46	52	2	26.00	2-52	–	–
Fisher, F.E.	1	2	–	14	23	11.50	–	–	–	204‡	78	1	78.00	1-78	–	–
Fleming, S.P.	4	8†	–	92	278	34.75	–	2	3	–	–	–	–	–	–	–
Foley, H.	1	2†	–	2	4	2.00	–	–	–	–	–	–	–	–	–	–
Franklin, T.J.	21	37	1	101	828	23.00	1	4	8	–	–	–	–	–	–	–
Freeman, D.L.	2	2	–	1	2	1.00	–	–	–	240	169	1	169.00	1-91	–	–
Gallichan, N.	1	2	–	30	32	16.00	–	–	–	264‡	113	3	37.66	3-99	–	–
Gedye, S.G.	4	8	–	55	193	24.12	–	2	–	–	–	–	–	–	–	–
Gillespie, S.R.	1	1	–	28	28	28.00	–	–	–	162	79	1	79.00	1-79	–	–
Gray, E.J.	10	16	1	50	248	15.50	–	1	6	2076‡	886	17	52.11	3-73	–	–

INDIVIDUAL CAREER RECORDS – NEW ZEALAND continued

				BATTING AND FIELDING						BOWLING						
	Tests	I	NO	HS	Runs	Avge	100	50	Ct/St	Balls	Runs	Wkts	Avge	BB	5wI	10wM
Greatbatch, M.J.	34	61†	5	146*	1858	33.17	3	9	25	6	0	0	–	–	–	–
Guillen, S.C.	3	6	1	41	98	16.33	–	–	4/1	–	–	–				
Guy, J.W.	12	23†	2	102	440	20.95	1	3	2	–	–	–				
Hadlee, D.R.	26	42	5	56	530	14.32	–	1	8	4883	2389	71	33.64	4-30	–	–
Hadlee, R.J.	86	134†	19	151*	3124	27.16	2	15	39	21918	9612	431	22.29	9-52	36	9
Hadlee, W.A.	11	19	1	116	543	30.16	1	2	6	–						
Harford, N.S.	8	15	–	93	229	15.26	–	2	–	–						
Harford, R.I.	3	5†	2	6	7	2.33	–	–	11	–						
Harris, C.Z.	5	10†	1	56	116	12.88	–	1	2	132	103	0	–	–	–	–
Harris, P.G.Z.	9	18	1	101	378	22.23	1	1	6	42	14	0	–	–	–	–
Harris, R.M.	2	3	–	13	31	10.33	–	–	–	–						
Hart, M.N.	6	10†	3	36	161	23.00	–	1	3	1439‡	563	11	51.18	3-47	–	–
Hartland, B.R.	9	18	–	52	303	16.83	–	1	5	–						
Haslam, M.J.	2	1†	1	3	3	3.00	–	–	2	300‡	153	1	153.00	1-33	–	–
Hastings, B.F.	31	56	6	117*	1510	30.20	4	7	23	22	9	0	–	–	–	–
Hayes, J.A.	15	22	7	19	73	4.86	–	–	3	2675	1217	30	40.56	4-36	–	–
Henderson, M.	1	2†	1	6	8	8.00	–	–	1	90‡	64	2	32.00	2-38	–	–
Horne, P.A.	4	7†	–	27	71	10.14	–	–	3	–						
Hough, K.W.	2	3	2	31*	62	62.00	–	–	1	462	175	6	29.16	3-79	–	–
Howarth, G.P.	47	83	5	147	2531	32.44	6	11	29	614	271	3	90.33	1-13	–	–
Howarth, H.J.	30	42†	18	61	291	12.12	–	1	33	8833‡	3178	86	36.95	5-34	2	–
James, K.C.	11	13	2	14	52	4.72	–	–	11/5	–						
Jarvis, T.W.	13	22	1	182	625	29.76	1	2	3	12	3	0	–	–	–	–
Jones, A.H.	37	70	7	186	2898	46.00	7	11	25	250	144	1	144.00	1-40	–	–
Kerr, J.L.	7	12	1	59	212	19.27	–	1	4	–						
Kuggeleijn, C.M.	2	4	–	7	7	1.75	–	–	1	97	67	1	67.00	1-50	–	–
Larsen, G.R.	1	2	–	8	10	5.00	–	–	2	268	116	2	58.00	2-116	–	–
Latham, R.T.	4	7	–	119	219	31.28	1	1	5	18	6	0	–	–	–	–
Lees, W.K.	21	37	4	152	778	23.57	1	1	52/7	5	4	0	–	–	–	–
Leggat, I.B.	1	1	–	0	0	0.00	–	–	2	24	6	0	–	–	–	–
Leggat, J.G.	9	18	2	61	351	21.93	–	2	–	–						
Lissette, A.F.	2	4	2	1*	2	1.00	–	–	1	288‡	124	3	41.33	2-73	–	–
Lowry, T.C.	7	8	–	80	223	27.87	–	2	8	12	5	0	–	–	–	–

INDIVIDUAL CAREER RECORDS – NEW ZEALAND continued

				BATTING AND FIELDING						BOWLING						
	Tests	I	NO	HS	Runs	Avge	100	50	Ct/St	Balls	Runs	Wkts	Avge	BB	5wI	10wM
McEwan, P.E.	4	7	1	40*	96	16.00	–	–	5	36	13	0	–	–	–	–
MacGibbon, A.R.	26	46	5	66	814	19.85	–	3	13	5659	2160	70	30.85	5-64	1	–
McGirr, H.M.	2	1	–	51	51	51.00	–	1	–	180	115	1	115.00	1-65	–	–
McGregor, S.N.	25	47	2	111	892	19.82	1	3	9	–	–	–	–	–	–	–
McLeod, E.G.	1	2†	1	16	18	18.00	–	–	–	12	5	0	–	–	–	–
McMahon, T.G.	5	7	4	4*	7	2.33	–	–	7/1	–	–	–	–	–	–	–
McRae, D.A.N.	1	2†	1	8	8	4.00	–	–	–	84‡	44	0	–	–	–	–
Matheson, A.M.	2	1	–	7	7	7.00	–	–	2	282	136	2	68.00	2-7	–	–
Meale, T.	2	4†	–	10	21	5.25	–	–	–	–	–	–	–	–	–	–
Merritt, W.E.	6	8	1	19	73	10.42	–	–	2	936	617	12	51.41	4-104	–	–
Meuli, E.M.	1	2	–	23	38	19.00	–	–	–	–	–	–	–	–	–	–
Milburn, B.D.	3	3	2	4*	8	8.00	–	–	6/2	–	–	–	–	–	–	–
Miller, L.S.M.	13	25†	1	47	346	13.84	–	–	1	2	1	0	–	–	–	–
Mills, J.E.	7	10†	1	117	241	26.77	1	1	2	–	–	–	–	–	–	–
Moir, A.M.	17	30	8	41*	327	14.86	–	–	2	2650	1418	28	50.64	6-155	2	–
Moloney, D.A.R.	3	6	–	64	156	26.00	–	1	3	12	9	0	–	–	–	–
Mooney, F.L.H.	14	22	2	46	343	17.15	–	–	22/8	8	0	0	–	–	–	–
Morgan, R.W.	20	34	1	97	734	22.24	–	5	12	1114	609	5	121.80	1-16	–	–
Morrison, B.D.	1	2†	–	10	10	5.00	–	–	1	186	129	2	64.50	2-129	–	–
Morrison, D.K.	35	51	16	42	260	7.42	–	–	13	7532	4181	120	34.84	7-89	8	–
Morrison, J.F.M.	17	29	–	117	656	22.62	1	3	9	264‡	71	2	35.50	2-52	–	–
Motz, R.C.	32	56	3	60	612	11.54	–	3	9	7034	3148	100	31.48	6-63	5	–
Murray, B.A.G.	13	26	1	90	598	23.92	–	5	21	6	0	1	0.00	1-0	–	1
Nash, D.J.	6	9	5	56	128	32.00	–	1	6	1296	651	21	31.00	6-76	2	–
Newman, J.	3	4	–	19	33	8.25	–	–	–	425‡	254	2	127.00	2-76	–	–
O'Sullivan, D.R.	11	21	4	23*	158	9.29	–	–	2	2744‡	1224	18	67.83	5-148	1	–
Overton, G.W.F.	3	6†	1	3*	8	1.60	–	–	1	729	258	9	28.66	3-65	–	–
Owens, M.B.	8	12	6	8*	16	2.66	–	–	3	1074	585	17	34.41	4-99	–	–
Page, M.L.	14	20	1	104	492	24.60	1	2	6	379	231	5	46.20	2-21	–	–
Parker, J.M.	36	63	2	121	1498	24.55	3	5	30	40	24	1	24.00	1-24	–	–
Parker, N.M.	3	6	–	40	89	14.83	–	–	2	–	–	–	–	–	–	–
Parore, A.C.	12	21	2	71	408	21.47	–	2	34/2	–	–	–	–	–	–	–
Patel, D.N.	25	47	6	99	848	20.68	–	3	8	4050	2030	45	45.11	6-50	3	–
Petherick, P.J.	6	11	4	13	34	4.85	–	–	4	1305	681	16	42.81	3-90	–	–
Petrie, E.C.	14	25	5	55	258	12.90	–	1	25	–	–	–	–	–	–	–

INDIVIDUAL CAREER RECORDS – NEW ZEALAND continued

			BATTING AND FIELDING							BOWLING						
	Tests	I	NO	HS	Runs	Avge	100	50	Ct/St	Balls	Runs	Wkts	Avge	BB	5wI	10wM
Playle, W.R.	8	15	–	65	151	10.06	–	1	4	–	–	–	–	–	–	–
Pocock, B.A.	6	12	–	34	135	11.25	–	–	1	12	10	0	–	–	–	–
Pollard, V.	32	59	7	116	1266	24.34	2	7	19	4421	1853	40	46.32	3-3	–	–
Poore, M.B.	14	24	1	45	355	15.43	–	–	1	788	367	9	40.77	2-28	–	–
Priest, M.W.	1	1†	–	26	26	26.00	–	–	–	72‡	26	1	26.00	1-26	–	–
Pringle, C.	11	16	2	24*	135	9.64	–	–	2	2505	1191	26	45.80	7-52	1	1
Puna, N.	3	5	3	18*	31	15.50	–	–	1	480	240	4	60.00	2-40	–	–
Rabone, G.O.	12	20	2	107	562	31.22	1	2	5	1385	635	16	39.68	6-68	1	–
Redmond, R.E.	1	2†	–	107	163	81.50	1	1	–	–	7	–	–	–	–	–
Reid, J.F.	19	31†	3	180	1296	46.28	6	2	9	18	–	0	–	–	–	–
Reid, J.R.	58	108	5	142	3428	33.28	6	22	43/1	7725	2835	85	33.35	6-60	1	–
Roberts, A.D.G.	7	12	1	84*	254	23.09	–	1	4	440	182	4	45.50	1-12	–	–
Roberts, A.W.	5	10	1	66*	248	27.55	–	3	4	459	209	7	29.85	4-101	–	–
Robertson, G.K.	1	1	–	12	12	12.00	–	–	–	144	91	1	91.00	1-91	–	–
Rowe, C.G.	1	2	–	0	0	0.00	–	–	1	–	–	–	–	–	–	–
Rutherford, K.R.	48	85	7	107*	2119	27.16	3	15	29	256	161	1	161.00	1-38	–	–
Scott, R.H.	1	1	–	18	18	18.00	–	–	–	138	74	1	74.00	1-74	–	–
Scott, V.J.	10	17	1	84	458	28.62	–	3	7	18	14	0	–	–	–	–
Shrimpton, M.J.F.	10	19	–	46	265	13.94	–	–	2	257	158	5	31.60	3-35	–	–
Sinclair, B.W.	21	40	1	138	1148	29.43	3	3	8	60	32	2	16.00	2-32	–	–
Sinclair, I.M.	2	4†	1	18*	25	8.33	–	–	1	233	120	1	120.00	1-79	–	–
Smith, F.B.	4	6	–	96	237	47.40	–	2	1	–	–	–	–	–	–	–
Smith, H.D.	1	1	–	4	4	4.00	–	–	–	120	113	1	113.00	1-113	–	–
Smith, I.D.S.	63	88	17	173	1815	25.56	2	6	168/8	18	5	0	–	–	–	–
Snedden, C.A.	1	–	–	–	–	–	–	–	–	96	46	0	–	–	–	–
Snedden, M.C.	25	30†	8	33*	327	14.86	–	1	7	4775	2199	58	37.91	5-68	1	–
Sparling, J.T.	11	20	2	50	229	12.72	–	1	3	708	327	5	65.40	1-9	–	–
Stirling, D.A.	6	9	2	26	108	15.42	–	–	1	902	601	13	46.23	4-88	–	–
Su'a, M.L.	11	15†	4	44	131	11.90	–	–	6	2298‡	1058	32	33.06	5-73	2	–
Sutcliffe, B.	42	76†	8	230*	2727	40.10	5	15	20	538‡	344	4	86.00	2-38	–	–
Taylor, B.R.	30	50†	6	124	898	20.40	2	2	10	6334	2953	111	26.60	7-74	4	–
Taylor, D.D.	3	5	–	77	159	31.80	–	1	2	–	–	–	–	–	–	–
Thomson, K.	2	4	1	69	94	31.33	–	1	–	–	–	–	–	–	–	–
Thomson, S.A.	11	22	4	120*	643	35.72	1	3	6	21	9	1	9.00	1-9	–	–
Tindill, E.W.T.	5	9†	1	37*	73	9.12	–	–	6/1	1318	659	13	50.69	3-63	–	–

INDIVIDUAL CAREER RECORDS – NEW ZEALAND *continued*

	Tests	I	NO	HS	Runs	Avge	100	50	Ct/St	Balls	Runs	Wkts	BOWLING Avge	BB	5wI	10wM
Troup, G.B.	15	18	6	13*	55	4.58	–	–	2	3183‡	1454	39	37.28	6-95	1	1
Truscott, P.B.	1	2	–	26	29	14.50	–	–	1	–	5	0	–	–	–	–
Turner, G.M.	41	73	6	259	2991	44.64	7	14	42	12						
Vance, R.H.	4	7	1	68	207	29.57	–	1	1							
Vaughan, J.T.C.	1	2†	1	17	17	17.00	–	–	1	84	56	0	–	–	–	–
Vivian, G.E.	5	6†	–	43	110	18.33	–	–	3	198	107	1	107.00	1-14	–	–
Vivian, H.G.	7	10†	–	100	421	42.10	1	5	4	1311‡	633	17	37.23	4-58	–	–
Wadsworth, K.J.	33	51	4	80	1010	21.48	–	5	92/4							
Wallace, W.M.	13	21	–	66	439	20.90	–	5	5	6	5	0	–	–	–	–
Ward, J.T.	8	12	6	35*	75	12.50	–	–	16/1	–						
Watson, W.	15	18	–	11	60	5.00	–	–	4	3486	1387	40	34.67	6-78	1	–
Watt, L.	1	2	–	2	2	1.00	–	–	–							
Webb, M.G.	3	2	–	12	12	6.00	–	–	1	732	471	4	117.75	2-114	–	–
Webb, P.N.	2	3	–	5	11	3.66	–	–	2							
Weir, G.L.	11	16	2	74*	416	29.71	–	3	3	342	209	7	29.85	3-38	–	–
White, D.J.	2	4	–	18	31	7.75	–	–	1	3	5	0	–	–	–	–
Whitelaw, P.E.	2	4	2	30	64	32.00	–	–	–	–						
Wright, J.G.	82	148†	7	185	5334	37.82	12	23	38	30	5	0	–	–	–	–
Young, B.A.	8	16	–	120	575	35.93	1	4	15	–						
Yuile, B.W.	17	33	6	64	481	17.81	–	1	12	2897‡	1213	34	35.67	4-43	–	–

INDIVIDUAL CAREER RECORDS – INDIA

INDIA (200 players)	Tests	I	NO	BATTING AND FIELDING HS	Runs	Avge	100	50	Ct/St	Balls	BOWLING Runs	Wkts	Avge	BB	5wI	10wM
Abdul Hafeez – *see* Kardar, A.H.																
Abid Ali, S.	29	53	3	81	1018	20.36	–	6	32	4164	1980	47	42.12	6-55	1	–
Adhikari, H.R.	21	36	8	114*	872	31.14	1	4	8	170	82	3	27.33	3-68	–	–
Amarnath, L.	24	40	4	118	878	24.38	1	4	13	4241	1481	45	32.91	5-96	2	–
Amarnath, M.	69	113	10	138	4378	42.50	11	24	47	3676	1782	32	55.68	4-63	–	–
Amarnath, S.	10	18†	1	124	550	30.55	1	3	4	11	5	1	5.00	1-5	–	–
Amar Singh, L.	7	14	1	51	292	22.46	–	1	3	2182	858	28	30.64	7-86	2	–
Amir Elahi	1	2	–	13	17	8.50	–	–	–							
Amre, P.K.	11	13	3	103	425	42.50	1	3	9							
Ankola, S.A.	1	1	–	6	6	6.00	–	–	–	180	128	2	64.00	1-35	–	–
Apte, A.L.	1	2	–	8	15	7.50	–	–	–							
Apte, M.L.	7	13	2	163*	542	49.27	1	3	2	6	3	0	–	–	–	–
Arshad Ayub	13	19	4	57	257	17.13	–	1	2	3663	1438	41	35.07	5-50	3	–
Arun, B.	2	2	1	2*	4	4.00	–	–	2	252	116	4	29.00	3-76	–	–
Arun Lal	16	29	1	93	729	26.03	1	6	13	16	7	0	–	–	–	–
Azad, K.	7	12	1	24	135	11.25	–	–	3	750	373	3	124.33	2-84	–	–
Azharuddin, M.	62	88	3	199	4020	47.29	14	13	61	7	12	0	–	–	–	–
Baig, A.A.	10	18	–	112	428	23.77	1	2	6	18	15	0	–	–	–	–
Banerjee, S.A.	1	1	–	0	0	0.00	–	–	3	306	181	5	36.20	4-120	–	–
Banerjee, S.N.	1	2	–	8	13	6.50	–	–	–	273	127	5	25.40	4-54	–	–
Banerjee, S.T.	1	1	–	3	3	3.00	–	–	–	108	47	3	15.66	3-47	–	–
Baqa Jilani, M.	1	2	–	12	16	16.00	–	–	–	90	55	0	–	–	–	–
Bedi, B.S.	67	101	28	50*	656	8.98	–	1	26	21364‡	7637	266	28.71	7-98	14	1
Bhandari, P.	3	4	1	39	77	19.25	–	–	1	78	39	0	–	–	–	–
Bhat, A.R.	2	3†	1	6	6	3.00	–	–	–	438‡	151	4	37.75	2-65	–	–
Binny, R.M.H.	27	41	5	83*	830	23.05	–	5	11	2870	1534	47	32.63	6-56	2	–
Borde, C.G.	55	97	11	177*	3061	35.59	5	18	37	5695	2417	52	46.48	5-88	1	–
Chandrasekhar, B.S.	58	80	39	22	167	4.07	–	–	25	15963	7199	242	29.74	8-79	16	2
Chauhan, C.P.S.	40	68	2	97	2084	31.57	–	16	38	174	106	2	53.00	1-4	–	–
Chauhan, R.K.	11	7	2	15*	58	11.60	–	–	8	2687	937	30	31.23	3-8	–	–
Chowdhury, N.R.	2	2	1	3*	3	3.00	–	–	–	516	205	1	205.00	1-130	–	–
Colah, S.H.M.	2	4	–	31	69	17.25	–	–	2							
Contractor, N.J.	31	52†	1	108	1611	31.58	1	11	18	186	80	1	80.00	1-9	–	–

INDIVIDUAL CAREER RECORDS – INDIA continued

	Tests	I	NO	HS	Runs	Avge	100	50	Ct/St	Balls	Runs	Wkts	Avge	BB	5wI	10wM
					BATTING AND FIELDING								BOWLING			
Dani, H.T.	1	–	–	–	–	–	–	–	–	60	19	1	19.00	1-9	–	–
Desai, R.B.	28	44	13	85	418	13.48	–	1	9	5597	2761	74	37.31	6-56	2	–
Dilawar Hussain	3	6	–	59	254	42.33	–	3	6/1	–						
Divecha, R.V.	5	5	–	26	60	12.00	–	–	5	1044	361	11	32.81	3-102	–	–
Doshi, D.R.	33	38†	10	20	129	4.60	–	–	10	9322‡	3502	114	30.71	6-102	6	–
Durani, S.A.	29	50†	2	104	1202	25.04	1	7	14	6446‡	2657	75	35.42	6-73	3	1
Engineer, F.M.	46	87	3	121	2611	31.08	2	16	66/16	–						
Gadkari, C.V.	6	10	4	50*	129	21.50	–	1	6	102	45	0	–	–	–	–
Gaekwad, A.D.	40	70	4	201	1985	30.07	2	10	15	334	187	2	93.50	1-4	–	–
Gaekwad, D.K.	11	20	1	52	350	18.42	–	1	5	12	12	0	–	–	–	–
Gaekwad, H.G.	1	2†	–	14	22	11.00	–	–	–	222‡	47	0	–	–	–	–
Gandotra, A.	2	4†	–	18	54	13.50	–	–	1	6‡	5	0	–	–	–	–
Gavaskar, S.M.	125	214	16	236*	10122	51.12	34	45	108	380	206	1	206.00	1-34	–	–
Ghavri, K.D.	39	57†	14	86	913	21.23	–	2	16	7036‡	3656	109	33.54	5-33	4	–
Ghorpade, J.M.	8	15	–	41	229	15.26	–	1	4	150	131	0	–	–	–	–
Ghulam Ahmed	22	31	9	50	192	8.72	–	1	11	5650	2052	68	30.17	7-49	4	1
Gopalan, M.J.	1	2	1	11*	18	18.00	–	–	3	114	39	1	39.00	1-39	–	–
Gopinath, C.D.	8	12	1	50*	242	22.00	–	1	2	11	11	1	11.00	1-11	–	–
Guard, G.M.	2	2†	–	7	11	5.50	–	–	2	396‡	182	3	60.66	2-69	–	–
Guha, S.	4	7	2	6	17	3.40	–	–	2	674	311	3	103.66	2-55	–	–
Gul Mahomed	8	15†	1	34	166	11.06	–	–	3	77‡	24	2	12.00	2-21	–	–
Gupte, B.P.	3	3	2	17*	28	28.00	–	–	–	678	349	3	116.33	1-54	–	–
Gupte, S.P.	36	42	13	21	183	6.31	–	–	14	11284	4403	149	29.55	9-102	12	1
Gursharan Singh	1	1	–	18	18	18.00	–	–	2	–						
Hanumant Singh	14	24	2	105	686	31.18	1	5	11	66	51	0	–	–	–	–
Hardikar, M.S.	2	4	1	32*	56	18.66	–	–	3	108	55	1	55.00	1-9	–	–
Hazare, V.S.	30	52	6	164*	2192	47.65	7	9	11	2840	1220	20	61.00	4-29	–	–
Hindlekar, D.D.	4	7	2	26	71	14.20	–	–	3	–						
Hirwani, N.D.	14	18	10	17	45	5.62	–	–	5	3872	1799	58	31.01	8-61	3	1
Ibrahim, K.C.	4	8	–	85	169	21.12	–	1	–	–						
Indrajitsinhji, K.S.	4	7	1	23	51	8.50	–	–	6/3	–						
Irani, J.K.	2	3	2	2*	3	3.00	–	–	2/1	–						
Jadeja, A.D.	3	5	1	43	99	24.75	–	–	–	–						

INDIVIDUAL CAREER RECORDS – INDIA continued

				BATTING AND FIELDING						BOWLING						
	Tests	I	NO	HS	Runs	Avge	100	50	Ct/St	Balls	Runs	Wkts	Avge	BB	5wI	10wM
Jahangir Khan, M.	4	7	1	13	39	5.57	–	–	4	606	255	4	63.75	4-60	–	–
Jai, L.P.	1	2	–	19	19	9.50	–	–	–						–	–
Jaisimha, M.L.	39	71	4	129	2056	30.68	3	12	17	2097	829	9	92.11	2-54	–	–
Jamshedji, R.J.D.	1	2	2	4*	5	–	–	–	2	210‡	137	3	45.66	3-137	–	–
Jayantilal, K.	1	1	–	5	5	5.00	–	–	–							
Joshi, P.G.	12	20	1	52*	207	10.89	–	1	18/9							
Kambli, V.G.	11	13†	1	227	965	80.41	4	3	5	–					–	–
Kanitkar, H.S.	2	4	–	65	111	27.75	–	1	–						–	–
Kapil Dev	131	184	15	163	5248	31.05	8	27	64	27740	12867	434	29.64	9-83	23	2
Kardar, A.H.	3	5†	1	43	80	16.00	–	–	1							
Kenny, R.B.	5	10	–	62	245	27.22	–	3	–	19	13	1	13.00	1-9	–	–
Kirmani, S.M.H.	88	124	22	102	2759	27.04	2	12	160/38	–					–	–
Kishenchand, G.	5	10	–	44	89	8.90	–	1	4							
Kripal Singh, A.G.	14	20	5	100*	422	28.13	1	2	4	1518	584	10	58.40	3-43	–	–
Krishnamurthy, P.	5	6	–	20	33	5.50	–	–	7/1							
Kulkarni, R.R.	3	2	–	2	2	1.00	–	–	1	366	227	5	45.40	3-85	–	–
Kulkarni, U.N.	4	8†	5	7	13	4.33	–	–	–	448‡	238	5	47.60	2-37	–	–
Kumar, V.V.	2	2	–	6	6	3.00	–	–	2	605	202	7	28.85	5-64	1	–
Kumble, A.	17	15	2	21*	132	10.15	–	–	8	5692	2101	86	24.43	7-59	5	1
Kunderan, B.K.	18	34	4	192	981	32.70	2	3	23/7	24	13	0	–	–	–	–
Lall Singh	1	2	–	29	44	22.00	–	1	1	–						
Lamba, R.	4	5	–	53	102	20.40	–	1	5	–						
Madan Lal	39	62	16	74	1042	22.65	–	5	15	5997	2846	71	40.08	5-23	4	–
Maka, E.S.	2	1	1	2*	2	–	–	–	2/1							
Malhotra, A.	7	10	1	72*	226	25.11	–	1	9	18	3	0	–	–	–	–
Maninder Singh	35	38	12	15	99	3.80	–	–	9	8218‡	3288	88	37.36	7-27	3	2
Manjrekar, S.V.	30	47	5	218	1676	39.90	4	6	18	17	15	0	–	–	–	–
Manjrekar, V.L.	55	92	10	189*	3208	39.12	7	15	19/2	204	44	1	44.00	1-16	–	–
Mankad, A.V.	22	42	3	97	991	25.41	–	6	12	41	43	0	–	–	–	–
Mankad, M.H.	44	72	5	231	2109	31.47	5	6	33	14686‡	5236	162	32.32	8-52	8	2
Mantri, M.K.	4	8	1	39	67	9.57	–	–	8/1	–						
Meherhomji, K.R.	1	1	1	0*	0	–	–	–	1							
Mehra, V.L.	8	14	1	62	329	25.30	–	2	1	36	6	0	–	–	–	–
Merchant, V.M.	10	18	–	154	859	47.72	3	3	7	54	40	0	–	–	–	–
Milkha Singh, A.G.	4	6†	–	35	92	15.33	–	1	2	6	2	0	–	–	–	–

INDIVIDUAL CAREER RECORDS – INDIA *continued*

	Tests	I	NO	HS	Runs	Avge	100	50	Ct/St	Balls	Runs	Wkts	Avge	BB	5wI	10wM
				BATTING AND FIELDING							*BOWLING*					
Modi, R.S.	10	17	1	112	736	46.00	1	6	3	30	14	0	–	–	–	–
Mongia, N.R.	4	5	1	45	159	39.75	–	–	10/2	–	–	–	–	–	–	–
More, K.S.	49	64	14	73	1285	25.70	–	7	110/20	12	12	0	–	–	–	–
Muddiah, V.M.	2	3	1	11	11	5.50	–	–	1	318	134	3	44.66	2-40	–	–
Mushtaq Ali	11	20	1	112	612	32.21	2	3	7	378‡	202	3	67.33	1-45	–	–
Nadkarni, R.G.	41	67†	12	122*	1414	25.70	1	7	22	9165‡	2559	88	29.07	6-43	4	1
Naik, S.S.	3	6	–	77	141	23.50	–	1	–	–	–	–	–	–	–	–
Naoomal Jeoomal	3	5	1	43	108	27.00	–	–	–	108	68	2	34.00	1-4	–	–
Narasimha Rao, M.V.	4	6	1	20*	46	9.20	–	–	8	463	227	3	75.66	2-46	–	–
Navle, J.G.	2	4	–	13	42	10.50	–	–	1	–	–	–	–	–	–	–
Nayak, S.V.	2	3†	1	11	19	9.50	–	–	1	231	132	1	132.00	1-16	–	–
Nayudu, C.K.	7	14	–	81	350	25.00	–	2	4	858	386	9	42.88	3-40	–	–
Nayudu, C.S.	11	19	3	36	147	9.18	–	–	3	522	359	2	179.50	1-19	–	–
Nazir Ali, S.	2	4	–	13	30	7.50	–	–	–	138	83	4	20.75	4-83	–	–
Nissar, Mahomed	6	11	3	14	55	6.87	–	–	2	1211	707	25	28.28	5-90	3	–
Nyalchand, S.	1	2†	1	6*	7	7.00	–	–	–	384‡	97	3	32.33	3-97	–	–
Pai, A.M.	1	2†	–	9	10	5.00	–	–	–	114	31	2	15.50	2-29	–	–
Palia, P.E.	2	4†	1	16	29	9.66	–	–	–	42‡	13	0	–	–	–	–
Pandit, C.S.	5	8	1	39	171	24.42	–	–	14/2	–	–				–	–
Parkar, G.A.	1	2	–	6	7	3.50	–	–	1	–	–				–	–
Parkar, R.D.	2	4	–	35	80	20.00	–	–	–	120‡	50	1	50.00	1-32	–	–
Parsana, D.D.	2	2†	1	1	1	0.50	–	–	–	–	–				–	–
Patankar, C.T.	1	2	1	13	14	14.00	–	–	3/1	–	–				–	–
Pataudi, *Nawab of, sr*	3	5	–	22	55	11.00	–	–	–	–	–				–	–
Pataudi, *Nawab of, jr*	46	83	3	203*	2793	34.91	6	16	27	132	88	1	88.00	1-10	–	–
Patel, B.P.	21	38	5	115*	972	29.45	–	5	17	–	–				–	–
Patel, J.M.	7	10	1	12	25	2.77	–	–	2	1725	637	29	21.96	9-69	2	1
Patel, R.	1	2	–	0	0	0.00	–	–	1	84‡	51	0	–	–	–	–
Patiala, *Yuvraj of*	1	2	–	60	84	42.00	–	1	2	–	–				–	–
Patil, S.M.	29	47	4	174	1588	36.93	4	7	12	645	240	9	26.66	2-28	–	–
Patil, S.R.	1	1	1	14*	14	–	–	–	1	138	51	2	25.50	1-15	–	–
Phadkar, D.G.	31	45	7	123	1229	32.34	2	8	21	5994	2285	62	36.85	7-159	3	–
Prabhakar, M.	33	48	7	95	1338	32.63	–	9	18	7133	3384	92	36.78	6-132	3	–
Prasanna, E.A.S.	49	84	20	37	735	11.48	–	–	18	14353	5742	189	30.38	8-76	10	2
Punjabi, P.H.	5	10	–	33	164	16.40	–	–	5	–	–				–	–

INDIVIDUAL CAREER RECORDS – INDIA continued

| | | | BATTING AND FIELDING | | | | | | BOWLING | | | | | | |
	Tests	I	NO	HS	Runs	Avge	100	50	Ct/St	Balls	Runs	Wkts	Avge	BB	5wI	10wM
Rai Singh, K.	1	2	–	24	26	13.00	–	–	–	–	–	–	–	–	–	–
Rajindernath	1	–	–	–	–	–	–	–	–/4	–	–	–	–	–	–	–
Rajinder Pal	1	2	1	3*	6	6.00	–	–	–	78	22	0	–	–	–	–
Rajput, L.S.	2	4	–	61	105	26.25	–	1	–	–	–	–	–	–	–	–
Raju, S.L.V.	18	22	8	31	188	13.42	–	–	5	5125‡	1810	61	29.67	6-12	3	1
Raman, W.V.	8	13†	1	96	367	30.58	–	3	5	258‡	66	2	33.00	1-7	–	–
Ramaswami, C.	2	4†	1	60	170	56.66	–	1	–	–	–	–	–	–	–	–
Ramchand, G.S.	33	53	5	109	1180	24.58	2	5	20	4976	1899	41	46.31	6-49	1	–
Ramji, L.	1	2	–	1	1	0.50	–	–	–	138	64	0	–	–	–	–
Rangachari, C.R.	4	6	3	8*	8	2.66	–	–	1	846	493	9	54.77	5-107	1	–
Rangnekar, K.M.	3	6†	–	18	33	5.50	–	–	1	–	–	–	–	–	–	–
Ranjane, V.B.	7	9	3	16*	40	6.66	–	–	1	1265	649	19	34.15	4-72	–	–
Razdan, V.	2	2	1	6*	6	6.00	–	–	–	240	141	5	28.20	5-79	1	–
Reddy, B.	4	5	1	21	38	9.50	–	–	9/2	–	–	–	–	–	–	–
Rege, M.R.	1	2	1	15	15	7.50	–	–	1	–	–	–	–	–	–	–
Roy, A.	4	7†	–	48	91	13.00	–	–	–	–	–	–	–	–	–	–
Roy, Pankaj	43	79	4	173	2442	32.56	5	9	16	104	66	1	66.00	1-6	–	–
Roy, Pranab	2	3	1	60*	71	35.50	–	1	1	–	–	–	–	–	–	–
Sandhu, B.S.	8	11	4	71	214	30.57	–	2	1	1020	557	10	55.70	3-87	–	–
Sardesai, D.N.	30	55	4	212	2001	39.23	5	9	4	59	45	0	–	–	–	–
Sarwate, C.T.	9	17	1	37	208	13.00	–	–	–	658	374	3	124.66	1-16	–	–
Saxena, R.C.	1	2	1	16	25	12.50	–	–	–	12	11	0	–	–	–	–
Sekar, T.A.P.	2	1	1	0*	0	–	–	–	–	204	129	0	–	–	–	–
Sen, P.	14	18	4	25	165	11.78	–	1	20/11	–	–	–	–	–	–	–
Sengupta, A.K.	1	2	–	8	9	4.50	–	–	–	–	–	–	–	–	–	–
Sharma, A.K.	1	2	–	30	53	26.50	–	–	1	24‡	9	0	–	–	–	–
Sharma, C.	23	27	9	54	396	22.00	1	1	7	3470	2163	61	35.45	6-58	4	1
Sharma, G.	5	4	1	10*	11	3.66	–	–	2	1307	418	10	41.80	4-88	–	–
Sharma, P.	5	10	–	54	187	18.70	–	1	–	24	8	0	–	–	–	–
Sharma, S.K.	2	3	1	38	56	28.00	–	–	1	414	247	6	41.16	3-37	–	–
Shastri, R.J.	80	121	14	206	3830	35.79	11	12	36	15751‡	6185	151	40.96	5-75	2	–
Shinde, S.G.	7	11	5	14	85	14.16	–	–	–	1515	717	12	59.75	6-91	1	–
Shodhan, R.H.	3	4†	1	110	181	60.33	1	1	1	60‡	26	0	–	–	–	–
Shukla, R.C.	1	–	–	–	–	–	–	–	–	294	152	2	76.00	2-82	–	–
Sidhu, N.S.	31	46	2	124	1789	40.65	5	9	7	6	9	0	–	–	–	–
Sivaramakrishnan, L.	9	9	1	25	130	16.25	–	–	9	2367	1145	26	44.03	6-64	3	1
Sohoni, S.W.	4	7	2	29*	83	16.60	–	–	2	532	202	2	101.00	1-16	–	–

INDIVIDUAL CAREER RECORDS – INDIA *continued*

	Tests	I	NO	HS	BATTING AND FIELDING Runs	Avge	100	50	Ct/St	Balls	BOWLING Runs	Wkts	Avge	BB	5wI	10wM
Solkar, E.D.	27	48†	6	102	1068	25.42	1	6	53	2265‡	1070	18	59.44	3-28	–	–
Sood, M.M.	1	2	–	3	3	1.50	–	–	–	–	–	–	–	–	–	–
Srikkanth, K.	43	72	3	123	2062	29.88	2	12	40	216	114	0	–	–	–	–
Srinath, J.	12	15	8	21	91	13.00	–	–	5	2886	1212	33	36.72	4-33	–	–
Srinivasan, T.E.	1	2	–	29	48	24.00	–	–	–	–	–	–	–	–	–	–
Subramanya, V.	9	15	1	75	263	18.78	–	2	9	444	201	3	67.00	2-32	–	–
Sunderam, G.R.	2	1	1	3*	3	–	–	–	–	396	166	3	55.33	2-46	–	–
Surendranath	11	20	7	27	136	10.46	–	–	4	2602	1053	26	40.50	5-75	2	–
Surti, R.F.	26	48†	4	99	1263	28.70	–	9	26	3870‡	1962	42	46.71	5-74	1	–
Swamy, V.N.	1	–	–	–	–	–	–	–	–	108	45	0	–	–	–	–
Tamhane, N.S.	21	27	5	54*	225	10.22	–	1	35/16	–	–				–	–
Tarapore, K.K.	1	1	–	2	2	2.00	–	–	–	114‡	72	0	–	–	–	–
Tendulkar, S. R.	32	45	5	165	2023	50.57	7	10	23	408	172	4	43.00	2-10	–	–
Umrigar, P.R.	59	94	8	223	3631	42.22	12	14	33	4725	1473	35	42.08	6-74	2	–
Vengsarkar, D.B.	116	185	22	166	6868	42.13	17	35	78	47	36	0	–	–	–	–
Venkataraghavan, S.	57	76	12	64	748	11.68	–	2	44	14877	5634	156	36.11	8-72	3	1
Venkataramana, M.	1	2	2	0*	0	–	–	–	1	70	58	1	58.00	1-10	–	–
Viswanath, G.R.	91	155	10	222	6080	41.93	14	35	63	70	46	1	46.00	1-11	–	–
Viswanath, S.	3	5	–	20	31	6.20	–	–	11	–						
Vizianagram	3	6	2	19*	33	8.25	–	–	1	–						
Wadekar, A.L.	37	71†	3	143	2113	31.07	1	14	46	61‡	55	0	–	–	–	–
Wassan, A.S.	4	5	1	53	94	23.50	–	1	1	712	504	10	50.40	4-108	–	–
Wazir Ali, S.	7	14	–	42	237	16.92	–	–	1	30	25	0	–	–	–	–
Yadav, N.S.	35	40	12	43	403	14.39	–	–	10	8349	3580	102	35.09	5-76	3	–
Yadav, V.	1	1	–	30	30	30.00	–	–	1/2	–						
Yajurvindra Singh	4	7	1	43*	109	18.16	–	–	11	120	50	0	–	–	–	–
Yashpal Sharma	37	59	11	140	1606	33.45	2	9	16	30	17	1	17.00	1-6	–	–
Yograj Singh	1	2	–	6	10	5.00	–	–	–	90	63	1	63.00	1-63	–	–

INDIVIDUAL CAREER RECORDS – PAKISTAN

PAKISTAN (132 players)	Tests	I	NO	HS	BATTING AND FIELDING Runs	Avge	100	50	Ct/St	BOWLING Balls	Runs	Wkts	Avge	BB	5wI	10wM
Aamer Malik	13	17	3	117	489	34.92	2	2	15/1	126	73	1	73.00	1-0	–	–
Aamir Nazir	2	4	2	6*	7	3.50	–	–	–	318	203	3	67.66	2-79	–	–
Aamir Sohail	16	29†	1	205	979	34.96	1	7	15	180‡	104	2	52.00	1-14	–	–
Abdul Kadir	4	8	–	95	272	34.00	–	2	–/1	–	–	–	–	–	–	–
Abdul Qadir	67	77	11	61	1029	15.59	–	3	15	17126	7742	236	32.80	9-56	15	5
Afaq Hussain	2	4	4	35*	66	–	–	1	2	240	106	1	106.00	1-40	–	–
Aftab Baloch	2	3	1	60*	97	48.50	–	1	3	44	17	0	–	–	–	–
Aftab Gul	6	8	–	33	182	22.75	–	1	3	6	4	0	–	–	–	–
Agha Saadat Ali	1	1	1	8*	8	–	–	–	3	–	–	–	–	–	–	–
Agha Zahid	1	2	–	14	15	7.50	–	–	–	–	–	–	–	–	–	–
Akram Raza	6	6	1	29*	85	17.00	–	–	8	908	428	11	38.90	3-46	–	–
Alimuddin	25	45	2	109	1091	25.37	2	7	8	84	75	1	75.00	1-17	–	–
Amir Elahi	5	7	1	47	65	10.83	–	–	–	400	248	7	35.42	4-134	–	–
Anil Dalpat	9	12	1	52	167	15.18	–	1	22/3	–	–	–	–	–	–	–
Anwar Hussain	4	6	–	17	42	7.00	–	–	–	36	29	1	29.00	1-25	–	–
Anwar Khan	1	2	1	12	15	15.00	–	–	–	32	12	0	–	–	–	–
Aqib Javed	14	12	3	10	29	3.22	–	–	1	2094	1051	25	42.04	4-100	1	–
A:if Butt	3	5	–	20	59	11.80	–	–	–	666	288	14	20.57	6-89	1	–
Ashfaq Ahmed	1	2	1	1*	1	1.00	–	–	–	138	53	2	26.50	2-31	–	–
Ashraf Ali	8	8	3	65	229	45.80	–	2	17/5	–	–	–	–	–	–	–
Asif Iqbal	58	99	7	175	3575	38.85	11	12	36	3864	1502	53	28.33	5-48	2	–
Asif Masood	16	19	10	30*	93	10.33	–	–	5	3038	1568	38	41.26	5-111	1	–
Asif Mujtaba	19	31†	3	65*	730	26.07	–	7	16	222‡	122	2	61.00	1-0	–	–
Ata-ur-Rehman	9	9	3	19	48	8.00	–	–	2	1272	720	21	34.28	3-28	–	–
Atif Rauf	1	2	–	16	25	12.50	–	–	–	–	–	–	–	–	–	–
Azeem Hafeez	18	21†	5	24	134	8.37	–	–	1	4351‡	2204	63	34.98	6-46	4	–
Azhar Khan	1	1	–	14	14	14.00	–	–	–	18	2	1	2.00	1-1	–	–
Azmat Rana	1	1†	–	49	49	49.00	–	–	–	–	–	–	–	–	–	–
Basit Ali	11	18	1	103	743	43.70	1	5	4	6	6	0	–	–	–	–
D'Souza, A.	6	10	8	23*	76	38.00	–	–	3	1587	745	17	43.82	5-112	1	–
Ehteshamuddin	5	3	1	2	2	1.00	–	–	2	940	375	16	23.43	5-47	1	–

INDIVIDUAL CAREER RECORDS – PAKISTAN continued

				BATTING AND FIELDING						BOWLING						
	Tests	I	NO	HS	Runs	Avge	100	50	Ct/St	Balls	Runs	Wkts	Avge	BB	5wI	10wM
Farooq Hamid	1	2	–	3	3	1.50	–	–	–	184	107	1	107.00	1-82	–	–
Farrukh Zaman	1	–	–	–	–	–	–	–	–	80‡	15	0	–	–	–	–
Fazal Mahmood	34	50	6	60	620	14.09	–	1	11	9834	3434	139	24.70	7-42	13	4
Ghazali, M.E.Z.	2	4	–	18	32	8.00	–	–	–	48	18	0	–	–	–	–
Ghulam Abbas	1	2†	1	12	12	6.00	–	–	–	–						
Gul Mahomed	1	2†	1	27*	39	39.00	–	–	–	–						
Hanif Mohammad	55	97	8	337	3915	43.98	12	15	40	206	95	1	95.00	1-1	–	–
Haroon Rashid	23	36	1	153	1217	34.77	3	5	16	8	3	0	–	–	–	–
Haseeb Ahsan	12	16	7	14	61	6.77	–	–	1	2835	1330	27	49.25	6-202	2	–
Ibadulla, K. – *see* Khalid Ibadulla																
Ijaz Ahmed	19	25	–	122	743	29.72	2	3	16	54‡	18	1	18.00	1-9	–	–
Ijaz Butt	8	16	2	58	279	19.92	–	1	5	–						
Ijaz Faqih	5	8	1	105	183	26.14	1	–	–	534	299	4	74.75	1-38	–	–
Imran Khan	88	126	25	136	3807	37.69	6	18	28	19458	8258	362	22.81	8-58	23	6
Imtiaz Ahmed	41	72	1	209	2079	29.28	3	11	77/16	6	0	0	–	–	–	–
Intikhab Alam	47	77	10	138	1493	22.28	1	8	20	10474	4494	125	35.95	7-52	5	2
Inzamam-ul-Haq	16	26	6	135*	910	45.50	3	3	17	–						
Iqbal Qasim	50	57†	15	56	549	13.07	–	1	42	13019‡	4807	171	28.11	7-49	8	2
Israr Ali	4	8†	1	10	33	4.71	–	–	1	318‡	165	6	27.50	2-29	–	–
Jalaluddin	6	3	2	2	3	3.00	–	–	–	1197	537	11	48.81	3-77	–	–
Javed Akhtar	1	2	1	2*	4	4.00	–	–	–	96	52	0	–	–	–	–
Javed Burki	25	48	4	140	1341	30.47	3	4	7	42	23	0	–	–	–	–
Javed Miandad	124	189	21	280*	8832	52.57	23	43	93/1	1470	682	17	40.11	3-74	–	–
Kabir Khan	1	–	–	–	–	–	–	–	–	60‡	39	1	39.00	1-39	–	–
Kardar, A.H.	23	37†	3	93	847	24.91	–	5	15	2712‡	954	21	45.42	3-35	–	–
Khalid Hassan	1	2	1	10	17	17.00	–	–	–	126	116	2	58.00	2-116	–	–
Khalid Ibadulla	4	8	1	166	253	31.62	1	1	3	336	99	1	99.00	1-42	–	–
Khalid Wazir	2	3	1	9*	14	7.00	–	–	–	–						
Khan Mohammad	13	17	7	26*	100	10.00	–	–	4	3157	1292	54	23.92	6-21	4	–
Liaqat Ali	5	7	3	12	28	7.00	–	–	1	808‡	359	6	59.83	3-80	–	–
Mahmood Hussain	27	39	6	35	336	10.18	–	–	5	5910	2628	68	38.64	6-67	2	–

INDIVIDUAL CAREER RECORDS – PAKISTAN continued

	Tests	I	NO	HS	Runs	Avge	100	50	Ct/St	Balls	Runs	Wkts	Avge	BB	5wI	10wM
					BATTING AND FIELDING								BOWLING			
Majid Khan	63	106	5	167	3931	38.92	8	19	70	3584	1456	27	53.92	4-45	-	-
Mansoor Akhtar	19	29	3	111	655	25.19	1	3	9	156	84	2	42.00	1-8	-	-
Manzoor Elahi	4	6	1	52	109	21.80	-	1	5	462	191	3	63.66	2-12	-	-
Maqsood Ahmed	16	27	1	99	507	19.50	-	2	13	161‡	102	3	34.00	2-59	-	-
Masood Anwar	1	2†	-	37	39	19.50	-	-	-	24	20	0	-	-	-	-
Mathias, W.	21	36	3	77	783	23.72	-	3	22	348	115	2	57.50	2-82	-	-
Miran Bux	2	3	2	1*	1	1.00	-	-	-	-	-	-	-	-	-	-
Mohammad Aslam	1	2	-	18	34	17.00	-	-	-	-	-	-	-	-	-	-
Mohammad Farooq	7	9	4	47	85	17.00	-	-	1	1422	682	21	32.47	4-70	-	-
Mohammad Ilyas	10	19	-	126	441	23.21	1	2	6	84	63	0	-	-	-	-
Mohammad Munaf	4	7	2	19	63	12.60	-	-	4	769	341	11	31.00	4-42	-	-
Mohammad Nazir	14	18	10	29*	144	18.00	-	-	4	3262	1124	34	33.05	7-99	3	-
Mohsin Kamal	7	7	5	13*	31	15.50	-	-	2	1024	597	17	35.11	4-127	1	-
Mohsin Khan	48	79	6	200	2709	37.10	7	9	34	86	30	0	-	-	-	-
Moin Khan	11	15	2	32	169	13.00	-	-	24/2	-	-	-	-	-	-	-
Mudassar Nazar	76	116	8	231	4114	38.09	10	17	48	5967	2532	66	38.36	6-32	1	-
Mufasir-ul-Haq	1	1	1	8*	8	-	-	-	1	222‡	84	3	28.00	2-50	-	-
Munir Malik	3	4	1	4	7	2.33	-	-	-	684	358	9	39.77	5-128	1	-
Mushtaq Ahmed	15	20	4	18	100	6.25	-	-	4	2575	1190	35	34.00	3-32	-	-
Mushtaq Mohammad	57	100	7	201	3643	39.17	10	19	42	5260	2309	79	29.22	5-28	3	-
Nadeem Abbasi	3	2	-	36	46	23.00	-	-	6	-	-	-	-	-	-	-
Nadeem Ghauri	1	1	-	0	0	0.00	-	-	-	48‡	20	0	-	-	-	-
Nadeem Khan	1	1	-	25	25	25.00	-	-	-	312‡	195	2	97.50	2-147	-	-
Nasim-ul-Ghani	29	50†	5	101	747	16.60	1	2	11	4406‡	1959	52	37.67	6-67	2	-
Naushad Ali	6	11	-	39	156	14.18	-	-	9	-	-	-	-	-	-	-
Naved Anjum	2	3	1	22	44	14.66	-	1	-	342	162	4	40.50	2-57	-	-
Nazar Mohammad	5	8	1	124*	277	39.57	1	1	7	12	4	0	-	-	-	-
Niaz Ahmed	2	3	3	16*	17	-	-	-	1	294	94	3	31.33	2-72	-	-
Pervez Sajjad	19	20	11	24	123	13.66	-	-	9	4145‡	1410	59	23.89	7-74	3	-
Qasim Omar	26	43	2	210	1502	36.63	3	5	15	6	0	0	-	-	-	-
Ramiz Raja	48	78	5	122	2243	30.72	2	16	27	-	-	-	-	-	-	-
Rashid Khan	4	6	3	59	155	51.66	-	1	2	738	360	8	45.00	3-129	-	-
Rashid Latif	11	14	3	68*	366	33.27	-	3	34/4	-	-	-	-	-	-	-
Rehman, S.F.	1	2	-	8	10	5.00	-	-	1	204	99	1	99.00	1-43	-	-

INDIVIDUAL CAREER RECORDS – PAKISTAN *continued*

	Tests	BATTING AND FIELDING								BOWLING						
		I	NO	HS	Runs	Avge	100	50	Ct/St	Balls	Runs	Wkts	Avge	BB	5wI	10wM
Rizwan-uz-Zaman	11	19	1	60	345	19.16	–	3	4	132	46	4	11.50	3-26	–	–
Sadiq Mohammad	41	74†	2	166	2579	35.81	5	10	28	200	98	0	–	–	–	–
Saeed Ahmed	41	78	4	172	2991	40.41	5	16	13	1980	802	22	36.45	4-64	–	–
Saeed Anwar	6	10†	–	169	522	52.20	2	2	3	6‡	4	0	–	–	–	–
Salahuddin	5	8	2	34*	117	19.50	–	1	3	546	187	7	26.71	2-36	–	–
Salim Altaf	21	31	12	53*	276	14.52	–	–	3	4001	1710	46	37.17	4-11	1	–
Salim Jaffer	14	14	6	10*	42	5.25	–	–	2	2531‡	1139	36	31.63	5-40	1	–
Salim Malik	77	111	19	165	4040	43.91	11	22	52	308	144	5	28.80	1-3	–	–
Salim Yousuf	32	44	5	91*	1055	27.05	–	5	91/13	–	–	–	–	–	–	–
Sarfraz Nawaz	55	72	13	90	1045	17.71	–	4	26	13951	5798	177	32.75	9-86	4	1
Shafiq Ahmed	6	10	1	27*	99	11.00	–	–	–	8	1	0	–	–	–	–
Shafqat Rana	5	7	–	95	221	31.57	–	2	5	36	9	1	9.00	1-2	–	–
Shahid Israr	1	1	1	7*	7	–	–	–	2	–	–	–	–	–	–	–
Shahid Mahboob	1	2†	–	–	–	–	–	–	–	294	131	2	65.50	2-131	–	–
Shahid Mahmood	1	1	–	16	25	12.50	–	–	–	36‡	23	0	–	–	–	–
Shahid Saeed	1	1	–	12	12	12.00	–	–	–	90	43	0	–	–	–	–
Shakil Ahmed	1	1	–	0	0	0.00	–	–	–	–	–	–	–	–	–	–
Sharpe, D.	3	6	–	56	134	22.33	–	1	2	–	–	–	–	–	–	–
Shoaib Mohammad	42	63	7	203*	2622	46.82	7	12	21	282	130	5	26.00	2-8	–	–
Shujauddin	19	32	6	47	395	15.19	–	–	8	2313‡	801	20	40.05	3-18	–	–
Sikander Bakht	26	35	12	22*	146	6.34	–	–	7	4870	2412	67	36.00	8-69	3	1
Tahir Naqqash	15	19	5	57	300	21.42	–	1	3	2800	1398	34	41.11	5-40	2	–
Talat Ali	10	18	2	61	370	23.12	–	2	4	20	7	0	–	–	–	–
Taslim Arif	6	10	2	210*	501	62.62	1	2	6/3	30	28	1	28.00	1-28	–	–
Tausif Ahmed	34	38	20	35*	318	17.66	–	–	9	7778	2950	93	31.72	6-45	3	–
Waqar Hassan	21	35	1	189	1071	31.50	1	6	10	6	10	0	–	–	–	–
Waqar Younis	31	37	6	29	276	8.90	–	–	4	6411	3382	180	18.78	7-76	19	4
Wasim Akram	55	71†	10	123	1205	19.75	1	4	19	12484‡	5378	235	22.88	7-119	16	3
Wasim Bari	81	112	26	85	1366	15.88	–	6	201/27	2	2	0	–	–	–	–
Wasim Raja	57	92†	14	125	2821	36.16	4	18	20	4082	1826	51	35.80	4-50	–	–
Wazir Mohammad	20	33	4	189	801	27.62	2	3	5	24	15	0	–	–	–	–
Younis Ahmed	4	7†	1	62	177	29.50	–	1	1	6‡	6	0	–	–	–	–

INDIVIDUAL CAREER RECORDS – PAKISTAN continued

	Tests	I	NO	HS	Runs	Avge	100	50	Ct/St	Balls	Runs	Wkts	Avge	BB	5wI	10wM
				BATTING AND FIELDING									BOWLING			
Zaheer Abbas	78	124	11	274	5062	44.79	12	20	34	370	132	3	44.00	2-21	–	–
Zahid Fazal	6	10	1	78	223	22.30	–	1	4	–						
Zakir Khan	2	2	2	9*	9	–	–	–	1	444	259	5	51.80	3-80	–	–
Zulfiqar Ahmed	9	10	4	63*	200	33.33	–	1	5	1285	366	20	18.30	6-42	2	1
Zulqarnain	3	4	–	13	24	6.00	–	–	8/2	–						

INDIVIDUAL CAREER RECORDS – SRI LANKA

SRI LANKA (63 players)	Tests	I	NO	HS	Runs	Avge	100	50	Ct/St	Balls	Runs	Wkts	Avge	BB	5wI	10wM
					BATTING AND FIELDING							*BOWLING*				
Ahangama, F.S.	3	3†	1	11	11	5.50	–	–	1	801	348	18	19.33	5-52	1	–
Amalean, K.N.	2	3	2	7*	9	9.00	–	–	1	244	156	7	22.28	4-97	–	–
Amerasinghe, M.J.G.	2	4†	1	34	54	18.00	–	–	3	300‡	150	3	50.00	2-73	–	–
Anurasiri, S.D.	17	21	4	24	88	5.17	–	–	3	3697‡	1442	37	38.97	4-71	–	–
Atapattu, M.S.	3	6	–	1	1	0.16	–	–	–	–						
Dassanayake, P.B.	9	15	2	36	188	14.46	–	–	12/4	–						
De Alwis, R.G.	11	19	2	28	152	8.00	–	–	21/2	–						
De Mel, A.L.F.	17	28	5	34	326	14.17	–	–	9	3518	2180	59	36.94	6-109	3	–
De Silva, A.M.	3	3	–	9	10	3.33	–	–	4/1							
De Silva, D.S.	12	22	3	61	406	21.36	–	2	5	3031	1347	37	36.40	5-59	1	–
De Silva, E.A.R.	10	16†	4	50	185	15.41	–	1	4	2328	1032	8	129.00	2-67	–	–
De Silva, G.R.A.	4	7†	4	14	41	8.20	–	–	–	962‡	385	7	55.00	2-38	–	–
De Silva, P.A.	43	74	3	267	2760	38.87	7	12	21	738	389	11	35.36	3-39	–	–
Dharmasena, H.D.P.K.	4	7	1	30	46	6.57	–	–	1	1178	457	14	32.64	6-99	1	–
Dias, R.L.	20	36	1	109	1285	36.71	3	8	6	24	17	0	–	–	–	–
Fernando, E.R.N.S.	5	10	–	46	112	11.20	–	–	–							
Goonasekera, Y.	2	4†	1	23	48	12.00	–	–	6							
Goonatillake, H.M.	5	10	2	56	177	22.12	–	1	10/3							
Guneratne, R.P.W.	1	2	2	0*	0	–	–	–	–	102	84	0	–	–	–	–
Gurusinha, A.P.	28	47†	7	137	1519	37.97	4	4	21	1108	539	18	29.94	2-7	–	–
Hathurusinghe, U.C.	18	30	1	81	840	28.96	–	5	2	1428	560	16	35.00	4-66	–	–
Jayasekera, R.S.A.	1	2	–	2	2	1.00	–	–	–							
Jayasuriya, S.T.	15	24†	5	81	601	31.63	–	4	17	558‡	333	4	83.25	2-46	–	–
Jeganathan, S.	2	4	–	8	19	4.75	–	–	2	30‡	12	0	–	–	–	–
John, V.B.	6	10	5	27*	53	10.60	–	–	2	1281	614	28	21.92	5-60	2	–
Jurangpathy, B.R.	2	4	–	1	1	0.25	–	–	2	150	93	1	93.00	1-69	–	–
Kalpage, R.S.	7	13†	1	63	251	20.91	–	2	6	845	374	6	62.33	2-27	–	–
Kaluperuma, L.W.	2	4	1	11*	12	4.00	–	–	2	162	93	0	–	–	–	–
Kaluperuma, S.M.S.	4	8	–	23	88	11.00	–	–	6	240	124	2	62.00	2-17	–	–

INDIVIDUAL CAREER RECORDS – SRI LANKA *continued*

	Tests	I	NO	BATTING AND FIELDING HS	Runs	Avge	100	50	Ct/St	BOWLING Balls	Runs	Wkts	Avge	BB	5wI	10wM
Kaluwitharana, R.S.	3	4	1	132*	177	59.00	1	–	6	–	–	–	–	–	–	–
Kuruppu, D.S.B.P.	4	7	1	201*	320	53.33	1	–	6	–	–	–	–	–	–	–
Kuruppuarachchi, A.K.	2	2	2	0*	0	–	–	–	1	272‡	149	8	18.62	5-44	1	–
Labrooy, G.F.	9	14	3	70*	158	14.36	–	1	3	2158	1194	27	44.22	5-133	1	–
Liyanage, D.K.	8	8†	–	23	66	8.25	–	–	–	1271	622	17	36.58	4-56	–	–
Madugalle, R.S.	21	39	4	103	1029	29.40	1	7	9	84	38	0	–	–	–	–
Madurasinghe, A.W.R.	3	6†	1	11	24	4.80	–	–	–	396	172	3	57.33	3-60	–	–
Mahanama, R.S.	29	48	–	153	1650	34.37	3	9	17	36	30	0	–	–	–	–
Mendis, L.R.D.	24	43	1	124	1329	31.64	4	8	9	–	–	–	–	–	–	–
Muralitharan, M.	14	16	10	20*	113	18.83	–	–	5	3678	1678	53	31.66	5-101	3	–
Pushpakumara, K.R.	1	2	–	6	6	3.00	–	–	–	156	145	4	36.25	4-145	–	–
Ramanayake, C.P.H.	18	24	9	34*	143	9.53	–	–	6	3654	1880	44	42.72	5-82	1	–
Ranasinghe, A.N.	2	4	–	77	88	22.00	–	1	–	114‡	69	1	69.00	1-23	–	–
Ranatunga, A.	51	86†	4	135*	2804	34.19	4	17	22	2096	911	14	65.07	2-17	–	–
Ranatunga, D.	2	3	–	45	87	29.00	–	–	–	–	–	–	–	–	–	–
Ranatunga, S.	1	2†	–	5	9	4.50	–	–	–	–	–	–	–	–	–	–
Ratnayake, R.J.	23	36	6	56	433	14.43	–	2	9	4961	2563	73	35.10	6-66	5	–
Ratnayeke, J.R.	22	38†	6	93	807	25.21	–	5	1	3833	1972	56	35.21	8-83	4	–
Samarasekera, M.A.R.	4	7	–	57	118	16.85	–	1	3	192	104	3	34.66	2-38	–	–
Samaraweera, D.P.	5	10	–	42	134	13.40	–	1	4	–	–	–	–	–	–	–
Senanayake, C.P.	3	5†	–	64	97	19.40	–	–	2	–	–	–	–	–	–	–
Silva, S.A.R.	9	16†	2	111	353	25.21	2	–	33/1	–	–	–	–	–	–	–
Tillekeratne, H.P.	25	41†	6	93*	1280	36.57	–	9	56	18	6	0	–	–	–	–
Vaas, W.P.U.C.J.	1	2†	–	4	4	2.00	–	–	–	132‡	80	0	–	–	–	–
Warnapura, B.	4	8	–	38	96	12.00	–	–	2	90	46	0	–	–	–	–
Warnaweera, K.P.J.	10	12†	3	20	39	4.33	–	–	–	2333	1021	32	31.90	4-25	–	–
Weerasinghe, C.D.U.S.	1	1	–	3	3	3.00	–	–	–	114	36	0	–	–	–	–
Wettimuny, M.de S.	2	4	–	17	28	7.00	–	–	2	–	–	–	–	–	–	–
Wettimuny, S.	23	43	1	190	1221	29.07	2	6	10	24	37	0	–	–	–	–
Wickremasinghe, A.G.D.	3	3	1	13*	17	8.50	–	–	9/1	–	–	–	–	–	–	–

INDIVIDUAL CAREER RECORDS – SRI LANKA *continued*

	Tests	I	NO	HS	BATTING AND FIELDING Runs	Avge	100	50	Ct/St	Balls	Runs	Wkts	BOWLING Avge	BB	5wI	10wM
Wickremasinghe, G.P.	13	20	4	22	129	8.06	–	–	7	2352	1294	26	49.76	5-73	1	–
Wijegunawardene, K.I.W.	2	4	1	6*	14	4.66	–	–	–	364	147	7	21.00	4-51	–	–
Wijesuriya, R.G.C.E.	4	7	2	8	22	4.40	–	–	1	586‡	294	1	294.00	1-68	–	–
Wijetunge, P.K.	1	2	–	10	10	5.00	–	–	–	312‡	118	2	59.00	1-58	–	–

INDIVIDUAL CAREER RECORDS – ZIMBABWE

ZIMBABWE (22 players)	Tests	BATTING AND FIELDING								BOWLING						
		I	NO	HS	Runs	Avge	100	50	Ct/St	Balls	Runs	Wkts	Avge	BB	5wI	10wM
Arnott, K.J.	4	8	1	101*	302	43.14	1	1	4	–						
Brain, D.H.	4	7	–	28	74	10.57	–	–	–	978‡	431	18	23.94	5-42	1	–
Brandes, E.A.	6	10	1	18	60	6.66	–	–	3	1264	598	17	35.17	3-45	–	–
Briant, G.A.	1	2	–	16	17	8.50	–	–	1	–						
Bruk-Jackson, G.K.	2	4	–	31	39	9.75	–	–	–							–
Burmester, M.G.	3	4	2	30*	54	27.00	–	–	1	436	227	3	75.66	3-78		
Campbell, A.D.R.	7	13†	1	75	478	39.83	–	5	5	6	0	0	–	–	–	–
Crocker, G.J.	3	4†	1	33	69	23.00	–	–	–	456‡	217	3	72.33	2-65	–	–
Dekker, M.H.	3	5	1	68*	143	35.75	–	2	1	–						–
Flower, A.	7	12†	3	115	499	55.44	1	5	14/2	1	0	0	–	–	–	–
Flower, G.W.	7	13	–	96	343	26.38	–	2	1	282‡	144	2	72.00	1-8	–	–
Houghton, D.L.	7	12	1	121	363	33.00	1	1	7	5	0	0	–	–	–	–
James, W.R.	1	1	–	8	8	8.00	–	–	3	–						–
Jarvis, M.P.	2	2	1	2*	2	2.00	–	–	1	451‡	198	4	49.50	3-38	–	–
Peall, S.G.	2	4†	1	11*	21	7.00	–	–	1	330	111	2	55.50	2-89	–	–
Pycroft, A.J.	3	5	–	60	152	30.40	–	1	2	–						–
Ranchod, U.	1	2	–	7	8	4.00	–	–	–	72	45	1	45.00	1-45	–	–
Rennie, J.A.	2	3	–	3	5	1.66	–	–	–	358	171	3	57.00	2-22	–	–
Shah, A.H.	2	3†	–	28	59	19.66	–	–	–	186	125	1	125.00	1-46	–	–
Streak, H.H.	3	5	1	19*	21	5.25	–	–	1	665	284	8	35.50	5-56	1	–
Traicos, A.J.	4	6	2	5	11	2.75	–	–	4	1141	562	14	40.14	5-86	1	–
Whittall, G.J.	3	5	–	33	66	13.20	–	–	–	263	92	1	92.00	1-26	–	–

COMPLETE TEST RECORD FOR PLAYERS REPRESENTING TWO COUNTRIES

				BATTING AND FIELDING						BOWLING						
	Teams	Tests	I	NO	HS	Runs	Avge	100	50	Ct/St	Balls	Runs	Wkts	Avge	BB	5wI	10wM
Amir Elahi	I/P	6	9	1	47	82	10.25	–	–	–	400	248	7	35.42	4-134	–	–
Ferris, J.J.	A/E	9	17†	4	20*	114	8.76	–	–	4	2302‡	775	61	12.70	7-37	6	1
Guillen, S.C.	WI/NZ	8	12	2	54	202	20.20	–	1	13/3	–					–	–
Gul Mahomed	I/P	9	17†	1	34	205	12.81	–	–	3	77‡	24	2	12.00	2-21	–	–
Hearne, F.	E/SA	6	10	–	30	168	16.80	–	–	3	62	40	2	20.00	2-40	–	–
Kardar, A.H.	I/P	26	42†	3	93	927	23.76	–	5	16	2712‡	954	21	45.42	3-35	–	–
Midwinter, W.E.	E/A	12	21	1	37	269	13.45	–	–	10	1725	605	24	25.20	5-78	1	–
Mitchell, F.	E/SA	5	10	–	41	116	11.60	–	–	2	–					–	–
Murdoch, W.L.	A/E	19	34	5	211	908	31.31	2	1	13/2	–					–	–
Pataudi, Nawab of, sr	E/I	6	10	–	102*	199	19.90	1	–	–						–	–
Traicos, A.J.	SA/Z	7	10	4	5*	19	3.16	–	–	8	1611	769	18	42.72	5-86	1	–
Trott, A.E.	A/E	5	9	3	85*	228	38.00	–	2	4	948	390	26	15.00	8-43	2	–
Wessels, K.C.	A/SA	40	71†	3	179	2788	41.00	6	15	30	90	42	0	–	–	–	–
Woods, S.M.J.	A/E	6	10	–	53	154	15.40	–	1	5	412	250	10	25.00	3-28	–	–

Index of Test Cricketers 1876-77 to 1994

INDEX OF TEST CRICKETERS

Every cricketer who appeared in official Test matches before September 1994 is listed alphabetically within his country's section of the index. Players who appeared for two countries are listed within both sections. The numbers in brackets show the total number of Test match appearances by the player for that country. The numbers that follow are the reference numbers of the matches in which he played; only the prefix of each match number is listed; e.g. *Test No. 596/102 (E420/SA163)* is shown as '596'.

ENGLAND (570 players)

ABEL, Robert; b Rotherhithe, Surrey 30 Nov 1857; d Stockwell, London 10 Dec 1936; (13) 28, 29, 30, 31, 32, 35, 36, 37, 50, 51, 52, 72, 73.

ABSOLOM, Charles Alfred; b Blackheath, Kent 7 Jun 1846; d Port-of-Spain, Trinidad 30 Jul 1889; (1) 3.

AGNEW, Jonathan Philip; b Macclesfield, Cheshire 4 Apr 1960; (3) 993, 994, 1020.

ALLEN, David Arthur; b Horfield, Bristol 29 Oct 1935; (39) 487, 488, 489, 490, 491, 495, 496, 507, 509, 510, 511, 512, 513, 514, 515, 516, 517, 518, 519, 530, 531, 532, 534, 539, 543, 544, 561, 571, 572, 573, 575, 597, 598, 599, 600, 602, 603, 604, 605.

ALLEN, George Oswald Browning; b Bellevue Hill, Sydney, Australia 31 Jul 1902; knighted for services to cricket 1986; d St John's Wood, London 29 Nov 1989; (25) 195, 209, 210, 211, 220, 221, 222, 223, 224, 225, 226, 227, 235, 237, 252, 253, 254, 255, 256, 257, 258, 259, 296, 297, 298.

ALLOM, Maurice James Carrick; b Northwood, Middlesex 23 Mar 1906; (5) 186, 187, 188, 189, 206.

ALLOTT, Paul John Walter; b Altrincham, Cheshire 14 Sep 1956; (13) 907, 916, 921, 928, 930, 991, 992, 993, 994, 1017, 1018, 1019, 1020.

AMES, Leslie Ethelbert George; b Eltham, Kent 3 Dec 1905; d Canterbury, Kent 26 Feb 1990; (47) 185, 190, 191, 192, 193, 209, 210, 211, 219, 220, 221, 222, 223, 224, 225, 226, 227, 228, 229, 233, 234, 235, 236, 237, 238, 239, 240, 241, 242, 243, 244, 246, 255, 256, 257, 258, 259, 260, 261, 262, 263, 264, 267, 268, 269, 270, 271.

AMISS, Dennis Leslie; b Harborne, Birmingham 7 Apr 1943; (50) 609, 619, 620, 623, 637, 687, 688, 689, 690, 703, 704, 705, 719, 720, 721, 722, 723, 724, 725, 726, 727, 731, 732, 733, 734, 735, 739, 740, 741, 742, 743, 744, 750, 752, 753, 754, 755, 758, 759, 760, 761, 781, 788, 789, 790, 791, 792, 803, 804, 805.

ANDREW, Keith Vincent; b Greenacres, Oldham, Lancashire 15 Dec 1929; (2) 391, 543.

APPLEYARD, Robert; b Wibsey, Bradford, Yorkshire 27 Jun 1924; (9) 388, 392, 393, 394, 395, 401, 402, 408, 425.

ARCHER, Alfred German; b Richmond, Surrey 6 Dec 1871; d Seaford, Sussex 15 Jul 1935; (1) 59.

ARMITAGE, Thomas; b Walkley, Sheffield, Yorkshire 25 Apr 1848; d Pullman, Chicago, USA 21 Sep 1922; (2) 1, 2.

ARNOLD, Edward George; b Exmouth, Devon 7 Nov 1876; d Worcester 25 Oct 1942; (10) 78, 80, 81, 82, 83, 84, 86, 87, 93, 94.

ARNOLD, Geoffrey Graham; b Earlsfield, Surrey 3 Sep 1944; (34) 622, 623, 658, 698, 701, 702, 703, 705, 706, 707, 719, 720, 721, 722, 723, 724, 725, 726, 727, 733, 734, 735, 740, 741, 742, 743, 744, 751, 753, 754, 755, 758, 759, 760.

ARNOLD, John; b Cowley, Oxford 30 Nov 1907; d Southampton, Hampshire 3 Apr 1984; (1) 209.

ASTILL, William Ewart; b Ratby, Leicestershire 1 Mar 1888; d Stoneygate, Leicester 10 Feb 1948; (9) 168, 169, 170, 171, 172, 190, 191, 192, 193.

ATHERTON, Michael Andrew; b Manchester 23 Mar 1968; (40) 1125, 1126, 1145, 1146, 1147, 1148, 1149, 1150, 1158, 1159, 1160, 1161, 1162, 1171, 1172, 1173, 1174, 1175, 1191, 1192, 1193, 1214, 1219, 1223, 1224, 1225, 1226, 1227, 1228, 1251, 1252, 1253, 1254, 1255, 1260, 1261, 1262, 1263, 1264, 1265.

ATHEY, Charles William Jeffrey; b Middlesbrough, Yorkshire 27 Sep 1957; (23) 885, 898, 899, 1047, 1048, 1049, 1050, 1051, 1058, 1059, 1060, 1061, 1062, 1075, 1076, 1077, 1078, 1084, 1085, 1086, 1090, 1091, 1101.

ATTEWELL, William; b Keyworth, Nottinghamshire 12 Jun 1861; d Long Eaton, Derbyshire 11 Jun 1927; (10) 17, 18, 19, 20, 21, 27, 33, 35, 36, 37.

BAILEY, Robert John; b Biddulph, Staffordshire 28 Oct 1963; (4) 1102, 1141, 1142, 1143.

BAILEY, Trevor Edward; b Westcliff-on-Sea, Essex 3 Dec 1923; (61) 314, 315, 316, 317, 323, 326, 327, 328, 329, 331, 332, 333, 334, 337, 372, 373, 374, 375, 376, 382, 383, 384, 385, 386, 387, 388, 389, 391, 392, 393, 394, 395, 401, 402, 408, 409, 410, 411, 412, 425, 426, 427, 428, 434, 435, 436, 437, 438, 439, 440, 441, 443, 454, 455, 456, 458, 464, 465, 466, 467, 468.

BAIRSTOW, David Leslie; b Horton, Bradford, Yorkshire 1 Sep 1951; (4) 854, 884, 885, 897.

BAKEWELL, Alfred Harry; b Walsall, Staffordshire 2 Nov 1908; d Westbourne, Dorset 23 Jan 1983; (6) 209, 210, 229, 232, 245, 246.

BALDERSTONE, John Christopher; b Longwood, Huddersfield, Yorkshire 16 Nov 1940; (2) 780, 781.

BARBER, Robert William; b Withington, Lancashire 26 Sep 1935; (28) 492, 512, 513, 514, 515, 516, 517, 518, 519, 565, 571, 572, 573, 574, 591, 592, 593, 594, 595, 596, 597, 598, 599, 600, 601, 608, 609, 637.

BARBER, Wilfred; b Cleckheaton, Yorkshire 18 Apr 1901; d Bradford, Yorkshire 10 Sep 1968; (2) 244, 245.

BARLOW, Graham Derek; b Folkestone, Kent 26 Mar 1950; (3) 788, 789, 804.

BARLOW, Richard Gorton; b Barrow Bridge, Bolton, Lancashire 28 May 1851; d Blackpool, Lancashire 31 Jul 1919; (17) 5, 6, 7, 8, 9, 10, 11, 12, 13, 14, 15, 16, 22, 23, 24, 25, 26.

BARNES, Sydney Francis; b Smethwick, Staffordshire 19 Apr 1873; d Chadsmoor, Staffordshire 26 Dec 1967; (27) 65, 66, 67, 72, 96, 97, 98, 99, 100, 103, 104, 105, 116, 117, 118, 119, 120, 122, 123, 124, 126, 128, 129, 130, 131, 132, 133.

BARNES, William; b Sutton in Ashfield, Nottinghamshire 27 May 1852; d Mansfield Woodhouse, Nottinghamshire 24 Mar 1899; (21) 4, 9, 10, 11, 12, 13, 14, 16, 17, 18, 19, 20, 21, 23, 24, 25, 28, 29, 30, 33, 34.

BARNETT, Charles John; b Fairview, Cheltenham, Gloucestershire 3 Jul 1910; d Stroud, Gloucestershire 28 May 1993; (20) 229, 230, 231, 232, 254, 255, 256, 257, 258, 259, 260, 261, 262, 263, 264, 265, 286, 287, 288, 299.

BARNETT, Kim John; b Stoke-on-Trent, Staffordshire 17 Jul 1960; (4) 1103, 1121, 1122, 1123.

BARRATT, Fred; b Annesley, Nottinghamshire 12 Apr 1894; d Nottingham 29 Jan 1947; (5) 184, 186, 187, 188, 189.

BARRINGTON, Kenneth Frank; b Reading, Berkshire 24 Nov 1930; d Needham's Point, Bridgetown, Barbados 14 Mar 1981; (82) 408, 409, 474, 475, 476, 477, 478, 487, 488, 489, 490, 491, 493, 494, 495, 496, 507, 508, 509, 510, 511, 512, 513, 514, 515, 516, 517, 518, 530, 531, 532, 534, 535, 536, 537, 538, 539, 540, 541, 542, 543, 544, 545, 546, 547, 553, 561, 562, 563, 564, 565, 571, 572, 573, 574, 575, 591, 593, 594, 595, 596, 597, 598, 599, 600, 601, 605, 606, 618, 619, 620, 621, 622, 623, 628, 629, 630, 631, 632, 638, 639, 640.

BARTON, Victor Alexander; b Hound, Netley, Hampshire 22 Oct 1867; d Belle Vue, Southampton, Hampshire 23 Mar 1906; (1) 38.

BATES, Willie; b Lascelles Hall, Huddersfield, Yorkshire 19 Nov 1855; d Lepton, Yorkshire 8 Jan 1900; (15) 5, 6, 7, 8, 10, 11, 12, 13, 17, 18, 19, 20, 21, 25, 26.

BEAN, George; b Sutton in Ashfield, Nottinghamshire 7 Mar 1864; d Mansfield, Nottinghamshire 16 Mar 1923; (3) 35, 36, 37.

BEDSER, Alec Victor; b Reading, Berkshire 4 Jul 1918; (51) 276, 277, 278, 279, 280, 281, 282, 283, 284, 285, 286, 299, 300, 301, 302, 303, 309, 310, 311, 312, 313, 314, 317, 324, 325, 326, 327, 328, 329, 330, 331, 332, 333, 334, 335, 336, 337, 338, 351, 352, 353, 354, 372, 373, 374, 375, 376, 388, 389, 391, 410.

BENJAMIN, Joseph Emmanuel; b Christ Church, St Kitts 2 Feb 1961; (1) 1265

BENSON, Mark Richard; b Shoreham, Sussex 6 Jul 1958; (1) 1048.

BERRY, Robert; b West Gorton, Manchester 29 Jan 1926; (2) 323, 324.

BICKNELL, Martin Paul; b Guildford, Surrey 14 Jan 1969; (2) 1226, 1227

BINKS, James Graham; b Hull, Yorkshire 5 Oct 1935; (2) 554, 555.

BIRD, Morice Carlos; b St Michael's Hamlet, Liverpool, Lancashire 25 Mar 1888; d Broadstone, Dorset 9 Dec 1933; (10) 106, 107, 108, 109, 110, 130, 131, 132, 133, 134.

BIRKENSHAW, Jack; b Rothwell, Yorkshire 13 Nov 1940; (5) 706, 707, 721, 734, 735.

BLAKEY, Richard John; b Huddersfield, Yorkshire 15 Jan 1967; (2) 1213, 1214.

BLIGH, *Hon.* Ivo Francis Walter (*became 8th Earl of Darnley in 1900*); b Westminster, London 13 Mar 1859; d Puckle Hill, Cobham, Kent 10 Apr 1927; (4) 10, 11, 12, 13.

BLYTHE, Colin; b Deptford, Kent 30 May 1879, d near Passchendaele, Belgium 8 Nov 1917; (19) 65, 66, 67, 68, 69, 85, 88, 89, 90, 91, 92, 93, 94, 95, 96, 101, 104, 109, 110.

BOARD, John Henry; b Clifton, Bristol 23 Feb 1867; d on board *SS Kenilworth Castle* (en route from South Africa) 15 Apr 1924; (6) 58, 59, 88, 89, 91, 92.

BOLUS, John Brian; b Whitkirk, Leeds, Yorkshire 31 Jan 1934; (7) 546, 547, 553, 554, 555, 556, 557.

BOOTH, Major William; b Pudsey, Yorkshire 10 Dec 1886; d near La Cigny, France 1 Jul 1916; (2) 130, 134.

BOSANQUET, Bernard James Tindal; b Bulls Cross, Enfield, Middlesex 13 Oct 1877; d Ewhurst, Surrey 12 Oct 1936; (7) 78, 80, 81, 82, 83, 84, 85.

BOTHAM, Ian Terence; b Heswall, Cheshire 24 Nov 1955; (102) 806, 807, 817, 818, 819, 825, 826, 827, 828, 829, 830, 834, 835, 836, 837, 838, 839, 851, 852, 853, 854, 868, 870, 872, 876, 880, 881, 882, 883, 884, 885, 896, 897, 898, 899, 903, 904, 905, 906, 907, 908, 912, 913, 914, 915, 916, 917, 921, 928, 929, 930, 931, 932, 933, 938, 939, 940, 941, 942, 957, 958, 959, 960, 975, 976, 977, 978, 989, 990, 991, 992, 993, 994, 1017, 1018, 1019, 1020, 1021, 1022, 1038, 1039, 1040, 1041, 1042, 1051, 1058, 1059, 1061, 1062, 1075, 1076, 1077, 1078, 1079, 1123, 1124, 1125, 1175, 1176, 1187, 1189, 1190.

BOWDEN, Montague Parker; b Stockwell, Surrey 1 Nov 1865; d Umtali, Mashonaland (*later Rhodesia*) 19 Feb 1892; (2) 31, 32.

BOWES, William Eric; b Elland, Yorkshire 25 Jul 1908; d Menston, Leeds, Yorkshire 5 Sep 1987; (15) 219, 221, 226, 234, 236, 237, 242, 244, 245, 246, 265, 266, 272, 273, 276.

BOWLEY, Edward Henry; b Leatherhead, Surrey 6 Jun 1890; d Winchester, Hampshire 9 Jul 1974; (5) 183, 184, 187, 188, 189.

BOYCOTT, Geoffrey; b Fitzwilliam, Yorkshire 21 Oct 1940; (108) 561, 563, 564, 565, 571, 572, 573, 574, 575, 591, 592, 594, 595, 597, 598, 599, 600, 601, 602, 603, 606, 607, 608, 609, 618, 620, 622, 628, 629, 630, 631, 632, 637, 638, 639, 653, 654, 655, 656, 657, 658, 674, 675, 676, 677, 678, 688, 689, 690, 698, 699, 722, 723, 724, 725, 726, 727, 731, 732, 733, 734, 735, 739, 806, 807, 808, 814, 815, 816, 817, 818, 819, 829, 830, 834, 835, 836, 837, 838, 839, 851, 852, 853, 854, 868, 870, 872, 876, 880, 881, 882, 883, 884, 885, 896, 897, 898, 899, 903, 904, 905, 906, 907, 908, 912, 913, 914, 915.

BRADLEY, Walter Morris; b Sydenham, Kent 2 Jan 1875; d Wandsworth Common, Surrey 19 Jun 1944; (2) 63, 64.

BRAUND, Leonard Charles; b Clewer, Berkshire 18 Oct 1875; d Putney Common, Surrey 23 Dec 1955; (23) 65, 66, 67, 68, 69, 70, 71, 72, 73, 74, 78, 79, 80, 81, 82, 93, 94, 95, 96, 97, 98, 99, 100.

BREARLEY, John Michael; b Harrow, Middlesex 28 Apr 1942; (39) 777, 778, 788, 789, 790, 791, 792, 803, 804, 805, 806, 807, 808, 814, 815, 825, 826, 827, 828, 829, 830, 834, 835, 836, 837, 838, 839, 851, 852, 853, 854, 868, 870, 872, 876, 905, 906, 907, 908.

BREARLEY, Walter; b Bolton, Lancashire 11 Mar 1876; d Middlesex Hospital, London W1 13 Jan 1937; (4) 86, 87, 103, 122.

BRENNAN, Donald Vincent; b Eccleshill, Bradford, Yorkshire 10 Feb 1920; d Ilkley, Yorkshire 9 Jan 1985; (2) 337, 338.

BRIGGS, John; b Sutton in Ashfield, Nottinghamshire 3 Oct 1862; d Cheadle, Cheshire 11 Jan 1902; (33) 17, 18, 19, 20, 21, 22, 23, 24, 25, 26, 27, 28, 29, 30, 31, 32, 35, 36, 37, 40, 41, 42, 43, 44, 45, 46, 51, 53, 54, 55, 56, 57, 62.

EMMETT, Thomas, b Halifax, Yorkshire 3 Sep 1841; d Leicester 30 Jun 1904; (7) 1, 2, 3, 5, 6, 7, 8.

EVANS, Alfred John; b Newtown, Hampshire 1 May 1889; d Marylebone, London 18 Sep 1960; (1) 141.

EVANS, Thomas Godfrey; b Finchley, Middlesex 18 Aug 1920; (91) 278, 280, 281, 282, 283, 284, 285, 286, 287, 288, 289, 295, 296, 297, 298, 299, 300, 301, 302, 303, 309, 310, 311, 314, 315, 316, 317, 323, 324, 325, 327, 328, 329, 330, 331, 332, 333, 334, 335, 336, 351, 352, 353, 354, 372, 373, 374, 375, 376, 382, 383, 384, 386, 387, 388, 389, 390, 392, 393, 394, 395, 401, 402, 408, 409, 410, 425, 426, 427, 428, 429, 434, 435, 436, 437, 438, 439, 440, 441, 442, 443, 454, 455, 456, 457, 458, 464, 465, 467, 474, 475.

FAGG, Arthur Edward; b Chartham, Kent 18 Jun 1915; d Tunbridge Wells, Kent 13 Sep 1977; (5) 253, 254, 255, 256, 273.

FAIRBROTHER, Neil Harvey; b Warrington, Lancashire 9 Sep 1963; (10) 1075, 1086, 1092, 1093, 1145, 1146, 1147, 1212, 1213, 1219.

FANE, Frederick Luther; b Curragh Camp, Ireland 27 Apr 1875; d Kelvedon Hatch, Brentwood, Essex 27 Nov 1960; (14) 88, 89, 90, 91, 92, 96, 97, 98, 100, 106, 107, 108, 109, 110.

FARNES, Kenneth; b Leytonstone, Essex 8 Jul 1911; d Chipping Warden, Northamptonshire 20 Oct 1941; (15) 233, 234, 238, 241, 258, 259, 263, 264, 265, 266, 267, 268, 269, 270, 271.

FARRIMOND, William; b Daisy Hill, Lancashire 23 May 1903; d Westhoughton, Bolton, Lancashire 14 Nov 1979; (4) 207, 208, 239, 243.

FENDER, Percy George Herbert; b Balham, Surrey 22 Aug 1892; d Exeter, Devon 15 Jun 1985; (13) 137, 138, 139, 143, 144, 148, 149, 150, 151, 152, 153, 154, 181.

FERRIS, John James; b Sydney, Australia 21 May 1867; d Pietermaritzburg, South Africa 17 Nov 1900; (1) 38. (*Also 8 Tests for Australia: 25-30, 33, 34*).

FIELDER, Arthur; b Plaxtol, Tonbridge, Kent 19 Jul 1877; d Lambeth, London 30 Aug 1949; (6) 79, 80, 96, 97, 98, 99.

FISHLOCK, Laurence Barnard; b Battersea, London 2 Jan 1907; d London 26 Jun 1986; (4) 253, 254, 278, 283.

FLAVELL, John Alfred; b Wall Heath, Staffordshire 15 May 1929; (4) 510, 511, 561, 563.

FLETCHER, Keith William Robert; b Worcester 20 May 1944; (59) 640, 647, 648, 649, 656, 657, 674, 675, 676, 678, 679, 685, 691, 692, 701, 703, 704, 705, 706, 707, 719, 720, 721, 722, 723, 724, 725, 726, 727, 731, 733, 734, 735, 739, 740, 741, 742, 743, 744, 750, 751, 753, 754, 755, 758, 759, 760, 762, 788, 791, 792, 803, 912, 913, 914, 915, 916, 917, 921.

FLOWERS, Wilfred; b Calverton, Nottinghamshire 7 Dec 1856; d Carlton, Nottinghamshire 1 Nov 1926; (8) 17, 18, 19, 20, 21, 25, 26, 39.

FORD, Francis Gilbertson Justice; b Paddington, London 14 Dec 1866; d Burwash, Sussex 7 Feb 1940; (5) 42, 43, 44, 45, 46.

FOSTER, Frank Rowbotham; b Deritend, Birmingham 31 Jan 1889; d Northampton 3 May 1958; (11) 116, 117, 118, 119, 120, 122, 123, 124, 126, 128, 129.

FOSTER, Neil Alan; b Colchester, Essex 6 May 1962; (29) 959, 975, 977, 979, 980, 990, 1008, 1009, 1018, 1040, 1041, 1042, 1048, 1049, 1075, 1076, 1077, 1078, 1079, 1084, 1085, 1090, 1101, 1102, 1103, 1121, 1122, 1124, 1224.

FOSTER, Reginald Erskine; b Malvern, Worcestershire 16 Apr 1878; d Kensington, London 13 May 1914; (8) 78, 79, 80, 81, 82, 93, 94, 95.

FOTHERGILL, Arnold James; b Newcastle upon Tyne, Northumberland 26 Aug 1854; d Newcastle upon Tyne 1 Aug 1932; (2) 31, 32.

FOWLER, Graeme; b Accrington, Lancashire 20 Apr 1957; (21) 933, 939, 940, 941, 957, 958, 976, 977, 979, 980, 989, 990, 991, 992, 993, 994, 1005, 1006, 1007, 1008, 1009.

FRASER, Angus Robert Charles; b Billinge, Lancashire 8 Aug 1965; (21) 1123, 1124, 1125, 1140, 1141, 1148, 1149, 1150, 1158, 1159, 1161, 1228, 1252, 1253, 1254, 1255, 1260, 1261, 1262, 1263, 1264.

FREEMAN, Alfred Percy; b Lewisham, Kent 17 May 1888; d Bearsted, Kent 28 Jan 1965; (12) 158, 160, 169, 170, 171, 172, 173, 174, 175, 183, 184, 185.

FRENCH, Bruce Nicholas; b Warsop, Nottinghamshire 13 Aug 1959; (16) 1047, 1048, 1049, 1050, 1051, 1075, 1076, 1078, 1079, 1084, 1085, 1086, 1090, 1091, 1092, 1093.

FRY, Charles Burgess; b West Croydon, Surrey 25 Apr 1872; d Hampstead, Middlesex 7 Sep 1956; (26) 47, 48, 60, 61, 62, 63, 64, 70, 71, 72, 84, 85, 86, 87, 93, 94, 95, 101, 103, 105, 122, 123, 124, 126, 128, 129.

GATTING, Michael William; b Kingsbury, Middlesex 6 Jun 1957; (74) 816, 819, 881, 882, 883, 884, 885, 897, 903, 904, 905, 906, 907, 908, 913, 914, 915, 916, 917, 931, 932, 933, 959, 960, 975, 976, 978, 979, 980, 990, 1005, 1006, 1007, 1008, 1009, 1017, 1018, 1019, 1020, 1021, 1022, 1042, 1046, 1047, 1048, 1049, 1050, 1051, 1058, 1059, 1060, 1061, 1062, 1075, 1076, 1077, 1078, 1079, 1084, 1085, 1086, 1090, 1091, 1092, 1093, 1098, 1100, 1122, 1212, 1213, 1214, 1219, 1223, 1224.

GAY, Leslie Hewitt; b Brighton, Sussex 24 Mar 1871; d Salcombe Regis, Devon 1 Nov 1949; (1) 42.

GEARY, George; b Barwell, Leicestershire 9 Jul 1893; d Leicester 6 Mar 1981; (14) 156, 165, 167, 168, 169, 177, 178, 179, 180, 184, 185, 196, 233, 234.

GIBB, Paul Antony; b Brandsby, Yorkshire 11 Jul 1913; d Guildford, Surrey 7 Dec 1977; (8) 267, 268, 269, 270, 271, 276, 277, 279.

GIFFORD, Norman; b Ulverston, Lancashire 30 Mar 1940; (15) 562, 563, 688, 689, 690, 691, 698, 699, 700, 705, 706, 720, 721, 722, 723.

GILLIGAN, Arthur Edward Robert; b Denmark Hill, Surrey 23 Dec 1894; d Mare Hill, Pulborough, Sussex 5 Sep 1976; (11) 148, 152, 153, 154, 155, 157, 158, 159, 160, 161, 162.

GILLIGAN, Alfred Herbert Harold; b Denmark Hill, Surrey 29 Jun 1896; d Shamley Green, Surrey 5 May 1978; (4) 186, 187, 188, 189.

GIMBLETT, Harold; b Bicknoller, Somerset 19 Oct 1914; d Verwood, Dorset 30 Mar 1978; (3) 252, 253, 272.

GLADWIN, Clifford; b Doe Lea, Derbyshire 3 Apr 1916; d Chesterfield, Derbyshire 10 Apr 1988; (8) 287, 289, 309, 310, 311, 312, 313, 315.

GODDARD, Thomas William John; b Gloucester 1 Oct 1900; d Gloucester 22 May 1966; (8) 197, 261, 262, 267, 268, 270, 273, 274.

GOOCH, Graham Alan; b Leytonstone, Essex 23 Jul 1953; (113) 760, 761, 826, 827, 828, 829, 830, 834, 835, 836, 837, 838, 839, 851, 852, 853, 854, 870, 872, 876, 880, 881, 882, 883, 884, 885, 896, 897, 898, 899, 903, 904, 905, 906, 907, 912, 913, 914,

GOOCH, Graham Alan – *continued*
915, 916, 917, 921, 1017, 1018, 1019, 1020, 1021,
1022, 1038, 1039, 1040, 1041, 1042, 1046, 1047,
1048, 1049, 1050, 1051, 1084, 1085, 1086, 1098,
1099, 1100, 1101, 1102, 1103, 1121, 1122, 1123,
1124, 1126, 1140, 1141, 1145, 1146, 1147, 1148,
1149, 1150, 1159, 1160, 1161, 1162, 1171, 1172,
1173, 1174, 1175, 1176, 1185, 1186, 1187, 1189,
1190, 1191, 1192, 1193, 1212, 1214, 1223, 1224,
1225, 1226, 1227, 1228, 1260, 1261, 1262, 1263,
1264, 1265.

GOUGH, Darren; b Barnsley, Yorkshire 18 Sep 1970; (4),
1262, 1263, 1264, 1265.

GOVER, Alfred Richard; b Epsom, Surrey 29 Feb 1908;
(4) 253, 260, 262, 278.

GOWER, David Ivon; b Tunbridge Wells, Kent 1 Apr
1957; (117), 825, 826, 827, 828, 829, 830, 834, 835,
836, 837, 838, 839, 851, 852, 853, 854, 868, 870,
872, 876, 880, 885, 896, 897, 898, 899, 903, 904,
905, 906, 907, 912, 913, 914, 915, 916, 917, 921,
928, 929, 930, 931, 932, 933, 938, 939, 940, 941,
942, 957, 958, 959, 960, 975, 976, 977, 978, 979,
980, 989, 990, 991, 992, 993, 994, 1005, 1006, 1007,
1008, 1009, 1017, 1018, 1019, 1020, 1021, 1022,
1038, 1039, 1040, 1041, 1042, 1046, 1048, 1049,
1050, 1051, 1058, 1059, 1060, 1061, 1062, 1075,
1076, 1077, 1078, 1079, 1098, 1099, 1100, 1101,
1121, 1122, 1123, 1124, 1125, 1126, 1148, 1149,
1150, 1158, 1159, 1160, 1161, 1162, 1191, 1192,
1193.

GRACE, Edward Mills; b Downend, Bristol 28 Nov 1841;
d Thornbury, Gloucestershire 20 May 1911; (1) 4.

GRACE, George Frederick; b Downend, Bristol 13 Dec
1850; d Basingstoke, Hampshire 22 Sep 1880; (1) 4.

GRACE, William Gilbert; b Downend, Bristol 18 Jul 1848;
d Mottingham, Kent 23 Oct 1915; (22) 4, 9, 14, 15,
16, 22, 23, 24, 28, 29, 30, 33, 34, 35, 36, 37, 40, 41,
50, 51, 52, 60.

GRAVENEY, Thomas William; b Riding Mill, Northumberland 16 Jun 1927; (79) 336, 340, 341, 342,
343, 351, 352, 353, 354, 372, 373, 374, 375, 376,
382, 383, 384, 385, 386, 388, 389, 390, 392, 395,
401, 402, 408, 409, 410, 411, 412, 425, 426, 440,
441, 442, 443, 454, 455, 456, 457, 464, 465, 466,
467, 468, 472, 473, 530, 531, 532, 533, 536, 538,
539, 606, 607, 608, 609, 618, 619, 620, 621, 622,
623, 628, 629, 630, 631, 632, 637, 638, 639, 640,
641, 647, 648, 649, 653.

GREENHOUGH, Thomas; b Cronkey Shaw, Rochdale,
Lancashire 9 Nov 1931; (4) 474, 475, 478, 496.

GREENWOOD, Andrew; b Cowmes Lepton, Huddersfield, Yorkshire 20 Aug 1847; d Huddersfield 12
Feb 1889; (2) 1, 2.

GREIG, Anthony William; b Queenstown, South Africa 6
Oct 1946; (58) 698, 699, 700, 701, 702, 703, 704,
705, 706, 707, 719, 720, 721, 722, 723, 724, 725,
726, 727, 731, 732, 733, 734, 735, 739, 740, 741,
742, 743, 744, 750, 751, 752, 753, 754, 755, 758,
759, 760, 761, 762, 763, 777, 778, 779, 780, 781,
788, 789, 790, 791, 792, 803, 804, 805, 806, 807,
808.

GREIG, Ian Alexander; b Queenstown, South Africa 8
Dec 1955; (2) 931, 932.

GRIEVE, Basil Arthur Firebrace; b Kilburn, Middlesex 28
May 1864; d Eastbourne, Sussex 19 Nov 1917; (2)
31, 32.

GRIFFITH, Stewart Cathie; b Wandsworth, Surrey 16 Jun
1914; d Felpham, Sussex 7 Apr 1993; (3) 296, 312,
313.

GUNN, George; b Hucknall Torkard, Nottinghamshire 13
Jun 1879; d Tylers Green, Cuckfield, Sussex 29 Jun
1958; (15) 96, 97, 98, 99, 100, 102, 116, 117, 118,
119, 120, 190, 191, 192, 193.

GUNN, John Richmond; b Hucknall Torkard, Nottinghamshire 19 Jul 1876; d Basford, Nottingham 21
Aug 1963; (6) 65, 66, 67, 68, 69, 83.

GUNN, William; b St Anne's, Nottingham 4 Dec 1858; d
Nottingham 29 Jan 1921; (11) 25, 26, 28, 30, 33, 34,
39, 40, 41, 50, 60.

HAIG, Nigel Esmé; b Kensington, London 12 Dec 1887; d
Eastbourne, Sussex 27 Oct 1966; (5) 141, 190, 191,
192, 193.

HAIGH, Schofield; b Berry Brow, Huddersfield, Yorkshire 19 Mar 1871; d Taylor Hill, Huddersfield 27
Feb 1921; (11) 58, 59, 84, 85, 88, 89, 90, 91, 92, 102,
126.

HALLOWS, Charles; b Little Lever, Lancashire 4 Apr
1895; d Bolton, Lancashire 10 Nov 1972; (2) 143,
173.

HAMMOND, Walter Reginald; b Buckland, Dover, Kent
19 Jun 1903; d Durban, South Africa 1 Jul 1965;
(85) 168, 169, 170, 171, 172, 173, 174, 175, 176,
177, 178, 179, 180, 181, 182, 183, 185, 194, 195,
196, 197, 198, 204, 205, 206, 207, 208, 209, 210,
211, 219, 220, 221, 222, 223, 224, 225, 226, 227,
228, 229, 233, 234, 235, 236, 237, 238, 239, 240,
241, 242, 243, 244, 245, 246, 253, 254, 255, 256,
257, 258, 259, 260, 261, 262, 263, 264, 265, 266,
267, 268, 269, 270, 271, 272, 273, 274, 276, 277,
278, 279, 280, 281, 282, 284.

HAMPSHIRE, John Harry; b Thurnscoe, Yorkshire 10
Feb 1941; (8) 654, 655, 678, 679, 685, 686, 702, 762.

HARDINGE, Harold Thomas William; b Greenwich,
Kent 25 Feb 1886; d Cambridge, Kent 8 May 1965;
(1) 142.

HARDSTAFF, Joseph, *sr*; b Kirkby in Ashfield, Nottinghamshire 9 Nov 1882; d Nuncargate, Nottinghamshire 2 Apr 1947; (5) 96, 97, 98, 99, 100.

HARDSTAFF, Joseph, *jr*; b Nuncargate, Nottinghamshire
3 Jul 1911; d Worksop, Nottinghamshire 1 Jan
1990; (23) 244, 252, 253, 255, 256, 257, 258, 259,
260, 261, 262, 265, 266, 272, 273, 274, 276, 277,
282, 295, 297, 298, 299.

HARRIS, *4th Lord (Hon.* George Robert Canning); b St
Anne's, Trinidad 3 Feb 1851 (*succeeded to title
1872*); d Belmont, Faversham, Kent 24 Mar 1932;
(4) 3, 4, 15, 16.

HARTLEY, John Cabourn; b Lincoln 15 Nov 1874; d
Woodhall Spa, Lincolnshire 8 Mar 1963; (2) 90, 92.

HAWKE, *7th Lord (Hon.* Martin Bladen); b Willingham,
Gainsborough, Lincolnshire 16 Aug 1860 (*suc-
ceeded to title 1887*); d West End, Edinburgh,
Scotland 10 Oct 1938; (5) 47, 48, 49, 58, 59.

HAYES, Ernest George; b Peckham, Surrey 6 Nov 1876; d
West Dulwich, Surrey 2 Dec 1953; (5) 88, 90, 91,
105, 128.

HAYES, Frank Charles; b Preston, Lancashire 6 Dec
1946; (9) 725, 726, 727, 731, 732, 734, 735, 779,
780.

HAYWARD, Thomas Walter; b Cambridge 29 Mar 1871;
d Cambridge 19 Jul 1939; (35) 47, 48, 49, 50, 52, 53,
54, 55, 56, 57, 60, 61, 62, 63, 64, 65, 66, 67, 68, 69,
74, 78, 79, 80, 81, 82, 83, 84, 85, 86, 87, 93, 94, 95,
102.

HEARNE, Alec; b Ealing, Middlesex 22 Jul 1863; d
Beckenham, Kent 16 May 1952; (1) 38.

LEVER, John Kenneth; b Stepney, London 24 Feb 1949; (21) 788, 789, 790, 791, 792, 803, 804, 805, 808, 814, 815, 816, 819, 835, 852, 872, 876, 880, 913, 914, 1047.

LEVER, Peter; b Todmorden, Yorkshire 17 Sep 1940; (17) 675, 676, 677, 678, 679, 685, 686, 687, 688, 689, 691, 700, 750, 755, 758, 759, 761.

LEVESON GOWER, Henry Dudley Gresham; b Titsey, Surrey 8 May 1873; knighted for services to cricket 1953; d Kensington, London 1 Feb 1954; (3) 106, 107, 108.

LEVETT, William Howard Vincent; b Goudhurst, Kent 25 Jan 1908; (1) 231.

LEWIS, Anthony Robert; b Uplands, Swansea, Wales 6 Jul 1938; (9) 703, 704, 705, 706, 707, 719, 720, 721, 722.

LEWIS, Clairmonte Christopher; b Georgetown, Guyana 14 Feb 1968; (25) 1147, 1148, 1149, 1158, 1174, 1175, 1176, 1185, 1186, 1189, 1190, 1191, 1192, 1193, 1212, 1213, 1214, 1219, 1223, 1224, 1251, 1252, 1253, 1254, 1255.

LEYLAND, Morris (*known as Maurice*); b New Park, Harrogate, Yorkshire 20 Jul 1900; d Scotton Banks, Harrogate 1 Jan 1967; (41) 175, 180, 181, 182, 183, 184, 185, 196, 197, 198, 204, 205, 206, 207, 208, 220, 221, 222, 223, 224, 227, 233, 234, 235, 236, 237, 238, 239, 240, 242, 243, 245, 246, 252, 254, 255, 256, 257, 258, 259, 266.

LILLEY, Arthur Frederick Augustus; b Holloway Head, Birmingham 28 Nov 1866; d Brislington, Bristol 17 Nov 1929; (35) 50, 51, 52, 61, 62, 63, 64, 65, 66, 67, 68, 69, 70, 71, 72, 73, 74, 78, 79, 80, 81, 82, 83, 84, 85, 86, 87, 93, 94, 95, 101, 102, 103, 104, 105.

LILLYWHITE, James, *jr*; b Westhampnett, Sussex 23 Feb 1842; d Westerton, Sussex 25 Oct 1929; (2) 1, 2.

LLOYD, David; b Accrington, Lancashire 18 Mar 1947; (9) 740, 741, 742, 743, 744, 751, 752, 753, 754.

LLOYD, Timothy Andrew; b Oswestry, Shropshire 5 Nov 1956; (1) 989.

LOADER, Peter James; b Wallington, Surrey 25 Oct 1929; (13) 390, 411, 435, 436, 437, 438, 442, 443, 454, 455, 456, 464, 465.

LOCK, Graham Anthony Richard; b Limpsfield, Surrey 5 Jul 1929; d Perth, Australia 13 Mar 1995; (49) 353, 354, 375, 376, 382, 383, 384, 385, 386, 410, 411, 412, 425, 427, 428, 429, 438, 439, 442, 443, 454, 455, 456, 457, 458, 464, 465, 466, 467, 472, 473, 508, 509, 511, 513, 514, 515, 516, 517, 518, 519, 530, 531, 533, 545, 546, 547, 631, 632.

LOCKWOOD, William Henry; b Old Radford, Nottinghamshire 25 Mar 1868; d Old Radford 26 Apr 1932; (12) 39, 40, 42, 43, 44, 45, 46, 64, 70, 71, 73, 74.

LOHMANN, George Alfred; b Kensington, London 2 Jun 1865; d Matjesfontein, Cape Province, South Africa 1 Dec 1901; (18) 22, 23, 24, 25, 26, 27, 28, 29, 30, 33, 34, 35, 36, 37, 47, 48, 49, 50.

LOWSON, Frank Anderson; b Bradford, Yorkshire 1 Jul 1925; d Pool in Wharfedale, Yorkshire 8 Sep 1984; (7) 337, 338, 339, 340, 342, 343, 411.

LUCAS, Alfred Perry; b Westminster, London 20 Feb 1857; d Great Waltham, Essex 12 Oct 1923; (5) 3, 4, 9, 14, 15.

LUCKHURST, Brian William; b Sittingbourne, Kent 5 Feb 1939; (21) 674, 675, 676, 677, 679, 685, 686, 687, 688, 689, 690, 691, 692, 698, 700, 701, 726, 727, 750, 751.

LYTTELTON, *Hon.* Alfred; b London 7 Feb 1857; d Marylebone, London 5 Jul 1913; (4) 4, 9, 15, 16.

MACAULAY, George Gibson; b Thirsk, Yorkshire 7 Dec 1897; d Sullom Voe, Shetland Islands 13 Dec 1940; (8) 149, 150, 151, 152, 155, 165, 227, 228.

MacBRYAN, John Crawford William; b Box, Wiltshire 22 Jul 1892; d London 14 Jul 1983; (1) 156.

McCAGUE, Martin John; b Larne, N Ireland 24 May 1969; (2) 1225, 1226.

McCONNON, James Edward; b Burnopfield, Co. Durham 21 Jun 1922; (2) 389, 390.

McGAHEY, Charles Percy; b Bethnal Green, London 12 Feb 1871; d Whipps Cross, Essex 10 Jan 1935; (2) 68, 69.

MacGREGOR, Gregor; b Merchiston, Edinburgh, Scotland 31 Aug 1869; d Marylebone, London 20 Aug 1919; (8) 33, 34, 35, 36, 37, 39, 40, 41.

McINTYRE, Arthur John William; b Kennington, London 14 May 1918; (3) 326, 327, 411.

MacKINNON, Francis Alexander (*The 35th MacKinnon of MacKinnon*) b Kensington, London 9 Apr 1848; d Drumduan, Forres, Morayshire, Scotland 27 Feb 1947; (1) 3.

MacLAREN, Archibald Campbell; b Whalley Range, Manchester 1 Dec 1871; d Warfield Park, Bracknell, Berkshire 17 Nov 1944; (35) 42, 43, 44, 45, 46, 51, 52, 53, 54, 55, 56, 57, 61, 62, 63, 64, 65, 66, 67, 68, 69, 70, 71, 72, 73, 74, 83, 84, 86, 87, 101, 102, 103, 104, 105.

McMASTER, Joseph Emile Patrick; b Gilford, Co. Down, Ireland 16 Mar 1861; d London 7 Jun 1929; (1) 32.

MAKEPEACE, Joseph William Henry; b Middlesbrough, Yorkshire 22 Aug 1881; d Spital, Bebington, Cheshire 19 Dec 1952; (4) 136, 137, 138, 139.

MALCOLM, Devon Eugene; b Kingston, Jamaica 22 Feb 1963; (28) 1125, 1140, 1141, 1142, 1143, 1145, 1146, 1147, 1148, 1149, 1150, 1158, 1159, 1160, 1161, 1162, 1171, 1172, 1190, 1191, 1193, 1212, 1213, 1219, 1228, 1251, 1260, 1265.

MALLENDER, Neil Alan; b Kirk Sandall, Yorkshire 13 Aug 1961; (2) 1192, 1193.

MANN, Francis George; b Byfleet, Surrey 6 Sep 1917; (7) 309, 310, 311, 312, 313, 314, 315.

MANN, Francis Thomas; b Winchmore Hill, Middlesex 3 Mar 1888; d Milton Lilbourne, Wiltshire 6 Oct 1964; (5) 148, 149, 150, 151, 152.

MARKS, Victor James; b Middle Chinnock, Somerset 25 Jun 1955; (6) 933, 957, 977, 978, 979, 980.

MARRIOTT, Charles Stowell; b Heaton Moor, Lancashire 14 Sep 1895; d Dollis Hill, Middlesex 13 Oct 1966; (1) 229.

MARTIN, Frederick; b Dartford, Kent 12 Oct 1861; d Dartford 13 Dec 1921; (2) 34, 38.

MARTIN, John William; b Catford, Kent 16 Feb 1917; d Woolwich, London 4 Jan 1987; (1) 285.

MASON, John Richard; b Blackheath, Kent 26 Mar 1874; d Cooden, Sussex 15 Oct 1958; (5) 53, 54, 55, 56, 57.

MATTHEWS, Austin David George; b Penarth, Glamorgan, Wales 3 May 1904; d Penrhyn Bay, Denbighshire, Wales 29 Jul 1977; (1) 262.

MAY, Peter Barker Howard; b Reading, Berkshire 31 Dec 1929; d Liphook, Hampshire 27 Dec 1994; (66) 337, 338, 351, 352, 353, 354, 372, 376, 382, 383, 384, 385, 386, 387, 388, 389, 390, 391, 392, 393, 394, 395, 401, 402, 408, 409, 410, 411, 412, 425, 426, 427, 428, 429, 434, 435, 436, 437, 438, 439, 440, 441, 442, 443, 454, 455, 456, 457, 458, 464, 465, 466, 467, 468, 472, 473, 474, 475, 476, 487, 488, 489, 508, 509, 510, 511.

MAYNARD, Matthew Peter; b Oldham, Lancashire 21 Mar 1966; (4) 1102, 1227, 1228, 1251.

MEAD, Charles Philip; b Battersea, London 9 Mar 1887; d Boscombe, Hampshire 26 Mar 1958; (17) 116, 117, 118, 119, 130, 131, 132, 133, 134, 143, 144, 148, 149, 150, 151, 152, 176.

MEAD, Walter; b Clapton, Middlesex 25 Mar 1868; d Chipping Ongar, Essex 18 Mar 1954; (1) 61.

MIDWINTER, William Evans; b St Briavels, Gloucestershire 19 Jun 1851; d Yarra Bend, Kew, Melbourne, Australia 3 Dec 1890; (4) 5, 6, 7, 8. (*Also 8 Tests for Australia; 1, 2, 13-16, 25, 26*).

MILBURN, Colin; b Burnopfield, Co. Durham 23 Oct 1941; d Newton Aycliffe, Co. Durham 28 Feb 1990; (9) 605, 606, 607, 608, 620, 621, 638, 641, 649.

MILLER, Audley Montague; b Brentry, Westbury-on-Trym, Gloucestershire 19 Oct 1869; d Clifton, Bristol 26 Jun 1959; (1) 47.

MILLER, Geoffrey; b Chesterfield, Derbyshire 8 Sep 1952; (34) 781, 805, 806, 814, 815, 816, 817, 818, 819, 825, 826, 827, 828, 829, 834, 835, 836, 837, 838, 839, 851, 852, 853, 868, 896, 929, 931, 938, 939, 940, 941, 942, 989, 990.

MILLIGAN, Frank William; b Aldershot, Hampshire 19 Mar 1870; d Ramatlabama, Bechuanaland 31 May 1900; (2) 58, 59.

MILLMAN, Geoffrey; b Bedford 2 Oct 1934; (6) 516, 517, 518, 519, 530, 531.

MILTON, Clement Arthur; b Bedminster, Bristol 10 Mar 1928; (6) 456, 458, 464, 466, 474, 475.

MITCHELL, Arthur; b Baildon, Yorkshire 13 Sep 1902; d Bradford, Yorkshire 25 Dec 1976; (6) 230, 231, 232, 244, 246, 252.

MITCHELL, Frank; b Market Weighton, Yorkshire 13 Aug 1872; d Blackheath, Kent 11 Oct 1935; (2) 58, 59, (*Also 3 Tests for South Africa; 121, 122, 125*).

MITCHELL, Thomas Bignall; b Cresswell, Derbyshire 4 Sep 1902; (5) 223, 226, 233, 236, 243.

MITCHELL-INNES, Norman Stewart; b Calcutta, India 7 Sep 1914; (1) 242.

MOLD, Arthur Webb; b Middleton Cheney, Northamptonshire 27 May 1863; d Middleton Cheney 29 Apr 1921; (3) 39, 40, 41.

MOON, Leonard James; b London 9 Feb 1878; d near Karasouli, Salonica, Greece 23 Nov 1916; (4) 89, 90, 91, 92.

MORLEY, Frederick; b Sutton in Ashfield, Nottinghamshire 16 Dec 1850; d Sutton in Ashfield 28 Sep 1884; (4) 4, 11, 12, 13.

MORRIS, Hugh; b Cardiff, Wales 5 Oct 1963; (3) 1174, 1175, 1176.

MORRIS, John Edward; b Crewe, Cheshire 1 Apr 1964; (3) 1148, 1149, 1150.

MORTIMORE, John Brian; b Southmead, Bristol 14 May 1933; (9) 468, 472, 473, 476, 477, 553, 556, 557, 564.

MOSS, Alan Edward; b Tottenham, Middlesex 14 Nov 1930; (9) 382, 425, 474, 475, 476, 487, 491, 493, 494.

MOXON, Martyn Douglas; b Barnsley, Yorkshire 4 May 1960; (10) 1049, 1050, 1079, 1090, 1091, 1092, 1093, 1099, 1100, 1125.

MUNTON, Timothy Alan; b Melton Mowbray, Leicestershire 30 Jul 1965; (2) 1191, 1192.

MURDOCH, William Lloyd; b Sandhurst, Victoria, Australia 18 Oct 1854; d Yarra Park, East Melbourne, Australia 18 Feb 1911; (1) 38. (*Also 18 Tests for Australia; 2-17, 33, 34*)

MURRAY, John Thomas; b North Kensington, London 1 Apr 1935; (21) 507, 508, 509, 510, 511, 512, 513, 514, 515, 532, 533, 534, 537, 540, 575, 603, 609, 618, 619, 620, 621.

NEWHAM, William; b Shrewsbury, Shropshire 12 Dec 1860; d Portslade, Brighton, Sussex 26 Jun 1944; (1) 27.

NEWPORT, Philip John; b High Wycombe, Buckinghamshire 11 Oct 1962; (3) 1103, 1121, 1162.

NICHOLS, Morris Stanley; b Stondon Massey, Essex 6 Oct 1900; d Newark, Nottinghamshire 26 Jan 1961; (14) 186, 187, 188, 189, 197, 229, 230, 231, 232, 242, 243, 244, 246, 274.

OAKMAN, Alan Stanley Myles; b Hastings, Sussex 20 Apr 1930; (2) 427, 428.

O'BRIEN, *3rd Baronet*; Timothy Carew; b Dublin, Ireland 5 Nov 1861; d Ramsey, Isle of Man 9 Dec 1948; (5) 14, 28, 47, 48, 49.

O'CONNOR, Jack; b Cambridge 6 Nov 1897; d Buckhurst Hill, Essex 22 Feb 1977; (4) 182, 190, 191, 193.

OLD, Christopher Middleton; b Middlesbrough, Yorkshire 22 Dec 1948; (46) 704, 705, 706, 707, 719, 723, 724, 726, 731, 732, 733, 734, 739, 740, 741, 742, 743, 744, 751, 755, 758, 760, 762, 763, 777, 778, 788, 789, 790, 791, 803, 804, 805, 814, 817, 818, 825, 826, 827, 828, 834, 884, 885, 896, 905, 906.

OLDFIELD, Norman; b Dukinfield, Cheshire 5 May 1911; (1) 274.

PADGETT, Douglas Ernest Vernon; b Dirk Hall, Bradford, Yorkshire 20 Jul 1934; (2) 495, 496.

PAINE, George Alfred Edward; b Paddington, London 11 Jun 1908; d Solihull, Warwickshire 30 Mar 1978; (4) 238, 239, 240, 241.

PALAIRET, Lionel Charles Hamilton; b Grange-over-Sands, Lancashire 27 May 1870; d Exmouth, Devon 27 Mar 1933; (2) 73, 74.

PALMER, Charles Henry; b Old Hill, Staffordshire 15 May 1919; (1) 383.

PALMER, Kenneth Ernest; b Winchester, Hampshire 22 Apr 1937; (1) 575.

PARFITT, Peter Howard; b Billingford, North Elmham, Norfolk 8 Dec 1936; (37) 516, 517, 518, 519, 530, 531, 532, 533, 534, 535, 537, 540, 541, 542, 555, 556, 557, 562, 563, 564, 565, 571, 572, 573, 574, 575, 592, 593, 595, 596, 602, 603, 604, 654, 700, 701, 702.

PARKER, Charles Warrington Leonard; b Prestbury, Gloucestershire 14 Oct 1882; d Cranleigh, Surrey 11 Jul 1959; (1) 143.

PARKER, Paul William Giles; b Bulawayo, Southern Rhodesia 15 Jan 1956; (1) 908.

PARKHOUSE, William Gilbert Anthony; b Swansea, Glamorgan 12 Oct 1925; (7) 324, 325, 328, 329, 333, 476, 477.

PARKIN, Cecil Harry; b Eaglescliffe, Co. Durham 18 Feb 1886; d Cheetham Hill, Manchester 15 Jun 1943; (10) 135, 136, 137, 138, 139, 141, 142, 143, 144, 153.

PARKS, James Horace; b Haywards Heath, Sussex 12 May 1903; d Cuckfield, Sussex 21 Nov 1980; (1) 260.

PARKS, James Michael; b Haywards Heath, Sussex 21 Oct 1931; (46) 389, 491, 492, 493, 494, 495, 496, 544, 545, 546, 547, 553, 554, 555, 556, 557, 561, 562, 563, 564, 565, 571, 572, 573, 574, 575, 591, 592, 593, 594, 595, 596, 597, 598, 599, 600, 601, 602, 604, 605, 606, 607, 608, 628, 629, 630.

PATAUDI, *Nawab of, sr* (Iftikhar Ali Khan); b Pataudi, India 16 Mar 1910; d New Delhi, India 5 Jan 1952; (3) 220, 221, 233. (*Also 3 Tests for India; 276-278*)

PAYNTER, Edward; b Oswaldtwistle, Lancashire 5 Nov 1901; d Keighley, Yorkshire 5 Feb 1979; (20) 211, 219, 222, 223, 224, 225, 226, 260, 261, 263, 264, 265, 266, 267, 268, 269, 270, 271, 272, 273.

PEATE, Edmund; b Holbeck, Leeds, Yorkshire 2 Mar 1855; d Newlay, Leeds 11 Mar 1900; (9) 5, 6, 7, 8, 9, 14, 15, 16, 22.

PEEBLES, Ian Alexander Ross; b Aberdeen, Scotland 20 Jan 1908; d Speen, Buckinghamshire 28 Feb 1980; (13) 168, 169, 170, 171, 197, 198, 204, 205, 207, 208, 209, 210, 211.

PEEL, Robert; b Churwell, Yorkshire 12 Feb 1857; d Morley, Yorkshire 12 Aug 1941; (20) 17, 18, 19, 20, 21, 27, 28, 29, 30, 33, 35, 36, 37, 39, 42, 43, 44, 45, 46, 52.

PENN, Frank; b Lewisham, Kent 7 Mar 1851; d Bifrons, Patrixbourne, Kent 26 Dec 1916; (1) 4.

PERKS, Reginald Thomas David; b Hereford 4 Oct 1911; d Worcester 22 Nov 1977; (2) 271, 274.

PHILIPSON, Hylton; b Tynemouth, Northumberland 8 Jun 1866; d Westminster, London 4 Dec 1935; (5) 37, 43, 44, 45, 46.

PIGOTT, Anthony Charles Shackleton; b Fulham, London 4 Jun 1958; (1) 976.

PILLING, Richard; b Bedford 5 Jul 1855; d Old Trafford, Manchester, Lancashire 28 Mar 1891; (8) 5, 6, 7, 8, 14, 22, 27, 30.

PLACE, Winston; b Rawtenstall, Lancashire 7 Dec 1914; (3) 295, 297, 298.

POCOCK, Patrick Ian; b Bangor, Caernarvonshire, Wales 24 Sep 1946; (25) 630, 632, 637, 647, 703, 704, 705, 707, 719, 720, 721, 731, 732, 733, 735, 778, 779, 992, 993, 994, 1005, 1006, 1007, 1008, 1009.

POLLARD, Richard; b Westhoughton, Lancashire 19 Jun 1912; d Westhoughton 16 Dec 1985; (4) 277, 284, 301, 302.

POOLE, Cyril John; b Forest Town, Mansfield, Nottinghamshire 13 Mar 1921; (3) 341, 342, 343.

POPE, George Henry; b Tibshelf, Derbyshire 27 Jan 1911; d Chesterfield, Derbyshire 29 Oct 1993; (1) 286.

POUGHER, Arthur Dick; b Aylestone Park, Leicester 19 Apr 1865; d Leicester 20 May 1926; (1) 38.

PRICE, John Sidney Ernest; b Harrow, Middlesex 22 Jul 1937; (15) 554, 555, 556, 557, 564, 565, 571, 572, 573, 574, 688, 690, 691, 692, 699.

PRICE, Wilfred Frederick Frank; b Westminster, London 25 Apr 1902; d Hendon, Middlesex 13 Jan 1969; (1) 265.

PRIDEAUX, Roger Malcolm; b Chelsea, London 31 Jul 1939; (3) 640, 647, 648.

PRINGLE, Derek Raymond; b Nairobi, Kenya 18 Sep 1958; (30) 928, 929, 930, 932, 938, 940, 941, 989, 990, 991, 1046, 1047, 1048, 1050, 1098, 1099, 1101, 1102, 1103, 1121, 1126, 1171, 1172, 1173, 1174, 1185, 1186, 1189, 1192, 1193.

PULLAR, Geoffrey; b Swinton, Lancashire 1 Aug 1935; (28) 476, 477, 478, 487, 488, 489, 490, 491, 492, 495, 496, 507, 508, 509, 510, 511, 512, 513, 514, 515, 518, 519, 530, 533, 535, 536, 537, 538.

QUAIFE, William George; b Newhaven, Sussex 17 Mar 1872; d Edgbaston, Birmingham, Warwickshire 13 Oct 1951; (7) 62, 63, 65, 66, 67, 68, 69.

RADFORD, Neal Victor; b Luanshya, Northern Rhodesia 7 Jun 1957; (3) 1048, 1049, 1092.

RADLEY, Clive Thornton; b Hertford 13 May 1944; (8) 818, 819, 825, 826, 827, 828, 829, 830.

RAMPRAKASH, Mark Ravin; b Bushey, Hertfordshire 5 Sep 1969; (14) 1171, 1172, 1173, 1174, 1175, 1176, 1189, 1192, 1193, 1228, 1252, 1253, 1254, 1255.

RANDALL, Derek William; b Retford, Nottinghamshire 24 Feb 1951; (47) 789, 790, 791, 792, 803, 804, 805, 806, 807, 808, 814, 815, 816, 817, 818, 819, 834, 835, 836, 837, 838, 839, 851, 852, 853, 868, 870, 928, 929, 930, 931, 932, 933, 938, 939, 940, 942, 957, 958, 960, 975, 976, 977, 978, 979, 980, 989.

RANJITSINHJI, Kumar Shri (*later H H Shri Sir Ranjitsinhji Vibhaji, Jam Sahib of Nawanagar*); b Sarodar, India 10 Sep 1872; inherited title 1907; d Jamnagar, India 2 Apr 1933; (15) 51, 52, 53, 54, 55, 56, 57, 60, 61, 62, 63, 64, 70, 71, 73.

READ, Holcombe Douglas; b Woodford Green, Essex 28 Jan 1910; (1) 246.

READ, John Maurice; b Thames Ditton, Surrey 9 Feb 1859; d Winchester, Hampshire 17 Feb 1929; (17) 9, 17, 18, 19, 20, 21, 25, 26, 27, 31, 32, 33, 34, 35, 36, 37, 39.

READ, Walter William; b Reigate, Surrey 23 Nov 1855; d Addiscombe, Surrey 6 Jan 1907; (18) 10, 11, 12, 13, 15, 16, 22, 23, 24, 27, 28, 29, 30, 33, 34, 38, 40, 41.

REEVE, Dermot Alexander; b Kowloon, Hong Kong 2 Apr 1963; (3) 1185, 1186, 1187

RELF, Albert Edward; b Burwash, Sussex 26 Jun 1874; d Wellington College, Crowthorne, Berkshire 26 Mar 1937; (13) 78, 79, 88, 89, 90, 91, 92, 102, 130, 131, 132, 133, 134.

RHODES, Harold James; b Hadfield, Glossop, Derbyshire 22 Jul 1936; (2) 476, 477.

RHODES, Steven John; b Bradford, Yorkshire 17 Jun 1964; (6) 1260, 1261, 1262, 1263, 1264, 1265.

RHODES, Wilfred; b Kirkheaton, Yorkshire 29 Oct 1877; d Branksome Park, Dorset 8 Jul 1973; (58) 60, 61, 64, 70, 71, 72, 73, 74, 78, 79, 80, 81, 82, 83, 84, 86, 87, 96, 97, 98, 99, 100, 101, 103, 104, 105, 106, 107, 108, 109, 110, 116, 117, 118, 119, 120, 122, 123, 124, 126, 128, 129, 130, 131, 132, 133, 134, 135, 136, 137, 138, 139, 140, 167, 190, 191, 192, 193.

RICHARDS, Clifton John; b Penzance, Cornwall 10 Aug 1958; (8) 1058, 1059, 1060, 1061, 1062, 1077, 1101, 1102.

RICHARDSON, Derek Walter; b Hereford 3 Nov 1934; (1) 441.

RICHARDSON, Peter Edward; b Hereford 4 Jul 1931; (34) 425, 426, 427, 428, 429, 434, 435, 436, 437, 438, 439, 440, 441, 442, 443, 454, 455, 457, 458, 464, 465, 467, 468, 472, 473, 512, 513, 514, 515, 516, 517, 518, 519, 545.

RICHARDSON, Thomas; b Byfleet, Surrey 11 Aug 1870; d St Jean d'Arvey, Savoie, France 2 Jul 1912; (14) 41, 42, 43, 44, 45, 46, 50, 51, 52, 53, 54, 55, 56, 57.

RICHMOND, Thomas Leonard; b Radcliffe on Trent, Nottinghamshire 23 Jun 1890; d Saxondale, Nottinghamshire 29 Dec 1957; (1) 140.

RIDGWAY, Frederick; b Stockport, Cheshire 10 Aug 1923; (5) 339, 340, 341, 342, 343.

ROBERTSON, John David Benbow; b Chiswick, Middlesex 22 Feb 1917; (11) 289, 295, 296, 297, 298, 315, 339, 340, 341, 342, 343.

ROBINS, Robert Walter Vivian; b Stafford 3 Jun 1906; d Marylebone, London 12 Dec 1968; (19) 182, 194, 195, 209, 219, 227, 228, 242, 245, 246, 252, 253, 255, 256, 257, 258, 260, 261, 262.

ROBINSON, Robert Timothy; b Sutton in Ashfield, Nottinghamshire 21 Nov 1958; (29) 1005, 1006, 1007, 1008, 1009, 1017, 1018, 1019, 1020, 1021, 1022, 1038, 1040, 1041, 1042, 1046, 1075, 1076, 1077, 1078, 1079, 1084, 1085, 1090, 1091, 1092, 1093, 1103, 1124.

ROOPE, Graham Richard James; b Fareham, Hampshire 12 Jul 1946; (21) 706, 707, 719, 720, 722, 723, 724, 725, 763, 807, 808, 814, 815, 816, 817, 818, 819, 825, 826, 827, 828.

ROOT, Charles Frederick; b Somercotes, Derbyshire 16 Apr 1890; d Wolverhampton, Staffordshire 20 Jan 1954; (3) 163, 164, 166.

ROSE, Brian Charles; b Dartford, Kent 4 Jun 1950; (9) 814, 815, 816, 817, 818, 882, 883, 884, 896.

ROYLE, Vernon Peter Fanshawe Archer (*Rev.*); b Brooklands, Cheshire 29 Jan 1854; d Stanmore Park, Middlesex 21 May 1929; (1) 3.

RUMSEY, Frederick Edward; b Stepney, London 4 Dec 1935; (5) 564, 591, 592, 593, 594.

RUSSELL, Charles Albert George (*also known as* Albert Charles Russell); b Leyton, Essex 7 Oct 1887; d Whipps Cross, Essex 23 Mar 1961; (10) 135, 136, 137, 139, 143, 144, 149, 150, 151, 152.

RUSSELL, Robert Charles; b Stroud, Gloucestershire 15 Aug 1963; (36) 1103, 1121, 1122, 1123, 1124, 1125, 1126, 1140, 1141, 1142, 1143, 1145, 1146, 1147, 1148, 1149, 1150, 1158, 1159, 1160, 1171, 1172, 1173, 1174, 1176, 1185, 1186, 1187, 1189, 1190, 1191, 1251, 1252, 1253, 1254, 1255.

RUSSELL, William Eric; b Dumbarton, Scotland 3 Jul 1936; (10) 512, 516, 596, 597, 602, 603, 604, 605, 607, 621.

SALISBURY, Ian David Kenneth; b Northampton 21 Jan 1970; (7) 1190, 1191, 1212, 1213, 1252, 1253, 1263.

SANDHAM, Andrew; b Streatham, Surrey 6 Jul 1890; d Westminster, London 20 Apr 1982; (14) 144, 148, 149, 150, 151, 152, 156, 157, 158, 162, 190, 191, 192, 193.

SCHULTZ, Sandford Spence (*later* STOREY); b Birkenhead, Cheshire 29 Aug 1857; d South Kensington, London 18 Dec 1937; (1) 3.

SCOTTON, William Henry; b Nottingham 15 Jan 1856; d St John's Wood, London 9 Jul 1893; (15) 5, 6, 7, 8, 16, 17, 18, 19, 20, 21, 22, 23, 24, 25, 26.

SELBY, John; b Nottingham 1 Jul 1849; d Nottingham, 11 Mar 1894; (6) 1, 2, 5, 6, 7, 8.

SELVEY, Michael Walter William; b Chiswick, Middlesex 25 Apr 1948; (3) 779, 781, 792.

SHACKLETON, Derek; b Todmorden, Yorkshire 12 Aug 1924; (7) 325, 338, 339, 544, 545, 546, 547.

SHARP, John; b Hereford 15 Feb 1878; d Wavertree, Liverpool, Lancashire 28 Jan 1938; (3) 103, 104, 105.

SHARPE, John William; b Ruddington, Nottinghamshire 9 Dec 1866; d Ruddington 19 Jun 1936; (3) 34, 35, 36.

SHARPE, Philip John; b Shipley, Yorkshire 27 Dec 1936; (12) 545, 546, 547, 553, 561, 562, 653, 654, 655, 656, 657, 658.

SHAW, Alfred; b Burton Joyce, Nottinghamshire 29 Aug 1842; d Gedling, Nottinghamshire 16 Jan 1907; (7) 1, 2, 4, 5, 6, 7, 8.

SHEPPARD, David Stuart (*Rt. Rev.*); b Reigate, Surrey 6 Mar 1929; ordained 1955; (22) 326, 330, 331, 333, 353, 354, 388, 389, 428, 429, 442, 443, 533, 534, 535, 536, 537, 538, 539, 540, 541, 542.

SHERWIN, Mordecai; b Kimberley, Nottinghamshire 26 Feb 1851; d Nottingham 3 Jul 1910; (3) 25, 26, 28.

SHREWSBURY, Arthur; b New Lenton, Nottinghamshire 11 Apr 1856; d Gedling, Nottinghamshire 19 May 1903; (23) 5, 6, 7, 8, 14, 15, 16, 17, 18, 19, 20, 21, 22, 23, 24, 25, 26, 27, 33, 34, 39, 40, 41.

SHUTER, John; b Thornton Heath, Surrey 9 Feb 1855; d Blackheath, Kent 5 Jul 1920; (1) 29.

SHUTTLEWORTH, Kenneth; b St Helens, Lancashire 13 Nov 1944; (5) 674, 675, 685, 686, 687.

SIDEBOTTOM, Arnold; b Shawlands, Barnsley, Yorkshire 1 Apr 1954; (1) 1019.

SIMPSON, Reginald Thomas; b Sherwood Rise, Nottingham 27 Feb 1920; (27) 309, 316, 317, 323, 325, 326, 327, 328, 329, 330, 331, 332, 333, 334, 335, 336, 351, 352, 372, 374, 375, 387, 388, 390, 391, 401, 402.

SIMPSON-HAYWARD, George Hayward Thomas (*name changed from* SIMPSON *in* 1898); b Stoneleigh, Kenilworth, Warwickshire 7 Jun 1875; d Icomb, Gloucestershire 2 Oct 1936; (5) 106, 107, 108, 109, 110.

SIMS, James Morton; b Leyton, Essex 13 May 1903; d Canterbury, Kent 27 Apr 1973; (4) 244, 254, 256, 257.

SINFIELD, Reginald Albert; b Beamington, Stevenage, Hertfordshire 24 Dec 1900; d Ham Green, Bristol 17 Mar 1988; (1) 263.

SLACK, Wilfred Norris; b Troumaca, St Vincent, 12 Dec 1954; d Banjul, The Gambia 15 Jan 1989; (3) 1039, 1042, 1047.

SMAILES, Thomas Francis; b Ripley, Yorkshire 27 Mar 1910; d Harrogate, Yorkshire 1 Dec 1970; (1) 276.

SMALL, Gladstone Cleophas; b St George, Barbados 18 Oct 1961; (17) 1050, 1051, 1061, 1062, 1099, 1126, 1140, 1141, 1142, 1143, 1145, 1146, 1147, 1158, 1160, 1161, 1162.

SMITH, Alan Christopher; b Hall Green, Birmingham 25 Oct 1936; (6) 535, 536, 538, 539, 541, 542.

SMITH, Charles Aubrey; b City of London 21 Jul 1863; knighted for services to Anglo-American amity 1944; d Beverly Hills, California, USA 20 Dec 1948; (1) 31.

SMITH, Cedric Ivan James; b Corsham, Wiltshire 25 Aug 1906; d Mellor, Lancashire 9 Feb 1979; (5) 238, 239, 240, 241, 261.

SMITH, Christopher Lyall; b Durban, South Africa 15 Oct 1958; (8) 959, 960, 975, 977, 978, 979, 980, 1047.

SMITH, Denis; b Somercotes, Derbyshire 24 Jan 1907; d Derby 12 Sep 1979; (2) 244, 245.

SMITH, David Mark, b Balham, London 9 Jan 1956; (2) 1038, 1041.

SMITH, David Robert; b Fishponds, Bristol 5 Oct 1934; (5) 513, 514, 515, 516, 517.

SMITH, Donald Victor; b Broadwater, Sussex 14 Jun 1923; (3) 440, 441, 442.

SMITH, Ernest James; b Birmingham 6 Feb 1886; d Northfield, Birmingham 31 Aug 1979; (11) 117, 118, 119, 120, 122, 123, 124, 126, 128, 129, 131.

SMITH, Harry; b Gloucester 21 May 1890; d Downend, Bristol 12 Nov 1937; (1) 173.

SMITH, Michael John Knight; b Westcotes, Leicester 30 Jun 1933; (50) 454, 455, 456, 477, 478, 487, 488, 489, 490, 491, 492, 493, 494, 496, 507, 512, 513, 514, 515, 517, 518, 519, 553, 554, 555, 556, 557, 571, 572, 573, 574, 575, 591, 592, 593, 594, 595, 596, 597, 598, 599, 600, 601, 602, 603, 604, 605, 698, 699, 700.

SMITH, Robin Arnold; b Durban, South Africa 13 Sep 1963; (53) 1101, 1102, 1103, 1121, 1122, 1124, 1125, 1126, 1140, 1141, 1142, 1143, 1145, 1146, 1147, 1148, 1149, 1150, 1158, 1159, 1160, 1161, 1162, 1171, 1172, 1173, 1175, 1176, 1185, 1186, 1187, 1189, 1190, 1191, 1192, 1193, 1212, 1213, 1214, 1219, 1223, 1224, 1225, 1226, 1227, 1251, 1252, 1253, 1254, 1255, 1260, 1261, 1262.

SMITH, Thomas Peter Bromly; b Ipswich, Suffolk 30 Oct 1908; d Hyères, France 4 Aug 1967; (4) 278, 280, 283, 284.

SMITHSON, Gerald Arthur; b Spofforth, Yorkshire 1 Nov 1926; d Abingdon, Berkshire 6 Sep 1970; (2) 295, 296.

SNOW, John Augustine; b Peopleton, Worcestershire 13 Oct 1941; (49) 592, 595, 607, 608, 609, 618, 619, 620, 621, 629, 630, 631, 632, 637, 638, 639, 640, 641, 648, 649, 653, 654, 655, 657, 658, 674, 675, 676, 677, 678, 679, 690, 692, 698, 699, 700, 701, 702, 722, 723, 724, 725, 760, 761, 762, 763, 777, 778, 780.

SOUTHERTON, James; b Petworth, Sussex 16 Nov 1827; d Mitcham, Surrey 16 Jun 1880; (2) 1, 2.

SPOONER, Reginald Herbert; b Litherland, Lancashire 21 Oct 1880; d Lincoln 2 Oct 1961; (10) 86, 87, 104, 105, 122, 123, 124, 126, 128, 129.

SPOONER, Richard Thompson; b Stockton-on-Tees, Co. Durham 30 Dec 1919; (7) 339, 340, 341, 342, 343, 385, 412.

STANYFORTH, Ronald Thomas; b Chelsea, London 30 May 1892; d Kirk Hammerton, Yorkshire 20 Feb 1964; (4) 168, 169, 170, 171.

STAPLES, Samuel James; b Newstead Colliery, Notting-hamshire 18 Sep 1892; d Nottingham 4 Jun 1950; (3) 170, 171, 172.

STATHAM, John Brian; b Gorton, Manchester 17 Jun 1930; (70) 332, 335, 336, 339, 340, 341, 342, 343, 373, 382, 383, 384, 385, 387, 388, 389, 390, 391, 392, 393, 394, 395, 401, 402, 408, 409, 411, 412, 426, 428, 429, 434, 435, 436, 437, 439, 440, 441, 457, 458, 464, 465, 466, 467, 474, 475, 478, 488, 489, 490, 492, 493, 494, 495, 496, 507, 508, 510, 511, 530, 532, 533, 535, 536, 537, 538, 539, 543, 547, 596.

STEEL, Allan Gibson; b West Derby, Liverpool, Lanca-shire 24 Sep 1858; d Hyde Park, London 15 Jun 1914; (13) 4, 9, 10, 11, 12, 13, 14, 15, 16, 22, 23, 24, 28.

STEELE, David Stanley; b Bradeley, Staffordshire 29 Sep 1941; (8) 761, 762, 763, 777, 778, 779, 780, 781.

STEPHENSON, John Patrick, b Stebbing, Essex 14 Mar 1965; (1) 1126.

STEVENS, Greville Thomas Scott; b Hampstead, Middlesex 7 Jan 1901; d Islington, London 19 Sep 1970; (10) 148, 166, 167, 168, 169, 170, 171, 172, 190, 191.

STEVENSON, Graham Barry; b Ackworth, Yorkshire 16 Dec 1955; (2) 876, 898.

STEWART, Alec James; b Merton, Surrey 8 Apr 1963; (43) 1140, 1141, 1142, 1143, 1145, 1146, 1147, 1158, 1159, 1160, 1161, 1162, 1175, 1176, 1185, 1186, 1187, 1189, 1190, 1191, 1192, 1193, 1212, 1213, 1214, 1219, 1223, 1224, 1225, 1226, 1227, 1228, 1251, 1252, 1253, 1254, 1255, 1260, 1261, 1262, 1263, 1264, 1265.

STEWART, Michael James; b Herne Hill, Surrey 16 Sep 1932; (8) 531, 532, 543, 544, 545, 546, 553, 554.

STODDART, Andrew Ernest; b Westore, South Shields, Co. Durham 11 Mar 1863; d St John's Wood, London 4 Apr 1915; (16) 27, 35, 36, 37, 39, 40, 41, 42, 43, 44, 45, 46, 50, 51, 55, 56.

STORER, William; b Butterley, Derbyshire 25 Jan 1867; d Derby 28 Feb 1912; (6) 53, 54, 55, 56, 57, 60.

STREET, George Benjamin; b Charlwood, Surrey 6 Dec 1889; d Portslade, Sussex 24 Apr 1924; (1) 150.

STRUDWICK, Herbert; b Mitcham, Surrey 28 Jan 1880; d Shoreham, Sussex 14 Feb 1970; (28) 106, 107, 108, 109, 110, 116, 130, 131, 132, 133, 134, 135, 136, 137, 139, 140, 141, 157, 158, 159, 160, 161, 162, 163, 164, 165, 166, 167.

STUDD, Charles Thomas; b Spratton, Northamptonshire 2 Dec 1860; d Ibambi, Belgian Congo 16 Jul 1931; (5) 9, 10, 11, 12, 13.

STUDD, George Brown; b Netheravon, Wiltshire 20 Oct 1859; d Pasadena, California, USA 13 Feb 1945; (4) 10, 11, 12, 13.

SUBBA ROW, Raman; b Streatham, Surrey 29 Jan 1932; (13) 457, 478, 490, 491, 492, 493, 494, 495, 507, 508, 509, 510, 511.

SUCH, Peter Mark; b Helensburgh, Dunbartonshire, Scotland 12 Jun 1964; (8) 1223, 1224, 1225, 1227, 1228, 1260, 1261, 1262.

SUGG, Frank Howe; b Ilkeston, Derbyshire 11 Jan 1862; d Waterloo, Liverpool, Lancashire 29 May 1933; (2) 29, 30.

SUTCLIFFE, Herbert; b Summer Bridge, Harrogate, Yorkshire 24 Nov 1894; d Crosshills, Yorkshire 22 Jan 1978; (54) 153, 154, 155, 156, 157, 158, 159, 160, 161, 162, 163, 164, 165, 166, 167, 168, 169, 170, 171, 172, 173, 174, 175, 176, 177, 178, 179, 181, 182, 183, 184, 185, 194, 196, 197, 198, 210, 211, 219, 220, 221, 222, 223, 224, 225, 226, 227, 228, 233, 234, 235, 237, 242, 243.

SWETMAN, Roy; b Westminster, London 25 Oct 1933; (11) 466, 468, 472, 473, 476, 477, 478, 487, 488, 489, 490.

TATE, Frederick William; b Brighton, Sussex 24 Jul 1867; d Burgess Hill, Sussex 24 Feb 1943; (1) 73.

TATE, Maurice William; b Brighton, Sussex 30 May 1895; d Wadhurst, Sussex 18 May 1956; (39) 153, 154, 155, 156, 157, 158, 159, 160, 161, 162, 163, 164, 165, 166, 167, 173, 174, 175, 176, 177, 178, 179, 180, 181, 182, 183, 194, 195, 196, 197, 198, 204, 205, 206, 207, 208, 210, 225, 245.

TATTERSALL, Roy; b Tonge Moor, Bolton, Lancashire 17 Aug 1922; (16) 330, 331, 332, 333, 334, 335, 336, 337, 338, 339, 340, 341, 342, 343, 372, 387.

TAVARÉ, Christopher James; b Orpington, Kent 27 Oct 1954; (31) 880, 881, 907, 908, 912, 913, 914, 915, 916, 917, 921, 928, 929, 930, 931, 932, 933, 938, 939, 940, 941, 942, 957, 958, 959, 960, 975, 976, 993, 994, 1123.

TAYLOR, Jonathan Paul; b Ashby-de-la-Zouch, Leices-tershire 8 Aug 1964; (2) 1212, 1261.

TAYLOR, Kenneth; b Primrose Hill, Huddersfield, Yorkshire 21 Aug 1935; (3) 474, 475, 563.

TAYLOR, Leslie Brian; b Earl Shilton, Leicestershire 25 Oct 1953; (2) 1021, 1022.

TAYLOR, Robert William; b Stoke-on-Trent, Staffordshire 17 Jul 1941; (57) 685, 814, 815, 816, 817, 818, 819, 825, 826, 827, 828, 829, 830, 834, 835, 836, 837, 838, 839, 851, 852, 853, 868, 870, 872, 876, 904, 905, 906, 912, 913, 914, 915, 916, 917, 921, 928, 929, 930, 931, 932, 933, 938, 939, 940, 941, 942, 957, 958, 959, 960, 975, 976, 977, 978, 979, 980.

TENNYSON, Hon. Lionel Hallam (*became 3rd Lord Tennyson in 1928*); b Westminster, London 7 Nov 1889; d Bexhill-on-Sea, Sussex 6 Jun 1951; (9) 130, 131, 132, 133, 134, 141, 142, 143, 144.

TERRY, Vivian Paul; b Osnabruck, West Germany 14 Jan 1959; (2) 991, 992.

THOMAS, John Gregory; b Trebanos, Glamorgan, Wales 12 Aug 1960; (5) 1038, 1039, 1040, 1041, 1050.

THOMPSON, George Joseph; b Cogenhoe, Northampton 27 Oct 1877; d Clifton, Bristol 3 Mar 1943; (6) 101, 106, 107, 108, 109, 110.

THOMSON, Norman Ian; b Walsall, Staffordshire 23 Jan 1929; (5) 571, 572, 573, 574, 575.

WATKIN, Steven Llewellyn; b Maesteg, Glamorgan, Wales 15 Sep 1964; (3) 1171, 1172, 1228.

WATKINS, Albert John (*known as* Allan John); b Usk, Monmouthshire, Wales 21 Apr 1922; (15) 303, 309, 310, 311, 312, 313, 315, 339, 340, 341, 342, 343, 351, 352, 353.

WATSON, William; b Bolton upon Dearne, Yorkshire 7 Mar 1920; (23) 334, 335, 336, 337, 338, 354, 373, 374, 375, 382, 383, 384, 385, 386, 412, 425, 426, 457, 458, 465, 467, 472, 473.

WEBBE, Alexander Josiah; b Bethnal Green, London 16 Jan 1855; d Abinger Hammer, Surrey 19 Feb 1941; (1) 3.

WELLARD, Arthur William; b Southfleet, Kent 8 Apr 1902; d Eastbourne, Sussex 31 Dec 1980; (2) 261, 264.

WHARTON, Alan; b Heywood, Lancashire 30 Apr 1923; d Colne, Lancashire 26 Aug 1993; (1) 314.

WHITAKER, John James; b Skipton, Yorkshire 5 May 1962; (1) 1060.

WHITE, Craig; b Morley Hall, Yorkshire 16 Dec 1969; (4) 1260, 1261, 1262, 1263.

WHITE, David William; b Sutton Coldfield, Warwickshire 14 Dec 1935; (2) 512, 519.

WHITE, John Cornish; b Holford, Somerset 19 Feb 1891; d Combe Florey, Somerset 2 May 1961; (15) 142, 174, 176, 177, 178, 179, 180, 181, 182, 183, 195, 204, 205, 206, 208.

WHYSALL, William Wilfrid; b Woodborough, Nottinghamshire 31 Oct 1887; d Nottingham 11 Nov 1930; (4) 160, 161, 162, 198.

WILKINSON, Leonard Litton; b Northwich, Cheshire 5 Nov 1916; (3) 267, 269, 270.

WILLEY, Peter; b Sedgefield, Co. Durham 6 Dec 1949; (26) 780, 781, 854, 868, 870, 872, 880, 881, 882, 883, 884, 885, 896, 897, 898, 899, 903, 904, 905, 906, 1017, 1038, 1039, 1040, 1041, 1049.

WILLIAMS, Neil FitzGerald; b Hope Well, St Vincent 2 Jul 1962; (1) 1150.

WILLIS, Robert George Dylan; b Sunderland, Co. Durham 30 May 1949; (90) 676, 677, 678, 679, 686, 727, 731, 732, 733, 739, 744, 750, 751, 752, 753, 754, 780, 781, 788, 789, 790, 791, 792, 803, 804, 805, 806, 807, 808, 814, 815, 816, 817, 818, 819, 825, 826, 827, 828, 829, 830, 834, 835, 836, 837, 838, 839, 851, 853, 854, 868, 870, 872, 880, 881, 882, 883, 903, 904, 905, 906, 907, 908, 912, 914, 915, 916, 917, 921, 928, 929, 930, 931, 933, 938, 939, 940, 941, 942, 957, 958, 959, 960, 975, 976, 977, 978, 989, 990, 991.

WILSON, Clement Eustace Macro (*Rev.*); b Bolsterstone, Yorkshire 15 May 1875, ordained 1899; d Calverhall, Shropshire 8 Feb 1944; (2) 58, 59.

WILSON, Donald; b Settle, Yorkshire 7 Aug 1937; (6) 553, 554, 555, 556, 557, 685.

WILSON, Evelyn Rockley; b Bolsterstone, Yorkshire 25 Mar 1879; d Winchester, Hampshire 21 Jul 1957; (1) 139.

WOOD, Arthur; b Fagley, Bradford, Yorkshire 25 Aug 1898; d Middleton, Ilkley, Yorkshire 1 Apr 1973; (4) 266, 272, 273, 274.

WOOD, Barry; b Ossett, Yorkshire 26 Dec 1942; (12) 702, 703, 704, 705, 721, 758, 759, 761, 762, 763, 778, 825.

WOOD, George Edward Charles; b Blackheath, Kent 22 Aug 1893; d Christchurch, Hampshire 18 Mar 1971; (3) 153, 154, 155.

WOOD, Henry; b Dartford, Kent 14 Dec 1853; d Waddon, Surrey 30 Apr 1919; (4) 29, 31, 32, 38.

WOOD, Reginald; b Woodchurch, Cheshire 7 Mar 1860; d Manly, Sydney, Australia 6 Jan 1915; (1) 26.

WOODS, Samuel Moses James; b Ashfield, Sydney, Australia 13 Apr 1867; d Taunton, Somerset 30 Apr 1931; (3) 47, 48, 49. (*Also 3 Tests for Australia: 28-30*)

WOOLLEY, Frank Edward; b Tonbridge, Kent 27 May 1887; d Halifax, Nova Scotia, Canada 18 Oct 1978; (64) 105, 106, 107, 108, 109, 110, 116, 117, 118, 119, 120, 122, 123, 124, 126, 128, 129, 130, 131, 132, 133, 134, 135, 136, 137, 138, 139, 140, 141, 142, 143, 144, 148, 149, 150, 151, 152, 153, 154, 155, 156, 157, 158, 159, 160, 161, 162, 163, 164, 165, 166, 167, 183, 184, 185, 186, 187, 188, 189, 194, 195, 209, 219, 237.

WOOLMER, Robert Andrew; b Kanpur, India 14 May 1948; (19) 761, 763, 777, 778, 779, 780, 781, 788, 790, 803, 804, 805, 806, 807, 808, 880, 881, 903, 904.

WORTHINGTON, Thomas Stanley; b Bolsover, Derbyshire 21 Aug 1905; d Kings Lynn, Norfolk 31 Aug 1973; (9) 186, 187, 188, 189, 253, 254, 255, 257, 259.

WRIGHT, Charles William; b Harewood, Yorkshire 27 May 1863; d Saxelby, Melton Mowbray, Leicestershire 10 Jan 1936; (3) 47, 48, 49.

WRIGHT, Douglas Vivian Parson; b Sidcup, Kent 21 Aug 1914; (34) 263, 264, 265, 268, 269, 271, 272, 273, 274, 276, 277, 279, 280, 281, 282, 283, 284, 286, 287, 288, 289, 300, 309, 310, 311, 317, 326, 327, 328, 329, 330, 331, 332, 333.

WYATT, Robert Elliott Storey; b Milford, Surrey 2 May 1901; (40) 168, 169, 170, 171, 172, 184, 185, 192, 193, 198, 204, 205, 206, 207, 208, 220, 221, 222, 223, 224, 225, 226, 228, 229, 234, 235, 236, 237, 238, 239, 240, 241, 242, 243, 244, 245, 246, 252, 258, 259.

WYNYARD, Edward George; b Saharanpur, Bengal, India 1 Apr 1861; d Knotty Green, Beaconsfield, Buckinghamshire 30 Oct 1936; (3) 52, 88, 89.

YARDLEY, Norman Walter Dransfield; b Gawber, Barnsley, Yorkshire 19 Mar 1915; d Lodge Moor, Sheffield, Yorkshire 4 Oct 1989; (20) 267, 279, 280, 281, 282, 283, 284, 285, 286, 287, 288, 289, 299, 300, 301, 302, 303, 323, 324, 325.

YOUNG, Harding Isaac; b Leyton, Essex 5 Feb 1876; d Rochford, Essex 12 Dec 1964; (2) 62, 63.

YOUNG, John Albert; b Paddington, London 14 Oct 1912; d St John's Wood, London 5 Feb 1993; (8) 288, 299, 301, 303, 312, 313, 314, 315.

YOUNG, Richard Alfred; b Dharwar, India 16 Sep 1885; d Hastings, Sussex 1 Jul 1968; (2) 96, 100.

AUSTRALIA (359 players)

A'BECKETT, Edward Lambert; b East St Kilda, Melbourne 11 Aug 1907; d Terang, Victoria 2 Jun 1989; (4) 178, 179, 196, 214.

ALDERMAN, Terence Michael; b Subiaco, Perth 12 Jun 1956; (41) 903, 904, 905, 906, 907, 908, 909, 910, 911, 918, 919, 922, 923, 924, 937, 938, 981, 982, 983, 997, 998, 999, 1112, 1113, 1121, 1122, 1123, 1124, 1125, 1126, 1131, 1132, 1133, 1134, 1136, 1144, 1158, 1159, 1160, 1162, 1170.

ALEXANDER, George; b Fitzroy, Melbourne 22 Apr 1851; d Melbourne 6 Nov 1930; (2) 4, 17.

ALEXANDER, Harry Houston; b Ascot Vale, Melbourne 9 Jun 1905; d East Melbourne 15 Apr 1993 (1) 224.

ALLAN, Francis Erskine; b Allansford, Victoria 2 Dec 1849; d Melbourne 9 Feb 1917; (1) 3.

ALLAN, Peter John; b Brisbane 31 Dec 1935; (1) 597.

ALLEN, Reginald Charles; b Glebe, Sydney 2 Jul 1858; d Sydney 2 May 1952; (1) 26.

ANDREWS, Thomas James Edwin; b Newtown, Sydney 26 Aug 1890; d Sydney 28 Jan 1970; (16) 140, 141, 142, 143, 144, 145, 146, 147, 160, 161, 162, 163, 164, 165, 166, 167.

ANGEL, Jo; b Subiaco, Perth 22 Apr 1968; (1) 1208.

ARCHER, Kenneth Alan; b Yeerongpilly, Brisbane 17 Jan 1928; (5) 328, 329, 330, 344, 345.

ARCHER, Ronald Graham; b Brisbane 25 Oct 1933; (19) 364, 374, 375, 376, 391, 392, 393, 394, 403, 404, 405, 406, 407, 425, 426, 427, 428, 429, 430.

ARMSTRONG, Warwick Windridge; b Kyneton, Victoria 22 May 1879; d Darling Point, Sydney 13 Jul 1947; (50) 66, 67, 68, 69, 70, 71, 72, 73, 74, 75, 76, 77, 78, 79, 80, 83, 84, 85, 86, 87, 96, 97, 98, 99, 100, 101, 102, 103, 104, 105, 111, 112, 113, 114, 115, 116, 117, 118, 119, 120, 135, 136, 137, 138, 139, 140, 141, 142, 143, 144.

BADCOCK, Clayvel Lindsay; b Exton, Tasmania 10 Apr 1914; d Exton 13 Dec 1982; (7) 255, 256, 259, 263, 264, 265, 266.

BANNERMAN, Alexander Chalmers; b Paddington, Sydney 21 Mar 1854; d Paddington 19 Sep 1924; (28) 3, 4, 5, 7, 8, 9, 10, 11, 12, 13, 14, 15, 16, 17, 19, 20, 21, 25, 27, 28, 29, 30, 35, 36, 37, 39, 40, 41.

BANNERMAN, Charles; b Woolwich, Kent, England 23 Jul 1851; d Surry Hills, Sydney, 20 Aug 1930; (3) 1, 2, 3.

BARDSLEY, Warren; b Nevertire, Warren, New South Wales 6 Dec 1882; d Collaroy, New South Wales 20 Jan 1954; (41) 101, 102, 103, 104, 105, 111, 112, 113, 114, 115, 116, 117, 118, 119, 121, 123, 125, 126, 127, 129, 135, 136, 137, 138, 139, 140, 141, 142, 143, 144, 145, 146, 147, 158, 159, 161, 163, 164, 165, 166, 167.

BARNES, Sidney George; b Annandale, Sydney 5 Jun 1916; d Collaroy, New South Wales 16 Dec 1973; (13) 266, 275, 279, 280, 281, 283, 292, 293, 294, 299, 300, 301, 303.

BARNETT, Benjamin Arthur; b Auburn, Melbourne 23 Mar 1908; d Newcastle, New South Wales 29 Jun 1979; (4) 263, 264, 265, 266.

BARRETT, John Edward; b South Melbourne 15 Oct 1866; d Peak Hill, Western Australia 6 Feb 1916; (2) 33, 34.

BEARD, Graeme Robert; b Auburn, New South Wales 19 Aug 1950; (3) 877, 878, 879.

BENAUD, John; b Auburn, New South Wales 11 May 1944; (3) 708, 709, 718.

BENAUD, Richard; b Penrith, New South Wales 6 Oct 1930; (63) 348, 361, 362, 363, 364, 372, 373, 375, 391, 392, 393, 394, 395, 403, 404, 405, 406, 407, 425, 426, 427, 428, 429, 430, 431, 432, 433, 444, 445, 446, 447, 448, 464, 465, 466, 467, 468, 479, 480, 481, 482, 483, 484, 485, 486, 502, 503, 504, 505, 506, 507, 509, 510, 511, 535, 536, 537, 538, 539, 548, 550, 551, 552.

BENNETT, Murray John; b Brisbane 6 Oct 1956; (3) 1000, 1001, 1022.

BLACKHAM, John McCarthy; b North Fitzroy, Melbourne 11 May 1854; d Melbourne 28 Dec 1932; (35) 1, 2, 3, 4, 5, 6, 7, 8, 9, 10, 11, 12, 13, 14, 15, 16, 17, 20, 22, 23, 24, 25, 27, 28, 29, 30, 33, 34, 35, 36, 37, 39, 40, 41, 42.

BLACKIE, Donald Dearness; b Bendigo, Victoria 5 Apr 1882; d South Melbourne 18 Apr 1955; (3) 177, 178, 179.

BONNOR, George John; b Bathurst, New South Wales 25 Feb 1855; d East Orange, New South Wales 27 Jun 1912; (17) 4, 9, 10, 11, 12, 13, 14, 15, 16, 17, 19, 20, 22, 23, 28, 29, 30.

BOON, David Clarence; b Launceston, Tasmania 29 Dec 1960; (89) 998, 999, 1000, 1001, 1017, 1018, 1019, 1020, 1029, 1030, 1031, 1032, 1033, 1034, 1035, 1036, 1037, 1052, 1053, 1054, 1058, 1059, 1060, 1061, 1087, 1088, 1089, 1090, 1094, 1104, 1105, 1106, 1110, 1111, 1112, 1113, 1114, 1121, 1122, 1123, 1124, 1125, 1126, 1131, 1132, 1133, 1134, 1135, 1144, 1158, 1159, 1160, 1161, 1162, 1166, 1167, 1168, 1169, 1170, 1177, 1178, 1179, 1180, 1181, 1194, 1195, 1196, 1204, 1205, 1206, 1207, 1208, 1215, 1216, 1217, 1223, 1224, 1225, 1226, 1227, 1228, 1235, 1236, 1237, 1242, 1243, 1244, 1256, 1257, 1258.

BOOTH, Brian Charles; b Perthville, Bathurst, New South Wales 19 Oct 1933; (29) 510, 511, 535, 536, 537, 538, 539, 548, 550, 551, 552, 561, 562, 563, 564, 565, 566, 567, 568, 569, 570, 583, 584, 585, 586, 587, 597, 598, 599.

BORDER, Allan Robert; b Cremorne, Sydney 27 Jul 1955; (156) 836, 837, 838, 849, 850, 855, 856, 857, 858, 859, 860, 867, 868, 869, 870, 871, 872, 877, 878, 879, 885, 890, 891, 892, 893, 894, 895, 903, 904, 905, 906, 907, 908, 909, 910, 911, 918, 919, 920, 922, 923, 924, 935, 936, 937, 938, 939, 940, 941, 942, 956, 970, 971, 972, 973, 974, 981, 982, 983, 984, 985, 997, 998, 999, 1000, 1001, 1017, 1018, 1019, 1020, 1021, 1022, 1029, 1030, 1031, 1032, 1033, 1034, 1035, 1036, 1037, 1052, 1053, 1054, 1058, 1059, 1060, 1061, 1062, 1087, 1088, 1089, 1090, 1094, 1104, 1105, 1106, 1110, 1111, 1112, 1113, 1114, 1121, 1122, 1123, 1124, 1125, 1126, 1131, 1132, 1133, 1134, 1135, 1136, 1144, 1158, 1159, 1160, 1161, 1162, 1166, 1167, 1168, 1169, 1170, 1177, 1178, 1179, 1180, 1181, 1194, 1195, 1196, 1204, 1205, 1206, 1207, 1208, 1215, 1216, 1217, 1223, 1224, 1225, 1226, 1227, 1228, 1235, 1236, 1237, 1242, 1243, 1244, 1256, 1257, 1258.

BOYLE, Henry Frederick; b Sydney 10 Dec 1847; d Bendigo, Victoria 21 Nov 1907; (12) 3, 4, 5, 6, 7, 8, 9, 13, 14, 15, 16, 17.

BRADMAN, Donald George; b Cootamundra, New South Wales 27 Aug 1908; knighted for services to cricket 1949; (52) 176, 178, 179, 180, 194, 195, 196, 197, 198, 199, 200, 201, 202, 203, 212, 213, 214, 215, 216, 221, 222, 223, 224, 233, 234, 235, 236, 237, 255, 256, 257, 258, 259, 263, 264, 265, 266, 279, 280, 281, 282, 283, 290, 291, 292, 293, 294, 299, 300, 301, 302, 303.

BRIGHT, Raymond James; b Footscray, Melbourne 13 Jul 1954; (25) 805, 807, 808, 867, 868, 877, 878, 879, 885, 904, 905, 906, 907, 908, 935, 936, 1030, 1032, 1033, 1034, 1036, 1037, 1052, 1053, 1054.

BROMLEY, Ernest Harvey; b Fremantle, Western Australia 2 Sep 1912; d Clayton, Victoria 1 Feb 1967; (2) 223, 234.

BROWN, William Alfred; b Toowoomba, Queensland 31 Jul 1912; (22) 233, 234, 235, 236, 237, 247, 248, 249, 250, 251, 257, 258, 263, 264, 265, 266, 275, 290, 291, 294, 299, 300.

BRUCE, William; b South Yarra, Melbourne 22 May 1864; d (*drowned*) St Kilda, Melbourne 3 Aug 1925; (14) 18, 21, 22, 24, 35, 36, 37, 39, 40, 41, 43, 44, 45, 46.

BURGE, Peter John Parnell; b Buranda, Brisbane 17 May 1932; (42) 395, 403, 425, 426, 427, 431, 432, 433, 444, 464, 479, 481, 485, 486, 505, 506, 507, 508, 509, 510, 511, 535, 536, 539, 548, 549, 550, 551, 552, 561, 562, 563, 564, 565, 566, 567, 568, 569, 597, 598, 599, 600.

BURKE, James Wallace; b Mosman, Sydney 12 Jun 1930; d Manly, Sydney 2 Feb 1979; (24) 330, 331, 346, 392, 394, 425, 426, 427, 428, 429, 430, 431, 432, 433, 444, 445, 446, 447, 448, 464, 465, 466, 467, 468.

BURN, Edwin James Kenneth; b Richmond, Tasmania 17 Sep 1862; d Hobart 20 Jul 1956; (2) 33, 34.

BURTON, Frederick James; b Collingwood, Victoria 2 Nov 1865; d Wanganui, New Zealand 25 Aug 1929; (2) 26, 27.

CALLAWAY, Sydney Thomas; b Sydney 6 Feb 1868; d Christchurch, New Zealand 25 Nov 1923; (3) 35, 36, 44.

CALLEN, Ian Wayne; b Alexandra, Victoria 2 May 1955; (1) 813.

CAMPBELL, Gregory Dale; b Launceston, Tasmania 10 Mar 1964; (4) 1121, 1133, 1135, 1144.

CARKEEK, William; b Walhalla, Victoria 17 Oct 1878; d Prahran, Melbourne 20 Feb 1937; (6) 121, 123, 125, 126, 127, 129.

CARLSON, Phillip Henry; b Kedron, Brisbane 8 Aug 1951; (2) 838, 839.

CARTER, Hanson; b Halifax, Yorkshire, England 15 Mar 1878; d Bellevue Hill, Sydney 8 Jun 1948; (28) 96, 97, 98, 99, 100, 101, 102, 103, 104, 105, 111, 112, 113, 114, 115, 116, 117, 118, 119, 120, 138, 139, 140, 141, 142, 143, 145, 147.

CHAPPELL, Gregory Stephen; b Unley, Adelaide 7 Aug 1948; (87) 675, 676, 677, 678, 679, 698, 699, 700, 701, 702, 708, 709, 710, 714, 715, 716, 717, 718, 728, 729, 730, 736, 737, 738, 750, 751, 752, 753, 754, 755, 760, 761, 762, 763, 764, 765, 766, 767, 768, 769, 793, 794, 795, 796, 797, 803, 804, 805, 806, 807, 808, 867, 868, 869, 870, 871, 872, 877, 878, 879, 885, 890, 891, 892, 893, 894, 895, 909, 910, 911, 918, 919, 920, 922, 923, 924, 938, 939, 940, 941, 942, 956, 970, 971, 972, 973, 974.

CHAPPELL, Ian Michael; b Unley, Adelaide 26 Sep 1943; (75) 570, 600, 601, 613, 614, 615, 616, 617, 624, 625, 626, 627, 637, 638, 639, 640, 641, 642, 643, 644, 645, 646, 665, 666, 667, 668, 669, 670, 671, 672, 673, 674, 675, 676, 677, 678, 679, 698, 699, 700, 701, 702, 708, 709, 710, 714, 715, 716, 717, 718, 728, 729, 730, 736, 737, 738, 750, 751, 752, 753, 754, 755, 760, 761, 762, 763, 764, 765, 766, 767, 768, 769, 870, 871, 872.

CHAPPELL, Trevor Martin; b Glenelg, Adelaide 21 Oct 1952; (3) 903, 904, 905.

CHARLTON, Percie Chater; b Surry Hills, Sydney 9 Apr 1867; d Pymble, Sydney 30 Sep 1954; (2) 33, 34.

CHIPPERFIELD, Arthur Gordon; b Ashfield, Sydney 17 Nov 1905; d Sydney 29 Jul 1987; (14) 233, 234, 235, 236, 237, 247, 248, 249, 250, 251, 255, 256, 258, 264.

CLARK, Wayne Maxwell; b Perth 19 Sep 1953; (10) 809, 810, 811, 812, 813, 820, 821, 822, 823, 849.

COLLEY, David John; b Mosman, Sydney 15 Mar 1947; (3) 698, 699, 700.

COLLINS, Herbert Leslie; b Darlinghurst, Sydney 21 Jan 1888; d Sydney 28 May 1959; (19) 135, 136, 137, 138, 139, 140, 143, 144, 145, 146, 147, 158, 159, 160, 161, 162, 163, 164, 167.

CONINGHAM, Arthur; b South Melbourne 14 Jul 1863; d Gladesville, Sydney 13 Jun 1939; (1) 43.

CONNOLLY, Alan Norman; b Skipton, Victoria 29 Jun 1939; (29) 548, 549, 550, 567, 568, 598, 624, 625, 626, 637, 638, 639, 640, 641, 642, 643, 644, 645, 646, 665, 666, 667, 668, 669, 670, 671, 672, 673, 676.

COOPER, Bransby Beauchamp; b Dacca, India 15 Mar 1844; d Geelong, Victoria 7 Aug 1914; (1) 1.

COOPER, William Henry; b Maidstone, Kent, England 11 Sep 1849; d Malvern, Melbourne 5 Apr 1939; (2) 5, 17.

CORLING, Grahame Edward; b Newcastle, New South Wales 13 Jul 1941; (5) 561, 562, 563, 564, 565.

COSIER, Gary John; b Richmond, Melbourne 25 Apr 1953; (18) 766, 767, 768, 793, 794, 795, 796, 797, 803, 809, 811, 812, 813, 820, 821, 822, 834, 835.

COTTAM, John Thomas; b Strawberry Hills, Sydney 5 Sep 1867; d Coolgardie, Western Australia 30 Jan 1897; (1) 26.

COTTER, Albert; b Sydney 3 Dec 1884; d Beersheba, Palestine 31 Oct 1917; (21) 81, 82, 83, 86, 87, 96, 97, 101, 102, 103, 104, 105, 111, 112, 113, 114, 115, 116, 117, 118, 119.

COULTHARD, George; b Boroondara, Victoria 1 Aug 1856; d Carlton, Melbourne 22 Oct 1883; (1) 6.

COWPER, Robert Maskew; b Kew, Melbourne 5 Oct 1940; (27) 563, 567, 568, 569, 570, 583, 584, 585, 586, 587, 597, 598, 599, 601, 613, 614, 615, 616, 617, 624, 625, 626, 627, 637, 638, 639, 640.

CRAIG, Ian David; b Yass, New South Wales 12 Jun 1935; (11) 364, 428, 429, 430, 431, 433, 444, 445, 446, 447, 448.

CRAWFORD, William Patrick Anthony; b Sydney 3 Aug 1933; (4) 426, 431, 432, 433.

DARLING, Joseph; b Glen Osmond, Adelaide 21 Nov 1870; d Hobart 2 Jan 1946; (34) 42, 43, 44, 45, 46, 50, 51, 52, 53, 54, 55, 56, 57, 60, 61, 62, 63, 64, 65, 66, 67, 70, 71, 72, 73, 74, 75, 76, 77, 83, 84, 85, 86, 87.

DARLING, Leonard Stuart; b South Yarra, Melbourne 14 Aug 1909; d Daw Park, Adelaide 24 Jun 1992; (12) 223, 224, 233, 234, 235, 236, 247, 248, 249, 250, 251, 257.

DARLING, Warrick Maxwell; b Waikerie, South Australia 1 May 1957; (14) 813, 821, 822, 823, 835, 836, 837, 838, 850, 856, 857, 858, 859, 860.

DAVIDSON, Alan Keith; b Lisarow, Gosford, New South Wales 14 Jun 1929; (44) 372, 373, 374, 375, 376, 392, 394, 395, 425, 429, 430, 432, 444, 445, 446, 447, 448, 464, 465, 466, 467, 468, 479, 480, 481, 482, 483, 484, 485, 486, 502, 503, 504, 506, 507, 508, 509, 510, 511, 535, 536, 537, 538, 539.

GROUBE, Thomas Underwood; b Taranaki, New Zealand 2 Sep 1857; d Glenferrie, Melbourne 5 Aug 1927; (1) 4.

GROUT, Arthur Theodore Wallace; b Mackay, Queensland 30 Mar 1927; d Brisbane 9 Nov 1968; (51) 444, 445, 446, 447, 448, 464, 465, 466, 467, 468, 479, 480, 481, 482, 484, 485, 486, 502, 503, 504, 505, 506, 507, 508, 509, 510, 511, 538, 539, 548, 549, 550, 551, 552, 561, 562, 563, 564, 565, 566, 569, 583, 584, 585, 586, 587, 597, 598, 599, 600, 601.

GUEST, Colin Ernest James; b Melbourne 7 Oct 1937; (1) 537.

HAMENCE, Ronald Arthur; b Hindmarsh, Adelaide 25 Nov 1915; (3) 283, 291, 292.

HAMMOND, Jeffrey Roy; b North Adelaide 19 Apr 1950; (5) 714, 715, 716, 717, 718.

HARRY, John; b Bendigo, Victoria 1 Aug 1857; d Canterbury, Melbourne 27 Oct 1919; (1) 44.

HARTIGAN, Roger Joseph; b Chatswood, Sydney 12 Dec 1879; d Brisbane 7 Jun 1958; (2) 98, 100.

HARTKOPF, Albert Ernst Victor; b North Fitzroy, Melbourne 28 Dec 1889; d Kew, Melbourne 20 May 1968; (1) 159.

HARVEY, Mervyn Roye; b Broken Hill, New South Wales 29 Apr 1918; (1) 282.

HARVEY, Robert Neil; b Fitzroy, Melbourne 8 Oct 1928; (79) 293, 294, 302, 303, 318, 319, 320, 321, 322, 327, 328, 329, 330, 331, 344, 345, 346, 347, 348, 360, 361, 362, 363, 364, 372, 373, 374, 375, 376, 391, 392, 393, 394, 395, 403, 404, 405, 406, 407, 425, 426, 427, 428, 429, 430, 431, 432, 433, 445, 446, 447, 448, 464, 465, 466, 467, 468, 479, 480, 481, 482, 483, 484, 485, 486, 502, 503, 504, 506, 507, 508, 509, 510, 511, 535, 536, 537, 538, 539.

HASSETT, Arthur Lindsay; b Geelong, Victoria 28 Aug 1913; d Batehaven, New South Wales 16 Jun 1993; (43) 263, 264, 265, 266, 275, 279, 280, 281, 282, 283, 290, 291, 292, 293, 299, 300, 301, 302, 303, 318, 319, 320, 321, 322, 327, 328, 329, 330, 331, 344, 345, 347, 348, 360, 361, 362, 363, 364, 372, 373, 374, 375, 376.

HAWKE, Neil James Napier; b Cheltenham, Adelaide 27 Jun 1939; (27) 539, 549, 550, 551, 552, 561, 562, 563, 564, 565, 566, 569, 570, 583, 584, 585, 586, 587, 597, 599, 600, 601, 613, 615, 627, 637, 638.

HAYDEN, Matthew Lawrence, b Kingaroy, Queensland 29 Oct 1971; (1) 1256.

HAZLITT, Gervys Rignold; b Enfield, Sydney 4 Sep 1888; d Parramatta, Sydney 30 Oct 1915; (9) 96, 97, 120, 121, 123, 125, 126, 127, 129.

HEALY, Ian Andrew; b Spring Hill, Brisbane 30 Apr 1964; (62) 1104, 1105, 1106, 1110, 1111, 1112, 1113, 1114, 1121, 1122, 1123, 1124, 1125, 1126, 1131, 1132, 1133, 1134, 1135, 1136, 1144, 1158, 1159, 1160, 1161, 1162, 1166, 1167, 1168, 1169, 1170, 1177, 1178, 1179, 1180, 1181, 1194, 1195, 1196, 1204, 1205, 1206, 1207, 1208, 1215, 1216, 1217, 1223, 1224, 1225, 1226, 1227, 1228, 1235, 1236, 1237, 1242, 1243, 1244, 1256, 1257, 1258.

HENDRY, Hunter Scott Thomas Laurie; b Woollahra, Sydney 24 May 1895; d Sydney 16 Dec 1988; (11) 140, 141, 142, 143, 145, 146, 158, 176, 177, 178, 179.

HIBBERT, Paul Anthony; b Brunswick, Melbourne, 23 Jul 1952; (1) 809.

HIGGS, James Donald; b Kyabram, Victoria 11 Jul 1950; (22) 820, 821, 823, 824, 834, 836, 837, 838, 839, 855, 856, 857, 858, 859, 860, 869, 870, 890, 891, 892, 893, 895.

HILDITCH, Andrew Mark Jefferson; b North Adelaide 20 May 1956; (18) 839, 849, 850, 855, 856, 857, 858, 859, 860, 1000, 1001, 1017, 1018, 1019, 1020, 1021, 1022, 1029.

HILL, Clement; b Hindmarsh, Adelaide 18 Mar 1877; d Parkville, Melbourne 5 Sep 1945; (49) 50, 51, 52, 53, 54, 55, 56, 57, 60, 61, 62, 65, 66, 67, 68, 69, 70, 71, 72, 73, 74, 75, 76, 77, 78, 79, 80, 81, 82, 83, 84, 85, 86, 87, 96, 97, 98, 99, 100, 111, 112, 113, 114, 115, 116, 117, 118, 119, 120.

HILL, John Charles; b Murrumbeena, Melbourne 25 Jun 1923; d Caulfield, Melbourne 11 Aug 1974; (3) 372, 374, 406.

HOARE, Desmond Edward; b Perth 19 Oct 1934; (1) 505.

HODGES, John Robart; b Knightsbridge, London 11 Aug 1855; d Collingwood 17 Jan 1933; (2) 1, 2.

HOGAN, Thomas George; b Merredin, Western Australia 23 Sep 1956; (7) 956, 972, 981, 982, 983, 984, 985.

HOGG, Rodney Malcolm; b Richmond, Melbourne 5 Mar 1951; (38) 834, 835, 836, 837, 838, 839, 849, 850, 855, 856, 857, 858, 859, 860, 867, 869, 891, 892, 893, 894, 903, 906, 940, 941, 942, 956, 970, 971, 972, 974, 981, 982, 983, 985, 997, 998, 999, 1000.

HOHNS, Trevor Victor; b Brisbane 23 Jan 1954; (7) 1113, 1114, 1122, 1123, 1124, 1125, 1126.

HOLE, Graeme Blake; b Concord West, Sydney 6 Jan 1931; d Adelaide 14 Feb 1990; (18) 331, 344, 345, 346, 347, 348, 360, 361, 362, 363, 372, 373, 374, 375, 376, 391, 392, 393.

HOLLAND, Robert George; b Camperdown, Sydney, 19 Oct 1946; (11) 998, 999, 1001, 1018, 1019, 1020, 1021, 1029, 1030, 1031, 1034.

HOOKES, David William; b Mile End, Adelaide 3 May 1955; (23) 803, 804, 805, 806, 807, 808, 867, 877, 938, 939, 940, 941, 942, 956, 981, 982, 983, 984, 985, 1030, 1031, 1032, 1033.

HOPKINS, Albert John Young; b Young, New South Wales 3 May 1874; d North Sydney 25 Apr 1931; (20) 68, 69, 70, 71, 72, 73, 74, 75, 76, 77, 78, 79, 80, 81, 82, 84, 85, 87, 104, 105.

HORAN, Thomas Patrick; b Midleton, Co. Cork. Ireland 8 Mar 1854; d Malvern, Melbourne 16 Apr 1916; (15) 1, 3, 5, 6, 7, 8, 9, 10, 11, 12, 13, 18, 19, 20, 21.

HORDERN, Herbert Vivian; b North Sydney 10 Feb 1883; d Darlinghurst, Sydney 17 Jun 1938; (7) 114, 115, 116, 117, 118, 119, 120.

HORNIBROOK, Percival Mitchell; b Obi Obi, Queensland 27 Jul 1899; d Spring Hill, Brisbane 25 Aug 1976; (6) 180, 194, 195, 196, 197, 198.

HOWELL, William Peter; b Penrith, New South Wales 29 Dec 1869; d Castlereagh, Penrith 14 Jul 1940; (18) 55, 56, 57, 60, 61, 62, 63, 64, 65, 66, 67, 68, 70, 76, 77, 78, 79, 80.

HUGHES, Kimberley John; b Margaret River, Western Australia 26 Jan 1954; (70) 808, 810, 812, 834, 835, 836, 837, 838, 839, 849, 850, 855, 856, 857, 858, 859, 860, 867, 868, 869, 870, 871, 872, 877, 878, 879, 885, 890, 891, 892, 893, 894, 895, 903, 904, 905, 906, 907, 908, 909, 910, 911, 918, 919, 920, 922, 923, 924, 935, 936, 937, 938, 939, 940, 941, 942, 970, 971, 972, 973, 974, 981, 982, 983, 984, 985, 997, 998, 999, 1000.

LEE, Philip Keith; b Gladstone, South Australia 15 Sep 1904; d Woodville South, Adelaide 9 Aug 1980; (2) 213, 224.

LILLEE, Dennis Keith; b Subiaco, Perth 18 Jul 1949; (70) 678, 679, 698, 699, 700, 701, 702, 708, 709, 710, 714, 750, 751, 752, 753, 754, 755, 760, 761, 762, 763, 764, 765, 766, 768, 769, 793, 794, 795, 796, 797, 803, 867, 868, 869, 870, 871, 872, 877, 878, 879, 885, 890, 891, 892, 893, 894, 895, 903, 904, 905, 906, 907, 908, 909, 910, 911, 918, 919, 920, 922, 923, 924, 938, 956, 970, 971, 972, 973, 974.

LINDWALL, Raymond Russell; b Mascot, Sydney 3 Oct 1921; (61) 275, 279, 281, 282, 283, 290, 291, 292, 293, 294, 299, 300, 301, 302, 303, 318, 319, 320, 321, 327, 328, 329, 330, 331, 344, 345, 346, 347, 348, 360, 361, 362, 363, 372, 373, 374, 375, 376, 391, 392, 393, 395, 403, 404, 405, 406, 407, 425, 427, 428, 429, 430, 431, 432, 433, 467, 468, 479, 481, 484, 486.

LOVE, Hampden Stanley Bray; b Lilyfield, Sydney 10 Aug 1895; d Mosman, Sydney 22 Jul 1969; (1) 223.

LOXTON, Samuel John Everett; b Albert Park, Melbourne 29 Mar 1921; (12) 294, 301, 302, 303, 318, 319, 320, 321, 322, 327, 328, 329.

LYONS, John James; b Gawler, South Australia 21 May 1863; d Magill, Adelaide 21 Jul 1927; (14) 26, 30, 33, 34, 35, 36, 37, 39, 40, 41, 42, 43, 46, 53.

McALISTER, Peter Alexander; b Williamstown, Melbourne 11 Jul 1869; d Richmond, Melbourne 10 May 1938; (8) 81, 82, 96, 97, 98, 99, 102, 103.

MACARTNEY, Charles George; b West Maitland, New South Wales 27 Jun 1886; d Sydney 9 Sep 1958; (35) 96, 97, 98, 99, 100, 101, 102, 103, 104, 105, 111, 112, 113, 115, 120, 121, 123, 125, 126, 127, 129, 135, 139, 140, 141, 142, 143, 144, 145, 147, 163, 164, 165, 166, 167.

McCABE, Stanley Joseph; b Grenfell, New South Wales 16 Jul 1910; d Beauty Point, Sydney 25 Aug 1968; (39) 194, 195, 196, 197, 198, 199, 200, 201, 202, 203, 212, 213, 214, 215, 216, 220, 221, 222, 223, 224, 233, 234, 235, 236, 237, 247, 248, 249, 250, 251, 255, 256, 257, 258, 259, 263, 264, 265, 266.

McCOOL, Colin Leslie; b Paddington, Sydney 9 Dec 1916; d Woy Woy, New South Wales 5 Apr 1986; (14) 275, 279, 280, 281, 282, 283, 290, 291, 293, 318, 319, 320, 321, 322.

McCORMICK, Ernest Leslie; b North Carlton, Melbourne 16 May 1906; d Tweed Heads, New South Wales 28 Jun 1991; (12) 247, 248, 249, 250, 251, 255, 256, 258, 259, 263, 264, 265.

McCOSKER, Richard Bede; b Inverell, New South Wales 11 Dec 1946; (25) 753, 754, 755, 760, 761, 762, 763, 764, 765, 766, 769, 793, 794, 795, 796, 797, 803, 804, 805, 806, 807, 808, 867, 870, 872.

McDERMOTT, Craig John; b Ipswich, Queensland 14 Apr 1965; (58) 1000, 1001, 1017, 1018, 1019, 1020, 1021, 1022, 1029, 1031, 1032, 1033, 1035, 1037, 1052, 1053, 1061, 1087, 1088, 1089, 1090, 1094, 1110, 1112, 1161, 1162, 1166, 1167, 1168, 1169, 1170, 1177, 1178, 1179, 1180, 1181, 1194, 1195, 1196, 1204, 1205, 1206, 1207, 1208, 1215, 1216, 1217, 1223, 1224, 1235, 1236, 1237, 1242, 1243, 1244, 1256, 1257, 1258.

McDONALD, Colin Campbell; b Glen Iris, Melbourne 17 Nov 1928; (47) 348, 360, 361, 362, 363, 364, 394, 395, 403, 404, 405, 406, 407, 425, 426, 427, 428, 429, 430, 431, 433, 444, 445, 446, 447, 448, 464, 465, 466, 467, 468, 479, 480, 481, 482, 483, 484, 485, 486, 502, 503, 504, 505, 506, 507, 508, 509.

McDONALD, Edgar Arthur; b Launceston, Tasmania 6 Jan 1891; d Blackrod, Lancashire, England 22 Jul 1937; (11) 137, 138, 139, 140, 141, 142, 143, 144, 145, 146, 147.

McDONNELL, Percy Stanislaus; b Kensington, London, England 13 Nov 1858; d Brisbane 24 Sep 1896; (19) 4, 5, 6, 7, 8, 10, 11, 12, 14, 15, 16, 17, 20, 25, 26, 27, 28, 29, 30.

McGRATH, Glenn Donald; b Dubbo, New South Wales 9 Feb 1970; (5) 1235, 1237, 1243, 1257, 1258.

McILWRAITH, John; b Collingwood, Melbourne 7 Sep 1857; d Camberwell, Melbourne 5 Jul 1938; (1) 24.

MACKAY, Kenneth Donald; b Windsor, Brisbane 24 Oct 1925; d Point Lookout, Stradbroke Island, Queensland 13 June 1982; (37) 426, 427, 428, 431, 432, 433, 444, 445, 446, 447, 448, 464, 465, 466, 467, 468, 479, 480, 481, 482, 483, 484, 485, 486, 502, 503, 504, 505, 506, 507, 508, 509, 510, 511, 535, 536, 538.

McKENZIE, Graham Douglas; b Cottesloe, Perth 24 Jun 1941; (60) 508, 509, 510, 535, 536, 537, 538, 539, 548, 549, 550, 551, 552, 561, 562, 563, 564, 565, 566, 567, 568, 569, 570, 583, 584, 585, 586, 587, 598, 599, 600, 601, 613, 614, 615, 616, 617, 624, 625, 637, 638, 639, 640, 641, 642, 643, 644, 645, 646, 665, 666, 667, 668, 669, 670, 671, 673, 674, 675, 676.

McKIBBIN, Thomas Robert; b Raglan, Bathurst, New South Wales 10 Dec 1870; d Bathurst 15 Dec 1939; (5) 46, 51, 52, 53, 54.

McLAREN, John William; b Toowong, Brisbane 24 Dec 1887; d Highgate Hill, Brisbane 17 Nov 1921; (1) 120.

MACLEAN, John Alexander; b Brisbane 27 Apr 1946; (4) 834, 835, 836, 837.

McLEOD, Charles Edward; b Port Melbourne 24 Oct 1869; d Toorak, Melbourne 26 Nov 1918; (17) 42, 53, 54, 55, 56, 57, 64, 65, 67, 80, 81, 82, 83, 84, 85, 86, 87.

McLEOD, Robert William; b Port Melbourne 19 Jan 1868; d Middle Park, Melbourne 14 Jun 1907; (6) 35, 36, 37, 39, 40, 41.

McSHANE, Patrick George; b Keilor, Melbourne 1857; d Kew, Melbourne 11 Dec 1903; (3) 21, 25, 27.

MADDOCKS, Leonard Victor; b Beaconsfield, Victoria 24 May 1926; (7) 393, 394, 395, 403, 427, 428, 432.

MAGUIRE, John Norman; b Murwillumbah, New South Wales 15 Sep 1956; (3) 973, 984, 985.

MAILEY, Arthur Alfred; b Waterloo, Sydney 3 Jan 1886; d Kirrawee, New South Wales 31 Dec 1967; (21) 135, 136, 137, 138, 139, 141, 142, 144, 145, 146, 147, 158, 159, 160, 161, 162, 163, 164, 165, 166, 167.

MALLETT, Ashley Alexander; b Chatswood, Sydney 13 Jul 1945; (38) 641, 642, 665, 666, 667, 668, 669, 670, 676, 678, 701, 702, 708, 709, 728, 729, 730, 736, 737, 738, 751, 752, 753, 754, 755, 760, 761, 762, 763, 764, 765, 766, 767, 768, 769, 871, 872, 885.

MALONE, Michael Francis; b Perth 9 Oct 1950; (1) 808.

MANN, Anthony Longford; b Middle Swan, Perth 8 Nov 1945; (4) 809, 810, 811, 812.

MARR, Alfred Percy; b Pyrmont, Sydney 28 Mar 1862; d Arncliffe, Sydney 15 Mar 1940; (1) 18.

MARSH, Geoffrey Robert; b Northam, Western Australia 31 Dec 1958; (50) 1032, 1033, 1034, 1035, 1036, 1037, 1052, 1053, 1054, 1058, 1059, 1060, 1061, 1062, 1087, 1088, 1089, 1090, 1094, 1104, 1105, 1106, 1110, 1111, 1112, 1113, 1114, 1121, 1122, 1123, 1124, 1125, 1126, 1134, 1135, 1144, 1158, 1159, 1160, 1161, 1162, 1166, 1167, 1168, 1169, 1170, 1177, 1178, 1179, 1180.

MARSH, Rodney William; b Armadale, Western Australia 11 Nov 1947; (96) 674, 675, 676, 677, 678, 679, 698, 699, 700, 701, 702, 708, 709, 710, 714, 715, 716, 717, 718, 728, 729, 730, 736, 737, 738, 750, 751, 752, 753, 754, 755, 760, 761, 762, 763, 764, 765, 766, 767, 768, 769, 793, 794, 795, 796, 797, 803, 804, 805, 806, 807, 808, 867, 868, 869, 870, 871, 872, 877, 878, 879, 885, 890, 891, 892, 893, 894, 895, 903, 904, 905, 906, 907, 908, 909, 910, 911, 918, 919, 920, 922, 923, 924, 935, 936, 937, 938, 939, 940, 941, 942, 970, 971, 972, 973, 974.

MARTIN, John Wesley; b Wingham, New South Wales 28 Jul 1931; d Burrell Greek, New South Wales 16 Jul 1992; (8) 503, 504, 506, 549, 566, 567, 569, 617.

MARTYN, Damien Richard; b Darwin 21 Oct 1971; (7) 1204, 1205, 1206, 1208, 1217, 1242, 1243.

MASSIE, Hugh Hamon; b near Belfast (*now* Port Fairy), Victoria 11 Apr 1854; d Point Piper, Sydney 12 Oct 1938; (9) 5, 6, 7, 8, 9, 10, 11, 12, 19.

MASSIE, Robert Arnold Lockyer; b Subiaco, Perth 14 Apr 1947; (6) 699, 700, 701, 702, 708, 710.

MATTHEWS, Christopher Darrell; b Cunderdin, Western Australia 22 Sep 1962; (3) 1058, 1059, 1110.

MATTHEWS, Gregory Richard John; b Newcastle, New South Wales 15 Dec 1959; (33) 973, 974, 985, 1000, 1020, 1029, 1030, 1031, 1032, 1033, 1034, 1035, 1036, 1037, 1052, 1053, 1054, 1058, 1059, 1060, 1061, 1158, 1159, 1160, 1161, 1162, 1166, 1167, 1194, 1195, 1196, 1204, 1206.

MATTHEWS, Thomas James; b Mount Gambia, South Australia 3 Apr 1884; d Caulfield, Melbourne 14 Oct 1943; (8) 118, 119, 121, 123, 125, 126, 127, 129.

MAY, Timothy Brian Alexander; b North Adelaide 26 Jan 1962; (19) 1088, 1104, 1105, 1106, 1110, 1111, 1114, 1207, 1224, 1225, 1226, 1227, 1228, 1236, 1237, 1242, 1243, 1244, 1256.

MAYNE, Edgar Richard; b Jamestown, South Australia 2 Jul 1882; d Carrum, Victoria 26 Oct 1961; (4) 125, 126, 146, 147.

MAYNE, Lawrence Charles, b Westonia, Western Australia 23 Jan 1942; (6) 583, 584, 585, 669, 672, 673.

MECKIFF, Ian; b Mentone, Melbourne 6 Jan 1935; (18) 444, 445, 447, 448, 464, 465, 466, 468, 479, 480, 482, 483, 484, 485, 486, 502, 504, 548.

MEULEMAN, Kenneth Douglas; b Melbourne 5 Sep 1923; (1) 275.

MIDWINTER, William Evans; b St Briavels, Gloucestershire, England 19 Jun 1851; d Yarra Bend, Kew, Melbourne 3 Dec 1890; (8) 1, 2, 13, 14, 15, 16, 25, 26. (*Also 4 Tests for England; 5-8*)

MILLER, Keith Ross; b Sunshine, Melbourne 28 Nov 1919; (55) 275, 279, 280, 281, 282, 283, 290, 291, 292, 293, 294, 299, 300, 301, 302, 303, 318, 319, 320, 321, 322, 327, 328, 329, 330, 331, 344, 345, 346, 347, 348, 360, 361, 362, 363, 372, 373, 374, 375, 376, 391, 393, 394, 395, 403, 404, 405, 406, 407, 425, 426, 427, 428, 429, 430.

MINNETT, Roy Baldwin; b St Leonards, Sydney 13 Jun 1888; d Manly, Sydney 21 Oct 1955; (9) 116, 117, 118, 119, 120, 121, 125, 127, 129.

MISSON, Francis Michael; b Darlinghurst, Sydney 19 Nov 1938; (5) 503, 505, 506, 507, 508.

MOODY, Thomas Masson; b Adelaide 2 Oct 1965; (8) 1131, 1132, 1133, 1136, 1181, 1194, 1195, 1196.

MORONEY, John; b Randwick, Sydney 24 Jul 1917; (7) 318, 319, 320, 321, 322, 327, 347.

MORRIS, Arthur Robert; b Dungog, New South Wales 19 Jan 1922; (46) 279, 280, 281, 282, 283, 290, 291, 292, 293, 299, 300, 301, 302, 303, 318, 319, 320, 321, 322, 327, 328, 329, 330, 331, 344, 345, 346, 347, 360, 361, 362, 363, 364, 372, 373, 374, 375, 376, 391, 392, 393, 394, 403, 404, 405, 407.

MORRIS, Samuel; b Hobart 22 Jun 1855; d Albert Park, Melbourne 20 Sep 1931; (1) 18.

MOSES, Henry; b Windsor, New South Wales 13 Feb 1858; d Strathfield, Sydney 7 Dec 1938; (6) 25, 26, 27, 35, 36, 45.

MOSS, Jeffrey Kenneth; b Melbourne 29 Jun 1947; (1) 850.

MOULE, William Henry; b Brighton, Melbourne 31 Jan 1858; d St Kilda, Melbourne 24 Aug 1939; (1) 4.

MURDOCH, William Lloyd; b Sandhurst, Victoria 18 Oct 1854; d Yarra Park, East Melbourne 18 Feb 1911; (18) 2, 3, 4, 5, 6, 7, 8, 9, 10, 11, 12, 13, 14, 15, 16, 17, 33, 34. (*Also Test No. 38 for England*)

MUSGROVE, Henry Alfred; b Surbiton, Surrey, England 27 Nov 1860; d Darlinghurst, Sydney 2 Nov 1931; (1) 18.

NAGEL, Lisle Ernest; b Bendigo, Victoria 6 Mar 1905; d Mornington, Victoria 23 Nov 1971; (1) 220.

NASH, Laurence John; b Fitzroy, Melbourne 2 May 1910; d Heidelberg, Victoria 24 Jul 1986; (2) 216, 259.

NITSCHKE, Holmesdale Carl; b Adelaide 14 Apr 1905; d Adelaide 29 Sep 1982; (2) 212, 213.

NOBLE, Montague Alfred; b Sydney 28 Jan 1873; d Randwick, Sydney 22 Jun 1940; (42) 54, 55, 56, 57, 60, 61, 62, 63, 64, 65, 66, 67, 68, 69, 70, 71, 72, 73, 74, 75, 76, 77, 78, 79, 80, 81, 82, 83, 84, 85, 86, 87, 96, 97, 98, 99, 100, 101, 102, 103, 104, 105.

NOBLET, Geffery; b Adelaide 14 Sep 1916; (3) 322, 346, 364.

NOTHLING, Otto Ernst; b Teutoburg (*now* Witta), Queensland 1 Aug 1900; d Chelmer, Brisbane 26 Sep 1965; (1) 177.

O'BRIEN, Leo Patrick Joseph; b West Melbourne 2 Jul 1907; (5) 221, 224, 250, 251, 256.

O'CONNOR, John Denis Alphonsus; b Sydney 9 Sep 1875; d Lewisham, Sydney 23 Aug 1941; (4) 98, 99, 100, 101.

O'DONNELL, Simon Patrick; b Deniliquin, New South Wales 26 Jan 1963; (6) 1017, 1018, 1019, 1020, 1021, 1030.

OGILVIE, Alan David; b Southport, Queensland 3 Jun 1951; (5) 809, 810, 811, 822, 824.

O'KEEFFE, Kerry James; b Hurstville, Sydney 25 Nov 1949; (24) 677, 679, 708, 709, 714, 715, 716, 717, 718, 728, 729, 730, 736, 737, 738, 793, 794, 795, 796, 797, 803, 804, 805, 806.

OLDFIELD, William Albert Stanley; b Alexandria, Sydney 9 Sep 1894; d Killara, Sydney 10 Aug 1976; (54) 135, 136, 137, 144, 146, 158, 159, 160, 161, 162, 163, 164, 165, 166, 167, 176, 177, 178, 179, 180, 194, 195, 196, 197, 198, 199, 200, 201, 202, 203, 212, 213, 214, 215, 216, 220, 221, 222, 224, 233, 234, 235, 236, 237, 247, 248, 249, 250, 251, 255, 256, 257, 258, 259.

O'NEILL, Norman Clifford; b Carlton, Sydney 19 Feb 1937; (42) 464, 465, 466, 467, 468, 479, 480, 481, 482, 483, 484, 485, 486, 502, 503, 504, 505, 506, 507, 508, 509, 510, 511, 535, 536, 537, 538, 539, 548, 550, 551, 552, 561, 562, 564, 565, 566, 567, 583, 584, 585, 586.

O'REILLY, William Joseph; b White Cliffs, New South Wales 20 Dec 1905; d Sutherland, New South Wales 6 Oct 1992; (27) 215, 216, 220, 221, 222, 223, 224, 233, 234, 235, 236, 237, 247, 248, 249, 250, 251, 255, 256, 257, 258, 259, 263, 264, 265, 266, 275.

OXENHAM, Ronald Keven; b Nundah, Brisbane 28 Jul 1891; d Brisbane 16 Aug 1939; (7) 178, 179, 180, 201, 202, 203, 212.

PALMER, George Eugene; b Mulwala, New South Wales 22 Feb 1859; d Baddaginnie, Benalla, Victoria 22 Aug 1910; (17) 4, 5, 6, 7, 8, 10, 11, 12, 13, 14, 15, 16, 17, 20, 22, 23, 24.

PARK, Roy Lindsay; b Ballarat, Victoria 30 Jul 1892; d Middle Park, Melbourne 23 Jan 1947; (1) 136.

PASCOE, Leonard Stephen (formerly DURTANOVICH); b Bridgetown, Western Australia 13 Feb 1950; (14) 804, 806, 807, 870, 871, 872, 885, 890, 891, 892, 893, 894, 895, 920.

PELLEW, Clarence Everard; b Port Pirie, South Australia 21 Sep 1893; d Adelaide 9 May 1981; (10) 135, 136, 137, 138, 140, 141, 142, 143, 144, 147.

PHILLIPS, Wayne Bentley; b Adelaide 1 Mar 1958; (27) 970, 971, 972, 973, 974, 981, 982, 983, 984, 985, 997, 998, 1017, 1018, 1019, 1020, 1021, 1022, 1029, 1030, 1031, 1032, 1033, 1034, 1035, 1036, 1037.

PHILLIPS, Wayne Norman; b Geelong, Victoria 7 Nov 1962; (1) 1181.

PHILPOTT, Peter Ian; b Manly, Sydney 21 Nov 1934; (8) 583, 584, 585, 586, 587, 597, 598, 599.

PONSFORD, William Harold; b North Fitzroy, Melbourne 19 Oct 1900; d Kyneton, Victoria 6 Apr 1991; (29) 158, 159, 160, 161, 162, 166, 167, 176, 177, 194, 195, 197, 198, 199, 200, 201, 202, 203, 212, 213, 214, 215, 220, 222, 223, 233, 235, 236, 237.

POPE, Roland James; b Ashfield, Sydney 18 Feb 1864; d Manly, Sydney 27 Jul 1952; (1) 18.

RACKEMANN Carl Gray; b Wondai, Queensland 3 Jun 1960; (12) 939, 970, 971, 984, 997, 1131, 1132, 1134, 1135, 1136, 1144, 1160.

RANSFORD, Vernon Seymour; b South Yarra, Melbourne 20 Mar 1885; d Brighton, Melbourne 19 Mar 1958; (20) 96, 97, 98, 99, 100, 101, 102, 103, 104, 105, 111, 112, 113, 114, 115, 116, 117, 118, 119, 120.

REDPATH, Ian Ritchie; b Geelong, Victoria 11 May 1941; (66) 549, 561, 562, 563, 564, 565, 566, 568, 569, 597, 613, 614, 615, 616, 617, 624, 625, 626, 637, 638, 639, 640, 641, 642, 643, 644, 645, 646, 665, 666, 667, 668, 669, 670, 671, 672, 673, 674, 675, 676, 677, 678, 679, 708, 709, 710, 714, 715, 716, 717, 718, 736, 737, 738, 750, 751, 752, 753, 754, 755, 764, 765, 766, 767, 768, 769.

REEDMAN, John Cole; b Gilberton, Adelaide 9 Oct 1865; d Gilberton, 23 Mar 1924; (1) 42.

REID, Bruce Anthony; b Osborne Park, Perth 14 Mar 1963; (27) 1032, 1033, 1034, 1035, 1036, 1037, 1052, 1054, 1058, 1059, 1060, 1061, 1062, 1087, 1088, 1104, 1105, 1106, 1158, 1159, 1160, 1161, 1168, 1169, 1178, 1179, 1204.

REIFFEL, Paul Ronald; b Box Hill, Victoria 19 Apr 1966; (12) 1181, 1215, 1216, 1217, 1226, 1227, 1228, 1235, 1236, 1242, 1244, 1258.

RENNEBERG, David Alexander; b Balmain, Sydney 23 Sep 1942; (8) 613, 614, 615, 616, 617, 624, 625, 626.

RICHARDSON, Arthur John; b Sevenhill, South Australia 24 Jul 1888; d Adelaide 23 Dec 1973; (9) 158, 159, 160, 161, 163, 164, 165, 166, 167.

RICHARDSON, Victor York; b Unley, Adelaide 7 Sep 1894; d Parkside, Adelaide 29 Oct 1969; (19) 158, 159, 160, 177, 178, 194, 195, 196, 197, 220, 221, 222, 223, 224, 247, 248, 249, 250, 251.

RIGG, Keith Edward; b Malvern, Melbourne 21 May 1906; (8) 203, 213, 214, 215, 216, 257, 258, 259.

RING, Douglas Thomas; b Hobart 14 Oct 1918; (13) 294, 303, 344, 345, 346, 347, 348, 360, 361, 362, 363, 364, 373.

RITCHIE, Gregory Michael; b Stanthorpe, Queensland 23 Jan 1960; (30) 935, 936, 937, 981, 982, 983, 984, 985, 1001, 1017, 1018, 1019, 1020, 1021, 1022, 1029, 1030, 1031, 1032, 1034, 1035, 1036, 1037, 1052, 1053, 1054, 1058, 1059, 1060, 1062.

RIXON, Stephen John; b Albury, New South Wales 25 Feb 1954; (13) 809, 810, 811, 812, 813, 820, 821, 822, 823, 824, 999, 1000, 1001.

ROBERTSON, William Roderick; b Deniliquin, New South Wales 6 Oct 1861; d Brighton, Melbourne 24 Jun 1938; (1) 18.

ROBINSON, Richard Daryl; b East Melbourne 8 Jun 1946; (3) 804, 806, 807.

ROBINSON, Rayford Harold; b Stockton, New South Wales 26 Mar 1914; d Stockton 10 Aug 1965; (1) 255.

RORKE, Gordon Frederick; b Mosman, Sydney 27 Jun 1938; (4) 467, 468, 482, 483.

RUTHERFORD, John Walter; b Bungulluping, Bruce Rock, Western Australia 25 Sep 1929; (1) 432.

RYDER, John; b Collingwood, Melbourne 8 Aug 1889; d Fitzroy, Melbourne 3 Apr 1977; (20) 135, 136, 137, 138, 139, 145, 146, 147, 160, 161, 162, 163, 164, 165, 166, 176, 177, 178, 179, 180.

SAGGERS, Ronald Arthur; b Sydenham, Sydney 15 May 1917; d Sydney 17 Mar 1987; (6) 302, 318, 319, 320, 321, 322.

SAUNDERS, John Victor; b Melbourne 21 March 1876; d Toorak, Melbourne 21 Dec 1927; (14) 68, 71, 72, 73, 74, 76, 77, 78, 79, 96, 97, 98, 99, 100.

SCOTT, Henry James Herbert; b Toorak, Melbourne 26 Dec 1858; d Scone, New South Wales 23 Sep 1910; (8) 14, 15, 16, 17, 19, 22, 23, 24.

SELLERS, Reginald Hugh Durning; b Bulsar, India 20 Aug 1940; (1) 568.

SERJEANT, Craig Stanton; b Nedlands, Perth 1 Nov 1951; (12) 804, 805, 808, 809, 810, 811, 812, 820, 821, 822, 823, 824.

SHEAHAN, Andrew Paul; b Werribee, Victoria 30 Sep 1946; (31) 624, 625, 626, 627, 637, 638, 639, 640, 641, 642, 643, 644, 645, 646, 665, 666, 667, 668, 669, 670, 671, 672, 673, 674, 675, 701, 702, 708, 709, 728, 729.

SHEPHERD, Barry Kenneth; b Donnybrook, Western Australia 23 Apr 1937; (9) 537, 538, 549, 550, 551, 552, 570, 586, 587.

SIEVERS, Morris William; b Wonthaggi, Victoria 13 Apr 1912; d Brunswick, Melbourne 10 May 1968; (3) 255, 256, 257.

SIMPSON, Robert Baddeley; b Marrickville, Sydney 3 Feb 1936; (62) 444, 445, 446, 447, 448, 465, 502, 503, 504, 505, 506, 507, 508, 509, 510, 511, 535, 536, 537, 538, 539, 548, 549, 550, 551, 552, 561, 562, 563, 564, 565, 566, 567, 568, 569, 570, 583, 584, 585, 586, 587, 598, 600, 601, 613, 614, 615, 616, 617, 624, 625, 627, 809, 810, 811, 812, 813, 820, 821, 822, 823, 824,

SOUTH AFRICA (257 players)

ADCOCK, Neil Amwin Treharne; b Cape Town 8 Mar 1931; (26) 377, 378, 379, 380, 381, 408, 409, 410, 411, 434, 435, 436, 437, 438, 444, 445, 446, 447, 448, 492, 493, 494, 495, 496, 523, 524.

ANDERSON, James Henry; b Kimberley 26 Apr 1874; d Melkamer, Bredasdorp, Cape Province 11 Mar 1926; (1) 76.

ASHLEY, William Hare; b Mowbray, Cape Colony 10 Feb 1862; d Plumtree, Southern Rhodesia 14 Jul 1930; (1) 32.

BACHER, Aron; b Roodepoort, Transvaal 24 May 1942; (12) 594, 595, 596, 613, 614, 615, 616, 617, 670, 671, 672, 673.

BALASKAS, Xenophon Constantine; b Kimberley 15 Oct 1910; d Johannesburg 12 May 1994; (9) 204, 205, 217, 218, 243, 249, 250, 251, 268.

BARLOW, Edgar John; b Pretoria 12 Aug 1940; (30) 520, 521, 522, 523, 524, 548, 549, 550, 551, 552, 558, 559, 560, 571, 572, 573, 574, 575, 594, 595, 596, 613, 614, 615, 616, 617, 670, 671, 672, 673.

BAUMGARTNER, Harold Vane; b Henley-on-Thames, Oxfordshire, England 17 Nov 1883; d Accra, Gold Coast 8 Apr 1938; (1) 130.

BEAUMONT, Rolland; b Newcastle, Natal 4 Feb 1884; d Durban 25 May 1958; (5) 121, 127, 128, 131, 132.

BEGBIE, Denis Warburton; b Middelburg, Transvaal 12 Dec 1914; (5) 309, 310, 311, 321, 322.

BELL, Alexander John; b East London 15 Apr 1906; d Mowbray, Cape Town 1 Aug 1985; (16) 182, 183, 184, 205, 206, 208, 212, 213, 214, 215, 216, 217, 218, 243, 244, 245.

BISSET, Murray; b Port Elizabeth 14 Apr 1876; knighted 1928; d Salisbury, Southern Rhodesia 24 Oct 1931; (3) 58, 59, 110.

BISSETT, George Finlay; b Kimberley 5 Nov 1905; d Botha's Hill, Natal 14 Nov 1965; (4) 169, 170, 171, 172.

BLANCKENBERG, James Manuel; b Claremont, Cape Town 31 Dec 1892; presumed dead; (18) 130, 131, 132, 133, 134, 145, 146, 147, 148, 149, 150, 151, 152, 153, 154, 155, 156, 157.

BLAND, Kenneth Colin; b Bulawayo, Southern Rhodesia 5 Apr 1938; (21) 520, 521, 522, 523, 524, 549, 550, 551, 552, 558, 559, 560, 571, 572, 573, 574, 575, 594, 595, 596, 613.

BOCK, Ernest George; b Kimberley 17 Sep 1908; d Springs, Transvaal 5 Sep 1961; (1) 248.

BOND, Gerald Edward; b Cape Town 5 Apr 1909; d Cape Town 27 Aug 1965; (1) 267.

BOSCH, Tertius; b Vereeniging, Transvaal 14 Mar 1966; (1) 1188.

BOTTEN, James Thomas; b Pretoria 21 Jun 1938; (3) 594, 595, 596.

BRANN, William Henry; b Port Elizabeth 4 Apr 1899; d Port Elizabeth 22 Sep 1953; (3) 148, 149, 150.

BRISCOE, Arthur Wellesley; b Johannesburg 6 Feb 1911; d near Dessie, Ethiopia 22 Apr 1941; (2) 248, 268.

BROMFIELD, Harry Dudley; b Mossel Bay, Cape Province 26 Jun 1932; (9) 520, 521, 522, 523, 524, 573, 574, 575, 594.

BROWN, Lennox Sydney; b Randfontein, Transvaal 24 Nov 1910; d Durban 1 Sep 1983; (2) 213, 218.

BURGER, Christopher George de Villiers; b Randfontein, Transvaal 12 Jul 1935; (2) 447, 448.

BURKE, Sidney Frank; b Pretoria 11 Mar 1934; (2) 522, 573.

BUYS, Isaac Daniel, b Somerset East, Cape Colony 4 Feb 1895; presumed dead; (1) 148.

CAMERON, Horace Brakenridge; b Port Elizabeth 5 Jul 1905; d Johannesburg 2 Nov 1935; (26) 168, 169, 170, 171, 172, 181, 182, 184, 185, 204, 205, 206, 207, 208, 212, 213, 214, 215, 216, 217, 218, 242, 243, 244, 245, 246.

CAMPBELL, Thomas; b Edinburgh, Scotland 9 Feb 1882; d Milndale, Natal 5 Oct 1924; (5) 106, 107, 108, 109, 122.

CARLSTEIN, Peter Rudolph; b Klerksdorp, Transvaal 28 Oct 1938; (8) 448, 492, 493, 494, 495, 496, 548, 551.

CARTER, Claude Paget; b Durban 23 Apr 1881; d Durban 8 Nov 1952; (10) 122, 124, 133, 134, 145, 146, 147, 155, 156, 157.

CATTERALL, Robert Hector; b Port Elizabeth 10 Jul 1900; d Johannesburg 2 Jan 1961; (24) 148, 149, 150, 151, 152, 153, 154, 155, 156, 157, 168, 169, 170, 171, 172, 181, 182, 183, 184, 185, 204, 205, 206, 207.

CHAPMAN, Horace William; b Durban 30 Jun 1890; d Durban 1 Dec 1941; (2) 133, 145.

CHEETHAM, John Erskine; b Mowbray, Cape Town 26 May 1920; d Johannesburg 21 Aug 1980; (24) 313, 318, 319, 320, 334, 335, 336, 337, 338, 360, 361, 362, 363, 364, 370, 371, 377, 378, 379, 380, 381, 408, 409, 412.

CHEVALIER, Grahame Anton; b Cape Town 9 Mar 1937; (1) 670.

CHRISTY, James Alexander Joseph; b Pretoria 12 Dec 1904; d Durban 1 Feb 1971; (10) 181, 182, 208, 212, 213, 214, 215, 216, 217, 218.

CHUBB, Geoffrey Walter Ashton; b East London 12 Apr 1911; d East London 28 Aug 1982; (5) 334, 335, 336, 337, 338.

COCHRAN, John Alexander Kennedy; b Johannesburg 15 Jul 1909; d Johannesburg 15 Jun 1987; (1) 208.

COEN, Stanley Keppel; b Heilbron, Orange Free State 14 Oct 1902; d Durban 28 Jan 1967; (2) 168, 172.

COMMAILLE, John McIllwaine Moore; b Cape Town 21 Feb 1883; d Cape Town 28 Jul 1956; (12) 106, 107, 108, 109, 110, 153, 154, 155, 156, 157, 168, 169.

CONYNGHAM, Dalton Parry; b Durban 10 May 1897; d Durban 7 Jul 1979; (1) 152.

COOK, Frederick J.; b in Java 1870; d Gallipoli, Turkey 30 Nov 1915; (1) 47.

COOK, Stephen James; b Johannesburg 31 Jul 1953; (3) 1200, 1201, 1232.

COOPER, Alfred Henry Cecil; b Johannesburg 2 Sep 1893; d Johannesburg 18 Jul 1963; (1) 130.

COX, Joseph Lovell; b Pietermaritzburg 28 Jun 1886; d Bulawayo, Rhodesia 4 Jul 1971; (3) 130, 131, 133.

CRIPPS, Godfrey; b Mussoorie, India 19 Oct 1865; d nr Adelaide, Australia 27 Jul 1943; (1) 38.

CRISP, Robert James; b Calcutta, India 28 May 1911; d Colchester, Essex, England 2 Mar 1994; (9) 242, 243, 244, 245, 246, 247, 248, 249, 251.

CRONJE, Wessel Johannes; b Bloemfontein 25 Sep 1969; (16) 1188, 1201, 1202, 1203, 1232, 1233, 1234, 1242, 1243, 1244, 1256, 1257, 1258, 1263, 1264, 1265.

CULLINAN, Daryll John; b Kimberley 4 Mar 1967; (8) 1203, 1232, 1233, 1234, 1242, 1243, 1244, 1265.

CURNOW, Sydney Harry; b Benoni, Transvaal 16 Dec 1907; d Perth, Australia 28 Jul 1986; (7) 204, 206, 207, 212, 214, 215, 216.

DALTON, Eric Londesborough; b Durban 2 Dec 1906; d Durban 3 Jun 1981; (15) 182, 208, 212, 213, 217, 218, 243, 244, 245, 246, 247, 267, 269, 270, 271.

DAVIES, Eric Quail; b King William's Town, Cape Colony 26 Aug 1909; d Port Alfred, Cape Province 11 Nov 1976; (5) 250, 251, 267, 268, 269.

DAWSON, Oswald Charles; b Rossburgh, Durban 1 Sep 1919; (9) 285, 286, 287, 288, 289, 309, 310, 311, 313.

DEANE, Hubert Gouvaine; b Eshowe, Zululand 21 Jul 1895; d Johannesburg 21 Oct 1939; (17) 153, 154, 155, 156, 157, 168, 169, 170, 171, 172, 181, 182, 183, 184, 185, 205, 206.

DE VILLIERS, Petrus Stephanus; b Vereeniging, Transvaal 13 Oct 1964; (9) 1242, 1243, 1244, 1256, 1257, 1258, 1263, 1264, 1265.

DIXON, Cecil Donovan; b Potchefstroom, Transvaal 12 Feb 1891; d Johannesburg 9 Sep 1969; (1) 132.

DONALD, Allan Anthony, b Bloemfontein 20 Oct 1966; (17) 1188, 1200, 1201, 1202, 1203, 1232, 1233, 1234, 1242, 1243, 1244, 1256, 1257, 1258, 1263, 1264, 1265.

DOWER, Robert Reid; b Kokstad, Cape Colony 4 Jun 1876; d Cape Town 15 Sep 1964; (1) 58.

DRAPER, Ronald George; b Oudtshoorn, Cape Province 24 Dec 1926; (2) 321, 322.

DUCKWORTH, Christopher Anthony Russell; b Que Que, Southern Rhodesia 22 Mar 1933; (2) 437, 438.

DUMBRILL, Richard; b Teddington, Middlesex, England 19 Nov 1938; (5) 594, 595, 596, 613, 614.

DUMINY, Jacobus Petrus; b Bellville, Cape Colony 16 Dec 1897; d Cape Town 31 Jan 1980; (3) 168, 171, 183.

DUNELL, Owen Robert; b Port Elizabeth 15 Jul 1856; d Lyons, France 21 Oct 1929; (2) 31, 32.

DU PREEZ, John Harcourt; b Salisbury, Southern Rhodesia 14 Nov 1942; (2) 616, 617.

DU TOIT, Jacobus Francois; b Jacobsdal, Orange Free State 5 Apr 1868; d Lindley, Orange Free State 10 Jul 1909; (1) 38.

DYER, Dennis Victor; b Durban 2 May 1914; d Durban 16 Jun 1990; (3) 287, 288, 289.

EKSTEEN, Clive Edward; b Johannesburg 2 Dec 1966; (1) 1232.

ELGIE, Michael Kelsey; b Durban 6 Mar 1933; (3) 520, 521, 522.

ENDEAN, William Russell; b Johannesburg 31 May 1924; (28) 338, 360, 361, 362, 363, 364, 370, 371, 377, 378, 379, 380, 381, 408, 409, 410, 411, 412, 434, 435, 436, 437, 438, 444, 445, 446, 447, 448.

FARRER, William Stephen; b King William's Town, Cape Province 8 Dec 1936; (6) 522, 523, 524, 558, 559, 560.

FAULKNER, George Aubrey; b Port Elizabeth 17 Dec 1881; d Walham Green, London, England 10 Sep 1930; (25) 88, 89, 90, 91, 92, 93, 94, 95, 106, 107, 108, 109, 110, 111, 112, 113, 114, 115, 121, 122, 124, 125, 127, 128, 154.

FELLOWS-SMITH, Jonathan Payn; b Durban 3 Feb 1932; (4) 492, 493, 494, 496.

FICHARDT, Charles Gustav; b Bloemfontein 20 Mar 1870; d Bloemfontein 30 May 1923; (2) 38, 47.

FINLASON, Charles Edward; b Camberwell, London, England 19 Feb 1860; d Surbiton, Surrey, England 31 Jul 1917; (1) 31.

FLOQUET, Claude Eugene; b Aliwal North, Cape Colony 3 Nov 1884; d Port Elizabeth 22 Nov 1963; (1) 108.

FRANCIS, Howard Henry; b Clifton, Gloucestershire, England 26 May 1868; d Cape Town 7 Jan 1936; (2) 58, 59.

FRANCOIS, Cyril Matthew; b Lewisham, Kent, England 20 Jun 1897; d Pretoria 26 May 1944; (5) 148, 149, 150, 151, 152.

FRANK, Charles Newton; b Jagersfontein, Orange Free State 27 Jan 1891; d Johannesburg 26 Dec 1961; (3) 145, 146, 147.

FRANK, William Hughes Bowker; b King William's Town, Cape Colony 23 Nov 1872; d Durban 16 Feb 1945; (1) 48.

FULLER, Edward Russell Henry; b Worcester, Cape Province 2 Aug 1931; (7) 363, 364, 370, 371, 408, 412, 445.

FULLERTON, George Murray; b Johannesburg 8 Dec 1922; (7) 288, 289, 321, 322, 334, 335, 336.

FUNSTON, Kenneth James; b Pretoria 3 Dec 1925; (18) 360, 361, 362, 363, 364, 370, 371, 377, 378, 381, 436, 437, 438, 444, 445, 446, 447, 448.

GAMSY, Dennis; b Durban 17 Feb 1940; (2) 670, 671.

GLEESON, Robert Anthony; b Port Elizabeth 6 Dec 1873; d Port Elizabeth 27 Sep 1919; (1) 47.

GLOVER, George Keyworth; b Wakefield, Yorkshire, England 13 May 1870; d Kimberley 15 Nov 1938; (1) 49.

GODDARD, Trevor Leslie; b Durban 1 Aug 1931; (41) 408, 409, 410, 411, 412, 434, 435, 436, 437, 438, 444, 445, 446, 447, 448, 492, 493, 494, 495, 496, 548, 549, 550, 551, 552, 558, 559, 560, 571, 572, 573, 574, 575, 613, 614, 615, 616, 617, 670, 671, 672.

GORDON, Norman; b Boksburg, Transvaal 6 Aug 1911; (5) 267, 268, 269, 270, 271.

GRAHAM, Robert; b Grahamstown, Cape Colony 16 Sep 1877; d Eastbourne, Sussex, England 21 Apr 1946; (2) 58, 59.

GRIEVESON, Ronald Eustace; b Johannesburg 24 Aug 1909; (2) 270, 271.

GRIFFIN, Geoffrey Merton; b Greytown, Natal 12 Jun 1939; (2) 492, 493.

HALL, Alfred Ewart; b Bolton, Lancashire, England 23 Jan 1896; d Johannesburg 1 Jan 1964; (7) 149, 150, 151, 152, 171, 172, 207.

HALL, Glen Gordon; b Pretoria 24 May 1938; d Ramsgate, Natal 26 Jun 1987; (1) 573.

HALLIWELL, Ernest Austin; b Ealing, Middlesex, England 7 Sep 1864; d Johannesburg 2 Oct 1919; (8) 38, 47, 48, 49, 59, 75, 76, 77.

HALSE, Clive Grey; b Empangeni, Natal 28 Feb 1935; (3) 550, 551, 552.

HANDS, Philip Albert Myburgh; b Claremont, Cape Town 18 Mar 1890; d Parys, Orange Free State 27 Apr 1951; (7) 130, 131, 132, 133, 134, 147, 156.

HANDS, Reginald Harry Myburgh; b Cape Town 26 Jul 1888; d in France 20 Apr 1918; (1) 134.

HANLEY, Martin Andrew; b Aliwal North, Cape Province 10 Nov 1918; (1) 311.

HARRIS, Terence Anthony; b Kimberley 27 Aug 1916; d Plettenberg Bay, Cape Province 7 Mar 1993; (3) 285, 286, 312.

HARTIGAN, Gerald Patrick Desmond; b King William's Town, Cape Colony 30 Dec 1884; d Durban 7 Jan 1955; (5) 121, 122, 130, 131, 132.

HARVEY, Robert Lyon; b Swinbourne, Orange Free State 14 Sep 1911; (2) 250, 251.

HATHORN, Christopher Maitland Howard; b Pietermaritzburg 7 Apr 1878; d Johannesburg 17 May 1920; (12) 75, 76, 77, 88, 89, 90, 91, 92, 93, 94, 95, 113.

HEARNE, Frank; b Ealing, Middlesex, England 23 Nov 1858; d Cape Town 14 Jul 1949; (4) 38, 47, 48, 49, (*Also 2 Tests for England: 31, 32*).

HEARNE, George Alfred Lawrence; b Catford, Kent, England 27 Mar 1888; d Barberton, Transvaal 13 Nov 1978; (3) 148, 149, 157.

HEINE, Peter Samuel; b Winterton, Natal 28 Jun 1928; (14) 409, 410, 411, 412, 434, 435, 436, 437, 438, 444, 446, 447, 448, 523.

HENRY, Omar; b Stellenbosch, Cape Province 23 Jan 1952; (3) 1200, 1202, 1203.

HIME, Charles Frederick William; b Bermuda 24 Oct 1869; d Pietermaritzburg 6 Dec 1940; (1) 47.

HUDSON, Andrew Charles; b Eshowe, Natal 17 Mar 1965; (16) 1188, 1200, 1201, 1202, 1203, 1232, 1233, 1234, 1242, 1243, 1244, 1256, 1257, 1258, 1263, 1264.

HUTCHINSON, Philip; b West Dean, Sussex, England 26 Jan 1861; d Durban 30 Sep 1925; (2) 31, 32.

IRONSIDE, David Ernest James; b Lourenço Marques, Mozambique 2 May 1925; (3) 378, 379, 380.

IRVINE, Brian Lee; b Durban 9 Mar 1944; (4) 670, 671, 672, 673.

JOHNSON, Clement Lecky; b Co. Kildare, Ireland 1871; d Maraisburg, Transvaal 31 May 1908; (1) 48.

KEITH, Headley James; b Dundee, Natal 25 Oct 1927; (8) 364, 409, 410, 411, 412, 434, 435, 436.

KEMPIS, Gustav Adolph; b Port Elizabeth 4 Aug 1865; d Chiloane Island, Mozambique 19 May 1890; (1) 31.

KIRSTEN, Gary; b Cape Town 23 Nov 1967; (9) 1242, 1243, 1244, 1256, 1257, 1258, 1263, 1264, 1265.

KIRSTEN, Peter Noel, b Pietermaritzburg 14 May 1955; (12) 1188, 1200, 1201, 1202, 1203, 1244, 1256, 1257, 1258, 1263, 1264, 1265.

KOTZE, Johannes Jacobus; b Hopefield, Cape Colony 7 Aug 1879; d Cape Town 7 Jul 1931; (3) 76, 77, 93.

KUIPER, Adrian Paul; b Johannesburg 24 Aug 1959; (1) 1188.

KUYS, Frederick; b George, Cape Colony 21 Mar 1870; d Oudtshoorn, Cape Province 12 Sep 1953; (1) 59.

LANCE, Herbert Roy; b Pretoria 6 Jun 1940; (13) 523, 524, 594, 595, 596, 613, 614, 615, 616, 617, 671, 672, 673.

LANGTON, Arthur Beaumont Chudleigh; (registered as Arthur Chudleigh Beaumont Langton) b Pietermaritzburg, Natal 2 Mar 1912; d Accra, Gold Coast 27 Nov 1942; (15) 242, 243, 244, 245, 246, 247, 248, 249, 250, 251, 267, 268, 269, 270, 271.

LAWRENCE, Godfrey Bernard; b Salisbury, Southern Rhodesia 31 Mar 1932; (5) 520, 521, 522, 523, 524.

LE ROUX, Frederick Louis; b Durban 5 Feb 1882; d Durban 22 Sep 1963; (1) 133.

LEWIS, Percy Tyson; b Cape Town 2 Oct 1884; d Durban 30 Jan 1976; (1) 130.

LINDSAY, Denis Thomson; b Benoni, Transvaal 4 Sep 1939; (19) 548, 551, 552, 558, 559, 560, 571, 572, 573, 594, 595, 596, 613, 614, 615, 616, 617, 672, 673.

LINDSAY, John Dixon; b Barkly East, Cape Colony 8 Sep 1908; d Benoni 31 Aug 1990; (3) 285, 286, 287.

LINDSAY, Nevil Vernon; b Harrismith, Orange Free State 30 Jul 1886; d Pietermaritzburg 2 Feb 1976; (1) 146.

LING, William Victor Stone; b Kimberley 3 Oct 1891; d Brakpan, Transvaal 26 Sep 1960; (6) 145, 146, 147, 148, 149, 150.

LLEWELLYN, Charles Bennett; b Pietermaritzburg 26 Sep 1876; d Chertsey, Surrey, England 7 Jun 1964; (15) 48, 58, 75, 76,77, 111, 112, 113, 114, 115, 122, 124, 125, 127, 128.

LUNDIE, Eric Balfour; b 15 Mar 1888; d near Ypres, Belgium 12 Sep 1917; (1) 134.

McCARTHY, Cuan Neil; b Pietermaritzburg 24 Mar 1929; (15) 309, 310, 311, 312, 313, 318, 319, 320, 321, 322, 334, 335, 336, 337, 338.

MACAULAY, Michael John; b Durban 19 Apr 1939; (1) 575.

McGLEW, Derrick John; b Pietermaritzburg 11 Mar 1929; (34) 334, 335, 360, 361, 362, 363, 370, 371, 377, 378, 379, 380, 381, 408, 409, 410, 411, 412, 435, 444, 445, 446, 447, 448, 492, 493, 494, 495, 496, 520, 521, 522, 523, 524.

McKINNON, Atholl Henry; b Port Elizabeth 20 Aug 1932; d Durban 1 Dec 1983; (8) 496, 522, 574, 575, 595, 596, 613, 614.

McLEAN, Roy Alastair; b Pietermaritzburg 9 Jul 1930; (40) 336, 337, 338, 360, 361, 362, 363, 364, 370, 371, 377, 378, 379, 380, 408, 409, 410, 411, 412, 434, 435, 436, 437, 438, 444, 445, 446, 447, 492, 493, 494, 495, 496, 520, 521, 522, 523, 524, 571, 572.

McMILLAN, Brian Mervin; b Welkom, Orange Free State 22 Dec 1963; (13) 1200, 1201, 1202, 1203, 1233, 1234, 1244, 1256, 1257, 1258, 1263, 1264, 1265,

McMILLAN, Quintin; b Germiston, Transvaal 23 Jun 1904; d Randfontein, Transvaal 3 Jul 1948; (13) 182, 185, 204, 205, 206, 207, 208, 212, 214, 215, 216, 217, 218.

MANN, Norman Bertram Fleetwood; b Brakpan, Transvaal 28 Dec 1920; d Johannesburg 31 Jul 1952; (19) 285, 286, 287, 288, 289, 309, 310, 311, 312, 313, 318, 319, 320, 321, 322, 334, 335, 336, 337.

MANSELL, Percy Neville Frank; b St George's, Telford, Shropshire, England 16 Mar 1920; (13) 337, 338, 360, 361, 362, 363, 364, 370, 371, 409, 410, 411, 412.

MARKHAM, Lawrence Anderson; b Mbabane, Swaziland 12 Sep 1924; (1) 312.

MARX, Waldemar Frederick Eric; b Johannesburg 4 Jul 1895; d Durban 2 Jun 1974; (3) 145, 146, 147.

MATTHEWS, Craig Russell; b Cape Town 15 Feb 1965; (11) 1201, 1202, 1203, 1242, 1243, 1256, 1257, 1258, 1263, 1264, 1265.

MEINTJES, Douglas James; b Pretoria 9 Jun 1890; d Johannesburg 17 Jul 1979; (2) 151, 152.

MELLE, Michael George; b Johannesburg 3 Jun 1930; (7) 321, 322, 338, 360, 361, 362, 363.

MELVILLE, Alan; b Carnarvon, Cape Province 19 May 1910; d Kruger National Park, Transvaal 18 Apr 1983; (11) 267, 268, 269, 270, 271, 285, 286, 287, 288, 289, 311.

MIDDLETON, James; b Chester-le-Street, Co. Durham, England 30 Sep 1865; d Newlands, Cape Town 23 Dec 1913; (6) 47, 49, 58, 59, 76, 77.

MILLS, Charles Henry; b Peckham, Surrey, England 26 Nov 1867; d Southwark, London, England 26 Jul 1948; (1) 38.

RICHARDSON, David John; b Johannesburg 16 Sep 1959; (17) 1188, 1200, 1201, 1202, 1203, 1232, 1233, 1234, 1242, 1243, 1244, 1256, 1257, 1258, 1263, 1264, 1265.

ROBERTSON, John Benjamin; b Wynberg, Cape Town 5 Jun 1906; d Cape Town 5 Jul 1985; (3) 247, 248, 249.

ROSE-INNES, Albert (*also known as* A.R.Innes); b Port Elizabeth 16 Feb 1868; d East London 22 Nov 1946; (2) 31, 32.

ROUTLEDGE, Thomas William; b Liverpool, Lancashire, England 18 Apr 1867; d Stockton-on-Tees, Co. Durham, England 9 May 1927; (4) 38, 47, 48, 49.

ROWAN, Athol Matthew Burchell; b Johannesburg 7 Feb 1921; (15) 285, 286, 287, 288, 289, 309, 310, 311, 312, 313, 334, 335, 336, 337, 338.

ROWAN, Eric Alfred Burchell; b Johannesburg 20 Jul 1909; d Johannesburg 30 Apr 1993; (26) 242, 243, 244, 245, 246, 247, 248, 249, 268, 269, 270, 271, 309, 310, 312, 313, 318, 319, 320, 321, 322, 334, 335, 336, 337, 338.

ROWE, George Alexander; b Grahamstown, Cape Colony 15 Jun 1874; d Cape Town 8 Jan 1950; (5) 48, 49, 58, 59, 75.

RUSHMERE, Mark Weir; b Port Elizabeth 7 Jan 1965; (1) 1188.

SAMUELSON, Sivert Vause; b York, Natal 21 Nov 1883; d Durban 18 Nov 1958; (1) 110.

SCHULTZ, Brett Nolan; b East London 26 Aug 1970; (5) 1200, 1202, 1232, 1233, 1234.

SCHWARZ, Reginald Oscar; b Lee, Kent, England 4 May 1875; d Etaples, France 18 Nov 1918; (20) 88, 89, 90, 91, 92, 93, 94, 95, 106, 107, 109, 110, 111, 112, 113, 114, 115, 121, 122, 125.

SECCULL, Arthur William; b King William's Town, Cape Colony 14 Sep 1868; d Johannesburg 20 Jul 1945; (1) 49.

SEYMOUR, Michael Arthur; b Kokstad, Cape Province 5 Jun 1936; (7) 548, 549, 551, 552, 571, 572, 670.

SHALDERS, William Alfred; b Kimberley 12 Feb 1880; d Cradock, Cape Province 18 Mar 1917; (12) 59, 75, 76, 77, 88, 89, 90, 91, 92, 93, 94, 95.

SHEPSTONE, George Harold; b Pietermaritzburg 8 Apr 1876; d Johannesburg 3 Jul 1940; (2) 48, 58.

SHERWELL, Percy William; b Isipingo, Natal 17 Aug 1880; d Bulawayo, Southern Rhodesia 17 Apr 1948; (13) 88, 89, 90, 91, 92, 93, 94, 95, 111, 112, 113, 114, 115.

SIEDLE, Ivan Julian; b Durban 11 Jan 1903; d Durban 24 Aug 1982; (18) 170, 183, 184, 185, 204, 205, 206, 207, 208, 242, 243, 244, 246, 247, 248, 249, 250, 251.

SINCLAIR, James Hugh; b Swellendam, Cape Colony 16 Oct 1876; d Yeoville, Johannesburg 23 Feb 1913; (25) 47, 48, 49, 58, 59, 75, 76, 77, 88, 89, 90, 91, 92, 93, 94, 95, 106, 107, 109, 110, 111, 112, 113, 114, 115.

SMITH, Charles James Edward; b Gamtoos River, Cape Colony 25 Dec 1872; d Johannesburg 27 Mar 1947; (3) 75, 76, 77.

SMITH, Frederick W.; *no details known*; (3) 31, 32, 48.

SMITH, Vivian Ian; b Durban 23 Feb 1925; (9) 285, 286, 288, 289, 318, 319, 320, 408, 444.

SNELL, Richard Peter; b Durban 12 Sep 1968; (4) 1188, 1233, 1234, 1244.

SNOOKE, Stanley Delacourte; b St Mark's, Tembuland, Cape Colony 11 Nov 1878; d Cape Town 4 Apr 1959; (1) 95.

SNOOKE, Sibley John; b St Mark's, Tembuland, Cape Colony 1 Feb 1881; d Port Elizabeth 14 Aug 1966; (26) 88, 89, 90, 91, 92, 93, 94, 95, 106, 107, 108, 109, 110, 111, 112, 113, 114, 115, 121, 122, 124, 127, 128, 150, 151, 152.

SOLOMON, William Rodger Thomson; b Fort Beaufort, Cape Colony 23 Apr 1872; d Cradock, Cape Province 12 Jul 1964; (1) 58.

STEWART, Robert Bernard; b in India 3 Sep 1856; d Cala, Cape Province 12 Sep 1913; (1) 31.

STRICKER, Louis Anthony; b Beaconsfield, Kimberley 26 May 1884; d Cape Town 5 Feb 1960; (13) 106, 107, 108, 109, 111, 112, 113, 114, 115, 124, 125, 127, 128.

SUSSKIND, Manfred John; b Johannesburg 8 Jun 1891; d Johannesburg 9 Jul 1957; (5) 153, 154, 155, 156, 157.

SYMCOX, Patrick Leonard; b Kimberley 14 Apr 1960; (5) 1232, 1233, 1234, 1242, 1243.

TABERER, Henry Melville; b Keiskammahoek, Cape Colony 7 Oct 1870; d Colesburg, Cape Province 5 Jun 1932; (1) 75.

TANCRED, Augustus Bernard; b Port Elizabeth 20 Aug 1865; d Cape Town 23 Nov 1911; (2) 31, 32.

TANCRED, Louis Joseph; b Port Elizabeth 7 Oct 1876; d Johannesburg 28 Jul 1934; (14) 75, 76, 77, 88, 89, 90, 91, 92, 94, 124, 125, 127, 128, 131.

TANCRED, Vincent Maximillian; b Port Elizabeth 7 Jul 1875; d Roodepoort, Transvaal 3 Jun 1904; (1) 58.

TAPSCOTT, George Lancelot; b Barkly West, Cape Province 7 Nov 1889; d Kimberley 13 Dec 1940; (1) 130.

TAPSCOTT, Lionel Eric; b Kimberley 18 Mar 1894; d Cape Town 7 Jul 1934; (2) 151, 152.

TAYFIELD, Hugh Joseph; b Durban 30 Jan 1929; d Durban 25 Feb 1994; (37) 318, 319, 320, 321, 322, 360, 361, 362, 363, 364, 370, 371, 377, 378, 379, 380, 381, 408, 409, 410, 411, 412, 434, 435, 436, 437, 438, 444, 445, 446, 447, 448, 492, 493, 494, 495, 496.

TAYLOR, Alistair Innes; b Johannesburg 25 Jul 1925; (1) 434.

TAYLOR, Daniel; b Durban 9 Jan 1887; d Durban 24 Jan 1957; (2) 133, 134.

TAYLOR, Herbert Wilfred; b Durban 5 May 1889; d Newlands, Cape Town 8 Feb 1973; (42) 121, 122, 124, 125, 127, 128, 130, 131, 132, 133, 134, 145, 146, 147, 148, 149, 150, 151, 152, 153, 154, 155, 156, 157, 168, 169, 170, 171, 172, 181, 184, 185, 205, 206, 207, 208, 212, 213, 214, 215, 216, 217.

THEUNISSEN, Nicolaas Hendrik Christiaan de Jong; b Colesburg, Cape Colony 4 May 1867; d Greylingstad, Transvaal 9 Nov 1929; (1) 32.

THORNTON, Patrick George; b Skipton, Yorkshire, England 24 Dec 1867; d London, England 31 Jan 1939; (1) 75.

TOMLINSON, Denis Stanley; b Umtali, Rhodesia 4 Sep 1910; d Durban 11 Jul 1993; (1) 242.

TRAICOS, Athanasios John; b Zagazig, Egypt 17 May 1947; (3) 671, 672, 673, (*Also 4 Tests for Zimbabwe; 1197-1199, 1218*)

TRIMBORN, Patrick Henry Joseph; b Durban 18 May 1940; (4) 615, 616, 617, 673.

TUCKETT, Lindsay; b Durban 6 Feb 1919; (9) 285, 286, 287, 288, 289, 309, 310, 312, 313.

TUCKETT, Lindsay Richard; b Durban 19 Apr 1885; d Bloemfontein 8 Apr 1963; (1) 132.

TWENTYMAN-JONES, Percy Sydney (*also known as* P.S.T.Jones); b Beaufort West, Cape Colony 13 Sep 1876; d Cape Town 8 Mar 1954; (1) 77.

VAN DER BIJL, Pieter Gerhart Vintcent; b Cape Town 21 Oct 1907; d Kalk Bay, Cape Province 16 Feb 1973; (5) 267, 268, 269, 270, 271.

VAN DER MERWE, Edward Alexander; b Rustenburg, Cape Transvaal 9 Nov 1904; d Johannesburg 26 Feb 1971; (2) 183, 251.

VAN DER MERWE, Peter Laurence; b Paarl, Cape Province 14 Mar 1937; (15) 548, 549, 550, 558, 559, 574, 575, 594, 595, 596, 613, 614, 615, 616, 617.

VAN RYNEVELD, Clive Berrange; b Cape Town 19 Mar 1928; (19) 334, 335, 336, 337, 338, 377, 378, 379, 380, 381, 434, 435, 436, 437, 438, 445, 446, 447, 448.

VARNALS, George Derek; b Durban 24 Jul 1935; (3) 571, 572, 573.

VILJOEN, Kenneth George; b Windsorton, Cape Province 14 May 1910; d Krugersdorp, Transvaal 21 Jan 1974; (27) 204, 207, 208, 213, 214, 215, 216, 218, 242, 244, 245, 246, 247, 249, 250, 251, 267, 269, 270, 271, 285, 286, 287, 288, 289, 312, 313.

VINCENT, Cyril Leverton; b Johannesburg 16 Feb 1902; d Durban 24 Aug 1968; (25) 168, 169, 170, 171, 172, 181, 183, 184, 185, 204, 205, 206, 207, 208, 212, 213, 214, 215, 216, 217, 218, 242, 244, 245, 246.

VINTCENT, Charles Henry; b Mossel Bay, Cape Colony 2 Sep 1866; d George, Cape Province 28 Sep 1943; (3) 31, 32, 38.

VOGLER, Albert Edward Ernest; b Swartwater, Queenstown, Cape Colony 28 Nov 1876; d Pietermaritzburg 9 Aug 1946; (15) 88, 89, 90, 91, 92, 93, 94, 95, 106, 107, 108, 109, 110, 111, 114.

WADE, Herbert Frederick; b Durban 14 Sep 1905; d Johannesburg 23 Nov 1980; (10) 242, 243, 244, 245, 246, 247, 248, 249, 250, 251.

WADE, Walter Wareham; b Durban 18 Jun 1914; (11) 267, 268, 269, 309, 310, 311, 312, 313, 318, 319, 320.

WAITE, John Henry Bickford; b Johannesburg 19 Jan 1930; (50) 334, 335, 336, 337, 360, 361, 362, 363, 364, 370, 371, 377, 378, 379, 380, 381, 408, 409, 410, 411, 412, 434, 435, 436, 437, 438, 444, 445, 446, 447, 448, 492, 493, 494, 495, 496, 520, 521, 522, 523, 524, 548, 549, 550, 552, 558, 559, 560, 574, 575.

WALTER, Kenneth Alexander; b Johannesburg 5 Nov 1939; (2) 520, 521.

WARD, Thomas Alfred; b Rawalpindi, India 2 Aug 1887; d East Springs, Transvaal 16 Feb 1936; (23) 121, 124, 125, 127, 128, 130, 131, 132, 133, 134, 145, 146, 147, 148, 149, 150, 151, 152, 153, 154, 155, 156, 157.

WATKINS, John Cecil; b Durban 10 Apr 1923; (15) 318, 319, 320, 360, 361, 362, 363, 364, 370, 371, 377, 380, 381, 434, 435.

WESLEY, Colin; b Durban 5 Sep 1937; (3) 493, 494, 495.

WESSELS, Kepler Christoffel; b Bloemfontein 14 Sep 1957; (16) 1188, 1200, 1201, 1202, 1203, 1232, 1233, 1234, 1242, 1243, 1256, 1257, 1258, 1263, 1264, 1265. (*Also 24 Tests for Australia; 939-942, 956, 970-974, 981, 982, 997-1001, 1017-1022, 1029*).

WESTCOTT, Richard John; b Lisbon, Portugal 19 Sep 1927; (5) 379, 380, 381, 445, 446.

WHITE, Gordon Charles; b Port St John's, Cape Colony 5 Feb 1882; d Gaza, Palestine 17 Oct 1918; (17) 88, 89, 90, 91, 92, 93, 94, 95, 106, 107, 108, 109, 121, 124, 125, 127, 128.

WILLOUGHBY, Joseph Thomas; b Aldershot, Hampshire, England 7 Nov 1874; d *circa* 1955; (2) 47, 49.

WIMBLE, Clarence Skelton; b Graaff-Reinet, Cape Colony 22 Apr 1861; d Johannesburg 28 Jan 1930; (1) 38.

WINSLOW, Paul Lyndhurst; b Johannesburg 21 May 1959; (5) 321, 322, 408, 410, 411.

WYNNE, Owen Edgar; b Johannesburg 1 Jun 1919; d (*drowned*) False Bay, Cape Province 13 Jul 1975; (6) 309, 310, 311, 318, 319, 320.

ZULCH, John William; b Lydenburg, Transvaal 2 Jan 1886; d Umkomaas, Natal 19 May 1924; (16) 106, 107, 108, 109, 110, 111, 112, 113, 114, 115, 131, 132, 134, 145, 146, 147.

WEST INDIES (205 players)

ACHONG, Ellis Edgar; b Belmont, Port-of-Spain, Trinidad 16 Feb 1904; d Port-of-Spain 29 Aug 1986; (6) 191, 227, 228, 229, 238, 239.

ADAMS, James Clive; b Port Maria, Jamaica 9 Jan 1968; (9) 1188, 1205, 1206, 1208, 1251, 1252, 1253, 1254, 1255.

ALEXANDER, Franz Copeland Murray; b Kingston, Jamaica 2 Nov 1928; (25) 442, 443, 449, 450, 451, 452, 453, 459, 460, 461, 462, 463, 469, 470, 471, 487, 488, 489, 490, 491, 502, 503, 504, 505, 506.

ALI, Imtiaz; b in Trinidad 28 Jul 1954; (1) 775.

ALI, Inshan; b Couva, Trinidad 25 Sep 1949; (12) 683, 694, 695, 697, 714, 716, 718, 725, 731, 735, 764, 801.

ALLAN, David Walter; b Hastings, Barbados 5 Nov 1937; (5) 527, 529, 587, 605, 606.

ALLEN, Ian Basil Alston; b Coull's Hill, St Vincent 6 Oct 1965; (2) 1172, 1173.

AMBROSE, Curtly Elconn Lynwall; b Swetes Village, Antigua 21 Sep 1963; (48) 1095, 1096, 1097, 1098, 1099, 1100, 1101, 1102, 1110, 1111, 1112, 1113, 1114, 1117, 1118, 1119, 1120, 1141, 1142, 1143, 1154, 1155, 1156, 1166, 1167, 1168, 1169, 1170, 1171, 1172, 1173, 1174, 1175, 1188, 1204, 1205, 1206, 1207, 1208, 1220, 1221, 1222, 1241, 1251, 1252, 1253, 1254, 1255.

ARTHURTON, Keith Lloyd Thomas; b Charlestown, Nevis 21 Feb 1965; (20) 1101, 1117, 1118, 1119, 1120, 1188, 1204, 1205, 1206, 1207, 1208, 1220, 1221, 1222, 1241, 1251, 1252, 1253, 1254, 1255.

ASGARALI, Nyron Sultan; b St James, Port-of-Spain, Trinidad 28 Dec 1920; (2) 440, 443.

ATKINSON, Denis St Eval; b Rockley, Christchurch, Barbados 9 Aug 1926; (22) 304, 305, 306, 308, 346, 348, 350, 383, 384, 385, 386, 403, 405, 406, 407, 421, 422, 423, 424, 439, 441, 449.

ATKINSON, Eric St Eval; b Rockley, Christchurch, Barbados 6 Nov 1927; (8) 449, 451, 453, 459, 462, 463, 470, 471.

AUSTIN, Richard Arkwright; b in Jamaica 5 Sep 1954; (2) 820, 821.

BACCHUS, Sheik Faoud Ahamul Fasiel; b Georgetown, British Guiana 31 Jan 1954; (19) 823, 824, 840, 841, 842, 843, 844, 845, 880, 881, 882, 883, 884, 886, 887, 888, 889, 918, 920.

BAICHAN, Leonard; b Rose Hall Village, Berbice, British Guiana 12 May 1946; (3) 756, 757, 769.

BAPTISTE, Eldine Ashworth Elderfield; b Liberta, Antigua 12 Mar 1960; (10) 964, 983, 984, 985, 989, 990, 991, 992, 993, 1143.

BARRETT, Arthur George; b Kingston, Jamaica 5 Apr 1942; (6) 680, 681, 732, 734, 745, 749.

BARROW, Ivan; b Kingston, Jamaica 6 Jan 1911; d Kingston 2 Apr 1979; (11) 193, 199, 200, 201, 202, 203, 227, 228, 229, 241, 272.

BARTLETT, Edward Lawson; b St Michael, Barbados 10 Mar 1906; d St Michael, Barbados 21 Dec 1976; (5) 175, 199, 200, 202, 203.

BENJAMIN, Kenneth Charlie Griffith; b St John's, Antigua 8 Apr 1967; (7) 1188, 1207, 1251, 1252, 1253, 1254, 1255.

BENJAMIN, Winston Keithroy Matthew; b St John's, Antigua 31 Dec 1964; (16) 1080, 1095, 1096, 1097, 1100, 1101, 1102, 1117, 1221, 1222, 1241, 1251, 1252, 1253, 1254, 1255.

BEST, Carlisle Alonza; b Bridgetown, Barbados 14 May 1959; (8) 1038, 1039, 1040, 1140, 1141, 1142, 1154, 1155.

BETANCOURT, Nelson; b in Trinidad 4 Jun 1887; d in Trinidad 12 Oct 1947; (1) 191.

BINNS, Alfred Phillip; b Kingston, Jamaica 24 Jul 1929; (5) 365, 403, 421, 423, 424.

BIRKETT, Lionel Sydney; b in Barbados 14 Apr 1904; (4) 199, 200, 201, 202.

BISHOP, Ian Raphael; b Port-of-Spain, Trinidad 24 Oct 1967; (18) 1117, 1118, 1119, 1120, 1140, 1141, 1142, 1143, 1154, 1155, 1156, 1204, 1205, 1206, 1207, 1208, 1220, 1221.

BOYCE, Keith David; b St Peter, Barbados 11 Oct 1943; (21) 682, 715, 716, 717, 718, 725, 726, 727, 731, 732, 734, 735, 745, 746, 748, 756, 757, 765, 767, 768, 769.

BROWNE, Cyril Rutherford; b Bridgetown, Barbados 8 Oct 1890; d Georgetown, British Guiana 12 Jan 1964; (4) 173, 174, 190, 192.

BUTCHER, Basil Fitzherbert; b Port Mourant, Berbice, British Guiana 3 Sep 1933; (44) 459, 460, 461, 462, 463, 469, 470, 471, 487, 488, 543, 544, 545, 546, 547, 583, 584, 585, 586, 587, 605, 606, 607, 608, 609, 610, 611, 612, 628, 629, 630, 631, 632, 642, 643, 644, 645, 646, 650, 651, 652, 653, 654, 655.

BUTLER, Lennox Stephen; b Woodbrook, Port-of-Spain, Trinidad 9 Feb 1929; (1) 404.

BUTTS, Clyde Godfrey; b Perseverance, British Guiana 8 Jul 1957; (7) 1014, 1056, 1057, 1072, 1081, 1082, 1083.

BYNOE, Michael Robin; b Christchurch, Barbados 23 Feb 1941; (4) 471, 610, 611, 612.

CAMACHO, George Stephen; b Georgetown, British Guiana 15 Oct 1945; (11) 628, 629, 630, 631, 632, 642, 643, 654, 655, 680, 681.

CAMERON, Francis James; b Kingston, Jamaica 22 Jun 1923; (5) 304, 305, 306, 307, 308.

CAMERON, John Hemsley; b Kingston, Jamaica 8 Apr 1914; (2) 272, 273.

CAREW, George McDonald; b Bridgetown, Barbados 4 Jun 1910; d in Barbados 9 Dec 1974; (4) 238, 296, 297, 306.

CAREW, Michael Conrad; b Woodbrook, Port-of-Spain, Trinidad 15 Sep 1937; (19) 543, 545, 606, 631, 642, 643, 644, 645, 646, 650, 651, 652, 653, 680, 682, 684, 693, 694, 695.

CHALLENOR, George; b Waterloo, Barbados 28 Jun 1888; d St Michael, Barbados 30 Jul 1947; (3) 173, 174, 175.

CHANDERPAUL, Shivnarine; b Unity Village, Guyana 18 Aug 1974; (4) 1252, 1253, 1254, 1255.

CHANG, Herbert Samuel; b in Jamaica 22 Jul 1952; (1) 843.

CHRISTIANI, Cyril Marcel; b Georgetown, British Guiana 28 Oct 1913; d Georgetown 4 Apr 1938; (4) 238, 239, 240, 241.

CHRISTIANI, Robert Julian; b Georgetown, British Guiana 19 Jul 1920; (22) 295, 296, 297, 298, 304, 305, 306, 307, 308, 323, 324, 325, 326, 344, 345, 346, 347, 348, 349, 366, 369, 384.

CLARKE, Carlos Bertram; b Bridgetown, Barbados 7 Apr 1918; d Putney, Surrey, England 14 Oct 1993; (3) 272, 273, 274.

SOBERS, Garfield St Aubrun; b Bay Land, Bridgetown, Barbados 28 Jul 1936; knighted for services to cricket 1975; (93) 386, 404, 405, 406, 407, 421, 422, 423, 424, 439, 440, 441, 442, 443, 449, 450, 451, 452, 453, 459, 460, 461, 462, 463, 469, 470, 471, 487, 488, 489, 490, 491, 502, 503, 504, 505, 506, 525, 526, 527, 528, 529, 543, 544, 545, 546, 547, 583, 584, 585, 586, 587, 605, 606, 607, 608, 609, 610, 611, 612, 628, 629, 630, 631, 632, 642, 643, 644, 645, 646, 650, 651, 652, 653, 654, 655, 680, 681, 682, 683, 684, 693, 694, 695, 696, 697, 725, 726, 727, 731, 732, 733, 735.

SOLOMON, Joseph Stanislaus; b Corentyne, Berbice, British Guiana 26 Aug 1930; (27) 460, 461, 462, 463, 469, 470, 471, 488, 489, 502, 503, 504, 505, 506, 525, 526, 527, 529, 543, 544, 545, 546, 547, 583, 584, 585, 586.

STAYERS, Sven Conrad; b in British Guiana 9 Jun 1937; (4) 525, 526, 527, 528.

STOLLMEYER, Jeffrey Baxter; b Santa Cruz, Trinidad 11 Apr 1921; d Melbourne, Florida, USA 10 Sep 1989; (32) 272, 273, 274, 295, 298, 304, 305, 307, 308, 323, 324, 325, 326, 344, 345, 346, 347, 348, 349, 350, 365, 366, 367, 368, 369, 382, 383, 384, 385, 386, 404, 405.

STOLLMEYER, Victor Humphrey; b Santa Cruz, Trinidad 24 Jan 1916; (1) 274.

TAYLOR, Jaswick; b in Trinidad 3 Jan 1932; (3) 453, 460, 469.

TRIM, John; b Corentyne, Berbice, British Guiana 25 Jan 1915; d in British Guiana 12 Nov 1960; (4) 297, 307, 308, 347.

VALENTINE, Alfred Lewis; b Kingston, Jamaica 29 Apr 1930; (36) 323, 324, 325, 326, 344, 345, 346, 347, 348, 349, 350, 365, 366, 367, 368, 369, 382, 383, 384, 403, 404, 406, 421, 422, 423, 424, 440, 441, 449, 502, 503, 504, 505, 506, 527, 529.

VALENTINE, Vincent A.; b Port Antonio, Jamaica 4 Apr 1908; d Kingston, Jamaica 6 Jul 1972; (2) 228, 229.

WALCOTT, Clyde Leopold; b Bridgetown, Barbados 17 Jan 1926; (44) 295, 296, 297, 298, 304, 305, 306, 307, 308, 323, 324, 325, 326, 344, 345, 348, 349, 350, 365, 366, 367, 368, 369, 382, 383, 384, 385, 386, 403, 404, 405, 406, 407, 439, 440, 441, 442, 443, 449, 451, 452, 453, 490, 491.

WALCOTT, Leslie Arthur; b in Barbados 18 Jan 1894; d in Barbados 27 Feb 1984; (1) 190.

WALSH, Courtney Andrew; b Kingston, Jamaica 30 Oct 1962; (65) 997, 998, 999, 1000, 1001, 1016, 1039, 1055, 1056, 1057, 1071, 1072, 1073, 1080, 1081, 1082, 1083, 1095, 1096, 1097, 1098, 1099, 1100, 1101, 1102, 1110, 1111, 1112, 1113, 1114, 1117, 1118, 1119, 1120, 1140, 1141, 1143, 1154, 1155, 1156, 1166, 1167, 1168, 1169, 1170, 1171, 1172, 1173, 1174, 1175, 1188, 1204, 1205, 1206, 1207, 1208, 1220, 1221, 1222, 1241, 1251, 1252, 1253, 1254, 1255.

WATSON, Chester Donald; b in Jamaica 1 Jul 1938; (7) 487, 488, 489, 490, 491, 503, 525.

WEEKES, Everton de Courcy; b Bridgetown, Barbados 26 Feb 1925; (48) 295, 296, 297, 298, 304, 305, 306, 307, 308, 323, 324, 325, 326, 344, 345, 346, 347, 348, 349, 350, 365, 366, 367, 368, 369, 382, 384, 385, 386, 403, 404, 405, 406, 407, 421, 422, 423, 424, 439, 440, 441, 442, 443, 449, 450, 451, 452, 453.

WEEKES, Kenneth Hunnell; b in USA 24 Jan 1912; (2) 272, 274.

WHITE, Anthony Wilbur; b Brighton, Bridgetown, Barbados 20 Nov 1938; (2) 583, 584.

WIGHT, Claude Vibart; b Georgetown, British Guiana 28 Jul 1902; d in Guyana 4 Oct 1969; (2) 175, 192.

WIGHT, George Leslie; b Georgetown, British Guiana 28 May 1929; (1) 368.

WILES, Charles Archibald; b Bridgetown, Barbados 11 Aug 1892; d Diego Martin, Trinidad 4 Nov 1957; (1) 228.

WILLETT, Elquemedo Tonitto; b Charlestown, Nevis 1 May 1953; (5) 715, 716, 717, 746, 747.

WILLIAMS, Alvadon Basil; b Kingston, Jamaica 21 Nov 1949; (7) 822, 823, 824, 840, 841, 842, 844.

WILLIAMS, David; b San Pernando, Trinidad 4 Nov 1963; (3) 1188, 1204, 1205.

WILLIAMS, Ernest Albert Vivian; b Bridgetown, Barbados 10 Apr 1914; (4) 273, 295, 296, 297.

WILLIAMS, Stuart Clayton; b Nevis 12 Aug 1969; (1) 1255.

WISHART, Kenneth Leslie; b in British Guiana 28 Nov 1908; d Georgetown, Guyana 18 Oct 1972; (1) 240.

WORRELL, Frank Mortimer Maglinne; b Bank Hall, Bridgetown, Barbados 1 Aug 1924; knighted for services to cricket 1964; d Mona, Kingston, Jamaica 13 Mar 1967; (51) 296, 297, 298, 323, 324, 325, 326, 344, 345, 346, 347, 348, 349, 350, 365, 366, 367, 368, 369, 383, 384, 385, 386, 403, 405, 406, 407, 439, 440, 441, 442, 443, 487, 488, 490, 491, 502, 503, 504, 505, 506, 525, 526, 527, 528, 529, 543, 544, 545, 546, 547.

NEW ZEALAND (190 players)

ALABASTER, John Chaloner; b Invercargill 11 Jul 1930; (21) 413, 416, 417, 418, 419, 424, 454, 455, 520, 521, 522, 523, 524, 540, 542, 633, 634, 635, 636, 693, 694.

ALLCOTT, Cyril Francis Walter; b Lower Moutere 7 Oct 1896; d Auckland 19 Nov 1973; (6) 188, 189, 209, 210, 211, 218.

ANDERSON, Robert Wickham; b Christchurch 2 Oct 1948; (9) 782, 783, 784, 817, 818, 819, 828, 829, 830.

ANDERSON, William McDougall; b Westport 8 Oct 1919; d Christchurch 21 Dec 1979; (1) 275.

ANDREWS, Bryan; b Christchurch 4 Apr 1945; (2) 728, 729.

BADCOCK, Frederick Theodore; b Abbottabad, India 9 Aug 1897; d South Perth, Australia 19 Sep 1982; (7) 186, 187, 188, 217, 218, 225, 226.

BARBER, Richard Trevor; b Otaki 3 Jun 1925; (1) 423.

BARTLETT, Gary Alex; b Blenheim 3 Feb 1941; (10) 520, 521, 522, 523, 524, 578, 602, 603, 634, 636.

BARTON, Paul Thomas; b Wellington 9 Oct 1935; (7) 520, 521, 523, 524, 540, 541, 542.

BEARD, Donald Derek; b Palmerston North 14 Jan 1920; d Lancaster, Lancashire, England 15 Jul 1982; (4) 349, 350, 423, 424.

BECK, John Edward Francis; b Wellington 1 Aug 1934; (8) 378, 379, 380, 381, 421, 422, 423, 424.

BELL, William; b Dunedin 5 Sep 1931; (2) 379, 381.

BILBY, Grahame Paul; b Wellington 7 May 1941; (2) 602, 603.

BLAIN, Tony Elston; b Nelson 17 Feb 1962; (11) 1051, 1108, 1109, 1216, 1217, 1235, 1236, 1237, 1248, 1249, 1250.

BLAIR, Robert William; b Petone, Wellington 23 Jun 1932; (19) 370, 371, 377, 378, 380, 381, 401, 421, 422, 455, 457, 458, 472, 473, 541, 542, 558, 559, 560.

BLUNT, Roger Charles; b Durham, England 3 Nov 1900; d London, England 22 Jun 1966; (9) 186, 187, 188, 189, 209, 210, 211, 217, 218.

BOLTON, Bruce Alfred; b Christchurch 31 May 1935; (2) 472, 473.

BOOCK, Stephen Lewis; b Dunedin 20 Sep 1951; (30) 817, 818, 819, 828, 829, 830, 846, 847, 848, 873, 874, 875, 976, 977, 986, 987, 988, 1002, 1003, 1004, 1010, 1011, 1013, 1014, 1015, 1030, 1071, 1072, 1093, 1116.

BRACEWELL, Brendon Paul; b Auckland 14 Sep 1959; (6) 828, 829, 830, 846, 890, 1012.

BRACEWELL, John Garry; b Auckland 15 Apr 1958; (41) 890, 891, 892, 902, 957, 958, 959, 960, 986, 988, 1003, 1004, 1016, 1030, 1031, 1036, 1037, 1049, 1050, 1051, 1071, 1072, 1073, 1074, 1087, 1088, 1089, 1091, 1092, 1093, 1107, 1108, 1109, 1115, 1116, 1137, 1138, 1144, 1145, 1146, 1147.

BRADBURN, Grant Eric; b Hamilton 26 May 1966; (5) 1151, 1152, 1153, 1163, 1210.

BRADBURN, Wynne Pennell; b Thames 24 Nov 1938; (2) 559, 560.

BROWN, Vaughan Raymond; b Christchurch 3 Nov 1959; (2) 1029, 1030.

BURGESS, Mark Gordon; b Auckland 17 Jul 1944; (50) 633, 634, 635, 636, 650, 652, 656, 657, 659, 660, 661, 662, 663, 664, 686, 693, 694, 695, 696, 697, 711, 712, 713, 722, 723, 724, 738, 770, 771, 772, 782, 783, 784, 785, 786, 787, 796, 797, 817, 818, 819, 828, 829, 830, 846, 847, 848, 890, 891, 892.

BURKE, Cecil; b Auckland 22 Mar 1914; (1) 275.

BURTT, Thomas Browning; b Christchurch 22 Jan 1915; d Christchurch 24 May 1988; (10) 284, 314, 315, 316, 317, 332, 333, 349, 350, 370.

BUTTERFIELD, Leonard Arthur; b Christchurch 29 Aug 1913; (1) 275.

CAIRNS, Bernard Lance; b Picton 10 Oct 1949; (43) 730, 759, 772, 783, 784, 785, 787, 797, 819, 828, 829, 846, 847, 848, 873, 874, 875, 890, 891, 892, 900, 901, 902, 922, 923, 924, 954, 955, 957, 958, 959, 960, 975, 976, 977, 986, 987, 1010, 1011, 1012, 1013, 1014, 1031.

CAIRNS, Christopher Lance; b Picton 13 Jun 1970; (10) 1131, 1165, 1185, 1186, 1187, 1215, 1216, 1235, 1237, 1248.

CAMERON, Francis James; b Dunedin 1 Jun 1932; (19) 520, 521, 522, 523, 524, 540, 541, 542, 558, 559, 560, 576, 577, 578, 582, 589, 590, 591, 592.

CAVE, Henry Butler; b Wanganui 10 Oct 1922; d Wanganui 15 Sep 1989; (19) 314, 315, 316, 317, 401, 402, 413, 414, 415, 416, 417, 418, 419, 420, 421, 423, 424, 454, 456.

CHAPPLE, Murray Ernest; b Christchurch 25 Jul 1930; d Hamilton 31 Jul 1985; (14) 371, 377, 378, 379, 380, 381, 401, 424, 522, 523, 558, 559, 560, 602.

CHATFIELD, Ewen John; b Dannevirke 3 Jul 1950; (43) 758, 796, 797, 818, 922, 954, 955, 957, 958, 959, 975, 976, 977, 987, 988, 1002, 1010, 1011, 1012, 1013, 1014, 1015, 1016, 1029, 1031, 1035, 1036, 1037, 1051, 1071, 1072, 1073, 1074, 1087, 1089, 1091, 1092, 1093, 1107, 1108, 1109, 1115, 1116.

CLEVERLEY, Donald Charles; b Oamaru 23 Dec 1909; (2) 217, 275.

COLLINGE, Richard Owen; b Wellington 2 Apr 1946; (35) 576, 577, 578, 579, 582, 588, 589, 591, 592, 593, 634, 635, 657, 685, 686, 711, 713, 722, 723, 724, 736, 737, 738, 758, 759, 770, 771, 772, 782, 784, 785, 817, 818, 819, 830.

COLQUHOUN, Ian Alexander; b Wellington 8 Jun 1924; (2) 401, 402.

CONEY, Jeremy Vernon; b Wellington 21 Jun 1952; (52) 729, 730, 736, 737, 846, 847, 848, 873, 874, 875, 891, 892, 900, 901, 902, 922, 923, 924, 954, 955, 957, 958, 959, 960, 975, 976, 977, 986, 987, 988, 1002, 1003, 1004, 1010, 1011, 1012, 1013, 1014, 1015, 1016, 1029, 1030, 1031, 1035, 1036, 1037, 1049, 1050, 1051, 1071, 1072, 1073.

CONGDON, Bevan Ernest; b Motueka 11 Feb 1938; (61) 576, 577, 578, 580, 581, 582, 590, 591, 592, 593, 602, 603, 604, 633, 634, 635, 636, 650, 651, 652, 656, 657, 658, 659, 660, 661, 662, 663, 664, 685, 686, 693, 694, 695, 696, 697, 711, 712, 713, 722, 723, 724, 728, 729, 730, 736, 737, 738, 758, 759, 770, 771, 772, 796, 797, 817, 818, 819, 828, 829, 830.

COWIE, John; b Auckland 30 Mar 1912; d Wellington 3 Jun 1994; (9) 260, 261, 262, 275, 284, 314, 315, 316, 317.

PAGE, Milford Laurenson; b Lyttelton 8 May 1902; d Christchurch 13 Feb 1987; (14) 186, 187, 188, 189, 209, 210, 211, 217, 218, 225, 226, 260, 261, 262.

PARKER, John Morton; b Dannevirke 21 Feb 1951; (36) 711, 722, 723, 724, 728, 729, 730, 736, 737, 738, 758, 759, 770, 771, 772, 782, 783, 784, 785, 786, 787, 796, 797, 817, 818, 819, 829, 830, 846, 847, 873, 874, 875, 890, 891, 892.

PARKER, Norman Murray; b Dannevirke 28 Aug 1948; (3) 784, 785, 786.

PARORE, Adam Craig; b Auckland 23 Jan 1971; (12) 1147, 1186, 1198, 1199, 1209, 1210, 1211, 1215, 1259, 1260, 1261, 1262.

PATEL, Dipak Narshibhai; b Nairobi, Kenya 25 Oct 1958; (25) 1071, 1072, 1073, 1087, 1088, 1089, 1115, 1131, 1151, 1152, 1153, 1164, 1165, 1185, 1186, 1187, 1198, 1199, 1211, 1215, 1216, 1217, 1235, 1236, 1237.

PETHERICK, Peter James; b Ranfurly, Otago 25 Sep 1942; (6) 782, 783, 785, 786, 787, 797.

PETRIE, Eric Charlton; b Ngaruawahia 22 May 1927; (14) 414, 415, 416, 417, 454, 455, 456, 457, 458, 472, 473, 602, 603, 604.

PLAYLE, William Rodger; b Palmerston North 1 Dec 1938; (8) 454, 455, 456, 457, 458, 540, 541, 542.

POCOCK, Blair Andrew; b Papakura 18 Jun 1971; (6) 1235, 1236, 1237, 1248, 1249, 1261.

POLLARD, Victor; b Burnley, Lancashire, England 7 Sep 1945; (32) 579, 580, 581, 582, 588, 589, 590, 591, 592, 593, 602, 603, 604, 633, 634, 635, 636, 650, 651, 652, 656, 657, 658, 660, 662, 663, 664, 685, 712, 722, 723, 724.

POORE, Matt Beresford; b Christchurch 1 Jun 1930; (14) 371, 377, 378, 379, 380, 381, 402, 413, 414, 415, 416, 417, 418, 420.

PRIEST, Mark Wellings; b Greymouth 12 Aug 1961; (1) 1145.

PRINGLE, Christopher, b Auckland 26 Jan 1968; (11) 1151, 1152, 1153, 1163, 1164, 1185, 1210, 1250, 1259, 1261, 1262.

PUNA, Narotam; b Surat, Gujarat, India 28 Oct 1929; (3) 602, 603, 604.

RABONE, Geoffrey Osbourne; b Gore 6 Nov 1921; (12) 314, 315, 316, 317, 349, 350, 371, 377, 378, 379, 401, 402.

REDMOND, Rodney Ernest; b Whangarei 29 Dec 1944; (1) 713.

REID, John Fulton; b Auckland 3 Mar 1956; (19) 848, 900, 901, 902, 986, 987, 988, 1002, 1003, 1004, 1010, 1011, 1012, 1029, 1030, 1031, 1035, 1036, 1037.

REID, John Richard; b Auckland 3 Jun 1928; (58) 316, 317, 332, 333, 349, 350, 370, 371, 377, 378, 379, 380, 381, 401, 402, 413, 414, 415, 416, 417, 418, 419, 420, 421, 422, 423, 424, 454, 455, 456, 457, 458, 472, 473, 520, 521, 522, 523, 524, 540, 541, 542, 558, 559, 560, 576, 577, 578, 579, 580, 581, 582, 588, 589, 590, 591, 592, 593.

ROBERTS, Andrew Duncan Glenn; b Te Aroha 6 May 1947; d Wellington 26 Oct 1989; (7) 771, 772, 783, 784, 785, 786, 787.

ROBERTS, Albert William; b Christchurch 20 Aug 1909; d Christchurch 13 May 1978; (5) 186, 217, 218, 260, 262.

ROBERTSON, Gary Keith; b New Plymouth 15 Jul 1960; (1) 1037.

ROWE, Charles Gordon; b Glasgow, Scotland 30 Jun 1915; (1) 275.

RUTHERFORD, Kenneth Robert; b Dunedin 26 Oct 1965; (48) 1013, 1014, 1015, 1016, 1035, 1036, 1037, 1049, 1071, 1072, 1074, 1087, 1092, 1093, 1107, 1108, 1137, 1138, 1139, 1144, 1146, 1147, 1151, 1152, 1153, 1163, 1164, 1165, 1186, 1187, 1198, 1199, 1209, 1210, 1211, 1215, 1216, 1217, 1235, 1236, 1237, 1248, 1249, 1250, 1259, 1260, 1261, 1262.

SCOTT, Roy Hamilton; b Clyde 6 May 1917; (1) 284.

SCOTT, Verdun John; b Devonport, Auckland 31 Jul 1916; d Devonport 2 Aug 1980; (10) 275, 284, 314, 315, 316, 317, 332, 333, 349, 350.

SHRIMPTON, Michael John Froud; b Feilding 23 Jun 1940; (10) 541, 542, 560, 602, 603, 604, 685, 686, 728, 729.

SINCLAIR, Barry Whitley; b Wellington 23 Oct 1936; (21) 540, 541, 542, 558, 559, 560, 576, 578, 579, 581, 588, 589, 590, 591, 592, 593, 602, 603, 604, 633, 636.

SINCLAIR, Ian McKay; b Rangiora 1 Jun 1933; (2) 422, 423.

SMITH, Frank Brunton; b Rangiora 13 Mar 1922; (4) 284, 314, 315, 349.

SMITH, Horace Dennis; b Toowoomba, Queensland, Australia 8 Jan 1913; d Christchurch 25 Jan 1986; (1) 225.

SMITH, Ian David Stockley; b Nelson 28 Feb 1957; (63) 890, 900, 901, 902, 922, 923, 924, 958, 959, 975, 976, 977, 986, 987, 988, 1002, 1003, 1004, 1010, 1011, 1012, 1013, 1014, 1015, 1016, 1029, 1030, 1031, 1035, 1036, 1037, 1049, 1050, 1071, 1072, 1073, 1074, 1087, 1088, 1089, 1091, 1092, 1093, 1107, 1108, 1109, 1115, 1116, 1131, 1137, 1138, 1139, 1144, 1145, 1146, 1151, 1152, 1153, 1163, 1164, 1165, 1185, 1187.

SNEDDEN, Colin Alexander; b Auckland 7 Jan 1918; (1) 284.

SNEDDEN, Martin Colin; b Mt Eden, Auckland 23 Nov 1958; (25) 900, 901, 902, 922, 923, 924, 954, 955, 960, 975, 1029, 1073, 1074, 1088, 1091, 1092, 1109, 1131, 1137, 1138, 1139, 1144, 1145, 1146, 1147.

SPARLING, John Trevor; b Auckland 24 Jul 1938; (11) 456, 457, 458, 472, 473, 520, 522, 524, 540, 558, 559.

STIRLING, Derek Alexander; b Upper Hutt 5 Oct 1961; (6) 1002, 1003, 1004, 1015, 1050, 1051.

SU'A, Murphy Logo; b Wanganui 7 Nov 1966; (11) 1186, 1187, 1198, 1199, 1209, 1210, 1211, 1215, 1217, 1235, 1236.

SUTCLIFFE, Bert; b Ponsonby, Auckland 17 Nov 1923; (42) 284, 314, 315, 316, 317, 332, 333, 349, 350, 370, 371, 377, 378, 379, 380, 381, 401, 402, 413, 414, 415, 416, 417, 418, 419, 420, 421, 422, 455, 456, 457, 458, 472, 473, 579, 580, 581, 582, 588, 589, 590, 591.

TAYLOR, Bruce Richard; b Timaru 12 Jul 1943; (30) 580, 581, 582, 588, 589, 590, 592, 593, 604, 633, 635, 636, 650, 651, 652, 656, 658, 659, 661, 663, 694, 695, 696, 697, 711, 712, 713, 722, 723, 724.

TAYLOR, Donald Dougald; b Auckland 2 Mar 1923; d Epsom, Auckland 5 Dec 1980; (3) 284, 423, 424.

THOMSON, Keith; b Methven 26 Feb 1941; (2) 634, 635.

THOMSON, Shane Alexander; b Hamilton 27 Jan 1969; (11) 1139, 1164, 1165, 1185, 1248, 1249, 1250, 1259, 1260, 1261, 1262.

TINDILL, Eric William Thomas; b Nelson 18 Dec 1910; (5) 260, 261, 262, 275, 284.

INDIA (200 players)

ABDUL HAFEEZ, *see* KARDAR, A.H.

ABID ALI, Syed; b Hyderabad 9 Sep 1941; (29) 624, 625, 626, 627, 633, 634, 635, 636, 659, 660, 661, 665, 680, 681, 682, 683, 684, 690, 691, 692, 703, 704, 706, 707, 739, 740, 741, 745, 746.

ADHIKARI, Hemchandra Ramchandra; b Baroda 31 Jul 1919; (21) 290, 291, 292, 293, 294, 304, 305, 306, 307, 308, 339, 340, 342, 352, 353, 354, 355, 357, 431, 432, 463.

AMARNATH, Lala; b Lahore 11 Sep 1911; (24) 230, 231, 232, 276, 277, 278, 290, 291, 292, 293, 294, 304, 305, 306, 307, 308, 340, 341, 343, 355, 356, 357, 358, 359.

AMARNATH, Mohinder; b Patiala 24 Sep 1950; (69) 669, 770, 771, 772, 773, 774, 775, 776, 785, 786, 787, 788, 790, 809, 810, 811, 812, 813, 831, 832, 833, 840, 845, 851, 853, 860, 943, 944, 945, 946, 947, 948, 949, 950, 951, 952, 953, 961, 962, 964, 965, 968, 995, 996, 1005, 1006, 1007, 1008, 1009, 1024, 1025, 1032, 1033, 1034, 1046, 1048, 1052, 1053, 1054, 1064, 1065, 1066, 1067, 1068, 1069, 1070, 1081, 1082, 1083.

AMARNATH, Surinder; b Kanpur 30 Dec 1948; (10) 770, 771, 772, 773, 774, 791, 792, 831, 832, 833.

AMAR SINGH, Ladha; b Rajkot 4 Dec 1910; d Jamnagar 20 May 1940; (7) 219, 230, 231, 232, 252, 253, 254.

AMIR ELAHI; b Lahore 1 Sep 1908; d Multan, Pakistan 28 Dec 1980; (1) 291. (*Also 5 Tests for Pakistan; 355-359*)

AMRE, Pravin Kalyan; b Bombay 14 Aug 1968; (11) 1200, 1201, 1202, 1203, 1212, 1213, 1214, 1218, 1229, 1230, 1231.

ANKOLA, Salil Ashok; b Sholapur 1 Mar 1968; (1) 1127.

APTE, Arvind Laxmanrao; b Bombay 24 Oct 1934; (1) 476.

APTE, Madhav Laxmanrao; b Bombay 5 Oct 1932; (7) 357, 358, 365, 366, 367, 368, 369.

ARSHAD AYUB; b Hyderabad 2 Aug 1958; (13) 1080, 1081, 1082, 1083, 1107, 1108, 1109, 1117, 1118, 1119, 1120, 1127, 1129.

ARUN, Bharathi; b Vijayawada 14 Dec 1962; (2) 1063, 1065.

ARUN LAL; b Moradabad, Uttar Pradesh 1 Aug 1955; (16) 934, 943, 944, 945, 1067, 1080, 1081, 1082, 1083, 1107, 1108, 1109, 1117, 1118, 1119, 1120.

AZAD, Kirtivardhan; b Purnea, Bihar 2 Jan 1959; (7) 900, 912, 913, 914, 963, 965, 966.

AZHARUDDIN, Mohammad; b Hyderabad 8 Feb 1963; (62) 1007, 1008, 1009, 1023, 1024, 1025, 1032, 1033, 1034, 1046, 1047, 1048, 1052, 1053, 1054, 1063, 1066, 1067, 1068, 1069, 1070, 1081, 1082, 1083, 1107, 1108, 1109, 1117, 1118, 1120, 1127, 1128, 1129, 1130, 1137, 1138, 1139, 1148, 1149, 1150, 1157, 1177, 1178, 1179, 1180, 1181, 1197, 1200, 1201, 1202, 1203, 1212, 1213, 1214, 1218, 1229, 1230, 1231, 1245, 1246, 1247, 1259.

BAIG, Abbas Ali; b Hyderabad 19 Mar 1939; (10) 477, 478, 482, 483, 484, 497, 498, 499, 610, 611.

BANERJEE, Sudangsu Abinash; b Calcutta 1 Nov 1919; d Calcutta 14 Sep 1992; (1) 306.

BANERJEE, Shute Nath; b Calcutta 3 Oct 1913; d Calcutta 14 Oct 1980; (1) 308.

BANERJEE, Subroto Tata; b Patna 13 Feb 1969; (1) 1179.

BAQA JILANI, Mohammed; b Jullundur 20 Jul 1911; d Jullundur 2 Jul 1941; (1) 254.

BEDI, Bishan Singh; b Amritsar 25 Sep 1946; (67) 611, 612, 618, 619, 620, 626, 627, 633, 634, 635, 636, 659, 660, 661, 665, 666, 667, 668, 669, 680, 681, 682, 683, 684, 690, 691, 692, 703, 704, 705, 706, 707, 739, 740, 741, 746, 747, 748, 749, 771, 772, 773, 774, 775, 776, 785, 786, 787, 788, 789, 790, 791, 792, 809, 810, 811, 812, 813, 831, 832, 833, 840, 841, 842, 852, 853, 854.

BHANDARI, Prakash; b Delhi 27 Nov 1935; (3) 400, 418, 433.

BHAT, Adwai Raghuram; b Puttur, Mangalore 16 Apr 1958; (2) 963, 964.

BINNY, Roger Michael Humphrey; b Bangalore 19 Jul 1955; (27) 861, 862, 863, 864, 865, 866, 876, 893, 900, 961, 962, 964, 965, 966, 967, 968, 969, 995, 1025, 1032, 1033, 1046, 1047, 1048, 1067, 1068, 1070.

BORDE, Chandrakant Gulabrao; b Poona 21 Jul 1934; (55) 459, 460, 462, 463, 474, 476, 477, 478, 482, 483, 484, 485, 486, 497, 498, 499, 500, 501, 513, 514, 515, 516, 517, 525, 526, 527, 528, 529, 553, 554, 555, 556, 557, 566, 567, 568, 579, 580, 581, 582, 610, 611, 612, 618, 619, 620, 624, 625, 626, 627, 633, 634, 635, 636, 665.

CHANDRASEKHAR, Bhagwat Subramanya; b Mysore 17 May 1945; (58) 554, 555, 556, 557, 567, 568, 581, 582, 610, 611, 612, 618, 619, 620, 624, 625, 690, 691, 692, 703, 704, 705, 706, 707, 739, 740, 745, 747, 748, 749, 770, 771, 772, 773, 774, 775, 776, 785, 786, 787, 788, 789, 790, 791, 792, 809, 810, 811, 812, 813, 831, 832, 833, 840, 841, 844, 845, 851.

CHAUHAN, Chetendra Pratap Singh; b Bareilly, Uttar Pradesh 21 Jul 1947; (40) 659, 660, 669, 705, 706, 810, 811, 812, 813, 831, 832, 833, 840, 841, 842, 843, 844, 845, 851, 852, 853, 854, 855, 856, 857, 858, 859, 860, 861, 862, 863, 864, 865, 866, 893, 894, 895, 900, 901, 902.

CHAUHAN, Rajesh Kumar; b Ranchi, Bihar 19 Dec 1966; (11) 1212, 1213, 1214, 1218, 1229, 1230, 1231, 1245, 1246, 1247, 1259.

CHOWDHURY, Nirode Ranjan; b Calcutta 23 May 1923; d Durgapur 14 Dec 1979; (2) 307, 339.

COLAH, Sorabji Hormasji Munchersha; b Bombay 22 Sep 1902; d Ahmedabad 11 Sep 1950; (2) 219, 230.

CONTRACTOR, Nariman Jamshedji; b Godra, Gujarat 7 Mar 1934; (31) 417, 418, 419, 420, 433, 459, 460, 461, 462, 463, 474, 475, 477, 478, 482, 483, 484, 485, 486, 497, 498, 499, 500, 501, 513, 514, 515, 516, 517, 525, 526.

DANI, Hemchandra Tukaram; b Dudhani, Maharashtra 24 May 1933; (1) 357.

DESAI, Ramakant Bhikaji; b Bombay 20 Jun 1939; (28) 463, 474, 475, 476, 477, 478, 482, 485, 486, 497, 498, 499, 500, 501, 513, 515, 516, 517, 525, 526, 527, 555, 556, 580, 581, 582, 625, 633.

DILAWAR HUSSAIN, b Lahore 19 Mar 1907; d Lahore, Pakistan 26 Aug 1967; (3) 231, 232, 254.

DIVECHA, Ramesh Vithaldas; b Bombay 18 Oct 1927; (5) 341, 343, 353, 354, 358.

DOSHI, Dilip Rasiklal; b Rajkot 22 Dec 1947; (33) 855, 856, 857, 858, 859, 860, 861, 862, 863, 864, 865, 866, 876, 893, 894, 895, 901, 902, 912, 913, 914, 915, 916, 917, 928, 929, 930, 934, 943, 944, 945, 946, 961.

DURANI, Salim Aziz; b Kabul, Afghanistan 11 Dec 1934;
(29) 484, 513, 514, 515, 516, 517, 525, 526, 527,
528, 529, 553, 554, 555, 556, 557, 566, 567, 568,
579, 580, 581, 610, 680, 681, 682, 704, 705, 707.

ENGINEER, Farokh Maneksha; b Bombay 25 Feb 1938;
(46) 514, 515, 516, 517, 525, 526, 527, 579, 580,
581, 582, 612, 618, 619, 620, 624, 625, 626, 627,
633, 634, 635, 636, 659, 660, 665, 666, 667, 668,
669, 690, 691, 692, 703, 704, 705, 706, 707, 739,
740, 741, 745, 746, 747, 748, 749.

GADKARI, Chandrasekhar Vaman; b Poona 3 Feb 1928;
(6) 365, 368, 369, 397, 398, 399.

GAEKWAD, Anshuman Dattajirao; b Bombay 23 Sep
1952; (40) 747, 748, 749, 773, 775, 776, 785, 786,
787, 788, 789, 791, 792, 813, 841, 842, 843, 844,
845, 851, 852, 949, 950, 951, 952, 953, 961, 962,
963, 964, 965, 966, 967, 968, 969, 995, 996, 1005,
1006, 1007.

GAEKWAD, Dattajirao Krishnarao; b Baroda 27 Oct
1928; (11) 351, 356, 359, 365, 366, 463, 474, 476,
477, 478, 500.

GAEKWAD, Hiralal Ghasulal; b Nagpur 29 Aug 1923; (1)
356.

GANDOTRA, Ashok; b Rio de Janeiro, Brazil 24 Nov
1948; (2) 661, 666.

GAVASKAR, Sunil Manohar; b Bombay 10 Jul 1949;
(125) 681, 682, 683, 684, 690, 691, 692, 703, 704,
705, 706, 707, 739, 740, 741, 745, 749, 770, 771,
772, 773, 774, 775, 776, 785, 786, 787, 788, 789,
790, 791, 792, 809, 810, 811, 812, 813, 831, 832,
833, 840, 841, 842, 843, 844, 845, 851, 852, 853,
854, 855, 856, 857, 858, 859, 860, 861, 862, 863,
864, 865, 866, 876, 893, 894, 895, 900, 901, 902,
912, 913, 914, 915, 916, 917, 928, 929, 930, 934,
943, 944, 945, 946, 947, 948, 949, 950, 951, 952,
953, 961, 962, 963, 964, 965, 966, 967, 968, 969,
995, 996, 1005, 1006, 1007, 1008, 1009, 1023, 1024,
1025, 1032, 1033, 1034, 1046, 1047, 1048, 1052,
1053, 1054, 1063, 1064, 1065, 1066, 1068, 1069,
1070.

GHAVRI, Karsan Devji; b Rajkot 28 Feb 1951; (39) 747,
748, 749, 786, 787, 788, 791, 792, 811, 812, 813,
833, 840, 841, 842, 843, 844, 845, 851, 852, 853,
854, 855, 856, 857, 858, 859, 860, 861, 862, 863,
864, 865, 866, 876, 893, 894, 895, 901.

GHORPADE, Jayasinghrao Mansingrao; b Panchgani,
Maharashtra 2 Oct 1930; d Baroda 29 Mar 1978; (8)
367, 369, 419, 432, 461, 475, 476, 478.

GHULAM AHMED; b Hyderabad 4 Jul 1922; (22) 306,
307, 308, 342, 343, 351, 352, 353, 354, 355, 356,
357, 359, 396, 397, 398, 399, 416, 431, 433, 460,
461.

GOPALAN, Morappakam Joysam; b Maduranthakam,
Madras 6 Jun 1909; (1) 231.

GOPINATH, Coimbatarao Doraikannu; b Madras 1 Mar
1930; (8) 340, 341, 343, 351, 358, 397, 398, 486.

GUARD, Ghulam Mustafa; b Surat, Gujarat 12 Dec 1925;
d Ahmedabad 13 Mar 1978; (2) 459, 484.

GUHA, Subroto; b Calcutta 31 Jan 1946; (4) 618, 666, 667,
668.

GUL MAHOMED; b Lahore 15 Oct 1921; d Lahore,
Pakistan 8 May 1992; (8) 276, 290, 291, 292, 293,
294, 355, 356. (*Also Test No. 430 for Pakistan*)

GUPTE, Balkrishna Pandharinath; b Bombay 30 Aug
1934; (3) 500, 557, 580.

GUPTE, Subhash Pandharinath; b Bombay 11 Dec 1929;
(36) 341, 357, 358, 365, 366, 367, 368, 369, 396,
397, 398, 399, 400, 416, 417, 418, 419, 420, 431,
432, 433, 459, 460, 461, 462, 463, 474, 475, 476,
477, 478, 497, 498, 499, 514, 515.

GURSHARAN SINGH; b Amritsar 8 Mar 1963; (1) 1139.

HANUMANT SINGH (*The Maharajkumar of Banswara*);
b Banswara, Rajasthan 29 Mar 1939; (14) 556, 557,
566, 567, 568, 579, 580, 581, 582, 611, 612, 618,
620, 659.

HARDIKAR, Manohar Shankar; b Baroda 8 Feb 1936; d
Bombay 4 Feb 1995; (2) 459, 460.

HAZARE, Vijay Samuel; b Sangli, Maharashtra 11 Mar
1915; (30) 276, 277, 278, 290, 291, 292, 293, 294,
304, 305, 306, 307, 308, 339, 340, 341, 342, 343,
351, 352, 353, 354, 355, 357, 358, 365, 366, 367,
368, 369.

HINDLEKAR, Dattaram Dharmaji; b Bombay 1 Jan
1909; d Bombay 30 Mar 1949; (4) 252, 276, 277,
278.

HIRWANI, Narendra Deepchand; b Gorakhpur, Uttar
Pradesh 18 Oct 1968; (14) 1083, 1107, 1108, 1109,
1117, 1118, 1119, 1137, 1138, 1139, 1148, 1149,
1150, 1157.

IBRAHIM, Khanmohammed Cassumbhoy; b Bombay 26
Jan 1919; (4) 304, 305, 306, 308.

INDRAJITSINHJI, Kumar Shri; b Jamnagar 15 Jun 1937;
(4) 566, 567, 568, 661.

IRANI, Jahangir Khan; b Karachi 18 Aug 1923; d Karachi,
Pakistan 25 Feb 1982; (2) 290, 291.

JADEJA, Ajaysingh Daulatsingh; b Jamnagar 1 Feb 1971;
(3) 1200, 1201, 1203.

JAHANGIR KHAN, Mohammed; b Jullundur 1 Feb 1910;
d Lahore, Pakistan 23 Jul 1988; (4) 219, 252, 253,
254.

JAI, Laxmidas Purshottamdas; b Bombay 1 Apr 1902; d
Bombay 29 Jan 1968; (1) 230.

JAISIMHA, Motganhalli Laxmanarsu; b Secunderabad 3
Mar 1939; (39) 475, 486, 498, 499, 500, 501, 513,
514, 515, 516, 517, 526, 527, 528, 529, 553, 554,
555, 556, 557, 566, 567, 568, 579, 580, 581, 582,
610, 611, 626, 627, 633, 634, 635, 636, 661, 680,
683, 684.

JAMSHEDJI, Rustomji Jamshedji Dorabji; b Bombay 18
Nov 1892; d Bombay 5 Apr 1976; (1) 230.

JAYANTILAL, Kenia; b Hyderabad 13 Jan 1948; (1) 680.

JOSHI, Padmanabh Govind; b Baroda 27 Oct 1926; d
Poona 8 Jan 1987; (12) 339, 342, 356, 365, 366, 368,
462, 474, 475, 477, 482, 497.

KAMBLI, Vinod Ganpat; b Bombay 18 Jan 1972; (11)
1212, 1213, 1214, 1218, 1229, 1230, 1231, 1245,
1246, 1247, 1259.

KANITKAR, Hemant Shamsunder; b Amravati, Vidarbha
8 Dec 1942; (2) 745, 746.

KAPIL DEV, Nikhanj; b Chandigarh 6 Jan 1959; (131)
831, 832, 833, 840, 841, 842, 843, 844, 845, 851,
852, 853, 854, 855, 856, 857, 858, 859, 860, 861,
862, 863, 864, 865, 866, 876, 893, 894, 895, 900,
901, 902, 912, 913, 914, 915, 916, 917, 928, 929,
930, 934, 943, 944, 945, 946, 947, 948, 949, 950,
951, 952, 953, 961, 962, 963, 964, 965, 966, 967,
968, 969, 995, 996, 1005, 1006, 1008, 1009, 1023,
1024, 1025, 1032, 1033, 1034, 1046, 1047, 1048,
1052, 1053, 1054, 1063, 1064, 1065, 1066, 1067,
1068, 1069, 1070, 1080, 1081, 1082, 1083, 1107,
1108, 1109, 1117, 1118, 1119, 1120, 1127, 1128,
1129, 1130, 1137, 1138, 1139, 1148, 1149, 1150,
1157, 1177, 1178, 1179, 1180, 1181, 1197, 1200,
1201, 1202, 1203, 1212, 1213, 1214, 1218, 1229,
1230, 1231, 1245, 1246, 1247, 1259.

KARDAR, Abdul Hafeez (*known until 1947 as* Abdul
Hafeez); b Lahore 17 Jan 1925; (3) 276, 277, 278,
(*Also 23 Tests for Pakistan; 355-359, 387-390, 396-
400, 413-415, 430, 449-453*).

KENNY, Ramnath Bhaura; b Bombay 29 Sep 1930; d
Bombay 21 Nov 1985; (5) 461, 483, 484, 485, 486.

KIRMANI, Syed Mujtaba Hussain; b Madras 29 Dec 1949;
(88) 770, 771, 772, 773, 774, 775, 776, 785, 786,
787, 788, 789, 790, 791, 792, 809, 810, 811, 812,
813, 831, 832, 833, 840, 841, 842, 843, 844, 845,
855, 856, 857, 858, 859, 860, 861, 862, 863, 864,
865, 866, 876, 893, 894, 895, 900, 901, 902, 912,
913, 914, 915, 916, 917, 928, 929, 930, 934, 943,
961, 962, 963, 964, 965, 966, 967, 968, 969, 995,
996, 1005, 1006, 1007, 1008, 1009, 1032, 1033, 1034.

KISHENCHAND, Gogumal; b Karachi 14 Apr 1925; (5)
290, 291, 293, 294, 356.

KRIPAL SINGH, Amritsar Govindsingh; b Madras 6 Aug
1933; d Madras 22 Jul 1987; (14) 416, 417, 418, 420,
431, 433, 462, 475, 513, 514, 515, 553, 556, 566.

KRISHNAMURTHY, Pallemoni; b Hyderabad 12 Jul
1947; (5) 680, 681, 682, 683, 684.

KULKARNI, Rajiv Ramesh; b Bombay 25 Sep 1962; (3)
1054, 1066, 1067.

KULKARNI, Umesh Narayan; b Alibagh, Maharashtra, 7
Mar 1942; (4) 624, 626, 627, 634.

KUMAR, Vaman Vishwanath; b Madras 22 Jun 1935; (2)
501, 513.

KUMBLE, Anil; b Bangalore 17 Oct 1970; (17) 1149,
1197, 1200, 1201, 1202, 1203, 1212, 1213, 1214,
1218, 1229, 1230, 1231, 1245, 1246, 1247, 1259.

KUNDERAN, Budhisagar Krishnappa; b Mangalore 2
Oct 1939; (18) 484, 485, 486, 500, 501, 513, 528,
529, 553, 554, 555, 556, 557, 580, 610, 611, 619,
620.

LALL SINGH; b nr Kuala Lumpur, Malaya 16 Dec 1909; d
Kuala Lumpur, Malaysia 19 Nov 1985; (1) 219.

LAMBA, Raman; b Meerut, Uttar Pradesh 2 Jan 1960; (4)
1063, 1064, 1065, 1080.

MADAN LAL Sharma; b Amritsar 20 Mar 1951; (39) 739,
740, 747, 748, 770, 771, 772, 773, 774, 775, 776,
785, 789, 790, 809, 810, 912, 913, 914, 915, 916,
917, 928, 929, 930, 934, 943, 944, 945, 952, 953,
961, 962, 963, 964, 965, 967, 996, 1047.

MAKA, Ebrahim Suleman; b 5 Mar 1922; (2) 358, 367.

MALHOTRA, Ashok; b Amritsar 26 Jan 1957; (7) 916,
917, 928, 967, 968, 969, 1009.

MANINDER SINGH; b Poona 13 Jun 1965; (35) 944, 945,
946, 947, 948, 949, 950, 951, 966, 967, 968, 969,
995, 1023, 1025, 1046, 1047, 1048, 1052, 1053, 1054,
1063, 1064, 1065, 1066, 1067, 1069, 1070, 1080,
1081, 1082, 1128, 1129, 1130, 1218.

MANJREKAR, Sanjay Vijay; b Mangalore 12 Jul 1965;
(30) 1080, 1117, 1118, 1119, 1120, 1127, 1128, 1129,
1130, 1137, 1138, 1139, 1148, 1149, 1150, 1157,
1177, 1178, 1179, 1180, 1181, 1197, 1200, 1201,
1202, 1203, 1245, 1246, 1247, 1259.

MANJREKAR, Vijay Laxman; b Bombay 26 Sep 1931; d
Madras 18 Oct 1983; (55) 341, 342, 351, 352, 353,
354, 355, 356, 359, 366, 367, 368, 369, 396, 397,
398, 399, 400, 416, 417, 418, 419, 420, 431, 432,
433, 459, 460, 461, 463, 474, 475, 497, 498, 499,
500, 501, 513, 514, 515, 516, 517, 525, 526, 527,
528, 529, 553, 554, 555, 557, 566, 567, 568, 579.

MANKAD, Ashok Vinoo; b Bombay 12 Oct 1946; (22)
659, 660, 665, 666, 667, 668, 669, 681, 682, 683,
690, 691, 692, 741, 748, 785, 786, 787, 790, 809,
811, 812.

MANKAD, Mulvantrai Himmatlal (*known as 'Vinoo'*); b
Jamanagar 12 Apr 1917; d Bombay 21 Aug 1978;
(44) 276, 277, 278, 290, 291, 292, 293, 294, 304,
305, 306, 307, 308, 339, 340, 341, 342, 343, 352,
353, 354, 355, 357, 358, 359, 365, 366, 367, 368,
369, 396, 397, 398, 399, 400, 416, 417, 419, 420,
431, 432, 433, 462, 463.

MANSUR ALI KHAN, *see PATAUDI, Nawab of, jr.*

MANTRI, Madhav Krishnaji; b Nasik, Maharashtra 1 Sep
1921; (4) 340, 351, 352, 396.

MEHERHOMJI, Kharshed Rustomji; b Bombay 9 Aug
1911; d Bombay 10 Feb 1982; (1) 253.

MEHRA, Vijay Laxman; b Amritsar 12 Mar 1938; (8) 417,
418, 516, 525, 528, 529, 553, 554.

MERCHANT, Vijay Madhavji; b Bombay 12 Oct 1911; d
Bombay 27 Oct 1987; (10) 230, 231, 232, 252, 253,
254, 276, 277, 278, 339.

MILKHA SINGH, Amritsar Govindsingh; b Madras 31
Dec 1941; (4) 485, 500, 501, 513.

MODI, Rusi Sheriyar; b Surat, Gujarat 11 Nov 1924; (10)
276, 277, 278, 304, 305, 306, 307, 308, 339, 357.

MONGIA, Nayan Ramlal; b Baroda 19 Dec 1969; (4)
1245, 1246, 1247, 1259.

MORE, Kiran Shankar; b Baroda 4 Sep 1961; (49) 1046,
1047, 1048, 1052, 1054, 1063, 1064, 1065, 1066,
1067, 1068, 1069, 1070, 1080, 1081, 1082, 1083,
1107, 1108, 1109, 1117, 1118, 1119, 1120, 1127,
1128, 1129, 1130, 1137, 1138, 1139, 1148, 1149,
1150, 1157, 1177, 1178, 1181, 1197, 1200, 1201,
1202, 1203, 1212, 1213, 1214, 1229, 1230, 1231.

MUDDIAH, Ventappa Musandra; b Bangalore 8 Jun
1929; (2) 482, 498.

MUSHTAQ ALI, Syed; b Indore 17 Dec 1914; (11) 231,
232, 252, 253, 254, 277, 278, 306, 307, 308, 343.

NADKARNI, Rameshchandra Gangaram; b Nasik,
Maharashtra 4 Apr 1932; (41) 418, 459, 474, 476,
477, 478, 482, 483, 484, 485, 486, 497, 498, 499,
501, 517, 525, 526, 527, 528, 529, 553, 554, 555,
556, 557, 566, 567, 568, 579, 580, 581, 582, 610,
624, 626, 627, 633, 634, 635, 636.

NAIK, Sudhir Sakharam; b Bombay 21 Feb 1945; (3) 741,
746, 747.

NAOOMAL JEOOMAL Makhija; b Karachi 17 Apr 1904;
d Bombay 18 Jul 1980; (3) 219, 231, 232.

NARASIMHA RAO, Madireddy Venkateshwar; b Secunderabad 11 Aug 1954; (4) 842, 843, 858, 859.

NAVLE, Janardhan Gyanoba; b Fulgaon, Maharashtra 7 Dec 1902; d Poona 7 Sep 1979; (2) 219, 230.

NAYAK, Surendra Vithal; b Bombay 20 Oct 1954; (2) 929, 930.

NAYUDU, Cottari Kanakaiya; b Nagpur 31 Oct 1895; d Indore 14 Nov 1967; (7) 219, 230, 231, 232, 252, 253, 254.

NAYUDU, Cottari Subbanna; b Nagpur 18 Apr 1914; (11) 231, 232, 252, 253, 276, 278, 290, 291, 292, 294, 342.

NAZIR ALI, Syed; b Jullundur 8 Jan 1906; d Lahore, Pakistan 18 Feb 1975; (2) 219, 232.

NISSAR, Mahomed; b Hoshiarpur, Punjab 1 Aug 1910; d Lahore, Pakistan 11 Mar 1963; (6) 219, 230, 231, 252, 253, 254.

NYALCHAND, Shah; b Dhangadhra, Saurashtra 14 Sep 1919; (1) 356.

PAI, Ajit Manohar; b Bombay 28 Apr 1945; (1) 659.

PALIA, Phiroz Edulji; b Bombay 5 Sep 1910; d Bangalore 9 Sep 1981; (2) 219, 252.

PANDIT, Chandrakant Sitaram; b Bombay 30 Sep 1961; (5) 1047, 1052, 1053, 1179, 1180.

PARKAR, Ghulam Ahmed; b Kalusta, Maharashtra 24 Oct 1955; (1) 928.

PARKAR, Ramnath Dhondu; b Bombay 31 Oct 1946; (2) 703, 704.

PARSANA, Dhiraj Devji; b Rajkot 2 Dec 1947; (2) 843, 844.

PATANKAR, Chandrakant Trimbak; b 24 Nov 1930; (1) 419.

PATAUDI, *Nawab of, sr* (Iftikhar Ali Khan); b Pataudi, Punjab 16 Mar 1910; d New Delhi 5 Jan 1952; (3) 276, 277, 278, (*Also 3 Tests for England; 220, 221, 233*)

PATAUDI, *Nawab of, jr* (Mansur Ali Khan); b Bhopal 5 Jan 1941; (46) 515, 516, 517, 527, 528, 529, 553, 554, 555, 556, 557, 566, 567, 568, 579, 580, 581, 582, 610, 611, 612, 618, 619, 620, 625, 626, 627, 633, 634, 635, 636, 659, 660, 661, 665, 666, 667, 668, 669, 705, 706, 707, 745, 747, 748, 749.

PATEL, Brijesh Parsuram; b Baroda 24 Nov 1952; (21) 739, 740, 745, 746, 749, 770, 771, 772, 774, 775, 776, 785, 786, 787, 788, 789, 790, 791, 792, 809, 810.

PATEL, Jasubhai Motibhai; b Ahmedabad 26 Nov 1924; d Ahmedabad 12 Dec 1992; (7) 400, 420, 431, 432, 483, 485, 486.

PATEL, Rashid; b Sabarkantha 1 Jun 1964; (1) 1108.

PATIALA, *Yuvraj of* (Yadavendra Singh) (*later HH Lt-Gen. Maharaja of Patiala*); b Patiala, Punjab 17 Jan 1913; d The Hague, Holland 17 Jun 1974; (1) 232.

PATIL, Sandeep Madhusudan; b Bombay 18 Aug 1956; (29) 865, 866, 876, 893, 894, 895, 900, 901, 902, 912, 913, 914, 915, 929, 930, 934, 943, 944, 945, 946, 961, 962, 963, 964, 966, 995, 996, 1005, 1006.

PATIL, Sadashiv Raoji; b Kolhapur, Maharashtra 10 Oct 1933; (1) 417.

PHADKAR, Dattatraya Gajanan; b Kolhapur, Maharashtra 12 Dec 1925; d Madras 17 Mar 1985; (31) 291, 292, 293, 294, 304, 305, 307, 308, 339, 341, 342, 343, 351, 352, 353, 354, 358, 359, 365, 366, 367, 368, 396, 399, 400, 416, 417, 419, 420, 432, 461.

PRABHAKAR, Manoj; b Ghaziabad, Uttar Pradesh 15 Apr 1963; (33) 1006, 1007, 1127, 1128, 1129, 1130, 1137, 1138, 1139, 1148, 1149, 1150, 1157, 1177, 1178, 1179, 1180, 1181, 1197, 1200, 1201, 1202, 1203, 1212, 1213, 1214, 1218, 1229, 1230, 1231, 1245, 1246, 1247.

PRASANNA, Erapally Anantharao Srinivasa; b Bangalore 22 May 1940; (49) 517, 526, 612, 618, 619, 620, 624, 625, 626, 627, 633, 634, 635, 636, 659, 660, 661, 665, 666, 667, 668, 669, 680, 681, 684, 704, 705, 706, 740, 741, 745, 746, 747, 748, 749, 770, 771, 772, 773, 789, 790, 791, 792, 809, 811, 812, 813, 831, 832.

PUNJABI, Pananmal Hotchand; b Karachi 20 Sep 1921; (5) 396, 397, 398, 399, 400.

RAI SINGH, Kanwar; b Darkati, Punjab 24 Feb 1922; (1) 292.

RAJINDERNATH; b Amritsar 7 Jan 1928; d Madras 22 Nov 1989; (1) 357.

RAJINDER PAL; b Delhi 18 Nov 1937; (1) 554.

RAJPUT, Lalchand Sitaram; b Bombay 18 Dec 1961; (2) 1023, 1024.

RAJU, Sagi Laksmi Venkatapathy; b Hyderabad 9 Jul 1969; (18) 1137, 1138, 1157, 1177, 1178, 1180, 1181, 1197, 1202, 1203, 1212, 1213, 1214, 1231, 1245, 1246, 1247, 1259.

RAMAN, Woorkeri Venkat; b Madras 23 May 1965; (8) 1083, 1107, 1119, 1137, 1138, 1139, 1197, 1202.

RAMASWAMI, Cota; b Madras 18 Jun 1896; (2) 253, 254.

RAMCHAND, Gulabrai Sipahahimalani; b Karachi 26 Jul 1927; (33) 351, 352, 353, 354, 355, 358, 359, 365, 366, 367, 368, 369, 396, 397, 398, 399, 400, 416, 417, 418, 419, 420, 431, 432, 433, 459, 460, 462, 482, 483, 484, 485, 486.

RAMJI, Ladha; b Pidhar, Gujarat 1900; d Rajkot 20 Dec 1948; (1) 230.

RANGACHARI, Commandur Rajagopalachari; b Mamandur, Madras 14 Apr 1916; d Madras 9 Oct 1993; (4) 293, 294, 304, 305.

RANGNEKAR, Khanderao Moreshwar; b in Maharashtra 27 Jun 1917; d Bombay 11 Oct 1984; (3) 290, 292, 293.

RANJANE, Vasant Baburao; b Poona 22 Jul 1937; (7) 460, 513, 514, 516, 529, 553, 566.

RAZDAN, Vivek; b Delhi 25 Aug 1969; (2) 1128, 1130.

REDDY, Bharath; b Madras 12 Nov 1954; (4) 851, 852, 853, 854.

REGE, Madhusudan Ramchandra; b Panvel, Maharashtra 18 Mar 1924; (1) 307.

ROY, Ambar; b Calcutta 5 Jun 1945; (4) 660, 661, 667, 668.

ROY, Pankaj; b Calcutta 31 May 1928; (43) 339, 340, 341, 342, 343, 351, 352, 353, 354, 355, 356, 359, 366, 367, 368, 369, 396, 397, 398, 399, 400, 416, 419, 420, 431, 432, 433, 459, 460, 461, 462, 463, 474, 475, 476, 477, 478, 482, 483, 484, 485, 486, 497.

ROY, Pranab; b Calcutta 10 Feb 1957; (2) 916, 917.

SANDHU, Balwinder Singh; b Bombay 3 Aug 1956; (8) 946, 947, 948, 949, 950, 951, 952, 966.

SARDESAI, Dilip Narayan; b Margao, Goa 8 Aug 1940; (30) 514, 525, 527, 528, 553, 554, 555, 556, 557, 566, 567, 568, 579, 581, 582, 610, 612, 619, 624, 625, 665, 680, 681, 682, 683, 684, 690, 691, 692, 703.

SARWATE, Chandrasekhar Trimbak; b Sangor, Vidarbha 22 Jun 1920; (9) 277, 290, 291, 292, 293, 294, 304, 306, 340.

SAXENA, Ramesh Chandra; b Delhi 20 Sep 1944; (1) 618.

SEKAR, Thirumalai Ananthan Pillai; b Madras 28 Mar 1956; (2) 947, 948.

SEN, Probir; b Comilla, Bengal 31 May 1926; d Calcutta 27 Jan 1970; (14) 292, 293, 294, 304, 305, 306, 307, 308, 341, 343, 353, 354, 355, 359.

SENGUPTA, A.K.; b Lucknow 3 Aug 1939; (1) 462.

SHARMA, Ajay Kumar; b Alwar, Rajasthan 3 Apr 1964; (1) 1083.

SHARMA, Chetan; b Ludhiana, Punjab 3 Jan 1966; (23) 995, 996, 1005, 1007, 1008, 1023, 1024, 1025, 1032, 1034, 1046, 1048, 1052, 1053, 1063, 1064, 1080, 1081, 1082, 1117, 1118, 1119, 1120.

SHARMA, Gopal; b Kanpur 3 Aug 1960; (5) 1009, 1023, 1068, 1069, 1157.

SHARMA, Parthasarthi; b Alwar, Rajasthan 5 Jan 1948; (5) 746, 747, 773, 788, 789.

SHARMA, Sanjeev Kumar; b Delhi 25 Aug 1965; (2) 1109, 1148.

SHASTRI, Ravishankar Jayadritha; b Bombay 27 May 1962; (80) 900, 901, 902, 912, 913, 914, 915, 916, 917, 928, 929, 930, 943, 948, 949, 950, 951, 952, 953, 962, 963, 964, 965, 966, 967, 968, 969, 995, 996, 1005, 1006, 1007, 1008, 1009, 1023, 1024, 1025, 1032, 1033, 1034, 1046, 1047, 1048, 1052, 1053, 1054, 1063, 1064, 1065, 1066, 1067, 1068, 1069, 1070, 1080, 1081, 1082, 1083, 1107, 1108, 1109, 1117, 1118, 1119, 1120, 1127, 1128, 1129, 1130, 1148, 1149, 1150, 1157, 1177, 1178, 1179, 1197, 1200, 1201, 1202.

SHINDE, Sadashiv Ganpatrao; b Bombay 18 Aug 1923; d Bombay 22 Jun 1955; (7) 276, 305, 339, 340, 342, 351, 352.

SHODHAN, Roshan Harshadlal; b Ahmedabad 18 Oct 1928; (3) 359, 365, 369.

SHUKLA, Rakesh Chandra; b Kanpur 4 Feb 1948; (1) 934.

SIDHU, Navjot Singh; b Patiala, Punjab 20 Oct 1963; (31) 966, 969, 1107, 1108, 1109, 1117, 1118, 1119, 1120, 1127, 1128, 1129, 1130, 1137, 1148, 1149, 1150, 1179, 1180, 1181, 1212, 1213, 1214, 1218, 1229, 1230, 1231, 1245, 1246, 1247, 1259.

SIVARAMAKRISHNAN, Laxman, b Madras 31 Dec 1965; (9) 953, 1005, 1006, 1007, 1008, 1009, 1024, 1033, 1034.

SOHONI, Sriranga Wasudev; b Nimbora, Maharashtra 5 Mar 1918; d Thane 19 May 1993; (4) 277, 278, 290, 340.

SOLKAR, Eknath Dhondu; b Bombay 18 Mar 1948; (27) 661, 666, 667, 668, 669, 680, 681, 682, 683, 684, 690, 691, 692, 703, 704, 705, 706, 707, 739, 740, 741, 745, 746, 748, 749, 775, 789.

SOOD, Man Mohan; b Lahore 6 Jul 1939; (1) 485.

SRIKKANTH, Krishnamachari; b Madras 21 Dec 1959; (43) 912, 913, 914, 915, 946, 947, 1008, 1009, 1023, 1024, 1025, 1032, 1033, 1034, 1046, 1047, 1048, 1052, 1053, 1054, 1063, 1064, 1065, 1066, 1067, 1068, 1069, 1070, 1080, 1081, 1082, 1083, 1107, 1108, 1109, 1127, 1128, 1129, 1130, 1177, 1178, 1180, 1181.

SRINATH, Javagal; b Mysore 31 Aug 1969; (12) 1177, 1178, 1179, 1180, 1181, 1197, 1200, 1201, 1203, 1229, 1230, 1259.

SRINIVASAN, Tirumalai Echambadi; b Madras 26 Oct 1950; (1) 902.

SUBRAMANYA, Venkataraman; b Bangalore 16 Jul 1936; (9) 582, 611, 612, 619, 620, 624, 625, 635, 636.

SUNDERAM, Gundibail Rama; b Udipi 29 Mar 1930; (2) 418, 419.

SURENDRANATH; b Meerut 4 Jan 1937; (11) 461, 462, 474, 475, 476, 477, 478, 482, 483, 499, 500.

SURTI, Rusi Framroz; b Surat, Gujarat 25 May 1936; (26) 497, 501, 525, 526, 527, 528, 529, 555, 567, 568, 579, 611, 612, 618, 619, 624, 625, 626, 627, 633, 634, 635, 636, 659, 660, 665.

SWAMY, Venkataraman Narayan; b Calicut, Karala 23 May 1924; d Dehra Dun, Uttar Pradesh 1 May 1983; (1) 416.

TAMHANE, Narendra Shankar; b Bombay 4 Aug 1931; (21) 396, 397, 398, 399, 400, 416, 417, 418, 420, 431, 432, 433, 459, 460, 461, 463, 476, 478, 483, 498, 499.

TARAPORE, Keki Khurshedji; b Bombay 17 Dec 1910; d Bombay 15 Jun 1986; (1) 304.

TENDULKAR, Sachin Ramesh; b Bombay 24 Apr 1973; (32) 1127, 1128, 1129, 1130, 1137, 1138, 1139, 1148, 1149, 1150, 1157, 1177, 1178, 1179, 1180, 1181, 1197, 1200, 1201, 1202, 1203, 1212, 1213, 1214, 1218, 1229, 1230, 1231, 1245, 1246, 1247, 1259.

UMRIGAR, Pahlan Ratanji; b Sholapur, Maharashtra 28 Mar 1926; (59) 305, 339, 340, 341, 342, 343, 351, 352, 353, 354, 355, 356, 357, 358, 359, 365, 366, 367, 368, 369, 396, 397, 398, 399, 400, 416, 417, 418, 419, 420, 431, 432, 433, 459, 460, 461, 462, 463, 474, 475, 476, 477, 482, 483, 484, 497, 498, 499, 500, 501, 514, 515, 516, 517, 525, 526, 527, 528, 529.

VENGSARKAR, Dilip Balwant; b Rajapur, Maharashtra 6 Apr 1956; (116) 770, 771, 772, 774, 776, 790, 809, 810, 811, 812, 813, 831, 832, 833, 840, 841, 842, 843, 844, 845, 851, 852, 853, 854, 855, 856, 857, 858, 859, 860, 861, 862, 863, 864, 865, 876, 893, 894, 895, 900, 901, 902, 912, 913, 914, 915, 916, 917, 928, 929, 930, 934, 943, 944, 945, 946, 947, 948, 949, 950, 951, 952, 953, 963, 964, 965, 967, 968, 969, 995, 996, 1005, 1006, 1007, 1008, 1009, 1023, 1024, 1025, 1032, 1033, 1034, 1046, 1047, 1048, 1053, 1054, 1063, 1064, 1065, 1066, 1067, 1068, 1069, 1070, 1080, 1081, 1082, 1107, 1108, 1109, 1117, 1118, 1119, 1120, 1138, 1139, 1148, 1149, 1150, 1157, 1177, 1178, 1179, 1180, 1181.

VENKATARAGHAVAN, Srinivasaraghavan; b Madras 21 Apr 1946; (57) 579, 580, 581, 582, 610, 611, 620, 660, 661, 665, 666, 667, 668, 669, 680, 681, 682, 683, 684, 690, 691, 692, 703, 707, 739, 741, 745, 746, 770, 774, 775, 776, 785, 786, 787, 788, 810, 840, 841, 842, 843, 844, 845, 851, 852, 853, 854, 855, 856, 857, 949, 950, 951, 952, 953, 961, 962.

VENKATARAMANA, Margasaghayam; b Secunderabad 24 Apr 1966; (1) 1120.

VISWANATH, Gundappa Ranganath; b Bhadravati, Mysore 12 Feb 1949; (91) 666, 667, 668, 669, 682, 683, 684, 690, 691, 692, 703, 704, 705, 706, 707, 739, 740, 741, 745, 746, 747, 748, 749, 770, 771, 772, 773, 774, 775, 776, 785, 786, 787, 788, 789, 790, 791, 792, 809, 810, 811, 812, 813, 831, 832, 833, 840, 841, 842, 843, 844, 845, 851, 852, 853, 854, 855, 856, 857, 858, 859, 860, 861, 862, 863, 864, 865, 866, 876, 893, 894, 895, 900, 901, 902, 912, 913, 914, 915, 916, 917, 928, 929, 930, 934, 943, 944, 945, 946, 947, 948.

VISWANATH, Sadanand; b Bangalore 29 Nov 1962; (3) 1023, 1024, 1025.

VIZIANAGRAM, *Maharajkumar of (Sir* Gajapatairaj Vijaya Ananda); b Vizianagram, Andhra 28 Dec 1905; d Benares, Uttar Pradesh 2 Dec 1965; (3) 252, 253, 254.

WADEKAR, Ajit Laxman; b Bombay 1 Apr 1941; (37) 610, 612, 618, 619, 620, 624, 625, 626, 627, 633, 634, 635, 636, 659, 660, 661, 665, 666, 667, 668, 669, 680, 681, 682, 683, 684, 690, 691, 692, 703, 704, 705, 706, 707, 739, 740, 741.

WASSAN, Atil Satish; b Delhi 23 Mar 1968; (4) 1137, 1138, 1139, 1150.

WAZIR ALI, Syed; b Jullundur 15 Sep 1903; d Karachi, Pakistan 17 Jun 1950; (7) 219, 230, 231, 232, 252, 253, 254.

YADAV, Nandlal Shivlal; b Hyderabad 26 Jan 1957; (35) 856, 857, 858, 859, 860, 861, 862, 863, 864, 866, 876, 894, 895, 902, 915, 967, 968, 969, 996, 1005, 1006, 1007, 1008, 1032, 1033, 1034, 1052, 1053, 1054, 1064, 1065, 1066, 1068, 1069, 1070.

YADAV, Vijay; b Gonda 14 Mar 1967; (1) 1218.

YAJURVINDRA SINGH; b Rajkot 1 Aug 1952; (4) 791, 792, 854, 855.

YASHPAL SHARMA; b Ludhiana, Punjab 11 Aug 1954; (37) 852, 853, 854, 855, 856, 857, 858, 859, 860, 861, 862, 863, 864, 865, 866, 876, 893, 894, 895, 901, 916, 917, 928, 929, 930, 934, 947, 948, 949, 950, 951, 952, 953, 961, 962, 963, 965.

YOGRAJ SINGH; b Chandigarh 25 Mar 1958; (1) 900.

PAKISTAN (132 players)

AAMER MALIK; b Mandi Bahauddin 3 Jan 1963; (13) 1085, 1086, 1097, 1104, 1115, 1116, 1127, 1128, 1129, 1130, 1134, 1136, 1156.

AAMIR NAZIR; b Lahore 2 Jan 1971; (2) 1221, 1250.

AAMIR SOHAIL; b Lahore 14 Sep 1966; (16) 1189, 1190, 1191, 1192, 1193, 1211, 1220, 1221, 1238, 1239, 1240, 1248, 1249, 1250, 1266, 1267.

ABDUL KADIR; b Karachi 10 May 1944; (4) 569, 570, 576, 577.

ABDUL QADIR Khan; b Lahore 15 Sep 1955; (67) 814, 815, 816, 861, 862, 863, 886, 887, 931, 932, 933, 935, 936, 937, 944, 945, 946, 947, 948, 970, 971, 972, 973, 974, 978, 979, 980, 996, 1002, 1003, 1004, 1010, 1011, 1026, 1027, 1028, 1043, 1045, 1055, 1056, 1057, 1066, 1067, 1069, 1076, 1077, 1078, 1079, 1084, 1085, 1086, 1095, 1096, 1097, 1104, 1105, 1106, 1115, 1116, 1127, 1128, 1129, 1130, 1151, 1152, 1154, 1156.

AFAQ HUSSAIN; b Lucknow, India 31 Dec 1939; (2) 512, 570.

AFTAB BALOCH; b Karachi 1 Apr 1953; (2) 664, 756.

AFTAB GUL; b Gujar Khan, Rawalpindi 31 Mar 1946; (6) 647, 649, 664, 687, 688, 689.

AGHA SAADAT ALI; b Lahore 21 Jun 1929; (1) 415.

AGHA ZAHID; b Lahore 7 Jan 1953; (1) 756.

AKRAM RAZA; b Lahore 22 Nov 1964; (6) 1129, 1155, 1182, 1249, 1250, 1266.

ALIMUDDIN; b Ajmer, India 15 Dec 1930; (25) 387, 388, 390, 396, 397, 398, 399, 400, 413, 414, 415, 430, 449, 450, 451, 452, 453, 470, 480, 498, 518, 519, 531, 532, 533.

AMIR ELAHI; b Lahore 1 Sep 1908; d Multan 28 Dec 1980; (5) 355, 356, 357, 358, 359. (*Also Test No. 291 for India*).

ANIL DALPAT Sonavaria; b Karachi 20 Sep 1963; (9) 978, 979, 980, 1002, 1003, 1004, 1010, 1011, 1012.

ANWAR HUSSAIN; b Lahore 16 Jul 1920; (4) 355, 356, 358, 359.

ANWAR KHAN; b Karachi 24 Dec 1955; (1) 846.

AQIB JAVED; b Sheikhupura 5 Aug 1972; (14) 1115, 1134, 1151, 1152, 1153, 1182, 1183, 1184, 1189, 1190, 1191, 1192, 1193, 1211.

ARIF BUTT; b Lahore 17 May 1944; (3) 570, 576, 577.

ASHRAF ALI; b Lahore 22 Apr 1958; (8) 926, 927, 995, 996, 1026, 1084, 1085, 1086.

ASHFAQ AHMED; b Lyallpur 6 Jun 1973; (1) 1239.

ASIF IQBAL Razvi; b Hyderabad, India 6 Jun 1943; (58) 569, 570, 576, 577, 578, 588, 589, 590, 621, 622, 623, 647, 648, 649, 662, 663, 664, 687, 688, 689, 708, 709, 710, 711, 712, 713, 719, 720, 721, 742, 743, 744, 756, 757, 782, 783, 784, 793, 794, 795, 798, 799, 800, 801, 802, 831, 832, 833, 847, 848, 849, 850, 861, 862, 863, 864, 865, 866.

ASIF MASOOD; b Lahore 23 Jan 1946; (16) 647, 649, 662, 687, 688, 689, 708, 709, 710, 721, 742, 743, 744, 756, 757, 794.

ASIF MUJTABA, Mohammad; b Karachi 4 Nov 1967; (19) 1056, 1057, 1084, 1189, 1190, 1191, 1192, 1193, 1211, 1220, 1221, 1222, 1238, 1239, 1240, 1248, 1249, 1266, 1267.

ATA-UR-REHMAN; b Lahore 28 Mar 1975; (9) 1189, 1220, 1221, 1222, 1238, 1239, 1240, 1248, 1249.

ATIF RAUF; b Lahore 3 Mar 1964; (1) 1250.

AZEEM HAFEEZ; b Karachi 29 Jul 1963; (18) 961, 962, 963, 970, 971, 972, 973, 974, 978, 979, 995, 996, 1002, 1003, 1004, 1010, 1011, 1012.

AZHAR KHAN; b Gujranwala 7 Sep 1955; (1) 879.

AZMAT RANA; b Lahore 3 Nov 1951; (1) 879.

BASIT ALI; b Karachi 13 Dec 1970; (11) 1220, 1221, 1222, 1238, 1239, 1240, 1248, 1249, 1250, 1266, 1267.

D'SOUZA, Antao; b Goa, India 17 Jan 1939; (6) 469, 518, 519, 530, 531, 534.

EHTESHAMUDDIN; b Lahore 4 Sep 1950; (5) 861, 864, 866, 878, 933.

FAROOQ HAMID; b Lahore 3 Mar 1945; (1) 570.

FARRUKH ZAMAN; b Peshawar 2 Apr 1956; (1) 783.

FAZAL MAHMOOD; b Lahore 18 Feb 1927; (34) 355, 356, 357, 358, 359, 387, 388, 389, 390, 396, 397, 398, 400, 413, 415, 430, 449, 450, 451, 452, 453, 469, 470, 471, 479, 481, 497, 498, 499, 500, 501, 519, 533, 534.

GHAZALI, Mohammad Ebrahim Zainuddin; b Gujarat, India 15 Jun 1924; (2) 388, 389.

GHULAM ABBAS; b Delhi, India 1 May 1947; (1) 623.

GUL MAHOMED; b Lahore 15 Oct 1921; d Lahore 8 May 1992; (1) 430 (*Also 8 Tests for India; 276, 290-294, 355, 356*).

HANIF MOHAMMAD; b Junagadh, Gujarat, India 21 Dec 1934; (55) 355, 356, 357, 358, 359, 387, 388, 389, 390, 396, 397, 398, 399, 400, 413, 414, 415, 430, 449, 450, 451, 452, 453, 469, 479, 480, 481, 497, 498, 499, 500, 501, 512, 518, 519, 530, 531, 532, 533, 534, 569, 570, 576, 577, 578, 588, 589, 590, 621, 622, 623, 647, 648, 649, 662.

HAROON RASHID Dar; b Karachi 25 Mar 1953; (23) 795, 798, 799, 800, 801, 802, 814, 815, 816, 825, 826, 827, 846, 850, 877, 878, 925, 926, 932, 935, 936, 937, 946.

HASEEB AHSAN; b Peshawar 15 Jul 1939; (12) 449, 452, 453, 470, 480, 497, 498, 499, 500, 501, 512, 519.

IJAZ AHMED; b Sialkot 20 Sep 1968; (19) 1066, 1076, 1077, 1078, 1079, 1084, 1085, 1086, 1095, 1096, 1104, 1105, 1106, 1134, 1135, 1136, 1151, 1152, 1153.

IJAZ BUTT; b Sialkot 10 Mar 1938; (8) 469, 470, 471, 479, 481, 530, 532, 534.

IJAZ FAQIH; b Karachi 24 Mar 1956; (5) 888, 910, 1069, 1095, 1096.

IMRAN KHAN Niazi; b Lahore 25 Nov 1952; (88) 687, 742, 743, 744, 782, 783, 784, 793, 794, 795, 798, 799, 800, 801, 802, 831, 832, 833, 847, 848, 849, 850, 861, 862, 863, 865, 866, 877, 879, 886, 887, 888, 889, 909, 910, 911, 927, 931, 932, 933, 935, 936, 937, 943, 944, 945, 946, 947, 948, 973, 974, 1026, 1027, 1028, 1043, 1044, 1045, 1055, 1056, 1057, 1066, 1067, 1068, 1069, 1070, 1075, 1076, 1077, 1078, 1079, 1095, 1096, 1097, 1115, 1116, 1127, 1128, 1129, 1130, 1134, 1135, 1136, 1154, 1155, 1156, 1182, 1183, 1184.

IMTIAZ AHMED; b Lahore 5 Jan 1928; (41) 355, 356, 357, 358, 359, 387, 388, 389, 390, 396, 397, 398, 399, 400, 413, 414, 415, 430, 449, 450, 451, 452, 453, 469, 470, 471, 479, 480, 481, 497, 498, 499, 500, 501, 512, 518, 519, 530, 531, 533, 534.

INTIKHAB ALAM Khan; b Hoshiarpur, Punjab, India 28 Dec 1941; (47) 481, 499, 500, 501, 512, 518, 530, 533, 534, 569, 570, 576, 577, 578, 588, 589, 590, 621, 622, 623, 647, 648, 649, 662, 663, 664, 687, 688, 689, 708, 709, 710, 711, 712, 713, 719, 720, 721, 742, 743, 744, 756, 757, 782, 783, 784, 799.

INZAMAM-UL-HAQ; b Multan 3 Mar 1970; (16) 1189, 1190, 1191, 1192, 1211, 1220, 1221, 1222, 1238, 1239, 1240, 1248, 1249, 1250, 1266, 1267.

IQBAL QASIM, Mohammad; b Karachi 6 Aug 1953; (50) 793, 794, 795, 799, 801, 814, 815, 816, 825, 826, 827, 831, 832, 833, 861, 862, 863, 864, 865, 866, 877, 878, 879, 886, 887, 888, 889, 909, 911, 925, 926, 927, 935, 936, 946, 947, 961, 1002, 1003, 1004, 1010, 1068, 1069, 1070, 1084, 1085, 1086, 1104, 1105, 1106.

ISRAR ALI; b Jullundur, Punjab, India 1 May 1927; (4) 355, 357, 479, 480.

JALALUDDIN; b Karachi 12 Jun 1959; (6) 937, 943, 944, 995, 996, 1026.

JAVED AKHTAR; b Delhi, India 21 Nov 1940; (1) 532.

JAVED BURKI; b Meerut, India 8 May 1938; (25) 497, 498, 499, 500, 501, 512, 518, 519, 530, 531, 532, 533, 534, 569, 570, 576, 577, 578, 588, 589, 590, 621, 622, 623, 664.

JAVED MIANDAD Khan; b Karachi 12 Jun 1957; (124) 782, 783, 784, 793, 794, 795, 798, 814, 815, 816, 825, 826, 827, 831, 832, 833, 846, 847, 848, 849, 850, 861, 862, 863, 864, 865, 866, 877, 878, 879, 886, 887, 888, 889, 909, 910, 911, 925, 926, 927, 931, 932, 933, 935, 936, 937, 943, 944, 945, 946, 947, 948, 961, 962, 963, 970, 971, 972, 973, 974, 995, 996, 1002, 1003, 1004, 1010, 1011, 1012, 1026, 1027, 1028, 1043, 1044, 1045, 1055, 1056, 1057, 1066, 1067, 1068, 1070, 1075, 1076, 1077, 1078, 1079, 1084, 1085, 1086, 1095, 1096, 1097, 1104, 1105, 1106, 1115, 1116, 1127, 1128, 1129, 1130, 1134, 1135, 1136, 1151, 1152, 1153, 1154, 1155, 1182, 1183, 1184, 1189, 1190, 1191, 1192, 1193, 1211, 1220, 1221, 1222, 1238, 1239, 1240.

KABIR KHAN; b Peshawar 12 Apr 1974; (1) 1267.

KARDAR, Abdul Hafeez; b Lahore 17 Jan 1925; (23) 355, 356, 357, 358, 359, 387, 388, 389, 390, 396, 397, 398, 399, 400, 413, 414, 415, 430, 449, 450, 451, 452, 453, (*Also 3 Tests for India; 276-278*)

KHALID HASSAN; b Peshawar 14 Jul 1937; (1) 388.

KHALID IBADULLA; b Lahore 20 Dec 1935; (4) 569, 578, 621, 622.

KHALID WAZIR Ali; b Jullundur, Punjab, India 27 Apr 1936; (2) 387, 389.

KHAN MOHAMMAD; b Lahore 1 Jan 1928; (13) 355, 387, 388, 396, 397, 399, 400, 413, 414, 415, 430, 451, 453.

LIAQAT ALI Khan; b Karachi 21 May 1955; (5) 757, 814, 815, 825, 826.

MAHMOOD HUSSAIN; b Lahore 2 Apr 1932; d Harrow, Middlesex, England 25 Dec 1991; (27) 356, 357, 358, 359, 389, 390, 396, 397, 398, 399, 400, 414, 449, 450, 451, 469, 470, 471, 497, 498, 499, 500, 501, 512, 530, 531, 532.

MAJID Jahangir KHAN; b Ludhiana, Punjab, India 28 Sep 1946; (63) 569, 588, 589, 590, 621, 622, 623, 647, 648, 649, 687, 688, 708, 709, 710, 711, 712, 713, 719, 720, 721, 742, 743, 744, 756, 757, 782, 783, 784, 793, 794, 795, 798, 799, 800, 801, 802, 831, 832, 833, 847, 848, 849, 850, 861, 862, 863, 864, 865, 866, 877, 878, 879, 886, 887, 888, 889, 909, 910, 911, 927, 933, 947.

MANSOOR AKHTAR; b Karachi 25 Dec 1957; (19) 886, 887, 909, 925, 931, 932, 933, 935, 936, 937, 943, 944, 945, 1075, 1076, 1077, 1078, 1079, 1134.

MANZOOR ELAHI; b Sahiwal 15 Apr 1963; (4) 996, 1003, 1069, 1070.

MAQSOOD AHMED; b Amritsar, India 26 Mar 1925; (16) 355, 356, 357, 358, 359, 387, 388, 389, 390, 396, 397, 398, 399, 400, 413, 414.

MASOOD ANWAR; b Khanewal 12 Dec 1967; (1) 1156.

MATHIAS, Wallis; b Karachi 4 Feb 1935; d Karachi 1 Sep 1994; (21) 415, 430, 449, 450, 451, 452, 453, 469, 470, 471, 479, 481, 497, 498, 499, 500, 501, 512, 530, 531, 534.

MIRAN BUX, Malik; b Rawalpindi 20 Apr 1907; d Dhok Rata, Rawalpindi 8 Feb 1991; (2) 398, 399.

MOHAMMAD ASLAM Khokhar; b Lahore 5 Jan 1920; (1) 388.

MOHAMMAD FAROOQ; b Junagadh, Gujarat, India 8 Apr 1938; (7) 497, 501, 531, 532, 588, 589, 590.

MOHAMMAD ILYAS; b Lahore 19 Mar 1946; (10) 570, 576, 577, 578, 588, 589, 590, 623, 647, 648.

MOHAMMAD MUNAF; b Bombay, India 2 Nov 1935; (4) 480, 481, 512, 518.

MOHAMMAD NAZIR (*also known as* NAZIR JUNIOR); b Rawalpindi 8 Mar 1946; (14) 662, 663, 664, 720, 886, 887, 888, 889, 961, 962, 963, 970, 971, 972.

MOHSIN KAMAL; b Faisalabad 16 Jun 1963; (7) 980, 1027, 1044, 1075, 1076, 1077, 1078.

MOHSIN Hasan KHAN; b Karachi 15 Mar 1955; (48) 816, 825, 826, 827, 846, 849, 910, 911, 926, 927, 931, 932, 933, 935, 936, 937, 943, 944, 945, 946, 947, 948, 961, 962, 963, 970, 971, 972, 973, 974, 978, 979, 980, 995, 996, 1002, 1003, 1010, 1011, 1012, 1027, 1028, 1043, 1044, 1045, 1055, 1056, 1057.

MOIN KHAN b Rawalpindi 23 Sep 1971; (11) 1155, 1156, 1182, 1183, 1184, 1189, 1190, 1191, 1192, 1220, 1221.

MUDASSAR NAZAR; b Lahore 6 Apr 1956; (76) 793, 814, 815, 816, 825, 826, 827, 832, 833, 846, 850, 861, 862, 863, 864, 865, 877, 878, 879, 909, 910, 911, 927, 931, 932, 933, 935, 936, 937, 943, 944, 945, 946, 947, 948, 961, 962, 963, 970, 971, 972, 973, 974, 979, 995, 996, 1002, 1003, 1004, 1010, 1011, 1012, 1026, 1027, 1028, 1043, 1044, 1045, 1055, 1057, 1075, 1076, 1077, 1078, 1079, 1084, 1085, 1086, 1095, 1096, 1097, 1104, 1105, 1106, 1115, 1116.

MUFASIR-UL-HAQ; b Karnal, India 16 Aug 1944; d Karachi 27 Jul 1983; (1) 578.

MUNIR MALIK; b Lieh 10 Jul 1934; (3) 481, 532, 533.

MUSHTAQ AHMED; b Sahiwal 28 Jun 1970; (15) 1135, 1154, 1155, 1189, 1190, 1191, 1192, 1193, 1211, 1220, 1238, 1240, 1248, 1266, 1267.

MUSHTAQ MOHAMMAD; b Junagadh, Gujarat, India 22 Nov 1943; (57) 471, 497, 498, 499, 500, 501, 512, 518, 519, 530, 531, 532, 533, 534, 621, 622, 623, 647, 648, 649, 662, 663, 687, 688, 689, 708, 709, 710, 712, 713, 719, 720, 721, 742, 743, 744, 756, 757, 782, 783, 784, 793, 794, 795, 798, 799, 800, 801, 802, 831, 832, 833, 846, 847, 848, 849, 850.

NADEEM ABBASI; b Rawalpindi 15 Apr 1964; (3) 1128, 1129, 1130.

NADEEM GHAURI; b Lahore 12 Oct 1962; (1) 1136.

NADEEM KHAN; b Rawalpindi 10 Dec 1969; (1) 1222.

NASIM-UL-GHANI; b Delhi, India 14 May 1941; (29) 449, 450, 451, 452, 453, 469, 470, 471, 479, 480, 497, 498, 499, 500, 518, 519, 530, 531, 532, 533, 534, 569, 570, 576, 577, 578, 621, 622, 710.

NAUSHAD ALI; b Gwalior, India 1 Oct 1943; (6) 576, 577, 578, 588, 589, 590.

NAVED ANJUM; b Lahore 27 Jul 1963; (2) 1128, 1153.

NAZAR MOHAMMAD; b Lahore 5 Mar 1921; (5) 355, 356, 357, 358, 359.

NIAZ AHMED; b Benares, Uttar Pradesh, India 11 Nov 1945; (2) 622, 648.

PERVEZ SAJJAD Hassan; b Lahore 30 Aug 1942; (19) 569, 576, 577, 578, 588, 589, 590, 648, 662, 663, 664, 687, 688, 689, 711, 712, 713, 719, 720.

QASIM Ali OMAR; b Nairobi, Kenya 9 Feb 1957; (26) 962, 970, 971, 972, 973, 974, 978, 979, 980, 995, 996, 1002, 1003, 1004, 1010, 1011, 1012, 1026, 1027, 1028, 1043, 1044, 1045, 1055, 1056, 1057.

RAMIZ Hasan RAJA; b Lyallpur 14 Jul 1962; (48) 978, 980, 1028, 1043, 1044, 1045, 1055, 1056, 1057, 1066, 1067, 1068, 1069, 1070, 1075, 1079, 1084, 1085, 1086, 1095, 1096, 1097, 1104, 1105, 1106, 1127, 1128, 1129, 1130, 1135, 1136, 1151, 1152, 1153, 1154, 1156, 1182, 1183, 1184, 1189, 1190, 1191, 1192, 1193, 1211, 1220, 1221, 1222.

RASHID KHAN; b Karachi 15 Dec 1959; (4) 925, 926, 971, 1012.

RASHID LATIF; b Karachi 14 Oct 1968; (11) 1193, 1211, 1222, 1238, 1239, 1240, 1248, 1249, 1250, 1266, 1267.

REHMAN, Sheikh Fazalur; b Amritsar, India 11 Jun 1935; (1) 452.

RIZWAN-UZ-ZAMAN; b Karachi 4 Sep 1962; (11) 909, 925, 926, 1056, 1066, 1067, 1068, 1069, 1070, 1115, 1116.

SADIQ MOHAMMAD; b Junagadh, Gujarat. India 3 May 1945; (41) 662, 663, 664, 687, 688, 689, 708, 709, 710, 711, 712, 713, 719, 720, 721, 742, 743, 744, 757, 782, 783, 784, 794, 795, 798, 799, 800, 801, 802, 814, 815, 825, 826, 827, 831, 864, 865, 866, 886, 888, 889.

SAEED AHMED; b Jullundur, Punjab, India 10 Oct 1937; (41) 449, 450, 451, 452, 453, 469, 470, 471, 479, 480, 481, 497, 498, 499, 500, 501, 512, 518, 519, 530, 531, 532, 533, 534, 569, 570, 576, 577, 578, 588, 589, 590, 621, 622, 623, 647, 648, 649, 689, 708, 709.

SAEED ANWAR; b Karachi 6 Sep 1968; (6) 1155, 1248, 1249, 1250, 1266, 1267.

SALAHUDDIN Mulla; b Aligarh, Uttar Pradesh, India 14 Feb 1947; (5) 588, 589, 590, 648, 663.

SALIM ALTAF Bokhari; b Lahore 19 Apr 1944; (21) 621, 623, 663, 664, 688, 689, 708, 709, 710, 711, 712, 713, 719, 720, 721, 793, 794, 798, 799, 800, 832.

SALIM JAFFER; b Karachi 19 Nov 1962; (14) 1057, 1067, 1070, 1086, 1097, 1105, 1106, 1115, 1116, 1128, 1152, 1153, 1183, 1184.

SALIM MALIK; b Lahore 16 Apr 1963; (77) 925, 926, 943, 944, 945, 946, 947, 948, 961, 963, 972, 973, 974, 978, 979, 980, 995, 996, 1002, 1003, 1004, 1010, 1011, 1012, 1026, 1027, 1028, 1043, 1044, 1045, 1055, 1066, 1067, 1068, 1069, 1070, 1075, 1076, 1077, 1078, 1079, 1084, 1085, 1086, 1095, 1096, 1097, 1104, 1105, 1106, 1115, 1116, 1127, 1128, 1129, 1130, 1135, 1151, 1152, 1153, 1154, 1155, 1156, 1182, 1183, 1184, 1189, 1190, 1191, 1192, 1193, 1211, 1248, 1249, 1250, 1266, 1267.

SALIM YOUSUF; b Karachi 7 Dec 1959; (32) 925, 1027, 1028, 1055, 1056, 1057, 1066, 1067, 1068, 1069, 1070, 1075, 1076, 1077, 1078, 1079, 1095, 1096, 1097, 1104, 1105, 1106, 1115, 1116, 1127, 1134, 1135, 1136, 1151, 1152, 1153, 1154.

SARFRAZ NAWAZ Malik; b Lahore 1 Dec 1948; (55) 649, 709, 710, 711, 712, 713, 719, 721, 742, 743, 744, 756, 757, 782, 783, 784, 793, 795, 798, 800, 801, 802, 814, 816, 825, 827, 831, 832, 833, 846, 847, 848, 849, 850, 877, 878, 879, 886, 889, 909, 910, 911, 932, 943, 944, 945, 946, 947, 948, 972, 973, 974, 978, 979, 980.

SHAFIQ AHMED; b Lahore 28 Mar 1949; (6) 742, 814, 815, 816, 888, 889.

SHAFQAT RANA; b Simla, India 10 Aug 1943; (5) 569, 647, 649, 663, 664.

SHAHID ISRAR; b Karachi 1 Mar 1950; (1) 784.

SHAHID MAHBOOB; b Karachi 25 Aug 1962; (1) 1129.

SHAHID MAHMOOD; b Lucknow, India 17 Mar 1939; (1) 533.

SHAHID SAEED; b Lahore 6 Jan 1966; (1) 1127.

SHAKIL AHMED; b Daska 12 Nov 1971; (1) 1222.

SHARPE, Duncan; b Rawalpindi 3 Aug 1937; (3) 479, 480, 481.

SHOAIB MOHAMMAD; b Karachi 8 Jan 1962; (42) 962, 963, 980, 1004, 1010, 1026, 1066, 1067, 1068, 1075, 1076, 1077, 1078, 1085, 1095, 1096, 1097, 1104, 1105, 1106, 1115, 1116, 1127, 1128, 1129, 1130, 1134, 1135, 1136, 1151, 1152, 1153, 1154, 1155, 1156, 1182, 1183, 1184, 1193, 1238, 1239, 1240.

SHUJAUDDIN Butt; b Lahore 10 Apr 1930; (19) 387, 389, 390, 396, 397, 398, 399, 400, 413, 414, 415, 469, 470, 471, 479, 480, 481, 518, 519.

SIKANDER BAKHT; b Karachi 25 Aug 1957; (26) 784, 802, 815, 816, 825, 826, 827, 831, 833, 846, 847, 848, 849, 850, 862, 863, 864, 865, 866, 887, 909, 910, 911, 931, 933, 945.

TAHIR NAQQASH; b Lahore 6 Jul 1959; (15) 925, 926, 927, 931, 932, 935, 936, 937, 943, 948, 961, 962, 963, 970, 1012.

TALAT ALI Malik; b Lahore 29 May 1950; (10) 708, 711, 719, 720, 721, 826, 827, 846, 847, 848.

TASLIM ARIF; b Karachi 1 May 1954; (6) 866, 877, 878, 879, 886, 887.

TAUSIF AHMED; b Karachi 10 May 1958; (34) 877, 878, 879, 925, 926, 927, 978, 979, 995, 1002, 1028, 1043, 1044, 1055, 1056, 1057, 1066, 1067, 1068, 1070, 1075, 1079, 1084, 1085, 1104, 1105, 1106, 1116, 1134, 1135, 1136, 1151, 1153, 1238.

WAQAR HASSAN; b Amritsar, India 12 Sep 1932; (21) 355, 356, 357, 358, 359, 387, 388, 389, 390, 396, 397, 398, 399, 400, 413, 414, 415, 430, 450, 471, 480.

WAQAR YOUNIS; b Vehari 16 Nov 1971; (31) 1127, 1130, 1134, 1135, 1136, 1151, 1152, 1153, 1154, 1155, 1156, 1182, 1183, 1184, 1189, 1190, 1191, 1192, 1193, 1211, 1220, 1221, 1222, 1238, 1239, 1240, 1248, 1249, 1250, 1266, 1267.

WASIM AKRAM; b Lahore 3 Jun 1966; (55) 1011, 1012, 1026, 1027, 1028, 1043, 1044, 1045, 1055, 1056, 1066, 1067, 1068, 1069, 1070, 1075, 1076, 1077, 1078, 1079, 1084, 1086, 1095, 1096, 1097, 1127, 1128, 1129, 1130, 1134, 1135, 1136, 1151, 1152, 1154, 1155, 1156, 1182, 1183, 1184, 1190, 1191, 1192, 1193, 1211, 1220, 1221, 1222, 1239, 1240, 1248, 1249, 1250, 1266, 1267.

WASIM BARI; b Karachi 23 Mar 1948; (81) 621, 622, 623, 647, 648, 649, 662, 663, 664, 687, 688, 689, 708, 709, 710, 711, 712, 713, 719, 720, 721, 742, 743, 744, 756, 757, 782, 783, 793, 794, 795, 798, 799, 800, 801, 802, 814, 815, 816, 825, 826, 827, 831, 832, 833, 846, 847, 848, 849, 850, 861, 862, 863, 864, 865, 866, 888, 889, 909, 910, 911, 931, 932, 933, 935, 936, 937, 943, 944, 945, 946, 947, 948, 961, 962, 963, 970, 971, 972, 973, 974.

WASIM Hasan RAJA; b Multan 3 Jul 1952; (57) 711, 712, 713, 719, 743, 744, 756, 757, 782, 798, 799, 800, 801, 802, 814, 815, 816, 825, 826, 827, 846, 847, 848, 849, 861, 862, 863, 864, 865, 866, 877, 878, 879, 886, 887, 888, 889, 909, 910, 911, 925, 926, 927, 931, 948, 961, 962, 963, 970, 971, 978, 979, 980, 995, 1004, 1010, 1011.

WAZIR MOHAMMAD; b Junagadh, Gujarat, India 22 Dec 1929; (20) 357, 389, 390, 396, 397, 398, 399, 400, 413, 414, 430, 449, 450, 451, 452, 453, 469, 470, 471, 479.

YOUNIS AHMED, Mohammad; b Jullundur, Punjab, India 20 Oct 1947; (4) 662, 663, 1068, 1069.

ZAHEER ABBAS, Syed; b Sialkot 24 Jul 1947; (78) 662, 687, 688, 689, 708, 709, 710, 711, 712, 713, 720, 721, 742, 743, 744, 756, 757, 782, 783, 784, 793, 794, 795, 800, 801, 802, 831, 832, 833, 847, 848, 849, 850, 861, 862, 863, 864, 865, 877, 878, 887, 888, 889, 910, 911, 927, 931, 932, 933, 935, 936, 937, 943, 944, 945, 946, 947, 948, 961, 962, 963, 970, 971, 972, 973, 974, 978, 979, 980, 995, 996, 1002, 1003, 1004, 1011, 1012, 1026, 1027.

ZAHID FAZAL; b Sialkot 16 Nov 1973; (6) 1154, 1155, 1156, 1182, 1183, 1184.

ZAKIR KHAN; b Bannu 3 Apr 1963; (2) 1045, 1130.

ZULFIQAR AHMED; b Lahore 22 Nov 1926; (9) 356, 358, 359, 387, 390, 413, 414, 415, 430.

ZULQARNAIN, b Lahore 25 May 1962; (3) 1043, 1044, 1045.

SRI LANKA (63 players)

AHANGAMA, Franklyn Saliya; b Colombo 14 Sep 1959; (3) 1023, 1024, 1025.

AMALEAN, Kaushik Naginda; b Colombo 7 Apr 1965; (2) 1045, 1094.

AMERASINGHE, Mudalige Jayantha Gamini; b Colombo 2 Feb 1954; (2) 986, 988.

ANURASIRI, Sangarange Don; b Panadura 25 Feb 1966; (17) 1044, 1045, 1065, 1074, 1176, 1182, 1183, 1184, 1194, 1195, 1196, 1209, 1210, 1241, 1245, 1246, 1247.

ATAPATTU, Marvan Samson; b Kalutara 22 Nov 1970; (3) 1157, 1194, 1247.

DASSANAYAKE, Pubudu Bathiya; b Kandy 11 Jul 1970; (9) 1232, 1233, 1234, 1241, 1245, 1246, 1247, 1266, 1267.

DE ALWIS, Ronald Guy; b Colombo 15 Feb 1959; (11) 954, 956, 986, 987, 988, 1044, 1045, 1063, 1064, 1065, 1094.

DE MEL, Ashantha Lakdasa Francis; b Colombo 9 May 1959; (17) 921, 925, 926, 927, 934, 956, 994, 1023, 1024, 1025, 1026, 1027, 1028, 1043, 1044, 1045, 1063.

DE SILVA, Ashley Matthew; b Colombo 3 Dec 1963; (3) 1219, 1229, 1230.

DE SILVA, Dandeniyage Somachandra; b Galle 11 Jun 1942; (12) 921, 925, 926, 927, 934, 954, 955, 956, 986, 987, 988, 994.

DE SILVA, Ellawalakankanamage Asoka Ranjith; b Kalutara 28 Mar 1956; (10) 1023, 1043, 1063, 1064, 1065, 1132, 1133, 1164, 1165.

DE SILVA, Ginigalgodage Ramba Ajith; b Ambalangoda 12 Dec 1952; (4) 921, 925, 926, 934.

DE SILVA, Pinnaduwage Aravinda; b Colombo 17 Oct 1965; (43) 994, 1023, 1024, 1025, 1026, 1027, 1028, 1043, 1044, 1045, 1063, 1064, 1065, 1094, 1103, 1132, 1133, 1157, 1163, 1164, 1165. 1176, 1182, 1183, 1184, 1194, 1195, 1196, 1209, 1210, 1219, 1229, 1230, 1231, 1232, 1233, 1234, 1241, 1245, 1246, 1247, 1266, 1267.

DHARMASENA, Handunettige Deepthi Priyantha Kumara; b Colombo 24 Apr 1971; (4) 1233, 1234, 1266, 1267.

DIAS Roy Luke; b Colombo 18 Oct 1952; (20) 921, 925, 926, 927, 934, 956, 987, 988, 994, 1023, 1024, 1025, 1026, 1027, 1028, 1043, 1063, 1064, 1065, 1074.

FERNANDO, Ellekutige Rufus Nemesion Susil; b Colombo 19 Dec 1955; (5) 954, 955, 956, 986, 987.

GOONASEKERA, Yohan; b Colombo 8 Nov 1957; (2) 954, 955.

GOONATILLAKE, Hettiarachige Mahes; b Kandy 16 Aug 1952; (5) 921, 925, 926, 927, 934.

GUNERATNE, Roshan Punyajith Wijesinghe; b Colombo 26 Jan 1962; (1) 956.

GURUSINHA, Asanka Pradeep; b Colombo 16 Sep 1966; (28) 1028, 1044, 1045, 1063, 1064, 1065, 1074, 1132, 1133, 1157, 1163, 1164, 1165, 1176, 1182, 1183, 1184, 1194, 1195, 1196, 1209, 1210, 1219, 1229, 1230, 1231, 1232, 1266.

HATHURUSINGHE, Upul Chandika; b Colombo 13 Sep 1968; (18) 1164, 1165, 1176, 1182, 1183, 1184, 1194, 1195, 1196, 1209, 1210, 1219, 1229, 1230, 1231, 1232, 1233, 1234.

JAYASEKERA, Rohan Stanley Amarasiriwardena; b Colombo 7 Dec 1957; (1) 927.

JAYASURIYA, Sanath Teran; b Matara 30 Jun 1969; (15) 1164, 1165, 1176, 1182, 1183, 1184, 1195, 1196, 1219, 1231, 1233, 1234, 1241, 1246, 1266.

JEGANATHAN, Sridharan; b Colombo 11 Jul 1951; (2) 954, 955.

JOHN, Vinothen Bede (*formerly* J.V.B.JEYARAJA-SINGHAM); b Colombo 27 May 1960; (6) 954, 955, 986, 987, 988, 994.

JURANGPATHY, Baba Roshan; b Colombo 25 Jun 1967; (2) 1025, 1064.

KALPAGE, Ruwan Senani; b Kandy 19 Feb 1970; (7) 1230, 1232, 1241, 1245, 1246, 1247, 1267.

KALUPERUMA, Lalith Wasantha; b Colombo 25 May 1949; (2) 921, 926.

KALUPERUMA, Sanath Mohan Silva; b Colombo 22 Oct 1961; (4) 986, 987, 988, 1094.

KALUWITHARANA, Romesh Shantha; b Colombo 24 Nov 1969; (3) 1194, 1195, 1231.

KURUPPU, Don Sardha Brendon Priyantha; b Colombo 5 Jan 1962; (4) 1074, 1094, 1103, 1176.

KURUPPUARACHCHI, Ajith Kosala; b Colombo 1 Nov 1964; (2) 1044, 1074.

LABROOY, Graeme Fredrick; b Colombo 9 Jun 1964; (9) 1063, 1094, 1103, 1132, 1133, 1157, 1163, 1164, 1165.

LIYANAGE, Dulip Kapila; b Kalutara 6 Jun 1972; (8) 1195, 1196, 1209, 1210, 1229, 1230, 1234, 1245.

MADUGALLE, Ranjan Senerath; b Kandy 22 Apr 1959; (21) 921, 925, 926, 927, 934, 954, 955, 956, 986, 987, 988, 994, 1023, 1024, 1025, 1026, 1027, 1028, 1074, 1094, 1103.

MADURASINGHE, Arachchige Wijayasiri Ranjith; b Kurunegala 30 Jan 1961; (3) 1103, 1194, 1194.

MAHANAMA, Roshan Siriwardene; b Colombo 31 May 1966; (29) 1044, 1045, 1074, 1094, 1132, 1133, 1157, 1163, 1176, 1183, 1184, 1194, 1195, 1196, 1209, 1210, 1219, 1229, 1230, 1231, 1232, 1233, 1234, 1241, 1245, 1246, 1247, 1266, 1267.

MENDIS, Louis Rohan Duleep; b Colombo 25 Aug 1952; (24) 921, 925, 926, 927, 934, 956, 986, 987, 988, 994, 1023, 1024, 1025, 1026, 1027, 1028, 1043, 1044, 1045, 1063, 1064, 1065, 1074, 1103.

MURALITHARAN, Muthiah; b Kandy 17 Apr 1972; (14) 1195, 1196, 1210, 1219, 1229, 1231, 1232, 1233, 1234, 1241, 1245, 1246, 1247, 1266.

PUSHPAKUMARA, Karuppiahyage Ravindra; b Panadura 21 Jul 1975; (1) 1267.

RAMANAYAKE, Champaka Priyadarshi Hewage; b Colombo 8 Jan 1965; (18) 1094, 1103, 1132, 1133, 1163, 1164, 1165, 1176, 1182, 1183, 1194, 1195, 1196, 1209, 1219, 1229, 1233, 1234.

RANASINGHE, Anura Nandana; b Colombo 13 Oct 1956; (2) 926, 934.

RANATUNGA, Arjuna; b Colombo 1 Dec 1963; (51) 921, 925, 926, 934, 956, 986, 987, 988, 994, 1023, 1024, 1025, 1026, 1027, 1028, 1043, 1044, 1045, 1063, 1064, 1065, 1074, 1094, 1103, 1132, 1133, 1157, 1163, 1164, 1165, 1182, 1183, 1184, 1194, 1195, 1196, 1209, 1210, 1219, 1229, 1230, 1231, 1232, 1233, 1234, 1241, 1245, 1246, 1247, 1266, 1267.

RANATUNGA, Dammika; b Colombo 12 Oct 1962; (2) 1132, 1133.

RANATUNGA, Sanjeeva; b Colombo 25 Apr 1969; (1) 1267.

RATNAYAKE, Rumesh Joseph; b Colombo 2 Jan 1964; (23) 954, 955, 956, 986, 1023, 1024, 1025, 1026, 1027, 1028, 1043, 1064, 1065, 1074, 1133, 1157, 1163, 1164, 1165, 1176, 1182, 1183, 1184.

RATNAYEKE, Joseph Ravindran; b Colombo 2 May 1960; (22) 925, 927, 934, 954, 955, 987, 988, 994, 1026, 1027, 1028, 1043, 1044, 1045, 1063, 1064, 1065, 1074, 1094, 1103, 1132, 1133.

SAMARASEKERA, Maitipage Athula Rohitha; b Colombo 4 Aug 1961; (4) 1103, 1132, 1157, 1182.

SAMARAWEERA, Dulip Prasanna; b Colombo 12 Feb 1972; (5) 1241, 1245, 1246, 1247, 1267.

SENANAYAKE, Charith Panduka; b Colombo 19 Dec 1962; (3) 1163, 1164, 1165.

SILVA, Sampathawaduge Amal Rohitha; b Moratuwa 12 Dec 1960; (9) 955, 994, 1023, 1024, 1025, 1026, 1027, 1043, 1103.

TILLEKERATNE, Hashan Prasantha; b Colombo 14 Jul 1967; (25) 1133, 1157, 1163, 1164, 1165, 1176, 1182, 1183, 1184, 1196, 1209, 1210, 1219, 1229, 1230, 1231, 1232, 1233, 1234, 1241, 1245, 1246, 1247, 1266, 1267.

VAAS, Warnakulasuriya Patabendige Ushantha Chaminda Joseph; b Colombo 27 Jan 1974; (1) 1267.

WARNAPURA, Bandula; b Rambukkana, Colombo 1 Mar 1953; (4) 921, 925, 927, 934.

WARNAWEERA, Khahakachchi Patabandige Jayananda; b Matara 23 Nov 1960; (10) 1043, 1157, 1163, 1209, 1210, 1219, 1229, 1230, 1231, 1266.

WEERASINGHE, Colombage Don Udesh Sanjeeva; b Colombo 1 Mar 1968; (1) 1024.

WETTIMUNY, Mithra de Silva; b Colombo 11 Jun 1951; (2) 954, 955.

WETTIMUNY, Sidath; b Colombo 12 Aug 1956; (23) 921, 925, 926, 927, 954, 955, 956, 986, 987, 988, 994, 1023, 1024, 1025, 1026, 1027, 1028, 1043, 1044, 1045, 1063, 1064, 1065.

WICKREMASINGHE, Anguppulige Gamini Dayantha; b Colombo 27 Dec 1965; (3) 1132, 1209, 1210.

WICKREMASINGHE, Gallage Pramodya; b Matara 14 Aug 1971; (13) 1182, 1183, 1184, 1194, 1230, 1231, 1232, 1233, 1241, 1245, 1246, 1247, 1266.

WIJEGUNAWARDENE, Kapila Indaka Weerakkody; b Colombo 23 Nov 1964; (2) 1176, 1184.

WIJESURIYA, Roger Garrad Christopher Ediriweera; b Moratuwa 18 Feb 1960; (4) 927, 1026, 1027, 1028.

WIJETUNGE, Piyal Kashyapa; b Badulla 6 Aug 1971; (1) 1232.

ZIMBABWE (22 players)

ARNOTT, Kevin John; b Salisbury 8 Mar 1961; (4) 1197, 1198, 1199, 1218.

BRAIN, David Hayden; b Salisbury 4 Oct 1964; (4) 1199, 1218, 1239, 1240.

BRANDES, Eddo Andre; b Port Shepstone, Natal, South Africa 5 Mar 1963; (6) 1197, 1199, 1218, 1238, 1239, 1240.

BRIANT, Gavin Aubrey; b Salisbury 11 Apr 1969; (1) 1218.

BRUK-JACKSON, Glen Keith; b Salisbury 25 Apr 1969; (2) 1238, 1239.

BURMESTER, Mark Greville; b Durban, South Africa 24 Jan 1968; (3) 1197, 1198, 1199.

CAMPBELL, Alistair Douglas Ross; b Salisbury 23 Sep 1972; (7) 1197, 1198, 1199, 1218, 1238, 1239, 1240.

CROCKER, Gary John; b Bulawayo 16 May 1962; (3) 1197, 1198, 1199.

DEKKER, Mark Hampton; b Gatooma 5 Dec 1969; (3) 1238, 1239, 1240.

FLOWER, Andrew; b Cape Town, South Africa 28 Apr 1968; (7) 1197, 1198, 1199, 1218, 1238, 1239, 1240.

FLOWER, Grant William; b Salisbury 20 Dec 1970; (7) 1197, 1198, 1199, 1218, 1238, 1239, 1240.

HOUGHTON, David Laud; b Bulawayo 23 Jun 1957; (7) 1197, 1198, 1199, 1218, 1238, 1239, 1240.

JAMES, Wayne Robert; b Bulawayo 27 Aug 1956; (1) 1240.

JARVIS, Malcolm Peter; b Fort Victoria 6 Dec 1955; (2) 1197, 1198.

PEALL, Stephen Guy; b Salisbury 2 Sep 1970; (2) 1238, 1239.

PYCROFT, Andrew John; b Salisbury 6 Jun 1956; (3) 1197, 1198, 1199.

RANCHOD, Ujesh; b Salisbury 17 May 1969; (1) 1218.

RENNIE, John Alexander; b Fort Victoria 29 Jul 1970; (2) 1238, 1240.

SHAH (*registered as OMARSHAH*), Ali Hassimshah; b Salisbury 7 Aug 1959; (2) 1198, 1218.

STREAK, Heath Hilton; b Bulawayo 16 Mar 1974; (3) 1238, 1239, 1240.

TRAICOS, Athanasios John; b Zagazig, Egypt 17 May 1947; (4) 1197, 1198, 1199, 1218. (*Also 3 Tests for South Africa: 671-673*)

WHITTALL, Guy James; b Chipinga 5 Sep 1972; (3) 1238, 1239, 1240.